Huang Di nei jing su wen
Volume I

BOOK

The Philip E. Lilienthal imprint
honors special books
in commemoration of a man whose work
at University of California Press from 1954 to 1979
was marked by dedication to young authors
and to high standards in the field of Asian Studies.
Friends, family, authors, and foundations have together
endowed the Lilienthal Fund, which enables UC Press
to publish under this imprint selected books
in a way that reflects the taste and judgment
of a great and beloved editor.

Huang Di nei jing su wen

An Annotated Translation of
Huang Di's Inner Classic – Basic Questions

Volume I
Chapters 1 through 52

Paul U. Unschuld and Hermann Tessenow
in Collaboration with Zheng Jinsheng

UNIVERSITY OF CALIFORNIA PRESS
Berkeley   Los Angeles

Acknowledgment

This annotated translation of the *Su wen* was made possible by a long-term commitment from the Volkswagen Foundation, following up an initial pilot phase funded by the German Research Association (DFG). It is with utmost gratitude that we acknowledge this generous support and an understanding of the complexities of our project.

University of California Press, one of the most distinguished university presses in the United States, enriches lives around the world by advancing scholarship in the humanities, social sciences, and natural sciences. Its activities are supported by the UC Press Foundation and by philanthropic contributions from individuals and institutions. For more information, visit www.ucpress.edu.

University of California Press
Berkeley and Los Angeles, California

University of California Press, Ltd.
London, England

Library of Congress Cataloging-in-Publication Data

Unschuld, Paul U., 1943–.
    Huang Di nei jing su wen: an annotated translation of Huang Di's Inner Classic — Basic Questions / Paul U. Unschuld and Hermann Tessenow in collaboration with Zheng Jinsheng. — 1st ed.
        p.   cm.
    Includes bibliographical references.
    ISBN 978-0-520-26698-8 (set)
    1. Su wen.   2. Medicine, Chinese—Early works to 1800.   I. Unschuld, Paul U. (Paul Ulrich), 1943-   II. Tessenow, Hermann, 1945-   III. Zheng, Jinsheng, 1946-   IV. Su wen. English.   V. Title: Annotated translation of Huang Di's Inner Classic — Basic Questions.
    R127.1.S93H7   2011
    616'.09—dc21   2010039378
Manufactured in the United States of America
19   18   17   16
10   9   8   7   6   5   4

The paper used in this publication meets the minimum requirements of ANSI/NISO Z39.48-1992 (R 1997) (Permanence of Paper).

CONTENTS
Volume I

P<small>ROLEGOMENA</small>

I.   On the Significance of the *Huang Di nei jing Su wen* / 10

II. Principles of Translation

1.   On Methodology / 12

2.   Individual Terms as Examples of Uncertainties as to which Translation Is Most Appropriate / 14

    2.1. *jing* 經 / 14
    2.2. *du mai* 督脈 and *ren mai* 任脈 / 15
    2.3. *fu* 府 and *zang* 臓 / 16
    2.4. *mu* 募 and *shu* 俞 / 18
    2.5. *rong* 榮/*ying* 營 / 18
    2.6. *ji* 肌 / 19
    2.7. Names of Needle Insertion Holes, *xue* 穴 / 19

3.   Individual Terms as Examples of Translation Difficulties: Alternative Meanings of the Same Term / 19

    3.1. *qi* 氣 / 19
    3.2. *bing* 病 / 20
    3.3. *mai* 脈 / 21
    3.4. Identical Terms Used for a Morphological Structure and an Insertion Point ("hole") / 21

III. Textual Structures in the *Su wen* Translation

1. *Textus Receptus* and Predecessors / 22

2. Structural Markers in the Translation / 23

IV. Italics, Upper Case and Lower Case Writings of Titles and Terms / 24

V. Footnotes / 24

ANNOTATED TRANSLATION OF *Su wen* 1 THROUGH 52

Chapter 1   Discourse on the True [Qi Endowed by] Heaven in High Antiquity / 29
Chapter 2   Comprehensive Discourse on Regulating the Spirit [in Accordance with] the Qi of the Four [Seasons] / 45
Chapter 3   Discourse on how the Generative Qi Communicates with Heaven / 59
Chapter 4   Discourse on the True Words in the Golden Chest / 83
Chapter 5   Comprehensive Discourse on Phenomena Corresponding to Yin and Yang / 95
Chapter 6   Discourse on the Division and Unity of yin and yang / 127
Chapter 7   Further Discourse on Yin and Yang / 137
Chapter 8   Discourse on the Hidden Canons in the Numinous Orchid [Chambers] / 155
Chapter 9   Discourse on the Six Terms [of a Year] and on Phenomena [associated with the Condition] of the Depots / 163
Chapter 10 The Generation and Completion of the Five Depots / 185
Chapter 11 Further Discourse on the Five Depots / 203
Chapter 12 Discourse on Different [Therapeutic] Patterns Suitable [for Use in Different] Cardinal Points / 211
Chapter 13 Discourse on Moving the Essence and Changing the Qi / 219
Chapter 14 Discourse on Decoctions and Wines / 233
Chapter 15 Jade Tablet Discourse on the Essentials / 247
Chapter 16 Discourse On The Essentials of Diagnosis and On Exhaustion in the Conduits / 257
Chapter 17 Discourse on the Essentials of Vessels and the Subtleties of the Essence / 273

Chapter 18   Discourse on Phenomena [Reflecting the Status of] Qi in a
             Normal Person   /   301
Chapter 19   Discourse on the Jade Mechanism and the True [Qi of the]
             Depots   /   323
Chapter 20   Discourse on the Three Sections and Nine Indicators   /   351
Chapter 21   Further Discourse on the Conduit Vessels   /   369
Chapter 22   Discourse on How the Qi in the Depots Follow the Pattern of
             the Seasons   /   383
Chapter 23   Wide Promulgation of the Five Qi   /   401
Chapter 24   Blood and Qi, Physical Appearance and Mind   /   413
Chapter 25   Discourse on Treasuring Life and Preserving Physical
             Appearance   /   419
Chapter 26   Discourse on the Eight Cardinal [Turning Points] and on
             Spirit Brilliance   /   433
Chapter 27   Discourse on the Division and Union of True [Qi] and Evil
             [Qi]   /   447
Chapter 28   Discourse Thoroughly Deliberating upon Depletion and
             Repletion   /   459
Chapter 29   Discourse on the Major Yin and on the Yang Brilliance
             [Conduits]   /   479
Chapter 30   Explanation of the Yang Brilliance Vessel   /   487
Chapter 31   Discourse on Heat   /   491
Chapter 32   To Pierce Heat   /   499
Chapter 33   Discourse Deliberating upon Heat Disease   /   515
Chapter 34   Discourse on the Assessment of Movements Contrary [to their
             Regular Course]   /   527
Chapter 35   Discourse on Malaria   /   535
Chapter 36   To Pierce Malaria   /   553
Chapter 37   Discourse on Qi Recession   /   567
Chapter 38   Discourse on Cough   /   575
Chapter 39   Discourse on Pain   /   583
Chapter 40   Discourse on Abdomen and Center   /   599
Chapter 41   To Pierce Lower Back Pain   /   613
Chapter 42   Discourse on Wind   /   625
Chapter 43   Discourse on Blocks   /   639
Chapter 44   Discourse On Limpness   /   653
Chapter 45   Discourse on Recession   /   665
Chapter 46   Discourse on Disease Manifestations   /   677
Chapter 47   Discourse on Strange Diseases   /   689
Chapter 48   Discourse on Very Strange [Diseases]   /   705
Chapter 49   Explanations on the Vessels   /   719
Chapter 50   Discourse on the Essentials of Piercing   /   733

Chapter 51 Discourse on the Restrictions of Piercing / 737
Chapter 52 Discourse on Prohibitions in Piercing / 741

BIBLIOGRAPHY

1. Dictionaries and Encyclopedias / 754

2. Monographs / 755

3. Articles / 761

PROLEGOMENA

This is the first of two volumes of an annotated English translation of the ancient Chinese life sciences text *Huang Di nei jing su wen* (short: *Su wen*). In contrast to the available translations, this version is the outcome of a full application of rigorous philological principles. Furthermore, as shall be indicated in detail below, it takes the views of numerous Chinese and Japanese scholarly and clinical authors into consideration so that readers of these volumes will always have a choice between our interpretation of debatable text passages, and the views of others. This translation was not prepared primarily with an eye on the contemporary clinical applicability of its physiological and pathological views, as well as the text's therapeutic advice, provided by the authors of the *Su wen* two millennia ago. Rather, it has been the task of this translation to introduce readers to ideas, and their linguistic expression, developed in the context of the manipulation of the length and the quality of human life in such a way that it lasted as long as possible with minimal physical and mental suffering.

If these ancient ideas are restored to life by our translation they will serve various useful purposes. First, these ideas will lend themselves to a comparison with similar traditions from the beginning of European medicine and may help us to gain a better understanding of "what is medicine".[1] For us to appreciate the basic differences and parallels between the more than two millennia of Western and Chinese medical traditions, access to English translations of the seminal life science texts of Chinese antiquity, unadulterated by modern biomedical concepts

---

1 Paul U. Unschuld, *What is Medicine? Eastern and Western Approaches to Healing*. University of California Press. Berkeley and Los Angeles, 2009.

and, is essential.[2] Second, it is only on the basis of such translations that the later development of Chinese medicine can be traced, in particular its recent redefinition as Traditional Chinese Medicine in contemporary China and abroad. The creative reception of so-called TCM in many Western countries has led to a conceptual and clinical reality that is rather distant from its beginnings in Han-dynasty China. It is through a comparison of today's realities with these beginnings that a real awareness may emerge of the process that Chinese medicine has undergone in its adaptation to the values and requirements of modern times.

Our project of preparing the first philologically rigorous English translation of the *Su wen* began in 1988. Two volumes have now been published by University of California Press; the first examines the origins and the history of the *Su wen*, and offers a survey of its contents.[3] The second is the first dictionary in Western Chinese studies devoted to a single life science text of Chinese antiquity.[4] It gives the meanings of all 1866 Chinese characters in more than 81000 positions forming the text. It includes, as an appendix, the complete Chinese reference text, and on a CD, a concordance.

I. On the Significance of the *Huang Di nei jing su wen*

During the 4th to 3rd centuries BCE a new view on nature emerged in China. Comparable to the emergence of a science in the Eastern Mediterranean only a few hundred years earlier, some Chinese philosophers began to perceive regularities in the daily workings of the universe that appeared to be governed by natural laws rather than numinous beings such as gods, ancestors, or ghosts. The assumption that such laws existed became closely tied to a vision of patterned relationships among all phenomena in the world, be they tangible or not. In China, the new world view found its most obvious expression in the theories of systematic correspondence known as Yin-Yang and Five-Agents doctrines respectively. Soon enough, the validity of these theories was extended to an understanding of the human organism. This was the origin of a medicine that developed in sharp contrast to earlier modes of interpreting and manipulating health and illness. There was a novel attempt at health management designed to rely exclusively on natural science in the construction of physiological and patholo-

---

2 See also, Paul U. Unschuld, *Nan-ching. The Classic of Difficult Issues*. University of California Press. Berkeley and Los Angeles, 1976.

3 Paul U. Unschuld, *Huang Di Nei Jing Su Wen. Nature, Knowledge, Imagery in an Ancient Chinese Medical Text*. University of California Press. Berkeley and Los Angeles, 2003.

4 Hermann Tessenow and Paul U. Unschuld, *A Dictionary of the Huang Di Nei Jing Su Wen*. University of California Press. Berkeley and Los Angeles, 2008.

gical theories, that is, in understanding what came to be considered normal and abnormal functions of the human organism.

For ancient Europe, the emergence of such a medicine is associated with the generation of texts that are widely known as the *Corpus Hippocraticum*. For ancient China, it is seen in the context of writings that were gathered into the textual corpus of the *Huang Di nei jing* and a few parallel compilations, during the first through third centuries CE. The early history of these ancient Chinese literary monuments of a new medicine needs not be recounted here; it has been elucidated in detail in the first volume of our *Huang Di nei jing su wen* project.

The *Huang Di nei jing su wen* constitutes, judged from a perspective of both historians and clinicians, the most valuable source available today, enabling readers to appreciate the intense intellectual dynamics in health care characteristic of the time of the earlier and later Han dynasties, and beyond. With an unclear history of transmission until the sixth century CE, when Quan Yuanqi 全元起 compiled a first commentated edition, the *textus receptus* has been identified by Chinese historians as a work of the Zhou-Qin-Han era since at least the 14th century; Chinese researchers of the 20th century see the original text as a product of the Han dynasty. Wang Bing in the ninth century rearranged the text, added commentaries, and amended it by another long text the origins of which have not been clearly identified to this day, i.e., the seven comprehensive discourses on the doctrine of the five periods and six *qi*. Finally, in the 11th century, an imperial editorial office added further comments and published a printed version of the *Huang Di nei jing su wen* that has remained the authoritative *textus receptus* to this day.

As early as the 14th century, the renowned literary critic Lü Fu 呂復, had realized that the *Suwen* was not the work of a single author. Rather, he stated, it combines texts written by numerous authors over an extended period of time. However, this "extended period of time" may, as we recognize today, have lasted for no more than two centuries. In the course of a most productive era, stimulated by the new yin-yang and five-agents outlook on the world, countless scholars, their names lost to posterity, sat down to apply the doctrines of systematic correspondences to many issues requiring an explanation. Many different schools appear to have sprung up, each with their own attempts at reconciling perceived reality with the new doctrines, and it may have been only in a second phase that these schools, confined to oral tradition at first, generated written texts to be distributed over larger geographical distances. The *Huang Di nei jing su wen*, much like the *Huang Di nei jing ling shu* (short: *Ling shu*), owes its existence to compilers who, beginning in the Han dynasty, excerpted text passages from a large pool of separate writings. They chose quotations that they considered representative of specific medical traditions or simply interesting and transformed them into textual corpora, each with its own characteristics and emphasis. The *Huang Di nei jing su wen* is worth special attention because more than all other compilations of the time it has retained its nature as an anthology. The compilators of the *Su wen*, as the title is generally abbreviated, avoided a complete obfuscation of the diverse origins of the many textual pieces they brought together. As a consequence, today's reader, even without much philological scrutiny, easily recognizes many of the "breaks" separating historical levels, or just indicating the transition from one author's text piece to the next. Conceptual contradictions, such as those between the holistic interpretation of *nue* 瘧 disease (malaria) in treatise 35 and an organ-centered interpretation in treatise 36, as well as differences in dialogue partners, and an oscillation between dialogue and non-dialogue chapters, all point to the compilers' reluctance to generate a monolithic, homogenous text. The application of philological expertise has brought to light many more such breaks and transitions. The heterogeneity and homogeneity of text parts are often obscured by editorial devices linking different text parts, by the intended as well as unintended re-arrangement of textual segments, by the integration of formerly separate commentaries into the main text, and by changes in pronunciation over time which makes it difficult to recognize the rhyming structure of text passages, to name the most common elements contributing to the internal structure of the *Su wen*.

No attempt has ever been made to prepare a philologically correct English translation of the *Su wen*, nor has an attempt been made to make the heterogeneous structure of the *Su wen* visible. The two volumes of an annotated English version of the *Su wen* presented here are meant to change this and to offer a quality of translation and annotation that will enable, for the first time, a wide range of readers without command of classical Chinese to conduct a comparative research on ancient Chinese and European medical classics. The following are the basic principles we have observed in the pursuance of our task.

II. Principles of Translation

1. On Methodology

It is a perfectly legitimate approach to re-examine the concepts and practices of health care of Chinese or European antiquity in the light of a 21st century understanding of human biology, and hence to rewrite ancient medical texts with a vocabulary based in modern biomedical notions. Such an attempt at re-contextualization may be helpful to those who are convinced of the truth of their current views and are eager to verify these views in the sources of the past. It is equally legitimate to strive to bring to light the ideas, theories and facts held and expressed by ancient authors on their own terms. For historians of ideas, and even for some clinicians of so-called Traditional Chinese Medicine, it should be of primary interest to reconstruct the perceptions of health and disease held by intellectuals of two millennia ago, and to ask what it was that shaped their thoughts and knowledge. This approach takes ancient literary (and other) sources seriously as such. It does not isolate them from their literary and cultural environments. Rather, it interprets them as indicators of an environment to which one otherwise has no access. It is only through such an approach that the history of culture in general, and of ideas and knowledge in particular can be written. And in the case of Traditional Chinese Medicine, it is only through this approach that the divergence of the present from the legacy of the past can be identified clearly.

This second approach lies at the basis of the translation of the *Su wen* as presented here. In fact, a translation, in our view, is worth its name only if it strives to reproduce a text in a target language as close to its original format and meaning as possible, without omissions and anachronistic interpretations and additions. We believe that an application of this principle is particularly justified in dealing with a text like the *Su wen*. Its origin lies more than two thousand years in the past. Many of its passages allow for different interpretations as to what the authors may have meant to say and what facts they were actually referring to. A translation such as ours demands a reader interested in obtaining a most faithful (albeit occasionally incomplete) image of the contents and structure of the original text. Our aim is to make the ideas, theories, and practices laid out in the text fully visible and conceivable again. However, it is not the translator's primary task, instead it is the reader's task, to reconstruct the ideas, theories, and practices laid down in the text. Where necessary, the translator may, of course, based on an intimate understanding of the text and its original cultural environment, offer his or her own views, separate from the translation, in footnotes or appendices.

While this may be the ideal approach, no translation that is intended to be readable can do without interpretative definitions and additions, and even if one intends to focus exclusively on the material and conceptual background of the time when the text was written, such definitions and additions will be projections that can never be entirely free of modern knowledge and concepts. We are fully aware of this dilemma and have identified as many such projections as possible in our translation. This includes the juxtaposition, in the footnotes, of our final translation with possible alternatives as seen by ourselves, or offered by Chinese and Japanese scholars.

The identification and translation of the technical terms of the text posed particular difficulty. It was our intention to use English equivalents intended to be as close as possible to the images conveyed by the original Chinese terms. That is, concomitant with the approach outlined above, we have not attempted to replace ancient Chinese technical terminology with modern biomedical terminology. For one thing, ancient Chinese technical terms are by no means so sufficiently well-defined for us to succeed with a one-to-one translation. Second, such an approach would obscure the original notions that determined the emergence of certain Chinese technical terms out of every-day language, most often through a metaphorical expansion of their initial meaning. The Chinese term *jing* 經, to be further discussed below, may serve as an example. The original literal meaning: warp of a loom, had already been long left behind in the usage of *jing* as a medical technical term. Hence we did not deem it suitable to recreate in our translation the earliest known significance of the term.

In a few cases, no English equivalent matches a Chinese original. This is either because the Chinese original has too many meanings to be expressed by a single English term, or because the original meaning remains too nebulous. Examples are *qi* 氣, but also Yin 陰 and Yang 陽. In these cases, we have chosen a *pinyin* transliteration based on current standard pronunciation. We are aware of a widespread hesitation to translate certain anatomical terms, such as *xue* 血 or *gan* 肝, with their English morphological equivalents blood or liver, respectively. The different physiological and pathological functions assigned to these and other fluids and tissues in ancient China have led many to prefer a *pinyin* transliteration over a literal translation. Our approach here takes a different path. If a morphological-anatomical unit has been identified as such in the Chinese text, it is translated with its vernacular equivalent in English. Functions assigned do change over time, and it is to be expected that a reader of a historical text will be aware of this. Hence *bi* 鼻, *mu* 目, *er* 耳 are translated with their vernacular English counterparts nose, eye, and ear, and the same applies to *gan* 肝 liver, *xue* 血 blood, and *nao* 腦 brain. The ancient Chinese naturalists had a very clear perception of nose and eyes and of liver and blood as distinct morphological/physical entities. But even a cursory reading of the text shows that the functions assigned to these entities in the ancient Chinese interpretation of the organism differ from today's understanding. It cannot be the task of a translation to reflect these dynamics by modifying the morphological terminology. The physiological concepts we associate with blood at the beginning of the 21st century differ greatly from the established knowledge of even as short a time ago as the 19th century. Still, we continue to speak of blood as far as the morphological fact is concerned. The same should apply to a translation of ancient Chinese morphological designations.

The following may serve to elucidate how we arrived at our choices in view of some particularly problematic instances.

2. *Individual Terms as Examples of Uncertainties as to which Translation Is Most Appropriate*

2.1. *jing* 經

As pointed out above, the original meaning of *jing* 經, warp, had already given way in literature contemporary with the *Su wen* to metaphorical expansion expressing the notion of "passing through" and "main supporting structure", as well as "vertical". In the ancient Chinese view of human morphology and an assumed network of vessels as the foundation of organism's physiology and pathology, the term *jing* 經 appears to have been chosen to denote the "main vessels", *jing mai* 經脈, passing through the body (seen from a standing position) vertically. These are distinguished from the so-called "network vessels", *luo mai* 絡脈, that were believed to mostly permeate the body horizontally. This is attested by many *Su wen* passages where the terms *jing mai* 經脈 and *luo mai* 絡脈 serve to denote these two types of vessels.

Five times in *Su wen* 62 and six times in different chapters of the *Huang Di nei jing ling shu*, a term *jing sui* 經隧 is used. Seen together with *jing mai* 經脈, *jing* 經 appears here merely as an adjective "main" (or "vertical"). *Jing mai*, then, would read "main (or: vertical) vessel"; *jing sui* would read "main (or: vertical) tunnel". The latter term is of particular interest as it seems to clearly express a notion of tube-like structures in the body where qi and blood are assumed to flow. Nevertheless, a meaning of *jing* 經 as "path" is attested since the Late Han era too. This suggests that an expression such as *shi yi jing* 十一經 is not merely an abbreviation of *shi yi jing mai* 十一經脈, "11 *jing*-vessels". Rather, we may read *jing* 經 as incorporating the meaning of the path of qi and blood. The long-established translation of *jing* 經 as "conduit(s)" that we continue here is an approximation. It fails to distinguish the *jing* 經 clearly from the *luo* 絡 as the latter are obviously defined as conduit-transmitters of *qi* and blood, too. We have chosen "conduit" in the sense of "main conduit" in our translation of *jing* nevertheless. This is because the *Su wen* does not permit a clear definition of *jing* 經 as meaning either "vertical" or "main structure". It may well be that *jing* 經 was then perceived as combining both these meanings. A certain hierarchy is achieved by translation of *luo mai* 絡脈 as "network vessels", that is, second-degree vessels serving as links between the main vessels.

2.2. *du mai* 督脈 and *ren mai* 任脈

These terms denote vessels passing through the back and front side (i.e. the yang and yin side, respectively) of the human body in a central line from head to genital organ. *Du* and *Ren* are terms borrowed by Han dynasty medical authors from the arena of state administration. *Du* vs. *ren* is the only pairing that has been rendered in English with a complete metaphorical equivalent for some time already; as is to be expected not by Chinese but by Western authors. Birch and Felt in their *Understanding Acupuncture* have chosen "governing vessel" vs. "controller vessel". The terminology chosen in our translation is "supervisor vessel" vs. "controlling vessel". One may assume that well-established hierarchical differences between administrative positions of *du* and *ren* stimulated Han dynasty authors to select this pairing in naming two important conduit vessels.

Du and *ren* signify tasks in an administration. Charles O.Hucker identifies *du* as "most commonly signifying that, without giving up his regular post, an official had been delegated to take temporary charge of another post."[5] One may detect mobility, and hence a *yang* quality, in "taking temporary charge of another post", but *ren* as the opposite can hardly be identified as a more stable position. Hence the choice of these terms may have been led by other considerations. Rather than choosing a pairing that suggested "movement" vs. "non-movement" to Han dynasty readers, two administrative terms were selected that reflect different echelons in a bureaucratic hierarchy. *Du* was definitely a higher ranking official than ren. A *du* could be in charge of, for example, an army division. A *du* was a leading position, such as a supervisor, or a general. In contrast, *ren* has the meaning "to shoulder", "to shoulder a task", "to assume an official position". A *ren* could be any lower official who was simply in charge of controlling the execution of some ordinary task.

Ren mai 任脈 is widely translated in TCM literature as "conception vessel". This interpretation is based on the fact that the *ren mai* is associated with functions of conception and pregnancy. Also, in non-medical literature, 任 is sometimes used in place of 妊, "pregnancy." However, the pairing of two metaphors selected from bureaucratic terminology appears to us much more convincing than the naming of one vessel after an office in bureaucracy, and the other after an alleged physiological function. The general principle in choosing terms for these pairings appears to have been to select two terms from one arena of public life known to all potential future users of these terms. The two terms chosen had to be rather close in their meanings, with a difference that enabled one to associate one of the two with a *yang* and the other with a *yin* meaning. The metaphorical rationale of juxtaposing *du* and *ren* in the context of human physiology seems to have been one of acknowledging a higher rank of *yang* phenomena in comparison with *yin* phenomena.[6]

2.3. *fu* 府 and *zang* 臟

Apparently, the Yin-Yang-Doctrine encouraged its followers to distinguish among functions and tangible components of the human body as being either of the yin or of the yang category. Thus, among the organs they expected to find some with a yin nature, i.e., those seen as quietly hiding their contents in the depth of the organism for a long time, and others with a yang nature, i.e., those associated with brief storage, passage, and location in the exterior of the human body. Hence, at least since the compilation of the *Huang Di nei jing* texts, *fu* 府

---

5 Charles O. Hucker, *A Dictionary of Official Titles in Imperial China*. Stanford University Press, Stanford, California, 1985, 535.

6 Paul U. Unschuld, Yin-Yang Theory, the Human Organism, and the *Bai hu tong*. A Need for Pairing and Explaining. *Asian Medicine*, in press.

and *zang* 臟 (in modern writing with the radical "flesh", 腑 and 臟) signify two groups of human/animal organs based on such reasoning. These are lung, heart, spleen, liver, and kidney(s) as the five *zang*, and stomach, gallbladder, small intestine, large intestine, bladder and a morphologically non-verifiable organ named *san jiao* ("triple burner") as the six *fu*.

While it is quite clear what *fu* 腑 and *zang* 臟 signify in non-medical contexts, the selection of just these terms in ancient China for morphological and physiological purposes, and their translation into English as "palace(s)" and "depot(s)" may require some explanation. In late Zhou and early Chinese vernacular language, both terms were used to refer to what one might call places of storage, such as granaries, depots, or reservoirs. *Fu* may have been places where funds, documents, victuals, and other items required by a bureaucracy, were stored temporarily. *Zang* were places to hide away particularly valuable, precious items. Such a reading of non-medical usage seems to parallel the distinction provided in *Su wen* 11, where the 6 *fu* are said to receive the more solid *qi* which they do not store for long but quickly release. In contrast, the five *zang* store the finest *qi*, which they do not normally or easily release. That is, the terms *zang* 臟 and *fu* 腑 were chosen as suitable because they carried the same basic meaning of storage but allowed a distinction to be made between alleged yin and yang natures of the organs.

There are no English terms to express conveniently using two single words this *fu-zang* antagonism of short-term and long-term storage, of transitory storage vs. fixed storage. *Zang* could be translated as "treasury" or "depository", or, as we have chosen, "depot" to approach the notion of a long-term storage. For *fu*, though, it is impossible to find a matching term. Also, during the late Zhou and early Han dynasty, the meaning of *fu* underwent an expansion from short-term storage facility to also signify venues of administration, and subsequently a palace where an administrator resides. A hint at this expansion of the meaning of *fu* is given in *juan* 8 of Ban Gu's 班固 *Bai hu tong yi* 白虎通義 of 79 CE. The relevant paragraph appears to have been written to help readers to ground certain moral values in human physiology and at the same time explain the specific relations between *zang* and *fu* organs. Apparently, at the time of the *Bai hu tong yi*, the designations of the two groups of organs in question, and their respective functions, already required an explanation. The interpretation chosen was one of considering the five *zang* as fulfilling central administrative functions in the body's economy, while the *fu* were seen as supporting units. The problem facing the authors of the *Bai hu tong yi* was how to reconcile their physiological understandings with the terms *zang* and *fu* that no longer exactly fit them. The image chosen is that of six *fu* as "palaces" (the text speaks of *gong fu* 宮府), each of which is attached to a *zang*. In view of this supplemental socio-metaphorical pairing and because of semantic ambiguity becoming associated with the term *fu* in the course of the Han era, one of us (PUU) has long ago chosen to refer to both metaphorical pairings by translating *fu* as palace and *zang* as depot. For want of a more convincing alternative, we have continued this choice.

2.4. *mu* 募 and *shu* 俞

Mu 募 and *shu* 俞 are designations of needle insertion points on the front and on the back of the human body. In current English acupuncture literature they are commonly rendered as "alarm" and "transportation" points respectively. The original pairing of these terms reflects, in our view, once again a yin-yang distinction. *Mu* 募 means "to levy", "to collect", which is a yin function that is to be expected for needle insertion holes located on the yin side, i.e., the front of the body; *shu* 俞 means "to transport", "to move" things. This is a yang function as one would expect due to its association with needle insertion holes located on the yang side, i.e., the back of the human body.

2.5. *rong* 榮/*ying* 營

The compound *ying qi* 營氣, widely translated as "constructive *qi*" in Western TCM literature, is seen once in the *Su wen*; the compound *rong qi* 榮氣, literally "flourishing *qi*", four times. More often *ying qi* 營氣 appears in the *Ling shu* and in the *Tai su*, at locations similar or identical with those of 榮氣 in the *Su wen*; *rong qi* 榮氣 does not appear in these compilations. One may assume that both writings were in use in ancient China. The question is which of these alternatives should be preferred in making a literal translation.

Both *rong qi* 榮氣 (or simply *rong* 榮) and *ying qi* 營氣 (or simply ying 營) appear regularly in a pairing of terms with *wei qi* 衛氣 (or simply *wei* 衛). The meaning of the latter is unambiguous. *Wei* 衛 is a Chinese term for "to protect", "to guard", and "a guard". *Wei qi* 衛氣, then, is a "protecting *qi*" or "guard *qi*". In view of the pairings examined above and the parallel passages in the *Ling shu* and in the *Tai su*, we have preferred to read *rong qi* 榮氣 as a variant of *ying qi* 營氣. Further research may examine whether the former is a variant of the latter only in medical contexts, or perhaps is preferred because of a taboo on the latter. *Rong qi* 榮氣 and *ying qi* 營氣 therefore appear in our translation as "camp *qi*". Both ying 營 and *wei* 衛 are military terms. The military here includes troops that guard through patrolling and others that wait in camps to be mobilized for action. These two functions may serve to denote two types of *qi* believed to exist in the human body to protect the organism and ward off intruders. The patrolling guards *wei* 衛 were seen as fulfilling a yang function, the stationary, walled-in troops in a camp *ying* 營 were seen as ideal to signify a yin function. Hence the meaning denoted in the pairing of *rong qi* 榮氣/ *ying qi* 營氣 and *wei qi* 衛氣 is "guard *qi*" and "camp *qi*", respectively.

2.6. *ji* 肌

This term is commonly translated as "muscle(s)". Some modern authors concluded that *ji* 肌 and *rou* 肉 refer to the same morphological entities, and suggested translating *ji* from ancient texts always as "flesh". The usage of the terms in the *Su wen* does not confirm this view. In many passages *ji* 肌 and *rou* 肉 appear together. They may have been deemed to be closely related, and yet rather than being used as synonyms they apparently were meant to denote different entities. *Su wen* 1-5-6 is an example. The text states: "Sinews and bones prosper in abundance, muscles and flesh are full and strong". To be sure, none of the four terms *jin* 筋, gu 骨, *ji* 肌 and *rou* 肉 is defined unambiguously, and they may not refer to the morphological structures of sinews, bones, muscles, and flesh respectively as understood today in one-to-one correspondences. Nevertheless, the vernacular English terms chosen here may come closest to what their Chinese equivalents were chosen to express in antiquity.

2.7. Names of Needle Insertion Holes, *xue* 穴

An enigma unsolved to this day is the origin and, in quite a few instances, the meaning of terms assigned by ancient Chinese authors to the *xue* 穴, that is, to holes in the skin deemed suitable for needle insertion. The *Su wen* offers names that appear to have been introduced prior to the Tang era. During the Tang era, Wang Bing, in his comments, mentioned further designations of *xue* 穴. We have not been able to identify a general rationale underlying all the pre-Tang and the Tang terms. Some of them go back to human and animal morphology, others are metaphors borrowed from geographical structures or administration, still others do not lend themselves to any meaningful categorization. We have considered various hypotheses such as, for example, that at least some of these terms are transcriptions of terms loaned from a foreign language. In our translation of these terms we have sometimes deviated from established English renderings. Nevertheless, various English readings are possible in several cases.

3. Individual Terms as Examples of Translation Difficulties: Alternative Meanings of the Same Term

3.1. *qi* 氣

It would be futile to search in Chinese for a conceptual equivalent to the European "spirit", as there is no Chinese term that could be used to include meanings ranging from Holy Spirit to methylated spirit. Similarly, the Chinese term *qi* 氣 has incorporated in the course of its two-millennia-long existence numerous conceptual layers that cannot be expressed by a single European word. Its late emergence in Chinese script in the final phase of the Zhou era, and its graphical composition suggest that the character was introduced to denote vapors, possibly in an early physiological context those vapors associated with food. Soon enough, the significance of the new graph was extended to include a wide range of phenomena among which, at least from hindsight, a clear demarcation appears impossible. We may assume that *qi*, despite its many diverse applications, always referred to a vague concept of finest matter believed to exist in all possible aggregate states, from air and steam or vapor to liquid and even solid matter. In the absence of a conceptual English equivalent, *qi* 氣 is one of the very few Chinese terms we have chosen to transliterate rather than to translate. It should be noted that the interpretation of *qi* 氣 as "energy", so widespread in TCM literature today, lacks any historical basis.

Some passages in the *Su wen* may tempt one to assign a specific meaning to *qi* 氣 and translate accordingly, for example: "breath" in phrases such as *shao qi* 少氣 or *qi shao* 氣少 ("short of breath"). Even in such instances one cannot be sure to what degree such a translation is appropriate. The phrases quoted may denote shortness of breath and at the same time conditions that are associated with a shortage of qi in the organism. Hence we have avoided a more specific translation here too.

3.2. *bing* 病

Bing 病 is found in the *Su wen* to denote two different concepts that may or may not have been recognized as such by the authors of the respective text passages. *Bing* appears in contexts suggesting a meaning of being ill from the perspective of a patient, and it was used in other contexts to denote what medical theory believes to be the pathological change or dynamics in an organism underlying visible or otherwise noticeable signs. These differences could be expressed through translations such as "to suffer from", or "suffering", "ailment", "illness" in terms of the feelings of a patient and the assessment of his status by his lay environment. The perspective of the trained physician on the patient's inner condition is now commonly expressed in English with the terms "disease" and "to have a (specific) disease".

Often the text mentions what we might call symptoms or "indicators", as we have preferred to translate the Chinese term *hou* 候, and then offers the name of the pathological state responsible for these signs. In such cases, the translation of *bing* 病 as "disease" is unproblematic. In other passages, an alternative translation, "to suffer from," is more plausible. The context of *bing* 病 in the *Su wen* does not always make it clear which of these meanings may have been intended. This is particularly true for the so-called seven comprehensive discourses developing the theories of five periods and six *qi* in *Su wen* 66-71 and 74. In these cases we have preferred the more neutral meaning of "illness" emphasizing the lay person's perspective. It appears less imbued with theory.

3.3. *mai* 脈

"Blood vessels", Donald Harper concluded in his analysis of the Mawangdui manuscripts of the late 3rd to early 2nd century BCE, "are the obvious original referent of *mai* 脈. ... As vessel theory developed, what held vapor was not clearly distinguished from what held blood". By the time that the *Su wen* texts were written, beginning with the 2nd and 1st century BCE, Chinese medical physiology and pathology had passed through its most creative and dynamic initial phase of conceptualization. The Yin-Yang and Five-Agents Doctrines of systematic correspondence had entered, at least on the level of theory, diagnosis and treatment. The simple mechanical diagnostic criteria recorded in the Mawangdui manuscripts for assessing the status of the vessels gave way to complicated parameters requiring a detailed examination of the flow of *qi* and blood in and along these vessels. Apparently, the use of the term *mai* 脈 was extended to embrace a second referent to meet the new requirements. In the *Su wen*, *mai* 脈 denotes two related but nevertheless separate concepts. These are, first, assumed diverse morphological structures believed to be passage-ways of blood and *qi*, and, second, certain attributes of movements in, or associated with, the vessels to be discerned through vessel diagnosis.

In most instances, context and also early commentaries leave little doubt as to which of these two referents is meant in the usage of *mai* 脈. We have translated *mai* 脈 accordingly either as "vessel(s)" or as "[movement(s) in the] vessels". In a few passages even early readers could not be certain as to which of the two meanings was intended. An example is the beginning of *Su wen* 7 where the text speaks of se *mai* 澀脈, "rough [movements in the] vessels" or "rough vessels". Any translation choice here will remain debatable.

3.4. Identical Terms Used for a Morphological Structure and an Insertion Point ("hole")

In some cases, the designations assigned by ancient Chinese authors to needle insertion holes are identical with the designations of morphological structures that are used in other contexts too. In most instances it is clear whether a compound term is meant, in a particular statement, to designate a specific needle insertion point. In such cases we have capitalized these designations. Where we were not so sure, we have preferred to identify such terms as designations of morphological structures, and have refrained from capitalization.

Finally, we wish to point out that we have striven to always use the same word in English for translating a Chinese term. We have chosen different English words only if we were certain that one and the same Chinese term was used in different contexts of the *Su wen* to signify clearly distinguishable meanings.

III. Textual Structures in the *Su wen* Translation

1. *Textus Receptus and Predecessors*

The present translation of the *Su wen* is based on a version of the received Chinese text derived from different ancient and more recent editions of the *Huang Di nei jing su wen*. Where necessary, notes attached to the translation explain our textual choices. The currently available Chinese edition closest to our reference text is the *Huang Di nei jing su wen* 黃帝內經素問 published by Ren min wei sheng chu ban she 人民衛生出版社, Beijing 1963, 5ᵗʰ printing, 1983. For easy reference and comparison of the Chinese with our English version, the entire Chinese reference text is reprinted and available in Hermann Tessenow and Paul U. Unschuld, *A Dictionary of the Huang Di Nei Jing Su Wen*, published by University of California Press in 2003 as the second volume of the *Huang Di nei jing su wen* project. To permit a rapid location, in the Chinese reference text, of any given section of our translation, we have divided the English text and the Chinese reference text by numbers referring to the pages and lines of the 1983 edition of the *Huang Di nei jing su wen* by Ren min wei sheng chu ban she 人民衛生出版社.

The Chinese reference text is printed, except for its division into chapters and sometimes paragraphs, without further significant structuring. In contrast, our translation has introduced numerous structural indicators leading quite often to very short lines.

Large parts of the *Su wen* were originally transmitted as rhymed couplets. Others have been compiled in rather schematic repetitions of identically or similarly structured statements; one may even speak here of tables in a modern sense. Both rhymed and tabular structures were presumably intended to facilitate oral transmission through memorization of the many rather brief individual texts that were later entered into the *Su wen*. Because of changes in character pronunciation over time the verses were not always recognizable as such in the received text of the *Su wen*. In many places, we have intended to recreate the spirit of the rhymed and tabular structures through the lengths of sentences and the word-wrap. The resulting visual appearance of the printed text permits greater clarity than an unstructured text and, hence, better comparability, for example, in cases where textual pieces written by different authors using different metric systems were added one upon the other by the compilers of the *Su wen*. Most important, though, such a structuring puts an end to one of the more serious misconceptions associated with previous attempts at providing an English version of the *Su wen*, that is the notion of a text written from begin to end as a more or less homogenous narrative.

Naturally, our translation has aimed at the *textus receptus*, not its textual predecessors. Nevertheless, at times it appeared feasible to us to hint at what we assume to be an earlier structure of a given segment of the text.

2. Structural Markers in the Translation

We have made use of markers in our translation to indicate, first, where we consider lacunae to be resulting from the loss of portions of the original text; second, where we believe there to be later additions to the original text, and third, where our translation has added wording without an exact correspondence in the Chinese text. In detail, these markers are as follows:

Assumed lacunae resulting from the loss of portions of the original text are marked by square brackets with blanks in between: [....].

Assumed additions to the original text are passages that obviously do not fit into their contexts. They may be regarded as later supplements. These are of three kinds. First, there are additions introduced by the compilers of the *Su wen*. That is, these changes were intended. We have, wherever we believe to have identified such additions, marked them with pointed brackets: < ...>. Additions to the original text may, second, be commentaries originally appearing separately from the main text (for example, by being written with smaller characters, in a different color, or between the columns of the main text). In the course of time, some of these commentaries appear to have been more or less unintentionally included in the main text. Wherever we believe this to have been the case, we have marked the passages with curly brackets: { ... }.

In addition, at times, such commentaries have been commented upon themselves, and these second generation commentaries later were included in the primary commentary. In these cases we have marked the secondary commentaries with double curly brackets: {{ ... }}.

Finally, the received text of the *Su wen* includes shorter or longer phrases that appear not to be connected to their contexts at all. These may be copy errors, or unintentional doublings of passages, or they result from an erroneous sequencing of whatever pieces of wood or other materials this portion of the text was originally written on. Such passages have been marked with reverse pointed brackets: > ... <.

It should be noted that these markings may serve only to alert to breaks in their immediate contexts. They are not meant to answer questions such as whether certain portions of the text originated from identical compilers/authors. We have not marked larger text portions, such as the introductory sections of the individual chapters and also many dialogues, that have certainly been compiled by later editors integrating older material. Hence it may well be that some of the additions to older text portions marked with pointed brackets <....> date from the same compilers who were also responsible for integrating the older materials into the introductory sections and dialogue structures.

Where the translation required an addition to construe a meaningful English sentence, or where for other reasons a supplement appears desirable, we have included our additions in square brackets: [ ]. Additional information that we considered to be required is inserted in round brackets: ( ). However, we have made use of round brackets in the text in only very few cases. For the most part, additional information required for a better understanding of a character or sequence of characters is found in the footnotes.

IV. Italics, Upper Case and Lower Case Writings of Titles and Terms

We have designated with italics Chinese titles of books and technical terms which, instead of translating, we present in *Pinyin* transcription. This does not apply to transcribed titles of book chapters and to terms such as qi, yin and yang, that have been accepted as loan words in English already.

We have capitalized the first letter of the first word of transcribed Chinese book and chapter titles.

We have used a small script to alert to commentaries added by later antique Chinese authors to the tables in *Su wen* 71.

V. Footnotes

The footnotes are designed for the most part to support a historical interpretation of the text. They do not attempt to offer an interpretation of physiological or pathological statements from a perspective of modern medical knowledge and practices. We have collected and evaluated more than 600 Chinese and Japanese monographs from the past 1600 years, and close to 3000 articles written by Chinese authors in the 20th century. Based on this we have included in the footnotes a large number of alternative views, taken from these monographs and papers, on the meaning of individual characters and shorter or longer text passages. Often the views of Chinese and Japanese commentators of the past offer alternatives to our interpretations. We have quoted them to provide readers with as much information on the different readings of the *Su wen* as possible. In many instances, the list of commentators excerpted begins with Wang Bing of the 9th century. The sequence of later commentators is not necessarily historical. For example, where commentators pursued different arguments we have placed together those with similar arguments before turning to another point of view. The bibliographic details of all monographs and papers cited in the footnotes of each of the two volumes of annotated translation are provided at the end of the respective volume. Annotated bibliographies of all the monographs and papers consulted by us, regardless of whether they found entrance in our footnotes have been added to this volume as a CD.

ANNOTATED TRANSLATION OF
SU WEN 1 THROUGH 52

Chapter 1
Discourse on the True [Qi Endowed by] Heaven[1] in High Antiquity

1-1-2

In former times there was Huang Di.

When he came to life, he had magic power like a spirit.[2]
While he was [still] weak[3], he could speak.
While he was [still] young[4], he was quick[5] of apprehension.

After he had grown up, he was sincere and skillfull.[6]
After he had matured[7], he ascended to heaven.[8]

---

1 2139/43: "The Daoists, in the *Huang ting jing* 黃庭經, have a saying 積精累氣以
為真 ("when the essence is concentrated and the qi is accumulated, this is the true
[state]"). The notion expressed here is that of essence and qi being unseparated. Now,
天真 refers to the essence qi acquired prior to one's birth; it is the primordial matter
underlying the vital activities of the human body."

2 Zhang Jiebin: "This is extreme intelligence." The following five lines are a quotation
either directly from ch.1 of the *Shi ji* of 90 B.C., from ch. 62 of the *Da Dai Li ji*,
from ch. 23 of the *Kong zi jia yu*, or from a text used by these compilations. The two
passages are identical except for the final two characters. See note 8.

3 1551/63: "In ancient times, children up to the age of 100 days were called 'weak.'"

4 Tanba: "Acording to the *Li ji*, 曲禮, the age of ten years is called 'youth.'"

5 Wang Bing: "徇 stands for 疾, 'quick.'" 1031/40: "徇 is identical with 循 in the
sense of 'complete,' 'comprehensive.' 齊 stands for 疾, 'quick.' Tanba comments: 'the
knowledge of the sage was comprehensive and his spirit was quick.'" 2753/62: "徇
stands for 侚, 'quick.'"

6 Wang Bing: "敦 stands for 信, 'sincere;' 敏 stands for 達, 'intelligent.'" Zhang Jiebin:
"敦 stands for 厚大, 'very sincere.'"

7 Most commentators interpret 成 as reference to the personal maturity of Huang
Di. In contrast, 1031/40 interprets 成 as 成道, in the sense of "having attained the
Way."

8 Wang Bing: "He casted a tripod at Tripod Lake Mountain. After he had it finished
(成), he rose to heaven in broad daylight (as an immortal)." In contrast, Zhang Jiebin
takes this story to be a fairy tale and interprets 登天 as "to die". Yu Yue argued that
Huang Di, if he had "risen to heaven", that is, if he had died, would not have been able
to ask Qi Bo any questions. Hence Yu Yue suggested to interpret 登天 as „assuming
the position of ruler" and he quoted the following statement from the *Yi jing* 易經,
Ming yi zhuan 明夷傳 to strengthen his point: 初登于天, 照四國也, „when he first

Now, he asked the Heavenly Teacher:[9]

"I have heard that
the people of high antiquity,
in [the sequence of] spring and autumn, all exceeded[10] one hundred years.
But in their movements and activities there was no weakening.
As for the people of today,
after one half of a hundred years, the movements and activities of all of them weaken.
Is this because the times are different?
Or is it that the people have lost this [ability]?"[11]

1-2-1
Qi Bo responded:
"The people of high antiquity,
those who knew the Way,[12]
they modeled [their behavior] on yin and yang[13] and
they complied with the arts and the calculations.[14]

---

ascended to heaven, he brought splendor on the four kingdoms", with „ascended to heaven" referring here to assuming the position of the ruler. Wang Hongtu et al./152 agreed. 925/11 and 1031/40 agree, most likely on the basis of an attempt to eliminate metaphysical elements from the text. Tanba Genkan argues that the end of this passage probably has been changed by Wang Bing who moved the text originally to be found in the 9th *quan* of Quan Yuanqi´s *Su wen* edition to the beginning of the *Su wen*. He adduces evidence from the almost identical passages *in the Shi ji* 史記, the *Da Dai li ji* 大戴禮記, and the *Jiayu* 家語. In all those sources, instead of 登天 the text reads 聰明, "[he was] clever." According to Tanba, Wang Bing who had a strong Daoist background changed this to 登天 in accordance with chapter 6 of the *Zhuang zi* where it is said that Huang Di "ascended to the cloudy heaven (登雲天)", and to other texts. 669/5 agrees. .

9 Wang Bing: "The 'Heavenly Master' is Qi Bo."

10 Ma Shi: "度 stands for 越, 'to surpass.'" Tanba follows the *Yu pian* 玉篇 and identifies 度 as 渡, 過, with the same meaning of 'to exceed.'"

11 Hu Shu: "人將失之耶 should be 將人失之耶. Further below the text states 將天數然也. In antiquity, 也 and 耶 were used interchangeably." See also Wang Hongtu et al./150.

12 Wang Bing: " 'To know the Way' is to know the Way of [self] cultivation."

13 Gao Jiwu/574: "法 is 效法, 'to imitate.' "

14 Wang Bing: " 'The numbers' refers to 保生之倫, 'the grand principles of protecting life.'" Ma Shi, Zhang Zhicong, *Gu dian yi zhu xuan* bianxiezu /56, and Gao Jiwu/234 agree. The *Kuang ya* states: 數 is 術. The *Han shu* 漢書, Yi wen zhi 藝文志,

[Their] eating and drinking was moderate.

[Their] rising and resting had regularity.

They did not tax [themselves] with meaningless work.[15]

Hence,

they were able to keep physical appearance and spirit together,[16]

---

states: 太史令尹咸校數術 (note: 數術 rather than 術數 as in *Su wen* 01). The commentary by Shi Gu 師古 states: "數術 refers to the books of prognostication, the art of prescribing, and to medical as well as pharmaceutical literature." The *Lei shuo* 類說, ch. 37, quotes 和 as 知. In this case, the phrase should read "They knew the arts and the calculations." Donald Harper wrote on the 數術 division of medical literature in the bibliographic section of the *Han shu*: " '*Shu shu*' is a grab bag of occult literature, including divination, demonology, and incantation. What appears to be a heterogeneous mixture makes sense when one realizes the chief criterion for classifying these books in the same division: they all concern techniques applied to dealing with particular areas of the natural world and spirit world. Thus the specialists in various fields of natural philosophy and occult knowledge were appreciated above all for the results of their *shu* 數, 'calculations', and *shu* 術, 'arts;' simultaneously, physicians were known by their *fang* 方, 'recipes', and *ji* 技, 'techniques.' " See Harper, 1998, 45f.

15 Lin Yi et al.: "Quan Yuanqi has 飲食有常節, 起居有常度, 不妄不作. The *Tai su* has this wording, too. Yang Shangshan stated: 'They chose sound and form, as well as fragrant flavors, on the basis of *li* 禮, [that is,] they were not reckless in what they observed and heard. When they moved they did so in accordance with *li*; they never performed activities beyond their province.' " 2168/6 agrees with a lengthy discussion. Hu Shu: "The [wording in the] Quan Yuanqi edition and in the version of Yang Shangshan is correct. 作 is identical with 詐, 'to pretend,' 'to deceive.' 作 was read like 胙, *zu*, in antiquity. The preceding three characters 者, 數, and 度 formed a rhyme [with 作] and they rhymed with 俱 and 去 below. When Mr. Wang changed 飲食有 常節, 起居有常度 to 飲食有節, 起居有常, the sentence structure no longer juxtaposed true and false. When he changed 不妄不作 to 不妄作勞, he misread 作 as the 作 of 作為, 'to work.' Yang Shangshan in his comment on the *Tai su* committed the same error. By linking 作 with 勞, Wang Bing completely distorted the meaning of the classic!" Following this argument, the passage should read: "In food and drinking they observed moderation. In rising and resting they observed regularity. Neither did they behave recklessly, nor did they commit any deceptive activities."

16 For an almost identical passage see *Huai nan zi* ch.2. However, in *Huai nan zi* the statement ends with the two characters 俱沒, 'perish together,' rather than with 俱 alone. "They were able to let the physical appearance (that is, the body) and spirit perish together" excludes two alternatives, that is, that the body dies while the spirit lives on or that the spirit dies while the body lives on. Both these possibilities were considered to happen and were feared. Whether the character 沒 was omitted here by mistake or purposely, or whether an educated reader, who knew this statement from the *Huai nan zi*, would consider the notion of "perish" implied in the present statement, remains open.

and to exhaust the years [allotted by] heaven.
Their life span exceeded one hundred years before they departed. [17]

The fact that people of today are different is because[18]
they take wine as an [ordinary] beverage,[19]
and they adopt absurd [behavior] as regular [behavior].[20]
They are drunk when they enter the [women's] chambers.[21]

Through their lust they exhaust their essence,
through their wastefulness they dissipate their true [qi].[22]

---

17 Wang Bing: "When physical appearance and spirit are kept together, this is identical with an endowment of utmost longevity. Because one carefully nourishes [body and spirit], one receives the true [qi] from heaven. Hence it is possible to make full use of the years allotted by heaven. 去 is to say: to leave the physical appearance. The *Ling shu* states: With the age of one hundred, the five depots are all depleted and all their spirit qi have departed. Only the physical appearance is left and its existence has reached its end. Because [the people in antiquity] knew the Way, their lifetime was extended. "Exceeded one hundred years" is to say, they turned one hundred and twenty years old. The *Shang shu*, Hong fan, 商書洪範, states: 'The first is named longevity.' [The commentary of Kong Anguo says:] 'That is 120 years of age.' (cf. Ruan Yuan 193 above)"

18 Wang Bing: "They have left the Way."

19 Wang Bing: "They are over-fond of drinking [wine]."

20 Wang Bing: "They show little fidelity." 526/6 follows *Jia yi jing* 甲乙經, ch. 11, nr. 7 and identifies 妄 as 安, in the sense of "leisure." In this case the passage should read: "They adopt leisure as a regular pursuit."

21 Wang Bing: "They indulge in too much sex." 666/41 points out that in symmetry with the preceding and the following passages 醉以 should be 以醉. 669/5 disagrees.

22 Wang Bing: "樂色, 'to take pleasure in sex,' is called 欲, 'desire.' 輕用, 'frivolous use,' is called 耗. To find pleasure in sex is called 'lust.' To make frivolous use [of one's essence] is called 'wastefulness.' If one takes pleasure in sex without limits, then one's essence will be exhausted. If one makes frivolous use [of one's essence] without end, then the true qi will be dissipated. Hence it is because the sages cherished [their] essence and carefully considered its use that their bones were full of marrow and strong. Lao zi has said: '[The Sages] weaken their wills and strengthen their bones.'" Lin Yi et al.: "The *Jia yi jing* has 好, 'to love,' 'to be fond of,' instead of 耗." 925/11 and Fang Wenhui/110 agree. In contrast, 669 relates 耗散 to all four preceding examples of misbehavior and interpretes these two characters as a consequence: "they waste and dissipate their true [qi]." Yu Yue: "The interpretation [of 耗] as 好, 'desire,' is correct. The meanings of 好 and 欲 are very close. 'Through their lust they exhaust their essence; through their desires they dissipate their true qi' is an identical meaning expressed in two different sentences. With the present wording 耗散其真 the purpose

They do not know how to maintain fullness and
they engage their spirit when it is not the right time.[23]
They make every effort to please their hearts, [but]
they oppose the [true] happiness of life.[24]
Rising and resting miss their terms.

Hence,
it is [only] one half of a hundred [years] and they weaken.[25]

---

of this statement is unclear. Wang Bing's comment is based on the error in the main
text." Wang Hongtu et al./153 agrees.

23 Wang Bing: "That is to say, they make frivolous use of and give free rein to their
desires. The *Lao zi* has stated: 持而盈之不如其已. That is to say: to cherish [one's]
essence and to protect the true [qi] (see *Lao zi* ch. 9) is like holding a vessel filled [with
liquid]. If one moves it without care it will turn over and the true [qi endowed by]
heaven will be spilled. *Zhen gao* 真誥 has stated: 'If one is unable to be continuously
careful in his activities, all kinds of diseases will arise. How could this be blamed on
the spirit-brilliance?' This is meant here." Lin Yi et al.: "Another version has 解 instead
of 時." Hu Shu: "The character 時 is correct; 解 is a mistake. 時 is identical with 善.
People in later times missed the present meaning of 時 and erroneously changed it
[to 解]." 925/12 follows Hu Shu in interpreting 時 as 善, "to be good at ...", a usage
of 時 attested in the *Shi jing* 詩經, Xiao ya 小雅, already. 2168/5 agrees and adduces
further evidence. Shen Zumian: "When Hu Shu followed the *Guang ya* to interpret
時 as 善, he was wrong. 時 should be interpreted as 期, in the sense of 'period.'"
Zhang Yizhi et al.: "時 should be interpreted as 待, in the sense of 'to stop.' .. These
two characters were pronounced identically in high antiquity. 御 has the meaning of
用, 'to employ.' 不時御神 has the meaning of 'they never ceased using the spirit.'"
Zhang Jiebin: "御 is 統御, 'to govern.'" Zhang Zhicong: "不時御神 is 不能四時調
御其神, 'unable to regulate his spirit.'" 699/12 reads 御 as 御用, "to manage," in the
sense of "they fail to use their essence spirit economically." Wang Shaozeng/213 and
Wang Shaozeng & Xu Yongnian/103 propose a missing character between 不 and 時,
that is: 按: "they did not guard their spirit in accordance with the [requirements of
the] seasons." Qian Chaochen-90/137: "御 is used here in the sense of 治, 'to order,'
主持, 'to direct.'"

24 Wang Bing: "To find pleasure in realizing one's heart's desires is to counteract the
happiness that can be obtained by nourishing one's life. *Lao zi* has stated: 'Extreme
love must result in great expenditure.'" 522/43 interprets 生樂 as 生活上的正常規律,
"the proper laws to be obeyed in life." In this case this passage should be read: "They
act contrary to the proper laws to be obeyed in life."

25 Wang Bing: "This state, too, is reached because of a dissipation [of the true qi].
Now, the Way – it cannot be left even for a short moment! To part from the Way results in an inability to make full use of the entire life span of years allotted by heaven.
Lao zi has stated: 'When something is strong, it will age,' and he termed this as 'not
the Way.' 'Not the Way' means to perish early. That is meant by 'to part from the Way.'"

1-3-2

Now,

when the sages of high antiquity taught those below,
they always spoke to them [about the following]. [26]

The depletion evil[27] and the robber wind,[28]
there are [specific] times when to avoid them.[29]
Quiet peacefulness, absolute emptiness
the true qi follows [these states].
When essence and spirit are guarded internally,
where could a disease come from?[30]

Hence,
the mind is relaxed and one has few desires.
The heart is at peace and one is not in fear.
The physical appearance is taxed, but is not tired. [31]

---

26 Lin Yi et al.: "The version commented by Quan Yuanqi has 上古聖人之教也
下皆為之, 'as for the teachings of the sages in high antiquity; all those below prac-
tised them.' The *Tai su* and the *Qian jin* have the same wording. Yang Shangshan
stated: 'When the Sages in high antiquity made people practice [something], they
themselves practiced it first. That was a teaching without words. A teaching without
words is superior to a teaching with words. It is therefore that all the people acted
accordingly. Hence, [the text] states: 'all those below practiced them.'" 2168/5 agrees
on the basis of further evidence. Hu Shu: "The wording in the Quan Yuanqi edition is
correct. 下皆為之 is 下皆化之, 'all those below transformed them.' .. Mr. Wang failed
to understand this. Hence, he exchanged the positions of 下 and 也, making 上古聖
人之教下也 a sentence, and linking the three characters 皆謂之 to the [eight charac-
ters] following below. He missed the meaning of the [original passage]."

27 Wang Bing: "When an evil takes advantage of a depletion to enter this [void], this
is called 'depletion evil.'" For a detailed discussion, see 428/7.

28 Wang Bing: "To intrude and injure equilibrium and harmony, that is called 'robber
wind.'"

29 Zhang Wenhu: "These three sentences do not fit into the text preceding and following them. Maybe some text has been omitted here."

30 Wang Bing: "恬惔虛無 is 靜, 'quiet.' If one follows the Way in all honesty and if,
therefore, the essence is kept inside, no evil qi is able to cause harm." Zhang Zhicong:
"'Empty nothingness' is 'not to be confused by items and desires.'" 2821/20 discusses
this concept in detail.

31 Wang Bing: "The inner mechanism is at rest, hence, the desires are few. The connections to the outer sphere are quiet, hence, the heart is at peace. Thus, affects and
desires have left, right and wrong form one line, and rising and resting are appropriate.
Hence, [the body may be taxed but] is not tired."

The qi follows [its appropriate course] and therefrom results compliance:
everything follows one's wishes;
in every respect one achieves what one longs for.[32]

1-3-5
Hence,
they considered their food delicious, [33]
they accepted their clothes,[34] and
they enjoyed the common.[35]
Those of higher and those of lower status did not long for each other.
The people, therefore, were called natural.[36]

Hence,
cravings and desires could not tax their eyes.
The excess evil could not confuse their hearts.

---

32 Wang Bing: "The mind is not covetous, hence, all desires are appropriate. The
heart is easily satisfied, hence, all demands must be fulfilled. Since there are no ex-
travagant requests, it is not difficult to meet them."

33 Wang Bing: "No matter whether it was fine or crude, they accepted it." Lin Yi et
al.: "Another version has 甘, 'sweet,' instead of 美." See *Lao zi, Dao de jing* 80, for an
almost identical statement.

34 Wang Bing: "No matter whether they were nice or bad, they went along with
them."

35 Wang Bing: "They eliminated all admiration [for the sophisticated]."

36 Wang Bing: "They had reached a state of no request. That is the so-called 'satisfaction of the heart.' Lao zi has stated: 'There is no greater catastrophy than not to know
satisfaction. And there is no greater calamity than to long for gains. Hence, those who
know the satisfaction of satisfaction, they will be satisfied constantly.' Hence, those
who do not speak of being satisfied with material items, they have knowledge of [true]
satisfaction. Those who are satisfied in their hearts, they know satisfaction. Not to give
free rein to desires, this is identical with the natural state of things. Hence, the Sages
stated: As long as we have no desires, the people will remain in a natural state." Lin Yi
et al.: "Another version has 日 instead of 曰." Lin Yi et al. may have had in mind here
Qian jin fang 千金方, ch. 27, nr. 1, where this passage reads: 故其民日朴, "the people
turned simpler day by day." 526/6 reads 曰 as 自, "from," "hence", and consideres the
character 日 in the *Qian jin fang* as a mistake, too. In this case the passage should read
"Hence, the people were simple." Gao Jiwu/176 and Gao Jiwu/606 reads: "故 is 固 in
the sense of 本來, 'formerly.' 曰 is 為, 'to be.'" In this case the passage should read: "In
former times people were simple." For a detailed discussion see 2705/59ff.

The stupid and the knowledgeable, the exemplary and the non-exemplary,
none was in fear of other beings.[37]

Hence,
they were one with the Way.

That by which all of them were able to exceed a lifespan of one hundred years,
while their movements and activities did not weaken,
[that was the fact that] their virtue was perfect and they did not meet with
danger."[38]

1-4-4
[Huang] Di:
"When someone is old in years and no [longer] has children,
is it that his strength is exhausted?[39]
Or is it that the heavenly numbers[40] are such?"[41]

Qi Bo:
"In a female,
at the age[42] of seven,

37 Gao Jiwu/574: "They did not suffer from gain or loss of external things." Following usages of 物 in the *Zuo zhuan*, 1551/64 proposes: "物 stands for 類, 'class.'" In
this case the passage would read: "No one cared whether he was classed as stupid or
knowledgable, exemplary or non-exemplary."

38 Wang Bing: "They never entered a dangerous situation. Hence, their virtue remained perfect. *Zhuang zi* has stated: 'Those who stick to the Way, their virtue is perfect. Those whose virtue is perfect, their physical appearance is perfect. Those whose
physical appearance is perfect, they have found the Way of the sages.' (See *Zhuang zi*
12 天地 , Chen Guying p. 351.) Further it is said: 'That someone refrained from active
interference and still did not enjoy a full life, this has never happened so far.'"

39 Wang Bing: "材 is 材幹, that is, the ability keep one's body standing upright."
JJZG: "材 is identical with 才. 材 (才) is 用, 'function.'"

40 Ma Shi: "These are all the numbers bestowed upon man by heaven." 1551/65:
" 'Numbers of heaven' is identical with 'the Way of heaven.'

41 Hu Shu: "將 is 抑, initial particle." Shen Zumian: "Hu Shu is wrong; 將 must not
be interpreted as 抑. 將 is 順, 'to comply with.'" Zhang Yizhi et al.: "Both sentences
are questions. Hence, to interpret 將 as 抑 is in accordance with the meaning. As for
材, the *Shuo wen* 說文 states '力 is 筋, 'sinew.'" Hence, 材力 ought to refer to the qi
of the kidneys."

42 384/58 points out that the character 歲 was used in the sense of "years of life" not
before the Han dynasty.

the qi of the kidneys abounds.
The [first] teeth are substituted and
the hair grows long.

With two times seven,
the heaven *gui*[43]
arrives,[44]
the controlling vessel is passable and

---

43 Wang Bing: "癸 is to say 壬癸, this is the water of the North, the name of one of the [heavenly] branches. The controlling vessel and the thoroughfare vessel are both extraordinary conduit vessels. When the qi of the kidneys is complete and abundant, the thoroughfare and the controlling vessel are passed by a flow. The menstrual blood gradually accumulates and moves down when its time comes. The thoroughfare is the sea of blood; the controlling [vessel] governs uterus and fetus. When both supply each other one may have children." Zhang Jiebin: "All [earlier] authors have explained the term 天癸 as referring to [male] essence and [female] blood. But if we analyse the text, where it states: 'In females, with two times seven the 天癸 arrives; .. the monthly affair moves down periodically. In males, with two times eight, the 天癸 arrives; .. the essence qi flows off,' then in both cases the 天癸 comes first and is then followed by essence and blood, respectively. There is a clear differentiation between what comes first and what comes second; each has its own meaning. How then could anyone say that 天癸 is essence and blood, or that blood and essence are 天癸! 癸, now, is the water of heaven; it is the name of a [heavenly] stem. The stems are the yang of the branches. The designation for the yang is qi. 癸 is the mate of 壬; the designation for the mate is yin. Hence, 天癸 refers to the yin qi of 天一. This qi changes to water. Hence, it is named 天癸." Ma Shi: "天癸 is the yin essence. The reason is, the kidneys belong to the water; the 癸, too, belongs to the water. It is generated from an accumulation of qi of the earlier dependencies." 2756/43: "The text of 上古天真論 does not have the two characters 天真. But these two characters in the title must have been taken from the contents of this treatise. Hence, we cannot but conclude that the two characters 天癸 must be a mistake for 天真." 925/13 agrees. 2756/44 and 2757/43 go further and interpret 天 as referring here to the "head" as opposed to 地 which, in the phrase 地道, 'the Way of the earth,' refers to the kidneys. Hence, according to 2756 and 2757, "heaven" and "earth" signify "above" and "below," that is, head and kidneys/genital region, in the body. *Su wen* 05 has 天地者萬物之上下也, "Heaven and earth constitute above and below of all creatures." Accordingly, 天真 is a "true qi produced in the brain of the head." Such a concept, though, is attested nowhere else. Yang Shangshan: "天癸 is the essence qi." Zhongyi yanjiuyuan...: " 'Heaven' stands for 天一; 癸 is one of the ten branches; it belongs to [the agent of] water. Tian yi generates water; hence, the name is 天癸, 'water of heaven.' " See also 1343.

44 496/54 quotes earlier commentators who have interpreted 至 here as 充, "full," "complete," and agrees on the basis that a meaning of "complete" is the opposite of 竭, "exhausted", further down. In this case the passage should read: "when the true [qi of] heaven is complete." See also 1530.

the great thoroughfare vessel[45] abounds [with qi].
The monthly affair moves down in due time and,
hence, [a woman] may have children.[46]

With three times seven,
the qi of the kidneys has reached its normal level.
Hence, the wisdom teeth[47] emerge and
[females] grow to their full size.

With four times seven,
the sinews and bones are firm and
the hair has grown to its full extent.
The body and the limbs are in a state of abundance and strength.

With five times seven,
the yang brilliance vessel weakens;
the face begins to dry out;
the hair begins to fall off. [48]

With six times seven,
the three yang vessels weaken {in the upper sections}.
The face is all parched, [49]
the hair begins to turn white.[50]

---

45 Lin Yi et al.: "Quan Yuanqi and *Tai su*, as well as *Jia yi jing*, have 伏衝之脈, 'vessel of the hidden thoroughfare.'" 925/14 identifies "great thoroughfare vessel" as "thoroughfare vessel." Yu Yue: "In the Han-era, the character 太 was occasionally written 伏. ... Later on, people did not recognize this character. They added a dot and wrote it as 伏, creating a different character."

46 Wang Bing: "What is called 'monthly affair' is a normal, harmonious qi that appears regularly every thirtieth day. When this period is extended, the [respective woman] is said to have a disease."

47 Wang Bing: "These are the teeth that grow at the very end. When the kidney qi is balanced and the wisdom teeth grow, that shows that the teeth are extensions of the bones." Tanba: "真 is identical with 齻."

48 Wang Bing: "The yang brilliance vessel supplies the face with qi. Hence, when it weakens, the hair falls off and the face dries out."

49 Zhang Yizhi et al.: "焦 is 憔, 'worn out by grief.' The *Han shu* 漢書, Xuzhuan 敘傳, states: 朝為榮華, 夕而焦瘁. 焦瘁 is 憔瘁, 'worn out by grief.'"

50 Wang Bing: "All the three yang vessels extend upwards to the head. Hence, when the three yang vessels weaken, then the face is all dried out and the hair begins to turn white. The reason for their weakness lies in the nature of females. They have a surplus

With seven times seven,
the controlling vessel is depleted and
the great thoroughfare vessel is weak and [its contents are] diminished.
The heaven *gui* is exhausted.

The way of the earth is impassable.
Hence, the physical appearance is spoilt and [a woman can] no [longer] have
children.⁵¹

1-5-4
In a male,
at the age of eight,
the qi of the kidneys is replete;
his hair grows and
the [initial] teeth are substituted.

With two times eight,
the qi of the kidneys abounds;⁵²
the heaven *gui* arrives and
the essence qi flows away.
Yin and yang find harmony. ⁵³
Hence, he can have children.

With three times eight,
the qi of the kidneys has reached its normal level.
The sinews and the bones are firm and strong.
Hence, the wisdom teeth emerge and
[men] grow to their full size.

---

of qi and a deficiency of blood, because [the latter] is frequently drained by way of
menstruation."

51 Wang Bing: "The menstruation stops. This is called 'the way of the earth is impassable.' Both the thoroughfare and the controlling [vessel] weaken. Hence, [the text]
states: the physical appearance is spoilt and a woman can no longer have children."

52 Gao Jiwu/236: "Guo Aichun-92 considers the three characters 腎氣盛 to be a
later addition."

53 Most Chinese authors interpret 陰陽和 as a reference to the sexual union of man
and woman. In contrast, the Japanese commentator 喜多村: "That is to say, in males,
with two times eight [years], yin and yang, that is, qi and blood, are blended harmoniously." 925 agrees.

With four times eight,
the sinews and the bones prosper in abundance.
The muscles and the flesh are full and strong.

With five times eight,
the qi of the kidneys weakens;
the hair falls off and
the teeth wither.

With six times eight,
the yang qi weakens and is exhausted in the upper sections.
The face dries out and
the hair on the head and on the temples shows streaks of white.[54]

With seven times eight,
the qi in the liver weakens;
the sinews can no longer move.[55]
The heaven *gui* is exhausted.
{The [remaining] essence is diminished}
The kidney depot is weak and
the physical body is completely exhausted.[56]

With eight times eight,
the teeth and the hair go.
The kidneys rule the water;
they receive the essence from the five depots and six palaces and they store it.
Hence, when there is abundance in the five depots, [essence] can flow away.
[At this age] now the five depots are all weak and the sinews and the bones
have become sluggish.

54 Tanba: "*Meng zi* has 頌白. Zhao Qi 趙崎 commented: 頌 is 斑, 'streaks.' That is,
half of the hair consists of white streaks." Zhang Yizhi et al.: "The *Tai ping sheng hui
fang* 太平聖惠方, quoting [this passage from the *Su wen*] does not have the character
頌. Neither does the character 頌 appear in Wang Bing's comment."

55 According to Ma Kanwen, the following text is "an example of obvious disar-
rangement of the original bamboo strips." He suggests to insert here the two characters 八八 from further below. See Ma Kanwen p.11.

56 Wang Bing: "The qi of the liver nourishes the sinews. [Now] the liver is weak,
hence, the sinews can no longer move. The qi of the kidneys nourishes the bones.
[Now] the kidneys are weak, hence, the body is extremely tired. The heaven *gui* is
exhausted. Hence, only little essence is left." Zhang Yizhi et al.: "The *Han shu* 漢書,
Xiong nu zhuan xia 匈奴傳下, states: 極 is 困, 'distress.' In a commentary to the *Lü
shi chun qiu* 呂氏春秋, Shi yin 適音, Gao You 高誘 stated: 極 is 病, 'disease.'"

The heaven *gui* is used up entirely.
Hence, the hair on the head and on the temples turns white and the body and
the limbs are heavy.
[A male of that age] no [longer] walks upright and no [longer] has children."

1-6-4
[Huang] Di:
"It happens that someone who is already old in years nevertheless has children,
how can that be?"

Qi Bo:
"In this case the life span [allotted] by heaven exceeds the norm.[57]
The qi passes through the vessels as usual and
the qi of the kidneys has a surplus.
Although [someone] has children,
males do not exceed the end reached at eight times eight and
females do not exceed the end reached at seven times seven,
when the essence qi of heaven and earth are all exhausted."[58]

[Huang] Di:
"Now,
those [who follow] the Way,
they all reach a number of one hundred years.
Can they have children?"

Qi Bo:
"Now,
those [who follow] the Way,
they can drive away old age and
they preserve their physical appearance.

---

57 Wang Bing: "That is, the true qi allotted by heaven is present in surplus from the
very beginning."

58 Wang Bing: "If one is old and begets children, the age of the children will not
exceed the numerical limits set by the heaven *gui*." In contrast to Wang Bing, most
later commentators have interpreted the phrase "when the essence qi of heaven and
earth are all exhausted" as characterizing the person who has children at a high age.
522/43 notices a contradiction here, because this same person is said to have a surplus
of kidney qi. On the basis of the meaning of "to carry" attested for 竭 in the *Shuo
wen* 說文 and other sources, Guan Jisheng suggests a meaning of "load", "stress" here:
"males who are beyond eight times eight, and females who are beyond seven times
seven, perceive reproduction as stress on their vigor." See also 772/34.

Although their body has lived a long life,
they are [still] able to produce children." [59]

1-6-10
Huang Di:
"I have heard,
in high antiquity there were true men.[60]
They upheld [the patterns of] heaven and earth and
they grasped [the regularity of] yin and yang.
They exhaled and inhaled essence qi. [61]
They stood for themselves and guarded their spirit.
Muscles and flesh were like one. [62]

Hence,
they were able to achieve longevity, in correspondence with heaven and earth.
There was no point in time when [their life could have] come to an end. [63]
Such was their life in the Way. [64]

---

59 Wang Bing: "These are the so-called people who have attained the Way."

60 Wang Bing: "True men are those who have attained the Way." For classic definitions of the "true men" see 莊子, 大宗師, and 淮南子, 本經訓, as well as 史記, 始皇
本紀.

61 442/34: " 'Exhaling and inhaling essence qi' is one of the ancient methods of
nourishing life. Another name is 行氣, 'to move the qi.' " See also 莊子, 刻意篇.

62 Lin Yi et al.: "Quan Yuanqi has 身肌宗一 instead of 肌肉若一; the *Tai su*, too.
Yang Shangshan comments: Muscles and stature of the true man's body are of identical quality with the Uppermost Pole. Hence, [the text] states: 'are of one kind with
the One.' "

63 Wang Bing: "Their body paralleled the Way and their longevity paralleled the Way.
Hence, they were able to live for an endless time in that their long life lasted through
the entire [existence of] heaven and earth. 敝 stands for 盡, 'to exhaust entirely.' " On
the basis of Huang's 皇 commentary on 論語, 為政 (蔽, 當也), *NJCD* explains 敝
as identical here with 蔽 in the meaning of 相當, "corresponding." In this case, the
passage reads: "Hence, they were able to have a long life corresponding to heaven and
earth." Gao Jiwu/9 agrees. Shen Zumian: "The character 敝 is a mistake; maybe this
should be the character 敵, 'to oppose.' Elsewhere it is stated that 敝 should be 適, 'to
correspond,' because 敝 and 適 have often been exchanged for each other in antiquity.
However, on the basis of character similarity, it should be 敵." In this case the passage
should read: "They were able to obtain longevity despite the limitations imposed by
heaven and earth on the lifespan of man." Such an interpretation is in keeping with
the following sentence.

64 Zhang Qi: "These four characters are an erroneous insertion." Zhang Yizhi et al.:
"These four characters make no sense; there must be an erroneous omission."

At the time of middle antiquity,
there were the accomplished men.
They were of pure virtue and they were entirely in accord with the Way. [65]
They adapted themselves to [the regularity] of yin and yang and
they lived in harmony with the four seasons.
They left the world and they departed from the common.[66]
They accumulated essence and preserved their spirit.
They roamed between heaven and earth and
their vision as well as their hearing went beyond the eight reaches.
This way, they added to their lifespan and were strong.
They, too, may be counted among the true men.

1-7-4
Next, there were the sages.
They lived in harmony with heaven and earth and
they followed the patterns of the eight winds. [67]
They accomodated their cravings and their desires within the world and the
common and their heart knew no anger.

In their activities they had no desire to disassociate themselves from the world;
in their <clothing and> bearing they had no desire to be observed by the common people. [68]

---

65 Lin Yi et al.: "Quan Yuanqi has 合于道數." 497/34 agrees on the basis that the
surrounding text abounds with "daoist" notions and identifies 道數 as "daoist arts and
numbers."

66 Gao Shishi: "With their body they were part of the customs of their days; with
their heart they transcended the customs of their days."

67 A concept referring to winds originating in the eight cardinal points East, South,
West, North, East-North, East-South, West-South, and West-North. See also *Suwen*
26, note 21.

68 At first glance, the three characters 被服章 make no sense here, and they do not
fit into the metrical structure of the preceding and the two following lines which are
composed of six characters each. Lin Yi et al. and various later commentators agree
that they represent accidental amendations. In contrast, 1715/80 proposes to move
被服章 in front of the line before last, 無恚嗔之心, to create two parallel strings of
eight characters with similar structure (適嗜 .. 之間 and 被服 .. 之心) and identifies
被 as preposition, reads 服 in the sense of 遵守, "to observe," and 章 in the sense of 章
法, 'law.' The entire eight character passage should read, according to 1715/80: "they
observed the constraints of the laws and had no angry feelings." 1208/131 leaves the
three characters 被服章 at their place and sees a string of four characters 被服章舉.
He identifies 章 as 彰, 'to display,' and, on the basis of 國語, 周語下, 舉 as 譽, 'praise.'
1208/131 reads the entire passage from 被 to 俗 as: "In the style and color of their

Externally, they did not tax their physical appearance with any affairs;
internally, they did not suffer from any pondering.

They made every effort to achieve peaceful relaxation and
they considered self-realization as success.
Their physical body did not deteriorate and
their essence and their spirit did not dissipate.
They, too, could reach a number of one hundred [years].

1-8-2
Next, there were the exemplary men.
They took heaven as law and the earth as rule;
their appearance resembled sun and moon.
They distinguished among and arranged the stars
[on the basis of their] movements contrary to or following [the movements of]
yin and yang. [69]
They distinguished among the four seasons.
They went along with high antiquity and
they acted in complete union with the Way.
They, too, were able to add to their long life and
to have their full time."

---

clothing they did not display the fashions of their days." 475/41 identifies 被 with 剪,
"to eliminate," and reads 服章 as 章服, "official dress," in the sense of "strict hierarchic
order." In this case the passage would read: "The Sages did away with rigid hierar-
chies." We consider the two characters 被服, 'clothing', a later insertion intended to
elaborate on the following statement. 章 was added to form together with 舉 a parallel
two character compound, 'bearing'.

69 Wang Bing: "星 refers to all the stars; 辰 refers to the pole star. 辯列 is to say: they
defined the sequence of the more distant and not so distant positions occupied by the
stars in the course of 365 days. 'They went against or they followed yin and yang' is
to say: by conducting an opposing and/or regular counting based on the six *jia* 六甲
[pattern] and other patterns they figured out subtle omens of luck or misfortune. *The
Yin Yang Scripture* 陰陽書 states: the *jia zi* 甲子 [cycle] of man and center starts from
jia zi 甲子 and is followed by *yi chou* 乙丑, etc., counting in accordance with the usual
sequence. The *jia zi* [cycle] of the earth and of that below starts from *jia xu* 甲戌 and
is followed by *gui you* 癸酉, counting against the usual sequence. That is meant by
'they went against or they followed yin and yang.'"

Chapter 2
Comprehensive Discourse on Regulating the Spirit
[in Accordance with] the Qi of the Four [Seasons]

2-8-6
The three months of spring,
they denote effusion and spreading.[1]
Heaven and earth together generate life;
the myriad beings flourish.[2]

Go to rest late at night[3] and rise early.[4]
Move through the courtyard with long strides.[5]
Dishevel the hair[6] and relax the physical appearance,[7]
thereby cause the mind [to orient itself on] life.

Give life and do not kill.
Give and do not take.
Reward and do not punish.

---

1 Wang Bing: "In spring the yang rises. The qi that was hidden [in winter] spreads out. It gives birth to all kinds of beings and displays their beautiful appearance. Hence, this is called 'outbreak and display.'" 2095/44: "發 stands for 揚, 'to spread,' 'to flourish.' 陳 stands for 布, 'to spread.'" In contrast, Zhang Zhicong: "發 stands for 啟, 'to open.' 陳 stands for 故, 'old.' The meaning is: 'to break up the old and follow the new.'" Yang Shangshan: "發 stands for 舊. That is, during the three months of spring all the old roots and old seeds of herbs and trees break out again." Tanba: "發陳 has the meaning of 發散, 'to spread,' and 陳敷, 'to distribute.' Zhang Zhicong interprets 陳 as 故. However, given the wordings 蕃秀 and 容平 below, the text obviously refers to qi. Hence, Wang Bing's commentary must be correct." Sun Yirang: "發陳 has the meaning of 'to break open the old and substitute it by the new.' Wang Bing's commentary missed this meaning." Zhang Yizhi et al.: "陳 is 舊, 'old.' 發陳 is: to eliminate the old and bring forth the new."

2 Wang Bing: "The qi of heaven is warm, the qi of the earth breaks out. The warmth [of the qi of heaven] and the outbreak [of the qi of the earth] merge. Hence, the myriad beings are nourished and flourish."

3 The *Tai su* has 晚, "late", instead of 夜.

4 Wang Bing: "Warm qi generates life; cold qi disperses. Hence, one goes to rest at night and rises early."

5 Zhang Zhicong equates 廣 with 緩, "leisurely."

6 Gao Jiwu/22 and others interpret 被 as 披, "to open", "to unroll."

7 Zhang Jiebin identifies 緩形 as 舉動和緩, "relaxed behavior."

This is correspondence with the qi of spring and
it is the Way to nourish life.

Opposing it harms the liver.
In summer, this causes changes to cold,[8] and
there is little to support growth. [9]

2-9-3
The three months of summer,
they denote opulence and blossoming.[10]
The qi of heaven and earth interact and
the myriad beings bloom and bear fruit.

Go to rest late at night and rise early.
Never get enough of the sun.[11]
Let the mind have no anger.
Stimulate beauty and have your elegance perfected.[12]

---

8 Zhang Zhicong: "When the wood is harmed, it cannot produce fire. Hence, in summer, which is the time when fire is in command, there are changes contrary [to the normal course of seasons] which generate cold disease."

9 Wang Bing: "逆 is to say: to carry out the orders of autumn in contrast [to the requirements of spring]. The liver corresponds to wood and flourishes in spring. Hence, to carry out the orders of autumn [in spring] causes harm to the qi of the liver. In summer fire flourishes and wood perishes. Hence, the disease develops in summer. Now, as for the qi of the four seasons, the qi of spring generates life and the qi of summer contributes to growth. If one counteracts [the orders of] spring and harms the liver, this results in diminished qi [with a reduced ability] to receive the order of growth in summer."

10 Wang Bing: "The generation of yang [qi] begins with spring. When it comes to summer, [the yang qi] abounds and all beings grow. Hence, [the text speaks of] 蕃秀. 蕃 is 茂, 'luxuriance,' 盛, 'abundance.' 秀 is 華, 'blooming,' 美, 'beauty.' "

11 Zhang Qi: "厭 is 倦, 'tired.' " Cheng Shide et al./23: "無厭于日 is to say: in summer the days are long and mankind does not get tired. That is, in summer the qi of growth rules, hence, the human qi should not be idle." Zhang Yizhi et al.: "厭 is 飽, 'satisfied.' 無厭于日 is: not satisfied with the work of one day." 542 interprets 壓日 as 安日, "to wait for the sun." See also 2770.

12 Cheng Shide et al./23: "The *Er ya* states: [The blossoms of] trees are called 華, those of herbs are called 榮. When there are fruits but no herbal blossoms, this is called 秀; when there are herbal blossoms but no fruits, this is called 英. Zhang Jiebin: "華英 is to say 神氣, 'spirit qi.' " Cheng Shide et al.: "成 is 盛, 'abundance.' "

Cause the qi to flow away,[13]
as if that what you loved were located outside.[14]

This is correspondence with the qi of summer and
it is the Way to nourish growth.
Opposing it harms the heart.[15]
In autumn this causes *jie* and malaria,[16] and
there is little to support gathering.
>Multiple disease [develops] at winter solstice.<[17]

2-10-1
The three months of autumn,

---

13 Shen Zumian: "This statement should follow the characters 使志無怒."

14 Wang Bing: "Mild yang qi causes the transformation of beings; a gentle mind causes qi to flow off. When the beings transform, then they bloom and abound. When the qi flows off, then the skin interstices open. The order of the season is to disperse yang. Hence, that what one loves goes along with the yang and is outside." Ma Shi: "When there is no anger, the qi risks being depressed. One must allow this qi to flow off."

15 Wang Bing: "逆 is to say: to carry out the orders of winter in contrast [to the requirements of summer]. The heart corresponds to fire and flourishes in summer. Hence, to carry out [in summer] the orders of winter this harms the qi of the heart. In autumn the metal flourishes and the fire perishes. Hence, the disease develops in autumn. Now, as for the qi of the four seasons, the qi of autumn gathers and the qi of winter stores. If one opposes [the orders of] summer and harms the heart, this results in diminished qi [with a reduced ability] to receive the order of gathering in autumn. The water of winter overcomes the fire [of summer]. Hence, at the time of winter solstice a serious disease develops."

16 The term *jie* 痎 appears four times in the *Su wen*, always in conjunction with *nüe* 瘧. *Jie* may have been a term for intermittent fevers breaking out every second day; *nüe* may have been used initially for all types of intermittent fevers. In later times, *nüe* was the only term used for what today is called malaria disease. The *SWJZ* defines 痎 as: "Every second day a malaria fever (瘧) breaks out once." Zhang Jiebin: "When the heart is harmed, the qi of summerheat avails itself [of the heart]. In autumn then, the qi of metal draws [everything] in and the evil of summerheat is depressed internally. Now the yin wishes to enter, but the yang wards it off. Hence, there is cold. The fire wishes to leave, but the yin ties it down. Hence, there is heat. Metal and fire struggle with each other. Hence, fits of cold and heat alternate and this is malaria."

17 Shen Zumian: "The four characters 冬至重病 do not fit the meaning of the text preceding and following them. They may be an erroneous insertion." Tanba had expressed the same opinion.

they denote taking in and balance.[18]
The qi of heaven becomes [19] tense.[20]
The qi of the earth becomes bright.

Go to rest early and rise early,
get up together with the chicken.[21]
Let the mind be peaceful and tranquil, so as
to temper the punishment carried out in autumn.[22]
Collect the spirit qi and
cause the autumn qi to be balanced.[23]
Do not direct your mind to the outside and
cause the lung qi to be clear.[24]

---

18 Wang Bing: "In summer the myriad beings grow and blossoms as well as fruits
have reached completion. Their 容狀, 'appearance,' does no longer change and is fixed
by autumn." Ma Shi: "The yin qi has started to rise already and the appearance of all
beings is finally determined. Hence, the image of the qi [in autumn] is called 'appearance settled.'" 2095: "容 is 收納, 'to take in,' and 平 is 平治, 'in peaceful order.'" Fang
Wenhui/110 identifies 容 as 搈 with the meaning of "movement", and 平 as 止, "to
stop", 靜, "quiet." In this case, the passage should read: "The three months of autumn,
this means: any movement ceases." Zhang Yizhi et al.: "Tanba interprets 容 as 盛,
'abundance.' This argument is based on the *Shuo wen*. The commentary in the *Sheng
ji jing* 聖濟經 states: 'At ease (容) and without hurry; balanced (平) and without bias.
That is to say 容平.' This is correct."

19 Gao Jiwu/568: "The *Guang shi ci* 廣釋詞 states: 以 is identical with 益, 'to increase.' It has the meaning here of 'ever more.'"

20 Wang Bing: "Winds blow with a cutting sound."

21 Wang Bing: "One fears to be struck by cold and dew. Hence, one goes to sleep
early. One wishes to establish peace and tranquility. Hence, one rises early."

22 Violent storms in autumn appeared like a "punishment". This was also the season,
in ancient China, to perform executions of criminals sentenced to capital punishment.
Wang Bing: "When the mental qi is hectic, one is not careful in his activities. If one is
not careful in his activities, one accentuates the severity of autumn punishments, goes
along with killing, and destroys life. Hence, one establishes a peaceful and tranquil
mind to soften the punishments carried out in autumn."

23 Wang Bing: "When the spirit is agitated, one's desires may be set aflame. When
the desires are set aflame, this harms the harmonious qi. When the harmonious qi is
harmed, the qi of autumn is no longer balanced. Hence, one preserves one's spirit qi
and this causes the qi of autumn to be balanced." Zhang Yizhi et al.: "Earlier the text
has 容平. The repetition of the character 平 here may be a mistake for 正, 'proper.'"

24 Wang Bing: "This too is in accordance with the gathering nature of autumnal qi."
Zhang Zhicong: "To preserve the spirit qi and not let the mind be directed to the

This is correspondence with the qi of autumn and
it is the Way to nourish gathering.
Opposing it harms the lung.
In winter this causes outflow of [undigested] food and
there is little to support storage.[25]

2-11-1
The three months of winter,
they denote securing and storing.[26]
The water is frozen and the earth breaks open.

Do not disturb the yang [qi].[27]
Go to rest early and rise late.
You must wait for the sun to shine.[28]

Let the mind enter a state as if hidden,
{as if shut in}[29]
as if you had secret intentions;[30]
as if you already had made gains. [31]

---

outside, all this is to follow the qi of gathering in autumn and causes the metal of the
lung to be clear and pure."

25 Wang Bing: "逆 is to say: to carry out the orders of summer in contrast [to the
requirements of autumn]. The lung corresponds to metal and flourishes in autumn.
Hence, to carry out [in autumn] the orders of summer, this harms the qi. In winter the
water flourishes and the metal perishes. Hence, the disease develops in winter. 飧泄
refers to the outflow of undigested food. If one opposes [the orders of] autumn and
harms the lung, this results in diminished qi [with a reduced ability] to receive the
order of storage in winter."

26 Wang Bing: "Herbs and trees wither. The insects leave. The openings of the earth
close. The yang qi goes into hiding."

27 Wang Bing: "The yang qi has moved into the depth. Water freezes and the earth
cracks. Hence, it is essential to close everything tightly. One does not wish to work to
fatigue. 擾 is to say: 煩, 'annoyed,' in the sense of 勞, 'fatigue.' "

28 Wang Bing: "To avoid the cold."

29 Qian Chaochen-88/232: "Various editions have 匪 instead of 匿. Tanba Genkan
has pointed out: '匿 and 得 rhyme,' that is, 匿 and 得 both belong to the 之 group of
rhymes. Hence, 匪 must be a mistake." Hu Shu: "匪 is a mistake introduced beginning
with the Song dynasty."

30 Hu Shu: "That is to say: as if one thought [only] of oneself."

31 Wang Bing: "All this is to say one does not wish to go out needlessly lest one is
struck by cold." *Tai su*, ch. 2, "Shun yang", 順陽, has 德, 'virtue,' instead of 得. The

Avoid cold and seek warmth and
do not [allow sweat] to flow away through the skin.
This would cause the qi to be carried away quickly.[32]

This is correspondence with the qi of winter and
it is the Way of nourishing storage.
Opposing it harms the kidneys.
In spring this causes limpness with receding [qi],[33] and
there is little to support generation.[34]

2-12-1

The qi of heaven is that which is clear and pure, lustrous and brilliant.
[Heaven] stores [its] virtue without end.[35]
Hence, it does not [let its virtue] move downwards.[36]

Ishimpo 醫心方 follows the wording in the *Tai su*. Hu Shu: "己 is 私. 若私有意 and 若己有得 are parallel statements."

32 Wang Bing: " 'To avoid cold and seek warmth' is to say: one stays deep inside the house. 無泄皮膚 is to say: one avoids sweating. Sweating is dispersing yang qi. When the yang qi is dispersed one is frequently attacked by cold qi. 亟 stands for 數, 'repeatedly.' " Zhang Yizhi et al.: "The *Tai su* has 不極 instead of 亟奪. 極, 匿, and 得 rhyme. Hence, one may agree [with the *Tai su* version]." Shen Zumian: "奪 does not rhyme with 匿 and 得. Maybe the two characters 極奪 have been reversed. 極, 匿, and 得 rhyme." *SWJZ*: "亟is 敏疾, 'fast.' " Gao Jiwu/257 considers 奪 to be a later erroneous addition and follows the *Yi xin fang* 醫心方 which has 使氣極." See also Qian Chaochen-88/63.

33 Yang Shangshan: "痿厥 is 'not able to walk.' "

34 Wang Bing: "逆 is to say: to carry out the orders of summer in contrast [to the requirements of winter]. The kidneys correspond to water and flourish in winter. Hence, to carry out [in winter] the orders of summer, this harms the qi of the kidneys. In spring the wood flourishes and the water perishes. Hence, the disease develops in spring. If one opposes [the orders of] winter and harms the kidneys, this results in diminished qi [with a reduced ability] to receive the order to generate life in spring."

35 The *Tai su* has 上, 'to ascend,' instead of 止: "The virtue is stored and does not rise."

36 Wang Bing: "The four seasons form a sequence and the seven luminaries move in a circle. That is to say: heaven has no physical appearance. This is hidden virtue. When virtue is invisible, then its application is inexhaustible. Hence, [the virtue] does not descend. *Lao zi* stated: 'Those who possessed utmost virtue, they did not [demonstrate their] virtue.' That is to say, heaven is extremely remote and high. Its virtue is invisible. The Way of the entire life, should it not follow heaven all the more?!" Zhang Canjia interprets 下 as 下泄, "to leak", in the sense of "the qi of heaven always remains in heaven; it never leaks." In contrast, Wang Qi identifies 下 as 去, "to go"; consequently,

When heaven were to shine, then sun and moon would not shine,[37] and evil
would harm the orifices.[38]

As for yang qi, when it is obstructed,
as for the qi of the earth, when its brilliance is covered,[39]
then clouds and fog are not clear.
As a result, corresponding above, white dew fails to descend.[40]

不下 would mean "it never goes", "it is eternal." Li Guoqing equals 下 with 少, "to
decrease", in the sense of "it never decreases."

37 Wang Bing: "Heaven hides [its] virtue, because it wishes to conceal its great brilliance. Because where great brilliance is visible, minor brilliance is eliminated. Hence,
the virtue of great brilliance must be hidden. If heaven itself were brilliant, then the
brilliance of sun and moon were concealed." In contrast, Li Guoqing: "明 is identical
with 萌. The *Jing ji zuan gu* 經籍纂詁 states: '萌 refers to 肓.' 肓 means 'confused,'
'benighted.' Hence, this sentence should be interpreted as follows: 'When the qi of
heaven is obscured, then yin fog spreads everywhere, so that during daytime one cannot see the sun and during nighttime one cannot see the moon. Sun and moon lose
their brilliant radiance and evil qi fills the void and causes harm.'" Similar, 2259/30
which adds a 不, 'not,' between 天 and 明: "If heaven does not shine, then sun and
moon cannot shine."

38 Yang Shangshan: "空竅 is to say: the 365 [needling] holes." Wang Bing: "If one
leaves the Way, then the depletion evil enters into the orifices." In contrast, Cheng
Shide et al.: "The meaning is, evil qi would fill the space between heaven and earth."

39 Wang Bing: "Yang [qi] is to say: the qi of heaven, that is, wind and heat. Earth
qi is to say: dampness, and this includes clouds and fog. When wind and heat have
harmed a person, then his nine orifices are shut and blocked. When fog and dampness
have caused a disease, then a shade on the eyes obscures vision."

40 Wang Bing: "Fog is of one kind with the clouds; dew is of one kind with rain.
Now, when the yang is abundant then the earth does not send [any qi] upwards to
respond; when the yin is depleted, heaven does not send [any qi] downwards to interact. When therefore clouds and fog do not transform the subtle and essence qi,
heaven corresponds to this above resulting in the calamity of a failure of white dew
to descend." Zhang Zhicong: "The qi of the earth rises and turns into clouds and fog.
The qi of heaven descends and turns into rain and clouds. When clouds and fog are
not pure, this is because the qi of the earth has not risen. When the qi of the earth
fails to rise, then the qi of heaven does not descend. Hence, the response above is such
that dew does not descend." Li Guoqing agrees: "精 is identical with 晴, 'clear sky.' The
Yü pian 玉篇 states: 'when the rain stops, [the sky] is clear and there are no clouds.'
Hence, the meaning of the present passage is: if the qi of heaven is not clear, then the
dew cannot descend. When the rising and descending of the qi of heaven and earth
lose their regular order, this is to say: 'the qi of the earth does not rise and the qi of
heaven does not descend.' The mechanism of coming to life, transformation, growth
and upbringing of the myriad beings does not function. Life cannot be bestowed and

Interaction fails to manifest itself.
The life of the myriad beings, hence, no [longer] receives any bestowals.[41]
When there are no bestowals, then many eminent trees die.[42]

2-12-4
Bad qi is not effused.[43]
Wind and rain are excessive.
White dew does not descend.

---

if even large trees die, it is even more difficult for the other living beings to survive."
2050/23: "The *Shi ji*, 天官書, has: 天精而見景星. The *Han shu*, 天文志, has 天晴而
見景星." Similarly, 703/37 identifies 精 as 晴, 'fair sky.' "

41 Wu Kun: "Mutual interaction is most important for the two qi of yin and yang. If
the interacting qi cannot manifest themselves freely in the outside, then the life of the
myriad beings has nothing to be supplied 施受 with, and if it has nothing to be supplied with, then tall trees respond first and many die." Following the *Shi jing*, 大雅, 皇
矣, where the passage 施于孫子 is commented as 涎及子孫也, Zhang Canjia prefers
to read 施 as *yi*, "to extend." Here: "Life is not extended." Li Guoqing agrees.

42 Wang Bing: "When clouds and fog fail to transform their essential and subtle
[qi], rain and dew fail to bestow moisture. That is [meant by] the qi of heaven fails
to descend. When the qi of the earth fails to rise, then the Way of change and transformation suffers. This leads to the destruction of the foundations of generation and
upbringing. Hence, when the myriad beings have no supplies to live, when they die it
is the 名木 that respond first. Hence, [the text] states: 'many 名木 die.' 名 is to say 名
果珍木, ' valuable fruit and precious wood.' 表 is to say: 'display their appearance.' "
Liu Zhenmin et al./72: "Wang Bing is wrong. 名 stands for 大, 'tall.' 名木 are the tall
trees.' " 670/7: "In antiquity, the meaning of 大, 'tall,' was occasionally expressed by the
term 名." See Zhang Yizhi et al./14 for further evidence.

43 Wang Bing: "惡 stands for 害氣, 'harmful qi.' 發 is to say 散發, 'to disperse.' ..
That is to say, harmful qi is concealed and stored and is not effused. [Hence,] wind
and rain exceed their standards and many fractures and injuries occur. Withered trees
form heaps and there is blossoming in spring." In contrast, Zhang Zhicong: "惡氣 is
忿怒之氣, 'the qi of anger.' "The "qi of anger", that is, violent storm and also capital
punishment, is associated with autumn and if it fails to develop the season does not
show its appropriate nature. The *Tai su* does not have the character 不; it states 惡
氣發, "Bad qi develops" and considers this as the second of altogether eight negative
consequences of the lack of "bestowals" listed in the following passages. Zhang Canjia
identifies 不 with 丕, "great": "Bad qi develops greatly." 2270/37 agrees on the basis of
evidence quoted from ancient texts. 2384, in a lengthy discussion, concludes: "惡 is a
mistake for 地, 'earth': 'The qi of the earth is not effused.' " Li Guoqing considers the
character 不 to be used here merely as a particle emphasizing the following character
發: "Bad qi develops!" 307/186 agrees.

As a result, gardens wither and there is no blossoming.[44]

Robber winds arrive often and
violent rains emerge frequently.
Heaven, earth, and the four seasons fail to maintain their mutual [relationship] and
lose their relationship with the Way.
As a result, before it has reached its middle, [life] is curtailed and extinguished.[45]

Only the sages follow the [Way];
hence, their bodies have no strange diseases. [46]

---

44 Wang Bing: "惡 is to say: a qi that harms. 發 is to say: disperse. 菀 is to say 蘊積, 'dense accumulation.' That is to say: Harmful qi lies hidden and does not disperse. Wind and rain are excessive and cause breaking and harm repeatedly. Dense accumulations of withered trees do not blossom in spring. How could this happen only to beings [other than humans]? When man leaves the Way, the same happens to him." Yang Shangshan: "菀 is 宛. 宛 has the meaning of 'rot and die.'" Liu Zhenmin et al./72: "菀槁: Grasses and trees rot and do not blossom.' 菀 stands for 郁結, 積滯, 'accumulation.'" 916/52 identifies 菀 with 郁 in the sense of 蘊結, "oppressed","sad." See also 692/41. 2268/34: "菀, in ancient times identical with 郁, is to describe the 'lush growth of herbs and trees.'" In contrast, 302 identifies 菀 as 宛, "exsiccated." In this case, the passage should read: "[Herbs and trees] dry out and wither." We read 菀 here as 苑 yuan, in the sense of 'garden'. (See WLGHYCD.)

45 Yang Shangshan: "未央 is 久, 'long.'" Wang Bing: "央 stands for 久, 'long,' 遠, 'far.' Hence, if one does not act in accordance with the four seasons and frequently encounters the harm of the eight winds and loses the relationship with the Way, then the true qi of heaven before long will end in destruction." Wu Kun agrees: "未央 is 未久, 'before long.'" In contrast, Zhang Jiebin: "央 stands for 中半, 'middle','half-way.'" Cheng Shide et al. follows an attested use of 央 for 盡, 'to complete,' 'to use up,' in the *Chu* ci 楚辭: "One dies before one has used up one's allotted time." Li Guoqing identifies 央 as 殃, "to end": "One dies before one has finished the years allotted by heaven." See also 307/184.

46 Several editions have 苛, "serious", instead of 奇, "strange." Li Guoqing agrees. In light of the definition of 苛 in the *Shuo wen* as "tiny grass", Ma Kanwen suggests to interpret 苛疾 as "slight illness". See Ma Kanwen p.14. With this reading an appropriate translation would be: "..their bodies will not have [even] minor diseases."

They do not neglect the myriad beings.[47]
Their generative qi does not exhaust itself.[48]

2-13-2
If one acts contrary to the qi of spring, then
the minor yang does not promote generation.
The liver qi changes internally.[49]

If one acts contrary to the qi of summer, then
the major yang does not stimulate growth.
The heart qi is empty internally.[50]

If one acts contrary to the qi of autumn, then
the major yin does not collect.
The lung qi burns and there is fullness.[51]

------

47 1552/135: "物 stands for 事, 'affair.'" In this case the passage should read: "They fail in none of their affairs."

48 Wang Bing: "The Way is not far away from man; man's heart is far away from the Way. Only the heart of the Sages is one with the Way. Hence, their longevity is endless. 從 is 順, 'in accordance with.' That is, they live in accordance with the orders of the four seasons. One must not oppose them. If one opposes them, then the five depots are harmed internally and various diseases emerge."

49 Wang Bing: "生 is to say: 動出, 'move and emerge.' When the yang qi does not emerge, because it is suppressed internally in the liver, then it mixes with the liver qi. [The latter] undergoes change and is harmed."

50 Wang Bing: "長 is to say: 外茂, 'external luxuriance.' 洞 is to say: 空, 'empty.' When the yang qi is not luxuriant outside, it presses against the heart internally. [Its] heat causes internal wasting. Hence, there is a hole in the heart." 526/6: "洞 may be a mistake for 動, 'to move.' In ch.26 of the *Tai ping sheng hui fang* 太平聖惠方, 治心勞諸方, 動 has the meaning of 痛. Wang Bing says: 洞 means 'the heart is empty inside.' Sun Dingyi 孫鼎宜 states: '洞 should be 恫, 'moaning with pain.'" *SWJZ*: "恫 is 痛, 'pain.'"

51 Wang Bing: "焦 stands for 上焦, 'upper burner.' The major yin passes the qi. It masters transformations in the upper burner. Hence, when the lung qi fails to collect, the upper burner is full." Lin Yi et al.: "The Quan Yuanqi edition has 進滿 instead of 焦滿. *Jia yi jing* and *Tai su* have 焦滿." Zhang Jiebin: "Autumn is associated with metal. The lung and the large intestine correspond with it. Hence, if one opposes the qi of autumn, then the order of great yang is not received, with the result that the lung has heat and its lobes burn. This causes distention and [a feeling of] fullness." Hu Shu: "焦 is correct. When the Quan Yuanqi edition has 進, this is an error because of a similarity of the two characters. 焦 corresponds to the statement 肺熱葉焦 in *Suwen* 44 246-10. 焦滿 parallels 濁沉, 'thick and deep,' further below. If 焦 stood for

If one acts contrary to the qi of winter, then
the minor yin does not store.
The kidney qi is turbid and in the depth.[52]

2-13-6
Now,
the yin and yang [qi] of the four seasons,
they constitute root and basis of the myriad beings.

Hence, the sages
in spring and summer nourish the yang and
in autumn and winter nourish the yin[53], and
this way they follow their roots.

Hence,
they are in the depth or at the surface with the myriad beings at the gate to life
and growth.[54]

上焦, this would not parallel the text below. Also, the 'upper burner' cannot simply be
termed 'burner.' That is an error."

52 Wang Bing: "沉 is 沉伏, 'hidden in the depth.' The qi of minor yin passes through
the kidneys internally. Hence, in case the minor yin does not lie hidden, the qi of the
kidneys is thick and in the depth." The *Tai su* and the *Jia yi jing* have 濁, "turbid",
instead of 獨, "solitary", "alone." Gao Jiwu/14 interprets both characters as a mistake
for 觸, "to run against", "to touch."

53 Wang Bing: "In spring they ate cool [food], in summer they ate cold [food],
to provide nourishment in the [period of] yang. In autumn they ate warm [food],
in winter they ate [hot] food, to provide nourishment in the [period of] yin." For a
discussion of this principle in treatment as opposed to prevention, see 1983. Ma Shi:
"The myriad beings come to life in spring, grow in summer, are gathered in autumn
and are stored in winter. These [regularities of] yin and yang in the course of the four
seasons are the root and the source of the myriad beings. Hence, in spring and summer
those sages who adhered to the Way of nourishing [their] genesis and growth, they
nourished [their] yang qi, while in autumn and winter those who adhered to the Way
of nourishing [their] gathering and storage, they nourished [their] yin qi. In contrast,
Wu Kun identified yin and yang with depots and palaces, respectively."

54 Hua Shou: "浮沉 is like 出入, 'to leave and to enter.'" Mori 森立之: "根 and 門
form a rhyme. 門 is another name for heaven; 根 is another name for the earth." Duan
Yishan/12: "沈浮 is to say 升降, 'to rise and to descend,' or 盛衰, 'abundance and
weakness.' *Zhuang zi*, in 知北遊, stated: '天下莫不沈浮, 終身不故; 陰陽四時運行,
各得其序, 'Everything under the sky moves to the depth or at the surface and has no
fixed position for its entire life. Yin and yang move throughout the four seasons; they
occupy specific [places] according to the sequence [of the seasons].'" 1552 separates

To oppose one's root,
is to attack one's basis
and to spoil one's true [qi]. [55]

2-14-1
Hence,
yin [qi], yang [qi], and the four seasons,
they constitute end and begin of the myriad beings,
they are the basis of death and life.
Opposing them results in catastrophe and harms life.
If one follows them, severe[56] diseases will not emerge.
This is called "to achieve the Way."

As for the Way,
the sages practice it;
the stupid wear it [for decoration only].[57]

If one follows yin and yang, then life results;
if one opposes them, then death results.
If one follows them, then order results;
if one opposes them, then disorder results.

---

between 以從其根 and 故于萬物, in the sense of: if one is at the mercy of seasonal changes in the same way as are herbs and trees, then this is because one has harmed one's root, which in turn has destroyed the true [qi] of heaven.

55 Duan Yishan/12: "真 is 真氣. Also, in *Zhuang zi*, 山木, there is a statement: 'Today I walked through [the park of] Diaoling and I forgot myself (吾身).' Sima Biao 司馬彪 commented: 'The character 身 is also written with the character 真.' Hence, the present passage 'destroys one's true [qi]' could also be read as 'destroys oneself/one's body.'"

56 Some editions have 奇, "strange", instead of 苛. See also Gao Jiwu/244. See also above, note 46, for a reading of 苛 as "slight; minor". With this reading an appropriate translation would be: "[Even] minor diseases will not emerge."

57 Duan Yishan/12: "佩 is identical with 倍, 'to oppose,' 'to turn one's back against.'" Liu Zhenmin et al./72 identifies 佩 as 背, 'to turn one's back against.'" 916/53 agrees, but identifies 佩 as 悖, "to rebel." For a detailed discussion, see 2194 and Wang Hongtu et al./150 where Hu Shu's reading of 佩 as 倍 is accepted as correct. In contrast, Yang Shangshan in the *Tai su*: "The sages .. move it through their body and treasure it in their heart; the stupid .. wear it on their clothes (佩之于衣裳)."

{To act contrary to what is appropriate, this is opposition.
This is called inner obstruction.}⁵⁸

2-14-5
Hence, [when it is said]
"the sages did not treat those already ill, but treated those not yet ill,
they did not put in order what was already in disorder, but put in order what
was not yet in disorder,"
then this means just the same.

Now,
when drugs are employed for therapy only after a disease has become fully
developed,
when [attempts at] restoring order are initiated only after disorder has fully
developed,
this is as if a well were dug when one is thirsty,
and as if weapons were cast when the fight is on.
Would this not be too late, too?

58 Wang Bing: "格 stands for 拒, 'to oppose.' That is to say, the inner nature opposes
the Way of heaven." See also 917/45.

Chapter 3
Discourse on how the Generative Qi Communicates with Heaven[1]

3-14-10
Huang Di:
"Now,
since antiquity, that wich communicates with heaven,
the basis of life,
is based in yin and yang.

Between heaven and earth and
within the six [cardinal points] uniting [the world]
all the qi within the nine regions <and the nine orifices>[2],
<the five depots, the twelve sections>[3]
communicate with the qi of heaven.[4]

---

1 "Heaven" to be understood here in the sense of "the universe."

2 Wang Bing: "九州, 'the nine regions,' refers to [the nine divisions set up by the Great Yu, that is] Ji 冀, etc. In the outer world the nine regions are spread out; internally the nine orifices correspond to them. Hence the text states "Nine regions, nine orifices." Hu Shu: "The two characters 九竅 are a later insertion. 'Nine regions' is 'nine orifices.' In a commentary to the *Er ya* 爾雅, shi xu pian 釋獸篇, Mr. Kuo's 郭 commentary stated: '州 is 竅.' .. Hence the idea of 'orifice' was expressed in antiquity with the character for 'region.' In the present passage, there is no need to state 九竅 in addition to 九州. I presume the two characters 九竅 are an ancient commentary that was erroneously inserted into the main text."

3 Wang Bing: "十二節, 'twelve sections,' refers to the twelve qi. The twelve sectional qi of heaven, the twelve conduit-vessels of man correspond to them outside. They all alike are controlled by heaven. Hence [the text] states: 'they all communicate with heaven.'" Gao Shishi: "十二節, 'twelve joints,' refers to the two hands, the two elbows, the two arms, the two feet, the two knees, and the two thighs." Fu Weikang & Wu Hongzhou/256: "The two wrists, the two elbows, the two shoulders, the two ankles, the two knees, and the two pelvic joints."

4 Wang Bing: "六合 is to say: the four cardinal directions (that is, North, West, South, East), as well as above and below. The nine regions are *ji* 冀, *yan* 兗, *yu* 豫, *qing* 青, *xu* 徐, *yang* 揚, *jing* 荊, *liang* 梁, and *yong* 雍. The nine regions are spread outside and the nine orifices correspond to them inside. Hence [the text] speaks of 'nine regions, nine orifices.' 'Five depots' refers to the five spirit depots. The five spirit depots include the liver storing the *hun*-soul, the spleen storing the will, the heart storing the spirit, the lung storing the *po*-soul, and the kidneys storing the mind. They form the physical appearance." Qian Chaochen-88/43 identifies 九竅 as a commentary placed by a later

<It generates five; its qi are three.>[5]

If this [qi of heaven] is offended repeatedly,
then evil qi harms man.
[Hence] this [qi of heaven] is the basis of one's lifespan.[6]

3-15-1
The qi of the hoary heaven,
it is clear and pure, and as a result the mind is in order.
If one lives in accordance with it, then the yang qi is strong.[7]

---

author behind 九州. By the time of the Tang dynasty, this commentary had become part of the text and was no longer recognized as such by Wang Bing and subsequent commentators. Both the Mawangdui manuscripts and the *Shan hai jing* 山海經 use 州 for 竅, "orifice." Yu Yue: "The two characters 九竅 are definitely later insertions. 九州 itself means 九竅. The Guo 郭 commentary to the *Er ya*, Shi shou pian 釋獸篇, states: 州 is 竅. .. Hence it is not necessary to repeat 九竅 following 九州." Shen Zumian: "州 is 尻. The Gao 高 commentary to the statement 許鄙相脈 in the *Lü shi chun qiu*, Guan biao pian 觀表篇, says: '脈 is the anus.' Later people no longer knew the meaning of the character 州 and interpreted it in the sense of 'the earth has nine regions.' Both the Mawangdui manuscripts and the *Shan hai jing* have 州 for orifice." *Huai nan zi*, Tian wen xun 天文訓, has: 蚑行喙息, 莫貴于人. 孔竅肢體, 皆通于天."

5 Fu Weikang & Wu Hongzhou/256: "Yin and yang generate the five agents and subdivide into the three yin and three yang qi." 692/41: "All authors interpret 其生五 as 五行, 'five agents.' This is certainly not wrong, but they have failed to make clear why 生 should be read as 行. 生 stands for 性, 'nature.' 性 can be read as 行." For a detailed justification of this argument, see there. *Su wen* 66 and 67 have 化生五味, "through transformation they generate the five flavors." Shen Zumian: "Spring-wood-liver, summer-fire-heart, autumn-metal-lung, and winter-water-kidneys, they all are generated by the fifth [agent] in the center. Hence [the text] states: 'They come to life through the fifth.' The fifth [agent] is the center-spleen-soil. 其氣三 has been interpreted by all authors on the basis of three yin and three yang. This is incorrect. Three yin and three yang together are six qi, not three qi. *Su wen* 9 has 三而成天, 三而成地, 三而成人. Hence heaven, earth, and man constitute the three qi."

6 Wang Bing: " 'To offend' is to say: evil qi offends the generative qi. When the evil qi offends [the generative qi] again and again, the generative qi is in danger. Hence the true [qi] of heaven is to be treasured and nourished as the basis of longevity."

7 Wang Bing: "Spring is the 'greenish heaven' (春為蒼天); it rules outbreak and generation. Yang qi is the qi of heaven." Mori: "The heaven is greenish (蒼). That is its proper color. When Wang Bing interprets this as the heaven in spring, this is incorrect." Zhang Yizhi et al.: "The *Shuo wen* states: 天 is 顚, 'summit,' 'top.' .. Hence in the present [statement] the 天 of 蒼天 is used metaphorically to denote the human head. Hence the following text states: 'When it is clear then sentiments and mind are

Even if there is a robber evil,
it cannot bring any harm.
This [is so because one] follows the sequence of the seasons.[8]

Hence, when the sages
concentrated essence and spirit,
and when they ingested the qi of heaven
they communicated with the spirit brilliance.[9]

If one misses the [sequence of the seasons],
then internally the nine orifices are closed,
and externally muscles and flesh are congested.
The guard qi dissipates.[10]
This is called[11] self injury;
it is the deletion of qi.[12]

3-15-4
As for the yang qi [in man],
this is like heaven and sun.

---

in order.'" We do not interpret 蒼天 here in the sense of a specific color of heaven or the sky. Rather, in this passage 蒼 seems to express the limitlessness and/or old age of heaven.

8 Wang Bing: "Because one follows the sequence of the qi of the four seasons, the qi of the robber evil cannot cause harm."

9 Wang Bing: "To be able to transmit essence and spirit, only the sages who have attained the Way are able to do this." Zhang Jiebin: "傳 is 受, 'to receive.' 服 stands for 佩, 'to respect.'" Yu Yue: "傳 should be read like 搏, 'to seize,' which means 'to collect.'" Zhang Zhicong: "Hence the sages transmitted essence and spirit and they ingested the clear qi of the hoary heaven, so as to have it communicate with their spirit-brilliance." Li Guoqing: "服 should be read as 順應, 'to act in accordance with.'" Hu Shu: "The character 傳 makes no sense. Wang Bing's commentary does not explain it. 傳 is most likely a mistake for 搏, which is identical with 專. That is to say, essence and spirit of the sages were concentrated. *Su wen* 78 has 精神不轉. *Su wen* 25 has 神無營 于眾物, 'the spirit does not pass to the multitude of beings.' The meaning is close. In ancient texts the characters 專一 were often written 搏." The *Tai su* has 搏.

10 Wang Bing: "'To miss' is to say: to counteract the principle of clarity and purity of the hoary heaven. The guard qi forms a union with the yang qi of heaven."

11 Gao Jiwu/464: "謂 stands for 為, 'is.'"

12 Wang Bing: "To counteract the qi of the hoary heaven and to oppose the principle of clarity and purity, causes elimination of the proper, true qi. This removal of the [proper qi] was not sent down by heaven, it was caused by man himself."

If [the sun] were to lose its location,
then this would reduce longevity [of man]
and [his physical appearance] would not look fine.[13]
The fact is,
the movements [of the celestial bodies] in heaven
require the sun to be lustrous and brilliant.[14]
Hence the yang [qi] follows [the sun] and rises;[15]
it is that which protects the outside.

3-16-1
As a result of cold,
[yang qi] tends to resemble a moving pivot.
Rising and resting are as if [that person] were frightened,
and the spirit qi drifts around.[16]

---

13 Wang Bing: "This is to explain the functions of the yang qi [indicated] above. That is, man has yang [qi] just like heaven has the sun. When heaven loses its position, then the sun is not bright. When man loses his position, then the yang [qi] is not stable. When the sun is not bright, then heaven is dark. When the yang [qi] is not stable, then man's life span is shortened." In contrast, Shi Changyong 史常永 in *Yi shi wen xian li lun cong kan* 醫史文獻理論叢刊, 1979, Nr.2, p.4. has suggested a punctuation following 所則, together with an interpretation of 則 as 法則, "rule." Based on the interpretation by Wang Bing, all other commentators separate this sentence between 所 and 則, interpreting 所 as "position" and 則 as "consequently." However, since it is not clear how heaven could lose its position, Wang Bing's interpretation may not be correct. One could also follow the *Tai su* which has 行, "to pass," instead of 所. Mori: "The version with 行 is correct. 行, 彰, and 明 form a rhyme. That is to say, because the sun is situated in the void and darkness of heaven, all stars and all beings are lighted and are supplied with a nourishment of warmth for their life."

14 Wang Bing: "That is to say, man's life must definitely avail itself of yang qi."

15 Yan Hongchen & Gao Guangzhen/22: " 'Moves upwards' is by no means to say that it moves up into the head and to the face. In terms of inner and outer, outer is 'above' inner. Hence the yang basically moves to the outer sections of the body."

16 Wang Bing: "欲如運樞 is to say 內動, 'internal movement.' 起居如驚 is to say 暴卒, 'sudden,' 'hectic.' That is, because the weather is cold one should stay inside, thickly covered all around. One moves inside like a pivot. One must see to it that [the cold] does not annoy the sinews and the bones lest yang qi flows away through the skin resulting in harm caused by cold poison. If one's rising and resting are hectic and if one runs around wildly to exhaustion, then the spirit qi drifts around and oversteps its borders, having no place where it may relax and find peace." Lin Yi et al.: "The *Tai su* has 連樞. Quan Yuanqi commented: 'The yang qi is fixed like a pivot, that is: its movement is fixed.'" Qian Chaochen-88/48: "According to Lin Yi et al., Quan Yuanqi had 欲如連樞. Also, *Tai su*, 調陰陽, has 連樞 with a commentary by Yang Shangshan: '連 stands for 數, often; 樞 stands for 動, movement.' Comment: 運 is a

As a result of summerheat {sweat},
if [the patient suffers from] uneasiness, he will pant with large noise;
if he is at peace, he [nevertheless] speaks a lot.[17]

---

mistake for 連 because the characters look quite similar. The character 連 is the older version of the younger character 輦, 'carriage.' That is to say, when someone is affected by wind and/or cold, he will react like the pivot of a carriage, which moves at the outside but is quiet inside. Hence the following passage warns: 'If rising and resting resemble surprise mo-vements, the spirit qi will drift around.' The phrase 'one tends to resemble the pivot of a carriage' is a metaphor." For textual evidence demonstrating the relationship between 連 and 輦, see Qian Chaochen-88/48. Zhang Wenhu: "Cold qi has a gathering effect. As a result, the yang [qi] is fastened and cannot move freely. Hence one is excited and the spirit qi cannot find rest. Wang Bing mistakenly takes 連, 'fastened,' as 運. His interpretation is forced and misses the meaning of the classic. The character 欲 may well be a mistake. Quan Yuanqi in his comment speaks of 動 [instead of 欲]." Yan Hongchen & Gao Guangzhen/117: "Zhu Danxi considers the twelve characters beginning with 欲如運樞 a later addition that should be deleted, while the two sentences 體若燔炭, 汗而而散 should be moved behind the three characters 因于寒. From the structure and the meaning of the entire text, these changes make sense." In contrast, 47/57: "Wu Kun suggested to move the twelve characters 欲如 ... 乃浮 behind 衛外者也. A careful reading suggests that these changes are not justified by the contents of the text. The meaning [of these twelve characters] follows 因于寒. On the basis of a comparative analysis of the three other passages, [these twelve characters] refer to a major sign resulting from an affection by cold."

17 Wang Bing: "If one was harmed by cold poison, in summer this will change to a summerheat disease. 煩 is 煩躁, irritated. 靜 is 安靜, 'at peace.' 喝 is 大呵出聲, 'a strong yawning producing a sound.' That is, if a disease results from summerheat, one should have [the patient] sweat to let [the heat] flow off. In case the heat is not released through the exterior, it will attack internally. Center and outside will both be hot. Hence [patients] are irritated, pant, with frequent forceful and noisy exhalation. In case [patients] are not irritated, they are hot inside and cold outside, the blocked heat attacks the center. Hence [patients] speak a lot without a pause. Instead of 喝 another edition has 鳴, 'sound.' " Zhang Jiebin: "Even those who are quiet cannot help but start talking a lot. The reason is, when evil heat harms the yin, essence and spirit inside will be confused. Hence one becomes extremely talkative." Zhang Zhicong: "If one is not uneasy but calm, then this evil is still in the qi section. That is, the qi is harmed and the spirit qi is depleted. Hence [such patients] speak a lot." Li Guoqing: "This disease emerges because the evil of summer-heat has harmed a person. Because the qi of the heart communicates with summer and because summerheat is the qi of summer, when the heat of summerheat abounds, then this harms the heart. In light cases the evil enters the qi section and generates irritation and vexation. One has high fever and is thirsty. In serious cases the heat affects the heart-enclosure and this may reach a degree where the spirit is confused and one talks incoherently. The spirit is confused. Hence one is not restless but calm. Incoherent speech means that one talks much. This is a sign of abundance and repletion with yang heat." *SWJZ*: "煩 is heated head with pain." Zhang Qi: "喝 is an error for 渴, 'thirsty.' 'Summerheat' is what the

The body resembles burning coal.
Sweat flow lets [the internal heat] disperse.[18]

As a result of dampness,
the head [feels] as if wrapped with something wet,
the heat is not driven out,[19]
the large sinews shrink and shorten;
the small sinews slacken and extend.[20]
{"Shrink and shorten" is cramp; "slacken and extend" is limpness.}

Jin gui calls sunstroke. According to the *Jin gui*, in case of a sunstroke, one must not induce sweating or draining. When Mr. Wang states that in case of a summerheat disease [patients] must sweat, this is an error." Yu Chang: "The character 汗 may be an insertion. Further down the text states 汗出而散. That is, the proper treatment of summerheat [disease] is to induce sweating. Why should [the text] here say: 'when they sweat and are excited, they will pant and exhale forcefully'? Also, the two characters 汗煩 make no sense themselves. 煩則喘喝 corresponds to the four character sentence 靜則言多 below. Hence to read 汗 as a one-character sentence is less plausible than to delete it."

18 Wang Bing: "This is to further elucidate the principle behind having [the patient] sweat [in case of summerheat disease]. When the body is hot like burning coal, how can [the heat] be eliminated? It must be driven out through sweating. This causes the heat to disperse. Another edition has 燥 instead of 燔. That is a mistake." Gao Jiwu/581 interprets 而散 as "and disperses the heat." 678/55-56 discusses two readings of this statement. While Wang Bing and Zhang Jiebin recommend sweating to disperse and eliminate the heat, Zhu Zhenheng and others hold that it would be an inappropriate therapy to cause a patient to sweat who resembles burning coal because he was affected by summerheat. These commentators suggest that the final four characters 汗出而散 are a mistaken insertion. Zhang Yizhi et al.: "汗, 喘, 言, 炭, and 散 form a rhyme."

19 *Gu dian yi zhu xuan* bianxiezu /38: "攘 has the meaning of 攘消除, 'to eliminate.'"

20 Wang Bing: "In case a disease is caused by heat in the outer regions of the body, it must be drained by sweat. If contrary to this the head [of the patient] is treated with dampness that is, if it is wrapped up with something wet, hoping thereby to eliminate the heat, the heat qi does not disperse. Rather, it combines with the dampness and attacks the interior. When the large sinews receive heat, they shrink and shorten; when the small sinews receive dampness, they relax and extend. When [the large sinews] shrink and shorten, they are cramped and cannot stretch. When [the small sinews] relax and extend, they weaken and have no strength. 攘 is 除, 'to eliminate.'" Yang Weijie/23 cites Zhu Zhenheng 朱震亨: " 'The large sinews shrink and shorten' [is to say]: when heat harms the blood, it cannot nourish the sinews. Hence they cramp. 'The small sinews relax and extend' [is to say]: when dampness harms the sinews, they cannot hold the bones. Hence limpness and weakness result." In contrast,

As a result of qi,[21]
[...]
This causes swelling.

If the four ropes substitute each other,
the yang qi is exhausted.[22]

Wang Shaozeng & Xu Yongnian/5: "Following a harm caused by dampness evil, the head is heavy as if wrapped up. If dampness and heat cannot be eliminated, large and small sinews shrink and shorten, or small and large sinews relax and extend." 630/39, 1127/11, 683/49, and 1126/12 agree with Wang Shaozeng & Xu Yongnian/5 in identifying this statement as an example of 互辭-style, i.e., "reciprocal phrasing."

21 Yao Shaoyu and others: "This qi is yang qi." Zhang Jiebin: "The guard qi, the camp qi, and the qi of the depots and palaces, they are all the qi [meant here]." Zhang Zhicong: "This is an external evil qi that harms the yang qi and causes harm to the yang qi so that it cannot move." Hu Shu: "This refers to heat qi. Above the text refers to cold, summerheat, and dampness. To speak of qi in general here, does not continue the structure of the previous argument. Hence it must be heat qi." Mori: "Above, the text speaks of cold, summerheat, and dampness. Here it says 'if this is followed by wind.' Qi refers to wind."

22 Wang Bing: "When the [movement of the] qi is habitually hasty [in a person] and if dampness and heat are added, then the qi, the dampness, and the heat struggle with each other and this causes swellings. In this situation, the evil qi gradually increases, while the proper qi slowly decreases, with the result that the sinews, the bones, the blood, and the flesh substitute each other in their functions. Hence [the text] states 'The four ropes substitute each other.' Zhang Jiebin: "If the guard qi, the camp qi, and to the qi of the depots and palaces are out of balance, each of them may cause a disease. 四維 stands for 四肢, the four limbs. 相代 means: 'they alternately fall ill.'" GSS: "Qi stands for 'wind.' *Su wen* 5 states: 'Yang qi is the designation for the swift winds of heaven and earth.' Hence [the text] does not speak of 'wind,' but speaks of 'qi.' 'As a result of qi, this causes swelling' is to say: When the wind is excessive, the extreme twigs/ends/points? (末) fall ill, and [accordingly] the four limbs swell. 四維相代 is to say: 'The four limbs cannot borrow strength for their movement anywhere, but must substitute each other.'" As for the four limbs, they are the basis of all [of the body's] yang. Now they have to substitute each other, and as a result, the yang qi is exhausted. ... It cannot guard the exterior [any more]." Yan Hongchen & Gao Guangzhen/117: "四維 stands for 四肢, 'the four limbs.' 相代 is 互相替代, 'to substitute each other.' [The meaning of this passage is:] 'If it results from a depletion of qi, the four limbs swell and become ill one after another.'" In contrast, 968/53: "The two characters 四維 do not constitute a compound here and they are not identical with the compound 四維 in *Su wen* 69. The 'four' refers to the four types of evil qi mentioned above, that is, wind, cold, summerheat, and dampness. 維 stands for 維系, 'connected,' 'tied.' When [the text] speaks of 四維相代, this is to say: 'the four types of evil qi, that is, wind, cold, summerheat, and dampness, are closely connected to each other and alternately harm a person.' As a result of such a situation, the yang qi of a person's body vanishes."

3-16-5

As for the yang qi,

in case of uneasiness and taxation, bloating[23] results.

Wu Kun: "四維 refers to blood, flesh, sinews, and bones. They are named 四維 because the hold the human body together." 1673/44: "Over time, the physicians have interpreted the statement 因于氣為腫四維相代陽氣為竭 in various ways. 1. The term 'qi' in this sentence was interpreted by Zhang Jiebin as 正氣, 'proper qi,' and by Gao Shishi as 邪氣, 'evil qi.' In my opinion, one should follow the latter. If one were to follow the former, this would destroy the entire context. The three qi 'cold,' 'warmth,' and 'dampness' mentioned above are external affections. If one were now to speak of a 'depletion qi,' this would not agree with the general argumentation of the text." In the context, the author says, there is always mentioned 'wind' as one of the four specific seasonal qi. 'Qi' should be understood here in the sense of 'wind'. 2. The statement 四維相代 is, in my opinion, a concluding remark concerning the previous passages 因于寒, 因于署, etc. Most commentators identify 四維 as the four extremities. The fourth edition of the teaching manual 內經選讀 speaks of 'four extremities' too. It suggests that it is because of the qi depletion that the disease causes swellings. If one notices surface swellings of the four extremities alternating in the four extremities, this is a sign of weakness and exhaustion of yang qi. In my opinion, this is not so, because in a clinical examination one rarely sees surface swellings alternatingly affecting the four extremities in cases of weakness and exhaustion of yang qi. .. In explaining 四維, one should follow the statement in *Su wen* 69: 四維 stands for 四角, 'the four corners,' that is, the cardinal directions North-West, South-West, South-East, and North-East. These for directions are associated with the four trigrams 乾, 坤, 巽, and 艮. From a statement in 九宮八風 (i.e., *Ling shu* ch. 77)... it is evident that the four corners are associated with the first 45, or 46, days of the four seasons spring, summer, autumn, and winter, and that the evil [qi] of the four seasons follow from the initial periods of the seasons and take their turns in accordance with the seasons. Hence 四維 must be interpreted as 'the four evil [qi] associated with the four seasons.' .. The meaning of the entire passage is: 'when the evil [winds] of the four seasons alternately harm man, this may lead to a situation where the yang qi vanishes.'"

23 Wang Bing: "張 is 脹, 'to swell,' 'to expand.'" Yan Hongchen & Gao Guangzhen/179: "張 is 向外擴張, 'to expand towards outside,' 'to disperse.'" Gao Jiwu/9: "To explain 張 on the basis of its extended meaning as 亢盛, 'abundant,' is quite appropriate. There is no need to interpret 張 as 脹, 'to expand.'" Qian Chaochen-88/46 points out that contrary to an assump-tion held by all other commentators, the character 張, with its general meaning "extension," was employed in Qin and early Han times to denote also a more narrow concept of extensions of body parts, that is, "swellings." The character 脹 appears to have been introduced only at some time later during the Western Han era. Hence 張 is the original character. 1580/3: "張 stands for 強." The meaning of the entire passage as suggested by 1580 is: "The yang qi is strong when vexation and fatigue [diminish the yin qi]." See there for a detailed justification. Yu Yue: "In front of the character 張 the character 筋, 'sinews,' is missing. 筋張 and 精絕 are two parallel structures. Now that the character 筋 is missing, the meaning of the statement is no longer clear. Since Wang Bing's commentary reads

The essence is cut short and evil accumulates.

In summer, this lets that person experience boiling recession.

The eyes are blind and cannot be used to look.

The ears are closed and cannot be used to hear.

[There are] *kui-kui* [sounds in the body] as if a city [wall] was destroyed;

[there are] *gu-gu* [sounds in the body like rushing water that] cannot be stopped. [24]

As for the yang qi,

in case of great anger,[25]

筋脈脹張, 精氣竭絕, it is obvious that [the character 筋] was not missing yet in the edition perused by Wang Bing." Given the structure of the "yang qi" statement further below, this argumentation is not convincing. Hence, Yu Chang: "Following 精絕 the character 而 may be missing. The structure 精絕而辟積于夏, 使人煎厥 is identical with the structure of the subsequent passage 氣絕而血菀于上, 使人薄厥." One may also consider 張 to be a mistake for an unknown character qualifying 精 here in the same way as the character 形 qualifies 氣 below.

24 Wang Bing: "In this case both the kidneys are harmed and the bladder is depleted. The conduits of the kidneys are tied to the center of the ears. The conduits of the bladder emerge from the canthi. Hence the eyes are blind and the ears are closed." Zhang Zhicong: "潰 stands for 漏, 'to drip.' That is to say, when the city [walls] are destroyed, they cannot store the essence. 汨汨 refers to 'flowing.' That is to say, the cold yin [seminal] essence flows away and cannot be stopped." 1192/4 criticizes Zhang Zhicong's view as narrowing down this issue to referring to males only, while, in fact, this passage was concerned with the qi of males and females alike. Ma Kanwen p. 12: "Yu Chang 于鬯, a noted Qing dynasty scholar well versed in phonology, gave a detailed commentary on the expression 壞都 ....都 should be explained as an equivalent to *zhu* 陼 which is the same as 渚 ('river bank,' 'islet')." 2802/47: "都 should be read as 渚. Gao Shishi interpreted 都 as 國都, 'state capital': 'Gushing water destroying a capital, is to say, ears and eyes are confused and the spirit loses its guarding function, as if the capital of a country was destroyed.' This does not appear suitable. When a capital is destroyed, how could this be the result of the strength of water gushing forth? The original meaning of 潰潰 is 'water bursting forth.' The extended meaning is 'to break up,' 'to destroy.'" See also 915/57 and 2167/49. Zhang Yizhi et al.: "潰潰, *kui-kui*, simulates the sound of breaking river banks. 汨汨, *gu-gu*, simulates the sound of gushing water."

25 1580: "If 怒 is interpreted here as one of the affects, that is, 'anger,' the meaning of this passage is difficult to explain. 怒 stands here for 甚, 'very.' 大 was used in ancient times for 太, 'overly.' 大怒 has the meaning here of 'too much.' 形氣 refers to the yin qi. If the yang qi is too strong, the yin liquids will vanish. Hence [the text states]: 形氣絕; 絕 means 'to vanish.'"

the qi of the physical appearance is cut short[26]
and the blood is densely compacted[27] above.[28]
It lets that person experience a beating recession.[29]

When there is harm to the sinews {they slacken},
they appear unable to function.[30]
When sweat seeps out on one side,
this lets that person experience unilateral withering.[31]

---

26 693/38: "The two characters 形氣 are, without any doubt, later amendations; they make absolutely no sense here. With these two characters the role of the three characters 陽氣者 as subject of this sentence is lost to 形氣. The [correct] meaning of this passage is that in case of great anger the [flow of the] yang qi is interrupted and blood accumulates above, so that the patient has 'receding [qi] resulting from pressing [qi].' The structure is identical with the structure of the passage further above: 陽氣者煩勞則張." See also note 23 above.

27 2753/62: "菀 stands for 鬱, 'dense growth.'" 2051/59: "汪認菴 in his *Su wen ling shu lei zuan yue zhu* 素問靈樞類纂約注, states: 菀 is equal with 鬱, 'dense growth.'"

28 Wang Bing: "This is yet another warning against unrestrained [affects such as] happiness or anger. Their excessive operation causes disease. Now, in case of anger the kidney receives harm; in severe cases the [flow of] qi is interrupted. In case of great anger the qi flows contrary to its normal direction and the yang [qi] cannot descend. Since the yang [qi] moves contrary to its normal direction, blood accumulates inside the heart and the chest. 'Above' refers to the heart and the chest." 2726/41: "'Above' refers to the brain."

29 Wang Bing: "Yin and yang [qi] battle each other, qi and blood race to unite. Because of their battling, a recession is generated. Hence [the disease] is called 'recession due to battling.'" *Gu dian yi zhu xuan* bianxiezu /42: "A disease where qi and blood battle each other and move upwards, contrary to their regular course, is called 'receding [qi] because of battling.'" 2225/3: "This is a type of receding [qi] resulting in dizziness, caused by great anger that lets the qi flow contrary to its regular course. See also *Su wen* 39: 'Anger causes the qi to flow contrary [to its regular course].'"

30 Wang Bing: "In case of excessive anger the qi may strike the sinews. When sinews and network vessels are harmed internally, the spring [in the body] relaxes and the physical body is in a state of limpness, seemingly unable to hold anything." *Gu dian yi zhu xuan* bianxiezu /42: "The sinews and vessels are paralysed, as if they did not accept the directions sent them by one's will." 1580/3: "若 is a mistake for 苦; 容 is to be explained as 用, 'function.' Following a 'receding [qi] because of striking,' the sinews and the vessels are relaxed and the limbs and the body are paralysed. Hence [the text] states: 'one suffers from a loss of functions.'"

31 Wang Bing: "沮 stands for 濕潤, 'to moisten.'" Lin Yi et al.: "The *Qian jin* has 祖 instead of 沮. The Quan Yuanqi edition has 恆." Wu Kun: "沮 stands for 止, 'to stop.'" Zhang Jiebin: "沮 stands for 傷, 'to harm,' 壞, 'to destroy.'" 1450/52: "沮 stands for 阻止, 'to block.' The meaning of the passage 汗出偏沮 is 'the sweat flow is regionally

When sweat flows and meets with dampness,
this generates pimples and heat rashes.[32]

In cases of changes associated with rich food,
the feet generate large boils.[33]
When [the hands] receive [something] it is as if one were holding nothing.[34]

---

blocked.'" See there for a detailed discussion. Gao Jiwu/797: "沮 has two readings here. One is as in 阻止, 'to stop,' the other is as in 濕潤, 'to moisten.' Ma Shi stated: 'When someone sweats on one side only, either on the left or on the right, then there is a blockage on one side and no sweat flows there. That half of the body which does not sweat will suffer from hemiplegia the next day.' Wu Kun, too, states: '沮 is identical with 止, 'to stop.'"

32 Wang Bing: "When yang qi is effused [through sweating] and is checked by cold water, then heat is suppressed internally and a surplus of heat is blocked in the skin. In serious cases this results in swellings and sores; in mild cases in pimple ulcers. 痱 are wind eruptions." Zhang Yizhi et al.: "The appearance of 沸瘡 resembles boiling water. Hence the term. This has been called 沸子 through the ages; the modern term is 痱子." *SWJZ*: "痤 is a small swelling."

33 Wang Bing: "高 is 膏, 'fat.' 梁, 'beam,' is 粱, 'delicious food.' When people without forbearance sweat profusely, [the sweat] will form knots and generate swellings and pimples. People who are used to rich food internally often have stagnating heat. Their skin is thick and their flesh is tightly sealed. Hence [the heat/sweat] changes to boils internally. .. The reason why boils emerge on the feet is that the four extremities are the sources of all yang. Because of an excessive waste of [yang qi] in the lower [regions, that is, the feet], the evil [qi] poison attacks the depleted area." Lin Yi et al. criticized Wang Bing: "When boils emerge, they are not often located on the feet. When rich food undergoes changes. large boils develop everywhere, not only on the feet." (See Qian Chaochen-88/152.) Qian Chaochen-90/63: "足 is an adverbial modifier in this sentence. It is to indicate that large boils generate often; it does not say that large boils grow on the feet. When Wang Bing identified 足 as 'feet,' this was wrong." 706/40: "姚止庵 of the Qing dynasty has commented '足生 is 足以生丁毒, 'it is quite sufficient to generate boil poison.' This is in perfect agreement with the general meaning of the text." 1580/3: "足 stands here for 多, 'many [times].' 丁 stands for 病, 'disease.' 大丁, then, should refer here to heat signs. The meaning is: 'In case rich food undergoes changes, often heat signs are generated.'" Beijing zhongyi xueyuan et al./63: "高 equals 膏. Fat meat is called 膏. Good nutrition is called 粱. 高粱 stands for delicious food." Yan Hongchen & Gao Guangzhen/198: "丁 is 疔, 'boils.'"

34 Wang Bing: "If external dampness intrudes it will clash with the heat in the center. One receives the poison of the evil [dampness qi] as if one were holding an empty container [only waiting for it]. Hence [the text] states '[One] receives [it] as if one were holding an empty [container].'" Wang Shaozeng/37: "As if one were holding an empty container filled with something."

If in a state of taxation one sweats and encounters wind,
and if cold strikes [against the skin], this leads to blotches;
in case it accumulates,[35] this generates pimples.[36]

3-17-5
As for the yang qi,
if it is firm, it nourishes the spirit;
if it is soft, it nourishes the sinews.[37]

If opening and closing [of one's pores] are not appropriate and
if cold qi follows this [opportunity to enter the body, then
this] generates a severe bending [of the body].[38]

---

35 In contrast, Qian Chaochen-88/61: "The character 鬱 is used in the entire *Suwen*
in the sense of 蘊結, 'depressed.'"

36 Wang Bing: "If one taxes one's body during the cold or cool seasons to a degree
that sweat effuses and if, at the same time, cold wind strikes the skin so that cold
comes to reside in the interstice structures, then fat and liquids congeal and collect
in the dark palaces. Because the flow through the openings dries up, blotch thorns
grow inside the skin. Their appearance resembles rice grain, or even needles. After
an extended period the location on top of them turns black. They are more than one
fen long and their color is white-yellow. 'Dark palaces' is to say: the openings through
which the sweat flows. 痤 is to say: red colored as swollen from anger, with blood and
pus inside. All these are caused by internal accumulations of yang qi."

37 Wang Bing: "This serves again to elucidate the movement of the yang qi [in the
body] and the nourishment it provides. .. When movement and resting are out of
proper balance, then this generates all sorts of disease." For an interpretation of 精
as 強, "strong," see Gao Jiwu/238. 678/55, listing six different meanings of the character used for "essence" in the *Neijing*, reads 精 here as 爽慧, "lively." Gao Jiwu/512:
"When the yang qi is strong (精強), then it is able to nourish the spirit. When it is soft
rather than hard, then it nourishes the sinews." See there for a detailed justification of
this interpretation. 1127/10: "'Essence' is to be interpreted here as 'clear and pure.'"
1126/11 agrees. 1580: "精 has the meaning here of 靜, 'quiet.' When the yang qi is
quiet and at peace, the spirit is clear. Hence [the text] states: 'nourishes the spirit.' 柔
is to be explained here as 安, 'peaceful.' It has the same meaning as 靜. When the yang
qi is at peace, the sinews and the vessels are passable. Hence [the text states]: 'when it
is soft, this nourishes the sinews.'"

38 Wang Bing: "開 is to say: [sweat] effuses through the skin interstices. 闔 is to say:
the dark palaces (that is, the openings in the skin through which sweat flows) are
tightly closed. Now, when effusion and closing lose their proper balance, they are attacked by cold. The sinews and network vessels deep inside [the body] experience accumulations of depletion cold. As a result, the sinews and network vessels cramp. [An
afflicted person] appears bent forward like a hunchback." Beijing zhongyi xueyuan et
al./78: "'If opening and closing are not appropriate' is to say that the sweat holes do

3-18-1
When the sunken vessels develop tumors, [this is because
the qi] stays for long[39] in the flesh and the interstice [structures].[40]
The qi of the transsporters is transformed and strikes [the depots].
Its transmission [in the organism] causes a tendency to be frightened and
the [patient] is shocked.[41]

When the camp qi does not follow [its regular course],
but proceeds contrary [to its regular course] in the flesh structures [underneath
the skin],
this then creates *yong*-abscesses and swelling.

If *po*-sweat flows without end,[42]
the physical form is weakened and the qi melts away.
Hence the holes and transporters are closed and this develops into wind-
malaria.[43]

---

not open or close properly; e.g., in summer they should open, but fail to open, and in
winter they should close, but fail to close."

39 Gao Jiwu/219: "留連 means 'it stays and does not leave.'"

40 In contrast, Wang Bing: "陷脈 is to say: cold qi causes a deficiency in the respective vessels. The cold accumulates and remains there. The blood in the conduits
congeals. Chronic blood clots strike against the interior and produce conglomerations
in the the flesh structures. Hence this results in a development of ulcers and tumors;
flesh and interstice [structures] become (closely) connected." For 陷脈, see also *Su
wen* 60-325-1.

41 Wang Bing: "That is to say: If cold enters the spine, the qi of the transportation
points changes and transforms and enters the depth [of the organism] where it strikes
the depots and palaces. This generates a tendency to be fearful and manifests itself as
shock."

42 Tanba: "魄 and 白 were used exchangeably in antiquity." In a commentary to the
occurrence of 'white sweat' in the *Zhan guo ce* 戰國策, Bao Biao 鮑彪 stated: "White
sweat is sweat that is not caused by summerheat." Beijing zhongyi xueyuan et al./78:
"Ancient physicians assumed that the appearance of sweat is related to the lung, because the lung is associated with the skin and the hair. In addition, the lung [was
thought] to store the *po*-soul. Body liquid that leaves through the pores is called sweat;
hence they called it 'sweat of the *po*-soul.'"

43 Wang Bing: "When one sweats incessantly, with the physical appearance weakened and the qi diminished, and if in this [situation] one is struck by wind and cold,
then the transportation holes close and the heat is stored inside and cannot leave.
In autumn, then, the autumn yang is taken in again. The two types of heat merge
and cause excitement. Spells of cold and heat follow each other. Because all this was

3-18-4
The fact is,
the wind is the origin of the one hundred diseases.[44]
In case [a person is] clear and calm, the flesh and the interstice [structures] are
firmly closed up and resist.
Even though there is a strong wind [which is] a violent poison,
it will be unable to harm that [person].
This is [so because one] follows the sequence of the seasons. [45]

The fact is,
when a disease persists over long time, it is transmitted [in the organism] and it
is transformed.[46]
When [a stage is reached where] above and below have lost their union,
then [even] a good physician cannot do anything about it.[47]

---

caused by wind, one speaks of wind-malaria." Beijing zhongyi xueyuan et al./78: "This
is one of the malaria diseases. It results from wind. This ailment often results from
an encounter with wind in a situation where one flees the heat and seeks a cold place
and sweats. The evil closes the pores and cannot flow off. This is always associated
with restlessness, headache, an aversion to cold with spontaneous sweating, and with
alternating feelings of first heat and then cold."

44 In contrast, Gao Jiwu/606: "Originally, wind-evil was the cause of many diseases."

45 Wang Bing: "If one's desires cannot fatigue one's eyes, if the evil of lewdness
cannot confuse one's heart, if no recklessness causes fatigue, this is 'clarity and purity.'
Because of one's clarity and purity, the flesh and the interstice [structures] are closed
and the skin is sealed tightly. The true and proper [qi] guards the interior and no depletion evil intrudes. .. Those who are 'clear and pure,' they follow the order/sequence
of the four seasons, .. they do not cause fatigue through reckless behavior, and rising
and resting follow certain rules. As a result, their generative qi is never exhausted and
they are able to preserve their strength forever."

46 For a reading of 傳化 as *zhuan hua*, "transform" see Hsü, 438. The term is also
used in *Su wen* 19, where a later commentary leaves no doubt that is was meant to be
read as *chuan hua*, expressing the meaning of "transmission and transformation." See
Su wen 19-125-2.

47 Wang Bing: "并 is to say: 氣交通, 'the qi communicate.' Now, when a disease
has persisted for long in the depth [of the organism], it changes, transforms, and is
transmitted further. Above and below fail to communicate; the [flow of] yin and yang
[qi] is blocked. Even if a physician were to employ the best [therapeutic] patterns, of
what use could they be?!"

The fact is,
when yang accumulates,[48] disease and death [result].
The yang qi will be barred [from flow].[49]
In case it is barred [from flow], it must be drained.
If no correct treatment is initiated quickly,
an uneducated [practitioner] will ruin the [patient].

The fact is,
the yang qi,[50]
during daytime,[51] it rules the exterior.
At dawn, the qi of man emerges.
At noon, the yang qi abounds.
When the sun is in the West, the yang qi is already depleted.
The qi gates close.[52]

Hence,
in the evening there is collection and resistance.[53]
One must not disturb sinews and bones;
one must not encounter fog and dew.

[If one's behavior] contradicts [the reqirements of] these three periods [of a day],
[one's] physical appearance will experience distress and weakening."[54]

3-19-5
Qi Bo:
"As for the yin, it stores the essence and rises quickly.[55]

---

48 2753/62: "畜 stands for 蓄, 'to accumulate.' "

49 Gao Jiwu/19: "當 stands for 擋, in the meaning of 擋住, 'to prevent.' "

50 2360/14: "Yang qi stands for guard qi here."

51 1580/4: "The character 一 is a simplification of the character 晝, 'daytime.' Daytime is yang and nighttime is yin."

52 Wang Shaozeng/34 interprets the 'qi gates' as the pores through which the sweat leaves. See also Yan Hongchen & Gao Guangzhen/6.

53 Yan Hongchen & Gao Guangzhen/6: "After sunset, the people go into their houses and separate themselves from the world outside."

54 Ma Shi and Gao Jiwu/259: "薄 stands for 衰, 'to weaken.' "

55 Wang Bing: "亟 stands for 數, 'repeatedly.' " Zhang Jiebin: "亟 is to be explained as 氣, qi. [This statement] is to show that yang can generate yin and that yin can generate yang. This way it makes sense. When all books interpret the character 亟 as 數, 'repeatedly,' then this makes no sense." Qian Chaochen-88/62: "When Zhang Jiebin

As for the yang, it protects the exterior and is firm.[56]

When the yin fails to dominate its yang,
then the [movement in the] vessels flows beating and hasty.
Merger results in craziness.[57]
When the yang does not dominate its yin,
then the qi of the five depots enter into a struggle.
The nine orifices are impassable.[58]

---

interprets 嘔 as 氣, these [two characters] may be interchangeable, but interchangeable is not the same as identical. In the ancient literature there is not a single instance where 嘔 stands for 氣. In the ancient pronunciation system, the two characters are very far apart from each other and cannot be exchanged for each other. In the *Suwen*, the character 嘔 appears eight times and it is employed with two meanings, that is, 'repeatedly,' and 'hurriedly.'" Gao Jiwu/584 interprets 起嘔 as "[the yin] supports the yang qi without interruption." *JJZG*: "嘔 is 急, 'quick.'" Zhang Yizhi et al.: "嘔 is identical with 極. The *Tai su* has 極. *Xun zi* 荀子, Fu 賦, has 出入甚極. Yang 楊 commented: "極 is to be read as 嘔, it means 急, 'quick.'"

56 In contrast, Gao Jiwu/584 interprets 為固 as "gives strength to the yin qi to guard the interior."

57 Wang Bing: "薄疾 is to say 'extremely depleted and rapid.' 并 is to say 'abundant and replete.' 狂 is to say 'to walk madly,' or 'to climb up crazily.' When the yang is '并' in the four limbs, one turns mad. *Su wen* 30 states: 'The four limbs are the origins of all yang. When the yang is abundant then the four limbs are replete. If they are replete one can climb on summits and sing. [The yang abundance causes] heat abundance in the body. Hence one throws off one's cloths and wishes to run.' All this happens because the yin cannot overcome the yang." For comparison, see *Su wen* 75: 三陽并至 .. 為巔疾. Gao Shishi: "薄 stands for 虛, 'depleted.' 疾 stands for 急, 'fast.'" Fu Weikang & Wu Hongzhou/259: "薄 stands for 迫, 'to press.' 并 stands for 合并, 'to unite.'" Mori: "并 is 并病, 'accumulation disease.' That is to say, when the yang qi is replete and accumulates in the section of yin [qi, that is, of] blood, then this often results in craziness. *Su wen* 62 states: 'When the blood collects in the yin [region] and qi collects in the yang [region], fright and craziness result.'"

58 Wang Bing: "The nine orifices are linked internally to the depots; externally they constitute officials [of the depots]. Hence, when the qi in the five depots enter into a struggle, then the nine orifices are impassable. When [the text] speaks of 'nine orifices,' this is to say: the front yin [orifice] and the back yin [orifice, that is, the orifices of stools and urine] are impassable. At the same time it refers to the seven orifices [in the head], that is, the eyes are the officials of the liver; the nose is the official of the lung; the mouth is the official of the spleen; the ears are the officials of the kidneys; the tongue is the official of the heart. The tongue, though, is not a passable orifice. The *Jin gui zhen yan lun* 金匱真言論 states: 'The red color of the South enters and penetrates the heart; its orifices are the ears. The black color of the North enters and penetrates the kidneys; their orifices are the two yin [openings].'" 1580/4: "爭 is a simplified ver-

Hence,
the sages arranged[59] yin and yang [in such a way that
their] sinews and vessels were in harmony,
[their] bones and marrow were solid and firm, and
[their] qi and blood both followed [their usual course].[60]
In such a situation,
inner and outer are balanced in harmony;
an evil cannot cause harm;
ears and eyes are clear;
the qi set-up is as usual. [61]

---

sion of 靜, 'quiet,' 'at peace.' It has the meaning of 'stagnation.' The preceding sentence
states that pathological changes towards an abundance of yang cause heat and movement. This sentence states that pathological changes towards a unilateral dominance
of yin qi causes stillstand and blockages. When the yin is abundant, the faculties of
the five depots weaken and a situation of blockages and impassability emerges. Hence
[the text] states: 'the nine orifices are impassable.'" In contrast, 4/37: "The interpretation of the passage 五藏氣爭 by previous authors has mostly not been helpful. The
Shuo wen 說文 states: '爭 has the meaning of 引, 'to pull.' Whenever the term 爭 is
used it means that something is pulled to return to oneself.' With this, the meaning
of 五藏氣爭 is not difficult to explain. The meaning of 五藏氣爭 is 五藏爭氣. And
which qi is pulled? It is the yang qi competed for by the five depots. 陽不勝其陰, 則
五藏氣爭九竅不通 is to say, when the body's yin abounds while the yang is depleted,
the five depots, abounding with yin, compete for the insufficient yang qi and from this
results that the functions of the five depots are not in mutual balance. The nine orifices
are connected with the five depots through the conduits and vessels and they depend
on the warmth provided by the yang qi and on the moist nourishment provided by the
yin qi of the five depots. Now that the five depots compete with each other for yang qi,
the balance is unobtainable and the nine orifices lose their functions."

59 Gao Shishi: "陳 stands for 敷布, 'to arrange.'"

60 Wang Bing: "從 is 順, 'to comply.' This is to say, if one follows the pattern of yin
and yang and approaches the Way of nourishing life, then the sinews, the vessels, the
bones, and the marrow are supplied with what is appropriate. As a result, both the
qi and the blood can comply with the annual seasons and are in harmony with the
[seasonal] qi." Mori: "If one sets forth [in his activities] the Way of yin and yang and
if he lives in accordance with the qi of heaven and earth, then the sinews, and the
vessels, the bones, and the marrow, the qi and the blood are soft and pliable, as well
as firm and hard."

61 Wang Bing: "Evil qi cannot conquer [the true qi]. Hence the true qi stands all by
itself and is in a regular state. If one misses the Way of the sages, then diseases approach the body. Hence the statement in the following text." 1580/4: "立 is a mistake
for 血, 'blood.' Statements in this treatise like 氣血皆從 and 氣血以流 may serve as
evidence. 故 is to be interpreted as 常, 'regular.'" In contrast, Gao Jiwu/719: "According to Gao You's 高誘 commentary on the *Lü shi chun qiu* 呂氏春秋, 立 stands for

3-20-3

When wind settles [in the body] and encroaches upon the [proper] qi,
then the essence vanishes,[62]
and the evil harms the liver.[63]
Subsequent[64] overeating [causes]
sinews and vessels to relax.
The intestines are flushed[65], and this leads to piles.[66]
Subsequent excessive drinking [causes]

行, 'to move.'" Zhang Yizhi et al. agrees. In this case the translation should read: "..
Ears and eyes are clear and the qi passes [through the body] as usual." Tanba: "Man
receives the qi of heaven and earth to establish (立) his existence. Hence [the text]
states 氣立."

62 Wang Bing: "The following four points outline the results of leaving the Way of
the sages. Wind qi corresponds to the liver. Hence, when the wind is excessive and
when the essence va-nishes, the liver receives harm." Zhang Jiebin: "淫氣 is disorderly
yin and yang qi. If the exterior is not balanced [in yin and yang qi], then wind evil
settles there. Wind is wood and generates fire. Excessive qi transforms into heat. The
heat harms the yin. As a result, the essence dissipates. Wind evil communicates with
the liver. Hence the liver receives harm first." Zhang Zhicong: "The [seminal] essence
flows away spontaneously." In contrast, Gao Jiwu/237: "'Essence' stands for 'blood.'
亡 means 'injured.'" Zhang Yizhi et al.: "淫 in the present context means 過分, 過度,
that is, 'excessive.' 淫氣 is an excessive qi harming the human body." Mori: "風客淫氣
is to say: wind evil settles in the body and encroaches upon the yang qi."

63 Gao Jiwu/436: ."·. the reason is that the external evil has harmed the liver."

64 *NJCD*: "因而 is 卒然, 'sudden.'"

65 Zhang Yizhi et al.: "澼 is the modern version of 辟. *Su wen* 7 has 陰陽虛腸辟死,
'when yin and yang are depleted, the intestines are flushed and one dies.'" Tanba: "The
character combination 腸澼 appears ten times in *Ling shu* and *Su wen*. They mostly
refer to red-white diarrhea. Only the present treatise speaks of 腸澼為痔, taking up
an ancient general expression for feces, pus and blood leaving the passageway of the
grains, (that is, the intestines)."

66 Wang Bing: "If one eats too much, then the intestines and the stomach are 橫滿,
'overly full.' When the intestines and the stomach are full, then the sinews and the
vessels relax and lose their connecting [functions]. Hence the intestines have a wash-
out and this leads to piles." Zhang Jiebin: "This passage and the following two are
secondary consequences of wind settling as visitor and excessive qi. Now, in case of excessive [qi] in the external regions [of the body], wind qi settles in the yang brilliance
[conduit] if one has eaten too much. This causes intestines and stomach to be overly
full. When they are overly full, they receive injury and harm. Hence the sinews and
vessels relax and the resulting disease is intestinal wash-out with piles. Diarrhea with
pus and blood is the consequence." Gao Shishi:"因而飽食者 is to say 'if [following
a harm caused to the liver by evil wind] one overeats [before the wind has left], then
...' Gao Jiwu/716 reads: "the sinews relax and the vessels deteriorate." Cheng Shide et

the qi to move contrary [to its regular course].
Subsequent exertion
causes harm to the qi of the kidneys, and
lets the high bones be spoiled.[67]

3-20-6
The essential principle in all [interactions] of yin and yang
is to have the yang [qi] sealed [in the body] and, thereby, to ensure its
firmness. [68]
When the two do not harmonize,[69]
this is as if there was spring but no fall;

---

al./49: "橫 is 不順理, 'not in correspondence with the pattern.' Here it has the meaning of 逆亂, 'counteracting and disorderly.'" *NJCD*: "橫 is 馳縱, 'lose,' 'relaxed.'"

67 Wang Bing: "強力 is to say: to overexert oneself in sexual intercourse. 'High bones'
are the prominent bones of the lower back. Now, if one overexerts oneself in sexual
intercourse, the essence vanishes. When the essence has vanished, the kidneys are
harmed. When the kidneys are harmed, the marrow qi dries up internally. Hence the
high bone is spoiled and cannot function any longer. When the sages had intercourse,
they did not behave like this. Hence the subsequent statement." For a discussion of
the wording of Wang Bing's commentary, see Qian Chaochen-88/279. *NJCD*: "高骨
refers to the spinal bones of the lumbar region."

68 Wang Bing: "The crucial point in the interactions of yin and yang lies truly in the
yang qi being tightly sealed so that it cannot flow away at random. If it is sealed and
does not flow away at random, the generative qi is strong and firm and can exist for
long. This is the Way of the sages." Wan Lanqing et al./2: "The crucial point in the
entire [situation of] yin and yang in the body is that the yang qi closes [the exterior]
and hence is able to provide external protection." *Gu dian yi zhu xuan* bianxiezu /5:
"密 stands for 嚴密, 'strong.' 固 stands for 堅固, 'firm.' 陽密乃固 has been interpreted
in two different ways. One says, when the yang qi is strong, the external protection [it
offers] is firm. The second says, when the yang in the external sections is strong, then
the yin in the internal sections is firm. Judged from the wording of this passage, the
first explanation is closer to the meaning of the text, but it refers only to the yang. If
judged from the fact that yin and yang are related to each other in that one forms the
basis of the other, then the second explanation is more appropriate." Gao Jiwu/720:
" 'The crucial point in the entire [situation of] yin and yang is such that if the yang qi
is quiet and settled, the yin qi is then able to firmly provide protection internally. 密
is to be explained as 安定, 'quiet and settled.' because an overly strong yang may harm
yin. Further below the text states: 'When the yang is strong, it cannot be secluded
and the [flow of the] yin qi is interrupted.' The meaning of 密 is 'secluded without
manifestation to the outside.'" Wang Shaozeng & Xu Yongnian/13 has 陰密陽固: "It
is crucial that the yin qi is quiet and that the yang qi is firm." For an analysis of this
passage on the basis of its rhyme structure, see 129/69.

69 Wang Bing: " 'The two' refers to yin and yang."

as if there was winter but no summer. [70]
If they are harmonized subsequently,
this is called [to follow the] standards[71] of the sages.

Therefore,
when the yang is strong[72] [to a degree that] it cannot be sealed [in the body],
then the [flow of] yin qi is interrupted.[73]
When the yin and yang are balanced and sealed,
then essence and spirit are in order.

3-21-2
When yin and yang are dissociated,
then the [flow of] essence qi is interrupted. [74]
If subsequently one exposes [oneself and is affected by] wind,
this generates cold and heat.[75]

Hence,
if one was harmed in spring by wind,
<the evil qi stays for long>

---

70 Wang Shaozeng & Xu Yongnian/13: "If either yin or yang dominate unilaterally, the balance is lost. This is as if within the course of one year there was only spring but no fall, or as if there was only winter but no summer. Hence, to balance yin and yang, this is the supreme method employed by the sages to nourish life."

71 *Gu dian yi zhu xuan* bianxiezu /5: "度 stands for 法度, 'law.'"

72 *Gu dian yi zhu xuan* bianxiezu /5: "强 stands for 亢盛, 'overbearing.'" See also Wang Shaozeng/107.

73 Wang Bing: "When the yang cannot be sealed because it is too strong, then the yin flows away and the essence qi is exhausted and cut off." 1580/4: "秘 does not mean 秘固, 'firmly sealed,' here; it stands for 溢 and has the meaning of 'flat,' 'quiet.'" We agree with Gao Jiwu/728 and also with 193/40 and associate 平 and 秘 with both yin and yang. The following passage may be seen as evidence.

74 Wang Bing: "When the yin [qi] is out of balance and when the yang [qi] is not firmly sealed and if [in such a situation] forceful [intercourse] causes an outflow [of essence], then this diminishes the true [qi] of heaven [one is endowed with] and the two qi [that is, yin and yang qi] dissociate and the conduits and network [vessels] are empty. Essence qi fails to transform and its flow is interrupted."

75 Wang Bing: "When one was affected by wind while he has exposed his naked body, the wind qi intrudes from outside and the yang qi resists from inside. Wind and yang [qi] clash against each other and this generates [alternating spells of] cold and heat."

then this causes a pipe flush.[76]

If one was harmed in summer by summerheat,
in autumn this causes *jie* and malaria.[77]

If one was harmed in autumn by dampness,
<[the qi] rises contrary [to its regular course] and one coughs> [78]
this develops to limpness with receding [qi].[79]

If one was harmed in winter by cold,
in spring he will develop a warmth disease.[80]

The qi of the four seasons
alternately harm the five depots.

3-21-6
That which comes to life through yin,
it originates from the five flavors.
The five mansions of the yin,
they [may also] receive harm from the five flavors.[81]

---

76 Tanba: "*Su wen* 5 has 飧泄, 'diarrhea.' *Ling shu* 4 states: '洞 is undigested food, it leaves the body as it is swallowed.' Now, 洞 and 筒 are identical. .. When food is un-digested, it [moves through the body] as if [the body] were a bottomless pipe. Hence [such diarrhea] is called 洞泄, 'pipe flush.'"

77 Wang Bing: "If in summer the heat was excessive and if autumnal yang is received [by the body] in addition, heat and [autumnal] yang attack each other and this causes malaria. 痎 is 老, 'old.' Another term is 瘦, 'emaciation.'"

78 Wang Bing: " 'Dampness' is the dampness qi of the earth. If the autumnal damp-ness dominates and if in winter water rules in addition, the water will avail itself of the lung. Hence a disease of [qi] moving contrary to its regular direction, that is, of cough, emerges."

79 Wang Bing: "When dampness qi attacks the depots and palaces internally, then cough moves contrary to the normal direction [of qi] and disperses in the sinews and vessels. This, in turn, results in paralysis and weakness."

80 Wang Bing: "The winter cold causes freezing; the yang qi in spring effuses. When the cold fails to open [the surface], the yang boils inside. Cold [qi] and boiling [yang qi] hold each other. Hence a warmth disease emerges."

81 Wang Bing: "This so-called 'yin' are the depots of the five spirits and these so-called 'mansions' are the residences of the five spirits. That is, that by which the five depots are generated has its basis in the five flavors. The transformation products of the five flavors are collected in the respective depots. Even though the [the depots] re-

Hence,
when the flavors [consumed] are excessively sour,
this causes the liver qi to overflow,[82] and
the [flow of the] spleen qi will be interrupted. [83]

When the flavors [consumed] are excessively salty,
the qi of the major bones[84] is fatigued,
the muscle[-flesh] is shortened and
the qi of the heart is repressed.[85]

When the flavors [consumed] are excessively sweet,
the qi of the heart pants and there is fullness;
the color is black.
The qi of the kidneys is not balanced. [86]

---

ceive life from the five flavors, it is also through the five flavors that they receive harm. Indeed, if that which is good is, at the same time, excessive, harm will appear. Hence the following statement." Gao Shishi: "The five flavors are the basis of the yin depots, but the yin depots may also be harmed by the five flavors, if consumed in excess. This is like water which may keep a boat afloat, but may also overturn it."

82 Zhang Jiebin: "津 is 溢, 'to overflow.' " Mori: "津 is 潤, 'moisture.' That is, if one eats too much sour flavor, then the qi of the liver will be moistened. The liver, that is, wood, abhors dryness and loves dampness. The spleen, that is, soil, abhors dampness and loves dryness. Hence in case the liver-wood is overly moist, then its qi, too, will be excessively moist. Because it causes the qi in the spleen conduits to stop circulation, diarrhea diseases emerge like a swarm of bees rises."

83 Wang Bing: "If one eats too much sour food, this lets a person develop protuberance illness. The urine fails to pass freely, and this causes the liver to accumulate too much liquid. When this liquid overflows internally it causes the lobes of the liver to rise. When the lobes of the liver rise, then the qi of the spleen conduit is cut off and does not move. Why is that? Because wood checks soil."

84 Gao Shishi: "大骨 refers to the bone of the lower back prominence." Gu Guang-guang: "大骨 is 高骨." Wang Ang: "This is the prominent bone in the lower back above the gate of life [acupuncture] opening." Mori: "This is the hip bone of the lumbar region. This is the region of the kidneys. That is, when the qi of the 'major bone 大骨' is fatigued, that is to say: the qi of the kidneys is fatigued." Zhang Yizhi et al.: "The *Tai su* has a character 則 above the character 大. The *Yun ji qi qian* 雲笈七籤 does not have the character 大. Hence 大骨氣勞 may be an error for 則骨氣勞, 'then the qi of the bones is fatigued.' "

85 Mori: "In antiquity, 肌 referred to 肌肉, that is, flesh. 短肌 is the opposite of 長肌肉; it means 'emaciated.' "

86 Wang Bing: "Consumption of too much sweet flavor causes a feeling as if the heart was pressed. The nature of sweet [flavor] is obstruction and retardation. Hence

When the flavors [consumed] are excessively bitter,
the qi of the spleen is not soggy,
and the qi of the stomach is strong.[87]

When the flavors [consumed] are excessively acrid,
sinews and vessels are worn out[88] and slacken,
and essence and spirit perish.[89]

3-22-4
Hence,
if one carefully balances the five flavors,
the bones are upright,[90] and the sinews are soft.
As a result, qi and blood flow,
and the interstice structures are closed.

If such [a state has been reached],
the bones and the qi will be[91] firm.

If the Way is carefully observed as the law [demands],
the mandate of heaven will last long."

---

it causes qi panting and fullness. Why, then, is the [qi of the] kidneys not balanced?
Because soil restrains water. 衡 is 平, 'balanced.'"

87 Wang Bing: "The nature of bitter [flavor] is hardness and dryness. Also, it nourishes spleen and stomach. Hence the spleen qi is not moist and the stomach qi is rich."

88 Zhang Jiebin: "泪 is 壞, 'worn out.'"

89 Instead of 央, the *Tai su* has 英. Yang Shangshan: "英 is 英盛, 'blossoming and abundant.'" *Guang ya*, Shi gu yi 廣雅, 釋詁一: "央 is 盡, 'exhausted.'" *Jiu ge* 九歌: "央 is 已, 'finished.'" Wang Bing: "泪 stands for 潤, 'to moisten.' 央 stands for 久, 'long.' The nature of acrid [flavor] is to moisten. It disperses in the sinews and nourishes them. Hence it lets the sinews be soft and the vessels be moist and essence and spirit will last long. Why? Because the acrid [flavor] supplements the liver." (This agrees with the description of drug properties to be found in *Su wen* chapter 22.) Lin Yi et al. criticized Wang Bing's interpretation of 央 as 久 as wrong: "央 stands for 殃, 'misfortune.'" Hu Shu: "The interpretation of 央 as 殃 is correct."

90 1580/4: "正 should be explained as 精; with the meaning: the bones are strong."

91 Gao Jiwu/478: "The 以 in 以精 stands for 已, 'already.'" We read 以 in the sense of 以是/是以, "on the basis of this".

Chapter 4
Discourse on the True Words in the Golden Chest

4-22-8

Huang Di asked:

"Heaven has eight winds.[1] The conduits have five winds.[2]

What does that mean?"

Qi Bo responded:

"The eight winds bring forth evil [qi].

They become the [five] winds in the conduits.

They affect the five depots.

The evil qi brings forth diseases.[3]

<As for the so-called 'to grasp the dominations among the four seasons,'

spring dominates late summer,

late summer dominates winter,

winter dominates summer,

summer dominates autumn and

autumn dominates spring.

These are the so-called 'dominations among the four seasons'>[4]

---

1 These are the winds originating in the South, the South-West, the West, the North-West, the North, the North-East, the East, and the South-East. See *Ling shu* 77.

2 Wang Bing: "經 refers to the conduit vessels. They are the passage ways through which the camp and the guard [qi], the blood and the qi flow." Zhang Jiebin: "經 refers to the conduit vessels. The 'five winds' are the winds of the five depots."

3 Wang Bing: "The final cause [of the diseases] named here is the evil emitted by the eight winds. When it was received by the conduit vessels it follows the [path of the] conduits and affects the five depots, because evil offends the proper. Hence it brings forth diseases." 475/41 quotes Ge Songping, *Huang Di nei jing su wen zhi gui* 黃帝內經素問指歸 which identifies 邪 as 耶, a final particle, and 以 as superfluous here and suggests the following reading: 八風發邪, 為經風, 觸五臟邪: "When the eight winds emerge, they become conduit winds; they affect the five depots.".

4 Wang Bing: "Spring is wood, summer is fire, late summer is soil, autumn is metal, winter is water. Each of them dominates that what it can overcome and kill. When it is said that the five seasons dominate each other, this is not to say that when the eight winds strike man, this results in disease. What it means is that whenever any of them meets that [seasonal qi] by which it cannot be dominated, then this brings forth disease." The *Tai su*, ch.3 "Yin yang za shuo" 陰陽雜說, has 脈 instead of 勝. Tanba suggested that the 32 characters from 所謂得 to 四時之勝也 are later insertions which make no sense here. A parallel statement appears in *Su wen* 09; there

4-23-3
The East wind is generated in spring;
[it causes] a disease in the liver.
The transporters[5] are in the neck.[6]

The South wind is generated in summer;
[it causes] a disease in the heart.
The transporters are in the chest and flanks.[7]

The West wind is generated in autumn;
[it causes] a disease in the lung.
The transporters are in the shoulders and back.[8]

The North wind is generated in winter;
[it causes] a disease in the kidneys.
The transporters are in the lower back and thighs.[9]

The center is the soil.
The diseases are in the spleen.
The transporters are in the spine.[10]

---

it is the begin of the dialogue. 526/5 agreed and suggested that the present passage constituted an erroneous insertion here taken from *Su wen* 09. In contrast, Fu Wei-kang & Wu Hongzhou/261 suggested the following interpretation: "Qi Bo replied: 'The eight abnormal climatic conditions in the natural world are pathogenic elements; by penetrating the conduit vessels of the human body they harm the five depots and bring forth the five winds. The diseases brought forth by these abnormal evil qi of the eight regions result from the relationships among the four seasons where a superior qi subdues that which it is able to subdue."

5 1072: "俞在頸項 refers to the location of the point to be selected for treatment."

6 Wang Bing: "The qi of spring stimulates flourishing on top of the myriad beings. Hence it is transported in the neck."

7 Wang Bing: "The heart minor yin conduit follows the chest and emerges in the flanks. Hence it is transported there."

8 Wang Bing: "The lung is located in the upper burner. The back is the palace of the chest. Shoulders and back follow each other. Hence it is transported there."

9 Wang Bing: "The lower back is the palace of the kidneys. The thighs are located next to it. Because their qi are linked, they are referred to here together."

10 Wang Bing: "Because the spine corresponds to the soil, it is said to be situated in the center."

4-23-6
Hence,
as for the qi of spring, [it causes] diseases in the head.[11]
As for the qi of summer, [it causes] diseases in the depots.[12]
As for the qi of autumn, [it causes] diseases in the shoulders and in the back.[13]
As for the qi of winter, [it causes] diseases in the four limbs.[14]

Hence,
in spring one tends to suffer from stuffy nose and nosebleed;[15]
in the middle [month] of summer[16] one tends to have diseases in chest and flanks;[17]
in late summer[18] one tends to suffer from vacating diarrhea and cold center;[19]

---

11 Wang Bing: "The qi of spring is to say: the liver qi. In each [case the generation of disease] follows the correspondence [among seasonal qi and] the qi in a specific depot." Zhang Jiebin: "Yang qi moves upwards."

12 Wang Bing: "It corresponds to the heart." Zhang Jiebin and Gao Shishi identify "depot" here as "heart." In contrast, Ma Shi: " 'The qi of summer, [it causes] diseases in the depots,' externally these are the chest and the flanks, internally these are the depots." 778/35: "Further down the text says that the qi of autumn causes diseases in the shoulders and the back and that the qi of winter causes diseases in the four limbs. The entire text here is a survey, then, of head, inner depots, four limbs, shoulders, and back. To explain 'depot' as 'heart' appears doubtful. Hence Ma Shi's comments are correct." Zhang Yizhi et al. agrees.

13 Wang Bing: "It corresponds to the lung."

14 Wang Bing: "The four limbs have little qi; cold poison prefers to cause harm there. The location of the disease is where the evil finds entrance." Ma Shi: "Above, the text spoke of lower back and thighs, here it speaks of the four limbs. It regards the four limbs as the ends, resembling the branches of trees who wither when affected by cold."

15 Wang Bing: "Because the qi is in the head. The *Li ji* 禮記, 'Yue ling' 月令, states: 'If autumn carries out the orders of summer, then people often suffer from blocked nose and from running nose.'" 778/35, 447/42: "鼽 is explained in the *Shuo wen* as 'blocked nose.;' 衄 is explained in the *Shuo wen* as 'nosebleed.'"

16 778/35: "The fifth month of the moon calendar."

17 Wang Bing: "Because the heart vessel passes through chest and flanks."

18 778/35: "The sixth month of the moon calendar."

19 Wang Bing: "The soil rules in the center. It is the storehouse for waste, water, and grain. Hence [the diseases are] vacating diarrhea and cold center." Yan Hongchen & Gao Guangzhen/9: "寒中 is 'cold qi is in the central burner.'"

in autumn one tends to suffer from wind-malaria;[20]
in winter one tends to suffer from block and receding [qi].[21]

Hence,
if in winter no pressing-lifting is conducted,
in spring there will be no stuffy nose and no nosebleed.[22]

---

20 Wang Bing: "This disease emerges because coolness curtails summerheat. The *Li ji* 禮記, 'Yue ling' 月令, states: 'If mid autumn carries out the orders of summer, then people often suffer from malaria." Gao Shishi: " 'Wind-malaria' means: one shivers from cold and one's shoulders and back tremble."

21 Wang Bing: "The blood corresponds to water. When it is cold, then water freezes. Because the flow of qi is striking, blockage and receding [qi] result." Zhang Jiebin: "The cold evil is in the four limbs." Wu Kun: " 'Blockage' and 'receding [qi]' are two different issues. The 'blockage' mentioned here is blockage due to cold and the 'receding [qi]' mentioned here is a recession because of cold." Zhang Zhicong: "The four limbs are the source of all yang. In winter, the yang qi moves downwards into storage and the conduits are depleted of qi in the outer regions. When wind enters the conduits, hands and feet suffer from receding [qi] with blockage as a result." 778/35: "The term 痹 is employed in the *Su wen* in four different meanings: First it is a general designation of diseases affecting the yin section. Second it has the meaning of 'obstruction,' as for instance in 食痹, 'food obstruction.' Third it is the 痹 of 麻痹, 'numbness,' and fourth it is rheumatism affecting the joints, as in the treatise 痹論 when it speaks of 行痹, etc.. As to 厥, the treatise 厥論 states: 'When the yang qi weakens in the lower [parts of the body], this is receding [qi] with cold. When the yin qi weakens in the lower [parts of the body], this is receding [qi] with heat.' Wang Bing states: '厥 indicates that the qi moves upwards, contrary to its regular course.' " See also 447/42.

22 Wang Bing: "按 is to say: 按摩, 'massage.' 蹻 is to say: hands and feet are lifted and moved like rapid tiptoeing. This is the so-called [technique of] 導引, 'guiding and pulling [of qi].' Now, when the sinews and bones are moved, then the yang qi does not remain stored. In spring, the yang qi rises. Strong heat steams the lung. The lung communicates with the nose. Hence diseases take shape there. Hence, if no massage is conducted in winter, there will be neither running nose nor nosebleed in spring. 鼽 is to say: water runs out of the nose. 衄 is to say: blood runs out of the nose." Zhang Jiebin: "按蹻 refers to the massage of extremities and joints, to conduct [the technique of] 導引, 'guiding and pulling [of qi].' During the three [months of] winter, the principal qi lies hidden and is stored in the yin. If sinews and bones are excited at a time when [the principal qi] should lie hidden and be stored, then essence qi will flow away excessively. As a result, in spring, summer, autumn, and winter the respective diseases emerge. Hence it is appropriate in winter to support storage. In spring, then, the yang qi is generated, but the yin essence is strong." Tanba: "按蹻 is 按摩矯揉, 'massage, straightening, and bending.' Wang Bing's commentary is far-fetched." See also 447/43.

If in spring there is no disease in the neck,[23] [then]
in the middle [month] of summer there will be no disease in the chest and in
the flanks,
in late summer there will be no such disease as vacating diarrhea and cold
center,
in autumn there will be no such disease as wind-malaria,
in winter there will be no such diseases as block, receding [qi], outflow of [un-
digested] food,[24] and sweating.[25]

4-24-3
Now,
the essence, it is the basis of the body.
Hence,
if there is storing of essence, there will be no warmth disease in spring;[26]
if in summer [despite] summerheat no sweat leaves [the body],

---

23 Tanba and 526/5 assume the five characters 春不病頸項 "If in spring there is no
disease in the neck" to be out of place here.

24 Lin Yi et al. assumes the six characters 飧泄而汗出也 "outflow of (undigested)
food and sweating" to be a later insertion that makes no sense here. Zhang Qi considers 飧泄 out of place here.

25 Wang Bing: "All the five sentences above refer to states that result if no massage
was conducted in winter." 2259/31 concluded that the entire passage from 故冬不按
蹻 down to 而汗出也 is a senseless listing here without inner coherence, that should
be deleted.

26 Wang Bing: "This is to say: if no massage was conducted in winter, then the essence qi remains hidden and stored. Hence the yang qi is not made to rise unnecessar-
ily, there will be no warmth disease in spring." "Essence" has been identified by some
commentators (including Tanba) here as a reference to seminal essence lost, first of
all, through excessive sexual intercourse. See 859/17 and 447/43. In contrast, Ma Shi,
Zhang Jiebin, and 678/55, following Wang Bing, relate the preservation of essence to
the absence of massage in winter. Zhang Jiebin: "The essence of the human body is
the true yin. It is the source of the principal qi. If one wastes one's essence, this causes
depletion of yin. When the yin is depleted, any yang evil may easily attack. Hence
there is a tendency towards warmth diseases. What this means here is that if there is
no massage in winter, then the essence qi will remain hidden and stored. And if the
yang is not brought to life wantonly, then there will be no warmth diseases in spring."
The *Tai su* has 清, "clear", instead of 精.

this generates wind-malaria[27] in autumn.[28]

{This is the law of [examining] <the vessels in> a normal person.}[29]

4-24-6

Hence it is said:

In yin is yin; in yang is yang.[30]

From dawn to noon, this is the yang of heaven;

it is the yang in the yang.

From noon to dusk, this is the yang of heaven;

it is the yin in the yang.[31]

---

27 447/43: "風瘧 stands for 瘧疾, 'disease of malaria.' The major reason is an affection by the cold wind of autumn. Hence it is called 'wind fever.' " Wu Kun: "If one was
harmed first by heat and then by cold, metal and fire fight each other, with the result
that cold and heat break out alternatingly in that person."

28 Wang Bing: "That is to say: because the qi of wind and coolness has curtailed the
sweating [caused by] summerheat." Zhang Jiebin: "If the summerheat is hidden [in
the body] during the months of summer, so that no sweat flows, then the summerheat
evil accumulates internally. When it comes to autumn, then, that is at a time when
cold presses on the [summerheat], cold and heat engage in a fight, and this leads to the
disease of wind-fever. Of the two paragraphs above, one says that in winter one should
close and store, the second says that one should open and drain. If in winter one does
not store the essence, one will have a warmth disease [later]. If in summer one does
not let the sweat flow, then one will suffer from malaria [afterwards]. Yin and yang
open and close and the same applies to the qi of the seasons. The [text] here speaks
only of winter and summer; autumn and spring are in between of them." Lin Yi et al.:
"The text from here on does not fit in with the preceding text."

29 Wang Bing: "That is to say, the patterns of the [movements in the] vessels of
healthy and sick persons." Wu Kun: "脈法 is to say 診法, 'the patterns of diagnosis.' "
Ma Shi: "All these are instances of diseases resulting from the seasons. It is essential
that one also knows the [movement in the] vessels." Zhang Jiebin: "The qi of the four
seasons, if one acts in accordance with them, this brings peace. If one acts contrary to
them, disease results. This is the vessel pattern of the healthy person. 'Vessel pattern'
refers to the reasons why conduit vesselss receive harm." 778/36: "The explanations
given by Wu Kun and Zhang Jiebin are forced; one should follow the comment offered by Lin Yi et al.." We consider the phrase to be a commentary. 脈, vessels, might
be a late insertion into this commentary. The reason for such an insertion could have
been the following: 平人, "the normal person", in the *Suwen* appears often (albeit not
always) in the context of vessel diagnosis, and 脈法 is used as a term elsewhere. The
Tai su has the same phrase but adds 地 after 法: 此平人脈法地也. This could be translated as: "This is how the vessels of a normal person take the earth as a pattern".

30 Wang Bing: "That is to say: as they are just emerging and as they flourish."

31 Wang Bing: "At midday, the yang [qi] abounds. Hence [the text] states: yang in
yang. At dusk, the yin [qi] abounds. Hence [this period] is called: yin in yang. Yang

From early evening[32] to the crowing of the cocks, this is the yin of heaven;
it is the yin in the yin.
From the crowing of the cocks to dawn, this is the yin of heaven;
it is the yang in the yin.[33]
The fact is,
man, too, corresponds to this.

4-24-9
Now,
speaking of the yin and yang of man,
then the outside is yang, the inside is yin.[34]
Speaking of the yin and yang of the human body,
then the back is yang, the abdomen is yin.
Speaking of the yin and yang among the depots and palaces of the human
body,
then the depots are yin and the palaces are yang.[35]

The liver, the heart, the spleen, the lung, and the kidneys,
all these five depots are yin.
The gallbladder, the stomach, the large intestine, the small intestine, the urinary
bladder, and the triple burner,
all these six palaces are yang.

Why would one want to know about yin in yin and yang in yang?
This is because
in winter, diseases are in the yin [sections];

---

qi rules daytime. Hence the entire period from dawn to dusk is called 'yang of heaven'
and within [this period] there is once again a differentiation between a yin and a yang
[period]."

32 148/52 and 484/12: "Mr. Yu Chang 于鬯 holds that the character 合 is a mistake
for 台, which in turn is an abbreviation of 始, 'begin.' 合夜, therefore, stands for 始夜,
'beginning night,' which means 'dusk.' "

33 Wang Bing: "Because at the time when the cocks crow the yang qi (here: the sun)
has not appeared yet. At dawn the yang qi has risen. Hence [this period] is called
'yang in yin.' "

34 1922/57: " 'Outside' refers to the physical shell of the body; 'inside' refers to the
inner organs."

35 Wang Bing: " 'Depot' is to say: where the five spirits are stored. 'Palace' is to say:
the palaces where the six transformations take place." 526/5: "The two characters 者
following 藏 and 府 are superfluous here. If one reads 藏為陰, 府為陽, the style is
identical with the passages above: 外為陽, 內為陰; 背為陽, 腹為陰."

in summer, diseases are in the yang [sections].³⁶
In spring, diseases are in the yin [sections];
in autumn, diseases are in the yang [sections].
In all cases one must look for their location to apply needles and [pointed]
stones.³⁷

Hence,
the back being yang, the yang in the yang is the heart.³⁸
The back being yang, the yin in the yang is the lung.³⁹
The abdomen being yin, the yin in the yin are the kidneys.⁴⁰
The abdomen being yin, the yang in the yin is the liver.⁴¹
The abdomen being yin, the extreme yin in the yin is the spleen.⁴²

4-25-8
All these are correspondences in the transportation [of qi] among yin and yang,
exterior and interior, inner and outer, female and male [regions].⁴³
Hence,
through these there is correspondence to the yin and yang of heaven."

---

36 448/40: " 'Yin' refers to the kidneys here, 'yang' to the heart."

37 It remains unclear whether 針石 refers to "needle stones", i.e., pointed stones, or
to "needles and [pointed] stones" reflecting the parallel existence of acupuncture by
needling and bloodletting by means of pointed stones during the Han era. See also
Su wen 11, 13, and 14.

38 Wang Bing: "The heart is a yang depot. It is situated in the upper burner region.
Because a yang [depot] is situated in a yang [region], it is called yang in yang."

39 Wang Bing: "The lung is a yin depot. It is situated in the upper burner region.
Because a yin [depot] is situated in a yang [region], it is called yin in yang."

40 Wang Bing: "The kidneys constitute a yin depot. They are situated in the lower
burner region. Because a yin [depot] is situated in a yin [region], they are called yin
in yin."

41 Wang Bing: "The liver is a yang depot. It is situated in the central burner region.
Because a yang [depot] is situated in a yin [region], is is called yang in yin."

42 Wang Bing: "The spleen is a yin depot. It is situated in the central burner region.
Because an extreme yin [depot] is situated in a yin [region], it is called extreme yin
in yin."

43 Zhang Zhicong: " 'Female and male' refers to the depots and palaces." See also
1166/14 for an examination of "female" and "male" as remnants of a more ancient
classificatory system.

[Huang] Di:

"The five depots correspond to the four seasons.

Do all of them have [something specific] that they collect and receive?"[44]

Qi Bo:

"Yes, they do.

The East; green-blue color.

Having entered it communicates with the liver;

it opens an orifice in the eyes.[45]

It stores essence in the liver.

The disease it brings forth is shock.[46]

Its flavor: sour;

its class: herbs and trees;

its domestic animal: chicken;

its grain: wheat.[47]

Its correspondence with the four seasons, above it is Jupiter.

{Hence the qi of spring is in the head.}

Its tone: *jue*;

its number: eight.

{Hence one knows that [its] diseases are located in the sinews.}

Its odor: fetid.

4-26-3

The South; red color.

Having entered it communicates with the heart;

---

44 Zhang Jiebin: "收受 is to say: like qi seek each other; each has a place to turn to. The East is the region where wood governs; the liver is the depot associated with the wood. Hence they communicate with each other." Wu Kun: "The colors of the five regions enter [man] and communicate with the five depots. This is called 收; each of the five depots stores its essence. This is called 受."

45 1748/50 interprets this passages as 肝開竅于目, 'the liver opens an orifice in the eyes,' or 'the liver has an orifice opening in the eyes.'" See there for a detailed discussion.

46 Lin Yi et al.: "In *Su wen* 70 there is a statement 其發為驚駭. The statement 其病 發驚駭 is superfluous here."

47 955/34, quoting Li Nian'e 李念莪 (=Li Zhongzi): "The 麥 is the first to ripe. Hence it corresponds to the East and to the qi of spring." For a discussion of the five types of grain, see 2243/5. An exact botanical identification of this crop is not possible.

it opens an orifice in the ears.[48]
It stores essence in the heart.
Hence the disease [it brings forth] is in the five depots.

Its flavor: bitter;
its class: fire;
its domestic animal: sheep.
Its grain: glutinous millet.
Its correspondence with the four seasons, above it is Mars.
{Hence one knows that its diseases are located in the vessels.}
Its tone: *zhi*;
its number: seven.
Its odor: burned.

The center; yellow color.
Having entered it communicates with the spleen.
It opens an orifice in the mouth.
It stores essence in the spleen.
Hence the disease [it brings forth] is at the base of the tongue.

Its flavor: sweet;
its class: soil.
Its domestic animal: ox;
its grain: panicled millet.
Its correspondence with the four seasons, above it is Saturn.
{Hence one knows that its diseases are in the flesh.}
Its tone: *gong*.
Its number: five.
Its odor: aromatic.

4-27-5
The West; white color.
Having entered it communicates with the lung.
It opens an orifice in the nose.
It stores essence in the lung.
Hence the disease [it brings forth] is in the back.

Its flavor: acrid,
its class: metal.

---

48 In contrast, *Su wen* 05 identifies the kidneys as the organ responsible for the ears.
1122 and 2437 offer discussions of this apparent contradiction.

Its domestic animal: horse;
its grain: rice.
Its correspondence with the four seasons, above it is Venus.
{Hence one knows that its diseases are in the skin and body hair.}
Its tone: *shang*;
its number: nine.
Its odor: fishy.

The North; black color.
Having entered it communicates with the kidneys.
It opens an orifice in the two yin [sites].[49]
It stores essence in the kidneys.
Hence the disease [it brings forth] is in the ravines.[50]

Its flavor: salty;
its class: water;
its domestic animal: the swine.
Its grain: the bean.
Its correspondence with the four seasons, above it is Mercury.
{Hence one knows that its diseases are in the bones.}
Its tone: *yu*;
its number: six.
Its odor: foul.

4-29-1
Hence,
those who are experts in the [examination of the] vessels,[51]
they carefully investigate the five depots and the six palaces,
whether [a movement] runs contrary to or follows [its regular course].

---

49 I.e., the outlets for urine and stool.

50 *Su wen* 58 has "The large meeting points of flesh are the valleys; the small meeting points of flesh are the ravines. It is in the parting of the flesh where the ravines and valley meeting points are located." 955/35: "谿谷 is the location in the flesh where water flows and stagnates. Hence in case of diseases affecting the spleen, these 'ravines' are influenced and edemas develop. Li Niane commented: '谿 is where the water flows and stagnates.'"

51 Wu Kun: "脈 stands for 診, 'to diagnose.'"

The arrangements of yin and yang, exterior and interior, female and male:
they store them in their bosom,[52]
and they link the heart with the essence.[53]

If it is not this kind of a person, do not teach him.
If it is not this kind of truth,[54] do not confer it.

This is called achieving the Way."

52 Tanba: "This 意 is not the 意 of 志意, 'intention.' In antiquity, 意 and 臆, 'breast,' 'heart,' 'thoughts,' were used exchangeably. 心意 is to say: 胸臆, 'bosom.' "

53 779; Fang Wenhui/147: "意 stands for 臆, 'the breast,' 'the heart.' " 1555/572: "心 意 stands for 心胸, 'heart and chest.' "The *Tai su* has 之 instead of 心: 藏之心意, 合之 于精. Gao Shishi: "藏之心意 is to say, the principles are extremely subtle and they are difficult to transmit to others by means of words. To join heart and essence is called 心意."

54 In contrast to the majority of commentators, Gao Jiwu/589 identifies 真 as "a person with a true heart sincerely loving the medical profession."

Chapter 5

Comprehensive Discourse on Phenomena Corresponding to Yin and Yang

5-31-1

Huang Di:

"As for yin and yang, they are

the Way of heaven and earth,[1]

the fundamental principles [governing] the myriad beings,[2]

father and mother to all changes and transformations,[3]

the basis and beginning of generating life and killing,[4]

the palace of spirit brilliance.[5]

To treat diseases, one must search for the basis.[6]

---

1 Wang Bing: "This is to say, the Way of change and transformation, of creation and completion."

2 Wang Bing: "This is their function of support and generation. The yang provides the [myriad beings] with proper qi so that they come to life and the yin provides them with support so that they may stand up. Hence [the text] states 'they are the web holding the myriad beings.'" For an etymology of 綱紀 and its interpretation as 綱領, see 448/41.

3 Wang Bing: "This is their function [in the generation of] strange classes [of beings]. Why? Now, hawks 鷹 are transformed to turtle-doves 鳩. Moles are transformed to quails. Rotten grass is transformed to fireflies. When small birds enter a large water, they become ge-mussels 蛤. When pheasants enter a large water, they become shen-mussels 蜃. This way all strange classes [of beings] are generated through changes and transformations [resulting from an interaction of yin and yang]."

4 Wang Bing: "This is their function [in the generation of] cold and summerheat. The myriad beings depend on the warmth of yang qi to come to life and they die because of the cold of yin qi. Hence it is obvious that the periodic movements of yin and yang [qi] are the source and origin of life and death."

5 Wang Bing: "府 is 宮府, 'palace.' That is to say, where many issues of life and death, of change and transformation are handled. Why? Because the spirit brilliance resides in them."

6 Wang Bing: "The association of yin and yang with the life and death, the change and transformation of the myriad beings, is reflected in the human body. Hence [to grasp] the Way of treating diseases, one must first of all search for this [association of yin and yang with life and death in the human body]." Zhang Jiebin: "本 is 'the source in yin and yang.' Man's depots and palaces, qi and blood, outer and inner, above and below, they all have their source in yin and yang. And outside and at the surface: the wind, the cold, the summerheat, and the dampness, as well as the the four seasons and the five agents, they all are associated with the two qi of yin and yang. When it comes

Hence,
the accumulation of yang, that is heaven;
the accumulation of yin, that is the earth.
Yin is tranquillity, yang is agitation.
Yang gives life, yin stimulates growth.
Yang kills, yin stores.[7]
Yang transforms qi, yin completes physical appearance.

5-32-1
Cold at its maximum generates heat;
heat at its maximum generates cold.
Cold qi generates turbidity;
heat qi generates clarity.

When clear qi is in the lower [regions of the body],
then this generates outflow of [undigested] food.
When turbid qi is in the upper [regions],

---

to the qi and flavors used in the treatment of disease, or to the left or right [side of the body] where the needles are applied, to the differentiation, in diagnosis, of complexion and [movement in the] vessels, to [therapeutic modes such as] pulling upwards or causing that which is above to move downwards, all these [phenomena] are part of the patterns of yin and yang. Hence [the text] states: 'In order to treat diseases, one must search for their source.' That is to say, one must search whether the source of the disease is a yin evil or a yang evil; one must search whether the disease is in the yang sector or in the yin sector, in the qi sector or in the blood sector. One must investigate which drugs are appropriate for use, whether it is the [ability of] qi to ascend, or of flavor to descend, of warmth to fill, or of bitter to drain." 448/42: "Why do we say that 本 stands for yin and yang? Because in *Su wen* 3 it says: '生之本,本于陰陽.'" (see 3-14-10) See also *Gu dian yi zhu xuan* bianxiezu /57: "'Source' refers to yin and yang." 1186: "In the course of time, the four most pertinent explanations of 本 have been the following: 1. 'The source is in yin and yang.' [examples follow] 2. 'The source is in the cause of the disease.' [examples follow] 3. 'The source is in spleen and kidneys.' [examples follow] 4. 'The source is in the six changes.' [example follows]. .. 本 is nothing but the basic nature of the disease. It does not simply refer to the cause of the disease and it does not refer to the location of the disease and it even less refers to one depot or another. 本 equals 証, 'disease sign.' To search for the source is to differentiate the disease signs." For details see there. See also 2129/43 for a detailed discussion.

7 683/50 interprets these two lines as examples of the 互文 ("reciprocal phrasing") style. Accordingly, the four activities of generation, stimulation of growth, killing, and storage should be associated with yin and yang alike. 684/46 agrees. Gao Jiwu/726 disagrees. See 2445 for an explanation of this passage as a reference to the functions of the four seasons. See also 448 and 1959 for detailed discussions.

then this generates bloating.[8]

These [are examples of] activities of yin and yang [qi] contrary [to their normal patterns],[9]
and of diseases opposing [the patterns of] compliance.[10]

5-32-4
The fact is,
the clear yang is heaven;
the turbid yin is the earth.
The qi of the earth rises and turns into clouds;
the qi of heaven descends and becomes rain.
Rain originates from the qi of the earth;
clouds originate from the qi of heaven.[11]

Hence,
the clear yang exits through the upper orifices;
the turbid yin exits through the lower orifices.[12]

---

8 Wang Bing: "When heat qi is in the lower part of the body, then food [lit: grains] does not transform. Hence there is outflow of [undigested] food. When cold qi is in the upper part of the body, then the qi fails to dissipate. Hence there is swelling. Why? Because yin is tranquillity, while yang is agitation." SWJZ: "膹 is 起, 'to rise.'" Guang yun 廣韻: "膹 is 'swollen flesh.'" Zhang Yizhi et al.: "脹 was originally written 張; another writing is 痕. The *Yu pian* 玉篇 states: '痕 is 滿, 'fullness.'"

9 Zhang Yizhi et al.: "反 is identical with 翻. 翻 has the meaning of 反復無常, 'backwards and forwards, without regularity.' 作 means 行, 'to pass,' 'to move.' 陰陽反作 is: the movement of yin [qi] and yang [qi] has lost its regularity." Yan Hongchen & Gao Guangzhen/162: "These are abnormal changes [in the interactions] of yin and yang."

10 Gao Jiwu/212: 逆縱 is 反常, 'contrary to the regular.'

11 Wang Bing: "Yin qi rises and congeals to clouds above. Yang qi dissipates and flows down as rain. Rain is a transformation product of clouds. Hence [the text] states: 'Rain originates from the earth.' Clouds are accumulations of qi. Hence [the text] states: 'Clouds originate from heaven.'"

12 Wang Bing: "Those qi that have their origin in heaven, they have a propensity towards what is above. Those qi that have their origin in the earth, they have a propensity towards what is below. Each follows its class. The upper orifices include ears, eyes, nose, and mouth. The lower orifices include the yin openings in the front and behind." Wan Lanqing et al./3: "'Clear yang' refers here to those light and clear elements in the subtle essence of water and grains that move upwards [in the body]. They are effused through the upper orifices and transform into breathing and sounds, as well as into the perceptive abilities of tasting, smelling, seeing, and listening." *Gu dian yi zhu xuan bianxiezu* /5: "Anus and urinary paths." Wan Lanqing et al./3: "'Turbid yin' refers to

The clear yang is effused through the interstice structures;
the turbid yin moves to the five depots.[13]
The clear yang replenishes the four limbs;
the turbid yin turns to the six palaces.[14]

5-32-7
Water is yin;
fire is yang.[15]
Yang is qi;
yin is flavor.[16]

Flavor turns to physical appearance.
Physical appearance turns to qi.
Qi turns to essence.[17]
Essence turns to transformation.[18]

---

the waste products and turbid liquids remaining after the digestion and resorption of
water and grains. After their transformation into feces and urine, they are discharged
through the two lower orifices."

13 Wang Bing: " 'Interstice structures' is to say: the gates of outflow. Hence the clear
yang [qi] can be effused through them. The five depots are the locations of storage.
Hence the turbid yin can go there."

14 Wang Bing: "The four limbs move on the outside. Hence clear yang fills them.
The six palaces transform inside. Hence the turbid yin turns there." Wan Lanqing et
al./4: " 'The clear yang is effused through the interstice structures,' and 'the clear yang
fills the four limbs' refers to the protective yang qi." Fang Wenhui/8: "支 was used in
ancient times for 肢, 'limbs.' "

15 Wang Bing: "Water is cold and tranquil. Hence it is yin. Fire is hot and agitated.
Hence it is yang."

16 Wang Bing: "Qi disperses only; hence it consists of yang. Flavor is tied to physical
appearance. Hence it consists of yin." Zhang Jiebin: "The qi has no physical appearance and rises, hence it is yang. The flavor has matter and descends, hence it is yin."
249/10: "The 'qi' in this statement refers to the [temperature] qi in drugs and food, i.e.,
cold, hot, warm, and cool [qi]. 'Flavor' is the flavor of drugs and food, i.e., sour, bitter,
sweet, acrid, salty, bland, etc.."

17 673: "This is to say, heaven nourishes man with the five qi."

18 Wang Bing: "Physical appearance feeds on flavor, hence 'flavor turns to physical
appearance.' Qi nourishes physical appearance. Hence 'physical appearance turns to
qi.' Essence feeds on qi. Hence 'qi turns to essence.' Transformation generates essence.
Hence 'essence turns to transformation.' Hence the following statement. Zhang Jiebin:
"歸 is 依投, 'to depend on.' " 249/10: "The original meaning of 歸 is 'to turn around.'
here it is extended to 'to nourish.' 形 refers to the physical body of man, including the

Essence is nourished by qi.
Physical appearance is nourished by flavor.[19]
Transformations generate essence.
Qi generates physical appearance.[20]
Flavor harms physical appearance.
Qi harms essence.[21]
Essence transforms into qi.
Qi is harmed by flavor.[22]

---

organs, etc.; 氣 refers to the principal qi of the human body. The meaning of the entire passage is: 'The flavors in food and drugs can nourish the human body; the human body, having been nourished this way, can bring forth the functions of qi transformation. ... The 'qi' is the qi of food and drugs; 'essence' refers to the yin essence of the human body. 歸 stands for 'nourish,' 'generate' ... . The meaning of the entire passage is: 'The qi of food and drugs can generate essence and blood of the human body; the generation of essence and blood depends on the process of qi transformation."

19 249/10: "The essence qi of the human body builds up through using up the qi of food and drugs. On the other hand, the essence splendor of the human body relies on the support provided by the qi of drugs and food. The physical body of man relies on consuming the flavor of food and drugs for its growth; that is, the physical body relies on nourishment provided by the flavor of food [and drugs]."

20 249/10: "This is a supportive statement to 'essence turns to transformations,' and 'the physical appearance turns to qi.' Essence turns to transformations, hence 'transformations generate essence.' Physical appearance turns to qi, hence 'qi generates physical appearance.' 'Transformation generates essence' is to say that the essential and subtle qi of food and drugs can transform into the essence qi of the human body. 'Qi generates physical appearance' is to say that the functions of qi transformation in the human body stimulate the growth and development of the human body. That is to say, the qi and the flavors of the environment cannot be transformed directly into the essence and the physical appearance required by the human body; they must go through the process of qi transformation in the body."

21 249/10: "That is, excesses in the qi and flavor of food and drugs produce pathological changes. Excesses in the flavor harm the physical appearance, excesses in the qi harm essence and blood."

22 249/10: "That is, the yin essence (a visible substance) can transform into the invisibal functions of qi transformation. Yin essence is the foundation of the activities of qi transformation; however if the flavors of food and drugs are excessive, this can harm the functions of qi transformation in the human body." Gao Jiwu/437: "The functions of the depots and palaces are harmed by beverages and food." For a detailed discussion with graph, see also Wan Lanqing et al./45.

5-33-3
Flavor is yin and exits through the lower orifices.
Qi is yang and exits through the upper orifices.[23]

That which is of strong flavor is yin;
that with weak [flavor] is yang of yin.
That which is of strong qi is yang;
that with weak qi is yin of yang.[24]

When the flavor is strong, then outflow [results];
when it is weak, then penetration [results].[25]
When the qi is weak, then it brings forth outflow;
when it is strong, then it brings forth heat.[26]

The qi of strong fire[27] weakens.
The qi of a small fire[28] gains in strength.[29]
Strong fire feeds on qi.

---

23 Wang Bing: "Flavors are material. Hence they flow downwards through the orifices of outflow causing relief. Qi has no physical appearance. Hence it rises and leaves through the gates of inhalation and exhalation."

24 Wang Bing: "Yang brings forth qi. A rich qi is pure yang. Yin brings forth flavor. A rich flavor is pure yin. Hence that which is weak in flavor is is yang in yin. What is weak in qi is yin in yang."

25 Gao Jiwu/258: "Drugs with weakly pronounced flavor have a diuretic effect."

26 Wang Bing: "Yin qi moistens what is below. Hence what is rich in flavor causes diarrhea. Yang qi flames upwards. Hence what is rich in qi is effused as heat/causes fever. Weak flavor is diminished yin. Hence it opens the way for outflow. Weak qi is diminished yang. Hence [it causes] sweat flow. 發泄 is to say: sweat flows." Gao Jiwu/258: "Li Gao, quoted in *Ben cao gang mu*, ch.1 part 2: "氣味陰陽, states 發 stands for 滲, 'to leak.'"

27 Yan Hongchen & Gao Guangzhen/24: " 'Strong fire' refers to an excessive presence of yang qi. It is a pathological sign."

28 Yan Hongchen & Gao Guangzhen/24: " 'Weak fire' is a gentle, not excessive yang qi."

29 Wang Bing: "When the strength of a strong fire is exhausted, it weakens. When the weakness of a small fire reaches its end, it gains in strength." Zhang Jiebin: "Fire is the yang qi of heaven and earth; without this fire, heaven cannot generate any beings; without this fire, man cannot live. .. However, a gentle fire generates beings; while, in contrast, a violent fire harms beings." Yan Hongchen & Gao Guangzhen/24: "An excessive yang qi can weaken the proper qi; a gentle yang qi can strengthen the proper qi."

Qi feeds on small fire.[30]
A strong fire disperses qi.
A small fire generates qi.[31]

Qi and flavor:
acrid [flavor] and sweet [flavor] are effused and disperse and are yang,
sour [flavor] and bitter [flavor] cause gushing up and outflow and are yin.[32]

5-33-7
When yin dominates, then the yang is ill;
when yang dominates, then the yin is ill.[33]
When the yang dominates, then there is heat;
when the yin dominates, then there is cold.[34]
Doubled cold results in heat;
doubled heat results in cold.[35]

---

30 Yan Hongchen & Gao Guangzhen/24: "Strong fire diminishes the proper qi; a small fire strengthens the proper qi." Hence, this statement could also be translated as: "A strong fire feeds on the [proper] qi; the [proper] qi is nourished by small fire." Fang Wenhui/26: "Excessive yang qi can diminish the principal qi."

31 Wang Bing: "Qi generates strong fire. Hence [the text] states: 'a strong fire feeds on qi.' A small fire nourishes qi. Hence [the text] states: 'Qi feeds on small fire.' Because a strong fire feeds on qi, when qi gets a strong fire, then [the qi] diminishes and disperses. Because a small fire increases qi, when qi gets a small fire, then [the qi] grows. The same applies to the strength or weakness of yang qi in man." For a discussion of 壯火散氣少火生氣 see 1510.

32 Wang Bing: "It is not only such that qi and flavor are classified as yin or yang respectively, among acrid, sweet, sour, and bitter [flavors] the difference between yin and yang qi exists, too. Why? Acrid [flavor] disperses and sweet [flavor] relaxes. Hence [the text states]: 'they are effused and disperse and are yang.' Sour [flavor] gathers and bitter [flavor] drains. Hence [the text states]: 'they cause gushing up and outflow and are yin.'"

33 Wang Bing: "What dominates will have no disease. What does not dominate will have disease." Yan Hongchen & Gao Guangzhen/19: "This is unilateral dominance and refers to evil qi." Gao Jiwu/595: "When the yin qi flourishes unilaterally, the yang is often harmed by cold; hence the yang qi weakens. When the yang qi flourishes unilaterally, the yin is often harmed by heat; hence the yin qi weakens."

34 Wang Bing: "Such [states] result from greatly excessive presence [of yin or yang qi]." Lin Yi et al.: "The *Jia yi jing* has 'a yin disease results in heat; a yang disease results in cold.' The wording is different, but the meaning is the same."

35 Wang Bing: "When something reaches its limits, it turns around. This is like a strong fire which has a weak qi and a small fire which has a strong qi." Zhang Jiebin: "重 has the meaning of 重疊, 'duplicated.' That is to say, when in a yin season one is, in addition, affected by cold, or when in a yang season one is, in addition, affected by

Cold harms the physical appearance;
heat harms the qi.[36]
Harmed qi causes pain;
a harmed physical appearance causes swelling.[37]
‹Hence,
when there is pain first and swelling afterwards,
qi has harmed the physical appearance.
When there is swelling first and pain comes afterwards,
the physical appearance has harmed the qi.›[38]

5-34-3
When wind dominates, then there is movement;[39]
when heat dominates, then there is swelling.[40]

---

heat. Or, if a heat qi of heaven harms the yang section of man; or, if a cold qi of heaven harms the yin section of man, all this is called 'duplication.'" Yan Hongchen & Gao Guangzhen/19: "重 stands for 極, 'peak,' 'extreme.'" Gao Jiwu/166: "重 can also be read 'zhong,' in the meaning of 'deep,' 'very,' 'extreme.' In this case the ideas would be that of things reaching an extreme and turning into their opposite."

36 Wang Bing: "In case of cold, the guard qi cannot flow freely. Hence the physical appearance is harmed. In case of heat, the camp qi dissipates internally. Hence the qi is harmed. Even though, in general, yin [qi] generates physical appearance and yang [qi] transforms to qi, once [yin and yang qi] are present in excess, physical appearance and qi are harmed [by them]." Yan Hongchen & Gao Guangzhen/119: "Cold is a yin evil; the physical body is associated with yin too. Hence cold evil easily harms the physical body. Heat is a yang evil. The qi is associated with yang too. Hence heat evil easily harms the qi sector."

37 Wang Bing: "When qi is harmed, then heat collects in the inner section and this results in pain. When the physical appearance is harmed, then cold strikes against the skin and this results in swelling." Gao Jiwu/484: "The character 則 has been omitted here [in front of the characters 痛 and 腫]." 307/185 agrees.

38 Wang Bing: "First there is a qi sign and [afterwards] the disease affects the physical appearance. Hence [the text] states: 'qi has harmed the physical appearance.' First there is a sign in the physical appearance and [afterwards] the disease affects the qi. Hence [the text] states: 'the physical appearance has harmed the qi.'" Gao Jiwu/437: "That is, the physical body has received harm first and this then has affected the qi sector."

39 Wang Bing: "When wind dominates, then all beings are shaken. Hence they move." The *Tai su* does not have the four characters 則動熱勝. Zhang Yizhi et al.: "動 is identical with 腫. The four characters 熱勝則腫 may be a commentary that was inserted into the main text."

40 Wang Bing: "When heat dominates, then the yang qi collects internally. Hence vast swelling occurs all of a sudden. In severe cases, the camp qi moves against the interstice structures. It accumulates there and causes a swelling of *yong*-abscesses with pus."

When dryness dominates, then there is aridity;
when cold dominates, then there is surface [swelling].⁴¹
When dampness dominates, then there is soggy outflow.⁴²

Heaven has the four seasons and the five agents.
It is through [the former that heaven causes] generation, growth, gathering, and storage.
It is through [the latter that it] generates cold, summerheat, dryness, dampness, and wind.⁴³

Man has the five depots;
they transform the five qi,⁴⁴
thereby generating joy, anger, sadness,⁴⁵ anxiety, and fear.⁴⁶

5-34-6
The fact is,
joy and anger harm the qi;

---

41 Wang Bing: "When cold dominates, then the yin qi congeals in the dark palaces [i.e., in the pores; see *Su wen* 61 and 62]. When the dark palaces are tightly closed, the yang qi attacks them from the inside. Hence swelling results." *Gu dian yi zhu xuan* bianxiezu /37: " 'When cold dominates, then there is swelling' refers here mainly to yang depletion with internal cold. The qi is transformed and does not move, with the result that the water stagnates and causes surface swelling."

42 Wang Bing: "When dampness dominates, it attacks spleen and stomach internally. When spleen and stomach receive dampness, then water and grain are not separated. When water and grain mix, they flow away through the transmission path of the large intestine. Because dampness abounds internally and flows out, this is called 'soggy outflow.'" *Gu dian yi zhu xuan* bianxiezu /37: "This is diarrhea."

43 Wang Bing: "Spring generates, summer brings growth, autumn gathers, winter stores; that is the so-called [sequence of] generation, growth, gathering, and storage in the course of the four seasons. Winter-water-cold, summer-fire-summerheat, autumn-metal-dryness, spring-wood-wind, later summer-soil-dampness; that is the so-called [sequence of] cold, summerheat, dampness, dryness, and wind [in the course] of the five agents." 527/47 proposes to move the two characters 五行 in front of 以 生寒暑.

44 In contrast, Gao Jiwu/396: "The human body has the five depots. They are able to create – by way of transformations – the five qi. As a result, the five states of mind joy, etc., are generated."

45 2104/5 identifies the character 悲 as an error for 思, "pensiveness," in correspondence with the listings further below.

46 Wang Bing: " 'The five depots' is to say: liver, heart, spleen, lung, and kidneys. 'The five qi' is to say: joy, anger, sadness, anxiety, and fear."

cold and summerheat harm the physical appearance.[47]
Violent anger harms the yin;
violent joy harms the yang.[48]

Receding qi moves upwards;
it fills the vessels and leaves the physical appearance.[49]

If joy and anger are unrestrained,[50]
if cold and summerheat[51] exceed the norms,
life no longer exists on a solid [foundation].

Hence,
doubled yin must [become] yang;
doubled yang must [become] yin.

Hence it is said:
If [a person] is harmed in winter by cold,
he will [suffer from] warmth disease in spring.[52]

---

47 Wang Bing: "Joy and anger are generated from qi. Hence [the text] states: 'joy and anger harm the qi.' When cold and summerheat dominate, they both dominate over the physical appearance. Hence [the text] states: 'cold and summerheat harm the physical appearance.' These are just examples; the same applies to all [other states of mind and seasonal qi]."

48 Wang Bing: "In case of anger, the qi rises. In case of joy, the qi descends. Hence if qi rises violently, then it harms the yin. When qi descends violently, it harms the yang."

49 Wang Bing: "厥 is 氣逆, 'qi moving contrary [to its proper course].' When qi moving contrary [to its proper course] rises and fills the conduits and network [vessels], then the spirit qi drifts around and leaves the body." On the concept of 'receding [qi]' in the *Nei jing*, see 1683. Zhang Jiebin: "The qi of cold, summerheat, joy, and anger, when they turn violent and move upwards, contrary to their regular course, then only the yang will be replete. Hence the vessels are filled. When the yang is strong, the yin leaves. Hence it leaves the physical appearance. This is a phenomenon of solitary yang."

50 Gao Jiwu/720: " 'Joy and anger' represent here all the seven emotions."

51 Gao Jiwu/720: " 'Cold and summerheat' represent here all the six qi."

52 A similar wording appears in *Su wen* 3, 21-5. Wang Bing: "Any harm caused by a qi associated with one of the four seasons may lead to disease. To be harmed by the poison of cold, though, this is the most fatal and violent qi. The moment one is struck [by cold], a disease sets in. Hence one speaks of 'harm caused by cold.' In those cases where [someone struck by cold] does not fall ill immediately, the cold poison is stored in the muscles and in the skin. In spring it changes to a warmth disease; in summer

If he is harmed in the spring by wind,
he will develop outflow of [undigested] food in summer.[53]
If he is harmed in summer by summerheat,
he will suffer from *jie* and malaria in autumn.[54]
If he is harmed in autumn by dampness,
he will develop cough in winter."[55]

5-35-5
[Huang] Di:
"I have heard, the sages of high antiquity
in discussing and structuring the physical appearance of man,
they arranged and distinguished among the depots and palaces,
they traced and connected the conduit vessels and
they combined [them to set up] the six unions.[56]
In each case they followed the respective conduits.

The qi holes where [the qi] are effused,
all their locations have a name.
The ravines, valleys[57], and the joints,[58]
all have a place where they emerge.
The divisions and the sections, opposition and compliance,

---

it changes to a summerheat disease. Hence those who are concerned with nourishing
their life, they must beware of harm by evil [qi]."

53 A similar wording appears in *Su wen* 3, 21-3. Wang Bing: "When wind strikes the
exterior, then the liver corresponds to this internally. The liver qi invades the spleen
and this results in outflow of [undigested] food."

54 A similar wording appears in *Su wen* 3, 21-4. Wang Bing: "If the summerheat in
summer was extreme and if in autumn further strong heat is added, the two heats attack each other and this results in intermittent *jie*-fever. *Jie* is 瘦, 'emaciation.'"

55 A similar wording appears in *Su wen* 3, 21-4. Wang Bing: "If in autumn there
was much dampness and if in winter dampness rules again, then water and dampness
merge and the lung qi weakens. Hence in winter severe cold causes cough."

56 Wang Bing: "六合 is to say: 'the [system of] unions of the twelve conduit vessels.'
The *Ling shu* states: 'Major yin and yang brilliance form one union (一合), minor yin
and major yang form one union, ... There are three [such unions] for the vessels of
both the hands and the feet; hence they are called 'six unions.'" Wang Qi: "These are
the associations of the twelve conduit vessels with yin and yang. There are three types
of associations [with yin and yang] of the conduit vessels of hands and feet. Hence
one speaks of 'six unions.'"

57 See *Su wen* 58.

58 Wang Bing: "屬骨 refers to the location where two bones meet."

all have their regular structures.
The four seasons and yin and yang,
all have their normal arrangements.
The correspondences of outer and inner,
all have exterior and interior.[59]
Is this true?"

5-35-8
Qi Bo responded:
"The East generates wind;
wind generates wood;
wood generates sour [flavor];
sour [flavor] generates the liver;
the liver generates the sinews;
the sinews generate the heart;
<The liver rules the eyes.>

In heaven it is darkness,
in man it is the Way,
on the earth it is transformation.
Transformation generates the five flavors;
the Way generates wisdom;
darkness generates the spirit.[60]

5-36-3
The spirit,
in heaven it is wind,
on the earth it is wood,
in man's body it is sinews.

Among the depots it is the liver;
among the colors it is greenish;
among the tones it is *jue*;
among the voices it is shouting;
among the movements [indicating] changes it is grasping;[61]

---

59 Wang Bing: "表裏: all yang conduits and vessels are 表, 'external;' all yin conduits and vessels are 裏, 'internal.'"

60 2520/50: "The 23 character passage 在天為玄 .. 玄生神, 神 was erroneously inserted here."

61 Wang Bing: "握 is that by which one brings things close together. (牽就)" 2725/49 disagrees and identifies 握 as the ability of the fist to grasp things.

among the orifices it is the eye;
among the flavors it is sour;
among the states of mind it is anger.

[If] anger [causes harm, it] harms the liver; sadness dominates anger.
[If] wind [causes harm, it] harms the sinews; dryness dominates wind.
[If] sour [flavor causes harm, it] harms the sinews;[62] acrid [flavor] dominates
sour [flavor].

The South generates heat;
heat generates fire;
fire generates bitter [flavor];
bitter [flavor] generates the heart;
the heart generates the blood;
the blood generates the spleen.
<The heart rules the tongue.>

In heaven this is heat;
on the earth it is fire;
in man's body it is the vessels.

Among the depots it is the heart;
among the colors it is red;
among the tones it is *zhi*;
among the voices it is laughing;

---

62 The system underlying the attribution to the five flavors to an ability to cause harm
in this and the following four paragraphs seems to be not homogenous. In the present paragraph it is stated that "sour [flavor] generates the liver; the liver generates the
sinews; .. sour [flavor] harms the sinews." Similarly, further below it is stated: "Sweet
[flavor] generates the spleen; the spleen generates the flesh; .. sweet [flavor] harms the
flesh." And: "Acrid [flavor] generates the lung; the lung generates the skin and the
body hair; .. acrid [flavothe qi of the wind

r] harms the skin and the body hair." According to these statements, the flavor generating a specific depot can also harm the body parts associated with this depot (probably because it might be excessive).However, in the remaining two paragraphs of this
table it is stated: "Bitter [flavor] generates the heart; the heart generates the blood; ..
bitter [flavor] harms the qi." And: "Salty [flavor] generates the kidneys; the kidneys
generate the bone and the marrow; .. salty [flavor] harms the blood." According to
these statements the flavor generating a specific depot can harm the body parts associated with the depot dominated by this depot. See notes 64 and 67 below.

among the movements [indicating] changes it is anxiety;[63]
among the orifices it is the tongue;
among the flavors it is bitter;
among the states of mind it is joy.

[If] joy [causes harm, it] harms the heart; fear dominates joy.
[If] heat [causes harm, it] harms the qi; cold dominates heat.
[If] bitter [flavor causes harm, it] harms the qi;[64] salty [flavor] dominates bitter [flavor].

5-39-1
The center generates dampness;
dampness generates soil;
the soil generates sweet [flavor];
sweet [flavor] generates the spleen;
the spleen generates the flesh;
the flesh generates the lung.
<The spleen rules the mouth.>

In heaven it is dampness;
on earth it is soil;
in man's body it is the flesh.

Among the depots it is the spleen;
among the colors it is yellow;
among the tones it is *gong*;
among the voices it is singing;
among the movements [indicating] changes it is hiccup;[65]
among the orifices it is the mouth;
among the flavors it is sweet;
among the states of mind it is pensiveness.

---

63 Wang Bing: "憂 helps to complete things." 2104/29 proposes the character 憂 to be an error for 噫, "to belch." This is on the basis of the association of "anxiety" with the lung below and of the identification of belching as a movement of the heart in *Su wen* 52. 2725/49 disagrees and identifies 憂 as the emotion "anxiety," associated with the heart, that causes changes in one's facial expression. For a detailed discussion, see also 673.

64 2725: "The qi in the two statements 熱傷氣 and 苦傷氣 may be a mistake for 血, 'blood.'" See notes 62 and 67.

65 Wang Bing: "噦 is to say 噦噫, 'to belch.' It emerges from cold in the stomach." 2725: "噦 is the so-called 'dry vomiting' of today." For a detailed discussion, see there.

[If] pensiveness [causes harm, it] harms the spleen; anger dominates pensiveness.
[If] dampness [causes harm, it] harms the flesh; wind dominates dampness.
[If] sweet [flavor causes harm, it] harms the flesh; sour [flavor] dominates
sweet [flavor].

5-40-2
The West generates dryness;[66]
dryness generates metal;
metal generates acrid [flavor];
acrid [flavor] generates the lung;
the lung generates skin and body hair;
skin and body hair generate the kidneys.
<The lung rules the nose.>

In heaven it is dryness;
on the earth it is metal;
on man's body it is skin and body hair.

Among the depots it is the lung;
among the colors it is white;
among the tones it is shang;
among the voices it is weeping;
among the movements [indicating] changes it is coughing;
among the orifices it is the nose;
among the flavors it is acrid;
among the states of mind it is anxiety.

[If] anxiety [causes harm, it] harms the lung; joy dominates anxiety.
[If] heat [causes harm, it] harms the skin and the body hair; cold dominates
heat.
[If] acrid [flavor causes harm, it] harms the skin and the body hair; bitter
[flavor] dominates acrid.

5-41-3
The North generates cold;
cold generates water;
water generates salty [flavor];
salty [flavor] generates the kidneys;

---

66 *Gu dian yi zhu xuan* bianxiezu /8: "The West controls the autumn; the climate
associated with this season is dryness."

the kidneys generate the bones and the marrow;
the marrow generates the liver.
‹The kidneys rule the ears.›

In heaven it is cold;
on the earth it is water;
in man's body it is the bone.

Among the depots it is the kidneys;
among the colors it is black;
among the tones it is *yu*;
among the voices it is groaning;
among the movements [indicating] changes it is shivering;
among the orifices it is the ear;
among the flavors it is salty;
among the states of mind it is fear.

[If] fear [causes harm, it] harms the kidneys; pensiveness dominates fear.
[If] cold [causes harm, it] harms the blood; dryness dominates cold.
[If] salty [flavor causes harm, it] harms the blood;[67] sweet [flavor] dominates
salty [flavor].

5-42-4
Hence it is said:
As for heaven and earth,
they are the above and the below of the myriad beings,[68]
as for yin and yang,
they are the male-female [couple] of blood and qi.[69]
As for left and right,

---

67 Lin Yi et al.: "According to the *Tai su*, 血 is 骨, 'bone.'" 2725: "The character for
'blood' is a mistake in these two statements; the character should be 'bone.'" For details of the argument, see there.

68 2956/44: "When the *Nei jing* and other texts of the Qin and Han era speak of
'myriad beings,' only living beings (all animals and plants) are meant. Hence when it
was said: 'the upper part of the myriad beings is called heaven,' this is to say, in animals
the head and in plants the branches and leaves are called 'heaven.' When it is said: 'the
lower part of the myriad beings is called earth,' this is to say, in plants the roots and in
animals the reproductive organs of the lower body are called 'earth.'"

69 In contrast, Gao Jiwu/558: "The character 之 is used here as conjunction, in the
sense of 与, 'and': 'yin and yang is blood and qi and male and female.' Qi and male
belong to the yang; blood and female belong to the yin."

they are the paths of yin and yang.[70]
As for water and fire,
they are the signs of yin and yang.[71]
As for yin and yang,
they are the beginning[72] of the myriad beings.

Hence it is said:
The yin is inside, it is the guardian of the yang;
the yang is outside, it is employed by the yin."[73]

---

70 Wang Bing: "The intermediary qi of yin and yang circulate on the left and on the right. Hence 'left and right constitute the paths of yin and yang.' " Zhang Jiebin: "Yang rises on the left; yin descends on the right." Yan Hongchen & Gao Guangzhen/13: " 'Left and right' refers to the passageways by which yin and yang rise and descend [in the organism]." Zhang Zhicong: "The South and the East are left, the North and the West are right. The two qi of yin and yang, rise and descend on all four sides, day and night they revolve in a circle. Man's yin and yang [qi], similar to the qi of heaven and earth, circulates day and night. Hence left and right are the passage-ways of yin and yang." Hu Tianxiong/47: "If one stands facing South, after midnight, the sun rises from one's left. After noon, the sun descends on one's right. When it rises, the yang qi gradually gains force; when it descends, the yin qi gradually gains force. The qi in man corresponds to this. Hence, in the morning the yang qi emerges; in the evening the yang qi is depleted. This is meant by 'left and right are the passageways of yin and yang.' "

71 Hu Shu: "The passage 陰陽之徵兆 was originally worded 陰陽之兆徵. Above, 下, 女 and 路 formed a rhyme. 徵 rhymed with 始."

72 Wang Bing: "That is to say: [yin and yang] are able (能) to constitute the origin (始元) of the emergence and completion of change and transformation." Zhang Jiebin: "[Yin and yang] can be the begin of change and transformation, of generation and completion. They can make [these processes] begin and they can make them end." Yan Hongchen & Gao Guangzhen/13: "能始 has the meaning of 原始, 'origin.' " Fang Wenhui/95: "In the *Shi ji*, 天官書, 三能 stands for 三台. The *Er ya*, 釋詁, states: '胎 is 始.' Hence 胎, 台, and 能 were used interchangeably in ancient times." 969/61 extends this argument with further evidence and rejects Wang Bing's equation of 能 with 能 夠. Qian Chaochen-90/94: "In antiquity the pronunciations of 能 and 始 were similar. The two characters must be seen as one expression; they cannot be separated into two. That is, the meaning of 能始 is that of 始, 'begin.' The present expression has nothing in common with an expression such as "they can make [processes] begin and they can make them end.' " 萬物能始 could also be read as "beginning of the potential of the myriad beings."

73 Wang Bing: "The yin is quiet; hence it is the guardian of the yang. The yang moves; hence it is employed as messenger by the yin." In contrast, Gao Jiwu/461: "This passage is to be read as 陰在內, 陽守之. 陽在外, 陰使之, 'The yin is inside, the yang guards it; the yang is outside, the yin employs it.' " 1753/27 agrees.

5-43-1
[Huang] Di:
"In what way can yin and yang be considered as laws?"

Qi Bo:
"When yang dominates, the body is hot and the interstice structures close.
Rough panting[74] makes one bend down and up.[75]
No sweat flows and one is hot.
The teeth are dry and [patients] experience vexation and grievance.[76]
If there is [a feeling of] fullness in the abdomen [this indicates imminent] death.
It can be endured in winter; it cannot be endured in summer.[77]

When yin dominates, the body is cold and sweat flows.
The body is permanently cool.[78]
One shivers frequently and feels cold.
In case of cold, receding [qi] results.
When receding [qi] occurs, there is [a feeling of] fullness in the abdomen and [this indicates imminent] death.[79]
This can be endured in summer; it cannot be endured in winter.[80]

---

74 Yan Hongchen & Gao Guangzhen/159: "The sound of the panting is rough."

75 Ma Shi: "The qi cannot come to rest, hence the body bends forward and backward."

76 Gao Jiwu/353: "以 equals 而, a conjunction: 'The heart has a feeling of uneasiness and the chest has a feeling of pressure.'" Gao Jiwu/11: "The *Tai su* has 煩悗, 'vexation.' The *Jia yi jing* has 悶, 'feeling of chest pressure.'" See 692/41, 1574/70, and Beijing zhongyi xueyuan et al./71 for discussions of the meaning of 煩冤.

77 2753/62: "能 stands for *nài* 耐, 'to endure.'" Yan Hongchen & Gao Guangzhen/159: "Because this disease is yang and goes along with heat, [the patient] can endure the cold of winter, but he cannot endure the heat of summer." Beijing zhongyi xueyuan et al./71: "Patients with excessive yang may stand this in winter, but when it comes to summer, when they are affected by the heat of summerheat, the disease will become more serious." For a detailed discussion, see also Wan Lanqing et al./5-6 and 419/4.

78 Beijing zhongyi xueyuan et al./71: "清 is to be interpreted here as 寒, 'cold.'"

79 Gao Jiwu/596: "When at the same time that the four limbs are cold because of [qi] moving contrary to its regular course, the abdominal region is distended and has a feeling of fullness, this is often an indication of [imminent] death following an excessive flourishing of yin and an interruption of yang [qi]." Also, 2619/52.

80 Yan Hongchen & Gao Guangzhen/159: "Because this disease is yin and goes along with cold, [the patient] can endure the heat of summer, but he cannot endure the cold of winter."

These are the changes in the alternating domination of yin and yang, [and their associated] disease manifestations."[81]

5-43-5
[Huang] Di:
"How are these two harmonized?"

Qi Bo:
"If one knows of the seven injuries and eight benefits,
then the two can be harmonized.[82]

---

81 Fang Wenhui/95 equates 病能 with 病態, "manifestation of a disease." See also 1312/41. In contrast, Yan Hongchen & Gao Guangzhen/159 and Beijing zhongyi xueyuan et al./71 interpret 能 as "the ability to endure seasonal influences."

82 See Wan Lanqing et al./7 for a listing of various interpretations in the course of time: Wang Bing, Gao Shishi , et al. refer to *Su wen* 01 where the life of females is periodized on the basis of the number seven and that of males on the basis of the number eight: In females it is most important that the monthly period descends in time, this is called 七損; in males it is most important that the seminal essence is complete, this is called 八益. Zhang Jiebin and Li Zhongzi interpret "seven" as an uneven number, referring to yang, and "eight" as an even number, referring to yin, with 損 standing for "decrease," and 益 standing for "growth" here. 七損八益 is, in the opinion of Zhang Jiebin and Li Zhongzi, a reference to the "waning and waxing of yin and yang." In contrast, Zhang Zhicong: "[The life of] females proceeds in periods of seven [years]; that of males in periods of eight [years]. 七損八益 means: if the yang has continuously surplus, one must take away from (i.e., "injure") it. If the yin is continuously insufficient, one must add to (i.e., "benefit") it." Tanba: "In females, at the age of five times seven the yang brilliance vessel weakens; at the age of six times seven the three yang vessels weaken above; at the age of seven times seven, the controlling vessel is depleted. These are the 'three injuries' affecting females. In males, at the age of five times eight, the qi of the kidneys weakens; at the age of six times eight, the yang weakens above; at the age of seven times eight, the qi of the liver weakens; at the age of eight times eight the qi of the kidneys weakens and the teeth fall out. These are the 'four injuries' affecting males. Three plus four is seven. In females, at the age of seven the qi of the kidneys flourishes; at two times seven, the true [qi] of heaven arrives; at three times seven the qi of the kidneys is balanced; at four times seven sinews and bones are firm. These are the 'four benefits' affecting females. In males, at the age of eight, the qi in the kidneys is replete. At two times eight, the qi of the kidneys flourishes; at three times eight the qi of the kidneys is balanced; at four times eight the sinews and bones are at the peak of their development. These are the 'four benefits' affecting males. Four plus four is eight." All interpretations listed above have been superseded now by the discovery of the term 七孫 (=損) 八益 in the Mawangdui manuscript 天下至道谈. Here the "seven injuries and eight benefits" are linked to sexual arts. See Ma Jixing 1992, 1027 and Harper 1998, 428. A purely sexual interpretation is suggested also by

If one does not know to employ these [principles],[83]
then the term of weakening will come early.

At the age of forty,
the yin qi has decreased to half of its own [former amount];[84]
one's daily activities[85] weaken.
At the age of fifty,
the body feels heavy;
the ears and the eyes are no longer clear.
At the age of sixty,
the yin [reaches a state of] limpness;[86]
the qi is severely weakened and the nine orifices are no [longer] freely passable.
Below is depletion; above is repletion.
Snivel and tears both flow.[87]

5-43-10
Hence it is said:
If one knows these [principles], then one remains strong;
if one does not know these [principles], then one turns old.[88]

Hence,
the origin is identical,
but the names are different.[89]

Wang Bing's comment unambiguously associating 用, in the following sentence, with sexual arts. See also 659, 815, 1878, 710, 2240, 1107, 813, and 2698.

83 Wang Bing: "用 refers to the sexual arts."

84 Gao Jiwu/384: "半 stands for 減半, 'decreased to its half.'"

85 lit.: "rising and resting."

86 Gao Jiwu/167: "A reference to the reproductive organs of males and females." See there for a detailed discussion. Wang Qi: "痿 stands for 萎, 'to wither.' 'The yin withers' means that the yin [seminal] essence has become weak."

87 On the character 泣, see 2586/334-335.

88 Wang Bing: " 'To know [it]' is to say: if one knows the seven [behaviors leading to] injury and the eight [behaviors leading to] benefit, then this is the Way how to keep the physical appearance whole and how to preserve one's nature."

89 Yu Chang: "出 is to be read as 生, 'come to life.' The preceding sentence states: 'those who know them, they are strong; those who do not know them, they are old.' The present sentence continues: '[those who know and those who do not know], they come to life alike but receive different names [i.e., strong or old] later on.'"The *Dao de jing*, ch.1, has a parallel statement: 此兩者同出而異名, referring to the identity in

Those who know, they investigate the identical;
those who are ignorant, they investigate the different.[90]
The ignorant have not enough;
those who know, they have surplus.[91]
If one has surplus,
then ears and eyes are clear;
the body is light and the limbs are strong.
Those who are old become strong again;
those who are strong can be treated [with] even better [results].

5-44-2
Hence,
the sages have acted on the basis of 'no intervention.'
They have enjoyed their ability to be peaceful and tranquil.[92]
They have followed their desires and their mind was pleased, maintaining
absolute emptiness.[93]

---

the origin of having no desires and being able to behold the subtleties of the Way and
of having desires and being able to see only its external boundaries. Wu Kun: "They
are identical in that their physical appearance was generated by the qi of heaven and
earth; this is called 'identical origin.' But there are also the differences of a long or
short life; this is called 'different names.'" 2260/33: "The so-called 'yin qi' refers to
the essence and to the blood of the human body. Essence and blood are the two most
precious things; they should be guarded. Hence [the text] states: 'those who know
it remain strong; those who do not know it become old.' Now, essence and blood is
one and the same thing, essence is a transformation of blood. Hence [the text] states:
'Equal origin and different names.'"

90 2260/33: "That is to say, the knowledgable, they know that essence and blood are
of identical origin; the ignorant, they believe [essence and blood] to be two separate
things."

91 2260/33: "The ignorant do not know how to protect and nourish essence and
blood; hence their body weakens early, that is, essence and blood are not enough.
Those who are knowledgable, they know how to protect and nourish themselves."

92 *Ling shu* 68 has a similar statement: "Quietness and non-intervention can keep
the qi moving." The character 憺 could be an error here for 恢, "silent." *Zhuang zi*,
Book 15: Ke yi 刻意, has a passage suggesting a close relationship to the entire present paragraph: 夫恬惔寂漠虛无无為, 此天地之本而道德之質也. 故聖人休焉, 休
則平易矣. 平易則恬惔矣. 平易恬惔則憂患不能入, 邪氣不能襲. 故其德全而神不
虧. And further down: 虛无恬淡乃合天德. (See Chen Guying p. 435, 436.)

93 Hu Shu and 1126/10: "守 is a mistake for 宇. The wording should be 虛無之宇.
..宇 is 居." 2529/58: "The character 守 is difficult to interpret here. Hu Shu states:
'The character 守 is out of place, it should be 宇. The passage 從欲快志于虛無之宇 is

Hence, [the fact that]
their lifespan has no limit,
and will end only with heaven and earth,[94]
this is [a result of the way] how the sages ordered their body.

Heaven is not sufficiently present in the North-West.[95]
Hence the North-West is yin,
and the ears and the eyes of man on the right are not as clear as on the left.
The earth is incomplete in the South-East.
Hence the South-East is yang,
and the hands and feet of man on the left are not as strong as on the right."

[Huang] Di:
"Why is this so?"

Qi Bo:
"The East is yang.
As for the yang, its essence collects above.
When it collects above, then the above is brilliant and there is depletion below.

---

similar in its meaning to a passage in *Huai nan zi*, treatise "Shu zhen" 俶真篇, 而徒倚
乎汗漫之宇. The commentary by 高誘 says: 宇 stands for 居, 'dwelling.'"

94 947/14: "The Sages, in treating their body, they followed their desires and acted in
accordance with the comfort their mind had achieved and they regarded emptiness as
the foundation of guarding their heart. There were no thoughts that could have tied
them. Hence their body was strong and their long life knew no limits. They could last
as long as do heaven and earth. Li Zhongzi: 從欲 is the 從所欲 of Confucius. (*Ana-
lects* II, iv, 6: 'At seventy I could follow what my heart desired, without transgressing
what was right.') 快志 is the 自慊 of the 'Great Learning' (See Legge, vol I, p. 366,
The Great Learning, Ch. VI, 1: What is meant by 'making the thoughts sincere,' is
the allowing no self-deception, as when we hate a bad smell and as when we love
what is beautiful. This is called *self-enjoyment*. Therefore, the superior man must be
watchful over himself when he is alone.) If one reaches utmost emptiness and guards
one's quietude, this is 'guarding emptiness.' That under heaven which receives harm is
solidity, is having. The body is identical with that of emptiness, but [the latter] is not
destroyed. Hence its long life has no limits and lasts as long as heaven and earth." See
also 2-906/11 for a detailed discussion.

95 419/5: "In Chinese medical thought, heaven represents yang, the earth represents
yin. Warm and hot climate is yang; cold and cool climate is yin. The North-Western
region is comparatively cold; in a comparatively cold region, warmth and heat are
comparatively rare. Hence [the text] states: "Heaven is not sufficiently present in the
North-West."

Hence,
this lets the ears and eyes be clear, while the hands and feet do not move comfortably.

The West is yin.
As for the yin, its essence collects below.
When it collects below, then there is abundance below and there is depletion above.
Hence,
the ears and eyes are not clear, while the hands and feet move comfortably.

Hence,
whenever one is affected by evil,
if it happens above, then it is serious on the right.
If it happens below, then it is serious on the left.

These are locations where the yin and yang of heaven and earth cannot be complete.
Hence,
the evil resides there.

The fact is,
heaven has the essence;
the earth has the physical appearance.
Heaven has the eight arrangements;[96]
the earth has the five structures.[97]

Hence,
[heaven and earth] can be father and mother of the myriad beings.
The clear yang rises towards heaven;
the turbid yin returns to the earth.

---

96 Wang Bing: "八紀 is to say 'the regular order of the eight seasonal turning points 八節.'" 1901/44: "These are the two equinoxes (spring and autumn), the two solstices (summer and winter), and the four seasonal beginnings (begin of spring, begin of summer, begin of autumn, begin of winter)."

97 Wang Bing: "The five agents are the 井里 ("villages") of birth and upbringing. 五里 refers to the neighborhoods (里) where the five agents give birth [to things]." Wang Qi: "五里 refers to the five cardinal points East, South, West, North, and center." Qian Chaochen-90/95: "紀 stands for 綱紀, 規則, 'basic rules,' 'basic principles.' 理 serves to express the same meaning with a different word."

5-45-1
The fact is,
the movement and resting of heaven and earth,
the spirit brilliance sets up their fundamental principles.[98]
Hence,
they are able to pass through generation, growth, gathering, and storage and
when the end is reached, to start anew.

Only the exemplary men
correspond to heaven above to nourish the head,
follow the image of the earth below to nourish the feet,
side with the affairs of man in the middle to nourish the five depots.

The qi of heaven communicates with the lung;
the qi of the earth communicates with the throat;
the qi of the wind communicates with the liver;
the qi of thunder communicates with the heart;
the qi of valleys communicates with the spleen;[99]
the qi of rain communicates with the kidneys.

The six conduits are streams;
the intestines and the stomach are the sea.
The nine orifices are where qi flows like water.[100]

5-45-6
One takes heaven and earth for yin and yang:
the sweat of yang, this is how one names the rain of heaven and earth;[101]

---

98 Wang Bing: "Clear yang rises to heaven; turbid yin turns to the earth. However, who is responsible for their moving and resting? The arrangements made by spirit brilliance. Earlier, the text spoke of 'the palace of spirit brilliance.' (see the beginning of *Su wen* 5). This may serve to explain the present [statement]."

99 Wang Bing: "The reason is that valleys are empty, and the spleen is something that receives." *Tai su* has 穀, grain, here instead of 谷, "valley".

100 Zhang Jiebin: "This should be 水氣之注, 'where water and qi flow.'"

101 Wang Bing: "When human sweat flows away through the interstice structures in the skin, that is an effusion of yang qi. Now, to take a metaphor from the realm between heaven and earth, clouds rise and rain falls. Hence the statement [in the text]."

the qi of yang, this is how one names the swift wind of heaven and earth.[102]
Violent qi[103] resembles thunder.
Qi moving contrary [to its regular course] resembles yang.[104]

Hence,
if treatment
does not take the arrangements of heaven as law and
if it does not employ the structures of the earth,
then catastrophe and harm will arrive.

The fact is,
the arrival of evil wind[105] is fast like wind and rain.[106]

Hence,
those who are experts in treatment,
they treat [a disease as long as it is in] the skin and the body hair.[107]
Next are those who treat [a disease when it is in] the muscles and skin.[108]
Next are those who treat [a disease when it is in] the sinews and vessels.[109]

---

102 Wang Bing: "Yang qi disperses through effusion. Fast wind soars. Hence this correspondence [suggested a naming of yang qi as 'fast wind']. The old [versions of the] classic did not have the two characters 名之; I have added them in parallel with the preceding statement." See also 648/66 and 246/14.

103 Fu Weikang & Wu Hongzhou/265: "Violent qi refers to the qi of anger."

104 Wang Bing: "Qi moving contrary [to its proper course] rises. So does yang [qi]."

105 *Gu dian yi zhu xuan* bianxiezu /57: " 'Evil wind' refers to the evil qi of the six excessives."

106 Wang Bing: " 'Arrival' is to say: the arrival at the physical appearance of the body." Yu Chang: "The text speaks of 'evil wind' and then it says 'fast as wind.' This makes no sense. All the preceding and the following statements refer to qi, not to wind. .. 'Evil wind' should be 'evil qi.' The present statement makes sense only when it is read: 'the arrival of evil qi occurs as fast as [the arrival of] wind and rain.' Further below the text says 'an affection by the evil qi of heaven harms the five depots in man.' The evil qi there is exactly the evil qi meant here." The *Tai su* does not have the character 邪; instead of 疾 it has 傍.

107 Wang Bing: "To stop it the moment it sprouts."

108 Wang Bing: "To eliminate what has just arisen." *NJCD*: "肌膚 is 肌肉, 'muscles and flesh.' " The character 膚, "skin", is also attested, in Chinese antiquity, in the sense of "minced meat" to be used in sacrifices. In the present statement, 膚 may simply be an erroneous writing of 肉, "flesh."

109 Wang Bing: "To attack what has become a disease."

Next are those who treat [a disease when it is in] the six palaces.[110]
Next are those who treat [a disease when it is in] the five depots.
When it comes to treating the five depots,
the [chances of the patient's] death and survival are half and half.

The fact is,
if man is affected by the evil qi of heaven,
then this harms his five depots.[111]
If one is affected by the cold or heat of water and grains,
then this harms the six palaces.[112]
If one is affected by the dampness qi of the earth,
then this harms the skin, the flesh, the sinews, and the vessels.[113]

5-46-7
Hence,
those who know well how to use the needles,
from the yin they pull the yang and
from the yang they pull the yin.[114]
With the right they treat the left and
with the left they treat the right.[115]
From this they know that;
from the exterior they know the interior.
By observing the structures of excess and inadequacy,

---

110 Wang Bing: "To treat what has become serious."

111 Wang Bing: "The qi of the four seasons and the wind of the eight cardinal points, they all constitute heavenly evil. *Su wen* 4 states: 'The eight winds bring forth evil [qi]. They become the [five winds] in the conduits. The winds affect the five depots.' Hence an affection by the evil qi of heaven causes harm to the five depots of man."

112 Wang Bing: "Heat harms the stomach and the bladder. Cold harms the intestines and the qi of the gallbladder."

113 Wang Bing: "When dampness qi dominates, then neither camp nor guard qi can pass. Hence an affection [by dampness qi] harms the skin, the flesh, the sinews, and the vessels."

114 Wang Shaozeng/123: "They pull out via the yin section the evil qi in the yang section and they pull out via the yang section the evil qi in the yin section."

115 *Gu dian yi zhu xuan* bianxiezu /6: "When the disease is on the left side, choose points on the right side for treatment and vice versa."

they see the minute and notice the excess.
When they apply the [needles], there will be no failure.[116]

Those who know well how to diagnose,
they inspect the color and press the vessels.
First they distinguish yin and yang.[117]
They investigate what is clear and turbid and know the section.[118]
They observe [the patient's] panting and breathing, they listen to the tones and voices and
they know what one is suffering from.
They observe the weight and the beam, the circle and the square and
they know which [qi] rule the disease.[119]

---

116 Wang Bing: "Because of their profound understanding." Gao Jiwu/552: "When they apply the needles, there can be no failure."

117 Wang Bing: "Through a differentiating [examination] in the yang [sector], they know the location of a disease. Through a differentiating [examination] in the yin [sector], they know the terms of death and survival."

118 Wang Bing: "That is to say, they examined the green-blue, red, yellow, white, or black coloring in [a patient's] complexion. 'Section' is to say: the location [of the disease in the] depots or palaces can be determined." *Gu dian yi zhu xuan* bianxiezu /47: " 'Clear and turbid' refers to the light or deep, bright or dark nature of one's complexion. When the complexion is light and bright, this is 'clear.' When it is deep and dark, this is 'turbid.' In general, when the complexion is clear and bright, the disease is in the yang section; when it is turbid and dark, the disease is in the yin section. 'Section' refers to the location of the disease." Yan Hongchen & Gao Guangzhen/202: " 'Section' refers to the sections in the face where the condition of the depots and palaces manifests itself." Zhang Yizhi et al.: "*Qian jin*, ch. 19, no. 5, Quan sheng zhi mi fang 全生指迷方, ch.1, quotes 部分 as 分部. *Su wen* 77 has 瀋于分部. 知病本始. 分部 refers to the network vessels under the surface in the skin. They are divided 分 into the three yin and three yang [categories] and each has its location 部位."

119 Wang Bing: "權 is to say: the weight of a balance. 衡 is to say 星衡, the horizontal bar [connecting] the *xing* (i.e., some stars of the *hydra* or of the *gemini*, or the middle star of the *ursa maior*?). 規 is to say: round shape. 矩 is to say: square shape. Now, the weight of a balance is that by which one examines inside and outside. The beam of a balance is that by which one determines [what is] high and low. The circle is that by which one displays [what is] soft and hollow. A square is that by which one elucidates [what is] strong and abundant. *Su wen* 17 has: '[The [movement in the] vessels rises and descends with the four [seasonal] changes: Hence,] in spring it should correspond to being struck by the circle.' That is to say: the yang qi is soft and pliable. 'In summer it should correspond to being struck by the square.' That is to say, the yang qi abounds and is strong. 'In autumn it should correspond to being struck by the beam.' That is to say: yin [qi] rises and yang [qi] descends. There is qi above on high and below. 'In winter it should correspond to being struck by the weight.' That is to say: the yang qi

They press at the foot-long section and at the inch,
they observe [whether the movement in the vessels] is at the surface or in the depth, smooth or rough, and
they know the location where the disease has emerged.[120]
[The fact that] in their treatment they commit no mistakes,
this is because in their diagnosis they do not miss [the point].

5-47-3
Hence it is said:
When a disease begins to emerge, one can pierce and [the disease] ends.
When it abounds, one must wait until it weakens and [the disease, when pierced,] ends.[121]

---

resides below. 所主之 is to say: whether the diseases that have emerged corresponding to the qi of the four seasons are above or below, in the center, or outside." *Gu dian yi zhu xuan* bianxiezu /47: "權衡規矩 refers to the different [movements in the vessels] normally occurring in the four seasons. 規 is the circular disk [or: circle]. In spring, the yang qi is gentle and the [movement in the] vessels should correspond by reflecting the roundness and smoothness of a circular disk. 矩 is the carpenter's square. In summer, the yang qi is strong and rich. The [movement in the] vessels should correspond by reflecting the vastness and rectangular nature of the square. 衡 is the beam of a balance used for weighing. In autumn, the yin rises and the yang descends. The [movement in the] vessels should respond by reflecting the balancing of high and low of the beam. 權 is the weight of the balance. In winter, the yang qi lies stored and is hidden. The [movement in the] vessels should respond by reflecting the heaviness and sinking down of the weight of a balance." Shen Zumian: "According to the *Han shu* 漢書, Lü li zhi 律歷志 and Wei xiang zhuan 魏相傳, weight, beam, circle, and square refer to the four seasons. The statement in *Su wen* 17 (see there and above in Wang Bing's comment) is the proof." See also Yan Hongchen & Gao Guangzhen/202.

120 Gao Jiwu/298: "They examine whether the skin is smooth or rough and whether the [movement in the] vessels at the inch-opening is at the surface or in the depth. This way they can diagnose the cause why a disease has emerged." See also Gao Jiwu/715. Various editions have a punctuation mark following 而知病所生以治. In contrast, we follow Lin Yi et al., 246/11, and other commentators, reading this passage as follows: 而知病所生, 以治無過, 以診則不失. The *Jia yi jing* has 病所在 instead of 病所生.

121 Wang Bing: "When disease [qi] is removed while it abounds, this will injure the true qi too. Hence in case of abounding [disease qi] one must wait until it weakens." Beijing zhongyi xueyuan (2): "When the strength of the disease has reached its peak, one should wait until it has decreased somewhat and then needle [the patient]. Only then one will achieve a cure." In contrast, 1603: "When the disease is in full force, one can needle it. Then wait until the evil qi weakens and retreats. One can eliminate a disease, when its nature has stabilized itself." 655/42 disagrees: "In addition to the present statement in *Su wen* 05, the doctrine not to needle at the time when a disease is in full force, appears in many treatises in the *Nei jing*. For example, in *Ling shu* 55:

Hence,
after it has become light, scatter it.[122]
After it has become heavy, eliminate it.[123]
After it has become weak, let it shine [again].[124]

'The superior practitioner needles when a disease has not emerged yet; next [is the practitioner who] needles when it is not in full force yet; next [is the practitioner who] needles when it already weakens. .. Hence it is said: At the moment when it is in full force, do not dare to cause any harm! Needle when it already weakens and the result will be brilliant!' "

122 Zhang Jiebin: "That which is light floats on the surface. Hence one must scatter it. 揚, 'to scatter,' stands for 散, 'to disperse.'" *Gu dian yi zhu xuan* bianxiezu /58: " 'Light' refers to the disease evil which is light and floats at the surface."

123 Zhang Jiebin: " 'When it is heavy' refers to inner repletion, a condition which must be diminished. 減 stands for 瀉, 'to drain.'" *Gu dian yi zhu xuan* bianxiezu /58: " 'Heavy' indicates that the disease evil has entered the interior. Because the strength of the disease has already entered the interior, it must be treated with the method of draining." 2138/38 points out a parallel passage in *Lü shi chun qiu*, "Jin shu" 盡數. Gu Guanguang: "In case of serious (lit.: "heavy") diseases it is difficult to achieve a quick cure with drugs. Hence they are to be eliminated gradually. When, eventually, the evil [qi] leaves and the proper [qi] is still weak, it must be made to flourish again." Shen Zumian: "In these three statements, 揚 and 彰 form a rhyme, while 減 appears out of place. Such structures never occurred in ancient rhymes. 減 may be a mistake here for 蕩, 'to dissipate.' "

124 Wang Bing: "Because the disease qi is weak, an attack causes the evil to leave. As a result, the true qi is firm and the complexion develops a brilliant shine again." Zhang Jiebin: " 'When it is weak' [refers to] depletion of qi and blood. Hence one must make it manifest again. To 'make it manifest' is to fill, to increase." 1739/48 disagrees with Zhang Jiebin and identifies the character 其 as a reference to the disease evil, not to qi and blood. For a detailed discussion see there. *Gu dian yi zhu xuan* bianxiezu /58: "彰 has the meaning here of 'to support.'" Beijing zhongyi xueyuan et al./115: "The strength of the disease decreases day by day and the proper qi too is increasingly insufficient. In treating such cases, a support of the proper qi must have priority and it must be combined with efforts to eliminate the evil. This is to cause the evil qi to leave [the body] entirely and to have the proper qi recover." In contrast, Yan Hongchen & Gao Guangzhen/257: "彰之 is to say, let the disease [causing] evil even more evidently weaken and retreat." Li Zhongzi: "When that which is weak is not filled, it will sink into darkness and hide in the depth. When it is filled, it comes to life again. Hence [the text] says 'let it be evident again.' This shows that the method of making something evident is nothing but the method of warming and filling." See 299/60 for a detailed discussion.

5-47-5

When the physical appearance has insufficiencies, warm it with qi.[125]
When the essence has insufficiencies, supplement it with flavor.[126]
When it is on high, trace [it] and disperse it.[127]
When it is down below, pull and eliminate it.[128]
In case of central fullness, drain it inside.[129]
When there is an evil, soak the physical appearance to induce sweating. [130]

---

125 Wang Bing: " 'Qi' refers to the guard qi. The *Ling shu* states: 'The guard qi serves to warm the seam of the flesh and to fill the skin. It enriches the interstice structures and is responsible for their opening and closure.' Hence, when the guard qi is warm the physical appearance is [supplied] sufficiently. *Su wen* 1 states: 'The kidneys rule the water; they receive the essence from the five depots and six palaces and they store it. Hence, when there is abundance in the five depots, [essence] can flow off.' From this follows that in case the essence is insufficient, one should fill the flavors in the five depots." *Gu dian yi zhu xuan* bianxiezu /58: "Most drugs that fill the qi have a warm nature. Hence [the text] states: 'warm them with qi.'" Wang Shaozeng/37-38: "One must use drugs with a strongly developed qi to warm and fill the [physical appearance]."

126 Wang Bing: " 'Flavor' refers to the flavors of the five depots." *Gu dian yi zhu xuan* bianxiezu /58: " 'When the essence has insufficiencies' refers to signs of depletion of the yin-essence. 'Flavor' refers to drugs with strongly pronounced flavor." See 470 for a detailed discussion.

127 Wang Bing: "越 is to say: 揚越, 'to scatter.'" Zhang Jiebin: "越 is 發揚, in the sense of 'to raise and disperse it, to have it rapidly flow out through vomiting.'" Zhang Yizhi et al.: "越 has the meaning of 散, 'to disperse.'" *Gu dian yi zhu xuan* bianxiezu /58: " 'High' refers to diseases in the upper part [of the body]. 越, 'to overstep,' refers to the method of causing someone to vomit." Beijing zhongyi xueyuan et al./115 quoting Li Zhongzi agrees.

128 Wang Bing: "引 is to say 泄引, 'to purge.'" *Gu dian yi zhu xuan* bianxiezu /58: " 'Below' refers to diseases in the lower part [of the body]. 'Pull and eliminate' is to say: guide the disease evil to leave from the lower part [of the body] by means of purgation.

129 Wang Bing: " 'Inside' is to say: inside the abdomen." *Gu dian yi zhu xuan* bianxiezu /58: " 'Central fullness' refers to an extended and full central burner region. 'Drain' refers to methods of eliminating the evil, not necessarily only to purgation." Fang Wenhui/17: "When the disease causes distension and fullness in the center, internally employ methods of drainage." Shen Zumian: "越 and 竭 form a rhyme, while 內 appears out of place. Also, the grammatical structure of this line differs from the two preceding. There must be a mistake here. I suggest [the following wording]: 中滿者寫 而洩之. This way, 越, 竭 and 洩 form a rhyme."

130 Wang Bing: " 'Evil' is to say: the qi of evil wind. When wind has struck the outer [regions of the body], then sweating is to be induced to effuse it." Yan Hongchen & Gao Guangzhen/257: "漬 is 'to soak in water.' The meaning of the entire sentence

Those in the skin, cause sweating and effuse them.
Those that are fierce, press and collect them.[131]
Those that are replete, disperse and drain them.[132]

Investigate their yin and yang [association],
to distinguish soft and hard [medication].[133]
In case of yang diseases, treat the yin;
in case of yin diseases, treat the yang.[134]

---

is to have the physical body soak in hot water to cause it to sweat. Just as Zhang Jiebin stated: 'The ancients used hot water for soaking to generate sweating with the aim of eliminating the evil.'" *Gu dian yi zhu xuan* bianxiezu /58: " 'Soak the physical appearance' is to employ medicinal decoctions to soak the human body." Beijing zhongyi xueyuan et al./115: "Steaming and warm baths are the methods of 'soaking the physical appearance.' That is, one employs the methods of steaming or of warm baths to cause sweating." See also 2171/14.

131 Wang Bing: "慓 stands for 疾, 'fast.' 旱 stands for 利, 'sharp.' When the signs indicate a qi that is fast and sharp, then apply pressure to arrest [it]." Yan Hongchen & Gao Guangzhen/257: "按 stands for 按摩, 'massage.' " In contrast, *Gu dian yi zhu xuan* bianxiezu /58: "按 stands for 抑制, 'to repress,' 'to restrain.' When the nature of a disease is rather violent, one must employ restraining methods to seize its strength." Beijing zhongyi xueyuan et al./115: "One applies massage to let the evil qi disperse and to hold the proper qi together." The *Tai su* has 投, "to remove," instead of 收. Yang Shangshan interpreted this as "first press [the location needled with a finger] and then remove [the needle]." In contrast, Mori: "安, 'to press' and 收, 'to collect,' are methods in the context of needling. That is, once a needle is withdrawn, [the insertion hole] is to be pressed with a finger lest the qi disperses." Our interpretation of 收之 follows the parallels in the structure of the present, the preceding and the following statement, i.e., 發之, 收之 and 泄之.

132 Wang Bing: "In case of yang repletion, [it is appropriate to] effuse and disperse [the qi]. In case of yin repletion, [it is appropriate to] guide and drain [the qi]. Hence the following statement."

133 Wang Bing: "Yin is soft; yang is hard." *Gu dian yi zhu xuan* bianxiezu /58: "柔 stands for 柔和, 'gentle.' This refers to the rather gentle manifestation of yin signs. 剛 stands for 剛烈, 'violent.' This refers to the rather violent manifestation of yang signs. Hence 'to distinguish soft and hard' means 'to distinguish yin and yang [diseases].' " Tanba: "Li comments: 'Examine whether a disease is yin or yang and then apply soft or hard drugs accordingly.' For 'soft medication and hard medication' see the biography of Bian Que in the *Shi ji* 史記."

134 Wang Bing: "This is what was worded above as 'from the yin they pull the yang and from the yang they pull the yin. With the right they treat the left and with the left they treat the right.' " *Gu dian yi zhu xuan* bianxiezu /58: "In case of disease signs indicating that yang heat has harmed the yin, one should employ methods filling the yin, and in case of disease signs indicating that yin cold has harmed the yang,

Stabilize blood and qi, so that
each keeps its native place.[135]
<When the blood is replete, one must open it;[136]
when the qi is depleted, one must pull it.>"[137]

---

one should employ methods filling the yang." For detailed discussions, see 1314 and 1433.

135 *JJZG*: "鄉 is like 居, 'residence'".... "鄉 is 所, 'location.'" The evidence is taken from the Han commentary of Zhao Qi 趙岐 to *Meng zi*, Gao zi shang 告子上, "莫知其鄉", and from the Mao commentary to *Shi jing* 詩經, Xiao Ya 小雅, Cai Qi 采芑. Wu Kun: "定 is 安, 'to pacify.' All conduits have blood and qi. It is necessary to settle them and to see to it that they stay at their places, lest they leave their position and intrude into or offend [a position not their own]." *Gu dian yi zhu xuan* bianxiezu /58: " 'Place' refers to the location of the disease. One must determine whether a disease is in the blood sector or in the qi sector and apply a treatment according to the location of the disease evil."

136 Wang Bing: "決 is to say: 決破其血, 'to cut the [patient's] blood.' *Gu dian yi zhu xuan* bianxiezu /58: " 'When the blood is replete' refers to signs of stagnating blood. 決 is to dissolve blockages in water; here it refers to methods transforming or breaking up stagnations." In contrast, Gao Jiwu/13 interprets 決之, lit. "to cut off," as a reference to bloodletting. See also Gao Jiwu/158 for further support of this argument. In contrast, Beijing zhongyi xueyuan et al./115: "One must stimulate the movement of the blood to eliminate the evil."

137 Wang Bing: "㸷 is to be read as 導, 'to guide.' If one applies 導引, 'massage,' the qi flows unimpeded." Qian Chaochen-88 supports Wang Bing and discusses his argument in detail. In contrast, Gao Jiwu/13 and also Gao Jiwu/158 identify this technique of "pulling" as as reference to an acupuncture technique of filling: "The previous sentence refers to the method of draining by means of bloodletting; the present statement refers to a method of filling by means of needling. Just as it is said in the *Tai su*: 'To fill is to pull (引) the qi by means of needling.'" *Gu dian yi zhu xuan* bianxiezu /58: " 'Pull' refers to methods of raising. When the qi is depleted and has sunk down, one employs methods of raising [the qi again]." Beijing zhongyi xueyuan et al./115 agrees: "When the qi is depleted and has sunken down, the yang qi must be raised again." Zhang Yizhi et al.: "㸷 is 掣, in the sense of 'to raise,' 'to lift.' Li Zhongzi 李中梓 has stated: '[This is] to raise it, just as one lifts something by hand.'" The parallel phrases in the *Tai su* and in the *Jia yi jing* have 掣 instead of 㸷. For a lengthy discussion see also 692/40.

Chapter 6
Discourse on the Division and Unity of Yin and Yang[1]

6-48-6
Huang Di asked:
"I have heard:
heaven is yang, the earth is yin;
the sun is yang, the moon is yin.
Longer months and shorter months, 360 days
constitute one year,[2] and
man corresponds to this too.[3]

Now,
the three yin and the three yang [of man] do not correspond to the [one] yin
and [one] yang [of heaven].
What is the reason for this?"

Qi Bo responded:
"As for the yin and yang [correspondences in man],
count their [associations] and [you] can [reach] ten;
expand these [associations] further[4] and [you] can [reach] one hundred.
Count these [associations] and [you] can [reach] one thousand;
expand them further and [you] can [reach] ten thousand.
The [associations] exceeding ten thousand are countless,
and still their essential [principle] is one.[5]

---

1 From the following text it is obvious that 離 refers to the countless applications of
a yin and yang categorization of all phenomena, while 合 refers to the idea that all
these countless applications, despite their seeming disparity, never leave the unity of
yin and yang.

2 Lin Yi et al.: "The passage from 天為陽 through 成一歲 appears in *Su wen* 09
too."

3 See 1166/14 for an examination of this statement in the light of ancient calendar
systems in China. See also 1371/13.

4 Huang Sanyuan/33: "推 stands for 推廣演繹, 'extend and deduce.'"

5 Wang Bing: " 'One' is to say 離合, 'division and unity.' " Wu Kun: "This is to say, the
Way of yin and yang begins with one. Inferences may result in ten, hundred, thousand,
ten thousand, or innumerable [applications], but the essential [principle] originates
from one yin and one yang." Zhang Jiebin: "The Way of yin and yang, all in all it is
one, applied individually it reaches ten, hundred, thousand, or ten thousand [applica-
tions], all of them did not exist if it were not for the changes and transformations of

6-48-10
Heaven covers [the myriad beings].
The earth carries [them].
When the myriad beings just come to life,[6]
before they emerge from the earth,
{this is called the location of yin,}[7]
this is called yin in the yin.[8]
When they emerge from the earth,
then this is called yang in the yin.[9]
Yang [qi] provides the [myriad beings] with proper [qi];
yin [qi] rules them.[10]

---

yin and yang. Hence, the obvious and the subtle, the large and the small, the count-less appearances and bodies, there is none which did not contain this principle. The changes and transformations may be many, but the essential [principle] is one; 'one' is the basic principle, 理, and nothing else."

6 Zhang Yizhi et al.: "方 is 將, 'about to,' here."

7 Wang Bing: "They exist in the yin, hence this is called 陰處."

8 Wang Bing: "When the physical appearance does not move yet and has not emerged yet, this too is yin. Because the yin resides in the yin, this is called yin in the yin."

9 Wang Bing: "When the physical appearance moves and emerges, this is yang. Be-cause the yang exists in the yin, this is called yang in the yin." Yu Yue: "則 should be 財, in the sense of 才出地者 'when they are just emerging from the earth.'" Shen Zumian: "Yu Yue is wrong. 則 should be 如. Above the text says 'not yet emerged from the earth,' here it states: 'even though they have emerged, their appearance is not complete yet.'"

10 Wang Bing: "When the yang confers the proper qi, the myriad beings come to life. When yin holds the control, then all physical appearances stand up." In con-trast, 2685/41: "[This passage] uses 正 and 主 to explain the mutual relationships and the individual functional characteristics of yin and yang within the laws of their interactions. Yin is the 主 'being in charge' of yang; yang is the 正, 'regulator,' of yin. 主 means 'to support', 'to take charge of;' that is, yin is the material basis for the dynam-ics between yin and yang. 正 is to prevent any excess or insufficiency. *Guan zi*, 法法, states: 'As for 正, it is that which stops excess and does not allow insufficiency.' That is, yang is the guiding factor in the dynamics of yin and yang." Gao Jiwu/553: "予 and 為 have identical meanings here: 'to provide with.' 之 is identical with 其 and refers to the myriad beings. 正 refers to 元氣, 'the principal qi;' 主 is to be interpreted as the 'major substance of all things,' i.e., yin essence. [The entire passage reads:] 'Yang provides the myriad beings with the principal qi; yin provides them with yin essence.' Another explanation identifies 正 as the qi of heaven, while yin refers to the qi of the earth." Zhang Yizhi et al.: "予 is identical with 與, 'to give.' 施 and 與 have the same meaning."

Hence,
they come to life through spring;
they grow through summer;
they are collected through autumn;
they are stored away through winter.[11]
If [their] regularity is lost, then the four [seasonal qi] of heaven and earth are obstructed.[12]
The changes of yin and yang, as far as they occur in man, if one puts them in numbers, they can be quantified too."[13]

6-49-3
[Huang] Di:
"I should like to hear about the division and unity of the three yin and three yang."

Qi Bo:
"When the sages stand facing the South,
the front side [of the body] is called broad brilliance;
the back is called great thoroughfare.[14]

---

11 Gao Jiwu/630: "The myriad beings come to life because of the warmth of spring qi; they grow because of the fire and heat of the summer qi; they are gathered because of the clarity of the autumn qi; and they are stored because of the cold of the winter qi."

12 Wang Bing: "Spring and summer are yang; hence they give birth and let grow. Autumn and winter are yin. Hence they collect and store. If this regular Way is lost, then spring does not give birth, summer does not let grow, autumn does not collect, and winter does not store. In this case, the qi of the four seasons are obstructed; the qi of yin and yang have nowhere to move."

13 Wang Bing: "The yin and yang [interactions] in heaven and on earth are countless, but it is quite possible to know the number of their operations in the physical appearance of man." The *Tai su*, ch. 5, Yin yang he 陰陽合, has 亦數之可散. Yang Shangshan commented: "散 is 分, 'to divide.'"

14 Wang Bing: "廣 stands for 大, 'grand.' The South is [the dual combination of the stems] *bing ding* and it is controlled by the position of fire. The yang qi is rich and brilliant. Hence it is called 'grand brilliance.' One regulates one's affairs facing the light. Hence the Sages stood facing South. When the *Yi* [*jing*] states: 'One meets at *li* 離,' then this is meant here. In the body, the depot heart is located in the South; hence [the text] states 前曰廣明, 'the front is named broad brilliance.' The thoroughfare vessel is located in the North; hence [the texts] states 後曰太衝, 'the back is named great thoroughfare.' Now, the great thoroughfare is rich and great because it is there that the vessel of the kidneys unites with the thoroughfare vessel. Hence it is called 'great thoroughfare.'" Ma Shi: "廣明 refers to the heart. The position of the heart is

The [vessel on the] earth[-side] of the great thoroughfare is called minor yin [vessel].[15]

[The vessel] above the minor yin [vessel] is called major yang [vessel].[16]

{The major yang [vessel] originates from the Extreme Yin [hole],[17] and ends in the gate of life.[18] It is called yang in the yin.}[19]

6-49-6

The [region from the] center of the body upwards is called broad brilliance. [The vessel] below the broad brilliance is called major yin [vessel].[20]

The [vessel in] front of the major yin [vessel] is called yang brilliance [vessel].[21]

---

the South; it is controlled by the position of the fire. The yang qi is rich and brilliant [there]. Hence it is called 'broad brilliance.'"

15 Wang Bing: "This proves once more that the two vessels form a union and constitute outer and inner."

16 Wang Bing: "The kidney depot is yin. The bladder palace is yang. The yin qi is below, the yang qi is above. These are the qi of the conduits that form 'one union' [of a yin and a yang vessel]."

17 Extreme Yin (至陰) is the name of an insertion point; it is located on the foot major yang conduit associated with the bladder. Wang Bing: "The name of a hole located at the outer side of the small toe."

18 Wang Bing: "The gate of life stores essence; it is the location of brilliant radiance. It is [a name for] the two eyes. The major yang vessel originates from the eyes and extends downwards to the feet. Hence its root is in the tips of the toes and its conclusion is in the eyes. The *Ling shu* states: 命門者目也, 'Gate of life is the eye.' The present [statement] coincides with the definition given in the *Ling shu*." 2271/39: "'Gate of Life' refers to the Essence Brilliance (精明) hole at the inner canthus. Hence it should be written 明門." 967/45 agrees that 命門 should be written 明門, but for other reasons: the eye is a "gate," and 明 stands for "to see." For details, see there. 2260/34 objects against Wang Bing's identification of the 'gate of life' as reference to the eyes and follows the eighth difficult issue in the *Nan jing*, as well as Xu Dachun, identifying the 'gate of life' as situated between the two kidneys. For details of his argument, see there.

19 Wang Bing: "Because the major yang [vessel] is located in the earth[-region] of the minor yin [vessel], it is called 'yang in the yin.'"

20 Wang Bing: "The *Ling shu* states: heaven is yang; the earth is yin. From the lower back upwards, this is heaven; from the lower back downwards, this is the earth. Hence the upper half of the body is associated with broad brilliance; what is below broad brilliance is associated with the major yin. Also, below the broad brilliance depot heart the major yin depot spleen is situated."

21 Wang Bing: "The stomach in the center of the human body is yang brilliance. Its vessel runs in front of the spleen vessel. The spleen is major yin; its vessel runs behind the stomach vessel."

{The yang brilliance [vessel] originates from the Grinding Stone Hole.
It is called yang in the yin.}[22]
The [vessel] outside of the ceasing yin [vessel] is called minor yang [vessel].[23]
{The minor yang [vessel] originates from the Orifice Yin [hole].
It is called minor yang in the yin.}[24]

Hence,
in the division and unity of the three yang [vessels],
the major yang is the opening;
the yang brilliance is the door leaf;
the minor yang is the pivot.[25]

---

22 Grinding Stone (厲兌) is an insertion point located on the foot yang brilliance
conduit, it is associated with the stomach. Wang Bing: "The name of a hole located at
the tip of the toe next to the big toe. Because the yang brilliance [vessel] is located in
front of the major yin [vessel], it is called yang in the yin."

23 Wang Bing: "The minor yang vessel of the gallbladder in the center of the human
body runs outside of the sector of the liver vessel. The ceasing yin vessel of the liver
runs inside the position of the gallbladder vessel. .. Hence the outside of the ceasing
yin is called minor yang."

24 Orifice Yin (竅陰) is an insertion point located on the foot minor yang conduit
and associated with the gallbladder. Wang Bing: "A hole located at the tip of the toe
next to the small toe. Because the minor yang is located at the outside of the ceasing
yin, it is called minor yang within yin."

25 Wang Bing: "離 is to say 別離應用, 'divided operation.' 合 is to say 配合, 'to unite.'
'Opening,' 'door leaf,' and 'pivot' is to say that the amounts of the three yang qi differ;
they also differ in movement and operation. Now, 'the opening' is the basis of the control of movement and standstill. 'The door leaf' is the force retaining one in custody.
'Pivot' is the secret [mechanism] governing movement and turnaround. It is from
these different [definitions] of the three qi that their [different] operations result."
The *Tai su* has 關, 'gate', instead of 開, 'opening'. Lin Yi et al.: "According to the *Jiu
xu* 九墟 (=*Ling shu*), the major yang is 'the gate.' The yang brilliance is 'the door leaf.'
The minor yang is the 'pivot.' Hence, when the 'gate' is broken, the flesh is destroyed
and the joints slow down and sudden illnesses emerge. Hence when one observes such
sudden diseases, they are to be eliminated through the major yang [vessel]. When the
'door leaf' is broken, the qi has nothing that could stop it and diseases of perturbed
breathing emerge. Hence such perturbations are to be eliminated through the yang
brilliance [vessel]. When the 'pivot' is broken, the bones are tossed and do not rest
firmly on the ground. Hence, in case of tossed bones, [the disease] is to be eliminated
through the minor yang [vessel]. The *Jia yi jing* has the same wording." The *Jia yi
jing* and the *Ling shu* available today have 開, just as the *Su wen*. Zhang Jiebin: "The
major yang is 'the opening;' it is the outside of the three yang. Yang brilliance is 'the
door leaf;' it is the inside of the three yang. Minor yang is the 'pivot.' That is to say, it
is yang qi between outside and inside. It can move outwards and it can move inwards;

[These] three [yang] conduits cannot lose each other.
If they beat, but not at the surface, this is called 'one yang.' "[26]

---

it resembles the functions of a pivot." Zhang Zhicong: "開 is 'to open,' and 闔 'to close,' like a door leaf; 樞, 'pivot,' is something that revolves back and forth. When the pivot['s activity] ceases, no opening or closing is possible. When opening and closing cease, there is nothing to move the pivot." 1837/50: "This is to say, 'opening,' 'closing,' and 'pivot' are three aspects of one and the same thing. Each has its individual task, but all of them are of use to each other. They support each other and it is impossible that one were omitted." Wu Kun: "The major yang [conduit] is outside; it distributes the yang qi and is called 'opening.' The yang brilliance [conduit] is inside; it takes yang qi in and is called 'door leaf.' The minor yang [conduit] is located between the outside and the inside; it moves the yang qi around. It resembles a pivot shaft and is called 'pivot.' " 2843/45: "In the *Nei jing*, [the concept of] 'opening,' 'door leaf,' and 'pivot' has two meanings. First it compares the relationships between the three yin and the three yang to 門栓, 'door pin,' 門闔, 'door leaf,' and 門軸, 'door pivot,' in order to explain that the relationships between the three yin and the three yang are of mutual utility and interdependence. Second [the *Nei jing*] employs [this concept] to outline the special characteristics of the [qi in] the three yin and the three yang [vessels]. 'The major yang is the opening' is to point out the characteristic of the major yang qi, i.e., to be at the surface, at the outside. 'The yang brilliance is the door leaf' is to point out the characteristic of the yang brilliance qi, i.e., to stick to the inside, to remain stored internally. 'The minor yang is the pivot' is to point out that the minor yang is situated between the realms of yin and yang, that it has capacity of a pivot to revolve, i.e, when it moves outwards it is yang, when it moves inwards it is yin." For detailed discussions see 2060, 2685, and 785. 2264 and 890 argue that the character 開 in the *Su wen* is an error and should be 關 in the sense defined in the *Shuo wen*, i.e., a horizontal bar used to block a door. Qian Chaochen-90/49, too, offers a detailed justification for interpreting the occurrence of 開 in the present context as a mistake for 關. This issue is also discussed in 735. According to the *Ling shu*, chapter 10, the minor yang vessel (i.e., the 'pivot') runs always between the major yang vessel and the yang brilliance vessel. This also fits the metaphor of a pivot.

26 Wang Bing: "When the arrival of the [qi in the] three [yang] conduits strikes the [fingers of one's] hand without any difference in their being light or heavy, then one is justified to speak of the qi of one yang. The [three yang conduits] do no longer send three [distinguishable] yang [qi] to move down." Zhang Yizhi et al.: "The *Tai su* has 傳 instead of 浮. Yang Shangshan commented: '搏 is 相得, 'correspondence.' 傳 is 失所守, 'to lose that which one guards.' " 2685/41: "浮, 'at the surface,' and [below] 沉, 'in the depth,' refer to characteristics in the nature of yin and yang; not to the nature of movements in the vessels. 浮, 'at the surface,' expresses the idea that the nature of yang is directed upwards and towards the outside. 沉, 'in the depth,' represents the nature of yin which is directed upwards and towards the inside. 傳 has the meaning of 聚, 'to assemble.' This is not the assembling of one yin and one yang; it is the assembling of the three yang that turn into one yang; it is the assembling of the three yin that turn into one yin. This is also the meaning of 'division and unity.' If divided, there are three yin and three yang; if assembled, there is one yin and one yang. In the present

6-50-4
[Huang] Di:
"I should like to hear of the three yin [vessels]."

Qi Bo:
"Those in the outer region, they are yang [vessels];
those inside, they are yin [vessels].

This being so,
the center is yin and
its thoroughfare [vessel] is below.
It is called major yin [vessel].²⁷
{The major yin [vessel] originates from the Hidden White [hole].
It is called yin in the yin.}²⁸
The [vessel] behind the major yin [vessel] is called minor yin [vessel].²⁹
{The minor yin [vessel] originates from the Gushing Fountain [hole].³⁰
It is called minor yin in the yin.}

The [vessel] in front of the minor yin [vessel] is called ceasing yin [vessel].³¹
{The ceasing yin [vessel] originates from the Large Pile [hole].³²

---

case, the division [of yin and yang] cannot be without limits; the yin qi and the yang qi of the human body are divided into three according to their amounts in the conduits and network [vessels]."

27 Wang Bing: "The thoroughfare vessel is located below the spleen; hence [the text] states: 'its thoroughfare is below.'"

28 Hidden White (隱白) is an insertion point located on the foot major yin conduit and associated with the spleen. Wang Bing: "隱白 is the name of a hole located on the tip of the big toe. Because the major yin is located in the yin, it is called the yin in the yin."

29 Wang Bing: "This is [a reference to] the relative positions of depots and conduit vessels. Major yin is the spleen; minor yin is the kidney. Below the depot spleen, a little to the back, is the position of the kidneys."

30 Gushing Fountain (涌泉) is an insertion point located on the foot minor yin conduit and associated with the kidneys. Wang Bing: "涌泉 is the name of a hole below the sole of the foot, in the fold that is formed when the foot is drawn in."

31 Wang Bing: "This too is [a reference to] the relative positions of depots and conduit-vessels. The 'minor yin' is the kidney; the 'ceasing yin' is the liver. In front of the depot kidney, a little upwards, is the position of the liver."

32 Large Pile (大敦) is an insertion point located on the foot ceasing yin conduit and associated with the liver. Wang Bing: "The name of a hole at the tip of the big toe, inside [the region of] the three hairs."

[It is the] 'cut yang of the yin.'[33]
It is called 'cut yin of the yin.' }[34]

Hence,
in the division and unity of the three yin,
the major yin is the opening;
the ceasing yin is the door leaf;
the minor yin is the pivot.[35]

6-51-5
These three [yin] conduits cannot lose each other.
If they beat, but not in the depth, this is called 'one yin.'[36]

---

33 Hua Shou's *Su wen chao*, 素問抄, does not have the four characters 陰之絕陽.

34 Wang Bing: "The two yin come together [here]. Hence [the text] states: 'cut yang of the yin.' 厥 is 盡, 'exhausted.' When the yin qi reaches here, it is exhausted. Hence [the text] states: 'Cut yin of the yin.'" Gao Shishi: " 'Ceasing yin' means complete exhaustion of yin. When [the text] states: 陰之絕陽, this is to say 'pure yin with absolutely no yang.'" Wu Kun: "The three yin and the three yang arrive at this conduit as their end point. Hence this is 'cut yang,' and it is also called 'cut yin.'" Yu Yue: "The meaning is unclear. Maybe the original wording was: 厥陰根起於大敦, 陰之絕陽, 名曰陰中之陰 ('The ceasing yin [conduit] emerges from the Large Pile [hole], the yin where the yang is cut. That is called yin in the yin'). Because the two yin merge here and because there is yin but no yang, it its called yin in the yin." Tanba: "Xu 徐 deleted the four characters 陰之絕陽. That was correct."

35 Wang Bing: "This too refers to unequal qi." Ma Shi: "The 'major yin' is the 'third yin.' It is the outer of the yin; its significance is 'opening.' The 'ceasing yin' is the 'first yin.' It is the end of the yin; its significance is 'door leaf.' The 'minor yin' is the 'second yin.' It is the center of the yin. Its significance is 'pivot.' Without pivot there would be nothing that could be in control; without door leaf there would be nothing that could enter; without opening there would be nothing that could leave. Division must go along with unity." Zhang Jiebin: "The 'major yin' is 'opening;' it resides at the outside of the yin sector. The 'ceasing yin' is 'the door leaf;' it resides inside the yin sector. The 'minor yin' is the 'pivot;' it resides in the center of the yin sector. 'Opening' controls leaving; 'door leaf' controls entering; the 'pivot' controls the space between leaving and entering." One would expect that similarly to the 3 yang, the 'pivot', i.e. the minor yin vessel, should run between the major yin and the ceasing yang vessels. However, according to the present TCM, the minor yin vessel never runs between these vessels. But this is not so clear in the *Ling shu*: The course of the 3 yin vessels described in chapter 10 implies the probability that at least in the abdominal region (a region which in *Su wen* 6 seems to be very important) the foot minor yin vessel runs between the other two foot yin vessels.

36 Wang Bing: "沈, 'in the depth,' is to say 殊見, 'distinguishable appearances.' This is similar to the [appearance of the] yang at the surface. When all the conduit qi arrive

Yin and yang move endlessly.
Repeated transmission constitutes one cycle.
The qi inside and the physical appearance outside,
they complete each other."[37]

in full accord, without there being any differences of [movements] at the surface or in the depth, then they can be said to be the qi of one single yin. The [three yin conduits] do no longer operate individually in sending three yang [qi] to move down."

37 Wang Bing: "䡖䡖 is to say 氣之往來, 'the coming and going of the qi.' 積 is to say 積脈之動, 'continuos movement in the vessels.' 傳 is to say 陰陽之氣流傳, 'transmission flow of yin and yang qi.' Now, the qi in the vessels comes and goes; it moves and does not stop. It adds one movement to the next. Qi and blood move in a circle. While the water sinks [in the clepsydra] by two marks, [qi and blood] complete one cycle in the body. Hence [the text] states: 'continuous transmission results in one circulation.' Now, the camp and the guard qi follow the breathing [of man] and flow everywhere in the outer region of one's physical appearance. They ward off depletion evil and [both] inside and in the outer region they exert their control. [Qi and physical appearance] support each other's position. Hence [the text] states: 'The qi inside and the physical appearance outside perfect each other.'" Zhang Jiebin: "The pysical form is generated from qi; the qi is accumulated in the physical appearance. Hence the qi moves inside and the physical appearance constitutes the outside. Each depends on the other. This is the Way of yin and yang and outer and inner, of division and unity, and mutual generation." On the etymology of 䡖䡖, see 2632/46 and 915/57.

Chapter 7
Further Discourse on Yin and Yang

7-52-2
Huang Di asked:
"Man has four regulars and twelve verticals.[1]
What does that mean?"

Qi Bo responded:
"The four regular [movements in the vessels] correspond to the four seasons;
the twelve vertical [vessels] correspond to the twelve months.
The twelve months correspond to the twelve vessels.[2]

The [movement in the] vessels may be yin or yang.
If one knows the yang [nature of a movement], one [also] knows the yin [nature of a movement];

---

1 Wang Bing: "經 is to say 經脈, 'regular [movements in the] vessels;' 從 is to say 順從, 'to go along with.'" Wu Kun: "The 'four 經' are liver-wood, heart-fire, lung-metal, and kidneys-water. [The text] does not speak of five 經 because the soil penetrates all five agents; it rules over the [remaining] four 經. 十二從 stands for 十二支, 'twelve branches.'" Li Guoqing: "The text states clearly that it is man's body which has 'twelve 從;' hence they cannot be interpreted as 'twelve branches.' 從 was identical, in former times, with 縱, 'vertical;' it stands in contrast to 橫, 'horizontal.' Hence it refers to the twelve conduit-vessels running up and down in the human body. The twelve conduit-vessels correspond to the twelve months, as for example, the hand-great-yin corresponds to the first month, [etc.]. The pathological changes in the twelve vessels correspond to the climatic changes during the twelve months." Mori: "四經 refers to the four regular (經常) appearances of the movement in the vessels in the course of the four seasons, i.e., string-like, hook-like, hair-like, and stone-like. 十二從 is another name for 十二脈, i.e., the paths of the twelve conduit vessels. 從 is to say: 縱, 'vertical.' It is a term used to denote the opposite of the network vessels, which run horizontally. When the text speaks first of 'twelve verticals' and then of 'twelve vessels,' these are not two different items." The *Tai su*, ch. 3 Yin yang za shuo 陰陽雜說, has 順, 'to comply, instead of 從.

2 Wang Bing: "In spring, the [movement in the] vessels is string-like; in summer, the [movement in the] vessels is vast; in autumn, the [movement in the] vessels is at the surface; in winter, the [movement in the] vessels is in the depth. These are the so-called 'regular [movements in the] vessels [associated with] the four seasons.' 從 is to say that the qi of heaven complies in its movement with the division [of the year] according to the twelve 辰-terms; hence it corresponds to the twelve months. 十二脈 is to say: the three yin vessels and the three yang vessels of the hands and the three yin vessels and the three yang vessels of the feet."

if one knows the yin [nature of a movement], one [also] knows the yang [nature of a movement].[3]

Altogether, there are five yang [movements in the vessels].

Five times five results in 25 yang [movements].[4]

{As for the so-called yin [qi], these are the true [qi of the] depots.

When they appear, this indicates destruction. Destruction entails death.[5]

As for the so-called yang [qi], this is the yang [qi] of the stomach duct.}[6]

---

3 Wang Bing: "Profound knowledge [of the yin and yang nature of the movement in the vessels] leads to a comprehensive understanding of [their] changes."

4 Wang Bing: " 'Five yang' refers to the yang qi of the five depots. The five depots correspond to the seasons. Each contributes to the appearance of a single [movement in the] vessels. [That is,] one single [movement in the] vessels comprises the yang [qi] of the five depots. Five multiplied by five is 25 yang [movements]." Gao Shishi: "The liver vessel [movement] corresponds to spring. The heart vessel [movement] corresponds to summer. The spleen vessel [movement] corresponds to late summer. The lung vessel [movement] corresponds to autumn. The kidney vessel [movement] corresponds to winter. In spring, the [movements in] the vessels of the liver, the heart, the spleen, the lung, and the kidneys all have a slightly string[-like] stomach vessel [movement]. In summer, they all have a slightly hook[-like] stomach vessel [movement]. In late summer, they all have a slightly relaxed stomach vessel [movement]. In autumn, they all have a slightly hair[-like] stomach vessel [movement]. In winter, they all have a slightly stone[-like] stomach vessel [movement]. This is 'five times five results in twenty five yang.' "

5 Wang Bing: "The five depots are yin. Hence [the text] states: 'As for the yin [qi], these are the true [qi of the] depots themselves.' 'When they appear' is to say: the [movement in the] vessels [associated with] the liver arrives tense in the center and in the outside. It is cutting as if [one's fingers] passed along the blade of a knife; as if one pressed the strings of a cither. The [movement in the] vessels [associated with] the heart arrives beating, firm and strung together, as if [one's fingers] moved along the seeds of *yi-yi*. The [movement in the] vessels [associated with] the lung arrives big and depleted; as if one were to touch someone's skin with fur or feathers. The [movement of the] vessels [associated with] the kidneys arrives beating and [occasionally] interruptet, [sounding] *bi-bi*, as if a finger hurled a stone. The [movement in the] vessels [associated with] the spleen arrives weak, at times coming in quick succession, at times coming with long intervals. Whenever such [movements in the] vessels appear, these are signs that the respective depot is destroyed and the spirit has left. Hence one must die." Cheng Shide et al.: "A [movement in the] vessels of the true [qi of the] depots is a [movement in the] vessels without stomach qi." Zhang Jiebin: " 'Yin' is to say 'without yang.' 'Without yang' is without the stomach qi of yang brilliance, i.e., when only the yin [movement in the] vessels of the [qi of the] depots themselves appears. Like, when only a string[-like] or a hook[-like movement appears], this is the true [qi of a] depot. [In such a case], the stomach qi is destroyed. Hence one must die."

6 Wang Bing: "The 'yang of the stomach duct' refers to the qi at man's facing (*ren ying*). One examines the qi at these [locations and investigates] whether the [move-

By differentiating at the yang,
one knows the location of the disease.
By differentiating at the yin,
one knows the times of death and survival.[7]
{The three yang are at the head;
the three yin are at the hands.
This is what is called 'one.'}[8]

---

ment in the] vessels [at man's facing] is moving or quiet, is big or small, and whether
it corresponds to [that felt at] the vessel openings [at the wrists] or not. The stomach is
the sea of water and grain. Hence one knows the location of a disease if one examines
its qi. The man's facing [locations] are at both sides of the throat. The movement in
the vessels [there] can be felt with the hands. The movement in the vessels [there] is
normally small on the left and big on the right side. The small [movement] on the left
usually serves to indicate the [condition of the] depots. The large [movement] on the
right usually serves to indicate the [condition of the] palaces. Another version has 胃
胞之陽. That is an error." Mori: "The *Tai su* has 胃胞 instead of 胃脘. 胃胞 and 胃脘
refer to the same meaning. 胃脘 is to say 胃氣, 'stomach qi;' 胃胞 is to say the 胃中,
'stomach center.' The *Shuo wen* states: '脘 is 胃府, 'stomach palace.' This is a new character; it is vulgarized seal script. The ancient character was 管, 'duct.' The [stomach's]
upper opening is the 上管, 'upper duct,' the center is the 中管, 'central duct,' and the
lower opening is the 'lower duct.' Hence the correct writing is 胃管, 'stomach duct.' To
write 胃脘 instead of 胃胞 is the same as to write 腧 instead of 輸穴, or 脈 instead of
脈張. Zhang Zhicong: "The so-called 'yang' is the yang qi generated by the stomach
duct." Tanba: "Wang Bing was wrong when he spoke of the qi at man's facing."

7 Wang Bing: "The yang [qi] protects the outside and provides firmness. Now, when
an external evil strikes, one differentiates at the [location where the] yang [qi moves]
and knows the location of the disease. The yin [depots] store the spirit and [their qi]
guards the interior. When one examines whether [a person's qi] is true and proper, or
whether it is in good shape or destroyed, one differentiates at the [location where the]
yin [moves] and knows the times of death and survival of the patient." Ma Shi: "In
man one only distinguishes at the yang conduits whether there is a disease and then
one knows the location where the disease emerged." 2868/28 points out a parallel passage in *Su wen* 19, but denies the possibility that the present passage in *Su wen* 07 has
been accidentally repeated in *Su wen* 19. For details, see there.

8 Wang Bing: " 'Head' is to say man's facing (*ren ying*); 'hands' is to say qi opening.
The two correspond to each other. If the [movement in the] vessels is equally big or
small [at both these locations], as if a rope of equal diameter were pulled [through
both locations], one speaks of a healthy person. Hence [the text] states: 'This is what
is called one.' The qi opening is located one inch behind the fish-line (separating wrist
and palm). The man's facing is located 1.5 inches to each side of the throat. All these
[locations] may serve to examine the qi of the depots and palaces." Zhang Jiebin:
" 'The three yang at the head' refers to the man's facing [location]; 'the three yin at the
hands' refers to the qi-opening. Now, the qi of the three yang have the yang brilliance
qi of the stomach as their source and the yang brilliance movement [in the] vessels

<By differentiating at the yang,
one knows the critical times of a disease;
by differentiating at the yin,
one knows the times of death and survival.>[9]

7-53-3
One should take care to become familiar with yin and yang and
one must not develop [therapeutic] schemes in the same way as ordinary [prac-
titioners].[10]

{As for the so-called yin and yang [associations],
that which leaves is yin;
that which arrives is yang.
That which is quiet is yin;
that which moves is yang.

---

appears at the man's facing [location] in a distance of one and a half inches on both
sides of the throat. Hence [the text] states: 'the three yang at the head.' The qi of the
three yin have the major yin qi of the spleen as their source. But the [movement in
the] vessels [associated with] the spleen does originally not appear at the qi opening.
How can it be 'at the hands'? In *Su wen* 11 it is said: 'The five flavors enter [the body
through] the mouth and they are stored in the stomach. They serve to nourish the qi
of the five depots and any changes become apparent in the qi opening. The qi opening
is the major yin.' Hence this is to say that the three yin are at the hands." 2130-6/3:
" 'Head' refers to the throat/neck. Duan Yucai 段玉裁 states: 頭 stands for 脰, 'nape'.
[Characters] with identical pronunciations but referring to different items have been
used to replace each other here.' 三陽在頭 is to say: if one wishes to diagnose whether
the three yang have depletion or repletion, one can examine the man's facing locations
at the throat."

9 Zhang Jiebin: "忌時 is to say: qi may be weak or abundant and a disease is at times
critical." Yu Yue: "忌 is an error for 起, 'to rise,' 'to emerge.' Above the text states: 'By
differentiating at the yang, one knows the location of the disease. By differentiating at
the yin, one knows the times of death and survival.' *Su wen* 19 states: 'By differentiating at the yang, one knows the origin of a disease. By differentiating at the yin, one
knows the times of death and survival.' The characters 來 and 期 form a rhyme. Hence
the two characters 處也 must be errors. Here [the text] states: 知病起時, paralleling
the statment 知病從來 [in *Su wen* 19]. 忌 was erroneously written for 起 because of
the similarity of the two characters."

10 Wang Bing: "If one carefully estimates the signs of the [condition of the] qi
and if one is familiar with yin and yang, all doubts concerning death or survival [of
a patient] will get resolved automatically and one will proceed along the proper path
without harboring any doubts. Of what use could all kinds of [further] deliberations
be?"

That which is retarded is yin;
that which is frequent is yang.}

7-53-5
Whenever one feels a [movement in a] vessel of a depot that is the [movement in the] vessels of this [depot's] true [qi, the following applies]:[11]
When the arrival of a liver [movement] is suspended and interrupted, {tense}[12] [the patient] will die after 18 days.
When the arrival of a heart [movement] is suspended and interrupted, [the patient] will die after 9 days.
When the arrival of a lung [movement] is suspended and interrupted, [the patient] will die after 12 days.
When the arrival of a kidney [movement] is suspended and interrupted, [the patient] will die after seven days.
When the arrival of a spleen [movement] is suspended and interrupted, [the patient] will die after four days."[13]

---

11 Wang Bing: "真脈之藏脈 is to say 真藏之脈, '[movement in] the vessels of the true [qi of a] depot.'"

12 The corresponding passage in the *Tai su* does not have the character 急; hence most commentators agree that it appears to be a mistaken addition here. For instance, 529/2: "急 was added here erroneously in accordance to a wording in *Su wen* 19: 真肝脈至中外急." 526/5: "懸絕 has the meaning here of 懸殊, 'separated.' 肝至懸絕 is to say: when the true liver [movement in the] vessels appears, then [this depot] is separated from the other parts [of the organism]." 533/18: "懸絕 appears to have the meaning of 懸殊, 'separated.' 肝至懸絕 is to say: in the liver section a [movement of the] true [qi of the] depot appears all alone; separated from the heart, lung, kidney, and spleen [movements in the] vessels. After 18 days, absolutely no stomach qi is left. Hence [the patient] will die. In earlier commentaries, 懸絕 was considered an appearance of the [movement in the] vessels. That was wrong." Tanba: "Hua Shou stated '懸絕 is: thin like a silk thread by which something is suspended and tending to rupture.' Mr. Wang 汪 [commenting on Hua Shou] wrote: '懸絕 is 止絕, 'interrupted.'" The *SWJZ* defines 絕 as 斷絲, 'a silk thread that is cut.'" See *Su wen* 79-563-2 for evidence of a usage of 懸絕 not as a binom but as a combination of two different pulse qualities.

13 Wang Bing: "'18 days' constitute excess beyond the completion numbers of metal and wood. '9 days' constitute excess beyond the completion numbers of water and fire. '12 days' constitute excess beyond the generation and completion numbers of metal and fire. '7 days' constitute excess beyond the generation numbers of water and soil. '4 days' constitute excess beyond the generation number of wood. Hence *Su wen* 18 states: If a liver [movement] appears, [the patient will] die at *geng xin*. If a heart [movement] appears, [the patient will] die at *ren kuei*. If a lung [movement] appears, [the patient will] die at *bing ding*. If a kidney [movement] appears, [the patient will] die at *wu ji*. If a spleen [movement] appears, [the patient will] die at *jia yi*. The reason

It is said:

"Diseases in the second yang break out in the heart and in the spleen.[14]

[As a result] one cannot [use] the hidden bend;

females do not have their monthly [period].[15]

---

is that in all these cases the arriving qi cannot be overcome at a certain date and hence [the patient] dies. Why? Because he cannot overcome the robber qi." Gao Shishi: "The soil is situated in the center and fertilizes the four sides. Fire above, water below, wood to the left, and metal to the right. When the qi of the soil cannot respond to all four [sides] death follows within four days." Tanba: "Wang Bing's comment fails to make clear why only in case of the spleen death occurs in connection with the generation number."

14 Wang Bing: "Second yang refers to the yang brilliance vessels of large intestine and stomach. When the intestines and the stomach develop a disease, the heart and the spleen receive it." Hua Shou: "心脾 should be 肺脾." Zhang Jiebin: "Second yang is yang brilliance. These are the two conduits of stomach and large intestine. Stomach and heart are mother and son. When a person's desires have first harmed the heart, the harm done to the mother injures also her son. Stomach and spleen are outside and inside. When a person's spleen was harmed by too much work, the harm done to the depot is transmitted also to the palace. Hence any internal harm to the essence, externally harms the physical appearance. Any disease affecting the stomach is a disease of the second yang. Hence it has arisen from heart and spleen." Ma Shi: "Second yang refers to the foot yang brilliance conduit of the stomach. It is the official of the granaries; it controls the intake of water and grains." 1938/18: "The *Tai su* in ch.3 has: '發心痺.' This is correct. The 脾 in the *Su wen* may very well be a mistake for 痺." 1938/18 sees two reasons justifying this statement: First, all the remaining five statements in this passage refer to diseases emerging from one of the yin or yang [conduits], none refers to the depots and palaces. The term 心痺 appears in *Su wen* 10 and *Su wen* 43 as well. Second, the *Tai su* is an older version than Wang Bing's edition and therefore closer to the original. For details see there. Mori: "The *Tai su* wording is to be followed. The reason is, 脾 is also used for 痺. For example, in ancient texts the term 麻痺 was also written 麻脾." 399/16+12 agrees with a detailed argumentation. 419/6 interprets 心痺 as "heart pain" in the sense of "stomach ache." See also 1721/35.

15 Wang Bing: "隱曲 is to say: 'concealed and intricate.' When the intestine and the stomach develop a disease, this is received by the heart and the spleen. When the heart receives it, then the blood does not flow; when the spleen receives it, the flavors are not transformed. When the blood does not flow, females do not have their monthly period. When the flavors are not transformed, males have less [seminal] essence. Hence they cannot perform those matters that are concealed and intricate." Zhang Jiebin: "不得隱曲 refers to a disease of the 陽道 (i.e., male member). The stomach is the sea of water and grains, of qi and blood. It controls transformation, construction, and protection and provides the male member with moisture. ... Here now, the source of all transformations has a disease. As a result, the male member is weakened externally. Hence it cannot be secretly bent." Yang Shangshan: "隱曲 refers to stools and urine." Tanba agrees. The Tang dynasty history, 唐書, 安祿山傳, has: 隱曲常瘡, "the private

Their transmission generates wind wasting.
[Further] transmission causes rapid breathing.
[Once this stage is reached, the patient] will die;
no cure is possible."[16]

7-54-1
It is said:
"When the third yang develops a disease, it breaks out as cold and heat.
Below this causes *yong*-abscesses and swelling.
It also causes limpness with receding [yang qi], as well as soreness in the calves.[17]

---

parts [i.e., the sexual organs] have ulcers." Li Guoqing: "隱曲 could be interpreted as the large intestine holding the stools and it could be interpreted as the bladder storing the urine." 10/2 follows the arguments voiced by Ma Shi, Zhang Shanlei and others: " 'Hidden and bent' refers to suppressed [sexual] desires. If this situation lasts for too long, the functions of the liver are affected and this in turn affects spleen and heart. Finally, the monthly period is blocked." 852/14 agrees and offers a historical survey of all interpretations offered in the course of the centuries. 1938/19: "Later authors have interpreted 隱曲 as 'unfulfilled desires.' This is wrong. In *Su wen* 42, Wang Bing has commented on 隱曲 in more detail ... making it clear that this term refers to urine and stools." 1317/45 holds the same view. For a discussion of the major four interpretations of 隱曲, i.e., sexual organ, sexual intercourse, (sexual) desires, and stools/urine, see 1508/11, 714/65, and also 2540/190, as well as 2260/34.

16 Wang Bing: "That is to say, when [a disease] has penetrated [the body] deeply over an extended period of time. When a stomach disease has penetrated [the body] deeply over an extended period of time, it is transmitted into the spleen and this generates [a condition] where wind heat causes consumption. When the large intestine is very ill, the disease is transmitted to the lung, where it causes panting and rapid breathing. Now, intestines, stomach, spleen, and lung band together and approach the heart. These are three depots and two palaces entering into a fight. Hence [the patient] dies and cannot be cured." Zhang Zhicong: "When essence and blood are depleted, heat is abundant and generates wind. Wind and heat set each other ablaze and as a result the liquids are dispersed increasingly." *Gu dian yi zhu xuan* bianxiezu /45: "This is to describe that the body is weakened and that the flesh is emaciated. As if wind blew against plants, which dry and shrivel as a result." Mori: "Both Wang Bing and Yang Shangshan interpret [wind consumption] as emaciation resulting from wind and heat. Now, the stomach rules the muscles and the flesh. When spleen and stomach are depleted, then the muscles and the flesh experience emaciation." Li Zhongzi: "When the stomach has a disease, the lung loses its nourishment. Hence the qi-breath is rapid."

17 Wu Kun: " 'Third yang' is the hand major yang vessel of the small intestine and the foot major yang of the bladder. The vessel of the small intestine emerges at the hands, follows the arms, winds around the shoulders, and turns to rise to the head. The vessel of the bladder originates at the head, divides to follow the spine, penetrates the thighs, enters the popliteal fossa, and follows the calfs. Hence when the disease is

Its transmission causes dispersing moisture.[18]
[Further] transmission causes breakdown illness with elevation illness."[19]

It is said:
"When the first yang develops a disease, one is short of qi and has a tendency to cough.
[There is also] a tendency to outflow.
Its transmission causes heart tugging.[20]
Its [further] transmission causes a barrier."[21]

---

in the upper section, it breaks out as [spells of] cold and heat. When it is in the lower section, it causes *yong*-abscesses and swelling in the calfs, etc. 痿 is absence of strength. 厥 is cold feet because of qi moving contrary [to its regular course]." Zhang Zhicong: "The major yang qi controls the outside. When evil [qi] hits man, it is first in the skin and the hair. Evil and proper [qi] strike at each other and this results in a disease of [alternating] cold and heat." The *Tai su*, ch. 3 Yin yang za shuo 陰陽雜說 has 喘悁. Yang Shangshan commented: "When the major yang [qi] breaks out, such diseases as [spells of] cold and heat emerge. 悁 is identical with 患, 'to suffer.'" With this wording the passage reads: "It also causes suffering from limpness, ceasing [yang qi], and panting." See Qian Chaochen-88/279 for an identification of 腨 as "calf of the leg."

18 Zhang Jiebin: "When yang evil generates heat on the [body's] outside, then all the moisture qi of the skin is dispersed. This is called 索澤, 'dispersing moisture.'" Cheng Shide et al.: "索, 'shrinking,' stands for 散, 'dissipate,' 盡, 'to end.'" 157/55: "The meaning of 索 here is 沒有, 'not to have.' (That is, the skin is dry) and has no moisture."

19 Wang Bing: "When the heat is extreme, then essence and blood dry. Hence the qi moistening the skin dissipates entirely. Now, the yang qi sinks while the [qi] of the yin vessels rises to enter into a struggle. When [the yin qi] struggles above, then much cold ensues. When [the yang qi] sinks, then the sinews slacken. Hence the testicles fall and become slack, and 癀疝 develops internally." Cheng Shide et al.: "癀 stands for 墮, 'to fall.'".... Zhang Zihe 张子和 in his *Ru men shi qin* 儒門事親: '癩疝 is a swelling of the scrotum. It may have the size of a pint or of a peck. It does not itch or ache.'" 482/42: "癀 stands for 隤, 'to break down.'"

20 Wang Bing: "'First yang' is to say minor yang vessel of the gallbladder and of the triple burner. The qi of the gallbladder occupies the stomach. Hence a tendency to outflow results. In case of a disease inside the triple burner, diminished qi results (i.e., one is short of breath). The yang soil steams the lung. Hence one wishes to drink. Why? Because the fire of the heart corresponds inside."

21 Wang Bing: "Barred qi occupies the heart. The heart is heat. Hence the yang qi is obstructed internally and the triple burner has agglomerations inside and is struck by heat. Hence a diaphragm blockage results and there is no possibility to relieve oneself." Wang Bing's commentary suggests that the original text may have spoken of *ge ge* 膈膈, "barred diaphragm". The first of these two characters may have been omitted from the text in later times. Zhang Jiebin: "When the heart fails to move peacefully, but rather as if it were pulled, this is called 心掣, 'dragged heart.' Because the wood avails

7-54-4
When the second yang and the first yin develop a disease,
it is responsible for shock and back pain.
[Patients] tend to belch;[22] [patients] tend to yawn.
{This is called "wind-recession."}[23]

When the second yin and the first yang develop a disease,
[patients] tend to experience distension;
the heart has [a feeling of] fullness;[24] [patients] tend to [pull in] qi.[25]

When the third yang and the third yin develop a disease,
this causes unilateral withering, limpness, and slackening.[26]

---

itself of the soil, the spleen and the stomach receive harm. This causes pathoconditions of a 'barrier.' "The *Tai su* has 瘛, 'to tug,' instead of 掣.

22 For a discussion of the different usages of the character 噫, 'to belch,' in the *Nei jing*, see 1813/40.

23 Wang Bing: " 'First yin' is to say: the ceasing yin [vessel], i.e. the vessels of the heart ruler and of the liver. The heart ruler vessel emerges from the chest center and is attached to the heart. ... When the qi of the heart is insufficient, [the heart] is intruded by the qi of the kidneys. The liver is responsible for fright. Hence, fright results, as well as a tendency to yawn. Now, the liver qi is wind. When the qi of the kidneys rises contrary to its regular course, then the wind recedes, too. Hence [the disease] is called 'wind receding.' " 2225: "These pathoconditions are caused by wind evil intruding into the yang brilliance and ceasing yin conduits and stimulating the qi of liver and stomach to move contrary to its normal course."

24 Cheng Shide et al.: "滿 is identical with 懣, 'chest pressure.' "

25 Wang Bing: " 'Second yin' is to say: the minor yin conduits of the heart and of the kidneys. When [the qi] of kidneys and gallbladder alike rise contrary [to their regular course], the triple burner cannot pass [its qi]. The qi accumulates above. Hence one [experiences a feeling of] fullness in the heart. The lower section [of the body] is depleted, while the [qi in the] upper section abounds. Hence there is an outflow of qi." Zhang Zhicong: "When the heart connection is tight, the passage through the qi path is restricted. Hence one sighs deeply to expand it. The qi concerned here is that of the triple burner. Hence it pulls at the triple burner." Tanba: "The *Li ji* has an expression 勿氣, Zheng 鄭 commented: 'That is to say: 鼻息, breathing through the nose.' Hence the interpretation given by Zhang Zhicong is acceptable." See also 371/41 for an identification of 氣 as 太息, 'to breath deeply.' "Ma Shi suggested an interpretation as 怒, "to get angry."

26 The meaning of the character 易 is unclear; see 148/52 for the rejection of an argument that 易 is a mistake for 瘍.

The four limbs [can]not be lifted.[27]

7-54-6
Drumming first yang is called hook[-like].[28]
Drumming first yin is called hair[-like].[29]
A drumming yang [qi] that dominates and is tense[30] is called string[-like].[31]
A drumming yang [qi] that arrives interrupted [into individual strokes] is called stone[-like].[32]
When yin and yang surpass each other, it is called stream[-like].[33]

---

27 Wang Bing: "When the [qi of the] third yin is insufficient, unilateral stiffness develops. When the [qi of the] third yang has a surplus, this causes changes to limpness. 易 is generally used for 變易, 'changes;' 痿 is 弱無力, 'weak, without strength.'" Sun Yirang interprets 易 as 弛, "relaxed." Gao Jiwu/715 agrees and interprets it as 弛緩. The term 痿易 may be an error here for 痿厥, "limpness with ceasing," which occurs in similar contexts in *Ling shu* 26 and in the *Jia yi jing*, ch.10/4. See also 543 and Wang Hongtu et al./155 f.

28 Following the character 鉤, the *Tai su* has the two characters 曰鼓. Yang Shangshan: "鼓 is the drumming movement in the vessels." On the interpretation here of "drumming" as a verb, see also 698/67. One should not exclude an interpretation of 鼓 as a transitive verb: "When [a disease] rouses the [qi of] first yang, [the resulting movement in the vessels] is called hook[-like]."

29 Mori: "The *Tai su* does not have the character 鼓 here; it was erroneously moved to the preceding statement."

30 527/45: "The character 急 is an error. The *Tai su* has 隱, this is a mistake, too. 急 should be 陰. 勝 stands for 多, 'plenty.' The so-called 鼓陽勝陰 string-like [movement in the] vessels; .. it appears as a yang movement with strong elements of yin."

31 The *Tai su* has 隱, "hidden", instead of 弦.

32 527/45: "The character 'yang' is a mistake here; it should be yin. 絕 stands for 極, 'extreme.' When yin reaches an extreme, freezing cold and frozen soil result. Hence the appearance of the [movement in the] vessels resembles stones. When yang reaches an extreme, the [movement in the] should be vast and frequent; why should [the text] speak of 'stone?'"

33 Wang Bing: "The first yang is to say: tripler burner; it is the palace of the heart vessel. If it is such that the first yang moves like drumming, then a hook[-like movement in the] vessels corresponds to it. A hook[-like movement in the] vessels is a heart [movement in the] vessels. That is to say, it can be observed directly. The first yin is the qi of ceasing yin, of liver and wood. A hair[-like movement] is the [movement in the] vessels [associated with] the lung, metal. When the metal [movement] arrives and drums on the wood, then this [movement in the] vessel is hair[-like]. When the metal qi invades inside, while the yang [qi] of the wood is still dominating, then a tense [situation] appears internally. Then the [movement in the] vessels is string[-like]. When the yang qi arrives and is tense, the vessel [movement] is named string[-like]

Yin struggles inside;
yang causes trouble outside.
[In this case] the *po*-sweat is not retained,[34] and
a four-fold countermovement emerges in the [limbs].
When it emerges, then it steams the lung,[35] and
lets that person pant with sounds.[36]
>As for the [qi] generated by the yin,
its harmonious basis are the flavors.<[37]

Hence,
when hard comes to hard,
yang qi breaks up and disperses and

---

and belongs to the liver. When the yang qi arrives and occasionally is like interrupted, the vessel [movement] is named stone[-like] and belongs to the kidneys. When the qi of yin and yang surpass each other, and when none of them can overcome the other, then the [movement in the] vessels resembles the flow of water." The *Tai su* has 彈, "bullet[-like]", instead of 溜.

34 On the various occurrences of the character 魄 in connection with sweating and pores, see 1324/12.

35 527/45: "熏 is a mistake. The *Tai su* has 動; [the former character] should be exchanged. The commentary by Zheng 鄭 on the *Li ji*, Yue ji 樂記, states '動 is written occasionally as 勳.' From this it is obvious that the character 熏 here is a corrupt version of 動, where the element 力 has been omitted mistakenly. Yang Shangshan interprets 動 as 傷, 'harm.' That is to say, 動 has the meaning of 痛, 'pain,' and 'pain' has the same meaning as 'harm.' " Accordingly, this passage should read: "When it emerges, it harms the lung."

36 Wang Bing: "In case the metal drums without end, [this indicates that] the yang qi has gained excessive dominance. The two qi act on each other with internal struggle and external fight. This leads to endless sweating. Hands and feet turn cold. If this [condition develops to an] extreme, the yang qi causes internal burning; sweat flows and cannot be retained. The heat, then, attacks the lung. It rises and steams the lung. This causes [the patient] to pant with sounds."

37 Wang Bing: " 'Yin' is to say: the five depots storing the spirits. That is to say, the harmonious qi that enables the five depots to generate and maintain the true [qi of] heaven has its name from its harmonious and tranquil nature." Mori: "The *Tai su* has 曰味 instead of 曰和. That is appropriate. The present wording in the *Su wen* is an error. Yang Shangshan commented: 'The basis for the generation of harmonious qi in the five depots are the five flavors. 曰 is identical with 為, 'to constitute.' " See also *Su wen* 3: 陰之所生本在五味, "that which comes to life through yin, it originates from the five flavors." We have changed the *Su wen* text here in accordance with the *Tai su* version.

the yin qi wastes away and perishes.[38]
<If it is muddy, then hard and soft are not in harmony;
the [movement of the] conduit qi is interrupted.>[39]

7-55-4
In cases of [diseases] belonging to the "killing yin" [type],
death follows within three days.[40]
In cases of [diseases] belonging to the "generating yang" [type],
death follows within four days.[41]

---

38 Wang Bing: " 'Hard' is to say: yang. That is to say, when yang qi steams the interior, this causes sweat to flow on the outside. If it burns without end, a yang dominance is increased by additional yang. Hence [the yang] abounds but cannot exist [like this] for long. As a result, the yang qi disperses by itself. When the yang is destroyed, the yin cannot exist alone. Hence, wen the yang qi is destroyed and dispersed, the yin qi dissipates, too. This is 'inviting defeat by striving for supremacy.' " Zhongyi yanjiuyuan…: " 'Hard' refers to yang qi. 'Hard comes to hard' means excessive flourishing of yang qi." 527/45: "The character 與 is a mistake for 愈, 'to increase,' 'to exceed.' "

39 Wang Bing: "When the blood is turbid, [this indicates that] the yang is dominant over an extended period of time. If one sees a patient with turbid blood, one should take great care to harmonize his qi and repeatedly stimulate its flow." *Ling shu* 67 has a passage reminiscent of the present statement suggesting a positive meaning of 淖, in the sense of mild, gentle, harmonious: 陰陽和調而血氣淖澤滑利 "Yin and yang are balanced harmoniously and the qi and the blood are gentle, moist, smooth, and unimpeded." *SWJZ*: "淖 is 泥, 'muddy.' " Zhang Yizhi et al: The *Yi qie jing yin yi* 一切經音義 quoting the *Zi lin* 字林 states: "Extreme moisture is called 淖." Wu Kun: "淖 is to say: great excess of yin qi resulting in 潦淖, 'flooding.' " Zhang Jiebin: "淖 is to say: disorderly passage of cold dampness because of yin qi dominance." Tanba: "Wu Kun and Zhang Jiebin interpret this as surplus of yin qi. That is correct. Gao Shishi interprets 淖 as 和, 'harmonious.' That is wrong." Tanba Genken 丹波元堅: "Yang Shangshan interprets 淖 as 亂, 'disorder,' in the sense of 'yang disperses and yin dissipates. Hence hard and soft are not in harmony. As a result [the movement in] the twelve conduits is interrupted.' I do not know the basis on which he interpreted 淖 as 亂. This remains to be investigated." See also Qian Chaochen-88/278 for a discussion of 淖.

40 Wang Bing: "That is, fire intrudes metal." Zhongyi yanjiuyuan…: "When a heart disease is transmitted to the lung, this is called 死陰 'killing yin.' As is stated in the text: 'When the heart proceeds to the lung, this is called 死陰.' "

41 Wang Bing: "That is, wood intrudes fire." Lin Yi et al.: "Another version has 四日而生, 'after four days [the patient returns to] life.' The Quan Yuanqi edition has 四日而已, 'after four days [the disease is] cured.' Both are identical [in their meaning]. A careful comparison with the preceding and following text suggests that those [editions] having 死, 'death,' are wrong." 2721 and 2282 agree. Yu Yue: "Further below the text states: 'When a liver [disease] approaches the heart, this is called 'generating yang.' When a heart [disease] approaches the lung, this is called 'killing yin.' Hence,

{As for the so-called "generating yang" and "killing yin,"
when [a disease in] the liver proceeds[42] to the heart,
this is called "generating yang;"[43]
when [a disease in] the heart proceeds to the lung;
this is called "killing yin."[44]
When [a disease in] the lung proceeds to the kidneys,
this is called "doubled yin."[45]
When [a disease in] the kidneys proceeds to the spleen,
this is called "rebelling yin."[46]
Death [is inevitable]; no cure [is possible].}

7-56-2
In case of conglomerated yang,

---

even though the terms 'generating yang' and 'killing yin' speak of killing and generating, in fact they both refer to deadly conditions. The comment of Lin Yi et al. is wrong. The 已 in the Quan Yuanqi edition is a mistake for 亡, 'to perish.'"

42 419: "The character 之 stands for 至, 'to approach.'"

43 Wang Bing: "The mother comes to take care of her son. Hence this is called 'generating yang.' But it is not only [called so] because wood produces fire. Another reason is that yang qi controls production/life." Zhongyi yanjiuyuan...: "When a liver disease is transmitted to the heart, this is called 生陽." Gao Jiwu/532: "When a liver disease is transmitted to the heart, this is wood generating fire and this is called 'generating yang.' When a disease of the heart is transmitted to the lung, this is fire subduing metal. This is called 'killing yin.'"

44 Wang Bing: "Yin (i.e., metal) controls punishment and killing. When fire repeatedly intrudes metal, metal is destroyed by fire. Hence [the text] states: 'dying.'"

45 Wang Bing: "This, too, is a mother-son [relationship]. Because both are yin qi the [text] states 'doubled yin.'" 2355: "When it emerges from a yin depot and is transmitted to a yin depot, this is called 'doubled yin.'"

46 Wang Bing: When the qi of soil is punished and put aside, the water can rise. Hence [the text] speaks of 辟陰. Gao Jiwu/24: "辟 is the ancient version of the modern 僻, 'mean,' 'perverted.'" This is in contrast to the passage further below where the same character suggests the meaning of "to open." Zhongyi yanjiuyuan...: "辟 has the meaning of 反克, 'to turn against and subdue.' When a kidney disease is transmitted to the spleen, the water of the kidneys rebels against the soil of the spleen. Hence this is called 辟陰, 'rebelling yin.'" 2355/10: "When it turns against [that depot] in the mutual transmission [by which it is normally controlled] and rebels against it, this is called 'rebelling yin.'" Tanba: "Zhang Jiebin interprets 辟 as 放辟: 'Originally, water is checked by soil. If, now, water rebels against the spleen, the water has nothing to fear. This is called 辟陰, 'freed yin.'" That seems to be correct." Yang Shangshan: "辟 is 重疊, 'duplicated.' It is extreme yin, major yin duplicated." Tanba Genken 丹波元堅: "Yang Shangshan's interpretation seems to be correct."

the four limbs swell.[47]
In case of conglomerated yin,
the stool has one pint of blood.
In case of two conglomerations, these are two pints;
in cases of three conglomerations, these are three pints.[48]

In cases of conglomerations where yin and yang [vessels branch out] diagonally, with more on the yin and less on the yang [part], this is called "stone water."[49] The lower abdomen is swollen.

Second yang conglomerations are called "wasting."[50]
Third yang conglomerations are called "barrier."[51]

---

47 Wang Bing: "This is because the four limbs are the sources of all yang." Zhongyi yanjiuyuan...: "結 means: the qi and the blood have formed conglomerations and cannot move freely." Fang Wenhui/8: "When evil qi has conglomerated in the yang conduits, the four limbs swell."

48 Wang Bing: "Because the yin controls the blood." Zhongyi yanjiuyuan...: "Evil qi conglomerates in the yin conduits. When the yin network vessels receive harm, blood passes down with the stools." Cheng Shide et al.: "The *Sheng ji zong lu* 聖濟總錄 states: 'In case of evil [qi] in the five depots, the [movement in the] yin vessels is not harmonious. When the [movement in the] yin vessels is not harmonious, then bloods stagnates in it. Diseases of conglomerated yin result from internal conglomerations of yin qi, keeping it from moving outside. Blood enters the intestines. Hence there is blood in the stool.' Conglomeration of yin is to say, then: conglomeration of blood in the yin vessels. Zhang Jiebin stated: 'In mild cases the stool has one pint of blood. This way the conglomeration evil is set free. If not and if there is a second conglomeration, then the stool has two pints. (Etc.)'"

49 This statement and the following statements may represent attempts to employ the yin and yang doctrine and vessel theory for an explanation of disease names in common use since before the introduction of the ideas of systematic correspondence. 527/46: "The *Tai su* has 者針 instead of 斜. The character 針 is a [mistaken] addition. The wording 陰陽結者 corresponds to the structure of the preceding passages. The identification of 斜 as 邪 is wrong."

50 Wang Bing: "'Second yang conglomerations' is to say that the stomach and the large intestine are both [affected by] heat conglomerations. When the intestines and the stomach harbor heat, they are likely to consume water and grains." Lin Yi et al.: "This should be 'second yin' [rather than 'second yang']" Zhongyi yanjiuyuan...: "Stomach and intestines have heat conglomerations. As a result they consume the grains and one is hungry."

51 Wang Bing: "This is to say, heat conglomerations in the small intestine and in the bladder. When the small intestine has heat conglomerations, the blood vessels dry. When the bladder has heat, the liquids dry. Hence a barrier results and the stools cannot pass." 527/46: "I assume that following the character 隔 the character 塞,

Third yin conglomerations are called "water."⁵²
First yin and first yang conglomerations are called "throat block."⁵³
When yin beats and yang branches out, this is called "to have a son."⁵⁴
When yin and yang are depleted and when the intestines [make noise

---

'blockage,' is missing." Tanba: "The *Tai su* has 'second yang conglomerations.' Yang
Shangshan commented: 'Stool and urine are blocked.' Mori: 'The wording "two" in the
Tai su is acceptable. It is to say, when heat conglomerates in spleen and stomach, then
stool and urine are blocked.' In today's version of the *Su wen* 'two' and 'three' have
been exchanged mistakenly. Wang Bing's comments are based on a mistaken version.
All later commentators followed him." Zhang Yizhi et al.: "The preceding statement
speaks of 'second yang.' Hence the 'two' in the *Tai su* should be 'three.' "

52 Wang Bing: "This is to say, the vessels of the spleen and of the lung are both [af-
fected by] cold conglomerations. When spleen and lung have cold conglomerations,
the qi is transformed into water." See also 94/52 for an identification of "water" as
"edema," following the statement in *Su wen* 74: "All instances of swelling and fullness
because of dampness are associated with the spleen." 983/35: "When spleen and lung
are affected by conglomerations, they are unable to move and to transform the liquids.
[As a result], the water qi stagnates and this causes a large swelling."

53 Wang Bing: " 'First yin' is to say: the vessels of the heart-master. 'First yang' is to
say: the vessels of the triple burner. Both the vessels of the triple burner and of the heart-master wind around the throat. Here now the qi is hot and conglomerates inside
[these vessels]. Hence this causes 'throat closure.' " 2475/158 points out a possibly
related passage in *Chun qiu fan lu* 春秋繁露: 陰陽之動使人足病喉痺, 'The movement of yin and yang lets man develop foot disease and throat block.'. 92: "結 has the
meaning of 'forming conglomerations,' as in 聚, 'to accumulate,' 合, 'to combine,' 凝
聚, or 'to congeal.' 一陰一陽結 is to say: the first yin and the first yang connect with
each other and hence cause the disease of throat closure." See also 1011/9.

54 Wang Bing: " 'Yin' is to say: in the foot-long section [near the wrist]; 'beat' is to
say: beat against the hand. When the [movement in the vessels] at the foot-long section beats differently from that at the inch opening, the yang qi stands out. This is a
sign of pregnancy. Why? Because there is yang branching out into the yin." Zhang
Jiebin: " 'Yin' stands first for the hand minor yin, but then it may also refer to the
foot minor yin. Now, the heart controls the blood; the kidneys control the uterus.
Both control pregnancy. 搏 stands for 'beat against the hand.' 陽別 is to say: the yin
[movement in the] vessels beats the hand and it appears like a yang evil. But its drumming movement is smooth and fluent, which basically is not an evil [movement in
the] vessels. That is, a yang [movement] appears in the yin and 'deviating [from the
rule]' (別) the appearance is one of harmony. This is called 陰搏陽別, 'yin beats and
deviating [from the rule] yang [appears].' " Zhang Zhicong: " 'Yin beats' [is to say: the
movement in] the vessels at the foot-long section is smooth and fluent and its strokes
can be felt with the hand. 'Yang branches out' [is to say:] the yang [movement] at
the inch-opening appears to emerge separately, unrelated to the other. This indicates
pregnancy." 1775/59: " 'Yin' refers to the [movement in the] vessels in the foot-long
section; 'yang' refers to the [movement in the] vessels in the inch section. When the

sounding] *bi*, [the patient] dies.[55]
When yang is added to the yin, this is called "sweat."[56]
When the yin is depleted and the yang beats, this is called "collapse."[57]

7-56-7
When all third yin beat, [the patient] dies within 20 days at midnight.[58]
When all the second yin beat, [the patient] dies at nighttime of the 13th day.[59]

---

beating of the yin [movement in the] vessels against the fingers is markedly different from the yang [movement in the] vessels, this is a sign of a pregnancy."

55 Wang Bing: "辟 stands for yin. Now, when the stomach qi does not stay and the intestines open without any restriction, the yin center has no supplies and the true qi is exhausted. Hence [the patient] dies." Lin Yi et al.: "The Quan Yuanqi edition has 澼, 'to wash clean,' instead of 辟." Mori: "When the yin and the yang conduits are depleted, neither spleen qi nor stomach qi is transformed. .. Hence the stool is not retained and diarrhea results. Wang Bing's comment interprets 辟 as 開, 'to open.' That is not correct."

56 Wang Bing: "The yang is below and the yin is above. When the yang qi rises and beats against the yin, [he latter] can enclose it firmly. As a result [the yang] causes steam and this produces sweat." 419/6: "The original meaning of this passage is to describe the appearance of [a movement in] the vessels [and call it 'sweat']. Nowadays it is interpreted as the [pathological] mechanism leading to sweat." See also 1705/12.

57 Wang Bing: "When the yin vessels have insufficiencies while the [movement in the] yang vessels beats with abundance, this results in an internal collapse, with blood flowing down." 1317: "The two qi of yin and yang must be balanced. When the yin [qi] is depleted, this may cause excessive activity of yang [qi]; when the yin [qi] is excessively abundant, this may cause depletion of yang [qi]. When the yin is not in harmony with the yang, the yang qi beats. When the blood is aroused by the yang, the blood receives heat and moves. When the blood is hot and moves irregularly, this may lead to a collapse with blood flowing down." 834/343: "Li Dongyuan comments on this passage: 'When females have blood collapsing, the reason is that the kidneys are depleted of water and yin [qi] and cannot check the minister fire in the [heart] enclosing network. Hence the blood moves away and collapses.'The term 崩中 is used nowadays to describe profuse uterine bleeding, i.e., metrorrhagia. This meaning may have been suggested here by Wang Bing. It was certainly known to Yang Shangshan already. He defined 崩 as 下血, "downpour of blood." For a detailed discussion see 2151/20.

58 Wang Bing: "This is exceeding the completion numbers of the spleen and of the lung. 搏 stands for 伏鼓, 'hidden drumming.' This is different from the normal signs. When the yin qi is extremely abundant, [the patient] dies at midnight."

59 Wang Bing: "This is the completion number of the heart and of the kidneys. The yin qi has not reached its peak yet. Hence death occurs in the evening."

When all the first yin beat, [the patient] dies within ten days.[60]
When all the third yang beat and drum, [the patient] dies within three days.[61]

7-57-2
When the third yin and the third yang beat together,
heart and abdomen are full.
If this develops to an extreme and
if [the patient] is unable to [use the] hidden bend,[62]
he will die within five days.

When all the second yang beat, the disease is warmth.[63]
Death [is inevitable,] no cure [is possible].
[The patient] dies within ten days.

---

60 Wang Bing: "These are the generation and the completion numbers of liver and heart." 2721/39 points out that the corresponding *Tai su* passage has 十日平旦死, '[the patient] dies at dawn of the tenth day.' The two characters 平旦 correspond to a specific daytime given in the previous prognostic statements. Hence they may have been mistakenly omitted here.

61 Wang Bing: "Because the yang qi is fast."

62 Wang Bing: "隱曲 refers to the passage of stools and urine." Ma Shi, Gao Shishi, and others agree. 601/45: "Where 隱曲 is used as a noun, it refers to the sexual organ; where it is used as a verb, it may mean 'the urine does not pass,' or 'disease of the yang paths.' Zhang Zhicong rearranges the wording to 心滿,腹發盡, 'the heart has [a feeling of] fullness; the abdomen is extremely distended.'" Wu Kun: "盡 is 極, 'extreme.' 發盡 is 'extreme distension and fullness.' Gao Jiwu/250: "Guo Aichun-92 states: 盡 appears to be a mistake for 疼, 'pain.'" This interpretation by Guo Aichun-92 may have been possible only on the basis of a comparison of the shortened version of 盡 with 疼." 852: "不得 has the meaning of 不能, 'to be unable.'"

63 The corresponding passage in *Tai su* ch.3 has 募, "to summon," instead of 其. Yang Shangshan: "When the qi of both yin and yang have accumulated, then yin and yang summon a disease." Mori: "Another version has 幕, 'curtain.' This may be a mistake for 暮, 'sunset,' 'evening.' 暮病溫 is to say: to develop fever at sunset."

Chapter 8
Discourse on the Hidden Canons in the Numinous Orchid [Chambers]¹

8-58-2
Huang Di asked:
"I should like to hear [the following]:
How do the twelve depots² engage each other,
and what is their hierarchy?"

Qi Bo responded:
"An encompassing question, indeed!
Please let me speak about them one by one.³

The heart is the official functioning as ruler.
Spirit brilliance originates in it.⁴
The lung is the official functioning as chancellor and mentor.
Order and moderation originate in it.⁵

---

1 2078/20: "This treatise was titled 十二藏相使 in the Quan Yuanqi edition."

2 ZZB: "藏 is to be read in the fourth tone. In terms of individual categorization, the 府 are yang and the 藏 are yin. Seen together, they all can be called 藏. This is analogous to the 藏 of 庫藏, 'depot,' because they store things."

3 *Su wen* 09, 69, and 71 have an identical wording. Wang Bing explained 遂 in *Su wen* 71 as 盡, "exhaustively." Another interpretation might be based a.) on the meaning "to comply" of 遂: "May I comply [with your wish] and speak about them," or b.) on the meaning "thereupon:" "May I speak about them immediately," or: "May I speak about them one by one."

4 Wang Bing: "It is responsible for establishing order among beings. Hence it is the official functioning as ruler. It is clear and quiet and houses one's magic power (靈). Hence [the text] states: 'Spirit brilliance originates in it.'" See 1365/24 for parallel identifications of body parts with "official" functions in pre-Han philosophical literature. *Su wen* 79 identifies the liver depot as most important; *Su wen* 44 identifies the lung as the head of all depots. 1694/12 explains why these should not be seen as contradictory statements. See also 1863/42.

5 Hucker does not list an official function named 相傅. Wang Bing: "Its position is high, but it is not the lord; hence it is the official functioning as Minister and Mentor. It is responsible for the passage of camp and guard [qi]; hence order and moderation originate in it." 2187/47: "治節 stands for 治理和調節, 'to rule and to regulate.'" 2493/531: "During the Han dynasty, the central [government] had a 相; [before that,] the royal kingdoms had established the position of 相, too. During the Han era the position of prime minister 丞相 was often associated with that of a 太傅,

The liver is the official functioning as general.
Planning and deliberation originate in it.[6]
The gallbladder is the official functioning as rectifier.
Decisions and judgments originate in it.[7]
The *dan zhong* is the official functioning as minister and envoy.
Joy and happiness originate in it.[8]

'Grand Mentor.' 相傅 is a position in the Han bureaucary." Zhen Lifen et al./77: "相傅 are ancient official titles. 相 stands for 宰相, 'Grand Councilor;' 傅 stands for 太傅, 'Grand Mentor,' and 少傅, 'Junior Mentor.' These were positions below the ruler and above all the other officials." See also 2187/47 for a similar opinion. Zhang Yizhi et al.: "Another name for 相傅 during the Han era was 相國, abbreviated as 相, 'Grand Councilor.'"

6 Wang Bing: "It is brave and able to pass decisions; hence [the text] states 'general.' It secretly develops that which has not sprouted yet; hence 'planning and deliberation originate in it.'" Hucker 694 (p. 140): "General: throughout history the most common term for the commander of a substantial body of troops." 961/25: "The term 將軍 dates from the Warring States period. In the *Shi zi* 尸子 [a work compiled during the Warring States period] it is said: 'An army of 100 000 without a 將軍 will behave disorderly.'" 226/66: "The *Lü shi chun qiu*, Zhi Yi 執一, states: 軍必有將."

7 Wang Bing: "It is tough, upright, and determined; hence it is the official functioning as rectifier. It is straightforward and knows no doubts; hence judments and decisions originate from there." Hucker 1534 (p.189): "Rectifier, from A.D.220 local dignitaries appointed in each Region, Commandery, and District to register and classify all males in their jurisdictions who were considered eligible for government office on the basis of their hereditary social status, assigning them to 9 ranks theoretically reflecting their meritoriousness." Zhen Lifen et al./77: "中正 is the title of an official responsible for assessing the moral standing of certain people." 1877/16: "The titles 中正, 相傅, 州都, etc. existed only beginning with the North-South [division of] Dynasties. From this one may know that the completion of this treatise occurred after the Han dynasty. 2298/53: "This treatise was compiled at the time of the Wei and Jin [dynasties]. The official title 中正 existed only beginning with the Cao Wei [dynasty]." 221/212 and 1198/2: "中正 has the meaning of 不偏不倚, 'impartial.'" 1582/47 disregards the social metaphor implied and reads 正 as 盛, with the meaning of 盛納 or 盛貯, 'to contain.' The author sees this interpretation justified by the 42ⁿᵈ difficult issue in the Nan jing where the text states: "[The gallbladder] 盛精汁三合 'is filled with three *he* of essence liquid.'" 1582/47 suggests that 決斷 should be read 泄止, "drain and stop," referring to the function of the gallbladder to excrete and store gall liquid.

8 Wang Bing: "This is the region in the chest between the two breasts. It is the 氣海, 'the sea of qi.' Now, the heart ruler is the lord, responsible for transmitting teachings and orders. The *dan zhong* rules the qi. It spreads the qi through the yin and yang [regions]. When the qi and the mind are in appropriate condition, good fortune and joy emerge as a result and are distributed to the yin and yang [regions]. Hence it is the official functioning as 'Minister and Envoy.'" Zhang Qi: "膻中 is the heart enclosing network. It represents the palace walls inside of which the heart ruler resides." Wang

The spleen and the stomach are the officials responsible for grain storage.
The five flavors originate from them.[9]
The large intestine is the official functioning as transmitter along the Way.
Changes and transformations originate in it.[10]
The small intestine is the official functioning as recipient of what has been perfected.
The transformation of things originates in it.[11]

8-58-8
The kidneys are the official functioning as operator with force.
Technical skills and expertise originate from them.[12]

Ang: "This is the heart enclosing network." Cheng Shide et al.: "The present treatise refers to a 膻中 but does not mention the heart enclosing network. In contrast, *Ling shu* 10 refers to the heart enclosing network but fails to mention a 膻中. Hence Li Zhongzi, Gao Shishi, and Wang Ang held that 膻中 is identical with the heart enclosing network." Zhang Jiebin: "In the list of outer and inner [depots and palaces associated with] the twelve conduits, there is a heart enclosing network, but no 膻中. The heart enclosure is located right above the diaphragm. It serves as a guardian of the heart. *Ling shu* 35 states: '膻中 is the palace wall of the heart ruler.' This conforms with the meanings which are expressed by means of the terms 'heart enclosure', 'minister', and 'envoy'." Tanba: "[To state] 'This is the heart enclosing network' is wrong. Even though both are located in the upper burner, the 膻中 is the formless basic qi, while the blood network vessels enclosing the heart constitute the heart enclosing network. How can the two be identified as constituting one and the same thing?" Yang Shangshan: "膻 stands for 胸中, 'chest center.'" See also *Su wen* 17-107-3.

9 Wang Bing: "They hold the five grains; hence they are the officials responsible for grain storage. They nourish the four sides; hence [the text] states: 'The five flavors originate from them.'"

10 傳道 may also be read as "path of transmission." Hence Wang Bing: "傳道 is to say: the path along which the unclean is transmitted. 變化 is to say: change and transformation of the physical appearance of things."

11 Wang Bing: "[The small intestine] takes orders from the stomach to receive and hold the waste. Once it has received [the waste], it transforms them anew and transmits them into the large intestine. *Gu dian yi zhu xuan* bianxiezu /11: "盛 is read like 成. The *Li ji* 禮記, Wang zhi 王制, has a term 受成. Kong Yingda 孔穎達 commented: '受成 refers to an acceptance and realization of plans completed by someone else.'"

12 Wang Bing: "They perform their operations with force; hence [the text] states 強作. They create physical appearance; hence [the text] speaks of 'technical skills and expertise.' In females 'technical skills and expertise' applies; in males it is truly 'operating with force.'" Tang Rongchuan 唐容川 in his *Yi jing jing yi* 醫經精義: "The marrow in the bones is generated from the essence in the kidneys. As long as there is sufficient essence available, the marrow is able to act. The marrow is in the bones. When the

The triple burner is the official functioning as opener of channels.
The paths of water originate in it.[13]
The urinary bladder is the official functioning as regional rectifier.[14]
The body liquids are stored in it.
<When the qi is transformed, then [urine] can originate [from there].>[15]
All these twelve officials must not lose [contact with] each other.

---

marrow acts, then the bones are strong. Hence they can 'operate with force.'" Gao Jiwu/27: "Nowadays, 伎 is written 技."

13　Wang Bing: "It guides yin and yang [qi] and opens blockages. Hence it is the official functioning as Opener of the ditches and the waterways originate from there." Wu Kun: "決 stands for 開, 'to open.' 瀆 stands for 水道, 'water way.'" See also 1899/43. Zhang Jiebin: "決 stands for 通, 'to penetrate,' 'to make passable.'"

14　This identification follows Hucker 1346 (p.179). Accordingly, the title 州都 was introduced during the North-South Division as a variant of the term Rectifier (see above) applied to the regional level. The Regional Rectifier was responsible for identifying and classifying all males considered qualified for government office. In contrast, one may also interpret this passage as "is the official functioning as provincial capital." Hence, Wang Shaozeng/175 identifies 州都 as 都會, "city." *Gu dian yi zhu xuan* bianxiezu /11 identifies 州都 as an "administrative region." Zhen Lifen et al./77: "州都: The *Shuo wen* states: 'A place amidst water where one can dwell is called 州. 都 is a dike keeping water off. This indicates that the urinary bladder is the organ responsible for gathering liquids."

15　Wang Bing: "When [the bladder] is supplied with transformed qi from the sea of qi (氣海) then the urine flows off from there. In case the qi arriving from the sea of qi is inadequate, then [the bladder] is closed tightly and blocked." 1148/46 suggests that 藏 is a mistake here for 出, "to originate." This way, the author Liu Changshou 劉昌壽 argues, the structure of the preceding eleven statements is repeated. Liu Changshou suggested therefore further to make a full stop before 氣化. The following sentence, he concluded does not refer solely to the bladder, as is suggested by all previous authors, but to all twelve depots. In his view, the passage should read as follows: "[As long as] qi is transformed, [spirit brilliance, order and economy, etc.] may originate from the [twelve depots]." 883/17 repeats this argument. 1032/60, in a direct reply, disagrees and interprets 氣化 as referring, in the present context, to the functions of the bladder and the triple burner. 2091/39: "出 stands for 傳泄, 'to discharge.'" *Su wen* 72 has a largely identical listing of the functions of the depots and palaces. Except for one occurrence in *Su wen* 03, the term 氣化 occurs once in *Su wen* 69, 23 times in *Su wen* 71, once in *Su wen* 72, and once in *Su wen* 74. Since treatises 69 through 74 are most likely additions of the Tang era, the six characters 藏焉氣化則能 may represent a later rephrasing and expansion of an original wording 津液出焉. In correspondence with the previous statements, the characterization of the bladder may have ended with the wording 津液出焉, "the body liquids emerge from there." See also 1019/47.

Hence,

if the ruler is enlightened, his subjects are in peace.

To nourish one's life on the basis of this results in longevity.[16]

There will be no risk of failure till the end of all generations.

Thereby ruling the world will result in a most obvious success.

If the ruler is not enlightened, then the twelve officials are in danger.[17]

This causes the paths to be obstructed and impassable.[18]

The physical appearance will suffer severe harm.

To nourish life on the basis of this results in calamities.

Thereby ruling the world will greatly endanger the ancestral temple.[19]

8-59-6

Beware, beware![20]

The perfect Way is subtle!

Its changes and transformations are inexhaustible.

Who would know its origin?[21]

How embarrassing:[22]

---

16 Wang Bing: "When the ruler is enlightened, punishments and rewards will be one and the same. When punishments and rewards are one and the same, the government officials will adhere to the law. When the government officials adhere to the law, the people will not commit offenses resulting from excessive behavior. Now when the ruler [i.e., the heart] is enlightened internally, it will weigh good and bad. When it weighs good and bad, it examines peace and danger. When it examines peace and danger, the body will not die early or be harmed by leaving the Way. Hence to nourish one's life on the basis of these [principles] brings longevity.

17 Wang Bing: " 'Ruler' is to say: the official function of the heart as ruler." 2655/19 draws attention to remarks by Zhao Xianke 趙獻可 to the effect that the heart cannot be the ruler meant here because if this were so the text should speak of only "eleven officials." Zhao Xianke suggested that the 命門 , "gate of life," was meant here as ruler.

18 Wang Bing: "使道 refers to the paths of spirit qi."

19 Wang Bing: "How could the ancestral temple remain in its position?!"

20 2568/49: "The character 之 has no grammatical meaning here; it is inserted here merely for the purpose of balancing the structure of the sentence."

21 Wang Bing: "This is to outline the application of the perfect Way. Seen in its small dimensions, it is so subtle and penetrates all that is minute. Seen in its large dimensions, it is wide and broad and its changes and transformations are without end. This being so, who could know or examine its profound essence?"

22 *SWJZ*: "窘 is 迫, 'embarrassed,' 'in trouble.' " Wang Bing: "窘 stands for 要, 'essential.' " 2261/33: "The 19 characters from 窘 down to 良 are not related to the meaning

[Even] the exemplary, they are helpless;[23]

---

of the preceding and following text; they have been erroneously inserted here and can be omitted."

23 The received text has 消者瞿瞿. We read 消 as 肖 in the sense of "to come close to the ideal", in contrast to 不肖, "to be far away from the ideal". Wang Bing: "瞿瞿 is 勤勤, 'diligent.' The essential in the human body, that is the Way. Now, it is by taking into regard the differences in their waxing and waning that one seeks [to understand] the principles of all living beings and wishes to recognize the final origin of their changes and transformations. Even though one is diligent in searching for an understanding, who could recognize the essential subtleties?" Lin Yi et al.: "The *Tai su* has 肖者濯濯." In the present *Tai su*, this passage is missing. 2719/6: "Wang Bing's interpretation contradicts the grammatical structure of this passage and leaves its meaning far behind. In contrast, the wording of the *Tai su* is most appropriate. 肖 is 似, 'to resemble.' 肖者 refers to things that resemble each other and are still slightly different. 濯濯 is 'a bald, bare appearance (光秃貌)'. *Meng zi*, Gao zi shang 告子上, states: 'When the people see its bareness, they assume it was never wooded. But is this the nature of the mountain?' The comment by Zhao Qi 趙崎 says: '濯濯 refers to an appearance without herbs and trees.' This is exactly the origin of the present statement.... The meaning here is: 'Similar facts and principles are as difficult to distinguish from each other as are bare mountain peaks.' This way, [this passage] can also be associated with the meaning of the following statement: 'who knows their essentials?' Hence Qi Bo continued with a sigh: 'How difficult!' Also, in terms of rhymes, 濯 .... rhymes with 要, 當 rhymes with 良, but 瞿 .... does not rhyme with 要. Furthermore, this four sentence passage [ending with 孰者為良] appears in a virtually identical version in *Su wen* 69.... It may well be that this is an ancient poem that was inserted wherever it was thought to fit.... To conclude, the *Tai su* passage 肖者濯濯 is the correct version." 2721/39 repeats this argument. 247/23 agrees. In contrast, 1949/45 quotes the *Ci hai* 辭海 definition of 肖 as "to resemble", but suggests a meaning here of 肖者 as "those who study medicine" and follows Wang Bing in interpreting 瞿瞿 as "diligent." In a direct comment to 2721/39, 144/33 stated: "孰 may be 熟, in the sense of 成熟 'ripe,' 'mature,' or 精熟, 'be minutely acquainted with'.... It may also be the interrogative particle 孰. The three occurrences of 孰 in this passage [beginning with 至道在微] offer both of these usages. In the statement 孰知其要, 孰 has the meaning of 'how is it possible?'. In the other two statements, 孰 has the meaning of 精熟, 'minutely acquainted with.' *Su wen* 69 has 莫, 'there is not,' instead of 孰. The characters differ, but the meaning is comparable. 消 and 肖 ... have the meaning of 衰微, 'weak,' 'insignificant.'... 消者 may have the metaphorical meaning of 'a person who knows very little.' Hence a 消者 (i.e., 'ignoramus,') is the opposite of a 孰者 (i.e., 'expert'). 瞿瞿 is the predicate of 消者; it describes a manner of nervously looking here and there.... Even though such a person looks here and there, he or she will grasp nothing nevertheless. Obviously [,as the text states,] 莫知其妙, 'he does not know the mysteries'." In contrast, 150/59: "孰 is an interrogative particle; 者 has no meaning itself and was added simply for stylistic reasons." 2802/47: "瞿瞿 appears to describe an emaciation (消瘦). The meaning is: 'the twelve officials (i.e., the twelve depots) have lost mutual contact and the physical appearance of [that] person becomes thin. Nobody knows

who [of them] knows its essentials?
In view of the unfathomable,
who can stand up to this?[24]

The numbers of the fleeting and of the indeterminable,[25]
they emerge from [the numbers of] the minutest length.[26]
The numbers of the minutest length,
they have their origin in measurement.

---

the cause.' 瞿瞿 stands for 癯癯 in the sense of 瘠, 'lean,' 'emaciated.'" For quotations justifying this interpretation, see there. 894/17: "瞿瞿 is to describe a physician who diligently studies medicine. 肖 refers to an outstanding physician. 當 is 值, 'happen to.'" *JJZG*: "瞿瞿 refers to an appearance of looking fixedly." Shen Zumian: "濯濯 makes no sense either. Wang Bing's interpretation of 瞿瞿 as 'diligent' is off the point, too. 瞿瞿 is identical with 矍矍, 'to look right and left in alarm.' *Su wen* 69 has 肖者瞿瞿. The character 肖 is correct. Maybe the present sentence and the subsequent statement were worded 瞿瞿者肖, 莫知其妙 originally. 肖 and 妙 form a rhyme." Zhang Yizhi et al.: "Based on the wording in the *Tai su*, the character 肖 should be regarded as correct. 肖 has the meaning of 小, 'small.' 肖者瞿瞿 is to say: A small man (or: the masses) whose perception of the Way is narrow and whose learning is shallow, may have his eyes and his mouth wide open, but will be unable nevertheless to reach an informed judgment." We read the phrase as 肖者瞿瞿, identical with the wording in *Su wen* 69. See also 69-417-3.

24 Wang Bing: "If thereby one whished to clarify the origins of change and transformation, even if he were to search with utter diligence, how could anybody get to know the essential subtleties! Not to understand them, on the contrary, results in a farreaching distance. 閔閔 stands for 深遠, 'deep and far.'" Gao Shishi and Zhang Zhicong identify 閔閔 as 憂, "grief." Gao Jiwu/208: "[This passage should read:] 'The deep and mysterious principles of medicine as well as the corresponding regular principles, in what way are they good?' 當 is 當道, 'the right Way.' 之 is a conjunction, functioning like 與, 'and.' The original meaning of 閔 was not 'deep and far.' The *Shuo wen* 說文 states: '閔 is to hang at a door.' Duan 段 commented: 'Its extended meaning is pain and sorrow.'" 915/56: "瞿瞿 refers to the appearance of someone hastily looking around. The *Li ji* states: '瞿瞿 is as if one searched for something without getting it.' 閔閔 alludes to a confused appearance. 閔 is identical with 泯, 'confused.' 要 refers to the essential and subtle issues of the Way. 當 has the meaning of 阻斷, 'to separate.' This is to say, the mutual stimulation of the twelve depots rests on a perfect Way that is subtle and undergoes endless changes and transformations. It is most difficult to perceive for anyone without an upright mind.'"

25 Wang Bing: "恍惚 is to say: it seems as if it existed and it seems as if it did not exist." See also Laozi 14 and 21 for the use of 恍惚 to describe the "undeterminable" nature of the Way.

26 毫氂, lit. "a tenth of a thousandth part of the length of a foot."

Increasing them thousandfold, increasing them ten thousandfold,[27]
can make them bigger and bigger.
Expanding them, enlarging them,
will build their physical appearance."[28]

8-60-2
Huang Di:
"Good!
I have heard
'the Way of the essence light,
this is the achievement of the great sages.'

But as far as [their] promulgation of the Great Way is concerned,
if it is not after [a period of] fasting and chastity and if [I] have not selected an
auspicious day,
[I] do not dare to accept it."

Huang Di, thereupon, chose an auspicious day and a good omen,
and stored these [teachings] in the Numinous Orchid Chamber[29]
to have them transmitted and treasured[30] there.

---

27 2568/49: "The character 之 has no grammatical meaning here; it was inserted
merely for the purpose of balancing the structure of the sentence." In contrast, 704/48:
"The numericals 'thousand' and 'ten thousand' have 之 as their object. Hence they are
used here as verbs, with the meaning 'increase them thousandfold; increase them ten
thousandfold.'"

28 475/41: "制 should be 晰. 制 finds no explanation here. ... 晰 has the meaning of
'clear.'" If one were to follow this argument, the passage would read: "The physical
form becomes apparent."

29 See 2493/531 for information on this chamber.

30 Yu Chang: "保 is to be read as 寶, 'treasure,' 'to treasure.'"

Chapter 9
Discourse on the Six Terms [of a Year] and on Phenomena [Associated with the Condition] of the Depots[1]

9-60-7
Huang Di asked:[2]
"I have heard:
In heaven one relies on six [times] six terms, <to complete one year>.[3]
on the earth one relies on nine [times] nine [geographic regions] to set up calculations.[4]
<Counting man, he, too, has 365 joints. Through this one establishes [a correspondence with] heaven and earth. This has always been so.>[5]

---

1 See 1375/394 for an analysis of relationships between this treatise and later treatises concerning the theory of the five periods and six qi.

2 137/12: "Beginning from 黃帝問曰 to 請陳其方, many statements have been forced into [the original text] and the reasoning is forced, too. These amendations have been made, without any doubt, by Daoists."

3 2026/28: "This is to say, six times the sixty [days] of a *jia zi* 甲子 [period] constitute one year." Cheng Shide et al./139: " 'Six [times] six,' this is six times the *jia zi* [period of sixty days]. Altogether these are 360 days, conforming to the number of the revolutions of heaven."

4 Further down the text repeats these phrases but has 地以九九 instead of 人以九九. Zhang Yizhi et al. suspects that in the present wording "earth" has been erroneously replaced by "man," because "man" is mentioned twice. We have changed the *Su wen* text accordingly. Most Chinese commentators, though, see 人以九九制會 as the original wording. E.g., Cheng Shide et al./139: "人以九九 refers to man's possessing nine orifices and nine depots. The passage of the qi in man corresponds to that of sun and moon in heaven. The qi of the nine orifices and nine depots can be investigated at the external signs revealing the condition of the depots at the nine indicators at three [wrist] sections. 制 is 正, 'to correct,' 裁斷, 'to determine.' 會 is to say 會通, 'to standardize.' Wu Kun: "In ancient times, the emperor met the feudal lords during his inspection tours and during hunting. All the pitch-pipes, the standards, the measures, the weights had to be equalized. This was named 會通, 'to adapt.' " In contrast to previous commentators, we read 會 as *kuai*, "to calculate." 制會 is: to set up a calculation, for example, to estimate annual harvest or tax income.

5 Cheng Shide et al./139: "*Ling shu* 01 states: 節之交, 三百六十五會, 'Where the sections join each other, these are 365 meeting places.' Also: 'The so-called joints are the locations where the spirit qi leaves and enters during its travels.' That is, 節 refers to the transportation points. Another possibility is to interpret '365 sections' as referring to the 365 sections of the skeleton."

I do not know what this means."[6]

Qi Bo responded:
"A brilliant question, indeed!
Please let me speak about them one by one.

Now,
as for 'six [times] six terms,'
as for 'nine [times] nine to set up calculations,'
it is with these [figures] that one determines the degrees of heaven and the
numbers of qi [terms].[7]

9-61-1
The 'degrees of heaven' is that by which the passage of sun and moon is determined.[8]

---

6 Wang Bing: " 'Six [times] six terms' is to say: to pass six times through the [sixty]
days of the six *jia* [terms] to complete the terms of a year. 九九制會 is to say: the
number of circling nine [times] through the 'nine fields' (i.e., the nine divisions of
earth) to establish a correspondence (制會通) of man's physical appearance [with
the earth]. In other words, [the question posed by Huang Di is as follows:] 'The correspondence of the 365 sections of man's [physical appearance] with the six [times]
six terms of heaven has [been referred to] for long. If now, in addition, an calculation
pattern of nine [times] nine is set up, then this [is to say that] two years and a greater
half are called one cycle.' [I] do not know the original source of this pattern." Lin Yi
et al.: "Wang Bing's commentary states 'Two years and a greater half are called one
cycle.' Now, 九九制會 should say: 'two years and one fourth of a year (i.e., 810 days)
are called one cycle.' "

7 Wang Bing: " 'Six [times] six terms' are the degrees of heaven; 九九制會 is the
number of qi [terms]. This so-called number of qi [terms] refers to the qi of generation
and completion. One celestial cycle consists of 365 degrees plus one forth of a degree.
If this is paralleled with the qi of the twelve [30 days] terms [of a year], then one year
ends after 360 days. If one combines them with the short months [of 29] days the
resulting number [of days] would even less be sufficient [to reach the number of 365]
Hence an intercalary [term] is added regularly after 64 qi [terms]." Gao Shishi: "天
度 refers to the 365 degrees passed by the circular movement of the sun. 氣數 is the
normal number of the 24 qi [terms in the course of one year]."

8 Zhang Jiebin: "制 is 節, 'to regulate,' 正, 'to order.' The width of the universe in itself
can not be measured. What can be measured, though, are the circular movements of
the constellations that are attached to heaven. Through the passage of these constellations, the path of heaven becomes obvious and the slower or faster course of the seven
celestial bodies (i.e., sun, moon, the five planets) has its [fixed] terms. By this, therefore, the movement of the sun and of moon can be de-termined." See also 705/54.

The 'numbers of qi [terms]' is that by which the operations of transformation and generation are arranged.⁹

Heaven is yang; the earth is yin.
The sun is yang; the moon is yin.
[Their] passage has separate arrangements.¹⁰
[Their] circulation¹¹ has paths and structures.¹²
[While] the sun passes through one degree,
the moon passes through thirteen degrees and has some odd [time left].

Hence,
[in the succession of] longer and shorter months,
365 days constitute one year,
with surplus of accumulated qi [that results in] intercalations.¹³

---

9 Wang Bing: "制 is to say 準度, 'to standardize measures.' 紀 is to say 綱紀, 'web,' 'fundamental principles.' Through establishing the standards of the passages of sun and moon, one knows whether the passage of sun and moon is retarded or fast. Through the operations of transformation and generation it becomes obvious that these [transformations and generations] correspond to the arrival of the [respective] qi. When qi [arrival] and corresponding [transformations and generations] show no discrepancy, then the pattern of generation and completion is not discontinued. The speed [of the passage of sun and moon] corresponds to the degrees [of heaven], the longer and shorter months arise from this." Zhang Jiebin: "紀 is 記, 'to record.' The number of qi [terms] has no physical appearance and is in itself difficult to examine. What can be examined, though, is the coming and going of yin and yang which is visible in the sequence of the [seasonal] terms. When the [seasonal] terms come in sequence, the seasons follow each other and the decay and growth of the myriad beings has its [fixed] periods. By this, therefore, the manifestations of transformations and generation can be recorded."

10 Cheng Shide et al./140: "分紀 is 分野紀度, 'separate the fields and record/calculate the degrees,' i.e., the areas and degrees drawn against the background of heaven. Zhang Zhicong comments: '行有分紀 is to say the movement of sun and moon follows distinct regions and marked degrees."

11 Cheng Shide et al./140: "周 is 環周, 'circulation.' 道理 refers to 軌道, 'track,' 'path.' That is to say, the circulatory passage of sun and moon follows a fixed path." Zhang Zhicong: "周有道理 is to say: the circular movement of sun and moon in heaven follows the paths of the Southern way and of the Northern way."

12 In contrast, 2308/47: "道理 is not the binomial expression of today and does not have the meaning of 'basic principle.' 理 stands for 通, 通行, 'to pass through;' it is used here as a verb. 道 stands for 道路, 'way;' it is a noun. 周有道理 is to say: sun and moon, in their circulation, pass along a fixed way."

13 Wang Bing: "The sun passes slowly. Hence in the time span of day and night it passes through one degree of heaven. After 365 days it has completed one cycle plus a

Place the end at the beginning.
Display the proper in the middle.
Push the remainder to the end,
and the degrees of heaven are completed."[14]

9-62-1
[Huang] Di:
"I have heard by now about the degrees of heaven.
I should like to hear [now] how the numbers of qi [terms] are matched with them."[15]

Qi Bo:
"In heaven one takes six [times] six [ten day terms] to arrive at the [number of its] terms.
On the earth one takes nine [times] nine [geographic sections] to set up a calculation.

Heaven has ten day [terms].
When the [ten] day [terms] have been completed six [times], the cycle returns to *jia*.[16]

---

fraction of a degree. The moon passes quickly. Hence in the time span of day and night it passes through thirteen degrees of heaven. Within 29 days it completes one cycle through heaven. When it is said 'through thirteen degrees and has some odd [time left],' that is to say: it passes through an additional 7/19 degrees."

14 Wang Bing: "端, end, is 首, 'head,' 'onset;' 始 is 初, 'beginning.' 表 is 彰示, 'to display.' 正 is 斗建, ' established by [the direction into which the handle of] the dipper (i.e, *ursa maior*) [points].' 中 is 月半, 'middle of the month.' 推 is 退位, 'to push away in its position'. The meaning [of this statement] is: place the first [annual] qi at the [first] day of the first of the [24 annual] *jie* 節 (terms); show the cardinal point that is established by the [direction into which the handle] of the dipper [points] in the middle of the month; move the remaining [days which are not covered by the twelve months] into the future." 2475/158 and 2138/38 point out a similar statement in the *Zuo zhuan*, first year of duke Wen左傳文元年: 先王之正時也, 履端于始, 居正于中, 歸余于終. (See Ruan Yuan 1836 below.)

15 Gao Jiwu/453: "I wish to know how the number of qi [terms] is combined with the degrees of heaven."

16 Wang Bing: " 'Ten days' refers to the days 甲, 乙, 丙, 丁, 戊, 已, 庚, 辛, 壬, and 癸. 'Ten' is the perfect number of heaven and earth. .. A cycle of sixty days, this is the [number of days of] one 甲子 [period]. Six cycles of 甲子 [periods] until a new onset, this completes the days of one year. This is the pattern of a year of 360 days; it is not the number of the [365] degrees of heaven. This is based on 12 months of 30 days each. If one subtracts the [missing days of the] short months [of 29 days], the dif-

When *jia* has been repeated six [times], one year is completed.
{This is a pattern of 360 days.}

9-62-4
"Now,
since antiquity, that wich communicates with heaven,
the basis of life,
is based in yin and yang.
All the [yin and yang] qi
within the nine regions <and the nine orifices>,
communicate with the qi of heaven.[17]

Hence,
its generations are five; its qi are three.[18]

---

ference is pronounced even more." 729/2: "周甲 stands for 六十甲子, 'the sixty [days from] *jia zi* [to *jia zi*].'"

17 Wang Bing: "通天 refers to the principal qi, i.e., the true [endowment received from] heaven. That is, physical appearance obtains life from the earth; fate is endowed only by heaven. Hence to receive vital qi represents a communication link with heaven. [Heaven] endows [one] with yin and yang [qi] and this is the root and foundation [of life]. *Su wen* 25 states: 'Man comes to life on the earth; his fate is tied to heaven. When heaven and earth combine their qi, this is called man.' The nine regions are Ji 冀, Yan 兖, Yu 豫, Qing 青, Xu 徐, Yang 揚, Jing 荊, Liang 梁, and Yong 雍. That is, the earth is divided into nine regions and man has nine orifices. [Here] the essence spirit moves in and out and the qi corresponds to it. Hence [the text] states: 'nine regions, nine orifices.' The *Ling shu* states: 'The earth has the nine regions; man has the nine orifices.' This is meant here. The first qi mentioned above refers to the qi of the true [endowment provided by] heaven; it is normally attached to the [body's] center. As long as [the supply] of qi by heaven is not interrupted, this true magic [endowment] remains attached to the interior. The movement and the resting in the passage through the depots, all this [depends on a] communication with [the qi of] heaven. Hence [the text] states: 'they all communicate with the qi of heaven.'"

18 See the initial statement in *Su wen* 03 for a parallel wording. Wang Bing: "The existence of physical appearance depends on the periodic operation of the five agents. To define their origins: it is from the three qi that their generation and completion results. Hence [the text] states: 'Its agents are five; its qi are three.' 2458/24: "To interpret [the three characters] 其氣三 one must take Daoist thinking into account. In the 42nd chapter of the *Dao de jing* 道德經 by Lao zi 老子 it is stated: 'The Way generated One. One generated Two. Two generated Three. Three generated the myriad beings. The myriad things shoulder the yin and embrace the yang; the penetrating qi accounts for harmony.' .. 'One' is the 太一, the 'great One.' .. 'Two' is yin and yang. .. 'Three' is yin qi, yang qi, and 和氣, 'harmonized qi.' .. 其氣三, therefore, refers to the three qi mentioned by Lao zi: yin qi, yang qi, and harmonized qi. .. The character 生 in 其生

9-63-1

Being three they form heaven;
Being three they form the earth;
Being three they form man.[19]
Three times three, together this makes nine.
Nine [serves] to divide [the earth] into the nine fields;
the nine fields are the nine depots."[20]
{The fact is,
the physical depots are four,
the spirit depots are five.[21]
Together this makes nine depots to correspond to them.}[22]

五 and the character 氣 in 其氣三 refer, in both cases, to 生氣, i.e., the qi generating the myriad beings."

19 Wang Bing: "It is not so that only man comes to life through the three qi. The same applies to the Ways of heaven and earth. Hence all the trigrams of the *Yi jing* must be composed of three [lines]."

20 Wang Bing: "The meaning is: the nine fields (lit.: wastelands) correspond to the nine depots. The *Erh ya* 爾雅 states: 'Outside of a city are the suburbs; outside of the suburbs is the 甸-region; outside the 甸-region are the pastures; outside of the pastures are the forests; outside of the forests are the deserts; outside the deserts are the fields (lit.: wastelands).' This serves to explain what is stated here."

21 Wang Bing: "The 'four physical depots' are, first, the temples at the head; second, the ears and the eyes; third, the mouth and its teeth; and, fourth, the chest and the center. They are named [physical depots] because segments of physical appearance constitute these depots. The 'five spirit depots' are, first, the liver; second, the heart; third, the spleen; fourth, the lung; and, fifth, the kidneys. They are named [spirit depots] because [each of them] stores a spirit inside. The liver stores the *hun*-soul, the heart stores the spirit, the spleen stores the sentiments, the lung stores the *po*-soul, the kidneys store the mind. Hence these two [types of depots] are distinguished." 1992/283: "Those [depots] storing formless qi transformation, they are called 'spirit depots.' Those [depots] storing physical matter, they are called 'physical depots,' or 'containers' (器). The stomach, the large intestine, the small intestine, and the triple burner, as well as the bladder, they are called 'containers,' or 'physical depots,' because their function is to digest the water and grains of beverages and food and to separate essence from dregs and at the same time to absorb essence as nourishment and to excrete the dregs in form of feces or urine. .. They do not participate in any functions of the essence spirit. The gallbladder occupies a special position between the physical and the spirit depots. It partakes in the functions of digestion and in the work of the essence spirit, the latter because it occupies the official position of Rectifier who is an expert in passing decisions."

22 1910/6: "The *Zhou li* 周禮, 天官疾醫職 speaks of 'nine depots.' Also, *Su wen* 06 and *Su wen* 20 both speak of 'five spirit depots and four physical depots, together this makes nine depots.' These nine depots are paralleled with the nine provinces and the

[Huang] Di:

"I have heard by now about the calculations of six [times] six and nine [times] nine.

You, Sir, have [also] spoken of accumulated qi [that results in] intercalations.

I should like to hear what is meant here by 'qi.'

Please release me from ignorance and disperse [my] delusions."

9-63-5

Qi Bo:

"This was kept secret by the Lords on High;

the teachers of former times have transmitted it."[23]

[Huang] Di:

"Please, let me hear about these [issues] one by one!"[24]

Qi Bo:

"[A duration of] five days is named *hou*;[25]

[a duration of] three *hou* [terms] (i.e., three times five days) is named *qi*;[26]

[a duration of] six *qi* [terms] (i.e., six times fifteen days) is named season;

[a duration of] four seasons is named year.

Each of them follows what is responsible for governing it.[27]

9-64-2

The five periods succeed each other;

---

nine wastelands. According to Zhang Zhicong, the nine depots are the five depots plus the four palaces stomach, small intestine, large intestine, and bladder."

23 Wang Bing: "上帝 refers to the ruler in high antiquity; 先師 refers to Jiu Daiji 僦 貸季, the teacher of an ancestor of Qi Bo. He has established, in high antiquity, the patterns of the complexions and of the [movements in the] vessels."

24 Wang Bing: "遂 stands for 盡, 'exhaustively.'"

25 917/44: "候 has three meanings in the medical literature; here it refers to a specific time period."

26 371/41: "氣 is 節氣, [a term of 15 days]; one year has 24 節氣. This is an astronomical concept, as are 候, 時, and 歲."

27 Wang Bing: "When the sun moves five degrees in heaven, this is [a term of] five days. Three *hou* [terms] constitute exactly fifteen days. The 'six qi [terms]' together constitute a 90 day [term and] this is exactly three months. Hence 18 *hou* [terms] constitute six qi [terms]. Six qi [terms] are called [one] season. Four seasons together constitute 360 days. Hence [the text] states: '[a term of] four seasons is named a year.' 各從主治 is to say: each day of a year is associated with one of the qi of the five agents, by which it is ruled. Hence the following statement."

each of them governs [one of] these [sections of the year].[28]
When the days of an annual cycle are completed,
this constitutes one cycle, after which it commences anew.
When a time period begins, the [respective] qi spreads.
Like a ring, this has no end."

<The *hou* [terms of five days] follow the same law, too.>

Hence it is said:
He who does not know
what a year contributes [to man's state of health],
how the qi abound and weaken,
and why repletion or depletion emerge,
he cannot serve as practitioner.[29]

[Huang] Di:
"The beginnings of the five periods,
this resembles a ring without end.
When their [qi] is greatly excessive or inadequate, how is that?"

Qi Bo:
"The five qi take their positions one after another;
each of them has [a qi] that it dominates.
The changes between [periods of] abundance and depletion,
this is their regularity."

---

28 See 2308/46. For an analysis of traces of early developmental stages of the theory of the five periods in this treatise, see 2026/28, also 1370/4.

29 Wang Bing: "五運 refers to the qi of the five agents as they correspond to the periodic movement of heaven and govern [all] transformation. 襲 is to say 承襲, 'to receive what is handed down.' In the sense of how a wife receives what is given to her [by her husband]. That is, the qi of the five agents is handed from father to son, [in the sense that the a father] rules [over a son]. This is so during all the days of one cycle and without break the cycle begins anew. 時 refers to the time before [the solar term] spring begins when [the qi] should arrive. 氣 refers to the qi in the vessels that should be ruling [at the time]. When the qi arrives before spring, the qi in the vessels arrives, too. Hence [the text] states: 'when the time is [spring] begins, the [respective] qi spreads.' 候 refers to the *hou* [period] of the sun moving five degrees. That is, during the [five] days of a *hou* [period] the five qi generate each other, too; any deviation in their arrival causes disease. 工 refers to those who are experts in restoration and nourishment; that is, one must know of this and only then one can roam through the empire."

[Huang] Di:
"What is a balanced qi?"

Qi Bo:
"One that is not excessive."

9-64-7
[Huang] Di:
" 'Greatly excessive' and 'inadequate,' what does that mean?"

Qi Bo:
"This is [outlined] in the classic."[30]

[Huang] Di:
"What is that to say:
'[Each of them has a qi] that it dominates'?"[31]

Qi Bo:
"Spring dominates late summer;
late summer dominates winter;
winter dominates summer;
summer dominates autumn;
autumn dominates spring."

This is what [is meant if one] says:
"If one encounters in a season a domination by an [excessive qi of one of] the
five agents, in each such case this qi serves to name the depot."[32]

---

30 Wang Bing: "Everything concerning balanced, excessive and inadequate statusses
of the five qi has been outlined in *Su wen* 19." Lin Yi et al.: "Wang Bing states: 'Everything has been outlined in *Su wen* 19.' However, that treatise speaks about excesses
and inadequacies in the vessels, not about excesses, inadequacies, and balanced status
of the five periods. [Wang Bing] should have said 'All has been outlined in *Su wen*
69 and 70.'"

31 The following statement occurs in a parallel passage in *Su wen* 04.

32 Wang Bing: "Spring corresponds to wood; wood dominates soil. Late summer
corresponds to soil; soil dominates water. Winter corresponds to water; water dominates fire. Summer corresponds to fire; fire dominates metal. Autumn corresponds to
metal; metal dominates wood. This is the normal [course]. Late summer was added
to the four seasons; hence [the text speaks of the] so-called [mutual] domination of
the seasons on the basis of the five agents.' The so-called 'late summer' is the sixth
month. Soil is generated by fire and grows during summer. When it is grown (長) it
rules. Hence one speaks of 長夏, (lit.: grown summer).' As for [the statement] 以氣命

9-65-2
[Huang] Di:
"How does one know [whether a qi] dominates?"

Qi Bo:
"Search for their arrival.
Always trace them to the begin of spring.[33]
When [a qi is] not yet [expected to] arrive, but arrives, this is called 'greatly excessive.'
As a result, it strikes against that which it [under normal conditions] does not dominate,[34]
and it harrasses that which it [normally simply] dominates.
This is called 'qi encroaching.'[35]
When [a qi is expected to] arrive, but fails to arrive, this is called 'inadequate.'

As a result,
that which it [under normal conditions] dominates moves recklessly, while
that which it generates is affected by disease;
that which it [under normal conditions] does not dominate it strikes against it.

藏, the wood of spring is associated internally with the liver; the soil of late summer is associated internally with the spleen; the water of winter is associated internally with the kidneys; the fire of summer is associated internally with the heart; the metal of autumn is associated internally with the lung. Hence [the text] states: 'In each case this qi serves to name the depot.'" For a suggestion that remnants of an ancient ten months sun calendar surface here, see 1064/2.

33 Wang Bing: " 'Begin of spring' refers to the day of [the solar term] 立春, 'spring begins.' Among the four seasons, spring is the superior. Hence for assessing qi one always returns to the day before [the solar term] 'spring begins.' " Gao Jiwu/258: "Whenever one calculates the arrival times of the qi of the depots, one must take [a time] before 'spring begins' as baseline. In case a season has not arrived yet, while its corresponding depot qi is already present, then this is called 'excessive.' An 'excessive' [qi] may contrary [to normal] dominate that qi by which it is usually dominated and it may rebel against that qi which it dominates. This then is called 'qi encroaching.' 薄, according to the *Kang xi zi dian* 康熙字典, is 侵, 'to invade.' "

34 Fang Wenhui/168 interprets 薄 as 侵犯, "to infringe upon."

35 We follow Chinese commentators who have identified the ten characters from 不分 to 能禁 as an erroneous insert here. They are repeated a few lines further down from where they may have inadvertently been copied here. Hence we have omitted them in the Chinese text quoted here. Wang Bing: "These ten characters result from an erroneous mix up of bamboo slips by someone in previous times. Further down, following [the characters] 五治, they make sense. Here [I] write them in red." See also 2520/50 and 2130/3.

This is called 'qi pressing.'
{When [the text] states "search for their arrival," this is the time of the arrival
of the qi.}

Carefully observe its [arrival] time.
[Then you] are able to predict the qi.³⁶
If [the arrival] misses [its proper] time and if the manifestations contradict [the
time] and
if one [is unable to] distinguish among the five governing [qi],
evil is generated internally and
no practitioner can stop it."³⁷

9-66-1
[Huang] Di:
"Does it happen, that [a qi] is not succeeded [by its proper successor]?"³⁸

Qi Bo:
"The qi of the hoary heaven, they must not leave their regular course.
When the qi [of the seasons] fail to succeed [each other], this is called irregular
and
irregularities result in changes."³⁹

---

36 Wang Bing: " 'Time' refers to the time of the arrival of the [respective] qi. For assessing the [qi of an entire] year, one starts on the day of 'spring begins.' For assessing
the [seasonal] qi, one starts at the fixed dates [marking the begin of each] of the four
seasons. For assessing the [qi of a particular] day, one follows the day on which the
assessment is to be conducted. Hence [the text states:] 'Carefully observe its [arrival]
time. [Then you] are able to predict the qi.' "

37 Wang Bing: "反 is to say 反背, 'to oppose.' 五治 is to say: the governing qi of an
entire year as they are ruled by the five agents. That is, if the five governing [qi] are
not separated [according to their respective seasons], one erroneously invites the eight
evils. If someone is unable to understand the periodic movement of the true qi of
heaven, how could he be in a position to develop an understanding of the origins of
disease?" *NJCD*: "The respective therapies chosen in accordance with the laws of the
ruling periods of the five depots." Yao Shaoyu: "The five depots are associated with the
five agents; externally they correspond to the four seasons. The times when diseases
occur differ and the therapeutic patterns differ, too. Hence [the text] speaks of 'five
treatments.' "

38 Wang Bing: "That is, can it happen that the qi of the five agents do not succeed
each other?"

39 Wang Bing: "That is to say, in changes in the regularity of heaven."

[Huang] Di:
"Irregularities leading to changes, how is that?"

Qi Bo:
"When changes occur in the arrival [of the qi], then this results in disease.
If [the qi that arrives is] that which is [normally] dominated [by the qi that
should have arrived, the disease] is slight;
if [the qi that arrives is] that which is [normally] not dominated [by the qi that
should have arrived, the disease] is serious.[40]
If subsequently [one suffers from] multiple affections by evil, then death follows."
{Hence,
if it is not its time, then [the disease] is slight.
If it is its time, then [the disease] is serious.}[41]

9-66-5
[Huang] Di:
"Good!
I have heard:

The qi unite and assume physical appearances.[42]

---

40 2840/9: "For instance, if in spring ([which is associated with the agent of] wood)
one is affected by the qi of dampness of late summer ([which is associated with the
agent of] soil), which is [a qi] that [spring qi normally] overcomes (wood overcomes
soil), then the disease is relatively minor. If one is affected by the dryness qi of autumn
(metal), which is [normally] not overcome [by wood] (metal overcomes wood), then
the disease is serious."

41 Wang Bing: "When the hoary heaven spreads qi it cannot leave [the laws of]
the five agents. Man exists within the qi; how could he not correspond to the Way
of heaven? Now, when man's qi is in disorder, it does not follow the regularities of
heaven. Hence this is manifested in disease and death. The *Zuo zhuan* 左傳 states:
'To oppose heaven brings misfortune.' That is the same [notion]. If in a year associated with wood the qi of fire arrives, two years later disease [will arrive]. If the qi of
soil arrives, three years later disease [will arrive]. If the qi of metal arrives, four years
later disease [will arrive]. If the qi of water arrives, five years later disease [will arrive].
If the true qi is insufficient and if one is repeatedly affected by evil, [then] the true
qi becomes insignificant internally. Hence a repeated affection by evil again results in
death. If one is attacked by a qi that is not in its ruling year, this will cause a slight
disease. It will not necessarily cause internal harm to the spirit depots. Hence [the text
states:] 'it is slight if it is not its time.'"

42 1513/1: "An extremely fine qi is the material element constituting everything
between heaven and earth."

One follows their changes in determining their names.[43]

The periods of heaven and earth,
the transformations of yin and yang,
their [influences] on the myriad beings,
which is less and which is more?
May [I] hear of this?"[44]

Qi Bo:
"An encompassing question, indeed!

The extension of heaven is broad to a degree that it cannot be estimated.
The extension of the earth is large to a degree it cannot be measured.

This is an inspired question worth a great spirit,
please let me delineate [the issue] in outlines [only].[45]

The herbs[46] generate[47] the five colors;
the changes undergone by the five colors
are more than one can see.
The herbs generate the five flavors;
the delicacies[48] of the five flavors

---

43 2300/48: "This is to say, nature generates the myriad beings through transformation of the principal qi. Because the physical appearances result from the conglomerations of qi, their names are different too." 1563/42: "因 is 根据, 'in accordance with.' 以 is 而."

44 Lin Yi et al.: "A careful examination shows that the passage beginning with 'Qi Bo: What a brilliant question!' down to here is missing in both the edition commented by Quan Yuanqi and the *Tai su*. It may have been added by Wang Bing."

45 137/12: "The text from 黃帝問曰 to 請陳其方 has many false conclusions; its underlying principles are forced. Without any doubt, [this text] was added by Daoists."

46 137/12: "[The text from] 草生五色 down to 凡十一藏取決于膽也 is the original text of this treatise."

47 1515/49: "生 can be interpreted as 有, 'to have.' In today's Chinese, this should read: 'the herbs have five colors, [and further down:] the herbs have five flavors.'" See there for a detailed listing and comparison of the various meanings of 生 in the *Nei jing*.

48 527/46: "美 should be 變, 'changes.' The two characters are very similar in handwriting and easily give rise to errors. Wang Bing comments: 'What the eyes can see and the flavors in one's mouth, this is beyond any enumeration.' The passage 'is beyond any enumeration' serves to explain the two usages of the character 變, 'changes.'"

exceed one's perception.[49]
The cravings and desires differ;
each has something it communicates with.[50]

9-67-2
Heaven feeds man with the five qi;
the earth feeds man with the five flavors.[51]
The five qi enter through the nose and
are stored in the heart and in the lung.
They cause the five complexions to be clear above,[52] and
the tones and voices can manifest themselves.

The five flavors enter through the mouth and
are stored in the intestines and in the stomach.

---

49 2138/38 and 2475/158 point out a parallel passage in the *Wen zhong zi zhong shuo* 文中子中說, 孫子病勢篇, by Wang Tong 王通 (584-618) of the Sui dynasty: 聲不過五, 五聲之變, 不可勝極也. 色不過五, 五色之變, 不可勝觀也. 味不過五, 五味之變, 不可勝嘗也.

50 391/7: "Because the 'cravings and desires' of individuals or of the depots and palaces differ, there are preferences in the reception of the qi and flavors." 520/17: "Several texts interpret 'cravings and desires' as those of man; in my opinion, this refers to the 'cravings and desires' of the plants: 'The desires of the plants for the qi of yin and yang of the natural world.'" For a detailed discussion of these eight characters, see 2217/1-4.

51 Wang Bing: " 'Heaven feeds man with the five qi,' that is, foul qi collects in the liver; burning qi collects in the heart; aromatic qi collects in the spleen; frowzy qi collects in the lung; rotten qi collects in kidneys. 'The earth feeds man with the five flavors,' that is, sour flavor enters the liver; bitter flavor enters the heart; sweet flavor enters the spleen; acrid flavor enters the lung; salty flavor enters the kidneys. The clear yang transforms to qi and rises to constitute heaven; the turbid yin becomes flavor and descends to become earth. Hence heaven feeds man with the qi and the earth feeds man with flavor." Gao Jiwu/168: "Very many authors follow the interpretation offered by Wang Bing, i.e., 'the five qi are foul, burning, aromatic, frowzy, and rotten.' Only Wu Kun assumed that these 'five qi' are the qi of the earth. 五味 is interpreted by all authors as 'five flavors sour, bitter, sweet, acrid, and salty.' If we examine 味, the *Shuo wen* 說文 states: 'These are 滋味, nourishing substances.' The *Ji yun* 集韻 says: '飲食之味, substances used to drink and eat.' 五 is an encompassing number, it means 'all kinds.' 五味 then refers to 'all kinds of beverages and food.' "

52 Gao Jiwu/174: "修 is left out of their explanations by quite a few authors; the general explanation is 明潤, 'clear and shining.' Only Guo Aichun 郭靄春 thinks 修 to be identical with the particle 攸. Also, the *Su wen xuan zhu* 素问选注 states: '修 is 善, 'beautiful.' 五色修明 means 'the complexion is beautiful and shining.' "

When the flavors have a place where they are stored,[53]
this serves to nourish the five qi.[54]
When the qi are generated in harmony and
when the body liquids complete each other,[55]
then the spirit will be alive by itself."[56]

9-67-5
[Huang] Di:
"What are the phenomena [associated with the condition] of the depots?"[57]

---

53 526/5: "The character 腸, 'intestines,' may be an erroneous insertion. ... *Su wen* 11
states: 五味入口藏于胃. The sentence structure is similar to the one here. Concerning the following passage 味有所藏, Sun Dingyi 孫鼎宜 said: '味 should be 胃.' If we
follow his argument, 胃有所藏 continues the [statement in the text] above and makes
it even clearer that the character 腸 is an erroneous insertion."

54 705/54: "In the food ingredients are stored that serve to nourish the qi of the
five depots."

55 Gao Jiwu/168: "生 is 養, 'to nourish.' 相 is 幫助, 'to assist.' 成 is 盛, 'abundant.'"

56 Wang Bing: "The heart is reflected in the complexion; the lung rules the sounds of
the voice. Hence when qi is stored in the heart and in the lung, above it lets the five
complexions be clear and distinguishable and it lets the [five] sounds of one's voice
be evident. The qi is the mother of the water. Hence when flavors are stored in the
intestines and in the stomach, they internally nourish the five qi. When the five qi are
transformed harmoniously, then the body liquids are generated. Qi and body liquids
together transform to completion. The spirit qi may then come to life and spread
and undergo transformations." From this commentary it appears that Wang Bing has
punctuated this statement differently from contemporary editions. He may have read
the text as follows: 氣和而生津液, 相成, 神乃自生.

57 Wang Bing: "象 is to say: that which can be seen and inspected from outside."
Wan Lanqing et al./11: "藏 refers to the internal depots, including the five depots
and six palaces. They are termed 藏 because they are located in the depth of the body.
象 is according to the commentary by Wang Bing: 'That which can be seen from the
outside; that which can be observed.' The meaning is, even though the depots and
palaces are located inside the human body, their physiological activities, as well as their
pathological changes, manifest themselves externally through signs. On the basis of an
examination of these signs it is possible to decide about the situation in the internal
depots and palaces." 391/7: "The meaning is: 'After the depots and palaces have taken
in and stored the qi and the flavors, which signs appear to demonstrate this?' The following text uses statements such as 其華, 其充, and 通于某氣 to answer the question
concerning the status of the depots and palaces after the intake and storage of qi and
flavors." For a historical survey of the development of the concept of 藏象 from its
meaning of "external image of storage" in the *Su wen* to its contemporary meaning of
"external signs of the condition of depots [and palaces]," i.e., from *cang xiang* to *zang
xiang*, see there. See also 2301/50 for a detailed discussion.

Qi Bo:

"The heart is the basis of life;[58]
it is [responsible for] changes of the spirit.[59]
Its effulgence is in the face.[60]
Its fullness [manifests itself] in the blood vessels.[61]
It is the major yang in the yang.
It communicates with the qi of summer.

The lung is the basis of the qi;
it is the location of the *po*-soul.
Its effulgence is in the body hair.
Its fullness [manifests itself] in the skin.[62]
It is the major yin in the yang.[63]
It communicates with qi of autumn.

---

58 941/59: "本 is 根本, 'basis.' In contrast, 1204/3: "The character 本, occurring in this section five times, should be read as 本性, 'basic nature.' 生 is 生長, 'generation and growth;' 神 is 變化, 'changes and transformations.' That is to say: 'The basic nature of the heart is to control generations and growth, as well as changes and transformations.' " For an elaboration of this argument, see there.

59 Wang Bing: "The heart is the official functioning as ruler; the spirit brilliance originates from it. Now, the prospering and the perishing of the myriad beings is closely tied to the ruler. Hence [the text] states: 'The heart is the basis of life; it is [responsible for] changes of the spirit.' " Lin Yi et al.: "The Quan Yuanqi edition and the *Tai su* have 神之處, '[it is the] location of the spirit.' " *Gu dian yi zhu xuan* bianxiezu /12 agrees: "This is correct in vision of the following text speaking of 魄之處, 精之處, 魂之居, etc.' " In contrast, Yan Hongchen & Gao Guangzhen/37: "神之變 is: 'Spirit-wisdom evolves through changes and transformations out of it.' "

60 Wang Bing: "The qi of fire flames upwards. Hence its effulgence is in the face."

61 Wang Bing: "The heart nourishes the blood; it rules the [movement in the] vessels. Hence [the text states]: 'Its fullness [manifests itself] in the blood vessels.' " In contrast, Yan Hongchen & Gao Guangzhen/37: "Because the heart rules the blood and the vessels, the heart is able to cause fullness and repletion in respect of the blood and its vessels."

62 Wang Bing: "The lung stores qi. Its spirit is the *po*-soul. It nourishes skin and hair. Hence [the text] states: 'The lung is the basis of qi; it is the location of the *po*-soul. Its effulgence is in the hair. Its fullness [manifests itself] in the skin.' "

63 Wang Bing: "The lung depot is ruled by the major yin qi. It rules in autumn." Lin Yi et al.: "As for 'major yin,' the *Jia yi jing* and the *Tai su* have 'minor yin.' [In the *Su wen* too] it should be 'minor yin.' Even though the lung is categorized among the twelve conduits as 'major yin,' within the yang section it should nevertheless be regarded as 'minor yin.' "

The kidneys are responsible for hibernation;
they are the basis of seclusion and storage.
They are the location of the essence.
Their effulgence is in the hair on the head.
Their fullness [manifests itself] in the bones.[64]
They are the minor yin in the yin.[65]
They communicate with the qi of winter.

9-68-2
The liver is the basis of exhaustion to the utmost.[66]

---

64 Wang Bing: "When the entrances to the earth are tightly sealed, the hibernating insects are stored in the depth. The kidneys are also responsible for the water [in the organism] and they receive and store the essence of the five depots and six palaces. The brain is the sea of marrow. The kidneys rule the bone marrow. The hair on the head is nourished by the brain. Hence 'their effulgence is in the hair of the head and their fullness [manifests itself] in the bones.'" Gao Jiwu/168: "The *Shuo wen* 說文 states: '蟄 is 藏, to store.' It refers to the hibernation of animals in winter. It is a metaphor here for man's hiding away."

65 Lin Yi et al.: "The Quan Yuanqi edition, the *Jia yi jing*, and the *Tai su* have 'major yin' instead of 'minor yin.' Even though the kidneys are categorized among the twelve conduits as 'minor yin,' within the yin section they should nevertheless be regarded as 'major yin.'"

66 1955/63: "罷 has the same pronunciation and meaning as 疲, 'fatigue.' Here it means 'weak.' 極 is the ridgepole; it stands for strength. Here it means 'strong.'" 706/39: "The character 罷 stands for 疲, 'fatigue.' The liver rules the sinews; they can endure fatigue and taxation. Hence [the text] speaks of the 'basis of fatigue.'" 1262/78: "The phrase 罷極 appears not only in the *Nei jing*, the *Shi ji* 史記, 淮陰侯列傳 has: '能千里而襲我亦已罷極.'" See also 2753/62. 692/41: "Some interpret 罷極 as 疲勞至極, 'extreme fatigue,' others consider 疲 and 極 as carrying the same meaning and see a binomial expression here. Others again edit 罷極 to 四極, in the sense of 'four extremities.' .. No matter whether we interpret it as 'extreme fatigue' or 'four extremities,' in comparison with the [concept of a] 'basis' associated with the other depots – 'the basis of life,' 'the basis of qi,' 'the basis of storage,' etc. – one might ask whether if there were no liver, there could be no fatigue? Could there be such a statement? We think the character 罷 should be read as is. The commentary by Duan 段 to the *Shuo wen* 說文 (i.e, *SWJZZ*) states: '罷 is 'to stop,' 'to rest.' This is correct. It is not necessary to change [the character]. ... Hence 罷極 is to say 'to stop fatigue.' Man's movement originates from his sinews. The sinews are generated and ruled by the liver; they are closely related to the liver. When the sinews become tired, the liver qi stops this." Gao Jiwu/159: "罷極 is interpreted by the Beijing zhongyi xueyuan (2) as 'ability to endure fatigue.' The *Ji yun* 集韻 states: '罷 is sometimes abbreviated to 羆' Hence Gao Shishi explained [this passage] in the following way: 'Like a bear endures taxation.' 羆 is a type of bear. 極 is explained in the *Shuo wen* 說文 as 棟, 'ridgepole.' The present statement is to express the meaning of an extraordinary endurance strength. Hence it could

It is the location of the *hun*-soul.
Its effulgence is in the nails.
Its fullness [manifests itself] in the sinews.
It serves to generate blood and qi.[67]
<Its flavor is sour; its color is greenish.>[68]
It is the minor yang in the yang.[69]
It communicates with the qi of spring.

---

be rendered as 'the liver is the basis of the endurance of taxation and of the shoulder-ing of hardships.'" See also 2888/60 and 1384/58 supporting this view. 969/63: "In the longterm process of transmitting the *Nei jing*, some of the contents of this text at some time became difficult to understand, with the result that some investigators made forced changes based on their own ideas. For example, the character 罷 in *Su wen* 09 may very well have been originally 能. Some scholars may not have been aware of the fact that 能 must be read as 耐, 'to endure,' and simply because they assumed that 能 極 is not an established compound and because they knew the ancient compound 罷 極, they added on top of the character 能 the character 罒 to create the character 罷." 2532/41 agrees. 1204/2: "罷極 is 罷極; 極 stands for 急, 'urgent.' That is to say, the basic nature of the liver is wild and urgent like that of a bear." 174/10 interprets 罷 as 弛緩, 'relaxed,' and 極 as 緊急, 'tight,' [i.e., the liver] is the basis of the relaxed or tight status of the sinews and membranes. This interpretation coincides with the physiology and the pathology of the liver." For details, see there. 476/32: "According to the *Kuang ya* 廣雅, 罷 is 勞, 'taxation.' 極 is read 亟, and can be interpreted as 受. 受 has the mean-ing of 用, 'function,' 'application.' The liver stores the blood and rules over the sinews. All the movements of the human body depend on a taxation of the liver's sinews and on the function of the liver's blood." 137/12: "膽者,罷極之本 should be 肝膽者, 罷極 之本." See also Fang Wenhui/104, 285/15, 1176/57, and 521/23. We follow 969/63.

67 Wang Bing: "Now, all the movements of man result from the strength of his sin-ews. The liver rules the sinews. Its spirit is the *hun*-soul. Hence [the text] states: 'The liver is the basis of 罷極, is the location of the *hun*-soul.' The nails are outgrowths of the sinews and the sinews are nourished by the liver. Hence 'its effulgence is in the nails. Its fullness [manifests itself] in the sinews.' The East is where life begins. Hence [the text states:] 'blood and qi are generated by [the liver].'"

68 Lin Yi et al.: "These six characters should be eliminated."

69 Lin Yi et al.: "The Quan Yuanqi edition, the *Jia yi jing*, and the *Tai su* have 'minor yang in the yin.' [The *Su wen* too] should have 'minor yang in the yin.' Wang Bing quotes *Su wen* 04 as evidence that [the liver] is 'the yang in the yang.' With this Mr. Wang meant to say that it is the minor yang in the yang. If we take a look at the text above where the heart depot is [identified as] major yang in the yang, Mr. Wang had adduced there the statement on the period from dawn to midday as evidence. Here once again he quoted it as evidence in the context of the description of the liver depot. He did not quote, though, the statement [in *Su wen* 04] that the period 'from the crowing of the cocks to dawn, this is the yin of heaven; it is the yang in the yin.' Hence the error in Wang's commentary is obvious. One should follow the Quan Yuan-qi edition, the *Jia yi jing*, and the *Tai su*, all of which have 'minor yang in the yin.'"

The spleen
<and the stomach, the large intestine, the small intestine, the triple burner, and
the urinary bladder>
is the basis of grain storage.[70]
It is the location of the camp [qi].[71]
{They are named containers. They are able to transform the dregs. They are [the
places] where the substances are turned and enter and leave.}[72]
Its effulgence is in the lips, and in the four white [sections in the eyes surrounding the pupils].[73]

---

70 526/5: "Neither the *Wu xing da yi* 五行大義, ch.3, no.4, nor the *Yun ji qi jian* 雲
笈七簽, ch.57, no.7, have the nine characters 胃大腸小腸三焦膀胱. This is correct. In
the *Wu xing da yi*, the sequence of the five depots is in the order of mutual production.
Later authors, who added the doctrine of the twelve official positions, changed the
sequence and also inserted the statement 'The eleven depots receives their decisions
from the gallbladder.' Then they further added the nine characters 胃大腸小腸三
焦膀胱 to arrive at a number of altogether eleven depots. Yu Chang 于鬯 considers
the character 一 to be an erroneous insertion." 2268/36: "The enumeration of the six
palaces in this passage has the character 脾, 'spleen,' which does not belong here, while
the character 膽, 'gallbladder,' is omitted. Obviously, this is a mistake. Hua Shou and
Wang Ji rearrange [the sequence of the characters to]: 脾者, 倉廩之本, 營之居也. 其
華在唇四白, 其充在肌, 此至陰之類, 通与土氣. 胃, 大腸, 小腸, 三焦, 膀胱, 能化糟
粕, 轉味而入出者也. In principle, I agree with the revision by Hua Shou and Wang
Ji, but some peculiarities need further discussion. Because among the six palaces the
character 膽 should not be missing, it is to be added. It is missing here because it was
added in the sentence further down: 凡十一藏取決于膽也, where the character 膽
should be the character 心, 'heart.' Also, following the text above, 'the kidneys are the
great yin within the yin,' 'the liver is the minor yin within the yin,' for the spleen it
should be stated: 'it is the extreme yin within the yin. The two characters 之類 are an
erroneous insertion and should be deleted. *Ling shu* 01 and *Ling shu* 41, as well as the
Jia yi jing, treatise Shi erh yuan 十二原篇, state: 'The spleen is the extreme yin within
the yin.' This can be taken as proof. Below the characters for 'bladder' a character 者
is missing and should be added."

71 *Gu dian yi zhu xuan* bianxiezu /12: "營 refers to the essence qi of water and grain
passing through the vessels." Fu Weikang & Wu Hongzhou/269: "The camp [qi]
emerges from the central burner. The central burner is the seat of spleen and stomach.
Hence spleen and stomach are the places where the camp qi is produced."

72 Wang Bing: "They all are able to receive and they move without break. Hence
'they are the basis of storage. They are named containers.' The camp qi emerges from
the central burner. The central burner is the location of spleen and stomach. Hence
[the text] states: 'They are the location of the camp [qi].'"

73 Wang Bing: "The mouth is administrated by the spleen. The spleen rules the muscles and the flesh. Hence [the text] states: 'their effulgence is in the lips and in the four
white. Their fullness [manifests itself] in the muscles.' 'Four white' is to say: the white

Its fullness [manifests itself] in the muscles.
<Its flavor is sweet; its color is yellow.>[74]
It is the category extreme yin.[75]
It communicates with the qi of soil.[76]

9-69-3
{Altogether eleven depots.[77]
They receive decisions[78] from the gallbladder.}[79]

---

colored flesh on the four sides of the lips." *Gu dian yi zhu xuan* bianxiezu /12: "唇四
白 refers to the white flesh surrounding the lips of the mouth." 1992/283: "The two
characters 四白 have been interpreted by most authors as the white flesh surrounding
the lips. In fact, though, the color of the lips is red. Hence Li Gao 李杲 stated that 四
白 should be 四紅. In my own opinion, the two characters are not essential. Hence I
omit them." Our translation of 四白 as "the white in the eyes surrounding the pupils"
is based on a use of this compound in Wang Fu 王符, *Qian fu lun* 潛夫論, 相列, a
work of the first century AD. See *HYDC* 3, 575.

74 Lin Yi et al.: "These six characters should be eliminated."

75 Fu Weikang & Wu Hongzhou/269: "The major yin is the first of the three yin.
Hence it is called 'extreme yin.' "

76 Gao Shishi: "[The passage from 脾胃大腸 down to 通于土氣] has been erroneously mixed up. [It should read:] 脾者倉廩之本, 營之居也. 其華在唇四白, 其充
在肌, 其味甘, 其色黃, 以至陰之類, 通于土氣. 胃, 大腸, 小腸, 三焦, 膀胱, 名曰器,
能化糟粕, 轉味而入出者也." Zhang Qi agrees. See also 2868/28.

77 137/15: "The 'palaces' can also be called 'depots,' as for example in *Su wen* 09
where [the text] speaks of 'eleven depots.' The 'depots,' though, are never called 'palaces.' " Yu Chang: "The character 一 is an erroneous addition. Not counting the gallbladder, there are altogether ten depots."

78 526/6: "Sun Dingyi 孫鼎宜 considers 決, 'decision,' to be a mistake for 足, 'sufficient.' "

79 Wang Bing: "From the heart to the gallbladder, these are eleven depots. Now, the
gallbladder is the rectifier, it passes resolute decisions without personal bias. Hence [the
text states]: "the eleven depots receive decisions from the gallbladder.' " Wan Lanqing
et al./12: "Li Dongyuan 李東垣 in his *Pi wei lun* 脾胃論 states: 'The gallbladder, this
is the minor yang qi that rises in spring. When the spring qi rises, the myriad [beings]
transform in peace. Hence when the qi of the gallbladder rises in spring, the remaining
depots follow it. When the qi of the gallbladder does not rise, frequent diarrhea occurs." 1501/39: "The statement 十一藏取決于膽 has been interpreted differently over
time. Most important are the following four versions. 1. 'The gallbladder is responsible
for decisions.' An example is the comment by Wang Bing [see above]. 2. 'The gallbladder is responsible for the qi generated in spring.' An example is the comment by Li
Dongyuan [see above]. However, *Su wen* 02 states: 'If one acts contrary to the qi of
spring, then the minor yang does not come to life and the qi of the liver changes inter-

Hence,
when [the movement in the vessels] at man's facing is once over [normal] fullness,
the disease is in the minor yang.
When it is twice over [normal] fullness,
the disease is in the major yang.
When it is three times over [normal] fullness,
the disease is in the yang brilliance.
When it is four times over [normal] fullness or more,
[the disease] is 'obstructed yang.'

When [the movement in the vessels] at the inch opening is once over [normal]
fullness,
the disease is in the ceasing yin;
When it is twice over [normal] fullness,
the disease is in the minor yin;
When it is three times over [normal] fullness,
the disease is in the major yin;

---

nally..'. This explains that the liver, too, is responsible for the qi emerging in spring,
not only the gallbladder. 3. 'The qi of the gallbladder serves to support the proper and
fight the evil.' .. This is difficult to reconcile with the meaning of the text here, because
courage and cowardice are not only related to the gallbladder, but also to the heart
and the liver. 4. 'The control of the gallbladder extends half to the outside, half to the
inside; it is able to penetrate the yin and the yang.' An example is the comment by
Zhang Jiebin: 'The foot minor yang is a conduit half outside, half inside. It is also said
to occupy the official position of Rectifier. Another name is extraordinary palace. This
is because it is able to penetrate the yin and the yang and all the eleven depots receive
their decisions from it.' " 2268/36: " 'The eleven depots receive decisions from the gallbladder,' this passage appears neither in the *Ling shu*, nor in the *Tai su*, or in the *Jia yi
jing*. Only *Su wen* 47 states: 'The liver is the leader of the center; it receives decisions
from the gallbladder...' This explains the mutual dependence of liver and gallbladder;
when the qi of the liver is suppressed, the liquid of the gallbladder flows away upwards
and the mouth has a bitter [flavor. This disease] is gallbladder obtusion. From a perspective of the overall relationships between depots and palaces, the heart is the ruler
of the entire body. [Various statements in the *Nei jing*] demonstrate that all thoughts
emerge from the heart and that the gallbladder does by no means pass all decisions."
244/68: "取 is an abbreviated version of 諏 and has the meaning of 謀, 'to plan.' [This
passage] should read: 'Of all the eleven depots, planning and decision making occur
in the gallbladder.' " For details of the argumentation, see there. 1582/47: " '十一藏取
決于膽' does not mean 'decisions are made in the gallbladder.' 決 has the meaning of
泄, 'to drain.' 取決 has the meaning of 取泄, 'receive drainage.' Of all the five depots
and six palaces, only the gallbladder is able to secrete gall liquid and it this way helps
the qi dynamics of the five depots and six palaces to [fulfill the function of] drainage."
See also 178/40, 2810/8, 127/95, 1471/60, 1694/12, and 551/6.

When it is four times over [normal] fullness or more,[80]
[the disease] is 'yin closure.'

9-69-6
When the [movements in the vessels that can be felt at] man's facing and at
the inch opening are both four times over [normal] fullness, or more,
this is 'closure and obstruction.' "[81]
{In cases of 'closure and obstruction,' the vessels are filled to the extreme.[82] [The
patient] cannot [live to the] limits of the essence qi [allotted to him] by heaven
and earth and will die.}[83]

---

80 916/54: "己 is identical with 以."

81 Tanba: " 'Closure and obstruction' is a sign of total interruption of [the movement]
between inner and outer, i.e., yin and yang sections. *Su wen* 17 states: 'When yin and
yang do not respond to each other, that is called closure and obstruction.' " Mori: "The
two characters 關格 have the meaning of 閉拒, 'to close and to ward off.' " 2393/21:
"The *ren ying* is a yang vessel; it is an indicator of the six palaces associated with the
three yang. When evil [qi] abounds in the depots, the yang qi is in the external sections, near the surface and cannot interact with the yin. This is called 'resisting yang.'
This is what is called 'overflowing yang causes external obstruction' in *Ling shu* 09. The
inch-opening is located on a yin vessel; it is an indicator of the five palaces associated
with the three yin. When evil [qi] abounds in the depots, then the yin qi is closed
in internally and cannot reach to the yang. This is called 'yin closure.' This is what is
called 'overflowing yin causes internal closure' in *Ling shu* 09. When evil qi abounds
both in the three yin and in the three yang, in the five depots and in the six palaces, so
that yin and yang, qi and blood are out of balance, the qi dynamics in the depots and
palaces are in disorder and this is 'closure and obstruction.' " For an analysis of the 關
格 disease from a contemporary clinical perspective, see 2621/27. See also 2721/40.

82 916/54: "羸 is identical with 盈, 'full.' " Mori: "The commentary by Wang Bing
informs us that his version had 羸, 'lean,' 'thin,' instead of 贏. Some Song author
changed this to 贏. If one reads it as 羸, it makes sense in connection with the subsequent statement. The patient is emaciated and cannot exhaust the time span allotted
to him by heaven; hence he dies. If one reads it as 贏, it makes sense in connection
with the preceding statement. In case of a movement [in the vessels] that is termed
closure and obstruction, the meaning is that the vessels are filled to the extreme."

83 Wang Bing: " 'Both full' is to say, the [movement] is four times stronger than
normal in both vessels. No being can endure such abundance for long; when it has
reached an extreme, weakening and destruction follow. Hence [the text states:] '[The
patient] cannot [live to the] limits of the essence qi [allotted to him] by heaven and
earth and will die.' " 2757/44: "This is to say, when the essence qi from the upper and
the lower sections of the human body do not communicate, death is inevitable."

Chapter 10
The Generation and Completion of the Five Depots

10-70-3
The correlate of the heart are the vessels;[1]
its splendor [appears in] the complexion;[2]
its ruler are the kidneys.[3]

The correlate of the lung is the skin;[4]
its splendor [appears in] the body hair;[5]
its ruler is the heart.[6]

---

1 Wang Bing: "The qi of fire moves hastily and the [movement in the] vessels always equals it. The heart depot corresponds to the fire. Hence [the text states: 'the heart] is the correlate of the [movement in the] vessels.'" Wu Kun: "The heart generates the blood and stores the spirit. Hence the [movement in the] vessels is material manifestation of the blood and the operation of the spirit. Hence [the text states:] 'The heart is the correlate of to the [movement in the] vessels.'" 527/47: "Following the character 合 a character 于 is missing; it should be supplemented on the basis of *Yun ji qi qian* 雲笈七籤 ch.57, nr.7. The same applies to the following wordings 合皮 etc." Yan Hongchen & Gao Guangzhen/39: "合 is 配合, 'to pair,' 'to mate.' For instance, the heart is inside, the vessels are outside. Inside and outside constitute a pair. Hence [the text states:] 'The heart and the vessels form a pair.'"

2 Wang Bing: "Fire flames upwards and has a red color. Hence its splendor appears in the face and [manifests itself in] a red complexion."

3 Wang Bing: "主 is to say: [the heart] stands in a relationship of fear with its ruler and the kidneys. Fire stands in a relationship of fear with fire. Water is its officer. Hence it stands in a relationship of fear with the kidneys." Zhang Zhicong: "The heart rules the fire and it is controlled by the kidneys, [i.e.,] water. Hence the kidneys are the ruler of the generation and transformation performed by the heart depot." 1028/2: "主 has the meaning here of 受制, 'to be controlled by,' or 被剋, 'to be subdued by.'" For a detailed etymology of 主 in the present context, see 2308/46.

4 Wang Bing: "The qi of metal is firm and fixed. The appearance of the skin is so, too. The lung depot corresponds to the metal. Hence it is a correlate of the skin."

5 Wang Bing: "Hair is attached to the skin. Hence it is where the splendor [of the lung] appears [externally]."

6 Wang Bing: "Metal stands in a relationship of fear with the fire. Fire is its officer; hence [the lung] stands in a relationship of fear with the heart."

The correlate of the liver are the sinews;[7]
its splendor [appears in] the nails;[8]
its ruler is the lung.[9]

The correlate of the spleen is the flesh;[10]
its splendor [appears in] the lips;[11]
its ruler is the liver.[12]

The correlate of the kidneys are the bones;[13]
their splendor is the hair on the head;[14]
their ruler is the spleen.[15]

10-70-6
Hence,
if one consumes large quantities of salty [food],
then the [contents of the] vessels will congeal so that [their flow] is impeded

---

7 Wang Bing: "The nature of wood [includes] being bent or straight. The physical appearance of the sinews is identical. The liver depot corresponds to the wood. Hence it is a correlate of the sinews."

8 Wang Bing: "Nails are outgrowths of the sinews. Hence they are where the splendor [of the liver] appears [externally]."

9 Wang Bing: "Wood stands in a relationship of fear with metal. Metal is its officer; hence [the liver] stands in a relationship of fear with the lung."

10 Wang Bing: "The nature of the soil is soft and thick. The physical appearance of the flesh is identical. The spleen depot corresponds to the soil. Hence it is a correlate of the flesh."

11 Wang Bing: "The mouth is the officer of the spleen. Hence the lips are where the splendor of the spleen appears [externally]. 'Lips' refers to the locations of the white-colored four boderlines. Not to the red [lips]."

12 Wang Bing: "The soil stands in a relationship of fear with the wood. Wood is its officer. Hence [the spleen] stands in a relationship of fear with the liver."

13 Wang Bing: "The nature of water is to flow and be moist. The essence qi is identical. Bones are penetrated by essence marrow. Hence [the kidneys] are linked to the bones."

14 Wang Bing: "The brain is the sea of marrow; it is ruled by the qi of the kidneys. Hence the hair on the head is where the splendor [of the kidneys] appears [externally]."

15 Wang Bing: "Water stands in a relationship of fear with the soil. The soil is its officer. Hence [the kidneys] stand in a relationship of fear with the spleen."

and the complexion changes.[16]
If one consumes large quantities of bitter [food],
then the skin will desiccate and the body hair is plucked out.[17]
If one consumes large quantities of acrid [food],
then the sinews become tense and the nails dry.[18]
If one consumes large quantities of sour [food],
then the flesh hardens and shows wrinkles and the lips peel.[19]
If one consumes large quantities of sweet [food],
then the bones will ache and the hair on the head falls off.[20]

These are the harms resulting from the five flavors.[21]

10-71-4
Hence,
the heart longs for bitter [flavor].[22]

---

16 Wang Bing: "The heart is related to the [movement in the] vessels; its splendor appears in in the complexion. Salty [flavor] benefits the kidneys, [and makes them] dominate the heart. The heart cannot prosper. Hence the [movement in the] vessels congeals and stagnates and the complexion changes." Zhang Jiebin: "泣 is identical to 澀, 'rough.' " Zhang Yizhi et al.: "泣 is identical to 立, 'to stand.' The character 泣 is an error here; it should be 立."

17 Wang Bing: "The lung is related to the skin; its splendor appears in in the hair on the skin. Bitter [flavor] benefits the heart, [and makes it] dominate the lung. The lung cannot prosper. Hence the skin desiccates and the hair on the skin is plucked out."

18 Wang Bing: "The liver is related to the sinews; its splendor appears in in the nails. Acrid [flavor] benefits the lung, [and makes it] dominate the liver. The liver cannot prosper. Hence the sinews become tense and the nails dry."

19 Wang Bing: "The spleen is related to the flesh; its splendor appears in in the lips. Sour [flavor] benefits the liver, [and makes it] dominate the spleen. The spleen cannot prosper. Hence the flesh hardens and shows wrinkles and the skin of the lips will crack." Cheng Shide et al./160: "The *Tong ya* 通雅 states: 胝: 皮肉生革不仁也. That is to say, the skin is thick. As for 䐈, the *Ji yun* 集韻 states: 皺也, 'these are wrinkles.' Wrinkles in the flesh are 䐈."

20 Wang Bing: "The kidneys are linked to the bones; their splendor is in the hair on the head. Sweet [flavor] benefits the spleen, [and makes it] dominate the kidneys. The kidneys cannot prosper. Hence the bones will ache and the hair on the head falls off.

21 Wang Bing: "The five flavors enter the mouth and are transported to the intestines and to the stomach. Internally they nourish the five depots. Each has a [specific depot] which it nourishes and which longs for it. The [depot] which longs for it is, in turn, harmed by it. Hence the subsequent statement."

22 Wang Bing: "Because it is related to fire."

The lung longs for acrid [flavor].[23]
The liver longs for sour [flavor].[24]
The spleen longs for sweet [flavor].[25]
The kidneys long for salty [flavor].[26]

This is what the five flavors conform with. {The qi of the five depots}.[27]

Hence,
if the complexion appears
green-blue like young grasses, death [is imminent];[28]
yellow like hovenia-fruit, death [is imminent];[29]
black like soot, death [is imminent];[30]
red like rotten blood, death [is imminent];[31]
white like withered bones, death [is imminent];[32]

This is how death is visible in the five complexions.[33]

---

23 Wang Bing: "Because it is related to metal."

24 Wang Bing: "Because it is related to wood."

25 Wang Bing: "Because it is related to soil."

26 Wang Bing: "Because it is related to water."

27 Lin Yi et al.: "The Quan Yuanqi edition has 此五味之合五藏之氣也. This is in agreement with the preceding text. The *Tai su* has this version too." This version has the following meaning: "These are the qi of the five depots the five flavors conform with."

28 Wang Bing: "兹 stands for 滋, 'to sprout.' That is to say, like the green-blue color of grasses that are just emerging." Wu Kun: "草滋: when herbs are provided with nourishment, their color is increasingly deep." Zhang Zhicong: "兹 is 蓐蓆, 'mat.' 草兹 refers to the color of dead rushes. It is green-blue with some white." See also Wang Hongtu et al. /198.

29 Wang Bing: "The color [of this fruit] is green-blue-yellow."

30 Wang Bing: "炱 stands for 炱煤, 'soot.'" Tanba: "The *Qian jin yi* [*fang*] 千金翼 [方] has the character 煤 following the character 炱." Zhang Yizhi et al.: "Judged from the structure of the preceding and of the subsequent text, there should be a character 煤 here."

31 Wang Bing: "衃血 is to say: rotten, coagulated blood; its color is red-black." *SWJZ*: "衃, this is coagulated blood."

32 Wang Bing: "Like the white of desiccated bones."

33 Wang Bing: "The depots are ruined hence a fatal complexion is visible." Zhang Zhicong: "The five complexions are desiccated and withered and in addition there is a complexion indicating defeat. Hence death [is imminent]."

10-72-1
[If the complexion appears]
green-blue like the feathers of the kingfisher, [the person will] survive;
red like a chicken comb, [the person will] survive;
yellow like the abdomen of a crab, [the person will] survive;
white like the lard of pigs, [the person will] survive;
black like the feathers of a crow, [the person will] survive.

This is how survival is visible in the five complexions.[34]

If [the complexion] is generated by the heart, it resembles vermilion wrapped up in white silk.[35]
If [the complexion] is generated by the lung, it resembles red wrapped up in white silk.
If [the complexion] is generated by the liver, it resembles virid wrapped up in white silk.[36]
If [the complexion] is generated by the spleen, it resembles a *gua-lou* fruit wrapped up in white silk.[37]
If [the complexion] is generated by the kidneys, it resembles violet wrapped up in white silk.[38]

These are the external splendors generated in the five depots.[39]

10-72-6
Complexions and flavors match the five depots.[40]

---

34 Wang Bing: "That is a shining [complexion]. Even though such a complexion is adorable, if it is somewhat obscured, this is even better. Hence the subsequent statement."

35 Wang Bing: "縞 is to say: white color." *JJZG*: "縞 is 素, 'plain,' 'pure.'" Tanba: 'The *Mai jing* has 綿, 'silk,' instead of 縞. The *Xiao er ya* 小爾雅 states: "縞 is fine silk."

36 Wang Bing: "紺 is a light green-blue color." *JJZG*: "紺 is 青, 'green-blue.'" *Shi ming* 釋名: "紺 is green-blue containing red."

37 Mori: "When the *gua-lou* fruit is ripe, it has a shining yellow color. Wrapped up in white silk, this color is pale yellow." The *Tai su* does not have the character 實 following *gua lou*.

38 Wang Bing: "This is the true appearance of a complexion of survival."

39 Wang Bing: "榮 stands for 美色, 'beautiful complexion.'" The *Tai su* does not have the character 外 following the character 之.

40 The *Tai su* does not have the character 色, 'complexion,' preceding the character 味. Zhang Zhicong: "當 is 合, 'to match.'"

White matches the lung and acrid.
Red matches the heart and bitter.
Green-blue matches the liver and sour.
Yellow matches the spleen and sweet.
Black matches the kidneys and salty.

Hence,
white matches the skin;
red matches the vessels;
green-blue matches the sinews;
yellow matches the flesh;
black matches the bones.[41]

All vessels are tied to the eyes.[42]
All marrow is tied to the brain.[43]
All sinews are tied to the joints.[44]
All blood is tied to the heart.[45]

---

41 Wang Bing: "Each [color] is associated with the qi of that depot that it nourishes."

42 Wang Bing: "The vessels are the palaces of the blood. *Su wen* 23 states: 'If one beholds [something] for long, this harms the blood.' From this it is evident that all vessels are tied to the eyes." Gao Shishi: "The five depots are located in the interior and the qi passes through the entire body. 'All vessels' refers to the vessel paths by which the blood vessels pass through the entire body. The essence brilliance of the five depots moves upwards and pours into the eyes. Hence all vessels are tied to the eyes." Wu Kun: "To prove this with the [courses of the] conduit vessels: The vessels of the bladder emerge from the inner canthi. The vessels of the stomach interconnect with the eyebrows. The vessels of the gallbladder emerge from the outer canthi. The vessels of the triple burner reach to the outer canthi. Also, the vessels of the heart are connected with the eye connection; the vessels of the liver are linked to the eye connection. That is, all vessels are tied to the eyes." 137/15: "The character 目 should be 腎, 'kidneys.'" Zhang Yizhi et al.: "屬于目 is 注于目, '[all vessels] pour into the eyes.'"

43 *Ling shu* 33: "The brain is the sea of marrow." Wang Bing: "The brain is the sea of marrow. Hence all marrow is tied to it."

44 Wang Bing: "The hard knottings of sinew qi form interconnections inside the joints of the bones. *Su wen* 23 states: 'If one walks for long, this harms the sinews.' From this it is evident that all the sinews are tied to the joints." 527/46: "The character 節, 'joints,' is a mistake. *Tai su* 17 has 肝, 'liver' instead of 節." 137/15 agrees. Beijing zhongyi xueyuan et al./11 explains "joints" as 骨節, "joints of bones."

45 Wang Bing: "The blood resides inside the vessels; it is tied to the heart. *Su wen* 26 states: 'Blood and qi are man's spirit. The spirit, though, is the ruler of the heart.' From this it is evident that all the blood is tied to the heart."

All qi is tied to the lung.[46]
This is the morning and the evening of the four limbs and the eight ravines.[47]

10-73-1
The fact is,
when man lies down the blood returns to the liver.[48]
When the liver receives blood one can see.[49]

---

46 Wang Bing: "This is because the lung depot rules the qi."

47 Wang Bing: "谿 is the name for the small folds in the flesh. The 'eight ravines' are the elbows, the knees, and the wrists/ankle joints [of hands and feet]. Qi and blood, sinews and vessels have alternating states of fullness and weakness here. Hence this is 'morning and evening.'" Zhang Zhicong: "This is the flesh of the four limbs, legs and arms." Zhang Jiebin: "The hands have elbows and armpits; the feet have the hip and the hollows under the knees. Morning and evening is to say, all the vessels, the marrow, the sinews, the blood, and the qi emerge from here and enter here [in the four limbs]; and neither in the morning nor in the evening does their movement leave [the four limbs]." Beijing zhongyi xueyuan et al./11 agrees with Zhang Jiebin. Cheng Shide et al./164: "*Ling shu* 71 states: 'When the lung and the heart are affected by evil qi, it settles in the two elbows. When the liver is affected by evil qi, it settles in the two armpits. When the spleen is affected by evil qi, it settles in the two hips. When the kidneys are affected by evil qi, it settles in the two hollows under the knees. All these eight hollows are chambers of motion and juncture, where the true qi passes and where the blood network takes its way.' From this it is apparent that the comment by Zhang Jiebin is correct." Wu Kun: "朝 is 會, 'meeting.' In ancient times, when the lords and the officials had their morning meetings this was called 朝. 夕 stands for evening meeting. That is to say, the vessels, the marrow, the sinews, the blood, and the qi – these five meet in the eight ravines of the four limbs in the morning and in the evening." Cheng Shide et al./164: "Another view is to identify 朝夕 with 潮汐, 'morning tide and evening tide.' In ancient times these characters were used interchangeably." Beijing zhongyi xueyuan et al./11, Gao Jiwu/8 and Fang Wenhui/5 et al. offer this latter view. Wang Hongtu et al./198: "朝夕 and 潮汐 were used interchangeably in ancient times. The morning tide is called 潮; the evening tide is called 汐. That is to say, the passage of qi and blood in the human body undergoes changes of abundance and weakness resembling the rising and falling of the ocean tides. Hence they follow a definite regularity."

48 Wang Bing: "The liver stores the blood; the heart makes it pass. When a person moves, the blood travels through all the conduits. When a person rests, the blood returns to the liver depot. Why this is so? Because the liver rules the sea of blood."

49 Wang Bing: "That is a reference to its operation. The eye is the officer of the liver. Hence one can see when the liver receives blood." Zhang Jiebin: "The orifice of the liver is the opening of the eyes. When the liver is supplied with blood, spirit gathers in the eyes. Hence one can see." Cheng Shide et al./164: "The following text refers to the feet, the palms, and the fingers. Hence Li Dongyuan 李東垣 in his *Pi wei lun* 脾胃論 states: '肝 should be 目, 'eye.'" 527/46 agrees. For detailed argumentation, see there.

When the feet receive blood, one can walk.[50]
When the palms receive blood, they can grasp.
When the fingers receive blood, they can hold.

When someone has lied down and then walks out and wind blows at him and
when the blood congeals in the skin, this is block.[51]
When it congeals in the vessels, this is retarded flow.[52]
When it congeals in the feet, this is receding [qi].[53]
In these three cases,
the blood has passed but cannot return to the void it [has left].[54]
Hence [this] leads to block and receding [qi].

10-73-5
Man has the twelve large valleys and

---

50 Wang Bing: "When the qi passes, the blood flows. Hence one can walk when the
feet receive blood."

51 Wang Bing: "This is to say 'numbness.'" 1187/69: "When one lies down the yang
qi turns inside. At the moment one [rises] and goes out, the guard qi has not yet returned to the muscular exterior and while the [qi in the] muscular exterior is [still] unbalanced, wind evil occupies the muscles, enters the human body and causes a block."
See also Gao Jiwu/405 for separating 臥 and 出.

52 Wang Bing: "泣 is to say: the passage of the blood is not free." Zhang Jiebin:
"When wind and cold attack [the body] from outside, the blood coagulates in the
vessels. As a result the vessel paths are blocked and this means disease." 2685/45: "The
character 泣 has three different readings in the *Nei jing*. The first is *qi* and refers to
tears. Another is identical in pronunciation and meaning with 澀, 'rough.' The third is
li and refers to stagnation of blood and qi. Yu Yue 俞樾 suggested that 泣 is an error
for 沍, 'frozen,' 'congealed.' The element 互 constituting the right side of the character
was erroneously written as 立." 2753/61: "泣 is identical to 澀, 'rough.'"

53 Wang Bing: "厥 is to say: the feet are cold because of ceasing [qi]." Zhang Jiebin:
"The four limbs are the basis of all yang. When wind and cold settle here and when
the blood coagulates in the feet, then the yang weakens and the yin flourishes. At the
same time, the qi moves [upwards] contrary [to its normal course] and this is ceasing."
Zhang Zhicong: "When the yin qi and the yang qi fail to interact, this is 'ceasing.' The
lower parts are yin and the blood is yin. When the blood coagulates in the lower parts,
then the yin and the yang of the upper and the lower parts do no longer interact and
this is 'ceasing.'" Cheng Shide et al./165: "This comment is based on chapter 厥陰 in
the *Shang han lun* 傷寒論."

54 Wang Bing: "空 [refers to] the paths where the blood flows. These are the large
conduit-tunnels." 916/53: "空 is identical to 孔, 'hole,' 'opening.'"

the 354 small ravines.
{Less twelve transporters.}⁵⁵

All these are locations
where the guard qi [can] come to a halt and
where the evil qi [can] settle as visitor.⁵⁶

55 In contrast, Wang Bing: "Where the large conduits meet, these [locations] are
called 'large valleys.' The 'twelve divisions' are the twelve conduit-vessel sections.
Where the small network [vessels] meet, these [locations] are called 'small ravines.'
Now, if one takes the 365 small network [vessels] into account and subtracts from
[this number] the twelve transportation [points] then there should be [left] 353
names. When the classic states '354,' this is a writing error in the transmission [of
the text]. 'Four' should be 'three.'" Wu Kun and Ma Shi agree. Zhang Jiebin: " 'Large
valleys' refers to the largest of the joints. The largest joints are in the four limbs. In
the arms these are the shoulder, the elbows, and the wrists. In the feet these are the
thigs, the knees, and the ankles. Each of the four limbs has three joints. This makes
twelve sections. 分 is 處, 'location.' All those comments are wrong that interpret 大
谷十二分 as sections of the twelve conduit vessels. 'Small ravines' refers to joints of
bones throughout the body." Lin Yi et al.: "Other text versions, including the Quan
Yuanqi edition and the *Tai su,* have 關, 'joints,' instead of 俞, 'transportation [point].'"
Zhang Zhicong: "These are the small interstices in the flesh. 名 stands for 穴, 'hole.'
The interstices in the flesh are [locations of] interaction. These locations of interaction have the names of [needling] holes." Gao Shishi: " 'Twelve transportation points'
is 'twelve clefts of the large valleys.'" Wu Kun: "The twelve transportation points are
not included in the 365 names [of needling holes]. Hence [the text] states: 'less the
twelve transportation points.'" Cheng Shide et al./166: "The four characters 少十二
俞 may be a commentary added by a later person on the side [of the text] which was
erroneously entered into the main text." 2721/40: "This text passage appears now in
Tai su 17 as follows: 人有大谷十二分, 小溪三百五十四, 名小十二關. Wang Bing
has erroneously interpreted 關 as 俞; he also erroneously interpreted 小 as 少 and he
further erroneously separated the sentence, adding 名 to 三百五十四. This way he
obscured the meaning of the text of the classic. Ma Shi, Wu Kun, Zhang Jiebin, and
Zhang Zhicong could not leave Wang Bing's mistakes behind because they had not
seen the *Tai su* yet. Yang Shangshan states: 'The twelve large joints of the hands and
feet are called twelve junctures.' Also, Gao Shishi stated: '十二俞 refers to the twelve
large valleys.' Tanba agreed with Gao Shishi and cited Lin Yi et al. as evidence. On
grammatical grounds, Yang Shangshan and Gao Shishi are right. The subject of 名小
十二關 is 大谷十二. Next I believe that 分 is not a numerical adjunct... [The passage]
reads: 人有大谷十二, 分小溪三百五十四, 名小十二關, 'Man has the twelve valleys,
branching out into 364 small ravines. They are named small twelve junctures.' 分 has
the meaning of 剖分, 'to divide,' 衍生, 'outgrowth.' Now, valleys are large and ravines
are small. Hence all the small ravines emerge from the large valleys."

56 Wang Bing: "When the guard qi passes in abundance, no evil qi can settle. When
the guard qi is deficient and comes to a halt, then the evil qi can settle as a visitor.
Hence [the text] states: 'this is where the evil qi settles as visitor.'"

Needles and [pointed] stones remove the [evil qi] in an encircling manner.[57]

For examining the onset of a disease,
the five decisive criteria are employed as basic rules.[58]
If one wishes to know its starting point,
one first establishes its mother.[59]
{The so-called 'five decisive criteria' are the five vessels.}[60]

---

57 Wang Bing: "緣 is to evoke the image of 夤緣, 'to leave by creeping along.' That is to say, when the evil qi settles as visitor and when the [movement of the] guard qi has come to a halt, pierce the respective valley and the evil qi will leave creeping along the vessels."

58 Wang Bing: "五決 is to say: one takes the [movement in the] vessels [associated with] the five depots as the basic rule to decide about survival or death [of the patient]."

59 Wang Bing: "建 is 立, 'establish.' 'Mother' is to say: the host qi corresponding to the season. First establish the host qi corresponding to the season and then seek for the evil and the proper qi." Wu Kun: " 'Mother' is the stomach qi corresponding to the season. That is, if in spring the [movement in the] vessels is slightly string-like; if in summer the [movement in the] vessels is slightly hook-like; if in late summer the [movement in the] vessels is slightly soft; if in autumn the [movement in the] vessels is slightly hair-like; if in winter the [movement in the] vessels is slightly stone-like, then one may speak of a balanced [movement] with the presence of stomach qi. The soil is the mother of the myriad beings; hence one calls it 'mother.' If a string-like [movement] is extreme, then one knows that the disease started from the liver; if a hook-like [movement] is extreme, then one knows that the disease started from the heart. If a soft [movement] is extreme, then one knows that the disease started from the spleen. If a hair-like [movement] is extreme, then one knows that the disease started from the lung. If a stone-like [movement] is extreme, then one knows that the disease started from the kidneys. Hence [the text] states: 'If one wishes to know its starting point, one first establishes its mother.' " 1899/43 supports Wu Kun. Ma Shi: " 'Mother' is the mother in the mutual occupation of the five depots. This is the true so-called starting point of a disease." Zhang Jiebin: " 'Mother' is the cause of a disease. If one cannot find this cause, then secondary and primary events cannot be distinguished. Hence one must first establish its mother, as is outlined in the text below: this or that depot, this or that conduit." Wang Hongtu et al. /198: " 'Mother' refers to the five depots here. When a disease in the conduit vessels turns worse, it will enter the depots. [The text states] 五決為紀. The 五決 are the five vessels. That is, as soon as one knows the status of the five vessels, one should also know the status of the five depots linked to these five vessels. The five depots are the source of the five vessels. Hence [the text] says 'mother.' "

60 Wang Bing: "These are the vessels associated with the five depots."

10-74-1
Hence,
headache and peak illness,
[this is] depletion below and repletion above.[61]
The excess is in the foot minor yin and great yang [conduits].
If it is serious, it enters the kidneys.[62]

Dizziness and shaking, blurred vision and deafness,
[this is] repletion below and depletion above.
The excess is in the foot minor yang and ceasing yin [conduits].
If it is serious, it enters the liver.[63]

Abdominal fullness, bloating, and
propping barriers in the upper and lower flanks,[64]

---

61 Zhang Jiebin: "Headache and peak illness is repletion above. In case of repletion above, there follows depletion below. The excess is located in the two conduits of the kidneys and bladder. The reason is, the foot major yang vessels move from the peak [of the skull] into the brain and the kidneys with the bladder represent outer and inner. Yin is depleted and yang is replete. Hence this disease."

62 Wang Bing: "The foot minor yin [conduit] is the vessel associated with the kidneys. The great yang [conduit] is the vessel associated with the bladder." 2940/40: "The reason is that the foot major yang vessel of the bladder proceeds from the peak [of the skull] to encircle the brain and at the same time it connects with the kidneys and is tied to the bladder. Kidneys and bladder constitute outside and inside. When the kidneys are depleted, they are unable to draw the qi of great yang. As a result, the major yang qi moves upwards contrary to its normal course and this results in headache and constitutes peak illness. If the disease is serious, it enters the kidneys."

63 Wang Bing: "徇 is 疾, 'fast.' 蒙 is 不明, 'not clear.' That is to say, all of a sudden the eyes have a disease and are no longer clear. 招 is to say 掉, 'to shake.' This is 'to shake and be restless.' 尤 is 甚 , 'very.' When the eye has the disease not to be clear and the head shakes strongly, this is a sudden disease. When the eyes turn blind and the ears become deaf, this is a gradual disease. The foot minor yang [conduit] is the vessel associated with the gallbladder. The ceasing yin [conduit] is the vessel associated with the liver." Yang Shangshan: "徇蒙 is 眩冒, 'dizzy.'" Cheng Shide et al./168: "尤 is identical to 搖, 'to shake.' Hua Shou comments: '招搖 is to say: the head shakes and cannot be held still.'" 1011/7: "徇 is 疾速, 'fast.'" Fang Wenhui/78: "徇蒙 is 眴矇, 'dizziness.'" 916/52: "徇 is 眩, 'dizzy.' 蒙 is 冒, 'blind.' 尤 is 搖, 'to shake.'" Wang Hongtu et al./199 agrees. For a summarizing discussion whether to identify 招尤 as a compound or as two separate concepts, see 148/52. See also 2418/428.

64 692/40: "The character 支 stands here for 槙膜, 'swelling.' The *Shuo wen* 說文 states: 膜, 'to rise.' Duan 段 commented (in his *SWJZZ*): 'This should be flesh rises.'" 526/6: "The character 脅 is an erroneous insertion. *Tai su* 15 has no 脅 following 胠. 脅 is a commentary noted to the side of 胠 which was then erroneously inserted into

[this is] receding [qi] below and dizziness above.
The excess is in the foot major yin and yang brilliance [conduits].[65]

Coughing with rising qi and
receding [qi][66] in the chest,
this is excess in the hand yang brilliance and major yin [conduits].[67]
In case the heart is vexed and one has headache,
the disease is in the diaphragm.
This is excess in the hand great yang and minor yin [conduits].[68]

10-75-1
Now,
the [movements in the] vessels
be they minor or big, smooth or rough, at the surface or in the depth,

---

the main text. It should be omitted. The character 支 has the meaning of 拄, 'to support.' 鬲 is identical to 膈, 'diaphragm.' 胠 refers to the upper flanks. The meaning of
the passage 支鬲胠 is to describe extreme uneasiness in the region of the diaphragm
and upper flanks." Zhongyi yanjiuyuan...: "支 has the meaning of 支撐, 'to prop up.'
鬲 is 隔塞, 'to block.' The region below the armpit is called 胠, 'upper flanks;' the
region below the 胠 is called 脅, 'lower flanks.' 支鬲胠脅 is: The region of the chest,
the diaphragm, and the flanks is affected by blockage and distension. 'Receding below'
refers to qi and blood moving upwards contrary to their normal course with the result
that the four limbs suffer from receding [qi] with cold. 'Dizziness above' refers to unclean qi that does not descend, with swellings in chest and abdomen." The *Jia yi jing*
has 支滿, 'propping fullness,' instead of 支鬲."

65 Wang Bing: "下厥上冒 is to say: the qi rises contrary [to its proper course] from
below and strikes the eyes. The foot major yin [conduit] is the vessel associated with
the spleen. The yang brilliance [conduit] is the vessel associated with the stomach."
Gao Shishi: "When the major yin spleen qi fails to rise, this leads to receding below.
When the yang brilliance stomach qi fails to descend, this leads to dizziness above."
Gao Jiwu/171: "The normal course is that the foot yang brilliance stomach [qi] moves
the unclean downwards. In the present case, it moves contrary [to its proper course]
and unclean qi affects the upper parts [of the body]. This results in dizziness and
blurred vision and similar conditions."

66 Lin Yi et al.: "The *Jia yi jing* has 病, 'disease,' instead of 厥."

67 Wang Bing: "The hand yang brilliance [conduit] is the vessel associated with the
large intestine. The major yin [conduit] is the vessel associated with the lung.

68 Wang Bing: "The hand great yang [conduit] is the vessel associated with the small
intestine. The minor yin [conduit] is the vessel associated with the heart." Lin Yi et al.:
"The *Jia yi jing* has: In case of pain in the chest, with propping fullness and the lower
back and the spine pulling each other with pain, this is excess in the hand minor yin
and great yang [conduits]."

they can be differentiated with the fingers.[69]
The phenomena [associated with the conditions] of the five depots,
they can be deduced from [objects of] the same kind.[70]
The five depots appearing in the tones,
they can be known by way of reasoning.[71]
As for the examination of the subtle appearances of the five complexions,
they can be inspected with the eyes.[72]

10-75-3
Those who are able to match the [movement in the] vessels and complexion,
they can achieve succes in a myriad cases.[73]

---

69 Wang Bing: " 'Minor' is to say 細小, 'fine.' 'Large' is to say 'full and large.' 'Smooth' is to say: it comes and goes fluently. 'Rough' is to say: its coming and going is blocked and has difficulties. 'At the surface' is: it floats under the hand. 'In the depth' is: you find it when you press. This way, even though all these [movements] have different appearances, a skilled hand and an investigative heart will nevertheless be able to differentiate them."

70 Wang Bing: "象 is to say 氣象, 'image of qi.' That is to say, although the five depots are hidden and invisible, the nature and operations of the images of their qi can be deduced from the similarity of [other] objects. How that? The image of the liver [qi] is the wood whose [nature includes being] bent or straight. The image of the heart [qi] is the fire which flames upwards. The image of the spleen is the soil which is quiet and does not move. The image of the lung is the metal which is hard and cutting. The image of the kidneys is the water which is moist and moves downwards."

71 Wang Bing: "音 is to say 五音, 'the five tones.' Now, the tone associated with the liver is *jue* [etc.]. These are the regular correspondences. Whether the tones of the voices that appear as a result of the mutual superiority and defeat [among the five agents/depots] are good or not, this can be discerned through reasoning by those who have a sharp ear and a judicious heart." 1445/55: "This is to say: the five depots are inside [the body] and cannot be seen. However, through physiognomy and tones [of the voice] they manifest themselves externally. This makes it clear that the essence qi of the five depots is the internal foundation of the five tones and of the five voices." Yu Chang: "音 is an error for 音. 音 stands for 倍. 倍 is to say 背, 'back.' 五藏相音 is 五藏相背, 'the five depots turn their backs at each other.' 'The five depots turn their backs at each other' is to say: the five depots no longer guard each other." The *Tai su* has 上醫, 'superior physician', instead of 五藏.

72 Wang Bing: "色 is to say 顏色, 'complexion.' Now, the color associated with the liver is green-blue, [etc.]. These are the regular colors. However, the interactions in the qi appearances – leading to favorable or unfavorable signs – are very subtle. They can be observed and recognized only with clear eyes able to look afar."

73 Wang Bing: "In case of a green-blue complexion the corresponding [movement in the] vessels is string-like. In case of a red complexion the corresponding [movement in the] vessels is hook-like. In case of a yellow complexion the corresponding [move-

If in case of a red [complexion the movement in the] vessels arrives
gasping and firm,
the diagnosis states: accumulated qi in the center.
<Occasionally this is a harm caused by food.>
It is called heart block.[74]
One gets it as an external disease.
One thinks and ponders and the heart is depleted.
Hence evil follows this [lead].

If in case of a white [complexion the movement in the] vessels arrives
gasping and at the surface,
this is depletion above and repletion below.
<One is frightened and there is accumulated qi in the chest.>

If it is gasping and hollow,[75]
this is called lung block, as well as cold and heat.[76]

---

ment in the] vessels is intermittent. In case of a white complexion the corresponding
[movement in the] vessels is hair-like. In case of a black complexion the corresponding [movement in the vessels is firm. These are the regular correspondences between
complexions and [movements in the] vessels. Those now who investigate aberrations
and similarities and who pass decisions on success or failure, if they are free of doubts in
their examinations, they will be successfull myriad times in myriad cases they take up."

74 Wang Bing: "喘 is to say the [movement in the] vessels arrives like hasty gasping.
When the vessels that are located high [in the body] have a disease, then the [move-
ment in the] vessels appears like gasping. Hence only the two depots heart and lung
are meant here. A gasping [movement in the vessels] indicates that the qi of the heart
is insufficient. A firm [movement in the vessels] indicates that there is a surplus of
disease qi. The heart vessel rises from the heart which is located in the center of the
chest. Hence [the text states:] 'accumulated qi in the center, occasional harm caused
by food.' 'Accumulation' is to say: disease qi accumulates. 'Block' is to say: the qi of the
depots does not pass." On "heart block" see 1938 and 399 for detailed discussions."

75 Mori: "虛 is 噓, in the sense of 噓吸, 'to inhale.'"

76 Wang Bing: " 'Gasping' means insufficient [qi]; 'at the surface' means lung depletion. When the lung [qi] is insufficient, this is to say: the heart is depleted. In case of
depletion above, there must be fullness below. Because of insufficient [qi] one is easily
frightened and qi accumulates in the chest. Now, when the [movement in the] vessels
is gasping and at the surface, in this case the lung itself has insufficient [qi]. When
[the movement in the vessels] is gasping and hollow, in this case the qi of the heart
moves upwards and occupies the lung. [Hence the lung] receives heat and its qi cannot circulate. Hence [this state] is called lung block with cold and heat [spells] on the
outside of the body." 2261/34: " 'Above' refers to the lung; 'below' refers to the heart.
That is to say, when the fire of the heart burns the lung, qi accumulates in the chest and
the qi in the lung is depleted, [which leads to] gasping. In front of the character 驚 the

One gets it when one is drunk and then sends inwards.[77]

10-76-3
If in case of a green-blue [complexion the movement in the] vessels arrives extended, rebounding left and right,
accumulated qi exist below the heart, with propping [fullness in the] upper flanks.
This is called liver block.[78]
One gets it from cold and dampness.
<The same law [of disease generation] applies to elevation illnesses.>
The lower back has pain; the feet are cool and the head aches.[79]

If in case of a yellow [complexion the movement in the] vessels arrives big and hollow,
accumulated qi exist in the abdomen and
there is receding qi.
This is called receding [qi] with elevation illness.[80]

---

character 善, 'to have a tendency,' is missing. From Wang Bing's comment 'Because of insufficiency one has a tendency to be frightened' one may learn that the text of the classic should have the character 善. The two characters 寒熱 should follow the characters 喘而虛 and should not come behind 'lung block.' This would correspond to the structure of the preceding and of the following text." Yu Chang: "The two characters 寒熱 should follow the characters 得之 (i.e., 'one gets it from cold and heat'). This matches the structure of the preceding and of the subsequent statements."

77 Wang Bing: "The flavor of wine is bitter and dry. Internally it benefits the heart. If one is very drunk and has sexual intercourse, the heart qi rises and occupies the lung." For an identification of 使內 as "to have sexual intercourse", see also *Su wen* 44-248-2.

78 Wang Bing: " 'The [movement in the] vessels is extended and rebounds' means that it is string-like and tight. Tightness indicates cold qi. To be struck by dampness results in a string-like [movement]. The liver controls the upper and lower sections of the flanks; it is close to the heart. Hence qi accumulates below the heart, causing propping [fullness in the] flanks."

79 Wang Bing: "A tight [movement in the] vessels indicates cold; an extended [movement in the] vessels indicates dampness. The elevation disease is generated by cold and dampness, too. Hence [the text] states: 'the pattern of the elevation disease is identical.' Cold and dampness are in the lower [parts of the body], hence the lower back aches. The liver vessel rises from the feet upwards to the head and emerges at the forehead. It meets with the controlling vessel at the peak. Hence in case of a disease [affecting the liver vessel] one has cold feet and headache. 清 stands also for 冷, 'cold.'"

80 Wang Bing: "When kidney qi moves upwards contrary [to its normal course], this is ceasing elevation disease." 2225/4 lists various occurrences of 厥 in the *Nei jing*, in-

<The same law [of disease generation] applies to women.>
One gets it if after quickly moving the four limbs – with sweat leaving [the body] – one encounters wind.[81]

10-76-6
If in case of a black [complexion the movement in the] vessels arrives firm and big above,
accumulated qi exist in the lower abdomen and in the yin region.
This is called kidney block.[82]
One gets it from washing oneself with cool[83] water and then going to lie down.[84]

10-76-8
Whenever one observes <strange [movements in the] vessels [associated with]> the five complexions,
when the face is yellow and the eyes are green-blue,
when the face is yellow and the eyes are red,
when the face is yellow and the eyes are white,
when the face is yellow and the eyes are black,
[the patient] will not die.[85]

---

cluding the present passage and concludes: "These refer either to the qi of depots and palaces moving contrary to its normal course, or to the conduit qi moving upwards contrary to its normal course. They all refer to the pathology of qi moving contrary to its normal course."

81 Wang Bing: " 'The pattern is identical to that in women' is to say: the signs [are identical]."

82 Wang Bing: " 'Above' is the inch-opening. The kidneys rule the lower burner. Hence, qi accumulates in the lower abdomen and in the yin [i.e., sexual] region." 2261/34: " 'Above' should be changed to 'below.' 'Below' refers to the [movement in the] vessels that appears in the foot-long section [of the lower arms]. The foot-long section serves to indicate the [condition of the] abdomen. It is an external indicator of the kidneys." 527/46 supports this view.

83 2049/43: "清 stands for 凊, 'cool.' "

84 Wang Bing: "When dampness qi harms the lower [body parts] this is because it turns to the kidneys; how then could one not become ill if one washes oneself and then goes to sleep?"

85 Wang Bing: " 'Strange [movement in the] vessels refers to those [movements] that do not parallel complexion. Whenever one sees a yellow complexion, this indicates the presence of stomach qi. Hence [that person] will not die." Lin Yi et al.: "The *Jia yi jing* does not have the three characters 之奇脈." Without these three characters, which do indeed seem to be later additions, the statement reads: "Whenever [one of] the [fol-

When the face is green-blue and the eyes are red,
when the face is red and the eyes are white;
when the face is green-blue and the eyes are black;
when the face is black and the eyes are white,
when the face is red and the eyes are green-blue,
in all these cases one must die.[86]

---

lowing] five complexions appears ... death is not imminent." 11/214 has omitted the
three characters 之奇脈 and interprets 相 as 視, "to observe," "to see." 2721/40: "In
comparison with the previous and the following text, the three characters 之奇脈 do
not belong here. I suspect the seven characters 凡相五色之奇脈 should be moved in
front of 赤脈之至也."

86 Wang Bing: "That all cases where no yellow complexion is present must die, that is
a consequence of the absence of stomach qi. The five depots have the qi of the stomach
as their basis. Hence death is imminent in all those cases with no presence of a yellow
complexion."

Chapter 11
Further Discourse on the Five Depots

11-77-3

Huang Di asked:

"I have heard:

of the prescription masters[1]

some consider the brain and the marrow to be depots; [2]

others consider the intestines and the stomach to be depots;

still others consider them to be palaces.

May I[3] ask about these contradictions;[4]

all say of themselves they are right.[5]

I do not know the Way of their [reasoning];

I should like to hear an explanation for this."

Qi Bo responded:

"The brain, the marrow, the bones, the vessels, the gallbladder,[6] and the female uterus,[7]

these six are generated by the qi of the earth.

Their storing is associated with yin;

their image is that of the earth.

---

1 Wang Bing: "方士 are scholars knowledgable of the prescription arts." See also Harper 1998, 51.

2 The *Tai su* has 或以為府 following 或以為腦髓為藏. In this case the opening statement reads: "Some consider the brain and the marrow to be depots; others consider them as palaces. Some consider the intestines and the stomach to be depots; others consider them to be palaces."

3 704/49: "敢 should be interpreted as 冒昧地, 'bold.'" Fu Weikang & Wu Hongzhou/272: "敢 has the meaning of confessing one's own ignorance."

4 Shanghai zhongyi xueyuan../12: "更 is 互相, 'mutual.'"

5 583/40: "皆自謂是 is a Han dynasty usage [of 是] in the meaning of 正確, 'correct.'"

6 2269/37 identifies a misplacement of the character 膽, "gallbladder," here and suggests that it should be moved down to precede the character 胃, "stomach." This way the text would speak of only five "extraordinary palaces" and of altogether six palaces transmitting the transformed. For details of the argument see there.

7 Zhang Jiebin: "女子胞 is 子宮, 'uterus.'" 1209: "女子胞 is also named 子宮. It brings forth and accepts essence qi and completes the fetus."

Hence,
they store and do not drain;[8]
they are called extraordinary palaces.[9]

11-77-7
Now,
the stomach, the large intestine, the small intestine, the triple burner, and the urinary bladder,
these five are generated by the qi of heaven.
Their qi resembles heaven.

Hence,
they drain and do not store.
They receive the turbid qi of the five depots.[10]
They are called palaces of transmission and transformation.

---

8 Fu Weikang & Wu Hongzhou/272: "瀉 has the meaning of 傳瀉, 'transmit and drain.'"

9 Wang Bing: "Even though the brain, the marrow, the bones, and the vessels are called 'palaces,' they do not really constitute outside and inside with the spirit depots. The gallbladder is related to the liver, but [its function] is different from transmission and drainage performed by the six palaces. Even though the uterus emits and receives – it receives in that it receives essence qi, and it emits in that it emits physical appearance', ... still, this operation of emitting and receiving is different from that of the six palaces. Hence [the text] states: 'store but do not drain. They are called extraordinary palaces.'" Zhang Jiebin: "All these six were originally not counted among the six palaces. Because they store yin essence they are said to have been generated by the earth qi and they are called palaces. The gallbladder is one of the six palaces. But because it stores and does not drain it is different from the remaining [five palaces with their functions of] transmitting the transformed. The uterus is different, too, because it emits and receives essence qi and completes the fetus." Ma Shi: "These palaces are single; they have nothing to be paired with." Cheng Shide et al./175: "奇 is 异, 'differen;' 恆 is 常, 'normal.' The extraordinary palaces are 'different from the normal' palaces." 2091/39 proposes that the gallbladder should not be counted among the 'extraordinary palaces,' and that the character 膽 is a mistake here for 卵, "testicles." One reason is that the six extraordinary palaces list a [female] uterus, but no male equivalent. Hence if males are supposed to have the same number of extraordinary palaces as females, the "gallbladder" is to be replaced by the "testicles." Second, the author sees a similarity between the ancient writings of the characters 胆 and 卵. For details of the argument, see there. For a detailed refutation of this argument, see 2938/38. 2755/9-11 suggests that the character 膽 should be 胸中, "chest center." For details of the lengthy argument see there. See also 2261/34 and 2228/150.

10 2379/17-18 suggests on grounds of the structure and of the meaning of the text to move the six characters 此受五藏濁氣 behind the statement 'they are called ex-

These are [locations] where nothing can stay for long, [but where things] are transported and drained."[11]

<The *po*-gate[12], too, is engaged by the five depots.
Water and grain cannot be stored [there] for long.>[13]

11-77-10
<As for the so-called five depots, they store the essence qi and do not drain [it].[14]
Hence, even if they are full, they cannot be replete.[15]

---

traordinary palaces,' and to interpret 濁氣 as 精氣, 'essence qi.'" For details of the argument see there.

11 Wang Bing: "That is to say, when water and grain enter [these palaces of transmitting the transformed], they are changed and transformed to dregs and they are then discharged. They cannot stay inside [of these palaces] for long. It is the task [of these palaces] to transport and drain and thereby to eliminate [from the body] what has been transformed completely, Because they transport and drain all [products of] transformation, they are called palaces transmitting the transformed."

12 Wang Bing: "This is to say: the anus. Internally it communicates with the lung. Hence it is called gate of the *po*-soul. It receives those things that have been transformed and drains them. They are sent there by the five depots. Water and grain (i.e., liquid and solid food) cannot be stored in there for long." Tanba: "魄 is identical to 粕, 'grain sediments in distilled liquor.' The treatise 'The Way of Heaven' (天道篇) in *Zhuang zi* 莊子 [has a passage]: 古人之糟魄已夫. Sima's 司馬 *Yin yi* 音義 states: 'Rotten food is called 魄;' elsewhere it is stated: 'spoiled dregs are 魄, or 粕.'"

13 2431/36: "This explains that the anus does not only serve as a gate of the lung and of the large intestine, but is also engaged for transmitting and transforming the dregs of the five depots." See 2150/52 and 461/33 for detailed discussions of this statement. The *Tai su*, ch. 6, links 魄門 to the preceding statement: 輸寫魄門, 為五藏使, "transport and drainage through the *po*-gate, initiated by the five depots." See also 2686/53.

14 2932/48: "'They do not drain' is to say: even though the five depots are said to store essence qi, it is not so that the essence qi stored by the depots is not drained. It is just not drained directly to the outside. Hence *Su wen* 01 states: 'The kidneys control the water; they receive essence from the five depots and six palaces and store it. Hence when the five depots have abundance, there can be drainage.' From this it is obvious that even though the main function of the five depots is to store, under specific circumstances they are nevertheless able to transport and drain essence qi towards the other depots and palaces."

15 Wang Bing: "Essence qi causes fullness; water and grain cause repletion. [The five depots] store nothing but essence qi. Hence they can be full but they cannot be replete." Lin Yi et al.: "The Quan Yuanqi edition, the *Jia yi jing*, and the *Tai su* have 精神, 'essence spirit,' instead of 'essence qi.'" Yang Shangshan: "Essence spirit is always present in the depots and does not leave them. Hence [the essence spirit] is

As for the six palaces, they transmit and transform things, but do not store [them].[16]
Hence, they [may be] replete, but they cannot be full.>[17]
{The reason is as follows.
When water and grain enter the mouth,
then the stomach is replete and the intestines are empty.
When the food moves down, then the intestines are replete and the stomach is empty.

---

not drained and [the depots] nevertheless are full. Even though they are full, they are regularly depleted. Hence [the text states:] 'not replete.'" Zhang Jiebin: "The constitution of essence qi is clear. [When the text states: 'the depots] store but do not drain,' this is because they merely have [immaterial] fullness rather than repletion from [material] accumulation." Wu Kun: "The essence qi is a subtle spirit; it functions without traces. Hence [the depots] are full but not replete." Yao Shaoyu: "The essence qi is most precious and any repletion is difficult to achieve."

16 182/39: "This is to say, the five palaces carry, in the process of vital dynamics, the responsibility of transporting and transmitting those items remaining after the transformation of water and grains. In concrete terms, beverages and food enter the body and are received and digested by the stomach and by the small intestine. Their essential subtle matter is then transported by the palaces responsible for transmitting the transformed to the remaining depots and structures, to support the functions of the organism. Their dregs are eliminated from the body by means of the large intestine and the bladder via the two yin [orifices] in the front and in the back." Yu Chang: "[When the text] states 'they transform things but do not store [them],' then this refers to the 'palaces of transmission and transformation' mentioned in the text above. The text above lists as palaces of transmission and transformation the stomach, the large intestine, the small intestine, the triple burner, and the bladder. These are only five palaces. It states further: 'The *po*-gate, too, is engaged by the five depots, water and grain cannot be stored [there] for long.' Hence the *po*-gate, too, is one of the palaces of transmission and transformation. Together these are six palaces. This list differs from the six palaces gallbladder, stomach, large intestine, small intestine, bladder, and triple burner listed in *Su wen* 4. The gallbladder appears in the preceding text, too; it is one of the extraordinary palaces, not one of the palaces of transmission and transformation. Hence the gallbladder was left out and replaced by the *po*-gate to arrive at the number of six palaces. ... Huang Di's question demonstrates that at that time there was disagreement as to the exact definition of depots and palaces."

17 Wang Bing: "Because they do not store essence qi, but merely receive water and grain." Zhang Jiebin: "The constitution of water and grain is turbid. [When the text states: 'the depots] transform things and do not store,' this is because they [may] be in a state of repletion from [material] accumulations but they cannot be full." Yao Shaoyu: "Transformed things are extremely filthy and [this] cannot be stored for long. ... Transformed things are things resulting from the transformation of water and grain."

Hence [the text] states:"replete but not full, full but not replete."}

11-78-3
[Huang] Di:
"How comes that only [the movement in the vessels that can be felt at] the qi-opening is ruled by the five depots?"[18]

Qi Bo:
"As for the stomach,
it is the sea of water and grain;
it is the great source [supplying] the six palaces.[19]
The five flavors enter the mouth.
They are stored in the stomach to nourish the five depot qi.[20]
{The opening of this qi is also at the major yin.}[21]

---

18 Wang Bing: "The 'qi-opening' is the 寸口, 'inch-opening;' another name is 脈口, 'vessel opening.' Because the inch-opening is [a location] where the abundance or weakness of qi can be examined, it is called 'qi-opening.' It is here where one can feel the movement or the resting of the [flow in the] vessels. Hence it is called 'vessel opening.' In all cases [the information] is taken from [a location] one inch behind the fish-line [at the wrist]. This, then, is the 'inch-opening.'" Zhang Jiebin: "The meaning of the inch-opening is expressed by three names. The hand major yin is the conduit vessel of the lung. The lung controls all qi. Whether the qi is abundant or weak is visible here. Hence it is called qi-opening. The lung is the meeting point of all vessels. It is here where all vessels come together. Hence it is called vessel opening. The vessels emerge [here] from the great abyss for a length of one inch and nine *fen*, hence it is called inch-opening. Even though these are three different names, they nevertheless refer to the same."

19 Wang Bing: "Man has four seas. The sea of water and grain is one of them. It receives water and grain to nourish the four sides. Because it is the source of movement and transformation, it is 'the grand source from which the six palaces are supplied.'" 2268/37: "In front of 'six palaces' the two characters 五藏, 'five depots,' have been omitted. From the following statement 'Hence the qi and the flavors of the five depots and six palaces, they [all] originate from the stomach' it is evident that the stomach is not only the source from which the six palaces are supplied. For further evidence see *Su wen* 29 and 19."

20 526/6: "The character 藏 is out of place here. *Tai su* 14 has no character 藏 following 五; it should be deleted. 'The five flavors enter the mouth; they are stored by the stomach to nourish the five qi' is identical to the meaning of 'the flavors are stored to nourish the five qi' in *Su wen* 09."

21 Wang Bing: "The vessel movement that is examined at the inch-opening is the passage of the qi in the hand major yin vessel. Hence [the text] states: 'the qi-opening is major yin, too.'" Zhang Jiebin: "The qi-opening is by definition associated with the major yin; so, why does [the text] state 'is associated with the major yin, too?' Now, the

Hence,
the qi <and flavors[22]> of the five depots and six palaces,
they originate from the stomach,[23]
and any changes appear at the qi-opening.[24]

Hence,
when the five qi enter the nose,
they are stored by <heart and> lung.
When <heart and> lung have a disease,
the nose is not free as a result.[25]

---

qi-opening is associated with the lung, which is hand major yin. When it distributes
stomach qi, then this is in the spleen which is foot major yin. *Ling shu* 18 states: 'The
grain enter the stomach, whence they are transmitted to the lung. From there all the
five depots and six palaces receive qi.' *Su wen* 45 states: 'The spleen is responsible for
passing on the liquids for the stomach.' *Su wen* 21 states: 'The beverages enter the
stomach. Essence qi flows off from there and is moved upwards to the spleen. The
spleen qi disperses and returns upwards to the lung.' Hence the stomach qi must turn
to the spleen; the spleen qi must turn to the lung and later passes through the depots
and palaces as camp and guard [qi]. Hence, even though the qi-opening belongs to
the hand major yin, [the qi] does in fact turn to the foot major yin. Hence [the text]
states: 'the qi-opening is major yin, too.'"

22 526/6: "The character 味 is out of place here. The Ming manuscript kept by the
Nanjing Library 南京圖書館 has no character 味, and the *Lei shuo* 類說, ch.37 has
no character 味 either."

23 Lin Yi et al.: "The Quan Yuanqi edition has 入, 'enter,' instead of 出."

24 Wang Bing: "The intake of grain is responsible for repletion in the paths of the
camp qi." (Lin Yi et al.: "Obviously, this comment by Wang Bing is based on the *Ling
shu*. However, 實 is written there 寶, 'treasure.'") The grain enter the stomach and
their qi is transmitted to the lung. The pure essence then follows the lung qi and passes
along the qi-opening. Hence [the text] states: 'its changes appear at the qi-opening.'"
Yang Shangshan: "The stomach is the sea of water and grain; it is the superior of the
six palaces. It brings forth the five flavors to nourish the five depots. The blood qi and
the guard qi proceed through the hand major yin vessels and arrive at the qi-opening.
Whether the [condition of the] five depots and six palaces is good or bad, all this is
conveyed here by the stomach qi; it comes together in the hand major yin and appears
at the qi-opening. Hence [the text] states: 'Any changes appear [at the inch-open-
ing].'"

25 Zhang Zhicong: "This is to say: When [the text states that] the five qi enter
through the nose and are stored in the heart and in the lung, these qi are yang. The
nose is the orifice of the lung; hence when the heart and the lung have a disease, the
nose is impassable as a result." Ma Shi: "Of the five depots, only heart and lung are located above the diaphragm and receive these five qi. Hence when heart and lung have
a disease, the nose is impassable as a result." Gao Jiwu/553: "為之 is 因此, 'because of

11-78-8
Whenever one treats a [patient's] disease,[26]
one must investigate his below,[27]
take into account [the movement in] his vessels,
observe his mind, and
relate [all this] to his disease.[28]

---

this.'" 2686/53: "The character 藏 should be interpreted as 深, 'deep.' This is to say, the clear qi that is inhaled enters deep into the heart and the lung." 526/6: "The character 心, 'heart,' is an erroneous addition. The orifice of the lung is the nose. Hence further down it is stated: 'when the lung has a disease, the nose is impassable.' If the character 心 is added, this is most difficult to explain. The *Lei shuo* 類說 has no character 心; it should be deleted."

26 137/15: "The paragraph beginning with 凡治病 can be deleted; it is out of place here."

27 Wang Bing: "下 is to say: 'whether it can be seen below the eyes or not.'" 2722/43: "Lin Yi et al. states: 'The *Tai su* has 必察其上下, 適其脈候, 觀其志意, 与其病能, 'Examine above and below, check the signs of the [movement in the] vessels, observe the sentiments and the will, and relate [all this] to the potential of the disease.'' The *Tai su* version is correct; Wang Bing's commentary is forced. Yang Shangshan states: 'For treating diseases it is essential to examine the *ren-ying* [points to the left and right of the throat] above and to investigate the inch-opening below, in order to check the signs of the [movement in the] vessels.' This statement comes close to the [meaning]. In fact, though, 'above' and 'below' do not necessarily have the meaning read into these terms by Yang Shangshan. 能 is 態, 'bearing.' That is, examine sentiments and will and the bearing of the disease." Ma Shi: " 'Observe the below' is to observe whether the lower orifices are passable or not." Zhang Jiebin: " 'Below' is to say: the two yin [orifices; i.e., the openings for urine and stools]. The two yin [orifices] are the orifices of the kidneys and the gate for [shutting or opening] the stomach. *Su wen* 17 states 'If the granaries cannot keep what they store, the doors are not under control.' Those who keep their guard survive; those who lose their guard, they die. Hence stools and urine are the lock to the stomach qi and they are closely linked to the uncritical or critical state of the principal qi of the entire body. Hence one must observe the 'below.'"

28 Wang Bing: "Examine whether the [movement in the] vessels is abundant or depleted; observe and estimate the evil and the proper in his sentiments and will and the requirements resulting from the disease being in the depth or superficial and from its being constructive or destructive and then stay with the [appropriate] pattern to treat it." Xue Xue: "適 is 測, 'to measure.' The [movement in the] vessels is the foremost [indicator] of the blood [and the] qi. Hence one takes only the inch-opening to decide about auspicious or inauspicious signs. ... Hence one must observe the [movement in the] vessels."

If[29] someone is in the grip of[30] demons or spirits,
it is impossible to talk to [him][31] about perfect virtue.[32]
If someone has an aversion to needles and [pointed] stones,[33]
it is impossible to talk to [him][34] about perfect skill.[35]

If the patient does not permit treatment,
the disease must not be treated.
If one treats it, there will be no success.[36]

---

29 527/47: "The *Tai su* has the character 乃 above 拘; it should be inserted here, too. 乃 has the meaning of 若, 'if.' The preceding paragraph 凡治病 .. outlines what is proper; this paragraph 乃拘于鬼神 outlines the opposite. These two paragraphs constitute a pair of opposites. If the character 乃 is omitted, the meaning is not clear."

30 Ye Gang/154: "於 is to be explained as 被, passive voice particle." See also 702/47.

31 702/47: "The character 之 is omitted after the 与."

32 Wang Bing: "If one's sentiments and will are heterodox, he will love prayers and sacrifices. If one were to speak to him about perfect virtue, he would certainly turn his back against this. Hence [the text states:] 'It is impossible to talk to him about perfect virtue.'" 217/7: "至德 is 'highest virtue.' Here it refers to medical theory." See also the Bian Que biography in *Shi ji* 史記, ch.109, for a similar opinion: "Those who believe in shamans and do not believe in physicians, they constitute the sixth group of patients that must not be treated."

33 It remains unclear whether 針石 refers to "needle stones", i.e., pointed stones, or to "needles and [pointed] stones" reflecting the parallel existence of acupuncture by needling and bloodletting by means of pointed stones during the Han era. See also *Su wen* 04, 13, and 14.

34 704/52: "The character 之 is omitted after the 与." Ye Gang/145: "与言 is 'to talk to someone.'"

35 Wang Bing: "When someone has an aversion to needles and/or stones, no skill can be applied. Hence [the text states:] 'it is impossible to talk to him about perfect skill.'"

36 Wang Bing: "If [a patient's] mind is set not to permit someone to treat him, he must die. A forced treatment would never be successful. Hence [the text] states: 'if one treats it there will be no success.'"

Chapter 12
Discourse on Different [Therapeutic] Patterns Suitable [for Use in Different] Cardinal Points

12-80-2
Huang Di asked:
"When physicians treat diseases,
one identical disease may be treated differently[1] in each case,
and is always healed. How is that?"

Qi Bo responded:
"Physical features of the earth let it be this way.[2]

The fact is,
the region of the East,[3]
this is where heaven and earth give life first.
[This is] the land of fish and salt;
beaches border on the water.

Its people eat fish and crave for salty [meals].
All of them consider their place of residence as comfortable and they regard their food as delicious.[4]

As for the fish, it lets one develop a heated center;[5]

---

1 Wang Bing: " 'Differently' is to say: with needle-stones, cauterisation, toxic drugs, physical exercises, and massage."

2 Wang Bing: "That is to say, [treatment] follows [locally characteristic] features of generation, growth, gathering, and storage stimulated by heaven and earth, and whether a region is high or low, dry or damp." Zhang Jiebin: "When the features of the earth differ, the customs differ too. Hence the therapeutic patterns follow [these differences] too, and are not alike."

3 Zhang Zhicong: "域 is 區界, 'region;' 宇內, 'within the universe.' "

4 1932/72: "They all are convinced that their residential area is peaceful and suitable and they are convinced that their food and beverages are exquisite." Gao Jiwu/418-419 and 157/56 agree.

5 Wang Bing: "When fish causes the development of ulcers, this is evidence of heat in the center. When salt causes the development of thirst, this is proof of blood being overpowered." Zhang Zhicong: "The nature of fish is associated with fire; hence [fish] causes heat in the center of man." Gao Jiwu/411: "Causes heat accumulation inside the body."

as for the salty [meals], they defeat the blood.[6]

Hence,
its people all have a black complexion and open [skin] structures.
their diseases are always yong-abscesses and ulcers.[7]
For their treatment, pointed stones are suitable.[8]

Hence,
it is for sure that [the therapy with] pointed stones originated in the East.[9]

12-80-7
The West,
this is the region of gold and jade.
It is the location of sand and stones.
It is where heaven and earth contract and pull [things together].[10]

Its people live in earthen mounds and the winds are frequent.[11]

6 Chen Zhuyou/30 and Huang Sanyuan/40: "勝 is 傷害, 'to harm.'" Gao Jiwu/484:
"Between 鹽者 and 勝血, the two characters 使人, 'cause man,' have been omitted."
536/33: "鹽 is a mistaken character here and should be 鹹, 'salty flavor.' 鹹者勝血 is
the same principle as 鹹走血, 'salty flavor moves to the blood,' in *Su wen* 23."

7 Wang Bing: "When the blood is weak and hot, one tends to develop abscesses
and ulcers."

8 Wang Bing: "砭石 is to say: needles made from stone. The *Shan hai jing* 山海經
states: The mountain of Mr.Gao has stones resembling jade. Needles can be produced
from them. These then are the pointed stones." Zhang Jiebin: "砭石 is 石針, 'stone
needles.' The people of the East have wide skin structures and they suffer from abscesses and ulcers. Their diseases are in the external muscles. Hence they use pointed
stones. The treatment carried out with pointed stones is shallow."

9 Wang Bing: "The people in the East use them [even] today."

10 Wang Bing: "Following the pattern of the [operation of the] qi of autumn. 引 is:
to pull and gather."

11 Wang Bing: "Their residences resemble earthen mounds. Hence [the text] states:
'they live in mounds.'" Lin Yi et al.: "Overall, the West is a region of high elevation
and the people live on high mounds. Hence winds are frequent. This does not mean
that their residences resemble earth mounds." Zhang Zhicong: "An elevated plain is
called 陸. A large 陸 is called 阜. A large 阜 is called 陵, 'mound.' Because they live
on mountains and mounds, winds are frequent." Yao Shaoyu: "The Western people
live in holes. This is so up to the very present. Because they use mounds as residences,
[the text] states: 陵居." Yu Chang in his *Xiang cao xu jiao shu* 香草續校書 points out:
"The [two characters] 其民 should be 其地, 'its land.' The text further down states for
the first time 'its people do not dress in clothes but in hair and grasses.' To connect

The water and the soil are hard and strong.[12]

Its people do not dress with clothes but wear garments of hair and grasses.[13]
Its people [enjoy] rich food and they are fat.[14]

Hence,
[external] evil cannot harm their physical body;[15]
their diseases emerge from within.[16]
For their treatment, toxic drugs are appropriate.[17]

---

the present statement with the subsequent [statements of 'its people ...'] is a mistake."
Cheng Shide et al./183 supports the interpretation offered by Yu Chang. For details
see there. See also Gao Jiwu/399.

12 Wang Bing: "The qi of metal is stern and kills. Hence 'water and soil are hard
and strong.'"

13 Wang Bing: "They do not dress in silk, hence [the text] states: 不衣. 褐 refers to
毛布, 'fabrics made of hair.' 薦 is to say: 細草, 'fine grasses.'" The *Shi jing* 詩經, Guo
feng 國風, Pin 豳, Qi yue 七月, has: "無衣無褐, 何以卒歲, without the [fine] clothes
and without the garments of hair, how could we get to the end of the year?" See Legge
Vol. IV, Part I, Bk xv, 1, p.226.

14 Wang Bing: "華 is to say: 鮮, 'delicious,' 美, 'rich,' 酥酪, 'koumiss,' and bones as
well as meat types [of food]."

15 Wang Bing: "The water and the soil are hard and strong; the beverages and the
food are fat; the interstices of the skin are tightly sealed; the blood and the qi are
replete. Hence evil cannot cause any harm." Chen Zhuyou/30: "形體 is 身體的表面,
'the outside of the body.'"

16 Wang Bing: " 'Within' is to say: excesses in joy, anger, sadness, grief, and fear, as
well as drinking and eating and sexual intercourse." Lin Yi et al.: "The 悲, 'sadness,' [in
Wang Bing's commentary] should be 思, 'pensiveness.'" Yao Shaoyu: "邪 is 外邪, 'external evil.' The evil of the six excesses must enter [the body] from outside. Here now,
the interstices are sealed because of the fat; the body is warm because of the [garments
made from] hair and grass. Hence the evil has no way to enter. Only if one overeats,
then fat and sweetness accumulates in the intestines and in the stomach. [Similarly,
excessive sexual] desires waste the true principal [qi. As a result,] the disease is not
outside, it is inside." Huang Sanyuan/40: "內 is 內因, 'internal cause.'"

17 Wang Bing: "If they are able to attack the disease, one calls them toxic drugs.
Because their blood and qi abound, because their muscles and flesh are hard, because
their beverages and their food are exquisite and because water and soil are strong,
hence in case of a disease prescriptions of toxic drugs are appropriate to check it.
'Drugs' is to say all those herbs, trees, insects, fish, birds, and quadrupeds that are able
to eliminate disease." Zhang Zhicong: "All drugs that are able to eliminate disease
are called 'toxic drugs.'" Zhang Jiebin: "The diseases emerge from inside. Hence they
cannot be treated by needles, cauterization, massage, or exercises. One must use toxic

Hence,
it is for sure that [the treatment with] toxic drugs originated in the West.[18]

12-81-3
The North,
this is the region where heaven and earth secure and store.

Its land lies at a high elevation,
[its people] live in earthen mounds.

Wind, cold, and piercing frost [dominate].[19]

Its people find joy in living in the wilderness and in consuming milk.

___

drugs." Zhang Zhicong: "毒藥: these are drugs containing poison. *Su wen* 70 states: 'If one treats diseases with strong poisons, one eliminates six out of ten. If one treats diseases with regular poisons, one eliminates seven out of ten. If one treats diseases with weak poisons, one eliminates nine out of ten.' Of those [substances] that were listed as 'without poison' as the upper class [of drugs in the herbal] of Shen Nong 神農, it was said that they could be taken for long and that they increased one's span of life, while those drugs with poison in the middle and in the lower class were used to treat diseases and to attack diseases." Yao Shaoyu: "The diseases of the depots and palaces cannot be treated with light and bland drugs; hence toxic drugs are suitable. 'Toxic drugs' are those with heavily pronounced qi and with a strongly developed flavor." 2262/43: "The so-called 'toxic drugs' are drugs whose [qi-]nature and flavor are violent and strongly pronounced. Hence one distinguishes between strong toxicity, regular toxicity, and minor toxicity. For example, [drugs] like *fu-zi* [aconite], *xi-xin* [rhizoma asari], and *gan-jiang* [dried ginger] are mostly very warm in their [qi-]nature; *huang-lian* [rhizoma coptidis], huang-qin [radix scutellariae baicalensis], or *huang-bo* [cortex phellodendri] are mostly very cold in their [qi-]nature. If they are used appropriately, they can cure diseases; if they are used inappropriately, they can kill a person. The *Shuo wen* 說文 states: 毒 is 厚, 'rich,' 'liberal.' The *Yi jing* 易經 [states]: 聖人以此毒天下, 而民從之, 'The sages presented this to the empire liberally and the people followed them.' From this it is obvious that the interpretation of 毒 as 厚, 'rich,' 'liberal,' is old. When the *Nei jing* states 'toxic drugs are suitable for their treatment,' this is to say: because these people live on high elevations in the mountains, their muscles and skin are thick and solid. Hence one must use drugs [whose properties are] violent and strongly pronounced to heal their diseases. It is not so that one must attack their diseases solely with such [toxic substances as are] *pi-shi* [arsenic] or *ba-dou* [croton seeds].

18 Wang Bing: "The prescription arts of the Westerners offer them [to us still] today."

19 Wang Bing: "Following the pattern of the [operation of the] qi of winter."

Their depots are cold and generate diseases of fullness.[20]
For their treatment, cauterization is appropriate.

Hence,
it is for sure that cauterization originated in the North.[21]

12-81-5
The South,
this is [the region] where heaven and earth bestow growth and nourishment;
it is the place where yang [qi] is present in abundance.

Its land lies low;
water and soil are weak.
It is [a region] where fog and dew assemble.[22]

Its people crave for sour [foods],[23] and they eat [food of] a strong odor.[24]

---

20 Lin Yi et al.: "The *Jia yi jing* 甲乙經 does not have the character 滿, 'fullness.'"
Zhang Jiebin: "To live in the wilderness and to consume milk, this is the nature of the
people in the North. In the land of the Hu 胡 this is so up to the very present. The qi
of the earth is cold [there] and the nature of milk is cold too. This causes man's depots
to be cold. When the depots are cold, one often has constipation. Hence such diseases
as swelling and fullness emerge."

21 Wang Bing: "To burn moxa is called 灸焫 (to cauterize). The Northerners practice
exactly this method." Zhang Zhicong: "Yang arises out of yin; fire emerges out of
water. With moxa one is able to reach to the true yang within the water. In the North,
only yin and cold are abundant, while the yang qi is secured and stored. If one burns
these [diseases] with moxa, one can reach to the principal yang below the extreme yin.
Hence the pattern of cauterization originated from the North."

22 Wang Bing: "Following the pattern of the [operation of the] qi of summer. 'Below the earth,' this is where the flowing water turns. There is much water. Hence 'the
soil is weak and fog and dew assemble.'" Gao Shishi: "The land caves in in the South-
East, hence [the text states:] 'the land there lies low.' When the land is elevated, it is
hard; when the land lies low, it is soft. Hence water and soil are weak. When the land
is low, the water and the dampness follow it. Hence dew and fog assemble there."

23 Gao Shishi: "The earth is weak in the South-East and [the people] therefore
prefer a flavor generating [the agent they] themselves [are dominated by]. The people there crave for sour [foods]; wood generates fire. The preceding text on the East
[states: the people there] crave for salty [foods]; water generates wood. The region of
the North-West has surplus. Hence [the text] does not state [what the people there]
prefer."

24 Wang Bing: "That is to say, what they eat does not have a pleasant aroma." Lin
Yi et al.: "The Quan Yuanqi edition has 食魚, 'they consume fish,' instead of 食胕."

Hence,
its people all [have] tight [skin] structures and a reddish complexion.[25]
Their diseases are cramps and block.[26]
For their treatment, fine[27] needles are appropriate.

Hence,
it is for sure that the nine needles have originated in the South.[28]

12-81-8
The center,
its land is flat and damp.
It is here that heaven and earth generate the myriad beings in large numbers.[29]

Its people eat diverse [foods] and are never fatigued.[30]

Zhang Jiebin: "胕 is 腐, 'rotten.'" 2753/62 agrees. For a detailed survey of the use of this character in the *Su wen*, see 1682/42.

25 Gao Shishi: "致理 is 腠理致密, 'the interstice structures are tight.'" Zhang Qi: "致理 may be a mistake. Red is the color of yang. The land is low and damp. Hence sinews and bones have diseases." 536/33: "It may well be that the character 致 should be 疏, 'distant,' 'relaxed.' This passage outlines the natural characteristics of the South, with its great dampness and abundance of heat. If [the text] had stated 'wide structures,' this might have been more appropriate."

26 Wang Bing: "Sour flavor is astringend; hence all the people have tightly sealed flesh structures. Because this is a place of yang abundance, the complexion is red. In case of internal fullness of dampness qi and when heat qi strikes internally, then the sinews get twisted and the vessels suffer from block."

27 Wang Bing: "微 is 細小, 'fine.' By means of fine needles one regulates weakness and abundance in the vessels."

28 Wang Bing: "The Southerners revere them greatly."

29 Wang Bing: "It follows the pattern of the [operation of the] virtue of soil. Hence it gives life to many beings. Now, in the East is the sea. The South is low. The West and the North are elevated. In the center, the land is flat and damp. With the topographical features differing to such a degree, the diseases that are generated vary too." Cheng Shide et al./186: "眾 is 多, 'often,' 'many.'"

30 Wang Bing: "This is the hub of the four cardinal directions and the myriad beings meet here. Hence the people have a diversified diet and do not [suffer from] fatigue."

Hence,
their diseases are often limpness with receding [qi], and [spells of] cold and
heat.[31]

For their treatment, guiding-pulling and pressing-lifting are appropriate.[32]

Hence,
it is for sure that guiding-pulling and pressing-lifting have originated in the
center.[33]

12-82-3
Hence,
the sages brought various [patterns] together in treatment;[34]
each [case] received what was appropriate for it.[35]

---

31 Wang Bing: "The dampness below causes frequent disease of limpness and weakness, of qi moving contrary to its proper course, and of spells of cold and heat."

32 Wang Bing: "導引 is to say: stimulation of the sinews and bones and movement of
the extremities and joints. 按 is to say: to press the skin and the flesh; 蹻 is to say: to
quickly raise hands and feet." Wu Kun: "導引 is to move the qi through the conduits,
lest blockages occur to generate a disease. . [按蹻] is to rub the sinews and the joints
to help the passage of the yang qi." For a more detailed explanation, see 447/43.

33 Wang Bing: "This is the proper Way employed by the people in the center to
nourish the spirit and to regulate the qi."

34 631/60: "The character 雜 does not mean 混雜, 'mixed,' or 雜亂, 'confused.' 雜合
以治 is 配合著治療, 'to bring together all types of treatment.'" Zhang Yizhi et al.:
"雜 is 集, 'to collect.' That is to say, 'they collected all therapeutic methods and applied
them in their treatments.'"

35 Wang Bing: "They used [the various therapeutic methods] in accordance with the
cardinal direction [where they treated a disease]. Hence they applied the appropriate
[therapy] in each case. Only the sages are able to follow this pattern." Zhang Zhicong:
"Heaven has the qi of the four seasons. The earth has the requirements of the five
directions. The people differ in where the live, how they dress, and what they eat. In
treatment one distinguishes between needling, cauterization, and drugs. Hence the
sages either orientated themselves on the qi of heaven, or they acted in accordance
with the requirements of the cardinal direction, or they followed the disease of the
respective person. Hence they sometimes used needles, cauterization, or toxic drugs, in
other cases [they treated with] exercises or massage." Gao Jiwu/542: "Guo Aichun-92
states: 'the character 所 is an erroneous addition.' Wang Bing in his commentary has
stated: 各得其宜. Hence the edition on which Wang Bing based his comments did
not have the character 所."

Hence,
if what one uses for treatment is different,
and the disease is healed in all [cases] nevertheless,
[then] one has grasped the nature of disease
and one knows the entire complex of treatment."[36]

---

36 Wang Bing: "Because they were aware of [different] dispositions." Zhang Zhicong: " 'One has grasped the nature of disease,' [is to say:] if one knows whether a disease was caused by the qi of heaven or by the qi of the earth or by man's desires, then
one has grasped the causality of a disease. Sometimes one uses one of the therapeutic
patterns of the five cardinal directions because the people come from five directions;
in other cases it is appropriate to employ needle-stones or cauterization, or toxic drugs
or massage, because the qi or the person [to be treated] is [in a state of] emergence,
growth, collection, or storage. This is the grand complex of treatment. By no means,
though, is it a must to treat with pointed stones in the East and with toxic drugs in
the West!"

Chapter 13
Discourse on Moving the Essence and Changing the Qi

13-82-7
Huang Di asked:
"I have heard that,

when [the people] in antiquity treated a disease,
they simply moved the essence and changed the qi.[1]
They were able to invoke the origin and [any disease] came to an end.[2]

---

1 Wang Bing: "移 is to say: 移易, 'change.' 變 is to say: 變改, 'to alter.' All [these activities] caused the evil not to harm the proper, so that the essence spirit recovered to strength and guarded the interior. *Su wen* 03 has: 'The sages transmitted the essence spirit and they ingested the qi of heaven.' *Su wen* 01 states: 'When the essence spirit guards the interior, where should a disease arrive from?'" Zhang Zhicong: "This is, they moved and increased the [patients'] essence and they transmitted and changed their qi." Wu Kun: "They altered the essence spirit and they transformed the qi in the depots. For instance, [by generating] anxiety they overcame anger; [by generating] fear they overcame joy; [by generating] anger they overcame pondering; [by generating] joy they overcame anxiety; [by generating] pondering they overcame fear and they guided the camp and the guard [qi through the organism] – all this was undertaken [in this context]." Gao Shishi: "導引, 'to guide,' is called 移; 振作, 'to stir up,' is called 變." 536/33: "其 has the meaning of 有, 'to have.' That is, 'in ancient times, for the treatment of disease, there existed only [the methods of] moving the essence and changing the qi.'" 移精變氣, "to move essence and change the qi", may be read as a refutation of macrobiotic practices in the treatment of illness. See also below, note 7.

2 Zhang Zhicong: "Words directed at the spirits are called 祝." Zhang Jiebin: "由 is where the disease emerged from." Ma Shi: "祝由 is to pray to the origin of the disease by speaking to the spirits. In high antiquity, before the emergence of toxic drugs, needles, and [pointed] stones, it was only through moving the essence and changing the qi, one could exorcise the origin of a disease and heal it." Wu Kun: "Whenever someone's affects leave the middle way and if one of the five sentiments is unilaterally pronounced and causes harm, disease emerges. For instance, in case of anger, the qi rises; in case of fear, the qi moves downwards. .. That is, when the qi has a disease, this generates all kinds of diseases. When the ancients treated [a patient], they clearly perceived his feelings and they prayed to the origin of the disease. That is to say, when a patient had a unilaterally [pronounced emotion], this caused a disease in his qi. They treated [the unilaterally pronounced emotion] by that [emotion] which overcomes it; and they harmonized it by that which generates it." 1033/259: "The term 祝由 has been interpreted by the majority of the commentators as a type of therapy whereby one prays to the spirits. Both in the *Gong yang zhuan* 公羊傳 and in the *Gu liang zhuan* 穀梁傳 , 祝 has the meaning of 斷, 'to cut.' 由 can be interpreted as 原因, 'cause,' 'reason.' 祝由, then, is to be interpreted as 'to cut the cause of the disease.'" For

When the people of nowadays treat a disease,
[they employ] toxic drugs to treat their interior and
[they employ] needles and [pointed] stones to treat their exterior.[3]

Some are healed; others are not healed.

Why is this so?"

13-82-9
Qi Bo responded:
"People in antiquity lived among their animals.
They moved and were active and this way they avoided the cold.
They resided in the shade and this way they avoided the summerheat.[4]
Internally, they knew no entanglements resulting from sentimental attachments;[5]

---

further details of this argument, see there. Similarly, 536/33 rejects the intepretation of 祝由 as referring to an invocation of spirits and quotes the *Guang ya* 廣雅, Shi gu yi 釋詁一, to support the interpretation of 祝 as 斷, "to cut." For details see there. Gao Jiwu/238: " 'I have heard when the physicians in ancient times treated a disease, they merely changed the thoughts and the spirit of the patient, [thereby] cutting the root of the disease to cure the disease.' " 137/13: "呼吸, 'to breathe,' is 祝; 遷徙; 'to move,' is 由. 祝由 is therefore an ancient method of 'moving to another place to find cure and nourishment.' Hence [the text] states 如日月光. 如 is 就, 'to approach.' This is to say: face the light of sun and moon to improve one's breathing." 2495/531: "From this it can be seen that by the time of the Warring States and earlier, shamanism and medicine were not yet separated, or that shamanism and medicine existed side by side." 1044/10: "祝由 is an ancient suggestive therapy. During the Ming era, Zhang Jiebin employed – on the basis of the ancient 祝由 – verbal suggestion and pharmaceutical drugs to treat mental disorders. He obtained excellent results." For an interpretation of 祝由 as an ancient psychological therapy, see 1385/70, 2432/4, and 1789/54. In contrast, 2660/9 in a lengthy argument rejects the psychological interpretation of 祝由 and identifies it as a shamanistic therapy which is no longer considered valid by the *Nei jing*.

3 It remains unclear whether 針石 refers to "needle stones", i.e., pointed stones, or to "needles and [pointed] stones" reflecting the parallel existence of acupuncture by needling and bloodletting by means of pointed stones during the Han era. See also *Su wen* 04, 11, and 14.

4 Wang Bing: "The ancients lived in caves. At night they went into seclusion; in the morning they [began to] move around. One can be certain that they [lived] amidst the animals. Now, when they moved, the yang was abundant and hence their body heat was sufficient to ward off the cold. Cool qi generates cold. Hence by residing in the shade, they were able to avoid the summerheat."

5 Gao Shishi: "眷慕 is 眷戀思慕, 'to think [of someone] with sentimental affection.' "

externally, they did not have the physical appearance of stretching towards officialdom.[6]

In this peaceful and tranquil world,
the evil was unable to penetrate deeply.
Hence toxic drugs were unsuited to treat their interior,
and needles and [pointed] stones were unsuited to treat their exterior.

Hence it was possible to move essence and invoke the origin and [any disease] came to an end.[7]

13-83-1
The people of today are different.
Anxiety and suffering encircle their interior;
exertion of the physical appearance harms their exterior.

---

6 Lin Yi et al.: "The Quan Yuanqi edition has 曳, 'to pull,' instead of 伸.Zhang Jiebin: "伸 is 屈伸, 'to bend and stretch.' 宦 is the strain of wealth and name." Wu Kun: "This is: searching entrance into officialdom." Gao Shishi's and Zhang Zhicong's editions have 官, 'official,' instead of 宦. Zhongyi yanjiuyuan...: "伸 is 伸曲, 'to stretch.' 宦 is 任宦, 'to serve as official.' 伸宦: to pursue fame and gain." 536/34: "伸官 may be an error for 憂患, 'suffering from anxiety.' 憂患 parallels the preceding 眷慕. In ancient times, 憂患 was written 憂悥. The *Shuo wen* 說文 states: '憂 is 愁, 'anxiety.' *Zhuang zi* 莊子, Ke yi 刻意, states: '平易恬惔, 則憂患不能入.' This meaning corresponds to that of the present treatise's 恬憺之世, 外無憂患之形." 2284/60: "伸官 should be 紳縉. 縉 refers to the capstrings/silk tassels of officials. Hence, 紳縉 stands for 仕宦, 'officials.' "

7 Wang Bing: "Their sentiments cast away all thoughts; hence their interior was not troubled by any affects. They eliminated all desires; hence externally they did not have the physical appearance of stretching themselves for officialdom. They quietly protected their true heavenly [endowment] and hence could not be overcome by evil. Hence they just moved the essence and changed the qi and did not rely on toxic drugs, or on invoking the cause of a disease. Neither did they work hard with needles and [pointed] stones and were healed [nevertheless]." Zhang Jiebin: "Internally they had no sentimental affects; externally there was no urge or pursuit. Hence [the text] states 'peaceful and tranquil world.' When [the world is] peaceful and tranquil, the true [endowment] of heaven is complete and firm; qi and blood are strong and replete and no evil can enter." 536/34: "It seems that following 移精 the two characters 變氣 have been omitted." 移精 parallels 移珍, "to offer/confer precious objects", which is attested for Han times (see the entry 移珍 in the *Han yu da ci dian* 漢語大辭典). Harper 1998, 119, states that *jing* 精 prior to the fourth century B.C. referred to "things that were pure and refined" and that were presented as offerings to the external

Also,
the [people] have lost [the knowledge how] to follow the four seasons and
they oppose the requirements of cold and summerheat.

The robber wind frequently reaches [them].
The depletion evil [is present] in the morning and in the evening;
internally it reaches to the five depots, to the bones and to the marrow;
externally it harms the orifices, the muscles, and the skin.

13-83-4
This is why
minor diseases inevitably develop into serious [problems];
serious diseases inevitably result in death.

Hence,
invoking the origin cannot end [a disease any longer]."

[Huang] Di:
"Good!

I wish to attend a patient and
when [I] observe [him to find out] whether [he must] die, or will survive,
[I should like to] cast away all doubts.[8]
[I] should like to know the essentials
- [they should be as clear] as the light of sun and moon.

May [I] hear [of this]?"

13-83-6
Qi Bo:
"Complexion and [movement in the] vessels, this is

---

spirits. Hence the phrase 移精祝由 may also be read as "to offer sacrifices to invoke
the [demonic] origin [of illness]" and, hence, as an indirect refutation of resorting to
the belief in demons in therapeutic attempts aiming at a restoration of health. For a
detailed interpretation of this passage, see Unschuld 2003, 327-331

8 Zhang Zhicong: "嫌疑 is: one cannot decide about [a patient's imminent] death or
survival." 2051/59: "嫌疑 is 狐疑, 'doubt.' Hence the comment by Zhang Zhicong."
For details of the argument, see there.

what the Lords on High valued;
the teachers of former times have transmitted it.

In high antiquity, Jiu Daiji was ordered
to establish the structure of the complexions and the [movements in the] vessels,[9] and [to reveal their]
communication with the spirit brilliance,[10] [by]
matching them with [the five agents] metal, wood, water, fire, and soil, and
with the four seasons, the eight winds and the six [cardinal points] uniting [the world].

Whether they did not leave their regular [patterns],[11]
and whether there were changes, transformations, and mutual shifts [of positions],
through [these parameters] he observed these mysteries and
knew the essentials of [death and survival].

---

9 Tanba, *Su wen shi*: "Luo Mi 羅泌 (of the Song dynasty) stated in his *Lu shi* 路史: 'Shen Nong established a prescription book. Then he ordered Jiu Daiji to structure the complexions and the [movements in the] vessels.'"

10 Wu Kun: "理色脈 is: he sought the patterns in the complexion and in the [movement in the] vessels. 通神明 is to say: the results of his examination of the complexion and of the [movement in the] vessels, he brought them together with spirit brilliance." Gao Shishi: "He established the Way of the complexion and of the [movement in the] vessels of the human body and he penetrated the spirit brilliance of sun and moon."

11 Wang Bing: "The former teachers related a white complexion and a hair[-like movement in the] vessels to [the agent] metal, corresponding to autumn. They related a virid complexion and a string[-like movement in the] vessels to wood, corresponding to spring. They related a black complexion and a stone[-like movement in the] vessels to water, corresponding to winter. They related a red complexion and a vast [movement in the] vessels to fire, corresponding to summer. They related a yellow complexion and an intermittent [movement in the] vessels to soil, corresponding to late summer. These are the four seasons. Now, they related these complexions and these [movements in the] vessels to inactive and active [stages of the] five agents below and to the coming and going of the four seasons above. Hence the eight winds and the crushing sounds [of thunder] within the six [cardinal points] uniting [the universe] did not leave the regularity expected [of them]. Everything could be predicted in its time [of arrival]. How? This was known from observing those changes and transformations. Hence the statement in the text below."

If one wishes to know the essentials of [death and survival],
then it is in the complexion and the [movement in the] vessels that they are [to be found].[12]

13-83-10
The complexion is that by which [a physician establishes] correspondences to the sun.
The [movement in the] vessels is that by which [a physician establishes] correspondences to the moon.

To permanently search for these essentials,
this, then, is the essential in the [prediction of death and survival].[13]

Now,
the changes and transformations of the complexion,
as they correspond to the [movements in the] vessels in the [course of the] four seasons,

---

12 Wang Bing: "This is to say why the complexion and the [movement in the] vessels are the means by which to recognize the essentials in the changes, transformations and mutual alterations in the qi of the four seasons and five agents." 583/40: "是 is not used as a pronoun here. Obviously, it is employed here as a copula with a judgmental function. This is certainly a usage of the Han era."

13 Wang Bing: "When [the text] states that the [movement in the] vessels corresponds to the moon, while the complexion corresponds to the sun, [it refers to] the standards of prognosis. To regularly search for aberrations in the complexion and in the [movement in the] vessels, this then is a necessity in the examination of healthy men." Yang Shangshan: "The physical appearance and the complexion appear outside and are yang, hence they correspond to the sun. The [movement in the] vessels and the blood appear inside and are yin, hence they correspond to the moon." Zhang Jiebin: "The complexion follows the categories of the five agents and changes in that it may be light or dark. The sun has the ten stems and changes in that it may be covered or shines. Hence the complexion corresponds to the sun. The vessels have the twelve conduits and they change in that they may be depleted or replete. The moon has the twelve branches and it changes in that it expands and contracts. Hence the [movement in the] vessels correspond to the moon." Zhang Zhicong: "Sun and moon are the essence of yin and yang of heaven and earth. Now, the complexion is yang and the [movement in the] vessels is yin, and in continuously searching for the essentials in the complexion and in the [movement in the] vessels, one never leaves the realm of yin and yang. Hence if one knows in what [terms] the complexion corresponds to the sun and in what [terms] the [movement in the] vessels corresponds to the moon, then the essentials [of diagnosis] lie in there."

this is what was valued by the Lords on High,
and [this is] by which they established links to spirit-brilliance.

This way they kept death at a distance and remained close to life.[14]

13-84-1
It is therefore that they extended the Way of life, [and hence]
they were called sage kings.[15]

When [the people] in middle antiquity treated a disease,
once it had arrived, they treated it by means of decoctions.[16]

It took ten days to remove the diseases of the eight winds and five blocks.[17]
If they had not ended after ten days,

---

14 Wang Bing: "They examined whether complexion and [movement in the] vessels was right or not and they knew the subtle omens of death and survival. Hence they were usually able to stay away from death and remain close to life."

15 Wang Bing: "The Lords in high [antiquity] listened to the Way and carefully practiced it. Hence they were able to extend the Way of life. Only the sage kings were able to do this."

16 Zhang Jiebin: "'Decoctions' are prepared from the five grains; they are not drugs."

17 Wang Bing: "The 'eight winds' are the winds of the eight cardinal points. 'Five blocks' is to say: the blocks of the skin, the flesh, the sinews, the bones, and the vessels. The *Ling shu jing* states: 'The wind coming from the East is called infant wind. When it harms man, this occurs externally in the sinews. Internally it settles in the liver. The wind coming from the South-East is called weakness wind. When it harms man, this occurs externally in the muscles. Internally it settles in the stomach. The wind coming from the South is called great weakness wind. When it harms man, this occurs externally in the vessels. Internally it settles in the heart. The wind coming from the South-West is called scheming wind. When it harms man, this occurs externally in the flesh. Internally it settles in the spleen. The wind coming from the West is called hardness wind. When it harms man, this occurs externally in the skin. Internally it settles in the lung. The wind coming from the North-West is called breaker wind. When it harms man, this occurs externally in the hand great yang vessels. Internally it settles in the small intestine. The wind coming from the North is called great hardness wind. When it harms man, this occurs externally in the bones. Internally it settles in the kidneys. The wind coming from the North-East is called violence wind. When it harms man, this occurs externally in the armpits and flanks. Internally it settles in the large intestine.' Also, the treatise *Su wen* 43 states: 'Harm caused by wind during the *jia-yi* period in spring is called sinew block. Harm caused during the *bing-ding* period in summer is [called] vessel block. Harm caused by wind during the *geng-xin* period in autumn is [called] skin block. Harm caused by evil during the *ren-gui* period in

they treated them with *cao-su*
and the branches of *cao-gai*,
and supported this with roots and ends.[18]

winter is bone block. If one encounters it during [the period of] extreme yin, this is
flesh block.' These are the so-called diseases of the eight winds and five blocks." Lin
Yi et al.: "The treatise 痺論 quoted in this commentary differs from the text of the
痺論 (*Su wen* 43) in the text as it is extent today. [Wang Bing's commentary] should
state: 'The [treatise] 風論 (*Su wen* 42) states: Harm caused by wind during the *jiayi* period in spring is liver wind. Harm caused by wind during the *bing-ding* period
summer is heart wind. Harm caused by evil during the *wu-ji* period in late summer is
spleen wind. Harm caused by evil during the *geng-xin* period in autumn is liver wind.
Harm caused by evil during the *ren-gui* period in winter is kidney wind. *Su wen* 43
states: When the three qi of wind, cold, and dampness arrive and unite [in the body],
this causes block. If one encounters [such a situation] in winter, this is bone block; if
one encounters it in spring, this is sinew block; if one encounters it in summer, this is
vessel block; if one encounters it in [the period of] extreme yin, this is muscle block;
if one encounters it in autumn, this is skin block.' "

18 The *Tai su* has 草荄 instead of 草蘇 and 眇, 'subtle,' instead of 助. Yang Shangshan commented: 荄 refers to roots and stems of herbs. 眇 is the essential in the treatment of disease by means of the roots and stems of herbal drugs." Wang Bing: "草
蘇 is to say: drug decoctions. 草荄 is to say: roots of herbs. 枝 is to say 'stems.' That
is, one brings the roots and sprouts of all the drugs together and prepares a decoction
from them, so that all of them assist each other and this then is taken in. In general,
among the drugs are those where one makes use of roots, those where one makes use
of stems, those where one makes use of branches, and those where one makes use of
flowers and fruits. There are also those where one makes use of roots, stems, branches,
flowers, and fruits [together]. If a decoction fails to eliminate [a disease], then all [the
parts of the plants] are employed. Hence [the text] states 'roots and ends offer support.' Ma Shi: "蘇 is 'leaf;' 荄 is 'root;' 枝 is 'stem.' 荄 is 本 'origin,' 枝葉, 'branches
and leaves,' are 末, 'ends.' These are decoctions of later times." Gao Shishi: "草蘇草荄
are toxic drugs. 荄枝 is 本, 'origin,' 蘇枝 is 末, 'end.' 本末為助 is: one employs them
to disperse the evil and support the proper [qi]." Zhang Zhicong: "This is to say, the
diseases have sign and origin and the herbs have origins and ends. 蘇 is 'stem;' 荄 is
'root.' 草蘇之枝 are the lateral branches of the stems. 草荄之枝 are the lateral roots
of the roots. Hence the 蘇荄 are considered 'origin,' and the lateral branches are the
'ends.' " Wu Kun: "*Cao-su* and *cao-gai* are two easily obtainable drugs. 枝 stands for
干, 'stem.' 本 is 'root,' 末 is 'sprout,' and 助 is 'support.' " Zhongyi yanjiuyuan...: "蘇
comes from 穌 and describes a comfortable, relaxed appearance. Its extended meaning
is 'leaf.' " Cheng Shide et al.: "荄 is interpreted in the *Shuo wen* 說文 as 根, 'root.' "
Gao Jiwu/558: "蘇 is 'herb leaves;' 荄 is 'herb root.' 枝 is 'herb stem.' 本 refers to roots;
末 refers to branches and leaves."

When tip and root match,
the evil qi will yield.[19]

13-84-4
When [the people of] later generations treated a disease,
then this was different.
The treatments were not based in the four seasons.[20]
They no longer knew of [the significance of] sun and moon.[21]
They did not recognize [whether the qi] moved contrary to or followed [its regular course].[22]

---

19 Wang Bing: "標本已得, 邪氣乃服 is to say, if the practitioner and the disease correspond in the treatment, then the evil qi weakens and after some time a favorable [situation results]. *Su wen* 14 states: 'The disease is 標, 'tip,' the practitioner is 本, 'root.' If tip and root do not fit, the evil qi does not yield.'" Lin Yi et al.: "The Quan Yuanqi edition states: 'If one gets a hold of tip and root, then the evil qi disperses [散].'" Wu Kun: "Diseases have tip and root. Where a disease is received [in the organism], this is the root; where it is transmitted, this is the tip. Now, if one gets a hold of the root and if one also gets a hold of the tip, then all evil qi will yield." Gao Jiwu/7: "服 is identical with 伏, 'to submit,' 'to yield.'"

20 698/67: "本四時 can be interpreted as 以四時為根据, 'to take the four seasons as a basis.'"

21 536/34: "'Sun and moon' refers to complexion and [movement in the] vessels."

22 Wang Bing: "All the qi of the four seasons have a place to be. If one recklessly carries out an attack without basing it on the location [of the qi], then this is contrary to the ancient [pattern]. *Su wen* 64 states: In spring, the qi is in the conduits and vessels; in summer, the qi is in the tertiary [conduits] and in the network [vessels]; in late summer, the qi is in the muscles; in autumn, the qi is in the skin; in winter, the qi is in the bones and in their marrow. When the practitioner subdues an evil he must do so always according to its present location. 'They do not know sun and moon' is to say: The sun has cold and warmth, light and darkness; the moon has emptiness and fullness, loss and gain. *Su wen* 26 states: All patterns of needling require an observation of the qi of sun and moon and stars and of the eight regulars of the four seasons. When the qi is determined, one [can] needle the [patient]. Hence, when heaven is warm and when the sun is bright, then the blood in man is rich in liquid and the guard qi is at the surface. Hence, the blood can be drained easily and the qi can be made to move on easily. When heaven is cold and the sun is hidden, then the blood in man congeals and the guard qi is in the depth. At time of beginning crescent moon, blood and qi originate as essence and the guard qi begins to move. When the disk of the moon is full, blood and qi are replete and muscles and flesh are firm. When the disk of the moon is empty, muscles and flesh wane, the conduits and network [vessels] are depleted and the guard qi leaves. The physical appearance exists all by itself own. It is therefore that one follows the seasons of heaven in regulating blood and qi. Hence, when the heaven is cold, do not needle. When heaven is warm, there are no coagula-

When a disease had already assumed physical manifestation, they wished [to use] fine needles to treat the exterior of the [patient] and decoctions to treat his interior.[23]

Uneducated practitioners behave very aggressively,
believing they can launch an attack.
Before the old disease has ended,
a new disease emerges in addition."[24]

13-85-3
[Huang] Di:
"I should like to hear the Way of the essential."

Qi Bo:
"The most essential in treatment is [the following]:
Not to miss [movement in the] vessels and complexion,[25] and
to make use of them without confusion,
that is the grand rule of treatment.[26]

If [acting] contrary to and [acting] in compliance with [the norms] are reversed,[27] and

---

tions. When the moon emerges, do not drain; when the moon is full, do not supply. At empty moon, do not apply any treatment. This is called: get a hold of the times and regulate the [disease]. 不審逆從 is to say: they do not examine whether a disease can be healed or not." 月郭空, "empty moon", refers to specific days associated with yang heavenly stems within a month.

23 2495/531: "The reliance on decoctions for internal treatments began with the Han era."

24 Wang Bing: "粗 is to say: 粗略, 'primitive.' 兇兇 is to say: they do not consider whether a measure is appropriate or not. What does that mean? If they let a hungry person who has lost physical appearance and qi to an extreme, [if they let such a person] eat to repletion, this must result in diarrhea!" Lin Yi et al.: "Another edition [of Wang Bing's commentary] has 害, 'harm,' instead of 霍, 'diarrhea'." Qian Chaochen-90/62: "*Xun zi* 荀子, Tian lun 天論, has 君子不為小人匈匈也輟行. The commentary states: '匈匈 is the sound of hubbub. It is identical with 訩. 粗工兇兇 is: uneducated practitioners generate hubbub without end." For 凶凶, see also 915/57.

25 The *Tai su* has 脈色 instead of 色脈. This is correct in that 色 forms a better rhyme with 極, and also with 惑, 則, 得, and 國. We have followed the text of the *Tai su* here.

26 Wang Bing: "惑 is to say: 惑亂, 'confusion.' 則 is to say: 法則, 'rule.'"

27 536/34: "The character 到 is an error; it should be 倒, 'on the contrary.'"

if tip and root do not match,
[in the course of the treatment the healer] loses his spirit, [just as in government the ruler] loses his country."²⁸

<Remove²⁹ the old and approach the new,
then you acquire the [status of the] true man.>³⁰

13-85-5
[Huang] Di:
"I have heard the essentials [of prognosis and treatment] from you, Sir.
In your statements, Sir, you have never left complexion and [movement in the]
vessels.
That I know."

Qi Bo:
"The utmost [principle] in treatment lies with the oneness."³¹

---

28 Wang Bing: "逆從倒行 is to say: to oppose the suitable is to act contrary. 標本
不得 is to say: the practitioner and the disease do not fit. Why [in such a situation]
should the spirit qi be harmed only in the treatment of people? If this were applied to
the assistance given to a ruler, the strength and the well-being of the throne would not
be maintained either." See also 1876/46.

29 2111/37: "去 is 棄, 'to discard.'"

30 Wang Bing: "If one fails to get a hold of tip and root, [i.e.,] when practitioner
and disease do not fit, one must remove the old, that is, the person acting contrary to
the patterns, and approach the new, that is, a knowledgable scholar. This way one gets
hold of a most truthful and refined person to complete the cure." Zhang Jiebin: " 'To
remove the old' is to remove the inadequacy of old practices; 'to approach the new'
is to approach the success of daily reform. If the new is continuously renewed, one's
studies will let one reach [the level of] the sages and the exemplary and achieve the
Way of the true man." Wu Kun: " 'To remove the old' is to remove the evil of the old
days; 'to approach the new' is to nourish the qi of new life. This is the task of moving
the essence and changing the qi. If one [acts] like this, one will achieve the Way of
the true men of high antiquity." Gao Jiwu/371: "Discard the old techniques and move
towards the new teachings, then you can acquire the doctrine how to nourish the life,
[developed by] the true men of high antiquity."

31 Gao Shishi: "The great rule of treatment, if one searches for its utmost [prin-
ciple], this is the principle of complexion and [movement in the] vessels. Hence [the
text states:] 'the utmost [principle] of treatment lies with the One.'"

[Huang] Di:
"What is that to say, the 'oneness'?"[32]

Qi Bo:
"There is oneness, and therefore one gets it."[33]

13-86-3
[Huang] Di:
"How?"

Qi Bo:
"Close the door and shut the windows,
tie yourself to the patient,
repeatedly inquire about [his] feelings,
adapt [your treatment] to his sentiments.[34]

If one gets a hold of the spirit,
the [patient] will prosper;

---

32 Zhang Zhicong: "The 'one' is the spirit. When the spirit is lost, one dies. That which has got a spirit, lives. When the spirit qi disperses, even a good practitioner cannot heal [a disease]."

33 Wang Bing: "What you have grasped following your questions." Zhang Yizhi et al.: "Wang Bing's comment suggests that the text he saw had the character 問 follow the character 因." Zhang Jiebin: "The One is the greatness of the Way; it is the source of the myriad things and of the myriad beings. If man can get a hold of the One, then the universe is in his hands. If man can know the One, then the myriad beings return to his heart. The One is the origin. 因 is 所因, 'that which follows.' If one gets a hold of that which follows, what could there be that one could fail to get a hold of?" Zhang Zhicong: "The 'One' is the spirit. If one gets a hold of the spirit, then one gets a hold of the complexion, the [movement in the] vessels, and the essence qi." Gao Shishi: "One gets it by following the sentiments of the patient." Tanba Genken 丹波元堅: "When during the Song dynasty Chen Yan 陳言 named his book 三因極一, he worded this title in view of the present paragraph. Hence the current character 因 refers to 'the causes of disease.'"

34 Wang Bing: "Enquire about his desires and observe whether they are permissible or not." Zhang Jiebin: "Shut the door, close the windows, and tie [yourself] to the patient. See to it that the [patient] is quiet and is not disturbed. Then [both sides are] relaxed and one can enquire about his feelings. Undertake every effort to follow his sentiments. The reason is that it is essential to achieve a welcoming mood [in the patient]. As a result, the one who asks does not feel awkward and the patient does not harbor any dislike. Hence one is able to examine the causal links from begin to end and the treatment will be faultless." Gao Jiwu/554: "意 is identical with 情, 'affects.'"

if the spirit is lost,
[the patient] perishes."[35]

[Huang] Di: "Good!"

---

35 536/34: "神 is by no means to say 神氣, 'spirit qi.' The statement 得神 summarizes
what was said on complexion and [movement in the] vessels above. In terms of fact,
when the facial complexion is shining and glossy and when the movement in the
vessels is balanced, then this is 得神, 'to be in possession of the spirit;' when the physical appearance is emaciated and the complexion is bad and when the [movement in
the] vessels is contrary to the four seasons, then this is 失神, 'to have lost the spirit.'"
1344/39: "神 is used in Chinese medicine in a wider and in a narrower sense. In a
wider sense, 神 refers to the entirety of the external appearance of the vital activities of
the human body, including the physical appearance, the facial complexion, the spirit
of the eyes, responsiveness and movement of limbs and body. The passage 得神者昌,
失神者亡 is an example of the usage of 神 in this wider sense." For a discussion of the
various meanings of 神, see also 1894/387 and 2528/10-11. Gao Jiwu/369: "When
the spirit qi of the patient prospers, prognosis is good; when the spirit qi of the patient
is weak, prognosis is bad."

Chapter 14
Discourse on Decoctions and Wines

14-86-7
Huang Di asked:
"To prepare decoctions and wines from the five grains,[1] how is that done?"[2]

Qi Bo responded:
"One must[3] take paddy,[4] and
burn paddy straw [to cook] it.
As for the paddy, it is complete;
as for the paddy straw it is hard."[5]

[Huang] Di:
"How can this be?"

Qi Bo:
"[Paddy] receives a harmonious [blend of the qi of] heaven and earth and
the appropriate [qi of] high and low,
hence it can reach completion.
[Paddy straw] is cut for harvest at the right time,
hence it can reach hardness."[6]

---

1 2243/5: "The 'five grains' include: 大麥, 'barley,' 小米, 'millet,' 高粱, 'Chinese sorghum,' 粳米, 'nonglutinous rice,' and 大豆, 'soybean.'" See this paper for a thorough discussion of the entire treatise.

2 Wang Bing: "液 refers to 清液, 'clear liquids.' 醪醴 refers to a type of wine." Zhang Jiebin: "湯液醪醴, these are all [different] types of wine. 湯液 refers to a kind of clear wine." 2686/53 reads this line as follows: 為五穀湯液, 為五穀醪醴, 奈何?

3 1716/79: "必 has the meaning of 組合, 'to form.'" For textual evidence, see there. In contrast, Gao Jiwu/482: "One must (必須) use paddy to prepare [the wine] and [one must] use paddy straw to boil it."

4 537/26: "In ch.10/2 of the *Sheng ji jing* 聖濟經, the commentary by Wu 吳 identifies 必 as 醴, 'wine.' 醴 stands for 蘊, 'to collect.' 醴以稻米 is to say: one prepares wine from collected paddy. The meaning of 醴 corresponds to that of 炊, 'to boil.' With the character 必, this passage is difficult to explain."

5 Wang Bing: " 'Hard' is to say: use [paddy straw] that is hard. 'Complete' is to say: take [paddy] that is complete. Complete [paddy] yields a clear, cold wine. Hard [paddy straw] results in a qi that moves quickly and brings about fast results."

6 Wang Bing: "Paddy grows from the essence of water, [which is] yin; on its head it carries the qi of the yang of heaven. When these two [i.e., essence of water and yang

14-86-10
[Huang] Di:
"When the sages in high antiquity made decoctions and wines,
they produced them but did not employ them.
Why was that?"

Qi Bo:
"Ever since antiquity, when the sages made decoctions and wines,
they did so only to be prepared.[7]

Now,
in high antiquity, when they made decoctions,
they produced them as a rule,[8] but did not consume them.[9]
As for the people of middle antiquity,
[their adherence to] Way and virtue had decreased and
evil qi occasionally reached [into the body].[10]
[People] consumed [decoctions and they still] achieved success in
a myriad cases."[11]

---

qi of heaven] are blended, [paddy] is generated through [their] transformation. Hence [the text] states: 'it can reach completion through the blending of heaven and earth.' The qi of autumn is quite unyielding. Frost and dew freeze. Paddy is harvested in winter. Hence [the text] states: 'when the harvest is cut, it has received the [nature of the] season and can reach hardness.' "

7 Wang Bing: "That is to say, the sages felt strongly for life. They warded off whatever [danger] was just emerging and they arranged their measures to be prepared for unexpected dangers." Wang Shaozeng/129: 以為 should be read as 以之為, 'they regarded them (i.e., the liquids and medicinal wines) as (ready for use).' "

8 1678/45, on the basis of the *Shuo wen*, interprets 故 as 故意, "intentionally." Gao Jiwu/605 interprets 故 as "before," "previously."

9 Wang Bing: "The sages did not treat what was ill already, they treated what was not ill yet. Hence they only prepared [decoctions and wines] for use, but did not consume them."

10 94/14: "The noun 時 used in front of a verb has the meaning 有時, 'occasionally,' 時時, 'frequently.' "

11 Wang Bing: "Even though [adherence to] Way and virtue had decreased and even though evil qi occasionally reached [the body], because the hearts [of the people] were still close to the Way, they could consume [decoctions and medical wines] and achieved a myriad cures." Zhang Jiebin: "[Adherence to] Way and virtue had decreased and the true [endowment received from] heaven was harmed. Hence evil could invade them. However, they had not lost the Way entirely. Hence they merely had to consume decoctions and wines and could reach perfect restoration again."

14-87-1
[Huang] Di:
"For the people of today, there would not necessarily be a cure.
Why?"[12]

Qi Bo:
"The people of today,
they must administer toxic drugs to attack in their center, as well as
chisel stones, needles, and moxa to treat their exterior."[13]

---

12 Wang Bing: "That is to say, it is not necessarily as it was during the times of middle
antiquity. Why?" Wu Kun: "已 stands for 止, 'to stop.' That is to say, to consume decoctions did not necessarily stop [the evil qi]." Yao Shaoyu: "This is to say: it is not
necessarily like in the old times."

13 Wang Bing: "That is, the [therapeutic] patterns differ from [those employed in]
ancient times." Zhang Jiebin: "齊毒藥 is: to use toxic drugs as remedies 劑." Zhang
Zhicong: "齊 stands for 疾, 'disease.' ... In today's world, one only knows how to
attack diseases, but one does not know how to nourish one's proper qi." *Han Fei zi*
韓非子, 喻老篇: "Bian Que said: 'When a disease is in the interstice structures, hot
water and poultices will reach it. When a disease is in the skin, needles and stones will
reach it. When [a disease] is in the intestines and in the stomach, fire preparations 火
齊 will reach it." Hence Sun Yirang: "The character 必 should be 火; the seal script
versions of these characters are similar. Hence this mistake arose." 2722/44 agrees:
"必齊 and 毒藥 are combined here to parallel 鑱石針艾." Wang Hongtu et al. /199
agrees. Ma Shi: "In later times, the evil qi became quite strong; only toxic drugs and
piercing were suitable now for treatment. However, in later times drugs were added
to the wines, while in high antiquity wines were made from the five grains only. The
latters' nature was rather pure, hence they were unable to treat the evil of the later
times." Yu Yue: "齊 should be read as 資 in the sense of 用, 'to employ.' That is, one
must employ toxic drugs etc. to attack and treat the inner and outer segments [of the
body]." 1716: "必齊 refers to a treatment with dietetic preparations. *Su wen* 15 states:
'If a faint complexion appears, decoctions will master the cure; an end is reached
within ten days. If a deep complexion appears, 必齊 will master the cure; an end is
reached within 21 days. If a very deep complexion appears, wines will master the
cure; an end is reached within 100 days.' These three expressions 湯液, 必齊, and 醪
酒 correspond to 必齊, 毒藥, ... 鑱石, and 針艾 in the present text. Hence there is no
doubt that 必齊 is a specific term. .. 必 has the meaning of 組, 'well-designed.' 必齊
stands for 組劑, 'well-designed recipes.'.... *Su wen* chapter 21 has the phrase: '調食
和藥', 'regulate with diet and harmonize through drugs' which has the same meaning.
Hence the entire phrase should be read in the sense of: 'They regulate with diet and
harmonize through drugs to attack in their center; they employ chisel stones, needles,
and moxa to treat their exterior.'" For textual evidence supporting this argument, see
there. 2463/34: "必 stands for 必須, 'must.' 齊 stands for 齊聚, 'to bring together,' 配
伍, 'to combine.' 毒藥 refers to 藥物, 'drugs.' 中 refers to the internal parts of the
body. The meaning of the entire phrase is: one combines various effective drugs and

[Huang] Di:
"When the physical appearance is destroyed and the blood is exhausted
and yet a [therapeutic] success is not established,
why is that?"[14]

Qi Bo:
"The spirit was not employed."[15]

14-87-3
[Huang] Di:
"What does that mean: 'the spirit was not employed?' "

Qi Bo:
"This applies to the Way of needles and [pointed] stones.[16]
When essence spirit fails to enter and

---

has the patient consume them to treat his internal disease." 916/54: "齊 stands for
制, 'to prepare.' " 698/66 agrees with the interpretation of 齊 as a verb in the present
context. 230/53: "鑱石 are needles made from stone." The character sequence 鑱石針
is rather unusual. One of these characters may be a later addition, even though it is
unclear which. The rhythm of the two statements 必齊 .. 其中, 鑱石 .. 外也 suggests
that it originally consisted of two strings of seven characters each. The combination 鑱
石 occurs only twice in the *Su wen*, once in the present treatise and later in treatise 47
in a phrase which appears to be a later commentary. A term 石針 does not appear in
the *Su wen*. A term 鑱針 appears once in *Su wen* 36. *Su wen* 04, 11, 13, as well as the
present treatise have the expression 針石 which may refer to needles and [pointed]
stones, or to needle[-sharp] stones.

14 Wu Kun: "That is, if a treatment was carried out with the [therapeutic] patterns
mentioned above, resulting in a destruction of the physical appearance and an exhaustion of the blood."

15 Wang Bing: "This is to say, the spirit cannot stimulate the excellent operation of
the needles and stones. Why? Because the will and the mind have turned their back
to the instructions offered by their teacher." Zhang Jiebin: "The Way of all treatments
of diseases is such that the evil is attacked with needles or drugs and that the drugs
are transported through the spirit qi. Hence, if one carries out a treatment from the
outside, the spirit responds inside. If one employs it to achieve a rising movement,
their will be a rising movement; if one employs it to achieve a descent, there will be
a descent. This is how the spirit can be employed. If one treats with drugs internally
but the qi of the depots fails to respond, if one treats with needles or moxa externally
but the qi of the conduits fails to respond, then the spirit has already left and there is
nothing that could be employed." 230/54: "使 is 使用, 'to make use of,' 'to employ.' "

16 537/26: "Following 針石, the character 者 is missing. It should be added in accordance with [the corresponding wording in] the *Tai su*, 知古今篇. 道 is identical with
導, 'to guide.' The meaning is: the only effect of needles and stones is to stimulate the

when the mind is in disorder,
a disease cannot be healed.[17]

---

blood and the qi. If one hopes to cure a disease, one must also cause the essence spirit to move freely and the mind to be settled in peace."

17 The Quan Yuanqi edition has a positive wording of this statement: 精神進, 志意定, 故病可愈, "the essence spirit enters, mind and sentiments are fixed, hence the disease can be healed." The *Tai su* wording is 精神越, 志氣散, 故病不可愈, 'the essence spirit transgresses [its limits], the mental qi disperses, hence the disease cannot be healed." Yu Yue: "The wording of the Quan Yuanqi edition fits best. If read in connection with the preceding text, Huang Di asks: What does that mean, 'the spirit was not employed'? Qi Bo: The needles and stones, this is the Way. [They make] essence and spirit enter and [they cause] mind and sentiments to be fixed. Hence a disease can be healed. That is, to enter the essence and the spirit and to fix mind and sentiments, that is the Way of the needles and stones, that is the so-called spirit. The present version, though, does not explain the Way of the needles and stones; it simply states why a disease cannot be cured. If [the Quan Yuanqi version is] read in connection with the subsequent text, [this makes sense, too]: '[The needles and stones make] the essence and the spirit enter and [they cause] mind and sentiments to be fixed. Hence a disease can be healed. In the present case, the essence is destroyed and the spirit has left. Camp and guard [qi] cannot be gathered again. Why? If one's desires have no limits and if one suffers without end, the essence qi will be destroyed, the camp [qi] stops its flow and the guard [qi] vanishes. Hence, the spirit leaves and the disease does not heal.' Why a disease does not heal is explained exactly with an argument opposite to why a disease can be healed. In today's version, the text is repetitive because it explains twice why a disease cannot be healed. Also, why would the argument need the character 今, if it were not to turn it into its opposite?" Gao Shishi: "The Way of applying the needles and stones is such that the essence spirit of the practitioner and the essence spirit of the patient, the mind of the practitioner and the mind of the patient – both must come together. In the present case, the essence spirit of the practitioner did not enter and [his] mind is in disorder. The practitioner and the patient/disease contradict each other. Hence the patient/disease is not healed." Zhang Zhicong: "This indicates that the practitioner did not guard the spirit. The classic states: 'Whenever one wishes to carry out a correct piercing, one must first order the spirit.' In the present case, a crude practitioner did not know the Way of the needles and stones." Hua Shou: "Without proper qi, drugs cannot move [through the body] and without proper qi, needles cannot eliminate [anything]. Hence it is stated: The Way of needles and stones is such that when the essence spirit enters and the mind is ordered, then a disease can be cured. If the essence spirit leaves [its proper realm] and if the mind dissipates, one may employ needle and stones, but the disease will not be healed." 986/38: "Because the patient does not know how to nourish his life, but gives rein to his desires, he causes his mind to weaken. His spirit qi disperses and his diseases cannot be cured. Hence it is clear why the nature of a disease in its initial phase appears as a weakening of the essence spirit which is unable to actively support the treatment. Subsequently, the spirit qi disperses and shows no reaction whatsoever to the treatment. Hence the meaning of 'the spirit does not effect [anything]' is: The essence spirit

In the present case, the essence is destroyed and the spirit has departed,[18]
the camp [qi] and the guard [qi] cannot be gathered again.
Why?[19]

14-87-6
If cravings and desires have no limits,
if anxiety and suffering find no end,
the essence qi will be destroyed,
the camp [qi] is impeded,[20] and
the guard [qi] vanishes.

Hence,
the spirit leaves and the disease does not heal."[21]

14-87-7
[Huang] Di:
"Now,
when a disease begins to emerge,

---

weakens, the spirit qi disperses and cannot provide any appropriate response to the treatment." 1670/37 agrees.

18 On the various meanings of 去 in the *Nei jing*, see 2111. The meaning it identifies here is that of 渙散, "to disperse."

19 This is a rare case of what appears to be a rhetorical question built in Qi Bo's argument. We have considered whether this is a corrupted passage originally worded 帝曰 何者岐伯曰嗜欲… However, nowhere else in the *Su wen* a question posed by Huang Di is worded 何者.

20 See Wang Bing's comment on the term 泣 in *Su wen* 10: 泣謂血行不利, "泣 is to say: the blood cannot pass freely."

21 Wang Bing: "Essence and spirit are the sources of life. Camp and guard [qi] are the rulers of the qi. When the rulers of the qi fail to assist [the therapy], when the sources of life are depleted again and again and when the spirit does not maintain its internal residence, how could a disease be healed?" Zhang Jiebin: "The kidneys store the essence; the essence is yin. The heart stores the spirit; the spirit is yang. When the essence is destroyed and when the spirit has left, then yin and yang are both ruined, outer and inner are both injured, camp and guard [qi] cannot fullfill their functions. This is the reason. Because today's people indulge in pleasures and suffer beyond limits and because they fail to receive [proper] nourishment, they arrive at a stage where the essence qi is destroyed, the [flow of the] camp [qi] is rough and the guard [qi] is eliminated, so that no strength is left."

it is extremely feeble and extremely fine[22] and
it will first enter the skin and produce conglomerations there.

Today, all the good practitioners state:
A disease that is fully developed is called 'opposition.'
At this time, needles and [pointed] stones[23] cannot [be employed to] restore
order and
good drugs cannot reach there.

Today, all the good practitioners
have grasped the [appropriate] laws and
they guard the respective numbers.[24]

Relatives, elder and younger brothers, persons far and near,[25]
their tones and voices are heard daily by one's ears and
the five [colors of their] complexion are seen daily by one's eyes,[26]

and if [their] diseases are not healed,
[one might ask], too, why [everyone remained] inactive, [and why] no [treat-
ment was carried out] early?"[27]

14-87-11
Qi Bo:
"[When it is said]

---

22 Gao Shishi: "微 stands for 輕, 'light;' 精 stands for 細, 'fine.' " Zhang Jiebin: "極微
is to say: light and superficial, not yet deep. 極精 is to say: whole, not yet in disorder.
At this time, treating the [disease] is very easy." Wu Kun: "That is to say, at a time
when the disease is very minute and easy to cure." Mori: "The *Guang ya* 廣雅 defines
精 as 小, 'small.' "

23 It remains unclear whether 鍼石 refers to "needle stones", i.e., pointed stones, or
to "needles and [pointed] stones" reflecting the parallel existence of acupuncture by
piercing and bloodletting by means of pointed stones during the Han era. See also *Su
wen* 04, 11, and 13.

24 Gao Jiwu/234: "數 stands for 術, 'technique.' "

25 Perhaps: persons who are more or less close to one.

26 Gao Jiwu/213 interprets 遠 as strengthening the meaning of 近, giving the phrase
the meaning of 親近.

27 Lin Yi et al.: "Another version has 謂, 'to say,' instead of 暇." Zhang Jiebin: "暇
stands for 慢事, 'acting slowly.' " 1609 agrees. Gao Jiwu/449: "何暇 stands for 可謂
'can be said.' " 230/54: "何暇不早乎 is: 'why is [a treatment] delayed and not [carried
out] early?' 暇 is 閑, 'unoccupied.' Here it has the meaning of 拖延, 'to delay.' "

'The disease is the root and
the practitioner is the tip.
If tip and root do not match,
the evil qi does not yield,'
[then] this means just the same."[28]

[Huang] Di:
"There are [diseases] which do not emerge from the finest body hair;
[instead,] the yang [qi] is exhausted in the five depots.[29]

The [body] liquids fill the bulwarks.[30]
The *po*-soul resides alone.

---

28 Wang Bing: "This is to say, the physician and the disease do not correspond to
each other." Yang Shangshan: "標 stands for 末, 'end.' Diseases caused by wind, cold,
summerheat, and dampness, they constitute the root; the needle-stones and liquid
drugs employed by the practitioner, they constitute the tip." Zhang Jiebin: "A dis-
ease/patient must receive treatment to be cured. Hence the disease is the root and the
practitioner is the tip. Now, when disease/patient and treatment/physician correspond
to each other, their sentiments penetrate each other and this leads to their victory.
There will be help and no disease will remain uncured. .. If they do not correspond to
each other, the evil qi cannot be subdued and this is the reason why the disease is not
cured." 2469/6: "病 refers to the patient; 工 refers to the physician." See also 1129/3
for a discussion of previous interpretations.

29 Lin Yi et al.: "The Quan Yuanqi edition and the *Tai su* have 傷, 'harmed,' instead of 陽, 'yang.' This makes sense, too." 972/47: "以 stands for 為; 竭 does not
mean 'exhausted' here, it stands for 阻塞, 'blocked.' It should be read as 遏, 'to block.'
Hence the entire phrase should read 五藏陽為遏, 'the yang [qi] in the five depots is
blocked.'" 1716/79: "以 was identical in ancient times with 已, 'already.' The character
links 'yang' with 'exhausted.'" 230/54: "That is, these diseases do not emerge because
of an affection from outside the body. Rather their origin lies in a blockage of the yang
qi in the five depots preventing its spread [through the organism]."

30 The *Tai su*, ch. 19, Zhi tang yao 知湯藥, has 虛廓 instead of 充郭. Yang Shangshan commented: "廓 is 空, 'empty.'" Zhang Jiebin: "郭 refers to chest and abdomen.
Su wen 35 states: 'Chest and abdomen are the bulwarks of the depots and palaces. ..
Today the yang qi is exhausted and cannot move through and harmonize the water
ways. Hence the [body] liquids move disorderly and fill the bulwarks." 916/52: "郭
stands for 韓, 'hides with the hair removed.' 充郭, therefore, is 充皮, 'fills the skin.'"
Gao Jiwu/42 agrees with the basic identity of 郭 with 韓, but acknowledges its meta-
phoric usage with the meaning of 'bulwark' here. Tanba: "Gao Shishi interpreted 郭
as identical with 廓, in the sense of 空廓, 'empty.' *Ling shu* 65 has 'The guard qi does
not circulate, hence 腸胃充郭, intestines and stomach are empty.' From this it appears
that Gao Shishi's commentary is correct."

The essence is weakened in the interior.[31]
The qi has vanished from the exterior.[32]

There is no use to protect the physical appearance with clothing.[33]
In this [situation the movements of] the four extremities are hectic and they excite the center.[34]

This is [a situation where] the qi is blocked inside,[35]
and the physical appearance is altered outside.[36]

---

31 537/26: "The two characters 孤精 have been mistakenly reversed in their sequence; it should be 精孤. 精孤 corresponds to the phrase 氣耗 further down. 孤 has the meaning of 虛, 'depleted.'" If one were to follow this argument, the phrase should read "The essence is depleted inside."

32 Zhang Jiebin: "When there is no qi in the essence, then the essence is solitary inside. When there is no yang in the yin, then the qi dissipates towards outside." Yang Shangshan: "Even though the essence of the five depots is present, there is little qi that is exhaled and inhaled outside. 耗 stands for 少, 'little.' The lung is harmed and exhausted."

33 Ma Shi: "In this case the solitary essence is present inside and the yang qi dissipates outside. The physical body is soft and weak and cannot be covered with clothing." Yang Shangshan: "When the skin is numbed and cannot be touched by clothing, the spleen is harmed and exhausted. 保 stands for 近, 'to approach.'" 1609/37: "That is to say, the body is swollen to such an extent that the clothes one used to wear do not fit any longer." Gao Jiwu/579: "與 is to be interpreted here as 被 (particle indicating passive voice): 'A swollen body cannot be covered by clothing.'"

34 Zhang Jiebin: "The four extremities are the basis of all yang. When the yang qi does not move, the four extremities have much yin and are swollen to tightness. These swellings result from yin blockages; because the yang qi inside the stomach cannot check the water and because lung and kidneys are both ill, this is followed by panting and coughing. Hence there is 'movement inside.'" Zhang Qi: "The 'four extremities' are hands and feet. 急 refers to a fast movement. When the four extremities are moved rapidly, the inner qi is set in motion and one pants hastily."

35 537/26: "拒 has the meaning of 困, 'besieged.' 拒 is identical here with 距, 'to oppose.' 氣拒于内 is to say: the qi is impeded inside; it cannot move normally."

36 Lin Yi et al.: "The character 施 may be a mistake." Qian Chaochen-88/279: "Lin Yi et al. states: 'The character 施 may be a mistake.' Mr Gu states: 'The character 施 stands for 弛, 'to relax.' It is not a mistake.'" Fu Weikang & Wu Hongzhou/274: "施 should be read as 易, 'to change,' 改變, 'to change.' The meaning is: the water qi causes changes in the physical body." Zhang Yizhi et al.: "The *Ji yun* 集韻 states: 施 is 改易, 'to alter.'" The *Er ya* 爾雅, Shi gu 釋詁, has: "弛 is 易, 'to change.'"

How is this treated?"[37]

14-88-3
Qi Bo:
"Restore the balanced order of weight and beam.[38]

---

37 Wang Bing: " 'Does not emerge via the body's finest hair' is to say: they emerge
from within [the body]. The yin qi abounds internally; the yang qi is exhausted. Because it is interrupted [in its flow], it cannot enter into the abdomen. Hence [the text]
states: 'the yang [qi] in the five depots is exhausted.' 'Liquids' refers to water. 充 is 滿,
'full.' 郭 is 皮, 'skin.' Yin [qi] accumulates in the center [of the body is to say: the center of the body] is filled with water qi causing distension. [The water qi] rises to attack
the lung; the lung qi is lost to a degree that is dangerous. The *po*-soul is the spirit of
the lung. When the kidneys are harmed by water, the child (i.e., the kidneys) fails to
assist its mother (i.e., the lung). Hence [the text] states: 'its *po*-soul resides by itself.'
Now, the yin essence is harmed and decreases inside; the yang qi vanishes outside. As
a result, the triple burner closes. There is overflow, but the water ways are impassable.
Water fills the skin; the body is clogged and swells. Hence [the text] states: 'The physical appearance cannot be covered with clothes.' In such situations, the [movement
in the] vessels in the four extremities is frequent and urgent and internally there is a
drumming movement in the lung. A 'lung movement' is to say: the [breathing of] qi is
urgent with coughing. That is, in all such cases water qi is closed in inside the abdominal membrane and swelling causes distension in the outside of the body's physical
appearance. One should carry out a thorough investigation of tip and root to grasp the
[nature of] the [situation]. 四極 refers to 四末, 'the four extremities.' "

38 Wang Bing: "平治權衡 is to say: investigate whether the [movement in the] vessels is at the surface or in the depth. When the [movement in the] vessels is at the
surface, [the disease] is in the outer regions; when the [movement in the] vessels is in
the depth, it is in the internal regions. When it is in the internal regions, drain it; when
it is in the exterior regions, [eliminate it] through sweating. Hence [the text] states
further below: 'open the demon gate, clear the pure depot.' "Wu Kun: "The pattern of
restoring the balance should resemble weight and beam. Yin and yang must be equally
balanced; neither should be lighter or heavier, fall or rise." 537: "The *Tai su*, 知湯藥,
has 卒治 instead of 平治... 平 is a mistake for 卒 and 卒, in turn, is a mistake for 雜.
For example, [the title] *Shang han za bing lun* 傷寒雜病論 has been changed to 傷
寒卒病論. Following the character 雜, the character 以 is missing. In ancient times
the character 於 was written as 于. 于 and 平 are very similar in form. Some copyist
has transferred the character 平 to the begin of the phrase and thereby created the
erroneous wording 平治於權衡. From the context [it is obvious that Huang] Di asks:
'How is this to be treated?' Qi Bo responds: '[There are] various [patterns] for treatment..'. This meaning corresponds to *Su wen* 12." For further details of the argument,

Remove what is densely compacted, cut out the old.[39]

---

see there. 475/42 identifies 平 as 卒, in the meaning of 急, "quickly." 1934/35: "平 is identical with 辨, 'to distinguish between.' .. In the author's preface to the *Shang han lun* it is stated: 并平脈辨証, 'Distinguish between the [movements in the] vessels and discrimate between pathoconditions.' This is an example of an identical usage of 平 and 辨. 平治於權衡 should be read as follows: 'In estimating (權衡)the nature of a disease, one should distinguish between pathoconditions and [then] conduct the treatment.'" 2049/43 and 1978/47 agree. In contrast, 2395/17 identifies the phrase 平治於權衡 as referring to a general therapeutic principle of restoring a balance (平) and calls attention to several related statements in *Su wen* treatises 20, 71, 74, and *Ling shu* 5.

39 Lin Yi et al.: "The *Tai su* has 莖, 'stem,' instead of 莝." Wang Bing: "去宛陳莝 is to say: remove water that has accumulated over long, just as one cannot allow grasses and stems to remain in the body for long." Zhang Jiebin: "宛 stands for 積, 'accumula-tion.' 陳 stands for 久, 'old.' 莝 stands for 斬草, 'to cut grass.' That is to say, eliminate long-term accumulations of water qi, that is, you wish to eliminate them as if you were cutting grass." 2767/39: "莝 is the verb and 陳 is the object. This corresponds to the verb-object relationship of 去宛. The entire phrase 去宛陳莝 has the meaning: 'discard coagulations of blood and eliminate accumulations of water.'" This argument is supported in 2767/39 by a reference to the rhyme structure of the phrase. See there for details. Zhang Yizhi et al.: "去 and 莝 are verbs; 宛 and 陳 are nouns. 去宛 is: remove blood clots. 莝陳 is: diminish accumulations of water. When the *Tai su* has 莖 instead of 莝, this is probably a mistake." Gao Shishi: "莝 stands for 腐, 'rotten.' 去宛陳莝 is to say: When the body liquids fill the bulwarks, one must eliminate that which has been rotten over a long time." Zhang Zhicong agrees. For a detailed argument supporting Gao Shishi and Zhang Zhicong, see 1446/58+40. See also 305 and 117. 1508/11: "Li Jinyong 李今庸 has pointed out: the three characters 去宛陳 originally constituted one sentence. This is a therapeutic pattern of bloodletting by piercing the network vessels. Hence the phrase 宛陳 is associated with blood clottings in the conduits and network [vessels]. But there are other scholars who identify 宛陳 as accumulations of water. Either [identification] makes sense." 1617/35, in a detailed argument, rejects the identification of a three character phrase 去宛陳; 962/58 and 3-748/56 support the identification of a three character phrase and identify 去宛陳 as a reference to an ancient blood-letting therapy. For details, see there. 1506/7 adduces textual evidence from the *Su wen* and *Ling shu* to support the blood-letting inter-pretation. A lengthy argument in favor of this interpretation is offered also in Wang Hongtu et al./199, pointing out the occurrence of a similar phrase 宛陳則除之 in *Su wen* 54, *Ling shu* 01, and *Ling shu* 03. 1595/45: "陳 has the meaning of 陣, 'to battle.' It is used here in the meaning of 'to attack.' 莝 means 'rotten.' Hence the entire phrase means: 'Eliminate accumulations and attack what is rotten.'" For a detailed discussion of various previous interpretations see 2864.

Slightly move the four extremities.[40]
[Let the patient wear] warm clothing.[41]

Apply a misleading piercing to the [pertinent][42] locations
to restore the [patient's] physical appearance.[43]
Open the demon gates and

---

40 Ma Shi: "四極 stands for 四支, 'the four limbs.'" Wu Kun: "Movement makes the liquids flow. Hence one asks [the patient] to slightly move the four extremities." 743 follows the *Shuo wen* and identifies 微 as 隱行, "hidden movement." Because of a close relationship between the four extremities and the spleen and because of clinical considerations, 743 suggests an interpretation of 微動四極 as a reference to stimulate the [hidden] movement of the yang qi in the spleen. For details see there. See also 2303/52. 1203/15, on the basis of ancient textual evidence, identifies 微 as a reference to edema and 動 as meaning 發生, "to emerge." 微動, therefore, means "edemas emerge." 莝, in the interpretation by 1203, has the meaning "to cut [grass]." Hence the entire phrase is to be read as 去宛陳, 莝微動, "remove accumulations and eliminate edemas." See there for details of the argument. 475/42: "In front of 微動四極, the two characters 是以, 'therefore,' are missing. The two characters 溫衣 are unrelated to the preceding and following text; maybe some text is missing here. According to the passages 寒飲食寒衣, 溫食熱衣, etc. in *Su wen* 22, the two characters 熱食, 'hot food,' may be missing in front of 溫衣." 1203/15 suggests a reading as 四極溫衣: "Because patients with edemas often suffer from an insufficiency of yang qi, the four extremities show signs of adversely moving cold. Hence one must keep the four extremities warm and apply a misleading piercing to them to let rotten liquids flow off."

41 Wang Bing: "微動四極 is to say: slightly move the four extremities and let the yang qi gradually move again. Hence [the text] states further: 'warm [with] clothing.'" Zhang Jiebin: "Warm clothing is to assist the yang in the external regions of the muscles. This way, yin coagulations are easily dispersed." 2414/68 reads "warm clothing, misleading piercing" as a reference to an acupuncture technique whereby the patient has to remain dressed and the needles are inserted through the clothing. The purpose is to have the needles remain inserted for an extended period without the patient catching a cold. For details, see there.

42 1193/8: "其 refers to the edema here." For an explanation of the notion of a "misleading piercing", see *Su wen* 63.

43 Wang Bing: "When the conduit vessels are full, there is an overflow in the network vessels. When there is an overflow in the network vessels, the [patient] is to be needled misleadingly to regulate his network vessels, so that his physical appearance returns to its original condition, with no swelling. Hence [the text] states: 'apply a misleading piercing to restore his physical appearance.'" Zhang Jiebin: "Then one carries out a misleading piercing in that one choses the left [side for piercing] to treat the right and choses the right [side for piercing] to treat the left. This way the stagnations in the large network [vessels] are eliminated."

clean the pure palace[44] and the
essence will recover in due time.[45]

When the five yang [qi] have spread [everywhere],
this clears the five depots and opens the passage through them.
Hence essence is generated by itself and

---

44 Zhang Jiebin: "The 'demon gates' refers to the openings for the sweat. The lung
controls the skin and the body hair; it stores the *po* and is associated with the yin.
Hence one speaks of 'demon gates.' The 'pure palace' is the bladder. Above it has no
entrance opening, but below it has an exit hole. Dregs and filth cannot enter it, hence
it is called the pure palace." Zhang Zhicong: "The 'demon gates' are the openings for
the body hair. 'To open the demon gates' is to induce sweating. 'To cleanse the pure
palace' is to drain the bladder. If one opens the demon gates, then the lung orifice
is passable and the water-liquids disperse. This is the so-called 'when the external
orifices are open, then the internal orifices are passable; when the upper orifices are
passable, then the lower orifices are drained.'" Zhang Qi: "This is the same meaning
as in the *Jin gui* [*yao lüe*] 金匱 [要略], [where it is stated:] 'In case of swelling above
the waist, one must induce sweating; in case of swelling below the waist, one must
stimulate urination.'" 17/37: "The *Ju yu* 舉隅 identifies the character 鬼 as a corrupt
version of 魄. 郭老 comments: But [the 'demon gate' here] is different from the 魄門
in *Su wen* 11. The 魄門 there refers to the 糟粕之門, the 'gate of the waste,' (i.e., the
anus). Here, the 魄門 refers to the openings through which the sweat leaves." 2767/38
agrees and refers to *Su wen* 3 and *Su wen* 9 for further evidence. In contrast, 1326/24
identifies the "demon gate" with the anus and interprets "to open the demon gates" as
referring to both induced sweating and induced urination and defecation." 1840/73:
"The character 鬼 has two pronunciations/meanings. The first is 魄, *po*. Because the
lung controls the skin and the body hair and because it stores the *po*, hence the pores
for the sweat are called 鬼/魄門, 'demon/*po* gate.' The second reading is 鬼, *gui*. In
ancient times, the people mentioned 神 and 鬼 as a pair of opposites. The 'spirit' was
yang and the 'demon' was yin. The lung controls the skin and the hair and is associated
with the yin. Hence the pores for the sweat are called 'demon gates.' Nowadays, both
readings exist in traditional Chinese medicine." 636/48 rejects the traditional reading
of "to open the demon gates" and "to cleanse the pure palace" as two separate therapeutic interventions, i.e., causing a patient to sweat and induce urination. Rather, the
author sees these two phrases a referring to one strategy against swellings caused by
water, i.e., stimulate the passage of lung qi and open the passageways of water. For
details, see there.

45 Zhang Zhicong: "服 stands for 復, 'to recover.' [That is] 'the essence will recover
over time.'" Zhang Qi: "[This is] 精自復, 'the essence will recover as a result.'" Zhang
Jiebin: "服 stands for 行, 'to move.' When the water qi is eliminated, the true essence
moves. When the yin evil is eliminated, then the five yang spread. 'The five yang' refers
to the stomach qi in the five depots." 1422/39: "服 can be read as 治, 'to govern,' 職,
'to be in charge,' here. Hence the entire passage should read: 'The essence of the five
depots rules internally when its time [of abundance] has come.'"

the physical appearance will be marked by itself by abundance [again].
Bones and flesh will protect each other and
the grand qi will be balanced."⁴⁶

[Huang] Di: "Good!"

<hr />

46 Wang Bing: " 'Open the demon gate' is: open the dark palaces and expel the qi.
'Five yang' refers to the yang qi of the five depots. 'Clean the pure palace' is to say:
drain water from the bladder. When the [movement in the] vessels has [returned to]
harmony, then the qi of the five essences will – after some time – yield to the authority
of the kidneys. Now, when the yang [qi] of the five depots gradually begins to flow
outside the five depots again, the unclean qi will be removed. This then causes the essence and the marrow to emerge again and the physical appearance as well as the flesh
will return to abundance. Once the depots and the palaces are back to harmony, the
qi of bones and flesh protect each other. The qi of the great conduit vessels is balanced
again." Zhang Jiebin: "服 is 行, 'to pass.' " Zhang Qi: "服 is 復, 'to return.' " Zhang Zhicong: "The 'grand qi' is the qi controlled by the major yang." Ma Shi: "The 'grand qi'
stands for 大氣, 'major qi.' This is the proper qi." Tanba agrees with Ma Shi. 537/27:
"巨氣 is 拒氣, 'to block the qi.' 拒氣乃平 is to say: originally the qi was impeded inside.
The triple burner failed to send [it through the organism] and this resulted in swelling.
After a harmonizing treatment, the qi dynamics reach everywhere and the water can
move downwards. Hence [the text] states: What is blocked is brought back to normal."

15-89-2
Huang Di asked:
"I have heard:
the [texts] *To Estimate and Measure* and *The Strange and the Normal*,
what they expound is not identical.[1]
How are their [contents] to be used?"[2]

Qi Bo responded:
"As for *To Estimate and Measure*,
this [text expounds how] to measure whether a disease is at the surface or in
the depth.
As for *The Strange and the Normal*, this [text] discusses strange diseases.[3]

Please, let me speak about the perfect numbers of the Way.[4]

---

1 Zhang Jiebin: "'What they signify is different' [is to say:] there are those that
discuss diseases, there are those that discuss vessel [movements] and complexion,
there are those that discuss the depots and palaces and there are those that discuss
yin and yang."

2 Wang Bing did not comment on the meaning of 揆度奇恆; from his comments
further below it appears, though, as if he had assumed a literal meaning: "to measure/
estimate what is normal and what is strange." In contrast, Ma Shi: "五色脈變 and 揆
度奇恆 are titles of ancient medical classics." 252/38: "It is not difficult to see that the
揆度 and the 奇恆 of which [Huang Di states] 'I have heard,' does not refer to an
oral transmission but to texts transmitted in writing. The answer given by Qi Bo is an
explanation of [the contents of these] texts." 1877/15 agrees.

3 Gao Jiwu/212: "*Su wen* 15 states: '奇恆 [discusses] strange diseases.' Hence Zhang
Zhicong: '奇恆 means: different from what is normal.' *Su wen* 63 also speaks of 奇病,
'strange diseases.' Wang Bing commented: 'Diseases in the blood network are called
奇邪, 'strange evil.'"" 2262/43: "In the sentence 奇恆者, 言奇病也 there must be some
part of the text missing. It should be 言奇病恆病也. 奇 and 恆 are opposites. Strange
diseases are 奇病, normal [diseases] are 恆病. If during a yang disease one notices a
yin [movement in the] vessels, this is 奇; if during a yang disease one notices a yang
[movement in the] vessels, this is 恆. The physician needs to recognize, from examining the [movement in the] vessels and the complexion, whether [the disease] is normal or strange and only then does he know whether prognosis is favorable or not."

4 The *Tai su* has 謂, 'to say,' instead of 請, 'please'. In this case, the subsequent phrase
could be read in conjunction with the preceding text: "As for *To Estimate and Measure*, this [text expounds how] to measure whether a disease is at the surface or in the

The Five Complexions,
The Changes in the [Movements in the] Vessels,
To Estimate and Measure, and
The Strange and the Normal,
the Way [expounded in all these texts] is one.[5]

The spirit turns around, it does not go backwards.
When it goes backwards, then it no [longer] turns around.
In this case [one] has lost [one's vital] mechanism.[6]

---

depth. As for *The Strange and the Normal*, this [text discusses] strange diseases. [Both texts] speak about the perfect numbers below heaven." Yang Shangshan: "數 is 理, 'principle.'" Zhang Yizhi et al.: "*Dao de jing* 5 has 多言數窮. A comment states: 數 is 理, 'principle.'"

5 Wang Bing: "一, 'One,' refers to the correspondence of complexion and [movement in the] vessels. If one knows the correspondence of complexion and [movement in the] vessels, then one is able to measure the strange and the normal." Lin Yi et al.: "According to the Quan Yuanqi edition, 請 is 謂." Zhang Jiebin: "The 一 is simply the 'spirit' referred to below." Ma Shi: "*Changes in the Five [Colors of] Complexion and in the [Movement in the] Vessels* and *To Estimate and Measure the Strange and the Normal* are book titles." Gu Guangguang agrees.

6 Wang Bing: "Blood and qi are the spirit qi. *Su wen* 26 states: 'Blood and qi are the spirit of man; they must be nourished carefully.' Now, as long as blood and qi follow their proper course, as long as the four seasons substitute each other [in their usual order], as long as the four rulings follow a circular sequence, and as long as the five qi do not usurp each other's function, under such circumstances 'the spirit follows a circular movement and does not turn back.' 回, 'to turn back,' is to say 卻行, 'to move backwards.' Now, blood and qi follow the rulings [of the five agents]; they do not [ordinarily] associate with a move backwards. If they move back, this is acting against normality; if they act against normality, then they turn back and do not continue their circulatory movement. If they turn back and do not continue their circulatory movement, then [the patient] has lost the dynamics of his vital qi. How to explain this? Now, when the wood weakens, then the fire rules. When the fire weakens, then the soil rules. When the soil weakens, then the metal rules. When the metal weakens, then the water rules. When the water weakens, then the wood rules. When this [cycle] comes to an end, it begins anew. When this circulation occurs, this is what is meant by 'the spirit is engaged in a circulatory movement and does not turn back.' If the wood weakens, and the water rules, if the water weakens and the metal rules, if the metal weakens and the soil rules, if the soil weakens and the fire rules, if the fire weakens and the wood rules, this is what is meant by 'it turns back and does not continue its circulatory movement.'" Zhang Jiebin: "The spirit is the principle of life and death; it is the force that does not cease. As long as the five qi continue their circular movement, and do not leave their regular order, the 'spirit circulates and does not turn back.' However, once it move backwards, it opposes its normal state and can no longer circulate. In this case it has lost its power of generating qi." Wu Kun: " 'Spirit' refers to the

15-89-5
The essentials of the perfect numbers are at hand and yet subtle.[7]
They are inscribed on jade tablets.

---

true and principal spirit of heaven. 轉 is to revolve like a handle. 回 is to oppose and to act against. 機 is 樞機, 'vital power.' This is to say, as long as the true and principal spirit of heaven revolves like a handle, and as long as there is no counteraction and opposition, the life creating power does not come to a halt. This is like the cycle of [the five agents] wood, fire, soil, metal, and water. When it has completed its cycle, it begins anew. This is [meant by] '[the spirit] continues a circular movement and does not turn back.' If among the five [agents] there is one instance of counteraction and opposition, then this is called 'moving back.' A backwards movement blocks further circular movement. The passage of the five agents comes to a halt, and the principle of life is destroyed. This then is the loss of the true vital powers of the movements and transformations of heaven." Zhang Zhicong: "As for 'spirit,' this is the spirit qi of the five depots and of the blood vessels. Now, the spleen is a solitary depot; it is the central soil and provides the four side [regions] with moisture. As long as the five depots are supplied with qi, they are involved in a circular movement and there is no turning back. If they oppose [the normal course] and transmit [qi] to that [agent] by which they are overcome, this is [what the text calls] 'they turn back and do not continue their circulatory movement.' In this case they have lost the dynamics of mutual generation and circular movement." 2030/56: "The meaning is: The fact that the periods of resting and dominance of the five agents in the qi of the depots of the human body can parallel, and do not oppose, the progression of the five agents [as it appears] in the four seasons depends on the correct adjustment of the 'spirit power' ruling the interior of the human body. Hence, phenomena indicating opposition, backward movement, or reverse circulation, demonstrate that the 'spirit power' has lost its proper function, which, in turn, is a sign of life coming to an end." See also 514 for a discussion of this passage within the context of notions of circulation in early Chinese philosophy. Zhang Yizhi et al.: "回 should be interpreted as 亂, 'disorder.'"

7 Wang Bing: "This is to say, the essential Way of the changes of the five complexions and five [movements in the] vessels is close to the normal course of heaven, and at the same time it is subtle and mysterious." Zhang Jiebin: "The meaning of 至數 is rather broad; it is outlined in *Su wen* 9, 66, 74, 68, 67, and 71. That is, the Way of heaven and man [is such that] if there is qi it will arrive, and if it arrives it follows [specific] numbers. The five complexions and the five [movements in the] vessels of man arrive only because of qi. Hence, no matter whether an excess or an insufficiency is concerned, there are always [specific] arrival numbers involved. If one knows the arrival numbers of heaven and earth, one can also know the arrival numbers in man." Cheng Shide et al.: "Lao zi comments: 數 is to say 理數, 'principal numbers.' 至數, then, are very important principal numbers. In the present context [至數] refers to complexion and [movement in the] vessels." Gao Jiwu/568: "以 has the meaning here of 可是, 'but,' 'nevertheless.'"

[The text] is named *Combined Jade Mechanism*.[8]
Appearance and complexion, how it appears above and below, on the left and on the right,
all this [can be found] in[9] these essentials.[10]

If a faint complexion appears, decoctions[11] will master the cure.
An end is reached within ten days.[12]
If deep complexion appears, one must [resort to] prescriptions to

---

8 Wang Bing: "玉機 is the name of a [*Su wen*] treatise. This is to say, these essential instructions on turning in and revolution have been inscribed on jade tablets in agreement with *Su wen* 19." Yu Yue: "The character 合 is an incorrectly written duplication of the character 命." Beginning with 至數, 五色脈變, this passage is identical with a passage in *Su wen* 19. There, however, the ending is more elaborate: 著之玉版, 藏之藏府, 每旦讀之, 名曰玉機, "they have been inscribed on jade tablets; they have been stored in the depots and palaces; they are read every morning. They are called *Jade Mechanism*." Since the structure of this passage corresponds, in *Su wen* 19, to a preceding paragraph, it may be assumed that it was quoted in *Su wen* 15 from *Su wen* 19. Hence, as Yu Yue pointed out already, the character 合 in the wording of *Su wen* 15 may be an erroneous insertion. However, Zhang Yizhi et al.: "The *Tai su* has 命曰合生機 instead of 命曰合玉機. Yang Shangshan commented: 'It was titled 合于養生之機也.' If one follows the *Tai su*, then the character 合 does not have to be discarded."

9 In contrast, Cheng Shide et al.: "在 stands for 察, 'to examine.' "

10 Wang Bing: "容色 is 他氣, 'other [than normal] qi.' For example, if a red, yellow, white or black complexion [rather than a green complexion] appears in the liver-wood section, these are all called 'other [than normal] qi.' The same applies to the remaining depots. Observations should be directed at the locations above and below, left and right of the hall of brilliance (i.e., the nose). Hence [the text] states: 'Each is at its essential [location].' " Wu Kun: "容 stands for 面容, 'facial expression.' 色 stands for the five complexions. 要 refers to the locations that are ruled by the outer manifestations of the [condition of the] depots. That is to say, in the facial expression, the five complexions appear externally, either above or below, either on the left or on the right. Each is ruled by its respective depot, and has its essential location." Lin Yi et al.: "The Quan Yuanqi edition had 客, 'visitor,' instead of 容." 1126/10: "容 is a mistake for 客, 'visitor.' " Qian Chaochen-90/85: "From Wang Bing's interpretation of 容色 as 他氣 it is obvious that the original text had 客色, 'visitor complexion.' When Wang Bing wrote his comment, the *Su wen* did not have the mistaken 容 yet. Today, even Wang Bing's comment has 容. This shows that after Wang Bing someone tried to 'correct' his statement, and erroneously exchanged 容 for 客." We interpret 要 as a reference to the "essentials of the perfect numbers" mentioned above.

11 Ma Shi: "According to *Su wen* 14, these liquids are prepared from the five grains; they are different from the liquid remedies of later times."

12 Wang Bing: "When the complexion is shallow, the disease is light. Hence it ends within ten days."

master the cure.[13]

An end is reached within twenty one days.

If a very deep [complexion] appears, wines[14] will master the cure.

An end is reached within one hundred days.

When the complexion has faded away and when the face is emaciated, do not treat.[15]

A complete end is reached within one hundred days.[16]

---

13 Wang Bing: "When the complexion is deep, the disease is serious." Zhang Jiebin interprets 齊 as identical with 劑, "prescription." Wu Kun interprets 齊 as "together:" "Above, the text [states:] when the complexion is shallow, one treats with liquids; further below the text [states:] when the complexion is very deep, one treats it with wines. Here [the text] states that the complexion is deep. That is, it is neither shallow nor very [deep]. Hence one must resort to liquids and wines, and apply both together in treatment. The time until the disease comes to an end is twice of that when [the complexion is] shallow." 2722/44: "必齊 is an error for 火齊. Above the text speaks of 湯液, below it refers to 醪醴. The argument is stringent only if we interpret 必齊 as 火齊, 'fire prescriptions.'" (See also *Su wen* 14) 1262/79: "A Japanese scholar has proposed to identify 必 as 泌, 'to gush forth.' 必齊, then, are the juices squeezed from fresh drugs for medicinal use. This makes some sense." Sun Yirang: "The character 必 expresses a necessity. 齊 stands for 和劑, 'formula.' 齊 and 劑 were used interchangeably in ancient times. These would be the common meanings. However, in the present context they make little sense. 必齊 is to be read in one line with 湯液 and 醪醴. Both here and in *Su wen* 14, 必 is to be read as 火; the shape of the two characters is very similar in seal script, hence such errors can occur easily. The *Shi ji* 史記, Cang gong zhuan 倉公傳, has 飲以火劑湯. 火劑湯 is to say: decoctions prepared by boiling several drugs. In the present treatise, 'hot liquids' are decoctions prepared from the five grains. 'Fire formulas' are decoctions prepared by boiling toxic drugs." Zhang Yizhi et al.: "酒 should be 醴." For the interpretation of 必齊, see also *Su wen* chapter 14, note 13.

14 537/27: "The character 酒 is an error for 醴."

15 Wang Bing: "If the complexion appears very deep, and gives an impression of destruction, and if the flesh of the face is emaciated, no treatment is possible." Yu Chang: "色夭 is: 色白, 'white complexion.' *Ling shu* 61 states: 色夭然白. That is the proof. The reason is, a white complexion must be accompanied by a qi of moisture and glossiness. In case of a white complexion that is not accompanied by a qi of moisture and glossiness, this is called 色夭." The *Tai su* has: 其色赤面兌, 不為治. Yang Shangshan commented: "兌 is 尖小. That is to say, the face is emaciated and has no flesh." Tanba Genken 丹波元堅: "Both main text and [Yang Shangshan's] commentary are difficult to follow."

16 Wang Bing: "When the complexion does not imply destruction, and when the face is not emaciated, a treatment may lead to an end [of the disease] within one hundred days." Lin Yi et al.: "When the complexion appears tender and the face emaciated, even though one does not treat, [the disease] will come to a complete end within 100 days." Zhang Jiebin: "When the complexion is tender and the face emaciated, the

15-90-1

When the [movement in the] vessels is short und the qi [flow] is interrupted, [this indicates] death.[17]

When the disease is warmth with extreme depletion, [this signals] death.[18]

>The complexion, how it appears above and below, on the left and on the right, all this [can be found] in these essentials.<[19]

Above is opposition; below is compliance.[20]

---

spirit qi has left. Hence no treatment is possible. In the preceding passage, [end] refers to the end of the disease; here it refers to the end of life. [These two readings] must not be confused." 537/27: "Above the two characters 百日 six characters may be missing: 色不夭, 面不脫. If these six characters are not added, what sense does this statement make? First it says 'do not treat' and then it states 'comes to an end within one hundred days.' This is certainly a contradiction! Wang Bing's commentary is worded as if those additional six characters were still present." 2855/53: "The character 面 is most likely a mistake for 血, 'blood.' Evidence may be found in *Ling shu* 30: 血脫者色白夭然不澤. If the passage were worded 色夭血脫不治, it corresponded to the following passage 脈短氣絕死. The meaning is: Those whose complexion is tender have lost blood, and cannot be treated. Those whose [movement in the] vessels is short have their qi [circulation] interrupted, and this is a sign of imminent death. In the former case one observes the complexion, in the latter one feels the [movement in the] vessels. In the former [the text] speaks of blood, in the latter it speaks of qi. Complexion and [movement in the] vessels are opposites, and so are blood and qi."

17 Wang Bing: "A short [movement in the] vessels already indicates depletion; if, in addition, [the movement] is interrupted, the true qi is exhausted, and hence [the patient] must die." Zhang Jiebin: "When the [movement in the] vessels is short, and when the qi is cut off, this indicates depletion in the center and a loss of yang." Wu Kun: "When the [movement in the] vessels arrives in short strides, if it appears above and does not reach to the gate, the yang qi is cut off; if it appears below and does not reach to the gate, the yin qi is cut off."

18 Wang Bing: "If in case of extreme depletion, one suffers from warmth, the warm qi dries up the essence and the blood internally. Hence [the patient] dies." Wu Kun: "Persons suffering from warmth have their essence and their blood extremely depleted. As a result, there is no yin to overcome the warmth and the heat."

19 We consider this statement an erroneous duplication of the identical statement above.

20 Wang Bing: "A complexion visible below [results from] a qi caused by a disease. Hence [the text speaks of] compliance. A complexion visible above is a sign of a harmed spirit. Hence [the text speaks of] opposition." Ma Shi: "When the complexion appears above, the strength of the disease is just at its height. Hence this is opposition. When the complexion appears below, the strength of the disease has already weakened. Hence this is compliance."

In females, on the right is opposition, on the left is compliance.
In males, on the left is opposition, on the right is compliance.[21]

15-90-4
A change
to doubled yang [qi, this indicates] death,
to doubled yin [qi, this indicates] death.[22]
In case yin and yang turn into another [state],[23] treat where weight and beam
have lost their balance.[24]

---

21 Wang Bing: "Left is yang. Hence in males, the right is compliance and the left
is opposition. Right is yin. Hence in females, right is opposition, and left is compliance."

22 Wang Bing: "When the complexion is visible in females on the left, or in males
on the right, this is a change. When the complexion appears on the left side in males,
this is called doubled yang; when in females the complexion appears on the right side,
this is called doubled yin. When the qi has reached its peak, it will reverse. Hence all
[such cases] die." Gu Guangguang: "The character 易 is an erroneous insertion." Mori:
"Wang Bing interprets 易 as 變易. This makes no sense. 易 stands for the character
亦, 'too.' In commentaries to *Su wen* 37 and 60, Wang Bing stated: '易 is 亦.' 易 and
亦 were used interchangeably in ancient times." Zhang Yizhi et al.: "The character
易 summarizes what is called opposition and compliance above. Hence Wang Bing's
commentary. .. These, then, are the 'strange states/affairs' mentioned further down in
the text."

23 Lin Yi et al.: "In accordance with *Su wen* 05 this should read 陰陽反作 (i.e., 'yin
and yang act against normal')." Zhang Yizhi et al.: "*Su wen* 05 proves that 他 should
be 作, in the sense of 行, 'to pass.' " 2722/44 substantiates this view in more detail. In
contrast, 28/1: "According to a traditional viewpoint of Chinese medicine, diseases
appearing within one and the same organism may under complicated circumstances
produce mutually contradictory pathological changes, e.g., external cold with internal
heat, heat above and cold below, depletion of proper [qi] with repletion of evil [qi],
harm to both yin and yang, ascending and descending [qi] accompanying each other,
and so on. This, then, is 陰陽反他, 'yin and yang turn into another [state].' Hence
Gao Shishi stated: 'when yin and yang agree with each other, this is conformity; when
they turn into another [state], this is opposition.' The character 逆, 'opposition,' simply
indicates a dual pathology existing within one and the same organism in that ant-
agonistic pathological dynamics, i.e., yin and yang turning into another [state] and
opposing [each other], appear."

24 Wang Bing: "權衡相奪 is to say: If the two qi of yin and yang fail to achieve a
suitable distribution above and below, this is an aberration from their normal state.
In this case one must measure the qi, and adjust it as is suitable." Zhang Jiebin: "治在
權衡相奪 is to say: measure what is light and what is heavy, and take away [from the
latter] to achieve a balance."

These matters are dealt with by [the text] The Strange and the Normal.
These matters are dealt with by [the text] To Estimate and Measure.

A beating [movement in the] vessels [indicates] block and lameness, as well as an interaction of cold and heat.[25]

When the [movement in the] vessels is solitary, this is [a sign of] dissipated qi.[26]
When [the movement in the vessels] is depleted and if there is outflow, this is [a sign of] lost blood.
To be solitary is opposition; depletion is compliance.[27]

---

25 Wang Bing: "When the [movement in the] vessels strikes against one's hand, and when one suffers from block and lame hands and feet, all this is caused by interactions of cold and hot qi, not by evil qi or depletions and repletions." Zhang Jiebin: "搏脈 is a [movement in the] vessels due to abounding evil [qi] and weakened proper [qi], with yin and yang [qi] playing havoc. Hence there is block, lameness, and spells of interacting cold and heat." Tanba: "Wang Bing identifies an interaction of cold and heat as the cause of the disease of beating [movement in the] vessels, block, and lameness. However, this does not agree with the subsequent text. Hence one should follow Zhang Jiebin." Mori: "搏脈 is to say: there is not just one [movement in the] vessels. There are two [movements in the] vessels beating against each other. All cases of block and lameness result from an affection of blood and qi by evil [qi], with evil and proper [qi] being engaged in a fight."

26 Wang Bing: "All the [movements in the] vessels that have only an external but not an internal aspect, or those that have only an internal but not an external aspect, they are called 'solitary.' If they have both an external and an internal aspect, while the qi is insufficient, this is always called 'depleted and weak qi.'" Zhang Jiebin: "孤 is to say: 偏絕, 'unilaterally cut off.' That what is cut off cannot come to life again. Hence this is opposition. 'Depletion' is a term for insufficiency. That what is insufficient can still be resupplied. Hence it is called compliance."

27 Wang Bing: "What is solitary has nothing to lean on; hence this is called opposition. What is depleted and weak may recover. Hence this is called compliance." Gao Shishi: "虛泄 is to say: the vessel qi is depleted internally. There is no drumming movement." The Wu Kun edition has 濇, "rough," instead of 泄. Wu Kun commented: "When such a [movement in the] vessels arrives it has external [aspects] but no internal [aspects], this is called depletion; that is, the yang is depleted. In case of depletion, [the movement in the vessels] must be rough, and the patient suffers from loss of blood." Cheng Shide et al.: "There is no basis for Wu Kun's changing 泄 into 濇." 2767/39: "The character 氣 in the passage 脈弧為消氣 is an erroneous insert. Between the two characters 虛泄 the character 為 was omitted. With the wording 脈弧為消, 虛為泄為脫血. 弧為逆, 虛為從 both the literary style and the medical reasoning are logical and coherent." Gao Jiwu/254: "For 虛泄, the *Tai su* has 虛泄. In accordance with the preceding sentence 脈弧為消氣, the character 脈 appears to be missing here in front of 虛."

15-90-7
To practice the law [laid down] in *The Strange and the Normal*, one starts from
the major yin.[28]

If the movement [of the disease proceeds to a depot] which [the transmitting
depot can]not dominate, this is called opposition.
Opposition results in death.[29]
If the movement [proceeds to a depot] which [the transmitting depot] can
dominate, this is called compliance.
Compliance results in survival.[30]

---

28 Wang Bing: "Whenever [one follows] the laws of measuring the strange and
the normal, one first determines the proper qi of the four seasons in the [movement
in the] vessels at the major yin [location] of the qi-opening. Then one measures the
strange or normal state of the qi."

29 Wang Bing: "If [in the agent of] wood one observes a metal [movement in the]
vessels, if [in the agent of] metal one observes a fire [movement in the] vessels, if [in
the agent of] fire one observes a water [movement in the] vessels, if [in the agent
of] water one observes a soil [movement in the] vessels, if [in the agent of] soil one
observes a wood [movement in the] vessels, in all these cases the movement is that
which cannot be overcome. Hence it is called counteraction. This is injury without
end, hence counteraction results in death."

30 Wang Bing: "If [in the agent of] wood one observes [movements in the] vessels
associated with water, fire, or soil; if [in the agent of] fire one observes [movement in
the] vessels associated with metal, soil, or wood; if [in the agent of] soil one observes
[movements in the] vessels associated with metal, water or fire; if [in the agent of]
metal one observes [movements in the] vessels associated with soil, wood, or water;
if [in the agent of] water one observes [movements in the] vessels [associated with]
metal, fire, or wood, all these are [movements in the] vessels that can be overcome.
Hence one speaks of compliance. In case of compliance there is nothing by which one
could be overcome, killed, harmed, or defeated. Hence compliance results in survival."
2840/9: "According to the association of the five depots with the five agents, and their
relationships of generation and destruction, if 'the movement is that which is not
overcome,' then this is [a movement of a agent] destroying the one that is present.
For instance, if in case of a liver disease a lung [movement in the] vessels occurs, or if
in spring an autumn [movement in the] vessels occurs. In this case the disease is opposition, and the prognosis is not good. If 'the movement is that which is overcome,'
then this is [a movement of an agent] that is destroyed by the present [agent]. For
instance, if in case of a liver disease a spleen [movement in the] vessels appears, or if
in spring a late summer [movement in the] vessels appears. In this case the disease
conforms [to the regular order] and prognosis is good."

The [cycle of the] domination of the eight winds and four seasons comes to its end and begins anew.[31]

Once an opposing movement occurs excessively, one cannot count again.[32]

The discourse on the essentials [written on the jade tablets] is finished."

---

31 Wang Bing: "This is because they do not leave the [circle of the] five agents. Hence, even though [the eight winds and four seasons] overcome each other, their circle begins anew once it has reached its conclusion."

32 Wang Bing: "過 is to say 遍, 'everywhere.' That is, as soon as the countermovement has affected the qi in all the five [depots, the situation] can no longer be counted as balanced and harmonious." The *Tai su* does not have the character 可 following the character 復, and it has 診 instead of 論. Yang Shangshan: "If the reverse movement results in one domination, this is 一過, 'one transgression.' A second transgression results in death. Hence it cannot be counted. For example, in case of a liver disease. When lung qi arrives to occupy the liver, this is 'one transgression.' A second transgression results in death. Hence it does not come to any counting. That is the peak of the essentials of diagnosis. Hence [the discourse] concludes with it." Mori: "Wang Bing's commentary is wrong here; one should follow Yang Shangshan. Also, to write 論要 instead of 診要, this, too, is an unjustified change introduced by Wang Bing. The title 玉版論要 is meaningless."

Chapter 16

Discourse on The Essentials of Diagnosis and on Exhaustion in the Conduits

16-91-4

Huang Di asked:

"The essentials of diagnosis, what are they like?"

Qi Bo responded:

"In the first month and in the second month,
the qi of heaven begins to spread;
the qi of the earth begins to be effused;
the qi of man is in the liver.[1]

In the third month and in the fourth month,
the qi of heaven spreads properly;
the qi of the earth is effused firmly;[2]
the qi of man is in the spleen.[3]

16-91-6

In the fifth month and in the sixth month,

---

1 Wang Bing: "方 stands for 正, 'just,' That is to say, the qi of heaven and earth is just bringing forth the myriad beings. The wood governs the East. It rules for 72 days. That is, 12 days into the third month. That is the time when the [qi of] wood operates. In terms of months, these are the first and the second month. At this time, the qi of man is in his liver." *NJCD*: "[方 stands for] 旺盛, 'abundant.' The *Guang ya* 廣雅 states: '方 is 大, large.'" 2204/38 quotes the *Shang shu* and the *Han shu* and concludes: "In antiquity, the meaning of 方 was identical with that of 放, 'to set free,' 'to effuse.' Wang Bing was not aware of the phonetic loan meaning of 方 and interpreted 方 as 正, 'just;' this is definitely wrong. In both sentences, 方 is used as a phonetic loan character for 放. 天氣始方 is to say: the yang qi begins to move. 天氣正方 is to say: the yang qi moves strongly." 2270/38 and 2263/37 agree.

2 2308/48: "方 has the same meaning as 發, 'to effuse.'" 正 and 定 are both adverbs of time. 正 stands for 正在, 'at the moment of;' 定 has the same meaning as 正. In ancient times, one did not like to repeat identical characters; rather one preferred different characters to express the same meaning." Fang Wenhui/12 agrees.

3 Wang Bing: "The qi of heaven spreads properly because the yang qi abounds in brilliance. The earth qi is effused firmly, causing the myriad beings to blossom and to wish to bear fruit. However, at the conclusion of this season, the soil rules. The [qi of] soil is generated in [times associated with the celestial stem] *bing*. Hence the qi of man is in the spleen."

the qi of heaven is abundant;
the qi of the earth has moved upward;
the qi of man is in the head.⁴

In the seventh month and in the eighth month,
the yin qi begins to kill;⁵
the qi of man is in the lung.⁶

In the ninth month and in the tenth month,
the yin qi begins to freeze;
the qi of the earth begins to be closed in;
the qi of man is in the heart.⁷

In the eleventh month and in the twelfth month,
the freezing is repetitive;⁸
the qi of the earth is enclosed;⁹

---

4 Wang Bing: "The yang [qi] of heaven abounds in luminosity; the earth [qi] blazes and ascends. Hence [the text] states: the qi of heaven abounds and the earth qi rises. The nature of fire is to flame upward. Hence the qi of man is in the head."

5 Zhang Zhicong: "始殺 is 'the qi begins a stern killing, 肅殺.' " See also Forke, *Lun Heng*, 'The yin principle is cold murder.' (陰道肅殺)

6 Wang Bing: "In the seventh month, the three yin [qi] emerge separately; in the eighth month they begin a stern killing. Hence [the text] states: the yin qi begins to kill. Now, the stern killing carried out by the yin qi corresponds to the [operation of] metal. The qi of the lung reflects the [operation of] metal. Hence the qi of man is in the lung."

7 Wang Bing: "When the the yin qi begins to coagulate and the qi of the earth begins to close in, this follows the return of the yang [qi] to the interior. Hence the qi of man is in the heart."

8 Zhongyi yanjiuyuan...: "復 is identical with 腹, 'abdomen,' which, in turn, stands for 厚, 'thick.' " 2263/37: "All authors have explained 冰復 as 水伏, 'the water is concealed.' Or they say 冰復 is: 'freezing and freezing again,' i.e., coagulation in extreme cold. All these explanations are wrong. The climatic conditions referred to here coincide with [statements in] the chapter Yue ling 月令 of the *Li ji* 禮記: 'In the second month of winter, the ice thickens and the earth cracks.' Elsewhere it states: 季冬之月, 冰方盛, 水澤腹堅 and the commentary says: 腹 is 厚, 'thick.' In the present text, 冰復 is a phonetic loan expression used for 冰腹 and it is an abbreviated version of 冰方盛, 水澤腹堅, 'ice abounds and the waters and marshes are thick and hard.' "

9 Wu Kun: "合 stands for 閉而密, 'tightly sealed.' "

the qi of man is in the kidneys.[10]

16-92-1
Hence,
in spring, pierce the scattered transporters,
and also the parting structures.[11]
Stop when blood comes out.[12]

<In severe cases the qi is transmitted;
in light cases [the disease lasts for one qi] circulation period.>[13]

---

10 Wang Bing: "The yang qi is deep inside, hence the qi [of man] is in the kidneys."
See 1457/11 for a discussion of this calendar.

11 Wang Bing: "散俞 is to say 間穴, 'holes far apart.' 分理 is to say 肌肉分理, 'parting structures between muscles and flesh.'" Lin Yi et al.: "The *Si shi ci ni cong lun* 四
時刺逆從論 (*Suwen* 64) states: In spring the qi is in the conduit vessels. The 散俞
[mentioned] here refer to the transporter [holes] on the conduit vessels." Gao Shishi:
"散俞 are the transporter [holes] on the network vessels." Wu Kun: "散俞 are the
transporter holes spread all over the back." Ma Shi: "散俞 are the holes spread over all
the conduits." Tanba: "散俞 are the opposite of 本輸, (i.e., the insertion holes on the
conduits in the four extremities between elbows and finger tips and between knees
and toes). For example, in view of the major yin conduit associated with the lung,
except for the [insertion holes] Lesser Shang (少商), Fish Border (魚際), Great Abyss
(太淵), Main Conduit Ditch (經渠), and Foot Marsh (尺澤), all other holes are 'holes
spread far apart.' They are called 散俞, 'scattered transporter [holes].'" Mori: "及与 is
not an established expression. 与 and 于 were used interchangeably in antiquity. What
[the text is] to say is: in spring one pierces the scattered transporter [holes], neither
[too] shallow, nor [too] deep. One just advances towards the parting structures with
the blood vessels. The white flesh on the outside of the muscles where one can pierce
without the appearance of blood, they are called 肌服, or 肌肉. Those [layers] where,
if pierced, blood appears, they are called 分肉, or 分理."

12 Zhang Zhicong: "In spring, the qi rises towards the outside. Hence one must apply a shallow piercing in the fossas of the transporter [holes] spread [over the conduit
vessels]. As soon as blood appears, the qi in the vessels passes and the disease has come
to an end."

13 *Lun yu* 論語, Zi han 子罕, has: 病間. The comment explains: "A light [ailment]
is called 間."(See Ruan Yuan 2490 below). Wang Bing: "One distinguishes whether
[the nature of] the pathological qi is light or serious. 傳 is to say 相傳, 'transmission
from one to the next.' 環 is to say 循環, 'to follow a circular movement.' 'Transmission from one to the next' means that [a qi is] transmitted into [a conduit/depot by]
which it cannot be overcome. 'Follows a circular movement' means that it completes
a full cycle through [the depots/conduits of all] the five qi." Lin Yi et al.: "The *Tai
su* has 環已, 'comes to an end within one circulation period', instead of 環也. Zhang
Jiebin: "傳 is 布散, 'to spread.' 環 is 周, 'cycle.' In case of severe diseases one lets the

In summer, pierce the transporters on the network [vessels].[14]
Stop when blood appears.
<After the [disease] qi has been [removed] entirely, there will be closure for
[one qi] circulation period.>
Pain and disease must subside.[15]

---

needle remain inserted for an extended period of time; hence one must wait until the
qi is transmitted. In case of light diseases, one simply waits until the qi has undergone
one circulation through the body. This takes about two quarters [of a double hour; i.e.
one hour]. Then the piercing can be finished." 2719/7: "It really does not make any
difference whether one reads 環已 here or 環也 if one isolates this passage from the
entire sentence; it cannot be determined which is right and which is wrong as long
as the meaning remains incomplete. In order to determine which version is correct,
one has to take the context into account. The 'in serious cases' above corresponds to
the 'in light cases' here; hence 傳氣 and 環也 may appear to be opposites, too. This,
however, is certainly not the case. We assume that 環已 is correct, with 已 meaning
'healed,' while 環也 is wrong. Once one reads the entire sentence it is obvious that 環
也 makes no sense: 'Hence in spring, one pierces the scattered transporters, advancing
to the parting structures. Stop when blood comes out. In severe cases one transmits
the qi; in light cases immediate.' Lin Yi and the other [Song editors] examined this
and drew on the 環已, '[the disease] is healed within one circulation period,' of the
Tai su to correct the mistaken 環也 of the *Su wen*." 2722/44: "已 is 愈, 'to heal.' That
is to say, in case of severe diseases, at the time of the piercing, one must wait until the
qi is transmitted to the conduits pierced; in case of light diseases, only one circulation
is necessary and [the disease is] healed. With 環也 the meaning of the text is unclear."
1321/41: "The character 環 is explained by some as 循環, 'to revolve,' by some as 周,
'a complete cycle,' and by still others as 環轉. They all fail in the explanation of the
meaning of this phrase. What this [passage] refers to is the time a needle is allowed
to remain [in the skin] during piercing; it is not whether a disease is light or severe.
All the commentators of the Ming and Qing stuck to Wang Bing's comments, hence
they had to force their explanations. In this treatise further down it says: 盡氣閉環,
環為咳嗽, and 中心者環死. The meaning of the character 環 is always identical. The
character 環 is interchangeable here with the character 旋, 'to revolve,' 'thereupon.'
間者環也 means: in case of light diseases do not let the needle remain [in the skin];
the needle is to be withdrawn as soon as the piercing was carried out. 環死 is: 'instant
death.'" In contrast: 475/42: "環 has the same meaning here as [further down] in 中
心者環死, i.e., 'the qi of the conduits moves through one cycle.'"

14 Zhang Jiebin: "絡脈 is to say: the holes on all the conduits' network [vessels] near
the surface. Because in summer the qi is in the 孫絡, 'tertiary vessels.'" Ma Shi: "From
the context one should conclude that these are the holes on the network [vessels associated with] the heart and the small intestine."

15 Wang Bing: "盡氣 is to say: when blood appears, [the disease qi is] eliminated entirely. One inserts the needle to remove the evil qi filling the diseased vessel. Once the
evil qi has been completely eliminated, the transporter opening must be thoroughly
closed. As a result, the circulation in the conduit vessels continues and the qi [respon-

16-92-3
In autumn, pierce the skin along the [parting] structures.
<The same law [applies] above and below.>
Stop when the spirit has undergone a change.[16]

In winter, pierce the transporter openings[17] at the parting structures.
In severe cases lower [the needle] in a straight manner.
In light cases [insert the needle] by lowering it in a scattering manner.[18]

Spring, summer, autumn, and winter,
each [season] has its specific location to be pierced.[19]

---

sible for the] pain and disease will be removed. Because [this is a case of] great abundance of yang qi, the piercing must follow this law." Zhang Jiebin: "盡氣 is: remove the evil blood and the evil qi entirely. 'Blood' stands for evil qi. 閉環 is to say: remove the needle and close the hole and allow the qi to complete one circular passage. [This way,] all pain and diseases will be eliminated (退下)."

16 Wang Bing: "循理 is to say: 循肌肉之分理, 'along the parting structures of the muscles and the flesh.' 上 is to say 'vessels of the hands;' 下 is to say 'vessels of the feet.' 神變 is to say 'the qi in the vessels has undergone changes and is different from the time before the piercing took place.' The [movement in the] vessels is an operation of the spirit. Hence [the text] has this statement." 2308/47: "The interpretation of the 下 in 痛病必下 is not identical with that of the 下 in 上下同法. The 下 in 下法 has the meaning of a noun of locality; the 下 in 必下, in contrast, has the meaning of 除, 'to eliminate.' 下 is like 去, 'to drive away.' .. The 上下 of 上下同法 refers to 淺深, 'shallow and deep.' The meaning of the entire sentence is: 'It is the same for [piercing] patterns remaining at the surface or reaching into the depth. In both cases one must observe the spirit-complexion of the patient. When the spirit-complexion of the patient undergoes a change, one must stop the piercing."

17 Zhang Jiebin: "Deep holes are called 竅. In winter the qi is in the bone marrow. Hence one must go into the depth and take [it from] the transporter openings in the parting structures." Zhang Zhicong: "The 俞竅 are the hole openings of all the transporters 諸俞之穴竅. They are deeper than the 'scattered transporters (散俞)' and they lie close to the sinews and bones." Similar: 1072/29.

18 Wang Bing: "直下 is to say to move it down directly; 散下 is to say to move it down by scattering and spreading it." Zhang Jiebin: "甚者直下 is to say:] examine where the evil is located and take it directly from its location in the depth. 間者散下 [is to say:] spread the needle to the left and to the right, upward and downward and do not proceed too fast."

19 For a discussion of the concept of four seasons (rather than five in accordance with the five agents) in the *Nei jing*, see 2499/15.

Take as pattern the [location] where it is situated.[20]

16-92-5
If in spring one pierces the summer section,
the [movement in the] vessels loses its order and the qi is feeble.
[The evil qi] invades the bones and their marrow and
the disease [that was to be healed] cannot heal.
[This] lets a person wish not to eat.
<In addition one is short of qi.>[21]

If in spring one pierces the autumn section,
the sinews will be cramped.
Qi moving contrary [to its regular course] causes coughing within one circulation period.[22]
The disease [that was to be healed] does not heal.
[This] lets a person frequently [show signs of] fright.
<In addition he weeps.>[23]

---

20 Cheng Shide et al./218: "法 is 取法, 'to take as pattern,' 依据, 'to follow.'" Zhang Jiebin: "Earlier, the text spoke of the rising and descending of the qi in the course of the twelve months. Here it speaks of the [location of the] qi in the depth and near the surface in the course of the four seasons. Hence [the text states:] each [season] has its location to be pierced; follow the location where it is situated." Ma Shi: "Follow the location of that person's qi and pierce there."

21 Wang Bing: "The heart rules the [movement in the] vessels. Hence when the [movement in the] vessels has lost its order and when the qi is minimal, then [this is a sign that] the water has received [supplementary] qi in summer. The kidneys rule the bones. Hence the evil enters the bones and the marrow. When the fire of the heart is minimal, then the soil of the stomach is insufficient. Hence one does not wish to eat and the qi is diminished." Gao Shishi: "If in spring one pierces the summer section, the qi of the heart moves wildly and is harmed. The heart is tied to the vessels; hence the [movement in the] vessels is disorderly. When the [movement in the] vessels is disorderly, then the qi has nothing to attach itself to. Hence the qi is minimal. When the [movement in the] vessels is disorderly and when the qi is minimal, evil finds its way into [the body] and brings the bad into the bones and their marrow. As a result, spring diseases cannot be healed. When the [movement in the] vessels is disorderly, this will cause that person to lose all appetite. Hence when food qi enters the stomach, turbid qi turns to the heart and bad essence is in the vessels. [In this case], not only will the qi be minimal, it will be diminished in addition."

22 Gao Shishi: "環 is 轉, 'to revolve.'"

23 Wang Bing: "The wood has received [supplementary] qi in autumn. The liver rules the sinews. Hence if [in spring] one pierces the autumn section, the sinews twist. When the qi moves contrary to the [normal] circulatory course, this results in cough.

If in spring one pierces the winter section,
the evil qi attaches itself to the depots.
[This] lets a person [show signs of] distension.
The disease [that was to be healed] does not heal.
<In addition, [that person] wishes to talk.>[24]

16-93-2
If in summer one pierces the spring section,
the disease [that was to be healed] does not heal.
[This] lets a person be sluggish.[25]

If in summer one pierces the autumn section,
the disease [that was to be healed] does not heal.
[This] lets a person have no desire in his heart to speak.
He is frightened as if someone were about to arrest him.[26]

If in summer one pierces the winter section,
the disease [that was to be healed] does not heal.

The liver rules the [emotion of] fear. Hence [the patient] is frequently fearful. The lung rules the qi. Hence when the qi moves contrary [to its normal course], this results in weeping." Wu Kun: "逆氣 is [to say:] The liver is ill and the qi moves upward contrary [to its normal course]. 環 is: the qi moves in one cycle through the body. 咳嗽 is: the qi moving contrary [to its normal course] hits the lung and [causes] coughing." Gao Shishi: "環 is like 轉, 'to revolve.' The liver stores the *hun*-soul; the lung stores the *po*-soul. When *hun*-soul and *po*-soul are not in peace, one cries." Ma Shi: "The sound stimulated by the liver is weeping. Hence one weeps." Gao Jiwu/32: "環 is identical with 還, *xuan*, in the meaning of 'immediately.'"

24 Wang Bing: "In winter, the yang qi is subdued and stored. Hence the evil attaches itself and is stored, [internally]. When the kidneys are replete, this causes swelling. Hence if [in spring] one pierces the winter section, then this causes swellings in that person. [This is a case where] the fire receives [supplementary] qi in winter. The heart rules the speech. Hence [the patient] has an urge to speak." Zhang Zhicong: "Spring rules emergence and rising; winter rules closure and storage. If in spring one pierces the winter section, blood and qi are guided contrary [to their normal course] and become attached internally. Hence this causes that person's abdomen to swell."

25 Wang Bing: "The liver nourishes the sinews. When the liver qi is insufficient, the strength of the sinews relaxes." Cheng Shide et al./220: "解 is identical with 懈, 'idle,' 㑊 is 惰, 'careless.' 懈㑊 is 倦怠無力, 'remiss without strength.'"

26 Wang Bing: "The wood of the liver is [responsible for] speech. If one harms the autumn section, then the wood of the liver is depleted. Hence [the patient] is in fear as if someone were about to arrest him. When the liver [qi] is insufficient, [the patient] prefers not to speak and frequently shows signs of fear."

[This] lets a person be short of qi.[27]
He frequently tends to become angry.[28]

16-93-4
If in autumn one pierces the spring section,
the disease [that was to be healed] does not end.
[This] lets a person be fearful.
He has a desire to do something,
but when he gets up he has forgotten it.[29]

If in autumn one pierces the summer section,
the disease [that was to be healed] does not end.
[This] lets a person increasingly desire to sleep.
<In addition he tends to have dreams.>[30]

---

27 538/37: "The character 少 could be a mistake here and should be the character 上, 'to move upward.' 上氣 corresponds to the 'tends to become angry' below. 上氣, then, is 上逆, 'moving upward, reversing [its normal direction].' *Su wen* 64 states: 'If in summer one pierces the sinews and the bones, the blood and the qi move upward, reversing [their normal directions]. This causes in that person a tendency to become angry.'"

28 Zhang Jiebin: "If in summer one harms the kidney qi, then the essence is depleted and cannot transform into qi. Hence this causes that person's qi to be diminished. When the water is deficient, the wood has nothing by which it could be nourished. As a result, the liver qi turns violent and tense. Hence this causes that person to have a tendency towards becoming angry." Ma Shi: "If in summer one pierces the winter section, the kidney water is drained and the heart fire flares up. Therefore, the disease cannot be healed. The principal qi is weakened and diminished while the fire qi blazes internally and comes to assist its mother qi. [As a result, that person] frequently tends to be angry."

29 Wang Bing: "The reason for this is a liver depletion." Zhang Jiebin: "This is harm to the liver qi. When the heart loses [contact to] its mother (i.e., the liver), its spirit is insufficient. Hence this causes that person to be fearful and also to be forgetful." Gao Shishi: "Autumn rules harvesting. If [in autumn] the spring section is pierced, the qi and the blood are guided contrary [to their normal course] to move upward. Hence this causes that person to be fearful. The lung is located high [in the body]; order and economy emerge from there. Hence if one wishes to be active and the qi received is spread out instead, one rises and forgets it."

30 Wang Bing: "When the qi of the heart is diminished, then the qi of the spleen is isolated. As a result, [the patient] wishes to lie down. The heart rules the dreams; the spirit creates them. Hence one tends to dream [in such a situation]."

If in autumn one pierces the winter section,
the disease [that was to be healed] does not end.
[This] lets a person shiver and frequently feel cold.[31]

16-93-7
If in winter one pierces the spring section,
the disease [that was to be healed] does not end.
[This] lets a person wish to lie down but he cannot sleep.[32]
Even if he falls asleep, there are [still things] he sees.[33]

If in winter one pierces the summer section,
the disease [that was to be healed] does not heal.
The qi rises and develops into various blocks.[34]

If in winter one pierces the autumn section,
the disease [that was to be healed] does not end.
[This] lets a person tend to be thirsty.[35]

---

31 Wang Bing: "The yin qi rushes upward. Hence one has repeated feelings of cold. '*Xian xian*' is a type of [being affected by] cold."

32 Ma Shi: "而 stands for 如, 'as if.' " Wan Lanqing et al./29: "In the *Nei jing*, 臥 has the meaning of 睡眠, 'to sleep.' "

33 Wang Bing: "The liver qi is diminished. Hence one wishes to lie down, but cannot sleep. The liver rules the eyes. Hence one sleeps and still it is as if one saw the appearance of things."

34 Wang Bing: "The reason is that the qi is drained from the vessels." Gao Shishi: "When the qi moves upward, the yang follows and moves upward [too] and this means leakage. As to 'various blocks develop,' in winter the qi should be stored but, on the contrary, is [caused to] leak. If this [situation] persists for hours and days, patho-conditions of all the blocks [caused by] wind, cold, and dampness develop." Wu Kun: "If [in winter] one pierces the summer section and causes harm to the heart, then the soil of the spleen loses [supplies by] its mother (i.e., the fire of the heart). The spleen is depleted, hence the qi rises and causes superficial swelling. When the spleen is strong, it is able to check dampness. When it is depleted, then it is unable to check dampness. Hence the disease of atony-block and numbness emerges."

35 Wang Bing: "The qi of the lung is insufficient. Hence thirst develops." Wu Kun: "If one pierces the autumn section and harms the metal of the lung, then the water of the kidneys loses [supplies by] its mother. The kidneys rule the five liquids. Hence [that person] tends to be thirsty."

16-94-2
Whenever one pierces the chest and the abdomen, one must stay clear of the five depots.[36]

If one hits the heart, this leads to death within a circulation [period].[37]
If one hits the spleen, this leads to death within five days.[38]
If one hits the kidneys, this leads to death within seven days.[39]

If one hits the lung, this leads to death within five days.[40]
If one hits the diaphragm, this causes always harm to the center.

---

36 Wang Bing: "Heart and lung are located above the diaphragm; kidneys and liver are located below the diaphragm. The spleen reflects [the agent] soil and is situated in the center. Hence when piercing the chest and/or the abdomen, one must stay clear of these [depots]. The five depots store the essence spirit, the *hun*-soul, the *po*-soul, the sentiments, and the mind. If they are harmed, the five spirits leave. When the spirits have left, death arrives. Hence one must be careful."

37 Wang Bing: "The qi moves through one [more] circulation [after the heart was struck by a needle] and then [the patient] dies. Correctly stated, this is a circulation of twelve double-hours (正謂周十二辰)." 475/42 agrees. Yu Chang: "It appears as if originally there has been a character 正 below the [character] 環. Hence Wang Bing stated: 正謂周十二辰. *Su wen* 52 states: 'If piercing hits the heart, one dies within one day.' Hence to die '環正' is to say: one dies within one day. One day has twelve double-hours. For instance, if someone dies today at the double-hour of *wu*, the cycle (環) continues until exactly (正) the double-hour of *wu* tomorrow and then [that person] will be dead. Hence it is a mistake to omit the character 正. When some later people claimed that the conduit qi circulated (環) through the body in one more grand cycle, this is not in agreement with 52." Hua Shou: "The qi circulates through the body for one day and then death [sets in]." Wu Kun agrees. Li Guoqing/84: "環 is identical with 還, 'immediately.' 環死 is 'instant death.' When the *Nei jing* refers to a period of one day and one night, it uses the term 一日; here the term 環死 is used and the meaning must be different. Given the low state of medicine in ancient times, instant death was, without any doubt, a consequence of accidentally piercing into the heart. It is certainly impossible that circulation of the conduit qi could be maintained for one more day."

38 Wang Bing: "The number [associated with the agent] soil is five."

39 Wang Bing: "The completion number of water is six. When the number [of days associated with] water is completed, death will follow on the seventh day. Another version has the characters 'ten days.' That is a mistake."

40 Wang Bing: "The generation number of metal is four. When the number [of days associated with] metal is completed, death will follow on the fifth day. Another version has 'three days.' That, too, is a mistake."

The disease may be healed, but [the patient] must die within one year.[41]
Those who stay clear of the five depots in piercing,
they know [what it means to act] contrary to and to comply with [the norms].
{So-called compliance [is to comply with] the locations of the diaphragm, as
well as of spleen and kidneys. Those who do not know [these locations], they
act contrary to these [requirements].}[42]

16-95-1
[Whenever] one pierces the chest and the abdomen,
one must bandage them with a hemp cloth.[43]
Then pierce from above the one-layered cloth.[44]

---

41 Wang Bing: "Together, the qi of the five depots rule the entire year. When the
diaphragm is harmed, the qi of the five depots attack each other. Hence death will
follow within one year." Zhang Jiebin: "The diaphragm: in the front it is on a level
with the turtledove's tail (i.e., the xiphoid process); in the back it is on a level with the
eleventh vertebra. Heart and lung are located above the diaphragm; liver and kidneys
are located below the diaphragm. The spleen is located below the diaphragm but very
close to it. The diaphragm is that which separates the clear from the turbid; it divides
the upper and the lower [part of the body] and serves as a boundary [between] the
five depots. The qi of the five depots rule the four seasons in turn. If the diaphragm is
harmed, then the yin and yang qi of the depots are mixed up with each other. This is
harm to the center. Hence death follows within one year." 2263/37: "The present listing of the number of days elapsing before one dies after [one of] the five depots has
been struck by a needle, is different from *Su wen* 52 and *Su wen* 64. Also, 'when the
liver is struck one dies within five days' is omitted altogether. .. The present passage,
therefore, must be completed on the basis of *Su wen* 52."

42 Wang Bing: "The kidneys are attached to the spine; the spleen is situated in
the center. The diaphragm is linked to the flanks. Those who know, they act accordingly; those who do not know, they act contrary [to the requirements] and harm the
depots."

43 布 appears to refer here to a cloth of a somewhat thicker tissue, i.e., made of hemp
or linen.

44 Wang Bing: "When [the position of their] physical appearance is determined, one
will not erroneously hit the five depots." Lin Yi et al.: "Other editions have 幑, 'bandages,' or 撤, 'screen,' instead of 愾." Zhang Jiebin: "幑 is read 皎, *jiao*. It stands for 布,
'to spread.' 著 is read 灼, *zhuo*. It stands for 被服, 'to be dressed.'" Wu Kun: "Because
the chest and the abdomen are close to the five depots, one protects them from wind
and cold." Ma Shi: "愾 should be 幑; it stands for 巾 *jin*, 'napkin.' It is spread between
chest and abdomen. One pierces from above the spread out [napkin]. The reason is:
one does not wish to enter deeply." 916/52 agrees. Shen Zumian: "愾 is identified as
'happy' in the *Shuo wen*, but that is not the meaning here. Here it stands for 竅, 'opening,' i.e., what is called 'transporter [hole]' today. That is to say, when piercing chest
or abdomen, one first presses the hole [to be pierced] with a piece of cloth and then

If [a first] piercing does not heal [the disease], pierce again.[45]
When piercing with the needle, [one] must be disciplined.[46]
When piercing swellings, one moves the needle here and there.[47]
For conduit piercing, one must not move [the needle] here and there.[48]
This is the Way of piercing."

16-95-4
[Huang] Di:
"I should like to hear:
what is it like when the [qi of the] twelve conduit vessels is exhausted?"[49]

Qi Bo:
"When the [qi of the] major yang vessel is finished,
the eyeball is turned upward,[50] [the spine] is bent backward,[51] and hands and
feet [change between] spasms and slackening.[52]
The complexion is white.[53]

---

pierces from above the cloth." We were unable to identify the meaning of the character 憿. It does not appear in our translation.

45 Wang Bing: "[The criterion of] success is the arrival of qi. The *Zhen jing* 鍼經 states: 'When the qi does not arrive after insertion of the needle, do pierce again – no matter how often – until the qi arrives. Only then withdraw [the needle] and do not pierce again.' (see *Ling shu* chapter 1.) This is meant here." Wang Shaozeng/27: "復 is 多次, 'often.'"

46 Wang Bing: "肅 stands for 靜肅, 'calm and respectful.' This way one determines whether the qi is still present or has been lost."

47 Wang Bing: "The reason is: one wishes to eliminate large amounts of pus and blood."

48 Wang Bing: "The reason is: one does not wish to drain qi from the conduits."

49 Wang Bing: "終 is to say: 盡, 'exhausted.'" Zhang Jiebin: " 'Twelve conduit vessels' refers to the qi of the twelve depots." Wu Kun: "終 is to say 敗絕, 'destroyed and interrupted.'"

50 Wang Bing: "戴眼 is to say: the eyeball fails to move around and the view is directed upward." 964/2: "Following *Huai nan zi*, 戴 means 上, 'upward.' 戴眼 is to say: 'the eyes of the patient have no spirit; they turn upward and cannot move around." For details and a lengthy discussion of the term 戴眼, see there. Qian Chaochen-88/255 agrees.

51 Zhang Zhicong: "反折 is: the back is bent backward."

52 Zhang Jiebin: "瘈 refers to tense sinews; 縱 refers to relaxed sinews."

53 Ma Shi: "The water of the major yang [conduit] of the feet rules black; the fire of the major yin [conduit] of the hands rules red. These two colors do not appear and

Interrupted [streams of] sweat leave [the body].[54]
When it has left, [the patient] will die.[55]

When the [qi of the] minor yang [vessel] is finished,
the ears are deaf and all the joints are loose.
The eyes stare [as if the patient had been] terrified; the connection is cut.[56]
One day and a half after the connection was cut [the patient] dies.
As for his death, first his complexion is green-white, then he will die.

When the [qi of the] yang brilliance [vessel] is finished, mouth and eyes move
in [senseless] activity.
[The patient] tends to be fearful and [utters] absurd words.
His complexion is yellow.
When his upper and lower conduits [appear filled to] abundance and
when numbness sets in, then the end has come.[57]

---

the complexion is simply white."

54 Beijing zhongyi xueyuan et al./95: "絕汗 is: the sweat flows like pearls."

55 2940/40: "The reason is that the vessel of the foot major yang bladder conduit rises from the eye and proceeds along the back. Its qi nourishes the exterior of the entire body. Hence, when the qi of the major yang conduit is finally cut off, the eyes lose their connection and the eyeballs move upward into a fixed gaze; the sinews lose their nourishment and are cramped. The external protection is disabled and intermittent sweat flows."

56 *SWJZ*: "睘 is 驚視, 'to stare in terror.'" Wang Bing: "睘 is to say: 'one stares straight ahead as if in a state of terror.'" Zhang Jiebin: "睘 is to stare straight ahead as if in a state of terror. The reason for this is that the minor yang connection is cut and [the eyes] cannot move around." Gao Jiwu/37 agrees: "The eyes stare straight ahead, as if in a state of terror. The eye-balls are unable to move around." Ma Shi: "目睘 is the same as if one were to say 眼圈, 'eye socket.' The so-called 系 is the 系 referred to in *Ling shu* 80." Wu Kun has 目環 instead of 目睘: "目環 is: one watches with revolving [eyes]." Li Guoqing/86: "According to *Ling shu* 09, 目睘系絕 should be 目系絕, 'the eye connection is cut.' 目系 is the vessel referred to by *Ling shu* 80 as connecting [the eyes] with the brain."

57 Yao Shaoyu: "'Above' refers to the *ren-ying* [point] to the sides of the Adam's apple; 'below' refers to the *fu-yang* [point]. 盛 means hasty movement. In ancient times, when someone was about to die, [his condition] was determined by examining these [locations]." Wu Kun: "'The conduits above and below' refers to the yang brilliance [conduits] of both hands and feet. 盛 means 'overly full.' Here it is to say: no stomach qi is present. 不仁 is: not to notice pain." Gao Shishi: "不仁 is: the body is cold and the skin is hard."

When the [qi of the] minor yin [vessel] is finished,
the face is black and the teeth grow long and are stained.
The abdomen distends and is closed.
When above and below no longer communicate, then the end has come.⁵⁸

16-96-2
When the [qi of the] major yin [vessel] is finished,
the abdomen distends and is closed.
One cannot breathe.
One tends to belch and one tends to vomit.
Once [the patient] vomits, a movement [of qi] contrary [to its regular course]
has set in.
In case of a movement [of qi] contrary [to its regular course] the face turns
red.⁵⁹
If there is no movement [of qi] contrary [to its regular course], then above and
below no longer communicate.
Once they no longer communicate, the face turns black, the skin and the body
hair [appear] parched, and the end has come.⁶⁰

---

58 Wang Bing: "When the qi [flow] in the hand minor yin [conduit] is interrupted,
then the blood does not flow [either]. When the qi [flow] in the foot minor yin [con-
duit] is interrupted, then the bones are no longer flexible. When the bones are hard,
then they break and are disclosed above. Hence the teeth [appear to] grow longer and
collect dirt. Sweat and blood deteriorate and the skin assumes a fatal color. Hence
the face is black like lacquer, but not red." Gao Shishi: "垢 is: face and teeth have no
luster." Wu Kun: "The minor yin kidney vessel passes inside the abdomen, hence it
causes the abdomen to swell. The openings of the kidneys are the two yin [orifices
for passing urine and stools], hence [the kidney vessel] causes their closure. Now, in
case of swelling and closure, above one cannot eat and below one cannot ease oneself.
Above and below are blocked; heart and kidneys are separated from each other and
death [is unavoidable]."

59 Zhang Jiebin: "When the abdomen is swollen and closed, then the upward and
downward movements are hampered. If one cannot breathe, the passage ways of the
qi are obstructed. This results in belching and vomiting. In case of vomiting, the qi
reverses [its normal flow] and moves upward. Hence the face turns red." Zhang Zhicong: "The foot major yin vessel enters the abdomen and connects with the spleen.
Hence it causes abdominal distension. The hand major yin vessel moves above the
diaphragm and connects with the lung. It rules inhalation and exhalation. Hence it is
responsible if one cannot breathe."

60 Wang Bing: "When [the patient] vomits, the [passageway] above is still open.
Hence his face is red. In case he does not vomit, then the [passageway] below is closed
and the one above is no longer passable either. The qi of the heart burns in the [body's]
outer regions; hence the skin and its hair are burned and the end has come." Wu Kun
identified "above and below are blocked" as referring to [a situation where] the qi of

16-96-4
When the [qi of the] ceasing yin [vessel] is finished,
central heat and a dry throat [result].
One has a tendency to urinate. The heart is vexed.
In severe cases the tongue curls up.
When the testicles are drawn in upward,[61]
the end has come.

These [situations reflect] the destruction of the twelve conduits."[62]

---

the spleen cannot rise, while the qi of the lung cannot descend, and "black face" as indicating that the water of the kidneys has been checked by the soil of the spleen: "If the
[qi] does not move reversely, a blockage exists in the center. The qi of the lung is above
and cannot descend; the qi of the spleen is below and cannot rise. Above and below
cannot communicate with each other. When there is no communication, the qi of the
soil is replete and the water of the kidneys receives evil. Hence the face turns black.
The hand major yin is the lung; it rules the skin and the body hair. Hence it causes the
skin and the body hair to become burned."

61 For an explicit interpretation of 卵 as "testicles," see 969/61.

62 Wang Bing: "敗 is to say: the qi is completely exhausted, hence there is destruction."

Chapter 17
Discourse on the Essentials of Vessels and the Subtleties of the Essence[1]

17-98-2
Huang Di asked:
"What are the laws of diagnosis?"

Qi Bo responded:
"The laws of diagnosis [are as follows].

As a rule, it is at dawn,[2]
before the yin qi has begun its movement,
before the yang qi is dispersed,
before beverages and food have been consumed,
before the conduit vessels are filled to abundance,
when the [contents of the] network vessels are balanced,
before the qi and the blood move in disorder,[3]

---

1 138/20: "The 脈要 in the title should be 診要, 'essential of diagnosis.' The patterns of 'observing [the complexions]' and of 'feeling [the movements in the vessels]' are outlined here. Together with 'listening/smelling' and 'asking' they constitute the so called 'four diagnostic [approaches].'" 180/8: "The two characters 脈 and 診 are regularly used for each other in the *Nei jing*." For a survey of the various meanings of 脈 in the *Nei jing*, see there.

2 705/52: "以 is used here for 于, 'at,' 'in.'"

3 Wang Bing: "動 is to say 動而降卑, 'downwards movement.' 散 is to say 散布而 出, 'flow out and disperse.'" Lin Yi et al.: "Early morning is the time of pure yang. The yin qi does not move yet. How can [Wang Bing in his comment] state that 未 動 has the meaning of 'downward movement'?" Ma Shi: "'Yin qi' is 營氣, 'camp qi.' 'Yang qi' is 衛氣, 'guard qi.'" Wu Kun: "未動 is 靜, 'quiet;' 未散 is 斂, 'to gather.' 未 盛 is 平, 'balanced.' 調勻 is 和, 'harmonious.' 未亂 is 治, 'in order.'" 950/715: "Li Zhongzi comments: 'The camp and the guard qi of the human body, during day time they pass through the yang section, during night time they pass through the yin section. In early morning they convene at the inch-opening. Hence the examination of the [movement in the] vessels should be carried out in the early morning, when the yin qi is tranquil and does not move yet, when the yang qi is about to abound and has not dispersed yet, and before beverages and food have been taken in. [At this time] depletion and repletion are easy to recognize." 538/37: "The two characters 'yin' and 'yang' have been erroneously substituted for each other. The early morning is the time when yin and yang are exchanged. The yin qi is just at its end; what does it mean: 'not yet moving?' The yang qi is just being received; what does it mean: 'not yet dispersed?' Maybe this should be: 'When the yang qi has not yet started its movement; when the

that, hence,
one can diagnose an abnormal[4] [movement in the] vessels.

17-98-4
Squeeze[5] the vessels [to determine whether their movement] is excited or quiet,
and
observe the essence brilliance.[6]
Investigate the five complexions.

Observe
whether the five depots have a surplus or an insufficiency,
whether the six palaces are strong or weak,[7] and
whether the physical appearance is marked by abundance or decays.

All this is brought together to reach a conclusion [concerning] a differentiation
between [the patient's] death and survival.[8]

---

yin qi is not yet dispersed.' 動 is to say: the manifestation of abundance; 散 is to say:
extreme weakness.'"

4 Wang Bing: "過 is to say 異于常候, 'abnormal signs.'"

5 Wang Bing: "切 is to say: 'sink the fingers [into the skin] to bring them close to
the vessels.'"

6 Wang Bing: "Essence Brilliance (精明) is the name of holes; they are located to
the left and to the right of the hall of brilliance (i.e., the nose) at the inner canthi of
both eyes. Because they are situated near the eyes, they are called 'essence brilliance.'"
Zhang Jiebin: "To observe the essence brilliance of the eyes is to diagnose the spirit
qi." Wu Kun: "The essence brilliance is the essence spirit in the pupils in the eyes." Yao
Shaoyu: "[Wang Bing's] comment interpreting 精明 as the name of a hole is incorrect. The essence spirit of man's entire body rises to the pour into the eyes. To observe
the essence brilliance is to say: to observe the luster in the eyes." 538/37: "視精明 refers
to an examination enquiring whether the spirit qi of one's vision is present or not. 精
明 is 精光." Gao Jiwu/240: "精明 is to say: the eyes. Sun Dingyi 孫鼎宜 has stated: "精
明 is to say 目, 'eye.'" 1126/11 agrees.

7 538/37: " 'Six' is a mistake for 'five.' This mistake results from attempts in pri-
vately transmitted manuscripts to avoid repeating the character 'five' of 'five depots'
above. In fact, though, these 'five palaces' have absolutely nothing in common with the
conventional 'six palaces.' The [conventional] 'six palaces' refer to gallbladder, stomach,
large and small intestine, urinary bladder, and triple burner. The 'five palaces' here refer
to the 'palace of essence brilliance,' 'the palace of the chest center,' the 'palace of the
kidneys,' 'the palace of the sinews,' and 'the palace of the marrow' mentioned below.
Both [concepts] must not be confused."

8 538/38: "參伍 should be read in connection with the following passage; there should
be no break in this sentence here. .. The two characters 以此 summarize the items

17-98-6
Now,
the vessels, they are the palaces of the blood.⁹

[The movement in the vessels]
if it is extended, then the qi is in order.
If it is short, then the qi has a disease.¹⁰
If it is frequent, then the heart is vexed.¹¹
If it is big, then a disease is advanced.¹²
If it is abundant above, then the qi is [situated] high [in the body].
If it is abundant below, then this is a distension [because of] qi.¹³

---

listed above: 'feel the [movement in the] vessels, etc..' 以此參伍決死生之分 is to say: in diagnosing a disease one should feel the [movement in the] vessels, observe essence brilliance, and investigate the complexion, examine the five depots, the five palaces, physical appearance and qi, and consider all this together to distinguish whether the patient will die or survive. 決 should be 訣 as in ch. 28 of the *Qian jin fang*."

9 Wang Bing: "府 stands for 聚, 'to gather.' That is, whether the blood is present in large or small amounts, it always gathers in the conduit vessels and appears there. Hence *Su wen* 53 states: 'when the vessels are replete, the blood is replete; when the vessels are depleted, the blood is depleted.'" 175/34: "All places where things accumulate or are stored can be called 府." See there for a detailed discussion of the meaning of 府 in the *Nei jing*.

10 Wang Bing: "When the [movement in the] vessels is extended, the qi is balanced and, hence, 'in order.' When it is short, [the qi] is insufficient and hence there is a disease. .. An 'extended [movement in the] vessels' is one that comes and goes in long [periods]. A 'short [movement in the] vessels' is one that comes and goes in short [periods]."

11 Wang Bing: "If it is frequent and urgent, this is heat. Hence the heart is vexed. A 'frequent [movement in the] vessels' is one that comes and goes urgently and fast."

12 Wang Bing: "If it is strong, evil [qi] abounds. Hence a disease is on the way. A strong [movement in the] vessels comes full and strong."

13 Wang Bing: " 'Above' refers to the 'inch opening;' 'below' refers to 'in the foot-long section.' " Zhang Jiebin: " 'Above' is the 'inch' [location at the wrists]; in the case of 'abundance above,' the evil causes blockages in the upper region. 'The qi is high' is to say: one coughs out of fullness [above]. The 'gate' [section] and the 'foot-long section' are 'below.' In the case of 'abundance below,' the evil causes blockages below. Hence the abdomen is distended and full." Ma Shi: " 'Above' is the 'inch;' 'above abounds' is: the qi resides in a high location. 'Below' is below the 'inch;' this is the 'gate.' 'Abundant below' is: the qi [causes] distension in the center." Wu Kun: "上 refers to a rising [movement in the] vessels. In the case of 'abundance above,' the disease qi is high. 'High' stands for 粗, 'rough.' 下 refers to a descending [movement in the] vessels. In the case of 'abundance below,' the disease qi [causes] distension." Tanba: "All authors

If it is intermittent, then the qi is decreased.[14]
If it is fine, then the qi is diminished.[15]
If it is rough, then the heart aches.
If it is torrential and arrives urgently, like a gushing fountain,[16] and
if, in case the disease advances and the complexion is spoilt, it is extremely thin,
resembling, upon leaving, a string that was cut, death [is imminent].[17]

17-99-2
Now,
the essence brilliance and the five complexions,

---

interpret 'above' and 'below' in the sense of 'inch' and 'foot-long section.' However,
even though the *Nei jing* has the term 'inch opening,' it does not have the doctrine
of the three sections 'inch,' 'gate,' and 'foot-long section.' That is, [all authors] have
drawn their conclusions from the *Nan jing* to interpret the [*Nei*]*jing*. They cannot be
followed. When [the text] speaks of 'above' and 'below' here, it refers to all the vessels
of the upper section and the lower section [of the body] respectively. For details, see
Su wen 20."

14 Wang Bing: " 'Intermittent' is to say: the movement stops in between and cannot
continue its circulation by itself."

15 Lin Yi et al.: "The *Tai su* has 滑, 'smooth,' instead of 細."

16 Wang Bing: "渾渾 is to say: the qi in the vessels is turbid and [moves] disorderly.
革至 is to say: the [movement in the] vessels arrives string-like and strong, replete and
extended. 'Gushing up like a fountain' is to say: [the movement in the vessels] arrives
confused, without any order. It leaves but does not return." Zhang Jiebin: "渾渾 is:
turbid and not clear. 革至 is: strong and tough like a hide." 538/38: "Following 革 a
second character 革 has been omitted; it should be supplemented again in accordance
with ch. 1/13 of the *Mai jing* and ch. 28/5 of the *Qian jin* [*fang*]. 渾渾革革 is a parallel to the statement 弊弊綽綽 below. The meaning of 渾渾革革 is to state that the
vigor of the [movement in the] vessels is excessive, indicating there is yang but no yin.
Hence [the text] states: 病進而危, 'a disease is on the way and this is dangerous.' " For
a detailed discussion, see also 2722/44.

17 Wang Bing: "綽綽 is to say: very feeble, as if there was something which, however,
does not strongly respond to [the fingers of one's] hand. 如弦絕 is to say: the [move-
ment in the] vessels is suddenly interrupted, like a string that is cut and vanishes. If
the signs of a disease advance day by day and the complexion takes a turn to the worse
and if this is accompanied by the [types of movement in the] vessels described here,
death is inevitable." 538/38: "色 is a mistake; in accordance with the *Mai jing* and the
Qian jin [*fang*], it should be 危, 'danger.' 病進而危, 'the disease advances and becomes
a danger,' is a complete sentence. The character 弊 should be read in connection with
the following passage and it should be followed by a second character 弊. 弊弊綽綽

they are the effulgence of the qi.[18]

A red [complexion] should resemble [something of] vermilion [color] wrapped up in white;[19]
it should not resemble ochre.

A white [complexion] should resemble goose feathers;
it should not resemble salt.

A green-blue [complexion] should resemble the gloss of greenish jade;
it should not resemble indigo blue.

A yellow [complexion] should resemble realgar wrapped up in gauze;
it should not resemble clay.

A black [complexion] should resemble the color of multi-layered lacquer;
it should not resemble the sallowness of earth.[20]

If the appearance of the five complexions is delicate and feeble,
that [person's] life will not last for long.[21]

---

parallels the phrase 渾渾革革 above. The character 者 following 弦絕 should be omitted. 弊弊 means that the bow string is destroyed already; 綽綽, *chuo chuo*, reflects the sound of a string that is cut."

18 Wang Bing: "The essential reflection of the five qi appears above in the changes of the five complexions in between the essence brilliance [holes]." 2767/39: "The two characters 精明 have been erroneously moved here from the passage further below: 夫精明者, 所以視萬物. Even though it is possible to interpret 精明 as 精細明察, 'to carefully investigate,' this would not make any sense here." 948/607: "Li Zhongzi commented: 'the essence brilliance appears in the eyes; the five complexions manifest themselves in the face. [The essence brilliance and the five complexions] all are reflections of the qi.' Ma Shi commented: 'The five complexions are ruled by the essence brilliance; the essence spirit manifests itself in the five complexions. Hence essence brilliance and the five complexions are the reflections of my proper qi.'" 1923/38: "精明 refers to the eyes. Wang Bing's explanation [of this term] as names of [acupuncture] holes is mistaken. Of course, there are holes named 精明 in the inner canthi of the eyes, but the present text does not refer to these holes; it refers to the eyes. The evidence for this is in the wording 夫精明者, 所以視萬物, 別黑白, .. The so-called 欲 'desired' and 不欲 'undesired' colors here are the colors of the eyes, not the colors of facial complexion." See there for a detailed discussion of this view.

19 Ma Shi: "白 should be 帛, 'silk.'"

20 65/4: "地蒼 is soil of bluish-black color. Both the *Mai jing* and the *Jia yi jing* have the character 炭, '(char)coal.' The meaning implied is: black and desiccated."

21 Wang Bing: "Complexions of ochre, salt, indigo blue, clay, and earth sallow, all these are manifestations of destruction visible in extreme feebleness. Hence the life of the [persons exhibiting these complexions] will not last long." 538/38: "微 may be a mistake for 危, 'danger.' The mistake may have resulted from identical pronunciation. The expression 'five complexions' summarizes the text above. Ochre, salt, indigo blue,

Now,
essence brilliance,
it is that by which one observes the myriad beings,
distinguishes white from black and
investigates short and long.
If long is regarded as short,
if white is regarded as black,
in this case the essence has decreased.[22]

17-99-7
As for the five depots,
they are the guardians of the center.[23]
When the center has abundance and when the depots are full and
when the qi dominates and one is harmed by fear,
when the voice sounds as if words came out of a room,
this is dampness of the central qi.[24]

---

clay, and earth sallow are spoilt appearances of the five complexions. 'Essence' means
'very.' According to the commentary by Gao 高 to the *Lü shi chun qiu*, 'Jiao zi 驕恣,'
危 is 敗, 'destroyed.' Hence the passage 五色精微象見矣 is to say: A sign of extreme
destruction of the five complexions is manifested externally. This, then, corresponds
to the meaning of the passage below: his life will not last for long." 2263/37: "Following 精微 a character 敗, 'destroyed,' has been omitted and should be supplemented. ..
Wang Bing's commentary proves that the version at his disposal still had the character
敗. 精微 should not be interpreted as referring to a bad color. If the character 敗 is
inserted, the meaning of the sentence becomes clear."

22 Wang Bing: "These are warnings of errors committed by the [physicians]. All
interpretations of a decay of essence brilliance based on such [erroneous diagnosis] are
wrong." 948/607: "Li Zhongzi: 'The essence qi of the depots and palaces gather above
in the eyes and cause its radiant brilliance. Hence one speaks of essence brilliance."
Zhang Zhicong: "The five depots rule the presence of essence. As long as essence is
present, one can see the myriad beings and distinguish long and short."

23 Wang Bing: "The center of the body's physical appearance is the location where
the five spirits are securely guarded." Lin Yi et al.: "*Jia yi jing* and *Tai su* have 府,
'palace,' instead of 守." Wang Hongtu et al. /149 suggested in comparison with the
passage 虛無之守, where Wang Hongtu et al. followed Hu Shu in interpreting 守 as
宇: "守 should be an error for 宇, 'location,' 'dwelling.'" See 2847/35 for a discussion.

24 Wang Bing: "中 is to say 'in the abdomen.' 盛 is to say: the qi abounds. 藏 is to say:
the lung depot. 氣勝 is to say: [the qi] overpowers exhalation and inhalation, causing
them to change to panting breath. That is, when the qi abounds in the abdomen, when
the lung depot is filled and when the qi overpowers [the patient's] breathing so that
it changes [to panting, in this condition the patient] tends to be harmed by fear and
his voice cannot be emitted; it is as if it were in a room. All this results from dampness

When the speech is feeble and
when it takes an entire day before he speaks again,
this is qi deprivation.[25]

When someone fails to tie his clothes [properly to his body],[26] and
when [this person] tends to use bad language,
without sparing those near and those distant to him,
this is a spirit brilliance disorder.[27]

17-100-2
When the granaries do not [keep what they] store,
in this case the doors are not under control.[28]

---

qi in his abdomen." Zhang Qi: "The five character passage beginning with 氣勝 is a later addition."

25 Wu Kun: "That is to say, [the patient's] speech is very weak and he has difficulties to continue [talking]. He must wait all day before he can talk again." Zhang Zhicong: "The meaning here is that the essence qi of the five depots is depleted and one brings forth one's voice as is described here. 微 refers to weakness of the qi of one's voice. In case '[the patient has to wait] all day before he can speak again,' the qi is interrupted. The *Shang han lun* states: 'repletion results in talkativeness; depletion results in 鄭聲.' 鄭聲 is 重語, 'to stammer.'" Yu Chang: "The character 日 is an erroneous insertion. 終 is [to say]: the end of a word, of a statement; not the end of the day." Li Guoqing: "終日而復言 is to say: one's speech does not continue. One must let a very long time elapse before one is able to continue one's words. In this case the qi is extremely depleted and it is insufficient to let one speak. It is not a 'stammering.'" 2855/53: "乃 also has the meaning of 難, 'difficult;' 復 also has the meaning of 再, 'again.' An appropriate explanation is: 'one has difficulties in continuing to speak.'" For a detailed discussion supporting Wu Kun's view, see 666/42.

26 Wu Kun: "衣被不斂 is: one does not feel ashamed to undress." Nei jing xuan du: "One does not know how to dress properly." 1934/35: "斂 is 覆蓋, 'to cover.' The meaning of the entire sentence is: 'The garments do not cover the body.'" For details of the argument, see there.

27 538/38: "不避 is: one cannot distinguish. 避 is identical with 辟. The *Guang ya*, Shi gu 釋詁 states 辟 is 半. The original character of 半 is 判 and 判 has the meaning of 別, 'to distinguish.'"

28 Wang Bing: " 'Granaries' refers to the spleen and to the stomach. 'Door' refers to the 魄門, which is the 肛門, 'anus.' 要 stands for 禁要, 'tight.' " Zhang Jiebin: "要 stands for 約束, 'controlled.' The 'dark gate' (i.e., the pylorus), the 'screen gate' (i.e., the lower opening of the small intestine) and the '*po* gate' (i.e., the anus), they all are door gates of the granaries. When the door cannot close tightly, then the intestines and the stomach cannot store. Hence uncontrollable diarrhea results." Yao Shaoyu: "When the granaries do not store, everybody blames this on the spleen and on the stomach, not knowing that if the stomach has a disease, it cannot take in, and if the spleen has

When the water fountain does not stop,
in this case the urinary bladder does not [keep what it] stores.[29]

Those who are able to guard, they live.
Those who fail to guard, they die.[30]

Now,
the five depots, they are [those providing] strength to the body.[31]

As for the head,
it is the palace of essence brilliance.[32]
When the head is bent and vision is in the depth,[33]
essence and spirit are about to be lost.

---

a disease, it cannot move [things] on. Here now it is neither such that nothing can be taken in, nor that nothing can be moved on. When the storage is not firm, the responsibility lies with the kidneys. Why? Because the kidney has the two yin [openings; i.e. the openings for urine and feces] as its orifices. When the kidneys are depleted, they are unable to firmly close [these orifices]." Zhang Canjia: "Spleen and stomach have the official position of granary: Hence 'granary' definitely refers to spleen and stomach. 'Door' refers to the anus. 要 has the meaning of 約束, 'restrained,' 'controlled.'" 1978/46 agrees. See also Zhao Yi's 趙翼 *Gai yu cong kao* 陔餘叢考 for the usage of 要 in the sense of 纏, "to bind."

29 Wang Bing: "'Water fountain' refers to the flow from the anterior yin [orifice]."

30 Wang Bing: "As long as the spirit qi is given a place to stay and as long as it is guarded there, one will live. Once it loses its guard, death is inevitable. Now, how does one know that the spirit qi is no longer guarded? When the clothes are not worn orderly and when one tends to badmouth others, regardless of whether they are relatives or distant persons, then these are signs of disorder. In case the disorder is extreme, the [spirit] is not guarded by the depots."

31 Wang Bing: "When the depots are in peace, then the spirit is protected. When the spirit is protected, then the body is strong. Hence [the text] states: 'the strength of the body.'" Gao Jiwu/163: "強 is also used to express the meaning of 保養, 'to nourish.' (Hence this passage should be interpreted as 'The five depots provide the body with nourishment.')" *Xun zi* 荀子, Tian lun 天論, has: 強本而節用, 則天不能貧, with 強 used in the sense of 加強, "to strengthen."

32 110/3: "The *Yu pian* 玉篇 states: 府 is 聚, 'to gather.' A commentary to the *Zhou li*, Tian guan, Ji yi 天官, 疾醫 states: 'They are called 'palace' because they collect to abundance.' .. Hence, the original meaning of 府 is 藏, 'to store.'"

33 Zhang Jiebin: "The eyes have sunk in and they have no luster." 324/51: "The verb 視 is used here as a noun; it has the meaning 'eyes' and serves as subject." 1932/69: "The eyes have sunk back into their caves and have lost their luster."

17-100-5
As for the back,
it is the palace of that which is in the chest.[34]
When the back is curved and the shoulders drop,[35]
the palace will soon be destroyed [36]

As for the lower back,
it is the palace of the kidneys.
When [a person] is unable to turn and to sway,
his kidneys will soon be worn out.[37]

As for the knees,
they are the palaces of the sinews.[38]
When [a person] cannot [freely] bend and stretch and
if while walking he is bent forward and leans [on a stick],[39]
his sinews will soon be worn out.

As for the bones,
they are the palace of the marrow.
When [a person] cannot stand for long and
if while walking he staggers back and forth,
his bones will soon be worn out.

---

34 175/34: "That is to say, the chest and the back region constitute the palace of the two organs situated in the chest, i.e., heart and lung."

35 *NJCD*, quoting the *Yi xue gang mu* 醫學綱目: "隨 is 垂, 'to drop'."

36 Duan Yishan/12: "In accordance with the following statements 府將壞 should be 胸將壞, 'the chest is about to be destroyed.'"

37 641/37: "This is to say, the function of the loins depends on the kidneys." Wu Kun: "憊 is identical with 敗, 'destroyed.'"

38 Zhang Jiebin: "Even though the sinews are controlled by the liver, but most important among those holding together the joints and thereby keeping the body upright are the sinews in the fold behind the knee. Hence the knee is the palace of the sinews."

39 Lin Yi et al.: "Another edition has 俯, 'to bow down,' instead of 附. The *Tai su* has 跗, 'instep.'" Wu Kun: "僂 is to bend one's body. 附 is: to be unable to walk by oneself; to walk by leaning on something." Tanba: "To read 附 as 俯 is correct. See *Zuo zhuan*, 7th year of duke Zhao 昭." Li Guoqing: "附 is identical with 俯. The *Shuo wen* states: '俯 is 俛病, 'to suffer from bowing down.' The *Guang ya* states: '俯 is 短, 'short.' 僂附 is 僂俯, 'to have the back curved and to bow the head.'" 693/37: "The *Shuo wen* states: '附 is 附婁, this is a small earthen hill.' That is, 行則僂附 is to describe that the shins are curved like a hill." For a detailed discussion of this passage, see there.

Those who are able to [maintain] strength, they live.
Those who fail to [maintain] strength, they die." [40]

[   ]

17-100-9
Qi Bo:[41]
"In all cases contrary to [what is to be expected in the course of] the four
seasons,
surplus generates essence,[42]
insufficiency generates wasting.[43]
Responding to great excess,
insufficiency generates essence.
Responding to insufficiency,
surplus generates wasting.
When yin and yang [qi] do not correspond to each other,
the name of the disease is closure and obstruction." [44]

---

40 Wang Bing: "強 is to say: the central qi is strong and firm to offer protection."
Gao Jiwu/163: "Those who receive nourishment will live; those who lose nourishment
will die."

41 Lin Yi et al.: "This statement by Qi Bo is not preceded by a question." Zhang Qi:
"The 39 character passage beginning with 岐伯曰 must have been moved here from
another section of the classic. No forced interpretation should be attempted." Tanba:
"The meaning of the two characters 精 and 消 is not very clear. Zhang Qi is right."

42 Yu Yue: "精 is 甚, 'very.' That is to say, in all instances of surplus there is an excess
very much [beyond normal]." See also Wang Hongtu et al. /153. 1583/59: "The *Nei
jing shi yi* 內經釋義 of Beijing Chinese Medical College comments: 'Essence is to
say: extreme evil.' The *Shen Nong ben cao jing* in its section on Dragon Bones (龍骨)
states: 'They master demon possession in heart and abdomen; essence beings and old
goblins.' And in the section on *xu chang qing* 徐長卿: 'It masters demonic beings,
the one hundred essences, and *gu*-poison.' All these instances are additional evidence
proving that 'essence' has the meaning of 'disease,' or 'evil.'" 65/6: " 'Essence' is to say:
strength. See the *Ji yun* 集韻. 有餘為精 is to say: when the [movement in the] vessels
has a surplus, then evil qi abounds."

43 65/7: "消 is 弱, 'weak.' See *Shi min shi ji bing* 釋名釋疾病. 不足為消 is to say:
when the [movement in the] vessels is insufficient, the proper qi is weak."

44 Wang Bing: " 'Contrary to the four seasons' is: all insufficiencies are decreases of
blood and qi; all surpluses are dominations of evil qi over the essence. When the qi
of yin and yang do not correspond to each other, they cannot circulate through each
other's [region]. Hence [the text] states: 'closure and resistance.' " Yu Yue: "Wang Bing
comments: 'all surpluses are dominations of evil qi over the essence.' Why, however,

17-101-2
[Huang] Di:
"The vessels,
how about their movement in the course of the four seasons?
How does one know where a disease is located?
How does one know what changes are caused by a disease?
How does one know whether a disease is active in the interior regions?[45]
How does one know whether a disease is active in the outer regions?
I should like to ask these five [questions];
may I hear [an answer]?"

Qi Bo:
"Please, let me speak about
the [movement in the vessels] as it is as grand as the revolving movement of
heaven;[46]
outside of the myriad beings and
inside the six [cardinal points] uniting [the world][47]
there are the changes of heaven and earth and
the correspondences with yin and yang.

---

does the text speak only of 精 rather than of 邪氣勝精? Wang Bing's comment is
wrong. 精 is to say 甚, 'very.'" Gao Shishi: "精 is 精强, 'pure strength.' 消 is 消弱,
'weakness.' The grand schema of the [movement in the] vessels is such that if there is
surplus, then this is essence [strength]; if there is insufficiency, then this is weakness.
If the [movement in the vessels] is in contrast to the four seasons, essence [strength]
and weakness lose their regularity. Hence, during the seasons of spring and summer,
the [movement in the] vessels should be of great excess. In the case of great excess
surplus should be considered as essence [strength]. Here now it should be great excess,
but insufficiency is considered as essence [strength]. During the seasons of autumn
and winter, the [movement in the] vessels should be insufficient. In the case of insufficiency insufficiency should be considered as weakness. Here now it should be insufficient, but surplus is considered as weakness. In this situation, the [movement in the]
vessels is not in mutual correspondence with the yin and yang of the four seasons and
the name of the disease is 'closure and obstruction.' 'Closure' is inability to urinate;
'obstruction' is vomiting."

45 65/7: "乍 stands for 作 in the sense of 'a disease breaks out.' 乍 is the original version of 作. The inscriptions on the bronze vessels of the Shang and Zhou era all have
乍 instead of 作."

46 Wang Bing: "He refers to those periodic circulatory movements of yin and yang
that can be observed and serve to explain [those movements] of yin and yang that
cannot be observed."

47 Wang Bing: "六合 is to say: the four cardinal points [plus] above and below."

The gentle warmth of the bygone spring
brings forth the summerheat of summer;
the indignation of a bygone autumn
brings forth the anger of winter.[48]

17-101-6
The movement [of the qi] during the four [seasonal] changes:
the [movement in the] vessels rises and descends with them.
Therefore,
in spring it should meet the circle;
in summer it should meet the square.
In autumn it should meet the beam;
in winter it should meet the weight.[49]

Hence,
during the 45 days [following the term] 'winter solstice,' the yang qi is feeble
and ascends and the yin qi is feeble and descends.
During the 45 days [following] 'summer solstice,' the yin qi is feeble and
ascends and the yang qi is feeble and descends.

---

48 Wang Bing: " 'Spring warmth becomes summerheat' is to say: the yang emerges
[in spring] and reaches abundance [in summer]. 'Autumn indignation and winter anger' is to say: the yin is minor [in autumn] and proceeds towards strenght [in winter].
Another [version] has 急, 'urgent,' instead of 忿. The meaning is: in autumn the qi is
strong and urgent."

49 Gao Shishi: "In spring, the qi of heaven begins to emerge. The [movement in
the] vessels should be soft, weak, at the surface, and smooth. If it is so, it revolves and
attains the measure of a circle. In summer, the qi of heaven is properly spread. The
[movement in the] vessels is vast, strong and reaches everywhere. That is, it is full and
attains the measure of the square. In autumn, the qi of heaven begins to descend. The
[movement in the] vessels should be balanced, quiet, light, and hollow. That is, it is
balanced and regular and attains the measure of the beam. In winter, the qi of heaven
is securely stored. The [movement in the] vessels should be in the depth, stone[-like],
and heavy. That is, it descends into the depth and attains the measure of the weight.
These are the movements of the four [seasonal] changes and the [movement in the]
vessels rises and descends with them." 65/7: "中 has the meaning of 合, 'to agree
with.' " For the use of 中 in the sense of 符合, "to correspond", see *Shang jun shu* 商
君書, Jun chen 君臣: 言不中法者不聽, 行不中法者不高, 事不中法者不為, "Words
that do not correspond to the rules, do not listen to them. A conduct that does not
correspond to the rules, do not revere it. Any business that does not correspond to the
rules, do not carry it out." Also, *Han Fei zi* 韓非子, Nan yi 難一, has 中程者賞, 不
中程者誅, "Those who correspond to the rules, they are rewarded. Those who do not
correspond to the rules, they are punished."

Yin and yang [qi] have their seasons;
their periodicity [of waxing and waning] corresponds with the [movements in the] vessels.
From the loss of mutual [correspondence between these] periodicities[50]
one knows [how far the movement in the] vessels has departed [from normal].
From the length of the time of the departure
one knows the time of death.[51]

17-102-1
The subtle and the mysterious [operation of yin and yang qi] occurs in the vessels,
it must be investigated.
The arrangement of this investigation
originates from yin and yang.
The norms of this origin
are generated by the five agents.
The measure of this generation,
the four seasons provide [its] numbers.[52]

<Supplementation and draining must not be carried out at random;
they should match heaven and earth as if one were one [with them].
Grasp the nature of this oneness
to know death and survival.>[53]

17-102-3
Hence,
the [pitches of one's] voice match the five [musical] tones.[54]

---

50 698/66: "期 has the meaning of 會合, 'to come together', 'to coincide.'"

51 Wang Bing: "If one observes the regularity in the rising and falling of yin and yang, one knows the external signs of the changes and shifts occurring in the conduit vessels. If one examines the irregularities in the changes and shifts of the climate, one knows the terms when qi and blood are separated from and united with [the climate]. The terms of this departure cannot vary; hence one knows the moment of death."

52 We follow the *Tai su* which has 數, "number," instead of 宜. Yu Yue: "作數 is correct. 度 and 數 form a rhyme." Tanba, Duan Yuzai, and Zhang Yizhi et al. agree.

53 Tanba: "The 33 characters beginning with 始之 do not appear in the *Jia yi jing*. The same applies to the 78 character passage beginning with 是知陰盛則夢. With these characters omitted, the flow of the text becomes meaningful."

54 65/7: "The five pitches are: shouting, laughing, singing, wailing, and groaning."

The complexions match the five agents.
The [movements in the] vessels match yin and yang.[55]

This is to know:[56]
When the yin [qi] abounds,
then one dreams of wading through a big water and is in fear.
When the yang [qi] abounds,
then one dreams of big fires burning.
When both yin and yang [qi] abound,
then one dreams of mutual killings and harmings.
When [the qi] abounds above,
then one dreams of flying.
When [the qi] abounds below,
then one dreams of falling.
When one has eaten to extreme repletion,
then one dreams of giving.[57]
When one is extremely hungry,
then one dreams of taking.[58]
When the liver qi abounds,
then one dreams of anger.
When the lung qi abounds,
then one dreams of weeping.
When there are many short worms,
then one dreams of crowds assembling.[59]

---

55 Wang Bing: "In one's voice one produces the tones *gong, shang, yue, zhi,* and *yu*. Hence they correspond to the five tones. In one's complexion one displays the colors green, yellow, red, white, and black. Hence they correspond to the five agents. In one's [movement in the] vessels one exhibits the resting or ruling of cold and summerheat. Hence it corresponds to the qi of yin and yang."

56 See 2475/158 for a comparison of the following statements with an almost identical passage in *Lie zi*, Mu wang 穆王. The following passage from 陰盛 to 則夢哭 is almost identical with a passage in *Ling shu* 43. It may have been moved here erroneously. If omitted, the argumentation of this treatise in view of an examination of the movement in the vessels appears more coherent. Lin Yi et al.: "This passage from 陰盛 to 則夢哭 has been erroneously moved here from the *Ling shu.*"

57 Wang Bing: "Because there is an internal surplus."

58 Wang Bing: "Because there is an internal insufficiency."

59 Wang Bing: "If there are many short worms inside the body, then one dreams of crowds assembling."

When there are many long worms,
then one dreams of fights and mutual harming.>[60]

17-103-1
Hence,
to feel [the movement in] the vessels has a Way:
emptiness and quietude are to be treasured.[61]
On spring days, it floats at the surface,
like a fish swimming in a wave.[62]
On summer days, it is in the skin,
overflowing;[63] the myriad beings are present in surplus
On autumn days, it descends into the skin.
The hibernating creatures will soon go [into hiding].[64]
On winter days, it is at the bones;
the hibernating creatures are firmly sealed in.[65]

---

60 Wang Bing: "When long worms move, then there is no peace inside [the body]. When there is no peace inside, then the spirit races in disturbance. Hence one has such dreams." Lin Yi et al.: "These two sentences should not appear here. They constitute a text moved here from somewhere else in the classic."

61 Lin Yi et al.: "The *Jia yi jing* has 實, 'to treasure,' instead of 保." Wang Bing: "Above, [the text] has elucidated the correspondences between [the movements in] the vessels [and the seasonal movement of yin and yang qi]. Here now it raises the issue of the origins of feeling the [movement in the] vessels. Now, the Way of feeling the [movement in the] vessels requires that one keeps one's heart empty (i.e., open) and that one keeps one's mind quiet. This way one secures gain and loss and does not lose anything." Fang Wenhui/74: "保 stands for 實, 'precious.' 'An unprejudiced mind and quietude are most valuable.'" 951/768: "Li Zhongzi comments: 虛 is 空心, 'open-minded,' 'unbiased.' 靜 is: the body should be still and one should refrain from noise and movement.'" 65/8: "虛 is 'without desires.'"

62 2284/60: "在波 should be 在皮, 'in the skin.' In ancient times, 皮 and 膚 were used separately. 皮 referred to the surface [skin] and 膚 to the deeper [skin]." Jiang Yongao: "在皮 is a later addition. The original rhyme ends with 游."

63 Wang Bing: "泛泛乎 is to describe a great abundance of yang qi, which is reflected by the qi in the vessels. 'The myriad beings are present in surplus' [is to say: the movement in the vessels] is to obtain easily; it is vast and big."

64 Wang Bing: "They follow the gradual descent of the yang qi. Hence [the text] states 'descent into the skin.' How does one know that the yang qi descends gradually? Because the hibernating creatures go into hiding." 668/72: "去 has the meaning here of 藏, 'to conceal,' 'to remove.'"

65 Wang Bing: "'In the bones' is to say: the [movement in the] vessels is in the depth. 'The hibernating creatures are firmly sealed in' is to say: the yang qi is hidden away."

<The gentleman resides in his chamber.>[66]

17-103-4
Hence it is said:
Those who know the interior, they press [the vessels] and sort out their [inner movements].
Those who know the exterior, having ended they begin it.[67]

These six [patterns],
[they constitute] the grand law of feeling the [movement in the] vessels:

When the beating in the vessels of the heart is firm and extended,[68]
[the patient] must suffer from a curled tongue and from an inability to speak.

Gu dian yi zhu xuan bianxiezu /53: "That is to say, the [movement in the] vessels is hidden in the depth. One has to press the fingers down to the bones to feel it."

66 From 持脈有道 to 君子居室 the text is worded in rhymes. For an analysis, see 1131/39.

67 Wang Bing: " 'To know the interior' is to say: to know the qi in the vessels. Hence one presses [vessels] and makes [the qi] the guiding principle. 'To know the exterior' is to say: to know the complexion as reflection [of internal conditions]. Hence one ends with the five colors and begins anew." Zhang Jiebin: " 'Interior' refers to the qi of the depots. The [external] manifestation of the [qi in the] depots occurs at [definite] locations. Hence one can press [the vessels at these locations] and record [the status of the movement passing through them]. 'Exterior' refers to the qi of the conduits. The [movement in the] conduit vessels follows a [definite] sequence. Hence it is possible to reach its end and begin it anew." Gao Shishi: "One heavily presses the vessels and records the arrival frequency [of the movement inside of them]. One begins with light pressure and ends with heavy pressure. From the heavy [pressure] one returns to the light [pressure]. This way one knows the [movements in the] exterior vessels. Hence, once one knows the exterior, one stops and begins it [anew]. When this pressing and recording of the interior and the exterior has ended and begun six times, one has acquired the grand pattern of grasping the [movement in the] vessels." Wu Kun: "The Way of feeling the [movement in the] vessels has end and has beginning. At the beginning, one takes the [movement] at the surface; in the end one takes it in the depth. The [movement] at the surface serves to indicate the [condition in the] exterior; the [movement] in the depth serves to indicate the [condition in the] interior. 終而始之 is to say: take its [movement in the] depth and then examine again at the surface." Wang Hongtu et al. /200-201: " 'Inner' refers to the conduit vessels here; 'outer' refers to the network vessels here."

68 Wang Bing: "搏 is to say: to beat against the hand. Whenever the beating of the vessels is firm and extended, the heart is overtaxed, and the qi in the depots and vessels is extremely depleted. The hand minor yin vessel of the heart rises from the heart

When it is soft and dispersed, he must [suffer from] wasting circle. [The disease] will end by itself.[69]

When the beating in the vessels of the lung is firm and extended,
[the patient] must suffer from spitting blood.[70]
When it is soft and dispersed, he must suffer from profuse sweating.
{Until this day[71] it did not break out again.}[72]

---

connection and moves on both sides of the throat. Hence it causes the tongue to curl up and shorten, with the result that [the patient] cannot speak any longer."

69 475/42: "In the wording 當消環自已, there seems to be an erroneous omission. All the examples above and below have 當病; in accordance with the *Mai jing*, [the character 病] should be supplemented. Also, Lin [Yi] in his commentary (Lin Yi et al.) points out: the *Jia yi jing* has 渴, 'thirst,' instead of 環. Ch.4 of the *Jia yi jing*, ch. 6 of the *Mai jing*, and ch. 15 of the *Tai su*, all have 消渴. This is evidence enough that following the character 消 the character 渴 is missing. However, in the *Jia yi jing*, the *Mai jing*, and the *Tai su*, following the character 渴 the character 環 was left out. This sentence should read as follows: 當病消渴, 環自已, 'one should suffer from wasting-and-thirst; it heals by itself after a short while.' " This suggestion is difficult to follow. If one assumes that wasting-and-thirst was used to designate diabetes in Chinese antiquity already, one may also assume that it was known that this disease does not heal by itself. Neither an explanation of 環 as "circulation" nor its interpretations as "immediate" make sense here. Hence we may leave the term as it is and hypothesize that it reflects an ancient disease term, comparable to 肺消, "wasting of the lung" and 消中, "wasting center", the meaning of which had been forgotten by the time of the *Mai jing*, the *Jia yi jing*, etc. It is therefore that we prefer a literal translation. Wang Bing: "Whenever the [movement in the] vessels is soft and dispersed, the qi is replete while the blood is depleted. 消 is to say: 消散, 'to disperse.' 環 is to say: 環周, 'circle.' That is to say, the flow of the qi in the conduits resembles a circular [movement]. It should disperse by itself when the fire rules."

70 Wang Bing: "In the case of an extreme depletion in the lungs, the [movement in the] network [vessels] is reverted. When this is the case, blood flows away. Hence [the patient] spits blood."

71 The *Lei jing* has 令 , "to let," instead of 今. Hence Zhang Jiebin: "Sweating is to lose large amounts of yang [qi]. Hence it cannot be dispersed further." – The reference edition used by us also has 令 instead of 今. However, the Renmin weisheng chubanshe edition with unabbreviated characters on which the reference edition is based has 今. Obviously, this sentence was written in antiquity as a commentary, a fact later editors were not aware of. Perhaps they modified the character to make this sentence fit better into its context.

72 Wang Bing: "When sweat flows away through the dark palaces, the bodily liquids rush to the interstice structures. When [a person] is washed in that cold water is poured over him, his skin closes tightly and the sweat will be kept inside. When because of that pouring the sweat is kept inside, the [text] states: 'Pouring [has caused]

When the beating in the vessels of the liver is firm and extended and
when the complexion is not green-blue,
[the patient] must suffer from a fall as if he had been beaten.
<Hence there is blood below the flanks, letting that person pant because of [qi]
moving contrary [to its regular course]>.[73]

When it is soft and dispersed and when the complexion is glossy,
he must suffer from spillage drink.
{'Spillage drink' is: one is extremely thirsty and drinks a lot and [the liquid]
easily enters[74] the muscles and the skin and the region outside of the intestines
and the stomach.}[75]

When the beating in the vessels of the stomach is firm and extended and
when the complexion is red,
[the patient] must suffer from a broken thigh bone.
When it is soft and dispersed,
he must suffer from food block.[76]

---

sweat not to effuse until to now.' 灌 is to say: 灌洗, 'to pour out to wash.' When summerheat abounds this is done quite often." In contrast, Yao Shaoyu: "灌汗 refers to a
profuse sweating, as if sweat had been poured over [a person]."

73 Wang Bing: "In all cases where the presence of the qi of the respective conduit
itself exhibited in the [movement in the] vessels fails to correspond to the complexion,
in all these cases the disease has not originated inside but has come to dominate from
outside. Now, the vessel of the liver depot is straight and long/extended. Hence [the
text] states: 'When the complexion is not green-blue, [the patient] must suffer from
a fall, as if he had been beaten. The liver rules the two flanks. Hence [the text] states:
'Hence there is blood below the flanks.' The ceasing yin vessel of the liver spreads
through the flanks and follows the back of the gullet. Its branches leave the liver, penetrate the diaphragm in separate courses and rise to pour their contents into the lung.
In the present case, blood is below the flanks. Hence the blood qi rises and steams the
lung. Hence it lets the patient pant because of reversely moving [qi]."

74 Lin Yi et al.: "The *Jia yi jing* has 溢, 'spillage,' instead of 易." 1126/9: "易 is 溢,
'to spill.'"

75 Wang Bing: "When the facial complexion reveals drifting moisture, this is a case
of being struck by dampness. When one is struck by dampness while the blood is
depleted, the water-liquid fails to dissipate. Hence [the text] states 'must suffer from
spillage drink.' Because one is full of water that one has drunk, [this water] spills over
into the muscles, the skin, as well as into [the regions] outside the intestines and the
stomach."

76 Wang Bing: "痺 is 痛, 'pain.' The yang brilliance vessel of the stomach .. enters
the broken basin, moves down to the diaphragm, ties up with the stomach and winds
around the spleen. Hence when eating one feels pain. [The patient] experiences chest

17-104-4
When the beating in the vessels of the spleen is firm and extended and
when the complexion is yellow,
[the patient] must suffer from being short of qi.[77]
When it is soft and dispersed and
when the complexion is not glossy,
he must suffer in his feet and shins[78] from swelling. {Resembling water}

When the beating in the vessels of the kidneys is firm and extended and
when the complexion is yellow and red,
[the patient] must suffer from a broken lower back.[79]
When it is soft and dispersed,
he must suffer from diminished blood."[80]

{Until this day[81] it did not [break out] again.}

17-105-1
[Huang] Di:
"When in diagnosis one notices a tense [movement in the] vessels of the heart,
which disease is that?
What manifestation does this disease assume?"

---

pressure; the qi fails to disperse." Lin Yi et al.: "If 痺 is explained as 痛, 'pain,' this passage makes no sense." Zhang Jiebin: "食痺 indicates the following: food is consumed
but not digested; when it is consumed one has chest pressure with pain and spits
liquid. One must vomit to stop [this feeling]." 538/38: "痺 is a mistaken character
and should be 痞. The *Shuo wen* states: 痞 is 痛, 'pain.' 痺 is a dampness disease; [the
character] does not carry the meaning of 'pain.'"

77 Wang Bing: "When the spleen is depleted, then the lung has nothing that nourishes it. The lung rules the qi. Hence the qi is diminished."

78 *SWJZ*: "胻 is 脛耑, 'the [upper] end of the lower leg.'" *NJCD* agrees and regards
胻 and 䯒 as conveying identical meanings.

79 Wang Bing: "When the color of the qi is yellow-red, then this is a sign that heart
and spleen attack the kidneys. The kidneys [as a result] receive visitor yang. Hence the
lower back feels as if broken."

80 Wang Bing: "The kidneys rule water to generate and transform the bodily liquids. Here now the kidney qi is not transformed. Hence [the patient] must suffer from
diminished blood."

81 See note 71. Here the *Tai su* has 今, too.

Qi Bo:
"The name of the disease is 'heart elevation illness.'
The lower abdomen will exhibit its manifestation."

[Huang] Di:
"How is this to be explained?"

Qi Bo:
"The heart is a male depot;
the small intestine serves as its messenger.
Hence one says:
The lower abdomen will exhibit its manifestation."[82]

17-105-4
[Huang] Di:
"When in diagnosis one notices a stomach [movement in the] vessels;
what manifestation does the disease assume?"

Qi Bo:
"If the [movement in the] vessels of the stomach is replete, then this is distension.
When it is depleted, then this is outflow."

[Huang] Di:
" 'When a disease is fully developed[83] a change occurs.'
What is that to say?"

Qi Bo:
"When wind is fully developed, it causes [fits of] cold and heat.[84]

82 Wang Bing: "The heart is a male depot; its qi should be yang. Here now the [movement in the] vessels, in contrast, [indicates] cold. Hence this results in elevation disease. All [movements in the] vessels that are forceful and urgent, are cold. 'Manifestation' is to say: manifestation of the disease." Gao Shishi: "The yang in the yang, that is the heart. Hence the heart is a 'male depot.' The heart connects with the small intestine; hence the small intestine serves as its messenger. In the case of 'heart elevation disease,' the small intestine does not serve as its messenger. Hence the lower abdomen should have a manifestation [revealing this]."

83 475/42: "The following five characters 成 should all be read as 盛, 'to abound.' In ancient times, 成 was often used to substitute 盛."

84 Zhang Jiebin: "In some cases the [wind] accumulates in the interior and, as a consequence, the yang is depleted. When the yang is depleted, then external cold is felt. In other cases the [wind] accumulates in the exterior and, as a consequence, the yang

When the solitary [heat] disease is fully developed, it causes a wasting center.[85]
When a recession is fully developed, it causes peak illness.[86]
Wind staying for long causes outflow of [undigested] food.[87]
Fully developed wind in the vessels causes *li*.[88]
The changes and transformations caused by diseases are innumerable."

[Huang] Di:
"Yong-abscesses, swelling, sinew cramps, and bone pain, how does all this emerge?"

---

is replete. When the yang is replete, this generates external heat." Ma Shi: "When stomach wind is fully developed, this results in a disease of alternating fits of cold and heat." Tanba: " 'Cold and heat' refers to the cold and heat of depletion and taxation. This is what was called later on 'wind taxation.' " Li Guoqing agrees: "The [following] text speaks of '..wasting center,' '.. peak illness,' '.. food outflow,' and '*li*,' always refer- ring to names of diseases. Accordingly, 'cold and heat' mentioned here does not refer to symptoms but to a 'cold heat disease.' This is consumption."

85 Wang Bing: " '*Dan*-disease 癉' is dampness with heat. The heat accumulates in- ternally; hence it changes to 'wasting center.' The signs of 'wasting center' are desire to eat and emaciation." Gao Shishi: " '*Dan*-disease' is a fire-heat disease. When the *dan*-disease is fully developed, then the internal liquids are exhausted. Hence a change towards 'wasting center' occurs." Yan Hongchen & Gao Guangzhen/113: " '*Dan*-dis- ease' is an accumulation of heat evil. 消 refers to excessive digestion of liquid and solid food. 中 refers to the central burner, spleen and stomach. 消中 is to say: one eats much and urinates frequently." For a detailed discussion of the term 癉 see *Suwen* 35, note 35.

86 Wang Bing: " 'Recession' is to say: qi moving in a reverse direction. When the qi moves in a reverse direction, it rises and fails to move down again. When this is completed it changes into a peak illness above." Gao Shishi: " 'Recession' refers to cold hands and feet because of receding [qi]. When the recession is complete, yin and yang are no longer in harmony. The qi rises but does not move down again. Hence there is a change to headache and peak illness."

87 Wang Bing: "Wind staying for long does not undergo a change. But the food in the stomach is not transformed and flows off in diarrhea." Gao Shishi: "If one was harmed by wind in spring, in summer this changes to food outflow."

88 Wang Bing: "*Su wen* 42 states: 'When wind cold settles in the vessels and does not leave, this is called *li*-wind.' " Gao Shishi: "When wind harms the conduit vessels, it changes into the *li* abscesses of the *lai* disease 癩. Hence vessel wind develops into *li*." Gao Jiwu/25: "癘 is the ancient version of today's 癩, 'leprosy.' " Zhang Yizhi et al.: "Wang Bing's comment in *Su wen* 42 has 脈風盛為癘. Obviously, 成 and 盛 were used interchangeably in ancient times."

Qi Bo:
"These are swellings [caused] by cold qi;[89]
changes of the eight winds are [responsible]."

17-106-1
[Huang] Di:
"How are they treated?"

Qi Bo:
"These are diseases [associated with the course] of the four seasons.
One heals them with a treatment relying on that by which they are domi-
nated."[90]

[Huang] Di:
"When there is an old disease which is activated in the five depots, and when,
as a result, harm [is manifested in the movement in the] vessels and in the
complexion,[91]
how can one know, in each such case, whether it is a chronic [disease], or one
that came about all of a sudden?"[92]

17-106-4
Qi Bo:
"An encompassing question, indeed!

If it is verified that the [movement in the] vessels is diminished and that the
complexion is not lost,
it is a new disease.[93]

---

89 538/38: "腫 is a mistake; it should be 鍾. 鍾 has the meaning of 'to gather.' 寒氣
之鍾 is to say: accumulations of cold qi."

90 Wang Bing: "勝 is 勝克, 'to subdue.' Like, metal overcomes wood; wood overcomes soil; soil overcomes water; water overcomes fire; fire overcome metal. This then
is [the order of] mutual overcoming."

91 In contrast: Gao Jiwu/454: "Huang Di asked: there are old diseases and there
are new diseases because the five depots were affected by some external evil. As a result, the pulse and the complexion show harm. How can one distinguish in each case
whether it is an old disease or one that was acquired recently."

92 538/38: "The character 至 is an erroneous insertion. Yang [Shang shan] in his
commentary on *Tai su* 15 states: 'How does one know the difference between an old
disease and a recent onset.' It appears as if the version of the *Tai su* on which Yang re-
lied did not have the character 至; hence he did not mention it in his commentary."

93 Wu Kun: "徵 is 驗, 'to examine.'"

If it is verified that the [movement in the] vessels is not lost and that the complexion is lost,
it is a chronic disease.
If it is verified that both the [movement in the] vessels and the five complexions are lost,
it is a chronic disease.
If it is verified that both the [movement in the] vessels and the five complexions are not lost,
it is a new disease.

When liver and kidney [movements in the] vessels arrive simultaneously and when the complexion is greenish-red,
[the patient] must suffer from injuries, [although] no blood is visible.
If blood is already visible,
there is dampness as if struck by water.[94]

17-106-8
{The inside of the foot-long section, on both sides,
this is [the region of] the free ribs.}[95]

---

94 Wang Bing: "The complexion [associated with the] liver is green; the complexion [associated with the] heart is red. When a red complexion appears, the corresponding [movement in the] vessels is vast. If a kidney [movement in the] vessels appears, the corresponding complexion is black. Here now a kidney [movement in the] vessels arrives but, in contrast [to what is appropriate] one observes a heart complexion. The reason is an injury, but no blood is visible. If blood is visible, then dampness qi and water are in the abdomen." Zhang Jiebin: "Whenever the sinews and bones are injured, regardless of whether blood appears or not, the blood will coagulate and the conduits will become blocked. When the qi and the blood are coagulated and blocked, the physical appearance will swell and show fullness as if there were dampness qi in the conduits and this will be similar to being struck by water." Tanba believes that the entire passage from 帝曰: 有故病 to 若中水也 does not fit with the preceding and the following text. Hence he assumes that some text was erroneously omitted. Zhang Qi: "The six character passage beginning with 不見血 is an erroneous insertion." 2855/54: "What connection could exist between 'blood is already visible' and 'dampness?' 濕 may be an error for 澀, 'rough.' For instance, *Ling shu* 36 has 氣濕不行 and this is 氣澀不行 in the *Tai su*. Also, 已 has the meaning of 'to eliminate.' There should be a stop behind 已, with the entire sentence reading as follows: 當病毀傷, 不見血, 已, 見血,澀若中水也, 'he should suffer from an injury. If no blood is visible, this can be healed. If blood is visible this may reach a situation where the passage of qi and blood is rough, similar to being hit by water qi.'"

95 Wang Bing: "'Inside the foot-long section' is to say: inside the foot marsh [region]. 'Both sides' is to say: the outer sides of the foot [marsh region]. The 'free ribs' are close to the kidneys. The foot-long section rules them. Hence inside the foot-long section,

The exterior of the foot-long section serves to examine the kidneys;
the interior of the foot-long section serves to examine the abdomen.

On the central instep,[96]
on the left,
the exterior serves to examine the liver;
the interior serves to examine the diaphragm.
On the right,
the exterior serves to examine the stomach;
the interior serves to examine the spleen.[97]

17-107-2
On the upper instep
on the right,
the exterior serves to examine the lung;

---

on both sides, are the free ribs." 950/716: "Li Zhongzi comments: 季脅 is 小肋, 'the free ribs.'" Zhang Yizhi et al.: "'Inside the foot-long section' refers to the inner side of the arms; it has nothing to do with the 'foot-long section' of the inch-gate-foot region [at the wrists] of later times." Mori: "This paragraph beginning with 尺內兩傍 differs greatly from the text in the *Tai su*; it may be an insertion by Wang Bing." The meaning of this statement remains unclear. It may make sense as an isolated statement pointing out that the lower arm (the foot-long distance between elbow and wrist) touches on the free ribs if held in front of the chest. Such a meaning, though, if correct, appears to be rather unrelated to the subsequent references to points inside and outside the "foot-long section" where the conditions of the kidneys and of the abdominal center can be examined.

96 According to Chinese dictionaries, this is the only known use of 附 in the sense of 跗, "instep". The recent *Tai su* editions have 腹中. 跗上. The 1983 edition by Ren min wei sheng chu ban she offers the same punctuation but includes the commentary of Shou Shange 守山閣 who in contrast would read this passage 以侯腹. 中附上. We follow this reading which is in accordance with the structure below (missing in the *Tai su* version): 以侯脾. 上附上. It remains unclear wether the diagnostic technique outlined in these paragraphs refers to an examination of pulses, or to an inspection of the condition of the skin. The latter possibility appears plausible in view of the distance of the "central instep" region from the wrists. Also, such ancient terms as 看脈, 'to inspect the vessels,' as well as some terms associated with the condition of the vessels, including 澀, "rough", and 滑, "smooth", suggest that feeling the condition of the skin above the vessels may have played a significant role in ancient diagnosis. "Rough" and "smooth" are primarily descriptions of a surface, not of a movement in the vessels.

97 Wang Bing: "The spleen is located in the center. Hence it is examined through the interior. The stomach is the market place. Hence it is examined through the exterior."

the interior serves to examine the chest center.[98]
On the left,
the exterior serves to examine the heart;
the interior serves to examine the *dan zhong*.[99]

The front serves to examine the front;
the back serves to examine the back.[100]

<The upper [part] of the upper end, this is where the affairs in the chest and in the throat [can be examined].[101]
The lower [part] of the lower end, this is where the affairs in the lower abdomen, the lower back, the thighs, the knees, the shins, and the feet [can be examined].>[102]

17-107-5
When [the movement in the vessels] is rough and big,
the yin is insufficient and the yang has surplus.
This is a heated center.

When [the movement in the vessels] comes hastily and leaves slowly,
with repletion above and depletion below,
this is recession with peak illness.

---

98 Wang Bing: "The lobes of the lung hang down towards the outside. Hence they are examined through the exterior. The chest center rules the qi pipe. Hence it is examined through the interior."

99 Wang Bing: "The *dan zhong* is the sea of qi; it is the throat." Lin Yi et al.: "Wang Bing considered the *dan zhong* to be the throat. He was wrong." 2755/11: "*Dan zhong* is in fact an old name for the throat." For a detailed argument, see there. See also *Su wen* 08, where Wang Bing interpreted *dan zhong* as a reference to the "see of qi" in the center of the chest. Yang Shangshan, too, had interpreted *dan zhong* as "chest center." Later commentators agreed to identify *dan zhong* as heart enclosure, heart enclosing network.

100 Wang Bing: "The upper front is to say: the left inch opening. The lower front is to say: the front of the chest, as well as the sea of qi. Upper back is to say: the right inch opening. Lower back is to say: the back of the chest, the spine, and the qi pipe."

101 Wang Bing: "上竟上 is: up to the fish line. 下竟下 is to say: the entire location of the foot-long section where the movement in the vessels appears."

102 See 950/716 for an explication of these locations and for an explanation of their rationale in terms of systematic correspondence.

When [the movement in the vessels] comes slowly and leaves hastily,
with depletion above and repletion below,
this is [being struck by] bad wind.
{The fact is,
when one is struck by bad wind, the yang qi receives it.}[103]

When all [the movements in the] vessels are in the depth, fine, and frequent,
this is minor yin recession.[104]

When they are in the depth, fine, frequent, and dispersed,
[this causes alternating fits of] cold and heat.[105]

When they are near the surface and dispersed,
this causes dizziness[106] and they fall to the ground.[107]

17-107-8
Whenever [the movement in the vessels] is near the surface and does not race,
[the evil] is always in the yang.
This then causes heat.
When it races, it is in the hand.[108]

Whenever [the movement in the vessels] is fine and in the depth,
[the evil] is always in the yin:

---

103 Wang Bing: "Because the upper regions are depleted; hence the yang qi receives
it."

104 Wang Bing: "When the [movement in the] vessels in the foot-long section is in
the depth, fine, and frequent, this is a receding movement of the minor yin qi of the
kidneys. Why? Because the [movement in the] vessels in the foot-long section must
not be frequent. Here now it is frequent. Hence [the text] states: 厥, 'recession.' "

105 Wang Bing: "The yang attacks the yin; the yin qi is insufficient. Hence [the patient experiences] cold and heat."

106 916/53: "眴 is identical with 眩, 'confused vision.' "

107 Wang Bing: "When this [movement in the] vessels is at the surface, that is [a
sign of] depletion. When it is dispersed, that is [a sign of] insufficiency. When the
qi is depleted and the blood is insufficient, the head experiences dizziness and [the
patient] falls to the ground."

108 Wang Bing: "That is to state the grand pattern. When [the movement in the
vessels] is at the surface and does not race, then the disease is inside the foot yang
vessels. When it races, the disease is in the hand yang vessels. Yang is fire. Hence it
causes heat."

This then causes pain in the bones.
When it is quiet, it is in the feet.[109]

When it is frequent and stops once in a while,
the disease is in the yang vessels.[110]
[There is] outflow; the stool [carries] pus and blood.
In all cases of excess, squeeze the [vessels].

In the case of rough [movements in the vessels], the yang qi is present in surplus;
in the case of smooth [movements], the yin qi is present in surplus.

When the yang qi is present in surplus, the body will be hot without sweating;
when the yin qi is present in surplus, one will sweat profusely and the body will be cold.
When yin and yang [qi] are present in surplus, one will be cold without sweating.

17-108-4
If one pushes it into the exterior and if it remains in the interior and does not move into the exterior, [then the patient] has accumulations in the heart and in the abdomen.
If one pushes it into the interior and if it remains in the exterior and does not move into the interior, then the body has heat.
If one pushes it upwards and if it moves upwards and does not move into the lower [part], then the lower back and the feet are cool.
If one pushes it downwards and if it moves downwards and does not move into the upper [part], then head and nape ache.[111]

---

109 Wang Bing: "When it is fine and in the depth and races, then the disease has emerged from within the hand yin vessels. When it [is fine and in the depth and] is quiet, the disease has emerged from within the the foot yin vessels. The yin [qi] rules the bones. Hence the bones ache."

110 Wang Bing: "代 is 止, 'to stop.' When it moves frequently and stops once in a while, that is a disease ruled by yang qi." *SWJZ*: "代 is 更, 'to replace.'"

111 Yang Shangshan: "If one pushes upwards what is below, the qi cannot move down. Hence one knows that lower back and feet are cold. If one pushes downwards what is above, the qi cannot rise. Hence one knows that head and nape ache." The *Jia yi jing* has 下而不上 instead of 上而不下 and it has 上而不下 instead of 下而不上. Yu Yue: "The *Jia yi jing* version is correct. Earlier the text says 推而外之, 内而不外, 有心腹積. 推而内之, 外而不内, 身有熱也. In these statements, 内而不外 as well as 外而不内 refer to states of disease. Hence the present two statements should follow the same structure. Otherwise, 'if one pushes it down, so that it moves down and does

If one presses [the vessels] down to the bones and if the qi in the vessels is diminished, then the lower back and the spine ache and the body experiences a block." [112]

not move up,' etc., why should there be a disease? Wang Bing's comment is based on a corrupt version of the text; his interpretation is forced."

112 Wang Bing: "This is so because of excessive yin qi."

Chapter 18
Discourse on Phenomena [Reflecting the Status of] Qi in a Normal Person

18-109-2
Huang Di asked:
"What is [the movement in the vessels of] a normal person [like]?"[1]

Qi Bo responded:
"In man,
during one exhalation, the vessels exhibit two movements.[2]
During one inhalation, the vessels exhibit two movements too.
Exhalation and inhalation constitute one standard breathing period.
If the vessels exhibit five movements,
this is an intercalation [of a fifth movement] because of a deep breathing.[3]

---

1 Wang Bing: "A 'normal person' is to say: someone whose qi signs are balanced." Gao Jiwu/483: "Following the character 人 a character 脈 was omitted. It should be 平人之脈何如, 'what is the [movement in the] vessels of a normal person like?'"

2 300/42: "再 is not 又, 'again,' but 兩, 'twice.'"

3 Zhang Jiebin: "To emit qi is called 呼, 'to exhale.' To take in qi is called 吸, 'to inhale.' One exhalation and one inhalation together are called one breathing. 動 is 至, 'to arrive.' 再動 is 兩至, 'to arrive twice.' A normal person's [movement in the] vessels arrives twice during one exhalation and it arrives twice again during one inhalation. 呼吸定息 is to say: the moment when one breathing is completed while the next breathing has not commenced yet. [At this moment] the [movement in the] vessels arrives another time. Hence [the text] speaks of five movements/arrivals. 閏 is 餘, 'surplus.' Just as one says 閏月, 'an intercalary moon.' That is to say, a normal person among his regular breathing, exhibits one very long breathing. This is [meant by] 閏以太息, 'insertion of a great breathing.' Still, the arrival [of movements in the vessels] is not restricted to just five. This is just the status of a normal person without disease. However, if one counts the moments between breathings and the deep breathings, roughly the [movement in the] vessels should arrive six times during one breathing. Hence *Ling shu* 15 says: During exhalation and inhalation, the movement in the vessels proceeds by six inches. Hence one arrival corresponds to one inch." Tanba: "閏 is 餘, 'excess.' Zhang Jiebin's comment is quite detailed and corresponds to the contents of the *Nan jing*. However, the *Nan jing* states: 'One exhalation, two movements. One inhalation, two movements. Between exhalation and inhalation, one movement. That is, during a standard breathing period: five movements.' Zhang Jiebin states that there are four movements during one breathing period and with another movement in between two breathing periods, this makes altogether five movements. This is slightly different [from the *Nan jing*]." Mori: "One breathing period with four movements [in the vessels], that is one standard breathing period. Between each exhalation and

That is called 'normal person.'[4]

{A 'normal person' is not ill.}

As a rule, one takes [someone] who is not ill [as a standard] to assess a patient's [condition].

The physician is not ill.

Hence one takes the normal breathing [of the healthy physician] as a pattern for assessing the patient's [condition].[5]

18-109-5

When man

exhales once and his vessels exihibit one movement and

when he inhales once and his vessels exhibit one movement,

that is called 'short of qi.'[6]

When man

exhales once and his vessels exhibit three movements and

when he inhales once and his vessels exhibit three movements and are racing,

with heat appearing in the foot-long section,

---

inhalation there is one [additional] movement. This accounts for five movements during one standard breathing period. 閏餘 has the same meaning as the 閏 in the term 閏月, 'intercalary month.' Hence, because in addition to the standard breathing period there is an additional breathing, it is called 'intercalary.' With this intercalary breathing added, [a person] is normal and exhibits five movements in the vessels during one breathing period. If one were to speak only of exhalation and inhalation, then there are four movements during one breathing period."

4 Wang Bing: "The total length of the conduit vessels for one circulation through the body is 162 feet. Both during exhalation and during inhalation two movements in the vessels [can be felt]. During a standard breathing period, [because] yet another movement in the vessels [arrives], there are altogether five movements. After altogether 270 standard breathing periods, the qi can complete one circulation. Fifty circulations, then, cover 13 500 standard breathing periods. [In this time], all the qi passes over a distance of 8100 feet. If this is the case, [the movement of the qi] corresponds to the regular measures of heaven and the qi in the vessels is neither insufficient nor greatly excessive. The phenomena [reflecting the status] of the qi are balanced and adjusted. Hence [the text] speaks of a 'normal person.'" The first chapter of the *Wai ke jing yi* 外科精義 quotes this passage, but has 為, 'constitutes,' instead of 閏.

5 We read this passage as 以平息調之為法.

6 Wang Bing: "If both during exhalation and inhalation the vessels exhibit one movement, this is less one half of [the status of] a normal person. During 270 standard breathing periods, the qi proceeds by 81 feet, that is 4050 feet during 13500 standard breathing periods. Hence the reason for speaking of 'diminished qi' is obvious."

that is called 'to suffer from warmth.'⁷
If the [skin in the] foot-long section is not hot and
if the [movement in the] vessels is smooth,
that is called 'ill from wind.'
If the [movement in the] vessels is rough,
that is called 'block.'⁸

18-109-7
When man
exhales once and his vessels exhibit four movements or more,
that is called 'fatal.'
If the [movement in the] vessels is interrupted and fails to arrive,
that is called 'fatal.'⁹
If at times it is spaced, at times frequent,¹⁰
that is called 'fatal.'

18-109-8
The regular qi of a normal person is supplied by the stomach.
{The stomach [qi] is the regular qi of the normal person.}
When someone has no stomach qi, that is called 'movement contrary [to a

---

7 Wang Bing: "躁 is 煩躁, 'perplexed.'" Gao Jiwu/162: "Wang Bing's comment is a misrepresentation of the ancient meaning [intended here]. The character 躁 in the present text should be interpreted as 急躁有力, 'racing with force.'"

8 Wang Bing: "If both during exhalation and inhalation the vessels exhibit three movements, this exceeds [the status of] a normal person by one half. During 270 standard breathing periods, the qi proceeds by 243 feet. The signs of the disease become apparent because of this [status]. Now, the foot-long section is a yin section, while the inch section is a yang section. When both the yin and the yang sections are hot, this is warmth. If only the yang section exhibits a hasty and abounding [movement], then this [is a sign of] wind hitting the yang. 'Smooth' is to say: yang abundance. Hence the disease is wind. 'Rough' is to say: absence of blood. Hence the disease is numbness-block." Beijing zhongyi xueyuan et al./106: "'Block' is a disease where the passage of blood and qi are blocked." 1484/388: "Symptoms of pain and numbness in the muscle flesh and joints resulting from disharmonies in qi and blood caused by affections by wind, cold, or dampness evil." For a comprehensive discussion of the meaning of 庳 in the *Nei jing*, see 1801/10.

9 Wang Bing: "When the [movement in the] vessels is interrupted and fails to arrive, the true qi of heaven is completely absent."

10 Wang Bing: "When the [movement in the] vessels is alternatingly spaced and frequent, the essence of the grain in the stomach has perished too. Hence these are all signs of [imminent] death. Hence the following statement." Gao Jiwu/236: "數 is to be interpreted as 細密, 'fine and close meshed.' It is to be read as *cu*."

regular course].'[11]

A movement contrary [to a regular course results in] death.

When in spring [the vessels have] stomach [qi and exhibit a] slightly string[-like movement],[12] that is called 'normal.'

If it is mostly string[-like] with diminished stomach [qi present], that is called 'liver disease.'

If it is only[13] string[-like] with no stomach [qi present], that is called 'fatal.'[14]

If stomach [qi is present] and if [the movement] is hair[-like], that is called 'autumn disease.'[15]

If it is very hair[-like], that is called 'present disease.'[16]

<[In spring,]

the true [qi of the] depots disperses into the liver.[17]

The liver stores the qi of sinews and membranes.>

18-110-4

When in summer [one feels] stomach [qi together with a] slightly hook[-like movement in the vessels],[18] that is called 'normal.'

If it is mostly hook[-like] with diminished stomach [qi present], that is called 'heart disease.'

If it is only hook[-like] with no stomach [qi present], that is called 'fatal.'

If stomach [qi is present] and if one has a stone[-like movement in the vessels],

---

11 Wang Bing: "逆 is to say: in opposition to the signs exhibited by a normal person." Gao Jiwu/162: "According to the *Shuo wen* 無 is 亡, in the sense of 失去, 'lost.' That is to say, originally stomach qi was present. Because of some reason it is 'lost' now."

12 Wang Bing: "This is to say: it appears slightly string[-like]; it does not say: it is feeble *and* string[-like]."

13 917/44: "但 is to be interpreted as 只, 'only,' here."

14 Wang Bing: "That is to say, it is tight and strong like a new bow string."

15 Wang Bing: " 'Hair[-like]' is the [movement in the] vessels of metal qi [associated with] autumn."

16 Wang Bing: "[In this case] the wood receives metal evil. Hence the disease is present now."

17 Wu Kun: "In spring, the liver-wood is active. Hence the true heavenly qi of the five depots is all dispersed into the liver." Yao Shaoyu: "The five depots require the stomach qi as their foundation. This stomach qi is the true qi of the five depots. Hence [the text] speaks of [stomach qi as] true [qi of the] depots."

18 Wang Bing: "[Hook-like] is curved at first and settled afterwards, like the hook holding a belt."

that is called 'winter disease.' [19]
If [the movement is] very stone[-like], that is called 'present disease.' [20]

<[In summer,]
the true [qi of the] depots penetrates into the heart.
The heart stores the qi of the blood and the vessels.>

18-110-6
When in late summer [one feels] stomach [qi together with] a slightly soft and
weak [movement in the vessels], that is called 'normal.'
If [the movement is] mostly weak, with diminished stomach [qi present], that
is called 'spleen disease.'
If it is only intermittent with no stomach [qi present], that is called 'fatal.' [21]
If [the movement is] soft and weak and also stone[-like], that is called 'winter
disease.' [22]
If it is very weak, that is called 'present disease.' [23]

<[In late summer,]
the true [qi of the] depots provides moisture to the spleen.
The spleen stores the qi of the muscles and of the flesh.>

18-110-9
When in autumn [one feels] stomach [qi together with] a slightly hair[-like
movement in the vessels], that is called 'normal.'
If [the movement is] mostly hair[-like] with diminished stomach [qi present],
that is called 'lung disease.'

---

19 Wang Bing: " 'Stone[-like]' is the [movement in the] vessels [associated with]
winter. It is the water qi."

20 Wang Bing: "Fire is invaded by the water. Hence the disease is present now."

21 Wang Bing: "That is to say, it moves and stops in the middle. It is [so weak that it
is] unable to return by itself." For a more detailed discussion of different interpretations of 代, see *Su wen* 23.

22 Wang Bing: " 'Stone[-like]' is the [movement in the] vessels of water qi [associ-
ated with] winter. In accordance with the sequence of [mutual] overcoming [among
the five agents], stone[-like] should be string[-like]. In late summer the soil is cut (i.e.,
the movement of the qi associated with soil/stomach/spleen is interrupted). Hence
[the text] states: 'stone[-like].' "

23 Wang Bing: "If it is very weak, the soil [qi] is insufficient. Hence the disease is
present now." Lin Yi et al.: "The *Jia yi jing* has 'stone[-like]' instead of 'weak.' "

If it is only hair[-like] with no stomach [qi present], that is called 'fatal.'[24]
If [the movement is] hair[-like] and if there is also a string[-like movement],
that is called 'spring disease.'[25]
If it is very string[-like], that is called 'present disease.'[26]

<[In autumn,]
the true [qi of the] depots rises high into the lung to stimulate the passage of
the camp [qi] and guard [qi], of yin and yang [qi].>[27]

18-111-2
When in winter [one feels] stomach [qi together with] a slightly stone[-like
movement in the vessels], that is called 'normal.'
If [the movement is] mostly stone[-like] with diminished stomach [qi] present,
that is called 'kidney disease.'
If it is only stone[-like] with no stomach [qi present], that is called 'fatal.'
If [the movement is] stone[-like] and if there is also a hook[-like movement],
that is called 'summer disease.'[28]
If it is very hook[-like], that is called 'present disease.'[29]

---

24 Wang Bing: "['Hair-like'] is to say: like a floating item, like hair blown by the
wind."

25 Wang Bing: " 'String[-like]' is the [movement in the] vessels [associated with]
spring; it is wood qi. In accordance with the sequence of [mutual] overcoming [among
the five agents], 'string[-like]' should be 'hook[-like].' [Here now,] metal qi presses
against the liver. As a result, the arrival of the [movement in the] vessels appears
string[-like]. Hence it is not hook[-like] but string[-like]."

26 Wang Bing: "If the wood qi moves contrary [to its normal course] and invades
the [region of] metal, then the disease is present now."

27 Wang Bing: "The lung is situated in the upper burner. Hence the true [qi of the]
depots rises high. The *Ling shu* states: Inside the path of the camp qi, the grains cause
repletion. The grains enter the stomach; its qi is transmitted to the lung. It flows
into the center and disperses to the outside. The pure essence moves in the conduits.
Because its distribution starts from the lung, hence [the text] states: 'it stimulates the
passage ...' "

28 Wang Bing: " 'Hook[-like]' is the [movement in the] vessels [associated with]
summer; it is fire [qi] combined with soil qi. In accordance with the sequence of [mu-
tual] overcoming [among the five agents], 'hook[-like]' should be weak. The soil rules
in late summer but its true appearance does not show. Hence [the movement in the
vessels] is stone[-like] and there is also a hook[-like] movement. It appears together
with the [qi of] soil."

29 Wang Bing: "The water receives evil [qi] of fire and of soil. Hence the disease is
present now."

<[In winter,]
the true [qi of the] depots descends into the kidneys.
The kidneys store the qi of the bones and of the marrow.>[30]

18-111-4
The large network [vessel] of the stomach
is called *xu li*.[31]

It penetrates the diaphragm and connects with the lung.
It surfaces below the left breast.
The movement in this [vessel] is reflected by [movements of] the garment.[32]
{This is [caused by] the basic qi in the vessels.}[33]

---

30 Wang Bing: "The kidneys are located in the lower burner. Hence [the text] states: 'the true [qi of the] depots descends.' The kidney [qi] transforms into bones and marrow. Hence 'they store the qi of bones and marrow.'"

31 Yang Shangshan: "虛理 is a location like a city or district. This large network [vessel] of the stomach is the location where the five depots and six palaces receive their supplies. Hence it is called *xu li*." 2269/37-38: "虛里 is not only 'a location like a city or district,' it is a general reference to human habitats which are summarily called 墟里. In his poem Gui yuan tian ju 歸園田居, Tao Yuanming 陶淵明 stated: 暖暖遠人村, 依依墟里烟. Obviously, 墟里 is a general designation for 里巷, 'villages and lanes.' Earlier commentators have adopted this usage in their interpretations of *xu li* in the present context. When in this paragraph the large network [vessel] of the stomach is called *xu li*, that is to say: the large network [vessel] of the stomach penetrates the *xu li*. In reality this designation refers to the heart. The ancients named the heart *xu li* because the heart has a left chamber and a right chamber, where it stores large amounts of blood. It constitutes a hollow pathway for the circulation of the entire body. Like 'villages and lanes,' [the blood] can enter and leave [the heart]. Hence it is called *xu li*." (For details, see there) Gao Shishi: "The [movement in the] vessels depends on the stomach. The stomach is the center, the soil. Its qi penetrates the four sides. Hence the large network [vessel] of the stomach is called *xu li*. 大絡 is the network vessel of the stomach. 虛理 has the meaning of 四通, 'penetrating the four [sides].'" Wang Qi: "The *xu li* is located below the left breast; this is the location of the apex beat." *Gu dian yi zhu xuan* bianxiezu /55: "Other names are 乳根, 'breast root,' and 氣眼, 'qi eye.'" See also 1720/14. We consider *xu-li* to be a transliteration of a foreign term, possibly related to the Greek *xulos*. See introductory section.

32 The *Jia yi jing* has 其動應手, "its movement can be felt by [one's] hand."

33 Wang Bing: "宗 is 尊, 'honorable,' or 主, 'ruler.' That is to say, this is the honorable ruler of the twelve conduit vessels." Gao Shishi: "This is to say, the balanced qi of the stomach network [vessel]." Zhang Zhicong: "This is to say, the [movement in the] vessels of the five depots depends on the stomach. And the stomach qi that penetrates the five depots, that is the 'venerable qi.'" *Gu dian yi zhu xuan* bianxiezu /55: "宗 has the meaning of 根本, 'basic.' The heart rules the blood vessels. Hence the 'basic' qi of

If it is abundant, panting,[34] frequent, and interrupted,[35] then the disease is in the center.[36]
In case of transverse knottings, the [qi] has accumulations.[37]

If it is interrupted and does not arrive at all, that is called 'fatal.'[38]

{As for the movement reflected by the garments below the breast, [if it is interrupted and does not arrive, in this case] the basic qi leaks.}[39]

---

the vessels is located in the heart." 701/4: "脈 is used as a verb here in the sense of 'to examine the pulse.' 脈宗氣 is: 'to examine the venerable qi.'" For details, see there. 2269/38: "The 'venerable qi' refers to the yang [qi] of the heart and to the qi of the lung." For details, see there.

34 Gao Jiwu/179: "The *Shuo wen* states: '喘 is 疾息, 'rapid breathing.' The *Su wen* employs 喘 in its original meaning of 喘症, 'condition of panting.' In addition, the meaning of 喘 is employed metaphorically to denote the running movement of the heart depot, to denote a running movement in the abdomen, to denote sounds in the intestines, and to denote a [movement in the] vessels indicating a disease of the heart." 2855/53: "喘 is 疾, 'fast,' it does not have the meaning of 喘息, 'panting,' here. 盛喘數絕 is to say: the [movement in the] vessels comes with abundant force, it is fast and frequent, and stops once in a while."

35 Wang Bing: "絕 is to say: 暫斷絕, 'temporarily cut off.'"

36 Wang Bing: "中 is to say: 腹中, 'in the abdomen.'"

37 Zhang Canjia: "結 is to say: the [movement in the] vessels comes retarded and stops at times. 橫 describes the extended and firm [nature] of the [movement in the] vessels." 682/28: "All previous commentaries suggest the following structure of this passage: 盛喘數絕者. 則病在中. 結而橫. 有積矣. 絕不至曰死. .. It should be: 盛喘數絕者, 則病在中結而橫有積矣; 絕不至曰死, 'if it is abundant, panting, frequent, and interrupted, then the patient suffers from knottings in the center, and there are transverse accumulations. If it is interrupted and does not arrive at all, that is called death.'" For details, see there. 114/40: "結 indicates that the movement comes to a halt now and then. 橫 is to indicate that the location shifts transversely. Tanba assumed: '橫 is to say: the movement shifts towards the left side.' In fact, this transverse shifting may be directed towards the upper left or towards the right in direction of the scrobiculus cordis."

38 Wang Bing: "All these are types of movements in the vessels [that can be felt] below the left breast."

39 Lin Yi et al.: "The Quan Yuanqi edition does not have these eleven characters. The *Jia yi jing* does not have them either. Given the meaning of the preceding and of the following text, these eleven characters should be omitted." 475/42 suggests to change the sequence of the characters as follows: 胃之大絡, 名曰虛里, 貫膈絡肺, 出于左乳下, 其動應手, 脈宗氣也, 其動應衣, 宗氣泄也, "The large network [vessel] of the stomach is called *xu li*. It penetrates the diaphragm and connects with the lung. It

18-111-8
If one wishes to know [the diseases associated with] great excess and inadequacy:

If the [movement in the] vessels at the inch opening strikes the hand as a short
[movement],
that is called: 'headache.'

If the [movement in the] vessels at the inch opening strikes the hand as an
extended [movement],
that is called: 'foot and shin pain.'[40]

If the [movement in the] vessels at the inch opening strikes the hand as press-
ingly beating upwards,[41]
that is called: 'shoulder and back pain.'[42]

If the [movement in the] vessels at the inch opening is in the depth and firm,
that is called: 'disease in the center.'

If the [movement in the] vessels at the inch opening is at the surface and
abundant,
that is called: 'the disease is in the outer [regions].'[43]

If the [movement in the] vessels at the inch opening is in the depth and weak,
that is called: 'cold and heat' and
'elevation conglomeration ill,' with pain in the lower abdomen.[44]

---

surfaces below the left breast. When its movement can be felt by [one's] hand, this is
the base qi in the vessels. When its movement is reflected by [a movement of one's]
garments, [this is a sign that] the basic qi leaks."

40 Wang Bing: " 'Short' means insufficient yang qi. Hence the disease is in the head.
'Extended' means greatly excessive yin qi. Hence the disease is in the legs."

41 Wang Shaozeng & Xu Yongnian/104: "In front of 上擊者 a character 而 is missing."

42 Wang Bing: "The yang abounds above. Hence shoulders and back have pain."

43 Wang Bing: " 'In the depth' and 'firm' are yin [qualities], hence the disease is in
the center. 'At the surface and abundant' are yang [qualities], hence the disease is in
the outer [regions of the body]."

44 Wang Bing: " 'In the depth' is cold; 'weak' is heat. Hence [the text] states 'cold and
heat.' Also, 'in the depth' is yin abundance; 'weak' is yang surplus. If abundance and
surplus hit each other, there should be cold and heat. There should be no elevation illness with conglomerations and pain in the lower abdomen. This [passage] must been

If the [movement in the] vessels at the inch opening is in the depth, with
transverse [knottings],
that is called: 'accumulations below the flanks.' There are transverse accumulations in the abdomen, with pain.[45]

If the [movement in the] vessels at the inch opening is in the depth and pants,
that is called: 'cold and heat.'

18-112-4
If the [movement in the] vessels is abundant, smooth, and firm,
that is called: 'disease in the outer [region].'

If the [movement in the] vessels is diminished, replete, and firm, the disease is
in the interior.[46]

If the [movement in the] vessels is diminished, weak, and rough,[47]
that is called 'chronic disease.'[48]

If the [movement in the] vessels is smooth, at the surface, and hasty,
that is called 'new disease.'[49]

If the [movement in the] vessels is tense,
that is called: 'elevation conglomeration ill' with pain in the lower abdomen.

---

mistakenly placed here in former times." Lin Yi et al.: "The *Jia yi jing* does not have
these 15 characters. Also, the text further down has 寸口脈沈而喘曰寒熱, 脈急者曰
疝瘕, 少腹痛. The passage here is superfluous and should be deleted." 964/1-2: "The
Shuo wen states: 疝 is 腹痛, 'abdominal pain.' Mr. Yan's (顏) commentary is: '疝: The qi
moves quickly up and down in the abdomen. 瘕 stands for 症, 'disease.' That is, 疝瘕 is
a conglomeration in the abdomen that can move around and causes pain."

45 Wang Bing: "These, again, are internal knottings of yin qi."

46 Wang Bing: " 'Abundant' and 'smooth' are yang; 'diminished' and 'replete' are
yin. In case of a yin disease, the disease is in the interior. In case of a yang disease, the
disease is in the outer [region]."

47 Gao Jiwu/353: "The character 以 is identical here with 而, 'and.' "

48 Wang Bing: " 'Diminished' means the qi is depleted. 'Rough' means there is no
blood. Because blood and qi are depleted and weak, [the text] speaks of an old disease
that has gone far."

49 Wang Bing: " 'Smooth' and 'near the surface' are yang sufficiency. A fast [movement in the] vessels is qi wholeness. Because there is yang sufficiency and qi wholeness, the [text] speaks of a new disease that has not penetrated deeply."

18-112-7
If the [movement in the] vessels is smooth,
that is called: 'wind.'

If the [movement in the] vessels is rough,
that is called: 'block.'[50]

If it is relaxed and smooth,
that is called: 'heated center.'
If it is abundant and tight,
that is called: 'distension.'[51]

If the [movement in the] vessels follows the yin and yang [nature of the disease],
the disease is easy to bring to an end.

If the [movement in the] vessels runs counter to the yin and yang [nature of the disease],
the disease is difficult to bring to an end.[52]

If the [movement in the] vessels agrees with the four seasons,
that is called: 'disease without other [damage].'[53]

---

50 Wang Bing: "Smooth is yang. When the yang receives a disease, then this is wind. Rough is yin. When the yin receives a disease, then this is block."

51 Wang Bing: "緩 refers to a relaxed appearance; it is not the slowness of a movement. The yang [qi] abounds in the center. Hence the vessels are smooth and relaxed. Cold qi causes blocks and fullness. Hence the vessels are abounding and tight. 盛緊 is 盛滿, 'full with abounding [qi].'"

52 Wang Bing: "When the [movement in the] vessels and the [nature of the] disease correspond to each other, that is called 從, 'coinciding.' When they oppose each other, that is called 逆, 'moving contrary to a regular course.'"

53 Zhang Jiebin: "If in spring one feels a string[-like], in summer a hook[-like], in autumn a hair[-like], and in winter a stone[-like movement in the vessels], that is called 'in accordance with the four seasons.' Even though one may say [the person] has a disease, there is no other problem present." *Ci yuan* 辭源: "無他 is 無害, 'no damage.'" See *Hou Han shu* 後漢書 13, biography of Wei Ao 隗囂.

If the [movement in the] vessels contradicts the four seasons,
<and if it does not skip a depot>
that is called: 'difficult to bring to an end.'⁵⁴

18-113-1
When the arms have many green-blue vessels,
that is called: 'lost blood.'⁵⁵

When the vessel [movement] in the foot-long section is relaxed and rough,⁵⁶

---

54 *Nan jing* 53 states: 間藏者傳其所生也, "[Diseases] that skip a depot [in their transmission through the organism] are transmitted to those [depots] which are generated [by the transmitting depot]." This refers to a transmission, for instance, from the lung to the kidneys. Since the lung [i.e., metal] is the mother depot [i.e., agent] of the kidneys [i.e., water], such diseases will not take the patient's life. The four characters 及不閒藏 appear to be a later insertion here, possibly as a comment. The structure of the present statement corresponds to that of a passage further below: 脈有逆從四時, 未有藏形 (see 18-114-3). In that case, too, the latter four characters appear to be a commentary inserted into the main text.

55 Wang Bing: "If there is only a little blood, the vessels are empty and as a consequence visitor cold enters. Cold makes the blood liquid coagulate. Hence the color of the vessels is bluish."

56 Wang Bing: "The foot-long section is a yin region; [the movement in the vessels there] is ruled by the abdomen and the kidneys. 'Relaxed' is heated center. 'Rough' is absence of blood." Yao Shaoyu: "There are two interpretations of 緩. One is 和緩, 'peaceful.' This applies to the situation called 'the vessels have stomach qi.' Another is 緩弱, 'tardy.' This is a situation where the principal qi is harmed and the [movement in the] vessels is insufficient. If seen from this perspective, 'rough' is to say: decreased blood, and 'relaxed' means, without any doubt, 'qi depletion.' Even though each of the three sections of the vessels has its characteristics, the foot-long section is often considered the 'root and basis.' Hence if [the movement in the vessels] is relaxed and rough in the foot-long section, one knows that the qi is depleted and the blood is decreased and that their root and basis has already received harm." Cheng Shide et al.: " 'Foot length' refers to the skin of the foot-long section; when the [movement in the] vessels of the foot-long section is relaxed and rough, the skin of the foot-long section is relaxed and rough [too]." Li Guoqing: "尺脈緩澀 should be 尺緩脈澀. This is to say, the skin and the muscle flesh in the foot-long section are relaxed without any strength and the [movement in the] vessels arrives rough, blocked, [i.e.] not unimpeded. All this is the result of insufficiencies of qi and blood." 475/43 agrees. The structure of the combination of 尺 and 脈 varies in the present and in the subsequent statements. Given the wording 寸口脈 above, 尺脈 may be the original, correct wording here. The wordings 尺澀, "the foot length is rough' and 尺寒, "the foot length is cold", below may be reminiscences of early difficulties to leave skin diagnosis completely in favor of pulse diagnosis.

that is called: *jie-yi*.[57]
[The patient] longs for sleep.[58]

When the [movement in his] vessels is abundant,
that is called: 'lost blood.'[59]

When the [skin in the] foot-long section is rough, while [the movement in
the] vessels is smooth,
that is called: 'profuse sweat.'[60]

When the [skin in the] foot-long section is cold, while the [movement in the]
vessels is fine,
that is called: 'outflow behind.'[61]

---

57 Wang Bing: "A cold which is not cold, a heat which is not hot, a weakness which
is not weak, a strength which is not strong. That is, diseases that cannot be named,
they are called 解㑊." Hua Shou: "懈倦之極, 'extremely remiss.'" Gao Shishi: "懈㑊
is like 懈怠, 'remiss.'" 2269/38: "㑊 is an alternative for 亦 and this 亦 is an ancient
version of 腋, 'armpit.' .. The ancients named [diseases] after their symptoms. Because
[in all the cases just mentioned] the two armpits and the four extremities appear as if
loosened, they were named 懈㑊." Yang Shangshan: "懈㑊 is 怠懈運動難, 'lazy,' 'to
have difficulties to move.'" In this case, the pinyin transliteration would be *xie-yi*. The
term *jie-yi/xie-yi* may be a transliteration of a technical term of non-Chinese origin,
the meaning of which was lost subsequently. See *Su wen* 37-214-1 for a similar term
食亦 which may likewise be a transliteration of a foreign term.

58 Gao Shishi: "安臥 is 嗜臥, 'one wishes to lie down.'" 475/43: "the two characters
安臥 are read linked to the preceding characters in *Tai su* 15. Following the style of
the phrases 謂之 .. below, it may be that 安臥 is an ancient commentary to 謂之解
㑊."

59 Wang Bing: "To sleep for long [indicates:] the qi is harmed. When the qi is
harmed, diagnosis should reveal a feeble [movement in the] vessels. If now the [move-
ment in the] vessels is abundant, not feeble, then the blood has left and the qi has
nothing it could rule.."

60 Wang Bing: "That is to say, the skin in the foot-long section is rough, with the
[movement in the] vessels in the foot-long section being smooth. When the skin is
rough, the blood is dried up inside. When the [movement in the] vessels is smooth,
the yang qi abounds internally. With the blood being dried up and the yang qi being
present in surplus, [the patient] sweats a lot and the [movement in the] vessels is as
is described here."

61 Zhang Jiebin: "When the skin in the foot-long section is cold, the yang of the
spleen is weak, because the spleen rules the muscle flesh and the four extremities.
When the [movement in the] vessels of the foot-long section is fine, the yang of the

When the movement [in the vessels in] the foot-long section[62] is coarse, with regular appearance of heat,
that is called: 'heated center.'[63]

18-113-4
If a liver [movement] appears, [the patient will] die at *geng* and *xin*.[64]
If a heart [movement] appears, [the patient will] die at *ren* and *kui*.[65]
If a spleen [movement] appears, [the patient will] die at *jia* and *yi*.[66]
If a lung [movement] appears, [the patient will] die at *bing* and *ding*.[67]
If a kidney [movement] appears, [the patient will] die at *wu* and *ji*.[68]
<That is to say,
whenever [a movement of] the true [qi of a] depot appears, [the patient will] die.>

When the neck vessel moves and [the patient] is panting fast and coughs,
that is called: 'water.'[69]

---

kidneys is weak, because the kidneys rule the two yin [openings] and the lower section [of the body]. Hence there is 'outflow behind.'"

62 Another interpretation might render "When the [movement in the] vessels and [the skin in] the foot-long section are rough, .."

63 Wang Bing: "That is to say, in the lower burner." Gao Shishi: "常熱 is 膚熱. The [movement in the] vessels is coarse and the skin is hot. This is an indication of a surplus of yang qi. Hence, it is called 'heated center.'"

64 Wang Bing: "*Geng xin* is metal; it fells the wood of the liver." Ma Shi: "This is to say, when a [movement of] true [qi of a] depot appears, the date of death is determined [on the basis of the order of] mutual overcoming [among the five agents]. *Geng xin* is a metal day. If a [movement of] true [qi of the] depot of the liver appears and has absolutely no stomach qi, death will follow on the *geng xin* day because metal dominates wood."

65 Wang Bing: "*Ren gui* is water; it inundates the fire of the heart."

66 Wang Bing: "*Jia yi* is wood; it subdues the soil of the spleen."

67 Wang Bing: "*Bing ding* is fire; it melts the metal of the lung."

68 Wang Bing: "*Wu ji* is soil; it punishes the water of the kidneys."

69 Wang Bing: "When the water qi rises to overflow, then the lung is steamed by heat and the yang qi rises contrary [to its normal course]. Hence the [movement in the] neck vessels drums in abundance and [the patient] coughs and pants. 'Neck vessels' refers to the *ren-ying* vessels below the ears to the side of the throat." The *Tai su* has 頸脈動疾喘咳, "the neck vessel moves fast and [the patient] pants and coughs." Hence, Mori: "The *Tai su* has 疾喘. That is correct. This statement refers to vessels and pathoconditions alike. 動疾, 'moves fast,' refers to the [movement in the] vessels;

When the eye lids are slightly swollen, resembling a silkworm rising from sleep,
that is called: 'water.'[70]
When the urine is yellow-red and one longs for sleep,
this is 'yellow solitary [heat] disease.'[71]
If after finishing one's meal [one has a feeling] as if one were hungry,
that is 'stomach solitary [heat] disease.'[72]

When the face is swollen,
that is called: 'wind.'[73]
When the feet and the shins are swollen,

喘咳, 'pants and coughs,' refers to the pathoconditions." Zhang Yizhi et al.: "Wang
Bing's commentary, too, refers to [movement in] the vessels and to pathoconditions.
Hence he must have based his comments on a correct version."

70 Yang Shangshan: "目裹 is 目上下瞼, 'the lids above and below the eye.'" Wang
Bing: "*Su wen* 33 states: 'Water is yin; [the region] below the eyes is also yin. The
abdomen is where the extreme yin resides. Hence water in the abdomen will necessarily cause swelling below the eyes." Zhang Jiebin: "目裹 is the lid below the eyes. The
stomach vessel reaches here and the spleen qi rules here. When one notices a slight
swelling resembling silkworms rising from sleep, the [reason] is that water qi has
inundated spleen and stomach." 916/53 identifies 裹 as 窠, "nest," "indentation," and
interprets 目裹 as "socket of the eyeball." The *Tai su* does not have the character 蠶,
"silkworm." *Ling shu* 74 has 如新臥起狀, "as if rising after just having fallen asleep."

71 Wang Bing: "疸 is 勞, 'taxation.' When the kidneys are taxed and the uterus is hot,
one's urine is yellow-red. The *Zheng li lun* 正理論 states: 'One calls this 勞癉 because
one gets it from taxing [intercourse] with women.'" Lin Yi et al.: "In his commentary,
Wang Bing considers 疸 to be 勞. This is not the meaning. When it is said: one gets
疸 from taxing [intercourse] with women, this is admissible; [but] if one considers
疸 to be 勞, then this is not correct." *SWJZZ*: "The pronunciations of 癉 and 疸 are
identical; the meanings, though, differ. As the commentary by Kuo 郭 to the *Shan hai
jing* 山海經 and the Shi Gu 師古 commentary to the *Han shu* 漢書 state: 疸 is 黃病,
'yellow disease.'" Zhang Yizhi et al.: "The *Shuo wen* states: 疸 is 黃病, 'yellow disease';
癉 is 勞病, 'taxation disease.'"

72 Wang Bing: "If this is so, then one's stomach has heat. If it has heat it digests
the grain. Hence after finishing a meal, one feels as if one were hungry." *Gu dian yi
zhu xuan* bianxiezu /51: "疸 is 癉, 'weariness.'" Tanba: "This is what was called 消中,
'wasting center,' in the preceding treatise."

73 Wang Bing: "If, in addition, the face is swollen, then the diagnosis is 'stomach
wind.' Why? The yang brilliance vessel of the stomach emerges from the intersection
of the nose with the central point between the eyebrows. It moves down outside the
nose. Hence this [situation emerges]."

that is called: 'water.'[74]
When the eyes are yellow,
that is called: 'yellow solitary [heat] disease.'[75]
When the hand minor yin vessels of women have a very [pronounced] movement,
that is [a sign of] pregnancy.[76]

---

74 Wang Bing: "This is to say: the lower burner has water. The minor yin vessel of
the kidneys emerges from the sole of the foot and moves upwards along the shinbone.
It passes the groin and rises from the kidneys to penetrate the liver and the diaphragm.
Hence when there is water in the lower burner, the feet and the shins swell."

75 Wang Bing: "When yang flames upwards, heat accumulates in the chest. When
yang qi burns above, the eyes become yellow."

76 Yang Shangshan: "The hand minor yin vessel is the heart conduit vessel. The
[movement in the] vessels associated with the heart is ruled by the blood. When a
woman is pregnant, her monthly blood is closed in and cannot leave towards outside.
Hence there is an abundance in the hand minor yin vessel which [in turn] causes this
type of a movement." Wang Bing: "The hand minor yin vessel is one whose movement
can be felt with the little finger in the fold behind the palm. 動 is to say: 動脈, 'moving
vessel.' A 'moving vessel' is as big as a bean." Lin Yi et al.: "The Quan Yuanqi edition
has 'foot minor yin.'" Ma Shi: "The inch section of the left [hand] is associated with
the hand minor yin [vessel] of the heart conduit and it is outside and inside with the
hand major yang vessel of the conduit of the small intestine. The *Mai fu* 脈賦 states:
A big [movement in the] major yang [conduit indicates] a pregnancy with a male
[child]. Hence one knows: when the [movement] in the hand minor yin vessels is very
[pronounced], this is a pregnancy with a male child." Gao Shishi: " 'Minor yin' is the
[movement in the] vessels in the foot-long section. From examining the [movement
in the vessels in the] foot-long section one knows the location of the disease and one
can also know whether a woman is pregnant. When there is an excessive movement
in the hand minor yin vessels in both hands of a woman, one knows that [her] kidney
qi has a surplus, [because] it was affected by the qi generated by Tian yi 天一. Hence
she is pregnant." Zhang Jiebin: "*Su wen* 17 states: 'On the outside on the left of the
upper [region] of the upper instep, one examines the heart.' Hence the heart should
be examined at the inch [section] on the left. A 'very [pronounced] movement' is a
movement of a free and smooth flow. The heart generates the blood. When the blood
increases the womb may become pregnant. In case the movement in the heart vessel
of a woman is very [pronounced], this is so because the blood is increased. Hence she
should be pregnant." Yao Shaoyu: "The Quan Yuanqi edition has 'foot minor yin,' and
here it is written 'hand minor yin.' The meaning of both [statements] is the same.
Now, the hand minor yin is the heart; the foot minor yin is the kidney. The kidneys
rule the essence; the heart rules the blood. When essence and blood mix, one may have
a child. Hence a very [pronounced] movement of the minor yin is a [movement in
the] vessels [indicating] pregnancy."

18-114-3
The [movement in the] vessels may be contrary to or in compliance with the four seasons.
When their physical appearance fails to [reflect the condition of] the depots, [i.e.]⁷⁷
when the vessels are lean in spring and summer, or
when they are at the surface and big in autumn and winter,
that is called: '[movement] contrary to the four seasons.'⁷⁸

If [one suffers from] wind⁷⁹ and heat while the [movement in the] vessels is quiet, or
[if one suffers from] outflow and loss of blood while the [movement in the] vessels is replete;⁸⁰
if the disease is in the center while the [movement in the] vessels is depleted;
if the disease is in the exterior, while the [movement in the] vessels is rough and firm,
all these [situations] are difficult to cure.⁸¹
{That is called '[movement] contrary to the four seasons.'}

18-115-1
Man requires water and grain as his basis.
Hence,

---

77 The 53 character passage beginning with 未有藏形 and ending with 皆難治 appears almost identically in *Su wen* 19.

78 Wang Bing: "'A lean [movement in the] vessels in spring and summer' is to say: in the depth and fine. If the movement is at the surface and big in autumn and winter, this is not in correspondence with these seasons. The grand pattern is such that in spring and summer it should be at the surface and big; instead, it is in the depth and fine. In autumn and winter it should be in the depth and fine, instead it is at the surface and big.. Hence [the text] states: it does not correspond to the seasons."

79 Lin Yi et al.: "*Su wen* 19 has 病, 'to suffer from,' instead of 風."

80 Lin Yi et al.: "*Su wen* 19 has 泄而脈大, 脫血而脈實, 'outflow and a big [movement in the] vessels; loss of blood and a replete [movement in the] vessels."

81 Wang Bing: "In case of wind heat, the [movement in the] vessels should be running, but, on the contrary, it is a quiet [movement]. In case of outflow and loss of blood, the [movement in the] vessels should be depleted, but, on the contrary, it is a replete [movement]. In case of evil qi in the interior, the [movement in the] vessels should be replete, but, on the contrary, it is a depleted [movement]. When the disease is in the exterior, [the movement in] the vessels should be depleted and smooth, but, on the contrary, it is a firm and rough [movement]. Hence all these [are situations which] are difficult to cure."

once man is cut off from water and grain, he will die.

Once the vessels contain no stomach qi, death [is imminent] too.

{What is referred to here as 'contain no stomach qi' is [a situation] where one can feel a [movement in the] vessels of only the true [qi of a] depot, but does not feel any stomach qi.}

{{When it is stated 'in [feeling the movement in] the vessels one does not feel any stomach qi,' [then this refers to situations where] a liver [movement] is not string[-like], a kidney [movement] is not stone[-like, etc.]}}}[82]

The arrival of a major yang [movement in the] vessels,
it is vast, big, and extended.[83]
The arrival of a minor yang [movement in the] vessels,
it is at times frequent,
at times spaced,
at times short,
at times extended.[84]
The arrival of a yang brilliance [movement in the] vessels,
it is at the surface, big, and short.[85]

18-115-6
Now,
the arrival of a vessel [movement indicating a] normal heart is [as follows]:
strung together, resembling a string of pearls;[86]

---

82 Zhang Jiebin: "Human life depends on water and grain. Hence the stomach has water and grain as its basis. And the five depots, in turn, have the stomach qi as their basis. If a [movement in the] vessels [shows] the absence of stomach qi and if only the [movement in the] vessels of true [qi of the] depots is apparent, [the patient] will die. This resembles what was called in the preceding treatise 'only string[-like] with no stomach [qi]; only stone[-like] with no stomach [qi].' But even though 'only string[-like]' and 'only stone[-like]' indicate the true [qi of the] depots, if the liver has no qi then there is no string[-like movement] and if the kidneys have no qi there is no stone[-like movement]. This, too, is the result of a failure of the stomach to supply the five depots with qi. It is the same as [in a situation where there is only] the true [qi of the] depots with no stomach [qi] present."

83 Wang Bing: "When the qi abounds [the movement in the vessels] can be like this."

84 Wang Bing: "Because the passage of the qi is at times free and at times it is not free."

85 Wang Bing: "Because [the vessels] are filled to abundance with grain qi."

86 Yao Shaoyu: "'String of pearls': It arrives continuously without intervals, and it has the slipperiness of jade."

[it feels] as if [one's fingers] passed over *lang gan* [jade].
That is called: the heart is normal.

<In summer take the [presence of] stomach qi as basis [of an assessment].>[87]

The arrival of a diseased heart [movement in the] vessels is [as follows]:
panting in sequence;
in between it is slightly curved.
That is called: the heart has a disease.

The arrival of a dying heart [movement in the] vessels is [as follows]:
curved in front and straight behind,
as if one grasped a hook holding a belt.[88]
That is called: the heart dies.

18-116-3
The arrival of a normal lung [movement in the] vessels is [as follows]:
faded, like the murmur (of trees)[89]
resembling the falling of elm seeds.
That is called: 'the lung is normal.'

<In autumn take the [presence of] stomach qi as basis [of an assessment].>[90]

---

87 Wang Bing: "When there is stomach qi in the vessels, the [movement] is strung together and slightly reminiscent of a string of pearls."

88 Wang Bing: "居 is: not moving." Wu Kun: "When the [movement in the] vessels arrives curved and not stretched at first and is later settled and immobile, its appearance is vast and big and not smooth and free." Zhang Jiebin: "前曲 is to say: under light pressure [the movement appears] firm, strong, and not soft. 後居 is to say: under heavy pressure [the vessels appear] unyielding, replete, and not moving." The *Tai su*, ch.15, has 初曲后直, 'curved in front and straight behind.'" Li Guoqing: "A 'hook[- like movement in the] vessels' is the manifestation of a heart [movement in the] vessels. No matter whether it is a [movement in the] vessels indicating balance, disease, or death, in each case it should be hook[-like]. The *Shuo wen* states: '句 is 曲..'. 居 is identical with 佢. In ancient scripts 句 and 佢 do often appear together. .. From this one knows 句 (曲) and 佢 (居) both have the meaning of 彎曲, 'curved.'" For philo- logical-etymological details, see there. 2051/58 agrees. 1454/54: "居 is 佢, in the sense of 直, 'straight.' Wang Bing's commentary '居 is: not moving' is wrong."

89 915/56: "厭厭 (*yān yān*) is 'faded color.' The biography of Li Xun 李尋 in the *Han shu* has 列星皆失色, 厭厭如滅, 'all the stars have lost their color; they are sallow, like fading light.' 聶聶 (*she she*) refers to weak sounds."

90 Wang Bing: "When there is stomach qi in the vessels, the [movement] is slightly reminiscent of the light and hollow [nature of] elm seeds."

The arrival of a diseased lung [movement in the] vessels is [as follows]:
neither rising nor descending; [it feels]
as if [one's fingers] passed over chicken feathers.
That is called 'the lung has a disease.'[91]

The arrival of a dying lung [movement in the] vessels is [as follows]:
resembling a floating item;
it is like body hair blown by the wind.
That is called 'the lung dies.'

18-116-5
The arrival of a normal liver [movement in the] vessels is [as follows]:
soft and weak and waving,
as if one were raising the tip of a long bamboo cane.[92]
That is called 'the liver is normal.'

<In spring take the [presence of] stomach qi as basis [of an assessment].>[93]

The arrival of a diseased liver [movement in the] vessels is [as follows]:
abundant, replete, and smooth,
as if [one's fingers] passed along a long bamboo cane.[94]
That is called 'the liver has a disease.'

The arrival of a dying liver [movement in the] vessels is [as follows]:
tense, with increasing force,

---

91 Wang Bing: "That is to say: it is firm in the center and depleted on both sides."

92 Wang Bing: "That is to say, extended and soft." Ma Shi: "招 is identical with 迢. The extreme tip of a long cane is 迢迢, that it, it is very soft and weak." 915/56: "招 招: to call someone with one's hand is 招." Fang Wenhui/61: "招 is used for 迢; its original meaning is 'elevated and remote.' Here it is to be interpreted as 'soft, weak, and pliant.'"

93 Wang Bing: "When there is stomach qi in the vessels, the [movement] is extended and soft like the tip of a bamboo cane."

94 Wang Bing: "It is long but not soft." Yu Chang: "The characters 竿 and 滑 do not rhyme. A bamboo cane is hollow inside, it is not 'abundant and replete/solid.' Also, it is not 'smooth.' Because the appearances of the two characters are very similar, 竿 must be a corrupted writing of the character 笄, 'hairpin.' Such hairpins are made either from jade or from ivory. This corresponds to the meaning 'abundant and replete, as well as smooth.' The ancients used two types of hairpins. One type was employed to fix the hair, the other to fix a cap. Those to fix the hair were short, those to fix the cap were long. Hence, a 'long hairpin' refers to a hairpin used to fix the cap."

like a bow string that is just being pulled.⁹⁵
That is called 'the liver dies.'

The arrival of a normal spleen [movement in the] vessels is [as follows]:
harmonious, soft, and distanced,
resembling chicken stepping on the earth.⁹⁶
That is called 'the spleen is normal.'

<In late summer take the [presence of] stomach qi as basis [of an assess-
ment].>⁹⁷

The arrival of a diseased spleen [movement in the] vessels is [as follows]:
replete, abundant, and frequent,
resembling chicken raising their legs.
That is called 'the spleen has a disease.'

The arrival of a dying spleen [movement in the] vessels is [as follows]:
pointed and firm,
like a crow's beak,
like a bird's spur,
like [water] dripping into a house,
like the flow of water.
That is called 'the spleen dies.'⁹⁸

18-117-3
The arrival of a normal kidney [movement in the] vessels is [as follows]:
panting and strung together,
like a hook.

---

95 Wang Bing: "勁 is to say: 勁強, 'unyielding and strong.' This is the highest degree
of tightness."

96 Wu Kun: "相離 is: the [movement in the] vessels arrives unconnected." 2268/35:
"According to the *Zhou li*, 離 is 麗, 'to be connected with.' Hence this 離 is to be interpreted as 附麗, 'joined to.' In the present passage 和柔相離 is to say: 'harmonious
and soft [movements] are closely connected.'"

97 Wang Bing: "When there is little stomach [qi], the [movement in the] vessels is
replete and frequent."

98 Wang Bing: " '[Like] a crow's beak, [like] a bird's spur' is to say: pointed and
firm. '[Like] the flow of water, [like water] dripping into a house' is to describe the
nature of its arrival. '[Like] the flow of water' is to say: the arrival is balanced, there is
no drumming. '[Like water] dripping into a house' is to say: at times it moves, then
it rests."

When one presses it, it is firm.
That is called 'the kidneys are normal.'⁹⁹

<In winter take the [presence of] stomach qi as basis [of an assessment].>¹⁰⁰

The arrival of a diseased kidney [movement in the] vessels is [as follows]:
as if one pulled a creeper.
When one presses it, it increases in firmness.
That is called 'the kidneys have a disease.'¹⁰¹

The arrival of a dying kidney [movement in the] vessels is [as follows]:
it manifests itself as if a rope was pulled away,¹⁰²
[it sounds like] *bi–bi* as if a stone was hurled.¹⁰³
That is called 'the kidneys die.' "¹⁰⁴

99 Wang Bing: "Like a [movement in the] vessels associated with the heart, but formed like a hook [rather than being straight]. Upon pressure it turns small and firm."

100 Wang Bing: "When there is little stomach [qi], the [movement in the] vessels [feels] hard even without being pressed."

101 Wang Bing: "The physical appearance resembles 'pulling *ge*-beans' is to say: without pressing it is obviously hard already. When pressed it is particularly hard."

102 Wang Bing: " 'Emerging as if a rope was pulled' is like the movement of a snake." Wu Kun: "When two persons pull [the ends of] a rope, it is drawn long and becomes firm and tense."

103 Wang Bing: " '*Bi–bi* as if a stone was hurled' is to say: pressing and firm at the same time." Gao Shishi: "辟辟 is: the coming and the going [of this movement] is irregular. 'Like a pellet' is: round and firm, not soft." 2165/39: "彈 is used here as a verb, 'to hurl.' 辟辟如彈石 is a pulse quality resembling in its firmness the 'pipi' sound produced by a hurled stone."

104 For a table including all the information on the various movements in the vessels in relation to the seasons and to the different states of health of the five depots, see Wan Lanqing et al./20.

Chapter 19
Discourse on the Jade Mechanism
and the True [Qi of the] Depots

19-118-2
Huang Di asked:
"In spring, the [movement in the] vessels resembles a string.
How can it be string[-like]?"

Qi Bo responded:
"In spring, the [movement in the] vessels is a liver [movement].
The East is wood;
this is whereby the myriad beings come to life first.
Hence, when this qi comes, it is soft, weak, light, depleted, and smooth.
It is straight and extended.
Hence, it is called 'string[-like].'
[A movement] contrary to this [indicates] disease."

[Huang] Di:
"How can it be contrary?"

19-118-5
Qi Bo:
"When this qi comes replete and strong,
this is called 'greatly excessive.'
The disease is in the exterior.

When this qi comes not replete and is feeble,
this is called 'inadequate.'
The disease is in the center."[1]

[Huang] Di:
"When in spring the [movement in the] vessels is greatly excessive or inadequate,
what are all the respective diseases like?"

---

1 Wang Bing: "In the case of qi surplus, the disease assumes shape in the exterior.
In the case of being short of qi, the disease is in the interior." Wu Kun: "When the evil
enters from the outside, then the disease is 'great excess.' When the evil emerges from
within, then the disease is 'insufficiency.'"

Qi Bo:

"When it is greatly excessive,

then this causes a person to be forgetful;[2]

he experiences vertigo and suffers from peak illness.[3]

When it is inadequate,

then this lets a person have chest pain pulling [also] on the back.

When it is below,

then there is fullness in the lower and upper flanks on both [sides]."[4]

[Huang] Di:

"Good!

In summer, the [movement in the] vessels resembles a hook. How can it be hook[-like]?"

19-119-1

Qi Bo:

"In summer, the [movement in the] vessels is a heart [movement].

The South is fire;

this is whereby the myriad beings abound and grow.

Hence, when this qi comes, it is abundant; when it leaves, it is weak.

Hence, it is called 'hook[-like].'

A [movement] contrary to this [indicates] disease."

[Huang] Di:

"How can it be contrary?"

---

2 *Su wen* 69 has 忽忽善怒. *Su wen* 22 has 肝病者, 兩脅下痛引少腹, 令人善怒. Hence Wang Bing: "忘 is most likely a mistake for the character 怒, 'anger.'" Lin Yi et al., Zhang Jiebin, Ma Shi, Wu Kun, and Tanba agree. In contrast, Gao Shishi and Zhang Zhicong accept 忘, "to forget." 965/40: "忘 is 恍, 'confused.' The following passage serves as proof." For a detailed discussion, see 959/42.

3 *SWJZ*: "忽 is 忘, 'to forget.'" Hence 1588/45 reads this passage: 令人善忘忽忽, 眩冒而..." In contrast, Wang Bing: "忽忽 is 不爽, 'not in good health.' 眩 is 目眩, 'giddiness.' One sees things as if they were revolving. 冒 is to say 冒悶, 'chest pressure.'" Cheng Shide et al.: "忽忽 is 恍忽, 'confused,' and 'the spirit is not clear.'" 1588/45: "忽忽 is to describe forgetfulness." Zhang Jiebin: " 'Peak illness' is a disease in the top [of the head]." Wu Kun: " 'Peak illness' is: to fall."

4 Wang Bing: "胠 refers to the ribs below the armpits." Tanba Genken 丹波元堅: "Yang Shangshan states: 'Three inches below the armpits, these are the 腋. Below the 腋 down to the outer side of the 8th vertebral intersection, these are the 胠.'"

19-119-3
Qi Bo:
"When this qi comes abounding and leaves abounding, too,
this is called 'greatly excessive.'
The disease is in the exterior.⁵

When this qi comes not abounding and leaves, on the contrary, abounding,
this is called 'inadequate.'⁶
The disease is in the center."

[Huang] Di:
"When in summer the [movement in the] vessels is greatly excessive or inadequate,
what are all the respective diseases like?"

19-119-5
Qi Bo:
"When it is greatly excessive,
then this lets a person's body be hot and his skin be painful.
This is soaking.⁷
When it is inadequate,
then it lets a person have a vexed heart.

---

5 Wang Bing: "When the [movement in the] vessels comes abounding and leaves abounding, too, that is yang abundance. The heart qi is present in surplus. Hence this is 'greatly excessive.'"

6 Zhang Jiebin: "This 'when it leaves, in contrast, it is abundant' does not refer to an abundance in strength. All [movements in the] vessels emerging from the section of the bones and of the flesh to the borderline of the skin, they are called 'coming.' Those returning from the borderline of the skin to the section of the bones and of the flesh, they are called 'leaving.' When their coming is not abundant while their leaving, in contrast, is abundant, this is to say: their coming is insufficient and when they leave they have a surplus."

7 The *Tai su* has 骨, 'bone,' instead of 膚, 'skin.' Gao Shishi: "When the [movement in the] heart vessels is greatly excessive, then the fire qi comes to the surface outside. Hence it causes the body to be hot and the skin to have pain. The heat harms the exterior of the skin. Hence this causes 'soaking' and results in ulcers." Wu Kun: " 'Soaking' is: the heat does not leave; it saturates [the body] and leads to excess. ['Soaking'] is a name for evil heat gradually penetrating deeper and deeper." Ma Shi: " 'Soaking' is: the pain flows through the entire body." Yao Shaoyu: " 'Soaking' is sweat. The fire presses on the lung and causes sweating." *Su wen* 69 has: 身熱骨痛, 而為浸淫.

Above there appears coughing and spitting;
below it is qi outflow."[8]

[Huang] Di:
"Good!
In autumn, the [movement in the] vessels is like [something] floating.
How can it be floating?"[9]

Qi Bo:
"In autumn, the [movement in the] vessels is a lung [movement].
The West is metal;
this is whereby the myriad beings are gathered after they have reached maturity.
Hence, when this qi comes, it is light, depleted, and floating.
It comes tense and leaves dispersed.
Hence, it is called 'floating.'[10]
A [movement] contrary to this [indicates] disease."

[Huang] Di:
"How can it be contrary?"

19-119-10
Qi Bo:
"When this qi comes hair[-like] and if it is firm in the center and depleted on both sides,
this is called 'greatly excessive.'[11]
The disease is in the exterior.

When this qi comes hair[-like] and is feeble,
this is called 'inadequate.'
The disease is in the center."

---

8 Wang Bing: "The heart minor yin vessel emerges from the center of the heart. It is tied to the heart connection, moves down through the diaphragm and encloses the small intestine. Also, another branch moves upwards from the heart connection into the lung. Hence, in the case of greatly excessive heart [qi], the body is hot, the skin aches, and soaking overflow spreads into the physical appearance section." Cheng Shide et al.: " 'Qi outflow' is: breaking a wind."

9 951/769: "Li Zhongzi: 'floating' is another term for 'light and depleted.' "

10 Wang Bing: "The [movement in the] vessels arrives light and depleted. Hence it is called 'floating.' When it comes tense, this is because the yang [qi] had not penetrated into the depth. When it leaves dispersed, this is because the yin qi rises."

11 81/37: "虛 means: depleted 空, soft and no strength."

[Huang] Di:

"When in autumn the [movement in the] vessels is greatly excessive or insufficient,

what are all the respective diseases like?"

19-119-13

Qi Bo:

"When it is greatly excessive,

then this lets a person's qi move contrary [to its regular course] and [causes] back pain.

[The person] feels uncomfortable.[12]

When it is inadequate,

then this lets a person pant;

he exhales and inhales being short of qi and coughs.

There is rising qi; blood appears.

Below one hears the disease sound."[13]

[Huang] Di:

"Good!

In winter, the [movement in the] vessels is as if encamped.

How can it be encamped?"

Qi Bo:

"In winter, the [movement in the] vessels is a kidney [movement].

The North is water;

---

12 *SWJZ*: "惋 is 怒, 'anger.'" According to *SWJZZ*, the *SWJZ* should be read as: "惋 is 怨, 'grievance.'" *Tai su*, ch. 14, 四時脈形, has 溫溫, "warm," instead of 惋惋. Cheng Shide et al.: "惋惋 means 鬱悶不舒, 'uncomfortable with chest pressure.'" 915/56: "惋 is 蘊, 'to collect.'" See 2764/22 for a detailed discussion of 溫 and 惋.

13 Wang Bing: "'Below one hears the disease sound' is to say: When the breathing is panting, there are sounds in the lung." Zhang Jiebin: "In the case of insufficiency, one pants, coughs and is short of qi. 'Below one hears the disease sound' is to say: If one's breath is panting, then there is a sound below the throat." Yao Shaoyu: "'The disease sounds' is: the qi flows out below and one frequently breaks wind." Hua Shou: "上氣 見血, 下聞病音 is to say: one pants and throws up blood and one coughs again and again. 下 is identical with 次, 'a series,' and 復, 'repeatedly.'" Gao Shishi: "When the coughing injures the network vessels of the lung, blood appears when the qi moves upwards. When the qi moves upwards but fails to move downwards, then one hears disease sounds below. 'Disease sounds' refers to groaning; this is [a sign of] depletion below." Wu Kun has changed 下聞病音 to 及聞病音, 'and one hears pathological sounds.'"

this is whereby the myriad beings are brought together and stored.
Hence, this qi comes in the depth and is beating.[14]
Hence, it is called 'encamped.' [15]
A [movement] contrary to this [indicates] disease."

[Huang] Di:
"How can it be contrary?"

19-120-4
Qi Bo:
"When this qi comes like a hurled stone,[16]
this is called 'greatly excessive.'
The disease is in the exterior.
When this [qi] leaves like [a movement that is] frequent,[17]

this is called 'inadequate.'
The disease is in the center."

---

14 Lin Yi et al.: "The *Jia yi jing* has 潤, 'to moisten,' instead of 搏. One should follow
the *Jia yi jing* and change it here to 潤." Wu Kun: "搏 is 伏鼓, 'hidden drumming.' "

15 Wang Bing: "That is to say, it strikes against the hands from the depth." *Nan jing*
15 has 石, "stone," instead of 營. Gao Shishi: "營 is like 石, 'stone.' It means 'stored in
the depth.' " Hua Shou: "營 is like the 營 in 營壘, 'entrenched camp.' It is a location
of assemblance. In the winter months, the myriad living beings are concealed. Hence
[the text] says 'encamped.' " Cheng Shide et al.: "營 is a military camp. Here it is a
metaphor for a concealed [movement in the] vessels during winter time. Even though
it is in the depth, hidden in it are nevertheless vital activities." Zhang Zhicong: "營 is
居, 'to dwell,' 'to rest.' That is to say, in winter the qi dwells peacefully in the interior."
951/770: "Li Zhongzi: 營 is 'to return to seclusion.' " 238/401: "Mr. Yü comments:
營 is to say: 回繞, 'to encircle.' The character is identical with 縈, 'to wind around.' In
winter, the [movement in the] vessels is in the depth, as if it were wrapped." Zhang
Yizhi et al.: "營 is identical with 旬

16 See the comments on this phrase in *Su wen* 18.

17 Zhang Yizhi et al.: "The *Tai su*, ch.14, has 毛, 'hair[-like],' instead of 數. Yang
Shangshan commented: 'The kidney qi is insufficient. Hence when this qi leaves,
pressing it feels like pressing on hair. .. Another version has 如數.' Presumably, 數
stands here for 縮. In his commentary on the *Zhou li* 周禮, Chun gong 春宮, Zheng
鄭 stated: 'In ancient texts 數 was written for 縮. Du Zichun 杜子春 said: 數 should
be 縮. The *Shuo wen* states: 縮 is 亂." Cheng Shide et al.: "如數 does not refer to a
frequent [movement in the] vessels as it is caused by repletion heat." Zhang Jiebin:
'Actually, a frequent [movement] is associated with heat. Here, though, is a [move-
ment in the] vessels of destroyed true yin and it should also be tight and frequent. The

19-120-6
[Huang] Di:
"When in winter the [movement in the] vessels is greatly excessive or inadequate,
what are all the respective diseases like?"

Qi Bo:
"When it is greatly excessive,
then this lets that person experience *jie-yi*.[18]
The vessels in the spine ache and being short of qi one does not wish to speak.

When it is inadequate,
this lets a person's heart become suspended.
{As if one suffered from hunger.}[19]
The lateral abdomen is cool.[20]
There is pain in the spine.
The lower abdomen is full.
The urine changes [its nature]."[21]

[Huang] Di:
"Good!"

19-120-10
[Huang] Di:
"In the sequence of the four seasons,
there are differences in the changes between opposition and compliance.

---

greater the depletion is, the more frquent [is the movement in the vessels]. Actually
this is not the frequent [movement] of strength, yang, repletion and heat. Hence [the
texts] states: 'like frequent.'"

18 For comments on the term *jie-yi*, see 18-113-1.

19 Yang Shangshan: "The kidney vessels extend upwards into the skin. When, therefore, the kidneys are depleted, the heart is as if suspended." Zhang Jiebin: "In the case
of this insufficiency, the true yin is depleted. With this depletion, heart and kidneys
cannot interact. Hence this causes that person to have his 'heart suspended' and become fearful, as if he suffered from hunger."

20 Wang Bing: "胁中 is the soft and hollow region below the small ribs on both sides
of the spine. It is located outside of the kidneys. Hence it should be cool."

21 Wu Kun: " 'Change' means it changes its normal appearance. It may become clear
in color, or it may be blocked, or it may flow incessantly." Yao Shaoyu: " 'The urine
changes' [is to say:] the color is yellow red; the water dries up and becomes turbid."

This being so,
the spleen [movement in the] vessels alone, how is it ruled?"[22]

Qi Bo:
"The spleen [movement in the] vessels is [associated with] the soil.
[The spleen] is a solitary depot[23] serving to pour [qi] into the four sides."[24]

[Huang] Di:
"This being so,
whether the spleen is in good or bad [condition],
can this be seen?"

Qi Bo:
"A good [condition] cannot be seen;
a bad [condition] can be seen."[25]

[Huang] Di:
"How can a bad [condition] be seen?"

---

22 Wang Bing: " 'Ruled' is to say: 'ruling season and months.' "

23 Wang Bing: "It receives water and grain, transforms [them] into the body liquids and pours [these liquids] into the liver, the heart, the lung, and the kidneys. Because it does not rule officially during [any of] the four seasons, it is called 'solitary depot.' " Zhang Jiebin: "The spleen is associated with the soil. The soil is the origin of the myriad beings. Hence it moves water and grains and transforms [them into] liquids which it pours into the four depots liver, heart, lung, and kidneys. The soil has no definite location of its own; its rule is distributed over the four seasons. Hence it is called 'solitary depot.' " Cheng Shide et al.: " 'Solitary depot' is not a designation specifically applied to the spleen; in *Su wen* 34 it refers to the kidneys."

24 Shen Zumian: "灌 is a mistake for 權, 'to weigh.' 四旁 refers to the four weft cords, 四維, mentioned in *Guan zi* 管子, You gong pian 幼宮篇. 灌四旁 should be 權四旁."

25 Wang Bing: "[The spleen] does not rule officially during [one specific] season, but extends its government over all four terms. Hence its goodness cannot be seen; its badness can be seen." Gao Shishi: "A good [condition] of the spleen [movement in the] vessels affects all depots; hence when [the spleen] is in good [condition] this can not be perceived. When the spleen [movement in the] vessels lacks moisture, then all the depots have either great excess or insufficiency. Hence when it is in bad [condition], this can be seen." Zhang Jiebin: "When the spleen has no disease, then it pours out [liquids] everywhere, the four depots are in peace and one does not know the strength of the spleen involved here. Hence its 'good' condition cannot be seen. When the spleen has a disease then, as a consequence, the four depots have diseases, too. Hence bad signs appear."

Qi Bo:

"If [the spleen movement in the vessels] comes like the flow of water, this is called 'greatly excessive.'

The disease is in the exterior.

If it resembles the beak of a bird, this is called 'inadequate.'

The disease is in the center."[26]

19-121-4

[Huang] Di:

"Sir, you say that the spleen is a solitary depot;

it is the center, [i.e.,] soil, from which [qi] is poured into the four sides.

When its [movement] is greatly excessive or inadquate,

what are all the respective diseases like?"

Qi Bo:

"When it is greatly excessive,

then this lets a person be unable to lift his four limbs;[27]

when it is inadequate,

then this let a person's nine orifices become impassable."

{This is called "heaviness and stiffness."}[28]

---

26 In accordance with *Su wen* 18, Zhang Qi: " 'Flowing water' and 'crow's beak' are spleen [movements in the] vessels indicating death. There may be a mistake here." Yao Shaoyu agrees. In contrast, Zhang Jiebin: "The terms are identical, but the meaning is different." Gao Shishi: "When the outpour [from the spleen] is greatly excessive, the spleen qi comes like a flow of water. In this case, dampness qi has occupied [the spleen] and this is called 'greatly excessive dampness in the soil.' The disease should be in the exterior. When the outpour [from the spleen] is insufficient, the spleen qi does not spread. 'When [the movement in the vessels] resembles the beak of a crow' then it is firm and stops by itself. This is called 'the qi of the soil is insufficient.' The disease should be in the center. All these [situations] can be seen."

27 Wang Bing: "Because [the spleen] rules the four limbs, when it has a disease, one cannot lift them."

28 Yang Shangshan: "When the spleen is depleted and receives a disease, it cannot pass qi to the nine orifices. Hence they are impassable. [The spleen] does not pass qi through the body. Hence the body becomes heavy (重) and is stiff (強)." Wang Bing: "The solitary depot of the spleen pours [liquid] into the four adjacent [depots]. In the case of disease [in the spleen], the five depots lose their harmony and, as a result, the nine orifices are impassable. 重 is to say: the qi of the depots is duplicated. 強 is to say: the qi is not in harmony." Gao Shishi: "重 is read in the second tone. 強 is read in the fourth tone. When the spleen [movement in the] vessels is out of harmony and when the nine orifices are impassable, then the spleen has a disease and above and below and all the four sides, all have a disease. Hence this is called 'repeated loss of harmony.' 強 is 不和, 'out of harmony.' "

19-121-7
When [Huang] Di rose he was startled.[29]
He paid reference twice knocking his head on the ground and said:
"Good!
I have received [your teachings on] the great essentials of the [movements in the] vessels and
on [the great essentials of] the perfect numbers in the world.
[And I have also heard that as far as the texts]
The Five Complexions,
The Changes in the [Movements in the] Vessels,
To Estimate and Measure, and
The Strange and the Normal [are concerned],
the Way [expounded in all these texts] is one.[30]

The spirit turns around, it does not go backwards.
When it goes backwards, then it no [longer] turns around.
In this case [one] has lost [one's vital] mechanism."[31]

The essentials of the perfect numbers are at hand and yet subtle.
He had them inscribed on jade tablets,[32] and
he had them stored in the depots and palaces.[33]
He read them every morning.

---

29 Wang Bing: "瞿 is 忙, 'in haste.'" Gao Shishi: "瞿 is 驚顧, 'startled.'"

30 210/43 does not accept the interpretation of these terms as titles of ancient scripts: "揆 means 揣測, 'to measure.' 奇恆 is 'normal and changed.' [This passage] points out: For [interpreting] the changes of the five complexions and of the five [movement in the] vessels it is essential to know their normal state and to measure their changes."

31 Wang Bing: "When the five qi continue their circulation in due time, this is [a situation where] the spirit qi flows in circulatory movement and does not return. If it turns backward, weakens and opposes the [passage of the] normal qi of heaven, then this [is a situation where] it turns back and fails to continue its circulatory movement. Because it turns back and fails to continue its circulatory movement, the dynamics of the vital qi are lost."

32 See *Han shu*, biography of Zhang Heng 張衡, for a use of the term 玉版 to designate an instrument employed in prognostication.

33 Gao Shishi: "藏府 is 密室, 'private quarters.'" *Han shu* 49, biography of Chao Cuo 晁錯, has 刻于玉版, 藏于金匱, "inscribe them on jade tablets and store them in the golden chest." In the introduction to the *Shi ji*, Si-ma Qian states: "故明堂石室, 金匱玉版, 圖籍散亂, 'the maps and scripts of the ancient Hall of Brilliance and Stone Chamber, of the Golden Chest and of the Jade Tablets were [all] scattered in chaos.'"

Their title is *Jade Mechanism*."³⁴

19-121-11
[Each of] the five depots receives qi from the [depot] which it generates;
it transmits it to the one which it dominates.
The qi rests in [that depot] by which [the transmitting depot] is generated.
Death results [when it is] in that [depot] which [the transmitting depot] cannot dominate.
<If a disease will result in death,
it must first be transmitted and pass [from one depot to another]. When it has
reached [a depot] which [the transmitting depot] cannot dominate, the patient
will die.>³⁵

{This is to say 'passage of qi contrary [to a regular course].'
Hence death [follows].}³⁶

---

34 See *Su wen* 15 and 63 for parallel passages. The *Tai su* has 生機, 'mechanism
of life', instead of 玉機. 2868/28 emphasises that such parallel passages must not
necessarily be interpreted as duplications of original *Nei jing* passages within the *Nei
jing*. Rather, these appear to be fragments of third texts quoted in similar or different
contexts in various treatises of the *Nei jing*. For details, see there. 138/19: "There may
have been a text of this title in ancient times. 玉機 is an instrument. In the same way
as the 'jade board' it served as a measure."

35 Wang Bing: "受氣所生 is to say: they receive disease qi from [a depot] which
they themselves generate. 傳所勝 is to say: they transmit [it to a depot] which they
themselves dominate. 氣舍所生 is to say: [the qi] rests in [a depot] by which [the
transmitting depot] itself is generated. 死所不勝 is to say: death occurs at [a depot]
by which [the transmitting depot] itself is dominated." Gao Shishi: "收 should be 授,
'to give.' The same applies to [the usages of 收] below. The qi given by the five depots
to those [depots] which they generate, this is the proper qi. It is given to the son one
generates. If it is transmitted to [a depot] which [the transmitting depot] dominates,
this is the disease qi of the five depots. [A depot] transmits it to [the depot] which it
dominates. I generate [something else] and [something else] generates me. Both are
[instances of] 'that which generates.' The qi which rests in the [depot] which gener-
ates/is generated, this is the proper qi of the five depots. It rests in the mother [depot]
which generates [the transmitting depot]. Death occurs at [a depot] by which [the
transmitting depot] is dominated, [this refers to] the fatal qi of the five depots. Death
occurs where one is subdued. This is the depot which [the transmitting depot] itself
cannot dominate. When a disease leads to death, this is not a sudden death. It must
first be transmitted to all the other depots. When it finally reaches the depot which
[the depot affected first] cannot dominate, then the disease will end in death."

36 969/61: "This is a 'reverse passage' of 'son transmits to the mother.' After a transmission through three [depots the qi] has reached [the depot] which cannot be dominated and death follows."

The liver
receives qi from the heart.
It transmits it to the spleen.
The qi rests in the kidneys.
Death occurs when it reaches the lung.

The heart
receives qi from the spleen.
It transmits it to the lung.
The qi rests in the liver.
Death occurs when it reaches the kidneys.

19-122-3
The spleen
receives qi from the lung.
It transmits it to the kidneys.
The qi rests in the heart.
Death occurs when it reaches the liver.

The lung
receives qi from the kidneys.
It transmits it to the liver.
The qi rests in the spleen.
Death occurs when it reaches the heart.

The kidneys
receive qi from the liver.
They transmit it to the heart.
The qi rests in the lung.
Death occurs when it reaches the spleen. "
{All these are cases of death from a [passage] contrary to [a regular course].}[37]

19-122-6
{One day and one night,
this [period] is divided by five.

---

37 969/61: "This is an ancient commentary which was later mixed up with the text."

It is by this that one predicts whether death or survival[38] will be early or late.}[39]

Huang Di:[40]
"The mutual communications and the transmissions [of diseases] among the
five depots,
they all follow a [specific] sequence.[41]
When [one of] the five depots has a disease,
it is always transmitted to the [depot] which [the transmitting] can dominate.[42]
If it is not cured [there],
the law is that after three months or six months,
or after three days or six days,
[the disease] is [further] transmitted among the five depots and then must
result in death."[43]

---

38 Lin Yi et al.: "The *Jia yi jing* has the character 者 instead of 生." (In this case the
passage reads as: "One may predict whether death will be early or late.") Wang Shaozeng & Xu Yongnian/45: "死生, the meaning emphasized here is 死, 'death.'"

39 Wang Bing: "[A disease transmitted initially by] the liver will end in death [when
it has reached the position of] the lung; i.e., in autumn [or during the period of] *geng
xin.* The same applies to the remaining four [possibilities]. Also, the morning is ruled
by [the term] *jia yi*; the daytime is ruled by *bing ding*; the four periods, soil, (some editions have 上; this is a mistake for 土, 'soil') are ruled by *wu ji*; late afternoon is ruled
by *geng xin*; night is ruled by *ren gui*. From these [relationships] it is possible to know
whether death or survival will be early or late." Gao Shishi: "The five divisions are: *yin
mao* is ruled by [the agent] wood; *si wu* is ruled by [the agent] fire; *shen you* is ruled by
[the agent] metal; *hai zi* is ruled by [the agent] water; *chen xu* and *chou wei* are ruled
by [the agent] soil. When [a disease transmitted by] the liver reaches the lung, [the
patient] dies. Death occurs in the period *shen you*. When [a disease transmitted by]
the heart (i.e., fire) reaches the kidneys (i.e., water), [the patient] dies. Death occurs
in the period *hai zi* (i.e., water). When [a disease transmitted by] the spleen (i.e., soil)
reaches the liver (i.e., wood), [the patient] dies. Death occurs in the period *yin mao*
(i.e., wood). When [a disease transmitted by] the lung (i.e., metal) reaches the heart
(i.e., fire), [the patient] dies. Death occurs in the period *si wu* (i.e., fire). When [a disease transmitted by] the kidneys (i.e., water) reaches the spleen (i.e., soil), [the patient]
dies. Death occurs in the periods *chen xu* and *chou wei* (i.e., soil)."

40 Zhang Qi and others consider the three characters 黄帝曰 to be erroneous insertions.

41 2215/28: "相通 is 相互貫通, 'mutual penetration.' 次 is 次序, 'sequence.'"

42 Wang Bing: "Because the text above has stated that death occurs as a result of
reverse transmission, here it states that this is a move contrary to the sequence of
transmission to the [depot] which can be dominated."

43 Wang Bing: " 'Three months' is to say: [the period required by] one single depot
for further transmission of a qi. 'Six months' is to say: [the period required by the qi]

This is in accordance with the sequence of transmission to the [depot] which can be dominated.[44]

19-122-10
Hence, when it is said:
'By differentiating at the yang,
one knows where the disease comes from.
By differentiating at the yin,
one knows the time of death and survival,'[45]

---

to reach the position of [that depot which is] dominated [by the transmitting depot]. 'Three days' refers to the number of the three yang [conduits] to match them with the days [of transmission]. 'Six days' counts them together with the three yin [qi]. *Su wen* 31 states: 'A harm caused by cold, within one day it is received by the great yang [conduit]. Within two days it is received by the yang brilliance [conduit]. Within three days it is received by the minor yang [conduit]. Within four days it is received by the major yin [conduit]. Within five days it is received by the minor yin [conduit]. Within six days it is received by the ceasing yin [conduit]. That is meant here.'

44 Lin Yi et al.: "These seven characters follow the preceding commentary [by Wang Bing]. They were erroneously incorporated into [the main text]. They are absent from the Quan Yuanqi edition and from the *Jia yi jing*." 458/12: "There is no doubt, [the seven characters 是順傳所勝之次] must be a commentary by Wang Bing, because Wang Bing has written in a commentary on the previous paragraph the following sentence: 是逆傳所勝之次, 'this is a move contrary to the sequence of transmission to the [depot] which can be dominated.'"

45 Lin Yi et al.: "An examination of an older [version] shows that a commentary was written here as [main text of] the classic. It should be reverted to a commentary." For an almost identical passage, see *Su wen* 07. Zhang Jiebin: " 'Yang' refers to the outside; this is to say: the external indicators. 'Yin' refers to the inside; this is to say, to the qi in the depots. Whenever an evil hits the body, it must assume physical appearance in the exterior and through examining the external signs one can know in which conduit the disease is located. Hence through differentiating at the yang one knows the origin of the disease. When a disease harms the qi in the depots, it must destroy its true [qi] and through examining its basis one can know on which day there will be a crisis. Hence through differentiating at the yin one knows the date of death or survival." Ma Shi: "If one differentiates at the yang conduits, one knows the origin of the disease, that is, from which yang conduit it has arrived at its present location. From differentiating at the yin conduits one knows the date of death or survival. This is what is said in *Su wen* 05: 'if next one treats the six palaces,' [the disease] must not necessarily end in death; 'if next one treats the five depots,' the chances of death or survival are half and half. Hence one can know the date of death or survival." Wu Kun: " 'Yang' is a [movement in the] vessels arriving in harmony; it has stomach qi. 'Yin' is a [movement in the] vessels arriving without harmony. Here the true [qi of a] depot dominates and no stomach qi is present. That is to say, that what can be differentiated in a harmonious yang [movement in the] vessels, this is: one knows the origin of the disease if one section

this is to say: one knows that he will die once it reaches that [depot] where it meets distress.[46]

19-123-1
Hence,
the wind is the chief [cause] of the one hundred diseases.[47]

Now,
when wind and cold settle in a person,
they let [this] person's entire finest body hair [stand up] straight.
The skin closes and develops heat.
At this time,
[the wind and the cold] can be effused through [induced] sweating.[48]

In some cases block, numbness, swelling, and pain [result].[49]
At this time,
it can be removed through hot water and poultices, as well as through fire cauterization and piercing.[50]

If no cure is achieved,
the disease enters the lung and lodges there.

---

is not in harmony. Through distinguishing the true [qi in the] depots in the five yin [movements in the] vessels one can know the date of death or survival in advance."

46 Wang Bing: "困 is: to reach [a depot] which cannot be dominated." Gao Shishi: "困 is 受剋, 'to be subdued.'"

47 *Su wen* 03 has: "The wind is the beginning of the hundred diseases." Fu Weikang & Wu Hongzhou/280: "長 is 首, 'head,' 'begin.'" Zhang Jiebin: "As for 客, [the wind and the cold] arrive from outside like visitors; where they settle is not their permanent [residence]."

48 Wang Bing: "客 is to say: 客止於人形, 'it settles in the physical appearance of man.' The wind strikes against the skin; the cold dominates the interstice structures. Hence the fine hair stands up straight, the dark palaces close and heat emerges."

49 Wang Bing: "These states result because the disease undergoes changes. When the heat strikes blood and qi, then blockage and numbness result. When the coldness qi harms the physical appearance, this causes swelling and pain."

50 Wang Bing: "That is to say, to disperse the cold evil and to spread the proper qi." Fu Weikang & Wu Hongzhou/280: "'Hot water' means: by washing with hot water. 'Poultice' means: by applying hot drugs on the skin. 火灸 is 用火燻灼, 'to cauterize with hot fumes.'"

It is [now] called 'lung block.' [51]
It develops cough and rising qi.

19-123-5
If no cure is achieved [at this stage],
then the lung will transmit [the disease] further and pass it to the liver.
The disease is [now] called liver block.
Another name is 'recession.' [52]
The flanks ache and food is thrown up.
At this time,
one can press as well as pierce. [53]

If no cure is achieved,
the liver transmits it to the spleen.
The disease is [now] called 'spleen wind.'
[The patient] develops solitary [heat] disease and has heat in the abdomen.
The heart is vexed and the discharge is yellow.
At this time,
one can press, one can give drugs, and one can bathe.

19-124-1
If no cure is achieved,
the spleen transmits it to the kidneys. [54]
The disease is [now] called 'elevation conglomeration ill.' [55]

---

51 Cheng Shide et al.: "痹 is 閉, 'closed.'" Zhang Zhicong: "The skin and the qi section are the yang [section]; the five depots are the yin [section]. When the disease is in the yang [section], it is called 'wind.' When it is in the yin [section], it is called 'blockage.' The disease has settled in the lung; hence it is called 'lung blockage.' 痹 is 閉, 'closed.' The evil is enclosed in the lung. Hence one coughs and [suffers from] rising qi."

52 Wang Bing: "The metal of the lung fells the wood. The qi moves down into the liver. Hence [the text] states: 'If no cure is achieved, [the lung] transmits it to the liver. The qi of the liver communicates with the gallbladder. The gallbladder tends to develop anger. In the case of anger, qi moves contrary [to its proper course]. Hence another name [of the disease] is 'recession.'"

53 Zhang Zhicong: "按 is 按摩導引, 'massage and physical exercise.'"

54 Gao Jiwu/557: "Some authors interprete 之 as 到, 'to reach.' In reality, though, 之 is identical with 于, 'to.' It may also be interpreted as 之于, '[transmit] it to.'"

55 964/2: "The *Shuo wen* states: 疝 is 'abdominal pain.' 疝瘕 is a disease of 'having lumps in the abdomen that can move and cause pain.'" For details, see there.

The lower abdomen feels pressed,⁵⁶ is hot and has pain.
One's discharge is white.
Another name is 'bug poison.'⁵⁷
At this time,
one can press and one can give drugs.

If no cure is achieved,
the kidneys transmit it to the heart.
One suffers from sinews and vessels pulling each other and becoming tense.⁵⁸
The disease is [now] called 'spasms.'⁵⁹
At this time,
one can cauterize and one can give drugs.
If no cure is achieved,
after [the disease] has lasted for ten days,
the law is that death must occur.

19-124-5
After the kidneys have transmitted [the disease] to the heart,
if the heart transmits it back to the lung,
[the patient] develops [feelings of] cold and heat.⁶⁰
The law is that after three years one must die.⁶¹

---

56 692/41: "冤 is the same principle as 郁, 'to feel pressed.'" 1574/70: "冤熱 is like 郁
熱, 'to feel pressed with heat.'" 970/4 has a detailed discussion on the meaning of 冤
in the present context and interprets 冤熱, in accordance with *Su wen* 35 and other
treatises, as 煩悗 , "annoyed, vexed."

57 Wang Bing: "This is as if one's flesh was eaten by some bug. It wastes away day by
day. Hence another name is 蠱, 'bug poison.'"

58 Wang Bing: "When the [qi of the] kidneys is insufficient, then no water is generated. When no water is generated, then the sinews desiccate and become tense. Hence
they pull each other. When the yin qi is weak internally and when the yang qi flames
up in the outer regions, the sinews and the vessels receive heat and cramp. Hence [the
disease] is named 'spasm.'"

59 1790/58: "瘈 is 拘攣 or 拘急, 'contraction,' 'to seize.'"

60 Wang Bing: "Because the kidneys transmit [the evil] to the heart and because
the heart cannot receive a disease, [the heart] transmits it back again to the metal of
the lung. The lung, now, is harmed a second time. Hence [the patient] experiences
cold and heat." Gao Shishi: "The heart rules the spirit-brilliance and usually does not
receive evil. Hence when the kidneys transmit the [disease] to the heart, the heart in
turn transmits it back and has it pass to the lung."

61 Wang Bing: "The [transmission from the] lung reaches the kidneys within one
year. [The transmission from] the kidneys reaches the liver within one year. [The

This is the sequence of the [transmission of] diseases.[62]

However, those [diseases] that develop all of a sudden,[63] they must not necessarily be treated [in accordance with the sequence of] transmission.[64]

In some cases, it happens that transmission and transformation [of the disease
through the depots] do not follow the [normal] sequence.[65]

Those that enter [the body] without following the sequence [of transmission],
are anxiety, fear, sadness, joy, and anger.
They are the cause that [diseases] are unable to follow this sequence [of trans-
mission].
Therefore they let a person have a serious disease.[66]

19-124-8
Hence, if a massive depletion [results
from] joy,
then the qi of the kidneys takes advantage [of this depletion];[67]
[from] anger,
then the qi of the liver takes advantage [of this depletion];[68]

---

transmission from] the liver reaches the heart within one year. The fire then avails itself of the lung. Hence [the text] states: 'three years.' "Hua Shou: " 'Three years' should
be 'three days.' "Wu Kun has 三噦, "three belches," instead of 三歲.

62 Wang Bing: "That is to say: transmission [by a depot] to that [depot which is]
dominated [by the former]."

63 Gao Shishi: "卒 is to be read as *cu* [in the sense of] 'suddenly.' "

64 Wang Bing: "They do not necessarily occur following a sequence of transmission. Hence it is not necessary to treat them in accordance with the [sequence of]
transmission."

65 Gao Jiwu/562: "以 is used here in the sense of 按照, 'in accordance with.' "

66 Wang Bing: "An outbreak of anxiety, fear, sadness, joy, or anger is not tied to any
regular division [of time]. As soon as one encounters [these emotions], an outbreak
follows. Hence their generation of disease qi does not follow any order either." Yao
Shaoyu: "Harm caused by [any of] the five emotions accumulates for long and then
breaks out all of a sudden. In the beginning it does not come in accordance with [an
established] order. Hence the disease does not follow any sequence [of depots]."

67 Wang Bing: "In the case of joy, heart qi is transferred to the lung. The heart qi is
not protected. Hence the kidney qi occupies/takes advantage of [the depletion]."

68 Wang Bing: "In the case of anger, the qi moves contrary [to its proper course].
Hence the liver qi occupies the spleen." The character 怒, "anger", appears to be a

[from] sadness,
then the qi of the lung takes advantage [of this depletion];⁶⁹
[from] fear,
then the qi of the spleen takes advantage [of this depletion];⁷⁰
[from] anxiety,
then the qi of the heart takes advantage [of this depletion].⁷¹
This is the Way of this.⁷²

Hence,
there are five diseases.
Five [diseases per] five [depots results in] 25 changes,
as well as in transformations [occurring in the process of] transmission.
{'Transmission' is the term [used here] for 'taking advantage.'}⁷³

19-125-3
When the major bones have dried and
when major [masses of] flesh have sunk down,⁷⁴
when the qi in the chest is full and
when the breath is panting and does not flow unimpeded,
while the qi moves one's physical appearance,

---

mistake for 思, "pensiveness." The qi of the liver, i.e., of wood, takes advantage of the void left by a depleted qi of the spleen, i.e., of soil. Pensiveness is the emotion associated with the agent soil.

69 Wang Bing: "In the case of sadness, the lung qi is transferred to the liver. The liver qi receives the evil [qi]. Hence the lung qi has occupied it." Zhang Zhicong: " 'Lung' should be 'liver.' 'Sadness' should be 思, 'pensiveness.' " The character 悲, "sadness", appears to be a mistake for 怒, "anger." The qi of the lung, i.e., of metal, takes advantage of the void left by a depleted qi of the liver, i.e., of wood. Anger is the emotion associated with the agent wood.

70 Wang Bing: "In the case of fear, the kidney qi is transferred to the heart. The qi of the kidneys is no longer protected. Hence the spleen qi occupies [the kidneys]."

71 Wang Bing: "In the case of anxiety, liver qi is transferred to the spleen. The liver qi is no longer protected. Hence the heart qi occupies [the liver]."

72 Wang Bing: "That is the normal path/way of [a transmission that does] not follow the [regular] sequence."

73 252/39: "This appears to be a commentary which later became mixed with the text."

74 Wang Bing: "When the skin is desiccated and sticks to the bones and when the flesh has sunk in, this is called 'the major bones have dried and the major [masses of] flesh have sunk down.'" Gao Shishi: " 'The major bones' and 'the major [masses of] flesh' refer to the bones and to the flesh of both arms and thighs."

death is to be expected within six months.[75]
If one notices a [movement of the] true [qi of a] depot [in the vessels],
one [can] inform [the patient] of the expected day [of his death].

When the major bones have dried and
when major [masses of] flesh have sunk down,
when the qi in the chest is full and
when one's breath is panting and does not flow unimpeded and
when internal pain pulls on the shoulders and the nape,
death is to be expected within one month.[76]
If one notices a [movement of the] true [qi of a] depot in the vessels,
one [can] inform [the patient] of the expected day [of his death].

19-125-6
When the major bones have dried and
when major [masses of] flesh have sunk down,
when the qi in the chest is full and
when one's breath is panting and does not flow unimpeded,
when internal pain pulls on the shoulders and the nape and
when the body is hot, with the flesh wasting away and the protuberant muscles
being destroyed and

---

75 Wang Bing: "When 'the qi in the chest is full and when one's breath is panting
and does not flow unimpeded,' then the lung has lost control. The lung is responsible
for order and regulation; the qi and the breathing originate from it. When its qi moves
the physical appearance, then this is [to say] the qi does not flow in succession. Hence
one raises shoulders and back to draw in the required qi from afar. In such a situation,
all the physical depots have already received harm and the spirit depots are injured,
too. When such signs appear, death can be predicted to occur within 180 days. If
the true [qi of the] depot appears in the vessels, then the [exact] day of death can be
given." Gao Shishi: "When 'the major bones have dried out,' this is a kidney disease.
When 'the great flesh has sunk down,' this is a spleen disease. When 'qi fills chest and
center and when one's breath is panting and does not flow unimpeded,' this is a lung
disease. 便 is like 利, 'unimpeded.' 'The qi moves the physical appearance' is to say: the
qi does not leave or enter the body unimpeded, hence it causes the body to shake."

76 Wang Bing: "When the fire essence leaves towards outside and when the yang
qi flames above, the metal has been affected by a fire disaster. Hence there is internal
pain and shoulders and nape are as described here. Death can be predicted within 30
days. The depot [referred to here is that] of the heart." Gao Shishi: "Following the
kidney disease, the spleen disease, and the lung disease mentioned above, [here now
the text] speaks of internal pain affecting shoulders and nape. In this case the disease
has proceeded along the conduits and has arrived in the wind palace now. Hence
death follows within one month." (The "wind palace" is a location at the back of the
skull, above the nape)

if one notices a [movement of the] true [qi of a] depot [in the vessels],
death [follows] within ten months.[77]

When the major bones have dried and
when major [masses of] flesh have sunk down,
when the shoulders [draw] inwards and when the marrow dissolves,
when one's movement and activities weaken increasingly and
if one notices the arrival of the true [qi of a] depot,
death is to be expected within one year.[78]
If one notices the true [qi of a] depot,
one [can] inform [the patient] of the expected day [of his death].

19-126-1
When the major bones have dried and
when major [masses of] flesh have sunk down,
when the qi in the chest is full and
when there is pain in the abdomen,
when one feels uneasy in the heart and
when the shoulders, the nape and the body are hot,
when the protuberant [muscles] are destroyed and when the flesh has wasted
away,
when the sockets of the eye have sunk in and
when one notices a true [qi of the] depots and
when [the patient's] eyes do not perceive anybody,
death is imminent.
If [the patient still] perceives someone,
he will die when the time is reached that cannot be dominated.[79]

---

77 Wang Bing: "The yin qi is weakened and the yang qi flames internally. Hence the
body is hot. 䐃 are the tips of the flesh. The spleen rules the flesh. Hence when the
flesh looks as if it had fallen off entirely, the 䐃 appear as if destroyed. When such signs
appear, death follows after 300 days. 䐃 refers to the flesh behind elbows and knees
resembling lumps." Gao Shishi: "The fat is called 䐃." Zhang Jiebin, Hua Shou, and
Wu Kun suggest "ten days" instead of "ten months."

78 Wang Bing: "肩髓內消 is to say: the broken basin (i.e., the supraclavicular fossa)
is deep. 'The activities weaken' is to say: the intercourse [with the other depots] weakens gradually. But the other depots have not been affected yet. Hence death is to be
predicted within 365 days. The depot [referred to] is that of the kidneys." Lin Yi et al.:
"The Quan Yuanqi edition and the *Jia yi jing* have 真藏未見 instead of 真藏來見. 來
is an error for 未, 'not yet.'" Wu Kun, Zhang Zhicong, and others agree.

79 Wang Bing: "The wood generates this fire; the liver qi passes through the heart
vessel to reach the lower abdomen. Above it spreads through the flanks and proceeds
along the back of the throat into the nape and into the forehead. Hence there is ab-

In case an acute depletion arrives in the body suddenly,
the five depots are closed, [because] they are cut off [from circulation],
the vessel paths are impassable and
the qi fails to come and go.
This is like falling or drowning;
one cannot determine the time [of death].[80]

19-126-5
When a [movement in the] vessels is interrupted and fails to arrive, or
when it arrives five or six times while a person breathes once,[81]
even if the flesh of his physical appearance has not wasted away and [82]
even if one does not notice a true [qi of a] depot [in the movement in the vessels],
[that person] must die nevertheless.[83]

---

dominal pain and uneasiness in the heart. Shoulders, nape, and the body are hot; the muscle lumps are destroyed and the flesh has fallen off. The liver rules the eyes. Hence the sockets of the eyes have sunk in. When [the patient] cannot see other persons any longer, death follows immediately. 'At a time which cannot be dominated' refers to the *geng xin* month. The depot [mentioned here is that] of the liver."

80 Wang Bing: "That is to say: When the five depots transfer [a disease] among each other, in cases [the disease] is transmitted to a depot which the transmitting depot cannot dominate, one can wait for the true qi of the depot [to arrive] in the vessels. Once it arrives, the day of death can be predicted. In case an acute depletion evil hits the interior of the body, the five depots are cut off [from circulation] and close [their entrances and exits]. The vessel paths are no longer passable and the qi does not move back and forth. Hence [the text] compares this with a fall or death from drowning; i.e., the days of death cannot be predicted here either."

81 Lin Yi et al.: "Why should a person die if the [movement in the] vessels arrives five or six times during one breathing period? The character 息 is a mistake for 呼, 'to exhale.' "

82 Yu Chang: "The first character 不 may be an erroneous insertion linked to the second character 不. Because the flesh of the physical appearance has fallen off, death is inevitable even though the true qi of that depot does not appear. If the statement were to say 'the flesh of the physical appearance has not fallen off,' there should be a 雖, 'even though,' in this sentence. It should be worded: 'Even though the flesh has not fallen off and even though the true qi of the depot does not appear.' Another [commentator] has stated the character 不 should be 已, 'completely.' *Su wen* 20 has a parallel wording: 形肉已脫, 九侯雖調, 猶死."

83 Wang Bing: "This is a [movement in the] vessels of 'dramatic depletion' and 'sudden arrival [of evil qi].' "

When a [movement of the] true [qi of the] liver arrives in the vessels,
which is tense in the center and in the outside
as if [one's fingers] passed along the blade of a knife, giving one a cutting sensation,
as if one pressed the strings of a cither,[84] and
when the complexion is green-white and not glossy,
with [the patient's] body hair breaking off,
then [the patient will] die.

When a [movement of the] true [qi of the] heart arrives in the vessels,
which beats and is firm and strung together,
as if [one's fingers] passed along [a line of] *yi yi* seeds,[85] and
when the complexion is red-black and not glossy,
with [the patient's] body hair breaking off,
then [the patient will] die.

When a [movement of the] true [qi of the] lung arrives in the vessels,
which is big and depleted,
as if one touched a person's skin with fur or feathers and
when the complexion is white-red and not glossy,
with the [patient's] body hair breaking off,
then [the patient will] die.

When a [movement of] the true [qi of the] kidneys arrives in the vessels,
with is beating and [occasionally] interrupted,
[sounding] *bi-bi* as if a finger hurled a stone and
when the complexion is black-yellow and not glossy,
with [the patient's] body hair breaking off,
then [the patient will] die.

When a [movement of] the true [qi of the] spleen arrives in the vessels,
which is weak and at times frequent, at times spaced, and
when the complexion is yellow-green and not glossy,
with [the patient's] body hair breaking off,
then [the patient will] die.

---

84 915/56: "責 is 嘖, 'to call out.' 嘖嘖 is the sound of the crow." 2662/22 separates between 責責然 and 如按.

85 Possibly the seeds of *Coix lacryma-jobi* L.var.mayuan (Roman) Stapf.

In all cases where one notices a [movement of the] true [qi of the] depots in the vessels, [the patients will] die and [can]not be cured."[86]

19-126-13
Huang Di:
"When one notices a [movement of the] true [qi of the] depots, this is called 'fatal.'
Why?"

Qi Bo:
"All the five depots are supplied with qi by the stomach.
[Hence] the stomach is the basis of the five depots.
The qi of the depots cannot arrive by itself at the hand major yin [conduit];
it is only because of the stomach qi that it can arrive at the hand major yin.[87]

Hence,
[the qi of] each of the five depots,
when its time [of dominance has come],
it is in its [specific] manner that it arrives at the hand major yin.[88]

19-127-3
Hence,
when evil qi dominates,
the essence qi is weakened.
Hence,
in the case of severe diseases, the stomach qi cannot arrive together with it at the hand major yin.

---

86 Lin Yi et al.: "Yang Shangshan has stated: 'Because it is not mixed with other qi, it is called true qi.' The qi of the five depots are all mixed with stomach qi; they are unable to operate alone. .. As long as the qi of the five depots is mixed with stomach qi one will live a long life. When the true qi [of a depot] appears alone, death is inevitable."

87 Wang Bing: "The normal [condition] of a balanced person is supplied with qi by the stomach. The stomach qi is the normal qi of a balanced person. Hence it is because of the stomach that the qi of the depots can arrive at the hand major yin [conduit]." Lin Yi et al.: "This is main text of *Su wen* 18 which was moved here as a comment by Wang Bing."

88 Wang Bing: "['By itself' means:] it arrives at the hand major yin [conduit] in its own specific manifestation." Gao Shishi: "The [qi of the] five depots liver, heart, spleen, lung, and kidneys arrive at the hand major yin [conduit], each at its time [of dominance] and when they cause [the movement of the qi in the vessels] to be string[-like], hook[-like], hair[-like], or stone[-like]."

Hence,
the true qi of the depot appears alone.
When it appears alone, the disease has dominated the depot.
Hence,
this is called 'fatal.'"

[Huang] Di:
"Good!"

19-127-7
Huang Di:
"For all treatments of diseases, one investigates the [patient's] physical appearance, his qi, and whether his complexion is glossy,
whether the [movement in the] vessels abounds or is weak,
whether the disease is new acquired or chronic and
then, in treating it, one does not act too late.[89]

When physical appearance and qi agree,
this is called 'curable.' [90]
When the complexion is glossy and [when the movement in the vessels] is at
the surface,[91]
this is called 'easily brought to an end.'
When the [movement in the] vessels conforms with the four seasons,
this is called 'curable.' [92]
When the [movement in the] vessels is weak and smooth,
then it has stomach qi.
This is called 'easy to cure.'

---

89 Wang Bing: "One strives to be ahead of its time when seizing it."

90 Wang Bing: "When the qi abounds and the physical appearance abounds; when
the qi is depleted and the physical appearance is depleted, this is 'they agree with each
other.'" Tanba Genken 丹波元堅: "The qi referred to here is the breath. One must
check the quiet or hasty nature of [a patient's] breathing and compare it with the lean
or fat status of his physical appearance, like outside and inside, and consider this as a
cornerstone in diagnosis."

91 Zhang Jiebin: "澤 is 潤, 'moist.' 浮 is 明, 'clear.' When the color is clear and moist,
the disease must be easily brought to an end."

92 Wang Bing: "When the [movement in the] vessels is string[-like] in spring,
hook[-like] in summer, floating in autumn, and encamped in winter, this is called
'coinciding with the four seasons.'"

Seize the [disease] in time.⁹³

19-128-1
When physical appearance and qi do not agree,
this is called 'difficult to cure.'⁹⁴
When the complexion has faded away⁹⁵ and is not glossy,
this is called 'difficult to bring to an end.'⁹⁶
When the vessels are replete and firm,
this is called 'increasingly serious.'⁹⁷
When the [movement in the] vessels opposes the four seasons,
[the disease] cannot be cured.⁹⁸
One must investigate [whether any of] these four difficulties [is present] and
clearly announce them [to the patient].⁹⁹

The so-called [movement] 'opposing the four seasons' [is as follows]:
In spring one notices a lung [movement in the] vessels;
in summer one notices a kidney [movement in the] vessels;
in autumn one notices a heart [movement in the] vessels;
in winter one notices a spleen [movement in the] vessels.

---

93 Wang Bing: "If one waits for the time when it can be seized and then seizes it,
then in thousand cases treated a myriad cures will be achieved. That is, one treats according to the location of blood and qi in the course of the four seasons." Gao Shishi:
"In treatment, one must not act too late. Hence [the text] states: 'seize it in time.'"
Wu Kun: "'Seize it in time' is: in spring, pierce the scattered transporters; in summer,
pierce the network transporters; in autumn, pierce the skin; in winter, pierce the transporter holes of the interstices."

94 Wang Bing: "When the physical appearance abounds while the qi is depleted, or
when the qi abounds while the physical appearance is depleted, all these are instances
of a failure to agree."

95 On the meaning of 夭 in the *Nei jing*, see 240/55. *SWJZ*: "夭 is 屈, 'to bend.'"
JJZG: "夭 is 災, 'catastrophe.'"

96 Wang Bing: "夭 is 不明而惡, not clear and bad. 不澤 is to say: withered and
desiccated."

97 Wang Bing: "When the vessels are replete and firm, the evil qi abounds. Hence,
[the disease] is increasingly serious."

98 Wang Bing: "The four preceding sentences are called 'the four difficulties.' Hence
the following statement."

99 Wang Bing: "These four, it is easy for the crude practitioner to talk about them
and it is difficult for the able practitioner to deal with them."

<All these [movements] arrive suspended and interrupted, and they are in the
depth and rough, hence
they are called 'opposing the four seasons.' >[100]
<When [the movement] does not show a [proper] manifestation of the depot,
[i.e.]
when in spring and summer the [movement in the] vessels is in the depth and
rough, or
when in autumn and winter [the movement in the] vessels is at the surface and
big,
then this is called 'opposing the four seasons.' >[101]

When the disease is heat but the [movement in the] vessels is quiet;
when [the disease] is outflow but the [movement in the] vessels is big;
when one has lost blood but the [movement in the] vessels is replete;
when the disease is in the center but the vessels are replete and firm;
when the disease is in the exterior but the vessels are not replete and firm,
all these [are situations that] are difficult to cure."[102]

Huang Di:
"I have heard:
depletion and repletion can serve to decide whether [a patient] will die or
suvive.
I should like to hear about the circumstances [of such decisions]."

Qi Bo:
"The five repletions are fatal and
the five depletions are fatal."[103]

[Huang] Di:
"I should like to hear about the five repletions and about the five depletions."

---

100 Wang Bing: "懸絕 is like an item that was suspended and has now been cut off."
See *Su wen* 07 for a parallel terminology. 533/18: "懸絕 appears to have the meaning
of 懸殊, 'separated.'"

101 Wang Bing: " 'Does not have [the physical appearance of the depot]' is to say: it
does not have the appearance of the [movement in the] vessels associated with that
depot."

102 Wang Bing: "They all are difficult to cure, because they do not agree with their
signs."

103 For detailed discussions of the concepts of "five repletions/depletions," see
1266/40, 1502/50, and 2840/11.

Qi Bo:
"An abounding [movement in the] vessels,
a hot skin,
an abdominal distension,
blockage in front and behind;
mental and physical pressure,
these are called the five repletions.[104]

A fine [movement in the] vessels,
a cold skin,
being short of qi,
unimpeded outflow in front and behind,
beverages or food do not enter [the stomach],
these are called the five depletions."[105]

19-129-2
[Huang] Di:
"Occasionally [people in such situations] survive.
Why?"

Qi Bo:
"When congee enters the stomach and
when the diarrheal outpour comes to a halt,[106]
then those with depletion will survive.
When the body sweats and
when they can [relieve nature] behind fluently,
then those with repletion will survive.
These are the manifestations of these [survivals]."

---

104 Wang Bing: " 'Repletion' refers to abundance and repletion of evil qi. Now, when the [movement in the] vessels abounds, [the evil is in] the heart. When the skin is hot, [the evil is in] the lung. When the abdomen is distended, [the evil is in] the spleen. When the front and the behind are impassable, these are the kidneys. In the case of chest pressure and dizziness, [the evil is in] the liver."

105 Wang Bing: " 'Depletion' refers to an insufficiency of true qi. Now, when the [movement in the] vessels is fine, [the evil is in] the heart; when the skin is cold, it is in the lung. When one is short of qi, it is in the liver. When there is outflow in front and behind, [it is in] the kidneys. When beverages and food do not enter [the body], [it is in] the spleen."

106 Gao Jiwu/252: "Guo Aichun-92 states: 注 is a mistake; it should be 利, 'free flow.' "

Chapter 20
Discourse on the Three Sections and Nine Indicators[1]

20-129-6
Huang Di asked:
"I have heard about the [art of the] nine needles from you, Sir.[2]
[Its applications] are manifold and comprehensive,
they are innumerable.

I should [now] like to hear the Way of the essential,
to entrust it to children and grandchildren;[3]
to transmit it to later generations;
to attach it to the bones and their marrow, and
to store it in liver and lung.

[I shall] smear blood around my mouth when [I] receive [this knowledge],[4]
[I will] not dare to let it leak [to others] carelessly.

---

1 A scroll with a fragmentary version of *Su wen* 20 – most likely copied during the middle of the Tang dynasty (8th century) – was discovered in the Dunhuang caves in 1899; it is now kept in the National Library in Paris (P.3287). A comparison of the Dunhuang version with the textus receptus in the *Su wen* was published by Wang Mimi in 1987 (see 1870/38). While no principle is apparent that could have led the compiler of the Dunhuang version in abridging the *Su wen* version, quite a few passages in the Dunhuang version are better understandable than in the *Su wen* version. For details, see 1870/38. Quan Yuanqi and Wu Kun have changed, in their editions of the *Nei jing*, the title of *Su wen* 20 to 訣生死論, "Discourse on how to decide about survival and death."

2 On the various meanings of the expression 'Nine Needles' in the *Nei jing*, see 799/16. The author categorizes all usages of 'Nine Needles' into four meanings: 1. As a reference to the art of piercing in general. 2. As a reference to a book title. 3. As a reference to the various types of needles. 4. As a reference to the numbers one to nine found in heaven and on earth. The present passage is identified as a reference to piercing in general. 802/190 grouped all usages of 'Nine Needles' according to three meanings: 1. As a reference to a book title. 2. As a reference to the art of piercing. 3. As a reference to the numbers constituting heaven and earth. Here, too, the present passage is identified as a reference to piercing in general.

3 Zhang Jiebin: "屬 is 付, 'to hand over.'" Ma Shi: "屬 is identical with 囑, 'to instruct.'" See also 916/54.

4 Wang Bing: "歃血 is 'to drink blood.'" This is a reference to an ancient ritual of smearing blood around one's mouth when taking an oath.

To have it conform to the Way of heaven,[5]
it must have an end and a beginning.
Above, it corresponds to the luminaries of heaven,
and to the calendrical arrangements of the stars.[6]
Below, it concurs with the four seasons and five agents. [Their qi] take their
positions of high and low rank one after another.[7]
In winter yin [qi dominates] and in summer yang [qi].
How does man correspond to this?
I should like to hear the method [to establish this correspondence]."

Qi Bo responded:
"A question touching the mysterious, indeed!
These are the perfect numbers of heaven and earth."[8]

20-129-11
[Huang] Di:
"I should like to hear about the perfect numbers of heaven and earth.
To have them match the physical appearance, the blood, and the qi of man and
to [be] always [able to] decide about [a patient's] death or survival,
how is that done?"

20-130-1
Qi Bo:
"The perfect numbers of heaven and earth,
they begin with one and
they end with nine.

---

5 Lin Yi et al.: "The Quan Yuanqi edition has 令合天地, 'let it agree with heaven
and earth.'"

6 Wang Bing: "天光 is to say: sun, moon, and the stars. 歷紀 is to say: the arrangement of the passage of sun and moon through the 28 [zodiacal] constellations and the
365 degrees of the sky."

7 Wang Bing: "The qi of the five agents ruling during [one of] the four seasons is of
'high rank.' That which assists is of 'low rank.'" See *Su wen* 22, where the metaphor of
'high and low rank' is unambiguously associated with the five agents. *Su wen* 25 has 更
立 instead of 更互. Gu Guanguang and others consider this to have been the original
wording of the present passage, too.

8 Wang Bing: "至數 is to say: 至極之數, 'the numbers reaching the final limits.'" Wu
Kun considered the preceding 99 characters as superfluous and omitted them from
his version.

One is heaven;
two is the earth,
three is man.

Subsequently they are multiplied by three
– three [times] three is nine –
to correspond to the nine fields.

Hence,
man has three sections.
[Each] section has three indicators.
They serve to decide about death or survival.
They serve to manage the one hundred diseases,
They serve to regulate [states of] depletion and repletion and
to eliminate evil and disease." ⁹

20-130-5
[Huang] Di:
"What is that to say: 'three sections'?"

Qi Bo:
"[Man]
has a lower section,
has a central section and
has an upper section.
Each section has three indicators.

The three indicators:
[one] is heaven,
[one] is earth and
[one] is man.
One must [use] one's finger to point them out [on the body] and
only then one can accept them as real.¹⁰

---

9 Wang Bing: "The so-called 'three sections' are the upper, central, and lower sections
of the human body; they are not the inch, gate, and foot-long sections [at the wrist].
The conduit paths originate from within these three sections. Hence all examinations
regarding [a patient's] death or survival are based on these [locations]. By piercing
them to achieve supplementation or drainage, evil diseases can be eliminated."

10 Wang Bing: "That is to say, they must be taught by a teacher." Zhang Jiebin: "指
而導之 is to say: one must receive instructions from a teacher." Gao Shishi: "指而導
之 is to say: one must follow [the vessels] with the fingers and press them." Tanba:
"Zhang Jiebin is right. 真 should be 質." 703/38: "A Ming manuscript edition has 質,

The heaven [indicator] of the upper section:
the moving vessels on the two [sides of the] forehead.[11]
The earth [indicator] of the upper section:
the moving vessels on the two [sides of the] cheeks.[12]
The man [indicator] of the upper section:
the moving vessels in front of the ears.[13]

The heaven [indicator] of the central section:
the hand major yin [locations].[14]
The earth [indicator] of the central section:
the hand yang brilliance [locations].[15]
The man [indicator] of the central section:
the hand minor yin [locations].[16]

The heaven [indicator] of the lower section:
the foot ceasing yin [locations].[17]
The earth [indicator] of the lower section:

'evidence,' instead of 真, 'true.' Also, Wang Bing in his comment states 質 is 成. Hence it is obvious that 真 is a mistaken character."

11 Wang Bing: "The movement of the qi of the foot minor yang vessels [can be felt] there."

12 Wang Bing: "This is the vessel movement to be felt on both sides, next to the grand crevice, below the nose holes. The movement of the qi of the hand yang brilliance vessels [can be felt] there."

13 Wang Bing: "The movement of the qi of the hand minor yang vessels [can be felt] there."

14 Wang Bing: "This is to say: the lung vessels. Their movement can be felt in the 'inch opening' behind the palm."

15 Wang Bing: "This is to say: the vessels of the large intestine. Their movement can be felt at the 'union valley' section at the junction of the bones between the thumb and the index finger."

16 Wang Bing: "This is to say: the heart vessels. Their movement can be felt at the 'spirit gate' section at the tip of the prominent bone (i.e., the styloid processus) behind the palm."

17 Wang Bing: "This is to say: the liver vessels. Their movement can be felt – it should be taken while the person lies down – at the 'five miles' section in the hollow one and a half inches below the Sheep Droppings (羊矢) [piercing hole] outside the [pubic] hair line."

the foot minor yin [locations].[18]
The man [indicator] of the lower section:
the foot major yin [locations].[19]

Hence, in the lower section
the heaven [indicator] serves to examine the liver.[20]
The earth [indicator] serves to examine the kidneys.[21]
The man [indicator] serves to examine the qi of spleen and stomach."[22]

20-131-3
[Huang] Di:
"How about the indicators of the central section?"

Qi Bo:
"It, too, has a heaven [indicator],
it, too, has an earth [indicator],
it, too, has a man [indicator].

The heaven [indicator] serves to examine the lung.[23]
The earth [indicator] serves to examine the qi in the chest.[24]
The man [indicator] serves to examine the heart."[25]

[Huang] Di:
"Through which [indicators] is the upper section examined?"

Qi Bo:
"It, too, has a heaven [indicator],

---

18 Wang Bing: "This is to say: the kidney vessels. Their movement can be felt at the 'big ravine (大溪)' section in the hollow behind the ankle and above the heel bone."

19 Wang Bing: "This is to say: the spleen vessels. Their movement can be felt at the 'winnower gate (箕門)' section directly below the 'five miles' [section] between the running sinews (趨筋) above the 'fish belly (魚腹)'."

20 Wang Bing: "The foot ceasing yin vessel passes through here."

21 Wang Bing: "The foot minor yin vessels passes through here."

22 Wang Bing: "The foot major yin vessel passes through here."

23 Wang Bing: "The hand major yin vessel is located here."

24 Wang Bing: "The hand yang brilliance vessel is located here. The classic states: 'intestines and stomach are examined together.' Hence [this location] is used to examine the chest-center."

25 Wang Bing: "The hand minor yin vessel is located here."

it, too, has an earth [indicator],
it, too, has a man [indicator].

The heaven [indicator] serves to examine the qi at the corners of the head.[26]
The earth [indicator] serves to examine the qi of mouth and teeth.[27]
The man [indicator] serves to examine the qi of ears and eyes.[28]

The three sections,
each has a heaven [indicator],
each has an earth [indicator] and
each has a man [indicator].

Being three they form heaven;
Being three they form the earth;
Being three they form man.

Three times three, together this makes nine.
Nine [serves] to divide [the earth] into the nine fields;
the nine fields are the nine depots.
{The fact is,
the spirit depots are five,
the physical depots are four.
Together this makes nine depots.}[29]

---

26 Wang Bing: "[This indicator] is situated at the corners of the head. Hence it serves to examine the qi of the corners of the head."

27 Wang Bing: "It is situated near mouth and teeth. Hence it serves to examine them."

28 Wang Bing: "It is located exactly in front of the ears and the vessels reach to the external canthi of the eyes. Hence it serves to examine the [qi of the ears and the eyes]."

29 Wang Bing: "As for the so-called 'spirit depots,' the liver stores the *hun*-soul, the heart stores the spirit, the spleen stores the sentiments, the lung stores the *po*-soul, the kidneys store the mind. Because spirit qi resides in each of them, the [text] speaks of 'five spirit depots.' The so-called four physical depots include, first, the corners of the head, second, the ears and the eyes, third, the mouth and its teeth, and fourth the chest-center." Lin Yi et al.: "The passage beginning with 三而成天 and ending with 合為九藏 is a repetition from *Su wen* 09. For commentaries on its meaning, see there." Zhang Zhicong: "The spirits of the five depots are generated by the liquids of the intestines and the stomach. The stomach rules the transformation of water and grains to the [body's] liquids. The large intestine rules the *jin*-liquids; the small intestine rules the *ye*-liquids; the bladder is the place where the liquids are stored. Hence these four palaces are the physical depots." 138/20: "Wang Bing's explanation is incorrect. [The

When the five depots have been ruined,
the complexion [of the patient] will fade away.[30]
When it has faded away, [the patient] will die."[31]

20-132-5
[Huang] Di:
"To conduct an examination,
how to proceed?"[32]

Qi Bo:
"One must first assess the physical appearance's fat or lean [condition]
to regulate depletion or repletion of the [patient's] qi.
In case of repletion, drain it.
In case of depletion, supplement it.[33]

20-132-6
One must first remove [an evil from] the blood vessels,
and only then one regulates any [depletion or repletion].
Regardless which disease is concerned,
[the treatment is continued] until a balance is reached."[34]

---

four physical depots] include the head with the brain, the skeletal structure, the sinews
with the vessels, and the skin with the flesh."

30 The Dunhuang version (see 1870/40) has a more concise wording of this passage:
九野為九藏, 神藏以敗, 刑(i.e.,形)藏以竭者, 其色必夭, "the nine fields are the nine
depots. When the spirit depots are ruined and when the physical depots are exhausted, the [patient's] complexion must have faded." The four characters 夭必死矣 do not
appear in the Dunhuang version.

31 Wang Bing: "夭 is to say: the complexion of death. It is an indicator of an abnormality. The complexion is the signal of the spirits; the depots are the abodes of
the spirits. Hence when the spirits leave, the depots are ruined. When the depots are
ruined, the complexion appears as an indicator of an abnormality and this is death."

32 Zhang Jiebin: "候 means examination (診候) of the nature of the disease." Zhang
Zhicong: "Examine the vessels at the nine indicators in the three sections and needle
them."

33 Wang Bing: "度 is to say: 量, 'to measure.'" Cheng Shide et al.: "調 is 調察, 'to
investigate.'"

34 Wang Bing: "When the blood vessels are full and hard, this is called: the evil
has settled down. Hence they are needled first to let blood. It is only then that [any
depletion or repletion] can be regulated. There is no need to enquire whether the
disease is an abundance or a depletion. The goal is to balance the qi in the vessels."
Zhang Jiebin: "Whenever there is stagnating blood in the vessels and when there are

[Huang] Di:
"To decide about [a patient's] death or survival,
how is that done?"

Qi Bo:
"When the physical appearance abounds, while the vessels are fine and
when one is short of qi [to a degree that] there is not enough for breathing,
[this indicates] danger.[35]

When the physical appearance is lean, while the vessels are big and
when there is much qi in the chest,
[this indicates] death.[36]

When physical appearance and qi agree,
[this indicates] survival.
When brought together but cannot be made to fit,
[this indicates] disease.[37]

When all the [movements in the vessels at the] nine indicators in the three sections do not conform with each other,
[this indicates] death.

---

obstructions, one must first needle [the vessels] and eliminate these obstructions and
it is only then that one can regulate any depletion or repletion." Yan Hongchen & Gao
Guangzhen/260: " 'Remove the blood vessels' is 'remove the stagnations in the blood
vessels.' Ma Shi states: 'In case of all these diseases there must be an evil. One must
first remove the knotted blood inside the vessels to remove this evil.' "

35 Lin Yi et al.: "The Quan Yuanqi edition and the *Jia yi jing*, as well as the *Mai
jing* have 死, 'death,' instead of 危." The Dunhuang version (see 1870/40), too, has
死, 'death,' instead of 危. Also, instead of 少氣 the Dunhuang version has 胸中氣少,
"the qi is diminished in the chest," or: "in the chest and in the center." Zhang Jiebin:
"When the physical appearance abounds while the [movement in the] vessels is fine
and while the qi is diminished so that it does not suffice for breathing, then the exterior has surplus and the center has an insufficiency, the branches and leaves abound,
while the roots are depleted. Hence a danger of perishing is near."

36 Wang Bing: "In this case the qi of the physical appearance is insufficient, while the
qi in the vessels has a surplus."

37 Wang Bing: "參 is to say: 參校, 'to examine.' 伍 is to say: 類伍, 'to categorize.' "
The expression 參伍 , also written參五, to be read "*san wu*" or "*can wu*", has been a
metaphor for "mismatched" and "confused" since its earliest usage in the *Yi jing*, in
Xun zi, Han Fei zi, and *Shi ji*. (See *CY* 241 and *HYDCD* 2, 840.) However, the usage
of 參伍 in the *Su wen* (*Su wen* 17-98-6, *Su wen* 26-166-9) suggest a meaning of "to
bring [various parameters] together [for assessment]".

When the [movements in the] vessels above and below, on the left and on the right
correspond to each other like the pounding in a mortar,
[this indicates that] the disease is severe.[38]

When [those movements in the vessels] above and below, on the left and on the right that do not conform are innumerable,
[this indicates] death.[39]

When the indicators in the central section – even if they alone are in agreement –
do not conform with [the status of] all the [other] depots,
[this indicates] death.

When the indicators in the central section show a diminished [qi] in comparison [with the remaining sections],
[this indicates] death."[40]
<When the eyes have sunk into [their sockets, this indicates] death.>[41]

20-133-5
[Huang] Di:
"How does one know the location of a disease?"

Qi Bo:
"Investigate the nine indicators.
If [the vessels at] any single one [of them] are small, [this indicates] disease.[42]

---

38 Wang Bing: "参春 is to say: a big and frequent drumming, like the up and down pounding of a pestle in a mortar." For a detailed discussion, see 2496/57.

39 Wang Bing: " 'Cannot be counted' is to say: [the movement in the vessels] arrives ten times or more during one breathing period."

40 Wang Bing: "減 is to say: 偏少, 'unilaterally diminished.' "

41 Wang Bing: "This refers to the major yang. The major yang vessel emerges from the inner canthus of the eye. When the eye sinks in, the major yang [movement in the vessels] has been interrupted." Zhang Jiebin: "The essence qi of the five depots and six palaces pour all into the eyes and give them clarity. When the eyes are sunk in, the yang essence is lost. Hence [the patient] must die."

42 Zhang Zhicong: "The [movements in the vessels at] the nine indicators [should] correspond to each other; above and below [should be] like one. They must not lose their correspondence. If one section alone differs, one knows where the disease is located and treats it according to the signs. 'Big' and 'small' refers to the appearance of the vessels themselves. 'Hasty' and 'retarded' refers to the frequency of qi [arrivals in

If [the vessels at] any single one [of them] are big, [this indicates] disease.
If [the movement in the vessels at] any single one [of them] is hasty, [this indicates] disease.
If [the movement in the vessels at] any single one [of them] is retarded, [this indicates] disease.
If [the skin of] any single one [of them] is hot, [this indicates] disease.
If [the skin of] any single one [of them] is cold, [this indicates] disease.
If one single [of them] has sunk down, [this indicates] disease.[43]

With [your] left hand on the foot, move up to a distance of five inches above
the ankle and press [the vessel] there.
Both at the right hand [and right] foot,
flip [the vessel] exactly at the ankle.[44]

If the [movement] responding [to one's finger] extends over five inches or
more,[45]
as if there were wriggling worms,
[this indicates] there is no disease.[46]

---

the vessels]. 'Cold' and 'hot' refers to the temperature of the skin in the three sections."
Tanba: " 'Hot' refers to a smooth [movement in the vessels]; 'cold' refers to a rough
[movement]. When Zhang Zhicong claims that 'hot' and 'cold' refer to the temperature of the skin, this, I fear, is wrong."

43 Zhang Jiebin: "陷下 is: [the movement in the vessels] is hidden in the depth and
does not rise." 1990/179 and 951/767 agree, with the former identifying 'has sunk
in' as indicating emaciation of the flesh at the location of any of the nine indicators.
For a detailed survey of the various meanings of the phrase 陷下 in the *Nei jing*, see
757/309. Tanba considered "hot" and "cold" as references to pulse qualities: " 'Hot' is
to say 'smooth [movement in the vessels],' 'cold' is to say 'tight [movement in the ves-
sels].' " See also 53/7 for a discussion of the significance of the appearance or absence
of identical movements at all nine indicators.

44 The *Jia yi jing* has the following version: 以左手于左足上去踝五寸按之, 以右手
當踝而彈之. The Dunhuang version is as follows: 以左手去足內踝上五寸, 指微案
(按)之, 以右手指當踝上微而彈之. Wang Bing: "The [movement] must be examined
both at the hands and at the feet. 'Above the ankle of the hand' is the hand major yin
[movement in the vessels], 'above the ankle of the foot' is the 'foot major yin' [move-
ment in the] vessels. The foot major yin vessel rules the flesh; it is felt in the lower
section. The hand major yin vessel rules the qi; it is felt in the central section. Hence
the text further down states: When the flesh has wasted away and when [the patient]
cannot walk [any longer], this is fatal." 1126/11: "當 is 對, 'against.' " For a description
of this technique of pulse feeling, see 733/8.

45 Zhang Jiebin: "應 is 動, 'to move.' "

46 Wang Bing: "Because the qi is harmonious."

If the [movement] responding [to one's finger] is hasty and
if it strikes the hand [like a] torrential [stream,
this indicates] disease.[47]

If it strikes the hand slowly,
[this indicates] disease.

If [the movement] responding [to one' finger] upwards fails to extend over [the
entire distance of] five inches, or
if upon flipping [the vessels] it does not respond [to one's finger at all,
this indicates] death.[48]

20-134-4
Hence,
when the flesh has wasted away and when the body [can] not move,
[this indicates] death.[49]
When [the movement] in the central section arrives at times spaced, at times
frequent,
[this indicates] death.[50]
<When the [movement in the] vessels there is intermittent and hook[-like],
the disease is in the network vessels.>[51]

---

47 Wang Bing: "渾渾 is 亂, 'chaotic.' " 915/56: "渾渾 refers to the appearance of a
strong water flow." For a detailed discussion see 1455/46.

48 Wang Bing: "The [movement of] qi is interrupted; hence, it cannot be felt."

49 Yang Shangshan: "去 is 行, 'to move.' When the flesh is lean and when the body
is weak and cannot move, this results in death." Wang Bing: "When the grain qi in
the [body's] exterior is weakened, the flesh appears as if it had fallen off entirely and
the true [qi endowed by] heaven is exhausted in the [body's] interior. Hence, the body
cannot move. When the true [qi] and the grain [qi] are both weakened, death is imminent. 去 is like 行去, 'to move.' " Zhang Zhicong: "This is to say, when the proper
qi is depleted, when the flesh has wasted away. The evil remains in the body and does
not leave (去). 2111/37: "去 is 行動, 'to walk and move.' 2284/60: "去 should be 夫,
'adult man.' That is, 'if the body is no [longer that of an] adult man, [the patient] will
die.' " For details, see there.

50 Wang Bing: " 'At times spaced, at times frequent' means that the qi is weakened
and chaotic. Hence death [follows]." Zhang Jiebin: " 'Central section' [refers to] the
vessels of the two hands."

51 Wang Bing: "A hook[-like movement in the vessels] is a summer [movement in
the] vessels. In addition, summer qi is in the network [vessels]. Hence the disease is in
the network vessels. When the network vessels receive an evil, then the conduit vessels
are blocked. Hence [the movement in the vessels] is intermittent and stops."

As for the mutual correspondence of the nine indicators,
above and below [should be] like one.
It must not be that they do not conform with each other.[52]

When [the movement at] one indicator is late,
then [this indicates] disease.
When [the movements at] two indicators are late,
then the disease is severe.
When they are late at three indicators,
then the disease is dangerous.[53]
{The so-called 'is late' means: [the movements] responding [to one's finger] do
not arrive together.}[54]

When investigating the [patient's] palaces and depots
to know the time of death or survival,[55]
one must first know the regular [movement in the] vessels,
and then one knows a disease [movement in the] vessels.[56]
When the true [qi] of a depot appears in the vessels,
[the patient will] die [when the disease has reached a depot, or continued until
a time] by which it is dominated.

Those whose [movement of the] qi of the foot major yang [vessel] has been
interrupted and who are unable to bend or stretch their feet,
they will die with their eyeballs turned upward."[57]

---

52 Wang Bing: " 'Above and below are like one' is to say: speed [of movement] and
size [of vessels] are identical."

53 Zhang Zhicong: "If no movement can be felt at one of the indicators, then one
of the qi of heaven, earth, and man is lost . Hence this indicates disease. If the movements at two of the indicators are late and cannot be felt, then two [of the qi] in the
three sections are lost. Hence this indicates a severe disease. If the movements at three
of the indicators cannot be felt, then [the qi] in all three [sections] are lost. Hence this
indicates a critical disease."

54 Wang Bing: "俱 is like 同, 'identical,' 一, 'one.' "

55 Wang Bing: "When the disease enters the palaces, then it [can be] cured. When it
enters the depots, then this is fatal."

56 Wang Bing: "A '[normal movement in the] vessels' is a [movement in the] vessels
of the five depots [in accordance with] the four seasons."

57 Wang Bing: "The foot major yang vessels start from the inner canthi of the eyes,
... they reach to the outer side of the feet. When the [movement of the] major yang qi
is interrupted, death [follows] as is outlined here."

20-135-1
[Huang] Di:
"[In] winter yin [qi dominates], in summer yang [qi].
How is that?"

Qi Bo:
"All [movements in the] vessels at the nine indicators that are in the depth,
fine, suspended, and interrupted, they are yin and they rule in winter.
Hence, [patients with such movements] die at midnight.
[All movements] that are abounding, racing, panting, and frequent, they are
yang and they rule in summer.
Hence, [patients with such movements] die at noon.

Hence,
those who suffer from cold and heat disease,
they die at dawn.
Those who have a heated center and who suffer from heat disease,
they die at noon.
Those who suffer from wind [intrusion],
they die at dusk.
Those who suffer from water [intrusion],
they die at midnight.
Those whose [movement in the] vessels is at times spaced, at times frequent, at
times retarded, and at times hasty,[58]
they may die in the final thirds of the four [quarters] of the entire day.[59]

20-136-1
When the physical appearance and the flesh have wasted away,
even if the [movements in the vessels at the] nine indicators are in agreement,
[the patient will] die.
Even if [one of] the seven diagnostic indicators [of death] appears,
as long as all the [movements in the vessels at the] nine indicators comply
[with the season],

---

58 Mori: "疏 and 數 have the same meaning as 遲 and 疾. Hence four of these eight
characters may be an insertion. Yang Shangshan refers, in his comment, only to 疏 and
數, not to 遲 and 疾. One may also say that 疏 and 數 refer to the appearance of the
[movement in the] vessels, while 遲 and 疾 refer to the strength of the [movement in
the] vessels. In this case there were no duplication and hence no later insertion."

59 We read 日乘 as 乘日, "an entire day long".

[the patient] will not die.⁶⁰

{As for the so-called 'will not die,' [this refers to] diseases of wind qi, and diseases associated with the monthly period.⁶¹

They appear like diseases of the seven diagnostic indicators [of death], but they are not. Hence, [the text] states: 'will not die.'}

If a disease of [one of] the seven diagnostic indicators [of death] is present, [the patient] will die if the [movement in] the respective vessels indicates destruction too.

{[The dying patient] will develop hiccup and belching.}⁶²

20-136-4

One must inquire about the [patient's] initial disease, and about the present disease.⁶³

---

60 Wang Bing: "In case of a wind disease, the vessels are big and [the arrival of qi in them is] frequent; in case of diseases associated with the monthly period, the vessels are small and tender. Even though these indicators are roughly identical with those of the seven diagnostic indicators [of death], the evidence they give of death or survival is different. Hence [the patient] will not die." Wu Kun: "When wind harms a person, the head will be affected first. Hence the vessels in the upper section alone are big, [the movement in them is] hasty and [the skin is] hot. In case of diseases [associated with] the monthly period, [despite a] surplus in the passage of blood, the vessels in the lower section are insufficient. Therefore they alone are small, or they alone have a retarded [movement], or they alone are cold, or they alone are sunk in. That is, all these [states] resemble disease vessels of the seven diagnostic indicators [of death], but they are not. Hence [the text] states: 'will not die.'" The Dunhuang version (see 1870/40) has 上七候, "the seven indicators [of death mentioned] above," instead of 七診. In fact, altogether eight indicators of death are mentioned in the preceding survey; also the wording 七診 appears in the following passage. Hence 上七候 may have been a change from 七診, the meaning of which may have been understood as little by the compiler of the Dunhuang version as it was by later commentators. See also 2017/5.

61 In contrast, Zhang Jiebin: "經月 is 'long term.'" Yao Shaoyu: "經 is 久, 'long time.' That is to say, the disease lasts longer than a month. An interpretation as 'monthly period' is wrong." Zhang Zhicong: "經月病 is 水病, 'water diseases.'" The Dunhuang version (see 1870/40) has 經間 instead of 經月. The meaning is not clear; it might parallel 經期 and 經時, "the menstrual period."

62 The Dunhuang version (see 1870/40) has 死者必發噦噫, "the dying [patient] will develop hiccup and belching." Wang Bing: "When the essence of the stomach is exhausted internally, the spirit not longer guards the heart. Hence this belching develops at the time when [the patient] dies." See *Su wen* 23 for the rationale of this statement.

63 Wang Bing: "方 is 正, 'right [now].'" Gao Shishi: "The Way of all examinations of diseases is such that 'one must ask about the initial disease' is [to say:] one must

Then one [must] squeeze all the vessels and
inspect the conduits and the network [vessels] near the surface and in the
depth.
One follows them upward and downward, contrary to and following [the flow
of their contents].⁶⁴

When the [movement in] these vessels is hasty, [this indicates] no disease.⁶⁵
When the [movement] in these vessels is retarded, [this indicates] disease.⁶⁶
When no [movement in the] vessels comes and goes, [this indicates] death.
When the skin sticks [to the bones, this indicates] death."⁶⁷

---

investigate the origin from which a disease arrived. 'One searches for the present
disease' is: one investigates its present signs." Zhang Zhicong: "The 'initial disease' is
a disease that has lasted for long and is in the depth. The 'present disease' is a recently
acquired evil; it has not penetrated [the body] deeply [yet]." The Dunhuang version
(see 1870/40) has 必須審諦問其所始, 若所始之病于今所痛異者, 乃定吉凶, "one
must investigate, through questioning, the beginning [of the disease]. If there is a difference between the disease at the beginning and where it hurts now, then one may
determine [whether the disease will have an] auspicious or unauspicious outcome."

64 Wu Kun: "各切 is: feel each of the nine indicators. To bring the fingers close to the
vessels, this is called 切; to follow the vessels with the fingers, this is called 循. Those of
the vessels that run straight [through the body], they are called 'conduits.' Those that
branch out and run transversely, they are the 'network [vessels].' Those visible at the
surface, they are the 'tertiary network [vessels].' Vessels in the outer parts are 'at the
surface;' those in the inner parts are 'in the depth.' Those located high [in the body]
are 'up;' those located below are 'down.' To move against them with the fingers is 'contrary;' to follow them is 'compliance.'" Most commentators, though, interpret the second 循 as a reference to treatment which should 'follow' the status of the movement
in the vessels. We follow Wu Kun since the present text is clearly divided into a diagnostic section, including this second 循, and a section devoted to treatment. Zhang
Zhicong: "In case of diseases that have lasted for long, the [movement in the] vessels
is in the depth and stands in opposition. In case of recent diseases, the [movement
in the] vessels is compliant and at the surface. Hence one must observe the conduits
and the network [vessels] near the surface and in the depth and [after investigating
whether the evil is] above or below and whether [the movement in the vessels] is in
opposition, or is compliant, [one carries out one's treatment] accordingly." See also *Gu
dian yi zhu xuan* bianxiezu /52.

65 Wang Bing: "Because the qi is strong and abounds."

66 Wang Bing: "Because the qi is insufficient."

67 Wang Bing: "The bones are dried out." Zhang Jiebin: "The blood and the liquids
have been lost completely. [Hence this is to] say: the skin is dried and sticks to the
bones."

20-136-7
[Huang] Di:
"Of these, the curable [diseases], how [are they treated]?"

Qi Bo:
"In case of diseases in the conduits, treat the conduit.
In case of diseases in the tertiary network [vessels], treat the blood in the tertiary network [vessels].[68]
In case of diseases in the blood and if the body has pain, treat the conduits and network [vessels].[69]
If the disease consists in an unevenly distributed evil, then carry out a misleading piercing with respect to the vessel affected by the unevenly distributed evil.[70]
If the [evil] stays [at one place, if the body] is lean, and [if the disease] does not move, pierce section by section.[71]

---

68 Wang Bing: "When blood stagnates [in the tertiary network vessels] pierce [the vessels] and let it [flow away]." Lin Yi et al.: "The *Jia yi jing* does not have the two characters 孫絡, 'tertiary.'"

69 Lin Yi et al.: "The *Jia yi jing* does not have the two characters 血病, 'blood disease.'"

70 Wang Bing: "奇 is to say 奇繆不偶之氣, 'a qi [affecting only] a single [conduit] not a pair [of conduits],' occupying a misleading location in the conduit vessels. Hence it is [treated by] 'misleading piercing.' 'Pierce it misleadingly' is: In piercing the network vessels, if [the evil is] on the left, take it from the right; if it is on the right, take it from the left." Zhang Jiebin: "奇邪, 'unevenly distributed evil,' does not enter the conduits; the disease is in the network [vessels]. When the evil resides in the big network [vessels], then from the left it flows into the right, from the right it flows into the left. This qi does not occupy a permanent location. Hence one must [treat] it by 'misleading piercing.'" Zhang Zhicong: "In case of 'unevenly distributed evil,' an evil does not enter the conduits but flows into the big network [vessels] and generates strange diseases." This commentary is supported by the wording in *Su wen* 63. Wu Kun: "奇邪 is an evil affecting only one of a pair of the single conduit [vessels]."

71 Wang Bing: "When the disease qi stagnates, when the physical appearance is lean and when the signs [of the disease] do not change, then follow the rhythm of [the patient's] breathing and apply a nourishing piercing." Cheng Shide et al.: "留 is: the evil qi stagnates. .. 不移 is to say: the disease evil does not move. 節 is 層次, 'levels.' Another opinion identifies 節 as 'joints.'" For example, Zhang Jiebin: "Whenever a disease evil stays for long and does not move, there must be accumulations in the eight folds of the four limbs. Hence one must search for them at the locations of the joints and needle there. This way the [qi] can be regulated." Zhang Zhicong: "When a disease is in the vessels and network [vessels], take it from the vessels; when a disease is in the bones and joints, treat the joints." 2284/60: "瘦 should be 廋, 'to be concealed.'" For details of this argument, see there.

20-137-1
In case of repletion above and depletion below,
squeeze [the vessels] and follow them [with the fingers],
search for their knotted network vessels,
pierce them and let their blood flow out,
so that they are made passable [again].[72]

Those whose pupils are high,[73] their major yang [qi] is insufficient.
Those whose eyeballs are turned upward,[74] their major yang [qi] is interrupted.

These are the essentials of how to decide about death and survival;
it is absolutely essential to investigate them."

>The fingers of the hand move five fingers above the outer ankle of the hand
and let the needle stay there.<[75]

---

72 The *Tai su* does not have the character 見. It says 以通之, "to make them passable [again]." Wang Bing: "結 is to say: the blood is knotted in the network [vessels].
When the blood has been eliminated, the conduits are passable [again]." Lin Yi et al.:
"The *Jia yi jing* has 以通其氣, 'to make its qi pass through [again]' instead of 以見
通之." Zhang Jiebin: "In case of repletion above and depletion below, there must be
a barrier. Hence one must feel [along] the vessels to search for it and one follows the
conduits to take it away. One tries to find out those of the network vessels that are
blocked by knottings, needles them and lets their blood flow out. When the knottings
blocking [the vessels] are eliminated, an open passage will be noticeable." On the various recommendations of bloodletting in the *Nei jing*, see 700/43.

73 Zhang Jiebin: "This is: to stare upward."

74 Cheng Shide et al.: "Their eyeballs are fixed staring upward."

75 The *Tai su* has 踝上五寸指間留針: "five *cun* above the ankle keep the needle between the fingers." Wang Bing: "This passage was mistakenly abridged." Gao Shishi:
"This is to say: when the [movement in the] foot major yang conduit vessel is insufficient, one must treat it by filling at the hand major yang [conduit]."

Chapter 21
Further Discourse on the Conduit Vessels

21-138-2

Huang Di asked:

"As for [the differences between] the places where people live, between their being active or quiet, brave or timid,[1]

does the [movement in the] vessels change, too, because of these [differences]?"

Qi Bo responded:

"Whenever a person is frightened, fearful, angry, or overworked,[2] whether one is active or quiet, all this causes changes.

Hence,

when one walks at night,

then the [resulting] panting originates from the kidneys.[3]

<Excessive qi brings disease to the lung.>[4]

---

1 Wu Kun: "Those who are strong, they are called 勇; those who are weak, they are called 怯." Cheng Shide et al.: " 'Brave and timid' refers here to strength and weakness in a person's physical constitution." 231/55 agrees.

2 2376/43 rejects the identification of 勞 as "overworked," "taxed," for most parts of the *Nei jing* and suggests, in the present context, an interpretation as 憂愁, "grief."

3 Wang Bing: "The kidneys rule at night; their qi associates with the darkness. Hence when one walks at night, the [resulting] panting originates from the kidneys." Zhang Qi: "Panting is always a lung disease, but it may have different reasons. That is, the qi of any of the five depots may enter the [lung] and then can cause panting." 1306/46: "This treatise discusses the [movement in the] conduit vessels; also, does it not begin with the statement: 'this causes changes in the [movement in the] vessels?' Hence, 'panting' is not the panting in one's breathing; it is a quality of the [movement in the] vessels." 920/35 discusses the three interpretations of "panting" as a quality of breathing, as a quality of the movement in the vessels, and as a substitute for 惝, "mournful," and agrees with the second. 1129/5 agrees.

4 Wang Bing: "Panting results from walking at night and straining the kidneys. When the qi is excessive and does not follow the [normal] sequence, then it will cause disease in the lung." Zhang Jiebin: "When the yin is harmed, the yang abounds. The qi moves contrary [to its normal course] and causes suffering. Lung and kidneys are mother and child depots and the minor yin vessel runs upward and enters into the lung. Hence the panting originates from the kidneys and the suffering from a disease occurs in the lung." Cheng Shide et al.: "淫氣 refers to a wildly moving, disorderly qi causing harm." 231/55: "淫 is 'greatly excessive,' 'not normal.'" Yao Shaoyu: "淫 is 溢, 'overflow.' It is the surplus qi of diseases."

When something makes one fall, [causing] fear [that one is injured],
the [resulting] panting originates from the liver.[5]
<Excessive qi harms the spleen.>[6]

When something makes one feel frightened, [causing] fear,
the [resulting] panting originates from the lung.[7]
<Excessive qi harms the heart.>[8]

When one crosses through water and when one stumbles and falls to the
ground,
the [resulting] panting originates from the kidneys and from the bones.[9]

---

5 Wang Bing: "Fear is generated in the liver. To fall down harms the sinews and
the blood. Hence one pants hastily and this [panting] originates, therefore, in the
liver." Gao Shishi: " 'To fall down and to have fear' is to have fear because one has
fallen down. To fall down harms the sinews. The liver rules the sinews. Hence the
panting originates from the liver." Zhang Qi: "Fear is associated with the kidneys and
the panting originates from the liver. That is, when one falls down and has fear, the
blood is harmed and the qi is in disorder. Hence [the panting] has its origin in the
liver." Tanba: "The association of the two characters 'to fall' and 'to have fear' is not
meaningful here. Also, further down [the text] mentions 'fright' and 'fear.' Hence the
character for 'fear' may be a mistake here."

6 Wang Bing: "When the [qi of the] liver, [i.e.,] the wood, moves uncontrolled, it
harms the spleen, [i.e.,] the soil."

7 Wang Bing: "In case of fright, the heart has nothing to lean on and the spirit has
nothing to return to. The qi in the chest is in disorder. Hence the [resulting] panting originates from the lung." Zhang Jiebin: "In case of fright and fear, the spirit qi
disperses in disorder. The lung stores the qi. Hence this panting originates from the
lung."

8 Wang Bing: "In case of fright, the spirit leaves [its residence]. Hence the qi overflows, turns against the heart and harms it." Yao Shaoyu: "The heart controls the spirit
brilliance. In case of fright and fear, the qi rushes upward against the lung. The spirit
brilliance rebels in disorder and the heart, contrary [to normal circumstances], is
harmed by it."

9 Wang Bing: "The humidity qi penetrates the kidneys and the bones. It is ruled by
the kidneys. Hence when one crosses water, stumbles and falls, the [resulting] panting
originates from the kidneys and the bones. 跌 is to say: 足跌, 'to slip.' 仆 is to say: 身
倒, 'to fall prostrate.'" Gao Shishi: "To cross water and to slip is to fall down and be
frightened. It is worse than walking by night. Hence the panting originates from the
kidneys and from the bones. [The qi] cannot move upward and join with the lung [qi];
[rather], perverse qi harms the bones. Hence [the text] states 'and [from the] bones.'"
Cheng Shide et al.: "度 is 渡, 'to cross over.'"

In such situations,
in those who are brave the qi [continues to] flow and [the panting] ends by
itself.
In those who are timid, the [qi] is stuck and this causes disease.[10]

Hence, when it is said:
'the Way of diagnosing disease:
to observe a person's brave or timid [nature],
[his] bones, [his] flesh, and [his] skin,
enables one to recognize his state,'
then this is to be considered the law of diagnosis.

21-138-8
Hence,
when one has drunk or eaten to extreme repletion,
the [resulting] sweat[11] originates from the stomach.[12]
When one was frightened and has lost essence,
the [resulting] sweat originates from the heart.[13]
When one bears a heavy load and walks over a long distance,
the [resulting] sweat originates from the kidneys.[14]
When one runs fast and is in fear,

---

10 Fang Wenhui/119: "著 is 'to attach to.'"

11 On the concept of "sweat" in the *Nei jing*, see 1102/10. 920/35 discusses the two
interpretations of sweat found in the secondary literature, i.e., literally as "sweat," and
as a substitute for 必傷, and rejects both. Rather, 920/35-36 argues, the definition
given in *Su wen* 33, 汗者精氣也, "sweat is essence qi," applies here: "The sweat mentioned here is not the sweat liquid on the outside of the skin; ['sweat'] refers to the
essence qi. This is sweat in a broader sense. The essence qi in the depots and palaces is
wasted because of excesses such as 'drinking and eating to extreme sufficiency,' 'scare
with loss of essence,' 'carrying heavy loads and walking over long distances,' (etc.)."

12 Wang Bing: "When one has eaten to extreme sufficiency, the stomach is full.
Hence the [resulting] sweat originates from the stomach."

13 Wang Bing: "Fright robs the heart of its essence. The spirit qi comes to the surface
and leaves [the heart]. Yang [qi] enters it. Hence the [resulting] sweat originates from
the heart." Gao Jiwu/238: " 'Essence' refers to 'spirit.' "

14 Wang Bing: "The bones are taxed, the qi rises excessively, and the kidneys are repeatedly strained beyond [their capacity]. Hence, when one carries a heavy load and
walks over a long distance, the [resulting] sweat originates from the kidneys." Zhang
Jiebin: "To carry a heavy load and walk over a long distance harms the bones. The
kidneys rule the bones. Hence the sweat originates form the kidneys."

the [resulting] sweat originates from the liver.[15]
When one agitates the body and works hard,
the [resulting] sweat originates from the spleen.[16]

Hence,
whenever in spring, autumn, winter, and summer,
[i.e.,] during the four seasons with their [rise and fall of] yin and yang [qi],
a new disease emerges because of overexertion,
[then] this is the rule.[17]

The qi of food enters the stomach.
[The stomach] spreads essence to the liver.
Excessive qi [flows] into the sinews.[18]

---

15 Wang Bing: "Sudden stress on the sinews extremely exhausts the liver qi. Hence when one runs fast and is in fear, the [resulting] sweat originates from the liver." Zhang Jiebin: "The liver rules the sinews and stores the *hun*-soul. Fast walking harms the sinews; fear harms the *hun*-soul. Hence the [resulting] sweat originates from the liver."

16 Wang Bing: " 'To agitate the body to fatigue' is to say: to exert oneself in work. It is not to run fast, or to walk over long distances. Now, when in working one exerts one's strength, then the essence of the grains spreads to the four [extremities]. The spleen transforms the water and the grains. Hence the [resulting] sweat originates from the spleen." Zhang Zhicong: "To agitate one's body and to tax one's physical appearance requires the presence of flesh. Only the spleen rules the muscles and the flesh. Hence the sweat originates from the spleen." Wu Kun: "To agitate the body to fatigue, is to exert oneself in work. The spleen rules the extremities. Hence the [resulting] sweat originates from the spleen." 419/5: "If the passage 飲食飽甚, ... 汗出于脾 is tied to the theories of traditional Chinese medicine, it simply makes no sense. There are many such passages in the *Nei jing*; their meaning awaits further research."

17 Wang Bing: "Not to act in accordance with one's nature and to force [activities on oneself], this is called 'beyond [one's capacity],' and causes disease. This is the normal principle involved here. When the five depots receive qi, they get their regular share. If the [qi] is used up beyond [the capacity of the depot involved], disease emerges as a result. Hence the following statement."

18 Wang Bing: "The liver nourishes the sinews. Hence when the stomach spreads the qi of the essence of the grains into the liver, then [this qi] is absorbed by the sinews and the network [vessels] as nourishment." Yao Shaoyu: "Disease qi is 淫. When the essence qi of food is also called 淫, then this designation is applied, in both cases, to a surplus." Cheng Shide et al.: "淫 is 甚, 'extreme.' Here it is to be interpreted as 滋養, 'to nourish.' The character is the same as in the preceding text, but the meaning is different." Ma Shi: "The qi of the grains enters the stomach and [the stomach] moves [the products of its] transformation to the spleen. The very finest qi is spread to the lung whence it flows, as nourishment, into the sinews."

The qi of food enters the stomach.

The turbid qi turns to the heart.

Excessive essence [flows] into the vessels.[19]

21-139-4

The qi in the vessels flows through the conduits.

The qi in the conduits turns to the lung.

The lung invites the one hundred vessels to have an audience with it.[20]

They transport essence to the skin and the body hair.

The hair vessels unite the essence and

they move qi to the palaces.[21]

---

19 Wang Bing: "濁氣 is the qi of the grains. The heart is located above the stomach. Hence the qi of the grains turns to the heart, from where [in turn] the finest essence flows into the vessels. Why so? Because the heart rules the vessels." Zhang Jiebin: " 'Turbid' is a reference to the substantial aspects of the qi of food." Zhang Zhicong: "The network [vessel] of the stomach moves upward to penetrate the heart. Hence the food qi that has entered the stomach turns to the heart. The child offers repletion to the mother."

20 Wang Bing: "That is to say, the flow of the qi in the vessels constitutes the big conduits. The qi of the conduits turns upward to the lung to make its court appearance there. The lung is the canopy [covering all other depots]. Its position is on high; ordering and rhythm originate from there. Hence it accepts the court appearance of the one hundred vessels." 2032/4: "肺朝百脈 has been explained, since Wang Bing and later by Zhang Jiebin, Wu Kun, Zhang Zhicong, Gao Shishi, and Ma Shi as 'the lung is where the hundred vessels meet.' .. It should not be interpreted as 'the hundred vessels meet at the lung;' it should be understood as 'the lung [qi] flows toward the blood vessels of the entire body to move the blood and to have the essence qi spread through the entire body.' " For details, see there. 866/3 agrees: "入, 流, 歸, 朝, 輸, 行, and 留, all these are verbs of directional motion; it is impossible that only 朝 could be an exception." For further details, see there. 1903/19 agrees: "肺朝百脈 is 肺使百脈如潮, 'the lung causes the [movement in the] vessels to flow like a wave.' " 721/52 offers a detailed argument supporting the identification of 朝 as 潮 in the sense of describing the movement of clouds, water, qi, blood, and other body liquids. In contrast, 1957/28: "This is to say: the blood liquid of the entire body returns, through its passageways, to the lung." 500/55: "朝 has the meaning of 聚會, 會見, 'to gather.' Only because the hundred vessel gather at the lung, [the lung] is able to make the qi of the spleen disperse and turn upward to the lung. 'One hundred vessels' does not mean 'all the body's vessels;' it means 'many vessels.' " *Gu dian yi zhu xuan* bianxiezu /20: " 'One hundred vessels' refers to all the vessels of the body." 499/38 opposes the identification of 朝 with 潮. A replique was published in 2466. For most extensive discussions of 肺朝百脈, see 112/5, 499/39, 2466/54, and 2465/32. Also: 848/6 and 2144/15.

21 Yang Shangshan: "毛脈 are the 孫脈, 'tertiary [network] vessels.' " Wang Bing: "府 is to say: a place where qi is accumulated; this is to say, the 'sea of qi' (氣海). It is located between the two breasts. It is [also] named 膻中.' " Zhang Jiebin: "The lung

21-139-6
If the essence[22] of the palaces and the spirit brilliance[23]
remain in the four depots,[24]
the qi turns to weight and beam.
Because [this lets] weight and beam be balanced,[25]

---

rules the body hair; the heart rules the vessels. The lung stores the qi; the heart generates the blood. Qi and blood are called father and mother. Only these two depots are
located in the chest; hence [the text] states: 'body hair and vessels unite [their] essence.'" Zhang Zhicong: "The skin rules the qi; the conduit vessels rule the blood. 毛
脈合精 is: blood and qi unite with each other. The six palaces are yang; hence they are
the first to receive the [qi]." Wu Kun: "A character 玄 should be added in front of 府.
The body hair is associated with the lung qi; the lung is associated with the heart and
the blood. When the body hair and the vessels join their essence, then the qi which
moves to the 'palaces' is the guard qi. The 玄府, 'dark palaces,' are the interstice structures (腠理)." Tanba: "When Wu Kun proposes to add the character 玄 and equates
玄府 with the interstice structures, that is a big mistake. 玄府 refers to the sweat holes;
this is something different than the interstice structures." Gao Shishi: "The hair on the
skin as well as the hundred vessels combine the essence moved by the lung and pass
qi to the six palaces." Yan Hongchen & Gao Guangzhen/44: "'Body hair' refers to the
lung; 'vessels' refers to the heart." 2593/46: "The qi and the blood in the skin and in
the body hair and in the conduit vessels of the human body come together and flow
into the *dan zhong* in the chest." For a detailed justification of Wang Bing's view, see
2541/55. 1284/11: "府 is 聚匯, 'to collect.' [The term] refers [here] to the larger blood
vessels." 2087/17 repeats and argues in favor of the interpretation of 毛脈 as "very fine
vessels." See also 175/33 for a detailed analysis. 506/62 discusses previous interpretations of 府 and identifies "palace" here as a reference to the heart.

22 1583/59: "精 is 強, 'strong.'"

23 1055/44: "[The term] 'spirit brilliance' is to denote the normal functioning of the
yang qi in the chest center." The entire passage is unclear. Even if "palace" is interpreted
here as "interstice structures" or "sweat holes", as some commentators have suggested,
the statement remains obscure. We cannot decide whether the first 府 was meant to
express the same meaning as the second.

24 *Gu dian yi zhu xuan* bianxiezu /20: "留 is 流, 'to flow into.'"

25 Wang Bing: "When the *dan zhong* spreads the qi [through the body], this occurs
by means of three separate ducts. One moving downward joins the 'qi street' (氣街).
One moving upward joins the 'breath way' (息道). The basic qi remains in a 'sea' and
accumulates in the chest center. This is called the 'sea of qi.' If [the qi] is distributed
this way, the four depots are settled peacefully and the triple burner is balanced. Center and outside, above and below, all receive their respective [share]." Zhang Zhicong:
"權衡 stands for 平, 'balanced.' 'Qi-opening' refers to the major yin vessel-openings of
both hands." Beijing zhongyi xueyuan et al./20: "'Weight and beam' has the meaning
of 'equilibrium.'"

at the qi-opening [a section of one] inch is established
to decide about [a patient's] death or survival.[26]

Beverages enter the stomach.
Overflowing essence qi
is transported upward to the spleen.[27]
The spleen qi spreads the essence,
which turns upward to the lung.[28]

---

26 Wang Bing: "The 'qi opening' is the grand important meeting point of the vessels.
All the one hundred vessels make their court appearance there. Hence this section
serves to decide about [a patient's] death or survival." Zhang Zhicong: "成寸 [is to
say:] one separates an inch section from the foot-long section. In other words, the five
depots and six palaces are supplied with qi by the grains and they send essence into
the vessels. All changes become apparent at the qi opening and this makes it possible
to decide about [a patient's] death or survival." Ma Shi: "The [qi opening] lies one
inch/*cun* away from the fish-line (i.e., the fold separating palm and wrist). Hence it
is named 成寸." 476/32: "The *Tai su*, ch. 16, has 氣歸于權衡, 以平氣口成寸, 以決
死生. 'Weight and beam' is a metaphor referring to the qi opening. *Guan zi*, 'Ming fa
jie' 明法解 states: '權衡者所以起輕重之數. Through diagnosis at the qi opening, one
is able to distinguish whether a disease is light or serious; hence 'weight and beam' is
used as a metaphor. The second mentioning of 'weight and beam' is an erroneous reit-
eration. 成寸 means: to determine 'inch,' 'gate,' and 'foot' within the one inch section
of the inch opening. 成 is 定, 'to determine.' The meaning of the entire phrase 以平
氣口成寸, 以決死生 is: 'On the basis of a diagnosis of the [movement of the] vessels
at the qi opening, distinguish the diseases of 'inch,' 'gate,' and 'foot' (representing the
depots and palaces) and determine the periods within which [the patient] will die or
survive.'"

27 Wang Bing: "Water [consumed as] beverage flows downward [in the body] and
reaches the triple burner. [There] the water is transformed to finest essence which rises
and turns into clouds and fog. Clouds and fog disperse and flow into the spleen. The
Ling shu states: 'The upper burner is comparable to fog; the central burner appears to
soak.' This explains what is said here." 529/3: "The character 漚 in Wang Bing's commentary is a mistake for 樞, 'pivot.' The upper burner is compared to fog; the lower
burner is compared to a ditch. Fog and ditch are nouns; to soak is a verb. This must be
a mistake. 'The central burner is comparable to a pivot' is to explain the important role
of stomach and spleen in moving [qi and essence] up and down in the body." Zhang
Jiebin: "游 is 游浮, 'to float.' 溢 is 涌溢, 'to flow away rapidly.'" Wu Kun: " 'Essence
qi' is the essence qi of the beverages." Cheng Shide et al.: "游溢 is to say: filled to
overflow with essence qi."

28 Li Zhongzi: "When water [consumed as] beverage enters the stomach, it is moved
first to the spleen. There it is used by the central burner for soaking. The spleen qi
[then] disperses [its] essence which meets [again] in the lung section. This is similar to
the qi of the earth which rises and then condensates to become clouds and fog. Hence
[the *Ling shu* states:] 'the upper burner is comparable to fog.'"

[The latter] frees and regulates the paths of the water, it transports [the water] downward to the urinary bladder.[29]

21-140-1
The essence of water is spread to the four [cardinal points],
it moves through all the five conduits simultaneously.[30]
When this [movement] conforms with the yin and yang [qi] of the four seasons and of the five depots, then
[the book] *Estimate and Measure* considers this as regular.[31]

---

29 Wang Bing: "[The qi of] water and soil are transformed together. They rise to nourish the metal of the lung. The metal qi penetrates to the kidneys. Hence [the text states:] it regulates the water ways. It turns around and flows into the lower burner. The urinary bladder stimulates transformations, which leads to urination. The *Ling shu* states: 'The lower burner is like a ditch.' This explains what is said here." Zhang Zhicong: "The lung corresponds to heaven and rules the qi. Hence it is able to clear and regulate the paths of water and to move [qi] downward into the urinary bladder. This is what is called 'the earth qi rises and turns into clouds; the heaven qi descends and turns into rain.'" 1903/19: "Because the phrase 通調水道 is preceded by the character 肺, all the physicians of later times have read this as 肺通調水道. However, a close reading of the *Nei jing* suggests that this [reading] should be reconsidered. ... The fact is that 脾氣, 'the qi of the spleen,' is the subject of the preceding sentence and also of 通調水道." For details, see there. In contrast, 1957/28: "This is to say: the lung is able to open and penetrate the water ways of the entire body." For a detailed discussion of 通調水道, see also 983/35.

30 Zhang Jiebin: "Water is generated out of qi; qi is the mother of water. Whenever lung qi arrives [in the urinary bladder], then the water essence is spread from there." Zhang Zhicong: "As for 五經并行, this is: [the water essence] pours into the conduit vessels of the five depots."

31 Wang Bing: "The qi in the conduits is the product of spreading the essence of the water. It makes the sinews and bones move and it completes the generation of blood and qi. When it corresponds to cold and summerheat in the course of the four seasons, to the state of yin and yang [qi] in the five depots, which are measured as abundance or depletion, then this is the normal Way in operation. 揆 is 量, 'to measure.' 以 is 用, 'to operate.'" Lin Yi et al.: "Another version has: 陰陽動靜." Such a wording would be considerably more meaningful than the present version. In this case one could read the entire passage beginning with 合於 as "coinciding with the [course of the] four seasons, the [state of the] five depots, the [presence of] yin and yang [qi], as well as the active or quiet [nature of the patient]." Ma Shi: "This is truly in accordance with the common meaning of the four seasons and five depots and of the ancient writings *Yin yang* and *Kui Du*." 394/54 identifies 揆度以為常也 as one sentence and interprets 揆度 as identical with today's 診斷, "to diagnose." 920/36 agrees. See *Su wen* 15, 46, and 77 for further interpretations of 陰陽 and 揆度 as book titles.

When only [the qi of] the major yang depot arrives,[32]
[accompanied by] receding [qi], panting, depletion,[33] and qi moving contrary
[to its proper course],
this is [a situation] of yin insufficiency and yang surplus.[34]
The exterior and the interior alike must be drained.
Take it at the lower transporters.[35]

21-140-4
When only [the qi of] the yang brilliance depot arrives,
this is [a situation] of doubled yang qi accumulation.[36]
The yang [qi] must be drained, the yin [qi] must be supplemented.
Take it at the lower transporters.

---

32 Zhang Qi: "獨至 is to say: the qi of one conduit abounds."

33 Zhang Qi: "The major yang rules the skin and the hair. Internally it is associated
with the lung. [Here now the major yang] conduit qi is particularly flourishing. Hence
[the patient] coughs, sighs and has reversely moving qi." Cheng Shide et al.: "虛 is
噓, 'to sigh.'"

34 Wang Bing: " 'Yin' is to say: the kidneys; 'yang' is to say: the bladder. Hence the
following statement."

35 Wang Bing: " 'Only [a movement of the major] yang arrives' is to say: the yang
qi arrives in abundance. When only yang [qi] arrives, the yang has a surplus. When
the yin [qi] is insufficient, then yang evil enters [the yin region]. Hence outer and inner sections must be drained. One selects the six transporters at the feet. The 'lower
transporters' are the transporters at the feet." Lin Yi et al.: "The character 六, 'six,' [in
Wang Bing's commentary] should be the character 穴, '[needling] hole.' For the [six]
palaces there are six transporters and for the [five] depots there are five transporters.
In the present case, both depots and palaces have to be drained; hence Wang Bing
should not state 'six transporters.' 'Six transporters' does not include the depots. If
[the commentary] stated 穴俞, this would refer to depots and palaces alike." Wu Kun:
"The major yang vessel rises from the Extreme Yin (*zhi yin* 至陰) [point] at the small
toe. Hence one must take the [major yang qi] from the lower transporters. 俞 is 俞穴,
'transportation hole.' "

36 Zhang Jiebin: "The yang brilliance is the foot yang brilliance conduit of the stomach. The yang brilliance is the sea [supplying] the twelve conduit vessels. It moves qi
to the three yang. When it arrives alone, then the yang qi has collected in the original
depot (i.e., the stomach) because of some evil. Hence one must drain the yang of the
stomach and fill the yin of the spleen. One selects the lower transporters. The yang
brilliance transporter is called 'Inundated Valley (*tao gu* 滔谷);' the major yin transporter is called 'Grand White.' " Wu Kun: "The major yang and the minor yang qi have
joined with the yang brilliance. Hence the yang surplus must be drained and the yin
insufficiency must be supplemented." Zhang Qi: "The yang brilliance is the richest
yang. When yang evil is transmitted to it, then this is called 'two yang have joined.' "

When only [the qi of the] minor yang depot arrives,
this is [a situation of] receding qi.
The region in front of the walker [vessel] is suddenly big.
Take it at the lower transporters.[37]
{When only the minor yang [qi] arrives,
this is [a situation of] excess of the first yang.}[38]

When the [qi of the] major yin depot [arrives] beating,
one carefully examines whether there is true [qi].[39]

When the qi in [all] the five vessels is diminished and
when the stomach qi is not balanced,
this is [a situation of excess of] the third yin.[40]
One should treat [this at] the lower transporters

---

37 Wang Bing: "蹻 is to say: the yang walker vessel. This is the foot minor yang vessel below the outer ankles of the feet. When the region in front of the walker is all of
a sudden big, then the minor yang qi abounds. Hence one selects the transporters at
the feet; [these] are the minor yang [transporters]." Zhang Jiebin: "The minor yang
is the foot minor yang conduit of the gallbladder. Diseases of the gallbladder conduit
are connected with the liver. Its qi tends to move reversely. When, therefore, minor
yang [qi] arrives alone, this is reversely moving qi. Now, reversely moving qi begins
below the feet. Hence it is to be examined in front of the walker. 'Walker' is the yang
walker; it is tied to the *shen mai* [transporter] of the foot major yang conduit. 'In
front' of the yang walker is the minor yang conduit. When the qi in the minor yang
[counduit] abounds, the region in front of the walker is suddenly big. Hence [for
treatment] one must select the lower transporters of the minor yang." Gao Shishi:
"卒 is 促, 'hasty.' 'Minor yang' is the beginning yang; it emerges from the ceasing yin.
'Minor yang arrives alone' [is to say:] the yang qi does not abound yet; it is a ceasing
yin qi. When the beginning yang fails to rise, then a hasty, big [movement appears]
in front of the walker. The minor yang conduit vessels is located in front of the yang
walker." Wu Kun: " 'Walker' refers to the ankles at the feet. The minor yang vessel of
the gallbladder emerges below in front of the outer ankle. Hence one suffers from a
sudden swelling in front of the walker."

38 Wang Bing: "The 'first yang' is the minor yang. 過 is to say 太過, 'greatly excessive.'
Because it is greatly excessive, the region in front of the walker is suddenly big."

39 Wang Bing: "When one notices a hidden drumming of the major yin [movement
in the] vessels, one must carefully examine it. If it is a [movement of the] true [qi of
the] depot, it should not be treated." Cheng Shide et al.: "搏 is to beat strongly; it is
identical with the 'hidden drumming' further down in the text. 省 is 察, 'to examine.' "

40 Wang Bing: " 'Third yin' is the major yin vessel of the spleen."

by supplementing the yang [qi] and draining the yin [qi].[41]

21-140-8
When the first yang [qi] hisses alone,
[this is a situation of] minor yang recession.[42]
The yang collects above and
the four vessels compete.[43]
The qi turns to the kidneys.[44]
One should treat [this at] the conduits and network [vessels]
by draining the yang [qi] and supplementing the yin [qi].[45]

When the first yin [qi] arrives,
this is because the ceasing yin governs.[46]
The true [qi] is depleted and makes the heart feel pain.[47]

---

41 Zhang Jiebin: "When a [movement of the] major yin depot strikes [one's fingers], then this is [a situation where] the major yin [qi] arrives alone. When the major yin [qi] arrives alone, then the qi is diminished in the vessels of all the five depots and the stomach qi is not balanced either. This is great excess of the third yin. Hence one must treat at its lower transporters, in that one fills the *xian gu* [transporter] of the foot yang brilliance [vessel] and the *tai bai* [transporter] of the foot major yin [vessel]."

42 Wang Bing: "嘯 is a sound in one's ear, like hissing. The vessels of the gallbladder and of the triple burner enter the ears. Hence if qi moves up in a reverse flow, one hears sounds in one's ears." Lin Yi et al.: "The minor yang is mentioned twice, the minor yin not at all. Hence 'first yang' may have been mistakenly written for 'second yin.' The Quan Yuanqi edition has 'minor yin recession' [instead of 'minor yang recession']. This should be sufficient evidence." Zhang Jiebin: "獨嘯 is 獨熾, 'to blaze alone.'" Cheng Shide et al.: "獨嘯 is 獨盛, 'abounds alone.'" Zhang Yizhi et al. quotes 孫鼎宜: "嘯 should be 肅, 'stern.' 'Stern alone' is equivalent to 'arrives alone.' This would parallel the wording in the preceding and in the subsequent statements."

43 Gao Shishi: "爭張 is 不和, 'out of harmony.'" We interpret 爭張 in the sense of 爭長.

44 Wang Bing: "When the four vessels of heart, spleen, liver, and lung compete for extension and when the yang [qi] has accumulated above, then the qi in the kidneys is insufficient. Hence qi turns to the kidneys."

45 Wang Bing: "When the yin qi is sufficient, then the yang qi will no longer accumulate above."

46 Zhang Jiebin: "'Arrives' means 'arrives alone.' 治 is 主, 'to rule.' 一陰 should have been followed by a character 獨."

47 Zhongyi yanjiuyuan...: "痏 is 酸痛, 'ache.'" Gao Jiwu/176: "痏心 is 心煩, 'vexed heart.'"

The receding qi remains [at one place] and beats.[48]
It develops into white sweat.[49]
[This is to be] regulated with diet and harmonized through drugs.
The treatment is to be conducted at the lower transporters."[50]

21-141-3
[Huang] Di:
"The [state of the] major yang depot, how is it reflected in an outer image?"

Qi Bo:
"It is reflected in the [qi] in the third yang [conduit] and [in a movement] at
the surface."[51]

---

48 Zhang Jiebin: "氣不散則留薄于經, 'if the qi does not disperse, it remains and
accumulates in the conduits.'"

49 2022/41: "魄, 白, and 迫 were used interchangeably in ancient times. 魄汗 is identical with the 白汗 mentioned in *Su wen* 21. Tanba quotes a commentary by Bao Biao,
鮑彪, to the *Zhan guo ce*: 'White sweat is sweat not caused by heat.'" 668/71: "魄汗 is
白汗 and is also 自汗, 'spontaneous sweat.'"

50 Wang Bing: "Another version has 'second [yin]' instead of 'first [yin];' this is a
mistake, though. The ceasing yin is the first yin. Above it is said: when the second yin
arrives, the minor yin must be treated. Below it is said: when the minor yin governs,
then the first yin should arrive. Now, the classics of the Three Grand [Emperors] have
been ruined by vulgar use for long. The people seldom open [the texts] and study their
characters. Hence there are many writing errors in their transmission." Zhang Jiebin:
"The 'first yin' is the foot ceasing yin conduit of the liver. 'Arrives' has the meaning
of 'arrives alone.' 治 is 主, 'to rule.' When liver evil arrives alone, the true qi must be
depleted. Wood and fire attack each other. Hence the heart feels pain. 'Ceasing qi' is reversely moving qi. When the ceasing qi fails to disperse, it remains in the conduits and
accumulates there. When the qi is depleted and not stable, then the [body's] outside
produces white sweat. 'Regulated with diet and harmonized through drugs' [is to say:]
one tries to get appropriate [drugs and diet]. If needles are used for treatment, [this
treatment] should be directed to the lower transporters. The ceasing yin transporter is
called *tai zhong*." Zhang Zhicong: "When reversely moving ceasing [yin] qi stays and
accumulates below the heart, it then moves upward against the lung, which therefore
effuses white sweat. Now, a depletion of true [qi] and a heart in pain, this is a disease
in the interior. When the conduit qi ceases and moves reversely, the disease is in the
exterior. Diseases in the interior are treated with drugs and diet; diseases in the exterior are treated with needles and sharpened stones." Cheng Shide et al.: "白汗 is 魄汗,
'*po* sweat.' 魄 and 白 were used interchangeably in ancient times."

51 Zhang Jiebin: "From here on downward the appearance of the sole arrival of [the
qi of one of] the six conduits is explained once again. As for 'the [state of the] major
yang [depot] is reflected in third yang [qi],' the yang [qi] moves in the outer sections
and [the major yang qi] is the apex of yang. Hence the [movement in the] vessels is

[Huang] Di:
"The [state of the] minor yang depot, how is it reflected in an outer image?"

Qi Bo:
"It is reflected in the first yang."
{As for the [movement of the qi of the] first yang depot, it is smooth and not replete.}⁵²

[Huang] Di:
"The [state of the] yang brilliance depot, how is it reflected in an outer image?"

Qi Bo:
"It is reflected in big [movements] near the surface."⁵³

<When a [movement of the qi of the] major yin depot beats [against one's fingers]
that is called 'hidden drumming.'⁵⁴
When a second yin [qi] arrives beating,
this is a kidney [movement] in the depth, not near the surface.>⁵⁵

---

at the surface in the exterior." Wu Kun: "The [*Nei*] *jing* states: when a major yang [movement in the] vessels arrives, it is vast, big, and extended. 'Vast' is a yang [movement]; 'big' is a yang [movement]; and 'extended' is a yang [movement]. Hence its appearance is three[fold] yang. The major yang rules the outer sections; hence the [movement in the] vessels is near the surface."

52 Ma Shi: "The minor yang is the interior of the yang and the exterior of the yin; it is what is called 'half exterior, half interior.' Its depot is where the yang emerges first. Hence the physical condition of its vessels is smooth and not solid." Wu Kun: " 'Smooth' is yang. It is smooth but not replete. Hence it is called first yang."

53 Lin Yi et al.: "Quan Yuanqi and *Tai su* have: 象心之大浮也, 'it is reflected in the big and superficial [appearance] of the [vessels associated with the] heart.' " Zhang Jiebin: "The yang brilliance, even though it is inside the major yang, it is, in fact, at the outside of the minor yang. In comparison with [a movement that is] smooth and not replete, it is big and at the surface." Zhang Zhicong: " 'Yang brilliance' is the union of the brilliance of the two yang (i.e., minor yang and major yang). When the yang qi are united, then yang heat abounds. Hence it appears as a big [movement] near the surface. 'Big and near the surface,' that is the qi of the second yang."

54 Zhongyi yanjiuyuan...: " 'Hidden drumming' means: even though the movement appears to be hidden, it nevertheless drums against the fingers."

55 Wang Bing: "This was written to elucidate once again the appearance of an isolated/solitary arrival of [the qi of individual depots in the] vessels."

Chapter 22
Discourse on How the Qi in the Depots Follow the Pattern of the Seasons

22-141-9
Huang Di asked:
"To correlate the physical appearance of man with the pattern of the four seasons and five agents and to treat [him accordingly],[1] how [should one proceed] to comply with [these] and how does one oppose [them]?

The meaning of achieving and of missing [a success],
I should like to hear about these matters!"

Qi Bo responded:
"As for the five agents,
these are metal, wood, water, fire, and soil.
Alternately they resume high and low ranks.
Through them one knows [whether a patient] will die or survive.
Through them one decides about completion or destruction and
[through them] one determines the [status of the] qi in the five depots,
the time when [a disease] is light or serious,[2] and
the time of [a patient's] death or survival."

22-141-12
[Huang] Di:
"I should like to hear about this comprehensively!"[3]

Qi Bo:
"The liver rules in spring.[4]

---

1 Guo Tian: "合 is 全, 整體, 'complete.' 法 is 則, 'rule.'" *NJCD*: "合 is 結合, 'to combine.'" Cheng Shide et al.: "合 is 應合, 'to agree'." The initial phrase of this paragraph remains unclear. If the first character 合 were correct, it should require two items to be "brought together." Here, however, the text names only one, i.e., the "physical appearance of man."

2 Zhang Zhicong: "間 is the time when a treatment can be achieved; 甚 is when [the disease] increases in severity." Cheng Shide et al.: "間甚 means 輕重."

3 Zhang Jiebin: "卒 is 盡, 'comprehensively.'"

4 Wang Bing: "Because it corresponds to wood."

The foot ceasing yin and the [foot] minor yang [conduits] rule [its] treatment.[5]
Its days are *jia* and *yi*.[6]
When the liver suffers from tensions,
quickly consume sweet [flavor] to relax [these tensions].[7]

The heart rules in summer.[8]
The hand minor yin and the [hand] major yang [conduits] rule [its] treatment.[9]
Its days are *bing* are *ding*.[10]
When the heart suffers from slackening,
quickly consume sour [flavor] to contract it again.[11]

22-142-2
The spleen rules in late summer.[12]

---

5 Wang Bing: "The [foot] ceasing yin [vessel] is the vessel of the liver; the [foot] minor yang [vessel] is the vessel of the gallbladder. Liver and gallbladder form a union. Hence their treatment is identical."

6 Wang Bing: "*Jia* and *yi* are wood; they are the [heavenly] stems of the East." Guo Tian: "*Jia* is yang; *yi* is yin. Hence the gallbladder is *jia* wood and the liver is *yi* wood." On the occurrence of the "heavenly stems" in the *Nei jing*, see 1576/42.

7 Wang Bing: "The nature of sweet [flavor] is harmonizing and relaxing." Lin Yi et al.: "The Quan Yuanqi edition has 肝苦急是其氣有餘, 'When the liver suffers from tensions. That is: its qi has surplus.'" The portion omitted in Wang Bing's version may have been an older commentary not considered essential by Wang Bing. Zhang Jiebin: "The liver has the official position of a military general. When the mind is angry the qi will be tense. When it is tense, it will inflict harm on [the liver] itself and [the liver] will suffer from this. [Hence] one consumes sweet [flavor] to relax these [tensions]. This way tensions can be balanced. Softness can check hardness."

8 Wang Bing: "Because it corresponds to fire."

9 Wang Bing: "The [hand] minor yin [vessel] is the vessel of the heart; the [hand] major yang [vessel] is the vessel of the small intestine. Hence their treatment is identical."

10 Wang Bing: "*Bing* and *ding* days are fire; they are the [heavenly] stems of the South."

11 Wang Bing: "The nature of sour [flavor] is to gather things together." Lin Yi et al.: "The Quan Yuanqi edition has 心苦緩是心氣虛, 'when the heart suffers from lack of tension. That is: a situation where the qi of the heart is depleted.'" Zhang Jiebin: "The heart stores the spirit. When its mind is joyful its qi will relax, the heart is depleted and the spirit disperses. Hence one should consume [sour] flavor to contract it again."

12 Wang Bing: "'Late summer' is to say: the sixth month." Lin Yi et al.: "The Quan Yuanqi edition states: 'The spleen rules during all four seasons. The sixth month is the

The foot major yin and the [foot] yang brilliance [conduits] rule [its] treatment.[13]
Its days are *wu* and *ji*.[14]
When the spleen suffers from dampness,
quickly consume bitter [flavor] to dry it.[15]

The lung rules in autumn.[16]
The hand major yin and the [hand] yang brilliance [conduits] rule [its] treatment.[17]
Its days are *geng* and *xin*.[18]
When the lung suffers from qi rising contrary [to its regular course],
quickly consume bitter [flavor] to drain it.[19]

---

place when the fire rules. Now, because the spleen rules the center and because the sixth month is in the middle of the twelve months, in the half of a year, it is therefore that the spleen rules during the sixth month.'" Guo Tian: " 'Late summer' refers to the sixth month; this is the season when the qi of the soil flourishes."

13 Wang Bing: "The [foot] major yin [vessel] is the vessel of the spleen; the [foot] yang brilliance [vessel] is the vessel of the stomach. Spleen and stomach form a union. Hence their treatment is identical."

14 Wang Bing: "*Wu* and *ji* are soil; they are the [heavenly] stems of the center."

15 Wang Bing: "The nature of bitter [flavor] is desiccating." Zhang Jiebin: "The function of the spleen is to move and transform the water and the grains and to keep the water under control. When dampness gains the upper hand, it harms the spleen, [i.e.,] the soil. [In such a situation] one should consume bitter [flavor] to dry it up."

16 Wang Bing: "Because it corresponds to metal."

17 Wang Bing: "The [hand] major yin [vessel] is the vessel of the lung; the [hand] yang brilliance [vessel] is the vessel of the large intestine. Lung and large intestine form a union. Hence their treatment is identical."

18 Wang Bing: "*Geng* and *xin* days are metal; they are the [heavenly] stems of the West."

19 Wang Bing: "The nature of bitter [flavor] is to drain off." Lin Yi et al.: "The Quan Yuanqi edition has 肺氣上逆是其氣有餘, 'when the lung suffers from qi rising in reverse movement {that is: its qi is present in surplus}.'" Zhang Jiebin: "The lung rules the qi. It carries out orders aimed at regulation and economy. When the qi has a disease, it rises in reverse movement to the lung. Hence one should qickly consume bitter [flavor] to drain it." Wu Kun: "The lung is the depot of purity and emptiness. It has the order of moving [qi] downwards. In the case of reversely upwards moving qi, the lung suffers from this. One should quickly consume sour [flavor] to drain the lung qi."

The kidneys rule in winter.[20]
The foot minor yin and the [foot] major yang [conduits] rule [its] treatment.[21]
Its days are *ren* and *gui*.[22]
When the kidneys suffer from desiccation,
quickly consume acrid [flavor] to moisten them.
{[Acrid flavor] opens the interstice structures, lets the body liquids reach [their destination] and [makes] the qi penetrate [the body].}[23]

22-142-6
When a disease is in the liver,
it will heal in summer.[24]
If it does not heal in summer,
it will become serious in autumn.[25]
If [the patient] does not die in autumn,

---

20 Wang Bing: "Because they correspond to water."

21 Wang Bing: "The [foot] minor yin [vessel] is the vessel of the kidneys; the [foot] major yang [vessel] is the vessel of the bladder. Kidneys and bladder form a union. Hence their treatment is identical."

22 Wang Bing: "*Ren* and *gui* are the [heavenly] stems of water and of the North."

23 Wang Bing: "The nature of acrid [flavor] is moistening. Now, when the interstice structures open and when [body] liquids arrive, then the lung qi flows downwards [with the result that] kidneys and lung communicate. Hence [the text] states: '[acrid flavor makes the liquids] communicate with the qi.'" Zhang Jiebin: "The kidneys are the depot of the water; they store the essence. In the case of yin diseases, they suffer from desiccation. Hence one should consume acrid [flavor] to moisten them. Now, acrid [flavor] is transformed out of metal which is the mother of water. It is able to open the interstice structures and reach to the body liquids because it is able to make the qi penetrate [the body]. Within the water is the true qi and only acrid [flavor] can reach to it. When the qi reaches the water, [the acrid flavor] reaches it, too." A number of authors have discussed the theoretical principle behind the recommendation to employ acrid flavor for moistening; see 82/8, 1120/54, 2197/116, 2900/57, 977/8, 2205/4, 976/13, and 639/56.

24 Wang Bing: "The son [of wood, i.e., fire] checks the demon [attempting to destroy the wood, i.e., metal]. The same principle applies to all the remaining healings [listed further down]." Zhang Jiebin: "Summer is associated with fire. [Fire] is generated by wood. The liver-wood fears the metal. Fire can balance [excessive] metal."

25 Wang Bing: "The son [of wood, i.e., fire] rests, but the demon [attempting to destroy the wood, i.e., metal] returns to dominance. The same principle applies to all the remaining cases of diseases turning more serious [listed further below]."

[the qi] will be maintained throughout winter.²⁶
[The patient] will rise in spring.²⁷
He must avoid to encounter wind.²⁸

Liver diseases are healed at *bing* and *ding* days.²⁹
If they are not healed at *bing* and *ding* days,
[the disease] will increase at *geng* and *xin* days.³⁰
If [the patient] does not die at *geng* and *xin* days,
[the qi] will be maintained through *ren* and *gui* days.³¹
[The patient] will rise at *jia* and *yi* days.³²

In the case of liver diseases,
[the patient] feels better at dawn.
[The disease] becomes serious in late afternoon.
At midnight [the disease] calms down.³³

The liver [qi] longs for dispersion.
[In case of a disease in the liver]

---

26 Wang Bing: "The demon [attempting to destroy the wood, i.e., metal] rests and
the mother [of wood, i.e., water] offers nourishment. Hence the qi is maintained in
the home territory of its parents. The same principle applies to all the remaining cases
of [qi] being maintained." Zhang Jiebin: "[In winter the liver-wood] is supplied with
qi of its mother. Hence it can be maintained without harm." Wang Ji: "執持 is 堅定,
'to maintain.' That is to say, there is neither addition, nor taking away. Rather, the balance is maintained."

27 Zhang Jiebin: "The period when wood rules." Mori: "起 is 回復, 'to recover.' "

28 Wang Bing: "Because wind qi communicates with the liver."

29 Wang Bing: "*Bing* and *ding* days corresponds to summer."

30 Wang Bing: "*Geng* and *xin* days corresponds to autumn."

31 Wang Bing: "*Ren* and *gui* days corresponds to winter."

32 Wang Bing: "[*Jia* and *yi* days] corresponds to spring and wood."

33 Wang Bing: "At the time [of the day] when the wood rules, [the patient] feels
better. At the time [of the day] when the metal rules, [the disease] becomes more serious. At the time [of the day] when the water rules, the [disease] subsides. The same
principle applies to all the remaining cases of [patients] feeling better or [diseases]
turning worse. Minor differences exist in view of at what time [a disease] subsides."
1311/44: "Yu Chang comments: 慧 should be 愈, 'to heal.' The *Fang yan* 方言, Chen
chu pian 陳楚篇, states: In Southern Chu, when a disease has healed, one sometimes
calls this 慧, 'to awake.' The *Guang ya* 廣雅, Shi gu 釋詁 states: 慧 is 瘉, 'to heal.' " In
contrast, Gao Jiwu/399: "The essence spirit of persons suffering from a liver disease is
comparatively clear at dawn."

quickly consume acrid [flavor] to disperse its [qi].[34]
Use acrid [flavor] to supplement it, sour [flavor] to drain it.[35]

22-143-5
When a disease is in the heart,
it will heal in late summer.[36]
If it does not heal in late summer,
it will become serious in winter.[37]
If [the patient] does not die in winter,
[the qi] will be maintained throughout spring.[38]
[The patient] will rise in summer.[39]
He must abstain from warm food[40] and from garments [causing] heat.[41]

Heart diseases are healed at *wu* and *ji* days.[42]
If they are not healed at *wu* and *ji* days,
[the disease] will increase at *ren* and *gui* days.[43]
If [the patient] does not die at *ren* and *gui* days,

---

34 Wang Bing: "Because the regular [nature] of the qi of this depot is to disperse, hence one employs acrid [flavor] to disperse it." Zhang Jiebin: "Wood should not form thickets. Hence one wishes to disperse it with acrid [flavor]."

35 Wang Bing: "Acrid flavor disperses, hence [it is employed] to supplement. Sour flavor collects, hence [it is employed] to drain." Zhongyi yanjiuyuan...: "The usage of 'supplement' and 'drain' here is not identical with the usual meaning of these concepts. As Wu Kun stated: 'Compliance with its nature is to supplement; to oppose its nature is to drain. The liver, [i.e.] the wood, favors acrid [flavor] and dispersion and dislikes sour [flavor] and [its function of] contracting [things].'" Lin Yi et al.: "The Quan Yuanqi edition has : 'Supplement it with sour [flavor]; drain it with acrid [flavor].'"

36 Zhang Jiebin: "Late summer, [i.e.] soil is the son of fire."

37 Zhang Jiebin: "Fire does not dominate water."

38 Zhang Jiebin: "This is when fire is generated."

39 Zhang Jiebin: "When fire rules."

40 Zhang Jiebin: " 'Warm' is to say: not hot." Gao Shishi: "濕食, 'damp food,' was erroneously changed to 'warm food' in ancient editions." Zhang Qi: "溫食 should be 冷食, 'cold food.' It generates cold and this is most harmful to the spleen." Li Guoqing agrees with Gao Shishi.

41 Wang Bing: "Heat makes the heart run fast. Hence it is strictly forbidden." Zhang Jiebin: "This might support the fire evil."

42 Wang Bing: "*Wu* and *ji* days corresponds to late summer."

43 Wang Bing: "*Ren* and *gui* days corresponds to winter."

[the qi] will be maintained through *jia* and *yi* days.[44]
[The patient] will rise at *bing* and *ding* days.[45]

In the case of heart diseases,
[the patient] feels better at noon.[46]
[The disease] becomes serious at midnight.[47]
At dawn [it] calms down.[48]

The heart [qi] longs for softness.
[In case of a disease in the heart,]
quickly consume salty [flavor] to soften its [qi].[49]
Use salty [flavor] to supplement it, sweet [flavor] to drain it.[50]

22-144-2
When a disease is in the spleen,
it will heal in autumn.[51]
If it does not heal in autumn,
it will become serious in spring.[52]
If [the patient] does not die in spring,
[the qi] will be maintained through summer.[53]
[The patient] will rise in late summer.[54]

---

44 Wang Bing: "*Jia* and *yi* days corresponds to spring."

45 Wang Bing: "Corresponds to summer and fire."

46 Zhang Jiebin: "The time [of the day] when fire rules."

47 Zhang Jiebin: "The time [of the day] when water gains the upper hand."

48 Zhang Jiebin: "The time [of the day] when fire is generated."

49 Wang Bing: "Because the regular [nature] of the qi of this depot prefers softness, hence one employs salty [flavor] to soften it." Zhang Jiebin: "When the heart fire is greatly excessive, [the heart] races beyond its limits. Hence one should quickly consume salty [flavor] to soften it. Now, salty [flavor] is transformed out of water; hence it can be of help here."

50 Wang Bing: "By supplementing with salty [flavor] one makes use of its softening [nature]. By draining with sweet [flavor] one makes use of its relaxing [nature]."

51 Zhang Jiebin: "Autumn is associated with metal, the son of soil."

52 Zhang Jiebin: "Soil does not dominate wood."

53 Zhang Jiebin: "Soil is generated by fire."

54 Zhang Jiebin: "When soil rules."

He must abstain from warm food and from overeating,
from damp earth and from soggy clothes.[55]

Spleen diseases are healed at *geng* and *xin* days.[56]
If they are not healed at *geng* and *xin* days,
[the disease] will increase at *jia* and *yi* days.[57]
If [the patient] does not die at *jia* and *yi* days,
[the qi] will be maintained through *bing* and *ding* days.[58]
[The patient] will rise at *wu* and *ji* days.[59]

In the case of spleen diseases,
[the patient] feels better when the sun begins to decline westwards.[60]
[The disease] becomes serious at sunrise.[61]
In the late afternoon it calms down.[62]

The spleen [qi] longs for relaxation.
[In case of a disease in the spleen],
quickly consume sweet [flavor] to relax its [qi].[63]

Use bitter [flavor] to drain it and sweet [flavor] to supplement it.[64]

---

55 Wang Bing: "Warmth, dampness, and eating to ample sufficiency, all alike harm the spleen qi. Hence they are strictly forbidden." Zhang Jiebin: " 'Warm' is to say: not hot. Thereby one prevents obstructions. Humid earth and soggy clothes represent yin cold. They all can cause disease in the spleen."

56 Wang Bing: "Corresponds to the qi of autumn."

57 Wang Bing: "Corresponds to the qi of spring."

58 Wang Bing: "Corresponds to the qi of summer."

59 Wang Bing: "Corresponds to late summer."

60 Zhang Jiebin: "The soil does not rule yet. Hence there is a turn for the better."

61 Zhang Jiebin: "Because wood dominates soil."

62 Wang Bing: "When the soil rules, [the patient] feels better. When the wood dominates [the soil], then [the disease] becomes more serious. When the metal supports it, then [the disease] subsides." Zhang Jiebin: "Its son aprroaches; hence it calms down."

63 Wang Bing: "The nature of sweet [flavor] is to harmonious and relaxed. It coincides with [the desire of the qi of the spleen to be] relaxed."

64 Wang Bing: "By draining with bitter [flavor] one makes use of its [nature to cause] hardening and to dry. By supplementing with sweet [flavor] one makes use of its pacifying and relaxing [nature]." Zhang Jiebin: "The nature of the spleen prefers to be relaxed. Hence one should consume sweet [flavor] to relax it. The spleen likes

22-144-7
When a disease is in the lung,
it will heal in winter.⁶⁵
If it does not heal in winter,
it will become serious in summer.⁶⁶
If [the patient] does not die in summer,
[the qi] will be maintained through late summer.⁶⁷
[The patient] will rise in autumn.⁶⁸
He must abstain from cold beverages or food and from wearing cold clothes.⁶⁹

Lung diseases heal at *ren* and *gui* days.⁷⁰
If they are not healed at *ren* and *gui* days,
[the disease] will increase at *bing* and *ding* days.⁷¹
If [the patient] does not die at *bing* and *ding* days,
[the qi] will be maintained through *wu* and *ji* days.⁷²
[The patient] will rise at *geng* and *xin* days.⁷³

In the case of lung diseases,
[the patient] feels better in the late afternoon.
[The disease] becomes serious at noon.
At midnight it calms down.⁷⁴

---

sweet [flavor] and abhors bitter [flavor]. Hence bitter serves to drain it; sweet serves to supplement it."

65 Zhang Jiebin: "The son of metal approaches."

66 Zhang Jiebin: "[Fire] cannot be dominated by metal."

67 Zhang Jiebin: "This is when metal qi is generated."

68 Zhang Jiebin: "This is when metal qi rules."

69 Wang Bing: "The lung dislikes cold qi. Hence [cold] clothing and food are strictly forbidden." Zhang Jiebin: "When the physical appearance is cold and when the beverages are cold, this harms the lung."

70 Wang Bing: "Corresponds to winter and water."

71 Wang Bing: "Corresponds to summer and fire."

72 Wang Bing: "This is late summer, soil."

73 Wang Bing: "Corresponds to autumn and metal."

74 Wang Bing: "When the metal rules, there is a turn to the better. When the water rules, the[diseases] calm down. When the fire rules then [the disease] becomes more serious."

The lung longs for contraction.
[In case of diseases in the lung],
quickly consume sour [flavor] to contract it.
Use sour [flavor] to supplement it and acrid [flavor] to drain it.[75]

22-145-3
When a disease is in the kidneys,
it will heal in spring.[76]
If it does not heal in spring,
it will become serious in late summer.[77]
If [the patient] does not die in late summer,
[the qi] will be maintained through autumn.[78]
[The patient] will rise in winter.[79]
He must strictly abstain from anything burning, from hot food, and from
warmth resulting from cauterization and clothes.[80]

Kidney diseases heal at *jia* and *yi* days.[81]
If they are not healed at *jia* and *yi* days,
[the disease] will become serious at *wu* and *ji* days.[82]
If [the patient] does not die at *wu* and *ji* days,
[the qi] will be maintained through *geng* and *xin* days.[83]
[The patient] will rise at *ren* and *gui* days.[84]

---

75 Wang Bing: "[The nature of] sour is to collect and harden. Hence it supplements. [The nature of] acrid is to disperse. Hence it drains." Zhang Jiebin: "The lung
corresponds to autumn; the qi [of autumn] rules the collection [of things]. Hence
one should consume sour [flavor] to collect it. The lung qi should be accumulated; it
should not be dispersed. Hence sour collects and serves to supplement; acrid disperses
and serves to drain."

76 Zhang Jiebin: "The domain of the son of water."

77 Zhang Jiebin: "Water does not dominate soil."

78 Zhang Jiebin: "This is when water is generated."

79 Zhang Jiebin: "This is when water rules."

80 Wang Bing: "The nature of the kidneys abhors dryness. Hence these things are
strictly forbidden."

81 Wang Bing: "Corresponds to spring and wood."

82 Wang Bing: "This is late summer, soil."

83 Wang Bing: "Corresponds to autumn, metal."

84 Wang Bing: "Corresponds to winter, water."

In the case of kidney diseases,
[the patient] feels better at midnight.
[These diseases] are severe during the final thirds of all four [quarters of a
day].[85]
In the late afternoon they calm down.[86]

The kidney [qi] longs for hardness.
[In case of diseases in the kidneys],
quickly consume bitter [flavor] to harden their [qi].[87]
Use bitter [flavor] to supplement them and salty [flavor] to drain them.[88]

22-145-8
Now, when evil qi has settled in the body,
[the resulting disease] will increase when [it meets] with [a time associated
with an agent that] dominates [the agent associated with the respective
depot].[89]

---

85 Zhang Jiebin: "Water rules at midnight; hence the turn to the better. The soil ruling through all four periods dominates the water; hence [kidney diseases] are serious
[throughout the final thirds of the four (quarters of a day)]." Zhongyi yanjiuyuan...:
" 'Final thirds of the four [seasons]' refers to the four quarters of a single day." The use
of 四季 in connection with the four quarters of a single day rather than of a year is
rare; in the *Su wen*, it is not attested elsewhere. See also *Su wen* 20-135-6.

86 Wang Bing: "At the time [of the day] when water rules [the patient] feels better.
At the time [of the day] when the soil rules [the disease] becomes more serious. At
the time [of the day] when metal rules [the disease] calms down."

87 For a detailed discussion of this principle, see 2206.

88 Wang Bing: "By supplementing with bitter [flavor] one makes use of its [nature
to cause] hardening. By draining with salty [flavor] one makes use of its [nature] to
soften." Zhang Jiebin: "The kidneys rule closure and storage; their qi appreciates complete seclusion. Hence if one wishes to harden the kidneys, one should consume bitter
[flavor] to harden them. Bitter [flavor] can harden; hence it serves to supplement.
Salty [flavor] can soften what is hard; hence it serves to drain."

89 Wang Bing: "邪, 'evil' includes everything that is not 'proper.' Wind, cold, summerheat, dampness, hunger, overeating, taxation, and idleness are all evil. Not only demons, poison, or epidemics." Wu Kun: "When the six excessives meet with a time
[associated with an agent] that dominates [the agent the excessives are associated
with], then they are enforced and cause disease in man."

When it reaches [a time associated with an agent] which [the agent associated with the respective depot] generates, it will be healed.[90]
When it reaches [a time associated with an agent] which [the agent associated with the respective depot] does not dominate, it will become more serious.[91]
When it reaches [a time associated with an agent] by which [the agent associated with the respective depot] is generated, it will be maintained.[92]
When it occupies its [proper] position [the patient] will rise.[93]

One must first determine the [movement in the] vessels of the five depots.
Then one is in a position to speak about the times when [a disease] is light or serious, and
about the times of [a patient's] death or survival.[94]

22-146-3
In the case of a liver disease,
there is pain below the two flanks and [this pain] pulls on the lower abdomen.
[The disease] lets that person develop a tendency to be angry.
In the case of depletion, the eyes become unclear and cannot see anything;

---

90 Wang Bing: "That is to say, when it reaches [into a time associated with an agent which the agent associated with the depot where the illness is situated] generates." Zhongyi yanjiuyuan...: "For instance, wood generates fire. Hence a liver (i.e., wood) disease will be healed in summer (i.e., a time associated with fire) and it will be healed at *bing* and *ding* days."

91 Wang Bing: "That is to say, when it reaches [into a time] the qi [of which is associated with an agent which] dominates [the agent associated with the depot where the illness is situated]." Zhongyi yanjiuyuan...: "For instance, liver diseases become more serious in autumn, they increase in strength at *geng* and *xin* days, because metal subdues wood."

92 Wang Bing: "That is to say, when it reaches [into a time] the qi [of which is associated with an agent which] generates [the agent associated with the depot where the illness is situated]." Zhongyi yanjiuyuan...: "For instance, liver diseases continue through winter and the [qi is] maintained through *ren* and *gui* days, because water can generate wood."

93 Zhongyi yanjiuyuan...: "For instance, [patients with] liver diseases will rise in spring, they will rise at *jia* and *yi days. Jia* and *yi* days and spring are periods of flourishing wood."

94 Wang Bing: "The [movements in the] vessels of the five depots is to say: the liver [movement] is string[-like]; the heart [movement] is hook[-like]; the lung [movement] floats at the surface; the kidney [movement] is encamped; and the spleen [movement] is intermittent. If one knows them one can speak about death and survival, minor and serious [states of illness]."

the ears cannot hear anything.
[The patient] tends to be fearful, as if someone were about to arrest him.

[For treatment] select the respective conduits,
[namely,] the ceasing yin and the minor yang [conduits].⁹⁵
If qi moves contrary [to its regular course], when
the head aches, the ears are deaf,
[or the hearing is] not clear, and the cheeks are swollen,
take those [with] blood.⁹⁶

22-146-6
In the case of a heart disease,
there is pain in the chest.
The flanks have propping fullness.⁹⁷
There is pain below the flanks.
There is pain between breast, back, shoulder, and shoulder blades.
There is pain inside of both arms.
In the case of depletion, chest and abdomen are enlarged.
The region below the flanks and the lower back pull each other and have pain.

[For treatment] select the respective conduits,
[namely,] the minor yin and the major yang [conduits], and
pierce those [with] blood below the tongue.⁹⁸
If [a heart disease] changes into [other] diseases, pierce in the cleft, those
[with] blood.⁹⁹

---

95 Wang Bing: " 'Conduits' refers to the conduit vessels; these are not diseases of the
network [vessels]. Hence [the text states:] 'Select the respective conduits.' One selects
the ceasing yin [conduit] to treat the liver qi; and one selects the minor yang [conduit]
to regulate reversely moving qi." Guo Tian: "取 is 治, 'to treat.' "

96 Wang Bing: "When the vessels are filled with blood to a degree that they differ
significantly from their regular status and if the qi is diagnosed as moving contrary [to
its normal course], one needles [the vessels for bloodletting] depending on where [the
problems is] on the left or on the right."

97 Wang Bing: "支 is 別, '[conduit] branches.' " *NJCD*: "支滿 is 支撐脹滿, 'propped
up and swollen.' "

98 Wang Bing: "The minor yin vessel rises from the heart connection and moves
along the throat. Hence [for treatment] one selects [a location] below the base of the
tongue."

99 Wang Bing: "The fold of the hand minor yin [vessel] is in the vessel behind the
palm, in a distance of half an inch from the wrist, exactly behind the small finger."

22-147-1
In the case of a spleen disease,
the body is heavy;
muscles and flesh tend to be limp.[100]
The feet cannot be contracted for walking.[101]
There is a tendency to spasms and
there is pain below the legs.[102]
In the case of depletion, the abdomen is full and
there are sounds in the intestines.
There is outflow of [undigested] food.
{The food is not digested.}[103]

[For treatment] select the respective conduits,
[namely] the major yin, the yang brilliance and the minor yin [conduits], those
[with] blood.[104]

22-147-4
In the case of a lung disease,
one pants and coughs from qi moving contrary [to its regular course].
There is pain in the shoulders and the back.
Sweat flows. The sacrum, the yin [region], the thighs, the knees, the thigh
bones, the calves, the shins, the feet – they all have pain.
In the case of depletion, and if one is short of qi,

This is a reference to the "Yin Cleft" needling point on the hand minor yin conduit
of the heart.

100 The *Jia yi jing* has 善飢, 肌肉痿, "a tendency to be hungry; the muscles and the
flesh [are marked by] limpness." Guo Tian: "善 is 多, 'often.'"

101 Wu Kun ends the sentence after 行; Wang Bing and Gao Shishi end the sentence after 收 and begin the next sentence with 行. Cheng Shide et al. agrees with
Gao Shishi. Guo Tian: "不收 is 不用, 'useless.'"

102 Paralleling the signs of diseases in the heart and in the liver listed above, 脚 could
be a writing error for 胠, "flank", "subaxillary region." See also *Su wen* 48-264-5, *Su
wen* 69-405-4, and *Su wen* 69-412-4.

103 In *Su wen* 2 this wording appears as part of a commentary by Wang Bing. Here,
too, it may be a commentary.

104 Wang Bing: "The minor yin [conduit] is the vessel of the kidneys. Because the
disease mentioned above involves sprasms when walking and pain in the lower [sec-
tions] of the feet, hence one selects it for letting blood. Whenever [vessels] are filled
with blood, one applies [blood]letting."

one is unable to breathe consecutively.[105]
The ears are deaf and the throat is dry.

[For treatment] select the respective conduits,
[namely] the major yin [conduits,] outside of the foot major yang [conduits]
and inside of the ceasing yin [conduits], those [with] blood.

22-147-6
In the case of a kidney disease,
the abdomen is enlarged and the shins are swollen.
[The patient] pants and coughs and the body is heavy.
Sweat flows during sleep;[106] [patients] dislike wind.
In the case of depletion, there is pain in the chest,
and there is pain in the upper and lower abdomen.[107]
[Patients suffer from] coolness [because of] receding [qi];[108] [their] sentiments
are unhappy.

[For treatment] select the respective conduits, [namely] the minor yin and
major yang [conduits], those [with] blood.[109]

---

105 Zhang Jiebin: "報 is 復, 'to return.' 不能報息 is to say: In exhaling and inhaling
one is short of breath/qi." Qian Chaochen-88/40: "Wang Bing fails to explain 報. In
the ancient literature, 報 was often used as a substitute for 赴, in the sense of 'fast.'"
For numerous examples, see there. *NJCD*: "報 is 接續, 'continue,' 'consecutively.'"

106 Wang Bing in a commentary to *Su wen* 71-498-11: "寢汗 is to say: while one
sleeps sweat leaves from the region of the chest, the throat, the neck and the armpits.
It is often erroneously called 盜汗, 'robber sweat.'" Guo Tian: "寢汗 is 盜汗, 'robber
sweat.'" 538/10: "寢汗 has been commented on in three ways. First, it has been interpreted as 盜汗, 'robber sweat,' i.e., sweat flowing while one sleeps. Second, it has been
interpreted as 浸, 'to flood.' This is to say: the body liquids flood [the body] and flow
off as sweat. The body is extremely saturated with dampness. Thirdly, authors have
avoided an interpretation. I think the interpretation of 寢汗 as 浸, 'to flood,' is correct.
The *Ji yun* 集韻 and the *Guang ya shu zheng* 廣雅疏証 both use 寢 identical with 浸;
the *Shuo wen* has 寢 as the original version of 浸." For further evidence, see there.

107 The *Jia yi jing* has 大腸小腸, "large intestine and small intestine", instead of 大
腹小腹.

108 Wang Bing: "清 is to say: 氣清冷, 'the qi is cool/cold.' 厥 is 氣逆, 'reversely moving qi.'"

109 Wang Bing: "The Way of all needling is such that in the case of depletion, one
supplements it and in the case of repletion, one drains it. In case there is neither abundance nor depletion, one selects the conduits for treatment. That is to say: [to treat
in] keeping with the Way. When there is blood in the conduits and network [vessels],
needle them to remove it. That is called 'protective pattern.' One must examine the

22-148-2

The liver [is associated with] the color green-blue;
[in the case of disease] one should consume sweet [flavor].
Non-glutinous rice, beef, dates, and the *kui* [herbs] are all sweet.[110]

The heart [is associated with] the color red;
[in the case of disease] one should consume sour [flavor].
Small beans,[111] dog meat, plums, and leek are all sour.[112]

The lung [is associated with] the color white;
[in the case of disease] one should consume bitter [flavor].
Wheat, mutton, apricots, and chives are all bitter.[113]

The spleen [is associated with] the color yellow;
[in the case of disease] one should consume salty [flavor].
Large beans, pork, chestnuts, and bean leaves are all salty.[114]

[patient's] physical appearance and identify the [status of his] qi. First remove the blood [from the] vessels and then balance surplus and insufficiency."

110 Wang Bing: "The nature of the liver includes a tendency to be tense. Hence one eats sweet things to make use of their relaxing [quality]."

111 The *Jia yi jing* has 麻, "hemp," instead of "small beans."

112 Wang Bing: "The nature of the heart includes a tendency to slacken. Hence one eats sweet things to make use of their contracting and hardening [qualities]." 韭 is identified nowadays as Allium tuberosum Rottler ex Sprengel, vernacular name: "Chinese leek". In a fresh state it is classified as 'acrid', in a boiled state as 'sweet'. It is not clear whether the plant that was named 韭 two millennia ago, and is listed as 'sour' in the present context, is identical with the item traded under this name today. Nevertheless, we have translated 韭 as "leek".

113 Wang Bing: "The nature of the lung includes a tendency towards qi moving contrary [to its normal course]. Hence one eats bitter things to make use of their transmitting and draining [qualities]." 薤 is identified nowadays as Allium macrostemon, vernacular name: "Chinese chives'". It is classified as 'acrid' and 'bitter'. It is not clear whether the plant that was named 薤 two millennia ago, and is listed as 'bitter' in the present context, is identical with the item traded under this name today. Nevertheless, we have translated 薤 as "chives".

114 Wang Bing: "An analysis of why these things should be eaten demonstrates that the purpose is to keep the mechanisms of the gates moving freely. The kidneys constitute the stomach gate. Spleen and stomach form a union. Hence one makes use of [the ability of] salty [flavor] to soften to make their gates move freely. When the gates move freely, the stomach qi passes [freely, too]. When the stomach [qi] passes, the spleen qi transform. Hence the flavors to be consumed for [treating] the spleen differ from all the others."

The kidneys [are associated with] the color black;
[in the case of disease] one should consume acrid [flavor].
Yellow glutinous millet, chicken meat, peaches, and onions are all acrid.[115]

22-149-1
Acrid [flavor] disperses;
sour [flavor] contracts;
sweet [flavor] relaxes;
bitter [flavor] hardens;
salty [flavor] softens.[116]

Toxic drugs attack the evil.[117]
The five grains provide nourishment.[118]
The five fruits provide support.
The five domestic animals provide enrichment.
The five vegetables provide filling.

When they are consumed in [appropriate] combinations of their qi and flavors,
they serve to supplement the essence and to enrich the qi."[119]

22-149-4
<These five [grains, fruit, domestic animals, and vegetables] have acrid, sour,
sweet, bitter, and salty [flavors].
Each exerts its [specific] benefit.

---

115 Wang Bing: "The nature of the kidneys includes a tendency towards drying up.
Hence one eats acrid things to make use of their moistening [qualities]."

116 Wang Bing: "These are their natural qi. However, the ability of acrid flavor and
bitter flavor is not limited to hardening and dispersing alone. Acrid [flavor] is also able
to moisten and to disperse; bitter [flavor] is also able to dry and to drain."

117 Wang Bing: " 'Drugs' is to say: metals, precious stones, minerals, herbes, trees,
vegetables, fruit, insects, fish, birds, and quadrupeds. They all can eliminate the evil
and nourish the proper [qi]. However, only toxic [drugs] are able to ward off evil and
to pacify the proper. Because of this ability, one always calls them 'toxic drugs.' " Zhang
Jiebin: " 'Poison' is to say: [a specific] qi or flavor is unilaterally strong."

118 2493/530: "The statement 'The five grains serve to nourish' originates from the
Zhou li."

119 Wang Bing: "Qi is a yang transformation; flavor is a yin application. When qi and
flavor are combined harmoniously, then they supplement and increase essence qi."

Some disperse, some contract; some relax, some tighten; some harden, some soften.[120]

As for the diseases of the four seasons and five depots, [they are treated] in accordance with the capabilities of the five flavors.>

---

120 Tanba: "Wang Bing failed to comment on the two characters 或急 and so did all other commentators. Because the preceding text lists nothing that has a tightening quality, these two characters may be an erroneous insertion." Zhang Yizhi et al.: "The [qualities] dispersing, contracting, relaxing, hardening, and softening correspond to the [flavors] acrid, sour, sweet, bitter, and salty [mentioned earlier]. There is nothing that corresponded to "some tighten." Hence this may be an erroneous insertion; the *Tai su* version may serve as proof."

Chapter 23
Wide Promulgation of the Five Qi[1]

23-150-2

Where the five flavors enter:

Sour [flavor] enters the liver.

Acrid [flavor] enters the lung.

Bitter [flavor] enters the heart.

Salty [flavor] enters the kidneys.

Sweet [flavor] enters the spleen.

These [relationships] are called "the five enterings."

When the qi in the five [depots] have a disease:[2]

In the heart it causes belching.[3]

In the lung it causes coughing.[4]

---

1 1764/53: "宣 is 發, 'to develop.' 明 is 顯, 'manifest.' 五氣 is 五藏本之氣, 'the qi of the five depots.'"

2 Zhang Jiebin: "The qi of the five depots cause diseases through reverse movements." Gao Jiwu/291: "The pathological changes resulting from a loss of balance of the qi of the five depots."

3 Wang Bing: "It reflects fire flaming upwards. Smoke leaves together with the flames. The heart does not accept anything dirty. Hence belching leaves from it." Zhang Jiebin: "噫 is 噯氣, 'belching.' One may examine the entire [Shen nong] ben jing 神農本經: it does not mention the sign 噯氣 even once and refers only to 噫. Hence the latter is the [former]. ... [These quotations from the Nei jing demonstrate:] the heart, the spleen, and the stomach, [diseases in all] these three depots have this sign. Because of an oppression of fire and soil the qi [of these depots] cannot expand freely. Hence this sign results." Zhang Zhicong: "The reason is that stomach qi rises contrary [to its normal direction] to the heart and thereby causes belching." SWJZ: "噫 is 飽食息, 'the breath [after one] has eaten to utter sufficiency.'" Gao Shishi: "噫 is 微噯氣, 'weak belching.'" Zhang Zhicong: "噫 is 不平之氣, 'unbalanced qi.'" Li Guoqing: "Following the statement in the Shuo wen, many authors have explained 噫 as 'belching.' In fact, though, (and apparent from references in the Guang yun 廣韻, the Ji yun 集韻, the Zhong hua da zi dian 中華大字典) 噫 means 'to sigh.' When the qi of the heart is oppressed and cannot move freely, one often notices the pathocondition of sighing. Hence 心為噫 should be interpreted as the sound of sighing." Based on a discussion of the association of the term 噫 with the three depots 'heart,' 'spleen,' and 'stomach' in the Nei jing, Gao Jiwu/40 suggest to interpret 噫 as 'belching' when it appears related to the stomach and the spleen, but as 'sighing' when it is related to the heart. Yao Shaoyu identifies 噫 as "[emitting] qi but no sound."

4 Wang Bing: "It reflects the unyielding hardness of metal. When one knocks at it it produces a sound. Hence when evil strikes the lung, coughing is the result."

In the liver it causes talkativeness.[5]
In the spleen it causes swallowing.[6]
In the kidneys it causes yawning <[and] it causes sneezing.>[7]
In the stomach it causes qi to move contrary [to its regular course], it causes
hiccup <[and] it causes fear.>[8]

---

5 Wang Bing: "It reflects the branches and twigs of trees and the branching off of
physical appearances. Speech displays what is hidden. Hence it leaves from the liver." Yao Shaoyu: "Talkativeness is that by which oppressions [of qi] in the center are
changed to expansions. The liver likes expansion and dislikes oppression. Hence it
generates talkativeness to change the oppression of the qi to expansion." Gao Shishi:
"語 is 多言, 'talkative.' "

6 Wang Bing: "It reflects the enclosing and containing carried out by the soil. All
things return to [its] interior and are accepted by it. Hence [the spleen qi] causes the
swallowing." Zhang Zhicong: "The main task of the spleen is to enable the stomach to
pass its liquids. When the qi of the spleen has a disease and is unable to pour liquids
into the [remaining] four depots, then these liquids, contrary [to their normal direction of movement], overflow at the mouth which is the orifice of the spleen. Hence
the sign of 'swallowing' results."

7 Wang Bing: "It reflects water flowing down. When it rises, it creates clouds and fog.
The qi is blocked in the stomach. Hence yawning is generated there. When the major
yang qi is balanced and unimpeded it fills the heart and leaves through the nose. This
then generates sneezing." Yao Shaoyu: "欠 is 呵欠, 'to yawn.' This is a disorderly and
indolent arrival of spirit qi. Now, the kidneys store the essence. When the essence is
depleted, the spirit qi becomes disorderly and indolent and this causes yawning. 嚏 is
噴嚏, 'to sneeze.' This is an arrival of lung qi proceeding to the outside. The kidneys
are associated with cold. [Their] qi easily freezes and coagulates. The kidneys are the
son [depot] of the lung. Their [qi] rises and moves to the mother [depot]. From there
it effuses and causes sneezing. Sneezing is caused not only by cold or wind-cold coming from the outside." Tanba: "*Ling shu* 78 does not have the two characters 為嚏, 'it
causes sneezing;' they may be an erroneous addition." 25/45: "I believe the two characters 為嚏 were meant to explain the two characters 為欠. This ancient commentary
was later erroneously inserted into the main text. The *Shuo wen* states: '欠, 張口氣
悟也.' The *Shuo wen* also states: '嚏, 悟, 解氣也.' 解氣 has the same meaning as 欠.
Hence 欠 and 嚏 can serve to explain each other."

8 Wang Bing: "[The stomach] is the sea of water and grains. The kidneys constitute
its gates. When the gates are closed and impassable, then the qi moves reversely and
rises. Because [the stomach] encloses and contains water and grains, its nature prefers
to accept cold. When cold and grains strike against each other, the result is burping.
When cold abounds, burping emerges; when heat abounds, fear emerges. Why so?
When the stomach is hot, the qi of the kidneys is feeble and weak. Hence this causes
fear." Zhang Jiebin: "The stomach is the sea of water and grains. When the stomach
has lost its harmony, then this causes the qi to [rise in a] reverse movement. 噦 is 呃逆,
'hiccough.' When cold has entered the stomach, this results in hiccough. 'Fear' is the
mental condition of the kidneys. The stomach is associated with the soil; the kidneys

In the large intestine and in the small intestine it causes outflow.[9]
In the lower burner, if it overflows it causes water.[10]
In the urinary bladder, if it does not pass freely it causes protuberance illness;
if it is unrestrained, it causes [involuntary] loss of urine.[11]
In the gallbladder, it causes anger.[12]

These are the so-called "the five diseases."[13]

---

are associated with the water. When soil evil harms the kidneys, then the spirit has
fear. Hence they all pass through the stomach." Yao Shaoyu: "When the kidneys are
depleted, fear results. Fear is not a disease of the stomach. Now, basically the stomach
has large amounts of qi and large amounts of blood. [In the present case] its fire is
most abundant. When the fire abounds, it diminishes the water. When the water is
depleted, the kidneys are weak. Now the kidneys are no longer a match for the stomach and hence they develop fear." Ma Shi: "When the stomach is hot then the kidney
qi becomes hot, too. Hence fear results." Zhang Zhicong: "When the stomach qi descends in reverse movement and accumulates in the kidneys, then this results in fear."
Neither *Ling shu* 78, nor the *Tai su* has the two characters 為恐, 'causes fear.' Hence
Tanba: "They may be an erroneous insertion." Li Guoqing agrees.

9 Wang Bing: "The large intestine is the palace representing a transmission route;
the small intestine is the palace of accepting riches. When the abundant qi received
[by the small intestine] is depleted and when the marshal of the transmission routes
is not restrained, then this results in outflow."

10 Wang Bing: "The lower burner is the location where the streams are separated.
When the qi chamber is not drained, there will be overflow and this generates water."
Cheng Shide et al.: "水 stands for 水腫, 'swellings from water.' Hence Zhang Zhicong: 'The lower burner is like a ditch; the water ways emerge from there. In the case
of disease, [the water] turns back and overflows and this results in water disease.'"

11 Wang Bing: "The urinary bladder is the palace of body liquids; the water originates
from it. Now, when the foot triple burner vessels are replete, this closes the lower
burner making them not passable. As a result [the patient] cannot urinate. When the
foot triple burner vessels are depleted and when the lower burner is not closed, then
[the patient suffers from involuntary] loss of urine." See also *Su wen* 49, note 55/56.

12 Wang Bing: "When the Central Rectifier passes decisions, he is neither selfish
nor biased. His nature is tough and decisive. Hence he causes anger."

13 2809/56: "The interpretations of this paragraph by the physicians have varied in
the course of time. In some cases they have interpreted these statements on the basis
of the theory of mutual control among the five agents. Examples are the comments
by Zhang Qi on the heart, by Zhang Jiebin on the stomach, and by Wu Kun on the
lung. ... For an explanation of other statements they have taken recourse to the theory
of the rising and descending of yin and yang. Examples are the comments by Zhang
Jiebin, Ma Shi, and Wu Kun on the kidneys. Nowadays, some commentators believe
that the entire passage from 胃為氣逆 to 膽為怒 is a commentary written by a later
author that was erroneously inserted into the main text. This author believes that this

23-151-2

The locations where the five essences collect:[14]
When essence[15] qi collects in the heart, joy results.[16]
When it collects in the lung, sadness results.[17]
When it collects in the liver, anxiety results.[18]
When it collects in the spleen, fright results.[19]
When it collects in the kidneys, fear results.[20]
These are the so-called "the five accumulations."
{In cases of a depletion mutual accumulations occur.}[21]

---

passage is intricately linked to the text and cannot be omitted." For a detailed analysis following this introduction, see there.

14 Zhang Jiebin: "并 is 聚, 'to collect.'" Yang Shangshan: "并 is 偏勝, 'unilateral domination.'" Wu Kun: "并 is 合而入之, 'to unite and enter.' As long as the essence qi of the five depots are stored in their respective depot, no disease results. But when they unite and agglomerate within one single depot, then they are evil qi causing a repletion there." Gao Jiwu/242: "The diseases resulting from accumulations of the essence qi of the five depots within one single depot."

15 1583/59: "In the present context, the character 精 carries the meaning of 過甚, 'overly excessive,' and may be explained as 病, 'disease.' 并 is to be interpreted as 甚, 'very much.' The idea is: when too much disease qi is present in the heart, joy results, etc. *Su wen* 17 states: 有餘為精, 'to have surplus creates essence.' This is interpreted by Beijing zhongyi xueyuan as follows: "'Essence' is to say: excessive evil.' The *Shen nong ben cao jing* states in its monograph on 'Dragon Bones:' 主心腹鬼疰精物老魅, 'they master demonic possession in the heart and in the abdomen, essence[-like] beings, and old goblins.' In all these cases 'essence' carries the meaning of 'disease' and 'evil.'"

16 Wang Bing: "'Essence qi' is to say: the essence qi of fire. When the lung is depleted and the essence of the heart accumulates there, then this causes [a person] to be joyful." Gao Jiwu/242: "When the essence qi accumulates in the heart, one is often joyful and laughs."

17 Wang Bing: "When the liver is depleted and the lung qi accumulates there, then this causes [a person] to be sad."

18 Wang Bing: "When the spleen is depleted and the liver qi accumulates there, then this causes [a person] to be grieved."

19 Wang Bing: "Another text has 飢 [instead of 畏]. When the kidneys are depleted and the spleen qi accumulates there, then this causes [a person] to be in fright."

20 Wang Bing: "When the heart is depleted and the kidney qi accumulates there, then this causes [a person] to be fearful."

21 1076/23: "This is to say: when the essence qi of one depot or palace is depleted, the remaining depots/palaces will – because of this depletion – send [their own] essence qi for assistance and pour it [into the depleted depot/palace]. This section of the [*Nei*] *jing* speaks only of some emotional changes accompanying the 'accumulation' of es-

What the five depots dislike:
The heart dislikes heat.[22]
The lung dislikes cold.[23]
The liver dislikes wind.[24]
The spleen dislikes dampness.[25]
The kidneys dislike dryness.[26]
These are the so-called "the five dislikes."

23-152-1
The fluids transformed by the five depots:[27]
The heart generates sweat.[28]

---

sence qi [in a specific depot] because [this depot] was 'depleted.' It does not elucidate why the essence qi through its accumulating in the heart, the lung, and the kidneys stimulates emotional processes characteristic of the respective depots, while its accumulation in the liver and in the spleen stimulates emotional processes not characteristic of these depots." For a discussion of this issue, see there. 331/3: "There are two major interpretations of this statement by later commentators. The first is represented by Yang Shangshan and considers 并 as referring to 偏勝, 'unilateral dominance.' That is, when the kidneys have a disease, they may exploit the fact of a depletion in the other depots. [Their qi] may unilaterally accumulate in [any of] the five depots and cause disease [there]. The second explanation is represented by Wang Bing and Zhang Jiebin and focusses on an accumulation between two depots in a relationship of [one] controlling [the other]. This generates emotional disease. This explanation interpretes 并 as 聚, 'to accumulate.' It assumes that the appearance of emotional disease is brought forth by [a situation where] one depot is replete, while that depot which [according to the five-agents theory] it can overcome, is depleted, so that of these two depots one is the origin and the other is the result." For further interpretations of 虛而相并, see there.

22 Wang Bing: "Heat causes the [movement in the] vessels to rush and become turbid."

23 Wang Bing: "Cold causes the qi to stagnate and obstruct [the vessels]."

24 Wang Bing: "Wind makes the sinews dry and tight."

25 Wang Bing: "Dampness makes the flesh weak and lets it swell."

26 Wang Bing: "Dryness causes the essence to dry up."

27 Zhang Zhicong: "Water and grain enter the stomach; their flavors are five. Each fluid moves through its particular passage-way. When the five depots receive the fluids of water and grains, they pour them to their external orifices and transform them to the five fluids."

28 Wang Bing: "It flows away through the skin interstices."

The lung generates snivel.[29]
The liver generates tears.[30]
The spleen generates saliva.[31]
The kidneys generate spittle.[32]
These are the so-called "the five fluids."

When the five flavors are to be avoided:
The acrid [flavor] moves to the qi;
in the case of diseases in the qi one must not consume acrid [flavor] in large
quantities.
The salty [flavor] moves to the blood;
in the case of diseases in the blood one must not consume salty [flavor] in large
quantities.[33]
The bitter [flavor] moves to the bones;
in the case of diseases in the bones one must not consume bitter [flavor] in
large quantities.[34]
The sweet [flavor] moves to the flesh;

---

29 Wang Bing: "It moistens the nostrils." 1803/6: "Throughout history physicians
have explained 涕 as 鼻涕, 'snivel.' For instance Zhang Jiebin: 'Snivel leaves from the
nose; [the nose] is the orifice of the lung.' I believe to explain 涕 solely as 'snivel' is
too overly restrict its meaning. In a broad sense, this term includes snivel and phlegm.
Anything excreted from the respiratory ducts is called 涕 and this includes in addition
to the snivel produced by the membranes in the nose (i.e., snivel in a narrow sense),
the phlegm produced by the laryngotracheal ducts and by the bronchi." For a detailed
discussion, see there.

30 Wang Bing: "They pour into the eyes."

31 Wang Bing: "It overflows lips and mouth." For a detailed discussion of this relationship, see 462/6.

32 Wang Bing: "It is generated by the teeth."

33 Lin Yi et al.: "Huangfu Shi'an 皇甫士安 (i.e., Huangfu Mi 謐) stated: 'Salty [fla-
vor] moves first to the kidneys. Here [the text] states: it moves to the blood. [The
reason for this discrepancy is:] The kidneys and the triple burner form a union. Even
though the blood vessels are tied to the liver and to the heart, they nevertheless constitute passage ways of the central burner. Hence salt moves to and enters the blood.'
In contrast, *Ling shu* 78 and *Tai su* 2.4 D (latter part) associate salty flavor with the
bones and bitter flavor with the blood. However, *Ling shu* 63 and *Tai su* 2.4D (earlier
part) list associations identical with those outlined here.

34 Wang Bing: "Bitter [flavor] moves towards the heart. Here [the text] states: it
moves to the bones. [The reason is:] water and fire assist each other. The qi of the
bones communicates with the heart."

in the case of diseases in the flesh one must not consume sweet [flavor] in
large quantities.
The sour [flavor] moves to the sinews;
in the case of diseases in the sinews one must not consume sour [flavor] in
large quantities.[35]
These are the so-called "the five interdictions."
{Do not let [the patient][36] eat large quantities.}

23-152-7
Where the five diseases break out:[37]
Yin diseases break out in the bones.
Yang diseases break out in the blood.[38]
Yin diseases break out in the flesh.
Yang diseases break out in winter.
Yin diseases break out in summer.[39]
These are the so-called "the five outbreaks."[40]

The disorders caused by the five evil [qi]:
When evil [qi] enters the yang [section], craziness results.

---

35 Wang Bing: "In all these cases [the flavors] cause a rapid movement of the respective qi. Hence one should not consume large quantities. If one consumes large
quantities, the disease becomes more serious. Hence patients should not consume
large quantities."

36 Gao Jiwu/482: "A 之 was omitted here, referring to the patient."

37 Zhang Zhicong: "The diseases of each of the five depots have specific locations
where they break out."

38 Wang Bing: "The bones and the flesh are yin and motionless; hence yang qi
moves there. The blood and the vessels are yang and show motion. Hence they are
occupied by yin qi."

39 Wang Bing: "In summer the yang qi abounds. Hence yin diseases break out in
summer. In winter the yin qi abounds. Hence yang diseases break out in winter. This
is so because the respective [qi] is diminished." Zhang Jiebin: "When yin dominates
then the yang is ill; when yang dominates then the yin is ill."

40 Gao Shishi: "The kidneys are yin; they rule the bones. Hence kidney-yin diseases
break out in the bones. The heart is yang; it rules the blood. Hence heart-yang diseases
break out in the blood. The spleen is yin; it rules the flesh. Hence spleen-yin diseases
break out in the flesh. The liver is yang; its season is spring. If winter fails to store,
spring has nothing with which to create life. Hence liver-yang diseases break out in
winter. The lung is yin; its season is autumn. If summer fails to bring growth, autumn
has nothing to harvest. Hence lung-yin diseases break out in summer."

When evil [qi] enters the yin [section], a block results.[41]
When it strikes at the yang, then this causes peak illness.[42]
When it strikes at the yin, then this causes muteness.[43]
When yang [qi] enters [the interior] and proceeds[44] to the yin [section], then this results in loss of motion.
When yin leaves [the interior] and proceeds to the yang [section], then this results in anger.[45]
These are the so-called "the five disorders."[46]

23-153-3
How the five evil [qi] appear:
When in spring one feels an autumn [movement in the] vessels,

---

41 Wang Bing: "When evil settles in the yang vessels, heat abounds in the four limbs. This results in craziness. When the evil enters the yin vessels then the [contents of the] six vessels coagulate, stagnate and [their flow] is blocked. Hence a block results."

42 Wang Bing: "When the evil internally strikes at the yang [section], then the speed of the flow in the vessels increases. This results in a disease rising to the peak." Zhang Jiebin: "搏 is 擊, 'to strike.' 巔 is 癲, 'peak disease.' When evil strikes against the yang, then the yang qi receives harm. Hence peak disease results. Earlier the text stated: 'when the evil enters the yang, craziness results.' In that case the evil supports the yang, the [resulting craziness] is a repletion of yang. Here [the text] states: 'when [evil] strikes against the yang, peak disease results.' In this case the evil attacks the yang; the [resulting peak disease] is a depletion of yang." For an analysis of the usage of the character 搏 in the ancient medical literature, see 1207/48 and 1205/42.

43 Wang Bing: "When the evil internally strikes the yin [section], then the [contents of the] vessels do no longer flow. This causes muteness, that is, inability to speak." 2196/7: "The type of 'muteness' referred to here resembles the stiffening of the tongue and the difficulties to speak caused by warmth diseases." For a detailed discussion of altogether seven meanings of 瘖 in the *Nei jing*, see there.

44 Wang Bing: "之 is 往, 'to proceed to.'" Gao Jiwu/557: "之 is used for 于, 'to,'" 2568/50 agrees. *Ling shu* and *Tai su* have 之於, "to move to."

45 Zhang Zhicong: "When an evil of the yang section enters the yin [section], then the resulting disease is a loss of motion. The reason is: yin abundance causes loss of motion. When an evil of the yin section enters the yang [section], then the resulting disease is frequent anger. This reason is: yang abundance causes anger."

46 One might arrive at a more meaningful interpretation if 搏 (see above) were to be read as 搏, "to accumulate." In this case, this paragraph describes, first, the consequences of evil qi entering the yang and the yin sections respectively; second, the consequences of evil qi accumulating in the yang and yin sections respectively; and third, the consequences of evil qi moving from the yang section into the yin and from the yin section into the yang section respectively.

when in summer one feels a winter [movement in the] vessels,
when in late summer one feels a spring [movement in the] vessels,
when in autum one feels a summer [movement in the] vessels,
when in winter one feels a late summer [movement in the] vessels.
{This is named: 'the yin [qi] leaves [the interior] and proceeds to the yang [section]. Patients tend to be angry.'⁴⁷ This is incurable.}
These are the so-called "the five evil [qi]."
{They all have the same fate; they die and cannot be cured.}⁴⁸

What the five depots store:
The heart stores the spirit.⁴⁹
The lung stores the *po*-soul.⁵⁰
The liver stores the *hun*-soul.⁵¹
The spleen stores the sentiments.⁵²
The kidneys store the will.⁵³
These are the so-called "what the five depots store."

What the five depots rule:
The heart rules the vessels.⁵⁴
The lung rules the skin.⁵⁵
The liver rules the sinews.⁵⁶

---

47 Lin Yi et al.: "[The passage] 陰出之陽病善怒 appears in the preceding passage already. Being repeated here it makes no sense. It must have been mistakenly inserted in an ancient [version of] the text." Without this insertion, the original text appears to have read: 名曰不治.

48 Beijing zhongyi xueyuan: "These six characters may have been a later commentary written on the margins of the text, that were still later erroneously copied into the main text." Yao Shaoyu: "The three characters 皆同命 are an erroneous insertion."

49 Wang Bing: "[The spirit] is a transformation product of the essence qi."

50 Wang Bing: "It assists the essence spirit."

51 Wang Bing: "It supports the essence spirit."

52 Wang Bing: "They record and do not let one forget."

53 Wang Bing: "It focusses the sentiments [on one goal] and does not let them shift elsewhere."

54 Wang Bing: "They block the camp qi. Their movement responds to one's breathing."

55 Wang Bing: "It encloses the sinews and the flesh. It wards off all evil."

56 Wang Bing: "They keep the motive apparatus tied together. Their movement follows the spirit."

The spleen rules the flesh.[57]
The kidneys rule the bones.[58]
These are the so-called "the five rulings."

23-154-3
The harms caused by the five taxations:[59]
To observe over a long time harms the blood.[60]
To lie down for a long time harms the qi.[61]
To sit for a long time harms the flesh.[62]
To stand for a long time harms the bones.[63]
To walk for a long time harms the sinews.[64]
These are the so-called "harms caused by the five taxations."

The phenomena reflecting the five [movements in the] vessels:[65]
The liver [movement in the] vessels is string[-like].
The heart [movement in the] vessels is hook[-like].
The spleen [movement in the] vessels is intermittent.[66]

---

57 Wang Bing: "It covers the depots, the sinews, and the bones. The guard qi passes through it."

58 Wang Bing: "They keep the sinews extended and they transform the marrow. They form the framework for keeping the body erect." For a detailed discussion of the relationship between "kidneys" and "bones," see 708/16.

59 Zhang Zhicong: "勞 is 太過, 'greatly excessive.'" *Gu dian yi zhu xuan* bianxiezu /41: "勞 is 疲勞過度, 'excessive fatigue.'"

60 Wang Bing: "This taxation affects the heart."

61 Wang Bing: "This taxation affects the lung."

62 Wang Bing: "This taxation affects the spleen."

63 Wang Bing: "This taxation affects the kidneys."

64 Wang Bing: "This taxation affects the liver."

65 Zhang Zhicong: "The [movements in the] vessels of the five depots, as they correspond to the images of the four seasons and five agents."

66 Wang Bing: "Soft and weak." Cheng Shide et al.: "The meaning of 代脈 has been [interpreted] differently. One opinion is that its meaning is 'stopping in between.' A second opinion is that its meaning is 'alternating between big and small.' A third opinion is that its meaning is 'substituting itself in the course of the four seasons.' All these are called 代. The substitution of 'substituting itself in the course of the four seasons' is a substitution in the climate. The substitution of 'stopping in between' is a substitution in the frequency of the arrivals. The substitution of 'alternating between big and small' is a substitution in the physical appearance of the [movements in the] vessels. The statement in the present paragraph refers to a substitution in the climate.

The lung [movement in the] vessels is hair[-like].[67]
The kidney [movement in the] vessels is stone[-like].[68]
These are the so-called "[movements in the] vessels of the five depots."

Hence Zhang Jiebin: '代 is 更代, to substitute. The spleen [movement in the] vessels is harmonious and soft. It conducts a separate rule throughout the four seasons. That is: in spring [the movement] should be harmonious, soft, and at the same time string[-like]. In summer it should be harmonious, soft, and at the same time hook[-like]. In autumn it should be harmonious, soft, and at the same time hair[-like]. In winter it should be harmonious, soft, and at the same time stone[-like]. [Different spleen movements] substitute each other in the course of the four seasons. Hence [the spleen movement] is called substitutive. [The term] does not refer to [the concept of] to stop in between [as in its meaning of intermittent, suggested by Wang Bing in his commentary to the occurrence of 代 in *Su wen* 18].'" 2902/39 distinguishes between a pathological movement in the vessels designated with the term 代 in the sense of 止, 'to stop,' and a normal movement associated with the spleen, designated with the term 代 in the sense of "representing the spleen throughout the four seasons." For details, see there. Zheng Jinsheng suggests that 代 may have been written 弋, 'wooden stick,' originally. He points out that the images associated with the movements in the vessels of the liver ("string"), the heart ("hook"), the lung ("hair"), and the kidneys ("stone") represent items of daily life. This may have been true also for the image associated with the movement in the vessel of the spleen.

67 Wang Bing: "It is light, drifts at the surface and is depleted/hollow, resembling hair or feathers."

68 Wang Bing: "It strikes in the depth and is hard. As if a stone was thrown."

Chapter 24
Blood and Qi, Physical Appearance and Mind

24-154-8
Now,
as far as the regular numbers of man are concerned:
The major yang [conduits] regularly [contain] much blood, little qi.
The minor yang [conduits] regularly [contain] little blood, much qi.
The yang brilliance [conduits] regularly [contain] much qi, much blood.
The minor yin [conduits] regularly [contain] little blood, much qi.
The ceasing yin [conduits] regularly [contain] much blood, little qi.
The major yin [conduits] regularly [contain] much qi, little blood.
These are the regular numbers of heaven.[1]

Foot major yang [conduits] and [foot] minor yin [conduits] constitute exterior
and interior.
[Foot] minor yang [conduits] and [foot] ceasing yin [conduits] constitute
exterior and interior.
[Foot] yang brilliance [conduits] and [foot] major yin [conduits] constitute
exterior and interior.
These are the yin and yang [conduits] of the feet.

Hand major yang [conduits] and [hand] minor yin [conduits] constitute exterior and interior.
[Hand] minor yang [conduits] and [hand] heart ruler constitute exterior and
interior.
[Hand] yang brilliance [conduits] and [hand] major yin [conduits] constitute
exterior and interior.
These are the yin and yang [conduits] of the hands.

Now, when one knows that from which the yin and yang [conduits] of hands
and feet suffer,

---

1 Wang Bing: "The quantities of blood and qi [in the conduits] represent the regular
numbers of heaven. Hence the Way of piercing is employed regularly to drain what is
[too] much." Gao Jiwu/232: "In accordance with the wording above, 'heaven' should
be 'man' here." Zhang Yizhi et al.: "The 52 character passage beginning with 夫人 appears with larger or smaller differences in the *Su wen*, the *Ling shu*, the *Jia yi jing*, and
the *Tai su*. All commentaries differ, too."

whenever one treats the disease, one must first remove their blood.[2]
That is,
remove that from which they suffer and
pay attention to what they long for.[3]
Then
drain what is present in surplus and
supplement what is insufficient.

24-155-6
If one wishes to know [the location of] the transporters on the back,[4]
one first measures[5] the distance between the two breast nipples [with a stalk of grass].
One breaks [this stalk] in the middle.
Again one takes another [stalk of] grass, measuring [the distance between the nipples], and removes one half of it.
After that one takes the two ends of the [remaining half] to support [the ends of the first stalk].[6]
Then one lifts [the resulting triangle] to measure this [person's] back.

---

2 Wang Bing: " 'One must first remove their blood' is to say: when the blood vessels appear filled beyond normal, then remove the [blood]. This is not to say that in a normal situation one has to remove the blood before piercing." Zhang Jiebin: "This is not to say that whenever one needles one must first remove blood." 2111/37: "去 is 解除, 'to eliminate.' "

3 Zhongyi yanjiuyuan...: "伺 is 觀察, 'to examine.' " Zhang Jiebin: "After the blood [causing] blockages has been removed, examine what the qi of the depots like. That is, the liver [qi] likes dispersion, the heart [qi] likes softness, the lung [qi] likes collection, the spleen [qi] likes dryness, the kidney qi likes hardness." Wu Kun: " '伺之所欲' [is to say]: wind, cold, summerheat, dampness, dryness, and fire, the patients may have an aversion to these [qi], or they may like them. One examines what they like and then one knows in which conduit the disease is located."

4 Ma Shi: "The 'transporters on the back' are the transporters of the five depots mentioned in the text further below. They below to the foot major yang conduit of the bladder. Because they are located on the back they are summarily called 'transporters on the back.' " Zhang Zhicong: "俞 is identical with 輸, 'to transport.' "

5 Wang Bing: "度 is 度量, 'to measure.' "

6 1263/16: "柱 is most likely a mistake for 拄, 'to oppose.' " Zhongyi yanjiuyuan...: "The meaning is that the first stalk is combined with the second, shorter stalk in such a way that an equilateral triangle results."

One lets one angle be situated upwards, on the same level as the great hammer on the spine.[7]
The [other] two angles are [situated] below.

Exactly at the location of the lower angles are the transporters of the lung.
One measurement[8] further down, [exactly at the location of the lower angles] are the transporters of the heart.
One measurement further down, at the left angle is the transporter of the liver; at the right angle is the transporter of the spleen.
One measurement further down are the transporters of the kidneys.
These [locations] are called "the transporters of the five depots."
These are the measurements[9] for cauterization and piercing.

24-155-11
When the physical appearance is joyful, while the mind suffers,
the disease emerges in the vessels.
Treat it with cauterization and piercing.[10]

When the physical appearance is joyful and the mind is joyful [too],
the disease emerges in the flesh.
Treat it with needles and [pointed] stones.[11]

---

7 There is a "Great Hammer" hole, i.e., GV-14. Probably what is meant here is not this hole, but rather the bone which lends his name to the hole.

8 Cheng Shide et al.: " 'Measurement' refers to the distance between the upper angle and the lower leg of the triangle."

9 Zhongyi yanjiuyuan...: "度 refers to 法度, 'pattern,' 'law,' here."

10 Wang Bing: "形 is to say 身形, 'the physical appearance of the body.' 志 is to say 心志, 'the mind.' 'The physical appearance is joyful' is to say: it is not overly exhausted. 'The mind suffers' is to say: to be engaged in pondering and deep thoughts. When [the physical appearance] is not overly exhausted, then the sinews and bones are balanced and in a state of normalcy. When someone is engaged in pondering and deep thoughts, then the camp and guard [qi] are obstinate, [i.e.,] qi and blood do not follow their regular courses. Hence the disease emerges from the vessels. Now, to drain abundance and to supplement depletion, that is the Way of cauterization and piercing." Zhang Jiebin: " 'The physical appearance is joyful' means: the body has no fatigue; 'the mind suffers' means: the heart ponders a lot. The heart rules the vessels. Deep thoughts and too much pondering cause disease in the vessels. When the vessels have a disease, one must treat the conduits and network [vessels]. Hence one cauterizes and needles in accordance with the requirements of each [case]."

11 Wang Bing: " 'The mind is joyful' is to say: one rejoices and forgets all grief. However, when the sinews and bones are not taxed and when heart and spirit rejoice, the structures of the flesh narrow down and the passageways of the qi become filled up.

When the physical appearance suffers while the mind is joyful,
the disease emerges in the sinews.
Treat it with poultices and pulling [exercises].[12]

When the physical appearance suffers and the mind suffers [too],
the disease emerges in the gullet and in the throat.[13]
Treat it with the one hundred drugs.[14]

The guard qi becomes disquieted and forms knottings. Hence the diseases emerge in the flesh. Now, when the guard qi stagnates and fills [the flesh] it is to be drained by means of needles. Knotted accumulations of pus and blood are to be broken up with stones. 'Stones' is to say: stone needles. These are sharpened stones." See also *Su wen* 04, note 37.

12 Zhang Jiebin: "熨 is to say 藥熨, 'medicinal poultice.' 引 is to say 導引, 'guiding and pulling exercises.'" Zhang Zhicong: "When taxation affects the physical appearance, then this harms the sinews; when the mind is idle and joyful, then the blood vessels have not been affected by a disease yet. Hence one treats [the harm done to the sinews] by means of poultices and gymnastics, thereby causing the blood vessels to nourish the sinews. As a result, health is restored." Yao Shaoyu: "When the sinews that are harmed [by taxation] encounter heat, they will relax; when they encounter cold, they will become tense. By applying poultice and guiding/pulling exercises, they are softened and do suffer neither from relaxation nor from tensions."

13 Mori: "咽 does not have the meaning of 'gullet' here. It is an alternative for 噎, 'to choke.' .. The meaning is: blocked throat and broken voice." That is to say: "The disease emerges from a blocked gullet."

14 Lin Yi et al.: "The *Jia yi jing* has 固竭, 'chronic exhaustion,' instead of 咽嗌, 'gullet and throat,' and 甘藥, 'sweet drugs,' instead of 百藥, 'the one hundred drugs.'" *Ling shu* 78, too, has 甘藥, "sweet drugs," instead of 百藥. Zhang Jiebin: "甘, 'sweet,' in former times was written 百. The *Ling shu* is correct. Hence [I] follow it." Wang Bing: "When one is engaged in serious studies and toils in one's profession, when one ponders and has deep thoughts, or when one is grieved, then the liver qi accumulates in the spleen. The lung and the gallbladder form a union; the throat serves as their emissary. Hence the diseases emerge from the throat." Zhang Zhicong: "To have the physical appearance and the mind suffer, there must be a lot of grief and thinking. Grief harms the lung, thoughts harm the spleen. Harm to the lung qi results in depletion and failure of passage. The qi must stagnate. The vessels of spleen and lung move upwards along the throat. Hence diseases emerge at the throat." Zhang Zhicong: "When physical appearance and mind suffer, this is to say: one hundred griefs affect the heart, ten thousand matters tax the physical appearance. As a result, yin and yang, blood and qi are harmed. Now, the throat rules the qi of heaven; the gullet rules the qi of the eart. [The qi of] heaven is the yang qi; [the qi of the] earth is the yin qi. Here now yin and yang, qi and blood are all harmed. Hence the disease emerges in the throat and in the gullet."

When the physical appearance is frequently affected by fright and fear,[15]
the conduit [vessels] and the network [vessels become] impassable.
The disease emerges from [sections that are] numb.
Treat it with pressing-rubbing and medicinal wines.[16]
These are the so-called five [combinations of] physical and mental appearances.[17]

24-156-4
Pierce the yang brilliance [conduits] to let blood and qi.
Pierce the major yang [conduits] to let blood, but abstain from [letting] qi.
Pierce the minor yang [conduits] to let qi, but abstain from [letting] blood.
Pierce the major yin [conduits] to let qi, but abstain from [letting] blood.
Pierce the minor yin [conduits] to let qi, but abstain from [letting] blood.
Pierce the ceasing yin [conduits] to let blood, but abstain from [letting] qi.[18]

---

15 Tanba: "Whether the character 形 is in place here can be doubted. Neither Wang
Bing, nor Wu Kun, or Zhang Jiebin refer to it in their commentaries. Ma Shi and
Gao Shishi add the character 苦 below 形." Mori: "數 refers to excessive bedroom
activities. Fear and fright are something different then 'the mind suffers.' That is to
say: heart and mind are in fear. The kidneys store the mind. Hence [the text] does not
refer to the mind separately." Zhang Yizhi et al.: "This paragraph speaks of five [states
of] physical appearance and mind. Apparently the character 志 was omitted. If it is
added, [the entire paragraph] acquires a stringent meaning. The character 數 need not
be changed."

16 Wang Bing: "In case of fright the qi in the vessels agglomerates; in case of fear the
spirit is not kept securely. When the [qi] in the vessels coagulates and the spirit travels,
then the conduits and network [vessels] are not passable and this results in a disease
of numbness. Now, pressing-rubbing serves to open what is blocked and to draw yin
and yang [qi through the body]. Medicinal wines serve to nourish the proper [qi] and
to remove the evil [qi], to regulate the center and to order the qi. 醪藥 is to say 酒
藥, 'wine drugs.'" Zhang Jiebin: "Fright brings the qi in disorder, fear causes the qi
to descend. In case of repeated fright and fear, qi and blood are dispersed in disorder
and the conduits and network [vessels] become inpenetrable. Hence one suffers from
numbness."

17 See Unschuld 2003, V.8.10., p. 227, for an interpretation of the term *xing zhi* 形
志 as a Chinese equivalent to the term somatopsychics.

18 Wang Bing: "This is to elucidate the rules for piercing the three yang and three yin
[conduits] with their different quantities of blood and qi, as outlined above." Zhang
Jiebin: "In general, [in piercing] the major yang and the ceasing yin [conduits], one
should let blood, but no qi. [In piercing] the minor yang, the minor yin, and the major
yin [conduits], one should let qi, but no blood. Only [when piercing] the yang brilliance [conduit] one can let blood and qi. This is exactly in accordance with the initial
paragraph." Lin Yi et al.: "The *Tai su* has: 'Needle the yang brilliance [conduit] to let
blood and qi; needle the major yin [conduit] to let blood and qi.' Yang Shangshan

Huang Di nei jing su wen

commented: 'Even though the yang brilliance [conduit] and the major yin [conduit] constitute exterior and interior, they equally abound with blood and qi. Hence blood and qi are to be drained from both of them.' That is, the major yin [conduit] and the yang brilliance [conduit] both alike have much blood and much qi. In earlier texts, it is said of the major yin: '[it contains] much blood, little qi' and elsewhere: 'much qi and little blood'. This does not tell us anything. If this is compared to the *Tai su*, then neither of these two statements is acceptable. ... This paragraph should follow the statement 'drain what is present in surplus and fill what is insufficient.' "

Chapter 25
Discourse on Treasuring Life
and Preserving Physical Appearance[1]

25-158-2
Huang Di asked:
"Covered by heaven and carried by the earth,
all the myriad beings have come to existence.
None has a nobler position than man.[2]

Man comes to life through the qi of heaven and earth;
he matures in accordance with the laws of the four seasons.[3]
Rulers and common people,
they all wish to preserve [their] physical appearance.[4]
[As far as] the diseases of the physical appearance [are concerned, though,]
no one knows their nature.
Excessive [qi] staying [in the body] move[5] deeper day by day.
They attach themselves to the bones and the marrow.
In my heart I ponder about this.[6]

---

1 2078/20: "This treatise was titled 刺禁, 'Prohibitions in piercing,' in the Quan Yu-anqi edition." 2687/55: "寶 is 保, 'to protect.' 寶命 is 保養生命, 'to protect and nour-ish life.' 全形 is 使形体健全, 'maintain the wholeness of the body.'"

2 Ye Gang/119: "於 is to be interpreted as 比, 'in comparison.'"

3 Wang Bing: "Heaven lets its virtue flow; the earth produces transformations with its qi. When virtue and qi form a union, [man] is brought to life." Zhang Jiebin: "Spring corresponds to the liver and supports coming to life; summer corresponds to the heart and supports growth; late summer corresponds to the spleen and supports transformation; autumn corresponds to the lung and supports harvest; winter corre-sponds to the kindeys and supports storage."

4 Wang Bing: "The noble and the common are different, but in their appreciation of life they are identical. Hence it belongs to the normal emotions of the noble and of the commoners to love life and to abhor death."

5 Zhang Jiebin: "When a disease is in the skin and its hair, it is at the surface and not yet in the depth. If one does not treat it early, then 'the excesses stay [in the body] and penetrate deeper day by day.'" Wu Kun: "When any of the six qi is present in excessive abundance, this is evil." Cheng Shide et al.: "淫 stands here for evil qi that has invaded the human body."

6 Lin Yi et al.: "The *Tai su* has 患, 'to suffer,' instead of 慮."

I wish [to employ] needles to remove these diseases.
How is this done?"[7]

25-158-5
Qi Bo responded:
"Now,
as for the salty flavor of salt, its qi lets liquids seep out of a container.[8]
As for a string which is cut, its sound is hoarse.[9]
As for the wood which has become old, its leaves are shed.[10]

---

7 Wang Bing: "When a depletion evil strikes a person, the evidence appears in the [patient's] complexion first. It cannot be recognized from [an altered state of] the body. [Sometimes] it has a physical appearance; [sometimes] it has not. Hence no one knows its circumstances. [The evil] remains [in the body] and does not leave. Day by day it moves deeper. The evil qi attacks the depletion. Hence it sticks to bones and marrow. [Huang] Di's compassion was immeasurable; hence he wished to apply the needle."

8 Wang Bing: " 'Salty' is to say: the flavor of salt. It is imbued with bitterness and makes things moist. Now, salty [flavor] is generated from bitter [flavor]. Salty [flavor] originates from water and contains water. It moistens the lower [parts of the body] and [its inherent] bitterness has a draining effect. Hence it is able to cause water liquid in containers to seep away. All [things] that are hollow and hold things are called 'container.' One that is on the outside of the body is the scrotum. Inside the body it is the same; there it is called bladder. Now, [speaking in terms of] diseases paired with the five depots, then [in the present case] the qi of the heart lies hidden in the kidneys and does not leave. This is what is meant here. Why? The kidneys reflect the water and their [associated] flavor is salty. The heart forms a union with the fire and its [associated] flavor is bitter. Bitter [flavor] causes sweat to flow; salty [flavor] moves to the bag. The fire seizes the water. Hence there is liquid outside the scrotum resembling sweat seeping away without end." 140/26: "The character 者 should be 着. The text should read: 夫鹽之味鹹, 着其氣, 令器津泄. In other words, 'the flavor of salt is salty. Salty flavor proceeds to the bones and roughens the blood. If one consumes large quantities of salt, heart and kidneys appropriate its salty qi and this can cause the liquid of the depot of the spleen to flow off.' "

9 140/26: " 'When a string is cut its sound is spoilt' [is to say:] When the kidney qi is weakened and spoilt, the lung connection (肺系, *Ling shu* 10, for "throat") loses its controlling force. Hence the vocal cord is cut internally and as a result its sound is silenced."

10 The *Tai su* has 木陳者其葉落發, "when the wood is old, the leaves fall off," instead of 木敷者其葉發. Wang Bing: "敷 is 布, 'to spread.' This is to say, the qi of the wood spreads .. the disease must break out in the lobes (葉) of the lung. Why? Because this is where the qi of wood disperses." Gao Shishi: "When the [qi of] wood disperses, then the branches and the leaves are not firm and fall off." Li Guoqing: "The *Tai su* interprets 發 as 廢, 'to do away with.' This is correct. 其葉發 is in reality 其葉廢, 'its

As for a disease which is in the depth [of the body], the sound it [generates] is hiccup.[11]

When man has these three [states],
this is called 'destroyed palace.'[12]
Toxic drugs do not bring a cure;
short needles cannot seize [the disease].

---

leaves fall off.'" For further evidence see there. 706/39 agrees: "發 is 廢." 674/160: "A comparison of the *Su wen* with the *Tai su* shows that the character 敷 in the *Su wen* is an obvious error. Now, 陳 and 敷 do not resemble each other, neither in their pronunciation nor in their written form. How could this error come about? .. The *Yü pian* 玉篇 states: 陳 is occasionally written 敷." 140: "This should be 木散者, 其葉撥, 'When the [qi of the] wood is dispersed, the leaves are shed.' The reason [for this metaphor] is the parallel between the leaves of trees and the lobes of the lung. The breathing of the lung resembles [that of] the leaves. To open up the branches is to harm the heart; to disturb the root is to shed the leaves." Fang Wenhui/27: "敷 stands for 腐, 'to rot.'" Yu Chang: "The meaning of 敷 is identical with that of 陳. … 敷 has the meaning of 陳布, 'to spread,' and of 久舊, 'old.' In the present context 敷 stands for 久舊, 'old.' The commentary by Yan 顏 to *Han shu* 漢書, Wen di ji 文帝紀, states: 陳 is 久舊, 'old.' That is correct and the same meaning applies to the phrase 木敷."

11 Yang Shangshan: "This is to say: if one wishes to recognize the subtleties of a disease, one should know [how to interpret] its signs. When a container is filled with salt, liquid flows off towards outside. One sees the liquid and knows of the salty [nature] of the salt. When the sound is hoarse, one knows a string of the lute is broken. When the leaves are shed, one knows that this is old wood already infested with insects. The evidence of the weakness and destruction of these three items is compared to the sound of belching; it is [likewise] a sign letting one know the disease in the depth. When a person emits belching sounds this is like the three examples given [before]: it signals that the palaces are destroyed. When the palaces in the center are destroyed, the disease is in the depth. Because the disease is in the depth, needles and drugs cannot seize [it]." Mori: "Qi, sound, leaves, and voice constitute four signs, referring to the diseases of four depots. 'Three' may be an error for 'four.'" Zhang Qi: "The character 三 is an erroneous insertion."

12 Wang Bing: "府 stands for 胸, 'chest,' because the lung is situated in the chest. 壞 is to say 損壞其府而取病, 'injure the palace and seize the disease.' *Bao pu zi* 抱朴子 states: '[Zhang] Zhongjing opened the chest to remove a red cake from it.' Hence one can open the chest and seize a disease." Yang Shangshan: "府 is 中府, 'central palace(s).' That is to say: the five depots." 140/27: " 'These three [states]' refers to the string that is cut, to the wood [qi] that is dispersed, and to the belching voice. The [disease] proposed here very much resembles tuberculosis: when the string is cut, this is the first stage; when the [qi of the] wood is dispersed, this is the second stage; when the voice sounds belching, this is the third stage. Hence [the text] states: poisonous drugs bring no cure; it cannot be seized with short needles."

[If applied they would achieve] nothing but to break[13] the skin and to injure the flesh.
Blood and [evil] qi would fight [each other] to blackness."[14]

25-159-3
[Huang] Di:
"When I think about the pain of the [people],
this disturbs my heart.
In my confusion, contrary to [my intentions I cause their pain] to increase in severity.
I am unable to substitute their diseases [with health].[15]

When the people hear this, they consider [me] cruel and destructive.[16]
What is to be done?"

---

13 546/43: "絕 has the meaning here of 損傷, 'to injure.' "

14 Wang Bing: "The disease leaks internally into the lung. Hence toxic drugs cannot produce a cure. Externally it is not in the conduits and network [vessels]. Hence short needles cannot seize it. Hence it is only with breaking the skin and harming the flesh that one can attack the [disease]. Since the bad blood was engaged in a struggle with the lung qi for a long time already, the blood is black when it becomes visible [in the surgical wound]." Yu Yue: "The ten characters 此皆絕皮傷肉血氣爭黑 should come in front of 有此三者. A 'broken skin' is the first; 'injured flesh' is the second, and 'blood and qi would fight each other to blackness' is the third. When these three are present, the disease is in the depth and the voice is belching. .. This is called 'destroyed palaces.' Toxic drugs cannot achieve a cure and short needles cannot seize it. This way the meaning is very clear. By reversing the order [of the characters], the meaning of this passage was lost."

15 Ma Shi: "The disease leaves the human body, as if it was removed through 'substitution (更代).' "

16 Wang Bing: "殘 is to say: 殘害, 'to harm;' 賊 is to say: 損劫, 'to rob.' In other words, '[I] fear to cross over to insensitivity and reach [a state] where I am hated by the people.' " Zhang Canjia: "殘賊 stands for 殘忍不仁, 'cruel and without compassion.' " Yu Chang: "The four characters 反其病 are to be read as one sentence. That is, because his mind is unsettled and confused when treating diseases he commits many errors. He is not only unable to remove their diseases, on the contrary, he even causes them to be more severe and is unable to substitute them. The meaning was quite clear originally. Wang Bing's comments are rather simple, leaving it open how he read [this passage]. Later authors have mistakenly read 心為之亂惑反甚 as one sentence and 其病不可更代 as a second sentence. .. They have disregarded the subsequent statement 'when the people hear this, they consider [me] cruel and destructive.' If he had been only unable to 'substitute a disease,' why should anyone have considered him cruel and destructive? They considered him cruel and destructive because he caused their diseases to become even more severe! And because he caused their diseases to

Qi Bo:

"Now,

man receives his life from the earth;

his fate depends on heaven.

When heaven and earth combine their qi,

that is called 'Man.' [17]

If someone is able to correspond to the four seasons,

heaven and earth are [his] father and mother.

If he knows the myriad beings,

one calls him Son of Heaven.

25-160-1

Heaven has yin [qi] and yang [qi];

man has the twelve sections.[18]

Heaven has cold and summerheat;

man has depletion and repletion.[19]

Those who are able to take the transformations of yin and yang of heaven and earth as guideline,

they do not miss the four seasons.

---

become even more severe, he would have liked to 'put himself into their place.' 更代, 'to substitute,' means: he would have liked to put his own body in place of the body of the diseased people."

17 140/27: "Wang Chong 王充 states in his *Lun heng* 論衡: 天地合氣, 人偶自生, 'Heaven and earth combine their qi, men come to life by the mating [of husband and wife]'. The present text, beginning with 夫人生于地 to 不可勝竭, is a later addition by Daoists."

18 Wang Bing: "節 is to say: 節氣, 'sectional qi.' Externally [man] corresponds through them to the twelve months; internally they constitute that which rules the twelve conduit vessels." Ma Shi: "Man has the twelve sections of the conduit vessels." Wu Kun: "Heaven has the six yin and the six yang; man also has the six yin and the six yang to correspond to them." *Su wen* 03 has 五藏十二節, "the five depots, the twelve joints." Gao Shishi: "The qi in the twelve skeletal joints of hands and feet in the human body are moved through the opening and closure [of these joints] like yin and yang [qi] through the opening of heaven at day and its closure during night."

19 Wu Kun: "Cold and summerheat [reflect] the waxing and waning of the yin and yang of heaven. Depletion and repletion [reflect] the waxing and waning of the yin and yang in man."

Those who know the structure of the twelve sections,
they cannot be fooled even by those with the most sagely wisdom.[20]

[Those who are] able to concentrate on the changes in the eight movements
and
on the five dominations taking their positions one after another and
those who are able to penetrate the numbers of depletion and repletion,
they emerge and they enter on their own.
When they open and close their mouth, [the words they say are] most subtle.
Autumn down is in their eye."[21]

---

20 Wang Bing: "經 stands for 常, 'regular.' In other words, those who are able to regularly correspond to the Way of yin and yang of heaven in nourishing [their lives], they agree with the requirements of birth and growth of the four seasons. Those who know the changes in the arrival of the qi of the twelve [annual] sections, they cannot even be insulted by and asked to follow the command of those with the most sagely wisdom." 698/65: "Some authors have interpreted 經 as 知道, 'to know.' This may be, but upon close analysis it appears better to replace 經 by 經紀 in the meaning of 治理, 'to bring under control.'" Yang Shangshan: "Even the wisdom of the sages is unable to add [to their's]. 欺 is 加, 'to add.'" Mori: "欺 and 加 were listed in the same rhyming category by the *Yun jing* 韻鏡. Their pronunciations were used interchangeably in antiquity." Zhang Yizhi et al.: "The *Lun yu* 論語, Gong zhi chang 公治長, has 我不欲人之加諸我者也. The comment says: 加 is 凌罵, 'to abuse.'"

21 The *Tai su* has a 者 following the character 變. Yang Shangshan: "'Eight movements' is to say: the qi of the eight seasonal junctures (八節). The qi of the eight seasonal junctures coincide with the qi of the five agents metal, wood, water, fire, and soil. Alternately they are abolished and established." Zhang Yizhi et al.: "The 'eight junctures' refers to the four [seasonal] beginnings, the two equinoxes, and the two solstices." Wang Bing: "存 is to say: 心存, 'to concentrate one's mind [on something];' 達 is to say 明達, 'to comprehend;' 呿 is to say: 欠呿, 'to yawn;' 吟 is to say: 吟嘆, 'to sigh.' 'Autumn downs in the eye' is to say: they certainly could examine even the finest details. 八動 is to say: 八節之風變動, 'the changing movements of the winds of the eight divisions/sections [of heaven].' 五勝 is to say: 五行之氣相勝, 'the mutual domination of the qi of the five agents.' 立 is to say: 當其王時, 'the time when [an agent] flourishes/rules.' 變 is to say: 氣至而變易, 'the qi arrives and undergoes/has undergone a change.' Once these three are known, the effects [of one's treatments] are obvious and they come as fast as shadow and echo. In all cases the spirit leaves or enters independently; even demonic beings are unable to summon it or chase it away." Mori: "存 is 察, 'to examine.'" *Huai nan zi* 淮南子, Tai zu 太祖, speaks of a legendary ruler of the past who did not speak for three years. Finally he slightly opened his lips 呿吟 and said only one word which was powerful enough, though, to cause a movement all over the world.

25-160-5
[Huang] Di:
"The physical appearance of human life,
it does not leave yin and yang.

Heaven and earth combine [their] qi,
separating it into the nine fields and
dividing it into the four seasons.[22]

The moon may be small or large;
a day may be short or long.[23]
When all the myriad beings arrive together,
their [multitude] is innumerable.[24]

[There is] depletion and repletion, opening and closing of one's mouth.
May I ask which method [is to be applied in therapy]?"[25]

Qi Bo:
"When wood meets metal, it is felled.
When fire meets water, it is extinguished.
When soil meets wood, it is penetrated.[26]

---

22 2209/40: " 'Nine fields' stands for the space per se; 'four seasons' stands for time."

23 2209/40: "The year has twelve months (月); a month may be 'large' or 'small.' The year has 365 days (日); a day may be 'short' or 'long.' "

24 2209/40: "至 should be interpreted here as 往復, 'to move back and forth.' "

25 Yang Shangshan: "方 is 道, 'Way;' " Cheng Shide et al.: "方 is 道, 'Way;' 法, 'law.' " 2209/40: "These two sentences are to say: 'Man's diseases include depletion and repletion; among the symptoms are yawning and sighing. The changes of diseases and symptoms correspond to the four seasons and to sun and moon, and – like the changes of the myriad beings – cannot be estimated. I should like to ask you: Are there any good patterns to be applied in their treatment?' 'Yawning and sighing' are the symptoms of depletion and repletion. 'Yawning' is the sound emitted with open mouth; 'sighing' is the sound emitted with the mouth closed." In view of the use of 呿吟 related in *Huai nan zi* (cf. note 21 above), this question may also be interpreted as an interest voiced by Huang Di in the principles of how to achieve a maximum of effect through a minimum of action.

26 The image referred to here may be that of a wooden spade or roots of trees penetrating soil. Wang Bing: "達 is 通, 'to penetrate.' " 148/52: "Wang Bing has interpreted 達 as 通, 'to penetrate.' Most later authors have blindly followed Wang Bing's commentary and have arrived at forced explanations of 達. Seen in its context, 達 should correspond to 伐, 'to fell,' 滅, 'to extinguish,' 缺, 'to break,' and 絕, 'to interrupt.' If

When metal meets fire, it is destroyed.
When water meets soil, it is interrupted [in its flow].[27]
These [five processes] apply to the [interactions among] all the myriad beings;
their [validity] is never exhausted.

25-160-10
Hence,
the [application of the] needles is based on five [principles] spread over the
world, but
the common people all [discard them like] leftovers from food.
No one knows them.[28]

---

explained as 'to penetrate,' it does not fit into this context. .. It should be interpreted
as 不通, 'impenetrable.'" 267/3, cover page: "達 should be read as 撻, 'to flog.' This is
to say: soil is conquered by wood." For details, see there. 969/62: "The *Shuo wen* 說文
states: 達 is 行不相遇 and this means 阻隔, 'to block.' 'To block' corresponds to the
meanings of 伐, 'to fell,' 滅, 'to extinguish,' 缺, 'to break,' and 絕, 'to interrupt' above
and below this passage." Yu Chang agrees, pointing out that the character 達 rhymes
with 伐, 災, 缺, and 絕, and that the meanings of all five are related, too." Zhang
Yizhi et al.: "The *Tai su* has 水 instead of 木. That is an error." See also 484/43 and
1312/40.

27 The image referred to here may be that of a dyke. 546/43: "絕 has the meaning
here of 遏抑, 'to restrain,' 'to check.'"

28 The *Tai su* has 飲食, "drink and eat," instead of 餘食. Yang Shangshan: "飲食 is 服
用, 'to apply.' The common people apply this Way, but they do not grasp its meaning."
Lin Yi et al.: "The Quan Yuanqi edition has 飽食, 'to eat to repletion,' instead of 餘
食. The commentary states: 'The ignorant people do not explain [anything in terms
of] yin and yang and they do not know the subtleties of piercing. They eat to repletion
all day, but no one [of them] knows the subtle benefits of their [food].'" Wu Kun: "黔
首, 'the black heads,' refers to the people with black hair." Zhang Jiebin: "The people."
2493/531: "The Period of the Warring States did not have the designation 黔首 for
the people. It was only in the 26th year of the rule of Qin Shi Huang (221 B.C.) that
a decree was issued: 'The designation of the people is changed to 黔首, 'black heads.'"
961/28: "According to the *Shi ji*, Liu guo nian biao, 史記, 六國年表, the decree was
issued in the 2nd year after the unification of China, i.e., in the 27th year of Qin Shi
Huang. However, in the *Lü shi chun qiu* 呂氏春秋, which was published in the 8th
year of Qin Shi Huang, the term 黔首 was employed at many places. Hence it was in
wide use already before the unification of the empire." Zhang Zhicong: "共 is 共同,
'general.' All the common people can do is cultivate their fields to pay their taxes; if
they have surplus grains they use it for their own nourishment. No one knows anything about the Way of treating [diseases] by means of needles." 2076/255 considers
this passage as a reference to the reaction of the people during the Qin dynasty to the
attempts by the government to standardize piercing by introducing so-called 官針,
"official piercing": "Quan Yuanqi's 飽食 is wrong. The 24th chapter of Lao zi's *Dao
de jing* 道德經 states: 自賤者無功, 自矜者不長. 其在道也曰: 餘食贅行, "He who

The first is: regulate the spirit.

The second is: know how to nourish the body.[29]

The third is: know [to decide] whether toxic drugs are reliable.[30]

The fourth is: prepare the pointed stones in small and large [sizes].[31]

The fifth is: know how to diagnose [the status of] blood and qi of the palaces and depots.

These five laws are all equally established;

each has its predecessor.[32]

---

praises himself will not be successful; he who brags of himself will not reach superiority. In terms of the Way this is called 'leftovers from food' and 'useless moves.'" With regard to the present paragraph of the *Su wen* this is to say, the people consider the regulations concerning the 'official piercing,' propagated throughout the empire, as superfluous. In fact, though, they do not know the deep meaning of it."

29 The *Tai su* has 形, "physical appearance", instead of 身, "body." Wang Bing: "To know the pattern of how to nourish one's own body is identical to [knowing] the Way how to nourish the people."

30 Wang Bing: "When evil is attacked by means of toxic drugs, they are to be employed in accordance with what is appropriate. The Way of proper and true [behavior] lies in here." Cheng Shide et al.: "真 has the meaning of 要領, 'essentials.' 毒藥為真 is to say: the physician must have grasped the essentials of the nature and function of poisonous drugs."

31 Wang Bing: "The ancients used pointed stones as needles. Hence [the text] does not refer to the nine needles; it simply speaks of pointed stones. One should prepare them in large and small sizes is to say: one employs them in accordance with the requirements of the disease." Lin Yi et al.: "Quan Yuanqi stated: pointed stones represent an ancient method of external treatment. They have three names: 1. needle stones, 2. pointed stones, and 3. chisel stone. In fact this is just one item. In ancient times [people] were unable to cast iron. Hence they used stones as needles. This is why they named them needle stones. That is to say, the workmen had to sharpen them and give them shapes of varying sizes in correspondence with the illnesses [to be treated]. Huang Di created the nine [types of] needles to replace the chisel stones. Those who carried out treatments in high antiquity, they always followed the requirements of the respective region. In the East, people often suffer from swelling due to accumulations. Hence [the use of] pointed stones emerged in the East." Shen Zumian: "This passage states that there are five [principles] of piercing spread all over the empire. As for the 1st, *shen*神, 2nd, *shen*身, 3rd, *zhen*真, and 5th, *zhen* 診, these words all belong to the same rhyming category. Only the 4th sentence, 四曰制砭石小大 , does not fit. Maybe two characters are missing. Perhaps the wording should be 四曰制砭石小大之瘨 ('.... prepare pointed stones for minor or serious *dian*'). This would parallel the structure of the subsequent sentence. The *Shuo wen* defines *dian* 瘨 as 病, 'disease.' Elsewhere it is defined as 腹張, 'bloated abdomen.'"

32 In the sense of: the sequence of these five steps must be observed.

The piercing in this final age[33] of today [is such that]
depletions are replenished and
what is full is drained.
All practitioners knows this [and nothing else].

Now,
when one takes heaven as law and the earth as rule and
when [one's] activities follow what is corresponding [to them, then]
harmony with [heaven and earth] will be like an echo and
following [heaven and earth] will be like a shadow.[34]
The Way does not include any demons or spirits;
one comes by oneself and one leaves by oneself."[35]

25-162-3
[Huang] Di:
"I should like to hear about this Way."

Qi Bo:
"For all piercing to be reliable,
one must first regulate the spirit.[36]
Once [the condition of] the five depots is determined and
once [the examination at] the nine indicators has been completed,
only then a needle can be applied.

One does not notice the [disturbing] multitude of the vessels;[37]
one does not pay attention to the [confusing] multitude of bad omina.
Outer and inner [should] agree with each other,

---

33 The expression 末世, "final age", contains a notion of decadence. In this case one
may wonder whether the author had a previous Golden Age of piercing in mind when
he referred to his own time as "final age." Final age may also simply have referred to a
tumultuous period near the end of a dynasty.

34 Wang Bing read 隋 and 應 separately: "隨應而動 is to say: its effects are like a
shadow, like an echo. That is to say: it is near like a shadow following a physical appearance, like an echo following a sound."

35 2138/37: "This passage is identical with the statement in *Guan Yin zi*, Wu jian
pian, 關尹子, 五鑒篇: 道無鬼神, 獨來獨往."

36 Wang Bing: "One must concentrate one's mind and be calm without motion. This
is the central point (真要) of piercing."

37 Wu Kun: "The deadly [movement in the] vessels of the depots themselves."

and no priority should be given to [the patient's] physical appearance.[38]
If he is able to handle the coming and going [of qi],
only then he should apply [the needle] to the person [he treats].[39]

Man has depletions and repletions.
The five depletions one does not approach;
the five repletions one does not stay away from. [40]

25-162-7
When [the moment] has come to deploy [the needle],
the interval [between decision and action] must not even [be as long as] as the blinking of an eye.[41]
The hand is moved with full concentration;[42]
the needle shines and [its shape] is even.[43]

---

38 Wu Kun: "One must not solely rely on an inspection of the physical appearance." Gao Jiwu/528: "無 stands for 毋, 'do not.'"

39 Wang Bing: "玩 is to say: 玩弄, 'to handle.' In other words: 精熟, 'to be familiar with.'" Wu Kun: "往 is to say: 病源, 'origin of a disease;' 來 is to say: 變病, 'the resulting disease.' In other words: When one is familiar with the origin whence a disease has come and the resulting diseases to be expected in the future, only then one may apply the needles in the treatment of man."

40 Yang Shangshan: " 'Five' is a reference to skin, flesh, vessels, sinews, and bones. When these five are depleted, do not approach them to drain them; when these five are marked by repletion, do not stay away from them and do not fail to drain them." Cheng Shide et al.: " 'Five depletions' refers to depletion of essence qi in the five depots. 'Five repletions' refers to repletions with evil qi in the five depots."

41 Cheng Shide et al.: "發 is 出針, 'deploy the needle.'" 900/69: "Instead of 瞚, the Quan Yuanqi edition and the *Tai su* have 眴. Both characters stand for 瞬, 'twinkling of an eye.' The *Jia yi jing* has 瞠; this is a mistake."

42 Wang Bing: "When the hand moves in the application of the needle, the [physician's] heart is as if concentrated on one single task." 140/27: "務 should be 鶩, 'ducks;' 耀 is 躍, 'to jump.' The five sentences 手動若鶩 ('the hand moves like a duck'), 針躍而勻 ('the needle [is inserted] in a quick and uniform push'), 伏如橫弩 ('it lies calm like a crossbow'), 起如發机 ('let [the needle] go like setting the mechanism [of the crossbow] into action') and 手如握虎 ('the hand is [firm] as if it held a tiger'), they express the most essential points of acupuncture. When Wang Bing commented [on 務 as] 'to concentrate' and [on 耀 as] 'the physical appearance of the needle is shiny and clean,' he read the characters literally and arrived at a mistaken explanation."

43 Wang Bing: "針耀而勻 is to say: the needle is clean and shining and its shape is even from top to bottom." Zhang Jiebin: "耀 is 清潔, 'clean.' 勻 is: the movement of one's fingers is relaxed." 1126/9: "耀 is a mistake for 搖, 'to shake.'" Mori: "耀 is identical with 搖 in the sense of 療治, 'to heal.' The *Fang yan* 方言, ch.10, has: 搖 is

The sentiments are calm and [one] concentrates on what is right to do [here].
[This way] one observes the changes as they happen.[44]

This is what is called 'obscure.'[45]
No one knows its physical appearance.[46]
One sees its *wu–wu,*
one sees its *ji–ji,*
from seeing it flying by
one does not know who it is.[47]

療治. Similarly, the *Guang ya* 廣雅, Shi gu san 釋詁三, has: 搖 is 療治. 針耀而勻 is
to say: At the moment the needle is to be inserted, [the physician's] manner should
be relaxed. When exhalation turns into inhalation he pierces [the needle] into [the
patient]. Such insertion follows certain rules; whether it remains near the surface or
reaches into the depth, that is in accordance with specific patterns."

44 Wang Bing: "One looks and breathes with a quiet mind and considers [the individual patient's case] with an upright attitude, and one observes the changes in the
conduit vessels that have been stimulated through one's regulation." Cheng Shide et
al.: "This is, one inspects the changes that occur after the needle has been inserted."
1126/9: "之 is a mistake for 知, 'to know.'"

45 *Xun zi* 荀子, Quan xue 勸學: 無冥冥之志者, 無昭昭之明, "those whose mind is
not secretive and trustworthy will not shine with glory." Wang Bing: "冥冥 is to say:
the changes and transformations of blood and qi remain invisible." 915/56 makes a
full stop behind 冥冥 and interprets 冥冥 as 精誠專一: "this is called sincereness and
concentration." See also *Su wen* 26.

46 Zhang Jiebin: "In other words, the changes in [the state of] blood and qi cannot
be seen as physical manifestations from the outside."

47 Wang Bing: "烏烏 is the [sound produced when] sighing because the qi has arrived; 稷稷 is the [sound produced when] regretting that it has already responded.
That is to say, success and failure in piercing appears to come out of the void. As if one
observed the coming and going of birds, how could anyone know who is responsible
for their moves? All one sees is whether the conduit vessels have signs of abundance
or depletion, and one trusts them. One does not know who has called them or sends
them away." Zhang Jiebin: "烏烏 is to say: the arrival of the qi resembles the flocking
together of crows. 稷稷 is to say: the qi is abundant like an amassing of millet. 從見其
飛 is to say: the coming and going of the qi resembles the flying around of the crows.
Now, all this has no center and it is impossible to find out who is in control of these
[movements]. Hence [the text] states: 不知其誰, 'one does not know who is [behind
of this].'" 915/56: "烏烏 is 循行貌, 'like one following another.' 稷 should be an error
for 夐. 夐夐 is 'quick.'" Yu Chang: "The character 從 is an error for 徒, 'only,' 'in vain.'
徒見其飛, 'it is of no use to watch them flying,' hence [the text] states: 'one cannot
recognize who they are.' By exchanging 從 with 徒, [the statement] lost its meaning. When Wang Bing interpreted 從 as 從, that was a big mistake." Mori: "Wang
Bing's interpretation of 烏烏 and 稷稷 is acceptable. All other authors have offered

[The needle] lies down like a cross-bow;
and it rises as if a trigger had been released."[48]

25-163-2
[Huang] Di:
"How about [treating] a depletion?
How about [treating] a repletion?"[49]

Qi Bo:
"When piercing a depletion wait for a repletion.
When piercing a repletion, wait for a depletion.[50]

---

wrong interpretations. Now, 烏烏 corresponds to the statement 'it lies down like a cross-bow' further on in the text; 稷稷 corresponds to the statement 'like setting the mechanism [of a cross-bow] in action.' In both cases this refers to the reaction of the qi to an insertion of a needle. 稷稷 is powerful, vigorous. 飛 has the meaning of 散飛, 'to disperse,' or 菲微, 'weak.' That is to say, when the qi comes it is weak and confused at the beginning. When it abounds, that is 稷稷嚴利. The physical appearance of the qi leaving and coming in abundance or marked by weakness cannot be named in its appearance. Hence [the text] states: 不知其誰. The *Yü pian* 玉篇 interprets 誰 as 何, 'what.' That is, one does not know its name." We interpret 烏烏 and 稷稷 as onomatopoetic expressions, invoking, though, in the Chinese reader an image of a movement in the vessels passing by like swiftly (稷稷) flying crows (烏烏).

48 14/28: "The meaning of this sentence is: As long as the qi has not arrived yet, one should let the needle remain [inserted] and wait for the qi just as one holds a crossbow down and waits to release [the arrow.] When the qi arrives, one must quickly withdraw the needle as fast as one releases the arrow of a cross-bow."

49 Gao Shishi: "[Above it was said:] The five depletions, they must not be approached; the five repletions, one must not stay away from them. That is, one pierces only the repletions, one does not pierce the depletions. [Huang] Di, however, wishes to pierce both depletions and repletions. Hence he asks how to treat a depletion and how to treat a repletion."

50 Wang Bing: "That is to say: one should regard the arrival of the [desired] qi as effect and conclude [the treatment]; one must not cling to the breathing frequency and regard it as a set pattern." All statements joined here in Qi Bo's response are commented upon in *Su wen* 54. Accordingly, the arrival of a yin qi results in depletion, the arrival of a yang qi results in repletion. Hence, this statement could be interpreted as "when piercing a depletion, wait for yang qi to arrive; when piercing a repletion, wait for yin qi to arrive." Another interpretation might be to read "wait for a repletion" as a reference to a solid status (實) of the blood vessels, and to read "wait for a depletion" as a reference to a hollow, spongy status (虛) of the blood vessels.

When the conduit qi has arrived,
guard it carefully, lest it is lost.[51]
Deep and shallow are at [one's] mind;
far and near are like one.
[One must be calm] as if one looked down into a deep abyss;
the hand [must be strong] as if it held a tiger.[52]
The spirit should not be confused by the multitude of things."[53]

---

51 Wang Bing: "Do not change the pattern lest the qi in the conduits is missed."

52 Mori: "The two characters 握虎 make no sense here. A tiger is not an item that could be held in one's hands. 虎 is an ancient character used for 琥, i.e., a piece of jade shaped like a tiger. 握虎 is to say: to hold the jade tally issued to deploy the military. It signals utmost care and precision." Zhang Yizhi et al. agrees.

53 Wang Bing: "That is to say, [one should act with] sincereness and concentration." Tanba Genken 丹波元堅: "營 is identical with 惑, 'to be confused.'" Zhang Yizhi et al.: "營 is identical with 熒, 'confused.'"

Chapter 26
Discourse on the Eight Cardinal [Turning Points] and on Spirit Brilliance[1]

26-164-1
Huang Di asked:
" 'The application of the needle,
it must be based on laws and rules.'[2]
Now, what are the laws and what are the rules?"

Qi Bo responded:
"[In piercing one should take] heaven as law and the earth as rule.
Combine them with 'the luminaries of heaven.' "[3]

[Huang] Di:
"I should like to hear of this comprehensively."

Qi Bo:
"All laws of piercing
require an observation of the qi of sun and moon and stars,
and of the eight cardinal [turning points] of the four seasons.[4]

---

1 140/27: "This treatise discusses piercing, but [its contents] have nothing to do with piercing. Because the *Needle Classic* was lost, the prescription masters of the Qin and Han took advantage of this void and inserted their compilations. However, they had no knowledge of the art and as a result their language is empty and wrong at many places."

2 The following appears to be a comment on a discourse recorded more succinctly in *Ling shu* 73; most of the following quotes refer to the text in *Ling shu* 73-452-5 ff. Wang Bing: "服 is 事, 'matter,' 'affair,' 'business.' 法 is 象, 'to imitate.' 則 is 準, 'standard'; it is 約, 'agreement,' 'treaty.' "

3 Wang Bing: "This is to say: one acts in conformity with the gradual movement of sun, moon, and stars." Zhang Jiebin: "The brilliance of heaven appears in sun and moon. They are called the 'luminaries of heaven.' " Zhang Zhicong: "One conforms with the cold and summerheat of heaven, with the cold and warmth of the sun, with the fullness and depletion of the moon, and with the movements of the stars."

4 Wang Bing: "四時八正 is to say: the regular qi of the four seasons and the winds of the eight seasonal junctures arrive to assemble at [the changing residences of] Tai yi. One carefully examines where the qi is situated and pierces this [location]." Ma Shi: "八正 is 'the regular qi of the eight seasonal junctures.' The beginnings of the four seasons, the two equinoxes, and the two solstices are called 'the eight cardinal [turning points].' "

When the qi is determined, one [can] pierce the [patient].[5]

Hence,
when heaven is warm and when the sun is bright,
then the blood in man is rich in fluid,[6]
and the guard qi is at the surface.
{Hence, the blood can be drained easily and
the qi can be made to move on easily.}

When heaven is cold and when the sun is hidden,
then the blood in man congeals so that [its flow] is impeded,[7] and
the guard qi is in the depth.

26-164-6
At the time of beginning crescent moon,
blood and qi originate as essence,[8] and
the guard qi begins to move.

---

5 Yang Shangshan: "As for 定, when one examines and recognizes the regular qi of heaven and earth, this is called 定, 'to determine.' Cheng Shide et al.: "定 is 定位, 'to determine a location.' In contrast, Wang Bing: "氣定乃刺之 is to say: When the wind qi of the eight seasonal junctures is calm and fixed, then one can pierce the conduit vessels and regulate depletion and repletion. Hence the *Li ji* 曆忌 states: 'Five days before and after the eight seasonal junctures one must not pierce or cauterize. [Otherwise] misfortune [results].' This is to say, the qi is not yet fixed. Hence one must not cauterize or pierce."

6 Zhang Jiebin: "淖 is 濡潤, 'rich.' When the sky is warm and the sun shines, the yang abounds and the yin is weak. The blood and the qi in man correspond to this. Hence the blood is imbued with liquid and is drained easily. The guard qi is at the surface and moves easily. When the sky is cold and the sun is hidden, the yang is weak and the yin abounds. Hence man's blood congeals and the guard qi is in the depth. When [the blood] is congealed, it is difficult to drain it. When [the guard qi] is in the depth, it has difficulties to move." Zhongyi yanjiuyuan...: "淖 has the meaning of 滑潤, 'smooth.'" Yu Chang: "淖液 stands for 潮汐, 'morning tides and evening tides.'" Mori: "淖液 stands for 淖澤, in the sense of 滋潤, 'rich.' Yang Shangshan interprets 液 as 津液; that is wrong."

7 Wang Bing: "泣 is to say: like snow in water." 238/401/ "泣 is 冱, 'congealed.'" Mori: "The *Tai su* has 涘泣 instead of 凝泣, in the sense of 澀, 'rough.'"

8 Yang Shangshan: "At new moon, the blood and the qi come to life anew. Hence one speaks of 精, 'essence.'" Zhang Jiebin: "精 is 正, 'regular,' is 流利, 'movable.'"

When the disk of the moon is full,[9]
blood and qi are replete;
the muscles and the flesh are firm.

When the disk of the moon is empty,
the muscles and the flesh wane,
the conduits and the network [vessels] are depleted and
the guard qi leaves.
The physical appearance exists all by itself.
It is therefore that one follows the seasons of heaven in regulating blood and qi.[10]

26-164-8
It is therefore that:
when heaven is cold, do not pierce,[11]
when heaven is warm, do not hesitate.[12]
At crescent moon, do not drain.
At full moon, do not supplement.
When the disk of the moon is empty, do not treat.
This is the so-called regulation at the right time.

One follows the sequence of [the qi of] heaven and
the times of abundance and depletion.
The position [of the qi] is determined in view of [the luminaries of heaven]
moving [the position of their] light;

---

9 Zhang Jiebin: "The moon belongs to the yin; it is the essence of water. Hence the up and down of the tides corresponds to the moon. The physical body of man belongs to the yin. The blood vessels belong to the water. Hence their [states of] depletion and repletion and [whether the qi is] in the depth or near the surface, also corresponds to the moon." Cheng Shide et al.: "郭 is identical with 廓. 月廓 is 望月, 'full moon.'"

10 1276/10: "天時 refers to the sequence of the four seasons spring, summer, autumn, and winter."

11 Wang Bing: "Because the blood is congealed and the guard qi is in the depth."

12 Wang Bing: "Because the blood is rich in liquid and the qi moves easily." Yang Shangshan: "When heaven is warm, blood and qi are rich. Hence one can pierce the [patient] and one must not harbor any doubts." In contrast, Zhang Jiebin, Ma Shi, Gao Shishi, and Zhang Zhicong read 疑 as 凝, "to congeal." Zhang Zhicong comments: "When heaven is warm and mild, then blood and qi do not coagulate and flow freely." Zhang Yizhi et al.: "Obviously, the version commented upon by Wang Bing had 凝, 'to congeal,' instead of 疑, 'to hesitate.'"

standing upright one waits for them.¹³

26-165-3
Hence it is said:
To drain at [beginning] crescent moon,
this is called 'depot depletion.'¹⁴

To supplement at full moon,
when blood and qi soar and overflow and
when the network [vessels] have resident blood,¹⁵
this is called 'doubled repletion.'¹⁶

To treat when the disk of the moon is empty,
this is called 'causing disorder in the conduits.'

Yin and yang [qi] mingle with each other;
true [qi] and evil [qi] are not separate.¹⁷
[The evil qi] moves into the depth to stay there;
external depletion [goes along with] internal disorder.

---

13 Wang Bing: "One observes the movement of the sun to determine the position of the qi. Facing the South and standing upright, one waits for the arrival of the qi and regulates it." Zhang Jiebin: "The position of the annual seasons is determined by means of the movement of the light of sun and moon. One faces the South, stands upright, waits [for the light] and examines it. Then one can perceive the indicators of the qi." See 395/42 for a discussion of the astronomical background.

14 Wang Bing: "[Because] blood and qi are weak." Lin Yi et al.: "The Quan Yuanqi edition has 減, 'to diminish,' instead of 藏, 'depot.' 藏 should be 減." Zhang Jiebin: "That is: one depletes a depletion." Zhang Yizhi et al. suggests to read 藏虛 as 重虛, 'doubled depletion,' in view of a warning in the *Tai su*, ch. 24: "At the time of crescent moon, the blood and the qi in the depots are feeble. Hence, piercing them causes doubled depletion." This reading parallels the term 重實, "doubled repletion", further below.

15 Wang Bing: "絡 elsewhere is 經, 'conduits.' That is wrong. Blood and qi are abundant. 留 elsewhere is 流, 'to flow.' This is incorrect." 2107/56: "The character 血, 'blood,' is a repetition of the previous character 血. *Tai su* ch. 24, 天忌, has 絡有留止, 'the network [vessels] have resident and stagnating [blood and qi].' The character 血, 'blood,' is a mistake for the character 止, 'to stop,' 'to stagnate.'"

16 Zhang Jiebin: "That is, one replenishes a repletion."

17 83/6: "真氣 is 正氣, 'regular qi.'"

As a result, excess evil rises."[18]

[Huang] Di:
"The stars and the eight cardinal [turning points], what is they examined through them?"[19]

26-165-6
Qi Bo:
"As for the stars,
it is with them that one determines the movement of sun and moon.[20]
As for the eight cardinal [turning points],
it is with them that one examines the depletion evils of the eight winds
as they arrive in due time.[21]
As for the four seasons,
it is with them that one distinguishes the location of the qi of spring, autumn, winter, and summer.

In that one makes adjustments to them in time,

---

18 Zhang Jiebin: "At the time of waning moon, blood and qi are weak. The regular does not overcome the evil. As a result, the evil qi stays in the depth and does not leave. If at this moment one applies the needles, yin and yang [qi] will mingle, true and evil cannot be distinguished and contrary [to one's intentions] excess evil will rise."

19 *Ling shu* 73 has: 上視天光，下司八正, "above inspect the celestial lights, below examine the eight regular [cardinal points]."

20 Wang Bing: "制 is 制度, 'rules,' 'system.' When one determines [the positions of] the stars, one can know the system behind the movement of sun and moon." Zhang Jiebin: "制 is 節制, 'to control.' One examines cold and heat by observing the color of the sun; one examines abundance and weakness by observing the light of the moon. One examines the alternation of abundance and depletion of sun and moon by observing the constellations. Hence [the text] states: 'As for the stars, it is with them that one determines the movement of sun and moon.'"

21 Wang Bing: "八正 is to say: 八節之正氣, 'the regular qi of the eight seasonal junctures.' The 'eight winds' include the 'infantile wind' of the East, the 'great weakness wind' of the South, the 'hardness wind' of the West, the 'great hardness wind' of the North, the 'bad omen wind' of the North-East, the 'weakness wind' of the South-East, the 'plotting wind' of the South-West, the 'breaking wind' of the North-West. 'Depletion evil' is to say: [an evil] taking advantage of a depletion in man and causing disease. 'To arrive in time' is to say: heaven corresponds to the movement of Tai-yi through his residences in that prior to and following the eight seasonal junctures the [respective] winds appear at the central palace." Zhang Jiebin: "The 八正 are the regular locations of the eight [cardinal] points. When the qi of the eight [cardinal] points arrives in time, one speaks of the 'eight winds.'"

{the depletion evils of the eight cardinal [turning points]}
one avoids them and thus does not offend them. [22]

When a depletion of the body
meets with a depletion of heaven,
the two depletions affect each other.
The respective [evil] qi reaches the bones.
When it enters, then it harms the five depots.
When a practitioner observes this [early] and stops it,[23]
it cannot harm.

Hence it is said:
'The prohibitions of heaven must be known.' "[24]

26-166-4
[Huang] Di:
"Good!
[How one takes] the stars as laws,
that I have heard by now.
I should like to hear [now how] 'to take the past as law.' "

Qi Bo:
"For 'to take the past as law,'

---

22 *Ling shu* 73 has: 無犯其邪. Wang Bing: "As for 'the location of the qi of the four seasons,' this is to say: In spring, the qi is in the conduit vessels. In summer, the qi is in the tertiary network [vessels]. In autumn, the qi is in the skin. In winter the qi is in the bones and in their marrow. Now, when one is affected by a depletion evil, this will excite and harm the true qi. If one [can] avoid an invasion [by this depletion evil], one will not become ill. The *Ling shu jing* states: The sages avoided the evil in the same way as they avoided arrows and stones. The reason is that [the evil] can harm the true qi." Wu Kun: "所在 [means the following]. During the first and second month, the qi of man is in the liver. During the third and fourth month, the qi of man is in the spleen. During the fifth and sixth month, the qi of man is in the head. During the seventh and eighth month, the qi of man is in the lung. During the ninth and tenth month, the qi of man is in the heart. During the eleventh and twelfth month, the qi of man is in the kidneys." The original passage may have had the wording 以時調之而避之勿犯 也. The character 也 of 調之也 may be a later addition inserted after what we identify as a later commentary had been added.

23 Wang Bing: "救 is 止, 'to bring to a halt.' "

24 *Ling shu* 73 has: 故曰必知天忌. Wang Bing: "Man observes prohibitions in view of heaven. Hence [the text] speaks of prohibitions of heaven. To oppose them results in disease. Hence one must know them."

one [should] first know the *Needle Classic*.[25]

'To apply it effectively today,'
one [should] first know of the cold and warmth of the sun and
of the empty and abounding state of the [disk of the] moon,
to examine whether the qi is at the surface or in the depth and
to adjust the body to these [conditions].
One will observe an immediate effect confirming these [laws].[26]

As for the 'observe its obscure [aspects],'
this is to say:
the qi of the physical appearance, the camp, and the guard [qi],
they have no physical appearance at the outside,
and only the practitioners know of them.[27]

26-166-8
The cold and warmth of the sun,
the empty and abounding state of [the disk of] the moon and
the presence of the qi at the surface or in the depth [in the course] of the four
seasons,
one brings everything together and assesses it.
The practitioner regularly sees this beforehand,
but it has no manifestation visible on the outside [of the body].
Hence [the text] states 'observing what is obscure.'

---

25 1073/31: "Huang-fu Mi 皇甫謐 (the author of the *Jia yi jing* of ca. A.D. 259)
called the *Ling shu* the 'Needle Classic.' *Ling shu* 1 has the phrase 先立針經. From
this can be seen that the *Ling shu* is older than the *Su wen*."

26 Wang Bing: "If in examining the qi one does not commit a mistake, there will
be immediate confirmation/an immediate effect." Zhang Zhicong: "If one observes
depletion and fullness of sun and moon in heaven and movement or calmness of the
channels and waters on the earth, to examine whether the qi is near the surface or in
the depth and whether the blood has congealed or flows gently, this is the so-called
'[In piercing one should take] heaven as law and the earth as rule to regulate the [qi
of the] body.'"

27 Wang Bing: "This is [a commentary] to elucidate the [passage of the] preceding
treatise (i.e., *Su wen* 25): 'The sentiments are calm and [one] concentrates on [one's]
duties. [This way] one observes the changes as they happen. This is what is called '[ob-
serving] the obscure. No one knows their physical appearance.' Even though the qi of
the physical appearance, the camp, and the guard [qi] do not have a physical appearance [themselves] that could become visible outside [of the body], the practitioner,
with the spirit brilliance of his heart, will reach an understanding; he alone knows
about their weakness or abundance."

As for 'penetrate the limitless,'
[this is to say:]
one can transmit [this knowledge] to later generations.[28]

It is therefore in this [respect] that the practitioners differ.[29]
But since it does not have a physical appearance visible at the outside,
not everybody can see it.[30]
One [tries to] observe it but it has no physical appearance;
one [tries to] taste it but it has no flavor.
Hence, it is called obscure; [it] is 'as fuzzy as the spirit.'[31]

As for the 'depletion evil,'
this is the depletion evil qi of the eight cardinal [turning points].[32]
As for the 'evil of the [eight] cardinal [turning points],'[33]
[this is to say:]
when the body is exerted and sweat flows and
when the interstice structures are open and
meet with depletion wind, then
the [latter] 'strikes man in a very subtle manner.'[34]

---

28 Wang Bing: "They stick to the written texts. Hence they can transmit [their knowledge] to later generations. Later generations will not interrupt [this tradition]. Hence it can exert its functions endlessly (lit.: penetrating through the limitless)."

29 Wang Bing: "Because it is they alone who see and know, the practitioners are different from [ordinary] people."

30 Wang Bing: "The [skilled] practitioner is different from the uneducated because all the uneducated cannot see it."

31 Gao Jiwu/219: "The *Shuo wen* has 仿佛 instead of 髣髴; it is also written as 方物, or 放物, 'to resemble an item.' Just as Zhang Jiebin stated: 'On the borderline of non-existence and existence.'" Tanba: "When the *Shuo wen* has 仿佛, this is to say: 仿 means 'to resemble;' 佛 means 'to behold but not to recognize.'" *NJCD*: "Not to recognize clearly." Zhang Yizhi et al.: "仿佛 is: to see things not clearly."

32 Wang Bing: "八正之虛邪 is to say: the depletion evil of the eight seasonal junctures. Because it comes from a depleted region, it follows the depletion [in man], enters there and causes illness. Hence it is called 'depletion evil of the eight cardinal [turning points].'" Yang Shangshan: "As for 'depletion evil,' this is wind coming from a region with depletion. Hence it is called 'depletion evil.'"

33 *Su wen* 80 has 八正邪, "the evil [qi] of the eight cardinal turning points."

34 *Ling shu* 4 and 73 has: 正邪之中人也微, "When the regular evil strikes man, this is subtle."

Hence, 'no one knows its nature;'
'no one sees its physical appearance.' [35]

26-167-4
'The superior practitioner stops its sprouts'
[is to say:]
he will certainly perceive first the qi at the nine indicators in the three sections
and
he comprehensively regulates what is not ruined and stops it.
Hence, he is called 'superior practitioner.'

'The inferior practitioner stops what has already fully developed'
[is to say:]
he [attempts to] rescue what is already ruined. [36]

'Stops what has already fully developed'
is to say:
he does not know that there are discrepancies among the nine indicators in the
three sections.
Hence, diseases [emerge] and ruin the [patient's physical appearance]. [37]

'To know where [the disease] is' is
to know how to diagnose, at the nine indicators in the three sections, the locations of the vessels having a disease and to treat them.
Hence, this is called 'to guard the doors.' [38]

---

35 Wang Bing: "Evil of the [eight] cardinal [turning points] does not come from
a depleted region. Because it hits man in a subtle way, no one knows its nature and
no one can see its physical appearance." Zhang Jiebin: " 'Regular evils' are the regular
winds of the eight points. ... Even though they are regular winds, they nevertheless may
harm man. Hence they are called 'regular evils.' They are also called 'depletion winds.'
They hit man in a subtle way, not as severely as a depletion evil or robber wind. Hence
no one knows its nature and man cannot perceive it."

36 *Ling shu* 73 has: 下工守其已成, 因敗其形, 'the inferior practitioner guards that
which has already formed, thereby ruining the [patient's] physical appearance."

37 Wang Bing: "The meaning of this [statement] will be outlined in full detail in *Su
wen* 27."

38 *Ling shu* 73 has: 是故工之用針也, 知氣之所在, 而守其門戶, "When, therefore,
the [superior] practitioner employs the needle, he knows where the qi is and guards
its door."

One does not know the nature [of this process],
but sees the physical appearance of the evil."[39]

26-167-8
[Huang] Di:
"I have heard of supplementation and draining,
but I have not yet grasped [their] meaning."

Qi Bo:
" 'For draining, one must employ the *fang* (方),'[40]
[this is to say:]
fang [is]
when the qi is just (*fang*) abounding,
when the month is just (*fang*) full,
when the sun is just (*fang*) warm,
when the body is just (*fang*) in peace,[41]
when the breathing is just (*fang*) [in a state of] inhaling,
then one inserts the needle.
Then one waits until it is just (*fang*) [in a state of] inhaling [again] and twists
the needle.
Then one waits again until it is just (*fang*) [in a state of] exhaling and slowly
pulls the needle [out].

---

39 In contrast, Wang Bing reads 知其所在者 to 而見邪形也 as one long sentence:
"The nine indicators in the three sections are the door for examining the [presence
of] evil. One 'guards the door,' and hence one sees an evil physical appearance. Since
it strikes man in a subtle manner, no one knows its nature and shape." Zhang Jiebin:
" 'To know where they are' is to know the place of the vessel having a disease. The nine
indicators in the three sections are the locations where the vessels having a disease
leave and enter. Hence they are called 'doors.' As for those whose [nature] is unknown
while their physical appearance can be seen, their physical appearance can be per-
veived here and hence their nature can be examined." Zhang Zhicong: "The superior
practitioner knows how to diagnose, at the nine indicators in the three sections, the
vessels having a disease. Hence he knows where they are and he treats them at the
location of the vessels having the disease. Hence when [the text] speaks of 'guarding
the doors,' this is to say: if one guards the true qi, the evil [qi] will leave by itself."

40 Yang Shangshan: "方 is 正, 'upright', 'proper.' " Wang Bing agrees. Cheng Shide
et al.: "方 refers here to 法則, 'rule,' 規律, 'law.' The meaning is: one must grasp the
rules." *Ling shu* 73 has 泄必用員, i.e., the opposite association of supplementation
and drainage with 方 and 員 respectively.

41 *SWJZ*: "定 is 安, 'peace.' "

Hence it is said:
For draining one must use *fang* (i.e., 'just [the right moment]).'
The [proper] qi will move there.[42]

26-167-12
'For supplementation one must employ the *yuan* (員).'[43]
[this is to say:]
Yuan is *xing* (行), 'to move;'
Xing is *yi* (移), 'to change location.'[44]

The piercing must hit the camp [qi].[45]
During inhalation one repeatedly pushes the needle [into the skin].[46]

Hence,
yuan and *fang* do not refer to the [shape of the] needles.

The fact is,
for nourishing the spirit,
one must know whether the physical appearance is fat or lean and
whether the camp and the guard [qi], the blood and the qi, abound or are weak.
Blood and qi, [they are] the spirit of man;
it is essential to nourish them carefully."[47]

26-168-2
[Huang] Di:
"A mysterious discourse, indeed!
When matching the physical appearance of man with yin and yang and the

---

42 Wang Bing: "When evil qi was drained to leave, true qi will move [again]."

43 916/54: "員 is identical with 圓, 'circular.' *Meng zi*, Bk.IV, states: 規矩方員之至
也, '[by the use of] circle and square [one arrives at] perfect rectangular and circular
[structures].'" (Meng zi IV, 1, 2 - cf. Legge vol.II, 292; see also IV,1, 1; IV, 1, 5.) *Ling
shu* 73 has 補必用方.

44 Wang Bing: "行 is to say: to transmit the qi which does not move."

45 Wang Bing: "When the needle enters the blood, this is called 中榮, 'to hit the
camp [qi].'"

46 Zhang Zhicong: "排 is 推, 'to push.'"

47 Wang Bing: "When the spirit is in peace, then one's life is extended over long
periods. When the spirit has left, then the physical appearance deteriorates. Hence
there is no way but to nourish [the spirit] carefully." 1055/45: "The 'spirit' here refers
to the blood and qi of man."

four seasons, when it comes
to their correspondences with depletion and repletion, and
to the prediction of what is obscure,
who except you, Sir, could penetrate this?

Now, Sir,
you have spoken several times of the physical appearance and of the spirit.
What does that mean: 'physical appearance;'
what does that mean: 'spirit'?
I should like to hear this comprehensively."

Qi Bo:
"Please, let me speak about the physical appearance.

The physical appearance, ah!, the physical appearance!
For the eyes it is obscure.[48]
One inquires about the location of the disease.[49]
One searches for it in the conduits.
It lies clearly perceivable in front of one,[50]
by pressing [though] one does not obtain a hold of it.
One does not recognize its nature.
Hence one speaks of 'physical appearance.' "

26-168-7
[Huang] Di:
"What does 'spirit' mean?"

Qi Bo:
"Please, let me speak about the spirit.

The spirit, ah!, the spirit!
The ears do not hear [it].

When the [physician's] eyes are clear, his heart is open and his mind goes
ahead,

---

48 For a discussion of the occurrence of the "A 乎 A" pattern in ancient Chinese literature, see 752/42.

49 Lin Yi et al.: "The *Jia yi jing* has 捫其所痛, 'one feels with the hand where it has
pain.' The meaning is the same."

50 Yu Yue: "慧然在前 was originally 卒然在前, 'suddenly in front of one.' "

he alone apprehends [it as if it were] clearly perceivable.[51]
But the mouth cannot speak [of it].[52]
Everyone looks out, [but] he alone sees [it].[53]
If one approaches it, it seems to be obscure,
[but to him] alone it is obvious [as if it were] clearly displayed.[54]
As if the wind had blown away the clouds.
Hence one speaks of a 'spirit.' "

<The nine indicators in the three sections:
treat them as the origin.
The discourse on the nine needles:
it it is not necessary to keep it.>[55]

---

51 Wang Bing: " 'The ears do not hear' is to say: the activities of the spirit are subtle and undisclosed. 'The eyes are clear, the heart is open and the mind is the first' is to say: the penetration [of things] by the heart is comparable to the unveiling of the hidden. The vision of the eyes is comparable to the opening of a thick screen."

52 Zhang Jiebin: "The miraculous cannot be transmitted through words."

53 80/447: "This is to say, when several persons behold one and the same object, it may well be that the result of their inspection differs."

54 Zhang Zhicong: "適 is 至, 'to arrive.' This is to say, when the qi arrives unclear, I am the only one who clearly perceives it." 1869/6: "This makes clear: this emergence of a new idea, of new images carries an accidental character. When a person is in the process of thinking, he is situated in a state of extreme clarity and lucidity. It is as if his ears did not hear anything, as if he were separated from everything in his environment and he achieves a state beyond ordinary thinking where he 'alone sees,' he 'alone reaches understanding,' he is 'alone in his perception.' "

55 Zhang Jiebin: "If one regards the nine indicators in the three sections as origins, then one can reach a spirit[-like] understanding. The discourse on the nine needles focusses on the physical substratum. Hence, if one has grasped the spirit, why should one rely on the [physical] substratum?"

Chapter 27
Discourse on the Division and Union of True [Qi] and Evil [Qi][1]

27-169-2
Huang Di asked:
"I have heard of [the art of] the nine needles [outlined in] nine chapters.[2]
You, Sir, have subsequently multiplied them by nine.[3]
Nine times nine is 81 chapters.
I have understood their meaning entirely.

The classic says:
[In case of] qi abundance and weakness,
[in case of] a shift towards imbalance left and right,
regulate the below with the above,
regulate the right with the left.

[In case] there are surplus and insufficiency,
supplement and drain at the brooks and transporters.[4]
This I have come to know.

All these shifts towards imbalance of the camp and guard [qi]
are generated by depletion and repletion,

---

1 See 451/39 for a discussion of the wording of this title. 478/33 and 541/1: "Lin Yi et al.: Originally there existed two chapters: 經合論 and 真邪論, with identical contents. Wang Bing eliminated the chapter 經合論 and established the new title 離合真邪論 [for the second]." Ma Shi: "[This chapter] discusses how the conduit (經) vessels conform (合) with the zodiacal constellations and the rivers, and it also deals with the meaning of true (真) qi and evil (邪) qi. Hence the title of this chapter." Wu Kun: "真 stands for 正氣, 'proper qi.' 邪 stands for 外邪, 'external evil.' When external evil enters [the body] and unites with the proper qi, this is called 合. To pierce such a [situation] and eliminate the evil, this is called 離." *NJCD* agrees.

2 For a discussion of the various meanings of the phrase "nine needles" in the *Nei jing*, see 802/10. The author interprets "nine needles" in the present context as the title of a scripture on acupuncture.

3 因而 is read here as 因之而, i.e. 根據九針九篇而 ..

4 The *Tai su* has 滎, 'brooks,' instead of 榮. We follow the *Tai su* and the 1983 edition by Ren min wei sheng chu ban she. Wu Kun: "All the twelve conduits have 滎, 'brooks,' and 輸, 'transporters.' Where they flow, these are the 滎; where they rush, these are the 輸."

not because an evil qi has entered the conduits from the outside.[5]

I should like to hear [the following]:
when evil qi is present in the conduits,
how does it cause diseases to a person,[6] and
how can it be seized?"

Qi Bo responded:
"Now,
the degrees and numbers introduced by the sages,
they definitely corresponded to heaven and earth.[7]
Hence,
heaven has the [lunar] lodges and the [365] degrees;
the earth has the main waters.
man has the [main] conduit vessels.[8]

27-169-8
When heaven and earth are warm and harmonious,
then the main waters are quiet and calm.
When heaven is cold and the earth is frozen,
then the main waters congeal so that [their flow] is impeded.[9]
When heaven has summerheat and the earth is hot,
then the main waters [gush forth as if] boiling and overflow.
When a sudden wind rises violently,
then the main waters gush up in breakers and rise [like] ridges [in the fields].[10]

---

5 Zhang Jiebin: "營衛傾移 is to say: in case of a unilaterial dominance of yin or yang, depletion and repletion emerge internally and cause disease. That is, there is no evil qi in the conduits."

6 病 is used here as a verb.

7 Compare with *Ling shu* 78: 聖人之起天地之數也.

8 Wang Bing: "宿 is to say: the 28 zodiacal constellations. 度 is to say: the 365 degrees of heaven. As for 經水, this is to say: the seas, the large rivers, the Wei [river], the lakes, the Mian [river], the Ru [river], the Yangzi [river], the Huai [river], the Lo [river], the [Huang-]he [river], the Zhang [river], and the Ji [river]. Because they correspond to the main conduit vessels in [the body], one calls them 經水, 'main waters.'"

9 Wang Bing: "泣 is to say: 血行不行, 'the blood flow does not flow.'" Zhang Jiebin agrees. Ma Shi: "泣 is read 澀, 'rough.'" Yu Yue and 2588/23: "The character 泣 should be the character 冱, 'to freeze,' 'to congeal.'" For detailed discussions of this argument, see there.

10 This metaphor refers to the common sight in agricultural regions where certain fields have alternating lines of mounds and drains, appearing like motionless waves

Now,
when evil enters the vessels,
if it is cold, then the blood congeals so that [its flow] is impeded.
If it is summerheat, then the qi is saturated with moisture.[11]
When subsequently a depletion evil enters [the vessels] and settles [there],
then this, too, is similar to when the main waters are affected by wind: [12]
The arrival of the vessel movement in the conduits,
at times it, too, rises [like] the ridges [in the fields].[13]
Its passage in the vessels is continuous.[14]

When it arrives at the inch opening and strikes the hand, at times it is big, at
times it is small.
{When it is big, then evil arrives;
when it is small, then it is balanced.}
Its passage has no permanent location.[15]
It is in the yin and in the yang [sections];
one cannot quantify its [advancement].[16]

---

and troughs. Cheng Shide et al.: "隴 is identical with 隆, 'eminent,' 'to exalt.'" 862/34:
"象波浪一樣涌起, 'to rush and rise like breakers.' 象畦壟一樣突起, 'to rise like the
ridges in the fields.'" Wang Bing: "When [wind] enters the conduit vessels, they react
in the same way."

11 Wang Bing (commenting on this phrase in *Su wen* 57): "淖 is 濕, 'moisture.' 澤 is
潤液, 'a moistening liquid.' This is to say: slightly moist."

12 Gao Jiwu/631: "Following the 因, a 之 is missing."

13 1193/8: "Guo Aichun of Tianjin reads 經之動脈 as 經脈之動, 'the movement
in/of the conduit vessels.'"

14 Wang Bing: "循循然 is 順動貌, 'to move along accordingly.' That is to say, it goes
along with the movement and resting of the conduit vessels; it follows the coming and
going of exhalation and inhalation." Zhang Zhicong: "循循 is 次序貌, 'in succession.'
That is, when the evil is in the conduits, even though at times it swells up, it nevertheless follows in its movement the sequence [of the conduits]. It has no permanent
location."

15 Wang Bing: "大 is to say: 大常平, 'bigger [than the] regular balanced [move-
ment].' To diagnose a 'small' [movement] is not to say a 'fine and small' [movement].
It is called 'small' in comparison with the 'big' [movement]. Now, as for the evil qi,
when it follows the [patient's] yin qi, then it enters the yin conduits; when it follows
the [patient's] yang qi, then it enters the yang vessels. Hence 'its passage has no permanent location.'"

16 Wang Bing: "Because it follows the flow moving through the conduit vessels."

27-170-2
Hence, one searches for the [evil]
at the nine indicators in the three sections and
if all of a sudden one encounters it,
one early blocks its road.[17]

[When the patient] inhales, insert the needle;[18]
do not let the [proper] qi revolt.[19]
[Hold the needle] calmly and let it remain [inserted] for a long time;
do not let the evil [qi] spread.
[When the patient] inhales, twist the needle
to get a hold of the qi.
Wait until [the patient] exhales to pull the needle [out].
When the exhalation is completed, [the needle] is removed.
Large [quantities of] qi leave.
Hence, this is called 'draining.'"[20]

27-170-5
[Huang] Di:
"What is insufficient is to be supplemented.
How?"

---

17 Wang Bing: "逢 is to say 逢遇, 'to meet.' 遏 is to say 遏絕, 'to interrupt.'" Zhang Jiebin: "遇 is 制, 'to check,' 'to control.'"

18 For a detailed discussion of the technique of relating insertion and withdrawel of the needle to inhalation and exhalation, see 1289/15 and 524/8.

19 Gao Jiwu/20: "The needle is inserted at the moment the patient inhales; one should not let the needle meet with a countermovement of the qi exhaled and inhaled."

20 Wang Bing: "The message of the classic is to supplement the true qi first and to drain the evil [qi] afterwards. Why? .. One must supplement first because the true qi is insufficient. If one were to drain it by means of the needle, then the conduit vessels would not be full and there would be nothing by which the evil qi could be flushed away/drained. Hence the true qi is supplemented first with the aim of generating a sufficient quantity of it. Then one drains to eliminate/flush away the evil [qi]. 引 is to say: 引出, 'to pull out.' 去 is to say: 離穴, 'to leave the hole.' One waits for [the patient to] exhale and pulls the needle to the door. When the exhalation is completed, then one leaves the hole opening. As a result, the [true] qi in the conduits will be given a balanced status, while there is nothing to detain the evil. Hence the grand evil qi follows the needle and leaves [the body]. 呼 is to say: the qi leaves; 吸 is to say: the qi enters; 'grand qi' is to say: the qi of a grand/significant evil qi, [i.e.] yin and yang [qi] being mixed up."

Qi Bo:

"It is essential to

first feel [the vessel] and move [the finger] along it;

[then] to squeeze it and disperse its [contents];

[then] to push and press it;

[then] to flip [a finger] against [it] and provoke it;

[then] to pull [the skin] up and lower the [needle into it].

[This way, one] comprehensively takes the [qi for supplementation].[21]

From the outside, pull the door[22]

to shut in its spirit.[23]

When an exhalation is completed, insert the needle.

[Hold the needle] calmly and let it remain [inserted] for long

to have the qi arrive.

As if one were waiting for someone of noble rank;

---

21 Wang Bing: "捫循 is to say: to feel with the hand. 切 is to say: to squeeze with the finger. To 'feel with one's fingers and follow it,' [is appropriate] if one intends to relax the qi. To 'squeeze and disperse it' causes [the qi] to pass through and disperse in the conduit vessels. To 'push and press it,' is to push and squeeze the [patient's] skin. To 'flip against and provoke it' lets the qi fill the vessel to distention. To 'pull [up the skin] and lower the [needle]' is to place the needle into the exact position. 'Comprehensively take it' refers to the usual way [of piercing]. To 'pull its door from the outside and to shut in its spirit' is to push and press it. That is to say, one presses the skin outside of the hole, exactly at the location to be pierced. When the piercing is completed, [the needle] is removed and the skin is not harmed. The reason is, when the door that is to be pierced is not opened, then the spirit qi is kept inside. Hence [the text] states: 'to shut in his spirit.'" Ma Shi: "Before one applies the needle, one 'must first feel and follow it' is to say: with one's finger one feels the hole [selected for piercing] and causes the qi to relax. 彈而怒之 is: one repeatedly presses it and causes an angry feeling in the patient, which [in turn] causes the qi to fill the vessels to distention. 抓而下之 is to say: with the nail of one's left hand one digs right into the hole [selected for piercing] and with the right hand one lowers the needle." Zhang Zhicong: "彈而怒之 is: once again one presses the hole with one's finger and the intention is to give the [patient's] mind something to concentrate on. As a result the qi will move there, causing the network vessels to be filled to distention, as if they had risen in anger."

22 Zhang Jiebin: "穴門也, 'this is the [piercing-]hole gate.'"

23 Ma Shi: "When the needle is inserted for the first time, it must penetrate [to the vessels] and seize the [qi]. That is, .. one waits until the qi has arrived and then pulls the needle towards outside up to the hole-gate. Then one pushes [the hole with one finger] and closes it, to keep the spirit qi shut in."

one does not know whether [he will come during] daytime or in the evening.²⁴
When the qi has arrived,²⁵
this is exactly the moment for which one has to be on the alert.²⁶

Wait for an inhalation and pull the needle.
The qi must not leave.
At each place [where a needle was inserted],
push [the hole] and close the door and
thereby let the spirit qi be preserved.
Large [quantities of] qi stay where they are.
Hence this is called 'supplementation.'"

27-171-3
[Huang] Di:
"To examine the qi, how is this done?"²⁷

Qi Bo:
"Now,
when the evil leaves the network [vessels],
it enters the conduits and
it lodges in the blood vessels.
Cold and warmth do not yet agree with each other.
[The evil] will rise like breakers gushing up.
At times it comes; at times it leaves.
Hence, it has no regular presence [anywhere].²⁸

---

24 Wang Bing: "暮 is 晚, 'evening.'"

25 The 以 stands for 已, "already."

26 The *Tai su* has 適人自護. Wang Bing: "適 is 調適, 'to harmonize.' 護 is 慎守, 'to guard carefully.' That is to say, when the qi is brought back into balance, one must guard it carefully and not let it undergo any changes which would mean that the disease emerges again. The *Needle Classic* states: 'When the conduit qi has arrived, guard it carefully, lest it is lost.' That is the meaning expressed here. As for 'to guard carefully,' that is outlined in the text below."

27 Wang Bing: "That is to say: to search for the qi that can be seized." Zhang Jiebin: "This is to search for the evil qi, not [to wait] for the arrival of the qi at the needle."

28 Wang Bing: "Because it circulates in the conduit vessel section of a length of 162 feet, it cannot remain forever at the location observed." Zhang Zhicong: "When cold and warm do still wish to find each other, then the true [qi] and the evil [qi] have not yet formed a union. Hence the evil qi swells up like breakers. It comes and goes in the conduit vessels and has no regular location."

Hence it is said:[29]
'Right at the moment it comes, it is essential to press [the vessel] and stop the [evil].
When it has been stopped, seize it.
Do not drain it by encountering its advancement.'[30]

27-172-1
{The true qi, this is the conduit qi.}[31]
The conduit qi is greatly depleted.

Hence [when] it is said
'it comes and cannot be met,'
[then] this means just the same.[32]

Hence, it is said:
'One examines the evil but [its status] cannot be recognized.
Large [quantities of] qi have passed by already.'[33]
If one were to drain in this [situation], then true qi would be lost.

---

29 Beginning here, almost all passages in this reply by Qi Bo marked '....' were quoted from a text also recorded in *Ling shu* 1.

30 In contrast, Wang Bing: "衝 is to say: balanced qi corresponding to the numbers of the clepsydra. The *Ling shu jing* states: When the water moves down one mark in the clepsydra, the qi of man is in the major yang. When the water has moved down two marks, the qi of man is in the minor yang. When the water has moved down three marks, the qi of man is in the yang brilliance. When the water has moved down four marks, the qi of man is in the yin section. Now, when the qi is in the major yang [section] then only the major yang [section] abounds with qi. When it is in the minor yang [section] then only the minor yang [section] abounds with qi. That is, if one observes that [a section] alone abounds [with qi] and if, therefore, one says 'evil has come' and pierces it to drain it, then, contrary [to one's intentions], one harms the true qi. Hence the subsequent statement." The *Jia yi jing* has 迎, 'to meet,' instead of 逢.

31 2744/419: "Obviously, 'true qi' is a general term used to designate the qi in the body." For a detailed discussion of the meaning of 'true qi' in the *Nei jing*, see also 83/6.

32 *Ling shu* 1 has 清靜而微, 其來不可逢, 其往不可追, "it is clear, calm, and feeble. When it comes, it cannot be met; when it departs, it cannot be pursued." A later commentary in *Ling shu* 3 reinterprets this metaphor and has 其來不可逢者, 氣盛不可補也, "as for 'it comes and cannot be met,' [that is to say:] the qi abounds and cannot be [further] supplemented."

33 Wu Kun: "大氣 is 人氣, 'the qi of man.'" Zhang Zhicong: "大氣 is the qi of the wind evil."

Once it is lost, it does not return.
The evil qi arrives again and the disease [qi] collects increasingly.

Hence, [when] it is said:
'it departs and cannot be pursued,'
[then] this means just the same.[34]

27-172-4
As for 'they cannot even tie it to a hair,'
[that is:] wait for the moment when the evil arrives and
deploy the needle to drain.[35]

'If [draining is performed] before or after' [the right moment],
blood and qi are exhausted, and
the disease cannot be brought down.[36]

---

34 Wang Bing: "It has departed already following the flow in the conduit vessels. Hence it cannot be pursued and is asked to return." *Ling shu* 3 has 其往不可追者, 氣虛不可瀉也, "as for 'when it departs it cannot be pursued,' [that is to say:] the qi is depleted and cannot be drained."

35 Yu Yue: "The six characters 不可挂以髮者 are a later insertion. 瀉 is an error for 焉. The original wording was 待邪之至時而發針焉, 'wait until the arrival of the evil [qi] and withdraw the needle from it.' The six characters were moved here erroneously from below; a meaning of this passage is not recognizable." Shen Zumian: "Yu Yue was wrong when he commented that these six characters are an erroneous insertion. Their meaning is: when inserting the needle, one must not make the slightest mistake. The presence of the two characters 故曰 makes it quite obvious, that these 6 characters are not an erroneous insertion. Also, 瀉 is not an error for 焉." Wu Kun "It appears that there is an omission of text that should precede these explanations." *Ling shu* 1 has 知機之道者, 不可掛以髮, 不知機道, 叩之不發, "Those who know the Way of the trigger, they cannot even tie a hair to it [without releasing it]. Those who do not know the Way of the trigger, they could not release it even if they knocked against it." As an alternative reading, the character 不 in the present wording 不可掛 may be identified as an erroneous later insertion. In this case, the original phrase would have meant "Those who know the Way of the trigger, they can [release it even by means of] a hair tied to it." The commentary in *Ling shu* 3 takes up the erroneous wording and has 不可掛以髮者, 言氣易失也, "as for 'it cannot be pulled by a hair,' that is to say: the qi is easily lost." The passage in the present version of the *Su wen* starts from this wording too. *Ling shu* 3 has: " 'When it departs it cannot be pursued' [is:] the qi is depleted and cannot be drained. 'It cannot be pulled with a hair' is to say: the qi is lost easily."

36 Wang Bing: "That is to say, if one takes it away when it cannot be taken away, one has missed the [right] time." Lin Yi et al.: "The Quan Yuanqi edition has 血氣已虛,

Hence it is said:
'To know [how] it can be seized,
is like releasing a trigger.
Not to know [how] it can be seized,
is like ramming a pestle.'[37]

Hence, [when] it is said:
'those who know the Way of the trigger,
they cannot even tie it to a hair;[38]
those who do not know the trigger,
they may ram it and it will not be released,'
[then] this means just the same."[39]

27-172-8
[Huang] Di:
"Supplementation and draining, how are they carried out?"

Qi Bo:
"This is [done by] attacking the evil.
Quickly remove [the needle][40] to remove abundant blood and
to have the [patient's] true qi return.[41]

'when blood and qi are already depleted.' The character 盡, 'exhausted,' should be the character 虛, 'depleted.' "

37 Zhang Jiebin: "機 is 弩機, 'the trigger mechanism of a cross-bow.' 椎 is 木椎, 'wooden pestle.' "

38 Chinese commentaries interpret this passage in the sense that one must not hesitate and should deploy the needle immediately once one notices the arrival of the evil qi.

39 Wang Bing: "機 is the subtle [mechanism] of a movement."

40 Gao Jiwu/477: "Following the character 出 a character 針 was omitted." Zhang Zhicong: "疾出其針, 'quickly remove the needle.' "

41 Wang Bing: "Observe where the blood is and take it." Zhang Jiebin: "That is, when one has been struck by evil, one must attack the evil. However, the treatment should be early and one must quickly have the evil leave, thereby removing [overly] abundant blood. As a result, the true qi will return by itself. This way, in the draining there is also supplementation."

This is, when an evil has just arrived as a visitor,

it [floats around] *rong-rong* [42] not occupying a definite location yet.

If one pushes it, then it will move forward;

if one pulls it, then it will stop.

Move [the needle] against [its flow] and pierce it.[43]

{This is warm blood.}

Pierce to let the [patient's] blood and

his disease comes to an end immediately."[44]

27-172-11

[Huang] Di:

"Good!

Now,

when true and evil [qi] have united,

and [yet the qi] does not rise [resembling] breakers [in the sea], or ridges [in the fields],

how is this to be examined?"

Qi Bo:

"Investigate abundance and depletion by feeling [the vessels at] all the nine

42 915/58: "溶溶 refers to the flow of water." The *Tai su* does not have the two characters 溶溶."

43 631/61: "逆 has the meaning here of 迎着, 'to move towards.' Everyone is familiar with the meaning 'counter,' 'to oppose' of 逆, but most people do not know that is also means 迎, 'to meet.' In fact, this is its basic meaning. The *Shuo wen* states: '逆 is 迎.'"

44 Wang Bing: "That is to say: The evil visitor has just arrived and has not found a permanent location yet. When pushing the needle to supplement [qi] at this moment, then [the visitor] is supplemented [too] and will move forward. If one pulls the needle to make it arrive, then it will follow this pulling and remain stopped [at one place]. If one does not cause the abounding blood to leave [the body] and, on the contrary, warms it, then the evil qi will dominate internally and, contrary [to one's intentions], the harm will be aggravated. Hence the subsequent statement of the text." Zhang Jiebin: "When evil [qi] has just intruded into a person, it is near the surface in the network [vessels] and has not settled at a definite location yet. If one pushes it, one can move it forward; if one pulls it, one can bring it to a halt. That is to say, it is very easy to seize it. Whenever one selects the network [vessels], one must take their blood. The evil [qi] leaves from the warm blood. [When the blood is let,] the evil must follow it and disappears. Hence the disease comes to an end immediately. 溫血 is 熱血, 'heats the blood.'" Wu Kun: "溫血 is 毒血, 'poisonous blood.'" Gao Shishi: "溫 is identical with 調, 'to regulate.'" Guo Aichun-81: "溫 is a mistake for 寫, 'to drain.'" Li Guoqing agrees. 2764/22: "The character 溫 should be read as 鬱, in the sense of 鬱積, 'thick and concentrated.'" For details, see there. Mori: "溫 is identical with 熅 and 蘊 in the sense of 郁血, 'stagnating blood.'"

indicators in the three sections and assess the [situation].⁴⁵
Investigate whether [the patient's] left and right, above and below have lost
mutual [balance] and, if so, which one is diminished in comparison with the
other.
Investigate which depot is affected by the disease, to predict [its future stages].

Those who do not know of the three sections,
they do not distinguish between yin and yang and
they do not separate heaven and earth.⁴⁶

The earth serves to examine the earth;
heaven serves to examine heaven;
man serves to examine man.

Harmonise the [situation in the] central palaces
to stabilize [the status in] the three sections.⁴⁷

Hence it is said:
if one pierces without knowing the nine indicators in the three sections and the
locations of the vessels affected by a disease,
even in the event of significant transgression
the practitioner is unable to stop it.

If one punishes where there is no transgression,
this is called a great error.
If one rebels against the grand norms,
the true [qi] cannot be restored.

If [a practitioner] treats a repletion as if it were a depletion,
if he considers evil [qi] as if it were true [qi] and
if he applies the needles disregarding what is right to do,

---

45 Wang Bing: "Drain what is abounding, supplement what is depleted. In case
there is neither abundance nor depletion, seize [the disease] at the conduits. That is
the pattern."

46 Yu Chang: "These 13 characters are erroneously misplaced here. They should follow the characters 以定三部 further below, preceding the characters 故曰刺不知三
部. Being moved to this place, the meaning of this passage is obscure."

47 Wu Kun: "The 'central storage place' is the stomach." Harper reads *zhong fu* in
a plural sense here as "referring to the internal organs in general." See Harper 1998,
420.

contrary [to his intentions] he will be a plunderer of qi
in that he removes the proper qi of [that] person.

27-173-7
He considers compliance to be opposition,
causing camp and guard [qi] to disperse in disorder.
The true qi has been lost already, while
the evil [qi] alone remains attached internally.
He interrupts the long life of [that] person,
conferring on [that] man the calamity of early death."[48]
{He does not know the three sections and the nine indicators. Hence, he cannot continue for long.}

<Because he does not know how to bring the [three sections and nine indicators] together with the four seasons and the five agents,
he will, as a consequence, contribute to their mutual domination.
He releases the evil to attack the proper, [thereby]
interrupting the long life of [that] person.>

<When the evil has come as a new visitor,
it has no definite location yet.
If one pushes it, it will move forward;
if one pulls it, then it will stop.
If one drains it as soon as one encounters it,
this disease will come to an end at once.>[49]

---

48 The *textus receptus* has 天殃, "calamities sent by heaven." In the present context this makes little sense. In agreement with the wording in *Su wen* 66-368-7, and also with the parallel text found in the *Tai su* and *Jia yi jing*, we read 天殃 as 天殃.

49 Zhang Qi: "These 26 characters are a later insertion." Mori: "When Zhang Qi states that these 26 characters are a later insertion, he is wrong. According to the wording in the *Tai su*, this is a separate paragraph, starting with the seven characters 黃帝問於崎伯曰. There is no repetition."

Chapter 28
Discourse Thoroughly Deliberating upon Depletion and Repletion

28-173-13
Huang Di asked:
"What is that to say: depletion, repletion?"

Qi Bo responded:
"When evil qi abounds,[1] then [this is] repletion.
When the essence qi is lost,[2] then [this is] depletion."[3]

[Huang] Di:
"[States of] depletion and repletion, what are they like?"

Qi Bo:
"A qi depletion is a lung depletion.
When the qi moves contrary [to its regular course], the feet are cold.[4]
When it is not its time, then [the patient] will survive.
When it is its time, then he will die.[5]

---

1 78/43: "盛 is 受, 'to receive,' to be pronounced as *cheng*. (For ancient examples, see there) Hence, the statement 邪氣盛則實 is to indicate 'when the body receives evil qi, repletion results.'"

2 Wang Bing: "奪 is to say: the essence qi decreases, as if it was taken away (奪去)." Zhang Jiebin: "奪 is to say: 失, 'to lose.'" 2107/56: "精 is a mistake for 正, 'regular.'" 668/73 agrees. 1788/44: "奪 has the meaning of 被奪, 'to be taken away.'"

3 Gao Shishi: "Depletion and repletion does not only refer to the depletion and repletion of blood and qi in the conduit vessels. When evil qi abounds in the body of man, then this is repletion; when the essence qi was taken away from the inner depots, then this is depletion."

4 Zhang Jiebin: "The lung rules the qi. Hence in the case of qi depletion, this is a lung depletion." 138/21: "The conduit vessels run in the interior; the network vessels can be seen at the outside. Hence a conduit depletion becomes apparent in the lung; and a network fullness starts in the feet."

5 Ma Shi: "When the lung is depleted and when the season [at the time one has this disease] is not [associated with an agent] overcoming [the agent associated with the depot afflicted], then [the patient] will survive. This is the case in spring, autumn, and winter. When [the disease] falls together with a season [associated with an agent that] overcomes [the agent associated with the afflicted depot], then [the patient] will die. This is, in the present case, the fire of summer." Wu Kun: "'Time' is the time when [the qi of a depot] should flourish. Like, in the summer months, all people have

The same applies to all the other depots."

[Huang] Di:
"What is that to say: 'doubled repletion'?"

Qi Bo:
"As for the so-called 'doubled repletion,'
that is to say: a severe heat disease.
[That is,] the qi is hot and the vessels are filled.
That is called 'doubled repletion.'" [6]

28-174-4
[Huang] Di:
"When all the conduits and the network [vessels] have a repletion, what is that like?
How is that to be treated?"

Qi Bo:
"When all the conduits and the network [vessels] have a repletion,
the vessels at the inch [section] are tense, while the foot-long section is relaxed. [7]

---

their qi depleted. In the winter months, all people have cold feet. Both [summer and winter] are not the seasons when the lung [qi] flourishes. If, however, one has the qi depletion and cold feet during the autumn months, then this is a time when the lung [qi] should flourish. This is an offense against a serious prohibition. Hence [that person] will die."

6 Gao Shishi: " 'Doubled repletion' is a disease of great heat in the human body. The qi abounds and is hot; the vessels abound [in their contents] and are full. When yin and yang, [i.e.,] qi and blood, are both replete, this is to say 'doubled repletion.' " Yao Shaoyu: "Inside and outside are both replete. Hence [the text] states 'doubled repletion.' "

7 Wang Bing: "脈急 is to say: 脈口; 'vessel opening.' " Zhang Jiebin: "This refers to the foot-long and inch [sections] of the vessel opening. It is there that one investigates the depletion or repletion of the conduits and network [vessels]." Ma Shi, Zhang Zhicong agree. Tanba: "Wang Bing states '脈急 is to say: 脈口; vessel opening,' but fails to explain the meaning of 尺緩. All authors consider [the latter] to refer to the vessels in the foot-long section. This is wrong. 尺緩 is to say: the skin of the foot-long section is relaxed. In the present paragraph, the vessel opening is used for examining the conduits, while the skin in the foot-long section is used for examining the network [vessels]. The conduits are yin and they are inside. These are the vessel paths. Hence they are examined at the inch opening. The network [vessels] are yang and they are located near the surface, not in the depth. Hence they are examined by means of the

All these [vessels] must be treated.[8]
{Hence it is said:
When it is smooth, then this is compliance;
when it is rough, then this is opposition.}[9]

Now,
all [instances of] depletion and repletion,
they originate from the grouping of related items.[10]
Hence when the five depots, the bones and the flesh are smooth and easy-
going, [the person concerned] can exist for long."[11]

[condition of the] skin in the foot-long section." Gao Jiwu/716: "The terms 寸 and
尺 do not correspond to 寸關尺, 'inch,' 'gate,' and 'foot' [where the pulse is felt at the
wrists]. Rather, 'inch' refers here to the vessel at the inch-opening, while 'foot' refers to
the condition of the skin in the foot-long section [between wrist and elbow]."

8 Zhang Jiebin: "When the [movement in the] vessels in the inch [section] is
tense, then evil [qi] resides in the conduits. When the [movement in the] vessels in
the foot-long section is relaxed, then heat abounds in the network [vessels]. In this
case, the conduits and the network [vessels] are all replete. They must all be treated.
'To treat' is to say: 'to drain.'"

9 Gao Shishi: "The conduits and network [vessels], internally they penetrate the
blood vessels, externally they penetrate the skin. When the conduits and the network
vessels abound [with contents], then the skin is glossy and moist. When the conduits
and network vessels are poor [in contents], then the skin is rough. Hence [the text]
states: 'When it is smooth, then this is compliance; when it is rough, then this is
opposition.'" *JJZG*: "從 is 順, 'to go along with,' 'to comply.'" Tanba: "The 31 characters from 故曰滑 down to 可以長久 may be an erroneous insertion. If moved down
to follow the statement 滑則生濇則死 the structure of the text would be fine."

10 Guo Tian: "物 is 形, 'physical appearance.' 類 is 相合, 'to agree.' The pathological
changes of depletion and repletion of the five depots inside the body can be reflected
in the external physical appearance of the body. Hence Chinese medicine assumes
that from a depletion or repletion of the physical body one can determine [condi-
tions of] depletion and repletion of the five depots. Vice versa, when the five depots
are balanced inside, then the bones and the flesh are moist and easily penetrable and
this indicates that that person is healthy." In contrast, *NJCD*: "物類 refers to living
beings including animals and plants." Gao Shishi: "始 is: 先見, 'appear first.' That is,
states of depletion and repletion can be see first in their corresponding external physical appearances." Tanba Genken 丹波元堅: "The *Jia yi jing* has 治, 'to treat,' instead
of 始. The meaning of this character appears to be suited best here." Zhang Yizhi et
al.: "Wang Bing did not refer to the character 類 in his commentary; it may not have
appeared in the version used by Wang Bing."

11 Wang Bing: "When living beings have just come to life, [their skin] is smooth
and [their bones, etc.] are easy-going; when they die, [their skin] is withered and
rough. Hence a rough [skin] is opposition, a smooth [skin] is compliance."

28-174-8
[Huang] Di:
"When the qi in the network [vessels] is insufficient,
while the qi in the conduits has a surplus,
how is that?"

Qi Bo:
"When the qi in the network [vessels] is insufficient,
while the qi in the conduits has a surplus,
the vessel opening is hot, while the foot-long section is cold.[12]
In autumn and winter this is opposition;
in spring and summer this is compliant.[13]

---

12 The *Tai su* does not have the character *kou* 口 following the character 脈. Gu
Guanguang: "The vessel passing straight through the inch [section] is the major yin
conduit. The vessel branching off from the yang brilliance [conduit] at the Broken Sequence (列缺) [hole] in the foot-long section is the major yin network vessel. Hence
the inch[-opening] is the location to examine the conduits; the foot-long section is
the location to examine the network vessels. This has nothing to do with yin and yang."
Tanba: "When Gao Shishi states: "Foot length' is to say: the skin in the foot-long
[section],' then he is quite right. However, the classic contains no evidence of 脈口,
'the vessel opening,' referring to the skin in the inch [section]."

13 Wang Bing: "In spring and summer, the yang qi has risen high. Hence when the
vessel opening is hot, while there is cold in the foot-long section, then this is 'compliant.' The 12 conduits and the 15 network vessels each follow a course on the left and
on the right [of the human body and each] experiences great excess or insufficiency
[of their contents]. The expert practitioner must search for what corresponds to them
best to apply needles or moxa. Hence [the text] states: 'treat those [locations] ruling
the disease.'" Zhang Jiebin: "A yang depletion fears a season of yin abundance. Hence
autumn and winter are 'opposition,' while spring and summer are 'compliant.'" Zhang
Zhicong: "When evil qi enters into [the body] from the outside, one sees to it that
proper qi moves from inside towards outside to ward off [the evil]. [The proper qi,
then,] causes the evil [qi] to leave from the skin, [i.e., from the] outer region. The
qi of autumn and winter sinks into the depth; it cannot cause the evil [qi] to leave
[the body] and disperse. Hence this is 'opposition.' The qi of spring and summer is at
the surface. Hence this is 'compliance.'" Gu Guanguang: "No treatise in the *Nei jing*
discussing the [movement in the] vessels links abundance and weakness in the foot
and inch [sections] to the four seasons. Hence Wang Bing's commentary is wrong.
.. Now, the network vessels are in the outside and they constitute yang. The conduits
are inside and they constitute yin. When the qi in the network vessels is insufficient,
while the conduit qi has surplus, then this is a situation of abounding yin [qi] and
depleted yang [qi]. Hence, such a situation can occur in summer, it cannot occur in
winter. When the conduits are depleted while the network vessels are filled, this is a
situation of abounding yang [qi] and depleted yin [qi]. Hence, such a situation can
occur in winter, but not in summer."

Treat that which rules the disease."[14]

[Huang] Di:
"When the conduits are depleted while the network [vessels] are full,
how is that?"

28-174-10
Qi Bo:
"When the conduits are depleted while the network [vessels] are full,
the foot-long section is hot and filled,
while the vessel opening is cold and rough.
If this [happens] in spring or summer, [the patient] will die;
if [this happens] in autumn or winter, [the patient] will survive."[15]

[Huang] Di:
"To treat these [states], how does one proceed?"

Qi Bo:
"When the network [vessels] are full while the conduits are depleted,
cauterize the yin and pierce the yang.
When the conduits are full while the network [vessels] are depleted,
pierce the yin and cauterize the yang."[16]

---

14 Zhang Jiebin: "This refers to the cauterization and piercing mentioned in the
text below." Ma Shi: "That is, any conduit having a surplus: it is drained; any conduit
having an insufficiency: it is filled."

15 Wang Bing: "In autumn and in winter, the yang qi has descended downwards.
Hence, if there is heat in the foot-long section while the vessel opening is cold, this is
'compliant.'" Zhang Jiebin: "When the conduits are depleted, while the network vessels are filled, the yin qi is insufficient and there is a surplus of yang evil. A depleted
yin fears the time of yang abundance. Hence [the patient] dies in spring and summer,
but survives in autumn and winter."

16 Wang Bing: "Because the yin section rules the network [vessels], while the yang
section rules the conduits." Zhang Jiebin: "In reality, the network [vessels] rule the
yang, while the conduits rule the yin. Cauterization is used to supplement; piercing
is used to drain." Tanba: "Wang Bing's association of yin and yang with the conduits
and network [vessels] is incorrect." 1951/29: "That is to say: the conduits belong to
the yin; the network [vessels] belong to the yang. And it is obvious, when they are
full, one pierces them; when they are depleted, one cauterizes them." Gu Guanguang:
"Cauterization is employed to supplement; piercing is employed to drain."

28-174-13
[Huang] Di:
"What is that to say: 'doubled depletion'?"

Qi Bo:
"The qi in the vessels is depleted above and it is depleted in the foot-long
section.
This is called 'doubled depletion.'"[17]

>[Huang] Di:
"How is it treated?"

Qi Bo:<
"As for the so-called qi depletion,
this is to say: there is no permanence [associated with it].[18]

When the foot-long section is depleted,
[the patient] walks timidly.[19]
When the vessels are depleted,

---

17 Wang Bing: "That is to say: the vessels are depleted both in the foot and in the
inch [section]." Lin Yi et al.: "The *Jia yi jing* has 脈虛氣虛尺虛, 'the vessels are depleted, the qi is depleted, the foot-long section is depleted. This is called doubled
depletion. [In the *Su wen*] here one character 虛 is less [than in the *Jia yi jing*] and
a character 上 is added. Wang Bing states in his comment: 'the vessels are depleted
both in the foot and in the inch [section].' But this does not [mean that] all the qi is
depleted. One should take into consideration the text above [stating] 'if one suffers
from a heat disease, when the qi is hot and when the vessels are full, this is a doubled
repletion.' Here now [the text states]: 'when the vessels are depleted, the qi is depleted,
and the foot-long section is depleted, then this is a doubled depletion.' That is, when
the vessels and the qi are all replete, then this is a doubled repletion. When they are
all depleted, then this is a doubled depletion. It is not so that only when both the foot
and the inch [section] are depleted a doubled depletion is present." Tanba: "Lin Yi et
al. is correct."

18 Yang Shangshan: "In the case of qi depletion, the qi of the chest center is unsettled." Wang Bing: "When the inch [sections show a] depletion, then the movement
in the vessels is abnormal."

19 Cheng Shide et al.: "恇 is 'timid,' and 'weak.'" Tanba: "*Ling shu* 74 has 尺肉弱
者解㑊安臥, 'the flesh of the foot-long [region] is weak; one experiences *jie-yi* and
sleeps peacefully.' The same meaning is expressed by 步行恇然, 'to walk timidly.' All
authors have interpreted 'foot-long' as part of [the diagnostic system of] inch [sec-
tion], gate [section], and foot-long section [where the movement in the vessels is to
be felt]. That is wrong."

this does not manifest itself in yin [or yang movements].[20]
In such cases,
if [the vessels] are smooth, then the [patient] will survive;
if they are rough, then he will die."

28-175-2
[Huang] Di:
"When cold qi rises violently and when the vessels are full and if there is
repletion,[21]
how is that?"

Qi Bo:
"If [the vessels] are replete and smooth, then [the patient] survives;

---

20 Yang Shangshan: "When the vessels at the inch-opening show depletion, then the
lung, which is [associated with the] hand major yin [conduit], is depleted. The yin qi
is insufficient. Hence [the text] states: 'no manifestation.'" Wang Bing: "It does not
manifest signs of the major yin. Why do I say so? The qi opening is the important
meeting point of the vessels; it is where the movement of the hand major yin [conduit
can be felt]." Zhang Jiebin: "The qi opening is the only location ruled by all five depots.
It is the important meeting point of [all] the vessels. The five depots are yin. When a
depot is depleted, then the [corresponding] vessel is depleted [too]. When a vessel is
depleted, then this manifests itself as yin deterioration. Hence [the text] states 'it does
not manifest the yin.'" Wu Kun: "The vessels are the palaces of the blood. When the
vessels are depleted, one knows that blood was lost. Hence [the text] states: it does
not manifest yin (i.e., blood)." Yu Chang: "The character 陽 appears to be missing
subsequent to the character 陰. 陽, 'yang' rhymes with the characters 常, *chang*, and 恇,
kuang, above. The omission of the character 陽 has destroyed the rhythm of the rhyme.
Also, a [movement in the] vessels cannot have only yin but no yang."

21 Both *Su wen* 48 and 62 suggest that the notion of "fullness" (滿) may have referred
to a tangible diagnostic parameter, i.e., to a physical condition noticeable to the patient and/or to the physician, while the notion of "repletion" (實) appears to have been
employed to refer to an abstract diagnostic parameter, i.e., to a condition defined in
theoretical terms. In the context of the present treatise the juxtaposition of "fullness"
and "repletion" may be based on a similar distinction. However, given a predominance
of vessel parameters in the present treatise suggesting traces of an older visual or tac-
tile examination of the skin above the vessels rather than a feeling of the movement
in the vessels, we cannot exclude the possibility of 實 having been employed here to
refer to a "solid" state of the vessels.

if they are replete and if [the movement in the vessel] is contrary [to its regular course],²² then [he] will die."²³

[Huang] Di:
"When the vessels are replete and full,
while the feet and the hands are cold,
and the head is hot,
how is that?"

28-175-5
Qi Bo:
"[If this happens] in spring or autumn, then [the patient] will survive;
if it happens in winter or summer, [he] will die."²⁴
<If the vessels are near the surface and rough, and
if they are rough and the body has heat, [then the patient] will die.>²⁵

---

22 Wang Bing: "逆 is to say: 濇, 'rough.'" Lin Yi et al.: "When Wang Bing interprets 逆 as 濇, then this is a gross mistake. The ancient texts are very concise; they often use reciprocal phrases. Above it is stated 'smooth' and below it is stated 'contrary [to its regular course].' Hence one easily knows that in case of 'smoothness' there is 'compliance,' and one sees that in case of 'movement contrary [to its regular course]' there is 'roughness.' This is not to say that 'movement contrary [to its regular course]' is 'roughness.'" 630/41: "The *Jia yi jing* and the *Mai jing* have 順滑/滑順 instead of 滑 and 逆濇 instead of 逆."

23 477/53: "The meaning of this sentence is: 'When the [movement in the] vessels is replete and smooth, then [the patient] will survive; when the [movement in the] vessels is replete and complies [with the signs of the disease], then he will survive, too. When the [movement in the] vessels is replete and in contrast [to the disease signs], then [the patient] will die. When it is replete and rough, he will die, too." 1133/31 agrees.

24 Wang Bing: "Generally speaking, when in summer hands and feet are cold, this is not a disease. This is summer carrying out the orders of winter. One acquires it in summer and dies in winter. When in winter the vessels are replete and full and when the head is hot, that, too, is not a disease. That is winter carrying out the orders of summer. One acquires it in winter and perishes in summer. If the same were said with summer and winter exchanged, then in no case one would die. If, though, one acquires these [states] in spring or autumn, that is a disease. Hence [whether a patient] survives or dies [is decided] in the middle month of a season."

25 Lin Yi et al.: "[These 11 characters from 脈浮而濇濇而身有熱者死] have been moved here [by Huangfu Mi in] the *Jia yi jing*. In older [versions of the *Su wen*] they followed [the statement below] 帝曰形度骨度 .. 以知其度也. The meaning of the following answer does not fit [that question]. Wang Bing was well aware of that erroneous insertion, but he did not know that Huangfu [Mi] had moved [these 11 characters] here. Now we have eliminated [this statement] from the paragraph further

[Huang] Di:
"When his physical appearance is completely filled,
how is that?"[26]

Qi Bo:
"When his physical appearance is completely filled,
the vessels are tense, big and firm.
The foot-long section is rough and does not correspond.[27]
In such a case, the fact is,
if there is compliance, then [the patient] survives;
if there is opposition, then [he] will die."[28]

---

down (i.e., 28-177-1) and we have moved it here." Ma Shi: "This passage is not part
of a question and answer dialogue; it may have been moved here erroneously." The *Tai
su*, ch. 30 "Shen du" 身度, still has this passage in what Lin Yi et al. refers to as an
"older version."

26 Gao Shishi: "形 is 身, 'body.' 滿 is like 實, 'replete.'" Zhang Zhicong: "The kidneys are the water depot; their qi is cold. The preceding paragraph stated that cold qi
suddenly rises, here now it speaks of an overflow from the water depot. Hence the
physical appearance is entirely filled. 'Physical appearance' is to say: skin and muscle
interstices. The space in the muscle interstices is ruled by qi which has no physical
appearance. When it is invaded by the blood which has physical appearance, then this
results in swellings."

27 Wang Bing: "形盡滿 is to say: the four tangible depots are completely filled."
(I.e., the stomach, the large intestine, the small intestine, and the bladder). Lin Yi et
al.: "The *Jia yi jing* and the *Tai su* have 滿, 'full,' instead of 濇, 'rough.'" Wu Kun: "形
refers to the four tangible depots. 滿 is: replete with evil qi. 脈 is the vessel in the inch
section. When the temples, the ears, the eyes, the mouth, the teeth, and the chest are
all filled with evil qi to repletion, then the inch vessel in the upper section must be
tense, big, and firm. The lower [part of the] body has no disease. Hence the vessel in the
foot-long section is rough and does not correspond to [the condition of the vessel]
in the inch [section]." Zhang Jiebin: "This refers to the signs of yang repletion and
yin depletion. The yang has a surplus, hence the physical appearance is entirely filled.
The vessels should be tense, big, and firm. The yin is insufficient. Hence the foot-long
section is rough and does not correspond [to the yang section]." Guo Tian: "不應 is:
the [movement in the] vessels and the physical body do not correspond." Tanba: "The
skin in the foot-long section is rough and the vessels are tense, big, and hard. These
[two parameters] do not correspond. The *Jia yi jing* and the *Tai su* have 滿, 'filled,'
instead of 澀, 'rough.'"

28 Guo Tian: "Smoothness is compliance; roughness is opposition. In the present
case, the [movement in the] vessels is tense, big, and firm. The foot-long section is
rough and does not correspond. This being so, if there were smoothness [in the foot-
long section], this would be compliance and [the patient] would survive. When there
is roughness, this is opposition and [the patient] will die."

28-175-8
[Huang] Di:
"What is that to say:
'if there is compliance, then [the patient] survives;
if there is opposition, then [he] will die?'"

Qi Bo:
"The so-called 'compliance,' [that is to say:] the hands and the feet are warm.
The so-called 'opposition,' [that is to say:] the hands and the feet are cold."

[Huang] Di:
"When a feeding mother[29] suffers from heat with her vessels being suspended[30]
and small,
how is that?"

Qi Bo:
"When her hands and feet are warm, then she will survive.
When they are cold, she will die."[31]

---

29 Zhang Jiebin: "乳子 is 嬰兒, 'infant.'" Wu Kun: "乳子 as 乳下孩, 'suckling.'"
86/345 identifies 乳子 as 嬰兒, 'infant.'" Yao Shaoyu: "乳子 is to say: a woman that
has given birth to a child and feeds it with milk." Cheng Shide et al.: "It is correct:
in ancient times, 乳子 referred to a woman feeding [her infant with] milk." Zhang
Qi and Tanba: "乳子 is 產後, '[a woman] after delivery.'" 966/33: "The *Shuo wen*
states: 'When humans or birds give birth to offspring, this is called 乳; for four-legged
animals it is [called] 產.' Hence there are many instances in ancient times where 乳
was interpreted as 產. (For a long list of examples from classical literature, see there)
To conclude, in the present text 乳子 has, without any doubt, the meaning of 產婦,
'lying-in woman.'" 1677/6 agrees with a detailed argument and concludes: "乳子 is
'giving birth to a child.' The term 乳子 was used in the meaning of 'infant' only after
the *Nei jing* was compiled, i.e., beginning with the Tang and Song." 960/40 agrees on
the basis of a detailed argumentation. 969/64: "The diseases of infants can be diagnosed only by an inspection of the network [vessels], not be feeling the pulse. Hence
one knows that Zhang Jiebin's identification of 乳子 as 'infant' is wrong." Li Guoqing
agrees.

30 Wang Bing: "懸 is to say: it moves like something that is suspended." Guo Tian:
"懸 is 絕, 'interrupted.'" Zhang Qi: "懸 is 弦, 'string[-like].' When subsequent to delivery blood and qi are depleted, [the woman] suffers from heat and has a string[-like]
and fine [movement in the] vessels, the string[-like movement] indicates stagnant
cold; the fine [movement] indicates diminished qi. That is, despite a yang disease a yin
[movement in the] vessels appears." Zhang Yizhi et al.: "懸 and 弦 were used interchangeably in ancient times. The *Mai jing* 脈經 has 弦 instead of 懸."

31 Lin Yi et al.: "The *Tai su* does not have the character 手. Yang Shangshan stated:
'When the feet are warm, the qi has descended. Hence [that person] survives. When

[Huang] Di:
"When a feeding mother was struck by wind and heat and
when she pants with sounds and breathes [by using her] shoulders,[32]
what are her vessels like?"

Qi Bo:
"When she pants with sounds and breathes [by using her] shoulders,
the vessels are replete and big.
When they are relaxed, then she will survive;
when they are tense, then she will die."[33]

[Huang] Di:
"In the case of intestinal flush with bloody stools,
how is that?"

Qi Bo:
"When the body is hot, then [the patient] will die;
when it is cold, he will survive."[34]

[Huang] Di:
"In the case of intestinal flush passing down white foam,
how is that?"

Qi Bo:
"When the vessels are in the depth, then [the patient] will survive;
when the vessels are near the surface, then [the patient] will die."[35]

---

the feet are cold, the qi does fails to descend. It moves contrary [to its normal direction] and this leads to death." This passage does not appear in the textus receptus of the *Tai su*.

32 Zhang Zhicong: "肩息 is 呼吸搖肩, 'to move one's shoulders up and down while breathing.'"

33 Wang Bing: " 'Relaxed' is to say: like a loose warp; 'tense' is to say: like a tense string. This is not the being relaxed or tense of the coming and going [of the movement in the vessels]."

34 Wang Bing: "[The body is] hot when the blood is destroyed. Hence [that person] will die. [When he body is] cold, the camp qi is present. Hence [that person] will survive."

35 Wang Bing: "This is a yin disease, but one observes a yang [movement in the] vesels. The [movement in the] vessels and the signs [of the disease] contradict each other. Hence [that person] will die."

28-176-8
[Huang] Di:
"In the case of intestinal flush passing down pus and blood, how is that?"

Qi Bo:
"When the vessels are suspended and interrupted,[36] then [the patient] will die;
when they are smooth and big, then he will survive."

[Huang] Di:
"In cases of [diseases] of the intestinal flush type,[37]
when the body is not hot and
when the [movement in the] vessels is not suspended and interrupted,
how is that?"

Qi Bo:
"When [the vessels] are smooth and big, this is to say: [the patient] will survive;
when they are suspended and rough, this is to say: he will die.
Predictions are made on the basis of which depot [is affected]."[38]

28-176-10
[Huang] Di:
"How about peak illness?"

Qi Bo:
"When the vessels are beating,[39] big and smooth,
[the disease will last] for a long time, [and then] end by itself.
When the vessels are small, firm and tense,
[the patient] will die and [can] not be treated."[40]

---

36 Guo Tian: "懸絕 is: extremely weak and interrupted."

37 Guo Tian: "屬 is 類, 'type.'"

38 Wang Bing: "When a liver [movement in the vessels] appears at a *geng xin* [date, the patient] will die. When a heart [movement] appears at a *ren gui* [date, the patient] will die. When a lung [movement] appears at a *bing ding* [date, the patient] will die. When a kidney [movement] appears at a *wu ji* [date, the patient] will die. When a spleen [movement] appears at a *jia yi* [date, the patient] will die. This is meant by 以 藏期之."

39 For a discussion of the usage and meaning of 搏 and 搏 in the *Nei jing*, see 1205/42.

40 Wang Bing: "A [movement in the] vessels that is small, firm, and tense, is a yin [movement]. It is a yang disease, but a yin [movement in the] vessels appears. Hence

[Huang] Di:

"When in the case of peak illness the vessels⁴¹ [show] depletion or repletion, how is that?"

Qi Bo:

"When [they show] depletion, [the patients] can be treated;
when [they show] repletion, then [the patient] will die."⁴²

[Huang] Di:

"When in the case of wasting solitary [heat] disease ⁴³ [the vessels show] depletion or repletion, how is that?"

Qi Bo:

"When the vessels [show] repletion and are big, the disease lasts for long and can be treated.
When the vessels are suspended, small, and firm,
the disease lasts for long and cannot be treated."⁴⁴

28-177-1
[Huang] Di:

"The measures of the physical appearance, [i.e.,] the measures of the bones, the measures of the vessels and the measures of the sinews,
how can these measures be known?"⁴⁵

[the patient] will die and cannot be treated."

41 In contrast, Guo Tian: "脈 refers here to diagnosis in general, not to an examination of some type of [movement in the] vessels."

42 Wang Bing: "Because [the movement in the vessels] is opposite to the signs [of the disease]."

43 Guo Tian: "癉 is read 丹, *dan*; it means 'heat.'"

44 Wang Bing: "In the case of a chronic disease, the blood and the qi weaken and the vessels should not be replete and big. Hence [the disease] cannot be cured." Lin Yi et al.: "The classic states: 'when the [movement in the] vessels [shows] repletion and is big and when the disease has lasted for a long time, it can be cured.' The commentary [by Wang Bing] implies 'it cannot be cured.' The *Jia yi jing*, the *Tai su* and also the Quan Yuanqi edition, they all have 'can be cured.'" 138/21: "The original text ends with 病久不可治. The subsequent text was misplaced here."

45 Wang Bing: "The 'measures of the physical appearance' are dealt with in the *San bei jing* 三備經 (a text no longer extant). The 'measures of the sinews, the measures of the vessels, and the measures of the bones' are all dealt with in the *Ling shu jing* 靈樞經. This present question would fit the beginning of those treatises in the [*Ling shu*] *jing*. Here it is an erroneous insertion. Another [version of the] classic has this

[   ]

[Huang] Di:

[   ]

[Qi Bo:]
"If in spring one hastily[46] treats the conduits and network [vessels],[47]
if in summer one hastily treats the transporters on the conduits, and
if in autumn one hastily treats the six palaces,
then, when it is winter, [the qi] will be obstructed.
When it is obstructed, employ drugs and, to a lesser degree, needles and
[pointed] stones.[48]
{When it is said [here]: 'to a lesser degree needles and [pointed] stones,' this
does not refer to [the treatment of] *yong*- and *ju*-abscesses.}[49]

---

question at the beginning of the treatise Ni cong lun 逆從論; that is a mistake." See
also note 25 above. Guo Tian: "度 is 量, 'measure.' 形度: The spleen and the lung rule
the physical appearance. This refers to the thick or thin, fat or lean condition of the
muscles, the flesh, and the skin. 骨度: The kidneys are linked to the bones. This refers
to the size and length of the bones. 脈度: The heart is linked to the vessels. This refers
to whether the vessels run from above downwards, or from below upward. 筋度: The
liver is linked to the sinews. The sinews can be measured in terms of depletion and
repletion, too."

46 Wang Bing: "亟 is like 急, 'tense.'" On the different meanings of 亟 in the *Nei jing*,
see Qian Chaochen-88/62-63. In contrast, Guo Tian: "亟 is 憊, 'exhausted,' 病, 'disease.'" In its treatises Jin ji xu 禁極虛 ("Avoidance of Extreme Depletion") and Shun
shi 順時 ("Going along with the Seasons"), the *Tai su* relates a prohibition to exhaust
yin or yang qi in the course of the four seasons. The present statement appears in this
context, with the character 亟 being replaced there by the character 極, "exhaustion."

47 Wang Bing: "閉塞 is to say: the door gate of the qi is closed." Guo Tian: "春亟 is
a disease of the liver/wood. At their beginning, liver diseases are still in the conduits-
network [vessels]. The disease is near the surface and hence the treatment is near the
surface. Hence one treats the respective conduit-network [vessels]."

48 Zhang Zhicong: "The qi of the winter season is closed in and stored inside. Hence
it is appropriate to employ drugs, and only to a lesser degree needles [and] stones. The
reason is: needles [and] stones regulate the outside; toxic drugs regulate the inside."

49 *Ling shu* 81 defines the terms 癰 and 疽 such that one is tempted to identify 癰 as
"abscess" and 疽 as "phlegmon." The term 癰疽, though, may refer to various types of
localized open or closed purulent processes in general. Wang Bing: "Even though the
qi gates are closed in winter, the qi of *yong*- and *ju*-abscesses is nevertheless violent
and creates large [amounts of] pus internally. If one does not quickly drain it then it
will putrefy the sinews and let the bones rot. Hence, even though it is winter time, it is

Yong- and *ju*-abscesses must not be given [even] a short time to return.[50]
If one does not know the location of an emerging *yong*-abscess and
if one presses for it but it does not respond to one's hand,
when at times it comes and at times [appears] not to exist any longer,
pierce three wounds[51] to the side[52] of the hand major yin [conduit] and
two on each of the capstring vessels.[53]

28-177-5
In the case of *yong*-abscesses in the armpits[54] together with massive heat,
pierce the foot minor yang [conduit] at five [locations].
If after the piercing the heat does not stop,
pierce the hand heart ruler [conduit][55] at three [locations] and

---

nevertheless appropriate to employ needles and stones for opening [the abscesses] and
for removing the [pus]." Guo Tian: "That is to say, in the case of abscesses associated
with the kidneys, one can still use needles [and/or] stones for treatment."

50 Wang Bing: "Why is it that the *yong*- and *ju*-abscesses, if one has acquired it in
winter, is to be treated by means of needles and/or stones? Because this disease, if only
a short time has passed without it having been drained, will cause sinews and bones
to rot internally and it will penetrate the depots and palaces." Guo Tian: 傾時 is 片
刻, 'a short while.' 回 is 深入, 'to enter deeply.' *Yong*- and *ju*-abscesses may be light,
nevertheless one must not let even a short time pass before treating them, lest the
disease deeply penetrates [the body] and reaches the depots." The *Tai su* has 不得須
時, 'do not wait any time.' Yang Shangshan commented: "Because abscesses are violent
diseases, one must not waste any time before applying the needle."

51 Ma Shi: "The wound caused by piercing is called 疻." Guo Tian: "This is the tiny
wound left after inserting a needle."

52 Guo Tian: "傍 is: on both sides."

53 Wang Bing: "One only has a feeling as if there were signs of *yong*- and *ju*-ab-
scesses, but one does not find out at which location they have emerged. Hence one
presses for it, but it does not respond to one's hand. 'At times it comes; at times it has
ended,' that is to say: One cannot identify a pain at a specific location. 'To the side of
the hand major yin [conduit]' is the foot yang brilliance vessel. That is to say, the six
holes including the Qi Door (氣戶) and others in the stomach section. The 'capstring
vessel' refers to the foot yang brilliance vessel, too. It is the vessel near the capstring,
hence it is called capstring vessel. 'Capstring' is to say; the band of the cap. Because
there is one on the left and one on the right, [the text] states 'two on each.'"

54 Wu Kun's edition has 腋 instead of 掖.

55 Guo Tian: "If after a [first] piercing the heat does not retreat, one must drain the
son [agent]. One inserts three needles into the heart enclosing network [vessel]. That
is, in the case of repletion, drain its son. One drains the heart fire."

pierce the hand major yin conduit-network [vessels] at the meeting point of the major bones at three [locations] each.[56]

When suddenly a *yong*-abscess [appears] and the sinews shrink and
in the case of sectionalized pain,[57] and
in the case of unending *po*-sweat,[58] and
when the uterus qi is insufficient,[59]
treat at the transporters of the conduits.[60]

28-177-8
When suddenly the abdomen is full and when pressure is unable to [push the abdominal wall] down,
[in such a situation] one selects the hand major yang conduit and network [vessels.
{These are the levy [holes] of the stomach.}[61]
[Also pierce at] the transporters on the minor yin [conduits]. Move three

---

56 Wang Bing: " 'The meeting point of the major bones' is the shoulder. That is to say: the Shoulder Truth (肩真) hole."

57 Guo Tian: "分 is read in the fourth tone. 隨分而痛: 'the locations harmed by the sudden rise of *yong* have pain.' "

58 Guo Tian: "魄汗 is 大汗, 'big sweat.' "

59 Zhang Jiebin: "胞氣不足 is: the water ways are impassable." Tanba: "胞 is 脬, 'urinary bladder.' This is the so-called yin bladder. Hence [the term] refers to the urinary bladder." Guo Tian: "胞氣 is 血海, 'the sea of blood.' That is to say, the evil enters the camp qi/the blood and causes severe harm." *NJCD* reads 胞 here as 脬, *pao*, "urinary bladder."

60 Wang Bing: "When suddenly an abscess emerges and spreads along a vessel, the sinews crossed spring up. They relax and become tense [alternately] and there is pain in the flesh section. Sweat flows as if it were never to end. If at the same time the uterine qi is insufficient, then in all such cases one can supplement or drain this at the transporters of the conduit vessel itself." Lin Yi et al.: "These two passages were distributed, in the old versions, at various places in this treatise; they have now been moved together to follow each other."

61 The *Tai su* has 取太陽經絡, "select the major yang conduits and network vessels." Wang Bing: " 'Major yang' is the hand major yang. The hand major yang emerges out of the minor yang conduits and network [vessels]. Hence, one selects the Central Duct (中脘) hole. This is the levy [hole] of the stomach." Lin Yi et al.: "The *Jia yi jing* states: 取太陽經絡血者則已, 'When one selects those parts of the major yang conduit and network [vessels] which contain blood, then [the disease] will be healed.' It does not have the characters 胃之募也."

inches to the side away from the vertebrae. [Conduct] five [piercings].
Employ the round-sharp needle.⁶²

28-178-1
In cases of cholera,⁶³
pierce five transporters on [both] sides and
three on both sides of the foot yang brilliance [conduit] and above.⁶⁴

To pierce convulsions resulting from fright, [select] five [locations on the] vessels:
pierce the hand major yin [conduits] at five [locations] each;
pierce the foot major yang [conduit] at five [locations];⁶⁵
pierce one [location] on both sides of the hand minor yin conduit-network
[vessels] and [also]
the foot yang brilliance [conduit at] one [location].
Move five inches upward from the ankle and pierce with three needles
[there].⁶⁶

28-178-3
As for all treatments directed at

---

62 Wang Bing: "The 'minor yin transporters' is to say: the transporters of the kidneys
on both sides [of the spine] below the 14th vertebra." 916/54: "員 is 圓, 'round.'" For
a description of the shape of the "round-sharp needle," and for its application in cases
of sudden qi accumulations, see *Ling shu* 1 and 7.

63 We read the Chinese characters *huoluan* 霍亂 as a possible transliteration of the
ancient Greek term *cholera* that was at the same time meant to reflect the dramatic
manifestation of the disease. Hence the meaning of the characters *huoluan*: "sudden
chaos." It is, of course, not possible to know whether the ancient Chinese used the
term "cholera" for the same disease as the ancient Greek. Nevertheless, the context of
vomiting and diarrhea here and in *Su wen* 71 appears to suggest at least a close proximity of the usages of the terms at the Western and Eastern end of a long trade route.
For a more detailed discussion, see Unschuld 2003, p. 204.

64 Wang Bing: " 'Foot yang brilliance' is to say: the transporters of the stomach. One
selects the stomach transporters and, in addition, one moves up to the third hole on
both sides of the minor yin transporters. These are the Stomach Granary (胃倉) holes."

65 Yang Shangshan: "經 is 足, 'foot.'" Wang Bing agrees. For a detailed discussion,
including an identification of 經 as 脛, 'lower leg,' i.e., 'foot,' see Yan Zhenhai/54.

66 Yan Zhenhai/54: "This passage has been read by Chinese commentators in basically three ways: (1) 刺癇驚脈五, 針手太陰各五, 刺經太陽五, 刺手少陰經絡傍者
一, 足陽明一, 上踝五寸刺三針. (2) 刺癇驚脈五: 針手太陰各五刺經, 太陽五, 刺手
少陰經絡傍者一, 足陽明一, 上踝五寸刺三針. (3) 刺癇驚脈五: 針手足太陰各五,
刺經, 太陽者五, 刺手少陰經絡傍者一, 足陽明一, 上踝五寸, 刺三針."

wasting solitary [heat] disease,[67] at
collapse resulting from stroke, at
unilateral withering,[68] at
limpness with receding [qi],[69] and at
qi fullness effused in a movement contrary [to its regular course],[70]
[if the patients are] well-nourished persons of noble rank,
then these are diseases brought forth by [the consumption of] rich food.

When the diaphragm is obstructed, with [the flow through it being] interrupted and
when there is no communication between above and below,
then this is a disease of sudden anxiety.

In the case of sudden recession accompanied by deafness, as well as
unilateral obstruction and impassability,[71]
the internal qi is suddenly beating.[72]
This is a disease which did not [emerge] from inside, [but] from outside
through being struck by wind.
Hence [the body] becomes lean; [the disease] stays and attaches itself [to one
location].[73]
When one walks lamely,
this is a disease of [being struck by] cold, wind, and dampness."[74]

---

67 2738/12: "消癉 is diabetes." 2583/8 agrees. Wang Bing (see below): "消 is to say:
內消, 'internal wasting.' 癉 is to say: 伏熱, 'hidden heat.'"

68 2741/10: "偏枯 is 半身不遂, 'hemiplegia.'"

69 Guo Tian: "The four limbs have reversely flowing [qi]."

70 Guo Tian: "Evil qi abounds and is effused upward in reverse flow."

71 Gao Jiwu/259: "Ma Shi: 偏 is 邊, 'side'. Accordingly, 偏塞閉 means 'blocked on
all sides, in front and behind'. Zhang Zhicong interprets 偏 as 偏于, 'unilaterally at
(one side).' Ma Shi's interpretation is to say: urine and stools do not flow. Zhang Zhicong divides the body, with 偏, into an upper and a lower part. When the upper part
is [unilaterally] blocked, 'there is a sudden recession with deafness, ...'" *NJCD*: "偏 is
便, 'urine and stools.'"

72 In contrast, Gao Jiwu/259: "薄 has the meaning of 迫, 'to press.'"

73 2687/35 parallels this phrase with a similar wording in *Su wen* 20: 留瘦不移.
While all previous authors have interpreted 瘦 as "emaciation," Hua Shou identified
瘦 as 廀, "concealed." In this case, 瘦留著 would have the meaning of "[the evil] remains hidden [in the body]." Guo Tian: "瘦 is 痺, 'lame.'"

74 Wang Bing: "消 is to say: 內消, 'internal wasting.' 癉 is to say: 伏熱, 'hidden heat.'
厥 is to say 氣逆, 'qi moving contrary [to its regular course].' 高 is 膏, 'fat.' 梁 is 粱,

28-178-7
Huang Di:
"Yellow solitary [heat] disease, violent pain, peak illness, and recession with craziness,
they are generated by [qi] moving contrary [to its regular course] for a long time.

When the five depots are not balanced,
this is generated by an obstruction of the six palaces.
When the head aches and when there is a ringing [sound] in the ears and when the nine orifices are not freely passable,
this is generated by the intestines and the stomach."[75]

'millet.' 蹠 is to say: 足, 'foot.' Now, fat [food] causes heat in man's center. [To consume] sweet [flavor] lets the center be full. Hence, when heat qi accumulates internally, it causes wasting-and-thirst as well as unilateral withering. The qi is filled and moves contrary [to its regular course]. To 'move contrary' is to say: it acts in opposition to its normal appearance; it is different in comparison with a normal person. In the case of anxiety, the qi is shut in and does not move. Hence the diaphragm is blocked and obstipated, and the qi vessels are interrupted so that there is no communication between the upper and the lower [parts of the body]. When the qi is firmly kept inside, then the passageways of the large and small conveniences are closed and there cannot be any outflow and drainage. When external wind strikes a person and hides in the depots without leaving again, then yang qi is received internally and causes heat. Externally it blazes in the muscles and in the flesh, causing wasting melting there. Hence when it stays and accumulates in the flesh section, wasting emaciation [results] and the skin attaches itself to the sinews and bones. When dampness overcomes the feet, then the sinews do not move freely; when cold overcomes the feet, then [the sinews] cramp and become tense. When wind, dampness, and cold overcome [the feet], then the guard qi conglomerates. When the guard qi has conglomerated, then the flesh has pain. Hence the feet are lame and one cannot walk."

75 Wang Bing: "The three yang [conduits] of the feet run from the head to the feet. However, in case [their qi] moves contrary [to its regular course] for a long time and fails to move downwards, then the qi accumulates in the upper burner and, hence, causes yellow solitary [heat] disease, with sudden pain, peak illness, crazy behavior, and reversely moving qi. Eating and drinking are out of order and lead to uncontrollable vomiting and diarrhea. Hence the six palaces close and cause disharmony in the qi of the five depots. When the intestines and the stomach are closed, then the qi cannot follow its course. When it cannot follow its course, then above and below, inside and outside fight for domination. Hence [the patient suffers from] headache, sounds in his ears, and closure of the nine orifices."

Chapter 29
Discourse on the Major Yin
and on the Yang Brilliance [Conduits]

29-179-4
Huang Di asked:
"The major yin [conduit] and the yang brilliance [conduit] constitute exterior
and interior; they are the vessels of spleen and stomach.
[And yet,] the diseases generated [in them] are different!
How is that?"[1]

Qi Bo responded:
"Yin and yang [conduits occupy] different positions.[2]
Alternately they are depleted or replete.[3]
Alternately [the movement of their contents] is contrary to or complies with
[the regular course].
Some [i.e., the yin vessels] follow the inside;
some [i.e., the yang vessels] follow the outside.
What they follow is not identical.
Hence [their] diseases have different names."[4]

---

1 Wang Bing: "The spleen depot and the stomach palace are both associated with
[the agent] soil. The diseases that emerge [in spleen and stomach] are different. Hence
[Huang Di] inquired about their not being alike."

2 Zhang Zhicong: " 'Yin and yang [occupy] different positions' is to say: the major
yin is located above and the yang brilliance is located below."

3 Zhang Zhicong: "That is to say: when the passage ways of yang are replete, the
passage ways of yin are depleted."

4 Wang Bing: "The spleen depot is yin; the stomach palace is yang. The yang vessels
move downwards; the yin vessels move upwards. The yang vessels follow the outside;
the yin vessels follow the inside. Hence [the text] states: 'what they follow is not the
same; the diseases have different names.'" Zhang Jiebin: "The robber wind and the
depletion evil are harm [caused] from outside; they are received by the yang and
they enter the five depots. Drinking and eating, rising and resting [may cause] harm
from inside. Hence the yin receives this [harm] and it enters the six palaces." Zhang
Zhicong: " 'They may follow the inside' is: some diseases of abdominal fullness with
outflow of [undigested] food result from immoderate drinking and eating, or from
untimely rising and resting. 'They may follow the outside' is: in some cases the body
becomes hot and one pants because of [the intrusion of] robber wind and depletion
evil. Hence these diseases have different names."

29-179-6
[Huang] Di:
"I should like to hear about their different appearances."

Qi Bo:
"The yang, that is the qi of heaven.
It rules the outside.
The yin, that is the qi of the earth.
It rules the inside.[5]
Hence,
the yang paths are [subject to] repletion;
the yin paths are [subject to] depletion.[6]
Hence,
when one is invaded by a robber wind or depletion evil,
the yang [conduits] receive it.
When food and drinks are [consumed] without restraint,
when rising and resting[7] occur out of time,

---

5 Wang Bing: "This is what is called [in the text]: 'Yin and yang [occupy] different positions.'"

6 Wang Bing: "This is what is called [in the text]: 'Alternately they are depleted or replete.'" Zhang Jiebin: "Yang is hardness; yin is softness." Wu Kun amended this to: "When the yang path is replete, the yin path is depleted; when the yin path is replete, the yang path is depleted." 137/16: "This is what is stated in *Su wen* 11 as follows: 'When the stomach is replete, the intestines are depleted; when the intestines are replete, the stomach is depleted.'" 1675/7: "'Yang' refers to the stomach palace; 'yin' refers to the spleen depot. 道 is 規律, 'law.' The five depots rule the storage of essence qi; they [can be] filled, but they [can] not be replete. Hence [the text] states: 陰道虛, 'the yin law is depletion.' The six palaces rule the transmission and transformation of things; they [can be] replete, but they [can] not be full. Hence [the text] states: 'the yang law is repletion.'" 804/54: "'Yang paths' and 'yin paths' refers to the passage ways of diseases caused by external affection or internal harm respectively." Mori: "The yang qi, which lacks physical appearance, nourishes the yin matter which has physical appearance. Hence, its regular state is repletion. The yin matter, which has physical appearance, receives yang qi which has no physical appearance. Hence, its regular state is depletion. As for qi and blood in the human body, [the former is] yang and is regularly replete in the outside regions [of the body]; [the latter is] yin and is regularly depleted in the inner regions [of the body]. Where there is depletion, the yang qi will occupy the depleted [region], to nourish the yin [qi, i.e.,] blood. Repletion is the result of yin [qi, i.e.,] blood receiving this replenishment [from the yang qi], and, hence, it contains yang qi. Hence, the regular state of the qi is repletion and that of the physical appearance is depletion."

7 "Rising and resting" is a general reference to the daily routine in one's home.

the yin [conduits] receive it.[8]

When the yang [conduits] receive it,
then it enters the six palaces.
When the yin [conduits] receive it,
then it enters the five depots.

29-180-1
When it enters the six palaces,
then the body becomes hot and one lies down when it is not the proper time.[9]
In the upper [part of the body this] causes panting exhalation.

When it enters the five depots,
then distension and obstruction result.
In the lower [part of the body this] causes outflow of [undigested] food.
If this lasts for long, it causes intestinal flush.[10]

Hence,
the throat rules the qi of heaven;
the gullet rules the qi of the earth.[11]
Hence,
the yang [conduits] receive the wind qi;
the yin [conduits] receive the dampness qi.[12]

---

8 Wang Bing: "This is what is called [in the text]: 'They may follow the inside; they may follow the outside.'"

9 2107/56: "[The meaning of] 不時臥 is not clear. The *Jia yi jing*, in [its section] 六經受病發傷寒，寒熱上 has: 不得眠, '[the patient] cannot sleep.' The meaning [of this wording] would be quite appropriate [in the present context]." Yu Chang: "This should be 身熱不得臥, 'the body is hot and [the patient] cannot sleep.'" Yan Hongchen & Gao Guangzhen/104: "不能按時安臥, '[the patient] cannot rest at the [proper] times.'" Yu Chang: "The character 時 may be an error; it should be 得, 'get,' 'be able to.'"

10 Wang Bing: "This is what is called [in the text]: 'What they follow is not the same. The names of the diseases differ.'" For a definition by Wang Bing suggesting a notion of "intestinal *pi*" as qi (i.e., gases) leaving the intestines, see *Su wen* 37.

11 Gao Shishi: "The 喉, 'throat,' controls exhalation and inhalation; it is the exit of the lung qi. Hence the throat rules the qi of heaven while the gullet controls water and grain." 58/30: "This explains most clearly that the 喉 is a part of the respiratory tract, while the 咽 is a part of the digestive tract. The 喉 is also the organ emitting sounds." For a discussion of these terms, see also 2755/12.

12 Wang Bing: "Similar qi search each other."

Hence,
the yin qi rises from the feet, moves upwards to the head,
and moves down along the arms to the tips of the fingers.
The yang qi moves up from the hands, reaches the head,
and moves down to the feet.[13]
<Hence it is said:
Yang diseases move up to the extreme [top] and descend.
Yin diseases move down to the extreme [bottom] and rise.>[14]

Hence,
if one was harmed by wind,
the upper [parts of the body] receive it first."
If one was harmed by dampness,
the lower [parts of the body] receive it first.[15]

29-180-7
[Huang] Di:
"When the spleen has a disease and the four limbs do not function,
how is that?"[16]

Qi Bo:
"All the four limbs are supplied with qi by the stomach,
but [the stomach qi] is unable to reach the conduits [directly].[17]
It is only because of the spleen that the [four limbs] get their supplies.[18]

---

13 Wang Bing: "This is what is called [in the text]: 'Alternately they move contrary to or along with [their regular course].'"

14 Wang Bing: "That is just to give a general outline. Now, the downward movement in the foot minor yin vessels differs from that of the qi in all the other yin [vessels]."

15 Wang Bing: "The yang qi flames upwards. Hence it receives wind. The yin qi moistens the below. Hence it receives dampness. The reason is: similar qi come together."

16 On the concept of 不用, see 1417/47.

17 Lin Yi et al.: "The *Tai su* has has 徑至, 'to proceed directly towards,' instead of 至經. Yang Shangshan states: 'The stomach supports the four limbs with water and grain, but [water and grain] cannot reach the four limbs directly. It is only through the spleen that the four limbs receive water and grain, *jin* and *ye* liquids, camp and guard qi."

18 Wang Bing: "The spleen qi transforms water and grain and distributes them as essence liquids. These then are taken in by the four limbs as their supplies."

Now, when the spleen has a disease and is unable to move the body liquids on
behalf of the stomach,[19]
the four limbs are not supplied with the qi of water and grain.
[Their] qi weakens day by day;
the vessel paths are no [longer] passable.[20]
The sinews and the bones, the muscles and the flesh,
none of them has qi to live.[21]
Hence, they do not function."

[Huang] Di:
"The spleen does not rule [a specific] season;[22]
how is that?"[23]

Qi Bo:
"The spleen, that is the soil.
It governs the center.[24]
Throughout[25] the four seasons it tends[26] the four depots.
In each [season] it is entrusted with government for 18 days;
it cannot rule an [entire] season by itself."[27]

---

19 For a discussion of the concept "on behalf of the stomach," see 110/2.

20 The *Jia yi jing* has 通, 'passable,' instead of 利..

21 Guo Tian: "生 is 養, 'for nourishment.' "

22 See 2114/4 and 2146/21 for discussions of parallels to this statement in Dong
Zhongshu's 董仲舒 *Chun qiu fan lu* 春秋繁露, Wu xing zhi yi 五行之義. For a detailed discussion of this concept, see 1249/58.

23 Wang Bing: "The liver rules [in] spring; the heart rules [in] summer; the lung
rules [in] autumn; the kidneys rule [in] winter. All [these] four depots have a regular
correspondence; the spleen, however, has no regular [season during which it might]
rule."

24 Wang Bing: "治 is 主, 'to rule.' "

25 2083/22: "常 is 長久, 'over long time,.' "

26 長 [*zhang*] is interpreted here in the sense of 撫養, "to bring up [like children]."
In contrast, Zhang Jiebin: "為四藏之長, 'it is the leader of the four depots.' " Ma Shi:
"長 is identical with 掌, 'to manage;' 主, 'to rule.' "

27 Guo Tian: "獨 is 偏, 'unilaterally.' Liver, heart, lung, and kidneys each rule one
season. Of the ninety days of each season, [the seasons] must be nourished for 18 days
by the qi of the soil. That is, the spleen rules [all] four seasons; it does not unilaterally
rule only one season, or one depot."

<As for the spleen depot,[28]
it permanently stores[29] the essence of the stomach, [i.e., of] soil.
As for the soil,
by generating the myriad beings,[30]
it takes heaven and earth as a law.
Hence, in the upper and lower [parts of the body] it reaches head and feet;
it cannot rule [only one specific] season.>

29-180-14
[Huang] Di:
"Spleen and stomach are connected through a membrane;[31] nevertheless [the former] can move the body liquids on behalf of the [stomach].
How is it that?"

Qi Bo:
"The foot major yin [conduit] is the third yin.
This vessel passes through the stomach, is connected with the spleen, and encloses the throat.
Hence, the major yin [conduit] moves qi on behalf of[32] the [stomach][33] to the three yin [conduits].[34]

---

28 The *Tai su* does not have the two characters 者 and 胃.

29 Wang Bing: "著 is to say: 常約著于胃, 'it is always tied to the stomach.' The soil qi assumes rule during the four seasons at the end of each season for 18 days. Hence each of the qi of the five agents rules for 72 days which adds up to the [number of] days of a complete year." Yang Shangshan explained 著 as 在, "to be present at." Gao Shishi: "著 is 昭著, 'evident.'" Guo Tian: "著 is 負荷, 'to carry.'" 1832/41: "著 is 昭著 于外, 'evident to the outside.'" Our reading of 著 in the sense of "to store" is based on such a usage in the Han text *Yen tie lun* 鹽鐵論, sect. Pin fu 貧富.

30 The *Tai su* has 主, 'to rule,' instead of 生.

31 Lin Yi et al.: "The *Tai su* has 以募相逆. Yang Shangshan states: 'The spleen is yin; the stomach is yang. The spleen is inside; the stomach is outside. Their positions are different. Hence [the text states:] 'mutual opposition.'"

32 Gao Jiwu/554: "為 is 給, 'for,' 'on behalf of.'"

33 Wu Kun: "為之 is 為胃, 'on behalf of the stomach.' 三陰 is major [yin], minor [yin], and ceasing [yin]. The spleen on behalf of the stomach moves qi to the three yin; it transports the yang brilliance qi into all [three] yin [conduits]."

34 Gao Shishi: "The ceasing yin is the first yin; the minor yin is the second yin; the major yin is the third yin. Hence the foot major yin is the third yin." Guo Tian: " 'Three yin' is: the five depots."

As for the yang brilliance [conduit], it is the outside.[35]
It is the sea for the five depots and six palaces.[36]
It, too, moves qi on behalf of the [stomach] to the three yang [conduits].[37]
The depots and the palaces, they all receive their qi from the yang brilliance
through these [two] conduits.[38]
Hence,
[it is they who] move the body liquids on behalf of the stomach."

>When the four limbs are not supplied with the qi of water and grain,
they will increasingly weaken day by day.
The yin paths[39] are no [longer] passable.
The sinews and the bones, the muscles and the flesh,
none of them has qi to live.
Hence, they do not function.<[40]

---

35 Wang Bing: "The stomach is the outside of the spleen."

36 Guo Tian: "The stomach receives water and grain and pours them into the depots and palaces. Hence it is the sea for the five depots and six palaces."

37 Zhang Jiebin: "The yang brilliance is the outside of the major yin. It rules the
reception of water and grain to pour them into the depots and palaces. Hence it is the
sea for the five depots and six palaces. Even though the yang brilliance moves qi to
the three yin, it, too, depends on the spleen qi for these movements. Hence [the text]
states 亦, 'too.'" 1009/45: "之 is the stomach; 'too' refers to the major yin alluded to
above." Wu Kun: "之 is the spleen."

38 Guo Tian: " 'Through this conduit' is 'through the spleen conduit.' "

39 Zhang Jiebin: "The 'yin paths' are the blood vessels.' " Gao Shishi: "The yin paths
are not free, that is: the vessel paths are not free." Guo Tian: "The 'yin paths' are the
conduit vessels."

40 Tanba: "The 28 characters beginning with 四肢不得稟水穀氣 repeat the text
from above. This is truly an erroneous addition."

Chapter 30
Explanation of the Yang Brilliance Vessel

30-181-8
Huang Di asked:
"When the foot yang brilliance vessel has a disease,
[the patient] has an aversion to [other] people and to fire.[1]
When he hears the sound of wood,[2] he is frightened to scare, and neither bells nor drums can make him move.
Why is it that he is frigthened when he hears the sound of wood?
I should like to hear the reason of this?"[3]

Qi Bo responded:
"As for the yang brilliance [conduit], this is the vessel of the stomach.
The stomach is soil. Hence, when [the patient] hears the sound of wood and is frightened,
this is because soil has an aversion to wood."[4]

[Huang] Di:
"Good!
When he has an aversion to fire, why is that?"

Qi Bo:
"The yang brilliance rules the flesh.
Its vessel abounds with blood and qi.[5]

---

1 For the symptoms, see virtually identical passages in the Mawangdui manuscript *MSI.B.3, Yin yang shi yi mai jiu jing, jia ben.* 阴阳十一脉灸经,甲本. See Harper 1998, 205 ff and Ma Jixing 1992, 232 f.

2 2018/5: "木 is a copying error of 水, 'water.'"

3 Wang Bing: "The preceding treatise stated: 'When it enters the six palaces, then the body turns hot and [the patient] lies down when it is not the right time. In the upper [part of the body this] causes panting exhalation.' Now, the yang brilliance [conduit] is the stomach vessel. In the present case the disease differs from the situation described in the preceding treatise. In contrast, the [patient] is frightened when he hears the sound of wood. Hence, [Huang Di] asks for the [reasons of this] difference."

4 Wang Bing: "The *Yin yang shu* 陰陽書 states: wood overcomes soil. Hence the soil has an aversion to wood."

5 139/23: "The [two characters] 其脈 should be linked to the following text, not to the preceding text. If they were linked to the preceding text, they may have been

When an evil settles in it, then heat results.
When the heat is extreme, then [the patient] has an aversion to fire."

[Huang] Di:
"When he has an aversion to people, why is that?"

Qi Bo:
"When the yang brilliance qi recedes,
then [the patient] pants and is distressed.
When he is distressed, then he has an aversion to people."[6]

30-182-1
[Huang] Di:
"Some pant and die;
others pant and survive.
How is that?"

Qi Bo:
"When [this] recession with countermovement involves[7] the depots, then [the patient] will die.
When it involves the conduits, then he will survive."[8]

30-182-2
[Huang] Di:
"Good!

---

mistakenly exchanged for 与肌. The *Jia yi jing* has 其肌 because the stomach rules the muscles (肌) and the flesh." The *Tai su* has 其血盛, 'its blood abounds,' instead of 其脈血氣盛."

6 Wang Bing: " 'Distressed' is to say: heat presses internally. Hence, [the patient] has an aversion to other people."

7 *NJCD*: "連 is 及, 'to reach,' 波及, 'to involve.' " Ma Shi: "When the reverse movement internally reaches the five depots, then the evil has already penetrated deeply. Hence [the patient] will die. When externally it has reached the conduit vessels, then the evil is still in the exterior, hence [the patient] will survive." Gao Shishi: "The network [vessel] of the stomach, above it is linked to the heart enclosure; to the side it penetrates the armpits. In the present case, now, the stomach qi flows reversely."

8 Wang Bing: "經 is to say: 經脈, 'conduit vessels.' 藏 is to say: 五神藏, 'the five spirit depots.' [The patient] dies when [the reverse flow] involves the depots because the spirit has left." Gao Shishi: "When the disease reaches the heart depot of the minor yin, then [the patient] will die; when it reaches the conduit vessel of the heart enclosure, then [the patient] will survive."

When the disease is severe, then [the patient] throws off his clothes and runs around.

He climbs on what is high and sings.

In some cases he even fails to eat for several days and [yet] he leaps over walls,[9] and he climbs on houses.

All the places he climbs on, he would ordinarily[10] not be able [to reach].

Being ill, though, he is able to do so.

Why is that?"

Qi Bo:

"The four limbs are the basis of all yang.[11]

When the yang abounds, then the four limbs are replete.

When they are replete, then one is able to climb on something high."

30-182-6

[Huang] Di:

"When he throws off his clothes and runs around,

why is that?"

---

9 Wang Bing: "踰垣 is 驀牆, 'to leap over walls.'"

10 Wang Bing: "素 is 本, 'originally.'"

11 Wang Bing: "The yang [conduits] receive their qi from the four limbs. Hence the four limbs are the origin of all yang." Gao Shishi: "The three hand yang [conduits] run from the hands to the head; the three foot yang [conduits] run from the head to the feet. Hence the four limbs are the origin of all yang." 941/59: "The four limbs are not at all 'the origin of all yang.' 四肢為諸陽之本 should be 四肢為諸陽之末, 'the four limbs are the final destination of all yang.'" 1662/43: "The spleen rules the four limbs. The four limbs depend, for their warmth, on all the yang qi generated through transformation by spleen and stomach. It is this way that their regular physiological functions can be maintained. .. Hence the present passage is to be read as follows: 'As for the four limbs, all yang is the foundation [of their functioning].'" 2750/21: "The character most easily exchanged for 本 is *tao* 夲. According to the *Shuo wen*, the meaning is 'to move forward,' 'fast.' This phrase, then, should be read as 'The yang qi of the entire body can quickly move forwards to the four limbs.'" 2434/3: "From the arguments listed above, 本 should be interpreted as 所在之處, 'location.' 諸陽 refers to the yang qi of spleen and stomach. [..] the entire phrase should be read: 'The four limbs are locations of the yang [qi of spleen and stomach].'" Li Guoqing: "本 has the meaning of 依据, 'basis,' 'foundation.' The phrase is to be read as 'The four limbs are the basis for examining the changes of the yang qi in the human body.'" For details of the arguments in all the papers quoted, see there. See also 527/14, 1935/7, 2656/47, 1831/78, 1182/34, 1061/31, 686/24, and 2688/13.

Qi Bo:
"The heat abounds in [his] body.
Hence he throws off his clothes and wishes to run around."

[Huang] Di:
"When he [utters] absurd words and voices insults,
without sparing those near or distant to him, and
when he sings,
why is that?"

Qi Bo:
"When the yang abounds, then this lets that person
[utter] absurd words and voice insults,
without sparing those near or distant to him, and
not to wish to eat.
When he does not wish to eat, he runs around wildly as a result."[12]

---

12 Wang Bing: "The foot yang brilliance vessel of the stomach descends through the diaphragm, touches the stomach, and encircles the spleen. The foot major yin vessel of the spleen enters the abdomen, touches the spleen, encircles the stomach, rises through the diaphragm, passes along the throat, connects with the base of the tongue, and disperses below the tongue. Hence, the diseases manifest themselves as is outlined here."

Chapter 31
Discourse on Heat[1]

31-183-2
Huang Di asked:
"Now,
as for heat diseases,
they all are of the type 'harm caused by cold.'[2]
Some are healed, some end in death.
When they end in death, this happens always within six or seven days.
When they are healed, this takes always ten days or more.
Why is that?
I do not know an explanation of this;
I should like to hear a reason for this."[3]

Qi Bo responded:
"As for the great yang [conduit],
it is connected with all the yang [conduits].[4]

---

1 Various Chinese commentators have focussed on the close relationships between the contents of *Su wen* 31 and of the *Shang han lun*. See especially 2506/1, 1690/13, 885/1, 2275/3, 2843/44, and 1248/13.

2 Yang Shangshan: "Extreme cold turns into heat. When the three yin or the three yang vessels, the five depots or the six palaces receive heat and develop a disease, this is called 'heat disease.' The 'heat disease' [discussed] here, though, has its origin in the reception of cold, in massive harm [caused by cold]. Because one was harmed by cold, one got this heat disease. It is named ['harm caused by cold'] because of its origin. Hence these heat diseases are said to belong to the group of 'harm caused by cold.'"

3 Wang Bing: "Cold is the qi of winter. In winter time there is severe cold and the ten thousand types [of living beings] are concealed in the depth. The gentleman is securely covered [with clothes] and is not harmed by the cold. If one is affected, then this is called 'harm caused by cold.' Harm caused by any of the qi of the four seasons can result in disease, but the harm caused by cold is the most poisonous. When one is struck by [this] deadly aggressive qi and falls ill, this is called 'harm caused by cold.' In those cases which do not fall ill immediately, the cold poison is stored in the muscles and in the skin until before summer arrives. Then it changes to a warmth disease. After summer has arrived, it changes to a heat disease. Its outbreak, then, is always brought about by a harm caused by cold. Hence [the text] states: 'All heat diseases do belong to the group of 'harm caused by cold.'"

4 Wang Bing: "巨 is 大, 'great.'" Guo Tian: "巨 is 太, 'major.'" Cheng Shide et al.: "巨 is 大, 'great.' In antiquity, 大 and 太 were identical. 巨陽, then, is 太陽." Zhang Zhicong: "屬 is 會, 'to meet.' That is to say, the major yang is the meeting point of all

Its vessel is linked to the wind palace.
Hence, it rules the qi of all the yang [conduits].[5]

When a person is harmed by cold,
then the disease he develops is heat.[6]
The heat may be extreme, but he will not die.[7]
In cases where one develops a disease because of double affection by cold, there
is absolutely no way to escape death."[8]

31-183-7
[Huang] Di:
"I should like to hear about the appearance of such a [diseases]."

Qi Bo:
"[In the case of] harm caused by cold,

---

the yang." Zhang Yizhi et al.: "屬 is identical with 注, 'to pour into.' .. That is, the great
yang [conduit] is where all yang is poured into."

5 Wang Bing: " 'Wind Palace (風府)' is the name of a hole [used for piercing]. It is located above the nape one body-standardized inch into the hair line." Guo Tian: "The
'Wind Palace' is a hole on the supervisor vessel. 'Supervisor' is ruler. The supervisor
vessel rules all yang vessels. Hence the Wind Palace is the meeting point of all yang.
The major yang is the meeting point of all the yang and it rules the camp and the
guard qi. Its physiological function is to ward off wind and cold." Hua Shou: "The 21
characters from 巨陽者 to 諸陽主氣也 should be moved to behind [the passage] 傷
寒一日, 巨陽受之." Cheng Shide et al.: "These 21 characters are a commentary to the
statement 'All heat diseases belong to the group of 'harm caused by cold." This is to
say, the major yang rules the qi of all the yang [conduits]; it oversees the exterior of
the entire body. When cold evil attacks the outside, it will harm first the major yang.
When the major yang has received the evil, the muscles and the exterior are closed
firmly and the yang qi cannot disperse. Hence it stagnates and causes heat."

6 Zhang Zhicong: "為 is to say: the major yang qi causes [the heat disease]."

7 Wang Bing: "When cold poison accumulates in the muscles and in the skin, the
yang qi cannot disperse [to the outside] and is oppressed internally. Hence despite one
was harmed by cold, the disease one develops is heat."

8 Wang Bing: "The depots and the palaces correspond to each other. When both
receive cold, this is called 'double affection.' " Gao Shishi: "The yang vessel receives
cold and the yin vessel receives cold, too. When yin and yang both receive [cold], the
depot and the palace are harmed alike. Hence there is no way to escape death." Guo
Tian: " 'Double affection by cold' is: cold harms the conduits of both the exterior and
the interior. 必 is 審, 'to examine.' [That is,] 'one must conduct a careful examination
to find out wether the disease will take a fatal turn or not.' "

on the first day, the great yang [conduits] receive it.[9]
Hence, the head and the nape have pain;
the lower back and the spine are stiff.[10]

On the second day, the yang brilliance [conduits] receive it.[11]
The yang brilliance rules the flesh;
its vessels line the nose on both sides and enclose the eyes.
Hence, the body is hot, the eyes have pain, and the nose is dry.
One cannot lie down.[12]

On the third day, the minor yang [conduits] receive it.
The minor yang rules the gallbladder;[13]
its vessels follow the flanks and enclose the ears.
Hence, the chest and the flanks have pain, and the ears are deaf.

31-184-4
When all three yang conduits and network [vessels] have received this disease,[14]
and before it has entered the depots,[15]

---

9 Wang Bing: "[This is] the qi of the third yang. The great yang vessel is near the
surface. A vessel which is near the surface is located in the outside [of the body] in the
skin and its hair. Hence when one is harmed by cold, on the first day the major yang
is the first to receive it." Guo Tian: " 'Great yang' is 'major yang.' "

10 Wang Bing: "Above, the text states: 'Its vessel is linked to the wind palace (風府).'
That is just roughly spoken. In detail, the foot major yang [conduit] starts from the
peak to enter and enclose the brain. It branches off and descends to the nape, follows
the shoulders inside the shoulder blades, parallels the spine, and touches the hips.
Hence the head and the nape have pain and the hips and the back are stiff." Guo Tian:
"強 is 強直, 'stiff.' "

11 Wang Bing: "Because the yang was affected by heat. Identical qi seak each other;
hence it moves from the major yang [conduits] into the yang brilliance [conduits]."

12 Wang Bing: "When the body is hot, this is because the flesh has received the evil.
When heat is in the stomach, one is vexed. Hence one cannot lie down. The remaining [symptoms] are generated in agreement with [those body parts] enclosed by the
[yang brilliance] vessel."

13 Lin Yi et al.: "The Quan Yuanqi edition has 'bones' instead of 'gallbladder.' " The
Tai su, the *Jia yi jing*, and Tanba all have "bones" instead of "gallbladder." For a detailed discussion, see 2418/428.

14 Guo Tian: " 'Three yang' refers to major yang, yang brilliance and minor yang."

15 Lin Yi et al.: "The Quan Yuanqi edition has 'palaces' instead of 'depots.' " Zhang
Zhicong: "藏 is 裏, 'interior,' 陰, 'yin.' This is to say, all the three yang conduits and
network [vessels] have received a heat disease. [The disease] at this point is still in the

one can [make the patient] sweat and [the disease] ends.[16]

On the fourth day, the major yin [conduits] receive it.[17]
The major yin vessels spread into the stomach and enclose the throat.[18]
Hence, the abdomen is full and the throat is dry.

On the fifth day, the minor yin [conduits] receive it.
The minor yin vessels penetrate the kidneys and enclose the lung.
They are attached to the base of the tongue.
Hence, the mouth is desiccated, the tongue is dry, and one has thirst.

31-184-7
On the sixth day, the ceasing yin [conduits] receive it.
The ceasing yin vessels move along the yin (i.e., sexual) organ and enclose the liver.
Hence, there is vexation and fullness,[19] and the scrotum shrinks.

When the three yin and the three yang [conduits], the five depots and the six palaces
have all received the disease,
then the camp and the guard [qi] no [longer] move,
the five depots are no [longer] passable, and
death results.[20]

In those cases where no double affection by cold has occurred,

---

exterior of the body and has not entered the interior, the yin [sections, of the body].
It can be dispersed through sweating." Guo Tian: "藏 is 裏, 'interior.'" Ma Shi: "The
so-called 'depots' here are not the internal depots; they are the three yin conduits. Because the three yin [conduits] are associated with the five depots, the character 'depot'
was used here to speak [of the three yin conduits]."

16 Wang Bing: "Because the disease is in the exterior, one can [cure it by causing
the patient to] sweat."

17 Wang Bing: "It has reached its peak in the yang [conduits], hence the yin [con-
duits] receive it."

18 Guo Tian: "嗌 is 喉, 'throat.'"

19 Cheng Shide et al.: "滿 is identical with 懣, 'depressed.'"

20 Wang Bing: "死 is 澌, 'to perish,' 'to die.' This is to say, the essence and the qi have
all perished. Hence such [patients] always die within the sixth or seventh day of the
disease." 307/183: "This is a statement concerning the sequence of the six conduits in
which transmission and transformation [of the disease] occurs; it would be a mistake
to restrict [the meaning of this statement] to a fixed number of days."

on the seventh day, the disease in the great yang [conduits] weakens.
The headache has somewhat abated.[21]

On the eighth day, the disease in the yang brilliance [conduits] weakens.
The body heat has somewhat abated.

On the ninth day, the disease in the minor yang [conduits] decreases.
The deafness abates and one [can] hear.[22]

On the tenth day, the disease in the major yin [conduits] weakens.
The abdominal [distension] decreases and [assumes a size] as before.
Then one thinks of drinking and eating [again].

On the eleventh day, the disease in the minor yin [conduits] weakens.
The thirst stops and there is no [longer a feeling of] fullness.
The dryness of the tongue ends and [the patient] sneezes.

On the twelfth day, the disease in the ceasing yin [conduits] weakens.
The scrotum slackens,[23] and the lower abdomen moves down slightly.[24]
Large [quantities of] qi depart.[25]
The disease reaches its end within a day."

31-185-4
[Huang] Di:
"To treat this, how does one proceed?"

Qi Bo:
"In treating this one always opens the passage through the depots and vessels.[26]

----

21 Wang Bing: "The evil qi gradually retreats and the conduit qi gradually returns to harmony. Hence [the headache] lessens."

22 In contrast, Guo Tian: "Hence the ears can hear a little."

23 Guo Tian: "縱 is 弛緩, 'to relax.'"

24 Guo Tian: "微下 is 松弛, 'to loosen.'"

25 In contrast, Wang Bing: "大氣 is to say: 大邪之氣, 'the qi of a severe evil.'" Zhang Zhicong: "The evil of harm caused by cold is a most dangerous poison. Hence it is called 大氣, 'great qi.'" *Ling shu* 49 has 大氣入藏府者不病而死, "when large [quantities of] qi enter the depots and the palaces, one is not ill and dies suddenly." Tanba interprets 大氣 here and in *Ling shu* 49 as 大邪之氣, "qi of great evil." For a detailed discussion, see 40/27.

26 Guo Tian: "通 is 疏解, 'to open.'"

The disease weakens and reaches its end within a day.
If [the disease] has not yet lasted for three days, one can [make the patient]
sweat and [the disease] ends.[27]
In cases where [the disease] has lasted for three days, one can drain and [the
disease] ends."[28]

[Huang] Di:
"When a heat disease has come to an end and was healed,
at times there are residuals.[29]
Why is that?"[30]

Qi Bo:
"All residuals [result from a situation where] the heat is extreme and yet one
forces the [patient] to eat.
Hence, there are residuals.
In these cases it is always such that the disease has already weakened, but there
is some heat that remains stored.
Because this [heat] strikes at the grain qi [consumed], the two heats merge.[31]
Hence, there is a residual."

31-185-9
[Huang] Di:
"Good!
To treat residuals, how does one proceed?"

Qi Bo:
"Observe whether the [patient suffers from] depletion or repletion and
assess whether [his qi] move contrary to or follow [their regular course].

----

27 Guo Tian: "Before three days are full, the disease is [still] in the three yang
conduits of the major yang, the yang brilliance, and the minor yang. Hence it can be
dispersed from the exterior [of the body] by means of sweating."

28 Guo Tian: "When three days are full, the disease evil has been transmitted into
the three yin conduits. The heat is in the interior now and one can drain the internal
heat from the three yin [conduits]."

29 Guo Tian: "遺 is 留, 'to remain.'"

30 Wang Bing: "When the evil qi weakens and leaves [the body], but does not
[leave] entirely, it is as if some of it was left behind in man."

31 1207/48: "相薄 is 相迫. 迫 is 附. 附 is 增益, 'to increase,' 'to add.' That is, the
residual heat and the heat of the grain qi add to each other."

This way [the disease] can be brought to an end."[32]

[Huang] Di:
"When the disease is heat, which restrictions [exist] in this [situation]?"[33]

Qi Bo:
"When a heat disease has somewhat abated,[34] and [if at this point] one eats meat, then [the disease] returns.
If one eats a lot, then a residual results.
These are restrictions that apply here."[35]

31-185-12
[Huang] Di:
"When the disease is double affection by cold,
how is this reflected by the [movement in the] vessels and
what is the physical appearance of the disease like?"

Qi Bo:
"In case of double affection by cold,
when the disease is in its first day, then the great yang [conduit] and the minor yin [conduit] both have the disease.
As a result, the head aches, the mouth is dry, and there is vexation and fullness.

[When the disease is] in its second day, then the yang brilliance [conduit] and the major yin [conduit] both have the disease.
As a result, the abdomen is full, the body is hot, [the patient] does not wish to eat, and his speech is incoherent.[36]

---

32 Wang Bing: "One examines whether the [patient suffers from] depletion or repletion and supplements or drains [accordingly]. Then [the disease] will come to an end."

33 Gao Jiwu/452: "何禁 is 禁何, 'what is to be avoided?'"

34 Gao Jiwu/475 interprets 少愈 as 稍有好轉, "has taken a slight turn to the better."

35 Wang Bing: "These are the so-called restrictions in food and toil. Although the heat has somewhat abated, it has not been eliminated entirely. The qi of spleen and stomach are depleted and [spleen and stomach] are, therefore, unable to digest. The meat [consumed] hardens and the food stays [in the stomach]. Hence the heat emerges again. 復 is to say: the old disease returns."

36 Wang Bing: "譫言 is to say: 妄謬而不次, 'false and disorderly.'" Lin Yi et al.: "Yang Shangshan states: 多言, 'verbose.'" See also 1509/3.

[When the disease is] in its third day, then the minor yang [conduit] and the ceasing yin [conduit] both have the disease.
As a result, [the patient] is deaf, the scrotum shrinks and recedes.
Water and [other] beverages do not enter and [the patient] fails to recognize people.

[When the disease is] in its sixth day,[37] [the patient] dies."[38]

31-186-2
[Huang] Di:
"When the five depots have been harmed already,
when the six palaces are not passable and
when the camp and the guard [qi] do not move,
when in such a situation [the patient] dies after three days,
why is that?"

Qi Bo:
"The yang brilliance [conduits] are the leaders of the twelve conduit vessels.[39]
[In the present case,] their blood and qi abound.
Hence, [the patient] does not recognize people.
Within three days, their qi is exhausted.
Hence, [the patient] dies."

<Whenever someone has a disease 'harm caused by cold' and develops warmth, those cases preceding summer solstice day, they constitute a suffering from warmth;
those cases following summer solstice day, they constitute a suffering from summerheat.
All summerheat must leave [the patient] through his sweating.
One must not stop [the sweating].>[40]

---

37 In contrast, Guo Tian: "六日 is 六經."

38 Wang Bing: "The great yang and the minor yin constitute outside and inside. The yang brilliance and the major yin constitute outside and inside. The minor yang and the ceasing yin constitute outside and inside. Hence in case of a double affection by cold qi, [outside and inside] both receive this evil."

39 Guo Tian: "長 is 養, 'to nourish.'" *NJCD*: "長 is 主, 'ruler.'"

40 Wang Bing: "The meaning of this [passage] is based on the presence of large or small quantities of heat, [i.e.,] whether it abounds or is weak. As long as yang heat does not abound, it is controlled by cold. Hence when it causes a disease, this is called 'warmth.' When the yang heat greatly abounds, the cold cannot control it. Hence when it causes a disease, this is called 'summerheat.' Now, summerheat diseases must

Chapter 32
To Pierce Heat

32-186-8
When the liver has a heat disease,
the urine turns yellow first.[1]
The abdomen has pain; [the patient] lies down often and the body is hot.[2]

When the heat is fought [by the proper qi],
[the patient] talks crazily and is frightened.
The flanks are full and have pain.
The hands and the feet move restlessly.
[The patient] cannot sleep peacefully.[3]

---

be cured by [letting the patient] sweat. One must not do the contrary and let [the heat] stop [in the body]. This would result in a severe [disease]." Lin Yi et al.: "Yang Shangshan states: 'If one was slightly harmed by cold in winter, this will develop into a warmth disease before summer arrives. If one was severely harmed by cold in winter, this will develop into a summerheat disease after summer has arrived." Guo Tian: "The evil is concealed in the interior and should be dispersed through sweating. One must not stop the sweating. Otherwise, the evil could not be removed [from the body]." Zhang Qi: "In the eight character [passage] 暑當与汗... there must be an erroneous omission."

1 Tanba: "On the basis of the wording in connection with the four depots further below, the character 先 should precede [the characters] 小便."

2 Wang Bing: "The liver vessel encircles the private organ, touches the lower abdomen, and rises [from there]. Hence [in the case of heat disease in this vessel] the urine does not pass and is yellow first, the abdomen has pain and one lies down a lot. When cold accumulates, it creates cold. Hence the body is hot." Zhang Qi: "The lower abdomen is the liver region. When the lower abdomen has heat, the urine is yellow as a result. Wood subdues the spleen; hence the abdomen has pain. The liver and the gallbladder share the same qi. When the gallbladder has heat, [the patient] loves to lie down. The minister fire rises to pour out. Hence the entire body is hot. The heat of the five depots is obviously emitted internally; it is not identical with an affection by heat from the outside." Zhang Zhicong: "'First' is to say: first there is this or that internally caused heat and first this or that pathocondition appears."

3 Wang Bing: "Even though the conduit and the network [vessels] have received heat, the spirit depots have not taken in an evil yet. The evil and the proper [qi] fight each other. Hence [the text] states 爭. Also, the liver vessel rises from the lower abdomen, passes by the stomach, penetrates the diaphragm, spreads into the flanks, follows the throat and then encloses the base of the tongue. Hence [the patient] speaks crazily, the flanks are full and have pain. The nature of the liver is quiet and it masters fright. Hence in the case of a disease [in the liver, the patient] is frightened, hands and feet

On *geng* and *xin* [days] this is severe;
On *jia* and *yi* [days the patient] sweats profusely.⁴
When the qi moves contrary [to its regular course], then death occurs on *geng* and *xin* [days].⁵
Pierce the foot ceasing yin and the [foot] minor yang [conduits].⁶
{When 'it moves contrary [to its regular course],' then [the patient] has headache and is dizzy.⁷ The vessel pulls on and rushes against the head.}⁸

---

are restless, [the patient] lies down, but cannot find peace." Zhang Jiebin: "When the [heat] qi fights against the liver, then the liver qi turns into disorder. Hence [the patient] talks crazily and is frightened. .. Extreme heat generates wind. Wind excess moves into the four limbs. Hence hands and feet are restless. When wood evil invades the soil, it will proceed to the stomach. When the stomach loses its harmony, one's sleep is not peaceful." Wu Kun: "When the heat is extreme, then it strikes against the qi of the depots. Evil and proper [qi] fight each other." Zhang Zhicong: "When man sleeps, then the blood returns to the liver. When the liver qi has received harm and cannot take in the blood, [the patient] cannot find sleep." Cheng Shide et al.: "熱爭 is to say: the evil and the proper [qi] fight each other."

4 Zhang Zhicong: " 'Profuse sweating' is to say: the proper overcomes the evil and [the evil] leaves [the body] to the outside."

5 Wang Bing: "The liver rules the wood; *geng* and *xin* [days] are metal. Metal overcomes wood. Hence [the disease] is serious and [the patient] dies on *geng* or *xin* [days]. *Jia* and *yi* [days] are wood. Hence a profuse sweating sets in on *jia* and *yi* [days]." Zhang Zhicong: " 'When the qi moves contrary [to its regular course],' [is to say:] the heat is excessive and moves contrary [to its regular course] in the interior, contrary [to its proper direction]." Shen Zumian: "In this treatise the five agents doctrine is employed to predict a person's survival or death. What it says is that because *jia* and *yi* are associated with the liver and because *geng* and *xin* dominate and harm *jia* and *yi*, sweat leaves [the body] and the qi of wood is weakened. Hence such signs are listed as evidence of imminent death."

6 Wang Bing: "The [foot] ceasing yin is the liver vessel; the [foot] minor yang is the gallbladder vessel." Zhang Jiebin: "The minor yang is the exterior to the ceasing yin. Both can serve to drain the evil heat."

7 Wang Bing: "員員 is to say: 似急, 'as if tense.' " Yang Shangshan: "員 is 頭切痛, 'extreme headache.' " Zhang Jiebin: "員員 is: 靡定貌, 'unsettled.' " Zhang Zhicong: "員員 is to say: 周轉, 'vertigo.' " Gao Jiwu/208: "員 is read 云, *yun*." The *Jia yi jing* has 貢貢 instead of 員員. Wu Kun: "員員 is 小痛, 'minor pain.' " Li Guoqing: "員員 is 眩暈, 'dizzy.' " Qian Chaochen-90/140: "員員 is to say: 紜紜, 'confused.' " The *Tai su* does not have the two characters 逆則.

8 Wang Bing: "The liver vessel rises from the base of the tongue following the back of the throat and emerges at the temples and meets with the supervisor vessel at the peak. Hence [in the case of heat disease in this vessel the patient] has headache and [feels] dizzy." Zhang Jiebin: "The liver vessel and the supervisor vessel (督脈) meet at the peak. Hence, when qi rises moving contrary [to its regular course], then the head

32-187-1
When the heart has a heat disease,
at first [the patient] is not happy;
then,⁹ after several days, the heat sets in.¹⁰

When the heat is fought [by the proper qi], then [the patient] suddenly has heartache.
[The patient experiences] vexation and has an urge to vomit.
The head aches, the face is red, and [the patient] does not sweat.¹¹

On *ren* and *gui* [days] this is severe.
On *bing* and *ding* [days the patient] sweats profusely.
When the qi moves contrary [to its regular course], then death occurs on *ren* and *gui* [days].¹²

---

aches and [the patient] is dizzy. This is [the so-called] 脈引衝于頭." Li Guoqing: "脈引衝頭 is: qi moving contrary [to its regular course] follows the conduit vessels upwards and strikes the head."

9 Gao Jiwu/625: "乃 is 才, 'then.'"

10 Wang Bing: "That which is responsible for governing living beings, that is called 'the heart.' When disease qi enters [its] conduit and network [vessels], then the spirit cannot govern in peace. Hence at first [the patient] is unhappy and the heat sets in after several days." Wu Kun: "When the heart [qi] is in harmony, then [the patient] is happy; when it is not in harmony, then [the patient] is not happy." Yao Shaoyu: " 'Not to be happy' is to say: rising and resting are not comfortable. The heart is the depot of fire. Its inherent qi is heat. When the heart has a disease, then the fire does not remain calmly at its location and heats the physical appearance. Hence, when the heart experiences a heat disease, before this heat becomes apparent, there is some [other] suffering first."

11 Wang Bing: "The hand minor yin vessel of the heart emerges from within the heart. It branches out and rises from the heart connection, passing by the throat. The straight passage of the minor yang vessel follows the throat downwards to the diaphragm and touches the stomach. An off branch comes from the broken basin, follows the neck upwards into the cheeks and reaches the outer canthi of the eyes. Hence [in the case of heat disease in this vessel] there is sudden heartache, [the patient] is vexed and has a tendency to vomit, the head aches, and the face is red. Among the liquids, the heart is represented by the sweat. Now that [the heart has] a disease, no sweat leaves [the body]."

12 Wang Bing: "The heart rules the fire. *Ren gui* [days] are water. Water extinguishes fire. Hence [the disease] is severe and [the patient] dies, on *ren* and *gui* [days]. *Bing* and *ding* [days] are fire. Hence [the patient] sweats profusely on *bing* and *ding* [days]. [A description of] the signs of qi moving contrary [to its regular course] is missing in the text."

Pierce the hand minor yin and the [hand] major yang [conduits].[13]

32-187-3
When the spleen has a heat disease,
at first the head [feels] heavy and the cheeks have pain.
The heart is vexed and the forehead is green-blue.[14]
[The patient] wishes to vomit and the body is hot.[15]

When the heat is fought [by the proper qi], then the lower back aches and [the patient] cannot use [it] to bend down and up.
The abdomen is full and has outflow.
The two jaws ache.[16]

On *jia* and *yi* [days], this is severe;

---

13 Wang Bing: "The [hand] minor yin is the heart vessel; the [hand] major yang is the vessel of the small intestine." Ma Shi: "The heart and the small intestine are exterior and interior. Hence one pierces the holes of these two conduits."

14 Cheng Shide et al.: "顏 refers to 額, 'the forehead.' It is also called 庭. *Ling shu* 49 states: '庭 is 顏.'"

15 Wang Bing: "The stomach vessel emerges at the junction of the nose and of the forehead. It descends along the outside of the nose and enters the upper teeth, encircling them. It appears again and passes by the mouth, encircling the lips, moves further down and joins the sauce receptacle. It follows the jaws backwards, descends further in an angle and reappears at the Great Facing (*da ying* 大迎). It follows the lower jawbone, rises to in front of the ears, exceeds the Visitor Host Person, and follows the hair line to the temples. Hence [in the case of heat disease in this vessel] the head [feels] heavy first, the cheeks have pain and the space between the eyebrows is greenish. An off branch of the spleen vessel once again emerges from the stomach. It rises to the diaphragm and pours into the heart. Its straight passage rises to the diaphragm and passes by the throat. Hence [the patient's] heart is vexed, he wishes to vomit and his body is hot."

16 Wang Bing: "An off branch of the stomach vessel emerges from the lower opening of the stomach. It moves down inside the abdomen, reaching into the qi street, and joins with the upper thigh. The qi street is located in front the lower back. Hence [in the case of heat disease in this vessel] the lower back aches. The spleen vessel enters the abdomen, links with the spleen and encloses the stomach. Also, the stomach vessel, after joining the sauce receptacle (*cheng jiang* 承浆, the infralabial fossa), it follows the jaws backwards, descends further in an angle and reappears at the Great Facing (*da ying* 大迎). It follows the lower jawbone. Hence [in the case of heat disease in this vessel] the abdomen is full and has outflow. The two jaws have pain." Zhang Jiebin: "The lower back is the palace of the kidneys. When heat fights the spleen, then the soil evil avails itself of the kidneys and will certainly flow into the lower back. Hence this causes pain in the lower back and [the patient] can not bow up and down."

on *wu* and *ji* [days the patient] sweats profusely.
When the qi moves contrary [to its regular course], then death occurs on *jia* and *yi* days.[17]
Pierce the foot major yin and the [foot] yang brilliance [conduits].[18]

32-187-6
When the lung has a heat disease,
at first [the patient] shivers,[19] there is receding [qi] and the finest body hair rises.
[The patient] has an aversion to wind and cold.
The upper surface of the tongue is yellow.
The body is hot.[20]

When the heat is fought [by the proper qi], then [the patient] pants and coughs.
Pain moves into the chest, the breast, and the back.[21]

---

17 Wang Bing: "The spleen rules the soil; *jia* and *yi* [days] are wood. Wood removes soil. Hence [the disease] is serious and [the patient] dies on *jia* or *yi* [days]. *Wu* and *ji* [days] is soil. Hence [the patient] sweats profusely on *wu* and *ji* [days]. The signs of qi moving contrary [to its regular course] are not discussed in the text."

18 Wang Bing: "The [foot] major yin is the spleen vessel; the [foot] yang brilliance is the stomach vessel."

19 Gao Shishi: "淅 has the meaning of sprinkling the body with water." Shanghai zhongyi xueyuan et al./149: "淅 is like being in fear of cold. 厥 has the meaning here of [being] cold." Tanba Genken 丹波元堅: "The *Tai su* does not have the characters 厥, 毫 and 寒. Yang Shangshan commented: 'The lung rules the hair and the interstice structures. When internal heat extends it causes the hair to rise and it causes an aversion to wind. The heat of the lung steams upwards, hence the top of the tongue is yellow. The lung is responsible for passing qi through the body. Hence the body turns hot.' Wang Bing does not refer to 毫 in his commentary. Hence his version may not have had this character either."

20 Wang Bing: "The lung rules the skin and externally it provides nourishment to the hair. Hence when heat strikes it, then there is first a shivering. [the patient] has an aversion to wind and cold and [this] makes the finest hair rise. The lung vessel emerges from the central burner, descends, encloses the large intestine and follows it to the stomach opening. In the present case, lung heat enters the stomach and the stomach heat rises. Hence [in the case of heat disease in this vessel] the top of the tongue is yellow and the body is hot."

21 Zhang Yizhi et al.: "The *Shuo wen* has: 膺 is 胸, 'chest.' The *Guang ya* agrees. The commentary by Gui 桂 quotes the *Cang ji pian* 蒼頡篇: '膺 are the bones above the breasts.' In a commentary to the *Han shu* 漢書, Wei Zhao 韋昭 stated: 'The chest is high on four sides. Where it goes down in the center, that is called 膺.'" Mori: "The

[The patient] cannot take deep breaths.
The head aches unbearably.
Sweat leaves [the body] and [the patient feels] cold.[22]

On *bing* and *ding* [days], this is severe.
On *geng* and *xin* [days the patient] sweats profusely.
When the qi moves contrary [to its regular course], then death occurs on *bing* and *ding* [days].[23]
Pierce the hand major yin and [hand] yang brilliance [conduits].
<[Let] blood in the size of a large bean come out.[24]
[The disease] comes to an end immediately.>[25]

32-188-4
When the kidneys have a heat disease,
at first the lower back aches and the shins hurt.
[The patient] suffers from thirst, drinks frequently and [his] body is hot.[26]

---

hollow space in the center below the heart is called 胸; the region to the left and right where the ribs form a barrier, that is called 膺." Zhang Zhicong: "膺 refers to the elevated regions on both sides of the chest."

22 Wang Bing: "The lung is situated above the diaphragm. The qi rules the chest. If it changes the [direction of its] movement repeatedly, this results in coughing. Also, [the lung] stores the qi and rules ex- and inhalation. The back, in turn, is the palace of the chest center. Hence [the patient] pants and coughs, pain moves into chest and back and [the patient] cannot take deep breaths. The network vessel of the lung moves upwards and meets with the center of the ear. It lets the heat qi rise and steam [the head]. Hence [the patient] has unbearable headache, sweat leaves [the body] and [the patient] is cold."

23 Wang Bing: "The lung rules the metal. *Bing* and *ding* [days] are fire. Fire melts metal. Hence [the disease] is serious and [the patient] dies on *bing* or *ding* [days]. *Geng* and *xin* [days] are metal. Hence [the patient] sweats profusely on *geng* and *xin* [days]. The signs of qi moving contrary [to its regular course] are missing in the classic; they were not recorded."

24 Tanba: "There is no word of blood letting in the case of heat disease in the remaining depots. [The text] speaks of [blood letting] only with regard to a heat disease in the lung. This can truly be doubted." Gao Shishi has moved the seven characters 出血如大豆立已 further down to follow the passage 刺足少陰太陽.

25 Wang Bing: "The [hand] major yin is the lung vessel; the [hand] yang brilliance is the vessel of the large intestine. One must observe which network vessels abound [with blood] and pierce them to let [the blood] come out."

26 Wang Bing: "The bladder vessel emerges from inside the shoulder blade, passes along the spine and moves into the lower back. Also, the lower back is the palace of the kidneys. Hence [in the case of heat disease in this vessel] at first the lower back

When the heat is fought [by the proper qi], then the nape aches and is stiff.
The shins are cold and they hurt.
The lower side of the feet is hot.
[The patient] does not wish to speak.[27]
<When [the qi] moves contrary [to its regular course], then the nape has pain,
[the patient feels] dizzy,[28] and [his mind is] agitated.>[29]

On *wu* and *ji* [days], this is extreme.
On *ren* and *gui* [days the patient] sweats profusely.
When the qi moves contrary [to its regular course], then death occurs on *wu*
and *ji* [days].[30]
Pierce the foot minor yin and the [foot] major yang [conduits].[31]
{Whenever [a patient] sweats, when [heat qi] reaches the day when [the agent
associated with the respective depot] dominates, the sweat will leave [the
body].}[32]

---

aches. Also, the kidney vessel follows the back of the inner ankle, rises inside the calf
and reappears in the inner curve of the bend of the knee. Also, its straight passage
rises from the kidneys, penetrates the diaphragm, enters the lung, follows the throat
and passes by the base of the tongue. Hence [in the case of heat disease in this vessel]
the shins ache, [the patient] suffers from thirst, [the patient] drinks frequently and
the body is hot."

27 Wang Bing: "The bladder vessel comes out of the brain and branches off down
the nape. Also, the kidney vessel emerges from below the small toe, runs diagonally
across the sole of the foot and reappears below the navicular bone. It follows the back
of the inner ankle and branches off into the heel whence it rises inside the shins. Also,
its straight course rises from the kidneys, penetrates liver and diaphragm, enters the
lung, follows the throat and passes by the base of the tongue. Hence [in the case of
heat disease in this vessel] the nape aches and is stiff. The shins are cold and have pain.
The lower side of the feet is hot and [the patient] does not wish to speak."

28 915/58: "員 is identical with 暈, 'to be dizzy.'" Shanghai zhongyi xueyuan et
al./149: "員員 has the meaning of 頻頻, 'agitated.'"

29 Tanba: "澹: The *Shuo wen* states: 澹 is 水搖, 'agitated water.' Wang Bing interpretes 澹 as 不定, 'unsettled.' The meaning is the same."

30 Wang Bing: "The kidneys rule the water. *Wu* and *ji* [days] are soil. The soil corrects
the water. Hence [the disease] is severe and [the patient] dies on *wu* or *ji* [days]. *Ren*
and *gui* [days] are water. Hence [the patient] sweats profusely on *ren* and *gui* [days]."

31 Wang Bing: "The [foot] minor yin is the kidney vessel; the [foot] major yang is
the bladder vessel."

32 Wang Bing: "On the day when the qi flourishes, that is [what the text calls] 所勝.
When it flourishes, then it dominates the evil. Hence it is always on those days when
the respective [qi] flourishes that [the patient] sweats." Gao Shishi: "This is an erro-

In the case of heat disease in the liver, the left cheek[33] becomes red first.[34]
In the case of heat disease in the heart, the forehead[35] becomes red first.[36]
In the case of heat disease in the spleen, the nose becomes red first.[37]
In the case of heat disease in the lung, the right cheek becomes red first.[38]
In the case of heat disease in the kidneys, the chin[39] becomes red first.[40]

Even though the disease has not broken out yet, as soon as one perceives a red color, one pierces it.
{This is called 'to treat what is not yet ill.'}[41]

32-189-4
Heat diseases emerging from specific locations[42] come to an end when they

---

neously inserted passage. Further down the text states 諸當汗者, 至其所勝日, 汗大出也. This passage was erroneously repeated here." The *Tai su* does not have the eleven character passage beginning with 諸汗者.

33 Yan Hongchen & Gao Guangzhen/213: "頰 is the lower region in front of the ears."

34 Wang Bing: "The liver qi is associated with the wood. Wood qi corresponds to spring. If one stands upright facing the South, then it is his left cheek."

35 Yan Hongchen & Gao Guangzhen/213: "顏 is the section above the two eyebrows up to the frontal hair line. It is commonly called 額頭."

36 Wang Bing: "The heart qi is associated with the fire. Fire qi flames upwards; it points to an indicator reflecting brilliance. Hence one examines it at the 顏. 顏 is 額, 'forehead.'" Gao Shishi: "The heart [is] fire [and] is located in the upper [part]. Hence in the case of a heat disease in the heart, the forehead becomes red first."

37 Wang Bing: "The spleen qi is associated with the soil. The soil flourishes in the center. The nose is located in the center of the face. Hence [the spleen qi] manifests itself through the nose."

38 Wang Bing: "The lung qi is associated with the metal. Metal qi corresponds to autumn. If one stands upright facing the South, then it is his right cheek." Gao Shishi: "The lung [is] metal [and] is located on the right. Hence in the case of a heat disease in the lung, the right cheek is red first."

39 Yan Hongchen & Gao Guangzhen/213: "頤 is the upper region of the chin (commonly called 下巴)."

40 Wang Bing: "The kidney qi is associated with water. Water moistens only that which is below; it produces clear signs. Hence its signs appear at the chin."

41 Wang Bing: "The sages did not treat what is ill; they treated what is not ill yet. .. That is meant here."

42 Yang Shangshan: "The 'specific locations' are the sections [in the face where changes in the] color [appear]." Yao Shaoyu: "部 refers to the sections in the face mentioned above."

have reached a [specific] time.[43]

In case the piercing was contrary [to the requirements, the disease nevertheless] comes to an end after three circulations.[44]

If there is multiple opposition, then [the patient] will die.[45]

{Whenever [a patient] should sweat, when [the heat qi] reaches the day when [the agent associated] dominates, sweat leaves [the body] profusely.}[46]

Whenever one treats a heat disease, one lets the [patient] drink cold water and only then one pierces him.

---

43 Wang Bing: "期 is the day of profuse sweating. That is, for the liver these days are the *jia* and *yi* days, for the heart these are the *bing* and *ding* days, for the spleen these are the *wu* and *ji* days, for the lung these are the *geng* and *xin* days and for the kidneys these are the *ren* and *gui* days."

44 Wang Bing: " 'Contrary' is to say: 'One removes a [specific] qi contrary [to the requirements]. That is, if in the case of a liver disease one pierces the spleen, if in the case of a spleen disease one pierces the kidneys, if in the case of a kidney disease one pierces the heart, if in the case of a heart disease one pierces the lung, if in the case of a lung disease one pierces the liver, then these are all [examples of] piercing the qi of the five depots contrary [to the requirements]. 三周 is to say: three circulations through the three yin and three yang vessels. Also, if in the case of a major yang disease one pierces and drains the yang brilliance; if in the case of a major yang disease one pierces and drains the yang brilliance; if in the case of a yang brilliance disease one pierces and drains the minor yang; if in the case of a minor yang disease one pierces and drains the major yin; if in the case of a major yin disease one pierces and drains the minor yin; if in the case of a minor yin disease one pierces and drains the ceasing yin, all these are [examples of] removing the qi of the three yin and three yang vessels contrary [to the requirements]." Zhang Jiebin: " 'Contrary [to the requirements]' is to say: to drain a depletion, or to fill a repletion. When a disease is treated contrary [to the requirements], this disease will become serious. If it is serious, the cure will set in, contrary [to one's expectations], only slowly. As for 三周, [the disease] will come to an end after it has passed, three times, the day when [the respective qi] dominates." Tanba: "If one examines Wang Bing's commentary, [the end of the disease] comes very fast. One should follow Zhang Jiebin's commentary."

45 Wang Bing: "If the first piercing was already contrary [to the requirements], the disease qi [continues] to flow and is transmitted further. If one pierces contrary [to the requirements] again, this is 'doubled opposition.' In the case of a single opposition piercing, [the disease qi] will nevertheless come to an end after three circulations. Through a doubled opposition, though, one inevitably generates evil."

46 Wang Bing: "When it flourishes, then it overcomes the evil. Hence in all cases it is such that when [the disease] has lasted until the day when [the respective qi] flourishes, [the patient] will sweat." Lin Yi et al.: "These 24 characters of commentating text are repeated here from above. They should be discarded. The *Jia yi jing* and the *Tai su* do not issue them twice." Zhang Zhicong: "勝日 is to say: the day when the [depot's] inherent qi dominates and flourishes."

One must provide him with cold clothing.
He [should] stay at a cold location.
When the body is cold, one stops.[47]

If in the case of heat disease, the chest and the flanks ache first and if the hands and the feet are restless,
pierce the foot minor yang [conduit] and supplement the foot major yin [conduit].[48]
When the disease is severe, conduct the fifty-nine piercings.[49]

---

47 Yang Shangshan: "All those suffering from heat disease are to be treated with cold. Altogether there are four different [approaches]. First, to drink cold water causes the interior [sections of the body] to become cold. Second, to pierce the holes lets the vessels become cold. Third, by means of cold clothing one lets the exterior [sections of the body] become cold. Fourth, by residing at a cold place, one lets the body become cold. With these four colds, one lets the interior and the exterior [sections of the] body become cold. Hence the heat disease ends." Wang Bing: "When cold water is in the stomach, the yang qi abounds in the external regions. Hence, one lets [the patient] drink cold [water] and then conducts the piercing. When the heat recedes, coolness emerges. Hence the body becomes cold and the piercing is stopped."

48 Wang Bing: "This gives an example of proper removal. That is, if in case the foot minor yang, the wood, has a disease, one drains the wood qi of the foot minor yang and one supplements the soil qi of the foot major yin, then this [procedure is chosen] because one fears that the wood transmits [the disease] to the soil." Lin Yi et al.: "The Quan Yuanqi edition and the *Tai su* have hand major yin instead of foot major yin." The *Tai su* does not have the character 補.

49 Wang Bing: " 'Fifty-nine piercings' refers to five lines on the head. These lines are five to expel the heat of all the yang [vessels] moving contrary [to its regular course]. Great Shuttle (大杼), Breast Transporter (膺俞), Broken Basin (缺盆), Back Transporter (背俞), these eight [holes] are employed to drain the heat from inside the chest. Qi Street (氣街), Three Miles (三里), Upper [and] Lower Edge of the Great Hollow (巨虛上下廉), these eight [holes] are employed to drain the heat from inside the stomach. Cloud Gate (雲門), Shoulder Bone (髃骨), Bend Middle (委中), Marrow Hollow (髓空), these eight [holes] are employed to drain the heat of the four limbs. The transporter[-holes] of the depots, [of which there are] five on both sides, these ten [holes] are employed to drain the heat of the five depots. All these fifty-nine holes control heat. Hence, when a disease is severe then one pierces these. Now, of the five lines on the head [the holes of] the line in the very middle are called: Upper Star (上星), Fontanel Meeting (顖會), Anterior Vertex (前頂), Hundred Convergences (百會), Posterior Vertex (後頂). The [holes on the] next two [lines] on the side are called: Fifth Place (五處), Receiving the Light (承光), Communication with Heaven (通天), Declining Connection (络却), Jade Pillow (玉枕). The [holes on the] next [lines] further [outside] are called: Approaching Tears (臨泣), Eye Window (目窗), Proper Camp (正營), Receiving the Numinous (承靈), Brain Hollow (腦空)." See 1861/10

32-190-1

If a heat disease begins with pain in the hands and arms, pierce the hand yang brilliance and the [hand] major yin [conduits] and as soon as sweat leaves [the body], stop [the piercing].

If a heat disease begins in the head, pierce the major yang [conduit] in the nape and as soon as sweat leaves [the body], stop [the piercing].

If a heat disease begins in the feet and shins, pierce the foot yang brilliance [conduit] and as soon as sweat leaves [the body], stop [the piercing].[50]

If in the case of a heat disease the body [feels] heavy first, if the bones ache and the ears are deaf and if [the patient] tends to experience blurred vision,[51] pierce the foot minor yin [conduit].[52]

When the disease is severe, conduct the fifty-nine piercings.[53]

If in the case of a heat disease [the patient] at first experiences vertigo and is hot and if his chest and flanks have [a feeling of] fullness, pierce the foot minor yin and the [foot] minor yang [conduits].

32-193-1

When a major yang [movement appears in the] vessels,[54] and

when the splendor [of a major yang] color shows in the [region of the] cheek bones,[55]

this is heat disease.[56]

---

for a comparative examination of the fifty-nine locations advocated for piercing in various *Su wen* and *Ling shu* treatises.

50 Lin Yi et al.: "Neither the *Su wen* nor the *Tai su* did originally have this statement; it was added now on the basis of the [version of the] *Jia yi jing*."

51 We read 瞑 as 瞋.

52 Wang Bing: "According to the classic, there are no regular holes ruling this. One must supplement and drain at the well and brook [holes]."

53 Zhang Qi: "Maybe the eight characters 身重骨痛耳聾 should follow the passage 腎熱病者先腰痛胻酸. The three characters 熱病先 and the twelve character passage beginning with 刺足少陰 are erroneous insertions." The *Tai su* has foot minor yang instead of foot minor yin.

54 In contrast, Gao Shishi: "脈 is 經脈, 'conduit vessel.'"

55 Wang Bing: "榮 is 飾, 'make up.' That is to say, red color appears on the cheek bones like make up. The so-called 'cheek bones' are located below the eyes at the outer canthus." Zhang Jiebin: "榮 is 發見, 'to become apparent.'"

56 Zhang Wenhu: "榮顴 refers to the complexion in the facial region. To speak of 顴 does not require one to speak of 骨." Yang Shangshan read: "Pierce the foot minor yin, minor yang and major yang vessels. When the complexion is beautiful in the cheeks,

If the splendor is not exchanged yet,[57] this is to say: there will be immediate sweating.[58]

Wait for [some] time and [the disease] will come to an end.[59]

---

this is a heat disease in the bones." He commented: "All these three vessels emerge from the bones. Hence when these three vessels have a disease and in case a red complexion is strongly developed in the cheek region, this is a heat disease in the bones." Yan Zhenhai/55: "There are two possibilities to read this passage in that the character 骨 is linked either to the preceding or to the following characters. Wang Bing, in his commentary, linked the character 骨 to the preceding text. Yang Shangshan commented: 有赤色榮顴者, 骨熱病也, 'if red color appears on the cheek bones, this is a heat disease in the bones.' That is, Yang Shangshan linked the character 骨 to the following text. Now, the meaning of 色榮顴 is sufficiently clear; it does not need the character 骨. 'A heat disease in the bones' belongs to the category of kidney diseases. Further down, the text of the [*Nei*] *jing* states: 'the heat disease has internally tied up with the kidneys.' This may serve as additional proof. The kidneys rule the bones. Hence a heat disease in the kidneys turns into a heat disease in the bones. Earlier, the [*Nei*] *jing* states: 'When the kidneys have a heat disease, the chin is red first.' Hence the character 顴 should be a mistake for 頤 here."

57 Wang Bing: "In another [version], the character 榮 is erroneously written 營, 'camp [qi].'" Lin Yi et al.: "The *Jia yi jing* and the *Tai su* have 榮未夭, 'the luster has not perished yet.'" Zhang Jiebin: "The 榮 here is different from the 榮 in the previous passage. Here it refers to the camp and guard [qi]. 榮未交 is to say: The evil has affected the guard [qi], but has not joined with the camp [qi] yet. The [evil] qi has not penetrated deeply yet." The Wu Kun edition has 營, 'camp [qi],' instead of 榮. Gao Jiwu/246: "榮 is to be interpreted as 'color,' especially as 'facial color.'" Cheng Shide et al.: "*Su wen* 19 has 色夭不澤, 'when the color has perished and is not glossy, this is to say: difficult to heal.' On the basis of this, 榮未夭 is to say: the color is glossy and is not spoiled yet. The disease qi is still minor and has not penetrated deeply. Hence one can bring [the disease] to an end by having [the patient] sweat." Yu Chang: "榮未交 should be read, as suggested by Lin Yi et al., in the wording of the *Jia yi jing* and of the *Tai su*: 榮未夭. That would be correct."

58 The *Tai su* has 日, "day," instead of 曰 and links it to the preceding characters. Instead of 今 it has 令, "to cause."

59 Wang Bing: "Whenever there is a 曰, this indicates that a pattern is quoted from an ancient classic. [This passage] is to say: the complexion may indicate abundance, but the qi of yin and yang do not mix. Hence the pattern states: Today [the patient] will sweat and [the disease] comes to an end. 'To wait for the time' is: if in the case of a liver disease one waits for a *jia* or *yi* day, if in the case of a heart disease one waits for a *bing* or *ding* day, if in the case of a spleen disease one waits for a *wu* or *ji* day, if in the case of a lung disease one waits for a *geng* or *xin* day and if in the case of a kidney disease one waits for a *ren* or *gui* day, then this is what is meant by 'one waits for the time.' As for 交, this refers to what is outlined in the following sentence." The *Tai su* and the *Jia yi* have 自已, "heals by itself," instead of 而已. The entire passage reads in the *Tai su* as follows: 榮未夭日, 令且得汗, "on a day when the luster (or: camp [qi]

If [however], a struggle with a ceasing yin [movement in the] vessels is apparent,

the time of death is no more than three days away.[60]

{When the heat disease has linked up internally with the kidneys,

[this is visible in a] minor yang [movement in the] vessels and in [a minor yang] color.}[61]

As for a minor yang [movement in the] vessels, when the splendor of its color shows in front of the cheeks, this is heat disease.[62]

If the splendor is not exchanged yet, this is to say: there will be immediate sweating.

Wait for [some] time and [the disease] will come to an end. 'If, however, a

---

has not perished yet, one must let [the patient] sweat. Wait for [some] time and [the disease] will heal by itself." This appears to be the original reading; the present version is corrupt and our translation is forced around this corruption. However, since the same passage is repeated a few lines further down in this treatise and appears – with minor differences only – twice in the *Tai su*, one may presume that both the compiler of the present treatise and of the *Tai su* quoted it from an even older source, with the *Tai su* quote remaining closer to the original version than the present quotes in the *Su wen*.

60 Wang Bing: "Externally the red color of the major yang appears; internally one feels a string-like ceasing yin [movement in the] vessels. Now, when the major yang has received a disease, it should transmit it into the yang brilliance. When in the present case now, in contrast, a ceasing yin [movement in the] vessels appears, then the soil is destroyed and the wood has robbed it. Hence [the patient] dies. Now, the soil qi is destroyed already, but the wood [qi] makes crazy moves here and there. The generation number of wood is three. Hence the time of death does not exceed three days."

61 Wang Bing: "病 may be a mistake for 氣, 'qi.' If a red color qi internally links the two sides of the nose, then this is the color of the minor yang vessels. It is not the color of the ceasing yin vessels. Why? The kidney section is located near the nose." Lin Yi et al.: "Older editions did not have the six characters 少陽之脈色也. They were added by Wang Bing. Wang Bing's comments are incorrect. One should follow the interpretation offered by Yang Shangshan." Wu Kun omitted these six characters from his edition.

62 The *Tai su* and the *Jia yi jing* have 筋, "sinews," instead of 前. Gu Guangguang: "The character 筋 is correct. The minor yang [region] forms the outer side of the liver. The liver rules the sinews. Hence this causes a heat disease in the sinews." Mori: "One should follow the *Tai su* which has 筋熱病. This wording parallels the wording 骨熱病 above."

struggle with a minor yin [movement in the] vessels is apparent,[63]
the time of death is no more than three days away.[64]

32-193-5
In the case of heat disease, the qi holes [to be treated are the following]:[65]
[Those] located[66] below the third vertebra rule heat in the chest.
[Those] located below the fourth vertebra rule heat in the [region of the]
diaphragm.
[Those] located below the fifth vertebra rule liver heat.
[Those] located below the sixth vertebra rule spleen heat.
[Those] located below the seventh vertebra rule kidney heat.[67]
{The splendor shows in the sacrum.}[68]

---

63 Gu Guanguang: "When the cheeks are red and when the jaws in the face are red,
too, in this case the minor yang and the minor yin exchange [their qi]. The two fires
flame vigorously and the yang [qi] in the kidneys dries up. Hence [the patient] dies."

64 Wang Bing: "When the minor yang [vessels] receive a disease, they should transmit it to the major yin [conduits]. In the present case, contrary to the normal course, a
minor yin [movement in the] vessels appears. Again the soil is destroyed and the wood
has robbed it. Hence death will occur within three days. This is the number associated
with wood." Lin Yi et al.: "Wang Bing's comments were not based on the original version. Neither the *Jia yi jing* nor the *Tai su* have the five characters 期不過三日."

65 Mori: "The *Tai su* does not have the passage 熱病氣穴. The *Jia yi jing* has it. Obviously, Wang Bing has inserted it here on the basis of the *Jia yi jing*."

66 Wu Kun: "To be at a [specific] location is called 間."

67 Zhang Jiebin: "Below the third vertrebra [to the side] is the [hole called] *Po*-Soul
Door (魄戶) Below the fourth vertebra, to the side, is the [hole called] *Gao Huang* (膏
肓). Below the fifth vertrebra, to the side, is the [hole called] Spirit Hall (神堂) . Below the sixth vertebra, to the side, is the [hole called] *Yi Xi* (譩譆). Below the seventh
vertebra, to the side, is the [hole called] Diaphragm Pass (膈關)." Ma Shi: "Below the
third vertebra [is the hole] called Body Pillar (神柱). Below the fourth vertebra there
is no hole. Below the fifth vertebra [is the hole] called Spirit Path (神道). Below the
sixth vertebra [is the hole] called Numinous Tower (靈臺). Below the seventh vertebra
[is the hole] called Extreme Yang (至陽)." Cheng Shide et al.: "The text of the classic
clearly states 'below the .. vertebra.' Zhang Jiebin's interpretation 'below the .. vertebra,
to the side' is a mistake."

68 Wang Bing: "The sections of the spine are called 椎, 'vertebra.' The end of the
spine is called 骶, 'sacrum.' This is to say, the heat qi of the kidneys penetrates, in the
exterior, the end of the spine." Zhang Jiebin: "That is, if one takes the yang qi from the
upper [end of the spine], one must supplement the yin qi at the lower [end]. Hence
[the text] states: 榮在骶, 'the yin qi is in the sacrum.'" Wu Kun: "The upper seven
vertebrae are the yang section; hence they rule heat diseases. The lower seven vertebrae
are the yin section. They rule the camp [qi and/i.e. the] blood. If one pierces them one

{Above the nape, the third vertebra, where the depression is, in the center.}[69]

<If there is a movement contrary [to its regular course] from below the cheeks [upwards] to the cheek bones, this is [a case of] serious conglomeration.[70]
If it moves down to the jaws, this is abdominal fullness.
If [it moves to] behind the cheek bones, this is pain in the flanks.
If [it moves to] above the cheeks, [the disease] is above the diaphragm.>[71]

---

depletes the yin. Hence [the text] states: 'the camp [qi] is in the sacrum.' The meaning is: one must not cause harm here." Cheng Shide et al.: "Zhang Jiebin advocates to fill the yin at the lower [end of the spine]; Wu Kun states one must not harm [this region]. The two statements contradict each other." For a radical reformulation of the text beginning with 太陽之脈色榮權骨, see 2317/6. Zhang Yizhi et al.: "The *Tai su* does not have the two characters 骶也 and it links the two characters 榮在 to the following characters. Sun Dingyi says: 'The *Tai su* version is correct. 骶 is 營. The *Guang ya* 廣雅, Shi gu yi 釋詁一, states: '營 is 度.' This refers to a pattern how to measure the vertebrae.'"

69 Wang Bing: "This mentions the important pattern of counting the vertebrae of the spine. That is to say, the intersection below the third vertebra rules the heat in the chest. How to count them? One must always take advantage of the clefts [between the vertebrae]. These are the locations where the qi effuses." Zhang Jiebin: "The 項上 三椎 are the three intersections of the nape bones, not the vertebra of the spine. In the cleft between the third vertebra, this is the first intersection. The name of the hole is Great Hammer (大椎). If one counts from this one downwards, one gets all the vertebra in their sequence."

70 Yao Shaoyu: "A 'movement contrary [to its regular course]' is from below upwards. The cheeks are below the cheek bones. 逆顴 is to say: it rises from the cheeks to the cheek bones. 瘕 is 氣塊, 'conglomeration of qi.'" Zhang Zhicong: "Below the cheeks is the chin. If the color below the cheeks rises in a movement contrary [to its regular course] to the cheek bones, this [indicates that] the kidney heat avails itself of the liver. This must result in large conglomerations with diarrhea (大瘕泄)." For the term 大瘕泄, see also *Nan jing* 57.

71 Zhang Zhicong: "When there is a movement contrary [to its regular course] to behind the cheek bones, this [indicates that] the heat evil has availed itself of the gallbladder. This causes the flanks to ache. In the case of a movement contrary [to its regular course] to above the cheek bones, this [indicates that the heat evil] is in the section of the heart and of the lung above the diaphragm."

Chapter 33
Discourse Deliberating upon Heat Disease

33-194-6
Huang Di asked:
"Someone suffers from warmth.
When sweat has left [his body], the heat returns always[1] and
the [movement in the] vessels races.
The disease is not weakened by the sweating.[2]
[The patient] utters crazy words and cannot eat.
What is the name of this disease?"

Qi Bo responded:
"The disease is named 'yin yang interaction.'
If it comes to [such] an interaction, [the patient] will die."[3]

[Huang] Di:
"I should like to hear an explanation of this."

---

1 Fu Weikang & Wu Hongzhou/290: "輒 has the meaning of 常常, 'often.'" 232/55:
"輒 has the meaning of 即, 'then.'"

2 In contrast, Gao Jiwu/438: "不能被發汗減輕, 'one must not diminish the essence
through causing [the patient] to sweat.' Another reading could be 不因發汗減輕,
'one [must] not diminish the essence by having [the patient] sweat.' 為 is interpreted
here as 因, 'because.'"

3 Yang Shangshan: "Sweat is a yin liquid; heat is abundance of yang qi. When the
yang [qi] abounds, there is no sweat. When sweat leaves [the body], then the heat
decreases. When in the present case, heat leaves [the body] while the heat fails to
decrease, this is [a situation where] the yang evil abounds and yin [qi] emerges anew.
The two interact with each other, hence the name [of the disease] is 'yin yang interaction.'" Wang Bing: "交 is to say 交合, 'to form a union.' The qi of yin and yang do not
separate." Wan Lanqing et al./26: " 'Yin' refers to the proper qi of yin essence; 'yang'
refers to the evil of yang heat. .. The yang evil enters the yin section. The evil abounds
and the proper [qi] is weak. Because the evil of the yang heat steams away the body
liquids, the [resulting] exhaustion of yin essence brings forth the most dangerous signs
of a loss of yin and also of a loss of yang. Hence [the text] speaks of 'death.'" 1502/50:
"陰陽交 is not a disease of its own; it is a serious pathological condition appearing
in the development of heat disease. It has its name because yang heat moves to the
interior and intrudes into the yin section, yin liquid flows off to the outside, with the
result that yin and yang mix with each other." 1966/55: "交 should be interpreted as
交爭, 'to interact with and battle against each other.'" See also 2286/40.

Qi Bo:

"That because of which sweat leaves man is generated by grain;
grain generates essence.[4]

Now, when evil [qi] and [proper] qi interact in a struggle[5] in the bones and in
the flesh and when this leads to sweating, [this indicates that] the evil retreats
and the essence[6] dominates.

When the essence dominates, then one should be able to eat and there should
be no returning heat.

{Returning heat is evil qi.}

{The sweat is essence qi.}

When, in the present case, after the sweat has left [the body], the heat always
returns,

this [indicates that] evil dominates.

When [the patient] cannot eat, the essence has nothing from which it [could]
emerge.[7]

---

4 Wang Bing: "The qi of the grains is transformed to essence. When the essence qi
dominates, it causes sweating." 246/10: "The 于 in 生于穀 is identical with 從, 'from.'
This is a very common meaning and Wang Bing did not add a comment. However,
the 于 in 穀生于精 is an auxiliary word, without any meaning of its own in this sentence. Hence Wang Bing comments this passage as 穀氣化為精 to point out to the
reader that the character 于 is not translatable here." Gao Jiwu/236 agrees. 2552/15:
" 'Essence' refers to the liquids inside the body here." 666/43: "汗生于穀, 穀生于精 is
to say: Sweat is a product of the transformation of water and grains. However, when
there is no essence qi for the transformation of water and grains, then the water and
the grains simply remain water and grains and there is nothing from which sweat
could be produced through transformation. This process can be summarized and put
in simple language as: sweat is generated by essence. Hence further on the text states:
'sweat is essence qi.' And it states also: 'If someone cannot eat, [his] essence has nothing that could add to it.' "

5 678/55 supports a reading of 邪氣 here as "evil [qi] and [proper] qi."

6 1583/59: "精 stands for 正, 'the proper.' "

7 Wang Bing: " 無俾 is to say: it has nothing that could stimulate it to become sweat.
When the grains are not transformed, then no essence is generated and no essence
is transformed into [something that can] flow. Hence 'it has nothing it could stimulate.' " The *Mai jing* has 裨, 'to benefit,' 'to aid,' instead of 俾." Gao Shishi: "俾 is 補益,
'to supplement.' " Gao Jiwu/16: "俾 is 裨, in the meaning of 增添, 'to add,' 'to increase.'
The *Shuo wen* states: 俾 is 益, 'to benefit.' " 1193/8: "The *Er ya*, Shi yan 釋言, states:
"俾 is 職, 'duty.' The Shi gu 釋詁 states: 俾 is 使, 'to send.' Hence the meaning of 精
無俾 is: the essence qi cannot fulfill its functions. The essence qi has been destroyed
by the evil qi. Hence it cannot carry out its duties and [the patient] is unable to eat. In
antiquity, [the notions of] essence, qi and spirit were not clearly distinguished. Hence
精無俾 is identical with 神不使 in *Su wen* 14." According to *HYDCD*, 俾 can have

When[8] the disease remains [in the body, the patient's] life can suddenly collapse.[9]

33-195-1
Also,[10]
the *Discourse on Heat*[11] states:
'When sweat leaves [the body] and the [movement in the] vessels nevertheless races and is abundant, [the patient] will die.'
When in the present case, the [movement in the] vessels does not correspond to the sweating,
this [is because the proper qi] does not overcome the disease. The [patient's imminent] death is obvious.[12]
Those who utter crazy words, they have lost their mind.
Those who have lost their mind, they die.[13]

In the present case, [all these] three [signs] appear; [hence, the patient must] die.[14]

---

the meaning of "be obedient, to follow", attested in the *Shu jing* 書經, Jun shi 君奭 (cf. Ruan Yuan 225 below). We interpret 俾 as "to emerge from", a meaning which could be derived from the meaning "to follow".

8 Gao Jiwu/504: "而 is 如果, 'if.' "

9 Wang Bing: "If there is such a situation that sweat leaves [the body] very fast, while [the disease] stays attached [to the interior] and does not depart, then this person's life may all of a sudden reach a state of great danger." The *Mai jing* 脈經, ch. 7, no. 18 has 汗而熱留者, "in case the heat stays despite sweating, .."

10 Gao Jiwu/494: "且 is 況且, 'furthermore.' "

11 Wang Bing:"This is a *Discourse on Heat* of high antiquity. After a sweating, the [movement in the] vessels should be retarded and calm. If, in contrast, it races and is tense because of abundance and fullness [in the vessels], then the true qi is exhausted and the evil abounds. Hence one knows [the patient] will die." Zhang Jiebin: "This is a reference to the treatise 熱病, 'heat disease,' of the *Ling shu*." The *Jia yi jing* does not have the four characters 夫熱論曰.

12 Wang Bing: "When the [movement in the] vessels is not calm but races and is abundant, this is a lack of mutual correspondence [with the fact that the patient is sweating]."

13 Wang Bing: "The mind resides in the essence. In the present case, the essence has nothing that could stimulate it. Therefore, the mind has no place where it could reside. When the mind does not stay at its residence, then [the patient] loses his mind."

14 In contrast, Yang Shangshan: "When sweat leaves [the body] and the heat fails to decrease, [imminent] death manifests itself in three signs: First, [the patient] cannot eat. Second, the [movement in the] vessels is hasty. Third, [the patient] loses his mind.

If only one [of these signs] were not to appear, [the patient would] survive.
Even though [the disease] improves a little,[15] [the patient] must die."[16]

[Huang] Di:
"Someone suffers from body heat.
Sweat leaves [the body; he experiences] vexation and fullnes.
The vexation and the fullness are not resolved by the sweating.[17]
What disease is this?"

Qi Bo:
"When sweat leaves [the body] and the body [remains] hot, this [disease] is
'wind.'
When sweat leaves [the body] and the vexation and the fullness are not re-
solved, this is 'recession.'
The disease is named: 'wind-recession.' "[18]

33-195-6
[Huang] Di:
"I should like to hear about it comprehensively."

When sweat leaves [the body] and when [at the same time the patient] is hot, if these
three signs of [imminent] death appear and no indication of life, [the patient] may be
cured and will die nevertheless. Another [interpretation] is: there are three deaths [out
of three cases] and one has not seen even one survival [out of three cases]." See also Fu
Weikang & Wu Hongzhou/290.

15 Wu Kun: "Even though they improve a little, they must die." Gao Jiwu/24: "愈 is
an old version of the character 癒, 'to heal.' "

16 Wang Bing: "When sweat leaves [the body] while the [movement in the] vessels races and is abundant, this is the first [reason why the patient] will die. When
the [proper qi] is unable to overcome the disease, this is the second [reason why the
patient] will die. When [the patient] speaks crazily and loses his mind, this is the third
[reason why he] will die."

17 Zhang Jiebin: "This is to say: after the sweating, the heat and the vexation are
not dispersed."

18 Ma Shi: "When the major yang is affected by wind and when the minor yin qi
recedes, this is called 'wind recession.' " 1623/15: "Because the wind rules drainage,
hence sweat leaves [the body] and the body turns hot. When the qi from the lower
[parts of the body] rises in reverse movement, then [the heart] is vexed, [one has a
feeling of] fullness and, at the same time, the feet are cold. The disease is brought
about by wind evil. Hence it is called 'wind recession.' " For 風厥, see also 2688/45
and 2225/6.

Qi Bo:

"The great yang rules the qi.

Hence it is the first to receive evil.

The minor yin and the [great yang] are exterior and interior.

When [the great yang qi] is affected by heat,

then [the minor yin qi] rises to follow it.

When it follows it, then this is recession."[19]

[Huang] Di:

"How to treat it?"

Qi Bo:

"Exterior and interior are to be pierced.

Have the [patient] drink and consume a decoction."[20]

33-195-9

[Huang] Di:

"When exhaustion wind causes a disease, how is that?"

Qi Bo:

"Exhaustion wind, as a rule[21] it is below the lung.[22]

---

19 Wang Bing: " 'Rises to follow it' is to say: the minor yin follows the major yang and rises."

20 Yang Shangshan: "One can pierce the exterior and interior vessels of the yin and yang to attack the exterior and one has the [patient] drink a decoction liquid to treat his interior." Wang Bing: "This is to say: one drains the major yang and supplements the minor yin. 'One [lets him] drink a decoction' is to say: one stops the kidney qi's reverse movement upwards.' " Zhang Jiebin: "When the yang evil abounds, the yin is definitely depleted. Hence one must drain the heat of the major yang and supplement the qi of the minor yin. 飲之服湯 has the meaning expressed in *Ling shu* 17: 'In case of depletion drink medicine for supplementation.' " Tanba: "Drug decoctions were, in antiquity, simply called 'decoction' (湯)." The *Tai su* does not have the character 服 following 飲之. Yang Shangshan: "Have [the patient] drink a decoction to cure his interior."

21 Guo Aichun-92: "法 should be 發, 'develops.' " 2378/50 agrees. In this case, this statement should read: "Exhaustion wind develops below the lung."

22 Wang Bing: "[This disease] emerges because of exhaustion wind. Hence it is called 'exhaustion wind.' 'Exhaustion' is to say: the kidneys are exhausted. The vessels of the kidneys rise from the kidneys, penetrate the liver and the diaphragm and enter the lung. Hence, when the kidneys are exhausted wind is generated, rises and resides below the lung." Gao Shishi: " 'Below the lung,' this is the heart. Exhaustion caused by vexation harms the heart." Zhang Qi: "Exhaustion harms the qi. When the lung depot

The disease resulting from this [exhaustion wind] lets a person stiffen above and causes blurred vision.[23]
What is spat resembles snivel [from the nose].[24]
[The patient] has an aversion to wind and shakes from cold.
This is the disease of exhaustion-wind."[25]

[Huang] Di:
"How to treat it?"

33-196-1
Qi Bo:
"To help [the patient] bend down and up,[26] pull [essence] from the great yang.

---

receives a disease, this is in the region between chest and diaphragm. Hence [the text] states: 'below the lung.'" Wu Kun: "In case of a disease of exhaustion wind, the evil is received below the lung, i.e., in the fourth, fifth, and sixth vertebra." Yao Shaoyu: " 'Below the lung' is to say: the disease rises from below the lung."

23 Wang Bing: "The bladder qi cannot rise to nourish [the upper part of the body]. Hence this person's head and neck stiffen and his vision is not clear. The lung is struck by the wind, [that is,] the exhaustion qi rises and steams [the lung]. Hence, it causes spittle to leave [the mouth] like mucus [leaves] the nose. The kidney qi is insufficient and the yang qi attacks the interior. Exhaustion [qi] and heat unite. Hence [the person] has an aversion to wind and shakes from cold." 693/37: "Yu Chang states in his *Xiang cao xu jiao shu* 香草續校書: " 'Stiffen above' makes no sense. 上 may be a mistake for 工 and 工 could stand for 項, 'neck.' 強工 is 強項, 'stiffens the neck.' Yu Chang's comment is quite adequate."

24 Tanba: "The character 痰, 'mucus,' 'phlegm,' did not exist in antiquity. When [the text] here states 'what is spat resembles snivel [from the nose],' then this is to say: [the patient] spits phlegm."

25 Gao Shishi: "勞 is 煩勞, 'exhaustion caused by vexation.' 勞風 [is to say:] exhaustion caused by vexation results in internal depletion and generates wind disease." 2376/43: "勞 has the meaning of 煩勞, 'exhaustion caused by vexation,' here." 2557/20: "The disease of 'exhaustion wind' is caused by exhaustion leading to depletion and subsequent affection by wind evil. The disease takes its seat in the lung." See also 1428/38.

26 Yang Shangshan: "This disease often causes [the patient] to move [his head] down and up again. Hence one stops this." Wang Bing: "救 is like 止, 'to stop.' This is to say: one stops bowing and stretching in [the patient's] activities so as to avoid that the exhaustion qi proliferates." Gao Jiwu/217: "俛 is identical with 俯, 'to move down.' " Gao Jiwu/571: "以 is identical here with 宜, 'it is advisable,' 'one should.' " Gao Shishi: "When the [contents of the] conduit vessels are in harmony [again], then [one's ability of] bowing down and bowing upwards is as it used to be and the 'stiffening of the above' can be healed." Mori: "*Su wen* 05 has 'When the yang dominates, then the body is hot. The interstice structures close. Rough panting makes [the patient] bend

For those with essence, [it takes] three days.[27]

---

down and up.' The meaning of the expression 俯仰 in *Su wen* 05 is identical with its usage here. Hence, the two characters 俯仰 have the meaning 'to pant.'" See also 2242/45. We interpret 救 as 援助, "to aid." This appears plausible given the first symptom mentioned above of the disease to be cured, i.e., "the person stiffens above."

27 Yang Shangshan: "In case one pierces to pull major yang essence, it takes three days. When [the patient is able to] bow up and down [again], he is healed. If one draws the yang brilliance [essence], it takes five days. If one draws [essence from] the minor yang, which has no essence, it will take seven days. As soon as green-yellow turbid snivel leaves [the body] through mouth and nose, the disease will be healed." Zhang Zhicong: "巨陽引精 is to say: The bladder is the palace where the liquids are stored. After they have been transformed through [an interaction with] qi, they leave [the body]. When the great yang qi abounds, it is able to draw the evil water of the kidney essence and make it leave [the body] through the urine. After three days [the disease] is cured. [For patients] in their midlife, whose essence qi is depleted, it takes five days. For old [people] whose essence qi is weak, it takes seven days." Wu Kun: "The great yang and the minor yin, [i.e.,] the kidneys, are exterior and interior. The kidneys are the palace of the essence. The essence is a yin entity. It cannot move by itself; it must be pulled by the qi of the great yang to be able to flow off. Hence [the text] states: 'the great yang draws the essence.'" 680/3: "The *Da ya mao zhuan* 大雅毛 傳 states: '引 is 長.' The meaning of 引精 is: 精力旺盛, 'the essence strength flourishes and abounds.' This is a reference to persons of young age and full of vigor." Zhang Qi: "This sentence cannot be interpreted; it may be corrupt." Yao Shaoyu: "The 21 characters of Qi Bo's answer from 以救 to 七日 make no sense. There must be some error included here." Gao Jiwu/238: "精 may refer to a strong body. Commenting on the statement 精者三日, 中年者五日, 不精者七日, Zhang Lu says: 'Even strong people must take drugs for three days until an effect appears. When one treats [patients] in their middle years, or those without strength, one must observe periods of five to seven days." 1127/10: "精者 refers to young age; 不精者 refers to old age." 1936/12: "巨陽 引 is a sentence of its own. This passage must be read: 歧伯曰: 以救俯仰, 巨陽引. 精 者三日, ... This way, the meaning of this passage is obvious. 以救俯仰, 巨陽引 refers to the aim and to the method of treating exhaustion wind. The 精 here in 精者 and 不精者 does not refer to 精氣, 'essence qi.' It refers to 精力, 'essence strength,' 精神, 'essence spirit.' 精者 are strong and vigorous persons; 不精者 are old persons. 巨陽 引 is to be interpreted as follows: by means of stretching [exercises] or piercing one guides the conduit qi in the major yang conduit and disperses the wind evil." 2085/42: "Following 巨陽引 a character 精 is left out to avoid a repetition of two identical characters." Accordingly, the passage should be read as 巨陽引精. 精者 ... "From the great yang draw essence. In those [patients] with essence, it takes .." 2378/50: "My personal opinion is to move 巨陽引 in front of 以救俛仰." For example, see 2861/45: "俯仰 is a metaphorical expression indicating the serious nature of the disease; it does not refer to the actual appearance/symptoms of a disease. It is placed here in front of 巨陽引 to emphasize it. The *Tai su*, Re bing lun 熱病論, has 以針引巨陽脈, 精者三 日, 俯仰即愈, that is, 'pull out [and eliminate the evil qi from] the great yang [vessel]. For those with essence the critical state will be healed within three days.'" 1134/7:

For those [patients] in their middle years,[28] [it takes] five days.
For those without essence, [it takes] seven days.

They cough out green-yellow snivel,[29]
which resembles pus;[30]
it assumes the size of pellets and leaves from the mouth as if it came from the nose.[31]
If no [mucus] leaves, then [this] harms the lung.
When the lung is harmed, then [the patient] will die."[32]

33-196-4
[Huang] Di:
"Someone suffers from kidney wind.

"The *Nei jing* frequently uses 引 to express the meaning of 'piercing.' 巨陽引 is: 'one pierces the foot major yang bladder conduit.' 以救俛仰 is: 'to treat the critical condition of bowing down and up because of his panting breathing.' " For details, see there. Hu Tianxiong: "All commentators have read 巨陽引精者三日 as one sentence; their interpretations, though, are forced. The *Yi tong* 醫通 considers the three characters 巨陽引 to constitute one sentence. This is correct. .. The disease had entered [the body] via the major yang; hence it is appropriate that it leaves via the major yang. Acupuncturists should pierce here in accordance with the principle outlined in *Ling shu* 5: 'In case of sudden disease, take it from the major yang.' The 精 in 精者三日 is 強, 'strong.' 精者 refers to persons with a strong body. 'Three days' and further below 'five days' and 'seven days' refers to the approximate period during which [a patient] expectorates green-yellow mucus."

28 The *Tai su* does not have the character 年.

29 384/58: "涕 has the meaning of 鼻涕, 'nose snivel.' "

30 The *Tai su* has 稠膿, "thick pus."

31 Gao Jiwu/354: "若 is 或, 'or.' "

32 Wang Bing: "The great yang [conduit] is the vessel of the bladder. The bladder and the kidneys are exterior and interior. Hence, the great yang [conduit] draws essence. .. Now, when the major yang vessels draws in essence qi and has it rise to attack the lung, then within three days – for those in the middle years within five days and for those whose natural constitution lacks essence qi within seven days – one coughs up thick snivel to leave [the nose]. Its color is green-yellow, resembling pus. Regular cough rises via the throat and leaves through the mouth. Sudden coughing rushes against the nostrils and leaves through the nose. All such cases are brought about by an exhaustion of the kidney qi and a depletion of the qi of the lung, with yang qi pressing against the latter. Hence, when [the snivel] does not leave [the body], it harms the lung. When the lung is harmed, the camp and the guard [qi] disperse and the *po*-soul does not govern internally. Hence [the patient] dies."

His face and instep have a *mang*-type congestion.[33]
His speech is impaired.[34]
Can this [patient] be pierced?"[35]

Qi Bo:
"A depletion must not be pierced.
If one must not pierce and pierces nevertheless, five days later this qi will arrive."[36]

[Huang] Di:
"When it arrives; how is that?"

---

33 Wang Bing: "瘲然 is 腫起貌, 'swollen.' 壅 is to say: obstruction below the eyes assuming the appearance of a lying silkworm." Zhang Jiebin: "胕 is 'swollen.' 瘲 is 'loss of color.' 壅 is 'turbid,' 'unclear.'" Ma Shi: " 'Face' is the face of the head; 胕 is the face of the feet." Zhang Zhicong: "The face and the feet are swollen." Gao Shishi: "[The region] inside the skin and outside the flesh is called 胕." Wang Qi: "胕 is 浮, 'floating,' 'excessive.' 面胕瘲然 is 顏面浮腫, 'the face is swollen near the surface.'" Beijing zhongyi xueyuan (2): "This is to describe a swelling of the face and of the feet." *JMZYCD*: "胕 is identical with 跗, 足背, 'the instep.'" The meaning of 胕 is unclear. Several readings are offered in Chinese dictionaries: (1) 腐, "to rot". (2) 浮, "superficial", "floating", "near the surface". (3) 跗, "instep". (4) 附, "attached". (5) 膚, "skin". Wherever no definite clue is available to favor any of these readings, we have decided to simply transliterate the character as *fu*[-type swelling]. No definition of 瘲然 is attested in ancient literature. *Su wen* 47-263-9 compares it to an edematose swelling, "as if one had water." 庬 and 厖, though, are attested with the meaning "thick" in early texts. Hence, the character with the disease radical may imply a swelling or something thick for other reasons.

34 Wang Bing: "The kidney vessel rises from the kidneys, penetrates the liver and the diaphragm and enters the lung. It continues along the throat and passes by the base of the tongue. Hence it causes harm to one's speech."

35 2270/38: "不 should be read as 否, 'or not.'"

36 Wang Bing: "至 is to say: the disease qi arrives. It stays with each depot for one day. On the fifth day it arrives at the kidneys. Now, the kidney [qi] was insufficient already and the wind strikes it internally. This is called 'doubled repletion' (the text has 種 instead of 重; that must be a mistake). If one causes a massive drainage by means of piercing, one will, contrary [to one's intentions], harm the [proper] qi of the depot. When the true qi is insufficient, it cannot return. Hence, five days after the piercing the respective [disease] qi will arrive." 704/47: "後五日其氣必至 is: 五日後病必加重, 'after five days, the disease will become more serious.'" Hu Tianxiong: "This character 至 should be interpreted as the 至 in 極至, 'extreme.' That is to say, if one pierces even though one must not pierce, five days later the disease qi will be extreme."

Qi Bo:
"When it arrives, [the patient] will be short of qi,[37] and he will be hot at times.

The heat rises from chest and back to the head.
Sweat leaves [the body] and the hands are hot.
The mouth is dry, has a bitter [taste and the patient is] thirsty.

The urine is yellow.
The region below the eyes is swollen.
There are sounds in the abdomen.

The body is heavy and [the patient] has difficulties walking.
The monthly affair does not come;
[the patient is] vexed and cannot eat.
He cannot lie flat on his back.
When he lies flat on his back, then he coughs.

The name of this disease is wind-water.
It is discussed in the *Laws of Piercing*."[38]

[Huang] Di:
"I should like to hear its explanation."

33-197-1
Qi Bo:
"Where evil [qi] collects,
the [proper] qi must be depleted [first].[39]
When the yin [qi] is depleted, yang [qi] will collect there.

---

37 704/47: "少氣 is: 呼吸不利, 'exhalation and inhalation cannot proceed freely.'"

38 Wang Bing: "刺法 is the name of a treatise which is lost today."

39 Tanba: "This does not mean: 'when evil accumulates, one must deplete it.' The meaning [of this passage] is: 'If there is a location where the qi is depleted, evil will accumulate there.'" 1700/23: "The passage 邪之所湊, 其氣必虛 has three meanings. 1.) The proper qi is depleted first and evil [qi] accumulates in its place. This causes disease. 2.) Evil qi abounds and, in contrast, the proper [qi] is depleted. The proper does not overcome the evil. This results in disease too. 3.) Evil qi intruces and the proper qi is increasingly depleted. This harms the human body." For a detailed outline of these three possibilities of interpretation, see there. 1701/23: "The character 湊 has the meaning here of 從外而進, 'to enter from the outside.'" Yan Hongchen & Gao Guangzhen/141: "The original meaning of 湊 is 聚集, 'to collect.' Here it is used in the sense of 侵犯, 'to encroach.'" See also 2030/55, 2560/7, 81/36, 377/41, and 353/22.

Hence,
[the patient is] short of qi, is hot at times, and sweat leaves [his body].

When the urine is yellow, [this is because] there is heat in the lower abdomen.
When [the patient] cannot lie flat on his back, [this is because] there is a disharmony in the stomach.[40]
When [the patient] lies flat on his back, then he coughs severely, [because qi]
rises and presses against the lung.[41]

Whenever someone has water qi, at first a slight swelling is visible below his
eyes."

33-197-4
[Huang] Di:
"How is this to be explained?"

Qi Bo:
"Water is yin.
[The region] below the eyes is yin, too.
The abdomen is where the extreme yin resides.[42]
Hence,
when there is water in the abdomen, it must cause swelling below the eyes.

The true qi rises contrary [to its regular course].
Hence,
the mouth has a bitter [taste] and the tongue is dry.
When [the patient] lies down, he cannot lie flat on his back.
When he lies flat on his back, then he coughs out clear water.[43]

---

40 Gao Jiwu/173: "不和 is 堅, 'hard.' This [hardness] is the result of swellings caused
by water evil filling [the abdomen]. Ma Shi's interpretation 'because the kidney vessel
pours into the chest' did not get the meaning of this [phrase]. Only Zhang Zhicong
pointed out 'water rises and avails itself of the stomach,' thereby coming much closer
to the heart of the matter than Gao Shishi whose interpretation was 'the soil qi in the
stomach is in disharmony.' "

41 411/25: "This is just to say, [the patient] sits upright and cannot lie flat."

42 Zhang Yizhi et al.: " 'Extreme yin' refers to spleen and kidneys."

43 Wan Lanqing et al./29: "不能平臥, 'to be unable to lie flat,' as if sleeping, is expressed in the *Nei jing* as 不能正偃. 臥 refers to sleeping here, not to lying flat in a posture
of sleep."

33-197-7
Whenever [someone has] a water disease, as a rule, he cannot lie down.
When he lies down, then he is scared.
When he is scared, then he coughs seriously.

When there are sounds in the abdomen,
the disease has its basis in the stomach.
When it strikes the spleen,
then [one is] vexed and cannot eat.
When the food does not move down,
[this is because] the stomach duct is barred.
When the body [feels] heavy and [the patient] has difficulties walking,
[this is because] the stomach vessel is in the foot.[44]
When the monthly affair does not arrive,
[this is because] the uterine vessel is closed."

{As for the 'uterine vessel,' it is connected with the heart and forms a network
inside the uterus.
In the present case, qi rises and presses against the lung.
The heart qi cannot pass through downwards.
Hence the monthly affair does not arrive.}[45]

[Huang] Di: "Good!"

---

44 Zhang Jiebin: "The stomach rules muscles and flesh; its vessel runs through the
foot. [Here now] water qi resides in the flesh. Hence the body [feels] heavy and one
cannot walk."

45 Wang Bing: "The text above is marked by omissions and errors."

Chapter 34
Discourse on the Assessment of Movements Contrary
[to their Regular Course][1]

34-197-14
Huang Di asked:
"When a person's body is unusually warm or unusually hot,[2]
what causes it to be hot,[3] and [why does he experience] vexation and fullness?"

Qi Bo responded:
"The yin qi is diminished and the yang qi dominates.
Hence, [the body] is hot, and [the patient experiences] vexation and fullness."[4]

[Huang] Di:
"When a person's body is not cold because of [inadequate] clothing and
when inside there is no cold qi,[5]

---

1 Guo Tian: "逆調 is to say: the qi of the depots have lost their regular order." 140/31:
"The manifestations of the diseases may be compliant or reverse. When the yang
abounds and [the patient] is hot, or when the yin abounds and [the patient] is cold,
this is normal. When the yin is depleted and [the patient] is (not) hot, or when the
yang is weak and [the patient] does not feel cold, then this is a change [from the nor-
mal]. A change from the normal is 'a movement contrary [to a regular course].' To
treat a change from the normal, this is called 'regulation of a movement contrary [to
its regular course].' When the disease is in the upper [part of the body] and one seeks
to treat it in the lower part, this, too, is called 'regulation of a movement contrary [to
its regular course].'" We read 調 as diào, "to assess."

2 Wang Bing: "非常 is 異于常候, 'different from normal appearance.' Hence [the
text] states 非常, 'unusual.'" Yu Chang: "常 was originally written 裳, 'clothes.' The
Shuo wen states: 常 is 下裙, 'lower skirt.' It is also written 裳. Hence 常 and 裳 are
one and the same character. .. Wang Bing's commentary is wrong. He did not take into
account the text below, stating 人身非衣寒也. .. In comparison with the expression
衣寒 there, it should be clear that 常溫 and 常熱 are 裳溫, 'to dress in warm clothes,'
and 裳熱, 'to dress in hot clothes,' respectively." See also 1312/41. 666/41: "Yu Chang
is wrong for three reasons. First, he does not take into account that the human body
has a certain normal warmth .. Second, he misinterprets a verb (衣) as a noun .. Third,
he confuses the meanings of 衣 and 裳. Wang Bing's commentary is correct." For the
detailed argument, see there. Ma Shi: "非常 is 極, 'extremely.'"

3 The Jia yi jing does not have the three characters 為之熱.

4 916/54: "滿 is identical with 懣, 'chest pressure.'"

5 Zhang Qi: "The character 中 may be a mistake." Gao Shishi: "中非有寒氣 is: there
is no cold qi inside." Guo Tian: "中 is 傷, 'to be harmed.'" 805/55: "中 is 傷, 'to be

how can cold emerge from inside?"[6]

Qi Bo:
"This person has much blocked qi.[7]
[His] yang qi is diminished; [his] yin qi is present in large quantities.
Hence, the body is as cold as if he had come out of water."

34-198-3
[Huang] Di:
"There are persons whose four limbs are hot and
who, when they encounter wind and cold,
[feel] as if burned, as if [scorched by] fire,
why is that?"[8]

Qi Bo:
"These persons' yin qi is depleted, while their yang qi abounds.

As for the four limbs, they are yang.

---

harmed.' 寒氣 is cold evil coming from outside."

6 Gao Shishi: "寒從中生者 is: cold qi emerges from the inside and leaves to the outside." Guo Tian: "中 is 裡, 'inside.'" 805/55: "寒從中生: the patient feels that the cold develops from his internal sections."

7 Zhang Jiebin: "痺氣 is: the proper qi does not move." Wu Kun: "痺氣 is: the qi does not flow freely and a block develops." 2491/45: "痺 is 閉, 'closure.' Evil qi remains in the body and, as a result, the qi and the blood cannot pass freely. This is outlined most clearly in *Su wen* 43." Guo Tian: "多 is 常, 'regularly,' 'often.'"

8 Lin Yi et al.: "The Quan Yuanqi edition does not have the two characters 如火. The *Tai su* states: 如炙于火, 'as if roasted by fire.' One should follow the *Tai su* text." 2085/42: "The statement of Lin Yi [in Lin Yi et al.] is very well suited. The original meaning of 炙 was 'to roast meat.' It did not have the meaning of roasting anything else. Later, this meaning gradually expanded. .. According to everybody's opinion as to the time of the compilation of the *Nei jing*, at that time it only had the meaning of 'to roast meat.' This is without any doubt. 如炙于火 is 'it appears like meat roasted on fire.' The patient's yang qi abounded unilaterally and [in this state] he encountered wind evil. .. The wind helps the fire to flare up and lets the yang qi abound even more. Just like meat roasted over fire, which the more it is roasted the more it shrinks, the physical appearance [of the patient] appears to waste away in its muscles and flesh and this is called 'the flesh melts away.'" Wu Kun: "如炙 is: one feels the heat oneself as if cauterized with hot fumes. 如火 is: one dreads one's own heat as one dreads fire." 805/56: "炙 is 燻炙, 'to cauterize with fumes.' 如炙 is: one feels hot oneself. 如火 is: one is considered hot by others." Guo Tian: "炙 is pronounced *zhi.*"

When two yang meet each other[9] while the yin qi is depleted and diminished, then the diminished water cannot extinguish the intensely burning fire and the yang governs alone."

{"Governs alone" is: it cannot [continue to] generate and stimulate growth. A domination that is isolated comes to a halt.}[10]

{"Encounters wind and [has a feeling] as if burned, as if [scorched by] fire" is: this person's flesh will melt away.}[11]

34-198-7
[Huang] Di:
"There are persons with a cold body.
Hot water or fire cannot heat them;
thick clothes cannot warm them.[12]
And yet, [these persons] do not tremble with cold.
Which disease is this?"

Qi Bo:
"Such persons have a habitual kidney qi domination and
their work has to do with water.[13]

---

9 Zhang Jiebin: "The four limbs are the origin of all yang. The wind is yang qi. When the four limbs are hot and encounter the wind outside, this is what is called 'two yang meet each other.'" Guo Tian: "得 is 合, 'to unite.'"

10 Wang Bing: "Water is yin and fire is yang. In the present case, the yang qi has a surplus, while the yin qi is insufficient. Hence [the text] states: 'diminished water cannot extinguish an intensely burning fire.' 治 is 主, 'to rule.' 勝 is 盛, 'abundant.'" 805/56: "When yin and yang [qi] of the human body are balanced in harmony, they are able to generate each other. In the present case, the yin is extremely depleted and the yang qi dominates the entire body alone. Yang [qi dominating] alone cannot give birth to and let grow [the yin qi]. Hence [the text] states: 'It dominates alone and comes to a stop.'" Wu Kun: "不能生長 is to say: unilaterally [dominating] yang cannot give birth to yin." The *Chun qiu Gu liang zhuan* 春秋穀梁傳, Duke Zhuang 莊公, 3, has: "獨陰不生, 獨陽不生, 獨天不生, 三合然後生, 'Yin does not generate by itself, yang does not generate by itself, heaven does not generate by itself, only after all three unite there is generation.'" (See Ruan Yuan 2381 above.)

11 Wang Bing: "爍 is 消, 'to waste away.'" Zhang Jiebin: "The flesh is yin. When the yang abounds, this harms the yin. Hence this lets the [affected] person's muscles and flesh waste away."

12 Gao Jiwu/416: "Following the characters 熱 and 溫 a character 之 is omitted here."

13 Wang Bing: "以水為事 is to say: his [sexual] desires abound." Yao Shaoyu: "Those who have a habitual kidney qi domination, they exploit this strength, and they give free rein to their desires. Hence [the text states]: 'it is with water that they manage

[Their] major yang qi is weak.
[Their] kidney fat[14] has dried away and does not stimulate growth.

34-198-10
>One water cannot dominate two fires.<[15]

The kidneys, they are water,
and they generate the bones.[16]
When the kidneys fail to generate,
then the marrow cannot be filled up.
Hence, extreme cold reaches the bones.

The reason why [this person] cannot tremble with cold is [as follows]:
The liver is the first yang,
the heart is the second yang.
The kidneys are a solitary depot.
One water cannot overcome two fires.
Hence, [the patient] cannot tremble with cold.

The disease is called 'bone block.'[17]

---

their affairs.'" Zhang Zhicong: "以水為事 [refers to] the domination of the water of the bladder. That is to say, this person's qi of water cold is unilaterally dominant." Zhang Qi: "以水為事 refers to such activities as wading through water or swimming." 419/4: "Not a few commentators explain 以水為事 as a reference to sexual habits. However, judging from the text of *Su wen* 43 (see there) 以水為事 is an obvious reference to persons whose work is conducted in water." 805/56: "素 is 平素, 'usually.'" Guo Tian: "素 is 向來, 'hitherto.'" Li Guoqing: "The Nan jing College of TCM explains this as unilateral addiction to tea and wine: 'If one loves to drink tea or wine, dampness abounds in [the body] unilaterally. This, too, is 以水為事 .'"

14 Guo Tian: "脂 stands for 水, 'water.'" *NJCD*: "脂 refers to the yin essence, (i.e., to the male semen)."

15 Gao Shishi: "These seven characters are mistakenly repeated here from further below."

16 Gao Jiwu/576: "生 is to be interpreted as 養, 'to nourish.' 于 is a fill word [with no meaning of its own]." Hu Tianxiong: "*Su wen* 5 states: 'The kidneys generate the bones and [their] marrow.' Further down [in the present treatise] it is stated: 'when the kidneys fail to produce, then the marrow cannot be filled up.' Hence it should be evident that the character 於 is an erroneous insertion. The *Jia yi jing* and the *Tai su* both have 主骨. Because in the old script 生 and 主 were very similar, this mistake may have resulted."

17 Gao Shishi: "When cold is in the bones, the disease is called 'bone stagnation.'" Guo Tian: "痺 is 不通, 'impassable.'"

A person with this [disease] will have tight joints."[18]

34-198-13
[Huang] Di:
"When a person's flesh is numb[19] and remains numb although[20] one dresses
[this person] tightly with padded clothes,
which disease is this?"[21]

Qi Bo:
"The camp qi is depleted;
the guard qi is replete.

When the camp qi is depleted, then [this results in] numbness.
When the guard qi is depleted, then [this results in] a loss of function.
When both the camp and the guard [qi] are depleted, then [this results in]
numbness together with a loss of function.[22]

---

18 Wang Bing: "When the kidneys do not produce, then the marrow is not filled
up. When the marrow is not filled up, then the sinews turn dry and shrink. Hence
the joints are tight." Zhang Jiebin: "In this case, the water does not control the fire.
As a result both the sinews and the bones lose their nourishment. Hence the joints
are tight."

19 Gao Jiwu/466: "This should be read as 肉苛之人, 'a person whose flesh is
numb.'"

20 307/183: "The *Li ji* 禮記, Tan gong shang 檀弓上, states: 伯魚之母死, 期而猶哭.
Zheng Xuan 鄭玄 commented: 猶 is 尚, 'still.'"

21 Wang Bing: "苛 is 瘖重, 'numb and heavy.'"

22 Zhang Jiebin: "When it is stated above that the guard qi is replete, then this is
to point out that the muscles and the flesh basically have no disease. When it states
below that the guard qi is depleted, this is really a reference to a disease of the guard
qi. When the camp and the guard qi are both depleted, then both the blood and the qi
have a disease. Loss of sensitivity is a result of blood depletion; loss of function is a result of qi depletion." Ma Shi: "The camp qi is yin qi. It moves in the interior [sections
of the body] and it is the guardian of the yang. Hence this qi is depleted. The guard qi
is yang qi. It moves in the exterior [sections of the body] and it is the messenger of the
yin. Hence this qi is replete... Hence the yang paths are replete and the yin paths are
depleted." Because of an apparent contradiction with the following statement, Tanba
considers the seven characters 榮氣虛, 衛氣實也 to be an erroneous later addition.
In contrast, 1272/9 and, in an almost identical wording 1800/78, following Zhang
Jiebin and Ma Shi, consider the first statement 榮氣虛, 衛氣實也 to be a reference
to a normal physiological condition, while they interpret the following statement as a
reference to a pathological state. For details, see there. See also 2083/23 for a defense
of the present wording of the passage. *Ling shu* 75 has 衛氣不行則為不仁, "when the

If the flesh is as usual [despite camp and guard qi being depleted],[23]
then a person's body and mind have no mutual [relationship],[24] and this is to
say: death."

34-199-2
[Huang] Di:
"There are persons who have qi moving contrary [to its regular course], who
cannot lie down and whose breathing is accompanied by noises;
[there are others] who cannot lie down and whose breathing is not accompanied by noises;
[there are others] whose rising and resting are as usual, while their breathing is
accompanied by noises;
[there are others] who can lie down and walk but who pant;
[there are others] who cannot lie down and cannot walk and who pant;
[and there are those] who cannot lie down and if they lie down they pant.
All these [states] are caused by which depot?

I should like to hear the reason for these [states]."[25]

Qi Bo:
"When someone cannot lie down and when his breathing is accompanied by
noises, this is [a case of] yang brilliance [qi] moving contrary [to its normal
course].

---

guard qi does not move, then this results in a loss of sensitivity." 641/38: "衛氣虛則不
用 is to say: when the guard qi is harmed, this can cause the four limbs to become soft
and weak and not to bend and stretch freely."

23 In contrast, the *Tai su* has 肉如苛 ("the flesh is numb") and links these three
characters to the preceding passage. Cheng Shide et al. agrees: "Because Huang Di
refers to 肉苛 in his question above, 肉如故 should be changed in accordance with the
wording in the *Tai su*." 2083/23: "肉如故 is the special characteristic of this disease;
肉苛 refers in the sphere of sensation to an inability to feel pain or temperatures and
in the sphere of functions to an inability to move according to one's will. Still, from
the outside, the flesh appears like normal. Hence [the text] states: 'The flesh is as
before.'"

24 Wang Bing: "When the body uses the mind, but [the mind] fails to respond and
when the mind is not attached to the body, this looks like 'the two do not have each
other.'" Lin Yi et al.: "The *Jia yi jing* has 三十日死, 'dies after 30 days,' instead of 死."
2050/24: "有 stands here for 友, 'to be in harmony with.'" Guo Tian: "不相有 is 不相
協調, 'out of mutual harmony.'"

25 1899/42: "The characters 臥 and 不臥 do not refer to 'sleeping,' but to 'lying
down.'" Wan Lanqing et al./29: "臥 is 'to sleep.' 臥不安 is 'not to sleep well.'"

The [qi in the] three foot yang [conduits] moves downwards.[26]
In the present case, it moves contrary [to its normal course] and rises.
Hence, the breathing is accompanied by noises.

The yang brilliance is the stomach vessel.
The stomach is the sea of the six palaces.
Its qi [usually] moves downwards, too.
When the [qi of the] yang brilliance moves contrary [to its normal course],
it cannot follow its [usual] path.
Hence, one cannot lie down.

When the *Lower Classic* states
'When the stomach is not in harmony, then one does not lie down peacefully,'[27]
then this means just the same.

34-199-9
Now,
when [someone] rises and rests as usual, with his breathing being accompanied
by noises, this is a case of a movement contrary [to its regular course] in the
network vessels of the lung.
The [qi in the] network vessels cannot rise or descend following the conduit.
Hence, it stays in the conduit and does not move.
Diseases of the network vessels affect a person only slightly.[28]
Hence, rising and resting are as usual, but the breathing is accompanied by
noises.

34-199-11
Now,
when someone cannot lie down and when, if he lies down, he pants,
this is a case of water qi settling.[29]

---

26 805/57: "足三陽者下行 is: the three yang conduits of the feet, they all rise from
the head and descend to the feet. Their qi should move downwards to maintain the
physiological state of rising yin and descending yang [qi]."

27 See 411/25, 2899/46, 438/13, 1929/41, and 2807/116 for discussions of this
statement.

28 324/51: "病人 is 使人病, 'causes a person to be ill.'"

29 Guo Tian: "客 is 寄, 'to lodge.' When the lung is harmed and cannot transform
water, the water settles and stays in the lung." Mori: "The character 客 may be an error
for 逆, 'to move contrary to a normal course.' 'Water qi' is to say: beverages."

Now,
water follows the body liquids in its flow.
The kidneys are the depot of water;
they rule the body liquids and
they rule [a person's] lying down and panting."

[Huang] Di:
"Good!"³⁰

---

30 Wang Bing: "On the basis of [those conditions] explained in the classic, not to be able to lie down and to breathe without noises, to be able to lie down and to walk with panting, and not to be able to lie down, not to be able to walk, together with panting, the meaning of these three [states] is not discussed. [A respective passage] was lost from [the text] in antiquity."

Chapter 35
Discourse on Malaria

35-200-2
Huang Di asked:
"Now,
all [cases of] *jie* and malaria are generated by wind.[1]
Their collecting and being active occurs at [specific] times.[2]
Why?"

Qi Bo responded:
"When malaria begins to break out,
it first emerges from the finest body hair.
[The patient] stretches and yawns and then [the disease] is active.
[The patient] shivers from cold and his jaws chatter.[3]
Both the lower back and the spine experience pain.

When the cold leaves, then [the patient feels] hot everywhere in the inner and outer [regions of his body].

---

1 *SWJZ*: "痎 is malaria breaking out every second day." Yang Shangshan: "When it breaks out once every second day, this is called 痎. As for 瘧, [this term refers in] the present classic only to a disease that breaks out in autumn after one has been harmed by summerheat in summer. Sometimes it is called 痎, sometimes it is only called 瘧. It must not break out each day, or every second day to be defined as 痎. Only when its appearance differs in the course of the four seasons, then this is considered 痎." Wang Bing: "痎 is identical with 老, 'old' (in the sense of 'chronic disease'). It is also [identical with] 瘦, 'emaciated.'" Zhang Jiebin: "痎 is 皆, 'all.' Malaria manifests itself in many conditions, all together they are called 痎瘧." Wu Kun: "痎 is malaria, too. When the disease [manifests itself] during nighttime, this is called 痎; when [it manifests itself] during daytime, this is called 瘧. The *Fang yan* 方言 says 痎市 instead of 夜市, 'night market.' This is based on that [meaning of the term]." Gao Shishi: "痎 is 陰瘧, 'yin [type] malaria.' 瘧 is yang [type] malaria." 1940/41: "*Su wen* 2 has 痎瘧; *Su wen* 35 has 痎瘧. Both characters are interchangeable. ... Also, *Ling shu* 79 discusses 瘧 many times, but it never uses the term 痎. The *Jia yi jing*, in ch. 7, quoting *Su wen* 35 夫痎瘧者皆生于風, states 瘧疾皆生于風. This shows that the meaning expressed by means of 瘧 in the *Ling shu* and in the *Jia yi jing* is identical with that expressed by means of 痎瘧 in the *Su wen*." The *Jia yi jing* has: 其以日作以時何也也, 'why is it that they are active each day, that their outbreak occurs in [specific] seasons?'"

2 Wu Kun: "蓄 is: the disease rests; the evil lies hidden. 作 is: the disease breaks out; the evil moves."

3 Wang Bing: "慄 is to say 戰慄, 'trembling with fear.' 鼓 is to say 振動, 'to shake.'"

His head aches as if it [were about to] burst.
He is thirsty and longs for cold beverages."

35-200-5
[Huang] Di:
"Which qi causes this to be so;
I should like to hear its Way."

Qi Bo:
"Yin and yang [qi] rise and descend, interacting in struggle.[4]
Depletion and repletion occur alternately.
The yin [qi] and the yang [qi] move into each other's [section].

When the yang [qi] collects in the yin [section],
then the yin [section] has a repletion, while the yang [section] is depleted.
When the yang brilliance is depleted,
then one shivers from cold and the jaws chatter.[5]

When the great yang is depleted,
then the lower back and the backbone, as well as the head and the nape have pain.[6]

When all three yang are depleted, then the yin qi dominates.
When the yin qi dominates, then the bones are cold and ache.
The cold is generated inside.

---

4 Wang Bing: "The yang qi moves down; when it has reached the extreme end it rises [again.] The yin qi moves upwards; when it has reached the extreme end it descends [again]. Hence [the text] states: 'Yin and yang rise and descend, interacting in struggle.'"

5 Wang Bing: "'The yang collects in the yin' is to say: yang qi enters the yin section. The yang brilliance [conduit] is the stomach vessel. It .. passes along the jaws .. Hence when its qi is insufficient, then [the patient] has an aversion to cold. He trembles and his jaws chatter." Zhang Zhicong: "When the evil and the guard qi accumulate internally, then the qi of the three yang collects in the yin [section]. When it collects in the yin [section], then the yin [section] is replete inside, while the yang [section] is depleted in the outside. The qi of the yang brilliance [conduit] rules the muscles and the flesh and [its] conduit vessels meet below the jaws. Hence [the patient] 'trembles with cold and his jaws chatter.'"

6 Wang Bing: "The great yang [conduit] is the bladder vessel. Its vessel originates from the head and divides to descend down the nape following inside the shoulder blades, passing along the spine reaching into the hips. Hence, when its qi is insufficient, then the hips, the back, the head, and the nape have pain."

Hence, the center and the outside are all cold.

When the yang abounds, then the outside is hot.
When the yin is depleted, then the inside is hot.
When outside and inside are both hot, then [the patient] pants and is thirsty.
Hence, he longs for something cold to drink.[7]

All these [states] are acquired from harm by summerheat during summer.
The heat qi abounds; it is stored inside the skin and outside of the intestines
and the stomach.
{This is where the camp qi lodges.}[8]
This lets the person's sweat openings widen.[9]
The interstice structures open.
If subsequently [that person] is affected by autumn qi, sweat leaves [the body]
and encounters wind.

35-201-5
One may also be affected by it through bathing.
[In this case] the water qi lodges inside the skin and
resides [there] together with the guard qi.
The guard qi moves through the yang [sections] during daytime and it moves
through the yin [sections] during the night.
When this qi meets the yang, it leaves to the outside;
when it meets the yin, it strikes at the inside.
The inside [qi] and the outside [qi] strike at each other.[10]

---

7 Wang Bing: "The heat has harmed the qi. Hence inside and outside are both hot.
As a result, one pants and is thirsty." Zhang Jiebin: "In this case the evil originates
from the yin section and joins with the yang section. When it joins with the yang
section, then the yang [qi] dominates. When the yang [qi] dominates, then both the
outside and the inside are hot and one pants, is thirsty and longs for cold [beverages]."
Gao Shishi: "The yang rules the outside; when the yang abounds then the outside is
hot. The yin rules the inside, when the yin is depleted, then the inside is hot. When
outside and inside are both hot, the yang qi abounds excessively. As a result, one pants
and is thirsty. Hence one yearns for something cold to drink."

8 Wang Bing: "The [region] outside of the intestines and the stomach is ruled by the
camp qi. Hence [the text] states: this is where the camp qi resides. 舍 is like 居, 'to
reside.'"

9 Lin Yi et al.: "The Quan Yuanqi edition has 汗出空疏, 'sweat leaves [the body];
the [sweat] openings widen.'" Cheng Shide et al.: "空 is identical with 孔, '[sweat]
hole.'"

10 The *Tai su* does not have these four characters.

Hence, [the disease] is active each day."[11]

35-201-7
[Huang] Di:
"When it skips a day [before it] is active [again],
why is that?"[12]

Qi Bo:
"When this qi lodges in the depth,[13]
it strikes at the yin [qi] internally.[14]
The yang qi breaks out alone,
the yin evil remains attached inside.
The yin [qi] struggles with the yang [qi] and cannot leave.
Hence, [the disease] skips a day [before it] is active [again]."

[Huang] Di:
"Good!
When it is active [progressively] later each day,[15] and [afterwards progressively]
earlier each day,
which qi causes it to be like this?"

Qi Bo:
"The evil qi settles in the wind palace [first, whence] it descends along the
spinal column.[16]
[Once in a cycle of] one day and one night, the guard qi has a big meeting at
the wind palace.

---

11 Wang Bing: "作 is 發作, 'to break out.'"

12 Wang Bing: "間日 is to say: 隔日, 'every second day.'"

13 Zhang Zhicong: "This is to say: the evil qi lodges in the depth."

14 Cheng Shide et al.: "內薄 is 內迫, 'internally presses.'"

15 Wang Bing: "晏 is 日暮, 'end of the day.'" Cheng Shide et al.: "The outbreak of the
malaria disease occurs later day after day. Hence [the text] states: 日晏." Gao Jiwu/16:
"晏 also has the meaning of 晚, 'late,' 遲, 'retarded,' as for instance in *Mo zi* 墨子,
Shang xian 尚賢: 蚤朝晏退."

16 Wang Bing: "脊 is 'both sides of the spine.'" Wu Kun, Ma Shi, Yao Shaoyu agree.
Zhang Jiebin: "脊 is identical with 呂. The backbone is called 呂." *SWJZ*: "呂 is
'backbone.'" *Guang ya* 廣雅: "呂 is 'flesh.'" Cheng Shide et al.: "On the basis of the
wordings 循脊而下 and, further down, 日下一節, the meaning of 脊 should be backbone."

The next day, [the evil qi] descends one [vertebral] joint each day.
Hence, it is active [progressively] later [each day].

< This [qi] at first settles in the backbone.
Everytime when it reaches the wind palace,
then the interstice structures open.
When the interstice structures open,
then [further] evil qi enters.
When [further] evil qi enters,
then the disease is active.
This way [the disease] is active a little later each day. >[17]

35-201-14
When the [evil qi] has left the wind palace, it descends one [vertebral] joint
each day.
After descending for 25 days it reaches the sacrum.
On the 26th day, it enters into the spine and pours into the vessel hidden in the
spinal column.[18]
The qi rises and on the ninth day it leaves through the broken basin.[19]

---

17 Wang Bing: "節 is to say: 脊骨之節, 'joint of the backbone.' Now, when the evil qi
has a long way [to go], its attendance in the meeting is retarded. Hence [the disease]
is active late in the day.'"

18 Wang Bing: "From the nape downwards to the sacrum are altogether 24 joints.
Hence when it descends by one joint each day, on the 25th day it reaches the sacrum.
On the 26th day it enters the spine and pours into the vessel hidden in the spine. As
for the 'vessel hidden in the spine,' this is to say: the hidden course of the kidney vessel among the sinews on both sides of the spine." Lin Yi et al.: "The Quan Yuanqi
edition has '21 days' instead of '25 days,' and '22 days' instead of '26 days.' The *Jia yi
jing* and the *Tai su* have identical wordings. Instead of 伏衝之脈 the *Jia yi jing* has 太
衝之脈, 'great thoroughfare vessel .'" Zhang Jiebin: "*Ling shu* 79 states: 'It enters the
spine and pours into the hidden thoroughfare vessel .' Now, the thoroughfare vessel
follows the spine in that it runs hidden in the backbone. Hence it is also called 伏衝,
'[vessel] hidden in the backbone.'" Cheng Shide et al.: "One should follow Zhang
Jiebin's interpretation." Yao Shaoyu: "The backbone itself has 21 vertebrae. When [the
evil] descends each day by one vertebra, it should take only 22 days. And to reach the
sacrum should take only 23 days. Now, Wang Bing's version has additional three days
because he adds the three vertebra of the nape. The Quan Yuanqi edition, the *Jia yi
jing*, and the *Tai su* all have 21 and 22 days respectively because they only speak of the
number of the [vertebrae of the] backbone itself. In reality, then, there is no difference
[between Wang Bing and the other versions]."

19 Tanba: "The 'broken basin' [here] is not the 'Broken Basin' of the yang brilliance
stomach conduit. .. [This term] refers to the 'Celestial Chimney (天突)' hole of the
controlling vessel."

The qi [ascends] higher each day.
Hence, it is active a little earlier each day."[20]

>As for "it skips a day [before it] is active [again],"
that is because the evil qi strikes at the five depots internally and attaches itself
horizontally to the membrane plain.[21]
Its path is far, the qi is in depth, and its movement is slow.
It cannot move alongside the guard qi.
It cannot leave together [with the guard qi].[22]
Hence, it skips a day [before it] is active [again].<[23]

35-202-4
[Huang] Di:
"[You,] Sir, have stated of the guard qi:
whenever it reaches the wind palace, then the interstice structures open.
When they are open, then evil qi enters.
When [evil qi] enters, then the disease is active.

Now, when the guard qi descends one joint each day, the outbreak of this qi
does occur not exactly at the wind palace.
When it is active daily, how is that?"

Qi Bo:
"In this case the evil qi has settled in the head and in the nape and descends
along the spinal column.
Hence,
depletion and repletion are not identical [everywhere in the body].
The evil strikes at different locations.
Therefore, it must not be exactly at the wind palace.

---

20 Zhang Jiebin: "The evil is in the vessel hidden in the spine and rises following
the backbone. ... Its qi moves higher each day and from the yin [section] it proceeds to
the yang [section]. The evil retreats day by day. Hence it is active progressively earlier
[each day]."

21 *Su wen* 39 has 膜原. Wang Bing: "募原 is to say: the '原系 ("base connection") of
the diaphragm membrane.'" For a detailed discussion of 募原, see also Qian Chao-
chen-88/149 and 1691/13.

22 Tanba: "The *Jia yi jing* has 偕, 'to accompany,' instead of 皆. This is probably correct."

23 The 44 characters from 其間日發者 to 故間日乃作也 are interpreted by Gao
Shishi and Tanba as a part of Qi Bo's answer to Huang Di's question 其間日而作者
何也, mistakenly moved here.

Hence,

when the evil strikes at the head and at the nape,

it is when the [guard] qi reaches the head and the nape that the disease [is active].[24]

When it strikes at the backbone, it is when the [guard] qi reaches the backbone that the disease [is active].

When it strikes at the lower back and at the spine, it is when the [guard] qi reaches the lower back that the disease [is active].

When it strikes at the hands and at the feet, it is when the [guard] qi reaches the hands and the feet that the disease [is active].[25]

Wherever the guard qi is located, it joins with the evil qi [to battle]. Then the disease is active.

Hence,[26]

the wind [that enters the body] has no permanent palace [there].[27]

Where the guard qi is effused,[28] the interstice structures must open.

Where it joins with the evil qi [to battle], that is its palace."[29]

35-202-12
[Huang] Di:
"Good!
Now,
wind and malaria resemble each other, and they belong to the same category.
However, only the wind is present permanently, while the malaria may rest at

---

24 Zhang Jiebin: "氣至 refers to the arrival of the guard qi." Ma Shi: "邪氣至, 'when the evil qi arrives.'" Cheng Shide et al.: "Below it is stated: 'When the location of the guard qi falls together with that of the evil qi, then the disease is active.' Hence 氣至 must refer to the arrival of the guard qi. Zhang Jiebin's comment is correct."

25 Wang Bing: "Hence the subsequent treatise [advocates] to always pierce the location where the evil [qi] resides."

26 Lin Yi et al.: "The Quan Yuanqi edition, the *Jia yi jing*, and the *Tai su* do not have the 88 characters from 此邪氣客于頭 to 則病作故." Tanba: "These 88 characters may be an ancient commentary."

27 Ma Shi: "The wind does not affect [the body] regularly at the same place. Hence 'it does not have a regular palace.' As for 府,' all places where things collect can be called 府. This is not the 'palace' of the 'wind palace.'" Cheng Shide et al.: "That is to say: this 'wind palace' is not the 'Wind Palace' [piercing] hole."

28 Tanba: "Below the text states: 衛氣應乃作. The 發 here should be 應." *Ling shu* 79 has 衛氣應乃作.

29 Lin Yi et al.: "The *Jia yi jing* has 其病作, 'the disease breaks out,' instead of 則其府也."The *Tai su*, ch. 25, has 舍 instead of 合; it does not have the character 邪. The Wu Kun edition and *Ling shu* 46 have 邪氣之所舍.

[specific] times.
Why?"[30]

Qi Bo:
"The wind qi stays at its location,
hence it is permanently present, while
the malaria qi following the conduits and network [vessels moves] deep to
strike from the inside.[31]
Hence, when the guard qi responds, then it is active."

[Huang] Di:
"[If in case of] malaria [the patient] is first cold and afterwards hot,
why is that?"

Qi Bo:
"When in summer someone is harmed by massive summerheat and
when his sweat leaves [the body] profusely, [then]
the interstice structures have opened to effuse [the sweat].
If subsequently he encounters a summer qi and also the chilling temperatures
of a water cold, [both] are stored in the interstice structures, in the skin.[32]
When in autumn he is harmed by wind, then the disease reaches completion.[33]

Now,
cold is a yin qi; wind is a yang qi.
[The patient] was first harmed by cold and afterwards he was harmed by wind.
Hence, he is cold first and hot afterwards.

---

30 Wang Bing: "Both wind and malaria may abound or be weak. Hence [the text]
states: 'resemble each other, same category.'" Zhang Jiebin: "This character 'wind'
refers to the pathoconditions [generated by] wind. The wind [disease] and the malaria
[disease] are both caused by wind. Seen from their origin, they belong to the same
category. However, a wind [disease] does not rest, while the malaria [disease] at times
comes to a halt. This is how one knows to distinguish them."

31 *Ling shu* 79 has 內搏.

32 Yu Chang: "The character 水 is without doubt a mistake for 小, 'little.' Lin [Yi
in Lin Yi et al.] quotes the *Jia yi jing* and the *Tai su* as evidence; they have 小寒迫
之. The two characters 迫之 are not necessary. Further evidence is a commentary by
Wang Bing on *Su wen* 69, where he states: 凄滄 is 薄寒, 'minor cold.' 薄寒 is nothing
but 小寒. Wang Bing explained 凄滄 as 薄寒 because the main text established such
an interpretation."

33 Wang Bing: "Summerheat is yang qi. A wind stroke is received by the yang qi.
Hence when someone is harmed by wind in autumn, the disease is complete."

The disease is active in a [specific] time [of the year].
It is called cold malaria."

35-203-8
[Huang] Di:
"When [the patient] is first hot and afterwards cold,
why is that?"

Qi Bo:
"In this case he was first harmed by wind and afterwards harmed by cold.
Hence, he is first hot and afterwards cold.
[In this case], too, it is active in a [specific] time [of the year].
It is called warmth malaria.

When [the patient experiences] only heat but no cold,
the [movement of the] yin qi was interrupted first and
the yang qi[34] is effused alone.
As a result, [the patient suffers from] shortness of qi, vexation, and grievance.
[His] hands and feet are hot and he has an urge to vomit.
[This disease] is named solitary [heat] malaria."[35]

35-203-12
[Huang] Di:
"Now,
the classic states:
'That which has surplus, drain it;
that which is insufficient, supplement it.'

Well,
heat is surplus, cold is insufficiency.
Now, as far as the cold of a malaria [disease] is concerned, hot water or fire
cannot warm it.

---

34 Ma Shi: "'Yang qi' is 'wind qi'"

35 Wang Bing: "癉 is 熱, 'heat.' Extreme heat causes it." Zhang Zhicong: "癉 is 單, 'singular.' This is to say, there is solely an outbreak of yang [qi] and one is ill with heat." Tanba: "[To explain] 癉 as having the meaning of 'solely yang,' this may be possible in reference to 'solitary [heat] malaria (癉瘧).' It is not possible, though, in reference to 'spleen *dan*,' 'gallbladder *dan*,' or 'wasting *dan*.' Wang Bing's interpretation of 癉 as 'heat' is quite clear. 癉 is a fire (燀) resulting from a disease. The *Shuo wen* states: 'It is 炊, to steam.' The *Guang yun* 廣韻 states: 'like rising fire.' The *Guo yu* 國語, Zhou yu 周語, states: Fire without flames [is] 癉. [Wang Bing's explanation of] 癉 as 'heat' has its origin here."

And as far as its heat is concerned, [even] ice water cannot cool it.

All these are types of surplus and insufficiency.
[However,] at this time,
[even] a good practitioner cannot stop [them].
He must wait until [the disease] weakens by itself and only then pierce it.

What is the reason for this?
I should like to hear an explanation."

Qi Bo:
"The classic states:
'Do not pierce [a patient with] an intensely burning heat.[36]
Do not pierce [a patient with] a torrential movement in the vessels.[37]
Do not pierce [a patient with] an incessant sweating.'[38]
Hence, it is because the disease is in full advance against [the proper qi] that it cannot be treated yet.[39]

Now,
when malaria breaks out first,
the yang qi collects in the yin [section].
At this time,
the yang [section] is depleted, while the [qi in the] yin [section] abounds.

---

36 Lin Yi et al.: "The Quan Yuanqi edition and the *Tai su* have 氣, 'qi,' instead of 熱." Zhang Jiebin: "熇熇之熱 is heat just abounding. One cannot pierce it. That is to say, one avoids a pointed [weapon] coming towards one."

37 Wang Bing: "渾渾 is: no beginning and no end." Zhang Jiebin: "In case of a '渾渾 movement in the vessels' it cannot be determined whether the yin or the yang are depleted or replete. One cannot find out the true conditions [of the patient] and one fears one may be wrong. Hence one cannot pierce." Ma Shi: "In case of a '渾渾 movement in the vessels' the vessels abound with evil [qi] and [the movement is] chaotic." 694/45: "渾 should be read 滾, 'water flowing rapidly.'" For a lengthy discussion of this term, see there.

38 This is a quotation from *Ling shu* 55 where a parallel is drawn between military tactics in case of an advancing enemy and therapeutic approaches in case of a disease in full development. Wang Bing: "漉漉 is profuse sweating." 2167/49: "This is a description of profuse sweating resembling water being strained. 漉 is 濾過, 'to strain.'" For a thorough discussion of the three metaphors employed here, see also 1455/46.

39 Ma Shi: "If one pierces at the moment when the strength of the disease is just abundant, then one moves against the disease qi. Hence one cannot treat yet." Cheng Shide et al.: "為其病逆 is 逆其病氣, 'to move against the disease qi.'"

The outside [section] has no qi.[40]
Hence, one is cold first and shivers.

The yin qi moves against [the yang qi in the yin section] in full advance. When this has reached its peak, then it will turn back. [Both yin and yang qi] leave [the yin section], and proceed to the yang [section].

When yang and yin [qi] collect again in the outside [region]
then the yin [section] is depleted, while the yang [section] is replete.
Hence, [the patient] is first hot,[41] and has thirst.

35-204-4
Now,
as for the malaria qi,
when it collects in the yang [section], then the yang [qi] dominates.
When it collects in the yin [section], then the yin [qi] dominates.
When the yin [qi] dominates, then [the patient feels] cold.
When the yang [qi] dominates, then [the patient feels] hot.

As for malaria, this is an irregular [presence] of the qi of wind and cold [in the body].
When the disease has reached its peak, then it will turn back.[42]
When it comes to the outbreak of the disease, this is like the heat of fire, like [the coming of] wind and rain: one cannot do anything against it.

Hence,
when the classic states
'[to pierce] right at the moment when [the disease] abounds must result in destruction;[43] [when a disease is pierced] after it has weakened, the success of

---

40 Wu Kun: "'The outside has no qi' is to say: the guard qi accumulates in the yin [region] and the exterior is depleted." Gao Jiwu/243: "'The outside has no qi' refers to [the absence of] yang qi."

41 Zhang Qi: "先 should be 後, 'later.'" Wu Kun agrees. The *Tai su* does not have the character 先.

42 The *Tai su* links the character 至 with the preceding characters: 病極則復至. In contrast, Wang Bing: "復 is 復舊, 'return to the old (i.e., original) state.' That is to say, when the qi has been effused entirely, it will return to its original state."

43 Wang Bing: "方 is 正, 'just.' If one drains it when it just abounds, one may cause harm to the true qi." Wu Kun: "That is to say, if one pierces the disease evil just at the moment when it abounds, one inevitably causes destructive harm to the proper qi."

an intervention will be most obvious,'⁴⁴
then this means just the same.

Now,
when the malaria [disease] has not broken out yet, [i.e.,]
when the yin [qi] has not collected in the yang yet, or
when the yang [qi] has not collected in the yin yet,
if one regulates the [situation] at this point [in time],
the true qi will find peace and the evil qi will perish.⁴⁵

Hence,
when the practitioner cannot treat that which has already broken out,
this is because⁴⁶ [at this time the disease] qi is in full advance against [the
proper qi]."⁴⁷

35-204-10
[Huang] Di:
"Good!
How to attack it?
What about earlier or later [outbreaks]?"

Qi Bo:
"When the malaria [disease] is about to break out,
yin and yang [qi] are about to change their locations.
This must start from the four extremities.⁴⁸
When the yang [qi] has been harmed, the yin [qi] will follow it.

---

44 *Ling shu* 55 has: 故曰: 方其盛也, 勿敢毀傷; 刺其已衰, 事必大昌, "Hence it is
said: 'At the moment when it abounds, do not dare [to pierce; this would result in]
destruction-harm. If one pierces [it when] it has already weakened, [one's] intervention will be most glorious.' "

45 Wang Bing: "That which is drained, it must be hit. That which is supplemented, it
must be met. Hence the true qi achieves peace and the evil qi will perish."

46 Gao Jiwu/559: "為 is 由于, 'because,' here."

47 Wang Bing: "The true qi pauses and the evil qi moves strongly. The true [qi] cannot dominate the evil. This is 逆, 'movement contrary [to a normal course].' " Wang
Bing's commentary is based on a purely physiological understanding of the wording
here while, in fact, the origin of the term 逆 may be a military metaphor: one does not
attack an enemy advancing in full strength. See *Ling shu* 79.

48 Zhang Jiebin: "Whenever a malaria [disease] is about to break out, the four extremities will have a sense of cold first."

Hence,
preceding this moment,
firmly bind the location of the [yin qi],
lest the evil qi is able to enter, or the yin qi to leave.[49]
An examination reveals that the [evil qi] can be seen in the tertiary network
[vessels]. Take it from all those that abound, are firm, and [have] blood.[50]
This way, the true [qi] moves there while [the evil qi] has not been able to collect yet."[51]

35-205-1
[Huang] Di:
"When a malaria [disease] fails to break out,
the corresponding [states] of this [stage], what are they like?"[52]

Qi Bo:
"As for malaria qi, its [presence] must alternate between abundance and
depletion,
corresponding to the location of the qi.

---

49 Wang Bing: "That is to say, one firmly binds the four extremities so that the qi remains at its place in each of them. As a result, the location where the evil resides will
become visible by itself. When it is visible, one pierces [the respective vessel] to let
the blood leave." Zhang Jiebin: " 'One firmly binds its location' is to say: [one ties the
extremities] above the joints to prevent the evil qi from flowing." Zhang Zhicong: "By
firmly binding the four extremities one prevents evil which is in this conduit to enter
another conduit and one prevents the conduit qi of that other conduit to leave there
and join [the evil] in this conduit."

50 Zhang Jiebin: "One examines which of the tertiary network [vessels] are firm and
abound [with blood], and takes the [blood] from them. The people in the North
practice this method often in that they let blood with pointed stones. It is called 'to
release the cold.' " Ma Shi: "One must conduct a careful examination. If one observes
that the evil is in the tertiary network vessels, one pierces those which are the richest
in contents and the firmest and lets the blood from them. This way the true qi will
come by itself and the evil has not been able to join [it]."

51 Wang Bing: "往 is 去, 'to move away.' " Lin Yi et al.: "The *Jia yi jing* has 其往, 'it
moves away,' instead of 真往. The *Tai su* has 直往, 'moves straight on.' " Zhang Jiebin:
"As a result, the true qi will come and go and the evil has no way to join it." Wu Kun:
"真 is 正邪, 'the proper evil.' " Yao Shaoyu: "真往未得并 is to say: if one can treat it
before it has broken out, then the true evil will leave by itself and cannot enter the
inside."

52 Zhang Jiebin: "瘧不發 is to say: before it has become active one wishes to see its
reflection to search for the location of the [evil] qi." Gao Shishi: "At the time when
the malaria disease has not broken out yet, how is [this latent disease] reflected in

When the disease is in the yang [section], then [the patient] is hot and the [movement in the] vessels is hasty.

When it is in the yin [section], then [the patient] is cold and the [movement in the] vessels is calm.

When it has reached its peak, then yin and yang are both weak and the guard [qi] and the [evil] qi have disassociated themselves from each other.[53]
Hence, the disease can rest.

When the guard [qi] and the [evil] qi gather [again], then the disease returns."[54]

35-205-5
[Huang] Di:
"At times [the disease] skips two days [before a renewed outbreak],
or it may even take several days before [the disease] breaks out [again].
In some cases [the patient] is thirsty, in others he is not thirsty.
What is the reason for this?"

Qi Bo:
"As for the days skipped [before a renewed outbreak],
the evil qi and the guard qi have settled in the six palaces,[55] and
there are times when they have lost each other and cannot find each other.
Hence, [the disease] rests for several days before it is active [again].

Malaria is an alternating domination of yin and yang [qi].
In some cases it is severe, in others it is not severe.

---

the [movement in the] vessels and other conditions?" Cheng Shide et al.: "應 has the meaning here of 表現, 'to manifest oneself.' "

53 Wu Kun: "When the activity of the disease has reached its peak, then both the yin blood and the yang qi are weakened and ruined. The true evil has departed from the guard qi. Hence the disease can enter a phase of rest." Gao Shishi: "When the disease is at its peak, then the qi of yin and yang is weak. When both the yin and the yang [qi] are weak, then the guard qi and the evil qi separate. Hence the disease can enter a phase of rest. This is why it does not break out." Yao Shaoyu: " '[When the disease is at its] peak, then yin and yang are both weak' is to say: when the disease has lasted for long then both the qi and the blood are depleted and the [movement in the] vessels at the foot and inch [locations] must be weak without strength."

54 Yao Shaoyu: "集 is to say: the evil qi joins once again with the guard qi." Hua Shou: "集 is to say: it meets with the evil [qi]."

55 Zhang Qi: "This sentence is corrupt. Nowhere in this treatise does one find the idea of 'to settle in the six palaces.' " Tanba: "The preceding text does not speak of a 'settling in the six palaces.' Maybe this is a mistake for 'wind palace.' "

Hence, some [patients] are thirsty, others are not thirsty."⁵⁶

35-205-8
[Huang] Di:
"A discourse states:
'If in summer [someone] was harmed by summerheat,
in autumn he will necessarily fall ill with malaria.'⁵⁷
If, now, [the outbreak of] the malaria does not necessarily correspond [to the arrival of autumn],
why is that?"

Qi Bo:
"This [statement in the discourse refers to diseases] corresponding to the four seasons.
When diseases assume a different manifestation,
these are cases contradicting the four seasons.⁵⁸

Those who fall ill in autumn, they will be very cold.⁵⁹
Those who fall ill in winter, they are not very cold.⁶⁰
Those who fall ill in spring, they have an aversion to wind.⁶¹

---

56 Wang Bing: "When the yang [qi] dominates the yin [qi] seriously, then [the patient] is thirsty. When the domination of the yang [qi] over the yin [qi] is not serious, then [the patient] is not thirsty. 'To dominate' is to say to abound in strength in comparison with the other qi."

57 For such statements, see *Su wen* 3 and 5. The character 病 here may be a mistake for 痎.

58 Zhang Jiebin: "If in summer one was harmed by summerheat and if in autumn one will fall ill with malaria. This is in correspondence with the four seasons. If someone falls ill with malaria in spring, summer, or winter, then the disease often takes a different appearance." Wu Kun: "'Contrary to the four seasons' is to say: In spring it should be warm, but, on the contrary, it is very cold. In summer it should be hot, but, on the contrary, it is very cold. In autumn it should be cool, but, on the contrary, it is very warm. In winter it should be cold, but, on the contrary, it is very hot. When the malaria disease assumes different appearances, it is because of this."

59 Wang Bing: "In autumn the qi is clear and cool. The yang qi descends. The heat is stored in the muscles and in the flesh. Hence [one feels] very cold."

60 Wang Bing: "In winter the qi is bitingly freezing; the yang qi lies hidden and is stored away. It does not struggle with the cold. Hence [one does] not [feel] very cold."

61 Zhang Jiebin: "In spring the yang qi flows off towards the outside. The interstice structures gradually widen, but the surplus cold has not departed yet. Hence the pa-

550

Those who fall ill in summer, they sweat profusely."[62]

35-205-12
[Huang] Di:
"Now,
if one is ill with warmth malaria or with cold malaria,[63] where are both [these
two diseases] lodged?
In which depot do they lodge?"[64]

Qi Bo:
"The warmth malaria is acquired in winter through being struck by wind.
The cold qi is stored in the bone and in the marrow.
By the time of spring, the yang qi is effused massively.
The evil qi cannot leave by itself.

If subsequently [the patient] encounters massive summerheat,
his brain and marrow melt; his muscles and flesh wane.
From the interstice structures emerges an outflow [of sweat].
Or [that person] exerts himself [and sweats].
The evil qi leaves together with the sweat.

This disease is stored in the kidneys;
its qi at first leaves from the inside and moves towards the outside.[65]

---

tient often has an aversion to wind."

62 Zhang Jiebin: "In summer, the heat is extreme; it steams the muscles and the
[body's] outside. Hence patients with this [disease] sweat a lot." Zhang Zhicong: "In
summer the yang qi flows off towards outside. The interstice structures open widely.
Hence one sweats a lot."

63 Cheng Shide et al.: "Zhou Xuehai stated: '寒 should be 癉.' The question refers to
warmth malaria and to cold malaria, while the answer refers to warmth malaria and to
solitary [heat] malaria. Hence Zhou Xuehai's statement appears to be correct."

64 Zhang Jiebin: "安舍 is to say: where does it lodge?"

65 Wang Bing: "The kidneys rule in winter. Winter rules the bone marrow. The brain
is the sea of marrow. Above and below correspond to each other. Receding heat steams
the upper [part of the body]. Hence the brain marrow melts. When it melts, then the
heat qi accumulates in the [body's] outside. Hence muscles and flesh waste away and
the disease is stored in the kidneys." Cheng Shide et al.: "The evil qi follows the sweat
from the kidneys and leaves towards the outside." Gao Shishi: "When the interstice
structures open in summer, or when one exerts oneself, then the evil qi in the bone
marrow leaves with the sweat and this causes malaria. That is, the disease evil is stored

In such a situation,
the [qi in the] yin [section] is depleted and the [qi in the] yang [section]
abounds.
When [the qi in] the yang [section] abounds, then [the patient] is hot.[66]
When it weakens, then the qi turns back again and enters [the inside].[67]
When it enters [the inside], then the yang [section] is depleted.
When the yang [section] is depleted, then [the patient] is cold.
Hence, he is first hot and cold afterwards.
[The disease] is named warmth malaria."

35-206-6
[Huang] Di:
"How about solitary [heat] malaria?"

Qi Bo:
"In case of solitary [heat] malaria the lung is habitually hot.
The qi abounds in the body.
When it comes to recession with countermovement, with [the qi] rushing
upwards, the central qi is replete and does not flow away towards the outside.[68]
If subsequently [the patient] exerts himself,
the interstice structures open.
Wind and cold lodge inside the skin, and within the partings of the flesh,

---

in the kidneys. The qi leaves first from the bone marrow inside through the muscles,
the flesh, and the interstice structures outside."

66 Wang Bing: "'The yin is depleted' is to say: the qi of the kidney depot is depleted.
'The yang abounds' is to say: the major yang qi of the bladder abounds."

67 Wang Bing: "'Weak' is to say: the disease weakens and retreats. 'It enters again'
is to say: it enters the yin vessels of the kidneys." Yao Shaoyu: "衰 is: it abounds to
an extreme and changes. The meaning is the same as that of 病極, 'the disease has
reached its extreme,' and 逆極, 'reverse movement to the extreme,' in the preceding
text. [Wang Bing's] comment implies that the disease weakens and retreats, that is,
the malaria is healed. [If this were so, though, the text, further down,] would not
speak of yang depletion resulting in cold." Hua Shou: "When the yang [qi] abounds
to an extreme then the yin must be depleted. The malaria, then, avails itself of this
depletion and once again enters the interior. The yang [qi] of the interior has already
been harmed by the malaria and is depleted. When the yang is depleted, then the yin
is replete. Hence [the patient] is cold again. This can be regarded as evidence of the
alternating abundance and depletion of the malaria qi."

68 Zhang Zhicong: "The lung rules the qi of the entire body. [In the present case,] the
lung habitually has heat, hence the qi abounds in the body. This qi recedes in a reverse
movement and rushes upwards, hence it does not flow off towards the outside and
causes repletion in the center. In this case there is repletion both inside and outside."

whence they effuse [internally].

When they are effused, then the yang qi abounds.

When the yang qi abounds and does not weaken, then [the patient] has developed a disease.

The qi fails to reach the yin [section]; hence [the patient] is hot only, but not cold.[69]

When the qi is stored internally in the heart,
and lodges outside in the partings of the flesh,
this lets the [afflicted] person's flesh waste away [as if] melting.
Hence, [this disease] is called solitary [heat] malaria."

[Huang] Di:
"Good!"

---

69 Zhang Jiebin: "The evil strikes the outside. It is only in the yang section and does not reach the yin. Hence [the patient experiences] only heat, no cold." Yao Shaoyu: "'The qi' is the disease qi. The disease is entirely in the yang [section]. Hence [the text] states: 'it does not reach the yin [section].'" Gao Shishi: "Above the text discusses the warmth malaria, stating 'the qi turns back again and enters; hence [the patient] is first hot and cold afterwards.' In case of the solitary (*dan*) [heat] malaria, the qi does not return to the yin, hence [the patient experiences] only (*dan*) heat and is not cold."

Chapter 36
To Pierce Malaria[1]

36-206-14
Malaria of the foot major yang [conduit]:
it lets a person have lower back pain and a heavy head.
Cold rises from the back.[2]
[Patients] are cold first and afterwards hot.[3]
The heat is intense as in harm caused by summerheat.
When the heat stops, sweat leaves [the body].

[This disease] is difficult to bring to an end.[4]
Pierce [the foot major yang conduit] into the cleft. Let blood.[5]

---

1 140/28: "The old name for 瘧 was 'spleen cold.' That is, the large network [vessel] of the spleen was [thought to be] affected by cold and dampness."

2 Wang Bing: "The foot major yang vessel originates from the top of the skull and enters and encircles the brain. It leaves [the brain] again and divides [into two branches] descending from the nape, passing inside the shoulder blade, following the spine and reaching the lower back. Another branch descends from within the shoulder blade to the left and to the right [of the spine], penetrates the buttocks and passes through the femoral prominence. Hence [malaria of the foot major yang vessel] causes the lower back to ache and gives one [a feeling of] a heavy head. Cold emerges from the back."

3 Wang Bing: "*Hao-hao* indicates the appearance of extreme heat. *Ye-ye*, too, is abounding heat. The major yang [qi] is insufficient. Hence one is first cold. When the cold has reached a peak, it generates heat. Hence one is hot afterwards."

4 Wang Bing: "Heat is generated because of qi depletion. When the heat stops, this is because the qi has returned. When the qi has returned and one sweats nevertheless, this is [a sign that] the evil qi abounds and that the true [qi] does not dominate. Hence this is difficult to cure."

5 Wang Bing: "The cleft of the major yang [conduit] is called Golden Gate (金門). The Golden Gate is located on the exterior side of the foot below the ankle. Another name is Pass Beam (關梁)... When piercing it, [the needle] can be inserted three parts of a standardized body inch deep." Ma Shi: "The center of the cleft is the Bend Middle (委中) hole." Cheng Shide et al.: "郄 stands for 隙, 'fissure.' This [term] refers to a hole [in general]; it does not necessarily specify the cleft hole." 742/46 interprets 郄中 as 委中, Bend Middle. It is questionable, though, whether a specific acu-point was recommended for blood letting in the oldest strata of the text. Hence we assume 郄中 to be a reference not to a specific point but to the short section of the vessel apparent "in the cleft," i.e., in the bend of the knee. This hypothesis is strengthened by the wording of the corresponding passage in the *Jia yi jing* which has 膕中, "in the hollow of the knee," (i.e., in the popliteal fossa) instead of 郄中.

Malaria of the foot minor yang [conduit]:
it lets a person's body experience jie-yi.[6]
Neither the cold nor the heat are severe.[7]
[Patients] hate to see [other] people.
If they see [other] people, their heart is scared,[8]
they develop plenty of heat and sweat leaves [their body] profusely.[9]

Pierce the foot minor yang [conduit].[10]

36-207-3
Malaria of the foot yang brilliance [conduit]:
It lets a person first be cold.
[Patients] shiver severely.
When the cold has been severe for a long time, it changes into heat.
When the heat goes, sweat leaves [the body].
[Patients] love to see the light of sun and moon.
[Exposure to] fire qi makes them happy.[11]

---

6 For a discussion of 解㑊, see *Su wen* 18-113-1.

7 Wang Bing: "The yang qi does not abound yet. This is the cause for this." Wu Kun: "When evil gathers in the interior, then the cold is extreme; when it gathers in the exterior, then the heat is extreme. The minor yang is half exterior, half interior. Hence neither cold nor heat are extreme."

8 Wang Bing: "The gallbladder forms a union with the liver. When the liver is depleted, one has fear. The evil presses against the [proper] qi. Hence [patients] hate to see [other] people and if they see [other] people, the heart is alarmed."

9 Wang Bing: "When the evil [qi] abounds, then there is much heat. One was struck by wind, hence sweat leaves [the body]." Wu Kun: "熱多 is: 熱勝, 'the heat dominates.'" Cheng Shide et al.: "The text says nothing of 'being struck by wind.' The basis of Wang Bing's comment is unclear."

10 Yang Shangshan: "One can select the Wind Pool (風池) and the Hill Ruins (丘墟) holes of the minor yang [conduit]." Wang Bing: "The Pinched Ravine (俠溪) [hole] masters this. .. This is the brook [transporter] of the minor yang. When piercing [it] one can insert [the needle] three parts of a standardized body inch deep and lets it remain for [a period of] three exhalations."

11 Wang Bing: "When the yang [qi] is depleted, then the outside is cold first. When the yang [qi] is extremely depleted, then it will return to abundance. Hence, after experiencing a long period of extreme cold [the patient] turns hot. When the heat disappears, the sweating ends. The yin is strong inside and the yang cannot dominate the yin. Hence [patients] love to see the light of sun and moon and they are happy when [they encounter] fire qi." Zhang Jiebin: "The yang brilliance [conduit] is a conduit with plenty of blood and qi. [Here] now cold evil dominates it. Hence one is first cold and after a long time [this changes to] heat. When the heat disappears, then the

Pierce the foot yang brilliance [conduit] on the instep.[12]

36-207-5
Malaria of the foot major yin [conduit]:
it lets a person be unhappy.
[Patients] tend to breathe deeply and do not wish to eat.[13]
They experience frequent [spells of] cold and heat, with sweat leaving [their body].[14]
When the disease arrives, then [patients] tend to vomit.
When the vomiting has ended, then [the disease] weakens.[15]

---

evil is released. Hence sweat leaves [the body]. *Ling shu* 10 states: 'When a yang brilliance disease arrives, one has an aversion to [other] people and to fire. In the present case, [the patient] loves to see the light of sun and moon, that is, he is happy when he is affected by fire qi. Why? Because when the yang brilliance receives yang evil, this is a repletion of the stomach. Hence one has an aversion to heat. When the yang brilliance receives yin evil, this is a depletion of the stomach. Hence one loves warmth."

12 Wang Bing: "This is the Surging Yang (衝陽) hole. .. When piercing [it], one can insert [the needle] three parts of a standardized body inch deep and lets it remain for [a period of] ten exhalations."

13 Wang Bing: "When the heart qi flows into the lung, then happiness follows. In the present case, the spleen depot has received disease [qi]. The heart, [its] mother, comes to stop it. Fire qi descends into the spleen, but does not move upwards into the lung. Also, a branch of the major yin vessel rises from the stomach to the diaphragm and pours into the heart. Hence [this disease] lets one be unhappy and [patients] tend to breathe deeply." Zhang Jiebin: "The spleen is the son of the heart. When the spleen has a disease, then the heart qi is uneasy. Hence one is unhappy."

14 Wang Bing: "The spleen rules the transformation of the grains; it supports the four sides. In the present case, evil [qi] has accumulated in it and the depots receive no supplies. The soil [qi] is present during [all] four seasons. When it flourishes it battles with the evil qi. Hence one does not wish to eat, experiences frequent spells of cold and heat and sweats." Zhang Jiebin: "When the spleen fails to transform, then the upper burner is blocked. Hence one tends to breathe deeply and has no appetite." Ma Shi: "The spleen rules the transformation of the grains. [In the present case,] evil qi accumulates in it. Hence one does not wish to eat."

15 Wang Bing: "The foot major yin vessel enters the abdomen, touches the spleen, encircles the stomach, rises to the diaphragm and parallels the throat. Hence, when disease qi arrives in it, one vomits. When the vomiting ends, [the disease qi] weakens and retreats." Gao Shishi: "When a malaria disease just arrives, the proper qi cannot move upwards and reach the outside. As a result one tends to vomit. When one vomits, then the qi of the major yin rises from below. Hence, when the vomiting ends [the disease] weakens."

That is [the moment] to seize it.[16]

36-208-1
Malaria of the foot minor yin [conduit]:
it lets a person vomit severely.
[Patients] experience frequent [spells of] cold and heat.
They are more often hot than cold.[17]
They wish to stay home, with doors and windows closed.

This disease is difficult to bring to an end.[18]

36-208-3
Malaria of the foot ceasing yin [conduit]:
It lets a person's lower back ache and gives
the lower abdomen [a feeling of] fullness.
The urine does not flow freely;
it resembles a protuberance illness, but it is no protuberance illness.[19]
[Patients] have a frequent [urge to] relieve themselves.
Their sentiments are fearful.

---

16 Wang Bing: "One waits until the disease has weakened and disappears and only
then seizes it. This is to say: when it has weakened one seizes it at the well transporters
and the Duke Grandchild (公孫) [hole]. .. One can pierce them four parts of a standardized body inch deep." Wu Kun: "取 is 'to select the conduit hole.' " Tanba: "The
Jia yi [*jing*] has the three characters 足太陰, 'foot major yin,' following this. Given the
examples of the text above, these three characters should be added."

17 Wang Bing: "The foot minor yin vessel penetrates the liver and the diaphragm. It
[then] enters the lung and follows the throat. Hence one vomits and spits severely and
experiences frequent spells of cold and heat. The kidney is a yin depot. Yin qi generates cold. In the present case, the yin qi is insufficient. Hence [patients] are more hot
than cold." Lin Yi et al.: "The *Jia yi jing* has 嘔吐甚多寒少熱." Zhang Jiebin: "When
the kidneys have a disease, then the yin is depleted. When the yin is depleted, [the
patient] is more hot than cold."

18 Wang Bing: "In case of a disease in the yang brilliance vessels of the stomach [pa-
tients] wish to be alone, to close the door and the windows and to stay at home. In the
present case, [the text] outlines signs of a disease of the stomach, [associated with the
agent of] soil, which, contrary [to what one should expect], appear in case of [a dis-
ease] in the kidneys, [associated with the agent of] water. Soil punishes water. Hence
this disease is difficult to heal." Zhang Jiebin: "When a disease is in the yin [section],
one enjoys quietude. Hence, one wishes to close doors and windows and stay at home.
The kidneys are the depot of extreme yin. When evil [qi] settles [in the kidneys], this
disease is difficult to heal."

19 See also *Su wen* 49, note 55/56.

The qi is insufficient.
In the abdomen there is uneasiness.[20]

Pierce the foot ceasing yin [conduit].

Lung malaria:
it lets a person's heart be cold.
When it is very cold [it changes to] heat.
While it is hot, [patients] tend to be frightened as if they had seen something [frightening].[21]

Pierce the hand major yin and yang brilliance [conduits].[22]

36-209-1
Heart malaria:
it lets a person's heart be very vexed.
[Patients] long for cool water.
Contrary [to what might be expected,] they are often cold and not very hot.[23]

---

20 Wang Bing: "The foot ceasing yin vessel .. encircles the yin organ and reaches into the lower abdomen. Hence the disease appears as is [outlined in the text]. 癃 is to say: one cannot pass urine. 悒悒 is 不暢, 'not joyous.'" *SWJZ:* "悒 is 不安, 'uneasy.'" Zhang Zhicong: "The wood rules the qi generated in spring. When the ceasing yin [vessel] has received evil [qi], the vital qi is insufficient. The wood stagnates and cannot reach out. Hence there is uneasiness in the abdomen." See also 2167/48.

21 Zhang Jiebin: "The lung is the canopy covering the heart. [In the present case] a cold evil [originating from the lung, i.e., the metal] has availed itself of [the heart, i.e., the fire] which it [usually] cannot overcome. Hence lung malaria causes the heart to be cold. When the cold has reached its peak, heat will return and the qi of the heart suffers harm. Hence, [patients] tend to be frightened as if they had seen something [frightening]."

22 Wang Bing: "The Broken Sequence (列缺) rules this [disease]. .. When piercing [it] one can insert [the needle] three parts of a standardized body inch deep and lets it remain for [a period of] six exhalations." Zhang Jiebin: "One must pierce the two conduits of the exterior and of the interior, to drain the repletion of the yang brilliance and to supplement the depletion of the major yin [conduits]."

23 Zhang Qi: "The heart has heat. Hence, [patients] are vexed and wish to consume cold beverages. [As a result] the heat is blocked [internally] and cannot move to the exterior [of the body]. Yin qi [dominates] the exterior surface. Hence [patients] are mostly cold, while the heat is not extreme."

Pierce the hand minor yin [conduit].[24]

Liver malaria:
it lets a person's complexion become greenish.[25]
[Patients] take deep breaths.
They resemble a corpse.
Pierce the foot ceasing yin. Let blood appear.[26]

Spleen malaria:
it lets a person be cold.
[Patients] have pain in the abdomen.
When they are hot, sounds occur in their intestines.
When these sounds come to an end, sweat leaves [the body].[27]

Pierce the foot major yin [conduit].[28]

36-209-5
Kidney malaria:
it lets a person shiver.
[Patients] writhe with pain in the lower back and in the spine.

---

24 Wang Bing: "The Spirit Gate (神門) rules this [disease]. ... When piercing [it] one can insert [the needle] three parts of a standardized body inch deep and lets it remain for [a period of] seven exhalations."

25 Zhang Jiebin: "The liver belongs to the wood. Hence the complexion is greenish. When the liver is blocked, then the qi moves reversely. Hence [patients] take deep breaths. When the wood has a disease, it is hard and stiff. Hence the [patients'] appearance is as if they were dead."

26 Wang Bing: "The Central Mound (中封) rules this [disease]. ... One pierces until the blood has left [the hole] and then stops. When piercing one can insert [the needle] four parts of a standardized body inch deep and lets it remain for [a period of] seven exhalations." Wu Kun: "The ceasing yin [conduit] contains much blood. Hence one removes blood from there to drain repletion evil."

27 Wu Kun: "'Lets a person be cold' is: lets a person first be cold. The spleen is [associated with] the center and the soil. Hence [patients] have pain in the abdomen. Pain is repletion with evil qi. 'When [the patient] is hot, then sounds occur in the intestines,' is: the spleen qi moves. 'When the noises stop, sweat leaves [the body],' is: the evil qi reaches the exterior."

28 Wang Bing: "The Shang Hill (商丘) rules this [disease]. ... When piercing [it], one can insert [the needle] three parts of a standardized body inch deep and lets it remain for [a period of] seven inhalations."

[Patients] have difficulties passing their stools.[29]
Their vision is dizzy.[30]
Hands and feet are cold.

Pierce the foot major yang and minor yin [conduits].[31]

Stomach malaria:
it lets a person have an ulcer disease.
[Patients] tend to be hungry but cannot eat.
When they eat, propping fullness results,[32] and the abdomen is enlarged.[33]

Pierce the foot yang brilliance and major yin transverse vessel. Let blood.[34]

36-209-8
In case malaria breaks out:

---

29 We follow here a passage in the *Chu ci* 楚辭, Yan ji 嚴忌: 愁脩夜而宛轉, "I felt worried for long and at night I turned back and forth." Wu Kun: "宛 is 似, 'to appear.' 轉 is 傳送, 'to transmit.' That is to say, it appears as if one could transmit, but the stools leave only under great difficulties." Zhang Jiebin: "When the lower back and the back are in pain, it hurts when one bends and turns the body around." Ma Shi: "宛 轉 is: 'one has difficulties to turn one's body.'" Yan Zhenhai/52: "The characters 宛 轉 belong to the preceding phrase. The *Wai tai mi yao* 外台秘要, '卒心痛方,' has 宛 轉痛. The meaning is identical with 痛宛轉. The three characters 大便難 represent a fixed phrase occurring in the *Nei jing* at various locations."

30 See 2167/48.

31 Wang Bing: "The Great Goblet (太鍾) rules this [disease]."

32 916/53: "支 is identical with 撐, 'to prop up.' 支滿 is to say: 䐜滿, 'dropsical swellings.' One feels as if one were supported by pillars."

33 Wang Bing: "The stomach has heat and the spleen is depleted. Hence one tends to be hungry, but cannot eat. If one eats, then propping fullness results and the abdomen becomes large." Lin Yi et al.: "The *Tai su* has 疽病, 'ulcers,' instead of 且病." Zhang Jiebin: "There are six palaces, but [the text] speaks only of a stomach[-malaria] because the stomach is the chief of the six palaces. When the evil is in the yang brilliance [conduit], then the stomach disease extends to the spleen. Hence one tends to be hungry but cannot eat and the limbs are full and the abdomen becomes large." Ma Shi: "且 is 將, 'about to.' When the disease is about to develop, one tends to be hungry but cannot eat."

34 Wang Bing: "The Grinding Stone (厲兌), the Ravine Divide (解谿), and the Three Miles (三里) rule this [disease]. .. For piercing [it] one can insert [the needle] one part of a standardized body inch deep and lets it remain for one [period of] exhalation."

when the body is just hot,[35]
pierce the moving vessel on the instep.
Open the hollow and let its blood.[36]
[The body will be] cold immediately.[37]

In the case of malaria:
when [the patient] is just about to become cold,[38]
pierce the hand yang brilliance and major yin [conduits], as well as the foot
yang brilliance and major yin [conduits].[39]

36-210-2
In the case of malaria:
when the vessels are full and big,
quickly pierce the transporters on the back.[40]
Select a medium [size] needle [to pierce] near the five upper flank transporters;
one [piercing] at each [of them].[41]

---

35 Zhang Jiebin: "'The body is just hot' is to say: before [the disease] has manifested itself, when the heat is about to become active."

36 Yang Shangshan: "'To open the hollow' is: one enlarges the hole by swinging [the needle] to and fro."

37 Wang Bing: "The yang brilliance vessel holds plenty of blood and plenty of qi. The heat abounds and the qi is strong. Hence if one lets its blood one can cause immediate cold."

38 Zhang Jiebin: "The cold is about to break out, but has not broken out yet." Zhang Zhicong: "This is, the evil is about to enter the interior, the yin."

39 Wang Bing: "This, too, is to say: open a hole and let its blood." Zhang Jiebin: "By piercing the yang brilliance [conduits] of the hands and feet, one can drain the heat. By piercing the major yin [conduits] of the hands and of the feet, one can supplement the yin."

40 Zhang Jiebin: "'Full, big, and tense' is: replete with yang evil. The back is where all the yang leaves. Hence one must pierce there, i.e., at the five upper flank transporters. 胠 is 脅, 'flanks.'" Gao Shishi: "中針 is a needle which is neither big nor small. 胠 is the part of the back alongside the flanks. When in the case of malaria the vessels are full, big, and tense, the conduit vessels have a surplus of qi. All the transporters of the five depots are on the back. Hence one pierces the 'transporters of the back.' The transporters of the five depots are arranged on the back on two lines. Outside of these two lines are two further lines. They are the so-called 胠." Tanba Genken 丹波元堅: "胠 refers to the flanks below the armpits."

41 Zhang Yizhi et al.: "傍五胠俞 refers to the five transporter holes near the upper flanks."

Let blood in accordance with whether [the patient is] fat or lean.[42]

36-210-3
In the case of malaria:
when the vessels are small and replete,
quickly cauterize the minor yin [conduit] at the shin and
pierce the well [hole] on the finger.[43]

>In the case of malaria:
when the vessels are full and big,
quickly pierce the transporters on the back.
Select the five upper flank transporters and the transporters on the back; one
[piercing] at each [of them].
Move [the needle] until the blood is reached.<[44]

In the case of malaria:
when the vessels are relaxed, big, and depleted,
then it is appropriate to employ drugs;
it is not appropriate to employ needles.[45]

---

42 Wang Bing: "When someone is lean, the piercing is shallow and only small amounts
of blood are let. When someone is fat, the piercing is deep and large amounts of blood
are let. 'Transporters on the back' is to say: the Great Shuttle (大杼) [holes]."

43 Wang Bing: "'Cauterize the shinbone minor yin' is to say: [cauterize] the Recover
Flow (復溜) [hole]. .. When piercing, one can insert [the needle] three parts of a
standardized body inch and lets it remain for [a period of] three exhalations. 'Pierce
the toe well' is to say: pierce the Extreme Yin (至陰) [hole]. The Extreme Yin [hole] is
located at the outer side of the small toe. .. It is the well [hole] of the foot major yang
[conduit]. When piercing, one can insert [the needle] one part of a standardized body
inch and lets it remain for [a period of] five exhalations." Zhang Zhicong: "When the
vessels are small, this is [because] the qi in the vessels is depleted."

44 Wang Bing: "This is to say: one adapts the deep or shallow [piercing] of the [pierc-
ing] hole to the fat or lean [status of the patient], .. and inserts the needle until it has
reached a blood vessel." Lin Yi et al.: "The 55 characters beginning with 瘧脈滿大急
including this commentary by Wang Bing should be deleted. They are a repetition of
what was said above and make no sense." Gu Guangguang: "Lin Yi et al. speaks of 55
characters. In its present version this passage has 57 characters. I suspect that the two
characters 背俞 following the characters 五胠俞 in the proper text are a later insertion. 用 should be 及, "and.""

45 Wang Bing: "'Relaxed' [is the result of being] hit by wind. 'Big' is a qi repletion.
'Depleted' is blood depletion. [In the present case], the blood is depleted and the qi is
replete and [the patient] was hit by wind. Hence one must treat with drugs to chase
away the evil. It would be inappropriate to drain with needles and let [the patient's]

36-210-5
Whenever in treating malaria
this [treatment] precedes an outbreak by the time span of a meal,
[the disease] can [still] be treated.
Once [this point in time] has passed, then one has missed the [right] moment.[46]

In all cases of malaria in which the vessels are not visible,
pierce between the ten fingers and let blood.[47]
When the blood has left, [the disease] will certainly end.
In cases where an initial observation shows that the body is red like small beans,
take the [blood] entirely.

As for the twelve malaria [diseases] their outbreaks occur all at a different time.[48]
Investigate the physical appearence the disease assumes, to recognize in which vessel the disease is.

---

blood." Zhang Jiebin: "The needles have [the function] to drain, not to supplement. Hence, in case the vessels are depleted it is not appropriate to employ needles. *Ling shu* 17 states: 'what abounds is to be drained; what is depleted is to be supplemented by consuming drugs.' This is meant here."

46 Wang Bing: "At the time before [the malaria] has manifested itself, true [qi] and evil [qi] reside at different places and no breakers rise at the banks. Hence one can [still] treat [the disease]. When this time has passed, then true and evil [qi] have merged. If one were to attack now, one would contrary [to one's intentions] harm the true qi. Hence [the text] states: 'one has missed the [right] moment.' "The passage beginning with 36-210-2 ("In the case of malaria: when the vessels are full and big, etc.") and ending here appears to be one of the few passages in the *Su wen* the relocation of which can be traced to Wang Bing. According to   Lin Yi et al., it was moved here from *juan* 4 of the Quan Yuanqi edition. It is interesting to note that the passage was moved here in its entirety, i.e., including what must be an erroneous earlier insertion.

47 Wu Kun: "When the vessels are invisible, the yang is excited and the vessels, nevertheless, are hidden. Hence one pierces between the ten fingers to drain the yang." Gao Shishi: "脈不見 is: one does not observe vessels that are full, big, and tense, or small, solid, and tense, or relaxed, big, and depleted. The disease is not in the vessels. All one has to do is to pierce the well holes between the ten fingers." Cheng Shide et al.: "Blood letting is a method to drain repletions. Hence one should follow Wu Kun's commentary."

48 Cheng Shide et al.: "These are the malaria of the six conduits, of the five depots and of the stomach, as outlined above."

If the piercing precedes the moment of its outbreak by a time span of a meal,
the first piercing will cause [the disease] to weaken,
a second piercing will cause it [to improve] noticeably,
a third piercing will cause it to end.[49]

If it does not end [after a third piercing],
pierce the two vessels below the tongue and let blood.
If it [still] does not end,
pierce the conduit abounding [with blood] in the cleft and let blood.[50]
Also, pierce below the nape on both sides of the spine.
This must cause [the disease] to end.
{As for 'the two vessels below the tongue,' these are the Ridge Spring [holes].}

36-211-3
To pierce malaria, it is essential to first ask where the disease broke out initially and
pierce there first.[51]
If it [appeared] initially as headache and heaviness,
first pierce on the head and in the region of the two [sides of the] forehead and at the two eyebrows. Let blood.
If it [appeared] initially as pain in the nape and in the back,
pierce there first.
If it [appeared] initially as pain in the lower back and in the spine,
first pierce into the cleft. Let blood.
If it [appeared] initially as pain in the hands and arms,
first pierce the hand minor yin and yang brilliance [conduits] between the ten fingers.
If it [appeared] initially as pain in the feet and shins,
first pierce the foot yang brilliance [conduit] between the ten toes. Let blood.[52]

---

49 Zhang Jiebin: "After one piercing the disease weakens but this is not yet noticeable. Hence one must pierce again. Only then one notices (知) an effect. After the third piercing the disease can come to an end." Zhang Zhicong: "According to ancient [terminology], when the urine flows unimpeded and when the abdomen is in harmony, this is '知.'" Yu Chang: "知 should be interpreted as 愈, 'healed.' The *Fang yan* 方言, Chen chu pian 陳楚篇, states: '知 is 愈.' [That is,] when in Southern Chu a disease was healed, they called it 知. 知 is a state between 'weakened' and 'ended.'"

50 Zhang Zhicong: "This is to say: blood and qi abound here."

51 Zhang Jiebin: "One attacks its base first."

52 Wang Bing: "In all cases one drains the evil from the locations it occupies."

36-211-7
Wind-malaria:
when the malaria breaks out,
then sweat leaves [the body] and [patients] have an aversion to wind.
Pierce those back transporters of the third yang conduit that have blood.[53]

When the shin aches so severely that pressing it causes unbearable [pain],
this is called 'disease attached to the marrow.'[54]
Employ the chisel needle to needle the Severed Bone and let blood.[55]
[The disease] will end immediately.

When the body has little pain, pierce the Extreme Yin.[56]
[Pierce also] the well holes of all the yin [conduits]. Do not cause blood to leave.
Pierce once every second day.[57]

When in the case of malaria [the patient] is not thirsty and if [the disease] is active every second day,
pierce the foot major yang [conduit].[58]

---

53 Wang Bing: "三陽 is the major yang." Zhang Jiebin: "The blood of the transporters of the three yang conduits/third yang conduit on the back is to say: the Bladder Transporter (膀胱俞) of the foot major yang, the Stomach Transporter (胃俞) of the foot yang brilliance, and the Gallbladder Transporter (膽俞) of the foot minor yang. They all are foot major yang conduit holes." Gao Shishi: "Wind-malaria is to have a malaria disease because [one was struck by] wind. When the malaria manifests itself, sweat leaves [the body] and one has an aversion to wind. The major yang is the third yang. By piercing the blood of the transporters of the third yang conduit on the back, one treats the wind-malaria of the major yang."

54 We assume 胕 to be an erroneous writing of 附 here.

55 Wang Bing: "This is the Yang Assistance (陽輔) [hole]."

56 The *Tai su* links 刺之 to the following sentence, instead of to 刺至陰. Lin Yi et al.: "The *Jia yi jing* does not have the two characters 至陰." Gao Shishi: "The body experiences a minor pain; it cannot be compared to the extreme pain felt in the shin-bones. The pain is not in the bones, it is in the major yang penetrating the body. Hence one pierces the Extreme Yin (至陰) of the major yang conduit."

57 Wang Bing: "All well [holes] are located at the tips of the fingers/toes. The well [hole] of the foot minor yin [vessel] is located in the indentation in the sole of the feet."

58 Zhang Jiebin: "Not to be thirsty [indicates] there is no evil in the interior; the evil is in the exterior. Hence, one must pierce the foot major yang [conduit]."

In case [the patient] is thirsty and if [the disease] is active every second day, pierce the foot minor yang [conduit].[59]
When in the case of warmth malaria no sweat leaves [the body], carry out the fifty-nine piercings.[60]

---

59 Zhang Jiebin: "In the case of thirst, the evil is in between the exterior and the interior. Hence one must pierce the foot minor yang."

60 See *Su wen* 32 for a listing of the fifty-nine holes. See also 1861/10 for a detailed survey.

Chapter 37
Discourse on Qi Recession

37-212-4
Huang Di asked:
"The five depots and six palaces, when they move cold and heat among each other,
how [is that]?"[1]

Qi Bo:
"When the kidneys move cold to the spleen,[2]
[this results in] *yong*-abscesses, swelling, and being short of qi.[3]

When the spleen moves cold to the liver,
[this results in] yong-abscesses, swelling, and sinew cramps.[4]

---

1 Zhang Jiebin: "相移 is to move a disease from its present location to another."

2 The textus receptus has 肝; the *Tai su* and the Quan Yuanqi edition have 脾 instead of 肝. Judged from the structure of the following discourse, "liver" appears indeed to be a mistake here for "spleen."

3 Wang Bing: "The liver stores the blood. However, when cold enters [the liver], then the yang qi is not dispersed. When the yang qi is not dispersed, then the blood collects and the [flow of the] qi roughens. Hence this results in abscesses and swellings and causes diminished qi (i.e., one is short of breath)." Lin Yi et al.: "The Quan Yuanqi edition and the *Jia yi jing* have 'moves cold to the spleen.' When Wang Bing based his comments on [the presence of the character] 'the liver,' he started from an erroneous version." Zhang Jiebin: "The spleen rules the muscles and the flesh. When it is affected by cold then [its] qi collects and hardens. When it has hardened and does not disperse, this causes swelling and boils. 'Diminished qi' [is to say:] when cold abounds, then the yang is depleted below. When the yang is depleted, then there is nothing that could be transformed into qi." Zhang Zhicong: "The spleen rules the muscles and the flesh. When cold qi transforms itself into heat, then the flesh rots and this causes boils and pus. The spleen collects the original and true qi. [Here] the spleen depot is affected by evil [qi], hence the [original and true] qi is diminished." Wu Kun: "'Diminished qi' [is to say:] The kidneys inhale yin qi. In the present case, the yin qi of the kidneys has moved [elsewhere] and has collected in the spleen. As a result, the yin qi of the kidneys is feeble. There is nothing [the kidneys] could inhale. Hence [the text speaks of] 'diminished qi.'" Hua Shou: "The flesh is transformed into pus; hence, this causes boils. The blood is harmed and the qi is diminished. Hence, [the text] states: 'diminished qi.'"

4 Wang Bing: "The spleen depot rules the flesh; the liver depot rules the sinews. When the flesh is warm, then the sinews are relaxed; when the flesh is cold, then the sinews are tense. Hence, the sinews are cramped. When the flesh is cold, then the guard qi accumulates. Hence this causes abscesses and swelling."

When the liver moves cold to the heart,
[this results in] craziness and *ge-zhong*.⁵

When the heart moves cold to the lung,
[this results in] *fei-xiao*.⁶

{As for *fei-xiao*, one drinks one [part] and urinates two [parts].
This is fatal and cannot be treated.}⁷

---

5 Wang Bing: "The heart is a yang depot; the spirit is located in it. When cold presses against it (or: accumulates in it), then the spirit becomes confused and leaves. Hence craziness results. The yang qi and the cold press against each other. Hence the diaphragm is blocked and the center is impassable." Zhang Jiebin: "When the liver moves cold to the heart, it transmits [the cold] to the [depot] it generates. The heart rules the fire; it stores the spirit. When it receives reversely moving cold of a liver evil the spirit becomes confused and craziness results." Zhang Qi: "隔中 is: the qi of the central burner does not flow freely." A literal translation of *ge-zhong* is "barred center". We consider this term to be a transliteration of an originally non-Chinese term the meaning of which was lost prior to the lifetime of Wang Bing.

6 Yang Shangshan: "The heart transmits cold to the lung. When the lung receives cold, it develops heat. When the lung burns, this results in thirst. This is called 'the lung dissolves.'" 2241/27: "消 is short for 消癉, 'wasting *dan*.' The three terms 肺消, 鬲消, and 消渴 refer to [the condition of] 上消, 'upper wasting,' when [a person] drinks a lot but his thirst does not end." We consider 肺消 to be a term of foreign or non-Han Chinese origin. A literal translation is "wasting lung", corresponding to the Greek term *phthisis*.

7 Wang Bing: "The heart is a yang depot. [Here now,] contrary [to what is normal] it has received cold. The cold qi does not dissipate [in the heart] and is moved to the lung. The cold follows the fire of the heart which internally melts the metal essence. [Here now,] the metal has received the fire evil. Hence it wastes away. When the lung melts away, [its] qi has nothing that could hold it. Hence one urinates twice as much as one drinks. Metal and fire destroy each other. Hence [the patient] dies and cannot be treated." Zhang Jiebin: "The heart and the lung are two yang depots. When the heart moves cold to the lung, the ruler fire is weak. When the heart fire is insufficient, then it cannot provide warmth and nourishment to the lung [which is associated with the agent] metal. When the lung qi is not warmed, then it cannot move and transform the body liquids. Hence one urinates twice as much as one drinks. Now, the lung is the mother of the water. When the water leaves in large quantities, then the lung qi is pulled out too. Hence this is called 'the lung wastes away.'" Zhang Qi: "When the lung depot receives cold, the spleen yang is damaged too. Beverages enter the stomach, but they are not transformed into essence. Rather they are passed on directly into the water palace." 307/184: "'One' and 'two' are used here as a comparison. 'One [part]' is to say: little; 'two [parts]' is to say: plenty."

37-212-7
When the lung moves cold to the kidneys,
this causes *yong-shui*.[8]

{As for *yong-shui*, one presses the abdomen and it does not feel hard. Water qi
has settled in the large intestine. If [the patient] moves quickly, then there is a
[gurgling in his abdomen] sounding *zho-zho* and resembling [sounds generated by] a fluid in a bag.
This is a water disease.}[9]

When the spleen moves heat to the liver,
then this causes fright and nosebleed.[10]

When the liver moves heat to the heart,
then [this results in] death.[11]

---

8 We consider this term to be a transliteration or translation of an originally non-
Chinese term the meaning of which was lost prior to the lifetime of Wang Bing. It is
translatable as "surging water."

9 Wang Bing: "The lung stores the qi. The kidneys rule the water. When lung cold
enters the kidneys, the kidney qi has a surplus. When the kidney qi has a surplus, then
it rushes upwards against the lung. Hence [the text] speaks of 'water bubbling up.' The
large intestine is the palace associated with the lung. When both the lung and the kidneys are affected by cold, there is no place to go to, neither above nor below. Hence the
water qi takes residence in the large intestine. When the kidneys receive freezing cold,
they cannot transform the liquids. The large intestine collects water which does not
flow further on. Hence, when one walks quickly, there are gurgling sounds resembling
a soft bag filled with thick fluid." Zhang Jiebin: "湧水 is: water rising upwards from
below, resembling the bubbling up of [water in] a spring." Mori: "濯濯, *zho-zho*, is,
without any doubt, the sound of water." The *Tai su* has 裹壺, "like enclosed in a jar."

10 Wang Bing: "The liver stores the blood. In addition, it rules the [emotion of]
fright. Hence, when heat presses against it (or: accumulates in it), then one [suffers
from] fright and blood leaves from the nose." Zhang Jiebin: "The liver rules the [emo-
tion of] fright. When evil heat presses against it, the *hun*-soul is restless. The liver
vessel rises to the peak of the skull; the nose is linked to the brain. When liver fire
rises, in a reverse movement, along the conduit, the blood is pressed by heat. Hence
nosebleed results."

11 Wang Bing: "Two yang merge. Fire burns wood. Hence, when liver heat enters the
heart, one must die." Zhang Zhicong: "The heart is responsible for the ruler fire and
does not receive evil. [Here now] evil heat occupies [the heart], hence one dies."

When the heart moves heat to the lung,
further transmission causes *ge-xiao*.[12]

37-213-2
When the lung moves heat to the kidneys,
[further] transmission causes *rou-zhi*.[13]

When the kidneys move heat to the spleen,
[further] transmission causes depletion and intestinal flush.
[The patient] dies and must not be treated.[14]

---

12 Wang Bing: "Between heart and lung is a slanting membrane. The lower end of
this membrane is tied to the diaphragm. Hence when heat from the heart enters the
lung and if transmission and transformation continue for long, this causes a heating
of the internal membranes (*ge*), with wasting (*xiao*) thirst, and one drinks a lot." We
consider this term to be a transliteration of an originally non-Chinese term the meaning of which was lost prior to the lifetime of Wang Bing. It is translatable as "wasting
diaphragm" and could correspond to the term *fei xiao* 肺消, "wasting lung", "*phthisis*",
above.

13 Wang Bing: "柔 is to say: the sinews are soft and have no strength. 痓 is to say: the
bones are/suffer from 痓 and do not follow [one's intentions]. The qi and the bones
are hot and the marrow does not fill the interior [of the bones]. Hence the bones are
stiff and cannot be lifted, while the sinews are soft and relaxed and have no strength."
Lin Yi et al.: "The Quan Yuanqi edition has 痙, 'convulsion,' instead of 痓." The *Tai
su* too. Tanba: "柔 has the meaning of 陰, 'yin.' The *Shang han lun* [states:] major yang
diseases with fever but without sweating and, contrary [to what one might expect]
with an aversion to cold, are called 剛痙. A major yang disease with fever and with
sweating and with no aversion to cold, is called 柔痙. Cheng Wu-ji 成無已 commented: The character 柔痓 is a mistake for 痙, 'convulsions.' The lung is associated
with the major yin; the kidneys are associated with the minor yin. [In the present case]
the lung moves heat to the kidneys and generates convulsions. Hence [the disease]
is called 柔痙, 'soft convulsions,' (i.e., 'yin convulsions'). The *Huo ren shu* 活人書
has 柔痙; it also speaks of 陰痙. This is correct." For a detailed argument in favor of
interpreting 痓 as 痙, see also Qian Chaochen-90/95f. We consider this term to be a
transliteration of an originally non-Chinese term the meaning of which was lost prior
to the lifetime of Wang Bing. It is translatable as "soft convulsion."

14 Wang Bing: "The spleen, [i.e.,] soil, restrains the water. When the kidneys, contrary [to what is normal], move heat to the [spleen], the spleen-soil is unable to restrain the water and receives the disease. If this transmission continues for long, the
result is depletion harm. As for 'intestinal [relief sounding like] *pi*. The patient dies,'
[the following is to say:] the kidneys rule the lower burner. They are the image of water
and [hence] they are cold. In the present case they move heat. That is, their essence qi
has been wasted inside and there is nothing to keep guard. Hence the intestines are
evacuated with [the sound] *pi* in that qi [leaves them and] cannot be stopped."

When the uterus moves heat to the urinary bladder,
then [this results in] protuberance illness and blood in the urine.[15]

When the urinary bladder moves heat to the small intestine,
[then this results in] barred intestines[16] with inability to relieve oneself.
Above it causes *kou-mi*.[17]

37-213-5
When the small intestine moves heat to the large intestine,
[then this] causes *fu-jia*.[18]

---

15 Wang Bing: "The urinary bladder is the palace of the [body] liquids. The uterus
is responsible for intake. Hence, when heat enters the urinary bladder, the uterus has
heat inside and outside. [This] spills over into the yin network [vessel]. Hence, one
cannot pass urine and if one passes urine it contains blood. "Wu Kun: "胞 is the yin-
uterus. In males it is the chamber holding the semen and in women it is the womb.
The urinary bladder is the storer into which the urine flows. When [the text] states
'the uterus moves heat into the bladder,' then the urine does not pass freely and this is
called 'protuberance illness.' In serious cases the urine contains blood." Ma Shi: "The
bladder is the palace of the [body] liquids. In addition, there is a uterus situated within
the bladder. .. When there is extreme heat in the uterus and when this heat is moved
into the bladder, the result is protuberance illness and if urine is passed it contains
blood." 1317/47: "胞 is an abbreviation for 女子胞, 'uterus.' .. The uterus is close to the
urinary bladder; one is in front and one is in the back. Also, both are linked to the kidneys. When evil from the womb is transmitted to the bladder, the qi transformation in
the urinary bladder is blocked by evil heat. This may lead to protuberance illness. The
heat harms the blood network [vessels] in the bladder. Hence hematuria results."

16 Fang Wenhui/91: "鬲 was identical in ancient times with 隔; it has the meaning
of 隔塞, 'blockage.'"

17 Wang Bing: "The vessel of the minor intestine encloses the heart. It follows the
throat, moves down to the diaphragm, meets with the stomach and touches the small
intestine. Hence, when it receives heat, it causes intestinal blockage below and one
cannot relieve oneself. Above the mouth develops abscesses and rots. 糜 is 爛, 'to
decay,' 'to rot.'" Fang Wenhui/91: "糜 is 麋, 'to dissolve.'" We consider this term to
be a transliteration of an originally non-Chinese term the meaning of which was lost
prior to the lifetime of Wang Bing. It is translatable as "oral putrescence."

18 Wang Bing: "When the heat of the small intestine is moved to the large intestine,
two heats press against each other. As a result, blood spills over and this causes hidden *jia*-accumulations. When the blood roughens and does not flow freely, then the
monthly affair is stopped in the depth and does not flow freely either. Hence [the text]
states: 'This is 虙瘕; this is in the depth.' 虙 is identical with 伏, 'hidden.' 瘕 is written 疝 elsewhere. This is a transmission error." Zhang Jiebin: "When the heat of the
small intestine passes down, it moves into the large intestine. When the heat collects
and does not disperse and when either qi or blood remain accumulated at a crooked

{That is the depth}.[19]

When the large intestine moves heat to the stomach,
one likes to eat, but [the person is] lean. >Enters<[20]
One calls this *shi-yi*.[21]

When the stomach moves heat to the gallbladder,
this, too, is called *shi-yi*.

---

location, then this is called 虙瘕. 虙瘕 is to say: [the blood or the qi accumulations] are secretly hidden in the depth and cannot be removed easily." We consider this term to be a transliteration of an originally non-Chinese term the meaning of which was lost prior to the lifetime of Wang Bing. The *Tai su* has 密疝.

19 Zhang Zhicong: "沉 is 痔, 'piles.' The small intestine rules the fire; the large intestine rules the metal. When fire heat affects metal in excess, then this causes intestinal piles." Gao Shishi added the character 痔 following 沉: "The fire heat moves down and causes deep-lying piles."

20 Wang Bing: "The stomach is the sea of water and grains. Its qi provides nourishment to the muscles and to the flesh in the outer regions. Heat dissolves the water and the grains and also it melts the muscles and the flesh. Hence, [patients] love to eat and emaciation sets in [nevertheless]." Lin Yi et al.: "The *Jia yi jing* has 又 instead of 入. Wang Bing's comment '[patients] love to eat and emaciation sets in' makes no sense whatsoever. It is not as plausible as the version of the *Jia yi jing* having a 又 which should be read in connection with the following (i.e., 又謂之 ..)." Yao Shaoyu: "Wang Bing's edition has 瘦入 instead of 瘦人, 'emaciated person.' This is difficult to understand. The *Jia yi jing* has 又 instead of 入 and connects it to the following text. However, since no name was given above, why should it say 'also [called]'? This makes no sense." 324/51: "瘦人 is 使人瘦, 'lets [that] person become emaciated.'" The *Tai su* has 食而瘦. 入胃之食亦, "one eats and is emaciated [nevertheless]. This is the *shi-yi* which enters the stomach."

21 Yang Shangshan: "亦 means 易, 'to change.' This is to say: there is heat in the stomach. Hence the food entering the stomach is transformed and dissolved entirely. It does not generate muscles and flesh. Hence emaciation results." Wang Bing: "食亦 is to say: food enters [the stomach] and is transformed excessively. It cannot generate muscles and flesh. 亦 is 易, 'to change.'" Zhang Jiebin interprets 食亦 as 遺食亦病, "even though one eats, one falls ill nevertheless." Zhang Zhicong: "亦 is 解㑊. This is to say, even though one is able to eat, the body slackens nevertheless." 1751/34: "Duan Yucai 段玉裁 (in his *SWJZZ*) has stated: '亦 is like 大, 'big,' 甚, 'very.'" This is correct. 食亦 is a repetition of 食; it means: one loves to eat and is easily hungry nevertheless. 解㑊 is a repetition of 懈怠; it means: the body is very weak, without any strength." For 解㑊 see also *Su wen* 18-113-2. We consider this term to be a transliteration of an originally non-Chinese term the meaning of which was lost prior to the lifetime of Wang Bing.

37-214-2

When the gallbladder moves heat to the brain,
then [this results in] *xin-e* and *bi-yuan*.[22]
{As for *bi-yuan*, that is turbid snivel flowing down without end.[23]
Further transmission causes nosebleed and blurred vision.}[24]
<The fact is, one acquires these [states] from qi recession.>"

---

22 *Xin-e* 辛頞 is translatable as "bitter bridge of the nose." *Bi-yuan* is translatable as
"nose abyss". We consider these terms to be transliterations of originally non-Chinese
terms the meaning of which was lost prior to the lifetime of Wang Bing.

23 Wang Bing: "When brain liquid seeps downwards it becomes turbid snivel. When
snivel [flows] downwards without end it is as if it came from a water fountain. Hence
this is called 鼻淵, 'nose abyss..'. 辛 is to say: 酸痛, 'pain.'" 1751/34: "The character 辛
should be 辛, with the meaning of 罪, 'to offend.' Because the gallbladder moves heat
to the brain, the heat evil above moves against (干) the forehead section and causes
the condition of 鼻淵."

24 Wang Bing: "衊 is to sweat blood." Cheng Shide et al.: "The *Shuo wen* states: '衊 is
汗血 'impure blood.'" Wu Kun: "When blood leaves through the nose, this is called
衄衊. Abundant [nosebleed] is 衄; weak [nosebleed] is 衊." Zhang Yizhi et al.: "Blood
leaving from the nose is called 衄; blood leaving from the eyes is called 衊. 衄衊 refers
to nose and eyes bleeding simultaneously."

Chapter 38
Discourse on Cough

38-214-5
Huang Di asked:
"When the lung lets a person cough,
how is that?"[1]

Qi Bo responded:
"The five depots and six palaces, they all [may] let a person cough, not only the lung."[2]

[Huang] Di:
"I should like to hear about the appearances of these [coughs]."

Qi Bo:
"Skin and body hair are the correlates of the lung.
Skin and body hair are the first to receive evil qi.
This way, the evil qi [enters the lung] from its correlates.[3]

When cold beverages or food have entered the stomach and
when [the cold] has followed the lung vessel to ascend to the lung,
then the lung is cold.
When the lung is cold, then both outside and inside [transmission] have come together.
Subsequently, the [two cold] evils settle in the [lung].
This, then, causes lung cough.[4]

---

1 Gao Jiwu/483: "Below the character for 'lung' the character for 'disease' was omitted: 'A lung disease can cause one to cough. Why?'"

2 Zhang Zhicong: "The lung rules the qi and its location is the highest. It is where the hundred vessels meet. Even though cough is a condition of the lung, the evil [qi] of all the five depots and six palaces are able to rise and turn to the lung and cause cough."

3 Wang Bing: "'Evil' is to say: cold qi." Zhang Jiebin: "'Evil qi' is wind cold. The skin and the body hair receive it first; then it enters the lung. Hence 'it follows the association.'"

4 Wang Bing: "The lung vessel emerges from the central burner. It descends and encircles the large intestine, turns around and follows the opening of the stomach, rises [through] the diaphragm and touches the lung. Hence [the text] states: 'it follows the lung vessel and rises to the lung.'"

38-214-9

Each of the five depots receives a disease [directly from the outside] when it is its season.

When it is not its season, it is always such that it is through transmission that [the disease] is brought to a [depot].[5]

Man is one with heaven and earth.

Hence each of the five depots receives the disease when it is affected by cold during the season its qi governs.[6]

[When the cold qi] is feeble, then it causes cough;

when it is severe, it causes outflow and pain.[7]

---

5 Wang Bing: "'Season' is to say: the months [a depot] rules. If it is not during the months it rules it cannot receive evil [qi]. Hence it transmits [any evil] further on and hands it over [to the depot whose season it is]." Zhang Jiebin: "For example, the liver should receive a disease in spring, because this is its season. Now, if the liver has a disease even though it is not the season during which the wood is in command, this is because the lung receives the evil first and is able to transmit it [to the liver]. The same applies to all the depots and palaces that receive evil [qi] even though it is not their season." Zhang Zhicong: "In autumn, the lung is the first to receive an evil. … If it is not in autumn, then the [remaining] five depots transmit their evil to the lung and cause coughing." Wu Kun: "In spring the liver is in charge. Hence the liver is the first to receive evil [qi]. If it happens to be cold evil, then [the liver] transmits it to the lung." Zhang Qi: "The three characters 非其時 are an erroneous insertion." 2030/55: "Each of the five depots receives evil and develops a disease in that season during which its qi is supposed to govern. If it is not the season during which its qi is supposed to go-vern and it develops a disease nevertheless, then the disease evil of this depot has been transmitted there from another depot. For example, if in spring it is not the liver that falls ill but the heart, then this is a situation where it is not the season [of the heart] and yet it develops a disease. Hence the evil must have been transmitted to the heart from another depot."

6 Zhang Jiebin: "治時 is the season during which its qi is in command. When the evil is feeble, [its penetration] is shallow and it remains in the outer section. Hence it causes cough. When it is serious, [its penetration] is deep and it enters the interior. Hence it causes outflow and pain." Gao Shishi: "When it is feeble, then the hand ma-jor yin [conduit] receives the cold and this causes cough. When it is serious, the foot major yin [conduit] receives the cold and this causes outflow and pain."

7 Wang Bing: "When the cold qi is feeble, then outside this is reflected by the skin and the hair, inside it penetrates to the lung. Hence [patients] cough. When the cold qi is severe, then it enters the interior. When the interior cracks, then [this causes] pain. When [the cold qi] enters the intestines and the stomach, then diarrhea-type outflow results."

If [the evil] avails itself of [a weakness in] autumn, then the lung is the first to
receive the evil.[8]
If [the evil] avails itself of [a weakness in] spring, then the liver is the first to
receive it.
If [the evil] avails itself of [a weakness in] summer, then the heart is the first to
receive it.
If [the evil] avails itself of [a weakness in] the [period of] extreme yin,[9] then
the spleen is the first to receive it.
If [the evil] avails itself of [a weakness in] winter, then the kidneys are the first
to receive it."[10]

38-215-4
[Huang] Di:
"How to distinguish these [situations]?"

Qi Bo:
"The appearance of lung cough:
[Patients] cough and their breath is panting with noises.
In severe cases, they spit blood.[11]

The appearance of heart cough:
When [patients] cough, then their heart aches.

---

8 Lin Yi et al.: "The Quan Yuanqi edition and the *Tai su* do not have the three characters 乘秋則. They may be an erroneous addition." Wang Bing: "It is the season when
they should operate. Hence, they are the first to receive evil qi."

9 2083/23: "Beijing zhongyi xueyuan (2) comments: '至陰 refers here to the season
of late summer.' The meaning of 至 is 'to reach.' Summer is yang; autumn is yin. Late
summer, then, is the period at the meeting of summer with autumn, when the yang
has reached its peak and the yin begins [its term]. It is the transition period from
summer to autumn, from yang to yin. Hence the name 至陰." See also 2107/25 citing
a similar example from *Su wen* 43.

10 Gao Shishi: "Even if the liver, the heart, the spleen or the kidneys receive the
[cold evil] first, they all transmit it to the lung and cause cough."

11 Wang Bing: "The lung stores the qi and regulates the breathing. Hence, in case
of coughing, the breathing is panting and there are noises in the throat. In serious
cases, there is a movement contrary [to the normal course] in the network [vessel]
of the lung. Hence [patients] spit blood." Zhang Jiebin: "The blood [patients] spit
is thrown out while they cough. The disease is in the lung. This is not the same as
vomiting blood."

They have an obstructing sensation in the throat, as if there was a stick.[12]
In severe cases, the gullet is swollen and the throat is blocked.[13]

The appearance of liver cough:
When [patients] cough, then they experience pain below the two flanks.
In severe cases, they cannot turn.
When they turn, there is fullness in the region below the two upper flanks.[14]

38-215-8
The appearance of spleen cough:
When [patients] cough, then the region below the right flank aches.[15]
Deep inside, [this pain] pulls on the shoulders and the back.[16]
In severe cases, [patients] cannot move.
When they move, then the cough turns violent.

---

12 Wu Kun: "介介 has the meaning of 'hardened and obstructed.'" 915/58: "介介 is to describe an obstruction. Zhang Zhicong commented: 'There is an obstruction in the throat as if there was a stick (如梗狀).' 梗 is identical with 鯁, 'fishbone.' 如梗狀 is: as if a fishbone got stuck [in one's throat]." 2802/47: "介介 is to describe an obstructed throat releasing 'croaking' (介介) sounds."

13 Wang Bing: "The hand heart ruler vessel emerges from the chest center and touches the heart enclosure. The minor yin vessel emerges from within the heart and touches the heart connection. Its branch rises from the heart connection and runs along the throat. Hence, the disease is as [is described] here." Wu Kun: "喉痺 is: the throat is swollen and has pain." Gao Jiwu/725: "咽腫喉痺 is 咽喉腫痺. 痺 is identical with 閉, 'closure.' One must not read this as 'the gullet is swollen but not closed; the throat is closed but not swollen.'"

14 Yang Shangshan: "Another version has 脅, 'flanks,' instead of 胠." Wang Bing: "The foot ceasing yin vessel rises, penetrates the diaphragm, spreads out in the flanks and follows the back of the gullet. Hence, [the disease is] as is [described] here." Zhang Jiebin: "'One cannot turn' is: one cannot bend up and down. The region below the flanks is called 胠."

15 Mori: "'Below the right flank' should be 'below the left flank.' The *Tai su* has 在, 'at,' above 右. Originally [在] was 左, 'left.' Later, 左 was mistakenly written 在. Later again, someone added the character 右. 'Right flank' does not make sense; hence all kinds of meaningless comments have been written."

16 Wang Bing: "The foot major yin vessel rises, penetrates the diaphragm and moves along the throat. Its branch emerges from the stomach and rises to the diaphragm. Hence the disease is as [is described] here. The spleen qi connects with the lung. Hence, the pain pulls on the shoulders and on the back. The spleen qi rules the right side. Hence, [the text refers to] the region below the right flank. 陰陰 is a deep, slow pain." Cheng Shide et al.: "陰陰 is 隱隱, 'concealed.'"

The appearance of kidney cough:
When [patients] cough, then the lower back and the backbone pull each other
and have pain.
In severe cases, they cough saliva."

38-215-10
[Huang] Di:
"The cough of the six palaces,
how about it?
Wherefrom do they receive the disease?"[17]

Qi Bo:
"When the coughing of [any of] the five depots extends over a long time,
then it is transmitted to [one of] the six palaces.

When spleen cough does not come to an end,
then the stomach receives it.
The appearance of stomach cough:
[Patients] cough and vomit.
When the vomiting is severe, long worms come out.[18]

When liver cough does not come to an end,
then the gallbladder receives it.
The appearance of gallbladder cough:
[Patients] cough and they vomit gall.[19]

---

17 150/59: "安 is used for 所, in the sense of 處所, 'location.' It should be read here
as 'where?'"

18 Wang Bing: "The spleen forms a union with the stomach. Also, the vessel of the
stomach follows the throat and enters the broken basin. It moves further down to
[penetrate] the diaphragm, touches the stomach and encloses the spleen. Hence, when
the spleen cough does not end, the stomach receives it. When the stomach [has re-
ceived] cold, then vomiting sets in. When the vomiting is severe, then the intestinal
qi move upwards in reverse flow. Hence, worms are thrown out." Zhang Jiebin: "長虫
stands for 蚘虫, '*hui*-worms.' They reside in the intestines and in the stomach. In case
of severe coughing they follow the qi and are thrown out above."

19 Wang Bing: "The liver forms a union with the gallbladder. Also, the vessel of the
gallbladder moves downwards from the broken basin into the chest center, penetrates
the diaphragm and encloses the liver. Hence, when liver cough does not end, the gallbladder receives it. The gallbladder qi tends to move contrary [to its regular course].
Hence, [patients] vomit warm, bitter juice."

When lung cough does not come to an end,
then the large intestine receives it.
The appearance of cough of the large intestine:
[Patients] cough and release stools.[20]

When heart cough does not come to an end,
then the small intestine receives it.
The appearance of cough of the small intestine:
[Patients] cough and release [intestinal] qi.
{Qi and cough are set free together.}[21]

38-216-5
When kidney cough does not come to an end,
then the urinary bladder receives it.
The appearance of urinary bladder cough:
[Patients] cough and lose urine.[22]

When the coughing extends over a long time and does not come to an end,
then the triple burner receives it.
The appearance of triple burner cough:

---

20 Wang Bing: "The lung forms a union with the large intestine. Also, the vessel of
the large intestine enters the broken basin and encloses the lung. Hence, when the
lung cough does not end, the large intestine receives it. The large intestine is the palace of transmission. Hence, when cold enters it, its qi cannot be stopped." Lin Yi et
al.: "The *Jia yi jing* has 遺矢, 'to release stools,' instead of 遺失." Cheng Shide et al.:
"The *Tai su*, too, has 遺矢. 矢 is identical with 屎, 'ordure.' 遺矢 is: stools pass unrestrained." See also 1978/46.

21 Wang Bing: "The heart forms a union with the small intestine. Also, the vessel of
the small intestine enters the broken basin and encloses the heart. Hence when heart
cough does not come to an end, the small intestine receives it. When the small intestine abounds with cold, [its] qi enters the large intestine. When [the patient] coughs,
then the qi of the small intestine rushes downwards. Hence it loses qi." Cheng Shide
et al.: "失氣 is 矢氣. This is commonly called 'to break wind.'" Gao Shishi: "失 is 散,
'to set free.'" Yao Shaoyu: "失氣 is 'the qi disperses.'"

22 Wang Bing: "The kidneys form a union with the urinary bladder. Also, the vessel
of the bladder passes from the shoulder blades along the spine into the lower back,
follows the backbone, encloses the kidneys and touches the bladder. Hence, when
kidney cough does not end, the bladder receives it. The bladder is the palace of the
[body] liquids. Hence one [coughs and] loses urine." Cheng Shide et al.: "遺溺 is:
urine flows unrestrained."

[Patients] cough and [experience] abdominal fullness.
They does not wish to eat or drink.

In all these cases [cold] assembles in the stomach and ties exist to the lung.
This lets a person develop plenty of snivel and spittle;[23]
the face has surface swelling [because of] qi moving contrary [to its regular course]."[24]

38-217-1
[Huang] Di:
"To treat this, how does one proceed?"

Qi Bo:
"For treating the depots, treat their [respective] transporters.[25]

---

23 1803/6: "The character 涕 refers to phlegm here. *Su wen* 33 has 咳出青黃涕, 其狀如膿, 'the coughing produces a greenish-yellow 涕; its appearance resembles pus.' Obviously, phlegm is meant here."

24 Wang Bing: "'Triple burner' does not refer to the hand minor yang; it really is to say: upper burner and central burner. Why? The upper burner leaves from the upper mouth of the stomach, follows the throat, penetrates the diaphragm, spreads into the chest center and reaches the armpits. The central burner, too, reaches the [upper] mouth of the stomach. It leaves from behind the upper burner. The qi it receives are the dregs rushing [down] and the [body] liquids rising upwards. [The central burner] transforms their subtle essence and pours them upwards into the vessel of the lung. There they are transformed into blood. Hence [the text] states: 'they all accumulate in the stomach and they are tied to the lung.' When the two burners receive a disease, then evil qi steams the lung and the lung is full of qi. Hence, it causes one to have plenty of tears and spittle. The face swells and the qi moves contrary [to its regular course]. 'The abdomen is full and [patients] do not wish to eat' is the result of cold in the stomach. The vessel of the stomach moves downwards from the broken basin into the breast, moves further down along the abdomen and reaches the qi street. Its branch starts from the lower mouth of the stomach, moves inside the abdomen and reaches the qi street where it unites [again with the main course of the vessel]. In the present case, the stomach receives evil. Hence, the disease is as [it is described] here." Gao Jiwu/173: "In all these cases, water evil collects in the stomach and rises to affect the lung." 1678/45: "關 should be interpreted here as 進入, 'to enter.' The *Shang shu* 尚書, 'Da zhuan' 大傳, comments: 關 is identical with 入, 'to enter.' (For further examples, see there)."

25 This metaphor may refer to the point in the course of a river where it becomes navigable.

For treating the palaces, treat their [respective] confluences.
In case of a surface swelling, treat their streams."[26]

[Huang] Di: "Good!"

---

26 Wang Bing: "All depot transporters are the third holes of the vessels. All palace
confluences are the sixth holes of the vessels. The streams are the fourth holes of
the vessels of the depots and the fifth holes of the vessels of the palaces. The *Ling
shu* states: where the vessels rush, these are the transporters; where they move, these
are the streams; where they enter, these are the confluences. This is meant here." In
contrast, Gao Shishi interpreted 俞 as "the transporter [holes] of the five depots on
the back," and 經 as "conduit vessels." Zhang Zhicong: "In case of cough in the five
depots, one must treat their respective transporters. The transporters of the five depots
are all located on the back."

Chapter 39
Discourse on Pain[1]

39-218-2
Huang Di asked:
"I have heard:
those who know how to speak about heaven,
they must have experienced man.
Those who know how to speak about the past,
they must have become one with the present.
Those who know how to speak about [other] people,
they must have dealt with themselves sufficiently.[2]

Thereby [their understanding of] the Way is free of confusion and the essential
numbers [can be known] to their full extent.
This is the so-called understanding.[3]

---

1 1160/50: "The meaning of 舉痛 has been interpreted in three ways: First, (舉) has
been interpreted as 舉例 or 例舉, 'to mention.' (See Yao Shaoyu and Gao Shishi).
Second, it has been interpreted as 辨議, 'to differentiate meanings.' (See Sun Yirang).
Third, it has been assumed that 舉痛 is an error for 卒痛, 'sudden pain.' Lin Yi et
al. stated: 'In this treatise, Huang Di asked about the diseases of sudden pain in the
five depots. 舉 may be an error for 卒.' Wu Kun agreed." See also 1138 for a detailed
discussion of this treatise.

2 In contrast, Wang Bing reads these three statements in the sense of: those who
know to speak about heaven (i.e., about the qi of the four seasons, etc.), they must
have success when they treat a person. Those who know how to speak about the past
(i.e., how the ancient sages nourished life), they must be able to act appropriately in
the present. Those who know man (i.e., his physical constitution, etc.), they must be
able to apply this to their own situation. 2114/2: "This corresponds to a statement by
Dong Zhongshu 董仲舒 in his *Ju xian liang dui ce san* 舉賢良對策三: 善言天者必
有征于人; 善言古者必有驗于今." Zhang Jiebin: "厭 is 足, 'sufficient.'" Gao Shishi:
"厭 is 棄, 'to discard.'" Tanba: "Zhang Jiebin's interpretation is correct." Yu Chang:
"厭 is to be read as 合. The *Shuo wen*, section 厂, states: '厭: elsewhere 合.' In his
commentary to the *Guo yu* 國語, Zhou yu 周語, Wei 韋 stated, too: '厭 is 合.' Wang
Bing's statement 靜慮於己, 亦與彼同, 'one thinks as calmly of oneself as one does of
others,' appears to have read [厭] as 同. 同 is 合. Because his interpretation was not
clearly pointed out as such, later authors have read it as 足, 'sufficient.' This is not as
good, though, as a reading as 合. Also, 厭 rhymes with 驗." For a similar passage, see
Su wen 69-418-10 ff.

3 Yang Shangshan: "To have grasped the most important principles, this is the reason
for a clear understanding." Cheng Shide et al.: "數 is 理, 'structure.'" Wang Bing:
"When these [three conditions are fulfilled], one knows the highest of the important
numbers of the Way and no doubt or delusion remains. One fully understands the fi-

Now I ask you, Sir:
to bring about [a situation where]
from words one can obtain knowledge,
from inspection one can obtain insights and
from feeling one can obtain a hold,[4]
[that is,] to bring about [a situation where] one has experienced oneself with
the effect that one is released from ignorance with all delusions dispersed,[5]
may I hear about this?"

Qi Bo paid reverence twice knocking his head on the ground and responded:
"Which Way is this question about?"

39-218-6
[Huang] Di:
"I should like to hear [the following]:
when man's five depots experience sudden pain,
which qi causes this?"[6]

Qi Bo responded:
"The flow in the conduit vessels does not stop.
It circulates without break.
When cold qi enters the conduits, stoppage and retardation result.[7]
[The contents of the vessels] are impeded to the degree that they fail to flow.

---

nal structures and therefore is able [to speak] like this." Gao Jiwu/234: "數 is identical with 度, to be interpreted as 'rules,' 'patterns.'"

4 Cheng Shide et al.: "言 refers to the diagnostic method of questioning. 視 refers to the diagnostic method of observing. 捫 refers to the diagnostic method of palpation/ [pulse] feeling.'"

5 Wang Bing: "That is to say, as if one opened the ears of the young and ignorant and freed a heart from its doubts and delusions, so that the eyes see and the hands feel, in order to understand each single principle by examination."

6 139/26: "'Sudden pain' is 'qi pain.' Qi pain is different from pain caused by wind and it is also different from other types of pain resulting from injuries." For an analysis of the pain section of this treatise, see also 2039/51.

7 *SWJZ*: "稽 is 留止, 'to stay [at one location].'"

When [the cold qi] settles outside the vessels, then the blood is diminished;
when it settles inside the vessels,[8] then the qi cannot pass through.
Hence,
there is sudden pain."[9]

39-218-9
[Huang] Di:
"This pain:
sometimes it stops all of a sudden,
sometimes a pain is severe and does not subside,
sometimes a pain is severe and [its location] cannot be pressed,
sometimes pressing it stops the pain,
sometimes pressing it is of no benefit,
sometimes a panting movement responds to the [pressure exerted by one's]
hand,[10]
sometimes heart and back pull each other [causing] pain,
sometimes the ribs in the flanks and the lower abdomen pull each other [causing] pain,

---

8 1079/1: "'The blood is diminished' does not mean that the blood is depleted. Rather this is to say that the cold causes the conduit vessels to contract with the result that the relative amount of blood and qi moved through the vessel paths is diminished."

9 Gao Shishi: "The twelve conduit vessels of the human body are the passageways where blood and qi leave and enter. Their flow does not come to a halt; it circulates without pause. When cold qi enters the conduits and the proper qi stops and is retarded, then the blood congeals and does not move. The qi moves outside of the vessels and the blood follows it. If now cold [qi] settles outside of the vessels, then the blood is diminished. The blood moves inside the vessels and the qi follows it. If now cold [qi] settles inside of the vessels, then the qi cannot pass. When cold [qi] settles in the conduit vessels, neither qi nor blood can flow and circulate. Hence there is sudden pain." Zhang Zhicong: "When cold qi settles outside of the vessels, then the vessels shrink and the blood is diminished. When it settles inside of the vessels, then the vessels become full and the qi cannot pass. Hence there is sudden pain."

10 Guo Aichun-92: "喘 is a mistake for 揣, 'to feel for.' 動 has the meaning of 痛, 'pain.'" Tanba: "This refers to a beating movement in the abdomen. 喘 is occasionally used identically with 蝡. For 蝡 the *Shuo wen* states: 動也, 'movement.'" Li Guoqing: "The *Guang ya* 廣雅 states: 揣 is 蠕動, 'to wriggle like a worm.'" 516/79: "The character 喘 may have the meaning of 震動, 'trembling movement.'" For a lengthy argument, see there. Hu Tianxiong: "喘 is 湍, 'the rushing of water.' That is to say, the [movement in the] vessels arrives like the rushing of a vast water."

sometimes there is pain in the abdomen pulling into the yin (i.e., inner side of the) thighs,[11]
sometimes a pain stays for a long time and generates accumulations,
sometimes there is sudden pain death with [the patient] not recognizing anybody, returning to life, though, after a short[12] while,
sometimes there is pain accompanied by vomiting,
sometimes the abdomen has pain with outflow from the behind and
sometimes there is pain with closure and impassability.

All these [types of] pain have a different manifestation.
How are they to be distinguished?"[13]

39-219-5
Qi Bo:
"When cold qi settles outside the vessels, then the vessels become cold.
When the vessels are cold, then they shrink.
When they have shrunk, then the vessels are curved and tense.[14]
When they are curved and tense, then they pull on the small network [vessels] outside.
Hence,
sudden pain results.
When they are given heat,
then the pain stops immediately.[15]

---

11 Yang Shangshan: "The outer side of the 股 is called 髀, 'outer thighs;' the inner side of the 髀 is called 股, 'inner thighs.' The [inner thighs] are situated below the yin [region]. [Hence] they are the 'yin thighs.'"

12 1678/45: "The *Gu shu xu zi ji shi* 古書虛字集釋 states: 有 is 又, 'again,' 'further.'"

13 Wang Bing: "[Huang Di] likes to know the locations where the different signs appear." Zhang Zhicong: "形 is 証, 'sign,' 'symptom.' That is to say, all these pain signs are different. How can they be distinguished?"

14 Cheng Shide et al.: "绌 is 屈曲, 'bent,' 'winding.' 急 is 拘急, 'cramped.'"

15 Wang Bing: "The vessels encircle [the body] on its left and on its right. Hence, when [the body] gets cold, then they shrink and cramp. When they have shrunk and are cramped, then the guard qi cannot pass through them. Hence, they pull on the small network vessels outside. When the guard qi cannot enter, the cold settles inside. The vessels are tight, not relaxed; hence, pain is generated. When they are given heat, then the guard qi moves again and the cold qi retreats. Hence, the pain stops." Yang Shangshan: "炅 is pronounced like 桂, *gui*; it is 'heat.'" Ma Shi: "If one happens to encounter heat qi, this may be fire or hot water, then the guard qi moves in the outside [regions] and the pain ends suddenly." Cheng Shide et al.: "炅 is identical with 炯7

Subsequent to multiple strikes by cold,
a pain will persist for long.[16]

When cold qi settles inside the conduit vessels and strikes against the heat qi
there, then the vessels become full.[17]
When they are full, then they ache and cannot be pressed.[18]

When cold qi stagnates and the heat qi follows [the cold qi] upwards,[19] then
the vessels are full and big and both the blood and the qi are in disorder.
Hence,
the pain is extreme and [the vessels] cannot be pressed.[20]

39-219-10
When cold qi settles in the region of the intestines and of the stomach,

---

, 'hot; brilliant.' Shen Zumian in his *Du Su wen yi duan* 讀素問臆斷 states: ' The *Yü
pian* 玉篇 states: <炅 is '[where] smoke leaves'> This is correct. 炅 refers to a method
of needling and burning. Its tradition was lost long ago.'" 139/26: "炅氣 is 熱氣, 'heat
qi.' [The text] speaks of 炅 instead of 熱 because [this heat] comes from inside." See
also 908/79 and 2268/35.

16 Zhang Zhicong: "If one is repeatedly affected by cold, then the yang qi receives
harm. Hence the pain lasts long and does not end."

17 1079/2: "相薄 means that cold and heat cannot maintain their mutual balance."

18 Wang Bing: "The rationale of why if one presses them the pain is extreme, this is
outlined in the subsequent text." Zhang Jiebin: "The yang qi moves inside the vessels.
When cold attacks it, then cold and heat press against each other. [Hence the yang qi]
remains [at one location] and does not move. As a result there is evil repletion in the
conduit. Hence the vessel is full and one feels pain. One cannot press this [location]."
1079/2: "滿 is identical with 悶. It means 紊亂, 'chaotic.'"

19 2767/38: "上 is a mistake for 之. In the seal script, these characters are very similar.
.. Hence this passage should read: 'The qi follows it.'" For details, see there.

20 Wang Bing: "Because the vessels are full and big and blood and qi are in disorder,
if one were to press them [in this situation], then the evil qi would attack internally.
Hence, they must not be pressed."

below the membrane plain,²¹ and the blood cannot disperse,²²
the small network [vessels] become tense and pull and, hence, there is pain.
When one presses [the location of the pain], then the blood and the qi disperse.
Hence,
pressing it ends the pain.

When cold qi settles in the vessels running on both sides of the spine,
then one may press deeply and is still unable to reach there.
Hence,
to press them is of no benefit.²³

---

21 Wang Bing: "膜 is to say: the membrane of the diaphragm; 原 is the root of
the diaphragm and 肓. (See Wang Bing's comment on the term 幕原 in *Su wen* 35
for Wang Bing's interpretation of 原 as 原系, "root connection.")" See 906/40 for a
detailed discussion of the terms 膏 (i.e., 膈)(interpreted as "diaphragm"), 肓 (interpreted as "peritoneum"), and 原 (interpreted as "source," "origin," "root"): "The Turtledove Tail (鳩尾) hole is the 'root of the diaphragm.' It is located below the processus
xiphoideus of the sternum. Hence it was considered the place where the diaphragm is
connected to [the body]. The Sea of Qi (氣海) hole is the 'root of the peritoneum.' It
is located below the navel. Hence it was considered the place where the peritoneum
was connected to [the body]." Zhang Zhicong: "膜原 is the fatty membrane attached
to the intestines and the stomach." 1691/13: "The *Zhong yi ming ci shu yu xuan shi* 中
醫名詞術語選釋 quotes the *Song Ya zun sheng shu* 嵩崖尊生書: 原 has the meaning
of 廣野, 'the deserts,' 'wilderness.' Also, from *Ling shu* 66 it is apparent that 膜原
does by no means specifically refer to a section between the pleura and the diaphragm,
but refers also to a location in the abdominal cavity."

22 Wang Bing: "'The blood cannot disperse' refers to the blood inside the small network vessels within the diaphragm membrane. When the network [vessels] are full,
they are tense. Hence they pull and pain develops. When one presses them with one's
hand, then the cold qi disperses and the small network [vessels] relax. Hence the pain
stops." The *Tai su* has 而, 'and,' instead of 血, 'blood.'" Mori: "This passage should be
read following the wording in the *Tai su*. The occurrence of the character for 'blood' in
the current version is a mistake. Because Wang Bing used a version with that mistaken
writing, he added the character 血 in the subsequent statement."

23 Yang Shangshan: "The supervisor vessel runs along the spine. Hence it is called
'vessel running along the spine.' The supervisor vessel runs upwards deep inside the
spine. Therefore no pressure reaches it. Hence to press it is of no benefit." Wang Bing:
"As for 'the vessels running along spine,' that is the supervisor vessel right in the
center. On both sides are the major yang vessels. The supervisor vessel runs inside the
spine; the major yang vessels pass through the sinews of the backbone. Hence, even if
one presses into the depth, one cannot reach them. If one presses right into the center
[of the spine], the sinews of the backbone become bent; if one exerts pressure to the
sides [of the spine], then the sinews of the backbone become cramped. In both cases,
when [the sinews] are bent or cramped, the guard qi can no longer move. Cold qi ac-

When cold qi settles in the thoroughfare vessel,
{the thoroughfare vessel emerges from the Pass Head,[24] and rises straight up along the abdomen}
when cold qi settles [in it], then this vessel is no [longer] passable.
When this vessel is no [longer] passable, then the qi moves accordingly.
Hence,
a panting movement responds to the [pressure exerted by the] hand.[25]

39-220-2
When cold qi settles in the vessels of the back transporters, then the [movement in the] vessels is impeded.
When the [movement in the] vessels is impeded, then the blood is depleted.
When the blood is depleted, then pain results.

---

cumulates increasingly and collects internally. Hence, 'to press them is of no benefit.'"
Zhang Jiebin: "That which runs along the spine is the foot major yang conduit. Those which are situated deepest are the hidden thoroughfare and the hidden supervisor vessels. Hence, no pressure can reach their location." Gao Shishi: "The 'vessel running along the spine' refers to the transporters of the five depots. Hence, when [cold qi] settles there, it is in the depth. Through pressing them one cannot reach the internal depots. Hence, to press them is of no benefit." Zhang Zhicong: "The 'vessel running along the spine' is the hidden thoroughfare vessel. The hidden thoroughfare vessel rises inside the spine. When evil settles in it, then it is deep (inside). Hence, to press it is of no benefit." Yao Shaoyu: "'Running along the spine' is the back. In the human body, only the back is thick and has depth. Hence, even though one presses there, this is of no benefit. To interpret 'running along the spine' as [a reference to] the supervisor vessel is a mistake. The supervisor vessel passes relatively near the surface. How can one call it 'deep?' When the text speaks of 'pressing' here, it can only refer to the flesh of the back."

24 Zhang Jiebin: "The Pass Head (關元) is a hole on the controlling vessel. It is located three inches below the navel."

25 Wang Bing: "The thoroughfare vessel is an extraordinary conduit vessel. 'Pass Head' is the name of a hole located three inches below the navel. When [the text] states 'it rises' from this point and then moves upwards along the abdomen, this is not [to say] it originates from there. Its final origin is below the kidneys. 直上 is to say: it rises and meets with the throat. 氣因之 is to say: when the thoroughfare vessel is blocked, the foot minor yin 'qi because of this' rises and causes fullness above. The thoroughfare vessel and the minor yin [vessel] run parallel. Hence, a panting movement can be felt with one's hand." Tanba rejects the interpretations of 喘動 by Wang Bing, Wu Kun, and Zhang Jiebin, who read 喘動 as a reference to a pulse quality, as wrong: "it refers, in the present context, to a pounding movement in the abdomen." Zhang Yizhi et al.: "喘 is identical with 湍, 'to rush [like water].' The *Shi ming* 釋名 states: '喘 is 湍, 湍 is 疾, 'fast'.' 揣, according to the *Ji yun* 集韻, is 搖. 搖, according to the *Shuo wen*, is 動, 'to move.'"

These transporters pour into the heart.
Hence, they pull each other and this [causes] pain.
If one presses them, then heat qi arrives.
When heat qi arrives, then the pain stops.[26]

39-220-4
When cold qi settles in the ceasing yin vessel,
{the ceasing yin vessel encloses the yin (i.e., sexual) organ and is tied to the liver}
when cold qi settles in this vessel,
then the [flow of the] blood is impeded and the vessel becomes tense.
Hence,
the ribs in the flanks and the lower abdomen pull each other [causing] pain.[27]

When receding qi[28] settles in the yin (i.e., inner side of the) thighs,[29]
cold qi rises into the lower abdomen.
The [flow of the] blood is impeded in the lower [region].
[Above and below] pull each other.

---

26 Wang Bing: "'Transporters of the back' is to say: the vessel of the transporters of the heart. It is also [called] the foot major yang vessel. Now, all the transporters communicate internally with the depots. Hence [the text] states 'these transporters pour into the heart. When they pull each other, there is pain.' When one presses them, then warmth qi enters. When warmth qi enters, then the heart qi effuses towards the outside. Hence, the pain stops." Zhang Jiebin: "'Transporters of the back' is to say: the transporters of the five depots. All of them are holes on the foot major yang conduit. The major yang vessel follows the spine to [the level of] the heart where it enters [the body] and disperses. Further above it appears [again] at the neck. Hence when cold settles then the vessel roughens and the blood is depleted. This has the effect that the back and the heart pull each other and pain results. The reason is that the transporters pour into the heart." See *Ling shu* 11. Hua Shou: "I am not sure what the 13 characters 按之 to 痛止矣 are meant to say." Gao Shishi has moved these 13 characters further up in the text to follow the passage 按之痛止. Tanba: "This way the line of the argumentation is upheld. Gao Shishi's version is correct."

27 Wang Bing: "The ceasing yin [vessel] is the vessel of the liver. It enters the [pubic] hair, encircles the private organ, moves into the lower abdomen, rises to pass through the liver and the diaphragm and spreads across the flanks."

28 Zhang Jiebin: "'Receding qi' is cold qi moving reversely." Yao Shaoyu: "This, too, is the qi of the ceasing yin liver vessel." Cheng Shide et al.: "The character 厥 and the character 寒 further below may have been exchanged." 1683/7: "厥 is identical here with 'cold.'"

29 Cheng Shide et al.: "This is the inner side of the upper thigh. Here it refers to the location crossed by the liver conduit."

Hence,
the abdomen has pain, pulling on the yin (i.e., inner side of the) thighs.[30]

When cold qi settles in the region between the small intestine and the membrane plain, in the blood of the network [vessels],
the [flow of the] blood is impeded and cannot pour into the large conduits.
The blood and the qi stagnate and cannot pass.
Hence,
[the blood and the qi] stay [at one location] for a long time and generate accumulations.[31]

39-220-9
When cold qi settles in the five depots,
a recession with countermovement [results in] outflow above.[32]
The yin qi is exhausted and the yang qi does not enter.
Hence,
[patients] experience sudden pain death and do not recognize anybody.
When the qi turns back again, then [the patient] will live.[33]

When cold qi settles in the intestines and in the stomach,
a recession with countermovement [results in] an exit above.

---

30 Wang Bing: "Here, too, the ceasing yin qi of the liver vessel is responsible. Because this vessel follows the yin [side of the] thighs, enters the [pubic] hair, encircles the private organ and proceeds to the lower abdomen, [the text] states: 'When ceasing yin settles in the yin [side of the] thighs, cold qi rises into the lower abdomen.'"

31 Wang Bing: "That is to say, the blood coagulates because of the cold qi and generates accumulations." Zhang Yizhi et al.: "The *Tai su*, ch. 27, has 卒然, 'sudden,' instead of 宿昔. This should be followed." Mori: "宿昔 stands for 昨昔, 'yesterday night.'"

32 Zhang Jiebin: "When cold harms the qi of the depots, then this qi cannot descend and rises in a reverse movement with an outflow above. As a result, the true yin is suddenly exhausted, while the yang qi has not entered yet. Hence there is sudden pain and death (i.e., unconsciousness)." Wu Kun: "'Outflow above' refers to a gushing vomiting. When the gushing reverse movement is extreme, the yin qi will be exhausted. Hence there is sudden pain and one falls unconscious." Guo Tian: "When the text further down speaks of 厥逆上出, it refers to vomiting. In the present sentence, 'outflow above' means sweating on one's head." For a discussion of the term 厥, see 2225/4.

33 Wang Bing: "That is to say, the qi of the depots is pressed into the stomach by the cold and does not move. As soon as the qi can pass again, [the disease] comes to an end." Lin Yi et al.: "Maybe the [phrase] 擁胃 in [Wang Bing's] comment should be 擁冒, 'is concealed,' 'is suppressed.'"

Hence,
there is pain accompanied by vomiting.[34]

When cold qi settles in the small intestine,
the small intestine cannot generate agglomerations.
Hence,
there is a [constant] outflow from one's behind and the abdomen has pain.[35]

When heat qi stays in the small intestine,
there is pain in the intestine.
The heat of solitary [heat] disease burns and dries out [the intestine],[36] and
as a result [the stools] harden and dry and cannot leave.
Hence,
there is pain with closure and impassability."[37]

39-221-2
[Huang] Di:
"This is the so-called
'from words one can obtain knowledge.'
'From inspection one can obtain insights,'
how is that?"[38]

---

34 Wang Bing: "When cold settles in the intestines and in the stomach and stays there, then the yang qi cannot flow downwards and, on the contrary, moves upwards. When the cold does not leave, then pain develops. When the yang [qi] moves upwards then [the patient] vomits. Hence one has pain and vomits."

35 Wang Bing: "The small intestine is the palace that receives abundance. When it is full inside, then the cold evil finds no place to settle. Hence it cannot accumulate and is transmitted further into the coiled intestine. The coiled intestine is the wide intestine. It is the palace responsible for transmission. [When the cold evil has arrived there] nothing can be retained in it and stay there for long. Hence, there is [constant] outflow from [the patient's] behind and [he feels] pain."

36 Zhang Zhicong: "癉 is 消癉, 'wasting *dan*.' The small intestine rules the liquids. In case of heat in the intestines, the liquids waste away and *dan* heat results." The *Tai su* has 竭, 'exhausted,' instead of 渴. Yang Shangshan: "When heat qi stays in the small intestine, then the interior of the small intestine is hot. The dregs dry out and harden. Hence constipation results." See also the notes on *dan* in *Su wen* 17, 19, and 35.

37 Wang Bing: "The heat causes the body liquids to flow away. Hence, the stools harden."

38 Wang Bing interprets this as a diagnostic statement, in the sense of "one inspects [a patient] and can see [his status]": "That is to say, one examines the complexion."

Qi Bo:
"The five depots and six palaces,
they definitely all have [corresponding] sections.[39]
When inspecting the five colors there,
yellow and red represent heat,[40]
white represents cold,[41]
green-blue color and black represent pain.[42]

This is the so-called
'from inspection one can obtain insights.'"

39-221-5
[Huang] Di:
"'From feeling one can obtain a hold,'
how is that?"[43]

Qi Bo:
"Inspect the vessel ruling the disease.
When it is firm and has blood, and when it has sunk down,[44] in both cases one gets a hold [of the disease] by feeling [the vessel]."

[Huang] Di:
"Good!

---

39 Wang Bing: "This is to say: the sections on the face." Zhang Zhicong: "The qi colors of the five depots and six palaces do all appear in the face and each of them rules a specific section." Yan Hongchen & Gao Guangzhen/213: "固 is 固定, or 一定, 'for sure.'"

40 Wang Bing: "When one was struck by heat, then the color is yellow-red."

41 Wang Bing: "When the yang qi is diminished, the blood cannot rise to supply the complexion. Hence, it is white."

42 Wang Bing: "When the blood congeals and is impeded, then it turns bad. Hence, the color is green-blue or black and as a result [the patient] feels pain."

43 Wang Bing: "捫 is 摸, 'to palpate.'" Zhang Zhicong: "This is to say: one presses the vessels and 'obtains' the disease."

44 Zhang Jiebin: "When the vessel is hard, this is an accumulation of evil. When the blood stays [at one location], the network [vessels] abound [with blood] and rise. When they sink down, [their contents of] blood and qi is insufficient. These are mostly yin signs."

I know that the hundred diseases[45] are generated by the qi.[46]

When one is angry, then the qi rises.
When one is joyous, then the qi relaxes.
When one is sad, then the qi dissipates.
When one is in fear, then the qi moves down.
In case of cold the qi collects;
in case of heat, the qi flows out.
When one is frightened, then the qi is in disorder.[47]
When one is exhausted, then the qi is wasted.
When one is pensive, then the qi lumps together.
These nine qi are not identical.
Which diseases generate [these states]?"

39-221-9
Qi Bo:
"When one is angry, then the qi moves contrary [to its regular course].
In severe cases, [patients] spit blood and there is outflow of [undigested] food.[48]
Hence,
the qi rises.[49]

When one is joyous, then the qi is in harmony and the mind is unimpeded.
The camp [qi] and the guard [qi] pass freely.

---

45 500/55: "'Hundred' does not mean 'all;' it means 'many.'"

46 See 494/53 for a detailed discussion of the meaning of qi in this statement.

47 Lin Yi et al.: "The *Tai su* has 憂, 'grief,' instead of 驚."

48 Lin Yi et al.: "The *Jia yi jing* and the *Tai su* have 食而氣逆, 'one eats and the qi moves reversely,' instead of 飧泄."

49 Wang Bing: "When [a person] is angry, then the yang qi rises contrary [to its normal course] and the liver qi occupies the spleen. Hence, in severe cases this causes [that person] to vomit blood and to have an outflow of [undigested] food. How to recognize this state? When [someone] is angry, then his face turns red. In extreme cases it turns green. The *Ling shu jing* states: 'When anger abounds and does not end, then it will harm the mind.' Obviously, in case of anger the qi rises contrary [to its normal course] and fails to descend." Zhang Jiebin: "Anger is a state of mind of the liver. When anger excites the liver, then the [liver] qi rises in a reverse movement. The qi compels the blood to rise. Hence, in severe cases [patients] vomit blood. The wood of the liver avails itself of the spleen. Hence, this results in an outflow of [undigested] food. The liver is yang in yin; its qi effuses downwards. Hence, [in case of anger] the [liver] qi rises."

Hence,
the qi relaxes.[50]

When one is sad, then the heart connection is tense.
The lobes of the lung spread open and rise and the upper burner is impass-
able.[51]
The camp [qi] and the guard [qi] do not disperse.
Heat qi is in the center.
Hence,
the qi dissipates.[52]

39-222-1
When one is in fear, then the essence withdraws.[53]

---

50 Wang Bing: "The qi and the vessels are in [a state of] harmonious balance. Hence,
the mind is unrestrained. The camp [qi] and guard [qi] pass freely. Hence, the [move-
ment of the] qi is slow and relaxed." Zhang Jiebin: "In case of extreme happiness the qi
slows down excessively and gradually reaches [a state of] dispersion. Hence, *Ling shu*
8 states: 'In case of happiness and joy, the spirit wears out and disperses and cannot
be kept.' [From this] the meaning [of the present passage] can be learned." Zhang Qi:
"All the nine qi [states listed here] refer to diseases. 緩 should have the meaning of 緩
散不收, '[the qi] disperses and can not be kept together.'"

51 Wang Bing: "布葉 is to say: 布蓋之大葉, 'the large lobes of a cover.'" Lin Yi et
al.: "The *Jia yi jing* and the *Tai su* have 'the two burners are impassable' instead of 'the
upper burner is impassable.' Also, Wang Bing's explanation of 布葉舉 as 布蓋之大葉
may not be correct. Quan Yuanqi states: 'When one is sad, then this harms the heart.
The heart connection becomes tense and, as a consequence, it excites the lung. When
the lung qi is tied down, [the movement in] all the conduits is reversed. Hence the
lung spreads out and its lobes are lifted. How could one state 肺布 is 'the large lobes
of the lung cover?'" Zhang Jiebin: "When sadness emerges from the heart, then the
heart connection becomes tense. When [it] sides with the lung, then the lobes of the
lung are lifted. Hence, *Su wen* 23 states: 'When essence qi agglomerates in the lung,
sadness results.' The heart and the lung are both situated above the diaphragm. Hence,
this causes the upper burner to be impassable." Gao Jiwu/725: "肺布葉舉 is 肺葉布
舉, 'The lobes of the lung spread open and rise.'"

52 Zhang Jiebin: "Sadness and grief harm the qi. Hence the qi dissipates." Zhang
Zhicong: "When the qi is retained in the center then it heats the center and the qi
does not move. Hence it hides away and dissipates." Cheng Shide et al.: "The text
states clearly: 'heat qi is in the center.' When Zhang Jiebin comments 'sadness and
grief harm the qi,' that is wrong. Also, 消 is identical with 銷, in the sense of 銷爍, 'to
melt.' *Su wen* 56 states: 'In case of strong heat, the sinews relax, the bones dissipate
and the flesh melts.' The 消 there is identical with the one here."

53 Zhang Jiebin: "When fear harms the kidneys, then it harms the essence. Hence,
this may reach [a state where] the essence withdraws."

When it withdraws, then the upper burner becomes closed.
When it is closed, then the qi turns back.
When it turns back, then the lower burner becomes distended.
Hence,
the qi does not move.[54]

When one is cold, then the interstice structures close and the qi does not move.
Hence,
the qi collects.[55]

When one is hot, then the interstice structures open and the camp [qi] and
guard [qi] pass through.
Sweat flows out profusely.
Hence,
qi flows out.[56]

---

54 Wang Bing: "When one is in fear, then the yang essence withdraws upwards and
fails to flow downwards. Hence, [the text states] 'when it withdraws, then the upper
burner becomes blocked.' When the upper burner is blocked and when the qi does not
flow, the yin qi of the lower burner revolves, too, and fails to disperse. It accumulates
and causes distention. Now, when the upper burner is firmly closed and the lower
burner qi revolves [where it is], both keep [their qi] at one location. Hence, the qi
does not move." Lin Yi et al.: "氣不行 should be 氣下行, 'to qi moves downwards.'"
Gao Shishi: "Fear harms the kidneys and the exchange between the upper and lower
[sections of the body] is interrupted. Hence, [the text states:] 'the qi does not move.'
'The qi does not move' is: it does not move upwards. Hence, in case of fear, the qi
moves downwards."

55 Wang Bing: "腠 is to say: the locations where the body liquids flow out [through
the skin]. 理 is to say: the central meeting points of the line structures [on the skin]
(文理逢會之中). 閉 is to say: 密閉, 'tightly closed.' Qi is to say: guard qi. Move is to
say: to flow. 收 is to say: 收歛 (possibly a writing error for 收斂, 'to gather'). When
the body is cold, the guard qi is in the depth. Hence, the line structures and the
locations of outflow in the skin close tightly and the qi cannot flow. The guard qi is
gathered inside and cannot disperse." Zhang Jiebin: "腠 is to say: the skin interstices
(膚腠), 理 is to say: the flesh structures (肉理). When cold tightens [the body] up
from outside, then the dark palaces (i.e., the pores) close and the yang qi cannot pass
through. Hence it collects in the interior and cannot disperse." Ma Shi: "When the
body is cold, then the interstice structures close and the guard qi cannot move towards
the outside. Hence the qi of the depots and palaces is gathered in the interior." Gao
Shishi: "In case of cold, the interstice structures close and as a result the qi of the triple
burner cannot pass through and gather in the muscles. Hence the qi does not move."

56 Wang Bing: "When a man is in the yang (i.e., the day section of day and night,
the light section of light and dark), he is relaxed; when he is in the yin (i.e., the night
section of day and night, etc.) he is afraid. Hence, when it is hot, then the structures of

39-222-4
When one is frightened, then
the heart has nothing to lean on,
the spirit has nowhere to return, and
one's deliberations have nowhere to settle.
Hence,
the qi is in disorder.[57]

When one is exhausted, then one's breath is panting and sweat leaves [the body].
Both outside and inside, [the limits] are exceeded.[58]
Hence,
the qi is wasted.[59]

When one is pensive, then the heart has a place to be,[60]
the spirit has a place to turn to and
the proper qi stays [at one location] and does not move.
Hence,
the qi lumps together."[61]

---

the skin open and [qi] effuses. Camp [qi] and guard [qi] proceed [through the body] massively and the body liquids flow away to the outside by way of massive sweating."

57 Zhang Jiebin: "When one is severely frightened, or has sudden fear, then the spirit-mind disperses, the blood and the qi separate and the yin and the yang [qi] disperse. Hence, 'the qi is in disorder.'" Zhang Zhicong: "One's thoughts and considerations are full of doubts and one cannot reach a decision." Gao Jiwu/530: "The *Shuo wen* defines 定 as 安, 'settled,' 'in peace.'"

58 Yan Hongchen & Gao Guangzhen/125: "When sweat leaves [the body], this is 'outside the limit is exceeded.' When one's breathing is panting, this is 'inside the limit is exceeded.'"

59 Wang Bing: "When one has exhausted one's strength, then the qi runs fast. Hence, one's breathing is panting. When the qi runs fast, then the yang effuses towards the outside. Hence, sweat leaves [the body]. Now, when one pants and when sweat leaves [the body, the qi] exceeds its limits in the interior and in the exterior. Hence, the qi diminishes."

60 Yan Hongchen & Gao Guangzhen/125: "存 is 寄存, 'to lodge.'"

61 Wang Bing: "When the heart is attached [to something] it does not disperse. Hence, the qi, too, remains at its place." Wu Kun: "結 is 不散, 'fails to disperse.'"

Chapter 40
Discourse on Abdomen and Center

40-223-2
Huang Di asked:
"Someone suffers from [the following]:
heart and abdomen[1] are full [to the extent that] if one has had breakfast, then he cannot eat in the evening.[2]
Which disease is that?"

Qi Bo responded:
"The name is drum[-like] distension."[3]

[Huang] Di:
"To treat it, how to proceed?"

Qi Bo:
"Treat it with wine made from chicken droppings.
One dosis [lets the disease improve] noticeably; a second dosis [lets the disease] end."[4]

---

1 Gao Shishi: "心腹 is: below the heart and above the abdomen. 滿 is 脹滿, 'distended.'" Zhang Zhicong: "'Heart and abdomen are full' is to say: the region between the chest and the diaphragm is the imperial city ruled by the heart; the abdomen is the city wall [surrounding] the depots and the palaces."

2 Ma Shi: "'If one eats in the morning, then one cannot eat in the evening,' that is, because of the swelling one cannot take another meal." Wu Kun: "'One eats in the morning; then one cannot eat in the evening,' is: [the disease] is light in the morning and has become critical at night."

3 Wang Bing: "Heart and abdomen are distended and [give a feeling of] fullness. [The patient] cannot eat anymore; his physical appearance is distended like a drum. Hence, the name [of the disease] is drum distension." The *Tai su* has 穀脹, grain distension, instead of 鼓脹. Zhang Qi: "It is solid outside and empty inside; its appearance resembles a drum."

4 Zhang Jiebin: "The nature of chicken droppings is able to dissolve accumulations and to make qi descend. It stimulates the passage of urine and stools. Hence it is a remedy to attack repletion evil. .. After one dosis one can know its effect." Cheng Shide et al.: "知 is 效, 'effect.'" Qian Chaochen-90/98: "To interpret 知 as 知銷, 'to know,' is a mistake. 知 has the same meaning as 已, 'to end.' Both serve to express that an illness has been cured. The *Guang ya shi gu* 廣雅釋詁 states: 已 and 知 are identical with 愈, 'to cure.' Also, the *Fan yan* 方言 states: 差, 間, and 知 are identical with 愈, 'to cure.' In Southern Chu, when a disease is cured, this is called 差, or 間, or 知." If one were to interpret 知 in the present context as identical with 已, 'to end,' or 愈, 'to

40-223-4
[Huang] Di:
"When occasionally it manifests itself again,
why is that?"

Qi Bo:
"In this case, beverages and food [have been consumed] without restraint.
Hence, occasionally one has [this] disease [again].

Neverthelesss, even if the disease has ended for the moment, occasionally [the
patient] must suffer as before. [This is because] qi has collected in the abdomen." 5

[Huang] Di:
"Someone suffers from [the following]: in his chest and flanks he feels prop-
ping fullness. His intake of food is impeded.
When the disease sets in, then a fishy and fetid odor is smelled first and clear
fluid leaves [the body].
In the beginning, [patients] spit blood and their four limbs are cool.
Their eyes are dizzy.6
They often pass blood in front and behind.7

---

cure,' it would be difficult to explain the meaning of "one dosis [lets the disease] end,
a second dosis [lets the disease] end", as Qian Chaochen prefers it.

5 Wang Bing: "When beverages and food are consumed immoderately, then this
harms the stomach. The stomach vessel descends inside the abdomen. Hence, when
beverages and food are consumed immoderately and when the disease from time
to time [occurs again], this is because disease qi has accumulated in the abdomen."
Instead of 時故當病, the *Jia yi jing* has 因當風, "following an encounter with wind,"
and the *Tai su* has 時當痛, "from time to time there is pain." Zhang Qi: "Either something has been omitted, or something was mistakenly added here."

6 Wu Kun: "If 'one first spits blood,' the liver has a disease and cannot store the
blood. Also, because the nature of the wood is to move upward, hence 'one first spits
blood.' As for 'the four limbs are cold,' the yang qi does not move to the four limbs,
rather it associates with the interior. The yin qi of the interior, in contrast, leaves for
the four limbs. 'The eyes are dizzy,' this is because one has lost large quantities of
blood and the orifice [associated with the] liver has lost its clarity." Gao Shishi: "The
lung vessel starts from the chest and moves into the hands; the liver vessel starts from
the feet and moves into the flanks. When both the lung and the liver have a disease,
the four limbs are cool as a result."

7 Yang Shangshan: "Blood leaves repeatedly with the urine and with the stools."

What is the name of [this] disease;
how is it acquired?"⁸

Qi Bo:
"The disease is named blood decay.⁹
It is acquired in younger years either [because of] a massive loss of blood or
[because] one has entered the [women's] chambers in a state of drunkenness
[with the result that]
the qi is exhausted and the liver is harmed.
Hence, the monthly affair is weak and diminished and fails to arrive."¹⁰

40-223-10
[Huang] Di:
"To treat it, how to proceed?

---

8 Wang Bing: "清液 is 清水, 'clear water,' also called 清涕, 'clear mucus.' 'Clear mucus' refers to dense fluid flowing downward from the secret funnel (that is, the vagina).
The water leaving [the body] is clear and cold." Zhang Jiebin: "The lung rules the qi.
Its odor is fishy. The liver rules the blood. Its odor is fetid. When the lung qi is unable to level the liver, then both the liver and the lung [qi] rise in a reverse movement.
The turbid qi does not descend and the clear qi does not rise. Hence one smells fishy
and fetid [odors] and spits clear fluid. From one's mouth one spits blood; the blood
does not return to the conduits." Wu Kun: "When clear fluids leave through the nose,
this is because there is no stomach qi in the lung to exert a harmonizing effect there.
Hence, the clear fluids of the lung, [that is, of] the metal, leave [the body]." Tanba:
"Given the preceding text, Zhang Jiebin's comment is correct."

9 Yang Shangshan: "The disease of 'blood decay' has eight different appearances:
1. Fullness of chest, flanks, and limbs. 2. Aversion to eat. 3. When the disease is about
to break out, there is first a qi of fishy and fetid odor [leaving the patient]. 4. Clear
fluids flow away. 5. The patient spits blood. 6. The four limbs are cold. 7. The eyes are
dizzy. 8. Blood leaves from time to time with urine and stools. These eight appearances are called the disease of blood decay. ... When the monthly period is diminished,
or fails to come at all, this is because this blood decay disease has formed." Zhang
Jiebin: "'Blood decay' means: the passage of the monthly water is interrupted." See
also 283/28.

10 Wang Bing: "When large amounts of blood leave [the body], this is called 脱血.
This [term refers] to blood leaving [the body] as downflow from the uterus, as nosebleed, or as vomiting alike. When one is drunk, then the vessels abound with blood.
When the vessels abound with blood, then the interior is hot. If then one enters the
bedroom (that is, engages in sexual intercourse), the marrow and [other] fluids flow
down. Hence, the qi in the kidneys is exhausted. The liver stores the blood. Smaller or
larger losses of blood harm the liver. Now, in males this leads to a weakening of the
essence fluid; in females, the monthly affair diminishes and does not arrive."

Recovery is achieved by which art?"[11]

Qi Bo:
"Take four black cuttlefish bones and one [measure/root of] madder,[12] combine these two items and form pills in the size of small beans using sparrow eggs.[13]
Five pills are to be taken before meals;
they are to be swallowed with abalone liquid.[14]
They clear the intestines and the center,[15] and
they reach a harmed liver."[16]

---

11 Another possible translation of this question could be based on an interpretation of 復 in the sense of 又, "again", rather than in the sense of 回復, "to recover": "Again, which technique is to be employed?"

12 Zhang Jiebin: "*lüru* 蘆茹 is also called *rulü* 茹蘆; this is 茜草, 'madder herb.' (*Rubia cardifolia* L.) It stops bleeding and heals uterine bleeding. It also can increase the essence qi, enliven the blood and penetrate the conduit vessels." The Mawangdui manuscript *Wu shi er bing fang* 五十二病方 recommends *rulu* 茹蘆, that is, madder root, against "dry itch." See Harper 1998, 297.

13 Zhang Jiebin: "雀 is 麻雀, 'sparrows.' Sparrow eggs can supplement and increase essence and blood."

14 Gao Shishi: "鮑魚 is 醃魚, 'dried, salted fish.'" Gao Shishi cites the widely attested ancient meaning of the term 鮑魚; *NJCD* agrees. If this were so, the liquid recommended here might be the brine obtained from an aqueous preparation of "dried, salted fish." However, as a pharmaceutical substance named 鮑魚汁 is recorded nowhere else in known ancient literature, we follow *HYDCD* and *ZGYXDCD* which identify 鮑魚 as 鰒魚, "abalone." See also note 16 below for Wang Bing's comment.

15 *Tai su*, ch. 30, has 脅中, "the flanks and the center," instead of 腸中. Lin Yi et al.: "Other versions have 傷中, 'injured center.'"

16 Wang Bing: "When the meal is second and the drugs are first, this is called 後飯, 'eat afterwards.' .. When one is drunk and taxes one's strength through sexual intercourse (lit.: through entering the bedroom), then the essence qi in the kidneys is exhausted and the monthly affair is diminished and fails to arrive. As a result, bad blood remains in one's center. When the essence qi is exhausted, then the yin [member] (that is, the penis) is limp and fails to rise and one has no [seminal] essence. When bad blood remains [in the center], then the blood is blocked in the center and does not disperse. Hence, one takes these four drugs before one enters the [women's] chambers (that is, has sexual intercourse; we read 入方 as 入房). The ancient *Ben cao jing* 本草經 states: 'black cuttlefisch bones, salty flavor, cold-balanced [nature], no toxicity. Main indication: blockage of bleeding of women. Madder, acrid flavor, cold-balanced, slight toxicity. Main indication: disperses bad blood. Sparrow eggs, sweet flavor, warm-balanced, no toxicity. Indication: strengthens the yin [member] in case of weakness and makes it rise. Provides heat, plenty of [seminal] essence, so that one has offspring. 鮑魚, acrid flavor, stench, warm-balanced, no toxicity. Main indication: stagnating blood, blocked blood in the four limbs which does not disperse.'"

[Huang] Di:

"A disease is [as follows]:

The lower abdomen [gives the patient a feeling of] abundance.

Above, below, to the left and to the right, everywhere are roots.[17]

Which disease is that?

Can it be treated, or not?"

Qi Bo:

"The name of the disease is hidden beams."[18]

40-224-3

[Huang] Di:

"Hidden beams, through which cause is this [disease] acquired?"

Qi Bo:

"[The lower abdomen] holds massive pus and blood, located outside of the intestines and the stomach.

This must not be treated.

If one treats it, each time one presses the [lower abdomen] this brings [the patient] closer to death."[19]

---

17 Wu Kun: "'Root' is where the disease ends." Zhang Zhicong: "'It has roots above and below, on the left and on the right,' [that is to say:] this disease is in the blood section and it is linked, through the network vessels, to above and below and [all] the four sides." "Root" may be interpreted as a reference to hardenings resembling roots that can be felt by palpating the abdomen.

18 Wang Bing: "[The term] 'hidden beams' [refers to] accumulations in the heart. ... The disease is named 'hidden beams' because above and below there are hardenings as if there were hidden beams." Lin Yi et al.: "This [disease of] hidden beams is very different from the hidden beams of the accumulations in the heart. These diseases have the same name, but in fact they differ and are not alike." Zhang Jiebin: "伏 is 藏 伏, 'hidden.' 梁 is to say: 彊梁堅硬 'violent and hard.'" Wu Kun: "伏梁 is to say: like hidden bridge beams. This name was chosen because the suffering is deep inside. The [occurrence of the term] here is not identical with the discourse on 'hidden beams' in the *Nan jing* (difficult issue 56). There it refers to accumulations in the heart, that is, to yin qi in the depots. Here it refers to accumulations of pus and blood, that is, to yang poison." See also 2822/1.

19 Wang Bing: "Because a package of large amounts of pus and blood is situated outside of the intestines and the stomach, which if pressed results in unbearable pain; whenever it is pressed, this leads to [the patient's] death." Zhang Jiebin: "按 is 抑, 'to press down with one's hand.' If one presses it firmly, this is to say, this is an overly wild attack. Hence [the patient] must die." Zhang Zhicong: "'It cannot be treated' is: it cannot be treated through pressure or rubbing (that is, massage). If one presses and rubs it because one wishes to disperse it quickly, this will result in pain and [the

40-224-4
[Huang] Di:
"How is that?"

Qi Bo:
"When this passes downward, then it is by way of yin [passageways].
It is inevitable that what is passed downward is pus and blood.
When this is moved upward, then it presses against the stomach duct where it
generates a barrier.
{[That is:] *yong*-abscesses inside the stomach duct, on both sides.}[20]

This is a chronic disease; it is difficult to cure.
When it resides above the navel,[21] this is opposition;
when it resides below the navel, this is compliance.[22]

---

patient] may wish to die. That is, any evil with a physical appearance is not easy to
disperse."

20 Wang Bing: "Because that section of the thoroughfare vessel that moves downward encloses the yin [member], and because that section that moves upward follows
the abdomen, [the pus and the blood] above, they rush against the stomach duct;
below they press against the yin member. When, therefore, they press against the
yin, then one passes pus and blood with the urine and the stools. When [the pus and
the blood] rush against the stomach, then the disease qi rises and leaves through the
diaphragm. Again, on both sides inside the stomach duct these abscesses grow. Why is
that so? Because originally a large amount of pus and blood was located outside of the
intestines and the stomach. 生 should be 出, 'to leave.'" Lin Yi et al.: "The *Tai su* has
使, 'to cause,' instead of 俠." Yang Shangshan may have felt compelled to change the
wording. His version reads: 出鬲. 使胃脘內癰, "It leaves [through] the diaphragm,
causing *yong*-abscesses in the stomach duct." Zhang Qi: "生 should be 至, 'to reach.'
俠 should be 使, 'to cause.'" Gao Shishi: "Everytime one presses severely to cause it
to move downward, [the patient] will pass pus and blood [with his urine and stools].
Everytime one presses severely to cause it to move upward, it will rush against the
stomach duct and this will generate a barrier and cause abscesses on both sides in the
stomach duct." This must be a very early commentary, since it appears in the *Tai su*,
too, albeit in a corrupted version. As an alternative to Wang Bing's interpretation, one
might read *ge-jia* as a foreign term the meaning of which was lost by the time of Yang
Shangshan and Wang Bing. In this case, the passage would read: "...where it presses
against the stomach duct and generates *ge-jia*," followed by a commentary "This is a
yong-abscess inside the stomach duct."

21 916/54: "齊 is identical with 臍, 'navel.'"

22 Wang Bing: "When a package of large amounts of pus and blood is situated above
the navel, then it will gradually harm the heart depot. Hence this is 'opposition.' If
it is situated below the heart, then it is a little further away from the heart and it can
gradually be attacked. Hence this is 'compliance.' 從 is 順, 'favorable.'" Zhang Jiebin:

Do not move [it]; quickly remove [it]." [23]
{This is discussed in the [treatise] Laws of Piercing.}[24]

40-225-2
[Huang] Di:
"Someone has his body and limbs {thigh bones, thighs, and shins} all swollen.
The region around his navel is painful.
Which disease is that?"

Qi Bo:
"The disease is named hidden beams.[25]
These are wind roots.[26]

"When it is situated above the navel, then it will gradually annoy the heart and the lung. Hence this is 'opposition.' When it is situated below [the navel], its force seems to relax. Hence this is 'compliance.' "

23 Wang Bing: "亟 is 數, 'frequent.' 奪 is 去, 'to remove.' That is to say, one must not move it; the only way is to remove it again and again [in smaller quantities]." Gao Shishi: "勿動亟奪 is to say: one must not forcefully press and rub to remove it." Wu Kun: "'Move' is to move the stomach qi, to move the stools. 亟 is 數, 'frequent.' 奪 is 下之, 'to pass downward.' [The passage] is to say: One must not activate the stomach qi to pass the stools; rather the [pus and the blood] have to be removed again and again." Ma Shi: "One must frequently drain [the patient] to remove the [pus and the blood]. This way one can gradually diminish them and prevents them from causing annoyance above."

24 1639/9: "This is an example for a comment that was later mistakenly inserted into the main text."

25 Wang Bing: "The preceding 26 characters have been erroneously inserted into *Su wen* 47. Without these 26 characters, the following text makes no sense." 2921/76: "It is generally assumed that these 26 characters have been inserted [here] by Wang Bing himself."

26 Wang Bing: "These four characters are originally part of this treatise; they appear in the treatise on 'Unusual diseases', too." Zhang Jiebin: "風根 is cold qi." Wu Kun: "That is to say because wind poison strikes roots in the center. When wind poison strikes roots in the center, pain results in the region surrounding the navel. The navel is the pivot of the human body. When the pivot has a disease, it cannot revolve the yin and the yang qi. Hence the body, the thigh bones, the thighs, and the shins all swell." Zhang Zhicong: "Wind is yang evil. It harms man's yang qi. In the present case, wind evil has harmed the qi and it stays in the region between the navel and the abdomen. Hence [the text] states: 'this has its roots in the wind.' " Wang Ji: "The four characters 此風根也 may be a [later] insertion." Li Guoqing: "風根 means: the wind is the cause." In keeping with the wording in 40-224-2, "above and below, to the left and to the right, everywhere are roots", we translate 風根 literally as "wind roots." This

The [wind] qi has spilled into the large intestine and has attached itself to the *huang*.
The plain of the *huang* is below the navel.[27]
Hence,
the region around the navel has pain.
One cannot move this [qi].[28] If one moves it, this causes the disease of rough-ened urination of water."[29]

40-225-5
[Huang] Di:
"You, Sir, have frequently stated [the following]:
in the case of heated center and in the case of wasting center, it is not advisable to consume rich food, aromatic herbs, and mineral drugs.[30]

---

may be a reference to a concept of accumulations or hardenings in the abdomen the meaning of which was lost in later centuries.

27 Wang Bing: "This, too, is the thoroughfare vessel . 'Below the navel' is to say: *bo yang* 脖胦; it is located two and a half standardized body inches below the navel." Wu Kun: "The empty space without flesh in the cavity [of chest and abdomen] is called *huang*. 原 is 源, 'origin.' 'Below the navel,' this is the sea of qi (氣海). Another name is *bo yang* 脖胦. *Ling shu* 1 states: 'The plain of the *huang* is called *bo yang* 脖胦.' This is meant here." Zhang Jiyou: "[*Huang*] refers here to the [region] inside the abdomen, outside the intestines." *NJCD:* "原 is 本原, 'origin.'" See also 906/40.

28 Mori: "'One must not move it' has the same meaning as the exhortation 'do not move it' in the preceding paragraph. That is to say, one must not apply massage to move the network vessels. All previous commentators have interpreted this in the sense of moving something down with purgatives. That was wrong."

29 Gao Shishi: "This disease is not associated with a qi having a physical appearance. Still, one cannot wildly attack [it] to agitate it. If one agitates it, then the qi fails to transform and the water does not pass. This then causes the disease of roughened [passage of the] water. This 'hidden beam' [disease] is situated in the qi section; it is not identical with the hidden beam [disease] of packages of large amounts of pus and blood."

30 Wang Bing: "If one drinks often and urinates frequently, this is called 'heated center.' If one eats often and urinates frequently, this is called 'wasting center.' To be often joyful, this is called 瘨. To be often angry, this is called 狂." Zhang Jiebin: "'Heated center' and 'wasting center' are diseases of internal heat." Wu Kun: "高 is like 膏, 'rich.'"

Mineral drugs [cause one to] develop madness;[31]
aromatic herbs [cause one to] develop craziness.[32]

Now,
heated center and wasting center all [occur in] the wealthy and noble.
In this case,
if one forbids [them to consume] rich food, this is not to their liking.
If one forbids [them to take] aromatic herbs and mineral drugs, the disease
cannot be healed.
I should like to hear an explanation of this."[33]

40-225-8
Qi Bo:
"Now,
the qi of aromatic herbs is fine;[34]
the qi of mineral drugs is fierce.
The qi of both is fast and strong.
Hence, any person who is not in a state of harmony and does not have a relaxed
mind, cannot take these two."[35]

---

31 674/161: "瘨 is 疽. Wang Bing identifies 瘨 as a mental disease. However, the *Jia yi jing*, ch.11, no. 6, has 石藥發疽. There are no records in the literature of mineral drugs causing mental disease, but there are records of mineral drugs causing abscesses." 2493/531: "瘨 is 癲." Gao Jiwu/25 and Fang Wenhui/164 agree. See also 1820/57.

32 On Wang Bing's comment see 528/20.

33 Wang Bing: "In case of 'heated center' and 'wasting center,' spleen qi pours upward and this is brought about by sweet and fat [food]. Hence, one forbids [the patient to consume] rich food and aromatic herbs. Now, people of high standing are proud and licentious. They disregard others and there is no way to prohibit them [from consuming rich food]. If one voices such prohibitions, this is against their will. If one gives in to their [preferences], then this adds to their disease."

34 674/161: "The character 美 is an error for 羑 , which is identical with 恢, 'to burn.'"

35 Wang Bing: "[In the present case] spleen qi pours out and generates the disease. If the qi [of the food/herbs consumed] is pleasant, it doubles the abundance in the spleen. The qi of wasting heat is rapid. [If one consumes food/herbs with] fierce qi, then this adds to the heat in the [spleen. ... Hence only people with a relaxed mind and being in harmony can consume these two [types of food/herbs]. 悍 is 利, 'cutting.' 堅 is 定, 'fixed,' 固, 'firm.' 勁 is 剛, 'unyielding.' That is to say, the qi of aromatic herbs and mineral drugs is firm, unyielding, and fierce."

[Huang] Di:
"Cannot take these two, why so?"

Qi Bo:
"Now,
the heat qi is fierce.
The qi of [those] drugs is so too.
When the two meet, it is to be feared that this harms the spleen in the interior.
The spleen is soil and has an aversion to wood.
For those who consume these drugs, when [the disease] lasts until a *jia* or *yi* day, [it is] discussed again."³⁶

40-226-3
[Huang] Di:
"Good!
Someone suffers from [the following]:
the breast is swollen; the neck aches, the chest is full, and the abdomen is distended.
What disease is that?
How is it acquired?"³⁷

40-226-4
Qi Bo:
"It is called recession with countermovement."³⁸

---

36 Wang Bing: "*Jia* and *yi* are wood. Hence when [the disease] lasts until a *jia* or *yi* day one will discuss again whether the disease has increased or decreased." Cheng Shide et al.: "Instead of the two characters 更論, the *Jia yi jing* has 當愈甚, 'it will be much more serious.' Wu Kun and Zhang Jiebin follow this version and interpret it as 病甚, '[on *jia* and *yi* days] the disease will be serious.' Wang Bing, Gao Shishi, Zhang Zhicong, Yao Shaoyu, and Ma Shi, they all comment: 'When the time has come, one will discuss [the further development of the disease] again.' The comments of the former are based on [the fact that] wood overcomes soil. Hence, on *jia* and *yi* days the disease will be severe. The latter assumed that the spleen is not necessarily harmed, because earlier it is stated: 'it is to be feared that the spleen is harmed.' Hence both interpretations are meaningful."

37 Wang Bing: "膺 are the sides of the chest. 頸 is the front side of the neck. 胸 is the space within the 膺." 1679/25: "Originally, the character 頸 referred to the front side of the neck. It is only since the Han dynasty that it referred to the neck. In the *Nei jing*, the character 頸 is often used in the sense of 'neck.' For instance, in *Su wen* 40."

38 Wang Bing: "It is generated by qi moving contrary [to its normal course]. Hence it is called 'recession with countermovement.'" Zhang Jiebin: "The yin [qi] sides with the yang and what is below moves against its normal direction to what is above. Hence

[Huang] Di:
"To treat it, how to proceed?"

Qi Bo:
"When the [patient] is cauterized, then he will turn mute;
when he is [treated with] stones, then he will become crazy.³⁹
Wait for his qi to merge.
Only then he can be treated."⁴⁰

40-226-6
[Huang] Di:
"How is that?"

Qi Bo:
"When yang qi doubles above, there is a surplus above.
If one cauterizes it, then the yang qi enters the yin.
When it has entered [the yin], then [the patient] will turn mute.⁴¹
If one treats him with stones, then the yang qi is depleted.
When it is depleted, then [the patient] becomes crazy.⁴²
Wait for his qi to merge; only then treating him can achieve the cure."⁴³

---

the disease is named 'recession with countermovement.' " Wu Kun: "That is to say, it is generated by qi moving contrary [to its normal course]. Minor cases are [called] 厥, 'receding;' serious cases are [called] 逆, 'movement contrary [to its normal course].' "

39 Wang Bing: " 'Stone' is to say: 'to open it with stone needles.' " Wu Kun: " 'Stone' is to say: 'to pierce it with sharpened stones.' " 1977/37: "石 is used here verbally in the sense of 'to pierce.' "

40 Cheng Shide et al.: " 'The qi merge' is: yin and yang qi unite."

41 Wu Kun: " 'Enters the yin' is: enters the interior." Zhang Jiebin: "When in a situation where the yang qi has a surplus above one still cauterizes, this is to support fire with fire. The yang reaches an extreme and occupies the yin. As a result the yin cannot offer any resistance. Hence, [the patient] loses his voice and turns mute."

42 Wang Bing: "When it is cauterized, then the qi of the fire supports the yang [qi]. When the yang abounds it enters the yin. When [it is treated with] stones, then the yang qi leaves [to the outside]. When the yang qi has left, then there is not enough inside. Hence, [patients] turn crazy." Zhang Jiebin: "When all the yang [qi] rises, there will be a depletion below. If one drains the [yang qi] with stones, then the yang qi will leave [the body] through the piercing. When it has left, then both the upper and the lower [sections] are depleted and the spirit has lost its guard. Hence [the patient] becomes crazy."

43 Wang Bing: "并 is to say: 并合, 'to merge.' When the two qi have merged by themselves, then they are both complete/healed. Hence, one can initiate a treatment.

[Huang] Di:
"Good!
How does one know that a pregnant [woman] will soon give birth?"⁴⁴

Qi Bo:
"The body has a disease, but there is no evil [movement in the] vessels."⁴⁵

40-226-10
[Huang] Di:
"When the disease is heat and when there are some locations that ache, why is that?"

Qi Bo:
"When the disease is heat, a yang [movement appears in the] vessels.⁴⁶

If this is not the case, then cauterizing them or treating them with stones causes unilateral dominance. Hence, a cure is impossible and [the erroneous treatment causes patients to turn] mute and crazy." Ma Shi: "It must be such that the yang qi descends from above and the yin qi rises from below. After the yin and the yang have united, one may treat the [disease] and will reach a cure regardless of whether one employs cauterization or piercing."

44 576/37: "生 has the meaning of 分娩, 'parturition.'" 1061/31 agrees. In contrast, 1317/47 and others interpret this passage in the sense of "How does one know that [a woman] who is pregnant will survive? Her body is ill but she has no evil [movement in the] vessels."

45 Wang Bing: "'Disease' is to say: menstruation is blocked. The *Mai fa* 脈法 states: 'When the arrival of the [movement in the] vessels in the foot [section] is interrupted, menstruation is blocked. .. When in the present case menstruation is blocked while the [movement in the] vessels, contrary [to what one should expect], is normal, then this is a sign that the respective woman is pregnant. Hence [the text] states: 'The body has a disease, but there is no evil [movement in the] vessels.'" Zhang Jiebin: "When the body is ill, the [movement in the] vessels should [reflect the] disease, too. If the six [movements in the] vessels are balanced and smooth, while the body has some unrest, this is caused, undoubtedly, by fetal qi." Wu Kun: "'The body has a disease' is to say: the body has some unrest. In such a situation there should be an evil [movement in the] vessels. Hence, one knows that the respective [woman] is pregnant and will live. 'Live' is: she will not suffer afterwards."

46 Zhang Jiebin: "A yang [movement in the] vessels is a fire evil. Whenever one is ill from heat, the cause must lie in the yang." Wu Kun: "That is to say: the yang vessels have received a disease." Gao Shishi: "Heat is a yang disease. When [one is affected by] heat the [movement in the] three yang conduit vessels is not harmonious. Hence [the text states:] when one is ill from heat, [this is because of] the [movement in the] yang vessels.

In terms of the movement of the three yang [conduits],[47]
when [the movement felt at] man's facing is once over [normal] fullness,[48] [the disease is in] the minor yang [conduit];
when it is twice over [normal] fullness, [the disease is in] the major yang [conduit];
when it is three times over [normal] fullness, [the disease is in] the yang brilliance [conduit],[49] and enters the yin.[50]
Now, [from the] yang it enters the yin.
Hence,
the disease is in the head and at the same time in the abdomen,
resulting in bloating and headache."[51]

[Huang] Di:
"Good!"

---

47 Wu Kun: "動 is: the [movement in the] vessels arrives very excited. The resulting disease is pain." Ma Shi: "An excited [movement in the] three yang conduits is evidence of an external affection."

48 1718/32: "That is to say: when the [movement in the] vessels at the *ren ying* point is twice as big as at the inch opening, the disease is in the minor yang."

49 This statement is an abridged version of a statement appearing at the end of *Su wen* 9.

50 Lin Yi et al.: "The *Jia yi jing* does not have the three characters 入陰也." Wu Kun has added the character 未, 'not yet:' 'It has not yet entered the yin.'"

51 Zhang Jiebin: "The head rules the yang; the abdomen rules the yin. When yang evil is in the head, this results in headache. When it enters the yin section, then the abdomen becomes distended." Zhang Qi: "陽入於陰 should be 陽不入於陰, 'from the yang it does not enter the yin.'" Mori: "The *Tai su* has 痛, 'pain,' instead of 病. This is acceptable. Headache is an outer yang condition; abdominal pain is a yin cold condition. The headache of a major yang disease and the abdominal pain of a minor yin disease, that is correct."

Chapter 41
To Pierce Lower Back Pain

41-227-5
When it is the foot major yang vessel that lets a person's lower back ache,
[then there is pain] pulling on the nape, the spine, the sacrum, and the back as
if there was a heavy [weight].[1]
Pierce the major yang [vessel] in the cleft right into the conduit. Let blood.[2]
In spring, avoid the appearance of blood.[3]

When it is the minor yang [vessel] that lets a person's lower back ache,
[then there is pain] as if someone had pierced with a needle into this [person's]
skin, and
[the patient is] continously unable to bend down and up and
cannot look back.[4]

---

1 Wang Bing: "The foot major yang vessel divides [into two courses] moving
downwards into the nape, following the shoulder, inside the shoulder blade, paralleling the spine on both sides, finally reaching the center of the lower back. It divides
and moves down to penetrate the sacrum. Hence, if it causes one to have lower back
pain, [the pain] pulls on the nape, the spine, the sacrum, and the back as if there was
a heavy weight."

2 "Cleft" is possibly a reference to the popliteal fossa.

3 Yang Shangshan: "The foot major yang qi is weak in winter and spring. To let blood
[at this time] may lead to depletion. Hence, [the text] warns against it." Wang Bing:
"'In the cleft' is the Bend Middle (委中) [hole]. It is located on the moving vessel in
the central line (i.e., fold) of the depression at the back of the knee, where the foot
major yang vessel enters. .. The major yang is linked to the kidneys. The kidneys rule
in winter. [Their] water is weakened in spring. Hence, in spring one should avoid the
appearance of blood."

4 Wang Bing: "The foot minor yang vessel makes a circle at the [pubic] hair line,
moves horizontally and enters the center of the concave part of the lower back. Hence,
it causes lower back pain as if one had been pierced with a needle into the skin. .. The
minor yang vessel emerges from the pointed canthus of the eye, reaches to the corners
of the [fore]head, descends behind the ear, follows the neck, runs in front of the hand
yang brilliance [conduit], reaches the shoulder and crosses over to behind the hand
yang brilliance [conduit]. Its branch course descends from below the pointed canthus
of the eye and enters the Great Facing (大迎) [hole], merges with the hand minor
yang [conduit] below the cheekbone, moves down, joins the cheek carriage (頰車),
descends along the neck and merges with the broken basin. Hence, one cannot look
back." Zhang Jiebin: "The minor yang qi corresponds to wind and wood; it is received
by the yang section. Hence, it is as if one had pierced a needle into the [patient's] skin.
循循然 is 遲滯貌, 'as if obstructed.' That is to say, [the patient] cannot lift [some-
thing], or move, with ease." Zhang Zhicong: "循循 is 漸次, 'gradually.'" Wu Kun: "循

Pierce the minor yang [vessel] at the tip of the support bone.[5] Let blood.
{The 'support bone' is the bone rising alone at the outer edge of the knee.}
In summer, avoid the appearance of blood.[6]

41-227-9
When it is the yang brilliance [vessel] that lets a person's lower back ache,
[then that person is] unable to look back and, when he looks back as if he had
seen [something], he tends to be sad.[7]
Pierce the yang brilliance [vessel] at the front side of the shins. [Generate]
three wounds[8]

循 is 漸. That is to say, [patients] are gradually unable to bown down and straighten
themselves again." The *Jia yi jing* has the two characters 左右 above the character 顧:
"One cannot turn left or right to look back." 2167/48: "循循然 is to describe a state
where any movement causes discomfort." *Huai nan zi*, Yuan dao 原道, has 循 in the
meaning of "to rub." In this sense, 循循然 may also be read here in conjunction with
the preceding statement as referring to a "pricking" sensation on or in the skin.

5 This could be a reference to the upper outer edge of the fibula.

6 Yang Shangshan: "The foot minor yang qi is weak from spring to summer. To let
blood [during this time] may lead to depletion. Hence, [the text] warns against it."
Wang Bing: "成骨 is to say: the depression holding a finger between the two prominent bones of the outside of the knee and the upper tip of the shinbone. The shinbone
supports (成柱) the knee and the thighs. Hence, it is called 'support bone' (成骨).
The minor yang is linked to the liver. The liver rules in spring. The wood weakens in
summer. Hence, one must avoid the appearance of blood [in summer]." Zhang Jiebin:
"The solitary prominence at the outer side of the knee is the upper tip of the shinbone.
It is called 'support bone' because it holds (成立) the body."

7 Wang Bing: "The foot yang brilliance vessel emerges from where the nose intersects
with the center [between the] brows. It descends along the outside of the nose, enters
the upper teeth, turns around, comes out, parallels the mouth on both sides, encircles
the lips, descends, crosses the sauce receptacle (承浆, the infralabial fossa), recedes
along the back of the jaw and comes out at the lower edge at the Great Facing (大
迎) [hole]. Its branch course moves from in front of the Great Facing [hole] down
to man's facing (人迎), follows the throat and enters the broken basin. Other branch
courses emerge from the lower opening of the stomach, follow the inside of the abdomen to the center of the qi street, merge again and descend to the lower back. Hence,
if [this vessel] causes one to have lower back pain, one cannot look back. If one turns
to look back as if one had seen something, the yang is depleted. Hence, one feels sad."
Wu Kun: "'As if one had seen something,' is what [Zhang] Zhong-jing calls: 'as if one
had seen a demonic appearance.'

8 As becomes more obvious from its usage in the text further below, we consider 痏
to refer here to the "wounds" caused by piercing. In contrast, Cheng Shide et al.: "The
Yü pian 玉篇 states: '痏 is 瘡, 'wound.' In the present context 痏 refers to the wounds
generated by cauterization."

<Above and below, balance them>
Let blood.
In autumn, avoid the appearance of blood.[9]

When it is the foot minor yin [vessel] that lets a person's lower back ache,
[then there is] pain pulling at the inner edge of the spine.[10]
Pierce the minor yin [vessel] above the inner ankle. [Generate] two wounds.
In spring, avoid the appearance of blood.
{If too much blood is let a recovery is impossible.}[11]

41-228-3
When it is the vessel of the ceasing yin that lets a person's lower back ache,
[then the patient has a feeling] in the lower back as if a string of a bow or
crossbow was pulled.[12]
Pierce the vessel of the ceasing yin [vessel] outside [the region of] calf and heel

---

9 Yang Shangshan: "The foot yang brilliance [qi] is weak from midsummer to autumn. To let blood [during this time] may lead to depletion. Hence, [the text] warns
against it." Wang Bing: "The yang brilliance [vessel] is tied to the spleen. The spleen
rules in late summer. The soil weakens in autumn. Hence, one should avoid the appearance of blood in autumn."

10 Wang Bing: "The foot minor yin vessel moves up inside the thighs at the back
edge, penetrates the spine and links up with the kidneys. Hence, when it causes one
to have lower back pain, the pain pulls [along] the inner edge of the spine." Lin Yi
et al.: "The Quan Yuanqi edition and the *Tai su* have 脊內痛, 'pain inside the spine,'
instead of 脊內廉.

11 Yang Shangshan: "The minor yin qi and the major yang qi are weak from winter
to spring. To let blood [during this time] may cause depletion. Hence, [the text] warns
against it." Zhang Jiebin: "In spring the wood flourishes and the water is weak. Hence,
in piercing the foot minor yin [vessel] one should avoid the appearance of blood in
spring. If one lets too much blood, then the kidney qi cannot recover." Zhang Zhicong: "The blood is generated out of the essence water. The kidneys are responsable for
storage to [be able] in spring to give out vital qi. If in spring one lets blood, then one
drains what [the kidneys] have stored. If this is too much, it cannot recover."

12 Wang Bing: "The foot ceasing yin vessel emerges from the yin [side of the] thigh,
encircles the yin (i.e., genital) organs and reaches the lower abdomen. It divides into
branch courses merging with the major yin and major yang [vessels] below the lumbar
vertebrae and paralleling the spine on both sides. Their holes are in the hollows of
the third and fourth vertrebrae; these are the Central Bone-Hole (中髎) [hole] and
the Lower Bone-Hole (下髎) [hole]. Hence, when the vessel of the ceasing yin lets a
person's lower back ache, one has [a feeling] in the lower back as if a string of a bow
or crossbow was drawn. 如張弦者 is to say: 強急之甚, 'extremely stiff and tense.'"
307/183: "The *Shuo wen* states: 'A crossbow is a bow with a handle.' Hence, 弩 and 弓
are used here alternatively [to express the same meaning]."

[i.e., outside of] the fish belly. Follow [the vessel with your fingers] and pierce where something appears strung together.[13]

If this disease causes a person to be talkative [or] to remain silent [as if that person were] not intelligent,[14]
pierce it to [generate] three wounds.[15]

---

13 Wang Bing: "'Calf and heel' refers to the vessel at the outer side of the calf moving down right into the heel. The shape of the calf is that of the belly of a fish lying on its side. Hence, [the text] states: 'at the outside of the fish belly.' If one follows the flesh [with his fingers] and reaches where the network [vessel holding the] blood appears as if something was strung together, pierce it to let the [blood]. This should occur exactly at the Woodworm Canal (蠡溝) hole of the foot ceasing yin network [vessel], located five inches above the inner ankle." Zhang Jiebin: "腨 is the calf of the leg. 踵 is the heel. [The text speaks of a] 'fish belly' because the the calves are shaped like a fish belly. Between the calf and the heel, at the outside of the fish belly, where, if one follows [the vessel with one's finger], it is as if something was strung together, this is the Woodworm Canal hole of the foot ceasing yin network [vessel]." Lin Yi et al.: "There is a discrepancy between the text and the commentaries, in that the text speaks of the ceasing yin vessel, while the commentaries refer to the ceasing yin network [vessel]. Maybe the character 脈 in the text should be 絡."Wu Kun: "累累 is as if the evil had formed knots in the network [vessel] resembling dikes built against breakers (波隴)."

14 Wang Bing: "The ceasing yin vessel rises behind the throat, enters the palate, and encircles the base of the tongue. Hence, if it has a disease [the patient] tends to be talkative. In cases of wind abundance, [patients] are confused. Hence they are not quick-witted."Wu Kun: "言 is 自言, 'to start speaking by oneself.' 善言 is: to start speaking by oneself without being asked. 默默不慧 is: if he is asked he remains silent as if he did not understand." Ma Shi: "The ceasing yin vessel follows the back of the throat and ascends into the forehead. Hence, when it has a disease [the patient] tends to be talkative. However, when wind abounds [in this vessel], then one is confused. Hence, one remains silent as if one were not intelligent." Zhang Zhicong: "The liver rules one's speech. Hence, if it has a disease it lets one tend to be talkative. 默默 is 'quiet.' That is to say, even though one tends to be talkative, [one's speech] is not disorderly. Liver diseases are caused by wind. Persons [afflicted by wind] are often confused. Hence, they appear not intelligent." Lin Yi et al.: "When the text states 善言默默然不慧, then the two diseases of 'tending to be talkative' and 'being silent' do not go together. The Quan Yuanqi edition does not have the character 善; this makes sense."The *Tai su* does not have the character 善 either. If the character 善 were left out, the passage could be translated as: "This disease lets a person's speech become silent."Tanba agreed: "All comments here seem forced. Only if the character 善 were omitted, the text would be meaningful." 2444/44: "善言者 is: one likes to talk; 默默然 is: one does not talk. The combination of these two [states] is a contradiction. The Quan Yuanqi edition does not have the character 善; hence, one knows that the character 善 is a later insertion."

15 Gao Shishi: "The pattern requires that the piercing is carried out at three wounds at the calf, at the heel and at the fish belly." Zhang Zhicong: "Pierce three wounds

41-229-1

When it is the separator vessel that lets a person's lower back ache,
[then there is] pain pulling on the shoulders and
the eyes are unclear and
[the patients] frequently lose urine [involuntarily].[16]
Pierce the separator vessel at the transverse vessel of the outer edge of the cleft
in the parting between sinews and flesh at the knee. Let blood .
Stop as soon as the blood changes [its color].

When it is the separator vessel that lets a person's lower back ache,
as if a belt was pulled [tightly],
[then there is] a permanent [feeling] as if the lower back was broken,[17] and
[the patient] tends to have fear.[18]
Pierce the separator vessel where there is, in the cleft, a knotted network [vessel] resembling a millet grain.
When piercing it, black blood will shoot out.
Stop as soon as the blood appears red.[19]

---

outside of the calf and the heel. 'Three wounds' is [to say:] one selects holes not on the [regular] conduits."

16 Wang Bing: "The 解脈 is a vessel moving in separate [strings]. That is to say, [these strings] are not united and move separately. The [vessel] concerned here is the foot major yang conduit. It emerges from the inner canthus of the eye, ascends to the forehead and crosses the top of the skull. It follows the shoulderblades, parallels the spine on both sides and reaches the center of the lower back. It enters, follows the paravertebral sinues, encircles the kidneys and ties up with the bladder. Further down, it enters the popliteal fossa. Hence, in the case of disease these signs appear. Also, its branch course emerges from the shoulder, divides and descends, penetrates the paravertrebral muscles, follows the outer back edge of the thighs and merges below with the popliteal fossa. The two vessels cut (解) the thighs like a rope. Hence, they are named 解脈, 'separator vessels.' Zhang Zhicong: "The 解脈 are the transversely spreading network vessels moving in separate [strings]. The conduit vessels are situated in the interior; those moving transversely at the surface are the network [vessels]. The network vessels spread transversely in the skin. Hence, they are called 解脈, 'spreading vessels.'" Wu Kun: "The 解脈 is a vessel branching off from the foot major yang [conduit]." Zhang Jiebin: "The separator vessel is associated with the bladder. Hence, [in the case of disease] it lets one urinate involuntarily." Gao Shishi: "The qi of the water palace of the bladder cannot leave through the skin. Hence, one frequently urinates involuntarily."

17 Lin Yi et al.: "The *Jia yi jing* has 如裂, 'as if cracked,' instead of 如引帶."

18 Lin Yi et al.: "The *Jia yi jing* has 善怒, 'one is likely to become angry,' instead of 善恐." The *Tai su*, too, has "one is likely to become angry."

19 Lin Yi et al.: "Quan Yuanqi states: 'These are two different references to the separator vessel as a source of disease. This may be an error. One cannot be sure.'"

41-229-5

When it is the yin companion vessel that lets a person's lower back ache,
[then there is] pain [generating a feeling] as if a small weight was in there,[20]
and
there is a swelling [resulting from] dammed up [qi].[21]
Pierce the yin companion vessel at the tip of the severed bone above the outer
ankle.[22] Generate three wounds.

When it is the yang rope vessel that lets a person's lower back ache,
[then there is] above the location of the pain[23] a swelling [resulting from]
dammed up qi.[24]
Pierce the yang rope vessel where the [yang rope] vessel and the major yang
[vessel] meet. Below the calf; one foot length distant from the ground.

41-230-3

When it is the transverse network vessel that lets a person's lower back ache,
[then the patient] cannot bend down and up,[25] and, when he bends up, he fears

---

20 Zhang Jiebin: "There is pain and [a feeling of] heaviness." Lin Yi et al.: "The *Tai su* has 小針, 'small needle,' instead of 小錘."

21 Wang Bing: "This is a network [vessel] branching off from the foot minor yang [conduit]. It moves parallel to the minor yang conduit. In a distance of five individually standardized body inches above the outer ankle, it divides and runs parallel with the ceasing yin conduit downwards to encircle the instep. Hence, it is called 'yin companion vessel.' 怫 is 怒, 'anger.' That is to say, swollen as if one were angry." Ma Shi: "The [term] yin companion vessel refers to the conduit vessel of the gallbladder. It parallels the foot ceasing yin liver conduit. ... Hence, it is called 'yin companion vessel.'" Gao Shishi: "The yang walker vessel emerges from the heel. It follows the outer ankle and rises to the Wind Palace (*feng fu* 風府). It originates from the yin and leaves for the yang. Hence, it is called 'with the yin.'" Wu Kun: "It is not clear what is meant by 同陰之脈. However, when [the text states that] the the tip of the severed bone at the outer ankle is to be pierced, this is a location reached by the foot minor yang vessel."

22 *YHHYZYCD*: "絕骨 refers to the region just superior to the lateral malleolus of the fibula."

23 痛上 could also be read as: "when the pain rises."

24 Wang Bing: "The yang rope emerges from the yang. It arises from the major yang. It is one of the eight single conduit vessels." Zhang Jiebin: "The yang rope is one of the extraordinary conduits. One calls it yang rope because it is the vessel tying all the yang vessels together." Zhang Zhicong: "The yang rope ties all the yang [vessels] of the entire body."

25 Wang Bing: "衡 is 橫, 'transverse.' That is to say, the network [vessel] to the outside of the major yang moves transversely from the lower back into the outer back edge of the thighs from where it descends and merges with the central conduit in

to fall to the ground.

<One gets this from an injury at the lower back which resulted from lifting something heavy.

The transverse network vessel is ruptured and [all] the bad blood turns there.>
Pierce it in the cleft between the yang sinews; move up from the cleft for several inches. [The locations to be pierced] are situated on a transverse line. Generate two wounds and let blood.

When it is the yin meeting vessel that lets a person's lower back ache,[26] [then] sweat [leaves the body] profusely above the location of the pain.[27] When the sweat has dried up, it lets that person have a desire to drink and, when the drinking is finished, he wishes to run.
Pierce above the straight yang vessel[28] [to generate] three wounds, on a transverse line above the walker [vessel], five inches below the cleft. Look for [locations] abounding [in blood] to let blood.[29]

41-231-2
When it is the flying yang vessel that lets a person's lower back ache,

the cleft behind the knee." Zhang Zhicong: "This is a discourse on lower back pain generated by a disease in the belt vessel. The belt vessel is a network [vessel moving] transversely in the lower back. Hence, it is called 'transverse network vessel.'"

26 Wang Bing: "This is the central [section] of the foot major yang conduit. This vessel follows the lower back downwards and meets with the yin [orifice] behind. Hence, it is called 'yin meeting vessel.' This vessel runs down from the lower back to the feet." Zhang Jiebin: "'Meeting of Yin (會陰)' is a hole on the controlling vessel. It is located in front of the anus and behind the scrotum. This is where the three vessels of the controlling, the thoroughfare, and the supervisor vessel meet. Hence, it is called 'Yin meeting.' The controlling [vessel] moves from here to the abdomen; the supervisor moves from here to the spine. Hence, [when they have a disease] they cause one to have lower back pain."

27 Or: "When the pain rises, sweat leaves [the body] profusely."

28 Wang Bing: "The straight yang vessel is the major yang vessel. It parallels the spine on both sides and moves downwards. It penetrates the sacrum, moves down and reaches the center of the popliteal fossa. It moves down along the calf and passes the back of the outer ankle. It moves in a straight course. Hence, it is called straight yang vessel. 蹻 stands for 陽蹻, 'yang walker [vessel]'" Zhang Zhicong: "The 'straight yang vessel' is the supervisor vessel. The supervisor vessel suvervises the yang of the entire body and it moves straight upwards through the spine. Hence, it is called 'straight yang.'"

29 Wang Bing: "'Walker' refers to the Extending Vessel (申脈) hole originating from the yang walker [conduit] below the outer ankle. 'Below the cleft' is below the fossa of the knee." The *Tai su* has "three inches."

[then], when the pain rises, [the patient feels] as if shaken.
In severe cases, [patients] are sad and have fear.[30]
Pierce the flying yang vessel five inches[31] above the inner ankle, in front of the
minor yin, where it meets with the yin rope [vessel].

When it is the shining yang vessel that lets a person's lower back ache,
[then there is] pain pulling on the breast.
The eyes are unclear.
In severe cases [patients] are bent backwards and
their tongue curls up and they cannot speak.[32]

---

30 Wang Bing: "This is the yin rope vessel. It passes five standardized body inches
above the inner ankle. In the region of the calf it rises paralleling the minor yin conduit. {The yin rope vessel moves in front of the minor yin vessel.} The foot minor
yin vessel rises from the kidneys, penetrates the liver and the diaphragm, enters the
lung, follows the throat and parallels the base of the tongue. Its branch course leaves
from the lung, encircles the heart and pours into the chest. Hence, if [the disease] is
serious, one is grieved and has fear. Fear is generated by the kidneys; grief is generated
by the heart." Zhang Jiebin: "'Flying Yang (飛陽)' is a hole on the network [vessel] of
the foot major yang." *Ling shu* 10 has: "The branch [course] of the foot major yang is
called 'flying yang.'" Gao Shishi: "怫怫 is 'as if angry.' The pain rises as if in anger and
causes swelling." 1659/38: "怫怫 is also written 怫怫. The meaning of 怫怫 in the *Su
wen* is 滿盛, 'full.' The meaning of this passage is: When the vessel of the flying yang
lets a person's lower back ache, this pain gives one a feeling of fullness.' One should
compare this with the passage 'the pain is as if a small weight was located inside.'
Here the feeling caused by the [lower back] pain is that of a small weight hidden inside. When Zhang Jiebin explained this feeling as 嗔憤, he did not have the modern
meaning of these characters, i.e. 'anger,' in mind. 嗔 is pronounced *tian* and means
'internal fullness.' 憤, too, means 'fullness.'" For details of the argument, see there.
1132/46: "The commentary to *Xun zi* 荀子, Fei shi er zi 非十二子: '佛 is read like
勃; 勃然 is the appearance of 'rising.'"

31 The *Jia yi jing* and the *Tai su* have "two inches."

32 Wang Bing: "This is the yin walker vessel. The yin walker vessel is a branch [vessel]
of the foot minor yin. It emerges from behind the navicular bone, rises to above the
inner ankle, moves straight up, follows the yin (i.e., inner side) of the thigh, enters the
yin [orifice] and continues [inside] the abdomen. It moves up into the chest, enters
the broken basin, rises, comes out in front of man's facing (*ren ying* 人迎), enters the
inner edge of the cheekbone and ties up with the inner canthus of the eye. [There] it
merges with the major yang and yang walker [conduits] to move up further. Hence,
the appearance of lower back pain [caused by this vessel] is as [is described] here." Ma
Shi: "'Shining Yang (昌陽)' is a name of a hole on the foot minor yin kidney vessel.
Another name is Recover Flow (復溜); it is also named Deep-lying White (伏白).
The straight course of the foot minor yin vessel rises from the kidneys, passes through
the liver and the diaphragm, enters the lung, follows the throat and moves along the
base of the tongue. Its branch [course] leaves from the lung, encloses the heart and

Pierce the inner sinews – generate two wounds – above the inner ankle in front
of the large sinew behind the major yin, two inches upwards from the ankle.

41-232-2
When it is the dispersing vessel that lets a person's lower back ache,
[then the patient develops] heat.
The heat, when it is extreme, generates vexation.
[Patients have a feeling] below the lower back as if a cross-beam was in there.
In extreme cases they lose urine [involuntarily].³³
Pierce the dispersing vessel in the parting between the bone and [muscle] flesh
on the front side of the knee.
{The binding vessel enclosing the outer edge}.³⁴ Generate three wounds.

When it is the vessel of the flesh structures that lets a person's lower back ache,
[then the patient] cannot cough.
When he coughs, the sinews shrink and become tense.³⁵
Pierce the vessel of the flesh structures – generate two wounds – at [a location]
outside the major yang [vessel] and behind the severed bone of the minor yang
[vessel].

---

pours into the chest. Hence, [in the case of disease] the vessel of the 'Shining Yang'
lets one have lower back pain."

33 Wang Bing: "The 'dispersing vessel' is a branch [course] of the foot major yin
[conduit]. It rises in dispersed courses, hence, its name. This vessel follows the inside of
the thigh, enters the abdomen and links with the minor yin and minor yang [vessels]
below the lumbar vertebrae inside the cavity of the bone. Hence, in the case of disease
one has [a feeling] as if a cross-beam was located in there." Zhang Zhicong: "This is a
discourse on lower back pain caused by a disease in the thoroughfare vessel. It enters
the chest and disperses. .. Hence, it is called 'dispersing vessel.' "

34 Wang Bing: "That is to say, at the frontal inner side of the knee. The 'bone and
flesh section' is to say: below the assisting bone in the knee, the two [regions] between
the lower edge [of the knee] and the flesh of the calf. 'Enclosing the outer edge' is
the network [vessel] of the major yin which appears here in a greenish color. At the
back below the assisting bone is a large sinew holding together (攜束) the bones of
the knee and of the shinbone. One selects the vessel located where this sinew and the
bones are bound together to eliminate this disease. After three piercings [the disease]
is healed. Hence, [the text] states: 'the binding vessel; generate three wounds in it.' "

35 Wang Bing: "The vessel inside the flesh emerges from the minor yang. It is where
the qi of the vessel of the yang rope is emitted. 里 is 裡, 'inside.' " Wu Kun: " 'The vessel of the flesh structures' is not clearly identifiable." See *Su wen* 3 for the occurrence
of a similar term: 肉理.

41-232-7
When the lower back pain [parallels] the spine on both sides and
when the pain reaches to the head so that one is stiff,[36] and
if the eyes are unclear and [the patient] tends to fall,
pierce the foot major yang [vessel] in the cleft. Let blood.

When in the case of lower back pain the upper [part of the body] is cold,[37]
pierce the foot major yang [vessel] and yang brilliance [vessel].[38]
When the upper [part of the body] is hot,
pierce the foot ceasing yin [vessel].
When [the patient] cannot bend down and bend up,
pierce the foot minor yang [vessel].
In case of central heat and when [the patient] pants,
pierce the foot minor yin [vessel].
Pierce in the cleft and let blood.

41-233-3
<When in the case of lower back pain the upper [part of the body] is cold and
[the patient] cannot look back,
pierce the foot yang brilliance [vessel].
When the upper [part of the body] is hot, pierce the foot major yin [vessel].
In case of central heat and when [the patient] pants,
pierce the foot minor yin [vessel].
When the stools [pass only] with difficulties,
pierce the foot minor yin [vessel].

---

36 Zhang Zhicong: "几几 is a bird with short feathers. [The term refers to an] image
of a stiff back that one wishes to stretch out." Qian Chaochen-90/97: "几几 should
be read *jin*. It is a loan character for the homophone 掔, in the sense of 'firm,' 'stiff.'"
For a lengthy argumentation, see there. Cheng Shide et al.: "几 should be read *shu*. It
describes a stiff back that cannot be stretched comfortably."

37 Qian Chaochen-88/125: "The 99 characters from 腰痛上寒 to 刺足少陰 have
been added by Wang Bing." This statement is questionable since the first part of this
passage occurs in the *Tai su* in the same context, too. For details, see Qian Chaochen-
88/125.

38 Zhang Jiebin: "上寒 and 上熱 do refer, in all the cases [listed here], to the upper
section of the body. In the case of cold, pierce the yang conduits to remove yin evil
from the yang section." Wu Kun: "When the lower back aches and when the skin
above has cold, this is cold enclosing heat. [In such cases] one should drain the outer
region. Hence, pierce the foot major yang and yang brilliance [conduits]." The following passage of 37 characters, beginning with 痛上寒, appears in *Ling shu* 26, too, with
only two characters being different: 刺 is replaced with 取, 'select,' and 郄 is replaced
with 膕, popliteal fossa."

When the lower abdomen is full, pierce the foot ceasing yin.
If [there is a feeling] as if [the lower back] was broken and [when the patient]
cannot bend down and up, and if he cannot lift [anything],
pierce the foot major yang [vessel].
When [the pain] pulls the inner edge of the spine,
pierce the foot minor yin [vessel].>

41-233-6
When lower back pain pulls the lower abdomen and draws on the lateral abdomen,[39] and
when [the patient] cannot bend up,
pierce where the lower back and the sacrum intersect, above the two hip bones
and the buttocks.
The number of wounds to be generated varies with the waxing or waning of the
moon.
When the needle is deployed, the pain ends immediately.
<If [the pain] is on the left, select the right;
if it is on the right, select the left.>[40]

---

39 Ma Shi: "胁 refers to the indented and soft region below the flanks."

40 Mori: "The *Tai su* does not have these six characters. They were inserted here by
Wang Bing paralleling a statement in *Su wen* 63."

Chapter 42
Discourse on Wind

42-236-2
Huang Di asked:
"When wind harms a person,
it may cause cold and heat; or
it may cause a heated center; or
it may cause a cold center; or
it may cause *li*-wind;[1] or
it may cause unilateral withering; or
it may cause wind.[2]

These diseases are all different.
Their names are not identical.
In some cases [the wind] internally reaches the five depots and six palaces.
I do not know any explanation of this;
I should like to hear an explanation of this."

Qi Bo responded:
"When wind qi is stored in the skin,
it cannot penetrate into the interior and
it cannot flow away to the outside.[3]

---

1 1488/611: "癘 has the meaning of 惡, 'bad.' 癘風 is commonly called 大麻風."

2 The *Tai su* has the character 賊, "robber," in front of the character for "wind." Tanba: "The following text has 'brain wind,' 'eye wind,' 'dripping wind,' 'inner wind,' 'head wind,' 'intestinal wind,' and 'outflow wind.' Presumably, a character was omitted between the [characters] 為 and 風." Hua Shou: "The character 或 should be 均, 'all [are caused by wind].'" Guo Aichun-92: "The 12 characters beginning with 或為 風也 represent a later insertion." 390/8: "One may wonder whether 'cold-heat' is the name of a disease or refers to disease signs. .. I think, 'cold-heat' is listed here in one line with 'heated center,' 'cold center,' etc. and should be interpreted as the name of a disease. This is demonstrated by the naming of *Ling shu* treatises 21 and 70 and by the naming of diseases in the *Su wen* as 'cold-heat.'" For a detailed discussion, see there.

3 Wang Bing: "When the interstice structures open, then evil wind enters. When the wind qi has all entered, the dark palaces close tightly. Hence, [the wind qi] cannot penetrate the interior and it cannot flow away to the exterior." Zhang Jiebin: "When wind cold attacks the skin interstices, then the dark palaces close tightly. Hence, [the wind cold] cannot penetrate the interior and it cannot flow away to the exterior. This is the beginning of an affection from the outside." Wu Kun: "This is to say, at the beginning when they have received wind, the evil is in the partings of the flesh." Zhang Qi:

Wind tends to move and to undergo frequent changes.[4]

When the interstice structures open, then [patients feel] cold as if [cold water] had been poured over them.

When [the interstice structures] are closed, then [patients are] hot and [suffer from] mental pressure.[5]

When [patients are] cold, then this decreases [their intake of] food and beverages;

when [patients are] hot, then this dissolves muscles and flesh.

Hence, [this condition] lets a person tremble and be unable to eat.

{It is named 'cold [and] heat.'}[6]

"This [passage] is a mistaken insert here. It should follow the passage 風氣与太陽俱入 ... 其道不利 [further below]."

4 Yao Shaoyu: "'Tends to move' is: there is nowhere where [the wind] does not reach. 'Undergoes frequent changes' is: the signs [of the disease] differ."

5 *SWJZ*: "洒 is 滌, 'to wash.'" Zhang Yizhi et al.: The *Zi lin* states: "洒 is 濯, 'to wash.'" The *Li ji* 禮記, Yü zao 玉藻, has 色洒如也. The commentary states: '洒 is 肅驚, 'respectful,' 'awful.'" Yang Shangshan: "如洗而寒, 'as if one was cold from washing.'" Wang Bing: "洒然 is to describe '[a feeling of] cold.' 悶 is to describe '[a state of] not feeling comfortable.' When the interstice structures are open, then the wind blows softly. Hence, [patients feel] cold. When the interstice structures are closed, then the wind moves wildly. Hence, [patients] do not feel comfortable.'" Zhang Jiebin: "The wind itself is a yang evil. The yang is responsible for relaxation and outflow. Hence, it causes the interstice structures to open. When they are open, then the guard qi is no [longer kept] firmly. Hence, [patients] shiver and [feel] cold. When cold dominates, then the interstice structures close. When they are closed, then the yang qi is blocked inside. Hence, [patients] feel vexed and hot and experience mental pressure."

6 Wang Bing: "Cold wind enters the stomach; hence, [the intake of] food and beverages decreases. Heat qi is stored internally; hence, it dissolves muscles and flesh. Cold and heat merge with each other; hence, one trembles and cannot eat. This is called 'cold [and] heat.' 怢慄 is to describe 'sudden trembling resembling a [shivering from] cold.'" Lin Yi et al.: "Instead of 怢慄, the Quan Yuanqi edition has 失味, while the *Jia yi jing* has 解㑊." Zhang Jiebin: "When cold evil harms the yang, then the stomach qi cannot transform [food and beverages]. Hence, [patients] eat and drink less. When cold and heat interact, then they tremble with cold." Yao Shaoyu: "怢 is 忽忘, 'to disregard,' 'to forget.' 慄 is 戰慄, 'awestruck.' That is to say, cold and heat agitate each other and one falls unconscious." Cheng Shide et al.: "怢 is identical with 佚, in the sense of 更替, 'to replace.' 慄 is 寒慄, 'to tremble because of cold.' 怢慄, then, is: 'cold and heat alternate.' Hence, the text states further down: 'This is named cold [and] heat.' Zhang Jiebin's comment is the most convincing."

42-236-8

When the wind qi enters the stomach alongside with[7] the yang brilliance
[conduit],
it follows the vessel and rises to the inner canthi of the eyes.
In case the [afflicted] person is fat, then the wind qi cannot flow away toward
outside.
This, then, causes a heated center and yellow eyes.
In case the [afflicted] person is lean, then [the wind qi] flows away toward
outside and [the patient feels] cold.
This, then, causes a cold center and tears to flow.[8]

When the wind qi enters alongside with the major yang conduit,
it moves to the transporters of all the vessels and
disperses into the partings of the flesh.
[There] it clashes with the guard qi, whose paths are no longer free.[9]

---

7 Cheng Shide et al.: "與 is 從, 'following.'" Gao Jiwu/579: "與 is used here identically with 以, 'by way of': The wind evil enters the stomach by way of the yang brilliance conduit."

8 Wang Bing: "'Yang brilliance,' that is the stomach vessel. The stomach vessel emerges from the junction of the nose and the forehead. It descends along the outside of the
nose and enters the upper teeth. It encircles [the teeth], leaves and parallels the mouth
on both sides. It encircles the lips, descends to meet with the sauce receptacle (*cheng
jiang* 承漿), moves back along the jaws, descends at the ridge, follows the throat into
the broken basin, descends to the diaphragm and touches the stomach. Hence, [when
the wind] enters the stomach by way of the yang brilliance [vessel], it follows this
vessel and rises to the inner canthi of the eyes. When the person [affected] is fat, then
the interstice structures are tightly closed. Hence, [the wind evil] cannot flow away
toward the outside and this results in a heated center and in yellow eyes. When the
person [affected] is lean, then the interstice structures are open and the wind can flow
away to the outside. As a result, the center is cold and tears leave [the eyes]." Zhang
Jiebin: "When wind qi has settled in the yang brilliance [vessel], it enters the stomach.
The stomach is situated in the central burner; its vessel rises and connects with the
eye connection. When the person [affected] is fat, then the interstice structures are
tightly closed. Hence, [the wind evil] cannot flow away toward the outside. It stays
and causes a heated center. Hence, the eyes are yellow." Zhang Qi: "Fat persons have
lots of dampness. [In the present case] dampness and heat merge with each other.
Hence, this results in a heated center and a yellow color appears in the eyes. The interstice structures of lean persons are wide open. The wind enters easily and it also flows
away easily. When the interior is depleted, then [this results in] cold. Tears often leave
the eyes because the wind has penetrated the liver."

9 Cheng Shide et al.: "相干 is 相互干擾, 'to offend each other.'"

Hence, it lets the muscles and the flesh develop a pressure distension[10] and have ulcers.

The guard qi congeals at these places and fails to move.

Hence, the flesh has [locations where it is] numb.[11]

42-237-3

In case of *li*[-wind], the camp qi is hot and rots. This qi is not clear.

Hence, it lets the nasal column decay and ruins the complexion.

The skin has ulcers and festers.[12]

<If wind and cold settle in the vessels and do not leave,

this is called '*li*-wind.'>

{It is also called 'cold and heat.'}[13]

---

10 Cheng Shide et al.: "憤 is 發, 'to effuse.' 膜 is 脹, 'to swell.' 憤膜 is 腫脹, 'swelling and distension.'" In our interpretation of 憤 as "pressure" we follow the definition offered by *HYDCD* which cites Zhu Xi's 朱熹 explanation of 憤 in the *Lun yu* 論語, ch.7, shu er 述而, paragraph 8: 憤者心求通而未得之意, "the meaning of 憤 is: the heart seeks a throughway but fails to achieve it yet."

11 Wang Bing: "Inside the partings of the flesh is where the guard qi moves. When wind and guard qi clash against each other, they both move in the partings of the flesh. Hence, the qi paths become rough and are impassable. When the qi paths are impassable, then the wind qi attacks internally and clinches the guard qi. Hence, the flesh swells and abscesses appear outside. 瘍 is 瘡, 'abscess.' When the guard qi cannot flow around and accumulates at one location, because the wind blows against it, then the flesh has certain locations where it is numb. 不仁: not to notice cold or heat, pain or itch." Zhang Jiebin: "The qi paths are rough and impassable. When they are impassable, then the wind evil collects. Hence, the muscles and the flesh swell as if there was 'pressure distension' (憤膜) and abscesses result." Zhang Qi: "Inside the parting of the flesh is where the guard qi moves. When wind settles there, it clashes with the [guard] qi. Hence, the qi paths are impassable."

12 Wang Bing: "When wind blows it enters the conduit vessels. The camp [qi] moves in the vessels. Hence, when wind enters the vessels, it attacks the blood internally and merges with the camp qi. This merger results in heat, [causing] the blood to rot and decay. 'This qi is not clear' is to say: it disperses disorderly. Now, when [the qi in] the blood vessels disperses disorderly, all the camp [qi] will join the wind and rise through the yang vessels into the head. The nose is the location where exhalation and inhalation occur. Hence, the nasal column decays and the complexion turns bad. The skin breaks open and festers." Zhang Jiebin: "When wind cold resides in the blood vessels for long and does not leave, then the camp qi transforms into heat. Hence, the skin rots and festers." Cheng Shide et al.: "癘風 is today's so-called 麻風病, 'leprosy.'" Gao Jiwu/25: "癘 is an ancient version of today's 癩, 'leprosy.'"

13 Wang Bing: "In the beginning, [this disease manifests itself as alternating spells of] cold and heat. When the heat has become manifest, it is called 癘風." Zhang Qi:

If one was harmed by wind in spring, at *jia* and *yi*, this causes liver wind.

If one was harmed by wind in summer, at *bing* and *ding*, this causes heart wind.

If one was harmed by evil in the final month of summer, at *wu* and *ji*, this causes spleen wind.

If one was struck by evil in autumn, at *geng* and *xin*, this causes lung wind.

If one was struck by evil in winter, at *ren* and *gui*, this causes kidney wind.[14]

42-237-7

When the wind strikes the transporters of the five depots and six palaces, this, too, causes wind of the depots and palaces.

In each case it enters through the respective door.[15]

Where it strikes unilateral wind results.[16]

"The 17 character passage beginning with 風寒客於脈而不去 should appear in front of the characters 癘者."

14 Zhang Zhicong: "'Wind' refers to an imaginary, improper evil wind. Hence, [the text] speaks of 'wind' and of 'evil,' of 'harm' and of 'strike.' That is to say, the harm caused by this improper wind at times it is minor, at times it is serious." Zhang Jiebin: "Spring, *jia*, and *yi* are wood; hence, the harm is directed at the liver. Summer, *bing*, and *ding* are fire; hence, the harm is directed at the heart. Late summer, *wu*, and *ji* are soil; hence, the harm is directed at the spleen. Autumn, *geng*, and *xin* are metal; hence, the strike is directed at the lung. Winter *ren*, and *gui* are water; hence, the strike is directed at the kidneys. This is to explain how wind evil reaches the five depots inside [the body]. When this passage associates the winds of the four seasons and ten stems with the five depots, this is not to say that in spring [the wind] must harm the liver on a *jia* or *yi* [day], or that in summer [the wind] must harm the heart on a *bing* or *ding* [day]. Within the course of each day, there, too, are qi of four seasons, and within the twelve [two hour] periods there, too, is a distinction of ten stems. Hence, if one meets with the qi of spring, it will enter the liver; and if one meets with the qi of *jia* or *yi*, this, too, will enter the liver. One must associate like with like and should not stick too closely [to the letter of the text]. This applies to all qi. Also, this passage speaks of 傷 ('harm') and 中 ('strike'). Originally, [these terms] were used interchangeably and they did not denote any difference in severity. In later times, 'struck by wind' was regarded a serious [disease], while 'harm caused by wind' was considered a minor [disease]. Originally, this meaning was not part of the classic; it was forced on it [only in later times]."

15 Yao Shaoyu: "The human body has transporter holes like a room has doors. When wind evil strikes a person, it must enter via the transporter holes. Hence, [the text] states 'enters through the respective doors.'"

16 Wang Bing: "It strikes [the patient] unilaterally through the transporters on the left or right and this then results in unilateral wind." Cheng Shide et al.: "This 'unilateral wind' is identical with the 'unilateral withering' in the initial paragraph. It results from wind evil striking one side only of the human body." 1488/611: "偏風 is a general

When the wind qi follows the wind palace and rises, then this causes brain wind.[17]

When the wind enters the connection with the head, then this causes eye wind. {The eyeballs are cold.}[18]

If someone drinks wine and is struck by wind, then this causes dripping wind.[19]

If someone enters the [women's] chambers and sweats and if he is struck by wind [in this situation], then this causes internal wind.[20]

If someone has just washed [his body] and is struck by wind, then this causes head wind.[21]

---

term for harm caused by wind evil to a specific tissue region, for instance: brain wind, eye wind, head wind."

17 Wang Bing: "'Wind palace (風府)' is the name of a hole. It is located just one inch inside the hair line in the neck, in the bend between the two large sinews. In this bend is the meeting point of the supervisor vessel and of the yang tie. Upwards from the Wind Palace is the brain entrance. The brain entrance is the meeting point of the supervisor vessel with the foot major yang [conduit]. Hence, when [the wind] follows the Wind Palace and rises, then this results in brain wind."

18 2741/11: "That is: the wind evil passes along the eye connection and enters head and brain."

19 Wang Bing: "In case of strong heat the interstices open. If one is struck by wind [in such a situation], sweat leaves [the body]. It [leaves in] large quantities, like a liquid dripping [from the skin]. Hence, this is called 'dripping wind.'" Zhang Jiebin: "The nature of wine is warm and dispersing and it tends to open the dark palaces (i.e., the pores). If one is struck by wind after having consumed wine, then sweat drips without end. Hence, this is called 'dripping wind.'" Yao Shaoyu: "The nature of wine is acrid and warm; it opens obstructions and makes the qi move. If on top of it one is affected by wind evil, then sweat liquid flows away to the outside and causes the true qi to drip away."

20 Wang Bing: "When someone exhausts his essence internally and when his interstice structures open externally, then the wind attacks the interior as a result. Hence, [the text] speaks of 'internal wind.'" Zhang Zhicong: "The interior is yin; the exterior is yang. The essence is yin; the qi is yang. The yang is the protector of the yin; the yin is the guardian of the yang. When one enters the bedroom, then the yin essence is exhausted internally; when sweat leaves [the body], then the yang qi relaxes externally. If in such [a situation] one is struck by wind, then the wind qi enters the interior straight away and causes 'internal wind.'"

21 Wang Bing: "When someone is struck by wind while he washes his hair, then [the wind] settles in his head. Hence, [the text] speaks of 'head wind.'" Zhang Zhicong: "To pour water over one's head is called 沐. When the head has just been washed, then its hair interstices are open. If [in such a situation] one is struck by wind, [the wind qi] enters the skin of the head and causes 'head wind.'"

When wind enters the center over a long period of time, then this causes intestinal wind. {Outflow of [undigested] food}.[22]

When it is externally in the interstice structures, then this causes outflow wind.[23]

Hence,

the wind is the chief [cause] of the one hundred diseases.[24]

When it comes to changes and transformations, other diseases result.[25]

It has no permanent cardinal point [where it comes from].

However, [whatever] sets in does so because of wind qi."[26]

---

22 Wang Bing: "When wind is in the intestines, it rises and steams the stomach. As a result, the food remains undigested and moves downwards to leave [the body]. 飧 泄 is: undigested food leaves [the body]." Zhang Jiebin: "When wind stays for a long time and does not disperse and enters the intestines and the stomach in the process of being transmitted [through the organism], then this will result in intestinal wind with blood flowing downwards if [it is associated with] heat, and it will result in an outflow of [undigested] food if [it is associated with] cold."

23 Wang Bing: "When wind resides in the interstice structures then the dark palaces open and are passable. The wind accumulates and sweat flows away. Hence, [the text] speaks of 'outflow wind.'"

24 Yang Shangshan: "The one hundred diseases are generated by wind. Hence, [the wind] is the chief [cause of the one hundred diseases]." Wang Bing: "長 is 先, 'first.' [The wind] is at the beginning of the one hundred diseases." For a detailed discussion, see 2718/40.

25 Zhang Jiebin: "When wind enters [the body], it moves from the surface into the depth. Once it is transmitted and transformed [inside the body], it will cause other diseases."

26 Zhang Jiebin: "無常方然 is to say: It is transmitted and transformed in many ways, but whichever [disease] emerges, it is always caused by wind qi." Zhang Zhicong: "方 is 處, 'location.' That is to say, when wind evil takes residence in man, it does not stay at a permanent location. For instance, when wind qi resides in the skin, this is/causes 'cold [and] heat.' When it resides in the vessels, then this is/causes 'cold center' or 'hot center.' When it resides in the depots and palaces, then this is/causes wind of the depots and/or palaces. When it follows the wind palace, then this is/causes brain wind. .. It has no permanent location and [whatever disease] comes up does so because of wind qi." Lin Yi et al.: "The Quan Yuanqi edition and the *Jia yi jing* have 故攻 instead of the character 致." Yu Chang: "Wu Kun has 自風氣也 instead of 有 風氣也. This should be followed. Above the text states: It has no permanent cardinal point [where it comes from]. Then, in contrast, the text states: 然致自風氣也. That is to say, even though [the wind] has no permanent cardinal direction [where it resides or comes from], when a disease sets in this is always because of wind. 自 has been erroneously exchanged with 有, with the result that the meaning has been obscured."

42-238-4
[Huang] Di:
"In what way do the physical manifestations of wind [affecting] the five depots differ?
I should like to hear about their diagnosis and about the manifestations of the [respective] diseases."²⁷

Qi Bo:
"The appearance of lung wind [is such]:
[patients] sweat profusely and have an aversion to wind.
Their [facial] color is a pale white.
They often cough and are short of qi.
During daytime [the disease] abates; at night it is severe.
It is diagnosed above the eyebrows; the color there is white.²⁸

The appearance of heart wind [is such]:
[patients] sweat profusely and have an aversion to wind.
When the burning is extreme, they tend to be angry and cry out.
Their [facial] color is red.

Hua Shou omitted the five characters 致自風氣也. The *Qian jin fang* 千金方 has 焉 instead of 然.

27 Wang Bing: "診 is to say: the [disease] signs that can be put into words. 能 is to say: the physical manifestation of the disease developing inside [the body]." 419/4: "The character 診 does not refer, here, to a diagnosis of the pulse or to an inspection of one's complexion. Rather, it is identical with the character 証, 'evidence,' 'sign.'" Fang Wenhui/95: "能 is identical with 態, 'behavior,' 'development.'"

28 Wang Bing: "Whenever large quantities of wind qi are inside [the body], then there is a surplus of heat. Heat causes the interstice structures to open. Hence, profuse sweating results. When wind accumulates inside, one has an aversion to wind as a result. 䏶 (*peng*) is to say: pale white. The color [associated with] the lung is white; when it is excited, this results in cough. [The lung] rules the storage of qi. [In the present case] wind accumulates inside it. Hence, [the patient's] color is pale white; he often coughs and [suffers from] short qi. During daytime the yang qi is in the exterior [regions of the body]; hence, [the disease] is inactive. At night the yang qi enters the interior and the wind inside follows it. Hence, [the disease becomes] severe. 'Above the eyebrows' is to say: the region of the Lookout Hall above the space between the eyebrows. This is where the [condition of the] lung can be examined externally." Guo Aichun-81: "For diagnosis one must pay attention to the region above the eyebrows." Gao Jiwu/21: "差 is an ancient version of today's 瘥, 'to cure.'"

When the disease is severe, [patients find] it impossible to speak cheerfully.
It is diagnosed at the mouth; the color there is red.[29]

The appearance of liver wind [is such]:
[patients] sweat profusely and have an aversion to wind.
They tend to be sad.
Their [facial] color is slightly greenish.
When the throat is dry, they tend to be angry.
At times they hate women.
It is diagnosed below the eyes; the color there is green-blue.[30]

42-239-1
The appearance of spleen wind [is such]:
[patients] sweat profusely and have an aversion to wind.
Their body is tired and [they are] lazy; their four limbs do not wish to move.
Their [facial] color is slightly yellow.

---

29 Wang Bing: "焦絕 is to say: The lips are burned and the line structures crack open because heat makes the skin peel. When wind accumulates in the heart, then the spirit behaves disorderly; hence, [patients] tend to be angry and to terrorize others. A branch course of the heart vessels moves upwards from the heart connection on both sides of the throat and rules the tongue. Hence, when the disease is severe, one cannot speak cheerfully any longer. The color of mouth and lips is red. Hence, diagnosis is conducted here. Red is the color of the heart." Lin Yi et al.: "The *Jia yi jing* does not have the character 嚇." Zhang Jiebin: "焦絕 is: the lips and the tongue are parched and the [supply of] liquids is interrupted." Yang Shangshan: "焦 is 'heat.' 絕 is 'does not pass.' That is to say: the heat does not pass." Zhang Jiebin: "Wind transforms wood; the heart is associated with the fire. When wind accumulates in the heart, then the evils of wood and fire merge and the spirit and the mind are confused. Hence, one may tend to be angry, or one may tend to be scared." Zhang Qi: "The character 嚇 is a later addition." Guo Aichun-92: "The 'tendency to be angry' does not correspond to the heart; This phrase seems to have been mistakenly exchanged with the phrase 善 悲, 'tendency to be sad,' listed further down in the section on liver wind." Fu Weikang & Wu Hongzhou/297: "絕 is 極, 'extreme.' 言不可快 is: The orifice of the heart is the tongue. Because the tongue is heavy one cannot speak comfortably."

30 Wang Bing: "When the liver has a disease, the heart receives no nourishment. When the heart qi is depleted, one tends to be sad. The liver is associated with the [agent] wood. The color of wood is green-blue. Hence, the color [of the patient] is slightly green-blue." Zhang Jiebin: "When qi gathers in the lung, one is sad; when the liver has a disease, the lung qi avails itself of the [void]. Hence, one tends to be sad. If one tends to be angry, this is the emotion of the liver. The liver is yang in yin; its vessel encircles the sexual organ. As long as [the liver] is strong, one loves sex; when it is ill, one becomes jealous. Hence, at times one hates women."

They do not wish to eat.
It is diagnosed above the nose; the color there is yellow.[31]

The appearance of kidney wind [is such]:
[patients] sweat profusely and have an aversion to wind.
Their face develops a surface swelling of the *mang*-type.[32]
The spine aches and they cannot stand upright.
Their [facial] color is [that of] soot.
The [passage through the] hidden bend is impeded.[33]
It is diagnosed above the cheeks;[34] the color there is black.

---

31 Wang Bing: "The qi of the spleen is associated with [the agent] soil; it rules the center. The nose is also located in the center of the face. Hence, one diagnoses [the condition of the spleen] there."

32 For a discussion of "*mang*-type", see translation *Su wen* 33, note 33.

33 Wang Bing: "痝然 is to say: swollen. The color of soot is black. The kidneys are yin. [The region] below the eyes is yin, too. Hence, when the depot of the kidneys receives wind, then the face is swollen 'like 痝.' The vessel of the kidneys .. passes through the spine. Hence, the spine aches and one cannot stand upright. 'Hidden bend' refers to the locations that are hidden and involved. The kidneys store the essence and their external reflection is the intercourse. In the present case, the depot [of the kidneys] was hit by wind and the essence qi inside it is diminished. Hence, the hidden and involved matters do not pass freely." 1661/45: "Yang Shangshan considers 隱曲 as a reference to urine and stools: '隱曲不利 is to say: urine and stools cannot pass.' In contrast, Wang Bing considers it as a reference to the frontal member and identifies 隱曲不利 as a weakening of one's sexual potency. Later authors, including Zhang Jiebin, Ma Shi, and Zhang Zhicong, all followed Wang Bing. .. In reality, though, the disease of kidney wind often goes along with anuresis and with irregular passage of stools. .. Hence, Yang Shangshan's interpretation is correct." 2538/34: "All five occurrences of 隱曲 in the *Nei jing* refer to urine and stools." 852/15: "The phrase 隱曲不利 refers in the present context only to a blocked passage of urine. To interpret 不得隱曲 as indicating a blocked passage of both urine and stools does certainly make sense. Seen from the present context, though, it mainly refers to a blocked passage of stools." 2540/190: "隱曲 does not have a fixed meaning. Sometimes it refers to sexual matters, sometimes it refers to urine and stools, sometimes it specifically refers to diseases of the frontal member. One must take the specific context into account in one's interpretation." See *Su wen* 7 for further comments on the meaning of 隱曲.

34 Wang Bing: "In the present situation, the essence is insufficient. Hence, the qi turns back internally to essence. The qi does not flow into the skin. As a result, black color appears above the muscles and the skin." Zhang Jiebin: "Basically, the muscles and the flesh are ruled by the spleen. In the present case, the combined evils of wind and water lash out against the soil. Hence, one diagnoses [in the flesh] above the muscles; the color [there] should be black." Gao Shishi: "䐃 was erroneously changed to 肌 in older editions. 䐃 refers to the flesh [above] the two cheekbones. 'Above the 䐃'

42-239-4
The appearance of stomach wind [is such]:
[patients] sweat profusely in the neck and have an aversion to wind.
Food and beverages do not move down; the diaphragm is obstructed and impassable.[35]
The abdomen has a tendency to fullness.
When they take off their clothes, then [one can see] a bloating.[36]
When they consume [something] cold, then there will be an outflow.
The evidence [of this disease] includes a lean physical appearance and an enlarged abdomen.[37]

The appearance of head wind [is such]:
[patients] sweat profusely on the head and in the face and have an aversion to wind.
One day prior to the [arrival of] wind, the disease is severe.

---

refers to the cheekbones. The 䐃 are ruled by the kidneys. The *Tai su* has 頤上, 'above the jaws.'" Zhang Qi: "*Su wen* 32 says that the state of the kidneys is to be examined at the jaws. Hence, 肌 is an error for 頤." Cheng Shide et al.: "Gao Shishi is correct." 2898/21: "Wang Bing's interpretation is farfetched. From the preceding and the following passages it is obvious that the state of the other four depots is diagnosed from those regions in the face which are ruled by the respective depots and palaces. Only for the kidneys it is 'above the muscles.' Now, the muscles are not even ruled by the kidneys. Yang Shangshan's statement 'one diagnoses above the muscles' is quite wrong."

35 See parallel wordings in *Su wen* 71-491-8 and 74-508-13.

36 Gao Jiwu/165: "失 is interpreted in the *Shuo wen* as 縱 and 縱 is interpreted as 捨, which in turn stands for 舍棄, 'to discard.'"

37 Wang Bing: "The branch course of the stomach vessel starts from the back of the jaws, moves down around the edge, passes through man's facing (*ren ying* 人迎), follows the throat, enters the broken basin, descends to the diagphragm, ties up with the stomach and encloses the spleen. The straight course descends from the broken basin to the inner edge of the breasts, passes on both sides of the navel and enters the qi street. The branch course emerges from the lower opening of the stomach, follows the inside of the abdomen and merges with the qi street. Hence, one sweats profusely in the neck; beverages and food do not move down; the [passage down] is stopped up and the abdomen tends to be full. If one takes off one's clothes, then one is cold outside and hot inside. Hence, the abdomen swells. If one consumes cold food, then cold items accumulate in the stomach and the yang cannot dissolve [the food] inside. Hence, there is diarrhea. The stomach and the spleen rule the flesh. In case the stomach qi is insufficient, the flesh does not grow. Hence, emaciation results. The wind qi collects in the stomach. Hence, the abdomen is enlarged."

They have headache and cannot leave the interior.
On the day the wind arrives, the disease will somewhat abate.[38]

42-240-2
The appearance of dripping wind [is such]:
it may entail profuse sweating.
[Patients] regularly cannot wear [even] thin clothes.
When they eat, then the sweat leaves [the body].
In severe cases the body sweats.[39] [The patients'] breath is panting.
They have an aversion to wind and their clothes are permanently soggy.[40]
Their mouth is dry and they tend to be thirsty.
They cannot perform any strenuous tasks.[41]

---

38 Wang Bing: "The head is the meeting point of all yang [vessels]. When wind takes residence there, the interstices of the skin relax. Hence, profuse sweating results on the head and in the face. Now, the yang qi of man is one with the wind outside. Hence, one day before the wind [qi manifest itself] one is severely ill. Because [the disease] is severe before the wind [qi manifests itself], it also weakens early. Hence, when it comes to the day the wind [qi manifests itself], the disease has somewhat abated already. 'Interior' is to say: 'inside the house.' One cannot leave the inside of the house because the headache is severe and one does not like the wind outside." Zhang Jiebin: "Whenever one suffers from head wind, remissions and outbreaks occur irregularly. Hence, whenever the wind qi is about to break out, one day before the wind [qi breaks out] one will be ill with extreme headache. This is because the yang evil resides in the yang section. The nature of yang is to be ahead and to be fast. What arrives first must weaken first. Hence, when the day of the wind arrives, the disease has somewhat improved already." Yao Shaoyu: "先風一日 is to say: at the time when the wind has just entered the head, while no signs have appeared yet. When wind affects a person, this person does not notice this immediately. All of a sudden his head aches. Only when sweat leaves [the body] and the face swells, it is then that he knows it is 'wind.' [At this moment, though,] the pain decreases already. That is, when the wind enters, [the pain] is extreme; when [the wind] reaches to the outside, [the disease] weakens."

39 Zhang Qi: "The two characters 身汗 are a later insertion." Gao Shishi's version has 自汗, 'spontaneous sweating,' instead of 身汗. Gao Shishi: "The wording 自汗 was erroneously changed to 身汗 in older versions. I have reversed this now. 甚則汗出 is to say: The body appears to lose no sweat. When [the patient] eats, then the sweat leaves [the body]. 甚則自汗 is to say: Occasionally [the body] sweats profusely. In severe cases there is spontaneous sweating. 甚 is 多, 'profuse sweating.'"

40 Tanba Genken 丹波元堅: "The *Tai su* has 裳, 'clothes on the lower half of the body,' instead of 常. Wang Bing's commentary, too, speaks of 衣裳濡. Hence, this may have been the original wording."

41 Yang Shangshan: "If one doubles one's clothes, one sweats; if one wears thin clothes, one feels cold." Wang Bing: "Spleen and stomach [have been affected by] wind heat. Hence, [patients] cannot wear [even] thin clothes. The interstice structures

The appearance of outflow wind [is such]:
[patients] sweat profusely.
When the sweat leaves [the body] it flows out to the surface of their clothes.
Their mouth is dry inside; the above is soaked.
When this wind[42] occurs, [patients] cannot perform any strenuous tasks.
When the entire body aches, then this is [caused by] cold."[43]

[Huang] Di:
"Good!"

relax and open; hence, when [such patients] eat, then sweat leaves [their body]. In severe cases the wind accumulates in the lung. Hence, the body sweats and the breathing is panting. [Patients] have an aversion to wind and their clothes are wet. Their mouth is dry and they tend to be thirsty. When they exert their physical appearance, then their breathing is a panting. Hence, they cannot perform any strenuous tasks." Lin Yi et al.: "Sun Si-miao states: 'If one puts on clothes, the body is hot like fire.'" Gao Shishi: "Excessive sweating is a sign of depletion. Hence, one wishes to wear thick clothes. Hence, [the text] states: 'Often one cannot [wear] thin clothes.'" Cheng Shide et al.: "常 was in antiquity identical with 裳, 'clothes.'" 704/43: "Very often (常常) one cannot have the patient wear thin clothes."

42 Zhang Qi: "The two characters 其風 are a later insertion." Tanba: "The four characters 上漬其風 are unclear. They may be a later erroneous insertion." Wu Kun: "'Above' refers to the upper half of the body. Profuse sweating [causes one to be wet] as if one had been soaked in water." Zhang Yizhi et al.: "A Ming manuscript does not have these four characters 上漬其風."

43 Wang Bing: "'The above is soaked' is to say: The surface of the skin is moist as if soaked with water. This is so because of profuse sweating. Because of the profuse sweating, the [body] liquids dry. Hence, the inside of the mouth is dry. When someone exerts his physical appearance, then sweat leaves [his body] profusely. Hence, he cannot perform strenuous tasks. The entire body aches because of the profuse sweating. Profuse sweating causes a loss of yang [qi]. Hence, [patients feel] cold." Cheng Shide et al.: "能 is identical with 耐, 'to endure': 'One cannot endure any strenuous tasks.' 'The above is soaked' is to say: the upper [part of the body] above the lower back sweats profusely."

Chapter 43
Discourse on Blocks

43-240-7
Huang Di asked:
"How does a block emerge?"[1]

Qi Bo responded:
"When the three qi wind, cold, and dampness arrive together,[2] they merge and cause a block.[3]
In case the wind qi dominates, this causes 'moving block.'
In case the cold qi dominates, this causes 'painful block.'
In case the dampness qi dominates, this causes 'attached block.'"[4]

---

1 The *Tai su* does not have the character 之. Wang Bing: "安 is identical with 何, 'how.'" Zhang Zhicong: "痺 is 閉, 'closure.' The evil [qi] is closed in and causes pain." Cheng Shide et al.: "痺 has the meaning of 閉阻, 'blocked,' 不通, 'impassable.'" 2539/18 agrees.

2 Gao Jiwu/314: "For 雜, the *Yü pian* 玉篇 states: 'is identical with 同, together.' The *Guang yun* 廣韻 states: 'is identical with 集, 'to gather.'" See also Gao Jiwu/159. The *Jia yi jing* has 合 instead of 雜 and 雜 instead of 合.

3 Zhang Jiebin: "When the three qi of wind, cold, and dampness arrive together, then they block the conduits and network [vessels]. Blood and qi cannot move and the resulting disease is 'block.'" Gui Fu: "The *Shuo wen* states: '痺 is a dampness disease.' The *Cang xie pian* 蒼頡篇 states: '痺 is loss of sensation in hands and feet.'"

4 Wang Bing: "Wind is received by the yang. Hence, this causes a block which moves. Cold is received by the yin. Hence, this causes a block which aches. Dampness is received by skin, flesh, sinews, and vessels. Hence, this causes a block which is attached and does not go away." Zhang Jiebin: "When the qi of yin cold settles in the region of muscles, flesh, sinews, and bones, then it has lumped together and does not disperse. The yang qi cannot move. Hence, an unbearable pain results. In the case of an 'attached block,' the limbs and the trunk of the body are heavy and immovable. In some cases this is painful; in others a loss of sensation results. Dampness is a transformation product of the soil. The disease often manifests itself in the muscles and in the flesh." Zhang Zhicong: "Wind tends to move and it undergoes frequent changes. Hence, the respective pain moves around and has no firm location. Cold is a yin evil; pain is yin. Hence, a dominant presence of cold qi causes a painful block. Dampness flows to the joints. Hence, this causes a block attached [to a specific location.]" Yan Hongchen & Gao Guangzhen/187: "著 is identical with 着. It has the meaning of 重着不移, 'attached and static.'"

[Huang] Di:

"That there are five [types] of this [disease], why is that?"[5]

Qi Bo:

"If one encounters these [qi] in winter,[6] this leads to bone block.

If one encounters these [qi] in spring, this leads to sinew block.

If one encounters these [qi] in summer, this leads to vessel block.

If one encounters these [qi] in [the period of] extreme yin, this leads to muscle block.[7]

If one encounters these [qi] in autumn, this leads to skin block."[8]

43-241-4

[Huang] Di:

"When [the disease] proceeds into the interior and lodges[9] in the five depots and six palaces, which qi causes that?"[10]

---

5 Wang Bing: "That is to say, the qi of wind, cold, and dampness are all different. That these three [qi] are able to generate five [types of] block, this is due to the dominance of which qi?"

6 Wang Shaozeng/126: "以 is 在, 'in.' "

7 Yang Shangshan: "至陰 [is] the sixth month; it is ruled by the spleen." Hu Tianxiong: "[The term] 至陰 appears in the [*Nei*] *jing* in three meanings: 1. It is the name of a hole [used for needling]. .. 2. The kidneys are 至陰. .. 3. The spleen is 至陰. The time it rules is late summer. *Su wen* 4 states: 'The extreme yin in the yin is the spleen.' In the present context it is obvious that 至陰 is late summer. Hence, Yang Shangshan is correct. Zhang Qi has changed 至陰 to 季夏, 'the last month of summer.' This is not necessary."

8 Wang Bing: "Winter rules the bones; spring rules the sinews; summer rules the vessels; autumn rules the skin; extreme yin rules the muscles and the flesh. Hence, [in] each [season the encounter with the three qi] results in a specific block. 至陰 is to say: the months *wu* and *ji* 戊己 and the months when the soil is entrusted with government." Ma Shi: "The emergence of the five [types of] block is linked to nothing but the three qi of wind, cold, and dampness. Because one may encounter these three qi in five seasons, the resulting diseases differ. It is not so that there are five qi which enter the five depots."

9 Wu Kun: "舍 is: the evil [qi] enters and takes residence there."

10 Wang Bing: "That is to say: the blocks in the skin, in the flesh, in the sinews, and in the vessels result from an external encounter, in the course of the five seasons, [with the three qi of wind, cold, and dampness]. However, when they settle internally in the depots and palaces, how do they get there?"

Qi Bo:
"Each of the five depots has a [specific] correlate;[11] when the disease [in the bones, sinews, etc.] lasts for a long time and does not go away, it [proceeds to the] interior and lodges in the [depot that is] the correlate [of the bones, sinews, etc.] respectively.[12]

Hence,
when a bone block has not ended yet and one is affected by evil [qi] again, [the evil qi proceeds to the] interior and lodges in the kidneys.
When a sinew block has not ended yet and one is affected by evil [qi] again, [the evil qi proceeds to the] interior and lodges in the liver.
When a vessel block has not ended yet and one is affected by evil [qi] again, [the evil qi proceeds to the] interior and lodges in the heart.
When a muscle block has not ended yet and one is affected by evil [qi] again, [the evil qi proceeds to the] interior and lodges in the spleen.
When a skin block has not ended yet and one is affected by evil [qi] again, [the evil qi proceeds to the] interior and lodges in the lung.
{The so-called 'block' is a multiple affection by the qi of wind, cold, and dampness, occurring for each [depot] during its respective season.}[13]

43-241-10
Whenever a block has settled in the five depots,
in the case of a lung block, [the patient experiences] vexation and fullness, [he] pants and vomits.[14]

---

11 i.e., the bones are the asscociates of the kidneys, the sinews are the correlates of the liver, etc.

12 Wang Bing: "The liver is linked to the sinews; the heart is linked to the vessels; the spleen is linked to the flesh; the lung is linked to the skin; the kidneys are linked to the bones. When the disease continues over a long time and does not leave, then it enters [the depots] in [accordance with] these [relationships]."

13 Wang Bing: "時 is to say: the month during which the qi rules. The liver [qi] rules during spring; the heart [qi] rules during summer; the lung [qi] rules during autumn; the kidney [qi] rules during winter; the spleen [qi] rules during the final month of each of the four seasons."

14 Gao Shishi: "The lung vessel emerges from the central burner; [the lung] is the canopy covering the heart. Hence, in the case of lung block, one is vexed. The lung rules in- and exhalation; its vessels pass by the stomach opening. Hence, in the case of lung block, one pants and vomits." Wu Kun: "When wind enters the lung, then one is vexed. When dampness enters the lung, then one has [a feeling of] fullness. When cold enters the lung, then one pants. The lung vessel encircles the stomach opening. Hence, one vomits. 嘔 is the term for [a vomiting] which produces sounds but does not throw up matter."

In the case of a heart block, the vessels are not passable.[15]
When [the patient] is vexed, then there is a drumming below the heart.
There is fiercely rising qi, and [the patient] pants.
The throat is dry and [the patient] tends to belch.[16]
When receding qi moves up, then [the patient] has fear.[17]

In the case of a liver block, at night when [the patient] lies down he is scared.
[The patient] drinks a lot and urinates frequently.[18]

---

15 Wang Bing: "The heart is linked to the vessels. When [the heart] receives evil [qi],
then the vessels are impassable."

16 Wang Bing: "Evil qi causes internal disturbance. Hence, one is vexed. The hand
heart ruler vessel of the heart enclosure emerges inside the chest. It comes out [of
there], touches the heart enclosure and moves down to the diaphragm. The hand minor yin vessel of the heart emerges inside the heart. It comes out of there, touches the
heart connection, moves down to the diaphragm and encloses the small intestine. Its
branch course rises from the heart connection along the throat. Its straight course, too,
rises from the heart connection [but moves] to the lung. Hence, if one is vexed, then
there is a drum[-like] fullness below the heart. Suddenly rising qi makes one pant
and dries the throat. .. Because there is drum[-like] fullness below, [patients] belch
to make the qi leave." Gao Shishi: "When the heart is depleted, then one is vexed.
Hence, [the text states:] in the case of vexation, there is drumming below the heart.
鼓 is identical with 動, 'movement.'" Hu Tianxiong: "心下鼓 is identical with 心下
悸, 'palpitation below the heart.' 煩 should be read as 勞, 'to toil,' or 動, 'to move.'"
Tanba: "Wang Bing's interpretation of 鼓 as 滿, 'fullness,' is wrong." Mori: "As for 心
下鼓, the *Tai su* does not have the character 心. That is, 下鼓, 'below: a drum,' has the
meaning of 'distended abdomen.' Wang Bing's commentary has something to it. The
reason is, when the heart is vexed, the intestines and the stomach in the lower part of
the body are closed and this results in a drum-like distension."

17 Wang Bing: "When qi moving contrary [to its proper direction] rises and occupies
the heart, then fear results."

18 Wang Bing: "The liver rules fright. The qi [of liver and fright] correspond to each
other. Hence, in the middle of the night one sleeps and then is scared. The vessel of the
liver follows the yin (i.e., inner side) of the thighs, enters the hair, encircles the yin (i.e.,
sexual) organ, reaches the lower abdomen, passes by the stomach, touches the liver,
encloses the gallbladder, rises, penetrates the diaphragm, spreads through the flanks,
follows upwards the back of the throat and enters the neck. Hence, one drinks a lot of
water and urinates frequently." Zhang Zhicong: "When the liver qi is closed in (痹閉),
then wood and fire are suppressed and heat [results]. Hence, above this lets one drink
a lot and below one urinates frequently." Wu Kun: "The liver stores the *hun*[-soul]. [In
the present case] the *hun*[-soul] is not in peace. Hence, this causes one to be scared.
The liver vessel follows the throat. When wind dominates, then the throat loses its
liquid. Hence, one drinks a lot. When dampness dominates, then the soil cannot hold
[the dampness] under control. Hence, one urinates frequently."

Above, [the abdomen] is stretched like during a pregnancy.[19]

In the case of a kidney block, [the patient] has a tendency to distension.[20]
The sacrum serves as heels; the spine serves as head.[21]

In the case of a spleen block, the four limbs are sluggish.
[The patient] coughs and vomits liquid.
Above, it causes a massive obstruction.[22]

---

19 Wang Bing: "Above [the liver vessel] pulls the lower abdomen, [creating a feeling]
as if one were pregnant." Wu Kun: "When cold dominates, then the sinews shrink
and become tense. Hence, above and below are pulled together, as if one carried something in one's bosom." Cheng Shide et al.: "All authors interpret 引 in the sense of 'to
pull.' However, a 'pulling' syndrome appears unrelated to the appearance and feeling
generated by a pregnancy. Hence, all these comments appear to be forced. Now, the
character 引 can be used as an adjective, as for instance in the expression 引滿之弓,
'a bow stretched to the full.' The *Shuo wen* interprets 引 as 'to stretch a bow.' 引如懷,
then, is to say: the abdomen is bloated like a fully stretched bow, resembling a pregnancy. The reason is that because of the disease of liver block, the qi flow is impeded
and the liquids stagnate. This condition manifests itself as a distented abdomen." The
Tai su has 演, "to widen", instead of 引如.

20 Wang Bing: "The kidneys are the gate of the stomach. When the gate is closed,
then the stomach qi cannot revolve. Hence, there is a tendency to distension."

21 Wang Bing: "'The sacrum serves as heels' is to say: the feet are cramped. 'The spine
serves as head' is to say: the body is bent." Cheng Shide et al.: "'The sacrum serves as
heels' is to say: one can sit, but cannot get up. 'The spine serves as head' is to say: one
can bow down one's head, but cannot lift it." Zhang Yizhi et al.: "The *Chu ci* 楚辭
states: '尻以安在?' The commentary reads: '尻 is the lowermost end of the spine.'"
The meaning of this statement is not clear; it may be related to a discourse in *Zhuang
zi* 莊子 6, 大宗師, where life and death are identified as nothing but two parts of one
"body" of existence: 以生為脊, 以死為尻, "Consider life as the spine and death as the
sacrum" and 尻以為輪, "The sacrum will be made into a wheel."(See Chen Guying p.
208.) The *Tai su* has 伐, '"to hit", instead of 代.

22 Wang Bing: "The soil rules the [final months of the] four seasons; externally it
rules the four limbs. Hence, the four limbs are weak and relaxed. The reason is that
its vessel emerges from the feet, follows the calves/shinbones and rises to the knees
and thighs. Now, the spleen vessel enters the abdomen, touches the kidneys, encloses
the stomach, rises to the diaphragm and parallels the throat. Hence, [in the case of
disease], one develops cough and vomits liquid. The spleen qi nourishes the lung and
the stomach; these, in turn, are connected with the throat. Hence, [in the case of
disease], this causes a massive obstruction above." Gao Shishi: "The soil [qi] pours
into the four directions. In the case of a block, the soil qi cannot pour out. The qi has
no way but to rise, contrary to its normal direction. Hence, this causes coughing. The
beverages entering the stomach need spleen qi to have their essence dispersed. In the

43-242-2
In the case of an intestinal block, [the patient] drinks frequently, but is unable
to discharge.
The central qi pants and struggles and at times it manifests itself as outflow of
[undigested] food.[23]

In the case of a uterus block, if one presses the lower abdomen and the urinary
bladder, this causes internal pain as if hot water had been poured over [the
lower abdomen].

---

case of a block, the essence cannot be dispersed. Hence, one vomits liquid. When the
spleen qi is unable to move around, then the lung cannot remain open. Hence, this
causes a massive obstruction above." Cheng Shide et al.: "'Above this causes a massive
obstruction' means: the upper burner is blocked and impassable." Guo Aichun-92: "大
should be 不. In antiquity, 不 was identical with 否. 否 is identical with 痞, 'stoppage.'
Accordingly, 大塞 should be 痞塞, 'blockade.'" The *Tai su* has 寒, "cold," instead of
塞, "obstruction."

23 Wang Bing: "The vessel of the large intestine enters the broken basin, encloses
the lung, descends to the diaphragm and touches the large intestine. The vessel of
the small intestine enters the broken basin, too, encloses the heart, follows the throat
downwards to the diaphragm, reaches the stomach and touches the small intestine.
When in the present case the small intestine harbors an evil [qi], then the [movement
in the] vessels cannot descend to the diaphragm. When the [movement in the] vessels
fails to descend to the diaphragm, then the intestines cannot transmit and transform
and the stomach qi accumulates and becomes hot. Hence, one drinks a lot of water and
is unable to discharge downwards. The yang qi in the intestines and in the stomach
and the evil [qi] move around hastily in mutual struggle. At times they find a throughway, but the spleen qi has not performed any transformation. Hence, when from time
to time a passage results, then this is an outflow of [undigested] food." Zhang Jiebin:
"'Intestinal block' refers to both the large and the small intestines. When the block
disease is located in the intestines, then the qi of the lower burner cannot perform
any transformations. Hence, one may drink frequently, but the water cannot be discharged. When the water cannot be discharged, then both beginning and end have
a disease. Hence, [the water] struggles with the central qi. Because the clear and the
turbid are not separated, at times one develops outflow of [undigested] food." Gao
Shishi: "The large intestine is the palace of the lung. When the large intestine has a
block, then the central qi moves upwards, contrary to its normal direction. Hence, one
pants." Cheng Shide et al.: "'The central qi pants and struggles' refers to intestinal
noises." 516/79: "The character 喘 includes [among others] the meaning of 震動, 'to
tremble.' For instance, in *Su wen* 43, 中氣喘爭: the yang qi in the intestines and in
the stomach struggles with the evil qi. Hence, the processes occurring in the abdomen
resemble a condition of peristaltic hyperfunction." Wang Shaozeng/220: "The *San yin
fang* 三因方 has 急, 'tense,' instead of 爭. Because the transformed qi cannot reach
the bladder, the water cannot pass down. It moves contrary to its normal direction and
invades the lung. Hence, the central qi 'pants and is tense.'"

Urination is rough.
Above, it causes clear snivel.[24]

<As for the yin qi,
if it is kept calm, then the spirit is stored;
if it is agitated, then it wastes away and perishes.[25]
Because beverages and food are doubled,[26]

---

24 Wang Bing: "The urinary bladder is the palace of the liquids. It keeps them inside an enclosure (胞). In the lower abdomen, it is located in the [region of the] Pass Head (關元) [hole]. In there the enclosing (胞) containers are stored... Here now the enclosure (胞) has received wind, cold, and dampness qi. As a result, the [contents of the] major yang vessel [associated with the] urinary bladder cannot flow downwards into the feet. Hence [the text states:] 'if one presses the lower abdomen and the urinary bladder, this causes internal pain, as if one had poured hot water [over the patient's lower abdomen]. Urination is rough.' When urination is rough, then this is [a sign that the contents of] the major yang vessel cannot move downwards. Hence, they rise and burn that [patient's] brain and cause clear liquid to leave through the nasal orifice. 沃 is identical with 灌, 'to pour over.'" Zhang Jiebin: "胞 is the balloon[-like physical organ] of the bladder. .. Because the bladder qi is blocked it hurts internally when [the physical organ] is pressed. When the water is closed in and cannot move, then accumulations result and cause heat. Hence, this [causes a feeling] as if one had been poured over with hot water." Wu Kun: "胞 is the chamber of the essence (i.e., the male semen); in women it is called the chamber of the blood. Hence, internal pain results if one exerts pressure at the location of the uterus in the lower abdomen. If [this pressure] remains at the surface, the exterior will have no pain." Gu Guangguang: "胞 refers to the urinary bladder here. *Ling shu* 63 has 膀胱之胞薄以懦. Later commentators have interpreted this as 'the urinary bladder constituting the room of the 胞,' or they have stated: 'the 胞 is located inside the bladder.' Both versions are wrong." The *Tai su* has 兩髀, "the two hip bones (feel as if poured over with hot water)", instead of 內痛.

25 Wang Bing: "'Yin' is to say: the five spirit depots. [The text] states 'the spirit is stored' and 'it wastes away and perishes' because when someone is peaceful and quiet and does not become involved with evil qi, then his spirit qi is tranquil and is stored internally. When someone acts hastily and clashes with evil qi, then his spirit is harmed; it will leave and disperse. As a result, the depots have lost their guard. Hence, [the text] states: 'wastes away and perishes.' This is to explain how the five depots receive evil [qi] and contract a block." Zhang Qi: "The palaces are yang; the depots are yin. Hence, the qi of the depots is called dying qi." Ma Shi: "'Yin qi' is the camp qi." Hu Tianxiong: "When the essence qi of the five depots wastes away and perishes, evil qi takes advantage of this [depletion] and enters [the five depots]. Hence, this results in blocks in the five depots."

26 Wang Shaozeng/220: "自 is a hypothetical conjunction: 'if.'"

the intestines and the stomach are harmed.>²⁷

43-243-1
When excessive qi[28] [causes] panting breath, a block has collected in the lung.
When excessive qi [causes] anxiety and pensiveness, a block has collected in the
heart.
When excessive qi [causes] an [involuntary] loss of urine,[29] a block has col-
lected in the kidneys.
When excessive qi [causes] fatigue and exhaustion,[30] a block has collected in
the liver.
When excessive qi [causes] muscle rupture,[31] a block has collected in the
spleen.[32]

---

27 Wang Bing: "The depots are harmed through hasty activities; the palaces receive
injuries through beverages and food. In each case this is to say: if they operate excessively, exceeding [the limits set by] their nature, then they receive evil [qi]. This is to
explain how the six palaces receive evil [qi] and contract a block." 938/23: "The five
sentence passage 陰氣者, 靜則神藏 .. 腸胃乃傷 is unrelated to the preceding and to
the following text. Hence, it was moved by Wu Kun into *Su wen* 3 to follow the statement 腎氣乃傷, 高骨乃壞."

28 Wang Bing: "'Excessive qi' is to say: those qi that move disorderly." Wu Kun:
"When the qi has lost its balance, it is called 'excessive qi.'" Zhang Qi: "'Excessive qi'
is evil qi." 139/28: "'Excessive qi' refers to the three qi of wind, cold, and dampness."
Wang Shaozeng/220: "'Excessive qi' refers to the evil qi that has caused the block.
When a panting breathing appears, the block has accumulated in the lung."

29 The *Tai su* has 歐唾, 'to vomit/spit,' instead of 遺溺.

30 The *Tai su* has 渴乏, "dried up/thirsty and weary," instead of 乏竭.

31 The *Tai su* has 淫氣飢絕, 痺聚在胃, 淫氣雍塞, 痺聚在脾, "when the excessive qi
[causes] hunger and exhaustion, a block has collected in the stomach; when the excessive qi [causes] obstruction, a block has collected in the spleen," instead of 淫氣肌絕.
546/43: "絕, in the present context, has the meaning of 瘦削, 'emaciation.'"

32 Lin Yi et al.: "The passage beginning from 凡痺之客五藏者 up to here was moved
by Wang Bing from *Su wen* treatise 陰陽別論 to the present location." Cheng Shide
et al.: "'Excessive qi' refers to the block evil. The evil [qi] that was in the skin, the flesh,
the sinews, and the bones moves to the [body's] interior. When panting occurs, then
this evil [qi] has accumulated in the lung. This then is a lung block." Hu Tianxiong:
"The use of 'excessive qi' here is identical with that elsewhere [in the *Su wen*]. The
difference is that elsewhere it results from wind taking residence, while here the three
qi of wind, cold, and dampness take residence together. In general, the essence qi is
depleted first and evil qi takes residence in the [depleted depots] afterwards. The [pas-
sage] 淫氣喘息 [means:] Because of panting breathing, the qi is wasted and the lung
qi is disturbed in the first place. Hence, evil qi takes residence in the lung and causes
a lung block."

In all cases of a block not having ended, [the disease] moves increasingly into the interior, too.
In case the wind qi dominates, the respective person's [disease] can easily be brought to an end."³³

43-243-4
[Huang] Di:
"In the case of block, occasionally
[the patient] dies, or
a pain continues over a long time, or
[the disease] is easily brought to an end.
What are the reasons [for these differences]?"

Qi Bo:
"When the [excessive qi] enters the depots, [this results in] death.
When it stays for long in the sinews and bones, [this results in] pain continuing over a long time.
When it stays in the skin, it is easily brought to an end."³⁴

[Huang] Di:
"When it settles in the six palaces, how is that?"

Qi Bo:
"In this case, too,³⁵ the [patient's] eating and drinking [habits], as well as his place of living, constitute the basis of his disease.

Of the six palaces, too,³⁶ each has its [respective] transporters.
When wind, cold, and dampness qi strike these transporters and if food and

---

33 Zhang Jiebin: "Wind is a yang evil; it can be dispersed. Hence, this is easy to cure. However, the two blocks caused by cold and dampness are more difficult to cure. The reason is, they are yin evils. When they settle and cause blockages, it is not easy to have them move on."

34 Wang Bing: "When it enters the depots and [the patient] dies, this is because the spirit leaves. When the sinews and bones ache over a long time, this is because it has firmly settled. When it is in the skin and can be cured easily, this is because it is at the surface. These differences result from its entering deeply or remaining at the surface."

35 Wang Shaozeng/220: "亦 has the same pronunciation as 以; 以 is identical with 由, 'because.'"

36 The *Tai su* does not have the character 亦.

beverages correspond to them,[37] they enter via the transporters and each [qi] lodges in its respective palace."[38]

43-243-9
[Huang] Di:
"To treat this with needles, how to proceed?"

Qi Bo:
"The five depots have transporters;
the six palaces have confluences.[39]

Follow the division of the vessels.
Each has a place where [its qi can be] effused.
Each [such place is to be needled] in accordance with [the nature of] the excess.[40]

---

37 Hu Tianxiong: "The preceding passage 'the qi of wind, cold, and dampness strike their transporters' refers to a harm caused to the outside; 'food and beverages correspond to them' refers to harm caused to the inside. When outside and inside have all received harm, then the evil [qi] enters the six palaces and causes a block."

38 Wang Bing: "The transporters of the six palaces are also called 'transporters of the back.' The transporters of the gallbladder are on [both] sides of the 10th vertebra. The transporters of the stomach are on [both] sides of the 12th vertebra. The transporters of the triple burner are on [both] sides of the 13th vertebra. The transporters of the large intestine are on [both] sides of the 16th vertebra. The transporters of the small intestine are on [both] sides of the 18th vertebra. The transporters of the bladder are on [both] sides of the 19th vertebra."

39 Yang Shangshan: "As for the 'transporters of the five depots,' according to the pattern of treating a block [in the five depots], one selects the transporter [holes] of the five depots. .. For treating a block in the six palaces, one must select their respective confluence [holes]." Zhang Jiebin: "The [statement] 'the five depots have transporters; the six palaces have confluences' applies to depots and palaces at the same time." Gao Shishi: "Not only the six palaces have transporter [holes], the five depots have transporter [holes, too]. Not only the five depots have confluence [holes], the six palaces have confluence [holes, too]." 1133/30: "Zhang Jiebin's comment is correct. The meaning is: The five depots as well as the six palaces have transporter holes and confluence holes that can be needled for treating the conditions associated with a block."

40 Lin Yi et al.: "The *Jia yi jing* has 治, 'treat [its faults],' instead of 隨." Cheng Shide et al.: "各隨其過 has been explained in three ways. A first opinion is to interpret 過 as a reference to the path crossed by the vessels. A second opinion interprets 過 as 過失, 'fault,' i.e., the location of the disease. A third opinion – proposed by Zhang Jiebin – starts from the phrase 所過為原 and interprets 過 as a reference to the 'plain holes.' (原穴)."

Then the disease will be healed."[41]

43-244-1
[Huang] Di:
"The camp and the guard qi, do they also let a person have a block?"[42]

Qi Bo:
"The camp [qi], that is the essence qi of water and grain.
When it is harmoniously balanced in the five depots,[43] and
when it is dispersed throughout the six palaces,[44]
then it can enter the vessels.
Hence, it follows the vessels upwards and downwards, penetrates the five depots and connects the six palaces.[45]

The guard qi, that is the violent qi of water and grain.
This qi is fast and unrestrained and cannot enter the vessels.

Hence, it moves inside the skin and in the partings of the flesh.
It steams against the *huang*-membrane and
it spreads in chest and abdomen.[46]
<To oppose this qi, results in disease.
To follow this qi, results in healing.> [47]

---

41 Cheng Shide et al.: "瘳 is 'cure.'"

42 Wang Shaozeng/220: "The *Tai su* has 合, 'to merge,' instead of 令. This is correct.
The character 人 is an abbreviated version of the character 為. This sentence should
read: 營衛之氣亦合為痺乎, 'do the camp and guard qi merge, too, to cause a block?'
This corresponds to the statement further below: 不與風寒濕氣合, 故不為痺."

43 Hu Tianxiong: "和 is identical with 合, 'to merge.' 調 is 和, 'to harmonize.' This
is to say, the camp qi is generated by the harmonious blending of the essence qi of the
five grains by the five depots."

44 This interpretation of 于 as "in" rather than as "by" is supported by 740/24.

45 Wang Bing: "The camp [qi] moves inside the vessels. Hence, there is no place it
does not reach."

46 Wang Bing: "'Inside the skin and in the parting of the flesh' is to say: outside
the vessels. '*Huang* membrane' is to say: the diaphragm, [i.e.,] the central membrane
separating the five depots." Yan Hongchen & Gao Guangzhen/59: "At some places
[this term] refers to the fatty membrane below the heart and above the diaphragm.
Elsewhere it refers to the fatty membrane outside the intestines." See 906/40 for a
discussion of 肓.

47 1801/10: "That is to point out: persons whose camp and guard qi is depleted easily
contract a block condition."

The [guard qi] does not merge with the qi of wind, cold, and dampness.
Hence, it does not cause a block."

43-245-5
[Huang] Di:
"Good!

In the case of block,
some [patients have] pain,
some [have] no pain;
some [patients experience] numbness.
Some are cold,
some are hot.
Some [patients experience] dryness;[48]
some [experience] dampness.
What are the reasons?"

Qi Bo:
"In the case of pain, much cold qi is present.
[Because] there is cold, hence, there is pain.[49]
In case there is no pain, [i.e., in the case of] numbness, the disease has persisted
for a long time and it has entered [the body] deeply.
The passage of the camp and guard [qi] is rough; the conduits and network
[vessels] are often slack.[50]
Hence, they are impassable.[51]
The skin is not provided with supplies.
Hence, [this] causes numbness.
When [the patient] is cold, the yang qi is diminished, while there are large
quantities of yin qi.

---

48 Wang Shaozeng/221: "The two characters 或燥 represent a later insertion. The
answer further down does not refer to 'dryness.' That is the evidence."

49 Li Zhongzi: "In the case of cold, the blood qi coagulates. Hence, there is pain."

50 Yan Hongchen & Gao Guangzhen/189: "疏 means 空虛, 'empty.'" Wang Shao-
zeng/221: "疏 is to be interpreted as 通, 'to penetrate.'"

51 Lin Yi et al.: "The *Jia yi jing* has 疏而不痛, 'relaxed with no pain,' instead of 疏故
不通." Zhang Jiebin: "通 should be 痛, 'pain.' 疏 is 空虛, 'empty.'"

[These two conditions] add to each other in connection with the [development of the] disease.[52]
Hence, [the patient] is cold.

When [the patient] is hot, the yang qi is present in large quantities, while the yin qi is diminished.
The disease qi dominates,[53] and
the yang [qi] meets the yin [qi].[54]
Hence, this leads to block[55] heat.

When [the patient] sweats profusely and is soggy, this is so because he has met with very [much] dampness.
The yang qi is diminished, while the yin qi abounds.
The two qi affect each other.
Hence, sweat leaves [the body] and [the patient is] soggy."

43-246-2
[Huang] Di:
"Now,
as for the disease of block, when it is without pain, how is that?"

Qi Bo:
"A block,
when it occurs in the bones, then [the body feels] heavy.
When it occurs in the vessels, then the blood congeals and does not flow.
When it occurs in the sinews, then [the body is] bent and cannot be stretched.
When it occurs in the flesh, then [the patient experiences] numbness.
When it occurs in the skin, then [the patient] is cold.
Hence, if [a patient] has any of these five [diseases], then he feels no pain.

---

52 Wang Bing: "Because the original disease was caused by the qi of wind, cold, and dampness, yin qi may add to it."

53 Wang Shaozeng/221: "The three characters 病氣勝 are a later insertion. These three characters do not appear in this passage as it is quoted in the 聖濟總錄."

54 Wang Bing: "遭 is 遇, 'to encounter.' That is to say, it encounters yin qi. The yin qi cannot overcome [the yang qi]. Hence, this results in heat." Lin Yi et al.: "The *Jia yi jing* has 乘, 'to occupy,' instead of 遭."

55 Wang Shaozeng/221: "The *Jia yi jing* does not have the character 痺 below 為. The statement above is 故為寒; this is the exact parallel to the present statement." Yan Hongchen & Gao Guangzhen/189: "痺熱 is 熱痺, 'heat block.'"

For all types of block [the following applies.]
When [the patient] encounters cold, then this results in [a sensation of crawling] insects;[56]
when he encounters heat, then this results in slackening."

[Huang] Di:
"Good!"

---

56 Wang Bing: "蟲 is to say: [a feeling] as if insects moved inside the skin." Lin Yi et al.: "The *Jia yi jing* has 急, 'tense,' instead of 蟲." Gao Shishi: "This is to say: cold merges with dampness, heat merges with dryness. When a dampness block meets with cold, then the cold and the dampness clash with each other and insects are generated as a result. When insects are generated, this results in itch." Sun Yirang: "虫 should be read as 疰. According to *SWJZZ*, 疰 is identical with 疼, 'pain.'" Li Guoqing and Qian Chaochen-88/42 agree; for a detailed argument, see the latter. 2636/51: "The *Jia yi jing* is correct; Wang Bing was wrong."

Chapter 44
Discourse on Limpness[1]

44-246-7
Huang Di asked:
"When the five depots let a person [suffer from] limpness,
how is that?"[2]

Qi Bo responded:
"The lung rules the body's skin and body hair.
The heart rules the body's blood and vessels.
The liver rules the body's sinews and membranes.
The spleen rules the body's muscles and flesh.[3]
The kidneys rule the body's bones and marrow.[4]

Hence,
when the lung is hot and when the lobes burn,
then the skin and the body hair are depleted and weak.
[The skin is] tense [and the body hair is] thin.
When [the heat] is stuck,[5]

---

1 Wang Bing: "痿 is to say: 痿弱無力以運動, 'weak, without strength to move.'"
Cheng Shide et al.: "痿 is identical with 萎, 'to dry.' That is, the four limbs dry and
lose their motility." *SWJZ*: "痿 is 痹, 'block.'" *Yu pian*: "痿 is inability to walk; 痹 is
dampness disease." Zhang Yizhi et al.: "痿 and 痹 refer to different [diseases]. Generally speaking, what is associated with pain, that is 痹; those without pain, but going
along with numbness and weakness, these are 痿 [diseases]."

2 Gao Jiwu/483: "五藏 should be 五藏熱邪, 'heat evil in the five depots.'"

3 *SWJZ* and *Guang ya*: "肌 is 肉."

4 Wang Bing: "[The body parts] ruled [by the depots] differ. Hence, when [the
depots] generate limpness, [these states] are associated with the [different body parts]
each of them rules."

5 Zhang Jiebin: "If the heat qi stays and does not leave and proceeds to the sinews,
vessels, bones, and flesh, then the disease of limpness and inability to walk develops."
Cheng Shide et al.: "著 means 留著不去, 'to stay and not to leave.'" 393/370: "The
Jia yi jing has: 故肺氣熱則葉焦. 焦則皮虛弱. 急薄著. 著則生痿躄矣. The *Tai su*
has: 故肺氣熱葉焦. 則皮毛膚弱急薄著. 則生痿辟. Yao Shaoyu has: 故肺熱葉焦則
皮毛虛. 弱急薄著. 則生痿躄也. Ma Shi has interpreted this as 'Hence, when the
lung is hot and the lobes burn, then the skin and the body hair are depleted, weak,
tense, and thinned out. When [the heat] stays, then this causes limpness and an inability to walk.' Most later commentators have adopted this interpretation, including
some of our own time. As far as I know, today it is only Wang Qi who reads 薄著 as
a sequence of separate meanings, and he comments on 急薄著 as follows: '急 is 急

then [this] causes limpness with an inability to walk.[6]

When the heart qi is hot,
then the [qi in the] lower vessels recedes and turns upwards.
When it turns upwards, then the vessels below are depleted.
When they are depleted, then [this] generates vessel limpness.

<The pivot is broken [; it cannot be employed to] raise [something].[7]
The shins are slack and [can]not be employed to [walk on] the earth.>[8]

迫 ("urgent," "pressing"); 薄 is 薄弱 ("weak"); and 著 refers to an evil that stays and does not leave.' My own opinion is that [the two characters] 薄著 should not be read separately. Except for the *Su wen*, this phrase also appears in *Ling shu* 5 where it is clearly a disyllabic expression. Also, it appears in [ancient] dictionaries, such as Liu Xi's 劉熙 *Shi ming* 釋名, Shi yan yu 釋言語, where it is stated: 縛, 薄也, 使相薄著也. From this it can be seen that this was a rather popular phrase at the time of the Han. It was only in later times that it became obsolete. Wang Xianqian 王先謙 of the Qing dynasty has stated in his *Shi ming shu zheng bu* 釋名疏証補: 薄著 is to say 附著, ('to adhere to.') The *Shuo wen* states: 急 is 褊 ('narrow'). Hence, 急 is 皺急 ('wrinkled') and has the same meaning as 薄著." Yan Hongchen & Gao Guangzhen/184: "急薄 refers to a dry skin."

6 *SWJZGL* vol. 11, p. 1203: 躄 does not occur in the *Shuo wen* but has the same meaning as 躃 which, according to the *Shuo wen* , is: "a person cannot walk." Wang Bing: "躄 is to say 攣躄; the feet cannot be stretched to walk." Zhang Jiebin: "'Lung limpness' is limpness of the skin and the body hair. When heat occupies the lung, [i.e. the agent] metal, then the lobes burn internally, while the skin and the body hair are depleted and weakened and turn tense and thin externally. When the heat stays and does not leave and when it proceeds to the sinews, the vessels, the bones, and the flesh, then the disease generates 'limpness and loss of motility.'" Ma Shi: "When the heat stays and does not leave, the lung is the mother, the kidneys are the son. The kidneys receive heat qi and the feet are bent and cannot be stretched. This results in the condition of 'limpness and loss of motility.'" Cheng Shide et al.: "When the four limbs are paralyzed and weak, this is called 痿; when the two feet cannot walk, this is 躄. 痿躄 is an encompassing term used here to denote a loss of function of the four limbs."

7 Yan Hongchen & Gao Guangzhen/184: "'Pivot' refers to the major joints here, such as the knees and the elbows. 折 is 斷折, 'to break,' or 脫位, 'dislocation.' The meaning is, one cannot move the joints as one would like to; it is as if they were broken or dislocated."

8 Wang Bing: "When the heat in the heart abounds, then the fire shines alone. When the fire shines alone, then it flames upwards internally. Normally the movement in the kidney vessels is directed downwards. In the present case, the fire abounds and flames upwards. Hence, the movement in the kidney vessels follows the fire and is reverted upwards, contrary to its normal direction. ... When the yin [qi] moves upwards to the diaphragm, the yang [qi] below has nothing to guard its residence. The heart qi penetrates the vessels; hence, [this] causes vessel limpness; the kidney qi rules the feet. Hence, the

When the liver qi is hot,
then the gall flows away.
The mouth has a bitter [taste]; sinews and membranes turn dry.
When sinews and membranes are dry,
then the sinews become tense and are cramped.[9]
This develops into sinew limpness.[10]

When the spleen qi is hot,
then the stomach dries and one is thirsty.
The muscles and the flesh are numb.
This develops into limpness of the flesh.[11]

---

axis of the knee joint is as if it were broken and cannot serve to raise [the feet]. The sinews of the shin slacken and cannot operate [to walk on] the earth." Zhang Jiebin: "In case of 'vessel limpness,' it appears as if the pivot was broken at all the joints of the four limbs. They cannot be raised. The feet and the shins slacken and cannot operate [to walk on] the earth." Cheng Shide et al.: "樞 is 樞紐, 'pivot,' 'axis.' Here [this term] refers to the joints. 挈 means 提挈, 'to raise.' The movement of the joints of the four limbs has lost its spirit; they cannot be raised. As if a pivot was broken." Hu Tianxiong: "The original text states 挈, not 不相. Where do the two characters 不相 in Wang Bing's commentary come from? Wang Bing has supplemented the text to explain it. Yang Shangshan, in his commentary, does not refer to the character 挈; he shortened the text to explain it. Hence, neither [Wang Bing's nor Yang Shangshan's comment] is acceptable. The character 折 has the meaning of 傷害, 'injury,' 'harm.' If one reads this passage as 'when the supporting ability of the joints is harmed, then the shins slacken and cannot operate [to walk on] the earth,' then the text appears meaningful." Zhang Jiyou: "挈 is used here in the sense of 垂解, 'slack.'" Tanba: "The *Shuo wen* states: 挈 is 懸持, 'to support through suspension.' Hence, Wang Bing is correct when he comments that the central part of the knee loses its ability to support [the body] through suspension [of the leg] as if it were broken." The monograph on *mu dan* 牡丹 in the *Shen Nong ben cao jing* 神農本草經 has 瘲 together with 痙 in the context of "convulsions," "spasms." Yu Chang: "Above the character 挈 a character 不, 'not,' appears to be missing. Hence Wang Bing comments: '.. cannot serve to raise [the feet].' Obviously, the version at the disposal of Wang Bing had 不挈. If the wording had been 挈 only, how could Wang Bing have meant to state 不相提挈? Also, the three characters 樞折挈 make no sense."

9 1588/45: "急 is 強急, 'tense;' 攣 is 攣縮, 'contracted.'"

10 Wang Bing: "The gallbladder is tied to the lobes of the liver and the flavor of its juice is extremely bitter. Hence, when the liver is hot, then the gall liquid overflows. When the gallbladder has a disease, then the mouth has a bitter taste. In the present case, the gall liquid overflows. Hence, the mouth has a bitter taste. The liver rules the sinews and the membranes. Hence, in case of heat the sinews and the membranes dry, cramp, and become tense. This develops into sinew limpness."

11 Wang Bing: "The spleen and the stomach are connected through a membrane. When the spleen qi is hot then the stomach liquid overflows. Hence, [the stomach]

When the kidney qi is hot,
then the lower back and the spine cannot be raised.
The bones dry and the marrow decreases.
This develops into bone limpness."[12]

44-247-2
[Huang] Di:
"How does one contract these [conditions]?"

Qi Bo:
"The lung is the chief of the depots.
It is the canopy covering the heart.[13]
In case of a loss, or in case one longs for something but does not get it,
then this manifests itself as lung noises.
When such noises [appear], then the lung is hot and the lobes burn.[14]

Hence, when it is said: 'Because the lung is hot and the lobes burn, the five
depots develop limpness with an inability to walk,' then this means just the
same.[15]

---

dries up and one is thirsty. The spleen rules muscles and flesh. In the present case,
heat accumulates inside of it. Hence, the muscles and flesh have no sensation and this
develops into flesh limpness."

12 Wang Bing: "The lower back is the palace of the kidneys. Also, the kidney vessels
ascend inside the thighs, penetrate the spine and touch the kidneys. Hence, when
the kidney qi is hot, then the lower back and the spine cannot be lifted. The kidneys
rule the bones and the marrow. Hence, in case of heat the bones dry and the marrow
decreases. This develops into bone limpness."

13 Wang Bing: "The position [of the lung] is high and it spreads its lobes through the
chest. Hence, it is the director of the depots and it is a canopy covering the heart."

14 Wang Bing: "One's mind is marked by bitterness and lack of joy because the qi is
suppressed. The lung stores the qi. When the qi is suppressed and cannot flow freely,
one pants as a result. The breathing is noisy and the lung is hot, its lobes burn."

15 Hu Tianxiong: "The *Jia yi jing* does not have the nine characters beginning with
故曰 and it does not have the characters 此之謂也. In the *Tai su*, only the character
曰 following the 故 is missing. Hence, this must be a quotation from an ancient classic
which was widely known at the time. Hence, it begins with 故曰 and ends with 此之
謂也. This is not a comment added by Wang Bing." 20/55: "Qian Xizuo 錢熙祚 holds:
'These nine characters are not necessary.' However, [this passage] conforms with the
text above; it should be explained as coherent with the text, not as a later insertion."

When sadness and grief are excessive,
then the network [vessels] of the uterus rupture.
When the network [vessels] of the uterus rupture,
then the yang qi is agitated internally.
When it is effused, then a collapse occurs below the heart.
[Patients] frequently pass urine with blood.[16]

44-247-7
Hence, the *Ben bing* states:
'When the large conduits are empty and depleted,
this develops into muscle block,[17]

---

16 Wang Bing: "When [someone] is grieved, then his heart connection is tense. The
lobes of the lung rise and the upper burner is impassable. The camp [qi] and the guard
[qi] fail to dissipate and heat qi is in the center. Hence, the [heart] enclosing network
ruptures and the yang qi moves drum[-like] internally. When this occurs, then there
is a collapse below the heart, with frequent passages of urine with blood. 'Collapse
below the heart' is to say: the heart enclosure breaks down internally and blood moves
downwards. 溲 is to say 溺, 'to urinate.'" Lin Yi et al.: "Yang Shangshan states: '胞絡
is the [heart] enclosing vessel above the heart.' Actually, the character 胞 should be 包.
The Quan Yuanqi version has 肌, 'muscles,' instead of 胞." Yao Shaoyu: "The function
of the enclosing network is to protect the heart. In case of excessive sadness and grief,
the qi is tense and the enclosing network is injured. When the network is injured, then
the heart falls ill. Now, the heart is associated with fire and it rules the blood. When the
heart is ill and fire is effused, then the blood cannot remain quiet. It flows downwards
to join the urine." Gao Shishi: "胞 is a mistake for 包. 包絡 is the network [vessel] of
the heart enclosure. When this enclosing network [vessel] ruptures, then blood flows
to the outside. 下崩 is a frequent passage of urine with blood." Cheng Shide et al.: "崩
is 'landslide.' Here it refers to a massive downflow of blood." Zhang Jiebin: "The 胞
絡 is the network vessel of the uterus." Wu Kun: " 胞 refers to the chamber of essence
(i.e., semen). In females, this is the sea of blood. 'The 胞絡 ruptures' is: the network
vessel of the enclosure ruptures. 心下崩 is: the blood of the heart rushes downwards
like a landslide." Zhang Zhicong: "胞絡 is the large network vessel of the enclosure,
i.e., the throughfare vessel. The throughfare vessel emerges from within the enclosure;
it is the sea of the twelve conduit vessels. The heart rules the blood [and the] vessels.
Hence, when the enclosing network ruptures, then the heart qi is depleted and there
is internal agitation." See *Su wen* 47-259-7/8 for a use of 胞之絡 and 胞絡 suggesting
that the term is not, or at least not always, used as a binome. Judged from the context
of *Su wen* 47, where a health problem of a pregnant woman is discussed, the meaning
here as there appears to be: "the network [vessels] of the uterus."

17 2107/56: "The *Tai su*, Wu zang wei 五藏痿, has 脈痺, "vessel block," instead of
肌痺. This passage discusses limpness as a result of heat in the heart. The heart rules
the blood vessels. Hence, the character 肌 is a mistake for 脈." Mori: "肌痺 makes no
sense. One should follow the version of the *Tai su*."

which is transmitted further to turn into vessel limpness.'¹⁸

When pondering is without limits,
when one does not get what one had longed for,
when [lewd] sentiments flow unrestrained to the outside and
when one enters the [women's] chambers excessively,
[then] the basic sinew slackens.
This develops into sinew limpness.¹⁹

---

18 Wang Bing: "*Ben bing* is the name of a treatise in an ancient classic. 'Large conduits' refers to the major conduit vessels. Because the heart breaks down and because of the passage of urine together with blood, the major conduits are empty. When the vessels are empty, then the heat collects internally. The guard qi abounds, while the camp qi is diminished. Hence, this develops into a muscle block. First one observes a muscle block, later this turns into a vessel limpness. Hence, [the text] states: 'is transmitted further to turn into vessel limpness.'" Zhang Zhicong: "'Large conduits' refers to the large network [vessels] of the uterus. The uterus is the blood chamber....The blood of the network [vessels] of the uterus moves half inside the vessels, half inside the skin interstices. When the blood outside the vessels is diminished, then this causes muscle block. When the blood inside the vessels is diminished, then this causes vessel limpness." Gao Shishi: "'The large conduits are empty and depleted' is compared to the rupturing of the [heart] enclosing network [vessel]. When the [heart] enclosing network [vessel] ruptures and blood flows down with the urine, then [the blood] cannot fill the muscles and flesh in the exterior. Hence, this develops into muscle block. Furthermore, it cannot circulate internally through the conduit vessels. Hence, it develops into vessel limpness." Cheng Shide et al.: "Wang Bing identifies 'large conduits' as the large conduit vessels; Zhang Zhicong interprets 'large conduits' as reference to the large network [vessels] of the uterus. Gao Shishi says it is the heart enclosing network. However, given that the first paragraph states 'the heart rules the blood vessels,' and 'when the heart qi is hot, this generates vessel limpness,' Wang Bing's comment is the most convincing." Hu Tianxiong: "The *Tai su* has 發為脈痺. Yang Shangshan commented: 'When urine is passed together with blood, this causes vessel depletion and develops into a vessel block.' Given that the text above has 'the large conduits are empty and depleted,' the version of the *Tai su* seems to be correct."

19 Gao Shishi: "That is, one has excessively exhausted oneself in sexual intercourse. Hence, the yin (i.e., sexual) organ is weak." Ma Shi: "*Su wen* 45 states: 'The front yin (i.e., the sexual organ) is where the basic sinews come together.' Hence, the sexual organ cannot be the basic sinew." Yu Chang: "宗 is to be interpreted as 眾, 'all.' The *Guang ya* 廣雅, Shi gu 釋詁, states: '宗 is 眾, 'all.' 宗筋 is like 宗讒, 'all slander.' 宗讒 is 眾讒; hence 宗筋 is 眾筋, 'all sinews.' Hence, further down the text states: 'The meeting of all the yin and the yang sinews.' And *Su wen* 45 states: 'The front yin is where all the sinews come together.' Where *Su wen* 45 has 宗, the *Jia yi jing* has 眾." Hu Tianxiong: "All commentators have assumed that 宗筋 refers to the sexual organ. Only Yu Chang has pointed out that 宗 is 眾. The arguments he quotes are quite strong. However, whenever the *Su wen* refers to 宗筋, this is in the context of

<It also causes white overflow.>[20]

Hence, the *Lower Classic* states:
'Sinew limpness is generated by <the liver> sending inwards.'[21]

When someone is submerged in dampness,
[because] his work has to do with water, and
if some [dampness] stays [in the body], or
when someone's place of living is damp,[22] and
his muscles and flesh are soggy,[23]

---

sexuality. Basically, it is without any doubt that the original meaning of 宗筋 is 眾筋, 'all sinews.' When 'all the sinews' slacken, then the front yin (i.e., the sexual organ), where 'all the sinews' meet, slackens, too. ... To avoid the term 'front yin,' and to say 'all vessels' instead is the same as to avoid the term 'go to the toilet,' and to say 'to change clothes' instead. *Ling shu* 28 has 目者宗脈之所聚, 'the eye is where all vessels gather,' and 耳者宗脈之所聚, 'the ear is where all vessel gather.' The ears and the eye are not termed 'all vessels' here because there is no distinction between vulgar and aesthetic designations [of these organs]. Hence, there is no need to avoid [the former]." *NJCD*: "宗筋 is 眾多筋, 'numerous sinews.'" We wonder wether 宗筋 is a transliteration or translation of a foreign term, the meaning of which was lost by the time comments began to be written on the text.

20 Wang Bing: "白淫 is to say: white matter overflows, resembling essence (i.e., semen). In men it moves down with the urine; in women it continuously moves down from the yin (i.e., sexual) organ."

21 Wang Bing: "*Lower Classic* is the title of an ancient classic. 'Sending inwards' is to say: to exhaust the yin (i.e., sexual) strength and to waste the essence qi." Hu Tianxiong: "The *Tai su* has 生于使內; the character 肝 is missing. This is the original text of the ancient classic *Lower Classic*. The character for 'liver' may have been inserted by some ignoramus later on the basis that the liver vessel encloses the sexual organ and rules the sinews. However, further down the text does not state 生于脾 where the flesh limpness is concerned and it does not state 生于腎 where the bone limpness is concerned. Hence, one should follow the *Tai su*. Yang Shangshan: "'Sending inwards' refers to entering the [women's] chambers (i.e., sexual intercourse)." Zhang Zhicong: "*Lower Classic* is the 73rd treatise further below, the 本病論; it is lost now."

22 Zhang Jiebin: "相 is 并, 'together with.'" Wu Kun: "相 is 伴, 'to go along with.'" Zhang Zhicong: "Inside and outside are both damp." Tanba: "The character 相 is difficult to explain." Zhang Qi: "Something is wrong with the four characters 居處相濕." Instead of 相, the *Jia yi jing* has 傷, 'receive harm.'" 2271/39: "The character 相 is a mistake; the *Jia yi jing* has 傷, 'receive harm.' 相 and 傷 have an identical vowel formation; hence, the mistake."

23 Yang Shangshan: "If one is soaked by staying at a damp location, this develops into a muscles and flesh block with a loss of sensation." Wu Kun: "漸 is 近, 'near,' 'to approach.'" Wang Bing: "If one works in a damp environment, or if one lives in the

a block [develops together with] numbness.
This develops into flesh limpness.[24]

Hence, the *Lower Classic* states:
'Flesh limpness is acquired on damp earth.'

44-248-5
It happens that someone walks a long distance and is exhausted to fatigue.
He encounters massive heat and becomes thirsty.
When he is thirsty, then the yang qi attacks internally.
When it attacks internally, then the heat lodges in the kidneys.
{The kidneys are the depot of water.}
Here now, the water does not dominate the fire.
As a result the bones dry and the marrow is depleted.
Hence, the feet cannot support the body.
This develops into bone limpness.[25]
Hence,
the *Lower Classic* states:
'Bone limpness is generated by massive heat.' "[26]

---

marshes, all this is 'one's work has to do with water.' When a healthy person stays idily
in such an environment for long and is affected by its [dampness, the resulting harm]
is particularly severe." Zhang Zhicong: " 'To have to do with water' is to prefer to drink
watery broths, with the damp turbidity staying in [the body]."

24 Wang Bing: "The flesh is associated with the spleen. The spleen qi has an aversion
to dampness. When dampness stays inside, then the camp qi cannot flourish. Hence,
the flesh develops limpness."

25 Wang Bing: " 'The yang qi attacks internally' is to say: it attacks the yin qi inside
the abdomen. The water cannot dominate the fire because the heat has settled in the
kidneys." Zhang Zhicong: "When one walks far and is tired to exhaustion, then this
harms the kidneys. When one encounters massive heat, then the summerheat/heat-
stroke harms the yin. When one is thirsty, then the yin liquid inside is exhausted. This
is because the qi of yang heat has internally attacked the yin and the heat has merged
with the kidneys. The kidneys are the depot of water. When the water abounds, then
it can control the fire. In the present case, the yang abounds and the yin is diminished.
The water cannot dominate the fire. Hence, the bones dry and the marrow is depleted.
The feet cannot operate [to walk on] the earth and this develops into bone limpness."

26 Wang Bing: "The kidneys, by their nature, hate dryness. Contrary [to what is normal, here now] heat resides inside of them. Because of this accumulation of heat the
bones dry. Hence, [this develops into] bone limpness, [i.e.,] an absence of strength."

44-248-9
[Huang] Di said:
"How to distinguish these [states]?"

Qi Bo:
"In case of lung heat,
the complexion is white and the body hair breaks.
In case of heart heat,
the complexion is red and the network vessels overflow.
In case of liver heat,
the complexion is greenish and the nails dry.
In case of spleen heat,
the complexion is yellow and the flesh [lets one feel a] wriggling movement.[27]
In case of kidney heat,
the complexion is black and the teeth wither."[28]

[Huang] Di:
"As you, Sir, have outlined it, this is alright.
The discourse[29] states:
'To treat limpness, select only the yang brilliance.'
Why is that?"[30]

Qi Bo:
"The yang brilliance [conduit],
it is the sea of the five depots and six palaces.[31]
It is responsible for keeping the basic sinews moist.[32]

---

27 Zhang Jiebin: "This is like a slight movement; it is also called 虫行, 'insects moving.'" The *Tai su* has 濡, "damp", instead of 蠕.

28 Ye Gang/59: "The 'color' referred to in these sentences is the complexion of the face."

29 Zhang Jiebin: "*Ling shu* 5 states: 'In case of limpness, take it from the yang brilliance.'" Wu Kun: "This, too, is an ancient discourse." Zhang Zhicong: "This is a quotation from *Su wen* 73."

30 For a justification of why only the yang brilliance conduit is suitable for a treatment of limpness, see 846/53. See also 287/29, 750/2, 467/29, 2932/46, and 39/22.

31 Wang Bing: "The yang brilliance [vessel] is the stomach vessel and the stomach is the sea of water and grain."

32 Cheng Shide et al.: "閏 is 潤. The *Tai su* has 潤 in the sense of 滋養, 'to nourish.'"

{The basic sinew is responsible for binding together the bones and for the free movement of the trigger joint.}³³

44-249-1
The thoroughfare vessel,
it is the sea of the conduit vessels.
It is responsible for pouring [liquid] into the ravines and valleys.³⁴
It unites with the yang brilliance [conduit] at the basic sinew.³⁵

The yin and the yang [conduits] are brought together at the meeting point with the basic sinew,
{This meeting takes place at the qi street},³⁶
and the yang brilliance [conduit] is their chief.³⁷

---

33 Wang Bing: "宗筋 is to say: the firm sinew above and below the transverse bone in the yin (i.e., pubic) hair. Above it connects the chest and the abdomen; below it penetrates the thighs. Also, it passes through the back and the abdomen upwards into the head and nape. Hence, the [text] states: 'The basic sinew is responsible for binding together the bones and for the free movement of the trigger joint.' Now, the lower back is the major joint of the body. It is by the [lower back] that bending and stretching are controlled. Hence, it is called 機關, 'trigger joint.'" Ma Shi: "It controls bending and stretching. Hence, it is called 機關."

34 Wu Kun: "The thoroughfare vessel is one of the [eight] extraordinary conduit vessels. It receives blood from the twelve [ordinary] conduits for the monthly affair of the women. Hence, it is the sea of the conduit vessels."

35 Wang Bing: "The thoroughfare vessel follows the abdomen and passes on both sides of the navel in a distance of five parts of an individually standardized body inch. The yang brilliance vessel, too, moves upwards on both sides of the navel, [however:] in a distance of one and five parts of an individually standardized body inch. The basic sinew vessel is in the middle. Hence, [the text] states: 'it merges with the yang brilliance at the basic sinew.' Since it is considered the 'sea of the twelve conduits,' it 'pours [its contents] into the ravines and valleys.' The large fissures of the flesh are the 'valleys;' the small fissures of the flesh are the 'ravines.'"

36 Wang Bing: "The qi street refers to the locations on both sides of the pubic hair where the movement in the vessels [can be felt]. The belt vessel encircles the body once on the level of the soft ribs and ties up with the supervisor vessel. The supervisor vessel rises and descends from the Pass Head (關元) [hole], along the abdomen. The supervisor vessel, the controlling vessel, and the thoroughfare vessel, these three vessels have the same starting point, but they differ in their further courses."

37 We follow the *Yu pian* 玉篇: "揔 is identical with 合, 'to merge.'" In contrast, Cheng Shide et al.: "揔 is identical with 總, 'all.'" Zhang Jiebin: "The front yin (i.e., the sexual organ) is the meeting place of the three yin vessels of the feet, of the yang brilliance, of the minor yang, of the thoroughfare, the controlling, the supervisor, and

They are all connected with the belt vessel,[38] and
they are connected with the supervisor vessel.
Hence, when the yang brilliance [conduit] is depleted,
then the basic sinew slackens and the belt vessel fails to pull [tight].[39]
Hence, the feet suffer from limpness and do not function."[40]

---

the walker [vessels, i.e, of] nine vessels. Among these nine [vessels], the yang brilliance is the sea of the five depots and six palaces. Since yin and yang [conduits] are
brought together (總) here, [the text] states 陰陽總宗筋之會." Wu Kun: "長 is like
主, 'to rule.'"

38 Wu Kun: "屬 is 受其管束, 'is under its control.'"

39 Wang Bing: "引 is to say: 牽引, 'to draw.'"

40 1926/46: "Qi Bo does not respond here to the question raised above: 'To treat limpness, one selects only the yang brilliance. Why is that?' Rather, he outlines the principle
mechanism of limpness resulting from a 'depletion of the yang brilliance.' One should
not forget, earlier he has outlined 'because the lung is hot and the lobes burn, the five
depots develop limpness and an inability to walk,' 'when sadness and grief are excessive,
then this develops into a muscle block. It develops into vessel limpness.' 'Sinew limpness is generated by the liver sending inwards,' [...] From this can be seen, the condition
of limpness does not emerge out of only one cause and for therapy one must not cling
to only one treatment pattern. It is therefore that Qi Bo states: 'always supplement [at]
their brooks and penetrate their transporters. Assess their depletions and repletions
and adapt them to those [movements] that are contrary to and in accordance with [the
normal flow]. When the sinews, the vessels, the bones, and the flesh [are treated] in
accordance with the season and month when they receive [their qi], then the disease
[can be] healed.' From the character 各 it may be realized that the yang brilliance is not
selected as the only [conduit] capable of [treating limpness]." 2227/21: "The character
獨 in 獨取陽明 is directed at the comparison of the major yang, the yang brilliance
and the minor yang in the treatise *Ling shu* 5; it is by no means to say that in treating
limpness one should select only the yang brilliance [conduit]. If the text were to claim
that 'only the yang brilliance [conduit] is to be selected for treatment,' wouldn't this
be a contradiction with the statement below: 'always supplement [at] their brooks and
penetrate their transporters. Assess their depletions and repletions and adapt them to
those [movements] that are contrary to and in accordance with [the normal flow].'?"
2195/8: "Over the centuries, physicians have disagreed whether the character 獨 in 獨
取陽明 is to be read as 儘取 ('merely select') or as 單獨取陽明 ('select nothing but').
For instance, Wang Kentang 王肯堂 of the Ming era stated: 'When any of the hundred body parts fails to be supplied with the qi of water and grain, it will lose its function and turn into a state of limpness. How could one treat limpness except by selecting
only the yang brilliance [conduit]?' ... My own humble opinion is: the character 獨 is
not to say that the yang brilliance is the only [conduit] to be selected, but that the yang
brilliance is to be selected as the main [conduit] for treatment. It is exactly as Zhang
Jiebin has said." See also 79/16.

44-249-4
[Huang] Di:
"To treat this, how to proceed?"

Qi Bo:
"In each case:
supplement [at] their brooks,
penetrate their transporters,[41]
assess their depletions and repletions and
adapt them to those [movements] that are contrary to and in accordance with
[the normal course].[42]

When the sinews, the vessels, the bones, and the flesh [are treated] in accordance with the season and months when they receive [their qi],
then the disease ends."[43]

[Huang] Di:
"Good!"

---

41 Zhang Jiebin: "'Supplementation' is to send qi; 'penetration' is to move qi. Above, the text states: 'one selects only the yang brilliance [conduit for treatment].' Here it states: 'supplement [at] the brooks and penetrate the transporters. That is, to treat limpness, one selects only the yang brilliance [conduit]. In addition, one must examine which conduit has received the disease and treat the respective [conduit/s], too. For example, in case of sinew limpness, one selects the brooks and transporters of the yang brilliance and ceasing yin [conduits]." Cheng Shide et al.: "One needles the brook holes to supplement the qi; one needles the transporter holes to open the passage of the qi."

42 Hu Tianxiong: "調 has the meaning of 'to examine.' 逆順 is 'to supplement and to drain.' 和 is 合, 'to combine,' 'in accordance.' That is to say: one first examines whether there is a depletion or repletion. Then, in accordance with whether a depletion or a repletion is present, one determines whether an intervention pattern of supplementation or draining is to be applied."

43 Wang Bing: "時受月 is to say: 受氣時月, 'the seaons and months when they receive qi.'" Zhang Jiebin: "The sinews, the vessels, the flesh, and the bones, they all have [specific] seasons, or months, when they receive [disease] qi. That is, diseases [of the season associated with the agent] wood appear in the sinews. Diseases [of the season associated with the agent] fire appear in the vessels. .. One should know whether the reception is at the surface or in the depth, to regulate a depletion or a repletion. One should know which seasonal qi abounds and which is weak, to know whether there is opposition or conformity. This way the disease can be cured." Cheng Shide et al.: "The *Tai su* has 日 instead of 月." Wu Kun changed 月 to 氣. Li Guoqing: "各以其時受月 should be interpreted as 各以其受氣之時月. This, then, refers to the months of the seasons when the qi of [one of] the five depots flourishes."

Chapter 45
Discourse on Recession

45-250-2
Huang Di asked:
"The cold and the heat [variants] of recession,
what [causes them]?"[1]

Qi Bo responded:
"When the yang qi weakens below,
then this causes cold recession;
when the yin qi weakens below,
then this causes heat recession."[2]

[Huang] Di:
"As for the heat of heat recession,
it always rises from the lower side of the feet.
Why?"

Qi Bo:
"The yang qi rises from the outside of the five toes.
The yin vessels gather at the lower side of the feet and come together in the center [of the sole] of the feet.
Hence,

---

1 Wang Bing: "厥 is to say: 氣逆上, 'qi moves upwards, contrary [to its regular direction].'" Zhang Zhicong: "厥 is 逆, 'countermovement.'" For a discussion of the meaning of the character 厥 in the *Nei jing*, see 2619/52, 1623/13, 1683/7, 2225/4, and 1081/45. For changes in the meaning of 厥 over time, see 2551/3. For a clinical perspective, see 855/1.

2 Yang Shangshan: "下 is to say: the feet. When the yang qi of the feet is depleted, yin qi takes advantage [of this depletion] and the feet become cold. This is called 'cold recession.' When the yin qi of the feet is depleted, yang qi takes advantage [of this depletion] and the feet become hot. This is called 'heat recession.'" Wang Bing: "'Yang' is to say: the three yang vessels of the feet. 'Yin' is to say: the three yin vessels of the feet. 'Below' is to say: the feet." 2619/52: "For the most part in the *Nei jing*, the character 厥 refers to pathoconditions. 'Cold recession' and 'heat recession' refer to pathoconditions resulting from excessive indulgence in wine or sex, or from physical exhaustion, injuring kidneys and spleen." See also 2583/6. For a comparative discussion of the meanings of the terms 'cold recession' and 'heat recession' in the *Nei jing* and in the *Shang han lun*, see also Wan Lanqing et al./38.

when the yang qi dominates,
then the lower side of the feet is hot."[3]

45-250-6
[Huang] Di:
"As for the cold of cold recession,
it always originates from the five toes and rises to the knees.
Why?"

Qi Bo:
"The yin qi emerges from the inside of the five toes.[4]
It gathers below the knees and comes together above the knees.
Hence,
when the yin qi dominates,
then there is cold originating from the five toes and reaching to above the knees."[5]
{This cold does not originate from outside; it always originates from inside.}[6]

---

3 Wang Bing: "This is a general outline. The foot major yang vessel emerges from the outer side of the tip of the small toe. The foot minor yang vessel emerges from the tip of the toe next to the small toes. The foot yang brilliance vessel emerges from the the tips of the middle toe and of the big toe. They all follow the yang side of the feet and move upwards [from there]. The vessels of liver, spleen, and kidneys gather on the lower side of the feet and come together in the center of the sole of the feet. When the yin [qi] is weak, then there is heat on the lower side of the feet." Lin Yi et al.: "The *Jia yi jing* has 陽氣走於足, 'the yang qi runs on the feet,' instead of 陽氣起 於足.' The character 起 should be 走." Cheng Shide et al.: "起 has the meaning here of 走, 'to run along,' or 運行, 'to pass along.' Zhang Jiebin: "The tips of the toes are called 表." Zhang Zhicong: "表 is 外側, 'the outer side.'" Zhang Qi: "The three yin vessels gather below the feet and come together at the soles of the feet. When yang qi dominates, then the yin qi is depleted and the yang proceeds there to take advantage of this [depletion]. Hence, the heat recession rises from below the feet."

4 Zhang Jiebin: "裡 is to say 內; this, too, refers to the lower side of the feet."

5 Wang Bing: "This, too, is but a general outline. The foot major yin vessel emerges from the inner side of the tip of the big toe. The foot ceasing yin vessel emerges from the three hairs at the tip of the big toe. The foot minor yin vessel emerges from below the small toe and moves diagonally across the sole of the foot. They all follow the yin side of the foot and move upwards [from there]. They follow the inner side of the thigh and enter the abdomen. Hence, [the text] states: 'gather below the knee and come together above the knee.'"

6 Yao Shaoyu: "When the yang is depleted, then the yin dominates; when the yin dominates, then there is cold. Now, this cold originates from a depletion of yang [qi]. Hence, [the text] states: 'from inside.'"

45-250-9
[Huang] Di:
"Cold recession, which fault has resulted in this [condition]?"⁷

Qi Bo:
"The front yin is where the basic sinews come together;
it is where the major yin and the yang brilliance [conduits] merge.⁸
In spring and summer much yang qi and little yin qi is present.
In autumn and winter the yin qi abounds and the yang qi is weak.

A person with this [disease may] be of sturdy constitution.
Because he has overtaxed himself in autumn and winter,⁹
the qi from below moves upwards to fight [with the proper qi for its space],¹⁰
[Hence, the proper qi above] cannot restore [its loss].

---

7 Zhang Zhicong: "Cold recession results from a loss of stored yang. Hence, [the text] says 失." Cheng Shide et al.: "失 is 丟失, 'to lose.'"

8 Wang Bing: "The basic sinew descends on both sides of the navel and merges with the yin (i.e., sexual) organ. Hence, [the text] states: 'The frontal yin is where the basic sinews come together.' The major yin [conduit] is the vessel of the spleen; the yang brilliance [conduit] is the vessel of the stomach. The vessels of the spleen and of the stomach are both attached to the basic sinew. Hence, [the text] states: 'this is where the major yin and yang brilliance [conduits] merge.'" Lin Yi et al.: "The *Jia yi jing* has 厥陰者眾筋之所聚, 'the ceasing yin [conduit] is the location where all sinews come together,' instead of 前陰者宗筋之所聚. The Quan Yuanqi edition states 前陰者厥陰也, 'the frontal yin is the ceasing yin.'" 1161/61: "宗筋 is 眾筋. The *Guang ya* 廣雅 states: '宗 is 眾, all.' In some passages 宗筋 refers to all the sinews of the entire body; in other passages it refers to the frontal yin (i.e., sexual organ). In the present passage the second meaning is intended." 139/29: "宗筋 refers to the extraordinary vessels; the kidneys are tied to the supervisor, the controlling, the thoroughfare, and the belt [vessels]." Tanba: "The frontal yin is where the 宗筋 meet; one cannot say: the frontal yin is the 宗筋." 2269: "Nowhere in the *Nei jing* is the sexual organ called 宗筋. It was only beginning with Yang Shangshan and Wang Bing that the 宗筋 was said to be the 'frontal yin.'"

9 Yang Shangshan: "The physical constitution of this person is strong and he gives free rein to his desires. He receives harm when he enters the [women's] chambers excessively in autumn and winter, i.e., at a time when the yang qi is weak. Hence, [the text] states: 'taken away through use.'" Wang Bing: "質 is to say 形質, 'physical condition.' 奪於所用 is to say: to have many desires and exhaust one's essence qi."

10 *SWJZ*: "爭 is 引, 'to pull.'" *SWJZZ* commented: "Whenever one speaks of 爭, this is to say: one pulls it to cause it to return to oneself."

The essence qi overflows and moves down;[11]
evil qi, then, follows it and moves upwards.
{The [evil] qi originates in the center.}[12]

The yang qi weakens and cannot pour into and provide with supplies the conduits and network [vessels].
The yang qi decreases day by day; only yin qi is present.
Hence,
it is therefore that the hands and the feet are cold."[13]

45-251-4
[Huang] Di:
"Heat recession, how does this [condition] come about?"

Qi Bo:
"When wine enters the stomach,
then the network vessels are full, while the conduit vessels are depleted.[14]
The spleen is responsible for moving the body liquids on behalf of the stomach.
When the yin qi is depleted, then the yang qi enters.
When the yang qi has entered, then the stomach is not in harmony.
When the stomach is not in harmony, then the essence qi is exhausted.
When the essence qi is exhausted, then it does not provide with supplies the
four limbs.[15]

---

11 Gao Jiwu/715: "This should be 精溢氣下, 'the essence overflows and the qi moves
down.'"

12 The *Tai su* has 氣居於中, 'the qi resides in the center.'" Yang Shangshan: "The qi
of cold evil moves upwards taking advantage of the depletion there and resides in the
center. Because the cold resides in the center, the depletion of the yang qi increases
day by day."

13 Yao Shaoyu: "The four limbs are the origins of all yang [conduits]. When the
yang is weak, then the yin dominates alone. Hence, the hands and feet are not warm,
but cold."

14 Wu Kun: "The conduits and the network [vessels] cannot be replete at the same
time. Hence, when the network vessels are full, then the conduit vessels are depleted."
Gao Shishi: "Yin depletion and yang abundance results in heat recession. Hence, [the
text] refers to wine drinking to make this clear. When wine enters the stomach, it
moves first through the skin and at first it fills the network vessels. As a result, the
network vessels are full while the conduit vessels are depleted."

15 Wang Bing: "The frontal yin [i.e., the sexual organ] is the place where the major
yin and the yang brilliance [conduits] merge. Hence, in case the stomach is not in

A person with this [disease] must have frequently entered the [women's] chambers drunk to intoxication or after having eaten to repletion.[16]
The qi has assembled in the spleen and cannot disperse.
The qi of the wine and the qi of the grain strike at each other.
Heat abounds in the center.
{Hence, heat is everywhere in the body. The interior is hot and the urin is red.}

Now,
when the qi of wine abounds and is fierce and
when the qi of the kidneys is weak,
the yang qi dominates alone.
Hence,
it is therefore that the hands and the feet are hot."[17]

45-251-10
[Huang] Di:
"Recession,
it may let a person have [a feeling of] abdominal fullness, or
it may let a person suddenly be unable to recognize people, or
it may be that after half a day, or even as long as after an entire day, he recognizes people again.
How is that?"

Qi Bo:
"When yin qi[18] abounds above, then it is depleted below.
When it is depleted below, then the abdomen is distended and [gives a feeling of] fullness.
When yang qi abounds above,[19] then qi from below has doubled above and the evil qi moves in full advance against it.

---

harmony, then the essence qi is exhausted. The essence is insufficient internally; hence there is no qi available to provide with supplies the four extremities."

16 In contrast, Gao Jiwu/570: "The 以 in 以入房 stands for 已 in the sense of 已經, sign of the past."

17 Wang Bing: "When someone enters the [women's] chambers intoxicated by wine or having eaten to repletion, he will lose his essence qi. Heat will enter his depleted center. Because of this, his kidneys weaken, his yang [qi] abounds and his yin [qi] is depleted. Hence, heat develops in his hands and feet."

18 Wang Bing: "Yin [qi] is to say: the qi of the foot major yin [conduit]."

19 Lin Yi et al.: "The *Jia yi jing* has the two characters 腹滿, 'the abdomen has [a feeling of] fullness,' instead of the five characters 陽氣盛於上. One should follow the version of the *Jia yi jing*." For a lengthy argument, see there.

When it moves in full advance against it, then the yang qi is in disorder.
When the yang qi is in disorder, then one does not recognize people."

45-251-14
[Huang] Di:
"Good!
I should like to hear [now] about the appearances of recession [affecting] the
six conduit vessels {that is, the manifestations of the disease}."[20]

Qi Bo:
"Recession in the great yang [conduit] results in [the following:]
the head is swollen.
The head [feels] heavy.[21]
The feet cannot move.
This [may] develop into dizziness and [patients] falling to the ground.

Recession in the yang brilliance [conduit] results in [the following:]
Peak illness; [patients] have an urge to run around and shout.[22]
They experience abdominal fullness and cannot lie down.
The face is red and hot.
[Patients] have hallucinations and [utter] absurd words.

Recession in the minor yang [conduit] results in [the following:]
sudden deafness; the cheeks are swollen and hot.
The flanks ache and the shins cannot be moved.

Recession in the major yin [conduit] results in [the following:]
abdominal fullness and bloating.
The behind is not freely passable.[23]

---

20 Wang Bing: "[Huang Di] asks to to be informed exhaustively about the recession [diseases] in each of the conduits." Wu Kun: "能 is 形, 'physical appearance.'" Zhang Yizhi et al.: "病能 is 病態, 'behavior/appearance of a disease.' From Wang Bing's commentary it appears that his version did not have the two characters 病能."

21 Wang Bing: "Another version has 踵, 'the heel,' instead of 腫. That is an error."

22 Wang Bing: "Another version has 巓 instead of 癲. That is an error." Wang Qi: "呼 is 呼叫, 'to shout.'"

23 Gao Jiwu/251: "The conditions listed in connection with the foot major yin vessel of the spleen include diarrhea; nowhere is a condition of constipation mentioned. 不利 may be explained as 滯下, 'stagnant [sensation] diarrhea.' See the paragraph on 'spleen diseases' in the *Qian jin yao fang* 千金要方."

[Patients] do not wish to eat and if they eat, they vomit.
They cannot lie down.

45-253-1
Recession in the minor yin [conduit] results in [the following:]
a dry mouth and red urine,
abdominal fullness and heartache.

Recession in the ceasing yin [conduit] results in [the following:]
the lower abdomen is swollen and has pain,
abdominal distension; the *jing* and the urine do not pass freely.[24]
[Patients] like to lie down with their knees bent.
The yin (i.e., the sexual organ) is shrunk and swollen.[25]
The shins are hot at their inner side.[26]

<When it abounds, then drain it.
When it is depleted, then supplement it.
When it is neither abundant nor depleted, take it from the [respective] con-
duits.>[27]

---

24 Tanba: "Zhang Jiebin states: '涇 (*jing*) is the name of a river. The meaning [of this
term here] is difficult to understand.' Wang Bing (commenting on *Su wen* 62) states:
'涇 is 'stools,' 溲 is 'urine." Yang Shangshan states: '涇 is 經, 'female menstruation."
Wu Kun states: '涇 is the normal flow of water. 溲 is 溺溲, urine. 涇溲不利 is to
say: the normal flow of the urine is blocked.' None of these explanations is reliable.
Ling shu 8, too, has 腹脹經溲不利. For 經 the *Jia yi jing* has 涇. Hence, 涇溲 is
'urine.' The *Ji yun* 集韻 states: 涇 is 泉, 'fountain.' 溲 is a general term referring to
stools and urine. Hence, the character 涇 was added to distinguish [urine here] from
stools." 1142/43: "Wang Bing's interpretation of 涇 as 'stools' has no basis. 涇 is a
loanword for 經 in the sense of 經常, 'normal.'" For the full argument, see there. Li
Guoqing: "涇溲不利 is: the monthly period, the stools, and the urine do not pass."
Gao Jiwu/252: "The *Tai su* has 水脹, 'dropsical swellings.' 溲不利 is 'the urine does
not pass freely.' 利 is to be read as 順利, 'unimpeded.' 不順利 is 'impeded; moving
down only with difficulties.'"

25 Zhang Qi: "This vessel encircles the yin organ. Hence, at times [the latter]
shrinks, at times it swells." Gao Shishi: "The frontal yin (i.e., male sexual organ) is
shrunk and the scrotum is swollen."

26 Wang Bing: "Another version has 'the shins are hot at the outer side.' That is a
copying error."

27 Wang Bing: "'Neither abundant nor depleted' is to say: the evil qi does not yet
abound and the true qi is not yet depleted." *Nan jing* 69: "One removes [an evil] from
the conduits [themselves] if neither a repletion nor a depletion is present, because [in

Recession with countermovement[28] in the major yin [conduit results in the
following]:[29]
the shins are tense and they cramp.
Heartache pulls on the abdomen.
Treat the [conduit] ruling the disease.[30]

Recession with countermovement in the minor yin [conduit results in the fol-
lowing]:
depletion[31] [occuring together with a feeling of] fullness,[32] vomiting,[33] and a
clear outflow downwards.[34]
Treat the [conduit] ruling the disease.

Recession with countermovement in the ceasing yin [conduit results in the
following]:
[patient suffer] cramps and their lower back aches.
Depletion [occurs together with a feeling of] fullness.

---

this case] a regular conduit has fallen ill by itself rather than as a result of having been
hit by an evil [transmitted from] another [conduit]."

28 995/29: "'Recession and countermovement' is an extreme state of recession."

29 The *Tai su* has 足太陰脈, "foot major yin vessel", and an identical "foot … vessel"
structure for the following five references to conduits too.

30 Wang Bing: "The major yin vessel passes on the left and on the right side [of
the body]. Examine which [side] has an excess [of qi] and remove it by letting it
effuse from there. Hence, [the text] states: 'Treat the [conduit] ruling the disease.'"
Zhang Jiebin: "治主病 is to say: all the holes to the left or right, above or below the
original conduit, as well as its 'plain' and 'transporter' holes, are appropriate for use
[in therapy]. One must examine which [hole] masters [the disease] and pierce it."
Zhang Zhicong: "This disease has emerged under the rule of the spleen. Hence, one
must treat the spleen ruling the disease." Cheng Shide et al.: "That is, treat the conduit
which has received the disease." Lin Yi et al.: "The entire text from 太陰厥逆 to the
end of this treatise appeared in ch. 9 of the Quan Yuanqi edition; it was moved here
by Wang Bing."

31 905/38: "This has been interpreted as a depletion of the kidneys, with an inability
to take in qi."

32 Wu Kun: "虛滿 is: depletion in the center and, nevertheless, a [feeling of] fullness."

33 Gao Shishi: "When receding qi moves contrary [to its regular direction] in the
minor yin conduit, [then] the minor yin fire qi is depleted above. Hence, there is an
abnormal condition (變証) of 'depletion with [a feeling of] fullness' as well as of an
urge to vomit."

34 The *Tai su* has 青, 'greenish,' instead of 清."

The frontal [yin organ] is closed;
the speech is incoherent.
Treat the [conduit] ruling the disease.

In case of countermovement in all three yin [conduits],[35] and if [nature] cannot
[be relieved] in front or behind,[36]
this lets a person's hands and feet be cold.
Death occurs within three days.[37]

Recession with countermovement in the major yang [conduit results in the
following]:
[patients] fall, vomit blood,[38] and tend to have nosebleed.
Treat the [conduit] ruling the disease.

45-254-2
Recession with countermovement in the minor yang [conduit results in the
following]:
the trigger joints do not move freely.
When the trigger joints do not move freely,
the lower back does not allow [one] to walk, and
the nape does not allow [one] to look back.
When this develops into intestinal *yong*-abscesses, [the patient] cannot be
treated.
[Patients who experience] fright, they die.[39]

---

35 995/31: "This is a reference to the three yin [conduits] of the feet, namely those
of the liver, the spleen and the kidneys.

36 Zhang Jiebin: "不得前後 is: either [stools and urine] are blocked and cannot pass,
or they flow off without restraint. This is to say, one cannot obtain a normal situation."

37 Wang Bing: "The three yin [conduits] are interrupted. Hence, [the patient] dies
within three days."

38 Yang Shangshan: "To fall backwards is called 僵; to fall forwards is called 仆. If
one was injured because of falling backwards or forwards, one vomits blood as a result." Zhang Qi: "The statement 'vomits blood' is a later addition." Wu Kun agrees.

39 Zhang Jiebin: "The trigger joints are the important meeting points of sinews and
bones; the gallbladder is associated with the sinews. In case of recession and countermovement in the minor yang [conduit], the sinews do not move freely. As a result, the
trigger joints, the lower back, and the nape are ill. When an intestinal ulcer develops
out of recession and countermovement in the minor yang [conduit], this is conglomerated poison of the minister fire. Hence, they cannot be treated. If [the patient] is

45-254-4
Recession with countermovement in the yang brilliance [conduit results in the following]:
[patients] pant and cough; their body is hot.
They tend to be frightened, to have nosebleed, and to vomit blood.[40]

Recession with countermovement in the hand major yin [conduit results in the following]:[41]
depletion, [a feeling of] fullness, and cough.
[Patients] tend to vomit foam.[42]
Treat the [conduit] ruling the disease.

Recession with countermovement in the hand heart ruler and minor yin [conduit results in the following]:
heartache pulling on the throat; the body is hot.
Death [is inevitable; the patient] must not be treated.[43]

Recession with countermovement in the hand major yang [conduit results in the following]:
the ears are deaf and tears flow.
The nape cannot [be turned for] looking back.

---

affected by fright, this poison ties up with the depots. Hence, death is inevitable." Wu Kun: "In case of fright, poison qi enters the heart. Hence, one dies."

40 Zhang Jiebin: "The yang brilliance vessel follows the throat, enters the broken basin and moves down to the diaphragm. Hence, it causes panting and coughing. The yang brilliance [conduit] rules the muscles and the flesh. Hence, it causes the body to be hot. .. The yang brilliance vessel emerges from the nose and ties up with the stomach. Countermovement of qi [in this vessel] causes nose bleeding and vomiting of blood." Tanba: "The [text] does not state 治主病者. [Some characters] may have been lost here."

41 The "foot" vessels above are not identified as such, in contrast to the following "hand" vessels.

42 Wang Bing: "This is so because the hand major yin vessel emerges from the central burner, moves down, encircles the large intestine, turns around, follows the opening of the stomach, rises to the diaphragm and ties up with the lung." Zhang Zhicong: "Recession and countermovement in the hand major yin [conduit] is a countermovement of lung qi. The lung rules the qi. Hence, [this results in] depletion [together with a feeling of] fullness and coughing. The water liquid cannot be dispersed. Hence, [patients] tend to vomit foam."

43 The *Tai su* has 死; 不熱可治, "death [is inevitable]; if there is no heat, [the disease] can be cured."

The lower back cannot be bent down and up.[44]
Treat the [conduit] ruling the disease.

Recession with countermovement in the hand yang brilliance and minor yang [conduits]:
it develops into a throat block,
a swollen throat region,[45] and a stiff [neck].[46]
Treat the [conduit] ruling the disease.

---

44 Wang Bing: "'The lower back cannot be employed for bending down and up' does not correspond to [the functions of] this vessel. [This statement] may have been erroneously inserted in ancient times." Wu Kun:"This vessel touches the small intestine. The small intestine is connected with the region of the lower back. Hence, the lower back cannot be bent down or up."

45 Zhongyi yanjiuyuan...: "嗌 has two meanings: 1. the upper opening of the esophagus and 2. the entire throat region."

46 Lin Yi et al.: "The Quan Yuanqi edition has 痓 instead of 痉." Yao Shaoyu: "痉 is a wind disease. The vessels of the large intestine and of the triple burner emerge from the broken basin and rise to the neck. Hence, in case of disease [the pathoconditions] are as [described in the text]. The Quan Yuanqi edition has 痓; Wang Bing has erroneously changed this to 痉. Later authors have interpreted 痓 as 痉. That was a result of this mistake." Wang Qi: "痓 is identical with 痉". Zhongyi yanjiuyuan...: "痓 refers to a stiff neck here."

Chapter 46
Discourse on Disease Manifestations[1]

46-256-2
Huang Di asked:
"When someone suffers from stomach duct[2] *yong*-abscess,
how is this to be diagnosed?"[3]

Qi Bo responded:
"To diagnose this [disease] one must examine the [movement in the] stomach vessel.[4]

[The movement in] this vessel should be in the depth and fine.
When it is in the depth and fine, the qi moves contrary [to its normal course].[5]
When it moves contrary [to its normal course], the [movement in the vessel at] man's facing is extremely abundant.
When it is extremely abundant, then there is heat.[6]
{Man's facing is [associated with] the stomach vessel.}

---

1 139/27: "病能 is equivalent to 病態, 'manifestation of a disease.'" See also 1401/66.

2 The *Tai su* has 胃管, "stomach tube", for both occurrences of 胃脘.

3 Wu Kun: "Below the respiration gate (i.e., the epiglottis) and above the strong gate (i.e., the cardia), the duct which receives water and grains is called 'stomach duct.' 癰 is 毒, 'poison.'" Zhang Zhicong: "The camp [qi] and the guard [qi], the blood and the qi, they are generated by the yang brilliance. In case the blood and the qi are blocked and move contrary [to their normal direction], then this is a disease of abscess-swelling. It is unlike an affection from the outside by the six excessives of the four seasons, or any internal harm by the five states of mind and seven emotions."

4 The *Tai su* has 得, "grasp", instead of 候.

5 Wang Bing: "The stomach is the sea of water and grains. It abounds with blood and its qi is strong. Here now, in contrast, the [movement in the] vessels is in the depth and fine. This is contrary to a normal state." Yao Shaoyu: "A stomach abscess is a sign of repletion heat; the [movement in the] vessels should be deep, fine, and strong. A strong [movement] is [a sign of] repletion heat. A deep and fine [movement indicates that] poison has accumulated internally. Even though the classic speaks only of a deep and fine [movement], it is without any doubt also a strong one."

6 Wang Bing: "'Deep and fine' are [signs of] cold. When cold qi blocks the yang, the vessel at man's facing abounds [with qi]. [The vessel at] man's facing is the yang brilliance vessel. Hence, when it abounds [with qi], then this is [a sign of] heat. 'Man's facing' is the designation of the vessel movement that can be felt on [both] sides of the throat." Zhang Qi: "The yang brilliance qi moves from the head to the feet. When [the movement] at the instep (*fu-yang* section/point) is deep and rough while at man's

Once there is a movement contrary [to its normal course] and abundance, then heat assembles at the stomach opening and does not move.
Hence,
the stomach duct develops a *yong*-abscess."[7]

[Huang] Di:
"Good!
Someone lies down to sleep and there is something which does not let him rest. Why is that so?"

Qi Bo:
"When the depots had been harmed and
the essence has [once again its] place it moves to to lean on, then [the patient] finds rest.[8]

---

facing it is extremely abundant, then [this is a sign indicating that] the conduit qi does not descend. Hence, one knows that heat accumulates in the stomach."

7 Wang Bing: "When blood and qi are strong and abound and are hit against by heat internally, the two qi combine their heat. Hence, they form an abscess." Zhang Jiebin: "When yang brilliance qi moves contrary [to its normal course] and abounds [at man's facing], then heat evil has gathered in the stomach duct. Hence, it forms abscesses where it stays."

8 These three lines do not appear to respond to Huang Di's question. In partial agreement with the *Tai su* version (see below) one could read: 藏有所傷, 及精有所之, 倚則不安, "The depots have been harmed somewhere and the essence has a place to move to. [Patients] lean on something and cannot find rest." Wang Bing interpreted the character 及 verbally as 及之, "to reach": "When the five depots are reached by something causing harm, the essence qi of water and grain have somewhere to move to and to settle [there]. If it supports them from below, then one lies down to sleep and finds rest. Because the harm has reached the depots, man cannot suspend the location of his disease somewhere in the empty space!" Ma Shi: "This is to say: someone lies down to sleep and cannot find rest, because the qi of his depots was harmed and the essence qi decreases. Now, the five depots are yin and each stores its specific essence. When the depots have received harm somewhere and the essence has 'somewhere to move to' - that means: it has a unilateral inclination - then the depots are harmed and the essence decreases. In such a situation, one lies down to sleep and cannot find rest. The essence must have a place to settle. When each [specific essence] is in its original depot and when there is no lack of it, then one finds rest. 寄 is 藏, 'to store.' As in 'the liver stores the *hun*, the lung stores the *po*,' etc." Lin Yi et al.: "The *Jia yi jing* has 情有所倚則臥不安, 'when the emotions have something they lean towards, then one lies down to sleep and cannot find rest,' instead of 精有所之寄則安. The *Tai su* has 精有所倚則不安, 'when the essence has somewhere it leans towards, then one cannot find rest.'" Wu Kun followed the *Tai su* version: "The depots are yin; they rule calmness. Hence, when the depots have received harm, then they suffer from insufficiency. When the yin es-

Hence, [in the present case] that person cannot suspend his disease."[9]

[Huang] Di:
"When someone is unable to lie on his back,
why is that?"

Qi Bo:
"The lung is the canopy covering the depots.[10]
When the lung qi abounds, then the vessels are big.

---

sence has somewhere it leans towards unilaterally, then this [results in] the problem of
extreme activity. This does not let man find rest at night." Fang Wenhui/127: "The *Jia
yi jing* is correct. 精 is identical with 情, 'emotion.' 寄 is identical with 倚 in the sense
of 偏, 'unilateral.'" The *Tai su* version edited by Renmin weisheng chubanshe has
精有所乏, 倚則不安, "when the essence has a place where it is exhausted, [patients]
lean on something and cannot find rest." Yang Shangshan: "If one enters the chamber
excessively, too much essence is drained and there is insufficiency. Hence, when one lies
down to sleep (倚臥), one cannot find rest." Hu Tianxiong: "[Huang] Di asked why,
when somene who lies down to sleep, he does not find rest; he did not ask why, when
someone lies down to sleep, he does find rest. The characters 精 and 情 are similar and
lend themselves to mistaken exchanges. There are many examples in the ancient literature. 倚 should be 依, in the sense of 依戀, 'to long for.' When one's emotions long for
something and one tosses to and fro, this is one of the commonly witnessed reasons for
sleeplessness. The meaning expressed in the *Jia yi jing* is the most adequate." 2284/61:
"傷 is an error for 傷, in the sense of 交易, 'to exchange.' That is, the depots and palaces
have a relationship of mutual exchange. Also, the essence spirit has a place to reside.
Hence, if one lies down, one finds rest."

9 Wang Bing: "Hence, one cannot suspend the location of one's disease in the air."
Zhang Jiebin: "Where could one suspend [one's disease] and stop suffering?" Ma Shi:
"懸 is 絕, 'to cut off.'" Yao Shaoyu: "懸 is like 運, 'to move.'" Cheng Shide et al.: "Given
the preceding wording in the *Jia yi jing* 情有所倚則臥不安, 'when the emotions have
something they lean towards, then one lies down to sleep and cannot find rest,' Yao
Shaoyu's explanation is most appropriate. The meaning is: if one cannot free oneself
from one's emotional ties, then one is equally unable to move away from the disease
of 'lying down to sleep but being unable to find rest.'" Hu Tianxiong: "In the *Tai su*,
in front of the character 懸 is a character 注. This passage cannot be explained. Given
the preceding wording in the *Jia yi jing*, the character 病 may be a mistake for 情,
'emotions.'" The *Tai su* wording 注懸 may be interpreted as "be hung in explaining",
i.e., that person should be certain about his disease.

10 Wang Bing: "[The lung] is situated high and spreads its lobes above the [remain-
ing] four depots situated below it. Hence, [the text] states: 'The lung is the canopy of
the depots.'"

When the vessels are big, then one cannot lie on one's back."[11]
{This is discussed in the [texts] *The Strange and the Normal* and *Yin and Yang*.}[12]

46-257-1
[Huang] Di:
"Someone suffers from recession.[13]
Examination [shows that] the [movement in the] vessels on the right is in the depth and tight, while on the left [the movement in] the vessels is at the surface and retarded.[14] If this is not so, which disease is responsable?"[15]

Qi Bo:
"If one examines the [patient] in winter,
the [movement in the] vessels on the right must be in the depth and tight under regular [circumstances].
This is in correspondence with the four seasons.
When the [movement in the] vessels on the left is at the surface and retarded, this is contrary to the [course of the] four seasons.

On the left, the responsibility for the disease should be with the kidneys.
There is an unbalanced connection with the lung.
There should be pain in the lower back."[16]

---

11 Wang Bing: "When the lung abounds with and is full of qi and one lies down to sleep, then the qi is hasty and one pants. Hence, one cannot lie on one's back." Zhang Jiebin: "'Abounds' is to say: replete with evil qi. Hence, the vessels are big."

12 Wang Bing: "奇恆 and 陰陽 are titles of chapters in ancient classics. They are no longer extant."

13 Zhang Zhicong: "This is to discuss a countermovement of kidney qi causing disease."

14 Gao Shishi: "The yang qi does not rise. Hence, on the right one diagnoses a deep and tight [movement in the] vessels. The yin qi does not descend. Hence, on the left one diagnoses a [movement in the] vessels that is at the surface and retarded."

15 Wang Bing: "不然 is 不沉, 'not deep.'" Lin Yi et al.: "The *Jia yi jing* has 不知, '[I] do not know,' instead of 不然." Zhang Jiebin: "The wording in the *Jia yi jing* offers a satisfactory meaning. One should follow it." Gao Shishi: "If one is ill with recession while the [movement in the] vessels is not such [that it indicates recession], then: where is [the conduit] responsible for the disease?" The *Tai su* does not have the two characters 不然.

16 Wang Bing: "'At the surface' is a [movement in the] vessels of the lung. Hence, [the text] states 'There is some connection with the lung.' The lower back is a palace of the kidneys. Hence, when the kidneys receive a disease, then there is pain in the

46-257-4
[Huang] Di:
"Why do [you] say so?"

Qi Bo:
"The minor yin vessel passes through the kidneys and encloses the lung.
In the present case one feels a lung [movement in the] vessels and it is there-
fore that the kidneys have a disease.
Hence, the kidneys have caused the disease of lower back pain."[17]

46-257-6
[Huang] Di:
"Good!
When someone suffers from a *yong*-abscess in his neck,
some treat it with stones, some treat it with needles or cauterization.
In all cases [the disease] ends.
Which of these [therapies] is reliable?"[18]

Qi Bo:
"This [*yong*-abscess] is an identical name for different types [of diseases].[19]

---

lower back."Wu Kun: "關 is 關系, 'connection.'"Tanba: "The *Jia yi jing* does not have
the character 關. *Su wen* 47 states: 其盛在胃, 頗在肺, 'it abounds in the stomach and
there is little in the lung.' The sentence structures are identical." Cheng Shide et al.:
"The character 關 should be deleted."

17 Wang Bing: "When the [movement in the] vessels on the left is at the surface
and retarded, it is not so that one observes the arrival of a lung [disease movement in
the vessels]. The [movement in the] vessels cannot be in the depth because the left
kidney has some insufficiency. Hence, one obtains a lung [movement in the] vessels,
but the kidneys have a disease." Zhang Jiebin: "Originally, the kidney vessel encloses
the lung. Here now, because it is a winter month, a lung [movement in the] vessels
appears at the position of the kidneys. That is, the kidney qi is insufficient. Hence, the
[movement in the] vessels cannot be in the depth; rather it appears at the surface and
is retarded. This is not a lung disease. The disease is in the kidneys. The lower back
is the palace of the kidneys. Hence, when kidney qi moves contrary [to its normal
course], the resulting disease will be pain in the lower back." 2568/47: "In the *Su wen*,
the character 之 appears 41 times as a demonstrative pronoun, comparable to today's
這樣, 'such.'"

18 Wang Bing: "That is to say: the [means of] attack differ, but the cure is identical."
Zhang Jiebin: "That is to say: which pattern is to be employed for a proper treatment?"
The *Jia yi jing* has 其治安在, 'where does one treat,' instead of 其真安在."

19 Wang Bing: "That is to say, even though in each case one speaks of an abscess in
the neck, but they differ in the skin; they are not of the same type. Hence, the subse-

Now,
in the case of a *yong*-abscess, the qi stagnates [at one place]. One must open it
with a needle to eliminate it.
Now,
when the qi abounds and blood has collected, one must drain it with a stone.
This is what is called 'different treatments for identical diseases.' "[20]

46-257-9
[Huang] Di:
"Someone suffers from anger and craziness;[21]
how does this disease emerge?"

Qi Bo:
"It emerges from the yang."

[Huang] Di:
"The yang? How can it let a person become crazy?"[22]

Qi Bo:
"As for the yang qi, because [its flow] was suddenly cut off and because [this
blockage] is difficult to open, one tends to be angry.[23]

---

quent statement." Zhang Zhicong: "The names of the abscesses are the same, but their
causes are all of a different type." Gao Shishi: "等 is 類, 'type.' " 2800/30 agrees.

20 Wang Bing: "息 is 瘜, which means 'dead flesh.' 'Stones' is 砭石, 'pointed stones.'
They can be used to open big abscesses and let the pus flow out. Nowadays, they have
been replaced by the sword needle." Zhang Jiebin: "息 is 止, 'to stop.' When in case of
an abscess the qi agglomerates, stays at one place and fails to disperse, one treats this
by employing a needle to open [the abscess] and eliminate this qi [agglomeration].
When the qi moves [again], then the abscess is cured." Wu Kun: "瘜 is 腐肉, 'rotten
flesh.' 針 is 鈹針, 'stiletto needle.' It is used to remove rotten flesh." Ma Shi: "Inside
an abscess there is qi 'at rest,' (頓息) it has not reached its extreme yet. When it is said
'one uses a stone to pierce and to drain it,' then this is because the qi abounds and
blood has accumulated." Gao Shishi: "氣之息 is 氣之止息, 'when the qi stops.' "

21 Lin Yi et al.: "The *Tai su* has 喜怒, 'tends to be angry,' instead of 怒狂." Zhang
Jiebin: "That is to say: [the patient] insults others regardless of whether they are closely related or distant [persons]."

22 Wang Bing: "When someone is angry, he does not take precautions against calamity. Hence, he is called 'crazy.' "

23 Gao Shishi: "決 is like 散, 'to disperse.' " Zhang Zhicong: "決 is 流行, 'to flow
on.' " Wu Kun: "The yang qi should rise. When all of a sudden it is blocked and
pressed down and when this [blockage] cannot be opened, then this causes one to

The disease is called 'yang recession.'" [24]

[Huang] Di:
"How does one know this?"

Qi Bo:
"The yang brilliance [qi] is in permanent movement.
The great yang [qi] and the minor yang [qi] do not move. [25]
While [usually] they do not move, [in the present case] they move with great speed.
This is the manifestation of that [disease]." [26]

46-258-1
[Huang] Di:
"To treat it, how to proceed?"

---

tend to be angry and [to act like] crazy." Mori: "The *Guang ya* 廣雅, Shi gu 釋詁 states: 折 is 曲, 'bent.'"

24 Wang Bing: "That is to say, the yang qi is blocked and cannot disperse. Such people are often angry. .. All these cases result from yang [qi] moving contrary [to its normal course, together with] extreme annoyance. Hence, the disease is called 'yang recession.'"

25 Zhang Jiebin: "These vessels exhibit a slight movement, but it is not very [strong]." Ma Shi: "The movement in the conduits of bladder and gallbladder is not as pronounced as in the conduit of the stomach."

26 Wang Bing: "That is to say, the vessels at the neck do always have a movement which does not stop. The normal movement of the yang brilliance [vessel], that is the movement at the sides of the throat. These are the individual locations called Man's Facing (人迎) and Qi Abode (氣舍). When the minor yang [vessel] has a movement, this movement is below the curve of the cheeks. These are the individual locations called Celestial Window (天窗) and Celestial Window (天牖). When the great yang [vessel] has a movement, this movement is in the fold in front of the large sinew on both sides of the neck. These are the individual locations called Celestial Pillar (天柱) and Celestial Countenance (天容). They should not move regularly. If now, on the contrary, they move strongly, this movement is [a sign of] a disease."   Lin Yi et al.: "In his comment, Wang Bing identifies the Celestial Window (天窗) as a minor yang position and the Celestial Countenance (天容) as a major yang position. In the *Jia yi jing*, the Celestial Window is where the qi of the major yang vessel effuses, while the Celestial Countenance is a location where the qi of the minor yang vessel effuses. The version of the *Jia yi jing* is correct."

Qi Bo:
"Deprive the [patient] of his food and [the disease] will end.[27]

Now,
food enters the yin,[28] and supports the growth of qi in the yang.
Hence,
if one deprives the [patient] of his food, [the disease] will end.[29]
Let the [patient] consume a drink of fresh iron flakes.[30]

Now,
fresh iron flakes cause qi to move down quickly."[31]

---

27 Wang Bing: "When one eats less, then the qi weakens. Hence, if one decreases his food to moderate amounts, the disease will come to an end by itself." Yang Shangshan: "衰其食 is 少食, 'to eat less.'" Lin Yi et al.: "The *Jia yi jing* and the *Tai su* have 衰, 'to weaken,' instead of 奪." Gao Jiwu/256: "Ever since Wang Bing explained this as 節去 其食, 'decreases his food to moderate amounts,' and since Ma Shi explained this as 'one must decrease his intake of food,' many later authors followed these statements. However, when those who suffer from craziness eat a lot, it is only with force that one can achieve anything. Since those suffering from craziness often eat a lot it is permissible to purposely deprive them of food. Hence, 奪 should be interpreted as 強硬禁止, 'prohibit by force.'" Yao Shaoyu: "This is: 'Forbid all food.' Hence, the text speaks of 奪." 1310/424: "奪其食, 'to deprive one of his food,' is 蕩滌腸胃, 'to flush the intestines and the stomach' by strong purgatives." 2053/79 agrees: "The original meaning of 奪 is a reference to a bird flying away from one's hand, that is, 'to lose something one has owned previously.' For instance, *Ling shu* 18 states: 奪血者無汗, 'those who have lost their blood, they cannot sweat.' This is different from 'to forbid' or 'to decrease.'" For a lengthy argument, see there.

28 Wang Shaozeng/167: "夫 is a demonstrative pronoun here, equivalent to 這個, 'this.'"

29 Zhang Jiebin: "The five flavors enter through the mouth and are transformed by the spleen. That is, food enters the yin [region]. It is stored in the stomach to nourish the qi of the five depots. That is, the qi is helped to grow in the yang [region]. When the food is reduced, then the qi is weakened. Hence, if one deprives [the patient] of his food and does not allow the stomach fire to continuously support the yang evil, then the anger and craziness resulting from yang recession can be brought to an end."

30 Lin Yi et al.: "The *Jia yi jing* has 落, 'to drop,' instead of 洛." Today's *Tai su* version, too. This drug consists of the bits and pieces ("flakes") falling to the ground when iron that has just left the furnace is hammered to assume a specific shape."

31 Wang Bing: "The flavor of iron droppings is acrid; [the qi] is slightly warm [to] balanced. Their main indication is to make qi move down. In vernacular language it is also called 'iron broth' (鐵漿). This is not 'fresh iron liquid' (生鐵液)." Zhang Jiebin: "These are iron pieces that have fallen down when raw iron is smelted in a furnace and hammered afterwards. They are soaked in water, which can be drunk. They are asso-

[Huang] Di:
"Good!
Someone suffers from [the following]: his body is hot and sluggish.
Sweat leaves [his body] as if he had taken a bath.
He has an aversion to wind and is short of qi.
Which disease is that?"

Qi Bo:
"The disease is called 'wine wind.'"[32]

46-258-5
[Huang] Di:
"To treat it, how to proceed?"

Qi Bo:
"Take ten parts each of *ze-xie* and *zhu* and five parts of *mi-xian*.
Mix and take before meals [as much as can be] taken up with three fingers."[33]

---

ciated with [the agent] metal; their qi is cold and heavy. They are very much capable of pressing down heat and of opening agglomerations, as well as of balancing the evil of wood and fire." Wu Kun: "This is 'fresh iron liquid.' It is cold and exerts heavy pressure. Hence, it moves qi down quickly. When the qi moves down the recession ends."

32 Wang Bing: "That is, one has drunken wine and was struck by wind. ... Now, in case of excessive drinking, the yang qi abounds, the interstice structures widen and the dark palaces open. When the yang [qi] abounds, then the sinews are marked by limpness and weakness. Hence, the body is sluggish. When the interstice structures widen, then wind enters and attacks the dark palaces. When [the dark palaces] open, then qi flows to the outside. Hence, sweat leaves as if one had taken a bath. When wind and qi strike from outside, the skin interstices open again and one sweats profusely. [This results in] internal depletion. *Dan*-heat steams the lung. Hence, one has an aversion to wind and is short of qi (i.e., breath). The disease resulted from wine. Hence, [the text] speaks of 'wine wind.'" Zhang Jiebin: "The basic nature of wine is hot. If one falls ill because of excessive drinking, the body is hot as a result. Dampness-heat harms the sinews; Hence, [the body is] indolent. Dampness-heat steams against the skin interstices. Hence, sweat leaves [the body] as if one had taken a bath. In case of profuse sweating, the guard [qi] is depleted. Hence, one has an aversion to wind. When the guard [qi] is depleted, then the qi is drained. Hence, one is short of qi."

33 Wang Bing: "The flavor of *zhu* is bitter; [its qi is] warm [to] balanced. Its main indications are serious [cases of] wind and to stop sweating. The flavor of *mi-xian* is bitter; [its qi is] cold and balanced. Its main indication is wind-dampness and sinew atony. The flavor of *ze-xie* is sweet; [its qi is] cold and balanced. Its main indication is wind-dampness and to increase the qi. ... If the meal is consumed afterwards and the medication is taken first, this is called 後飯, 'before meals.'"

>{The so-called 'fine' [movement felt] in the depth, it strikes the hand like a needle.[34]
Rub it, squeeze it.
In case of [qi] agglomerations, [the movement is] firm.
In case of widespread [qi, the movement is] big.}<[35]

>{The *Upper Classic* speaks of how qi communicates with heaven.
The *Lower Classic* speaks of changes and transformations of diseases.
The *Golden Chest* decides about death and survival.
The *To Estimate and Measure* [expounds how] to squeeze [the vessels] and assess them.
The *The Strange and the Normal* speaks of strange diseases.[36]

As for the so-called 'strange,'
in case of strange diseases, one cannot die in correspondence with the four seasons.
In case of normal [diseases], one can die in correspondence with the four seasons.
As for the so-called 'estimate,' this is just to squeeze [the vessels] and search for it.

---

34 Gao Jiwu/558: "The character 之 is used here for 而." 2568/50: "The character 之 is used here as a conjunction, in the sense of 和 or 與."

35 Gao Shishi has moved these 24 characters to the beginning of this treatise to follow the characters 故胃脘為癰也: "深 is 沉, 'in the depth;' 博 is 散, 'dispersed.' Above, the text states: 'The [movement in the] vessels should be deep and fine.' The statement [here] 沉之細者 is to say: this [movement] strikes the hand fine and deep like a needle. When the stomach duct has a *yong*-abscess, one must palpate it, or feel it by pressure, from the outside. When one palpates it, or feels it by pressure, if there are accumulations, that is the hardness of the abscess; if there is no accumulation and if there is a dispersion instead, that is the largeness of the abscess."

36 Yang Shangshan: "From the lower back upwards, .. these are the 'upper conduits.' (上經) From the lower back downwards, these are the 'lower conduits.' (下經) The upper conduits communicate with the qi of heaven; the lower conduits exhibit its changes." Zhang Zhicong: "The 上經 are the *Su wen* treatises 1 and 3, as well as 9 and 22, discussing the depots and the palaces, yin and yang of man, as well as the nine administrative regions and nine non-administrated sectors of the earth. All their qi communicates with heaven. As for the 下經, these are the treatises *Su wen* 28 through 49. They discuss pathological changes." Gao Shishi: "The 'upper classic' may refer to the *Ling shu jing*, while the 'lower classic' may refer to the *Mai jing* 脈經." Ma Shi: "The *Upper Classic*, the *Lower Classic*, the *Golden Chest*, the *Estimate and Measure*, as well as the *Strange and Normal*, these are titles of ancient books which have long been lost.

{This is to say, one squeezes the vessels to search for the structure of their [movement].}

As for 'assess,' one finds the location of the disease and assesses it in on the basis of the four seasons.}<³⁷

---

37 See 394/55 for a discussion of the term 度. Wang Bing: "All statements [beginning with the characters] 所謂 are explanations of unclear meanings. As for the present 所謂, [I] have searched the entire text of the classic but there is nothing that could be linked to the meaning of the present treatise. It appears as if the entire meaning expounded in these few sentences was meant to explain some additional text of the classic [which is not part of the current text]. In all versions available at present, the two treatises of the seventh [chapter] are missing. [The present commentaries] may be text passages of the lost [treatises of the] classic erroneously inserted here. The ancient text was cut apart and [these sections] have been erroneously added here."

Chapter 47
Discourse on Strange Diseases

47-259-6
Huang Di asked:
"Someone has a doubled body. In the ninth month [that person] turns mute.[1]
Why is that?"

Qi Bo responded:
"The network vessel of the uterus[2] has been interrupted."[3]

[Huang] Di:
"Why do you say so?"

Qi Bo:
"The network [vessel] of the uterus is tied to the kidneys.
The minor yin vessel penetrates the kidneys and is tied to the base of the tongue.
Hence, [that person] cannot speak."[4]

---

1 The *Shi jing* 詩經, Da ya 大雅, Wen Wang 文王, Da ming 大明, has: "大任有身, 生此文王, "Daren was pregnant and gave birth to our king Wen." (See Legge, Vol. IV, Part III, Bk I, 2., p. 432.) The commentary of the Mao 毛 edition of the Han era states: "身, 重也", and the interpretation by Zheng Xuan 鄭玄 states: "重 is to say: pregnancy." See Ruan Yuan, 上, p.507. Given the absence of a term 重身 from ancient literature, the original wording of the *Su wen* may have been 人有身, which, apparently, by the Han era needed an interpretation. Hence, someone added a 重, creating the term *chóng shen*, "doubled body." Wang Bing: "重身 is to say: inside the body is another body, that is a pregnancy. .. During the ninth month of a pregnancy, the foot minor yin vessel nourishes the fetus. When the [flow of] qi is almost cut off, [the expecting mother] turns mute and cannot speak." Wang Shaozeng/204 and Wang Shaozeng & Xu Yongnian/93: "When a pregnant woman in the ninth month speaks but fails to emit any sound, what is the cause?" Cheng Shide et al.: "瘖 is 子瘖, 'child[bearing] muteness.'" See also 574/29.

2 Wu Kun: "胞 is 子室, 'uterus.'"

3 Wang Bing: "絕 is to say: the flow [of qi in] a vessel has been cut and cannot pass through it [any longer]. Hence, when [the mother] cannot speak, it is not so that the [flow of the] true qi of heaven had been interrupted." The *Huai nan zi* 淮南子, Ben jing 本經, has: 江河山川絕而不流, "the [Long] River, the [Yellow] River, and the mountain streams are all 絕 and do not flow." The commentary explains: "[絕] is 竭, 'exhausted,' 'worn out.'" Ma Shi: "This is the 絕 of 阻絕, 'obstructed,' not of 斷絕, 'severed.'"

4 Wang Bing: "The minor yin [vessel] is the kidney vessel. If it is not supplied with qi, the tongue cannot [be employed for] speaking."

47-259-8
[Huang] Di:
"To treat this, how to proceed?"

Qi Bo:
"Do not treat.
Recovery will set in in the tenth month.[5]

The *Laws of Piercing* states:
Do not [further] diminish an insufficiency;
[do not further] add to any surplus.
This would serve to establish these [conditions] as a *chen*-disease.[6]

{After that regulate it.}[7]

47-259-10
As for the so-called 'do not diminish an insufficiency,'

---

5 Wang Bing: "In the tenth month the fetus has departed and the network [vessel] of the uterus is passable again. The kidney vessel supplies the upper [regions]. Hence, [a person] speaks as before."

6 Wang Bing: "疹 is to say: chronic disease. If a treatment is conducted contrary to the [correct] pattern, the fetus dies and does not leave. This then results in a long-lasting, chronic disease." Gao Shishi: "疹 is equivalent to 病, 'disease.'" Tanba: "The *Guo yu* 國語 states: 孤子寡婦疾疹, 'orphans and widows who have suffered from catastrophes.' The *Shang han lie* 傷寒例 has: 小人觸冒必嬰暴疹, 'when the little ones are attacked by the adverse, they will suddenly fall ill.' Wang Bing may be wrong." Cheng Shide et al.: "One should follow Gao Shishi." 916/54: "疹 is identical with 疢, 'fever.'" Zhang Yizhi et al.: "The *Jia yi jing*, ch.12/10 has 辜 instead of 疹. 辜 is identical with 故 and 故 has the same meaning as 久, 'old.'" See also 2885/212.

7 Lin Yi et al.: "The *Jia yi jing* and the *Tai su* do not have the four characters 然後調之. Now, Quan Yuanqi wrote in his commentary: 'when it is said "do not treat", that is to say: when someone is pregnant in the ninth month, [this person] must not be treated. One must wait until the conclusion of the tenth month, when, after [the child] was born, the original condition has returned. After that one regulates the [condition of the mother].' That is, these four characters were part of the comment added by Quan Yuanqi and have been erroneously inserted into the main text later on. They should be deleted." Ma Shi: "One must wait until the tenth month has passed and then regulates the [condition of the woman]." Hu Tianxiong: "Above the text states 'do not treat;' then it discusses treatment nevertheless. There is a contradiction here. ... Further below the four characters 然後調之 should follow the earlier statement 當十月復. The meaning is: at first one must not treat; after delivery one can regulate [the problem]. Then the *Laws of Piercing* are quoted to explain why the text initially stated 'do not treat.'"

when the body is lean, do not employ the chisel stone.⁸
'Do not add to any surplus' [is to say]:
when there is [something with] physical appearance in the abdomen and one drains the [abdomen].⁹
When one drains it, then the essence leaves and the disease alone seizes¹⁰ the center.
Hence, [the *Laws of Piercing*] states: 'a *chen*-disease is established.' "¹¹

47-260-2
[Huang] Di:
"When [someone] suffers from fullness below the flanks, with qi moving contrary [to its normal course] for two or three years without end, which disease is that?"

---

8 Wang Bing: "After nine months of pregnancy, the sinews and the bones are thin and worn out. The strength is diminished, the body [feels] heavy, and [that woman] has an aversion to [consuming] grain. Hence, the physical appearance of the body is lean and should not be [further] harmed with the chisel needle."

9 Hu Tianxiong: "When the text states: 'When the body is emaciated, do not employ the chisel needle,' this is to explain the [earlier statement] 'do not harm the insufficient.' Here now it says 'drain it,' which does not fit the [corresponding statement] '[do not] add to a surplus.' According to Sun Dingyi 孫鼎宜, '泄之' should be changed to '補之'. However, if in the following sentence 泄之則精出 were changed to 補之則精出, this would not make sense. I suspect some other text has been erroneously inserted here."

10 Zhang Zhicong: "The proper qi has left and – contrary [to one's intentions] – the evil disease alone occupies the [patient's] center." Cheng Shide et al.: "擅 is 盤据, 'to seize.' The *Zhan guo ce* 戰國策, Qin ce san 秦策三, has: 昔者中山之地, 方五百里, 趙獨擅之, 'In ancient times the *Zhongshan* region covered a size of 500 square *li*. Zhao alone occupied it.'"

11 Wang Bing: "When the fetus strangles the network [vessel] of the uterus, the qi of the kidneys cannot pass through. Hence, if one drains it, the kidney essence will leave as a result. The essence liquid will be exhausted internally and the fetus cannot reach completion. The fetus dies and remains stuck in the abdomen and does not leave. Because of this, '[the disease] seizes [the patient] alone.' Hence, a chronic disease forms." Zhang Zhicong: "'To drain' is to say: to drain by means of a needle. Now, the uterus and any accumulations in the abdomen, they all have a physical appearance. When it is in the female uterus, [the text] states: do not add to that which has surplus. In case of breath accumulation it states: do not cauterize or pierce. In case of hidden beams it states: do not move it. That is, in all cases where there is something with a physical appearance in the abdomen, one must not pierce and drain it. Even though the piercing may hit the disease, but the item with a physical appearance will not leave. As a result, contrary [to one's intentions] one drains the [patient's] essence

Qi Bo:

"The disease is named breath accumulation.[12]

Here the intake of food is not impeded,

one must not cauterize or pierce.[13]

[Let the patient] practice [exercises of] guiding-pulling continuously and [let him] take drugs.

Drugs alone do not suffice for the treatment."[14]

---

qi." Cheng Shide et al.: "Beginning with 所謂無損不足 all commentaries disagree. Especially when [the classic] employs the passage 腹中有形而泄之 to explain 無益有餘, the meaning does not fit. Hence, Zhang Qi stated: 'This section is a displaced passage from another [part of the] classic.'"

12 Zhang Jiebin: "When an accumulation occurs not in the center but below the flanks, which is very small in the beginning and increases in size over time, then the flanks have [a feeling of] fullness and the qi moves contrary [to its normal flow]. One pants hastily and has difficulties in breathing. Hence, the name [of this condition] is 'breath accumulations.'" Wu Kun: "息積 is 息賁, 'running breath,' 肺積, 'lung accumulation.'" Cheng Shide et al.: "The *Jia yi jing* has 息賁, 'running breath.' Wu Kun's commentary appears to be most appropriate." Zhang Zhicong: "This is a disease resulting from lung accumulations. The lung rules the qi and by controlling exhalation and inhalation, it determines [one's] breathing. Hence, accumulations in the lung are called 'running breath.' The classic speaks of 'breath accumulations.'"

13 Zhang Jiebin: "In case of panting cauterization is contraindicated since it may support the fire evil. In case of emaciation piercing is contraindicated since it may drain the stomach qi." Wu Kun: "The metal of the lung fears fire; hence, one cannot cauterize. The disease is not in the conduits; hence, one cannot pierce. Piercing it will merely harm the conduit qi."

14 Wang Bing: "While there is nothing in the abdomen with physical appearance, a fullness of [qi] moving contrary [to its proper course can be felt] below the flanks. If it is not cured for several years, the breath follows the qi of the physical form to move contrary [to its normal flow. As a result,] breathing is difficult. Hence, one calls this 'breath accumulation.' The qi is not in the stomach. Hence, [the patient] is not opposed to food. To cauterize this will cause the heat of the fire to flame up internally and the qi will be transformed to wind. To pierce this will drain the conduits and this, in turn, generates depletion and destruction. Hence, one can neither cauterize nor pierce. All one can do is continuously practice [exercises of] guiding-pulling and cause the qi to flow away. If one attacks the interior by means of drugs to dissolve obstructions, then [a cure] is possible. If one relies only on drugs, though, and does not continuously practice [exercises of] guiding-pulling, the drugs alone will not be able to cure the [patient]." Zhang Jiebin: "One must continuously practice [exercises of] guiding-pulling and carry them out for a long, long time, to open the obstructions. Then one employs drugs to harmonize the qi. If these two [approaches] are applied together the disease can be healed. If one relies on drugs only and fails to continuously practice [exercises of] guiding-pulling, then the drugs alone will not be able to achieve the cure. Obviously, a successful therapy of this disease is not easy." Gao Shishi: "積

47-260-5
[Huang] Di:
"Someone has his body and limbs {thigh bones, thighs, and shins} all swollen,
with pain around his navel.
Which disease is that?"

Qi Bo:
"The disease is named hidden beams.[15]
These are wind roots.[16]
This [wind] qi has spilled into the large intestine and has attached itself to the
huang.[17]
The plain of the *huang* is below the navel.
Hence, the region around the navel has pain.[18]

One cannot move this [qi]. If one moves it, this causes the disease of rough-
ened urination of water."[19]

---

is 漸次, 'continuously.' One must continuously practice [exercises of] guiding-pulling and take drugs. 導引 is 運行, 'movement.' Through movement one can restore
destructions in the conduit vessels."

15 Wang Bing: "This is called 'hidden beams' because it is a disease of the thoroughfare vessel ."

16 For an identical phrase and its commentaries, see 40-225-3.

17 No satisfactory identification of the term 肓 has been offered so far. We consider
this term as a transliteration of a non-Chinese reference to an anatomical detail no
longer known.

18 Wang Bing: "'Large intestine' refers to 'wide intestine' (廣腸, i.e., the colon).
When the classic speaks of 'large intestine,' this should be read as 'winding intestine'
(迴腸). Why? The *Ling shu jing* states: 'The winding intestine encircles the navel to its
right. It winds in circles and descends [in the form of] leaves heaped upon each other.
The wide intestine is attached to the spine and receives [the contents of] the winding
intestine. It encircles [the navel] to the left [and it, too, has the form of] leaves heaped
upon each other. With the former and the latter [terms], one avoids the [character]
'great.'' If one investigates [the statement in the classic on this basis], then [large in-
testine] here is winding intestine; it should not say large intestine."

19 Wang Bing: "動 is to say: to strike against and move it by means of toxic drugs,
to cause a heavy diarrhea." Beginning with 帝曰: 人有身體髀股 .. up to here the text
repeats a passage from *Su wen* 40 (225-2 to 225-5). See there for comments.

47-260-8
[Huang] Di:
"Someone has a very frequent [movement in the] vessels in the foot-long section.[20]
The sinews are tense and visible.
Which disease is that?"[21]

Qi Bo:
"These are the so-called '*chen*-diseased sinews.'[22]
The abdomen of that person must be tense.
When white color and black color appear, then the disease is severe."[23]

---

20 Tanba: "The 13th difficult issue of the *Nan jing* states: 'If the [movement in the] vessels is frequent, the skin of the foot-long section should also be marked by frequency.' On this Ding [Deyong] commented: '"Frequent", that is the heart. Hence, the skin of the inner side of the arm is hot.' The meaning here is identical." Yao Shaoyu: "The foot-long section is [associated with the] kidneys which rule the water. The liver is [associated with the] wood and rules the sinews. In the present case, the vessel [movement] in the foot-long section is extremely frequent. The reason is that the water is depleted and cannot nourish the wood." Zhang Qi: "When the [movement in the] vessels is frequent, this is heat. When the [movement in the] vessels in the foot-long section is frequent, this is heat in the kidneys." Wu Kun: "When the [movement in the] vessels in the foot-long section is extremely frequent, the water of the kidneys is depleted." Hu Tianxiong: "Except for the treatises added by Tang and Song authors and except for this phrase here, the phrase 尺脈 is mentioned nowhere in the entire *Nei-jing*. Obviously, at the time [of its compilation] there existed no doctrine yet of inch, gate, and foot. The statement in *Su wen* 18 '尺脈緩澀' was mistakenly inverted and should read '尺緩脈澀, the [skin of the] foot-long [section] is soft, while the [movement in the] vessels is rough.' The *Tai su* has 尺數甚 which cannot be explained either. Only the *Jia yi jing* has 尺膚緩甚 and this may be close to the meaning intended by the classic." Mori: "Whenever the classic speaks of 'foot' and 'inch,' these are references to the vessels at the inch opening and foot marsh."

21 Wang Bing: "'The sinews are tense' is to say: the two sinews in the foot-long section behind the palm are tense."

22 Zhang Jiebin: "疹筋 is: the disease is in the sinews." Mori: "疹筋 is identical with 筋病, 'sinew disease.'"

23 Wang Bing: "'The abdomen is tense' is to say: the sinews on both sides of the navel and the kidneys are tense. Because the [condition of the] abdomen is investigated in the foot-long section, there must be tensions in the abdomen if one observes tense sinews in the foot-long section. 'Colors appear' is to say: they appear in the face section. Now, in the observation of the five colors/complexions, white indicates cold and black indicates cold. Hence, when these two colors appear, the disease is severe." Wu Kun: "If in case of a sinew disease a white complexion appears, the metal has overcome the wood. If in case of a kidney disease one observes a black complexion, the qi of that

47-261-2
[Huang] Di:
"Someone suffers from headache which does not end for many years.[24]
How did he get it?
What is the name of that disease?"[25]

Qi Bo:
"He must have been invaded by massive cold.
Internally, it has reached the bones and the marrow.

The marrow is ruled by the brain.
[In the present case,] the brain [has been affected by qi] moving contrary [to its regular course].[26]
Hence, this causes headache.
The teeth ache, too.[27]
The disease is named recession with countermovement."

[Huang] Di:
"Good!"

47-261-6
[Huang] Di:
"Someone suffers from sweet [taste] in his mouth.
What is the name of that disease?
How did he get it?"

---

depot is lost." Ma Shi: "If this person exhibits a white and black complexion in his face, then [these] white and black [complexions] indicate cold."

24 Hu Tianxiong: "以 is 至, 'up to.'" Gao Jiwu/568: "以 is 而且, 'and furthermore.'"

25 Wang Bing: "A disease of headache should not remain uncured for months or several years. Hence, [Huang Di] was curious and posed this question."

26 Zhang Zhicong: "When marrow evil rises in counterflow, then it enters the brain. Hence, headache results which does not end for several years." Zhang Jiebin: "When strong cold reaches the marrow, it rises to enter the head and causes pain. The evil is in the depth. Hence, [the pain] does not end for several years."

27 Wang Bing: "The brain is the master of the marrow; the teeth are continuations of the bones. When the brain is affected by a reverse movement of cold, the cold enters the bones, too. Hence, it causes headache and the teeth ache, too." Zhang Jiebin: "The marrow is ruled by the brain; all marrow is associated with the brain." The *Tai su*, ch. 30, has 令人頭痛, 齒亦當痛. It does not have the eight character passage 病名曰厥 逆. 帝曰善.

Qi Bo:

"This is an overflow of the five qi.[28]

The name [of the disease] is spleen solitary [heat] disease.[29]

Now,

the five flavors enter the mouth and
they are stored in the stomach.

The spleen moves the essence qi on behalf of the [stomach].

The body liquids are located in the spleen.

Hence, they let that person have a sweet [taste] in his mouth.[30]

---

28 Yang Shangshan: "The five qi are the qi of the five grains." Zhang Jiebin: "The five qi are the transformation products of the five grains." Ma Shi: "The five qi are the qi of the five depots." Wu Kun: "The five qi include fishy, burned, aromatic, putrid, and foul smells." Zhang Zhicong: "The 'five qi' refers to the qi of the soil. The soil is located in the center. Its number is five. Its flavor is sweet. Its smell is aromatic. Its depot is the spleen. Its orifice is the mouth. If one frequently consumes sweets and delicacies, then the smell and the flavor stay in the spleen. The spleen qi overflows and the resulting signs appear in the external orifices." 2529/59: "Zhang Jiebin is correct. The five flavors enter the mouth and are stored in the stomach. They are transformed by the spleen and their qi rises to overflow. Hence, they cause the mouth to have a sweet [taste]." Cheng Shide et al.: "All these commentaries disagree. Given the fact that the text further down states 'the name is spleen *dan*,' Zhang Zhicong is correct. However, one can also follow the comments by Zhang Jiebin and Yang Shangshan. Wu Kun and Ma Shi are both wrong. Zhang Qi states: '五 should be 脾, spleen.' One may think about this [suggestion]." Hu Tianxiong: "The text below states 五味入口. Hence, Zhang Jiebin's interpretation of 'five qi' is correct." Gu Guanguang: "五氣 should be 五味之氣, 'the qi of the five [types of] grain.'" Tanba: "The *wanli* edition of the *Yi shuo* 醫說 writes 土氣, 'soil qi,' [instead of 五氣]."

29 Wang Bing: "癉 is 熱, 'heat.' When the spleen is hot, then the [remaining] four depots are all supplied alike. Hence, the five qi rise and overflow. This happens because of spleen heat. Hence, it is called 'spleen *dan*.'" See also 2303/53.

30 The *Tai su* has 液 instead of 津液. Yang Shangshan: "The liquid in the spleen is the liquid of the five grains." Zhang Zhicong: "The spleen is responsible for moving the body liquids on behalf of the stomach. The five flavors enter the mouth and each of the liquids moves its specific way. Bitter [liquids] first enter the heart. Sour [liquids] first enter the liver. Sweet [liquids] first enter the spleen. Acrid [liquids] first enter the lung. Salty [liquids] first enter the kidneys. In case the liquids cannot spread through the five depots and remain solely in the spleen, the spleen qi rises to overflow and causes a sweet [taste] in one's mouth." Hu Tianxiong: "*Su wen* 45 states: 'The spleen is responsible for moving the liquids on behalf of the stomach.' And the following sentence states: 'When the stomach is out of harmony, then the essence qi is exhausted.' From this it is obvious that in such statements 精氣 and 津液 refer to the subtle essence of food."

This is an effusion of fat and delicious [food].[31]
This person must have frequently consumed sweet and delicious [food] and [his diet] was mostly fat.
A fat [diet] lets man [experience] internal heat;
sweet [food] lets man have central fullness.[32]
Hence, this qi rises and overflows; it turns and causes wasting-and-thirst.[33]
Treat this with orchids. Eliminate the old qi."[34]

47-262-1
[Huang] Di:
"Someone suffers <a bitter [taste] in his mouth, select the Yang Mound Spring.>[35]

---

31 Lin Yi et al.: "The *Tai su* has 致, 'to bring forth,' instead of 發."

32 Wang Bing: "When the food is fat, then the interstice structures close tightly and the yang qi cannot flow away towards the outside. Hence, fat lets one be hot inside. The nature and the qi of sweet [taste] are harmonious and relaxed and dispersing. Hence, in case of counterflow, sweet [flavor] causes one to have [a feeling of] fullness in the center." Zhang Qi: "If one's diet is fat, then the qi stagnates and cannot penetrate [the body]. If one's diet is sweet, the central qi is slowed down [in its movement] and tends to rest [at one location]. Hence, the center [exhibits a feeling of] fullness."

33 Wang Bing: "In case of internal heat the yang qi flames upwards. When it flames upwards, one wishes to drink and the throat is dry. In case of fullness in one's center, there is a surplus of old qi. When there is a surplus, then the spleen qi rises and overflows. Hence, [the text] states: 'this qi rises and overflows and in turn causes wasting-and-thirst.'" Zhang Jiebin: "If heat stays and fails to leave, after some time this will harm the yin. This qi rises to overflow and changes into the disease of wasting-and-thirst." 2241/27: "'Wasting-and-thirst' is: one drinks a lot, but the thirst does not end." See there for a general discussion of the meaning of 消.

34 Wang Bing: "蘭 is to say 蘭草 (various Eupatorium plants). 除 is to say 去, 'to remove.' 陳 is to say 久, 'old.' That is to say, *lan* is able to remove old untransformed qi of sweet [flavor] and fat because of the effusing and dispersing ability of its acrid [flavor]." See also 1807/22.

35 Lin Yi et al.: "Neither the Quan Yuanqi edition nor the *Tai su* have the six characters 口苦取陽陵泉. Judging from the textual structure preceding and following [these characters] they appear to be a mistake." Zhang Qi: "These six characters are a displaced passage." Hu Tianxiong: "These six characters are not missing from the *Jia yi jing*. The Yang Mound Spring (陽陵泉) is the confluence hole of the gallbladder conduit; a bitter taste in one's mouth is [the result of] a ball bladder disease. *Ling shu* 4 states: 'At the confluences one treats the inner palaces.' *Su wen* 38 states: 'To treat the palaces, one treats at the confluences.' Hence, the Yang Mound Spring cannot be omitted in case of a gallbladder *dan*. .. It may be that the *Jia yi jing* took these six characters from the *Ming tang kong xue zhen jiu zhi yao* 明堂孔穴針灸治要 and that during the Tang or Song someone, in turn, took the [text of the] *Jia yi jing* to supple-

from a bitter [taste] in the mouth, what is the name of that disease? How did he get it?"

Qi Bo:
"The disease is named gallbladder solitary [heat] disease.[36]

Now,
the liver is the general in the center.
It receives its decisions from the gallbladder.
The gullet serves as its messenger.[37]
Such a person has frequently planned and deliberated without reaching a decision.
Hence, the gallbladder is depleted.[38] Its qi has risen and overflows [into that patient's mouth], and because of this [the patient feels a] the bitter [flavor] in his mouth.[39]

---

ment the *Su wen*. Wang Bing only commented on gallbladder *dan* and on the bitter taste in the mouth; he did not refer to the Yang Mound Spring. From this it is obvious that Wang Bing's version of the text did not have these six characters."

36 Wang Bing: "[癉], again, is 熱, 'heat.' The flavor of gall is bitter. Hence, one has a bitter [taste] in one's mouth."

37 Wang Bing: "*Su wen* 8 states: 'The liver is the official functioning as general. Planning and deliberation originate in it. The gallbladder is the official functioning as rectifier. Decisions and judgments originate in it.' Liver and gallbladder share [their] qi; they agree in their nature. Hence, all planning and deliberation takes its decision from the gallbladder. The throat and the gallbladder correspond with each other. Hence, the throat acts as messenger." Lin Yi et al.: "The *Jia yi jing* states: 'The gallbladder is the palace of the central essence; the five depots take [their] decisions from the gallbladder. [The phrase] 'the throat is its messenger' may be an erroneous insertion." Yu Zihan et al./100: "The *Han shi wai zhuan* 韓詩外傳 has: 'What are the so-called six palaces? [Answer:] The throat is the palace of measuring and intake; the stomach is the palace of the five grains; the large intestine is the palace of distribution and transportation; the small intestine is the palace of receiving the abundant; the gallbladder is the palace of collecting the essence; the bladder is the palace of the liquids.' The present treatise (*Su wen* 47) has: 'the liver is the general in the center; it takes its decisions from the gallbladder; the throat is its messenger.' That makes it clear that the *Su wen* occasionally refers to the throat as one of the palaces."

38 Cheng Shide et al.: "The *Jia yi jing* does not have the character 虛. Tanba states: 'If one frequently plans and deliberates without reaching a decision, the gallbladder qi will gush up.' Hence, the *Jia yi* [*jing*] appears to be correct."

39 Zhang Zhicong: "When pondering does not lead to a decision, then the liver qi is blocked and the gallbladder qi is depleted. The depletion qi of the gallbladder rises to overflow and hence the mouth experiences a bitter [taste]. The preceding paragraph

Treat it through the levy [holes] and transporter [holes] of the gallbladder."[40]
{The treatment is [outlined] in the [treatise] *Mutual Engagement among the Twelve Officials of Yin and Yang*.}[41]

47-262-5
[Huang] Di:
"Someone with protuberance illness urinates tens of times per day. {This is an insufficiency.}[42]
His body is hot like charcoal.
His neck and breast are as if obstructed.[43]
[The movement in the vessels at] man's facing races and is abundant.[44]
The breath is panting and qi moves contrary [to its regular course]. {This is a surplus.}[45]

---

discussed a repletion of spleen qi; the present one discusses a gallbladder qi depletion. The qi of both depletion and repletion can cause heat and generate *dan*." Zhang Qi: "When a gallbladder block is not resolved, the minister fire flares upwards. As a result, gallbladder qi overflows."

40 Wang Bing: "On chest and abdomen [the holes] are called 'levy [holes];' on the back they are called 'transporter [holes].'"

41 Wang Bing: "That is to say: the treatment pattern was outlined in that treatise; in the current [version of the] classic it is no longer extant." Zhang Jiebin: "治 should be 論. This refers to *Su wen* 8." Wu Kun, Gao Shishi agree with Zhang Jiebin.

42 Wang Bing: "癃 is inability to pass urine. 溲 is to pass urine." Wu Kun: "If in case of protuberance illness one passes urine tens of times each day, this is because of a depletion and weakening of the central qi. One wishes to relieve oneself, but is unable to pass [any urine]. When it leaves, it does not leave entirely. After a short while one wishes to pass urine again, but the amount that leaves is not large." See also *Su wen* 49, note 55/56.

43 Wang Bing: "頸膺如格 is to say: neck and anterior chest are separated from each other and do not properly correspond." Zhang Jiebin: "頸 refers to the throat; 膺 refers to the breast. 如格 is to say: the above and the below do not correspond, as if there was a blockade." Wu Kun: "The body is hot like coal because the stomach rules the muscles and the flesh. The neck and the chest are as if separated because the stomach vessel follows the throat and moves downwards through the inner curve of the breast." Mori: "格 is explained by the *Shuo wen* as 'like a long [piece of] wood.' The *Guang yun* 廣韻 states: 'branch of a tree.' Hence, 如格 is to say: the qi cannot communicate between neck and chest; [the patient cannot turn or bow flexibly; he is stiff like a tree."

44 Wang Bing: "人迎躁盛 is to say: The movement of the vessels on both sides of the throat is abundant, full, tense, and frequent. It runs abnormally fast. This is the stomach vessel."

45 Lin Yi et al. deleted the following 15 characters from the *Su wen*: 是陽氣太盛於外, 陰氣不足, 故有餘也, "In this case, the yang qi is overly abundant in the exterior,

The [movement in the] major yin vessels is subtle and fine like a hair. {This is an insufficiency.}

Where is this disease?
What is the name of this disease?"[46]

Qi Bo:
"The disease is in the major yin [conduits].
There is an abundance [of qi] in the stomach and some is in the lung.
The disease is named recession.
[The patient] dies and [can]not be treated.[47]
This is the so-called 'got five that have surplus and two that are insufficient.'"

---

while the yin qi is insufficient. Hence, this is a surplus." Lin Yi et al.: "These 15 characters have been written as main text in older versions. Neither the *Jia yi jing* nor the *Tai su*, though, have this passage. Further examination has revealed that it is a comment written by Quan Yuanqi which was erroneously inserted into the main text by people later on. Here, now, we have written it as a commentary again." Hence, in the present edition, these 15 characters do no longer appear in the *Su wen* text.

46 Wang Bing: "'The [movement in the] major yin vessels is subtle and fine like a hair' refers to the lung vessel located one individually standardized body inch at the elevated bone behind the thumb. This is where the qi of the proper hand major yin vessel flows; one can examine the five depots there."

47 Wang Bing: "When one suffers from protuberance illness with frequent urination, when the body is hot like coal, when neck and bosom appear like separated, when the breath pants and the qi flows contrary [to its regular course], in all these cases the [movement in the] hand major yin vessel should be vast, large, and frequent. Since in the present case the [movement in the] major yin vessel is, on the contrary, subtle and fine like a hair, vessel [movement] and disease are opposed to each other. How does this come about? The lung qi has moved contrary [to its normal flow] and has invaded the stomach whence it rises and causes the [movement at] man's facing to race and to be abundant. Hence, [the text] states: 'the disease is in the major yin; the [qi] abounds in the stomach.' Because the breath pants and the qi flows contrary [to its regular course], [the text] states: 'there is little [qi] also in the lung.' The cause of the disease is qi moving contrary [to its regular course]. The signs [of the disease, though,] do not correspond [to the cause of the disease]. Hence, the name of the disease is 'recession.' [The patient] dies and cannot be treated." Zhang Jiebin: "The yin [qi] does not enter the yang. Hence, it abounds in the stomach. The yang [qi] does not enter the yin. Hence, the [movement in the] major yin [conduit] is fine and subtle. The disease is named 'recession' because both the yin and the yang [qi] move contrary [to their normal flow]." Yao Shaoyu: "厥 is to refer here to 竭, 'exhaustion.' Qi and blood are both exhausted. Hence, all [disease] signs are bad and [the patient must] die and cannot be treated." Wu Kun: "厥 is 逆. That is to say, the disease is contrary to what is normal." Gao Shishi: "When the qi of yin and yang do not communicate and unite,

47-263-3
[Huang] Di:
"What is that to say 'five that have surplus and two that are insufficient'"?

Qi Bo:
"As for the so-called 'five that have surplus,' [that is to say]:
the qi of the five diseases have a surplus.
As for the 'two that are insufficient,'
these, too, are insufficiencies of disease qi.[48]

If, now, from outside one has acquired the five that have surplus and if from inside one has acquired the two that are insufficient, in this [case], the body is no [longer separated into] exterior or interior.
Evidently, it is quite normal that [the patient] will die."[49]

47-263-6
[Huang] Di:
"A person from birth on suffers from peak illness.

---

the name of the disease is 'recession.' This is the recession of protuberance illness. [The patient] dies and cannot be treated." Li Guoqing: "厥 has the meaning of 缺乏, 'to lack,' 不足, 'insufficient.'"

48 Tanba: "The *Jia yi [jing]* does not have the last character 五." Zhang Qi: "The two latter characters 五 and the last character 二 are all later insertions."

49 Wang Bing: "'The five external surplusses' [are the following]: First, the body is hot like coal. Second, neck and bosom appear as if separated. Third, the [movement in the vessels at] man's facing is hurried and abundant. Fourth, the breath pants. Fifth, the qi moves contrary [to its regular course]. 'The two internal insufficiencies' [include the following]: First, to suffer from protuberance illness and to pass urine tens of times per day. Second, the [movement in the] major yin vessel is subtle and fine like hair. Now, when it is said 'the disease is in the exterior,' then the two insufficiencies exist internally. When it is said in such cases 'the disease is in the interior,' then the exterior has acquired the five surplusses. One cannot rely on interior and exterior [here] and it is most difficult to establish a pattern of supplementing or draining. Hence, [the text] states: 'In this [case] the body [can] not [be separated into] exterior or interior. Evidently, [the patient] must die.'" Zhang Jiebin: "In case of the [former] five diseases, the evil qi has a surplus. In case of the [latter] two diseases, the proper qi is insufficient. If one were to try to drain the evil, a yin depletion would result in the interior. If one were to try to supplement the depletion, a yang repletion would result in the exterior. It is impossible to help in the interior and it is equally impossible to treat the exterior. This is a disease which is neither specifically in the interior nor in the exterior. It is of the type where yang signs appear together with a yin [movement in the] vessels. Death results and nothing can be done." The *Jia yi jing* has 死証 instead of 正死. Ma Shi: "正以必死而不疑也, 'must truly die, there is no doubt about it.'"

What is the name of this disease?
How did he acquire it?"[50]

Qi Bo:
"The disease is named fetal disease.
It is acquired in the mother's abdomen.
When the mother was extremely frightened, the qi rises and does not move down.
It takes residence together with the essence qi.
Hence, this lets the child develop peak illness."[51]

47-263-9
[Huang] Di:
"Someone suffers from a *mang*-type [disease], as if he had water.[52]
Squeezing his vessels [shows that] they are big and tight.[53]

---

50 Wang Bing: "Now the one hundred diseases are all generated by wind, rain, cold, summerheat, yin, yang, joy, or anger. However, when someone was just born and his physical [body] has not been invaded by evil qi and [this child] suffers from peak disease already nevertheless, how can evil qi cause harm from the very beginning? Hence, [Huang Di] poses this question. 巔 is to say 上巔, 'peak,' that is the 'head.'" Zhang Jiebin: "'Peak disease' is 癲癇, 'convulsions.'" Ma Shi: "'Peak illnesses' are all diseases affecting the peak, not only headache." Gao Shishi: "巔, 'peak', is 癲, 'peak illness.'" See also 1775/60.

51 Wang Bing: "'Essence qi' is to say: the essence qi of the yang." Zhang Jiebin: "In case of fright, the qi behaves disorderly and moves contrary [to its regular course]. Hence, the qi rises but fails to descend. When the qi behaves disorderly, then the essence follows it. Hence, essence and qi together proceed to the fetus and cause the child to acquire the disease of peak illness (癲)." Zhang Zhicong: "In case of a strong fright, the qi violently rises but fails to descend. Now, the essence serves to nourish the fetus and [in the present case] essence and qi cluster together. The mother has been frightened and her qi has risen. As a result the essence of the child, too, moves contrary [to its regular course]. As a result, the child develops peak disease."

52 Wang Bing: "痝然 is to say: the face is swollen, the eyes protrude and the complexion is unspecific." Zhang Jiebin: "It appears like water, but is not water." Zhang Zhicong: "'As if there was water' [is to say]: water qi rises and settles [in the face]; this is not the water having a physical appearance."

53 Wang Bing: "大緊 is to say: like the string of a bow. 'Big' refers to the qi; 'tight' refers to the cold. When cold qi strikes the interior and, contrary [to what one should expect], there is no pain, this is different from what happens normally. Hence, [Huang Di] poses this question." Zhang Zhicong: "'Big' refers to the wind; 'tight' refers to the cold." Ma Shi: "In case of wind heat the [movement in the] vessels is big; when wind and water clash then the [movement in the] vessels is tight."

The body has no pain,[54]
the physical appearance is not lean,[55]
and [the patient] cannot eat, and if he eats, the quantities [consumed] are small,
how is that disease called?"

Qi Bo:
"This disease emerges from the kidneys.
It is called kidney wind.[56]
In case of kidney wind one cannot eat and tends to be frightened.
When the fright has ended and the qi of the heart is in a state of limpness, [the patient] dies."[57]

[Huang] Di:
"Good!"

---

54 Wu Kun: "The disease is not linked to the outside region; hence, the body experiences no pain."

55 Zhang Zhicong: "The water qi has risen to settle [in the face]. Hence, the physical appearance is not emaciated." Gao Shishi: "The physical appearance is not emaciated [because] the disease is near the surface."

56 Wang Bing: "When the [movement in the] vessels is big and also tense like the string of a bow, then taxation qi has accumulated internally and struggles with the cold. The taxation qi strikes against the cold. Hence, it changes to wind. The wind dominates the kidneys. Hence, [the text] states: 'Kidney Wind.'" Hu Tianxiong: "The 'kidney wind' is discussed in *Su wen* 33, 42, and here; the description of the physical appearance of the disease is different each time. Only the swelling of the face is referred to in all three treatises alike. When Zhang Zhicong comments 'this is not an affection by wind from the outside,' then this is an incomplete statement that cannot serve as an explanation."

57 Wang Bing: "The kidney water receives wind; the heart fire is characterized by limpness and weakness. Fire and water are both in trouble. Hence, one must die." The *Tai su* has: 驚以心痿者死, "in cases of fright [patients] die because of limpness of their heart."

Chapter 48
Discourse on Very Strange [Diseases][1]

48-264-4
Liver fullness, kidney fullness, and lung fullness are all [instances of] repletion.
{That is, they cause swelling.}[2]
Lung congestion: [the patient] pants and [experiences] fullness in the two upper flanks.[3]
Liver congestion: [the patient experiences] fullness in the two upper flanks.
When he lies down to sleep, he is frightened.
He is unable to pass urine.[4]

---

1 Gui Fu suggests an interpretation of 奇 in the sense of 棄, "to abandon", "to die." In this case, the title of the present treatise should be read as "Discourse on Extremely Fatal [Diseases]."

2 Wang Bing: "滿 is to say: the vessels are full and replete with qi. 腫 is to say: 癰腫, 'yong-abscess-swelling.' When the depots are filled with qi, then [the consequences] are like this." Zhang Jiebin: "This is to say, the conduits of liver, kidneys, and lung can all be 'full.' When their vessels are replete, they must be at the surface and swollen. One distinguishes [which of the three depots is affected] as is outlined in the text below." Cheng Shide et al.: "滿 is: the conduits of the liver, the kidneys, and the lung are filled with evil qi. Hence, the vessel qi is filled to repletion. The sign for this is that [the vessel] is near the surface and swollen. Wang Bing's commenting on 腫 as 癰腫, 'yong-abscess-swellings,' is probably wrong." The Jia yi jing has 則, "then," instead of 即; the Tai su has 皆, "all." Yang Shangshan: "When these three depots are filled to repletion, it always results in yong-abscess-swelling." Guo Aichun-92: "It seems that 滿 should be 脈, 'vessel,' parallel with 肝脈 and 心脈 later on. The pronunciations of 滿 (man) and 脈 (mai) are very close and lend themselves to errors." If one followed the interpretation of Guo Aichun-92, the initial sentence of this treatise should read: "When the liver vessel, the kidney vessel, and the lung vessel are all replete, then they are swollen." Zhang Yizhi et al.: "腫 is an error for 雍, 'congestion.' The listing of 肺雍, 肝雍 and 腎雍 in the text further below may serve as proof."

3 Wang Bing: "The lung stores the qi and outside it is responsible for the breathing. Its branch vessel moves crosswise from the lung to below the armpits. Hence, [in case of its congestion] there is panting and there is fullness in the two upper flanks." Lin Yi et al.: "For 肺之雍, 肝雍 and 腎雍, the Jia yi jing always has 癰, 'abscess.'" The Tai su also has 癰. Zhou Xuehai: "To interpret 雍 as 癰 is wrong." Cheng Shide et al.: "雍 is 壅, 'congestion.'" Ma Shi: "The three conduits of lung, liver, and kidneys cannot generate abscesses, this 雍 should be 壅, 'congestion.' What it says is: the qi is blocked. .. 壅 has the meaning of 滿, 'filled.'" 1508/10: "雍 is 癰. 雍, 壅 and 癰 were used interchangeably in ancient times."

4 Wang Bing: "The vessel of the liver follows the yin (i.e., inner side) of the thighs, enters the (pubic) hair, encircles the yin (i.e., sexual) organ, reaches the lower abdomen, rises to penetrate the liver and the diaphragm and spreads out in the ribs. Hence,

Kidney congestion: [the patient experiences] fullness from the lower [sections of the] flanks to the lower abdomen.[5]
Of the [two] lower legs, [one is] large and [one is] small.
The thigh bones and the shins experience severe lameness. [The disease] changes into unilaterial withering.[6]

When the heart vessel is full and big,
[this goes along with] convulsions and spasms; the sinews are cramped.[7]

[in case of its congestion] there is fullness in the upper flanks and one is unable to pass urine. The liver masters fright. Hence, when they lie down to sleep, [patients] are frightened." Cheng Shide et al.: "胠 is the region of the ribs below the armpits. When the lung qi is blocked and cannot descend, one pants and the two upper flanks experience fullness."

5 Lin Yi et al.: "The *Jia yi jing* has 胠下, 'below the upper flanks,' instead of 腳下. 腳 should be 胠; one cannot say 'from below the feet to the lower abdomen.'" Ma Shi: "The kidney vessel passes along the back of the inner ankle. One branch course enters the heels and ascends into the calves and appears again at the inner edge of the hollow behind the knee. It rises at the inner back edge of the thigh, passes through the spine, links with the kidneys and encloses the bladder. Its straight course ascends from the kidneys, penetrates the liver and the diaphragm and enters into the lung. A side course leaves the lung, encloses the heart and pours into the chest. Hence, there must be swelling and fullness from below the feet to the lower abdomen."

6 Wang Bing: "When qi and blood undergo changes (變易), unilateral withering is the result." Yao Shaoyu: "That is to say, when the kidney qi is blocked, one suffers not only from distension and fullness below the upper flanks; in addition, both feet are affected by limping which changes into unilateral withering. The kidneys are the source of the vital qi. Hence, when they are congested, the qi congeals and the blood stagnates. The resulting disease is as is described here. The [portion of the leg] above the knee is the 髀, the [portion of the leg] below the knee is the 胻. 脛 is identical with 胻." Cheng Shide et al.: "大小 is to say: the two lower limbs differ in size. 易 is to say: sometimes [the unilateral withering develops] on the right, sometimes on the left." Hu Tianxiong: "Wang Bing's interpretation is wrong; all diseases can be said to result in changes of blood and qi, not only unilateral withering! One must read the four characters 跛易偏枯 as one sentence and one should follow Sun Yirang in reading 跛易 as 跛弛, 'at ease,' 'slack.'" *Su wen* 7 has 三陽三陰發病為偏枯痿易. *NJCD*: "易 is identical with 㑊, 'slack.'"

7 Wang Bing: "When the heart vessel is full and big, then the liver qi flows downwards and heat qi collects internally. The sinews dry up and the blood hardens. Hence, convulsions and spasm result and the sinews are cramped." Zhang Jiebin: "The heart is associated with fire. When the fire has a surplus, then the vessels are full and big. Their blood dries up. Hence, convulsions and spasm result and the sinews are cramped." Wu Kun: "An abounding fire generates wind. Hence, this lets one have convulsions and causes one to fall down. One develops spasms and the sinews are cramped." Gao

When the liver vessel is small and tense,
[this goes along with] convulsions and spasms; the sinews are cramped.[8]

48-264-7
When the [movement in the] liver vessel gallops violently,
[this indicates that] there is something that has shocked [the patient].[9]
When the [movement in the] vessels does not arrive and when [the patient] is
mute, do not treat. [The disease] will end by itself.[10]

When the kidney vessel is small and tense,
when the liver vessel is small and tense and
when the heart vessel is small and tense,
and if there is no drumming,
all these [conditions] are [signs of] conglomeration ills.[11]

Shishi: "The heart is where the spirit resides. When the heart vessel is full and big,
then the spirit cannot function smoothly. Hence, convulsions and spasm result and
the sinews are cramped. When the spirit qi does not penetrate the heart bladder, then
convulsions result. When the spirit qi not reach the joints of the bones, spasms
result. In case of convulsions, the sinews are cramped internally; in case of spasm, the
sinews are cramped externally."

8 Wang Bing: "The liver nourishes the sinews; internally, it stores the blood. [In the
present case] the liver qi receives cold; hence, convulsions and spasm result and the
sinews are cramped. When the vessel is small and tense, this is [a sign of] cold." Zhang
Jiebin: "The liver stores the blood. When [the vessel] is small, the blood is insufficient.
When it is tense, the evil has a surplus. Hence, this disease results. Now, convulsions,
spasm, and cramped sinews are one identical disease, but the two conduits of the heart
and of the liver can both have it. In one case the cause is heat, in the other case it is
wind and cold. Cold and heat are not the same, but [their effects in] weakening the
blood are the same. Hence, in both cases this disease results."

9 Wang Bing: "驚 is 馳, 'to go quickly, as a horse.' 驚 is to say: the [movement in the
vessel] is fast and tense. Yang qi collects internally. Hence, a gallopping [movement in
the vessels] results." Cheng Shide et al.: "驚 is 亂奔, 'to run wildly.' "

10 Wang Bing: "When the liver qi recedes, this recession causes the vessel to be
impassable. When the recession recedes, the vessel is passable again." Yao Shaoyu: "In
case it 'does not arrive,' the [movement in the] vessels is hidden in the depth. 瘖 is:
one cannot speak. In case of extreme fright, the [movement in the] vessel is hidden
and the mouth cannot speak. When the fright subsides, recovery comes by itself. One
must not treat."

11 Wang Bing: " 'Small and tense' refers to extreme cold. When there is no drumming, then the blood does not flow. When the blood does not flow and when cold
gathers, the blood coagulates internally and causes conglomeration ills as a result." Ma
Shi: "瘕 is 假, 'unreal.' The lump seems to have form; its disappearance or visibility

<When the [vessels of] both the kidneys and the liver are in the depth,
this is stone water.[12]
When they are both at the surface,
this is wind water.[13]
When they are both depleted,
this is [an indication of impending] death.[14]
When they are both small and string[-like],
[the patient] tends to be frightened.>[15]

---

are irregular. Hence, it is called 瘕. The vessels themselves are tense. If now within this tension they are also small and if they do not drum against one's hand, then they are in the depth. There must be a conglomeration inside." Mori: "瘕 is a conglomeration, caused be an internal knotting of water and blood. Hence, the [*Zhu*] *bing yuan* [*hou lun*] 諸病源候論 states: 瘕 diseases are caused by an imbalance of cold and warmth. Beverages and food are not digested and they strike against the qi of the depots, forming accumulations in the abdomen, with tangible lumps. They move together with the qi and they are named because of their elusiveness. Hence, [the text] states: 'are [signs of] conglomeration ills.'" *Yu pian* 玉篇: "瘕 are diseases in the abdomen."

12 Wang Bing: "The liver vessel enters the yin (i.e., sexual) organ and penetrates the lower abdomen. The kidney vessel penetrates the spine and encloses the bladder. Both these depots store qi. The thoroughfare vessel descends from the kidneys and encloses the uterus. In the present case, the water does not move and transforms itself. Hence, there are hardenings and knots. Now, the kidneys rule the water. In winter, the water freezes. The water originates from the kidneys. The kidneys are reflections of the [agent] water and they are located in the depth. Hence, when the qi conglomerates and is in the depth, this is called 'stone water.'" Zhang Jiebin: "The kidneys and the liver are located in the lower region [of the body]. The liver rules the wind. The kidneys rule the water. When [the movements in the vessels associated with] the liver and the kidneys are both in the depth, this is a yin in yin disease. One will suffer from stone water. Stone water refers to coagulations and knottings in the lower abdomen. It is in the depth, hard, and occupies the lower region." See also *Su wen* 7.

13 Wang Bing: "When the vessel is at the surface, this is [a sign of] wind. The lower burner rules the water. Wind accumulates in the lower section. Hence, this is called wind water." Zhang Jiebin: "When the [movements in the vessels associated with the] liver and the kidneys are both near the surface, this is a disease of yang in yin; one will suffer from wind water. Wind water travels through the four limbs. It is near the surface and occupies the upper region."

14 Wang Bing: "The kidneys are the root of the five depots. The liver rules wether [things] come to life. When the [qi of the] two is insufficient, life and rule are both weak. Hence, [the patient] dies."

15 Wang Bing: "When [the movement in] the vessels is small and string[-like], the [qi of] liver and kidneys is insufficient. Hence, it is like this." Lin Yi et al.: "The Quan Yuanqi edition has the passage 腎肝并沈 to 小弦欲驚 in the section 厥論, 'Discourse on Recession.' It was moved here by Wang Bing." The *Tai su* has this passage in *juan*

When the kidney vessel is large, tense, and in the depth and
when the liver vessel is large, tense, and in the depth,
all these [conditions] are [signs of] elevation illnesses.[16]

When the heart vessel beats and is smooth and tense,
this is [a sign of] heart elevation illness.[17]
When the lung vessel is in the depth and beats,
this is [a sign of] lung elevation illness.[18]

48-265-5
<When the third yang [vessel] is tense,
this is conglomeration ill.[19]
When the third yin [vessel] is tense,
this is elevation illness.[20]
When the second yin [vessel] is tense,
this is convulsion and recession.

26, at the and of the section 經脈厥. Zhang Jiebin: "When the [movements associated with the] liver and the kidneys are both small, the true yin is depleted. When it
is small and also string[-like], the wood evil dominates. When the qi is depleted and
the gallbladder is timid, one tends to be frightened." The *Tai su* has 亦, 'too,' instead
of 欲. Zhang Yizhi et al.: "欲 should be 為, 'is,' in correspondence with the wordings
為石水, 為風水, 為死 above."

16 Wang Bing: "疝 are caused by knottings and accumulations of cold qi. When
the vessel is in the depth, this is [a sign of] repletion. When the vessel is tense, this
is [a sign of] pain. When the qi is replete and when cold accumulates, this causes a
strangling pain, it causes 疝." Hu Tianxiong: "Wang Bing considers 疝 to refer to
pain." *SWJZ*: "疝 is [associated with] abdominal pain." Mori: "疝 is a disease associated with pain in the lower abdomen. 瘕 is a disease associated with pain in the upper
abdomen."

17 Zhang Jiebin: "When someone suffers from elevation illness and the beating of
his heart vessel is tense and smooth, cold has availed itself of the heart together with
evil qi." Zhang Zhicong: "Heart elevation illness assumes physical form in the lower
abdomen. The respective qi rises and strikes against the heart. Hence, the beating of
the heart vessel is smooth and tense."

18 Wang Bing: "In both these cases cold accumulates in the depots."

19 1011/13: "瘕 is: alternating conglomeration and dispersion without any regular
order."

20 Wang Bing: "When the major yang [conduit] receives cold, the blood coagulates
and this is a conglomeration ill. When the major yin [conduit] receives cold, the qi
accumulates and this is elevation illness."

When the second yang [vessel] is tense,
this is fright.> 21

When the spleen vessel drums outside and is in the depth,
this is intestinal flush.
After a long time this will end by itself.22

48-265-7
When the liver vessel is small and relaxed,
this is intestinal flush.
It is easy to cure.23

When the kidney vessel is small and beats in the depth,
this is intestinal flush with blood being passed down.24
Those whose blood is warm and whose body is hot, they will die.25

---

21 Wang Bing: "The second yin is the minor yin. The second yang is the yang brilliance." Zhang Jiebin: "When the vessels are tense, this is [a sign of] wind cold. The
evil has availed itself of the heart and of the kidneys. Hence, this results in convulsions
and recession. When wood evil avails itself of the stomach, this results in fright."

22 Wang Bing: "'Drums outside' is to say: the drumming movement is on the outer
side of the arms." Zhang Jiebin: "'In the depth' is in the inside. If, at the same time,
there is external drumming, the evil is not very deep. Even though this goes along with
an intestinal flush, after a long time it will heal by itself." Ma Shi: "In case of intestinal
flush, the intestine has some accumulation which is now moved down. What is moved
down may be blood, white foam, or pus and blood. The disease is in the intestine and
one always speaks of intestinal flush."

23 Wang Bing: "When the liver vessel is small and relaxed, this is [a sign of] the
spleen [qi] availing itself of the liver. Hence, it is easy to cure."

24 Wang Bing: "'Small' indicates an insufficiency of yin qi. 'Beats' is: yang qi avails
itself of [its territory]. [As a result], heat is in the lower burner. Hence, blood is passed
down." Zhang Zhicong: "The qi of yang heat accumulates below in the kidneys.
Hence, this results in intestinal flush with a downward passage of blood."

25 Wang Bing: "When the blood is warm and the body hot, in this case the yin qi is
destroyed. Hence, [the patient] dies." Gao Shishi: "When the blood is warm inside,
while the body is hot outside, the fire flares up and the blood is exhausted. Hence, [the
patient] dies." Hu Tianxiong: "The two characters 血溫 are doubtful. *Su wen* 28 states:
'In case of intestinal flush with a passing of blood, when the body is hot, then [the
patient] will die.' That is, in case of incessant diarrhea and fever, the cause is poison
that has originated from within the organs. Hence, these are often signs of impending
death. This has nothing to do with the two characters 'warm blood.'"

48-266-1
When in case of a heart and liver flush blood is passed down, too,[26]
both depots have a disease alike.
This is curable.[27]

<When the vessel is small, in the depth, and [the skin above it] is rough,
this is intestinal flush.>[28]
Those whose body is hot, they will die.
When the heat is manifest over seven days, [the patient will] die.[29]

48-266-3
When the stomach vessel is in the depth and drums and [when the skin above
it is] rough, or
when the stomach [vessel] drums outside and is big,[30] or
when the heart vessel is small, firm, and tense,
all these [are signs of] a barrier[31] and unilateral withering.

---

26 Wang Bing: "The liver stores the blood; the heart nourishes the blood. Hence,
in case of flush blood is passed down." Zhang Zhicong: "The heart is responsible for
generating the blood, the liver is responsible for storing the blood. When, therefore,
the two depots of the heart and of the liver receive qi of yang abundance causing intestinal flush, blood will move down, too."

27 Wang Bing: "The heart is fire; the liver is wood. Wood generates fire. Hence, one
can heal this."

28 Zhang Jiebin: "When the [movements in the vessels of] heart and liver are small,
in the depth, and rough, this is because the yin is insufficient and the blood has received harm. Hence, this causes intestinal flush." Wu Kun: "Small, in the depth, and
rough are all yin [movements]. In case the yin abounds and there is no yang to harmonize it, this causes cold flush." The *Tai su* does not have the eight characters 其脈
小沉濇為腸澼.

29 Wang Bing: "In case of intestinal flush with a downward passage of blood and a
hot body, the fire qi has been cut internally. It leaves the heart and turns to the outside.
Hence, [the patient] dies. Fire is associated with the number seven. Hence, [patients]
die after seven days." Zhang Jiebin: "When the [movement in the] vessels is in the
depth and fine, [the patient] should not be hot. In the present case the [movement
in the] vessels is small and the body is hot. This is countermovement. Hence, [the
patient] must die. He dies when the heat lasts until the seventh day because the six
yin have been destroyed entirely."

30 Wang Bing: "外鼓 is to say: The drumming does not occur at the foot or inch
[locations]; rather, it beats against the outer side of the arm."

31 Guo Aichun-92: "The character 鬲 is a mistake for 為. The ancient forms of these
characters resembled each other and lent themselves to mistakes. 皆為偏枯 would

In males [these signs] develop on the left;
in females they develop on the right.

Those who are not mute and whose tongue can [still] be turned, they can be
cured.
They will rise within 30 days.[32]
Those who comply, [even] if they are mute, they will rise within three years.[33]

Those who have not completed their 20th year of life, they will die within three
years.[34]

48-266-6
When the [movement in the] vessels arrives beating, [patients] who experience
nosebleed and a hot body, they will die.[35]

---

parallel the previous statements 皆為瘕 and 皆為疝." Hu Tianxiong: "Guo Aichun-
92 is correct."

32 Wang Bing: "In case someone with a unilateral withering suffers from muteness and cannot speak, the vessels of the kidneys and of the uterus are interrupted
internally. The vessel of the uterus is linked to the kidneys. The vessel of the kidneys
rises from the kidneys, penetrates the liver and the diaphragm, enters the lung, follows the throat and runs on both sides of the base of the tongue. Hence, if its [flow
of] qi is interrupted internally, [the patient] is mute and cannot speak." Zhang Jiebin:
"If one is not mute and as long as the tongue can be turned, even though there is a
countermovement in the conduits, it has not reached the depth of the depots and can
be healed. [The patient] will rise within a month. If, though, [the patient] suffers from
unilateral withering and is mute, the kidney qi is exhausted internally which leads to
these results. This disease is severe."

33 Wang Bing: "從 is to say: males develop [this disease] on the left, females develop
it on the right. When the disease follows these [associations of] left and right, even
if [the patient is] mute and cannot speak, a therapy will [nevertheless] enable him to
rise within three years."

34 Wang Bing: "Because their five depots have just been stabilized and their blood
and qi have just hardened. The depots that have just been stabilized, they can be
harmed easily; the qi that has just hardened is wasted excessively. Because [the de-
pots] are harmed easily and because [the qi] is wasted excessively, [the patient] will
die within three years."

35 Wang Bing: "Nosebleed causes the vessel to be depleted; hence, it should not
beat. If now, in contrast, the vessel beats, this is because of an extreme [flow of] qi.
Hence, [the patient must] die." Zhang Jiebin: "The true yin is lost. Hence, one must
die." Zhang Zhicong: "When blood is lost, there should be no beating in the vessels.
In case there is beating, this is qi moving to the outside excessively." Hu Tianxiong:
"而 is 如, 'as if,' 'like.'"

{When the [movement in the] vessels arrives suspended, hook[-like], and at the surface, this is a regular [movement in the] vessels.}
When the [movement in the] vessels arrives as if panting, this is called 'sudden recession.'[36]
{Those with 'sudden recession' do not know how to speak with other persons.}
When the [movement in the] vessels arrives as if frequent and when it lets one be extremely frightened,
this will come to an end by itself within three to four days.[37]

When the [movement in the] vessels arrives at the surface and linked {'at the surface and linked' is the same as 'frequent,'[38] [i.e.,] it arrives ten times or more during each breathing},
<in this case the contribution of qi to the conduits is insufficient>[39]

---

36 Wang Bing: "喘 is to say: It arrives suddenly, abounding, and tense. When it leaves it is weak. Just like someone who pants." Zhang Jiebin: "This is sudden recession (i.e., one falls unconscious) and one does not recognize anybody." Cheng Shide et al.: "喘 refers to a tense and hurried appearance of the [movement in the] vessels." Hu Tianxiong: "All authors have interpreted 喘 as the 喘 in 喘促, 'hurried.' That is wrong. 喘 is 湍, 'the rushing of water.' This is a metaphor indicating a vast and abounding [movement in the] vessels." The *Tai su* has 氣厥, "qi recession", instead of 暴厥.

37 Wang Bing: "A 'frequent' [movement in the] vessels is [a sign of] heat. Heat excites the liver and the heart. Hence, [the patient] is frightened. A frequent [movement in the] vessels is [a movement of the] heart vessel; the disease is such that the wood is offended by the fire. As long as the liver does not generate [the disease], it will not merge with the evil. Hence, after three days, on the fourth day, it will leave by itself. This is so because the generation number of wood is 'three.'" Zhang Qi: "'As if frequent' is to say: it appears like frequent, but is not. A frequent [movement] is [a sign of] heat. If it is 'as if frequent,' the liquids of the liver and of the heart are diminished. .. Hence, the spirit is confused and [the patient] is frightened easily. One must wait quietly until yin rises and yang descends. Then the [movement in the] vessels is balanced [again] and the fright subsides."

38 In contrast, 2268/35: "Zhang Jiebin interprets 如 as 'like.' This is wrong. 如 is 而, 'and.' For 脈至如喘 and 脈至如數, the *Jia yi jing* has 脈至而喘, etc. This may serve as evidence." For details, see there.

39 Zhang Jiebin: "When during one breathing ten or more [movements] arrive, this appears as if it were a frequent [movement], while in fact it is not a frequent [movement in the] vessels caused by heat. It is [a sign of] extreme weakness of the conduit qi." 2268/35: "予 is identical with 於, and 於 is used for 之, 'of.'" For details, see there. We interpret 予 as 給與, "to give", "to contribute." The wording 氣予不足 or 精予不足 in eight statements is difficult to interpret. It can mean "contribution of qi/essence by (the heart, the liver, the stomach, etc.)" or "contribution of qi/essence to (the heart, the liver, the stomach, etc.)." A concept of a "contribution" of qi or essence to or by an organ is attested nowhere else in the *Su wen* or any other ancient text. Hence one

ninety days after the slight appearance[40] [of such a movement the patient] will die.[41]

When the [movement in the] vessels arrives like burning fuel,[42]
<in this case the contribution of essence to the heart is lost>[43]
[the patient] will die when the herbs dry.[44]

48-267-4
When the [movement in the] vessels arrives like scattered leaves,[45]
<in this case the contribution of qi to the liver is depleted>
[the patient] will die when the leaves of the trees fall.

---

can only speculate what "contribution of qi to the stomach" or "contribution of qi by the stomach" was supposed to mean. While in this case the latter version makes some sense in that the stomach is commonly supposed to transform food and beverages and transmit their qi to further locations in the organism, one may wonder what the muscles or the twelve transporters may have to contribute and where their contribution is received. For the most part, the organs and body parts listed below might be more plausibly considered to be recipients than contributors. Hence we have chosen a tentative rendering expressing this interpretation.

40 Wu Kun: "微見 is 始見, 'first appearance.' That is to say, after this [movement in the] vessel has appeared for the first time, it takes 90 days until [the patient] dies."

41 Wang Bing: "浮合 resembles the continuing (合) [arrival] of drifting (浮) waves: those coming later traverse those in front. They are fast and their movement is irregular." Cheng Shide et al.: "This describes the appearance of the [movement in the] vessels as resembling breakers; suddenly they separate, suddenly they merge. It is most difficult to distinguish [one from the next]."

42 Gao Jiwu/23: "然 is the modern form of 燃, 'to burn.'" 1649/35: "火 is a noun used here as verb. 如火薪然 should be interpreted as 如燒柴禾的樣子, 'like burning fuel.' '然 is not the modern form of 燃, 'to burn;' it is used here in the meaning of 樣子, i.e., as a suffix to an adjective."

43 Wang Bing: "A fire of 'burning fuel' blinks and has no stable appearance; it is easily extinguished." Zhang Jiebin: "It comes as pointed as a flame and it leaves as fast as if it were extinguished. This is a [movement in the] vessels, where the fire depot has no root and where the essence qi of the heart conduit has been lost." Gao Jiwu/255: "奪 is 脫, 'deprived.'" The character 之 may be a later insertion; all comparable statements in this passage have 精予不足 or 氣予不足.

44 Zhang Qi: "The herbs dry in winter. Cold water passes the cold. The qi of the heart is cut off." Ma Shi: "When the essence of the heart is lost, the flourishing of the fire in summer can still be upheld. When it comes to the close of autumn and the beginning of winter, the qi of the heart is used up entirely. Hence, [the text] states: [the patient] dies when the herbs dry."

45 Wang Bing: "Like scattered leaves following the wind. It has no regular appearance."

When the [movement in the] vessels arrives like an inquiring visitor {as for 'inquiring visitor,' [this is to describe a situation, where] the vessels are obstructed and drum},
<in this case the contribution of qi to the kidneys is insufficient>[46]
[the patient] will die when the date flowers are about to fall down.[47]

When the [movement in the] vessels arrives as sticky as pills,
<in this case the contribution of essence to the stomach is insufficient>
[the patient] will die when the elm seeds fall.[48]

When the [movement in the] vessels arrives resembling crosspieces [in a ladder],
<in this case the contribution of qi to the gallbladder is insufficient>
[the patient] will die when the crops are ripe.[49]

---

46 Zhang Jiebin: "省客 is like a visitor who comes to inquire [about the wellbeing of the landlord]. He comes and then he goes again." Ma Shi: "The [movement in the] vessels is blocked at first and then there is a drumming against the finger again." Hu Tianxiong: "The two characters 省客 are difficult to explain. Sun Dingyi 孫鼎宜 states: '省客 (*sheng ke*) is 塞 (*se*). When the two characters are combined, they sound like *se*.' Sun is correct." 476/32: "The *Tai su* 15 has 省容 instead of 省客. That seems to be correct. 省 alludes to the meaning of 循摩, 'to feel;' 容 is 容刀, 'a blunt knife.' .. That is, the [movement in the] vessels described as 循摩容刀 is to convey the meaning of 'firm,' and 'hard.'" Tanba: "The *Tai su* is correct. 省容 is 'emaciated appearance.'"

47 Wang Bing: "懸 is to say: like something suspended. When this thing is moved, it falls down." Zhang Jiebin: "The time of the date flowers is the period of beginning summer. 懸 is: the flowers open; 去 is: the flowers fall. That is to say, at the time when the date flowers open and fall, the fire flourishes and the water withdraws. [The patient] dies when the kidneys are depleted." 2111/37: "去 is 掉落, 'to fall.'" 476/32: "According to Gao's (高) comment on the *Huai nan* (*zi*), 'Jing shen xun' (精神訓), 懸 is 視, 'to observe.' The meaning of this passage is: 'As soon as one sees the date flowers fall, [the patient] will die.'"

48 Wang Bing: "丸泥 is to say: like rolling pearls." Zhang Zhicong: "丸泥 is to say: like the paste of pills, i.e., not smooth. The stomach is yang and soil. It is located in the center. Its nature is soft and its physical appearance is round. Hence, it is said: when the [movement in the] vessels is weak and smooth, this is because it contains stomach qi. .. 'It resembles the paste of pills' is it does not appear moving smoothly. This is a sign that the stomach will perish." Zhang Jiebin: "They fall in spring. This is the time of flourishing wood. When the soil is destroyed, [the patient] dies."

49 Zhang Jiebin: "橫格 is like a cross-beam offering resistance to one's finger. It is long and it is firm. This is the true [qi of the] depot of the wood and the gallbladder qi is insufficient. The crops mature in autumn. This is [the time] when the metal flourishes. Hence, the wood is destroyed and one dies."

When the [movement in the] vessels arrives like a hank of strings,
<in this case the contribution of essence to the uterus is insufficient> and
when the patient is talkative, he will die when frost descends.
If he does not speak, he can be cured.[50]

48-267-9
When the [movement in the] vessels arrives like [streaks of] intersecting
lacquer {'[streaks of] intersecting lacquer' is [to describe a movement] arriving
from the left and from the right side},
[the patient] will die thirty days after its slight appearance.[51]

When the [movement in the] vessels arrives like [water] gushing from a
fountain,[52]
at the surface, and drumming in the muscles,
<in this case the contribution of qi to the major yang is insufficient>
qi and flavor are diminished.
[The patient] will die when the leek blossoms.[53]

---

50 Wang Bing: "The vessel of the bladder is linked to the kidneys; the vessel of the
kidneys passes on both sides of the base of the tongue. When a person's qi is insufficient, then he should be unable to speak. In the present case, on the contrary, he
loves to speak. This is [a sign] of the true qi being interrupted internally. It leaves the
kidneys and turns to the tongue [in the body's] exterior. Hence, [the patient] dies."
Zhang Jiebin: "胞 is 'uterus.'" Wu Kun: "胞 is 精室, 'chamber of essence.'" Cheng
Shide et al.: "That is, in females this is the uterus, in males it is the chamber where the
essence (i.e., semen) is stored."

51 Wang Bing: "左右傍至 is to say: like drips of lacquer intersecting left and right,
turning back and forth." Lin Yi et al.: "The *Jia yi jing* has 交棘, 'crossing thorns,'
instead of 交漆." Zhang Jiebin: "'Like intersecting lacquer' is like the intersecting
of [drips of] lacquer flowing away. They touch each other to the left and right, are
closely interwoven and are not clearly [distinguishable from each other]." Wu Kun:
"交 should be 絞, 'to twist.' 絞漆 is: yin and yang are messed up. From the first appearance of this [movement in the] vessels, it takes 30 days until [the patient] dies."

52 Wang Bing: "It leaves only, but does not enter."

53 Gao Shishi: "The qi is yang and the flavor is yin. The major yang [conduit] harbors
cold and heat, [i.e.] yin and yang qi. [Here now] the major yang is depleted. Hence,
the qi and the flavor are diminished. 英 is 盛, 'to abound.' 韭英 is: the final month of
spring is the time when the soil flourishes. When the leeks abound [the patient] dies
because soil overcomes water." Wu Kun: "'Diminished qi' is: the qi is insufficient. 'Diminished flavor' is: the liquids are insufficient. Leek blossoms in late summer." Tanba:
"[The meaning of] 少氣味 is not clear."

48-268-1

When the [movement in the] vessels arrives like loose soil {one presses it, but does not get it},
<in this case the contribution of qi to the muscles is insufficient> and
if, of the five colors, black is the first to appear,
[the patient] will die when the white *lei* blossoms.[54]

When the [movement in the] vessels arrives like a suspended jar[55] {as for 'suspended jar,' if one feels [this movement] at the surface it becomes bigger and bigger},
<the contribution of [qi to the] twelve transporters is insufficient>
[the patient] will die when the water freezes.

When the [movement in the] vessels arrives like a knife with its sharp edge turned upside {'a knife with its sharp edge turned upside' is: [if one feels it] at the surface it is small and tense; if one presses it, it is firm, big, and tense},[56] the

---

54 Wang Bing: "'Like loose soil (頹土)' is to say: big at the surface but hollow and soft [inside]. If one presses [the vessel] then there is nothing". *Jia yi jing, Mai jing*, and *Tai su* all have 委土 instead of 頹土. Mori: "頹土 has the same meaning as 委土. 頹 may be a mistaken writing of 頹. 委土 has the meaning of loosely gathered soil; it is soft, not hard. Hence, [the text] states: 'one presses it, but does not get it.'" Zhang Jiebin: "If a black color appears like that of water, the soil is ruined to an extreme and water turns against it to occupy it. Hence, [the patient] must die." According to Zhang Jiebin, 蔂 signifies a climbing plant which exists in five types: "the white ones of which come out in spring. This is the season when the wood flourishes. Soil will be defeated."

55 Cheng Shide et al.: "This is the uvula (懸雍垂) in the throat. Its shape is big above and small below. Here it is used to describe a [movement in the] vessels which appears big if felt at the surface, but is small when a little pressure is applied." Gao Jiwu/8: "雍 is 癕, 'yong-abscess.' The *Shuo wen* states: 癕 is 腫, 'swelling.'" 916/54: "雍 is 癕, 'yong-abscess.'" 2444/43: "The *Tai su* has 懸離 instead of 懸雍. .... 離 and 鷟 were used interchangeably in ancient times. Hence, 懸離 can also be written 懸黎. 懸黎 is a name of jade stones. .... When the *Su wen* speaks of 脈至如懸黎, this is to say it uses the metaphor of a jade pendant to refer to a [movement in the] vessels that is suspended at the surface but turns hard when it is pressed." The translation of 懸雍 as 'suspended jar' here follows the *Zheng yi* (正義) comment on the naming of a 懸雍 mountain in the *Shan hai jing* 山海經: "雍 is a modification of 甕. 雍 is an abbreviation of 甕, 'earthen jar.'" See also Tanba.

56 Zhang Jiebin: "偃刀 is 臥刀, 'a knife lying on its back.' At the surface it is small and tense, like the edge of a knife. Under pressure it feels firm, big, and tense, like the back of a knife." Gao Shishi: "偃 is 息, 'to rest'; 刀 is a metal tool." Tanba: "I do not understand what Gao Shishi's statement is meant to say." Mori: "偃刀 is 仰刀, 'a knife

[contents of the] five depots are densely compacted and boil.[57]
<Cold and heat collect only in the kidneys>
In such a state, the person cannot sit.
[The patient] will die at spring begins.[58]

48-268-6
When the [movement in the] vessels arrives like a pill that is smooth and does
not meet the hand {'does not meet the hand,' [that is,] one presses it but cannot get it},
<the contribution of qi to the large intestine is insufficient>
[the patient] will die when the date leaves grow.[59]

When the [movement in the] vessels arrives like flowers, this [disease] lets a
person tend to be fearful. He does not wish to sit or lie down. When he walks
or stands, he permanently listens.
<In this case the contribution of qi to the small intestine is insufficient>

[The patient] will die in the final month of autumn.[60]

---

pointed upwards.' It refers to the uppermost point of the edge of a knife. .. All commentators speaking of a 'knife lying on its back' etc. are wrong."

57 Wang Bing: "菀 is 積, 'to collect.' 熟 is 熱, 'heat.'"

58 Zhang Jiebin: "The lower back is the the palace of the kidneys; when the yin
of the kidneys is ruined, then one cannot get up or sit. At spring begins the yang
abounds, while the yin weakens day by day. Hence, [the patient] must die."

59 Zhang Jiebin: "如丸 is: short and small. 直 is 當, 'it fits.' That is to say, it is smooth
and small and has no root and cannot resist pressure. The large intestine corresponds to
[the celestial stem] *geng* and to metal. The date leaves grow in early summer. [At that
time] the fire flourishes and, as a result, the metal weakens. Hence, [the patient] dies."
Fang Wenhui/55: "直 is 應, 'corresponds to.'" 916/54: "直 is 值, 值 is 遇, 'to meet,' is 應."

60 Wang Bing: "'The [movement in the] vessels arrives like a flower' is: it resembles
the hollowness and weakness of flowers; one cannot really grasp it. The vessel of the
small intestine moves upwards into the ear. Hence, [in case of insufficient qi] one frequently hears [something]." Zhang Zhicong: "'The [movement in the] vessels arrives
like flowers' is: as light as flowers. The small intestine is the palace of the heart and
is associated with the [celestial stem] *bing* and with fire. Its [movement in the] vessels should arrive abounding. Here, though, it resembles flowers. That is, [its] qi is insufficient. When the qi of the palace is insufficient, the qi of the depot is depleted, too.
When the spirit is depleted, one is fearful. When the spirit and the mind are unsettled,
one cannot sit or sleep peacefully as a result. The vessel of the small intestine enters
the ear and touches the auditory palace (*ting gong* 聽宮). When [a patient] frequently
hears something in his ear resembling the singing of cicadas, or the sound of a bell,
these are signs of a depletion."

Chapter 49
Explanations on the Vessels[1]

49-268-11
Major yang:

As for the so-called "swollen lower back and buttock pain,"[2] [that is to say:]
The first month is major yang, is *yin*. {*Yin* is major yang.}[3]
In the first month the yang qi comes out above while the yin qi abounds.
The yang has not reached its own turn [of domination] yet.[4]

---

1 252/38: "This treatise quotes, following 34 所謂 phrases, statements also found in other sections of the *Nei jing* and provides them with an explanation. This includes 23 passages from *Ling shu* 10, two passages from *Ling shu* 13, and one passage each from the *Su wen* treatises 71, 48, 31, 40, 34, 62, as well as from *Ling shu* 57. In addition, there are two passages of unclear origin." Since the *Ling shu* is a compilation based on the same pool of original writings as the *Su wen*, the passages introduced here by the phrase 所謂 must be considered as originating in these (lost) original writings, not in the *Ling shu*. The parallel passages in the *Ling shu* are not always identical in their wording with the passages quoted in *Su wen* 49. For an investigation of parallels in the present treatise and the relevant Mawangdui manuscripts, see 905/37. See also 1375/393. 963/29 offers a table comparing the present treatise with *Ling shu* 10.

2 Wang Bing: "脽 is to say: 臀肉, 'the buttocks.'" If one follows *SWJZZ*, this definition is in accordance with *SWJZ*.

3 The *Tai su*, ch.8, has 大 instead of 太. Yang Shangshan: "In the eleventh month, the first yang is generated. In the twelfth month, the second yang is generated. In the first month, the third yang is generated. The third yang is generated during the *yin* 寅 season. At this time the presence of yang [qi] is massive already. Hence, [the text] speaks of 大陽, 'massive yang.'" Wang Bing: "During the first month, the third yang [qi] is generated. It is responsible for setting up the *yin* [as the first month of the year.] The third yang [qi] is called major yang [qi]. Hence, [the text] states: '*Yin* is major yang [qi].'" *JJZG*: "The *Shi ming shi tian* 釋名釋天 has: 寅 is 演, that is: 演生物, 'to generate things/beings.'" Yu Chang: "The first two characters 太陽 may be an erroneous duplication of the subsequent 太陽. [The original wording was:] 正月寅, 寅, 太陽也, 'The first month is *yin*. *Yin* is major yang.' That is, 'major yang' was meant to explain the meaning of *yin*. The duplication of 'major yang' in the present version makes no sense."

4 Wang Bing: "During the first month, even though the third yang [qi] is generated, the qi of heaven is still cold nevertheless. Because it is still cold, [the text] states: The yin qi abounds and the yang qi has not reached its turn yet. 次 is to say: to occupy the ruling position." Yu Chang: "次 should be read as 恣. The *Shuo wen* interprets 恣 as 縱, 'lax,' 'to let go.'"

Hence,
[people suffer from] "swollen lower back and buttock pain."[5]

49-269-1
As for the disease "unilateral depletion causing limping,"[6] in the first month,
the frozen yang qi breaks open and the earth qi comes out.[7]

As for so-called "unilateral depletion," [that is to say:][8]
The winter cold is unbalanced and there are insufficiencies.
Hence,
[people suffer from] "unilateral depletion causing limping."[9]

As for the so-called "stiffness above pulling the back,"[10] [that is to say:]
The yang qi moves upwards massively and struggles [there].
Hence,
[people suffer from] "stiffness above."

As for the so-called "ringing in the ears," [that is to say:]

---

5 Ma Shi: "The qi of the bladder should abound but is depleted in fact. In the present situation, the proper qi of the bladder is depleted. Lower back and buttocks swell and have pain because the vessel of the [bladder] moves down from within the lower back along the spine, penetrates the kidneys, enters the popliteal fossa and passes by the hip joint. Hence, it causes a disease as described here to emerge." Zhang Qi: "When a qi abounds that is yin and cold, the qi in the conduits does not move."

6 Wu Kun: "The major yang vessel moves along both feet. Hence, a unilateral depletion causes a limp." Gao Shishi: "偏虛 is 偏枯, 'unilateral withering.'" Gao Shishi moved the two characters 所謂 to in front of 病偏虛. Tanba agreed: "In an older version, the two characters 所謂 were erroneously moved behind 出也."

7 Wu Kun omitted the character 而: 凍解地氣出. Tanba agreed.

8 Tanba: "The two characters 所謂 have been omitted here by Gao Shishi; that was correct."

9 Yang Shangshan: "In the first month the third yang is present already. Hence, the frost breaks; the yang qi leaves the earth. Earlier, there was the third yin. Hence, if it is as if the winter cold was still present, the yang qi is insufficient. The same applies to the human body. In one half the yang is insufficient; hence this is unilateral depletion. 'To limp' is to say: the left foot limps unilaterally."

10 Wang Bing: "強上 is to say: the neck is stiff. In severe cases it pulls the back." Yu Chang: "上 may be a mistake for 工 and 工 stands for 項, 'the neck.' 強工 is 強項, 'stiff neck.'" 2378/51: "強上 is: the lower back section is stiff like wood and this reaches upwards to the neck."

The yang qi in the myriad beings abounds above and jumps.[11]

Hence,

[people suffer from] "ringing in the ears."[12]

49-269-4

As for the so-called "when it is extreme, then craziness and peak illness result,"

[that is to say:]

The yang [qi] is exhausted above and the yin qi follows [there] from below.

[As a result,] the below is depleted, while the above is replete.

Hence,

[people suffer from] "craziness and peak illness."[13]

As for the so-called "[a movement] near the surface is [a sign of] deafness,"

[that is to say:]

[The reason] lies always with the qi.[14]

---

11 Zhang Jiebin: "The two characters 萬物 are a later insertion."

12 Wang Bing: "This is so because a branch of the [major yang] vessel moves from the top of the head to the upper edge of the ear."

13 Yang Shangshan: "To drop the clothes and climb on elevated places, to run around wildly and utter meaningless words, this is called 狂. To fall prostrate, this is called 顛." Wang Bing: "Because the [major yang] vessel moves upwards through the forehead to the top of the head, where it enters the brain, encircling it before it appears again, and because its branch moves from the top of the head to the upper edge of the ear, hence, craziness and peak illness result." Zhang Zhicong: "In case of the so-called 狂 顛 disease, the yang qi is quite depleted above. The yin qi moves to [the location of the yang qi] from below but is unable to merge with the yang qi. [Hence,] depletion below and repletion above [result] and this causes the 狂顛 disease. The classic in question (i.e., the *Su wen*) states: 'When the yang qi abounds, then one is crazy.' (For similar statements, see *Su wen* 3, 19 - 6 and *Su wen* 30, 182 – 5 .) And it states elsewhere: 'When the qi rises and fails to descend, headache and peak-illness [result]. ' (The last statement is to be found in *Su wen* 80, 568-3)" Wu Kun: "As for the 狂 顛 disease, this is 狂躁, 'craziness,' and 巔頂痛 'vertex pain.'" Yao Shaoyu: "The *Zhu bing* [*yuan hou lun*] does not have the term 狂顛. The [*Nei*] *jing* mentions the two [characters] in conjunction, but they refer to two items. 狂 is 癲狂. [In this case,] the fire qi abounds unbalanced, the spirit brilliance is confused and in disorder. This is the so-called craziness of doubled yang. 巔 is 頂巔, 'vertex.' The head is where all the yang comes together. When the yang [qi] is exhausted above, the resulting diseases are many. They are called summarily 巔疾, 'peak disease.' "

14 Wang Bing: "Again, this is because the [major yang] vessel reaches the ear." Zhang Jiebin: "When the yang is replete above, then the qi is blocked and this causes deafness. Again, this is because the [major yang] vessel reaches the ear." Gao Shishi: "The 經脈論 states: 'the hand major yang vessel enters the ear. The disease it generates is deafness.' This explains that the phrase 所謂浮為聾者 is to say: the qi moves upwards

As for the so-called "when it enters the center, this causes muteness," [that is to say:]
When the yang abounds, it weakens already.
Hence,
"this causes muteness."[15]
In case of internal deprivation[16] and [subsequent] recession, muteness and lameness results. {This is a kidney depletion.[17] When the minor yin fails to arrive, this is "recession."}[18]

---

to the surface contrary [to its normal flow] and causes deafness. [The reason] lies always with the qi." Gao Jiwu/484: "Following 氣, the central character 病, 'disease,' is omitted."

15 Wang Bing: "When the yang qi is replete, enters the center and accumulates in the bladder and in the kidneys, then the qi cannot pass the network [vessels] of the bladder and of the kidneys. Hence, muteness results. The vessel of the bladder is tied to the kidneys. The vessel of the kidneys passes on both sides of the base of the tongue. Hence, muteness results, i.e., one cannot speak." Ma Shi: "Because the qi of the bladder is weakened already, it cannot support the kidney qi when it enters the center. Hence, the qi of the kidneys, whose vessel passes on both sides of the base of the tongue, cannot pass and this causes muteness." Zhang Jiebin: "Sounds are emitted through qi. The qi is yang. When the yang abounds, then the sound is big; when the yang is depleted, then the sound is weak."

16 Zhang Jiebin: "When the essence is lost, then the qi is lost and recession results. Hence, one is mute above and physical destruction results below." Wu Kun: "內 stands for 房, 'chamber,' (i.e., sexual intercourse); 奪 is: to waste one's yin (i.e., semen)."

17 Wang Bing: "俳 is 廢, 'destruction.' The kidney vessel together with the thoroughfare vessel leaves the qi street, follows the inner edge of the yin (i.e., inner side) of the thighs, moves transversely and enters the popliteal fossa, follows the inner edge of the shins, reaches the back of the inner ankle and enters the sole of the foot. Hence, when the kidney qi is lost in the interior, then the tongue is mute and the feet are destroyed. Hence, [the text] states: 'This is kidney depletion.'" The *Tai su* has 痱 instead of 俳. Cheng Shide et al.: "俳 is 痱; it refers to the disease of 瘖痱, that is muteness, i.e., inability to speak and inability to move the four limbs." Gao Jiwu/12 agrees. Shen Zumian: "俳 should be 痱. The *Shuo wen* interprets 痱 as 風病; nowadays it is generally called 沙病, 'sand disease' (a skin disease with sand-like eruptions)."

18 Zhang Jiebin: "This is to explain the meaning of the phrase 內奪而厥 above. The minor yin [conduit] is the vessel of the kidneys. It is with the major yang like outer and inner. When the kidney qi is lost internally, then the minor yin [qi] does not arrive. When the minor yin [qi] does not arrive, this is because the yin is depleted and there is no [yin] qi. When there is no [yin] qi, then the yang weakens. This is the result of recession." Zhang Zhicong: "The minor yin qi rules the kidneys. As the text above implies, when the kidneys are depleted because no minor yin qi arrives, then the hands and the feet [suffer from] recession and are cold."

Minor yang:
As for the so-called "the heart and the flanks ache," that is to say:
The minor yang abounds.
{As for "abounds," that is an external sign [of the condition] of the heart.}[19]
In the ninth month the yang qi is exhausted and the yin qi abounds.
Hence,
"the heart and the flanks ache."

49-270-3
As for the so-called "cannot turn to the side," [that is to say:]
The yin qi stores the beings.
When the beings are stored, then they do not move.
Hence,
[people] "cannot turn to the side."

As for the so-called "when it is extreme, then it jumps,"[20] [that is to say:]
In the ninth month the myriad beings have all weakened.
When all the herbs fall and the trees drop [their leaves], then the qi leaves the yang [region] and proceeds to the yin [region].
The qi abounds [in the yin region] and the yang moves downwards to [cause] growth [there].

---

19 The *Tai su* has 言少陽戌也戌者... instead of 言少陽盛也盛者... Yang Shang-shan: "The hand minor yang vessel encloses the heart enclosure; the foot minor yang vessel follows the inside of the flanks. Hence, in case of a minor yang disease the heart and the flanks ache. 戌 is the ninth month; during the ninth month the yang is diminished. Hence, [the text] states: 'minor yang.'" Cheng Shide et al.: "Following the previous statement 正月太陽寅 and the statements further below 陽明者午也, 太陰子也, 厥陰者辰也, the present 盛 should be 戌." The erroneous replacement of 戌 with 盛 must have occurred prior to the time of Wang Bing; he commented: "When the heart qi moves contrary [to its normal flow], then the minor yang abounds. The heart qi takes advantage of the wood and melts the metal of the lung in the exterior. Hence, [the text states]: 'As for abounds, that is an external sign of the heart.'" Ma Shi: "The vessel of the gallbladder moves in the flanks and the vessel of the heart appears in the armpits; [these locations] represent the 'outer' of the heart." Wu Kun: "The minor yang is wood; wood can generate fire. In the present case, the minor yang abounds; hence, the fire of the heart affects the outside." Zhang Jiebin: "The minor yang is associated with the wood. Wood generates fire. Hence, when the evil abounds, the origin lies in the gallbladder and the manifestation occurs in the heart. 表 is 標, 'sign.'"

20 Wang Bing: "躍 is 跳躍, 'to jump.'" Beijing zhongyi xueyuan: "There must be an erroneous insertion here; this statement makes no sense." Guo Aichun-92: "Seen in the light of all the other entries, 躍 should refer to a disease. It is unclear, though, to which disease 躍 could refer." Li Guoqing: "躍 could be explained through 跳. The *Shuo wen* states: 跳 is 蹶, 'to stumble.'"

Hence,
[the text] says "jumps."[21]

Yang brilliance:

As for the so-called "shiver and shake from cold," [that is to say:]
The yang brilliance is *wu*.[22] The fifth month is the yin of the abounding yang.
[At this time] the yang abounds and yin qi is added to it.
Hence,
"[people] shiver and shake from cold."[23]

49-270-8
As for the so-called "the shins are swollen and the thighs [can]not be con-
tracted," that is [to say:]
The fifth month is the yin of the abounding yang.[24]
When the yang weakens in the fifth month and when the first yin qi rises[25] it
starts to struggle with the yang.
Hence,
"the shins are swollen and the thighs [can]not be contracted."[26]

As for the so-called "pants above and this causes water," [that is to say:]
When the yin qi has descended it rises again.

---

21 Wu Kun: "'The qi abounds' is: the qi abounds in the yin [region]. 下 is the lower
region of the body. 陽之下 is to say: the yang qi moves downwards. For example, the
vessel of the minor yang [qi] appears at the outer edge of the knee and moves to the
two feet. 長 is 生長, 'come to life and grow.' The yang makes things move. Hence,
when it grows in the two feet, it lets one jump."

22 Yang Shangshan: "The yang brilliance is the head of the three yang. 午 is the fifth
month; that is the time when the yang abounds and when it is extensive and brilliant.
Hence, [the text] states: 'yang brilliance.'"

23 Wang Bing: "The yang qi descends and the yin qi rises. Hence, [the text] states:
'the yang abounds and yin qi is added to it.'"

24 Yao Shaoyu: "In the fifth month, the yang reaches its utmost abundance and the
first yin begins to emerge. The yang, in turn, enters the yin."

25 The *Tai su* has 而陰氣一下. This suggests a reading of the *Su wen* passage as 而
陰氣一上 as "and as soon as the yin qi rises."

26 Yang Shangshan: "The region above the lower back is yang; the region below the
lower back is yin. In the fifth month, the qi of first yin begins to emerge below and
enters into a struggle with the yang. The yang is strong and replete above, while the
yin is weak and depleted below. Hence, 'the shins are swollen and the thighs [can]not
be contracted.'"

When it rises, then the evil settles in the region of the depots and palaces.
Hence,
[it is said:] "this causes water."[27]

As for the so-called "chest pain and being short of qi," [that is to say:]
Water qi is in the depots and palaces.
As for "water, that is the yin qi. Yin qi is in the center.
Hence,
[people suffer from] "chest pain and being short of qi."[28]

49-271-1
As for the so-called "when it is extreme, then there is recession. [Patients] have

---

27 Wang Bing: "The 'depot' referred to here is the spleen; the 'palace' referred to
here is the stomach. The foot major yin vessel moves from the feet to the abdomen;
the foot yang brilliance vessels moves from the head to the feet. In the present case,
some yin qi descends and the major yin rises. Hence, [the text] states: 'the yin qi
descends and rises again.' When it 'rises again,' then the qi that has descended fails
to disperse; rather it settles in the region of spleen and stomach and transforms itself
into water." Zhang Jiebin: "When the yang brilliance, which is soil, has a disease, then
it is unable to control the water. Hence, the yin evil rises from below and settles in
the region of the depots and palaces, where it then transforms itself into water. The
basis of the water is in the kidneys; its extension is in the lung. When secondary and
primary location both have a disease, then this results in panting above." Yao Shaoyu:
"The water is associated with the yin. When the yin rises from below, then water evil
settles in the lung and causes panting." Zhang Zhicong: "'The yin qi descends and
rises again' is to say: at winter solstice the first yang begins to emerge and the yin qi
descends. When the fifth month is reached, the yin qi rises again. 'Evil' refers to water
evil. That is to say, the yin qi descends and returns to the water depot. When the yin
qi moves up again and gradually reaches abundance, then the water evil follows the
[yin] qi and rises, [too]. Above it settles in the region of the depots and palaces. Hence,
one pants and water [accumulations] occur." Zhang Qi: "復 is 反. The yin qi should
descend but, in contrast, rises. As a result, water evil settles in the region of the depots
and palaces, [that is,] water qi pours into the lung and the stomach qi moves contrary
[to its normal flow], too. Hence, there is 'panting above.'" Wu Kun: "The 'depot' [re-
ferred to here] is the lung; the 'palace' is the stomach. When the stomach, i.e., the soil,
cannot control the dampness, then [the latter] rises, enters the lung and causes water
[accumulations] as well as panting."

28 Wang Bing: "When the water stagnates below, then the qi accumulates above.
When the qi accumulates above, then the lung is full. Hence, the chest aches and is
short of qi (i.e., of breath)." Zhang Jiebin: "This is the yin of water evil, it is not true
yin. Yin evil is in the center and this causes chest pain. When the yin abounds, then
the yang weakens. Hence, one is short of qi. When one is short of qi, then the qi (i.e.,
the breath) is short and one pants."

an aversion to other people and to fire. When they hear the sound of wood,[29]
they are scared and frightened", [that is to say:]
Yang qi and yin qi strike at each other.[30]
Water and fire hate each other.
Hence, "they are scared and frightened."[31]

As for the so-called "they wish to be alone and to stay home with doors and
windows closed," [that is to say:]
The yin [qi] and the yang [qi] strike at each other.
The yang is exhausted and the yin abounds.
Hence, "they wish to be alone and to stay home with doors and windows
closed."

As for the so-called "when the disease is extreme, then they wish to climb on
elevations and to sing, to run around with their clothes thrown off," [that is to
say:]
Yin and yang repeatedly fight each other and come together in the exterior, in
the yang [region].
Hence,
this causes them "to run around with their clothes thrown off."

As for the so-called "when it settles in the tertiary vessels, then [patients suffer
from] head ache, stuffy nose, and swollen abdomen," [that is to say:]
Yang brilliance [qi] collects in the upper [region].
{"upper [region" refers to] the [patient's] tertiary network [vessels].}
>Major yin<[32]
Hence, the [patients suffers from] head ache, stuffy nose, and swollen
abdomen.[33]

---

29 2018/6: "木聲 is a mistake for 水聲." For a detailed argument, see there.

30 Zhang Jiebin: "薄 is: 氣相迫, 'the [two] qi strike against each other.'" Wu Kun: "薄 is 摩蕩, 'to rub off.'"

31 Zhang Jiebin: "When the [relationship between] yin qi and the yang qi is proper, then they are united; when it is evil, then they hate each other. [In the present case] yin evil strikes against the yang brilliance. Hence, one is scared and has fear."

32 Zhang Jiebin: "'Major yin' is to say: yin evil abounds; this is not a reference to the yin conduits. The text above always speaks of the evil of yin abundance. Hence, the meaning of the present phrase is evident." Tanba: "'Major yin' is difficult to explain here; [the two characters] may be an insertion." Probably these two characters have been erroneously copied from the the following passage (see below: 'Major yin, etc.').

33 Zhang Jiebin: "When cold evil settles in the yang brilliance [conduit], then this causes pain in the head, blockage in the nose, and distension in the abdomen. This

49-271-7
Major yin:

As for the so-called "[someone] suffers from distension," [that is to say:]
The major yin is *zi*.[34] In the eleventh month the qi of the myriad beings is all
stored in the center.
Hence,
[the text] states: "[someone] suffers from distension."[35]

As for the so-called "it moves upwards to the heart and causes belching," [that
is to say:]
The yin abounds and moves upwards to the yang brilliance.
The yang brilliance network [vessel] is connected with the heart.
Hence,
[the text] states "it moves upwards to the heart and causes belching."

As for the so-called "when they eat, then they vomit," [that is to say:]
When something abounds to fullness, it rises and overflows.
Hence,
[that person] "vomits."[36]

As for the so-called "when they are able [to relieve nature] behind and [pass]
qi,[37] then they experience a comfortable as if [a burden] had decreased," [that is

---

disease arises because yin qi moves upwards and accumulates in the tertiary network
[vessels] of the respective conduit. 'Major yin' is to say: abundance of yin evil; it does
not refer to the [respective] yin conduit."

34 Wu Kun: "In the eleventh month, the yin qi greatly abounds. Hence, [the text]
states: 'major yin.'"

35 Wang Bing: "Because the [major yin] vessel enters the abdomen, ties up with the
spleen and encloses the stomach, distension results when it has a disease."

36 Yang Shangshan: "When the stomach is full of food, then the yang qi dissolves it. In
the present case, in the eleventh month, the first yang is weak; it is not yet able to dissolve
[the food]. Hence,, when the stomach is full and overflows, this is called 'vomiting.'"
Wang Bing: "This is so because the [major yin] vessel is tied to the spleen, encloses the
stomach, rises to the diaphragm and passes on both sides of the throat." Zhang Jiebin:
"Spleen and stomach are outer and inner to each other. The stomach receives the water
and the grains. When the spleen is unable to move [things] on, then there is an abundance, a fullness, and an overflow of [these] things. Hence, this results in vomiting."

37 Zhang Zhicong: "得後 is to say: able to relieve [nature] behind. 氣 is: to break
a wind." Zhang Yizhi et al.: "The *Tai su* has 而 instead of 如. 而 and 如 were used
interchangably in ancient times."

to say:]
In the twelfth month[38] the yin qi descends and weakens and the yang qi is
about to come out.
Hence,
[the text] states "when they are able [to relieve nature] behind and [pass] qi,
then they experience a comfortable feeling as if [a burden] had decreased."

49-271-13
Minor yin:

As for the so-called "lower back pain," [that is to say:]
The minor yin, that is the kidneys[39]
In the tenth month[40] all the yang qi of the myriad beings is harmed.
Hence,
[people suffer from] "lower back pain."[41]

As for the so-called "they vomit and cough; rising qi [occurs together with]
panting," [that is to say:]

The yin qi is in the lower [region] and the yang qi is in the upper [region].
All the yang qi is near the surface and there is nothing that it might lean on or
follow.

---

38 Cheng Shide et al.: "The *Tai su* has 'eleventh month' instead of 'twelfth month.'
On the basis of the pathoconditions listed with regard to the remaining five conduit
vessels and if one takes into account the statement below: 'the yin qi descends and
weakens and the yang qi is about to come out,' this is a reference to the winter solstice.
Hence, one should follow the *Tai su*."

39 Hu Tianxiong: "In accordance with the preceding and the following text, 腎
should be 申. The *Tai su* has the same mistake."

40 Ma Shi: "The minor yin is the beginning yin. The tenth month is the second
month of winter; it, too, is minor yin." Cheng Shide et al.: "The *Tai su* has 'seventh
month' instead of 'tenth month.' Yang Shangshan states: 'In the seventh month, the
autumn qi begins to arrive. Hence, [the text] states: minor yin.' Also, since the text
states further below: 'the autumn qi begins to arrive and a slight frost begins to descend,' it is quite safe to follow the *Tai su*."

41 Wang Bing: "The minor yin is the vessel of the kidneys. The lower back is the
palace of the kidneys. Hence, [in case of disease in the minor yin vessel], the lower
back aches." Zhang Jiebin: "When cold evil enters the kidneys, then the lower back
aches. The pure yin is in the lower region; hence it corresponds to the qi of the tenth
month." Zhang Qi: "When the kidney yang is weak, [lower back] pain results because
the lower back is the palace of the kidneys."

Hence,

"they vomit and cough; rising qi [occurs together with] panting."[42]

As for the so-called "they are restless;[43] they cannot stand for long or sit for long; when they rise, then their eyes become unclear and they do not see anything,"[44] [that is to say:]

The yin and the yang of the myriad beings is undetermined and there is no ruler yet.

When the autumn qi begins to arrive, a slight frost begins to descend and immediately kills the myriad beings. Yin and yang are lost internally.

Hence,

"the eyes become unclear and do not see anything."

---

42 Wang Bing: "This is so because the [respective] vessel rises from the kidneys, passes through the liver and the diaphragm and enters the lung." Zhang Jiebin: "The yang is rooted in the yin; the yin is rooted in the yang. Both depend on each other. If there is no yang in the yin, [the yin] is in the depth and does not rise. As a result, there is solitary yang above. [The solitary yang] is at the surface and does not descend and there is nothing that follows it. Hence, one vomits, throws up qi, and pants."

43 Cheng Shide et al.: "The *Tai su* has 邑邑 instead of 色色. One should follow the *Tai su*." Yang Shangshan: "[邑邑 is:] sad because of disappointment." Gao Shishi: "The two characters 色色 are a later insertion." Zhang Jiebin: "[The two characters] 色色 are a mistake. This should be 邑邑, 'uneasy.'" Tanba: "邑 is 悒, 'unrest.'" We follow the *Tai su* version in the interpretation of Tanba. An early text using 邑 in the sense of 悒 is the *Shi ji*.

44 The *Tai su* does not have the character 久 in front of 坐. Hu Tianxiong: "The character 久 is a later insertion. The *Tai su* [version] is correct. The [Mawangdui manuscript] 陰陽脈灸經 has: 坐而起則目䀮如毋見. This can serve as evidence." Gao Shishi: "'One cannot stand for long or sit for long' means: one sits and wishes to rise. *Ling shu* 10 states: 'One sits and wishes to rise. The eyes turn unclear as if one were blind.'" Cheng Shide et al.: "Zhang Jiebin and Ma Shi read this like 不能久立久坐, 起目䀮䀮無所見, 'one cannot stand or sit for long. If one rises, then the eyes turn unclear and one does not see anything.' Yang Shangshan and Wu Kun read as follows: 不能久立, 久坐起目䀮䀮無所見, 'one cannot stand for long. If one has sat for a long time and rises, then the eyes turn dizzy and one does not see anything.' Yang Shangshan states: 'In the seventh month, the rule of yin or yang is not determined yet. The autumn qi begins to arrive and the yang qi begins to disappear. Hence, one is sad and disappointed. One cannot stand up for long. Also, neither yin nor yang are present internally in sufficient quantities. Hence, if one rises from one's seat, the eyes become unclear and one does not see anything.'"

49-272-4

As for the so-called "they are short of qi and they tend to be angry,"[45] [that is to say:]
The yang qi does not govern.
When the yang qi does not govern, then the yang qi cannot leave.
The liver qi should govern but is not yet able to do so.
Hence,
"they tend to be angry."
{As for "they tend to be angry," this is called "boiling recession."}[46]

As for the so-called "they are in fear as if someone were about to arrest them,"
[that is to say:]
[Under the dominance of] the autumn qi the myriad beings have not com-
pletely vanished yet.
The yin qi is present in small quantities and the yang qi enters [the interior].
Yin and yang [qi] strike at each other.
Hence,
[people suffer from] "fear."

As for the so-called "they hate to smell the odor of food," [that is to say:]
The stomach has no qi.
Hence,
"they hate to smell the odor of food."[47]

As for the so-called "the face is black like the color of earth," [that is to say:]
The autumn qi has been lost inside.

---

45 Gao Shishi: "'Short of qi,' [is to say:] the qi accumulates below. *Su wen* 62 states:
'when the blood accumulates above and when the qi accumulates below, the heart is
vexed and one tends to be angry."

46 The *Tai su* has 前, 'frontal,' instead of 煎. Guo Aichun-92: "煎 should be 前. 前
厥 is 前仆, 'to fall down forwards.'"This view is supported by 30/20. 2225/5: "煎厥 is
a mental confusion resulting from qi moving contrary [to its normal flow] because of
an excessively active yang qi 'boiling' the yin essence." See also 2669/21.

47 Zhang Jiebin: "When there is no stomach qi, the stomach qi is dispersed. The
stomach qi is destroyed because the kidneys have affected the stomach. [That is,]
the true fire in the kidneys is insufficient and cannot warm and nourish the source of
transformation. Hence, the stomach qi is depleted and one hates to smell the odor of
food. This is the same meaning as expressed in the previous treatise by the phrase 'one
is hungry but does not wish to eat.'" Yao Shaoyu: "The stomach is depleted. Hence,
there is no qi and one cannot distinguish the five flavors. As a result, one hates to smell
[the odor of food]."

Hence,
a change occurs in one's color.[48]

As for the so-called "when they cough, then there is blood," [that is to say:]
The yang vessels have been harmed.[49]
The yang qi does not yet abound above, but the vessels are full.[50]
When they are full, then [the patient] coughs.
Hence,
blood appears from the nose.[51]

49-272-11
Ceasing yin:

As for the so-called "breakdown illness with elevation illness, in women the lower abdomen is swollen,"[52] [that is to say:]
Ceasing yin is *chen*; the third month is the yin in the yang.
The evil is in the center.

---

48 Gao Shishi: "The color of the soil is the color of soil sallowness." Zhang Qi: "The color is a manifestation of changes in the qi. When the qi is lost internally, then the color of the respective depot appears. Hence, the face turns black." Hu Tianxiong: "The B-version of the [Mawangdui manuscript] 陰陽脈灸經 has 炧, 'the ashes of a pastille,' instead of 地. 地, therefore, is a mistake for 炧."

49 Zhang Jiebin: "'The yang vessels are harmed,' [is to say:] the vessels of the upper burner are harmed." Wu Kun: "[The text speaks of] yang vessels because these vessels move through the upper half of the body."

50 Zhang Qi: "The character 未 is a later insertion." Mori agrees. Tanba: "The *Tai su* has 'abdominal fullness' instead of 'the vessels are full.' Both [versions] are difficult to follow."

51 Zhang Qi: "The yang rises contrary [to its normal flow], hence one coughs. When the network [vessels] are harmed, then blood appears in the nostrils."

52 Gao Shishi: "癩疝 is like 癀疝; it refers to a swelling." *NJCD:* "癩疝 refers to a swollen scrotum." *Ling shu* 10 has: "When the foot ceasing yin vessel of the liver ... is excited, then the lower back aches and one cannot bend down and up. Males suffer from 癩疝; females suffer from abdominal swelling." Hu Tianxiong: "癩疝 refers to an elevation illness of males; a distension of the lower abdomen refers to an elevation illness of females. 頹 is 墮, 'to break down.' 疝 is 痛, 'pain.' In a commentary on *Su wen* 7, Wang Bing states: 'the yang qi falls down; the yin [movement in the] vessels rises to fight [it]. When [the yin] rises to fight, then there is much cold; when the [yang qi] falls, then the sinews relax. Hence, the scrotum hangs down and slackens.'"

Hence, [the text] states: "breakdown illness with elevation illness, the lower abdomen is swollen."[53]

As for the so-called "pain in the lower back and in the spine; [patients] are unable to bend down and up," [that is to say:]
In the third month, when everything is excited to blossom,[54]
once the myriad beings are bent down they do not return to an upright position.

49-272-13
As for the so-called "breakdown illness, protuberance illness,[55] elevation illness, and skin distension," [56] that is to say:
The yin abounds, too,[57] and the vessels are distended and impassable.
Hence,
[the text] states: "breakdown illness, protuberance illness, and elevation illness."

As for the so-called "when it is severe, then the throat is dry and the center is heated," [that is to say:]
Yin and yang [qi] strike at each other and heat [results].
Hence,
"the throat is dry."

---

53 Wang Bing: "This is so because the [ceasing yin] vessel follows the yin (i.e., the inner side) of the thighs, enters the region of the pubic hair, encircles the yin (i.e., sexual) organ and reaches the lower abdomen." Zhang Zhicong: "The third month is a time when the yang abounds while the ceasing yin rules the qi. Hence, this is yin in yang. 'Evil' is to say: yang qi. The qi of ceasing yin is in the interior and cannot yet leave [the body] entirely. Hence, it causes breakdown and elevation illnesses and abdominal swelling."

54 Zhang Jiebin: "三月一振 is: the yang qi is excited." Cheng Shide et al.: "振 is 振作發生, 'to stir up.'"

55 The present context suggests that 癃, like the other three diseases named here, refers to a health problem associated with some bulging or distension. Since this term was used in other contexts for what may have been complete or near-complete anuria, one may wonder whether it could have been designed to signify an enlarged prostate leading to an inability to pass urine.

56 Zhang Zhicong: "The yin (i.e., sexual) organ is swollen and one cannot pass urine." Gao Shishi: "When the yin organ is swollen and one cannot pass urine, then the skin is distended."

57 Wu Kun has 由, "resulting from," instead of 曰. Zhang Jiebin: "This again explains that the origin of the swellings accompanying protuberance and elevation illness lies in an abundance of yin evil. When yin [evil] abounds, then the yang qi does not move. Hence, these pathoconditions emerge." Tanba: "Wu Kun's version is correct."

Chapter 50
Discourse on the Essentials of Piercing

50-273-2
Huang Di asked:
"I should like to hear about the essentials of piercing."

Qi Bo responded:
"The diseases include [those] at the surface and [others] in the depth;
piercing includes shallow [piercing] and deep [piercing].
Always go to the respective structures;[1]
never go too far on this way.[2]
If one goes to far on this [way], then [this results in] internal harm;
if one does not reach it, then [this] generates external congestion.
Once there is a congestion, then evil will follow there.[3]

When [the proper measure of] shallow or deep [piercing] is not achieved,
contrary [to one's intentions] this will cause severe injury and
excites the five depots internally.
This will generate a serious disease subsequently.[4]

---

1 Gao Shishi: "各至其理 is: always reach the line structures (文理) of the skin, the flesh, the vessels, the sinews, and the bones." Cheng Shide et al.: "理 refers to the flesh section."

2 Wang Bing: "'Way' refers to the passage ways of the qi." Zhang Jiebin: "If one should [apply a] shallow [piercing] but does not do so, or if one should [apply a] deep [piercing] but fails to do so, that is alway 過其道. " Zhang Yizhi et al.: "理 and 道 have corresponding meanings. In *Meng zi* 孟子, Gao zi 告子 it is stated: 理義之悅我心. The commentary states: 理者，得道之理, '*li* is to grasp the structures of the Way.' "

3 Wang Bing: "'If one moves beyond [the necessary], then [this results in] internal harm' because [one had pierced] too deep. 'If one stays short [of the necessary], then [this] generates external congestion' because one has unreasonably enriched the qi of another section. When the qi is enriched so that external congestion results, evil qi will move to the depleted [region]." Zhang Jiebin: "If one [pierces] too deep, then this harms the qi in the interior. If [the piercing] is erroneously shallow, then this brings the qi to the outside. Hence, congestion-swelling results and the evil, contrary [to one's intentions] moves there." Zhang Zhicong: "In case of 壅 the blood and the qi do not move." Cheng Shide et al.: "壅 is 阻塞, 'blockage.' "

4 Wang Bing: "賊 is to say: 私害, 'self-inflicted harm.' 動 is to say: 動亂, 'to disturb.' 'External blockage' and 'internal harm' are the consequences of a 'severe disease.' Hence, [the text] states: 'later generates a severe disease.' " Cheng Shide et al.: "動 is 傷, 'to harm.' " 900/69 points out the rhyme structure of these 16 characters.

50-273-5
Hence,
it is said:

Among the diseases are
those in the finest body hair and interstice structures,
those in the skin,
those in the muscles and flesh,
those in the vessels,
those in the sinews,
those in the bones and
those in the marrow.[5]

Hence,
when piercing the finest body hair and the interstice structures, do not harm
the skin.
When the skin is harmed, then internally this excites the lung.
When the lung is excited, then [that person] will suffer from warmth-malaria
in autumn.
He shivers from cold in a *su*-manner.[6]

50-273-8
When piercing the skin, do not harm the flesh.
When the flesh is harmed, then this excites the spleen internally.

---

5 Wang Bing: "Long body hair is called 毫. The line structures (文理) of the skin
are called 腠理. Both can be seen on the skin." Zhang Zhicong: "'To pierce the finest
hair and the interstice structures' is the most shallow piercing."

6 The *Jia yi jing* has 淅淅, that is the soughing sound of the wind. Both the *su-su* of
the *Su wen* and the *xi-xi* of the *Jia yi jing* may be attempts at imitating the sounds
voiced when a person feels bitter cold. For this interpretation see also Gao Jiwu/42.
However, the appearance of 泝然 in *Su wen* 56 suggests another interpretation. Thus,
Zhang Zhicong reads 泝 as 溯, "to move against the stream", which is the original
meaning of that term: "To move upwards against the stream is called 泝. 泝泝然
is: the qi moves upwards against [its normal course] and one feels cold." This view is
also supported by 2167/49. 965/39 sees no connection between a countermovement
of qi (as implied by an interpretation of 泝泝 as 溯) and a feeling of cold: "The two
characters 泝泝 are corrupted versions of 淅淅." 969/63 agrees. 915/58: "泝泝然 is
identical with 肅肅然, 'pulling together' / 'stern'. *Zhuang zi* 莊子, 'Tian zi cai' 天
子才 has: 至陰肅肅. Cheng Xuan-ying 成玄英 commented: '肅肅 is the cold of yin
qi.'" 2165/40: "The 淅淅 of *Ling shu* 26, the 洒洒 of *Su wen* 49, and the 泝泝 of *Su
wen* 50 refer to different degrees of feeling cold. .. 泝泝 refers to a shivering from severe cold. One experiences a cold as if confronted by an influx of water. 泝 is identical
with 溯."

When the spleen is excited, then [that person] will suffer from abdominal
distension, vexation, and a lack of appetite for 72 days,
{during the months constituting the final thirds of the four [seasons]}.[7]

When piercing the flesh, do not harm the vessels.
When the vessels are harmed, then internally this excites the heart.
When the heart is excited, then [that person] will suffer from heartache in
summer.[8]

When piercing the vessels, do not harm the sinews.
When the sinews are harmed, then internally this excites the liver.
When the liver is excited, then [that person] will suffer from heat and slack-
ened sinews in spring.[9]

---

7 Wang Bing: "The spleen is linked to the flesh; it rules throughout the four seasons.
Also, the respective vessel moves [upwards] from the frontal edge of the inner thigh
into the abdomen, touches the spleen, encloses the stomach, rises to the diaphragm,
parallels the throat on both sides, connects with the base of the tongue and disperses
below the tongue. Its branch section, too, rises from the stomach to the diaphragm
and enters the heart. Hence, when the flesh is harmed, then this excites the spleen.
When the spleen is excited, then one suffers from a distended abdomen, vexation,
and a lack of appetite during the months of the four seasons. '72 days, the months
constituting the final thirds of the four [seasons]' is to say: in each the third month,
the sixth month, the ninth month, and the twelfth month when the soil rules for 18
days after the [first] twelve days." Wu Kun: "The spleen rules the central mansion.
Hence, the abdomen is swollen. When the spleen qi fails to move, then the central qi
is not transformed. This causes vexation. When the spleen is ill, then it fails to rub [the
stomach]. This causes one to lack appetite." 2038/10: "四季 refers to the last months
of each of the four seasons: 季春, 季夏, 季秋, 季冬. " Wang Bing, following the last
part of this sentence (probably an early commentary appended to the text) appears to
have based his calculations on a four-fold division of a year. Thus, he divided 72 by 4
and arrived at the number of 18 days at the end of each season. However, we assume
that the number of 72 days is based on a five-fold division of a year. That is, the entire
year has 360 days. One fifth amounts to 72 days. This way, each season is associated
with one of the five agents, with each agent being equally represented in the course of
an entire year. The season referred to here corresponds to the spleen.

8 Wang Bing: "The heart is linked to the vessels; it is ruled by the summer qi. The
minor yin vessel of the true heart emerges from within the heart and touches the heart
connection and the heart enclosure. The vessel of the heart master emerges from the
chest and touches the heart enclosure. *Su wen* 18 states: 'The true [qi] of the depots
penetrates into the heart.' Hence, when the vessels are harmed, then this excites the
heart. When the heart is excited, then one suffers from heartache in summer."

9 Wang Bing: "The liver is linked to the sinews; it is ruled by the spring qi. The *Zhen
jing* 鍼經 states: 'In case of heat the sinews slacken.' (This is a reference to a statement

When piercing the sinews, do not harm the bones.
When the bones are harmed, then internally this excites the kidneys.
When the kidneys are excited, then [that person] will suffer from distension and lower back pain in winter.[10]

When piercing the bones, do not harm the marrow.
When the marrow is harmed, then it melts away and the shins turn sore.
The body turns *jie-yi*-like and [one can]not go away."[11]

---

found in *Ling shu* chapter 13.) Hence, when the sinews are harmed, then this excites the liver. When the liver is excited, then one suffers from heat and slackened sinews in summer. 弛 is 縱緩, 'relaxed.'"

10 Wang Bing: The kidneys, too, are linked to the bones; they are ruled by the winter qi. The lower back is the palace of the kidneys. Hence, when the bones are harmed, then this excites the kidneys. When the kidneys are excited, then one suffers from lower back pain in winter. The straight line of the kidney vessel ascends from the kidneys and penetrates the liver and the diaphragm. Hence, [in case of a disease in this vessel] distension results." Yao Shaoyu: "One suffers from distension because the qi in the human body originates from the gate of life. When the kidneys are harmed, then the gate of life is no longer able to transform qi. [The qi is] blocked and cannot move on. Hence, distension results. [Wang Bing in his] comment states: '[The kidney vessel] penetrates the liver and the diaphragm.' Now, how could a distension emerge just because [the kidney vessel] penetrates the liver and the diaphragm?"

11 Wang Bing: "The marrow is that which fills the bones. The *Zhen jing* states: 'When the sea of marrow is filled insufficiently, then the brain revolves, the ears buzz, the shins turn sore, and one's vision is dizzy.' (See end of *Ling shu* 33.) Hence, when the marrow is harmed, then the brain and the marrow melt away, the shins turn sore, and the body slackens and cannot move. 銷鑠 is to say: the brain and the marrow melt away. .. when the brain and the marrow have melted away, then the bones are empty." Zhang Jiebin: "The marrow is the filling of the bones; it is associated with the essence; it is that which is situated in the greatest depth. When the essence and the marrow are harmed, such diseases as desiccation and withering, melting away, and sore shins result. 解㑊 is a term indicating fatigue and weakness; it is a yin depletion. When the yin is depleted, then the qi is depleted. When the qi is depleted, then one cannot move. That is what is meant by 不去." Hu Tianxiong: "去 is 除, 'to remove.' 不去 is 'cannot be removed.' That is to say, when the lung is excited, one falls ill in autumn and this can be healed at winter solstice. When the heart is excited, one falls ill in summer and this can be healed at autumn begins, etc. In case one pierces the bones and harms the marrow, causing the essence marrow to melt away, the shins will turn sore and the body is tired as a result. This disease is difficult to remove. Hence, when the text above speaks of harm to the five depots, it always mentions a time of the year when the disease breaks out. Only when a piercing of the bones has harmed the marrow, then there is no such [date]. This is proof enough." Zhang Yizhi et al.: "銷鑠 is 焦枯, 'to dry.'" See also *Su wen* 18-113-1.

Chapter 51
Discourse on the Restrictions of Piercing[1]

51-274-6
Huang Di asked:
"I should like to hear about piercing the shallow and the deep sections."[2]

Qi Bo responded:
"When piercing the bones, do not harm the sinews.
When piercing the sinews, do not harm the flesh.
When piercing the flesh, do not harm the vessels.
When piercing the vessels, do not harm the skin.[3]
When piercing the skin, do not harm the flesh.
When piercing the flesh, do not harm the sinews.
When piercing the sinews, do not harm the bones."[4]

Huang Di:
"I have not yet understood what that is to say.
I should like to hear its explanation."

---

1 Yao Shaoyu: "齊 is 一; that is, the piercing follows definite principles. One must not exceed and one must not stay short [of the necessary]." Hu Tianxiong: "齊 is 分限. 分限 refers to an amount (see *Zhou li*, Tian guan, Heng ren 周裡，天管，亨人); in the present context it refers to the degree of depth. When the *Ling shu* 9 states 刺肥人者以秋冬之齊，刺瘦人者以春夏之齊, then this is the meaning of 刺齊 here. Yao Shaoyu was wrong when he identified the present 齊 as the 齊 pronounced in the even tone." Ma Shi: "齊 is identical with the 劑, 'prescription,' of later times. Piercing requires 'prescriptions' in the same way as prescriptions are written out for medicinal drugs. Hence, the name of this treatise."

2 Wang Bing: "That is to say, the sections of the skin, the flesh, the sinews, the vessels, and the bones."

3 Gao Shishi: "That is to say, when it is appropriate to pierce into the depth, one must not apply shallow [piercing]; if one applies shallow [piercing], then [one hits] the wrong section."

4 Gao Shishi: "That is to say, when it is appropriate to apply shallow [piercing], one must not pierce into the depth; if one pierces into the depth, then [one hits] the wrong section." 1114/41: "This is to explain, the most important criterion for [determining] the depth of piercing is the location of the disease-evil. When the disease is in the depth, one pierces into the depth. When the disease is near the surface, one pierces near the surface."

51-274-9
Qi Bo:
" 'When piercing the bones, do not harm the sinews,' [warns against the following:]
the needle reaches the sinews and is withdrawn; it does not approach the bones.[5]
'When piercing the sinews, do not harm the flesh,' [warns against the following:]
[the needle] reaches the flesh and is withdrawn; it does not approach the sinews.
'When piercing the flesh, do not harm the vessels,' [warns against the following:]
[the needle] reaches the vessels and is withdrawn; it does not approach the flesh.
'When piercing the vessels do not harm the skin,' [warns against the following:]
[the needle] reaches the skin and is withdrawn; it does not approach the vessels.[6]

51-275-3
As for the so-called 'when piercing the skin, do not harm the flesh,' the disease is in the skin.
Insert the needle into the skin; do not harm the flesh.

---

5 Gao Shishi: "When it is said 'When piercing the bones, do not harm the sinews,' that is to say: if the needle reaches the sinews and is withdrawn and does not approach the bones, then this harms the sinews. Etc."

6 Wang Bing: "All this is to say [how] one misses the evil. Now, since the sinews are affected by cold evil, the flesh is affected by wind evil, the vessels are affected by dampness evil, and the skin is affected by heat evil, [these evils] are missed as is [described in the text]. The so-called 'evil' is always an attack by an improper qi." Zhang Jiebin: "When the disease is in the bones, one must pierce the bones directly and one must avoid harming the sinews. When the needle reaches the section of the sinews, pulls out qi [there] and is withdrawn again, but does not approach the bones, one harms the sinews because no disease is in the liver and by [piercing the sinews] one does not attack an excess there." In contrast, Ma Shi: "'When piercing the bones, the sinews are not harmed,' is: when the needle reaches the sinews and is withdrawn and does not approach the bones, then the disease in the bones heals by itself and the sinews are not harmed. 'When piercing the sinews, the flesh is not harmed,' is: when the needle reaches the flesh and is withdrawn and does not approach the sinews, then the disease in the sinews heals by itself and the flesh is not harmed. .. All these therapies take a 'not approaching [the location of the disease]' as their main [principle]."

'When piercing the flesh, do not harm the sinews,' [warns against the following:]
[to insert the needle] beyond the flesh and to hit the sinews.
'When piercing the sinews, do not harm the bones,' [warns against the following:]
to insert [the needle] beyond the sinews and to hit the bones.[7]
This would be called acting contrary to [what is appropriate]."[8]

---

7 Cheng Shide et al.: "'When piercing the bones do not harm the sinews' is by no means to say that the needle is to be withdrawn when it has reached the section of the sinews, so to avoid that by reaching into the depth of the bones one harms – contrary [to one's intentions] – the qi of the sinews. Rather one should 'pierce the bones directly, without harming the sinews.'"

8 Mori: "The first section of this text outlines four [types of piercing] that do not reach their destination; the latter section of the text outlines three [types of piercing] that exceed their proper limits. Hence, all [seven] are called 'acting against [what is appropriate].'"

Chapter 52
Discourse on Prohibitions in Piercing[1]

52-275-8
Huang Di asked:
"I should like to hear about prohibited techniques [in piercing]."[2]

Qi Bo responded:
"[Each] depot has an important [location where it can be] harmed;[3]
[these locations] must be inspected!

The liver generates life on the left;[4]
the lung stores on the right.[5]

---

1 For a detailed clinical discussion of the prohibitions mentioned below, see 1065/19.

2 Yang Shangshan: "數 is 法, 'method.'" *NJCD:* "數 is 術, 方法, 'technique, method'" Gao Jiwu/232: "數 is to be explained as 几, 'how many?' As Zhang Zhicong commented: 'That is to say: how many locations exist that one must not pierce?'" Gao Shishi: "數 is 條目, 'entry.'"

3 Gu Yanwu 顧炎武 stated in his *Ri zhi lu* 日知錄: "The *Nan yue* 南越, Wei tuo zhuan 尉佗傳, states: '發兵守要害處.' A comment to the *Han shu* 漢書, Xi nan yi zhuan 西南夷傳, states: Shigu said: 'The 要害 [places] are those that are important for me and where the enemy inflicts harm.' This commentary does not suffice. 要害 is to say: place to attack and to defend. [At such places] I can harm someone else and someone else can harm me. That is called 'harm.' The human body, too, has 要害 [places]."

4 Wang Bing: "The liver reflects the wood; it flourishes in spring. The spring is yang and brings [things] to life. Hence, it generates life on the left."

5 Wang Bing: "The lung reflects the metal; it flourishes in autumn. The autumn is yin; it gathers and kills. Hence, it stores on the right." Gao Shishi: "When man faces South, the East is to his left and the West is to his right. The liver rules the qi generated in spring; it is located in the East. Hence, 'the liver generates life on the left.' The lung rules the qi gathered in autumn; it is located in the West. Hence, 'the lung stores on the right.'" Wan Lanqing et al./51: "The meaning of these two statements is: the qi generated by the liver rises on the left; the clear qi of the lung descends on the right. One should realize that the ancients determined left and right in that they faced the South and turned their back against the North. .. The liver is associated with the East and the wood; the lung is associated with the West and the metal. The East is on the left; the West is on the right. The sun rises in the East; it descends in the West. .. The liver is the minor yang in the yin. It rules the generation of qi in the human body and

The heart commands in the exterior;[6]
the kidneys govern the interior.[7]
The spleen serves as their messenger;[8]
the stomach serves as their marketplace.[9]

---

is linked to the East. The East is on the left. Hence, its qi rises on the left." 2891/8: "The qi generated by the liver conduit starts on the left and rises; the qi stored by the lung conduit starts on the right and descends." 725/20: "These two statements refer to the anatomical positions of liver and lung. 'Left' and 'right' stand for 'below' and 'above,' respectively. That is, 'the liver exists below [the diaphragm]; the lung is stored above [the diaphragm].'" For details of the argument, see there. See also 1667/10. For a rejection of the 'anatomical' interpretation, see also 267.

6 Yang Shangshan: "The heart is the commander-ruler (部王) of the five depots. Hence, it is said 'to command.'" Wang Bing: "The yang qi rules the exterior; the heart reflects the fire." Ma Shi: "The heart is associated with the yang; it is located above the diaphragm. Hence, 'the heart is positioned in the exterior.'"

7 Yang Shangshan: "The qi moving between the [two] kidneys serves to govern the interior. Hence, [the text] states 'governs.'" Wang Bing: "The yin qi rules the interior; the kidneys reflect the water." Ma Shi: "The kidneys are associated with the yin; they are located below the diaphragm. Hence, 'the kidneys govern the interior.'" 1185/3: "'Interior' refers to the depots and palaces, to the bones and the marrow here. The kidneys store the essence and they rule the water. They nourish the depots and palaces with moisture and they fill and supply the bones and the marrow. Hence, [the text] states: 'The kidneys govern the interior.'"

8 Yang Shangshan: "The spleen is soil; it flourishes during [all] the four seasons. The spleen moves the grain qi to supply the four [remaining] depots. Hence, it is considered to be the 'messenger.'" Wang Bing: "It transports, without ceasing, the dregs, the water, and the grains. Hence, it is the 'messenger.'" Yao Shaoyu: "To run without a break, this is called a 'messenger.' The spleen is responsible for transporting and transforming the water and the grains to nourish the entire body. This is why it is considered the 'messenger.'"

9 Yang Shangshan: "The stomach is the palace of the spleen; The stomach stores the five grains; it delivers [their] qi to the spleen to supply the four [remaining] depots. Hence, it is the 'market.'" Wang Bing: "This is where the water and the grains turn to; all the five flavors enter here. It resembles the variety [of food] at the market. Hence, it is the 'market.'" Yao Shaoyu: "Where the one hundred goods are brought together, this is called a 'market.' The stomach is called 'sea of water and grains.' It serves to transform the five flavors. This is why it is considered the 'market.'" 725/20: "The two statements 'the spleen serves as its messenger; the stomach serves as its marketplace' have always been explained as references to the physiological functions of spleen and stomach. In fact, though, these statements refer to the anatomical positions of spleen and stomach. The *Er ya* 爾雅, Shi gu 釋詁, states: 使 is 從, 'to follow.' The statement 脾為之使 follows immediately after the statement 腎治于裡. This is to say, spleen and kidneys are associated with yin and with the interior. .. 'Market' refers to yang

Above the *ge-huang*, in the middle there are father and mother.[10]
To the side of the seventh joint, in the middle there is the small heart.[11]

---

and to exterior. Hence, 胃為之市 is to say: the stomach is associated with the yang and with the exterior." 2179/8: "The liver is located in the body on the right. The text says 生于左, it does not say 居于左, 'is located on the left.' 生左 is to say: the liver itself is located on the right, but its left lobe reaches to the left." 2763/41: "'Left and right' refers to yin and yang." See also 61/7.

10 Yang Shangshan: "Below the heart and above the diaphragm is the *huang*. The heart is yang; it is the father. The lung is yin; it is the mother. The lung rules the qi; the heart rules the blood. Together they provide nourishment and protection to the body. Hence, they are father and mother." Wang Bing: "Above the *ge-huang*, the sea of qi is located in the center. 'Qi' is the source of life; 'life' rules one's existence. Hence, the sea of qi is father and mother of man." Zhang Jiebin: "鬲 is 鬲膜, 'the diaphragm.' 肓 is [the region] below the heart and above the diaphragm. 'Above the 鬲肓, this is where the heart and the lung are located. The heart is the yang in the yang; the lung is the yin in the yang. The heart rules the blood; the lung rules the qi. They serve to build and protect the body. Hence, they are called 'father and mother.'" Wang Shaozeng & Xu Yongnian/28: "Above the *ge-huang* are the two depots maintaining life, i.e., heart and lung." 906/40: "鬲肓之上 is 鬲上, 'above the diaphragm.'" See there for a detailed discussion of 膏肓 and 鬲肓. Zhang Zhicong: "Yin and yang are father and mother of [all] transformation. Water and fire are the manifestations of yin and yang. 'In the center are father and mother' is to say: the heart is a yang depot; it is located above the diaphragm. The kidneys are a yin depot; they are located above the 肓." Gao Shishi: "鬲 is 胸鬲, 'chest diaphragm.' 肓 is the 肓-transportation point to the side of the navel. Above the diaphragm is the lung; it is heaven. Above the 肓 is the spleen; it is earth. The heaven is the father; the earth is the mother."

11 Wang Bing: "小心 is to say 真心, 'true heart.'" Lin Yi et al.: "The *Tai su* has 志心, 'mind-heart,' instead of 小心." Yang Shangshan: "The spine has three times seven, i.e., 21, joints. The kidneys are located to the side of the seventh joint of the lower [segment of the spine]. The spirit of the kidneys is called 志, 'mind.' The spiritual [forces] of the five depots are all called 神, 'spirit.' That by which the spirit manages things, it is called 'mind.' It is the spirit of the heart." Ma Shi: "Below the heart is the heart enclosing network; from its physical appearance it is yellow fat covering the heart. It is tied to the ceasing yin conduit. The [heart] enclosing network occupies a location from the fifth vertebra to the seventh [spine] joint. Hence, [the text] states: 'to the side of the seventh [spine] joint, in the center, is the small heart.' Now, the heart is the ruler, it is the big heart; the enclosing network is the official; it is the small heart." Wu Kun: "The spine has altogether 21 joints. What is referred to here as the seventh joint is the seventh joint of the lower segment. To the side [of the seventh joint] are the two kidneys; the left is the kidney, the right is the gate of life. The gate of life is the minister fire. The minister fire carries out tasks on behalf of the heart ruler. Hence, it is called 'small heart.'" Gao Shishi: "'To the side of the seventh joint [of the spine],' now, if counted from above downwards, to both sides of the seventh joint are

To take these [morphologies] into account entails happiness;
to oppose [them] entails calamity.[12]

52-276-2
When a piercing hits the heart, death occurs within one day.
If the [heart] was [merely] excited, this causes belching.[13]
When a piercing hits the liver, death occurs within five days.
If the [liver] was [merely] excited, this causes talkativeness.[14]
When a piercing hits the kidneys, death occurs within six days.[15]
If the [kidney] was [merely] excited, this causes sneezing.[16]
When a piercing hits the lung, death occurs within three days.

---

the Diaphragm Transporter (膈輸) holes. 'Small' is: extremely fine. 'In the center is
the small heart' is to say: the qi of the heart leaves [the body] through the Diaphragm
Transporter hole; it is extremely fine." Tanba: " 'Small heart' must refer to something
else." Cheng Shide et al.: "The 'seventh joint above' refers to the vertebrae of the neck;
it does not refer to the vertebrae of the spine. To the side of the vertebrae of the neck
is the location of the brain, i.e., medulla oblongata. Hence, 'small heart' is a metaphor
referring to the brain. By suggesting an analogy with the heart, the importance [of the
brain] is emphasized." 965/39: "The insertion holes to the side of the seventh vertebra,
both if counted from above or below, have nothing to do with the heart function of
storing the spirit. Hence, this 七 must be an error for 十, 'ten.' " See also 326/31,
145/6, 2711/49, and 219/18 for detailed discussions.

12 Wang Bing: "從 is to say: 隨, 'to follow,' 順, 'to adapt.' These eight are those by
which man comes to life and by which his physical appearance is perfected. If one
adapts to them, then happiness is prolonged. If one opposes them, then calamity arrives." See 900/68 for an identification of these statements as ancient rhymes.

13 Zhang Jiebin: "The heart is the ruler of the five depots and six palaces. Hence, if it
is hit death follows very quickly before a single day has passed. The qi associated with
the heart is 'belching.' When one notices belching, then the heart qi is interrupted."

14 Lin Yi et al.: "The Quan Yuanqi edition and the *Jia yi jing* have 欠, 'yawning,'
instead of 語. .. Wang Bing has changed 欠 to 語." Tanba: "*Su wen* 23 states: '[The
qi of the heart] is belching; [the qi of the] liver is talkativeness.' Hence, 語 is correct
[here]." Zhang Jiebin: "語 is to say: to speak disorderly without reason. The qi associated with the liver is 'talkativeness.' When one notices talkativeness, then the liver qi
is interrupted." Ma Shi: " 'Five days' should be 'three days' because [three] is the number generated by wood." Zhang Zhicong: "One's voice complies with the five tones.
'Five days' corresponds to the number of the five tones."

15 Lin Yi et al.: "The Quan Yuanqi edition and the *Jia yi jing* have 'three days' instead of 'six days.' "

16 25/45: "嚏 stands for 欠, 'yawning.' The meaning is identical." For a detailed discussion of 嚏 and 欠 see *Su wen* 23.

If the [lung] was [merely] excited, this causes coughing.[17]

When a piercing hits the spleen, death occurs within ten days.[18]

If the [spleen] was [merely] excited, this causes swallowing.

When a piercing hits the gallbladder, death occurs within one and a half days.

If the [gallbladder] was [merely] excited, this causes vomiting.[19]

52-276-5

If one, when piercing the instep, hits the large vessel and if blood leaves [the body] and does not stop, [the patient will] die.[20]

If one, when piercing the face, hits the stream vessel, in unfortunate [cases this] causes blindness.[21]

If one, when piercing the head, hits the Brain's Door [hole], if [the needle] enters the brain, [the patient] dies immediately.[22]

52-277-2

If one, when piercing below the tongue, hits the vessels excessively and if blood leaves [the body] and does not stop, this causes [patients] to be mute.[23]

---

17 Ma Shi: "'Three' should be five. [Five] is the number generated by metal. When the fourth day has come to an end and when the fifth day arrives, [the patient] dies. That is correct."

18 Lin Yi et al.: "The Quan Yuanqi edition and the *Jia yi jing* have '15 days' instead of 'ten days.'" Gao Shishi: "'Ten' is the completion number of [the agent] soil."

19 Wang Bing: "The qi of the gallbladder is courage. Hence, [exciting it] causes vomiting."

20 Wang Bing: "When the large vessel is excited [and bleeds] without coming to a stop, then this is [a reference to] the large conduit of the stomach. The stomach is the sea of water and grains. When blood leaves [the conduit of the stomach] without coming to a stop, then the stomach qi is poured out. The sea is exhausted and the qi is lost. Hence, [the patient] dies." Gao Shishi: "中大脈 is 中傷大指之經脈, 'to strike and injure the conduit vessel of the big toe.'"

21 Wang Bing: "The stream vessel in the face is the junction of the hand major yang [vessel] and of the controlling vessel. The hand major yang vessel starts from the cheekbones and moves diagonally to the inner canthi of the eyes. The controlling vessel rises on both sides of the nose to below the pupils. Hence, when piercing the stream vessel in the face, in unfortunate cases [the patient] may turn blind."

22 Wang Bing: "'Brain's Door (腦戶)' is the name of a hole [used for piercing]. Above the pillow bone (i.e., the occipital bone) it provides an entry into the brain. Now, the brain is the sea of the marrow. It is where the true qi is accumulated. When a needle enters the brain, then the true qi flows away. Hence, [the patient] dies immediately."

23 Wang Bing: "The vessel below the tongue is the spleen vessel. .. When blood leaves from below the tongue without coming to a stop, then the spleen qi can no longer

If one, when piercing the network [vessels] spreading on the lower side of the feet, hits a [major] vessel and the blood does not leave [the body], this causes a swelling.[24]

If one, when piercing the cleft, hits the large vessel, this causes that person to fall to the ground and lose his color.[25]

If one, when piercing the qi street, hits the vessel and the blood does not leave [the body], this causes a swelling. {A mouse is attached.}[26]

---

supply the tongue. Hence, [the patient] turns mute and cannot speak."

24 Wang Bing: "The 'spreading network' is to say: the network [vessel] spreading into various directions in the hollow below the foot just in front of the inner ankle. This is exactly the location of the Blazing Valley (然谷) hole. The 'vessel enclosing the center' is the thoroughfare vessel. The thoroughfare vessel descends together with the minor yin conduit behind the inner ankle to below the foot. If one pierces it and no blood leaves, then the qi of the kidney vessel and of the thoroughfare vessel have turned together into the Blazing Valley. Hence, they cause swelling." Obviously, Wang Bing reads 刺絡中脈 as "when one pierces the vessel enclosing the center" while we read 刺絡中脈 as "if, when piercing the network, one hits the vessel." A similar difference in our and Wang Bing's reading appears to apply to all the 刺 .. 中 .. statements here.

25 Wang Bing: "The large vessel in the cleft is the foot major yang conduit vessel. The vessel of the foot major yang emerges from the inner canthi of the eyes .. rises to the head and descends along the neck to the feet. Hence, if one neglects this prohibition in piercing [this vessel], then this causes that person to fall to the ground and lose the color of his face." "Cleft" may refer to the popliteal fossa here.

26 Wang Bing: "These are the vessels of the gallbladder and of the stomach located on the qi street. The gallbladder vessel follows the inside of the flanks and appears at the qi street. The vessel of the stomach passes on both sides of the navel and enters into the qi street. Its branch course emerges from the lower opening of the stomach and moves inside the abdomen until it reaches into the qi street where it merges [again with the main course]. If it is pierced as [outlined] here and no blood leaves, then the qi in the blood vessel has gathered inside. Hence, internal knottings occur, resulting in a swelling assuming the shape of a hidden mouse. The qi street is located in a distance of four inches on both sides of the navel below the abdomen. It is the moving vessel that can be felt with one's hand one inch above the 'attached mouse' (鼠僕.)" Lin Yi et al.: "Another version has 鼠鼷, (lit.: 'mouse,' here: 'groin') instead of 鼠僕. A commentary to *Su wen* 59 states: 'The qi street is located one inch above the groins at the two ends of the transverse bone (i.e., pubic bone) below the navel.'" Zhang Zhicong: "鼠僕 is to say: The swelling is between the groin 鼠鼷 and the Subservient Visitor (僕參) [hole]." Gao Shishi: "' qi street' is the pathway of the qi of the lower leg. If one pierces the qi street and hits the vessel, one harms the foot major yang and yang brilliance conduit vessels. If one harms these vessels in a way that the blood does not leave [the body], then this causes 'swelling at the *shu* and *pu* [holes].' If one harms the yang brilliance vessels, then the swelling occurs at the groin (鼠鼷); if one harms the major yang vessel, then the swelling occurs at the Subservient Visitor [hole]." Tanba: "It is not necessary to change 僕 to 鼷. From [passages in] the *Shuo wen,* the *Jia yi*

If one, when piercing between [the segments of] the spine, hits the marrow, this makes [the patient] become hunchbacked.[27]

If one, when piercing above the breasts, hits the breast chamber, this causes a swelling. {The root is eaten away.}[28]

If one, when piercing into the broken basin, sinks in [too deeply], with qi flowing out, this causes that person to pant and cough, with [his qi] moving contrary [to its regular course].[29]

If one, when piercing the fish belly of the hand, sinks in [too deeply], this causes a swelling.[30]

52-278-1
Do not pierce [anyone who is] heavily drunk; [lest] you let that person's qi move disorderly.[31]

---

jing, and in Chao Yuanfang's book (i.e., Chao Yuanfang's 巢元方 *Zhu bing yuan hou lun* 諸病源候論) it is obvious that 僕 and 鸞 are identical." (For details, see there.) Hu Tianxiong: "Tanba's statement elucidates what was never elucidated before; it eliminates all uncertainties. Even though Wang Bing has stated 'The qi street is located .. one inch above the 鼠僕, ' his comment is nevertheless: 'Internal knottings occur, resulting in a swelling assuming the shape of a hidden mouse.'"

27 Wang Bing: "脊閒 is to say: in the joints of the bones of the spine. If one pierces [there] and hits the marrow, then the essence qi of the bones flows away. Hence, [the patient] becomes hunchbacked."

28 Wang Bing: "Both above and below the breast is the foot yang brilliance vessel. When the milk in the milk chamber flows out, the qi and the blood in the chest come together there from outside [the milk chamber]. That is, when a piercing hits the milk chamber, then qi and blood mingle and amass [there]. Hence, a massive swelling results. Inside is pus rooted in the interior. It consumes the muscles and the skin and transforms them to pus water [resulting in a condition] that lasts long and cannot be healed." Zhang Zhicong: "根蝕 refers to a painful itching as if an insect was eating up [the breast]." Tanba: "'Root' refers to the root of the milk chamber (i.e., base of the breasts); it is not the Breast Root (乳根) hole." Mori: "跟食 is like 內食, 'internal consumption.' There is no need to identify this as 'root of the milk chamber.' The signs are those of an abscess in the breast."

29 Wang Bing: "The lung is the canopy covering the five depots; the broken basin is their path. The lung stores the qi and rules the breathing. Also, the [corresponding] qi is the cough. If in piercing into the broken basin, one sinks in [too deeply], then the lung qi flows away to the outside. This causes that person to pant and cough, [with his qi] moving contrary to [its regular course]."

30 Wang Bing: "The flow of the lung vessel proceeds inside the fish belly of the hand. Hence, if in piercing it one sinks in [too deeply], then this causes a swelling."

31 Wang Bing: "[The movement in] the vessels is excessively frequent [when one is drunk]. Hence, if pierced [in this condition] it runs disorderly." Lin Yi et al.: "The

Do not pierce [anyone who is] very angry; [lest] you let that person's qi move contrary [to its regular course].[32]
Do not pierce anyone who is very tired.[33]
Do not pierce anyone who has just eaten to repletion.[34]
Do not pierce anyone who is very hungry.[35]
Do not pierce anyone who is very thirsty.[36]
Do not pierce anyone who is extremely frightened.[37]

52-278-4

If one, when piercing the yin (i.e., inner side of the) thighs, hits the large vessel and if blood leaves [the body] and does not stop, [the patient will] die.[38]
If one, when piercing the Visitor-Host-Person [hole], sinks [the needle] into the interior and hits the vessel, this causes internal leaking and deafness.[39]
If one, when piercing the knee cap,[40] makes fluid leave [the knee], this causes [the patient] to limp.[41]
If one, when piercing the arm major yin vessel, [causes] blood to leave profusely, [the patient will] die immediately.[42]

Ling shu jing has 脈, 'vessel,' instead of 氣. "

32 Wang Bing: "When one is angry, the qi moves contrary [to its regular course]. Hence, if pierced [in this condition, this countermovement] is increased even more."

33 Wang Bing: "The conduit qi is overly exhausted."

34 Wang Bing: "The qi is filled to abundance."

35 Wang Bing: "The qi is insufficient."

36 Wang Bing: "The blood vessels are dry."

37 Wang Bing: "The spirit is overly unsettled and the qi is in disorder."

38 Wang Bing: "Inside the yin [side] of the thigh is the vessel of the spleen. The spleen is the center, the soil, the solitary depot pouring [its qi] to all four sides. If, now, blood leaves [the spleen vessel] without coming to a stop, the qi of the spleen will be exhausted. Hence, [the patient] dies."

39 Wang Bing: "陷脈 is to say: to pierce very deeply. If one pierces [the Visitor-Host-Person hole] very deeply, one destroys the junction of the hand minor yang and foot yang brilliance vessels in the hollow that opens in front of the ears when one opens the mouth. Hence, the ears leak. When the vessels leak internally, then the qi cannot be supplied [to the ears]. Hence, [the patient] turns deaf."

40 Gao Jiwu/41: "臏 is 髕, 'knee cap.'"

41 Wang Bing: "The knee is the palace of the sinews. The sinews meet inside of it. If fluid leaves [the knee], then the sinews dry. Hence, [the patient] limps."

42 Wang Bing: "The major yin [vessel] in the shoulder is the lung vessel. The lung rules the movement of the camp and guard [qi]. The orderly regulation of yin and

52-279-1
If one, when piercing the foot minor yin vessel, [causes] a doubled depletion and makes blood leave [the body], this causes the tongue to have difficulties in speaking.[43]
If one, when piercing into the center of the breast, sinks [the needle into the interior] and hits the lung,[44] this causes [the patient] to pant with [qi] moving contrary [to its regular course]. [The patient] breathes in an upright position.[45]
If one, when piercing into the elbow, sinks [the needle] into the interior [too deeply], the qi will turn there and as a result [the patient] cannot bend or stretch [the elbow any longer].[46]

52-279-3
If one, when piercing three inches below the yin (i.e., inner side of the) thigh, sinks [the needle] into the interior [too deeply], this lets that person experience [involuntary] loss of urine.[47]
If one, when piercing into the flanks below the armpit, sinks [the needle] into

---

yang originates from it. If blood leaves [the major yin vessel] in large amounts, then [the movement of] the camp and of the guard [qi] is interrupted. Hence, [the patient] dies immediately."

43 Wang Bing: "The foot minor yin [vessel] is the kidney vessel. The foot minor yin vessel penetrates the kidneys, encloses the lung and ties up with the base of the tongue. Hence, if [one, in piercing the foot minor yin vessel, causes] a doubled depletion, with blood leaving, then the tongue has difficulties in speaking."

44 For a reading of 膺中陷 as "depression in the center of the breast", see *Su wen* 60-325-2.

45 Wang Bing: "This is the result of lung qi rising and flowing away contrary [to its regular course]." Zhang Qi: "肺, 'lung' is an error for 脉, 'vessel.'" Mori: "The *Jia yi jing* does not have the character 中 and for 'lung' it has 'vessel.' The wording 中肺 in the present version may be an error."

46 Wang Bing: "肘中 is to say: the central location where the elbow bends, into the Foot Marsh (尺澤) hole. If one pierces too [deeply] and enters the vessel, bad qi will turn there. [This] qi hardens the joints. Hence, [the patient] cannot bend or stretch [his elbow any longer]."

47 Wang Bing: "Three inches below the [upper end of the] thigh is the network [vessel] of the kidneys. Both the thoroughfare vessel and the network [vessel] of the minor yin emerge from the kidneys, descend, appear at the qi street and follow the yin [side of the] thighs. Their ascending [branches] appear at the urinary bladder. Hence, if one, when piercing [the yin side of the thigh], sinks into the vessel, then this causes that person to lose urine."

the interior [too deeply], this lets that person cough.⁴⁸

If one, when piercing the lower abdomen, hits the urinary bladder and if urine leaves [the body], this lets that person's lower abdomen experience fullness.⁴⁹

If one, when piercing the calf, sinks [the needle] into the interior, this causes a swelling.⁵⁰

52-279-5
If one, when piercing above the eye socket, sinks [the needle] into the bone and hits the vessel, this causes leakage, [which, in turn,] causes blindness.⁵¹

If, when piercing into a joint, fluid leaves [the body, the patient] will not be able to bend and stretch [the respective joint any longer].⁵²

---

48 Wang Bing: "Below the armpit is the lung vessel. The vessel of the lung moves transversely from the lung connection and appears below the armpit. The straight moving vessel of the true heart depot rises from the heart connection and appears below the armpit. If one, when piercing [below the armpit], [hits] the interior and sinks into [these] vessels, then both the heart and the lung are excited and [the patient] coughs as a result."

49 Wang Bing: "The qi of the urinary bladder flows away towards the outside and grain qi turns there. Hence, the lower abdomen experiences fullness. 'Lower abdomen' is to say: below the navel."

50 Wang Bing: "In the calf is the foot major yang vessel. If [as a result of piercing there] major yang qi flows away, this causes a swelling."

51 Wang Bing: "The vessel in the eye socket bone is the eye connection, the vessel of the liver. If one, when piercing [there], [hits] the interior and sinks in [too deeply], then the eye connection is severed. Hence, the eyes leak and turn blind."

52 Wang Bing: "All sinews are tied to the joints; body liquids flow out [of the sinews] to moisten [the joints]. If fluid leaves [the joints], then the sinew membranes dry up. Hence, [the joints] cannot be bent or stretched."

BIBLIOGRAPHY

Vol. 1 *Su wen* Chapters 1-52

The following list of Chinese dictionaries, encyclopedias, monographs, and articles includes data from an encompassing bibliography we have prepared to include close to 3000 articles written by Chinese authors over the past decades and more than 600 Chinese and Japanese monographs from the past 1600 years that appeared to us relevant, and were consulted by us, for a better understanding of the history and contents of the *Huang Di nei jing su wen*. We have excerpted here for easy reference only those titles that we considered sufficiently essential to enter our annotations to our translation of *Su wen* chapters 1-52. Chinese dictionaries and encyclopedias are quoted in the notes by abbreviations combining the first letters of the words constituting their titles. Chinese and Japanese monographs, and those few written by Western authors, are quoted by the names of their authors, or, in cases of anonymous Chinese compilations, by the name of the academic units identified as editors. As for ancient Chinese works, e.g. the dynastic histories, philosophical texts, or ancient medical compilations apart from the *Su wen*, these are identified by their titles. Finally, articles are quoted in the annotations by their number in the comprehensive bibliography. These numbers are also provided in the listing below. Where necessary, references to page numbers follow the names of authors/compilers (in the case of monographs) or the title numbers from the encompassing bibliography (in the case of articles), separated by a slash. All Chinese monographs that examine and annotate the received text of the *Su wen* in the present sequence of its contents are quoted simply by the name of the author/compiler without page numbers. The complete bibliography of articles and monographs, except for commonly known texts such as the Han dynastic history or works by Chinese philosophers with no special reference to the *Su wen*, is added on a CD to the first volume of the present *Su wen* translation.

1. DICTIONARIES AND ENCYCLOPEDIAS

– *CY*: Wu Ziyan 吳澤炎 et al., *Ci yuan (xiu ding ben)* 辭源(修定本). Beijing 北京: Shangwu yinshu guan 商务印书馆 1998

– *GHYZD*: Zhang Yongyan 张永言 et al., *Jian ming gu han yu zi dian* 简明古漢語字典. Chengdu 成都: Sichuan renmin chubanshe 四川人民出版社 1986

– *HDNJCD*: Guo Aichun 郭霭春, Li Siyuan 李思源 et al., *Huang Di nei jing ci dian* 黄帝内经辞典. Tianjin 天津: Tianjin Science and Technology Press 天津科学技术出版社 1991

– *HYDCD*: Luo Chufeng 罗竹风 et al., *Han yu da ci dian* 漢語大詞典. Shanghai 上海: *Han yu da ci dian* chubanshe 漢語大詞典出版社 1986 - 1994

– *JJZG*: Ruan Yuan 阮元 et al., *Jing ji zuan gu* 經籍纂詁. Beijing: Zhonghua shuju 1982

– *JMZYCD*: Zhongyi da cidian bianji weiyuanhui 中医大辞典编辑委员会, *Jian ming zhong yi ci dian* 简明中医词典. Beijing 北京: People's Hygiene Press 人民卫生出版社 1986

– *NJCD*: Zhang Dengben 张登本, Wu Changchun 武长春 et al., *Nei jing ci dian* 内经词典. Beijing 北京: People's Hygiene Press 人民卫生出版社 1990

– *SWJZ*: Xu Shen 許慎, *Shuo wen jie zi* 說文解字. Beijing 北京: Zhonghua shuju 中华书局 1981

– *SWJZGL*: Yang Jialuo 楊家駱 et al., *Shuo wen jie zi gu lin zheng bu he bian* 說文解字詁林正補合編. Taipei 臺北: Ding wen shuju 鼎文書局 1983

– *SWJZZ*: Duan Yucai 段玉裁, *Shuo wen jie zi zhu* 说文解字注. Shanghai 上海: Shanghai guji chubanshe yingyin 上海古籍出版社影印 1988

– *SWTXDS*: Zhu Junsheng 朱骏声, *Shuo wen tong xun ding sheng* 说文通训定声. Wuhan 武汉: Wuhanshi guji chubanshe 武汉市古籍出版社影印. Cited according to Zhang Yizhi et al.

– *TPYL*: Li Fang 李昉 ed., *Tai ping yu lan* 太平御覽. Taipei 臺北: Taiwan shangwu yinshu guan 臺灣商務印書館 1967

– *WLGHYZD*: Wang Li 王力 ed., *Wang Li Gu han yu zi dian* 王力古漢話字典. Beijing 北京: *Zhonghua Shuju* 中華書局 2000

– *YHHYZYCD*: Wiseman, Nigel: *Ying-Han/ Han-Ying zhong yi ci dian = English-Chinese/ Chinese-English Dictionary of Chinese Medicine*. Hunan 1995

– *ZGYXDCD*: Xie Guan 謝觀 et al., *Zhong guo yi xue da ci dian* 中國醫學大辭典. Taipei 臺北: Taiwan shangwu yinshu guan 臺灣商務印書館 1982

2. MONOGRAPHS

– Beijing zhongyi xueyuan: 北京中医学院, *Nei jing shi yi* 内经释义. Shanghai 上海: Shanghai kexue jishu chubanshe 上海科学技术出版社 1978

– Beijing zhongyi xueyuan (2): 北京中医学院, *Nei jing xuan du* 内经选读. Shang hai 上海: Shanghai kexue jishu chubanshe 上海科学技术出版社 1978

– Beijing zhongyi xueyuan et al.: 北京中医学院, 北京市中医学校, *Zhong yi yuan zhu xuan du* 中医原著选读. Beijing 北京: Beijing renmin chubanshe 北京人民出版社 1978

– Chen Guying 陈鼓應, *Zhuang zi jin zhu jin yi* 莊子今註今譯. Taipei 臺北: Taiwan shangwu yinshu guan 臺灣商務印書館本之木 1981

– Chen Menglei 陈梦雷, *Yi bu quan lu* 醫部全錄. Beijing 北京: People's Hygiene Press 人民卫生出版社 1963

– Chen Zhuyou 陈竹友, *Yi yong gu han yu* 医用古汉语. Fuzhou 福州: Fujian renmin chubanshe 福建人民出版社 1981

– Cheng Shide 程士德 et al., *Su wen zhu shi hui cui* 素问注释汇粹. Beijing 北京: People's Hygiene Press 人民卫生出版社 1982

– Cullen, Christopher: Some Further Points on the Shih. *Early China* 6, 1980-81, p. 39

– Duan Yishan 段逸山, *Yi gu wen* 医古文. Beijing 北京: People's Hygiene Press 人民卫生出版社 1986

– Fang Wenhui 方文辉, *Zhong yi gu ji tong jie gu jin zi li shi* 中医古籍通借古今字例释. Guangzhou 广州: 科学普及出版社广州分社 1982

– Fang Yaozhong 方药中 & Xu Jiasong 许家松, *Huang Di nei jing su wen yun qi qi pian jiang jie* 黄帝内经素问运气七篇讲解. Beijing 北京: People's Hygiene Press 人民卫生出版社 1984

– Fu Weikang 傅维康 & Wu Hongzhou 吴鸿洲, *Huang Di nei jing dao du* 黄帝内经导读. Chengdu 成都: Bashu Books 巴蜀书社 1987

– Gao Jiwu 高纪武, *Yi gu wen yu fa yu xiu ci* 医古文语法与修辞. Xining 西宁: Qinghai renmin chubanshe 青海人民出版社 1987

– Gao Shishi 高世栻, *Huang Di su wen zhi jie* 黄帝素问直解 (or *Su wen zhi jie* 素问直解). Beijing 北京: Beijing kexue jishu wenxian chubanshe 北京科学技术文献出版社 1980

– *Gu dian yi zhu xuan* bianxiezu: Quanguo zhongdeng weisheng xuexiao shiyong jiaocai *Gu dian yi zhu xuan* bianxiezu 全国中等卫生学校试用教材《古典医著选》编写组, *Gu dian yi zhu xuan* 古典医著选. Chenyang 沈阳: Liaoning renmin chubanshe 辽宁人民出版社 1979

- Gu Guanguang 顾观光, *Su wen jiao kan ji* 素问校勘记. Cited according to Zhang Yizhi et al.

- Gu Yanwu 顧炎武, *Ri zhi lu* 日知錄. Cited according to Zhang Yizhi et al.

- Guan Jisheng 管济生, "*Su wen shang gu tien zhen lun" yi shi er ze*《素问·上古天真论》异释二则. *Guo yi lun tan* 国医论坛 1989 期 2(14), 43

- Gui Fu 桂馥, *Shuo wen jie zi yi zheng* 说文解字义证. Cited according to Zhang Yizhi et al.

- Guo Aichun-81: Guo Aichun 郭蔼春, *Huang Di nei jing su wen jiao zhu yu yi* 黄帝内经素问校注语译. Tianjin 天津: Tianjin kexue jishu chubanshe 天津科学技术出版社 1981

- Guo Aichun-92: Guo Aichun 郭蔼春, *Huang Di nei jing su wen jiao zhu* 黄帝内经素问校注. Beijing 北京：People's Hygiene Press 人民卫生出版社1992

- Guo Tian 郭霑, *Nei jing jiang yi* 内经讲义. Beijing: People's Hygiene Press 人民卫生出版社 1989

- *Han Fei zi*: Shao Zenghua 邵增樺, *Han Fei zi jin zhu jin yi* 韓非子今註今譯. Taipei: Taiwan shangwu yinshu guan 臺灣商務印書館1983

- *Han shu*: Ban Gu 班固, Han shu 漢書. Beijing: Zhonghua shuju 1987

- Harper 1998: Harper, Donald: *Early Chinese Medical Literature*. London: Kegan Paul International 1998

- Harper 1978-79: Harper, Donald: The Han Cosmic Board. *Early China* 4, p.1-10

- Harper 1980-81: Harper, Donald: The Han Cosmic Board - A Response to Christopher Cullen. *Early China* 6, p. 50 – 51

- *Hou Han shu*: Fan Ye 范曄, *Hou Han shu* 後漢書. Beijing: Zhonghua shuju 1973

- Hsü, Elisabeth: Yinyang and Mao's Dialectics in Traditional Chinese Medicine. *Asiatische Studien/Études Asiatiques*, LII, 2, 1988, p. 438.

- Hu Shu 胡澍, *Su wen jiao yi* 素问校义, *Huang Di nei jing su wen jiao yi* 黄帝内经素问校义. Cited according to Cheng Shide et al. and Zhang Yizhi et al.

- Hu Tianxiong 胡天雄, *Su wen bu shi* 素问补识. Beijing 北京: Chinese Medical and Pharmaceutical Science and Technology Press 中国医药科技出版社1991

- Hua Shou 滑寿, *Du su wen chao* 读素问钞. Cited according to Cheng Shide et al.

- *Huai nan zi*: Liu An 劉安, *Huai nan zi* 淮南子. *Er shi er zi* 二十二子, *p.* 1204-1308. *Shanghai*: Shanghai guji chubanshe 上海古籍出版社 1986

- Huang Sanyuan 黄三元, *Zhong yi gu wen ji chu* 中医古文基础. Taipei台北：Bade jiaoyu wenhua chubanshe 八德教育文化出版社1983

- Hucker, Charles O.: *A Dictionary of Official Titles in Imperial China*. Stanford 1985

– *Jia yi jing*: Huangfu Mi 皇甫謐, *Huang Di zhen jiu jia yi jing* 黄帝針灸甲乙經. Taipei: Tailian guofeng chubanshe yinxing 台聯國風出版社印行 1975

– *Lao zi*: Wang Bi王弼, *Lao zi dao de jing zhu* 老子道德經注. *Wang Bi ji jiao shi* 王弼集校釋, shang ce 上册. Beijing: Zhonghua shuju 1980

– Legge, James: *The Chinese Classics in Five Volumes.* Taipei: SMC Publishing Inc 1991

– Li Guoqing 李国清, *Su wen yi shi* 素问疑识. Harbin 哈尔滨: Heilongjiang renmin chubanshe 黑龙江人民出版社1988

– Li Jinyong 李今庸, *Xin bian Huang Di nei jing gang mu* 新编黄帝内经纲目. Shanghai上海: Shanghai Science and Technology Press 上海科学技术出版社 1988

– Li Zhongzi 李中梓 (= Li Nian'e 李念莪), *Nei jing zhi yao* 内经知要. (Written in 1642.) Shanghai上海：上海商务印书馆1955

– Lin Yi et al. 林億等 (Song commentators of Wang Bing´s *Su wen* edition), *Xin jiao zheng* 新校正. Cited according to our editions of Wang Bing 王冰, *Huang Di nei jing su wen* 黄帝内經素問, see below.

– *Ling shu*: Dai Xinmin 戴新民, *Huang Di nei jing zhang ju suo yin* 黄帝内經章句索引, p. 263-482 Ling shu jing 靈樞經. Taipei台北: Qiye shuju 啓業書局 1987

– Liu Zhenmin et al. 刘振民等, *Yi gu wen ji chu* 医古文基础. *Beijing* 北京：人民卫生出版社1980

– Ma Jixing 马继兴, *Ma wang dui gu yi shu kao shi* 马王堆古医书考释. Changsha 长沙: Hunan kexue jishu chubanshe 湖南科学技术出版社1992

– Ma Kanwen 马堪温, "Classic Chinese Medical Literature in Contemporary China: Texts Selected for Modern Editions, and Problems Associated with this Work". In Paul U. Unschuld, ed., *Approaches to Traditional Chinese Medicine.* Dordrecht: Kluwer Academic Press 1989, p. 7

– Ma Shi 马莳, *Huang Di nei jing su wen zhu zheng fa wei* 黄帝内经素问注证发微. (Written in 1586.) Beijing 北京：科学技术文献出版社1999. Normally cited according to Cheng Shide et al.

– *Mai jing*: Wang Shuhe王叔和, *Mai jing* 脈經. Fuzhou shi renmin yiyuan 副州市人民醫院, *Mai jing jiao shi* 脈經校釋. Beijing: People's Hygiene Press 人民卫生出版社1988

– Mori: Mori Risshi (or Tatsuyuki) 森立之, *Somon Kôchû* 素问考注. Cited according to Zhang Yizhi et al.

– *Nan jing*: Hua Shou 滑壽, *Nan jing ben yi, nan jing gu yi* 難經本義, 難經古義. Taipei: Wenguang tushu youxian gongsi yinxing 文光圖書有限公司印行 1984

– Nanjing zhongyi xueyuan: Nanjing zhongyi xueyuan yijing jiaoyanzu 南京中医学院医经教研组, *Huang Di nei jing su wen yi shi* 黄帝内经素问译释. Shanghai上

海: Shanghai kexue jishu chubanshe 上海科学技术出版社 1959 Cited according to Cheng Shide et al

— Qian Chaochen-88: Qian Chaochen 钱超尘, *Zhongyi guji xungu yanjiu* 中医古籍训诂研究. Guiyang 贵阳: Guizhou renmin chubanshe 贵州人民出版社 1988

— Qian Chaochen-90: Qian Chaochen 钱超尘, *Nei jing yu yan yan jiu* 内经语言研究. Beijing 北京: People's Hygiene Press 人民卫生出版社 1990

— Ruan Yuan 阮元 et al., *Shi san jing zhu shu* 十三經注疏. Beijing: Zhonghua shuju 1987

— Shanghai zhongyi xueyuan: Shanghai zhongyi xueyuan yiguwen jiaoyanzu 上海中医学院医古文教研组, *Gu dai yi xue wen xuan* 古代医学文选. Shanghai 上海: Shanghai kexue jishu chubanshe 上海科学技术出版社 1980

— Shanghai zhongyi xueyuan et al.: Shanghai zhongyi xueyuan, Zhejiang zhongyi xueyuan 上海中医学院、浙江中医学院, *Yi gu wen* 医古文. Shanghai 上海: Shanghai kexue jishu chubanshe 上海科学技术出版社 1978

— *Shen Nong ben cao jing*: Wang Jumo 王筠默, Wang Hengfen 王恒芬, *Shen Nong ben cao jing jiao zheng* 神農本草經校證. Changchun 長春: Jilin kexue jishu chubanshe 吉林科学技术出版社 1988

— Shen Zumian 沈祖绵, *Du su wen yi duan* 读素问臆断. Cited according to Zhang Yizhi et al.

— *Shi ji*: Sima Qian 司馬遷, *Shi ji* 史記. Beijing: Zhonghua shuju 1989

— Soothill, W. E.: *The Hall of Light*. New York 1952

— Sun Dingyi 孙鼎宜, *Huang Di nei jing zhang ju* 黄帝内经章句. Cited according to Zhang Yizhi et al., Hu Tianxiong, etc.

— Sun Yirang 孙诒让, *Su wen Wang Bing zhu jiao* 素问王冰注校. Cited according to Zhang Yizhi et al.

— *Tai su*: Yang Shangshan 楊上善 (ed.), *Huang Di nei jing tai su* 黄帝内經太素. Critical edition by Xiao Yanping 萧延平 (1924). Beijing: Renmin weisheng chubanshe yingyin 人民卫生出版社影印 1955-1958

— Tanba: Tanba Genkan 丹波元简, *Somon Shi* 素問識. Beijing 北京: 人民卫生出版社 1984

— Tanba Genken 丹波元堅, *Somon Shôshi* 素問紹識. Cited according to Cheng Shide et al. and Zhang Yizhi et al.

— Tang Rongchuan 唐容川, *Yi jing jing yi* 醫經精義. Cited according to Cheng Shide et al.

— Unschuld, Paul U. 2003: *Huang Di nei jing su wen - Nature, Knowledge, Imagery in an Ancient Chinese Medical Text*. Berkeley: University of California Press 2003

– Wan Lanqing 万兰清 et al., *Zhong yi si da jing dian zhu zuo ti jie* 中医四大经典著作题解. Nanchang 南昌: Jiangxi renmin chubanshe 江西人民出版社 1982

– Wang Ang 汪昂, *Su wen ling shu lei zuan yue zhu* 素问灵枢类纂约注, or *Su ling lei zuan* 灵素类纂. Shanghai 上海：上海科学技术出版社1959

– Wang Bing 王冰 (ed.), *Huang Di nei jing su wen* 黄帝内經素問 (ed. 762). Taipei 台北: 国立中国医药研究所影印明嘉靖顾从德本1960

– Wang Bing 王冰 (ed.), *Huang Di nei jing su wen* 黄帝内經素問. Beijing 北京：People's Hygiene Press 人民卫生出版社1963/ 1983

– Wang Hongtu 王洪图 et al., *Huang Di nei jing yan jiu da cheng* 黄帝内经研究大成. Beijing 北京: Beijing chubanshe 北京出版社1997

– Wang Ji 汪机, *Xu su wen chao* 续素问钞. Cited according to Cheng Shide et al.

– Wang Qi 王琦 et al., *Su wen jin shi* 素问今释. Guiyang 贵阳：Guizhou renmin chubanshe 贵州人民出版社1981

– Wang Shaozeng 王绍增, *Yi gu wen yu fa* 医古文语法. Harbin 哈尔滨: Heilongjiang kexue jishu chubanshe 黑龙江科学技术出版社1983

– Wang Shaozeng 王绍增 & Xu Yongnian 徐永年, *Yi gu wen xiu ci* 医古文修辞. Harbin 哈尔滨：Heilongjiang kexue jishu chubanshe 黑龙江科学技术出版社 1985

– Wu Kun 吴崐: *Nei jing su wen Wu zhu* 内经素问吴注. Jinan 济南: Shandong kexue jishu chubanshe 山东科学技术出版社 1984

– *Xun zi*: Zhang Shitong 章诗同, *Xun zi jian zhu* 荀子簡注. Shanghai: Shanghai renmin chubanshe 上海人民出版社1974

– Xue Xue 薛雪, *Yi jing yuan zhi* 医经原旨. Cited according to Cheng Shide et al.

– Yan Hongchen 阎洪臣 & Gao Guangzhen 高光振, *Nei nan jing xuan shi* 内难经选释. Chang chun 长春：Jilin renmin chubanshe 吉林人民出版社 1979

– Yan Zhenhai 严振海, *Gu yi ji de ju dou biao dian* 古医籍的句读标点. Shanghai 上海：Shanghai kexue jishu chubanshe 上海科学技术出版社1987

– Yang Shangshan 楊上善 (ed.), *Huang Di nei jing tai su* 黄帝内經太素. Taipei 台北: Wenguang Tushu Ltd. 文光圖書有限公司 1990

– Yao Shaoyu 姚紹虞 (*zi*: Zhi'an 止庵), *Su wen jing zhu jie jie* 素問經注節解. (Written in 1669.) Beijing 北京: Renmin weisheng chubanshe 人民卫生出版社, 1963 . Normally cited according to Cheng Shide et al.

– Yang Weijie 楊維傑, *Huang Di nei jing su wen yi jie* 黄帝内經素問譯解. Taipei: 樂群出版公司1977

– Ye Gang 叶岗, *Zhong yi gu ji yue du tan* 中医古籍阅读谈. Guangzhou 广州：Guangdong keji chubanshe 广东科技出版社 1980

– Yu Chang 于鬯, *Xiang cao xu jiao shu – Su wen jiao* 香草续校书，素问校. Cited according to Zhang Yizhi et al.

– Yu Yue 俞樾, *Nei jing bian yan* 内经辩言. Cited according to Zhang Yizhi et al.

– Yu Zihan et al. 余自汉等, *Nei jing ling su kao* 内经灵素考. Beijing 北京: Zhongguo zhongyiyao chubanshe 中国中医药出版社 1992

– Zhang Canjia 张灿玾, *Huang Di nei jing su wen jiao shi* 黄帝内经素问校释. Beijing 北京: People's Hygiene Press 人民卫生出版社 1980

– Zhang Jiyou 张继有, *Huang Di nei jing su wen Wu zhu ping shi* 黄帝内经素问吴注评释. Beijing 北京: Chinese Ancient Literature Press 中医古籍出版社 1986

– Zhang Jiebin 张介宾, *Lei jing* 類經. Beijing 北京: Renmin weisheng chubanshe 人民卫生出版社 1957

– Zhang Jiebin (2): 张介宾, *Lei jing tu yi* 類經圖翼. Beijing 北京: Renmin weisheng chubanshe 人民卫生出版社 1985

– Zhang Qi 张琦, *Su wen shi yi* 素问释义. Cited according to Cheng Shide et al. and Zhang Yizhi et al.

– Zhang Wenhu 张文虎, *Shu yi shi xu bi – nei jing su wen* 舒艺室续笔·内经素问. 同治十三年金陵冶城刊本. Cited according to Zhang Yizhi et al.

– Zhang Yizhi 张毅之 et al., *"Nei jing su wen" yi nan wen ti zhu du*《内经·素问》疑难问题助读. Beijing 北京: Zhongguo yiyao keji chubanshe 中国医药科技出版社 1993

– Zhang Zhicong 张志聪 (=Zhang Yin'an 张隐庵), *Huang Di nei jing su wen ji zhu* 黄帝内经素问集注, or *Su wen ji zhu* 素问集注. Taipei 台北：Wenguang tushu youxian gongsi yingyin 文光图书有限公司影印 1982

– Zhen Lifen et al. 陈丽芬等, *Yi wen jing hua* 医文精华. Shanghai 上海：Shanghai kexue jishu chubanshe 上海科学技术出版社 1986

– Zhongyi yanjiuyuan: Zhongyi yanjiuyuan zhongyi yanjiushengban 中医研究院中医研究生班, *Huang Di nei jing zhu ping* 黄帝内经注评. Published in Beijing by Research Class in Chinese Medicine of the Academy of Chinese Medicine 1980

– Zhou Fengwu 周凤梧 et al., *Huang Di nei jing su wen bai hua jie* 黄帝内经素问白话解. Beijing 北京: People's Hygiene Press 人民卫生出版社 1958

– Zhou Xuehai 周学海, *Nei jing ping wen* 内经评文. Cited according to Cheng Shide et al.

3. ARTICLES

4. Bai Junfeng 白峻峰 1987. "Wu zang qi zheng" xin shi "五藏气争"新释. *Guang ming zhong yi* 光明中医 3, 37

10. Ban Xiuwen 班秀文 1985. Shi tan *Nei jing* you guan fu ke de lun shu 试探《内经》有关妇科的论述. *Guang xi zhong yi yao* 广西中医药 3, 1-3, 13

11. Ban Zhaoxian 班兆贤 1987. Lian zhu yu hui huan xiu ci fa zai *Nei jing* zhong de ying yong 联珠与回环修辞法在《内经》中的应用. *Bei jing zhong yi xue yuan xue bao* 北京中医学院学报 4, 42-44

14. Ban Zhaoxian 班兆贤 1985. *Nei jing* xiu ci yan jiu – bi yu, dui ou ji pai bi《内经》——比喻、对偶及排比. *Shan dong zhong yi xue yuan xue bao* 山东中医修辞研究学院学报 9, 3, 26

17. Bao Laifa 包来发 1986. Ye tan *Nei jing* nei zheng jiao kan 也谈《内经》内证校勘. *Shang hai zhong yi yao za zhi* 上海中医药杂志 9, 36-37

20. Bao Laifa 包来发 1985. *Huang Di nei jing* zhu shi fen qi yuan yin qian xi《黄帝内经》注释分歧原因浅析. *Zhong yi za zhi* 中医杂志 11, 54-55

25. Bao Xiaodong 鲍晓东 1986. "Shen wei qian wei ti" bian "肾为欠为嚏"辨. *Zhe jiang zhong yi xue yuan xue bao* 浙江中医学院学报 4, 45

28. Bei Runpu 贝润浦 1984. Lun "yin yang fan ta, zhi zai quan heng xiang duo" 论"阴阳反他,治在权衡相夺". *Zhe jiang zhong yi xue yuan xue bao* 浙江中医学院学报 6, 1-3

30. Bi Xianhua 毕献华 1989. Qian tan *Nei jing* lun zhong fen zheng zhi 浅谈《内经》论中风证治. *Tian jin zhong yi* 天津中医 3, 20, 18

39. Cai Dingfang 蔡定芳 1981. "Zhi wei du qu yang ming" de ti hui he yin zheng "治痿独取阳明"的体会和印证. *Zhe jiang zhong yi xue yuan xue bao* 浙江中医学院学报 4, 22-24

40. Cai Fatian 蔡发田 1986. "Da qi ru yu zang fu zhe, bu bing er cu si" ping jie "大气入于脏腑者,不病而卒死"评解. *Hei long jiang zhong yi yao* 黑龙江中医药 4, 27, 37

47. Cai Xu 蔡旭 1987. Dui Wu Kun gai *Su wen* sheng qi tong tian lun zhong yi jing wen de kan fa 对吴昆改《素问·生气通天论》中一经文的看法. *An hui zhong yi xue yuan xue bao* 安徽中医学院学报 3, 57-58

53. Cao Hongxin 曹洪欣 1990. Bian zhen fa tan xi 遍诊法探析. *Zhong yi yao xin xi* 中医药信息 4, 7-8

58. Cao Zhenfen 曹振芬 1988. Qian tan *Nei jing* dui er bi hou ke xue de lun shu 浅谈《内经》对耳鼻喉科学的论述. *Tian jin zhong yi* 天津中医 6, 30-31

61. Chai Kefu 柴可夫 1990. Gan sheng fei jiang li lun de yuan liu 肝升肺降理论的源流. *Zhong yi yao xue bao* 中医药学报 2,7-9

65. Chang Senyuan 常森元 1983. *Huang Di nei jing su wen xi yi* xuan deng《黄帝内经素问析义》选登. *Shaan xi zhong yi han shou* 陕西中医函授 1,3-11

78. Chen Gang 陈钢 1987. Cong "you wu", "you yu bu zu" kan xu shi zheng de han yi 从"有无"、"有余不足"看虚证实证的涵义. *Liao ning zhong yi za zhi* 辽宁中医杂志 8,42-44

79. Chen Gang 陈钢 1990. Lun *Nei jing* bian zang fu jing mai lun zhi yu bian bing shi zhi 论《内经》辨脏腑经脉论治与辨病施治. *Shan dong zhong yi xue yuan xue bao* 山东中医学院学报 1,14

80. Chen Gang 陈钢 1987. Lun *Nei jing* zhen fa xue shuo zhong de "guan cha" 论《内经》诊法学说中的"观察". *Shaan xi zhong yi* 陕西中医 10,446-447

81. Chen Gang 陈钢 1989. *Nei jing* "xu" "shi" xi yi《内经》"虚" "实"析义. *Shaan xi zhong yi han shou* 陕西中医函授 5,36-37

82. Chen Gang 陈钢 1990. You tan "xin yi run zhi" 又谈"辛以润之". *Si chuan zhong yi* 四川中医 8,8

83. Chen Gang 陈钢 1990. *Nei jing* zhi "zhen qi" ji shi zheng qi《内经》之"真气"即是正气. *Zhong yi han shou tong xun* 中医函授通讯 6,6-7

86. Chen Guiting, Zhu Jinshan 陈贵廷,朱锦善 1981. *Nei jing* zhong you guan er ke xue de lun shu《内经》中有关儿科学的论述. *Zhe jiang zhong yi za zhi* 浙江中医杂志 8,344-345

94. Chen Junwen 陈俊文 1983. "Qi ben zai shen, qi mo zai fei" jie xi "其本在肾,其末在肺"解析. *Hu bei zhong yi za zhi* 湖北中医杂志 3,51-52

110. Chen Ming 陈明 1986. *Nei jing* zang fu cang xie lun bian《内经》脏腑藏泻论辨. *He nan zhong yi* 河南中医 6,1-4

112. Chen Ming 陈明 1989. Shi tan "fei chao bai mai" 试谈"肺朝百脉". *He nan zhong yi* 河南中医 6,5-7

114. Chen Nong 陈农 1986. *Nei jing* zhong you guan "xin jian bo dong de ji zai《内经》中有关"心尖搏动"的记载. *He nan zhong yi* 河南中医 5,40

117. Chen Nong 陈农 1988. "Qu wan chen cuo" xi "去宛陈莝"析. *Shang hai zhong yi yao za zhi* 上海中医药杂志 6,38

127. Chen Shuzhen 陈树珍 1988. "Qu jue yu dan" chu yi "取决于胆"刍议. *Shaan xi zhong yi* 陕西中医 2,95

129. Chen Siduan 陈四端 1958. Wo dui "san jiao" de ti hui 我对"三焦"的体会. *Fu jian zhong yi yao* 福建中医药 6,33

137. Chen Wujiu 陈无咎 1983. *Nei jing bian huo ti gang* 内经辨惑提纲. *Zhe jiang zhong yi za zhi* 浙江中医杂志 1, 9-16

138. Chen Wujiu 陈无咎 1983. *Nei jing bian huo ti gang* 内经辨惑提纲. *Zhe jiang zhong yi za zhi* 浙江中医杂志 2, 17-24

139. Chen Wujiu 陈无咎 1983. *Nei jing* bian huo ti gang 内经辨惑提纲.内经辨惑提纲. *Zhe jiang zhong yi za zhi* 浙江中医杂志 3, 25-32

140. Chen Wujiu 陈无咎 1983. *Nei jing bian huo ti gang* 内经辨惑提纲. *Zhe jiang zhong yi za zhi* 浙江中医杂志 4, 25-32

144. Chen Xianping 陈贤平 1986. "Xiao zhe qu qu shu zhi qi yao" zhi wo jian "消者瞿瞿，孰知其要"之我见. *Shang hai zhong yi yao za zhi* 上海中医药杂志 1, 33

145. Chen Xinsheng 陈新生 1965. Shi lun ming men 試論命門. *Ha er bin zhong yi* 哈尔滨中医 8, 6-10

148. Chen Yiting 陈贻庭 1988. Ping Yu Chang *Xiang cao xu jiao shu* dui *Su wen* de jiao shi 评于鬯《香草续校书》对《素问》的校释. *Fu jian zhong yi yao* 福建中医药 2, 51-52

150. Chen Yiting 陈贻庭 1990. *Nei jing* yi wen ci yu yong fa kao cha《内经》疑问词语用法考察. *Fu jian yi yao* 福建中医药, 4, 59

157. Chen Zengying 陈增英 1983. Ju zhong ci yi de que ding 句中词义的确定. *Xin zhong yi* 新中医 3, 55-56

174. Cheng Zhaozhi 成肇智 1988. "Ba/pi ji zhi ben" zheng yi "罢极之本" 正义. *He nan zhong yi* 河南中医 5, 10

175. Cheng Zhaozhi 成肇智 1980. *Nei jing* xi yi er ze《内经》析疑二则. *Hu bei zhong yi za zhi* 湖北中医杂志 1, 32-34

178. Cheng Zhaozhi 成肇智 1989. "Shi yi zang qu jue yu dan" de zhi yi he kan wu "十一脏取决于胆"的质疑和勘误. *Shang hai zhong yi yao za zhi* 上海中医药杂志 9, 40-42

180. Cheng Zhaozhi 成肇智 1983. *Nei jing* "mai" zi jian xi《内经》"脉" 字简析. *Zhe jiang zhong yi za zhi* 浙江中医杂志 1, 8-9

182. Cheng Zhaozhi et al. 成肇智 等 1984. *Nei jing* ti jie《内经》题解. *Hu bei zhong yi za zhi* 湖北中医杂志 4, 38-40

193. Cheng Shide 程士德 1984. Xin bian *Nei jing jiang yi* fu dao jiang zuo (ctd.) 新编《内经讲义》辅导讲座 (续). *Bei jing zhong yi xue yuan xue bao* 北京中医学院学报 2, 39-42

210. Cheng Shide 程士德 1987. *Nei jing* zi xue ti yao — bing zheng zhen zhi yang sheng bu fen《内经》自学提要(三)——病证诊治养生部分. *Zhong yi jiao yu* 中医教育 4, 42-45

217.   Cheng Shide, Guo Xiazhen 程士德, 郭霞珍 1982. *Nei jing* li lun ti xi de ji ben xue shu si xiang《内经》理论体系的基本学术思想. *Bei jing zhong yi xue yuan xue bao* 北京中医学院学报 3, 6-10

219.   Cheng Zhao 程昭 1986. Ming men xue shuo yan jiu yu lin chuang ying yong 命门学说研究与临床应用. *Xin jiang zhong yi yao* 新疆中医药 2, 18-21

221.   Cheng Zhaohuan 程昭寰 1981. Lüe lun "shi yi zang qu jue yu dan" ji qi lin chuang yi yi 略论 "十一脏取决于胆" 及其临床意义. *Zhe jiang zhong yi za zhi* 浙江中医杂志 5, 212-214

226.   Chi Huaji 迟华基 1989. "Gan zhe, jiang jun zhi guan" bu shi "肝者, 将军之官" 补释. *Shan dong zhong yi xue yuan xue bao* 山东中医学院学报 3, 66, 8

230.   Chi Huaji 迟华基 1983. Lesson 11: Biao ben de, shen qi shi, xie qi fu, ji bing yu — *Su wen* Tang ye lao li lun 第十一讲: 标本得神气使邪气服疾病愈——《素问·汤液醪醴论》. *Shan dong zhong yi za zhi* 山东中医杂志 5, 53-55

231.   Chi Huaji 迟华基 1984. Lesson 15: Chu yu chang tan lun jing mai, zai yan qi kou jue ji xiong — *Su wen* "Jing mai bie lun" 第十五讲: 出于常谈论经脉再言气口决吉凶——《素问·经脉别论》. *Shan dong zhong yi za zhi* 山东中医杂志 3, 55-57, 43

232.   Chi Huaji 迟华基 1985. Lesson 19: Ping re bing jin tui, lun zheng xie xiao zhang — *Su wen* "Ping re bing lun" 第十九讲: 评热病进退 论正邪消长——《素问·评热病论》. *Shan dong zhong yi za zhi* 山东中医杂志 1, 55-57, 54

238.   Chu Jinxiang 褚谨翔 1980. Yu Yue yu *Nei jing bian yan* 俞樾与《内经辩言》. *Zhe jiang zhong yi za zhi* 浙江中医杂志 9, 400-401

240.   Chu Xuanren, Wang Tianru 褚玄仁, 王天如 1982. Ye tan "qi zeng er jiu, yao zhi you ye" 也谈 "气增而久, 夭之由也". *Jiang su zhong yi za zhi* 江苏中医杂志 1, 55-56

244.   Cui Boying 崔伯瑛 1989. *Nei jing* jie gu san ze《内经》解诂三则. *Shan dong zhong yi xue yuan xue bao* 山东中医学院学报 3, 68-69

246.   Cui Xizhang 崔锡章 1986. Zen yang yue du gu yi shu de zhu shi 怎样阅读古医书的注释. *Guang ming zhong yi* 光明中医 3, 8-15

247.   Cui Xizhang 崔锡章 1984. Tan Lin Yi dui *Nei jing* de jiao kan yu xun gu 谈林亿对《内经》的校勘与训诂. *Gui yang zhong yi xue yuan xue bao* 贵阳中医学院学报 1, 21-23

249.   Cui Yanghong 崔扬红 1988. Shi xi "qi, wei, jing, xing" 试析 "气、味、精、形". *Zhong yi han shou tong xun* 中医函授通讯 3, 10

252.   Cui Zhongping 崔仲平 1986. *Nei jing* ben wen xun gu chu tan (1)《内经》本文训诂初探(上). *Ji lin zhong yi yao* 吉林中医药 2, 38-39

267. De Yi 得一 1961. Du shu sui ji — *Su wen* shi yi 讀书随記——素問釋义. *Jiang su zhong yi* 江苏中医 7, 封三

283. Dong Hanliang 董汉良 1982. *Nei jing* xue ku fang zheng zhi tan shi《内经》血枯方证之探释. *Shaan xi zhong yi* 陕西中医 3, 28-29

285. Dong Huxing 董胡兴 1981. *Nei jing* jiao xue guan jie liu fa《内经》教学贯解六法. *Xin zhong yi* 新中医 8, 47-51

287. Dong Qisheng 董其圣 1984. Zhi wei du qu yang ming zhi wo jian 治痿独取阳明之我见. *Shang hai zhong yi yao za zhi* 上海中医药杂志 7, 29-30

299. Duan Qizhong 段其忠 1982. Qian tan "zhang zhi zhi fa" 浅谈 "彰之之法". *Ji lin zhong yi yao* 吉林中医药 4, 60

300. Duan Yishan 段逸山 1982. Yi gu wen shu ci biao shi fa shu li 医古文数词表示法述例. *Shang hai zhong yi yao za zhi* 上海中医药杂志 11, 42-43

302. Duan Yishan 段逸山 1987. Yu gao 菀槀. *Shang hai zhong yi yao za zhi* 上海中医药杂志 6, 48

307. Duan Yishan 段逸山 1981. Gu yi jing te shu yu wen xian xiang ju yu (ctd.) 古医经特殊语文现象举隅 (续). *Zhong hua yi shi za zhi* 中华医史杂志 3, 183-186

324. Fang Wenhui 方文辉 1983. Shi ci huo yong qian xi (2) 实词活用浅析 (二). *Xin zhong yi* 新中医 2, 51-52

326. Fang Yaozhong 方药中 1980. "Ge huang zhi shang, zhong you fu mu, qi jie zhi bang, zhong you xiao xin" shi "鬲肓之上, 中有父母, 七节之傍, 中有小心" 释. *Cheng du zhong yi xue yuan xue bao* 成都中医学院学报 4, 31-32

331. Fang Yaozhong 方药中 1982. Tan "xu er xiang bing" 谈 "虚而相并". *Si chuan zhong yi* 四川中医 创刊号, 3-5

353. Fang Yaozhong, Xu Jiasong 方药中, 许家松 1986. Lun zhong yi li lun ti xi de ji ben nei han ji qi chan sheng de wu zhi ji chu 论中医理论体系的基本内涵及其产生的物质基础. *Tian jin zhong yi xue yuan xue bao* 天津中医学院学报 2-3, 14-27

371. Fang Zhaoqin 方肇勤 1983. Fen yun bu xi tan qi yi 纷纭不息探气义. *Shang hai zhong yi yao za zhi* 上海中医药杂志 11, 40-41

377. Feng Tailai 封太来 1983. Qian tan "feng yi sheng shi" 浅谈 "风以胜湿". *Shaan xi zhong yi* 陕西中医 3, 23-24

384. Feng Songjie 冯松杰 1986. Cong ci yi bian hua kan *Nei jing* cheng shu shi dai 从词义变化看《内经》成书时代. *Nan jing zhong yi xue yuan xue bao* 南京中医学院学报 3, 57-58

390. Fu Youfeng 符友丰 1988. *Su wen* Feng lun zha ji《素问·风论》札记. *Hei long jiang zhong yi yao* 黑龙江中医药 2, 8-9

391.   Fu Youfeng 符友丰 1989. Lüe lun zang xiang wen ti 略论脏象问题. *Hei long jiang zhong yi yao* 黑龙江中医药 3,7-9

393.   Fu Youfeng 符友丰 1985. *Su wen* "Wei lun" xun gu zha ji《素问·痿论》训诂札记. *Shaan xi zhong yi* 陕西中医 8,370-371

394.   Fu Youfeng 符友丰 1986. *Su wen* "Jing mai bie lun" zha ji — shi "kui duo yi wei chang ye"《素问·经脉别论》札记——释"揆度以为常也". *Zhong yi yao xue bao* 中医药学报 3,54-56

395.   Fu Qiang 府强 1986. Shi shu zi wu liu zhu na zhi fa de xing cheng yu fa zhan 试述子午流注纳支法的形成与发展. *Tian jin zhong yi xue yuan xue bao* 天津中医学院学报 4,40-42

399.   Fu Jingchun 傅景春 1982. "Er yang zhi bing fa xin pi" qian yi "二阳之病发心脾"浅议. *Guang xi zhong yi yao* 广西中医药 2,16,12

411.   Fu Zhenliang 傅贞亮 1980. Lun "wei bu he ze wo bu an" 论"胃不和则卧不安". *Shaan xi zhong yi* 陕西中医 2,25-26

419.   Fu Zhenliang 付贞亮 1979. Zen yang xue xi *Nei jing* 怎样学习《内经》. *Shaan xi zhong yi xue yuan xue bao* 陕西中医学院学报 1,1-7

428.   Gao Bozheng 高伯正 1986. "Xu xie" xiao yi "虚邪"小议. *Si chuan zhong yi* 四川中医 7,7

438.   Gao Feng 高峰 1988. "Wei bu he ze wo bu an" xiao yi "胃不和则卧不安"小议. *Shan dong zhong yi za zhi* 山东中医杂志 1,13

442.   Gao Guangzhen 高光震 1985. *Nei jing ci yu ci dian* yang gao xuan deng (3)《内经词语辞典》样稿选登(三). *Ji lin zhong yi yao* 吉林中医药 2,34

447.   Gao Guangzhen 高光震 1985. *Nei jing ci yu ci dian* yang gao xuan deng (8)《内经词语辞典》样稿选登(八). *Ji lin zhong yi yao* 吉林中医药 1,42-44

448.   Gao Guangzhen 高光震 1985. *Nei jing ci yu ci dian* yang gao xuan deng (9)《内经词语辞典》样稿选登(九). *Ji lin zhong yi yao* 吉林中医药 2,40-42

451.   Gao Guangzhen 高光震 1983. Pai jue yin ao, duo suo fa ming 排抉隐奥多所发明. *Shang hai zhong yi yao za zhi* 上海中医药杂志 5,38-39

458.   Gao Hesheng 高和声 1980. Wo dui *Nei jing* de ji dian ren shi 我对《内经》的几点认识. *Zhe jiang zhong yi xue yuan xue bao* 浙江中医学院学报 2,10-13

461.   Gao Jiashu 高甲成 1980. Dui "po men yi wei wu zang shi" de ren shi 对"魄门亦为五脏使"的认识. *Shan dong zhong yi xue yuan xue bao* 山东中医学院学报 4,33-34

462.   Gao Lili 高莉莉 1988. Lüe lun "pi wei xian" 略论"脾为涎". *Liao ning zhong yi za zhi* 辽宁中医杂志 9,6

467. Gao Qingtong 高庆通 1986. Tan "zhi wei du qu yang ming" de lin chuang ying yong 谈 "治痿独取阳明" 的临床应用. *Xin zhong yi* 新中医 8, 29-30

470. Gao Sihua 高思华 1982. Lun "xing bu zu zhe wen zhi yi qi, jing bu zu zhe bu zhi yi wei" 论 "形不足者温之以气精不足者补之以味". *Shan dong zhong yi xue yuan xue bao* 山东中医学院学报 2, 11-19

475. Gao Wenzhu 高文柱 1985. *Su wen* jiao du zha ji《素问》校读札记. *Tian jin zhong yi* 天津中医 4, 41-43

476. Gao Wenzhu 高文柱 1989. *Su wen* jiao du sui bi《素问》校读随笔. *Tian jin zhong yi* 天津中医 5, 32

477. Gao Wenzhu 高文柱 1986. Lin yi *Su wen* jiao kan yu xun gu zhi yan jiu 林亿《素问》校勘与训诂之研究. *Tian jin zhong yi xue yuan xue bao* 天津中医学院学报 2-3, 50-56

478. Gao Wenzhu, Guo Aichun 高文铸, 郭霭春 1990. Li dai jiao kan zhu shi *Huang Di nei jing su wen* gai shu (1) 历代校勘注释《黄帝内经素问》概述 (一). *Tian jin zhong yi xue yuan xue bao* 天津中医学院学报 1, 31-33, 4

482. Gao Yuemin 高越敏 1985. Guan yu *Su wen* zhong de tong jia zi 关于《素问》中的通假字. *Zhe jiang zhong yi xue yuan xue bao* 浙江中医学院学报 3, 41-43

484. Gao Yuemin, Hu Bin 高越敏, 胡滨 1986. Biao ge zi yu xun gu 标格资于诂训. *Zhe jiang zhong yi xue yuan xue bao* 浙江中医学院学报 4, 42-44

494. Geng Yinsuo 耿银锁 1984. Dui "bai bing sheng yu qi ye" de ren shi 对 "百病生于气也" 的认识. *He bei zhong yi* 河北中医 2, 53-54

496. Gong Shiming 龚仕明 1982. "Tian gui zhi" xi "天癸至" 析. *Jiang su zhong yi za zhi* 江苏中医杂志 1, 54

497. Gong Yun 龚云 1986. *Su wen* "Shang gu tian zhen lun" Lin jiao fang fa qian xi《素问·上古天真论》林校方法浅析. *Ji lin zhong yi yao* 吉林中医药 6, 34

499. Gong Zhanyue 龚占悦 1985. "Fei chao bai mai" bian "肺朝百脉" 辨. *Zhong yi yao xue bao* 中医药学报 5, 38-39, 35

500. Gong Zhanyue 龚占悦 1986. Ping "Fei chao bai mai" zai bian shi 评《"肺朝百脉" 再辨识》. *Zhong yi yao xue bao* 中医药学报 4, 55-56, 46

506. Gu Tieguang 谷铁光 1986. *Nei jing* bian xi san ze《内经》辨析三则. *Fu jian zhong yi yao* 福建中医药 3, 61

514. Gu Yulong 顾玉龙 1989. "Shen zhuan bu hui" yu yuan dao shuo "神转不回" 与圆道说. *An hui zhong yi xue yuan bao* 安徽中医学院学报 2, 5

516. Gu Yulong 顾玉龙 1981. *Nei jing* "chuan" zi han yi xi《内经》"喘" 字含义析. *Zhong yi za zhi* 中医杂志 4, 79

520. Guan Fengling 关凤岭 1988. "Shi yu" bing fei ren du ju "嗜欲" 并非人独具. *Bei jing zhong yi xue yuan xue bao* 北京中医学院学报 3, 17

521. Guan Fengling, Guan Fengshan 关凤岭, 关凤山 1989. "Ba/pi ji" bie jie "罢极" 别解. *Bei jing zhong yi xue yuan xue bao* 北京中医学院学报 2, 28

522. Guan Jisheng 管济生 1989. *Su wen* "Shang gu tian zhen lun" yi shi er ze 《素问·上古天真论》异释二则. *Guo yi lun tan* 国医论坛 2, 43

524. Guan Zunhui 管遵惠 1986. *Nei jing* bu xie shou fa tan shu《内经》补泻手法探述. *Yun nan zhong yi za zhi* 云南中医杂志 4, 7-9

526. Guo Aichun 郭霭春 1981. *Su wen* yan wu tuo dao ju li《素问》衍误脱倒举例. *Gui yang zhong yi xue yuan xue bao* 贵阳中医学院学报 3, 4-7

527. Guo Aichun 郭霭春 1981. *Su wen* yan wu tuo dao ju li (2)《素问》衍误脱倒举例 (下). *Gui yang zhong yi xue yuan xue bao* 贵阳中医学院学报 4, 45-48

528. Guo Aichun 郭霭春 1985. *Su wen* jiao kan ju li《素问》校勘举例. *Tian jin zhong yi xue yuan xue bao* 天津中医学院学报 1, 18-20, 44

529. Guo Aichun 郭霭春 1986. *Su wen* jing zhu guan kui 素问经注管窥. *Tian jin zhong yi xue yuan xue bao* 天津中医学院学报 2-3, 1-3

533. Guo Aichun 郭霭春 1987. Du *Su wen* sui bi (ctd.3) 读《素问》随笔 (续三). *Zhong yi yao yan jiu* 中医药研究 4, 18-19

536. Guo Aichun 郭霭春 1988. Du *Su wen* sui bi (ctd.6) 读《素问》随笔 (续六). *Zhong yi yao yan jiu* 中医药研究 1, 33-34

537. Guo Aichun 郭霭春 1988. Du *Su wen* sui bi (ctd.7) 读《素问》随笔 (续七). *Zhong yi yao yan jiu* 中医药研究 2, 26-27

538. Guo Aichun 郭霭春 1988. Du *Su wen* sui bi (ctd.8) 读《素问》随笔 (续八). *Zhong yi yao yan jiu* 中医药研究 4, 37-38

541. Guo Aichun, Gao Wenzhu 郭霭春, 高文柱 1984. Wang Bing zheng li ci zhu *Su wen* gai shu 王冰整理次注《素问》概述. *Ji lin zhong yi yao* 吉林中医药 1, 1-2

542. Guo Aichun, Zhao Yuyong 郭霭春, 赵玉庸 1965. Du *Su wen* sui bi 讀 "素問" 随筆. *Ha er bin zhong yi* 哈尔滨中医 6, 8-11

543. Guo Aichun, Zhao Yuyong 郭霭春, 赵玉庸 1965. Du *Su wen* sui bi (ctd.1) 讀 "素問" 随筆 (續一). *Ha er bin zhong yi* 哈尔滨中医 8, 1-2

546. Guo Bingneng 郭冰能 1986. *Nei jing* "jue" "jie" er zi yong yi li shi《内经》"绝" "竭" 二字用义例释. *Bei jing zhong yi xue yuan xue bao* 北京中医学院学报 2, 43

551. Guo Chunde 郭春德 1986. "Shi yi zang qu jue yu dan" qian shi "十一脏取决于胆" 浅识. *Yun nan zhong yi za zhi* 云南中医杂志 1, 6-7

574. Ha Xiaoxian 哈孝贤 1985. "Jiu yue er yin" zhi guan jian "九月而瘖" 之管见. *Cheng du zhong yi xue yuan xue bao* 成都中医学院学报 3, 29

576. Ha Xiaoxian 哈孝贤 1986. *Nei jing* lun fu ke yuan wen li ce《内经》论妇科原文蠡测. *Tian jin zhong yi* 天津中医 3, 35-37

583. Han Baoxian 韩葆贤 1985. *Nei jing* cheng shu yi zi kao《内经》成书年代一字考. *Shang hai zhong yi yao za zhi* 上海中医药杂志 8, 40

601. Hao Baohua, Zhang Hongyin 郝葆华, 张宏印 1981. "Er yang zhi bing fa xin pi" xi yi "二阳之病发心脾" 析疑. *Shaan xi zhong yi xue yuan xue bao* 陕西中医学院学报 4, 44-45

630. He Cun 河村 1985. Gu yi ji "hu wen" shuo lüe 古医籍 "互文" 说略. *He nan zhong yi* 河南中医 3, 39-42

631. He Cun 河村 1983. Gu yi ji "fan xun" qian tan 古医籍 "反训" 浅谈. *Shaan xi zhong yi han shou* 陕西中医函授 5, 59-63

636. Hong Jinshui 洪金水 1987. "Kai gui men, jie jing fu" chu yi "开鬼门, 洁净腑" 刍议. *Zhe jiang zhong yi xue yuan xue bao* 浙江中医学院学报 4, 48-49

639. Hong Qinguo 洪钦国 1987. Shen ku zao, ji shi xin yi run zhi 肾苦燥, 急食辛以润之. *Guang zhou zhong yi xue yuan xue bao* 广州中医学院学报 2, 56

641. Hu Chunshen 胡春申 1985. Shi lun *Nei jing* wei qi yu qi gong ying gong 试论《内经》卫气与气功硬功. *Shang hai zhong yi yao za zhi* 上海中医药杂志 5, 36-38

648. Hu Haitian 胡海天 1962. Wu yun liu qi (xu) 五运六气 (續). *Guang dong zhong yi* 广东中医 4, 40

655. Hu Jianbei 胡剑北 1986. "Qi sheng ke dai shuai er yi" bu yi yi jie "其盛, 可待衰而已" 不宜异解. *Shan xi zhong yi* 山西中医 4, 42

659. Hu Jiangong 胡健公 1957. Wo dui "qi sun ba yi" de kan fa he shang que 我对 "七损八益" 的看法和商榷. *Zhe jiang zhong yi za zhi* 浙江中医雜誌 12, 34-37

666. Hu Tianxiong 胡天雄 1989. Guan yu *Xiang cao xu jiao shu Nei jing su wen* zhong ji ge wen ti de ping shi 关于《香草续校书·内经素问》中几个问题的评释. *Bei jing zhong yi xue yuan xue bao* 北京中医学院学报 1, 41-43

668. Hu Tianxiong 胡天雄 1980. Tan tan *Nei jing* jiao xue de wen ti 谈谈《内经》教学的问题. *Hu nan zhong yi xue yuan xue bao* 湖南中医学院学报 3, 70

669. Hu Tianxiong 胡天雄 1982. *Su wen* zha ji (1): Shang gu tian zhen lun pian 素问札记(一)上古天真论篇. *Hu nan zhong yi xue yuan xue bao* 湖南中医学院学报 2, 4-8

670.   Hu Tianxiong 胡天雄 1982. *Su wen* zha ji (2): Si qi tiao shen da lun pian 素问札记(二)四气调神大论篇. *Hu nan zhong yi xue yuan xue bao* 湖南中医学院学报 4, 5

673.   Hu Tianxiong 胡天雄 1987. *Su wen bu zhi* yin yang ying xiang da lun (abstr.)《素问补识·阴阳应象大论》(摘要). *Hu nan zhong yi xue yuan xue bao* 湖南中医学院学报 1, 9-11

674.   Hu Tianxiong 胡天雄 1990. *Su wen* wu wen li shi《素问》误文例释. *Hu nan zhong yi xue yuan xue bao* 湖南中医学院学报 3, 160-162

678.   Hu Tianxiong et al. 胡天雄 等 1980. Wen ti jie da 问题解答. *Zhong yi za zhi* 中医杂志 6, 55-56

680.   Hu Xiaochen 胡晓晨 1990. *Nei jing* "jing" zi qian xi《内经》"精"字浅析. *Zhong yi han shou tong xun* 中医函授通讯 1, 2-3

682.   Hu Yongnian 胡永年 1985. *Su wen* zheng du yi ze《素问》正读一则. *He nan zhong yi* 河南中医 1, 28

683.   Hu Yongnian 胡永年 1985. *Nei jing* "hu wen" "dao zhi" yi xun ju yu《内经》"互文""倒置"义训举隅. *Hei long jiang zhong yi yao* 黑龙江中医药 2, 49-50

684.   Hu Yongnian 胡永年 1983. *Nei jing* xi yi san ze《内经》析义三则. *Hu bei zhong yi za zhi* 湖北中医杂志 6, 45-46

686.   Hu Yongnian 胡永年 1982. *Nei jing* xi yi er ze《内经》析义二则. *Shaan xi zhong yi* 陕西中医 2, 24

692.   Hu Zhixi 胡止犀 1986. Yi ji xun gu ju yu (1) 医籍训诂举隅(一). *Hu bei zhong yi za zhi* 湖北中医杂志 3, 40-41

693.   Hu Zhixi 胡止犀 1986. Yi ji xun gu ju yu (2) 医籍训诂举隅(二). *Hu bei zhong yi za zhi* 湖北中医杂志 4, 37-39

694.   Hu Zhixi 胡止犀 1986. Yi ji xun gu ju ju (3) 医籍训诂举隅(三). *Hu bei zhong yi za zhi* 湖北中医杂志 5, 45-46

698.   Hua Tiefeng, Ban Jiqing 华铁峰, 班吉庆 1982. *Su wen* zhong ming ci huo yong zuo dong ci de bian shi he fan yi《素问》中名词活用作动词的辨识和翻译. *Shan dong zhong yi xue yuan xue bao* 山东中医学院学报 4, 64-67

699.   Huang Aiping 黄爱萍 1983. Lun *Nei jing* yang sheng xue shuo de te dian 论《内经》养生学说的特点. *Xin zhong yi* 新中医 8, 11-15

700.   Huang Biyu 黄碧玉 1987. Lüe lun *Nei jing* ci xue liao fa 略论《内经》刺血疗法. *Fu jian zhong yi yao* 福建中医药 5, 42-43

701.   Huang Bin 黄斌 1986. Guan yu "mai zong qi" zhi shang que 关于"脉宗气"之商榷. *He nan zhong yi* 河南中医 6, 4

702. Huang Changjie 黄长捷 1983. *Nei jing* chang jian xi guan ju shi jie《内经》常见习惯句式解. *Bei jing zhong yi xue yuan xue bao* 北京中医学院学报 1, 46-47

703. Huang Changjie 黄长捷 1986. Li yong jiu zhu bian xi *Nei jing* yi yi zhi guan jian 利用旧注辨析《内经》疑义之管见. *Shaan xi zhong yi* 陕西中医 1, 37-38

704. Huang Changjie 黄长捷 1983. *Nei jing xuan du* se ci yin yi ji nan ju yu fa ji jie (2)《内经选读》涩词音义及难句语法集解(二). *Shaan xi zhong yi han shou* 陕西中医函授 1, 47-51

705. Huang Changjie 黄长捷 1982. Lüe tan *Nei jing xuan du* zhong ji ge xu ci de yong fa 略谈《内经选读》中几个虚词的用法. *Shaan xi zhong yi xue yuan xue bao* 陕西中医学院学报 4, 52-54

706. Huang Changjie 黄长捷 1983. *Nei jing* xun gu shi li ju yu《内经》训诂释例举隅. *Shaan xi zhong yi xue yuan xue bao* 陕西中医学院学报 4, 39-40

708. Huang Duoxiang 黄铎香 1980. "Shen zhu gu" chu tan "肾主骨"初探. *Xin zhong yi* 新中医 4, 16

710. Huang Guangyuan 黄广元 1983. "Qi sun ba yi" xi yi "七损八益"析疑. *Guang xi zhong yi yao* 广西中医药 4, 16

714. Huang Hailong et al. 黄海龙 等 1983. *Nei jing* wen ti jie da《内经》问题解答. *Jiang xi zhong yi yao* 江西中医药 2, 65, 61

721. Huang Jianzhuang 黄建庄 1990. Ye tan "fei chao bai mai" 也谈 "肺朝百脉". *Zhong yi yao xue bao* 中医药学报 3, 52-53

725. Huang Jingxian 黄景贤 1989. "Gan sheng yu zuo, fei cang yu you" qian shi "肝生于左, 肺藏于右"浅识. *Zhong yi yao xue bao* 中医药学报 2, 20

729. Huang Liuquan 黄柳泉 1986. Shi lun *Nei jing* de zi ran ke xue ji chu (3) 试论《内经》的自然科学基础(三). *Xin zhong yi* 新中医 6, 1-4

733. Huang Minggui 黄明贵 1988. Zhen luo mai fa ji qi ying yong 诊络脉法及其应用. *Yun nan zhong yi za zhi* 云南中医杂志 2, 5-9

735. Huang Ruzhen 黄儒珍 1962. Tan tan san yin san yang yu kai, he, shu wen ti 谈谈三阴三阳与开、阖、枢问题. *Shang hai zhong yi yao za zhi* 上海中医药杂志 10, 8-10

740. Huang Suping 黄素平 1964. *Nei jing* "ying wei" sheng li jian yao tu shuo《內經》"营卫"生理簡要圖說. *Zhe jiang zhong yi za zhi* 浙江中医杂志 2, 23-24

742. Huang Yanling 黄延龄 1982. Lüe tan *Nei jing* dui fang xue liao fa de lun shu 略谈《内经》对放血疗法的论述. *Zhong yi za zhi* 中医杂志 2, 46-47

743.   Huang Yuxi 黄玉玺 1985. Shi tan "Wei dong si ji" yu shui zhong de zhi liao 试谈 "微动四极" 与水肿的治疗. *Guang zhou zhong yi xue yuan xue bao* 广州中医学院学报 3,44-46

748.   Huang Ziyuan 黄自元 1984. *Huang Di nei jing* yin yang ping heng de zhe li tan tao《黄帝内经》阴阳平衡的哲理探讨. *Gui yang zhong yi xue yuan xue bao* 贵阳中医学院学报 增刊,9-11

750.   Huang Zongxu 黄宗勖 1989. "Zhi wei du qu yang ming" de lin chuang yun yong ti hui "治痿独取阳明" 的临床运用体会. *Fu jian zhong yi yao* 福建中医药 2,2-3

752.   Hui Qun 惠群 1981. "Shen hu shen ke zai men" ju du bian "神乎神客在门" 句读辨. *Zhong yi yao xue bao* 中医药学报 3,41

757.   Ji Xiaoping 纪晓平 1983. "Xian xia ze jiu zhi" shi yi "陷下则灸之" 释疑. *Zhe jiang zhong yi za zhi* 浙江中医杂志 7,309

772.   Jiang Chunhua 姜春華 1956. *Huang Di nei jing* xian dai yu jie shi (2) 黄帝内經現代語解釋 (二). *Xin zhong yi yao* 新中醫藥 2,32-34

778.   Jiang Chunhua 姜春華 1956. *Huang Di nei jing* xian dai yu jie shi (8) 黄帝内經現代語解釋 (八). *Xin zhong yi yao* 新中醫藥 11,35-37

779.   Jiang Chunhua 姜春華 1956. *Huang Di nei jing* xian dai yu jie shi (9) 黄帝内經現代語解釋 (九). *Xin zhong yi yao* 新中醫藥 12,24-26

785.   Jiang Daqi, Yang Yunzhang 姜达歧, 杨允璋 1980. Shi lun kai he shu 试论开合枢. *Zhe jiang zhong yi za zhi* 浙江中医杂志 9,429-430

799.   Jiang Jingbo 江静波 1953. Guan yu "jiu zhen" zai *Nei jing* li de yi xie kao ju 關於 "九針" 在内經裏的一些考據. *Bei jing zhong yi* 北京中醫 8,16

802.   Jiang Jingbo 江静波 1953. Jiu zhen shi shen me? 九針是什麽?. *Xin zhong yi yao* 新中醫藥 10,10

804.   Jiang Xiuzhen 江秀贞 1984. Lesson 17: Tai yin yang ming lun pi wei, na gu yun hua hou tian ben — *Su wen* "Tai yin yang ming lun pian" 第十七讲: 太阴阳明论脾胃 纳谷运化后天本——《素问·太阴阳明论篇》. *Shan dong zhong yi za zhi* 山东中医杂志 5,54-56

805.   Jiang Xiuzhen 江秀贞 1985. Lesson 20: Yin yang qi xue tiao he shun, ni yu tiao she ze wei bing — *Su wen* Ni tiao lun 第二十讲: 阴阳气血调和顺逆于调摄则为病——《素问·逆调论篇》. *Shan dong zhong yi za zhi* 山东中医杂志 2,55-57

813.   Jiang Jinbo 蒋劲柏 1964. *Su wen* "qi sun ba yi" ying gai zen yang li jie《素問》"七损八益" 应該怎样理解. *Jiang su zhong yi* 江苏中医 7,39

815.   Jiang Jinbo 蒋劲柏 1957. *Nei jing* zhong "qi sun ba yi" de yi yi dai shang 内經中 "七損八益" 的疑义待商. *Zhe jiang zhong yi za zhi* 浙江中醫雜誌 4,191-192

834. Jin Jiling 金季玲 1986. Shi lun *Nei jing* dui fu ke xue de gong xian 试论《内经》对妇科学的贡献. *Shaan xi zhong yi* 陕西中医 8, 342-343

846. Ke Mengbi 柯梦笔 1980. Tan zhi wei du qu yang ming 谈治痿独取阳明. *Jiang su zhong yi za zhi* 江苏中医杂志 3, 53-54

848. Ke Xinqiao 柯新桥 1985. "Jing qi gui yu fei, fei chao bai mai" qian shi "经气归于肺,肺朝百脉" 浅识. *He bei zhong yi* 河北中医 2, 6

852. Kong Lingxu 孔令诩 1981. Dui *Nei jing* zhong "yin qu" yi ci de tan tao 对《内经》中"隐曲"一词的探讨. *Guang xi zhong yi yao* 广西中医药 4, 14-15

855. Kong Qingxi 孔庆玺 1981. Jue zheng tan tao (2)厥证探讨 (下). *Yun nan zhong yi xue yuan xue bao* 云南中医学院学报 2, 1-5

859. Kuang Jiezhao 邝杰钊 1989. *Nei jing* "yin jing" li lun chu tan《内经》"阴精" 理论初探. *Xin zhong yi* 新中医 5, 17-19

862. Lan Xingsheng 蓝醒生 1981. *Nei jing* ci lei huo yong qian xi《内经》词类活用浅析. *Fu jian zhong yi yao* 福建中医药 6, 33-35

866. Lei Ping 雷平 1990. Ye tan "fei chao bai mai" 也谈 "肺朝百脉". *Si chuan zhong yi* 四川中医 11, 3

883. Li Bojian 李博鉴 1985. Pang guang qi hua zhi wo jian 膀胱气化之我见. *Bei jing zhong yi za zhi* 北京中医杂志 5, 17

885. Li Changyuan 李昌源 1982. *Shang han lun* yuan yuan yu *Nei jing* zhi wo jian《伤寒论》渊源于《内经》之我见. *Gui yang zhong yi xue yuan xue bao* 贵阳中医学院学报 增刊, 1-5

890. Li Chu 李锄 1980. "Kai he shu" yu "guan he shu" bian "开、阖、枢" 与 "关、阖、枢" 辨. *Shang hai zhong yi yao za zhi* 上海中医药杂志 3, 32-34

894. Li Congming, Zhou Shucheng 李从明,周书成 1991. *Su wen* die yin ci lei shi《素问》迭音词类释. *Yi gu wen zhi shi* 医古文知识 4, 15

900. Li Ding 李鼎 1982. *Nei jing* yun yu chu tan《内经》韵语初探. *Shan dong zhong yi xue yuan xue bao* 山东中医学院学报 4, 68-69

905. Li Ding 李鼎 1979. *Su wen* mai jie pian xin zheng — Du *Bo shu jing mei pian* zha ji《素问·脉解篇》新证——读《帛书经脉篇》札记. *Shang hai zhong yi yao za zhi* 上海中医药杂志 1, 37-39

906. Li Ding 李鼎 1983. "Gao huang" hai shi "ge huang" "膏肓" 还是 "膈肓". *Shang hai zhong yi yao za zhi* 上海中医药杂志 4, 40

908. Li Ding 李鼎 1984. "Jiong" yu "re" "炅" 与 "热". *Zhong yi za zhi* 中医杂志 6, 79

915. Li Guang 李广 1981. *Huang Di nei jing su wen* zhong de die zi《黄帝内经素问》中的迭字. *Shan dong zhong yi xue yuan xue bao* 山东中医学院学报 2, 55-59

916. Li Guang 李广 1982. *Nei jing* tong jia zhi yi bie《内经》通假之一瞥. *Shan dong zhong yi xue yuan xue bao* 山东中医学院学报 增刊, 52-54

917. Li Guang 李广 1982. Yi ji chang yong zi gu jin yi cha yi er shi li 医籍常用字古今义差异二十例. *Shan dong zhong yi xue yuan xue bao* 山东中医学院学报 3, 44-45

920. Li Guoqing, Cao Hongxin 李国卿, 曹洪欣 1989. "Jing mai bie lun" yi shi san ze《经脉别论》疑识三则. *Guo yi lun tan* 国医论坛 6, 35-36

925. Li Guoqing et al. 李国卿 等 1988. *Su wen* yi nan qian shi《素问》疑难浅识. *Zhong yi yao xue bao* 中医药学报 3, 11-14

938. Li Jiren et al. 李济仁 等 1987. Wu Kun he *Su wen zhu* 吴昆和《素问吴注》. *An hui zhong yi xue yuan xue bao* 安徽中医学院学报 3, 22-24

941. Li Jigui 李继贵 1982. "Si zhi wei zhu yang zhi ben" xi yi "四肢为诸阳之本"析疑. *Zhong yi za zhi* 中医杂志 5, 59

947. Li Jianyi 李健颐 1957. *Nei jing zhi yao* qian zhu (3) 内經知要淺註 (三). *Xin zhong yi yao* 新中醫藥 10, 13-17

948. Li Jianyi 李健颐 1958. *Nei jing zhi yao* qian zhu (6) 内經知要淺註 (六). *Xin zhong yi yao* 新中醫藥 1, 23-24

950. Li Jianyi 李健颐 1958. *Nei jing zhi yao* qian zhu (8) 内經知要淺註 (八). *Xin zhong yi yao* 新中醫藥 3, 31-34

951. Li Jianyi 李健颐 1958. *Nei jing zhi yao* qian zhu (9) 内經知要淺註 (九). *Xin zhong yi yao* 新中醫藥 4, 34-38

955. Li Jianyi 李健颐 1958. *Nei jing zhi yao* qian zhu (13) 内經知要淺註 (十三). *Xin zhong yi yao* 新中醫藥 9, 31-35

959. Li Jinyong 李今庸 1984. *Su wen* jie yi yi ze《素问》揭疑一则. *Bei jing zhong yi xue yuan xue bao* 北京中医学院学报 5, 42-43

960. Li Jinyong 李今庸 1985. *Su wen* jie yi yi ze《素问》揭疑一则. *Bei jing zhong yi xue yuan xue bao* 北京中医学院学报 1, 40

961. Li Jinyong 李今庸 1981. *Huang Di nei jing* de cheng shu nian dai he cheng shu di dian kao《黄帝内经》的成书年代和成书地点考. *He nan zhong yi* 河南中医 3, 25-28

962. Li Jinyong 李今庸 1976. *Nei jing* xi yi san ze《内经》析疑三则. *He nan zhong yi xue yuan xue bao* 河南中医学院学报 4, 57-59

963. Li Jinyong 李今庸 1980. Dui suo wei "shi dong" "suo sheng bing" jie shi de yi dian shang que 对所谓 "是动"、"所生病" 解释的一点商榷. *Hu bei zhong yi za zhi* 湖北中医杂志 3, 26-29

964. Li Jinyong 李今庸 1984. Zhong yi gu dai bing zheng ming ci kao 中医古代病证名词考. *Hu bei zhong yi za zhi* 湖北中医杂志 2, 1-3

965. Li Jinyong 李今庸 1985. Jiao kan fa zhong de li jiao zuo yong 校勘法中的理校作用. *Hu bei zhong yi za zhi* 湖北中医杂志 3, 39-40

966. Li Jinyong 李今庸 1990. *Su wen* "ru zi" ci yi kao bian《素问》"乳子" 词义考辨. *Hu bei zhong yi za zhi* 湖北中医杂志 4, 33

967. Li Jinyong 李今庸 1983. *Huang Di nei jing* jie yi san ze《黄帝内经》揭疑三则. *Ji lin zhong yi yao* 吉林中医药 3, 44-46

968. Li Jinyong 李今庸 1978. *Nei jing* xi yi wu ze《内经》析疑五则. *Shan dong zhong yi xue yuan xue bao* 山东中医学院学报 4, 50-54

969. Li Jinyong 李今庸 1979. *Huang Di nei jing* yue du zhi dao《黄帝内经》阅读指导. *Shan dong zhong yi xue yuan xue bao* 山东中医学院学报 4, 60-64, 57

970. Li Jinyong 李今庸 1983. Yi xue sui bi san ze 医学随笔三则. *Tian jin zhong yi xue yuan xue bao* 天津中医学院学报 1, 4-7

972. Li Jinyong 李今庸 1981. *Su wen* xi yi er ze《素问》析疑二则. *Zhe jiang zhong yi xue yuan xue bao* 浙江中医学院学报 4, 47

976. Li Jun 李筠 1989. "Shen ku zao, ji shi xin yi run zhi" xiao yi "肾苦燥, 急食辛以润之" 小议. *Liao ning zhong yi za zhi* 辽宁中医杂志 9, 13-14

983. Li Laitian 李莱田 1982. Fei "tong tiao shui dao" chu tan 肺 "通调水道" 初探. *Shan dong zhong yi xue yuan xue bao* 山东中医学院学报 3, 35-37

986. Li Miaozhu 李妙珠 1983. Qian tan "shen bu shi" 浅谈 "神不使". *Fu jian zhong yi yao* 福建中医药 5, 37-39

995. Li Qingping 李庆坪 1958. *Nei jing* zhong guan yu niao de ji zai 内經中关于尿的记载. *Zhe jiang zhong yi za zhi* 浙江中医杂誌 5, 27-34

1009. Li Shupei 李树沛 1984. Tan "yi wei zhi xing qi yu san yang" 谈 "亦为之行气于三阳". *Hu nan zhong yi xue yuan xue bao* 湖南中医学院学报 10, 45

1011. Li Sichi 李斯熾 1959. "*Su wen xuan ji yuan bing shi*" de tan tao (xu wan) "素问玄机原病式" 的探討 (續完). *Cheng du zhong yi xue yuan xue bao* 成都中医学院学报 1, 4

1019. Li Tingyu 李庭玉 1977. "Qi hua" tan tao "气化" 探讨. *Xi zhong yi* 新中医 2, 47

1028. Li Weipu 李蔚普 1956. Nan chang xi yi xue xi zhong yi ban *Nei jing* jiang zuo (ctd.) 南昌西医学习中医班内經講座 (續). *Jiang xi zhong yi yao* 江西中医药 12, 2-41

1031. Li Weipu 李蔚普 1959. *Nei jing* qian jie 内經浅解. *Jiang xi zhong yi yao* 江西中医药 9, 40-44

1032. Li Wenjiang 李文江 1986. Du "pang guang qi hua zhi wo jian" yi wen de kan fa 读 "膀胱气化之我见" 一文的看法. *Bei jing zhong yi za zhi* 北京中医杂志 4, 60

1033. Li Wenxu 李文旭 1981. "Zhu you" bian xi "祝由" 辨析. *Zhe jiang zhong yi za zhi* 浙江中医杂志 6, 259

1044. Li Xingmin 李兴民 1981. *Nei jing* yu yi xue xin li xue《内经》与医学心理学. *Guang xi zhong yi yao* 广西中医药 3, 9-11

1055. Li Yan, Yan Xiaotian 李雁, 阎晓天 1987. *Nei jing* zhong "shen" de gai nian《内经》中 "神" 的概念. *He bei zhong yi* 河北中医 6, 42-45

1061. Li Yisheng 李益生 1989. *Su wen* xi yi san ze《素问》析疑三则. *Shaan xi zhong yi han* shou 陕西中医函授 4, 31-32

1064. Li Yingjun 李应钧 1988. *Huang Di nei jing* yu *Xia xiao zheng* ji shi yue tai yang li《黄帝内经》与《夏小正》及十月太阳历. *Zhong yi yao xue bao* 中医药学报 2, 1-2

1065. Li Yingfen, Sun Shousheng 李映芬, 孙守生 1983. Cong jie po xue jiao du qian xi *Su wen* "Ci jin lun" pian 从解剖学角度浅析《素问·刺禁论》篇. *Shaan xi zhong yi xue yuan xue bao* 陕西中医学院学报, 1983 期 3, 19

1072. Li Yuanji 李元吉 1958. Guan yu *Nei jing* zhong shu zi yi yi de tan tao 关于内经中俞字意义的探討. *Guang dong zhong yi* 廣東中醫 5, 29-31

1073. Li Yuanji 李元吉 1958. *Ling shu* shou yao gang rou pian yu yi 灵樞寿夭剛柔篇語譯. *Zhe jiang zhong yi za zhi* 浙江中医杂志 9, 31-34

1076. Li Zhenbin 李振彬 1984. Ye tan "xu er xiang bing" 也谈 "虚而相并". *Shan dong zhong yi xue yuan xue bao* 山东中医学院学报 4, 23-25

1079. Li Zhengdong, Wang Xiuzhen 李正东, 王秀珍 1987. *Nei jing* teng tong ji zhi quan shi《内经》疼痛机制诠释. *Zhong yi yao xin xi* 中医药信息 6, 1-3

1081. Li Zhijian 李志坚 1986. *Nei jing* jue zheng qian shi《内经》厥证浅识. *Shan dong zhong yi xue yuan xue bao* 山东中医学院学报 4, 45-46

1102. Liang Yinghuan, Liang Yingtao 梁映寰, 梁映涛 1982. Tan tan *Nei jing* de "han" 谈谈《内经》的 "汗". *Xin zhong yi* 新中医 7, 10-14

1107. Liao Jiaxing 廖家兴 1957. Wo yi tan tan "qi sun ba yi" 我亦談談 "七損八益". *Zhe jiang zhong yi za zhi* 浙江中医雜誌 9, 37-38

1114. Lin Hong 林红 1988. Qian tan *Nei jing* zhen ci shen qian yuan ze 浅谈《内经》针刺深浅原则. *Cheng du zhong yi xue yuan xue bao* 成都中医学院学报 1, 40 (40)

1120. Lin Qingzhou 林庆洲 1985. "Xin neng run zao" qian xi "辛能润燥"浅析. *Fu jian zhong yi yao* 福建中医药 6, 54

1122. Lin Tiandong 林天东 1986. "Xin kai qiao yu er" xiao yi "心开窍于耳"小议. *Bei jing zhong yi za zhi* 北京中医杂志 5, 21-22

1126. Ling Yaoxing 凌耀星 1981. Jiao xue *Nei jing* de ti hui 教学《内经》的体会. *Shan dong zhong yi xue yuan xue bao* 山东中医学院学报 4, 9-17

1127. Ling Yaoxing 凌耀星 1979. Tan bao yu tiao ci, wen li yu yi li 探宝与挑疵 文理与医理. *Shang hai zhong yi yao za zhi* 上海中医药杂志 3, 9-11

1129. Ling Yaoxing 凌耀星 1982. *Nei jing* xi yi si ze《内经》析疑四则. *Shang hai zhong yi yao za zhi* 上海中医药杂志 3, 3-5

1131. Ling Yaoxing 凌耀星 1988. *Nei jing* yun jiao liang li《内经》韵校两例. *Shang hai zhong yi yao za zhi* 上海中医药杂志 1, 39

1132. Ling Yaoxing 凌耀星 1988. Ye tan *Nei jing* xue hai you yu yu bu zu — yu Wang Xinhao tong zhi shang que 也谈《内经》血海有余与不足——与王心好同志商榷. *Shang hai zhong yi yao za zhi* 上海中医药杂志 11, 45-46

1133. Ling Yaoxing 凌耀星 1986. *Huang Di nei jing* zhong de hu wen jian yi《黄帝内经》中的互文见义. *Tian jin zhong yi xue yuan xue bao* 天津中医学院学报 2-3, 29-31

1134. Ling Yaoxing 凌耀星 1987. *Huang Di nei jing* ju dou zhi yi《黄帝内经》句读质疑. *Tian jin zhong yi xue yuan xue bao* 天津中医学院学报 2, 4-8

1138. Ling Yaoxing 凌耀星 1979. *Su wen* "ju tong lun" bei ke bi ji《素问·举痛论》备课笔记. *Zhe jiang zhong yi xue yuan xue bao* 浙江中医学院学报 3, 52-55

1142. Liu Aimin 刘爱民 1987. "Jing sou bu li" shi "泾溲不利"释. *Shang hai zhong yi yao za zhi* 上海中医药杂志 2, 43

1148. Liu Changshou 刘昌寿 1982. *Nei jing* "qi hua ze neng chu yi" zhi wo jian《内经》"气化则能出矣"之我见. *Cheng du zhong yi xue yuan xue bao zeng kan* 成都中医学院学报 增刊, 46-47

1160. Liu Chengcai 刘承才 1985. Lesson 22: Ju han lun tong chan bing ji, jiu qi wei bing yi xu zhi — *Su wen* ju tong lun (jie xuan) 第二十二讲: 举寒论痛阐病机 九气为病医须知——《素问·举痛论》(节选). *Shan dong zhong yi za zhi* 山东中医杂志 4, 50-53

1161. Liu Chengcai 刘承才 1986. Di er shi wu jiang: wu wei jie you fei re sheng. Zhi wei zhong zai qu yin yang 第二十五讲: 五痿皆由肺热生 治痿重在取阴阳. *Shan dong zhong yi za zhi* 山东中医杂志 1, 60

1166. Liu Chuanzhen 刘传珍 1989. Shi yue tai yang li zai *Nei jing* zhong de yi ji 十月太阳历在《内经》中的遗迹. *Guo yi lun tan* 国医论坛 3, 14-15

1176. Liu Hong 刘鸿 1989. "Ba/pi ji zhi ben" xin jie "罢极之本"新解. *Zhong yi za zhi* 中医杂志 7, 57-58

1182. Liu Hui 刘辉 1986. *Shi po jie zi du ben zi* shang que yi ze《识破借字读本字》商榷一则. *Shang hai zhong yi yao za zhi* 上海中医药杂志 1, 34

1185. Liu Jiayi 刘家义 1987. Tan tan "shen zhu wai" 谈谈"肾主外". *Hu bei zhong yi za zhi* 湖北中医杂志 1, 2-3

1186. Liu Jiayi 刘家义 1984. Shi lun "zhi bing bi qiu yu ben" 试论"治病必求于本". *Shan dong zhong yi xue yuan xue bao* 山东中医学院学报 4, 19

1187. Liu Jiayi 刘家义 1985. "Xie zhi suo cou, qi qi bi xu" bie shi "邪之所凑, 其气必虚" 别识. *Shan dong zhong yi xue yuan xue bao* 山东中医学院学报 2, 69-70

1192. Liu Jianxin 刘建新 1987. Zai lun *Nei jing* jing qi 再论《内经》精气. *Hu nan zhong yi xue yuan xue bao* 湖南中医学院学报 1, 3-4

1193. Liu Jianxin, Fu Shuang 刘建新, 符霜 1988. Mao se dun kai, ning zhi jie tong, xi du *Su wen bu shi* shu gao 茅塞顿开 凝滞皆通——喜读《素问补识》书稿. *Hu nan zhong yi xue yuan xue bao* 湖南中医学院学报 2, 6-8

1198. Liu Jinwen 刘荩文 1988. Jian shu liu fu gong neng bu zheng 简述六腑功能补正. *Zhong yi han shou tong xun* 中医函授通讯 1, 2-4

1203. Liu Lianqun 刘联群 1989. Ying yi "Qu yu chen, cuo wei dong" duan ju, *Su wen* yi duan jing wen tan tao 应以"去菀陈, 莝微动"断句——《素问》一段经文探讨. *He nan zhong yi* 河南中医 1, 15

1204. Liu Lianqun 刘联群 1989. Gan wei "Ba/pi ji zhi ben" xin tan 肝为"罢极之本"新探. *He nan zhong yi* 河南中医 4, 2-4

1205. Liu Lianqun 刘联群 1984. Zhong yi han zi bian xiao 6. "Bo" "tuan" bian yong 中医汉字辨淆 6."搏""抟"辨用. *Si chuan zhong yi* 四川中医 4, 42-43

1207. Liu Lianqun 刘联群 1984. Zhong yi han zi bian xiao 8. "Bo" "bo" bu tong 中医汉字辨淆 8. "薄""搏"不通. *Si chuan zhong yi* 四川中医 6, 48-49

1208. Liu Lianqun 刘联群 1987. Bei fu zhang san zi fei yan wen《被服章》三字非衍文. *Zhe jiang zhong yi za zhi* 浙江中医杂志 3, 131

1209. Liu Ling 刘伶 1988. *Nei jing* you guan fu ke lun shu chu yi《内经》有关妇科论述刍议. *Zhong yi han shou tong xun* 中医函授通讯 18 (162)

1248. Liu Xinsheng 刘新生 1982. Tan tan shen cang zhi, kong shang shen de lin chuang yi yi 谈谈肾藏志、恐伤肾的临床意义. *Shaan xi zhong yi* 陕西中医 2, 25-26

1249. Liu Xinya 刘新亚 1986. Cong "pi bu zhu shi" tan tiao yang pi wei de zhong yao yi yi 从"脾不主时"谈调养脾胃的重要意义. *Fu jian zhong yi yao* 福建中医药 5, 58-59

1262. Liu Yichao 刘奕超 1981. Gu yi ji yi zhu yao zhong shi xun gu 古医籍绎注要重视训诂. *Zhong yi za zhi* 中医杂志 6, 78-79

1263. Liu Ying 刘英 1987. *Huang Di nei jing su wen* fan qie zhu yin kao bian《黄帝内经素问》反切注音考辨. *Bei jing zhong yi xue yuan xue bao* 北京中医学院学报 2, 16-18

1266. Liu Youping 刘幽萍 1981. Dui "wu xu" "wu shi" de ti hui 对"五虚""五实"的体会. *Zhe jiang zhong yi xue yuan xue bao* 浙江中医学院学报 4, 40-41

1272. Liu Yukun 刘玉坤 1989. "Rong qi xu, wei qi shi" chu yan "荣气虚, 卫气实"刍言. *Xin jiang zhong yi yao* 新疆中医药 2, 9

1276. Liu Yukun, Zhang Lixia 刘玉坤, 张立侠 1990. *Nei jing* fa shi er zhi si xiang chu lun《内经》法时而治思想刍论. *He nan zhong yi* 河南中医 6, 9-11

1284. Liu Changhua 柳长华 1987. *Nei jing* yi yi ju li《内经》疑义举例. *Shan dong zhong yi xue yuan xue bao* 山东中医学院学报 3, 11

1289. Lou Baiceng 樓百层 1964. Shi lun *Nei jing* zhen ci bu xie (2) 試論《內經》針刺補泻 (下). *Zhe jiang zhong yi za zhi* 浙江中医杂志 4, 15-17

1306. Lu Yanxin 陆严心 1985. *Nei jing* xi yi yi ze《内经》析疑一则. *Guang xi zhong yi yao* 广西中医药 5, 46

1310. Luo Jin 罗进 1984. *Su wen* "duo qi shi" shi yi《素问》"夺其食"释义. *Zhe jiang zhong yi za zhi* 浙江中医杂志 9, 424

1311. Luo Ronghan 罗荣汉 1985. *Nei jing* xun gu chu tan (shang)《内经》训诂初探(上). *Ji lin zhong yi yao* 吉林中医药 3, 43

1312. Luo Ronghan 罗荣汉 1985. *Nei jing* xun gu chu tan (xia)《内经》训诂初探(下). *Ji lin zhong yi yao* 吉林中医药 4, 40-41

1314. Luo Xianchu 罗贤初 1985. "Yang bing zhi yin, yin bing zhi yang" guan jian "阳病治阴、阴病治阳"管见. *Hu nan zhong yi xue yuan xue bao* 湖南中医学院学报 1, 47

1317. Luo Yuankai 罗元恺 1986. *Nei jing* you guan fu chan ke tiao wen chan shi《内经》有关妇产科条文阐释. *Xin zhong yi* 新中医 8, 43-47

1321. Luo Yu 洛雨 1986. "Huan" zi xiao kao "环"字小考. *Ji lin zhong yi yao* 吉林中医药 1, 41

1324. Luo Sanzhui 雒三椎 1983. Dui "kai gui men" de yan tao 对"开鬼门"的研讨. *Zhe jiang zhong yi za zhi* 浙江中医杂志 1, 12

1326. Lü Jiaxiang 吕家祥 1983. Qian tan *Nei jing* zhi shui san fa de li lun ji lin chuang ti hui 浅谈《内经》治水三法的理论及临床体会. *Shaan xi zhong yi han shou* 陕西中医函授 1, 24-27

1343. Ma Jian 马坚 1989. Shi "tian gui" 释 "天癸". *Si chuan zhong yi* 四川中医 10, 封三

1344. Ma Jun 马骏 1988. Qian tan "fan ci zhi fa, bi xian ben yu shen" 浅谈 "凡刺之法、必先本于神". *Hei long jiang zhong yi yao* 黑龙江中医药 2, 39-40

1365. Meng Naichang 孟乃昌 1988. Ming men xue shuo xin kao, zai liang qian nian de zheng heng zhong xing cheng 命门学说新考——在两千年的争衡中形成. *Shan xi zhong yi* 山西中医 4, 24-26

1370. Meng Qingyun 孟庆云 1981. Lun *Nei jing* yun qi xue shuo dui zhong yi li lun de gong xian ji qi ju xian xing 论《内经》运气学说对中医理论的贡献及其局限性. *He nan zhong yi* 河南中医 5, 4-6,3

1371. Meng Qingyun 孟庆云 1983. *Huang Di nei jing* de shi kong guan 黄帝内经的时空观. *Hu bei zhong yi za zhi* 湖北中医杂志 3, 17-19

1375. Meng Qingyun 孟庆云 1980. Wang Bing bu zhu yun qi qi pian bian shi 王冰补注运气七篇辨识. *Zhe jiang zhong yi za zhi* 浙江中医杂志 9, 392-395

1384. Ni Fachong 倪法冲 1981. "Ba/pi — ji" kao, jian lun "gan zhe ba/pi ji zhi ben" de sheng li gai nian "罢极"考——兼论 "肝者, 罢极之本" 的生理概念. *Fu jian zhong yi yao* 福建中医药 1, 57-58

1385. Ni Jianwei, Zhong Lei 倪健伟, 钟雷 1986. Zhu you bian xi 祝由辨析. *Zhong yi za zhi* 中医杂志 5, 70

1401. Ouyang Qi 欧阳锜 1983. *Nei jing* bing neng lei bu《内经》病能类补. *Cheng du zhong yi xue yuan xue bao* 成都中医学院学报 1, 66

1417. Pan Wenkui 潘文奎 1990. Qian lun "pi bing er si zhi bu yong" de zheng zhi 浅论 "脾病而四肢不用" 的证治. *Jiang su zhong yi* 江苏中医 11, 47-48

1422. Pan Yuangen 潘远根 1987. *Nei jing* zhu shi bian yi《内经》注释辨疑. *Zhe jiang zhong yi xue yuan xue bao* 浙江中医学院学报 2, 38-39

1428. Peng Jianzhong 彭建中 1985. *Nei jing* "lao feng" qian xi《内经》"劳风" 浅析. *Jiang su zhong yi za zhi* 江苏中医杂志 1, 39-40

1433. Peng Junfeng 彭俊峰 1986. "Yang bing zhi yin, yin bing zhi yang" chu yi "阳病治阴,阴病治阳" 刍义. *Guang xi zhong yi yao* 广西中医药 3, 41-42

1445. Qi Nan 齐南 1987. *Nei jing* wen zhen chu tan《内经》闻诊初探. *Bei jing zhong yi za zhi* 北京中医杂志 5, 55-56

1446. Qi Nan 齐南 1986. Tan "qu yu chen cuo" 谈 "去菀陈莝". *Jiang xi zhong yi yao* 江西中医药 1, 58-59

1450. Qi Tianshou 祁天寿 1984. Shi "pian ju" shi "偏沮". *Nan jing zhong yi xue yuan xue bao* 南京中医学院学报 4, 52

1454. Qian Chaochen 钱超尘 1983. Zhong yi yu xun gu 中医与训诂. *Bei jing zhong yi* 北京中医 2, 52-54,29

1455. Qian Chaochen 钱超尘 1982. *Su wen* jie gu liang ze《素问》解诂两则. *Bei jing zhong yi xue yuan xue bao* 北京中医学院学报 1, 46-47

1457. Qian Chaochen 钱超尘 1986. *Nei jing* han li kao lüe《内经》汉历考略. *Bei jing zhong yi xue yuan xue bao* 北京中医学院学报 1, 10

1471. Qian Su 虔素 1982. "Fan shi yi zang, jie qu jue yu dan" qian shi "凡十一藏, 皆取决于胆" 浅识. *Fu jian zhong yi yao* 福建中医药 5, 60

1484. Qin Bowei 秦伯未 1956. *Nei jing zhi yao* qian jie "内經知要" 淺解. *Zhong yi za zhi* 中医雜誌 7, 386

1488. Qin Bowei 秦伯未 1956. *Nei jing zhi yao* qian jie (ctd.) "内經知要" 淺解 (續). *Zhong yi za zhi* 中医杂誌 11, 603-612

1501. Qiu Xingfan 邱幸凡 1980. Shi lun "shi yi zang qu jue yu dan" 试论 "十一脏取决于胆". *Hu bei zhong yi za zhi* 湖北中医杂志 4, 39-41

1502. Qiu Xingfan 邱幸凡 1985. *Nei jing* ti jie《内经》题解. *Hu bei zhong yi za zhi* 湖北中医杂志 5, 50-51

1506. Qiu Xingfan 邱幸凡 1981. *Nei jing* luo mai li lun chu tan《内经》络脉理论初探. *Liao ning zhong yi za zhi* 辽宁中医杂志 2, 5-7

1508. Qiu Xingfan 邱幸凡 1983. *Nei jing* duo yi zi ci xi yi《内经》多义字词析义. *Zhe jiang zhong yi za zhi* 浙江中医杂志 1, 10-11

1509. Qiu Yongzhong 邱永忠 1990. "Zhan yu" chu tan "谵语" 初探. *Shaan xi zhong yi xue yuan xue bao* 陕西中医学院学报 2, 3-5

1510. Qiu Yunxian 邱云先 1987. "Zhuang huo san qi, shao huo sheng qi" qian xi "壮火散气、少火生气" 浅析. *Hu bei zhong yi za zhi* 湖北中医杂志 3, 封三

1513. Qu Feng 曲峰 1984. *Huang Di nei jing* de ren shi lun《黄帝内经》的认识论. *Nan jing zhong yi xue yuan xue bao* 南京中医学院学报 3, 1-4

1515. Qu Jiantong 曲见通 1986. "Sheng" zai *Nei jing* zhong de yun yong "生" 在《内经》中的运用. *Bei jing zhong yi xue yuan xue bao* 北京中医学院学报 3, 47-49

1530. Ren Jixue 任继学 1984. Du *Su wen* ji ze xiao yi 读《素问》几则小议. *Ji lin zhong yi yao* 吉林中医药 1, 3-4

1551. Ren Yingqiu 任应秋 1958. *Su wen* yi zhu 素問譯註. *Zhong yi za zhi* 中医杂誌 1, 62-66

1552. Ren Yingqiu 任应秋 1958. *Su wen* yi zhu (ctd.) 素問譯註(續). *Zhong yi za zhi* 中医杂志 2, 133-135

1555. Ren Yingqiu 任应秋 1958. *Su wen* yi zhu (ctd.)素問譯註(續). *Zhong yi za zhi* 中医杂志 8, 568-572

1563. Rong Hong 荣鸿 1986. Yi ji yi shi ying zhu zhong xu ci 医籍译释应注重虚词. *Shang hai zhong yi yao za zhi* 上海中医药杂志 2, 42-43

1574. Shao Guanyong 邵冠勇 1979. Yi jing kao yi shu ze 医经考异数则. *Shan dong zhong yi xue yuan xue bao* 山东中医学院学报 4, 68-71

1576. Shao Guanyong 邵冠勇 1983. Tian gan di zhi ji qi zai yi jing zhong de ying yong 天干地支及其在医经中的应用. *Shan dong zhong yi xue yuan xue bao* 山东中医学院学报 3, 40-44

1580. Shen Hongyan 申鸿砚 1984. "Sheng qi tong tian lun" xi yi《生气通天论》析疑. *He bei zhong yi* 河北中医 2, 3-4

1582. Shen Hongyan 申鸿砚 1988. "Dan zhu jue duan" xin shi "胆主决断" 新识. *He nan zhong yi* 河南中医 2, 47

1583. Shen Hongyan 申鸿砚 1984. *Nei jing* "jing" zi shi san yi《内经》"精"字十三义. *Jiang su zhong yi* 江苏中医 1, 59

1588. Shen Benyan 沈本琰 1983. Lu Yuanlei *Zhong yi sheng li shu yu jie* xuan zai 陆渊雷《中医生理术语解》选载. *Shang hai zhong yi yao za zhi* 上海中医药杂志 3, 43-45

1595. Shen Qilin 沈其霖 1985. "Qu yu chen cuo" guan jian "去菀陈莝" 管见. *Bei jing zhong yi xue yuan xue bao* 北京中医学院学报 1, 45

1603. Shi Daqing 师大庆 1986. "Qi sheng ke dai shuai er yi" yi jie "其盛, 可待衰而已" 异解. Shan dong zhong yi 山西中医 2, 42

1609. Shi Guanqing, Wu Mingqin 石冠卿, 武明钦 1979. *Nei jing su wen*: "Tang ye lao li lun" shi《内经·素问·汤液醪醴论》释. *He nan zhong yi xue yuan xue bao* 河南中医学院学报 1, 33-37

1617. Shi Jiping, Liu Donghan 时吉萍, 刘东汉 1989. "Qu yu chen cuo" zhi guan jian "去菀陈莝" 之管见. *Gan su zhong yi xue yuan xue bao* 甘肃中医学院学报 2, 35

1623. Shi Zhensheng 时振声 1983. Dui *Nei jing* jue zheng de tan tao 对《内经》厥证的探讨. *Hei long jiang zhong yi yao* 黑龙江中医药 1, 13-17

1639. Shu Youyi 舒有艺 1983. "Qi sun ba yi" xiao kao "七损八益" 小考. *Shaan xi zhong* yi 陕西中医 1, 40-41

1649. Song Shugong 宋书功 1987. Gu jin zi, yi ti zi, tong jia zi bian xi (1) 古今字、异体字、通假字辨析(一). *Bei jing zhong yi xue yuan xue bao* 北京中医学院学报 1, 34-35

1659. Song Ziran 宋子然 1985. *Su wen* "bi bi" ci yi bian xi《素问》"拂拂"词义辨析. *Bei jing zhong yi xue yuan xue bao* 北京中医学院学报 3, 38

1661. Su Li 苏礼 1981. *Nei jing* "yin qu" yi ci bian xi《内经》"隐曲"一词辨析. *Shaan xi zhong yi* 陕西中医 4 (10), 44

1662. Su Li, Hong Wenxu 苏礼, 洪文旭 1983. "Si zhi zhe, zhu yang zhi ben" shu zheng "四肢者, 诸阳之本" 疏证. *Shang hai zhong yi yao za zhi* 上海中医药杂志 7, 43

1667. Sun Daizong 孙岱宗 1979. Tan tan zu guo yi xue "zuo gan you fei" zhi shuo 谈谈祖国医学 "左肝右肺" 之说. *Yun nan zhong yi xue yuan xue bao* 云南中医学院学报 3, 10-11

1670. Sun Guangren (transl.) 孙广仁 译 1978. "Bi qi" jie "必齐" 解. *Shan dong zhong yi xue yuan xue bao* 山东中医学院学报 4, 77

1673. Sun Hongsheng 孙洪生 1985. "Si wei xiang dai" shi "四维相代" 释. *Bei jing zhong yi xue yuan xue bao* 北京中医学院学报 5, 44

1675. Sun Lijun 孙理军 1988. *Nei jing* yi nan ming ju xuan shi (ctd.1)《内经》疑难名句选释 (续一). *Shaan xi zhong yi han shou* 陕西中医函授 6, 6-8

1677. Sun Lin 孙林 1988. *Su wen* "ru zi" bian《素问》"乳子" 辨. *He nan zhong yi* 河南中医 2, 6

1678. Sun Manyun 孙曼云 1984. *Nei jing* xun gu zha ji san ze《内经》训诂札记三则. *Bei jing zhong yi xue yuan xue bao* 北京中医学院学报 4, 45

1679. Sun Manzhi 孙曼之 1987. *Huang Di nei jing* de ci yu te dian ji qi zhu zuo nian dai chu tan《黄帝内经》的词语特点及其著作年代初探. *Bei jing zhong yi xue yuan xue bao* 北京中医学院学报 5, 25-26

1683. Sun Shifa 孙世发 1986. Shi lun *Nei jing* jue zheng de cheng yin ji zheng xing 试论《内经》厥证的成因及证型. *Hei long jiang zhong yi yao* 黑龙江中医药 4, 7-9

1690. Sun Tong 孙桐 1982. Qian lun *Nei jing* yu *Shang han lun* de guan xi 浅论《内经》与《伤寒论》的关系. *Nan jing zhong yi xue yuan xue bao* 南京中医学院学报 4, 13-14

1691. Sun Tong 孙桐 1983. "Mo yuan" quan shi "膜原" 诠释. *Nan jing zhong yi xue yuan xue bao* 南京中医学院学报 4, 13, 30

1694. Sun Tong 孙桐 1983. Ru he li jie "fan shi yi zang qu jue yu dan" 如何理解 "凡十一脏取决于胆". *Shaan xi zhong yi xue yuan xue bao* 陕西中医学院学报 12, 12-13

1700. Sun Wenfa 孙文发 1961. Lun "xie zhi suo cou, qi qi bi xu" 論 "邪之所凑, 其气必虚". *Fu jian zhong yi yao* 福建中医药 4, 23 (155)

1701. Sun Wenfa 孙文发 1963. Zai lun "xie zhi suo cou, qi qi bi xu" 再論 "邪之所凑, 其气必虚". *Fu jian zhong yi yao* 福建中医药 5, 23-24

1705. Sun Yan 孙燕 1986. "Yang jia yu yin wei zhi han" ji qi lin chuang yi yi "阳
加于阴谓之汗" 及其临床意义. *Hei long jiang zhong yi yao* 黑龙江中医药
3, 12-13

1715. Sun Yulong 孙玉龙 1981. *Su wen* yi yi liang ze shi xi《素问》疑义两则试
析. *Zhong yi za zhi* 中医杂志 6, 79-80

1716. Sun Yulong 孙玉龙 1982. "Tang ye lao li lun" xi yi san ze《汤液醪醴论》
析疑三则. *Zhong yi za zhi* 中医杂志 5, 79-80

1718. Sun Yuxin 孙玉信 1989. "Yin bo yang bie" xiao yi "阴搏阳别" 小议.
Shaan xi zhong yi han shou 陕西中医函授 1, 31-32

1720. Sun Zhongnian 孙忠年 1988. Qian xi *Nei jing Nan jing* lun fu zhen 浅析
《内经》《难经》论腹诊. *Shaan xi zhong yi xue yuan xue bao* 陕西中医学
院学报 4, 11-16

1721. Sun Zhuxi 孙竹溪 1961. Dui "er yang zhi bing fa xin pi" de ti hui 对 "二
阳之病发心脾" 的体会. *Fu jian zhong yi yao* 福建中医药 1, 35-36

1739. Tan Deying 覃德英 1983. Dui *Nei jing xuan du* zhong ji ju jing wen yu yi
zhi bu tong kan fa 对《内经选读》中几句经文语译之不同看法. *Guang
xi zhong yi yao* 广西中医药 6, 48

1748. Tang Xuezeng 唐学曾 1978. Shi tan "gan kai qiao yu mu" 试谈 "肝开窍于
目". *Zhe jiang zhong yi xue yuan xue bao* 浙江中医学院学报 3, 50

1751. Tang Zaiyu 唐再予 1964. *Su Ling* xiao shi (to be ctd.) 素灵小識 (待續).
Jiang su zhong yi 江苏中医 4, 33-38

1753. Tao Guangzheng 陶广正 1985. Tan tan Lao zi de zhe xue si xiang zai
Huang Di nei jing zhong de fan ying 谈谈老子的哲学思想在《黄帝内经》
中的反映. *Guang ming zhong yi* 光明中医 3, 26-28

1764. Tian Daihua 田代华 1984. Lesson 16: Xuan ming wu zang qi, zhen zhi de
suo yi, *Su wen* "Xuan ming wu qi pian" (jie xuan) 第十六讲: 宣明五脏气 诊
治得所宜——《素问·宣明五气篇》(节选). *Shan dong zhong yi za zhi* 山
东中医杂志 4, 53-56

1775. Wan Benshan 万本善 1984. *Nei jing* tai yun li lun ji yao《内经》胎孕理论
辑要. *Fu jian zhong yi yao* 福建中医药 5, 59-61

1788. Wang Hong 汪红 1988. Fan xun zi ou she 反训字偶拾. *Zhe jiang zhong yi
xue yuan xue bao* 浙江中医学院学报 1, 44-45

1789. Wang Kemin et al. 汪克敏 等 1985. Cong pian ming kan *Nei jing* xin li xue
si xiang de xi tong xing 从篇名看《内经》心理学思想的系统性. *Cheng
du zhong yi xue yuan xue bao* 成都中医学院学报 2, 53-55

1790. Wang Pengmei 汪朋梅 1980. Bing ji shi jiu tiao you guan tiao wen zhi yi
yi 病机十九条有关条文之疑议. *Zhe jiang zhong yi za zhi* 浙江中医杂志
4, 58-59, 63

1800. Wang Changrong 王长荣 1985. "Rong qi xu, wei qi shi" xi yi "荣气虚, 卫气实" 析疑. *Zhong yi za zhi* 中医杂志 5, 78

1801. Wang Chengde 王承德 1985. *Nei jing* lun bi《内经》论痹. *Shan xi zhong yi* 山西中医 2, 10

1803. Wang Chunsheng 王春生 1988. *Nei jing* "fei wei ti" tan xi《内经》"肺为涕" 探析. *Liao ning zhong yi za zhi* 辽宁中医杂志 7, 6-7

1807. Wang Duanwen 王端文 1984. "Zhi zhi yi lan" guan jian "治之以兰" 管见. *Shan dong zhong yi xue yuan xue bao* 山东中医学院学报 1, 22

1810. Wang Fengqi 王凤岐 1982. Qin Bowei lao shi dui *Nei jing* zhi yan jiu 秦伯未老师对《内经》之研究. *Zhe jiang zhong yi za zhi* 浙江中医杂志 5, 193-194

1813. Wang Guanhui 王官惠 1985. *Nei jing* "yi" zi bian xi《内经》"噫" 字辨析. *Hu bei zhong yi za zhi* 湖北中医杂志 3, 40-41

1820. Wang Hai'ou 王海鸥 1982. *Nei jing* lun jing shen bing《内经》论精神病. *Hu nan zhong yi xue yuan xue bao* 湖南中医学院学报 2, 56-59

1831. Wang Hongtu 王洪图 1984. Shi xi si zhi wei zhu yang zhi ben 试析四肢为诸阳之本. *Zhong yi za zhi* 中医杂志 8, 78

1832. Wang Hongtu, Che Baoping 王洪图, 车保平 1985. Cong *Ming tang wu zang lun* qian tan zang fu bie cheng 从《明堂五藏论》浅谈脏腑别称. *Bei jing zhong yi xue yuan xue bao* 北京中医学院学报 1, 41-42

1837. Wang Hongtu, Che Baoping 王洪图, 车保平 1984. Tan *Huang Di nei jing* zhi liu jing 谈《黄帝内经》之六经. *Bei jing zhong yi za zhi* 北京中医杂志 4, 49-53

1840. Wang Hongtu et al. 王洪图 等 1985. Zi xun xin xiang 咨询信箱. *Zhong yi za zhi* 中医杂志 11, 73

1861. Wang Lijun, Zhang Jinju 王立君, 张金菊 1988. Shi lun *Nei jing* wu shi jiu ci 试论《内经》五十九刺. *Cheng du zhong yi xue yuan xue bao* 成都中医学院学报 2, 10-11

1863. Wang Lin 王琳 1981. "Fei zhu zhi jie" qian lun "肺主治节" 浅论. *Shan dong zhong yi xue yuan xue bao* 山东中医学院学报 3, 42-44

1869. Wang Miqu 王米渠 1985. *Nei jing* "shen" de fan chou tan tao《内经》"神" 的范畴探讨. *Hu bei zhong yi za zhi* 湖北中医杂志 3, 5-6

1870. Wang Mimi 王咪咪 1987. Dun huang juan zi *Nei jing* kao 敦煌卷子《内经》考. *Shang hai zhong yi yao za zhi* 上海中医药杂志 3, 38-40

1877. Wang Minghui 王明辉 1983. Cong cheng shu nian dai zhi zheng kan *Nei jing* de xue shu fa zhan 从成书年代之争看《内经》的学术发展. *He nan zhong yi* 河南中医 4, 15-17, 23

1878. Wang Minghui 王明辉 1984. Ru he li jie *Nei jing* de "qi sun ba yi" 如何
理解《内经》的 "七损八益". *Jiang su zhong yi za zhi* 江苏中医杂志
3, 42-43

1894. Wang Pengyu 王鹏宇 1980. *Nei jing* sheng ming guan chu tan《内经》生
命观初探. *Zhe jiang zhong yi za zhi* 浙江中医杂志 9, 386-388

1899. Wang Qi 王琦 1979. Guan yu ru he xue xi *Nei jing* wen ti de tao lun ji
yao 关于如何学习《内经》问题的讨论纪要. *Zhong yi za zhi* 中医杂志
7, 41-47

1901. Wang Qi et al. 王琦 等 1979. Lüe lun *Nei jing* zhong de yi xue yu qi xiang
wen ti 略论《内经》中的医学与气象问题. *Shang hai zhong yi yao za zhi*
上海中医药杂志 5, 44-49

1903. Wang Qiang 王强 1990. Fei zhu tong tiao shui dao bian xi 肺主通调水道
辨析. *Bei jing zhong yi za zhi* 北京中医杂志 5, 19

1910. Wang Qingqi 王庆其 1987. *Nei jing* "ge jia xue shuo" ju yu《内经》"各家
学说" 举隅. *Xin zhong yi* 新中医 7, 6-8

1922. Wang Ruoquan 王若铨 1963. Guan yu *Ling shu* "Jing mai pian" "shi dong
suo sheng bing" zhi wo jian 关于《灵枢·經脈篇》"是动、所生病" 之我
见. *Ha er bin zhong yi* 哈尔滨中医 1, 55-57, 37

1923. Wang Ruoquan 王若铨 1966. "Jing ming wu se" bian "精明五色" 辨. *Hei
long jiang zhong yi yao* 黑龙江中医药 3, 38-39

1926. Wang Sanhu 王三虎 1983. Xue xi *Nei jing* yi de 学习《内经》一得. *Shaan
xi zhong yi* 陕西中医 4, 46

1929. Wang Sanshan 王三山 1985. "Wei bu he ze wo bu an" bian "胃不和则卧不
安" 辨. *Bei jing zhong yi xue yuan xue bao* 北京中医学院学报 2, 41

1932. Wang Shaozeng 王绍增 1983. Zhong yi gu ji de shi ci huo yong 中医古籍
的实词活用. *Hei long jiang zhong yi yao* 黑龙江中医药 4, 69-73

1934. Wang Shicheng 王石成 1985. *Su wen* ping yi zhi ci wu zhu bian zheng si
ze《素问》平易之词误注辨正四则. *Guang xi zhong yi yao* 广西中医药
4, 34-35

1935. Wang Shicheng 王石成 1986. "Si zhi zhe zhu yang zhi ben ye" bian xi "四
肢者诸阳之本也" 辨析. *He bei zhong yi* 河北中医 1, 7

1936. Wang Shicheng 王石成 1986. "Ju yang yin jing zhe" bian xi "巨阳引精
者" 辨析. *He nan zhong yi* 河南中医 1, 12-13

1938. Wang Shifu 王士福 1962. Dui *Su wen* "er yang zhi bing fa xin pi" jie shi de
shang que 对素問 "二阳之病发心脾" 解釋的商榷. *Fu jian zhong yi yao*
福建中医药 3, 18-19

1940. Wang Shifu 王士福 1960. *Su wen* "jie nue" zhu jie kao lüe 素問 "痎疟" 註
解考略. *Jiang xi zhong yi yao* 江西中医药 10, 41-42

1949. Wang Shoufeng 王守锋 1984. *Su wen* qian tan yi ze《素问》浅探一则. *Bei jing zhong yi xue yuan xue bao* 北京中医学院学报 4, 45

1951. Wang Shudong 王树栋 1990. *Nei jing* jiu fa qian shi《内经》灸法浅识. *Liao ning zhong yi za zhi* 辽宁中医杂志 6, 28-30

1955. Wang Tongling 王桐龄 1983. You guan *Nei jing* yi ju bian xi ju li 有关《内经》疑句辨析举例. *Hei long jiang zhong yi yao* 黑龙江中医药 2, 62-63

1957. Wang Wanjie 王万傑 1957. *Su wen* wu zang sheng li zuo yong de fen xi 素問五臟生理作用的分析. *Shan dong yi kan* 山东医刊 2, 27-28

1959. Wang Wang 王汪 1980. "Yang sheng yin zhang, yang sha yin cang" shi yi "阳生阴长,阳杀阴藏"释义. *Shaan xi zhong yi xue yuan xue bao* 陕西中医学院学报 4, 54-55

1966. Wang Xiaoping 王小平 1989. "Yin yang jiao" xiao yi "阴阳交"小议. *Shan dong zhong yi xue yuan xue bao* 山东中医学院学报 1, 55

1977. Wang Yicheng 王义成 1989. *Nei jing* ming ci dong hua liu fa《内经》名词动化六法. *Guo yi lun tan* 国医论坛 5, 37-38

1978. Wang Yicheng, Guo Huixiong 王义成, 郭辉雄 1988. *Nei jing* zhong gu yin tong jia qian tan《内经》中古音通假浅谈. *Hu bei zhong yi za zhi* 湖北中医杂志 2, 46-48

1983. Wang Yuxian 王与贤 1982. Dui "chun xia yang yang, qiu dong yang yin" de ti hui 对"春夏养阳、秋冬养阴"的体会. *Nei meng gu zhong yi yao* 内蒙古中医药 1, 34-35

1990. Wang Yugao 王宇高 1957. Mai zhen (1) (*Nei jing zhi yao* tong su jiang hua 4) 脈診(上)(内經知要通俗講話之四). *Zhe jiang zhong yi za zhi* 浙江中医雜誌 4, 178-179

1992. Wang Yugao 王宇高 1957. Zang xiang (1) (*Nei jing zhi yao* tong su jiang hua 6) 藏象 (上) (内經知要通俗講話之六). *Zhe jiang zhong yi za zhi* 浙江中医雜誌 6, 282-284

2017. Wang Yuchuan 王玉川 1990. Qi zhen yu qi chuan ming yi shi tong lun 七诊与七传名异实同论. *Bei jing zhong yi xue yuan xue bao* 北京中医学院学报 2, 5-7,23

2018. Wang Yuchuan 王玉川 1990. "Wen mu sheng er jing" bian yi "闻木声而惊"辨疑. *Bei jing zhong yi xue yuan xue bao* 北京中医学院学报 4, 5-8

2022. Wang Yuchuan 王玉川 1981. Xue xi *Su wen* "Sheng qi tong tian lun" fu dao cai liao 学习《素问·生气通天论》辅导材料. *Shaan xi zhong yi* 陕西中医 3 (9), 38

2026. Wang Yuchuan 王玉川 1986. Zhong yi yin yang xue shuo fa zhan shi qian shuo (ctd.2) 中医阴阳学说发展史浅说 (续二). *Zhong yi jiao yu* 中医教育 4, 26-28

2030.   Wang Yuchuan 王玉川 1984. Guan yu wu xing xiu wang wen ti 关于五行
         休王问题. *Zhong yi za zhi* 中医杂志 10, 54-57

2032.   Wang Yusheng 王玉生 1990. "Fei chao bai mai" xi yan lu "肺朝百脉" 析
         验录. *Liao ning zhong yi za zhi* 辽宁中医杂志 11, 4-5

2038.   Wang Zhao 王钊 1989. *Nei jing* zhong de si shi he si ji《内经》中的四时
         和四季. *Bei jing zhong yi xue yuan xue bao* 北京中医学院学报 2, 10

2039.   Wang Zhenbang 王振邦 1987. Tan *Nei jing* "wu zang cu tong" 谈《内
         经》"五藏卒痛". *Jiang xi zhong yi yao* 江西中医药 6, 51-52, 35

2049.   Wang Zhumin 王筑民 1982. *Nei jing* tong jie zi li shuo《内经》通借字例
         说. *Gui yang zhong yi xue yuan xue bao* 贵阳中医学院学报 1, 42-44

2050.   Wang Zhumin 王筑民 1986. *Nei jing* tong jie zi xu shi《内经》通借字续
         释. *Gui yang zhong yi xue yuan xue bao* 贵阳中医学院学报 4, 23-24

2051.   Wang Zhumin 王筑民 1982. Gu yi ji yin xun li shuo 古医籍音训例说.
         Zhong yi za zhi 中医杂志 4, 58-59

2053.   Wang Zimo 王子谟 1984. "Duo qi shi" zhi yi "夺其食" 质疑. *Zhong yi za
         zhi* 中医杂志 3, 79

2060.   Wei Beihai, Yu Rencun 危北海, 郁仁存 1963. Dui kai he shu wen ti de
         shang que 对开阖枢问题的商榷. *Shang hai zhong yi yao za zhi* 上海中医
         药杂志 5, 23-27

2076.   Wei Yaoxi 魏尧西 1981. *Ling shu* wei Qin shi huang shi dai guan xiu yi
         dian《灵枢》为秦始皇时代官修医典. *Zhe jiang zhong yi za zhi* 浙江中医
         杂志 6, 254-255

2078.   Wei Yiguang 魏贻光 1984. Wang Bing yu *Su wen ci zhu* 王冰与《素问次
         注》. *Fu jian zhong yi yao* 福建中医药 6, 19-22

2083.   Wen Changlu 温长路 1983. *Nei jing xuan du* ruo gan wen ti zhi guan
         jian《内經选讀》若干問題之管見. *He nan zhong yi* 河南中医 3, 22-24

2085.   Wen Changlu 温长路 1983. Guan yu *Huang Di nei jing* ruo gan wen ti
         yi xun zhi qian jian 关于《黄帝内经》若干问题义训之浅见. *Shan dong
         zhong yi xue yuan xue bao* 山东中医学院学报 2, 40-43

2087.   Weng Gongqing 翁工清 1983. Mao mai he jing de wo jian 毛脉合精的我
         见. *Zhong yi yao xue bao* 中医药学报 2, 17-19

2091.   Wu Guochuan 吴国传 1988. Bian xi "dan" "luan" hua qi heng 辨
         析 "胆" "卵" 话奇恒. *Shang hai zhong yi yao za zhi* 上海中医药杂志
         3, 39-40

2095.   Wu Ji'an 吴缉庵 1982. *Nei jing* zhai wen yi xi《内经》摘文译析. *Fu jian
         zhong yi yao* 福建中医药 4, 44-46

2104.   Wu Kaopan 吴考槃 1964. Dui *Su wen* zhong ruo gan ju wen ji zhu jie de
        wo jian 对《素問》中若干句文及註解的我見. *Shang hai zhong yi yao za
        zhi* 上海中医药杂志 7, 29-30

2107.   Wu Kaopan 吴考槃 1986. *Su wen* kao ding《素问》考定. *Zhong yi yao
        xue bao* 中医药学报 5, 56,25

2111.   Wu Liu Chunhua 吴刘春华 1987. *Nei jing* "qu" zi yong yi li shi《内
        经》"去"字用义例释. *Guang ming zhong yi* 光明中医 5, 37

2114.   Wu Miman 吴弥漫 1989. Han chu jing xue dui *Nei jing* xue shu de ying
        xiang 汉初经学对《内经》学术的影响. *Tian jin zhong yi xue yuan xue bao*
        天津中医学院学报 3, 1-5

2129.   Wu Runqiu, Yang Haibin 吴润秋, 杨海滨 1984. Dui *Nei jing* "zhi bing bi
        qiu yu ben" de tan tao 对《内经》"治病必求于本"的探讨. *Ji lin zhong yi
        yao* 吉林中医药 4, 43-44

2130.   Wu Shiji 吴仕骥 1987. Lüe tan Wang Bing zhu shi *Su wen* de gong xian 略
        谈王冰注释《素问》的贡献. *He nan zhong yi* 河南中医 6, 2-5

2138.   Wu Wending 吴文鼎 1982. *Huang Di nei jing* yu "Huang Lao xue pai"
        – *Nei jing* cheng shu nian dai bie kao《黄帝内经》与"黄老学派"——
        《内经》成书年代别考. *Shang hai zhong yi yao za zhi* 上海中医药杂志
        9, 36-38

2139.   Wu Wending 吴文鼎 1979. *Su wen* "Shang gu tian zhen lun" bei ke bi ji《素
        问·上古天真论》备课笔记. *Zhe jiang zhong yi xue yuan xue bao* 浙江中医
        学院学报 4, 43-46

2144.   Wu Xu 吴旭 1983. Qian yi "fei chao bai mai" 浅议"肺朝百脉". *Nan jing
        zhong yi xue yuan xue bao* 南京中医学院学报 1, 14-15

2146.   Wu Yiyuan, Yu Zihan 吴一渊, 余自汉 1983. Du *"Huang Di nei jing* cheng
        shu nian dai zhi yi" he "Zhi yi bu zheng" zhi wo jian 读《"黄帝内经"成书年
        代质疑》和《质疑补正》之我见. *He nan zhong yi* 河南中医 6, 20-23

2150.   Wu Yong 吴勇 1989. Xi "po men yi wei wu zang shi, shui gu bu de jiu cang" de
        han yi 析"魄门亦为五藏使,水谷不得久藏"的涵义. *Fu jian zhong yi yao*
        福建中医药 2, 52

2151.   Wu Yunyao 吴允耀 1983. Shi lun "yin xu yang tuan wei zhi beng" 试论"阴虚
        阳抟谓之崩". *Jiang xi zhong yi yao* 江西中医药 3, 20-22

2165.   Xia Xuechuan 夏学传 1985. Shi tan *Nei jing* zhong de chong yan ci 试谈《内
        经》中的重言词. *He nan zhong yi* 河南中医 5, 38-41

2167.   Xia Xuechuan 夏学传 1985. *Nei jing* "chong yan ci" qian shi (2)《内经》"重
        言词"浅释(下). *Ji lin zhong yi yao* 吉林中医药 2, 48-49

2168.   Xia Xuechuan 夏学传 1986. Shi shu Hu Peng jiao gu *Su wen* zhi fang fa 试述
        胡澎校诂《素问》之方法. *Si chuan zhong yi* 四川中医 12, 5-6

2171. Xiang Ping 项平 1983. *Nei jing* zhong de wai zhi fa《内经》中的外治法. *Nan jing zhong yi xue yuan xue bao* 南京中医学院学报 3, 13-15

2179. Xiao Xi 蕭熙 1931. *Nei jing* gan zang jin shi (1) 内經肝臟今釋 (上). *Yi jie chun qiu* 醫界春秋 63, 8-10

2187. Xiao Hanzhong 肖汉忠 1985. "Fei zhe, xiang chuan (fu)zhi guan, zhi jie chu yan" shi xi "肺者,相传(傅)之官,治节出焉" 试析. *Nei meng gu zhong yi yao* 内蒙古中医药 3, 47

2194. Xiao Zuotao 肖佐桃 1980. "Dao zhe sheng ren xing zhi, yu zhe pei zhi" bian "道者圣人行之,愚者佩之" 辩. *Hu nan zhong yi xue yuan xue bao* 湖南中医学院学报 3, 75

2195. Xie Qiu 解秋 1990. *Nei jing* zhi wei zhi guan jian《内经》治痿之管见. *Si chuan zhong yi* 四川中医 12, 8-10

2196. Xie Bangyong 谢邦永 1983. *Nei jing* Yin de han yi《内经》瘖的含义. *Zhe jiang zhong yi za zhi* 浙江中医杂志 1, 7-8

2197. Xie Chunguang 谢春光 1988. "Xin run" qian xi "辛润" 浅析. *Shaan xi zhong yi* 陕西中医 3, 117-118

2204. Xie Jiguang 谢继光 1986. Lun *Nei jing* zhen jiu shi zhi de xian hou ci xu 论《内经》针灸施治的先后次序. *Shang hai zhen jiu za zhi* 上海针灸杂志 4, 39-41

2205. Xie Jianjun 谢建军 1984. Xin wei neng "run" bian xi 辛味能 "润" 辨析. *Shaan xi zhong yi* 陕西中医 8, 4-5

2206. Xie Jianjun 谢建军 1986. Qian tan "ku neng jian yin" 浅谈 "苦能坚阴". *Shaan xi zhong yi* 陕西中医 8, 368-369

2209. Xie Yufan 谢浴凡 1985. Wu xing yu yu yin yang zhong — *Su wen* "Bao ming quan xing lun" jie yi 五行寓于阴阳中——《素问·宝命全形论》节译. *Shang hai zhong yi yao za zhi* 上海中医药杂志 7, 40-41

2215. Xing Yurui 邢玉瑞 1989. *Nei jing* yi nan ming ju xuan shi《内经》疑难名句选释. *Shaan xi zhong yi han shou* 陕西中医函授 1, 26-28

2217. Xing Yurui 邢玉瑞 1987. Shi lun "shi yu bu tong ge you suo tong" 试论 "嗜欲不同 各有所通". *Shaan xi zhong yi xue yuan xue bao* 陕西中医学院学报 1, 1-4

2225. Xiong Jibo 熊继柏 1985. Lüe tan *Nei jing* zhong "jue" de han yi 略谈《内经》中 "厥" 的含义. *Zhe jiang zhong yi xue yuan xue bao* 浙江中医学院学报 6, 4-6

2227. Xiong Jibo 熊继柏 1990. Shi lun *Nei jing* jiao xue san jie he 试论《内经》教学三结合. *Zhong yi jiao yu* 中医教育 3, 20-22

2228. Xu Ailiang 徐爱良 1989. She li "qi heng zhi fu bian zheng" chu yi 设立 "奇恒之腑辨证" 刍议. *Hu nan zhong yi xue yuan xue bao* 湖南中医学院学报 3, 150-151

2240. Xu Rongzhai 徐荣斋 1981. *Nei jing* shi xiao lu (ctd.2)《内经》识小录 (续二). *He nan zhong yi* 河南中医 3, 46

2241. Xu Rongzhai 徐荣斋 1981. *Nei jing* shi xiao lu (ctd.3)《内经》识小录 (续三). *He nan zhong yi* 河南中医 4, 27-28

2242. Xu Rongzhai 徐荣斋 1981. *Nei jing* shi xiao lu (the end)《内经》识小录 (续完). *He nan zhong yi* 河南中医 6, 45

2243. Xu Rongzhai 徐荣斋 1981. *Su wen* "Tang ye lao li lun" "zhi ze bu fen" shi xi《素问·汤液醪醴论》"治则部分" 试析. *Liao ning zhong yi za zhi zhuan ji zeng kan* 辽宁中医杂志专辑增刊, 5-9

2259. Xu Xiangting 徐湘亭 1958. *Nei jing* kao ding 內經考訂. *Jiang su zhong yi* 江苏中医 1, 29-31

2260. Xu Xiangting 徐湘亭 1958. *Nei jing* kao ding (ctd.) 內經考訂 (續). *Jiang su zhong yi* 江苏中医 2, 33-34

2261. Xu Xiangting 徐湘亭 1958. *Nei jing* kao ding (ctd.) 內經考訂 (續). *Jiang su zhong yi* 江苏中医 3, 33-34

2262. Xu Xiangting 徐湘亭 1958. *Nei jing* kao ding (ctd.) 內經考訂 (續). *Jiang su zhong yi* 江苏中医 5, 43

2263. Xu Xiangting 徐湘亭 1958. *Nei jing* kao ding (ctd.) 內經考訂 (續). *Jiang su zhong yi* 江苏中医 7, 37-38

2264. Xu Xiangting 徐湘亭 1983. Lun *Su wen* "kai he shu" yu *Tai su* "guan he shu" zai yi yi shang de cha bie 论《素问》开阖枢与《太素》关阖枢在意义上的差别. *Jiang su zhong yi za zhi* 江苏中医杂志 2, 4-5

2268. Xu Xiangting 徐湘亭 1982. Shi lun *Nei jing* de xun gu yu jiao kan 试论《内经》的训诂与校勘. *Shang hai zhong yi yao za zhi* 上海中医药杂志 4, 34-38

2269. Xu Xiangting 徐湘亭 1983. *Nei jing* ruo gan ming ci kao zheng《内经》若干名词考证. *Shang hai zhong yi yao za zhi* 上海中医药杂志 9, 37-39

2270. Xu Xiangting 徐湘亭 1984. Du yi jing yao bian bie gu zi yi yi 读医经要辨别古字意义. *Shang hai zhong yi yao za zhi* 上海中医药杂志 11, 37-38

2271. Xu Xiangting 徐湘亭 1985. Bian *Nei jing* he *Nan jing* suo cheng "ming men" de cha bie 辨《内经》和《难经》所称 "命门" 的差别. *Shang hai zhong yi yao za zhi* 上海中医药杂志 9, 39

2275. Xu Youling 徐有玲 1960. Jian shu shang han yu *Nei jing* wen bing zhi jian de guan xi 簡述伤寒与内經温病之間的关系. *Bei jing zhong yi xue yuan xue bao* 北京中医学院学报 1, 3-4

2282. Xu Jingsheng 许敬生 1987. *Su wen* Quan Yuan qi ben yi wen chu tan《素问》全元起本佚文初探. *He nan zhong yi* 河南中医 1, 40-42

2284. Xu Kongzhang 许孔璋 1984. *Su wen* zhui shi《素问》缀諟. *An hui zhong yi xue yuan xue bao* 安徽中医学院学报 3, 59-61

2286. Xu Shibiao 许士骠 1987. Zhen yu chu tan "yin yang jiao" 诊余初探 "阴阳交". *Shang hai zhong yi yao za zhi* 上海中医药杂志 2, 40-41

2298. Xu Qi 项祺 1986. *Nei jing* wen ti jie da《内经》问题解答. *Shan xi zhong yi* 山西中医 1, 52-53

2300. Xu Qi 项祺 1986. *Nei jing* de xue shu si xiang《内经》的学术思想. *Shan xi zhong yi* 山西中医 4, 48-50

2301. Xu Qi 项祺 1987. Dui *Nei jing* zang xiang xue shuo de tan xi 对《内经》藏象学说的探析. *Shan xi zhong yi* 山西中医 4, 50-52

2303. Xu Qi 项祺 1988. *Nei jing* bing zheng xue shuo de gai shu《内经》病证学说的概述. *Shan xi zhong yi* 山西中医 4, 50-53

2308. Xue Fengkui 薛凤奎 1984. Shi ci yi xiang de xuan ze fang fa 实词义项的选择方法. *Liao ning zhong yi za zhi* 辽宁中医杂志 8, 46-48

2317. Xue Tongquan 薛彤权 1988. *Huang Di nei jing* bu fen jing wen zhi yi《黄帝内经》部分经文质疑. *Tian jin zhong yi xue yuan xue bao* 天津中医学院学报 1, 5-7

2355. Yang Li 杨力 1986. *Nei jing* bing chuan li lun tan tao《内经》病传理论探讨. *Hei long jiang zhong yi yao* 黑龙江中医药 1, 9-10

2360. Yang Qikuan 杨齐宽 1983. Wei qi de te xing 卫气的特性 *Cheng du zhong yi xue yuan xue bao* 成都中医学院学报 4, 12-14

2376. Yang Xiaoqi 杨孝麒 1983. *Huang Di nei jing su wen* "lao" zi kao shi《黄帝内经素问》"劳"字考释. *Shang hai zhong yi yao za zhi* 上海中医药杂志 8, 43-44

2378. Yang Xu 杨旭 1985. *Su wen* "Ping re bing lun" lao feng tiao qian shi《素问·评热病论》劳风条浅识. *Zhong yi yao xue bao* 中医药学报 3, 50-52

2379. Yang Xu, Wang Fei 杨旭, 王非 1988. "Ci shou wu zang zhuo qi" bian shi "此受五脏浊气" 辨识. *Zhong yi yao xue bao* 中医药学报 5, 17

2384. Yang Yuejin 杨跃进 1983. *Su wen* xi yi yi ze《素问》析疑一则. *Shan dong zhong yi xue yuan xue bao* 山东中医学院学报 3, 11

2393. Yang Zejun 杨泽君 1980. Guan ge yu ge se 关格与隔塞. *Gui yang zhong yi xue yuan xue bao* 贵阳中医学院学报 4, 21-23

2395. Yang Zhenping 杨振平 1988. Shi xi *Su wen* "Tang ye lao li lun" de zhi liao xue si xiang 试析《素问·汤液醪醴论》的治疗学思想 *Zhong yi han shou tong xun* 中医函授通讯 4, 16-17

2414. Ye Youxin 叶又新 1981. Shi shi Dong Han hua xiang shi shang ke hua de yi zhen — jian tan jiu zhen xing cheng guo cheng 试释东汉画象石上刻划的 医针——兼探九针形成过程. *Shan dong zhong yi* xue yuan xue bao 山东中 医学院学报 3, 60-68

2418. Yi Zheng'an 衣正安 1980. *Nei jing* "shao yang zhu gu" de tan tao《内 经》"少阳主骨"的探讨. *Zhe jiang zhong yi za zhi* 浙江中医杂志 9, 428

2431. Yin Mengfan 阴孟凡 1983. Cong "shi er zang xiang shi" tan zang xiang xue shuo de zheng ti guan 从"十二脏相使"谈脏象学说的整体观. *Fu jian zhong yi yao* 福建中医药 5, 35-37

2432. Yin Mengfan 阴孟凡 1981. Cong *Huang Di nei jing* kan jing shen yin su zai ji bing fang zhi zhong de zhong yao yi yi 从《黄帝内经》看精神因素 在疾病防治中的重要意义. *Ji lin zhong yi yao* 吉林中医药 2, 1-4

2434. Yin Xueping 尹雪萍 1986. "Si zhi zhe, zhu yang zhi ben ye" zhi wo jian "四肢者, 诸阳之本也"之我见. *Shan dong zhong yi za zhi* 山东中医杂志 1, 2-4

2437. Yuchi Jing 尉迟静 1985. "Xin ji qiao yu er" de li lun chu tan "心寄窍于 耳"的理论初探. *Bei jing zhong yi xue yuan xue bao* 北京中医学院学报 3, 37

2444. Yu Tiecheng 于铁成 1986. *Su wen* Quan Yuan qi ben yu xin jiao zheng Wang Bing zhu ben hu kan yan jiu《素问》全元起本与新校正王冰注本互 勘研究. *Tian jin zhong yi xue yuan xue bao* 天津中医学院学报 2-3, 41-49

2445. Yu Weidong 于卫东 1983. Shi "yang sheng yin zhang, yang sha yin cang" 释 "阳生阴长, 阳杀阴藏". *He nan zhong yi* 河南中医 2, 22

2458. Yu Zihan 余自汉 1982. *Nei jing su wen* "qi qi san" qian shi《内经·素 问》"其气三"浅释. *He nan zhong yi* 河南中医 4, 24

2463. Yu Zihan 余自汉 1980. Guan yu *Nei jing su wen* Tang ye lao li lun shi" de ji chu zhu shi 关于"《内经·素问·汤液醪醴论》释"的几处注释. *He nan zhong yi xue yuan xue bao* 河南中医学院学报 1, 34-35

2465. Yu Zihan 余自汉 1984. "Fei chao bai mai" bian shi "肺朝百脉"辨识. *Zhong yi yao xue bao* 中医药学报 2, 32, 36

2466. Yu Zihan 余自汉 1986. "Fei chao bai mai" zai bian shi — jian da Gong Zhangyue tong zhi de shang que "肺朝百脉"再辨识——兼答龚占悦同 志的商榷. *Zhong yi yao xue bao* 中医药学报 4, 53-54, 35

2469. Yu Changrong 俞长荣 1982. Shi lun *Nei jing* de fang zhi xue si xiang 试论 《内经》的防治学思想. *Fu jian zhong yi yao* 福建中医药 1, 2

2475. Yu Shenchu 俞慎初 1957. *Huang Di nei jing* de kao zheng ji qi jia zhi 黄帝 内經的考証及其价值. *Zhe jiang zhong yi za zhi* 浙江中医雜誌 4, 158-160

2491. Yue Shouli 岳守礼 1982. Cong *Ling shu jing* kan zu san li de zhu zhi zuo yong 从《灵枢经》看足三里的主治作用. *Zhong yi za zhi* 中医杂志 8, 44-46

2493. Zeng Fanfu 曾凡夫 1981. *Su wen* cheng shu nian dai kao《素问》成书年代考. *Zhe jiang zhong yi za zhi* 浙江中医杂志 12, 530-531

2495. Zeng Zhaoqi 曾昭耆 1957. Xie zai *Nei jing zhi yao* "Zang xiang" pian hou 寫在内經知要 "藏象" 篇后. *Zhong yi za zhi* 中医杂誌 1, 54

2496. Zhai Fuxing, Zhai Linhai 翟福兴, 翟林海 1989. *Su wen* "ru can chong" xiao yi《素问》"如参舂" 小议. *Zhong yi za zhi* 中医杂志 7, 57

2499. Zhai Shuangqing 翟双庆 1988. Shi lun *Nei jing* wu xing xue shuo de ge zhong bu tong xue shuo 试论《内经》五行学说的各种不同学说. *Bei jing zhong yi xue yuan xue bao* 北京中医学院学报 5, 15-17

2506. Zhang Juying, Yu Erxin 章巨膺, 于尔辛 1963. Tan tao *Shang han lun* yun yong he fa zhan *Nei jing* de li lun 探討《伤寒論》运用和发展《内經》的理論. *Jiang su zhong yi* 江苏中医 10, 1-4

2520. Zhang Canjia 张灿玾 1986. Xue xi *Nei jing* bi xu zhu yi de ji ge wen ti 学习《内经》必须注意的几个问题. *Fu jian zhong yi yao* 福建中医药 5, 50-53

2528. Zhang Canjia 张灿玾 1984. Shi shu *Huang Di nei jing* de yi ban bian zheng yuan ze 试述《黄帝内经》的一般辨证原则. *Zhong yi yao yan jiu za zhi* 中医药研究杂志 创刊号, 9-11

2529. Zhang Canjia et al. 张灿玾 等 1981. *Huang Di nei jing su wen* jiao shi hou ji《黄帝内经素问》校释后记. *Shan dong zhong yi xue yuan xue bao* 山东中医学院学报 3, 55

2532. Zhang Chaoling, Shao Douchun 张朝灵, 邵斗春 1986. "Gan zhe Pi ji zhi ben" zhi wo jian "肝者罢极之本" 之我见. *Bei jing zhong yi xue yuan xue bao* 北京中医学院学报 3, 41

2538. Zhang Dajun 张大君 1980. Tan tan "er yang zhi bing fa xin pi" 谈谈 "二阳之病发心脾". *Shaan xi zhong yi* 陕西中医 3, 34-35

2539. Zhang De'er 张德二 1980. *Nei jing* zhong de ruo gan qi xiang xue wen ti《内经》中的若干气象学问题. *Jiang su zhong yi za zhi* 江苏中医杂志 2, 42-45

2540. Zhang Defu 张德付 1989. *Su wen* "yin qu bu li" du yan《素问》"隐曲不利" 读研. *Shaan xi zhong yi* 陕西中医 4, 190

2541. Zhang Defu, Han Can 张德付, 韩璨 1989. *Nei jing* "xing qi yu fu" zhi "fu" zi kao《内经》"行气于府" 之 "府" 字考. *Hu nan zhong yi za zhi* 湖南中医杂志. 2, 55

2551. Zhang Dengben 张登本 1980. Gu jin lun jue zhi yi tong 古今论厥之异同. *Shaan xi zhong yi xue yuan xue bao* 陕西中医学院学报 3, 3-8

2552. Zhang Dengben 张登本 1981. Han de sheng li yu ji bing de guan xi — xue xi *Nei jing* de ti hui 汗的生理与疾病的关系——学习《内经》的体会. *Shaan xi zhong yi xue yuan xue bao* 陕西中医学院学报 2, 15-18, 43

2557. Zhang Dengben, Dang Binglin 张登本, 党炳琳 1986. *Nei jing jiang yi* yuan wen zi xue lan yao (ctd.1)《内经讲义》原文自学览要 (续一). *Shaan xi zhong yi han shou* 陕西中医函授 3, 16-24

2560. Zhang Dengben et al. 张登本 等 1986. *Nei jing jiang yi* fu xi ti jie da xuan zai《内经讲义》复习题解答选载. *Shaan xi zhong yi han shou* 陕西中医函授 3, 1-15

2568. Zhang Dongda 张东达 1986. *Su wen* zhong "zhi" zi yong fa qian yi《素问》中 "之" 字用法浅议. *Shaan xi zhong yi xue yuan xue bao* 陕西中医学院学报 1, 45-50

2575. Zhang Haifeng 張海峰 1956. Nan chang xi yi xue xi zhong yi ban *Nei jing* jiang zuo 南昌西医学习中医班内經講座. *Jiang xi zhong yi yao* 江西中医药 7, 6-13

2583. Zhang Ji 张吉 1980. Dui *Nei jing* jue zheng de chu bu tan tao 对《内经》厥证的初步探讨. *Bei jing zhong yi xue yuan xue bao* 北京中医学院学报 2, 5-9

2586. Zhang Ji 张吉 1982. *Nei jing* qi, pei er zi jie bian《内经》泣、佩二字解辨. *Zhe jiang zhong yi za zhi* 浙江中医杂志 7, 334-335

2588. Zhang Ji 张吉 1982. Dui *Nei jing* zhong "qi" "pei" zhu jie bian 对《内经》中 "泣" "佩" 注解辨. *Zhong yi yao xue bao* 中医药学报 2, 23-24

2593. Zhang Jinliang 张金良 1983. Bian "shen ming" 辨 "神明". *Bei jing zhong yi xue yuan xue bao* 北京中医学院学报 3, 45

2619. Zhang Qixian 张启贤 1983. *Nei jing* "jue" zi qian shi《内经》"厥" 字浅识. *Hu bei zhong yi za zhi* 湖北中医杂志 4, 52-53

2621. Zhang Renyu 张仁宇 1963. Shi lun "guan ge" bing 試論 "关格" 病. *Zhong yi za zhi* 中医杂志 9, 27-29

2632. Zhang Shanlei 张山雷 1983. Du *Su wen* shi xiao lu (3) 读素问识小录 (三). *Zhe jiang zhong yi xue yuan xue bao* 浙江中医学院学报 4, 46-49

2636. Zhang Shanlei 张山雷 1984. Du *Su wen* shi xiao lu (8) 读素问识小录 (八). *Zhe jiang zhong yi xue yuan xue bao* 浙江中医学院学报 6, 50-51

2655. Zhang Xikui, Wang Xuli 张喜奎, 王旭丽 1989. Shi cong *Nei jing* tan nao wei sheng ming zhi ben 试从《内经》谈脑为生命之本. *Tian jin zhong yi* 天津中医 3, 19

2656. Zhang Xiaobo 张晓波 1983. "Si zhi wei zhu yang zhi ben" de jie yi "四肢为诸阳之本" 的解疑. *Nei meng gu zhong yi yao* 内蒙古中医药 1, 47-48

2660.   Zhang Xinyu 张新渝 1986. "Zhu you" bian xi "祝由" 辨析. *Cheng du zhong yi xue yuan xue bao* 成都中医学院学报 3, 9-10

2662.   Zhang Xinyu 张新渝 1984. Bian "ti ruo fan tan , han chu er san" 辨 "体若燔炭、汗出而散". *He nan zhong yi* 河南中医 6, 21-22

2669.   Zhang Yi 张毅 1990. "Jian jue" xi yi "煎厥" 析疑. *Zhong yi han shou tong xun* 中医函授通讯 1, 21

2685.   Zhang Zhenyu 张珍玉 1984. Du *Nei jing* zha ji (3) 读《内经》札记(三). *Shan dong zhong yi xue yuan xue bao* 山东中医学院学报 2, 41-45

2686.   Zhang Zhenyu 张珍玉 1984. Du *Nei jing* zha ji (4) 读《内经》札记(四). *Shan dong zhong yi xue yuan xue bao* 山东中医学院学报 3, 53-57

2687.   Zhang Zhenyu 张珍玉 1984. Du *Nei jing* zha ji (5) 读《内经》札记(五). *Shan dong zhong yi xue yuan xue bao* 山东中医学院学报 4, 53-57

2688.   Zhang Zhenyu 张珍玉 1985. Du *Nei jing* zha ji (6) 读《内经》札记(六). *Shan dong zhong yi xue yuan xue bao* 山东中医学院学报 1, 43-46

2698.   Zhang Zongdong 张宗栋 1986. Ye tan ru he li jie *Nei jing* de "qi sun ba yi" 也谈如何理解《内经》的 "七损八益". *Jiang su zhong yi za zhi* 江苏中医杂志 8, 45-47

2705.   Zhao Bo 赵博 1988. *Su wen* "pu" shi《素问》"朴" 释. *Gui yang zhong yi xue yuan xue bao* 贵阳中医学院学报 1, 59

2711.   Zhao Dihua 赵棣华 1974. "Ming men" tan tao "命门" 探讨. *Xin zhong yi* 新中医 1, 49-51, 40

2718.   Zhao Guoren 赵国仁 1983. *Su wen* "Feng lun" xue xi ti hui《素问·风论》学习体会. *Zhe jiang zhong yi xue yuan xue bao* 浙江中医学院学报 6, 40-41

2719.   Zhao Huixian 赵辉贤 1980. *Huang Di nei jing tai su* yi wen kao bian《黄帝内经》太素遗文考辨. *Gui yang zhong yi xue yuan xue bao* 贵阳中医学院学报 4, 6-11

2720.   Zhao Huixian 赵辉贤 1983. *Su wen* ruo gan zi yi jie huo《素问》若干字义解惑. *Shang hai zhong yi yao za zhi* 上海中医药杂志 7, 38

2721.   Zhao Huixian 赵辉贤 1984. *Su wen* ruo gan zi yi jie huo《素问》若干字义解惑. *Shang hai zhong yi yao za zhi* 上海中医药杂志 11, 39-40

2722.   Zhao Huixian 赵辉贤 1985. *Su wen* ruo gan zi yi jie huo (3)《素问》若干字义解惑(三). *Shang hai zhong yi yao za zhi* 上海中医药杂志. 5, 43-45

2725.   Zhao Huixian 赵辉贤 1981. "Yin yang ying xiang da lun" yi yi bian xi《阴阳应象大论》疑义辨析. *Zhe jiang zhong yi xue yuan xue bao* 浙江中医学院学报 4, 49-50

2726.   Zhao Jiaqi, Zhang Linying 赵家祺, 张琳瑛 1985. Nao yu zang fu xiang guan lun chu tan 脑与脏腑相关论初探. *Tian jin zhong yi* 天津中医 6, 39-42

2738. Zhao Mingshan 赵明山 1982. *Nei jing* zhong de shen jing jing shen bing zheng chu tan《内经》中的神经精神病症初探. *Liao ning zhong yi za zhi* 辽宁中医杂志 11, 12-14

2741. Zhao Mingshan 赵明山 1988. Lun *Nei jing* zhong de feng xie yu feng bing (ctd.) 论《内经》中的风邪与风病 (续). *Liao ning zhong yi za zhi* 辽宁中医杂志 6, 10-12

2744. Zhao Mingshan 赵明山 1985. *Nei jing xuan du* shi yi (1)《内经选读》释疑(一). *Zhong yi han shou tong xun* 中医函授通讯 4, 418-420

2750. Zhao Xixin 赵喜新 1983. Si zhi zhe zhu yang zhi tao ye 四支者诸阳之本 (音滔tao)也. *He nan zhong yi* 河南中医 2, 21

2753. Zhao Yifu 赵益夫 1981. Gu yi ji tong jie zi li shi 古医籍通借字例释. *Zhong yi za zhi* 中医杂志 8, 61-63

2755. Zhao Youchen 赵有臣 1987. Lun "Wu zang bie lun" zhong de "dan" — qi heng zhi fu zhong de "dan" ying wei "shan zhong" 论《五脏别论》中的"胆"——奇恒之腑中的"胆"应为"膻中". *Liao ning zhong yi za zhi* 辽宁中医杂志 9, 9-12, 8

2756. Zhao Youchen 赵有臣 1987. Tian gui xin tan — jian lun zai zhong yi xue li lun shang de yi yi 天癸新探——兼论在中医学理论上的意义. *Shang hai zhong yi yao za zhi* 上海中医药杂志 9, 42-44

2757. Zhao Youchen 赵有臣 1989. Zai lun tian gui wei tian zhen zhi chuan wu — da Wang, Chen zhi "shang que" 再论天癸为天真之传误——答王、陈之"商榷". *Shang hai zhong yi yao za zhi* 上海中医药杂志 5, 43-44

2763. Zhao Zhengyuan 趙正元 1959. Guan yu *Nei jing* "Ci jin lun" gan ju yu zuo de tan tao 关于内經刺禁論肝居于左的探討. *Ha er bin zhong yi* 哈尔滨中医 8, 41-42

2764. Zhao Zhonghua 赵中华 1986. "Wen" zi shi yi "温"字释义. *Bei jing zhong yi xue yuan xue bao* 北京中医学院学报 6, 22

2767. Zheng Bangben 郑邦本 1985. *Nei jing* nei zheng jiao kan ju ju《内经》内证校勘举隅. *Shang hai zhong yi yao za zhi* 上海中医药杂志 4, 38-40

2770. Zheng Enze 郑恩澤 1958. Du "*Su wen* yi zhu si qi tiao shen da lun" hou de ji dian yi jian 讀"素問譯註四气調神大論"后的几点意見. *Zhong yi za zhi* 中医杂志 9, 11

2800. Zheng Shouzeng 郑守曾 1982. *Nei jing* lei gai nian yan jiu (jie lu)《内经》类概念研究(节录). *Cheng du zhong yi xue yuan xue bao* 成都中医学院学报 1, 28-32

2802. Zheng Xiaochang, Song Ziran 郑孝昌, 宋子然 1984. *Nei jing* chong yan (2)《内经》重言(下). *Cheng du zhong yi xue yuan xue bao* 成都中医学院学报 4, 45-47, 60

2807. Zhi Dao 植道 1984. Xiao yi "wei bu he ze wo bu an" 小议 "胃不和则卧不安". *Zhe jiang zhong yi za zhi* 浙江中医杂志 3,116

2809. Zhong Darui 钟大瑞 1984. "Wu qi suo bing" shi lun shu zang fu xiang guan de bing li ji zhi "五气所病" 是论述脏腑相关的病理机制. *Guang xi zhong yi yao* 广西中医药 4,56-57

2810. Zhong Jiaxi et al. 钟嘉熙. 等 1988. "Shi yi zang qu jue yu dan" chu yi "十一脏取决于胆" 刍议. *Xin zhong yi* 新中医 9,8

2821. Zhou Cheng, Zhu Changgang 周骋, 朱长刚 1988. "Tian dan xu wu" xin shi "恬惔虚无" 新识. *Bei jing zhong yi xue yuan xue bao* 北京中医学院学报 3,20

2822. Zhou Guoqi 周国琪 1987. Shi lun *Nei jing* ji ju zheng 试论《内经》积聚证. *Ji lin zhong yi yao* 吉林中医药 3,1-2

2840. Zhou Xuesheng 周学胜 1989. *Nei jing* "jue si sheng" fang fa qian xi《内经》"决死生" 方法浅析. *Shan dong zhong yi xue yuan xue bao* 山东中医学院学报 2,8-11

2843. Zhou Zongyao 周宗尧 1986. Shi lun *Nei jing* he *Shang han lun* liu jing zhong shao yang de wei zhi 试论《内经》和《伤寒论》六经中少阳的位置. *He nan zhong yi* 河南中医 3,44-47

2847. Zhu Baozhong 朱宝忠 1982. Dao shi "wu xing" shi you xing — san jiao bie lun 道是 "无形" 实有形——三焦别论. *Shang hai zhong yi yao za zhi* 上海中医药杂志 11,35-37

2855. Zhu Guangren 朱广仁 1981. *Su wen* jiao shi jie xuan《素问》校释节选. *Jiang su zhong yi za zhi* 江苏中医杂志 6,53-54

2861. Zhu Qian, Xia Qing 朱倩, 夏庆 1991. "Yi jiu fu yang, ju yang yin" kao ding "以救俛仰,巨阳引" 考订. *Guo yi lun tan* 国医论坛 5,45

2864. Zhu Shengquan 朱生全 1986. "Qu yu chen cuo" bian xi "去宛陈莝" 辨析. *Shaan xi zhong yi* 陕西中医 4,150-151

2868. Zhu Weichang 朱伟常 1983. He Xu Xiangting tong zhi shang que 和徐湘亭同志商榷. *Shang hai zhong yi yao za zhi* 上海中医药杂志 9,28-29

2885. Zhu Ziqing 朱子青 1956. Lüe shu *Su wen* bian zheng de ke xue xing yu li shi jia zhi 略述素問辨症的科学性与曆史價值. *Zhong yi za zhi* 中医雜誌. 4,210-213

2888. Zhu Jianping 竹剑平 1985. Gao Shizong zhu shi *Nei jing su wen* xue shu cheng jiu 高士宗注释《内经素问》学术成就. *Yun nan zhong yi za zhi* 云南中医杂志 1,60-61

2891. Zhu Jinmei 祝蓋梅 1956. Di shi yi shi er jiang *Nei jing* 第十一、十二講内經. *Shang hai zhong yi yao za zhi* 上海中医藥杂誌 9,2 (386)

Huang Di nei jing su wen
Volume II

BOOK

The Philip E. Lilienthal imprint
honors special books
in commemoration of a man whose work
at University of California Press from 1954 to 1979
was marked by dedication to young authors
and to high standards in the field of Asian Studies.
Friends, family, authors, and foundations have together
endowed the Lilienthal Fund, which enables UC Press
to publish under this imprint selected books
in a way that reflects the taste and judgment
of a great and beloved editor.

Huang Di nei jing su wen

An Annotated Translation of
Huang Di's Inner Classic – Basic Questions

Volume II
Chapters 53 through 71, and 74 through 81

Paul U. Unschuld and Hermann Tessenow
in Collaboration with Zheng Jinsheng

UNIVERSITY OF CALIFORNIA PRESS
Berkeley   Los Angeles

Acknowledgment

This annotated translation of the *Su wen* was made possible by a long-term commitment from the Volkswagen Foundation, following up an initial pilot phase funded by the German Research Association (DFG). It is with utmost gratitude that we acknowledge this generous support and an understanding of the complexities of our project.

University of California Press, one of the most distinguished university presses in the United States, enriches lives around the world by advancing scholarship in the humanities, social sciences, and natural sciences. Its activities are supported by the UC Press Foundation and by philanthropic contributions from individuals and institutions. For more information, visit www.ucpress.edu.

University of California Press
Berkeley and Los Angeles, California

University of California Press, Ltd.
London, England

© 2011 by the Regents of the University of California

Library of Congress Cataloging-in-Publication Data

Unschuld, Paul U., 1943–.
    Huang Di nei jing su wen: an annotated translation of Huang Di's Inner Classic — Basic Questions / Paul U. Unschuld and Hermann Tessenow in collaboration with Zheng Jinsheng.
— 1st ed.
    p.   cm.
    Includes bibliographical references.
    ISBN 978-0-520-26698-8 (set)
    1. Su wen.   2. Medicine, Chinese—Early works to 1800.   I. Unschuld, Paul U. (Paul Ulrich), 1943-   II. Tessenow, Hermann, 1945-   III. Zheng, Jinsheng, 1946-   IV. Su wen. English.   V. Title: Annotated translation of Huang Di's Inner Classic — Basic Questions.
    R127.1.S93H7   2011
    616'.09—dc21   2010039378
Manufactured in the United States of America
19   18   17   16
10   9   8   7   6   5   4

The paper used in this publication meets the minimum requirements of ANSI/NISO Z39.48-1992 (R 1997) (Permanence of Paper).

CONTENTS
Volume II

PREFATORY NOTES TO VOL. II

ANNOTATED TRANSLATION OF *Su wen* 53 THROUGH 71, 74 THROUGH 81
Chapter 53   Discourse on the Aims of Piercing   /   11
Chapter 54   Explanations on the Needles   /   15
Chapter 55   Discourse on Rules of Extended Piercing   /   25
Chapter 56   Discourse on Skin Sections   /   35
Chapter 57   Discourse On Conduits and Network [Vessels]   /   43
Chapter 58   Discourse on Qi Holes   /   47
Chapter 59   Discourse on Qi Palaces   /   61
Chapter 60   Discourse on Bone Hollows   /   73
Chapter 61   Discourse on Holes [to treat] Water and Heat   /   89
Chapter 62   Discourse on Regulating the Conduits   /   101
Chapter 63   Discourse on Misleading Piercing   /   131
Chapter 64   Discourse on Opposition and Compliance in Piercing in
             [the Course of] the Four Seasons   /   149
Chapter 65   Discourse on Tip and Root and on the Transmission of Disease
             [Inside the Organism]   /   159
Chapter 66   Comprehensive Discourse on Arrangements of the Principal [Qi]
             of Heaven   /   173
Chapter 67   Comprehensive Discourse on the Progression of the Five
             Periods   /   189
Chapter 68   Comprehensive Discourse on the Subtle Significance of the Six
             [Qi]   /   213
Chapter 69   Comprehensive Discourse on Changes [resulting from] Qi
             Interaction   /   241

Chapter 70   Comprehensive Discourse on the Five Regular Policies   /   285
Chapter 71   Comprehensive Discourse on the Policies and Arrangements of
              the Six Principal [Qi]   /   357
Chapter 74   Comprehensive Discourse on the Essentials of the Most
              Reliable   /   535
Chapter 75   Discourse on Making Known the Perfect Teachings   /   643
Chapter 76   Discourse on Demonstrating a Natural Approach   /   651
Chapter 77   Discourse on Expounding the Five Faults   /   665
Chapter 78   Discourse on Evidence of the Four Failures   /   679
Chapter 79   Discourse on Yin and Yang Categories   /   687
Chapter 80   Discourse on Comparing Abundance and Weakness   /   705
Chapter 81   Discourse on Explaining the Subtleties of Essence   /   719

BIBLIOGRAPHY

1.   Dictionaries and Encyclopedias   /   732

2.   Monographs   /   733

3.   Articles   /   739

PREFATORY NOTES TO VOL. 2

The present translation of the *Su wen* is based on a version of the original Chinese text derived from different ancient and more recent editions of the *Huang Di nei jing su wen*. Where necessary, notes attached to the translation explain our textual choices.

Readers of the present translation may wish to also consult the introductory volume to this project, i.e., Paul U. Unschuld, *Huang Di Nei Jing Su Wen. Nature, Knowledge, Imagery in an Ancient Chinese Medical Text*, published by University of California Press in 2003. Its survey of the contents of the *Su wen* may be especially helpful for comprehending the doctrine of "the five periods and six qi" outlined in *Su wen* treatises 66 through 71, and 74, that comprise about one third of the entire text of the *Su wen*.

The currently available Chinese edition closest to our reference text is the *Huang Di nei jing su wen* 黃帝內經素問 published by Ren min wei sheng chu ban she 人民衛生出版社, Beijing 1963, 5th printing, 1983. For easy comparison of the subsequent English translation of the *Huang Di Nei jing su wen* with the original Chinese text, the entire Chinese reference text is reprinted and available in Hermann Tessenow and Paul U. Unschuld, *A Dictionary of the Huang Di Nei Jing Su Wen*, published by University of California Press in 2003 as the second volume of the *Huang Di nei jing su wen* project. To permit a rapid location, in the Chinese reference text, of any given section of our translation, we have divided the present English text and the Chinese reference text in the appendix to the Dictionary by numbers referring to the pages and lines of the 1983 edition of the *Huang Di nei jing su wen* by Ren min wei sheng chu ban she 人民衛生出版社. Thus, 54-281-6 is: *Su wen* chapter 54, page 281, line 6.

ANNOTATED TRANSLATION OF *SU WEN* 53 THROUGH 71, 74 THROUGH 81

Chapter 53
Discourse on the Aims of Piercing[1]

53-279-8
Huang Di asked:
"I should like to hear about the essentials of depletion and repletion."

Qi Bo responded:
"When the qi is replete, the physical appearance is replete;
when the qi is depleted, the physical appearance is depleted.
That is the regular [association]; [any situation] contrary to this is disease.[2]

When the grain abounds, the qi abounds;
when the grain is depleted, the qi is depleted.
That is the regular [association]; [any situation] contrary to this is disease.

When the vessels are replete, the blood is replete;
when the vessels are depleted, the blood is depleted.
That is the regular [association]; [any situation] contrary to this is disease."[3]

53-280-3
[Huang] Di:
"How can it be 'contrary'?"

---

1 Ma Shi: "志 is 記, 'to record.' This treatise discusses the essentials of depletion and repletion and also the patterns of draining a repletion and of supplementing a depletion. These must be recorded and should not be forgotten. Hence, the name of the treatise." 2690/43 agrees. Yao Shaoyu: "Except for the final four sentences, the entire treatise has nothing to do at all with piercing and it is not clear why it is named 刺志." 2723/6: "志 is the old version of the character 識. 識 is 記, 'to record,' 知, 'to know.'" We follow the usage of 志 in the sense of "aim", "to aim at", as attested in the *Shu jing* 書經, Pan geng shang 盤庚上: 若射之有志, "when shooting at him, there is an aim", and also in the *Zuo zhuan* 佐傳, 8th year of duke Ding 定公八年: 顏息射人, 中眉, 退曰: 我無勇, 吾志其目也, "Yan Xi shot a person and hit an eyebrow. He turned back saying: 'I have no courage; I aimed at his eye.'"(See Ruan Yuan 170 above and 2142 above.)

2 Wang Bing: "反 is to say: 不相應合, 'lack of mutual correspondence,' 失常平之候, 'loss of signs of normality.' Physical appearance and qi are opposed to each other; hence, a disease emerges. 氣 is to say: the qi in the vessels; 形 is to say: the physical appearance of the body."

3 Wang Bing: "The vessels constitute the palace of the blood. Hence, depletion and repletion appear in both [the vessels and the blood] alike. When [the states of vessels and of the blood] oppose each other, then this constitutes a disease."

Qi Bo:

"When the qi is depleted and the body is hot [nevertheless], that is called 'contrary.'[4]

When grain enters [the body] in large quantities and the qi is diminished [nevertheless], that is called 'contrary.'[5]

When grain does not enter [the body] and the qi is plentiful [nevertheless], that is called 'contrary.'[6]

When the [contents of the] vessels abound, while the blood is diminished, that is called 'contrary.'

When the [contents of the] vessels are diminished,[7] while the blood is plentiful, that is called 'contrary.'[8]

53-280-6

When the qi abounds, while the body is cold, this is acquired through harm caused by cold.

When the qi is depleted while the body is hot, this is acquired through harm caused by summerheat.[9]

When grain enters [the body] in large quantities and the qi is diminished [nevertheless], this is acquired because of a loss of blood. Dampness resides in

---

4 Wang Bing: "Qi depletion is an insufficiency of yang qi. When the yang qi is insufficient, the body should be cold. When the body is hot, the qi in the vessels should abound. When the [qi in the] vessels does not abound and the body is hot [nevertheless], then these are signs that do not agree. Hence, this is called 'contrary.'" The *Jia yi jing* has: 氣盛身寒, 氣虛身熱, 此謂反也. Lin Yi et al.: "One should follow the *Jia yi jing* and add the four characters 氣虛身熱.

5 Wang Bing: "The qi of grain leaves the stomach and is distributed through the conduit vessels. Grain enters the stomach and [its qi] is dispersed through the vessel paths. If, in the present case, grain enters [the stomach] in large quantities while qi [is distributed through the vessels] in small quantities nevertheless, then stomach qi is not dispersed. Hence, this is called 'contrary.'"

6 Wang Bing: "The stomach qi disperses in the exterior and is joined by the [qi of the] lung."

7 Gu Guanguang: "少 should be 小, 'small.'"

8 Wang Bing: "The conduit vessels move the qi; the network vessels receive the blood. The conduit qi enters the network [vessels]; the network [vessels] receive the conduit qi. [In the present case] the signs do not agree. Hence, this is a [situation] contrary to normality."

9 Wang Bing: "傷 is to say 觸冒, 'reckless offense.' Cold harms the physical appearance. Hence, the qi abounds and the body is cold. Heat harms the qi. Hence, the qi is depleted and the body is hot."

the lower [section of the body].[10]

When grain enters [the body] in small quantities and the qi is plentiful [nevertheless], evil is situated in the stomach and also in the lung.[11]

53-281-1

In case the vessels are small, while the blood is plentiful, this is because of heat in the beverages.[12]

In case the vessels are big, while the blood is diminished, wind qi is situated in the vessels.

[Hence,] water and [other] beverages do not enter.

This is what is meant [by 'contrary'].”[13]

53-281-2

<Now,

as for repletion, that is: qi enters;

---

10 Wang Bing: “A loss of blood results in blood depletion. When the blood is depleted, then the qi abounds internally and is transformed into body liquids which flow downwards into the lower burner. Hence, [the text] states: ‘dampness resides in the lower [section of the body].’” Ma Shi: “If grain enters [the body] in large quantities and – contrary [to what one should expect] – qi is present in small quantities [only], this is because [the patient] has lost blood. When too much blood was lost, then the qi is diminished [too]. Also, dampness resides in the lower [section of the body]. If this dampness dominates, then the conduit vessels are blocked and this, too, causes a decrease of qi.” Cheng Shide et al.: “When the spleen loses its ability to transport, water-dampness stagnates internally. The nature of dampness is heavy and turbid; it flows down into the lower burner. Hence, ‘dampness resides in the lower [section of the body].’”

11 Wang Bing: “When the stomach qi is insufficient, lung qi flows downwards into the stomach. Hence, evil is situated in the stomach. However, when lung qi enters the stomach, then the lung qi does not guard [the lung] itself. When the [lung] qi fails to guard [the lung] itself, then evil qi will move there as a result. Hence, [the text] states: ‘Evil is situated in the stomach and also in the lung.’” In contrast, 307/183: “According to the *Er ya* 爾雅, Shi gu xia 釋詁下, 及 is identical with 與.” Yu Chang: “These two characters have an identical meaning; this duplication goes back to the ancients themselves. Wu Kun has omitted the character 與; that was unnecessary.”

12 Wang Bing: “飲 is to say: 留飲, ‘stagnant beverages.’ When beverages stagnate in the spleen and/or in the stomach, then the spleen qi overflows. When the spleen qi overflows, then this causes heat in the center.” Tanba agrees.

13 Wang Bing: “When [the vessels] are filled to repletion with wind qi, then water and broths cannot enter the vessels.”

as for depletion, that is: qi leaves.[14]
As for qi repletion, that is heat;
as for qi depletion, that is cold.[15]

In case [a needle] is inserted [to treat] repletion, the left hand opens the
needle hole.[16]
In case [a needle] is inserted [to treat] depletion, the left hand closes the
needle hole.>[17]

---

14 Wang Bing: "To enter is yang; to leave is yin. Yin [qi] is generated inside; hence,
it 'leaves'; yang [qi] is generated outside; hence it 'enters.'"

15 Wang Bing: "[In the former situation], the yang [qi] abounds and the yin [qi]
is closed in internally. Hence, [the body is] hot. [In the latter situation], the yin [qi]
abounds and the yang [qi] is present in minimal quantities in the external [sections of
the body]. Hence, [the body] is cold." In contrast, 638/9 interprets "that is heat" and
"that is cold" as references to the causes of qi repletion and qi depletion respectively.
For both arguments, see 638/3.

16 The *Jia yi jing* has 孔, "hole", instead of 空.

17 Wang Bing: "That is to explain the application of a needle to supplement or drain,
respectively. The right hand holds the needle and the left hand plucks [the skin at] the
hole [to be pierced]. Hence, in case of repletion, the left hand opens the hole pierced
to drain there. In case of depletion, the left hand closes the hole pierced to supplement there." Zhang Jiebin: "入實 is: 'to pierce a repletion.' One holds the needle with
one's right hand and twirls [the needle] to enlargen its path. This is [meant by] 'the
right hand opens the hole pierced.' 入虛 is: 'to pierce a depletion.' After the needle is
withdrawn, one presses and closes the opening with one's left hand. This is [meant by]
'the left hand closes the hole pierced.'" Hu Tianxiong: "The character 左 (for 'left') in
'the left hand opens the hole pierced' is probably a mistake. Zhang Jiebin followed the
comments by Hua Shou and Wu Kun and changed the character to 右 (for 'right');
that was correct." 524/9: "When treating a condition of repletion by piercing, the left
hand opens the hole pierced after the needle is withdrawn; it must not apply any pressure and close [the hole]. When treating a condition of depletion, the left hand should
press and close the hole pierced after the needle is withdrawn." See also 1289/16.

Chapter 54
Explanations on the Needles

54-281-6
Huang Di asked:
"I should like to hear
an explanation of the 'nine needles' and
the Way of depletion and repletion."[1]

Qi Bo responded:
"As for
'when piercing a depletion, then replenish it,'
[that is, pierce until] there is heat below the needle.
{When the qi is replete, then heat is present.}[2]

As for
'when there is fullness, then discharge it,'
[that is, pierce until] there is cold below the needle.
{When the qi is depleted, then cold is present.}[3]

As for
'what is densely compacted and old, eliminate it,'
[that is,] let the bad blood.[4]

---

1 The following phrases ending with the character 者 may be quotations from a larger text named 九鍼 *Jiu zhen*, "The Nine Needles." This text appears to have also been the basis of *Ling shu* 1, titled 九鍼十二原. From 刺虛則實之者 to 九針之名各不同形者 these phrases are to be found in *Ling shu* 1 without commentary. A large part of *Su wen* 54 is a commentary to this text (see also note 15 below).

2 Zhang Jiebin: " 'There is heat below the needle' is: the cold turns into heat. When [the region below the needle] is hot, then the proper qi has arrived and the depletion has been replenished. Hence, this is a supplementation."

3 Zhang Jiebin: " 'There is cold below the needle' is: the heat turns into cold. When [the region below the needle] is cold, then the evil qi has arrived and the repletion has been depleted. Hence, this is a drainage."

4 Wang Bing: "菀 is 積, 'accumulation.' 陳 is 久, 'old.' 除 is 去, 'to remove.' That is to say, when blood has accumulated in the network vessels for a long time, one pierces [these vessels] with a needle and removes it." 971/56: "This makes it very clear that the phrase 去菀陳 (in *Su wen* 14) is a therapy whereby blood is let by piercing the network vessels." See also 1617/35, 919/1, and 117/38.

As for
'in case evil dominates, deplete it,'
[that is,] remove the needle and do not press [the hole pierced].⁵

As for
'slow and quick results in repletion,'
[that is,] slowly remove the needle and quickly press the [hole pierced].⁶

As for
'quick and slow results in depletion,'
[that is,] quickly remove the needle and slowly press the [hole pierced].⁷

54-282-1
As for
'when one speaks of
'repletion and depletion,''⁸
these are [differences in the] quantities of cold and warm qi.⁹

As for
'sometimes it is not present, sometimes it is present,'
that is, it is fast and cannot be recognized.¹⁰

---

5 Wang Bing: " 'Evil' is a term for what is not proper. When qi is present which is not [the qi] of the respective conduit, then this [qi] is called 'evil.' This is not a reference to a domination by an evil which is the essence of a demonic poison. When the needle is withdrawn, one must not press the hole; rather the transporter is to be opened to achieve a conduit depletion in that the evil qi is drained through effusion."

6 Wang Bing: " 'Slowly remove [the needle]' is to say: one removes it only after one has had a hold of the conduit qi for quite a while. 'Quickly press' is to say: Once the needle has been completely removed from the hole, one quickly presses it. This prevents the proper qi from flowing away and safeguards the completion of the conduit-vessel qi. Hence, [the text states:] 'slow and quick results in replenishment.' "

7 Wang Bing: " 'Quickly remove the needle' is to say: When the needle has been inserted into the hole to a degree where it has reached the conduit-vessels, then it is quickly removed again. 'Slowly press' is to say: When the needle has been removed from the hole entirely, one slowly presses it. This allows the evil qi to flow away and the essence qi to stabilize. Hence, [the text states:] 'quick and slow results in depletion.' "

8 This quotation from the text which appears in *Ling shu* 1 (see note 1 above) may itself be regarded as a commentary to an earlier text.

9 Wang Bing: " 'Cold' and 'warm' refer to the yin and yang qi of the conduit-vessels."

10 Wang Bing: "That is to say: those who are ignorant cannot recognize it immediately. Now, since it cannot be recognized immediately, 'it is as if it were not present.' "

As for
'investigate later and earlier,'
this is to get to know the earlier and later [course] of a disease.

As for
'those who cause depletion and repletion,'
[that is,] the practitioner must not miss the [appropriate therapeutic] law.

As for
'sometimes one obtains a gain, sometimes one causes a loss,'
this is [the result of] departing from the [appropriate therapeutic] law.[11]

54-282-3
As for
'in view of the essentials of [treating] depletion and repletion, the nine needles
are most miraculous,'
that is, for each [disease] there is an appropriate [needle].[12]

As for
'the times of supplementing and draining,'
that is, [the piercing should] coincide with the opening and closure of the qi.[13]

For those who are wise and possess divine intelligence it is 'as if it were present.'"
Cheng Shide et al.: "The feelings of cold and heat [in the region] where the needle is
inserted change quickly."

11 Wang Bing: "If one erroneously supplements what is replete, the result is 'as if one
had obtained a gain.' If one erroneously drains what is depleted, the result is 'as if one
had caused a loss.'"

12 Wang Bing: "In case of heat in head and body, the chisel needle is appropriate.
In case of qi fullness in the flesh section, the round needle is appropriate. When the
vessel qi is depleted or diminished, the arrowhead needle is appropriate. To drain heat,
let blood and discharge through effusion obstinate diseases, the lance-point needle is
appropriate, ... That is to say: 'for each [disease] there is an appropriate [needle].'"

13 Wang Bing: "When the [movement of the] qi coincides with the time marks, this
is called 'open.' When [the time marks] have been passed and [the qi] has not yet arrived nevertheless, that is called 'closed.' As for 'time marks,' when the water [of the
clepsydra] has fallen by one mark, the qi of man is in the major yang [conduit]. When
[the water] has fallen to the second mark, the qi of man is in the minor yang [conduit].
When the water has fallen to the third mark, the qi of man is in the yang brilliance
[conduit]. When the water has fallen to the fourth mark, the qi of man is in the yin
section. As the water falls without end, the qi moves without end. Hence, when [the
arrival of the qi] coincides with the time marks, one calls this 'open.' When the [water]
has passed the time mark and [the qi] has not arrived yet, this is called 'closed.'" Zhang

54-282-5
As for
'the names of the nine needles, each [refers to] a different shape,'
that is, [before using] the needles investigate carefully where supplementation
or draining are required. ¹⁴

As for
'when piercing a repletion, wait for a depletion,'¹⁵
that is, let the needle remain until yin qi arrives aboundingly and then remove
the needle.¹⁶

As for
'when piercing a depletion, wait for a repletion,'
that is, when yang qi arrives aboundingly and when there is heat below the
needle, then remove the needle.

54-283-1
As for
'when the conduit qi has arrived, guard it carefully lest it is lost,'
that is, do not make any changes.¹⁷

As for
'deep and shallow are at [one's] mind,'

Jiebin: "When the qi arrives in time, that is called 'open.' When [the time] is over and
it has not arrived yet, that is called ' closed.'"

14 Wang Bing: "窮其補寫 is to say: each [needle] is employed in accordance with
one's therapeutic [intention]." The *Tai su* has 其所之當補瀉也, '[one must carefully
examine] the suitability of supplementation or draining at these locations."

15 This and the following 7 quotations (to 神無營於眾物) are excerpts from a text
which appears, without commentary, in *Su wen* 25-163-3 to 25-163-5 and in *Tai su*
19, 16A, 125b-2 to 125b-6. This text, too, may have been part of the text named 九
鍼 (see note 1 above).

16 Zhang Zhicong: "One lets the needle remain [in the skin] to wait for the qi to
arrive. When ample yin qi arrives, the [region where] the needle is inserted turns cold
and the yang qi has receded entirely. The repletion has changed into a depletion."

17 Wang Bing: "That is to say: when one has obtained the qi in that it has arrived,
one must carefully guard it and not change the method. Otherwise one invites harm."
Zhang Zhicong: "One must prevent that the qi undergoes any changes." Cheng Shide
et al.: " 'Change' refers to a change in the methods of piercing. Wang Bing is correct."

that is, one [must] know whether the disease is located in the inner or outer [regions].[18]

As for
'near and far are like one,'
that is, no matter whether [a disease] is deep or shallow, examination is identical.[19]

As for
'as if one looked down into a deep abyss,'
that is, do not dare to be careless.

54-283-4
As for
'the hand [must be strong] as if it held a tiger,'
that is, one wishes it to be strong.[20]

As for
'the spirit should not be confused by the multitude of things,'
that is, have a tranquil mind and observe the patient, look neither to the left nor to the right.[21]

As for
'do what is right to do, no what is evil, when lowering the needle,'
that is, one should [hold the needle] upright and properly.[22]

---

18 Wang Bing: "Instead of 志, another copy has 意, 'sentiment.' Both 志 and 意 refer to the application of the needle." Ma Shi: "That is to say, when the disease is in the depth, then the needle is to be inserted deeply. When the disease is near the surface, then the insertion of the needle is shallow."

19 Wang Bing: "That is to say: there may be differences in that the qi is near or distant. Nevertheless, a successful examination (測候) is always built on the [quality of the] arrival of the qi." In contrast, Cheng Shide et al.: "候 is 候氣, 'to wait for the qi.'"

20 Wang Bing: " 'Strong' is to say: it holds the needle firmly."

21 End of list of seven annotated phrases also found in *Su wen* 25 (see note 15 above).

22 Wang Bing: "正 refers to 直, 'straight.' When piercing with the needle, one [moves it] neither left nor right." Cheng Shide et al.: "義 is a proper conduct. Here it refers to the proper method of inserting the needle. 邪 is 斜, 'slanting.' 義無邪下 is: one must be correct in inserting the needle."

As for
'one must rectify his spirit,'
that is, one must look into the eyes of the patient and control his spirit, thereby
letting the qi flow easily.[23]

54-283-7
As for the so-called
'three miles,'
this is [a location] three inches below the knee.

As for the so-called
'*fu-zhi,*'
lift the knee and the parting is easily visible.[24]

As for
'great hollow,'
this is the single depression at the shin [that is visible] if one raises one's foot.[25]

---

23 Wang Bing: "[One must] concentrate [the patient's] essence spirit lest it disperses.
As a result, the spirit will cause a regulation of the qi in the center and in the external
regions."

24 Wang Bing: " 'Three Miles' (三里) is the name of a hole. It is located exactly three
inches below the knee, in the flesh parting between the two sinews outside of the shin.
If one presses it very hard, then the moving vessel on the instep is arrested. Hence,
[the text] states: 'Lift the knee and the parting is easily visible.' " Lin Yi et al.: "In
accordance with *Su wen* 60 this should be 跗上." Gao Shishi: "Older versions have
mistakenly replaced 上 by 之. 跗上 refers to the moving vessel at the Surging Yang (衝
陽) [hole]." Ma Shi: "跗上 is the Surging Yang hole of the foot yang brilliance conduit
of the stomach." Guo Aichun-81: "膝 is a mistake for 脈, 'vessel;' 分 is a mistake for
則. In hand-writing, 分 and 則 are very similar and can easily be mistaken for each
other. 舉膝分易見 should therefore be 舉脈則易見, that is to say, one looks for the
moving vessel and the Surging Yang hole is easily visible." Wu Kun: "跗 is 拊 in the
sense of 'to press firmly.' 拊之 is: to press firmly at the Three Miles (三里) divide."
Tanba: "The [text] does not say 'press the Three Miles.' Hence, one cannot follow
[Wang Bing's] statement regarding 'the moving vessel on the instep is arrested.' It may
be that in front of 跗 the character 低 ('to lower,' 'to bend down') was left out and that
in front of the character 之 the character 取 is missing. *Ling shu* 4 has: 取之三里者
低跗, 取之巨虛者舉足, 'to remove it from the Three Miles, bend down the instep; to
remove it from the Great Hollow, lift the foot.' This may serve as evidence." Lin Yi et
al.: "The Quan Yuanqi edition has 低骺, 'Bend down the shins,' instead of 跗之. The
Tai su has 付之.' "

25 Wang Bing: " 'Great Hollow (巨虛)' is the name of a hole. 蹻 is to say 舉, 'to lift.'
To select the Lower Edge of the Great Hollow (巨虛下廉) [hole] for treatment, let

As for
'lower edge,'
this is what has sunk down."²⁶

54-283-9
[Huang] Di:
"I have heard [the following:]
the nine needles correspond above to heaven and earth, to the four seasons and
to yin and yang.
I should like to hear the methods [underlying] their [use] so that they may be
transmitted to later generations to serve as rules."

54-284-1
Qi Bo:
"Now,
one [is] heaven,
two [is] the earth,
three [is] man,
four [are the] seasons,
five [are the] tones,
six [are the] pitchpipe tones,
seven [are the] stars,
eight [are the] winds,
nine [are the] fields.

The body corresponds to these [numbers], too.

Each of the needles has what it is appropriate for.
Hence, it is said: nine needles.

Man's skin corresponds to heaven.²⁷

---

the patient] lift the foot. It is below the depression between the two sinews on the
outer side of the shinbones."

26 Wang Bing: "If one wishes to know where the Lower Edge hole is located, its
place is below the singular depression between the two sinews on the outer side of
the shinbones."

27 Wang Bing: "It covers all beings. That is the image of heaven." Ma Shi: "The skin
of man corresponds to heaven. Heaven covers the myriad things; the skin is the screen
protecting the body." Zhang Zhicong: "Now, the One is heaven. Heaven is yang. Of
the five depots lung corresponds to heaven. The lung is the canopy covering the five

Man's flesh corresponds to the earth.[28]
Man's vessels correspond to man.[29]
Man's sinews correspond to the seasons.[30]
Man's voice correspond to the tones.[31]

When yin and yang in man merge [their] qi, this corresponds to the tones of the pitchpipes.

Man's teeth, face, and eyes correspond to the stars.[32]
The qi leaving and entering man corresponds to the winds.[33]
Man's nine orifices and 365 network [vessels] correspond to the fields.[34]

54-284-6
Hence,
the first needle [serves to pierce] the skin.
The second needle [serves to pierce] the flesh.
The third needle [serves to pierce] the vessels.
The fourth needle [serves to pierce] the sinews.
The fifth needle [serves to pierce] the bones.
The sixth needle [serves to] regulate yin and yang.
The seventh needle [serves to] increase the essence.
The eighth needle [serves to] eliminate wind.
The ninth needle [serves to] open the nine orifices and to eliminate the qi from the 365 joints.
That is meant [when it is said:] Each has that which it rules.[35]

---

depots and six palaces. The skin is linked to the lung; it is the yang of man. Hence, the skin of man corresponds to heaven."

28 Wang Bing: "It is soft and thick, peaceful and quiet. That is the image of the earth."

29 Wang Bing: "They change between abundance to weakness; that is the image of man."

30 Wang Bing: "They are firm and stable. That is the image of the seasons."

31 Wang Bing: "Because it comprises all the five tones."

32 Wang Bing: "The human face corresponds to the stars because it has seven openings."

33 Wang Bing: "[Man's qi] leaves, goes, and returns. That is the image of the wind."

34 Wang Bing: "The exterior of the physical appearance of man is the image of the fields."

35 Wang Bing: "The first needle is the chisel needle. The second needle is the round needle. The third needle is the arrowhead needle. The fourth needle is the lance needle.

Man's heart and sentiments correspond to the eight winds.[36]
Man's qi corresponds to heaven.[37]
Man's hair, teeth, ears, eyes, and five sounds correspond to the five tones and to the six tones of the pitchpipe.[38]
Man's blood and qi in his yin and yang vessels correspond to the earth.[39]
Man's liver and eyes, one lets them correspond to nine."[40]
{The nine orifices and 365.}[41]

54-285-1
[The] man [section in man], in addition, may serve to observe movement and resting.
[The] heaven [section in man], second, may serve to examine the five colors.
{The seven stars, one lets them correspond to them.}
[...] may serve to examine whether the hair has no shine.
The five [human] tones, in addition, may serve to examine *gong, shang, jue, zhi, yu.*
{The six pitchpipe tones, their surplus and insufficiency correspond to them.}

54-285-3
<Two,> the earth [section in man], in addition, may serve to examine whether high and low have surplus.
The nine fields [in man], in addition, {the joint transporters correspond to them} may serve to examine the closed joints.

The fifth needle is the sword needle. The sixth needle is the round-sharp needle. The seventh needle is the fine tipped needle. The eighth needle is the long needle. The ninth needle is the large needle."

36 Wang Bing: "They move and rest without physical appearance. That is the image of the wind."

37 Wang Bing: "It moves without pause. That is the image of heaven."

38 Wang Bing: "The hair and the teeth are generated and grow; the ears and the eyes are clear and penetrable. The five sounds respond to their likes. Hence, they correspond to the five tones and to the six sounds of the pitchpipe."

39 Wang Bing: "Man's yin and yang [qi] may meet and they generate and complete [things]. The blood and the qi in the vessels may be depleted, or they abound. Hence, they correspond to the earth.

40 Wang Bing: "The liver qi communicates with the eyes. The generation number of wood is three. Three multiplied by three corresponds to nine."

41 Lin Yi et al.: "The Quan Yuanqi edition does not have these seven characters."

<Three> Man's changes.

The first division, in man [it may serve] to examine the teeth.⁴²

Much outflow, little blood.

The tenth division, [it may serve to examine] changes of *jue*.

The fifth division may serve to examine [whether the movement in the vessels is] relaxed or tight.

The sixth division [may serve to examine an] insufficiency.

The third division [may serve to examine the presence of] cold in the joints.

The ninth division [may serve to examine] in man cold, warmth, dryness, and dampness in the course of the four seasons.

{The four seasons, in addition, correspond to this.

This may serve to examine whether they are mutually opposed.}

{In addition, the four cardinal points.}

Each serves as explanation.⁴³

---

42 The *Tai su* has 以候 instead of 人候.

43 Wang Bing: "[Beginning with 九竅三百六十五] these 124 characters are entirely corrupt; their meaning is incomplete and cannot be researched." Lin Yi et al.: "Wang Bing speaks of 124 characters. The present text comprises only 123 characters. One character was lost."

Chapter 55
Discourse on Rules of Extended Piercing[1]

55-285-8

In case an expert in piercing does not[2] diagnose [but prefers to] listen to the patient's statement: "It is in the head. The head has an illness, pain."[3] and if on

---

1 Gao Shishi: "長 is like 廣, 'to broaden.' As for 長刺節, starting from the locations of the diseases, [the present treatise] formulates rules of piercing these [locations]. For instance, in case of headache, fits of cold and heat, putrefied swelling, (etc.), the piercing to remove the [disease] is always carried out at the location of the disease. Hence [the present treatise] extends piercing beyond the five rules (outlined in *Ling shu* 75) and the twelve rules (outlined in Ling shu 7) and it is therefore that its title refers to 'Extended Rules of Piercing.'" We do not consider the present treatise as an extension of Ling shu 7 and 75. Rather, it appears to us that 長 refers to a technique of piercing outlined in this treatise whereby the needle is left in the skin for an "extended" period of time, or is inserted several times, until a therapeutic effect can be observed.

2 Zhang Jiebin: "Those who are good in piercing, they must not take recourse to diagnosis [by feeling the movement in the vessels]. They only listen to what the patients say and whatever they undertake will be effective. This, however, is a statement with regard to those only who have a miraculous command of piercing; it is not to say that experts in piercing must not diagnose at all [by feeling the movement in the vessels]. Nowadays the masters of later times are neither excellent in piercing, nor do they know how to diagnose [by feeling the movement in the vessels]. Hence, when it comes to supplementing a depletion or to draining a repletion, how could they avoid committing mistakes? When the treatise in *Ling shu* 1 states: 'Whenever one is about to employ the needle, one must first diagnose [by feeling the movement in] the vessels and examine whether the [movement of the] qi [indicates] a severe problem or [a disease which is] easy to handle. Only then one may commence the treatment,' then the meaning of the present [passage] can be understood." Wu Kun: "That is to say: experts in piercing must not cling to the patterns of diagnosing [by feeling the movement in the vessels]. It is sufficient to listen to the patients and to pierce in accordance with what they say about their ailments." Yao Shaoyu: "When someone is good in diagnosing [by feeling the movement in] the vessels but is not good in employing the needles, then he is not good at all. Hence, when the classic states 'does not diagnose [by feeling the movement in the vessels],' it is not [to say] that one should not diagnose [by feeling the movement in the vessels], rather it is to say that one should not concentrate on such diagnosis alone." Li Guoqing: "Sun Dingyi 孫鼎宜 has: 不 should be 來, 'in order to.' ['In order to carry out a diagnosis, the expert of piercing [should] listen to what the patients say.'] In fact, though, 不 is merely an interjection, as is frequently the case in the Nei jing. Hence, 刺家不診 is 刺家診. This is a reference to those who are especially gifted in piercing." 1895/47 agrees: "The character 不 has no meaning here." For evidence see there.

3 The *Tai su* has 在頭疾頭痛, "[I have] an illness in the head. [My] head has pain." 1569/18: "The first 頭 is a noun used here as an adjective in the sense of 'being at the

behalf of this he needles him <the depot>,⁴ when the piercing reaches to the bones, the disease ends.

<Above, do not harm the bones, the flesh, and the skin>⁵
{As for the skin, it is the way.}⁶
<To conduct a yin piercing, insert [the needle] into one [central] and four neighboring locations.>⁷

---

head.' The second 頭 is a noun meaning 'head.'"

4 Wang Bing: "藏 is equal to 深, 'deep.' That is to say: pierce deeply. Hence, the statement in the text later on." Zhang Jiebin: "藏 is 裡, 'inside.' That is to say: he inserts the needle deeply." Lin Yi et al.: "The Quan Yuanqi edition does not have the character 藏." The character 藏 appears to be a later insert, possibly added to interpret the phrase 為針之 in view of the subsequent advises 刺大藏, "pierce the big depots," and 刺之迫 藏, "pierce close to the depots."

5 The *Tai su* does not have the character 上. Wu Kun and Ma Shi have 止, 'to stop,' instead of 上. If this were the original version, 止 should be read as the last character of the preceding sentence; together with 已 it would form the compound 已止, 'to end'. Zhou Xuehai: "It must be the character 止." See also the appearance of 止 in line 285-11 below for further evidence. Wu Kun: "傷 does not mean 損傷, 'to injure.' If one pierces to the bones, how could one avoid harming the bones, the flesh, and the skin? The meaning is: one must not move [the needle] carelessly lest one harms the true qi in the bone section, the flesh section, or the skin section." We interpret the reference to "above" as a warning not to harm the bones in the head section, i.e., in the "upper" sections of the body.

6 Wang Bing: "The skin is the way taken by the needle. Hence, when piercing the bones one must not harm the bones, the flesh, or the skin." Zhang Jiebin: "Skin and flesh are the way by which the needle is inserted."

7 The *Tai su* has 陽刺 instead of 陰刺 , and it does not have the character 處. Yang Shangshan: "Originally the text had 陰刺, but that was a mistaken character." Wang Bing: "When the head experiences [feelings of] cold and heat, one treats it by means of the yin piercing pattern. 'Yin piercing' is to say: to pierce it comprehensively, at as many [locations as is mentioned] here." Lin Yi et al.: "Other editions [of Wang Bing's commentary] have 平刺 , 'balanced piercing,' instead of 卒刺 , 'comprehensive piercing'. The *Jia yi jing* states: 'Yang piercing is to insert [one needle] into one central [location] and into four neighboring [locations]. Yin piercing is to pierce to the left and right, everywhere.' Hence, the 'yin piercing' here may in fact be a 'yang piercing.'" *Ling shu* 7 has 揚刺, 'raising piercing' instead of 陽刺: "'Raising piercing' is to insert [a needle] into one central [location] and into the four sides [of that location] and to withdraw it to a shallow position." Wu Kun: "Movement is yang, quietude is yin. Yin piercing is to insert the needle and not to twirl it or move it here and there." *Ling shu* 7 refers to "yin piercing" as the tenth of the twelve categories of piercing. Yin piercing is defined there as "piercing left and right [ankle] together to treat cold recession. To

55-285-10
For treating cold and heat which have entered the depth [of the organism and]
have concentrated [there], pierce the large depots.⁸
When [the cold or heat] have come near the depots, pierce the back.⁹
{These are the transporters on the back.¹⁰ For piercing an [evil] near the depots,
[pierce] the Depot Meeting [hole].}¹¹
When cold and heat in the abdomen have left, stop [the piercing].¹²
Also, pierce it in the lower back.¹³
Deploy the needle into a shallow [position] and let blood.

55-286-3
For treating putrefied swellings, pierce above the putrefaction.¹⁴

---

be struck by cold recession [affects] the minor yin [conduit] behind the ankle." The
present reference to a yin piercing appears unrelated to this *Ling shu 7* account.

8 Yang Shangshan: "大藏 refers to the lung. The shape of the lung is larger than that
of the remaining four depots. Hence, it is called 'large depot.'" Wang Bing: "When
a disease qi of cold or heat has entered the depth [of the body] and has attacked the
center to gather there, one must pierce the five depots to ward it off." Zhang Jiebin:
"The evil qi has entered [the body] deeply and [has affected] one depot in particular.
For treatment one must find out this great depot and remove [the evil] directly from
it." Ma Shi: "The five depots are the 'great depots.'" 419/4: "Given the preceding and
the following passages, the character 大 may be an error for 內, 'internal.' The seal
characters of 大 and 內 resemble each other." Hu Tianxiong: "From here on down to
與刺之要, the text is difficult to explain. All commentators disagree and have their
own opinion. What they say is farfetched."

9 Wang Bing: "迫 is 近, 'near.'"

10 The *Tai su* has 迫藏刺背俞也, '..near the depots, pierce the back transporters.'

11 Wang Bing : "When it is said: 'pierce close to the depots,' why is that? Because
it is there that the qi of the depots meets and effuses." Wu Kun: "One pierces those
transporters located near the [affected] depot because it is there that the depot qi accumulates."

12 Wang Bing: "That is to say: when piercing the transporters on the back, one stops
the piercing only when the cold or heat has been removed, regardless of how often
one has to pierce."

13 The *Tai su* has 腰, lower back, instead of 要.

14 Wang Bing: " 'Putrefied swelling' is to say: the flesh inside the swelling has rotted
and changed into pus and blood. Small abscesses are pierced with a shallow [insertion
of the needle]; large abscesses are pierced with a deep [insertion of the needle]." Lin
Yi et al.: "Both the Quan Yuanqi edition and the *Jia yi jing* have 癰 instead of 腐."

Find out whether the *yong*-abscess is small or large and conduct a deep or shallow piercing.[15]

When piercing large [abscesses] there is much blood;
in the case of small ones,[16] insert [the needle] more deeply.
[In each case] one must aim at inserting the needle straight [downwards] and
stop [at the bottom of the abscess].

55-286-1
When the disease consists of accumulations in the lower abdomen, pierce from
the skin fat down to the lower abdomen and stop.[17]
[Also,] pierce on both sides along the spine in the region of the fourth
vertebra.[18]

---

15 In the *Tai su*, this sentence contains no 刺. Accordingly, it should be rendered as:
"Examine whether the *yong*-abscess is small or large, deep-lying or at the surface."

16 *Tai su* and *Jia yi jing* do not have the two characters 小者. Wang Bing interprets
端 as "straight": "In case of large *yong*-abscesses one lets large amounts of blood; in
case of small *yong*-abscesses all that is required is to insert the needle straight [downwards]."

17 Wang Bing: " 'Accumulations in the lower abdomen' is to say: accumulations of
cold and/or heat qi. 皮髓 is the line running horizontally five individually standardized body inches below the navel. One must pierce carefully and cannot insert [the
needle] too deeply. *Su wen* 52 states: 'If one pierces the lower abdomen and hits the
bladder, urine leaves and fills the lower abdomen of that person.' Hence, one must not
insert [the needle] deeply." Lin Yi et al.: "According to the *Shi yin* 釋音, 皮髓 is 皮
骷, read *kuo*. 骷 is the tip of a bone. Hence, 皮骷 is the tip of the pubic bone below the
navel. The Quan Yuanqi edition has 皮髓." Cheng Shide et al.: "Ma Shi reads 髓 as 脂
– it means 'fat' – and he quotes a passage from the *Zuo chuan*, 6th year of Duke Huan.
He is perfectly right. The character 髓 has the three different versions of 骷 in the *Shi
yin*, 髓 in the Quan Yuanqi edition, and of 脂 in Ma Shi's commentary. Its meanings
are two: the first is tip of a bone, the other is fat. Together with 皮 it cannot, of course,
refer to the tip of a bone. However, if read as 'fat,' where should this location be? To
sum this up: all interpretations are forced. The *Tai su*, ch. 雜刺, has 腹齊 instead of the
two characters 皮髓. Yang Shangshan commented: 'In case of accumulations in the
lower abdomen, one pierces from the navel downwards to the lower abdomen.' One
should follow the *Tai su*."

18 Wang Bing: "According to the classic, there is no transporter 'on both sides of
the spine in the region of the fourth vertebra.' I suspect that [the text should be] 'in
the region of the fifth vertebra.' Below the fifth vertebra on both sides [of the spine]
are the transporters of the true heart. The heart corresponds to the lower abdomen.
Hence, [the text] should state 'in the region of the fifth vertebra.'" Ma Shi and Gao
Shishi: "This is the transporter-hole of the heart enclosure [which is associated with

[Also,] pierce into the bone-holes in the two pelvic bones and into the free ribs.[19]

[All these piercings serve] to guide the abdominal qi.

When the heat has descended, [the disease] ends.

55-286-4

When the disease is in the lower abdomen, [with the patient experiencing] abdominal pain and an inability to pass stools or urine,

<The name of the disease is elevation illness; it is acquired because of cold.>

pierce between the lower abdomen and the two thighs.

[Also,] pierce between the lower back and the hip bones.

Pierce many times.

When [the region pierced] is all hot, the disease ends.

55-286-6

When the disease is in the sinews, [with the patient experiencing] sinew cramps, pain in the joints, so that they do not allow [one] to walk,

<This is called sinew block.>

aim at piercing above the sinews.

Pierce into the parting of the flesh.

One must not hit the bones.

When the disease emerges, the sinews are hot.

When the disease ends, stop [the piercing].[20]

55-287-2

When the disease is in the muscles and in the skin, [with the patient experiencing] pain all over the muscles and the skin,

<This is called muscle block. [It results from] harm caused by cold and dampness.>

---

the] ceasing yin." Wu Kun and Zhang Zhicong: "These are the *Gao Huang* (膏肓) holes on both sides of the fourth vertebra."

19 Wang Bing: "骼 refers to the bones of the lower back. 髎 is written 髀 in other versions. That is a mistake resulting from the similar shapes of these characters. 髎 refers to the Squatting Bone-Hole (居髎) hole on the side of the lower back. 季脅 肋間 should be: one must pierce the Capital Gate (京門) hole in the region of the free ribs."

20 Wang Bing: "When the sinews are cold the [sinew] block emerges. Hence, when the sinews have become hot, the disease is healed and one stops [the treatment]." The Wu Kun edition has omitted the two characters 病起.

pierce the large partings and the small partings [of the flesh].[21]
Deploy the needle many times and insert it deeply aiming at [generating] heat.

Do not harm the sinews and the bones.
When the sinews and the bones are harmed, *yong*-abscesses develop resembling [pathological] changes.[22]

When all partings [of the flesh] are completely hot, the disease has ended. Stop [the piercing].[23]

55-287-5
When the disease is in the bones,
[with the patient experiencing his] bones being so heavy that he cannot lift them and bones and marrow being sore and in pain,
<[This results] from extreme cold qi. [The disease] is named bone block.>
when [the disease] is in the depth, piercing must aim at not to harm the vessels or the flesh.[24]

The ways [along which to insert the needle] are the large partings and the small partings [of the flesh].
When the bones have become hot, the disease ends. Stop [the piercing].[25]

55-287-7
When the disease is in all the yang vessels [with the patient experiencing] alternate fits of cold or heat,[26]

---

21 Wang Bing: " 'Large parting' is to say: Large flesh parting; 'small parting' is to say: small flesh parting."

22 Mori: "The meaning of 若變 is not clear. 變 may be an erroneous writing of 攣. That is to say, when the sinews and the bones have been harmed seriously and in the depth, this leads to abscesses. When they have been harmed only slightly and near the surface, this results in cramps. Hence, harm done to the bones results in abscesses; harm done to the sinews results in cramps." Zhang Yizhi et al.: "The *Jia yi jing* has 寒, 'cold,' instead of 癰. That appears to be correct."

23 Wang Bing: "Heat can dissolve cold. Hence, [heat signals that] the disease has ended and [the therapist] stops [the piercing]."

24 Ma Shi: "為故 is 為復其舊, 'to restore its former [condition].' "

25 Wang Bing: "How is it [possible] not to harm the vessels and the flesh when piercing a bone block? By inserting the needle into the large and small partings of the flesh that are penetrated by the qi."

26 Wang Shaozeng/116: "且 ... 且 ... is 有時 ... 有時 ... , 'at times ... at times ...' "

{when it is in all the partings [of the flesh, with the patient experiencing] alternate fits of cold or heat,}
<This is called craziness.>²⁷
pierce it at the depleted vessels.
Inspect the partings [of the flesh]; when they have turned hot entirely, the disease ends. Stop [the piercing].²⁸

55-287-8
When the disease breaks out for the first time, it breaks out once in a year.
If not treated, it breaks out once in a month.
If not treated [even then], it breaks out four, five times in a month,
<[This] is called peak illness.>²⁹
pierce all the partings [of the flesh] and all the vessels.³⁰

---

27 Wang Bing: "The [movement of the] qi is crazy and disorderly."

28 Gao Shishi: "This is the pattern of piercing the disease of craziness. 'When the disease is in all the yang vessels, with alternating fits of cold and heat,' then the evil qi has occupied the conduit vessels. 'When it is in all the partings [of the flesh] with alternating fits of cold and heat,' then the evil has occupied the partings of the flesh. When the evil of the partings of the flesh and the evil of the conduit vessels interact and unite, the [resulting] disease is called craziness. 'One pierces it to deplete the vessels' [is to say:] one does not let the evil occupy the conduit vessels." Hu Tianxiong: " 'Alternating fits of cold and heat' is a sign of a disease in the yang conduits. If one were to follow Gao Shishi's comments, one would not know how to distinguish between the alternating fits of cold and heat [resulting from a disease] in all the yang [conduits] and those [resulting from a disease] in all the partings [of the flesh]. If these [states] cannot be distinguished, then statements such as 'the evil qi has occupied the conduit vessels' and 'the evil qi has occupied all the partings [of the flesh]' are nothing but bookish speculation. Now, when an evil is in the partings of the flesh with alternating fits of cold and heat, this is a sign of a disease being present in all the yang [conduits]. The first four characters 且寒且熱 are an erroneous repetition of the phrase following below; they are to be deleted. The ancients believed that fever brought evil to the outside, causing yang abundance. [They also believed] that fear of cold resulted from evil moving to the inside, causing yang depletion. The 之 here in 刺之虛脈 is 其, [that is,] one searches for all those yang vessels which are depleted and supplements them, thereby causing all the partings [of the flesh] to be hot and have no cold."

29 Zhang Jiebin: "When yin dominates, this causes a peak disease. In case it breaks out once a year or once a month, the qi is in the depth and the way is far and it has a base to lodge. Hence, a treatment is not easy. When it breaks out four or five times a month, it is violent and fast. It comes quickly and leaves quickly, too. This is a curable [disease]."

30 Hu Tianxiong: "The two characters 諸脈 are difficult to interpret. The *Jia yi jing* has 刺諸分, 其脈尤寒, 以鍼補之, 'pierce all the partings, and if the vessels there are

In case there is no cold, regulate it by means of needles.
When the disease [ends]³¹ stop [the piercing].³²

55-287-11
When the disease is wind, [with the patient experiencing] alternate [fits of]
cold and heat and with hot sweat leaving [the body] many times each day,³³
first pierce the network vessels in all parting structures.

When sweat leaves and [the patient] feels cold and hot alternately,
pierce once every third day.
After one hundred days [the disease] ends.³⁴

55-287-12
When the disease is massive wind,
[with the patient experiencing] his bones and joints to be heavy and beard and
eyebrows to fall off,
<This is called massive wind.>³⁵
piercing aims at the muscles and the flesh.

---

particularly cold, supplement them by means of needles.' One should follow the *Jia yi jing* ."

31 The *Tai su* has 已, "end."

32 Zhang Jiebin: " 'In case there is no cold,' then even the peak disease results from a yang evil. One either drains or supplements; [in any case,] one employs the needles to regulate this." Gao Shishi: " 'All partings' is: all partings of the flesh; 'all vessels' is: all conduit vessels. 'In case there is no cold,' is to say: In case there is neither cold nor heat. This is different from the alternate fits of cold and heat in case of suffering from craziness. The craziness disease is yang; the peak disease is yin. Yang is associated with surplus; yin is associated with insufficiency. Hence, one must employ the needles to regulate or supplement such [conditions]." Ma Shi: "When it is stated here 'in case there is no cold,' [that is to say the following:] when the disease is in the yin section, there is only cold and no heat. When it reaches a state of 'no cold,' then this is a sign that the disease is healed." Hu Tianxiong: "病已 does not mean that the disease is healed; it means that the signs of the disease are healed."

33 550/31: "數過 is 數次, 'many times.'"

34 Yao Shaoyu: "The wind is a yang evil, hence, it lets a person [feel alternately] cold and hot. When wind enters the finest openings, then the dark palace opens and sweat leaves frequently. However, if it enters deeply, then the sweat may leave but the cold and the heat are not eliminated entirely nevertheless. One must pierce frequently, even up to one hundred days, before this is finished."

35 Cheng Shide et al.: "大風 is 大麻風, 'leprosy.'"

Sweat will leave for one hundred days.[36]
Pierce the bones and the marrow, [once again causing] sweat to leave for one hundred days.[37]

Altogether these are two hundred days. When the beard and the eyebrows grow [again], stop the needling.[38]

---

36 Wang Bing: "This serves to drain the boiling heat of the protective qi."

37 Wang Bing: "This serves to drain the boiling heat of the camp qi."

38 Wang Bing: "When all the boiling heat has left, the yin qi is restored internally. Hence, lots of sweat leaves [the body] and the beard and the eyebrows grow again." Zhang Jiebin: "[Evil which] is present in the shallow regions fills all the interstice structures. Hence, one must pierce the muscles and the flesh to drain the poison from the yang section. The wind follows the sweat and disperses. When piercing into the depth one must approach the bones and the marrow to drain the wind poison from the yin section. When the wind poison has been eliminated entirely, the [flow of the] camp and of the guard qi is restored. Eyebrows and beard grow again and the disease is completely healed. At that moment one can stop the piercing." Zhang Zhicong: "Because the evil has entered [the bones and the marrow] through the muscles and the flesh, one must pierce the muscles and the flesh first and see to it that sweat leaves for one hundred days. Next one pierces the bones and the marrow and again sees to it that sweat leaves for one hundred days."

Chapter 56
Discourse on Skin Sections

56-289-2

Huang Di asked:

"I have heard [the following]:

the skin has divisions and sections,[1]

the vessels are arranged as conduits,[2]

the sinews have knots and form networks,[3] and

the bones have measures [of varying lengths].

The diseases generated in these [body parts] are all different.

They are distinguished in accordance with the divisions and sections where they are situated,

wether they are on the left or on the right, above or below, in a yin or in a yang [section].

The begin and the end of the diseases,

I should like to hear the Way of this."[4]

---

1 Ma Shi: "The skin of the human body is divided into separate sections. For example, in the center of the back, this is the course of the supervisor vessel. To both sides of the supervisor vessels are four courses associated with the foot major yang conduit. [The section] behind the ribs and to the side of the back is associated with the foot minor yang conduit. The ribs are associated with the foot ceasing yin conduit and so on."

2 Gao Shishi: "The vessel paths covering the body include the conduits (經) running straight [through the extremities and the body] and the connections (紀) forming a transverse network. Hence, [the text states:] 脈有經紀."

3 Zhang Zhicong: "結 is 結系, 'to tie in knots;' 絡 is 連絡, 'to connect.' That is to say, the sinews are tied to the flesh divides and connected with the bones." Gao Shishi: "The twelve conduit-sinews [listed in treatise 13] of the *Ling shu* do all have something they are knotted to and they are connected among each other. Hence, [the text states:] 筋有結絡."

4 Zhang Zhicong: "When evil is present in the skin, the flesh, the sinews, the bones, the network vessels, the depots or the palaces, it may be near the surface or in the depth in each of these. Hence, this may cause sinew cramp or pain in the bones, wasting flesh, or breaking [muscle] lumps; or it may enter the depots and palaces and cause diseases in the depots and palaces. If one distinguishes which section of the network vessels above or below, on the left or on the right is involved, and [if one distinguishes] the presence of [the evil] in a yin or yang [category] of the twelve conduits, one knows the begin and the end of the disease."

56-289-4
Qi Bo responded:
"If [you] wish to know the skin sections,
take the conduit vessels as their arranging [structure].⁵
‹This applies to all the conduits.›⁶

The yang [skin section] of the yang brilliance [conduit] is called *hai fei*.⁷
‹The same law [applies] above and below.›⁸

---

5 Zhang Zhicong: "紀 is 記, 'mark.' If one whishes to know the sections of the skin, one should divide the [skin] on the basis of the network vessels that can be seen. In addition, though, the conduit vessels serve as ordering structures, too."

6 Wang Bing: "If one follows the vessels where they pass and where they end, and what they rule, then the skin sections can be known. 'All conduits' is to say: the twelve conduit vessels. This applies to all the twelve conduit vessels."

7 Wang Bing: "蚩 is 生化, 'generation and transformation.' 害 is 殺氣, 'killing qi.' When a killing qi moves, then generation and transformation end. Hence, [the text] states 害蚩." Wu Kun: "害 is identical with 闔, 'door-leaf,' 'to shut'; 蚩 is 蠢動, 'wriggling movement.' Now, the yang brilliance [section] is the face. The face is *wu* (午). In the fifth month the yang qi [commences] a wriggling movement, and as soon as yin qi rises, it begins to struggle with the yang. That is, it shuts in the yang. Hence, [the text] states 害蚩." Zhang Jiebin: "害 is 損; 蚩 is an old version of the character 飛, 'to fly.' That is to say, the yang abounds and comes to the surface. Whenever something abounds extremely, it will receive harm. Hence, yang abundance occurs in the yang brilliance and harm to the yang occurs in the yang brilliance, too. Hence, the yang of the yang brilliance is called 害蚩." Tanba: "In ancient times, 害, 盍, and 闔 were used for each other. The *Er ya*: 闔 is 扉, 'door leaf' or 閉 'to close.' The *Shuo wen* states: 闔 is 門扇, 'door leaf.' 害蚩 is 闔扉, that is: 門扇, 'door leaf.' *Su wen* 6 states: 陽明為闔. The meaning is the same." Li Guoqing: "害蚩 has the meaning of the 關門, 'to shut a door.' As the other names given below, 害蚩 serves to explain physiological and pathological characteristics [in this case] of the yang brilliance. The yang brilliance resides between the two yang; it masters closure. When it closes in the qi of the major yang and of the minor yang, the result is that the qi of major [yang] and minor [yang] are both in one conduit. This is called 'combined brilliance of the two yang.' Hence, when 害蚩 is interpreted as 'door leaf' by Tanba, this corresponds both to the meaning of the term itself and to medical theory." See also 674/162.

8 Wang Bing: " 'Above' is to say: the hand yang brilliance [conduit]; 'below' is to say: the foot yang brilliance [conduit]." Wang Bing's interpretation of this statement and its five repetitions may be correct. Still, they appear to us as early insertions with a political undertone in that they were meant to convey a central request of Legalist philosophy: "The same law applies to above and below," i.e., to the upper and lower echelons in society.

The network [vessels] observed in this section near the surface[9] are all yang brilliance network [vessels].

56-289-6
If their color is
mostly green-blue, then pain [is present],
mostly black, then a block [exists],
yellow and red, then heat [is present],
mostly white, then cold [is present].
If all the five colors are visible, then cold and heat [are present].

When the network [vessels] abound [with qi],
then [the evil] has entered the conduit [vessels] to settle there.
<The yang rules the exterior;
the yin rules the interior.>[10]

56-289-8
The yang [skin section] of the minor yang [conduit] is called *shu chi*.[11]
<The same law [applies] above and below.>
The network [vessels] observed in this section near the surface are all minor yang network [vessels].
When the network [vessels] abound [with qi],
then [the evil] has entered the conduit [vessels] to settle there.
<The fact is,
that which is in the yang [section], it rules the entering;
that which is in the yin [section], it rules the leaving.[12]
From there it seeps into the interior.
The same applies to all the conduits.>[13]

---

9 Wu Kun: "These are the network vessels near the surface in the skin section."

10 Wang Bing: " 'Yang' is to say: the yang network [vessels]; 'yin' is to say: the yin network [vessels]. This is a general statement. It applies to the conduits and network [vessels] visible in hands and feet and the sections of the body alike." Li Guoqing: "The network vessels are in the exterior and belong to the yang; the conduit vessels are in the interior and belong to the yin."

11 Wang Bing: "樞 is to say: 樞要, 'pivotal base;' 持 is to say: 執持, 'to maintain.'" Wu Kun: "樞 is 樞軸, 'pivot.' That is the so-called 'the minor yang is the pivot.' 持 is 把持, 'to hold.' Now, the minor yang resides between outside and inside. This is like 'holding the pivot.'"

12 The *Jia yi jing* has 外, 'outside,' instead of 出.

13 Zhang Jiebin: "Evil always enters the conduits through the network [vessels]. Hence, [when the text states] 在陽者主內, that is to say: [the evil] enters the interior

56-289-11
The yang [skin section] of the major yang [conduit] is called *guan shu*.[14]
<The same law [applies] above and below.>
The network [vessels] observed in this section near the surface are all major yang network [vessels].
When the network [vessels] abound [with qi], then [the evil] has entered the conduit [vessels] to settle there.

56-290-2
The yin [skin section] of minor yin [conduit] is called *shu ru*.[15]

---

from the yang section. 在陰者主出以滲于內 is to say: [the evil] leaves the conduits and seeps into the depots. This sequence [in the passage] of evil qi applies to all the conduits alike." Hu Tianxiong: "Hua Shou, Wu Kun, Zhang Qi, Sun Dingyi and others consider these 19 characters to be an erroneus insertion. Probably they have been moved here from their original position further down, where they followed the statement 從陰內注於骨."

14 Wang Bing: "The 關, 'gate,' controls the movement in the exterior. Its function is to keep things quiet and to ward off [enemies]. It resembles the turning around of a pivot. [When it fulfills its function,] then the qi is harmonious and balanced." Wu Kun: "關 is 固衛, 'to protect firmly.' The minor yang is the pivot; it turns around and spreads the yang qi. The major yang binds and firmly protects the yang [qi] turned around and spread [by the minor yang]. Hence, it is called 關樞." Zhang Zhicong: "The major yang rules all the yang qi and it rules the outside. Yang qi emerges from within the yin; when the pivot revolves, it leaves to the exterior. The major yang qi leaves from the interior and firmly protects the exterior. Hence, it is called 關樞." For an extensive discussion of the meaning of 關 in the present context, see 2264/5.

15 Wang Bing: "儒 is 順, 'to go along with.' To guard what is important and be in agreement with yin and yang, that is the operation of opening and closing." Lin Yi et al.: "The *Jia yi jing* has 橋 instead of 儒." The *Tai su* also has 橋. For a discussion of the meaning of 橋 see below. Wu Kun: "儒 should be 腝, (a character composed of the components 'flesh' and 'soft'). The hand minor yin vessels move down along the back edge inside the shoulder. The foot minor yin vessels rise along the back edge of the inner thigh. All these are locations where soft flesh dominates. Hence, they are called 腝, 'soft parts.' 樞腝 is the movement of the pivot mechanism inside the upper arms." Zhang Jiebin: "儒 is explained by the *Shuo wen* as 柔, 'soft.' Wang Bing says 'adaptive.' The minor yin is the pivot opening or closing the three yin and the yin qi is soft and adaptive. Hence, the name 樞儒." Gao Shishi: "The yin of the minor yin rises from the calf and the popliteal fossa and pours into the chest where it ends. [Like] a magic mechanism of a revolving pivot it separates water and fire. Hence, it is called 樞儒. 儒 is like 區, 'to separate.'" Tanba: "The 橋 [of the *Jia yi jing*] is pronounced 軟. Other versions are 楔 and 桷 ("a small post"). The *Er ya* identifies 桷 as 槸, 'support beam.' The commentary states: 'This is the 櫨, 'support beam.' .. The yin of the minor yin is named after the support beam above the pivot. Hence, it is called 樞橋." Li Guoqing: "Tanba is right." Mori: "樞儒 is identical with 樞杼, 'pivot and shuttle.' Now, both

<The same law [applies] above and below.>

The network [vessels] observed in this section near the surface are all minor yin network [vessels].

When the network [vessels] abound [with qi], then [the evil] has entered the conduit [vessels] to settle there.

{When it enters the conduits, it is from the yang section that it pours into the conduits.[16]

When it leaves [the conduits], it is from the yin [section] that it pours into the bones.}[17]

56-290-4

The yin [skin section] of the heart ruler [conduit] is called *hai jian*.[18]

<The same law [applies] above and below.>

The network [vessels] observed in this section near the surface are all heart ruler network [vessels].

When the network [vessels] abound [with qi], then [the evil] has entered the conduit [vessels] to settle there.

---

the minor yin and the minor yang [vessels] reside in the center: Hence, [the text] states: both minor yin and minor are the pivot, or: the pivot shuttle. The meaning is the same."

16 Yang Shangshan: "From the network section, which is yang, [the disease evil] pours into the conduits, which are yin."

17 Zhang Jiebin: " 'When it leaves, it pours from the interior, which is yin, into the bones,' that is to say: the [evil] leaves the conduits and enters the bones."

18 Wang Bing: "The vessel of the heart ruler enters [the body] below the armpit. When the qi [in this vessel] is not in harmony, then this hampers and harms the movement of the shoulders and armpits." Cheng Shide et al.: "The yin of the heart ruler is the yin of the ceasing yin." Ma Shi: "肩 is 重, 'heavy.' The ten thousand things sink into the depth because of yin; and this yin qi is present to kill them. Hence, it is called 害肩." Wu Kun: "The heart ruler is the hand ceasing yin. Its vessel rises to below the armpit. Hence, it is called 害肩. 害 is identical with 闔, 'to shut in.' That is to say, it collects and encloses yin qi in the section of the shoulders and armpits." Zhang Jiebin: "肩 is 任, 'to bear,' 戴, 'to carry.' The yang rules movement; the yin rules carrying. When yin abundance has reached an extreme, the [yin] qi will be harmed. That is, the yin abundance occurs in the ceasing yin and harm to the yin occurs in the ceasing yin, too. Hence, it is called 害肩." Tanba: "肩 is identical with 楣, it is identical with 枅. 闔楣 is the beam above a door leaf holding the pivot." For details of this argument, see there. 674/161: "肩 is a mistaken writing of 扉, 'door leaf.'"

56-290-6
The yin [skin section] of major yin [conduit] is called *guan zhe*.[19]
<The same law [applies] above and below.>
The network [vessels] observed in this section near the surface are all major yin
network [vessels].
When the network [vessels] abound [with qi], then [the evil] has entered the
conduit [vessels] to settle there.

56-290-8
The altogether twelve conduit and network vessels constitute the sections of
the skin.[20]

Hence, the first emergence of the one hundred diseases must begin in the skin
and its hair.

When the evil strikes there, then the interstice structures open.
When they are open, then [the evil] enters the network vessels and settles
there.

If it stays there and is not [made to] leave, it will be transmitted into the
conduits.
If it stays there and is not [made to] leave, it will be transmitted into the palaces where it accumulates in the intestines and in the stomach.

56-290-11
When evil begins to enter the skin, in a *su*-manner it raises the finest body hair
and it opens the interstice structures.[21]

---

19 Lin Yi et al.: "The *Jia yi jing* has 執, 'to hold,' instead of 蟄." The *Tai su* has 關樞.
Zhang Jiebin: "A gate serves to protect externally; the hibernating insects lie hidden
inside. The yin rules the depots and the major yin protects them. Hence, it is called
關蟄." Zhang Zhicong: "蟄 refers to torpid insects hibernating in seclusion. That is,
when the qi is stored in the yin [section] and wishes to move to the outside, it is shut
in by the major yin. Hence, [the yin of the major yin] is called 關蟄." Tanba: "蟄 is
槷, 'peg.' The *Shi wen* 釋文 states: '槷 is 門橜, 'gate peg.' 關槷 refers to the peg in the
center of a gate, that is the location where the left and right leafs come together." For
details of the argument, see there.

20 2435/15: "The meaning is: 'The network vessels of the twelve conduits mentioned
above have their corresponding sections among the skin sections.'"

21 Wang Bing: "*Su* 泝 is an aversion to cold. 'To rise' is: the body hair rises and stiffens. 'Interstice structures' always refers to the holes and the line structures of the skin."
The *Jia yi jing* has 淅然, "like the soughing of wind." Tanba: "The *Jia yi jing* is correct."

When [the evil] has entered the network [vessels], then the network vessels abound [with evil] and their color changes.[22]

When [the evil] has entered the conduits and has settled there, then [the conduits] experience depletion and [the vessels] sink down.[23]

When it stays in the region of sinews and bones,

in case it [consists of] plenty of cold, then this causes sinew cramp and the bones to have pain.

In case it consists of plenty of heat, then this causes the sinews to slacken and the bones to waste,[24] the flesh to melt away, and the protuberant [muscles] to be destroyed.

The body hair [stands up] straight and breaks."

56-290-14
[Huang] Di:
"Now,
you, Sir, have outlined the twelve sections of the skin.

How is it that diseases emerge in them?"

Qi Bo:
"The skin consists of sections [made up] by the vessels.[25]

Zhang Jiebin: "溯然 is: [the body hair] stiffens and rises, as if one were shivering from cold."

22 Wang Bing: " 'Abound' is to say: they are full. 'Changes' is to say: different from normal."

23 Wang Bing: "When a conduit is depleted, it is entered by evil. Hence, [the text] states: 感虛, '[the conduits] experience depletion.' The vessels are depleted and the [proper] qi is diminished. Hence, [the vessels] 'form a depression downwards.'" The *Tai su* has 減, 'to diminish,' instead of 感. Yang Shangshan: "When the qi is diminished, a depletion results. There is little blood and the vessels sink in." Hu Tianxiong: "Both 感 and 減 are wrong; [感 and 減] are mistaken writings of the character 藏, 'depot.' 陷下 is to say: it is transmitted internally into the depots. When the depots are depleted, a transmission occurs towards the interior. When the depots are replete, then [the evil] is not transmitted to the interior and stays in the section of the sinews and bones, as the text states further below."

24 Zhang Jiebin: "消 is 枯渴, 'to dry up.'"

25 Wang Bing: "Whether the qi in the vessels stays for a while or moves, this is always such that the yin and yang qi follow the course of the conduits and rule a [particular] section. Hence, [the text] states: 'sections made up by the vessels.'"

When evil settles in the skin, then the interstice structures open.
When they have opened, then the evil enters the network vessels and settles there.
When the network vessels are full, then it pours into the conduit vessels.
When the conduit vessels are full, then [the evil] enters the palaces and depots and lodges there.

56-291-3
Hence,
the skin has divisions and sections;
if one does not [treat] accordingly, serious diseases will emerge."[26]

[Huang] Di:
"Good!"

---

26 Wang Bing: "Each vessel passes in the skin through its respective section. When a vessel receives an evil qi, then a disease is generated as a result. It is not such that [a disease] can be generated by a skin qi." Yang Shangshan: "If one does not heal [a disease] as long as it is near the surface, it will develop into a serious disease later on. 與 is 療, 'to heal.'" Zhang Jiebin: "If one does not treat in advance (預), then the evil will penetrate deeper day by day and develop into a serious disease. 與 is identical with 預, 'in advance.'" Zhang Zhicong: "不與 is 不及, 'inadequate.' That is to say, the outside qi of the skin and of the hair is depleted and lets evil enter the conduits, resulting in a dangerous disease involving the depots." Tanba: "The *Jia yi jing* has 不愈, 'not healed.' This meaning is very clear."

Chapter 57
Discourse On Conduits and Network [Vessels]

57-291-6
Huang Di asked:
"Now,
the network vessels differ with respect to the five colors they manifest.[1]
They vary in that they are green-blue, yellow, red, white, or black.
What is the reason?"

Qi Bo responded:
"The conduits have a regular color,
while the network vessels have no regular [color. Their color] undergoes changes."[2]

[Huang] Di:
"What are the regular colors of the conduits like?"

Qi Bo:
"The [color associated with the] heart is red.
The [color associated with the] lung is white.
The [color associated with the] liver is green-blue.
The [color associated with the] spleen is yellow.
The [color associated with the] kidneys is black.
All these [colors] are also reflected in the colors of the respective conduit vessels."

57-291-9
[Huang] Di:
"Do the yin and yang [sections] of the network [vessels] reflect [the colors of] these conduits, too?"

---

1 Hu Tianxiong: "見也 should be understood as 見者."

2 Wang Bing: "The conduits move the qi. Hence, they appear in the regular colors corresponding to the [four] seasons. The network vessels rule the blood. Hence, when they receive evil [qi] their color changes to more than one." Gao Shishi: "The conduit vessels are tied to the palaces and depots internally; hence, they display the regular colors of the five agents. The network vessels, in contrast, are at the surface and can be seen from outside. Their [color] is not regular and undergoes frequent changes."

Qi Bo:
"The colors of the yin network [vessels] reflect those of the respective conduits;
the colors of the yang network [vessels] change. They have no permanence.
[The colors] are activitated in accordance with the four seasons.[3]

57-291-11
When there is plenty of cold, [the contents of the vessels] congeal so that [their
flow] is impeded.
When they have congealed so that [their flow] is impeded, then [the vessels
assume a color of] green-blue to black.
When there is plenty of heat, [the contents of the vessels] are saturated with
moisture.[4]
When they are saturated with moisture, then [the vessels assume a color of]
yellow to red.

---

3 Zhang Zhicong: "The yin-network [vessels] are the network [vessels] of the six yin
conduits; they correspond to the conduits of the five depots. Each has its regular color
which does not change. The yang-network [vessels] are the network [vessels] of the
six yang conduits. They are tied to the yang of the six palaces. They undergo changes in
accordance with the [pairings of] spring-green-blue, summer-red, autumn-white, and
winter-black." Zhang Jiebin: "*Ling shu* 17 states: The conduit vessels are inside; those
[vessels] branching away and running transversely are the network [vessels]. Those
parting from the network [vessels] are the tertiary [vessels]. Hence, if stated in terms
of conduits and network [vessels] seen together, then the conduits are inside and yin
and the network [vessels] are outside and yang. If stated only in terms of the network
vessels, one distinguishes again between the large network [vessels] and the tertiary
network [vessels], between those in the interior and those in the exterior. Those located in the depth and in the interior, these are the yin network [vessels]. The yin
network [vessels] are located close to the conduits. Hence, they correspond to them
in their colors. Hence, their colors are regular, in accordance with the association of
the five agents with the five depots. Those located near the surface and in the exterior,
these are the yang network [vessels]. The yang network [vessels] are visible near the
surface; their color does not correspond to the conduits. Hence, it changes irregularly
in accordance with the coming and going of the qi of the four seasons." Hu Tianxiong:
"How can Zhang Jiebin say 'it changes irregularly' when [these changes occur] 'in accordance with the coming and going of the qi of the four seasons'? This paragraph is
corrupt; Zhang Jiebin's mistake results from his closely following, in his commentary,
the [present version of the] text." Li Guoqing: "Zhang Jiebin's comments are most accurate and should be followed." These observations on a regularity despite the preceding affirmation of the lack of a regularity, may have been added by a later author.

4 Wang Bing: "淖 is 濕, 'damp.' 澤 is 潤液, 'moist.' That is to say, 'slightly moistened.'"
Cheng Shide et al.: "The *Zi lin* 字林 states: 'Extreme moisture is called 淖.' [The
term] is used here in the sense of 濡潤, 'moisture.' 淖澤 is to be explained here as 滑
利, 'smooth and easy going.'"

All these are regular colors.
Such [a status] is called 'free of disease.'⁵
When all the five colors appear, this is called 'cold and heat.'"⁶

[Huang] Di:
"Good!"

5 Ma Shi: "The eight characters 此皆常色謂之無病 should follow the phrase 從四時而行也." Wu Kun and Zhang Zhicong agreed. Tanba: "Zhang Jiebin and Gao Shishi have followed in their interpretations the present version of the text. They were wrong." The *Tai su* has 此其常色者, 謂之無病, "those displaying these regular colors are said to have no disease."

6 Zhang Jiebin: "When the five colors appear together, then yin and yang [qi] have changed to disorder and they have lost their regular status. Hence, the disease of an alternating emergence of cold and heat results." Mori: "寒熱 is to say: an evil qi of an aversion to cold accompanied by fever."

Chapter 58
Discourse on Qi Holes

58-291-15
Huang Di asked:
"I have heard, there are 365 qi holes[1] to correspond to one year.
I do not know their locations yet.
I should like to hear about them comprehensively."

Qi Bo paid reverence twice knocking his head on the ground and responded:
"An embarrassing question, indeed![2]
Who except a sage emperor could penetrate this Way so thoroughly.
Therefore,
please, let me pour out my thoughts,[3]
and provide a complete account of all their locations."

58-292-2
[Huang] Di brought his hands up to his chest, went to and fro, and rejected
[Qi Bo's praise]:
"That you, Sir, have opened the Way for me [was as follows].
Even though my eyes had not yet seen these locations and
even though my ears had not yet heard these numbers,
it is because of [your teachings] that [my] eyes have become clear and
it is because of [your teachings] that my ears have been sharpened."

Qi Bo:
"This is what is called
'with the sages it is easy to talk;
a good horse is easy to control.'"

58-292-5
[Huang] Di:
"'With the sages it is easy to talk' does not apply to me.
A common saying is
'the true numbers open a person's thoughts.'
What I ask now are the true numbers

---

1 Zhang Jiebin: "All holes in the human body are locations of the qi."

2 Cheng Shide et al.: "窘 has the meaning of 為難, 'causing distress,' 'embarrassing.'"

3 Yang Shangshan: "溢意 is 縱志, 'to free the determination.'"

to release me from ignorance and to disperse [my] delusions.[4]
[I am] not sufficiently [equipped] yet in this discourse.[5]

58-292-7
Therefore,
I should like to listen to you, Sir, when you pour out your mind and provide a
complete account of all these locations so that their meaning unfolds.
Please, let me [record them and] store this [knowledge] in the Golden Chest;
I shall not dare to take it out again."

Qi Bo paid reverence twice and rose:
"Please, let [me your] subject, speak about this.
‹When back and heart[6] draw each other and have pain, the locations to treat
are the Celestial Chimney and [the Central Pivot below the] tenth vertebra,[7] as
well as the Upper Regulator.[8]

---

4 Zhang Jiebin: "The ‘true numbers’ are the numbers [obtained through] investigating the [true nature of] things and [through] thorough penetration of their principles."

5 2493/531: "The *Qi fa* 七發 by Mei Cheng 枚乘 of the Han era has 發蒙解惑, 不足
以言也. The present text states 發蒙解惑, 未足以論也. This parallel indicates that the
Su wen is a product of the Han era." See also 409/4 for literary parallels.

6 Zhang Zhicong: " ‘Heart’ refers to heart and chest here."

7 Wang Bing: "According to the *Jia yi jing* and to the *Jing mai liu zhu kong xue tu
jing*, there should be no hole below the tenth vertebra. This may be [an error for]
‘seventh vertebra.’" Ma Shi: "The 十 in 十椎 should be 大, ‘Great Hammer (大椎)
[hole].’" Zhang Zhicong: "The tenth vertebra is located seven vertebrae below the
great hammer. This is the Extreme Yang (至陽) hole of the supervisor vessel; it is the
meeting point of the supervisor vessel with the yang binding [vessel]. Because another
three vertebrae are located above the great hammer, the total number is ten vertebrae."
Zhang Jiebin: "The ‘tenth vertebra’ refers to the Central Pivot (中樞) [hole] of the
supervisor vessel. This hole is not listed in the literature with the exception of *Su wen*
59 where Wang Bing in his comment on the section discussing the effusion of the qi
of the supervisor vessel states: ‘The Central Pivot [hole] is located in the joint below
the tenth vertebra.’ This corresponds without any doubt to the present [statement]."
Tanba followed Zhang Jiebin.

8 The *Tai su* has 上紀下紀. The following *Su wen* text, an ancient commentary, refers
to both to "the Upper Regulator 上紀" and "the Lower Regulator 下紀." It may be that
the *Tai su* wording is correct.

{The 'Upper Regulator' is the Stomach Duct;[9]
the 'Lower Regulator' is the Pass Head.}[10]

58-292-11
The back and the chest are connected diagonally,
[and so are] yin and yang [regions], left and right.[11]
This way, their diseases [cause] pain and roughness in the front and in the back.
The chest and the flanks have pain so that [the patient] is unable to breathe
and he cannot lie down.
[He experiences] rising qi, shortness of qi, and unilateral pain.[12]

58-293-2
The vessels are full and rise diagonally from the sacrum vessel.
They enclose the chest and the flanks, prop the heart, penetrate the diaphragm,
rise to the shoulder and join with the Celestial Chimney.
They diagonally descend from the shoulder and intersect below the tenth
vertebra.>[13]

---

9 Wang Bing: "That is to say: the Central Duct (中脘) [hole]. The Central Duct [hole] is a levy [hole] of the stomach."

10 Wang Bing: "The Pass Head (關元) [hole] is a levy [hole] of the minor yang."

11 Ma Shi "邪 is identical here with 斜." Zhang Zhicong: "This is to explain the text above. The evil of back and chest is linked to the yin and yang and it pulls on the left and right." Tanba: "Ma Shi is correct."

12 Zhang Zhicong: "The reason for 'one is unable to breath and one cannot lie down; the qi rises, the qi is short,' is [as follows]: the supervisor vessel penetrates on its rise heart and diaphragm and enters the throat. The controlling vessel enters the chest center and rises to the throat. The reason for the 'unilateral pain' is that the vessel 'emerges diagonally from the sacrum and encloses the flanks, rises to the shoulder and descends diagonally again.'"

13 Lin Yi et al.: "[The passage] beginning with 背與心相控而痛 and ending here may have been moved here erroneously from *Su wen* 60." Hu Tianxiong: " Lin Yi et al. is correct. *Su wen* 58 is concerned with qi holes; its emphasis lies in the sentence 'provide a complete account of their locations.' [Huang Di] did not ask for [information about] treatment." Zhang Zhicong: "This means: when yin and yang are affected by evil, and when chest and back pull each other, this is because the controlling and supervisor vessels are linked to each other. The controlling and the supervisor vessels are united because the great network [vessel] of the supervisor [vessel] intersects with the controlling vessel. The great network [vessel] of the supervisor [vessel] is called 'extended strength' (長強). It rises on both sides of the spine to the nape and disperses on the head. It descends along the shoulder-blades to the left and to the right, with one branch passing along the major yang [conduit] and running through the backbone. The so-called great network [vessel] resembles a separate stream branching off

Depot transporters: 50 holes,[14]
palace transporters: 72 holes,[15]
heat transporters: 59 holes,[16]
water transporters: 57 holes.[17]

58-297-1
There are five [conduit] lines on the head: [each] line has five [holes]; five
[times] five is 25 holes.[18]
On both sides of the central spine there are five [holes]; altogether ten holes.[19]

---

from a stream. When the conduit vessels are full, then they pour [their contents] into
the great network [vessels]. Hence, [the text states:] when the supervisor 'vessel is full
then [its contents] appear diagonally in the sacrum vessel.' That is, the branch [ves-
sel] of the supervisor vessel 'leaves diagonally from the sacrum and encloses the chest
and the flanks.' Its network [vessel] 'props the heart and penetrates the diaphragm,
rises to the shoulder blades' and intersects with the controlling vessel at the Celestial
Chimney (天突). It descends again from the shoulder diagonally and intersects with
the supervisor vessel below the tenth vertebra. Hence, chest and back pull on each
other and have pain. The treatment is conducted at the Celestial Chimney and at the
tenth vertebra because these are the locations where the great network [vessel of the
supervisor vessel] passes through and intersects with [the supervisor and the controlling vessels]."

14 Wang Bing: " 'Depots' is to say: the five depots of liver, heart, spleen, lung, and kidneys. They do not include the four physical depots (i.e., temples, ears and eyes, mouth
and teeth, chest center). 'Transporters' is to say: well, brook, transporter, stream, and
confluence. This is not [a reference to] the transporters on the back." See *Su wen* 20,
note 29, and *Su wen* 09, note 21.

15 Wang Bing: " 'Palace' is to say: the six palaces. They do not include the nine physical palaces. 'Transporters,' once again, is to say: well, brook, transporter, stream, and
confluence. Not the transporters on the back."

16 Cheng Shide et al.: "These are the transporter holes where heat is treated." For a
detailed analysis of which holes may be meant here, see 1861/10.

17 Cheng Shide et al.: "These are the holes where diseases of swellings [caused by]
water [accumulations] are treated." Wang Bing: "[The heat transporters and the water
transporters] have all been outlined in *Su wen* 61."

18 Wang Bing: "They, too, are included in the fifty-nine heat transporter holes."

19 Wang Bing: "That is to say: the transporters on the back associated with the five
depots. The lung transporters are located on both sides below the third vertebra. The
heart transporters are located on both sides below the fifth vertebra. The liver transporters are located on both sides below the ninth vertebra. The spleen transporters are
located on both sides below the eleventh vertebra. The kidney transporters are located
on both sides below the fourteenth vertebra. Each of these transporters of the five
depots is located in a distance of one and a half standardized body inches away from

On both sides above the great hammer there is one [hole]; altogether two
holes.[20]
[On the level of] the eye there are the two holes of Pupil [Bone-Hole] and
Floating White.[21]
The depressed locus in the parting of the two thigh bones: two holes.[22]
The two Calf's Nose holes.

58-298-1
The two In-the-ear-there-is-a-lot-to-hear holes.[23]
The two Eyebrow Base holes.[24]
The two Completion Bone holes.
One hole in the center of the nape.[25]
The two Pillow Bone holes.
The two Upper Pass holes.
The two Great Facing holes.
The two Lower Pass holes.

---

the spine. They fall together with the meeting points (i.e., holes) on the foot major
yang vessels." Zhang Zhicong: "胎 is 脊, 'backbone.'"

20 Wang Bing: "Neither the *Jia yi jing* nor the *Jing mai liu zhu kong xue tu jing* 經
脈流注孔穴圖 list [these holes]. It is not clear which transporters [are meant here]."
Lin Yi et al.: "Above the great hammer on [both] sides there are no holes. The holes
on [both] sides below the great hammer are called Great Shuttle (大杼) and Posterior
Presence (後有). Hence, Wang Bing states 'it is not clear [what is meant here].'"Wu
Kun: "These should be the two Celestial Pillar (天柱) holes. They are located in the
depressions at the outer edges of the large sinews protruding on both sides of the nape
at the hair line."

21 Zhang Zhicong: "The Pupil Bone-Hole (瞳子髎) [holes] are located in the canthi; the Floating White (浮白) holes are located one inch inside the hair line behind
the ears. One to the left and one to the right. Altogether these are four holes. They all
belong to the foot-minor yang conduit of the gallbladder."Wu Kun has 值, "to meet,"
instead of 目: "Those 'corresponding to the pupil,' are the two Floating White holes
one inch inside the hairline behind the ears. They correspond (值) to the pupils at the
front side [of the head]."

22 Wang Bing: "That is to say: the Ring-shaped Hoe (環銚) holes."The meaning of
厭 in the present context remains unclear. Combinations of 厭 with terms for bones
(髀厭 and 骸厭) occur several times in the *Su wen* and in the *Ling shu*. They do not
clarify the issue either. Our translation is based on the attested meaning of 厭 "to
press down."

23 Wang Bing: "That is to say: the Auditory Palace (聽宮) holes."

24 Wang Bing: "That is to say: the Bamboo Gathering (攢竹) holes."

25 Wang Bing: "That is the Wind Palace (風府) hole."

58-299-1
The two Celestial Pillar holes.
The four holes of the Upper Edge and Lower Edge of the Great Hollow.
The two Bent Teeth holes.[26]
The one Celestial Chimney hole.
The two Celestial Palace holes.
The two Celestial Window (I) holes.
The two Supporting Protuberance holes.
The two Celestial Window (II) holes.
The two Shoulder Divide holes.[27]
The one Pass Head hole.
The two Bend Yang holes.
The two Shoulder Truth holes.
The one Muteness Gate hole.
The one navel hole.[28]

58-300-1
Chest transporters: twelve holes.[29]
Back transporters: two holes.[30]
Breast transporters: twelve holes.[31]
Parting of the flesh: two holes.[32]
Two holes in the transverse line above the ankle.[33]
The four yin and yang walker [vessel] holes.

---

26 Wang Bing: "These are the Cheek Carriage (頰車) holes."

27 Wang Bing: "These are the Shoulder Well (肩井) holes."

28 Wang Bing: "This is located in the navel. It is a forbidden [hole]; it must not be pierced. Piercing it would cause bad ulcers in that person's navel; when it is opened so that feces leaves, [the patient] will die and cannot be treated. Moxibustion is possible."

29 Wang Bing: "These are the Transporter Palace (俞府), the Luxurious Center (彧中), the Spirit Depots (神蔵), the Magic Ruins (靈墟), the Spirit Seal (神封), and the Covered Walk (步廊) [holes] to the left and to the right, altogether twelve holes."

30 Wang Bing: "These are the Great Shuttle (大杼) holes."

31 Wang Bing: "That is to say: the Cloud Gate (雲門), the Central Palace (中府), the Encircling Brook (周滎), the Chest Village (胸鄉), the Celestial Ravine (天谿/溪), and the Food Outlet (食竇) [holes] to the left and to the right, altogether twelve holes."

32 Lin Yi et al.: "The *Jia yi jing* does not have a hole [named] Parting of the Flesh. From its location it may be the Yang Assistance (陽輔) hole."

33 Wang Bing: "That is the Exchanging Messages (交信) [hole]."

The water transporters are located in all the partings [of the flesh].³⁴
The heat transporters are in the qi holes.³⁵

The cold and the heat transporters in the depressed locus of the two lower leg bones: two holes.³⁶

58-301-2
Great prohibition: 25; five inches below the Celestial Palace.³⁷

Altogether these are 365 holes;
it is from [these locations] that the needles are set in motion."³⁸

---

34 Wang Bing: " 'Partings' is to say: in the structures dividing the flesh. One takes them for treating water."

35 Wang Bing: "One takes them for draining heat."

36 Wang Bing: "骸厭 is to say: in the 骸厭 along the knee on the outer side of the knees." *SWJZ*: "骸 is 脛骨, 'lower leg bone.'" Tanba: "Zhang [Jiebin] states: '兩骸厭 中.' That is to say: in the 厭 on the outer side below the knee. These are the Yang Pass (陽關) holes of the foot minor yang [vessels]."

37 Wang Bing: "These are the Five Miles (五里) holes. The [text] speaks of 'great prohibition' because it is forbidden to pierce there. The *Zhen jing* 鍼經 (i.e., the *Ling shu*) states: 'Confront it (i.e., the evil qi) at the Five Miles [holes]. Stop in the middle of the way. Go there five [times] and this is the end of it. Five outpours will exhaust the qi of the depots. Hence, after five times five, [i.e.,] 25 [outpours] these transporters will be exhausted. This is why [the text] speaks of these ['25 great prohibitions']. It states further: 'The Five Miles [holes] are the Five Miles [holes] behind the foot marsh.'" Zhang Jiebin: "The 'great prohibitions' are holes that are forbidden to pierce. These are the Five Miles [holes] of the hand yang brilliance [conduit] five inches below the Celestial Palace (天府) hole [which is situated] on the lung conduit. One on the left and one one the right; together two holes." In the following, Zhang Jiebin repeats the *Ling shu* text quoted by Wang Bing, together with Wang Bing's conclusion. Gao Shishi: " 'Great prohibition, 25 [holes] refers to the well, brook, transporter, stream, and confluence [holes] of the five depots; these are prohibitions concerning five [times] five [,i.e.,] 25 transporters. 'Five inches below the Celestial Palace,' that is: below the Celestial Palaces, in a distance of five inches, these are the Five Miles holes on the left and right. *Ling shu* 2 states: 'The moving (i.e., pulsating) vessel of the foot-length [-section] at the Five Miles [hole], this is where it is forbidden [to pierce] the five transporters.'" Zhang Zhicong: "That is to say: each of the five depots has five transporters. When five transporters are pierced five times, this amounts to 25 piercings. As a result, the qi of [all] the five depots is exhausted. Hence, when [the texts] states 'great prohibition: 25,' what it says is: 'it is prohibited to conduct 25 piercings.'"

38 Lin Yi et al.: "From 'Depot Transporters: 50 holes' up to here, including all holes that are named repeatedly, the total adds up to 360 holes. If the holes above and below the Celestial Chimney (天突) at the tenth vertebra are included, this adds up to 365

58-301-3
[Huang] Di:
"I know by now the locations of the qi holes and
the locations where to move the needles.[39]
I should like to hear whether the tertiary network [vessels],[40] the ravines, and
the valleys, too, have something they correspond to."

Qi Bo:
"The 365 holes of the meeting points of the tertiary network [vessels],[41] they,
too, correspond to one year.

They serve as an overflow [reservoir] of an unevenly distributed evil;
They serve as passage [ways] of the camp and the guard [qi].[42]

---

holes. If those are omitted that are listed repeatedly, the real number of holes listed
is 313."

39 Zhang Zhicong: "居 is 止, 'to halt.' That is to say: the location where the needle
halts. 游針 is to say: one finds the path where the needle [should enter] and moves
into it with genius resembling [the famous cook who was able to] let a blade roam
[through the flesh] with ample free space." Hu Tianxiong: "居 is 處, 'location.' Above
it says 氣穴之處, 'location of the qi holes,' here it says 游針之居, 'location where the
needle moves.' The *Nei jing* calls the insertion of a needle into a qi hole 游針, 'to move
the needle.'"

40 Wang Bing: "The 孫絡 are small network [vessels]; that is to say, they branch off
from the network [vessels]."

41 Wu Kun: "The tertiary network [vessels] also have 365 holes, thereby corresponding to one year." Zhang Jiebin: "[The text] speaks of 穴會, 'meeting points of the
holes,' of the tertiary network [vessels] because [these] network [vessels] 'meet' with
the [insertion] holes. The holes are deep inside; the network [vessels] are at the surface
outside. Inside and outside meet each other; Hence, [the text] speaks of 'meeting
points of the holes.' This is not to say that in addition to the qi holes there exist another 365 network [vessel] holes." Gao Shishi: "That is to say: all the tertiary network
[vessels] of the body are linked to the 365 [insertion] holes."

42 Ma Shi: "奇邪 is an uncommon evil. As soon as one has contracted this evil, one
develops fever in the outside and shortness of qi inside. One must not lose any time
and drain [this unevenly distributed evil] immediately to free the passage of the camp
and guard [qi]." Gao Shishi: "As for '奇邪' *Su wen* 63 states: 'When an evil enters the
tertiary network, settles there and does not enter the conduits, it will flow into the
great network and cause strange diseases. 奇邪 corresponds to 奇病, 'strange diseases.'
The strange evil is present in the network [vessels] because it has flowed there from
the tertiary network [vessels]. 溢 is 泛溢, 'to flow,' in the sense of 外出, 'to leave to the
outside.' The strange evil flows out of the tertiary network because it is linked to the
great network and because it is passed through by the camp and by the guard [qi]."

58-301-6
When the camp and the guard [qi] stagnate,
when the guard [qi] disperses and when the camp [qi] overflows, and
when the qi is exhausted and the blood is stuck,⁴³ then
externally this causes the development of heat and
internally this causes one to be short of qi.⁴⁴
Then drain quickly; do not lose any time
to free the passage of the camp and guard [qi].
Drain it where it appears;
do not care about the meeting points."⁴⁵

Zhang Jiebin: "溢 is 注, 'to flow,' 滿, 'full.' 奇 is 异, 'different.' When an evil starting
from the skin and its hair pours into the network [vessels], it flows from the left to the
right and from the right to the left. Its qi occupies no permanent location and does
not enter the conduits. This is an extraordinary evil." Tanba: "The four characters 以通
榮衛 may be a later insertion." Hu Tianxiong: "One must read 奇 as the 奇, 'unpaired,'
in 奇偶. 奇邪 is 余邪, 'surplus evil.' The 奇邪 is an evil qi which does not flow inside
the conduit vessels but has flown out into [the region] outside of the conduit vessels.
This type of evil qi does not follow the conduit vessels in its movement. It may rise to
the orifices, or it may lump together in the blood network. Ma Shi, Gao Shishi, Zhang
Zhicong are all wrong. 'The unpaired evil overflows through them,' this is a reference
to the tertiary network [vessels] from a perspective of pathology; 'the camp and the
guard [qi] pass through them,' this is a reference to the tertiary network [vessels] from
a perspective of physiology. There is no need to assume that the latter sentence is a
later insertion." We follow the interpretation introduced by Hu Tianxiong. However,
we read "unpaired" as "unevenly distributed".

43 Hu Tianxiong: "This may be a comment written in the margins of the text that
was later erroneously inserted into the main text. When 'the guard [qi] is dispersed,'
then 'the qi is exhausted.' When 'the camp [qi] has flowed off,' then the blood is
stuck."

44 Zhang Zhicong: "The blood and the qi of the great network [vessels] appear outside in the skin, and they meet with the tertiary network [vessels]. Hence, the guard
[qi] outside of the vessels and the camp [qi] inside the vessels interact with each
other in the tertiary network [vessels] in the skin. The tertiary network [vessels] pass
through the skin outside and they connect with the conduit vessels inside to pass the
camp and the guard [qi]. Hence, when evil settles in [the tertiary network vessels],
then the camp and the guard [qi] are impeded in their flow. They cannot interact and
do not move. As a result, the qi is exhausted and the blood stagnates. When evil qi is
present in the external section, then this causes fever and the proper qi is impeded in
its flow. Inside this causes shortness of qi."

45 Wang Bing: "When the camp [qi] accumulates and the guard [qi] stagnates and
when inner and outer fight each other, then this will become evident in the blood
network. At this time one must drain them immediately, without asking where the
transportation [holes] and meeting points of the vessels are." Zhang Zhicong: "One

58-302-2
[Huang] Di:
"Good!
I should like to hear about the meeting points of the ravines and valleys."

Qi Bo:
"The large meeting points of the flesh are the valleys;
the small meeting points of the flesh are the ravines.
In the partings of the flesh, [this is where] the ravines and valley meeting
points are located.[46]

They serve as passage [ways] of the camp and the guard [qi] and
they serve to assemble large [quantities of] qi.[47]

When evil overflows [from the tertiary network vessels], the [paths of the] qi
are congested.
The vessels turn hot and the flesh rots.
The camp and the guard [qi] do not move.
This will cause pus [to develop].

---

must drain quickly and not lose any time, to free the passage of the camp and of the
guard qi. One pierces to drain at locations where one sees that blood stagnates and
that the color has changed. One does not ask where the transportation holes and the
meeting points are."

46 Zhang Zhicong: "The flesh has large partings and small partings. The large partings, as for instance at the flesh of thighs and arms, all have passages along the boundaries [of the individual flesh sections]. The small partings are located in the muscle
flesh; they all have linear structures. Now, even though the [flesh sections] are divided
by structures or open passages, they are nevertheless linked to each other. Hence, the
locations of great parting are also locations of great meeting; the locations of small
parting are also locations of small meeting. The partings of the flesh divides serve to
pass the camp and the guard qi. Hence, they are called 'ravines' and 'valleys.'" Zhang
Jiebin: "The meeting points of the flesh are attached to the bones; the meeting points
of the bones are the joints. Hence, the large joints and the small joints are at the same
time the locations of the large meeting points and of the small meeting points and the
ravines and valleys emerge from within them." See also 2417/50 for a comparison of
various occurrences of the terms "ravines" and "valleys" in the *Nei jing*.

47 Lin Yi et al.: "The *Jia yi jing* has 以舍大氣, 'to accomodate great [amounts of]
qi.'" Zhang Zhicong: "大氣 is 宗氣, 'basic qi.'" Hu Tianxiong: "大氣 is 正氣, 'proper
qi.'" 969/60 agrees. See there for a detailed discussion.

Internally [the evil] melts away the bones and their marrow;
externally it destroys the big protuberances of the muscles.[48]

58-302-5
If [the evil] remains in the joints and interstice [structures], it will cause destruction.[49]

When accumulated cold lodges [in the ravines and valleys],
the camp and the guard [qi] will not find a place to halt,
the flesh will curl up and the sinews will shrink.[50]
>The ribs< The elbows cannot be stretched.[51]
Internally this results in bone block;
externally this causes numbness.[52]
This is called insufficiency."
<Massive cold stays in the ravines and valleys.>

58-302-8
The 365 holes of the meeting points of the ravines and valleys, they, too, correspond to a year.

---

48 Wang Bing: "This happens because of excessive heat." Wu Kun has exchanged 腘 for 䐃. Zhang Jiebin: "腘 must be 䐃. This is a mistake because one can speak of 'great 䐃' but not of great 腘." Cheng Shide et al.: "The *Guang yun* 廣韻 defines 腘 as '[fossa] in the bend of the leg.' 䐃 refers to protruberances of flesh. Hence, it is correct to exchange 腘 for 䐃."

49 Wang Bing: "When it stagnates in the bone junctures, which is a location where liquids are retained, then the marrow and the liquids in the bone junctures will rot and turn into pus. Hence, destruction of the sinews and bones is inevitable and one will not be able any longer to bend or stretch [them]."

50 Lin Yi et al.: "The Quan Yuanqi edition has 寒肉縮筋, 'the flesh is cold and the sinews shrink.'"

51 Yu Chang: "The character 肘 is an erroneous insertion connected to the character 筋 in the preceding text. The preceding and the following text consists of four character statements. There should not be one additional character just here." 2623/67: "The *Tai su* has 時不得伸, 'at times cannot stretch.' 時 and 肘 are similar in shape and have been mistakenly exchanged. Hence, it is clear that the character 肘 is an erroneous insertion."

52 Zhang Zhicong: "The evil closes the outside; hence a 'bone block' develops internally. The camp and the guard [qi] move contrary [to their normal flow] in the inside; hence numbness develops outside."

< Their small blocks spread everywhere;
following the vessels they come and go.
They can be reached by the fine needle.
[Their treatment] is in agreement with the laws [of piercing].>⁵³

[Huang] Di then dismissed his entourage and rose. He paid reverence twice
and said:
"Today you have released me from ignorance and you have dispersed [my]
delusions.
I shall store [this knowledge] in a golden chest;
I shall not dare to take it out again."⁵⁴
Then he stored it in the Golden Orchid Chamber,⁵⁵ and gave it the title *The
Locations of the Qi Holes.*⁵⁶

58-302-11
<Qi Bo:
"As for the tertiary network vessels branching out from the conduits, those
whose blood abounds and should be drained. {They, too, are 365 vessels.} They
all pour into the network [vessels], whence [their content] is transmitted to

53 Wang Bing: "When the qi of a minor cold flows through the vessels moving back
and forth and causing block diseases, this can be regulated with the needle. This corresponds to the regular laws [of piercing]." Zhang Zhicong: " 'Small blocks' is to say:
when evil has just begun to enter the skin, before it has caused harm to the sinews
and bones. 'Vessels' is to say: the tertiary network [vessels]. When evil is present in the
skin and moves here and there following the [tertiary network] vessels, it is drained
where it is observed. This is identical to the laws of treating the tertiary network [ves-
sels]." Mori: "The *Tai su* has 與法相思 instead of 與法相同. The commentary by Yang
Shangshan explains it as 與法相司. Hence, the version used by Yang Shangshan had
司. In the present version of the *Tai su* this was erroneously written 思 because of the
identical pronunciation; it was erroneously written 同 in the present version of the *Su
wen* because of the similarity of the characters 司 and 同. Wang Bing's commentary
was wrong. 與法相司 is to say: the regular pattern of [using] the small needle agrees
with the main indications outlined in the work *Ming tang* 明堂. Hence, it controls
the disease (與病相司)."

54 Fang Wenhui/113: "It should be stored in a treasure chest and no one unauthor-
ized shall lightly take it out again."

55 Zhang Zhicong: "Zhang Taohuang: 'That is, he stored it in his heart.' " 2493/531:
"The 'Golden Chest' appears in the 'Annals of Emperor Gao' in the Dynastic History
of the Han. It is the most sacred place in the palace in the Han era. The 'Orchid Ter-
race' is the place where in the Han era palaces the literature was stored."

56 Wu Kun and and Yao Shaoyu omit the 23 character passage beginning with 辟
and ending with 乃. They consider it to be an erroneous insertion.

pour into the twelve network vessels.

{These are not solely the 14 network vessels.}[57]

Internal divisions where [the blood can be] drained to the inside, [these are] ten vessels."> [58]

---

57 Wang Bing: " '14 network [vessels]' is to say: the twelve conduit network [vessels] and the network [vessels] of the controlling vessel and of the supervisor vessel. The large network [vessel] of the spleen emerges from the spleen. Hence, it is not included here." The Gao Shishi edition has "twelve" instead of "14." Zhang Yizhi et al. quotes Sun Dingyi 孫鼎宜: "絡 is an error for 經, 'conduit.' "

58 Wang Bing: "解 is to say: the conduits and network [vessels] in the bone divides. Even though their courses are separate, the evil received is drained into the vessels of the five depots following [these courses], too." Zhang Jiebin: "解 is 解散, 'to open and disperse.' 瀉 is 'to eliminate a repletion through draining.' 中 is 'the five depots.' That is to say, even though there are twelve network [vessels], they are linked separately with the five depots. Hence, one can drain [their] contents into the center." Hu Tianxiong: "Yao Shaoyu has deleted the three characters 歧伯曰 and has placed the following 46 characters in front of the statement '[Huang] Di dismissed ..' He ends this treatise with the statement 'and titled it *The locations of the qi holes*.' From the structure of the text, Yao Shaoyu's rearrangement makes sense. However, the meaning of these seven sentences consisting of more than 40 characters is hard to explain. Perhaps these are teachings transmitted by a teacher, hence an explanation was not included. It may have been difficult to relate these statements [to a passage in any of the treatises], hence it was recorded here for the time being." The insert makes sense once it is understood as a compiler's devise to bridge treatises 58 and 59. The "ten vessels" reappear in the subsequent treatise.

Chapter 59
Discourse on Qi Palaces[1]

59-303-3
There are 78 holes on the foot major yang vessel where qi is effused:[2]

One each at the tips of the two eyebrows.[3]

Into the hair and to the nape [in a mutual distance of] three and a half inches, [there are] five [holes] side by side, three inches away from each other .[4]

---

1 Li Guoqing: "The [term] 'qi palaces' refers to the locations where the qi of the conduit vessels meet and interact." Ma Shi: "The previous [treatise, i.e., *Su wen* 58] discusses holes. Hence, it is called 'Qi Holes.' The present [treatise] discusses the locations where the qi of the vessels is effused. Hence, it is called 'Qi Palaces.'" Gao Shishi: "The three yang vessels of the hands and feet are ruled by the six palaces. Hence, the locations where the qi of the vessels is effused are called 'qi palaces.'" 1794/34: " 'Qi palace' has two meanings. One is: the palaces where the qi is effused at the meeting points of the conduit vessels. The meaning of 府 in this case is that of 庫府, 'storehouse' or 'treasury.' The second is: the holes where the vessel qi of the three yang vessels of the hands and of the feet associated with the six palaces is effused. The term 'qi palace' appears nowhere else in the *Su wen*. It is a general term for locations where the vessel qi is effused; it is not another term for transporters or qi holes." For details, see there.

2 The *Tai su* has "73 holes." Wang Bing: "If those [holes] are included where qi floating at the surface passes in smallest quantities, one should speak of 93 holes, not of 78 holes. The proper conduits and vessels have 78 holes where [qi] meets and effuses; [in addition] there are 15 holes where smallest quantities pass. [Together] they amount to this number [of 93]." Wu Kun: "If one checks [the holes listed below] one reaches [a number of] 91 holes, 13 holes more [than the 78 mentioned in the text]. This [number] differs from [the number of holes known] today. Nowadays one counts on the left and on the right altogether 126 holes." The Gao Shishi edition has "76 holes." See the end of note 10 below.

3 Wang Bing: "I.e., the Bamboo Gathering (攢竹) holes. The applications and the locations of cauterization and piercing [should follow] a law identical with [the one mentioned in the treatise] on Qi holes."

4 The *Tai su* has "two" instead of "three." Wang Bing: "Two holes each, i.e., the Great Shuttle (大杼) and Wind Gate (風門) [holes]. The applications and the locations of cauterization and piercing [should follow] a law identical with [the one mentioned in the treatise] on Qi holes." 693/38: "The meaning of 灸刺分壯 in Wang Bing's commentary is: 灸壯刺分, applications of cauterisation and locations of piercing'." Lin Yi et al.: "Another edition states: 'Into the hair and to the nape [in a mutual distance of] three inches.' And another commentary [by Wang Bing] states: ' "Inch" refers to the individually standardized body inch. All inches [should be measured following]

{Those [lines] where floating qi is in the skin⁵ are altogether five lines. [Each] line has five [holes]. Five times five are 25.}

---

an identical law.' This is entirely different from the present commentary. The present commentary [by Wang Bing] states: 'Two holes each, i.e., the so-called Great Shuttle and Wind Gate [holes]. The locations and the quantities of cauterization and piercing [to be applied here should follow] a law identical with the [treatise] on "Qi holes."'" In today's "Qi hole" treatise there is no mentioning of a Wind Gate hole. Hence, when the commentary states 'the law [should be] identical with [that in the "Qi holes" treatise],' it is obvious that this comment is wrong. This is not the fault of Wang Bing, it is the fault of some later person. Taking a close look at [the statement] 'Into the hair and to the nape [in a mutual distance of] three and a half inches, [there are] five [holes] side by side, separated from each other by three inches,' this refers to the following passage on the qi floating in the skin in five lines, with each line having five holes. Hence Wang Bing did not comment on it. All he said was 'inch refers to individually standardized body inch.' However, [the character] 頂 ("top of the head") was erroneously changed to 項 ("nape") here and the character 半 is a [later] addition. Hence, if [the text] said 'Into the hair and to the top of the head,' then this would be the three inches from the Fontanel Meeting (顖會) hole to the Hundred Convergences (百會) hole on the top of the head and three further inches from the Hundred Convergences [hole] backwards to the Posterior Vertex (後頂) [hole]. Hence, [the text] states 'Into the hair and to the vertex [in a mutual distance of] three inches.' As for [the characters] 傍五, this number includes the central line and [two each] on each side. As for [the characters] 相去三寸, that is to say: from the Hundred Convergences (百會) [hole] in the center of the vertex to the front and to the back, to the left and to the right, always in a distance of three inches, there are five vessels, each having five [holes]; together these are 25 holes. When later people misinterpreted 頂 as 項 and thought this referred to the Great Shuttle and Wind Gate [holes], this was a serious mistake. The Great Shuttle [holes] are located below the first vertebra on both sides [of the spine]; the Wind Gate [holes] are located below the second vertrebra. They are more than just three and a half inches distant from the hairline. Hence, the error is most obvious." Zhang Jiebin and Gao Shishi followed Lin Yi et al. and exchanged 項 for 頂. Tanba agreed. Ma Shi: " 'Into the hair' is: Into the hairline on the back [of the head]." Hu Tianxiong: "The statements of Wang Bing and Ma Shi are both incomprehensible, with Ma Shi's statement being especially wrong. This paragraph discusses where the qi of the foot major yang vessel is effused. Starting from the tip of the eyebrows and ending to the side of the small toes, this conduit vessel passes from the front to the back, from above to below – that is obvious. Hence, 'into the hair and to the nape' refers to the frontal hair line. .. One should eliminate the characters 'three and a half inches,' and the text will have a proper meaning."

5 Wang Bing: "浮氣 is to say: by causing the qi to pass through [the skin] floating at the surface, it is possible to eliminate heat." Wu Kun: "That is [to say:] the yang qi floats on top of the skull." Zhang Jiebin: "That is to say: the vessel qi that floats on top of the head." Mori: "浮氣 is equivalent to 浮脈, 'floating [movement in the] vessels.' At these 25 holes the qi in the vessels flows near the surface in the skin. Hence, [the text] states 'floating qi.' This corresponds to the [concept of] 浮絡 in *Su wen* 58."

One each on both sides of the large sinews in the center of the nape.[6]
One each on both sides of the wind palace.[7]
One each on both sides of the spine[8] in the gaps [between the ribs attached] to
15 of the altogether 21 joints [from the Great Pillar] down to the sacrum.[9]
<Five transporters of the five depots and six transporters of the six palaces (on
each side).>[10]

---

6 All commentators agree in identifying these two holes as the Celestial Pillar (天
柱) holes. In contrast, Gao Shishi: "These are the Wind Pool (風池) [holes]." Hu
Tianxiong: "In the development of the doctrine of the conduit vessels, the [knowledge
on] conduit vessels came first. Then there were holes and finally there were names
for these holes. The two moxa manuals among the Mawangdui silk manuscripts only
state 'cauterize vessel xxx' or 'treatment through vessel xxx,' but they do not refer to
specific locations. The *Su wen* often refers to locations of holes, but does not mention
names."

7 All commentators agree in identifying these two holes as the Wind Pool (風池)
holes. In contrast, Gao Shishi: "These are the Celestial Pillar (天柱) [holes]."

8 Tanba: "The *Tai su* has 背 ('back') instead of 脊 ('spine')." Wang Bing has 背 in his
commentary.

9 Wang Bing: "As for 'one in each gap between the 15 [ribs],' these are the 13 holes
listed nowadays in the *Zhong gao kong xue tu jing* 中誥孔穴圖經; these are to the left
and right altogether 26 holes. Namely, the Attached Branch (附分), *Po*-Soul Door (魄
戶), Spirit Hall (神堂), *Yi Xi* (譩譆), Diaphragm Pass (膈關), *Hun*-Soul Gate (魂門),
Yang Headrope (陽綱), Thought Dwelling (意舍), Stomach Granary (胃倉), *Huang*
Gate (肓門), Will Chamber (志室), Bladder *Huang* (胞肓), and the Sequence End
(秩邊) [holes]." Zhang Jiebin: "If one examines the *Jia yi* [*jing*] and the other classics, one finds 14 holes. Namely, the Great Shuttle (大杼), Attached Branch, *Po*-Soul
Door, Spirit Hall, *Yi Xi*, Diaphragm Pass, *Hun*-Soul Gate, Yang Headrope, Thought
Dwelling, Stomach Granary, *Huang* Gate, Will Chamber, Bladder *Huang*, and the
Sequence End [holes]. Nowadays the *Gao Huang* (膏肓) hole was added to reach the
number 15. However, this hole was not mentioned before the Jin 晉 era. Hence, the
original number [of holes] to the left and right was 28."

10 The *Tai su* does not have these 12 characters. Mori: "These 12 characters may have
been inserted [as a commentary] by Wang Bing in red script." Gao Shishi: "From both
sides of the Wind Palace (風府) downwards alongside the spine, [i.e.,] from the great
hammer down to the sacrum one counts 21 joints. Within [the total span of] these 21
joints, there is one [hole] on each (side) located in 15 of the interspaces, namely, the
Lung Transporter (肺俞), the Ceasing Yin Transporter (厥陰俞), the Heart Transporter (心俞), the Diaphragm Transporter (膈輸), the Liver Transporter (肝俞), the
Gallbladder Transporter (膽俞), the Spleen Transporter (脾俞), the Stomach Transporter (胃俞), the Triple Burner Transporter (三焦俞), the Kidney Transporter (腎
俞), the Large Intestine Transporter (大腸俞), the Small Intestine Transporter (小腸
俞), the Bladder Transporter (膀胱俞), the Transporter Inside the Central Spine (中
脊内俞), and the White Ring Transporter (白環俞). Altogether these are 30 holes.

Six transporters each on both sides from the Bend Middle down to the side of the [tip of the] small toe.[11]

59-305-2
There are 62 holes[12] on the foot minor yang vessel where the qi is effused:

Two each above both corners [of the forehead].[13]
Five each exactly above the eyes into the hairline.[14]
One each above the corners [of the forehead] in front of the ears.[15]
One each below the corners [of the forehead] in front of the ears.[16]
One each below the ear locks.[17]
One Visitor-Host [hole] on each [side].[18]
One each in the depression behind the ears.[19]
One Lower Pass [hole] on each [side].[20]

[On one level with] the 15 interspaces are the transporters of the five depots, i.e., lung, heart, liver, spleen, and kidneys, these are five both on the left and on the right and the transporters [of the six palaces], i.e., gallbladder, stomach, triple burner, large intestine, small intestine, and bladder. These are six both on the left and on the right. The five transporters of the depots and the six transporters of the palaces (on each side) are included in the total of 15 interspaces and these 15 interspaces in turn are included in the total of 21 joints." In contrast, Zhang Jiebin did not include the altogether 22 transporters of the depots and palaces into the total of, as he counted, 28 holes located on the level of the 15 interspaces.

11 Wang Bing: "I.e., the six Bend Middle (委中), Kunlun Mountains (崑崙), Capital Bone (京骨), Bundle Bone (束骨), Valley Passage (通谷), and Extreme Yin (至陰) holes."

12 The *Tai su* speaks of 52 holes.

13 Wang Bing: "I.e., the Celestial Thoroughfare (天衝) and the Temporal Hairline Curve (曲鬢) holes, two each on the left and on the right." Gao Shishi: "角 is 頭角, 'corners of the head.'"

14 Wang Bing: "I.e., the Approaching Tears (臨泣), Eye Window (目窗), Proper Camp (正營), Receiving the Numinous (承靈), and Brain Hollow (腦空) holes on the left and on the right."

15 Wang Bing: "I.e., the two Jaw Pressure (頷厭) holes."

16 Wang Bing: "I.e., the two Suspended Grain (Weight) (懸釐) holes."

17 Wang Bing: "I.e., the two Harmony Bone-Hole (和髎) holes."

18 Wang Bing: " 'Visitor-Host-Person (客主人)' is the name of holes."

19 Wang Bing: "I.e., the two Wind Screen (翳風) holes."

20 Wang Bing: " 'Lower Pass (下關)' is the name of holes."

One each behind the jaws below the ears.[21]
One each in the broken basins.[22]
Three inches below the armpits, from below the flanks [up] to the upper flanks, one each in the eight gaps.[23]
One each at the center and to the side of the thigh pivots.[24]
Six transporters each on both [legs] from the knees down to the toe next to the small toe.[25]

59-307-2
There are 68 holes on the foot yang brilliance vessel where the qi is effused:

Three each to the side of the hairline at the forehead and at the skull.[26]
One each in the facial cheek bone hollows.[27]

---

21 Wang Bing: "I.e., the two Cheek Carriage (頰車) holes."

22 Wang Bing: " 'Broken Basin (缺盆)' is the name of holes."

23 In contrast, Wang Bing: "Below the armpits, these include the Armpit Abyss (淵腋), Immobile Sinew (輒筋), and Celestial Pool (天池) [holes]. From below the flanks to the upper flanks, these include the Sun and Moon (日月), Camphorwood Gate (章門), Belt Vessel (带脉), Fifth Pivot (五樞), Linking Path (維道), and Squatting Bone-Hole (居髎) holes. These are nine holes on the left and on the right; together 18 holes." The text refers to only eight "gaps", i.e. (if one counts the holes on both sides), to altogether 16 holes. The "Squatting Bone-Hole holes" mentioned by Wang Bing are not located in the region of the flanks but near the thigh pivot (see the following footnote).

24 Wang Bing: "I.e., the two Ring-shaped Hoe (環銚) holes." The two "Squatting Bone-Hole holes" should be added here (see the preceding note). See also Lin Yi et al.

25 Wang Bing: "I.e., the six Yang Mound Spring (陽陵泉), Yang Assistance (陽輔), Hill Ruins (丘墟), Approaching Tears (臨泣), Pinched Ravine (俠溪) and Orifice Yin (竅陰) holes. To the left and right, these are twelve holes."

26 Wang Bing: "I.e., the Suspended Skull (懸顱), Yang White (陽白), and Head Corner (頭維) [holes]. To the left and right, altogether six holes."

27 Yang Shangshan: "䪼 is 鼻表, 'outside of the nose.'" Wang Bing: "I.e., the Four White [Sections] (四白) hole." Wang Bing further down: "䪼 is 頄. 頄 is 面顴, 'facial cheek.'" Tanba: "This may be a mistake for 頰, 'cheek.' The *Shi gu* 釋骨 of Mr. Shen 沈氏 states: 'the bone rising below the eye is called 頄 . That which is located below to the side and is prominent and big, is called 面䪼骨; other names are 顴骨 and 大顴.' 䪼 and 頄 were used identically in ancient times." Gao Jiwu/32: "䪼 has two meanings: 1. it refers to diseases of the nose, such as running nose. 2. it refers to a location, as in the present passage." 1508/10: "䪼 refers, first, to the nose, second, to the cheek bones, and third, to a stuffed nose or running nose." For details, see there.

One Great Facing [hole] in the bone hollow on each [side].[28]
One Man's Facing [hole] on each [side].[29]
One each in the bone hollow outside the broken basin.[30]
One each in the gaps between the [rib] bones in the center of the breast.[31]
Five each outside on both sides of the turtledove tail (i.e., sternum) and exactly
three inches below the breast [nipple], on both sides of the stomach duct.[32]
Three each three inches apart on both sides of the navel.[33]
Three each on both sides two inches below the navel.[34]
One each at the qi street moving vessels.[35]
One each above the crouching rabbit.[36]
Eight transporters each from the Three Miles [hole] down to the middle toe.[37]
‹The holes located in the partings.›[38]

---

28 Wang Bing: " 'Great Facing (大迎)' is the name of holes."

29 Wang Bing: " 'Man's Facing (人迎)' is the name of holes."

30 Wang Bing: "I.e., the two Celestial Bone-Hole (天髎) holes."

31 Yang Shangshan: "Breast Window (膺窗) and Breast Center (乳中), to the left
and to the right two holes." Wang Bing: "I.e., the six holes of Breast Window (膺窗),
… Qi Door (氣户), Storeroom (庫房), Roof (屋翳), Breast Center (乳中), Breast
Root (乳根)."

32 Wang Bing: "I.e., the five holes Not Contained (不容), Assuming Fullness (承滿),
Beam Gate (梁門), Pass Gate (關門), and Supreme Unity (太一)." Gao Shishi: "俠 is
并, 'to parallel.' That is, paralleling the sternum on both sides."

33 Yang Shangshan: "I.e., the three holes Supreme Unity (太一), Slippery Flesh Gate
(滑肉門), and Celestial Pivot (天樞)." Wang Bing: "廣 is to say: away from the navel
on a transverse line… I.e., the Slippery Flesh Gate, Celestial Pivot, and Outer Mound
(外陵) [holes]."

34 Wang Bing: "I.e., the Great Gigantic (大巨), Water Way (水道) and Return (歸
來) [holes]."

35 Wang Bing: " 'Qi Street' is the name of holes."

36 Wang Bing: "I.e., the two holes of Thigh Joint (髀關)." The character 菟 may be
a variant here of 兔.

37 Wang Bing: "I.e., the eight holes of Three Miles (三里), Upper Edge (上廉), Lower Edge (下廉) Ravine Divide (解谿), Surging Yang (衝陽), Inundated Valley (滔谷),
Inner Court (内庭), Grinding Stone (厲兑)."

38 Wang Bing: "As for 分之所在穴空, the foot yang brilliance vessel departs (分) at
the Three Miles (三里) hole and passes downwards, while the straight course [of this
vessel] follows the shins, moves beyond the instep and enters the middle toe, at the
end of which, i.e., at the Grinding Stone (厲兑) [hole], it reappears. Its branch courses
move, together with the straight course, to the top of the instep and enter between the
middle toe and the adjacent toes. Hence, [the text] states 分之所在穴空, 'the holes at

59-310-1

There are 36 holes[39] on the hand major yang vessel where the qi is effused:

One each at the inner canthi of the eyes.[40]
One each outside the eyes.[41]
One each below the cheek bone.[42]
One each above the auricles.[43]
One each in the center [in front of the] ears.[44]
One Great Bone hole on each [side].[45]
One hole each in the bone above the curved armpit.[46]
One each in the depression [on both sides] above the clavicle.[47]
One each four inches above the celestial window.[48]
One each in the shoulder divide.[49]
One each three inches below the shoulder divide.[50]
Six Transporters each from the elbow down to the base of the small finger.[51]

---

the location where the branch courses move to.' 之 is 往, 'to proceed towards.' That is to say, [the vessel] is divided into several lines all of which proceed to the holes located between the toes."

39 The *Tai su* has "26" instead of "36." Yang Shangshan: " '30 was mistakenly changed to 20.' "

40 Wang Bing: "I.e., the two Bright Eyes (睛明) holes."

41 Wang Bing: "I.e., the two Pupil Bone-Hole (瞳子髎) holes."

42 Wang Bing: "I.e., the two Cheek Bone-Hole (顴髎) holes."

43 Wang Bing: "I.e., the two Grandchildren of the [Forehead] Corner (角孫) holes."

44 Wang Bing: "I.e., the two Auditory Palace (聽宮) holes."

45 Wang Bing: " 'Great Bone (巨骨)' is the name of [these two] holes."

46 Wang Bing: "I.e., the two Upper Arm Transporter (臑俞) holes."

47 Wang Bing: "I.e., the two Shoulder Well (肩井) holes."

48 Wang Bing: "I.e., the four holes of Celestial Window (天窗) and Orifice Yin (竅陰)."

49 Wang Bing: "I.e., the two Grasping the Wind (秉風) holes."

50 Wang Bing: "I.e., the two Celestial Ancestor (天宗) holes."

51 Wang Bing: "I.e., the six holes of Small Sea (小海), Yang Valley (陽谷), Wrist Bone (腕骨), Back Ravine (後溪), Front Valley (前谷), and Lesser Marsh (少澤). If those to the left and right are counted together, these are altogether twelve holes."

59-311-2
There are 22 holes on the hand yang brilliance vessel where the qi is effused:

Two each at the outer edge of the nostrils and above the nape.[52]
One Great Facing [hole] in the bone hollow on each side.[53]
One each at the meeting points of the pillar bones.[54]
One each at the meeting points of the shoulder bones.[55]
Six transporters each from the elbow down to the base of the finger next to the thumb.[56]

59-312-1
There are 32 holes on the hand minor yang vessel where the qi is effused:

One each below the cheek bone.[57]
One each behind the eyebrows.[58]
One each above the corners [of the forehead].[59]
One each behind the lower completion bone.[60]
One each in the center of the nape in front of the foot major yang [conduit].[61]
One each on both sides of the supporting protuberance.[62]

---

52 Wang Bing: "I.e., Welcome Fragrance (迎香) and Supporting Protuberance (扶突), two holes each."

53 Wang Bing: " 'Great Facing (大迎)' is the name of holes."

54 Wang Bing: "I.e., the two Celestial Tripod (天鼎) holes." Gao Shishi: "This is the nape bone. 'Meeting points of the pillar bones' refers to the points where nape and shoulders meet. These are the two Celestial Tripod holes." Zhang Zhicong: "The pillar bone is the nape bone situated above the shoulderblade."

55 Wang Bing: "I.e., the two Shoulder Bone (肩髃) holes."

56 Wang Bing: "I.e., the Three Miles (三里), Yang Ravine (陽溪), Union Valley (合谷), Third Space (三間), Second Space (二間), and Shang-Yang (商陽) holes."

57 Wang Bing: "I.e., the two Cheek Bone-Hole (顴髎) holes."

58 Wang Bing: "I.e., the two Silk Bamboo Hollow (絲竹空) holes."

59 Wang Bing: "I.e., the two Suspended Grain (Weight) (懸釐) holes." Lin Yi et al.: "In outlining the [holes on the] foot minor yang vessel, [this hole] is said to be located below the corners [of the forehead]. Here it [says] 'above the corners' and this may be wrong."

60 Wang Bing: "I.e., the two Celestial Window (天牖) holes."

61 Wang Bing: "I.e., the two Wind Pool (風池) holes."

62 Wang Bing: "I.e., the two Celestial Window (天窗) holes."

One Shoulder Truth [hole] on each [side].⁶³
One each in the partings three inches below the Shoulder Truth [holes].⁶⁴
Six transporters each from the elbow down to the base of the finger next to the small finger.⁶⁵

59-313-1
There are 28 holes on the supervisor vessel where the qi is effused:

Two in the center of the nape.⁶⁶
Eight in the center backwards from the hairline.⁶⁷
Three in the face.⁶⁸
15 holes from the great hammer down to the sacrum and on the side.⁶⁹
{Down to the sacrum there are altogether 21 joints.
This is the law of [determining holes according to] the vertebrae.}

59-314-2
There are 28 holes on the controlling vessel where the qi is effused:

---

63 Wang Bing: " 'Shoulder Truth (肩真)' is the name of holes."

64 Wang Bing: "I.e., the Shoulder Bone-Hole (肩髃), Upper Arm Convergence (臑會), and Dissipating Luo [River] (消濼); two holes each."

65 Wang Bing: "I.e., the six holes of Celestial Well (天井), Branch Ditch (支溝), Yang Pool (陽池) Central Islet (中渚), Fluid Gate (液門), and Pass Thoroughfare (關衝). If those to the left and right are counted together, these are altogether twelve."

66 Wang Bing: "I.e., the two Wind Palace (風府) and Mute's Gate (瘖門) holes."

67 Wang Bing: "I.e., the eight holes of Spirit Court (神庭), Upper Star (上星), Fontanel Meeting (顖會), Anterior Vertex (前頂), Hundred Convergences (百會) Posterior Vertex (後頂), Unyielding Space (强間), and Brain's Door (腦户)."

68 Wang Bing: "I.e., the three holes of White Bone-Hole (素髎), Water Trough (水溝), Gum Intersection (斷交)."

69 Wang Bing: "I.e., the 15 transporters of Great Hammer (大椎), Kiln Path (陶道), Body Pillar (神柱), Spirit Path (神道), Numinous Tower (靈臺), Extreme Yang (至陽), Sinew Contraction (筋縮), Central Pivot (中樞), Spinal Center (脊中), Suspended Pivot (懸樞), Life Gate (命門), Yang Pass (陽關), Lumbar Transporter (腰俞), Long Strong (長强), and Meeting of Yang (會陽)." Hu Tianxiong: "In accordance with the preceding and the following text, these should be 16 holes." For details, see there.

Two in the center of the throat.[70]
One each in the depressions between the bones in the center of the breast.[71]
One [each] for [each of the] three inches from the turtledove tail downwards,[72] for [each of the] five inches in the stomach duct [region],[73] and for [each of the] six and a half inches from the stomach duct down to the transverse bone.[74] {This is the law of [determining holes according to the position of] the abdominal vessels.}
[Between the two] lower yin [orifices] there is one separate [hole].[75]
There is one each below the eyes;[76]
one below the lip;[77]
one Gum Intersection [hole].[78]

---

70 Wang Bing: "I.e., the two Ridge Spring (廉泉) and Celestial Chimney (天突) holes."

71 Wang Bing: "I.e., the six holes of Swivel Mechanism (旋機), Florid Canopy (華蓋), Purple Palace (紫宮), Jade Hall (玉堂), *Dan Zhong* (膻中), and Central Court (中庭)." Hu Tianxiong: "This 膺中, 'in the center of the breast', means 胸中, 'in the center of the chest.' This is different from the statement in *Su wen* 58: 'Breast transporters: twelve holes.'"

72 Wang Bing: "I.e., the Turtledove Tail (鳩尾), Great Tower Gate (巨闕), and Upper Duct (上腕) holes." Hu Tianxiong: "The meaning of the twelve characters from here down to 六寸半一 is difficult to understand. All commentators have read them in a different way. .. The text is corrupt here."

73 Wang Bing: "I.e., the Central Duct (中腕), Interior Strengthening (建里), Lower Duct (下腕), Water Divide (水分), and Center of the Navel (臍中) holes."

74 Wang Bing: "I.e., the Yin Intersection (陰交), *Bo Yang* (脖胦), Cinnabar Field (丹田), Pass Head (關元), Central Pole (中極), and Curved Bone (曲骨) holes."

75 Wang Bing: "I.e., the Meeting of Yin (會陰) hole."

76 Wang Bing: "I.e., the two Tear Container (承泣) holes."

77 Wang Bing: "I.e., the Sauce Receptacle (承漿) hole."

78 Wang Bing: " 'Gum Intersection (齗交)' is the name of this hole." Gao Shishi: "The seam of the teeth intersects with the controlling vessel. Hence, this is called 'Gum Intersection.'" Wu Kun: "The 'Gum Intersection' is located inside the lip in the seam of the upper teeth. This is where the controlling and the supervisor vessels meet." Zhang Zhicong: "The Gum Intersection hole is located in the gum seam below the teeth inside the lips. In ancient times, there were two gum intersections. The gum intersection of the supervisor vessel entered the upper teeth; the gum intersection of the controlling vessel entered the lower teeth. These are [locations] where above and below the gums and the teeth intersect. Hence, they are called gum intersections."

59-316-2
There are 22 holes on the thoroughfare vessel where the qi is effused:

One for [each] inch downwards from a half inch on both sides outside of the turtledove tail down to the navel.[79]
One for [each] inch downwards from five *fen* on both sides of the navel to the transverse bone.[80]
{This is the law of [determining holes according to the position of] the abdominal vessels.}

59-316-4
There is one each on the foot minor yin [vessels] below the tongue,[81] and on the tense vessels of the ceasing yin [vessels] in the [pubic] hair.[82]
One each on the hand minor yin [vessels].[83]
One each on the yin and yang walker [vessels].[84]

[Together with] all locations on the fish lines of the hands and feet where the qi of the vessels is effused,
there are altogether 365 holes.[85]

---

79 Wang Bing: "I.e., the six holes of Dark Gate (幽門), Valley Passage (通谷), Yin City (陰都), Stone Pass (石關), Shang Bend (商曲), and *Huang* Transporter (肓俞). To the left and to the right, these are altogether twelve holes."

80 Wang Bing: "I.e., the five holes of Central Flow (中注), Marrow Palace (髓府), Uterine Gate (胞門), Great Manifestation Yin Pass (陰關), and Lower Pole (下極). To the left and to the right, these are altogether ten holes." *Fen* is a measure of length here. It corresponds to a tenth of an inch.

81 Wang Bing: "The two holes of the foot minor yin [conduit] below the tongue are the two Sun and Moon Origin (日月本) holes to the left and to the right in front of the moving vessel in the depression in front of man's facing."

82 Wang Bing: "The tense vessels are in the yin (i.e., pubic) hair. Above the yin (i.e., sexual) [organ], on both sides in a distance of 2 1/2 individually standardized body inches. If one touches it cautiously with one's finger, it feels hard. If one touches it forcefully, pain will extend upwards and downwards."

83 Wang Bing: "I.e., the hand minor yin cleft holes. This is the hand minor yin cleft located one half individually standardized body inch behind the wrist."

84 Wang Bing: "The one on the yin walker [vessel] is also called Exchanging Messages (交信) hole. The one on the yang walker [vessel] is also called Yang Attachment (附陽) hole."

85 Wang Bing: "Those existing on the conduits exceed [this number] by altogether 19 holes. These are the so-called qi palaces." Wu Kun: "All locations on the hands and feet where there are partings between dark and white flesh, resembling the borderlines of

color on the abdomen of fish, they are called 'fishline.'" Zhang Jiebin: "The prominent flesh locations to both sides of the hands and feet are all called 'fish.' When here all fishlines are referred to, that is because the four extremities are the origins of the twelve conduit vessels. Hence, this wording serves to elucidate the basic line connecting the qi palaces of all the conduits."

Chapter 60
Discourse on Bone Hollows[1]

60-318-2
Huang Di asked:
"I have heard, the wind is the origin of the one hundred diseases.[2]
To treat it with needles, how to proceed?"

Qi Bo responded:
"When wind enters [the body] from the outside,
it lets a person shake from cold.
Sweat leaves [the body] and the head aches.
The body [feels] heavy and has an aversion to cold.[3]

Treat [this] at the Wind Palace.
Regulate the [patient's] yin and yang.[4]

---

1 Gao Shishi: "The 'bone hollows' are the holes at the bone joints all over the body."

2 Wang Bing: "始 is 初, 'beginning.'" Zhang Jiebin: "When wind hits a person, it will first [affect] the skin and its hair and later proceed to the conduits and network [vessels], to the depots and palaces. From the shallow [regions] it enters the deeper [regions]; from a slight [affection] it turns into a serious [disease]. In its course it tends to make frequent changes. Hence, it is the begin of the one hundred diseases. When the sages avoided wind in the same way as they avoided arrows and stones, this was in fact to prevent even a slight [affection]." Gao Shishi: "Of the evil of the six excesses, the wind occupies the top position. Hence, 'the wind is the begin of the one hundred diseases.'"

3 Wang Bing: "When wind hits the physical body, the interstice structures close tightly and the yang qi takes up the internal defense. When the cold repeatedly dominates externally, dominating [cold] and defending [yang qi] fight each other. [As a result] the camp and the guard [qi] lose their positions. Hence, a situation as described here emerges." Zhang Jiebin: "Wind evil attacks from the outside; yang qi defends inside. Evil and proper [qi] battle each other, hence, one shakes from cold. The wind harms the guard [qi], hence, one sweats. The evil settles in the three yang [conduits], hence, one has head ache and the body [feels] heavy. When the guard [qi] is harmed, then the outside is timid. Hence, one has an aversion to cold." Hu Tianxiong: "The *Tai su* has 惡風寒. *Su wen* 42 states: 'Whenever one has a wind disease, one sweats massively and has an aversion to wind.' Hence, when the *Tai su* has the character for 'wind' following the character for 'aversion,' that is correct."

4 Wang Bing: " 'Wind Palace (風府)' is [the name of] a hole. It is located in the nape, one half individually standardized body inch into the hair line in the [central] fold."

If there is an insufficiency, supplement [it];
if there is a surplus, drain [it].

60-318-5
When massive wind [causes] neck pain,
pierce the Wind Palace.[5]
{The Wind Palace is at the upper hammer.}[6]

When massive wind [causes] sweat to leave [the body],
cauterize the *yi-xi* [hole].
{The *yi-xi* [hole] is located in the back, below, paralleling the spine on both
sides [in a distance of] three inches. If one presses[7] there and lets the patient
shout *yi-xi*, the *yi-xi* [hole] will correspond to one's hand.}[8]

60-318-7
When it is because of wind that someone hates wind,
pierce at the tips of the eyebrows.[9]

When [his neck] cannot touch the pillow,[10]
[pierce] on the shoulder between the transverse bones.[11]

---

5 See 2689/57 for a discussion of "wind" terms in the *Nei jing*.

6 Wang Bing: "上椎 is to say: 大椎上, 'above the great hammer,' one half individually standardized body inch into the hair line."

7 916/54: "厭 is 壓; 壓 is 按捺, 'to press heavily.'"

8 Wang Bing: "*Yi Xi* (譩譆) is [the name of two] holes. They are located at the inner edges of the shoulder blades, parallel to [the spine] below the sixth vertebra on
both sides in a distance of three individually standardized body inches. When one
presses them with the hand and lets the patient make an *yi-xi* sound, then one will
feel a movement under one's finger." 1720/13: "One lets the patient make a sound of
yi and/or *xi*."

9 Gao Shishi: "從 is 迎, 'to receive.'" Ma Shi: "That is to say, in case of being affected by wind and in case of aversion to wind." Cheng Shide et al.: " 'Tips of the
eyebrows' refers to the Bamboo Gathering (攢竹) holes." Wang Qi: "從風憎風 is a
disease caused by a wind evil. It manifests itself as an aversion to wind."

10 失枕, lit.: "to lose/miss the pillow," is identified today as crick in the neck. Wu
Kun: "The wind is in the neck. The neck aches and does not move freely; it cannot be
laid on the pillow."

11 Wang Bing: "I.e., the Broken Basin (缺盆) hole." Ma Shi: "This is the Great Bone
(巨骨) hole." Zhang Jiebin: "This should be the Outer Shoulder Transporter (肩外
俞) of the hand major yang [conduit] above the shoulder bone in the back. Or it is

When [the patient] is bent [forwards], let [him] lift his forearm.
Exactly on one level with the elbow cauterize the Spinal Center.[12]

60-319-1
When the network in the lateral abdomen and free ribs pulls on the lower
abdomen, resulting in pain and distension,
pierce the *yi-xi* [hole].[13]

When there is pain in the lower back so that one cannot turn around and sway,
[and if this pain] pulls tightly on the testicles,
pierce the eight bone-holes and [also the location on the skin] above the pain.[14]

---

the Shoulder Well (肩井) hole of the foot minor yang [conduit]; it, too, masters pain
in the neck."

12 The present text and the *Tai su* have 揄, 'to lift,' instead of 榆 as found in some
other versions. Wang Bing: "榆 is read as 搖. 搖 is to say 搖動, 'to wave.' In case of a
crick in the neck, do not only select the transverse bone on the shoulder. One should
also cauterize the center of the spine with [the patient] assuming an upright posture.
To verify the [proper location] let [the patient] make his arm make a waving movement and ask him to bend his elbow. From the neck downwards on one level with
the tip of his elbow exactly in the center, this is the [proper] location. It is called Yang
Pass (陽關)." Gao Shishi: "When one sleeps at night and has no head rest, then one
suffers between the transverse bones on the shoulders. One cannot stretch comfortably; hence, [one has a feeling] as if [something was] broken. If [it appears to be]
broken, one cannot lift the arm. In this case the patient must wave the arm until it
forms one level with the elbow to correct it. When the patient waves the arm to one
level with the elbow, there is a hollow in the spine. It is exactly at this location that one
must cauterize in the center of the spine and one must not look for any other place."
Zhang Zhicong: "折 is to say: the back is bent in an obtuse angle 磬折 and cannot be
stretched comfortably. .. One moves the arm so that it is on one level with the tip of
the elbow. The corresponding location [on the same level] in the center of the spine,
this is where the vertebral hole of the spine center is to be cauterized." Ma Shi: "This
is a statement on the cauterization pattern to be applied when an arm is broken.
Whenever someone has broken an arm, one lets this person wave his arm and bring it
into a bent position. Then [the patient should] raise his arm to one level with the elbow. Then one cauterizes him in the spine to let the qi of elbow and arm pass freely."

13 Wang Bing: "胗 is to say: the soft locations paralleling the spine on both sides. 少
腹 is [the region] below the navel." Gao Shishi: "The tip of the ribs is called 胗 . 胗絡
refers to the network [vessels] at the tips of the ribs."

14 2424/24: "The 'eight bone-holes' are the [two] upper, next, central, and lower
bone-holes. They are located at the end of the spine to the left and to the right in the
four sacrum hollows."

{The eight bone-holes are located in the partings of lower back and sacrum.}[15]

60-319-3

In case of a mouse fistula[16] with [alternating fits of] cold and heat,
[let the patient] turn [to the side] and pierce the Cold Palace.
{The Cold Palace is located in the camp in the [bone] divide close to the outside of the knee.}[17]
{When selecting [for treatment] the outside above the knee, let the [patient
lean forwards as if he] paid reverence;[18]
When selecting [for treatment] the center [of the sole] of the feet, let the
[patient] kneel down.}[19]

60-319-5

<As for the controlling vessel, it emerges from below the Central Pole,[20] rises to

---

15 Wang Bing: " 'Parting' is to say: the location below the depression in the sinew and
the parting of the flesh between lower back and sacrum."

16 Zhang Jiebin: "鼠瘻 is 瘰癧, 'scrofulous lumps.'" Zhang Zhicong: "鼠瘻寒熱 is
one disease. Its origin is in the depots. Its end develops between the neck and the
armpits." "鼠瘻寒熱 is poison in the water of the kidney depot which passes upwards
along the vessels."

17 Wang Bing: "This is between the bones on the outside of the knee, where bending
and stretching take place. Cold qi tends to enter there. Hence, it is called 'cold palace.'
解 is to say: 骨解, 'bone division.' 營 is to say: one must pierce into the depth and hit
the [patient's] camp [qi]." Zhang Jiebin: "The 'cold palace' is located below the knee in
the divide [between the knee and] the outer assisting bone (i.e., the fibula). All cold qi
moving upwards from below must accumulate in the knees. Hence, the knee cap is extremely cold. Hence, the name 'cold palace.' 營 is 窟, 'dwelling.' This is the Yang Pass (陽
關) hole of the foot minor yang conduit. When a mouse fistula is located between neck
and armpits, this disease has its origins in liver and gallbladder. Hence, one must select
these [locations] for treatment." Gao Shishi: "The 'cold palace' is the major yang vessel.
附膝外 is: the outer side of the knee. 解 is 骨解, 'bone divide.' Hence, this is the bone
seam at the outer side of the knee. 營 is 營俞, 'brook transporter' (apparently, 營 is used
here for 滎). This is the Valley Passage (通谷) hole at the base joint of the small toes."

18 Wang Bing: "[To let the patient lean forward as if he] paid reverence for seizing
[the disease], causes the knee hole to open."

19 Wang Bing: "[To let the patient] kneel for seizing [the disease] lets the soles of the
feet be visible." Zhang Zhicong: "When one lets [the patient] kneel, then the foot is
bent and the Gushing Fountain (涌泉) hole is easily accessible in the transverse line
of the sole of the foot."

20 Zhang Jiebin: " 'Central Pole (中極)' is the name of a hole of the controlling vessel. It is located one inch above the curved bone (i.e., the anteromedial portion of the
pubic bone)."

the [pubic] hairline, follows the inside of the abdomen, rises to the Pass Head, reaches to gullet and throat, rises [further] to the chin, follows the face, and enters the eyes.[21]

As for the thoroughfare vessel, it emerges[22] from the qi street[23] and merges with the minor yin conduit,[24] rises on both sides of the navel, reaches the chest center and disperses.[25]

When the controlling vessel causes a disease,
in males these are internal knottings and the seven elevation illnesses.
In females these are conglomerations below the belt.[26]

---

21 Lin Yi et al.: "The *Nan jing* and the *Jia yi jing* do not have the six characters 上 頤循面入目." Of the editions presently extant, the *Nan jing*, 28th difficult issue, does not have these six characters, while the *Jia yi jing* has them.

22 Zhang Jiebin: "起 is to say where the vessel appears on the outside; this is not to say where it has its source from which it emerges."

23 Wang Bing: "Qi Street (氣街) is the name of [two] holes located in the [pubic] hair line on both sides one individually standardized body inch above the groins." Gao Shishi: "The qi street is the thoroughfare of the abdominal qi. Its location is in the moving vessels (i.e., arteries) to the left and right of the navel." Zhang Zhicong: "氣 街 is 氣沖. These are holes of the foot yang brilliance conduit. They are located on the lower abdomen in the hair, two inches on both sides, at the two tips of the transversal bone."

24 Lin Yi et al.: "The *Nan jing* and the *Jia yi jing* have 'yang brilliance' [instead of 'minor yin.']."

25 Wang Bing: "The controlling vessel and the thoroughfare vessel are extraordinary vessels. The controlling vessel rises exactly from the navel. The thoroughfare vessel rises on both sides of the navel. The Central Pole (中極) is a location four individually standardized body inches below the navel. When [the text] says 'below the Central Pole,' then that is to say: the controlling vessel rises from inside the lower abdomen and appears at the hair line whence it rises further. This is not to say that it originates here."

26 Wang Bing: "The supervisor vessel is an extraordinary vessel, too. However, the controlling vessel, the thoroughfare vessel, and the supervisor vessel are three branches originating from one source. (For a discussion of the concept of "one source, three branches," see 296/69 and 2563/53). Hence, the [*Nei*] *jing* occasionally states: the thoroughfare vessel is the supervisor vessel. How to explain this? The *Jia yi* [*jing*] and the ancient *Jing mai liu zhu tu jing* 經脈流注圖經 call the controlling vessel passing along the back 'supervisor vessel,' and the [vessel] rising straight from the lower abdomen is called 'controlling vessel' and it is also called 'supervisor vessel.' These names, then, are based on a differentiation of back and abdomen as yang and yin [respectively]. Because the controlling vessel rises from the uterus, passes the belt vessel and

When the thoroughfare vessel causes a disease,
[this lets] the qi move contrary [to its regular course] and [causes] internal
tightness.[27]

When the supervisor vessel causes a disease,
[this causes] the spine to be stiff and to be bent backwards.>[28]

60-320-2
As for the supervisor vessel, it emerges[29] from the lower abdomen and then
moves down to the center of the [pubic] bone.

In females it enters and ties up with the court cavity.[30]
{This cavity is the tip of the urinary cavity.}[31]

---

penetrates the navel before it rises further, when it has a disease, in males this causes
internal knottings and the seven elevation illnesses, in females it causes [disease] in
the region below the belt, [i.e.,] conglomerations." Wu Kun: "帶下 are red and white
[vaginal] discharges." Tanba: "[The term] 'red and white [vaginal] discharges' appears
first in [Chao Yuan-fang's 巢元方 *Zhu*] *bing yuan* [*hou lun*] 諸病源候論. In ancient
times the term 帶下 carried the meaning of 'below lower back and belt.' All diseases
related to the monthly period are summarily called 'below the belt.' In the *Shi ji* 史記,
Bian Que 扁鵲 is called 帶下醫, 'physician [treating diseases] below the belt.' The *Jing
gui* [*yao lue*] has 36 entries on disease 'below the belt.'"

27 Wang Bing: "Because the thoroughfare vessel passes on both sides of the navel; it
rises together with the minor yin conduit and reaches the chest center, hence, when
the thoroughfare vessel has a disease, then qi moves contrary [to its regular course]
and there is internal tightness."

28 Wang Bing: "Because the supervisor vessel rises inside the spine, hence, when the
supervisor vessel has a disease, the spine is stiff and bent backwards."

29 Wang Bing: " 'Emerges' is not to say 'originates.' [The term is used here] like in the
statement 'controlling vessel and thoroughfare vessel emerge from the uterus.'"

30 Wang Bing reads 繫廷孔 as forming one term: "attachment to the court cavity":
"The 'attachment to the court cavity' is the hidden outlet which is close to the so-
called frontal yin hole. It is named 'attachment-to-the-court-cavity' because the yin
court is attached to it."

31 Wang Bing: " 'Cavity' is 窈漏, 'hidden outlet.' In this hidden outlet, there is in the
upper part the urinary cavity (溺孔). 'Tip' is to say: the tip above this urinary cavity in
the yin court." Zhang Jiebin: "廷 is 正, 'true,' 直, 'straight.' 廷孔 is to say: the straight
cavity in the true center, i.e., the urinary cavity." Zhang Zhicong: " 'The tip at the
urinary cavity' is the birth gate inside the yin [i.e., female sexual organ]." Tanba: "廷 is
挺, 'to stick out.' The birth gate bulges out, hence, it is called 廷孔. Zhang Zhicong's
comment is correct. When Zhang Jiebin interprets [廷] as 正 and 直 and considers
[the 廷孔] to be the urinary cavity, this is wrong."

Its network [vessels] follow the yin (i.e., sexual) organ [with the various branches] uniting again in the region of the perineum.[32]

They wind around to behind the perineum, separating into branches winding around the buttocks and reaching the network [vessels] between the [foot] minor yin and the [foot] great yang [conduits]. They merge with the [foot] minor yin [conduit] and rise on the inner back edge of the upper thighs, penetrate the spine, are connected with the kidneys, emerge together with the major yang [conduit] from the inner canthi of the eyes, rise to the forehead, intersecting [with the major yang conduit] on the peak of the skull, enter and enclose the brain, return to the outside and branch out to descend along the nape, follow the inside of the shoulderblades, move on both sides of the spine and reach the center of the lower back. They enter and follow the spinal column and enclose the kidneys.

60-321-2
In males it follows the stalk and descends to the perineum; [their further course] equals that in females.
That course of it which rises straight upwards from the lower abdomen, it penetrates the navel center, rises and penetrates the heart, enters the throat, rises to the lower cheek, winds around the lips, rises and ties up with the center below both eyes.

When it generates a disease,
there is pain from the lower abdomen rushing upwards to the heart.
[Patients] cannot [relieve nature] in front and behind.
This causes the surging elevation illness.[33]

---

32 Wang Bing: "The network [vessels] branching away from the supervisor vessel leave from the tip of the urine opening, move down along the private organ and unite at the perineum again. The so-called 閒 refers to the 'space between' the frontal and the dorsal yin [openings] (i.e., between sexual organ and anus)."

33 Wang Bing: "An examination of the generation of this disease reveals that it is situated in the controlling vessel. When the classic states 'it causes surging elevation illness,' this makes it very clear that it is ruled by a vessel apart from the supervisor vessel. Why? If each vessel has each qi and if there is no such situation where yin and yang rule differently, then the disease generated should include pain in both the heart and the back. How could it only 'surge upwards to the heart and cause elevation illness'?"

In females [this disease] prevents them from becoming pregnant.
[Also, it leads to] protuberance illness,[34] piles, [involuntary] loss of urine, and
dry throat.[35]

60-321-6
When the supervisor vessel generates a disease,
treat the supervisor vessel.
Treat it above the [pubic] bone.[36]
In severe cases [treat] at the camp below the navel.[37]

When [the patient experiences] rising qi with sounds,
treat in the center of the throat.
{This is in the midst of the broken basins.}[38]

When the [patient] suffers from [qi] rushing upwards to the throat,
treat at the advance.
{As for 'advance,' this is the rise [of the vessels] on both sides of the chin.}[39]

---

34 See also *Su wen* 49, note 55/56.

35 Wang Bing: "The reason is, once again, that the thoroughfare vessel and the controlling vessel rise together from the lower abdomen to the throat. Also, because the
supervisor vessel follows the private organ, meets at the perineum, ... hence, [females]
cannot become pregnant. .. The reason it is called 任脈 is that females have it for the
nourishment [of the fetus in the womb] (任養; see *Bai hu tong* 白虎通, Li yue 禮樂:
任養萬物, "to nourish the myriad beings").

36 Wang Bing: " This is also a branch of the controlling vessel. The thoroughfare,
the controlling [vessel], and the supervisor vessel, these three have different names but
they constitute one body. This is clear. 'Above the bone' is to say: the Curved Bone (曲
骨) hole in the pubic hair above the transverse bone in the lower back."

37 Yang Shangshan: "As for 'camp below the navel,' that is the base of the supervisor
vessel. 營, too, is the location of a hole." Wang Bing: " 'Below the navel' is to say: the
Yin Intersection (陰交) hole one individually standardized body inch straight below
the navel." Zhang Jiebin: "營 is 窟, 'cave.'" Cheng Shide et al.: " 'Camp below the navel' refers to a transporter hole in the lower abdomen below the navel."

38 Wang Bing: "中 is to say: the Celestial Chimney (天突) hole in the center between the two broken basins. It is located four individually standardized body inches
below the Adam's apple in the central cavity at the meeting of the yin binder and the
controlling vessels."

39 Wang Bing: "The yang brilliance vessel advances upwards to the chin and encircles the lips. Hence, the passage on both sides of the chin is called 'advance.' What
is meant here is the Great Facing (大迎) hole." Zhang Jiebin: "When, in case of qi
fullness, one pants and [the qi] rushes upwards to the throat, one must treat the Great
Facing holes of the foot yang brilliance conduits on both sides of the chin. The yang

60-322-1

In case of lameness,

when the knee can be stretched but cannot be bent,

treat the [patient's] bolt bone.[40]

When [the patient] sits and his knee aches,

treat its trigger.[41]

When [the patient] stands and has summerheat in the divide,

treat the bone joint.[42]

When the knee aches and when the pain reaches into the big toe,[43]

treat the [patient's] knee bay.[44]

When the [patient] sits and his knee aches as if something was hidden in it,[45]

treat the [patient's lower thigh bone] joints.[46]

---

brilliance vessel advances upwards from there to the chin and [through] the face. Hence, the sides of the chin are named 'advance.' Zhang Zhicong: "As for 漸, this is to say: the supervisor vessel enters the throat, rises to the lips and to the teeth and advances further divided into two branches. It passes by the sides of the chin and enters the eyes. One must pierce it at the location where it advances upwards to the sides of the chin."

40 Wang Bing: "蹇膝 is to say: the knee aches and bending and stretching are difficult because of lameness."

41 Zhang Jiebin: "The moving location of the bone seam on both sides of the buttocks is called 機. This is the Ring-shaped Hoe (環銚) hole of the foot minor yang [vessel]." Gao Shishi: "機 is 機關, 'trigger joint.' When the knee aches while one sits, the joint is not in order." 2424/27: "These should be the Thigh Joint (髀關) [holes]."

42 Wang Bing: "署 is 熱, 'heat.' When [a patient] with pain in his knee stands up and has heat in the divide of the knee bones, one treats this at the bone gate. 'Bone gate' is to say: the knee divide. Another edition has 起而引解, 'one rises and it pulls the divide.' That is to say: when the knee aches and one rises, the pain is drawn into the divide of the knee bones." Tanba: "The other edition quoted by Wang Bing appears to be correct." 2424/27: "These should be the Knee Eye [holes]."

43 Yang Shangshan: "拇指 is the small toe." Gao Shishi: "拇指 is the big toe." Tanba: "The *Shuo wen* states: 拇 is 將指. The commentary by Yan Shi-gu 顏師古 in the *Ji jiu pian* 急就篇 states: 拇 is 大指, 'big toe;' another name is 將指."

44 Wang Bing: "膕 is to say: the Bend Middle (委中) hole in the curvature of the leg behind the knee divide."

45 Gao Shishi: "隱 is identical with 藏, 'to store.' 'The knee aches as if something were hidden in it,' is: it aches and there is a swelling." Wu Kun: " 'As if something were hidden in it,' that is where the evil has attached itself."

46 Wang Bing: "The joint is above the knee bay, exactly behind the thigh bone." Ma Shi: " 'One must treat its joint' may refer to the Support (承扶) hole. It belongs to the foot major yang conduit of the bladder. It is located in the hidden line below the

When the knee aches and cannot be bent and streched,
treat in the [patient's] back.[47]

60-322-4
When that which connects [the knee] with the shin [feels] as if broken,
treat the transporter bone-holes on the yang brilliance [conduit].[48]
[If the pain] is as if [a bone] was severed,
treat the brook [holes] on the great yang and minor yin [conduits].[49]

---

buttocks." Zhang Jiebin: "Above the knee bay is a joint. This joint is the bone divide
in the knee bay."

47 Yang Shangshan: "That is, in the back transporters of the foot major yang [con-
duit]." Wang Bing: "That is to say: the Great Shuttle (大杼) hole." Gao Shishi: "The
knee aches and the sinews are not soft and pliable. Hence, the spine can not be bent or
stretched. The disease has emerged in the sinews governed by the major yang. Hence,
one must treat in [the region of] the back and stretching and bending will be as before." 2424/27: "Perhaps these are the Yin Mound Spring (陰陵泉) [holes]."

48 治陽明中俞髎: Some commentators read 中俞 as a compound 'central transporter'. Yang Shangshan: "One treats the central transporter of the foot yang brilliance conduit. That is the Upper Edge of the Great Hollow (巨虛上廉)." Wang Bing:
"When the knee aches and one cannot bend or stretch it and if that [part which] connects [the knee with] the shin has pain, as if broken, then one pierces the central transporter bone-holes of the yang brilliance vessel. That is, one selects the Three Miles (三
里) hole." Gao Shishi: "髎 is 骨穴, 'bone-hole.' 'Central transporter' is a transporter of
the foot yang brilliance [conduit]. Of the five transporter holes, the well and the brook
are in front, the stream and the confluence at at the end. The transporter is in the center. Hence, [Wang Bing and Yang Shangshan] state 'central transporter bone-hole'.
That is to say: the Sunken Valley (陷谷) hole in the region of the middle toe." Zhang
Jiebin: "Wang Bing interpretes [this location] as the Three Miles (三里) [holes]. I say
[the text] refers to the transporter holes of the yang brilliance [conduit]. These should
be the Sunken Valley (陷谷) [holes]." 2424/27: "These are the Three Miles [holes]."
On the other hand, Wu Kun: " 'Transporter bone-holes' refers to the six transporter
holes of well, brook, transporter, plain, stream, and confluence. One selects the one
which is appropriate."

49 Wang Bing: "When there is pain and when the knee [feels] as if it was cracked
(膝如別離), one treats the brook [holes] of the foot major yang and minor yin [con-
duits]. The brook [hole] of the foot major yang is the Valley Passage (通谷) [hole]; the
brook [hole] of the foot minor yin is the Blazing Valley (然谷) [hole]." Zhang Jiebin:
"If one searches for yet another therapy pattern, then the Valley Passage brook hole
of the foot major yang [conduit] and the Blazing Valley brook hole of the foot minor
yin [conduit] may both serve to treat the afore[mentioned] condition." Tanba: "From
the meaning of the text, Zhang Jiebin is correct." 2424/27: "This refers to the Valley
Passage and Blazing Valley [holes]; both may be pierced for bloodletting."

In case [someone suffers of] *yin-luo* and soreness in the shins and cannot stand
up for long,
treat the network [vessel][50] of the minor yang [conduit].[51]
{It is located five inches above on the outside.}[52]

60-323-1
<Above the assistant bone, below the transverse bone, this is the 'bolt bone.'[53]
That which is on both sides of the hip bone is called 'trigger.'
The knee divide is the 'lower leg bone joint.'
The bone on both sides of the knee is the connection with the lower leg bone.
Below the lower leg bone is the 'assistant [bone].'
Above the assistant [bone] is the 'knee bay.'
Above the knee bay is the 'joint.'
The transverse bone of the head is the 'pillow [bone].'>

60-323-4
<As for the 57 water transporters:
There are five lines above the sacrum, [each] line has five [holes].
There are two lines above the crouching rabbit, [each] line has five [holes].
There is one line each to the left and to the right. [Each] line has five [holes].
There is one line above each ankle. [Each] line has six holes. >

There are marrow hollows. They are located three *fen* behind the brain.
{They are located below the pointed bone at the [lower] borderline of the
skull.}[54]
One is located below the base of the gums.

---

50 Lin Yi et al.: "維, 'rope', is an error for 絡, 'network [vessel].'" We have followed
this suggestion, and have replaced 維 with 絡.

51 Wang Bing: "淫濼 is to say: [the knee feels] sore and painful and has no strength."
Zhang Jiebin: "淫濼 is involuntary emissions of semen." (In commenting on *Ling shu*
24, 風痺淫濼, Zhang Jiebin states: 淫濼 is 'to intrude deeper day by day.') Gao Shishi:
"淫 is 极, 'extreme;' 濼 is 寒, 'cold;' 維 is 絡, 'network [vessel].' 淫濼胻痠 is 'extreme
cold and cutting pain in the shinbone.'" Cheng Shide et al.: "Zhang Jiebin's comment
on *Ling shu* 24 appears to be correct."

52 2424/27: "These should be the Bright Light (明光) [holes]. Other editions identify them as Yang Assistance (陽輔) [holes]. The two are located one inch apart." The
Tai su has 在外踝上五寸, "five inches above the outer ankle." This makes more sense
than the current version of the *Su wen*.

53 Cheng Shide et al.: "楗 is 股骨, 'thighbone.'"

54 Wang Bing: "That is to say, the Wind Palace (風府) [hole]. It penetrates right
into the brain."

One is in the center behind the nape, below the covered bone.[55]
One is the upper hollow of the spinal bones
{It is located above the Wind Palace.[56] The lower hollow of the spinal bones is the hollow below the sacrum bone.}[57]

There are several marrow hollows in the face, located on both sides of the nose.[58]
There are also bone hollows located below the mouth exactly [on the level of] the two shoulders.[59]
There are two shoulderblade bone hollows, located at the yang (i.e., outer side) of the center of the shoulderblade.[60]

60-324-1
There is a forearm bone hollow, located at the yang [side] of the arm.
{In a distance of four inches from the [wrist] ankle in the hollow between the two bones.}[61]

There is the upper hollow of the thigh bone, located at the yang [side] of the thigh.
{It comes out four inches above the knee.}[62]

---

55 Wang Bing: "That is to say, the Mute's Gate (瘖門) hole." Zhang Jiebin: "復 is 伏, 'hidden.'" Mori: "復 is 枕骨, 'pillow bone' (i.e., the occipital bone). The pillow bone is located below the skull. They truly repeat each other. Hence, it is called 'repetitive bone.'"

56 Wang Bing: "'Above' is to say, the Brain's Door (腦戶) hole."

57 Wang Bing: "It does not respond to therapy. Hence, the classic omits its name."

58 Wang Bing: "That is to say, the Cheek Bone-Hole (顴髎) hole and others. The classic does not list these unimportant locations one by one."

59 Wang Bing: "That is to say: the Great Facing (大迎) holes." Ma Shi, Zhang Jiebin, Wu Kun agree. Zhang Zhicong: „That is to say: of the bone hollows at numerous locations in the face, some are located below the mouth and communicate with the shoulder bones."

60 Wang Bing: "Near the Shoulder Bone (肩髃) [hole]. The classics have no name [for this hole]."

61 Wang Bing: "One individually standardized body inch above the Branch Ditch (支溝) [hole]. It is called Connect Between (通間) [hole]."

62 Wang Bing: "Above the Yin Market (陰市) [hole] and below the Crouching Rabbit (伏兔) [hole]."

There is a shin bone hollow, located at the upper end of the assistant bone.[63]
There is a bone hollow of the thigh borderline, located in the [pubic] hair
below the moving [vessel].[64]

60-324-4
There are the sacrum bone hollows, located behind the thigh bone.
{In a distance of four inches.}[65]

<The flat bones have structures [enabling a] seeping in; [they serve to] collect.[66]
They do not have marrow cavities.>
{change to: the marrow has no hollows.}[67]

60-324-7
The law of cauterizing cold and heat:

---

63 Wang Bing: "That is to say: the Calf's Nose (犢鼻) hole. It is located below the knee
cap and above the shinbone."

64 Wang Bing: "The classics lack the name [of this hole]." The *Tai su* has 動脈下,
"below the moving vessel."

65 Wang Bing: "These are the eight bone-holes at the sacrum."

66 The *Tai su* does not have the character 湊.

67 Wang Bing: "The 'flat bones' are the flat bones in the region of the sacrum. There
are line structures on these bones where [the marrow] seeps in and collects in them.
There are no additional cavities for the marrow. 易 is 亦, 'also.' When the bones have
cavities, the marrow has cavities [where it is stored]; when the bones have no cavities,
the marrow has no cavities either." Zhang Jiebin: " 'Flat bones' is to distinguish [these
bones] from the round bones. All round bones have marrow in them. Where there
is marrow, there are also cavities for the marrow. In the cases of the flat bones, they
have only structures where [blood] can seep into them through blood vessels, and they
have no marrow. Hence in all flat bones the marrow has been replaced by the [blood]
seeping in, so that these bones have no marrow, and also no hollows. These are all the
bones of the type of the lower ribs." Gao Shishi: "扁骨 are the bones of the ribs situated where chest and spine meet. "易 is 交易, 'to exchange.' The 'flat bones' have line
'structures' where a tranquil 'seeping' occurs. They 'collect' in chest and spine. Inside
they 'do not have marrow hollows.' This makes it clear: 滲理湊 is the exchange of the
marrow. 無髓孔 is: there are no hollows at the two ends [of the bones]." Zhang Qi:
"The four characters 易髓無空 are a later insertion." 2270/38: "The 'flat bones' are the
lower ribs. The three characters 無髓孔 may be a comment written by a later person in
the margins that was erroneously inserted into the proper text. They should be deleted.
If not, they repeat the meaning of the subsequent phrase. 易髓無空 should be 易無
髓空. 易 is to be read as 平易, 'flat.'" We read 易髓無空 as an editorial note that was
erroneously not deleted.

First cauterize the great hammer in the nape.[68]
Base the number of cauterizations applied on the age [of the patient].
Next cauterize the peg bone.[69]
Base the number of cauterizations applied on the age [of the patient].
Look for depressions at the locations of the transporters on the back and cauterize there.[70]
Raise the arm and cauterize the depression on the shoulder.[71]
Cauterize between the two free ribs.[72]
Cauterize the tip of the severed bone above the outer ankle.[73]
Cauterize between the small toe and the next toe.[74]
Cauterize the vessel in the depression below the calf.[75]
Cauterize behind the outer ankle.[76]
Cauterize the location above the broken basin bone which if squeezed feels hard and generates pain as if it were a sinew.
Cauterize in the depression in the center of the breast between the bones.[77]
Cauterize below the bundle bone of the palm.[78]
Cauterize three inches below the navel, the Pass Head.

---

68 2204/40: "The Great Hammer is passed by the yang qi of the entire body; it is a hole where the supervisor vessel and all the yang conduits intersect. It has the function of draining heat and opening the outside, of warming the yang and of dispersing cold."

69 Wang Bing: "The end of the spine is called 橛骨, 'peg bone' (i.e., the coccyx)."

70 Zhang Jiebin: "The transporters of the back are all holes of the foot major yang conduit. At locations where there is a depression, the qi of the conduit is insufficient. Hence, one must cauterize there."

71 Wang Bing: "This is the Shoulder Bone (肩髃) hole." Gao Shishi: "The transporters of the five depots and six palaces are all located on the back. Hence, if upon inspection one notices that there are depressions at the locations of these transporters, one cauterizes them on the left and right. The method of searching for these [depressions] is such that one lifts the arms and the shoulders and cauterizes the depressed locations [that appear] on the back."

72 Wang Bing: "This is the Capital Gate (京門) hole; a levy hole of the kidneys."

73 Wang Bing: "This is the Yang Assistance (陽輔) hole."

74 Wang Bing: "This is the Pinched Ravine (俠溪) hole."

75 Wang Bing: "This is the Sinew Support (承筋) hole."

76 Wang Bing: "This is the Kunlun Mountains (崑崙) hole."

77 Wang Bing: "This is the Celestial Chimney (天突) hole."

78 Wang Bing: "This is the Yang Pool (陽池) hole."

Cauterize the moving vessel at the [pubic] hairline.[79]
Cauterize in the parting three inches below the knee.[80]
Cauterize the moving vessels of the foot yang brilliance [vessel] on the instep.[81]
Apply one cauterization on the peak of the skull.[82]

60-326-1
At the location where one was bitten by a dog,
apply three cauterizations.[83]
{For it is in accordance with the laws [to treat] diseases resulting from harm
caused by dogs that one applies the cauterization.[84] Altogether 29 locations
must be cauterized}.[85]

In the case of harm caused by food, cauterize it. If [the disease] does not come
to an end, it is essential to look for those conduits excessively [filled] with yang
[qi].
Pierce the respective transporters several times and give [the patient] drugs.[86]

---

79 Wang Bing: "This is the Qi Thoroughfare (氣街) hole."

80 Wang Bing: "This is the Three Miles (三里) hole."

81 Wang Bing: "This is the Surging Yang (衝陽) hole." See also 1682/43 for a discussion of the notion of "instep," and for a confirmation of Wang Bing's interpretation.

82 Wang Bing: "This is the Hundred Convergences (百會) hole." See also 1616/484 for a confirmation.

83 692/40: "Duan Yucai 段玉裁 (in his *SWJZZ*), in a comment on the *Shuo wen* 說文 explanation of 灼 as 灸, states: 'The medical literature calls the cauterization of the body with moxa 壯.'

84 Wang Bing: "When one was harmed by a dog and develops [alternating fits of] cold and heat, one must cauterize the [patient] in accordance with the laws applied in cases of harm caused by dogs; one applies three cauterizations." Zhang Jiebin: "Harm caused by a dog lets one [develop alternating fits of] cold and heat. Hence, this law of cauterization exists." 1110/372: "The level of this therapeutic method is comparable to that of the [Ma Wang Dui manuscript] 'Prescriptions against 52 Ailments' (*Wu shi er bing fang* 五十二病方)."

85 The *Tai su* has "27 locations."

86 Ma Shi: "When someone was harmed by food and develops [alternating fits of] cold and heat, one cauterizes him. When one cauterizes him and [the alternating fits of] cold and heat do not come to an end, one must look for all yang conduits that have a disease and pierce their transporters several times and one [must] apply drugs to regulate this. As a result, the [fits of] cold and heat will vanish." Li Jinyong: "*Su wen* 2 has 夫病已成而後藥之 with 藥之 in the sense of 治之. Hence, in *Su wen* 60 one should read 數刺其俞而治之, 'treat it by frequently piercing the respective transport-

ers.'" Zhang Zhicong: "When cauterization has not ended [the disease, this is a sign that] the qi of yin poison abounds. Hence, one must look for the locations where the yin conduits pass through the yang and drain them by frequently piercing the respective transporters there. This way the poison of the yin depots is cut off from [flowing into] the yang and if, in addition, one [has the patient] consume drugs dissolving the poison to treat the yin, this is a complete pattern for treating scrofula and [alternating fits of] cold and heat." Hu Tianxiong: "The character 'yang' has been interpreted by all authors differently. Some have interpreted it as 'yang conduits,' some as 'yang heat' (in the sense of: "one must search where the conduits have excessive yang heat"), others have interpreted it as 'yang abundance.' Su wen 61 states: 'The so-called conduits abounding [with contents], these are the yang vessels.' Hence, 'yang' has the meaning of 盛, 'abounding [with contents]' here."

Chapter 61
Discourse on Holes [to treat] Water and Heat.

61-326-5
Huang Di asked:
"The minor yin, how is it that it rules the kidneys;
The kidneys, how is it that they rule the water?"

Qi Bo responded:
"The kidneys are the extreme yin.
Extreme yin is abundant water.
The lung is the major yin.
Minor yin is a winter vessel.[1]
Hence, its basis is in the kidneys,
its end is in the lung.[2]
Both accumulate water."[3]

---

1 Hu Tianxiong: "The *Tai su* has the four characters 腎者少陰 (instead of 肺者太陰). In the preceding paragraph, [Huang] Di asks two questions. First, 'how is it that the minor yin rules the kidneys?' and second, 'how is it that the kidneys rule the water?' In the preceding passage, Qi Bo has already answered the question 'how is it that the kidneys rule the water?' Hence, the subsequent passage should respond to the question 'how is it that the minor yin rules the kidneys?' The [*Tai su*] phrasing 'the kidneys are minor yin; minor yin is a winter [movement in the] vessels' answers this question. I should also like to point out here the difference between [the statements] 'the kidneys are minor yin' and 'the kidneys are extreme yin.' 'Extreme yin' refers to the climate. The kidneys rule [in] winter; the command of winter is severe cold. Hence, [the text] states: 'the kidneys are extreme yin.' 'Minor yin' refers to the conduit vessels, as is said in *Ling shu* 10: 'The foot minor yin vessel of the kidneys [emerges from ...].' Hence, [the text] states: 'the minor yin is the winter vessel.'" 脈 may stand here for 氣, "qi." See also Hu Tianxiong in note 34.

2 Hu Tianxiong: "The character 其 is a pronoun for 'minor yin vessel.' Hence, the [subsequent] commentary by Wang Bing."

3 Wang Bing: " 'Yin' is to say: cold. The winter months [are marked by] extreme cold; the kidney qi corresponds to them. Hence, [the text] states: 'The kidneys are the extreme yin.' Water governs in winter. Hence, [the text] states: 'Extreme yin is abounding water.' The minor yin vessel of the kidneys rises from the kidneys, penetrates liver and diaphragm and enters the lung. Hence, [the text] states: 'Its origin is in the kidneys; its end is in the lung.' When the kidney qi rises contrary [to its normal flow], water settles in the lung as a result. Hence, [the text] states: 'They all collect water.'" Zhang Jiebin: "The kidneys correspond to the qi of the North; their depot is located in the lower part [of the body]. Hence, they are called 'extreme yin.' The water

61-326-7
[Huang] Di:
"The kidneys, how can they generate diseases by assembling water?"

Qi Bo:
"The kidneys are the gates of the stomach.[4]
Hence, when the gates do not [open] freely,
water assembles and follows its type.[5]

61-326-11
Above and below it spills into the skin;

---

governs in winter and the kidneys rule it. Hence, [the text] says 'abound with water.'"
For a detailed discussion of 其本在腎, 其末在肺 see also 94/51.

4 Zhang Jiebin: "The 關 ('gate') is the place where the door leafs must meet. Hence, it
controls opening and closing, leaving and entering. The kidneys rule the lower burner;
their openings are the two yin [openings]. Water and grains enter the stomach. The
clear [parts] leave through the frontal yin [opening]; the turbid [parts] leave through
the yin [opening] in the back. When the kidney qi undergoes transformation, then the
two yin [openings] are passable. When the kidney qi does not undergo transformation, then the two yin [openings] close. .. Hence, [the text] states: the kidneys are the
gate of the stomach." Hu Tianxiong: "The *Tai su* has 關閉, 'the gate is closed,' instead
of 關. Yang Shangshan commented: 'The stomach rules water and grain. When the
stomach qi is shut in and cannot move freely, the kidneys accumulate water.' That is,
Yang Shangshan considers the stomach as the gate of the kidneys, while Wang Bing
considers the kidneys as the gate of the stomach. One should follow Wang Bing's
comment."

5 Wang Bing: "The 關 is that by which one controls leaving and entering. The kidneys rule the lower burner. The bladder is its palace. It controls the [kidneys'] separate
outflow through the gate openings, [i.e.,] the two yin [openings.]. Hence, when the
kidney qi undergoes transformation, then the two yin [openings] are passable; when
the two yin [openings] are closed, then the stomach fills up to fullness. Hence, [the
text] states: the kidneys are the gate of the stomach. When the gate is closed, then
water collects. When water collects, then the qi stagnates. When the qi stagnates,
then water is generated. When water is generated, then the qi overflows. Qi and water
are of the same type (同類). Hence, [the text] states: 'When the gate is closed so that
there is no free flow, the water accumulates and follows its type.'" Hu Tianxiong: "The
Tai su has 關閉不利, 'the gate is closed, no free flow,' (instead of 關門不利). If one
examines Wang Bing's comment stating 關閉則水積 and also his comments in *Su
wen* 23, it is obvious that the original text had 關閉不利. Lin Yi et al. has no editorial
comment on this; hence, this is a copy error from after the Song." *Gu dian yi zhu xuan
bianxiezu* /14: " 'Follows its type,' the kidneys are the water depot; water returns to the
water depot. Hence, [the text] states 'follows its type.'"

hence, [this] leads to *fu*-swelling."[6]
{As for '*fu*-swelling,' that is a disease resulting from the assembling of water.}

61-326-12
[Huang] Di:
"Is all water generated by the kidneys?"

Qi Bo:
"The kidneys constitute a female depot.[7]
When the qi of the earth rises, it associates with the kidneys and generates water fluid.
Hence, it is called 'extreme yin.'

61-327-1
When one does something with resolve and taxes oneself to the extreme, then sweat leaves from the kidneys.
When sweat leaves the kidneys and encounters wind, internally it cannot enter the depots and palaces and

---

6 Wang Bing: "'Above' is to say: the lung; 'below' is to say: the kidneys. Both the lung and the kidneys overflow. Hence, water accumulates in the abdomen and generates disease." Yang Shangshan: "胕 has the same meaning as 腐, 'rotten flesh.'" Zhang Jiebin: "Surface swelling of muscles and skin is called 胕. The spleen rules the muscles and the flesh; it is [associated with] the foot major yin [conduit]. When it is attacked by cold and water, contrary [to what is normal] it accumulates water and generates a disease." Zhang Zhicong: "胕腫 is 脹, 'swelling.' The skin is linked to the lung. When water has accumulated below, it will contrary [to its normal direction] overflow and rise. Hence, it causes swelling in the skin. Hence, it is because of water accumulation that this disease emerges." Gao Shishi: "胕腫 is: skin and muscles are swollen to fullness. The water qi does not move." Wu Kun: "浮腫, 'superficial swelling,' is called 胕." *NJCD* and *GHYZD* agree. *GHYZD*: The *Shan hai jing* 山海經, Xi shan jing 西山經, has 浴之已疥, 又可已胕, "to use it for washing cures scabies and it is able to cure surface swelling, too." Cheng Shide et al.: "胕 is 膚, 'skin.'" The *Zhan guo ce* 戰國策, Chu ce 楚策, has 尾湛胕漬, "the tail is soaked; the skin is drenched." 1798/36: "The use of 胕腫 in the *Nei jing* refers to 浮腫, 'superficial swelling,' or 膚腫, '*fu*-swelling,' but never to 足腫, 'swollen feet.'" Zhang Yizhi et al.: "胕 is 膚, 'skin.'" For a detailed discussion, see there. See also 1682/42. The meaning of 胕 is unclear. As can be seen from the commentaries quoted above and elsewhere, the following readings are offered in Chinese dictionaries: (1) 腐, "to rot". (2) 浮, "superficial", "floating", "near the surface". (3) 跗, "instep". (4) 附, "attached". (5) 膚, "skin". Wherever no definite clue is available to favor any of these readings, we have decided to simply transliterate the character as *fu*[-type swelling].

7 Wang Bing: "牝 is 'yin.' Also, [the kidneys] rule a yin position. Hence, they are called 'female depot.'"

externally it cannot transgress beyond the skin.
It settles in the dark palaces and[8]
moves inside the skin.
Its transmission leads to *fu*-swelling.
This is based in the kidneys.
The name is wind water."[9]
{As for the so-called 'dark palace,' [this term refers to] the sweat openings.}[10]

61-327-4
[Huang] Di:
"The fifty-seven water transporter locations,
what do they rule?"

Qi Bo:
"The fifty-seven kidney transporter holes,[11]
this is where the accumulated yin assembles.

---

8 The *Tai su* has 六府 instead of 玄府. See also below note 10.

9 Wang Bing: " 'To exert and tax onself to the extreme' is to say: forceful sexual inter-course. When sweat leaves [the body] because of taxing exertion, then the dark palaces (i.e., the pores) open. When the sweat leaves [the body] and encounters wind, then the dark palaces close again. When the dark palaces are closed, then the remaining sweat cannot leave, hides internally in the skin and transforms into water. This water has resulted from [an encounter of sweat with] wind. Hence, it is called 'wind water.' "

10 Wang Bing: "The color of sweat fluid is dark. It leaves [the body] through open-ings. Because the sweat accumulates inside of them, one calls them 玄府. 府 is 聚, 'accumulation.' " Zhang Jiebin: "Sweat belongs to the water. The color of water is dark. Hence, the residence of the sweat is called 'dark palace.' [The sweat] leaves via openings. Hence, one speaks of 'sweat openings.' However, sweat results from qi transformation. When it leaves [the body] it is scarcely perceptible. This is another meaning of 玄府." Hu Tianxiong: "The *Tai su* does not have these eight characters. In the preceding text it has 客于六府, 'it settles in the six palaces,' instead of 客于玄府. When sweat leaves [the body] and encounters wind, the sweat fluid cannot enter the [body's] interior and it cannot leave for the outside. All it can do is settle in the dark palaces (i.e., in the pores). It cannot settle in the six palaces, as should be obvious on first glance. Hence, the character 六 in the *Tai su* is a mistake for 玄. These eight characters may be a comment by someone in antiquity that was later erroneously inserted into the main text." Mori: "玄府 refers to something extremely dark and fine, i.e., to something even the eyes cannot perceive. The openings through which the sweat leaves [the body] are extremely fine, no human eye can see them. Hence, they are called 'dark palaces.' " See also 2186/64 for a detailed discussion of the concept of "dark palace."

11 Hu Tianxiong: " 'Kidney transporters' stands for 'water transporters.' "

It is here where the water leaves or enters.[12]

>From the sacrum upwards the five [conduit] lines,
with [each] line having five [holes],
these are the kidney transporters.<[13]

61-327-7
As a fact, water diseases,
below they cause *fu*-swelling in the upper abdomen,
above they cause panting exhalation.[14]

---

12 Zhang Jiebin: "All these fifty-seven holes are locations where the collected yin accumulates and where the water leaves or enters [the body]. The kidneys rule the water. Hence, they are all called 'kidney transporters.'" Gao Shishi: "The fifty-seven kidney transporter holes extend from the sacrum to the feet. They are located in the lower half of the body and they are ruled by the qi of the earth. Hence, [the text] states: this is where the collected yin accumulates. Where the collected yin has accumulated, the water qi moves there too. Hence, it is through them that the water leaves or enters [the body]."

13 Wang Bing: "Altogether there are five lines of transporters on the back. The one exactly in the center is where the qi of the supervisor vessel is effused. The next four lines, [two] on both sides, this is [where] the qi of the foot major yang vessel [is effused]." Zhang Jiebin: "As for 'each line has five [holes],' the five holes of the central line are the Long Strong (長強), Lumbar Transporter (腰俞), Gate of Life (命門), Suspended Pivot (懸樞), and Spinal Center (脊中) [holes]. Each of the adjacent two lines has five holes; these are the White Ring Transporter (白環俞), Transporter Inside the Central Spine (中膂内俞), Bladder Transporter (膀胱俞), Small Intestine Transporter (小腸俞), and Large Intestine Transporter (大腸俞). Each of the further two adjacent lines has five holes; these are the Sequence End (袟邊), Bladder *Huang* (胞肓), Will Chamber (志室), *Huang* Gate (肓門), and Stomach Granary (胃倉). Altogether, these five lines have 25 holes. They are all located in the [region of the] lower burner and they rule the water. Hence, they are all called 'kidney transporters.'" Hu Tianxiong: "The *Tai su* has the five characters 此皆腎輸也, 'all these are kidney transporters.' Yang Shangshan commented: 'Because they are located close to the kidneys and also because they are situated in the kidney region and are reached by the kidney qi, hence, they are all called kidney transporters.' However, the fifty-seven kidney transporters listed above are by no means all located in the kidney region, nevertheless they are called 'kidney transporters.' Yang Shangshan's comment is wrong. The ten characters beginning with 尻上 up to here may be an erroneous insertion. They should be moved down to follow the passage 水氣之所留也 and to precede (the passage beginning with) 伏菟."

14 Wang Bing: "When water resides in the kidneys below, then there is a *fu*-swelling in [the region from] the abdomen to the feet. When above it enters the lung, then pant-breathing, hasty and tense, as well as strong exhalations result."

If [the patient] cannot lie down,
tip and root both have the disease.[15]

As a fact,
the lung causes panting exhalation and
the kidneys cause water swelling.[16]
The lung causes a [qi movement] contrary [to its normal course and
the patient] cannot lie down.[17]

61-327-9
[Lung and kidneys] are distinguished in [what] they transport.
For both of them [applies] that what they receive[18]
is that what is being retained of water and of qi.[19]

<Above the crouching rabbit the two lines on each side,
with [each] line having five [holes],
these are the streets [of the qi] of the kidneys.[20]

---

15 Wang Bing: "As for 'tip and root,' the lung is the tip; the kidneys are the root. [The situation being] as [described] here, lung and kidneys both have a disease because of water."

16 Wang Bing: "The lung causes panting exhalation, qi moving contrary [to its normal course] and inability to sleep because it rules the breathing. The kidneys cause water swelling because they rule the water."

17 Wang Bing: "The lung causes panting exhalation, qi moving contrary [to its normal course], and inability to sleep because it rules breathing. The kidneys cause water swelling because they rule the water."

18 The *Tai su* has 分之相輸受者. Yang Shangshan: "Because the kidneys rule the water and the lung rules the qi, hence, [the text] states 'divides them.' The two yin accumulate together, hence, [the text] states: 'they transport and receive [water and qi] to/from each other.' 相輸受 is: water and qi are retained and stagnate together." Hu Tianxiong: "According to the *Tai su*, this passage 分為相輸 should be linked to the three characters 俱受者 below. Yang Shangshan's comment is very appropriate. Because the lung moves the qi it controls to the kidneys and because the kidneys move the water they control to the lung, hence, 'the parts transport (water and qi) to each other.'" For a detailed discussion of 水氣 as "water qi," see 59/10.

19 Ma Shi: "The two conduits form separate parts which originally transport [qi] to each other and correspond to each other. When they both receive this disease, it is because water qi stagnates [in them]."

20 Wang Bing: "The regular transporters in the abdominal region [are arranged in] altogether five lines. The two lines on both sides adjacent to the navel, this is where the qi of the foot minor yin vessels of the kidney depot and of the thoroughfare vessel effuses. The next two on both sides are [lines] where the qi of the foot yang brilliance

{This is where the three yin [conduits] intersect in the legs.} [21]

From the ankles upwards one [conduit] line each,
with [each] line having six [holes],
these are the downward lines of the kidney vessels.[22]
{They are called great thoroughfares.}>[23]

The altogether fifty-seven holes, they all are [locations] on the yin network [vessels] of the depots, locations where the water settles."[24]

---

vessels of the stomach palace effuses. The holes of these four lines are located above the crouching rabbit (i.e., the anterior thigh)." Tanba: "All authors have identified 伏 兔 as a hole on the foot yang brilliance conduit. That may be wrong. This is a [protuberance of] flesh rising above the knee, shaped like a rabbit. Hence, the name."

21 Zhang Jiebin: "The three yin include the three yin [conduits] of the liver, the spleen, and the kidneys." This commentary might have been displaced from the following period, because in fact, these three yin intersect in the lower leg, above the ankle.

22 Wang Bing: "As for 'above each ankle is one line, each line has six [holes],' on the inside of the feet above the ankle are the foot minor yin and yin walker vessels. Together they move upwards along the calves. The foot minor yin vessel has the three holes of Great Thoroughfare (太衝), Recover Flow (復溜), and Yin Valley. The yin walker vessel has the three holes of Shining Sea, Exchanging Messages (交信), and Guest House. The yin walker [vessel] is a branch of the foot minor yin vessel." Zhang Jiebin: "'Above each ankle is one line,' this can only refer to the foot minor yin conduit of the kidneys. The six holes on each line are the Great Goblet, Shining Sea, Recover Flow, Exchanging Messages, Guest House, and Yin Valley." Gao Shishi: "'Above the ankle,' this is the outer ankle of the feet. 'Above each ankle there is one [conduit] line, with each line having six [holes],' is to say: the six holes of Yin Intersection (陰 交), Leaking Valley, Shang Hill, Gentleman's Grandchild, Great White, and Great Metropolis. To the left and to the right, these are twelve holes. The kidney vessel rises from the feet; it can also [be seen as] moving downwards along the lower leg. Hence, [the text] states: 'These are downward lines of the kidney vessel.'"

23 Ma Shi: "The kidney and the thoroughfare vessels move together downwards to the feet. There they unite and abounding [with contents they form a] large [vessel]. Hence, [the text] speaks of a 'great thoroughfare.'" Gao Shishi: "The kidney vessel moves upwards from the feet. It can also move downwards along the lower leg. Hence, [the text] states: 'These are downward lines of the kidney vessel.'"

24 Wu Kun: "'Depot' is the kidney depot. 'Network' is 支絡, 'branch network [vessels].'" Zhang Zhicong: "All these fifty-seven holes are located on yin network [vessels] of the water depots, where the water resides. 'Reside' is to say: it has settled in the network of the vessels; it has not entered the inside of the vessels." Hu Tianxiong: "The *Tai su* has 皆藏陰之終 instead of 皆藏之陰絡. Regardless of which version is concerned, both cannot be interpreted."

61-328-1
[Huang] Di:
"In spring, [it is said,]
take the network vessels in the partings of the flesh.[25]
Why is that?"

Qi Bo:
"In spring, the wood begins to govern.
The qi of the liver begins to stimulate generation.
The liver qi is tense; the wind of this [season] is swift.

The regular [location] of the conduit vessels is in the depth.
Their qi is diminished.
One must not enter the depth.
Hence,
take the network vessels in the partings of the flesh."

61-330-1
[Huang] Di:
"In summer, [it is said,]
take the conduits abounding [with qi] at the interstice [structures].
Why is that?"

Qi Bo:
"In summer, the fire begins to govern.
The qi of the heart begins to stimulate growth.

The vessels are lean and the qi is weak.[26]
The yang qi remains [at its place] and overflows.[27]
The heat steams the interstice [structures];
internally it reaches the conduits.

Hence,
take the conduits abounding [with heat] at the interstice [structures]."

---

25 Zhang Qi: "This [portion of the] text may have been erroneously moved here from *Su wen* 64."

26 Zhang Zhicong: "The South generates heat; heat generates fire; fire generates the heart; and the heart rules the blood vessels. [In summer] the heart qi begins to grow. Hence, the vessels are still lean and the qi is still weak."

27 Lin Yi et al.: "Another edition has 流, 'to flow,' instead of 留." Gao Jiwu/11: "The *Tai su* and the *Jia yi jing* have 流, 'to flow,' instead of 留. 流 is correct."

{When the disease leaves at the moment the skin is opened,[28] the evil has resided in the shallow regions.}

{As for the so-called 'conduits abounding [with heat],' these are the yang vessels.}

61-330-4
[Huang] Di:
"In autumn, [it is said,]
take the conduit transporters.[29]
Why is that?"

Qi Bo:
"In autumn, the metal begins to govern.
The lung is about to gather and kill.[30]

The metal is about to dominate the fire.[31]
The yang qi is at the confluences and
the yin qi begins to dominate.
Dampness qi reaches the body.[32]
The yin qi does not abound yet;
it cannot enter deeply yet.

Hence,
take the transporters to drain the yin evil,

---

28 Wang Bing: "絕 is to say: 絕破 ('to break open'), to allow the disease to leave [the body]." Hu Tianxiong: "絕 is 過, 'to pass through.' When the needle passes through the skin, the disease is healed."

29 Ma Shi: "These are the stream (經) holes and transporter (俞) holes of each conduit."

30 Wang Bing: "The three yin [qi] have risen entirely. Hence, they are about to gradually gather and to kill." Gao Shishi: "收 is 收斂, 'to collect.' 殺 is 肅殺, 'very stern.'" Zhang Zhicong: "Autumn is the official responsible for capital punishment. Its season is [that of] metal; its order is to confine and to return to submission. Hence, the lung qi will confine [things] and the myriad beings will be killed."

31 Wang Bing: "When metal flourishes, the fire is weak. Hence, [the text] states: 'The metal is about to dominate the fire.'" Gao Shishi: "The fire qi of summer vanishes. Hence, the metal is about to dominate the fire."

32 Wang Bing: "Because there is a gradual increase in rain, dampness, fog, and dew. Hence, [the text] states: 'Dampness qi gradually reaches the body.'" Zhang Jiebin: "The yang qi is still at the confluences of all the conduits. The yang qi begins to weaken; and the yin qi begins to dominate. Hence, the qi of cold and dampness reaches the body."

take the confluences to clear [the body] of yang evil."³³
{The yang qi begins to weaken; hence, take it from the confluences.}

61-330-8
[Huang] Di:
"In winter, [it is said,]
take the wells and brooks.
Why is that?"

Qi Bo:
"In winter, the water begins to govern.
The kidneys are about to stimulate closure.
The yang qi is weak and diminished;
the yin qi is firm and abounds.
The great yang hides in the depth and
the yang vessels leave.³⁴

Hence,
take the wells to bring the yin countermovement down,
take the brooks to replenish the yang qi."³⁵

---

33 Zhang Jiebin: "The yin qi is not in the depth yet; it is still in the yang section. Hence, one takes the streams and transporters to drain the yin evil. The yang qi begins to weaken; the evil is about to disappear. Hence, one takes confluence holes to clear [the body] of the yang evil." Gao Shishi: "When the yin qi begins to dominate, then the yin qi does not abound yet. When dampness qi reaches the body, then it cannot enter deeply yet. Hence, one selects the transporters to drain the evil of yin and dampness. 'Transporters' is streams and transporters. .. However, in autumn one may also have diseases resulting from an intrusion of yang evil. If the yang qi is at the confluences, one selects the confluences to clear [the body] of the yang evil. The reason is that in autumn the yang qi begins to weaken. Hence, one must select the confluences too and not only the streams and transporters."

34 Wang Bing: "去 is to say: to move downwards." Hu Tianxiong: "陽脈 is 陽氣, 'yang qi.' In ancient times, 脈 and 氣 were used interchangeably."

35 Zhang Zhicong: "The kidneys are the depot of water; the command of winter is closure and storage. The yang qi has become weak, while the qi of yin and cold is strong and abounds outside. When the major yang qi hides in the depth, the respective yang vessels leave the yang region, too, and turn to the interior. Hence, one must select the wells [for treatment] to down the adversely rising yin qi and one selects the brook [holes] to supplement the yang that lies hidden in the depth. This [approach] corresponds to the command of the season. Now, the well [holes] are [associated with the agent of] wood. Wood is generated by water. Hence, one selects the wells, [i.e.,] the wood, to down the yin qi so as not to let it develop and rise contrary [to its normal flow]. The brooks are [associated with the agent of] fire. Hence, one selects

{Hence, when it is said
'in winter take the wells and brooks,
in spring there will be no stuffy nose and nosebleed,'
then this means just the same.}[36]

61-330-11
[Huang] Di:
"Now, you, Sir, have told [me] of the fifty-nine transporters where heat diseases
are treated;
I have discussed [with you] their significance.
I have not been able yet [to follow] your instructions [on how] to distinguish
their locations.
I should like to hear where they are located and
then hear about their significance."

Qi Bo:
"The five [conduit] lines on top of the head,
with five [holes] per line,
they serve to disperse heat [qi] moving contrary [to its regular course] in all the
yang [conduits].

61-330-13
Great Shuttle, Breast Transporter, Broken Basin, and Back Transporter,
these eight [holes] serve to drain heat from inside the chest.[37]
Qi Street, Three Miles, Upper Edge and Lower Edge of the Great Hollow,

---

the brook holes to supplement the yang qi, thereby assisting that which is hidden and
confined."

36 Zhang Zhicong: "Now, the command of winter is closure and storage to supply
the qi of generation in spring. Hence, if in winter one selects the wells and the brooks
[for treatment], one assists in storing the major yang and the minor yin qi. When in
spring the yang qi moves to the outside, the outer guard [qi] is firm and does not allow
wind evil to harm the skin, the interstice structures, and the network vessels. Hence,
there is no stuffy nose and nosebleed in spring." Cheng Shide et al.: "In autumn one
selects the stream holes and the transporter holes; in winter one selects the well holes
and the brook holes. The decision [where to treat] is made on the basis of man's correspondence with the four seasons in that there are differences in the rule of the qi of
the five depots and in the abundance and weakness of the qi of yin and yang." For a
detailed discussion of "if in winter one selects the wells and brooks, in spring there will
be no stuffy nose and nosebleed," see 2790/84.

37 Zhang Jiebin: "These eight holes are all located in front and in the back of the
chest. Hence, one can drain heat in the chest [through them]."

these eight [holes] serve to drain heat from inside the stomach.[38]
Cloud Gate, Shoulder Bone, Bend Middle, and Marrow Hollow,
these eight [holes] serve to drain heat from the four limbs.[39]
Five transporters of the five depots on [each] side [of the spine],[40]
these ten [holes] serve to drain heat from the five depots.
All these fifty-nine holes are [holes] on the left and on the right [side for treating] heat."

61-332-3
[Huang] Di:
"When someone was harmed by cold and
in [the course of its] transmission [the disease changes to] heat,
why is that?"

Qi Bo:
"Now,
when cold abounds, then it generates heat."

---

38 Zhang Jiebin: "These eight [holes] are all holes of the foot yang brilliance conduits. Hence, one can drain heat in the stomach [through them]."

39 Zhang Jiebin: "Cloud Gate (雲門), and Shoulder Bone (髃骨) form links with the hands; Bend Middle (委中) and Marrow Hollow (髓空) form links with the feet. Hence, these eight holes can [serve to] drain heat from the four limbs."

40 Wang Bing: " 'Five transporters on [each] side' is to say: the five holes *Po*-Soul Door (魄户), Spirit Hall (神堂), *Hun*-Soul Gate (魂門), Thought Dwelling (意舍), and Will Chamber (志室). They are located on both sides of the spine in a distance of three individually standardized body inches. They coincide with locations where the qi of the foot major yang vessels is effused."

Chapter 62
Discourse on Regulating the Conduits

62-334-2
Huang Di asked:
"I have heard of a statement in the *Laws of Piercing*:
'A surplus, drain it;
An insufficiency, supplement it.'
What is that to say: 'surplus'?
What is that to say: 'insufficiency'?"

Qi Bo responded:
"There are five [states of] surplus and
there are also five [states of] insufficiency.
What is it that [you, Huang] Di, would like to ask?"

62-334-4
[Huang] Di:
"I should like to hear all about it."

Qi Bo:
"The spirit [may] be present in surplus and it [may] be insufficient.
The qi [may] be present in surplus and it [may] be insufficient.
The blood [may] be present in surplus and it [may] be insufficient.
The physical appearance [may] be present in surplus and it [may] be insufficient.
The will [may] be present in surplus and it [may] be insufficient.
In all these ten [states] the qi differs."[1]

62-334-6
[Huang] Di:
"Man has the essence qi and the body liquids,
the four limbs and the nine orifices,

---

1 Wang Bing: "The spirit is associated with the heart; the qi is associated with the lung; the blood is associated with the liver; the physical appearance is associated with the spleen; and the will is associated with the kidneys. Since each of them has its [own] affiliation, [their qi states] differ." Gao Shishi: "The spirit, the qi, the blood, the physical appearance, and the will, each may be in [a state of] surplus, each may be in [a state of] insufficiency. The [states of] qi differ in all these [states of] surplus and insufficiency, hence, this is discussed in detail in the text below."

the five depots and the 16 sections,[2]
as well as the 365 joints;[3]
they [may] develop the one hundred diseases.

When the one hundred diseases develop,
there is always a depletion or a repletion [involved].

Now,
you, Sir, tell me there are [only] five [states of] surplus and
there are also five [states of] insufficiency.
How are they generated?"[4]

62-334-9
Qi Bo:
"All [these states] are generated by the five depots.[5]

Now,
the heart stores the spirit,
the lung stores the qi,
the liver stores the blood,
the spleen stores the flesh,
the kidneys store the will,
and this completes the physical appearance.[6]

---

2 Yang Shangshan: "The nine orifices and the five depots add up to 14. The four
limbs together are the hands and feet. Hence, there are 16 sections." Wang Bing: "As
for the '16 sections,' the hands and feet are two, the nine orifices are nine and the five
depots are five. Together this adds up to 16 regions." Gao Shishi: "The 16 sections of
the physical body include the two elbows, the two arms, the two popliteal fossae, the
two thighs, the body's front and back, left and right, as well as the head's front and
back, left and right." Zhang Zhicong: "The 16 sections are the conduit vessels of the
16 regions. There are twelve conduit vessels of the hands and feet, two walker vessels,
one supervisor vessel, and one controlling vessel, altogether 16 sections." Tanba: "Gao
Shishi's remarks are superior to the ancient commentaries."

3 Wang Bing: " '365 joints' does not refer to the bone joints; these are the [365] locations where the spirit qi leaves and enters [the body]."

4 Wang Bing: "That is to say, the number of diseases the body may have is large, but
the number of diseases mentioned [by Qi Bo] is small. How is this to be explained?"

5 Wang Bing: "That is, by the five spirit depots."

6 Wang Bing: "That is to say: Why are all the diseases generated by the five depots?
Because they store the spirits and form the physical appearance." Gao Shishi: "The
generation of the one hundred diseases is always tied to the five depots. Hence, all are

{The mind penetrates [everything], in the interior it links up with bones and marrow, thereby completing the physical appearance of the body. >The five depots.<}⁷

The paths of the five depots,
they all emerge from the conduit tunnels with
[the latter] serving to pass the blood and the qi.
When blood and qi are not in harmony,
then the one hundred diseases cause change and transformation.
Hence, guard the conduit tunnels."⁸

---

generated by the five depots.' 藏 (*zang*), 'depot,' is 藏 (*cang*), 'to store.' Now, the heart stores the spirit; hence, when the spirit has a surplus or is insufficient, this is ruled by the heart. The lung stores the qi; hence, when the qi has a surplus or is insufficient, this is ruled by the lung. .. When spirit, qi, blood, flesh, and will are collected, this constitutes the physical appearance." Zhang Qi: "The four characters 而此成形 are a later insertion." Cheng Shide et al.: "The *Jia yi jing* does not have these four characters; hence, one can follow the comment by Zhang Qi." Yu Chang: "The sequence of the two characters 此成 should be reversed. 此 refers to the five depots: 成此形 is: 'complete the physical appearance of the five depots.'"

7 Wang Bing: "志意 is an encompassing reference to the five spirits. 'Bone and marrow' is an encompassing reference to the completion and transformation of outside and inside. That is to say, when all the five spirits prosper, when the transformation of the bones and the marrow is complete, then the physical appearance of the body is established and the five depots exist in mutual interdependence." Lin Yi et al.: "The *Jia yi jing* does not have the two characters 五藏." Gao Shishi: "The two characters 五藏 may be a later insertion. I presume the following two characters 五藏 may have been erroneously repeated here. The kidneys store the will and they also store the essence. The spleen stores the sentiments and it also stores the flesh. When will and sentiments pass freely, then they link the bones and the marrow of the kidneys and of the essence and they form the body's physical appearance of the spleen and of the flesh. This makes it clear that when the will passes freely, then the marrow is freely passable; and when the sentiments pass freely, then the physical appearance is freely passable. This argument may be extended to the heart: when the spirit passes freely, then the vessels are freely passable. To extend it to the lung: when the qi passes freely, then the *po*-soul passes freely, [too]. To extend it to the liver, when the blood passes freely, then the *hun*-soul passes freely, [too]. These words are not spelled out [in the text], but their meaning is completely present."

8 Wang Bing: "隧 is 潜道, 'hidden passageways.' The conduit vessels pass hidden [through the body] and cannot be seen. Hence, one calls them conduit-tunnels. As for the blood and the qi, they constitute the spirit of man. When they are invaded by an evil, then the blood and the qi are not in order. When the blood and the qi are not in order, there will be changes and transformations and the one hundred diseases emerge as a result. Now, it is in the conduit vessels that death or survival are determined, where the one hundred diseases are located and where a depletion or repletion

62-335-4
[Huang] Di:
"When the spirit has [assumed a state of] surplus or insufficiency,
how is that?"

Qi Bo:
"When the spirit has [assumed a state of] surplus,
then one laughs without end;
when it has [assumed a state of] insufficiency,
then one is sad.[9]

When blood and qi have not collected yet,
the five depots are in peace and stable.[10]
[But] the evil has settled in the physical appearance.
[A feeling of] shivering emerges from the finest body hair."

---

is regulated. Hence, one guards the conduit tunnels." Lin Yi et al.: "The *Jia yi jing* has 經渠, 'conduit gutter.' The meaning is the same." 2566/13: "The meaning of the character 守 is 遵循, 'to adhere to,' 掌握, 'to control,' 'to master.' 經隧 is 通道, 'throughway.' Zhang Jiebin states: 'The conduit vessels move hidden in the depth; hence, they are called 'conduit tunnels.' 守經隧, therefore, is: to recognize and treat diseases, one must master the knowledge on the relevant conduit vessels."

9 Wang Bing: "This is the depot of the heart. The *Zhen jing* 鍼經 (i.e., the *Ling shu*) states: 'The heart stores the vessels; the vessels house the spirit. When the heart qi is depleted, then one experiences sadness. When it is replete, then one laughs without end.' (See *Lingshu* 8.) Instead of 悲, other editions have 憂, 'anxiety.' That is a mistake." Lin Yi et al.: "The *Jia yi jing*, the *Tai su*, and the Quan Yuanqi edition have 憂, 'anxiety,' instead of 悲. Huang-fu [Mi] stated in his comment: 'When the heart is depleted, then one experiences sorrow. When one experiences sadness, then one is anxious. When the heart is replete, then one laughs, when one laughs, then one is happy."

10 Wang Bing: "并 is to say: 并合, 'to unite;' 'to come together.' It has not united with the evil yet. Hence, [the text] states: 'has not come together yet.'" Zhang Jiebin: "并 is to say: 偏聚, 'unilateral accumulation.' When evil strikes man, [remains in his body] for long and does not disperse, then it unites either with the qi or with the blood. [At this stage] the disease is serious. In the present situation, neither the blood nor the qi have united [with the evil] because the evil has not entered deeply yet. Hence, the five depots are in peace and stable." Gao Shishi: "When the blood or the qi have collected and when they have excited the five depots internally, the resulting disease is severe. When blood or qi have not collected yet and at a time when the five depots are in peace and stable, an evil may have settled in the physical body, when the [feeling of] cold and shivering emerges from the finest hair, this is a slight evil, it has not entered the conduits and network [vessels] yet." *Su wen* 3 has 并乃狂, "union results in craziness." Wang Bing commented: "并 is 盛實, 'abundant and replete.'" See also *Su wen* 23 and 331/3 for the concept of 并.

<It has not entered the conduits and network [vessels] yet. Hence, [this state] is
termed 'slight [disease] of the spirit.'>[11]

62-335-7
[Huang] Di:
"To supplement or drain, how to proceed?"

Qi Bo:
"When the spirit has [assumed a state of] surplus,
then drain blood from the small network [vessels].[12]
When letting blood, do not push deeply.
Do not hit the large conduits.
As a result, the spirit qi will be balanced.[13]

When the spirit [has assumed a state of] insufficiency,
look for the [patient's] depleted network [vessels],

---

11 Wang Bing: "When [the disease] emerges from the finest hair and is still in the
small network [vessels], this is a slight disease of the spirit. Hence, [the text] states
'slight [disease] of the spirit.'" Lin Yi et al.: "The *Jia yi jing* has 悽厥, 'grief recession,'
instead of 洒淅. The *Tai su* has 㴇泝. Yang Shangshan: 㴇 is 'the hair openings.' When
water flows backwards, this is called 泝. That is to say, the evil qi enters the interstice
structures like water flowing reversely into the hair openings." Zhang Jiebin: "When
the [feeling of] cold and shivering emerges from the finest hair and has not reached
the conduits and network [vessels] yet, this is because a slight surface evil is present in
the outside of the vessels. This is a slight disease of the spirit. Hence, [the text] states:
神之微."

12 Ma Shi and others have exchanged the character 血 for 脈, vessel: "Drain the vessels of the small network to let blood." Such a wording appears to be confirmed by the
subsequent comment by Wang Bing.

13 Wang Bing: "The evil enters the small network. Hence, one can drain the vessels of
the respective small network to let their blood. One must not push the needle deeply.
When the needle enters deeply, it harms the flesh. Since the evil resides in the small
network [vessels], one should not let the needle hit the big conduits. Once the blood
has left the network [vessels], the spirit qi will be balanced as a result. 斥 is 推, 'to
push.' The 'small network [vessels]' are the tertiary network [vessels]. 平 is to say: 平
調, 'adjusted.'" Zhang Jiebin: "斥 is 棄除, 'to remove.' The heart rules the blood vessels
and stores the spirit. The spirit itself has no physical appearance. Hence, when the
spirit has [assumed a state of] repletion, all one has to do is to drain the blood from
the small network [vessels]. One must not remove the blood from too great a depth
and hit the conduits there. The spirit will be balanced as a result." Qian Chaochen-
90/137: "斥 is used here in the sense of 推進, 'push forward,' not in the sense of 丟
棄, 'to abandon.'"

press them so that [the qi] arrives and
pierce to free [the flow].

Do not let the [patient's] blood and
do not drain the [patient's] qi.
This way one will make the conduits passable,
and the spirit qi will be balanced."[14]

62-336-2
[Huang] Di:
"To pierce a slight [affection], how to proceed?"[15]

Qi Bo:
"Press and rub [the affected area] continuously and [at the same time]
apply[16] the needle without pushing [into the depth].[17]
[In this way] move the qi to the [place of] insufficiency[18]
and the spirit qi may recover."[19]

62-336-4
[Huang] Di:
"Good!

---

14 Wang Bing: "All that is required is to open the conduit vessels and ensure a harmonious free flow. Press the depleted network vessels to cause its qi to arrive. Because
the spirit is insufficient, do not let blood or drain qi." Ma Shi: "When the spirit is
insufficient, the respective conduit [vessels] must be depleted. 利 is 和, 'harmonize.'"
Hua Shou: " 'Depleted network [vessels] refers to network vessels that have sunk in
because they are depleted."

15 Wang Bing: "Again, [Huang Di raises the issue of affections] that have just arisen
from the finest hair, without entering the conduits and network [vessels] yet."

16 Zhang Zhicong: "着針 is to say: as if one applied bandages and inserted the needle
through only one single layer of cloth. That is, one must pierce extremely shallow; the
needle must not be pushed into the depth.

17 Wu Kun: "無釋 is 無已, 'without end.' 無斥 is 無深, 'do not insert deeply.'"

18 Lin Yi et al.: "The *Jia yi jing* and the *Tai su* have 移氣于足, 'move the qi to the
feet.' They do not have the character 不. Yang Shangshan: 'Apply massage to move the
qi to the heels.'" Zhang Qi: "The character 不 is a later insertion."

19 Wang Bing: "One applies a massage to the location affected by the disease without
letting one's hands go. One applies the needle at the location affected by the disease,
again without pushing it. This way one causes the spirit qi of that person to move

When the qi[20] has [assumed a state of] surplus or insufficiency,
how is that?"

Qi Bo:
"When the qi has [assumed a state of] surplus,
then one pants and coughs, and there is rising qi.
[In a state of] insufficiency, the breathing is free
and one is short of qi.[21]

When blood and qi have not collected yet,
the five depots are in peace and stable.
[But] the skin has a slight disease."
<This is called 'slight outflow of white qi.'>[22]

62-336-6
[Huang] Di:
"To supplement or drain, how to proceed?"

Qi Bo:
"When the qi has [assumed a state of] surplus,
then drain the [patient's] conduit tunnels.
Do not harm the conduits,
do not let the [patient's] blood and
do not drain the [patient's] qi.

---

internally to the needle. By moving the spirit qi of that person one causes (今 interpreted as an error for 令) it to fill up by itself. As a result, slight diseases will leave by
themselves and the spirit qi can recover to normal."

20 Cheng Shide et al.: "The original text does not have the character 氣 in front of
有. The *Tai su* has it. Given the preceding and the subsequent [structure of the] text,
it has been supplemented here." 2317/7 agrees.

21 Wang Bing: "This is the depot of the lung. The lung stores the qi. When the
breathing is not free, then one pants." Zhang Zhicong: "The lung rules the qi and
controls exhalation and inhalation. Hence, in case of surplus one pants and coughs
[because of] adversely rising [qi]. In case of insufficiency, exhalation and inhalation
do not occur freely and one [suffers from] being short of qi (i.e., dyspnoe)." Gao
Jiwu/249: "息利 should be 息不利."

22 Wang Bing: "The lung forms a union with the spleen; its [associated] color is
white. Hence, a slight disease of the skin is called 'slight outflow of white qi.'" Cheng
Shide et al.: " 'White qi' is to say: 'lung qi.'" Gao Shishi: " 'Slight outflow' is equivalent
to 'slight depletion.'"

[In a state of] insufficiency,
supplement the [respective] conduit tunnels, but
do not [allow] qi to leave."[23]

[Huang] Di:
"To pierce a slight [affection], how to proceed?"

62-337-1
Qi Bo:
"Press and rub [the affected area] continuously,
produce a needle, show it [to the patient] and tell him:
'I shall insert it deeply.'
Once one approaches that person [with the needle] he will undergo a change;
his essence qi will hide itself [internally].
The evil qi will disperse in disorder.
It will find no place to rest and
it will flow away through the interstice structures.
The true qi will find together [again]."[24]

---

23 Wang Bing: " 'Qi' is to say 'camp qi.' When the needle draining harms the conduit, then blood leaves and the camp qi flows away. Hence, one should not let blood and drain qi. All one wants is to drain the guard qi. On the other hand, in case of needle supplementation, one should carefully close the transporter hole; one should not even let the guard qi flow away." Yang Shangshan: " 'Conduit tunnels' refers to a branch of the hand major yin [conduit here]; it proceeds to the hand yang brilliance [conduit]. Hence for supplementing and draining one always resorts to such branches of the regular conduits. .. One must not harm the regular conduits."

24 Yang Shangshan: "革 is 改, 'to change.' When someone hears something enjoyable, his body and his heart will be full of delight; when he hears something painful, then his body and his emotions will undergo a change. In the case of joy, the entire body is relaxed; in the case of change, the emotions and the will assume a posture of defense. Once there is this defense, the evil qi will dissolve and hide away." Wang Bing: "This, too, is to say: one applies massage to the location affected by the disease. 革 is 皮, 'skin,' 'hide.' 我將深之適人必革 is to say: [one announces a piercing into] the depth, but pierces only superficially. This forces the respective person to develop fear. Hence, his essence qi hides away in the depth. Because one applies a regulating therapy to the skin and because the essence qi lies hidden in the depth, the evil has no basis to hold on to. It disperses in disorder and finds no place to rest. [Hence] it effuses and flows away through the interstice structures. Once the evil qi has flowed away, the true qi and the skin interstices find together again (相得)." Zhang Jiebin: "適 is 至, 'to reach.' 革 is 變, 'to change.' First one applies massage to make the qi of the skin move. Next one produces a needle, lets the [patient] see it and states: 'I shall insert it deeply.' The aim is that one frightens [the patient] so that his essence qi hides away internally. 適人必革 is to say: when one approaches the respective person with the needle, one

[Huang] Di:
"Good!
When the blood has [assumed a state of] surplus or insufficiency, how is that?"

Qi Bo:
"When the blood has [assumed a state of] surplus,
then one is angry;
[when it has assumed a state of] insufficiency,
then one is in fear.[25]

When blood and qi have not collected yet,
the five depots are in peace and stable.
[But] the tertiary network [vessels] overflow to the outside,
and the conduits have resident blood."[26]

62-337-6
[Huang] Di:
"To supplement or drain, how to proceed?"

Qi Bo:
"When the blood has [assumed a state of] surplus,
then drain the respective conduits abounding [with blood], to let this blood.

[In a state of] insufficiency,
look for those conduits that are depleted and insert the needle.
Let it remain in the vessels for long,

---

changes [the meaning of] what one said before and pierces only superficially." Zhang Zhicong: "出針 is: one produces the [needle] and inserts it superficially. 視之 means: one inspects the depth [of the insertion]."

25 Wang Bing: "This is the depot of the liver. The *Zhen jing* 鍼經 states: 'The liver stores the blood; when the liver qi is depleted, then one is in fear. When it is replete, then one is angry.' (See *Lingshu* 8.)" Lin Yi et al.: "The Quan Yuanqi edition, the *Jia yi jing*, and the *Tai su* all alike have 悲, 'sadness,' instead of 恐."

26 Wang Bing: "When the network [vessels] abound with evil, [the latter] will enter the conduits. Hence, [the text] states: 'When the water of the tertiary network [vessels] overflows, then the conduits have resident blood.'" Cheng Shide et al.: "The *Jia yi jing*, the *Tai su*, as well as the editions compiled by Zhang Jiebin and Wu Kun, all have 外, 'to the outside,' instead of 水." 849/151: "When [the contents of] the tertiary vessels flow away to the outside, then this occurs in one's sputum, through nosebleeding, and through one's stools and urine."

and as soon as [you] see that the vessels become big,[27]
quickly withdraw the needle.
Do not let blood flow out."[28]

62-337-9
[Huang] Di:
"To pierce resident blood, how to proceed?"

Qi Bo:
"Look for the blood network [vessels],
pierce them and let their blood.
Do not allow bad blood to enter the conduits and
generate a disease there."[29]

[Huang] Di:
"Good!
When the physical appearance has [assumed a state of] surplus or insufficiency,
how is that?"

Qi Bo:
"When the physical appearance has [assumed a state of] surplus,
then the abdomen is distended and the *jing* and the urine do not pass freely.[30]

---

27 Lin Yi et al.: "The *Jia yi jing* has 久留血至, 'one lets it remain for long until the blood arrives.' The *Tai su* agrees [with the *Jia yi jing*]." Yu Chang: "The two characters 內針 form a sentence of their own."

28 Wang Bing: "When the vessels are full, then the blood is present in surplus. Hence, one lets it. When the conduit qi is depleted, then the blood is insufficient. Hence, one does not allow the blood to flow away. To let [the needle] remain for long and then quickly withdraw it, is to say: to supplement it." Zhang Jiebin: "The method of supplementing a depletion is such that one lets the needle remain [in the skin] for long and waits for the qi [to arrive]. This is the so-called 'as if one were waiting for a noble person; one does not know whether he comes during daytime or in the evening.' When the needle has remained [in the skin] for long, one just looks whether the respective vessel has become big. This is [the sign that] the qi has arrived. Then one quickly withdraws the needle. If blood were to leave, the depletion would become more serious. Hence, one must not let blood flow away."

29 Wang Bing: "When the network vessels are full of blood, one pierces and squeezes them to let it. This way blood of a bad color will not enter the conduit vessels."

30 For a similar phrase, see *Su wen* 45, 253-2, and note 24. Yang Shangshan: "涇 is 經, i.e., the monthly period of women." Wang Bing: "This is the depot of the spleen. 涇 is 大便, 'stools;' 溲 is 小便, 'urine.'" Wu Kun: "涇 is the normal flow of water." Tanba: "涇溲 is 小溲. The *Ji yun* states: '涇 is 泉, (a spring of water.)' 涇 is 徑, 'a short

[When it has assumed a state of] insufficiency,
then the four limbs do not function.
When blood and qi have not collected yet,
the five depots are in peace and stable.
[But] the muscles and the flesh [let one feel a] wriggling movement."
< This is called 'slight wind.' > [31]

62-338-2
[Huang] Di:
"To supplement or drain, how to proceed?"

Qi Bo:
"When the physical appearance has [assumed a state of] surplus,
then drain its yang conduits.
[In a state of] insufficiency,
supplement its yang network [vessels]." [32]

[Huang] Di:
"To pierce a slight [affection], how to proceed?"

Qi Bo:
"Select the region of the partings of the flesh.
Do not hit the [patient's] conduits and
do not harm the [patient's] network [vessels].

---

cut;' that is to say, a passageway. 溲 is a general reference to stools and urine. Hence, the character 涩 was added to distinguish [the urine here] from the stools." 1142/43: "涩 is 經, as in 經常, 'regularly.' This passage should be read as 'stools and urine are regularly blocked.'" For a detailed discussion of 涩溲, see there and also 1150/42.

31 Wang Bing: "When evil gathers in the partings of the flesh, the guard qi cannot pass through. The yang qi causes internal drumming. Hence, the flesh has [a feeling as if there was] a wriggling movement." Zhang Jiebin: "This is an outside evil of the spleen conduit. The spleen rules the muscles and the flesh. Hence, a slight evil that has not entered deeply yet causes only a wriggling movement in the region of the muscles and the flesh, resembling the slight movement of bugs. The spleen is soil and fears the wind which is wood. The wind controls the movement. Hence, one speaks of 'slight wind.'"

32 Wang Bing: "These are the conduits and network [vessels] of the stomach." Gao Shishi: " 'Yang conduits' refers to the yang brilliance conduits; 'yang network [vessels] refers to the yang brilliance network. When the physical appearance, the flesh, has a surplus, then the soil qi is replete. Hence, one drains the yang brilliance conduit. To drain a conduit is to let [qi] move from inside to the outside. This is the method of how to drain a surplus. When the physical appearance, the flesh, is insufficient, then

[This way,] the guard qi can recover,
while the evil qi will disperse."³³

62-338-5
[Huang] Di:
"Good!
When the will has [assumed a state of] surplus or insufficiency,
how is that?"

Qi Bo:
"When the will has [assumed a state of] surplus,
then the abdomen is distended and there is outflow of [undigested] food.³⁴
[When it has assumed a state of] insufficiency,
then recession results.³⁵
When blood and qi have not collected yet,
the five depots are in peace and stable.
[But] the bone joints have a movement."³⁶

---

the soil qi is depleted. Hence, one supplements the yang brilliance network [vessels].
To supplement network [vessels] is to let [qi] move from outside to the inside. This is
the method of supplementing an insufficiency."

33 Wang Bing: "The guard qi serves to warm the partings of the flesh and to fill
the skin; to fatten the interstice structures and to control their opening and closure.
Hence, if the flesh has a [feeling as if there was a] wriggling movement, one takes
it from the region of the partings of the flesh. To let the evil [flow away], one only
opens the flesh section. Hence, one must not hit the conduits and one must not harm
the network [vessels]. [Once] the guard qi returns to its earlier status, the evil qi
disperses entirely." Cheng Shide et al.: "A comment to the *Li* [*ji*] 禮記 states: 索 is
散, 'disperse.'" Gao Shishi: "The partings of the flesh are located outside the conduits
and inside the network [vessels]. Hence, to pierce it, one must not hit the conduits
internally and one must not harm the network [vessels] externally. 索 is 消, 'to melt;'
'to disperse.'"

34 Zhang Jiebin: "The kidneys store the will; [the will] is the essence of the water.
Water transforms into cold. Hence, when the kidney evil has a surplus, then there is
cold qi in the abdomen and causes abdominal distension as well as outflow of [undi-
gested] food." Zhang Zhicong: "The kidneys are the gate of the stomach. When the
gate does not move freely, then water collects and causes the abdomen to swell and
food to flow away [undigested]."

35 Wang Bing: "This is the depot of the kidneys. 厥 is 逆行上衝, 'to rise moving
contrary [to a regular course] and to rush upwards.'"

36 The *Jia yi jing* has 有傷, 'has been harmed,' instead of 有動. Wang Bing: "The kidneys are united with the bones. Hence, when the bones are attacked by evil, then the
bone joints have a drumming movement, or there is a feeling as if there was something

[Huang] Di:
"To supplement or drain, how to proceed?"

Qi Bo:
"When the will has [assumed a state of] surplus,
then drain the blazing sinews, where they have blood.[37]
[When it has assumed a state of] insufficiency,
then supplement at the Recover Flow [hole]."

62-339-1
[Huang] Di:
"To pierce a situation when [the blood and the qi] have not collected yet, how
to proceed?"

Qi Bo:
"Seize it immediately.
Do not hit the [patient's] conduits.
[This way,] the location of the evil can be depleted at once."[38]

[Huang] Di:
"Good!
I have heard by now of the physical appearances of depletion and repletion,
but I do not know why they come about."

Qi Bo:
"When qi and blood collect,[39] and

---

drumming in the bone joints." Cheng Shide et al.: "動 is 鼓動, 'drumming movement.'
That is, one has a feeling as if there was a drumming movement in the joints."

37 Yang Shangshan: "然筋 should be 然谷." Wang Bing and Zhang Jiebin agree:
"This is a brook hole of the foot minor yin [conduit]. By letting its blood, one can
drain a kidney repletion." Lin Yi et al.: "An examination of all occurrences of 然谷
shows that often the following phrasing is used: 然骨之前者. Maybe in the present
statement the two characters 骨之 are missing and the character 前 was erroneously
written as 筋."

38 Wang Bing: "One does not search for an [appropriate] transporter hole, but selects
the location where the evil resides. Hence, [the text] states: 即取." Lin Yi et al.: "The
Jia yi jing has 以去其邪, 'to remove the evil,' instead of 邪所." The *Tai su* has 以邪
instead of 邪所: "This way the evil can be depleted immediately."

39 Cheng Shide et al.: "并 is 合并, 'to unite.' This is a metaphor for unilateral abundance." 234/57: "Qi and blood have undergone unilateral accumulations."

when yin and yang have lost their balance,⁴⁰
[then] the qi acts disorderly in the guard [region], and
the blood moves contrary [to its regular course] in the conduits.
Blood and qi reside in separate locations,
resulting in a repletion here and a depletion there.⁴¹

62-339-5
When the blood collects in the yin [region] and
qi collects in the yang [region],
this, then, leads to fright and craziness.⁴²

When the blood collects in the yang [region] and
qi collects in the yin [region],
this, then, leads to a heated center.⁴³

---

40 Cheng Shide et al.: "傾 is 傾陷, 'to fall in;' 傾斜, 'to overturn.' Here it refers to 失
調, 'lose [their] balance.'" 234/57: "Yin and yang have lost their equilibrium."

41 Zhang Zhicong: "When the blood leaves its residence, then the blood is depleted
and the qi is replete. When the qi leaves its residence, then the qi is depleted and the
blood is replete. Hence, [the text] states: 'one replete; one depleted.'" Gao Shishi:
"When qi and blood mingle with each other, depletion and repletion are generated."
234/57: "When the qi collects in the blood [region], then the qi [region] is depleted
and the blood [region] is replete; when the blood collects in the qi [region], then the
blood [region] is depleted and the qi [region] is replete. When yin and yang fall into
each other's [region], [that is,] when yin [qi] falls into the yang [region], then the
yin [region] is depleted and the yang [region] is replete; when yang falls into the yin
[region], then the yang [region] is depleted and the yin is replete. This is meant by 'one
is replete, one is depleted.'"

42 Wang Bing: "When the qi collects in the yang [region], then the yang qi abounds
externally. Hence, fright and craziness result." Zhang Jiebin: "When the blood collects
in the yin [region], this is a [state of] doubled yin. When the qi collects in the yang
[region], this is a [state of] doubled yang. Doubled yin is peak illness; doubled yang
is craziness. Hence, this causes 'fright and craziness.'" 140/31: "That is, the qi and the
blood are separated."

43 Wang Bing: "When the qi collects in the yin [region], then the yang qi abounds
internally. Hence, this causes a heated center." Zhang Jiebin: "When the blood collects in the yang [region], the yin [qi] is in the outside; when the qi collects in the yin
[region], the yang [qi] is inside. Hence, this causes a 'heated center.'" 140/31: "That is,
the qi and the blood mix with each other." 234/57: "The blood is originally in the interior and is associated with the yin. When it collects in the yang [region], then the yin
[region] is depleted and the yang [region] is replete. This causes internal heat. The qi is
originally in the exterior and it is associated with the yang. When it collects in the yin
[region], then the yang [region] is depleted and the yang qi abounds internally. Hence,

When the blood collects above and
qi collects below,
the heart is vexed and [the patient] tends to be angry.[44]

When the blood collects below and
qi collects above,
[patients] behave disorderly and tend to forget."[45]

62-339-8
[Huang] Di:
"When the blood collects in the yin [region] and
the qi collects in the yang [region],
then this is a case of blood and qi residing in separate locations.
What is it that causes repletion and
what is it that causes depletion?"

Qi Bo:
"The blood and the qi prefer warmth and have an aversion to cold.
In case of cold, they are impeded and cannot flow.
Warmth, then, dissolves [these impediments] and removes them.[46]

---

when blood collects in the yang [region] and when qi collects in the yin [region], both
these [conditions] can generate internal heat. 中 is 内, 'internal.'"

44 234/57: "The blood is ruled by the heart and it is stored by the liver. When the
blood collects in the upper [region], it rushes against the heart and vexation as well as
chest pressure result. The liver loses its nourishment and the qi dynamics are blocked.
The qi collects in the lower [region] and as a result the liver qi abounds alone. Hence,
one tends to be angry."

45 Wang Bing: " 'Above' is to say: above the diaphragm; 'below' is to say: below the
diaphragm." Zhang Jiebin: "When the blood collects in the upper [region], then the
yin evil oppresses the heart. Hence, [the heart] is vexed and alarmed. When the qi
collects in the lower [section], then fire moves against the liver. Hence, one tends to
be angry. When the blood collects in the lower [section], then the yin qi does not rise;
when the qi collects in the upper [section], then the yang qi does not descend. Yin [qi]
and yang [qi] are separated and disperse. Hence, the spirit is in disorder and one tends
to forget." Zhang Zhicong: "血并于下 is: the blood accumulates in the lower [section]
and one tends to forget. 氣并于上 is: the qi rises adversely and causes perturbation
and disorder." 234/57: "When the blood collects in the lower [region], the heart spirit
loses its nourishment. When the qi collects in the upper [region], this perturbs the
heart spirit. Hence, one is confused and tends to be forgetful."

46 Wang Bing: "泣 is to say: as if snow in water caused [the latter] to congeal and be
impeded [in its movement]."

Hence,
where the qi collects, a depletion of blood develops;
where the blood collects, a depletion of qi develops."[47]

62-339-11
[Huang] Di:
"Man has only blood and qi.
Now, you, Sir, tell me:
when the blood collects, this causes a depletion and
when the qi collects, this causes a depletion, [too].

Is that [to say] there is no repletion?"

Qi Bo:
"To be present is repletion;
not to be present is depletion.[48]

Hence,
when qi collects, then there is no blood;
when blood collects, then there is no qi.
If, now, blood and qi lose each other's presence,
then this will result in a depletion.[49]

Both the network [vessels] and the tertiary vessels transport [their contents]
into the conduits.
When the blood and the qi collect [simultaneously],
then this causes a repletion there.

---

47 Wang Bing: "When the qi collects in the [region of the] blood, then the blood is
diminished. Hence, the blood is depleted. When the blood collects in the [region of
the] qi, then the qi is diminished. Hence, the qi is depleted." 1911/11: "氣并 is 氣偏
盛, 'the qi abounds unilaterally.'"

48 Wang Bing: "When qi collects in the [region of the] blood, then there is no blood
[any longer]. When blood collects in the [region of the] qi, then there is no qi [any
longer]."

49 Wang Bing: "When qi collects in the [region of the] blood, then the blood loses
its qi. When blood collects in the [region of the] qi, then the qi loses its blood. Hence,
[the text] states: 'Blood and qi lose each other.'" Ma Shi: "When the qi collects in the
yang [section], then qi is present while blood is not present. That is, the qi is replete
and the blood is depleted. When blood collects in the yin [section], then the blood is
present while the qi not present. That is, the blood is replete and the qi is depleted.

When the blood and the qi both move upwards,[50]
then this is a massive recession.
[Massive] recession causes sudden death.[51]
When the qi turns back again, [the patient] will live;
when it does not turn back, then [he] will die."[52]

62-340-2
[Huang] Di:
"Repletions, by which paths do they arrive?
Depletions, by which paths do they leave?
It is the essentials of depletion and repletion of which I should like to hear the
principles."

Qi Bo:
"Now,
yin [conduits] and yang [conduits], they all have transporters and meeting
points.

When the yang [qi] pours into the yin [conduits, then]
the yin [conduits] are full [and the qi] moves to the outside,[53]
then yin and yang are evenly balanced,
the physical appearance is filled.

{If [the movement in the vessels at] the nine indicators is identical,
this is called "normal person."}

---

50 Gao Jiwu/242: "與 is 隨, 'to follow,' 'together with.'"

51 1946/5: "This is a pathocondition of repletion where both the blood and the qi
abound. Blood and qi together fill and block the cinnabar field. Hence, the spirit is
confused and one does not recognize persons or anything else." Yan Hongchen & Gao
Guangzhen/180: "In case of 'massive recession,' one is suddenly unconscious and does
not recognize persons or anything else."

52 Zhang Jiebin: "When the blood and the qi together move upwards, then there is
repletion above and depletion below. In case of depletion below, the yin is lost. When
the yin is lost, then the root is cut away and recession below goes along with exhaustion above. This is 'massive recession.' Hence, sudden death results. When the qi has
reached a peak and turns around, then the yin can gradually return. Hence, one can
recover. When it leaves entirely and does not turn around, one cannot live."

53 Zhang Jiebin: "When yang pours into the yin, then it turns from the conduits
into the depots. When yang fills the outside, then it leaves the depots and reaches the
conduits."

Now,
when evil emerges,
it either emerges in the yin or
it emerges in the yang.
When it emerges in the yang,
it was acquired through wind, rain, cold, or summerheat.
When it emerges in the yin,
it was acquired through beverages or food, the place of living, [sexual union of]
yin and yang,[54] or through [emotions such as] joy or anger."[55]

62-340-7
[Huang] Di:
"How is it that wind and rain harm a person?"

Qi Bo:
"When wind and rain harm a person,
they first settle in the skin,
whence they are transmitted into the tertiary vessels.
When the tertiary vessels are full,
then [the evil] is transmitted into the network vessels.
When the network vessels are full,
then [the evil] is transported into the large conduit vessels.

When blood and qi collect with evil and settle in the interstice [structures],
the vessels there will be firm and big.
Hence, this is called 'repletion.'"
<In case of repletion, the outer [vessels] are firm and full and cannot be pressed.
If one presses them, then this causes pain.>

---

54 Tanba: "This 'yin and yang' refers to sexual intercourse." Zhang Qi: "The 'yin and yang, joy and anger' is to say: a person's own qi is either unilaterally yin or unilaterally yang and, hence, the seven emotions do unilaterally dominate, too."

55 Yang Shangshan: "Wind, rain, cold, and summerheat, these external evils come from the outside and enter the six palaces first. Hence, [the text] states 'emerges in the yang.' Beverages and food, rising and resting, male and female [intercourse], as well as joy and anger, these internal evils emerge in the five depots. Hence, [the text] states 'emerge in the yin.'" Zhang Jiebin: "Wind, rain, cold, and summerheat emerge from the outside; they are external affections. Hence, they are called yang. Beverages and food, one's place of living, [the union of] yin and yang, joy and anger, emerge from inside. They constitue internal harm. Hence, they are called yin."

62-340-11
[Huang] Di:
"How is it that cold and dampness harm a person?"[56]

Qi Bo:
"When cold and dampness strike a person,
the skin does not contract,[57] [but]
the muscles and the flesh are firm and tight,
the camp blood is impeded and
the guard qi leaves.
Hence, this is called 'depletion.'"
<In case of depletion, [the skin is] wrinkled and folded, the qi is insufficient.[58]
If one presses [the vessels], then the qi suffices to give them warmth. Hence,
[the patient] is happy and feels no pain.>[59]

---

56 Zhang Qi: "Above, [the text] referred to 'cold and summerheat'; here it refers to
'cold and dampness.' The character [for 'dampness'] is a mistake."

57 Lin Yi et al.: "The Quan Yuanqi edition has 不仁, 'numb,' instead of 不收." The
Jia yi jing and the *Tai su* do not have the character 不. Yang Shangshan: "皮膚收 is:
the skin is tight and drawn together." Gao Shishi: "不收 is: sweat leaves [the pores];
they do not close." 2270/37: "不 is 丕, 'great,' here. In ancient times, the two characters were used interchangeably. The passage should read 皮膚大收, 'the skin contracts
massively.'" Zhang Jiebin: "When cold and dampness strike a person, this will harm
the guard qi. Hence, the skin does not contract and slackens." 2855/53: "不 is a corrupted version of 束, 'to bind together.' The ancient script versions of these characters
are similar." For a detailed discussion see also 971/57.

58 Wang Bing: "聶 is 聶皺, 'wrinkled,' 'folded'; 辟 is 辟疊, 'folded.'" Ma Shi: "That
means: the flesh is 僻積, 'wrinkled.'" Zhang Jiebin: "When one speaks in a low voice,
that is called 聶. When the feet are weak and cannot move, that is called 辟. In each
case the qi is insufficient." Zhang Zhicong: "聶 is identical with 儡; 辟 is 積, 'to collect.'" Cheng Shide et al.: "According to the meaning of the text, [these characters]
refer to wrinkled skin. Hence, one should follow Wang Bing's commentary." Qian
Chaochen-90/140: "辟 is 襞, 'fold.' .. When cold and dampness strike a person, this
causes the skin to slacken. .. Hence, 聶辟 must refer to 皮膚不收, 'the skin does not
contract. Because the skin fails to contract, many wrinkles and folds appear.'" The *Tai
su* and the *Jia yi jing* have 攝辟. Also, in the *Tai su* the characters 不足 are followed
by the two characters 血泣, in the *Jia yi jing* they are followed by the two characters
血濇. The *Su wen* always has 泣 where other texts have 濇; hence the two characters
血泣, "the [flow of] blood is rough", appear to be missing here.

59 Zhang Jiebin: "When the qi is depleted and one has pain, one presses the respective [location] so that qi arrives. When the qi has arrived, then yang [qi] collects and
yin [qi] disperses. Hence, [the patient] can be happy and the pain ends."

62-340-16
[Huang] Di:
"Good!
How is it that yin [qi] generates a repletion?"⁶⁰

Qi Bo:
"If joy or anger are unrestrained, then the yin qi⁶¹ rises contrary [to its regular course].⁶²
When it rises contrary [to its regular course],
then a depletion results below.
When a depletion exists below,
then yang qi moves there.
Hence, this is called 'repletion.' "⁶³

62-340-18
[Huang] Di:
"How is it that yin [qi] generates a depletion?"⁶⁴

Qi Bo:
"When [a person is full of] joy, then the qi descends.⁶⁵
When he is sad, then the qi dissolves.
When it dissolves, then the vessels are depleted. {Empty.}

When because of cold beverages or food

---

60 Wang Bing: " 'Repletion' is to say: abounding evil qi." Ma Shi: "That is to say: The yin conduit has a depletion or repletion disease." Cheng Shide et al.: " 'Yin' refers to the yin conduits."

61 Cheng Shide et al.: "In this case the yin qi is the qi of the liver conduit."

62 Zhang Qi: "The characters 喜 and 不節 are later additions." Tanba: "Further down the text states: 喜則氣下. Hence, the present character 喜 is a later insertion."

63 Yang Shangshan: "When someone cannot control his anger, then the yin qi rises. When the yin qi rises, then this is an adverse rising. One vomits or cannot eat. When the yin qi has risen, then a depletion exists below. When a depletion exists below, then the yang qi seizes [the depleted region]. Hence, this is called 'yin repletion.'"

64 Wang Bing: " 'Depletion' is to say: the essence qi is lost."

65 528/20: "喜則氣下 and *Su wen* 39 恐則氣下, 'in case of fear, the qi descends,' are contradictory theoretical statements. We think the present 喜 is an error for the character 恐, 'fear.' Zhang Qi has: This should be 喜則氣緩, 'in case of joy, the qi slows down.' In view of the preceding and the following passages, though, *Su wen* 39 is correct. Hence, 喜 should be changed to 恐."

the cold qi vapor fills [the vessels],[66]
then the blood is impeded and the qi leaves.
Hence, this is called 'depletion.'"

62-341-2
[Huang] Di:
"The classic states:
'When the yang is depleted, then the outside is cold;
when the yin is depleted, then the inside is hot.
When the yang abounds, then the outside is hot;
when the yin abounds, then the inside is cold.'[67]

This I have heard already.
But I do not know why it is so."

Qi Bo:
"The yang receives its qi from[68] the upper burner.
[This qi] serves to warm the region of the skin and the parting of the flesh.

If, now, cold qi prevails in the [body's] outside,
then the upper burner is blocked.
When the upper burner is blocked,
then the cold qi remains in the outside alone.
Hence, [patients] are cold and shiver."[69]

62-341-6
[Huang] Di:
"How is it that a yin depletion generates internal heat?"

Qi Bo:
"When one is exhausted to fatigue and
when the qi of the physical appearance is weak and diminished and
when the grain qi does not abound, [then]

---

66 The *Jia yi jing* has 動藏, 'excites the depots,' instead of 熏滿. The *Tai su* has 熏
藏, 'to fill the depots with vapor.'" Cheng Shide et al.: "The version of the *Jia yi jing*
is correct."

67 For a detailed comparison of the following explanation of this quotation by Qi Bo
with the current understanding of the concepts yin/yang depletion/abundance as well
as internal/outside heat/cold, see Wan Lanqing et al./40.

68 Wang Shaozeng/134: "于 is equivalent to 從, 'from,' here."

69 Wang Bing: "慄 is 振慄, 'to shiver from cold.'"

the upper burner does not move [its qi] and
the lower [stomach] duct is blocked.[70]
As a result, the stomach qi is hot and
the heat qi steams into the chest.
Hence, [patients experience] internal heat."[71]

62-341-8
[Huang] Di:
"How is it that yang abundance generates outside heat?"

Qi Bo:
"When the upper burner is not freely passable,
then the skin is contracted tightly.
The interstice structures are obstructed.
The dark palaces[72] are impassable.
[As a result] the guard qi cannot flow out transgressing [the skin].
Hence, [there is] outside heat."[73]

---

70 Lin Yi et al.: "The *Jia yi jing* has 'the lower burner is impassable.'"

71 Zhang Jiebin: "The 'qi of one's physical appearance' is the yin qi. The qi of the upper burner is a transformation product of the essence of water and grain. In the present case someone was careless in exhausting himself to fatigue and the qi of his physical appearance is weak and diminished. Hence, when the spleen yin is harmed, the grain qi does not abound and the [qi of the] upper burner does not move. When [the qi] above does not move, the duct below is impassable. As a result heat is blocked in the stomach palace and steams the chest [and the] center. This is how a yin depletion generates internal heat." Zhang Zhicong: "When [the text] states 'yin depletion causes internal heat,' this is because the center, [i.e.,] the soil has received harm. [Excessive] drinking and eating, as well as fatigue harm the spleen. The spleen rules the muscles and the flesh. Hence, the qi of one's physical appearance decreases. Water and grain enter the stomach; they are transmitted further by the spleen qi. When the spleen does not transmit, then the grain qi does not abound. The upper burner cannot transmit the flavors of the five grains; the lower burner cannot receive the essence of water and grain. The stomach is the palace of yang heat. When the qi remains [where it is] and does not move, then the heat steams into the chest and causes internal heat." See 2582/7 for a detailed discussion of 陰虛生內熱.

72 Lin Yi et al.: "The *Jia yi jing* and the *Tai su* do not have the two characters 玄府, 'dark palace.'" 458/13: "The two characters 玄府 were added by later persons as an explanation of 腠理, 'interstice structures.'"

73 Wang Bing: "In case of a harm caused by cold coming from the outside, when the poison collects in all yang [conduits] inside and when cold abounds in the [body's]

62-341-10
[Huang] Di:
"How is it that yin abundance generates internal cold?"

Qi Bo:
"When receding qi[74] rises contrary [to its regular course],
cold qi accumulates inside the chest and does not flow away.
When it does not flow away, then the warmth qi leaves.
When the cold [qi] remains alone,
then the blood congeals so that [its flow] is impeded.
When it congeals, then the vessels are blocked.[75]
[As a result,] these vessels abound with contents, are big, and rough.
Hence, the center is cold."[76]

62-341-13
[Huang] Di:
"When yin [qi] and yang [qi] collect and
when, therefore, blood and qi have collected and

---

exterior, then the skin contracts. When the skin has contracted, then the interstice structures are tightly closed. Hence, the guard qi accumulates and has no way to flow. The cold qi accumulates in the exterior and the yang qi struggles inside. The collected fire burns inside; hence, this generates 'external heat.'" Zhang Jiebin: "The qi of the upper burner rules the yang section. Hence, in case of external harm caused by cold evil, the upper burner is no longer passable. The outside of the muscle [flesh] is closed and the guard qi accumulates through stagnation. It can flow nowhere and causes external heat. When it is said 'when someone is harmed by cold, then he suffers from heat,' this is a pathocondition caused by an affection from the outside." Gao Shishi: "The yang rules the above and it rules the exterior. When the upper burner is not freely passable, then the skin in the exterior closes tightly and, hence, internally the interstice structures are blocked and the dark palaces are not passable. As for the 'interstice structures,' these are the line structures of the interstices in the flesh. As for the 'dark palaces,' these are the sweat holes of the hair openings. When the dark palaces, the skin and the interstice structures do not [allow] communication among each other, then the guard qi is blocked and cannot flow away. Hence, there is yang abundance and external heat as a result."

74 Zhang Jiebin: "This is the qi of cold recession." Zhang Zhicong: "the yin qi of the lower burner rises adversely in recession."

75 Lin Yi et al.: "The *Jia yi jing* has 腠理不通, 'the interstice structures are not passable,' instead of 脈不通.'"

76 Wang Bing: " 'Warmth qi' is to say: yang qi. When yin [qi] rises moving contrary [to its regular course], then the yang leaves to outside the skin."

when, therefore, the disease has assumed a manifestation,
to pierce such [a condition], how to proceed?"

Qi Bo:
"To pierce such [a condition],
take it from the conduit tunnels.
Take the blood from the camp [region] and
take the qi from the guard [region].[77]

Take the manifestation [of the disease] into consideration.
Follow the quantity and the higher or lower location [of qi in the body] in the
course of the four seasons."[78]

62-342-1
[Huang] Di:
"When blood and qi have collected,
when the disease has assumed a physical manifestation, and
when yin and yang have lost their balance,
to supplement and drain [in such a situation], how to proceed?"[79]

---

77 Ma Shi: "The blood may be depleted or replete and the camp qi belongs to the
yin. Blood is generated by the camp [qi]. Hence, for piercing the blood, one simply
takes it from the camp qi. The qi may be depleted or replete and the guard qi belongs
to the yang. The qi also belongs to the yang. Hence, to pierce the qi, one simply takes
it from the guard qi."

78 Wang Bing: "The camp [qi] controls the blood; it is a yin qi. The guard [qi] controls the qi; it is a yang qi. Hence, for applying the Way of piercing, one must first
know whether [the patient's] physical [body] is long or short and whether his bone
[structure] is wide or narrow." Ma Shi: "The physical body of man differs in that it
may be long or short, fat or lean, large or small. In the course of the four seasons the
[climate] may be cold or hot, warm or cool. One must take the physical appearance
of man and the seasons into account to decide the amount and the level of piercing."
Zhang Zhicong: "用 is 以, 'to take [into account).' .. One must take into account
whether the seasonal qi rises or descends, is at the surface or in the depth, whether it
is present in larger or smaller amounts, on which level [in the body it has settled]. For
instance, when it is said (in *Su wen* 63) that the number of wounds [to be created with
a needle] depends on the waxing and waning of the moon, then this is what is meant
by 'amount.' Or, [when it is said (in *Su wen* 4)] in spring [one pierces the] transporters
in the neck, in summer in the chest and flanks, in autumn in the shoulders and back
and in winter in the lower back and thighs, then this is meant by 'level.'"

79 Hu Tianxiong: "以 is 已, 'already.'"

Qi Bo:

"To drain a repletion, insert the needle when the qi abounds.[80]
The needle enters together with the qi.
This serves to open the gate[81] as if [82] a doorleaf was made to move freely.[83]
When the needle leaves together with the qi,[84] the essence qi is not harmed
and the evil qi is brought down.

Do not close the outside gate,[85]
so that the disease is made to leave.
Widen its path by moving [the needle] here and there,
as if its road was made passable.
{This is called 'massive drainage.'}
It is essential to squeeze [the location pierced] and make [the qi] leave.[86]
[As a result], large [quantities of] qi will yield."[87]

[Huang] Di:

"To supplement a depletion, how to proceed?"

Qi Bo:

"Hold the needle but do not position it yet.

---

80 Zhang Jiebin: "That is, the needle is inserted when the patient has inhaled." Ma
Shi: "One waits until the evil qi is just abounding and then lets the patient inhale qi
before one inserts the needle."

81 1134/5: "門 refers to the transporter holes of the human body."

82 Qian Chaochen-88/282: "The *Jia yi jing* has 而, 'and,' instead of 如. In ancient
times these characters were equivalent."

83 Wu Kun: "One pierces the transporter holes to open a door through which the evil
[may] leave. When the evil is blocked and replete, it wishes to leave but has no door.
This [piercing] serves to free its door."

84 Zhang Jiebin: " 'Needle and qi leave both' is: one waits until the patient exhales qi
and removes the needle."

85 Cheng Shide et al.: "The 'outside gate' is the piercing hole."

86 Wang Bing: "That is to say, one wishes to open the hole and drain its qi. 切 is to
say: 急, 'urgent,' 'quickly.' That is to say: one quickly withdraws the needle." Gao Shishi: "切 is 按, 'to press.' 必切而出 is to say: the right hand holds the needle, the left
hand must press the hole and cause the [needle] to leave [the hole]." Cheng Shide et
al.: "One should follow Gao Shishi's interpretation."

87 Wang Bing: "大氣 is 大邪氣, 'massive evil qi.' 屈 is to say: 退屈, 'to withdraw.'"

In this way stabilize [your] intentions.[88]
Wait for an exhalation to insert the needle.
When the qi leaves [the patient's mouth], introduce the needle.

62-342-7
The needle hole is obstructed on four [sides],[89] and
the essence [qi] has no [possible exit] from which it could leave.
Right at the moment of repletion, quickly remove the needle.
When the qi enters [the patient's mouth], withdraw the needle,
lest the heat returns.[90]
Obstruct its gate.
The evil qi will disperse.
As a result, the essence qi is preserved.
To move the qi, wait for the [proper] time.[91]
The qi nearby is not lost.[92]
As a result, the qi from far away will arrive.[93]
This is called 'pursuing it.'"[94]

62-342-9
[Huang] Di:
"You, Sir, have said:
there are ten depletions and repletions,[95]

---

88 Wu Kun: "When the [patient's] sentiments are stabilized, his true qi will be stabilized, too."

89 Cheng Shide et al.: "That is: the needle fits the hole tightly. This is the opposite of the earlier statement: 'through moving [the needle] here and there one creates a big passageway.'"

90 Zhang Qi: "This sentence is an erroneous insertion."

91 Wang Bing: "One wishes to move the qi and achieve a supplementation. When supplementing one must always watch the clepsydra [to determine] where the qi is and only then the piercing is to be carried out. That is meant by 'wait for the [proper] time' to regulate it." Lin Yi et al.: "The *Jia yi jing* and the *Tai su* have 動無後時, 'for moving, one must not be behind the time.'"

92 Wang Bing: "The 'qi nearby' is the qi that has already arrived."

93 Wang Bing: "The 'qi far away' is the qi that has not yet arrived."

94 Wang Bing: "That is to say: the hole is to be sealed closely lest its qi disperses and flows away. 追 is to say: 補, 'to supplement.'" 307/184: "追 is like 送, 'to send away.' The meaning is 瀉, 'to drain.'"

95 Ma Shi: "The spirit, the qi, the blood, the flesh, and the will, each may be depleted or replete. Hence, this adds up to ten."

generated in the five depots.
{The five depots are nothing but the five vessels.}

Now,
all the twelve conduit vessels generate their diseases;
Here, you, Sir, only refer to the five depots.

62-342-11
Now,
the twelve conduit vessels, they encircle all the 365 joints.[96]
When the joints have a disease, it must reach the conduit vessels.[97]
The diseases of the conduit vessels do always consist of depletion or repletion.
How can this be brought together?"[98]

62-342-13
Qi Bo:
"The fact is, the five depots have the six palaces to form exterior and interior
with [them].[99]
The conduits and network [vessels], the limbs and the joints,
they all develop depletion and repletion.
Follow the location of the disease and regulate there.

When the disease is in the vessels,
regulate it through the blood.[100]
When the disease is in the blood,

---

96 Zhang Jiebin: "The so-called 'joints' are the locations where the spirit qi meets. This
is a reference to the transporter holes, hence, there are 365 joints."

97 Wu Kun: "被 is 及, 'to arrive.'"

98 Zhang Jiebin: "何以合之 is to say: how can all [these diseases] be associated with
the five depots?" Gao Shishi: "Above, Qi Bo stated: 'There are five [types of] surplus
and there are five [types of] insufficiency; they all are generated by the five depots.'
[Huang] Di spoke of the five depots and [identified them] only with the five vessels.
The [states of] depletion and repletion of the five vessels, how can they be brought to
together with [those of] the twelve conduit vessels?"

99 Tanba: "The *Tong ya* 通雅 states: 'In ancient times, 固 and 故 were identical."
Zhang Yizhi et al.: "與 is identical with 以."

100 Wang Bing: "The vessels are the palace of the blood. When the vessels are replete,
the blood is replete; when the vessels are depleted, the blood is depleted. Hence, when
a disease is in the vessels, one regulates it through the blood." Lin Yi et al.: "The Quan
Yuanqi edition and the *Jia yi jing* have 病在血調之脈, 'when the blood has a disease,
regulate it through the vessels.'"

regulate it through the network [vessels].[101]
When the disease is in the qi,
regulate it through the guard [region].[102]
When the disease is in the flesh,
regulate it through the parting of the flesh.[103]
When the disease is in the sinews,
regulate it through the sinews.[104]
When the disease is in the bones,
regulate it through the bones.[105]

62-343-2
With a heated needle apply a robbing piercing[106] below them and also where
[the sinews are] tense.[107]
When the disease is in the bones,
[apply] a fire needle and poultices prepared from drugs.[108]
When in case of a disease the location of the pain is unknown,

---

101 Wang Bing: "When the blood has a disease, the network vessels change [their appearance]. Hence, one regulates [the diseases of the blood] through the network [vessels]." Ma Shi: "When the blood has a disease, nottings form in the network vessels." Hu Tianxiong: "The *Tai su* has 病在血調之脈; it does not have the six characters 病在脈調之血. In accordance with the earlier statement 取血於營 and also in accordance with the following passage 病在氣調之衛, this passage here should read 調之營, 'regulate it through the camp [region].'"

102 Wang Bing: "The guard [region] rules the qi. Hence, when the qi has a disease, one regulates it through the guard [region]."

103 Wang Bing: "One waits for [alternating fits of] cold and heat and removes it."

104 Wang Bing: "In accordance with the relaxed or tense [status of the sinews], one applies piercing or hot poultices."

105 The *Tai su* does not have the six characters 病在骨調之骨. Hu Tianxiong: "These six characters should follow the characters 調之筋."

106 *NJCD*: "A piercing pattern whereby the needle is not left to remain in the skin; it is quickly inserted and quickly removed again." Zhang Zhicong: " 'Robbing piercing' is: one pierces with the force of a robber and immediately withdraws [the needle] again."

107 Wang Bing: "When the sinews are tense, then one heats the needle and applies a robbing piercing." Zhang Jiebin: "燔針 is: after the needle has been inserted, one heats it with fire to warm it. .. When the sinews are cold, they become tense. Hence, a robbing piercing with a heated needle is applied." Gao Shishi: "及與急者 is to say: 筋痺, 'sinew block.'"

108 Wang Bing: "This is a pattern to regulate the bones. 焠針 is 火針, 'fire needle.'" Zhang Jiebin: "When the disease is in the bones, its qi is in the depth. Hence, one

[to pierce] the two walker [vessels] is best.
When the body has pain,
while no disease [is detectable] at the nine indicators,
then pierce it by applying a misleading [piercing].[109]
When the pain is on the left,
while the [movement in the] vessels on the right [is marked by] disease,
apply a grand piercing.[110]

It is essential to carefully investigate the nine indicators.
[This way] the Way of the needles will be perfect."

---

must apply a heated needle for piercing it and one employs drugs of an acrid and hot [nature] to disperse it."

109 Wang Bing: " 'Misleading piercing' is piercing the network vessels. When the pain is on the left, one needles on the right; when the pain is on the right, one needles on the left."

110 Wang Bing: " 'Grand piercing' is piercing the conduit vessels. When the vessels ache on the left, one needles on the right; when the pain is on the right, one needles on the left." For a detailed outline of the difference of 'misleading' and 'grand' piercing, see also 29/31.

Chapter 63
Discourse on Misleading Piercing[1]

63-344-2
Huang Di asked:
"I have heard about misleading piercing, but
I have not grasped its meaning yet.
What is that to say: misleading piercing?"

Qi Bo responded:
"Now,
when an evil settles in the physical appearance,
it will first lodge in the skin and its hair.
It stays there [for a while] and does not leave.
Then it enters [more deeply] and lodges in the tertiary vessels.
It stays there [for a while] and does not leave.
Then it enters [further] and lodges in the network vessels.
It stays there [for a while] and does not leave.
Then it enters [further] and lodges in the conduit vessels.
It links up with the five depots internally and spreads into the intestines and the stomach.
With both the yin and the yang [regions] being affected,
the five depots will be harmed.

---

1 Wang Bing: "繆刺 is to say: the holes to be pierced should be employed as if one committed an error (紕繆) in applying the [normal] principles." Zhang Jiebin: "繆 is 異, 'another.' When the disease is on the left, one pierces on the right; when the disease is on the right, one pierces on the left. The piercing is conducted at another place [than the location of the disease]. Hence, it is called 繆刺." Hu Tianxiong: "繆刺 is: the piercing is applied on the basis of a crosswise connection between left and right." Gao Shishi: "繆刺 is to say: to pierce the network [vessels]. .. One pierces before the evil has penetrated [the body] deeply. The meaning is that of 綢繆, 'to apply preventive measures [before a catastrophe has occurred].'" 140/29: "繆刺 is to say: the disease is in the network vessels but the piercing is directed at the conduits; or the disease is on the left and the piercing is conducted on the right. Because conduits and network vessels are intertwined, the needle is applied [at a location] removed [from the location of the ailment]. In ancient literature, 繆 and 穆 were used identically. Hence, [繆 has] the meaning of 沕穆高遠, 'profound and far away.' Wang Bing's comment is incorrect." We read 繆 as 謬, "to mislead." See also 2857/49, 944/52, 29/31, and 241/42.

That is the sequence whereby an evil enters through the skin and its hair and finally reaches the five depots.[2]
In such cases, then, treat the respective conduits.

Now,
when an evil has settled in the skin and its hair,
it will enter [the body] to lodge in the tertiary network [vessels].
There it stays and does not leave.
If [its further passageways] are obstructed and impassable,
it cannot enter the conduits.
[Rather,] it overflows into the large network [vessels],
generating strange diseases.[3]

62-344-8
Now,
when an evil has settled in the large network [vessels,
and cannot enter the conduits,
from] the left it pours to the right,
[from] the right it pours to the left.
Above and below, left and right
it clashes against the conduits and
spreads into the four extremities.[4]

This [evil] qi has no permanent location and
it does not enter the transporters of the conduits.
[Treating such an evil] is called: misleading piercing."

63-344-10
[Huang] Di:

---

2 Tanba: "極 is 至, 'to reach an end.'"

3 Wang Bing: "When a disease is situated in the blood network [vessels], that is called 'strange disease.'" Lin Yi et al.: "The Quan Yuanqi edition has 十五絡, '15 network [vessels],' instead of 大絡." Hu Tianxiong: "When the present [text] speaks of an evil qi that does not enter the conduits but flows into the large network [vessels] and generates 奇病 instead, these 奇病 are exactly the 奇邪 of which *Ling shu* 5 says 'it leaves the conduits.' The present 奇 is the 奇 of 奇偶, 'odd and even.' It is different from the 奇 in [the heading of *Su wen* 47] 奇病論 which is the 奇 of 奇恆, 'abnormal.'" Zhang Zhicong: "奇病 is to say: the disease qi is on the left and the signs [of the disease] appear on the right; [or] the disease qi is on the right and its signs appear on the left."

4 Ma Shi: "The evil clashes against the conduits but cannot enter them. Hence, it spreads into the four limbs."

"I should like to hear [the following]:
in misleading piercing
given [a disease is] on the left, one selects the right, while
given [a disease is] on the right, one selects the left.
Why is that?
And how is this to be distinguished from grand piercing?"[5]

Qi Bo:
"When an evil settles in the conduits,
[first] there is abundance on the left, then [in addition] a disease develops on
the right, or
[first] there is abundance on the right, then [in addition] a disease develops on
the left.

63-344-12
There are also [situations] where it changes its location.[6]
The pain[7] on the left has not ended yet and the vessels on the right have a
disease before [the problem has subsided on the left].
Such cases must [be treated] with a grand piercing.[8]
One must hit the respective conduits, not the network vessels.[9]

The fact is,
when the network [vessels] have a disease,[10]
the locations of the pain and of the conduit vessels are misleading.
Hence, [this type of piercing] is called misleading piercing."

---

5 Cheng Shide et al.: "Grand piercing and misleading piercing are identical in that
when the disease is on the left, one takes [it from] the right; and when the disease is
on the right, one takes [it from] the left. The difference is that in grand piercing one
pierces the large conduits, while in misleading piercing one pierces the large network
[vessels]. Hence, Wu Kun states: '巨刺 is piercing the large conduits.'" Mori: "巨 may
be a mistake for 互, 'reciprocal'; this would be identical with the meaning of 繆."

6 Lin Yi et al.: "The *Jia yi jing* has 病易且移, 'the disease undergoes changes and
moves [to another location].'"

7 The *Tai su* has 病, 'disease,' instead of 痛.

8 Zhang Zhicong: "巨 is 大, 'big.' That is to say, one must remove the [evil] with a
long needle."

9 Wang Bing: "先病 is to say: Elsewhere the pain has not ended yet and here a
diseases exists already to succeed it."

10 Wang Bing: "'Network' is to say: the side branches of the proper conduits; not the
proper branches."

63-345-1
[Huang] Di:
"I should like to hear [the following:]
To conduct a misleading piercing, how to proceed?
To seize [the disease], what is to be done?"

Qi Bo:
"When an evil has settled in the network [vessels] of the foot minor yin [con-
duits],
it lets the [affected] person experience sudden heartache and violent distension.
Chest and flanks [suffer from] propping fullness.[11]

If no accumulations exist,
pierce in front of the blazing bone to let blood.[12]
[The disease] comes to an end in the time span of a meal.[13]
<If it does not end,>[14]

---

11 Wang Bing: "Because the network branches of the [foot minor yin conduit] rise
together with the proper conduit from the kidneys, penetrate the liver and the diaphragm and move to the heart enclosure, hence, an evil settling in them causes a
disease with such [signs]."

12 Wang Bing: " 'In front of the blazing bone' is the Blazing Valley (然谷) hole. ... For
piercing one can enter [the needle] three parts of an individually standardized body
inch." Hu Tianxiong: "Wang Bing's comment is wrong. To pierce the Blazing Valley
[hole] and enter [the needle] three parts of an individually standardized body inch
would be a [therapy] law of striking the conduits by means of grand piercing. This is
not a misleading piercing. For misleading piercing one should pierce the respective
network [vessels]. When the [text] states 'pierce in front of the blazing bone and let
blood there,' this is [an advice] to pierce the respective blood network [vessels]." Gao
Shishi exchanged the 骨 for 谷, 'valley,': "In case of distension and fullness, there are
accumulations and one must pierce chest and flanks. If no accumulations are present,
the disease is in the network [vessels] of the minor yin [conduits] and rises to the heart
enclosure. Hence, one must pierce in front of the Blazing Valley of the foot minor
yin [conduit]. 'In front of the Blazing Valley' is the blazing bone." Tanba: "*Ling shu*
2 states: 'The [qi of the] kidneys ... flows into the blazing valley. The blazing valley is
located below the blazing bone.' Hence, there is no need to change a character." Cheng
Shide et al.: "One should follow Wang Bing."

13 In contrast, Wang Bing: "[The treatment] lets one be hungry and long for food
immediately."

14 Cheng Shide et al.: "The *Jia yi jing* does not have the two characters 不已." The
Tai su does not have them either. Tanba: "This [treatment] is already concerned with
a network disease. Why should one wait and see whether it is not healed and apply a
misleading piercing only then? The *Jia yi* [*jing* version] is correct."

[when the disease is on] the left, select [for treatment] the right,
[when the disease is on] the right, select [for treatment] the left.[15]
In case the disease has just broken out,
five days [after] seizing [the evil],[16] [the disease] will have ended.

63-345-4
When an evil has settled in the network [vessels] of the hand minor yang
[conduits],
it lets the [affected] person experience throat block and a curled tongue.
The mouth is dry and the heart is vexed.
The outer edges of the arms ache.
The hands do not reach to the head.[17]

63-345-6
Pierce the finger next to the middle finger above the nail,[18]
generating one wound each [the width of] one leek leaf away from the [finger]
tip.[19]
[In patients] with a strong [constitution, the disease] will end at once;
in older [patients] it will end after a while.
[When the disease is on] the left select [for treatment] the right;
[when the disease is on] the right select [for treatment] the left.
If this is a new disease, it will end after several days.

---

15 Wang Bing: "That is to say, when the pain is on the left, seize it at the right; when
the pain is on the right, seize it at the left."

16 Cheng Shide et al.: "The *Jia yi jing* and the *Tai su* do not have the character 取; it
may be a later insertion."

17 Wang Bing: "Because this vessel follows the outer side of the hands, leaves to the
outside of the arms, rises to the shoulders, enters the broken basin, spreads to the *dan
zhong* and encircles the heart enclosure and because its branch course rises from the
dan zhong, emerges at the broken basin, rises further to the nape and also because the
heart rules the tongue, hence, the disease [causes a condition] as is described here."
Cheng Shide et al.: " 'The hands cannot reach the head' is: one lifts both hands but
cannot reach the head because the outer edges of the arms ache."

18 Lin Yi et al.: "According to the *Jia yi jing*, the Pass Thoroughfare (關衝) hole is
located at the tip of the finger next to the small finger. When the present [version]
states 'middle finger,' that is a mistake." The *Tai su* has 小指次指, "the finger next to
the small finger." Zhang Qi: "中 should be 小."

19 Wang Bing: "That is to say, [pierce at] the Pass Thoroughfare (關衝) hole. It is the
well hole of the minor yang [conduit]. .. Pierce at both the left and the right hand.
Hence, [the text] states 'one wound each.' 疛 is 瘡, 'sore.'"

63-345-8
When an evil has settled in the network [vessels] of the foot ceasing
yin [conduits],
it lets the [affected] person experience sudden elevation illnesses and
violent pain.[20]

Pierce above the nail of the big toe where it meets with the flesh,
generating one wound each.[21]
In males [the disease] will end immediately;
in females it will end after a while.[22]
[When the disease is on] the left select [for treatment] the right;
[when the disease is on] the right select [for treatment] the left.

63-346-1
When an evil has settled in the network [vessels] of the foot major
yang [conduits],
it lets the [affected] person experience pain in the head, the nape, and the
shoulders.
Pierce above the nail of the small toe where it meets with the flesh,
generating one wound each.[23]
[The disease] will end immediately.
If it does not end, pierce three wounds below the outer ankles.
[When the disease is on] the left select [for treatment] the right;
[when the disease is on] the right select [for treatment] the left.
[The disease] will end in the time span of a meal.[24]

---

20 Wang Bing: "Because this network leaves the minor yang [conduit] in a distance
of five individually standardized body inches above the inner ankle and because its
branch follows the shins, rises to the testicles and forms a knot around the stalk,
[when an evil settles in it] this causes sudden elevation illness and violent pain." Hu
Tianxiong: "Chao Yuan[fang] 巢源[方] (*Zhu bing yuan hou lun* 諸病源候論) states:
疝 is 痛, 'pain.' Hence, 卒疝 and 暴痛 are mutually explanatory phrases. .. 卒疝 refers
to males; 暴痛 refers to females."

21 Wang Bing: "That is to say, [pierce at] the Large Pile (大敦) hole. It is the well
hole of the ceasing yin [conduit]."

22 Zhang Zhicong: "The blood in males abounds; hence, they are healed immediately. The life of females is characterized by an insufficiency of blood. Hence, it takes
a while."

23 Wang Bing: "That is to say, [pierce at] the Extreme Yin (至陰) hole; it is the well
hole of the the major yang [conduit]."

24 Wang Bing: "That is to say: [pierce at] the Golden Gate (金門) hole in the cleft of
the foot major yang [conduit]."

63-346-3

When an evil has settled in the network [vessels] of the hand yang brilliance [conduits],

it lets the [affected] person experience qi fullness inside of his chest.

His breath is panting and he has a [feeling of] propping [fullness] in his upper flanks.

The chest is hot inside.

Pierce the fingers next to the thumb above the nail,

generating one wound each [the width of] a leek leaf away from the [finger] tip.

[When the disease is on] the left select [for treatment] the right;

[when the disease is on] the right select [for treatment] the left.

[The disease] will end in the time span of a meal.[25]

63-346-6

When an evil has settled in the region of arm and palm and

[when the arm] cannot be bent,

pierce behind the respective ankle.[26]

At first press this [location] with a finger.

When it aches, then pierce it.

The number [of wounds to be generated][27] follows the waxing and waning of the moon.

<At the time of crescent moon, [generate]

one wound on the first day,

two wounds on the second day, [and so forth until]

15 wounds on the 15th day, [then]

14 wounds on the 16th day, [and so forth].>

---

25 Wang Bing: "That is to say, [pierce at] the Shang-Yang (商陽) hole; this is the well hole of the hand yang brilliance [conduit]."

26 Lin Yi et al.: "The Quan Yuanqi edition states: 'This is the ankle at the joint at the base of the human hand.'"

27 *Su wen* 41 has 痏數, "number of wounds." Cheng Shide et al.: "痏 is 瘢, 'a scar/ mark on the skin caused by piercing.'" 2414/66-67: "At the time of the Eastern Han emperor He (89 – 105 CE) an imperial physician named Guo Yu 郭玉 pointed out that the holes to be pierced are very small points that must not be missed with even the slightest aberration. A little later at the time of Emperor He, a book entitled *Yi shi* 乙石 gave an illustration of one hole holding several needles. On the right sits a female patient pierced at three locations, with each location having 'three wounds,' i.e., three needles were pierced into one hole. .. These doctrines are reflected in the *Ling shu* and in the *Su wen*." 1749/7: "The original meaning of 痏 was 'wound created by piercing.' Here it refers to the number of times a needle is inserted."

63-346-9
When an evil has settled in the foot yang walker vessels,
it lets the [affected] person have eye pain starting from the inner canthus.[28]
Pierce two wounds each one half inch below the outer ankles.[29]
[When the eye pain] is on the left, pierce on the right;
when it is on the right, pierce on the left.
After a time it takes to walk ten miles has elapsed, [the disease] has come to an end.

63-347-2
When a person has fallen,
when bad blood remains inside,
when the abdomen is full and distended and
when he can [relieve nature] neither in front nor behind,
[let him] first drink drugs freeing the passage.[30]

In this case the ceasing yin vessel has been harmed above; the minor yin network [vessel] has been harmed below.[31]

63-347-3
Pierce the blood vessel[32] below the inner ankle, in front of the blazing bone, to let blood,[33] and

---

28 Wang Bing: "Because this vessel emerges from the feet and rises to the head where it touches the inner canthi of the eyes. Hence, such a disease lets the patient experience eye pain starting from the inner canthi."

29 Wang Bing: "That is to say, [pierce at] the Extending Vessel (申脈) hole, this is where the yang walker [conduit] emerges."

30 Wu Kun: "[The patient] should first consume a medication to free the passage of blocked blood." Gao Jiwu/253 agrees: "Drugs causing the blood to move."

31 Gao Shishi: "When someone falls, this harms the sinews which are ruled by the liver and the bones which are ruled by the kidneys. When [it is stated] here 'the ceasing yin vessel has been harmed above,' this is the liver vessel, and 'the minor yin network [vessel] has been harmed below,' this is the kidney network [vessel]. The liver is associated with wood; its nature is to move upwards. Hence, [the text] states: 'above.' The kidneys are associated with water; its nature is to move down. Hence, [the text] states: 'below.'"

32 Lin Yi et al.: "The character 脈 in 血脈出血 may be [an error for] the character 絡, 'network [vessel].'"

33 Wang Bing: "That is the network [vessel] of the minor yin [conduit]."

pierce the moving vessel of the foot on the instep.³⁴
If [the disease] does not end, pierce one wound each above the three hairs.³⁵
When blood appears, stop [the treatment] immediately.
When [the disease] is on the left, pierce on the right;
when it is on the right, pierce on the left.³⁶

<When someone tends to have sadness and be frightened and is unhappy,
pierce according to the prescription [outlined] above, too.>

63-347-6
When an evil has settled in the network [vessels] of the hand yang brilliance
[conduits],
it lets the [affected] person become deaf in that occasionally he does not hear a
sound.
Pierce the finger next to the thumb above the [finger] nail,
generating one wound each [the width of] one leek leaf away from the [finger]
tip.³⁷
[The patient] will hear [again] immediately.
In case [the disease] does not end, pierce above the nail of the middle finger
where it meets with the flesh.³⁸
[The patient] will hear [again] immediately.
<Those who never hear anything, they cannot be pierced.³⁹

---

34 Wang Bing: "That is to say, [pierce at] the Surging Yang (衝陽) hole; this is the
plain [hole] of the stomach."

35 "Three hairs" denotes the region just proximal to the base of the nail of the big
toe.

36 Wang Bing: "That is to say, [pierce at] the Large Pile (大敦) hole; that is the well
hole of the ceasing yin [conduit]."

37 Wang Bing: "At the Shang-Yang (商陽) hole, as outlined above."

38 Wang Bing: "That is to say, [pierce at] the Central Thoroughfare (中衝) hole; this
is the well hole of the hand heart ruler [conduit]."

39 Wang Bing: "In this case the [flow of] qi in the network [vessels] has been interrupted completely. Hence, one cannot [achieve a cure through] piercing." Zhang
Zhicong: "This is a sign of deafness resulting from an inner harm; piercing is possible
only when [deafness results from] an evil having settled in the network [vessels]."

Those in whose ears wind emerges, they, too, are pierced in accordance with
this technique.>⁴⁰
When [the disease] is on the left, pierce on the right;
when it is on the right, pierce on the left.

63-348-1
Whenever [someone experiences] blocks that come and go, that move and do
not occupy a permanent location,
pierce where the pain is in the parting of the flesh.⁴¹
The number [of wounds to be generated] follows the waxing and waning of the
moon.
<In the application of the needle, the number of wounds [generated] follows
the [changes in the] abundance and weakness of the qi.
When the [number of wounds] needled exceeds the number of the days
[counted after new moon], then qi is lost.
When it does not reach the number of the day, then the qi is not drained.⁴²
When [the disease] is on the left, pierce on the right;
when it is on the right, pierce on the left.
[As soon as] the disease has ended, stop [the treatment].
If it does not come end, pierce it again in accordance with the law [just
outlined].

During crescent moon, [generate]
one wound on the first day,

---

40 Cheng Shide et al.: " 'Wind emerges in the ears' refers to sounds appearing in
one's ears." Yang Shangshan: "When a person has a feeling as if wind left from his
ears, then evil has settled in the network [vessels] of his hand yang brilliance [con-
duits]. Hence, the same [therapeutic] law is to be applied."

41 Gao Shishi: "All blocks that come and go are called 行痹, 'passing blocks.' When
they pass [here and there] and do not occur at a specific location, the evil is situated
in the flesh divides and does not pour into the conduit vessels." Zhang Jiebin: "This is
to say: Follow the location of the pain, search for the respective network [vessel] and
apply a misleading piercing there."

42 Gao Shishi: "When the moon is in a state of growth, the qi abounds; when the
moon is in a state of waning, the qi is weak. In the number of wounds to be generated,
the application of the needles follows the abundance or weakness of the human qi.
When the qi is weak, the [number of] needles should be small. In case the [number
of] needles [applied] exceeds the number [assigned to a] day [in the sequence of
growing and waning of the moon], then the qi is lost and a depletion results. When
the qi abounds, then the [number of] needles [applied] should be large. When the
[number of] needles is less than the number [assigned to a] day [in the sequence of
growing and waning of the moon], then the evil qi cannot be drained."

two wounds on the second day, and
{increase [the number of wounds] gradually up to}
15 wounds on the 15th day, [then]
14 wounds on the 16th day,
{[whereafter the number of wounds generated] is gradually decreased again}.>⁴³

63-348-6
When an evil has settled in the foot yang brilliance conduit,⁴⁴
it lets the [affected] person have a stuffy nose and nosebleed and the upper
teeth become cold.
Pierce above the nail of the toe next to the middle toe,⁴⁵ one wound each where
it meets with the flesh.
When [the disease] is on the left, pierce on the right;
when it is on the right, pierce on the left.

63-348-8
When an evil has settled in the network [vessels] of the foot minor yang [con-
duits],
it lets the [affected] person have pain in the flanks so that he is unable to
breathe.
He coughs and sweats.⁴⁶
Pierce above the nail of the toe next to the small toe, one wound each where
[the nail] meets with the flesh.⁴⁷
The inability to breathe will end immediately.
The sweating will stop immediately.

Those who cough, they should wear warm cloths and consume [warm] beverages and food;

---

43 Wang Bing: "This way the piercing will never exceed or fall short of the [required]
number."

44 Lin Yi et al.: "The Quan Yuanqi edition and the *Jia yi jing* have 陽明之絡, 'network [vessel] of the yang brilliance [conduit],' instead of 陽明之經." The *Tai su*, too,
has 絡 instead of 經. Ma Shi, Wu Kun, and Zhang Jiebin agree.

45 Wang Bing: " 'Middle [toe]' should be 'big [toe].'" The *Tai su* has "it lets the [af-
fected] person have stuffy nose and nosebleed and the lower teeth become cold. One
pierces the middle finger above the nail."

46 Gao Jiwu/405: "咳 is used here as an adverbial modifier indicating the circumstances under which sweating occurs."

47 Wang Bing: "That is to say, [pierce at] the Orifice Yin (竅陰) hole; that is the well
hole of the minor yang [conduit]."

[the cough] will end within one day.[48]
When [the disease] is on the left, pierce on the right;
when it is on the right, pierce on the left.
The disease will end immediately.
When it does not end, pierce again in accordance with the law [just outlined].

63-348-11
When an evil has settled in the network [vessels] of the foot minor yin
[conduits],
it lets the [affected] person have pain in his throat so that he is unable to take
in any food.
He will tend to be angry without cause.
The qi moves upwards to above the diaphragm.[49]
Pierce three wounds each in the vessel in the center of the lower side of the
feet.[50]
Together, [these] six piercings will [cause the disease] to end immediately.
When [the disease] is on the left, pierce on the right;
when it is on the right, pierce on the left.[51]

---

48 Zhang Zhicong: "In case of coughing, the evil is in the lung. Hence, one should
wear warm cloths and consume warm food and beverages. If the physical appearance
is cold and one drinks cold, this would double the harm."

49 Wang Bing: "賁 is 氣奔, 'the qi rushes.'" Lin Yi et al.: "Wang Bing's interpreta-
tion of 賁 as 氣奔 is wrong. According to the *Nan jing*, the stomach is the 賁門.
Yang Xuancao 楊玄操 said: 賁 is 膈, 'diaphragm.' What [the text] says is: 氣上走膈
上, 'the qi moves upwards beyond the diaphragm.' Since the [*Nei*]*jing* states 氣上走,
'the qi moves upwards,' why should one interpret 賁 as 'evil rushing upwards'?" Zhang
Zhicong: "賁 is to say 賁門, 'strong gate.' The kidney qi rises through the stomach.
Hence, 'the qi rises and moves above the strong [gate].'" Mori: " In a commentary to
Su wen 17, Wang Bing has stated: 肝主賁, 賁, 膈也." "膈上, above the diaphragm,' is
also called 賁上."

50 Wang Bing: "That is to say, [pierce at] the Gushing Fountain (涌泉) hole; that is
the well hole of minor yin [conduit]."

51 Gao Shishi: "The six characters 左刺右右刺左 are a later insertion." Tanba agrees.
Mori: "There is no doubt that the [three characters] 凡六刺 have come down from
antiquity. The statement following these three was written later by someone in the
margins and was erroneously entered into the [main text thereupon]. It can be eliminated. What the text is meant to say is: In all these six piercings, it is only through
misleading piercing that the disease can be eliminated."

<In cases of a swelling in the throat,
if one is unable to swallow saliva,[52] and
if at times one is [even] unable to produce saliva,
apply a misleading piercing in front of the blazing bone to let blood.
[The disease] ends immediately.
When [the disease] is on the left, pierce on the right;
when [the disease] is on the right, pierce on the left.[53]>

63-349-5
When an evil has settled in the network [vessels] of the foot major yin [conduits],
it lets the [affected] person have lower back pain pulling[54] on the lower abdomen and drawing on the lateral abdomen.[55]
He cannot breathe in an upright position.[56]
Pierce the divide between lower back and sacrum,[57] above the two buttocks.
{This is the transporter in the lower back.}[58]
The number of wounds [to be generated] follows the waxing and waning of the moon.
When the needle is deployed, [the disease] ends immediately.
When [the disease] is on the left, pierce on the right;
when [the disease] is on the right, pierce on the left.[59]

63-349-8
When an evil has settled in the network [vessels] of the foot major yang [conduits],

---

52 In contrast, Gao Shishi: "內 is equivalent to 咽, 'throat.'" Cheng Shide et al.: "內唾 refers to saliva in the throat."

53 Wang Bing: "That, too, is a network [vessel] of the foot minor yin [conduit]. This is so because this network [vessel] parallels the large conduit [running along] the throat." Zhang Yizhi et al.: "The 29 characters 嗌中腫 .. 右刺左 appear in both the *Tai su* and the *Jia yi* [*jing*] in front of the passage 邪客於足少陰太陰足陽明絡."

54 Zhang Jiebin: "控 is 引, 'to pull.'"

55 Wang Bing: "胂 is to say: the hollow, soft region below the small ribs."

56 Gao Jiwu/404: "One cannot thrust the chest forward to breath."

57 Cheng Shide et al.: "The final section of the spine is called 尻. Where the bones meet, this is called 解."

58 Lin Yi et al.: "According to the Quan Yuanqi edition, the three characters 是腰俞 were not part of the old versions."

59 Wang Bing: "The region between the lower back and the sacrum is called 'divide.' Right in its center is the transporter of the lower back."

it lets the [affected] person have a cramp and tightness in his back, which pull
on the flanks and create pain.

When piercing this, [move down] starting from the nape several vertebrae on
both sides of the spine.

Quickly press there and if [a location] responds to the hand with pain, pierce to
the side [of this location generating] three wounds.

[The disease] ends immediately.

63-350-3

When an evil has settled in the network [vessels] of the foot minor yang [con-
duits],

it lets the [affected] person have persistent pain in the pivot;[60]

the thigh bone cannot be raised.

Pierce into the pivot with a hairfine needle.

In case of cold, the needle is to remain for long.

The number [of wounds to be generated] follows the waxing and waning of
the moon.

[The disease] ends immediately.[61]

63-350-5

<For treating all the conduits pierce them [directly].

If there is no disease where [the conduit] passes,

then apply a misleading piercing.>[62]

<In case of deafness, pierce the hand yang brilliance [conduit].

---

60 Wang Bing: "Because this conduit emerges from the qi street, winds around the
hair line and moves transversely to enter the hip joint, hence, the pain [occurs there].
.. 樞 is 髀樞, 'hip pivot.'"

61 Wang Bing: "Behind the thigh pivot is the Ring-shaped Hoe (環銚) hole. .. This
is a hole where the qi of the foot minor yang vessel effuses."

62 Wang Bing: "When the conduit has no disease, then the evil is located in the
network. Hence, it is to be pierced misleadingly. When the location where the conduit
crosses has a disease, in that case it is a conduit disease and one must not conduct a
misleading piercing." Zhang Jiebin: "That is to say: the disease is not in the conduits
but in the network [vessels]. Hence, one conducts a misleading piercing. When the
disease is in the conduits, that is called 巨刺, 'grand piercing.'" Gao Shishi: "治諸經刺
之 is to say: for treating any disease of the conduits, one pierces the respective conduit
directly. 所過者不病 is to say: no evil has settled on the way passed by the conduit
and it has no disease. When it has no disease, then the disease is situated only in the
network [vessels]. Hence, pierce it misleadingly."

If [the disease] does not end, pierce where the vessel passing through there emerges in front of the ear.[63]

In case of toothache, pierce the hand yang brilliance [conduit].

If [the disease] does not end, pierce where the vessel enters the teeth and [the disease] ends immediately. >

63-351-1

When an evil has settled in the region of the five depots, the disease is such that the vessels have a pulling pain.

At times it comes and at times it stops.[64]

Find out the [location of the] disease and apply a misleading piercing above the nails of hands or feet.[65]

Find out the vessel [that is afflicted] and let its blood.

Pierce once every second day.

If the [disease] has not ended after one piercing,

it will end after five piercings.[66]

If [the evil] is transmitted misleadingly[67] and

pulls on the upper teeth and

if the teeth and lips are cold and have pain,

---

63 Wang Bing: " 'Hand yang brilliance [conduit]' is to say: At the front of the hand at the finger next to the thumb [the width of] one scallion leaf away from the tip. This [hole] is called Shang-Yang (商陽)." The *Jia yi jing* has 過脈 instead of 通脈.

64 Wu Kun: " 'In the five depots' is to say: in the network [vessels] of the five depots." Zhang Jiebin: "When an evil settles in the five depots, it will, in each case, pull on the respective conduit and cause pain [there]." Gao Shishi: "When an evil settles in the five depots, the [resulting] disease is such that the conduit vessels and the network vessels pull each other and have pain. Sometimes [the evil] appears in the network vessels, sometimes it stops only in the conduit vessels. Hence, 'at times it comes and at times it stops.' "

65 Wang Bing: "In each case pierce their well holes. When [the disease] is on the left, select [for treatment] the right; when [the disease] is on the right, select [for treatment] the left."

66 Wang Bing: "If there are blood vessels, then pierce them according to the technique mentioned here."

67 Zhang Zhicong: "That is to say, an evil of the hand yang brilliance [conduit] is adversely transmitted to the foot yang brilliance vessel." Cheng Shide et al.: "When [an evil] should not be transmitted and is transmitted nevertheless, that is called 'adverse transmission.' "

find out which vessels on the back of the hand have blood and remove it.⁶⁸
[Pierce] one wound above the nail of the middle toe into the foot yang brilliance [conduit] and
one wound each above the nail on the fingers next to the thumb.
The [disease] will end immediately.
When [the disease] is on the left, select [for treatment] the right;
when [the disease] is on the right, select [for treatment] the left.⁶⁹

63-351-6
When an evil has settled in the network [vessels] of the hand and foot minor
yin and major yin as well as of the foot yang brilliance [conduits],
{All these five network [vessels] meet in the ear and rise to encircle the left
corner [of the forehead].⁷⁰
In this case all the five network [vessels] are exhausted.}
this lets all the [affected] person's body's vessels have a movement while his
physical appearance has no sensitivity.
<They resemble a corpse.
Sometimes it is called corpse[-like condition because of] receding [qi].⁷¹>

---

68 Wang Bing: "When the disease is transmitted misleadingly and pulls on the upper
teeth and in case the teeth and lips are cold and have pain, pierce the yang brilliance
network on the back of the hand." Zhang Zhicong: "One must first inspect the vessels
on the back of the hand and eliminate the [blood] from those where blood stagnates.
This is to drain evil from the branches of the hand yang brilliance conduits."

69 Wang Bing: "That is to say, [pierce at] the Grinding Stone (厲兌) hole at the second finger."

70 Wang Bing: "The hand minor yin true heart vessel, the foot minor yin kidney vessel, the hand major yin lung vessel, the foot major yin spleen vessel, and the foot yang
brilliance stomach vessel, these five network [vessels] meet in the center [in front] of
the ear. They appear there and encircle the left frontal angle."

71 Wang Bing: "That is to say, [the patient] feels sudden chest pressure and has an appearance like a corpse. The body and the vessels, though, are those of a normal person
and move. When yin qi abounds above, then the qi below steams upwards and evil qi
rises contrary [to its regular course]. When evil qi rises contrary [to its regular course],
then the yang qi is in disorder. When the yang qi is in disorder, then the five networks
close and are not passable. Hence, the respective [person] resembles a corpse. Because
this [condition] is a result of receding [qi], one speaks of 'corpse recession.'" Zhang
Zhicong: "When all five network [vessels] are exhausted, then the camp and guard
[qi] do not move. This, then, lets [the affected] person's body and vessels tremble
and his physical appearance become unconscious. Now, a person's life depends on his
breathing qi and on the fluidity of his blood. When blood and qi do not move, then
his physical appearance resembles a corpse."

Pierce above the nail to the inner side of the big toe, [the width of] one leek leaf away from the tip.[72]
Then pierce the center [of the sole] of the feet.[73]
Then pierce above the nail of the middle toe; one wound each.[74]
Then pierce on the inner side of the thumb [the width of] one leek leaf away from the tip.[75]
Then pierce [into] the <hand heart ruler [conduit and the]>[76] minor yin [conduit], one wound each at the tip of the pointed bone.[77]
[The disease] ends immediately.
If it does not end, use a bamboo tube to blow into both the [patient's] ears.[78]
Shave the hair of a square inch [sized field] at the [patient's] left corner [of the forehead] and process [the hair] by burning it.[79]

---

72 Wang Bing: "That is to say, [pierce at] the Hidden White (隱白) hole; that is the well hole of the foot major yin [conduit]."

73 Wang Bing: "That is to say, [pierce at] the Gushing Fountain (涌泉) hole; that is the well hole of the foot minor yin [conduit]."

74 Wang Bing: "That is to say, [pierce at] the well hole of the foot yang brilliance [conduit] on the second toe."

75 Wang Bing: "That is to say, [pierce at] the Lesser Shang (少商) hole; that is the well hole of the hand major yin [conduit]."

76 Wang Bing: "That is to say, [pierce at] the Central Thoroughfare (中衝) hole; that is the well hole of the hand heart ruler [conduit]." Lin Yi et al.: "The *Jia yi jing* does not advice to pierce the hand heart ruler. The five network [vessels] listed above do not include the hand heart ruler either. If it were to be pierced as is recommended here, this would sum up to six network vessels" Zhang Qi: "The two characters 心主 are a [later] addition." Tanba: "The text above does not include a reference to the heart ruler ceasing yin [vessels]. Hence, this is a mistake which must be deleted. Lin Yi et al. is correct."

77 Wang Bing: "That is to say, [pierce at] the Spirit Gate (神門) hole; that is the transporter of the hand minor yin [conduit] behind the palm in the depression at the tip of the pointed bone." The *Tai su* does not have these five characters.

78 Wang Bing: "That is to say: one lets qi enter the ear and assist the five network [vessels] internally to have the qi pass again. One inserts the tube into the ear, tightly seals it with one's fingers lest any qi flow away and then blows with utmost [force]. The qi will force its way into the network vessels and penetrate them."

79 Wang Bing: "The hair at the left [frontal] angle is an outgrowth of the blood of the five network [vessels]. Hence, one removes it by shaving and prepares it [for intake] by burning." 1681/78: "The 燔治 of the *Nei jing* is identical with the 燔治 of the Mawangdui silk manuscripts. The meaning of 治 is identical with 碎, 'to break into small pieces,' (i.e., to process)."

Let [the patient] drink one cup of the [processed hair] with good wine.[80]
Into those who cannot drink it, it is poured [by force].
The [disease] ends immediately.

63-352-4
As for the technique of piercing,[81] first observe the conduit vessels.
Squeeze them and follow them [with the fingers].[82]
Investigate whether they are depleted or replete and regulate them.

To those that [can] not be regulated, a conduit piercing is applied.[83]
To those that have pain [only] while the conduits do not have a disease, apply a
misleading piercing. Hence, look for those [locations] where the respective skin
section has network [vessels] with blood, and
select all of them [for treatment].

That is the technique[84] of misleading piercing."

80 Wang Bing: "Wine is employed to transport the strength of drugs. Also, it flares
upwards and enters the heart. The heart rules the vessels. Hence, one has [the patient]
consume the [drugs] with good wine." Zhang Jiebin: "One [asks the patient] to drink
wine to assist the drug effects to pass through blood and qi."

81 Yang Shangshan: "數 is 法, 'method.'" *NJCD*: "數 is 術, 'technique,' 方法, 'method.'" (This meaning of 數 is to be seen clearly in *Su wen* 52-275-8 and 63-348-1.)

82 The *Jia yi jing* has 循, "to follow," instead of 從.

83 Cheng Shide et al.: "經刺 is 巨刺, 'grand piercing.'"

84 Wang Qi: "數 has the meaning of 原則, 'principle.'"

Chapter 64
Discourse on Opposition and Compliance in Piercing in [the Course of] the Four Seasons

64-352-8

When the ceasing yin [qi] is present in surplus,[1] the [resulting] disease is a yin block.[2]

When it is present insufficiently, the disease generated is heat block.[3]

When [the vessels] are smooth, then the disease is fox [type] elevation illness wind.

When they are rough, then the disease is accumulated qi in the lower abdomen.[4]

---

1 Lin Yi et al.: "The passage from 'When the ceasing yin [qi] is present in surplus ..' to 'Frequently the sinews are tight and the eyes ache' appears in the Quan Yuanqi edition in ch. 6."

2 Wang Bing: " 'Block' is to say: 'pain.' 'Yin' is to say: 'cold.' 'To be present in surplus' is to say: the ceasing yin qi abounds and fills [the vessels]. Hence, yin [qi] effuses to the outside and causes cold block." Lin Yi et al.: "Wang Bing's interpretation of 'block' as 'pain' cannot be followed." Zhang Zhicong: "痹 is 閉, 'closure.' Blood and qi remain attached to the region of skin, flesh, sinews, and bones and cause pain." Zhang Jiebin: " 'Ceasing yin' is the qi of wind and wood. When wind and wood are present in surplus, then evil collects in the liver. The vessels of the liver conduit form knottings in all yin sections. Hence, the [resulting] disease is 'yin block.'"

3 Wang Bing: "When the yin [qi] is present insufficiently, then the yang is present in surplus. Hence, this causes a heat block." Yu Chang: "From Wang Bing's commentary it appears that the character 生 is a later insertion." Zhang Yizhi et al.: "Wang Bing did not refer to the character 生; obviously the version he used did not have the character 生."

4 Yang Shangshan: "A fox cannot urinate at night; only when the sun comes out [the fox] is able [to urinate]. This disease in humans is identical with the [situation of the] fox. Hence, it is called 'fox elevation illness.'" Wang Bing: "The ceasing yin vessels follow the thighs and enter the [pubic] hair. They encircle the yin (i.e., sexual) organ and reach the lower abdomen. Its network [vessels] branch off and follow the lower leg upwards to the testicles where they tie up with the penis. Hence, [a ceasing yin disease] causes fox[-type] elevation illness and accumulated qi in the lower abdomen." Zhang Jiebin: "疝 is pain in the frontal yin (i.e., sexual organ) and in the abdomen. In both males and females all five depots may have it. The fox lies hidden during daytime and comes out in the night; it is a yin animal. When the 疝 is in the ceasing yin [vessels], the leaving and entering, rising and descending [of its qi] is irregular, resembling a fox. Hence, [the text] speaks of 'fox elevation illness-wind.' This is not a wind that has entered [the body] from the outside; what is meant here is a liver evil." Yu Chang: "In

64-353-1
When the minor yin [qi] is present in surplus, the [resulting] disease is skin block {inconspicuous papules}.[5]
When it is present insufficiently, the [resulting] disease is lung block.[6]

When [the vessels] are smooth, then the disease is lung wind elevation illness. When they are rough, then the disease is accumulation [resulting in a] passing of urine with blood.[7]

When the major yin [qi] is present in surplus, the [resulting] disease is flesh block {cold center}.
When it is present insufficiently, the [resulting] disease is spleen block.[8]

---

its subsequent statements, the text always refers to some wind elevation illness. Hence, the sequence of the two characters 疝風 should be reversed." See also Harper 1998, 209-210, for a possible derivation of 狐疝 from the term *pian shan* 偏疝, "inguinal swelling on one side", in one of the Ma wang dui manuscripts.

5 Ma Shi: "This should be 癗疹." Wu Kun: "隱疹 is 癗疹." 916/54: "軫 is identical with 疹, 'pustule.' The *Yu pian* 玉篇 states: '癗疹 are small elevations on the outside of the skin.'" Cheng Shide et al.: "隱軫 is 隱疹. This [term] refers to small papules appearing on the skin."

6 Wang Bing: "The reason is that kidney water moves contrary [to its regular course] and ties up with the lung, which is its mother. The foot minor yin vessel rises from the kidneys, penetrates liver and diaphragm and enters the lung. Hence, when [minor yin qi] is present in surplus, the [resulting] disease is skin block and insignificant papules. In case of insufficiency the [resulting] disease is lung block." Gao Shishi: "The minor yin is [associated with] fire. [In the course] of the four seasons, fire is [associated with] summer. When the minor yin [qi] is present in surplus, then the fire qi flames to the outside. Hence, the [resulting] disease is skin block and insignificant papules. When the minor yin [qi] is present insufficiently, then the fire qi is depleted internally. Hence, the [resulting] disease is lung block."

7 Wang Bing: "Because the proper [minor yin] conduit enters the lung, penetrates the kidneys and encircles the bladder, hence [when it causes a disease] this is lung elevation illness [in the one case] and accumulation [together with] hematuria [in the other case]." Zhang Jiebin: "A rough [movement in the vessels] indicates that heart blood is insufficient. Hence, the conduit [passage] is obstructed and this results in accumulations. The blood is in disorder and this results in a passage of urine with blood."

8 Wang Bing: "The spleen rules the flesh; hence [the disease] is like this." Wu Kun: "The major yin [qi] is the qi of dampness and soil. When this qi is present in surplus, then dampness prevails. The spleen rules the muscles and the flesh. Its position is in the center. Hence, [the resulting disease is] flesh block and cold center." Zhang Jiebin: "Cold and dampness are present in the spleen. Hence, this causes 'cold center.'"

When [the vessels] are smooth, then the disease is spleen wind elevation illness. When they are rough, then the disease is accumulation [resulting in] frequent fullness experienced by heart and abdomen.[9]

64-353-4

When the yang brilliance [qi] is present in surplus, the [resulting] disease is vessel block. {The body experiences frequent heat.}
When it is present insufficiently, the [resulting] disease is heart block.[10]

When [the vessels] are smooth, then the disease is heart wind elevation illness. When they are rough, then the disease is accumulation [resulting in] a frequent tendency to be frightened.[11]

64-353-5

When the major yang [qi] is present in surplus, the [resulting] disease is bone block. {The body is heavy.}
When it is present insufficiently, the [resulting] disease is kidney block.[12]

---

9 Wang Bing: "The major yin vessel enters the abdomen, touches the spleen and encircles the stomach. Its branch rises from the stomach to the diaphragm and attaches itself to the heart center. Hence, [when it causes a disease] this is spleen elevation illness and frequent fullness in heart and abdomen."

10 Wang Bing: "When the stomach has a surplus, then [its contents/qi] rise and turn to the heart. When it experiences insufficiency, then there is a block below the heart. Hence, it is like this." Zhang Jiebin: "The yang brilliance [qi] is the qi of dryness and metal. It is associated with the large intestine and with the stomach. When the dryness qi is present in surplus, then the blood vessels are depleted and the yin water is weak. Hence, the [resulting] disease is vessel block and the body is frequently hot." Ma Shi: "Yang brilliance [refers to] the foot yang brilliance conduit of the stomach. The stomach is the son of the heart. When [its qi] is present in surplus, then the [resulting] disease is vessel block. The reason is that the heart rules the vessels. The vessels are half in the outside [region of the body]. When [the stomach qi] is present insufficiently, then the [resulting] disease is heart block. The heart rules the interior."

11 Wang Bing: "The vessel of the heart ruler rises from the chest center, touches the heart enclosure, descends to the diaphragm and encircles the triple burner. Hence, [when it causes a disease] this is heart elevation illness and a frequent tendency to be scared." Zhang Jiebin: "When [the vessels] are smooth, then dryness and heat generate wind. Heat is ruled by the heart. Hence, [the resulting disease] is heart wind elevation illness. When [the vessels] are rough, then the stomach is depleted and obstructed. Hence, the disease is accumulation. When the stomach is depleted, [the qi of] wind and wood seize it. Hence, one tends to be scared."

12 Wang Bing: "The major yang and the minor yin constitute outer and inner. Hence, whether it is a surplus or an insufficiency, the [resulting] diseases do always concen-

When [the vessels] are smooth, then the disease is kidney wind elevation illness. When they are rough, then the disease is accumulation [resulting in] a tendency to frequent peak illness.[13]

When the minor yang [qi] is present in surplus, the [resulting] disease is sinew block. {The flanks experience fullness.}
When it is present insufficiently, the [resulting] disease is liver block.[14]

When [the vessels] are smooth, then the disease is liver wind elevation illness. When they are rough, then the disease is accumulation [resulting in] frequent tightness of the sinews and aching eyes.[15]

64-353-8
Hence,
in spring the qi is in the conduit vessels.
In summer the qi is in the tertiary network [vessels].
In late summer the qi is in the muscles and in the flesh.
In autumn the qi is in the skin.
In winter the qi is in the bones and in the marrow.

[Huang] Di:
"I should like to hear the reason of this."

Qi Bo:
"In spring,
the qi of heaven begins to [disperse into] the open;

---

trate on the kidneys." Zhang Jiebin: "In case of insufficiency, the kidney qi is weak. Hence, the [resulting] disease is kidney block."

13 Wang Bing: "The major yang vessels cross the peak of the head. They enter [the head], encircle the brain, descend following the spine and encircle the kidneys. Hence, [when they cause a disease] this is kidney wind and peak illness."

14 Wang Bing: "The minor yang and the ceasing yin constitute outer and inner. Hence, the [resulting] disease turns to the liver." Zhang Jiebin: "When the minor yang [qi] is present insufficiently, then the qi of the liver depot is depleted. Hence, the [resulting] disease is liver block."

15 Wang Bing: "The liver rules the sinews. Hence, the sinews are frequently tight. The ceasing yin vessel rises and appears at the forehead; it meets with the supervisor vessel at the peak of the head. Its branch descends from the eye connection. Hence, the eyes ache." Zhang Jiebin: "When [the vessels] are rough because the blood [flow] is obstructed, the disease is liver accumulation. The liver rules the sinews; its orifices are the eyes. Hence, the sinews are tight and the eyes ache."

the qi of the earth begins to flow out.
What is frozen breaks open; the ice melts.
The water flows and the conduits are passable.
Hence, the human qi is in the vessels.[16]

64-354-1
In summer,
the conduits are full and the qi overflows.
It enters the tertiary network [vessels] which [thereby] receive blood.
The skin is filled and replete.[17]

In late summer,
the conduits and the network [vessels] all abound [with contents] which internally overflow into the muscles.[18]

In autumn,
the qi of heaven begins to contract [things].
The interstice structures are obstructed and the skin is pulled together tightly.[19]

In winter,
[everything is] covered and stored away.
Blood and qi are in the center.
They are attached to the bones and the marrow internally and penetrate the five depots.

Hence,
evil qi regularly follows the [flow of proper] qi and blood of the four seasons when it enters [the body] and settles in it.

---

16 Zhang Jiebin: "In spring time, the qi of heaven and earth moves. The water springs flow. Hence, the human qi, too, is in the conduit vessels." Zhang Qi: "The rise and fall of the qi in the human body follows the qi of heaven and earth."

17 Ma Shi: "In summer qi is present in the tertiary network [vessels] because in summer time the conduit vessels are filled to the extreme and the qi of the [conduit vessels] overflows into the tertiary network [vessels]. The tertiary network [vessels] receive blood and the skin on the outside is entirely filled, hence the human qi is in the tertiary network [vessels]."

18 Ma Shi: "In late summer, the qi is in the muscles and in the flesh. This is just because in late summer the conduit vessels and the network vessels abound [with qi] which overflows into the muscles. Hence, the human qi is in the muscles and in the flesh."

19 Wang Bing: "引 is 牽引, 'to pull.'"

[However,]
when it comes to changes and transformations,
they cannot be quantified [in terms of regular time periods].[20]
This being so,
one must act in compliance with the regular qi and punish and eliminate
the evil.[21]
When the evil is eliminated, disorderly qi will not be generated."[22]

64-354-7
[Huang] Di:
"To oppose the four seasons and generate disorderly qi, how is that?"

Qi Bo:
"When in spring one pierces the network vessels,
[then] blood and qi overflow to the outside.
This lets that person be short of qi.[23]

When in spring one pierces the muscles and the flesh,
[then] blood and qi circulate contrary [to their regular course].
This lets that person experience rising qi.[24]

---

20 Gao Shishi: "The host qi of the four seasons, they all have their regular time periods. The transformations and changes of the evil qi, though, they cannot be calculated
[in terms of regular appearances]."

21 Ma Shi: "辟 is identical with 闢, 'to open.'" Cheng Shide et al.: "辟除 has the
meaning of 祛除, 'to eliminate.'"

22 Zhang Jiebin: "When the evil has left, the qi is regulated. Hence, it does not reach
a situation where disorder is generated."

23 Wang Bing: "When blood and qi overflow to the outside, then the center is
marked by insufficiency. Hence, one is 'short of qi.'" Ma Shi: "In spring one should
pierce the conduit vessels. If one pierces the network vessels, that is, if one pierces in
spring what should be pierced in summer, then blood and qi flow away to the outside
and large [quantities of] qi are diminished in the center." Zhang Jiebin: " 'Short of qi'
should be 'short of qi and blood.'"

24 Zhang Jiebin: "This is piercing in spring [what should be pierced] in late summer.
In spring the wood rules while the soil qi is depleted. If one repeatedly pierces the
muscles and the flesh and [thereby] repeatedly harms the original [qi] of the spleen,
the circulation of blood and qi will be reversed. Hence, panting, fullness, and rising
qi result."

When in spring one pierces the sinews and the bones,
[then] the blood and the qi are attached internally.
This lets that person have abdominal distension.[25]

64-354-9
When in summer one pierces the conduit vessels,
then blood and qi are exhausted.
This lets that person experience *jie-yi*.[26]

When in summer one pierces the muscles and the flesh,
[then] the blood and the qi withdraw[27] to the interior.
This lets that person tend to be fearful.[28]

When in summer one pierces the sinews and the bones,
[then] blood and qi rise contrary [to their regular course].
This lets that person tend to be angry.

---

25 Wang Bing: "[Blood and qi] remain attached internally and do not disperse. Hence, distention results." Zhang Jiebin: "This is piercing in spring [what should be pierced] in winter. In spring the qi effuses and moves to the outside. If nevertheless one enters deeply and selects the sinews and bones [for treatment], one harms the yin. Hence, blood and qi remain attached internally and this causes that person's abdomen to be distended."

26 Wang Bing: "Blood and qi are diminished or exhausted. Hence, one experiences *jie-yi*. However, the [resulting state] cannot be named. 解㑊 is to say: cold [but] not cold; hot [but] not hot; strong [but] not strong; weak [but] not weak. Hence, one cannot name this [state]." Cheng Shide et al.: "解 is to be interpreted as 懈, 'inattentive.' Hence, the meaning of 解㑊 is 懈惰, 'lazy,' 'indifferent.'" Hu Tianxiong agrees; see there for details. Zhang Zhicong: "In summer the qi abounds and blood and qi have left already to the outside [to pour into] the tertiary network [vessels]. If they are removed, once again, from the conduit vessels, then blood and qi are exhausted internally. This lets that person be tired." For further comments, see also *Su wen* 18-113-1.

27 Wang Bing: "郤 is 閉, 'close.' When blood and qi are closed in internally, then the yang qi cannot pass through [the body]. Hence, one tends to be fearful." Cheng Shide et al.: "郤 is 退, 'to retreat.'"

28 Wang Bing: "When blood and qi rise contrary [to their regular course], then the qi of anger corresponds. Hence, one tends to be angry." Zhang Jiebin: "When in summer one pierces the winter section, then the yin will be depleted internally and the yang dominates in the outside. This causes that person's blood and qi to move contrary [to their regular course] and results in a tendency to be angry."

When in autumn one pierces the conduit vessels,
[then] blood and qi rise contrary [to their regular course].
This lets that person be forgetful.[29]

64-354-12
When in autumn one pierces the network vessels,
[then] the qi does not move in the [body's] outside.
This lets that person lie down; he does not wish to move.[30]

When in autumn one pierces the sinews and bones,
[then] blood and qi disperse internally.
This lets that person shiver from cold.[31]

64-355-1
When in winter one pierces the conduit vessels,
[then] blood and qi are all lost and
this lets that person's eyes become unclear.[32]

---

29 Wang Bing: "Blood and qi rise contrary [to their regular course, generating] fullness in the lung. Hence, one tends to be forgetful." Wu Kun: "The heart generates the
vessels. When in autumn one pierces the conduit vessels and depletes the respective
conduits, then the conduit vessels are depleted and the heart qi is depleted, too. Hence,
one is forgetful." Zhang Qi: "When in autumn a disease is in the lung and contrary [to
an appropriate treatment] one harms the liver and the blood, the [liver] qi is brought
into disorder, moves adversely to the lung and cannot interact with the lower region.
Hence, one is forgetful."

30 Lin Yi et al.: "Another version has 血氣不行, 'blood and qi do not move.' The
Quan Yuanqi edition and the *Tai su* have 氣不衛外, 'the qi does not guard the exterior.'" Zhang Jiebin agrees: "Autumn is the time of collecting and securing; the qi
leaves already the network [vessels]. If one pierces them nevertheless, then the qi is
depleted and cannot protect the exterior. The qi belongs to the yang; when the yang is
depleted one lies down and does not wish to move."

31 Wang Bing: "When blood and qi are dispersed internally, then the central qi is
depleted. Hence, one is cold and shivers." Zhang Qi: " 'Dispersed internally' should be
'dispersed externally.' Both lung and kidneys have a disease and the yang qi flows out
to the exterior. Hence, one is cold and shivers."

32 Wang Bing: "Because there is neither blood nor qi that could nourish them."
Zhang Zhicong: "Winter rules closure and storage to supply the qi of spring creation.
If [at a time] when there should be storage, in contrast one conducts a drainage, then
this results in a complete loss of blood and qi inside and this causes that person's eyes
to be unclear. The reason is, all the essence of the five depots pours into the eyes and
allows them to see. In winter, blood and qi are in the center. They are attached to the
bones and the marrow in the interior and they penetrate the five depots. If blood and

When in winter one pierces the network vessels,
[then] the internal qi flows away to the outside.
[That which] stays causes a massive block.[33]

When in winter one pierces the muscles and the flesh,
[then] the yang qi is exhausted and interrrupted [in its flow].
This lets that person be forgetful.[34]

All these [mistaken] piercings in the course of the four seasons [constitute] the
fault of massive opposition.[35]
It is impossible not to conform [to the four seasons].
To act contrary to them generates diseases of disorderly qi encroaching into
another [territory].[36]

64-355-5
Hence,
if one pierces without knowing the course of the four seasons,
and what has generated the diseases,[37] and
if one considers compliance as opposition,
[then] the proper qi is in disorder internally and
strikes at the essence.
It is essential to investigate the nine indicators.

---

qi are lost internally, then all the five depots are depleted. This causes that person's eyes
to be unclear."

33 Zhang Zhicong: "In case of a 'great block,' the qi of the depots is depleted and
the evil is blocked in the five depots." Zhang Jiebin: "If at a time when the yang qi
lies hidden in storage one pierces the yang section, then the yang qi flows out to the
outside. [As a result,] the yang is depleted and the yin dominates. Hence, a 'great
block' results." Mori: " 'Internal qi flows away to the outside' is to say: yang qi appears
outside. The blood, which is yin, does not move. Hence, this causes a block." Zhang
Yizhi et al.: "The character 内 is an error for 血, 'blood.' "

34 Wang Bing: "When the yang qi is not strong [in winter], it will be exhausted in
spring. Hence, one is forgetful."

35 Or: "[cause] diseases of massive movements contrary [to a regular course]." Lin Yi
et al.: "The Quan Yuanqi edition has 六經之病, 'diseases of the six conduits.' " Mori:
"大逆之病 does not fit the context. One should follow the Quan Yuanqi edition."

36 Wang Bing: "淫 is 不次, 'not in [proper] succession.' When their movement does
not proceed in [proper] succession, then [the qi] invade each other's [territory] and are
mixed up and this generates disease."

37 Gao Jiwu/259 interprets: "Hence, if in piercing one does not know where the
regular qi is and what the reasons are for diseases to appear, .."

When the proper qi is not in disorder,
essence and qi do not turn around."[38]

64-355-7
[Huang] Di:
"Good!"

In piercing the five depots,
if one hits the heart, death occurs within one day.
Its excitement leads to belching.[39]

If one hits the liver, death occurs within five days.
Its excitement leads to talkativeness.

If one hits the lung, death occurs within three ays.
Its excitement leads to coughing.

If one hits the kidneys, death occurs within six days.
Their excitement leads to sneezing {yawning}.[40]

If one hits the spleen, death occurs within ten days.
Its excitement leads to swallowing.

64-356-1
To injure in the course of piercing [one of] a person's five depots must result
in death.
If [any of the depots] is excited, then it is from the manifestations of change
associated with each depot that one knows [the period after which] the [pa-
tient] will die.

---

38 Wang Bing: " 'Does not turn around' is to say: 不逆轉, 'does not turn around
moving contrary [to a regular course].' " Gao Shishi: " 'Does not turn around' is 內存,
'is present inside.' " Hu Tianxiong: "Tanba wonders whether the character 轉 may not
be an error for 薄, 'clash.' This is very appropriate. Above the text states: 'the proper
qi is in disorder inside; it clashes with the essence.' Here it states: 'The proper qi is
not in disorder, it does not clash [with] the essence.' The error arose because the two
characters 轉 and 薄 are quite similar."

39 See *Su wen* 52 for an almost identical set of statements.

40 25/45: "欠 and 嚏 have the same meaning, i.e., 'to yawn.' " For details, see there.

Chapter 65
Discourse on Tip[1] and Root and on the Transmission of Disease [Inside the Organism]

65-356-4
Huang Di asked:
"Diseases have tip and a root;[2]
in piercing there is opposition and compliance.[3]
How is that?"

Qi Bo responded:
"All formulas of piercing
require one to distinguish yin and yang.[4]
Front and back correspond to each other,[5]

---

1 *Guan zi*, "Ba Yan" 管子霸言: 大本小標, "Large base [of a tree], small tips [of the branches]."

2 Wang Bing: "本 is the first disease; 標 is a later disease." Zhang Jiebin: "標 is 末, 'end;' 本 is 原, 'origin.' This is just like a tree has roots and branches. If referred to separately, then root and branches have different shapes; if referred to together, then the tips originate from the root." Ma Shi: "標 is the later development of a disease; 本 is the first manifestation of a disease." For a detailed discussion of the concept of "tip and root", see 1817/37.

3 Ma Shi: " 'Opposition,' this is when the disease is at the root and one tries to stop it at the tip, or when the disease is at the tip and one tries to stop it at the root. 'Compliance,' this is when it is at the root and one tries to stop it at the root, or when it is at the tip and one tries to stop it at the tip. These are different therapeutic patterns." 1610/48: "When the disease is at the root and one treats the tip; or when it is at the tip and one treats the root, this is opposing therapy. When the disease is at the root and one treats the root, or when it is at the tip and one treats the tip, this is compliance therapy."

4 Ma Shi: "One must distinguish whether the disease is in the yin conduits or in the yang conduits." Zhang Jiebin: "The [meaning] encompassed by the two characters yin and yang is broad, [including], for example, conduits and network [vessels], the seasons, qi and blood, as well as the [categorization of the] diseases. There is nothing that is not included." 1610/48: "One must distinguish whether this disease is in the depots or in the palaces, whether the disease is in the yin conduits or in the yang conduits, whether the disease is in the qi or in the blood and whether the pathoconditions are yin or yang."

5 Ma Shi: " 'Front' and 'behind' are abdomen and back. The conduits and network [vessels] of [abdomen and back] correspond to each other." Wu Kun: "That is to say: if one pierces the conduit holes in the front and on the back, their qi correspond to

opposition and compliance can be applied.⁶
Tip and root mutually shift [positions].⁷

Hence, it is said:
in some cases, it is at the tip and it is searched for at the tip;
in some cases, it is at the root and it is searched for at the root;
in some cases, it is at the root and it is searched for at the tip;
in some cases, it is at the tip and it is searched for at the root.

65-356-7
Hence,
in treatment,
in some cases, one achieves a success by selecting [for treatment] the tip;
in some cases, one achieves a success by selecting [for treatment] the root;

[That is,]
in some cases, one achieves a success by selecting [a treatment] that is an
opposition;
in some cases, one achieves a success by selecting [a treatment] that is a
conformance.⁸

Hence,
if one knows opposition and comformance,

---

each other." Zhang Zhicong: " 'Front and behind correspond to each other' is: some
diseases come first and some diseases come later."

6 Wu Kun: " 'Opposition' is paradox treatment; 'compliance' is proper treatment. 得
施 is to say: one applies treatments without failure." Zhang Jiebin: "Sometimes one
opposes, sometimes one complies; one must apply the [appropriate] pattern." On the
concepts of 逆治 and 從治, see a detailed discussion in 1399/43.

7 *Gu dian yi zhu xuan* bianxiezu /62: "Wu Kun: 'In piercing, sometimes one treats the
tip and sometimes one treats the root. One shifts to and fro.' The meaning is: there
is no fixed order whether to treat diseases at the tip or at the root first or later. When
the tip disease is serious, one treats the tip first; when the root disease is serious, one
treats the root first." See also 2766/9.

8 Wang Bing: "If one has grasped the nature of a disease and if one knows the main
points of treating it, then both opposition and compliance can be applied and must
lead to success." *Gu dian yi zhu xuan* bianxiezu /62: "The former is: when [the disease]
is at the root, one takes it at the tip; when it is at the tip, one takes it at the root. The
latter is: when [the disease] is at the tip, one takes it at the tip; when it is at the root,
one takes it at the root."

a proper practice [results by itself] without one having to worry about it.⁹
Those who know tip and root,
they take up a myriad [cases] and achieve a myriad successes.
Not to know tip and root,
that is called an absurd practice.¹⁰

65-356-10
Now,
as for the Way of yin and yang, opposition and compliance,¹¹ tip and root,
[it may seem] small but it is big.
A statement on one [disease] results in knowledge on the harm¹² caused by the
one hundred diseases.¹³
[It may seem] diminished but it is plentiful.
[It may seem] shallow but it is wide.
One can make a statement on one [example] and knows one hundred.
By [examining] the shallow, know [what is in] the depth;
by investigating the near, know [what is] far away.

---

9 Wang Bing: "When no doubts are harbored concerning the Way, the knowledge
will be deep and clear and, as a result, no questions are posed to other people and the
conduct will be proper." Ma Shi: "Then [one is able to conduct] a pattern of proper
action and does not have to ask other people." 1126/11: "當 is to be interpreted as 正
確, 'correct.'"

10 306/122: "不知標本 should be 不知標本逆從."

11 1610/49: " 'Yin and yang' refers to the pathoconditions; 'opposition and conformity' refers to the therapeutic patterns."

12 1610/49: "害 is 要害, 'vital,' 關鍵, 'key.' That is to say: if one only discusses the
question of tip and root, one understands the key elements of all kinds of diseases."

13 Wang Bing: "That is to say, [when one] distinguishes between yin and yang and
knows opposition and conformity, the patterns [of therapy] are obvious and the essential subtleties are visible. One observes where [a disease] commences and at this
point it is minor/small (小). One follows where it flows and then it is serious/big (大).
This way, it is obvious. Hence, [the text] states: 'A statement on one [disease] results in
knowledge on the harm caused by the one hundred diseases.' " Wu Kun: " 'One' refers
to the root; 'one hundred' refers to the tip." Ma Shi: "One discusses one disease and
then knows the harm caused by the hundreds of diseases." Gao Shishi: "One discusses
tip and root, opposition and compliance in view of one single [disease] and knows
the harm caused by the hundreds of diseases." See *Su wen* 74-534-4 for an almost
identical statement.

65-356-12
[When people] speak of tip and root,
this is easy and yet they do not reach [the core of it].[14]

To treat contrary to [the requirements], that is opposition;[15]
to treat in agreement with [the requirements], that is compliance.[16]

When the disease is first and a movement contrary [to its regular course] occurs afterwards,
treat its root.[17]
When a movement contrary [to its regular course] is first and the disease occurs afterwards,
treat its root.

65-356-14
When the cold is first and a disease emerges afterwards,
treat its root.

---

14 Wang Bing: "Even though something is extremely deep and obscure, people do not even go a short way [to reach it]. They penetrate everything by relying on that which is shallow and near. Thus, the Way of tip and root, even though it is easy to put it in words, the ordinary people neither in their knowledge nor in what they see are in a position to reach it." Zhang Jiebin: "This Way of tip and roots, of opposition and compliance, of yin and yang appears shallow and within reach. [However,] even though talking about it may be easy, in reality one never reaches it." Cheng Shide et al.: "That is, the Way of tip and root, of opposition and compliance appears easy to understand. However, to grasp its application in concrete situations is not so easy." 1610/49: "That is to say: The principles of tip and root are easy to understand; however, when to be applied in clinical practice, they are not so easy to grasp." *Su wen* 74-534-5 has 易而勿損, "it is easy and one will not cause harm."

15 1610/49: " 'To act contrary to [the requirements]' is to act contrary to the manifestation of the disease. For instance, if one treats a disease of cold nature with heating drugs; or if one treats and disease of hot nature with cold or cool drugs."

16 Zhang Jiebin: "得 is 相得, 'suited,' 'agreeable.' It is identical with 順, 'appropriate,' 'to fit.'" Gao Shishi: "Not to know tip and root and treating the [disease] contrary to [what is required], that is opposition. To know its tip and root and to treat it appropriately, that is compliance."

17 Zhang Jiebin: "逆 is a movement of blood and qi contrary [to their regular course]." Wu Kun: "逆 is 嘔逆, 'vomiting [because of] adverse movement.'" Zhang Qi: "逆 is 厥逆, 'receding movement contrary [to a regular course].'" Cheng Shide et al.: "Further down the text states 有先逆而後病. Hence, the meanings suggested by Wu Kun and Zhang Qi make sense, but they are not as convincing as the interpretation offered by Zhang Jiebin."

When the disease is first and cold emerges afterwards,
treat its root.

When the heat is first and a disease emerges afterwards,
treat its root.
When the heat is first and central fullness emerges afterwards,
treat its tip.[18]

When the disease is first and outflow occurs afterwards,
treat its root.
When an outflow occurs first and another disease emerges afterwards,
treat its root.
{One must regulate it for the moment and then treat the other disease.}[19]

When the disease is first and central fullness emerges afterwards,
treat its tip.
When central fullness is first and a vexed heart [emerges] afterwards,
treat its root.

{Man has visitor qi and identical qi.}[20]

---

18 Zhang Jiebin: "In all cases of disease, one first treats the root. Only in the case of central fullness, one first treats its tip. The reason is, when the disease is central fullness, the evil is in the stomach. The stomach is the root of the depots and palaces. When the stomach is full, then the qi of drugs and food cannot move and all the depots and palaces lose their provisions. Hence, if one treats the [stomach] first this, too, is treating the root." Hua Shou: "This sentence should read 先病而後生熱者治其標, 'When the disease is first and heat is generated afterwards, one treats its tip,' because from the sentence in the text further down 'When the disease is first and if central fullness develops afterwards, one treats its tip' it is obvious that the present [version] is a mistake." *Ling shu* 25, in a parallel passage, has "disease" instead of "heat."

19 Gao Shishi: "If an outflow occurs first and if other diseases are generated afterwards, one treats the root of this initial outflow. If an outflow occurs first, then the center, [i.e.,] the soil, is depleted first. Hence, one treats its root. One must regulate it [first] and treat the other diseases later, thereby giving priority to the center, [i.e.,] the soil."

20 Lin Yi et al.: "The Quan Yuanqi edition has 固, 'firm,' instead of 同." Tanba: "The Quan Yuanqi edition appears to be correct. 'Visitor qi' refers to an evil qi; 'firm qi' refers to the true qi." Zhang Jiebin: "'Visitor qi' is a passing periodic qi; it comes and leaves irregularly. Hence, it is called 'visitor qi.' The 'identical qi' is the host qi of the four seasons. It is identical year after year. Hence, it is called 'identical qi.'" Ma Shi: "In case there are two disease qi, with the roots of the [two] diseases not being identical, the [qi] that is transmitted from one to the other, it is called 'visitor qi.' In case there are the qi of two diseases whose roots are identical, the [qi] that is transmitted

When urine and stools do not pass freely,
treat its tip.
When urine and stools pass freely,
treat its root.[21]

65-357-7
When a disease breaks out and there is a surplus,
[view] this as root and tip. {First treat its root and afterwards treat its tip.}
When a disease breaks out and there is an insufficiency,
[view] this as tip and root. {First treat its tip and afterwards treat its root.}[22]

from one to the other, it is called 'identical qi.'" Gao Shishi: "As for 'visitor qi,' these
are the qi of wind, heat, dampness, fire, dryness, and cold when they enter the human
body and cause disease. As for 'identical qi,' the qi of ceasing yin of the human body is
identical with the wind; the qi of minor yin is identical with the heat. The qi of major
yin is identical with the dampness; the qi of minor yang is identical with the fire; the
qi of yang brilliance is identical with the dryness; the qi of major yang is identical with
the cold. The proper qi of the three yin and three yang have the identical qi of wind,
heat, dampness, fire, dryness, and cold that cause their diseases." Zhang Zhicong: "As
for 'visitor qi,' that is to say: the six qi of heaven. As for 'identical qi,' that is to say:
in my body these six qi exist, too. They are identical with the qi of heaven." Nanjing
zhongyi xueyuan: "All authors differ in their comments on what is 客氣 and 同氣;
also, their comments are mostly far-fetched. We think that one should change 同
to 固 according to the old version of the text. 'Visitor qi' refers to a newly acquired
evil qi; 'firm qi' (固氣) refers to evil qi originally present in the body already. When
the disease is acquired first, then it is the root; a disease acquired afterwards, that is
the tip. Hence, the visitor qi is the tip; the firm qi is the root. This sentence holds the
meaning of the preceding and introduces the meaning of the following text." Cheng
Shide et al. and 1610/50 agree. Mori: "同氣 is supposed here to refer to the opposite
of 'visitor qi.' Hence it refers to true qi, proper qi, yang qi. .. The visitor qi is a qi that
has left its proper position and has moved to other locations." *Ling shu* 25 does not
have the character 人.

21 Wang Bing: " 'Root' is the first disease; 'tip' is the later disease. One must carefully
investigate [which is which]." Zhang Jiebin: "If one first had another disease and if
urine and stools do not pass freely afterwards, one first treats the tip. In all other cases
one first treats the root; only in the present case one [first] treats the tip. The reason
is, when urine and stools do not pass freely, these are signs of danger. Even though
[blockage of urine and stools] is a tip disease, one must treat it first, nevertheless. This
is [an example for] the saying: 'in the case of emergence, treat its tip.'"

22 Wang Bing: "本而標之 is to say: there is an initial disease and, in addition, there
is a later disease. Because there is a surplus, one first treats the root and afterwards
treats the tip. 標而本之 is to say: first a light, minor, and slow [disease] develops and
afterwards a serious, major, and urgent [disease] develops. Because there is an insuf-
ficieny, one first treats its tip and afterwards treats the root." Zhang Jiebin: "If the
disease is provoked by a surplus of [a pathogenic] qi, then [this qi] will rebel against

Carefully investigate whether it is light or serious;
regulate it on the basis of reasoning.²³

In light cases move [against all of them] jointly;
in serious cases move [against each of them] alone."²⁴

---

the other qi of the other depots, and because it is transmitted from the root to the tip,
hence, one must first treat its root. If the disease is provoked by an insufficiency of qi,
then it will become the subject of a rebellion of the other qi of the other depots, and
because they are transmitted from the tip to the root, hence, one must first treat the
tip." Gao Shishi: "When a disease develops and the evil qi has a surplus, then .. one
first treats the root of the evil qi and afterwards treats the tip of the proper qi. That
is the pattern of treating a surplus [because of evil qi]." 1109/28: "I assume that the
original text is corrupt. If one exchanges 有餘 and 不足, the meaning of this phrase
can be interpreted as follows: If the disease develops because of an insufficiency of
proper qi, then the insufficiency of the proper qi is the root and the disease evil is the
tip. One first treats the root, i.e., supports the proper qi and then treats the tip, i.e.,
eliminates the disease evil. If the disease develops because of a surplus of evil qi, i.e.,
when evil qi abounds, then the abundance of the evil qi is the tip and the proper qi is
the root. One first treats the tip, i.e., removes the evil qi, and then treats the root, i.e.,
calms down the proper qi. This way, one takes the evil qi as the tip and the proper qi
as the root, the earlier disease as root and the later disease as tip. This corresponds to
the general idea of tip and root."

23 Wang Bing: "間 is to say 多, 'many.' 甚 is to say 少, 'few.' 'Many' is to say: [there are]
many physical signs but [the disease] is light and easy [to heal]. 'Few' is to say: [there
are] few physical signs but [the disease] is serious and difficult [to cure]. 以意調之 is
to say: one examines whether [the disease is at the] tip or [at the] root; whether it is
a state of insufficiency or of surplus. It is not to say: one [may] relinquish the patterns
and act wantonly according to one's own considerations." Zhang Jiebin: "間 refers to
a light disease; 甚 refers to a serious disease." Zhang Yizhi et al.: "The sequence of 多
and 少 in Wang Bing's comment appears to have been reversed. It should have been
'間 is to say: 少, few; 甚 is to say 多, many.'"

24 Wang Bing: "并 is to say: another vessel, too, has taken in evil qi and they have a
joint disease. 獨 is to say: only one conduit has acquired the disease and there are no
other qi involved. If the joint [appearance of diseases in several vessels] is serious, then
[the diseases] are transmitted from one [vessel] to another. When this transmission is
fast, [patients] will die, too." Zhang Jiebin: "When the diseases are light, one can heal
them together. Hence, [the text] says 'move together.' When a disease is serious, it is
difficult to tolerate disorder. Hence, [the text] states 'move alone.' *Gu dian yi zhu xuan
bianxiezu* /63: "When the disease is light, one can treat root and tip simultaneously;
When the disease is serious, one must take the circumstances into regard and either
treat only the root, or treat only the tip, to concentrate the force [of the treatment] on
solving the major contradiction."

>When urine and stools do not pass freely first and
a disease emerges afterwards,
treat its root.<[25]

65-357-10
Now,
as for the transmission of the diseases,[26]
in the case of a heart disease, first [the patient experiences] heartache.
[After] one day he coughs.[27]
[Within the next] three days the flanks [experience] propping [fullness and]
pain.[28]
[Within the next] five days there is obstruction and impassability; the body
aches and the limbs are heavy.[29]
If [the disease] has not ended [within the next] three days [the patient will] die,
in winter at midnight, in summer at noon.[30]

---

25 Zhang Qi: "This passage has been erroneously moved here. It should follow the
passage 小大利治其本."

26 Shen Zumian: "Both in the title and in this sentence, the character 傳 should
be read as 轉, .. [in the sense of] 'coming and going, without a permanent place to
stay.'"

27 Wang Bing: "The heart fire dominates the metal [of the lung. Hence, the disease]
is transmitted to the lung. The lung, when excited, produces coughing. Hence, this
[state results]."

28 Wang Bing: "The lung metal dominates the wood [of the liver. Hence, the disease]
is transmitted to the liver. Because the respective vessel passes along the flanks, hence,
this [states results]." Ma Shi: "Another three days, this adds up to four days."

29 Wang Bing: "The liver wood dominates the soil [of the spleen. Hence, the disease]
is transmitted to the spleen. The nature of the spleen is peace and subjection. Because
the qi of wood seizes it, closure results which does not permit free passage; the body
has pain and [feels] heavy." Ma Shi: "Another five days, this adds up to nine days."

30 Wang Bing: "That is to say, exactly at the hours of *zi* (11 p.m. – 1 a.m.) and *wu*
(11 a.m. – 1 p.m.). Elsewhere it is stated: [To state] a difference between [the times of
death in] winter and summer is incorrect. It is quite obvious that this refers to noon
and midnight." Zhang Jiebin: "The heart fire fears water. Hence, [the patient] will
die in winter at midnight. The yang evil is excessively active. Hence, in summer [the
patient] will die at noon. That is, extreme weakness ends in death and extreme abundance ends in death." Mori: "Midnight is [associated with] water; and at midnight in
winter the dominance of water is especially pronounced. Since water overcomes fire,
hence, [patients] die. Midday is [associated with] fire; and during midday in summer
the domination of fire is especially pronounced. Because the fire of the heart has been
extinguished entirely, it cannot stand any [additional] fire. Hence, [patients] die at
this time, too."

65-358-1
In the case of a lung disease, [the patient] pants and coughs.
[After] three days the flanks will experience propping fullness and pain.[31]
[Within] one [further] day the body is heavy and the limbs ache.[32]
[Within the next] five days distensions occur.[33]
If [the disease] has not ended [within the next] ten days, [the patient] will die, in winter at sunset, in summer at sunrise.[34]

65-358-3
In the case of a liver disease, [the patient] feels dizzy in head and eyes and experiences propping fullness in his flanks.
[Within] three days the limbs are heavy and the body has pain.[35]
[Within the next] five days distensions occur.[36]
[Within the next] three days, the lower back, the spine, and the lower abdomen have pain and the shins are sore.[37]

---

31 Wang Bing: "The lung transmits [the disease] to the liver."

32 Wang Bing: "The liver transmits [the disease] to the spleen."

33 Wang Bing: "Because [the disease] was transmitted to the [respective] palace."

34 Wang Bing: "In the first month of winter sunset occurs at eight marks [of the clepshydra] (刻) and three *fen* 分 after *shen* (3-5 p.m.). In the second month of winter sunset occurs at seven marks and three *fen* after *shen*. In the final month of winter sunset occurs at shen, identical with the first month [of the following season]." In the first month of summer sunrise occurs at eight marks and one *fen* after *yin* (3-5 a.m.). In the second month of summer sunrise occurs at seven marks and three *fen* after *yin*. In the final month of winter sunset occurs at yin, identical with the first month [of the following season]." Zhang Jiebin: "These are the hours of *mao* (5-7 a.m.) and *you* (5-7 p.m.); they are associated with the transformations of dryness and metal. The lung rules the qi; when it loses its protection, then death occurs." Ma Shi: "In winter sunset is at *shen* (3-5 p.m.). Even though *shen* belongs to metal, the metal is weak and cannot be upheld. In summer the sun rises at *yin* (3-5 a.m.). [At that time] the wood flourishes and fire is about to emerge. The [flow of the] lung qi has been interrupted already and cannot wait for the emergence of the fire."

35 Wang Bing: "The liver transmits [the disease] to the lung."

36 Wang Bing: "Because [the disease] was transmitted to the palace."

37 Wang Bing: "That is to say: the stomach transmits [the disease] to the kidneys. Because the respective vessel rises from the foot, follows the interior of the calf, emerges at the inner ridge of the popliteal fossa, rises at the inner back ridge of the thighs, passes through the spine, touches the kidneys and winds around the bladder, hence, this [state results]. The lower back region is the palace of the kidneys. Hence, the lower back aches."

If [the disease] has not ended [within the next] three days, [the patient] will die, in winter at sunset,[38] in summer at [the time of] breakfast.[39]

In the case of a spleen disease, one's body aches and the limbs feel heavy. [After] one day distensions occur.[40]
[Within the next] two days the lower abdomen, the lower back, and the spine have pain and the shins are sore.[41]
[Within the next] three days the backbone and the sinews have pain and [the path of] urination is closed.[42]
If [the disease] has not ended [within the next] ten days, [the patient] will die, in winter when people are at rest, in summer at meal time.[43]

65-359-2
In the case of a kidney disease, the lower abdomen, the lower back, and the spine have pain and the shins are sore.
[After] three days the backbone and the sinews have pain and [the path of] urination is closed.[44]
[Within the next] three days, the abdomen is distended.[45]

---

38 Lin Yi et al.: "The *Jia yi jing* has 日中, 'noon.'"

39 Wang Bing: "早食 is to say: earlier than meal time. Exactly at the hours of *mao* (5-7 a.m.)." Ma Shi: "In winter the sun sets at *shen* (3-5 p.m.); [death occurs] because the metal flourishes and the wood is weak. In summer breakfast time is at *mao* (5-7 a.m.); [death occurs] because the wood flourishes, while the [flow of the] qi, in contrast, is interrupted."

40 Wang Bing: "Because [the disease] was transmitted to the palace."

41 Wang Bing: "The stomach transmits it to the kidneys."

42 Wang Bing: "Because [the disease] was transmitted to the palace, it has reached the backbone." Ma Shi: "Because the kidneys transmit it to their palace, [i.e.,] the bladder, hence, the backbone and the sinews ache and the [path of the] urine is closed."

43 Wang Bing: "人定 is to say: 25 marks after *shen* (3-5 p.m.). 晏食 is to say: 25 marks (i.e., quarter hours) after *yin* (3-5 a.m.)." Cheng Shide et al.: "人定 is the time at night when people go to sleep. 晏食 refers to the evening meal." Zhang Jiebin: "These are the hours of *si* (9-11 a.m.) and *hai* (9-11 p.m.). They control the transformation of wind and wood; hence, a spleen disease fears them." Gao Shishi: "In winter, people go to rest at *xu* (7-9 p.m.); in summer the evening meal is at *xu* (7-9 p.m.), too. The soil does not flourish and [the patients] die." Ma Shi: "In winter [people] goes to rest at *hai* (9-11 p.m.); [patients die] because soil does not dominate water. In summer the 晏食 is at *yin* (3-5 a.m.). [Patients die] because wood comes to check the soil."

44 Wang Bing: "Because [the disease] was transmitted to the palace."

45 Wang Bing: "The bladder transmits it to the small intestine." Wu Kun "The abdomen is distended because both the kidneys and the bladder have the disease. The

[Within the next] three days, the two flanks have propping [fullness and] pain.[46]

If [the disease] has not ended [within the next] three days, [the patient] will die, in winter in the early morning, in summer in the late afternoon.[47]

65-359-4

In the case of a stomach disease, [the patient] experiences distension and fullness.[48]

[After] five days the lower abdomen, the spine, and the lower back have pain and the shins are sore.[49]

[Within the next] three days the backbone and the sinews have pain and [the path of] urination is closed.[50]

[Within the next] five days the body and the limbs feel heavy.[51]

If [the disease] has not ended [within the next] six days, [the patient] will die, in winter after midnight, in summer at the time when the sun begins to decline westwards.[52]

---

central mansion cannot transform qi and the minister fire in the kidneys is depleted and weak and does not generate the soil of the stomach. Hence, this [state] results."

46 Wang Bing: "The palace transmits it to the depot." Zhang Jiebin: "Within three days it rises to the heart. The proper [conduit] of the hand heart master branches out to descend [on both sides] to three inches below the Armpit Abyss (淵掖) where it enters the chest. Hence, both flanks ache."

47 Wang Bing: "大晨 is to say: nine marks after *yin* (3-5 a.m.). That is the time of great brilliance [of coming daylight]. 晏晡 is to say: nine marks after *shen* towards the time of dusk."

48 Wang Bing: "Because the respective vessel follows the abdomen. Hence, this [state results]."

49 Wang Bing: "The stomach transmits it to the kidneys."

50 Wang Bing: "Because [the disease] is transmitted to the palace, it reaches the backbone."

51 Wang Bing: "The bladder is the palace of water; it transmits [the disease] to the spleen."

52 Wang Bing: " 'After midnight' is to say: eight marks (i.e., quarter hours) after *zi* (11 p.m.-1 a.m.), exactly at *chou* (1-3 a.m.). 'When the sun beings to decline westward' is to say eight marks after *wu* (11 a.m.-1 p.m.), exactly at *wei* (1-3 p.m.)." Ma Shi: "Midnight is at *zi*; [patients die because] soil does not dominate water. In summer the sun begins to decline westward at *wei*; this is just the time when the soil is weak."

In the case of bladder disease, [the path of] urination is closed.[53]
[After] five days the lower abdomen is distended, the lower back, and the spine have pain and the shins are sore.[54]
[Within] one [further] day, the abdomen is distended.[55]
[Within] one [further] day, the body and the limbs ache.[56]
If [the disease] has not ended [within the next] two days, [the patient] will die, in winter when the cocks crow, in summer in late afternoon.[57]

65-360-2
All diseases are transmitted according to a [fixed] order.
When [the transmission occurs] in this way,
each [disease] has a [fixed] time when [the patient] will die.
One cannot pierce.[58]

---

53 Wang Bing: "This is the palace of body liquids. Hence, this [state results]."

54 Wang Bing: "Because [the disease] turns to the depot."

55 Wang Bing: "The kidneys, in turn, transmit [the disease] to the small intestine." Wu Kun: "Abdominal distension is a stomach disease."

56 Wang Bing: "The small intestine transmits it to the spleen." Zhang Jiebin: "Within the next day it reaches the heart; from the palace it is transmitted to the depot. The heart rules the blood vessels. Hence, the body aches." Wu Kun: "When the body has pain, this is a spleen disease." Ma Shi: "The small intestine transmits [the disease] to the spleen. Hence, the body aches."

57 Wang Bing: " 'The cocks crow' refers to the crowing of the cocks in the morning. This is exactly at *chou* (1-3 a.m.); 下晡 is to say: the sun declines in the afternoon, five marks after *shen* (3-5 p.m.)." Ma Shi: "In winter the cocks crow at *chou*; at *chou* the soil dominates the water. Late afternoon in summer is at *shen* (3-5 p.m.). [At that time] the metal is weak and cannot generate water." Wu Kun: "In winter the cocks crow at *chou*; in summer afternoon is at *wei* (1-3 p.m.)."

58 Wang Bing: "When the five depots shift [diseases] among each other, it is always as [outlined] here. Transmission may be slow or fast. Slow [transmissions] take one, two, or three years until [the patient] dies. Next come those that take three to six months until [the patient] dies. Fast [transmissions] take one, two, three, four days, or five or six days until [the patient] dies. An investigation of the patterns of these disease transmissions [demonstrates that] they always [follow the relationships among the] qi of the five agents. [However,] if one examines the numbers of days, they do not correspond to these principles. Now, to follow the arrangement of the five agents, the number [of days associated with the agent] which is not dominated [is required] for a transmission to [that depot] which it dominates. That is to say, fire transmits to the metal; [the text] should state 'one day' [and so it does]. Metal transmits to the wood; [the text] should state 'two days' [but it speaks of 'three days']. Wood transmits to soil; [the text] should state 'four days' [but it speaks of 'five days'] (etc.).."

If in the course [of the transmission, the disease] skips one depot[59] and comes to a halt,
and if it [eventually continues and] reaches the third or fourth depot,
then one can pierce."

---

59 Wang Bing: "間一藏止 is to say: [the disease] passes by the next depot ahead (in the sequence of mutual generation), but is not transmitted further. That is, wood transmits to soil; [or] soil transmits to water; [or] water transmits to fire; [or] fire transmits to metal; [or] metal transmits to wood and then [transmission] stops. In each case one depot is passed by. As for 'it reaches the third or fourth depot,' that is to say: [transmission] proceeds to the third or fourth depot ahead. All transmissions to the third depot involve a qi which the [original depot] itself does not dominate. Whenever the fourth depot is reached, then father and mother are reached who generate the [original depot] itself. When there is no domination, then there is no harm by another [depot]. Generation occurs in [a relationship of] father and son; it does not aim at a destructive fight. The movement of the qi follows [the rules]. Hence, it is possible to pierce such [situations]." Cheng Shide et al.: "*Ling shu* 42 and the *Jia yi jing* do not have the character 止. They seem to be correct." The 53rd difficult issue of the *Nan jing* states: "間藏 is transmission to its son [depot]."

Chapter 66
Comprehensive Discourse on Arrangements
of the Principal [Qi] of Heaven.

66-361-2
Huang Di asked:
" 'Heaven has the five agents;
they control¹ the five positions.²
Thereby [the five agents] generate cold, summerheat, dryness, dampness, and wind.³
Man has the five depots;
they transform⁴ the five qi,
thereby generating joy, anger, pensiveness, anxiety, and fear.'⁵

The discourse states:
'The five periods succeed each other and each of them governs [one of] these [segments of the year].
When the days of an annual cycle⁶ are completed, the cycle commences anew.'⁷
That I have come to know already. I should like to hear [now] how this is linked to the manifestations of the three yin and three yang."

66-361-5
Gui Yuqu paid reverence twice knocking his head on the ground and responded:
"A brilliant question, indeed!

---

1 Wang Bing: "御 is 臨御, 'to control.'" Wang Qi: "御 is 恰, 'proper;' it has the meaning here of 支配, 'to allocate,' 分佈, 'to spread.'"

2 Wang Qi: " 'The five positions' are the five cardinal points of East, South, West, North, and Center."

3 218/45: "*Su wen* 5 states: 'the East generates wind, .. the South generates heat, ..' Because the five qi of cold, summerheat, dryness, dampness, and wind are the qi ruling the five different seasons, the present [expression] 'five positions' includes the five seasons."

4 Wang Bing: "化 is to say: 生化, 'generate and transform.'"

5 See *Su wen* 5 for an almost identical statement.

6 Wang Qi: "終朞 is 'one year.'"

7 Quotation from *Su wen* 9 or a predecessor text.

Now, the five periods and yin-yang, they are the Way of heaven and earth,[8]
'the fundamental principles [governing] the myriad beings,
father and mother to change and transformation,
basis and beginning of generating life and killing,'
they are the palace of spirit brilliance.[9]
Is it possible not to understand them!

The fact is,
'When a being comes to life, this is called transformation.
When a being reaches the extreme point [in its development], this is called
[the point of] change.[10]
That which cannot be fathomed in [the alternation of] yin and yang, it is called
spirit.[11]
Where the operation of the spirit follows no prescribed method, this is called
sagehood.'[12]

---

8 696/35: " 'Way' refers to the laws underlying the variations in the progression of
the (five) periods."

9 See *Su wen* 5 for an identical statement, except for the reference to the five periods.
Wang Bing: " 'Way' is to say: the Way of generation through transformation. 綱紀 is
to say: the principles governing generation, transformation, completion, gathering,
and storage. 'Father and mother' is to say: that which is prior to the physical appearance of the myriad beings. 'Basis and beginning' is to say: it is because of them that
all generation and killing exist. Now, never has there been a physical appearance that
depended on qi but was not maintained [in its existence] by the [qi of the] five periods
as well as of yin and yang. Why is it that creation and transformation [through the qi
of the five periods and of yin and yang] occurs unendingly and that they can be the
origin of the generation and transformation of the myriad beings? Because they are
the palace of spirit brilliance. After all, that union and dispersion [of qi] are immeasurable, that generation and transformation [of the myriad beings] are inexhaustible,
all this is possible only because of the movement of the spirit brilliance."

10 Zhang Zhicong: "When an abundance has reached its extreme, it will [be followed by] weakness; when a weakness has reached its extreme, it will [be followed by]
abundance."

11 Cf. *Yi jing, Xi ci* 易經, 繫辭: 陰陽不測之謂神.

12 Wang Qi: "方 is 常規, 'common rule.' " Fang Yaozhong: "方 has the meaning of 違,
'to oppose,' or 逆, 'to counteract.' 聖 refers to 高明, 'outstanding brilliance.' The meaning of the phrase 神用無方謂之聖 is: the laws of nature cannot be opposed. Those
who are able to act in accordance with the laws of nature, they are persons of outstanding brilliance." We interpret the phrase 無方 in accordance with *Xun zi*, Dalue 大略:
"博學而無方." See *GHYZD* 167.

66-362-1
Now, as for the operation of change and transformation,
'in heaven it is darkness,[13]
in man it is the Way,[14]
on the earth it is transformation'.[15]

Transformation generates the five flavors.[16]
The Way generates wisdom.[17]
The darkness generates the spirit.[18]

The spirit,
in heaven it is wind, on the earth it is wood.
In heaven it is heat, on the earth it is fire.
In heaven it is dampness, on the earth it is soil.
In heaven it is dryness, on the earth it is metal.
In heaven it is cold, on the earth it is water.'[19]

The fact is,
'in heaven it is qi;
on the earth it turns into physical appearance.[20]

---

13 Wang Bing: "玄 is 遠, 'far away.' The Way of heaven is dark and distant; [its] changes and transformations are inexhaustible. The [*Zuo*] *zhuan* states: 'The Way of heaven is distant; the Way of man is near.'"

14 Wang Bing: "道 is to say: 妙用之道, 'the Way of miraculous operations.'"

15 Wang Bing: "化 is to say: 生化, 'generation and transformation.' In the generation of the myriad beings, the substance of physical appearance cannot be completed if the earth is not fecundated by the qi of the soil."

16 Wang Bing: "The sour and bitter, sweet and bland, acrid and salty [flavors of] metals and stones, herbs and trees, roots and leaves, flowers and fruits, are all generated through qi transformation. They exist when it is their time."

17 Wang Bing: "Wisdom penetrating the miraculous operations can be generated only by the Way." Zhang Jiebin: "Because there is the Way, there is activity; because there is activity, there is knowledge. Hence the Way generates knowledge." Wu Kun: "Man gathers experience and then has knowledge. [Hence] the Way generates knowledge."

18 Wang Bing: "Darkness is distance, is hidden, and deep. Hence it generates the spirit."

19 Beginning with 在天為玄 quoted from *Su wen* 5 or a predecessor text.

20 Wang Bing: "'Qi' is to say: wind, heat, dampness, dryness, and cold. 'Physical appearance' is to say: wood, fire, soil, metal, and water."

Physical appearance and qi affect each other and [thereby]
they generate, through transformation, the myriad beings.'²¹

66-363-1
This being so,
'heaven and earth are the above and the below of the myriad beings.
Left and right are the paths of yin and yang.²²
Water and fire are the signs of yin and yang.²³
Metal and wood are the end and the begin of generation and completion.'²⁴

'Qi may be present in large or small quantities;
a physical appearance may be [in a state of] abundance or weakness.
Above and below call on each other;
hence decrease and increase are obvious.' "²⁵

---

21 Zhang Jiebin: " 'Physical appearance' is yin; qi is yang. 'Physical appearance and
qi affect each other' is [to say]: yin and yang unite. When they unite, then the myriad
beings come to life through transformation."

22 1667/11: "This is so because in ancient times they stood facing the South. Hence
the East was to their left and the West was to their right. To the left is the path where
major yang and major yin rise from the East; to the right is the path where major
yang and major yin descend towards the West." Zhang Jiebin: "The left is yang; it rules
ascension; hence the path of yang proceeds through the South. The right is yin; it rules
descend. Hence the path of yin proceeds through the North. These are 'the pathways
of yin and yang.' "

23 Cheng Shide et al.: "徵 is 証, 'evidence,' 驗, 'to prove effective.' 兆 is 預見, 'to
foresee.' " Zhang Jiebin: "The evidence of yin and yang appears in water and fire; the
operation of water and fire appears in cold and summerheat. Hence the coming and
going of yin and yang is manifested in [the coming and going of] cold and summerheat. That is meant here."

24 See *Su wen* 5 for an identical statement. Fang Yaozhong: " 'Wood' symbolizes
'life,' 'sprouting' here; 'metal' symbolizes 'gathering,' 'maturity.' That is to say, the entire
existence of a living being is a process starting from sprouting and proceding through
growth, maturity, withdrawal to renewed existence and growth. The origin of all this
is movement."

25 Wang Bing: " 'Qi may be present in large or small quantities' is to say: the quantities of yin and yang are different on the three levels [ceasing yin, minor yin, major
yin, and minor yang, yang brilliance, major yang]. 'A physical appearance may be [in a
state of] abundance or weakness' is to say: the qi of the five periods may be excessive
or insufficient. Because of these large or small quantities, these abundancies and weak-
nesses, heaven and earth call on each other and harm or benefit caused to yin and yang
are clearly visible." *Su wen* 68 has: "When the qi of heaven descends, the qi flows on

66-363-4
[Huang] Di:
"I should like to hear how the five periods rule the seasons."²⁶

Gui Yuqu:
"The periodical progression of each of the five qi spans the days of a complete annual cycle; they do not rule only a season."²⁷

66-364-1
[Huang] Di:
"I should like to hear what that is to say."

Gui Yuqu:
"[I, your] subject, have continuously studied the text of the *Book on the Supreme Beginning and on the Principal [Qi] of Heaven*²⁸ where it is stated:
'The extension of the Great Void is boundless;
it is the basis of [all] founding and it is the principal [source] of [all] transformation.²⁹

---

the earth. When the qi of the earth rises, the qi surges to heaven. Hence those on high and those below call on each other."

26 Wang Bing: "時 is 四時, 'the four seasons.'"

27 Wang Bing: "The days of one period are 365 days and one quarter." Fang Yao-zhong: "終朞 is an alternative version of 期; in general it refers to a period of time. The meaning of this phrase is: the changing climatic manifestations of wind, fire, dampness, dryness, and cold all have their specific time periods (when they dominate). Speaking in terms of one year, each year can be divided into the five seasons of spring, summer, late summer, autumn, and winter; each season is slightly more than 73 days long. .. In terms of climate, each year is different. A onesided dominance of wind, fire, dampness, dryness, or cold is a regular phenomenon. For instance, if the present year is characterized by much wind, the next year will have much rain and the following year will be rather dry. These phenomena of onesided dominance do, in general, apply to a period of one year and they progress in a fixed sequence. Because the "progression of the five qi" can refer to the climate of each season in the course of a year, and also to the characteristic changes dominating an entire year, the original text states 'The progression of each qi covers the days of an entire period; it does not rule only one season.'"

28 Wang Bing: "The *Book of the Principal [Qi] of Heaven* records the arrangements of the movement of the true principal qi of heaven." For a discussion of conceptual parallels in the *Yi jing*, see 882/5.

29 Wang Bing: " 'Great Void' is to say: the region of emptiness and darkness; that which is filled by the true qi; the palace of the spirit brilliance. The true qi is infinitesimal; nothing is too far for it to reach. Hence it can constitute the basis and beginning

The myriad beings depend on [the Great Void] to come into existence,
[and it is because of the Great Void that] the five periods complete their course
in heaven.[30]
[The Great Void] spreads the true magic power of qi,[31]
and it exerts control over the principal [qi] of the earth.[32]
[Hence] the nine stars are suspended [in heaven] and shine and
the seven luminaries revolve in a cycle.[33]

---

of generation and transformation and the true principal [source] of the periods and
qi. 基 is 本, 'root.'" Zhang Jiebin: "肇 is 始, 'begin.' 基 is 立, 'to stand up,' 'to establish.'
化元 is 造化之本原, 'the origin of creation.'" Cheng Shide et al.: "That is to say, the
universe is the foundation of the origin of generation and transformation."

30 Wang Bing: "五運 is to say: the periods of wood, fire, soil, metal, and water. 終天
is to say: one year, (i.e.,) 365 days and one quarter. End and begin follow each other;
when a cycle is completed, it begins anew. That is to say: the five periods govern in the
Great Void alternately in succession; in the course of the four seasons they move along
the regions and return [to their starting point]. The six qi rule differently at separate
locations. The myriad beings follow them in their generation and transformation. ..
Hence [the text] states: the myriad beings depend on it in their beginning."

31 Wang Bing: "The true qi of the Great Void reaches everywhere. The [true] qi
supports generation and existence. Hence anything that depends on qi and contains
magic power embraces true qi to be alive." Wang Qi: "The essence qi of the true magic
power of heaven and earth is spread to the myriad beings."

32 Wang Bing: "揔統坤元 is to say: The principal qi of heaven constantly control
the qi of the earth. That is the Way of generation through transformation." Wang Qi:
"坤元 refers to the basis of the generation and transformation of the myriad beings
by the great earth. The meaning is: The basis of the generation and transformation of
the myriad beings through the great earth ruled by the principle qi of heaven." Cheng
Shide et al.: "坤元 is to say, the virtue of the earth is the basis of the generation and
growth of the myriad beings." Zhang Zhicong: "真靈 refers to man and the myriad
beings. 總統坤元 is to say, the earth resides within heaven, heaven encloses the earth
on the outside."

33 Wang Bing: " 'Nine stars,' that is in the time of high antiquity. In high antiquity,
the disposition of the time was such that the people were pure; they turned to the real
and reverted to the simple. The nine stars were suspended to shine and the five periods
extended evenly. In middle antiquity, Way and Virtue had somewhat weakened, the
marker stars of the dipper hid the luminaries. Hence only seven stars were visible. The
nine stars are called *tian peng* 天蓬, *tian rui* 天芮, *tian chong* 天衝, *tian fu* 天輔, *tian
qin* 天禽, *tian xin* 天心, *tian ren* 天任, *tian zhu* 天柱, and *tian ying* 天英. ..... The seven
luminaries are sun, moon, and the five stars (i.e., planets)." 597/43: "Terms like 九星,
'nine stars,' 太虛, 'great void,' and 七曜, 'seven luminaries,' have all been introduced to
China from Western regions. They are not documented in the literature of the Eastern
Han or earlier. .. The statement 九星懸朗 seems to refer to the characteristics of the
fixed stars. Wang Bing's commentary draws farfetched comparisons." This statement

66-364-4
[This] is called yin; [this] is called yang.
[This] is called soft; [this] is called hard.[34]
[Hence] when that which is in the dark and that which is obvious have assumed their positions,
there is cold and summerheat, relaxation and tension.[35]

Generation [follows upon] generation, transformation [follows upon] transformation,
[with the result that] all the things come into open existence.'[36]

[My forefathers and I, your] subject, have [transmitted] this [text] for ten generations; it explains what [you have asked]."[37]

66-365-2
[Huang] Di:
"Good!
What does that mean 'Qi may be present in large or small quantities; a physical appearance may be [in a state of] abundance or weakness'?"

---

needs to be corrected insofar as the term 太虛, 'great void,' is attested in *Zhuang zi* already.

34 Based on *Yi jing*, Shuo gua 說卦. See Ruan Yuan 1, 93 below: "聖人...立天之道, 曰陰與陽, 立地之道, 曰柔與剛". Wang Bing: "Yin and yang are the Way of heaven; soft and hard are the Way of the earth. Heaven generates by means of yang and causes growth by means of yin; the earth transforms by means of softness and achieves completion by means of hardness."

35 Wang Bing: " 'The hidden and the obvious have assumed their positions' is to say: [all] men and [all] spirits have found their [proper] residences. 'Cold, summerheat, relaxed, tense' is to say: Yin and yang do not miss their proper [sequence]. When all men and spirits stick to their places of residence, there will be no mutual attack; when yin and yang do not miss their [proper] sequence, [all] beings receive what they need. That is the Way of heaven and earth; the principles [underlying the wellbeing] of the humans and of the spirits are the same."

36 Based on the *Yi jing*, hexagram *gou* 姤卦. (See Ruan Yuan 1, 57 center: "天地相遇品物咸章.") Gao Jiwu/22: "品物 is 萬物, 'the myriad things.' 品 is explained as 眾, 'all.'" 1779/43: "章 is 印章, 'mark,' 'seal.' 品物咸章 is to explain that all living beings are constrained by the laws of nature." Cheng Shide et al.: "章 has the meaning of 昭, 'luminous.'"

37 Wang Bing: "This text was transmitted to Gui Yuqu through ten generations."

Gui Yuqu:
"The qi of both yin and yang may be present in large or small quantities.
Hence one speaks of the three yin and three yang.

'The physical appearance may be [in a state of] abundance or weakness,' that
is to say: the government of each of the five agents may be [marked by] great
excess and inadequacy. Hence when at the beginning [of a cycle, one agent]
leaves in surplus, it will be followed by insufficiency; when it leaves insufficiently, it will be succeeded by surplus.[38]

66-365-5
'If one knows [the qi] that has come up and [the qi] that will follow,
the qi can be predicted.'"[39]
<Correspondence to heaven, this is 'heavenly complements';[40] a year that fol-

---

38 Wang Bing: "始 is to say: a *jia zi* year. *Su wen* 68 states: 'The qi of heaven starts
with *jia*; the qi of the earth starts with *zi*. *Zi* and *jia* combined are called 歲立 ("begin
of years").' This explains [what is meant] here. Now, the qi supporting the 365 days
of the initial *jia zi* year should be insufficient. This can be deduced for all six [recur-
rences of] *jia* years. Hence, when [a period of] surplus has come to an end, then [it
will be followed by] insufficiency. When [a period of] insufficiency has come to an
end, then there will be surplus. There are also annual periods which are characterized
neither by surplus nor by insufficiency. This happens when heaven and earth undergo
common transformations. When [a period of] suplus comes to an end and there is
surplus again, or when [a period of] deprivation has come to an end and there is little
deprivation again, then the Way of heaven and earth has taken a change [away] from
the normal; catastrophes and diseases emerge [as a consequence]."

39 Zhang Zhicong: "迎 is 往, 'to go away.' 隨 is 來, 'to come.' If the coming and
going of the years is known, then it is possible to determine in advance the excess or
insufficiency of any qi." Zhang Jiebin: "迎 is 迎其至, 'to meet its arrival'; 隨 is 隨其
去, 'to follow its departure.' For example, a seasonal command may be abounding or
weak. Hence [it is essential] to inspect whether its arrival is slow or fast. Whether
it arrives or fails to arrive, that is to be known in advance. That is 'to know what lies
ahead.' The qi periods have dominance and retaliation. When a domination is slight,
retaliation will be slight, too. When a domination is severe, retaliation will be severe,
too. Whether [domination and retaliation] are slight or severe, that is to be known
in advance. That is 'to know what follows.'" Cheng Shide et al.: "Zhang Jiebin's comments are superior."

40 Wang Bing: "應天 is to say: If in a year of the period of wood, the ceasing yin
appears above; if in a year of the period of fire, the minor yang and the minor yin appear above; if in a year of the period of soil, the major yin appears above; if in a year
of the period of metal, the yang brilliance appears above; if in a year of the period of
water the major yang appears above, then in these five [combinations] the qi of heaven

lows [its orders],[41] this is 'year that is straight.'[42] When three come together, this is order.>[43]

66-366-1
[Huang] Di:
" 'Above and below call on each other,' what does that mean?"

Gui Yuqu:
"Cold, summerheat, dryness, dampness, wind, and fire, these are the yin and yang of heaven. The three yin and three yang, they act on behalf of the above.[44]

Wood, fire, soil, metal, water, <and [minister] fire,> these are the yin and yang of the earth.
Generation, growth, transformation, gathering, and storage, they correspond to them below.[45]

---

descends in complete agreement with the [respective] periods. Hence [the text] states: 應天為天符."

41 Zhang Jiebin: "承 is 下奉上, 'that which is below accepts an order from that which is above and acts accordingly.' 直 is 會, 'to meet.'" Cheng Shide et al.: "Another name for 歲直 is 歲會."

42 Wang Bing: "承歲 is to say: when in a year of the period of wood the year corresponds to *mao*; when in a year of the period of fire the year corresponds to *wu*; when in a year of the period of soil the year corresponds to *chen, xu, chou*, and *wei*; when in a year of the period of metal the year corresponds to *you*; when in a year of the period of water the year corresponds to *zi*. These five [combinations] are those in which a year is straight, 歲之所直. Hence [the text] states: 'Years following [their orders] are years that is straight' 承歲為歲直. 歲直 is also called 歲位, 'year in position.'"

43 Wang Bing: "三合 is to say: When in a year of the period of fire the minor yin appears above and the branch of the year coming down is *wu*. When in a year of the period of soil the major yin appears above and the branches of the year coming down are *chou* and *wei*. When in a year of the period of metal the yang brilliance appears above and the branch of the year coming down is *you*. In these three [instances] the qi of heaven, the period qi, and the branch of the year do all meet. Hence [the text] states: when the three come together, this is order. 三合 [i.e., years when these three come together] are also 天符, 'heavenly complements' [years]."

44 Wang Bing: "Major yang is cold; minor yang is summerheat; yang brilliance is dryness; major yin is dampness; ceasing yin is wind; minor yin is fire. They all have their origin in heaven. Hence [the text] states: they are the yin and yang of heaven."

45 Wang Bing: "Wood is the initial qi. Fire is the second qi. The minister fire is the third qi. Soil is the fourth qi. Metal is the fifth qi. Water is the final qi. Because they correspond to heaven on earth, [the text] states: 'they correspond below.'" 171/1: "Basically there are three opinions as to the different meanings of 變 'change' and 化 'trans-

'Heaven employs yang [qi] to generate, yin [qi] to stimulate growth.
Earth employs yang [qi] to kill, yin [qi] to store.'⁴⁶

66-366-4
<Heaven has yin and yang; the earth has yin and yang, too.
Wood, fire, soil, metal, water, <and [minister] fire,>
these are the yin and yang of the earth.
Generation, growth, transformation, gathering, and storage [result from
them].>⁴⁷

The fact is, in yang there is yin; in yin there is yang.⁴⁸
Therefore, those who wish to know the yin and yang of heaven and earth, [they

---

formation.' The first is: a variation of a character is a change; a variation of a physical
appearance is a transformation. The second is: a slow variation is called change; an
abrupt variation is called transformation. The third is: 'In heaven it is change; on the
earth it is transformation; with respect to yang the term is change; with respect to yin
the term is transformation; in spring and summer it is change; in autumn and winter
it is transformation.' Obviously, the meanings of both 'change' and 'transformation'
include a variation of quantity and of character, gradual variation and abrupt variation,
while 'transformation,' in addition, also includes the meaning of female reproduction.
Hence the *Nei jing* has 'generation, growth, transformation, gathering, and storage,'
rather than 'generation, growth, change, gathering, and storage.'"

46 Wang Bing: "Generation and growth are the Way of heaven; storage and killing
are the Way of the earth. Heaven is yang; it rules generation. Hence 'it generates by
means of yang; it causes growth by means of yin.' The earth is yin; it rules killing.
Hence 'it kills by means of yang; it stores by means of yin.' Heaven and earth are
different in that the one is above and the other below. Nevertheless, the circulatory
movement of yin and yang applies to both of them." We follow 19/141, identifying
this statement as an example of "reciprocal phrasing" (互文). In contrast, 982/37: "殺
is not the 殺 of 'to kill'; it should be read as 洒 in the sense of 'weaken,' 'decrease.' ..
When the yang [qi] is generated and the yin [qi] grows afterwards, this is a natural
phenomenon of the first half of each year; when the yang [qi] decreases and the yin
[qi] hides afterwards, this is a natural phenomenon of the second half of each year. The
qi of heaven rules the first half of the year; the qi of the earth rules the second half of
the year. Hence *Su wen* 66 has 'Heaven generates with yang [qi] and lets grow with
yin [qi]; the earth decreases [the living beings] with yang [qi] and stores them with
yin [qi]." 1581/20: "殺 is 收, 'to gather.'" See also 2445/22.

47 Zhang Jiebin omitted these 16 characters in the *Lei jing*.

48 Wang Bing: "If either the qi of yin or [the qi of] yang reaches an [uncontrolled]
maximum, it will be excessively active. Hence both must be present in combination.
Su wen 5 states: 'Cold at its maximum creates heat; heat at its maximum creates cold.'
Elsewhere it states: 'Double yin must [become] yang; double yang must [become] yin.'
That is to say: when a qi has reached a maximum, then this results in change. Hence

should be aware of the following].
'The qi corresponding to heaven,
they move without break.'
{Hence [after] five years there is a move to the right.}

The qi corresponding to the earth,
they are quiet and keep their position.
{Hence after six annual cycles [the cycle] returns to meet [its starting point].}[49]

Movement and resting call on each other;[50]
above and below come down on each other.

---

in yang there is also yin and in yin there is also yang. Among the diagrams of the *Yi* [*jing*], [the diagram] *li* contains depletion and [the diagram] *kan* contains repletion. These are visual signs of the meaning indicated here." Zhang Jiebin: "Heaven is basically yang; nevertheless there is yin in yang. The earth is basically yin; nevertheless there is yang in yin. That is the Way of yin and yang being hidden in each other. Hence in water there is brilliance and in fire there is darkness. It is only because there is yin in yang that the qi of heaven can descend and it is only because there is yang in yin that the qi of the earth can rise. That is the basis of [the statement] 'above and below call on each other.'"

49 Wang Bing: "Heaven has the six qi; the earth has the five positions. Heaven approaches the earth with its six qi from above; the earth receives [the qi of] heaven at its five positions. Now, the qi of heaven are not met [from below] by a [a qi corresponding to the] ruler fire. If six [qi] are received by five [positions], then after five years there is a surplus of one [heavenly] qi. Hence there is a shifting by one position. If at five [positions] six [qi] are received, then it regularly takes six years to fully complete [one cycle] of the principal qi of heaven. Hence after six years the [cycle] 'returns to meet [its starting point].' This is what was called [earlier] 'this constitutes one cycle, after which it commences anew.' The qi of the earth proceed to the left. They move on and do not turn back. The qi of heaven turn round to the East. As a rule, one counts five years beginning with the period of fire. When [these five years] are complete, the next qi [in the series of the periods of the heavenly qi] should be above the ruler fire. This is a pattern not [permitting] that what comes down meets [that which is below]. Hence there is a move to the right to above the ruler fire qi. Thereby it comes down to the right from qi to come down to above the minister fire. Hence [the text] states: 'After five years they move to the right.' Because of these movements [of the qi of heaven] and the steadiness [of the positions of the earth] and because above meets with below, the dynamics of the changes in the nature of the myriad beings in heaven and on earth become apparent." For a completely different interpretation of this passage see: Fang Yaozhong, p.48.

50 Zhang Zhicong: "That is, the qi of heaven and earth affect each other."

Yin and yang mingle with each other.
That is where changes result from."⁵¹

66-367-6
[Huang] Di:
"The circular arrangements of above and below, do they have any numbers?"⁵²

Gui Yuqu:
" 'Heaven employs [the number] six to generate terms.
The earth employs [the number] five to cause restraint.'

As for the qi completing a circle around heaven, six annual cycles constitute
one perfection.
For a complete arrangement of the earth, five years constitute one cycle.⁵³

{The ruler fire relies on being honored; the minister fire relies on [its] position.}⁵⁴

---

51 Zhang Zhicong: "The five qi of heaven control the five agents of the earth below.
Wood, fire, soil, metal, water, and fire of the earth approach the six qi of heaven above.
Hence [in one case] heaven has five and the earth has six, [in the other case] heaven
has six and the earth has five. When these yin and yang [qi] intermingle, this results
in an arrangement of 30 years, or in one cycle of 60 years."

52 Fang Yaozhong: " 'Above' refers to the six qi of heaven; 'below' refers to the five
agents of the earth, i.e., the five periods of wood, fire, soil, metal, and water. 周 is 'to
revolve in a cycle.' 紀 is 規律, 'order.' 上下周紀, then, refers to the order of the revolving movement of the five periods and the six qi."

53 Wang Bing: " 'Six sections' is to say: the division into the six qi; 'five orderings' is
to say: the division into the five positions (i.e., cardinal directions). One position corresponds to one year. [Its] qi governs one entire year. Hence five years constitute one
cycle; six years constitute one perfect [cycle]. 'Perfect [cycle]' is to say: perfect succession of the qi of heaven; 'cycle' is to say: circulatory movement through the positions of
the earth. The reason that only five positions of the earth are referred to even though
there are six is that the qi of heaven does not come down to the ruler fire."

54 The textus receptus has 君火以明. Wang Bing and Lin Yi et al. read 君火以名 (as
for Lin Yi et al., see *Suwen* 74 504-7, note 11; translated in our note 22). - 967/45
agrees: "The ruler fire is situated to the right of the minister fire. However, the position of the ruler is established only by a name, not by the annual qi. Hence the six qi
of heaven do not meet with its qi to carry out the policy of the ruler fire; [the minister
fire] sticks to its position and receives the orders of heaven to spread the orders of
the fire. It is [only] by name [that the ruler fire] is bestowed with [the qi of] heaven.
Hence [the text] states: 'the ruler fire [exists] by name.' [The minister fire] guards its

When five and six are merged,
this results in 720 qi,
which constitutes one arrangement.
{Altogether thirty years.}
1440 qi
{Altogether sixty years.}
constitute one cycle.
Inadequacy and great excess can all be seen in this [cycle]."⁵⁵

66-368-2
[Huang] Di:
"Sir, your words,
[in view of the] above they have exhaustively covered the qi of heaven;
[in view of the] below they have said everything about the arrangements of the earth.

That can be called encompassing!
I should like to hear and store that [which will allow me]

'to employ [it] above to govern the people and
to employ [it] below to regulate the body,
to let the people acquire an understanding,
and above and below to be harmonious and intimate.
[So that] favours will flow downwards;
children and grandchildren will experience no anxiety and
the transmission of this [knowledge] to later generations
will never end.'
May [I] hear [it]?"

---

position and is granted an order. Hence [the text] states: 'the minister fire [exists] by position.'" For a literal interpretation, see 2643/60. 1293/15: "君火以明 is to say: it is above; 相火以位 is to say: it is below. .. 明 refers to 神明, 'spirit brilliance.'" – The *Li ji*, Liyun, has a meaning of 明 as 'to honor': "故君者所明, 非明人者也 – It is the ruler who must be honoured [by the common people], and it is not the common people who must be honoured by him." (See Ruan Yuan vol.2 p. 1422 above). Our reading follows the latter *Li ji* meaning of 明.

55 Wang Bing: "According to the calendrical pattern, one [period of] qi comprises 15 days. Hence if these [15 day periods] are added up to 720 qi [periods], then these are 30 years. If added up to 1440 qi [periods], these are 60 years. The classic states: 'Surplus is followed by insufficiency; insufficiency is followed by surplus.' Hence within [a period of] 60 years there will appear [periods of] insufficiency and of excess."

66-368-6
Gui Yuqu:
" 'The mechanism of the perfect numbers
is at hand and yet subtle.
That which arrives, it can be seen.
That which leaves, it can be pursued.

Those who respect them, they prosper.
Those who treat them with contempt, they perish.
Not to follow the Way but to pursue one's personal ends,
this must result in the calamity of early death.'[56]

[I] have attentively accepted the Way of heaven; please let me speak about what
is truly important."

66-368-8
[Huang] Di:
" 'Those who know to speak of the beginning, they will understand the end;
those who know to speak of what is near, they will know what is far away.'
Hence if the perfect numbers [are known] to their full extent and if the Way [is
followed] without confusion, this is called enlightenment.
I should like you, Sir, to extend [these numbers] and put them into sequence.

'Let them have a regular structure and
let [your language] be simple but not deficient.
[Then their transmission] will last long and be interrupted[57] at no time.
Easy to use and difficult to forget,
they will become fundamental principles [to act after].'
The essentials of the perfect numbers, I should like to hear them all."

66-368-11
Gui Yuqu:
"How brilliant a question is this, indeed! How brilliant is the Way, indeed!
Like a drum responding to the drumstick, like the echo responding to the
sound.

[I, your] subject, have heard the [following]:
Years [classified] *jia* and *ji* are governed by the soil period.
Years [classified] *yi* and *geng* are governed by the metal period.

---

56 240/55 reads 天 here as 災害, "disaster."

57 546/43: "絕 is 消亡, 'to perish.'"

Years [classified] *bing* and *xin* are governed by the water period.
Years [classified] *ding* and *ren* are governed by the wood period.
Years [classified] *wu* and *gui* are governed by the fire period."

[Huang] Di:
"How do they conform with the three yin and three yang?"

Gui Yuqu:
"In *zi* and *wu* years, the minor yin appears above.[58]
In *chou* and *wei* years, the major yin appears above.
In *yin* and *shen* years, the minor yang appears above.
In *mao* and *you* years, the yang brilliance appears above.
In *chen* and *xu* years, the major yang appears above.
In *si* and *hai* years, the ceasing yin appears above."

{The minor yin is that which is called 'tip.'[59] The ceasing yin is that which is called 'end.'}

66-369-5
What is above in ceasing yin [years], the wind qi rules it.
What is above in minor yin [years], the heat qi rules it.
What is above in major yin [years], the dampness qi rules it.
What is above in minor yang [years], the minister fire rules it.
What is above in yang brilliance [years], the dryness qi rules it.
What is above in major yang [years], the cold qi rules it."

{[These are] what is called 'root'; these are the so-called "six principal [qi]."}[60]

---

58 Cheng Shide et al.: "'Above' refers to the qi governing heaven of the visitor qi." Zhang Jiebin: "'Above' is to say: governs heaven. For instance, in a *zi* or *wu* year, the minor yin [qi] appears above to control heaven."

59 Zhang Jiebin: "標 is 首, 'head.' The yinyang sequence of a 60 years [cycle] begins with a *zi* or *wu* (year), hence the minor yin is the 'tip'; it reaches its completion with a *si hai* (year); hence the ceasing yin is called 'end.'"

60 Wang Bing: "The three yin and the three yang constitute the 'tip.' Cold, summer-heat, dryness, dampness, wind, and fire constitute the 'root.' Hence [the text] states: 'These are what is called root.' The true principal qi of heaven undergo six transformations to govern the principal [qi] of the earth in its functions of generation and completion. Following their respective requirements, the six transformations have different roots. That which generates them are indeed all the true principal qi. Hence [the text] states: 'six principal [qi].'" See, *Su wen* 71, note 1.

[Huang] Di:

"Bright is this Way, indeed! Brilliant is this discourse, indeed! Please let me inscribe this on jade tablets and store them in the Golden Chest.[61] I'll give it the title *Arrangements of the Principal [Qi] of Heaven*."

---

61 2493/531: „The Golden Chest is mentioned in the Dynastic History of the Han, Records on Emperor Gao (漢書, 高帝紀). It was the most sacred place in the palaces of the Han era."

Chapter 67
Comprehensive Discourse on the Progression
of the Five Periods[1]

67-369-11
Huang Di sat in the Hall of Light.[2]
In the beginning he rectified the mainstay of heaven.[3]
He looked down [from his elevated seat] and observed the eight farthest [regions].[4]
Having carried out investigations, he established the five constants.[5]

---

1 In contrast, 359/154 and 338/41 read 五 as "five agents" and 運行 as 運動變化, "movement and change." For a general discussion of the contents of *Su wen* 67 see there.

2 Cheng Shide et al.: "The Hall of Light (明堂) is the location where in ancient times the emperor and his officials gathered for discussions." – See also the following note.

3 Cheng Shide et al.: "正天綱 is to inspect the orbits of the celestial bodies." – The metaphorical usage of 綱 here is closely linked to the original meaning of the character, i.e., the main rope holding together a net. Donald Harper renders 天綱 as "the Mainstay of Heaven." By comparing Han and Pre-Han sources and pointing to similar Babylonian and Indian concepts, Harper showed that the primary reference of 天綱 was to the fixed stars of the *Big Dipper* (*ursa maior*) which were conceived of as a "support-cord for the multitude of stars" and as holding the heaven together. See his papers in *Early China* 4 (1978-79), p. 3 and in *Early China* 6 (1980-81), p.50-51. Harper (EC 6, p.51) stated: "The idea that in its function as the Mainstay of Heaven the Big Dipper regulates celestial movements entered into the political theories of the period. This idea underlies the ancient tradition that the ruler was to occupy the chamber inside the Hall of Light (明堂) which corresponded to the direction indicated by the handle of the Dipper during each of the twelve calendar months (see Soothill p. 93)." Moreover, the action of 正天綱, similar to the action of 在璿璣玉衡以齊七政 mentioned in the *Shang shu, Yao dian*, was probably linked to "the initiation of a new reign by a ritual act which aligns the new monarch with the model of Heaven" (being a model of the Dipper, which represented Heaven). "An adjustment in the calendar for ritual purposes is probably involved as well." See Harper 1980-81, EC 6 p. 51 and Cullen, EC 6, p. 39 .

4 Wang Bing: "八極 is 八方, 'eight cardinal points.'"

5 Wang Bing: "五常 are the five qi moving in between heaven and earth." Cheng Shide et al.: "That is, he examined and established the regularities of the policies and orders [issued] by the periodical qi [associated with] the five agents." In various contexts outside of the *Su wen*, 五常 also refers to the five moral virtues and to the five basic social relationships. The latter meaning may be implied here, too. The term 五常 appears in the *Su wen* only twice, here and in *Su wen* 71.

67-370-1
He summoned the Heavenly Teacher and asked him:[6]
"A discourse states:
'the movement and resting in heaven and on the earth,
the spirit brilliance sets up their arrangement.
As for the rise and descent of yin and yang,
cold, summerheat [and the remaining of the six qi] appear as their manifestations.'[7]

I have heard from you, Sir, the numbers [associated with] the five periods.[8]
But in your [words,] Sir, [you] have spoken only of how each of the five qi rules
over one year. {The first *jia* determines [all] periods.}[9] This is why I would like
to discuss this [with you]. Gui Yuqu has said:

'Soil rules *jia* and *ji* [years].
Metal rules *yi* and *geng* [years].
Water rules *bing* and *xin* [years].
Wood rules *ding* and *ren* [years].
Fire rules *wu* and *gui* [years].[10]

What is above in *zi* and *wu* [years], minor yin rules it.
What is above in *chou* and *wei* [years], major yin rules it.
What is above in *yin* and *shen* [years], minor yang rules it.
What is above in *mao* and *you* [years], yang brilliance rules it.
What is above in *chen* and *xu* [years], major yang rules it.
What is above in *si* and *hai* [years], ceasing yin rules it.'[11]

---

6 Cheng Shide et al.: " 'Heavenly Teacher' is an honorary designation of Qi Bo."

7 See *Su wen* 5 (5-45-1) and *Su wen* 69 (69-414-4) for textual parallels. The second
line of this quote reads 神明為之綱紀 in *Su wen* 5.

8 Cheng Shide et al.: "This refers to *Su wen* 9."

9 Wang Bing: " 'First *jia*' is the beginning of [a cycle of] six *jia* [years]; it is the *jia
zi* year."

10 Zhang Jiebin: "These are the five periods. 首甲定運 is to say: a cycle of 60 years
begins with a *jia zi* [constellation]. It serves to determine [all subsequent] periods."

11 Zhang Jiebin: "This is [a listing of the periods] ruled by the three yin and three
yang. 主 is 司天, 'to control heaven.' " Cheng Shide et al.: "This is identical to the
statement in *Su wen* 66: 子午之歲, 上見少陰..."

These are not the [usual] pairings with yin and yang. What is the reason for this?"[12]

67-370-8
Qi Bo:
"The Way of these [instructions by Gui Yuqu] is brilliant. These are [pairings with] the yin and yang in heaven and earth.[13]
Now, those that can be quantified by putting them in numbers, they are the yin and yang in man.[14]
Those paired like this, they can be grasped by counting.

Now,
'as for the yin and yang [correspondences in man],
count their [associations] and [you] can [reach] ten;
expand these [associations] further and [you] can [reach] one hundred.
Count these [associations] and [you] can [reach] one thousand;
expand them further and [you] can [reach] ten thousand.'[15]

[In contrast, the manifestations of] the yin and yang of heaven and earth cannot be counted and further extended [through enumerations]; they are referred to by images."[16]

---

12 Cheng Shide et al.: "That is to say, there are some instances where the six qi of yin and yang and the five periods do not overlap [in their associations]. For instance, *jia* and *ji* rule the soil period, but in terms of the five agents *jia* is associated with wood and *ji* is associated with soil. *Hai* and *zi* are both associated, in terms of the five agents, with water, but in terms of the six qi *hai* is ceasing yin, wind, and wood, while *zi* is minor yin and ruler fire."

13 In the preceding enumeration of the heaven stems, *jia* is equal to 1 which is yang, while *ji* is equal to 6 which is yin. Hence the pairing of *jia* and *ji* is a pairing of yang and yin. The same applies to all the remaining pairings. In contrast, in the enumeration of the earth branches, *zi* (the first earth branch) and *wu* (the seventh earth branch) are both yang because they represent odd numbers (1 and 7) in the sequence of the twelve branches, *chou* and *wei* are both yin (2 and 6) and so on. Qi Bo's reply refers to the fact that *zi* and *wu* may nevertheless be identified as a yang and yin pairing. The first six earth branches (*zi, chou, yin, mao, chen,* and *si*) are categorized as yang (= heaven), while the second six earth branches (*wu, wei, shen, you, xu,* and *hai*) are categorized as yin (= earth).

14 Cheng Shide et al.: "The first character 數 is 數目, 'number.' The latter character 數 is 計算, 'to count.'" Zhang Jiebin: "The yin and yang in man, that which is near can be counted and is easy to know for man."

15 See *Su wen* 6 for an identical statement.

16 Wu Kun: "That is to say, the yin and yang [associations] of heaven can be extended indefinitely. They cannot be searched for through enumeration; they must be searched

67-370-11
[Huang] Di:
"I should like to hear what this begins with."

Qi Bo:
"A brilliant question, indeed!
[I, your] subject, have read the text of the *Book on the Supreme Beginning and on the Principal [Qi] of Heaven*, [stating]:

'The qi of a vermilion heaven passes through the [stellar divisions of] *niu* and *nü* and [through those of] the *wu* section.
The qi of a yellow heaven passes through the [stellar divisions of] *xin* and *wei* and [through those of] the *ji* section.
The qi of a greenish heaven passes through the [stellar divisions of] *wei* and *shi* and [through those of] *liu* and *gui*.
The qi of white heaven passes through [the stellar divisions of] *kang* and *di* and [through those of] *mao* and *bi*.
The qi of a dark heaven passes through [the stellar divisions of] *zhang* and *yi* and [through those of] *lou* and *wei*.'[17]

---

for through [their] images." Zhang Jiebin: "The yinyang [associations] of heaven and earth are inexhaustible. It is impossible to trace them with a limited number of numbers. Hence they must be searched for through their images." See also 2007/13 and 1908/35. For a discussion of the various meanings of 象 in the *Neijing*, see 329/7 and 1376/9.

17 Cheng Shide et al.: " 'Vermilion heaven' is the red colored qi of fire. 'Yellow heaven' is the yellow colored qi of the soil. 'Greenish heaven' is the green-blue colored qi of wood. 'Clear heaven' is the white colored qi of metal. 'Dark heaven' is the black colored qi of water. Tradition has it that when the ancients inspected the images in heaven, they saw periodic qi in five colors. Hence an opinion resulted that qi in the five colors of vermilion, yellow, greenish, clear, and dark pass along heaven. 牛, 女 und 心, 尾, 危, 室, 柳, 鬼, 亢, 氐, 昴, 畢, etc. are the designations of the 28 stellar divisions. Because the celestial bodies revolve without ever coming to an end, the 28 stellar divisions are used to determine the locations of the celestial bodies. The 28 stellar divisions that appear in spring serve as starting point. 角, 亢, 氐, 房, 心, 尾, 箕 are located in the East; they are called the seven Eastern divisions. 斗, 牛, 女, 虚, 危, 室, 壁 are located in the North; they are called the seven Northern divisions. 奎, 婁, 胃, 昴, 畢, 觜, 參 are located in the West; they are called the seven Western divisions. 井, 鬼, 柳, 星, 張, 翼, 軫 are located in the South, they are called the seven Southern divisions. The segment of *wu* 戊 is the position of the two stellar divisions of *kui* 奎 and *bi* 壁; the segment of *ji* 己 is the position of the two stellar divisions of *jiao* 角 and *zhen* 軫." 1166/15: "Obviously, the *Tai shi tian yuan ce* continues a ten months solar calendar."

{As for the so-called *wu* and *ji* sections, these are [the positions of the stellar divisions of] *kui* and *bi* and of *jiao* and *zhen*, respectively. They are the gates of heaven and earth.}[18]

67-371-3
Now, where the manifestations begin, the Way [of understanding] emerges. That must be comprehended."[19]

[Huang] Di:
"Good!

A discourse states:
'Heaven and earth,
they are the above and the below of the myriad beings;
left and right,

---

18 Cheng Shide et al.: "The sun is seen in its movement at the position of the two stellar divisions of *kui* and *bi* exactly at the time of the transition from spring to summer; it is at the position of the two stellar divisions of *jiao* and *zhen* exactly at the time of the transition from autumn to winter. Summer is the yang in yang; winter is the yin in yin. Hence the ancients called *kui bi* and *jiao zhen* (i.e., the sections of *wu* and *ji*) the 'gates of heaven and earth.'" 263/15: "The stellar divisions of *kui* and *bi* are located at [the borderline of] West and North, right at the [trigram] *qian* 乾 of the eight trigrams, at the position of *wu* and soil. The stellar divisions of *jiao* and *zhen* are located at [the borderline of] East and South, right at the [trigram] *xun* 巽 of the eight trigrams, at the position of *ji* and soil. .. [As for] 'the *wu* section is the entrance of heaven, the *ji* section is the gate of the earth,' the entrance of heaven masters opening; the gate of the earth masters storage. The entrance of heaven and the gate of the earth are the entrance gates where the yin and yang [qi] of heaven and earth rise and descend. They are the turning points for the external appearance of cold and warmth." For further details and a graph, see there. Zhang Jiebin: "That the days become longer, that the seasons become warmer and that the myriad beings come to life and develop, all this has its begin with *kui* and *bi*. That the days become shorter, that the seasons become colder and that the myriad beings are stored away, all this has begin with *jiao* and *zhen*."

19 263/14: "This makes it very clear that the transformations and movements of the ten stems have been determined on the basis of the positions of the 28 stellar constellations in the sky. The qi of a vermilion heaven is to say: the transformations of the five agents appear in the sky as fire qi. The color of fire is vermilion-crimson. Hence [the text] speaks of 'vermilion heaven..'.." For further details see there. *NJCD*: "候 is 物候." 353/26: "候 signifies all kinds of external manifestations. 道 is law and rule. Hence the meaning of this passage is: On the basis of the external manifestations of things it is possible to formulate the laws inherent in things."

they are the paths of yin and yang.'[20]
I do not know what that is to say."[21]

67-371-5
Qi Bo:
"As for the so-called above and below,
these are the locations where yin and yang are seen in the upper and lower
[halves] of a year.

As for the [so-called] left and right, [the following applies]:
'Whenever the ceasing yin appears above, the minor yin is to the left and the
major yang is to the right.
Whenever the minor yin appears [above], the major yin is to the left and the
ceasing yin is to the right.
Whenever the major yin appears [above], the minor yang is to the left and the
minor yin is to the right.

67-371-8
Whenever the minor yang appears [above], the yang brilliance is to the left and
the major yin is to the right.
Whenever the yang brilliance appears [above], the major yang is to the left and
the minor yang is to the right.
Whenever the major yang appears [above], the ceasing yin is to the left and the
yang brilliance is to the right.'"

{When it is said 'face the North and name their position,' [then] this is to state
how it is perceived}[22]

---

20 See *Su wen* 5 and *Su wen* 66 for textual parallels.

21 Zhang Zhicong: "This is another discourse on the [positions of the] six qi above
and below, on the left and on the right. The [qi] controlling heaven is above, the [qi]
at the fountain is below. The generation and transformation of the myriad things occurs in between. Hence heaven and earth are the above and the below of the myriad
things. 'Left and right' refers to the intervening qi. The intervening qi mark the steps
[between the qi controlling heaven and the qi at the fountain]; hence they are called
the paths of yin and yang."

22 Wang Bing: "This statement is made from a position facing North. 'Above' is the
South; 'below' is the North. To the left is the West; to the right is the East." Cheng
Shide et al.: " 'Face the North and name their positions' is to explain that the [posi-
tions of] left and right to the [qi] governing heaven are the left and right that are
determined while facing the North."

67-371-10
[Huang] Di:
"What does 'below' mean?"[23]

Qi Bo:
"When the ceasing yin is present above,[24] then the minor yang is present below,[25] the yang brilliance is to the left and the major yin is to the right.
When the minor yin is present above, then the yang brilliance is present below,
the major yang is to the left and the minor yin is to the right.
When the major yin is present above, then the major yang is present below, the
ceasing yin is to the left and the yang brilliance is to the right.

When the minor yang is present above, then the ceasing yin is present below,
the minor yin is to the left and the major yang is to the right.
When the yang brilliance is present above, then the minor yin is present below,
the major yin is to the left and the ceasing yin is to the right.
When the major yang is present above, then the major yin is present below, the
minor yang is to the left and the minor yin is to the right.

{When it is said 'face the South and name their positions,' [then]
this is to state how it is perceived.'}[26]

67-371-15
'The above meets with the below;[27]
cold and summerheat come down on each other.[28]

---

23 Cheng Shide et al.: " 'Below,' the position of the [qi] controlling heaven is above,
while the position of the [qi] at the fountain is below. This 'below' here refers to the
[qi] at the fountain."

24 i.e., in the upper half of a year.

25 i.e., in the lower half of that year.

26 Wang Bing: "That which rules the year is positioned in the South. Hence [an
oberserver] takes a position facing North and states what is on the left and on the
right. As for 'that which is below,' its position is in the North. Hence [an observer]
takes a position facing South and states what is on the left and on the right. 'Above'
is the position of heaven; 'below' is the position of the earth. When facing the South,
the East is to the left, the West is to the right."

27 Zhang Jiebin: "遘 is 交, 'to meet.'" Cheng Shide et al.: " 'Above' refers to the visitor
qi; 'below' refers to the host qi. 上下相遘 is: the visitor qi that control heaven or are at
the fountain interact (相交) with the qi ruling a season."

28 Zhang Zhicong: "相臨 is to say: 加臨之六氣, 'the six qi joining from below and
coming down from above.'" Cheng Shide et al.: "寒署相臨 refers to the joining from

When the qi agree with each other, then this results in harmony.
When they do not agree with each other, then this results in disease.' "[29]

[Huang] Di:
"When the qi agree with each other and a disease [appears nevertheless], how is that?"

Qi Bo:
"That is because [that which is] below comes down on [what is] above; it does not occupy its proper position."[30]

67-372-1
[Huang] Di:
"How do they move or rest?"[31]

Qi Bo:
" 'Those above, they pass to the right.
Those below, they pass to the left.
To the left and to the right, they complete one circle around heaven.

---

below and coming down from above of the qi controlling heaven, of [the qi] being at the fountain and of the intervening qi to the left and to the right to the six qi that rule the seasons. 'Cold' and 'summerheat' refer here to the six qi in general."

29 Wang Bing: "When wood comes down on fire, when metal comes down on water, when water comes down on wood, when fire comes down on soil, when soil comes down on metal, [then these are relationships where their qi] fit each other (because wood generates fire, metal generates water, etc.). When wood comes down on soil, when soil comes down on water, when water comes down on fire, when fire comes down on metal, when metal comes down on wood, [then these are relationships where their qi] do not fit each other (because wood dominate soil, soil dominates water, etc.). When the above comes down on the below, that is an appropriate [movement]. When the below comes down on the above, that is a countermovement. Countermovement is also an oppression. Hence disease is generated."

30 Wang Bing: "If soil comes down on fire, fire comes down on wood, wood comes down on water, water comes down on metal and metal comes down on soil, these are all [relationships of] the below descending to the above. That does not conform to their position. The meaning [implied here is that] of father and son. The son is below and the father is above. If the son descended to the father, would not this be a countermovement, too?"

31 Wang Bing: "That is to say: the movement of heaven and earth to the left and to the right."

[When they enter the] next [circle] they meet anew [with the original starting point].'"[32]

[Huang] Di:
"I have heard Gui Yuqu say:
'The [qi] corresponding to the earth, they rest [at one place and keep their position].'[33]

Now you, Sir, state: 'Those below pass to the left.' I do not know what that is to say. I should like to hear how this is generated."[34]

67-372-5
Qi Bo:
"[As far as] the movement and resting in heaven and on earth,
and the replacement and return of the five agents [are concerned],
although Gui Yuqu did nothing but examine the [heaven] above, he was still unable to reach a comprehensive understanding.

Now,
in the operations of change and transformation,
heaven hangs the images,
while the earth completes the physical appearances.

---

32 Wang Bing: " 'Above' is heaven; 'below' is the earth. 周天 is to say: heaven encircles the positions of the five agents of the earth. Heaven bestows six qi [on the earth]; the earth spreads the five agents. .. 周天 does not refer to the six qi encircling heaven." Zhang Jiebin: " 'Those above pass to the right' is to say: the qi of heaven move to the right. From the East [they move] to the West and descend to the earth. 'Those below pass to the left' is to say: the qi of the earth revolve to the left. [They move] from the West to the East and rise to heaven. Hence the [qi] controlling heaven in the upper [half of the year] will pass through *si, wu, wei,* and *shen* and descend in the West. The [qi] at the fountain in the lower [half of the year] will pass through *hai, zi, chou,* and *yin* and rise in the East." 314/13: "That is to say: the intervening qi [to the side] of [the qi] controlling heaven passes from the right to the left; the intervening qi [to the side] of [the qi at] the fountain passes from the left to the right. Also, yin passes to the left; yang passes to the right." 339/34: "周 is 圓周, 'circumference' in the sense of 環繞, 'encircle,' 'surround.' 餘 is: after one full circle has been completed. 復會 is: return to the starting point again."

33 *Su wen* 66-367-3.

34 *SWJZ*: "Movement emerges out of resting. Hence [the text] says '生.'"

The seven luminaries are threaded in the [Great] Void;[35]
the five agents are attached to the earth."[36]

{The earth is [the foundation] which carries all physical appearances that come
to life and reach maturity.
The [Great] Void is that by which the essence qi corresponding to heaven are
arranged in order.[37]
The movements of physical appearances [in relation to] essence [qi] resemble
the relationship of root and base with branches and leaves.[38]
[You] look up to these images; although they are far away, they can be recognized.}

[Huang] Di:
"Is it not so that the earth is below?"[39]

Qi Bo:
"The earth is below man and within the Great Void."[40]

---

35 Zhang Zhicong: "緯虛 is to say: they [move] lengthwise and crosswise through
the Great Void." *SWJZ*: "[The luminaries move] lengthwise and crosswise [經緯]
through the Great Void and they wind around the earth."

36 Wang Bing: "To observe the returning movement of the five stars in the East lets
the principles of the passage to the left of the earth become exceedingly clear. 麗 is 著,
'to be attached.'" Cheng Shide et al.: "The *Zheng yun* 正韻 says '麗 is 附, 'to attach.'
That is, the five agents are attached to the earth and complete its physical appearance."
The *Yi jing* 易經 definition added to hexagram *li* 離: 日月麗乎天, 百穀草木麗乎地,
"sun and moon are attached to heaven, the one hundred grains, herbs, and trees are
attached to the earth."

37 677/396: "The 'essence qi corresponding to heaven' is a yang qi. Gao You 高誘,
commenting on the *Lü shi chun qiu*, 'Yuan dao,' 呂氏春秋, 圜道, stated: '精 is the light
of sun and moon.'" We interpret "essence qi" here as a reference to sun, moon, and the
stars, based on *Huai nan zi, juan* 3, "Tian wen xun" 天文訓: 火氣之精者為日 .. 水氣
之精者為月, 日月之淫為精者為星辰, "The essence of the fire qi generated the sun,
.. the essence of the water qi generated the moon. The essence of the surplus [qi] of
sun and moon generated the stars."

38 Zhang Zhicong: "The earth is static like a root; the qi at the fountain moves like
branches and leaves." Zhang Jiebin: "The seven luminaries [move lengthwise and]
crosswise through the [Great] Void like roots; the five agents are attached to the earth
like branches and leaves." 2568/49: "猶根本之與枝業 is 猶根本與枝業."

39 Wang Bing: "That is to say, it revolves and does not rest. How can it be 'below'?"

40 Wang Bing: "It is where man resides; [hence] it can be said to be 'below.' In the
final analysis, though, [the earth] is a thing in the Great Void."

[Huang] Di:
"Is it supported?"[41]

67-373-1
Qi Bo:
"The Grand Qi holds it.[42]

'By dryness it dries it.
By summerheat it steams it.
By wind it moves it.
By dampness it moistens it.
By cold it hardens it.
By fire it warms it.' " [43]

67-373-3
{The fact is,
wind and cold are below; dryness and heat are above. Dampness qi is in the

---

41 Wang Bing: "That is to say: the Great Void is limitless; how can the physical body
of the earth be supported and stay at one place?" Zhang Jiebin: "That is to say: the
earth is amidst the Great Void and does not fall down nevertheless. Hence is it attached to something?" Fang Wenhui/21: "馮 was [used] in ancient times for 憑." See
also 169/52.

42 Wang Bing: " 'Grand Qi' is to say: the qi of creation; it is the [qi] sustaining the
Great Void. The reason why the Great Void does not contract, why the earth [ex-
ists over] long, and heaven continues forever lies in the [fact that] the qi of creation
sustains it. If the qi were to transform and undergo changes [itself] and if it were
not to sustain the [Great Void] any longer, the containers [suspended] in the Great
Void would be destroyed, too. Now, when leaves drop and fly through the open space
without falling [to the earth] quickly, that is because they ride on the qi. Hence they
cannot gain speed. Everything residing on the earth with physical appearance is sus-
tained by the qi of creation. However, there are large and small containers and their
destruction may be slow or fast. However, if no qi is present to sustain them, the destruction of large and small [items] is all the same." Zhang Jiebin: "The 'grand qi' is the
principal qi of the Great Void. All the myriad things depend on it. Hence the earth is
located in the middle of the Great Void because it is supported by the principal qi."
2315/12: " 'Grand qi' refers to the six qi." 1735/39: "Heaven encloses the earth like an
egg containing a yolk."

43 Zhang Jiebin: "These are transformations of the grand qi. That is, the activities
of the six qi between heaven and earth." Zhang Zhicong: "That is to say how the six
qi move between heaven above and earth below. Wind, cold, summerheat, dampness, dryness, and fire are qi without physical appearance in heaven. Drying, steaming,
moving, moistening, hardening, and warming are [their] corporal manifestations on
the earth."

middle. The fire vacillates among them.[44]
Hence when cold, summerheat, [etc., i.e.,] the six [qi] enter, they let the
[Great] Void generate and transform [things].}[45]

{Hence
when dryness dominates, then the earth is dry.
When summerheat dominates, then the earth is hot.
When wind dominates, then the earth moves.
When dampness dominates, then the earth turns muddy.
When cold dominates, then the earth cracks.
When fire dominates, then the earth hardens.}

[Huang] Di:
"The qi of heaven and earth, by which [manifestations] are they examined?"

Qi Bo:
"The workings of domination and revenge[46] of the qi of heaven and earth, they
do not manifest themselves [in signs that can] be examined.[47]

When the *Laws of [Examining] the Vessels* states:
'The changes of heaven and earth cannot be examined in the [movement in
the] vessels,'
then this means just the same."

---

44 Zhang Jiebin: "Cold resides in the North; the wind resides in the East. [They
move] from the North to the East. Hence [when the text] states 'wind and cold are
below,' that is 'those below pass to the left.' Heat resides in the South; dryness resides
in the West. [They move] from the South to the West. Hence [when the text] states
'dryness and heat are above,' that is because 'above' is 'pass to the right.' The earth is
soil. Soil transforms into dampness. Hence [the text] states: 'the dampness qi is in the
center.' Only the fire has two. The ruler fire resides above the dampness; the minister
fire resides below the dampness. Hence [the text] states 'the fire vacillates among
them.'"

45 Zhang Jiebin: "Without the [Great] Void, where should the qi be? Without the qi
how could there be transformation and generation?" Zhang Zhicong: "The six qi enter
the earth. Hence they let the corporal earth receive non-corporal qi of the [Great]
Void and thereby generate and transform the myriad things."

46 Cheng Shide et al.: "復 is 復氣; that is the 報復之氣, 'qi of revenge.'"

47 Wang Bing: "That is to say: the balanced qi and the [qi of] domination and revenge can be investigated through their physical appearances; they cannot be recognized through diagnostic examination."

67-373-8
[Huang] Di:
"How about the intervening qi?"

Qi Bo:
" 'Following the location of the qi,
one predicts [the intervening qi] on the left and on the right.' "[48]

[Huang] Di:
"How can they be predicted?"

67-373-10
Qi Bo:
"When [the intervening qi] follow the qi [that controls heaven], then there is harmony.
When they oppose the qi [that controls heaven], then there is disease.[49]
When they do not occupy their proper position, [this indicates] disease.[50]

---

48 Wang Bing: "[The qi] are examined at the four locations of foot and inch on the left and on the right to realize whether they correspond or not, whether there is excess or not."

49 Wang Bing: "That is to say, [the movement in the vessels] should be deep, but is not deep; it should be at the surface, but is not at the surface; it should be rough, but is not rough; it should be hook[-like] but is not hook[-like]; it should be string[-like] but is not string[-like]; it should be big but is not big, etc." Lin Yi et al.: "*Su wen* 74 states: "When a ceasing yin [qi] arrives, the [corresponding movement in the] vessels is string[-like]. When a minor yin [qi] arrives, the [corresponding movement in the] vessels is hook[-like]. When a major yin [qi] arrives, the [corresponding movement in the] vessels is deep. When a minor yang [qi] arrives, the [corresponding movement in the] vessels is big and at the surface. When a yang brilliance [qi] arrives, the [corresponding movement in the] vessels is short and rough. When a major yang [qi] arrives, the [corresponding movement in the] vessels is big and extended. When [the movement] that arrives is harmonious, then there is peace. When [the movement] that arrives is extreme, then there is a disease. When [the movement] that arrives is contrary [to what it should be like], there is a disease. When [the movement should] arrive but fails to arrive, there is a disease. When [a movement should] not arrive but does arrive, there is a disease. When yin and yang have exchanged [their positions], that is dangerous."

50 While the *Su wen* appears to refer to the general concepts of the five periods and six qi and of intervening qi appearing to the left and to the right of the qi "controlling heaven" or appearing "at the fountain," some commentators have interpreted this passage and the following statements in a narrow sense as related to pulse diagnosis.

When they change their positions, [this indicates] disease.[51]
When they fail to guard their position, this is dangerous.[52]

<When [the movements in the vessels in] the foot-long section and in the inch
[section] are reversed, this [indicates] death.[53]
Yin yang interaction [indicates] death.>[54]

'First one establishes which year it is,
to recognize which qi [dominates].
[The intervening qi] on the left and on the right can be seen in accordance.
Afterwards one can make a statement
concerning opposition or compliance [resulting] in death or survival.'"

Wang Bing: "When it appears at another position." Zhang Jiebin: "When that which
should be on the left is on the right and when that which should be on the right is on
the left, when that which should be above is below and when that which should be
below is above." Gao Shishi: "不當其位 is what was stated above: 'when [that which
is] below comes down on [what is] above that does not conform to its position.'"

51 Wang Bing: "That is to say: at the left a [movement in the] vessels of the right
appears, or at the right a [movement in the] vessels of the left appears. In such a case
the qi [of left and right] are confused. Hence [this indicates] disease." Cheng Shide et
al.: "迭 is 更, 'to alternate,' 'to change.' That is, left and right are reversed."

52 Wang Bing: "It already appears in another district and the palace in the respective
[district] is confronted with a qi of theft and killing. Hence the disease is dangerous."

53 Wang Bing: "The four years with a *zi, wu, mao,* or *you* [branch in their constellation of stems and branches] have such 'reverse' [qi]. That is to say, according to the
[constellation of a specific] year, a yin [movement] should appear at the inch [section
near the wrist]. Reversely, however, it appears at the foot-long [section]. According to
the [constellation of that same] year, a yang [movement] should appear at the foot-
long [section]. Reversely, however, it appears at the inch [section]. [In this case] both
the [movements at the] inch and at the foot-long [sections] are called 'reverse.' If this
were to apply only to the foot-long [section] or only to the inch [section], this would
be 不應, 'lack of correspondence,' it would not be 反, 'reverse.'"

54 Wang Bing: "The eight years with a *yin, shen, si, hai, chou, wei, chen,* or *xu* [branch
in their constellation of stems and branches] have such 'exchanged' [qi]. That is to say,
according to the [constellation of a specific] year, a yin [movement] should appear at
the right [wrist]. Reversely, however, it appears at the left. According to the [constella-
tion of that same] year, a yang [movement] should appear at the left [wrist]. Reversely,
however, it appears at the right. [The movement at] the left and at the right appear
'exchanged.' That is called 交, 'exchanged.' If this were to apply only to the left or to the
right, this would be 不應, 'lack of correspondence,' it would not be 交, 'exchanged.'"

67-374-4
[Huang] Di:
"Cold, summerheat, dryness, dampness, wind, and fire, what can they be correlated with in man?[55]
How do they contribute to the generation and transformation of the myriad beings?"

Qi Bo:
" 'The East generates wind.
Wind generates wood.
Wood generates sour [flavor].[56]
Sour [flavor] generates the liver.[57]
The liver generates the sinews.[58]
The sinews generate the heart.'[59]

67-375-1
'In heaven it is darkness;
in man it is the Way;
on the earth it is transformation.

Transformation generates the five flavors.
The Way generates wisdom.

---

55 Wang Bing: "合 is to say: 中外相應, 'center and outside correspond to each other.'" Qian Chaochen-90/136: "The extended meaning of 合 employed here is 應, 'to correspond,' 答, 'to respond.' The *Shi ji*, Le shu, 史記, 樂書, has: 合生氣之和. The zheng yi 正義 commentary states: 合 is 應, 'to correspond.'"

56 Wang Bing: "All those of the myriad beings that have a sour flavor, they originate from a generation and transformation of wood qi."

57 Wang Bing: "When sour flavor enters the stomach, it provides the liver depot with nourishment."

58 Wang Bing: "When the sour flavor enters the liver, it is further distributed by the liver depots to generate, through transformation, the sinews and membranes."

59 Wang Bing: "When the sour qi has nourished the sinews and membranes, it will flow on, transform and enter the heart." Zhang Zhicong: "The five cardinal points generate the five qi of heaven. The five qi generate the five agents of the earth. The five agents generate the five flavors and the five depots. The five depots generate the five body parts associated with them externally. Hence man depends on the qi and flavors of the five directions to come into being and to mature." See *Su wen* 5 for statements identical to major segments of this and the following passages. These passages are indicated by inverted commas.

Darkness generates the spirits.'
<Transformation generates qi.>

'The spirit,
in heaven it is wind,
on the earth it is wood,
in man's body it is the sinews,
<Among the qi it is softness.>
among the depots it is the liver.'

Its nature is warm.[60]
Its virtue is harmony.
Its operation is movement.
'Its color is greenish.'
Its transformation is blossoming.
{Its creatures are hairy.}
Its policy is dispersion.

67-376-3
Its commands are spreading and effusion.
Its causing changes is to break [things] and pull [them].
Its causing a calamity[61] is making [things] fall.

'Its flavor is sour.
Its state of mind is anger.

Anger harms the liver;
sadness dominates anger.
Wind harms the liver;[62]
dryness dominates wind.
Sour [flavor] harms the sinews;[63]

---

60 Wang Bing: "喧 is 溫, 'warm.'"

61 Cheng Shide et al.: "The *Shuo wen* states: '眚 is; the eye has a disease of screen growth.' The *Guang yun* 廣韻 states: 過也, 災也, 'this is excess; this is calamity.' It should be interpreted here as 'calamity,' 'misfortune.'"

62 Wang Bing: "Just like wind breaks the trees."

63 Wang Bing: "Sour [qi] drains the liver qi. If this drainage is excessive, then the [liver] qi will be harmed."

acrid [flavor] dominates sour [flavor].'⁶⁴

67-377-2
'The South generates heat.
Heat generates fire.
Fire generates bitter [flavor].⁶⁵
Bitter [flavor] generates the heart.⁶⁶
The heart generates the blood.⁶⁷
The blood generates the spleen.⁶⁸

In heaven it is heat;
on the earth it is fire;
in man's body it is the vessels.
<Among the qi it is breath.>⁶⁹
Among the depots it is the heart.'

67-378-1
Its nature is summerheat.
Its virtue is clarity.
Its operation is dryness.
'Its color is red.'
Its transformation is lushness.
{Its creatures are feathered.}
Its policy is brilliance.

---

64 Wang Bing: "Acrid is the flavor of metal. Hence it dominates sour which is the qi of wood. An excess of sour [qi] should be dominated with acrid [qi]."

65 Wang Bing: "All things with a bitter flavor originate from the generation and transformation of fire. When something sweet is brought into fire, its substance, after being burned, is bitter. That can be taken as evidence that bitter [flavor] is the result of a transformation by fire."

66 Wang Bing: "When bitter [things] enter the stomach, they transform and enter the heart."

67 Wang Bing: "When the transformation of the bitter flavor through the heart is complete, it is spread out to generate the blood and the vessels."

68 Wang Bing: "When the bitter flavor has completed its nourishing the blood, it flows from the blood, transforms and generates as well as nourishes the spleen."

69 Wang Bing: "息 is 長, 'growth.'" Zhang Jiebin: "When the blood and the qi are balanced, the breathing is regulated." Cheng Shide et al.: "息 has the meaning of coming into existence and [subsequent] growth. Wang Bing's comment is correct."

Its commands are pressure and steam.[70]
Its causing changes is [to generate] flames and melting.
Its causing a calamity is [to cause] burning heat.

'Its flavor is bitter.
Its state of mind is joy.

Joy harms the heart;
fear dominates joy.
Heat harms the qi;
cold dominates heat.
Bitter [flavor] harms the qi;
salty [flavor] dominates bitter [flavor].'

67-379-3
'The center generates dampness.[71]
Dampness generates soil.[72]
Soil generats sweet [flavor].[73]
Sweet [flavor] generates the spleen.[74]
The spleen generates the flesh;[75]
the flesh generates the lung.[76]

In heaven it is dampness;
on the earth it is soil;

---

70 Qian Chaochen-88/61: "Wang Bing interprets 鬱 as 盛, 'rich,' and 蒸 as 熱, 'hot.'
That is, 'the qi is very hot, like steam.' This is not correct. Throughout the *Su
wen*, the meaning of 鬱 is 'to collect,' 'to press together.' Why should the present statement be
an exception?"

71 Wang Bing: " 'Center' is the soil. The soil in the high mountains is damp. The
water in the soil emerges from springs."

72 Wang Bing: "When dampness qi accumulates in the interior [of the earth], the
physical body of the soil is all damp. As a result, the soil comes to life. When the soil
dries, it dies."

73 Wang Bing: "All things with a sweet flavor originate from a generation and transformation of soil."

74 Wang Bing: "When sweet things enter the stomach, they first enter the spleen."

75 Wang Bing: "Sweet flavor enters the spleen. From the spleen depot it is spread and
transforms to let the fat and the flesh develop and grow."

76 Wang Bing: "When the sweet qi has completed its nourishing the flesh, it flows
from the flesh, transforms and generates and nourishes the lung depot."

in man's body it is the flesh.
<Among the qi it is fullness.>
Among the depots it is the spleen.'

Its nature is resting and union.
Its virtue is sogginess.
Its operation is transformation.
'Its color is yellow.'
Its transformation is fullness.
{Its creatures are naked.}
Its policy is tranquility.

Its commands are clouds and rain.
Its causing changes is [to generate] movement and outpour.
Its causing a calamity is [to generate] excessive [rain]⁷⁷ and massive flooding.

67-381-1
'Its flavor is sweet.
Its state of mind is pensiveness.

Pensiveness harms the spleen;
anger dominates pensiveness.⁷⁸
Dampness harms the flesh;⁷⁹
wind dominates dampness.⁸⁰
Sweet [flavor] harms the spleen;⁸¹
sour [flavor] dominates sweet [flavor].'⁸²

---

77 Zhang Jiebin: "霖淫, 'rain,' and 崩溃, 'landslip,' are the calamities associated with soil." Cheng Shide et al.: "淫 is 'continuous rain.' 溃 is 'landslip.'"

78 Wang Bing: "Those who are angry do not think. Anger lets [a person] forget [all] calamities. Hence it is obvious that [anger] dominates [pensiveness]. If someone thinks [about a calamity] excessively, this is checked by arousing anger."

79 Wang Bing: "Excessive dampness is water. When water collects it causes swelling."

80 Wang Bing: "Wind is the qi of wood. Hence it dominates soil. Excessive dampness is checked with wind."

81 Wang Bing: "Only if it is excessive."

82 Wang Bing: "Excess sweetness is checked with sour [qi]. This serves to save the spleen qi."

'The West generates dryness.
Dryness generates metal.
Metal generates acrid [flavor].[83]
Acrid [flavor] generates the lung.[84]
The lung generates the skin and the body hair.[85]
The skin and the body hair generate the kidneys.[86]

In heaven it is dryness;
on the earth it is metal;
on man's body it is the skin and its hair.
<Among the qi it is completion.>
Among the depots it is the lung.'

Its nature is coolness.
Its virtue is clearness.
Its operation is hardening.[87]
'Its color is white.'
Its transformation is contraction.
{Its creatures are armored.}
Its policy is force.[88]

Its commands are fog and dew.
Its causing changes is [to cause] sternness and killing.
Its causing a calamity is [to cause] aging and falling.

67-383-2
'Its flavor is acrid.
Its state of mind is anxiety.

---

83 Wang Bing: "All things with an acrid flavor originate from a transformation of metal."

84 Wang Bing: "When acrid things enter the stomach, they first enter the lung."

85 Wang Bing: "Acrid flavor enters the lung. From the lung depot it is spread and transforms to generate the skin and the hair."

86 Wang Bing: "From the skin and the body hair the acrid qi flows on, transforms and generates qi that enters the kidneys."

87 Wang Bing: "固 is 堅定, 'hard.'" Fang Yaozhong: "固 refers to 堅固, 'hard,' and also to 保衛, 'protection.'"

88 Zhang Zhicong: "勁 is 堅銳, 'hard and piercing.'" Cheng Shide et al.: "勁 is 勁急, 'tense.'"

Anxiety harms the lung;[89]
joy dominates anxiety.
Heat harms the skin and the body hair;[90]
cold dominates heat.
Acrid [flavor] harms the skin and the body hair;[91]
bitter [flavor] dominates acrid [flavor].'[92]

67-383-4
'The North generates cold.
Cold generates water.
Water generates salty [flavor].[93]
Salty [flavor] generates the kidneys.[94]
The kidneys generate the bones and the marrow.[95]
The marrow generates the liver.[96]

In heaven it is cold;
on the earth it is water;
in man's body it is the bones.
<Among the qi it is hardness.>
Among the depot it is the kidneys.'

Its nature is piercing cold.
Its virtue is cold.

---

89 Wang Bing: "In case of anxiety the flow of qi is blocked. When it is blocked, the qi of the lung depot cannot pass either. Hence anxiety harms the lung."

90 Wang Bing: "When fire qi is present in abundance, things burn and desiccate. Hence when heat qi abounds, the skin and the body hair are harmed."

91 Wang Bing: "Only if it is excessive."

92 Wang Bing: "Bitter is the flavor of fire. Hence it dominates acrid [flavor] which is [a qi of] metal."

93 Wang Bing: "All things with a salty flavor originate from a transformation of water."

94 Wang Bing: "When salty things enter the stomach, they first turn to the kidneys."

95 Wang Bing: "Salty flavor enters the kidneys. From the kidney depot it is spread and transforms to generate the bones and their marrow."

96 Wang Bing: "From the bones and the marrow, the salty qi flows on, transforms and generates qi that enters the liver."

Its operation is [...]⁹⁷
'Its color is black.'
Its transformation is sternness.⁹⁸
{Its creatures are scaly.}
Its policy is resting.

Its commands [...]⁹⁹
Its causing changes is [to cause] piercing frost.
Its causing a calamity is [to cause] ice and hail.

67-385-2
'Its flavor is salty.
Its state of mind is fear.

Fear harms the kidneys;¹⁰⁰
pensiveness dominates fear.¹⁰¹
Cold harms the blood;¹⁰²
dryness dominates cold.
Salty [flavor] harms the blood;
sweet [flavor] dominates salty [flavor].' ¹⁰³

The five qi are positioned one after another. Each has [one] which precedes it.¹⁰⁴

---

97 Wang Bing: "Corruption of the original text." Zhang Jiebin: "Its operation is storage." Gao Shishi: "Its operation is drying, in the sense of hardening."

98 Wang Bing: "肅 is 靜, 'resting.'"

99 Wang Bing: "Corruption of the original text." Zhang Jiebin: "Its commands are closure." Gao Shishi: "Its commands are severity."

100 Wang Bing: "Extreme fear moves the center and thereby harms the kidneys."

101 Wang Bing: "Pensiveness reveals the dynamics of a calamity. Hence there is no fear."

102 Wang Bing: "When the cold is extreme, the blood congeals. Hence it harms the blood."

103 Wang Bing: "Sweet is the flavor of the soil. Hence it dominates salty [flavor which is associated with] water."

104 Zhang Zhicong: "The five qi are the qi of the five cardinal points. 更立 is: the alternation of the four seasons. As for 各有所先, the wind of spring, the heat of summer, the coolness of autumn, and the cold of winter, they all arrive prior to their respective [seasonal] terms."

When they are not at their position, then this is evil. When they [occupy] their proper position, then this is proper." [105]

67-385-4
[Huang] Di:
"The changes that result from a disease, what are they like ?"

Qi Bo:
"When the qi fit each other, then [diseases are] slight.
When they do not fit each other, then they are severe." [106]

[Huang] Di:
"How about [the qi] ruling a year?"

67-386-2
Qi Bo:
"When the qi has a surplus, then it restrains that which it [normally] dominates and insults that which it [normally] does not dominate. [107]

---

105 1126/11: "當 is 在, 'at.'"

106 Wang Bing: "When wood resides at the position of fire, when fire resides at the position of soil, when soil resides at the position of metal, when metal resides at the position of water, when water resides at the position of wood, when wood resides at the position of ruler, such [situations] are 'fitting,' (because wood is the parent of fire, fire is the parent of soil, etc.). Also, when wood resides at the position of water, when water resides at the position of metal, when metal resides at the position of soil, when soil resides at the position of fire, when fire resides at the position of wood, such [situations] are 'fitting.' In the final analysis, though, these are [situations where] a child wrongly assumes the position of father-mother, where what is below insults the above, and this resembles a minor counteraction. When wood resides at the position of metal or soil, when fire resides at the position of metal or water, when soil resides at the position of water or wood, when metal resides at the position of fire or wood, and when water resides at the position of fire and soil, such [situations] are 'not fitting.' Hence the disease is severe. Always determine the period qi and the qi controlling heaven first. Then it is possible to know whether the presence of the qi is 'fitting' or 'not fitting.'" 1028/3: "The meaning of 相得 is: the five agents should maintain a certain balance. If this balance is destroyed, pathological signs of unilateral strength will appear. That is to say: 'when they do not agree with each other, then it is severe.'" Fang Yaozhong: "That is, in a season of identical host qi and visitor qi, the climate (i.e., the qi manifestations) are regular and any disease remains minor. In a season when host qi and visitor qi are not identical, the climate is irregular and diseases tend to be severe."

107 Zhang Jiebin: "When the qi of wood has a surplus, then it restrains that which it [usually] dominates, [i.e.,] the soil is overcome by it and the transformation [of soil qi]

When it is inadequate, then that which it [normally] cannot dominate insults and harrasses it and it is treated lightly and insulted by that which it [normally] dominates."[108]

That which has insulted is affected by evil in turn.[109]
{That which has insulted is affected by evil because there is little fear.}[110]

[Huang] Di: "Good!"

---

to dampness is weak. It insults that which it [usually] does not dominate, [i.e.,] contrary [to what is normal] the metal is humiliated by the wood and the transformation [of metal qi] to wind is quite strong." See also 1412/2. Fang Yaozhong: "侮 applies when those who are below insult those who are above."

108 Wang Bing: "When the wood [qi] has surplus, it restrains the soil [qi] and thinks lightly of the metal [qi]. Since the metal does not take up a fight, the wood relies on its surplus and insults [the metal]. Also, when the wood [qi] is diminished and when the metal [qi] dominates, the soil [qi] contrary [to its normal relationship] insults the wood because the wood [qi] is insufficient [to dominate the soil]. Hence the soil turns reckless and insults the [wood]."

109 Zhang Zhicong: "That is to say: it occupies and insults [another depot] and is [then] affected by its revenge in turn. For instance, when the wood [qi] is insufficient, then the metal qi, which [the wood qi] cannot overcome, insults and occupies [the depot associated with the wood]. As a result, the location of the metal [qi] itself is depleted. When the season of autumn arrives, the depleted metal qi is affected by a revenge by the son of wood [i.e., by fire]. Hence fire heat melts the metal. That is meant by 'that which has insulted is affected by evil in turn.'"

110 Wang Bing: "'To be affected by evil' is always to say: to be affected by an evil from [an entity] oneself cannot dominate. If [someone] leaves his own dwelling and goes elsewhere, if he appears strong on the outside but is exhausted inside, if evil [qi] abounds while the [true] qi is weak and if there is little respect or fear, then [that person] takes in evil. Hence [the text states]: 'there is little fear.'" Wang Bing may have had an episode related in the *Zuo zhuan* 佐傳, Duke Xi 僖公, 15th year, in mind. Here the marquis of Jin was warned by one of his advisors not to employ, in an impending battle, horses raised in a foreign territory: 外彊內乾 "they appear strong outside but are exhausted inside." Also, the marquis of Jin had sought refuge in Qin and later showed neither respect nor fear in view of Qin, despite Qin having helped him in a time of famine. Hence he met defeat when Qin eventually decided to invade the territory of Jin. (See Legge, vol. V, 167 – 168.)

Chapter 68
Comprehensive Discourse on the Subtle Significance of the Six [Qi]

68-386-7
Huang Di asked:
"Alas! Profound is the Way of heaven, indeed!

'As if one faced drifting clouds,
as if one looked into a deep abyss.'

[However,]
when looking into a deep abyss, it is still possible to fathom [its depth];
when facing drifting clouds, no one knows their farthest extension.[1]

You, Sir, have repeatedly[2] spoken about the Way of heaven which should
be attentively accepted. I have heard [it] and [I have] stored it. In my heart,
[though,] I feel strange about it. I do not know what it means. I should like
you, Sir, to pour out your mind and provide a complete account of all these
issues.

'Let them never disappear,
so that they are not interrupted for a long time to come.'

May [I] hear about the Way of heaven?"

Qi Bo paid reverence by knocking his head on the ground twice and responded:

"It is brilliant, indeed, to ask about the Way of heaven!

---

1 Wang Bing: "A deep abyss is quiet and clear. Hence when inspecting it it is possible to fathom its depth. Drifting clouds move here and there; they unite and disperse.
Hence when looking up to them it is impossible to point out their exact borderlines.
That is to say, the images of the blue sky are like an abyss and can be inspected. The
Way of the movement and transformation of the [creatures with] scales and shells
resembles the clouds. No one can fathom how they go or stay in place." See *Su wen* 77
for an almost identical beginning, with 際 instead of 極.

2 Cheng Shide et al.: "數 is 頻, 'frequently.'"

These [activities]
'follow the sequence in heaven,[3] and the times of abundance and weakness.'"[4]

68-387-4
[Huang] Di:
"I should like to hear
why there is abundance and weakness in the course of the six [times] six [ten day] terms of the Way of heaven."[5]

Qi Bo:
"Above and below have [their fixed] positions;
left and right are [firmly] arranged.[6]

Hence
the [term] to the right of minor yang [qi], it is governed by the yang brilliance [qi].
The [term] to the right of yang brilliance [qi], it is governed by the major yang [qi].
The [term] to the right of major yang [qi], it is governed by the ceasing yin [qi].
The [term] to the right of ceasing yin [qi], it is governed by the minor yin [qi].
The [term] to the right of minor yin [qi], it is governed by the major yin [qi].
The [term] to the right of major yin [qi], it is governed by the minor yang [qi].

---

3 354/47: "因 is 根据, 'in accordance with,' 'on the basis of.' 時 is 'season' or 'period.' 'Abundance and weakness' refers to the abundance and weakness of yin and yang [qi]."

4 Zhang Zhicong: " 'Abundance' and 'weakness' refer to the insufficient or excessive presence of the six qi."

5 Zhang Zhicong: " 'Six six' is to say: the three yin and three yang [qi] controlling heaven are combined above with the six qi." 360/194: "The first six refers to the six qi, the second six refers to the three yin and three yang." 354/48: "The changes in the climatic conditions of wind, heat, fire, dampness, dryness, and cold within one year can be distinguished by means of the three yin and three yang [classification] into six terms on the basis of the different quantities of yin and yang [qi] present during these seasons." For a detailed discussion and also for a refutation of interpretations of 六 六 as six times sixty days, as, for instance, in *NJCD*: "One 'term' comprises 60 days", see there.

6 Wang Bing: " 'Above' and 'below' refers to the two qi controlling heaven and earth: 'left' and 'right' refers to the four qi to the left and right of the annual [qi]." Zhang Jiebin: "That refers to the sequence of the six locations to elucidate the abundance and weakness of the visitor qi."

{These are the so-called qi tips.⁷ That is, [one sees them in that sequence if one] faces the South and waits.⁸
Hence when it is said:
'Follow the sequence in heaven and the times of abundance and weakness. The positions of the qi are determined in view of [the luminaries in the sky] moving [the position of their] light. Stand upright and wait for them,'
then this means just the same.}⁹

68-387-10
The upper [half] of the minor yang [term] is governed by the fire qi. At midterm, the ceasing yin [qi] appears.¹⁰
The upper [half] of the yang brilliance [term] is governed by the dryness qi. At midterm, the major yin [qi] appears.¹¹

---

7 Wang Bing: "標 is 末, 'farthest end.'" Zhang Jiebin: "The three yin and three yang [qi] have the six qi as their root; the six qi have the three yin and three yang [qi] as tip."

8 Wang Bing: "The sages faced the South and stood this way to observe the arrival of the qi."

9 Wang Bing: "移光 is to say 日移光: the sun moves its light. 定位 is to say: when facing the South and observing the qi, stand upright and observe the arrival of the various qi in the course of the year. This way the qi can be awaited." Cheng Shide et al.: "移光定位, 正立而待之 is an ancient method for measuring [the movement in] heaven to determine the seasonal qi. Most often a 'wooden staff was planted' to observe the shadow caused by the sun and, thereby, to determine the seasonal qi." For an identification of the method referred to here with the ancient astronomical method of setting up a 圭表, 'sundial,' see also 597/46, 354/49, and 1901/44.

10 Wang Bing: "The minor yang [qi] is the fire in the South. Hence one sees that the above is governed by the qi of fire. It is linked to the [qi of] ceasing yin. Hence ceasing yin [qi, i.e., wind] appears at midterm." Zhang Jiebin: "From here on downwards [the text] speaks of the three yin and three yang. Each has its exterior and interior. Their qi communicate with each other. Hence each has a central qi (中氣) which is rooted in the other. The basic [qi] of minor yang is fire. Hence fire qi appears above. [The minor yang] and the ceasing yin constitute exterior and interior. Hence in the midst a ceasing yin [qi] appears." 354/49: "中氣 is 中見之氣, 'qi appearing in the center.' That is a qi which can be seen within the root qi. The 中氣 is a qi that is related to or stands in opposition to the root qi. .. Why is it that a related or opposite qi appears amidst the root qi? The reason is: when the six qi have developed to a certain degree it can often be seen that they turn into their opposites. E.g., heat can turn into cold and cold can turn into heat. Hence [the text] states: 'The upper [half] of minor yin is governed by heat; major yang appears in between. ...'" 418/18: "中氣 is an abbreviation of 中見之氣, 'qi appearing in the center.'" See also 914/5, 490/4, 271/30, and 897/7.

11 Wang Bing: "The yang brilliance [qi] is the metal in the West. Hence the above is governed by dryness qi. It is linked to the [qi of] major yin. Hence following the

The upper [half] of the major yang [term] is governed by the cold qi. At mid-term, the minor yin [qi] appears.[12]

The upper [half] of the ceasing yin [term] is governed by the wind qi. At mid-term, the minor yang [qi] appears.[13]

The upper [half] of the minor yin [term] is governed by the heat qi. At mid-term, the major yang [qi] appears.[14]

The upper [half] of the major yin [term] is governed by the dampness qi. At midterm, the yang brilliance [qi] appears."[15]

{These are the so-called roots. Subsequent to the root [qi], the [qi] of the mid-term appear. That [which appears] subsequent to this appearance, that is the tip of the qi.[16]

---

dryness qi, the major yin [qi, i.e., dampness] appears at midterm." Zhang Jiebin: "The basic [qi] of yang brilliance is dryness. Hence dryness qi appears above. [The yang brilliance] and the major yin constitute exterior and interior. Hence in the midst a major yin [qi] appears."

12 Wang Bing: "The major yang [qi] is the water in the North. Hence the above is governed by cold qi. It is linked to minor yin [qi]. Hence following the cold qi, the minor yin [qi, i.e., ruling fire] appears at midterm." Zhang Jiebin: "The basic [qi] of major yang is cold. Hence cold qi appears above. [The major yang] and the minor yin constitute exterior and interior. Hence in the midst a minor yin [qi] appears."

13 Wang Bing: "The ceasing yin [qi] is the wood in the East. Hence the above is governed by wind qi. It is linked to minor yang [qi]. Hence following the wind qi, the minor yang [qi, i.e., minister fire] appears at midterm." Zhang Jiebin: "The basic [qi] of ceasing yin is wind. Hence wind qi appears above. [The ceasing yin] and the minor yang constitute exterior and interior. Hence in the midst a minor yang [qi] appears."

14 Wang Bing: "The minor yin is the ruler fire in the South-East. Hence the above is governed by heat qi. It is linked to major yang [qi]. Hence following the heat qi, the major yang [qi, i.e., cold] appears at midterm." Zhang Jiebin: "The basic [qi] of minor yin is fire. Hence fire qi appears above. [The minor yin] and the major yang constitute exterior and interior. Hence in the midst a major yang [qi] appears."

15 Wang Bing: "The major yin is the soil in the South-West. Hence the above is governed by dampness qi. It is linked to yang brilliance [qi]. Hence following the dampness qi, the yang brilliance [qi, i.e., dryness] appears at midterm." Zhang Jiebin: "The basic [qi] of major yin is dampness. Hence dampness qi appears above. [The major yin] and the yang brilliance constitute exterior and interior. Hence in the midst a yang brilliance [qi] appears."

16 Wang Bing: "本 is to say: principal qi." Zhang Jiebin: "The six qi of the above constitute the roots of the three yin and three yang [qi]. The three yin and three yang [qi] of the below constitute the tip of the six qi."

Root and tip are not identical, their qi correspond to different images.}[17]

68-388-3
[Huang] Di:
"When its [time] has arrived and [the qi] arrives,
when [its time] has arrived and [the qi] does not arrive,
when [its time] has arrived and [the qi] is greatly excessive,
why is that?"[18]

Qi Bo:
"When [its time] has arrived and [the qi] arrives, that is harmony.
When [its time] has arrived and [the qi] does not arrive, the incoming qi is inadequate.
When [its time] has not yet arrived and [the qi] has arrived, the incoming qi has a surplus."[19]

---

17 Zhang Jiebin: " 'Root and tip are not identical,' in terms of the three yin and three yang [qi] this is as follows. The major yang has cold as its root and yang as its tip. The minor yin has heat has its root and yin as its tip. In terms of the qi that appear in the middle, when the minor yang [qi] arrives the fire comes to life and in the middle there is wind. When the yang brilliance arrives dryness comes to life and there is dampness in the middle. When the major yang [qi] arrives cold comes to life and there is heat in the middle. When the ceasing yin [qi] arrives wind comes to life and there is fire in the middle. When the minor yin [qi] arrives heat comes to life and there is cold in the middle. When the major yin [qi] arrives dampness comes to life and there is dryness in the middle. Hence if in any year an abnormal occurrence of cold or heat appears, the diagnostic pattern is based on [the possibility that] the [movement in the] vessels agrees with [the external situation] while the disease is opposed to it. The disease may have emerged because of the root [qi], because of the tip [qi], or because of the qi in the middle. A successful therapy may be directed at the root, at the tip, or at the qi in the middle. All these are [examples] of tip and root being different."

18 Wang Bing: "This refers to the six qi of heaven. The first qi emerges fifteen days prior to spring begins. The remaining second, third, fourth, fifth, and final qi arrive successively, each ruling for 60 days plus 87 and one half *ke*." Zhang Jiebin: "The following passage is to explain abundance and weakness in the manifestations of the qi. Each of the six qi ruling a year has its specific season. From the belated or early arrival of the qi it can be seen whether it is abundant or weak."

19 Wang Bing: "When the time has arrived and the [corresponding] qi arrives, that is a harmonious correspondence. This then is a balanced year (平歲). If [for instance] the qi of a *jia zi* year has a surplus it arrives prior to its time during the [preceding] *gui hai* year, [i.e.,] during a period when it should not arrive yet. If the qi of an *yi chou* year is insufficient it arrives after its time during the period when the [qi of the following] *jia zi* year should arrive. Hence [the text] states: 'the incoming qi is insufficient; the incoming qi has a surplus.' That is to say, when the period of arrival of the first qi is

68-389-1
[Huang] Di:
"When [its time] has arrived and [the qi] does not arrive;
when [its time] has not yet arrived and [the qi] arrives,
what is that?"

Qi Bo:
"When there is correspondence, then there is compliance.
If this is not so, then there is opposition.
When there is opposition, then this gives rise to changes.
When there are changes, then there is disease."[20]

[Huang] Di:
"Good!
Please speak about those correspondences."

Qi Bo:
"It is in the generation of things that those correspondences [appear];
it is in the qi and [its movement in] the vessels that those correspondences
[appear]."[21]

---

like that, the arrivals of all the remaining of the six qi of a year will be prior to their
[appropriate] time. When the annual qi is insufficient, the arrivals of [all] the six qi
will be late. No matter whether [the qi of] a subsequent time arrives early, or whether
[the qi of] a previous time arrives late, the difference amounts always to thirteen
days." Zhang Jiebin: "When the season has arrived while the [corresponding] qi has
not arrived, the incoming qi is insufficient. When the qi arrives before the [respective]
seasons has arrived, the incoming qi has a surplus."

20 Wang Bing: "When [the qi arrives] right in time, that is 'correspondence.' When
the time [the qi arrives] outside its time, then 'it is not so.' .. When the changes in
heaven and on earth lose their regularity, then all the myriad things fall ill." Zhang
Jiebin: "In case of correspondence there is compliance and the proper qi of generation
and transformation are present. In case it is not so, then there is opposition and the
qi of domination and revenge emerge. Changes result in heaven and on earth and the
myriad beings become ill, too." 355/49: "When climate and season correspond, this is
regularity. [Such regularity] is beneficial to the regular generation and growth of the
myriad things in nature."

21 Wang Bing: "The generation and blossoming of things occur at their regular times.
The arrival of the [movement in the] vessels occurs in regular intervals. In case [the
annual qi] has surplus, the year begins early; when it is insufficient, the year begins
late."

68-389-4
[Huang] Di:
"Good!
I should like to hear how the structures of the earth correspond to the positions
of the qi during the six [seasonal] terms."[22]

Qi Bo:
"To the right of obvious brilliance,[23]
that is the position of the ruler fire.[24]
To the right of the ruler fire,
retreating one step,
that is the [position] governed by the minister fire.
Moving one step further,
that is the [position] governed by the soil qi.
Moving one step further,
that is the [position] governed by the metal qi.
Moving one step further,
that is the [position] governed by the water qi.
Moving one step further,
that is the [position] governed by the wood qi.
Moving one step further,
that is the [position] governed by the ruler fire.

---

22 Zhang Jiebin: "The host qi do not move and keep their positions. Hence [the text]
speaks of 'six positions.' They are also called 'six steps.' These are the positions governed
by the six qi." Cheng Shide et al.: "六節氣位 refers to the six qi ruling a season. Because the host qi does not change year after year it is called 地理之應."

23 Wang Bing: "Where the sun comes out, that is called 'obvious brilliance.'" Zhang
Jiebin: "A little more than 60 days after vernal equinox." 355/50: "That is, from vernal
equinox onwards, the periods of daylight become gradually longer and the temperature of the qi gradually increases. Generation and transformation of the myriad things
gradually increases in richness and abundance. All these phenomena are signs of an
increasing brilliance of yang qi. Hence the term following vernal equinox and ending at summer begins is called 'obvious brilliance.' .. Hence this period is associated
with the minor yin ruler fire. 'Right' refers to a person facing South and naming its
position."

24 Zhang Jiebin: "To retreat one step is to retreat one step to the right of the ruler
fire." Cheng Shide et al.: "The three yin and three yang [qi, i.e.,] the six qi rule a part
of one year. That is, one year is divided into six steps. Each qi rules over one step. To
move one step to the right is to retreat one step."

68-390-2
Subsequent to the minister fire, the water qi succeeds it.[25]
Subsequent to the position of water, the soil qi succeeds it.[26]
Subsequent to the position of soil, the wind qi succeeds it.[27]
Subsequent to the wind qi, the metal qi succeeds it.[28]
Subsequent to the position of metal, the fire qi succeeds it.[29]
Subsequent to the ruler fire, the yin essence succeeds it."[30]

68-391-2
[Huang] Di:
"Why?"

Qi Bo:
" 'Excessive activity results in harm.
Succession provides restraint.'[31]

---

25 Wang Bing: "When heat abounds water succeeds it. Sprouts and shoots are tender and weak. Heavy rain brings overflow. The image of water is obvious." 355/51: 承 has the meaning of 制止, 'to check,' 'to curb,' or 抵御, 'to resist.' That is to say, each of the five agents has one [agent] by which it is checked. Such as, water can check fire, soil can check water, wood can check soil, .. 承 also has the meaning of 承襲, 'follow,' 'inherit.' That is to say, each of the five agents is closely followed by one which it cannot dominate."

26 Wang Bing: "When cold is extreme, the things harden und water freezes. All streams dry up. It is obvious that the image of of soil appears [to succeed the water] here."

27 Wang Bing: "Subsequent to speedy winds it is often such that rain falls. That is, dampness is transformed to rain by the blowing of wind."

28 Wang Bing: "When the wind blows the qi is clear and the myriad things are all dry. These are obvious images of metal succeeding wood."

29 Wang Bing: "To forge metal one generates heat. That is, fire makes the metal flow. [The fact that the metal] rides on top of the fire does not falsify the principle."

30 Wang Bing: "At the location of the ruler fire no great heat moves. The reason is that yin essence controls and succeeds it." Zhang Zhicong: "The preceding paragraph outlined the emergence of the six qi out of each other for ruling over one season [each]. The present [paragraph outlines] the restraint exerted by the six qi [upon each other, permitting] generation and transformation. Now, among the five agents there is generation and transformation, restraint and overcoming. In case there is no restraint, with [a qi's] activity reaching an extreme, harm results. If, however, there is restraint and overcoming, then there is generation and transformation. 承 is to say: to take over that which precedes and restrain it. Yin essence is the essence water generated by *tian yi* 天乙."

31 Wang Bing: "亢 is extreme excess. Things have an aversion to extremes." Zhang Jiebin: "亢 is extreme abundance. 制 is: to curb [a qi] because it has reached an ex-

When there is restraint, then there is generation and transformation.[32]
Externally abundance and weakness are arranged in sequence.[33]
When there is harm, then there is destruction and disorder;
generation and transformation are [marked by] serious disease."[34]

68-391-3
[Huang] Di:
"What about the causes of abundance and weakness?"

Qi Bo:
"When they are not at their positions, then they are evil.
When they occupy their proper positions, then they are proper.[35]

---

treme." *Gu dian yi zhu xuan* bianxiezu /8: "承 is 隨即, 'immediately,' 接着 'to follow.'"

32 Zhang Jiebin: "When extreme abundance is restrained, then there is no harm
resulting from excessive activity. When there is no harm resulting from excessive activity, then generation and transformation occur as a matter of course."

33 Zhang Jiebin: "When [a qi] should be abundant and is abundant, when [a qi]
should be weak and is weak, when the [proper] sequence is maintained and everything
is at its place, that is called 外列盛衰. 外列 is to say: 發育之多, 'massive production
and nourishment.'"

34 Zhang Jiebin: "If there is excessive activity without restraint, then this causes
harm. Harm is destruction, disorder, and abnormality. There is no generation and
transformation of proper qi and evil qi emerges instead. Hence this results in 'great
disease.'" Zhang Zhicong: "外列盛衰 is to say: the external succession of the qi ruling
a year is marked by abundance or weakness. When a qi ruling a year interacts with
an [identical] qi ruling a season, with the result that the excessive activity [of this qi]
reaches an extreme, then this will end in severe harm. Hence [the text] states: 'When
there is harm, then there is destruction and disorder; generation and transformation
are marked by great disease.'"

35 356/45: "當位 is present when the five agents association of the major period of a
given year is identical to the five agents association of the [earth] branch of that same
year. A 當位 year is called 歲會, 'the year meets.' 非位 is present when the five agents
association of the major periode of a given year is not identical to the five agents association of the earth [branch] of that year, but with the five agents association of the
qi controlling heaven in that year. Such a year is called 天符, 'heavenly complements.'"
In contrast, Cheng Shide et al. reads the earth branches as referring to cardinal points:
"'When they are at their position' refers to the proper positions of the four cardinal
points of *zi, wu, mao,* and *you. Chen, xu, chou,* and *wei* belong to the central positions
and soil. 'When they are not at their position' refers to *yin, shen, si,* and *hai* which are
not located at the proper positions of the five cardinal directions."

[When the qi are] evil, then changes are severe.
[When the qi are] proper, then [changes are] slight."

[Huang] Di:
"What is it to say, 'occupy their proper positions'?"

Qi Bo:
"When the wood period comes down on *mao*,
when the fire period comes down on *wu*,
when the soil period comes down in the final thirds of all the four [seasons],
when the metal period comes down on *you*,
when the water period comes down on *zi*."

This is what is called "the year meets."[36] {This is a balance of the qi.}[37]

[Huang] Di:
"When they do not occupy [their correct] positions, how is that?"

Qi Bo:
"In this [case] the year does not meet with them."[38]

---

36 Zhang Jiebin: "In this case the annual period and the annual branch are of identical qi. Hence [such years] are called 'the year meets.'" Cheng Shide et al.: "Whenever
the five-agents associations of the heaven stems and earth branches of a given year
are identical and if such coincidences converge with the proper positions of the five
cardinal points, that is called 'the year meets.' For example, in a *ding mao* year, *ding*
is a wood period, *mao* is the proper position of the cardinal point East and of wood.
Hence 'the wood period sides with *mao*.' Within a cycle of 60 years this applies to
eight years." The *Zhou li*, Tian guan, Si kuai 司會, uses the compound 歲會 (here to be
read '*sui kuai*') in the sense of "annual accounts" (see Ruan Yuan vol I, p. 679 below).

37 Wang Bing: "Neither excessive nor insufficient, that is called 'a balanced period
rules a year.' In a balanced year the generation of beings and the way the [movement in
the] vessels responds [to pulse feeling] should all correspond to the respective period
of time and there should be no [too] early or [too] late." Lin Yi et al.: "When a wood
period comes down on *mao*, that is a *ding mao* year. When a fire period comes down
on *wu*, that is a *wu wu* year. When a soil period comes down on [the final thirds of]
the four seasons, these are *jia chen, jia xu, ji chou*, and *ji wei* years. When a metal period comes down on *yu*, that is an *yi you* year. When a water period comes down on *zi*,
that is a *bing zi* year. Among them *wu wu, ji chou, ji wei*, and *yi yu* [years] are 'Tai-yi
heavenly complements' [years]."

38 Zhang Jiebin: "When the annual period does not converge with the earth branch,
then it may happen that the qi is not balanced."

68-391-8
[Huang] Di:
"If in a year of a soil period, one sees major yin [qi] in the upper [half of that year],

if in a year of a fire period, one sees minor yang [qi] and minor yin [qi] in the upper [half of that year],[39]

if in a year of a metal period, one sees yang brilliance [qi] in the upper [half of that year],

if in a year of a wood period, one sees ceasing yin [qi] in the upper [half of that year],

if in a year of a water period, one sees major yang [qi] in the upper [half of that year],

how is that?"[40]

Qi Bo:
"[In these cases the qi controlling] heaven meets with the [first half of a year].[41] Hence the *Book on the Principal [Qi] of Heaven* calls this 'heavenly complements.'"

68-392-2
[Huang Di:]
"How about [a year which is both] 'heavenly complements' and 'the year meets'?"

Qi Bo:
"This is a convergence of the '*tai-yi* heavenly complements' [type]."[42]

[Huang] Di:
"How about their hierarchy?"

---

39 Wang Bing: "Both the minor yin [qi] and the minor yang [qi] are fire qi."

40 Cheng Shide et al.: " 'Soil period,' 'fire period,' and so forth refer to the period [ruling an entire] year. 'Upper' refers to the [qi] controlling heaven. When the qi of a period [ruling an entire] year and the qi controlling heaven [during the first half of that year] correspond to each other, that is called 'heavenly complements.' For example, in a *ji chou* year, the *ji* is a soil period; the *chou* is major yin dampness [qi associated with the agent of] soil controlling heaven. Within the cycle of 60 years, twelve years are 'heavenly complements' years."

41 Wang Bing: "That is when the heavenly qi and the period qi converge with each other."

42 Wang Bing: "That is to say: three come together. The first is 'heaven meets.' The second is 'the year meets.' The third is 'the period meets.'" We read *tai-yi*, the "great one", not as a reference to Tai-yi, a numinous entity.

Qi Bo:

" 'Heavenly complements' upholds the law.

The 'the year meets'⁴³ carries out orders.

The '*tai-yi* heavenly complements' is the nobleman."⁴⁴

68-392-4

[Huang] Di:

"To be struck by [their] evil, how is that?"

Qi Bo:

"If someone is struck by [the official] upholding the law, the [resulting] disease is fast and dangerous.⁴⁵

If someone is struck by [the official] carrying out orders, the disease is slow and protracted.⁴⁶

If someone is struck by a nobleman, the disease is violent and fatal."⁴⁷

---

43 The textus receptus has 歲位. The context suggests that it should be read as 歲會.

44 Wang Bing: " 'To uphold the law' is equal to [the duties of] a minister. 'To carry out orders' is equal to [the duties of] a governor. 'Noblemen' are equal to rulers." Zhang Jiebin: "Those upholding the law are positioned above; that is equal to government administration. Those carrying out orders are positioned below; that is equal to all kinds of officials. Noblemen combine above and below. They correspond to rulers."

45 Wang Bing: "The standards of an official [supposed to] uphold the law are appropriate. He is able to deal with evil deeds on his own. Hence, the disease [caused by his intervention] is fast and dangerous."

46 Wang Bing: "A governor does not have the authority to uphold the law. Hence harm or disease [caused by his intervention] is not fast. It merely holds [the patient] in its grip (執持)."

47 Wang Bing: "[Noblemen are] righteous and do not carry out unjustified attacks. Hence when [their intervention causes] a disease, it is violent and leads to death." Zhang Jiebin: "When someone is struck by those who uphold the law, that is a clash with the qi controlling heaven. Heaven is the root of life. Hence such diseases are fast and dangerous. When someone is struck by those who carry out orders, that is a clash with the qi of the earth branches. The [resulting] harm is slightly less [severe]. Hence such diseases are slow and protracted. 持 is: evil and proper hold each other; the chances of a lucky or unlucky outcome are half and half. When someone is struck by a nobleman, that is a clash with both the qi of heaven and that of the earth. Hence [such diseases] are violent and lead to death. Now in these three cases the earth regards heaven as ruler. Hence to be struck by [the evil qi of] 'heavenly complements' is more severe than [to be struck by the evil qi of] the 'the year meets.' In a '*tai-yi* heavenly complements' [year] three [identical] qi come together. It should be obvious that [the diseases resulting from being struck by the qi of that year] are even more serious. Hence not to clash [with such qi] means health; when it comes to a clash there

68-392-6
[Huang] Di:
"When the positions are exchanged, how is that?"

Qi Bo:
" When the ruler takes the position of the official,
then this is compliance.
When the official takes the position of the ruler,
then this is opposition.

When there is opposition,
then disease is near,
and harm sets in fast.

When there is compliance,
then disease is far away,
and harm is slight."[48]

---

is no way to solve [the resulting problems]. When a person is affected [by such evil],
nothing can be done about it."

48 Wang Bing: "When the minister fire resides at the [location of the] ruler fire that
is [as if] an official took the place of the position of a ruler. Hence [such a situation is
identified as] 'opposition'. When the ruler fire resides at the [location of the] minister
fire, that is [as if] a ruler took the position of an official, [as if] the ruler came down
to inspect the position of an official. Hence [such a situation is identified as] 'compliance'. 'Distant' is to say: geographically distant; 'near' is to say: geographically near."
Zhang Jiebin: " 'Ruler' is ruler fire; 'official' is minister fire. When the ruler takes the
position of the official, that is, for instance, when [a year with] minor yin [qi] as visitor
[qi] comes together with minor yang [qi] as host [qi]. In this case the ruler is above
and the official is below. Hence this is 'compliance'. In a situation of 'compliance' diseases are far away and any harm [resulting from a disease] is minor. When the official
takes the position of the ruler, that is, for instance, when [a year with] minor yang [qi]
as visitor [qi] comes together with minor yin [qi] as host [qi]. In this case the official
is above and the ruler is below. Hence this is 'opposition'. In a situation of 'opposition' the time of a disease is near and harm [resulting from it] arrives fast." 356: "The
character 'position' refers to a meeting of visitor and ruler here. That is, the visitor qi is
added on top of the position of the host qi. Host qi refers to the regular qi ruling the
seasons in the course of one year. Visitor qi refers to the characteristic qi of each year.
When a visitor qi is added on top of the host qi, that is 客主加臨. .. 君位臣 refers to
[a situation where] the visitor qi is ruler fire which is added on top of the host qi which
is minister fire. 臣位君 is the opposite; it refers to [a situation where] the visitor qi is
the minister fire which is added on top of the host qi which is ruler fire. The effects [of
the former] are not serious. Hence one speaks of 順, 'compliance'; the effects [of the
latter] are severe. Hence they are called 逆, 'opposition.'"

{This refers to the so-called two fires.}

[Huang] Di:
"Good!
I should like to hear about their steps, how about them?"[49]

Qi Bo:
"A so-called step covers 60 degrees and some odd [parts of a degree].[50]
Hence, after 24 steps [these odd parts] add up to one hundred marks and
constitute one [full] day."[51]

68-393-3
[Huang] Di:
"What are the changes resulting from the correspondences of the six qi to the
five agents?"

Qi Bo:
" 'The positions [of the qi] have an end and a begin.
[Each] qi [term] has a first [half] and a [second half following] midterm.[52]
The upper [half] and the lower [half] are not alike.
To search them is different, too.' " [53]

---

49 356/47: " 'Their' refers to the six qi. 'Steps' refers to positions and time periods."

50 Wang Bing: "奇 is to say: 87.5 *ke*." Cheng Shide et al.: "60 degrees are 60 days.
One heavenly cycle covers 365 1/4 degrees. [One year] is divided into six steps, with
each step covering 60 degrees plus 87 1/2 *ke*. Hence [the text] states '[one] step is 60
degrees and some odd [parts of a degree].'"

51 Wang Bing: "This is a statement on the surplus of the heavenly degrees. An entire
heavenly cycle has 365 plus 1/4 degrees. 24 steps are exactly four years. 1/4 degree
amounts to 25 *ke*. Within four years the sum of all [surplus] qi adds up to 100 *ke*.
Hence this completes one day. One degree is one day."

52 Wang Bing: "位 is 地位, 'earth position.' 氣 is 天氣, 'heavenly qi.' Qi and position
alternate with each other. Hence during the first qi [term], heaven is in charge; during
the [second term subsequent to the] midterm of qi, the earth rules. When the earth
rules, then the qi flows on the earth. When heaven is in charge, then the qi ascends
to heaven. .. The first [term and the second term following] midterm are both 30 days
plus 43 and 3/4 *ke* long." Gao Shishi: " 'Position' is to say: the fixed positions of seasons
governed [by a qi]." Cheng Shide et al.: "These are the six steps."

53 Cheng Shide et al.: "There are two interpretations of 上下. According to the first,
上 refers to the visitor qi and 下 refers to the host qi. As in Zhang Zhicong's comment: 'Above and below are not identical is to say: the visitor qi is added above, the
host qi rules below. Each should be different; hence [the approaches] to examine
them are different, too.' According to the second, 上 refers to the heaven stems and

68-393-4
[Huang] Di:
"How to search them?"

Qi Bo:
"The qi of heaven starts with *jia*;
the qi of the earth governs under *zi*.⁵⁴
The combination of *zi* and *jia*
is called 'annual set-up.'⁵⁵
Carefully observe this time [of 'annual set-up'].
[Then you] are able to predict the qi [of each year].'"⁵⁶

68-393-6
[Huang] Di:
"I should like to hear about these years.
What is the starting point and what is the end of the [cycle of the] six qi;
what about 'early' and what about 'late'?"

Qi Bo:
"A brilliant question, indeed!

In a *jia zi* year,
the initial qi [term] {heavenly number} begins with the water [in the clepsydra]
sinking from the first mark and it ends after [60 days and] 87 and a half marks.
The second qi [term] begins at the 87th mark and six parts and it ends after
[further 61 days and] 75 marks.
The third qi [term] begins at the 76th mark and it ends after [further 61 days
and] 62 and a half marks.
The fourth qi [term] begins at the 62nd mark and six parts and it ends after

---

下 refers to the earth branches. Each year the heaven stems and the earth branches
are different. Hence [the text] states: above and below are not identical. See *Su wen
yi shi* 素问译释."

54 The original text had 地氣治 instead of 地氣始. Beginning with the Yuan era,
all important editions decided to change 治 to 始. The 1983 edition by Ren min wei
sheng chu ban she reinstated the reading of 治. See Zhang Canjia, vol. 2, p. 906-908.

55 Zhang Jiebin: "The qi of heaven has ten stems and begins with *jia*; the qi of the
earth has twelve branches and begins with *zi*. When *zi* and *jia* are combined, that is a
jia zi [year]. Through the combination of stems and branches the annual qi of a [cycle
of] 60 years are established."

56 Zhang Jiebin: "When the annual qi are established, then the individual seasons
can be observed and the respective qi can be predicted."

[further 61 days and] fifty marks.

The fifth qi [term] begins at the 51st mark and it ends after [further 61 days and] 37 and a half marks.

The sixth qi [term] begins at the 37th mark and six parts and it ends after [further 61 days and] 25 marks.

{These are the so-called "the first six";[57] they constitute numbers of heaven.}

68-394-3

In an *yi chou* year,

the initial qi [term] {heavenly number} begins with [the water sinking from] the 26th mark and it ends after [61 days and] 12 and a half marks.

The second qi [term] begins at the 12th mark and six parts and it ends after [61 days] when the water has sunk by 100 marks.

The third qi [term] begins at the first mark and it ends after [further 61 days and] 87 and a half marks.

The fourth qi [term] begins at the 87th mark and six parts and it ends after [further 61 days and] 75 marks.

The fifth qi [term] begins at the 76th mark and it ends after [further 61 days and] 62 and a half marks.

The sixth qi [term] begins at the 62nd mark and six parts and it ends after [further 61 days and] fifty marks.

{These are the so-called "the second six"; they constitute numbers of heaven.}

68-395-1

In a *bing yin* year,

the initial qi [term] {heavenly number} begins with [the water sinking from] the 51st mark and it ends after [61 days and] 37 and a half marks.

The second qi [term] begins at the 37th mark and six parts and it ends after [further 61 days and] 25 marks.

The third qi [term] begins at the 26th mark and it ends after [further 61 days and] twelve and a half marks.

The fourth qi [term] begins at the 12th mark and six parts and it ends after [61 days] when the water has sunk by 100 marks.

The fifth qi [term] begins at the the first mark and it ends after [further 61 days and] 87 and a half marks.

---

57 Possibly a reference to the *Yi jing* where the six lines constituting a hexagram were named "nine" (if they were yang lines changing to yin) or "six" (if they were yin lines changing to yang). "First six", then, refers to a changing yin line which is the first line at the bottom of the hexagram.

The sixth qi [term] begins at the 87th mark and six parts and it ends after [further 61 days and] 75 marks.

{These are the so-called "the third six"; they constitute numbers of heaven}

68-395-7
In a *ding mao* year,
the initial qi [term] {heavenly number} begins with [the water] sinking from the 76th mark and it ends after [61 days and] 62 and a half marks.
The second qi [term] begins at the 62nd mark and six parts and it ends after [further 61 days and] fifty marks.
The third qi [term] begins at the 51st mark and it ends after [further 61 days and] 37 and a half marks.
The fourth qi [term] begins at the 37th mark and six parts and it ends after [further 61 days and] 25 marks.
The fifth qi [term] begins at the 26th mark and it ends after [61 days and] 12 and a half marks.
The sixth qi [term] begins at the 12th mark and six parts and it ends after [61 days] when the water has sunk by 100 marks.

{These are the so-called "the fourth six." They constitute numbers of heaven}

Next is the *wu chen* year.
Its initial qi [term] once again begins at the first mark.

It is always like this, without end.
Once a cycle is completed, it begins again."

68-396-6
[Huang] Di:
"I should like to hear how these years are examined?"[58]

Qi Bo:
"An encompassing question, indeed!

---

58 Zhang Jiebin: "As for 歲候, that is a large term covering an entire year." Gao Shishi: "One year constitutes one 候; 60 years constitute 60 候."

When the sun passes through the first cycle,[59] the heavenly qi begins with the first mark.[60]

When the sun passes through the second cycle, the heavenly qi begins [after 365 days] at the 26th mark.[61]

When the sun passes through the third cycle, the heavenly qi begins [after the next 365 days] at the 51st mark.[62]

When the sun passes through the fourth cycle, the heavenly qi begins [after the next 365 days] at the 76th mark.[63]

When the sun passes through the fifth cycle, the heavenly qi once again begins at the first mark."[64]

{That is what is called 'one arrangement.'}[65]

68-397-1
Hence,
the convergences of qi in *yin, wu,* and *xu* years are identical.
The convergences of qi in *mao, wei,* and *hai* years are identical.
The convergences of qi in *chen, shen,* and *zi* years are identical.
The convergences of qi in *si, you,* and *chou* years are identical.

When [a cycle] has reached its end, it begins anew.

[Huang] Di:
"I should like to hear about their operation."[66]

Qi Bo:
"When talking of heaven, search for it at the roots.

---

59 Zhang Jiebin: "'One cycle' is one cycle through heaven. That is to say, the *jia zi* year is the first year." 356/55: "'One cycle' is one year."

60 Wang Bing: "That is the *jia zi* year."

61 Wang Bing: "That is the *yi chou* year."

62 Wang Bing: "That is the *bing yin* year."

63 Wang Bing: "That is the *ding mao* year."

64 Wang Bing: "That is the *wu chen* year. The remaining 55 years repeat this cycle and then start from the beginning again."

65 Wang Bing: "The law regards four years as 'one arrangement.'"

66 Gao Shishi: "用 is change and transformation, movement and standstill, rise and descent, leaving and entering."

When talking of the earth, search for it at the positions.
When talking of man, search for it at the qi interaction."⁶⁷

68-397-4
[Huang] Di:
"What is it to say: 'qi interaction'?"

Qi Bo:
"Amidst the interaction of the qi of the positions of above and below, that is
where man resides.⁶⁸

Hence when it is said:
'What is the upper [section of the] celestial axis, the heavenly qi rules it.
What is the lower [section of the] celestial axis, the qi of the earth rules it.
The section of qi interaction, the human qi follows it,
the myriad beings originate from it,'⁶⁹
then this means just the same."⁷⁰

---

67 Wang Bing: "本 is to say: the six qi of heaven, [i.e.,] cold, summerheat, dryness,
dampness, wind, and fire. It is through their transformations that the three yin and
yang [qi] emerge. Hence they are called 'root.' They are the so-called six principal [qi].
位 is to say: metal, wood, fire, soil, water, and ruler fire. Where the qi of heaven and
earth interact from above and below, that is where man resides." 357/47: "天 is 天氣,
'qi of heaven.' 本 refers to the six qi. That is to say, most important in the examination
of the changes and transformations in the natural climate is to examine the changes
and transformations of the six qi. 位 refers to the six steps, i.e., the positions associated with the 24 climatic terms in the course of one year. That is, when examining the
phenomena of transformation among all kinds of things on earth, it is important to
investigate the relationships between the succession of seasons and the phenomena of
transformation of all things on the basis of the six steps." "Roots" refers to 六元, i.e.,
the six climatic qi. See *Su wen* 66-369-7.

68 Wang Bing: "That is the sphere where the qi below heaven and above the earth
interact and unite. Man resides on the earth. Hence it is in the [sphere] where the qi
interact and unite that man resides. Hence all transformations and generations, as well
as changes, do occur in the [section of] qi interaction." 343/31: "上 refers to the qi of
heaven; 下 refers to the qi of the earth."

69 In view of a partially parallel statement in 71-475-12, the first two lines of this
quotation could also be read as "The upper [half] of the heavenly axis, the heavenly qi
rules it. The lower [half] of the heavenly axis, the qi of the earth rules it." The ancient
cosmological dimension of this statement was not taken into account by Wang Bing
and Zhang Jiebin. See next note.

70 Wang Bing: "The 'heavenly axis' is situated exactly to the sides of the navel. It is the
so-called half-way of the body. When the arms are stretched pointing towards heaven,

68-397-7
[Huang] Di:
"What is it to say: 'first' and 'middle'?"

Qi Bo:
"The 'first' [term] altogether [lasts for] 30 degrees and some odd [parts of a degree]. The qi [term after the] middle follows the same pattern."[71]

[Huang] Di:
"What is the reason [for distinguishing between] 'first [term]' and '[term after the] middle'?"

Qi Bo:
"They serve to distinguish between [the qi of] heaven and earth."[72]

68-397-9
[Huang] Di:
"I should like to hear about this comprehensively."

---

then [the level of the navel] is exactly half-way of the body. If one breaks it up into three sections, the upper section corresponds to heaven, the lower section corresponds to the earth, and the mid-section corresponds to qi interaction. The borderline of the interaction and union of the qi of heaven and earth, that is where the changes and transformations in terms of domination and revenge of cold, summerheat, dryness, dampness, wind and fire occur. Hence this is where the human qi comes from, this is where the myriad beings emerge out of transformation, with union and dispersion [of qi]." Zhang Jiebin: "樞 is 樞機 'central force,' 'controlling power.' That which is above the center, the qi of heaven rules it; that which is below the center, the qi of the earth rules it. The section where the qi [of heaven and earth] interact, that is the central position. Now, when physical appearance and qi affect each other, when above and below side with each other, the central palace corresponds to all these [situations] and acts as their marketplace. Hence this is where the qi of man comes from and this is where the myriad beings emerge from and this is where change and transformation become apparent."

71 Wang Bing: " 'Some odd [parts of a degree]' is to say: 30 days plus 43 and 3/4 *ke*. The first [term] and the [second term following] midterm combined last for 60 days and 87 1/2 *ke*. Each [term] has 3/4 *ke* in excess [to 30 days plus 43 *ke*]. Hence [the text] states 'the same pattern.'" Zhang Jiebin: "[One] 'degree' is [one] day. One step covers 60 days and 87 1/2 *ke*. If divided into two, the first half step starts from its first [day]. That is the first qi. It lasts for 30 degrees and some odd [parts of a degree]. .. The second half step begins at midterm. It is called midterm qi. Its number [of days] is the same as that of the first [term]. Hence [the text] states: 'the same pattern.'"

72 Wang Bing: "Thereby it is possible to know whether a qi on high or down below is responsible for the generation of human disease."

Qi Bo:
"The 'first [term]' is the [term of the] qi of the earth. The '[term after the] middle' is the [term of the] qi of heaven."[73]

[Huang] Di:
"How do they rise and descend?"

Qi Bo:
"The rise and descent of qi are alternating operations of heaven and earth."[74]

[Huang] Di:
"I should like to hear what these operations are like."

Qi Bo:
"When a rise is complete, the descent [begins]. That which descends is called [qi of] heaven.
When a descent is complete, the rise [begins]. That which rises is called [qi of] the earth.
When the qi of heaven descends, the qi flows on the earth.
When the qi of the earth rises, the qi surges to heaven.

The fact is,
'the [qi] on high and down below call on each other;

---

73 Wang Bing: "During the first [term of a] qi heaven is in charge. When heaven is in charge, then the qi of the earth rises into the Great Void. The [term of] qi [after] midterm is governed by the qi of the earth. When the qi of the earth rules, then the qi of heaven descends to that which has physical appearance." Wu Kun: "It is always such that qi rises first and descends afterwards. Hence the first [qi] is the qi of the earth, the midterm [qi] is the qi of heaven." Zhang Jiebin: " 'First and midterm' serve to distinguish between yin and yang. Each single qi degree must have an earlier and a later [part]. When it has an earlier and a later [part] then the earlier is yang and the later is yin. Yang rules progress; that is a movement upwards from below. Hence the first [qi] is the qi of the earth. Yin rules retreat; that is a movement downwards from above. Hence the midterm [qi] is the qi of heaven."

74 Wang Bing: " '升' is to say: 'rise upwards.' 降 is to say: 'descend downwards.' When [something] has risen to its extreme, then it descends; when [something] has descended to its extreme, then it will rise again. Rise and descent have no end, hence they reflect the alternating operations of heaven and earth." Zhang Zhicong: "The qi of heaven rules descend. However, descend results from rise. Hence the qi that descends has risen from the earth. The qi of the earth rules rise. However, rise results from descend. Hence the qi that rises has descended from heaven. That is the miracle of heaven and earth operating through each other (相用)."

rise and descent follow each other,
and this is the way that changes occur.' "75

68-398-5
[Huang] Di:
"Good!

'Cold and dampness meet each other.
Dryness and heat come down on each other.
Wind and fire come into contact.'
Is there anything in this that [I] should hear about?"76

Qi Bo:
"The [sequence of the] qi has [activities of] dominating [others] and of [being dominated as] revenge.
The activities of domination and revenge are marked by virtue77 and transformation, by operation and change.
When there is change, then evil qi resides there."78

68-398-7
[Huang] Di:
"What is it to say, 'evil'?"79

---

75 Wang Bing: "There are [terms of] qi domination and [those of] revenge. Hence changes result." Zhang Zhicong: "The qi of heaven flows on the earth; the qi of the earth surges to heaven. The qi of heaven up on high and of the earth down below affect each other. Descent follows rise; rise follows descent. When rise and descent follow out of each other, changes and transformations occur."

76 Zhang Jiebin's version has 間 instead of 聞. He interpreted 間 as 異, 'different.' Wang Bing's comment (see below) appears to refer to a reading of 間 instead of 聞, too. Wang Bing, though, interpreted 間 as "in between."

77 Cheng Shide et al.: "德 is 特性, 'special characteristics.'"

78 Wang Bing: "Clapping hands generate a sound; a fire causes water to boil. When things interact and unite, images [of such interaction and union] emerge from between them. The same is true for the results of all kinds of interactions and unions. When heaven and earth interact and unite, then the eight winds are excited to cause destruction and the six qi interact and pass quickly here and there between them. Hence no proper qi can establish itself; on the contrary, this results in evil qi."

79 Wang Bing: " 'Evil' is a designation of that which is not proper. In the [alternation of] domination and revenge of [the qi of] heaven and earth, the six qi of cold, summerheat, dryness, dampness, wind, and fire are each other's evil."

Qi Bo:
"Now,
the generation of beings results from transformation.
The extreme point [in the development] of beings results from change.[80]
When change and transformation strike at each other,
this is where completion and destruction originate from.[81]

The fact is,
'the qi may leave or return;
[its] operation may be slow or fast.
With [these] four being present,[82]
there is transformation and change.
That is the origin of the winds.'"[83]

---

80 Cheng Shide et al.: "極 is the final stage in the development of things; this is the point of weakening and destruction."

81 Wang Bing: "Now, when qi comes into existence and undergoes transformations, its physical appearance is invisible and its nature remains unknown, so that it is impossible to assess where it emerges and to inspect where it comes to a halt. The myriad beings come to life by themselves and they undergo transformations by themselves. They near completion without ever reaching an apex. That is called 'heavenly harmony.' [However] when its images are visible and when it manifests its movement as shaking, fiery, unyielding, violent, whirling, roving, quick, sudden, pulling, hard, breaking, spoiling, tearing, exciting, that is called 'evil qi.' Hence the generation of things occurs through silent transformation; their destruction is rapid change. Hence coming to life is a result of transformation; reaching an apex [in a development] is based on change. When change and transformation never cease, then the origins of completion and destruction are present all the time." Zhang Jiebin: "Of all the experts who have interpreted this, there are those who state 'if there is a periodic movement of yin and yang, then there is transformation, when [beings] come to life in spring and decay in autumn, then this is change.' Others state: 'when the myriad beings come to life and rest [later on], then this is transformation, when cold and summerheat alternate, then this is change.' Others state: 'to assume another corporal appearance is transformation; to alter a physical appearance is change.' Others state: 'when something comes into existence out of non-existence and when something enters non-existence out of existence, then this is transformation; when something small becomes strong and when something strong becomes aged, then this is change.' Hence when change or transformation affect a thing, generation is a result of transformation, in which case the qi advances, while destruction is a result of change, in which case the qi retreats. Hence [the text] states: 'the mutual affecting of change and transformation is the origin of completion and destruction.' 薄 is 侵迫, 'to invade and harass.'"

82 2568/48: "四者之有 is 有四者."

83 Wang Bing: "Heaven and earth change their positions; cold and summerheat move to different locations; water and fire change their locations. At the moment these

68-399-1
[Huang] Di:
" 'Slowness and speed, leaving and returning [of qi],
where the wind emerges from,
as well as any transformation and change,'
the fact is, they result from the changes of [qi from] abundance to weakness
[and vice versa] and nothing else.

How is it that the mutual conditioning of completion and destruction roams in
the middle [of all that]?"[84]

Qi Bo:
"The mutual conditioning of completion and destruction emerges out of movement.
'When there is unending movement,
then changes occur.' "

68-399-3
[Huang] Di:
"Is there a time limit [to movement]?"

---

movements occur, the slow or high speed of qi and the going forward and returning
are, hence, not regular. Even though it is impossible to investigate and recognize the
final principles [behind all this], [it is obvious, nevertheless,] that transformations
and changes result from these activities which may be mild or severe and that the
winds originate from them." Zhang Jiebin: " 'Qi may go or return,' that is, it advances
forward or retreats. '[Its] operation may be slow or fast,' that is, it may be abundant
or weak. When these four are present, transformations and changes occur. However,
proper wind is the outcome of transformations; evil wind is the outcome of changes."

84 Wang Bing: "倚伏 are the early signs of misfortune and happiness. Misfortune is
the foundation of happiness; happiness has misfortune lying in waiting. Hence misfortune and happiness condition each other. What is abundant will weaken; utmost
happiness will turn into grief. Hence utmost happiness is the foundation of misfortune, .. happiness lies hidden in utmost misfortune." 2530/18: "*Lao zi* 58 has: 禍兮福
所倚, 福兮禍所伏, 'misfortune: it is the basis for happiness; happiness: misfortune
lies hidden in it'. Because 倚 stands for 禍 and 伏 stands for 福, the basic meaning of
倚伏 is 禍福, 'misfortune and happiness.' " Cheng Shide et al.: "倚伏 has the meaning
of 'being the cause of each other.' "

Qi Bo:
"When there is no generation and no transformation, that is the time of resting."[85]

[Huang] Di:
"No generation, [no] transformation?"[86]

Qi Bo:
" 'When leaving and entering ceases,
then the transforming activity of the spirit mechanism vanishes.[87]
When rise and descent stop,
then the qi set-up is solitary and in danger.'[88]

---

85 Zhang Jiebin: "The preceding text states that the mutual conditioning of completion and destruction arises out of movement; this, then, is the time of movement. When movement has reached an extreme this will result in change and when a situation of no generation and no transformation is reached, then this is a time of standstill. Heaven and earth have spring and summer for movement, autumn and winter for standstill. Man has life for movement, death for standstill."

86 Wang Bing: "Can it be that there is no coming into existence and no transformation?"

87 *NJCD*: "化 is 死, 'to die.' The *Huai nan zi*, 'Jing shen xun,' 淮南子, 精神訓, has: 故形有摩而神未嘗化者. The commentary says: 化 is like 死."

88 Wang Bing: "出入 is to say: breathing. 升降 is to say: qi transformation. Now, the vital qi [needed by all the animals], whether they have fur or feathers, whether they are naked or have scales or shells, to fly, run, or crawl or walk, has its origin in the body and it is their spirit that is responsible for their movement or standstill. Hence [the text] speaks of a 'spirit mechanism.' However, as for metal, jade, soil and stones, [one uses] herbs or trees for melting [them] or making pottery. In all this cases, vital qi comes from the outside. One borrows [external] qi to complete their setup and manage [melting, making pottery, etc.]. Hence [the text] speaks of a 'qi set-up.' When *Su wen* 70 states: 'That which has its origin inside, it is called spirit mechanism. When the spirit has left, then the mechanism comes to a standstill. That which has its origin outside, it is called qi set-up. When the [movement of the] qi comes to a halt, then the transformations are interrupted,' then this means just the same." Zhang Zhicong: " 'Leaving and entering' is opening and closing. 機 is 樞機, 'axis mechanism.' 神機 is the unfathomable change and transformation of yin and yang. Now, opening and closing resembles the leafs of a door; an axis is the bolt that turns. Now, without axis, [a door] cannot open or close; and without opening and closing, there is nothing that could turn the axis. Hence, without leaving and entering, the transformations of the spirit mechanism subside. Rise and descent are the going and coming of cold and summerheat. Now, all the rise and descent of yin and yang [qi] takes its origin from the earth. Heaven encloses the earth on the outside. Therefore, when rise and descent subside, the qi on the outside is unprotected and in danger. When it is unprotected and in danger, then it does not generate [things]." 1196/5 associates 出入 with ani-

68-399-6
Hence,
when there is neither leaving nor entering,
then there is nothing by which there could be generation, growth, adulthood,
aging, and ending.
When there is neither rise nor descend,
then there is nothing by which there could be generation, growth, transformation, gathering, and storage.[89]

{Therefore, 'rise and descent, leaving and entering, that is what every container
has.' Hence the container is the location of generation and transformation.
When the container disperses, then it dissipates [its contents], and generation
as well as transformation come to a halt.}[90]

---

mals and man and 升降 with plants only: "That is to explain, animals require qi to
leave and enter [their bodies] to come to life, grow, mature, age, and perish. Plants
require the qi only to rise and to descend to come to life, grow, transform, be harvested,
and be stored." Wang Qi: "The ancients believed that the vital qi of all living bodies
of blood and flesh originates from inside and that the spirit rules all vital processes.
Hence they spoke of 神機, 'spirit mechanism.' [In contrast,] the vital qi of non-living
items such as minerals and plants originates from their outside. They take qi [from
the outside] to have their completion set up. Hence this is called 氣立, 'qi set-up.'"
445/38: "The present 氣立 has a meaning which differs somewhat from the meaning
of 氣立 in *Su wen* 3. As Wang Bing points out in his comment, only when [gold, jade,
etc.] receive qi from the natural world for nourishment can they reach completion (氣
立) and exist." See also 1397/21 for a discussion of 神機 and 氣立.

89 683/49: "This is an example of the style of literary parallelism. The passage should
be read: "when leaving and entering end, and when rise and descent come to a halt,
then there is nothing by which there could be generation, growth, maturing, aging,
and vanishing, and there is nothing by which there could be generation, growth, transformation, harvesting, and storage." See also 2154/45, 630/39, 1127/11, and 1126/11
for discussions of this paragraph.

90 Wang Bing: "器 is to say: heaven, earth and all bodies. 宇 is to say 屋宇, 'residence.'
Because the way in which the physical bodies enclose the palaces and depots and
receive their spirits is identical to heaven and earth, hence they are all called 'containers.' All bodies are small container-locations of generation and transformation;
the Great Void is the large container-location of generation and transformation. No
matter whether these containers are small or large, they all disperse. The life of any
container, be it small or large, is limited; [it is just that the moment of] dispersion may
be far away or near."

{Hence there is nothing without leaving and entering, nothing without rise and descent.⁹¹ Transformations may be small and they may be large. Time limits [of existence] may be near and they may be far away. In the presence of these four, maintaining their regularity is to be regarded most important.⁹² When this regularity is contravened, then catastrophes and harm arrive.}⁹³

{Hence when it is said:
'Without physical appearance there is no suffering,'
then this means just the same.}"⁹⁴

68-401-1
[Huang] Di:
"Good!
Can it be that there is no generation and no transformation?"

Qi Bo:
"An encompassing question, indeed!
To act in complete union with the Way, only the true men [are able to do this]."⁹⁵

[Huang] Di:
"Good!"

---

91 Wang Bing: "Even if true life is set up, all physical containers must have these two."

92 Wang Bing: " 'These four' is to say: leaving and entering, rise and descent." 1397/23: "常守 is to follow the laws in the regularity of yin yang and of the five agents."

93 Wang Bing: "Leaving and entering, rise and descent are the origin of generation and transformation. Hence they must be present. If this regular Way is contravened, then the spirit leaves its chamber and generation and transformation are reduced and finally cease. This must end in disaster.

94 Wang Bing: "When Lao zi said: 'The reason why I suffer greatly is because I have a body,' and 'If I had no body, where should I suffer?' then this explains [what was said above]." See *Dao de jing* 道德經 13.

95 Wang Bing: "The body of the true man is invisible and it is impossible to assess whether he leaves or enters heaven or earth, inside or outside. To follow the Way and approach truth in order to live, that is small. [To follow the Way] to enter the nothing, that is great. Who could be able to pass beyond the boundaries of the void and not be one with the Way?!"

Chapter 69
Comprehensive Discourse on Changes [resulting from] Qi Interaction

69-402-2
Huang Di asked:
"The five periods govern successively.[1]
Above they correspond to the annual cycles of heaven.[2]
Yin and yang leave and return;[3]
cold and summerheat, if one comes up the other will follow.[4]

True [qi] and evil [qi] strike at each other.[5]
Inner and outer [regions] part from [each other].[6]
The [contents of the] six conduits are stirred like waves.
The five qi shift towards imbalance.[7]

Great excess and inadequacy,
domination alone and appropriated [territory],[8]

---

1 Zhang Zhicong: "That is, the five periods succeed each other and rule alternately."

2 Wang Bing: "朞 is 365 days and a quarter day."

3 Zhang Zhicong: "When [a yin or yang qi] having surplus moves on, it is followed by [a yin or yang qi] that is insufficient. When [a yin or yang qi] being insufficient moves on, it is followed by [a yin or yang qi] that has surplus."

4 Zhang Zhicong: "迎隨 is 往來, 'to go and come.'"

5 Fang Wenhui/162: "相薄 is 相搏鬥, 'to fight each other.'"

6 Zhang Jiebin: "分離 is 不相保, 'do not protect each other.'" Zhongyi yanjiuyuan…: "At times of irregular climatic changes, unilaterally dominant evil qi may appear. It struggles with the proper qi of the human body. This, in turn, causes a failure in the coordination of the functions among the body's inner and outer sections with the result that yin and yang lose their balance."

7 Zhang Zhicong: "That is to say: people are affected by the qi of domination and revenge and fall ill." Cheng Shide et al.: "The 'five qi' refers to the qi of the five depots." Zhongyi yanjiuyuan…: "That is, because evil qi has invaded [the body] and because the yin and yang [qi] in the body have lost their balance, the qi and the blood in the six conduits flow rapidly and roaring like waves and billows. That is similar to the water of a river that has been struck by sudden gales. Similarly the five depots of the human body display unilateral domination and unilateral weakness."

8 Wang Bing: "專勝 is to say: excessive rule of [the qi of one of] the five periods over a year. 兼并 is to say: [the qi] ruling a year is insufficient." Cheng Shide et al.: "專勝 is: one qi is present in excess and abounds alone. 兼并 is: one qi is inadequate and two

I should like to speak about their beginning,[9]
and also about their regular designations.
May [I] hear [about them]?"[10]

69-402-5
Qi Bo paid reverence by knocking his head to the ground twice and responded:
"A brilliant question, indeed! This is the brilliant Way.
This is what the Lords on High valued, what the teachers of former times have transmitted.
[I, your] subject, though not intelligent, have heard their instructions in the past."[11]

[Huang] Di:
"I have heard [the saying]
'To meet the [right] person but not teach [him],
that is called losing the Way.
To transmit [the doctrine] to someone who is not the [right] person,
that is to treat the heavenly treasure without respect.'

My own virtue is surely undeveloped,
and not sufficient yet to receive the perfect Way.
Still, my people are grieved that their [life may] not continue to [its natural] end;
I should like you, Sir, [to make sure that]
it is protected without end and that
it flows to the limitless.

[other] qi usurp its [territory]." Zhongyi yanjiuyuan...: "When only one qi abounds and invades [the territory of] other qi, that is called 專勝. When only one qi is weak and when [its territory] is appropriated by two [other] qi simultaneously, that is called 兼并. 專勝 is excess; 兼并 is inadequacy. For example, in a year when the [qi of] wood is present in excess, it seizes the [territory of the] soil and humiliates the metal. That is 專勝. In a year when the [qi of] wood is inadequate, then it is humiliated by the [qi of] soil and [its territory is] seized by the [qi of] metal. That is 兼并."

9 Zhongyi yanjiuyuan...: "始 is 'starting point.'" 始 may be a mistake for 治, "to rule." Above, some versions have 五運更始, others have 五運更治.

10 Zhang Zhicong: "The [course of the] qi of heaven begins with *jia*; the [course of the] qi of the earth begins with *zi*. With the combination of *zi* and *jia* [the succession of] the annual periods is set up."

11 Zhongyi yanjiuyuan...: "旨 is to be interpreted as 美, 'beautiful': 'I have studied this beautiful knowledge in the past.'"

If I take control of these affairs and [if I wish to] handle them in agreement with rules, how [should I proceed]?"[12]

69-402-9
Qi Bo:
"Please, let me speak about these [issues] one by one.[13]

When the *Upper Classic* states:
'Now, [to know] the Way [is]
to know the line patterns in heaven above,
to know the structures of the earth below, and
to know the affairs of man in the center.
[Someone with this knowledge] can exist for long,'[14]
then this means just the same."[15]

[Huang] Di:
"What is that to say?"

Qi Bo:
"[That statement] is based in the position of the qi.

What is positioned in heaven,
these are the line patterns of heaven.
What is positioned on the earth,
these are the structures of the earth.
What is penetrated by the changes and transformations of the human qi,
these are the affairs of man."[16]

---

12 Zhang Zhicong: "則 is 法, 'law.'" See also 155/15.

13 Zhongyi yanjiuyuan...: "遂 is 盡, 'exhaustively.'"

14 Wang Bing: "Now, the Way, there is nothing too big that it did not embrace and there is nothing too fine that it could not enter. Hence the line patterns of heaven, the structures of the earth, and the affairs of man, they all are penetrated [by the Way]." The passage 道者 ... 長久 appears also in *Su wen* 75-547-8.

15 For a discussion of the Daoist context of this quotation, see 635/10.

16 Wang Bing: "The three yin and the three yang control heaven and earth. It is through them that the arrangement of the generation and transformation of yin and yang is manifested. That is called: 'Positioned in heaven and positioned on the earth.' The five periods reside in the center; they govern the changes and transformations of the human qi. Hence [the text] states: 'Penetrated by the human qi.'"Yao Shaoyu: "The qi of heaven, earth, and man have their fixed position. That is their 本, 'base.'The 'line patterns of heaven' include the stars and the other heavenly bodies, wind, rain,

The fact is
that which is in great excess, it precedes heaven;
that which is inadequate, it is behind heaven.[17]
That is what is called 'government and transformation to which man corresponds.'[18]

69-403-4
[Huang] Di:
"In the transformations [caused] by the five periods,[19]
if there is great excess, how is that?"[20]

Qi Bo:
"If in a year [associated with wood] there is great excess [of the qi] of wood,
wind qi prevails everywhere.
The spleen, [which is] soil, receives evil.[21]

People suffer from
outflow of [undigested] food and they eat less.
Their bodies are heavy. [They suffer from] vexation and grievance,
intestinal sounds, and propping fullness in the abdomen.[22]

---

cold, and summerheat. Their qi is based in heaven; it is positioned above. The 'structures of the earth' include mountains, rivers, birds, fishes, animals, and plants. Their qi is based on the earth; it is positioned below. The 'affairs of man' include qi and blood, depletion and repletion, outside and inside, countermovement and obedience. Their qi is based in man; it is positioned in the center."

17 Wang Bing: "先天 and 後天 refer to the times of the changes and transformations of the qi of generation and transformation. In a year of great excess, transformations set in before their time has arrived; in a year of insufficiency, transformations set in only after their time has arrived."

18 Zhang Jiebin: "Heaven governs and transforms above; man corresponds to that below."

19 Zhongyi yanjiuyuan...: " 'Transformation' is 'transformation of the qi.'"

20 Wang Bing: " 'Great excess' is to say: the qi of that year has a surplus." Cheng Shide et al.: " 'Great excess' refers to years associated with a yang stem. All years associated with the yang stems *jia*, *bing*, *wu*, *geng*, and *ren* are years where the 'annual period is marked by great excess.'"

21 Wang Bing: "When the [qi of] wood is present in surplus, the qi of the soil yields." Zhang Jiebin: "These are the six *ren* years. The transformation of wood is wind. When wood dominates, then it overcomes the soil. Hence the spleen depot receives evil."

22 Wang Bing: "飧泄 is to say: the food leaves the body without having been transformed. [As a result] the spleen [qi] is depleted. Hence [people affected] eat less and

<Jupiter corresponds above.²³>

69-403-7
When [the excess of the qi of wood] is severe, then
[the patients] are confused²⁴ and they tend to become angry.
Vertigo and peak illness occur.²⁵

The policy of the qi of transformation is not enacted;
the qi of generation governs alone.²⁶
[As a result,] cloudy things fly by.
Herbs and trees are kept in constant motion.
In severe cases, they are shaken and fall down.²⁷

---

their bodies are heavy. [They experience] vexation and grievance, intestinal sounds, and propping fullness in the abdomen." Zhang Jiebin: "Water and grain do not transform, hence there is outflow of [undigested] food. The spleen is depleted and does not move, hence [the patients] eat less. The spleen rules the muscles and the flesh. When its qi is weakened, the body [feels] heavy as a result. The vessel of the spleen rises in one branch from the stomach to the diagphragm and pours into the heart. Hence [patients experience] vexation and grievance."

23 Wang Bing: "In a year with greatly abounding wood qi the light of Jupiter is bright."

24 Gao Jiwu/210: " 'To be unhappy' is described by 忽忽."

25 Wang Bing: "When oppression and invasion [by the qi of wood] are extremely severe, then it is countered by [the qi of] metal. Hence [the wood] falls ill itself." Zhang Zhicong: "That is to say: when anything is overly excessive, then it will harm itself. A tendency to be angry is a disease of the affects associated with the liver. The ceasing yin [conduit] and the supervisor vessel meet at the top of the head. Hence [patients] experience vertigo and suffer from peak disease." Zhang Jiebin: "When wood [qi] abounds, then the liver is strong. Hence there is a tendency to become angry."

26 Zhang Jiebin: "The 'qi of transformation' is the qi of soil. The 'qi of generation' is the qi of wood. When the wood abounds, then the soil is weak. Hence the qi of transformation cannot extend its policy over the myriad things and the qi of generation, i.e., the wood [qi], governs alone."

27 Zhang Jiebin: "When the wind does not act virtuously, then clouds and things in the Great Void 'fly and move.' Herbs and trees are not calm. When the [qi of] wood dominates unendingly, then the [qi of] metal will succeed it. Hence when a situation is reached where herbs and trees are shaken and fall, this is because of the qi of metal."

[Illnesses] contrary [to normal are:]
pain in the flanks and severe vomiting.[28]
If [in such cases the movement in] the surging yang is interrupted, [the patient] will die and [can] not be treated."[29]

<Venus corresponds above.[30]>

69-404-1
If in a year [associated with fire] there is great excess [of the qi] of fire,
flaming summerheat prevails everywhere.
The lung, [which is] metal, receives evil.[31]

People suffer from
malaria, being short of qi, coughing and panting.

---

28 Zhang Jiebin: "The liver vessel spreads through the flanks. When the [qi of] wood is strong, then the [qi of the] liver moves contrary (逆) [to its normal direction]. Hence the flanks have pain. In case of severe vomiting, wood evil has harmed the stomach."

29 Wang Bing: "The 'surging yang' (衝陽) is [situated on] the stomach vessel." Zhang Zhicong: "The surging yang is located on the stomach vessel. [In the present case], the wood [qi] is present in excess and the [flow of the] qi of the soil has been interrupted. Hence a fatal condition has arisen that cannot be treated."

30 Wang Bing: "This applies to all *ren* years. Wood [qi] is present in surplus, while the soil [qi] is repressed. Hence [the latter] cannot spread its command to the myriad beings. The qi of generation is the qi of wood. Since it is greatly excessive, it rules alone in generation and transformation. The wind does not act virtuously; it moves without diverging [into different directions]. Hence cloudy things in the Great Void fly by, herbs and trees do not stand motionless; [that is,] they move and do not stand still and metal overcomes them. Hence in severe cases, herbs and trees are shaken and fall down. When the flanks, contrary to what is normal, ache, the wood has seized the [territory of the] soil. The 'surging yang' (*chong yang* 衝陽) is the stomach vessel. The wood qi dominates and the [movement of the] soil qi is interrupted as a result. Hence [the patient] dies. The metal takes revenge and Venus moves contrary to its regular course. Those [sections on the earth] associated with the stars [passed through by Venus] experience disaster. The harm resulting from such disaster emerges in the East. Correspondingly, internally the spleen is harmed first and afterwards the liver." Zhang Jiebin: "The metal restrains the domination of the wood. Hence the light of Venus is bright, it corresponds to the qi of the [metal]."

31 Wang Bing: "If the fire does not act on the basis of its virtues, then [it is] evil and harms the metal. If it acts on the basis of virtue, then its command is harmonious and balanced." Zhang Jiebin: "This applies to the six *wu* years. The transformation of fire is summerheat. When the fire dominates, then it overcomes the metal. Hence the lung depot receives evil."

There is blood overflow, blood outflow, and outpour below.
The throat is dry and the ears are deaf.
There is central heat, and there is heat in the shoulders and the back.[32]

<Mars corresponds above.>

When [the excess of the qi of fire] is severe, then
there is pain in the chest.
The flanks have propping fullness and the flanks have pain.
There is pain in the region of breast, back, shoulders, and shoulderblades.
There is pain in the inner side of both arms.
The body is hot, the bones ache, and there is soaking.[33]

The qi of gathering is not active;
the qi of growth is bright alone.
[As a result,] there is rain, water, frost, and cold.[34]

---

32 Wang Bing: "少氣 is to say: The qi is diminished and insufficient for breathing. 血
泄 is to say: blood dysentery, blood in the stool. 血溢 is to say: blood moves upwards
and leaves [the body] through the seven orifices. 注下 is to say: watery dysentery. 中
熱 refers to the center of the chest and heart [region]. 'Back' is to say: the palace of the
chest center. The shoulders are adjacent to it. Hence the chest and the heart center, as
well as the shoulders and the back are hot. When the qi of fire greatly abounds, then
the light of Mars shines far and moves towards [the observer] contrary [to its normal
direction]. Those sections [on the earth] associated with the lodges [passed through by
Mars] experience disaster." Zhang Jiebin: "Fire evil harms the yin. Cold and heat fight
each other. Hence this results in malaria. Strong fire consumes qi. Hence [patients
experience] diminished qi. The [qi of] fire occupies the [territory of the] lung, i.e., the
metal. Hence [patients] cough and pant. The [qi of] fire is forced to move without
order. Hence it rises and overflows through mouth and nose and it descends and flows
off through the two lower orifices. The nature of fire is hasty and fast. Hence there is
watery dysentery and outpour below. Dry throat, deaf ears, heat in the center, as well
as heat in the shoulders and in the back do all result from burnings caused by rising
fire and flames."

33 Wang Bing: "When the fire [acts] without virtue, it gives rein to heat and harms
the metal. Water acts in revenge. Hence the fire falls ill itself." Zhang Jiebin: "The fire
abounds, hence the body is hot. The water is diminished, hence the bones ache. Heat
flows through the entire body, hence 'soaking' [ulcers] emerge." Zhongyi yanjiuyuan...:
"浸淫 is to say: 浸淫瘡, 'sores because of soaking.' This disease results from the poison
of fire heat invading the heart conduit and breaking out through the skin." For 浸淫,
see also *Su wen* 19-119-6.

34 Wang Bing: "The character 水 should be 冰, 'ice.'" Zhang Jiebin: "The 'qi of gathering' is the qi of metal. The 'qi of growth' is the qi of fire. When the fire abounds, then
the metal is weak. Hence the qi of gathering is not active and the qi of growth shines

<Mercury corresponds above.[35]>

69-404-5
<If in the upper [half of the year] minor yin or minor yang come down [to join
the excess of the qi of fire],[36]
then fire with burning heat [causes] water fountains to dry up,
things burn and wither.>

Illnesses contrary [to what is normal are:]
absurd speaking, jumping in craziness,
coughing, and panting breath with sounds,
severe diarrhea, as well as endless overflow and outflow of blood.[37]
If [in such cases the movement in the vessels at] the great abyss is interrupted,
[the patient] will die and cannot be treated.[38]

<Mars corresponds above.[39]>

---

alone. When fire does not act virtuously, it is succeeded by water. Hence there is rain,
water, frost, and cold." Zhang Zhicong: "In this case the qi of metal is suppressed and
the qi of water takes revenge. .. Rain, water, frost, and cold result from the qi of cold
and water taking revenge."

35 Wang Bing: "When the qi of metal abates, the qi of fire acts alone and the qi
of water diminishes it. Hence rain, dew, ice, and hail appear, and frost and cold descend everywhere and kill things. Water takes revenge against fire and the celestial
images correspond to that. When Mercury moves contrary [to its normal direction],
cold disaster befalls [all] beings. Upon observation, Mercury is situated 30 degrees
ahead or behind of the sun..The disaster caused [by Mercury] is oriented towards the
South. Correspondingly, in man the lung is harmed first and, in a backlash, the heart
is harmed afterwards."

36 Zhongyi yanjiuyuan...: "上臨 refers to the 'qi controlling heaven.'"

37 Zhang Zhicong: "As for 病反, the fire is extremely active and contrary [to what
might be expected] harms itself. Incoherently speaking and jumping in craziness
are conditions resulting from extreme heat. Coughing, panting, and breathing with
sounds result from fire flaming upwards and melting the metal."

38 Wang Bing: "The great abyss (太溪) is [situated on] the lung vessel." Cheng Shide
et al.: " 'Great Abyss' is the name of a hole on the hand major yin lung conduit." Zhang
Zhicong: "The fire is extremely active and the [flow of the] qi of metal has been interrupted. Hence a fatal condition that cannot be treated has arisen."

39 Wang Bing: "This applies to all *wu* years. In *wu wu* and *wu zi* years the minor yin
appears in the upper [half of the year]; in *wu yin* and *wu shen* years the minor yang
appears in the upper [half of the year]. These are called 'years of heavenly tallies.' The
great abyss is [situated on] the lung vessel. The fire [qi] dominates and the [movement
of the qi of] metal is interrupted. Hence [the patients] die. Because the fire is greatly

69-405-2
If in a year [associated with soil] there is great excess [of the qi] of soil,
rain and dampness prevail everywhere.
The kidneys, [which are] water, receive evil.[40]

People suffer from
abdominal pain,
coolness and receding [yang qi in the limbs],
unhappy sentiments,
a heavy body, as well as vexation and grievance.[41]

<Saturn corresponds above.[42]>

When [the excess of the qi of soil] is severe, then
the muscles and the flesh decay.
The legs limp and [can] not be contracted.
When walking [people] tend to [suffer from] spasm.
There is pain below the feet.
[Spillage] drink develops,[43] and there is central fullness; [people] eat less.
The four limbs cannot be raised.[44]

---

excessive and, in addition, fire heat arrives in the upper [half of these years], the two
fires merge. Hence the corporal appearance manifests signs such [as described in the
text]. When Mars moves contrary [to its normal direction], that which is associated
with its lodges is in danger."

40 Wang Bing: "This is so because the soil [acts] without virtue." Zhang Jiebin: "These
are the six *jia* years. Soil transforms into dampness. When the [qi of] soil dominates,
then it overcomes water. Hence the kidney depot receives evil."

41 Wang Bing: " 'Abdominal pain' is to say: the upper and the lower abdomen ache.
清厥 is to say: countermoving frigidity in the legs. 'Unhappy sentiments' are like hidden grief. The soil [qi] comes to punish the water [qi] and the [celestial] images correspond to this." Zhang Jiebin: "These diseases emerge because soil evil harms the
kidneys."

42 Wang Bing: "When Saturn moves contrary [to its normal direction], that which is
associated with the lodges invaded [by Saturn] experiences disaster."

43 This reading of 飲 as 溢飲, "spillage drink", is based on what must be an early commentary documented in the main text of *Su wen* 17-104-2.

44 Wang Bing: "The spleen rules the muscles and the flesh; the [condition of the]
four limbs corresponds [to it] externally. Also, its vessel rises from the ends of the
central toes, passes diagonally along the inner side of the node bone (核骨, lateral
malleolus), appears at the outside and winds around the instep. Hence the disease is as

69-405-5
When these changes occur, [the soil] occupies its position.[45]
The qi of storage hides away,
the qi of transformation governs it alone.

[As a result, water] gushes up from fountains and rivers inundate [the land].
What had dried up becomes humid [again] and generates fish.
When wind and rain arrive massively,
soil collapses because of flooding.
Scaly animals are seen on the land.

Illnesses [contrary to normal are:]
abdominal fullness, semiliquid stools, and intestinal sounds.
If [someone suffers] contrary [to what is normal] from severe diarrhea,[46] and
if [the movement in the vessels at] the great ravine is interrupted, [the patient]
dies and [can] not be treated.

<Jupiter corresponds above.[47]>

---

outlined here." Zhang Jiebin: "In extreme cases, the soil evil is present in surplus and
the spleen conduit falls ill itself."

45 Wang Bing: "得位 is to say: in the [third] month of [each] season." Lin Yi et al.:
"In the outline of transformations occurring in years of great excess, a statement such
as 變生得位 is found only here because one such reference is sufficient to characterize
the remaining four qi, too." Zhang Jiebin: "The soil has no fixed position. Whenever
soil evil causes changes during the four seasons, this is the time when it occupies its
position." Zhang Zhicong: "The 18th day of the final months of the four seasons is the
time when the soil qi occupies its position and, contrary [to what is normal], causes
changes and generates these diseases." Yao Shaoyu: "得位 is to say: in the [third]
month of [each] season. That is the time when the soil rules. The rule of the soil is
distributed through the four seasons. When changes appear that are caused by the soil,
these must occur at times when the [soil] rules."

46 Zhang Jiebin: "All these are [conditions resulting from] harm received by the soil,
i.e., dampness, itself."

47 Wang Bing: "This applies to all _jia_ years. The [qi of] storage is the qi of water; the
[qi of] transformation is the qi of soil. [In the present case the qi of] transformation is
greatly excessive. Hence the water [qi] is stored and hidden and the qi of transformation rules alone. When soil dominates, the wood comes to take revenge. Hence wind
and rain arrive massively. Water gushes up from springs. Rivers and gutters overflow.
What was dry becomes moist again and generates fish. Dampness is extreme... The
great ravine (太溪) is [situated on] the kidney vessel. [In the present case] the soil [qi]
dominates and the [movement of the qi of] water is interrupted. Hence [the patients]
die. When wood comes to break the soil, the heavenly images [correspond to this]."

69-406-1
If in a year [associated with metal] there is great excess [of the qi] of metal,
dryness qi prevails everywhere.
The liver, [which is] wood, receives evil.[48]

People suffer from
pain below the two flanks and in the lower abdomen.
The eyes are red and have pain; the canthi develop ulcers.
The ears hear nothing.[49]

If sternness and killing are severe,
then the body is heavy and there is vexation and grievance.
There is chest pain which pulls on the back.
The two flanks are full and they have pain which pulls on the lower abdomen.

<Venus corresponds above.[50] >

69-406-4
When [the excess of the qi of metal] is severe, then
panting and coughing occur and qi moves contrary [to its regular course].
The shoulders and the back have pain.

Zhang Jiebin: "[Jupiter] is the star associated with wood. [In the present case] the soil dominates and the wood succeeds it. Hence the light of Jupiter is bright; it corresponds to the qi [of wood]."

48 Zhang Jiebin: "These are the six *geng* years. The transformation of metal is dryness. When the metal dominates, then it overcomes the wood. Hence the liver depot receives evil."

49 Zhongyi yanjiuyuan...: "The two flanks, the lower abdomen, the ears, and the eyes are locations passed by the conduit vessels of liver and gallbladder. When the qi of metal dominates, then the liver and the gallbladder, i.e., the depot and palace associated with wood, receives harm. Hence these diseases emerge."

50 Wang Bing: "The qi of metal is excessive already and sternness and killing are severe in addition. The qi of wood develops fears and doubts internally and the diseases [outlined in the text] emerge [as a result]. When the [qi of] metal abounds, that corresponding in heaven, [i.e.] Venus, is bright. It adds [its light] massively to the lodges [it passes through]. Those [sections on the earth] associated [with these lodges] and the heart experience disaster." Cheng Shide et al.: "Venus is the star associated with metal."

The sacrum, the yin [region], the thighs, the knees, the thigh bones, the calves, the shins, and the feet all suffer.[51]

<Mars corresponds above.[52]>

The qi of gathering is violent;
the qi of generation lies down.[53]

69-406-5
[As a result], the herbs and the trees shrink;
there is aging and drying; withering and falling.

Illnesses contrary [to what is normal are:]
violent pain,[54]
inability in the upper and lower flanks to lean back and to turn to the side,
coughing with [qi] moving severely contrary [to its regular course], and blood
overflow.[55]

---

51 Wang Bing: "Fire qi takes revenge against the [metal qi]; hence [the metal qi]
itself develops a disease. The heavenly images correspond in that Mars moves against
[its] normal course. Those [sections on earth] associated with [Venus which] protects
[metal] are to be pitied." Zhang Jiebin: "When [the Great Excess] is severe, then the
metal evil is present in surplus. The lung conduit falls ill itself. Hence [patients] pant
and cough [because of] qi moving contrary [to its normal direction]. The metal cannot generate water and this may cause a disease in the kidneys, i.e., yin [region], too.
Hence the sacrum, the yin [region], the thighs, the knees, and what is further below
are all ill." Zhang Zhicong: "When sternness and killing [on the side of the metal]
are too severe, then the qi of metal is depleted itself and the qi of fire comes to take
revenge. Panting, coughing, and adversely moving qi are [the manifestations of] lung
diseases. The transportation holes of the lung are located on the shoulders and on the
back. Hence the shoulders and the back have pain."

52 Zhang Jiebin: "When metal dominates, then the fire takes revenge. Hence the
light of Mars is bright; it corresponds to the qi of the [fire]."

53 Zhang Jiebin: "The 'qi of gathering' is the qi of metal. The 'qi of generation' is the
qi of wood."

54 Lin Yi et al.: "[The text] does not state where the sudden pain occurs. *Su wen* 74
states: 'heart and flanks experience sudden pain, with an inability in the lower flanks
to lean back and to turn to the side.' Hence in the present [context] heart and flanks
experience sudden pain."

55 Zhang Zhicong: "Sudden pain in the flanks and an inability to turn to the side
are [manifestations of] diseases of the liver and of the gallbladder. The liver vessel
penetrates the center of the lung. Hence [patients experience] severe coughing and

If [in such cases the movement in the vessels at] the great thoroughfare is interrupted, [the patient] dies and [can] not be treated.[56]

<Venus corresponds above.[57]>

If in a year [associated with water] there is great excess [of the qi] of water, cold qi prevails everywhere.
The evil harms the heart, [i.e.,] the fire.[58]

People suffer from
body heat and a vexed heart. [The movement in the vessels] races and [patients] feel excited.
There is yin recession; above, below, and center are cold.
[Patients] speak incoherently, the heart aches.

Cold qi arrives early.[59]

<Mercury corresponds above.[60]>

69-407-1
When [the excess of the qi of water] is severe, then the abdomen is enlarged and the shins are swollen.

---

adversely [rising qi]. The liver is responsible for storing the blood. Hence blood overflows."

56 Zhongyi yanjiuyuan...: "The great thoroughfare (太衝) is [situated on] the liver vessel. When metal is active, then the liver is destroyed. Hence when the [movement at the] great thoroughfare is interrupted, this is fatal and cannot be treated."

57 Wang Bing: "This applies to all *geng* years. When the qi of metal is violent, the qi of wood is punished. As long as the [qi of] fire has not arrived yet to take revenge, [illnesses] such as [outlined] here occur. 斂 is to say: branches and leafs that have emerged already attach themselves to the trunk. The great thoroughfare is [located on] the liver vessel. When the [qi of] metal dominates, the [flow of the qi of] wood is interrupted. Hence [patients die]."

58 Wang Bing: "The water does not act virtuously." Zhang Jiebin: "This applies to the six *bing* years. The transformation of water is cold. When water dominates, then it overcomes fire. Hence the heart depot receives evil."

59 Zhang Zhicong: "Cold qi rises and occupies [the territory above]. It presses the fire qi to flame towards outside. Hence the body is hot."

60 Wang Bing: "悸 is racing heart movement. 譫 is incoherent language. When the qi of heaven abounds with water, Mercury is bright and lustrous."

[Patients suffer from] panting and coughing.
Sweat leaves [their bodies] during sleep; they dislike wind.[61]

Massive rain arrives.
Dust and fog [generate] haziness and pressure.[62]

<Saturn corresponds above.[63] >

<If in the upper [half of the year] major yang [qi] come down [to join the excess of the qi of water], then
rain, ice, snow, and
frost descend when it is not their time.
Dampness qi changes things.[64]>

69-407-3
Illnesses contrary [to what is normal are:]
abdominal fullness, intestinal sounds,
semiliquid stools, failure to digest food,
thirst and confusion.[65]
If [in such cases the movement in the vessels at] the spirit gate is interrupted,
[the patient] dies and [can] not be treated.[66]

---

61 Zhang Zhicong: "Because the [qi of] water is severely excessive, it has received harm itself. That is the so-called 'fullness invites injury.'"

62 Zhang Zhicong: "Water [qi is present in] excess and the qi of soil takes revenge."

63 Wang Bing: "When [the qi of] water abounds without end [its territory] is occupied by soil. Hence when signs are displayed such as dust and fog [generating] haziness and density, [this is because of] the qi of soil. The kidney vessel originates from below the feet, moves upwards into the abdomen, continues upwards from the kidneys, penetrates the liver and the diaphragm, enters the lung and follows the throat. Hence it generates illnesses such as [described here]. The kidneys are yin. Hence sweat leaves [the body] during sleep and [the patients] have an aversion to wind. The illness of lying down to sleep and have sweat leave [the body] emerges because the qi of the soil dominates and reduces the water. Correspondingly, Saturn is bright and shining."

64 Cheng Shide et al.: "These are *bing chen* and *bing xu* years, when the major yang qi of cold and water controls heaven."

65 Zhang Zhicong: "All these are conditions of lacking water and destroyed soil. The soil of the spleen is unable to move its humors around. Hence [patients are] thirsty."

66 Zhang Zhicong: "The spirit gate (神門) is [situated on] the heart vessel. Because the qi of water is overly strong, Mars corresponds above in that it loses its color while Mercury increases its brilliance."

<Mars and Mercury correspond to this above.⁶⁷>

69-408-1
[Huang] Di:
"Good!
When [in the transformations caused by the five periods] there is inadequacy,
how is that?"⁶⁸

Qi Bo:
"An encompassing question, indeed!

If in a year [associated with wood the qi of] wood is inadequate,
dryness prevails everywhere.⁶⁹
The generation loses its correspondence.⁷⁰

[Hence] herbs and trees blossom late.⁷¹

---

67 Wang Bing: "This applies to all *bing* years. In *bing chen* and *bing xu* years major
yang appears in the upper [half of the year]. Such [years] are called 'years of heavenly
complements.' The qi of cold is very strong. Hence rain transforms into ice and snow.
When rain turns into ice, then this is hail. Frost descends frequently. [All these] are
signs of the cold. Soil takes revenge against water. Hence massive and incessant rain
sets in and dampness qi penetrates deeply inside [of things]. As a result, all things turn
damp. The spirit gate (神門) is [situated on] the heart vessel. Because water [qi] dominates, the [movement of the qi of] fire is interrupted. Hence [patients] die. When
water abounds very greatly, then Mars decreases in luster while Mercury is bright."

68 Wang Bing: "That is to say: when transformations resulting from a command are
few." Zhongyi yanjiuyuan...: "不及 has two meanings. The first is 不足, 'insufficiency,'
as is expressed in Wang Bing's commentary. The second is 不至, 'fails to arrive,' as is
indicated by the *Ci yuan* 辭源: 後時則曰不及, 'to be behind time is called 不及.' The
present passage combines both meanings."

69 Wang Bing: "When a time of coolness and frigidity has arrived to which is added
strong cold, then this is called dryness qi. Dryness is the qi of metal." Zhang Jiebin:
"These are the six *ding* years." Zhongyi yanjiuyuan...: "When [the qi of wood in] a year
associated with wood is inadequate, the [qi of] metal occupies [its territory]. Dryness
is the command given by metal. Hence dryness exerts massive activites."

70 Some versions have 氣 instead of 其.

71 Wang Bing: "To be behind the time is called 'to lose correspondence.'"

If sternness and killing are severe, then
hard trees are punished at the [branches and leaves] attached to them.[72]
There is softening and withering; aging and drying.

<Venus corresponds above.[73]>

69-408-3
People suffer from
coolness in the center,
the upper and the lower flanks ache,
the lower abdomen has pain.[74]
[They experience] intestinal sounds and semiliquid stools.

Cool rain arrives frequently.

<Venus corresponds above. >

<Its grain are greenish.>[75]

---

72 Zhang Zhicong: "Even hard trees receive its punishment and are harmed."

73 Wang Bing: "辟著 is to say: branches and stems dry out but [the leafs] do not fall down. 柔 is 耎, 'soft.' 蒼 is 青, 'green-blue.' The green color of the leafs of soft trees does not change but they dry out and roll up [nevertheless]. When the qi of wood is inadequate, the qi of metal occupies its [territory]. The light of Venus is bright and illuminates what is hollow."

74 Wang Bing: "These are liver illnesses [resulting from] metal qi occupying the wood. When [the liver] is occupied by the qi [of metal], sounds emerge in the intestines and semiliquid stools develop. These are not illnesses of pain in the upper and lower flanks, or in the abdomen. .. When the qi of summer arrives, [the illness] will come to an end by itself. When it meets the qi of autumn [the illness] returns. 'Coolness and rain 時至' is to say: they arrive in correspondence to their season. Metal and soil transform alike hence coolness and rain move together. The fire qi comes to take revenge. As a result, there is little rain in summer." Zhang Zhicong: "Pain in the flanks and in the lower abdomen are [manifestations of] diseases of the liver, [which is associated with] wood. [Under normal conditions] food qi enters the stomach. [The stomach] disperses the essence [of the food] to the liver. [The liver] moves qi to the sinews. [Here now] the liver qi is depleted and moves contrary [to its normal direction]; in addition, it meets cool [qi] in the center. Hence [patients suffer from] sounds in the abdomen and from semiliquid stools. The qi of metal is clear and cool. Hence when cool rain arrives frequently, that is because metal can generate water."

75 Wang Bing: "When metal [qi] dominates the entire year and when fire qi does not take revenge, then the greenish colored grain does not develop fruits."

69-408-5
<If in the upper [half of the year] yang brilliance comes down [to join the inad-
equacy of wood qi], the qi of generation loses [its rank as] policy [maker].
Herbs and trees blossom twice.[76]
In this case the qi of transformation is fast.[77]>

<Venus and Saturn correspond to this above.>

<Under its rule [things turn] old early.>[78]

When it comes to revenge, then
there is flaming summerheat [as if there were] fire flowing.
That which is of damp nature dries out;
herbs and trees that are soft and brittle, they are scorched and wither.
From their lower body [sections] they come to life again.[79]
Flowers and fruit transform simultaneously.[80]

----

76 Zhongyi yanjiuyuan...: "The qi of spring and generation, which is associated with
wood, cannot take over control. Because the qi of wood is weak, the blossoming of
herbs and trees in spring is curtailed. Only in summer and autumn, when fire and soil
rule, the myriad things flourish in abundance. Hence herbs and trees, too, blossom a
second time."

77 Zhongyi yanjiuyuan...: "The qi of transformation is the qi of dampness, i.e., of
soil."

78 Wang Bing: "This applies to all *ding* years. When in *ding mao* and *ding you* years
yang brilliance [qi] appears in the upper [half of the year], then these are called 'years
of heavenly punishment.' The qi of metal takes over [control] and dominates wood
under heaven. Hence the qi of generation loses its command and herbs and trees
flourish twice. Because the qi of generation loses its command, the tree blossoms open
late. Because the qi of metal curbs the wood, the [trees] begin to blossom and develop
ripe fruits only in autumn and summer. Because the qi of transformation is urgent and
fast, a success is achieved [even] that late. When the qi of metal dominates the wood,
heaven corresponds to this. Hence the light of Venus is very bright. Because the qi of
wood is diminished, the qi of the soil remains unrestrained. As a result, the qi of transformation causes fast generation and growth. When the [qi of] wood is diminished
and the [qi of] metal dominates, the qi of heaven corresponds to this. Hence Saturn
and Venus are shiny and bright. When greenish colored things age and fall down early,
this is also because the wood has little [qi] and is occupied by metal."

79 Zhongyi yanjiuyuan...: "The wood is weak, the metal dominates, and the qi of fire
comes to take revenge."

80 Zhongyi yanjiuyuan...: "Blossoming and fruit bearing appear at the same time."

[People] suffer from cold and heat, sores and ulcers, heat rashes[81] and papules, *yong*-abscesses, and pimples.

<Mars and Venus correspond to this above.[82]>

<Its grain are white and hard.>[83]

69-409-2
<White dew descends early.
The qi of gathering and killing prevails.
Cold and rain harm the things.
The creatures eat what is sweet and yellow.[84]
The spleen, which is soil, receives evil.
The red qi transforms late.
The qi of the heart governs late.
Above [it] dominates the lung, i.e., the metal.
Hence white qi yields.
Its grain do not reach maturity.
[People suffer from] cough and stuffy nose. >[85]

<Mars and Venus correspond to this above.[86]>

69-409-6
If in a year [associated with fire the qi of] fire is inadequate,

---

81 *NJCD*/355: "痱 is 痱子, 'heat rashes.'"

82 Zhang Zhicong: "Mars increases in light; Venus loses it luster."

83 Wang Bing: "When fire qi takes revenge against metal, massive heat develops in summer. Hence those of the myriad things that are damp in nature change to dryness. Flowing fire melts things. Hence all soft and brittle herbs and trees, as well as climbing plants, dry out and die in their upper parts while below their bodies come to life again. When the heat is moderate, few die; when the heat is strong, many die." Zhongyi yanjiuyuan...: "White is the color of metal. 堅 has the meaning of hard and full. Grains that are white and hard belong to the metal. The metal is punished by fire. Hence they may blossom, but they cannot develop fruits."

84 Zhang Jiebin: "When [the qi of] metal dominates, [the qi of] fire is bound to be weak. When [the qi of] fire is weak, [the qi of] soil is bound to have no strength. Hence creatures eat things that are sweet in taste and yellow in color because sweet and yellow are associated with soil.

85 Wang Bing: "鼽 is: Water leaves from inside the nose." Zhang Jiebin: "鼽 is 'stuffy nose.'" 1508/10: "鼽 refers to 'stuffy nose' or 'running nose' here."

86 Zhongyi yanjiuyuan...: "Mars increases in brilliance; Venus turns dark."

cold prevails everywhere.[87]
The policy of growth does not operate.[88]
Once things have blossomed they fall down.
If the freezing cold is severe, then
the yang qi fails to transform.
[The cold] breaks what blossoms and what is beautiful.

<Mercury corresponds above.[89]>

People suffer from
pain in the chest;
the flanks have propping fullness.
The two flanks ache.
There is pain in the breast, the back, in the region of the shoulder and shoul-
derblades and inside the two arms.
[The qi is] oppressed [in the body]. [Patients experience] dizziness and their
eyes are clouded.
The heart aches and there is sudden muteness.
The chest and the abdomen are enlarged.
The region below the flanks, the lower back, and the back pull on each other
and have pain.
[When this is] severe, then
[the body] is bent and cannot be stretched.
The pelvic bone and the thigh bone [feel] as if severed.[90]

<Mars and Mercury correspond to this above.[91]>

<[The color of] its grain is vermilion.>

---

87 Zhang Jiebin: "These are the six *gui* years. The [qi of] fire is inadequate and the [qi
of water] occupies its [territory]. Hence cold prevails everywhere."

88 Zhongyi yanjiuyuan...: "The qi of growth, i.e., of summer cannot take over control."

89 Wang Bing: "The fire is diminished and water dominates. Hence cold moves everywhere. When the command of growth is not realized, then the appearance of the
things deteriorates and they fall down. Because the qi of fire is diminished, the qi
of water abounds vastly. Of the images appearing in heaven, Mercury is particularly
bright."

90 Wang Bing: "This applies to all *gui* years. The [patients] suffer at locations passed
by the [movement in the respective] vessels."

91 Zhongyi yanjiuyuan...: "Water dominates and occupies the fire. Hence Mars turns
dull and loses its luster while Mercury is bright and shiny."

69-410-3
When it comes to revenge, then
dust [causes] pressure.
Also, massive rain arrives. ⁹²
Black qi is disgraced as a result.⁹³

[People]
suffer from duck-like semiliquid stools and from abdominal fullness.
Food and beverages do not move down.
[They suffer from] cold center and intestinal sounds,
from diarrheal outpour and abdominal pain,
from sudden cramps, limpness, and blocks.
The feet [can] not support the body.

<Saturn and Mercury correspond to this above. >

<Dark grain do not ripen. >⁹⁴

69-410-6
If in a year [associated with soil the qi of] soil is inadequate,
wind prevails everywhere.⁹⁵
The qi of transformation cannot give commands.
Herbs and trees are lush and blossom.

---

92 Zhang Zhicong: "埃 is 土, 'soil.' 鬱 is 烝, 'steam.' The qi of dampness, i.e., of soil
steams upwards hence massive rain is bound to come. That is what is called 'the qi of
the earth rises and forms clouds and rain.'"

93 Zhang Zhicong: " 'Black qi' is the qi of water. 辱 is 下, 'to put down.' The qi of soil
returns in revenge and the qi of water hides."

94 Wang Bing: "Dust, haziness, clouds, and rain are realizations of soil [qi]. To take
revenge against cold qi, [soil qi] is bound to do so with dampness. When dampness qi
floods the interior, then this generates abdominal disease and the body becomes heavy.
Hence there are symptoms as [described] here. 'Black qi' is the qi of water. 辱 is 屈辱,
'to insult.' 鶩 is 鴨, 'duck.' The soil takes revenge against the water. Hence the light of
Saturn is bright and shiny. When it comes down [to join the inadequacy of the qi of
fire] from above, then in the [sections on earth] associated with the lodges invaded [by
Saturn] people are affected by disease and disaster."

95 Zhang Jiebin: "These are the six *ji* years. The [qi of] soil is inadequate and the [qi
of wood] occupies its [territory]. Hence wind prevails."

If there whirling and surging are severe, then
[the plants] blossom, but do not develop fruits.[96]

<Jupiter corresponds above.[97]>

People suffer from
outflow of [undigested] food and cholera.
The body is heavy; the abdomen has pain.
The sinews and bones shake back and forth.[98]
The muscles and the flesh twitch and are sore. [People] tend to be angry.[99]

The qi of storage[100] controls the affairs.
Hibernating creatures hide away early.
Everybody suffers from cold center.

<Jupiter and Saturn correspond to this above.[101]>

<Its grain are yellow.>[102]

69-410-9
When it comes to revenge, then

---

96 Zhang Zhicong: "The soil is responsible for the maturing of things. Hence herbs
and trees may blossom, still they do not generate fruits."

97 Wang Bing: "Wood acts without virtue. Wood qi prevails, hence the qi of transformation cannot give orders. The qi of generation assumes authority alone. Hence herbs
and trees flourish profusely. When wind blows and [things are] whirled up severely,
that is because the qi of wood does not act virtuously. The qi of soil is diminished.
Hence no fruits develop. When the [qi of] soil is inadequate, [the qi of] wood occupies its [territory]. Hence Jupiter appears in brilliance."

98 Wang Bing: "繇 is 搖, 'to shake.'" See 1179/49 and 916/52 for evidence.

99 Zhongyi yanjiuyuan...: "All these are [signs of] harm caused by wind, i.e., wood
to the soil. The liver rules the sinews and it controls free outflow. Among the affects
it [is in charge of] anger."

100 Zhongyi yanjiuyuan...: "This refers to the qi of winter, cold, and water."

101 Zhongyi yanjiuyuan...: "Saturn is dark and Jupiter is bright."

102 Wang Bing: "This applies to all *ji* years. Wind takes residence in the stomach.
Hence [people] suffer from illnesses as [described] here. The qi of soil is inadequate
and water causes transformations together with it. Hence the qi of storage assumes
control. Hibernating creatures hide early at the location of the yang qi and all people
suffer from cold center. 繇 is 搖, 'to shake.'" Lin Yi et al.: "*Su wen* 74 has 筋骨繇併.
Hence the character 復 may be an erroneous writing of 併, 'to have a cramp.'"

the policy of gathering is harsh and violent.
The eminent trees age and wither.[103]
Chest and flanks have violent pain,
pulling downwards on the lower abdomen.
[Patients] tend to breathe deeply.[104]

69-410-10
<The creatures eat what is sweet and yellow;
Qi settles in the spleen.
Yellow grain are diminished.
People eat little; [food] has lost its flavor.[105]
Greenish grain are harmed. >[106]

<Venus and Jupiter correspond to this above.[107]>

<If in the upper [half of the year] ceasing yin [qi] comes down [to join the
inadequancy of the qi of soil],
flowing water does not freeze to ice.
The hibernating creatures appear.

---

103 670/7: "In antiquity, the meaning of 大, 'tall,' was occasionally expressed by the
term 名." See also *Su wen* 2-12-4, note 42.

104 Zhongyi yanjiuyuan...: "Wood is active [against soil] and [the child of soil, i.e.,]
metal takes revenge. [Hence] liver and gallbladder fall ill. The vessels of liver and gallbladder spread into chest and flanks. Hence chest and flanks experience sudden pain.
The liver vessel encircles the yin [i.e., sexual] organ and arrives in the lower abdomen.
Hence the pain moves downwards and pulls on the lower abdomen."

105 Zhongyi yanjiuyuan...: "When the [qi of] metal flourishes, the [qi of] fire is
bound to be weak. When the [qi of] fire is weak, the [qi of] soil is bound to have no
strength. When the spleen, i.e., soil, is depleted and has no strength, people suffer in
that they eat and drink less."

106 Wang Bing: "The qi of metal takes revenge against the wood. Hence eminent trees
age and wither. Metal enters the soil. That is, the mother embraces her child. Hence
creatures eat the inside of sweet and yellow things. Metal enters the soil. Hence [met-
al] qi takes residence in the spleen. When the qi of metal arrives in massive quantities,
it takes revenge against the enemies of soil, [i.e., against wood]. Hence yellow grain
have less fruits and greenish grain do not ripen."

107 Zhongyi yanjiuyuan...: "Metal dominates and restrains wood. Hence Venus increases its luster while Jupiter loses its brightness."

The qi of storage does not operate.[108]
The white [qi] does not take revenge.[109]>

<Jupiter corresponds above.[110]>

<In this case people are healthy.>[111]

69-411-4
If in a year [associated with metal the qi of] metal is inadequate,
flaming fire prevails.[112]
The qi of generation operates.
The qi of growth dominates alone.
Hence all things are lush,
hence dryness melting prevails.[113]

<Mars corresponds above.[114]>

---

108 Zhongyi yanjiuyuan...: "When ceasing yin [qi] arrives in the upper [half of the year], then minor yang [qi] is at the fountain. When the second half of the year is ruled by the minister fire of minor yang, then winter cannot give its order of cold. This, in turn, causes that flowing waters cannot freeze to ice and the hibernating creatures leave their hiding places."

109 Zhongyi yanjiuyuan...: "White is the color of metal. In the second half of the year the qi of wood has been pacified already. Hence the qi of metal does not come again to take revenge."

110 Zhongyi yanjiuyuan...: "Because the qi of metal does not come to restrain the [qi of] wood, the light of Jupiter is bright."

111 Wang Bing: "In *ji hai* and *ji si* years the ceasing yin appears in the upper [half] of the year; the minor yang is at the fountain. [That is,] fire is in control on the earth. Hence the hibernating creatures come out and flowing water does not turn into ice. Metal cannot take revenge. Hence the appearance of the stars in that year is as usual; people are healthy and do not suffer from illness." Zhongyi yanjiuyuan...: "When in autumn and winter the qi of wood is pacified and the qi of metal does not come to take revenge, people live amidst a pacified qi. Hence they are healthy and generate few diseases."

112 Zhang Jiebin: "These are the six *yi* years. The [qi of] metal is inadequate and the [qi of] fire occupies its [territory]. Hence flaming fire prevails."

113 Zhongyi yanjiuyuan...: "爍 is 燒灼, 'to burn.'"

114 Wang Bing: "Fire does not act virtuously and attacks metal. Perilous flames flow around so that great heat develops in summer. .. The images in heaven correspond to this. Hence Mars appears in great brilliance." Zhang Zhicong: "Metal cannot restrain wood. Hence the qi of wood, [i.e., the qi of] generation is realized, and the qi of fire,

People suffer from
pressure and heaviness in their shoulders and back, from
stuffy nose and from sneezing. Blood stools pour out below.[115]
The qi of gathering is belated.[116]

<Venus corresponds above.[117] >

<Its grain are hard and have awns.>[118]

69-411-6
When it comes to revenge, then
cold rain arrives all of a sudden.
This [causes] ice, hail, frost, and snow to fall and kill things.[119]

[People suffer from] yin recession and barrier.
Yang [qi] contrary [to its regular course] moves upwards;
head and brain's door[120] have pain.
It spreads to the fontanella peak, and heat develops.

<Mercury corresponds above. >

[i.e., the qi of] growth dominates alone. Because the qi of generation and growth abound, all things flourish. Because the qi of fire dominates alone dryness melting prevails. Mars corresponds above in that its light rays multiply."

115 Wang Bing: "This applies to all *yi* years. 瞀 is 悶, 'a feeling of pressure in the chest.' This disease results from taking in heat evil." See *Su wen* 71 for 瞀悶. In contrast to Wang Bing, Zhang Zhicong: "To look down and bow the head is called 瞀. Stuffy nose is a [manifestation of a] disease in the lung. When blood stools flow out downwards, [that is because] fire presses blood liquid to flow downwards."

116 Wang Bing: "[The qi of] gathering is the qi of metal. Fire qi dominates first; hence the qi of gathering is belated." Zhang Zhicong: "Metal is restrained by [fire]. Hence the qi of gathering prevails only late in autumn."

117 Wang Bing: "When fire qi dominates metal, metal cannot abound. When Mars moves contrary to [its] regular course, then the sections [on earth] associated with the lodges [passed through by Mars] experience disease." Lin Yi et al.: "Wang Bing's reference to Mars suggests that his *Su wen* text included a statement about Mars." Zhang Zhicong: "Venus corresponds above in that it loses its color."

118 Zhang Zhicong: "That is, they develop fruits."

119 Cheng Shide et al.: "When [the qi of] metal is weak and [the qi of] fire is active, the qi of water, which is the child of metal, arrives to take revenge."

120 Possibly a reference to a location above the neck at the back of the skull where an acupuncture point of identical designation is situated.

<Grain of vermilion color do not ripen.>
<People [suffer from]
sores in the mouth.
In severe cases, the heart aches.[121]>

69-412-2
If in a year [associated with water the qi of] water is inadequate,
dampness prevails everywhere.[122]
The qi of growth operates contrary [to what is normal].
Transformations enacted by it are fast.
Summerheat and rain arrive frequently.

<Saturn corresponds above.[123]>

People suffer from
abdominal fullness and heavy body, from
soggy outflow and from cold ulcers with water running out.
The lower back and thighs develop pain.
The knee bays, the calves, the thighs, and the knees do not move comfortably.
[They suffer from] vexation and grievance; the feet limp and are cool because
of receding [yang qi].
Their legs ache below.

69-412-4
[When this is severe], then

---

121 Wang Bing: "When cold qi diminishes the fire, then ice, hail, frost, and snow appear. ... 'Yin recession' is to say: cold moves contrary [to its normal direction]. 格 is 至,
'to approach'; it is also 拒, 'to resist.' When water moves to diminish fire in order to
save the metal from its hardship, the images of heaven correspond to this. Hence Mercury is bright. Grain of vermilion color is destroyed by frost and hail." Zhang Jiebin:
"厥 is 逆, 'countermovement.' 格 is 拒, 'to ward off.' When cold dominates below, then
yin [qi] recedes and wards off yang qi which [in turn] rises contrary [to its normal
direction]. That is called 'fire without root.'"

122 Zhang Jiebin: "These are the six *xin* years. The [qi of] water is inadequate and [the
qi of] soil occupies [its terriotry]. Hence dampness prevails everywhere."

123 Wang Bing: "Dampness prevails everywhere, that is to say: it rains frequently.
'Transformations are fast' is to say: things ripen early. Fire and dampness do both
transform. Hence the qi of transformation, [i.e., the qi of] soil acts fast. Summerheat
and rain arrive frequently. When [the qi of] water is inadequate and [the qi of] soil
dominates it, then the image of Saturn increases in brightness."

the instep is swollen.[124]
The qi of storage is not [in the rank of] policy [maker].
The kidney qi is not balanced.

<Mercury corresponds above.>

<Its grain are black millet.>[125]

<If in the upper [half of the year] major yin [qi] comes down [to join the inad-
equacy of the qi of water],
then massive cold sets in frequently.
The hibernating creatures hide away early.
The earth accumulates solid ice.[126]
Yang light does not govern.
People suffer from cold disease in the lower sections.
[When this is] severe, then the abdomen is full and there is surface swelling.>

---

124 Zhongyi yanjiuyuan...: "The [qi of] water is inadequate and [the qi of] soil occupies its [territory]. When the [qi of] soil flourishes overly excessive, the conduit of
the spleen itself will fall ill. The spleen rules the muscles and the flesh. In case of spleen
disease, dampness stays in the muscles and in the flesh and spreads to the sinews and
vessels. As a result lameness in the feet and a heavy body appear. When the movement
of the spleen loses its regularity, then this results in moist outflow and abdominal fullness. The essence of the spleen cannot be transported further to be spread [through
the body]; on the contrary it transforms into phlegm turbidity which follows the
spleen conduit to pour upwards into the chest. There it influences the qi dynamics
which results in vexation. The activity of the spleen, [i.e., the qi of] soil, harms the
yang [qi] of the kindeys. When the yang [qi] of the kidneys is depleted, it cannot generate warmth. Hence the four limbs turn 'cold because of receding [yang qi],' as well
as cold ulcers and running water. The conduit vessels of the kidneys encircle the lower
back, the thighs, the calves, the knees, and the soles of the feet, .. hence the lower back
and the thighs develop pain, the knee bays, the thighs, and the knees do not move
comfortably, the upper side of the feet is swollen and the legs ache below." 1682/43:
"跗腫 is 足腫, 'swollen feet.'"

125 Wang Bing: "The qi of storage is unable to spread its commands. Hence the kidney qi cannot cause harmony inside. 衡 is 平, 'balanced.' Mercury corresponds in that
its brilliance decreases. Sometimes it meets with Saturn. The [sections on earth] associated with the lodges [passed through by Mercury and Saturn] experience disaster."

126 Gao Jiwu/719: "地積堅冰 is: 'The water accumulated on the earth turns into
thick ice.'"

<Saturn corresponds above.>
<It is responsible for yellow grain.>[127]

69-412-8
When it comes to revenge, then
strong wind emerges suddenly.
The herbs are bent down and the [leaves of the] trees fall.
The young and the grown do not appear fresh.
The facial complexion changes frequently.[128]
Sinews and bones both[129] receive punishment.[130]
The flesh twitches and has spasms.
Eye vision is unclear.
Things break open and crack.[131]
The muscles and the flesh develop papules.
The qi collects in the diaphragm and
there is pain in the heart and in the abdomen."[132]

---

127 Wang Bing: "This applies to all *xin* years. In *xin chou* and *xin wei* years major yin appears in the upper [half of the year] and major yang appears at the fountain. Hence massive cold occurs frequently. The soil qi abounds alone. Hence Saturn increases in brilliance."

128 Zhongyi yanjiuyuan...: "The facial region is traversed mainly by the yang brilliance conduit vessels. The yang brilliance [qi] is associated with soil. When [the qi of] water is weak and [the qi of] soil dominates, [the qi of] wood arrives to take revenge. This affects the qi of the liver in the human body. As a result, the [qi of the] liver flourishes and occupies the stomach, [i.e., the territory of the qi of] soil. This [in turn] causes the facial region to change its color frequently."

129 Fang Wenhui/151: "并 is 皆, 'all.'" In contrast, Zhongyi yanjiuyuan...: "并 refers to 拘挛, 'crooked,' 'cramped.'"

130 Fang Wenhui/151: "辟 is identical to 僻, used here as a verb in the sense of 受邪, 'to receive evil.'"

131 Zhongyi yanjiuyuan...: "疎 is 分开, 'to open.' 壨 refers to things that crack because they were exposed to wind."

132 Zhongyi yanjiuyuan...: "The [qi of] soil flourishes and the qi of wood takes revenge. [The qi of] wood in heaven is wind. Wind evil attacks from the outside and harms the muscles and the skin. It accumulates and develops wind pustules. The qi of wood penetrates the liver. The qi of the liver gathers in the diaphragm. When the dynamics do not move on, then this generates pain in the [region of the] heart and in the abdomen."

<The yellow qi is harmed.
Its grain do not ripen.>
<Jupiter corresponds above.[133]>

69-413-1
[Huang] Di:
"Good!
I should like to hear about the respective seasons."

Qi Bo:
"An encompassing question, indeed!

[In a year] when the [qi of] wood is inadequate,
if in spring there is transformation [resulting in] pleasant tones [produced by] singing twigs,[134]
then in autumn there is a policy of fog and dew and coolness.
If in spring there is a domination of chilling temperatures, which injures and destroys,
then in summer there is a revenge [resulting in] flaming summerheat, burning, and melting.[135]

---

133 Wang Bing: "Wood takes revenge against soil. Hence yellow qi is harmed and yellow grain does not ripen. That is to say, when the fruits do not ripen, then there is nothing to put into (登) the sacrificial containers." Lin Yi et al.: "This should be 'Jupiter and Saturn correspond to this above.'"

134 Zhongyi yanjiuyuan...: "鳴條 refers to the sounds generated by wind blowing into the branches (枝條) of trees. 律 symbolizes ancient music." Cheng Shide et al.: "鳴條律暢 refers to the sounds generated by wind making trees move. These sounds are 'regular' (條) and 'pleasant' (暢)."

135 Zhang Jiebin: "When [the qi is] harmonious, then this results in 'transformation' and 'policy' as the regular course of the periods. When [the qi is] not harmonious, then this results in 'domination' and 'revenge' as changes of the qi. For example, if in a year [associated with] wood [the qi of wood] is inadequate, [the qi of] metal should overcome it. If the [qi of] metal does not arrive to overcome [the qi of wood] and if the qi of wood is not harmed, then in spring transformation [results in] regular and pleasant sounds and tones. When fall arrives, [the qi of] metal is not affected by any revenge and it can realize its policy of dew and fog, clarity and coolness. That is a harmonious [succession of] qi."

Its disasters[136] occur in the East.[137]
Its depot is the liver.
Its diseases
internally lodge in the upper and lower flanks;
externally they are in the joints.[138]

69-413-4
[In a year] when the fire [qi] is inadequate,
if in summer transformation [results in] lucidity and brilliance, luminosity and clearness,
then in winter there is a policy of harsh sternness and frost and cold.
If in summer there is a domination of chilling temperatures and of piercing frost,
then there is a revenge [resulting in] darkness caused by dust and massive rain that may occur when it is not their time.

Its disasters occur in the South.[139]
Its depot is the heart.
Its diseases
internally lodge in the breast and in the flanks;
externally they are in the conduits and network [vessels].[140]

69-413-7
[In a year] when the soil [qi] is inadequate,

---

136 Zhang Jiebin: "眚 is 災眚, 'catastrophic disaster.'"

137 Wang Bing: "Transformation refers to a harmonious qi. Domination refers to the qi of metal. Revenge refers to the qi of fire. When fire takes revenge against metal it is always because of [a weakness of] wood. Hence all catastrophes occur in the East. The same applies to all the other catastrophes [mentioned below]."

138 Zhongyi yanjiuyuan...: "The liver vessel spreads through the lower and upper flanks. Hence liver disease can lodge in the lower and upper flanks internally. The liver rules the sinews. The joints are the palaces of the sinews. Hence liver diseases can be situated in the joints externally."

139 Wang Bing: "Transformation refers to the virtue of fire. Domination refers to ravaging of water. Revenge refers to change caused by the soil. The South refers to [associated with] fire."

140 Zhongyi yanjiuyuan...: "The heart rules the blood vessels; their courses pass through chest and flanks. Hence its diseases lodge in the chest and in the flanks internally; externally they are situated in the conduits and network [vessels]."

if at the [ends of the] four ropes[141] transformation [results in] clouds of dust
and moisture,
then in spring there is a policy of singing twigs and drumming and breaking
open.
If at the [ends of] the four ropes there appears a change to shaking and pulling,
whirling and surging,
then in autumn there is a revenge [resulting in] sternness and killing and in
long lasting rain.

Its disasters occur at the [ends of the] four ropes.
Its depot is the spleen.
Its diseases
internally lodge in the heart and abdomen;
externally they are in the muscles, in the flesh, and in the four limbs.[142]

69-413-10
[In a year] when the metal [qi] is inadequate,
if in summer there is a command of luminosity and clearness, pressure, and
steam,
then,
then in winter there is a response of harsh freezing, correction, and sternness.
If in summer there is a change to flaming, melting, burning and blazing,
then in autumn there is a revenge [resulting in] ice, hail, frost, and snow.

---

141 Wang Bing: "The [four ropes] are the South-East, the North-East, the South-
West, and the North-West. 維 is 隅, 'corner.' That is to say: the sun is in the four cor-
ner-months" 26/46: "四維 is 四隅月, 'the four corner months,' i.e., the final 18 days of
each season when the soil qi rules." Zhongyi yanjiuyuan...: "A second meaning refers
to the four months *chen*, *xu*, *chou*, and *wei* in the course of the seasons, i.e., the third,
ninth, twelfth, and sixth months. They, too, are called 四維. A third meaning refers to
the four terms when the spleen, [i.e., the qi of] soil, flourishes [in the course of the
seasons]. A fourth meaning refers to the four limbs of the human body. In the present
context, 四維 refers to the seasons." See also 1673/44 for a detailed discussion.

142 Sun Yirang: "*Su wen* 70 has 發生之紀, 其德鳴靡啟坼. *Su wen* 71 has 其化鳴紊
啟坼. These passages and the present wording 鳴條鼓坼 are only slightly different;
their meaning is the same. I suspect that 鳴條 should be 鳴璺, 'the sound of cracking,' and 鼓 should be 啟, 'to open.' .. 條, 紊, and 靡 are all erroneous characters [for
鳴璺]." Wang Hongtu et al. /158: "Neither 鳴條, nor 鳴靡, nor 鳴紊 are established
expressions; if they were read as 鳴璺, they would make sense." If one were to follow
Sun Yirang and Wang Hongtu et al., the wording should be "In spring there is the
sound of cracking and stretching." Wang Bing: "The four ropes and the center are
ruled by the spleen."

Its disasters occur in the West.
Its depot is the lung.
Its diseases
internally lodge in the breast, in the flanks, in the shoulder, and in the back;
externally they are in the skin and the body hair.[143]

[In a year] when the water [qi] is inadequate,
if at the [ends of the] four ropes transformation [results in] torrential flooding
and moisture and in clouds of dust,
then there is a response of mild wind, of generation and development that may
occur when it is not their time.
If at the [ends of the] four ropes there appears a change to darkness because of
dust and to flooding because of rainstorms,
then there is a revenge [resulting in] whirling and moving here and there, in
shaking and pulling that may occur when it is not their time.

Its disasters occur in the North.[144]
Its depot are the kidneys.
Its diseases
internally lodge in the lower back, the spine, the bones and the marrow;
externally they are in the ravines and valleys [of the flesh], in the calves and
knees.[145]

69-414-2
Now,
the policies of the five periods
are like weight and beam [of a balance].

---

143 Zhongyi yanjiuyuan...: "The lung is associated with metal; it gives its orders in
autumn. The breast, flanks, shoulders, and back are regions surrounding it. Skin and
hair are its external associates. Hence when [a person] suffers from a disease [in the
lung], this may manifest itself in the regions surrounding the lung and in its external
associates."

144 Wang Bing: "Whirling, moving here and there, shaking and pulling are all caused
by strong winds." Lin Yi et al.: "In these accounts of [years when the qi of] metal and
water are inadequate, the transformations, commands, and responses caused by fire
and soil are listed first. Hence there is no need to speak of consequences in autumn
and winter. Next are discussed the changes resulting from fire and soil as they are
engaged in domination and revenge."

145 Wang Bing: "Large junctions of flesh are called 谷, 'valleys'; small junctions of flesh
are called 谿, 'ravines.'"

'What is up on high, they press it down;
what is below, they raise it.'
'What transforms, they correspond to it;
what changes, they revenge it.'[146]

That is the structure of generation, growth, transformation, completion, gathering, and storage; that is the regularity of qi.
When this regularity is lost, then the four [seasonal qi] of heaven and earth are obstructed.[147]

Hence when it is said:
'Movement and resting in heaven and on the earth,
the spirit brilliance sets up their arrangement.
As for the leaving and returning of yin and yang,
cold and summerheat [and the remaining six qi] appear as their manifestations,'[148]
then this means just the same."

69-414-6
[Huang] Di:
"What you, Sir, have stated about the changes of the five qi,
and about the responses in the four seasons,
can be called encompassing.

Now, when the movement of the qi is in disorder and
when it is active only accidentally,
when it develops irregular events and
when catastrophes come together suddenly,
how can this be predicted?"

---

146 Zhang Jiebin: "Now, the Way of heaven and earth, of yin and yang resembles the balance of weight and beam: there must not be the slightest deviation. Hence what is high up and excessively active, it must be pressed down because this is [a sign of] excess. What is low and moves down must be lifted because this is [a sign of] inadequacy. What is correct and transforms, that is followed by what corresponds to it. There is no animosity among the [earlier and the latter]. What is evil and causes changes, that is followed by what takes revenge. [Evil] is succeeded by restraint."

147 Wang Bing: "When the structure of regularity is lost, then the qi of the four seasons of heaven and earth are obstructed and have nowhere to move. Hence movement must come to rest and domination must be overcome by revenge."

148 For textual parallels, see *Su wen* 67-370-1.

Qi Bo:
"Now, the movements of the qi [indicating] changes
have never been regular;
virtues, transformations, policies, commands, catastrophes, and changes
are the different manifestations of [movements indicating changes]."

[Huang] Di:
"What is that to say?"

69-414-9
Qi Bo:
"The East generates wind.
Wind generates wood.
Its virtue is to extend harmony.[149]
Its transformation [brings about] generation and blossoming.[150]
Its policy is unfolding and opening up.[151]
Its command is wind.
Its change [to the extreme causes] shaking and effusion.[152]
Its catastrophes are dispersion and falling down.[153]

The South generates the heat.
Heat generates fire.
Its virtue is obviousness and clarity.
Its transformation [brings about] opulence and lushness.
Its policy is brilliance and luster.
Its command is heat.
Its change [to the extreme causes] fusing and melting.
Its catastrophe is burning heat.

The center generates dampness.
Dampness generates soil.
Its virtue is humidity and steam.[154]
Its transformation [brings about] prosperity and perfection.

---

149 Wang Bing: "敷 is 布, 'to spread.' 和 is 和氣, 'harmonious qi.'"

150 Wang Bing: "榮 is 榮滋, 'prosperous.'"

151 Wang Bing: "舒 is 展, 'to unfold,' 'to develop.' 啟 is 開, 'to open.'"

152 Wang Bing: "振 is 怒, 'excitement,' 'anger.' 發 is 出, 'to appear,' 'to leave.'"

153 1788/45: "The meaning of 落 in the present context is 'to fall down' (降落) and 'to stay at one place' (留止)."

154 Wang Bing: "溽 is 濕, 'dampness.' 蒸 is 熱, 'heat.'"

Its policy is peace and resting.
Its command is dampness.
Its change [to the extreme causes] floodings because of rainstorms.[155]
Its catastrophes are continuing rain and massive flooding.

69-415-2
The West generates dryness.
Dryness generates metal.
Its virtue is clearness and cleanliness.
Its transformation [brings about] tightness and contraction.[156]
Its policy is force and cutting.[157]
Its command is dryness.
Its change [to the extreme causes] sternness and killing.
Its catastrophes are aging and falling down.[158]

The North generates cold.
Cold generates water.
Its virtue is chilling temperature.[159]
Its transformation [brings about] clarity and tranquility.[160]
Its policy is freezing and sternness.
Its command is cold.
Its change [to the extreme causes] piercing cold.
Its catastrophes are ice, snow, frosts, and hail.

Hence through investigating their movement,
there is virtue and there is transformation,
there is policy and there is command,
there is change and there are catastrophes [to be recognized],
and [how all] things originate from them,
and [how] man corresponds to them."[161]

---

155 Wang Bing: "驟注 is 急雨, 'heavy rain.'"

156 Wang Bing: "緊 is 縮, 'to bind tight.' 斂 is 收, 'to accumulate.'"

157 Wang Bing: "勁 is 銳, 'piercing,' 'resolute.' 切 is 急, 'urgent.'"

158 Wang Bing: "When the killing qi is too extreme, then trees wither and fall down."

159 Wang Bing: "凄滄 is 薄寒, 'weak cold.'"

160 Wang Bing: "謐 is 靜, 'no motion.'"

161 Wang Bing: "Virtue, transformation, policy, and command are [manifestations of] a harmonious qi. Whether it moves or pauses, dominates or takes revenge, all this is conferred upon the myriad beings for their generation and perfection. Changes and

[Huang] Di:
"You, Sir, have outlined the manifestations of [each] year.
When their [qi] is inadequate or present in great excess,
to this the five stars correspond above.

Now, if
virtue and transformation, policy and command,
catastrophes and disasters,¹⁶² changes and alterations
occur irregularly and
make sudden movements,
do they (i.e, the five stars) change [their movement] because of this?"

69-415-9
Qi Bo:
"They follow heaven and carry out its [commands].
Hence there is no random movement and
there is nothing that fails to correspond.¹⁶³

When it comes to sudden movements,
these are changes in the interaction of qi.
In this case the [stars] do not correspond to it.

Hence when it is said:
'Correspondence is with the regular; there is no correspondence with the sudden,'
then this means just the same."¹⁶⁴

---

catastrophes are [manifestations of] a killing qi. It emerges suddenly; it moves violently and its passage causes harm. Even though all these are realizations of intrinsic movement and tranquility of heaven and earth, there are, nevertheless, some things that cannot bear such movement. They receive harm, they fall ill, and they die."

162 變易 interpreted here as 變異.

163 Zhang Jiebin: "承天而行 is to say: the manifestations [indicating excessive or inadequate presence of qi] of a year follow the periods of heaven. Hence there is no disorderly movement of qi and as far as the appearance of the five stars is concerned, they correspond to any movement."

164 Zhang Zhicong: " 'Sudden movements' are changes in the qi interactions in the course of the four seasons. Above they have no correspondence in [the appearance of] the five stars. Hence when [the text] states 'correspondence is with the regular, there is no correspondence with the sudden,' this means just the same."

[Huang] Di:

"When they correspond, how is that?"

Qi Bo:

"They always follow the transformation of the respective qi."[165]

69-416-1
[Huang] Di:

"When they pass [along heaven] slow or fast,[166] contrary [to their regular course] or in accordance [with it], how is that?"[167]

Qi Bo:

"When in pursuing their path they remain stationary [at one place] for a long time, or when they move contrary [to their regular course] and keep [their position for a while] and decrease in size, this is called 'they inspect what is below.'[168]

When in pursuing their paths they vanish, when after they have vanished they come [back] fast and when they pass through in curves, this is called 'they inquire about neglect and transgressions.'

---

165 Wang Bing: "The transformations of Jupiter correspond to the wind; the transformations of Mars correspond to heat; the transformations of Saturn correspond to dampness; the transformations of Venus correspond to dryness; the transformations of Mercury correspond to cold. When the qi changes, then [the five stars] correspond. Hence each star transforms following [the respective] qi. Earlier the text stated that revenge and domination all have their correspondences [in the five stars] above. Here now it states: [the stars] correspond to the regular, they do not correspond to the sudden. That is, as long as no major changes occur, [the stars above] do not correspond."

166 2568/49: "The use of 之 in the middle of this sentence is simply for stylistic reasons. 之 has no meaning here whatsoever." We read 之 as a genitive marker.

167 See 595/47 for a detailed discussion of the astronomical notions presented in the following statements.

168 Wang Bing: "以道 is 順行, 'to pass along [a given way].' 留久 is to say: 過應留之日數也, 'to exceed the number of days [a star] should remain [at a certain place]. 省下 is to say: To examine whether the common people and the noblemen under heaven act virtuously or commit transgressions." Cheng Shide et al.: "When they move from West to East, that is 順, 'in accordance' [with their normal direction]; from East to West, that is 逆, 'contrary' [to their normal direction]. When they are stationary and do not move, that is 留, 'to remain' [at one position]. When the time they are stationary is long, that is called 守, 'they keep' [their position]."

When they remain stationary for a long time and then [return in] a circle, when they alternately leave and come close [again], this is called 'they deliberate upon catastrophes [to be imposed on the people] in relation to their virtue.'[169]

69-416-5
When it responds to something near, then [the star] is small; when it responds to something far away, then [the star] is big.[170]

When the rays [of the stars] are twice as big in size as normal, the transformations [they cause] will be severe.[171]

When they are three times as big as normal, the disasters [they cause] will be about to break out.

When they are half as small as normal, the transformations [they cause] will be diminished.

---

169 Wang Bing: "環 is to say: 如環, 'to pursue a curved route like a ring, ever circulating and never leaving.'" Zhang Zhicong: "That is to say: when the people have committed offenses, they deliberate whether to send disasters down on them. When [the people] have displayed virtue, they deliberate whether to send good fortune down on them."

170 Wang Bing: " 'Near' is to say: the planets invading [the lodges] are constantly present; 'far away' is to say: the planets invading [the lodges] have left for a long time. 大小 refers to joyful events and to punishment." Zhang Jiebin: "When the reaction to something is near and minor, the respective star is small. When the reaction to something is far and severe, the respective star is big." Fang Yaozhong: "This sentence refers to the relationships between the sizes of the stars as they can be seen by the naked eye and the changes taking place on earth. If stars appear relatively small to the naked eye, the changes on the earth will be relatively small and the period during which these changes occur will be relatively short. When the size of the stars appears relatively big, then the changes on the earth will be relatively big and the period during which these changes occur will be relatively long. The size of the stars and their distance from the earth are closely related. When the distance is short, then they appear big; when the distance from the earth is far, then they appear small. In other words, when the star of a period is far away from the earth, the changes corresponding to it on the earth will be minor. When the distance from the earth is short, the changes occurring on the earth in correspondence are big."

171 Wang Bing: " 'Severe' is to say: policies and commands are passed with full strength. 發 is to say: 起, 'to emerge.' 即 is 至, 'to arrive.'" 597/47

When they are a third as small as normal,[172]
this is called 'to come down and observe.'

These are inquiries into the transgressions and the virtues of that below.[173]

69-416-8
Those who display virtue, they are rewarded with good luck;
those who commit transgressions, they are punished.[174]

<Hence, the perception of the images [of the stars] is as follows:
When they are high and far away, then they are small.
When they are low and near, then they are big.
The fact is,
when they are big, then joy and anger are close.
When they are small, then misery and luck are far away.>[175]

When the [qi associated with an] annual period is greatly excessive, then the
star [associated with this] period moves away to the North.[176]
When the period and the qi agree with each other, then each [star] moves
along its path.[177]

---

172 For a dating of this passage as Sui or Tang dynasty astronomy, see 597/47.

173 Wang Bing: "省 is to observe (省察) whether people, officials, princes, and kings
in the myriad countries act virtuously or have committed transgressions. Hence, how
could princes and kings, common people and officials not be deeply concerned about
sincerity and carefully guard themselves against evil."

174 Wang Bing: "Where there is virtue, heaven sends down luck to reward it. Where
there are transgressions, heaven sends down misfortune to harm them. From this it is
obvious, misfortune and luck are invited by man himself."

175 Wang Bing: "When the images [in heaven] appear high up and small, then neither misfortune nor luck have arrived. When the images [in heaven] appear low and
big, luck is not far away and misfortune is not far away either."

176 Zhang Jiebin: "It leaves its proper path and approaches the North. The reason is,
the North is the place where Ci-wei 紫微 and Tai-yi 太乙 reside. When a star [as-
sociated with a] period does not keep its proper path but leaves it towards the North,
it is obvious that it holds a strongly aggressive qi."

177 Wang Bing: "As long as there is no dislike that manifests itself in [mutual] destruction or attack, the rules are observed and everything moves along the middle
way." Wu Kun: "相得 is: no domination, [no] revenge. When this is the case, all five
stars move along their proper paths."

The fact is,
when [the qi associated with an] annual period is greatly excessive,
[then] the star that is in fear [of the dominant agent] loses its color and adopts
[that of] its mother.¹⁷⁸
When [the qi associated with an annual period] is inadequate,
then it adopts the color of that [agent] which it cannot dominate.¹⁷⁹

69-417-3
'[Even] the exemplary are helpless.
No one knows its mysteries.
In view of the unfathomable,
who can stand up to this?'¹⁸⁰
[There are those who] conduct false practices, not taking into regard evidence.
Thereby [they] deeply impress princes and kings."¹⁸¹

69-417-4
[Huang] Di: "When they correspond with catastrophes, how is that?"

Qi Bo:
"Here too they always follow the transformations of the [annual qi].
Hence,
the arrival of the seasons may go along with abundance or weakness.
Encroaching may be contrary to or in accordance with [the rules].

---

178 Wang Bing: "When the wood [star] loses its color, it adopts [the color] black.
When the fire [star] loses its color, it adopts [the color] greenish. When the soil [star]
loses its color, it adopts [the color] red. When the metal [star] loses its color, it adopts
[the color] yellow. When the water [star] loses its color, it adopts [the color] white."

179 Wang Bing: "The wood [star] adopts the color white. The fire [star] adopts the
color black. The soil [star] adopts the color greenish. The metal [star] adopts the color
red. The water [star] adopts the color yellow. That is to say: 'adopt [the color of] what
cannot be dominated.'"

180 Zhongyi yanjiuyuan...: "肖 is 取法, 'to take as example.' 瞿瞿 is 'to look timidly
left and right.' 閔閔 is 'to be grieved often.' The meaning of these four sentences is:
Those people who take heaven and earth as a model, they may nervously look here
and there and yet, the principles of heaven are inexhaustible and it is impossible to
know all their secrets. Hence in their hearts they ponder and ponder in grief and do
not know how they should behave best." This four sentence passage appears in *Su wen*
8-59-7, too. For further comments, see there .

181 Wang Bing: "They do not know the meaning of heaven and assess it on the
grounds of their personal opinion. They speak of catastrophes without evidence and
this is just sufficient to proclaim omina that cause fear in marquises and kings and to
nourish confusion in the common people."

Remaining [at one place] and keeping [a location] may take more or less
[time].
The visible manifestation may be good or bad.
[Sections on the earth] associated with the lodges [passed through by the plan-
ets] may encounter domination or defeat.
Corresponding evidence may be auspicious or inauspicious."[182]

[Huang] Di:
"Good or bad [manifestation], what is that to say?"

Qi Bo:
"They may be joyful or angry,
they may be anxious or mournful,
they may be humid or dry.
These are regular [manifestations] of the [heavenly] images.
They must be investigated carefully."[183]

---

182 Zhang Jiebin: "時至 is the successive arrival of the annual seasons. When the
movement of the five stars corresponds to the respective seasons, then this is 'abundance.' When it does not correspond to the season, then this is 'weakness.' When
they retreat towards East to punish, the stars pass along heaven slowly. Hence this
is in accordance [with their normal direction] and [corresponding] catastrophes are
mild. When they advance towards West to punish, the stars pass along heaven quickly.
Hence this is contrary [to their normal direction] and [corresponding] catastrophes
are serious. When [stars] are stationary and keep one position for many days, the
[corresponding] catastrophes are deep-reaching; when they are stationary and keep
one position for only a few days, the [corresponding] catastrophes remain superficial.
When the physical appearance displays a joyful and shiny color, this is a good [sign];
when the physical appearance has an angry, dry, or mournful color, this is a bad [sign].
宿屬 is to say: each of the 28 constellations and twelve heavenly bodies has a different
association with the five agents. Whenever in the arrival of the five stars excess is met
by abundance, or inadequacy is met by weakness, the [corresponding] catastrophes
will be even more severe. When excess meets with restraint and when inadequacy
receives support, the [corresponding] catastrophe will be mild. That is 'domination'
and 'defeat.'"

183 Wang Bing: "These are the appearances of the five stars. They are observed in
deep night. When a person observing them is joyful, that is because the star is happy.
When [a person] observing them is fearful, that is because the star is angry. When
the light [emitted by the stars] is alternately bright and dark, that is because the star is
sad. When the light [emitted by the stars] is remote and does not shine and when it is
different from the others, that is because the star mourns. When the light [emitted by
the star] is round and bright, when it is neither too full nor shrunk, when it is pleased
and lustrous, that is because the star is happy. If the light [of the star] comes down on

69-418-1
[Huang] Di:
"Do these six [types of manifestations] differ [in accordance with the stars being situated] high or low?"

Qi Bo:
"[No matter] whether the images appear high or low,
what they correspond to is one and the same.
Hence man corresponds to them, too."

69-418-3
[Huang] Di:
"Good!
How about movement and resting, decrease and increase in regard of the virtues, transformations, policies and commands [mentioned above]?"

Qi Bo:
"Now,
as for virtue, transformation, policy, command, catastrophes and changes,
they cannot enhance each other.[184]
Domination and revenge, abundance and weakness
cannot increase each other.[185]
Coming and going, small and big
cannot exceed each other.[186]
Rise and descent in [their] operation,

---

man suddenly and if its rays are full of light and if its image appears to tremble, that is because the star is angry."

184 Wang Bing: "In the movement and resting of heaven and earth, as well as in the going and coming of yin and yang, virtue is retributed with virtue and transformation is retributed with transformation. The same applies to policy and command, catastrophe and disaster, as well as to movement and revenge. Hence [the text] states 不能相加也, 'cannot enhance each other.'"

185 Wang Bing: "A domination [by a qi that] abounds is met by a revenge of [a qi that] abounds [too], and a domination [by a qi that] is mild is met by a revenge of [a qi that] is mild [too]. It should not be such that abundance is requitted with mildness, and transformation is requitted with change. Hence the text states 不能相多也, 'cannot increase each other.'"

186 Wang Bing: "The number of days of domination and revenge cannot differ." Gao Shishi: "The coming and going and the sizes of the five stars cannot be exceeded."

one cannot be without the other.[187]
All [the qi] do is to follow the respective movement of the others and take
revenge."[188]

[Huang] Di:
"The diseases generated by them, what are they like?"

Qi Bo:
"Virtue and transformations are the good luck [bestowed] by the qi;[189]
policy and command are the manifestations of the qi.
Changes and alterations are the arrangements of revenge.[190]
Catastrophes and disasters are the beginning of harm.
When the qi dominate one another, this is harmony.
If there is no mutual domination, this is disease.[191]

---

187 Wang Bing: "When wood dominates, metal is bound to take revenge. The same
applies to fire, soil, metal, and water. It has never happened that there was domination without [later] requittal. Hence no qi can cause another [qi] to be eliminated
completely." Fang Yaozhong: 用 is 作用, 'effect.' Here it refers to the effects of the
five qi and the five stars. Because the changes of the five stars are closely related to the
phenomena of change of the climate and of all things on the earth, in broad terms it is
possible to say that they are effected by wind, fire, dampness, dryness, and cold, and by
generation, growth, transformation, gathering, and storage. 升降 refers to movement
and it also refers to the phenomena of waxing and waning, of advance and retreat
within the natural processes of change."

188 Wang Bing: "A movement is bound to be followed by a revenge. [Hence] the
movement is examined to make a statement on [what can be expected to] be the
revenge." In contrast, Fang Yaozhong: 各 refers to the five stars, the five seasons, and
the five qi. 復 is to return to the original situation. This statement is to say: The pattern
of the movement of the five stars, the five seasons, and the five qi is one of coming and
going in a circle. Once a circle is completed it begins anew."

189 Fang Yaozhong: "The meaning is: the phenomena of life in nature are the outcome
of regular climatic conditions."

190 Wang Bing: 祥 is 善應, 'positive response.' 章 is 程, 'rule,' 式, 'pattern.' 復紀 is to
say: the laws of requittal and revenge."

191 Fang Yaozhong: " 'Qi' refers to the six qi. 相勝 is to say: when a particular qi
dominates unilaterally, that qi which it cannot dominate arrives to restrain it. 和 is 正
常, 'regular.' 不相勝 is to say: no qi arrives to restrain a unilaterally dominant qi. 病 is
to say: 'irregular.' "

When there is multiple affection by the evil, then [the resulting disease will be] severe."¹⁹²

69-418-9
[Huang] Di:
"Good!

This is [meant when it] is said:
'the discourse on the essence light,
this is the occupation of the great sages.
It promulgates the Great Way,
it penetrates the inexhaustible, and
it proceeds to the limitless.'

I have heard this:
'Those who know to speak about heaven,
they must have a corresponding [knowledge] about man.
Those who know to speak about the past,
they must have experienced the present.
Those who know to speak about the qi,
they must have a clear knowledge about [concrete] things.'¹⁹³

'Those who know to speak about the correspondences,
they are one with the transformations of heaven and earth.
Those who know to speak about transformation and about change,
they penetrate the structures of spirit brilliance.'¹⁹⁴

Who except you, Sir, is able to speak about the perfect Way?!"

69-419-2
Then [Huang Di] selected [an auspicious day with] a good omen and stored

---

192 Wang Bing: "重感 is to say: when the annual qi itself is inadequate and when, in addition, a qi appears in heaven that overcomes and kills [the annual qi], that is 'double affection.'"

193 2683/36: "That is to say: even though the qi is invisible and intangible, it can associate itself with material bodies to give expression to its functions."

194 691/56: "That is to say: Heaven and mankind, corporal appearance and qi, affect and response (應), changes/transformations and spiritual brilliance are all closely related, are all based on identical laws." See also 352/42.

[the discourse] in the numinous chamber.[195] Every morning he read it. He gave
it the title *Changes resulting from Qi Interaction.*

If one has not undergone [a period of] fasting and chastity, one dares not open
it. One must be cautious about transmitting it.

---

195 Wang Bing: "靈室 is 靈蘭室, 'numinous orchid chamber'; that is the imperial
library."

Chapter 70
Comprehensive Discourse on the Five Regular Policies

70-419-6
Huang Di asked:
"The extension of the Great Void is boundless.
The five periods turn [around in cycles, one] pressing [another].[1]
They differ in their weakness and abundance;
decrease and increase follow each other.

I should like to hear: what are the names, what is the arrangement of the [years of] balanced qi?"

Qi Bo responded:
"A brilliant question, indeed!

[A year of the] wood [period with balanced qi] is called 'extended harmony.'[2]
[A year of the] fire [period with balanced qi] is called 'ascending brilliance.'[3]
[A year of the] soil [period with balanced qi] is called 'perfect transformation.'[4]
[A year of the] metal [period with balanced qi] is called 'secured balance.'[5]
[A year of the] water [period with balanced qi] is called 'quiet adaptation.'"[6]

[Huang] Di:
"How about [years of] inadequacy?"

Qi Bo:
"[A year of the] wood [period with inadequate qi] is called 'discarded harmony.'

---

1 Zhang Jiebin: "回 is 循環, 'to move in a circle.' 薄 is 迫切, 'pressing.'" Cheng Shide et al.: "回薄 is: [the periods] move in an endless circle and they press one each another [forward]."

2 Wang Bing: "It spreads harmonious qi; hence beings come to life and flourish."

3 Wang Bing: "The qi of fire rises high and is brilliant."

4 Zhang Jiebin: "The soil contains the myriad beings; there is nothing that is not prepared in it. The soil generates the myriad beings; there is nothing it does not transform."

5 Wang Bing: "The qi of metal is clear; it strives for balance and stability."

6 Wang Bing: "The body of the water is clear and quiet and it adapts to [the shape of] things [in it]."

[A year of the] fire [period with inadequate qi] is called 'hidden brilliance.'
[A year of the] soil [period with inadequate qi] is called 'inferior supervision.'[7]
[A year of the] metal [period with inadequate qi] is called 'accepted change.'[8]
[A year of the] water [period with inadequate qi] is called 'dried-up flow.'"

[Huang] Di:
"[Years of] great excess, what is that to say?"

Qi Bo:
"[A year of the] wood [period with excessive qi] is called 'effusive generation.'
[A year of the] fire [period with excessive qi] is called 'fire-red sunlight.'
[A year of the] soil [period with excessive qi] is called 'prominent mound.'[9]
[A year of the] metal [period with excessive qi] is called 'firm completion.'[10]
[A year of the] water [period with excessive qi] is called 'inundating flow.'"

70-420-5
[Huang] Di:
"The arrangements of the three qi,[11] I should like to hear about their manifestations."[12]

Qi Bo:
"An encompassing question, indeed!

---

7 Wang Bing: "Even though the [qi of] soil is diminished, it nevertheless oversees the generation and transformation of the myriad beings."

8 Wang Bing: "It follows changes [made to its appearances] and hardens to form a myriad beings." Zhang Jiebin: "The original nature of metal is hardness. When [its qi is] inadequate, then it submits to transformation caused by fire and changes [its appearance]." Fang Yaozhong: "從 is 順從, 'to obey'; 革 is 改革, 'reform.'"

9 Wang Bing: "敦 is 厚, 'thick.' 阜 is 高, 'high.' The [qi of] soil is present in surplus; hence it is 'high' and 'thick.'"

10 Zhang Jiebin: "The nature of metal is hard; its operation forms things. When its qi is present in surplus, then its hardness and formation to [things] are particularly abundant."

11 Gao Shishi: " 'Three qi' refers to balanced [qi], excessive [qi], and inadequate [qi]."

12 Cheng Shide et al.: "On the basis of the subsequent text, 'manifestations' should be 'manifestations of things' (物候)."

In an arrangement of extended harmony,
the virtue of wood[13] prevails everywhere.
Yang [qi] unfolds and yin [qi] spreads.
The five transformations are spread widely and balanced.[14]

Its qi is uprightness.[15]
Its nature is adaptive.[16]
Its operation [manifests itself in what is] curved and straight.[17]
Its transformation brings [beings] to life and makes them flourish.[18]
Its class is <herbs and> wood.[19]
Its policy [brings about] effusion and dispersion.[20]
Its [climatic] manifestation is warmth and harmony.[21]
Its [seasonal] command [brings about] wind.

Its depot is the liver.
{As for the liver, it fears coolness.}[22]
It rules the eye.

---

13 Cheng Shide et al.: " 'Virtue of wood' refers to the transformations stimulated by the qi of wood."

14 Wang Bing: "It occupies its own location and does not struggle with others. Hence the transformations of the five qi do all spread their policies and commands to the four cardinal points and there is no mutual attack or invasion." Cheng Shide et al.: "The five transformations are generation, growth, transformation, gathering, and storage."

15 Cheng Shide et al.: "The qi of wood."

16 Wang Bing: "It adapts to the transformations of things." Zhang Zhicong: "It is soft and adaptive."

17 Wang Bing: "Curved and straight trunks of trees are all operations [of the qi of wood]."

18 Wang Bing: "When the transformations of wood extend everywhere, then beings come to life, flourish, and are beautiful."

19 The character 草 appears to be a later addition. Obviously a copyist did not see that in this table 木 represents the agent wood. Elsewhere the combination 草木 stands for "herbs and trees."

20 Wang Bing: "The qi of spring effuses and disperses."

21 Wang Bing: "Harmony is the qi of spring."

22 Wang Bing: "Coolness is [brought about by the seasonal] command issued by metal. The nature of wood is warmth. Hence it fears coolness." Gao Shishi: "The liver fears coolness just like the wood fears metal."

Its grain is sesame.²³
Its tree-fruit is the plum.²⁴
Its fruit are [those with a] kernel.²⁵
Its corresponding [season] is spring.
Its creatures²⁶ are hairy.²⁷
Its domestic animal is the dog.²⁸
Its color is greenish.
It nourishes the sinews.²⁹
Its illness is internal tightness and propping fullness.³⁰
Its flavor is sour.
Its tone is *jue*.³¹
Its [material] items are firm in the center.³²
Its number is eight.

70-422-1
In an arrangement of ascending brilliance,

---

23 Wang Bing: "The color [of sesame] is greenish." Gao Shishi: "The body of sesame is straight and its color is greenish. It is the first of the five grains." See 2016/8 on differences in the association of the five types of grain with the five agents and the five flavors in *Su wen* 4, 22, and 70, and *Ling shu* 56 and 65, respectively.

24 Wang Bing: "Its flavor is sour." Cheng Shide et al.: "sour is the flavor [associated] with wood. Hence 'its tree-fruit is the plum.'"

25 Wang Bing: "These are those with a hard kernel in the center." All [fruit with] kernels are associated with [the agent] wood; their substance is strong." Gao Shishi: "Inside the kernels is a seed which is the origin from which trees emerge. Hence 'its fruit are [those with] kernel.'"

26 Fang Yaozhong: "虫 refers to all animals, including man, in the realm of nature."

27 Wang Bing: "When the transformations of wood extend everywhere, then hairy creatures come to life." Zhang Jiebin: "Hair is straight like trees. This is the same kind of qi." Gao Shishi: "Hairy creatures have hair all over their bodies, resembling a luxurious growth of trees. Hence 'its creatures are hairy.'"

28 Wang Bing: "[Dogs] resemble growth of herbs and trees as there is no place they avoid." Zhang Zhicong: "The nature of dogs is to advance forward with courage." Zhang Jiebin: "The flavor of dog [meat] is sour." See 2016/9 on differences in the association of domestic animals with the five agents and the five flavors in *Su wen* 4 and 70, and *Ling shu* 56, respectively.

29 Wang Bing: "Sour [flavor] enters the sinews."

30 Wang Bing: "Generated by the qi of wood."

31 Wang Bing: "Tempered and proper."

32 Wang Bing: "Like soil that has wood in it."

the proper yang governs.³³
The virtue [of fire] is applied ubiquitously.³⁴
The five transformations are evenly balanced.

Its qi is highness.³⁵
Its nature is fast.³⁶
Its operation [manifests itself in] burning.
Its transformation [brings about] opulence and lushness.
Its class is fire.
Its policy [brings about] brilliance and luster.
Its [climatic] manifestation is flaming summerheat.
Its [seasonal] command [brings about] heat.

Its depot is the heart.
{As for the heart, it fears cold.}³⁷
It rules the tongue.³⁸
Its grain is wheat.³⁹
Its tree-fruit is the apricot.⁴⁰
Its fruit are [those with a] network.⁴¹
Its corresponding [season] is summer.
Its creatures are feathered.⁴²

---

33 Zhang Jiebin: "Fire rules the South. Hence it is called 'proper yang.'" Cheng Shide et al.: "The 'proper yang' is the South."

34 Zhang Jiebin: "Its qi reaches everywhere. Hence [the text] says 周普."

35 Wang Bing: "Fire flames upwards."

36 Wang Bing: "The nature of fire is hurried and fast."

37 Wang Bing: "Cold is [brought about by the seasonal] command issued by water. The nature of the heart is the heat of summerheat. Hence it fears cold." Zhang Zhicong: "The heart fears cold just like fire fears water."

38 Wang Bing: "Because the fire illumines the dark; it causes the tongue to stretch and be lighted."

39 Wang Bing: "The color [of wheat] is red." Gao Shishi: "Wheat comes to life in spring and ripens in summer. Hence 'its grain is wheat.'"

40 Wang Bing: "Its taste is bitter." Gao Shishi: "The color of apricots is red."

41 Wang Bing: "These are those with a branching network inside." Gao Shishi: "Network vessels stretch horizontally everywhere, resembling the spreading of fire."

42 Wang Bing: "Wings are the image of fire. When the transformations of fire extend everywhere, then feathered creatures come to life." Gao Shishi: "Feathered creatures fly soaring to the heavens, resembling fire flaming upward."

Its domestic animal is the horse.[43]
Its color is red.
It nourishes the blood.
Its illness is twitching [flesh] and [muscle] spasms.[44]
Its flavor is bitter.
Its tone is *zhi*.[45]
Its [material] items have vessels.[46]
Its number is seven.

70-423-2
In an arrangement of perfect transformation,
the qi is in harmony and heaven is beautiful.[47]
The virtue [of soil] flows into the four policies.[48]
The five transformations are equally refined.[49]

Its qi is balance.
Its nature is adaptive.
Its operation [manifests itself] high and below.
Its transformation [brings about] prosperity and copiousness.[50]
Its class is soil.

---

43 Wang Bing: "[Horses] are robust, determined, and fast. They are of one kind with the fire." Gao Shishi: "Horse is an image of heaven. It rules heaven. Heaven is lighted because of the sun. Hence 'its domestic animal is the horse.'"

44 Wang Bing: "These are movements [dictated by] the nature of fire." Zhang Zhicong: "When the conduit vessels are affected by the qi of fire, they shrink and become tense."

45 Wang Bing: "Harmonious and beautiful."

46 Wang Bing: "Inside of them are many vessel branches; they are operations of the fire."

47 Cheng Shide et al.: "協 is 調協, 'harmonized,' 融合, 'blended.'"

48 Cheng Shide et al.: " 'Four policies' are the policies of the four cardinal points, i.e., East, South, West, and North."

49 Wang Bing: "The virtue of soil is resting; it assists each of the four cardinal points and it helps the policies of metal, wood, water, and fire to accomplish their ends. The qi of soil is 'thick'; it corresponds to the qi of heaven that is beautiful and harmonious, to [make beings] come to life, grow, be gathered, be stored, end, and begin [their cycle of existence] anew. Hence the five transformations are equally refined."

50 Wang Bing: "It is only through the transformations of the soil that the myriad beings can prosper and become copius."

Its policy [brings about] peace and resting.[51]
Its [climatic] manifestation is humidity and steam.
Its [seasonal] command [brings about] dampness.

Its depot is the spleen.
{As for the spleen, it fears wind.}[52]
It rules the mouth.[53]
Its grain is panicled millet.[54]
Its tree-fruit is the date.[55]
Its fruit are [those with] flesh.[56]
Its corresponding [season] is late summer.
Its creatures are naked.[57]
Its domestic animal is the ox.[58]
Its color is yellow.
It nourishes the flesh.[59]
Its illness is blockage.[60]
Its flavor is sweet.
Its tone is *gong*.[61]

---

51 Wang Bing: "The physical body of the soil is thick; the virtue of the soil is resting. Hence the transformations brought about by its policy are those described here."

52 Wang Bing: "Wind is [brought about by the seasonal] command issued by wood. Even though the nature of the spleen combines the four [remaining] qi, its ruling [qi, i.e., that of soil] fears wood." Zhang Zhicong: "It fears wind because wood dominates soil."

53 Wang Bing: "The mouth rules the intake."

54 Wang Bing: "Its color is yellow."

55 Wang Bing: "Its flavor is sweet." Gao Shishi: "The flavor of dates is sweet and their flesh is yellow."

56 Wang Bing: "These are those with flesh inside." Zhang Jiebin: "The soil rules the muscles and the flesh."

57 Wang Bing: "They have no hair, wings, scales or shell, and resemble the physical appearance of soil." Gao Shishi: "Naked creatures have no hair on their body, resembling the yielding and moist [appearance] of soil. Hence 'its creatures are naked.'"

58 Wang Bing: "It is used for husbandry which is an operation of soil."

59 Wang Bing: "What is nourished [by it] is thick and motionless."

60 Wang Bing: "The nature of soil is to wrap and to obstruct."

61 Wang Bing: "Massive and heavy."

Its [material] items have a skin.[62]
Its number is five.

70-424-3
In an arrangement of secured balance,
there is gathering but no fight;
killing but no invasion.
The five transformations are widely promulgated.[63]

Its qi is cleanliness.
Its nature is hard.
Its operation [manifests itself in] dispersion and downfall.
Its transformation [brings about] firmness and contraction.
Its class is metal.
Its policy is forceful and stern.
Its [climatic] manifestation is clear and cutting.[64]
Its [seasonal] command [brings about] dryness.

Its depot is the lung.
{As for the lung, it fears heat.}[65]
It rules the nose.[66]
Its grain is rice.[67]
Its tree-fruit is the peach.[68]

---

62 Wang Bing: "Things endowed with the qi of perfect transformation have many muscles and much flesh." Cheng Shide et al.: "膚 is 肌肉, 'muscles and flesh.'"

63 Zhang Zhicong: "Metal is the image of weapons. When the qi of metal is harmonious and balanced, then there is gathering and no fighting."

64 Wang Bing: "清 is 大涼, massive coolness'; 切 is 急, 'tense'; it is the sound generated by wind."

65 Wang Bing: "Heat is [brought about by the seasonal] command of fire. The nature of the lung is coolness. Hence it fears the heat of fire." Zhang Zhicong: "The lung fears heat just like metal fears fire."

66 Wang Bing: "The lung stores the qi; the [qi] passes the nose for breathing."

67 Wang Bing: "Its color is white." Zhang Zhicong: "This is a grain maturing in autumn."

68 Wang Bing: "Its flavor is acrid." Gao Shishi: "桃 is 胡桃, 'walnut.'" Zhang Zhicong: "The color of peaches is white and they have hair. [Hence] this is the fruit [associated with the] lung."

Its fruit [are those with] a shell.[69]
Its corresponding [season] is autumn.
Its creatures are armored.[70]
Its domestic animal is the chicken.[71]
Its color is white.
It nourishes the skin and the body hair.
Its illness is cough.[72]
Its flavor is acrid.
Its tone is *shang*.[73]
Its [material] items are firm on the outside.[74]
Its number is nine.

70-425-4
In an arrangement of quiet adaptation,
there is storage but no injury.
There is order and benevolence [extends to those] below.
All the five transformations occur unimpaired.[75]

Its qi is brilliance.[76]
Its nature is to move downward.
Its operation [manifests itself in] pouring and inundation.
Its transformation [brings about] congealing and firmness.[77]

---

69 Wang Bing: "These are those with a hard shell on the outside." Gao Shishi: "A shell encloses [things] on the outside [resembling] armors made of metal."

70 Wang Bing: "These are those covered with a shell."

71 Wang Bing: "Its nature is that it loves to fight and to injure. It resembles the use of metal."

72 Wang Bing: "Illnesses causing sounds correspond to metal." Gao Shishi: "Its illness is cough because the lung qi cannot flow freely."

73 Wang Bing: "Unimpeded and high."

74 Wang Bing: "When the transformations of metal extend everywhere, then the physical body of things hardens on the outside." Gao Shishi: "All metallic things are hard on the outside."

75 Wang Bing: "治 is 化, 'transformation.' The nature of water is to move down. The reason why streams and seas rule all valleys is because they tend to move down into them." Cheng Shide et al.: "整 is 齊, 'even.'"

76 Wang Bing: "Clearness, purity, brilliance, and luster are ruled by the qi of water." Gao Shishi: "That is the clearness of water."

77 Wang Bing: "When the qi of storage spreads transformation, then watery things congeal and harden.

Its class is water.
Its policy [brings about] extensive flow.[78]
Its [climatic] manifestation is freezing and sternness.[79]
Its [seasonal] command [brings about] cold.[80]

Its depot are the kidneys.
{As for the kidneys, they fear dampness.}[81]
They rule the two yin [openings].
Its grain is the bean.[82]
Its tree-fruit is the chestnut.[83]
Its fruit [are those with] moisture.
Its corresponding [season] is winter.
Its creatures are scaly.[84]
Its domestic animal is the swine.[85]
Its color is black.
It nourishes the bones and the marrow.[86]
Its illness is recession.[87]
Its flavor is salty.

---

78 Wang Bing: "Wells and springs are not exhausted; rivers flow without interruption. That is the meaning of 'extensive flow.'"

79 Wang Bing: "凝 is 寒, 'cold.' 肅 is 靜, 'resting.'"

80 Wang Bing: "When the [seasonal] command issued by water extends everywhere, then cold rules the transformations of things."

81 Wang Bing: "Dampness is the qi of soil. The nature of the kidneys is cold. Hence they fear the dampness of soil." Zhang Zhicong: "The kidneys fear dampness just like water fears soil."

82 Wang Bing: "Its color is dark." Gao Shishi: "The bean reaches down [into the earth] deeply and its nature is cold."

83 Wang Bing: "Its flavor is salty." Gao Shishi: "The shell of the chestnut is vermilion and its shape resembles the kidneys."

84 Wang Bing: "Scales are generated through transformations of water." Gao Shishi: "They are born in water and they grow in water."

85 Wang Bing: "It prefers to [dig] downward." Zhang Jiebin: "The color [of swines] is mostly dark."

86 Wang Bing: "Its qi enters [bones and marrow]."

87 Wang Bing: "厥 is 氣逆, 'qi moving contrary [to its normal direction].'" Zhang Zhicong: "The kidneys are the source of the generative qi. Hence when [the kidneys] have an illness, then hands and feet turn cold because of receding [qi]."

Its tone is *yu*.[88]
Its [material] items have moisture.
Its number is six.

Hence
when there is generation without killing,
when there is growth without punishment,
when there is transformation without restraint,
when there is gathering without harm,
when there is storage without repression,
this is called 'balanced qi.'

70-427-2
An arrangement of discarded harmony,
that is to say: dominated generation.[89]
The qi of generation does not carry out its policy,
while the qi of transformation soars.[90]
The qi of growth is balanced by itself.

Under these circumstances, the [seasonal] command of gathering [arrives]
early.[91]
Cool rain falls frequently.
Winds and clouds rise together.[92]

---

88 Wang Bing: "Deep and harmonious."

89 Cheng Shide et al.: "When the [qi of the] wood period is inadequate, metal comes to conquer wood and soil comes to humiliate wood. Conquering and humiliation are both called 勝, 'domination.' Because the generative qi of wood is inadequate and is dominated and humiliated by the qi of soil and metal, hence [the text] speaks of 勝生." Zhang Jiebin: "The generative qi cannot carry out its policy. The qi of collecting dominates it. Hence [the texts] speaks of 勝生."

90 Wang Bing: "The [qi of] wood is diminished, hence the qi of generation does not carry out its policy. The [qi of] soil abounds, hence the qi of transformation soars." Zhang Zhicong: "When the policy of wood is not proclaimed, then the qi of soil has nothing to fear and the qi of transformation soars."

91 Wang Bing: "Fire is not malicious and does not commit any transgression; hence the qi of growth balances itself. Because the qi of wood is diminished, the policy of gathering [arrives] early."

92 Wang Bing: "Coolness is [brought about by] a transformation of metal; rain is the qi of dampness. Wind is [brought about by] a transformation of wood. Clouds are the qi of dampness." Gao Shishi: "[When the qi of] wood is inadequate, then the [qi of] metal dominates and the [qi of] soil has nothing to fear. Hence all three qi

Herbs and trees blossom late.
There is aging and drying, withering and falling to the ground.[93]
The things flourish and bear fruit.
The skin and the flesh are full internally.[94]

Its qi is contraction.
Its operation [manifests itself in] agglomeration.[95]
The movement it [generates causes] contractions and contortions, cramp, and slackening.[96]
The effusion it [generates causes] shock.[97]

Its depot is the liver.
Its tree-fruits are date and plum.[98]

---

are active simultaneously. Now, coolness is metal qi; clouds and rain are soil qi and wind is wood qi. Hence coolness and rain descend frequently and wind and clouds rise together."

93 Wang Bing: "The reason is: the qi of metal is present in surplus and the [qi of] wood cannot dominate." Lin Yi et al.: "In an arrangement of discarded harmony the [qi of] wood is inadequate and the qi of metal seizes its [territory]. Hence, there is aging and falling to the ground. It is not such that the qi of metal is present in surplus and that the [qi of] wood cannot dominate. In fact, the [qi of] wood is insufficient and the [qi of] metal dominates it." Zhang Zhicong: "The qi of generation does not carry out its policy, hence herbs and trees blossom late; the policy of gathering is early, hence there is aging and drying and falling to the ground." 1186/147: "實 should be 成熟, 'to reach completion.'"

94 Wang Bing: "Even though [the qi of] generation is late in such years, what reaches completion is full of fruit. The reason is: the qi of transformation, [i.e., the qi of] soil, acts quickly."

95 Zhang Jiebin: "When wood and metal transform simultaneously, the qi of agglomeration dominates." Gao Shishi: "Metal rules agglomeration and collecting, hence 'its qi is collecting.' Wood rules generation and agglomeration, hence 'its operation is agglomeration.'"

96 Wang Bing: "緛 is 縮短, 'to shorten.' 戾 is 了戾, 'to end.' 拘 is 拘急, 'to have a cramp.' 緩 is 不收, 'inability to contract.'" We interpret 戾 as "to turn into its opposite."

97 Wang Bing: "When a massive contraction ends in a sudden stretching, this resembles [jumping up in] fright." Zhang Jiebin: "Wind, the qi of wood, is weak. [Hence] liver and gallbladder are both ill."

98 Wang Bing: "Dates are fruit [associated with] soil; plums are fruit [associated with] wood." Lin Yi et al.: "李 should be 桃, 'peach.' Wang Bing's comment is wrong, too." Zhang Jiebin: "Dates are fruit [associated with] soil; plum should be peach,

Its fruit [are those with] kernel and shell.⁹⁹
Its grain are panicled millet and rice.¹⁰⁰
Its flavors are sour and acrid.¹⁰¹
Its colors are white and greenish.¹⁰²
Its domestic animals are the dog and the chicken.¹⁰³
Its creatures are hairy and armored.
It is responsible for fog and dew and chilling temperatures.¹⁰⁴
Its tones are *jue* and *shang*.¹⁰⁵
Its illnesses are swaying movement, outpour, and fear.¹⁰⁶
{They follow transformations of metal.}¹⁰⁷

70-428-2
<[A year of] minor *jue* is identical to one half of *shang*.¹⁰⁸

---

which is a fruit [associated with] metal. Because the [qi of wood] is inadequate, the two fruit of soil and metal abound."

99 Wang Bing: "Kernels are ruled by wood; shells are ruled by metal."

100 Wang Bing: "These are the grains [associated with] metal and soil [respectively]." Zhang Jiebin: "Panicled millet is [a grain associated with] soil; rice is [a grain associated with] metal. When [the qi of] wood is inadequate, then these two grain will ripen."

101 Wang Bing: "When sour things are boiled they become acrid at the same time." Zhang Jiebin: "What is sour is weak and what is acrid dominates. These are simultaneous transformations of wood and metal."

102 Wang Bing: "When greenish things are boiled they become white at the same time." Zhang Jiebin: "White is the color of metal; greenish is the color of wood. White abounds in comparison with greenish."

103 Zhang Jiebin: "The dog is the domestic animal [associated with] wood; the chicken is the domestic animal [associated with] metal."

104 Wang Bing: "These are transformations of metal."

105 Gao Shishi: "These are the tones of wood and metal, respectively."

106 Wang Bing: "That is: the wood has received evil." Zhang Jiebin: "A shaking movement is an illness of the sinews; outflow and fear are illnesses of liver and gallbladder." Gao Shishi: "A shaking movement is the image of wind and wood/trees. Shaking movement, outflow, and fear, water occur because water does not generate wood."

107 Wang Bing: "The wood does not carry out its own policy; hence [all] transformations follow the metal."

108 Wang Bing: "[A year of] minor *jue* [is a year of] inadequate [qi of] wood. Hence one half of [its transformations] are identical to the transformations of metal. 判 is 半, 'half.'" Lin Yi et al.: "This should be 少角與少商同. Why does [the text] not say 少商? The reason is: there are altogether six years with a 少商 period. In the *ding si*

[A year of] upper *jue* is identical to [a year of] proper *jue*.[109]
[A year of] upper *shang* is identical to [a year of] proper *shang*.>[110]

---

and the *ding hai* [years, transformations] are identical to [those in] the upper *jue* and the proper *jue* [years]. In the *ding mao* and the *ding yu* [years, transformations] are identical to [those in] the upper *shang* and the proper *shang* [years]. In the *ding wei* and the *ding chou* [years, transformations] are identical to [those in] the upper *gong* and the proper *gong* [years]. [In] these six years [transformations] are always identical to [those of] other [tones]. However these are not identical to the minor periods of fire, soil, metal, and water. Hence [the text] does not say 'identical to minor *shang*,' it merely makes a general statement when it says 半從商化, 'one half follows the transformations of *shang*.'" Cheng Shide et al.: "*Jue* is the tone of wood. When the [arrangement of the] period of wood is one of extended harmony, the tone is proper *jue*. When it is endangered harmony, it is minor *jue*. When it is effusive generation, it is major *jue*. The 'proper' in proper *gong*, proper *shang*, etc. in the text below always has the same meaning. 判 is 半. *Shang* is a metal tone. 'Half *shang*' is minor *shang*. When [the qi of a] wood period is inadequate, metal comes to conquer wood. One half of the qi of wood follows the transformations [stimulated] by metal. Hence the minor *jue* and the halved *shang* are identical." Fang Yaozhong: "宮, *gong*, 商, *shang*, 角, *jue*, 徵, *zhi*, and 羽, *yu*, are the five tones representing the five periods soil, metal, wood, fire, and water. Among the five periods, 'balanced qi,' 'excessive [qi],' and 'inadequate [qi]' are distinguished. Hence among the five tones one also distinguishes among 'proper,' 'minor,' and 'major.' 'Proper' stands for balanced qi. 'Minor' stands for inadequate [qi]. 'Major' stands for excessive [qi]. *Jue* represents the wood period. 'Minor' represents inadequate [qi]. Hence the 'minor *jue*' mentioned here refers to a year of inadequate [qi] of a wood period. 判 is a phonetic loan character for 半, 'half.' *Shang* represents the metal period. 判金 is 'half a metal period.' The meaning of 'minor jue is identical to half *shang*' is: in a year of the wood period with inadequate [wood qi], because the qi of metal comes to take over, the [climatic] qi manifestation representing the wood itself is not very pronounced. For one half [of that] year they resemble the [climatic] manifestations of qi and the manifestations in things, representative of metal. That is what is meant by 'follows transformations of metal' above."

109 Wang Bing: "When in the upper [half of a year] a ceasing yin [qi] appears, the transformations are identical to those in [a year of] extended harmony. That is to say, what appears in the upper [half] of *ding hai* and *ding si* years." Gao Shishi: "When the qi of wood controls heaven, this is called 'upper *jue*.' When the qi of metal is balanced, this is called 'proper *shang*.' When [the qi of a] wood period is inadequate and receives assistance from [the qi] controlling heaven, then the qi of wood establishes harmony. Hence upper *jue* and proper *jue* are identical."

110 Wang Bing: "When in the upper [half of a year] a yang brilliance [qi] appears, then the transformations are identical to those in a year of balanced metal. In *ding mao* and *ding you* years yang brilliance [qi] appears in the upper [half of the year]." Gao Shishi: "When the qi of metal controls heaven, this is called upper *shang*. When the qi of metal is balanced, this is called proper *shang*. When metal dominates the wood and when, in addition, metal qi happens to control heaven, metal alone is in charge of all affairs. Hence upper *shang* is identical to proper *shang*."

<Its illnesses are worn out limbs, *yong*-abscesses, swelling, sores, and ulcers.>[111]
>Its sweet creatures<[112]
{The evil harms the liver.}[113]
<[A year of] upper *gong* is like [a year of] proper *gong*.>[114]

70-428-4
If there is whistling of autumn winds,[115] sternness and killing, then flames and redness of fire, boiling and bubbling [appear in revenge].[116]

Disasters occur in three.[117]

---

111 Wang Bing: "That is, metal punishes wood." Zhang Jiebin: "When wood is punished by metal, the conduits and sinews fall ill. Excessive wind agitates the branches [of the trees]. Hence the [people's] limbs are worn out. When the limbs are worn out, then the ravines, valleys, and joints experience blockages and it is from them that *yong*-abscesses, swelling, sores, and ulcerations develop."

112 Zhang Jiebin: "What is sweet easily develops creatures (or: bugs). This is because the metal dominates the wood and there is nothing that could restrain the soil." Wu Kun: "This statement is a later insertion."

113 Wang Bing: "Even though all transformations are identical to [those of] metal [years], harm is directed at the liver [which is associated with] wood." Zhang Jiebin: "When the qi of wood is inadequate, then harm delivered by the evil occurs in the liver."

114 Gao Shishi: "When the qi of soil controls heaven, this is called upper *gong*. When the qi of soil is balanced, this is called proper *gong*. When the [qi of wood during a] wood period is inadequate, the soil has nothing to fear. When at the same time the qi of soil controls heaven, then the qi of soil is responsible for [all] transformations. Hence upper *gong* and proper *gong* are identical."

115 Gao Jiwu/25: "蕭飋 is to describe the winds prevalent in autumn. The *Yu pian* 玉篇 states: 飋 is 秋風, 'autumn wind.'"

116 Wang Bing: "Stern frost and stern killing are [signs of] metal acting without virtue. Flames and brightness, boiling and bubbling are [signs of] revenge taken by fire."

117 Wang Bing: "Fire takes revenge [against metal] for [harm done by metal to] wood. The resulting disasters occur in the East. 'Three' is the East." Cheng Shide et al.: " 'Three' refers to the third mansion. That is the *zhen* (震) position in the East." Gao Shishi: "If there is [wind] whistling and soughing and if it displays sternness and killing, then wood is punished by metal. Hence [the text] states: 'Its Disasters occur in three.' Now, the East resides in the third mansion, in the *zhen* position. This is wood. The South resides in the ninth mansion, in the *li* (離) position. This is fire. The center resides in the fifth mansion, in the soil position. These are the four corners. The West resides in the seventh mansion, in the *dui* (兌) position. This is metal. The North resides in the first mansion, in the *kan* (坎) position. This is water."

{This is so-called revenge.}[118]
This is responsible for [the appearance of] flying [creatures], moths, maggots,
and pheasants.[119]
Then there is thunder and tremor.[120]

70-429-2
An arrangement of hidden brilliance,
that is to say: dominated growth.[121]
The qi of growth is not spread widely.
On the contrary, the qi of storage is distributed.[122]
The qi of gathering enacts its own policies and
the [seasonal] command of transformation is balanced.[123]

Cold and clearness set in frequently;
the [seasonal] command issued by summerheat is weak.[124]

---

118 Wang Bing: "復 is 報復, 'to requite an injury.'"

119 Wang Bing: "飛 refers to feathered creatures. 蠹 are creatures generated inside.
蛆 are generated by flies. These are transformations that occur within things themselves. Pheasants are bird pests." Gao Shishi: "When [the fire] takes revenge, then the
qi of fire abounds. Now, [creatures] that fly are fire creatures. Moths are generated by
wood; they are fire generated by wood. Maggots are offspring of flies, they are generated by fire creatures. Pheasants, too, are fire creatures."

120 Gao Shishi: "Thunder is [a sign of] oppressed wood and effused fire."

121 Wang Bing: "The qi of storage dominates [the qi of] growth. That is to say: in
gui you, gui wei, gui si, gui mao, gui chou, gui hai years." Cheng Shide et al.: "When the
[qi of the] fire period is inadequate, water comes to conquer fire and metal comes to
humiliate fire. Because the qi of growth of fire is inadequate and because it is dominated and humiliated by the qi of water and metal [respectively], the [text] speaks of
'dominated growth.'"

122 Wang Bing: "The qi of growth, [i.e., of] fire, cannot arrange transformations.
Hence contrary [to what is normal] the qi of storage, [i.e., of] water is distributed
during that time."

123 Wang Bing: "The [qi of] metal and soil do not plan any attack or invasion against
the qi of that year. Hence metal issues its own policies and soil balances its own qi."
Zhang Jiebin: "Metal has nothing to fear. Hence the qi of gathering enacts its own
policies. There is nothing that could generate soil. Hence the policy of transformation
is balanced only."

124 Wang Bing: "The qi of fire does not operate." Gao Shishi: "Cold is the qi of water; clearness is the qi of metal. The qi of water dominates and metal has nothing to
fear. Hence cold and clearness come up frequently. Summerheat is the qi of fire. [The
qi of] fire is inadequate. Hence the policy carried out by summerheat is weak."

Transformation is continued and beings come to life.
When they have come to life, they do not grow.
When they mature, their fruits are tender.
As soon as they experience transformation, they turn old.[125]
The yang qi has yielded and is hidden;
the hibernating creatures hide away early.[126]

70-429-5
Its qi is oppression;
its operation [manifests itself] violently.[127]
The movement it [generates causes] changes and alterations from obviousness
to hiding.[128]
The effusion it [generates causes] pain.[129]

Its depot is the heart.[130]
Its tree-fruit are the chestnut and the peach.[131]
Its fruit [are those with] network and moisture.[132]

---

125 Wang Bing: "The [seasonal] command of fire is not activated. Hence all beings
that come to life by way of continuing transformation do not grow." Zhang Zhicong:
"Because they continue to receive the balanced qi of transformation of soil, beings
come to life. Because the qi of growth is not diffused, they come to life but do not
grow. Because they come to life but do not grow, they bear fruits even though they
are small. When they encounter the transformation qi of late summer, they turn old."

126 Gao Shishi: "The fire is inadequate. Hence the yang qi is crouched and hidden.
Water is in charge. Hence the hibernating creatures hide away early."

127 Wang Bing: "That is: fast." Zhang Zhicong: "Its qi is oppressed because water
restrains its fire. Its operation is violent because the fire wishes to be effused."

128 Gao Shishi: "The qi of fire cannot flow freely. Hence its movement displays internal hiding and changes occur to cold." Zhang Zhicong: "Obviousness is the policy
and command of fire. When the obviousness is concealed, then a change occurs to
cold. Hence 'The effusion it [generates causes] pain.' That is, pain emerges because
cold dominates."

129 Wang Bing: "Pain is generated by the heart." Gao Shishi: "The qi of fire is depleted and cold. The resulting illness is pain. Hence [the text states:] 'The effusion it
[generates causes] pain'"

130 Wang Bing: "The qi of the period of that year penetrates the heart."

131 Wang Bing: "The chestnut is a fruit [associated with] water; the peach is a fruit
[associated with] metal." Zhang Jiebin: "Because [the qi of] fire is inadequate these
two fruit ripen."

132 Wang Bing: "絡 are 支脈, 'branching vessels.' 'Moisture' is [to say:] they have
juice." Zhang Jiebin: "Network corresponds to fire; moisture corresponds to water."

Its grain are beans and rice.[133]
Its flavors are bitter and salty.[134]
Its colors are dark and vermilion.[135]
Its domestic animals are the horse and the swine.[136]
Its creatures are feathered and scaly.[137]
It is responsible for [the appearance of] ice, snow, frost, and cold.[138]
Its tones are *zhi* and *yu*.[139]
Its illnesses are confusion, sadness, and forgetfulness.[140]
{These are transformations resulting from [the qi of] water.}[141]

70-430-3
<[A year of] minor *zhi* is identical to [a year of] minor *yu*.[142]
[A year of] upper *shang* is identical to [a year of] proper *shang*.>[143]
{The evil harms the heart.}

---

133 Wang Bing: "Beans are [grain associated with] water; rice is [grain associated with] metal."

134 Wang Bing: "They are bitter and salty at the same time." Zhang Jiebin: "bitter is weak; salty dominates."

135 Wang Bing: "When things of vermilion color are boiled, they become dark at the same time." Zhang Jiebin: "The vermilion abounds; red is weak."

136 Zhang Jiebin: "Horses are domestic animals [associated with] fire; they should be diminished. Swine are domestic animals [associated with] water; they should abound."

137 Zhang Jiebin: "Wings/feathers belong to fire; scales belong to water. They abound and are diminished [respectively]."

138 Wang Bing: "These are the qi of water."

139 Gao Shishi: "These are [the tones of] fire and water."

140 Gao Shishi: "When [a person] suffers from spirit depletion, then he/she will be confused; when [a person] suffers from heart depletion, then [that person] will be sad and forgetful."

141 Wang Bing: "The fire is weak and the water is strong. Hence half the [transformations in a year of an] arrangement of hidden brilliance follow the transformations resulting from the policy of water."

142 Wang Bing: "Fire is diminished; hence one half is identical to the transformations of water." Zhang Zhicong: "This is a general statement on the six *gui* years. *Zhi* is the sound of fire. The [qi of the] fire period is inadequate, hence [the text] says 'minor *zhi*.' The water is in charge at the same time. Hence minor *zhi* and minor *yu* transformations occur alike."

143 Zhang Zhicong: "That upper *shang* and proper *shang* are identical, applies to the two years of *gui mao* and *gui you*. They are joined from above by yang brilliance [qi]

If there is freezing and piercing cold, then violent and long lasting rain [appear in revenge].¹⁴⁴

Disasters occur in nine.¹⁴⁵
This is responsible for [the appearance of] flooding because of rainstorms, [as well as for the appearance of] thunder, tremor, and shaking [of the earth] to the extent that one is frightened,
heavy overcast, and excessive rain.¹⁴⁶

70-430-6
An arrangement of inferior supervision,
that is to say: diminished transformation.¹⁴⁷
The qi of transformation does not issue the [seasonal] command;
the policy of generation manifests itself alone.¹⁴⁸

The qi of growth is in good condition;
rain is excessive;
the qi of gathering is balanced.¹⁴⁹

---

controlling heaven. Hence [the text speaks of] upper *shang*. Metal has nothing to fear and, in addition, it receives support from [the qi] controlling heaven. That is, in an arrangement of the fire period, [only] a carefully balanced policy [of fire qi] is carried out. Hence a year of upper *shang* is identical to the qi of proper *shang*. Metal and water dominate at the same time. [Hence] evil harms the heart."

144 Wang Bing: "Freezing, bitter and piercing cold are [signs of] water acting without virtue. Violent and long lasting rain are [signs of] revenge taken by soil." Zhang Jiebin: "'Freezing, bitter and piercing cold occur because water dominates fire."

145 Wang Bing: " 'Nine' is the South."

146 Wang Bing: "The qi of heaven and earth fight each other and generate these changes."

147 Wang Bing: "That is to say: the qi of transformation is diminished. This applies to *ji si, ji mao, ji chou, ji hai, ji you*, and *ji wei* years."

148 Wang Bing: "The [qi of] soil is diminished; only the [qi of] wood operates."

149 Wang Bing: "In case there is no mutual attack and invasion, then there is balance and uprightness. The qi of transformation is diminished. Hence rain extends beyond its period." Gao Shishi: "When only the policy of generation is displayed, then wood generates fire. Hence the qi of growth is in good condition and the qi of transformation cannot carry out its policy. As a result, the qi of the earth does not rise; hence rain extends beyond its period. Soil cannot generate metal, hence the qi of gathering is balanced."

Wind and cold rise together.[150]
Herbs and trees blossom and are beautiful.[151]
They flourish but do not bear fruits;
their maturing is incomplete.[152]

Its qi is dispersion.
Its operation [manifests itself in] resting and stabilisation.[153]
The movement it [generates causes] ulcers, gushing up, cracking, welling *yong*-
abscesses, and swelling.[154]
The effusion it [generates causes] sogginess and stagnation.[155]

70-431-3
Its depot is the spleen.
Its tree-fruit are plum and chestnut.[156]
Its fruit [are those with] moisture and kernel.[157]

---

150 Zhang Jiebin: "The soil is weak and the wood acts recklessly. The water has nothing to fear. Hence wind and cold rise together."

151 Wang Bing: "Wind is wood; cold is water. The [qi of] soil is diminished, hence
the qi of cold can move. The qi of growth is displayed alone, hence herbs and trees
flourish and are beautiful.

152 Wang Bing: "The qi of transformation is incomplete. Hence the fruits are hollow
inside." Gao Shishi: "When the qi of growth is in good condition, then herbs and trees
blossom and are beautiful. When the qi of gathering is balanced, then they ripen but
do not develop fruits."

153 Wang Bing: "Even though [the qi of soil] cannot carry out its policy alone, occasionally it operates nevertheless. [Such operations] are grounded in the virtue of soil
and are marked by resting and stabilisation." Zhang Zhicong: "Effusion is the qi of
wood. Resting and fixation are operations of soil."

154 Wang Bing: "瘍 is 瘡, 'abscess.' 涌 is 嘔吐, 'to vomit.' 分 is 裂, 'to crack.' 潰 is 爛,
'to rot.' 癰腫 is 膿瘡, 'suppurating abscesses.'"

155 Wang Bing: "That is the nature of soil. 濡 is 濕, 'dampness.'" Cheng Shide et al.:
"That is, the qi of water fails to move."

156 Wang Bing: "The plum is a fruit [associated with] wood; the chestnut is [a fruit
associated with] water." Zhang Jiebin: "When [the qi of] soil is inadequate, then these
two fruits ripen."

157 Wang Bing: " 'Moisture' is: those having juice inside; 'kernel' is: those having
something hard in their center." Zhang Jiebin: "Moisture corresponds to water; kernels correspond to wood."

Its grain are bean and sesame.[158]
Its flavors are sour and sweet.[159]
Its colors are greenish and yellow.[160]
Its domestic animals are ox and dog.[161]
Its creatures are naked and hairy.[162]
It is responsible for the effusion of raging tornados and shaking.[163]
Its tones are *gong* and *jue*.[164]
Its illnesses are stagnation, fullness, and constipation.[165]
{These are transformations resulting from [the qi of] wood.}[166]

70-431-6
<[A year of] minor *gong* is identical to [a year of] minor *jue*.[167]
[A year of] upper *gong* is identical to [a year of] proper *gong*.[168]

---

158 Wang Bing: "Beans are grain [associated with] water; sesame are grain [associated with] wood."

159 Wang Bing: "If sweet things are boiled, they become sour at the same time." Zhang Jiebin: "Sour [flavor] dominates; sweetness is weak."

160 Wang Bing: "Things that are yellow are green outside at the same time." Zhang Jiebin: "Mostly green; a little yellow."

161 Zhang Jiebin: "Oxes are domestic animals [associated with] soil; they should be diminished. Dogs are domestic animals [associated with] wood; they should abound."

162 Zhang Jiebin: "Nakedness belongs to soil; hair belongs to wood. They abound and are weak [respectively]."

163 Wang Bing: "These are operations of the qi of wood."

164 Gao Shishi: "Their tones *gong* and *jue* are [those of] soil and wood [respectively]."

165 Wang Bing: "Because the qi of soil embraces and obstructs." Zhang Jiebin: "Because the [qi of] soil is insufficient the [qi of the] spleen does not [move things]."

166 Wang Bing: "[The qi of soil] does not dominate. Hence this [year] follows the transformations of the [qi of] wood."

167 Wang Bing: "The [qi of] soil is diminished. Hence one half [of the year] follows the transformations of the [qi of] wood." Zhang Zhicong: "This is a general reference to the six *ji* years. *Gong* is the sound of soil. When the [qi of the] soil period is inadequate, this is minor *gong*. Wood is in charge, too. Hence minor *gong* and minor *jue* transformations occur alike."

168 Wang Bing: "When major yin [qi] appears in the upper [half of the year], then generation and transformation are identical to those in a period of balanced soil [qi]. This occurs in *ji chou* and *ji wei* years."

[A year of] upper *jue* is identical to [a year of] proper *jue*.>[169]
<Its illnesses are outflow of [undigested] food.>[170]
{The evil harms the spleen.}

70-432-2
If there is shaking and pulling, whirling and surging, then aging and drying, dispersion and falling to the ground [appear in revenge].[171]

Disasters occur at the four ropes.[172]
This is responsible for ruin and destruction [caused by] tiger and wolf.[173]

<Then cool qi operates.
The policy of generation is disgraced.[174]>

70-432-4
An arrangement of accepted change,
that is to say: diminished gathering.[175]
The qi of gathering is belated;

---

169 Wang Bing: "When a ceasing yin [qi] appears in the upper [half of the year], then this is always an arrangement of extended harmony. This occurs in *ji hai* and *ji si* years."

170 Wang Bing: "That is a domination of wind."

171 Wang Bing: "Shaking and pulling, [wind] gusting and whirling up are [signs of] wood acting without virtue. Aging and drying out, dispersion and downfall are [signs of] metal taking revenge."

172 Wang Bing: "These are the South East and the South West, the North East and the North West, [i.e.,] the locations of [the qi of] soil." For a discussion of the meaning of 四維 in the *Su wen*, see 26/46.

173 Wang Bing: "Tiger, wolf, monkey, [etc.], all these quadrupeds come to life in that they cause harm to the abundance of grain." Gao Shishi: "Tiger and wolf are animals [associated with] the West and with metal." Zhang Jiebin: "When tiger and wolf do much harm, these are always transformations of the qi of metal seeking revenge."

174 Wang Bing: "When the qi of metal moves, then the qi of wood is subdued." Gao Shishi: "The qi of metal dominates, hence cool qi operates. Metal can level wood. Hence the policy of generation is restrained."

175 Wang Bing: "The fire diminishes the qi of gathering which is [associated with] metal. That applies to *yi chou*, *yi hai*, *yi you*, *yi wei*, *yi si*, and *yi mao* years." Cheng Shide et al.: "折 is 減折, 'to diminish.' When the metal period fails to arrive in time, fire dominates to overcome metal, and wood comes to oppose and humiliate [the metal]. Hence the qi of gathering is diminished."

the qi of generation soars.[176]
Growth and transformation combine their virtues.
The policy of fire is spread widely.[177]
Hence all classes [of beings] are plentiful.[178]

Its qi soars.[179]
Its operation [manifests itself in] racing and cutting.[180]
The movement it [generates causes] clanking, stoppage, impairment of vision, and recession.[181]
The effusion it [generates causes] coughing and panting.[182]

70-432-6
Its depot is the lung.
Its tree-fruit are the plum and the apricot.[183]
Its fruit are [those with] shell and network.[184]

---

176 Gao Shishi: "The qi of gathering is belated because the qi of metal is depleted. The qi of generation moves freely because the wood has nothing to fear."

177 Wang Bing: "宣 is 行, 'to move.'"

178 Gao Shishi: " 'Growth' is the qi of fire; 'transformation' is the qi of soil. When the metal is inadequate, then fire dominates and generates soil. Hence [the qi of] growth and transformation join their virtues. Because the qi of fire is present in surplus, the policy of fire spreads. When the policy of fire spreads, then all things are plentiful."

179 Wang Bing: "It follows the fire."

180 Wang Bing: "Even though it is diminished and even though its operation is belated, when it operates then this is cutting and urgent, in accordance with the racing of fire." Zhang Zhicong: " 'Racing and cutting' are operations of metal."

181 Wang Bing: "鏗 is the sound of coughing. 禁 is to say: the two yin [openings] are blocked (禁止). 瞀 is 悶, 'depression.' 厥 is: qi rises contrary [to its normal direction]." Zhang Jiebin: "禁 is: no sound leaves [the body]. When the [qi of] metal is insufficient, the lung corresponds to this. The lung rules the qi. Hence illnesses emerge as described here."

182 Wang Bing: "Coughing is the sound of metal; panting results from the lung storing qi." Zhang Zhicong: "Coughing and panting result from fire punishing the lung."

183 Wang Bing: "The plum is the fruit [associated with the] wood; the apricot [is the fruit associated with the] fire."

184 Wang Bing: "These are those which a shell on the outside and a branching network inside." Zhang Jiebin: "Shells are associated with metal; network [vessels] are associated with fire."

Its grain are sesame and wheat.[185]
Its flavors are bitter and acrid.
Its colors are white and vermilion.[186]
Its domestic animals are the chicken and the sheep.[187]
Its creatures are armored and feathered.[188]
It is responsible for brilliance and luster, and for flames and melting.[189]
Its tones are *shang* and *zhi*.
Its illnesses are sneezing, coughing, stuffy nose, and nosebleed.[190]
{These are transformations resulting from [the qi of] fire.}

70-433-3
<[A year of] minor *shang* is identical to [a year of] minor *zhi*.[191]
[A year of] upper *shang* is identical to [a year of] proper *shang*.[192]
[A year of] upper *jue* is identical to [a year of] proper *jue*.>[193]
{The evil harms the lung.}

---

185 Wang Bing: "Sesame is the fruit [associated with] wood; wheat is [the fruit associated with] fire. The color of wheat is red."

186 Zhang Jiebin: "Mostly red, a little white."

187 Zhang Jiebin: "Chicken are the domestic animals [associated with] metal; they should be diminished. The sheep are the domestic animals [associated with] fire; they should abound."

188 Zhang Jiebin: "Armored creatures are [those associated with] metal. Feathered creatures are [those associated with] fire."

189 Gao Shishi: "Because the qi of fire dominates."

190 Wang Bing: "These are illnesses of the metal."

191 Wang Bing: "The [qi of] metal is diminished. Hence for one half its transformations are identical to those of [the qi of] fire." Zhang Zhicong: "This is a general reference to the six *yi* years. *Shang* is the tone ruling metal. When the metal period is inadequate, this is minor *shang*. Fire is in charge at the same time. Hence minor *zhi* [years] have the same transformations."

192 Wang Bing: "When yang brilliance [qi] appears in the upper [half of the year], then generation and transformation are identical to those in a period of balanced metal [qi]. This occurs only in *yi mao* and *yi you* years."

193 Wang Bing: "When ceasing yin [qi] appears in the upper [half of the year], then generation and transformation are identical to those in a period of balanced wood [qi]. This occurs in the upper [half of] *yi si* and *yi hai* years."

If there is flaming light and fiery redness, then ice, snow, frost, and hail [appear in revenge].[194]

Disasters occur in seven.[195]
This is responsible for the hiding away of scaly [animals], swine, and mouse.[196]

If the annual qi (of the following year) arrives early,
then this generates massive cold.[197]

70-434-2
An arrangement of dried-up flow,
that is to say: rebelling yang.[198]
The [seasonal] command of storing is not put forth,
[but] the qi of transformation prospers.[199]
The qi of growth is widely promulgated.

The hibernating creatures do not hide.[200]
The soil is moist and the water fountains decrease.
Herbs and trees grow tall and are lush;
they blossom and flourish to full completion.[201]

---

194 Wang Bing: "Fierce flaming with light and brightness are [signs of fire] acting without virtue. Ice, snow, dew, and hail are [signs of] revenge taken by water."

195 Wang Bing: " 'Seven' is the West."

196 Gao Shishi: "The son of metal is water. When its qi abounds it takes revenge against the fire. Hence it is responsible for [the appearance of] scaly [animals] lying in ambush, for swines and mice. Scaly [animals] are water creatures. 伏 is identical to 復, 'taking revenge.' Swine and mouse are associated with water."

197 Wang Bing: "That is a transformation of water."

198 Wang Bing: "The yin qi is inadequate and contrary [to what is normal] the yang qi takes its place. That applies to *xin wei, xin si, xin mao, xin you, xin hai,* and *xin chou* years." Zhang Zhicong: "Water and cold are inadequate."

199 Wang Bing: "The [qi of] water is diminished while [the qi of] soil flourishes." Gao Shishi: "The qi of storing does not come up because the [qi of] water is inadequate. Hence the qi of transformation prospers because the qi of soil abounds."

200 Zhang Zhicong: "When the water does not carry out its policy, then the fire has nothing to fear. Hence the qi of growth is spread widely and contrary [to normal] the yang [qi, i.e.,] heat, abounds. It is therefore that the hibernating creatures do not hide."

201 Gao Shishi: "When the soil dominates, the water crouches. Hence the soil is moist. When the water springs diminish, the qi of soil enacts its policy alone. Hence herbs and trees grow tall and flourish; they blossom and grow to full completion."

70-434-4
Its qi is stagnation.
Its operation [manifests itself in] seeping outflow.
The movement it [generates causes] firmness and stoppage.[202]
The effusion it [generates causes] dryness and withering.[203]

Its depot are the kidneys.
Its tree-fruit are dates and apricots.[204]
Its fruit [are those with] moisture and flesh.[205]
Its grain are glutinous millet and panicled millet.[206]
Its flavors are sweet and salty.[207]
Its colors are yellow and dark.[208]
Its domestic animals are the swine and the ox.[209]
Its creatures are scaly and naked.[210]
It is responsible for dust [causing] dense [air], [resulting in] a dark screen.[211]
Its tones are *yu* and *gong*.

---

202 Wang Bing: "This refers to urination. Water is diminished, hence desiccation and firmness result, causing a stoppage."

203 Wang Bing: "Because the yin [qi] is diminished and the yang [qi] abounds."

204 Wang Bing: "Dates are tree-fruit [associated with] soil; apricots are [fruit associated with] fire."

205 Wang Bing: "Moisture is a transformation of water; flesh is a transformation of soil." Zhang Jiebin: "Moisture corresponds to water and is weak; flesh corresponds to soil and abounds."

206 Wang Bing: "Glutinous millet is a grain [associated with] fire; panicled millet is a grain [associated with] soil." Lin Yi et al.: "Above the text states: 'Wheat is the grain [associated with] fire.' Here it states 'glutinous millet.' 黍 may be a mistake for 麥, 'wheat.'"

207 Zhang Jiebin: "Sweet [flavor] dominates; salty [flavor] is weak."

208 Wang Bing: "That is: yellow with dark." Zhang Jiebin: "Mostly yellow; a little dark."

209 Zhang Jiebin: "Swines are domestic animals [associated with] water; they should be diminished. Oxes are domestic animals [associated with] soil; they should abound."

210 Zhang Jiebin: "Scaly creatures are [those associated with] water; naked creatures are [those associated with] soil."

211 Wang Bing: "That is a domination of [the qi of] soil."

Its illnesses are limpness with receding [qi], and firmness below."²¹²
{These are transformations resulting from [the qi of] soil.}

70-435-1
<[A year of] minor *yu* is identical to [a year of] minor *gong*.²¹³
[A year of] upper *gong* is identical to [a year of] proper *gong*.>²¹⁴

<Its illnesses are protuberance illness and constipation.>²¹⁵
{The evil harms the kidneys.}

If there is darkness because of dust, and if there are squalls of rain, then shaking
and pulling, breaking and plucking [appear in revenge].²¹⁶

Disasters occur in one.²¹⁷
This is responsible for the appearance of hairy [animals like] fox and racoon
dog, and for changing and transforming without storing.²¹⁸

---

212 Wang Bing: "That is the result of a union of [the qi of] water and soil." Gao Shishi: "That is because the qi of water does not moisten. When the four limbs are not
penetrated harmoniously by the body fluids, then this results in limpness with receding [qi]. When the qi of water does not pour into the two yin [openings], then this
results in firmness below."

213 Wang Bing: "Both water and soil are responsible for one half of transformations."
Gao Shishi: "The water period is inadequate. Hence [the text] speaks of minor *yu*. Soil
is in charge at the same time. Hence minor *yu* and minor *gong* transformations occur
simultaneously." Cheng Shide et al.: "These are the six *xin* years."

214 Wang Bing: "When major yin [qi] appears in the upper [half of the year], then
generation and transformation are identical to those in a period of balanced soil [qi].
This occurs in the upper [half of] *xin chou* and *xin wei* years." Gao Shishi: "When the
qi of soil controls heaven, that is called upper *gong*. Soil is in charge at the same time,
and above receives assistance by [the qi] controlling heaven. Hence upper *gong* and
proper *gong* [transformations] occur alike."

215 Wang Bing: "癃 is: the urine does not pass; 閟 is: the stools are dried and do not
pass freely." See also *Su wen* 49, note 55/56.

216 Wang Bing: "Darkness because of dust and squalls of rain are [signs of] ravaging
soil. Shaking and pulling, breaking and plucking are [signs of] wood taking revenge."

217 Wang Bing: " 'One' is the North."

218 Nanjing zhongyi xueyuan: "Hairy creatures are creatures ruled by the wood period.
They appear even though it is not their time. The fox-racoon is a very suspicious animal that likes to move around. It symbolizes the unsteady movements of wood."

Hence [the dominating qi] takes advantage of a weakness and moves;
it arrives without invitation.
If it displays violent ravaging without virtue,
catastrophes will strike it in response.
Slight [transgressions] are met by slight revenge.
Severe [transgressions] are met by severe revenge.
This is the regularity of the qi.

70-436-1
An arrangement of effusive generation,
that is to say: to open up and to develop.[219]
<The soil cracks and is drained;
greenish qi reaches [everywhere].>[220]
The yang [qi] is in harmony; it spreads and transforms.
The yin qi follows.[221]
The qi of generation transforms in purity;[222]
the myriad beings blossom as a result.[223]

Its transformation [brings about] generation.
Its qi is beauty.
Its policy [brings about] dispersion.
Its command is to penetrate and be unimpeded.[224]

---

219 Wang Bing: "Things rely on the qi of wood to grow effusively and develop their nature."

220 Wang Bing: "The qi of generation rises and is effused. Hence the body of the soil breaks open and is drained. Because the wood enacts its policy alone, green qi rises and reaches [everywhere]. 達 is 通, 'to penetrate.'" Gao Shishi: "[The qi of] wood abounds and [the qi of] soil is weak. Hence the soil opens and is drained. Green qi is the qi of wood. Because [the qi of] wood abounds, green qi reaches everywhere." For discussions of the meaning of 疏泄, see also 63/2, 2277/41, 2069/45, 64/41, 1440/38, and 1381/39.

221 Wang Bing: "The minor yang [qi] emerges first and is effused in the outside of the myriad beings. The ceasing yin [qi] follows and moves inside the myriad images." Zhang Jiebin: "When the yang qi advances day by day, then the yin qi withdraws day by day. 乃隨 is equivalent to saying 乃後, 'is late therefore.'"

222 Cheng Shide et al.: "淳 is 厚, 'rich.'"

223 Wang Bing: "If in a year [associated with wood the qi of] wood is present in surplus and if the metal does not come to dominate it, the command of generation spreads transformation [everywhere]. Hence the beings open and blossom."

224 Wang Bing: "條 is 直, 'straight,' 理, 'structure.' 舒 is 啟, 'to open.'"

The movement it [generates causes] swaying, dizziness, and peak illness.[225]
Its virtue is singing [twigs],[226] dividing, opening up, and breaking open.[227]
Its change [to the extreme causes] shaking and pulling, breaking and plucking.

70-436-4
Its grain are sesame and rice.
Its domestic animals are chicken and dog.[228]
Its tree-fruit are plum and peach.[229]
Its colors are green-blue, yellow, and white.[230]
Its flavors are sour, sweet, and acrid.[231]
Its image is spring.
Its conduits are the foot ceasing yin and [foot] minor yang [conduits].[232]
Its depots are the liver and the spleen.[233]
Its creatures are hairy and armored.
Its [material] items are firm inside and outside.[234]
Its illness is anger.[235]

---

225 Zhang Jiebin: "When wind and [the qi of] wood are greatly excessive, illnesses emerge as outlined here."

226 Zhang Jiebin: "This is the sound of wind and trees." In comparison with similar passages in *Su wen* 69 and 71, Sun Yirang suggested to read 鳴靡 as 鳴璺, "the sound of cracking." See also Wang Hongtu et al. /158.

227 Wang Bing: "Generated by the qi of wind."

228 Zhang Jiebin: "The chicken is a domestic animal [associated with] metal. Dogs are domestic animals [associated with] wood."

229 Zhang Jiebin: "Plums are fruits [associated with] wood. Peaches are fruits [associated with] metal."

230 Zhang Jiebin: "Wood can overcome soil and equal metal. Hence these three colors appear."

231 Zhang Jiebin: "These three flavors, too, [correspond to] wood, soil, and metal."

232 Wang Bing: "The ceasing yin [conduit] is the vessel of the liver; the yang brilliance [conduit] is the vessel of the gallbladder."

233 Wang Bing: "The liver dominates the spleen."

234 Wang Bing: "Things with a kernel that are hard inside are equivalent to those that have a skin or shell."

235 Wang Bing: "Because of a surplus of [the qi of] wood." Gao Shishi: "Anger is an illness of the liver."

<[A year of] major *jue* is identical to [a year of] upper *shang*.[236]
[If a year is] upper *zhi*, then its qi moves contrary [to its regular course].>
<Its illnesses are vomiting and free flow.>[237]

If it fails to live up to its virtue, then the qi of gathering takes revenge.
The qi of autumn is forceful and cutting.
In severe cases sternness and killing result.[238]
Cool qi arrives massively;
herbs and trees wither and fall.
{The evil harms the liver.}[239]

70-437-5
An arrangement of fire-red sunlight,
that is to say: opulence and lushness.[240]
The yin qi [causes] transformations inside and
the yang qi [causes] blossoming outside.
Flaming summerheat causes transformations.
Hence [all] beings achieve prosperity.[241]

---

236 Wang Bing: "The transformations of a greatly excessive qi of wood are equivalent to those of [the qi of] metal." Lin Yi et al.: "This is the only instance in the section on excessive periods where a statement of this type is found that major *jue* is identical to upper *shang*. There is no such statement in regard to the remaining four periods. Hence the present passage may be a later addition." In the received text, such a statement is missing only in one period.

237 Wang Bing: "When minor yin or minor yang [qi] appears above, then these qi move contrary [to their proper direction]. In *ren zi* and *ren wu* years minor yin [qi] appears in the upper [half of the year]; in *ren yin* and *ren shen* years, minor yang [qi] appears in the upper [half of the year]. Because a surplus of wood [qi] meets with fire, the qi is inappropriate."

238 On the meaning of 'killing,' see 1556/71.

239 Wang Bing: "[The wood] relies on itself excessively and invades the [territory of the] soil. The qi of soil is amassed extremely and the metal takes revenge. Metal enacts a policy of killing. Hence evil harms the liver, [i.e.,] wood."

240 Wang Bing: "When things meet with the abounding yang [qi] then luxuriance and richness result. This applies to the years of *wu chen*, *wu yin*, *wu zi*, *wu xu*, *wu shen*, and *wu wu*." Zhang Zhicong: "In a year when [the qi of] fire is greatly excessive, the qi of growth abounds. Hence herbs and trees appear in luxuriant richness."

241 Wang Bing: "That is so because of massive presence of the qi of growth."

Its transformation [brings about] growth;
its qi is highness.²⁴²
Its policy [brings about] movement.²⁴³
Its command [brings about] singing and clearness.²⁴⁴
The movement it [generates causes] flaming, burning, absurd behavior, and disturbance.²⁴⁵
Its virtue is warmth and summerheat, pressure and steam.
Its change [to the extreme causes] flaming and fieriness, boiling and bubbling.²⁴⁶

70-438-2
Its grain are wheat and beans.
Its domestic animals are sheep and swine.²⁴⁷
Its tree-fruit are apricot and chestnut.
Its colors are red, white, and dark.
Its flavors are bitter, acrid, and salty.
Its image is summer.
Its conduits are the hand minor yin and [hand] major yang,²⁴⁸ the hand ceasing yin and [hand] minor yang.²⁴⁹
Its depots are the heart and the lung.²⁵⁰
Its creatures are feathered and scaly.

---

242 Wang Bing: "When growth and transformations are enacted, then the appearance of things is big." Zhang Zhicong: "The qi of fire rises. Hence 'its qi is high.'"

243 Wang Bing: "The [things] are altered; their appearance is irregular."

244 Wang Bing: "The operation of fire brings about sounds; when fire burns its appearance is bright and nothing remains dark. 顯 is 露, 'disclosed.'" Zhang Jiebin: "The sound of fire is strong; the light of fire is brilliant."

245 Wang Bing: "妄 is 謬, 'error,' 'exaggeration.' 擾 is 撓, 'to disturb.'" Zhang Jiebin: "These are harms resulting from abounding fire."

246 Wang Bing: "Domination and revenge reach their extremes here."

247 Lin Yi et al.: "Earlier in this discourse the text lists 'horse' as domestic animal associated with fire. Hence 羊 may be an error for 馬, 'horse.' Even though *Su wen* 4 and 22 have 'sheep', too, the present passage should follow the version in this discourse."

248 Wang Bing: "The minor yin [conduit] is the heart vessel; the major yang [conduit] is the vessel of the small intestine."

249 Wang Bing: "The ceasing yin [conduit] is the vessel of the heart enclosure. The minor yang [conduit] is the vessel of the triple burner."

250 Wang Bing: "The heart dominates the lung."

Its [material] items have vessels and moisture.²⁵¹
Its illnesses are laughing and malaria, sores and ulcers, blood flow, craziness and absurd behavior, as well as red eyes.²⁵²

70-438-5
<[A year of] upper *yu* is identical to [a year of] proper *zhi*.>²⁵³
<Its gathering is evenly [distributed].
Its illness is stiffness.>²⁵⁴
<In [a year of] upper *zhi* the qi of gathering is belated.>²⁵⁵

If its policy [brings about] violence and fieriness,
then the qi of storing will [come up as] revenge.

---

251 Wang Bing: "Vessels are fire things; moisture is a water thing. Water and fire are equally present." Lin Yi et al.: "脈 is 絡, 'network [vessels].' The characters are different, but the meaning is the same."

252 Wang Bing: "Because fire abounds."

253 Wang Bing: "If major yang [qi] appears in the upper [half of the year] then the qi of heaven is restrained. Hence a greatly excessive fire causes generation and transformation identical to a period of balanced fire. It is [the qi that] appears above in *wu chen* and *wu xu* years. If [the qi of a year] is identical to that in balanced fire periods, then the five regular qi do not invade each other's [domain]. Hence the generation and transformation caused by the qi of gathering, [i.e., the qi of] metal, are on the same level." Gao Shishi: "In *wu chen* and *wu xu* years, [the qi of] major yang, cold, and water controls heaven. That is called upper *yu*. When the fire period is greatly excessive and when it is joined in the upper [half of the year] by [the qi of] cold and water, then the qi of fire is balanced. Hence it is identical to the proper *zhi* of rising brilliance."

254 Gao Shishi: "Because the qi of fire is balanced and [the qi of] metal does not receive harm; the [qi of] gathering is sufficient. 齊 is 足, 'sufficient.' Fire rules the conduits and vessels. When it is joined by cold and water in the upper [half of the year], then the qi of fire receives harm. Hence the resulting illness is stiffness. Stiffness is an illness of the conduits and vessels." Zhang Jiebin: "In case of 痓, [the patient suffers from] lockjaw like in convulsions. Limbs and body have a cramp and are stiff."

255 Wang Bing: "If minor yin or minor yang [qi] appear in the upper [half of the year], then generation and transformation follow their own policy and the qi of metal cannot transform on the same level with them. If in *wu zi* and *wu wu* years minor yin [qi] appears in the upper [half of the year] and if in *wu yin* and *wu shen* years minor yang [qi] appears in the upper [half of the year], fire abounds. Hence the transformations of the qi of gathering are belated." Gao Shishi: "In *wu zi*, *wu wu*, *wu yin*, and *wu shen* years the ruler and the minister fire control heaven. That is called upper *zhi*. When the fire period is greatly excessive and when it receives assistance by [the qi] controlling heaven, then the qi of metal receives harm and the qi of gathering is belated."

Freezing cold appears often.
In severe cases there are rain, water, frost, hail, and cutting cold.
{The evil harms the heart.}[256]

70-439-2
An arrangement of prominent mound,
that is to say: wide-reaching transformation.[257]
[It is characterized by] pronounced virtue, clearness and resting,
adaptation, growth, and fullness.[258]
Extreme yin fills the inside;
the transformation of beings reaches completion and perfection.[259]

Smoke and dust, haziness and pressure
appear in thick soil.[260]
Massive rain prevails often.
Hence dampness qi operates and,
as a result, the policy of dryness is withdrawn.

70-439-4
Its transformation [brings about] roundness.
Its qi is prosperity.[261]

---

256 Gao Shishi: "When the qi of fire is greatly excessive, its policy is violent. In the beginning, the fire is unrestrained. Later, the water dominates. Hence the qi of storing takes revenge. In severe cases, water abounds and the fire is extinguished. Hence rain, frost, hail, and cutting cold appear and the evil harms the heart."

257 Wang Bing: "The [qi of] soil is present in surplus. Hence the qi of transformation is widely applied to things. This refers to *jia zi, jia xu, jia shen, shen wu, shen chen,* and *shen yin* years."

258 Wang Bing: "The nature of soil is to follow. Its operation does not entail fighting with other beings. Hence its virtue is strongly pronounced and it lacks agitation. When it follows the fire in causing growth and nourishment, this lets the myriad beings transform and to be full of qi."

259 Wang Bing: "至陰 is the essence qi of soil. That is, the reason why the myriad beings transform and reach completion is that the qi of magic strength (靈氣) of extreme yin generates transformations inside of them." Gao Shishi: "The qi of soil is major yin. Major yin is extreme yin."

260 Wang Bing: " 'Thick soil' are mountains. 'Smoke and dust' are the qi of soil."

261 Gao Shishi: " 'Its transformation is roundness,' that is the ubiquity of soil; 'its qi is prosperity,' that is the thickness of soil."

Its policy [brings about] resting.[262]
Its command [brings about] ubiquitous perfection.[263]
The movement it [generates causes] a storing up of accumulated moisture.
Its virtue is tender moisture and doubled mud.
Its change [to the extreme causes] shaking [of the earth] to the extent that one
is frightened, tornado and rainstorm, and landslips because of flooding.[264]

70-439-6
Its grain are panicled millet and sesame.
Its domestic animals are ox and dog.
Its tree-fruit are date and plum.
Its colors are yellow, dark and greenish.
Its flavors are sweet, salty and sour.[265]
Its image is late summer.[266]
Its conduits are the foot major yin and [foot] yang brilliance.[267]
Its depots are the spleen and the kidneys.[268]
Its creatures are naked and hairy.[269]

---

262 Wang Bing: "What is resting can exist for long. Hence its policy is persistent."
Zhang Jiebin: "Its virtue is thick and heavy. Hence its policy brings about peace and
resting."

263 Wang Bing: "The qi is relaxed. Hence it causes ubiquitous perfection." Zhang
Jiebin: "The soil rules during [all] four seasons and fills the myriad beings. Hence [the
text] speaks of ubiquitous perfection."

264 Wang Bing: "Shock and fright are caused by thunder. Tornados and rainstorms
are the onset of violent wind and rain. When massive rain rushes down violently, then
mountains break down and the soil flows away together with the water." Zhang Jiebin:
"These are transformations resulting from excessive [qi of] soil and simultaneous revenge by [the qi of] water."

265 Gao Shishi: "[The qi of] soil may be greatly excessive, nevertheless, when something greatly excessive moves on, it is followed by something inadequate. Hence the
three qi of soil, wood, and water are in charge together. Its grain pannicled millet and
sesame, its domestic animals ox and dog, as well as its tree-fruit date and plum are
[associated with] soil and wood [respectively]. Its colors yellow, dark, and green, and
its flavors sweet, salty, and sour, are [associated with] soil, water, and wood."

266 Gao Shishi: "Late summer is associated with soil."

267 Wang Bing: "The major yin [conduit] is the vessel of the spleen; the yang brilliance [conduit] is the vessel of the stomach."

268 Wang Bing: "The spleen dominates the kidneys."

269 Zhang Jiebin: "When the qi of soil is present in surplus, naked and hairy [crea-
tures] are transformed equally."

Its [material] items have flesh and kernel.[270]
Its illnesses are abdominal fullness and inability to lift the four limbs.[271]
[...]
Strong winds arrive with great speed.
[...]
{The evil harms the spleen.}[272]

An arrangement of firm completion,
that is to say: contracting and pulling.[273]
The qi of heaven is clean;
the qi of the earth is brilliant.
The yang qi is followed by
the yin [qi] in governing the transformations.[274]

Dryness carries out its policy.
Because of this control, the beings reach completion.
The qi of gathering spreads luxuriously;
transformations penetrate everywhere without coming to an end.[275]

---

270 Wang Bing: "Muscles are [transformations of] soil; kernels are [transformations of] wood."

271 Wang Bing: "The nature of soil is resting. Hence illnesses [during such an arrangement] are like this." Zhang Zhicong: "These are illnesses caused by water, dampness."

272 Wang Bing: "Wood [qi] abounds and is angry. Hence the soil, [i.e.,] the spleen receives harm." Gao Shishi: "In the beginning, [the qi of] soil is unrestrained. Later then [the qi of] wood dominates. Hence strong winds arrive with great speed."

273 Wang Bing: "引 is 敛, 'to contract.' Yang qi gathers and yin qi operates. Hence the myriad beings are gathered and contracted. This refers to *geng wu, geng chen, geng yin, geng zi, geng xu*, and *geng shen* years." Zhang Zhicong: "The policy of autumn controls gathering. Hence [the text] says 收引." Zhang Jiebin: "As for 引, yin [qi] abounds and yang [qi] is weak. The myriad beings pull each other and retreat."

274 Gao Shishi: "Summer is yang; autumn is yin. When autumn arrives, then the qi of yang heat is followed by transformations governed by yin [qi]."

275 Wang Bing: "The qi of gathering and killing arrives early; the transformations of the [qi of] soil cannot complete their operation." Lin Yi et al.: "The character 繁 may be an error." Gao Shishi: "As for 化治, the qi of transformation penetrates the myriad beings. The qi of autumn arrives early. Hence the penetration by the qi of transformation has not ended." Zhang Jiebin: "When dryness enacts its policy, the transformations of [its] qi bring about firmness. Hence it controls the ripening of the myriad beings. When the qi of gathering [associated with] metal abounds and spreads early, then the qi of transformation [associated with the] soil cannot carry out its policy to its end."

70-440-6
Its transformation [brings about] completion;
its qi is deletion.
Its policy [brings about] sternness.
Its command [brings about] sharpness and cutting.[276]
The movement it [generates causes] sudden breaking, ulcer, and infixation.[277]
Its virtue is fog and dew, and the whistling of cold winds.[278]
Its change [to the extreme causes] sternness and killing, withering and falling.[279]

70-441-1
Its grain are rice and glutinous millet.[280]
Its domestic animals are chicken and horse.
Its tree-fruit are peach and apricot.
Its colors are white, green-blue, and vermilion.
Its flavors are acrid, sour, and bitter.[281]
Its image is autumn.[282]
Its conduits are the hand major yin and [hand] yang brilliance.[283]

---

276 Wang Bing: "蕭 is 清, 'clearness,' 靜, 'resting.'" Gao Shishi: " 'Its transformation brings about completion,' that is the gathering of what has ripened in autumn. 'Its qi is deletion,' that is the deletion of things by means of metal. 'Its policy [brings about] sternness,' that is the clearness and sternness of metal. 'Its command [brings about] sharpness,' that is the hardness and strength of metal."

277 Zhang Jiebin: "Violent breaking occurs when the qi of metal is present in surplus. Ulcers and infixation are skin illnesses." Ma Shi: "Metal rules the skin."

278 Wang Bing: "These are transformations of dryness. 蕭飋 are sounds produced by wind. When it is motionless, this results in fog and dew; when it operates, then wind is generated."

279 Zhang Jiebin: "The policy of killing is carried out."

280 Lin Yi et al.: "Above the text states 'wheat is the grain of fire.' Here it should say 'its grain are rice and wheat.'"

281 Gao Shishi: "[The qi of] metal may be greatly excessive, nevertheless, when something greatly excessive moves on, it is followed by something inadequate. Hence the three qi of metal, wood, and fire are in charge together. Its grain rice and glutinous millet, its domestic animals chicken and horse, as well as its tree-fruit peach and apricot are [associated with] metal and fire [respectively]. Its colors white, green, and red, and its flavors acrid, sour, and bitter, are [associated with] metal, wood, and fire."

282 Gao Shishi: "Autumn is associated with metal."

283 Wang Bing: "The major yin [conduit] is the vessel of the lung; the yang brilliance [conduit] is the vessel of the large intestine."

Its depots are the lung and the liver.[284]
Its creatures are armored and feathered.[285]
Its [material] items have shells and networks.[286]
Its illness is panting with large noise; one has [a feeling of] fullness in the chest and breathes in an upright position.[287]

70-441-4
<[A year of] upper *zhi* is identical to [a year of] proper *shang.*>[288]
<Its generation is equal.[289]
Its illness is cough.>[290]

If the policy [of metal brings about] sudden change,
then the eminent trees do not blossom.[291]
What is soft and brittle has scorched tops.
The qi of growth comes to rescue [them].
[Hence] massive fire prevails;
also, flames and melting arrive.

---

284 Wang Bing: "The lung dominates the liver."

285 Wang Bing: "The [qi of] metal is present in surplus. Hence armored and feathered [creatures] are raised alike."

286 Wang Bing: "Shells are [a transformation of] metal; network [vessels] are a transformation of fire."

287 Wang Bing: "Because the qi of metal is present in surplus." Zhang Zhicong: "Hence the lung qi is replete."

288 Gao Shishi: "When in the upper [half of a year] minor yin or minor yang [qi] appear to control heaven, that is called upper *zhi*. When [the qi of] metal is greatly excessive and when fire controls heaven, then the qi of metal will become balanced and [the year is] identical to one of proper *shang.*"

289 Zhang Jiebin: "The qi of metal is balanced, [hence] the wood does not receive harm. As a result, the qi of generation can equally enact its transformations." Zhang Qi: "The three characters 其生齊 are a later insertion."

290 Wang Bing: "If minor yin or minor yang [qi] appear in the upper [half of the year], then the qi of heaven appears restrained. Hence its generation and transformation are identical to those of a year of balanced metal. If in the upper [half] of *geng zi* and *geng wu* years minor yin [qi] appears, or if in the upper [half] of *geng yin* or *geng shen* years minor yang [qi] appears, the fire restrains the metal. Hence the qi of generation transforms together with it. Fire occupies [the territory of] the metal, [i.e.,] the lung. Hence the illness is coughing."

291 670/7: "In antiquity, the meaning of 大, 'tall,' was occasionally expressed by the term 名." See also *Su wen* 2-12-4, note 42.

Winding plants will wither.
{The evil harms the lung.}²⁹²

70-442-1
An arrangement of inundating flow,
that is to say: seclusive storage.²⁹³
Cold controls the transformation of beings;
heaven and earth are extremely frozen.²⁹⁴
The policy of storing is widespread;
the command of growth does not soar.²⁹⁵

Its transformation [brings about] piercing cold.
Its qi is firmness.²⁹⁶
Its policy [brings about] tranquility.
Its command [brings about] outpour.²⁹⁷
The movement it [generates causes] drifting, outflow, pouring, and gushing
up.²⁹⁸
Its virtue is freezing cold and cold fog.²⁹⁹
Its change [to the extreme causes] ice, snow, frost, and hail.³⁰⁰

---

292 Wang Bing: " 'Change' is to say: 太甚, 'excessive.' When the policy is carried out
excessively, then the qi of generation is restrained. Hence the trees do not blossom and
the heads of herbs burn and die. When the violence of the policy does not come to an
end, then the qi of fire develops anger. Hence fire rages, and flames and melting arrive.
All brittle [things] like soft twigs and climbing herbs dry and die. Fire occupies the
[territory of] the metal qi. Hence the lung is harmed."

293 Wang Bing: "When yin qi acts massively, then its transformation is such that
heaven and earth [execute] seclusive storage. This applies to *bing yin, bing zi, bing
xu, bing shen, bing wu*, and *bing chen* years." Zhang Zhicong: "Winter policy [entails]
seclusive storage. Hence [this arrangement] is called 'seclusive storage.'"

294 Wang Bing: "Because of yin qi."

295 Wang Bing: "When the qi of storage operates, then growth and transformation
come to a halt. Hence the command [of growth] cannot develop." Gao Shishi: "Water
dominates the fire. Hence the command of growth cannot pass freely."

296 Wang Bing: "When cold qi arrives, things harden."

297 Wang Bing: "That is the image of water."

298 Zhang Jiebin: "漂 is 浮於上, 'to drift on the surface.' 泄 is 瀉於下, 'to flow off
downward.' 沃 is 灌, 'to pour down.' 涌 is 溢, 'to overflow.'"

299 Wang Bing: "These are transformations of cold."

300 Wang Bing: "They appear when it is not their time." Zhang Zhicong: "When
cold reaches an extreme, then [such] changes occur."

70-442-4
Its grain are bean and panicled millet.
Its domestic animals are swine and ox.
Its tree-fruit are chestnut and date.
Its colors are black, vermilion, and yellow.
Its flavors are salty, bitter, and sweet.[301]
Its image is winter.[302]
Its conduits are the foot minor yin and [foot] major yang.[303]
Its depots are the kidneys and the heart.[304]
Its creatures are scaly and naked.[305]
Its [material] items have moisture and are full.[306]
Its illness is distension.[307]

<{In [a year of] upper *yu*, the qi of growth does not transform.>[308]

If the policy [of water] is excessive, then the qi of transformation comes up massively.

---

301 Gao Shishi: "[The qi of] water may be greatly excessive, nevertheless, when something greatly excessive moves on, it is followed by something inadequate. Hence the three qi of water, soil, and fire are in charge together. Its grain bean and pannicled millet, its domestic swine and ox, as well as its tree-fruit water chestnut and date are [associated with] water and soil [respectively]. Its colors black, red, and yellow, and its flavors salty, bitter, and sweet, are [associated with] water, fire, and soil."

302 Gao Shishi: "Winter is associated with water."

303 Wang Bing: "The minor yin [conduit] is the vessel of the kidneys; the major yang [conduit] is the vessel of the bladder."

304 Wang Bing: "The kidneys dominate the heart."

305 Wang Bing: "The [qi of] water is present in surplus. Hence scaly and naked [creaturs] are raised alike."

306 Wang Bing: "Moisture is [a transformation of] water; fullness is a transformation of soil." Zhang Jiebin: " 'Fullness' should be flesh; it is a transformation of soil."

307 Wang Bing: "Water is present in surplus." Zhang Zhicong: "Water abounds and occupies the [territory of the] soil."

308 Wang Bing: "If major yang [qi] appears in the upper [half of the year], then the fire cannot spread its transformation to [let things] grow. If this appears in the upper [half of] *bing chen* and *bing xu* years, this is a 'heavenly complements water period.'" Gao Shishi: "If it is joined in the upper [half of the year] by [the qi of] major yang-cold-water, this is called upper *yu*. When [the qi of] water is greatly excessive and when it is joined by [qi of] water in the upper [half of the year], then the qi of growth cannot cause transformations. The qi of growth is the qi of fire."

Hence dust and darkness [occur in the section of] qi interaction.[309]
Massive rain falls frequently.
{The evil harms the kidneys.}[310]

70-443-2
Hence when it is said:
'If [the qi of a year] does not perpetuate its virtue, then [that qi] by which it is
dominated comes to take revenge.
If a policy perpetuates its principles, then [that qi] by which it is dominated is
identical in its transformations,'
then this means just the same."[311]

[Huang] Di:
"Heaven is insufficient in the North-West.
Cold is to the left and coolness to the right.
The earth is incomplete in the South-East.

---

309 The term 交 was used in the *Zuo zhuan*, Duke Xi 僖公, 5th year, in the sense
of " point of transition (from the ninth to the tenth month)". (See Ruan Yuan 1796
above). In the present context, this could refer to the point in time when the rule by
the qi of heaven of the first half of a year is followed by the rule by the qi of the earth
of the second half of that year. Our translation as "[qi] interaction" is based on the notion that in the middle of a year a short period of transition is ruled by both the qi of
heaven and the qi of the earth.

310 Wang Bing: "When violent cold sets in frequently, that is called 'excessive policy.'
The fire is invaded by the water and the soil comes to take revenge. Hence heaven and
earth are clouded and dark, the qi of soil and water interact. Massive rain falls and the
evil [qi of soil] harms the kidneys." Gao Shishi: "When the policy of water is greatly
excessive, then, in the beginning, [the qi of] water is unrestrained. Later on, the soil
dominates. Hence the qi of transformation comes up massively and the qi of dust and
darkness interact. When the qi of dust and darkness interact, this is earth qi rising.
When earth qi rises, massive rain falls frequently. Because the qi of soil is present in
surplus, evil harms the kidneys."

311 Wang Bing: "不恆.. is to say: to rely on oneself having surplus and to invade [the
territory of] that by which oneself cannot be dominated. 恆.. is to say: to hold on to
regular transformations and not to impose severe punishment. In this case the qi by
which oneself can be overcome will pursue identical government and transformation
throughout the year."

Heat is to the right and warmth is to the left.[312]
What is the reason for this?"[313]

Qi Bo:
"[The reason is] the qi of yin and yang,
the structure of being high or low,
the difference of excessive and diminished [qi].[314]

The South-East is yang.
As for the yang, its essence is bestowed to the below.
Hence there is heat on the right and warmth on the left.[315]

The North-West is yin.
As for the yin, its essence is presented to the above.
Hence there is cold on the left and coolness on the right.[316]

---

312 Gao Shishi: "Heaven is yang; yang qi is warm and hot. The earth is yin; yin qi is cold and cool. When [the qi of] heaven is insufficient in the North-West, then yang qi is diminished in the North-West. Hence there is cold and coolness to the left and to the right respectively. When the [qi of the] earth is not fully present in the South-East, then the yin qi is diminished in the South-East. Hence there is warmth and heat to the left and to the right respectively." Cheng Shide et al.: " 'Left and right' refers to cardinal points. In the North-West, 'right' is the West; it is associated with metal and corresponds to autumn. Hence its qi is coolness. The 'left' of the North-West is the North; it is associated with water and corresponds to winter. Hence its qi is cold. The 'left' of the South-East is the East; it is associated with wood and corresponds to spring. Hence its qi is warmth. The 'right' of the South-East is the South; it is associated with fire and corresponds to summer. Hence its qi is heat."

313 Wang Bing: "This is said facing the South-East."

314 Wang Bing: " 'High and low' refers to the physical appearance of the earth; 'Major and minor' refers to the differences in the abundance or weakness of the qi of yin and yang. Now, the physical appearance of the central plain (i.e., China) is such that the land in the North-West is high, while in the South-East it is low; in the West it is cool, in the North it is cold, in the East it is warm, and in the South it is hot."

315 Wang Bing: "The yang essence descends. Hence the earth corresponds below by turning warm. Yang qi is generated in the East and it abounds in the South. Hence the warmth in the East and the heat in the South is obvious evidence of the presence of more or less [yang] qi."

316 Wang Bing: "The yin essence rises. Hence the earth corresponds above by turning cold. Yin qi is generated in the West and abounds in the North. Hence the West is cool and the North is cold. The lord speaks facing the South-East; the official responds facing the North-West."

Hence the earth has highlying and lowlying [regions];
among the qi there is warm [qi] and cool [qi].
In the highlying [regions], the qi is cold;
in the low-lying [regions], the qi is hot.

70-443-9
Hence
those who go where it is cold and cool, they experience distension.[317]
Those going where it is warm and hot will suffer from sores.
Purging them ends the distension.
Letting them sweat ends the sores.[318]
This is nothing but the regularity in the opening and closing of the interstice
structures and the difference between excessive and diminished [qi]."

[Huang] Di:
"How does this affect longevity and early death?"

Qi Bo:
"Where yin essence is presented [from below], the people enjoy longevity.
Where yang essence is bestowed [from above], the people experience early
death."[319]

---

317 306/120: "The *Shuo wen* states: 適 is 之, 'to move toward.'"

318 Wang Bing: "In cold and cool regions, the interstice structures are rarely open
and mostly closed and the yang qi cannot disperse. Hence those who happen to meet
cold or coolness will experience a distended abdomen. In regions that are damp and
hot, the interstice structures are open often and are closed only rarely. When they
open often, then the yang [qi] disperses. Hence if it is alternatingly warm and hot, the
skin will develop sores. When [the former patients] are subjected to purgation, the
central qi will no longer be present in surplus; hence the distension is ended. When
[the latter patients] are subjected to sudorification, the yang qi is drained towards the
outside. Hence the sores are healed." Gao Shishi: "下之 means: the qi of heaven descends. When yin cold is met by yang heat, then the distensions end. 汗之 means: the
qi of the earth rises. When yang heat is met by yin cold, then the sores are healed."

319 Wang Bing: " 'Where yin essence is presented' that is high-lying land. 'Where
yang essence descends' that is low-lying land. In yin regions the yang [qi] is not drained
recklessly and the cold qi is kept outside. The evil [qi] does not strike frequently and
the proper qi is guarded firmly. Hence life extends for long. In yang regions the yang
qi is dispersed and effused beyond measure. [People] are frequently struck by dampness and wind. The true qi is exhausted unilaterally. Hence they die early. This can be
proven by the facts: in today's China, all people in the North-West enjoy a long life,
while all people in the South-East die early." 2643/60: " 'Yin essence' refers to yin qi,
[i.e.,] cold. 奉 is 上升, 'to rise.' 'Yang essence' refers to yang qi, [i.e.,] heat."

[Huang] Di:

"Good!

Their illnesses, how are they treated?"

Qi Bo:

"The qi of the North-West must be dispersed and cooled.

The qi of the South-East must be gathered and warmed.

{This is the so-called 'identical illnesses, different treatments.'}[320]

70-445-4

Hence it is said:

'Cold qi and cool qi,

treat [them] with cold and coolness;

soak them in running water.[321]

Warm qi and hot qi,

treat [them] with warmth and heat;

strengthen their being guarded internally.[322]

It is essential to adapt to the respective qi;

---

320 Wang Bing: "The interstice structures of the skin of the people in the West and in the North are tightly closed and they all eat hot food. Hence [their qi] must be dispersed and it must be cooled. The skin of the people in the East and in the South is relaxed and their interstice structures are open and they all eat cold food. Hence [their] qi must be gathered and it must be warmed." Zhang Jiebin: "In the North-West the qi is cold. When cold closes the outside, then heat accumulates inside. Hence it is necessary to disperse the outside cold and to cool the inner heat. In the South-East, the qi is heat. When the qi flows of to the outside, then cold emerges in the center. Hence it is necessary to hold what flows off toward outside and to warm the cold in the center. That is, the illnesses are identical but the treatments are different."

321 Zhang Jiebin: "In the North-West, there is cold qi and coolness qi. The people often eat hot food and their inner heat abounds. Hence it is appropriate to treat them with cold or coolness by soaking them in running water. That is to say, they are soaked in water to disperse their outer cold." In contrast: Yan Hongchen & Gao Guangzhen/269: "行 is 施行, 'to apply.' 水漬 is: 'soak in warm or hot water.' That is the [therapeutic] method of warm baths." 2171/14: "Zhang Zhicong states: '漬 is 浸, to soak, to immerse.' That is, water or drug extracts are employed to soak/immerse a specific location of the human body."

322 Zhang Jiebin: "In the South-West, there is warmth qi and heat qi. The people often eat cool food and develop cold internally. Hence it is appropriate to treat them with warmth and heat. Also, it is essential to strengthen their being guarded internally. If one aims at keeping the yang qi from flowing off, it is necessary to strengthen the center."

thereby it is possible to achieve a balance.
In case of false [heat or cold], act contrary to the [rule]."³²³

70-445-6
[Huang] Di:
"Good!
The qi of one single district [brings about]³²⁴ differences in generation and
transformation, in longevity and early death.
What is the reason for this?"

Qi Bo:
"The [differences in the] structures of highlying and lowlying [regions] are
caused by [differences in] the physical features of the earth.

The highest [regions] are governed by the yin qi.
The lowest [regions] are ruled by the yang qi.
When the yang [qi] dominates, it precedes heaven.
When the yin [qi] dominates, it is behind heaven.³²⁵

That is the regularity of the structures of the earth and the Way of generation
and transformation."

70-446-1
[Huang] Di:
"And their longevity and early death?"

---

323 Wang Bing: "[To employ] cold prescriptions to [treat] cold [qi], [to employ] hot
prescriptions to [treat] hot [qi], [to employ] warm prescriptions to [treat] warm [qi],
[to employ] cool prescriptions to [treat] cool [qi], that is the proper pattern; that is
[relying on] identical qi. .. If in case [people] in the West or in the North suffer from
cold illness, [treatment] relies (假) on hot and warm [prescriptions] to eliminate the
[cold], and if in case [people] in the East or in the South suffer from heat illness, it is
essential to [rely] on cool or cold [prescriptions], then this is treating them contrary
to the proper pattern outlined above." Fang Yaozhong: "假 refers to false images, like:
false cold or false heat. 反 refers to the pattern of 'opposing therapy' here. That is what
the *Neijing* calls 'apply cold [qi] in cases of [false] cold.'"

324 See 2493/531 for alluding to the use of 州, government district, here as one of 14
points suggesting a Han origin of the *Su wen*.

325 Wang Bing: "先天 is to say: preceding the celestial seasons; 後天 is to say: be
later than the celestial seasons. All this refers to the earlier or belated occurrence
of generation, blossoming, withering, and falling down on the earth. This applies to
things and it applies to human beings, too."

Qi Bo:

"Those [living] in highlying [regions], their qi gives them longevity.

Those [living] in lowlying [regions], their qi lets them die early.

There are differences depending on the smaller or larger [distances of the regions] of the earth.

When the [distances] are small, the differences are small.

When the [distances] are large, the differences are large.[326]

Hence those treating an illness,

they must comprehend the Way of heaven and the structure of the earth,

the alternating domination of yin and yang,

the earlier or later [arrival] of the qi,

human longevity and early death, and

the recurring times of generation and transformation.

This way they are able to understand human physical appearance and qi."

70-446-6

[Huang] Di:

"Good!

If in a specific year [the arrangement is such that there should] be no illness,[327] and yet the qi in the depots does not correspond. [The qi of that year] does not operate, why is that?"

Qi Bo:

"The qi of heaven restrains it. The qi have something they follow."[328]

[Huang] Di:

"I should like to hear this comprehensively."

---

326 Wang Bing: " 'Large' is to say: the South-East and the North-West are about ten thousand miles apart from each other. 'Small' is to say: residences in highlying [on the one side] and low-lying [regions] [on the other side] appromixately twenty or thirty miles, or even one hundred miles apart."

327 Fang Yaozhong: "不病 is 正常, 'regular,' 'normal.' ('The [qi of a given] year is normal')"

328 Wang Bing: " 'Follow' is to say: to act on behalf of someone else and not to attend to one's own interests." Zhang Jiebin: "歲有不病不應不用 is to say: in a [specific] annual period there should be illness, but there is no illness; the qi of the depots should correspond and should operate, but fails to correspond and fails to operate. 天氣制之 氣有所從之 is to say: when [the qi] controlling heaven restrains it, then it follows the qi of heaven. Hence it happens that it does not follow the [qi of that] year." Cheng Shide et al.: " 'Qi' refers to the qi of the five depots." Fang Yaozhong: " 'Qi of heaven' is the qi controlling heaven. 'Qi' refers to the qi of the annual period."

Qi Bo:
"When the minor yang [qi] controls heaven and
when fire qi comes down, then
the lung qi rises to follow.
White [qi] rises and metal operates.
[Hence] herbs and trees are met by disasters.[329]

Fire appears with burning heat;
it alters metal. It even makes it vanish.
Hence massive summerheat prevails.
[People suffer from] cough, sneezing, stuffy nose, nosebleed,
nasal congestion, from oral ulcers,
cold and heat, as well as *fu*-swelling.[330]

70-446-10
Wind prevails on the earth;
dust and sand fly whirling up.
[People suffer from] heartache and stomach duct pain,
from recession with countermovement, from barriers and impassability.
Its rule is violent and fast.[331]

---

329 Cheng Shide et al.: " 'Minor yang controls heaven' refers to *yin* and *shen* years. 'White' symbolizes the qi of dryness and metal. 'White [qi] rises and metal operates' [is to say:] the qi of dryness and metal, being in charge of affairs, receives the influence of fire."

330 Wang Bing: "These are indicators of *yin* and *shen* years. 臨 is to say: 御於下, 'to superintend what is below.' 從 is to say: 從事於上, 'to tend to the affairs of what is above.' 起 is to say: expensive on the market. 用 is to say: to carry out punishment. 'Coming down' and 'following,' 'rising' and 'operation' are to be seen together. 革 is 'animal hide' and it is 'to alter.' The qi of fire blazes. Hence [the text] states: it generates ulcers. 瘡 are ulcers on the body; 瘍 are ulcers on the head. 'Cold and heat' is to say: [the patient feels] cold first and hot afterwards. That is malaria. When the lung is harmed by fire, the water comes to rescue it. The water protects the lung and the center. Hence it causes swellings. 肘腫 is a swelling which after being pressed down does not rise again. This is generated by the qi of heaven." Lin Yi et al.: "[Wang Bing] refers in his comment to 瘡 and to 瘍. The current version of the text only has 瘍. The character 瘡 may have been dropped. As for 曰, other versions have 口, 'mouth.'" On the basis of Wang Bing's comment, 2637/48 reads 曰瘍 as 瘡瘍. See also 1798/36 for a discussion of the meaning of 胕 in the *Neijing*. We read 曰 as 口, and have changed the text accordingly.

331 Wang Bing: "Because ceasing yin [qi] is at the fountain, wind prevails on the earth. Because of this domination of excessive wind, these illnesses appear. The transformations of minor yang and ceasing yin [qi] are urgent and fast. Hence the illnesses [they cause] emerge fast, too. Hence [the text] states: its rule is violent and fast."

70-446-11
When the yang brilliance [qi] controls heaven, and
when dryness qi comes down, then
liver qi rises to follow.
Greenish [qi] rises; wood operates <and stands up>.
Hence soil is met by disasters.³³²

70-447-1
Chilling temperatures arrive frequently.
The trees are felled and the herbs wither.
[People suffer from] aching flanks and red eyes,
from swaying and shaking, from chattering [teeth] and shivering.
Their sinews are limp and they cannot stand up for long.³³³

Violent heat arrives and,
as a result, the soil is [struck by] summerheat.
Yang qi, oppressed [before by the cold, now] is effused.

The urine changes.
[Patients experience feelings of] cold and heat, like in malaria.
In severe cases the heart aches.

Zhang Jiebin: "Whenever minor yang [qi] controls heaven, then ceasing yin [qi] is
at the fountain. Hence wind prevails on the earth. In case of a domination of unrestrained wind, illness occurs in the ceasing yin [region]. The ceasing yin vessels pass
by the stomach, touch the liver and penetrate the diaphragm. Hence illnesses emerge
as listed here."

332 Cheng Shide et al.: "Yang brilliance [qi] controls heaven in *mao* and *you* years."

333 Wang Bing: "These are indicators of *mao* and *you* years. Another expression for
木用 is 木功, 'works of wood.' The illnesses [described] here are generated by the qi
of the heaven." Gao Shishi: "Yang brilliance is dryness and metal. Hence the qi of
dryness comes down. The qi controlling heaven restrains the human body. Because
the human beings experience this restraint, the qi of the liver rises to follow [the qi
controlling heaven]. The color of the liver is green and it belongs to wood. Hence
green [qi] rises and [the qi of] wood operates. When green [qi] rises and when [the qi
of] wood operates, then soil experiences a disaster, that is, wood punishes soil. When
extreme cold arrives frequently, that is a domination of the qi of metal. The trees are
cut and the herbs wither because metal punishes the wood. Aching flanks and red eyes
are illnesses of the liver, [i.e.,] of wood. Swaying and shaking, chattering teeth and
trembling are illnesses of liver depletion. The sinews lame and one cannot stand up for
long because the liver rules the sinews."

Fire spreads where [the herbs and trees] have withered.
Flowing water does not freeze.
Hence hibernating creatures appear.[334]

70-447-4
When the major yang [qi] controls heaven and
when cold qi comes down, then
the heart qi rises to follow.
Also, the fire is brilliant.[335]
Vermilion [qi] rises.
Hence metal is met by disasters.[336]

>Cold and coolness set in frequently.
When [they] dominate, then the water freezes.<

The fire qi rises high and is brilliant.
>The heart is hot and vexed.<
The throat is dry and [patients] tend to be thirsty.
[They suffer from] stuffy nose and sneezing.
They tend to be sad and yawn frequently.

Heat qi moves in an absurd manner.
Hence cold [returns in] revenge.
Frost descends when it is not its time.
[People] are forgetful.
In severe cases the heart aches.[337]

---

334 Wang Bing: "When minor yin [qi] is at the fountain, heat controls the earth and
a situation as described here emerges. The illnesses [described] here are generated by
the qi of the earth." Zhang Jiebin: "Whenever yang brilliance [qi] controls heaven,
then minor yin [qi, i.e.,] ruler fire, is at the fountain and heat prevails on the earth.
Hence the corresponding signs [of illness] emerge as is described here. When fire appears in the yin section, then cold and heat struggle. Hence [patients] feels cold as if
they suffered from malaria. The fire is repressed and cannot extend. Hence the heart
aches. Fire is dryness. Hence it causes withering."

335 Lin Yi et al.: "The three characters 火且明 should be 火用, 'the fire operates.'"

336 Cheng Shide et al.: "Major yang [qi] controls heaven in *chen* and *xu* years."

337 Wang Bing: "These are indicators of *chen* and *xu* years. When cold and coolness
arise frequently, this is the policy carried out by major yang. 'Fire qi rises high and is
brilliant' is to say: it burns on things. 'When it is not its time' is to say: too early and
unilateral harm. The illnesses that emerge are generated by the qi of heaven." Gao
Shishi: "Major yang [qi] is [the qi of] cold and water. Hence cold qi comes down to

The soil, then, is moist;
the water abounds and inundates [the land].
Cold arrives as a visitor.
Heavy overcast transforms [things];[338]
dampness qi changes beings.
Water drunk accumulates inside [the body].
There is central fullness and [people] do not eat.
The skin is numb and the flesh is insensitive.
The sinews and the vessels are not free.
In severe cases there are *fu*-swellings; the body's behind has *yong*-abscesses.[339]

70-447-9
When the ceasing yin [qi] controls heaven and
when wind qi comes down, then
the spleen qi rises to follow.
Also, the soil is heaped.
Yellow [qi] rises.
Hence water is met by disasters.[340]

The operation of soil is changed.
The body is heavy. The muscles and the flesh decay.
[People] eat less and their taste is impaired.
The wind moves through the Great Void;

---

join. The qi controlling heaven restrains the human body. Because the human beings receive this restraint, the qi of the heart follows above. The heart is associated with fire; its color is red. When the brilliance and redness of fire [qi] rises, then metal is met by disasters because fire punishes the metal. Cold and coolness come up frequently. Because of their domination, water freezes. That is the qi controlling heaven."

338 沈陰, lit.: "deep yin", "deep shadow"; a term used to denote "heavy overcast" in *Li ji* 禮記, 'Yue ling' 月令 already (see Ruan Yuan 1364 below). *NJCD*: "沈陰 is 'deep-reaching, dense yin clouds.'"

339 Wang Bing: "When the major yin [qi] is at the fountain, dampness controls the earth and a situation as described here emerges. The origin of the illness [described here] is generated by the qi of the earth." Lin Yi et al.: "身後癰 should be 身後難, 'the body has difficulties passing stools.'" Zhang Jiebin: "Whenever major yang [qi] controls heaven, then major yin [qi] is at the fountain and dampness prevails on the earth. Hence the indicators and the illnesses appear that are listed here. 肉苛 is 'numbness.' Because the flesh is numb and swollen, one cannot move and sits on the mat for long times. Hence the body develops abscesses and ulcers on the buttocks and on the back. All this is evidence of [illnesses of] the spleen, [i.e.,] of soil. They have arisen because of the qi of the earth."

340 Cheng Shide et al.: "Ceasing yin [qi] controls heaven in *si* and *hai* years."

the cloudy things [show] a swaying movement.
The eyes roll and there is a ringing [sound] in the ears.[341]

70-447-12
Fire gives rein to its violence.
Hence the earth is [struck by] summerheat.
Massive heat [makes things] waste away [as if] melting.
Red pours down.[342]
Hibernating creatures appear frequently.
Flowing water does not freeze.[343]
[...]
It is as fast as if a trigger had been released.[344]

---

341 Wang Bing: "These are indicators of *si* and *hai* years. 土用革 is to say: The qi of
soil is employed to cause changes in the respective bodies. 雲物搖動 is to say: winds
are high (i.e., strong). The illnesses [described] here are generated by the qi of heaven."
Gao Shishi: "Ceasing yin is the wind qi. Hence wind qi comes down to join. The qi
controlling heaven restrains the human body. Because the human beings experience
this restraint, the spleen qi rises to follow [the qi controlling heaven]. The spleen is
associated with soil; its color is yellow. In the present case [the qi of] soil abounds
and yellow [qi] rises. When [the qi of] soil abounds and yellow [qi] rises, then water
experiences catastrophes because soil punishes water. Because the qi of wind, [i.e.] of
wood abounds, the operation of [the qi of] soil is abandoned. When the body is heavy
and muscles as well as flesh decay, these are illnesses of the spleen. 食減口爽 is to say:
[people] eat less and their taste is satisfied nevertheless. That is made clear: when they
eat to sufficiency, this will not please their palate. This, too, is a spleen illness. When
the wind qi rises, then the wind passes through the Great Void and cloudy things
move and are shaken. In human beings this leads to turning eyes and ringing ears."

342 Wu Kun: "This is urine leaving with blood." Cheng Shide et al. cites *Su wen yi
shi* 素问译释: "This is red colored diarrhea." Zhou Fengwu et al.: "Blood leaves from
mouth and nose."

343 Wang Bing: "When minor yang [qi] is at the fountain, fire controls the earth
and a situation as described here emerges. The illnesses are generated by the qi of the
earth." Gao Shishi: "When ceasing yin [qi] controls heaven, then minor yang [qi] is at
the fountain. Minor yang [qi] is the qi of fire. Hence fire gives rein to its violence and
the earth experiences summerheat. When the earth experiences summerheat, then
great heat melts the [body] liquids. When the [body] liquids are subjected to heat,
then redness pours down. The qi of fire rules the opening. Hence hibernating creatures
appear frequently. The nature of fire is warm and hot. Hence flowing waters do not
freeze."

344 Wang Bing: "Changes and transformations caused by minor yang and ceasing
yin qi are very fast; they occur as fast as if a trigger had been pulled. Hence [the text]
states 'it is effused trigger-fast.'"

70-448-1
When the minor yin [qi] controls heaven and
when heat qi comes down, then
the lung qi rises to follow.
White [qi] rises; metal operates.
[Hence] herbs and trees are met by disasters.[345]

[People suffer from] panting and vomiting, from [alternating feelings of] cold
and heat,
from sneezing, stuffy nose, nosebleed, and nasal congestions.
Massive summerheat prevails everywhere.[346]
In severe cases, sores and ulcers [develop].
Burning [causes] metal to melt and stones to flow.

The earth is [struck by] dryness and coolness.
Chilling temperatures arrive frequently.
The flanks ache. [People] tend to breathe deeply.
Sternness and killing prevail.
Herbs and trees change.[347]

70-448-5
When the major yin [qi] controls heaven and
when dampness qi comes down, then

---

345 Cheng Shide et al.: "Minor yin controls heaven in *zi* and *wu* years."

346 Wang Bing: "These are indicators of *zi* and *wu* years. Because heat controls the
qi of heaven, these illnesses are generated by the qi of heaven." Gao Shishi: "Minor
yin [qi] is the ruler fire. Hence heat comes down to join. The qi controlling heaven restrains the human body. Because the human beings experience this restraint, the qi of
the lung rises to follow [the qi controlling heaven]. White begins [to function, the qi
of] metal operates, herbs and trees are met by disasters. This is identical to [a situation
where] minor yang qi controls heaven. That, too, is [a situation] where the qi of metal
follows [the qi of] fire and where metal punishes wood. Panting and vomiting, [alter-
nating feelings of] cold and heat, running nose, nosebleed, and blocked nose are also
illnesses of the lung. When great summerheat prevails everywhere, heat qi abounds."

347 Wang Bing: " 'Change' is to say: Change their appearance. Pain in the flanks and
deep breathing are [illnesses] generated by the qi of the earth." Gao Shishi: "When
minor yin [qi] controls heaven, then the yang brilliance [qi] is at the fountain. Yang
brilliance [qi] is [the qi of] metal. This qi is dry and cool Hence the earth [is struck
by] dryness and coolness. With dryness and coolness present, severe cold arrives frequently. Metal punishes the wood. Hence the flanks have pain and the liver is ill.
[People] tend to breathe deeply and to have gallbladder illnesses. Sternness and killing
prevail and herbs and trees change [their appearance]."

the kidney qi rises to follow.
Black [qi] rises.
[...]
Water experiences changes.[348]
Dust covers [the earth]; clouds and rain [appear].
[The passages] in the chest are not free.[349]
The yin (i.e., the sexual organ) is limp; [its] qi is weakened massively and it does not rise. It does not function.[350]
If exactly at this time, contrary [to what should be expected], the lower back and the buttocks ache,[351] {movement and turning are uncomfortable} [then this is] recession with countermovement.[352]

70-448-7
The earth stores the yin [qi];

---

348 Lin Yi et al.: "Judged from the preceding and following structure of the text, the three characters 火迺眚, 'and, as a result, fire is met by disasters' appear to be missing here." Cheng Shide et al.: "Major yin controls heaven in *chou* and *wei* years."

349 Gao Jiwu/251: "不利 refers to a condition of 'fullness and a feeling of pressure in the chest.'"

350 Lin Yi et al.: "The two characters 不用 should be 水用, 'water operates.'"

351 Wang Bing: "These are indicators of *chou* and *wei* years. 水變 is to say: sweet fountains change to salty [flavor]. 'Dust' is fog [rising from the] soil. 冒 is 不分遠, 'no dispersing widely.' Clouds and rain are transformations of soil. 膗 is 臀肉, 'buttocks.' The illnesses that appear are generated by the qi of heaven."

352 Lin Yi et al.: "Maybe these two characters should be linked to the preceding text." Gao Shishi: "The major yin [qi] is the qi of dampness. Hence dampness qi comes down to join. The qi controlling heaven restrains the human body. Because the humans experience this restraint, the kidney qi rises to follow [the qi controlling heaven]. The color of the kidneys is black; they are associated with water. Hence black [qi] rises and water changes [its appearance]. When black [qi] rises, then there is fine dust resembling a smoke screen. When water changes [its appearance], then clouds and rain appear. When water restrains the fire, then the [passages in the] chest are not free and the yin [organ] is lame. 'Yin' refers to the anterior yin [organ]. When the yin [organ] is lame, then the qi is greatly weakened and the qi generating yang does not emerge and does not operate. At the time when black [qi] rises and when water changes [its appearance], it is not only fire that experiences these catastrophes, contrary [to what might be expected] the lower back and the buttocks ache and movement and turning are not comfortable. When the lower back and the buttocks ache, then the essence in the kidneys is depleted. When the essence in the kidneys is depleted, then movement and turning are uncomfortable. All this results from non-interaction of yin and yang [qi]. Hence [the texts] speaks of 'recession with countermovement.'" Cheng Shide et al.: "當其時 is: at the time when the [qi of] soil flourishes."

also, massive cold arrives and
the hibernating creatures hide away early.
Below the heart is blockage and pain.³⁵³
The earth cracks; the ice is firm.
The lower abdomen aches.
[People] are frequently harmed by food.
When [the cold] harrasses the metal, then standing water increases.
Its flavor, then, is salty.
Running water decreases."³⁵⁴

70-448-10
[Huang] Di:
"[Each] year it happens that there are embryos which are not born.
When treating them, one does not achieve complete success.³⁵⁵
Which qi causes this?"

Qi Bo:
"The six qi and the five classes,
they dominate and restrain each other.³⁵⁶
<What is identical, let it abound.

---

353 916/53: "否 is 痞, 'blockage.'"

354 Wang Bing: "止水 is water in wells and springs. 流水 is rivers flowing profusely.
Even waters of extended [surface] change their regular sweet and appealing flavor to
salty flavor. The illnesses that are present are generated by the qi of the earth." Gao
Shishi: "When major yin [qi] controls heaven, then major yang [qi] is at the fountain.
Major yang [qi] is [the qi of] cold and water. Hence the earth stores the yin [qi].
Massive cold arrives, [that is,] the qi of cold is early. Hence the hibernating creatures
hide away early. The qi of fire is depleted, hence there is blockage and pain below the
heart. Cold water freezes, hence the earth cracks and the ice hardens. When the qi
of cold and water moves downward contrary to its normal direction, then the lower
abdomen is cold. When the qi of cold and water stays in the center, then [patients] are
frequently harmed by food. When the qi of cold and water rises to occupy the lung,
[i.e.,] metal, then the qi of water and heaven move together. Hence, when [the qi of
cold and water] occupies the [territory of] metal, then metal generates the water and
the water increases and the flavor is salty." Obviously, in contrast to Wang Bing, Gao
Shishi reads 乘金則止; 水增. Cheng Shide et al.: "附 has the meaning of 俯伏, 'to
lie prostrate.'"

355 Zhang Jiebin: "治 is: the qi governing a year."

356 Cheng Shide et al.: "The 'six qi' are the six qi controlling heaven and at the fountain. The 'five categories' are the five categories of animals generated by the five agents,
i.e., hairy, feathered, naked, armored, and scaly animals."

What differs, let it weaken.>[357]
That is the Way of heaven and earth; that is the regularity of generation and transformation.

Hence,
when ceasing yin [qi] controls heaven,
hairy creatures rest,
feathered creatures are born,
armored creatures do not reach completion.[358]

[When ceasing yin qi is] at the fountain,
hairy creatures are born,
naked creatures are diminished,
feathered creatures are not born.[359]

---

357 Cheng Shide et al.: " 'Identical' refers to situations where the six qi and the periodic qi belong to an identical category. 'Different' is when they do not belong to the same category. Zhang Zhicong: "When the [qi of the] five periods and the six qi are identical, the living beings ruled [by the respective periodical qi] abound. When the [qi of the] five periods and the six qi differ, then the living beings ruled [by the respective periodical qi] are weak."

358 Wang Bing: "That is to say: in *yi si, ding si, ji si, xin si, gui si, yi hai, ding hai, ji hai, ji hai, xin hai,* and *gui hai* years. 靜 is to say: 'to make no sound.' It also is to say: 'to retire.' Feathered [creatures] are fire creatures; their qi is identical to that of the earth (i.e., fire). Fire restrains the transformations of metal. Hence armored creatures do not reach completion. That is to say: only a few creatures that are of white color and have scales are conceived and given birth to." Zhang Jiebin: "When ceasing yin [qi, i.e., the qi of] wind and wood, controls heaven, then the minor yang [qi, i.e., the] minister fire, is at the fountain. [The qi of] hairy creatures is identical to the qi of heaven. Hence they are peaceful and quiet and do not cause injuries. [The qi of] feathered creatures is identical to the qi of the earth. Hence many of them are born. Fire restrains the transformations of metal. Hence armored creatures do not mature."

359 Wang Bing: "The qi of the earth restrains the soil; [hence] what is yellow and naked is diminished and receives harm. This will be especially severe when [the qi of] that year is taken over by the wood period. Feathered creatures are not born because their [generation is] repressed by minor yang [qi] itself. This applies to the five *yin* and five *shen* years. Whenever [the text] has 不孕 or 不成, that is to say 'few [are born/completed]'; it does not say that there are none at all." Zhang Jiebin: "When ceasing yin [qi, i.e., the qi of] wind and wood, is at the fountain, [the qi of] hairy creatures is identical to that qi; hence they are born. Wood overcomes soil. Hence naked creatures are diminished. When wood is oppressed below, fire cannot be generated. Hence feathered animals may come to life but are not born."

70-449-1
When minor yin [qi] controls heaven,
feathered creatures rest,
armored creatures are born,
hairy creatures do not reach completion.[360]

[When minor yin qi is] at the fountain,
feathered creatures are born,
armored creatures are diminished and are not born.[361]

70-449-3
When major yin [qi] controls heaven,
naked creatures rest,
scaly creatures are born,
feathered creatures do not reach completion.[362]

[When major yin qi is] at the fountain,
naked creatures are born,
scaly creatures[363] [are diminished and] do not reach completion.[364]

---

360 Wang Bing: "This refers to *jia zi, bing zi, wu zi, geng zi, ren zi, jia wu, bing wu, geng wu,* and *ren wu* years. When in such years dark colored hairy creaturs are born, only a few reach completion." Zhang Jiebin: "When minor yin [qi, i.e.,] ruler fire, controls heaven, [the qi of] feathered creatures is identical to the qi of heaven. Hence they are peaceful and quiet. [The qi of] armored creatures is identical to the qi of the earth. Hence they are born. When the qi of metal prevails on earth, then the [qi of] wood is weak. Hence hairy creatures are conceived but do not reach completion."

361 Wang Bing: "The qi of the earth restrains the metal; [hence] white, armored creatures are not born. This will be especially severe when [the qi of] that year is taken over by the fire period. This applies to the five *mao* and five *you* years." Zhang Jiebin: "[The qi of] feathered creatures is identical to that qi. Hence they are born. [The qi of] armored creatures experiences this [qi's] restraint; hence they are diminished and are not born."

362 Wang Bing: "This refers to *yi chou, ding chou, ji chou, xin chou, gui chou, yi wei, ding wei, ji wei, xin wei,* and *gui wei* years. 'Naked creatures' refers to [creatures] such as human beings and frogs. 'Feathered creatures' refers to those of green color, like parrots, woodpeckers, et al." Zhang Jiebin: "[The qi of] naked creatures is identical to the qi of heaven. Hence they are peaceful and quiet and do not cause injuries. [The qi of] scaly animals experiences this [qi's] restraint. Hence they do not reach completion."

363 Lin Yi et al.: "The character 耗, 'diminished,' is missing here."

364 Wang Bing: "The qi of the earth restrains the water; [hence] dark, scaly [creatures] are not born. This will be especially severe when [the qi of] that year is taken over by a soil period. This applies to the five *chen* and five *xu* years." Zhang Jiebin:

When minor yang [qi] controls heaven,
feathered creatures rest,
hairy creatures are born,
naked creatures do not reach completion.[365]

[When minor yang qi is] at the fountain,
feathered creatures are born,
armored creatures are diminished,
hairy creatures are not born.[366]

70-449-6
When yang brilliance [qi] controls heaven,
armored creatures rest,
feathered creatures are born,
armored creatures do not reach completion.[367]

"[The qi of] feathered creatures is identical to the qi of heaven; hence they rest. [The qi of] hairy creatures is identical to the qi of the earth. Hence they are born. When [the qi of] wood at the fountain abounds, then [the qi of] soil weakens. Hence naked creatures do not reach completion."

365 Wang Bing: "This refers to *jia yin, bing yin, wu yin, gen yin, ren yin, jia shen, bing shen, wu shen, geng shen*, and *ren shen* years. 'Naked creatures' is to say: those of green-blue color. 'Feathered creatures' is to say: all those of dark color."

366 Wang Bing: "The qi of the earth restrains the metal. White, armored [creatures] receive harm. This will be especially severe when [the qi of] that year is taken over by a fire period. When hairy creatures are not born, this is because they are restrained by the qi of heaven. This applies to the five *si* and five *hai* years." Zhang Jiebin: "[The qi of] feathered creatures is identical to this qi; hence they are born. The [qi of] armored creatures experiences this [qi's] restraint; hence they are diminished. When [the qi of] fire is at the fountain, then the qi of wood retreats. Hence hairy creatures are not born either."

367 Wang Bing: "This refers to *yi mao, ding mao, ji mao, xin mao, gui mao, yi you, ding you ji you, xin you*, and *gui you* years. 'Feathered [creature]' refers to fire creatures. Hence many of them are born. 'Armored creatures' are those with a red armor. When [creatures] with a red shell are not born, this is because they are restrained by the qi of heaven." In our opinion this should be "the qi of the earth", i. e., fire. Zhang Jiebin: "[The qi of] armored creatures is identical to the qi of heaven. Hence they rest. [The qi of] feathered creatures is identical to the qi of the earth. Hence they are born. [The text] repeats that armored creatures do not reach completion. Even though their qi is identical to that of heaven, they are, in fact, restrained by the qi of the earth."

[When yang brilliance qi is] at the fountain,
armored creatures are born,
hairy creatures are diminished,
feathered creatures do not reach completion.[368]

70-450-1
When major yang [qi] controls heaven,
scaly creatures rest,
naked creatures are born.[369]
[...]

[When major yang qi is] at the fountain,
scaly creatures [are born.
Feathered creatures] are diminished.
Naked creatures are not born.[370]

---

368 Wang Bing: "The qi of the earth restrains the wood; [hence] dark colored hairy creatures are diminished. Harm will be especially severe when [the qi of] that year is taken over by a metal period. This applies to the five *zi* and five *wu* years. Feathered creatures do not reach completion because minor yin [qi] appears in the upper [half of the year]." Zhang Jiebin: "[The qi of] armored creatures is identical to this qi, hence they are born. [The qi of] hairy creatures experiences this [qi's] restraint. Hence they are diminished. The qi of fire and metal are not in harmony with each other. Hence feathered creatures do not reach completion."

369 Wang Bing: "This refers to *jia chen, bing chen, wu chen, geng chen, ren chen, jia xu, bing xu, wu xu, geng xu,* and *ren xu* years. Naked creatures are born because the qi of the earth agrees. 'Scaly creatures rest' is to say: yellow scales do not operate. In such years thunder is rare because it is repressed by the qi of heaven." Lin Yi et al.: "This should say: 'Scaly creatures do not reach completion.'" Zhang Jiebin: "[The qi of] scaly creatures is identical to the transformations [stimulated by the qi] of heaven; hence they rest. [The qi of] naked creatures is identical to the transformations [stimulated by the qi] of the earth. Hence they are born."

370 Wang Bing: "The qi of heaven restrains by what it is dominated. Yellow, dark and scaly [creatures] are diminished. This applies to the five *chou* and five *wei* years." Lin Yi et al.: "This should say: 'Scaly creatures are born, feathered creatures are diminished, naked creatures are not born.' The character 'scaly' in [Wang Bing's] commentary should likewise be 'feathered.'" Zhang Jiebin: "[The qi of] scaly animals is identical to this qi; hence they are born. [The qi of] feathered creatures experience this [qi's] restraint. Hence they are diminished. The qi of water and soil are not in harmony with each other. Hence naked creatures are not born."

70-450-2

<Whenever there is a [qi] that takes advantage of the [weakness of the] period which does not reach completion, then this will be severe.>[371]

Hence,
the rule of qi has something it restrains;
the annual set-up has something it generates.[372]
The earth qi restrains that which it dominates itself.
The qi of heaven restrains that by which it is dominated itself.[373]

---

371 Wang Bing: "When it is a period taking advantage of wood (the character 水 is a mistake here), naked creatures will not reach completion. When it is a period taking advantage of fire, armored creatures will not reach completion. When it is a period taking advantage of soil, scaly creatures will not reach completion. When it is a period taking advantage of metal, hairy creatures will not reach completion. When it is a period taking advantage of water, feathered creatures will not reach completion. In such years, similar to the text above, only small numbers are born and brought up." Cheng Shide et al.: "Whenever [one of] the six qi takes advantage of a periodic qi, then those [beings] that do not reach completion will, as a result of encountering this [qi], not even be able to reach pregnancy or birth." Zhang Jiebin: "When [the qi of] wood takes advantage of the wood period, then naked creatures will not reach completion. When [the qi of] fire takes advantage of the fire period, then armored creatures will not reach completion. When [the qi of] soil takes advantage of the soil period, then scaly creatures will not reach completion. When [the qi of] metal takes advantage of the metal period, then hairy creatures will not reach completion. When [the qi of] water takes advantage of the water period, then feathered creatures will not reach completion."

372 Zhang Zhicong: "氣主 is to say: The five periods are the rulers of the five qi. 歲立 is to say: the first half of each year is ruled by the qi of heaven; the second half of each year is ruled by the qi of the earth. Because a year is established by the six qi controlling heaven and being at the fountain, the six qi have something they generate and the five periods have something they restrain. Hence it may be that [certain creatures] are not born, or do not reach completion." Zhang Jiebin: "氣主 is: The six qi are ruled by heaven and earth. 歲立 is a combination of branches and stems. The annual qi is established by the central period. 制 is the mutual restraint between what abounds and what is weak. 生 is the origin of generation and transformation."

373 Gao Shishi: " 'The qi of the earth' is the qi at the fountain. 'The qi of the earth restrains that which the respective agent dominates itself' [is to say], as stated in the text above, when ceasing yin [qi] is at the fountain, naked creatures are diminished; (etc.) 'The qi of heaven' is the qi controlling heaven. 'The qi of heaven restrains that by which the respective agent is dominated itself' [is to say], as stated in the text above, when minor yang or minor yin [qi] control heaven, then fire and heat come down. Hence white [qi] rises and [the qi of] metal operates. (etc.)"

Heaven restrains the colors.
The earth restrains the physical appearance.³⁷⁴
Whether the five classes [of creatures] are weak or abound,
this depends always on what is appropriate for the respective qi.

70-450-4
Hence,
when it happens that embryos are not born,
and if treating these [cases] does not result in complete success,
this is a regular [feature] of the qi.³⁷⁵
That is the so-called 'inner root'.³⁷⁶

---

374 Zhang Jiebin: "Colors are transformations of qi; their image is empty. Emptiness has its origin in heaven. Physical appearance consists of substance. Its body is solid. Solidity originates from the earth. Hence the qi controlling heaven restrain the five colors; the qi at the fountain restrain the five physical appearances." Gao Shishi: "The qi of heaven restrains above/in the upper [half of the year], and when the colors of white, green, red, yellow, and dark emerge and correspond to them, these are [examples of the qi of] heaven restraining the colors. The qi of the earth restrains below/in the second half [of the year], and whether all kinds of creatures are diminished, are not born, or do not reach completion, these are [outcomes of] the [qi of the] earth restraining physical appearance." Fang Yaozhong: "The generation and formation of the color of all living beings is associated with the qi controlling heaven in the first half of a year. The completion and maturing of all living beings with physical appearance is associated with the qi at the fountain in the second half of a year."

375 Wang Bing: "All living beings between heaven and earth are grouped into these five classes. 'Five [classes of creatures]' is to say: hairy, feathered, naked, scaly, and armored [creatures]. 'Creature' refers to anything with physical appearance that crawls, walks, flies, runs, pant-breathes, womb-breathes, is large or small, high or low, green-blue, yellow, red, white, or dark, and has a body clad in hairy [fur], feathers, scales, or shells. Those who do not have these four [types of cover] are the naked creatures. All five, though, can be born from the womb, out of eggs, out of dampness, or out of transformation."

376 Wang Bing: "When the root and base of the generative qi emerges from the center of the physical appearance of the body, then this is the 'inner root.' If something does not belong to these five classes, then the generative qi depends on external things to be established. When these [external things] are removed, then the generative qi is cut off." Zhang Jiebin: "The origin of the generative qi of all animals that have blood, qi, a heart, and consciousness is stored in the five internal [depots]. Because the spirit qi is the ruler, hence [the text speaks of] inner root." This is reminiscent of the Buddhist term *zhong gen* in the meaning of "ordinary natural disposition".

Those rooted in the exterior, they, too, are five.³⁷⁷

Hence the differences in generation and transformation go along with the five qi, the five flavors, the five colors, the five classes,³⁷⁸ and the five correspondences."³⁷⁹

70-451-2
[Huang] Di:
"What is that to say?"

Qi Bo:
"What is rooted inside, that is called spirit mechanism; when the spirit leaves, then the mechanism stops.³⁸⁰

---

377 Wang Bing: "That is to say: those like the five flavors and five colors. Now, any physical appearance of [the five agents of] wood, fire, soil, metal, and water borrows from 'external things that are completed already' and only then it can come to life and transform. When the external things are removed, then the generative qi is cut off. Hence they all are rooted in the exterior." Lin Yi et al.: "The two characters 色藏 should be 己成, 'completed.'" Zhang Jiebin: "The origin of the generation and transformation of all unconscious plants is based in transformations of external qi. Because their life depends on skin and shell, they are 'rooted in the exterior.'"

378 Wang Bing: "These 25 [categories] are present in all those [beings] that are rooted in the center and that are rooted in the exterior. 'Five qi' is to say: fetid [odor], burned [odor], aromatic [odor], fishy [odor], and putrid [odor]. 'Five flavors' is to say: sour, bitter, acrid, salty, and sweet. 'Five colors' is to say: green-blue, yellow, red, white, and dark. There are two 'five classes': One is: hairy, feathered, naked, scaly, and armored. The other is: dryness, dampness, liquid, firmness, softness. Since these are equally distributed among the myriad beings, mutual suitabilities exist."

379 Zhang Jiebin: "All beings, regardless of whether they are animals or plants, are differentiated according to the five agents in their generation and transformation. For instance, fetid, burned, aromatic, fishy, and putrid odor, these are the five qi. Sour, bitter, sweet, acrid, and salty, these are the five flavors. Green-blue, red, yellow, white, and dark, these are the five colors. All beings have a category they belong to and nothing can be outside of these five [categories]. In the similarities and differences among things each has its correspondences." Cheng Shide et al.: "宜 is 相應, 'mutual correspondence.'"

380 Wang Bing: "All classes [of beings] that have physical appearance and are rooted in the center, their life source is tied to heaven. All their movement and resting is triggered by the rule of the spirit qi. What causes this remains unknown to the beings themselves. Hence when the spirit leaves, then the Way of its triggering activities stops." Zhang Jiebin: "Those beings that have their roots inside of them, they are ruled by the spirit. All their consciousness and movement are brought about by the spirit mechanism. Hence, when the spirit leaves, then the mechanism follows it and stops." For a discussion of 神機, see also 1656/10.

What is rooted in the exterior, that is called qi set-up; when the qi [flow] comes to a halt, then the transformations are interrupted.[381]

Hence,
all [things] have [something by which they are] restrained,
all [things] have [something by which they are] dominated,
all [things] have [something by which they are] generated,
all [things] have [something by which they are brought to] completion."[382]

Hence when it is said
'[Those who] do not know what a year contributes and
[those who do not know] whether the qi are identical or differ,
they are not sufficiently equipped to discuss with them generation and transformation,'
then this means just the same."[383]

70-451-7
[Huang] Di:
"When the qi begins there is generation and transformation;
when the qi disperses, there is physical appearance;
when the qi spreads, there is opulence and parturition;
when the qi ends, the images change.

[The qi] causing this is one.[384]

---

381 Wang Bing: "The life source of those [beings] that are rooted in the exterior is tied to the earth. Hence their generation, growth, transformation, completion, collection, and storage are all set up by the qi of creation. The emergence of this [qi of creation] is also unknown to the beings themselves. Hence when the qi [of creation] halts [its activities], then the Way of generation, transformation, and completion is interrupted." Zhang Jiebin: "Those beings that have their roots outside of them, they necessarily depend on external qi in their existence, and their generation, growth, collection, and storage are set up by the qi of transformation. Hence, when the qi [of transformation] halts [its activities], then all transformations are interrupted as a consequence, too. Hence when the spirit of animals leaves, they die. When the skin of plants is flayed, they die. That is how animals and plants differ in their roots of generation and transformation."

382 Wang Bing: "No matter whether they are rooted in their own center or in the exterior, this applies to all [things]."

383 For a textual parallel, see *Su wen* 9-64-3.

384 Wang Bing: "始 is to say: 始發動, '[the qi] begins to be effused and to move.' 散 is to say: 流散於物中, '[qi] flows and disperses into the things.' 布 is to say: 布化 於結成之形, '[qi] spreads transformations resulting in complete physical form.' To

However,
those [things] that are endowed with the five flavors,
their generation and transformation may be weak or strong,
those reaching completion and maturity may be few or many.
End and begin are not identical.
What is the reason for this?"

Qi Bo:
"The qi of the earth restrains them.
It is not that heaven does not generate [them], or
that the earth does not [let them] grow."385

70-452-2
[Huang] Di:
"I should like to hear the Way of this."

Qi Bo:
"Cold, heat, dryness and dampness,
they differ in the transformations [they cause].

'reach its end' is to peak in being gathered and stored. Hence, when [the qi] begins
to move, [this leads to the] generation and transformation [of beings]. When it flows
and disperses, [beings] assume physical appearance. When it spreads transformations,
[beings will] form fruit. When it reaches its final peak, all the myriad phenomena
undergo changes." Zhang Jiebin: "That is to say: the beginning and ending, the dispersion and the spreading of the myriad beings do all originate from one identical qi.
However, their generation, transformation, formation [of fruits], and completion may
differ in that these [processes] may be vast or poor, [resulting in] few or many."

385 Wang Bing: "Heaven and earth do not apply any emotions to generation and
transformation; the qi of generation and transformation differ or are identical out
of themselves. Why? Because inside the body of the earth there are the six [qi that]
enter [all beings]. Because the qi are identical or differ, there may be generation and
transformation and there may be no generation and no transformation. There may be
little generation and little transformation and there may be widespread generation
and widespread transformation. Hence between heaven and earth there is nothing
that must be generated, that must be transformed, or that must not be generated, that
must not be transformed, that must be generated in small quantities or [that must]
be transformed in small quantities, or that must be generated on a broad scale, or that
must be transformed on a broad scale. Everything [is generated and transformed] according to its qi." Gao Shishi: "Whether generation and transformation are poor or
vast and whether those that form [fruits] and mature are few or many, that is because
the qi of the earth restrains these [processes]. It is not such that the qi of heaven does
not generate [these things]. The fact is that the qi of the earth restrains them so that
they fail to grow."

Hence,
when the minor yang [qi] is at the fountain,
cold poison is not generated.[386]
Its [suppressed] flavor is acrid.
It governs bitter and sour [flavor].
Its grain are greenish and vermilion.[387]

70-452-4
When the yang brilliance [qi] is at the fountain,
dampness poison is not generated.
Its suppressed flavor is sour.
Its qi is dampness.[388]
It governs acrid, bitter, and sweet [flavor].
Its grain are vermilion and white.[389]

---

386 Gao Shishi: "毒 is like 獨, 'solitary.' When yin and yang are not [balanced] harmoniously, their unilateral domination is 'poison.'"

387 Wang Bing: "These are transformations of the qi of *si* and *hai* years. Now, a poisonous effect is displayed by any qi of the five agents that is present in abundance and that exhibits ferocity. In the present case, fire is in the earth. Its qi is properly hot. The qi of things with cold poison differs from [the qi of] the earth; they differ in how they come to life and die. Hence only a few [substances with cold poison] are generated. Fire restrains the qi of metal. Hence those [things] with acrid flavor do not transform. The minor yang qi is confronted in the upper [half of the year] with ceasing yin [qi]. Hence in this year transformations to bitter and sour [flavors] occur. The six qi rule over the years. In this year, though, there is harmony throughout; wood and fire succeed each other. Hence there is no intermediary qi. Bitter and vermilion are transformations resulting from the qi of the earth; sour and greenish are generated by the qi of heaven." Zhang Jiebin: "When fire is in the earth, then no things of cold poison are generated. When the qi of fire restrains metal, then things with an acrid flavor correspond to this. The upper [half of a year with] minor yang [qi at the fountain] is ruled by ceasing yin [qi]. [That is], there is fire in the lower [half of the year] and wood in the upper [half of the year]. Hence it governs bitter and sour [flavor] and its grain are greenish and vermilion. Bitter and vermilion are associated with fire; they are transformations of the qi of the earth. Sour and greenish are associated with wood; they are generated by the qi of heaven."

388 Lin Yi et al.: "Only in the two cases of years with yang brilliance and major yin [qi] at the fountain does [the text] state 'its qi is dampness' or 'its qi is heat.' The reason is that [in times of] dampness and dryness cold qi and warmth qi do not appear. Hence [the text] mentions 'these qi' once more."

389 Wang Bing: "These are transformations of the qi of *zi* and *wu* years. Dryness is in the earth; its qi is cool. Hence few drugs are generated and transformed with dampness and warmth poison. Metal and wood restrain each other. Hence few [drugs] with a sour flavor transform. The yang brilliance qi is confronted in the upper [half of

When the major yang [qi] is at the fountain,
heat poison is not generated.
Its suppressed flavor is bitter.
It governs bland and salty [flavor].
Its grain are yellow and [of] black-millet [color].³⁹⁰

70-453-1
When the ceasing yin [qi] is at the fountain,
cool poison is not generated.
Its [suppressed] flavor is sweet.
It governs sour and bitter [flavor].
Its grain are greenish and red.³⁹¹
Its qi is concentrated;
its flavor is proper.³⁹²

---

the year] with minor yin [qi]. Hence in this year transformations to acrid and bitter [flavors] occur. Acrid and white are [transformations of] the qi of the earth; bitter and vermilion are the qi of heaven. Sweet is the intermediary qi. It is that by which the domination of metal by fire is accompanied. Hence [yang brilliance qi] simultaneously rules sweet [flavor]." Gao Shishi: "Acrid is a metal flavor; bitter is a fire flavor. Sweet is a soil flavor. Vermilion is a fire color. White is a metal color."

390 Wang Bing: "These are transformations of the qi of *chou* and *wei* years. Cold is in the earth; its transformations differ from [those of heat]. Hence in this year things with heat poison are not generated. Water dominates fire, hence the flavor is bitter. The major yang qi is confronted in the upper [half of the year] with major yin [qi]. Hence in this year transformations generate bland and salty [flavors]. The qi of major yin, [i.e., of] soil, is generated above in heaven. [Heaven] is far away and high. Hence the transformation to sweet [flavor] is poor and [the resulting flavor is] bland. Bland flavor is associated with sweet flavor. Blandness and yellow are transformation of [the qi of] heaven; salty [flavor] and black are transformations of [the qi of] the earth." Lin Yi et al.: "The phrase 味故當苦, 'hence the flavor is bitter', in [Wang Bing's] commentary should be: 故味苦者不化, 'hence those with a bitter flavor are not transformed.' This is a copying error."

391 Wang Bing: "These are transformations of the qi of *yin* and *shen* years. Warmth is in the earth; its nature differs from that of coolness. Hence in this year things with coolness poison are not generated. Wood dominates this [year's] soil. Hence there are only a few transformations to [drugs] with sweet flavor. The ceasing yin qi is united in the upper [half of the year] with minor yang [qi]. The qi that are united do not exhibit any mutual hostility. Hence they rule the transformation of sour and bitter [flavors]. Sour and greenish are transformations of [the qi of] the earth; bitter and red are transformations of [the qi of] heaven. There is no domination and subduing among these qi. There is no intermediary qi to stimulate transformation to sweet [flavor]."

392 Wang Bing: "In years with ceasing yin [qi] and minor yang [qi] at the fountain, all qi transformations are concentrated and the flavor is pure and proper. In all the

When the minor yin [qi] is at the fountain,
cold poison is not generated.
Its [suppressed] flavor is acrid.
It governs acrid, bitter, and sweet [flavor].
Its grain are white and vermilion.³⁹³

70-453-3
When the major yin [qi] is at the fountain,
dryness poison is not generated.
Its [suppressed] flavor is salty.
Its qi is heat.
It governs sweet and salty [flavor].
Its grain are yellow and [of] black-millet [color].³⁹⁴

---

other years the upper and the lower [halves of the year are dominated by] qi that dominate and subdue each other. Hence they all have intermediary qi and intermediary flavors." Gao Shishi: "When ceasing yin [qi] is at the fountain, because wind qi is associated with yang, no coolness poison is generated. Wood restrains the soil; [hence] those [substances] with sweet flavor are not generated either. When ceasing yin [qi] is at the fountain, this goes along with minor yang [qi] in the upper [half of the year]. Hence this [year] governs sour and bitter [flavors] and its grain are greenish and red. When the minor yang [qi] is in charge in the upper [half of the year], then ceasing yin [qi] is at the fountain. That which appears in the center, is ceasing yin [qi], too. What appear at the fountain and in the center are not two [different] qi. Hence these qi are concentrated. What appear at the fountain and in the center are not two [different] flavors. Hence these flavors are proper. 'Concentrated' is: not two. 'Proper' is: not biased unilaterally."

393 Wang Bing: "These are transformations of the qi of *mao* and *you* years. Heat is in the earth; its transformations differ from [those of] cold. Hence in this year drugs with cold poison are very rare. Fire qi melts metal. Hence there are only few transformations to [drugs] with acrid [flavor]. Minor yin [qi] and yang brilliance [qi] rule heaven and they rule the earth. Hence they govern bitter and acrid [flavors]. Bitter and vermilion are brought forth by the qi of the earth; acrid and white are generated by the qi of heaven. Sweet [flavor] is the separating qi because it serves to separate [the antagonists] and to bring their fighting to a halt." Gao Shishi: "Minor yin and minor yang are both associated with fire. Hence no cold poison is generated. The [suppressed] flavor [of minor yin] is acrid; that is the same as that of minor yang [qi]."

394 Wang Bing: "These are transformations of the qi of *chen* and *xu* years. Dampness is in the earth; [its transformations] differ from [those of] dryness. Hence [in this year] things with dryness poison are not generated or transformed. Soil restrains water. Hence there are few transformations to [drugs] with a salty flavor. The qi of major yin succeeds the major yang qi in the upper [half of the year]. Hence in this year transformations to [drugs with] sweet and salty [flavors] occur. Sweet and yellow are transformations of the [qi of the] earth; salty and black are transformations of the [qi

<When transformation is pure, then the salty maintains [its position]; when the qi is concentrated, then the acrid transforms and both govern together.>³⁹⁵

Hence it is said:
'To supplement what is above and below, follow them;
to put to order what is above and below, oppose them.
Regulate them in accordance with the presence of cold or heat, abundance or weakness.'³⁹⁶

---

of] heaven. Cold and dampness do not exhibit extraordinary mutual hostility; hence their intermediary qi go together and [drugs] with a heat qi correspond to them."

395 Wang Bing: "淳 is 和, 'harmony.' 化淳 is to say: in a year with minor yang [qi] at the fountain, fire comes to settle in the [territory of the] water. Contrary [to what might be expected, the water] can transform and procreate nevertheless. The reason is that water and salty [flavor] guard their own [locations] and do not engage in a fight with the fire. 氣專 is to say: in a year with ceasing yin [qi] at the fountain, wood [qi] settles in the [territory of the] water and descends repeatedly to cause transformations. The metal is not harmed. Hence acrid [flavor] is generated and transformed repeatedly and rules together with salty [flavor]. Only in these two years the qi of the upper and of the lower [half of the year] are not engaged in mutual fighting. Hence acrid and salty [flavors] can flourish alike. In all the other years there are changes resulting from domination and subduing among the upper and the lower [halves of the year]. In their center sweet [flavor] is transformed simultaneously to smoothen their [mutually] restraining [each other]. [Sweet flavor] differs in its generation and transformation from the remaining three flavors, (i.e., bitter, salty, and sour). Hence among the drugs between heaven and earth, most are acrid and sweet." Zhang Jiebin: "Among the six qi, only the major yin [qi] is associated with soil. When major yin [qi] controls the earth, soil is brought into position. Hence its transformations are pure. 'Pure' is 厚, 'rich,' 'strongly pronounced.' Of the five flavors, only salty [flavor] is associated with water. Its nature favors outflow. When pure soil restrains it, it will be guarded. Soil is associated with the position of soil. Hence [the text] says: 'the qi is concentrated.' Abounding soil generates metal. Hence [it] governs together with acrid transformations. 'Govern together' is to say: acrid, sweet, and salty [flavor] operate to govern together. That is, acrid is associated with metal, which is the son of soil and the mother of water. It can mediate between water and soil. Hence, when major yin [qi] is at the fountain, it governs the flavor between sweet and salty. Now, major yin and major yang are related like above and below. In both cases the application [of acrid flavor] is appropriate. However, when the major yin [qi] is at the fountain, acrid transformations are rich, when major yang is at the fountain, acrid transformations are weak."

396 Wang Bing: " 'Above' is to say: 'controlling heaven.' 'Below' is to say: 'at the fountain.' When the qi controlling heaven and earth are greatly excessive, then [it is necessary] to oppose their flavor so as to return them to order. When the qi controlling heaven and earth are inadequate, then [it is necessary] to go along with their flavor so as to harmonize them. 從 is 順, 'to go along with.'" Zhang Jiebin: "From here on down therapy patterns are discussed. 'Supplement' is: to supplement what is insufficient.

Hence when it is said:
'Take the above, take the below,
take the inside, take the outside,
to seek its excess.
For those who can stand poison, employ strong drugs;
for those who [can]not stand poison, use weak drugs,'³⁹⁷
then this means just the same.³⁹⁸

70-454-3
In case the qi moves in an opposite direction,
if the illness is above, take it from below, and
if the illness is below, take it from above.
If the illness is in the center, take it from its adjoining regions.³⁹⁹

'Treat' is: to treat that which has surplus. 從之 is to say: [treat] with identical qi. E.g.,
supplement lung [qi] with acrid [qi], or supplement the spleen [qi] with sweet [qi]. 逆
之 is to say: [in treating] act contrary to the [depot's] qi. E.g., treat the lung with bitter
[qi] or treat the spleen with sour [qi]. In all cases regulation follows the location of the
illness and is based on the requirements of cold and heat, abundance and weakness."

397 Cheng Shide et al.: "'Poison' means drastic. All drugs with drastic effects are
called 'poisonous drugs.'"

398 Wang Bing: "上取 is to say: restrain an excessive qi by means of drugs. If such
[effort to restrain an excessive qi] does not lead to obedience, then [the patient] is
made to vomit. 下取 is to say: remove illnesses in the lower [parts of the body] by
means of drastic drugs. If they do not leave despite such an attack, then they are to
be purged downwards. 內取 is to say: when food is consumed for medicinal purposes,
check its cold or hot [nature] and balance it. 外取 is to say: balance the illness qi
by medicinal poultices. When it should be cold but is hot, harmonize it with cool
[drugs]. When it should be hot but is cold, harmonize it with warmth. An unending
abundance above is removed by [making the patient] vomit; an unending abundance
below is removed by causing downward purgation. That is called 'the Way of getting
a hold of qi excesses.' 'Strong [drugs], weak drugs' is to say: they are rich or weak in
terms of qi and flavor."

399 Wang Bing: "下取 is to say: when cold moves adversely below and heat attacks
above, then the passage is not free below and qi abounds above, and warmth is applied below to regulate this. 上取 is to say: when cold accumulates below and is not
removed by an application of warmth, [i.e.] if the yang [qi] stored is insufficient, then
this yang [qi] is to be supplemented. 傍取 is to say: If qi collects on the left, then a
medicinal poultice is to be applied on the right; when qi collects on the right, then a
medicinal poultice is to be applied on the left to harmonize this." Gao Shishi: "'When
the illness is above it must be taken from below' is to say: when the qi is blocked above,
it is necessary to make it descend. 'When the illness is below it must be taken from
above' is to say: when the qi is blocked below, it is necessary to make it rise. 'When
the illness is in the center, it is necessary to take it from the outside, and it is taken

70-454-4

When heat is treated with cold, apply it warm.

When cold is treated with heat, apply it cool.

When warmth is treated with coolness, apply it cold.

When coolness is treated with warmth, apply it hot.[400]

---

from the left or right side,' is to say: when qi moves contrary [to its normal course] in the center, the respective conduits and vessels are to be opened so that it reaches the sides." Zhang Jiebin: "氣反 is: The root is here and the tip is elsewhere. .. 'When the illness is in the center, it is to be taken from the sides' is to say: the illness is generated internally and related, through the conduits, to the outside. In such cases [treatment is applied] eigher by needling or by cauterization, by hot poultices, or by massage, in accordance to the location [of the illness]." 2058/12: "That is: the basic location of the pathological changes is not identical to the location where the illness manifests itself." Zhang Zhicong: "氣反 is to say: the illness qi above and below, inside and outside are contrary to each other. For instance, when there is domination below and an illness, to the contrary, [manifests itself] above, it must be taken from (i.e., treated) below." *Gu dian yi zhu xuan* bianxiezu /61: "That is: the location where the illness manifests itself is not identical to the [location to expect given its] pathological process." 582/6: "氣反 must be interpreted in relation to 氣立. [In the present statement] 反 is not the opposite of 正, 'proper'; it is to be interpreted in the sense of 漫衍, 'to overflow.' The meaning resembles that of 泛, 'to inundate.' Above, the text has 氣專則辛化俱治, 'when the qi is concentrated, then the acrid transforms and both govern together.' By collateral evidence, 氣反 is the opposite of 氣專. When the 'concentration' is lost, an 'inundation' results. 氣反 does not refer to an illness, it refers to the effect of the yin and yang qi of heaven and earth on the human body. .. 'Above' and 'below' do not refer to 'above' and 'below' of the human body; these [terms] should be interpreted in the present sentence as references to the periodic qi. When the qi controlling heaven loses its 'concentration' (專) and leaves its position, that is 病在上, 'the illness is above.' Treatment must not be focussed on its [original] position; a therapy is to be directed at the qi at the fountain. That is 取之下, 'regulate it below.' When the qi at the fountain loses its 'concentration' (專) and leaves its position, that is 病在下, 'the illness is below.' Treatment must not be focussed on its [original] position; a therapy is to be directed at the qi controlling heaven. That is 取之上, 'regulate it above.' As for 'the illness is in the center,' that is to say: an illness has been caused because the intermediary qi has lost its 'concentration.' A treatment is to be applied through the neighboring intermediary qi. 傍 is 近, 'near.'" See also 88/4, 66/4, 1524/7, 223/20, and 2470/35.

400 Gao Shishi: "That is to elucidate: in cases of cold and heat, abundance and weakness patterns of complementary treatment and patterns of opposing treatment are used. When heat is treated with cold, cold drugs are employed to treat heat illness. 溫而行之 [is to say: cold] drugs taken [for the treatment of heat] should be warmed. When they are warmed, cold drugs move into the heat section and restore order there. .." Zhang Jiebin: "Whenever [the nature of] drugs is opposed to the [nature of the] illness, chances are that [the former] will not enter [the domain of the latter]. Hence [the drugs] are adapted to the qi of the [illness] to make them move. That is the Way of pretending."

Hence [laws exist]
to dissolve it, to delete it,
to emit it through vomiting, to purge it,
to supplement it, and to drain it.
Chronic and newly acquired [illnesses are treated] following the same laws."

[Huang] Di:
"If an illness is in the center and if [a person feels] neither a repletion nor a firmness,
if at times it assembles and at time disperses,
what is to be done?"

Qi Bo:
"An encompassing question, indeed!
For those without accumulations, search their depots [for treatment].
When they are depleted, supplement them.⁴⁰¹
[Employ] drugs to eliminate the [illness].
[Employ] a diet as a follow up to the [treatment].
Running water will soak it.
By harmonizing the [patient's] center and exterior,
it is possible to achieve a complete cure."⁴⁰²

70-455-2
[Huang] Di:
"[Some drugs] have poison, [others] have no poison.
Are there any essential rules as to their intake?"⁴⁰³

Qi Bo:
"Among the illnesses are those which are chronic and those which were newly acquired;
among the prescriptions are those that are large and those that are small.
[Among the drugs] are those that have poison and [others that] have no poison.

---

401 Wang Bing: "Where the illness is situated, name the depot and supplement there." Zhang Jiebin: "積 are illnesses with physical appearance."

402 Zhang Jiebin: " 'Drugs are employed to eliminate it' is: to remove the illness. 'Diet is employed to follow up' is: to nourish the [patient's] qi. 'Running water serves to soak it' is: the [patient's] conduits are made passable. If such an approach is employed, center and exterior are harmonized and the illness can be healed."

403 Gao Shishi: "約 is 規則, 'rules.'" *Gu dian yi zhu xuan* bianxiezu /64: "約 is 約束, 'restriction.'"

[In their application] it is definitely necessary to follow the regular compositions.[404]

If an illness is treated with [drugs of] massive poison, remove six [parts] of ten.
If an illness is treated with [drugs of] regular poison, remove seven [parts] of
ten.
If an illness is treated with [drugs of] weak poison, remove eight [parts] of ten.
If an illness is treated with [drugs] containing no poison, remove nine [parts]
of ten.
Employ a diet of grain, meat, tree-fruit, and vegetables to complete [the cure].

Do not permit these [limits] to be exceeded,
lest the proper [qi] is harmed.
If [the cure] is incomplete,
apply [a treatment] again in accordance with the laws [of therapy, but]
it is essential to first [acquire an understanding of the] annual qi.

70-455-7
Do not attack the harmony of heaven,[405]
Do not make the abundant [even more] abundant,
do not deplete what is depleted,
[lest you] submit that person to the calamity of early death.[406]

---

404 Zhang Jiebin: "When the illness is serious, [the treatment/prescription] should
be massive. When the illness is light, it should be minor. [Substances] that are not
poisonous should be used in large numbers; those that are poisonous should be used in
small numbers. These are the restrictions suggested by well-established conventions."
Gu dian yi zhu xuan bianxiezu /64: 制 is 有法度, 'to follow a law.'"

405 Zhang Zhicong: "It is essential before [treatment] to know whether [the qi of]
an annual period abounds or is weak. When it is weak, it has to be supplemented;
when it abounds, it must be drained. For supplementation, [drugs are used with a qi]
complementary [to the periodical qi]. For draining, [drugs are used with a qi] opposing [the periodical qi]. This way the central harmony of the heavenly periods is not
affected." 2889/18: 歲氣 refers to generation, growth, gathering, and storage in the
course of the four seasons. 毋伐天和 corresponds to the saying in the West: 'Physicians are the servants of nature.'"

406 Wang Bing: "If [a therapist] does not examine whether [a patient] suffers from
a depletion or repletion and if [that therapist] thinks of nothing but attack, then what
abounds will turn out to be even more abundant and what is depleted will turn out
to be even more depleted. Myriads of illnesses in their beginnings will become more
severe because of such [erroneous treatments]. The true qi will decrease day by day, the
strength of the illness will encroach upon [the patient] day by day, and it will be dif-

Do not invite the evil [qi],
do not lose the proper [qi],
[lest you] cut a person's long life."[407]

70-456-1
[Huang] Di:
"When someone has had an illness for long and
is not healthy even though [that person's] qi follows [its regular course again]
and
if [that person] is emaciated even though the illness has left [already], why is
that?"

Qi Bo:
"A brilliant question of a sage, indeed!
It is impossible to substitute the transformations [of nature by one's own activi-
ties];
it is impossible to disobey time![408]

Now,
once the conduits and network [vessels] have become passable and
once [the patient's] blood and qi follow [their regular courses again],
[the patient's] insufficiencies return to normal and
[his state will be] identical to that of all [healthy people].

[When this state is reached,] nourish the [patient] and harmonize the [organ-
ism].

---

ficult to escape the arrival of misfortune and of early death. So sad!" The *textus receptus*
has 天殃, "calamities sent by heaven." In the present context this makes little sense.
In agreement with the wording in *Su wen* 66-368-7, we read 天殃 as 天殃. Wang
Bing, referring in his commentary to 夭, "early death", may have used a text with the
wording 夭殃.

407 Wang Bing: "That is what is called 'destruction of heavenly harmony.' To attack
a depletion and call it a repletion is an 'invitation to evil [qi].' Not to recognize the
depletion of a depot, that is 'to lose the proper [qi].' The loss of proper qi is the origin
of death."

408 Wang Bing: "化 is to say 造化, 'creation.' Those who try to do the work of a mas-
ter-carpenter will most likely injure their hands; how could human strength substitute
the qi of creation? Now, generation, growth, gathering, and storage corresponds to
the transformations of the four seasons. Even those of greatest wisdom cannot reach
[these steps] ahead of time. Obviously, [these developments] do not arise from human
strength. Hence the generation, growth, gathering, and storage of things must wait
for their time."

Rest and wait for the time [of recovery].
Carefully guard the [patient's] qi,
lest it moves towards imbalance.
This way the [patient's] physical appearance will look fine and [his] generative
qi will grow.
[A healer who achieves this] is called sage king.

70-456-5
Hence when the *Great Essential* states:
'Do not substitute the transformations [of nature by your own activities];
do not disobey time.
It is essential to nourish and it is essential to harmonize,
and to wait for it to recover,'
then this means just the same."

[Huang] Di:
"Good!"

Chapter 71
Comprehensive Discourse on the Policies and Arrangements of the Six Principal [Qi].[1]

71-457-2
Huang Di asked:
"The transformations of the six [qi] and the [catastrophic] changes of the six [qi],[2] domination and revenge, excess and order,[3]
the earlier and the belated[4] [formation of] sweet, bitter, acrid, salty, sour and bland [flavors],[5] –
I have come to know all this.

Now,
the transformations of the five periods,

---

1 Cheng Shide et al.: "The 'six principal [qi]' include the six 'principals' of climatic changes, i.e., wind, fire, dampness, heat, dryness, and cold. In other words, these are the six qi ruling a year. 正 is 政, 'policy.' 紀 is 記其事, 'to record these events.' From how the present chapter records how the six qi control heaven above and are at the fountain below, how the intervening [visitor] qi are arranged to the left and to the right, as well as how the periods and the qi govern together and how the visitor and the host [qi] join from the above, it appears that 30 years represent one 'arrangement' and 60 years constitute one 'cycle.' Within these [years] there is transformation and change, there is domination and revenge, there is operation and illness. The laws of the development and changes of their respective policies and manifestations differ. Hence the name of this chapter is 'Recording the policies of the six principal [qi].'"

2 Zhang Zhicong: "The 'six transformations' is to say: the six qi controlling heaven and at the fountain do all undergo transformations. The 'six changes' is to say: the changes of restraint and domination." Cheng Shide et al.: " 'Six transformations' [refers to the] generation and transformation of the six qi. 'Six changes' [refers to the changes in the] abundance and weakness of the six qi." Fang Yaozhong: " 'Six transformations' refers to the regular changes of the six qi. 'Six changes' refers to the abnormal changes of the six qi."

3 Cheng Shide et al.: "勝 refers to 勝氣, 'dominating qi'; 復 refers to 復氣, 'qi taking revenge.' 淫 is 'excessive evil causing illness'; 治 is 治理, 'to govern.'" Fang Yaozhong: "淫 refers to disproportionate domination or excess. 治 refers to normal."

4 Fang Yaozhong: " 'Earlier and later' is to say that the generation and maturing of the five flavors do not occur at the same time each year; sometimes they occur earlier, sometimes they occur belated."

5 Fang Yaozhong: " 'Sweet, bitter, acrid, sour, salty' refers to the five flavors and also to all kinds of food and medicinal drugs."

sometimes they follow the qi of heaven,[6]
sometimes they oppose the qi of heaven;[7]
sometimes they follow the qi of heaven and oppose the qi of the earth;[8]
sometimes they follow the qi of the earth and oppose the qi of heaven;
sometimes they agree, sometimes they do not agree.[9]
These issues I cannot understand yet.

---

6 Lin Yi et al.: "五氣 may be an error for 天氣. This would link it to the following text." Zhang Jiebin: "五氣 should be 天氣." Cheng Shide et al.: " 'They follow the qi of heaven' is: the transformations of the five periods parallel the qi of heaven. 'Qi of heaven' refers to the qi controlling heaven." We agree with Lin Yi and Zhang Jiebin and have read 五氣 as 天氣.

7 Gao Shishi: "The transformations of the five periods, sometimes they follow the qi controlling heaven, sometimes they oppose the qi controlling heaven." Cheng Shide et al.: " 'Oppose the qi of heaven' is: the five periods and the qi controlling heaven are contradictory."

8 Gao Shishi: "Sometimes they follow the qi controlling heaven and oppose the earth qi at the fountain. Sometimes they follow the earth qi at the fountain and oppose the qi of heaven controlling heaven. 從 is like 同, 'to be identical to,' 'to agree with.' 逆 is like 異, 'to differ from.' "

9 Wang Bing: "When the qi are identical, that is called 從, 'to follow.' When the qi differ, that is called 逆, 'to oppose.' In case there is domination or restraint, that is 不相得, 'they do not agree.' When they generate one another, that is 相得, 'they agree.' Treatment patterns exist for [situations where] the qi controlling heaven and earth exceed or dominate one another, or seek revenge. If one wishes to balance and adjust the natures of the qi, it is not advisable to act against the qi of heaven and earth. [This way it is possible] to achieve quietude and peace." Zhang Zhicong: " 'Sometimes they agree, sometimes they do not agree' refers to the qi of the four seasons. That is, when [the presence of] wind and warmth is identical to the transformations occurring in spring, when [the presence of] heat and steam is identical to the transformations occurring in summer, when [the presence of] coolness and dew is identical to the transformations occurring in autumn, when [the presence of] clouds and rain is identical to the transformations occurring in late summer and when [the presence of] ice and snow is identical to the transformations of winter, all these cases constitute an 'agreement' of visitor qi and seasonal qi. When the host qi is insufficient while the visitor qi, contrary [to the rule], dominates, in such a case the visitor qi and the seasonal qi do not agree." Fang Yaozhong: " 'Five periods' refers to the five periods of wood, fire, soil, metal, and water. 'Transformation' refers to generation through transformation, i.e., to the phenomenon of the generation, growth, transformation, collection, and storage of the myriad beings. 'Five qi' is explained in two ways: One is to explain ['five qi'] as an error for 'qi of heaven.' A second is to explain ['five qi'] as a reference to a year with balanced qi throughout [all] five periods. We agree with the former. 'Five qi' should be 'qi of heaven,' i.e., the qi controlling heaven. Therefore, the meaning of this passage is: there are some years when the association of the annual period with the five agents is identical to that of the qi controlling heaven of that same year. 'Sometimes they

71-457-5
I should like
to comprehend the arrangements of heaven and
to follow the structures of the earth,[10]
to live in harmony with the respective periods and
to adjust to their transformations,
to let
above and below combine their virtues,
and no one violates each other's hierarchical position;
[to let]
heaven and earth [have their qi] rise and descend,
and no one misses what befits them;[11]
[to let]
the five periods enact [their policies],
and no one violates their policies.
To adjust to them [by means of] proper flavors,
what complies with and what opposes [the five periods]?"[12]

Qi Bo paid reverence twice knocking his head on the ground and responded:
"A brilliant question, indeed!

These are the fundamental principles [governing] heaven and earth,
they constitute the profound source of change and transformation.
Who except a sage emperor could penetrate these utmost structures thoroughly?!

Although [I, your] subject, am not intelligent,
[I] request to expound this Way,

---

oppose the qi of heaven' is: there are years when the association of the annual period with the five agents is opposed to that of the qi controlling heaven. 'Sometimes they follow the qi of heaven and oppose the qi of the earth' is: there are some years when the association of the annual period with the five agents is identical to that of the qi controlling heaven, while it is opposed to that of the qi at the fountain. (Etc.) 'Sometimes they agree' refers to [years] when the visitor qi and the host qi are identical."

10 Fang Yaozhong: " 'Heaven' refers to the seasons of heaven. 通天之紀 is, '[I wish to] understand the laws of the climatic changes.' 從地之理 is: '[I wish to] act in accordance with the conditions resulting from the structures of the earth.' "

11 Fang Yaozhong: "宜 is 正常, 'regular.' "

12 In contrast, Gao Shishi: "從逆 refers to treatments in accordance with or opposed to [the nature of the illness]."

so that it will never vanish, and
for a long time to come it will not undergo any change."

71-458-1
[Huang] Di:
"I should like you, Sir, to expand [these periods] and put them into sequence,
[and in your presentation you should]
follow the order of related [subjects],
distinguish the rulers of each section,
differentiate their basic controllers,
elucidate the numbers of the qi,[13] and
clarify the proper transformations.[14]
May [I] hear [this]?"

Qi Bo:
"First determine[15] the [set up of a] year to understand its qi,[16]

---

13 Wang Bing: "部主 is to say: that which is ruled, in separate sections, by the individual six qi. 宗司 are the positions corresponding with the course taken by the five [period] qi. 氣數 is to say: the proper numbers [of days] of the alternating operations of the five periodic qi of heaven and earth." Wu Kun: "As for 宗司, a general classification is 宗, a separation is 司. As for 'qi and numbers,' each of the six qi has its number. That is to say: each qi rules over 60 days." Wang Qi: "部主: heaven, earth, above, below, left, right if distinguished on the basis of the three yin and three yang constitute six 'sections.' Each section has its host qi. For example, the ceasing yin [section] is ruled by wind qi; the minor yin [section] is ruled by ruler fire; etc. 宗 is 總, 'to unite,' 統, 'to gather into one.' This refers to the qi ruling over an entire year. 司 is to say 分司, 'to control separate [units].' This refers to those qi that control one of the four seasons."

14 Wang Bing: "正化 is to say: the sour, bitter, sweet, acrid, and salty [flavors] and the cold, warm, frigid, and hot [qi] commensurable with the true qi and flavors associated with a specific year." Zhang Jiebin: "Those who occupy their respective position are 'proper'; those not occupying their position are evil." Cheng Shide et al.: "正化 is to say: transformations brought forth by the orders of the six qi occupying their proper positions."

15 The *Hou han shu* 後漢書, biography of Lang Kai 郎凱傳, has 主名未立. The commentary states: 立猶定, " 'to set up' is like 'to determine.'" *Ling shu* 46 has a parallel statement: 先立其年以知其時.

16 1074/5: "That is, the future course and direction taken by an illness is determined by calculating the abundance or weakness of the period qi of the four seasons of the year when a person has fallen ill and, then, by taking into account the relationships of mutual generation or overcoming among the positions taken by the illness in the depots and palaces on the one side and the period qi of the four seasons on the other side."

the numbers of the periodical progression of metal, wood, water, fire, and soil,[17] and

the transformations resulting from the coming down, and assuming control, of cold, summerheat, dryness, dampness, wind, and fire.[18]

Then
it is possible to perceive the Way of heaven and [as a consequence]
it is possible to adjust the qi of the people;[19]
how yin and yang curl up and unroll,
this is easy to understand and leaves no uncertainty.

Those that can be quantified by putting them in numbers,
please, let me speak about them one by one."[20]

71-458-6
[Huang] Di:
"The policy of major yang [qi], what is it like?"[21]

---

17 Fang Yaozhong: " 'Numbers' is to be explained here as 'laws.' That is, once a particular year has been determined, it is possible, on the basis of the heavenly stems of that year, to calculate the laws underlying the changes in the course of the annual period of that year on the basis of its heavenly stems."

18 Zhang Zhicong: "The six qi may come down to control heaven above and they may rule at the fountain below. There are the host qi of the four seasons and there are the visitor qi coming down to join [them]." Cheng Shide et al.: "臨御之化 are the transformations of [the qi] controlling heaven and [of the qi] at the fountain." Fang Yaozhong: "Cold, summerheat, dryness, dampness, wind, and fire are the six qi. 臨 refers to 降臨, 'to descend,' or 來臨, 'to come down.' Here it refers to 'visitor qi.' 御 refers to 駕御, 'to drive a carriage.' Here it refers to the 'host qi.' That is, once a particular year has been determined, it is possible, on the basis of the earth branches of that year, to calculate the laws underlying, in the course of the six qi in that year, the changes and transformations in the movement of host qi, visitor qi, intervening [visitor] qi, [the qi] controlling heaven and [the qi] at the fountain, as well as the joining below or coming down from above of visitor and ruling [qi]."

19 See 635/10 for a discussion of a reflection of Lao zi's philosophy in this statement.

20 Wang Bing: "遂 is 盡, 'exhaustively.'" Fang Yaozhong: "The first 數 is 規律, 'laws'; the second 數 is 數目, 'number.' 遂 is an adverb in the sense of 就, 'just.'"

21 Fang Yaozhong: "Beginning with this section the characteristics of climate, objects, and illnesses of each year in a cycle of 60 years are listed like in a table."

Qi Bo:
"These are the arrangements including *chen* and *xu* [earth branches].[22]

[The first two arrangements include the years when]
major yang [controls heaven], major *jue* [is the central period], major yin [is at
the fountain].[23]
[They are designated] *ren chen* and *ren xu*.[24]

71-458-8
Their period [manifests itself as] wind.[25]
The transformations [caused by] them include sounds of a chaotic opening and
breaking.[26]

---

22 Fang Yaozhong: "*Chen* and *xu* refer to the [earth] branches of each year. The
meaning of 辰戌之紀 is: in all years with *chen* and *xu* earth branches, the major yang
[qi], [i.e., the qi of] cold and water, controls heaven."

23 Cheng Shide et al.: " 'Major yang' is to say: [the qi of] major yang, i.e., cold and
water, controls heaven. 'Major yin' is: [the qi of] major yin, i.e., dampness and soil, is
at the fountain. 'Major *jue*' refers to an excess of the annual period, [i.e.,] the period of
wood. When the following text speaks of 'major *zhi*,' 'major *gong*,' 'major *shang*,' and
'major *yu*,' these are references to excesses of the periods of fire, soil, metal, and water
respectively as annual periods."

24 Fang Yaozhong: "This section is to say: because in *ren chen* and *ren xu* years the
annual stem is in both cases *ren* and because both *ding* and *ren* transform wood, these
two years are associated with periods of wood. *Ren* is associated in the sequence of
heavenly stems with an odd number; hence it is a yang stem. A yang stem stands for
excess. Hence [*ren* years] are years of excessive wood periods. The ancients used the
five musical notes *gong*, *shang*, *jue*, *zhi*, and *yu* to symbolize the five periods. Among
them, *gong* stands for the soil period, *shang* stands for the metal period, *jue* stands for
the wood period, *zhi* stands for the fire period, and *yu* stands for the water period.
Also, 太, 'major,' stands for 太過, 'excess,' and 少, 'minor,' stands for 不及, 'insufficiency.' The idea is that 'major' and 'minor' always follow each other. Because *ren chen*
and *ren xu* years are years of an excessive wood period, they are also 'major *jue*' years.
In *chen* and *xu* years, the major yang [qi, i.e., the qi of] cold and water controls heaven.
When major yang [qi] controls heaven, major yin [qi] must be at the fountain. Hence
ren chen and *ren xu* years are years when the major yin [qi, i.e., the qi of] dampness
and soil, is at the fountain."

25 Zhang Jiebin: "Wind is a transformation of wood." Fang Yaozhong: " 'Period' refers to the annual period. 'Wind' refers to a disproportionate dominance of wind qi."

26 Zhang Jiebin: " 'Sound' is the sound of wind and wood/trees. 紊 is 繁盛, 'abundant.' 啟拆 is: sprouts develop and the vessels of the earth open. This is to outline only
the proper transformations of the wind period of *ren* years. The statements below
follow the same structure." In comparison with corresponding passages in *Su wen* 69

The changes [caused by] them include shaking, pulling, breaking, plucking.[27]
The illnesses [caused by] them include dizziness, swaying, and blurred vision.[28]

[The sequence of visitor periods is as follows:]
- Major *jue* begin [of the sequence of host periods,] proper [start of the sequence of visitor periods][29]
- minor *zhi*
- major *gong*
- minor *shang*
- major *yu* end [of the sequence of host periods][30]

---

and 70, Sun Yirang reads 鳴紊 as 鳴璺, "the sound of cracking." Wang Hongtu et al. /158 agrees.

27 Zhang Jiebin: "振 is 撼動, 'to shake.' 拉 is 支離, 'to break off.' 摧 is 敗折, 'to be destroyed.' 拔 is 發根, 'to unroot.' *Ren* is yang and water. An excessive wind period is followed by the orders of metal. Hence these changes occur." Fang Yaozhong: "變 refers to catastrophic changes. Fierce winds destroy houses and unroot trees."

28 Zhang Jiebin: "When the eyes move, that is called 眩, 'dizziness.' When the head shakes, that is called 掉, 'swaying.' When the eyes do not open, that is called 瞑, 'blurred vision.' The wood period is excessive, hence such wind and wood illnesses occur." Fang Yaozhong: "In years with excessive wood [qi] and disproportionately dominant wind qi, the human body easily develops liver illnesses. Hence liver illnesses such as swaying, dizziness, and blurred vision manifest themselves clinically."

29 Beginning with this section, in the received text there are some commenting terms linked to the *Su wen* text which are printed in small letters (but not supposed to belong to Wang Bing's commentary). These parts are printed in small letters in the translation, too.

30 Zhang Jiebin: "This is the sequence, in the present year, of the five periods with their host qi and visitor qi. Their order is that of mutual generation. The host periods of the four seasons of each year [follow each other in such a way that] in spring there is the association with wood. It must begin with *jue* and end with *yu*. Hence the character 初 ('begin') is written as a commentary below [the character] 角 and the character 終 ('end') is written as a commentary below 羽. That is a listing of the host periods. The visitor periods follow the transformations of the heavenly stems. E.g., a *ren* year is yang and wood and begins with major *jue*. A *ding* year is yin and wood and begins with minor *jue*. A *wu* year is yang and fire and begins with major *zhi*. A *gui* year is yin and fire and begins with minor *zhi*. Each year [the arrangement] differs. Only in *ding* and *ren* years of the wood agent host and visitor both begin with *jue*. Hence the character 正, 'proper,' is also noted below the musical note *jue*. That is to say: [in such years] the [visitor] qi of the four seasons agree with the proper [qi, i.e., the host qi]. The same applies to the listings below." Cheng Shide et al.: "*Jue, zhi, gong, shang,* and *yu* are the five musical notes of ancient times. Here they symbolize wood, fire, soil, metal, and water." Fang Yaozhong: "This listing refers to the sequence and to the changes in the course of host periods and visitor periods of *ren chen* and *ren xu* years. The so-called

71-460-1

[The second two arrangements include the years when] major yang [controls heaven], major *zhi* [is the central period], major yin [is at the fountain]. [They are designated] *wu chen* and *wu xu.*[31] They are identical to proper *zhi.*[32]

'visitor periods' refer to the five seasons in the course of one year, i.e., to the specific climatic changes in the course of spring, summer, late summer, autumn, and winter. The calculation method for the visitor periods is such that one starts from the annual period of a given year. The annual period associated with a given year is the initial period of the visitor periods of that year. The following periods elapse in the sequence of mutual generation of the five agents. Because in *ren chen* and *ren xu* years the annual period is an excessive wood period, the initial visitor period of these two years is an excessive wood period, too, that is, 'major *jue*.' The second [visitor] period is a fire period. Because the sequence of the [visitor] periods as symbolized by the five musical notes follows a 'mutual generation of major and minor,' an excessive [visitor period] is followed by an insufficient [visitor period]. Hence the second [visitor] period is an insufficient fire period, that is, 'minor *zhi*.' The third [visitor] period is an excessive wood period, that is, 'major *gong*.' The fourth period is an insufficient metal period, that is, 'minor *shang*.' The fifth period is an excessive water period, that is, 'major *yu*.' That is the meaning of the sequence 'major *jue*, minor *zhi*, ..' listed above. The so-called host periods refer to the general climatic changes in the course of the five seasons of a given year. These general seasonal changes follow the mutual generation sequence of the five agents, i.e., wood/wind, fire/heat, soil/dampness, metal/dryness, and water/cold. This course is the same year after year. Hence the calculaton method of the host periods is quite simple. The initial period is wood; the second period is fire; the third period is soil; the fourth period is metal; the final period is water. Hence the listing can also express the sequence of the host periods. To the right of 'major *jue*' are the two characters 'begin' and 'proper.' 'Begin' refers to the initial period in the course of the host periods. 'Proper' refers to proper *jue*, to distinguish between *jue* [as the proper beginning of the sequence of host periods] and *jue* in the sequence of visitor periods. To the right of 'major *yu*' is the character 'end.' It refers to the final period in the sequence of the host periods. There is no difference of major or minor in the sequence of the host periods. Hence when seen as referring to the course of the host periods, the listing should be read simply as *jue, zhi, gong, shang, yu.*"

31 Fang Yaozhong: "This table is to be read in the same manner as the preceding table. One should first read *wu chen* and *wu xu* and afterwards read 'major yang, major *zhi*, major yin.' In *wu chen* and *wu xu* years, the annual stem is *wu. Wu* and *gui* transform fire. *Wu* is a yang stem. Hence *wu chen* and *wu xu* years are years with excessive fire, i.e., they are 'major *zhi*' years. The annual branches of *wu chen* and *wu xu* years are *chen* and *xu*. In *chen* and *xu* years, major yang [qi, i.e.,] cold and water, control heaven. When major yang [qi] controls heaven, major yin [qi] is at the fountain. Hence in *wu chen* and *wu xu* years, the major yang [qi, i.e.,] cold and water, controls heaven, and the major yin [qi, i.e.,] dampness and soil, are at the fountain."

32 Zhang Jiebin: "The fire period is excessive in that year and is restrained by [the qi of] cold and water controlling heaven. As a result, the fire is subdued. Hence [the

Their period [manifests itself as] heat.
The transformations [caused by] them include warmth, summerheat, [qi] op-
pression,³³ and damp heat.³⁴
The changes [caused by] them include flaming, fieriness, boiling, bubbling.³⁵
The illnesses [caused by] them are heat oppression.³⁶

[The sequence of visitor periods is like follows:]
- Major *zhi*
- minor *gong*
- major *shang*
- minor *yu* end [of the sequence of host periods]
- minor *jue* begin [of the sequence of host periods]³⁷

---

text] states: 'identical to proper *zhi*.'" Fang Yaozhong: " 'Proper *zhi*' refers to a year
with a period of balanced fire qi. That is, even though *wu chen* and *wu xu* years, judged
from their annual period, are years of an excessive fire period, still – judged from the
annual qi – the major yang [qi, i.e.,] cold and water, controls heaven. The excessive
fire period is subdued by the qi controlling heaven. Hence the text says 'identical to
proper *zhi*.'"

33 Qian Chaochen-88/61: "The meaning of 郁 in the *Su wen* is always 蘊結, 'to
collect,' 'to press together.'" See also *Su wen* 67.

34 Zhang Zhicong: "These are transformations of heat."

35 Fang Yaozhong: " 'Changes' refers to catastrophic changes. Because these are
years of an excessive fire period, climatic phenomena of fierce heat appear."

36 Zhang Jiebin: "Such an illness occurs because the heat period is excessive." Fang
Yaozhong: " 'Heat blockage' is: heat is blocked inside. That is, in *wu chen* and *wu xu*
years, the illnesses of the human body manifest themselves mainly through pathoconditions of internal heat."

37 Fang Yaozhong: "This listing refers to the sequence and to the changes in the
course of host periods and visitor periods of *wu chen* and *wu xu* years. According to
this listing the visitor periods of *wu chen* and *wu xu* years are the following: The initial
period is a period of excessive fire, that is, 'major *zhi*.' The second period is a period of
insufficient soil, that is, 'minor *gong*.' The third period is a period of excessive metal,
that is, 'major *shang*.' The fourth period is a period of insufficient water, that is, 'minor
yu.' The final period is one of insufficient wood, that is, 'minor *jue*.' The host periods
follow the sequence of all other years, that is, the initial [host] period is *jue*, the second
period is *zhi*, the third period is *gong*, the fourth period is *shang*, and the final period
is *yu*, in accordance with the [mutual generation order of the five agents, i.e.,] wood,
fire, soil, metal, and water. Two special points are to be explained here. First, the association of the five musical notes with the [visitor] periods follows a sequence of 'major
generates minor' and 'minor generates major.' The present listing, though, ends with
a sequence of minor *yu* followed by minor jue. The reason is that *wu chen* and *wu xu*
years are years of an excessive fire period, i.e., years of major *zhi*. Major *zhi* must be

71-458-14
[The third two arrangements include the years when] major yang [controls heaven], major *gong* [is the central period], major yin [is at the fountain]. [They are designated] *jia chen* – the year meets identical to heavenly complements – and *jia xu* – the year meets identical to heavenly complements.³⁸

Their period [manifests itself as] overcast and dust.³⁹
The transformations [caused by] them include tender moisture and doubled fertility.⁴⁰
The changes [caused by] them include shaking [of the earth] to the extent that

---

preceded by 'minor *jue*.' If it were 'major *jue*,' the subsequent agent should be 'minor *zhi*' which does not agree with the actual situation. Hence in *wu chen* and *wu xu* years, the final visitor period must be a minor *jue* [period] to conform with the rule. That is, in the course of one year, the initial period is decisive. Second, the statements 'minor *yu*, end' and 'minor *jue*, begin' were written to omit one listing. 'Minor *yu*, end' refers to the final period [in the sequence] of the host periods. That is, the final period is water, i.e., *yu*. 'Minor *jue*, begin' refers to the initial period of the host periods. That is, the initial period is wood, i.e., *jue*."

38 Fang Yaozhong: "The meaning of the entire statement is: *Jia chen* and *jia xu* years are years of an excessive soil period. The major yang [qi, i.e.,] cold and water, controls heaven; the major yin [qi, i.e.,] dampness and soil is at the fountain. '*Jia chen*, the year meets; *jia xu*, the year meets' is to say: even though *jia chen* and *jia xu* years are years of an excessive soil [period], nevertheless [the following applies]. The annual stems of *jia chen* and *jia xu* years are *jia*. *Jia* and *ji* transform soil. Hence they are associated with soil periods. The annual branches [of these two years] are *chen* and *xu*. *Chen, xu, chou,* and *wei* are originally associated with the agent soil among the five agents. That is, the five agents association of the large period and the original five phases association of the annual branches are identical. Hence the two years of *jia chen* and *jia xu* are 'the year meets' years. Also, the large period in both *jia chen* and *jia xu* years is an excessive soil period. The qi at the fountain [in these two years] is also associated with the agent soil of the five agents. According to the principle of 'if an excess is increased [that is] identical to heavenly complements' mentioned further below, *jia chen* and *jia xu* years can be called years 'identical to heavenly complements.'"

39 Zhang Zhicong: "In a later section it says 'yin and rain.'" Cheng Shide et al.: "陰埃 is a mistake for 陰雨, 'yin and rain.'" Fang Yaozhong agrees.

40 Cheng Shide et al.: "'Tender humidity and doubled fertility' has the meaning: appropriate winds and suitable rain fertilize the myriad beings." Fang Yaozhong: "柔潤 refers to 滋潤, 'moist,' 'to moisten.' 重澤 is 水多, 'plenty of water.' The meaning is, in *jia chen* and *jia xu* years, the soil period is excessive and the climate is characterized by disproportionate dampness. Hence it rains relatively often."

one is frightened, tornados, and rainstorms.⁴¹
The illnesses [caused by] them include dampness and heaviness below.⁴²

[The sequence of visitor periods is as follows:]
- Major *gong*
- minor *shang*
- major *yu* end [of the sequence of host periods]
- major *jue* begin [of the sequence of host periods]
- minor *zhi*⁴³

71-459-4
[The fourth two arrangements include the years when] major yang [controls heaven], major *shang* [is the central period], major yin [is at the fountain]. [They are designated] *geng chen* and *geng xu*.⁴⁴

Their period [manifests itself as] coolness.⁴⁵
The transformations [caused by] them include fog, dew, and whistling of cold wind.⁴⁶
The changes [caused by] them include sternness, killing, withering, and falling.
The illnesses [caused by] them include dryness, back pressure and [a feeling of] fullness in the chest.⁴⁷

---

41 Zhang Jiebin: "When the soil period is excessive, it is followed by [the commands of] wind and wood. Hence such changes occur."

42 Zhang Jiebin: "These are illnesses of [the qi of] soil and dampness." Fang Yao-zhong: " 'Dampness' is to say: the body retains liquids. 'Heavy below' is to say: the lower limbs ache and are swollen."

43 Fang Yaozhong: "In *jia chen* and *jia xu* years, the initial period of the visitor periods is major *gong*, the second period is minor *shang*, etc. The initial period of the host periods is *jue*, the final host period is *yu*."

44 Fang Yaozhong: "This listing is to say: *geng chen* and *geng xu* years are years of excessive metal. Hence they are also years of major *shang*, with major yang [qi, i.e.,] cold and water, controlling heaven, and major yin [qi, i.e.,] dampness and soil, at the fountain."

45 Fang Yaozhong: "That is, the climate of these two years is characterized by disproportionate coolness."

46 Zhang Jiebin: "These are the proper transformations of the metal period of a *geng* year." Cheng Shide et al.: " 'Whistling of cold wind' are the sounds of autumn winds."

47 Zhang Jiebin: "The metal period is stern and kills; the myriad beings wither and fall to the ground. [An excess of] metal is followed by the qi of fire, which results in the image of yang killings. Because of excessive metal qi [people suffer from] dryness

[The sequence of visitor periods is as follows:]
- Major *shang*
  - minor *yu* end [of the sequence of host periods]
  - minor *jue* begin [of the sequence of host periods]
- major *zhi*
- minor *gong*

71-459-7
[The fifth two arrangements include the years when] major yang [controls heaven], major *yu* [is the central period], major yin [is at the fountain]. [They are designated] *bing chen* – heavenly complements – and *bing xu* – heavenly complements.[48]

Their period [manifests itself as] cold.
The transformations [caused by] them include freezing and piercing cold.[49]
The changes [caused by] them include ice, snow, frost, hail.[50]

---

illness. [With the subsequent advent of fire qi] the lung, [which is] metal, receives an illness. Hence there is a [feeling of] pressure in the back and a [feeling of] distension and fullness in the chest." Zhang Zhicong: "瞀 conveys the image of drooping eyes." Fang Yaozhong: "背瞀 refers to 背部悶滿, '[a feeling of] pressure and fullness in the back.' Because these are years of an excessive metal period, the human body easily develops lung illnesses manifesting themselves clinically as dry mouth and throat and [a feeling of] pressure and fullness in the chest and in the back."

48 Gao Shishi: "*Bing* is a water period. *Chen* and *xu* are [associated with the] control of heaven by major yang, cold, and water. Hence both *bing chen* and *bing xu* [years] are [years of] 'heavenly complements.'" Fang Yaozhong: "*Bing chen* and *bing xu* years are years of an excessive water period, i.e., major *yu*. The major yang [qi, i.e.,] cold and water, controls heaven, the major yin [qi, i.e.,] dampness and soil is at the fountain. Because in *bing chen* and *bing xu* years the heavenly stem is *bing*, because *bing* and *xin* transform water, and because *bing* is a yang stem, *bing chen* and *bing xu* years are years associated with an excessive water period, i.e., they are major *yu* years. In *bing chen* and *bing xu* years, the annual branches are *chen* and *xu*. In *chen* and *xu* years, the major yang [qi, i.e.,] cold and water, controls heaven. The annual period is water and the qi controlling heaven is water. The five agents association of the annual period and of the qi controlling heaven is identical. Hence *bing chen* and *bing xu* years are years of 'heavenly complements.'"

49 Zhang Jiebin: "These are the proper transformations of the water period of a *bing* year." Cheng Shide et al.: " 'Freezing and piercing cold' describe the transformations of cold and water."

50 Zhang Jiebin: "An excess of [the qi of] water is followed by [an arrival of the] qi of soil. Hence such changes occur. Ice and hail are phenomena [associated with] soil."

The illness [caused by] them is massive cold staying in the ravines and valleys.[51]

[The sequence of visitor periods is as follows:]
- Major *yu* end [of the sequence of host periods]
- major *jue* begin [of the sequence of host periods]
- minor *zhi*
- major *gong*
- minor *shang*

71-460-1
Whenever there is such a policy of major yang [qi] controlling heaven,
the transformations of the [six] qi and the movement of the [five] periods
precede heaven.[52]

The qi of heaven is stern;
the qi of the earth rests.[53]

Cold comes down to the Great Void.
The yang qi does not issue commands.[54]
Water and soil combine [their] virtues.[55]

---

51 Zhang Jiebin: " 'Ravines and valleys' are the locations where sinews and bones meet in the joints. In case of excessive water period, cold is extreme and the qi coagulates. Hence such illnesses occur." Fang Yaozhong: " 'Massive cold' refers to illnesses of congealing and stagnating qi and blood. 'Ravines and valleys' are intersections in the muscles and flesh of the human body and they are locations where qi and blood flow."

52 Wang Bing: "The qi of the six steps [of development, i.e.,] generation, growth, transformation, completion, gathering, and storage, should all arrive prior to the heavenly seasons." Cheng Shide et al.: " 'Precede heaven' refers to [fact that] excessive qi arrives prior to the [respective] heavenly seasons."

53 Zhang Zhicong: "[The qi of] major yang, [i.e.,] cold and water, controls heaven. Hence the qi of heaven is stern. [The qi of] major yin, [i.e.,] dampness and soil, is at the fountain. Hence the qi of the earth is quiet."

54 Fang Yaozhong: " 'The yang qi does not issue its orders' is: the yang qi is insufficient."

55 Fang Yaozhong: " 'Water' refers to the qi controlling heaven, i.e., to the major yang [qi, that is,] cold and water. When major yang qi controls heaven, major yin [qi, i.e.,] dampness and soil, must be at the fountain. 'Soil' refers to the major yin [qi] at the fountain. 'Combine their virtue' refers to the phenomena in the transformation of the climate and of things following the joint effects of the qi controlling heaven and of the qi at the fountain."

<Mercury and Saturn correspond to this above.>[56]
<Its grain are dark and yellow.>[57]

71-460-3
Its policy is sternness;
its command is slowness.[58]

The policy of cold is carried out massively.
[There is] humidity; there is no yang flame.[59]
Hence fire [must] wait for its [proper] season to break out.[60]
When in the middle [of a year] the minor yang governs,

---

56 Wang Bing: "They are bright and big." Fang Yaozhong: "Mercury is the water star; Saturn is the soil star. Because major yang [qi] controls heaven and because major yin [qi] is at the fountain, the climatic changes of these years are characterized by disproportionate cold in the first half of the year and by disproportionate dampness in the second half of the year. These types of climatic changes are believed to be closely related to the course of the water star and of the soil star among the celestial bodies."

57 Wang Bing: "It is the proper qi of heaven and earth that generates them, lets them grow, transform, and ripen." "Zhang Jiebin: " 'Dark' corresponds to [the qi] controlling heaven; 'yellow' corresponds to [the qi] at the fountain. [These grain] are transformations of the proper qi of that year." Fang Yaozhong: "Dark and yellow grain are the 'grain of the year' of such years. 'Grain of the year' is to say: they grow relatively well in such years." Zhang Zhicong: "Those grain that are mainly dark and yellow, they ripen. They are affected by the qi controlling heaven and at the fountain. They are the so-called 'grain of the year.'"

58 Zhang Zhicong: " 'Sternness' refers to the policy of heaven; 'slowness' refers to the orders issued by the earth."

59 Zhang Zhicong: " 'There is humidity, but no yang flame' is to say: the yang emerging within the yin is kept down by [the qi of] cold and water." Fang Yaozhong: "In years when the major yang [qi, i.e.,] cold and water, controls heaven, the climate is cold and it appears as if there were only water, no fire."

60 Fang Yaozhong: "This statement continues the preceding statement. 'Break out' is the opposite of 郁, 'oppressed.' 'Fire [must] wait for [its proper] season to break out' means the following: In a year when the major yang [qi, i.e.,] cold and water, controls heaven, the first half of the year is characterized by unilateral cold. The initial qi of the host qi, that is, the ceasing yin [qi, i.e.,] wind and wood and the second qi, that is, the minor yin [qi, i.e.,] the ruler fire, are both oppressed by cold qi. When it should be warm, it is not warm. When it should be hot, it is not hot. Hence [the text stated]: 'the policy of cold is carried out massively; there is humidity but no yang flame.' However, the theory of the [five] periods and [six] qi assumes where there is 'oppression,' there will eventually be an 'outbreak.' When oppression has reached an extreme, an outbreak will follow. That is, at a certain time, the oppressed fire will break out. Hence [the text] states: 'the fire [must] wait for its time to break out.'"

seasonal rain has a limit.⁶¹
Once it has reached the maximum, the rain disperses.⁶²
There is a turn to the major yin.⁶³
When the clouds go to audience with the Northern Pole,⁶⁴
the transformation of dampness is widespread and
humidity flows to the myriad beings.⁶⁵

---

61 Zhang Jiebin: " 'Minor yang governs in the middle [of the year]' is: the third host qi. When the minister fire rules and the visitor [qi of] cold and water overcomes its ruling [qi], seasonal rain arrives. 涯 is 水際, 'rain period.' That is to say: rain arrives." Fang Yaozhong: " 'Minor yang' refers to the minor yang [qi, i.e.,] minister fire, among the six qi. In the sequence of the six qi ruling the six steps [of development], the initial qi is the ceasing yin [qi, i.e.,] wind and wood. The second qi is the minor yin [qi, i.e.,] the ruler fire. The third qi is the minor yang [qi, i.e.,] the minister fire. Hence, when [the present text] refers to 'minor yang,' it refers to the third qi of the host qi. 中治 refers to the qi controlling heaven among the visitor qi. When visitor and host qi meet from below and above, the qi controlling heaven is added on top of the third qi of the host qi, that is on top of the positon of the minor yang [qi, i.e.,] minister fire. The third qi occupies the third step of the altogether six steps. Its position is in the center of the six steps. Hence [the text] speaks of 'governs in the middle [of the year].' 時雨 refers to regular rain fall. In the present context it refers to the rainy season. It also refers to the seasonal qi associated with the fourth qi among the host qi, i.e., e major yin [qi, that is,] dampness and soil. 涯 refers to a border line. The meaning of the entire passage is: In a year when the major yang [qi, i.e.,] cold and water, controls heaven, the qi of heaven of the first half of the year is characterized by disproportionate cold. The initial qi of the host qi, i.e., the ceasing yin [qi, which is] wind and wood and the second qi, i.e., the minor yin [qi, that is] the ruler fire, are oppressed by the qi controlling heaven. When it should be warm, it is not warm; when it should be hot, it is not hot. The third qi, i.e., the minor yang [qi, that is,] the minister fire, is just at the position of the qi controlling heaven. Hence it, too, is disproportionately cold. When it should be hot, it is not hot. Because the qi controlling heaven is responsible for the first half of the year, the [effect of the] major yang qi, [i.e.,] cold, comes to a halt immediately after the [rule of the] third qi is over. At the time when the fourth qi, the major yin [qi, i.e.,] dampness and soil, begins to rule, the effect of the qi of cold and water has ended. That is meant by the text when it states: 'the seasonal rain has reached its limits.' "

62 Fang Yaozhong: "雨散 is hard to explain. All previous commentators have omitted this phrase. We wonder whether it is a mistake for 寒, 'cold.' "

63 Zhang Jiebin: "The second half of a year is ruled by the qi of the earth. Once the [influence of the] third qi has stopped at its final end and after the rain has dispersed, a transition occurs to the fourth qi. Subsequently, the [qi] at the fountain is in charge and the major yin [qi] resides in its position."

64 Wang Bing: "The Northern Pole is the palace of rain."

65 Fang Yaozhong: "That is, when the minor yin [qi, i.e.,] dampness and soil, is at the fountain, the generation and growth of the myriad beings is influenced by dampness."

Cold extends in the upper [half of the year];
thunder moves in the lower [half of the year].⁶⁶
The qi of cold and dampness
are held in [the sphere of] qi interaction.⁶⁷

71-460-6
People suffer from cold and dampness;
they develop decay of muscles and flesh.
The feet limp and [can] not be contracted.
There is soggy outflow and blood overflow.⁶⁸

The initial qi:
the qi of the earth has left its position.
Hence the qi is very warm;
the herbs blossom early.⁶⁹

---

66 Zhang Jiebin: " 'Thunder moves in the lower [half of the year]' is: the oppressed
fire breaks out." Zhang Zhicong: " 'Thunder moves in the lower [half of the year]' is:
the fire qi of minor yin is situated to the right of the major yin. Its effusion begins with
the advent of the fifth qi."

67 Fang Yaozhong: "In a year when the major yang [qi, i.e.,] cold and water, control
heaven, because the major yin [qi, i.e.,] dampness and soil, is at the fountain, the climate is characterized by cold and dampness."

68 Zhang Jiebin: " 'Blood overflow' is an illness of oppressed fire; it is always caused
by cold and dampness." Fang Yaozhong: " 'Moist outflow' is diarrhea. 'Blood overflow'
is bleeding. These pathoconditions are often associated with the spleen (i.e., the soil
depot) and in the kidneys (i.e., the water depot), if we look at the seat of the illness,
and with the cold and dampness, if we look at the nature of the illness."

69 Fang Yaozhong: "In the preceding section, the general circumstances have been
outlined of the changes in the appearance of things and climate in years when the
major yang [qi, i.e.,] cold and water, control heaven. In the following section, the
concrete circumstances of the changes in the appearance of things and climate during each step of the six steps ruling a season in years of major yang [qi, i.e.,] cold and
water. 'Initial qi' refers to [the following]: In a year when the major yang [qi, i.e.,] cold
and water, controls heaven, the initial qi of the intervening qi of the visitor qi coming
down to join [the annual qi] is the minor yang [qi, i.e.,] minister fire. 'The qi of the
earth has left its position' refers [to the following]: the minor yang [qi, i.e.,] minister
fire, is the initial qi in a year when the major yang [qi, i.e.,] cold and water, controls
heaven, because the qi at the fountain in the preceding year has left its position. In the
year preceding a year when the major yang [qi, i.e.,] cold and water, controls heaven,
the yang brilliance [qi, i.e.,] dryness and metal, controls heaven and the minor yin [qi,
i.e.,] ruler fire, is at the fountain. In a year when the major yang [qi, i.e.,] cold and
water, controls heaven the minor yin [qi, i.e.,] ruler fire, which was at the fountain in
the previous year, moves to the position of fifth qi. Hence the minor yang [qi, i.e.,]

Hence people are affected by epidemics,
and warmth diseases break out.
The body is hot; the head aches and
[patients] vomit.
The muscle[-flesh] and the interstice [structures] develop sores and ulcers.[70]

71-460-9
The second qi:
Massive coolness arrives contrary [to the regular order].
People experience chilling temperatures.
The herbs meet cold;
the qi of fire is pressed down then.[71]

People suffer from qi oppression and central fullness.

Cold begins.[72]

---

minister fire, can move to the position of initial qi in the present year from the position of second qi in the preceding year. 'The qi is very warm' is: in a year when the
major yang [qi, i.e.,] cold and water, controls heaven the initial qi is minor yang. Minor yang controls fire. Hence in the time period associated with the initial qi, which
in this year lasts from [the solar term] Great Cold to [the solar term] Excited Insects,
i.e., approximately from the twelve month to the second month of the lunar calendar,
the climate is very warm." Zhang Jiebin: "The final qi of the preceding year is [the qi
of] ruler fire; the initial qi of the present year is [the qi of] minister fire. When these
two qi interact, the qi is very warm. Hence herbs blossom early."

70 Zhang Jiebin: "The visitor qi is [the qi of] minister fire; the host qi is [the qi of]
wind and wood. Wind and fire strike each other, hence these illnesses appear."

71 Fang Yaozhong: " 'Second qi' refers to [the following]: In a year when the major
yang [qi, i.e.,] cold and water, control heaven, the second qi of the intervening qi of
the visitor qi coming down is the yang brilliance [qi, i.e.,] dryness and metal. 'Great
coolness arrives contrary [to the regular order]' is: because the yang brilliance [qi]
rules coolness and dryness, the climate is disproportionately cool in the time period
associated with the second qi, which in this year lasts from Vernal Equinox to Grain
Fills, that is, approximately from the latter ten days of the second month to the first
ten days of the fourth month of the lunar calendar. This period is the transition from
spring to summer; [the former] should be warm but is not warm; [the latter] should
be hot but is not hot. The generation and growth of herbs and trees is slowed down."
Zhang Zhicong: "Great cold arrives contrary [to the regular order] and transforms
heat to coolness prior to the middle of the year."

72 Gao Shishi: "Illnesses of [qi] oppression and fullness originate from cold. Hence
[the text] states: 'cold is at the begin.'" Fang Yaozhong: " 'Cold begins' refers [to the
following]: In a year when the major yang [qi, i.e.,] cold and water, controls heaven,
the climate in the first half of the year is disproportionately cold. However, because

The third qi:
The policy of heaven is widespread.
Cold qi prevails.
Hence rain falls.[73]

People suffer from cold;
contrary [to what one might expect], they have a heated center.[74]
[They suffer from] *yong-* and *ju*-abscesses and from outpour below.
The heart [feels] hot. [Patients suffer from] physical and mental pressure.
Those who are not treated die.[75]

71-460-12
The fourth qi:
Wind and dampness interact in a struggle.
The wind transforms to rain.
Hence there is growth, transformation, and completion.[76]

---

the initial qi is the minor yang [qi, i.e.,] minister fire, in reality [the climate] cannot become too cold. Hence the appearance of truly disproportionate cold begins only with the onset of the second qi."

73 Fang Yaozhong: "In a year when the major yang [qi, i.e.,] cold and water, controls heaven, the third of the visitor qi is the major yang [qi, i.e.,] cold and water. 'The policy of heaven is widespread' is: when in a year when major yang [qi, i.e.,] cold and water, controls heaven the position of the third qi of the six steps of the visitor qi, is taken by the qi controlling heaven. 'Cold qi prevails' is: major yang rules cold. On top of this, this step is ruled by the qi controlling heaven. Hence the climate is very cold in the time period associated with the third qi, which in this year lasts from Grain Fills to Great Heat, that is, approximately from the latter ten days of the fourth month to the first ten days of the sixth month of the lunar calendar."

74 Gao Shishi: "That is, they suffer from cold outside and, in contrast, are hot inside." Zhang Jiebin: "Cold and water offend the yang. Hence fire is affected everywhere. If this is not treated, the [flow of] yang [qi] will be interrupted and [the patient] dies."

75 Wang Bing: "When [people] should feel cold but, on the contrary, develop heat, that is contrary to the regularity of heaven. When heat develops from the heart, then the spirit is in utmost danger. If no assistance is given to the spirit immediately, it must perish. Hence those who receive treatment will live; those who do not receive treatment will die."

76 Zhang Zhicong: "At the intersection of summer and autumn, the host qi is that of dampness and soil. Hence there is growth, transformation, and completion. That is, summer rules growth, autumn rules completion, and late summer rules transformation." Fang Yaozhong: "In a year when the major yang [qi, i.e.,] cold and water, controls heaven, the fourth qi of the intervening qi of the visitor qi coming down is the ceasing yin [qi, i.e.,] wind and wood. 'Wind and dampness engage in struggle' is:

People suffer from massive heat and being short of qi;
the muscles and the flesh decay.⁷⁷ The feet are limp.
There is outpour below; it is red and white.

The fifth qi:
The yang returns to transform.
Hence the herbs experience growth, transformation, and completion.

People feel comfortable.⁷⁸

71-461-2
The final qi:
The qi of the earth [occupies its] proper [position].
The command of dampness prevails.⁷⁹

---

because the ceasing yin rules wind and warmth, the climate of the time period associated with the fourth qi, which in this year lasts from Great Heat to Autumn Equinox, that is, approximately from the last ten days of the sixth month to the first ten days of the eighth month in the lunar calendar, is disproportionately warm and is disproportionately dominated by wind."

77 Zhang Jiebin: "The ceasing yin qi, [i.e.,] wood, is in charge of the period of great heat. Wood can generate fire. Hence people suffer from great heat. Because the visitor [qi] overcomes the ruling [qi], the spleen, [i.e.,] the soil, receives harm. Hence such pathoconditions like diminished qi and flesh decay emerge."

78 Wang Bing: "Massive fire comes down to take control. Hence the myriad beings feel comfortable and flourish." Fang Yaozhong: "In a year when the major yang [qi, i.e.,] cold and water, controls heaven, the fifth qi of the intervening qi of the visitor qi coming down is the minor yin [qi, i.e.,] ruler fire. 'The yang returns to transform' refers [to the following]: because the minor yin rules the ruler fire and heat, the climate of the time period associated with the fifth qi, which in this year lasts from Autumn Equinox to Little Snow, that is, approximately from the last ten days of the eighth month to the first ten days of the tenth month in the lunar calendar, is disproportionately hot. 'People feel comfortable' is: the yang qi oppressed in the human body can be effused and flows off because of the turn of the climate to heat and does no longer cause irritations inside. Hence [people] feel happy."

79 Fang Yaozhong: " 'The final qi' is: in a year when the major yang [qi, i.e.,] cold and water, controls heaven, the final qi of the visitor qi is the minor yin [qi, i.e.,] dampness and soil. 'The qi of the earth [occupies its] proper [position]' is: this [major yin qi] also occupies the position of the qi at the fountain. 'The order of dampness prevails' is: when the major yin [qi, i.e.,] dampness and soil, is at the fountain, the dampness qi is disproportionately dominant in the second half of this year. Dampness qi is especially dominant in the time period associated with the final qi, which in this year lasts from Little Snow to Great Cold, that is, approximately from the final ten days of the tenth month to the first ten days of the twelfth month of the lunar calendar."

The clouds are are condensed in the Great Void;[80]
dust [causes] darkness in the wastelands.

People experience chilling temperatures.
Cold and wind arrive.
Contrary to [the regular order,] embryos die.[81]

71-461-4
Hence
this year it is appropriate [to employ]
bitter [flavor] to dry the [dampness] and to warm the [cold].[82]

It is necessary to break the qi oppressing it[83] and

---

80 Fang Yaozhong: "Heaven is covered by clouds."

81 Zhang Jiebin: "When the major yin [qi, i.e.,] dampness and soil, is at the fountain, this is the proper earth qi. Hence the order of dampness prevails, clouds are
condensed in the Great Void and dust darkens the waste lands. People prefer yang
and have an aversion to yin. Hence they feel miserably cold. Because [at this time] the
order of dampness [prevails] and cold wind arrives, the wind can dominate the dampness. Hence [the text] says 'contrary': 'When [wind dominates dampness] contrary [to
the order of the season] those who are pregnant will die.' This is so because man is a
naked creature, [generated] through a transformation of soil. When wind, [i.e.,] wood,
is added [to soil] out of season, then, as a result, the transformation [products] of soil
cannot proliferate." Zhang Zhicong: "The soil rules the transformation and prolifera-
tion of naked creatures, and man is the supreme creature among the naked creatures.
When cold wind arrives, the soil is dominated by wind, [i.e.,] wood. Hence pregnan-
cies do not reach completion. That is called: an untimely evil dominates the qi [sup-
posed to] rule a season." Fang Yaozhong: "Such a year is characterized by a cold and
damp climate. All living beings that are able to adapt [the diet, etc.] to these climatic
characteristics, will be able to grow, to have offspring, to proliferate. 'In contrast,' those
living beings that are not able to adapt to these climatic characteristics, will not grow,
have no offspring, and do not proliferate. That is, those who are pregnant will die."

82 Lin Yi et al.: "The nine characters 故歲宜 .. 之溫之 must follow the passage 以
安其正 further below; they have been moved here erroneously." Zhang Zhicong: "Bitter is the flavor of fire, fire can warm cold. Bitter [flavor] can dry dampness."

83 Zhang Jiebin: " 'Break the oppressing qi is: drain what is present in surplus."
Gao Shishi: "As for 郁氣, 'oppressed qi,' when water dominates, then fire is oppressed;
when soil dominates, than water is oppressed. Hence it is necessary to 'break the
oppressing qi.' Oppression is the basis of revenge. If one wishes to 'break' a [oppress-
ing qi], it is necessary, first of all, to nourish the source of its transformation. If one
wants to break its fire, one nourishes first its wood. If one wants to break its water,
one nourishes first its metal. [Wood and metal] are the sources of the generation and
transformation [of fire and water, respectively]." Fang Yaozhong: 郁氣, 'oppressing

to supply the source of its transformation first,[84]
to press down its [excessive] period and qi, and
to support that which does not dominate in that [particular year].[85]
Do not permit a violent transgression leading to the emergence of the respective diseases.

---

qi,' refers to a qi causing an oppression, i.e., a disproportionately dominant qi. 'One must break the oppressing qi' means [the following]: when a qi is present in surplus and exhibits disproportionate domination, the qi that is dominated will be oppressed internally. For example, when cold qi is disproportionately dominant, the fire qi will be supressed internally; etc. Hence for treatment one must first of all take care of the disproportionately dominant qi. Only when this disproportionately dominant qi has been brought back to order, the qi that was dominated inside can recover and resume its normal functions."

84 Wang Bing: " 'Source of transformation is to say: in the ninth month. One seizes it by moving towards it. This serves to supplement the fire of the heart." Lin Yi et al.: "Water is about to dominate. 先於九月迎取其化源 Before the ninth month [one has to] prevent it by taking away the source of its transformation, i.e, by draining the source of the [water, i.e., the] kidneys first. The reason is, water rules in the tenth month. Hence it is to be taken away before the ninth month. Because the water is drained, the fire is supplemented." Fang Yaozhong: "Wang Bing's commentary is to say: In the tenth, the eleventh, and the twelfth months, [i.e.,] the three winter months, the climate is very cold. Abounding cold qi can oppress the fire of the heart internally. Hence it is necessary to supplement the fire of the heart prior to the advent of winter, lest the fire of the heart is tied down by the cold evil."

85 Wang Bing: In the major *jue* year, the spleen does not dominate. In a major *zhi* year, the lung does not dominate. In a major *gong* year, the kidneys do not dominate. In a major *shang* year, the liver does not dominate. In a major *yu* year, the heart does not dominate. That is how it should be in these years. However, when major yang [qi] controls heaven, no matter which of the five annual qi is present it is always appropriate to assist the heart first and to support the qi of the kidneys afterwards." Fang Yaozhong: "抑 refers to 抑制, 'to restrain.' 其 refers here to a year in which major yin [qi] controls heaven. 運 refers to the annual period. 氣 refers to the annual qi. In a year with major yang [qi] controlling heaven, seen from the annual period, the ten years with major yang [qi] controlling heaven are years of greatly excessive annual periods. Seen from the annual qi, in years when the major yang [qi, i.e.,] cold and water, control heaven, the cold qi is disproportionately dominant. When the major yin [qi, i.e.,] dampness and soil, is at the fountain, dampness qi is disproportionately dominant. Hence when treating illnesses, it is necessary to 'restrain the periodic [qi] and the [annual] qi and to support that which does not dominate.'"

Consume the grain [associated with] that year to preserve its true [qi].
Avoid depletion evil to secure its proper [qi].⁸⁶

71-461-6
Depending on⁸⁷ whether the qi agrees with or differs from [the proper qi of
this year], [apply] more or less restraint to it.⁸⁸
When they agree in cold and dampness, dryness and heat serve to achieve
transformations.
When they differ in cold and dampness, dryness and dampness achieve trans-
formations.⁸⁹

Hence
in case of agreements, increase it;
in case of differences, diminish it.⁹⁰

---

86 Wang Bing: "When the [qi of] wood is present in excess, then spleen illnesses
emerge. When the [qi of] fire is present in excess, then lung illnesses emerge. When
the [qi of] soil is present in excess, then kidney illnesses emerge. When the [qi of]
metal is present in excess, then liver illnesses emerge. When the [qi of] water is present in excess, then heart illnesses emerge. The same applies when the qi of heaven and
earth are present in excess. 'Grain associated with that year' is to say: [grain] of yellow
color and of black color. 'Depletion evil' is to say: wind that comes from unexpected
directions." Fang Yaozhong: " 'Depletion evil' is 'depletion wind.' Regular wind is wind
that blows in spring from the East, in summer from the South, etc. Irregular wind
is wind that blows in spring from the West, in summer from the North. If one faces
the South and a northerly wind blows, if one faces the North and a southerly wind
blows, etc., that is what is called 'the wind comes from unexpected directions.' That is
a depletion wind."

87 Zhang Jiebin: "適 is 酌所宜, 'to deliberate what is suitable.'" 2289/22: "適 is
視, 'to observe,' 'to investigate.' The meaning here is 'on the basis of,' 'in accordance
with.'"

88 Fang Yaozhong: "適 has the meaning of 酌量, 'to consider.' 氣 refers to the annual qi, which is also the qi controlling heaven. 同異 refers to agreements or differences in the climate calculated in comparison of the annual period and the annual qi.
多少 refers to the degree of agreements and differences."

89 Wang Bing: "Major *gong*, major *shang*, and major *yu* years agree [with the annual
qi] in terms of cold and dampness. It is appropriate to treat with dryness and heat to
achieve transformations. Major *jue* and major *zhi* years differ [from the annual qi]
in terms of cold and dampness. It is appropriate to treat dampness with dryness to
achieve transformations."

90 Wang Bing: " 'Increase' refers to dryness and heat. 'Diminish' refers to dryness
and dampness. The amount of a qi to be employed depends on the [nature of the
respective] year." Zhang Zhicong: " 'Agree in cold and dampness' is to say: the ruling

When employing cold, stay away from cold.[91]
When employing coolness, stay away from coolness.
When employing warmth, stay away from warmth.
When employing heat, stay away from heat.
Food requirements [are based on] the same law.

In cases of false [heat or cold] act contrary to [this] rule.[92]

---

periods major *yu* and major *gong* are identical to the [qi of] cold and dampness controlling heaven and at the fountain. Hence it is necessary to employ more substances with a qi of dryness and heat to curb transformations [of cold and dampness]. That is, dryness is employed to restrain dampness and heat is employed to transform cold. The ruling periods major *zhi*, major *jue*, or major *shang* always differ from the qi of cold and dampness. Still, small amounts of [substances with a] qi of dryness and dampness are to be employed to transform them. Hence dampness is employed to enrich the qi of dampness and heat and dryness is used to restrain the evil of wind and wood." Fang Yaozhong: " 'Increase' and 'diminish' refer to the amounts of warm, hot, dry, or damp drugs employed. That is, when the annual period and the annual qi are entirely identical, one employs large quantities of warm, hot, dry, or damp drugs. In case they are not identical, because the annual qi is cold and dampness, it is not entirely possible not to consider the issue of cold and dampness. However, because they are not identical, warm, hot, dry, or damp drugs are employed in comparatively small amounts only."

91 Zhang Jiebin: "遠 is 避, 'to avoid.' In the application of cold drugs it is essential to avoid the cold of the annual qi. In the application of cool drugs, it is essential to avoid the coolness of the annual qi. Etc. The same law applies to drinking, eating, and housing." Fang Yaozhong: "遠 has the meaning of 疏遠, 'to separate,' 'to create a distance,' or 回避, 'to avoid.' That is, in the course of seasons characterized by cold, or when treating pathoconditions of cold, it is advisable either not to employ cold and cool drugs at all, or to use them cautiously." 732/3: "That is, in seasons of cold climate drugs of a cold or cool nature are to be avoided."

92 Zhang Jiebin: "That is to say: A qi is adopted that is contrary to the regular order. For example, in summer it should be hot, but, on the contrary, it is cold." Fang Yaozhong: "The character 假 is explained in two ways. According to the first, it refers to 假借, 'to make use.' That is, whatever a season is like, one can always 'make use' of cold or cool drugs to treat pathoconditions of heat, or 'make use' of hot or warm drugs to treat pathoconditions of cold. According to the second [explanation], the character 假 refers to 假象, 'false appearance.' That is to say, cold, heat, warmth, and coolness can appear as false phenomena, or it may be that the climate does not parallel a season. Hence treatment must not be tied too closely to the season or to external phenomena. The treatment must be directed at the nature [of the illness] underlying the pathoconditions." 1833/17: "When the climate is irregular (有假), the treatment should be based on an unusual approach (反之)." See also 315/7 and 2305/49 for a detailed discussion of the therapeutic principles outlined here.

If one acts contrary to this, illness [emerges].⁹³
This is a so-called seasonal [illness]."⁹⁴

71-462-1
[Huang] Di:
"Good!
The policy of yang brilliance, what is it like?"⁹⁵

Qi Bo:
"These are the arrangements including *mao* and *you* [earth branches].⁹⁶

[The first two arrangements include the years when] yang brilliance [controls heaven], minor *jue* [is the annual period], and minor yin [is at the fountain].⁹⁷
Coolness domination and heat revenge are identical [in both minor *jue* years].⁹⁸

---

93 Zhang Jiebin: " 'Those acting contrary fall ill' because they act contrary to the respective season. Later on, [the text] states 'the host qi is insufficient; the visitor qi dominates. That is meant here.' " Fang Yaozhong: "That is to say: those acting contrary to the therapeutic principles outlined in the preceding sentence, they fall ill." In comparison with parallel statements in the text later on it is obvious that this statement makes sense only if it is preceded by the four characters 此其道也, "that is the Way of this." Cf. *Su wen* 71-465-3, 71-470-15, 71-473-8, 71-475-3.

94 Wang Bing: "時 is to say: In the presence of spring, summer, autumn, and winter [qi], and of the intervening [visitor] qi, stay away from [drugs of] identical qi [for treating an illness]. That is, if [any of] the six qi has come down to take control and one makes use of cold or heat, warmth or coolness to eliminate the [resulting] illnesses regardless of the season, then this is not 'staying away' from them. For instance, when the major yang [qi, i.e., cold,] controls heaven and cold causes an illness, if one makes use of heat to cure this, then the application of heat is not 'staying away' from summer. The same applies to all the other qi. Hence [the text] speaks of 'making use of what is contrary to the regular [order].' [The application of a] diet is identical to [the application of] drug laws."

95 Fang Yaozhong: "The 'policy of yang brilliance' refers to a year when the yang brilliance [qi, i.e.,] dryness and metal, control heaven."

96 Fang Yaozhong: "The meaning is: in all years with *mao* and *you* earth branches the yang brilliance [qi], [i.e., the qi of] dryness and metal, controls heaven."

97 Fang Yaozhong: " 'Yang brilliance' refers to [the qi of] yang brilliance, [i.e.,] dryness and metal, controlling heaven. 'Minor *jue*' refers to years with an inadequate wood period. 'Minor yin' refers to [the qi of] minor yin, [i.e.,] the ruler fire, at the fountain."

98 Wang Bing: "Coolness dominates minor *jue*; heat takes revenge at coolness. Hence [the text] states: 'Coolness and heat dominate and take revenge the same way.' The same applies to all remaining minor periods." Fang Yaozhong: " 'Coolness' refers

[Both these years have conditions] identical to [those in] proper *shang* [years].⁹⁹
[They are designated] *ding mao* – the year meets – and *ding you*.¹⁰⁰

Their period [manifests itself as] wind, coolness, and heat.¹⁰¹

[The sequence of visitor periods is as follows:]
- Minor *jue* begin [of the sequence of host periods,] proper [begin of the sequence of visitor periods]
- major *zhi*
- minor *gong*
- major shang
- and minor *yu* end [of the sequence of host periods].¹⁰²

---

to the qi of coolness; in the present context it refers to the qi of yang brilliance, [i.e., of] dryness and metal, that controls heaven. In a year when the wood period is in-adequate, in spring when it should be warm in spring it is not warm; the climate is disproportionately cold. Because of the principle that the overall course of the seasons is balanced, with the arrival of summer the climate will be disproportionately hot." Zhang Zhicong: "When the wood period is inadequate, the cool qi of metal domi-nates it. Where there is domination, there must be revenge. [Hence] fire comes to take revenge."

99 Wang Bing: "As for 'identical to proper *shang*,' when yang brilliance [qi] appears in the upper [half of the year], upper *shang* is identical to proper *shang*. That is to say: the [qi of] wood of that year is inadequate. The same applies to all the other [situ-ations]." Fang Yaozhong: " 'Proper *shang*' is a year of a metal period with balanced qi. 'Identical to proper *shang*' refers to a year with an inadequate wood period where metal comes to avail itself of the wood. If, at the same time, this is a year with yang brilliance [qi, i.e.,] dryness and metal, controlling heaven, then subduing is added on top of subduing."

100 Fang Yaozhong: "All years with a five agents association of the annual period which is identical with the original five phases association of the branches of these years, are 'the year meets' years. The heavenly stem of a *ding mao* year is *ding*. *Ding* and *ren* transform wood; they are associated with the wood period. The branch of this year is *mao*. *Yin* and *mao* are associated with wood. Hence the annual period and the branch of that year have identical five agents associations."

101 Fang Yaozhong: "Wind is associated with wood; coolness is associated with metal; heat is associated with fire. When in a year with an inadequate wood period spring should be warm but is not warm, with the climate being disproportionately cool, it appears as if it were autumn. When it comes to summer the climate changes to disproportionate heat because of the mutual regulation of the seasons among each other."

102 Fang Yaozhong: "This listing is to say: In *ding mao* and *ding you* years, the first of the visitor periods is minor *jue*, the second is major *zhi*, the third is minor *gong*, the

71-462-6
[The second two arrangements include the years when] yang brilliance
[controls heaven], minor *zhi* [is the central period], and minor yin [is at the
fountain].[103] Cold domination and rain revenge is the same [in both minor *zhi*
years].[104] [Both these years have conditions] identical to [those in] proper *shang*
[years].[105] [They are designated] *gui mao* identical to the year meets and *gui you*
identical to the year meets.

Their period [manifests itself as] heat, cold, and rain.[106]

[The sequence of visitor periods is as follows:]
- Minor *zhi*
- major *gong*
- minor *shang*
- major *yu* end [of the sequence of host periods]
- major *jue* begin [of the sequence of host periods].

71-462-9
[The third two arrangements include the years when] yang brilliance [controls
heaven], minor *gong* [is the central period], and minor yin [is at the fountain].
Wind domination and coolness revenge is the same [in both minor *gong*
years].[107] [They are designated] *ji mao* and *ji you*.

---

fourth is major *shang*, the final is minor *yu*. The host periods follow the regular order
without change."

103 Fang Yaozhong: " 'Minor *zhi*' refers to years with inadequate fire period. That is,
in *gui mao* and *gui you* years with an inadequate fire period, the qi controlling heaven
is the yang brilliance [qi, i.e.,] dryness and metal, and the qi at the fountain is the
minor yin [qi, i.e.,] the ruler fire."

104 Zhang Zhicong: " 'Cold' is the qi of cold and water; 'rain' is the qi of dampness
and soil. When cold dominates the minor *zhi*, soil comes to take revenge it."

105 Fang Yaozhong: "In years with an inadequate fire period, the fire cannot subdue
the metal. If in the same year, on top of this, the qi controlling heaven is the yang
brilliance [qi, i.e.,] dryness and metal, the qi controlling heaven controls everything.
Hence the summer of that year should be hot but is not hot; there should be growth,
but there is no growth. [Summer] appears like autumn."

106 Zhang Jiebin: " 'Heat' is the period of minor *zhi*. 'Cold' is the dominating qi.
'Rain' is the qi of revenge."

107 Zhang Zhicong: "When a soil period is inadequate, wind, contrary [to the regular order of seasons] dominates it. The metal qi of coolness comes to take revenge."

Their period [manifests itself as] rain, wind, and coolness.[108]

[The sequence of visitor periods is as follows:]
- Minor *gong*
- major *shang*
- minor *yu* end [of the sequence of host periods]
- minor *jue* begin [of the sequence of host periods]
- major *zhi*.

71-462-12
[The fourth two arrangements include the years when] yang brilliance [controls heaven], minor *shang* [is the central period], and minor yin [is at the fountain].[109] Heat domination and cold revenge is the same [in both minor *shang* years].[110] [Both these years have conditions] identical to [those in] proper *shang* [years]. [They are designated] *yi mao* – heavenly complements[111] – and *yi you* – the year meets and *tai-yi* heavenly complements.[112]

---

108 Gao Shishi: "Minor *gong* soil periods are *ji mao* and *ji you* years. 'Their period is rain' is a *gong* and soil period. [The presence of] wind is a domination of wood; coolness indicates that metal takes revenge. These qi characterize the entire year."

109 Fang Yaozhong: " 'Yang brilliance' refers to the yang brilliance [qi, i.e.,] dryness and metal, controlling heaven. 'Minor *shang*' refers to years of an inadequate metal period. 'Minor yin' refers to the minor yin [qi, i.e.,] ruler fire, at the fountain. That is, in *yi mao* and *yi you* years of an inadequate metal period, the qi controlling heaven is the yang brilliance [qi, i.e.,] dryness and metal, and the qi at the fountain is the minor yin [qi, i.e.,] the ruler fire."

110 Gao Shishi: "[In years] when the minor *shang* metal period is inadequate, the heat qi of fire will dominate in the beginning. Later on, the qi of water and cold takes revenge. The dominating qi and the qi taking revenge rule the entire year."

111 Fang Yaozhong: "Any year when the annual period is identical in its five agents association with the qi controlling heaven, is a 'heavenly complements' year. The heavenly stem of *yi mao* years is *yi*; *yi* and *geng* transform metal. The annual [earth] branch of *yi mao* years is *mao*. In *mao* and *you* [years] the yang brilliance [qi, i.e.,] dryness and metal control heaven. The annual period is metal and the qi controlling heaven is metal, too. Because the annual period and the annual qi are identical, this *yi mao* year belongs to the 'heavenly complements' [years]."

112 Fang Yaozhong: "Years with identical five agents associations of the annual period and of the [earth] branch of that year belong to the 'the year meets' years. The heavenly stem of an *yi you* year is *yi*; *yi* and *geng* transform metal. The [earth] branch of that year is *you*. *Shen* and *you* are associated with [the agent] metal. The annual period is metal and the five agents association of the [earth] branch of that year is metal, too. Because the five agents association of the annual period and the original five agents association of the branches of these years are identical, an *yi you* year belongs to

Their period [manifests itself as] coolness, heat, and cold.[113]

[The sequence of visitor periods is as follows:]
- Minor *shang*
- major *yu* end [of the sequence of host periods]
- major *jue* begin [of the sequence of host periods]
- minor *zhi*
- major *gong*.

71-463-2
[The fifth two arrangements include the years when] yang brilliance [controls heaven], minor *yu* [is the central period],[114] and minor yin [is at the fountain]. Rain domination and wind revenge is the same [in both minor *yu* years].[115]

[Both these years have conditions] identical to [those in] minor *gong* [years].[116] [They are designated] *xin mao* and *xin you*.[117]

Their period [manifests itself as] cold, rain, and wind.[118]

---

the 'the year meets' years. Now, in terms of the qi controlling heaven, an *yi you* year is identical to an *yi mao* year. That is, the qi controlling heaven in an *yi you* year is metal, too. Hence an *yi you* year is also a year of 'heavenly complements.' Because it is a year of 'heavenly complements' and, in addition, belongs to the 'the year meets' years, it is called '*tai-yi* heavenly complements' [year]."

113 Zhang Jiebin: "Coolness is the qi of minor *shang*; heat is the dominating qi; cold is the qi taking revenge."

114 Fang Yaozhong: "Minor *yu* refers to years of an inadequate water period."

115 Gao Shishi: "In [a year of] minor *yu* when the water period is inadequate, the rain qi of soil dominates in the beginning. Later on the wind qi of wood takes revenge. The qi of domination and revenge rule the entire year."

116 Some editions have here the characters 辛卯少宮同. Fang Yaozhong: "The meaning of 辛卯少宮同 is: A *xin mao* year is identical in terms of changes affecting climate and objects with a year of an inadequate soil period."

117 Zhang Jiebin: "This paragraph says only *xin mao*, it does not say *xin you*. Perhaps this is an error that has been handed down for long." Some *Su wen* editions have the two characters *xin mao* twice. First, prior to the characters 少宮同 and, second, subsequent to 辛酉.

118 Fang Yaozhong: "In a year of an inadequate water period, the soil comes to take advantage [of this inadequacy]. 'Wind' refers to wood. When soil is greatly excessive because it has taken advantage of [the inadequacy of] water, then wood comes to take revenge. That is, in *xin mao* and *xin you* years much rain falls in winter and winds blow frequently next spring."

[The sequence of visitor periods is as follows:]
- Minor *yu* end [of the sequence of host periods]
- minor *jue* begin [of the sequence of host periods]
- major *zhi*
- minor *gong*
- major *shang*.

Whenever there is a policy of this yang brilliance controlling heaven,
the transformations of the [six] qi and the movement of the [five] periods are
behind heaven.[119]

The qi of heaven is tense;
the qi of the earth is bright.[120]
The yang alone issues its commands;
flaming summerheat prevails everywhere.[121]

---

119 Wang Bing: "As for the qi of the six steps, of generation, growth, transformation and completion, the movement and resting of all things are behind the heavenly
seasons. The same applies to the remaining 'minor' years." Fang Yaozhong: "The ten
years when yang brilliance [qi, i.e.,] dryness and metal, control heaven are years of an
inadequate annual period because their heavenly stems are always yin stems. Hence in
these years climate and seasons do not agree entirely."

120 Zhang Zhicong: "When the yang brilliance [qi] controls heaven, then the minor
yin [qi] is at the fountain. The order of metal rules the upper [half of the year]; hence
the qi of heaven is strong and unyielding. The ruler fire is present in the lower [half of
the year]; hence the qi of the earth is brilliant."

121 Fang Yaozhong: "From here on the following few sentences are difficult to explain. Hence former commentators either have not commentated on them at all, or
their explanations are rather confused. Zhang Jiebin states: 'In all years when yang
brilliance [qi] controls heaven, the qi of metal is insufficient and fire will take advantage of this [insufficiency]. Hence only yang [qi] issues its orders and flaming summerheat prevails greatly.' This explanation of years when yang brilliance [qi] controls
heaven as characterized by insufficient qi of metal does not agree with the spirit of
the *Nei jing*. Zhang Zhicong further confuses the [*Nei jing*] statement: 'Yang brilliance [qi is present] in the upper [half of the year] and the ruler fire [is present] in the
lower [half of the year]. Hence yang [qi, i.e.,] heat abounds and causes things to dry
and harden.' Gao Shishi agrees. However, why should 'only yang issue its orders and
flaming summerheat prevail greatly' when yang brilliance [qi is present] in the upper
[half of the year] and the ruler fire in the lower? That remains unclear. It is our opinion
that these two sentences should be interpreted from a perspective of domination and
revenge. In a year when the yang brilliance [qi] controls heaven, the qi of metal is disproportionately dominant in the first half of the year. The climate is disproportionately
cool. When it should be warm it is not warm; when it should be hot it is not hot. That
is meant by the statement 天氣急 above. When the qi of metal is disproportionately

The things dry and harden.
Pure wind governs.[122]

71-463-6
Wind and dryness move uncontrolled and
flow through [the sphere of] qi interaction.[123]
There is much yang [qi] and little yin [qi].
The clouds rush[124] to the rain palace,
hence the transformation to dampness is extensive.[125]
When dryness reaches its maximum [it changes to] humidity.[126]

<Its grain are white and vermilion.>[127] {These are the intervening [qi] grain

---

dominant, then fire comes to revenge it. Hence, in contrast [to the beginning of the
first half of the year], the climate of the summer of that year may exhibit great heat."
In our opinion, the explanations of Zhang Jiebin, Zhang Zhicong and Gao Shishi are
not confused at all. They are based, first, on the fact that all years in which yang brilliance controls heaven are associated with yin stems and branches – and consequetly,
the qi controlling heaven is to be regarded as inadequate in these years. Second, they
are based on the fact that minor yin qi, i.e., ruler fire, which in the same years is at the
fountain, is associated with the yang branches *zi* and *wu* – and consequently, the qi at
the fountain is to be regarded as excessive in these years.

122 Cheng Shide et al.: "淳風 refers to 淳和之風, 'a wind that is well balanced.'"
Fang Yaozhong: " 'Pure wind' is a regular wind. In the first half of the year the climate
is disproportionately cool and dry. Hence only grain and fruit with hard shells outside
grow well." Zhang Zhicong: "The initial qi of the qi ruling the seasons is the ceasing yin [qi, i.e.,] wind and wood. In all years of great excess, the visitor qi dominates
and most [things or developments] follow [the orders of] the visitor qi. In years of
inadequacy, the visitor qi is weak and the [orders of the] host qi are followed, too.
Hence when 'pure wind governs' that is a transformation of the initial qi, [i.e.,] wind
and wood."

123 For a definition of 氣交 as "the section where the qi of heaven and earth interact", see 68-397-3.

124 On this and other metaphors in the *Su wen*, see 15/37.

125 Wang Bing: " 'Rain palace' is the location of the major yin." Zhang Jiebin: " 'Rain
palace' is a location of rich soil and accumulated dampness."

126 Fang Yaozhong: "澤 is 水, 'water.'"

127 Wang Bing: "They are generated through transformation of the proper qi of
heaven and earth." Gao Shishi: "When they are affected by the [qi of] metal controlling heaven, then they turn white. When they are affected by the [qi of] fire then they
turn vermilion. These are the so-called 'grain of the year.'" Fang Yaozhong: "In a year
when the yang brilliance [qi, i.e.,] dryness and metal, controls heaven and when the
minor yin [qi, i.e.,] ruler fire, is at the fountain, the first half of the year is dispropor-

which are called major.}[128]
<That which causes destruction are the white and armored things and those feathered.>[129]

71-464-1
Metal and fire combine [their] virtues.[130]
<Venus and Mars correspond to this above.>[131]

---

tionately cool. This has a positive effect on the generation and completion of white grain. The second half of the year is disproportionately hot. This has a positive effect on the generation and growth of vermilion grain."

128 Wang Bing: "命太者 is to say: those [generated through] transformations of the 'major' *jue* and ['major'] *shang* qi mentioned in the text above, they are generated through transformations of the intervening [visitor] qi. Hence [the text] speaks of 'intervening [qi] grain.'" Zhang Jiebin: "In addition to the annual grain [that are products of] transformation of the proper [qi of a year], there are the intervening [qi] grain as [products of] transformation of the four intervening [visitor] qi to the left and to the right [of the qi controlling heaven and at the fountain]. 命 is 天賦, 'heavenly endowment.' 太 is: a qi that has surplus. Whenever the [qi] controlling heaven is a 'major' [qi, the qi] at the fountain must be a 'minor' [qi] and vice versa. For instance, in *mao* and *you* years when yang brilliance [qi] controls heaven, a 'minor' [qi] rules in the first half [of the year]. The minor yin [qi] is at the fountain, that is, a 'major' [qi] rules in the second half [of the year]. 命其太 is: the grain are to be named after the ['major'] intervening [visitor] qi at the fountain." Ma Shi: "Intervening [qi] grains are named after the intervening [visitor] qi of the major [*jue* and *shang*]."

129 Our translation of 耗 as "that which causes destruction" is based on the logic of the context. Metal dominates and white grain flourish, hence "white things" dominate, too, and cause destruction. In contrast, Gao Shishi: "When yang brilliance [qi] controls heaven, the qi of metal is inadequate. Hence feathered and hairy beings of white color and armored [creatures] and metal items dissipate and do not accumulate." Fang Yaozhong: "Yang brilliance [qi, i.e.,] dryness and metal, controls heaven and minor yin [qi, i.e.,] ruler fire, is at the fountain. Fire overcomes metal. Hence living beings associated with metal, such as those of white color or those armored, they receive great harm. They may be born but do not mature; they grow but do not breed."

130 Zhang Jiebin: "Above (i.e., in the upper half of the year) is metal; below (i.e., in the lower half of the year) is fire. Hence [the text] states: 'combine [their] virtues.'" Fang Yaozhong: " 'Metal' refers to the yang brilliance [qi, i.e.,] dryness and metal. 'Fire' refers to the minor yin [qi, i.e.,] ruling fire. 'Combine virtues' is: they influence each other and are effective together."

131 Wang Bing: "They appear large and brilliant."

Its policy is cutting;
its command is violent.[132]

The hibernating creatures appear and
the flowing water does not freeze.

People suffer from cough and obstructed throat.
Cold and heat develop, [leading to]
violent shaking and shivering. There is protuberance illness and constipation.[133]

71-464-3
Coolness is forceful at the beginning;
hence the hairy creatures die.[134]
Heat comes afterwards and is violent.
Hence the armored creatures perish.[135]
<These outbreaks are hasty.>
The activities of domination and revenge
cause disturbance and massive disorder.[136]

---

132 Zhang Zhicong: "Clear and cutting, that is the policy of metal. Fast and violent, that is the command of fire." Fang Yaozhong: " 'Its policy is cutting' refers to the natural phenomenon that the climate is disproportionately cool in the first half of a year in years when the yang brilliance [qi, i.e.,] dryness and metal, controls heaven. 'Its command is violent' refers to the natural phenomenon of very hot climate at the time when fire qi comes to take revenge because the qi of metal is disproportionately dominant."

133 Zhang Jiebin: "All these are illnesses [associated with the qi] of metal and fire, i.e., dryness and heat." For 癃, see also *Su wen* 49, note 55/56.

134 Fang Yaozhong: "Coolness is associated with metal. Hairy creatures are associated with wood. When 'hairy creatures die because of unyielding coolness in the beginning,' the meaning is: metal overcomes wood."

135 Zhang Jiebin: "After fire qi has taken residence at the fountain, metal receives its restraint. Hence armored creatures perish." Fang Yaozhong: "Armored creatures are associated with metal; the underlying meaning is: fire dominates metal."

136 Wang Bing: "At first the metal dominates and this causes harm to the wood. Hence hairy creatures die. Subsequently, fire dominates and metal does not dominate. Hence it is now that armored creatures perish. Those who dominate carry out killing. Feathered [creatures] have vanished. Those taking revenge come later; those that are strong die nevertheless. How should such qi be called if not 'disorderly'?"

The qi of coolness and heat
are held in the [sphere of] qi interaction.[137]

71-464-5
The initial qi:
The qi of the earth has left its position.[138]
The clouds are condensed in the beginning.
The qi is stern in the beginning.
Hence the water freezes;
cold and rain transform.[139]

---

137 Zhang Zhicong: "Yang brilliance qi and minor yin qi are both responsible for
hasty [actions]. Hence 'their outbreak is hasty.' When fire dominates metal in the first
half of the year, then water comes to take revenge against fire in the second half of the
year. Hence [the text speaks of] 'activities of domination and revenge,' and the annual
qi is in 'great disorder.' 氣交 is: the qi controlling heaven and the qi at the fountain,
[i.e.,] above and below, interact with each other." Fang Yaozhong: " 'The qi of coolness
and heat' refers to the yang brilliance qi, [i.e.,] dryness and metal, controlling heaven
and to the minor yin qi, [i.e.,] ruling fire, at the fountain. 持于氣交 refers to the time
between the first and the second half of a given year. The entire passage has the following meaning: In a year when the yang brilliance [qi] controls heaven, in the time
between the first and the second half of the year, in particular between the third and
the fourth qi, the climate is extremely unstable in that at times it is cool, at times it
is hot."

138 Fang Yaozhong: " 'Initial qi' refers to a year when the yang brilliance [qi, i.e.,]
dryness and metal, controls heaven and when the initial visitor qi coming down to join
[the host qi] is the major yin [qi, i.e.,] dampness and soil. 'The qi of the earth has left its
position' refers to the fact that in a year when the yang brilliance [qi, i.e.,] dryness and
metal, controls heaven, major yin is the initial qi because the qi at the fountain in the
preceding year has left its position. In the year prior to the year when yang brilliance
[qi] controls heaven, minor yang [qi, i.e.,] minister fire, controls heaven and ceasing
ying [qi, i.e.,] wind and wood, is at the fountain. In a year when yang brilliance controls
heaven, the ceasing yin [qi] which was at the fountain in the previous year has moved
to the position of fifth qi in the present year. Hence major yin can move from the position of second qi in the previous year to the position of initial qi in the present year."

139 Zhang Jiebin: "When major yin is active as initial qi, the climate is cold and
the qi is damp. Hence 'the clouds are condensed.' Dryness and metal control heaven,
hence 'the qi is stern.' When water freezes, this is because the qi is stern; cold and rain
are transformations of dampness." Fang Yaozhong: "This is a year when the yang brilliance [qi, i.e.,] dryness and metal, control heaven. The initial qi is the major yin [qi].
Major yin [qi] controls dampness. Dampness is a yin evil. Hence in the time period
associated with the initial qi, which in this year lasts from [the solar term] Great Cold
to [the solar term] Excited Insects, i.e., approximately from the final ten days of the
twelve month to the first ten days of the second month of the lunar calendar, the qi of
heaven is dark and damp, with cold and relatively frequent rain."

Its illnesses include central heat and distension.
The face and the eyes have surface swelling;
[patients] tend to be sleepy.
[They suffer from] stuffy nose, nosebleed, sneezing, yawning, and vomiting.
The urine is yellow-red.

In severe cases strangury results.[140]

71-464-7
The second qi:
Now the yang is widespread.
As a result, people feel comfortable,
and the beings come to life and blossom.[141]
Epidemics come about massively.
People are prone to sudden death.[142]

The third qi:
The policy of heaven is widespread.

---

140 Wang Bing: "These are major yin transformations." Lin Yi et al.: "Given that the 'qi is stern' and 'water freezes,' these may not be major yin transformations after all." Zhang Jiebin: "The host qi is wind and the visitor qi is dampness. Wind is yang; dampness is yin. When wind and dampness affect [a person], spleen and kidneys receive harm. Hence all these illnesses emerge." Gao Shishi: "The illnesses [caused by] them are central heat and distension because the dampness qi cannot reach the exterior. Face and eyes are swollen because the dampness qi cannot move downwards. [Patients] tend to be sleepy because the movement of the qi from inside to outside and from above to below is blocked. All these are illnesses of dampness, [i.e.,] of the spleen, [i.e.,] of major yin [qi]. Nosebleed, sneezing, and yawning are illnesses of dryness, [i.e.,] of the lung, [i.e.,] of major yin [vessels]."

141 Zhang Zhicong: "With the second [qi] the two fires of ruler and minister [meet] as ruling [qi] and visitor [qi]. Hence yang qi can spread widely. As a result, people feel comfortable and [all] things grow and blossom." Fang Yaozhong: "In the time period associated with the second qi, which in this year lasts from Vernal Equinox to Grain Fills, that is, approximately from the latter ten days of the second month to the first ten days of the fourth month of the lunar calendar, people feel comfortable because the climate of continuous rain and disproportionate domination of dampness of the preceding time period has changed to a climate of warmth and heat. Because the climate has turned warm, plants grow and flourish."

142 Wang Bing: "The reason is that the minister has taken the position of the ruler."

Hence coolness prevails.[143]
Dryness and heat interact and merge.

When the dryness has reached its maximum, it [changes to] humidity.[144]
People suffer from cold and heat.[145]

The fourth qi:
Cold and rain descend.
[People] suffer from sudden falls, as well as
from shaking, shivering [from cold], incoherent and absurd speech,
from being short of qi, and dry throat, and they drink [large quantities].
Also, they develop illnesses of heartache, *yong*-abscesses, swelling, sores, ulcers,
malaria, and cold.
The bones are limp;[146] the stools have blood.[147]

---

143 Fang Yaozhong: "In a year when the yang brilliance [qi, i.e.,] dryness and metal,
controls heaven, the third of the visitor qi is the yang brilliance [qi, i.e.,] dryness and
metal. 天 is 'qi controlling heaven.' 'The policy of heaven is widespread' means: the qi
controlling heaven is active – unlike the other intervening [visitor] qi – not only during the time period is associated with; it rules the entire year, especially so the first half
of that year. 'Hence cold prevails' is: in a year when the yang brilliance [qi] controls
heaven, the climate is disproportionately cool in the first half of that year, especially in
the time period associated with the third qi, which lasts in this year from Grain Fills
to Great Heat, that is, approximately from the final ten days of the fourth month to
the first ten days of the sixth months of the lunar calendar the climate is very different
from what should be expected as normal, i.e., it is very cool."

144 Zhang Jiebin: "This is a time when the host qi, i.e., minister fire, should issue its
orders. Hence dryness and heat merge. At the end of the [time period of the] third
qi at the intersection with the fourth qi, the host qi is major yin and the visitor qi is
major yang. Hence dryness reaches its maximum and changes to humidity. Because
at a time when yang abounds the qi of metal and coolness prevails, people suffer from
[alternate feelings of] cold and heat."

145 Wang Bing: " 'Cold and heat' is malaria."

146 Wang Bing: " 'The bones are limp' is: they have no strength."

147 Zhang Zhicong: "The fourth visitor qi coming down to join [the host qi] is the
major yang [qi, i.e.,] cold and water. The host qi is the major yin [qi, i.e.,] dampness
and soil. Hence cold and rain descends. After mid-year, the minor yin, i.e. ruler fire,
rules the qi. Still, cold and dampness join each other. Hence people suffer from illnesses such as shaking and shivering, disorderly speech, dry throat, and hematuria. The
reason for all these conditions is that cold congeals outside while heat is oppressed
inside."

71-464-11
The fifth qi:
The command of spring prevails contrary [to normal].
Hence herbs emerge and blossom.
The qi of the people is harmonious.[148]

71-464-12
The final qi:
Yang qi is widespread.
Contrary [to normal, the] manifestation [of the qi] is warmth.
Hibernating creatures appear.
The flowing water does not freeze.
Hence people are healthy and balanced.
The illnesses [caused by] it are warmth [illnesses].[149]

Hence [it is appropriate]
to consume the grain of the year to pacify the [patients'] qi[150] and
to consume the intervening [qi] grain to remove their evil.[151]

[This] year it is appropriate
to use salty, bitter, and acrid [flavor]
to sweat it out, to cool it, to disperse it.

---

148 Zhang Jiebin: "The ceasing yin [qi, i.e.,] wind and wood, is active and is met by
the warmth of the ruler fire at the fountain. Hence contrary to normal the order of
spring prevails, herbs are generated and blossom." Fang Yaozhong: " 'The qi of the
people is harmonious' cannot entirely be interpreted as the people are healthy and
have no illness. Because at the intersection of autumn and winter when it should be
cool but is not cool, when there should be gathering but is no gathering, then this is
abnormal. Hence the human qi cannot be balanced and normal, be healthy and have
no illness."

149 Wang Bing: "These are transformations of the ruler [fire]." Gao Shishi: "As final
visitor qi the minor yin [qi, i.e.,] ruler fire, comes down to join [the host qi]. Hence
yang qi is widespread and contrary [to normal] the climate is warm. When it is warm
in winter rather than cold, the hibernating creatures reappear and the running waters
do not freeze."

150 Fang Yaozhong: " 'Grain of the year' are grain that have grown under the influence of the qi controlling heaven and at the fountain of that year. In a year when the
yang brilliance [qi] controls heaven, the grain of the year are white grain and vermilion
grain."

151 Fang Yaozhong: " 'Intervening [qi] grain' are grain that have grown under the
influence of the intervening [visitor] qi to the left and to the right."

Adapt to the period and to the qi.
Do not permit the reception of evil.¹⁵²
Break the qi oppressing it and
supply the source of its transformation.¹⁵³

71-464-15
Depending on the light or heavy [presence of] cold and heat apply more or less restraint to them.
When there is agreement in terms of heat,
more heaven [qi is employed to cause] transformation.

When there is agreement in terms of coolness, more earth [qi is employed to cause] transformation.¹⁵⁴

---

152 Fang Yaozhong: "安 has the meaning here of 'to adapt.' That is, in a year when the yang brilliance [qi] controls heaven and it is known that the climate is disproportionately cool in the first half and disproportionately hot in the second half, it is essential to adapt to the climatic characteristics of such a year in one's lifestyle, emotions, and diet. This serves to prevent that one is affected by an outside evil."

153 Wang Bing: " 'Source of its transformation' is to say: in the sixth month. One seizes it by moving towards it." Lin Yi et al.: "Metal rules in the seventh month. Hence it is confronted in the sixth month to drain the qi of metal." Fang Yaozhong: " 'Break the oppressing qi' is: in treatment it is essential to deal with the disproportionately dominant qi that appeared in the human body as a result of the activities of the cause that led to the illness. 'Support the source of its transformation' is: supplement the oppressed qi and support the proper qi. Wang Bing's comment is to say: the climate of the three months of autumn, i.e., the seventh, the eighth, and the ninth month, is disproportionately cool. A greatly abounding cool qi is able to oppress wind qi inside [the body]. Hence it is advisable to supplement the liver, i.e., wood, prior to autumn to prevent that the liver, i.e., wood, is seized by dryness, i.e., metal."

154 Wang Bing: "Minor *jue* and minor *zhi* years are identical in terms of heat. The prescriptions employed mostly rely on the transformation of the cool [qi] of heaven to treat the [heat]. Minor *gong*, minor *shang*, and minor *yu* years are identical in terms of coolness. The prescriptions employed mostly rely on the transformation of the heat [qi] of the earth to treat the [coolness]. Fire is on the earth; hence in those [years] that are identical in coolness one mostly [uses] the transformations of [the fire qi of] the earth. Metal is in heaven; hence in those [years] that are identical in heat one mostly [uses] the transformations of [the metal qi of] heaven." Fang Yaozhong: "寒熱輕重 refers to the severity of cold or heat [displayed by a patient] as clinical condition. 少多其制 refers to the amounts of drugs used in therapy. 同熱者 refers to situations where the heat of the climate corresponds to that of the patient's pathoconditions. 多天化 is: one uses drugs that are transformation products of the qi controlling heaven. In the present context, these are drugs with a cooling function."

When employing coolness, stay away from coolness.
When employing heat, stay away from heat.
When employing cold, stay away from cold.
When employing warmth, stay away from warmth.
Food requirements [are based on] the same law.

In cases of false [heat or cold], act contrary to this [rule].
That is this Way.
Acting contrary to this [Way]
brings disorder into the norms set by heaven and earth and
disturbs the arrangement of yin and yang."

71-465-4
[Huang] Di:
"Good!
The policy of minor yang, what is it like?"[155]

Qi Bo:
"These are the arrangements including *yin* and *shen* [earth branches].[156]

[The first two arrangements include the years when] minor yang [controls
heaven], major *jue* [is the central period], and ceasing yin [is at the fountain].
[They are designated] *ren yin* identical to heavenly complements and *ren shen* identical to heavenly complements.[157]

Their period [manifests itself as] winds drumming.[158]
The transformations [caused by] them include sounds[159] of a chaotic opening

---

155 Fang Yaozhong: "That is in a year when minor yang [qi, i.e.,] minister fire, controls heaven."

156 Fang Yaozhong: "All years associated with *yin* and *shen* branches are years with
minor yang [qi, i.e.,] minister fire, controlling heaven."

157 Fang Yaozhong: "In *ren yin* and *ren shen* years, the heavenly stems are *ren. Ding*
and *ren* transform wood. *Ren* is a yang stem. Hence *ren yin* and *ren shen* years are years
with an excessive wood period, i.e., major *jue* years. In *ren yin* and *ren shen* years, the
annual branches are *yin* and *shen*. In *yin* and *shen* [years], minor yang [qi, i.e.,] minister fire, controls heaven, and ceasing yin [qi, i.e.,] wind and wood, is at the fountain.
The five agents association of the annual period and of the qi at the fountain is identical. Hence *ren yin* and *ren shen* years are 'identical to heavenly complements' years."

158 Fang Yaozhong: "運 refers to the annual period. 鼓 refers to 鼓動, 'to rouse.' Here
it refers to disproportionate domination."

159 Wu Kun: "紊 is 亂, 'disorder.'"

and breaking.

The changes [caused by] them include shaking, pulling, breaking, plucking.

The illnesses [caused by] them include swaying, dizziness, propping [fullness in the] flanks, fright, and shock.

[The sequence of visitor periods is as follows:]

- Major *jue* begin [of the sequence of host periods,] proper [begin of the sequence of visitor periods]
- minor *zhi*
- major *gong*
- minor *shang*
- major *yu* end [of the sequence of host periods].

71-465-10

[The second two arrangements include the years when] minor yang [controls heaven], major *zhi* [is the central period], ceasing yin [is at the fountain]. [They are designated] *wu yin* – heavenly complements- and *wu shen* – heavenly complements.[160]

Their period [manifests itself as] summerheat.

The transformations [caused by] them include warmth, noise,[161] [heat] oppression, and damp heat.

The changes [caused by] them include flaming, fieriness, boiling, bubbling.

The illnesses [caused by] them include heat oppression in the upper [sections of the body], blood overflow, blood outflow, heartache.[162]

The sequence of visitor periods is as follows:]

- Major *zhi*
- minor *gong*
- major *shang*
- minor *yu* end [of the sequence of host periods]
- minor *jue* begin [of the sequence of host periods].

---

160 Fang Yaozhong: "In *wu yin* and *wu shen* years, the heavenly stem is *wu*. *Wu* and *gui* transform fire. Hence the annual period of *wu yin* and *wu shen* years is a fire period. The qi controlling heaven is fire, too. Because the five agents association of the annual period and of the qi controlling heaven is identical, *wu yin* and *wu shen* years are years of 'heavenly complements.'"

161 Zhang Jiebin: "喧嚣 is the appearance of intense fire."

162 Gao Shishi: "These are illnesses of fire moving contrary [to its regular course]." Fang Yaozhong reads: 其病上熱, 郁血, 溢血, 血泄, 心痛.

[The third two arrangements include the years when] minor yang [controls heaven], major *gong* [is the central period], ceasing yin [is at the fountain]. [They are designated] *jia yin* and *jia shen*.[163]

Their period [manifests itself as] overcast and rain.
The transformations [caused by] them include tender moisture and doubled fertility.
The changes [caused by] them include shaking [of the earth] to the extent that one is frightened, tornados, and rainstorms.
The illnesses [caused by] them include a heavy body, *fu*-swelling, and blockage [resulting from spillage] drink.[164]

[The sequence of visitor periods is as follows:]
- Major *gong*
- minor *shang*
- major *yu* end [of the sequence of host periods]
- major *jue* begin [of the sequence of host periods]
- minor *zhi*.

71-466-1
[The fourth two arrangements include the years when] minor yang [controls heaven], major *shang* [is the central period], ceasing yin [is at the fountain]. [They are designated] *geng yin* and *geng shen* – identical to proper *shang*.[165]

Their period [manifests itself as] coolness.
The transformations [caused by] them include fog, dew, and extreme coolness.

---

163 Fang Yaozhong: "In *jia yin* and *jia shen* years, the heavenly stem is *jia*. *Jia* and *ji* transform soil. *Jia* is a yang stem. Hence these two years are years with an excessive soil period. Their qi controlling heaven is the minor yang [qi, i.e.,] minister fire; the qi at the fountain is the ceasing yin [qi, i.e.,] wind and wood."

164 Cheng Shide et al.: "胕腫 is 浮腫, 'surface swelling.' 痞飲 is abdominal distension because of stagnating liquid." Fang Yaozhong: "胕腫 is 足腫, 'swollen foot.'" For a detailed discussion of the occurrences of the term 胕腫 in the *Su wen* and its interpretation in most cases as 浮腫, in the sense of edema caused by an accumulation of water, see 1682/42. See also, *Su wen* 69-405-4.

165 Fang Yaozhong: "'Major *shang*' refers to a year of an excessive metal period. In *geng yin* and *geng shen* years, the annual stem is *geng*. *Yi* and *geng* transform metal. *Geng* is a yang stem. Hence *geng yin* and *geng shen* years are years of an excessive metal period. The qi controlling heaven is minor yang [qi, i.e.,] minister fire; the qi at the fountain is the ceasing yin [qi, i.e.,] wind and wood. 'Proper *shang*' is a year with balanced qi of a metal period. 'Identical to proper *shang*' is: even though *geng yin* and

The changes [caused by] them include sternness, killing, withering and falling.
The illnesses [caused by] them are in the shoulders, back, and chest.

[The sequence of visitor periods is as follows:]
- Major *shang*
- minor *yu* end [of the sequence of host periods]
- minor *jue* begin [of the sequence of host periods]
- major *zhi*
- minor *gong*.

71-466-4
[The fifth two arrangements include the years when] minor yang [controls heaven], major *yu* [is the central period], ceasing yin [is at the fountain]. [They are designated] *bing yin* and *bing shen*.[166]

Their period [manifests itself as] cold and sternness.
The transformations [caused by] them include freezing and piercing cold.
The changes [caused by] them include ice, snow, frost, and hail.
The illnesses [caused by] them include cold and surface swelling.

[The sequence of visitor periods is as follows:]
- Major *yu* end [of the sequence of host periods]
- major *jue* begin [of the sequence of host periods]
- minor *zhi*
- major *gong*
- minor *shang*.

71-466-8
Whenever there is a policy of this minor yang controlling heaven,

---

geng shen years are [years] with an excessive metal period, still, because their annual branches are *yin* and *shen* and because [at the time of] *yin* and *shen* [branches] minor yang [qi, i.e.,] minister fire, controls heaven, the metal period of an excessive annual period is restrained by the qi of fire controlling heaven. Hence these two *geng yin* and *geng shen* years are years of balanced qi of a metal period."

166 Fang Yaozhong: "Major *yu* refers to a year with an excessive water period. The annual stem of bing *yin* and bing *shen* years is *bing*. *Bing* and *xin* transform water. *Bing* is a yang stem. Hence these two years are years of an excessive water period. The qi controlling heaven is the minor yang [qi, i.e.,] minister fire; the qi at the fountain is the ceasing yin [qi, i.e.,] wind and wood."

the transformations of the [six] qi and the movement of the [five] periods precede heaven.[167]

The qi of heaven is proper;
the qi of the earth is disturbed.[168]
Violent winds rise.
Trees are bent down and sand flies.
Flaming fire prevails.[169]
Yin carries out yang transformations.
Rain corresponds frequently.[170]
Fire and wood combine [their] virtues.[171]
<Mars and Jupiter correspond to this above.>[172]
<Its grain are vermilion and greenish.>[173]

71-466-10
Its policy is harsh;
its command is disturbing.[174]

---

167 Fang Yaozhong: " 'Precede heaven' refers to an excessive annual period. The climate precedes the [respective] season."

168 Zhang Jiebin: "When the fire qi of minor yang controls heaven, the yang has found its [proper] position. Hence [the text states] 'the qi of heaven is proper.' When the ceasing yin [qi, i.e.,] wind and wood, is at the fountain, wind moves below. Hence 'the earth qi is disturbed.'" Fang Yaozhong: "In a year when the minor yang [qi, i.e.,] minister fire, controls heaven, the qi controlling heaven occupies the position of third qi. That is the proper position of the host qi minor yang, [i.e.,] minister fire."

169 Gao Shishi: "Ceasing yin [qi] is wind; hence 'violent winds occur.' Minor yang [qi] is fire; hence 'flaming fire prevails.'"

170 Fang Yaozhong: " 'Yin' refers to autumn and winter here. 'Yin carries out yang transformations' is to point out that autumn and winter are as hot as spring and summer."

171 Fang Yaozhong: " 'Fire' refers to minor yang [qi, i.e.,] minister fire, here. 'Wood' refers, in the present context, to ceasing yin [qi, i.e.,] wind and wood. 'Virtue' refers to function here. That is, in a year when the minor yang [qi, i.e.,] minister fire controls heaven, ceasing yin [qi, i.e.,] wind and wood, is at the fountain. Fire rules heat; wind rules warmth. Heat and warmth belong to one group. Hence their functions are basically identical."

172 Wang Bing: "They appear brilliant and big."

173 Zhang Jiebin: " 'Vermilion' corresponds to [the qi] controlling heaven; 'greenish' corresponds to [the qi] at the fountain."

174 Zhang Zhicong: " 'Harsh' is the policy of fire; 'disturbing' is the command issued by wind."

Hence
wind and heat unite and spread;
cloudy things surge [as if] boiling.¹⁷⁵
Major yin flows uncontrolled.¹⁷⁶
Cold arrives frequently.
Coolness and rain emerge together.¹⁷⁷

People suffer from cold center.
Externally sores and ulcers break open;
internally this causes outflow and fullness.¹⁷⁸

{Hence,
when the sages meet such [a situation],
they seek to create harmony and do not fight.}

If [cold and heat] leave and return [alternately],¹⁷⁹
people suffer from cold and heat, malaria and outflow,
deafness, blurred vision, vomiting.
Above, there is a swelling [because of] dammed up [qi]. The color changes.¹⁸⁰

---

175 Zhang Zhicong: "The qi of minor yang and ceasing yin interact and unite."

176 Fang Yaozhong: " 'Major yin' refers to the qi of rain and dampness. Here it is to say: in a year when the minor yang [qi, i.e.,] minister fire, controls heaven, the climate of the entire year is disproportionately hot. Because heat generates dampness, rain falls comparatively often."

177 Fang Yaozhong: "When fire qi is disproportionately dominant, cold qi will come to take revenge. Hence in the same year there may also be sudden changes to a cold climate. Cold and coolness evil, as well as rain and dampness evil will frequently appear at the same time."

178 Zhang Jiebin: "Fire abounds outside, hence people suffer from cold inside. Thus, the outside heat causes sores and ulcers, while the inside heat causes outflow and fullness."

179 Gao Shishi: "If there are no Sages [to create harmony], then heat comes when cold goes and cold returns when the heat leaves." Fang Yaozhong: "往復 is: cold and heat occur alternately. That is, in a year when the minor yang [qi] controls heaven, there is cold and there is heat. Cold and heat occur alternately and the climate undergoes great changes. At times it is cold; at times it is hot. [The climate] is extremely unstable."

180 Gao Shishi: " 'Outflow' is: the proper qi is depleted. 'Deafness and blurred vision' is: the orifices are not freely passable. 'Vomiting' is: [the qi of] the center, [i.e., of] soil, is depleted." Fang Yaozhong: "怫 is 怫郁, 'pressed.' Here it is to say: qi and blood can-

71-466-14
The initial qi:
The qi of the earth leaves its position.[181]
The wind dominates and makes [things] shake.
Then the cold leaves,
and [the initial qi] manifests itself as strong warmth.
The herbs and the trees blossom early.
Cold may come but does not kill.
Hence warmth diseases emerge.

The illnesses it [causes are those of] dammed up qi above.
Blood overflows [causing] red eyes.
[People suffer from] cough, countermovement, headache, and
hemorrhage; the flanks [have a feeling of] fullness.
Sores develop in the skin interstices.[182]

71-467-2
The second qi:
The fire, contrary [to the regular order], is oppressed.[183]
White dust rises at all four [cardinal points].
Clouds rush to the rain palace.[184]

not flow freely. That is, qi and blood are blocked in the facial region. Hence it swells
and the complexion changes." For a similar wording, 怫然種, see *Su wen* 41-230-1.

181 Fang Yaozhong: "'Initial qi' refers to a year when the minor yang [qi, i.e.,] minister fire, controls heaven and when the initial qi of the intervening qi of the visitor qi
coming down to join [the host qi] is the minor yin [qi, i.e.,] ruling fire. 'The qi of the
earth has left its position' refers to the fact that in a year when the minor yang [qi, i.e.,]
minister fire, controls heaven, minor yin, ruling fire is the initial qi because the qi at the
fountain in the preceding year has left its position. In the year prior to the year when
minor yang [qi, i.e., minister fire] controls heaven, major yin [qi, i.e.,] dampness and
soil, controls heaven and major yang [qi, i.e.,] cold and water, is at the fountain. In a
year when minor yang,[i.e.,] minister fire, controls heaven, the major yang [qi, i.e., cold
and water,] which was at the fountain in the previous year has moved to the position of
fifth qi in the present year. Hence minor yin [qi, i.e.,] ruler fire, can move from the position of second qi in the previous year to the position of initial qi in the present year."

182 Wang Bing: "These are transformations of minor yin."

183 Wang Bing: "This is so because it is the major yin section."

184 Fang Yaozhong: "The time period associated with the second qi, which lasts from
Vernal Equinox to Grain Fills, that is, approximately from the latter ten days of the
second month to the first ten days of the fourth month of the lunar calendar, right at
the intersection of spring and summer, this is a time ruled by the minor yin [qi, i.e.,]
ruler fire. In general, the climate [at this time] should be warm and mild. However,

Wind does not dominate the dampness;
hence there is rainfall.
People are healthy.

The illnesses [caused by] it are heat oppression above;
coughing, countermovement, vomiting.
Sores develop in the center.
Chest and throat are not free.
[People suffer from] headache, body heat,
mental confusion, and purulent sores.

The third qi:
The policy of heaven is widespread.
Flaming summerheat arrives.
The minor yang [qi] comes down [to take its position] above.
The rain has a limit.[185]

People suffer from heated center,
deafness, blurred vision, blood overflow, and
purulent sores, from cough, and vomiting, from
stuffy nose, nosebleed, thirst, sneezing, yawning, and
throat block, as well as from red eyes.
[Patients] tend to die suddenly.

---

because this is a year when minor yang [qi, i.e.,] minister fire, controls heaven and because the second visitor qi is major yin [qi, i.e.,] dampness and soil, spring experiences continuous rain and severe cold. When it should be warm, it is not warm. Hence the text states 'the fire, contrary to normal, is oppressed.' 'White dust rises at all four cardinal points' is to describe how the qi of dampness and soil rises, like white smoke or fog, from the earth and turns into clouds. 'Clouds rush to the rain palace' is: there are many clouds in the sky and they change into rain."

185 Fang Yaozhong: "In a year when minor yang [qi, i.e.,] minister fire, controls heaven, the third of the visitor qi is the minor yang [qi, i.e.,] minister fire. 'The policy of heaven is widespread' is: minor yang [qi, i.e.,] minister fire, controls heaven. 'Flaming summerheat arrives' is: because minor yang rules fire and because, in addition, the host qi of this step is the minor yang [qi, i.e.,] minister fire, the host qi and the visitor qi are all fire and heat. Hence in the time period associated with the third qi, that is, from Grain Fills to Great Heat, which is approximately from the final ten days of the fourth month to the first ten days of the sixth month, the climate is particularly hot. 'Above' is the qi controlling heaven."

71-467-6
The fourth qi:
Coolness arrives.[186]
Flaming summerheat transforms intermittently.[187]
White dew falls.
The qi of the people is harmonious and balanced.

The illnesses [caused by] it include fullness and a heavy body.

The fifth qi:
The yang leaves.
The cold comes.
Rain falls.
The qi gates are closed;
hard trees wither early.[188]

People avoid the cold evil;
the gentleman [stays in a] firmly closed [house].

71-467-9
The final qi:
The qi of the earth assumes its proper [position].
Hence the wind arrives.
The myriad beings, contrary [to the regular order], come to life.
Dense fog prevails.[189]

---

186 Fang Yaozhong: "In a year when minor yang [qi, i.e.,] minister fire, controls heaven, the fourth, i.e., an intervening qi of the visitor qi coming down to join [the qi controlling heaven] is the yang brilliance [qi, i.e,] dryness and metal. 'Coolness arrives' is: because yang brilliance [qi] rules coolness and dryness, hence in the time period associated with the fourth qi, that is, from Great Heat to Autumnal Equinox, approximately from the final ten days of the sixth month to the first ten days of the eighth month, the climate is disproportionally cool."

187 Zhang Jiebin: "間 is: at times it is active, at times it stops."

188 Zhang Zhicong: "The fifth, i.e., an intervening [visitor] qi is the major yang [qi, i.e.,] cold and water. Hence the yang heat leaves and the cold comes. Because at the intersection of autumn and winter the order of closure and storage is issued, the qi gates are closed, and it is advisable to close oneself off entirely so as to avoid [being struck by] cold evil." Fang Yaozhong: " 'Qi gates' refers to the sweat openings in the skin."

189 Fang Yaozhong: "In a year when the minor yang [qi, i.e.,] minister fire, controls heaven, the final visitor qi is the ceasing yin [qi, i.e.,] wind and wood. 'The earth qi is proper' is: It occupies the location of the qi at the fountain. 'Wind arrives' refers to the

The illnesses [caused by] it include
an inability to keep locked what should be locked,
heartache, >no storage of yang qi < and cough.[190]

Press down [the excessive] period and qi;
support that which does not dominate [in that year].[191]
It is necessary to break the qi oppressing it and
to seize the source of its transformation first.[192]
If sudden excesses are not generated,
severe diseases do not emerge.[193]

---

ceasing yin [qi, i.e.,] wind and wood, at the fountain. In the second half of this year, the climate is disproportionately warm and the wind qi dominates disproportionately. Especially in the time period associated with the final qi, that is, from after Little Snow to before Great Cold, from the final ten days of the tenth month to the first ten days of the twelfth month, the climate is disproportionately warm. When it should be cold, it is not cold. Because the climate is disproportionately warm, [i.e.,] winter carries out orders that should be issued by spring, hence herbs and trees sprout and grow early."

190 Zhang Zhicong: "This is the season of closure and storage. Nevertheless, the order of effusion and generation is issued. Hence the illnesses of this [time] are 'inability to restrain what should be closed in.'" Fang Yaozhong: "關閉 refers to the storage of yang qi inside [the body]. 不禁 refers to an inability to control something. The meaning is: in the time period of the final qi, when the order of winter is issued, the yang qi should be stored inside [the body]. However, because the ceasing yin [qi, i.e.,] wind and wood, is at the fountain and because the wind rules the movement, hence the yang qi that should be stored is not stored." *NJCD*: "關 is 氣門, 'gates of qi' (i.e., pores)." See above, *Su wen* 71-467-8. Apparently, the phrase 陽氣不藏, "no storage of yang qi", has been moved here from the line before. Style and contents are very similar to the second line, 關閉不禁.

191 Zhang Zhicong: "In a year [associated with the heavenly stem] *ren* the *jue* period is greatly excessive. Hence the qi of soil cannot dominate. In a *wu* year the period of fire is greatly excessive. Hence the qi of metal cannot dominate. It is therefore advisable to curb what is greatly excessive and to support what cannot dominate." Fang Yaozhong: "運氣 refers to the annual period and to the four intervening [visitor] qi of [the qi] controlling heaven and [of the qi] at the fountain."

192 Zhang Zhicong: "In *geng yin* and *geng shen* years minor yang [qi] controls heaven. Hence the *shang* period is oppressed. In *jia yin* and *jia shen* years ceasing yin [qi] is at the fountain. Hence the *gong* period is oppressed. In such situations the oppressed qi must be broken open and the source of the transformation of these two periods is to be treated first."

193 Wang Bing: "苛 is 重, 'serious.'" Fang Yaozhong: "暴過 refers to an acute illness." Zhang Jiebin: "If one is able to act in accordance with the laws outlined above, the qi will be in harmony by itself. Hence there will be no suffering from sudden excesses or severe illnesses." Compare with *Su wen* 71-461-5 and 71-473-3.

Hence
in this year it is appropriate
[to employ] salty and acrid [flavors] and it is appropriate [to employ] sour
[flavor]
to let it seep and to drain it,
to soak the [patient] and to effuse it.[194]

One observes whether the qi is cold or warm to regulate where there is excess.
When there is agreement of wind and heat, [employ] more cold [qi to cause]
transformation.
When there are differences in terms of wind and heat, [employ] less cold [qi to
cause] transformation.[195]

When employing heat, stay away from heat.
When employing warmth, stay away from warmth.
When employing cold, stay away from cold.
When employing coolness, stay away from coolness.
Food requirements [are based on] the same law.
>This is the Way.<[196]

In cases of false [heat or cold], act contrary to it.
Acting contrary to this [Way] is a cause of illness."

---

194 Fang Yaozhong: " 'Salty' refers to the cooling [nature of] salty [flavor]; 'acrid'
refers to the dispersing [nature of] acrid [flavor]; 'sour' refers to the collecting [nature
of] sour [flavor]. 滲 is 利尿, 'to stimulate urination.' 泄 is to stimulate the passage
of stools. 漬 is: to immerse in hot water. 發之 is: to cause sweating. The meaning is:
In a year when the minor yang [qi, i.e.,] minister fire, controls heaven and when the
ceasing yin [qi, i.e.,] wind and wood, is at the fountain, the climate of the entire year
is disproportionately warm and hot. The human body, too, easily contracts illnesses
caused by heat and warmth evil. Hence for therapy the drugs to be selected should be
salty to generate cold and sour to collect, so that the inner heat is cooled and the yin
[qi] is kept together. Also, drugs are to be employed that make urine and stools pass
so that the inside is cooled and the heat is drained. Acrid drugs that disperse are to
be used and the body is to be immersed in hot water, to make [the patient] sweat and
thereby to let the heat effuse to the outside."

195 Wang Bing: "Major *jue* and major *zhi* years are in agreement with [their nature
in terms of] heat and wind and cold is employed in large quantities to cause [their]
transformation. Major *gong*, major *shang*, and major *yu* years deviate from [their nature in terms of] wind and heat and coolness is used to balance their excesses."

196 The four characters 此其道也 should follow the subsequent statement 有假者反
之. Cf. *Su wen* 71-465-3, 71-470-15, 71-473-8, 71-475-3.

71-468-5
[Huang] Di:
"Good!
The policy of major yin, what is it like?"[197]

Qi Bo:
"These are the arrangements including *chou* and *wei* [earth branches].

[The first two arrangements include the years when] major yin [controls heaven], minor *jue* [is the central period],[198] and major yang [is at the fountain]. Coolness domination and heat revenge is the same [in both minor *jue* years].[199] [Both these years have conditions] identical to [those in] proper *gong* [years].[200] [They are designated] *ding chou* and *ding wei*.

Their period [manifests itself as] wind, coolness, and heat.

[The sequence of visitor periods is as follows:]
- Minor *jue* begin [of the sequence of host periods,] proper [begin of the sequence of visitor periods]
- major *zhi*
- minor *gong*
- major *shang*
- minor *yu* end [of the sequence of host periods].

[The second two arrangements include the years when] major yin [controls heaven], minor *zhi* [is the central period],[201] and major yang [is at the foun-

197 Fang Yaozhong: "That is a year when major yin [qi, i.e.,] dampness and soil, controls heaven."

198 Fang Yaozhong: " 'Minor *jue*' refers to a year with an inadequate wood period."

199 Fang Yaozhong: "In a year with an inadequate wood period, in spring, when it should be warm, it is not warm; the climate is disproportionately cool. In summer, however, there is more heat than usual. These are the characteristics of climatic changes in years with an inadequate wood period."

200 Gao Shishi: "When the soil period is inadequate, then the wind qi of wood is dominant in the beginning. Later the cool qi of metal takes revenge. Domination and revenge together rule the qi of the entire year." Fang Yaozhong: "A 'proper *gong*' year is a year of a soil period with balanced qi. If in a year with an inadequate wood period major yin [qi, i.e.,] dampness and soil, controls heaven, then in this year, because the wind qi is inadequate, the qi of dampness is disproportionately dominant in spring. Spring carries out the order of late summer; hence it rains frequently."

201 Fang Yaozhong: " 'Minor *zhi*' refers to years with an inadequate fire period."

tain]. Cold domination and rain revenge is the same [in both minor *zhi* years].²⁰² [They are designated] *gui chou* and *gui wei*.

Their period [manifests itself as] heat, cold, and rain.²⁰³

[The sequence of visitor periods is as follows:]
- Minor *zhi*
- major *gong*
- minor *shang*
- major *yu* end [of the sequence of host periods]
- major *jue* begin [of the sequence of host periods].²⁰⁴

71-468-13
[The third two arrangements include the years when] major yin [controls heaven], minor *gong* [is the central period],²⁰⁵ and major yang [is at the fountain]. Wind domination and coolness revenge is the same [in both minor *gong* years].²⁰⁶ [Both these years have conditions] identical to [those in] proper *gong* [years].²⁰⁷ [They are designated] *ji chou* – *tai-yi* heavenly complements – and *ji wei* – *tai-yi* heavenly complements.²⁰⁸

---

202 Zhang Zhicong: "The fire period is inadequate. Cold moves against it to dominate. Soil and rain come to take revenge."

203 Gao Shishi: " 'Its period is heat,' that is the period of *zhi* and fire. 'Cold' [refers] to a domination of water. 'Rain' is the revenge taken by soil."

204 All editions of the textus receptus known to us lack the character 初; we see no reason, though, why it should not be expected to appear here.

205 Fang Yaozhong: " 'Minor *gong*' refers to years with an inadequate soil period."

206 Gao Shishi: "When the soil period is inadequate, then the wind qi of wood dominates in the beginning. Later on the coolness qi of metal takes revenge. Domination and revenge together rule the qi of that entire year."

207 Fang Yaozhong: " 'Proper *gong*' is a year with a soil period of balanced qi. Even though *ji chou* and *ji wei* years, if judged from their heavenly stems, belong to the years with an inadequate soil period, still, because the annual branches of these two years are *chou* and *wei*, major yin [qi, i.e.,] dampness and soil, control heaven. According to the principle 'when the period is inadequate, it receives support,' the inadequate soil period of *ji chou* and *ji wei* years can receive the support of the qi controlling heaven which leads to a balanced qi."

208 Fang Yaozhong: "[Years] with an identical five agents association of the annual period and of the qi controlling heaven are the so-called 'heavenly complements.' [Years] with an identical five agents association of the annual period and of the original five phases association of the branches are called 'the year meets.' [Years] that are

Their period [manifests itself as] rain, wind, and coolness.²⁰⁹

[The sequence of visitor periods is as follows:]
- Minor *gong*
- major *shang*
- minor *yu* end [of the sequence of host periods]
- minor *jue* begin [of the sequence of host periods]
- major *zhi*.

71-468-16
[The fourth two arrangements include the years when] major yin [controls heaven], minor *shang* [is the central period],²¹⁰ and major yang [is at the fountain]. Heat domination and cold revenge is the same [in both minor *shang* years]. [They are designated] *yi chou* and *yi wei*.

Their period [manifests itself as] coolness, heat, and cold.²¹¹

[The sequence of visitor periods is as follows:]
- Minor *shang*
- major *yu* end [of the sequence of host periods]
- major *jue* begin [of the sequence of host periods]
- minor *zhi*
- major *gong*.

71-468-19
[The fifth two arrangements include the years when] major yin [controls heaven], minor *yu* [is the central period],²¹² and major yang [is at the fountain].

---

both 'heavenly complements' and 'the year meets,' they are '*tai-yi* heavenly complements.' Climatic changes in '*tai-yi* heavenly complements' years are quite severe."

209 Gao Shishi: " 'Its period is rain,' that is the period of *gong* and soil. 'Wind' [refers] to a domination of wood. 'Coolness' is the revenge taken by metal."

210 Fang Yaozhong: " 'Minor *shang*' refers to years with an inadequate metal period."

211 Fang Yaozhong: " 'Coolness' refers to the metal period. Here it refers to *yi chou* and *yi wei* years with an inadequate metal period. The meaning is: In *yi chou* and *yi wei* years with an inadequate metal period, fire comes to seize it. Because of the [rules of] domination and revenge, when fire qi is disproportionately active, water qi must come to take revenge. Hence the special feature of these years is that in autumn, when it should be cool, it is not cool. The climate is disproportionately hot. However, in winter it will be colder than usual."

212 Fang Yaozhong: " 'Minor *yu*' refers to years with an inadequate water period."

Rain domination and wind revenge is the same [in both minor *yu* years]. [Both these years have conditions] identical to [those in] proper *gong* [years]. [They are designated] *xin chou* identical to the year meets and *xin wei* identical to the year meets.[213]

Their period [manifests itself as] cold, rain, and wind.[214]

[The sequence of visitor periods is as follows:]
- Minor *yu* end [of the sequence of host periods]
- minor *jue* begin [of the sequence of host periods]
- major *zhi*
- minor *gong*
- major *shang*.

Whenever there is such a policy of major yin controlling heaven,[215]
the transformations of the [six] qi and the movement of the [five] periods are behind heaven.[216]

The yin alone carries out its policy;
the yang qi retreats into hiding.
Strong winds emerge frequently.[217]

---

213 Fang Yaozhong: "[Years] when the five agents association of the annual period and of the qi at the fountain is identical and when, in addition, the annual period is inadequate, are called 'identical to the year meets.'"

214 Fang Yaozhong: " 'Cold' refers to the water period. Here it refers to the inadequate water period of *xin chou* and *xin wei* years. 'Rain' refers to soil; 'wind' refers to wood. That is, in *xin chou* and *xin wei* years, when the water period is inadequate, soil comes to seize it. When the soil qi is disproportionately dominant, the qi of wind must come to take revenge. Hence the special feature of these years is that in winter, when it should be cold, it is not cold and it rains comparatively often. However, in the spring of the following year, the wind qi is disproportionately dominant and only little rain falls."

215 Fang Yaozhong: "These are years when the major yin [qi, i.e.,] dampness and soil, control heaven."

216 Wang Bing: "All generation, growth, transformation, and completion of the myriad beings is behind the heavenly seasons."

217 Zhang Jiebin: "When the soil is inadequate, it is seized by the qi of wind. Hence strong winds emerge frequently." Fang Yaozhong: "The 時起 of 大風時起 is: 應時而起, 'emerge in due time.' All years when the major yin [qi, i.e.,] dampness and soil, controls heaven are [characterized by] ceasing yin [qi, i.e.,[wind and wood, because the first visitor qi and the host qi are identical. Hence in the time period associated

>The qi of heaven descends;
the qi of the earth surges.<[218]
The plains and wastelands are dark and hazy.
White dust rises at the four [cardinal points].
Clouds rush to the Southern Pole.
Cold and rain arrive frequently.[219]
The beings are completed at the turn from summer to autumn.[220]

71-469-6
People suffer from cold and dampness and abdominal fullness.
The body suffers from distension pressure, *fu*-swelling,
blockage and countermovement, cold recession, cramp and tension.[221]

Dampness and cold combine [their] virtues.
Yellow and black dust [causes] darkness[222] and
prevails everywhere [in the section of] qi interaction.[223]
<Saturn and Mercury correspond to this above.>[224]

---

with the initial qi, which is the early time of spring, the qi of wind is disproportionately dominant."

218 The statement 天氣下降地氣上騰 should follow the statement 氣化運行後天 in *Su wen* 71-469-3. Cf. 71-460-1, 71-463-5, 71-466-8.

219 Fang Yaozhong: "This is a description of natural phenomena appearing in years when the major yin [qi, i.e.,] dampness and soil, control heaven, while the major yang [qi] is at the fountain. 原野昏霧 refers to a hazy and foggy qi of heaven."

220 Wang Bing: "The Southern Pole is the palace of rain. 差夏 is to say: the eleven days following 'autumn begins.'" Zhang Jiebin: "差 is 參差, 'irregular,' here. [The period stretching] from the very end of summer to the begin of autumn is called 差夏."

221 Zhang Zhicong: "All these conditions arise from affections by cold and dampness."

222 Wang Bing: " 'Yellow and black darkness and dust' is to say: the killing qi moves from the North and the West to the East and the South."

223 Gao Shishi: "When the qi controlling heaven and at the fountain merge and interact, then 'dampness and cold combine [their] virtues.'" Fang Yaozhong: " 'Dampness' refers to the major yin qi, [i.e.,] dampness and soil, controlling heaven. 'Cold' refers to the major yang qi, [i.e.,] cold and water, at the fountain. 'Yellow' refers to the major yin qi of dampness and soil; 'black' refers to the major yang qi of cold and water." For a definition of 氣交 as "the section where the qi of heaven and of the earth interact and unite", see *Su wen* 68-397-3.

224 Wang Bing: "Their appearance is large and brilliant."

Its policy is stern;
its command is calm.[225]
<Its grain are yellow and dark.>[226]

Hence
clouds are condensed above;
cold accumulates below.[227]
When cold water dominates fire,
then ice and hail result.
The yang light does not govern.
Hence killing qi prevails.[228]

<Hence
when there is surplus, to be high is appropriate;
when there is inadequacy, to be low is appropriate.
When there is surplus, to be late is appropriate;
when there is inadequacy, to be early is appropriate.[229]

---

225 Zhang Zhicong: " 'Sternness' is the policy of the soil; 'calmness' is the order of water." Gao Shishi: "Yin alone is in command; hence its policy is stern. Yang qi is on the retreat; hence its policy is calm." Fang Yaozhong: "肅 has the meaning of 清冷, 'chilly,' and of 肅清, 'to eliminate.' That is, in years when the major yin [qi, i.e,] damp-ness and soil, controls heaven and when the major yang [qi, i.e.,] cold and water, is at the fountain, the climate is characterized by cold and coolness and generation as well as growth of things is deficient. 寂 is 孤寂, 'lonely,' 靜止, 'motionless.' That is, the generation and growth of plants is slow; they lack in liveliness."

226 Wang Bing: "They are brought forth by the proper qi." Fang Yaozhong: "Because the climate is disproportionately cold and damp, the generation and growth of yellow and dark grain is favored. Hence they are the annual grain of years when major yin [qi] controls heaven and when major yang [qi] is at the fountain."

227 Gao Shishi: "Major yin [qi] controls heaven; hence yin condenses above. Major yang [qi] is at the fountain; hence cold congeals below."

228 Fang Yaozhong: "Plants do not grow well, or do not come to life and grow at all."

229 Zhang Jiebin: "Surplus and inadequacy refer to the qi of grain here. The colors, flavors, and the consistency of annual grain and intervening [qi] grain may differ in that their qi is weak or abounds. In the present year the policy of cold is excessive. Hence those grain that have a surplus of qi should [be grown in locations of] high [altitude] and they should [be grown] late because they are able to overcome the cold. Those with inadequate [qi], they should [be grown] early and they should [be grown] in lowlying [regions], because they cannot overcome the cold." Ma Shi: "Whenever one sows grain, in years with a surplus [of qi] their soil should be heaped high, in years with inadequate [qi] their soil should be low. Those with high soil, they should [ap-pear] late; those with low soil, they should [appear] early." Zhang Zhicong: "The soil

The benefits derived from the soil are
transformations of qi.
The qi of people follows these [laws], too.>

>{Intervening [qi] grain are called those which are major.}<[230]

71-469-11
The initial qi:
The qi of the earth has left its position.[231]
Hence the cold leaves.

---

in the five cardinal points differs in that it is either high or low, thick/rich or thin/poor.
Hence when the annual qi is present in surplus, the soil of the earth should be high
and thick/rich; when the annual qi is inadequate, the soil of the earth should be inferior and low. That is, a qi of great excess should [be helped to] be retarded, while an
inadequate qi should [be helped to] arrive early. When the soil is high and rich, the qi
will leave it slowly; when the earth is low, the qi rises easily. When the qi has a surplus,
one should see to it that it is perfected late; when it is inadequate, one should see to
it that it is perfected early." Gao Shishi: "In regions of high elevation, the qi is cold
and things are generated slowly. In regions of low elevation, the qi is warm and things
are generated early. In years when the qi has a surplus, it will arrive prior to its season.
Hence in such years it is appropriate to seek high elevations. [Here] the generation
of things is slow and their qi is perfected early. [Hence the perfection of things] will
not be too slow. In years when the qi is inadequate, it will arrive later than its season.
Hence in such years it is appropriate to seek low elevations. [Here] the generation of
things is early and their qi is perfected late. [Hence the generation of things] will not
be too early."

230 Gao Shishi: "Those [grain] that are generated and reach completion because they
are affected by the intervening [visitor] qi to the left or right of the [qi] controlling
heaven, they are called 'intervening [visitor] qi.'" – This passage should appear following 其穀黅玄 in *Su wen* 71-469-8. It appears to have been moved here erroneously
first and was corrupted by later editors because its meaning as a commentary to 其穀
黅玄 was no longer understood. For the original phrasing and position, see *Su wen*
71-463-8 and 71-474-10.

231 Fang Yaozhong: " 'Initial qi' refers to a year when the major yin [qi, i.e.,] dampness
and soil, controls heaven and when the initial qi of the intervening qi of the visitor
qi coming down to join [the host qi] is the ceasing yin [qi, i.e.,] wind and wood. 'The
qi of the earth has left its position' refers to the fact that in a year when the major yin
[qi, i.e.,] dampness and soil, controls heaven, ceasing yin [qi, i.e.,] wind and wood is
the initial qi because the qi at the fountain in the previous year has left its position. In
the year prior to the year when major yin [qi, i.e.,] dampness and soil, controls heaven,
minor yin [qi, i.e.,] ruler fire, controls heaven and yang brilliance [qi, i.e.,] dryness and
metal, is at the fountain. In a year when major yin [qi, i.e.,] dampness and soil, controls
heaven, the yang brilliance [qi, i.e.,] dryness and metal, which was at the fountain
in the previous year has moved to the position of fifth qi in the present year. Hence

The qi of spring [occupies its] proper [position].
Hence wind comes.[232]
Generation is widespread and the myriad beings blossom.

The qi of the people passes through and is unimpeded.
Wind and dampness strike at each other.
Hence the rain is belated.[233]

People suffer from blood overflow;
their sinews and network [vessels] have a cramp and are stiff.
Their joints do not move freely;
the body is heavy and the sinews are limp.[234]

71-469-14
The second qi:
Massive fire [occupies its] proper [position].[235]

---

ceasing yin [qi, i.e.,] wind and wood, can move from the position of second qi in the previous year to the position of initial qi in the present year."

232 Fang Yaozhong: " In a year when the major yin [qi, i.e.,] dampness and soil, control heaven, because the host qi and the visitor qi of the initial qi are ceasing yin [qi, i.e.,] wind and wood, the climate of that year in spring is basically a 'proper' climate."

233 Fang Yaozhong: " 'Late' refers to 'belated' here; the meaning is: 'insufficient.' In years when the major yin [qi, i.e.,] dampness and soil controls heaven, generally speaking the climate in the first half of the year is disproportionately damp and disproportionately large amounts of rain should fall. However, because the host qi and the visitor qi of the initial qi are ceasing qin [qi, i.e.,] wind and wood, wind qi dominates disproportionately. Wind is able to dominate dampness. Hence in the time period of the initial qi there is not only not much rain and water, on the contrary, there is very little. Hence the text states: 'Wind and dampness strike at each other; hence the rain is late.'"

234 Zhang Jiebin: "Wind illnesses manifest themselves in the sinews; dampness illnesses manifest themselves in the flesh. Hence all these conditions emerge. 'Blood overflow' results from wind harming the liver." Fang Yaozhong: "In a year when the major yin [qi, i.e.,] dampness and soil, controls heaven, the initial qi, which is wind qi, is disproportionately dominant. Hence the human body corresponds and manifests phenomena of a unilateral domination of liver qi and wind qi easily. Clinically this domination manifests itself in conditions such as bleeding and difficulties in movement." Gao Jiwu/248: " 'Blood overflow' is: blood leaves [the body] through mouth and nose."

235 Gao Shishi: "The host qi and the visitor qi of the second qi are both minor yin [qi, i.e.,] ruling fire. Hence 'great fire occupies its proper [position].'"

The beings [undergo] continued transformation.
Hence the [qi of] the people is harmonious.[236]

The illnesses [caused by] it are warmth epidemics. They prevail everywhere
far and near all alike.[237]
Dampness and steam strike at each other;
hence rain falls frequently.[238]

The third qi:
The policy of heaven is widespread.[239]
Dampness qi descends;
the qi of the earth surges.
Hence rain falls frequently and
cold follows it.[240]
When people are affected by cold and dampness,

---

236 Gao Shishi: "Fire generates soil. Hence the things are transformed and people are
harmonious." Fang Yaozhong: " 'Things' refers to living beings. 'Transform' is: they are
generated through transformation. 'People are harmonious' is: they are healthy, i.e.,
their state is normal."

237 Fang Yaozhong: "In a year when the major yin [qi, i.e.,] dampness and soil, controls heaven, the climate in the second qi [time period] is disproportionately hot.
Hence people's bodies are easily affected by warmth evil and [easily] develop warmth
illness. Also, this is easily transmitted. 咸若 means 'all like this.' That is, the illnesses
emerging in many places are all alike."

238 In contrast, Wang Bing: "When it corresponds to the regular schedule of heaven
and does not exceed its season, that is called 'it rains in time.'" Fang Yaozhong: "In a
year when the major yin [qi, i.e.,] dampness and soil, controls heaven, the climate in
the first half of the year is disproportionately damp and there should be disropor-
tionately large quantities of rain. However, the initial qi is the ceasing yin [qi, i.e.,]
wind and wood, and wind qi is disproportionately dominant. Wind can dominate
dampness. Hence the quantities of rain are diminished. The second qi is minor yin [qi,
i.e.,] ruling fire. Fire can generate soil. Hence the amount of rain fall is brought back
to normal. 'Dampness and steam strike at each other' is to say: the major yin [qi, i.e.,]
dampness and soil, controlling heaven and the second qi, that is, minor yin [qi, i.e.,]
ruling fire, affect each other."

239 Fang Yaozhong: "In a year when major yin [qi, i.e.,] dampness and soil, controls
heaven, the third qi of the visitor qi is major yin [qi, i.e.,] dampness and soil. Because
major yin qi is also, in that year, the qi controlling heaven, the text states: '[In the time
period of] the third qi the policy of heaven is widespread..'"

240 Zhang Jiebin "When the major yin [qi] controls heaven, dampness and soil are
in charge of affairs. Hence dampness qi descends, earth qi surges, and this causes rain.
Subsequent to the third qi, major yang [qi] is at the fountain. Hence 'cold follows it.'"

then they suffer from a heavy body and from *fu*-swelling.
Chest and abdomen are full.

71-470-1
The fourth qi:
Frightening fire comes down;
humidity and steam transform.[241]
The qi of the earth surges.
The qi of heaven is blocked.
There is cold wind in the morning and in the evening.
Steam and heat strike each other.
Herbs and trees [are enclosed by] congealing smoke.
When dampness transforms and does not flow,[242]
then white dew and clouds are widespread
to complete the command of autumn.[243]

People suffer from heat in the interstice structures,
sudden blood overflow, and malaria.
Heart and abdomen are full and hot. The abdominal wall is distended.[244]
In severe cases, there will be *fu*-swelling.[245]

The fifth qi:
The command of chilling temperatures prevails already.[246]
Cold and dew come down.
Hence frost descends early.

---

241 Fang Yaozhong: "In a year when the major yin [qi, i.e.,] dampness and soil, control heaven, the fourth, i.e., an intervening qi of the visitor qi coming down to join [the host qi] is the minor yang [qi, i.e.,] minister fire. 'Frightening fire' is the minor yang minister fire. Because the minor yang minister fire is an charge of affairs as fourth qi, the climate is hot to a degree that arouses fear.

242 Fang Yaozhong: " 'Smoke' is fog. Fog results from accumulations of dampness qi. Dampness qi, in turn, accumulates because the dampness does not flow off."

243 Wang Bing: "The myriad beings receive it to reach completion."

244 Zhang Jiebin: "膟 is 皮, 'skin.' Elsewhere it is said the abdominal front is called 膟."

245 Fang Yaozhong: "胕 is 膚, 'skin.'"

246 Fang Yaozhong: "In a year when the major yin [qi, i.e.,] dampness and soil, controls heaven, the fifth, i.e., an intervening of the visitor qi coming down to join [the host qi] is the yang brilliance [qi, i.e.,] dryness and metal. 'Chilling temperatures' is the order issued by autumn."

Herbs and trees turn yellow and [their leaves] fall.²⁴⁷
Cold qi reaches to the body.
The gentleman [stays in a] firmly closed [house].

People are affected by illnesses in the skin interstices.²⁴⁸

71-470-6
The final qi:
Cold comes up massively.²⁴⁹
Dampness transforms massively.²⁵⁰
Hence, frost accumulates and
clouds are condensed.
The water hardens to ice.
The yang light does not govern.

When people are affected by cold,
then they suffer from stiff joints.
The lower back and the buttocks ache.
{Cold and dampness are pushed²⁵¹ into the [sphere of] qi interaction, and cause disease}.²⁵²

---

247 Gao Jiwu/716: "Herbs turn yellow and the leaves of the trees fall."

248 Zhang Zhicong: "Yang brilliance qi rules the skin. Hence illnesses appear in the skin interstices." Fang Yaozhong: "The skin interstices are closely associated with the lung."

249 Fang Yaozhong: "In a year when the major yin [qi, i.e.,] dampness and soil, controls heaven, the final visitor qi is the major yang [qi, i.e.,] cold and water. In the time period associated with the final qi, i.e., between [the solar terms] Small Snow and Great Cold, that is, approximately between the final ten days of the tenth month to the first ten days of the twelfth month in the lunar calendar, the climate is very cold because in that time period both the major yang [qi, i.e.,] cold and water, is in charge both as host qi and as visitor qi."

250 Gao Shishi: "That is, dampness transforms to water."

251 *NJCD*: "推 is 遷移, 'to move to another place.'"

252 Fang Yaozhong: "This is to explain the origin and the nature of the illnesses listed above. 'Cold' refers here to the major yang [qi, i.e.,] cold and water. 'Dampness' refers to the major yin [qi, i.e.,] dampness and soil. 氣交 refers to [the space] between the qi of heaven and the qi of the earth. *Su wen* 68 states: 'At the position above [the earth] and below [heaven], amidst the interaction of the qi [of heaven and earth], that is where man resides.' The meaning of the entire sentence is: In a year when the major yin [qi, i.e.,] dampness and soil, controls heaven and when the major yang [qi, i.e.,] cold and water, is at the fountain, the climatic changes are characterized by cold and

It is necessary to break the qi oppressing it,
to seize the source of its transformation,²⁵³ and
to increase the annual qi.
One must not permit the evil to dominate.²⁵⁴
Consume the grain of the year to preserve its true [qi].²⁵⁵
Consume intervening [qi] grain to protect the [body's] essence.²⁵⁶

Hence
this year it is appropriate
to use bitter [flavor] to dry it, to warm it.
In severe cases, effuse it, drain it.²⁵⁷
If one fails to effuse and to drain,
then the dampness qi will overflow to the outside.
[As a result], the flesh rots and the skin breaks open and water and blood flow
into each other.
One must support the [patient's] yang fire and [thereby]
let the extreme cold be restrained.

---

dampness. Hence the illnesses named above, like stiff joints and pain in the lower back
and vertebras, are often the result of an affection by cold and dampness."

253 Gao Shishi: "Oppression is the basis of revenge. Hence one must break the qi oppressing it and regulate the source of its transformation to support it." Fang Yaozhong:
"The tenth through the twelfth months are the three months of winter. In a year when
the major yin [qi, i.e.,] dampness and soil, control heaven and when the major yang
[qi, i.e.,] cold and water, is at the fountain, the winter is extremely cold. Hence it is
advisable in the ninth month, prior to the advent of winter, to supplement the fire of
the heart to support the yang qi, that is, to treat before an illness has emerged."

254 Zhang Zhicong: "The annual period is inadequate. Hence one must add to it. Evil
qi is that qi which oneself is unable to overcome." Fang Yaozhong agrees.

255 Zhang Jiebin: " 'Annual grain' are the yellow and dark grain mentioned above."
Fang Yaozhong: " 'Annual grain' are the grain that grow under the influence of the
qi controlling heaven and of the qi at the fountain in a given year. In years when the
major yin qi controls heaven and the major yang qi is at the fountain, yellow and dark
grain are of a better quality than usual. Hence in such years one should consume much
of them to support the regular vital processes of the human body."

256 Fang Yaozhong: " 'Intervening [qi] grain' are the grain that grow under the influence of the intervening [visitor] qi to the left and to the right. Because the nature of
the intervening [qi] grain differs from the qi controlling heaven and at the fountain,
the grain that are affected by the intervening [visitor] qi have different effects, too."

257 Zhang Jiebin: "Bitter [flavor] is a transformation product of fire. [It is employed]
for drying to treat the dampness. Warm [flavor] serves to treat cold. Effusion can
remove cold; drainage serves to eliminate dampness."

71-470-12
Following the differences and agreements in the qi,
diminish or increase the deviation.²⁵⁸
When they agree in cold, use heat to achieve transformations.
When they agree in dampness, use dryness to achieve transformations.
In case of differences, diminish it;
in case of agreements, increase it.²⁵⁹

When employing coolness, stay away from coolness.
When employing cold, stay away from cold.
When employing warmth, stay away from warmth.
When employing heat, stay away from heat.
Food requirements [are based on] the same law.

In cases of false [heat or cold] act contrary to this [rule].
This is the Way.
If one acts contrary to this [Way], illness [emerges]."

71-470-16
[Huang] Di:
"Good!
The policy of minor yin, what is it like?"²⁶⁰

Qi Bo:
"These are the arrangements including *zi* and *wu* [earth branches].

[The first two arrangements include the years when] minor yin [controls heav-
en], major *jue* [is the central period],²⁶¹ and yang brilliance [is at the fountain].
[They are designated] *ren zi* and *ren wu*.

---

258 Fang Yaozhong: " 'Qi' refers to the annual qi. 'Differences and agreements' refers
to differences and agreements between the annual qi and the annual period. 少多
refers to the quantities of drugs of a special nature used in treatment. 判 is explained
by Zhang Zhicong as 分, in the sense of 區分, 'distinguish.'"

259 Fang Yaozhong: " 'Difference' refers to years when the annual qi and the annual
period do not have the same [climatic features]. 'Agreement' refers to years when they
do have the same. 'Diminish' and 'increase' refers to the amount of drugs employed for
warming the center, for dispersing cold, and for drying dampness."

260 Fang Yaozhong: "That is a year when the minor yin [qi, i.e.,] ruler fire, controls
heaven."

261 Fang Yaozhong: "Major *jue* refers to years of an excessive wood period. Here it
refers to *ren zi* and *ren wu* years."

Their period [manifests itself as] winds drumming.
The transformations [caused by] them include sounds of a chaotic opening and breaking.
The changes [caused by] them include shaking, pulling, breaking, plucking.
The illness [caused by them] is [a feeling of] propping fullness.

[The sequence of visitor periods is as follows:]
- Major *jue* begin [of the sequence of host periods,] proper [begin of the sequence of visitor periods]
- minor *zhi*
- major *gong*
- minor *shang*
- major *yu* end [of the sequence of host periods].

[The second two arrangements include the years when] minor yin [controls heaven], major *zhi* [is the central period],[262] yang brilliance [is at the fountain]. [They are designated] *wu zi* – heavenly complements – and *wu wu* – *tai-yi* heavenly complements.

Their period [manifests itself as] flaming summerheat.
The transformations [caused by] them include warmth, radiance, [heat] oppression, and damp heat.
The changes [caused by] them include flaming, fieriness, boiling, bubbling.
The illnesses [caused by] them include heat in the upper [sections of the body] and overflowing blood.

[The sequence of visitor periods is as follows:]
- Major *zhi*
- minor *gong*
- major *shang*
- minor *yu* end [of the sequence of host periods]
- minor *jue* begin [of the sequence of host periods].

71-471-7
[The third two arrangements include the years when] minor yin [controls heaven], major *gong* [is the central period],[263] yang brilliance [is at the fountain]. [They are designated] *jia zi* and *jia wu*.

---

262 Fang Yaozhong: " 'Major *zhi*' refers to a year with an excessive fire period." Here it refers to *wu zi* and *wu wu* years."

263 Fang Yaozhong: " 'Major *gong*' refers to years with an excessive soil period."

Their period [manifests itself as] overcast and rain.

The transformations [caused by] them include tender moisture and frequent rain.[264]

The changes [caused by] them include shaking [of the earth] to the extent that one is frightened, tornados, and rainstorms.

The illnesses [caused by] them include central fullness and a heavy body.

[The sequence of visitor periods is as follows:]
- Major *gong*
- minor *shang*
- major *yu* end [of the sequence of host periods]
- major *jue* begin [of the sequence of host periods]
- minor *zhi*.

71-471-10

[The fourth two arrangements include the years when] minor yin [controls heaven], major *shang* [is the central period],[265] yang brilliance [is at the fountain]. [They are designated] *geng zi* identical to heavenly complements – and *geng wu* identical to heavenly complements.[266] They are identical to proper *shang*.[267]

---

264 Lin Yi et al.: "Two [parallel passages] have 重澤 instead of 時雨. The two characters 時雨 may be a mistake." Fang Yaozhong interprets 時雨 as regular seasonal rain. Hence: "In years with an excessive soil period, more rain falls than usual. Hence we agree with Lin Yi et al.; the statement 重澤, 'double moisture,' (in previous listings of such years) is appropriate."

265 Fang Yaozhong: " 'Major *shang*' refers to years with an excessive metal period."

266 Fang Yaozhong: "Years with an excessive annual period the five agents association of which is identical to the five agents association of the qi at the fountain of the same year are called years 'identical to heavenly complements.' In *geng zi* and *geng wu* years, the annual stem is *geng*. *Yi* and *geng* transform metal. *Geng* is a yang stem. Hence *geng zi* and *geng wu* years are years with an excessive metal period. The annual branches of *geng zi* and *geng wu* years are *zi* and *wu*. In *zi* and *wu* years, the minor yin [qi], ruler fire, controls heaven and the yang brilliance [qi], dryness and metal, is at the fountain. That is, the five agents association of the qi at the fountain in *geng zi* and *geng wu* years is metal. Also, *geng zi* and *geng wu* years are years with an excessive metal period as annual period. Hence they are years 'identical to heavenly complements.' "

267 Fang Yaozhong: " 'Proper *shang*' refers to years with a metal period of balanced qi. *Geng zi* and *geng wu* years are basically years with an excessive metal period. However, because in these years the minor yin [qi, i.e.,] ruler fire, controls heaven and because fire can overcome metal, Hence the excessive metal period is constrained by the fire qi controlling heaven."

Their period [manifests itself as] coolness and force.
The transformations [caused by] them include fog, dew, and whistling of cold wind.
The changes [caused by] them include sternness, killing, withering, and falling.
The illness [caused by them] is coolness in the lower [parts of the body].²⁶⁸

[The sequence of visitor periods is as follows:]
- Major *shang*
- minor *yu* end [of the sequence of host periods]
- minor *jue* begin [of the sequence of host periods]
- major *zhi*
- minor *gong*.

[The fifth two arrangements include the years when] minor yin [controls heaven], major *yu* [is the central period],²⁶⁹ yang brilliance [is at the fountain]. [They are designated] *bing zi* – the year meets – and *bing wu*.

Their period [manifests itself as] cold.
The transformations [caused by] them include freezing and piercing cold.
The changes [caused by] them include ice, snow, frost, hail.
The illness [caused by] them is cold in the lower [part of the body].²⁷⁰

[The sequence of visitor periods is as follows:]
- Major *yu* end [of the sequence of host periods]
- major *jue* begin [of the sequence of host periods]
- minor *zhi*
- major *gong*
- minor *shang*.

71-472-2
Whenever there is such a policy of minor yin controlling heaven,
the transformations of the [six] qi and the movement of the [five] periods precede heaven.

---

268 Zhang Jiebin: "下清 is cold [induced] drainage from the two lower orifices and cold in the lower parts of the body." Fang Yaozhong: "These are changes in the climate and in things, as well as illnesses in the human body, resulting from a disproportion-ately dominant coolness qi in years with an excessive metal period."

269 Fang Yaozhong: " 'Major *yu*' refers to years with an excessive water period."

270 Fang Yaozhong: "These are changes in the climate and in things, as well as ill-nesses in the human body, resulting from a disproportionately dominant cold qi in years with an excessive water period."

The qi of the earth is stern;
the qi of heaven is bright.[271]

Cold interacts with summerheat;
dryness is added to heat.[272]

Clouds gallop towards the rain palace.
Hence dampness transformation prevails and
rain falls frequently.[273]

Metal and fire combine [their] virtues.[274]
<Mars and Venus correspond to this above.>[275]

---

271 Zhang Zhicong: "Dryness and metal [qi] is at the fountain; 'the qi of the earth
is stern.' The ruler fire [controls] heaven, hence 'the qi of heaven is brilliant.'" Fang
Yaozhong: "The 'qi of the earth' refers to the qi at the fountain. In years when the
minor yin [qi] controls heaven and the yang brilliance [qi, i.e.] dryness and metal, is
at the fountain, because the nature of metal is cool and stern, the climate in the second half of the year is disproportionately cool. 'Qi of heaven' refers to the qi controlling heaven. In years when the minor yin [qi] controls heaven, the ruler fire controls
heaven, because the nature of fire is brilliant, the climate in the first half of the year is
disproportionately hot.

272 Lin Yi et al.: "寒交暑 is to say: the final qi of the preceding year is minor yang
[i.e., minister fire]. The first qi of this year is major yang. That is, the major yang cold
interacts with the summerheat of the preceding year." Zhang Jiebin: "The yang brilliance [qi, i.e.,] dryness and metal, is at the fountain. Hence the qi of the earth is stern.
The minor yin [qi, i.e.,] ruler fire, controls heaven. Hence the qi of heaven is brilliant.
Metal is cold and dryness; fire is summerheat and heat. When the lower approaches
the upper, that is called 交, 'interaction.' When the upper approaches the lower, that is
called 加, 'to join.'" Gao Shishi: "When the minor yin [qi, i.e.,] fire and heat, is above
(i.e., controls heaven in the first half of the year) and when the major yang [qi, i.e.,]
cold and water, is the initial visitor qi, that is [an example of] cold interacting with
heat."

273 Gao Shishi: "The fourth visitor qi is the major yin [qi, i.e.,] dampness and soil.
Hence [the text] states: 'clouds gallop towards the rain palace. Hence dampness transformations prevail.'" Fang Yaozhong: "In a year when the minor yin [qi, i.e.,] the ruler
fire, controls heaven and when the yang brilliance [qi, i.e.,] dryness and metal is at the
fountain, major yin [qi, i.e.,] dampness and soil, is in charge both as the host qi and the
visitor qi of the [time period of the] fourth qi. Hence it rains relatively often."

274 Fang Yaozhong: "That is: the minor yin [qi, i.e.,] ruler fire, controlling heaven
and the yang brilliance [qi, i.e.,] dryness and metal, at the fountrian, influence each
other."

275 Wang Bing: "Their appearance is brilliant and large."

71-472-4
Its policy is brilliant;
its command is cutting.[276]
<Its grain are vermilion and white.>
[...]
Water, fire, cold, and heat
are held in the [sphere of] qi interaction,
and cause illnesses to commence.[277]
Heat illness emerges from above;
coolness illness emerges below.
Cold and heat encroach upon each other and struggle in the center.[278]

People suffer from cough and panting,
blood overflow, blood outflow, stuffy nose, sneezing,
red eyes, and ulcers in the canthi.
Cold recession enters the stomach.
The heart aches and the lower back has pain.
The abdomen is enlarged, the throat is dry. There is swelling above.[279]

71-472-8
The initial qi:

---

276 Zhang Jiebin: "Fire is brilliant, metal is cutting."

277 Zhang Jiebin: "Minor yin [qi] controls heaven and yang brilliance [qi] is at the fountain. Hence water and fire, cold and heat, cause illness in the [sphere of] qi interaction."

278 I.e., at the end of the first and at the beginning of the second half of the year. All Chinese commentators relate 'upper,' 'lower,' and 'center' to the course of a year. One should not exclude the possibility, though, that these references were meant to indicate bodily locations, too. See the following comment by Zhang Zhicong.

279 Zhang Zhicong: "Cough and panting, blood overflow, stuffy nose, sneezing, red eyes, ulcers in the canthi, dry throat, as well as swelling above are heat illnesses emerging above. Blood outflow and cold recession are coolness illnesses emerging below. [When the evil] enters the stomach, when the heart aches, and the lower back has pain, as well as when the abdomen is enlarged, that is because cold and heat struggle in the center and cause illness [there]." In contrast, Gao Shishi and Fang Yaozhong do not separate 寒厥 from 入胃. Fang Yaozhong: "Because the human body was affected by external cold, or because its proper qi was depleted or weakened, [i.e.,] because the yang qi was insufficient, the functions of spleen and stomach are harmed. This is manifested by all the illnesses listed below."

the qi of the earth has left its position.[280]
Dryness is about to leave.[281]
Hence cold begins.
The hibernating creatures hide again.
Water freezes,
frost descends again.
Wind arrives.
Yang qi is oppressed.[282]

People, contrary [to the regular order, stay in] firmly closed [houses].
The joints are stiff.

---

280 Fang Yaozhong: " 'Initial qi' refers to [the following]: In a year when the minor yin [qi, i.e.,] ruler fire, controls heaven, the initial qi of the intervening qi coming down as visitor qi to join [the host qi] is the major yang [qi, i.e.,] cold and water. 'The qi of the earth leaves its position' refers [to the following]: the major yang [qi, i.e.,] cold and water, is the initial qi in a year when the minor yin [qi, i.e.,] ruler fire, controls heaven because the qi at the fountain in the preceding year has left its position. In the year preceding a year when the minor yin [qi, i.e.,] ruler fire, controls heaven, the ceasing yin [qi, i.e.,] wind and wood, controls heaven and the minor yang [qi, i.e.,] minister fire, is at the fountain. In a year when the minor yin [qi, i.e.,] ruler fire, controls heaven the minor yang [qi, i.e.,] minister fire, which was at the fountain in the previous year, moves to the position of fifth qi. Hence the major yang [qi, i.e.,] cold and water can move to the position of initial qi in the present year from the position of second qi in the preceding year."

281 Lin Yi et al.: "Prior to a year when the yang brilliance [qi] is at the fountain, the minor yang [qi is at the fountain]. Minor yang is summerheat. As the text stated above 'cold interacts with summerheat.' Hence summerheat leaves and cold commences. That is, the character 'dryness' should be 'summerheat.'" Zhang Jiebin agreed. Ma Shi: "The leaving year is a *ji hai* year. The [qi] at the fountain in a *ji hai* [year] is the minor yang [qi]. That is, summerheat leaves and yang brilliance [qi] is at the fountain. Hence dryness will arrive. 去 should be 至, 'to arrive.'" Gao Shishi: "The initial visitor qi is major yang [qi, i.e.,] cold and water. 'The qi of the earth leaves its position' [is to say:] from yang brilliance it moves to major yang. The dryness of the yang brilliance [qi] leaves and the cold of the major yang [qi] begins. Hence [the text states:] 'Dryness will leave.'"

282 Fang Yaozhong: "Each year in the time period associated with the initial qi, the ceasing yin [qi, i.e.,] wind and wood, is in charge as host qi. When easterly winds arrive, the climate begins to turn warm and mild. Hence the text states: 'wind arrives.' However in a year when the minor yin [qi, i.e.,] ruler fire, controls heaven, the visitor qi in the time period associated with the initial qi is the major yang [qi, i.e.,] cold and water. In other words, [in such a year] spring, which should be mild, is cold in contrast because it is influenced by the visitor qi. The warm and mild qi is oppressed by the cold qi. Hence the text states: 'The yang qi is oppressed.'"

The lower back and the buttocks ache.[283]
Flaming summerheat is about to rise.
In the center and in the exterior sores and ulcers [develop].[284]

71-472-10
The second qi:
Yang qi is widespread.
Hence wind prevails and
the spring qi [occupies its] proper [position].
The myriad beings correspond [to this] and flourish.
Cold qi arises frequently.[285]
At this time, [the qi of] the people is harmonious.

---

283 Gao Shishi: "These are illnesses resulting from cold taking residence [in the body]."

284 Zhang Jiebin: "The minor yin [qi, i.e.,] ruler fire, controls heaven. It is also the second host qi. Hence flaming summer heat will emerge." Fang Yaozhong: " This statement has two meanings. First, the initial host qi is the ceasing yin [qi, i.e.,] wind and wood. The ceasing yin rules warmth. Because the visitor qi is the major yang [qi, i.e.,] cold and water, the warmth is oppressed by the cold. This results in cold outside and warmth inside, or cold transforms to heat which manifests itself clinically as fever. Second, the second host qi in a year when the minor yin [qi, i.e.,] ruler fire, controls heaven is the minor yin [qi, i.e.,] ruler fire. The visitor qi is the ceasing yin [qi, i.e.,] wind and wood. Both the ruler and the visitor qi are associated with warmth and heat. Hence the human body may be affected by heat evil from the outside and develops heat conditions. Sores are generally considered as heat conditions."

285 Zhang Jiebin: "The ruler fire controlling heaven does not abound yet. Hence 'cold qi arrives frequently.'" Gao Shishi: "The second visitor qi is the ceasing yin [qi, i.e.,] wind and wood. Wind is yang qi. Hence 'yang qi spreads' and 'wind prevails.' When the yang qi spreads and wind prevails, then this is the proper qi of spring. Hence the myriad beings correspond with blossoming. Nevertheless, the qi of heaven is cold. Hence when cold qi arrives frequently, people feel well." Fang Yaozhong: "寒氣時至 should be interpreted as 復氣, 'qi taking revenge.' The reason is, first, in a year when the minor yin [qi, i.e.,] ruler fire, controls heaven, the qi controlling heaven in the time period associated with the second qi is minor yin ruler fire and the host qi is minor yin ruler fire, too. Minor yin rules heat. The visitor qi is the ceasing yin [qi, i.e.,] wind and wood. Ceasing yin rules warmth. Warmth and heat belong to one class. In other words, in that time period the qi controlling heaven, the host qi, and the visitor qi all are associated with heat. Hence the climate should be very hot. It cannot be that 'the fire does not abound yet' or that 'the qi of heaven is cold.' Second, because in that time period the qi controlling heaven, the host qi, and the visitor qi all are associated with heat and the climate is very hot, climatic changes will follow with cold qi arriving to take revenge."

The illnesses [caused by] it include strangury,
blurred vision, and red eyes.[286]
The qi presses above and there is heat.[287]

The third qi:
The policy of heaven is widespread and
massive fire prevails.[288]
All classes [of beings] are plentiful and fresh.
Cold qi arrives frequently.[289]

People suffer from qi recession and heartache, from
alternate outbreaks of cold and heat, from
coughing, panting, and red eyes.

71-472-14
The fourth qi:
Humidity and summerheat arrive.[290]
Massive rain prevails often.
Cold and heat arrive alternately.[291]

---

286 Zhang Zhicong: "Strangury and obscured vision are illnesses caused by cold qi.
Red eyes are [caused by] the qi of ruler fire." Fang Yaozhong: "In a year when the minor yin [qi, i.e.,] ruler fire, controls heaven, the climate in the time period associated
with the second qi is disproportionately hot, and wind qi dominates disproportionately. The human body is easily affected by wind and heat from the outside. Clinical
manifestations are pathomanifestations of wind and heat, such as strangury, obscured
vision, and red eyes."

287 Zhang Jiebin: "These illnesses are caused by the ruler fire." Zhang Zhicong: " 'The
qi oppresses the above and there is heat' is: cold qi has moved upwards to seize [terri-
tory there]." Gao Shishi: "These are illnesses caused by the heat of minor yin fire."

288 Zhang Zhicong: "Both the ruler and the minister fire are present; hence the policy
of heaven spreads and massive fire prevails." Fang Yaozhong: "The third visitor qi is
the minor yin [qi, i.e.,] ruler fire."

289 Zhang Jiebin: "When fire reaches an extreme water takes revenge; when heat
reaches an extreme cold emerges. Hence 'cold qi arrives frequently.'"

290 Fang Yaozhong: "The fourth, i.e., an intervening qi of the visitor qi coming down
to join [the host qi] is the major yin [qi, i.e.,] humidity and soil."

291 Fang Yaozhong: "Minor yin [qi] controls heaven. Hence the climate is disproportionately hot in the first half of the year. Yang brilliance [qi, i.e.,] dryness and metal,
is at the fountain; hence the climate is disproportionately cool in the second half of
the year."

People suffer from cold and heat,
dry throat, yellow solitary [heat] disease,[292]
stuffy nose, and nosebleed; [spillage] drink develops.[293]

The fifth qi:
Frightening fire comes down.
Summerheat arrives contrary [to the regular order].[294]
Hence the yang transforms.

The myriad beings come to life, grow, and flourish.[295]
Hence people are healthy.[296]

---

292 A similar term, 黃疸, appears in *Su wen* 18 and *Su wen* 28. *SWJZGL* vol. 6, p. 891: "疸 and 癉 are borrowed for each other." Yellow *dan* is used today for jaundice.

293 Zhang Jiebin: "These are illnesses [caused by] heat." Fang Yaozhong: "寒熱 is: fever with an aversion to cold; here it refers to malaria. 飲發 is 水飲發作, 'water drink (i.e., stagnation of water in the body) develops.' Some of these conditions are associated with dampness and heat, some are associated with cold and dampness. In a year when the minor yin [qi, i.e.,] ruler fire, controls heaven and yang brilliance [qi, i.e.,] dryness and metal, is at the fountain, the first half of that year is disproportionately hot, while the second half is disproportionately cool. In the time period associated with the fourth qi the major yin [qi, i.e.,] dampness and soil, is in charge both as host qi and as visitor qi. Hence, because in this time period cold and heat arrive together, at times it is cold, at times it is hot, and dampness qi is disproportionately dominant. [People] may be affected from the outside by cold and dampness or by dampness and heat with the conditions listed here emerging as a result."

294 Fang Yaozhong: "In the time period associated with the fifth qi, that is from [the solar term] Autumnal Equinox to [the solar term] Little Snow, approximately in the time from the final ten days of the eighth month to the first ten days of the tenth month, the yang brilliance [qi, i.e.,] dryness and metal, is in charge as host qi. The climate should be disproportionately cool in general but because this is a year with the minor yin [qi, i.e.,] ruler fire, controlling heaven, the minor yang [qi, i.e.,] minister fire, coming down to join the fifth qi, the climate, contrary to [what one might expect], is very hot. Even though it is autumn, the order of summer prevails. Hence the text states 'summerheat arrives contrary to [the regular order].'"

295 Fang Yaozhong: "As for 陽乃化, 'yang' refers to a disproportionate domination of yang qi, that is, the climate is very hot. 'Transformation' refers to 化生, 'generation through transformation.'"

296 Zhang Jiebin: " 'Frightening fire' is the minister fire. That is the season of autumn harvest and yang qi transformation. Hence the myriad beings blossom and people are healthy." Cheng Shide et al.: "The fifth visitor qi is the minor yang [qi, i.e.,] minister fire."

{The illnesses [caused by] it are warmth [illnesses].}

71-472-16
The final qi:
The command of dryness prevails.²⁹⁷
Residual fire offers inner obstruction.
Swellings occur above.
[People suffer from] coughing and panting.
In severe cases, there is blood overflow.²⁹⁸

When cold qi comes up frequently,
then there is a screen of dense fog.²⁹⁹
Illnesses develop in the skin interstices.
Inside they lodge in the flanks.
Below they link up with the lower abdomen
and generate a cold center.
{The [qi of the] earth is about to change.}³⁰⁰

---

297 Fang Yaozhong: "In a year when the minor yin [qi, i.e.,] ruler fire, controls heaven, the final visitor qi is the yang brilliance [qi, i.e.,] dryness and metal."

298 Gao Shishi: "胵 should be 衝, 'to rush through.' The final visitor qi is the yang brilliance [qi, i.e.,] dryness and metal. Hence the order of dryness prevails. From above [i.e., from the previous time period] it inherits the fifth visitor qi which is associated with the minor yang [qi]. Hence 'residual fire is blocked internally.' Because it is blocked internally, it rushes upwards and causes coughing as well as panting. In serious cases blood overflow results."

299 Gao Shishi: "The qi in heaven is hazy."

300 Fang Yaozhong: " 'Earth' refers to the qi at the fountain. In a year when the minor yin [qi, i.e.,] ruler fire, controls haven, the yang brilliance [qi, i.e.,] dryness and metal, is at the fountain. The time period associated with the final qi is also the position occupied by the qi at the fountain. However, in terms of the host qi the time periods of the final qi is [associated with] the major yang [qi, i.e.,] cold and water. Coolness and cold belong to the same class, even though their intensity differs. Because the time period of the final qi falls together with severe cold and because the order of winter rules cold,, the yang brilliance [qi, i.e.,] dryness and metal, must change and transform into major yang [qi, i.e.,] cold and water. Hence the text at first states 'cold qi comes up frequently' and then says 'develops cold in the center.' Hence the statement 'the earth will change' is to say: the yang brilliance [qi] changes and transforms into major yang [qi]; the dryness qi changes into cold qi."

It is necessary to press down its [excessive] period and qi and
to supply that which is dominated in that year,³⁰¹
to break [the qi] oppressing it and [have it] effused and
to seize the source of transformation first
lest violent excesses lead
to the emergence of the respective illnesses.³⁰²

Consume the grain of the year to preserve the true qi.
Consume intervening [qi] grain to ward off depletion evil.

This year it is appropriate
[to use] salty [flavor] to soften it, and
to regulate the above.
In severe cases, employ bitter [flavor] to effuse it.³⁰³
Employ sour [flavor] to contract it,
and to pacify the below.
In severe cases, employ bitter [flavor] to drain it.³⁰⁴

71-473-5
Depending on whether the qi agrees with or differs from [the proper qi of this
year],
increase or diminish it.
In case of agreements with the qi of heaven, use cold and coolness to cause a
transformation.
In case of agreements with the qi of the earth, use warmth and heat to cause a
transformation.

When employing heat, stay away from heat.
When employing coolness, stay away from coolness.
When employing warmth, stay away from warmth.

---

301 Compared with *Su wen* 71-461-4 and 71-467-11, in this statement the character
不 ("not") appears to have been erroneously replaced by the character 歲.

302 All parallel statements have 折其鬱氣. The character 發 may be an erroneous
replacement for 氣."

303 Zhang Jiebin: "Salty [flavor] is a transformation product of water. Hence it is able
to regulate the ruler fire above. Effusion with bitter [flavor] serves to disperse fire."
Fang Yaozhong: "上 refers to the upper half of the year here."

304 Zhang Jiebin: "By collecting it with sour [flavor] it is possible to supplement the
metal. In that the ruler fire of the upper [half of the year] is balanced, the dryness and
metal [qi] of the lower [half of the year] is pacified. When dryness and heat are severe,
only drainage with bitter and cold [substances] will do."

When employing cold, stay away from cold.
Food requirements [are based on] the same law.

In cases of false [heat or cold], act contrary to this.
This is the Way.
Acting contrary to this [Way will cause] illnesses to break out."

71-473-9
[Huang] Di:
"Good!
The policy of ceasing yin, what is it like?"[305]

Qi Bo:
"These are the arrangements including *si* and *hai* [earth branches].

[The first two arrangements include the years when] ceasing yin [controls heaven], minor *jue* [is the central period],[306] and minor yang [is at the fountain]. Coolness domination and heat revenge is the same [in both minor *jue* years]. [Both these years have conditions] identical to [those in] proper *jue* [years].[307] [They are designated] *ding si* – heavenly complements – and *ding hai* – heavenly complements.[308]

Their period [manifests itself as] wind, coolness, and heat.[309]

[The sequence of visitor periods is as follows:]
- Minor *jue* begin [of the sequence of host periods,] proper [begin of the sequence of visitor periods]
- major *zhi*
- minor *gong*

---

305 Fang Yaozhong: " 'The policy of ceasing yin' refers to a year when ceasing yin [qi, i.e.,] wind and wood, controls heaven."

306 Fang Yaozhong: " 'Minor *jue*' refers to a year with an inadequate wood period."

307 Gao Shishi: "When the wood period is inadequate, then metal qi dominates in the beginning. Later the heat qi of fire takes revenge. Domination and revenge together rule the qi of the entire year. The minor *jue* wood period receives assistance from [the qi] controlling heaven. Hence it is identical to proper *jue*."

308 Fang Yaozhong: "When the annual period and the qi controlling heaven are identical in their five agents association, the year is called 'heavenly complements.'"

309 Gao Shishi: " 'Their period is wind' because it is a period of *jue*, [i.e.,] wood. Coolness results from a domination of metal; heat results from revenge taken by fire."

- major *shang*
- minor *yu* end [of the sequence of host periods].

71-473-14
[The second two arrangements include the years when] ceasing yin [con-
trols heaven], minor *zhi* [is the central period],[310] and minor yang [is at the
fountain]. Cold domination and rain revenge is the same [in both minor *zhi*
years].[311] [They are designated] *gui si* identical to the year meets and *gui hai*
identical to the year meets.

Their period [manifests itself as] heat, cold, and rain.[312]

[The sequence of visitor periods is as follows:]
- Minor *zhi*
- major *gong*
- minor *shang*
- major *yu* end [of the sequence of host periods]
- major *jue* begin [of the sequence of host periods].

[The third two arrangements include the years when] ceasing yin [controls
heaven], minor *gong* [is the central period],[313] and minor yang [is at the foun-
tain]. Wind domination and coolness revenge is the same [in both minor *gong*
years]. [Both these years have conditions] identical to [those in] proper *jue*
[years].[314] [They are designated] *ji si* and *ji hai*.

Their period [manifests itself as] rain, wind, and coolness.[315]

---

310 Fang Yaozhong: " 'Minor *zhi*' refers to a year with an inadequate fire period."

311 Gao Shishi: "When the fire period is inadequate, then the cold qi of water dominates in the beginning. Later the rain qi of soil takes revenge. Domination and revenge together rule the qi of the entire year."

312 Zhang Jiebin: "Heat is the period qi; cold is the dominant qi; rain is the qi taking
revenge."

313 Fang Yaozhong: " 'Minor *gong*' refers to a year with an inadequate soil period."

314 Gao Shishi: "When the soil period is inadequate, then wind qi of wood dominates in the beginning. Later the coolness qi of metal takes revenge. Domination and
revenge together rule the qi of the entire year. The wood qi is depleted by now and
receives assistance from [the qi] controlling heaven in the upper [half of the year].
Hence [the situation] is identical to proper *jue*."

315 Zhang Jiebin: "Rain is the period qi; wind is the dominant qi; coolness is the qi
taking revenge."

[The sequence of visitor periods is as follows:]
- Minor *gong*
- major *shang*
- minor *yu* end [of the sequence of host periods]
- minor *jue* begin [of the sequence of host periods]
- major *zhi*.

71-474-1
[The fourth two arrangements include the years when] ceasing yin [controls heaven], minor *shang* [is the central period],[316] and minor yang [is at the fountain]. Heat domination and cold revenge is the same [in both minor *shang* years]. [Both these years have conditions] identical to [those in] proper *jue* [years].[317] [They are designated] *yi si* and *yi hai*.

Their period [manifests itself as] coolness, heat, and cold.[318]

[The sequence of visitor periods is as follows:]
- Minor *shang*
- major *yu* end [of the sequence of host periods]
- major *jue* begin [of the sequence of host periods]
- minor *zhi*
- major *gong*.

71-474-4
[The fifth two arrangements include the years when] ceasing yin [controls heaven], minor *yu* [is the central period],[319] and minor yang [is at the fountain]. Rain domination and wind revenge is the same [in both minor *yu* years].[320] [They are designated] *xin si* and *xin hai*.

---

316 Fang Yaozhong: " 'Minor *shang*' refers to a year with an inadequate metal period."

317 Gao Shishi: "When the metal period is inadequate, then heat qi of fire dominates in the beginning. Later the cold qi of water takes revenge. Domination and revenge together rule the qi of the entire year. The wood qi controls heaven and the metal period is inadequate. Hence [the situation] is identical to proper *jue*."

318 Zhang Jiebin: "Coolness is the period qi; heat is the dominant qi; cold is the qi taking revenge."

319 Fang Yaozhong: " 'Minor *yu*' refers to years with an inadequate water period."

320 Gao Shishi: "When the water period is inadequate, then the rain qi of soil dominates in the beginning. Later the wind qi of wood takes revenge. Domination and revenge together rule the qi of the entire year."

Their period [manifests itself as] cold, rain, and wind.[321]

[The sequence of visitor periods is as follows:]
- Minor *yu* end [of the sequence of host periods]
- minor *jue* begin [of the sequence of host periods]
- major *zhi*
- minor *gong*
- major *shang*.

Whenever there is such a policy of ceasing yin controlling heaven,
the transformations of the [six] qi and the movement of the [five] periods are
behind heaven.[322]

<In all [years] identical with proper years,
the transformations of the [six] qi and the movements of the [five] periods
agree with heaven.>[323]

The qi of heaven is disturbed;
the qi of the earth is proper.[324]

Wind emerges; it is high and [reaches] far away.
Flaming heat follows it.[325]

---

321 Zhang Jiebin: "Cold is the period qi; rain is the dominant qi; wind is the qi taking
revenge."

322 Fang Yaozhong: "Because the annual stems in the ten years when the ceasing
yin [qi] controls heaven are all yin stems and because all these years are years of an
inadequate annual period, the climatic changes in these years cannot completely agree
with their respective seasons. They occur later than usual; they should arrive but do
not arrive [yet]."

323 Wang Bing: "In years of great excess, the transformations of the periods and the
passage of the qi precede the heavenly seasons. In years of inadequacy, transformation,
generation, and completion occur later than the heavenly seasons. In years coinciding with the proper [qi], transformation, generation, and completion occur as much
delayed or speeded up as the 24 qi [terms] of heaven; there is no preceding or being
late." Fang Yaozhong: "諸同正歲 refers to all years with a balanced qi. 天 is 'heavenly
season.'"

324 Gao Shishi: "擾 is 'excited by wind.'"

325 Fang Yaozhong: "Minor yang [qi] is at the fountain; fire qi is disproportionately
dominant [in the second half of the year]."

The clouds rush to the rain palace.
Hence dampness transformation prevails.³²⁶

Wind and fire combine [their] virtues.³²⁷
<Jupiter and Mars correspond to this above.>

71-474-9
Its policy is disturbance;
its command is speed.³²⁸

<Its grain are greenish and vermilion.>
{These are the intervening [qi] grain which are called major.}

{That which causes destruction are things with line patterns and horns and
those which are feathered.}

Wind and dryness, fire and heat
dominate and return in revenge and are active alternately.³²⁹
The hibernating creatures appear;
the flowing water does not freeze.
Heat illnesses prevail below;

---

326 Fang Yaozhong: "In a year when the ceasing yin [qi] controls heaven and the minor yang [qi] is at the fountain, the climatic changes of the entire year are characterized by a disproportionate domination of wind and heat. In the first half of the year,
the wind qi is disproportionately dominant. Wind can overcome dampness. Hence
there is comparatively little rain in the first half of the year; there is no dampness
when there should be dampness. In the second half of the year the fire qi is disproportionately dominant; in winter it is not cold when it should be cold. The qi of water is
inadequate. When the qi of water is inadequate, then soil [qi] arrives to seize [its ter-
ritory]. Hence 'clouds rush to the rain palace and dampness transformation prevails,'
that is, there is much rain."

327 Fang Yaozhong: "Wind qi dominates in the first half of the year; fire qi dominates in the second half of the year. Under the combined influence of wind qi and fire
qi, the climate of the entire year is characterized by wind and heat."

328 Fang Yaozhong: "Wind rules movement; hence 'the policy is disturbance.' The
nature of fire is speed; hence 'its order is speed.'"

329 Zhang Jiebin: "When the winds are severe, then dryness dominates. When
dryness dominates, then heat takes revenge. Hence dominance and revenge occur
alternatively as is outlined here." Fang Yaozhong: "Wind is associated with wood;
dryness is associated with metal; heat is associated with fire. When the qi of wood is
disproportionately dominant, metal comes to curb the wood. When the qi of metal is
disproportionately dominant, fire, in turn, curbs the metal."

wind illnesses prevail above.
Domination and revenge of wind and dryness assume shape in the center.

The initial qi:
In the beginning, when cold still has sternness,
in that moment the killing qi arrives.[330]
People suffer from cold in the lower [section] of their right.[331]

The second qi:
the cold does not leave.[332]
The flowers are covered with snow; the water freezes.
The killing qi enacts transformations.[333]
Hence frost descends and
the eminent herbs are scorched in their upper [parts].
Cold and rain arrive frequently;
the yang transforms in revenge.
People suffer from heat in the center.

---

330 Zhang Zhicong: "In the [time period associated with the] initial qi, yang brilliance [qi, i.e.,] coolness and metal, controls heaven. Hence in the beginning the cold is stern and the killing qi arrives." Fang Yaozhong: "In spring the qi is disproportionately cool; there is no generation [at a time] where there should be generation. On the contrary, phenomena of a stern and killing qi of coolness appear as if it were autumn. That is, in a year when the ceasing yin [qi, i.e.,] wind and wood, control haven, in the [time period associated with the] initial qi the yang brilliance [qi, i.e.,] dryness and metal, is in charge. The yang brilliance [qi] rules coolness. Hence in the time period associated with the initial qi, i.e., from [the solar term] Great Cold to [the solar term] vernal equinox, approximately from the final ten days of the twelfth month to the first ten days of the second month of the lunar calendar, the climate is disproportionately cool. Even though it is spring, the order of autumn prevails."

331 Fang Yaozhong: "The phrase 右之下 means 'below the major yang [qi], the intervening [visitor qi] to the right of the [qi] controlling heaven. That is, in fact, a reference to the initial qi. The meaning is: in years when the ceasing yin [qi, i.e.,] wind and wood, control heaven, in the time period associated with the initial qi, because the climate is disproportionately cool, the human body is easily affected by cold evil and develops pathoconditions of cold."

332 Gao Shishi: "The second visitor qi is the major yang [qi, i.e.,] cold and water. Hence 'cold does not leave.'"

333 Gao Shishi: "華雪 is 雪花, 'snow flowers.'" Fang Yaozhong: "In a year when the ceasing yin [qi, i.e.,] wind and wood, controls heaven, the major yang [qi, i.e.,] cold and water, is in charge as second qi. The climate is cold. The living beings should come to life, but do not come to life; they should grow, but do not grow. The order of winter prevails in spring."

The third qi:
The policy of heaven is widespread.[334]
Hence, wind rises frequently.
People suffer from tearflow; [they hear] a ringing [sound] in the ears. They
sway and are dizzy.[335]

71-474-16
The fourth qi:
Humidity and summerheat; dampness and heat strike each other.
The struggle occurs above the left.[336]
People suffer from yellow solitary [heat] disease,
and there is *fu*-swelling.

The fifth qi:
Dryness and dampness dominate alternately.

---

334 Fang Yaozhong: "The third visitor qi is the ceasing yin [qi, i.e.,] wind and
wood."

335 Fang Yaozhong: "In a year when the ceasing yin [qi, i.e.,] wind and wood, controls
heaven, the wind qi is disproportionately dominant, especially so during the time
period associated with the third qi. Hence the human body is easily affected by wind
evil from the outside, or it may be that the liver qi is disproportionately strong because
of climatic reasons, which leads to the illnesses listed here." Zhang Zhicong: "Wind
illnesses prevail above."

336 Fang Yaozhong: " 'Fourth qi' refers to the fourth visitor qi, minor yin ruling fire,
coming down to join [the host qi] in a year when the ceasing yin [qi, i.e.,] wind and
wood, controls heaven. 左之上 refers to the intervening [visitor qi] to the left of [the
qi] controlling heaven. The direction of the intervening [visitor qi] to the left of [the
qi] controlling heaven is to the left and the position is above. Hence it is called 'above
the left.' The initial qi is on the left side of the [qi at the] fountain. The second qi is
to the right side of [the qi] controlling heaven. The third qi is exactly on the position
above [the qi] controlling heaven. The fourth qi is on the left side of [the qi] controlling heaven. The fifth qi is on the right side of the [qi at the] fountain. The final qi is
exactly on the position above [the qi] at the fountain. That is, in a year when the ceasing yin [qi, i.e.,] wind and wood, controls heaven, [in the time period associated with]
the fourth qi the host qi is the major yin [qi, i.e.,] dampness and soil, and its climatic
manifestation is disproportionate dampness. The visitor qi is the minor yin [qi, i.e.,]
ruler fire, and its climatic manifestation is disproportionate heat. Hence in this time
period of the fourth qi, that is, from [the solar term] Great Heat and Autumn Equinox, approximately from the final ten days of the sixth month to the first ten days of
the eighth month, the climate is disproportionately damp and hot. Summerheat and
dampness struggle with each other."

Hence heavy overcast[337] is widespread.[338]
Cold qi reaches the body.
Hence wind and rain prevail.

The final qi:
Frightening fire controls the command.
Hence the yang transforms massively.
The hibernating creatures appear.
The flowing water does not freeze.
The qi of the earth breaks out massively.
Herbs come to life.[339]
Hence people feel comfortable;
the diseases [caused by] it are warmth epidemics.

71-474-20
It is necessary to break the [respective] oppressing qi and
to supply the source of transformation.
Support the period qi,
lest the evil dominates.[340]

This year it is appropriate
to employ acrid [flavor] to regulate the above and

---

337 *NJCD*: "沈陰 is 'deep-reaching, dense clouds.'"

338 Gao Shishi: "The fifth visitor qi is the major yin [qi, i.e.,] dampness and soil. The host qi is the yang brilliance [qi, i.e.,] dryness and metal. Hence dryness and dampness dominate alternatively. The qi of soil and of metal are both associated with yin and cold. Hence 'heavy clouds are widespread.'"

339 Zhang Zhicong: "The final host qi is the major yang [qi, i.e.,] cold and water. It is joined by the minister fire coming from above. Hence 'frightening fire controls the orders.' Because the visitor dominates the host, yang qi causes massive transformations. The running water does not freeze. The minor yang [qi] at the fountain is effused greatly; the herbs are affected by the qi of generation and growth and come to life. People are affected by the qi of warmth and feel comfortable."

340 Zhang Zhicong: "The 'source of transformation' is the source of the generation of the five periods and six qi. For example, in a minor *gong* period, the ceasing yin [qi] controls heaven and the qi of soil is oppressed as a result. In a minor *shang* period, the minor yang [qi] is at the fountain and the qi of metal is oppressed as a result. Hence it is essential to break the qi causing the oppression to assist the source of the transformations of the five periods. The same applies to the six qi. When an annual period is inadequate, it is necessary to support the period qi lest it will be dominated by the qi that is [normally] unable to dominate it. The same applies to the three inadequate qi."

to employ salty [flavor] to regulate the below.³⁴¹

The qi of frightening fire
must not be offended recklessly.³⁴²

71-475-1
When employing warmth stay away from warmth.
When employing heat stay away from heat.
When employing coolness stay away from coolness.
When employing cold stay away from cold.
Food requirements [are based on] the same law.

In cases of false [heat or cold], act contrary to the regular [laws].
This is the Way.
Acting contrary to this [Way leads to] illness."

71-475-4
[Huang] Di:
"Good!

---

341 Gao Shishi: "The qi of wood is [active] in the upper [half of the year. Hence] it is advisable to employ the acrid flavor of metal to regulate its upper [half]. The qi of fire is [active] in the lower [half of the year. Hence] it is advisable to employ the salty flavor of water to regulate its lower [half]." Fang Yaozhong: " 'Above' refers to the first half of the year. In a year when the ceasing yin [qi, i.e.,] wind and wood, controls heaven, wind qi is disproportionately dominant in the first half of the year. 'Wind' is closely associated with the 'liver' in the human body. In *Su wen* 22 the following therapeutic principle is outlined: 'The liver [qi] wishes to disperse; [in case of an illness in the liver,] one should quickly consume acrid [flavor] to disperse its [qi] and one employs acrid [flavor] to fill it.' Hence it is advisable to select drugs or food of acrid flavor and warm nature to regulate the [qi of the] liver in the human body. 'Salty' refers to drugs or food of a salty flavor and cold nature. 'Below' refers to the second half of the year. In a year when the ceasing yin [qi, i.e.,] wind and wood, controls heaven, the minor yang [qi, i.e.,] minister fire, is at the fountain. [Hence] the climate in the second half of that year is disproportionately hot. 'Fire' is closely associated with the 'heart' in the human body. According to the therapeutic principle outlined in *Su wen* 22, 'the heart [qi] wishes to be soft. [In case of an illness in the heart] one should quickly consume salty [flavor] to soften its [qi] and one employs salty [flavor] to fill it,' it is advisable to select drugs or food with a salty flavor and with a cold nature to regulate the [qi of the] heart in the human body."

342 Zhang Jiebin: "Whether the minister fire is depleted or replete is very difficult to distinguish. Hence [the text] states: 'the qi of frightening fire must not be offended recklessly.'"

What you, Sir, have outlined can be called encompassing.
But how is it possible to gain an understanding of these correspondences?"[343]

Qi Bo:
"A brilliant question, indeed!
Now, the six qi,
in their movement they follow a [specific] sequence;
when they stop they occupy a [specific] position.[344]

Hence
they are always observed in the first month, at dawn of the new moon.
Look for their position to know where they are.[345]

When a period has a surplus, it arrives early;
when a period is inadequate, its arrival is belated.[346]
That is the Way of heaven and the regularity of the qi.

When a period neither has a surplus, nor is insufficient,
that is called a proper year. This [period] arrives exactly in time."

---

343 Zhang Jiebin: "This is to ask for a verification of the qi correspondences outlined in the preceding section." Fang Yaozhong: "明 has the meaning here of 証明, 'to
prove,' or 驗証, 'to verify.'"

344 Zhang Jiebin: "次 is 序, 'order,' 'sequence.' 位 is 方, 'cardinal point.'" Fang Yaozhong: " 'Six qi' refers to ceasing yin [qi, i.e.,] wind and wood, minor yin [qi, i.e.,] ruling fire, minor yang [qi, i.e.,] minister fire, major yin [qi, i.e.,] dampness and soil, yang
brilliance [qi, i.e.,] dryness and metal, and major yang [qi, i.e.,] cold and water."

345 Wang Bing: "When yin is present, heaven responds with clouds; when yang is
present, heaven responds with clarity and quietude." Zhang Jiebin: "The six host qi
and the six visitor qi follow each other in a certain sequence and they occupy specific
locations. Hence to know their positions it is advisable to observe them in the early
morning of the first day of the first month to find out the locations of yin (i.e., cloudy
sky) and yang (i.e., bright sky), darkness and brilliance, cold and warmth, as well as of
wind qi to learn about the climate of the [subsequent] year. This is the beginning of
the days and of the seasons [of the entire year] and may, therefore, be read as an omen
for the entire year." Fang Yaozhong: " 覵 其位 may refer to an inspection of changes in
the direction pointed at by the handle of the Big Dipper." For a detailed justification
of this interpretation, see there.

346 Zhang Jiebin: " 'It arrives early' is: the qi arrives prior to the onset of [its cor-
responding] solar term; 'its arrival is late' is: the qi arrives after the onset of [its cor-
responding] solar term." Fang Yaozhong: " 'Period' refers to the annual period; 'has
surplus' refers to a year with a greatly excessive [annual period]. 'Inadequate' refers to
a year with an inadequate [annual period]."

71-475-9
[Huang] Di:
"The qi of domination and revenge
are present in regular [sequence];
catastrophes and disasters come about occasionally.
How can they be known in advance?"

Qi Bo:
"When the wrong qi transforms,
that is called 'catastrophe.'"

[Huang] Di:
"The numbers of heaven and earth,
when do they end and when do they begin?"³⁴⁷

Qi Bo:
"An encompassing question, indeed! The [underlying] Way is brilliant.

71-475-12
The beginning of the numbers
starts from the upper [half of the year] and ends with the lower [half].
The [time period] before the middle of a year, that is the [time period] ruled by
the qi of heaven.
The [time period] following the middle of a year, that is the [time period] ruled
by the qi of the earth.
[The time period] when the upper and the lower [halves of the year] interact
and exchange [their qi] is ruled by the qi interaction.³⁴⁸
[This way] the arrangement of a year is complete."

---

347 Zhang Jiebin: "[The qi] controlling heaven and [the qi] at the fountain rule for
a [certain] number [of days]." Fang Yaozhong: "數 is 規律, 'law.'" Zhang Zhicong:
"'Heaven' is to say: [the qi] controlling heaven; 'earth' is to say: [the qi] at the fountain."

348 Wang Bing: "'Middle of the year' refers to the day 'Autumn Begins.'" Zhang
Jiebin: "'Qi interaction' is: the qi of heaven and the qi of the earth exert joint effects.
氣交主之 is: at the time of the third and fourth qi the qi of heaven and the qi of the
earth interact. That is, the [time periods of the] third and fourth qi are the [time periods of] qi interaction of a given year. Hence whether a year has droughts or flooding,
whether it is characterized by abundance or dearth, and the generation, growth, collection and completion of things, [all these phenomena] are tied to these altogether
four months or 120 days from the middle of the fourth month to the middle of the
eighth month." Fang Yaozhong: "'Qi interaction' refers to the interaction of the qi of
heaven and of the earth. In the present statement it refers to the time period between

Hence when it is said
'when the positions are clear and their qi are obvious,
the months can be known,'
then this is what is called qi [here].[349]

71-476-1
[Huang] Di:
"Whenever I take control of an issue,
[I shall] carry it out in agreement with [these] rules.
If they do not match these numbers, how is that?"[350]

Qi Bo:
"The operation of the qi may be more or less;
the governing of transformations may abound or be weak.

---

the third and the fourth qi. 上下交互, 氣交主之 is: each year in the time period of
the third and fourth qi, that is each year from [the solar term] Grain Fills to [the
solar term] Autumnal Equinox, i.e., approximately in the time period from the final
ten days of the fourth month to the first ten days of the eighth month of the lunar
calendar, both the qi controlling heaven and the qi at the fountain exert an influence
on what is produced at this time."

349 Zhang Jiebin: "When the positions above and below, left and right are clear, then
the variations in the end and in the beginning of the six qi and twelve months can all
be known. These are the so-called qi of heaven and earth." Gao Shishi: "In the course
of one year, each of the four seasons [includes] six positions. The twelve months include altogether 24 qi [terms]. Hence [the text] states: 位時 (sic; changed by Gao)氣
月可知乎, 'by the positions and seasons the qi and the months can be known.'." Fang
Yaozhong: "位 refers to the positions and time periods associated with the six qi in the
course of one year. 明 stands for 明确, 'clear.' Gao Shishi has changed 明 to 時, 'season.' That, however, is unjustified. 氣 is 節氣, 'qi of a [solar] term.' The entire sentence
has the following meaning: once the positions and time periods occupied by each of
the six qi are known, the characteristics of the climatic changes of each solar term and
of each month are known, too."

350 Gao Shishi: "[Huang] Di at first established the stems and branches; he ordered
the calendar and clarified the seasons. Hence [the text] states: 'I have managed the
events [in the course of the years] and I have applied them as laws. If the events in the
course of a year do not agree with the numbers of the qi, what is the reason?'" Fang
Yaozhong: "則 has the meaning of 法則, 'rule'; in the present context it can be read as
'in accordance.' 數 refers to the 'numbers of heaven and earth' mentioned above. The
meaning of the entire sentence is: if one compares the actual conditions to the laws
outlined above, sometimes they do not agree with these laws."

The extent of this weakness or abundance [should]
agree with the transformations."³⁵¹

[Huang] Di:
"I should like to hear what 'agreement with the transformations' is like."

71-476-4
Qi Bo:
"Wind and warmth agree with the transformations [evoked by] spring.³⁵²
Heat, the red-yellow [color of] dusk, and fire agree with the transformations
[evoked by] summer.³⁵³
<Domination and revenge agree.>³⁵⁴

---

351 Zhang Jiebin: "治 is 合, 'to unite.'" Gao Shishi: "Within the course of one year,
the activities of the six qi, [i.e.,] wind, heat, dampness, fire, dryness, and cold, may be
excessive or inadequate. 'More' is excessive; 'less' is inadequate. The transformations
of the five periods govern the myriad beings; there may be surplus and there may be
insufficiency. 'Abundance' is surplus; 'weakness/dearth' is insufficiency. The abundance
or weakness in how the transformations govern [the myriad beings] and the increase
or decrease in the activities of the qi, they all agree with the transformation orders
issued by the four seasons, as is outlined in the text below."

352 Gao Shishi: "同化 is: the qi of the six qi and the qi of the five periods agree with
the transformations of the five agents in the course of the four seasons. Hence the
wind and warmth of the ceasing yin qi, i.e., wood, are identical to the tansformations
[evoked by] spring which are associated with *jue* and wood. The heat and the red-yellow [color of] dust and the fire of the minor yin and minor yang [qi] are identical
to the transformations [evoked by] summer which are associated with *zhi* and fire."
Fang Yaozhong: "化同 is: their effects on the transformation and generation of living
beings are identical. That is, in spring easterly winds blow strongly, the climate is warm
and mild, and spring rules generation. Even though 'spring,' 'warmth,' and 'wind' are
three different concepts, their effects on the transformation and generation of things
are identical. Hence their basic natures are identical, too, and can be categorized into
one group."

353 Fang Yaozhong: "曛 has the meaning of 薰蒸, 'steam.' 昏 is 昏迷, 'coma.' That
is, because in summer the sun burns and the climate is very hot the human body is
easily affected by heat or sunstroke and falls unconscious. Even though 'heat,' 'steam,'
'coma,' 'fire,' and 'summer' are different concepts, they are all related to fire and heat
nevertheless. Hence their basic natures are identical, too, and can be categorized into
one group."

354 Gao Shishi: "The domination of any of the six qi and the revenge taken by any
of the six qi, go along with the four seasons and with the five agents. Hence 'domination and revenge agree.' For example, the domination of wind agrees with spring, i.e.,
wood. The domination of heat agrees with summer, i.e., fire. Revenge taken by wind
agrees with spring, i.e., wood. Revenge taken by heat agrees with summer, i.e., fire."

Dryness and coolness, smoke and dew agree with the transformations [evoked by] autumn.

Clouds, rain, haziness, darkness, and dust agree with the transformations [evoked by] late summer.

Cold qi, frost, snow, and ice agree with the transformations [evoked by] winter."

These are the transformations of the five periods and six qi of heaven and earth. This is the regular order of the alternating operation of abundance and weakness.

71-476-7
[Huang] Di:

"When the progression of the five periods agrees with the transformations of heaven, that is called 'heavenly complement.'[355] This I have come to know.

I should like to hear what it means 'it agrees with the transformations of the earth.'"[356]

Qi Bo:

"There are three [possibilities] that great excess agrees with the transformations of heaven.[357] There are also three [possibilities] that inadequacy agrees with the

---

355 Fang Yaozhong: " 'Progression of the five periods' refers to the movement of the five periods wood, fire, soil, metal, and water. 'Agree with the transformations of heaven' is: they are identical to the qi controlling heaven in that same year. That is, when the annual period and the qi controlling heaven in that same year agree, that is called 同天化, 'agree with the transformations of heaven.' A year where there is 'agreement with the transformations of heaven' is called 'heavenly complement.'"

356 Fang Yaozhong: " 'Earth' refers to the qi at the fountain. 'Agree with the transformations of the earth' is: the five agents association of the annual period and of the qi at the fountain in that same year agree."

357 Fang Yaozhong: " 'Great excess' refers to years with a greatly excessive annual period. Within the 60 years of a *jia zi* circle, there are three groups [of years] that are associated with a greatly excessive annual period and where the five agents association of the annual period is identical to that of the qi controlling heaven in that same year. The first [group] comprises *wu zi* and *wu wu* years. *Wu* 戊 years belong to the years with a greatly excessive fire period. In *zi* and *wu* years minor yin [qi, i.e.,] ruler fire, controls heaven. [Hence in *wu zi* and *wu wu* years] the five agents association of the annual period and of the qi controlling heaven are identical. The second group are the *wu yin* and *wu shen* years. .. In *yin* and *shen* years minor yang [qi, i.e.,] minister fire, controls heaven. .. The third group are the *bing chen* and *bing xu* years. *Bing* 丙 [years] belong to years with a greatly excessive water period. In *chen* and *xu* years major yang [qi, i.e.,] cold and water, controls heaven. .. These three groups comprise altogether 6 years."

transformations of heaven.[358]

There are three [possibilities] that great excess agrees with the transformations of the earth.[359] There are also three [possibilities] that inadequacy agrees with the transformations of the earth.[360]

Altogether these are 24 years."

---

358 Fang Yaozhong: " 'Inadequate' refers to years with an inadequate annual period. Within the 60 years of a *jia zi* circle, there are three groups of years that are associated with an inadequate annual period and where, at the same time, the five agents association of the annual period is identical to that of the qi controlling heaven in the same year. One group comprises *ding si* and *ding hai* years. *Ding* years belong to the years with an inadequate wood period. In *si* and *hai* years, the ceasing yin [qi, i.e.,] wind and wood, controls heaven. [Hence in *ding si* and *ding hai* years] the five agents association of the annual period and of the qi controlling heaven are identical. The second group are the *yi mao* and *yi you* years. .. In *mao* and *you* years yang brilliance [qi, i.e.,] dryness and metal, controls heaven. .. The third group are the *ji chou* and *ji wei* years. *Ji* 己 [years] belong to years with an inadequate wood period. In *chou* and *wei* years major yin [qi, i.e.,] dampness and soil, controls heaven. .. These three groups comprise altogether 6 years."

359 Fang Yaozhong: " 'Great excess' refers to years with a greatly excessive annual period. 'Agree with the transformations of the earth' is: the five agents association of the annual period and of the qi at the fountain of the same year are identical. Within the 60 years of a *jia zi* circle, there are three groups [of years] that are associated with a greatly excessive annual period and where, at the same time, the five agents association of the annual period is identical to that of the qi at the fountain in that same year. The first [group] comprises *jia chen* and *jia xu* years. *Jia* 甲 years belong to the years with a greatly excessive soil period. In *chen* and *xu* years major yang [qi, i.e.,] cold and water, controls heaven, while major yin [qi, i.e.,] dampness and soil, is at the fountain. [Hence in *jia chen* and *jia xu* years] the five agents association of the annual period and of the qi controlling heaven are identical. The second group are the *ren yin* and *ren shen* years. .. In *yin* and *shen* years minor yang [qi, i.e.,] minister fire, controls heaven, while the ceasing yin [qi, i.e.,] wind and wood, is at the fountain. .. The third group are the *geng zi* and *geng wu* years. *Geng* 庚 [years] belong to years with a greatly excessive metal period. In *zi* and *wu* years minor yin [qi, i.e.,] ruler fire, controls heaven, while the yang brilliance [qi, i.e.,] dryness and metal, is at the fountain. The five agents association of the annual period and of the qi at the fountain in the same year is identical. .. These three groups comprise altogether 6 years."

360 Fang Yaozhong: " 'Inadequate' refers to years with an inadequate annual period. Within the 60 years of a *jia zi* circle, there are three groups of years that are associated with an inadequate annual period and where, at the same time, the five agents association of the annual period is identical to that of the qi at the fountain in the same year. One group comprises *gui si* and *gui hai* years. *Gui* years belong to the years with an inadequate fire period. In *si* and *hai* years the ceasing yin [qi, i.e.,] wind and wood, controls heaven, while the minor yang [qi, i.e.,] minister fire, is at the fountain. [Hence in *gui si* and *gui hai* years,] the five agents association of the annual period

71-476-10
[Huang] Di:
"I should like to hear what that is to say."

Qi Bo:
"In a *jia chen* [year] or a *jia xu* [year], the major *gong* [period] is joined by
major yin [qi] in the lower [half of the year];³⁶¹
in a *ren yin* [year] or a *ren shen* [year], the major *jue* [period]³⁶² is joined by
ceasing yin [qi] in the lower [half of the year];
in a *geng zi* [year] or a *geng wu* [year], the major *shang* [period]³⁶³ is joined by
yang brilliance [qi] in the lower [half of the year].
There are three of this type.

In a *gui si* [year] or a *gui hai* [year], the minor *zhi* [period]³⁶⁴ is joined by minor
yang [qi] in the lower [half of the year];
in a *xin chou* [year] or a *xin wei* [year], the minor *yu* [period]³⁶⁵ is joined by
major yang [qi] in the lower [half of the year];
in a *gui mao* [year] or a *gui you* [year], the minor *zhi* [period]³⁶⁶ is joined by

---

and of the qi at the fountain are identical. The second group are the *xin chou* and *xin
wei* years. .. In *chou* and *wei* years, major yin [qi, i.e.,] dampness and soil, controls
heaven, while major yang [qi, i.e.,] cold and water, is at the fountain. .. The third group
are the *gui mao* and *gui you* years. *Gui* 癸 [years] belong to years with an inadequate
fire period. In *mao* and *you* years, yang brilliance [qi, i.e.,] dryness and metal, controls
heaven, while minor yin [qi, i.e.,] ruler fire, is at the fountain. .. These three groups
comprise altogether 6 years."

361 Zhang Jiebin: "下加 is: that which is above is joined by that which is below. That
is to say: the central period is joined from below by [the qi] at the fountain. Major
gong is joined from below by major yin [qi]; both are soil. Major *jue* is joined from
below by ceasing yin [qi]; both are wood. Major *shang* is joined from below by yang
brilliance [qi]; both are metal. 'Three' is major yin, ceasing yin, and yang brilliance
[qi]." Fang Yaozhong: " 'Major *gong*' refers to a year with a greatly excessive soil period.
下 is the qi at the fountain. 加 is: the annual period and the qi at the fountain join
each other, that is, the five agents association of the annual period and of the qi at the
fountain is identical."

362 Fang Yaozhong: " 'Major *jue*' refers to a year with a greatly excessive wood period."

363 Fang Yaozhong: " 'Major *shang*' refers to a year with a greatly excessive metal
period."

364 Fang Yaozhong: " 'Minor *zhi*' refers to a year with an inadequate fire period."

365 Fang Yaozhong: " 'Minor *yu*' refers to a year with an inadequate water period."

366 Fang Yaozhong: " 'Minor *zhi*' refers to a year with an inadequate fire period."

minor yin [qi] in the lower [half of the year].
There are three of this type.[367]

71-476-14
In a *wu zi* [year] or a *wu wu* [year], the major *zhi* [period], [is joined by] minor yin [qi] coming down in the upper [half of the year];[368]
in a *wu yin* [year] or a *wu shen* [year], the major *zhi* [period], [is joined by] minor yang [qi] coming down in the upper [half of the year];
in a *bing chen* [year] or a *bing xu* [year], the major *yu* [period], [is joined by] major yang [qi] coming down in the upper [half of the year].
There are three of this type.[369]

In a *ding si* [year] or a *ding hai* [year], the minor *jue* [period], [is joined by] ceasing yin [qi] coming down in the upper [half of the year];
in a *yi mao* [year] or a *yi you* [year], the minor *shang* [period], [is joined by] yang brilliance [qi] coming down in the upper [half of the year];
in a *ji chou* [year] or a *ji wei* [year], the minor *gong* [period], [is joined by] major yin [qi] coming down in the upper [half of the year].
There are three of this type.[370]

---

367 Zhang Jiebin: "Minor *zhi* is joined from below by minor yang [qi]; both are fire. Minor *yu* is joined from below by major yang [qi]; both are water. Minor *zhi* is joined from below by minor yin [qi]; both are fire."

368 Fang Yaozhong: "*Wu zi* and *wu wu* years are years with a greatly excessive fire period. In *zi* and *wu* years, the minor yin [qi, i.e.,] ruler fire, controls heaven. The annual period is a greatly excessive fire period; the qi controlling heaven is the minor yin [qi, i.e.,] ruler fire. When the five agents association of the annual period is identical to that of the qi controlling heaven, that is a year of 'heavenly complement.' Hence *wu zi* and *wu wu* years are years of 'heavenly complement.'"

369 Zhang Jiebin: "上臨 is: that which is below [is joined] by the above coming down. That is, the [qi] controlling heaven comes down to [join] the central period. When minor yin and minor yang [qi] come down to [join] minor *gong*, they are all fire. When major yang [qi] comes down to [join] major *yu*, they are both water. 'Three' are minor yin, minor yang, and major yang [qi]." Fang Yaozhong: "上臨 is the [qi] controlling heaven."

370 Zhang Jiebin: "When minor *jue* is joined by ceasing yin [qi] coming down in the upper [half of the year], both are wood. When minor *shang* is joined by yang brilliance [qi] coming down in the upper half of the year, both are metal. When minor *gong* is joined by major yin [qi] coming down in the upper half of the year, both are soil. 'Three' refers to ceasing yin, yang brilliance, and major yin [qi]."

Outside of these 24 years, there is no joining [from below] and no coming
down."³⁷¹

71-476-18
[Huang] Di:
" 'Joining [from below],' what is that to say?"

Qi Bo:
"When great excess is joined [from below] [by the qi at the fountain, that is]
'identical to heavenly complement.'³⁷²

---

371 Zhang Jiebin (2): "When the text speaks of 24 years, this includes only the twelve
'heavenly complement' years and the twelve 'identical to heavenly complement' and
'identical to the year meets' years. These are altogether 24 years. The text does not
speak of 'the year meets' and '*Tai-yi* heavenly complement' [years]." (*Lei jing tu yi*;
Tian fu sui hui tu shuo 類經圖翼. 天符歲會圖說, p..69) Ma Shi: "A circle of 60
years includes four '*tai-yi* heavenly complement' years, twelve 'heavenly complement'
years, eight 'the year meets' years, six 'identical to heavenly complement' years, and six
'identical to the year meets' years. Seen separately, these are altogether 36 years; seen
jointly, these are only 32 years. The classic speaks of 24 years because it does not include the eight 'the year meets' years." Zhang Zhicong: "In altogether 24 years, the [qi]
of the upper and of the lower [halves of the year] join or come down to [the central
period]. This is not the case in the remaining 36 years." Fang Yaozhong: "Within a
circle of 60 years, there are only 28 years with [the central period] being joined from
below or being flanked from above [by the qi at the fountain or by the qi controlling
heaven]. Among them only four years belong to nothing but the group of 'the year
meets' [years], i.e., *ding mao, bing zi, xin hai*, and *geng shen* [years]. *Su wen* 68 states:
'the so-called 'the year meets' is balanced qi.' That is, years of balanced qi belong to
the 'proper years.' Hence years that are purely 'the year meets' need not be considered
among the years [where the central period] is joined from below or is flanked from
above [by the qi at the fountain or controlling heaven]; they can be excluded. When
these four years are subtracted from the above-mentioned 28 years, only 24 years do
in fact remain."

372 Zhang Jiebin: "When the six years [whose central period is] greatly excessive are
joined [from below], in the lower [half of the year by the qi] at the fountain, they are
called 'identical to heavenly complement.' When the six years [whose central period
is] inadequate are joined [from below] in the lower [half of the year by the qi] at the
fountain, they are called 'identical to the year meets.' " Fang Yaozhong: "Years with a
greatly excessive annual period where the five agents association of the annual period
is identical to the five agents association of the qi at the fountain of the same year,
they are called 'identical to heavenly complement' years. To take a *geng zi* year as an
example, the heavenly stem of *geng zi* years is *geng. Yi* and *geng* transform metal. *Geng*
is a yang stem and is associated with great excess. Hence *geng zi* years belong to [the
group of] years with a greatly excessive metal period. The annual branch of *geng zi*
years is *zi*. In *zi* and *wu* [years], the minor yin [qi, i.e.,] ruler fire, controls heaven and

When inadequacy is joined [from below by the qi at the fountain], that is 'identical to the year meets.'"³⁷³

[Huang] Di:
"'Coming down,' what is that to say?"

Qi Bo:
"Great excess and inadequacy are both called heavenly complement.³⁷⁴
However, [it is in accordance with] the extent of the changes in the movements [of the periods, that]
the manifestation of the illnesses is slight or severe and
the [occurrences of] survival and death are early or late."³⁷⁵

---

the yang brilliance [qi, i.e.,] dryness and metal, is at the fountain. The annual period is a greatly excessive metal period and the qi at the fountain is the yang brilliance [qi, i.e.,] dryness and metal. The annual period is greatly excessive and the five agents associations of the the annual period and of the qi at the fountain [of that year] are identical. Hence *geng zi* years are 'identical to heavenly complement' years."

373 Fang Yaozhong: "Years with an inadequante annual period where the five agents associations of the annual period and of the qi at the fountain are identical, they are called 'identical to the year meets' years. To take *xin chou* years as an example, in *xin chou* years, the annual stem is *xin*. *Bing* and *xin* transform water. *Xin* is a yin stem and is associated with inadequacy. Hence *xin chou* years are years with an inadequate water period. The annual brance of *xin chou* years is *chou*. In *chou* and *wei* [years] the major yin [qi, i.e.,] dampness and soil, controls heaven, while the major yang [qi, i.e.,] cold and water, is at the fountain. The annual period is an inadequate water period; the qi at the fountain is major yang [qi, i.e.,] cold and water. The annual period is inadequate and the five agents associations of the annual period and of the the qi at the fountain is identical. Hence *xin chou* years are 'identical to the year meets' years."

374 Fang Yaozhong: "Regardless of whether years with [an annual period of] great excess or inadequacy are concerned, as long as the five agents association of the annual period and of the qi controlling heaven is identical, they are all called years of 'heavenly complement.'"

375 Fang Yaozhong: "Generally speaking, when the climatic changes are drastic, the illnesses of the human body are comparatively serious, too. If a year belongs to those 'heavenly complement' [years] whose annual period is inadequate, then, in general, the climatic changes are minor, the illnesses are comparatively light, and the danger to one's life is relatively small. In contrast, if a year belongs to those 'heavenly complement' [years] whose annual period is greatly excessive, then the climatic changes are comparatively strong, the illnesses are comparatively serious, and the danger to one's life is comparatively great."

71-476-21
[Huang] Di:
"You, Sir, have said:
when employing cold stay away from cold; when employing heat stay away from heat.[376]
I did not know yet that this is so. I should like to hear what 'stay away' means."

Qi Bo:
"[When employing] heat, one should not offend the heat; [when employing] cold, one should not offend the cold.[377]
To follow [this principle results in] harmony; opposition results in illness.
One must respect and fear [cold and heat] and stay away from them."[378]
{This is the so-called "[each] season flourishes at [one of] the six positions."}[379]

---

376 Wang Shaozeng/38: "遠 is an adjective used as verb here in the sense of 避免, 'to avoid.'"

377 Fang Yaozhong: "The first character 熱 refers to the nature and effects of drugs and food employed in therapy; the second character 熱 refers to the nature of a season or of an illness. The same applies to the first and second character 寒. If one offends heat with heat, or cold with cold, that is 逆, 'opposition.'"

378 Wang Bing: "During the months when one of the four seasonal qi rules it is advisable to avoid drugs, food and clothing that are equally cold, hot, warm, or cool. If one employed those [drugs, etc.] which are identical to the four seasons, that would be an offence. I.e., one were to increase water by water, or to aid fire by fire. [Such behavior] must generate illness."

379 Zhang Jiebin: "時 is: the four seasons, i.e., the host qi. 位 is to say: 六部, i.e., the visitor qi. One has to stand in awe of both the host and the visitor qi; not to offend them is 從, 'to follow'; to offend them is 逆, 'opposition.'" Zhang Zhicong: "興 is 起, 'to rise.' The general meaning here is: within the course of one year six positions come up in correspondence with the seasons. Each rules for 60 days plus 87 1/2 *ke*. Each has the four qi cold, hot, warm, and cool; it is advisable to stay away from them and not to offend them. For example, in [the time period associated with] the initial qi, the qi of heaven is still cold and it is advisable to employ hot [drugs]. If at that time the minor yang [qi, i.e.,] minister fire, is in control and issues orders, one should stay away from it rather than offend it. Another example, in [the time period associated with] the second qi, the qi of heaven has warmed up already and it is advisable to employ cool [drugs]. If at that time the major yang [qi, i.e.,] cold and water, issues orders, one should stay away from this position and [not (error corrected by Fang Yaozhong)] employ cool [drugs]. The same applies to all six qi within the course of a year. To follow results in harmony; opposition causes illness. One must respect them and stay away from them." Cheng Shide et al.: "Zhang Jiebin reads 興 as 與. Nevertheless, we read it as 興 and follow the commentary by Zhang Zhicong." Fang Yaozhong: "時 refers to the four seasons here. I.e., these are the positions and time periods occupied within the course of one year by the six qi. These are the 'six steps' (六步) mentioned above. 興

71-477-3
[Huang] Di:
"How about warm and cool [drugs]?"³⁸⁰

Qi Bo:
"If the qi controlling [heaven] is heat, one must not offend it when employing
heat;

if the qi controlling [heaven] is cold, one must not offend it when employing
cold;

if the qi controlling [heaven] is coolness, one must not offend it when employing coolness;

if the qi controlling [heaven] is warmth, one must not offend it when employing warmth.³⁸¹

If the intervening [visitor] qi is identical to the host [qi], one must not cause an
offense.

If [the intervening visitor qi] differs from the host [qi], then one may cause a
little offense.³⁸²

---

has the meaning of 興起, 'to rise,' or 旺盛, 'flourish.' That is, in the course of the four
seasons of one year both the host qi and the visitor qi rule these seasons in six steps.
Hence in treating illnesses and in regulating [the body] by means of drink and food
one must act in accordance with the characteristics of each climatic step."

380 Wang Bing: "Warm and cool [drugs] are less strong than hot and cold [drugs]; is
it possible to employ them for only a slight offence?"

381 Cheng Shide et al.: "司氣 refers to the qi controlling heaven and earth. 無犯 is to
say: cold, hot, warm, and cool [drugs] must not offend the qi in control. That is, when
they must be employed, they must not be employed excessively." Zhang Zhicong:
"When the minor yin [qi] is active in the upper [half of the year], the qi in control is
heat. If [at that time] one employs heat [in therapy] it is nevertheless essential to stay
away from the heat of minor yin and cause no offence."

382 Zhang Jiebin: " 'Intervening qi' are the four intervening visitor qi to the left and
to the right. When the host qi and the intervening visitor qi are identical, the [force
of the] qi is strong; hence it must not be offended. When they differ, [i.e.] the host is
cold and the visitor is heat, or the host is heat and the visitor is cold, the qi is divided,
the evil is not unified. Hence it may be offended a little because its strength [is weak]."
Fang Yaozhong: " 'Intervening qi' are the four intervening [visitor] qi to the left and
right apart from the qi controlling heaven and at the fountain. When the intervening [visitor] qi is entirely identical to the host qi, then it is not advisable to offend
heat with heat, or to offend cold with cold. That is, when the intervening [visitor] qi
is minor yin [qi, i.e.,] ruler fire, and when the host qi is minor yin [qi, i.e.,] ruler fire,
or minor yang [qi, i.e.,] minister fire, then warm or hot drugs can only be used with
great care or in small amounts during that time period. Similarly, in food and in rising
and resting, warmth and heat should be avoided, too. When the intervening [visitor]

These are called 'the four fears.'
This must be investigated carefully."

71-477-6
[Huang] Di:
"Good!
If it comes to an offense, how does one proceed?"[383]

Qi Bo:
"When the qi of heaven is contrary to the season, then one can still follow the [requirements of the] season.[384]
When it comes to [a season] when the [visitor qi] dominates the host [qi], then [the visitor qi] can be offended.[385]

---

qi differs from the host qi, [warm or hot drugs, etc.] may be employed in accordance with the nature of the visitor qi; the restrictions mentioned above, i.e., not to offend heat with heat and not to offend cold with cold, do not apply here. For example, when the host qi is minor yin [qi, i.e.,] ruler fire, while the visitor qi is major yang [qi, i.e.,] cold and water, or yang brilliance [qi, i.e.,] dryness and metal, then it is possible in this time period, because the visitor qi is associated with cold and cool, to employ warm or hot drugs in appropriate quantities for treatment."

383 Wang Bing: "In case an offence is unavoidable."

384 Zhang Jiebin: " 'Qi of heaven' is the visitor qi; 'season' is the host qi. When the visitor [qi] does not agree with the host [qi], that is called 'in contrast to the season.' Because the host qi follows its regular course while the visitor qi is slightly unstable, [a treatment] must follow the host [qi]." Gao Shishi: "The 'qi of heaven' is the proper qi ruling a season. 'It is in contrast to the season' is: it is cold when it should be hot; it is hot when it should be cold. 'Then one can still follow the [requirements of the] season' is to say: when it is cold while it should be hot, cold is treated with heat. when it is hot while it should be cold, heat is treated with cold." Fang Yaozhong: "When the climate does not agree with the orders issued by a given season, in general the climate that should be present in that season should be taken as guideline."

385 Fang Yaozhong: "This refers to a serious discrepancy between a season and its actual climate. For example, when spring carries out the orders of autumn, or when autumn carries out the orders or summer, or when winter carries out the orders of spring, in such cases it is not advisable to base [a treatment] entirely on [the climate that should be present in] that season, rather it is advisable to proceed in accordance with the actual changes. I.e., in summer it should be hot but is not hot. Under normal conditions the characteristics of summer should be taken into account [in a treatment], that is, when employing heat stay away from heat. However, if there is a serious discrepancy, if summer carries out the orders of winter, if snow falls in the sixth month, then it is impossible to cling to the principles outlined above mechanically."

One does this until a balance is reached. [This limit] must not be exceeded."³⁸⁶
< This is [a situation] called 'the evil qi, contrary [to the regular order], domi-
nates.' > ³⁸⁷

71-477-9
Hence when it is said:
'Not to lose the trust in heaven and
not to oppose the requirements of the qi,
so as not to give wings to its dominating [qi] and
not to support its revenge,'
[then] this is what is called 'perfect treatment.' "³⁸⁸

71-477-11
[Huang] Di:
"Good!
Is the arrangement of the five periods and of the movements of the [six] qi as
they rule a year,
based on regular numbers?"³⁸⁹

Qi Bo:
"Please let [me, your] subject, list them one by one.

---

386 Wang Bing: "When the qi is balanced, then [the treatment] is to be stopped. Excessive [treatment] generates illness. Excessive treatment resulting in illness is identical to an offence."

387 Fang Yaozhong: " 'Dominates' is to say: a visitor qi dominates the host qi."

388 Wang Bing: "天信 is to say: the arrival time must be fixed." Zhang Jiebin: "The
periods of visitor and host qi should arrive 'in time'; that is 'the trust of heaven.' When
they do not agree with the qi of a given season, the trust of heaven is lost. The realization of cold, heat, warmth, and coolness should be in time; that is the requirement of
the qi. Not to care about whether [a therapy] opposes or follows [the seasonal qi] is
to oppose the requirements of the qi. To give wings to the dominating [qi] and heat;
or to employ cold to offend cold and to disregard the [usual] restrictions. The same
applies to warmth and coolness."

389 Cheng Shide et al.: "The numbers applied here originate from the 'generation'
and 'completion' numbering of the five agents in the *River Map* (河圖) [diagram].
Like: 'Heaven, one, generates water. The earth, six, completes it. The earth, two, generates fire. Heaven, seven, completes it. Heaven, three, generates wood. The earth, eight,
completes it. The earth, four, generates metal. Heaven, nine, completes it. Heaven, five,
generates soil. The earth, ten, completes it.' The 'generation' number of water is one;
its 'completion' number is six. The 'generation' number of fire is two; its 'completion'
number is seven, and so on."

Jia zi and *jia wu* years:

In the upper [half of the year]: minor yin, fire.
In the center: major *gong*, soil period.
In the lower [half of the year]: yang brilliance, metal.[390]

Heat transformation: two.
Rain transformation: five.
Dryness transformation: four.[391]
These are the so-called days of proper transformation.[392]

---

390 Gao Shishi: "In *zi* and *wu* years minor yin [qi] controls heaven. Hence [the text states:] 'In the upper [half of the year]: minor yin, fire.' *Jia* stands for a greatly excessive soil period. Hence [the text states:] 'In the center: major *gong*, soil period.' When minor yin [qi is active] in the upper [half of a year], then yang brilliance [qi is active] in the lower [half of a year]. Hence [the text states:] 'In the lower [half of the year]: yang brilliance, metal.'" Fang Yaozhong: "上 refers to the qi controlling heaven. 少陰火 is: minor yin [qi, i.e.,] ruler fire. 中 refers to the central period, i.e., the annual period. 'Major *gong*' is a year with a greatly excessive soil period. 下 refers to the qi at the fountain. 陽明金 is: yang brilliance [qi, i.e.,] dryness and metal. The meaning of the entire sentence is: *Jia zi* and *jia wu* years are years with a greatly excessive soil period. Minor yin [qi, i.e.,] ruler fire, controls heaven; yang ming [qi, i.e.,] dryness and metal, is at the fountain."

391 Cheng Shide et al.: "The generation number of fire is two; hence 'heat transformation: two.' Five is the number of soil; hence 'rain transformation: five.' Four is the generation number of metal. Hence 'dryness transformation: four.'" Fang Yaozhong: "熱化 refers to the qi controlling heaven in *jia zi* and *jia wu* years. In *jia zi* and *jia wu* years minor yin [qi, i.e.,] ruler fire, controls heaven. Minor yin rules heat. Hence in the upper half of *jia zi* and *jia wu* years, the climate is disproportionately hot and the transformation and generation of the myriad beings is affected by the qi of heat. 雨化 refers to the annual period of *jia zi* and *jia wu* years. *Jia zi* and *jia wu* years are years with a greatly excessive soil period. Soil rules dampness. Hence in the summer time of *jia zi* and *jia wu* years dampness qi is disproportionally abundant; rain and water increase disproportionately and the transformation and generation of the myriad beings is affected by the qi of dampness. 燥化 refers to the qi at the fountain in *jia zi* and *jia wu* years. In *jia zi* and *jia wu* years yang brilliance [qi, i.e.,] dryness and metal, is at the fountain. Yang brilliance rules coolness and it rules dryness. Hence in *jia zi* and *jia wu* years, the climate is disproportionally cool and disproportionally dry in the lower half of the year and the transformation and generation of the myriad beings is affected by cool qi and by dryness qi."

392 Wang Bing: "These are the transformations of the proper qi." Zhang Jiebin: "This is a summary of the preceding three sentences elucidating the [time] limits of the proper transformations of the three qi in the upper [half of a year], the center, and the lower [half]. Proper transformations are transformations of the proper qi. 度 is 日, 'day'; 日 is 度; [日] refers to the date when a specific qi command is activated." In

These transformations
in the upper [half of the year require] salty [flavor] and cold,
in the center [require] bitter [flavor] and heat,
in the lower [half of the year require] sour [flavor] and heat.
These are the so-called requirements of drugs and food.[393]

71-478-4
Yi chou and *yi wei* years:

In the upper [half of the year]: major yin, soil.
In the center: minor *shang*, metal period.
In the lower [half of the year]: major yang, water.[394]

Heat transformation, cold transformation; domination and revenge are identical [in these two years].[395]
These are the so-called days of evil qi transformation.[396]

Catastrophes occur in the seventh mansion.[397]

---

an astronomical context, 度 refers to one day in the solar calendar. See below *Su wen* 71-482-8 (see note 442).

393 Zhang Zhicong: "Ruler fire controls heaven; hence it is advisable to employ salty [flavor] and cold to restrain its transformation. The major yin, [i.e.,] dampness and soil, period transforms in the center. Hence it is advisable to employ bitter [flavor] to dry the dampness and to employ heat to warm the yin. Yang brilliance [qi, i.e.,] coolness, is at the fountain. Hence it is advisable to employ sour [flavor] to assist gathering and to employ heat to warm the coolness. Both drugs and food must be appropriate."

394 Fang Yaozhong: "Major yin [qi, i.e.,] dampness and soil, controls heaven. 'In the center minor *shang*, metal period' refers to a year with an inadequate metal period. Major yang [qi, i.e.,] cold and water, is at the fountain. The entire sentence states: *Yi chou* and *yi wei* years are years of an inadequate metal period. The major yin [qi, i.e.,] dampness and soil, controls heaven, while the major yang [qi, i.e.,] cold and water, is at the fountain."

395 Cheng Shide et al.: "The metal period is inadequate. Hence there are heat transformations because fire qi arrives to dominate. Domination must be followed by revenge. Heat qi dominates metal. Hence there are cold transformations because the water qi arrives to take revenge. 同 refers to the fact that these qi of domination and revenge are present in the two years *yi chou* and *yi wei* alike."

396 Cheng Shide et al.: "邪化 refers to the qi of domination and revenge; neither is associated with the proper transformations of the body itself."

397 Cheng Shide et al.: " 'Seventh mansion' refers to the proper West." Fang Yaozhong: "The meaning is: in *yi chou* and *yi wei* years natural catastrophes occur in the West."

Dampness transformation: five.
Coolness transformation: four.
Cold transformation: six.
These are the so-called days of proper transformation.[398]

These transformations
in the upper [half of the year require] bitter [flavor] and heat,
in the center [require] sour [flavor] and harmonious [nature],
in the lower [half of the year require] sweet [flavor] and heat.
These are the so-called drug and food requirements.[399]

71-478-9
Bing yin and *bing shen* years:

In the upper [half of the year]: minor yang, minister fire.
In the center: major *yu*, water period.
In the lower [half of the year]: ceasing yin, wood.[400]

Fire transformation: two.
Cold transformation: six.

---

398 Fang Yaozhong: "濕化 refers to the qi controlling heaven in *yi chou* and *yi wei*
years. In *yi chou* and *yi wei* years major yin [qi] controls heaven. Minor yin rules
dampness. Hence in the upper half of *yi chou* and *yi wei* years, the climate is disproportionally damp and the transformation and generation of the myriad beings in this
time period is affected by the qi of dampness. 清化 refers to the annual period of *yi
chou* and *yi wei* years. *Yi chou* and *yi wei* years are years with an inadequate metal period. Metal rules coolness and it rules dryness. Because the metal period is inadequate,
the climate in *yi chou* and *yi wei* years is not cool even though it should be cool and it
is not dry even though it should be dry and this has an influence on the regular generation and growth of living beings in autumn. 寒化 refers to the qi at the fountain in
yi chou and *yi wei* years. In *yi chou* and *yi wei* years major yang [qi] is at the fountain.
Major yang rules cold. Hence in *yi chou* and *yi wei* years, the climate is disproportionally cold in the second half of the year. As a result, the myriad beings receive too much
cold and their generation as well as growth stop."

399 Fang Yaozhong: "Bitter [flavor] is able to dry dampness; warmth can transform
dampness. Drugs and food with a sour flavor can assist in the gathering of yang qi.
Sweet [flavor] and heat can disperse cold and warm the center."

400 Fang Yaozhong: "*Bing yin* and *bing shen* years are years with a greatly excessive
water period. Minor yang [qi, i.e.,] minister fire, controls heaven, and ceasing yin [qi,
i.e.,] wind and wood, is at the fountain."

Wind transformation: three.[401]
These are the so-called days of proper transformation.

These transformations
in the upper [half of the year require] salty [flavor] and cold,
in the center [require] salty [flavor] and warmth,
in the lower [half of the year require] acrid [flavor] and warmth.[402]
These are the so-called requirements of drugs and food.

71-479-4
Ding mao the year meets and *ding you* years:

In the upper [half of the year]: yang brilliance, metal.
In the center: minor *jue*, wood period.

---

401 Fang Yaozhong: "火化 refers to the qi controlling heaven in *bing yin* and *bing shen* years. In *bing yin* and *bing shen* years minor yang [qi, i.e.,] minister fire, controls heaven. Minor yang rules fire. Hence in the upper half of *bing yin* and *bing shen* years, the climate is disproportionally hot and the transformation and generation of the myriad beings in this time period is affected by the qi of flaming heat. 寒化 refers to the annual period of *bing yin* and *bing shen* years. *Bing yin* and *bing shen* years are years with a greatly excessive water period. Water rules cold. Hence in the winter of *bing yin* and *bing shen* years, the climate is very cold and the transformation and generation of the myriad beings comes to a halt because they are affected by too much cold. 風化 refers to the qi at the fountain in *bing yin* and *bing shen* years. In *bing yin* and *bing shen* years ceasing yin [qi, i.e.,] wind and wood, is at the fountain. Ceasing yin rules wind. Hence in *bing yin* and *bing shen* years, there is a disproportionate dominance of wind, together with a disproportionately warm climate, in the second half of the year. As a result the transformation and generation of the myriad beings is affected by the qi of wind."

402 Fang Yaozhong: "上鹹寒 is: because the minor yang [qi, i.e.,] minister fire, rules heaven in the upper half of the year, the climate is disproportionally hot. Hence in treating illnesses and regulating [the organism] through food and drink, it is appropriate to employ drugs or food with a salty flavor and with cold nature. The reason is that salty [flavor] is able to drain heat and that cold can bring down fire. 中鹹溫 is: because these are years of a greatly excessive water period, the climate is disproportionately cold. Cold can harm the kidneys. Hence in treating illnesses and regulating [the organism] through food and drink, it is appropriate to employ drugs or food with a salty flavor and with warm nature. The reason is that salty [flavor] can enter the kidneys, while warmth can disperse cold. 下辛溫 is: because in the second half of the year ceasing yin [qi, i.e.,] wind and wood, is at the fountain, wind qi dominates disproportionately, and the climate is disproportionately warm. On the basis of the therapeutic principles of 'do not offend heat with heat' and 'do not offend cold with cold,' it is advisable under these circumstances to employ drugs or food of an acrid flavor and cool nature when treating illnesses or regulating through food and drink."

In the lower [half of the year]: minor yin, fire.⁴⁰³

Coolness transformation, heat transformation; domination and revenge are identical [in these two years].⁴⁰⁴
These are the so-called days of evil qi transformation.

Catastrophes occur in the third mansion.⁴⁰⁵

Dryness transformation: nine.
Wind transformation: three.
Heat transformation: seven.⁴⁰⁶
These are the so-called days of proper transformation.

These transformations
in the upper [half of the year require] bitter [flavor] and slight warmth,
in the center [require] acrid [flavor] and harmonious [nature],

---

403　Fang Yaozhong: "*Ding mao* and *ding you* years are years of an inadequate wood period. Yang brilliance [qi, i.e.,] dryness and metal, controls heaven, while minor yin [qi, i.e.,] ruler fire, is at the fountain."

404　Fang Yaozhong: "清化 refers to years with an inadequate wood period. In spring it is not warm when it should be warm; the climate is disproportionately cool. Speaking in terms of the five agents doctrine, when the qi of wood is inadequate, metal (i.e., coolness) comes to seize it. 熱化 refers to years with an inadequate wood period. Metal comes to seize the wood. However, when the qi of metal has assumed disproportionate domination, fire qi will arrive to take revenge."

405　Fang Yaozhong: " 'Third mansion' refers to the East."

406　Fang Yaozhong: "燥化 refers to the qi controlling heaven in *ding mao* and *ding you* years. In *ding mao* and *ding you* years yang brilliance [qi, i.e.,] dryness and metal, controls heaven. Yang brilliance rules coolness and it rules dryness. Hence in the upper half of *ding mao* and *ding you* years, the climate is disproportionally cool and it is disproportionately dry and the transformation and generation of the myriad beings is affected by the qi of dryness. 風化 refers to the annual period of *ding mao* and *ding you* years. *Ding mao* and *ding you* years are years with an inadequate wood period. Wood rules wind and it rules dampness. Because the wood period is inadequate, in *ding mao* and *ding you* years spring is not warm even though it should be warm. The climate is disproportionately cool and this has an influence on the sprouting, generation, and transformation of the living beings. 熱化 refers to the qi at the fountain in *ding mao* and *ding you* years. In *ding mao* and *ding you* years minor yin [qi, i.e.,] ruler fire, is at the fountain. Minor yin rules heat. The transformation and generation of the myriad beings is affected by the qi of wind."

in the lower [half of the year require] salty [flavor] and cold.[407]
These are the so-called requirements of drugs and food.

71-479-9
Wu chen and *wu xu* years:

In the upper [half of the year]: major yang, water.
In the center: major *zhi*, fire period.
In the lower [half of the year]: major yin, soil.[408]

Cold transformation: six.
Heat transformation: seven.
Dampness transformation: five.[409]
These are the so-called days of proper transformation.

---

407 Fang Yaozhong: "上苦小溫 is: because the yang brilliance [qi, i.e.,] dryness and
metal, rules heaven in the upper half of the year, the climate is disproportionately cool.
Hence in treating illnesses and regulating [the organism] through food and drink, it
is appropriate to employ drugs or food with a bitter flavor and with warm nature. The
reason is that warmth is able to dominate coolness. 中辛和 is: because these are years
of an inadequate wood period, the climate is not warm when it should be warm and
the liver qi is inadequate. Hence in treating illnesses and regulating [the organism]
through food and drink, it is appropriate to employ drugs or food with an acrid flavor
and with a comparatively warm and harmonious nature. The reason is that 'the liver
[qi] wishes to disperse. Hence one quickly consumes acrid flavor to disperse it.' 下
鹹寒 is: because in the second half of the year minor yin [qi, i.e.,] ruler fire, is at the
fountain, the climate is disproportionately hot. Hence it is advisable to employ drugs
or food of a salty flavor and cold nature when treating illnesses or regulating through
food and drink."

408 Fang Yaozhong: "*Wu chen* and *wu xu* years are years of a greatly excessive fire
period. Major yang [qi, i.e.,] cold and water, controls heaven, while major yin [qi, i.e.,]
dampness and soil, is at the fountain."

409 Fang Yaozhong: "寒化 refers to the qi controlling heaven in *wu chen* and *wu
xu* years. In *wu chen* and *wu xu* years major yang [qi, i.e.,] cold and water, controls
heaven. Major yang rules cold. Hence in the upper half of *wu chen* and *wu xu* years,
the climate is very cold and the transformation and generation of the myriad beings
in this time period is affected by the qi of great cold. 熱化 refers to the annual period
of *wu chen* and *wu xu* years. *Wu chen* and *wu xu* years are years with a greatly excessive fire period. Water rules heat. Hence in the summer of *wu chen* and *wu xu* years,
the climate is very hot and the transformation and generation of the myriad beings
is affected by flaming heat. 濕化 refers to the qi at the fountain in *wu chen* and *wu
xu* years. In *wu chen* and *wu xu* years major yin [qi, i.e.,] dampness and soil, is at the
fountain. Major yin rules dampness. Hence in *wu chen* and *wu xu* years, there is a disproportionate abundance of dampnness qi, together with a disproportionate increase

These transformations
in the upper [half of the year require] bitter [flavor] and warmth,
in the center [require] sweet [flavor] and harmonious [nature],
in the lower [half of the year require] sweet [flavor] and warmth.[410]
These are the so-called requirements of drugs and food.

71-480-1
Ji si and *ji hai* years:

In the upper [half of the year]: ceasing yin, wood.
In the center: minor *gong*, soil period.
In the lower [half of the year]: minor yang, minister fire.[411]

Wind transformation, coolness transformation; domination and revenge are
identical [in these two years].[412]
These are the so-called days of evil qi transformation.

---

in rain and water, in the second half of the year. The transformation and generation of
the myriad beings is affected by the qi of wind."

410 Fang Yaozhong: "上苦溫 is: because the major yang [qi, i.e.,] cold and water, rules
heaven in the upper half of the year, the climate is disproportionately cold. Hence in
treating illnesses and regulating [the organism] through food and drink, it is appropriate to employ drugs or food with a bitter flavor and with warm nature. The reason
is that cold can harm the kidneys and that bitter [flavor] can supplement the kidneys. 中甘和 is: because these are years of a greatly excessive fire period, the climate
is disproportionately hot. Hence in treating illnesses and regulating [the organism]
through food and drink, it is appropriate to employ drugs or food with a sweet flavor
and with cold nature that are relatively balanced [in their qi]. The reason is that sweet
[flavor] and cold [nature] can cool heat. 下甘溫 is: because in the second half of the
year major yin [qi, i.e.,] dampness and soil, is at the fountain, dampness qi dominates
disproportionately. Hence it is advisable to employ drugs or food of a sweet flavor and
warm nature when treating illnesses or regulating through food and drink, because
dampness can harm the spleen, sweet [flavor] can supplement the spleen, and warmth
can transform dampness."

411 Fang Yaozhong: "*Ji si* and *ji hai* years are years with an inadequate soil period.
Ceasing yin [qi, i.e.,] wind and wood, controls heaven, while minor yang [qi, i.e.,]
minister fire, is at the fountain."

412 Fang Yaozhong: "*Ji si* and *ji hai* years are years of an inadequate soil period.
Because the soil period is inadequate, wood comes to seize it. Hence in the summer
of these years wind qi dominates disproportionately, while rain and water are diminished. However, because of the principle of domination and revenge, when wind qi
dominates disproportionately, the qi of coolness and metal must come to take revenge.
Hence in the subsequent autumn the climate is cooler than in ordinary years."

Catastrophes occur in the fifth mansion.⁴¹³

Wind transformation: three.
Dampness transformation: five.
Fire transformation: seven.⁴¹⁴
These are the so-called days of proper transformation.

These transformations
in the upper [half of the year require] acrid [flavor] and coolness,
in the center [require] sweet and harmonious [nature],
in the lower [half of the year require] salty [flavor] and cold.⁴¹⁵
These are the so-called requirements of drugs and food.

---

413 Fang Yaozhong: "This is the central mansion; it symbolizes the center."

414 Fang Yaozhong: "風化 refers to the qi controlling heaven in *ji si and ji hai* years. In *ji si* and *ji hai* years ceasing yin [qi, i.e.,] wind and wood, controls heaven. Ceasing yin rules wind and it rules warmth. Hence there is a disproportionate domination of wind in the upper half of *ji si* and *ji hai* years and the climate is disproportionately warm. Because the climate is warm and mild and because of a disproportionate domi-nation of wind, the myriad beings come to life and grow. 濕化 refers to the annual period of *ji si* and *ji hai* years. *Ji si* and *ji hai* years are years with an inadequate soil period. When the soil period is inadequate, strong winds blow. Hence there is not much rain and water in late summer of these two years. It should be damp, but it is not damp. Droughts occur. The transformation and generation of the myriad beings is influenced by the lack of rain and water. 火化 refers to the qi at the fountain in *ji si* and *ji hai* years. In *ji si* and *ji hai* years minor yang [qi, i.e.,] minister fire, is at the fountain. Minor yang rules fire and it rules heat. Hence there is a disproportionate domination of fire qi in the lower half of *ji si* and *ji hai* years and the climate is dis-proportionately hot. Because the climate is disproportionately hot, the myriad beings come to life and grow."

415 Fang Yaozhong: "上辛涼 is: because the ceasing yin [qi, i.e.,] wind and wood, rules heaven in the upper half of the year, the climate is disproportionately warm and there is a disproportionate domination of wind qi. Hence in treating illnesses and regulating [the organism] through food and drink, it is appropriate to employ drugs or food with an acrid flavor and with cool nature. The reason is that acrid [flavor] is able to scatter wind and that coolness can dominate warmth. 中甘和 is: because these are years of an inadequate soil period, in treating illnesses and regulating [the organism] through food and drink, it is appropriate to employ drugs or food with a sweet flavor and with a harmonious nature. The reason is that sweet [flavor] is the flavor of soil. Because the soil qi is inadequate, the soil is to be supplemented by means of drugs or food with a sweet flavor. 下鹹寒 is: because in the second half of the year minor yang [qi, i.e.,] minister fire, is at the fountain, the qi of fire dominates disproportionately. Hence it is advisable to employ drugs or food of an salty flavor and cold nature when treating

71-480-6
Geng wu identical to heavenly complements and *geng zi* years identical to heavenly complements:

In the upper [half of the year]: minor yin, fire.
In the center: major *shang*, metal period.
In the lower [half of the year]: yang brilliance, metal.⁴¹⁶

Heat transformation: seven.
Coolness transformation: nine.
Dryness transformation: nine.⁴¹⁷
These are the so-called days of proper transformation.

These transformations
in the upper [half of the year require] salty [flavor] and cold,
in the center [require] acrid [flavor] and warmth,
in the lower [half of the year require] sour [flavor] and warmth.⁴¹⁸
These are the so-called requirements of drugs and food.

---

illnesses or regulating through food and drink. The reason is that salty [flavor] can dominate fire and that cold can dominate heat."

416 Fang Yaozhong: "*Geng wu* and *geng zi* years are years with a greatly excessive metal period. Minor yin [qi, i.e.,] ruler fire, controls heaven, while yang brilliance [qi, i.e.,] dryness and metal, is at the fountain."

417 Fang Yaozhong: "熱化 refers to the qi controlling heaven in *geng wu* and *geng zi* years. In *geng wu* and *geng zi* years minor yin [qi, i.e.,] ruler fire, controls heaven. Minor yin rules heat. Hence in the upper half of *geng wu* and *geng zi* years, the climate is disproportionately hot and the transformation and generation of the myriad beings is affected by the qi of fire and heat. 清化 refers to the annual period of *geng wu* and *geng zi* years. *Geng wu* and *geng zi* years are years with a greatly excessive metal period. Metal rules coolness and it rules dryness. Hence in the autumn of *geng wu* and *geng zi* years, the climate is cool and dry and the normal generation and growth, as well as collection and completion, of the myriad beings is influenced by this qi of coolness and dryness. 燥化 refers to the qi at the fountain in *geng wu* and *geng zi* years. In *geng wu* and *geng zi* years yang brilliance [qi, i.e.,] dryness and metal, is at the fountain. Hence in *geng wu* and *geng zi* years, the climate is disproportionately cool and disproportionately dry in the second half of the year. The generation, growth, collection, and completion of the myriad beings is influenced by this."

418 Fang Yaozhong: "上鹹寒 is: because the minor yin [qi, i.e.,] ruler fire, rules heaven in the upper half of the year, the climate is disproportionately hot. Hence in treating illnesses and regulating [the organism] through food and drink, it is appropriate to employ drugs or food with a salty flavor and with cold nature. The reason is that cold can dominate heat. 中辛溫 is: because these are years of a greatly excessive metal pe-

71-480-10
Xin wei identical to year meets and *xin chou* years identical to year meets:

In the upper [half of the year]: major yin, soil.
In the center: minor *yu*, water period.
In the lower [half of the year]: major yang, water.[419]

Rain transformation, wind transformation; domination and revenge are identical [in these two years].[420]
These are the so-called days of evil qi transformation.

Catastrophes occur in the first mansion.[421]

Rain transformation: five.
Cold transformation: one.[422]
These are the so-called days of proper transformation.

---

riod, the climate is disproportionately cool. Hence in treating illnesses and regulating [the organism] through food and drink, it is appropriate to employ drugs or food with a acrid flavor and with warm nature. The reason is that warmth can dominate coolness. 下酸溫 is: because in the second half of the year yang brilliance [qi, i.e.,] dryness and metal, is at the fountain, the climate is disproportionately cool. Hence it is advisable to employ drugs or food of a sour flavor and warm nature when treating illnesses or regulating through food and drink. Because metal can dominate wood, coolness can harm the liver; sour [flavor], in turn, can supplement the liver and warmth can dominate coolness."

419 Fang Yaozhong: "*Xin wei* and *xin chou* years are years with an inadequate water period. Major yin [qi, i.e.,] dampness and soil, controls heaven, while major yang [qi, i.e.,] cold and water, is at the fountain."

420 Fang Yaozhong: "雨化 refers to the major yin qi, [i.e.,] dampness and soil. 風化 refers to the ceasing yin qi, [i.e.,] wind and wood. *Xin wei* and *xin chou* years are years with an inadequate water period. When the water period is inadequate, soil comes to seize it. Hence the initial period of the visitor periods, as well as winter, of such years can display phenomena of disproportionately dominant dampness qi. However, because of the principle of domination and revenge, at a time when dampness qi is disproportionately dominant, wind qi will come to take revenge. Hence occasionally climatic changes towards a disproportionate domination of wind qi may occur."

421 Fang Yaozhong: "The 'first mansion' refers to the North."

422 Fang Yaozhong: "雨化 refers to the qi controlling heaven in *xin wei* and *xin chou* years. In *xin wei* and *xin chou* years major yin [qi, i.e.,] dampness and soil, controls heaven. Major yin rules dampness. Hence there is a disproportionate domination of dampness in the upper half of *xin wei* and *xin chou* years. The transformation and generation of the myriad beings is affected by this qi of rain and dampness. 寒化

These transformations
in the upper [half of the year require] bitter [flavor] and heat,
in the center [require] bitter [flavor] and harmonious [nature],
in the lower [half of the year require] bitter [flavor] and heat.[423]
These are the so-called requirements of drugs and food.

71-481-3
Ren shen identical to heavenly complements and *ren yin* years identical to heavenly
complements:

---

refers to the annual period of *xin wei* and *xin chou* years. *Xin wei* and *xin chou* years
are years with an inadequate water period. Water rules cold. Hence in *xin wei* and *xin
chou* years, the orders or winter arrive late; it is not cold when it should be cold. Also,
the myriad beings that should be stored are not stored and they are influenced by this
in their transformation and generation. What remains to be pointed out is that the
regular number of the qi at the fountain is not listed in this section. The reason is that
the regular number of the qi at the fountain is identical to that of the annual period.
Hence it did not have to be listed separately. The qi at the fountain in *xin wei* and
xin chou years is major yang [qi, i.e.,] cold and water, and the final qi of the host qi is
major yang [qi, i.e.,] cold and water, too. The qi at the fountain is also major yang [qi,
i.e.,] cold and water. Hence the climate should be disproportionately cold, but because
the annual period is an inadequate water period, the order of winter should be cold,
but is not cold. Hence it is only the generation number of water that could be listed
as the regular number of the qi at the fountain, 'cold transformation: one,' rather than
the completion number."

423 Fang Yaozhong: "上苦熱 is: because the major yin [qi, i.e.,] dampness and soil, rules
heaven in the upper half of the year, the climate is disproportionately damp. Hence
in treating illnesses and regulating [the organism] through food and drink, it is appropriate to employ drugs or food with a bitter flavor and with hot nature. The reason
is that bitter [flavor] is able to dry dampness and that heat can transform dampness.
中苦和 is: because these are years of an inadequate water period, dampness prevails
massively. It is not cold when it should be cold and the climate is disproportionately
hot. Dampness and heat interact [and generate] steam. Hence in treating illnesses and
regulating [the organism] through food and drink, it is appropriate to employ drugs
or food with a bitter flavor and with a balanced and harmonious nature. The reason
is that bitter [flavor] can dry dampness and is able to cool heat. 下苦熱 is: because in
the second half of the year major yang [qi, i.e.,] cold and water, is at the fountain, the
climate should be cold. However, because the annual period is an inadequate water
period and because, as a result, dampness prevails massively, it is advisable to employ
drugs or food of an bitter flavor and hot nature when treating illnesses or regulating
through food and drink. The reason is that bitter [flavor] can dry dampness, that heat
can dominate cold, and that heat can transform dampness. To summarize, the climatic
changes in *xin wei* and *xin chou* years are dominated by dampness and heat. Hence [in
treating illnesses] bitter/warm and bitter/hot drugs and food are most important."

In the upper [half of the year]: minor yang, minister fire.
In the center: major *jue*, wood period.
In the lower [half of the year]: ceasing yin, wood.[424]

Fire transformation: two.
Wind transformation: eight.[425]
These are the so-called days of proper transformation.

These transformations
in the upper [half of the year require] salty [flavor] and cold,
in the center [require] sour [flavor] and harmonious [nature],
in the lower [half of the year require] acrid [flavor] and coolness.[426]
These are the so-called requirements of drugs and food.

---

424 Fang Yaozhong: "*Ren shen* and *ren yin* years are years with a greatly excessive wood period. Minor yang [qi, i.e.,] minister fire, controls heaven, while ceasing yin [qi, i.e.,] wind and wood, is at the fountain."

425 Fang Yaozhong: "火化 refers to the qi controlling heaven in *ren shen* and *ren yin* years. In *ren shen* and *ren yin* years minor yang [qi, i.e.,] minister fire, controls heaven. Minor yang rules fire. Hence in the upper half of *ren shen* and *ren yin* years, the climate is disproportionately hot and the transformation and generation of the myriad beings is affected by the qi of fire and heat. 風化 refers to the annual period of *ren shen* and *ren yin* years. *Ren shen* and *ren yin* years are years with a greatly excessive wood period. Wood rules wind and it rules warmth. Hence in the autumn of *ren shen* and *ren yin* years, the order of spring arrives early; the qi of wind dominates disproportionately and the climate is disproportionately warm. The transformation and generation of the myriad beings is affected by this disproportionately dominating qi. In *ren shen* and *ren yin* years, the qi at the fountain is ceasing yin [qi, i.e.,] wind and wood; the annual period is a greatly excessive wood period and the qi at the fountain is ceasing yin [qi, i.e.,] wind and wood, too. Hence in the second half of [*ren shen* and] *ren yin* years, the qi of wind dominates disproportionately and the climate is disproportionately warm; it should be cold but is not cold; [the things] should be stored but are not stored. Hence the generation number of wood should be listed as its regular number, that is: 'wind transformation: eight.' Because this number is identical to the regular number of the annual period, is was not listed here separately."

426 Fang Yaozhong: "上鹹寒 is: because the minor yang [qi, i.e.,] minister fire, rules heaven in the upper half of the year, the climate is disproportionately hot. Hence in treating illnesses and regulating [the organism] through food and drink, it is appropriate to employ drugs or food with a salty flavor and with cold nature. The reason is that salty [flavor] can dominate fire and that cold can dominate heat. 中酸和 is: because these are years of a greatly excessive wood period, the wind qi dominates disproportionately and the climate is disproportionately warm. The liver qi in the human body corresponds to this by disproportionate domination. Hence in treating illnesses and regulating [the organism] through food and drink, it is appropriate to employ drugs

71-481-7
Gui you identical to year meets and *gui mao* years identical to year meets:

In the upper [half of the year]: yang brilliance, metal.
In the center: minor *zhi*, fire period.
In the lower [half of the year]: minor yin, fire.[427]

Cold transformation, rain transformation; domination and revenge are identical
[in these two years].[428]
These are the so-called days of evil qi transformation.

Catastrophes occur in the ninth mansion.[429]

Dryness transformation: nine.
Heat transformation: two.[430]
These are the so-called days of proper transformation.

These transformations
in the upper [half of the year require] bitter [flavor] and slight warmth,
in the center [require] salty [flavor] and warmth,

---

or food with a sour flavor and with a balanced and harmonious nature. The reason is
that sour [flavor] can drain and also nourish the liver. 下辛涼 is: because in the second
half of the year ceasing yin [qi, i.e.,] wind and wood, is at the fountain it is advisable
to employ drugs or food of an acrid flavor and cool nature when treating illnesses or
regulating through food and drink. The reason is that acrid [flavor] can scatter the
wind and that coolness can dominate warmth."

427 Fang Yaozhong: "*Gui you* and *gui mao* years are years with an inadequate fire
period. Yang brilliance [qi, i.e.,] dryness and metal, controls heaven, while minor yin
[qi, i.e.,] ruler fire, is at the fountain."

428 Fang Yaozhong: "寒化 refers to the major yang qi, [i.e.,] cold and water. 雨化
refers to the major yin qi, [i.e.,] dampness and soil. *Gui you* and *gui mao* years are years
with an inadequate fire period. When the fire period is inadequate, water comes to
seize it. Hence the time period associated with the initial period of the visitor periods,
as well as summer, of such years can display climatic changes of violent cold. However,
because of the principle of domination and revenge, at a time when cold qi is disproportionately dominant, dampness qi will come to take revenge. Hence occasionally
climatic changes towards a disproportionately damp or hot climate may occur."

429 Fang Yaozhong: "The 'ninth mansion' refers to the South."

430 Fang Yaozhong: "燥化 refers to the qi controlling heaven in *gui you* and *gui mao*
years. In *gui you* and *gui mao* years yang brilliance [qi, i.e.,] dryness and metal, controls

in the lower [half of the year require] salty [flavor] and cold.⁴³¹
These are the so-called requirements of drugs and food.

71-481-12
Jia xu year meets identical to heavenly complements and *jia chen* years year meets identical to heavenly complements:

---

heaven. Yang brilliance rules collness and it rules dryness. Hence there the climate is disproportionately cool and dry in the upper half of *gui you* and *gui mao* years. The generation growth of the myriad beings is influenced by this disproportionately cool and dry climate. 熱化 refers to the annual period of *gui you* and *gui mao* years. *Gui you* and *gui mao* [years] are years with an inadequate fire period. Hence in these two years, the orders or summer arrive late; it is not hot when it should be hot. Hence the myriad beings that should be hot are not hot and they are influenced by the disproportionately cool climate in their generation and growth. .. The regular number of the qi at the fountain is left out in this section. This cannot be explained here by referring to an identical regular number of the annual period. .. The nature of the qi at the fountain in *gui you* and *gui mao* years is not entirely identical to the fire qi of the annual period. .. Presumably the regular number of the qi at the fountain was omitted erroneously. It should be 'heat transformation: seven.'"

431 Fang Yaozhong: "上苦小溫 is: because the yang brilliance [qi, i.e.,] dryness and metal, rules heaven in the upper half of the year, the climate is disproportionately cool. Hence in treating illnesses and regulating [the organism] through food and drink, it is appropriate to employ drugs or food with a bitter flavor and with a slightly warm nature. The reason is that warmth is able to dominate coolness. Because the initial visitor qi in the upper half of the year is ceasing yin [qi, i.e.,] wind and wood, the second qi is minor yin [qi, i.e.,] ruler fire, and the third qi is minor yang [qi, i.e.,] minister fire, the host qi is disproportionately warm, or disproportionately hot. Hence even though one should employ disproportionately warm drugs and food for regulation because the climate is disproportionately cool since the visitor qi controlling heaven is yang brilliance [qi, i.e.,] dryness and metal, one should still take into account that the host qi is disproportionately warm and therefore not employ [drugs and food that are] very warm or very hot. All that is needed are drugs and food of a bitter [flavor] and of slight warmth. 中鹹溫 is: because *gui you* and *gui mao* years are years of an inadequate fire period, the climate is disproportionately cool. It is not hot when it should be hot. The heart qi of the human body is insufficient, hence in treating illnesses and regulating [the organism] through food and drink it is appropriate to employ drugs or food with a salty flavor and with a warm nature. The reason is that salty [flavor] is able to supplement the [qi of the] heart and that warmth can dominate coolness. 下鹹寒 is: because in the second half of the year minor yin [qi, i.e.,] ruler fire, is at the fountain, the climate is disproportionately hot. Hence it is advisable to employ drugs or food of an salty flavor and cold nature when treating illnesses or regulating through food and drink. The reason is that salty [flavor] can dominate fire and that cold can drain heat.

In the upper [half of the year]: major yang, water.
In the center: major *gong*, soil period.
In the lower [half of the year]: major yin, soil.[432]

Cold transformation: six.
Dampness transformation: five.[433]
These are the days of proper transformation.

These transformations
in the upper [half of the year require] bitter [flavor] and heat,
in the center [require] bitter [flavor] and warmth,
in the lower [half of the year require] bitter [flavor] and warmth.[434]
These are the requirements of drugs and food.

---

432 Fang Yaozhong: "*Jia xu* and *jia chen* years are years with a greatly excessive soil period. Major yang [qi, i.e.,] cold and water, controls heaven, while major yin [qi, i.e.,] dampness and soil, is at the fountain."

433 Fang Yaozhong: "寒化 refers to the qi controlling heaven in *jia xu* and *jia chen* years. In *jia xu* and *jia chen* years major yang [qi, i.e.,] cold and water, controls heaven. Major yang rules cold. Hence there is a disproportionate domination of cold qi in the upper half of *jia xu* and *jia chen* years and the climate is disproportionately cold. The generation and growth of the myriad beings is influenced by the cold and coolness of the climate, when it is not warm while it should be warm. 濕化 refers to the annual period of *jia xu* and *jia chen* years. *Jia xu* and *jia chen* years are years with a greatly excessive soil period. Hence there is a disproportionate domination of rain and dampness in late summer and in the time period associated with the initial qi of the visitor qi of these years. The transformation and generation of the myriad beings is affected the qi of this rain and of this dampness."

434 Fang Yaozhong: "上苦熱 is: because the major yang [qi, i.e.,] cold and water, rules heaven in the upper half of the year, the climate is disproportionately cold. In addition, the annual period is a greatly excessive soil period, and the visitor period is a disproportionately dominant dampness qi. The climate is marked by cold and dampness. Hence in treating illnesses and regulating [the organism] through food and drink, it is appropriate to employ drugs or food with a bitter flavor and with hot nature. The reason is that bitter [flavor] can dry dampness and that heat can disperse cold. 中苦溫 is: because these are years of a greatly excessive soil period, the qi of dampness dominates disproportionately. Hence in treating illnesses and regulating [the organism] through food and drink, it is appropriate to employ drugs or food with a bitter flavor and with a warm nature. The reason is that bitter [flavor] can dry dampness and that warmth can transform dampness. 下苦溫 is: because in the second half of the year major yin [qi, i.e.,] dampness and soil, is at the fountain, there is a disproportionate domination of dampness qi. This is identical to the annual period."

71-482-3
Yi hai and *yi si* years:

In the upper [half of the year]: ceasing yin, wood.
In the center: minor *shang*, metal period.
In the lower [half of the year]: minor yang, minister fire.[435]

Heat transformation, cold transformation; domination and revenge are identical [in these two years].[436]
These are the days of evil qi transformation.

Catastrophes occur in the seventh mansion.[437]

Wind transformation: eight.
Coolness transformation: four.
Fire transformation: two.[438]
These are the degrees of proper transformation.[439]

---

435 Fang Yaozhong: "*Yi hai* and *yi si* years are years with an inadequate metal period. Ceasing yin [qi, i.e.,] wind and wood, control heaven, while minor yang [qi, i.e.,] minister fire, is at the fountain."

436 Fang Yaozhong: "熱化 refers to the qi of minor yin, [i.e.,] ruler fire, or of minor yang [i.e.,] minister fire.. 寒化 refers to the major yin qi, [i.e.,] cold and water. *Yi hai* and *yi si* years are years with an inadequate metal period. [When the metal] period is inadequate, fire comes to seize it. Hence in this year autumn should be cool but is not cool; the climate is disproportionately hot. However, because of the principle of domination and revenge, water qi will come to take revenge. Hence this year's winter may exhibit climatic changes to a disproportionate cold."

437 Fang Yaozhong: "In *yi hai* and *yi si* years natural catastrophes occur mainly in the Western regions."

438 Fang Yaozhong: "風化 refers to the qi controlling heaven in *yi si* and *ji hai* years. In *yi si* and *ji hai* years ceasing yin [qi, i.e.,] wind and wood, controls heaven. Ceasing yin rules wind and it rules warmth. Hence there is a disproportionate domination of wind in the upper half of *yi si* and *ji hai* years and the climate is disproportionately warm. The myriad beings are affected in their transformation and generation by this disproportionate domination of wind. 清化 refers to the annual period of *yi si* and *ji hai* years. *Yi si* and *ji hai* years are years with an inadequate metal period. Metal rules coolness and it rules dryness. Hence in *yi si* and *yi hai* years autumn should be cool but is not cool; there should be gathering [of crops] but there is no gathering. Hence the regular generation, growth, gathering, and completion of the myriad beings is influenced."

439 One 度, "degree", exactly corresponds to a 24 hours period and is to be regarded as a more exact technical term based in astronomy for the colloquial "day." One may

These transformations
in the upper [half of the year require] acrid [flavor] and coolness,
in the center [require] sour [flavor] and harmonious [nature],
in the lower [half of the year require] salty [flavor] and cold.⁴⁴⁰
These are the requirements of drugs and food.

71-482-8
Bing zi year meets and *bing wu* years:

In the upper [half of the year]: minor yin, fire.
In the center: major *yu*, water period.
In the lower [half of the year]: yang brilliance, metal.⁴⁴¹

Heat transformation: two.
Cold transformation: six.

---

assume that beginning with the eleventh period, i.e., *jia xu* and *jia chen* years, a different copy of the text of this table was added to the preceding ten periods. Perhaps the
person responsible for combining the two parts began exchanging "day" against "degree" but, for reasons unknown, did not carry this on after two periods. It is obvious,
though, that this person read 度 in the sense of 日. The break between the two sections
in the text is also indicated by the continuous appearance of the characters 所謂 in the
phrasing of the first ten periods and their absence in the subsequent text.

440 Fang Yaozhong: "上辛涼 is: because the ceasing yin [qi, i.e.,] wind and wood, rules
heaven in the upper half of the year, there is a disproportionate domination of wind qi
and the climate is disproportionately warm. Hence in treating illnesses and regulating [the organism] through food and drink, it is appropriate to employ drugs or food
with an acrid flavor and with cool nature. The reason is that acrid [flavor] is able to
dominate wind and that coolness can dominate warmth. 中酸和 is: because *yi si* and
yi hai years are years with an inadequate metal period, the climate is disproportionately warm and the liver qi in the human body dominates disproportionately. Hence
in treating illnesses and regulating [the organism] through food and drink, it is appropriate to employ drugs or food with a sour flavor and with a harmonious nature. The
reason is that sour [flavor] is able to drain and to nourish the liver. 下鹹寒 is: because
in *yi si* and *yi hai* years minor yang [qi, i.e.,] minister fire, is at the fountain, the climate
is disproportionately hot. Hence it is advisable to employ drugs or food of an salty flavor and cold nature when treating illnesses or regulating through food and drink. The
reason is that salty [flavor] can drain fire and that cold can dominate heat."

441 Fang Yaozhong: "*Bing zi* and *bing wu* years are years with a greatly excessive
water period. Minor yin [qi, i.e.,] ruler fire, controls heaven, while yang brilliance [qi,
i.e.,] dryness and metal, is at the fountain."

Coolness transformation: four.
These are the degrees of proper transformation.[442]

These transformations
in the upper [half of the year require] salty [flavor] and cold,
in the center [require] salty [flavor] and heat,
in the lower [half of the year require] sour [flavor] and warmth.[443]
These are the requirements of drugs and food.

71-483-1
Ding chou and *ding wei* years:

---

442 Fang Yaozhong: "熱化 refers to the qi controlling heaven in *bing zi* and *bing wu* years. In *bing zi* and *bing wu* years minor yin [qi, i.e.,] ruler fire, controls heaven. Minor yin rules heat. Hence in the upper half of *bing zi* and *bing wu* years, the climate is disproportionally hot and the transformation and generation of the myriad beings in this time period is affected by a disproportionate domination of heat qi. 寒化 refers to the annual period of *bing zi* and *bing wu* years. *Bing zi* and *bing wu* years are years with a greatly excessive water period. Water rules cold. Hence in the winter of *bing zi* and *bing wu* years, the climate is very cold. 清化 refers to the qi at the fountain in *bing zi* and *bing wu* years. In *bing zi* and *bing wu* years yang brilliance [qi, i.e.,] dryness and metal, is at the fountain. Yang brilliance rules coolness and it rules dryness. Hence in *bing zi* and *bing wu* years, the climate is disproportionately cool in the second half of the year." Beginning with this passage, the term 度, 'degree', is used instead of 日, 'day' contained in all similar passages above. Apparently, the meaning is the same. See note 392 above.

443 Fang Yaozhong: "上鹹寒 is: because in *bing zi* and *bing wu* years minor yin [qi, i.e.,] ruler fire, controls heaven, the climate in the upper half of the year is disproportionately hot. Hence in treating illnesses and regulating [the organism] through food and drink, it is appropriate to employ drugs or food with a salty flavor and with cold nature. The reason is that salty [flavor] can dominate fire and that cold can dominate heat. 中鹹熱 is: because *bing zi* and *bing wu* years are years of a greatly excessive water period, the climate in the time period associated with the initial period of the visitor periods as well is in winter of these years is very cold. Cold can harm the kidneys and it can harm the heart. Hence in treating illnesses and regulating [the organism] through food and drink, it is appropriate to employ drugs or food with a salty flavor and with a hot nature. The reason is that salty [flavor] can enter the kidneys and is able to supplement the heart and that heat can dominate cold. 下酸溫 is: because in *bing zi* and *bing hai* years yang brilliance [qi, i.e.] dryness and metal, is at the fountain, the climate in the lower half of the year is disproportionately cool and disproportionately dry. Coolness can harm the liver; dryness can dominate wind. Hence it is advisable to employ drugs or food of a sour flavor and warm nature when treating illnesses or regulating through food and drink. The reason is that sour [flavor] can nourish the liver and that warmth can dominate coolness."

In the upper [half of the year]: major yin, soil.
In the center: minor *jue*, wood period.
In the lower [half of the year]: major yang, water.[444]

Coolness transformation, heat transformation; domination and revenge are
identical [in these two years].[445]
These are the degrees of evil qi transformation.

Catastrophes occur in the third mansion.[446]

Rain transformation: five.
Wind transformation: three.
Cold transformation: one.[447]
These are the degrees of proper transformation.

---

444 Fang Yaozhong: "*Ding chou* and *ding wei* years are years with an inadequate
wood period. Major yin [qi, i.e.,] dampness and soil, controls heaven, while major
yang [qi, i.e.,] cold and water, is at the fountain."

445 Fang Yaozhong: "*Ding chou* and *ding wei* years are years with an inadequate wood
period. When the wood period is inadequate, fire comes to seize it. Hence even though,
generally speaking, in *ding chou* and *ding wei* years, the climate in spring is disproportionately cool, it should be warm but is not warm. However, because the metal qi
is disproportionately dominant, the qi of fire will come to take revenge. Hence the
summer of *ding chou* and *ding wei* years can exhibit phenomena of disproportionate
heat to achieve self regulation."

446 Fang Yaozhong: "In *ding chou* and *ding wei* years, natural catastrophes occur in
the Eastern regions."

447 Fang Yaozhong: "雨化 refers to the qi controlling heaven in *ding chou* and *ding
wei* years. In *ding chou* and *ding wei* years major yin [qi, i.e.,] dampness and soil, controls heaven. [Hence] the climate in the upper half of the year is disproportionately
damp and much rain falls. 風化 refers to the annual period of *ding chou* and *ding wei*
years. *Ding chou* and *ding wei* years are years with an inadequate wood period. Spring
should be warm but is not warm; there should be generation, but there is no generation. 寒化 refers to the qi at the fountain in *ding chou* and *ding wei* years. In *ding chou*
and *ding wei* years major yang [qi, i.e.,] cold and water, is at the fountain. The climate
in the lower half of the year is disproportionately cold. Basically this statement should
list the 'completion' number of water to make it clear that cold qi is greatly excessive. However, because in *ding chou* and *ding wei* years 'coolness transformation, heat
transformation. [These processes are] like domination and revenge,' there is an aspect
of fire qi coming for revenge included here. Hence the cold qi cannot become overly
abundant in the winter of these years and it is therefore that the 'generation' number
of water is listed here."

These transformations
in the upper [half of the year require] bitter [flavor] and warmth,
in the center [require] acrid [flavor] and warmth,
in the lower [half of the year require] sweet [flavor] and heat.[448]
These are the requirements of drugs and food.

71-483-6
Wu yin and *wu shen* years heavenly complements:

In the upper [half of the year]: minor yang, minister fire.
In the center: major *zhi*, fire period.
In the lower [half of the year]: ceasing yin, wood.[449]

Fire transformation: seven.
Wind transformation: three.[450]
These are the degrees of proper transformation.

---

448 Fang Yaozhong: "上苦溫 is: because in *ding chou* and *ding wei* years major yin [qi, i.e.,] dampness and soil, controls heaven, dampness qi dominates disproportionately in the upper half of the years. Hence in treating illnesses and regulating [the organism] through food and drink, it is appropriate to employ drugs or food with a bitter flavor and with warm nature. The reason is that bitter [flavor] is able to dry dampness and that warmth can transform dampness. 中辛溫 is: because *ding chou* and *ding wei* years are years with an inadequate woodl period, it is not warm when it should be warm and the climate is disproportionately cool. The liver qi in the human body is inadequate, with scattering and draining suspended as a result. Hence in treating illnesses and regulating [the organism] through food and drink, it is appropriate to employ drugs or food with an acrid flavor and with a warm nature. The reason is that acrid [flavor] is able to scatter wind and that warmth can dominate coolness. 下甘熱 is: because in *ding chou* and *ding wei* years major yang [qi, i.e.,] cold and water, is at the fountain, the climate is disproportionately cold. Hence it is advisable to employ drugs or food of a sweet flavor and hot nature when treating illnesses or regulating through food and drink. The reason is that sweet [flavor] can supplement the center and that heat can dominate cold."

449 Fang Yaozhong: "*Wu yin* and *wu shen* are years of a greatly excessive fire period. Minor yang [i.e.,] minister fire, controls heaven, while ceasing yin [qi, i.e.,] wind and wood, is at the fountain."

450 Fang Yaozhong: "火化 refers to the qi controlling heaven in *wu yin* and *wu shen* years. In *wu yin* and *wu shen* years minor yang [qi, i.e.,] minister fire, controls heaven. [Hence] the climate in the upper half [of the year] is disproportionately hot. 風化 refers to the qi at the fountain in *wu yin* and *wu shen* years. Because in *wu yin* and *wu shen* years the ceasing yin [qi, i.e.,] wind and wood, is at the fountain, the climate is disproportionately warm and there is a disproportionate domination of wind qi. In *wu yin* and *wu shen* years, the fire period is greatly excessive, minor yang [qi, i.e.,] minister

These transformations
in the upper [half of the year require] salty [flavor] and cold,
in the center [require] sweet [flavor] and harmonious [nature],
in the lower [half of the year require] acrid [flavor] and coolness.[451]
These are the requirements of drugs and food.

71-483-10
Ji mao and *ji you* years:

In the upper [half of the year]: yang brilliance, metal.
In the center: minor *gong*, soil period.
In the lower [half of the year]: minor yin, fire.[452]

Wind transformation, coolness transformation; domination and revenge are
identical [in these two years].[453]

---

fire, controls heaven and ceasing yin [qi, i.e.,] wind and wood, is at the fountain. The
climate of the entire year is marked by warmth and heat. Hence the 'completion' number of wood should be listed here, that is 'wind transformation: seven' would be reasonable. However, only the 'generation' number of wood is listed in the text, referring
to an inadequate presence of wind qi. We assume that this is related to the principle
of domination and revenge. When fire qi is disproportionately dominant, water qi will
come to seize (to take revenge??) it. For reasons of self regulation, the lower half of *wu
yin* and *wu shen* years cannot be too hot. Hence the 'generation' number is listed in the
text, not the 'completion' number."

451 Fang Yaozhong: "上鹹寒 is: because in *wu yin* and *wu shen* years minor yang [qi,
i.e.,] minister fire, controls heaven, the climate is disproportionately hot. Hence in
treating illnesses and regulating [the organism] through food and drink, it is appropriate to employ drugs or food with a salty flavor and with cold nature. The reason is
that salty [flavor] can cool the heat and drain the fire. 中甘和 is: because *wu yin* and
wu shen years are years of a greatly excessive fire period, summer is very hot. Hence in
treating illnesses and regulating [the organism] through food and drink, it is appropriate to employ drugs or food with a sweet flavor and with a cold nature. The reason
is that sweet [flavor] and cold [nature] can nourish the yin and cool the heat. 下辛
涼 is: because in *wu yin* and *wu shen* years ceasing yin [qi, i.e,] wind and wood, is at
the fountain, the climate is disproportionately warm and the qi of wind dominates
disproportionately. Hence it is advisable to employ drugs or food of a acrid flavor and
cool nature when treating illnesses or regulating through food and drink. The reason is
that acrid [flavor] can scatter wind and that coolness can dominate warmth."

452 Fang Yaozhong: "*Ji mao* and *ji you* years are years with an inadequate soil period.
Yang brilliance [qi, i.e.,] dryness and metal, controls heaven, while minor yin [qi, i.e.,]
ruler fire, is at the fountain."

453 Fang Yaozhong: "風化 refers to ceasing yin qi, [i.e.,] wind and wood. 清化 refers
to yang brilliance qi, [i.e.,] dryness and metal. In *ji mao* and *ji you* years, the annual

These are the degrees of evil qi transformation.

Catastrophes occur in the fifth mansion.⁴⁵⁴

Coolness transformation: nine.
Rain transformation: five.
Heat transformation: seven.⁴⁵⁵
These are the degrees of proper transformation.

These transformations
in the upper [half of the year require] bitter [flavor] and slight warmth,
in the center [require] sweet [flavor] and harmonious [nature],
in the lower [half of the year require] salty [flavor] and cold.⁴⁵⁶
These are the requirements of drugs and food.

---

period is soil and is inadequate. Hence wind prevails greatly. In these years, summer should be damp but is not damp and there is less rain than usual. The wind qi is disproportionately dominant. Because of the principle of domination and revenge, when wind qi is disproportionately dominant, metal qi will come to take revenge. Hence in autumn of these years, the climate is disproportionately cool in comparison with regular years, seeking self regulation."

454 Fang Yaozhong: "In *ji mao* and *ji you* years natural catastrophis occur mainly in the central region."

455 Fang Yaozhong: "清化 refers to the qi controlling heaven in *ji mao* and *ji you* years. In *ji mao* and *ji you* years yang brilliance [qi, i.e.,] dryness and metal, controls heaven. [Hence] the climate in the upper half of the year is disproportionately cool. 雨化 refers to the annual period of *ji mao* and *ji you* years. *Ji mao* and *ji you* years are years with an inadequate soil period. Hence in these two years in late summer it is not damp when it should be damp. Rain and water are diminished and the qi of wind is disproportionately dominant. Signs of drought appear. 熱化 refers to the qi at the fountain in *ji mao* and *ji you* years. In *ji mao* and *ji you* years minor yin [qi, i.e.,] ruler fire, is at the fountain. The climate in the lower half of the year is disproportionately hot. 'Seven' is the 'completion' number of fire. Why this 'completion' number is listed here, is difficult to interpret. We should think that the 'generation' number of fire was appropriate. The reason is: in *ji mao* and *ji you* years yang brilliance [qi, i.e.,] dryness and metal, controls heaven. The qi controlling heaven does not only govern the upper half of the year but has a definite influence on the entire year. Also, given that 'wind transformation, coolness transformation. [These processes are] like domination and revenge,' the lower half of the year cannot be too hot. Hence we belief that it would have been more reasonable to list the 'generation' number of fire here."

456 Fang Yaozhong: "上苦小溫 is: in *ji mao* and *ji you* years yang brilliance [qi, i.e.,] dryness and metal, controls heaven. The climate in the upper half of the year is disproportionately cool. Hence in treating illnesses and regulating [the organism] through food and drink, it is appropriate to employ drugs or food with a bitter flavor and

71-484-3
Geng chen and *geng xu* years:

In the upper [half of the year]: major yang, water.
In the center: major *shang*, metal period.
In the lower [half of the year]: major yin, soil.[457]

Cold transformation: one.
Coolness transformation: nine.
Rain transformation: five.[458]
These are the degrees of proper transformation.

These transformations
in the upper [half of the year require] bitter [flavor] and heat,
in the center [require] acrid [flavor] and warmth,
in the lower [half of the year require] sweet [flavor] and heat.[459]
These are the requirements of drugs and food.

---

with a slightly warm nature. 中甘和 is: because *ji mao* and *ji you* years are years of an inadequate annual soil period and because sweet is the flavor of soil, hence in treating illnesses and regulating [the organism] through food and drink, it is appropriate to employ drugs or food with a sweet flavor and with a harmonious nature. 下鹹寒 is: because in *ji mao* and *ji you* years minor yin [qi, i.e.,] ruler fire, is at the fountain, the climate is disproportionately hot in the lower half of the year. Hence it is advisable to employ drugs or food of a salty flavor and cool nature when treating illnesses or regulating through food and drink."

457 Fang Yaozhong: "*Geng chen* and *geng xu* years are years with a greatly excessive metal period. Major yang [qi, i.e.,] cold and water, controls heaven, while major yin [qi, i.e.,] dampness and soil, is at the fountain."

458 Fang Yaozhong: "寒化 refers to the qi controlling heaven in *geng chen* and *geng xu* years. In *geng chen* and *geng xu* years major yang [qi, i.e.,] cold and water, controls heaven. Hence in the upper half [of *geng chen* and *geng xu* years] the climate is disproportionally cold. 清化 refers to the annual period of *geng chen* and *geng xu* years. *Geng chen* and *geng xu* years are years with a greatly excessive metal period. In the autumn [of *geng chen* and *geng xu* years] the climate is disproportionately cool. 雨化 refers to the qi at the fountain in *geng chen* and *geng xu* years. In *geng chen* and *geng xu* years major yin [qi, i.e.,] dampness and soil, is at the fountain. Hence in the lower half of [*geng chen* and *geng xu*] years, the climate is disproportionately damp and much rain falls."

459 Fang Yaozhong: "上苦熱 is: in *geng chen* and *geng xu* years major yang [qi, i.e.,] cold and water, controls heaven. The climate [in the upper half of the year] is disproportionately cold. Hence in treating illnesses and regulating [the organism] through food and drink, it is appropriate to employ drugs or food with a bitter flavor and with a hot

71-484-7
Xin si and *xin hai* years:

In the upper [half of the year]: ceasing yin, wood.
In the center: minor *yu*, water period.
In the lower [half of the year]: minor yang, minister fire.[460]

Rain transformation, wind transformation; domination and revenge are identical [in these two years].[461]
These are the degrees of evil qi transformation.

Catastrophes occur in the first mansion.[462]

Wind transformation: three.
Cold transformation: one.
Fire transformation: seven.[463]
These are the degrees of proper transformation.

---

nature. Since the host qi of the upper half of the year is, generally speaking, disproportionately warm, why should one have to employ bitter [flavor]? The reason is that bitter [flavor] is able to drain heat. However, since the visitor qi controlling heaven is major yang [qi, i.e.,] cold and water, the climate should also be disproportionately cold or cool. Hence [drugs with] a hot [nature] are to be employed nevertheless because heat can dominate cold. 中辛溫 is: because *geng chen* and *geng xu* years are years of a greatly excessive annual metal period, the climate in autumn is disproportionately cool. Hence in treating illnesses and regulating [the organism] through food and drink, it is appropriate to employ drugs or food with an acrid flavor and with a warm nature. The reason is that acrid [flavor] can scatter the wind and warmth can dominate coolness. 下甘熱 is: because in *geng chen* and *geng xu* years major yin [qi, i.e,] dampness and soil, is at the fountain, the climate is disproportionately damp [in the lower half of the year]. Hence it is advisable to employ drugs or food of a sweet flavor and hot nature when treating illnesses or regulating through food and drink. The reason is that sweet [flavor] can enter the spleen and that heat can transform dampness."

460 Fang Yaozhong: "*Xin si* and *xin hai* years are years with an inadequate water period. Ceasing yin [qi, i.e.,] wind and wood, controls heaven, while minor yang [qi, i.e.,] minister fire, is at the fountain."

461 Fang Yaozhong: "雨化 refers to the major yin qi, [i.e.,] dampness and soil. 風化 refers to the ceasing yin qi, [i.e.,] wind and wood. In *xin si* and *xin hai* years, the water period is inadequate and soil comes to seize it. When soil qi dominates disproportionately, wood, in turn, comes to take revenge."

462 Fang Yaozhong: "Natural catastrophes occur mainly in the Northern regions."

463 Fang Yaozhong: "風化 refers to the qi controlling heaven in *xin si* and *xin hai* years. In *xin si* and *xin hai* years ceasing yin [qi, i.e.,] wind and wood, controls heaven.

These transformations
in the upper [half of the year require] acrid [flavor] and coolness,
in the center [require] bitter [flavor] and harmonious [nature],
in the lower [half of the year require] salty [flavor] and cold.⁴⁶⁴
These are the requirements of drugs and food.

71-484-12
Ren wu and *ren zi* years:

In the upper [half of the year]: minor yin, fire.
In the center: major *jue*, wood period.
In the lower [half of the year]: yang brilliance, metal.⁴⁶⁵

Heat transformation: two.
Wind transformation: eight.

Hence in the upper half [of *xin si* and *xin hai* years] the qi of wind dominates disproportionately and the climate is disproportionately warm. 寒化 refers to the annual
period of *xin si* and *xin hai* years. *Xin si* and *xin hai* years are years with an inadequate
water period. In the winter [of *xin si* and *xin hai* years, the climate] should be cold but
is not cold; there should be storage but there is no storage. 火化 refers to the minor
yang [qi, i.e.,] minister fire, at the fountain in *xin si* and *xin hai* years. In the lower half
of [*xin si* and *xin hai*] years, the climate is disproportionately hot."

464 Fang Yaozhong: "上辛涼 is: in *xin si* and *xin hai* years ceasing yin [qi, i.e.,] wind
and wood, controls heaven. The climate in the upper half of the year is disproportionately warm and the qi of wind is disproportionately dominant. Hence in treating
illnesses and regulating [the organism] through food and drink, it is appropriate to employ drugs or food with an acrid flavor and with a cool nature. 中苦和 is: because *xin
si* and *xin hai* years are years with an inadequate water period, the climate in winter is
disproportionately hot. There is no storage when there should be storage; the kidney depot in the human body fails to fulfill its functions and the minister fire moves recklessly.
Hence in treating illnesses and regulating [the organism] through food and drink, it is
appropriate to employ drugs or food with a bitter flavor and with a harmonious nature.
The reason is that bitter [flavor] can harden the kidneys and is able to drain fire. 下
鹹寒 is: because in *xin si* and *xin hai* years minor yang [qi, i.e,] minister fire, is at the
fountain, the climate is disproportionately hot [in the lower half of the year, i.e.,] the qi
of fire is greatly excessive. Hence it is advisable to employ drugs or food of a salty flavor
and cold nature when treating illnesses or regulating through food and drink. The reason is that salty [flavor] can drain the fire and that cold can dominate heat."

465 Fang Yaozhong: "*Ren wu* and *ren zi* years are years with a greatly excessive wood
period. Minor yin [qi, i.e.,] ruler fire, controls heaven, while yang brilliance [qi, i.e.,]
dampness and metal, is at the fountain."

Coolness transformation: four.[466]
These are the degrees of proper transformation.

These transformations
in the upper [half of the year require] salty [flavor] and cold,
in the center [require] sour [flavor] and coolness,
in the lower [half of the year require] sour [flavor] and warmth.[467]
These are the requirements of drugs and food.

71-485-1
Gui wei and *gui chou* years:

In the upper [half of the year]: major yin, soil.
In the center: minor *zhi*, fire period.
In the lower [half of the year]: major yang, water.[468]

---

466 Fang Yaozhong: "熱化 refers to the qi controlling heaven in *ren wu* and *ren zi* years. In *ren wu* and *ren zi* years minor yin [qi, i.e.,] ruler fire, controls heaven. Hence in the upper half [of *ren wu* and *ren zi* years] the climate is disproportionally hot. 風 化 refers to the annual period of *ren wu* and *ren zi* years. *Ren wu* and *ren zi* years are years with a greatly excessive wood period. In the spring [of *ren wu* and *ren zi* years] the qi of wind is disproportionately dominant and the climate is disproportionately warm. 清化 refers to the qi at the fountain in *ren wu* and *ren zi* years. In *ren wu* and *ren zi* years yang brilliance [qi, i.e.,] dryness and metal, is at the fountain. Hence in the lower half of [*ren wu* and *ren zi*] years, the climate is disproportionately cool and disproportionately dry."

467 Fang Yaozhong: "上鹹寒 is: in *ren wu* and *ren zi* years minor yin [qi, i.e.,] ruler fire, controls heaven. The climate in the upper half of the year is disproportionately hot. Hence in treating illnesses and regulating [the organism] through food and drink, it is appropriate to employ drugs or food with a salty flavor and with a cold nature. 中酸 涼 is: because *ren wu* and *ren zi* years are years with a greatly excessive annual wood period, the qi of wind dominates disproportionately and the climate is disproportionately warm. Hence in treating illnesses and regulating [the organism] through food and drink, it is appropriate to employ drugs or food with a sour flavor and with a cool nature. 下酸溫 is: because in *ren wu* and *ren zi* years yang brilliance [qi, i.e,] dryness and metal, is at the fountain, the climate is disproportionately cool in the lower half of the year. Hence it is advisable to employ drugs or food of a sour flavor and warm nature when treating illnesses or regulating through food and drink."

468 Fang Yaozhong: "*Gui wei* and *gui chou* years are years with an inadequate fire period. Major yin [qi, i.e.,] dampness and soil, controls heaven, while major yang [qi, i.e.,] cold and water, is at the fountain."

Cold transformation, rain transformation; transformation and revenge are
identical [in these two years].[469]
These are the degrees of evil qi transformation.

Catastrophes occur in the ninth mansion.[470]

Rain transformation: five.
Fire transformation: two.
Cold transformation: one.[471]
These are the degrees of proper transformation.

These transformations
in the upper [half of the year require] bitter [flavor] and warmth,
in the center [require] salty [flavor] and warmth,
in the lower [half of the year require] sweet [flavor] and heat.[472]
These are the requirements of drugs and food.

---

469 Fang Yaozhong: "寒化 refers to the major yang qi, [i.e.,] cold and water. 雨化
refers to the major yin qi, [i.e.,] dampness and soil. In *gui wei* and *gui chou* years, the
fire period is inadequate and water comes to seize it. When water qi dominates disproportionately, soil qi, in turn, comes to take revenge."

470 Fang Yaozhong: "Natural catastrophes occur mainly in the Southern regions."

471 Fang Yaozhong: "雨化 refers to the qi controlling heaven in *gui wei* and *gui chou*
years. In *gui wei* and *gui chou* years major yin [qi, i.e.,] dampness and soil, controls
heaven. Hence in the upper half [of *gui wei* and *gui chou* years] the climate is disproportionately damp. 火化 refers to the annual period of *gui wei* and *gui chou* years.
Gui wei and *gui chou* years are years with an inadequate fire period. In the summer
[of *gui wei* and *gui chou* years, the climate] should be hot but is not hot; there should
be growth but there is no growth. 寒化 refers to the qi at the fountain in *gui wei* and
gui chou years. In *gui wei* and *gui chou* years major yang [qi, i.e.,] cold and water, is at
the fountain. The climate in the lower half of [*gui wei* and *gui chou*] years is disproportionately cold."

472 Fang Yaozhong: "上苦溫 is: in *gui wei* and *gui chou* years major yin [qi, i.e.,] dampness and soil, controls heaven. The climate in the upper half of the year is disproportionately damp. Hence in treating illnesses and regulating [the organism] through
food and drink, it is appropriate to employ drugs or food with a bitter flavor and
with a warm nature. 中鹹溫 is: because *gui wei* and *gui chou* years are years with an
inadequate annual fire period, [the climate in] summer should be hot but is not hot.
Hence in treating illnesses and regulating [the organism] through food and drink, it
is appropriate to employ drugs or food with a salty flavor and with a warm nature. 下
甘熱 is: because in *gui wei* and *gui chou* years major yang [qi, i.e.,] cold and water, is at
the fountain, the climate is disproportionately cold in the lower half of the year. Furthermore, because of the influence of the qi taking revenge, the climate exhibits at the
same time changes to a disproportionate dampness. Hence it is advisable to employ

71-485-6
Jia shen and *jia yin* years:

In the upper [half of the year]: minor yang, minister fire.
In the center: major *gong*, soil period.
In the lower [half of the year]: ceasing yin, wood.[473]

Fire transformation: two.
Rain transformation: five.
Wind transformation: eight.[474]
These are the degrees of proper transformation.

These transformations
in the upper [half of the year require] salty [flavor] and cold,
in the center [require] salty [flavor] and harmonious [nature],
in the lower [half of the year require] acrid [flavor] and coolness.[475]
These are the requirements of drugs and food.

---

drugs or food of a sweet flavor and hot nature when treating illnesses or regulating through food and drink."

473 Fang Yaozhong: "*Jia shen* and *jia yin* years are years with a greatly excessive soil period. Minor yang [qi, i.e.,] minister fire, controls heaven, while ceasing yin [qi, i.e.,) wind and wood, is at the fountain."

474 Fang Yaozhong: "火化 refers to the qi controlling heaven in *jia shen* and *jia yin* years. In *jia shen* and *jia yin* years minor yang [qi, i.e.,] minister fire, controls heaven. Hence in the upper half [of *jia shen* and *jia yin* years] the climate is disproportionally hot. 雨化 refers to the annual period of *jia shen* and *jia yin* years. *Jia shen* and *jia yin* years are years with a greatly excessive soil period. In the late summer [of *jia shen* and *jia yin* years], the climate is disproportionately damp and much rain falls. 風化 refers to the qi at the fountain in *jia shen* and *jia yin* years. In *jia shen* and *jia yin* years ceasing yin [qi, i.e.,] wind and wood, is at the fountain. Hence in the lower half of [*jia shen* and *jia yin*] years, the qi of wind is disproportionately dominant and the climate is disproportionately warm."

475 Fang Yaozhong: "上鹹寒 is: in *jia shen* and *jia yin* years minor yang [qi, i.e.,] minister fire, controls heaven. The climate [in the upper half of the year] is disproportionately hot. Hence in treating illnesses and regulating [the organism] through food and drink, it is appropriate to employ drugs or food with a salty flavor and with a cold nature. 中鹹和 is: because *jia shen* and *jia yin* years are years with a greatly excessive annual soil period, the climate is disproportionately damp. Hence in treating illnesses and regulating [the organism] through food and drink, it is appropriate to employ drugs or food with a salty flavor and with a harmonious nature. However, it is not easy to understand why during a greatly excessive soil period drugs and food of a salty [flavor] and harmonious [nature] should be employed. This differs from the advices of

71-485-10
Yi you tai-yi heavenly complements and *yi mao* years heavenly complements:

In the upper [half of the year]: yang brilliance, metal.
In the center: minor *shang*, metal period.
In the lower [half of the year]: minor yin, fire.[476]

Heat transformation, cold transformation; domination and revenge are identical [in these two years].[477]
These are the degrees of evil qi transformation.

---

what drugs and what food should be taken in years with a greatly excessive soil period as outlined above. Above the text stated for *jia zi* and *jia wu* years that the drugs and food '[required] in the center are bitter and hot' and for *jia chen* and *jia xu* years that the drugs and food '[required] in the center are bitter and warm. Only here [the drugs and food 'required] in the center are salty and harmonious.' Perhaps this is related to the annual qi. In *jia zi* and *jia wu* years, the annual soil period is greatly excessive, minor yin [qi, i.e.,] ruler fire, controls heaven and yang brilliance [qi, i.e.,] dryness and metal, is at the fountain. The [climate] in the upper half of the year is disproportionately hot, in the lower half of the year it is disproportionately cool. During the entire year dampness qi abounds disproportionately. 'Bitter and hot' [drugs and food] are required because bitter [flavor] can dry dampness and heat can dominate coolness. In *jia chen* and *jia xu* years, the annual soil period is greatly excessive, major yang [qi, i.e.,] cold and water, controls heaven, major yin [qi, i.e.,] dampness and soil, is at the fountain. The climate of the entire year is disproportionately cold and damp. 'Bitter and warm' [drugs and food] are required because bitter [flavor] can dry dampness and warmth can dominate cold. In *jia shen* and *jia yin* years, the annual soil period is greatly excessive, minor yang [qi, i.e.,] minister fire, controls heaven and ceasing yin [qi, i.e.,] wind and wood, is at the fountain. Both the qi controlling heaven and the qi at the fountain are disproportionately warm or hot. The entire year is ruled by warmth and heat. 'Salty and harmonious' [drugs and food] are required in such a situation because salty [flavor] can dominate fire and can drain heat. 下辛涼 is: because in *jia shen* and *jia yin* years ceasing yin [qi, i.e,] wind and wood, is at the fountain, the climate is disproportionately warm [in the lower half of the year]. Hence it is advisable to employ drugs or food of an acrid flavor and cool nature when treating illnesses or regulating through food and drink."

476 Fang Yaozhong: "*Yi you* and *yi mao* years are years with an inadequate metal period. Yang brilliance [qi, i.e.,] dryness and metal, controls heaven, while minor yin [qi, i.e.,] ruler fire, is at the fountain."

477 Fang Yaozhong: "熱化 refers to the minor yin qi, [i.e.,] ruler fire, and to the minor yang qi, [i.e.,] minister fire. 寒化 refers to the major yang qi, [i.e.,] cold and water. In *yi you* and *yi mao* years, the metal period is inadequate and fire comes to seize it. When fire qi dominates disproportionately, water qi comes to take revenge."

Catastrophes occur in the seventh mansion.⁴⁷⁸

Dryness transformation: four.
Coolness transformation: four.
Heat transformation: two.⁴⁷⁹
These are the degrees of proper transformation.

These transformations
in the upper [half of the year require] bitter [flavor] and slight warmth,
in the center [require] bitter [flavor] and harmonious [nature],
in the lower [half of the year require] salty [flavor] and cold.⁴⁸⁰
These are the requirements of drugs and food.

71-486-2
Bing xu heavenly complements and *bing chen* years heavenly complements:

In the upper [half of the year]: major yang, water.

---

478 Fang Yaozhong: "Natural catastrophes occur mainly in the Western regions."

479 Fang Yaozhong: "燥化 refers to the qi controlling heaven in *yi you* and *yi mao* years. In *yi you* and *yi mao* years yang brilliance [qi, i.e.,] dryness and metal, controls heaven. Hence in the upper half [of *yi you* and *yi mao* years] the climate is disproportionately cool and disproportionately dry. 清化 refers to the annual period of *yi you* and *yi mao* years. *Yi you* and *yi mao* years are years with an inadequate metal period. In the autumn [of *yi you* and *yi mao* years] the climate should be cool but is not cool. 熱化 refers to the qi at the fountain in *yi you* and *yi mao* years. In *yi you* and *yi mao* years minor yin [qi, i.e.,] ruler fire, is at the fountain. The climate in the lower half of [*yi you* and *yi mao*] years is disproportionately hot."

480 Fang Yaozhong: "上苦小溫 is: in *yi you* and *yi mao* years yang brilliance [qi, i.e.,] dampness and soil, controls heaven. The climate in the upper half of the year is disproportionately cool. Hence in treating illnesses and regulating [the organism] through food and drink, it is appropriate to employ drugs or food [with a bitter flavor and] with a disproportionately warm [nature]. However, because the host qi of the upper half the year is disproportionately warm and because in terms of the annual period the aspect of fire coming to seize metal has to be taken into account, [the nature of] the drugs and food must not be too warm. Hence the text states: 'bitter, slightly warm.' 中苦和 is: because *yi you* and *yi mao* years are years with an inadequate annual metal period and because fire qi comes to seize [the metal], the climate is disproportionately hot. Hence in treating illnesses and regulating [the organism] through food and drink, it is appropriate to employ drugs or food with a bitter flavor and with a harmonious nature. 下鹹寒 is: because in *yi you* and *yi mao* years minor yin [qi, i.e.,] ruler fire, is at the fountain, the climate is disproportionately hot in the lower half of the year. Hence it is advisable to employ drugs or food of a salty flavor and cold nature when treating illnesses or regulating through food and drink."

In the center: major *yu*, water period.
In the lower [half of the year]: major yin, soil.[481]

Cold transformation: six.
Rain transformation: five.[482]
These are the degrees of proper transformation.

These transformations
in the upper [half of the year require] bitter [flavor] and heat,
in the center [require] salty [flavor] and warmth,
in the lower [half of the year require] sweet [flavor] and heat.[483]
These are the requirements of drugs and food.

71-486-6
Ding hai heavenly complements and *ding si* years heavenly complements:

In the upper [half of the year]: ceasing yin, wood.
In the center: minor *jue*, wood period.

---

481 Fang Yaozhong: "*Bing xu* and *bing chen* years are years with a greatly excessive water period. Major yang [qi, i.e.,] cold and water, controls heaven, while major yin [qi, i.e.,] dampness and soil, is at the fountain."

482 Fang Yaozhong: "寒化 refers to the qi controlling heaven in *bing xu* and *bing chen* years. In *bing xu* and *bing chen* years, major yang [qi, i.e.,] cold and water, controls heaven. The climate in the upper half of the year is disproportionately cold. 雨 化 refers to the qi at the fountain in *bing xu* and *bing chen* years. In *bing xu* and *bing chen* years, the qi at the fountain is major yin [qi, i.e.,] dampness and soil. The climate in the lower half of the year is disproportionately damp. This section has no listing of the regular number of the annual period. The reason is that in *bing xu* and *bing chen* years, the annual water period is greatly excessive, its regular number should be 'cold transformation: six.' This is identical to the regular number of the qi controlling heaven. Hence it was omitted."

483 Fang Yaozhong: "上苦熱 is: in *bing xu* and *bing chen* years major yang [qi, i.e.,] cold and water, controls heaven. The climate [in the upper half of the year] is disproportionately cold. Hence in treating illnesses and regulating [the organism] through food and drink, it is appropriate to employ drugs or food with a disproportionately hot [nature]. 中鹹溫 is: because *bing xu* and *bing chen* years are years with a greatly excessive annual water period, the climate is particularly cold. Hence in treating illnesses and regulating [the organism] through food and drink, it is appropriate to employ drugs or food with a salty flavor and with a warm nature. 下甘熱 is: because in *bing xu* and *bing chen* years major yin [qi, i.e,] dampness and soil, is at the fountain, [the climate] is disproportionately damp in the lower half of the year. Hence it is advisable to employ drugs or food of a sweet flavor and hot nature when treating illnesses or regulating through food and drink."

In the lower [half of the year]: minor yang, minister fire.⁴⁸⁴

Coolness transformation, heat transformation; domination and revenge are
identical [in these two years].⁴⁸⁵
These are the degrees of evil qi transformation.

Catastrophes occur in the third mansion.⁴⁸⁶

Wind transformation: three.
Fire transformation: seven.⁴⁸⁷
These are the degrees of proper transformation.

These transformations
in the upper [half of the year require] acrid [flavor] and coolness,
in the center [require] acrid [flavor] and harmonious [nature],
in the lower [half of the year require] salty [flavor] and cold.⁴⁸⁸
These are the requirements of drugs and food.

---

484 *Ding hai* and *ding si* years are years with an inadequate wood period. Ceasing
yin qi, i.e., wind and wood, controls heave, while minor yang qi, i.e., minister fire, is
at the fountain.

485 Fang Yaozhong: "清化 refers to the yang brilliance qi, [i.e.,] dryness and metal.
熱化 refers to the minor yin qi, [i.e.,] ruler fire. In *ding hai* and *ding si* years, the wood
period is inadequate and metal comes to seize it. When metal qi dominates disproportionately, fire qi comes to take revenge."

486 Fang Yaozhong: "Natural catastrophes occur mainly in the Eastern regions."

487 Fang Yaozhong: "風化 refers to the qi controlling heaven in *ding hai* and *ding
si* years. In *ding hai* and *ding si* years, ceasing yin [qi, i.e.,] wind and wood, controls
heaven. The climate in the upper half of the year is disproportionately warm and the
qi of wind is disproportionately dominant. 火化 refers to the qi at the fountain in *ding
hai* and *ding si* years. In *ding hai* and *ding si* years, the qi at the fountain is minor yang
[qi, i.e.,] minister fire. The climate in the lower half of the year is disproportionately
hot. This section has no listing of the regular number of the annual period. The reason
is that *ding hai* and *ding si* years are years with an inadequate annual wood period. Its
regular number should be 'wind transformation: three.' This is identical to the regular
number of the qi controlling heaven. Hence it was omitted."

488 Fang Yaozhong: "上辛涼 is: in *ding hai* and *ding si* years ceasing yin [qi, i.e.,] wind
and wood, controls heaven. The climate in the upper half of the year is disproportionately warm and the qi of wind is disproportionately dominant. Hence in treating
illnesses and regulating [the organism] through food and drink, it is appropriate to
employ drugs or food with an acrid flavor and with a cool nature. 中辛和 is: *ding hai*
and *ding si* years are years with an inadequate annual wood [period]. The [climate in]
spring should be warm but is not warm. The qi of the wind is inadequate. Hence it

71-486-11
Wu zi heavenly complements and *wu wu* years *tai-yi* heavenly complements:

In the upper [half of the year]: minor yin, fire.
In the center: major *zhi*, fire period.
In the lower [half of the year]: yang brilliance, metal.[489]

Heat transformation: seven.
Coolness transformation: nine.[490]
These are the degrees of proper transformation.

These transformations
in the upper [half of the year require] salty [flavor] and cold,
in the center [require] sweet [flavor] and cold,
in the lower [half of the year require] sour [flavor] and warmth.[491]
These are the requirements of drugs and food.

---

is advisable to employ drugs or food of an acrid flavor and of a warm nature when treating illnesses or regulating through food and drink. 下鹹寒 is: because in *ding hai* and *ding si* years minor yang [qi, i.e.,] minister fire, is at the fountain, the climate is disproportionately hot [in the lower half of the year]. Hence it is advisable to employ drugs or food of a salty flavor and cold nature when treating illnesses or regulating through food and drink."

489 Fang Yaozhong: "*Wu zi* and *wu wu* years are years with a greatly excessive fire period. Minor yin [qi, i.e.,] ruler fire, controls heaven, while yang brilliance [qi, i.e.,] dryness and metal, is at the fountain."

490 Fang Yaozhong: "熱化 refers to the qi controlling heaven in *wu zi* and *wu wu* years. In *wu zi* and *wu wu* years, minor yin [qi, i.e.,] ruler fire, controls heaven. The climate in the upper half of the year is disproportionately hot. 清化 refers to the qi at the fountain in *wu zi* and *wu wu* years. In *wu zi* and *wu wu* years, the qi at the fountain is yang brilliance [qi, i.e.,] dryness and metal. The climate in the lower half of the year is disproportionately cool. This section has no listing of the regular number of the annual period. The reason is that in *wu zi* and *wu wu* years the annual fire period is greatly excessive, its regular number should be 'fire transformation: seven.' This is identical to the regular number of the qi controlling heaven. Hence it was omitted."

491 Fang Yaozhong: "上鹹寒 is: in *wu zi* and *wu wu* years minor yin [qi, i.e.,] ruler fire, controls heaven. The climate [in the upper half of the year] is disproportionately hot. Hence in treating illnesses and regulating [the organism] through food and drink, it is appropriate to employ drugs or food with a salty flavor and a cold nature. 中甘寒 is: because *wu zi* and *wu wu* years are years with a greatly excessive annual fire period, [the climate in] summer is particularly hot. Hence in treating illnesses and regulating [the organism] through food and drink, it is appropriate to employ drugs or food with a sweet flavor and with a cold nature. 下酸溫 is: because in *wu zi* and *wu wu* years yang brilliance [qi, i.e.,] dryness and metal, is at the fountain, the climate is dispro-

71-487-2
Ji chou *tai-yi* heavenly complements and *ji wei* years *tai-yi* heavenly complements:

In the upper [half of the year]: major yin, soil.
In the center: minor *gong*, soil period.
In the lower [half of the year]: major yang, water.[492]

Wind transformation, coolness transformation; domination and revenge are
identical [in these two years].[493]
These are the degrees of evil qi transformation.

Catastrophes occur in the fifth mansion.[494]

Rain transformation: five.
Cold transformation: one.[495]
These are the degrees of proper transformation.

---

portionately cool in the lower half of the year. Hence it is advisable to employ drugs
or food of a sour flavor and cool nature when treating illnesses or regulating through
food and drink."

492 Fang Yaozhong: "*Ji chou* and *ji wei* years are years with an inadequate soil period.
Major yin [qi, i.e.,] dampness and soil, controls heaven, while major yang [qi, i.e.,]
cold and water, is at the fountain."

493 Fang Yaozhong: "風化 refers to the ceasing yin qi, [i.e.,] wind and wood. 清化
refers to the yang brilliance qi, [i.e.,] dryness and metal. In *ji chou* and *ji wei* years,
the soil period is inadequate and wood comes to seize it. When wood qi dominates
disproportionately, metal qi comes to take revenge."

494 Fang Yaozhong: "Natural catastrophes occur mainly in the central regions."

495 Fang Yaozhong: "雨化 refers to the qi controlling heaven in *ji chou* and *ji wei*
years. In *ji chou* and *ji wei* years, major yin [qi, i.e.,] dampness and soil, controls heav-
en. The climate in the upper half of the year is disproportionately damp. 寒化 refers
to the qi at the fountain in *ji chou* and *ji wei* years. In *ji chou* and *ji wei* years, the qi
at the fountain is major yang [qi, i.e.,] cold and water. The climate in the lower half
of the year is disproportionately cold. 'One' is the 'generation' number of water. Why
this is applied here is difficult to understand. In terms of the host qi, the fifth qi is
yang brilliance [qi, i.e.,] dryness and metal, and the final qi is major yang [qi, i.e.,] cold
and water. [Hence] the lower half of the year is disproportionately cold. In terms of
the visitor qi, major yang [qi, i.e.,] cold and water, is at the fountain, [hence for this
reason the lower half of the year] should be disproportionately cold, too. Hence the qi
of cold in the lower half of *ji chou* and *ji wei* years should not be inadequate; it should
be greatly excessive. If one were to refer to a relationship with the annual period, in
ji chou and *ji wei* years, the annual [period, i.e.,] wood is insufficient. Major yin [qi,
i.e.,] dampness and soil, controls heaven. Upper *gong* and proper *gong* are identical.

These transformations
in the upper [half of the year require] bitter [flavor] and heat,
in the center [require] sweet [flavor] and harmonious [nature],
in the lower [half of the year require] sweet [flavor] and heat.⁴⁹⁶
These are the requirements of drugs and food.

71-487-7
Geng yin and *geng shen* years:

In the upper [half of the year]: minor yang, minister fire.
In the center: major *shang*, metal period.
In the lower [half of the year]: ceasing yin, wood.⁴⁹⁷

Fire transformation: seven.
Coolness transformation: nine.
Wind transformation: three.⁴⁹⁸
These are the degrees of proper transformation.

The [annual] period is inadequate and receives assistance. [Hence such years] belong
to the years with a balanced soil period. This cannot have an influence on the qi at the
fountain. Hence we believe that the listing of the 'generation' number here is an error
in the text; it should be 'cold transformation: six.'"

496 Fang Yaozhong: "上苦熱 is: in *ji chou* and *ji wei* years major yin [qi, i.e.,] dampness
and soil, controls heaven. The climate in the upper half of the year is disproportionately damp. Hence in treating illnesses and regulating [the organism] through food
and drink, it is appropriate to employ drugs or food with a bitter flavor and with a hot
nature. 中甘和 is: *ji chou* and *ji wei* years are years with an inadequate annual [period
of] soil. Hence it is advisable to employ drugs or food of a sweet flavor and of a harmonious nature when treating illnesses or regulating through food and drink. 下甘
熱 is: because in *ji chou* and *ji wei* years major yang [qi, i.e,] cold and water, is at the
fountain, the climate is disproportionately cold in the lower half of the year. Hence
it is advisable to employ drugs or food of a sweet flavor and hot nature when treating
illnesses or regulating through food and drink."

497 Fang Yaozhong: "*Geng yin* and *geng shen* years are years with a greatly excessive
metal period. Minor yang [qi, i.e.,] minister fire, controls heaven, while ceasing yin [qi,
i.e.,] wind and wood, is at the fountain."

498 Fang Yaozhong: "火化 refers to the qi controlling heaven in *geng yin* and *geng
shen* years. In *geng yin* and *geng shen* years, minor yang [qi, i.e.,] minister fire, controls
heaven. The climate in the upper half of the year is disproportionately hot. 清化 refers
to the annual period of *geng yin* and *geng shen* years. In *geng yin* and *geng shen* years,
the annual [period of] metal is greatly excessive. The climate in autumn is disproportionately cool. 風化 refers to the qi at the fountain in *geng yin* and *geng shen* years. In

These transformations
in the upper [half of the year require] salty [flavor] and cold,
in the center [require] acrid [flavor] and warmth,
in the lower [half of the year require] acrid [flavor] and coolness.[499]
These are the requirements of drugs and food.

71-487-11
Xin mao and *xin you* years:

In the upper [half of the year]: yang brilliance, metal.
In the center: minor *yu*, water period.
In the lower [half of the year]: minor yin, fire.[500]

Rain transformation, wind transformation; domination and revenge are identical [in these two years].[501]
These are the degrees of evil qi transformation.

Catastrophes occur in the first mansion.[502]

---

geng yin and *geng shen* years, the qi at the fountain is ceasing yin [qi, i.e.,] wind and wood. The climate in the lower half of the year is disproportionately warm."

499 Fang Yaozhong: "上鹹寒 is: in *geng yin* and *geng shen* years minor yang [qi, i.e.,] minister fire, controls heaven. The climate [in the upper half of the year] is disproportionately hot. Hence in treating illnesses and regulating [the organism] through food and drink, it is appropriate to employ drugs or food with a salty flavor and a cold nature. 中辛溫 is: because *geng yin* and *geng shen* years are years with a greatly excessive annual [period of] metal, [the climate in] autumn is disproportionately cool. Hence in treating illnesses and regulating [the organism] through food and drink, it is appropriate to employ drugs or food with an acrid flavor and with a warm nature. 下 辛涼 is: because in *geng yin* and *geng shen* years ceasing yin [qi, i.e,] wind and wood, is at the fountain, the climate is disproportionately warm in the lower half of the year. Hence it is advisable to employ drugs or food of an acrid flavor and cool nature when treating illnesses or regulating through food and drink."

500 Fang Yaozhong: "*Xin mao* and *xin you* are years with an inadequate water period. Yang brilliance [qi, i.e.,] dryness and metal, controls heaven, while minor yin [qi, i.e.,] ruler fire, is at the fountain."

501 Fang Yaozhong: "雨化 refers to the major yin qi, [i.e.,] dampness and soil. 風化 refers to the ceasing yin qi, [i.e.,] wind and wood. In *xin mao* and *xin you* years, the water period is inadequate and soil comes to seize it. When soil qi dominates disproportionately, wind qi comes to take revenge."

502 Fang Yaozhong: "Natural catastrophes occur mainly in the Northern regions."

Coolness transformation: nine.
Cold transformation: one.
Heat transformation: seven.[503]
These are the degrees of proper transformation.

These transformations
in the upper [half of the year require] bitter [flavor] and slight warmth,
in the center [require] bitter [flavor] and harmonious [nature],
in the lower [half of the year require] salty [flavor] and cold.[504]
These are the requirements of drugs and food.

71-488-3
Ren chen and *ren xu* years:

In the upper [half of the year]: major yang, water.
In the center: major *jue*, wood period.
In the lower [half of the year]: major yin, soil.[505]

Cold transformation: six.
Wind transformation: eight.

---

503 Fang Yaozhong: "清化 refers to the qi controlling heaven in *xin mao* and *xin you* years. In *xin mao* and *xin you* years, yang brilliance [qi, i.e.,] dryness and metal, controls heaven. The climate in the upper half of the year is disproportionately cool. 寒化 refers to the annual period of *xin mao* and *xin you* years. In *xin mao* and *xin you* years, the annual [period of] water is inadequate; winter should be cold but is not cold. 熱化 refers to the qi at the fountain in *xin mao* and *xin you* years. In *xin mao* and *xin you* years, the qi at the fountain is minor yin [qi, i.e.,] ruler fire. The climate in the lower half of the year is disproportionately hot."

504 Fang Yaozhong: "上苦小溫 is: in *xin mao* and *xin you* years yang brilliance [qi, i.e.,] dryness and metal, controls heaven. The climate in the upper half of the year is disproportionately cool. Hence in treating illnesses and regulating [the organism] through food and drink, it is appropriate to employ drugs or food with a disproportionately warm [nature]. 中苦和 is: *xin mao* and *xin you* years are years with an inadequate annual [period of] metal. In winter it should be cold but is not cold. Hence it is advisable to employ drugs or food of a bitter flavor and of a harmonious nature when treating illnesses or regulating through food and drink. 下鹹寒 is: because in *xin mao* and *xin you* years minor yin [qi, i.e,] ruler fire, is at the fountain, the climate is disproportionately hot in the lower half of the year. Hence it is advisable to employ drugs or food of a salty flavor and cold nature when treating illnesses or regulating through food and drink."

505 Fang Yaozhong: "*Ren chen* and *ren xu* years are years with a greatly excessive wood period. Major yang [qi, i.e.,] cold and water, controls heaven, while major yin [qi, i.e.,] dampness and soil, is at the fountain."

Rain transformation: five.[506]
These are the degrees of proper transformation.

These transformations
in the upper [half of the year require] bitter [flavor] and warmth,
in the center [require] sour [flavor] and harmonious [nature],
in the lower [half of the year require] sweet [flavor] and warmth.[507]
These are the requirements of drugs and food.

71-488-7
Gui si identical to year meets and *gui hai* [years] identical to year meets:

In the upper [half of the year]: ceasing yin, wood.
In the center: minor *zhi*, fire period.
In the lower [half of the year]: minor yang, minister fire.[508]

---

506 Fang Yaozhong: "寒化 refers to the qi controlling heaven *ren chen* and *ren xu* years. In *ren chen* and *ren xu* years, major yang [qi, i.e.,] cold and water, controls heaven. The climate in the upper half of the year is disproportionately cold. 風化 refers to the annual period of *ren chen* and *ren xu* years. In *ren chen* and *ren xu* years, the annual [period of] wood is greatly excessive. [The climate in] spring is disproportionately warm; the qi of wind dominates disproportionately. 雨化 refers to the qi at the fountain in *ren chen* and *ren xu* years. In *ren chen* and *ren xu* years, the qi at the fountain is major yin [qi, i.e.,] dampness and soil. The climate in the lower half of the year is disproportionately damp."

507 Fang Yaozhong: "上苦溫 is: in *ren chen* and *ren xu* years major yang [qi, i.e.,] cold and water, controls heaven. The climate [in the upper half of the year] is disproportionately cold. Hence in treating illnesses and regulating [the organism] through food and drink, it is appropriate to employ drugs or food with a disproportionately warm [nature]. 中酸和 is: because *ren chen* and *ren xu* years are years with a greatly excessive annual [period of] wood, the qi of wind dominates disproportionately in spring. Hence in treating illnesses and regulating [the organism] through food and drink, it is appropriate to employ drugs or food with a sour flavor and with a harmonious nature. 下甘溫 is: because in *ren chen* and *ren xu* years major yin [qi, i.e,] dampness and soil, is at the fountain, the climate is disproportionately damp in the lower half of the year. Hence it is advisable to employ drugs or food of a sweet flavor and warm nature when treating illnesses or regulating through food and drink."

508 Fang Yaozhong: "*Gui si* and *gui hai* years are years with an inadequate fire period. Ceasing yin [qi, i.e.,] wind and wood, controls heaven, while minor yang [qi, i.e.,] minister fire, is at the fountain."

Cold transformation, rain transformation; domination and revenge are identical
[in these two years].[509]
These are the degrees of evil qi transformation.

Catastrophes occur in the ninth mansion.[510]

Wind transformation: eight.
Fire transformation: two.[511]
These are the degrees of proper transformation.

These transformations
in the upper [half of the year require] acrid [flavor] and coolness,
in the center [require] salty [flavor] and harmonious [nature],
in the lower [half of the year require] salty [flavor] and cold.[512]
These are the requirements of drugs and food.

---

509 Fang Yaozhong: "寒化 refers to the major yang qi, [i.e.,] cold and water. 雨化
refers to the major yin qi, [i.e.,] dampness and soil. In *gui si* and *gui hai* years, the fire
period is inadequate and water comes to seize it. When water qi dominates disproportionately, soil comes to take revenge."

510 Fang Yaozhong: "Natural catastrophes occur mainly in the Southern regions."

511 Fang Yaozhong: "風化 refers to the qi controlling heaven in *gui si* and *gui hai*
years. In *gui si* and *gui hai* years, ceasing yin [qi, i.e.,] wind and wood, controls heaven.
The climate in the upper half of the year is disproportionately warm; the qi of wind
dominates disproportionately. 火化 refers to the annual period of *gui si* and *gui hai*
years. In *gui si* and *gui hai* years, the annual period, [i.e.,] fire, is inadequate. In summer
it should be hot but is not hot. Because in *gui si* and *gui hai* years the annual [period
of] fire is inadequate, the 'generation' number of fire is listed in the text to signify that
the qi of fire is inadequate. This section has no listing of the regular number of the
qi at the fountain. The reason may be that *gui si* and *gui hai* years are years with an
inadequate annual [period of] fire. When the annual [period of] fire is inadequate,
water comes to seize it. Winter is disproportionately cold. Hence, even though minor
yang [qi, i.e., minister fire] is at the fountain, the qi of fire cannot become greatly
excessive nevertheless. Hence the regular number of the qi at the fountain should be
the 'generation' number of fire and this is identical to the regular number of the annual
period. Hence it was omitted here."

512 Fang Yaozhong: "上辛涼 is: in *gui si* and *gui hai* years ceasing yin [qi, i.e.,] wind
and wood, controls heaven. The climate in the upper half of the year is dis_propor-
tionately warm and the qi of wind dominates disproportionately. Hence in treating
illnesses and regulating [the organism] through food and drink, it is appropriate to
employ drugs or food with an acrid flavor and with a cool nature. 中鹹和 is: *gui si* and
gui hai years are years with an inadequate annual [period of] fire. In summer it should
be hot but is not hot. The qi of the heart of the human body is inadequate. Hence it is
advisable to employ drugs or food of a salty flavor and of a harmonious nature when

All these
arrangements determining recurring times,[513]
[all] domination and revenge, as well as the proper transformations,
they all have [their] regular numbers.[514]
It is absolutely essential to investigate them.

Hence [when it is stated]
'Those who know the essentials of this,
they make one statement and have said it all.
Those who do not know the essentials of this,
[their words] drift around without ever exhausting [the topic]',
then this means just the same."

71-488-15
[Huang] Di:
"Good!
The qi of the five periods,
will they also take revenge against [the qi dominating] a year?"[515]

---

treating illnesses or regulating through food and drink. 下鹹寒 is: because in *gui si* and *gui hai* years minor yang [qi, i.e,] minister fire, is at the fountain, the climate is disproportionately hot [in the lower half of the year]. Hence it is advisable to employ drugs or food of a salty flavor and cold nature when treating illnesses or regulating through food and drink."

513 Zhang Zhicong: "That is to say, the qi of heaven begins with *jia*; the branches of the earth begin with *zi*. When [the series of] *zi* and *jia* are brought together, 30 years constitute one 紀, 60 years constitute one 周." Fang Yaozhong: " 'Fixed time periods' refers to the 60 years of a *jia zi* cycle."

514 Zhang Zhicong: "[Years of] domination and revenge are years of inadequacy; [years of] proper transformation are years of great excess." Fang Yaozhong: "Zhang Zhicong's comment does not reflect the spirit of the *Neijing*. ... It is obvious that when the qi of a period is disproportionately dominant, there will not only be dominance, there will be revenge, too."

515 Wang Bing: "復 is 報, 'to retribute.'" Zhang Jiebin: "This is to ask whether the qi of the five periods appear in the course of a year in [a succession of] dominance and revenge as do the six qi." Fang Yaozhong: "This sentence asserts in the style of a question that among the five periods whenever a phenomenon of disproportionate dominance occurs, a phenomenon of revenge will follow."

Qi Bo:
"What is under maximum pressure will break out;
wait for its time and it will become active."⁵¹⁶

[Huang] Di:
"I should like to ask what this is to say."

Qi Bo:
"The qi of the five regular [periods]
are greatly excessive or inadequate;
their outbreaks differ [accordingly]."⁵¹⁷

[Huang] Di:
"I should like to hear this comprehensively."

Qi Bo:
"When they are greatly excessive, [their outbreak is] violent;
when they are inadequate, [their outbreak is] slow.
When [their outbreaks] are violent: the illnesses [they cause] are severe.
When [their outbreaks] are slow: the illnesses [they cause] continue for
long." ⁵¹⁸

---

516 Zhang Jiebin: "When any of the five periodic [qi] is dominated [by another] too
much, its oppression will reach an extreme. Extreme oppression must be followed by
revenge. The outbreak of each [period qi] occurs at a specific time." Fang Yaozhong:
"E.g., water can subdue fire. In case of very strong water qi, the qi of fire will be oppressed and is oppressed to collect inside. However, when the oppression of fire has
reached an extreme degree, it is able to violently break the restraints placed on it by
water and to break out with the force of a prairie fire. One difference of the 'revenge'
in the context of 'oppression and outbreak' here and in the context of the 'domination
and revenge' listed above should be pointed out. The revenge in the context of 'oppression and outbreak' is taken by what was oppressed itself. As in the example just given,
the fire was oppressed and takes revenge itself. In contrast, in the case of disproportionate dominance, that which is dominated does not take revenge itself. Hence in
the current context, the character 復 can be interpreted as 恢復, 'to restore,' that is, to
restore a regular condition through a process of self regulation."

517 Wang Bing: "In years with a greatly excessive [period] the outbreak of the respective [qi] occurs early; in years with an insufficient [period] the outbreak of the
respective [qi] is belated." In contrast, Gao Shishi: "When the regular qi of wood, fire,
soil, metal, and water are greatly excessive or inadequate, their outbreaks are irregular.
異 is 不常, 'irregular.'"

518 Zhang Jiebin: "持 is: they advance and return, and linger for long."

[Huang] Di:
"Great excess and inadequacy, what are their numbers?"

Qi Bo:
"When they are greatly excessive, their numbers are completion [numbers];
when they are inadequate, their numbers are generation [numbers].
The soil is always [associated] with a generation [number]."519

71-489-5
[Huang] Di:
"Their outbreaks, how do they occur?"

Qi Bo:
"The outbreak of oppressed soil [qi is as follows]:520
Mountain valleys shake to the extent that one is frightened;521
tremendous thunder [occurs in the section of] qi interaction.522

---

519 Zhang Jiebin: "成 is: abundance of qi; 生 is: slight presence of qi. The qi of soil is generated and grows in all four seasons. Hence it is always associated with a 'generation' number and does not reach 'completion.'"

520 For a discussion of the following listing of the five "oppressions" see 2337/10, 1188/44, 2682/1, and 1497/10.

521 Zhang Jiebin: "Mountain valleys are locations deep inside the soil. 'Shaking to the extent that one is frightened' refers to the outbreak of the qi of the soil. 'Qi interaction' is amidst rise and descent; it is also the period of the third and fourth qi. That is, when fire and dampness join their qi, the effusion [of that qi] is thunder. Hence there is ample [thunder] during the seasons of fire and dampness.

522 Wang Bing: "鬱 is: extremely oppressing heavenly qi. Hence even though it is the heavenly qi, it has its constraints, too. When a share is used up, it weakens. Hence even though [soil qi] is oppressed, when it turns angry it [is able to] break out. The transformations of the soil do not prevail, the flaming is excessive, and there is no rain. [The qi of] wood abounds beyond extreme. Hence the oppressed [qi of soil] turns angry and breaks out. The nature of soil is resting and stability. When [the soil] is made to move, thunder and rain are activated massively and the qi of wood and soil holding on to each other are set free. When the *Yi[-jing]* states 'The activities of thunder and rain are released,' then this is [explained by what was] said above. Even though the soil is very angry, it is nevertheless restrained by wood. Hence all that occurs is shaking to the extent that it is frightening in the [region of] qi interaction and the sound [of the thunder] fails to reach high or wide. 'Qi interaction' is to say: above the soil, as high as the mountains." Zhang Jiebin: "殷 is 盛, 'abundant.'" Zhang Zhicong: "Thunder is the qi of fire. The third qi rules the fire; the fourth qi rules the soil. Hence when there is massive thunder at the time of the soil, fire and soil merge and an outbreak occurs at the [time of the] interaction of third and fourth qi. White is the qi of metal. When the [qi of] soil is unimpeded, metal transforms."

There is dust and darkness [which may be] yellow or black,
transforming into white qi.[523]
Tornados and rainstorms [affect] highlying [regions] and low altitudes.[524]
They hit the stones [making them] fly into the sky.
This is followed by flooding.
The flow of the rivers inundates [the environment], spreading everywhere.
The fields and pastures [are covered with] soil colts.[525]
At this time the transforming qi [of the soil] begins to extend [its reach].
There is a tendency to frequent rain.
[Everything] begins to come to life, begins to grow,
begins to transform, and begins to reach completion.[526]

Hence people suffer from
distension of heart [region] and abdomen;
[they experience] intestinal sounds and [relieve themselves] behind frequently.
In severe cases, the heart aches and the flanks are distended.
[Patients] vomit and have "cholera."

---

523 Fang Yaozhong: " 'Dust and darkness, yellow or black' refers to heavy overcast at the time of strong thunder and rain. 'They transform into white qi' refers to image of dense smoke and fog at the time of strong thunder and rain."

524 Zhang Zhicong: "高深 is: between high mountains and deep valleys."

525 Wang Bing: "After the flooding has abated, stones and soil are spread like a herd of colts put out to graze on the fields and waste lands. Whenever [the text] speaks of 'soil' this is identical to 'sand' and 'stones.'" Gao Shishi: "土駒 is: lumps of soil resembling young horses."

526 Wang Bing: " 'Transformation' refers to transformation of soil [qi]. When the soil [qi] is restrained, the qi of transformation cannot spread. When misfortune has reached an extreme, it will change to good fortune. What is curved to an extreme will stretch. When [the qi of soil] is able to react against being harrassed, the qi of transformation will be activated as a consequence. Hence it can spread to all classes [of things] and rain will provide herbs and trees with moisture in time to let them complete [their growth]. The qi of transformation, then, is diminished while the qi of growth has passed its zenith. Hence when [the text] states that the myriad beings begin to come to life, begin to grow, begin to transform, and begin to reach completion, these four [references to] 'begin' make it very clear that the transformation and completion of the myriad beings is belated." Zhang Jiebin: "When the qi of soil is oppressed, all transformations of things come to a halt. However, the outbreak of oppressed soil [qi] must occur at the time of the third and fourth qi. Hence [things] may still come to life, grow, transform, and reach completion without missing their [proper] seasons."

[Spillage] drink develops[527] and there is outpour below.
There are *fu*-swellings; the body is heavy.[528]

71-490-3
When the clouds rush towards the rain palace,
when colorful skies embrace the morning side of hills,[529] and
when mountains and marshes are darkened by dust,
then an outbreak [is imminent].
This occurs at the [time of the] fourth qi.[530]
When the clouds are stretched in front of heaven and mountains,
when they float and drift, emerge and disappear,
these are the first signs of a dammed up [soil qi ready to break out].[531]

---

527 See *Su wen* 69-405-4.

528 Zhang Jiebin: "All these are illnesses [associated with] dampness and soil. With dampness in the upper and central burners, there is distension in the heart [region] and in the abdomen. With dampness in the lower burner, there is frequent diarrhea. The heart is seized by dampness, hence it has pain. The liver is humiliated by dampness, hence the flanks are distended. 䐜 is 脹, 'to distend.' Noisy [vomiting] is 嘔; [throwing up] things is 吐. 霍亂 is when someone throws up and has diarrhea at the same time, with both his heart and his eyesight suffering from confusion. 飲 is 痰飲, 'phlegm drink (i.e., spillage drink stagnating in the body and assuming a viscosity of phlegm; see *Su wen* 17-104-2). Dampness qi harms the flesh. Hence there is *fu*-swelling and the body is heavy. All these are pathoconditions resulting from an effusion of dampness evil from the soil."

529 2493/531: "This is the style of Han poetry; it is definitely not the unsophisticated style of learned discourses of the Warring States period."

530 Wang Bing: "The 'rain palace' is the location of the major yin. 埃 is white qi resembling thin clouds. 'Fourth qi' is to say: from the 31. day after summer solstice to the day of autumnal equinox." Zhang Jiebin: "埃昏 is the turbid qi of soil. The soil rules the fourth qi. [It is active during] the sixty and some odd days subsequent to the [solar term] Great Heat in the sixth month. Hence the outbreak of oppressed soil [qi] occurs during the fourth qi."

531 Zhang Jiebin: "浮游 is 蜉蝣, 'dung gnats.' They come to life at sunrise and die at sunset. It is because of yin [qi] that they leave. The text says: [Things] as big as clouds stretching along the skies and mountains and as small as dung gnats that come to life and perish [soon after again], are all transformations of dampness alike. When these two appear then the oppressed [qi of] soil is about to break out; they are the first signs. 怫 is 鬱, 'oppressed.'" Zhang Zhicong: "This is the first sign of anxious and oppressed [soil qi] breaking out." Fang Yaozhong: "Following Zhang Zhicong's comment we assume that an interpretation of 怫 as 復, 'to take revenge,' is best."

71-490-4
The outbreak of oppressed metal [qi is as follows]:
The heaven is clean; the earth is brilliant.
The wind is cool;[532] the qi is cutting.
Massive coolness sets in.
Herbs and trees are engulfed by floating mist.[533]
Dryness qi prevails.
Dense fog rises frequently.
Killing qi arrives.
Herbs and trees age and dry out.
Hence the metal makes sounds.[534]

Hence the people suffer from
cough and countermovement [of qi];
the heart [region] and the flanks are full and pull on the lower abdomen.
There is a tendency to violent pain.
One cannot turn to the side.
The throat is dry, the face [assumes the color] of dust. The complexion is bad.[535]

---

532 Fang Yaozhong: "That is, the wind is cool."

533 Wang Bing: " 'Massive coolness' comes close to cold. 舉 is 用事, 'to be active.' 浮煙 is 'dryness qi.'" Zhang Jiebin: "浮煙 is the gathering qi of metal." Cheng Shide et al.: "浮煙 is thin fog." Fang Yaozhong: "浮煙 refers to the floating movement of mist."

534 Wang Bing: " 'Killing qi' is the miasma of frost. Genuine killing qi arrives at the *chou* hour (i.e., 1-3 a.m.). When its duration is extended, it may last until the hours of *mao* and *chen* (i.e., 5-7 a.m. and 7-9 a.m., respectively). With the advent of this qi, a mix of yellow, red, and black colors sets in, too. Those things that fail to dominate [this qi] are killed. Hence herbs and trees wither and dry. 蒼 is a weak greenish color." Zhang Jiebin: " 'Killing qi' is yin qi. 蒼乾 is 凋落, 'to fade away and fall down.' " Fang Yaozhong: " 'Metal' refers to autumn; 'sound' refers to the sound of autumnal wind."

535 Wang Bing: "Metal dominates and wood falls ill." Zhang Zhicong: "Coughing and dry throat are illnesses of the lung." Gao Shishi: "When oppressed metal [qi] breaks out, then dryness qi dominates. Hence people suffer from illnesses such as coughing and countermovement [of qi]. The [region of the] heart and of the flanks experiences fullness which pulls on the lower abdomen because the upward and downward movement of qi is out of balance. There is a tendency to violent pain and [patients] cannot move to the side because the inner and outer movement of qi is blocked. The face assumes a dusty color, i.e., the complexion is bad, because dryness qi dominates. All these are illnesses associated with dryness and metal."

When mountains and marshes dry out and
when the soil is frozen, with frost [resembling] salt,[536]
then the outbreak of the harrassed [metal qi] is [imminent].
The qi [when it breaks out] is the fifth.[537]
At night white dew descends.[538]
Wailing sounds [are heard] in the forest thickets.[539]
These are signs of harrassed [metal qi ready to break out].[540]

71-490-9
The outbreak of oppressed water [qi is as follows]:
Yang qi has left.
Yin qi comes up violently.
Massive cold arrives.
Rivers and marshes freeze severely.
Cold fog congeals to turn into frost and snow.[541]
In severe cases,
a dark screen of yellow or black [dust]
prevails everywhere in the [section of] qi interaction.[542]

---

536 Further below the text states 土浮霜鹵. Both 凝, "to freeze", and 浮, "surface", make sense. Still, one may be a corrupted quotation of the other.

537 Wang Bing: "The fifth qi [is the period lasting] from autumnal equinox to the fifteenth day after [the solar term] winter begins."

538 Wang Bing reads 零 as 濡, 'moist.' Zhang Jiebin: "The character 零 should be changed to 雪, 'snow.'" Zhang Zhicong: "Dew descends thick as snow." Cheng Shide et al.: "零 has the meaning of 'to descend.'"

539 Fang Yaozhong: "林莽 is 樹林, 'forests.' 林莽聲悽 is: the autumnal winds cause wailing sounds in the forests." 2493/531: "This is the style of Han poetry; it is definitely not the unsophisticated style of learned discourses of the Warring States period."

540 Fang Yaozhong: "怫 is 復, 'revenge.' That is, when frost and dew descend at night and when the sounds of autumn rise on all sides, then these are the first signs that the qi of metal is about to arrive and take revenge."

541 Wang Bing: "寒雾 is white qi. It has the appearance of fog but fails to float. It sits on the earth like frost or snow. It dries up in the sun." Zhang Jiebin: "When soil dominates and restrains water, then water is oppressed. When oppressed water breaks out, cold transformations prevail massively and the yang qi flees."

542 Zhang Jiebin: "Yellow is the color of soil; black is the color of water. Water is oppressed by soil and breaks out now. Hence the two colors appear together at the interaction of [these two] qi." Gao Shishi: " 'Qi interaction' is the interaction of winter and spring. [At this time] ice and snow transform to rain and water." Zhang Zhicong: " 'Qi interaction' is the interaction of summer and autumn, i.e., the period following minister fire." Fang Yaozhong: "*Su wen* 68 states: 'At the positions of above and below,

This results in frost that kills.
When water appears, that is an auspicious sign.[543]

71-491-2
Hence the people suffer from
cold having settled [in their body] and from heartache.
The lower back and the buttocks ache.
The large joints do not move freely.
Bending and stretching is not comfortable.
There is a tendency towards recession [of yang qi] with countermovement.
Blockages and hardenings [occur, as well as] abdominal fullness.[544]

When the yang light does not govern and
when heavy overcast[545] accumulates in the sky with
white dust causing haziness and darkness,
then the outbreak is [imminent].
The qi [when it breaks out] is the one before or after the second fires.[546]

---

amidst the interaction of the qi, that is where man resides.' Hence 'qi interaction' refers
to the natural environment in which man lives."

543 Zhang Jiebin: "祥 is 災異, 'disaster.' All good and bad omina are called 祥." Fang
Yaozhong: "Zhang Jiebin's comment does not agree with the spirit of the *Nei jing* and
it does not offer an explanation of 水迺見祥. Hence we do not follow it."

544 Zhang Jiebin: "All these are illnesses caused by cold and water. Fire fears water.
Hence the heart aches. Cold enters the kidneys. Hence the lower back and the buttocks have pain. Qi and blood stagnate under the influence of cold, sinews and vessels
become tense. Hence the joints do not move freely, stretching and bending are not
comfortable. The yin qi dominates and the yang qi fails to move. Hence [patients
experience] recession with countermovement, blockages and hardenings, as well as
abdominal fullness."

545 *NJCD*: "沈陰 is 'deep-reaching, dense yin clouds.'"

546 Fang Yaozhong: " 'Second fire' refers to the ruler fire of minor yin and to the
minister fire of minor yang. That is to say, the outbreak of oppressed water [qi] occurs
mainly around the times when the minor yin ruler fire, i.e., the first fire or the minor
yang minister fire, i.e., are in charge. In other words, when the minor yin [qi, i.e.,]
ruler fire controls a season, i.e., when the qi of fire is excessive and the qi of water is
oppressed, then the oppressed water can break out before the minor yang [qi, i.e.,]
minister fire controls a season. That is, there will be a phenomenon of cold qi arriving
to take revenge in the period following the second qi. When the minor yang [qi, i.e.,]
minister fire, controls a season, i.e., when the qi of fire is excessive and the qi of water
is oppressed, then the phenomenon of cold qi arriving to take revenge can be observed
following the period controlled by the minor yang [qi, i.e.,] minister fire, that is, dur-

When the Great Void is deep dark,
when the [cloud] qi resembles powdered hemp,
which is hardly visible, and
when its color is black and slightly yellow,
these are the first signs of harrassed [water qi ready to break out].547

71-491-6
The outbreak of oppressed wood [qi is as follows]:
The Great Void is darkened by dust;
cloudy things are disturbed.
Strong winds arrive.
They tear open houses548 and break trees.
The wood undergoes changes.549
Hence the people suffer from
pain in the stomach duct, exactly in the heart [region].
Above there is propping [fullness in] the two flanks.
The diaphragm and the gullet are impassable;
food and beverages do not move down.

In severe cases,
[patients hear] a ringing [sound] in the ears and [they experience] dizziness
and vertigo.

---

ing the period following the third qi. Hence the text states 'its qi [occurs] before and
after the second fire.'"

547 Wang Bing: "深玄 is to say: far up and deeply black. 'Qi resembles spread out
hemp' is: it is barely visible." Zhang Jiebin: "麻散 is: resembling the appearance of
scattered hemp [seeds]. They are small and barely visible. In general, the observation
of qi is carried out in the early morning hours. As for "its color is black and slightly
yellow," yellow is the color of the soil, black is the color of water. When it is slightly
yellow and black at the same time, this is a sign that the oppressed water is about to
break out."

548 2530/20: "This should be 發屋. The order [of the two characters] was erroneouly
reversed." 13/10 agrees.

549 Wang Bing: "屋發 is to say: it removes the figures of the fish with uplifted tail
from the roofs. 變 is to say: the soil brings forth strange trees of abnormal appearance." Zhang Jiebin: "When metal dominates and restrains wood, this is 'oppression of
wood.' When the oppressed [qi of] wood breaks out, wind qi moves massively. Hence
[the skies are] darkened by dust and the clouds are scattered. Torn open roofs and
broken trees are signs of changes caused by the [qi of] wood." Fang Yaozhong: "The
木 in 木有變 refers to wind qi. 變 refers to abnormalities or mishaps. That is, when
the oppressed [qi of] wood breaks out, the wind qi changes to abnormal [strength and
movements] and causes mishaps."

Their eyes fail to recognize other persons.
They tend to suddenly fall.[550]

71-491-9
When the Great Void [is filled with] greenish dust,
when heaven and the mountains have one color,
or when the qi has a turbid color,
such as a yellow-black color as if the qi were oppressed,
or when there are stretched clouds failing to produce rain,
then the outbreak is [imminent].[551]
The qi [when it breaks out] is irregular.[552]

When the herbs [on the banks] of long rivers are bent down,
when soft leaves display their dark [side],
when the pines moan in the high mountains, and
when tigers roar in the mountain canyons,[553]

---

550 Wang Bing: "Sinews and bones stiffen and fail to function. [Patients] suddenly fall down and are unconscious." Zhang Jiebin: "All these are illnesses caused by wind-wood-liver evil. The ceasing yin vessel passes along the stomach and penetrates the diaphragm. Hence there is pain in the stomach duct right at the heart, the gullet is barred, and neither food nor drink moves down. The two flanks are propped above because the liver qi moves contrary to its normal direction. The liver conduit follows the throat, enters the forehead, links up with the eye connection, and meets with the top of the skull. Hence [its qi] causes such signs as tinnitus, dizziness, and vertigo, as well as an inability to recognize other people by sight." Fang Yaozhong: "胃脘當心而痛 is pain in the upper abdomen. 上支兩脅 is pain in the two flanks."

551 Wang Bing: "The qi appears like dust or like clouds, [its color] sometimes being yellow or black. 'Oppressed' is: it appears as if it were held in the Great Void." The second part of this sentence is read differently by various commentators. Zhang Jiebin: 或氣濁色, 黃黑鬱若, 橫雲不起雨乃發也. Chen Menglei: 或氣濁色黃黑鬱若, 橫雲不起雨, 而乃發也. Gao Shishi: 或氣濁色, 黃黑鬱若, 橫雲不起雨, 而乃發也. Nanjing zhongyi xueyuan: 或氣濁色黃黑, 鬱若橫雲, 不起雨, 而乃發也.

552 Fang Yaozhong: "The outbreak of the oppressed [qi of] wood does not occur at specific times." Gao Shishi: "Wind is generated by the movement of wood [qi] during all four seasons. Hence [the text states:] 'its qi has no regularity.'"

553 Fang Yaozhong: "There is a common saying: 'when the tigers roar, wind comes up.' Hence [this saying] refers to the majestic strength of tigers. In the present context, though, it refers to the disproportionate domination of wind qi." 2493/531: "This is the style of Han poetry; it is definitely not the unsophisticated style of learned discourses of the Warring States period."

then these are the first signs of a harrassed [qi of wood ready to break out].[554]

71-491-12
The outbreak of oppressed fire [qi is as follows]:
The Great Void is [darkened by] a dense screen.
The great brilliance does not shine.[555]
Flaming fire prevails;
massive summerheat arrives.
Mountains and marshes burn and blaze.
Liquid flows from the timber.
Smoke surges from large mansions.
The soil is covered by salt [resembling a white layer of] frost.
Standing waters decrease.
Winding plants and herbs are scorched and turn yellow.
Wind prevails. The words spoken [by people] are confused.
The transformation of dampness is belated.[556]

71-492-4
Hence the people suffer from
being short of qi,
sores and ulcers, *yong*-abscesses, and swellings.
The flanks, the abdomen, the chest, and the back,
the face, the head, and the four limbs
experience distension pressure;

---

554 Wang Bing: " 'Herbs bend down' is to say: they bend down by themselves even though there is no wind. 'Soft leaves' is to say: the leaves of white willows. When the backside of all the leaves can be seen even though there is no wind, that is called 'to show the yin [side].' " Zhang Jiebin: "When herbs are met by wind, they must bend down. 呈陰 is: soft leaves hang down. Because of the wind they are turned around and their lower side can be seen." Fang Yaozhong: "松吟 is the moaning sound generated by pines under the impact of wind." Cheng Shide et al.: "The herbs are bend down by the wind and resemble the flowing water in a long river."

555 Wang Bing: "腫翳 is to say: red qi. 大明 is the sun." Zhang Jiebin: "The character 腫 is an error. It should be 曛, 'dusk.' " Zhang Zhicong: "大明 refers to the brilliance of sun and moon. When the oppressed [qi of] fire breaks out [it generates] a dark screen above with the effect that the brilliance of sun and moon cannot shine." Fang Yaozhong: "腫翳 refers to darkness."

556 Wang Bing: "The water in the wells vanishes. [People] tell false stories. Rain is overdue." Ma Shi: "The qi of fire [rises like] steamy vapor and winds blow. The words (言) spoken by people are difficult to understand. Misunderstandings (惑) are bound to happen." Gao Shishi: "惑 is 眩亂, 'confused.' " Fang Yaozhong: "風行 is 流行, 'to be widespread.' That is, confused words are widespread."

the abdominal wall is distended.
Ulcers, heat rashes, vomiting, and countermovement occur,
as well as [changes between] spasms and slackening, and pain in the bones.
The joints move [involuntarily].
There is outpour below, warmth-malaria, and
violent pain in the abdomen,
as well as blood overflow and outpour.
The essence fluid is diminished.
The eyes are red and the heart is hot.
In severe cases there is
physical and mental pressure, and vexation.
[Patients] tend to die suddenly.⁵⁵⁷

71-492-8
When at the end of [all] water clock marks⁵⁵⁸ strong warmth [causes]
sweat to make the dark palaces soggy,⁵⁵⁹
then the outbreak is [imminent].
The qi [when it breaks out] is the fourth.⁵⁶⁰

---

557 Wang Bing: "The effects of fire are fast. Hence [patients] tend to die suddenly."
Zhang Jiebin: "All these are illnesses caused by an abundance of fire. Strong fire consumes qi; hence the qi is diminished. Fire can make things rot. Hence ulcers and
abscesses develop. Because yang evil is present in surplus, [patients] suffer from swellings, blockages, and mental pressure, from distension of the abdomen, etc. Fire qi
surges upwards, hence [patients] vomit and experience countermovement [of qi]. Fire
harms the bones, hence the bones ache and have difficulties to fulfill their propping
function. Fire settles in the joints, hence the joints move [involuntarily]. When fire is
in the intestines and in the stomach, this leads to diarrhea. When fire is in the minor
yang [region], then warmth malaria results. When there is fire repletion in the abdomen, then the abdomen experiences violent pain. When fire enters the blood section,
then blood overflows. When fire burns the yin section, then the essence liquids are
diminished. When fire enters the liver, then the eyes turn red. When fire enters the
heart, then the heart turns hot. When fire flames in the upper burner, then loss of sight
and mental pressure result. The nature of fire is urgent and fast. When the [flow of
the] true yin is interrupted, sudden death results."

558 "The end of [all] water clock marks" refers to the conclusion of a day and night
cycle.

559 Zhang Jiebin: "玄府 are the sweat openings." Fang Yaozhong: " 'Sweat makes the
dark palaces soggy' is to say: sweat flows incessantly."

560 Fang Yaozhong: "The period of the fourth qi lasts from [the solar term] Great
Heat to [the solar term] Autumnal Equinox. Basically the fourth qi is a period ruled
by the major yin [qi, i.e.,] dampness and soil. Generally speaking, the qi of dampness
should dominate disproportionately. However, because of the outbreak of the op-

When movement meets with revenge, then [this results in] resting.
When the yang has reached its peak, it returns to yin.
The command of dampness [activates] transformations and completion.⁵⁶¹

When [at a time] when the blossoms break open the water freezes,
when mountains and rivers have ice and snow and
when flaming yang [warms the] Southern waters,
then these are the first signs of harrassed [fire qi ready to break out].⁵⁶²

71-492-9
[First] there are [phenomena] corresponding to the harrassed [qi],
then comes the retribution.
It is always such that when one observes the peak of the [pressure,
then] the outbreak occurs.
The outbreak of wood is not tied to a specific time.
Water follows the fire.⁵⁶³

Carefully observe the times [of harrassment and outbreak].
[Then you] are able to predict illnesses.
[When harrassment and outbreak] miss [their proper] times and contradict the
[nature of the] year,
when the five qi are not active [in time, then]
generation and transformation, and collecting and storage,
[these] policies cannot be perpetuated [either]."

---

pressed [qi of] fire, this period of the fourth qi may exhibit a hot climate nevertheless.
It should rain but does not rain."

561 Gao Shishi: "復 is 伏, 'to lie hidden.'" Zhang Jiebin: "When the yang has reached
an extreme, a reversion occurs to yin. The qi of soil becomes active and the order of
dampness returns. Hence the myriad beings are transformed and reach completion."

562 Zhang Jiebin: "When all blossoms open, that is a sign of the [presence of the]
second qi, i.e., ruler fire. 午澤 refers to moist regions in the South. When at the time
when the blossoms open, water freezes and if there is ice and snow, then this is a visible manifestation of an oppression of the qi of fire. When the flaming yang appears
above the moist regions in the South, this is a first sign that the oppressed [qi of] fire
is about to break out."

563 Wang Bing: "The [phenomena] corresponding 應 [to an oppressed qi] are the
first signs. Once they have appeared, the outbreak will occur. Hence the [phenomena]
corresponding [to an oppressed qi] appear first and the outbreak occurs afterwards.
There is nothing that could maintain its strength forever. When it is obvious that a
strength has reached its apex, the oppressed qi will become active soon afterwards.
What is oppressed will break out. That is a regular feature of qi."

[Huang] Di:
"When water breaks out and hail and snow [appear],
when soil breaks out and tornados and rainstorms [appear],
when wood breaks out and [houses] are destroyed and [trees] are broken,
when metal breaks out and clear [skies] and brilliant [earth appear],
when fire breaks out and red-yellow [color]⁵⁶⁴ obscures [vision],
which qi causes it to be this way?"

71-493-3
Qi Bo:
"The quantities of the [harrassed] qi differ and [hence] their outbreak is slight or severe.
In case of a slight [outbreak], only the respective qi itself [will appear];
in case of severe [outbreaks, the respective qi will appear] together with the subsequent [qi].
Once there is evidence of visible subsequent qi, [a severe outbreak] can be known [in advance]."⁵⁶⁵

---

564 Wang Bing: "曛 is: red-yellow color." Zhang Jiebin: "曛 is: heat qi."

565 Zhang Jiebin: "This serves to explain the meaning of 承制, 'succession and re-straint.' 氣有多少 is: [qi may be present] in excess or insufficiently. An outbreak may be mild or severe. When an oppression is mild, then the outbreak is mild [too]; when an oppression is severe, then the outbreak is severe [too]. 微者當其氣 [is:] the [op-pressed] qi itself appears. 甚者見其下 [is:] the succeeding qi appears, too. That is, subsequent to the position of water there is the soil qi that succeeds it. Subsequent to the position of soil there is the wood qi that succeeds it. Subsequent to the position of wood there is the metal qi that succeeds it. Subsequent to the position of metal there is the fire qi that succeeds it. Subsequent to the position of fire there is the water qi that succeeds it. Hence a mild outbreak of [oppressed qi of] water leads to cold; a severe [outbreak] leads to hail and snow. That is, soil [qi, i.e., dampness, appears], too, because the substance of hail and snow corresponds to [the dampness of] soil. A mild outbreak of [oppressed qi of] soil leads to dampness; a severe [outbreak] leads to tornados and hailstorms. That is, wood [qi, i.e., wind, appears], too, because wind rules tornados and hailstorms. A mild outbreak of [oppressed qi of] wood leads to wind; a severe [outbreak] leads to the destruction [of houses] and the breaking [of trees]. That is, metal [qi appears], too, because metal rules killing and cutting. A mild outbreak of [oppressed qi of] metal leads to dryness; a severe [outbreak] leads to clar-ity and brilliance. That is, fire [qi appears], too, because fire rules light and brilliance. A mild outbreak of [oppressed qi of] fire leads to heat; a severe [outbreak] leads to fumes obscuring vision. That is, water [qi appears], too, because water rules twilight and darkness. 徵 is 証. Through observing whether the qi succeeding is present or not, the mild or severe nature of an oppression and outbreak can be recognized." Fang Yaozhong: "當其氣 is: the outbreak occurs at a time when the [oppressed] qi itself is set to rule. As for instance, the outbreak of oppressed [qi of] soil occurs at the time of

[Huang] Di:
"Good!
If an outbreak of one of the five qi
does not occur at its proper position, how [can this be specified]?"

Qi Bo:
"By naming its delay."566

71-493-6
[Huang] Di:
"Can this delay be quantified?"

Qi Bo:
"[In case of a delay, the arrival of the qi] is always belated by 30 degrees and
some odd [parts of a degree]."567

[Huang] Di:
"The arrival of a qi may be earlier or later [than expected]; why is that?"

Qi Bo:
"When a period is greatly excessive, then it arrives early;
when a period is inadequate, then it arrives late.
This is the regularity of their manifestations."

[Huang] Di:
"When it arrives just in time, how is that?"

Qi Bo:
"When it is neither greatly excessive nor inadequate, then it arrives just in time.
Otherwise disasters occur."

---

the fourth qi, the outbreak of oppressed [qi of] metal occurs at the time of the fifth
qi and so forth. 兼其下 is to say: the outbreak occurs in the period subsequent to that
ruled by the [oppressed] qi itself. That is, when the quantity of oppressed qi is small,
its outbreak affects only the period ruled by that qi itself."

566 Zhang Jiebin: "命 is 令, 'order.'" Zhang Zhicong agrees. Gao Shishi: "差 is 不
及, 'inadequate.'"

567 Wang Bing: " 'Degree' is 'day.'" Zhang Jiebin: "30 degrees and some odd [parts of
a degree] is the length of a month."

[Huang] Di:

"Good!

If a qi causes transformation even though it is not its time, why is that?"

Qi Bo:

"When [a period] is greatly excessive, [the qi causes transformation] exactly when it is its time; when [a period] is inadequate, it turns to that by which itself is dominated."[568]

71-494-3

[Huang] Di:

"The qi of the four seasons

their arrival may be early or belated, they may occur up on high or below, to the left or to the right.

What are the manifestations of these [differences] like?"

Qi Bo:

"The movement [of the qi] may be contrary to or in accordance with [its regular course];

its arrival may be slowed down or speeded up.

Hence

in case of a greatly excessive [qi], transformations precede [the course of] heaven;

in case of inadequacy, they are behind [the course of] heaven."[569]

71-494-5

[Huang] Di:

"I should like to hear what this 'movement' is to say."

Qi Bo:

"The qi of spring moves to the West.

---

568 Wang Bing: "When it rains in winter, when it is cool in spring, when it is hot in autumn, and when it is cold in summer, all these [are examples of seasonal qi] turning to that [qi] by which it is is dominated." Fang Yaozhong: "Wang Bing interprets 己 勝 as 'that which the respective [qi] itself cannot dominate.' That is, when it rains in winter, [the qi of] soil has come to subdue [the qi of] water. When it is cold in spring, [the qi of] metal has come to subdue [the qi of] wood. When it is hot in autumn, [the qi of] fire has come to subdue [the qi of] metal. When it is cold in summer, [the qi of] water has come to subdue [the qi of] fire."

569 Wang Bing: "When the qi is present in surplus, its transformations precede [its proper season]. When the qi is inadequate, its transformations are belated."

The qi of summer moves to the North.
The qi of autumn moves to the East.
The qi of winter moves to the South.[570]

Hence
the qi of spring starts from below.
The qi of autumn starts from above.
The qi of summer starts in the center.
The qi of winter starts from the outside.[571]

---

570 Gao Shishi: "The qi of spring breaks out in the East. Hence the qi of spring moves from the East to the West. The qi of summer breaks out in the South. Hence the qi of summer moves from the South to the North. The qi of autumn breaks out in the West. Hence the qi of autumn moves from the West to the East. The qi of winter breaks out in the North. Hence the qi of winter moves from the North to the South." Fang Yaozhong: "The qi of spring starts from the East and gradually moves towards the West. Hence the qi of spring warmth and of spring generation abounds in the East and is weak in the West. Hence in terms of climate, it is disproportionately warm in the East and disproportionately cool in the West. In terms of things, generation and growth abound in the East, while generation and growth are minimised in the West. The qi of spring warmth and spring generation arrives early in the East and late in the West. Summer qi starts from the South and gradually moves towards the North. Hence the qi of summerheat and summer growth abounds in the South and is weak in the North. Hence in terms of climate, it is disproportionately hot in the South and disproportionately cold in the North. In terms of things, generation and growth are luxurious in the South, while they are retarded in the North. The qi of summerheat and summer growth arrives early in the South and late in the North. The qi of autumn starts in the West and gradually moves towards the East. Hence the qi of autumn coolness and autumn harvest abounds in the West and is weak in the East. Hence in terms of climate, the West is disproportionately cool and the East is disproportionately warm. In terms of things, the West is desolate and the East flourishes. The qi of autumn coolness and autumn harvest arrives early in the West and late in the East. The qi of winter starts from the North and gradually moves towards the South. Hence the qi of winter cold and of winter storage abounds in the North and is weak in the South. Hence in terms of climate, the North is disproportionately cold and the South is disproportionately hot. In terms of things, generation and growth are comparatively deficient in the North, while generation and growth abound in the South. The qi of winter cold and winter storage arrives early in the North and late in the South."

571 Fang Yaozhong: " 'Below' refers to lowlying regions; 'above' refers to high altitudes. 'Center' refers to inside; 標 is 表, 'outside.' That is, the qi of spring warmth and spring generation starts from lowlying regions. In other words, in lowlying regions spring arrives relatively early. The qi of autumn coolness and autumn harvest starts from high altitudes. That is, in highlying regions autumn arrives relatively early. .. The qi of summer fire starts from the center and spreads to the outside; the qi of winter storage starts from the outside and turns to the interior."

The qi of spring starts from the left.
The qi of autumn starts from the right.
The qi of winter starts behind [its time].
The qi of summer starts ahead [of its time].[572]

This is the regular [course] of the transformations of the proper [qi] in the course of the four seasons.

<Hence,
at an extremely high location, winter qi will be there permanently.
At an extremely lowlying location, spring qi will be there permanently.>[573]

This must be investigated carefully.”

[Huang] Di:
“Good!“

71-494-11
Huang Di asked:
“The appearances corresponding to the five periods and to the six qi,
the policies of the transformations of the six [qi] and
the arrangements of the [catastrophic] changes of the six [qi],[574]
how are they?”

Qi Bo responded:
“Now,
the policies and arrangements of the six qi [are such that]
they undergo transformations and they undergo changes; [575]
they have their [periods of] domination and those of revenge;
they have their [normal] operation and they may be marked by defects.
The manifestations of all these [processes and phenomena] are different.[576]

---

572 Fang Yaozhong: “ ‘Left’ refers to the East; ‘right’ refers to the West. ‘Behind’ refers to the North; ‘in front’ refers to the South.”

573 Wang Bing: “High mountain ranges are covered by snow even in mid summer; plants come to life and grow at low-lying rivers and in the wetlands even during a severe winter.”

574 For the reading of 正 as 政, see the title and note 1.

575 For the reading of 正 as 政, see the title and note 1.

576 Gao Jiwu/455: “不同其候 is 其候不同, ‘all these manifestations differ.’”

what would [you, Huang] Di, like [to have explained]?"⁵⁷⁷

71-494-13
[Huang] Di:
"I should like to hear an all encompassing [explanation]."

Qi Bo:
"Please, let me speak about these [issues] one by one.

Now, the arrival of the qi [is as follows]:
Where the ceasing yin [qi] arrives, there is harmonious balance.
Where the minor yin [qi] arrives, there is warmth.
Where the major yin [qi] arrives, there is dust and humidity.
Where the minor yang [qi] arrives, there is flaming summerheat.
Where the yang brilliance [qi] arrives, there is coolness and force.
Where the major yang [qi] arrives, there is cold and fog.⁵⁷⁸

This is the regular [course of] seasonal transformation.

71-495-3
Where the ceasing yin [qi] arrives, there is the wind palace; it causes cracking and opening up.
Where the minor yin [qi] arrives, there is the fire palace; it causes unfolding and flourishing.
Where the major yin [qi] arrives, there is the rain palace; it causes roundness and fullness.

---

577 Fang Yaozhong: 六氣正紀 refers to the laws underlying the regular changes and transformations of the six qi. 化 refers to generation through transformation; 變 refers to changes to catastrophe. 病 refers to illnesses of the human body."

578 Gao Shishi: "Ceasing yin [qi] is wind; it rules the [period of the] initial qi. Hence where the ceasing yin [qi] arrives, there is harmony. 和平 is 舒遲, 'quiet and refined.' Minor yin [qi] is heat; it rules the [period of the] second qi. Hence where the minor yin [qi] arrives, there is warmth. 暄 is 溫熱, 'warmth and heat.' Major yin [qi] is dampness; it rules the [period of the] third qi. Hence where the major yin [qi] arrives, there is dust and humidity. 埃 is equivalent to 土, 'soil.' 溽 is 濕熱, 'dampness and heat.' Minor yang [qi] is fire; it rules the [period of the] fourth qi. Hence where the minor yang [qi] arrives, there is flaming summerheat. Flaming summerheat is the qi of fire. Yang brilliance is coolness; it rules the [period of the] fifth qi. Hence where the yang brilliance [qi] arrives, there is coolness and stiffness. Late autumn and early winter is [a time of] coolness and stiffness. Major yang [qi] is cold; it rules [the period of] the final qi. Hence where the major yang [qi] arrives, there is cold fog. Cold fog collects as frost and snow."

Where the minor yang [qi] arrives, there is the heat palace; it causes movement
and departure.
Where the yang brilliance [qi] arrives, there is the palace that controls the killing; it causes change and aging.
Where the major yang [qi] arrives, there is the cold palace; it causes return and
storage.[579]

This is the regular [course of the qi] controlling transformations.

71-495-6
Where the ceasing yin [qi] arrives, there is generation and wind shaking
[things].[580]
Where the minor yin [qi] arrives, there is flourishing and visible manifestation.[581]
Where the major yin [qi] arrives, there is transformation, as well as clouds and
rain.[582]
Where the minor yang [qi] arrives, there is growth, as well as opulence and
freshness.[583]

---

579 Gao Shishi: "Ceasing yin [qi] rules wind. Hence where the ceasing yin [qi] arrives, there is the wind palace, there is splitting and opening. 璺 is 剖, 'to split.' 啟 is
開, 'to open.' Minor yin [qi] rules fire. Hence where the minor yin [qi] arrives, there is
the fire palace, there is spreading and flourishing. 舒 is 舒展, 'to spread out.' 榮 is 榮
華, 'splendor.' Major yin [qi] rules dampness. Hence where the major yin [qi] arrives,
there is the rain palace, there is perfection and fullness. 員 is 周, 'perfect'; 盈 is 滿, 'fullness.' Minor yang [qi] rules heat. Hence where the minor yang [qi] arrives, there is the
heat palace, there is moving and departure. 'Moving and departure' is: it appears outside. Yang brilliance [qi] rules collection. Hence where the yang brilliance [qi] arrives,
there is the palace directing the killing, there is change and aging. 庚 is 更, 'change';
蒼 is 老, 'aging.' Major yang [qi] rules cold. Hence where the major yang [qi] arrives,
there is the cold palace, there is return and storage. 'Return and storage' is: returning
to the inside and being firmly stored away.'" On 璺 see also 694/45.

580 Wang Bing: "These are transformations of [the qi of] wood." Zhang Jiebin: "The
qi of wood rises. Hence it rules generation. The nature of wind is movement. Hence
it shakes [things]."

581 Wang Bing: "These are transformations of [the qi of] fire." Zhang Jiebin: "At this
time the yang qi is just about to abound. Hence the things flourish and their manifestations are visible." Fang Yaozhong: "Minor yin refers to the second qi. 形見 refers to
generation and growth with great speed."

582 Wang Bing: "These are transformations of [the qi of] soil." Zhang Jiebin: "Soil
can transform to generate the myriad beings; clouds and rain are its qi."

583 Wang Bing: "These are transformations of [the qi of] fire." Zhang Jiebin: "The
yang qi abounds massively. Hence the things grow and are luxuriant and fresh." Fang

Where the yang brilliance [qi] arrives, there is gathering, as well as fog and dew.[584]

Where the major yang [qi] arrives, there is storing and firm closure.[585]

This is the regular [course of] transformations [caused by the] qi.[586]

71-495-9
Where the ceasing yin [qi] arrives, there is generation of wind;
in the end there is sternness.[587]
Where the minor yin [qi] arrives, there is the generation of heat;
in the middle there is cold.[588]
Where the major yin [qi] arrives, there is the generation of dampness;
in the end there is pouring rain.[589]

Yaozhong: "鮮 is 艷, 'beautiful.'"

584 Wang Bing: "These are transformations of [the qi of] metal." Gao Shishi: "Yang brilliance [qi] rules autumn. Hence when yang brilliance [qi] arrives, it brings about collection/harvesting. 雾露 is 清寒, 'coolness and cold.'"

585 Wang Bing: "These are transformations of [the qi of] water." Gao Shishi: "Major yang [qi] rules winter."

586 Zhang Jiebin: "The two [categories of] transformations listed above refer to [the effects of transformations on] plants."

587 Wang Bing: "The generation [of a qi] resulting from a transformation of wind is 風生, 'wind generation.' 蕭 is 靜, 'quiet.'" Gao Shishi: "生 is equivalent to 本, 'to originate.' 終 is equivalent to 極. The ceasing yin qi originates in wind. Hence when it arrives it is 風生, 'generated by wind.' 蕭 is 清蕭, 'clear and impressive.'" Zhang Zhicong: "Wind can generate the myriad beings; in the end it is, nevertheless, a qi of sternness and killing. That is, wind qi occurs during all four seasons. Hence [wind] is able to bring about generation and growth, as well as collection and killing, of the myriad beings." Fang Yaozhong: "風生 refers to a windy and warm climate. 終 is identical here with 中, 'in the middle.' It parallels the phrases 中為寒, 中為溫, etc., below. 蕭 is 蕭殺, 'stern and killing.' Wang Bing's comment is too vague; it explains nothing. Lin Yi et al. and Zhang Jiebin do not provide clear interpretations either. Zhang Zhicong's comments are appropriate.

588 Wang Bing: "The generation [of a qi] resulting from a transformation of heat is 熱生, 'heat generation.' Yin essence succeeds the upper [half of the year]. Hence in the middle [of that year] there is cold." Zhang Jiebin: "*Su wen* 68 states: 'The upper [half] of the minor yin [term] is ruled by the heat qi. At midterm the major yang [qi] appears.' Hence the minor yin [period] is marked by heat in the beginning and cold at midterm." Fang Yaozhong: "Minor yin refers to the second qi. 熱生 is to say: the climate changes to warmth and heat. 中為寒 is: in between there may be spells of cold."

589 Wang Bing: "The generation [of a qi] resulting from a transformation of dampness is 濕生, 'dampness generation.' Major yin [qi] rules in the upper [half of the year].

Where the minor yang [qi] arrives, there is the generation of fire;
in the end there is steam and humidity.⁵⁹⁰
Where the yang brilliance [qi] arrives, there is the generation of dryness;
in the end there is coolness.⁵⁹¹
Where the major yang [qi] arrives, there is the generation of cold;
in the middle there is warmth.⁵⁹²

This is the regular [course of] transformations [resulting from] the virtue [of
each of the six qi].

Hence there is pouring rain in the end." Gao Shishi: "The major yin qi originates from
dampness. Hence when it arrives, it is 'generated by dampness' (濕生). In the end rain
pours. Pouring rain is an excessive outpour of dampness." Fang Yaozhong: "濕生 refers to a disproportionately damp climate. 終 in the present context has the meaning
of 'develops' or 'results in.' That is, during this period there may be thunderstorms or
heavy rains."

590 Wang Bing: "The generation [of a qi] resulting from a transformation of fire is
火生, 'fire generation.' [Minor] yang [qi rules] in the upper [half of the year]. Hence
there is steam and humidity in the end." Zhang Zhicong: "Minor yang [qi, i.e.,] minister fire, is generated by damp regions. Hence in the end there is steam and humidity."
Fang Yaozhong: "In this period of the third qi, the qi of heaven is flaming heat. Because the weather is hot and because of massive rainfalls, a damp climate develops."

591 Wang Bing: "The generation [of a qi] resulting from a transformation of dryness
is 火生, 'dryness generation.' Yin [qi rules] in the upper [half of the year]. Hence there
is coolness in the end." Lin Yi et al.: "In this paragraph it is always such that first the
transformations of the respective qi itself are listed and then those of the opposing qi.
And only with respect to the yang brilliance qi [the text] speaks of 'generated by dryness' and 'in the end there is coolness.' The opposing qi does not appear. Judged from
the preceding and the following text, this passage should read: 'When the yang brilliance [qi] arrives, it is generated by coolness; in the end there is dryness. The reason is,
the position of metal is succeeded by the qi of fire. Hence yang brilliance qi is generated by coolness and turns into dryness in the end." Gao Shishi: "The yang brilliance
qi originates in dryness. Hence when it arrives it is 'generated by dryness' (燥生). In
the end there is coolness. Coolness is the clarity and cutting of metal."

592 Wang Bing: "The generation [of a qi] resulting from a transformation of cold is
寒生, 'cold generation.' [Major] yang [qi rules] the interior. Hence there is warmth
in the middle." Lin Yi et al.: "*Su wen* 68 states: 'The upper [half] of the major yang
[term] is ruled by the cold qi. At midterm the minor yin [qi] appears.' Hence it is
generated by cold and there is warmth in the middle." Fang Yaozhong: " 'Major yang'
refers to the final qi. 寒生 refers to a cold climate. 中為溫 is: there may be spells of
warmth in between. This may also be interpreted as: cold outside and heat inside; yin
outside and yang inside. This is the meaning of Wang Bing's comment."

71-496-3

Where the ceasing yin [qi] arrives, there is transformation affecting the hairy [creatures].

Where the minor yin [qi] arrives, there is transformations affecting the feathered [creatures].

Where the major yin [qi] arrives, there is transformations affecting the naked [creatures].

Where the minor yang [qi] arrives, there is transformations affecting the feathered [creatures].

Where the yang brilliance [qi] arrives, there is transformations affecting the armored [creatures].

Where the major yang [qi] arrives, there is transformations affecting the scaly [creatures].

This is the regular [course of] transformations [resulting from] the virtue [of each of the six qi].593

71-497-1

Where the ceasing yin [qi] arrives, there is transformation resulting in generation.

Where the minor yin [qi] arrives, there is transformation resulting in flourishing.

Where the major yin [qi] arrives, there is transformation resulting in sogginess.

Where the minor yang [qi] arrives, there is transformation resulting in lushness.

Where the yang brilliance [qi] arrives, there is transformation resulting in firmness.

Where the major yang [qi] arrives, there is transformation resulting in storage.

This is the regular [course of] the spreading of the [respective] policy.594

---

593 Gao Shishi: "Hairy creatures are associated with wood. Hence when ceasing yin [qi] arrives, there is transformations of the hairy [creatures]. Feathered creates are asociated with fire. Hence when minor yin or minor yang [qi] arrive, [they] both bring about transformations of feathered [creatures]. Naked creatures are associated with soil. Hence when major yin [qi] arrives, this brings about transformations of naked [creatures]. Armored creatures are associated with metal. Hence when yang brilliance [qi] arrives, there is the transformation of armored [creatures]. Scaly creatures are associated with water. Hence when major yang [qi] arrives, this brings about the transformation of scaly [creatures]. That is, the gestation and coming to life of all creatures is a regular feature of the transformations of the special virtues of each of the six qi."

594 Zhang Jiebin: "When the myriad beings come to life, this is the spread of warmth (溫) [qi] transformations. When the [myriad] beings flourish, this is the spread of warmth (暄) [qi] transformations. When the [myriad] beings are moistened, this is

Where the ceasing yin [qi] arrives, there is the rage of tornados, [followed by] massive coolness.

Where the minor yin [qi] arrives, there is massive warmth, [followed by] cold.

Where the major yin [qi] arrives, there is thunder and tremor, [followed by] flooding because of rainstorms and [by] fiery wind.

Where the minor yang [qi] arrives, there are tornados as well as burning and blazing, [followed by] frost and congealing.

Where the yang brilliance [qi] arrives, there is dispersion and falling [of leaves, followed by] warmth.

Where the major yang [qi] arrives, there is cold and snow, ice and hail, [followed by] white dust.

This is the regular [course of] qi changes [to the abnormal].[595]

71-497-7
Where the ceasing yin [qi] arrives, there is disturbance and movement, as well as coming up and following.[596]

Where the minor yin [qi] arrives, there are high and brilliant flames, as well as

---

the spread of dampness [qi] transformations. When the [myriad] beings abound, this is the spread of heat [qi] transformations. When the [myriad] beings harden, this is the spread of metal [qi] transformations. When the [myriad] beings are stored, this is the spread of water [qi] transformations. When a qi spreads, the [myriad] beings follow its transformation. Hence this is called 'policy.'"

595 Zhang Zhicong: "'The rage of tornados' is a change of wind [to the abnormal]. Coolness is the [restraint exerted by the] succeeding metal [on this excessive qi of wood, i.e., on the wind]. Great warmth (大暄) is an extreme presence of fire [qi]. Cold is the [restraint exerted by the] succeeding yin essence [on this excessive qi of fire]. Thunder and violent outpour are changes of the dampness [qi of] soil [to the abnormal]. When [such changes] reach an extreme, [the excessive qi of soil] is succeeded by wind qi [i.e., the qi of wood]. As for tornados, wind is a product of fire. Blazing and burning is an excessive flaming. When it has reached an extreme, it is succeeded by [freezing frost, i.e.,] the qi of water. Dispersion and the falling [of leaves] is [a change brought forth by] extreme sternness and killing [caused by the qi of metal]. Warmth is [the restraint exerted by the] succeeding qi of fire [on this excessive presence of the qi of metal]. Cold, snow, ice, and hail are [changes brought forth by] an extreme [presence of the qi of water, i.e., of] cold. When [this excess] has reached an extreme, it is succeeded by the qi of soil. That is, when [the presence of] a qi has reached an extreme, then changes occur resulting in harm. The succeeding [qi] will restrain [these extremes]."

596 Wang Bing: "That is the nature of wind." Zhang Jiebin: "迎隨 is the nature of wood." Fang Yaozhong: "迎 is 來, 'to come'; 隨 is 去, 'to go.' In the time period of the initial qi, the qi of wind dominates disproportionately; herbs and trees wave following the coming and going of the wind."

red-yellow [color].⁵⁹⁷

Where the major yin [qi] arrives, there is heavy overcast, white dust, as well as haziness and darkness.⁵⁹⁸

Where the minor yang [qi] arrives, there is luminosity and clearness, red clouds, as well as red-yellow [color].⁵⁹⁹

Where the yang brilliance [qi] arrives, there is smoke[-like] dust, frost, force and cutting, as well as wailing sounds.⁶⁰⁰

Where the major yang [qi] arrives, this results in inflexibility, in hardness and awns, as well as in standing.⁶⁰¹

This is the regular [course of] the prevailing commands issued [by the qi].⁶⁰²

71-498-2

Where the ceasing yin [qi] arrives, there is internal tightness.⁶⁰³

Where the minor yin [qi] arrives, there are ulcers and papules, as well as body heat.⁶⁰⁴

Where the major yin [qi] arrives, there is accumulation of beverages, as well as blockage.⁶⁰⁵

---

597 Wang Bing: "焰 is 陽焰, 'yang/sun flames.' 曛 is red-yellow color." Zhang Jiebin: "高明焰 is 陽光, 'yang/sun light.' 曛 is heat qi." Fang Yaozhong: "In the time period of the second qi, yang qi comes to abound and the climate turns to great heat."

598 Gao Shishi: "Heavy overcast, white dust, as well as haziness and darkness are manifestations of [the qi of] soil."

599 Wang Bing: "光顯 is 電, 'lightning.' 肜 is red color. This is identical to the minor yin qi." Zhang Zhicong: "Humid qi steams upward and turns into clouds."

600 Wang Bing: "That is the qi of killing." Gao Shishi: "'Smoke[-like] dust' is the dryness of metal. 'Frost' is the cold of metal. 'Forceful cutting' is the hardness of metal. 'Wailing sounds' is the sternness of metal."

601 Wang Bing: "These are the transformations of cold." Fang Yaozhong: "堅芒 refers here to the hardening and sharpening resulting from the freezing of ice and snow. 立 means: everything is quiet and does not move."

602 Wang Bing: "When commands are passed, nothing dares to withstand." Zhang Jiebin: "The qi proceeds and nothing dares to oppose it. Hence [the text] speaks of 'commands.'"

603 Wang Bing: "The sinews shrink. Hence they are tense."

604 Wang Bing: "[These illnesses] are generated by the qi of fire." Zhang Jiebin: "When the ruler fire is in charge, then the blood vessels are hot. Hence ulcers, eruptions, and body heat emerge." Fang Yaozhong: "肜 is 疹, 'papules.'"

605 Wang Bing: "These are obstructions by [the qi of] soil." Zhang Jiebin: "When [the qi of] soil, [i.e.,] dampness, is in charge, then the spleen will often be marked

Where the minor yang [qi] arrives, there is sneezing and vomiting, sores and ulcers.[606]
Where the yang brilliance [qi] arrives, there is floating hollowness.[607]
Where the major yang [qi] arrives, there is impeded bending and stretching.[608]

This is the regular [sequence] of illnesses [in the course of the six qi].

71-498-5
Where the ceasing yin [qi] arrives, there is propping [fullness and] pain.[609]
Where the minor yin [qi] arrives, there is fright and uncertainty, aversion to cold, trembling and shivering, as well as incoherent and absurd speech.[610]
Where the major yin [qi] arrives, there is accumulation and fullness.[611]
Where the minor yang [qi] arrives, there are violent illnesses such as fright, overexcitement, and visual distortion.[612]

---

by dampness obstruction. Hence [the flow of] drink comes to a halt; there are obstructions [in the passage downward]." Fang Yaozhong: "積 is 停積, 'accumulations because of halted flow.'"

606 Wang Bing: "[These illnesses] are generated by the qi of fire." Zhang Jiebin: "The minister fire flames upward. Hence there is sneezing and vomiting. The heat harms the skin structure; hence there are sores and ulcers."

607 Wang Bing: " 'Floating hollowness' is a slight swelling. After being pressed down, it rises again." Zhang Jiebin: "When the yang brilliance [qi] is in charge, 淫虛 appears. Skin and hair are associated with metal." Fang Yaozhong: "Only Wang Bing offers a meaningful explanation. A second interpretation could be to identify 'overflow' and 'hollow' as qualities marking the movement in the vessels. This is [a movement in the] vessels which is excessive and lacks strength nevertheless."

608 Zhang Jiebin: "When [the qi of] water, [i.e.,] cold, is in charge, the illnesses are in the bones. Hence bending and stretching is impeded."

609 Zhang Jiebin: "The ceasing yin [qi] rules the liver. Hence there is propping [fullness and] pain in the two flanks."

610 Zhang Jiebin: "The minor yin [qi] rules the heart. Hence it causes fright and uncertainty. When heat has reached an extreme, it turns into cold. Hence [patients] have an aversion to cold and they shake and tremble. Hyperactive yang harms the yin. Hence the mind [of the patients] is confused and they utter incoherent and absurd words."

611 Fang Yaozhong: "Water and drink accumulation results in distension and fullness."

612 Zhang Jiebin: "The minor yang [qi] rules the gallbladder. When it is invaded by fire, this causes fright and vexation. Fire is yang outside and yin inside. Hence [patients suffer from] chest pressure and dizziness. [The nature of] minister fire is urgent and fast. Hence it causes violent illness."

Where the yang brilliance [qi] arrives, the nose is stuffed, and there are illnesses
at the sacrum, the yin (region, i.e. the sexual organs), the thighs, the knees, the
thigh bone, the calves, the shins, and the feet.[613]
Where the major yang [qi] arrives, there is lower back pain.[614]

This is the regular [sequence] of illnesses [in the course of the six qi].

71-498-8
Where the ceasing yin [qi] arrives, there are contractions and contortions.[615]

---

613 Zhang Jiebin: "The yang brilliance stomach conduit rises from the nose. Hence it
causes a stuffy nose. Its [branches] meet at the qi street and gather at the ancestral sinew whence they move down to the feet. Hence the sacrum, the yin [parts], the knee,
and the feet are all ill." Gao Shishi: "The yang brilliance [qi is associated with the]
large intestine; it rules illnesses generated by the body liquids. When the body liquids
are depleted and cold, this results in a stuffy nose. The yang brilliance stomach vessel
moves downward to the Thigh Joint (髀關) [hole], touches on the Crouching Rabbit
(伏兔) [hole], moves down further into the knee cap, moves down further along the
outer ridge of the calves, and moves down into the instep. Hence the sacrum, the yin
[i.e., sexual organs], the thighs, the knees, the buttocks, the calves, the shins, and the
feet are all ill." Fang Yaozhong: "䪼 refers to the nose here. 尻 is the sacrum at the
end of the spine. 'Yin' refers to the external yin [i.e., genitals]. 足 is the sole of the
foot. That is, during the time period associated with the fifth qi, the above mentioned
locations of the human body develop illnesses because the climate is particularly cool
and particularly dry. However, the relationship between the affected body parts and
the yang brilliance [qi] is difficult to explain. Wang Bing and Zhang Zhicong do not
offer any explanations at all. The comments offered by Zhang Jiebin and Gao Shishi
are based on the course of the [yang brilliance] conduit. Such an interpretation, first,
does not agree with the general spirit of this section which discusses the manifestations of the six qi, the proper transformations of the six qi, and the arrangements of
the changes of the six qi in the course of the five periods. It does not discuss conduits.
Second, to rely on the course of the conduit does not explain all the locations of illnesses mentioned above. For instance, it is too far-fetched to explain illnesses at the
nose or at the buttocks with the course of the yang brilliance stomach conduit. Any
explanation must remain close to the original text. The locations where these illnesses
emerge are determined mainly by the lung; the nature of these illnesses is determined
mainly by coolness and dryness."

614 Zhang Jiebin: "The major yang urinary bladder vessel passes along both sides of
the spine to touch on the lumbar region. Hence it causes lumbar pain."

615 Zhang Jiebin: "Illnesses brought about by [the qi of] wood, i.e., ceasing qin [qi],
are located in the sinews. Hence they cause limbs and trunk to be pulled in. The [sin-
ews] no longer fulfill their functions of supporting [the body]." Fang Yaozhong: "戾
has the meaning of 捩 in the sense of 扭轉, 'to turn round.' Here it indicates that the
limbs and the trunk have a cramp."

Where the minor yin [qi] arrives, there is sadness and absurd behavior, as well as nosebleed.[616]

Where the major yin [qi] arrives, there is central fullness, cholera, vomiting, and diarrhea.[617]

Where the minor yang [qi] arrives, there is throat block, ringing in the ears, and vomiting gushing up.[618]

Where the yang brilliance [qi] arrives, there is chapped and peeling [skin].[619]

Where the major yang [qi] arrives, there is sweat flow during sleep and tetany.[620]

This is the regular [course] of illnesses.

71-498-11

Where the ceasing yin [qi] arrives, there is pain in the flanks, vomiting, and outflow.[621]

Where the minor yin [qi] arrives, there is [excessive] speech and [excessive] laughing.[622]

Where the major yin [qi] arrives, there is heaviness and *fu*-swelling.[623]

---

616 Wang Bing: "衄 is 污血, 'impure blood'; it also refers to fat." Zhang Jiebin: "Fire causes illness in the heart and accumulates in the lung. Hence sadness and absurd behavior result. The fire pushes the blood and causes it to move disorderly. Hence there is nosebleed which is [called] 衊 and there is impure blood which is [called] 衄." Wu Kun (see *Su wen* 37, note 24): "Abundant nosebleed is 衄; weak nosebleed is 衊."

617 Zhang Jiebin: "Because the [qi of] soil, [i.e.,] dampness, has harmed the spleen."

618 Wang Bing: "涌 is to say: food overflows and does not move down."

619 Zhang Jiebin: "These are illnesses resulting from dryness."

620 Wang Bing: " 'Sleep sweat' is to say: while one sleeps sweat leaves from the region of the chest, the throat, the neck, and the armpits. It is often erroneously called 盗汗, 'robber sweat.'" Zhang Jiebin: "[The qi of] water, [i.e.,] cold, is in charge; hence [patients] sweat in bed." 1979/10: "寢 is 浸, 'to soak' (in the sense of 'soaking sweat')."

621 Zhang Jiebin: "It is because the wood itself has an illness that the flanks have pain. The [qi of the] spleen has taken over the liver; hence [patients suffer from] vomiting and diarrhea."

622 Zhang Jiebin: "The minor yin [qi] rules the heart. The heart stores the spirit. When spirit is present in surplus, then [people] laugh incessantly." Gao Shishi: "Speech and laughing are ruled by the heart. When the heart qi is replete, then [people] will talk and laugh a lot." Fang Yaozhong: " 'Speech' refers here either to hampered or to abnormal speech. 'Laughing' refers here to abnormal laughing."

623 Wang Bing: "The flesh is like mud; when pressed, it does not rise again." Zhang Jiebin: "When the qi of soil, [i.e.,] dampness, is blocked in its flow, then the body becomes heavy and the flesh swells at the surface. That is called 胕腫." Fang Yaozhong:

Where the minor yang [qi] arrives, there is violent outpour, twitching and spasms, as well as sudden death.[624]

Where the yang brilliance [qi] arrives, [people experience] a stuffy nose and sneezing.[625]

Where the major yang [qi] arrives, there is outflow and halting.[626]

This is the regular [course] of illnesses.

71-499-3
In all these 12 [types of] change,
virtue is retributed with virtue;
transformation is retributed with transformation;
policy is retributed with policy;
command is retributed with command.
When the qi [in nature] is high, then [in man, too,] it is high.
When the qi [in nature] is below, then [in man, too,] it is below.
When the qi [in nature] is behind [its time], then [in man, too,] it is behind [its time].
When the qi [in nature] is ahead [of its time], then [in man, too,] it is ahead [of its time].
When the qi [in nature] is in the center, then [in man, too,] it is in the center.
When the qi [in nature] is outside, then [in man, too,] it is outside.

"重 is: [patients] have a feeling as if their body was very heavy. 胕 is 足種, 'swollen feet.'"

624 Zhang Jiebin: "When the minister fire invades the [territory of] metal and is received by the large intestine, then this causes violent diarrhea. When it invades the spleen, then this causes the muscles to twitch. When it invades the liver, then the limbs and the trunk, the sinews and the vessels suffer from convulsions. The nature of minister fire is urgent and violent. Hence it causes sudden death."

625 Zhang Jiebin: "The qi of metal is cold, stern, and unyielding. Hence it causes sniveling and sneezing."

626 Zhang Jiebin: "When cold qi moves downward, it can cause outflow. Hence [the text states] 流泄. When yin, [i.e.,] cold, [makes things] freeze and pull together and when the yang qi fails to transform, then this may cause an obstruction of the flow of urine and stools and it may prevent the sweat orifices from opening. Hence [the text states] 禁止." Gao Shishi: "流泄 is: sweat flows toward the outside. 禁止 is: blocked urine." Fang Yaozhong: "The explanations offered by Zhang Jiebin and Gao Shishi are not satisfying. In general, urination is not diminished in winter, it is increased. We believe, 流泄 can be interpreted as diarrhea or increased flow of urine. 禁止 can be interpreted as blocked movement of the joints."

This is the regular [correspondence] of the positions [of the qi].⁶²⁷

71-499-6
Hence
when wind dominates, then [this results in] movement;
when heat dominates, then [this results in] swelling;
when dryness dominates, then [this results in] aridity;⁶²⁸
when cold dominates, then [this results in] surface [swelling];⁶²⁹
when dampness dominates, then [this results in] soggy outflow.
<In severe cases the [path of] water is closed and *fu*-swelling occurs.>⁶³⁰

---

627 Wang Bing: " 'Above,' 'below,' 'in front,' 'behind,' 'in the center,' and 'outside' refers
to the locations where illnesses emerge. The qi in the hand yin and yang [conduits] is
'high.' The qi in the foot yin and yang [conduits] is 'below.' The qi in the foot major
yang [conduit] is in the back of the body. The qi in the foot yang brilliance [conduit] is
in the front of the body. The qi in the foot major yin, foot minor yin, and foot ceasing
yin [conduits] is in the center of the body. The qi in the foot minor yang [conduit] is
in the sides of the body. The illnesses caused by changes of qi find their expressions
in locations corresponding to those of the qi." Fang Yaozhong: "The initial qi is the
ceasing yin [qi, i.e.,] wind and wood. Its location is below. Hence in the time period
associated with the initial qi, the climate is warm and mild and the wind dominates
disproportionately. That is meant by the text when it states 氣下則下. The second qi
is the minor yin [qi, i.e.,] ruler fire. Its location is above. Hence in the time period
associated with the second qi, the climate turns hot and heat qi dominates disproportionately. That is meant by the text when it states 氣高則高. The third qi is the minor
yang [qi, i.e.,] minister fire. Its location is above and in front. Hence in the time period
associated with the third qi, the climate is hot and the qi of fire dominates disproportionately. That is meant by the text when it states 氣前則前. The fourth qi is the major
yin [qi, i.e.,] dampness and soil. Its location is above and in the center. Hence in the
time period associated with the fourth qi, the climate is hot and damp and dampness
qi dominates disproportionately. That is meant by the text when it states 氣中則中.
The fifth qi is the yang brilliance [qi, i.e.,] dryness and metal. Its location is below and
outside. Hence in the time period associated with the fifth qi, the climate is cool and
dry and both cold qi and dryness qi dominate disproportionately. That is meant by the
text when it states 氣外則外. The final qi is the major yang [qi, i.e.,] cold and water. Its
location is below and in the back. Hence in the time period associated with the final
qi, the climate is cold and cold qi dominates disproportionately. That is meant by the
text when it states 氣後則後."

628 Wang Bing: "External dryness causes the skin to crack. Internal dryness dries the
essence and the blood. When dryness affects the qi and the body liquids, then the
flesh dries and the skin clings to the bones."

629 Wang Bing: "浮 is 浮起, 'to swell.' When pressed a mark remains visible."

630 Wang Bing: " 'Soggy outflow' is a water dysentery. In case of 胕種 the flesh resembles mud; when pressed it has a dent which does not rise again. When water is

[One needs] only to follow the location of the qi
[and will be able] to state these changes [in a person's condition]."⁶³¹

71-499-8
[Huang] Di:
"I should like to hear about the operations of the [six qi]."⁶³²

Qi Bo:
"Now,
the operations of the six qi [are such that]
each turns to [that qi] by which it cannot be dominated and causes transformations there.⁶³³

Hence,
the transformations of the major yin [qi, i.e.,] rain, are applied to major yang
[qi],⁶³⁴

---

blocked, it stays idly in the skin." Zhang Jiebin: "Wind moves and it changes [its
strength and direction] frequently. Hence wind domination causes movement. Ulcers,
abscesses, and swellings are fire illnesses When essence, blood, and the body liquids
dry out inside and when the skin and the flesh chap and crack outside, then all these
illnesses are caused by dryness. When the abdomen [suffers from] fullness and when
the body is bloated, then these are illnesses caused by yang insufficiency and cold. 水
閉胕種 is: the water ways are blocked and the muscles as well as the flesh are swollen
and dinstended."

631 Fang Yaozhong: " 'Qi' refers to climate; 'presence' refers to season. 'Changes' refers to
pathological changes. That is, each of the six qi wind, heat, fire, dampness, dryness, and
cold, is associated with a specific season and has its specific presence [in the course of
the seasons]. Hence they all are associated with illnesses of different natures." Zhang
Zhicong: "所在 is: wind qi is present in spring, heat qi is present in summer, dryness
qi is present in autumn, cold qi is present in winter, and dampness qi is present during
all four seasons. Each rules 72 days plus a fraction of a day."

632 Wang Bing: "用 is to say: 'to apply its transforming qi [to another qi].'"

633 Fang Yaozhong: "不勝 is the qi by which a qi cannot be dominated. For instance,
wind can dominate dampness. Hence wind is the qi which cannot be dominated by
dampness. Heat dominates coolness and dryness. Hence heat is the qi which cannot
be dominated by coolness and dryness. Etc."

634 Gao Shishi: "In the operation of the six qi, restraint and transformation are of
primary importance. Hence each [qi] turns to that by which it cannot be dominated
and causes transformations there. Hence the transformation of the major yin [qi, i.e.,]
rain, is soil. When [soil] exerts an effect on the major yang [qi], then soil restrains
water. Because the son of soil is metal which, in turn, generates water, [soil] cannot be
dominated [by water] and causes [water] to transform." Fang Yaozhong: "施於 is 作

the transformations of the major yang [qi, i.e.,] cold, are applied to minor yin [qi],[635]
the transformations of the minor yin [qi, i.e.,] heat, are applied to yang brilliance [qi],[636]
the transformations of the yang brilliance [qi, i.e.,] dryness, are applied to ceasing yin [qi],[637]
the transformations of the ceasing yin [qi, i.e.,] wind, are applied to major yin [qi].[638]

用於, 'to exert an effect on.' That is, the dampness qi among the six qi can exert an effect on the cold qi among the six qi. It restrains the cold qi and prevents it from being disproportionately dominant. In terms of the five agents, dampness is associated with soil; cold is associated with water. That is, [the statement] 'the transformations of the major yin [qi, i.e.,] rain are applied to major yang [qi]' is [based on the principle of] 'soil can dominate water.'"

635 Lin Yi et al.: "This should be 'minor yin and minor yang [qi].'" Gao Shishi: "The transformation of major yang [qi, i.e.,] cold, is water. When [water] exerts an effect on the minor yin [qi], then water restrains fire. The son of water is wood which, in turn, generates fire." Fang Yaozhong: "The cold qi among the six qi can exert an effect on the heat qi or qi of fire among the six qi. It restrains the heat qi/qi of fire and prevents it from being disproportionately dominant. In terms of the five agents, cold is associated with water; heat is associated with fire. That is, [this statement] is [based on the principle of] 'water can dominate fire.'"

636 Gao Shishi: "The transformation of minor yin [qi, i.e.,] heat, is fire. When [fire] exerts an effect on the yang brilliance [qi], then fire restrains metal. The son of fire is soil which, in turn, generates metal." Fang Yaozhong: "The heat qi among the six qi can exert an effect on the coolness qi/dryness qi among the six qi. It restrains the coolness qi/dryness qi and prevents it from being disproportionately dominant. In terms of the five agents, heat is associated with fire and coolness/dryness is associated with metal. That is, [this statement] is [based on the principle of] 'fire can dominate metal.'"

637 Gao Shishi: "The transformation of yang brilliance [qi, i.e.,] dryness, is metal. When [metal] exerts an effect on the ceasing yin [qi], then metal restrains wood. The son of metal is water which, in turn, generates wood." Fang Yaozhong: "The coolness qi among the six qi can exert an effect on the warmth/wind qi among the six qi. It restrains the warmth/wind qi and prevents it from being disproportionately dominant. In terms of the five agents, coolness/dryness is associated with metal and warmth/wind is associated with wood. That is, [this statement] is [based on the principle of] 'metal can dominate wood.'"

638 Gao Shishi: "The transformation of ceasing yin [qi, i.e.,] wind, is wood. When [wood] exerts an effect on the major yin [qi], then wood restrains soil. The son of wood is fire which, in turn, generates soil." Fang Yaozhong: "The wind/warmth qi among the six qi can exert an effect on the dampness qi among the six qi. It restrains it and prevents it from being disproportionately dominant. In terms of the five agents,

In each case, naming their location provides evidence of [the time and location of] their [future operation]."⁶³⁹

71-499-11
[Huang] Di:
"When each of them occupies its [proper] position, how is that?"

Qi Bo:
"When each of them occupies its [proper] position, that is the regular [course of the] transformations."⁶⁴⁰

[Huang] Di:
"I should like to hear where they are present."

Qi Bo:
"Name their position
and [their] cardinal point and the months [where they operate] can be known [in advance]."⁶⁴¹

71-500-3
[Huang] Di:

---

wind is associated with wood; dampness is associated with soil. That is, [this statement] is [based on the principle of] 'wood can dominate soil.'"

639 Zhang Jiebin: "命 is 命其名也, 'name its name.'" Fang Yaozhong: "For example, the 'position' associated with fire is South; the 'month' associated with fire is the [time period of the] third qi. Hence in the South and in the time period associated with the third qi the climate is comparatively hot. The 'position' associated with water is the North; the 'month' associated with water is [the time period of the] final qi. Hence in the North and in the time period associated with the final qi the climate is comparatively cold."

640 Fang Yaozhong: "That is, in the time period associated with the initial qi, wind qi is disproportionately dominant. In the time period associated with the second qi, heat qi is disproportionately dominant. In the time period associated with the third qi, fire qi is disproportionately dominant. Etc. 常化 refers to the normal climatic changes in the course of a year."

641 Zhang Jiebin: "位 is the position a [qi] should occupy above or below. 方 is 方隅, 'place of residence.' 月 is 月令, 'season.' 'To name its position' is to name its halting place. When its halting place is named, then the locations where it settles and the months it rules, do all correspond and the regular changes [from one to the next] can be known." Fang Yaozhong: "Once the positions associated with the six qi are determined, the cardinal points and the annual seasons where the six qi are present can be identified accordingly."

"The qi [appearing] in the six positions,
they may abound or be depleted, how is that?"[642]

Qi Bo:
"There is the difference between excessive and diminished.
An excessive [qi] arrives slowly, but is present permanently;
a diminished [qi arrives] violently, but vanishes [soon afterwards]."[643]

[Huang] Di:
"The qi of heaven and earth,
how is it that they abound or are depleted?"

---

642 Zhang Zhicong: "These are the six qi ruling their respective seasons."

643 Wang Bing: "The application of great strength cannot last long. Hence it is violent [first] and vanishes [soon afterwards]. 亡 is 無, 'to be not present.'" Zhang Jiebin: "The six yang years are called 'major'; the six yin years are called 'minor.'" Zhang Zhicong: "A greatly excessive qi comes slowly and stays for long; an inadequate qi comes swiftly and stays for only a short time." Cheng Shide et al.: "'Major' refers to great excess; 'minor' refers to inadequacy. 亡 is 短, 'short.'" Fang Yaozhong: "太少 refers to the greatly excessive or inadequate nature of the five periods. For instance, a greatly excessive wood period is called 太角, 'major *jue*.' An inadequate metal period is called 少商, 'minor *shang*.' 太少異也 is to say: even though each of the six qi has its appropriate position and season, each season itself is associated with specific climatic changes. To take *ren chen* and *ding mao* years as examples, the annual stem of *ren chen* years is *ren*. *Ding* and *ren* are transformations of wood. *Ren* is a yang stem. [Hence] it is associated with a greatly excessive wood period. Hence *ren chen* years are major *jue* years. The initial period of the visitor periods in major *jue* years is major *jue*, too; it rules greatly excessive wind qi. The time period associated with the initial visitor qi and the time period associated with the season ruled by the initial qi of the six qi are largely identical. The initial qi [of the six qi] is the ceasing yin [qi, i.e.,] wind and wood. [Hence this time period] in itself is marked by a disproportionate domination of wind already. If now, in addition, it falls together with an initial visitor period in a major *jue* year, i.e., with a time period of greatly excessive wind qi, then the time period of the initial qi [of the six qi] of that year may have greatly abounding wind qi. That is the meaning of 'rich.' In *ding mao* years, the annual stem is *ding*. *Ding* and *ren* are transformations of wood. *Ding* is a yin stem. [Hence] it is associated with an inadequate wood period. Hence *ding mao* years are minor *jue* years. The initial visitor period of minor *jue* years is minor *jue*, too; it rules inadequate wind qi. When the ceasing yin [qi] is effective as initial qi [of the six qi], even though this means that wind qi is disproportionately dominant, nevertheless because the wind qi of the initial visitor period is inadequate, the one diminishes the other. Hence the time period of that year associated with the initial qi is characterized by inadequate wind qi. That is meant by 'depleted.' 徐而常 is to say: the impact on living beings is not very strong; 暴而亡 is to say: the impact on living beings is very strong; it may even prevent them from generation and growth."

71-500-5
Qi Bo:
"When the qi of heaven is insufficient, the qi of the earth will follow it.
When the qi of the earth is insufficient, the qi of heaven will follow it.
The period [qi] is located in between [the qi of heaven and earth] and
it is always the first [to be determined].⁶⁴⁴

[A qi] hates [the qi] which it does not dominate and
turns to what it agrees with.
Following the associations of the period [qi],
it generates its illnesses .⁶⁴⁵

71-500-7
Hence,
when there is domination in the upper [half of the year],
then the qi of heaven descends into the lower [half of the year];

---

644 Wang Bing: "運 refers to [the periods of] wood, fire, soil, metal, and water each of
which rules a year. When the qi of the earth dominates, then the annual period [qi]
rises. When the qi of heaven dominates, then the annual qi descends. In this rise and
descent, the period qi is usually the first to be removed and to be downed." Zhang
Jiebin: " 'Qi of heaven' is the [qi] controlling heaven; 'qi of the earth' is the [qi] at the
fountain. 'Period' refers to the annual period. The annual period resides in the center
of above and below, in the section of the qi interaction. Hence when the qi of heaven
is about to descend, then the period [qi] must descend first. When the qi of the earth
is about to rise, then the period [qi] will rise first." Fang Yaozhong: "天氣不足 refers
to an insufficient qi controlling heaven; 地氣隨之 is: the qi at the fountain is insufficient, too. 地氣不足 refers to an insufficient qi at the fountain. 天氣從之 is: the qi
controlling heaven will be insufficient, too. That is, when the climate in the first half
of a year is inadequate, the climate in the second half of that year will be inadequate,
too, and display abnormal changes. For instance, when the climate in the first half
of a year should be warm but is not warm, or should be hot but is not hot, then the
climate that should be cool in the second half of that year is not cool and the climate
that should be cold is not cold. Conversely, when the climate in the second half of a
year is inadequate, the climate in the first half of that year will be inadequate, too, and
display abnormal changes."

645 Zhang Jiebin: "This, too, refers to the central period. For example, in case a wood
period meets with dryness [qi, i.e., the qi of] metal, controlling heaven or earth, then
[metal] is that which [wood] cannot dominate; hence [the wood qi] hates it. When it
meets with water or fire controlling heaven or earth, this is a congenial and harmonious relationship, and it turns to them. That which cannot be dominated will subject
it to restraint; that which is congenial will support its domination. All such situations
can generate illness. Hence [the text] states: 'Illnesses are generated in accordance
with the movement of the period [qi].'"

when there is domination in the lower [half of the year],
then the qi of the earth leaves its position and rises into the upper [half of the year].[646]

In accordance with the increased or diminished [rise or descent of a qi], the [time] sections differ.[647]
In case of a slight [increase or diminishment in the rise or descent of a qi], the difference is minor;
in case of a severe [increase or diminishement in the rise or descent of a qi], the difference is large.[648]

In case of a severe [increase or diminishment, the respective qi] changes its position altogether. The exchange occurs at the qi interaction.
As a result, massive changes occur and illnesses break out.[649]

When the *Great Essential* states:
'In an arrangement of severe [increase or diminishment, the difference amounts to] five sections;
in an arrangement of slight [increase or diminishement, the difference amounts to] seven sections.

---

646 Wang Bing: "勝 is to say: 多, 'increased.' When [the qi] is increased above, it will descend by itself. When it is increased below, it will rise by itself. The movement of increased and diminished [qi] among each other is the regular behavior of the qi." Gao Shishi: "The first half of a year is ruled by the qi controlling heaven. 上勝 is: the qi controlling heaven is present in surplus. Hence in a situation of 'domination above' the surplus qi of heaven will descend. 降而下 is to say: it will flow into the second half of that year. The second half of a year is ruled by the qi at the fountain. 下勝 is: the qi at the fountain is present in surplus. Hence in a situation of 'domination below,' the qi of the earth will leave its position and rise. 遷而上 is: it will move into the first half of that year."

647 Wang Bing: "In case they are increased, then rise and descent will be increased, too. When they are diminished, then rise and descent will be diminished, too. In correspondence with their increased or diminished presence, there are slight or severe differences [in their time sections]."

648 Fang Yaozhong: "That is, the difference between the climate that should appear in a specific time period and the climate that does appear in fact."

649 Zhang Jiebin: "In case of severe [increase or diminishement], the exchange of the positions above and below takes place at the boundary line of qi interaction."

The differences are obvious,'
then this means just the same."⁶⁵⁰

71-500-11
[Huang] Di:
"Good!

The discourse states:
'Heat must not offend heat; cold must not offend cold.'

If [in a treatment] I do not intend to stay away from cold, or to stay away from
heat, how [can I proceed]?"⁶⁵¹

Qi Bo:
"An encompassing question, indeed!

If [you wish to] open the [body's] exterior, you do not [need to] stay away from
heat;
if [you wish to] attack the interior, you do not [need to] stay away from cold."⁶⁵²

71-500-13
[Huang] Di:
"If I do not [intend to] open [the body's outside] and if I do not [intend to]

---

650 Gao Shishi: "甚紀五分 is to say: five parts remain at their original position and
five parts are removed. 微紀七分 is to say: seven parts remain at their original position
and three parts are removed." Fang Yaozhong: "差 is 差距, 'difference.'"

651 155/14: "奈何 has the meaning here of 'what is to be done,' 'how to treat this.'"

652 Wang Bing: "To cause sweating one employs heat and does not [need to] stay
away from heat. To cause a diarrhea one employs cold and does not [need to] stay
away from cold. The reason is in both cases that [the heat or cold employed] will not
remain in the center [of the body]. Under such circumstances it is possible to employ
heat in summer and to employ cold in winter. However, if there is no [therapeutic goal
of] effusing [sweat] or of causing a diarrhea and if the [above mentioned] restrictions
are violated nevertheless, that is called foolish neglect of restrictions imposed by the
pattern." Gao Shishi: "When during a hot season a cold evil is in the [body's] outer
regions and if [in such a situation] one employs acrid and hot drugs to effuse the
[cold], then this is [an example of] 'opening the outside and not staying away from
heat.' When during a cold season a heat evil is inside [the body] and cold, draining
drugs are employed to attack it, then this is [an example of] 'attacking the inside and
not staying away from cold.'" Fang Yaozhong: "In case of pathoconditions affecting
the outer regions of the human body, patterns 'to open the outside' can be employed at
any time, even when the climate is hot."

carry out an [internal] attack and offend cold or offend heat nevertheless, what [happens]?"[653]

Qi Bo:
"Cold or heat would cause internal injuries. The illness [you try to heal] will become even more severe."[654]

[Huang] Di:
"I should like to hear what happens [if I were to wrongly employ heat or the cold] when [the person] has no illness."

Qi Bo:
"If there was no [illness, that person will] generate one;
if there was an [illness already,] it will become more serious."[655]

71-501-2
[Huang] Di:
"If one is generated, which one is it?"

Qi Bo:
"If one does not stay away from heat,
then heat will set in;
if one does not stay away from cold,
then cold will set in.
When cold sets in,
then firmness, blockage, and abdominal fullness,
pain, tightness, and diarrhea – such illnesses will be generated.

---

653 Zhang Jiebin: "If it is not because one intends to open the outside that heat is offended and if it is not because one intends to attack internally that cold is offended, what illnesses will result?" Cheng Shide et al.: "犯 has the meaning here of 'it should not be used and is used nevertheless.'"

654 Wang Bing: "If water is added to water, if fire is added to fire, this is truly appropriate to generate new illnesses; why should only the illness become more severe that is present already?" Gao Shishi: "If it is inappropriate to attack or effuse/open the outside and one employs cold or heat nevertheless, that is called 內賊, 'internal destruction.'"

655 Wang Bing: "In case there was no illness in the first place and one violates these restrictions nevertheless, such an approach is truly able to generate new illnesses. How much more difficult will it be [to cure a person] if [that person] has an illness that was not alleviated or entirely healed yet!"

When heat sets in,
then the body turns hot.
Vomiting, diarrhea, cholera,
yong-abscesses, *ju*-abscesses, sores, ulcers,
oppression, and outpour below,
twitching and spasm, swelling and distension,
vomiting, stuffy nose, nosebleed, headache,
changes of the bones and joints, pain in the flesh,
blood overflow, and blood outflow, as well as
strangury and constipation – such illnesses are generated."⁶⁵⁶

71-501-6
[Huang] Di:
"How to treat such [conditions]?"

Qi Bo:
"One must act in accordance with the seasons.
Treat that which you have offended with [a qi] that [can] dominate it."⁶⁵⁷

---

656 964/1: "The term 淋閟 does not appear in any other chapter; 淋 should be 癃. 癃 and 淋 were pronounced identically and used interchangeably in ancient times. During the Eastern Han 癃 was changed to 淋 because of a taboo placed on the name of Emperor Liu Long 劉隆. The present chapter correctly refers to 癃閟 following the line 凡此陽明司天之政 and *Su wen* 70, under the arrangement of 'dried up flow,' lists 癃閟, too. As for the meaning of 閟, the *Shuo wen* states: 'closed door.' 閟 stands for 閉. Hence 癃閟 is 癃閉."

657 Wang Bing: "In spring it is appropriate [to treat with] cool [drugs]; in summer it is appropriate [to treat with] cold [drugs]; in autumn it is appropriate [to treat with] warm [drugs]; and in winter it is appropriate [to treat with] hot [drugs]. These are [treatments] suiting a season; one must act accordingly. Now, if [one has generated heat by] offending heat, a treatment is to employ cold; if [one has generated cold by] offending cold, a treatment is to employ heat. If [one has generated warmth by] offending spring one should employ cool [drugs]. If [one has generated coolness by] offending autumn, one should employ warm [drugs]. The reason is that [the latter] dominates [the former]. If [one has generated heat by] offending heat, a treatment is to employ salty and cold [drugs]. If [one has generated heat by] offending cold, a treatment is to employ sweet and hot [drugs]. If [one has generated heat by] offending coolness, a treatment is to employ bitter and warm [drugs]. If [one has generated heat by] offending warmth, a treatment is to employ acrid and cool [drugs]. Such an [approach], too, is based on the principle of domination."

Huang Di asked:
"When a woman has a doubled body,[658]
how about [treating her with drugs containing] poison?"

Qi Bo:
"If there is a hardening,[659] there will be no harm [to the woman] and [the fetus]
will not be harmed either."[660]

[Huang] Di:
"I should like to hear what 'hardening' is meant to say."

Qi Bo:
"Massive accumulations; massive agglomerations.
They can be offended.
Weaken them to a degree of just over one half and then stop [the treatment].
If this [limit] is exceeded, [mother and child] will die."[661]

---

658 See an identical expression for "pregnancy", with historical comments, in *Su wen*
47-259-6.

659 We read 故 here as 固.

660 Wang Bing: "故 is to say: in case [a pregnant woman] suffers from large hardenings, from concretions, and conglomerations, with unbearable pain, then she is to be
treated with drugs breaking accumulations and curing concretions. In other words,
without such assistance all [women] will perish. If assisted this way, most will be kept
alive. Even though she consumes toxic drugs, she will not die. The first 無殞 means
'the mother will be healed'; 亦無殞 means: 'the child will not die either.'" Zhang
Jiebin: "Specific drugs are to be used for specific reasons. That is to say, if there is a
[specific] illness, then this illness will be the recipient [of its specific drugs]. Hence a
pregnant woman will not be harmed and the fetus will not be harmed either." *Gu dian
yi zhu xuan* bianxiezu /64: "重身 is 'pregnancy.' 故 is 'origin,' 'cause,' referring here
to an illness. 殞 is 'to perish,' 'to die,' and 'to fall.' The first 無殞 means 'do not harm
the pregnant woman'; the second 無殞 means: 'do not abort the fetus.' [The meaning
of the entire sentence is:] When a pregnant woman falls ill, is it allowed to use toxic
drugs for treatment? Answer: When a pregnant woman falls ill, even though one uses
toxic drugs, they are unable to harm that pregnant woman, or to cause an abortion of
the fetus." 1892/45: "故 is 變故, 'unforeseen misfortune.' The six characters 無殞亦無
殞也 make no sense. They must contain an error. The second 無 should be 有, 'to have':
'when treating a pregnant woman, [her fate is unforeseeable]; it may be that she does
not die; it may also be that she dies.'" See also 1620/24, 1099/40, and 2694/55.

661 Wang Bing: "To weaken them just over one half is not sufficient to cause harm
to the life [of mother and child]." Lin Yi et al.: "This section on the treatment of a
pregnant woman does not fit the contents of the preceding and of the following text.
It may have been moved here from another chapter."

[Huang] Di:

"Good!

If [a qi in the body] is extremely oppressed, how can it be treated?"

71-501-11
Qi Bo:

"When the wood [qi] is oppressed, open its way.[662]

When the fire [qi] is oppressed, effuse it.[663]

When the soil [qi] is oppressed, take it away.[664]

When the metal [qi] is oppressed, drain it.[665]

When the water [qi] is oppressed, break it.[666]

---

662 Wang Bing: "達 is to say: vomit it; free its way." Zhang Jiebin: "All illnesses of wood oppression are associated with wind. Now, wood prefers to move freely and to find its way. Hence it is necessary to free the conduits in the [body's] outside and to open the depots in the inside. To free the movement of the qi, that is called 達. All specialists identify 達 as emetic treatment. How could such [an approach] suffice to achieve a comprehensive success!" For a detailed discussion, see 1391/12.

663 Wang Bing: "發 is to say: sweat it; let it effuse." Zhang Jiebin: "All illnesses of fire oppression are associated with yang [qi] and with heat. Wherever there are accumulations because fire has settled down at a specific locations, it would be wrong to conceal them or to try to check them. In accordance to the strength [of the fire] it must be set free, it must be dispersed, it must be made to rise. This is like opening a window, like lifting the bed-clothes. All these activities are called 發; [a treatment] must not be limited to letting [the patient] sweat." For detailed discussions, see 1004/25, 1167/19, 1329/13, and 2043/20.

664 Wang Bing: "奪 is to say: purge it downwards; let there be no obstructions." Zhang Jiebin: "奪 is to take [something] away. All illnesses of soil oppression are associated with dampness obstructions. Whenever an obstruction occurs in the upper [part of the body], it must be taken away above; to have [the patient] vomit is appropriate. When an obstruction occurs in the central [part of the body], it must be taken away from the center. To attack it is appropriate. When an obstruction occurs in the lower [part of the body], it must be taken away below; to drain it downwards is appropriate. [A treatment] must not be limited to purging downward."

665 Wang Bing: "泄 is to say: drain it. Open the [body's] outside and stimulate urination." Zhang Jiebin: "All illnesses of metal oppression are associated with accumulations and stoppage, with dryness, and blockage. Hence [for treating them] one either opens [the patient's] outside, or breaks his/her qi [accumulations], or frees the way of his/her urine. No matter whether [a treatment is carried out] in the [body's] outside or inside, above or below, it can always be called 'draining.'"

666 Wang Bing: "折 is to say: curb it; check its countermovement." Zhang Jiebin: "折 is 調製, 'to regulate.' All illnesses of water oppression are associated with cold and with water. The nature of water is to flow. One must prevent inundations. Patterns of 'breaking' [include the following]. By nourishing the qi it is possible to transform

Now, to regulate these qi:
if they are excessive, break them
with that [qi] which they fear."667
{This is called 'to discharge them.'}

[Huang] Di:
"If [the qi is] false, how about that?"

Qi Bo:
"If the qi is false, then the restrictions need not be observed."668
{That is called: 'the host qi [of a season] is insufficient and the visitor qi dominates.'}

71-502-4
[Huang] Di:
"Accomplished is the Way of the sages!
The massive transformations in heaven and earth,
the [time] terms of the periodical progression [of the five periods],

---

water; the treatment is directed at the lung. By supplementing soil it is possible to check the water; the treatment is directed at the spleen. By strengthening the fire it is possible to dominate the water; the treatment is directed at the gate of life. Through strengthening its own [depot] it is possible to guide the water; the treatment is directed at the kidneys. All these [approaches] are called 折; not just 'curbing'!" Gao Shishi: "In older versions 折 was erroneously written 析, 'to split.'" In contrast, 913/37 considers 折 to be an error for 析 in the sense of "to free a passage": "The passage of the liquids is blocked; it must be 'opened'"

667 Wang Bing reads 然調其氣. 過者折之以其畏也: "With the help of all five patterns [listed above] the qi can be balanced. Once [the oppression] has been regulated, one examines whether there is a depletion or abundance and regulates [accordingly]. 'Excessive' is: greatly excessive. [A qi that is] greatly excessive is to be drained with its [corresponding] flavor. The kidneys are drained with salty [flavor]. Sour [flavor] drains the liver. Acrid [flavor] drains the lung. Sweet [flavor] drains the spleen. Bitter [flavor] drains the heart." Zhang Jiebin: "折 is 折抑, 'to restrain.' Restrain it with that which it fears."

668 Wang Bing: "In case the proper qi is insufficient, the qi coming down from above will dominate it. One makes use [假] of cold, hot, warm, or cool [drugs] to support the four proper qi. This way it is quite permissible to offend heat with heat, to offend cold with cold, to offend warmth with warmth, and to offend cool with coolness." Zhang Jiebin: "假 is 假借, 'to falsely assume another's identity.' It happens that a qi assumes a false identity. It should be hot, but is cold; it should be cold, but is hot. In such cases it is possible to match the false [qi with an identical qi] to treat it. Hence it is possible to employ heat to offend heat or to employ cold to offend cold, and to disregard the [usual] restrictions. The same applies to warmth and coolness."

the arrangements of [the qi] coming down and assuming control,
the policies of yin and yang, and
the commands of cold and summerheat,
who except you, Sir, could penetrate all this!

Please let [me] store this in the Numinous Orchid Chamber and
give it the title *The Policies and Arrangements of the Six Principal [Qi].*[669]
[I] shall not dare to display it without having undergone [a period of] fasting
and chastity.
One must be cautious about transmitting it."

---

669 For the reading of 正 as 政, see the title of chapter 71 and the corresponding
note.

Chapter 74
Comprehensive Discourse on the Essentials
of the Most Reliable

74-503-2
Huang Di asked:
"The five qi interact and unite and
they may abound or be depleted alternately.
This I have come to know.[1]
The six qi govern separate [time sections].
When they control heaven and earth,
what [effects are brought about] by their arrival?"[2]

Qi Bo paid reverence twice and responded:
"A brilliant question, indeed!
The great arrangements of heaven and earth,
this is what all men and spirits correspond to."

[Huang] Di:
"I should like to hear,
'upper conjunction [results in] luminosity,
lower conjunction [results in] obscurity.'
what does that mean?"[3]

---

1 Cheng Shide et al.: "五氣 refers to the qi of the five periods." In contrast, Fang Yaozhong: "五 refers to the five periods; 氣 refers to the six qi."

2 Zhang Jiebin: "'Arrive' is to say: 'occupy their positions.'" Fang Yaozhong: "司天地者 is: the qi controlling heaven and the qi at the fountain."

3 Fang Yaozhong: "'Obvious' refers to that which is visible in the regular course of natural change and transformation, i.e., spring, summer, autumn, and winter, dawn and dusk, day and night, wind, rain, darkness and light, etc. 'Obscure' refers to that wich is not easily perceivable in the regular course of natural change and transformation, i.e., the generation of the five flavors and five colors, that which suits the five depots, differences in the qualities of drugs and food, etc." Our translation of 上合 and 下合 as "upper conjunction" and "lower conjunction", respectively, is based in the astronomical terminology attested in the Song dynastic history; it may have been in use already prior to the Song dynasty. In cases of "upper conjunction", an inner planet vanishes, seen from the earth, behind the sun. In cases of "lower conjunction", an inner planet passes, seen from the earth, in front of the sun.

Qi Bo:
"This is ruled by the Way.
It is something which practitioners are uncertain about."⁴

74-503-6
[Huang] Di:
"I should like to hear about this Way."

Qi Bo:
"When the ceasing yin controls heaven, its transformations are [apparent in] wind.⁵
When the minor yin controls heaven, its transformations are [apparent in] heat.⁶
When the major yin controls heaven, its transformations are [apparent in] dampness.⁷
When the minor yang controls heaven, its transformations are [apparent in] fire.⁸
When the yang brilliance controls heaven, its transformations are [apparent in] dryness.⁹

---

4 Zhang Jiebin and Zhang Zhicong have 道之所生, "this is generated by the Way." Zhang Zhicong: "That which is generated by the Way; what is generates is only one. When practitioners do not know its essentials, [their words] flow erverywhere without ever exhausting [this topic] and they are constantly in doubt." Cheng Shide et al.: " 'Way' refers to medical theory here."

5 Fang Yaozhong: "All years associated with the branches *si* or *hai* are years when the ceasing yin [qi, i.e., wind and wood] controls heaven. In such years, the appearances of the transformations of things are closely related to a disproportionate dominance of wind qi."

6 Fang Yaozhong: "All years associated with the branches *zi* or *wu* are years when the minor yin [qi, i.e.] ruler fire, controls heaven. In such years, the appearances of the transformations of things are closely related to a disproportionate dominance of heat qi."

7 Fang Yaozhong: "All years associated with the branches *chou* or *wei* are years when the major yin [qi, i.e.,] dampness and soil, controls heaven. In such years, the appearances of the transformations of things are closely related to a disproportionate dominance of dampness qi."

8 Fang Yaozhong: "All years associated with the branches *yin* or *shen* are years when the minor yang [qi, i.e.] minister fire, controls heaven. In such years, the appearances of the transformations of things is closely related to a disproportionate dominance of fire qi."

9 Fang Yaozhong: "All years associated with the branches *mao* or *you* are years when the yang brilliance [qi, i.e.] dryness and metal, controls heaven. In such years, the

When the major yang controls heaven, its transformations are [apparent in] cold.[10]

On the basis of the positions of the depots where [the qi] has come down to, [it is possible to] name their diseases."[11]

74-504-1
[Huang] Di:
"What about the transformations of the earth [qi]?"[12]

Qi Bo:
"[Their] manifestations are identical to those resulting from the [qi] controlling heaven. The [manifestations of the] intervening qi are all identical, [too]."[13]

[Huang] Di:
" 'Intervening qi,' what does that mean?"

---

appearances of the transformations of things is closely related to a disproportionate dominance of dryness qi."

10 Fang Yaozhong: "All years associated with the branches *chen* or *xu* are years when the major yang [qi, i.e.] cold and water, controls heaven. In such years, the appearances of the transformations of things is closely related to a disproportionate dominance of cold qi."

11 Wang Bing: "Liver and wood, their location is the East. Heart and fire, their location is the South. Spleen and soil, their location is the South-West, as well as the four corners. Lung and metal, their location is the West. Kidneys and water, their location is the North. These are the fixed locations of the five depots. However when the [terms] controlled by the six qi and the [locations] arrived at by the five periods do not agree, than this results in disease. In case they agree, there is harmony. Hence one first takes [the positions] which the six qi have come down to and then discusses the diseases of the five depots." Fang Yaozhong: "藏位 refers to the locations of the depots in the human body. All diseases appearing at a time associated with spring and in a climate associated with a disproportionate dominance of wind qi, and which in their clinical manifestation resemble wind diseases as outlined above, permit one to state that they are located in the liver or gallbladder and that they have a wind nature. Etc."

12 Wu Kun: "地化 refers to transformations at the fountain." Fang Yaozhong: "This refers to the relationships between the qi at the fountain and the generation and transformation of the myriad beings."

13 Wang Bing: "Because the nature of the six qi is regular, even though they may appear at different positions, their transformations and their government is always the same."

Qi Bo:
"Those to the left and the right of the [qi] controlling [heaven and earth],
they are called 'intervening qi.' "[14]

74-504-3
[Huang] Di:
"How can they be distinguished?"

Qi Bo:
"Those [qi] ruling over an [entire] year, they [are responsible for] arranging that
year.
As for the intervening qi, they [are responsible for] arranging the [seasonal]
steps [within a year]."[15]

---

14 Wang Bing: "The regularity of the separate transformations of the six qi is such
that two of them control heaven and earth; they constitute [those] above and below,
good and evil, domination and revenge, host and visitor. The remaining four qi are distributed to the left and to the right." Zhang Jiebin: "Each of the six terms [of a year] is
ruled by one of the six qi. That above is called 'controlling heaven'; that below is called
'at the fountain.' The remaining four are called 'intervening qi.' Those above include
the intervening [qi] to the left of the [qi] controlling heaven and the intervening [qi]
to the right of the [qi] controlling heaven. Those below include the intervening [qi]
to the left of the [qi] at the fountain and the intervening [qi] to the right of the [qi]
at the fountain."

15 Wang Bing: "One year consists of 365 days plus one quarter of a day. One [sea-
sonal] step consists of 60 days plus 87 and one half *ke*. All days of the [seasonal] steps
added result in one year." Fang Yaozhong: "主歲 refers to the qi controlling heaven
and at the fountain. 紀歲 is: they rule the climatic changes of that year. Generally
speaking, the qi controlling heaven rules the climatic changes in the first half of a
year. The qi at the fountain rules the climatic changes in the second half of a year.
Hence the text states: '[The qi] ruling a year are [responsible for the] arrangement of
that year.' 間氣 are the qi to the left and right of the [qi] controlling heaven and at
the fountain. 紀步 is: they rule the climatic changes of each season in the course of a
year. The intervening [qi] to the left of the [qi] controlling heaven rules the changes
in climate and things during the time period associated with the fourth qi of a year.
The intervening [qi] to the right of the [qi] controlling heaven rules the changes in
climate and things during the time period associated with the second qi of a year. The
intervening [qi] to the left of the [qi] at the fountain rules the changes in climate and
things during the time period associated with the initial qi of a year. The intervening
[qi] to the right of the [qi] at the fountain rules the changes in climate and things
during the time period associated with the fifth qi of a year. Hence the text states: 'the
intervening [qi] are responsible for the arrangement of the [seasonal] steps.' That is,
when examining the changes in the climate and in the things of each season and each
year, in addition to taking into account the qi controlling heaven and at the fountain,
it is also essential to consider the intervening qi to the left and right and other relevant

74-504-4
[Huang] Di:
"Good!
How is it that a year is ruled?"

Qi Bo:
"When the ceasing yin controls heaven, it causes a transformation to wind.[16]
When it is at the fountain, it causes a transformation to sour [flavor].[17]
As controlling qi it causes a transformation to greenish [color].[18]
As intervening qi it causes a transformation to movement.[19]

---

aspects. Only on the basis of such a holistic consideration will it be possible to arrive at a realistic judgment concerning the changes in climate and things and the nature of diseases during a given year."

16 Wang Bing: "In *si* and *hai* years, the wind qi reaches high and far. Clouds fly and things are whirled up. These are transformations of wind."

17 Wang Bing: "In *yin* and *shen* years, wood controls the earth qi. Hence the transformations of things go along with sour [flavor]."

18 Wang Bing: "The qi of the wood period, in *ding* and *ren* years."

19 Wang Bing: "Their overall rule extends over 60 days plus 87 and one half *ke*." Lin Yi et al.: "In *chou* and *wei* years, the ceasing yin [qi] is the initial qi. In *zi* and *wu* years it is the second qi. In *chen* and *xu* years it is the fourth qi. In *mao* and *you* years it is the fifth qi." Fang Yaozhong: "In all years associated with *si* or *hai* branches, because the ceasing yin [qi, i.e.,] wind and wood, controls heaven, wind qi is disproportionately dominant in the first half of that year. In all years associated with *yin* or *shen* branches, the minor yang [qi, i.e.,] minister fire, controls heaven and the ceasing yin [qi, i.e.,] wind and wood, is at the fountain. Because the ceasing yin [qi, i.e.,] wind and wood, is at the fountain, those foods with a disproportionately sour flavor grow particularly well in the second half of that year. 司氣 has been interpreted by [former] commentators in terms of transformations of the five periods. We believe that such an explanation does not correspond to the meaning of the text. ... The present paragraph discusses the six qi, certainly not the five periods. ... We believe, 'controlling qi' refers here to both the qi controlling heaven and the qi at the fountain, and is identical in meaning here with the above-mentioned 'annual qi' (歲氣) and '[qi] ruling a year ' (主歲). 司氣為蒼化, then, is: because the qi controlling heaven and the qi at the fountain influence each other, regardless of whether it is a year with ceasing yin [qi, i.e.,] wind and wood, controlling heaven, or a year with ceasing yin [qi, i.e.,] wind and wood, at the fountain, all changes in climate and things in such years bear the characteristics of wood transformations. That is, in terms of climate, the wind qi dominates disproportionately, in terms of things, sour and green grain and fruit grow particularly well, and in terms of diseases liver and gallbladder diseases tend to develop. 動化, too, refers to wood transformations and wind transformations. That is, at a time when the ceasing yin [qi, i.e.,] wind and wood, constitutes the intervening qi, changes in climate and things manifest the characteristics of wood transformations and of wind transformations."

74-504-6
When the minor yin controls heaven, it causes a transformation to heat.[20]
When it is at the fountain, it causes a transformation to bitter [flavor].[21]
It does not control qi transformation,[22] but
as resident qi it causes a transformation to burning.[23]

---

20 Wang Bing: "In *zi* and *wu* years, the sun shines brightly; warmth and summerheat spread widely. These are transformations of heat."

21 Wang Bing: "In *mao* and *you* years fire controls the qi of the earth. Hence things come to life because of bitter [flavor]."

22 Wang Bing: "The ruler [fire] does not rule a period." Lin Yi et al.: "*Su wen* 66 states: 'The ruler fire [exists] by name; the minister fire [exists] by position.' That is to say, the ruler fire does not rule a period." Zhang Jiebin: "The difference between the five periods and the six qi is that the periods are based on the heavenly stems. Hence there are only five periods. The [six] qi are based on the earth branches. Hence there are six qi. Each of the five [periods] is associated with one of the five agents. Among the six [qi], the fifth is divided into ruler [fire] and [minister] fire. Hence among the six qi there are differences in the rule by the ruler fire and the minister fire, while among the five periods, the fire occupies only one position. There is one less in comparison with the six [qi]. Hence only the ruler fire does not control qi changes among the five periods." Cheng Shide et al.: " 'Resident qi' is used here for 'intervening qi.' Because the minor yin [qi] is the ruler fire, it is revered as 'resident qi.' "

23 Wang Bing: "This extends over 60 days plus 87 and a half [*ke*]. When ruler fire resides at its proper location, then it is considered as resident [qi], and it should not be considered as intervening [qi]. Lin Yi et al.: "In respect of the minor yin [qi, the text] does not speak of 'intervening qi'; it speaks of 'resident qi.' The reason is, the ruler fire is revered for residing everywhere; it should not be considered as intervening [qi]. Wang Bing has commented: 'When it resides at its proper location, then one should not consider it as intervening [qi].' From this it would follow: if it were to reside at another location, it would not be considered as resident [qi] and could be considered as intervening [qi]. In *yin* and *shen* years, [the minor yin qi] is the initial qi. In *chou* and *wei* years it is the second qi. In *si* and *hai* years it is the fourth qi. In *chen* and *xu* years it is the fifth qi." Fang Yaozhong: "In all years associated with *zi* and *wu* branches, because the minor yin [qi, i.e.,] ruler fire, controls heaven, heat qi is disproportionately dominant in the first half of these years. In all years associated with *mao* and *you* branches, the yang brilliance [qi, i.e.,] dryness and metal, controls heaven while minor yin [qi, i.e.,] ruler fire, is at the fountain. Because the minor yin [qi, i.e.,] ruler fire, is at the fountain, the climate is disproportionately hot in the second half of such years. Food and drugs with a disproportionately bitter flavor grow particularly well. As for 不司氣化, because the minor yin [qi, i.e.,] ruler fire controls heaven or is at the fountain, the climate in the first half of the year is entirely different from the second half of that year. Hence it is impossible to clearly state what the annual qi or the ruling qi of that year in its entirety is like. That is, in a year when the minor yin [qi, i.e.,] ruler fire, controls heaven, the climate in the first half of that year is disproportionately hot. However, when the minor yin [qi] controls heaven, yang brilliance [qi] must be at

When the major yin controls heaven, it causes a transformation to dampness.²⁴
When it is at the fountain, it causes a transformation to sweet [flavor].²⁵
As controlling qi it causes a transformation to yellow [color].²⁶
As intervening qi it causes a transformation to softness.²⁷

---

the fountain. Hence the climate in the second half of that year is disporportionately cool. On the other hand, when minor yin [qi, i.e.,] ruler fire, is at the fountain, yang brilliance [qi, i.e.,] dryness and metal, must control heaven. That is, the climate in the second half of that year is disproportionately hot and the climate in the first half of that year is disproportionately cool. At one time it is cool and at one time it is hot; hence it is hard to say which qi is the ruling qi of that entire year. Hence the text states 'it does not control the qi transformations.' 居氣 refers to the location where the ruler fire resides. In years when the minor yin [qi, i.e.,] ruler fire, controls heaven or is at the fountain, because 'it does not control the qi transformations' in such years, the place where the minor yin [qi, i.e.,] ruler fire, resides must be taken as a guideline when analysing the changes in climate and things in such years. When the minor yin [qi, i.e.,] ruler fire, controls heaven, the climate in the first half of that year is disproportionately hot. When the minor yin [qi] is at the fountain, the climate in the second half of that year is disproportionately hot and grain of the fire type grow particularly well. When the minor yin [qi] appears as an intervening qi, then the climate in the time period associated with that intervening qi is disproportionately hot and grain of the fire type grow particularly well. This is meant by the statement 'the resident qi causes burning transformations' in the text. Still, even though we have thought about this interpretation repeatedly, we cannot be sure whether it is accurate."

24 Wang Bing: "In *chou* and *wei* years, dense dust causes dim light. Clouds and rain are transformations of humidity/dampness."

25 Wang Bing: "This applies to *chen* and *xu* years. The soil controls the qi of the earth. Hence sweetness generations are generated prevail at this [time]."

26 Wang Bing: "This is the qi of the soil period, in *jia* and *ji* years."

27 Wang Bing: "When dampness transformations prevail, all things turn soft." Lin Yi et al.: "The major yin [qi] is the initial qi in *mao* and *you* years. It is the second qi in *yin* and *shen* years. It is the fourth qi in *zi* and *wu* years. It is the fifth qi in *si* and *hai* years." Fang Yaozhong: "In all years associated with *chou* and *wei* branches, because the major yin [qi, i.e.,] dampness and soil, controls heaven, dampness qi is disproportionately dominant in the first half of these years. In all years associated with *chen* and *xu* branches, major yang [qi, i.e.,] cold and water, controls heaven while major yin [qi, i.e.,] dampness and soil, is at the fountain. Because the major yin [qi, i.e.,] dampness and soil, is at the fountain, the climate is disproportionately damp in the second half of such years. Food with a disproportionately sweet flavor grows particularly well. When the major yin [qi, i.e.,] dampness and soil, is an intervening qi, then the climate and the things in that time period display the characteristics of a disproportionate dominance of dampness qi."

74-505-1
When the minor yang controls heaven, it causes a transformation to fire.[28]
When it is at the fountain, it causes a transformation to bitter [flavor].[29]
As controlling qi it causes a transformation to vermilion [color].[30]
As intervening qi it causes a transformation to brilliance.[31]

When the yang brilliance controls heaven, it causes a transformation to dryness.[32]
When it is at the fountain, it causes a transformation to acrid [flavor].[33]
As controlling qi it causes a transformation to white [color].[34]
As intervening qi it causes a transformation to coolness.[35]

---

28 Wang Bing: "These are *yin* and *shen* years. They are glowing hot and marked by burning. These are transformations of fire."

29 Wang Bing: "These are *si* and *hai* years. Fire controls the qi of the earth. Hence transformations to bitterness prevail at this [time]."

30 Wang Bing: "The qi of the fire period, in *wu* and *gui* years."

31 Wang Bing: "明 is 炳明, 'luminous.'" Zhang Jiebin: "When the fire period controls the qi, then colors change to red." Fang Yaozhong: "In all years associated with *yin* and *shen* branches, because the minor yang [qi, i.e.,] minister fire, controls heaven, fire qi is disproportionately dominant in the first half of these years. In all years associated with *si* and *hai* branches, ceasing yin [qi, i.e.,] wind and wood, controls heaven while minor yang [qi, i.e.,] minister fire, is at the fountain. Because the minor yang [qi, i.e.,] minister fire, is at the fountain, the climate is disproportionately hot in the second half of such years. Food with a disproportionately bitter flavor grows particularly well. The meaning of the entire sentence is: in years when the minor yang [qi, i.e.,] minister fire, controls heaven, or when minor yang [qi, i.e.,] minister fire, is at the fountain, the entire year is characterized by a disproportionate dominance of warm or hot climate. In the realm of things, those plants with a red color and with a bitter flavor grow particularly well. When the minor yang [qi, i.e.,] minister fire, is an intervening qi, then the climate and the things in that time period display the characteristics of the luminosity of fire transformations."

32 Wang Bing: "These are *mao* and *you* years; they are marked by fog and dew and chilling temperature. These are transformations of dryness." Zhang Jiebin: "When the qi of metal is [controlling] heaven, it causes transformations to dryness. As a result, [things] turn cool and stiffen. This is the case in *mao* and *you* years when yang brilliance [qi] controls heaven."

33 Wang Bing: "These are *zi* and *wu* years. Metal controls the qi of the earth. Hence transformations to acrid [flavor] prevail."

34 Wang Bing: "The qi of the metal period, in *yi* and *geng* years."

35 Wang Bing: "Winds rise high and are strong; the herbs and trees are affected by chilling temperature. These are transformations of coolness." Fang Yaozhong: "In all

74-505-4

When the major yang controls heaven, it causes a transformation to cold.[36]
When it is at the fountain, it causes a transformation to salty [flavor].[37]

---

years associated with *mao* and *you* branches, because the yang brilliance [qi, i.e.,] dryness and metal, controls heaven, dryness qi and cool qi are disproportionately dominant in the first half of these years. In all years associated with *zi* and *wu* branches, minor yin [qi, i.e.,] ruler fire, controls heaven while yang brilliance [qi, i.e.,] dryness and metal, is at the fountain. Because the yang brilliance [qi, i.e.,] dryness and metal, is at the fountain, the climate is disproportionately cool and disproportionately dry in the second half of such years. Food with a disproportionately acrid flavor grows particularly well. 素化 refers to white color. White is the color of metal. Hence 'white transformations' are 'metal transformations.' 清 is 'cool.' Coolness is the nature of metal. Hence 'coolness transformations' are 'metal transformations.' Literally, the meaning of the entire sentence is: in years when the yang brilliance [qi, i.e.,] dryness and metal, controls heaven, or when the yang brilliance [qi, i.e.,] dryness and metal, is at the fountain, the entire year is characterized by a disproportionate dominance of cool or chilly climate. In the realm of things, those grain with a white color and with an acrid flavor grow particularly well. However, the contents of this paragraph are basically identical to those of the preceding paragraph 'when the minor yin [qi] controls heaven this causes transformations to heat; when it is at the fountain this causes transformations to bitter.' The reason is that in years when the yang brilliance [qi, i.e.,] dryness and metal, is at the fountain, the minor yin [qi, i.e.,] ruler fire, must control heaven and that in years when the minor yin [qi, i.e.,] ruler fire, is at the fountain, yang brilliance [qi, i.e.,] dryness and metal, must control heaven. However, when the text of the former paragraph states 'It does not control the qi transformations; the resident qi causes a transformation of burning,' while the latter paragraph states 'the qi controlling [the year] causes transformations to pale; the intervening qi causes transformations to coolness,' then this is difficult to explain. We believe it is best to attempt an explanation on the basis of the former statement, that is, in all years when the yang brilliance [qi, i.e.,] dryness and metal, controls heaven, or is at the fountain, because such a year 'does not control the qi transformations,' hence the analysis of changes in climate or in the realms of things in such years must start from where the yang brilliance [qi, i.e.,] dryness and metal resides. When the yang brilliance [qi, i.e.,] dryness and metal controls heaven, then the climate is disproportionately cool in the first half of such years. When the yang brilliance [qi, i.e.,] dryness and metal, is at the fountain, then the climate is disproportionately cool in the second half of such years. Grain associated with metal grow particularly well. When the yang brilliance [qi, i.e.,] dryness and metal, is an intervening qi, then in the time period associated with this intervening qi, too, the climate is disproportionately cool and grain associated with metal grow particularly well."

36 Wang Bing: "These are *chen* and *xu* years. They are characterized by extreme cold, freezing, and hardening. These are the transformations of cold."

37 Wang Bing: "In *chou* and *wei* years. The water controls the qi of the earth. Hence transformations follow [the nature of] salt."

As controlling qi it causes a transformation to darkness.[38]
As intervening qi it causes a transformation to storage."[39]

Hence those who treat diseases,
they must understand the governings of separate [time sections] by the transformations of the six [qi],
what the five flavors and the five colors generate and
what is befitting the five depots.
[Only] then can they talk about the principles of fullness and depletion, as well
as of the generation of disease."[40]

74-506-2
[Huang] Di:
"When the ceasing yin is at the fountain, transformations to sour [flavor] are
predominant. This I have come to know.

If transformations to wind prevail, how is that?"

---

38 Wang Bing: "The qi of the water period; these are *bing* and *xin* years."

39 Wang Bing: "Chilliness causes freezing; all things are taken in." Zhang Jiebin:
"When the water period controls the qi, then all colors change to dark and black. This
is so in *bing* and *xin* years." Fang Yaozhong: "In all years associated with *chen* and *xu*
branches, because the major yang [qi, i.e.,] cold and water, controls heaven, cold qi
is disproportionately dominant in the first half of these years. In all years associated
with *chou* and *wei* branches, major yin [qi, i.e.,] dampness and soil, controls heaven
while major yang [qi, i.e.,] cold and water, is at the fountain. Because the major yang
[qi, i.e.,] cold and water, is at the fountain, the climate is disproportionately cold in
the second half of such years. Food with a disproportionately salty flavor grows particularly well. The meaning of the entire sentence is: in years when the major yang [qi,
i.e.,] cold and water, controls heaven, or when major yang [qi, i.e.,] cold and water, is at
the fountain, in terms of climate the entire year is characterized by a disproportionate
dominance of cold qi. In the realm of things, those grain associated with water grow
particularly well. When the major yang [qi, i.e.,] cold and water, is associated with the
time ruled by an intervening qi, then the climate and the things in that time period
display the characteristics of cold transformations."

40 Zhang Jiebin: "In the treatment of diseases it is always essential to search for their
origins; the [origins] are the six transformations." Fang Yaozhong: "The meaning of
the entire sentence is: a physician must know the relationships between changes in
climate and in [the appearance of] things. He must know the causes of the emergence
of the five flavors and of the five colors, their functions and their close relationships
with the prevention and treatment of disease in the human body."

Qi Bo:
"When wind prevails on the earth, then this is the so-called 'basis.'[41]
The same law applies to all the remaining qi.[42]

<That which originates in heaven is the qi of heaven;
that which originates on the earth is the qi of the earth.[43]

Heaven and earth unite [their] qi,
the six [seasonal] terms separate and
the myriad beings are generated through transformation.>[44]

Hence when it is said
'carefully examine the requirements of the qi;
do not neglect the trigger of the disease,'[45]
then this means just the same."

[Huang] Di:
"How do the [controlling qi] rule diseases?"[46]

Qi Bo:
"If [pharmaceutical] substances are prepared [in accordance with the qi] controlling a year, then that which rules [the diseases] will not be neglected."[47]

---

41 Wu Kun: "Wind is the 'origin' of sour [flavor]. The reason is: if there is wind first,
then [transformations to] sour [flavor] follow."

42 Wang Bing: "When the ceasing yin [qi] is at the fountain, wind prevails on the
earth. When the minor yin [qi] is at the fountain, heat prevails on the earth. When
the major yin [qi] is at the fountain, dampness prevails on the earth. When the minor
yang [qi] is at the fountain, fire prevails on the earth. When the yang brilliance [qi]
is at the fountain, dryness prevails on the earth. When the major yang [qi] is at the
fountain, cold prevails on the earth. Hence [the text] states: 'the remaining qi follow
the same law.' 'Basis' is to say: the principal qi above the six qi."

43 Wang Bing: "That which transforms in heaven is the qi of heaven; that which
transforms on the earth is the qi of the earth."

44 Wang Bing: "The myriad beings reside between heaven and earth; all their generation and transformation depends on the six qi."

45 Wu Kun: "病機 is the trigger causing a disease to emerge. All the hundreds of
diseases emerge because of the six qi. Hence the six qi are the triggers of disease." Fang
Yaozhong: "病機 is the mechanism and principle behind the emergence of disease."

46 Zhang Zhicong: "主病 is to say: the pharmaceutical substances to treat diseases."

47 Wang Bing: "If that which is generated and transformed by the [qi] controlling
heaven and earth is carefully taken into account, then the flavors [of the substances

74-506-7
[Huang] Di:
"What are 'substances [prepared in accordance with the qi] predominant in a year'?"[48]

Qi Bo:
"[They contain that year's] concentrated essence of heaven and earth."[49]

[Huang] Di:
"What about the 'controlling qi'?"[50]

Qi Bo:
"The 'controlling qi' is identical with [the period] ruling a year. However, it may be present in surplus or it may be insufficient."[51]

74-506-9
[Huang] Di:
" 'Substances not [affected by the qi] controlling a year,' what does that mean?"

---

selected] are in complete agreement with the respective years." Zhang Jiebin: "Each year one of the qi of heaven and earth is in control. If drugs are prepared in accordance with the qi in control, then that which rules the diseases will not be missed. That is, when the ceasing yin [qi] controls a year, sour substances are to be prepared. When the minor yin and the minor yang [qi] control a year, bitter substances are to be prepared. When the major yin [qi] controls a year, sweet substances are to be prepared. When the yang brilliance [qi] controls a year, acrid substances are to be prepared. When the major yang [qi] controls a year, salty substances are to be prepared. These are the so-called 'substances of the year.' When substances of the year are prepared, then the application of the five flavors is perfect."

48 Lin Yi et al.: "Maybe 先歲 should be 司歲, '[the qi] controlling a year.'" 司歲物 is in keeping with the wording 非司歲物 below. Hence in our translation we follow Lin Yi et al.. In contrast, see the comment by Zhang Jiebin in the following note.

49 Zhang Jiebin: "The 'substances of a year' are affected by the transformations of the [qi controlling] heaven and earth characteristic [of that year]. Their qi is complete and their strength is fully developed. Hence they are to be prepared 'ahead of time' (or 'predominantly')."

50 Wang Bing: "This is the qi controlling a period."

51 Wang Bing: "In their ruling a year the five periods may be marked by excessive or insufficient [qi]. In comparison with the 'substances of a year,' there may be 'drugs of a year' whose special essence is meagre or is present in surplus."

Qi Bo:

"[The qi] is dispersed.[52]

Hence the material substance is identical, but the quality is different.[53]

[When it says:]

'Qi and flavor [of identical substances] may be weak or strong;

nature and operation may be hasty or calm;

treatment and protection [offered] may be plenty or little;

force and transformation may be superficial or thorough',[54]

then this means just the same."

74-507-3

[Huang] Di:

"A year is responsible for harming a depot, what does that mean?"

Qi Bo:

"One determines that on the basis of what a [depot can]not dominate. This is what is essential here."[55]

[Huang] Di:

"How to treat such [harm suffered by the depots]?"

---

52 Wang Bing: "If a substance does not contain the concentrated essence [of the qi controlling a year], then it is [marked by] dispersed qi. When the qi is dispersed, this substance is not pure."

53 Wang Bing: "The physical appearance is identical but their strengths and functions differ. Hence they are not highly estimated."

54 Cheng Shide et al.: "力化 is identical to saying 'where the force of a drug extends.'"

55 Wang Bing: "For example, wood cannot dominate metal. Metal cannot dominate fire." Zhang Jiebin and others interpret 歲主 as 主歲, "[the qi] ruling a year." Hence they read this passage as "[the qi] ruling a year causes harm in the depots, what does that mean?" Zhang Jiebin: "That is to say, heaven has the qi of the year, man has the qi of the depots. The [qi of the] year is responsible for causing harm in the five depots in as much as the latter cannot dominate [the former]. For example, when wood qi is present in excess, then the [qi of the] spleen cannot dominate. When soil qi is present in excess, then the [qi of the] kidneys cannot dominate. Etc. These are the essential principles of harm caused to the depots." In contrast, Wu Kun: "[Huang] Di asks how it is that the drugs [affected by the qi] controlling a year rule the treatment of harm suffered by the five depots." Cheng Shide et al.: "Seen from the statement 所勝治之 further below, Wu Kun's comments are correct."

Qi Bo:
"When the above encroaches upon the below,
that which dominates it, balance it.
When the exterior encroaches upon the interior,
that which dominates it, bring it back to order."⁵⁶

74-507-5
[Huang] Di:
"Good!
To balance the qi, how to proceed?"⁵⁷

Qi Bo:
"Carefully investigate where yin and yang are present and regulate them
until a balance is reached.⁵⁸
Normal [diseases] are given a normal treatment;
[diseases] contrary [to the rule] are treated contrary [to the rule]."⁵⁹

---

56 Wang Bing: " 淫 ('encroach') is to say: to move there where oneself cannot be
overcome. 'The above has encroached upon the below' refers to the qi of heaven; 'the
outside has encroached upon the inside' refers to the qi of the earth. Make use of that
which restrains the dominating [qi] to balance it, or to bring it back to order. To restrain the dominating is to say: the five flavors as well as cold, heat, warmth, and coolness, use them in accordance with [their potential to] dominate." Zhang Jiebin: "淫 is
excess that causes harm. 上淫于下 is to say: heaven sends the six qi to cause disease
in the six conduits. 外淫于内 is to say: the earth causes diseases in the five officers (五
管; i.e., the five depots)."

57 Zhang Jiebin: "The question raised here is: how should a treatment be conducted
when a disease emerges even though the qi of that year is balanced."

58 206/5: "期 is 目的, 'aim.'" Lit.: "Regard a balanced [qi] as aim [of the treat-
ment]."

59 Wang Bing: "To know the positions of yin and yang is to know the correspondance
or failing correspondance [of the movements in the vessels] at the foot and inch [sec-
tions]. Not to know the locations of yin and yang is to take a gain for a loss and to take
opposition for compliance. Hence a careful examination is essential. When the disease
is in the yin [section], not in the yang [section], or when it is in the yang [section], not
in the yin [section], this is a 'normal disease.' It is to be treated 'normally.' That is to say:
heat is to be treated with cold and cold is to be treated with heat. If the yin [disease]
appears to have taken a position in the yang vessels, or if the yang [disease] appears
to have taken a position in the yin vessels, this is called 'irregular disease'; it is to be
treated 'irregularly.' That is to say: cold is to be treated with cold; heat is to be treated
with heat." Wu Kun: " 'Yin and yang' refers to the yin and yang [categorization] of
the conditions of the [movements in the] vessels." Fang Yaozhong: "The first 正 is to
say: someone was affected by heat and displays pathoconditions of heat; or someone
was affected by cold and displays pathoconditions of cold. The second 正 is to say: in

74-507-7
[Huang] Di:
"[You,] Sir, have said 'investigate where yin and yang are present and regulate
them.'

The discourse states
'[The movements in the vessels] at man's facing and at the inch opening correspond to each other.
As if one pulled a rope of equal diameter [through both locations]. This is
called balanced.'⁶⁰

Where yin [qi] is present, how [can this be felt] at the inch opening?"⁶¹

Qi Bo:
"Find out whether a year [is governed by the policy] of the South or of the
North and this can be known."⁶²

---

case of pathoconditions of heat, cold or cool drugs are employed for treatment. In case
of pathoconditions of cold, warm or hot drugs are employed for treatment. The first
反 is to say: someone was affected by heat and displays pathoconditions of cold, or
someone was affected by cold and displays pathoconditions of heat. The second 反 is
to say: someone was affected by heat, displays pathoconditions of cold and is treated
with cold or cool drugs, or someone was affected by cold, displays pathoconditions of
heat and is treated with warm or hot drugs."

60 Lin Yi et al.: " 'The discourse states' refers to *Ling shu* 48 where it is stated: 'The
inch opening masters the center; man's facing masters the exterior. The [movements
in the vessels] at these two [locations] correspond to each other; they go together and
they come together. They are of equal size, like a rope that is pulled [tight].' " Zhang
Jiebin: "Man's facing is located at the head; the inch opening is located at the hand.
When yin and yang correspond to each other, then the sizes [of the vessel movement]
are identical [at both locations]. That is called 'balanced.' "

61 Wang Bing: "When yin [qi] is present, the [movement in the] vessels is in the
depth and does not correspond [to the touch of the fingers]." Wu Kun: " 'Yin' is to
say: The [movement in the] vessels is deep and fine and does not correspond [to the
touch of the fingers]." Zhang Jiebin: " 'Yin' refers to minor yin. In case of a presence
of a minor yin [qi], the [movement in the] vessels at the inch opening does not correspond [to the touch of the fingers]. A [close] examination is necessary." Cheng Shide
et al.: "Even though the comments by Wang Bing and Wu Kun make sense, too, only
Zhang Jiebin's comment closely corresponds to the statement further below: 'In a year
of Northern policy, when the minor yin [qi] is at the fountain, then [the movement
in the vessels at] the inch opening does not correspond [to the touch of the fingers].' "
Fang Yaozhong: " 'Yin' refers to the five depots here."

62 Cheng Shide et al.: "南北 refers to the 南政 ('Southern policy') and 北政
('Northern policy') of the text below. There are two explanations: The first assumes

74-508-1
[Huang] Di:
"I should like to hear about this comprehensively."

Qi Bo:
"In a year of Northern policy,
when the minor yin is at the fountain,
then [the vessel movement at] the inch opening does not respond [to the
physician's fingers].⁶³
When the ceasing yin is at the fountain,
then [the vessel movement on] the right does not respond.⁶⁴
When the major yin is at the fountain,
then [the vessel movement on] the left does not respond.⁶⁵

---

that except for the *jia* and *ji* periods of soil, which are 'Southern policy,' all the remaining are 'Northern policy.' As Zhang Jiebin commented: 'The two years of *jia* and
ji [association] are Southern policy; the eight years of *yi, geng, bing, xin, ding, ren,*
wu, and *gui* are Northern policy. Among the five periods, the soil [period] is the one
most revered. Hence only [those years that are associated with] *jia* and *ji,* [i.e., with]
the soil period, they are 'Southern policy.' All the remaining are 'Northern policy.' The
second explanation assumes that [years associated with] *wu* and *gui,* [i.e., with] fire
periods, are Southern policy, the remaining being Northern policy. As Zhang Zhicong
stated: 'Among the five periods, *wu* and *gui* transform fire. Hence *wu* and *gui* years are
Southern policy. *Jia, yi, bing, ding, ji, geng, xin,* and *ren* [years] are Northern policy.'
The majority of [later] commentators followed the comments by Zhang Jiebin." Fang
Yaozhong: "A third explanation assumes that those years associated with the branches
hai, zi, chou, yin, mao, and *chen* are associated with Southern policy, while [those associated with the branches *si, wu, wei, shen, you,* and *xu* are associated with Northern
policy. A fourth explanation assumes that annual periods with greatly excessive [qi]
are Southern policy, while annual periods with inadequate [qi] are Northern policy."

63 Wang Bing: "In years [associated with] wood, fire, metal, and water periods the qi
is taken in by facing North. A qi that is at the fountain cannot be recognized [by the
movement in the vessels at the inch opening]. Only the qi to the left and to the right
appear in the vessels. When the qi is good, it cannot be recognized; when it is bad, it
can be recognized. Diseases are identified as to whether the qi arrives as visitor or host,
encroaches or dominates. The same applies to the qi of heaven." Zhang Jiebin: "不應
is: the [movement in the] vessels is deep, fine, and hidden. It does not respond to the
fingers [of the physician]."

64 Wang Bing: "Because the minor yin is on the right." Wu Kun: "'Right' refers to
the inch [opening] on the right. When the ceasing yin is at the fountain, then the
minor yin is at the inch [opening] on the right. Hence it does not respond [to the
physician's fingers]."

65 Wang Bing: "Because the minor yin is on the left." Zhang Jiebin: "When in years
of Northern Policy the major yin is at the fountain, then the minor yin is at the inch

In a year of Southern policy,
when the minor yin controls heaven,
then [the vessel movement at] the inch opening does not respond.[66]
When the ceasing yin controls heaven,
then [the vessel movement on] the right does not respond.[67]
When the major yin controls heaven,
then [the vessel movement on] the left does not respond.[68]

As for all these cases of no response, that which is contrary to these diagnoses will be [easily] visible."[69]

74-508-5
[Huang] Di:
"What about the manifestations [of a disease] in the foot-long section?"

Qi Bo:
"In a year of Northern policy,
when [any of] the three yin is below [at the fountain],
then the [movement in the vessels at the] inch [opening] does not respond [to

[opening] on the left. Hence it does not respond [to the physician's] fingers."

66 Wang Bing: "In years [associated] with a soil period orders are issued facing South. Hence when the minor yin controls heaven, then the [movement in the vessels at] the two inch openings of the hands do not respond [to the fingers of the physician]."

67 Zhang Jiebin: " 'Right' is the inch [opening] of the right [hand]. When in a situation of Southern policy ceasing yin controls heaven, then minor yin is at the right inch [opening]. Hence [the movement in the vessels there] does not respond [to the fingers of the physician]."

68 Zhang Jiebin: " 'Left' is the inch [opening] of the left [hand]. When in a situation of Southern policy major yin controls heaven, then minor yin is at the left inch [opening]. Hence [the movement in the vessels there] does not respond [to the fingers of the physician]."

69 Wang Bing: "The [movement in the] vessels does not respond because it is in the depth. When the [movement in the] vessels has sunk into the depth, the hand faces upward and [the movement is] in the depth. When the hand is turned around, then what is in the depth comes to the surface and a fine [movement] turns into a strong movement." Zhang Jiebin: "[A movement in the vessels] responding [to the fingers of the physician] at the inch [opening] under Southern policy will respond at the Foot [location] under Northern policy. That which responds at the inch [opening] under Northern policy will respond at the foot [location] under Southern policy. If an examination is carried out on the basis of the fact that North and South are opposites, then all [qi] can be detected even though there is no response either at the inch [opening] or at the foot [location]."

the physician's fingers].[70]
When [any of] the three yin is above [controlling heaven],
then the [movement in the vessels in the] foot-long section does not respond.[71]

74-508-6
In a year of Southern policy,
when [any of] the three yin is in heaven,
then the [movement in the vessels at the] inch [opening] does not respond [to
the physician's fingers].
When [any of] the three yin is at the fountain,
then the [movement in the vessels in the] foot-long section does not respond.

This is the same for the left and the right [hand]."

Hence when it is said
'Those who know the essentials of this,[72]
they make one statement and have said it all.
Those who do not know the essentials of this,
[their words] drift around without ever exhausting [the topic],'
then this means just the same.

[Huang] Di:
"Good!
When the qi of heaven or earth encroach upon the interior and [cause a] dis-
ease, how is that?"[73]

Qi Bo:
"When, in a year when the ceasing yin [qi] is at the fountain,
wind encroaches upon what it dominates,
then the qi [above the] earth is not bright,

---

70 Fang Yaozhong: " 'When any of the three yin is below' is to say: in years when the
ceasing yin, the minor yin, or the major yin [is at the fountain]."

71 Wang Bing: "To control heaven is called 'above'; to be at the fountain is called
'below.' "

72 Wang Bing: " 'Essentials' is: to know the presence of yin and yang. Those who
possess this knowledge will have no doubts left when they employ it."

73 Zhang Jiebin: "淫 is 邪勝, 'dominance of the evil.' 內淫 is: it enters the interior
from the exterior."

the plain fields are dark, and
the herbs flourish early.⁷⁴

74-508-12
People suffer from shivering and shaking with cold.
They tend to stretch and yawn frequently.⁷⁵
The heart aches and the [chest has a feeling of] propping fullness.⁷⁶
The two flanks have internal tightness.
Beverages and food do not move down.
The diaphragm and the gullet are impassable;
Eating results in vomiting.
The abdomen is distended and one tends to belch.
If one can [relieve nature] behind and [passes] qi, [this]
causes a comfortable feeling as if [a burden] had been decreased.
Body and limbs are all heavy.⁷⁷

---

74 Fang Yaozhong: "Because the wind qi is disproportionately dominant in the second half of years when the ceasing yin [qi] is at the fountain, the climate is disproportionately warm and winter issues the orders of spring. Hence some plants that should, under normal conditions, begin to sprout and grow in spring, they sprout and grow earlier at this time already."

75 Wang Bing: "伸 is to say: [patients] have a desire to stretch and strain their sinews and bones." Wu Kun, following *Ling shu* 10, has 呻, "to groan", instead of 伸, "to stretch", and interprets 欠 as "to bend and stretch the limbs and the body" because: "wind and wood make sounds. Hence [patients] tend to groan; trees are curved. Hence [patients] frequently bend and stretch."

76 Fang Yaozhong: "心痛 is stomach pain."

77 Wang Bing: "This applies to *jia yin, bing yin, wu yin, geng yin, ren yin, jia shen, bing shen, wu shen, geng shen,* and *ren shen* years. 昧 is 暗, 'dark.' 脅 is to say: [the region] from below the two breasts to outside the flanks." Zhang Jiebin: "The ceasing yin liver vessel penetrates the diaphragm and spreads through the flanks. Hence it causes such pathoconditions as heartache and propping fullness. In all these cases, the disease has resulted from an excessive domination of wood evil causing harm to spleen and stomach." Wu Kun: "Diaphragm and flanks have a disease, hence beverages and food cannot move downward. When diaphragm and gullet are impassable, food once eaten will be thrown up again. When [the qi of] wind and wood intrudes upon the spleen, then the abdomen distends. When [the qi of] wind and wood attacks the heart, then [patients] tend to belch. Because of a continuous repletion with the qi of wood, a comfortable feeling sets in, as if [the abdominal distension] had decreased, once [patients are able] to pass stools and break a wind. The ceasing yin rules the sinews. When the sinew qi is weak, the body feels heavy all over."

74-509-1
When, in a year when the minor yin [qi] is at the fountain,
heat encroaches upon what it dominates,
then flames float over rivers and marshes and,
contrary [to regular conditions], dark locations are well lit.[78]

People suffer from permanent sounds in the abdomen.
The qi rises and rushes upward to the chest.
They pant and cannot stand for long.
[They experience fits of] cold and heat. The skin is painful.
Vision is blurred. The teeth ache and the facial prominence is swollen.[79]
[Patients have] an aversion to cold associated with fever, resembling malaria.
They experience pain in the lower abdomen; the abdomen is enlarged.
<The hibernating creatures do not remain hidden.>[80]

74-509-4
When, in a year when the major yin [qi] is at the fountain,
<in this case, the herbs flourish early>[81]
dampness encroaches upon what it dominates,

---

78 Zhang Zhicong: "In *mao* and *you* years, the minor yin [qi] is at the fountain. The
minor yin [qi, i.e.,] ruler fire, is generated out of water. Hence 'flames float over rivers
and marshes.' The minor yin [qi] is outwardly yin but it is basically fire. Hence 'yin
locations, contrary [to normal], are well lit.'"

79 "Facial prominence" refers to the lower orbital region.

80 Wang Bing: "This applies to *yi mao, ding mao, si mao, xin mao, gui mao, yi you,
ding you, si you, xin you,* and *gui you* years. 'Yin locations' refers to the Northern regions. [Patients] cannot stand for long because their feet have no strength. 'The abdomen is enlarged' is to say: the qi of the heart is insufficient. The reason is that metal
and fire strike at each other." Wu Kun: "The nature of fire and flames is to rise. Hence
qi rushes upward and strikes the chest. Fire intrudes upon the lung. Hence [patients]
pant. The yin essence is burned up by fire. Hence there is nothing left to nourish the
bones. Hence [patients] cannot stand for long. When fire reaches an extreme, it will
transform itself. Hence [patients] experience fits of cold and heat. The skin is associated with the metal. [Here now] fire intrudes upon the metal. Hence the skin is
painful. When fire reaches an extreme, one longs for the yin. Hence vision is impaired.
Because heat qi intrudes upon the yang brilliance [conduit], the teeth ache and the
lower orbital regions are swollen. Yang brilliance rules metal. Because metal and fire
fight each other, [patients] have an aversion to cold and develop fever resembling
malaria. The minor yin vessel winds around the small intestines. Hence [patients]
experience pain in the lower abdomen. The yang [qi] is constantly present in surplus.
Hence the abdomen is enlarged."

81 Lin Yi et al.: "The four characters 草乃早榮 may be a later insertion."

then dust causes darkness in the mountain valleys.
What is yellow appears, contrary [to regular circumstances], black.⁸²
{Interaction with the extreme yin.}

People suffer from beverage accumulations⁸³ and heartache,
deafness with torrential and massive [movement in the ears].
The throat region is swollen and the throat is blocked.
The yin [openings] suffer from bleeding.
The lower abdomen has pain and is swollen.
[Patients] are unable to urinate.
[Hence] they suffer from [water qi] rushing upward and [generating] head-
ache.
The eyes [feel] as if they were to fall out [of their sockets];
the nape [feels] as if pulled at;
the lower back [feels] as if broken.
The thigh bones cannot be turned.
The knee bay [feels] as if knotted;
the calves [feel] as if severed. ⁸⁴

---

82 Zhang Jiebin: "Mountain valleys are locations rich of soil. Hence 'dust causes darkness in the mountain valleys.' Yellow is the color of the soil; black is the color of water. The soil dominates and the dampness is excessive. Hence [what should be] yellow appears black." Fang Yaozhong: "Black is the color of water and represents cold. In case of a disproportionate domination of dampness, rainfall is excessive and the climate may change from damp heat to cold."

83 An inability to transform/digest liquids leads to their accumulation in the body.

84 Wang Bing: "This applies to *jia chen, bing chen, wu chen, geng chen, ren chen, jia xu, bing xu, wu xu, geng xu*, and *ren xu* years. Major yin is [associated with] soil; its [corresponding] color that should appear in heaven is yellow. In contrast, black locations appear in the North. Water and soil appear together. Hence [the text] speaks of an 'interaction of the extreme yin.' That is, they combine their qi and their colors. 'Rush against the head, causing headache there' is to say: the pain is at the back of the brain and between the eyebrows." Wu Kun: "The major yin vessel passes along the gullet and ties up with the base of the tongue. Hence the throat region is swollen and the throat is blocked. The yin [orifices] suffer from bleeding because the dampness turns into heat and excites the blood. Blood strangury and bloody stool are the types [of conditions referred to here]. Dampness and heat pour into the bladder. Hence the lower abdomen is swollen and aches and [the patients] are unable to urinate. Dampness moves contrary [to its normal direction] upward; hence [patients] suffer from headache. The dampness evil causes harm to the major yang conduit with the effect that the eyes [give a feeling] as if falling out of their sockets, the nape [gives a feeling] as if pulled at, and the lower back [gives a feeling] as if broken. The upper thighs cannot be turned around; the knee bay [feels] like knotted and the calves [feel] as if

74-509-8

When, in a year when the minor yang [qi] is at the fountain,
fire encroaches upon what it dominates,
then flames light the wasteland.
Cold and heat arrive alternately.[85]

People suffer from red and white diarrheal outpour.[86]
The lower abdomen aches. The urine is red.
In severe cases, the stools have blood.
The manifestations are identical to [a year when] the minor yin [is at the
fountain].[87]

When, in a year when the yang brilliance [qi] is at the fountain,
dryness encroaches upon what it dominates,
then dense fog, coolness, and darkness occur.[88]

People suffer from a tendency to vomit.
When they vomit [they feel] a bitter [flavor].
They tend to breathe deeply.
Heart and flanks ache.[89] They cannot turn to the side.

---

severed." Fang Yaozhong: " 'Knee bay' refers to the knee joint here. Its movement is
impaired."

85 Wang Bing: "This applies to *yi si, ding si, ji si, xin si, gui si, yi hai, ding hai, ji hai,
xin hai,* and *gui hai* years."

86 Fang Yaozhong: "注泄赤白 refers to red and white diarrhea."

87 Zhang Jiebin: "All the remaining diseases manifest themselves in signs identical to those mentioned above for periods when the minor yin [qi] is at the fountain."
Fang Yaozhong: " 'Minor yin' refers to years when the minor yin [qi, i.e.,] ruler fire, is
at the fountain. 候 refers to 氣候 ('climate'), 物候 ('appearances of things'), and 病候
('signs of diseases'). Because minor yin [qi, i.e.,] ruler fire, and minor yang [qi, i.e.,]
minister fire, are both associated with fire, in years when the minor yin [qi] is at the
fountain and in years when the minor yang [qi] is at the fountain, the climate is disproportionately hot and people develop fire or heat diseases comparatively often."

88 Wang Bing: "This applies to *jia zi, bing zi, wu zi, geng zi, ren zi, jia wu, bing
wu, wu wu, geng wu,* and *ren wu* years. 'Haziness' and 'fog' is to say: it is impossible to
decide whether it is fog or darkness; it seems like fog. 清 is: slight cold. That is to say:
fog rises and causes darkness which makes it impossible to distinguish the shapes of
things, and it is slightly cold."

89 Wang Bing: "心脅痛 is to say: There is pain to the side of the heart in the flanks."
Fang Yaozhong: "This is pain in the stomach and in the flanks."

In severe cases, the throat is dry and there is dust on the face.[90]
The body lacks glossiness.[91]
Contrary [to what should be expected] the outside of the feet is hot.[92]

74-510-4
When, in a year when the major yang [qi] is at the fountain,
cold encroaches upon what it dominates,
then there is freezing and sternness, chilling temperature and shivering.[93]

People suffer from [pain in the] lower abdomen drawing the testicles in and
pulling on the lower back and the spine.
[The qi of the lower abdomen] rushes upward and [causes] heartache.
Blood appears.
The throat has pain and the jaws are swollen."[94]

---

90 Wang Bing: "That is to say: the face has a color as if soiled by dust."

91 *NJCD*: "膏澤 is 潤澤, 'moist', 'shiny.'"

92 Wu Kun: "That which is vomited has a sour flavor because when the qi of dryness, [i.e., of] metal, intrudes upon the gallbladder, it causes vomiting and the gall fluid rises upward. Hence it causes a bitter taste. The liver is located in the lower section [of the body]; its path is long. Metal rules killing. One's mind is sad. Hence [patients] draw in their breath for long. The yang brilliance vessels move downward to the inner edge of the breasts. The minor yang vessels penetrate the diaphragm and spread in the flanks. Hence there is pain in [the region of] the heart and of the flanks and [patients] are unable to turn to the side. The yang brilliance [qi] rules dryness. Hence the throat is dry and the face is dusty. The body lacks the glossiness of fat. The yang brilliance vessels run on the outside of the feet; their qi is cool and stern. Their illnesses should be those of coolness and frgidity. In the present case, though, heat appears. Hence [the text] speaks of 反熱, 'heat contrary [to what is normal].'"

93 Wang Bing: "This applies to *yi chou, ding chou, ji chou, xin chou, gui chou, yi wei, ding wei, ji wei, xin wei*, and *gui wei* years.

94 Wu Kun: "When cold qi enters the interior, it will cause harm [to regions] related to it, i.e., to the bladder and the kidneys. The bladder is associated with the abdomen, hence the lower abdomen aches. The kidneys rule the testicles. Hence [the pain] 'draws on the testicles.' The lower back is the palace of the kidneys; the major yang vessels pass along the spine and reach into the lower back. Hence [the pain] pulls on the lower back and the spine. The kidney vessels encircle the heart. Hence when [the qi] rushes upward it causes pain in the heart. The heart stores the blood, hence blood appears. The reason is that fire fears water. The hand major yang vessels follow the throat and rise to the submandibular region. Hence the throat aches and the submandibular region swells."

74-510-6
[Huang] Di:
"Good!
How to treat these [conditions]?"

Qi Bo:
"[As for] all the qi at the fountain,
if wind has encroached upon the interior,
this is treated with acrid [flavor] and cool [qi].
To assist use bitter [flavor].
Use sweet [flavor] to relax it;
use acrid [flavor] to disperse it.[95]

If heat has encroached upon the interior,
this is treated with salty [flavor] and cold [qi].
To assist use sweet and bitter [flavor].
Use sour [flavor] to contract it;
use bitter [flavor] to release it.[96]

If dampness has encroached upon the interior,
this is treated with bitter [flavor] and hot [qi].
To assist use sour and bland [flavor].

---

95 Wang Bing: "The nature of wind prefers warmth and has an aversion to coolness. Hence coolness is used to bring it back to order. A qi is employed here that dominates [the excessive qi]. Bitter [flavor] is employed to assist. This follows [the principle of selecting a flavor] that is of help [to the dominating qi]. When wood suffers from tension, sweet [flavor] is employed to relax it. When it suffers from repression, then acrid [flavor] is employed to disperse it."

96 Wang Bing: "The nature of heat has an aversion to cold. Hence cold is used to bring it back to order. If heat abounds in the [body's] outer regions, bitter [flavor] is used to effuse it. In case this does not solve the problem entirely, cold is employed again to restrain it. If cold does not restrain it entirely, bitter [flavor] is used in turn to effuse it." Wu Kun: "Heat is fire qi; water can dominate it. Hence [its excess] is treated with salty [flavor] and cold. This is assisted with sweet [flavor] because sweet [flavor] dominates salty [flavor], thereby preventing its excess. Sweet [flavor] must be accompanied by bitter [flavor] to prevent an an excess of salty [flavor] and also to drain a repletion caused by heat qi. When heat disperses throughout all conduits, it is gathered again by means of sour [flavor]. In case the heat lumps together and fails to disperse, bitter [flavor] is used to effuse it."

Use bitter [flavor] to dry it;
use bland [flavor] to drain it.⁹⁷

74-511-2
If fire has encroached upon the interior,
this is treated with salty [flavor] and cold [qi].
To assist use bitter and acrid [flavor].
Use sour [flavor] to contract it;
use bitter [flavor] to release it.⁹⁸

If dryness has encroached upon the interior,
this is treated with bitter [flavor] and warm [qi].
To assist use sweet and acrid [flavor].
Use bitter [flavor] to bring it down.⁹⁹

If cold has encroached upon the interior,
this is treated with sweet [flavor] and hot [qi].
To assist use bitter and acrid [flavor].
Use salty [flavor] to discharge it.
Use acrid [flavor] to moisten it.
Use bitter [flavor] to harden it."¹⁰⁰

---

97 Wang Bing: "Dampness and dryness are opposites. Hence [excessive dampness] is treated with bitter [flavor] and with heat, which are assisted by sour [flavor] and bland [flavor]. Dryness eliminates dampness. Hence this dampness is dried by means of bitter [flavor]. Bland [flavor] opens the orifices. Hence bland [flavor] is used for draining." Zhang Jiebin: "Dampness is the qi of the soil; dryness can eliminate it. Hence [its excess] is treated with bitter [flavor] and heat. Sour transforms out of wood; it is able to restrain soil. Hence [bitter flavor and heat] are assisted by sour [flavor] and bland [flavor]. [Dampness is] dried by means of bitter [flavor] because bitter [flavor] is a transformation product of fire."

98 Wang Bing: "Fire qi moves through the heart and the abdomen. The heart is the location where anger emerges. The nature of salt is to soften. Hence it is employed for treating [exciessive fire qi]." Zhang Zhicong: "Bitter [flavor] is able to drain; acrid [flavor] can disperse. Hence bitter [flavor] and acrid [flavor] are used to assist [salty flavor]."

99 Wu Kun: "Dryness is the qi of metal. Fire can dominate it. Hence [dryness] is treated with bitter [flavor] and warmth because bitter [flavor] and warmth are transformation products of fire. Sweet [flavor] and acrid [flavor] are warmth, too. In case of dryness with some cold in it, it is appropriate to [use them] for assistance. The dryness of dryness heat can be purged with bitter [flavor]."

100 Wang Bing: "To treat cold by means of heat is to put a squeeze on the dominant [qi], to break the manifestation of [that] qi, thereby curtailing its abundance."

74-511-5
[Huang] Di:
"Good!
What about the changes [caused by] the qi of heaven?"¹⁰¹

Qi Bo:
"When, [in a year when] the ceasing yin [qi] controls heaven,
wind encroaches upon what it dominates,
then the Great Void is darkened by dust.
Cloudy things are disturbed.
When the cold generates the qi of spring,
flowing waters do not freeze [any longer].

People suffer from pain in the stomach duct, exactly in the heart [region].
Above, there is propping fullness in the two flanks.
The diaphragm and the gullet are impassable;
[hence] beverages and food do not move downward.
The base of the tongue is stiff.
What is eaten is thrown up again.
[Patients suffer from] cold outflow, distended abdomen,
semiliquid stools, conglomerations, and strangury.
<The hibernating creatures do not leave.>¹⁰²

These illnesses originate in the spleen.¹⁰³

---

101 Zhang Jiebin: "From here on illnesses are discussed that result from an excessive dominance of the [qi] controlling heaven."

102 Zhang Jiebin, Gao Shishi, and Wu Kun have 出 instead of 去. Wu Kun: "When the [qi of] wood is overly active, then [the qi of] metal succeeds it and issues orders of coolness and sternness. Hence the hibernating creatures do not come out." Fang Yao-zhong: "In years when the ceasing yin [qi] controls heaven, the orders of spring arrive early and the climate warms up early. How could it be that the climate is warm and, still, the hibernating creatures do not come out? *Su wen* 70 states: 'When the ceasing yin [qi] controls heaven, .. the hibernating creatures appear in large numbers and the flowing waters do not freeze.' Something must be wrong with the present statement. Also, its position amidst the listing of diseases is inappropriate. Zhang Jiebin was right when he moved it behind the statement 流水不冰."

103 Wang Bing: "This refers to *yi si, ding si, ji si, xin si, gui si, yi hai, ding hai, ji hai, xin hai,* and *gui hai* years. In such years people suffer from accumulations in their center." Fang Yaozhong: "In years when the ceasing yin [qi] controls heaven, the wind qi is disproportionately dominant. Hence the qi of the liver, which corresponds [to the wind], is disproportionately dominant, too. When the liver dominates, it will invade

If the [movement at the] surging yang is interrupted,
[the patient] dies and is not treated.[104]

74-512-3
When, [in a year when] the minor yin [qi] controls heaven,
heat encroaches upon what it dominates,
[then] dammed up heat arrives
[because] the fire carries out its policy.[105]

People suffer from vexation and heat in the chest;
the throat is dry.
The upper flank on the right is full.
The skin aches. [People suffer from alternating fits of] cold and heat, coughing,
and panting.

If, in addition, massive rains arrive,
[people] spit blood, [and suffer from] blood outflow,
stuffy nose, nosebleed, sneezing, and vomiting.
The urine changes its color.

In severe cases, sores, ulcers, and *fu*-swellings [develop], as well as
pain in the shoulders, the back, the arms, the calves, and the broken basin.
The heart aches and the lung is distended.
The abdomen is full and enlarged.
Panting and coughing [sound like] 'peng,' 'peng.'

These illnesses originate in the lung.[106]

---

the spleen. Hence the above mentioned clinical conditions of spleen disease may easily appear."

104 Wang Bing: "The surging yang is the moving vessel on the upper side of the
feet. The stomach qi can be felt [there]. When [the movement in] the surging yang
vessel is weak, then [this indicates that] food and beverages have decreased. When it
is interrupted, then [this indicates that] neither drugs nor food can enter [the body].
What is swallowed is thrown up again. Any attack [by means of drugs] will not enter
[the body]; any [attempt to] nourish [the body] will not generate anything. The evil
qi gains strength every day, while [the movement of] the true qi is interrupted. Hence
[such patients] are bound to die and are not treated."

105 Zhang Zhicong: "怫 is 郁, 'oppressed.' The reason is: the fire of minor yin develops within the yin. Hence it is a 'oppressed fire.'"

106 Wang Bing: "This applies to the *jia zi, bing zi, wu zi, geng zi, ren zi, jia wu, bing
wu, wu wu, geng wu*, and *ren wu* years. .. In such years people suffer from accumula-

If the [movement at the] foot marsh is interrupted,
[the patient] dies and is not treated.[107]

74-513-1
When, [in a year when] the major yin [qi] controls heaven,
dampness encroaches upon what it dominates,
then, heavy overcast spreads, too.[108]
Rain [causes catastrophic] changes [which in turn cause] desiccation.[109]

[People suffer from] *fu*-swellings,[110] bone pain, yin blocks, {as for 'yin blocks,'
these are those that are not felt by pressing [a location]}, as well as
pain in the lower back, the spine, the head, and the nape.
[Patients suffer from] frequent dizziness and
from difficulties in passing stools.
The yin qi does not operate.
[People are] hungry but do not wish to eath.
When they cough and spit, then this is accompanied by blood.
The heart [feels] as if suspended.[111]

---

tions in their right." Zhang Jiebin: "All conditions such as vexation and heat in the
chest, dry throat, and so on, result from harm to the metal that is caused by a flaming
up of the ruler fire. The qi of metal rules the right side, hence the flank on the right
experiences fullness."

107 Wang Bing: "The foot marsh is the moving vessel in the large fold at the inner
angle of the elbow. The qi of the lung can be felt [here]. When fire melts the metal,
then [the latter] follows the command of heaven and the [flow of the] qi of metal is
interrupted internally. Hence [the patient] is in serious danger of perishing. When the
[movement] at the foot marsh does not arrive, the [movement of the] qi of the lung
has been interrupted and there is nothing that could rule the movement of the the
camp and of the guard qi. The true qi is exhausted internally. How could the [body]
be kept alive?"

108 Zhang Jiebin has 旦, "[every] day", instead of 且."

109 Lit.: "deep yin"; "deep shadow", a term used to denote "heavy overcast" in pre-*Su
wen* texts already. Zhang Jiebin: "In case of heavy overcast and [catastrophic] changes
caused by rain, [things are] soaked to a degree that they are harmed. Hence many
things wither and desiccate."

110 1682/42: "胕腫 is 浮腫, 'surface swelling.'" For a detailed discussion of the occurrences of 胕腫 and 跗腫 see there.

111 Wu Kun: " 'Peope suffer from *fu*-swellings': the flesh is like mud and remains
indented if pressed. The excess evil of dampness, [i.e.,] the qi of soil, has invaded the
water of the kidneys. The kidneys rule the bones. Hence the bones ache. The kidneys
rule storage. Hence yin blocks arise. The kidneys rule the supervisor vessel. Hence the
lower abdomen, the spine, the head, and the nape ache. The color of the kidneys is

These illnesses originate in the kidneys.[112]

If the [movement at the] great ravine is interrupted,
[the patient] dies and is not treated.[113]

74-513-4
When, [in a year when] the minor yang [qi] controls heaven,
fire encroaches upon what it dominates,
then, warmth qi prevails everywhere.
The policy of the metal is not balanced.

People suffer from headache and
malaria [which goes along] with fever and an aversion to cold.
The heat rises. The skin aches and
its color changes to yellow and red.
Transmission turns [this disease] into a water [disease].
The body and the face have *fu*-swellings;
the abdomen is full and [patients] breathe adopting an upright position.
[People suffer from] diarrheal outpour which is red and white,
from sores and ulcers, and from coughing and spitting [accompanied by] blood.
The heart is vexed and there is heat in the chest.

In severe cases, [patients suffer from] stuffy nose and nosebleed.

These illnesses originate in the lung.[114]

---

black. Hence vision is obscured and at times [patients experience] dizziness. The kidneys rule the fluids. When the fluids are lost the passage of stools turns difficult. The kidneys rule inhalation. When the kidneys are weak, inhalation is impossible. Hence [patients] may be hungry but do not wish to eat nevertheless."

112 Wang Bing: "This refers to *yi chou, ding chou, ji chou, xin chou, gui chou, yi wei, ding wei, ji wei, ji wei, xin wei,* and *gui wei* years. When the kidneys are affected by evil, there is no water to moisten and the lower burner turns dry. Hence the passage of stools is difficult."

113 Wang Bing: "The great ravine is a moving vessel at the inside of the feet behind the ankle, above the heel bone. The qi of the kidneys can be felt here. The soil evil dominates the water and the internal [flow of the] kidney qi is interrupted. The evil [qi] is present in excess, while the proper [qi] is weak. Prescriptions are of no use."

114 Wang Bing: "This refers to *jia yin, bing yin, wu yin, geng yin, ren yin, jia shen, bing shen, wu shen, geng shen,* and *ren shen* years. When the fire arrives to be in charge, the qi of metal is affected by evil. Hence [the text] states: 'the policy of metal is not balanced.'" Wu Kun: "Fire flames upward, hence the head aches. The qi of fire is heat, the qi of metal is cold. Metal and fire struggle with each other. Hence [patients] de-

If the [movement at the] celestial palace is interrupted,
[the patient] dies and is not treated.[115]

74-513-8
When, [in a year when] the yang brilliance [qi] controls heaven,
dryness encroaches upon what it dominates,
then, the trees flourish late and
the herbs come to life late.
Sinews and bones change internally.

People suffer from pain in the upper flank and lower flank on the left and
from cold and coolness in the center.
This affection results in malaria.
The massive coolness changes the manifestations [of the heavenly qi].
Coughing. Sounds in the abdomen.
Diarrheal outpour; duck-like semiliquid stools.

The eminent trees shrink;
life concentrates in [their] lower parts;
the herbs are scorched in their upper ends.

Violent pain in the heart and in the flanks.
One cannot turn to the side.
The throat is dry, the face [is covered with] dust, the lower back aches.
Males suffer from breakdown illness with elevation illness.
Females have pain in the lower abdomen.
Vision is impaired, the canthi have ulcers;
[patients suffer from] sores, pimples, and *yong*-abscesses.

<The hibernating creatures appear.>

---

velop fever and an aversion to cold, which is malaria. The skin is associated with metal.
Metal fears fire. Hence the skin aches when it meets with fire. The color changes to
yellow-red because of the fire. .. When lung heat produces snivel, that is called 軌.
When the nose bleeds, that is called 衄. All these conditions result from fire evil af-
fecting the lung. Hence [the text states:] 'these illnesses originate in the lung.'" Fang
Yaozhong: "軌衄 is nosebleed."

115 Wang Bing: "The celestial palace is the moving vessel three individually standardized body inches below the armpit above the inner side behind the elbow. The
qi of the lung can be felt here. Because the fire dominates, the [flow of] metal qi is
interrupted. Hence [patients] die."

These illnesses originate in the liver.[116]

If the [movement at the] great thoroughfare is interrupted,
[the patient] dies and is not treated.[117]

74-514-1
When, [in a year when] the major yang [qi] controls heaven,
cold encroaches upon what it dominates,
then, cold [qi] arrives, contrary [to normal circumstances].
Also, the water freezes,
<The blood changes in the center and
develops into *yong*-abscesses and ulcers.>

People suffer from recession heartache,[118]
blood vomiting, blood outflow, stuffy nose, nosebleed, and
a tendency to sadness. Occasionally they experience dizziness and fall to the
ground.

>If the [annual] period is fiercely flaming fire,[119]
then violent rains and hail occur.<[120]

The chest and the abdomen are full;
the hands are hot; the elbows have a cramp; the armpits are swollen.[121]
The heart is disturbed and moves strongly.
[Hence] the chest, the flanks, and the stomach duct are not at peace.

---

116 Wang Bing: "This refers to *yi mao, ding mao, ji mao, xin mao, gui mao, yi you, ding you, ji you, xin you*, and *gui you* years. Metal dominates, hence herbs and trees come to life and flourish late."

117 Wang Bing: "The great thoroughfare is the moving vessel two inches behind the base joint of the large toes. The [movement of the] qi of the liver can be felt here. When metal arrives to cut the wood, [then the flow of] the liver qi is interrupted internally. The true [qi] cannot dominate the evil [qi]. Death is inevitable."

118 Fang Yaozhong: "Headache combined with cold extremities."

119 Fang Yaozhong: "These are years with a greatly excessive fire period."

120 Zhang Jiebin has moved these eight characters behind 寒氣反至, 水且冰. Zhang Jiebin: "If [a year when the major yang qi controls heaven] happens to be a fire period with fiercely flaming fire qi, then water and fire struggle with each other. Hence violent rainfalls and hail occur."

121 916/52: "掖 is identical to 腋, 'the armpits.'" Commentators agree that 衝 is most likely an error for 腫.

The face is red and the eyes are yellow.
There is a tendency to belch and the throat is dry.

In severe cases, the color turns dark like soot.
[Patients are] thirsty and wish to drink.

These illnesses originate in the heart.[122]

If the [movement at the] spirit gate is interrupted,
[the patient] dies and is not treated."[123]

{From the so-called 'moving qi' it is possible to recognize the [condition of the] depots.}[124]

74-515-1
[Huang] Di:
"Good!
How to treat these [conditions]?"

---

122 Wang Bing: "This applies to *jia chen, bing chen, wu chen, geng chen, ren chen, jia xu, bing xu, wu xu, geng xu,* and *ren xu* years. When the major yang [qi] controls heaven, cold qi spreads and transforms. Hence the water freezes and the blood congeals. Inside the skin the guard qi accumulates, hence ulcers are generated. If [such a situation] falls together with a fire period, then the fiercely flaming fire heat will enter into a fight with the water. Hence violent rainfalls and hail occur, with balls the size of half pearls. The qi associated with the heart is belching. Hence [patients] tend to belch." Wu Kun: "The water does not rise and the fire does not descend. Hence chest and abdomen are full. The fire is oppressed in the center; hence the hands are hot. The cold resides in the network [vessels], hence the elbows are bent. The heart vessel emerges from the armpits, hence the armpits are swollen. 澹澹, 'disturbed,' indicates movement. Fire fears the water, hence [the heart] is disturbed and moves strongly. Because of this strong movement, chest, flanks, and stomach duct are not at peace. In case of severe fire the five fluids dry up. Hence [patients] are thirsty and wish to drink. All this is the result of cold evil affecting the heart. Hence [the text] states: these illnesses originate in the heart."

123 Wang Bing: "The spirit gate is the moving vessel at the tip of the pointed bone behind the palm. The qi of the true heart can be felt here."

124 Wang Bing: "How is it that a diagnosis enables one to know beforehand whether [a patient] will die? It is always such that from the moving qi in the conduit vessels associated with the depots it can be learned whether the spirit stored in these depots is [still] present or has vanished."

Qi Bo:
"[As for] the qi controlling heaven,

when wind encroaches upon what it dominates,
this is balanced with acrid [flavor] and coolness.
To assist use bitter [flavor] and sweet [flavor].
Use sweet [flavor] to relax it;
use sour [flavor] to discharge it.

When heat [as the qi controlling heaven] encroaches upon what it dominates,
this is balanced with salty [flavor] and cold.
To assist use bitter [flavor] and sweet [flavor].
Use sour [flavor] to contract it.

When dampness [as the qi controlling heaven] encroaches upon what it dominates,
this is balanced with bitter [flavor] and heat.
To assist use sour [flavor] and acrid [flavor].
Use bitter [flavor] to dry it;
use bland [flavor] to drain it.

If the dampness rises severely and if heat [develops],
this is treated with bitter [flavor] and warmth.
To assist use sweet [flavor] and acrid [flavor].
This is to induce sweating. Then one stops.   .

74-516-1
When fire [as the qi controlling heaven] encroaches upon what it dominates,
this is balanced with sour [flavor] and cold.
To assist use bitter [flavor] and sweet [flavor].
Use sour [flavor] to contract it;
use bitter [flavor] to effuse it.
Use sour [flavor] to restore it.
{This is identical to the [treatment in cases of] encroaching heat.}

When dryness [as the qi controlling heaven] encroaches upon what it dominates,
this is balanced with bitter [flavor] and dampness.
To assist use sour [flavor] and acrid [flavor].
Use bitter [flavor] to purge it.

When cold [as the qi controlling heaven] encroaches upon what it dominates,
this is balanced with acrid [flavor] and heat.
To assist use sweet [flavor] and bitter [flavor].
Use salty [flavor] to discharge it."

74-516-4
[Huang] Di:
"Good!
If contrary [to the regular qi controlling earth] an evil qi dominates, how are
[such conditions] treated?"[125]

Qi Bo:
"When wind controls on the earth and
coolness, contrary [to normal], dominates it,
this is treated with sour [flavor] and warmth.
To assist use bitter [flavor] and sweet [flavor].
Use acrid [flavor] to balance it.[126]

When heat controls on the earth and
cold, contrary [to normal], dominates it,
this is treated with sweet [flavor] and heat.
To assist use bitter [flavor] and acrid [flavor].
Use salty [flavor] to balance it.[127]

---

125 Wang Bing: "[The proper qi] is unable to encroach upon and dominate the other
qi and, in contrast, the qi that cannot dominate turns evil and dominates the [proper
qi]." Zhang Jiebin: "反勝 is to say: because the qi [controlling] heaven and earth
are insufficient, an intervening qi intrudes upon the depleted [region] and dominates
contrary [to what is normal]."

126 Wang Bing: "When the ceasing yin [qi] is at the fountain, then wind is in control
on the earth. This applies to the five *yin* and to the five *shen* years." Fang Yaozhong:
"In years when the ceasing yin [qi] is at the fountain, the wind should be disproportionately dominant and the climate should be disproprortionately warm in the second
half of such years. In reality, though, dryness qi dominates disproportionately and the
climate is disproportionately cool."

127 Wang Bing: "When the minor yin [qi] is at the fountain, then heat is in control
on the earth. This applies to the five *mao* and to the five *you* years. The evil [qi] is to
be drained first; the proper qi is to be balanced afterwards." Fang Yaozhong: "In years
when the minor yin [qi] is at the fountain, the heat qi or the qi of fire should be disproportionately dominant and the climate should be disproprortionately hot in the
second half of such years. In reality, though, cold qi dominates disproportionately and
the climate is disproportionately cold."

74-516-7
When dampness controls on the earth and
heat, contrary [to normal], dominates it,
this is treated with bitter [flavor] and cold.
To assist use salty [flavor] and sweet [flavor].
Use bitter [flavor] to balance it."[128]

When fire controls on the earth and
cold, contrary [to normal], dominates it,
this is treated with sweet [flavor] and heat.
To assist use bitter [flavor] and acrid [flavor].
Use salty [flavor] to balance it.[129]

When dryness controls on the earth and
heat, contrary [to normal], dominates it,
this is treated with balanced [qi] and cold.
To assist use bitter [flavor] and sweet [flavor].
Use sour [flavor] to balance it.

<To use harmonizing [substances] is beneficial.>[130]

When cold controls on the earth and
heat, contrary [to normal], dominates it,
this is treated with salty [flavor] and cold [qi].

128 Wang Bing: "When the major yin [qi] is at the fountain, then dampness is in
control on the earth. This applies to the five *chen* and to the five *xu* years." Fang Yaozhong: "In years when the major yin [qi] is at the fountain, the dampness qi should
be disproportionately dominant and there should be more rainfall than usual in the
second half of such years. In reality, though, the climate is disproportionately hot."

129 Wang Bing: "When the minor yang [qi] is at the fountain, then fire is in control
on the earth. This applies to the five *si* and to the five *hai* years." Fang Yaozhong: "In
years when the minor yang [qi] is at the fountain, the fire qi should be disproportionately dominant and the climate should be flamingly hot in the second half of
such years. In reality, though, cold qi dominates disproportionately and the climate is
disproportionately cold."

130 Wang Bing: "When the yang brilliance [qi] is at the fountain, then dryness is in
control on the earth. This applies to the five *zi* and to the five *wu* years." Fang Yaozhong: "In years when the yang brilliance [qi] is at the fountain, the dryness qi should
be disproportionately dominant and the climate should be cool in the second half of
such years. In reality, though, the climate is disproportionately hot." Gao Jiwu/253:
"利 is 宜, 'suitable.'"

To assist use sweet [flavor] and acrid [flavor].
Use bitter [flavor] to balance it.[131]

74-517-3
[Huang] Di:
"If the [qi] controlling heaven is dominated by an evil [qi], how [to treat] that?"

Qi Bo:
"When wind transforms in heaven and
coolness, contrary [to normal], dominates it,
this is treated with sour [flavor] and warmth.
To assist use sweet [flavor] and bitter [flavor].[132]

When heat transforms in heaven and
cold, contrary [to normal], dominates it,
this is treated with sweet [flavor] and warmth.
To assist use bitter [flavor], sour [flavor], and acrid [flavor].[133]

When dampness transforms in heaven and
heat, contrary [to normal], dominates it,
this is treated with bitter [flavor] and cold.
To assist use bitter [flavor] and sour [flavor].[134]

---

131 Wang Bing: "When the major yang [qi] is at the fountain, then cold is in control on the earth. This applies to the five *chou* and to the five *wei* years. When [the text] states 'treat,' this is [a request] to drain the dominating evil that has settled [in the body]. When it states 'assist,' this is [a request to use substances] that are beneficial. When it states 'balance,' this is [a request] to supplement the proper qi when it has weakened already." Fang Yaozhong: "In years when the major yang [qi] is at the fountain, the cold qi should be disproportionately dominant and the climate should be cold in the second half of such years. In reality, though, the climate is disproportionately hot."

132 Wang Bing: "These are *hai* and *si* years." Fang Yaozhong: "In years when the ceasing yin [qi] controls heaven, the wind qi should be disproportionately dominant and the climate should be disproportionately warm, in the first half of such years. In reality, though, the dryness qi is disproportionately dominant and the climate is disproportionately cool."

133 Wang Bing: "These are *zi* and *wu* years." Fang Yaozhong: "In years when the minor yin [qi, i.e.,] ruler fire, controls heaven, the heat qi should be disproportionately dominant and the climate should be disproprortionately hot, in the first half of such years. In reality, though, cold qi dominates disproportionately and the climate is disproportionately cold."

134 Wang Bing: "These are the *chou* and *wei* years." Fang Yaozhong: "In years when the major yin [qi, i.e.,] dampness, controls heaven, the dampness qi should be dispro-

When fire transforms in heaven and
cold, contrary [to normal], dominates it,
this is treated with sweet [flavor] and heat.
To assist use bitter [flavor] and acrid [flavor].¹³⁵

74-517-8
When dryness transforms in heaven and
heat, contrary [to normal], dominates it,
this is treated with acrid [flavor] and cold.
To assist use bitter [flavor] and sweet [flavor].¹³⁶

When cold transforms in heaven and
heat, contrary [to normal], dominates it,
this is treated with salty [flavor] and cold [qi].
To assist use bitter [flavor] and acrid [flavor]."¹³⁷

74-517-10
[Huang] Di:
"What about the mutual domination of the six qi?"¹³⁸

Qi Bo:
"When the ceasing yin dominates,
[patients hear] ringing [sounds] in the ears and the head is dizzy.

---

portionately dominant and there should be more rainfall than usual, in the first half of
such years. In reality, though, heat qi dominates disproportionately."

135 Wang Bing: "These are the *yin* and *shen* years." Fang Yaozhong: "In years when
the minor yang [qi] controls heaven, the fire qi should be disproportionately dominant
and the climate should be disproportionately hot, in the first half of such years. In
reality, though, cold qi dominates disproportionately and the climate is disproportionately cold."

136 Wang Bing: "These are *mao* and *you* years." Fang Yaozhong: "In years when the
yang brilliance [qi] controls heaven, the dryness qi should be disproportionately dominant and the climate should be disproportionately cool, in the first half of such years.
In reality, though, heat qi dominates disproportionately."

137 Wang Bing: "These are *chen* and *xu* years." Fang Yaozhong: "In years when the
major yang [qi] controls heaven, the cold qi should be disproportionately dominant
and the climate should be disproportionately cold in the first half of such years. In
reality, though, the climate is disproportionately hot.

138 Fang Yaozhong: "The six qi include wind, heat, fire, dampness, dryness, and
cold."

They feel nauseous and wish to vomit.[139]
The stomach is barred as if [it contained] cold.

Strong winds rise frequently.
The naked creatures do not proliferate.[140]

The qi collects in the upper flanks and in the lower flanks;
it transforms to heat.
The urine is yellow and red.
There is pain in the stomach duct, exactly in the heart [region].
[The pain] rises and there is propping [fullness] in the two flanks.
[Patients experience] intestinal sounds and an outflow of [undigested] food.
The lower abdomen aches.
There is red and white outpour below.

In severe cases, there is vomiting;
The diaphragm and the gullet are impassable.[141]

74-518-1
When the minor yin dominates,
there is heat below the heart. [Patients] tend to be hungry.
There is a countermovement below the navel.
The qi travels through the triple burner.[142]

Flaming summerheat arrives.
Hence the trees [effuse] liquid;[143]
the herbs wither.

---

139 Zhang Jiebin: "憒憒 is 心亂, 'heart trouble.'"

140 Fang Yaozhong: "Within the five agents, naked creatures are associated with soil; their generation and growth is closely related to dampness. In a climatic environment where dampness qi dominates disproportionately, [naked creatures] come to life and grow relatively well. Wind dominates dampness; hence in years when the ceasing yin [qi] is the ruling qi the generation and growth of naked creatures is not good."

141 Wang Bing: "These are the five *si* and the five *hai* years. Below the heart and above the navel is the stomach section. 胃鬲 is to say: above the stomach duct and below the great diaphragm. 鬲咽 is to say: beverages and food consumed are thrown up again."

142 Cheng Shide et al.: " 'Qi' refers to the heat qi of the minor qin [i.e.,] the ruler fire."

143 Wu Kun: "The liquids flow from the trees." Zhang Zhicong: "[The trees] are nourished by the yin water of the minor yin [qi]."

[People suffer from] vomiting, movement [of qi] contrary [to its regular course], overexcitement, vexation,
abdominal fullness, pain, and semiliquid stools.
Transmission turns this into a red downpour.[144]

74-518-3
When the major yin dominates,
if the fire qi is oppressed internally,
sores and ulcers are in the center.
[If the fire] spreads to the outside,
the disease is in the upper and lower flanks.

In severe cases, there is heartache and the heat is barred [from effusion].
[People suffer from] headache, throat block, and stiff nape.
When [the major yin qi] dominates alone,[145] then the dampness qi is oppressed internally and
cold presses against the lower burner.
Pain stays in the top of the skull and
there is a mutual pulling [between the top and the region] between the eyebrows.
The stomach [has a feeling of] fullness.

Rain arrives frequently.
Hence dryness transformations appear.[146]

The lower abdomen is full.
The lower back and the buttocks are heavy and stiff.
[Patients] feel uncomfortable internally,[147] and
they tend to [suffer from] diarrheal outpour.
The lower side of the feet is warm.
The head is heavy. The feet and the shins have *fu*-swellings.

---

144 Wang Bing: "These are the five *zi* and five *wu* years. 沃 is 沭, 'a stream.'" Zhang Jiebin: "赤沃 refers to bloody diarrhea and red urine." In a comment to *Su wen* 70, Wang Bing identifies 沃 as 沫, "foam."

145 Zhang Jiebin: "There is no heat and dampness dominates alone."

146 Zhang Jiebin: "'Dryness' should be 'dampness.'"

147 Wang Bing: "'Uncomfortable' is to say: the lower back [feels] heavy and is stiff. Bending and stretching is difficult." Wu Kun: "内不便 is to say: sexual intercourse is not convenient."

Beverages are effused in the center.
Fu-swelling develops above.[148]

74-518-8
When the minor yang dominates,
heat settles in the stomach.
The heart is vexed and has pain.
The eyes are red. [Patients] wish to vomit.
What is vomited has a sour [flavor]. [Patients] tend to be hungry.
The ears have pain; the urine is red.
[Patients] tend to be frightened and to make incoherent and absurd speeches.

Violent heat [causes] wasting away [as if] melting.
The herbs wither and the water dries up.
The armored creatures crouch.

The lower abdomen has pain;
the downpour is red and white.[149]

74-518-11
When the yang brilliance dominates,
coolness is effused in the center.
The upper and the lower flanks on the left have pain. [Patients suffer from] semiliquid stools.
Internally this causes throat obstruction;
externally this is effused as breakdown illness with elevation illness.[150]

Massive coolness; sternness and killing.
The flowers change their outer appearance.
The hairy creatures perish.

---

148 Wang Bing: "These are the five *chou* and the five *wei* years. When dampness dominates above, then the qi of fire is oppressed internally. When [dampness] dominates in the center, then cold strikes the lower burner. 脽 is to say: 臀肉, 'the flesh of the upper thighs.' 'Swelling above' is to say: on the head and in the face."

149 Wang Bing: "These are the five *yin* and the five *shen* years. Armored creatures are metal transformations. When the fire qi dominates strongly, the shelled insects crouch and lie down."

150 Fang Yaozhong: "癲疝 is the name of a disease. It manifests itself clinically as enlarged testicles."

[Patients] feel uncomfortable in the chest.
The throat is obstructed and they cough.[151]

74-518-13
When the major yang dominates,
freezing and also extreme cold arrive.
The water freezes even though this is not its time.
The feathered [creatures] transform later.

Piles and malaria develop.
Cold recession enters the stomach.
As a result, heartache emerges internally,[152] and
there are ulcers in the yin (i.e., the sexual organs).
The hidden bend is impeded.[153]
There is a mutual pulling [between the hidden bend and] the yin (i.e., inner
side of the) thighs.
The sinews have a cramp and the flesh is numb.[154]
The blood congeals in the vessels so that [its flow] is impeded.
The network [vessels] are full and the color changes.
Occasionally blood outflow results.
The skin is blocked and swollen.
The abdomen is full and [patients] eat less.
The heat, contrary [to normal], moves upward.

---

151 Wang Bing: "These are the five *mao* and the five *you* years." Wu Kun: "Yang
brilliance [qi] is a metal transformation. When it dominates, then coolness and cold
develop in the center. When metal dominates, then wood is harmed. Hence the upper
and the lower flanks on the left have pain. Because of coolness in the center, the stool
is semiliquid. The virtue of metal is to draw together. Hence the throat is blocked.
Hardness is a metal transformation. Hence breakdown and elevation illnesses appear.
Hairy creatures are associated with wood. Hence they perish when they encounter
metal. The chest center is the location of the lung, [i.e., of] metal. In case of severe
dryness, the lung contracts and cannot function any longer. The result is [a feeling of]
discomfort, a blocked throat, and cough."

152 Fang Yaozhong: " 'Heartache' refers to pain in the chest and in the abdomen."

153 Wu Kun: "俯首, 'to bow the head,' is 隱; 鞠躬, 'to bend the body,' is 曲." Fang
Yaozhong: "隱曲 refers to strangury and to sexual weakness and efflux in males, as
well as irregular menstruation in women." Guo Aichun-92: "The urine does not flow
freely." For a detailed discussion of 隱曲, see *Su wen* 7, also 852/14.

154 Wang Bing: "苛 is 重, 'heavy.'" Gao Shishi: "When the flesh experiences violent
pain, that is called 苛." Fang Yaozhong: "苛 is 'pain.'" Cheng Shide et al.: "苛 is 'numbness.'"

There is pain in the head and in the nape {at the fontanella peak and at the
Brain's Door}.¹⁵⁵
The eyes [ache] as if they were to fall out.
Cold enters the lower burner.
Transmission turns it into soggy outflow."¹⁵⁶

74-519-4
[Huang] Di:
"How to treat these [conditions]?"

Qi Bo:
"When the ceasing yin dominates,
this is treated with sweet [flavor] and coolness.
To assist use bitter [flavor] and acrid [flavor].
Use sour [flavor] to discharge it.¹⁵⁷

When the minor yin dominates,
this is treated with acrid [flavor] and cold.
To assist use bitter [flavor] and salty [flavor].
Use sweet [flavor] to discharge it.¹⁵⁸

74-519-7
When the major yin dominates,
this is treated with salty [flavor] and heat.

---

155 "Brain's Door (腦戶)" is the name of an insertion hole used for acupuncture needling. It is located above the os occipitalis.

156 Wang Bing: "These are the five *chen* and five *xu* years."

157 Wang Bing: "All the six dominations turn first on [that qi] by which they themselves cannot be dominated. Hence that which cannot dominate must be drained first
to clear their way. Second, the dominating qi is to be drained to have it retreat. If that
which dominates is treated without being driven away, then the dominating qi will
return to abundance and cause all kinds of internal diseases." Wu Kun: "When the
wood dominates, it defeats the soil. This is treated with sweet [flavor] to supplement
the soil. Cool [drugs] are employed to balance the wood. [Drugs of] bitter and acrid
[flavor] are employed to assist; they disperse wind and heat. Because the qi of wood
has generated a repletion, it is discharged by means of sour [flavor]."

158 Zhang Jiebin: "When heat dominates, it encroaches upon the metal. This is
treated with acrid [flavor] and cold to disperse the heat. Bitter and salty [flavors] are
employed to discharge the heat. The [heat] is drained with sweet [flavor] because the
proper flavor of fire is drained with sweet [flavor]."

To assist use acrid [flavor] and sweet [flavor].
Use bitter [flavor] to discharge it.¹⁵⁹

When the minor yang dominates,
this is treated with acrid [flavor] and cold.
To assist use sweet [flavor] and salty [flavor].
Use sweet [flavor] to discharge it.¹⁶⁰

When the yang brilliance dominates,
this is treated with sour [flavor] and warmth.
To assist use acrid [flavor] and sweet [flavor].
Use bitter [flavor] to drain it.¹⁶¹

When the major yang dominates,
this is treated with sweet [flavor]¹⁶² and heat.
To assist use acrid [flavor] and sour [flavor].
Use salty [flavor] to discharge it."¹⁶³

---

159 Zhang Jiebin: "When soil dominates, then dampness is present in excess. This is treated with salty [flavor] and heat. Salty [flavor] can moisten what is below; heat can dry the dampness. When dampness dominates, then the soil turns cold. [Hence treatment] is assisted by means of acrid and sweet [flavor]. Acrid [flavor] can warm the soil; sweet [flavor] can supplement the soil."

160 Wu Kun: "When fire dominates, it encroaches upon the metal. This is treated with acrid [flavor] and cold. Acrid [flavor] can disperse fire; cold can check fire. Sweet and salty [flavors] are employed to assist because sweet [flavor] calms down the urgency of the qi of fire and salty [flavor] softens the repletion of dryness caused by the qi of fire. [The text] refers to sweet [flavor] again to drain [the fire]. This is the drainage caused by repeated [dosages of] sweet [flavor]."

161 Zhang Jiebin: "When dryness, [i.e.,] metal, dominates, illnesses emerge in lung and liver. This is to be treated with sour [flavor] and warmth to moisten what is dry and to warm the lung. Acrid and sweet [flavors] are employed for assistance to drain the lung und to supplement the liver. Bitter [flavor] is employed to drain it because bitter [flavor] is a transformation of fire. It is able to drain repletions caused by dryness evil."

162 Lin Yi et al.: "甘 may be an error for 苦, 'bitter [flavor].'"

163 Wu Kun: "Major yang [qi] is cold and water. It is treated with sweet [flavor] to increase soil to [enable it to] ward off water. [Also,] heat is employed for treatment to support the yang and to disperse the cold. Acrid [flavor] is employed to assist lest the sweet [flavor] causes obstructions. Sour [flavor] is employed to assist lest the heat causes dryness. When cold qi enters the interior, it changes to heat and causes repletion with dryness. Hence salty [flavor] is employed to drain it."

74-519-10
[Huang] Di:
"The revenge taken by the six qi, what is it like?"[164]

Qi Bo:
"An encompassing question, indeed!

When the ceasing yin [qi] takes revenge,[165]
the lower abdomen hardens and [has a feeling of] fullness.
There is internal tightness and violent pain.
It makes the trees bend down and the sand fly.

The naked creatures do not blossom.
[The qi] recedes and the heart aches.[166]
Sweat is effused [from the body] and vomiting sets in.
Beverages and food do not enter [the body];
when they are [made to] enter, they come out again.
Sinews and bones sway. [Patients suffer from] dizziness, they feel cool, [because
the qi] recedes.

In severe cases, [the ceasing yin qi] enters the spleen.
The [passage of the] food is blocked and [anything eaten is] thrown up.[167]

---

164 Wang Bing: "復 is to say: 報復, 'revenge'; to avenge a domination. Any domination is sure to be followed by revenge." Fang Yaozhong: "For example, when wind qi
dominates disproportionately, dryness qi and coolness qi arrive to take revenge. When
the qi of fire or the qi of heat dominate disproportionately, cold qi arrives to take revenge. When the qi of dampness dominates disproportionately, the qi of wind arrives
to take revenge. Etc."

165 Fang Yaozhong: "Any disproportionate domination by the qi of dampness will
generate phenomena of wind qi taking revenge. For instance, in case of excessive rain
and dampness, wind appears. Wind functions to stop the rain and to disperse the
clouds. Thus, dampness is changed to dryness."

166 *Ling shu* 24: "厥心痛 is a pain as if one had been stabbed into the heart. .. The
complexion turns greenish as if [the patient] were to die."

167 Wang Bing: " 'Internal' is 'inside the abdomen and the flanks.' The trees are bent
and the sand flies because of strong winds. Wind indicates domination by [the qi
of] wood. Hence the soil cannot flourish. The qi 'recedes' is to say: the qi rushes into
the chest and flanks and advances to the heart. The stomach is affected by qi flowing
contrary to its usual course and carrying out an upward attack against the heart. This
causes pain. 清厥 is to say: hands and feet are cold. 食痹 is to say: after meals a pain is
felt below the heart. [This pain] is obscure and cannot be named; also, it is unbearable.

If the [movement at the] surging yang is interrupted,
[the patient] dies and is not treated.[168]

74-520-4
When the minor yin [qi] takes revenge,
pressing heat is generated internally.
[Patients] are vexed and overexcited; they [suffer from] stuffy nose and sneezing.
They experience strangling pain in the lower abdomen.
Fire appears with burning heat.
The throat is dry.
There is sectional outpour, stopping at times.[169]
The qi moves on the left;
it rises on the right.[170]
[The patients] cough and
their skin has pain.
Suddenly [they] turn mute and their heart aches.
Their [qi is] oppressed, they are dizzy, and do not recognize people.
Then they shake and shiver [from cold] and make incoherent and absurd
speeches.
When the cold ends, they turn hot.
They are thirsty and wish to drink.
They are short of qi,[171] and their bones turn limp.
[They suffer from] barred intestines and an inability to relieve themselves.
Externally this causes surface swelling, hiccup, and belching.

Once [the patient] has vomited, [the pain] stops. The reason is that stomach qi moves
contrary to its normal course and fails to flow downward."

168 Wang Bing: " 'Surging yang' is the qi of the stomach vessel."

169 Wang Bing: "分注 is to say: both urine and stools move downward." Zhang
Jiebin: "分注時止 is to say: at times the large intestine experiences outpour, while
the bladder is blocked. Fire resides in both." Wu Kun: "分注 is to say: the urine does
not flow freely, while the stools are discharged regularly, as if there were a 'separate
outpour.'"

170 Wang Bing: "The qi of fire and heat moves from the small intestine to the left
below the navel into the large intestine and rises to the left flank. In severe cases, it
moves upward to the right and enters the lung. Hence [the text] states: 'it moves on
the left and rises on the right.'"

171 They are short of breath.

The transformation of the red qi is belated;[172]
the flowing waters do not freeze.
Heat qi prevails everywhere.
The armored creatures [can]not recover.[173]

[Patients] suffer from heat rashes and papules, sores and ulcers,
from *yong*-abscesses and *ju*-abscesses, pimples, and piles.

In severe cases, [the minor yin qi] enters the lung.
[This leads to] coughing and *bi-yuan*.[174]

If the [movement at the] celestial palace is interrupted,
[the patient] dies and is not treated.[175]

74-521-1
When the major yin takes revenge,
[catastrophic] changes to dampness set in.[176]
The body is heavy and there is central fullness.
Food and beverages are not transformed.
The yin qi rises in recession.
[Patients] do feel uncomfortable in the chest.
Beverages are effused in the center.
[Patients] cough and pant with sounds.[177]

---

172 Zhang Jiebin: "The yang brilliance [qi] dominates first and the minor yin [qi] takes revenge afterwards." Fang Yaozhong: " 'Red qi' is 'heat qi.' That is, because of a disproportionate domination of the qi of coolness, heat qi arrives to take revenge."

173 Zhang Jiebin: "不復 is 不福, 'are not allotted wellbeing.'"

174 *Su wen* 34 has an ancient commentary on the term *bi-yuan*, interpreting it as turbid snivel leaving from the nose. Whether this was the original meaning intended by this term remains unclear. Its appearance in *Su wen* 34 suggests an origin from a foreign or non-Han Chinese language context.

175 Wang Bing: " 'celestial palace' is the qi of the lung vessel."

176 Zhang Jiebin: "皋 is 發, 'to develop.'" Fang Yaozhong: "That is, a disproportionate domination by dampness qi will generate new disaster."

177 Wu Kun: "Major yin is [the qi of] dampness and soil. When soil is present in surplus, it is associated with images of consolidation and accumulation. Hence the body turns heavy and the center experience fullness. The spleen resides in the central mansion; it is clear that it cannot restrain the dampness. When the central mansion is dominated by dampness, beverages and food do not transform and extreme dampness

Massive rain prevails often and
[lets] the scaly [creatures] appear on the land.

The top of the head aches and is heavy.[178]
Swaying and spasms are particularly severe.
[Patients] vomit and seclude themselves in silence.[179]
They spit clear fluid.

In severe cases, [the major yin qi] enters the kidneys.
As a consequence [patients suffer from] outflow from the [lower] orifices
beyond measure.

If the [movement at the] great ravine is interrupted,
[the patient] dies and is not treated.[180]

74-521-5
When the minor yang takes revenge,
massive heat will arrive,
[causing] withering, dryness, and blazing.[181]
The armored creatures vanish.

[People suffer from] fright, spasms, coughing, and nosebleed;
their hearts are hot, vexed, and overexcited.
They frequently relieve themselves and they dislike wind.
Receding qi moves upward.
The face looks as if covered by dust.
The eyes have twitching and spasms.
Fire qi is effused internally and

---

collects in the center. This is called 'yin qi.' When the yin qi rises and moves contrary
to its normal course, then [patients experience] pressure and a feeling of discomfort in
their chest. The reason is that dampness is effused in the center, with the effect that the
passages of the qi are not free. Hence [patients] cough and pant with sounds."

178 Lin Yi et al.: "頂 may be an error for 項, 'nape.'"

179 Wang Bing: "They wish to live in quietude." Zhang Zhicong: "密默 is: [patients]
wish to close doors and windows and reside alone."

180 Wang Bing: " 'Great ravine' is the qi of the kidney vessel."

181 Fang Yaozhong: "In all years when cool qi dominates disproportionately, at a
certain point the qi of fire will come to take revenge. The climate changes from cool
to hot."

causes oral putrescence[182] because of vomiting and [qi] moving contrary [to its regular course].
[Patients suffer from] blood overflow and blood outflow.

When [the fire qi] is effused it causes malaria.
[Patients have] an aversion to cold. [Their teeth] chatter and [the body] shivers.
When the cold has reached its peak, heat returns.
The network [vessels] of the throat burn and dry out.
[Patients are] thirsty; they drink water and [other] beverages [in large quantities].
The color changes to yellow and red.
They are short of qi and the vessels decay.[183]
[The heat] may transform into a water [disease];
transmission may generate *fu*-swelling.[184]

In severe cases, [the minor yang qi] enters the lung,
[leading to] coughing and blood outflow.[185]

If the [movement at the] foot marsh is interrupted,
[the patient] dies and is not treated.[186]

74-521-10
When the yang brilliance takes revenge,
cool qi comes up massively.[187]

---

182 We follow Wang Bing and have translated *kou mi* (Wang Bing: *kou she mi lan* 口舌糜爛) as "oral putrescence" here. See also *Suwen* 74 521-7 for a very similar term: 口麋.

183 Fang Yaozhong: "少氣 is qi depletion; 脈萎 is blood depletion."

184 Wang Bing: "胕 is to say: the skin is swollen. If pressed, a dent forms like in clay and [the skin] does not rise again." Fang Yaozhong: "That is, heat can harm the qi and it can diminish the blood. In a situation where both the qi and the blood are depleted, liquid retention may appear which generates swelling. That is the explanation of the earlier statement 'heat domination causes swelling.'"

185 Wang Bing: "All these conditions are generated by the qi of fire."

186 Wang Bing: " 'Foot marsh' is the qi of the lung vessel."

187 Fang Yaozhong: "In all years associated with a disproportionate domination of wind qi and warm qi, at a certain point the qi of dryness and cool qi arrive to take revenge."

The forest trees age and dry out.[188]
The hairy creatures are decimated.[189]

Illnesses emerge in the upper and lower flanks.
The qi turns to the left.[190]
[Patients] tend to breathe deeply.

In severe cases, they [suffer from] heartache with blockage and fullness,[191]
from abdominal distension and outflow.
They vomit bitter [flavor] and they cough and suffer from hiccup. They [experience] a vexed heart.
The disease is located in the diaphragm and in the center. [Patients suffer from] head ache.

In severe cases, [the yang brilliance qi] enters the liver.
[Patients experience] shock; their sinews have a cramp.[192]
If the [movement in the] great thoroughfare [vessel] is interrupted,
[the patient] dies and is not treated.[193]

74-522-3
When the major yang takes revenge,
receding qi moves upward.[194]

---

188 Wang Bing: "Killing qi surges massively and the trees cannot stand up to it. Hence green and fresh leaves do not [develop to a point where they turn] yellow, but dry out.

189 Fang Yaozhong: " 'Hairy creatures' are animals preferring warmth."

190 Zhang Zhicong: "The qi turns to the left because metal encroaches upon the wood." Fang Yaozhong: " 'Left' refers to the liver here. The meaning is, in case of revenge taken by the yang brilliance [qi, i.e., metal], because a dominating metal will encroach upon the wood, the human body may easily develop liver diseases."

191 2753/61: "否 is 痞, 'blockage.'"

192 Fang Yaozhong: "Shock and sinew cramp are clinical manifestations of liver disease."

193 Wang Bing: " 'Great thoroughfare' is the qi of the liver vessel."

194 Fang Yaozhong: "In all years associated with a disproportionate domination of heat qi and fire qi, at a certain point cold qi appears to take revenge. The climate changes from heat to cold."

The water freezes; rain [turns into] ice.[195]
The feathered creatures die.[196]

Heart and stomach generate cold.
Chest and diaphragm are not freely passable.
[Patients suffer from] heartache[197] with blockage and fullness.
They have headache and they tend to be sad.
[They suffer from] frequent dizziness and they fall to the ground.
They eat less.
The lower back and the buttocks, contrary [to normal], ache.
Bending and stretching is not comfortable.

The earth cracks, the ice is firm.
The yang light does not govern.[198]

There is [pain in] the lower abdomen drawing the testicles in and
pulling on the lower back and on the spine.
Above [the cold qi] rushes upward to the heart.[199]
[Patients] spit clear water and
they hiccup and belch.

In severe cases, [the major yang qi] enters the heart.
[Patients] are forgetful and they tend to be sad.

If the [movement at the] spirit gate is interrupted,
[the patient] dies and is not treated."[200]

74-522-8
[Huang] Di:
"Good!
How to treat these [conditions nevertheless]?"

Qi Bo:
"When the ceasing yin takes revenge,

195 Wang Bing: "雨冰 is to say: hail." Fang Yaozhong: "It snows."

196 Fang Yaozhong: "Feathered creatures prefer heat."

197 Fang Yaozhong: "This refers to pain in the chest and in the abdomen."

198 Fang Yaozhong: "That is, the climate is cold."

199 For an identical phrase 少腹..衝心, see *Su wen* 74-510-5.

200 Wang Bing: " 'Spirit gate' is the qi of the true heart vessel."

this is treated with sour [flavor] and cold.[201]
To assist use sweet [flavor] and acrid [flavor].
Use sour [flavor] to discharge it;
use sweet [flavor] to relax it.

When the minor yin takes revenge,
this is treated with salty [flavor] and cold.
To assist use bitter [flavor] and acrid [flavor].
Use sweet [flavor] to discharge it;
use sour [flavor] to contract it.[202]
Use acrid [flavor] and bitter [flavor] to effuse it.[203]
Use salty [flavor] to soften it.[204]

74-522-11
When the major yin takes revenge,
this is treated with bitter [flavor] and heat.
To assist use sour [flavor] and acrid [flavor].[205]
Use bitter [flavor] to discharge it,
to dry it, and
to drain it.

---

201 Lin Yi et al.: "Other editions have 'treated with acrid [flavor] and cold' in instead of 'treat with sour [flavor] and cold.'"

202 Gao Shishi: "Salty [flavor] is the flavor of water; cold is the qi of water. By treating with salty [flavor] and cold, the qi of fire is diminished. If the qi of fire is depleted excessively, [the treatment] is assisted with bitter [flavor]. Bitter [flavor] is the flavor of fire and it [can be] employed to help the fire. In case the qi of fire is excessively abundant, [the treatment] is assisted with acrid [flavor]. Acrid [flavor] is the flavor of metal; it [can be] employed to generate water. Another possibility is to drain it with sweet [flavor] and thereby to balance the water, or to contract it with sour [flavor] and thereby to generate fire."

203 Zhang Jiebin: "That is, to disperse the oppressed fire." Wu Kun and Zhang Jiebin have 以苦發之.

204 Zhang Jiebin: "That is, to dissolve accumulations of heat."

205 Wu Kun: "Major yin conducts its policy with dampness; this is treated with bitter [flavor] and heat to dry the dampness. Sour [flavor] is a transformation [product] of wood; it is able to balance the sweetness of dampness and soil. Acrid [flavor] is a transformation [product] of metal; it is able to disperse stagnating dampness and soil." Gao Shishi: "Bitter [flavor] is the flavor of fire; heat is the qi of fire. A treatment with bitter [flavor] and heat supports the qi of soil. In case the qi of fire is unsufficient, [the treatment is] assisted with sour [flavor], because wood generates fire. In case the qi of fire is greatly excessive, [the treatment is] assisted with acrid [flavor], because metal generates water."

When the minor yang takes revenge,
this is treated with salty [flavor] and cold.
To assist use bitter [flavor] and acrid [flavor].[206]
Use salty [flavor] to soften it;
use sour [flavor] to contract it.
Use acrid [flavor] and bitter [flavor] to effuse it.

When effusing it there is no need to stay away from the heat.[207]
Warmth and coolness must not be offended.[208]
The same law applies to the minor yin.

74-523-2
When the yang brilliance takes revenge,
this is treated with acrid [flavor] and warmth.
To assist use bitter [flavor] and sweet [flavor].[209]
Use bitter [flavor] to drain it;
use bitter [flavor] to purge it;
use sour [flavor] to supplement it.[210]

When the major yang takes revenge,
this is treated with salty [flavor] and heat.

---

206 Gao Shishi: "The treatment employs salty [flavor] and cold to diminish the qi of fire. When the qi of fire is overly depleted, [the treatment is] assisted with bitter [flavor]. When the qi of fire abounds excessively, [the treatment is] assisted with acrid [flavor]."

207 Fang Yaozhong: "Generally speaking, at a time of a disproportionate abundance of fire qi it is not advisable to add [to the fire by] employing warm or hot drugs. However, in case of an external affection by cold evil, when the cold ties together the external regions and produces signs of a disproportionate domination of fire qi, in that case it is quite appropriate to employ acrid, i.e., dispersing drugs for treatment."

208 Fang Yaozhong: "The meaning is: when the minor yang has arrived to take revenge, generally speaking, warm or hot drugs must not be used. On the other hand, the degree of cold or coolness [of the drugs employed] must be taken into consideration. That is, if salty and cold drugs are to be used at a time when minor yang takes revenge, the drugs employed should be very cold or cool. It would be inappropriate to use drugs of ordinary cold or coolness."

209 Zhang Jiebin: "A revenge by yang brilliance [qi, i.e.,] dampness and metal, is treated with acrid [flavor] and warmth. The proper flavor of metal is drained with acrid [flavor]. The coolness and dryness of metal is overcome by warmth. [The treatment is] assisted with bitter [flavor] and sweet [flavor]. Bitter [flavor] is a transformation [product] of fire; [hence] bitter [flavor] checks metal. Wood is harmed by metal; [hence] sweet [flavor] is employed to relax what is tense."

210 Gao Shishi has "sweet [flavor] is employed to supplement it."

To assist use sweet [flavor] and acrid [flavor].[211]
Use bitter [flavor] to harden it.

The treatment of all [conditions of] domination or revenge is [as follows]:
what is cold, heat it;
what is hot, make it cold;
what is warm, cool it;
what is cool, warm it;
what is dispersed, contract it;
what is pressed down, disperse it;
what is dry, moisten it;
what is tense, relax it;
what is firm, delete it;
what is crisp, make it firm;
what is weak, supplement it;
what is strong, discharge it.

Always pacify the respective qi.
It must be cleared and it must be calmed.
As a result, the disease qi will weaken and leave and
return to its origin.[212]
This is the entire complex of therapy."

74-523-9
[Huang] Di:
"Good!

The being 'above' and 'below' of the qi, what does that mean?"[213]

Qi Bo:
"The upper half of the body,
its qi are three;

---

211 Wu Kun: "Major yang is cold and water. To treat it with salty [flavor] is a treatment conforming with [the dominating qi]. To treat it with heat is a proper treatment. To assist [the treatment] with sweet [flavor] and acrid [flavor] is to make use of their dispersing capabilities."

212 Wang Bing: "宗 is 屬, 'to belong to.' If the regulation is reasonable then the surplus qi will by itself return to where it belongs and the diminished qi will by itself keep its residence in peace."

213 Zhang Jiebin: "The 'qi above and below' [refers to the qi] controlling heaven and at the fountain. [The qi of] the human body corresponds to this."

this is the section of heaven.
The qi of heaven rules it.

The lower half of the body,
its qi are three;
this is the section of the earth.
The qi of the earth rules it.[214]

Use the terms to name the qi;
use the qi to name their locations.
Then [it is possible] to speak of their illnesses.[215]

74-524-2
{'Half' refers to the celestial axis.}[216]

Hence
when the above dominates and the below is all ill,
use [the qi of] the earth to name it.[217]

---

214 Fang Yaozhong: "Beginning with Wang Bing, all commentators have interpreted 身半 as 'midline of the human body' and 天樞 as the 'heavenly pivot' points on both sides of the navel. We do not agree with this interpretation because 身 does not refer to the human body only; it also refers to the major part of things. Furthermore, the text discusses the relationships between [the qi] controlling heaven and at the fountain in terms of domination and revenge. Neither the preceding nor the following text talk about the human body. Hence it is impossible that the present paragraphs discuss any issues concerning the upper and the lower halves of the human body."

215 Wang Bing: "Names are used to talk about the qi; the qi are used to talk about the locations, and the locations of the qi, as well as cold and heat, are used to talk about the physical manifestations and the pathoconditions of the diseases." Zhang Jiebin: "以名命氣 is to say: define the terms and each qi has its association. For example, the three yin and the three yang, these are the terms. Once the terms are set, then each of the six qi has what it rules. 以氣命處 is to say: each of the qi of the six conduits has its location. An examination whether the qi is in the center or in the exterior, in the front or behind, above or below, on the left or on the right, lets one know the location of the disease."

216 Wang Bing: "The midline of the body is in the navel. It is also possible to take the lower back as the midline of the body. The meaning is that [both the navel and the lower back] are located in the middle [of the body]. .. The 'Celestial Pivot (天樞)' [refers to two points] in a distance of two individually standardized body inches on both sides of the navel." Wang Shaozeng & Xu Yongnian/101: "半 is 身半, 'midline of the body.'"

217 Wang Bing: "When the above (i.e., the qi controlling heaven in the first half of a year) dominates, then the below (i.e., the qi at the fountain in the second half of the

When the below dominates and the above is all ill,
use [the qi of] heaven to name it.²¹⁸

[As for] the so-called 'dominating [qi] arrives,' that is [to say:]
the retributing qi yields and hides and is not effused yet.

When revenge [qi] arrives, then [the resulting situation] should not be given
different names on the basis of [which qi controls] heaven and [which is at the
fountain on the] earth.
Always take [the arrival of] the revenge qi as pattern [of their designation]."²¹⁹

---

year) suffers from oppressed earth qi. Hence the naming of the diseases of the earth
(i.e., the diseases in the second half of the year) is based on the [fact that] the earth
[qi] (i.e., the qi at the fountain) is oppressed. When the below (i.e., the qi at the fountain) dominates, then the above (i.e., the qi controlling heaven) suffers from blocked
heavenly qi. Hence the naming of the diseases of heaven (i.e., of the qi controlling
heaven in the first half of a year) is based on the blocked [qi of] heaven." Zhang Zhicong: "For example, when the wood or the fire qi dominate in the upper half of the
body and when the three qi of soil, metal, and water in the lower half of the body all
have a disease, then this is named as earth [disease], that is to say: the disease is on the
earth." Fang Yaozhong: "下俱病者 is to say: the qi controlling heaven exerts a direct
influence on the second half of a given year. 'Earth' refers to the 'qi at the fountain.'
以地命之 has the meaning: the qi controlling heaven of a given year turns out to be
the qi at the fountain in that same year, too. For example, when the yang brilliance
[qi, i.e.,] dryness and metal, controls heaven, the climate in the upper/first half of
that year is disproportionately cool. When the yang brilliance [qi] controls heaven,
then the minor yin [qi] is at the fountain and the climate in the second half of that
year should be disproportionately hot. However, the real conditions of that year are
different: the second half is disproportionately cool, too. Hence one cannot say that
the climate of the second half is disproportionately hot because the minor yin [qi] is
at the fountain; on the contrary, the situation generated is 上勝而下俱病, 'the above
(i.e., the qi controlling heaven in the first half of a year,) dominates and the below (i.e.,
the qi at the fountain in the second half of that year,) is affected by disease.' [That is,]
the qi at the fountain is affected by the qi controlling heaven, which is the yang brilliance [qi, i.e.,] dryness and metal; hence the climate [in the second half of the year]
is disproportionately cool."

218 Fang Yaozhong: "上俱病者 is to say: the qi at the fountain exerts a direct influence on the first half of that year. 'Heaven' refers to the 'qi controlling heaven.' 以天
命之 has the meaning: the qi at the fountain of a given year turns out to be the qi
controlling heaven in that same year, too."

219 Wang Bing: "When a dominating [qi] has arrived and the revenge [qi] has not
[arrived] yet, the resulting illnesses are given differential names on the basis of whether it is the [qi of] heaven or earth [which dominates]. This is the pattern. However, as
soon as the revenge qi is effused, the [illnesses] generated are all named in regard of
the revenge qi as responsible for illnesses of cold or heat, regardless of whether the [qi

[Huang] Di:
"The movement of the dominating [qi] and of [the qi of] revenge,
do the times [when they occur] have any regularity?
Is the [arrival of these] qi a must?"

Qi Bo:
"The times [of their movement] occupy regular positions,
but the qi do not necessarily [move]."²²⁰

74-525-2
[Huang] Di:
"I should like to hear the Way of this."

Qi Bo:
"[From] the first qi and ending with the third qi,
that is the [term] ruled by the qi of heaven.
This is the regular [time of the] dominating [qi].

[From] the fourth qi and ending with the final qi,
that is the [term] ruled by the qi of the earth.
This is the regular [time of the] revenge [qi].²²¹

---

controlling heaven] above (i.e., in the first half of the year) or the [qi at the fountain]
below (i.e., in the second half of the year) had dominated [and therefore provoked a
revenge]."

220 Wang Bing: "Even though the positions [allotted to the movements of the qi of
domination and revenge] follow a regular sequence, it cannot be predicted for sure
whether a movement sets in or not." Gao Shishi: "One year has six seasons; the first
is [governed by] ceasing yin [qi], the last by major yang [qi]. [In the course of a year]
these seasons have their regular positions. In contrast, domination and revenge of the
qi are such that revenge follows domination. But this cannot be predicted for sure."

221 Zhang Jiebin: "The first half of a year is ruled by the qi of heaven; the second
half of a year is ruled by the qi of the earth. Domination comes first, revenge follows.
Hence from the initial qi through the third qi, that is the time ruled by the qi controlling heaven. In case of excess it will dominate that by which it cannot be dominated
itself. In case of inadequacy that by which it can be dominated arrives to dominate.
That is the regularity of domination. From the fourth qi through the final qi, that is
the time ruled by the qi at the fountain. In case of excess it will restrain that which
receives its orders. In case of inadequacy the son will take revenge for [what happened
to] his mother. That is the regularity of revenge. Hence [the text] states 'the times have
regular positions.'"

Where there is domination, there will be revenge;
where there is no domination, there will be no [revenge]."

74-525-5
[Huang] Di:
"Good!
When a revenge is completed and [another] domination [occurs], how is that?"

Qi Bo:
"When a dominating [qi] has arrived, then a revenge [qi will follow].
There is no regular number as to how frequently [this repeats itself].
Only when [the dominating qi and the qi taking revenge have] weakened, the
[cycle of domination and revenge] will come to an end.²²²

When after the revenge is completed, there is domination [again]
which is not followed by revenge, this will cause harm."
{This harms life.}²²³

74-525-7
[Huang] Di:
"If there is revenge and if contrary [to the rule], a disease [emerges neverthe-
less], how is that?"

Qi Bo:
"It occupies a position which is not its own.
[The qi and the position it occupies] do not agree with each other.²²⁴

---

222 Wang Bing: "When the domination is weak then the revenge will be weak, too.
Hence when the revenge is completed another domination occurs. When the domination is severe, then the revenge is severe, too. Hence when the revenge is completed
then it is very rare that another domination occurs. Now, even though the Way of
domination and revenge does not follow any regular number of occurrences, when
[the qi] has reached a state of weakness, [the sequence of] domination and revenge
will end by itself."

223 Wang Bing: "When a domination is not followed by revenge, this is because the
revenge qi has weakened. When it has weakened, it cannot take revenge. That is, the
true qi of heaven has received severe harm and life comes to an end."

224 Zhang Zhicong: "For instance, when fire qi takes revenge and occupies the position of metal; when metal qi takes revenge and occupies the position of fire. All these
are [examples of the revenge qi] occupying a position other than its own. [Qi and
position] do not match."

If massive revenge is taken against a domination, then the host [qi] will domi-
nate the [qi taking revenge].
Hence, contrary [to the rule], a disease [emerges]."[225]
{This applies to fire, dryness, and heat.}[226]

74-525-9
[Huang] Di:
"How to treat such [conditions]?"

Qi Bo:
"Now, when a qi dominates,
if [this domination] is slight, go along with it;
if it is severe, restrain it.[227]

When a qi takes revenge,
if [this revenge] is harmonious, balance it;
if it is violent, remove it.[228]

---

225 Wu Kun: "In case of massive revenge taken against a domination, the [qi taking
revenge] will be depleted itself. Once it is depleted, it will be encroached upon by the
host qi. Hence, contrary [to normal], there is disease."

226 Wang Bing: "Minor yang [qi] is fire. Yang brilliance [qi] is dryness. Minor yin
[qi] is heat. When minor yin or minor yang [qi] are at the fountain, this is fire residing
at the location of water. When yang brilliance [qi] controls heaven, this is metal residing at the location of fire. When metal has taken revenge against what it itself dominates, then fire, as host, will dominate it (i.e., the fire). When fire has taken revenge
against what it itself dominates, then water, as host, will dominate it (i.e., the fire).
As for domination and revenge by the remaining qi, there is no disease qi originating
from the existence of a host who dominates them. Hence [the text] states: 'this applies
to fire, dryness, and heat.'"

227 Zhang Jiebin: "微者隨之 is: go along with that qi to keep it in peace. 甚者制之
is: restrain it by employing that which it fears." Fang Yaozhong: "In case of weak domination, there is no need to intervene; just let it follow its natural course. According to
the laws of domination and revenge, a weak domination is followed by a weak revenge.
The influence of the qi taking revenge on the human body is not strong. Hence there
is no need to intervene. When the dominating qi is strong, the subsequent revenge
will be strong, too, and the influence on the human body will also be strong. Hence it
is necessary to counteract."

228 Wang Bing: "平 is to say: 平調, 'to adjust.' 奪 is to say: remove the qi that
abounds." Fang Yaozhong: "In case the qi taking revenge is not strong, some adjusting
harmonization suffices for the time being; no intervention is necessary."

Always follow the [strength or weakness of the] dominating qi.
Pacify what has yielded and gone into hiding.
Do not care about the number [of treatments];
[continue the treatment] until a balance is reached.²²⁹
This is the Way of this [treatment]."

74-526-1
[Huang] Di:
"Good!
What about domination and revenge [in the relationship] between visitor [qi]
and host [qi]?"

Qi Bo:
"The visitor qi and the host qi,
they dominate [when it is their time], but [such domination] is not [followed
by] revenge."²³⁰

74-526-2
[Huang] Di:
"What about their opposition and compliance?"

Qi Bo:
"When the host dominates, this is opposition.
When the visitor dominates, this is compliance.
That is the Way of heaven."²³¹

---

229 Zhang Zhicong: "Do not ask how many circles of domination and revenge have
passed; when the qi is balanced, this should be the end of it." Fang Yaozhong: "數
refers to the light or strong, slow or urgent nature of an intervention. That is, when
intervening against a dominating qi, there is no fixed rule as to whether [the interven-
tion] should be light or strong, slow or urgent. The goal to be reached is a normaliza-
tion of a person's physiological processes."

230 Zhang Jiebin: "The visitor qi moves and undergoes changes; the host qi is quiet
and regular. When a qi is strong, then it dominates; when a season has passed, [the respective qi] vanishes, too. Hence it is only because of changing abundance and weakness that one rules over the other; there is no revenge." Gao Shishi: "The six qi pass
through domination and revenge. However, visitor qi and host qi appear at the same
time at the same location. The [appearance of the] host qi is fixed; the [appearance of
the] visitor qi is irregular. Hence [in the relationship between visitor qi and host qi]
there is only domination, but no revenge."

231 Wang Bing: "The visitor receives the heavenly mandate to rule different cardinal
points. The host is situated below of it. Hence it should receive the heavenly mandate
with awe. If it does not go along with it and achieves domination, then the heavenly

[Huang] Di:
"How does this [influence the] generation of disease?"

Qi Bo:
"When the ceasing yin [qi] controls heaven,
in case the visitor [qi] dominates,
then [people suffer from] ringing [sounds] in the ears and from swaying and
dizziness.
When [the domination is] severe, then [the patients] cough.[232]

In case the host [qi] dominates,
then there is pain in the chest and in the flanks and
the tongue has difficulties in speaking.[233]

74-526-5
When the minor yin [qi] controls heaven,
in case the visitor [qi] dominates,
then [people suffer from] stuffy nose and sneezing. Their neck is stiff;
shoulders and back feel pressure with heat.
[People suffer from] headache, being short of qi, fever, deafness, and blurred
vision.

In severe cases, there is *fu*-swelling, blood overflow,
sores, ulcers, coughing, and panting.[234]

---

mandate is not carried out. Hence this is [called] 'counteraction.' When the visitor
dominates the host it has received [a mandate by] heaven and carries out the Way
along the principles. Hence this is [called] 'conformance.'"

232 Zhang Jiebin: "The initial qi through the third qi are ruled by the qi of heaven.
In *si* and *hai* years ceasing yin [qi] controls heaven. The visitor [qi of] wind and wood
are added to the host [qi] of ceasing yin, minor yin, and minor yang. When the visitor
[qi] dominates, then the qi of wood moves above and wind evil dominates. Hence
[people suffer from] ringing in the ears, swaying and dizziness, and in severe cases
from coughing.

233 Wang Bing: "These are the five *si* and five *hai* years." Zhang Zhicong: "The host
qi of a year include the three [qi of] ceasing yin [qi, i.e.,] wind and wood (as the initial
qi) and the ruler as well as the minister fire (as the second and third qi). Pain in the
chest and in the flanks results from excessive initial qi; difficulties [in moving] the
tongue for speaking result from a domination of the two fire qi."

234 Zhang Zhicong: "In a year when the minor yin [qi] controls heaven, the initial
qi is the major yang [qi, i.e.,] cold and water. The second qi is the ceasing yin [qi, i.e.,]
wind and wood. The third qi is the minor yin [qi, i.e.,] ruler fire. Stuffy nose, ringing
in the ears, and impaired vision result from a domination of ceasing yin [qi]. Pain in

In case the host [qi] dominates,
then the heart is hot, vexed, and overexcited.
In severe cases, [people suffer from] pain in the flanks and from propping fullness.[235]

When the major yin [qi] controls heaven,
in case the visitor [qi] dominates,
then [people suffer from] *fu*-swellings on the head and in the face.
They pant while exhaling and inhaling qi.[236]

In case the host [qi] dominates,
then chest and abdomen experience fullness.
After meals there is a feeling of pressure.[237]

74-526-9
When the minor yang [qi] controls heaven,
in case the visitor [qi] dominates,
then vermilion papules are effused externally.
<It also causes vermilion gangrene, sores and ulcers.>
[Patients] vomit because of a movement [of qi] contrary [to its regular course]
and [they suffer from] throat block,
headache and swollen throat region,
deafness and blood overflow.
Internally [the visitor qi] causes [changes between] spasms and slackening.

In case the host [qi] dominates,
then [people experience a feeling of] fullness in the chest. They cough and they
breathe adopting an upright position.
In severe cases, blood appears.
The hands are hot.[238]

---

head and nape, pressure and heat in the shoulders and in the back, and in severe cases
swelling, result from a domination of major yang [qi, i.e.,] cold and water. Diminished
qi, fever, blood overflow, abscesses, ulcers, cough, and panting, result from a domination of the ruler fire."

235 Wang Bing: "These are the five *zi* and five *wu* years."

236 Zhang Jiebin: "When in *chou* and *wei* years major yin [qi] controls heaven, the
visitor [qi] of dampness and soil is added to the host [qi] of wood and fire. When the
visitor [qi] dominates, then dampness and heat rise. Hence the head and the face are
swollen and [people] cough."

237 Wang Bing: "These are the five *chou* and five *wei* years."

238 Wang Bing: "These are the five *yin* and five *shen* years."

When the yang brilliance [qi] controls heaven,
coolness [qi] repeatedly has surplus internally.
As a result, [people suffer from] coughing, nosebleed, and obstructed throat, as
well as
heat in the heart and diaphragm [region].
If the cough does not end and if white blood comes out, [the patient] will die.[239]

When the major yang [qi] controls heaven,
in case the visitor [qi] dominates,
then [passage ways] inside the chest are not freely passable.
Clear snivel comes out.
[Once people are] affected by cold, then they cough.

In case the host [qi] dominates,
then there are sounds in the throat and in the throat region.[240]

74-526-14
When the ceasing yin [qi] is at the fountain,
in case the visitor [qi] dominates,
then the large joints do not move freely;[241]
internally this causes tetany and stiffness, cramp and spasms.
Externally [the sinews] do not move comfortably.[242]

In case the host [qi] dominates,
then the sinews and bones shake or have a cramp.
Lower back and abdomen have frequent pain.[243]

---

239 Wang Bing: " 'White blood' is to say: blood of a light red color is coughed up,
resembling [the color of] flesh, or that of the lung. These are the five *mao* and five *you*
years." Lin Yi et al.: "This paragraph does not mention a visitor [qi] domination and
also no host [qi] domination. Metal occupies the position of fire and a domination by
the visitor [qi] would be unreasonable. Hence [the text] does not refer to it."

240 Wang Bing: "These are the five *chen* and five *xu* years."

241 Wang Bing: "The large joints are the lower back and the knees."

242 Zhang Zhicong: "不便 is: the sinews do not move freely."

243 Wang Bing: "These are the five *yin* and five *shen* years." Fang Yaozhong: "Each
year the fourth host qi is the major yin [qi, i.e.,] dampness and soil, the fifth [host] qi
is the yang brilliance [qi, i.e.,] dryness and metal, and the final [host] qi is the major
yang [qi, i.e.,] cold and water. The meaning of the entire sentence is: in years when the
ceasing yin [qi] is at the fountain, in the second half of that year, at the time of a disproportionate domination of the fourth and the final of the host qi, pathoconditions
of diseases affecting the spleen or the kidneys, such as pain in the lower back, pain in

When the minor yin [qi] is at the fountain,
in case the visitor [qi] dominates,
then the lower back has pain.
The sacrum, the thighs, the knees, the thigh bones, the calves, the shins, and the
feet are ill.
They experience pressure with heat and soreness.
[People suffer from] *fu*-swelling and cannot stand for long.
Urine and stools change [color].

In case the host [qi] dominates,
then recession qi moves upward.
The heart aches and fever develops.
{[This is] *ge-zhong*.}²⁴⁴
All types of blocks emerge;
[the qi] is effused in the upper and lower flanks.
Po-sweat does not [remain] stored.
A fourfold countermovement emerges [in the limbs].²⁴⁵

74-527-4
When the major yin [qi] is at the fountain,
in case the visitor [qi] dominates,
then the feet are limp and the lower [part of the body feels] heavy.
Stools and urine do not pass on time.
Dampness has settled in the lower burner.
It is effused as soggy outflow,
and it causes the disease of swollen hidden bend.²⁴⁶

In case the host [qi] dominates,
then the cold qi moves moves in full advance against [it] and causes fullness.

---

the abdomen, etc., may appear. At a time when the fifth host qi dominates disproportionately, pathoconditions of a liver disease, such as 'sinews and bones shake and have
a cramp' may appear because the dominating metal has encroached upon the wood."

244 We consider *ge-zhong* 鬲中 as a transliteration of a foreign term. A literal translation is "barred center". See *Su wen* 37 for an appearance of the variant form 隔中 in
a context with further examples of terms of possibly foreign origin.

245 Wang Bing: "These are the five *mao* and five *you* years."

246 Wang Bing: " 'Illnesses of the hidden bend' is to say: illnesses at locations that
are hidden and bent." Fang Yaozhong: "This refers to irregular menstruation and stan-
gury." Zhang Zhicong: "隱曲 refers to the frontal private parts of men and women."
For a detailed discussion, see also Gao Jiwu/250, 601/45, 852/14, and 1508/11.

Food and beverages do not move down.
In severe cases, this leads to elevation illness.[247]

74-527-7
When the minor yang [qi] is at the fountain,
in case the visitor [qi] dominates,
then lower back and abdomen have pain and, contrary [to normal, people have]
an aversion to cold.
In severe cases, they pass down white [stools] and they urinate white [liquid].[248]

In case the host [qi] dominates,
then heat rises contrary [to its normal course] and settles in the heart.
The heart aches and fever develops.
A barrier in the center causes vomiting.

{The same manifestations appear as in case of the minor yin [qi at the foun-
tain].}[249]

74-527-9
When the yang brilliance [qi] is at the fountain,

in case the visitor [qi] dominates, then cool qi moves down.
The lower abdomen is firm and full and [patients suffer from] frequent passages of urine and stools.

In case the host [qi] dominates,
then the lower back is heavy and the abdomen has pain.
The lower abdomen develops cold.
Below this causes duck-like semiliquid stools.
As a result, there is cold recession in the intestines.
It rushes upward into the chest.
In severe cases, [people] pant and cannot stand for long.[250]

---

247 Wang Bing: "These are the five *chen* and five *xu* years." Fang Yaozhong: " 'Elevation illness' refers to pain in the lower abdomen and in the scrotum."

248 Zhang Zhicong: " 'To urinate white [liquid]' is to say: the qi does not transform
and the urine is not clear. 'To pass white [stool] ' is to say: The qi of soil has been
harmed and the stool turns white."

249 Wang Bing: "These are the five *si* and the five *hai* years."

250 Wang Bing: "These are the five *zi* and the five *wu* years."

74-527-11
When the major yang [qi] is at the fountain,
cold is repeatedly present in surplus internally.
As a result, the lower back and the sacrum have pain.
Bending and stretching are not free.
[People have] pain in the thighs, the shins, the feet, and the knees."²⁵¹

74-527-13
[Huang] Di:
"Good!
How to treat these [conditions]?"

Qi Bo:
"What is up on high, press it down;²⁵²
what is below, raise it;²⁵³
what is in surplus, break it;²⁵⁴
what is insufficient, supplement it.²⁵⁵
Assist with what is beneficial;
harmonize with what is suitable.
It is necessary to pacify the respective host [qi] and visitor [qi].
Act in accordance with their cold or warmth.²⁵⁶

---

251 Wang Bing: "These are the five *chou* and five *wei* years." Lin Yi et al.: "This paragraph does not refer to dominations of visitor and host [qi]. The reason is, with the [presence of the] major yang, water resides at the position of water. Hence [the text] does not speak [of a domination of visitor and host qi]."

252 Wang Bing: "Curb its domination." Zhang Zhicong: "That is to say: the host qi moves contrary [to its normal course] and rises."

253 Wang Bing: "Supplement its weakness."

254 Wang Bing: "Curb its ardor."

255 Wang Bing: "Complete its qi." This appears to be a quote from *Lao zi Dao de jing* 77: "高者抑之, 下者舉之, 有餘者損之, 不足者補之, '(The Way of Heaven) pulls down what is high, it lifts what is low, it diminishes what has a surplus, it supplements what is insufficient.'"

256 Zhang Zhicong: " 'Harmonize with what is beneficial' is: [harmonize with what] benefit [the depots] wish. For example, [*Su wen* 22 states]: 'The liver [qi] wishes to disperse; [in case of a disease in the liver] one should quickly consume acrid [flavor] to disperse its [qi].' Hence in a situation when the ceasing yin [qi] dominates, [a treatment] is assisted with [food/drugs of] bitter and acrid [flavor]. ... 'Keep the host [qi] and the visitor [qi] in peace' is: see to it that each of them keeps its original position. ... 'Act in accordance with cold and warmth' is: treat cold with heat and treat heat with cold.

What is in agreement, oppose it;
what is different, follow it."²⁵⁷

74-527-15
[Huang] Di:
"Treat cold with heat;
treat heat with cold.
Where the [host qi and the visitor] qi agree, oppose them.
If they do not agree, follow [each of] them.
This I have come to know by now.
How does this relate to the proper flavors [to be applied here]?"

Qi Bo:
"When the host [qi] occupies the position of wood,
for its discharge use sour [flavor],
for its supplementation use acrid [flavor].²⁵⁸

When the host [qi] occupies the position of fire,
for its discharge use sweet [flavor],
for its supplementation use salty [flavor].²⁵⁹

---

257 Zhang Zhicong: " 'What is in agreement oppose it' is: when the [host qi and
the visitor] qi agree, a treatment is suitable that opposes them. For example, if both
the host [qi] and the visitor [qi] control fire and heat, a treatment must employ salty
[flavor] and cold. If both of them control cold and water, then a treatment must employ acrid [flavor] and heat. 'What is different, conform to it' is: if [the host qi and the
visitor qi] do not agree, a treatment is suitable that conforms to [the status of both
of] them. For example, when [a visitor qi of] cold and water controls heaven on top
of a host qi of any of the two fires (i.e., ruler fire and minister fire), then in view of the
domination of the visitor [qi] it is essential to conform to the heat of the two fires to
treat the cold and in view of the domination of the host [qi] it is essential to conform
to the cold of the [qi] controlling heaven to treat the heat."

258 Wang Bing: "The position of wood is [occupied by] the initial qi of the first 61
days of spring." Cheng Shide et al.: "This is the position of the initial qi [i.e.,] ceasing
yin [qi, i.e.,] wind and wood."

259 Wang Bing: The position of the ruler fire is [occupied by] the second qi of the
final 61 days of spring. The position of the minister fire is [occupied by] the third qi of
the thirty days each preceding and following summer solstice. The qi of the two fires
are different, but their functions are identical."

When the host [qi] occupies the position of soil,
for its discharge use bitter [flavor],
for its supplementation use sweet [flavor].[260]

When the host [qi] occupies the position of metal,
for its discharge use acrid [flavor],
for its supplementation use sour [flavor].[261]

When the host [qi] occupies the position of water,
for its discharge use salty [flavor],
for its supplementation use bitter [flavor].[262]

When the visitor [qi] is ceasing yin,
use acrid [flavor] to supplement it;
use sour [flavor] to discharge it;
use sweet [flavor] to relax it.

When the visitor [qi] is minor yin,
use salty [flavor] to supplement it;
use sweet [flavor] to discharge it;
use salty [flavor] to contract it.[263]

When the visitor [qi] is major yin,
use sweet [flavor] to supplement it;
use bitter [flavor] to discharge it;
use sweet [flavor] to relax it.

74-528-8
When the visitor [qi] is minor yang,
use salty [flavor] to supplement it;

---

260 Wang Bing: "The position of soil is [occupied by] the fourth qi of the first 61 days of autumn."

261 Wang Bing: "The position of metal is [occupied by] the fifth qi of the final 61 days of autumn."

262 Wang Bing: "The position of water is [occupied by] the final qi of the thirty days each preceding and following winter solstice."

263 Lin Yi et al.: "*Su wen* 22 states: 'When the heart suffers from lack of tension, one should quickly consume sour [flavor] to contract it again. The heart [qi] wishes to be soft. [In case of a disease in the heart, patients] should quickly consume salty [flavor] to soften its [qi].' Here [the text] states 'employ salty [flavor] to contract it.' That is a mistake."

602 Huang Di nei jing su wen

 Huang Di nei jing su wen

use sweet [flavor] to discharge it;
use salty [flavor] to soften it.

When the visitor [qi] is yang brilliance,
use sour [flavor] to supplement it;
use acrid [flavor] to discharge it;
use bitter [flavor] to drain it.

When the visitor [qi] is major yang,
use bitter [flavor] to supplement it;
use salty [flavor] to discharge it;
use bitter [flavor] to make it firm;
use acrid [flavor] to moisten it.[264]
{It opens the interstice structures,
lets the body liquids reach [their destinations] and makes the qi penetrate [the body].}"

[Huang] Di:
"Good!
I should like to hear what 'yin and yang are three' is to say."

Qi Bo:
"The operations of the [yin and yang] qi differ depending on their different quantities."[265]

74-529-1
[Huang] Di:
"What is 'yang brilliance' to say?"

---

264 Wang Bing: "The periods ruled by the visitor qi extend over 61 days each; however, [the visitor qi] do not settle at any location permanently. [Where they settle] differs from year to year. When a visitor [qi] dominates, then the visitor [qi] is to be drained and the host [qi] is to be supplemented. When a host [qi] dominates, then the host [qi] is to be drained and the visitor [qi] is to be supplemented. A treatment should also follow the need to relax or to tighten."

265 Wang Bing: "The major yin [qi] is the proper yin. The major yang is the proper yang. The next smaller is the minor yin. The next smaller is the minor yang. Again the next smaller is the yang brilliance. And again the next smaller is the ceasing yin. Ceasing yin has the meaning of 'exhausted [yin].'"

Qi Bo:
"Two yang [qi] combine [their] brilliance."²⁶⁶

[Huang] Di:
" 'Ceasing yin,' what is that?"

Qi Bo:
"Both yin [qi] are equally exhausted."²⁶⁷

74-529-3
[Huang] Di:
"The qi is present in different quantities,
the disease [qi] may abound or be weak,
the treatment may be relaxed or urgent,
the prescriptions may be large or small,
I should like to hear about the essentials of these [issues]."

Qi Bo:
"Among the qi are those high and those below.
Among the diseases are those distant and those near.
The evidence [of a disease] may be inside or outside.

---

266 Zhang Jiebin: "This is a brilliance resulting from a union of two yang [qi]. It is yang abundance." Gao Shishi: "There is the yang of minor yang and there is the yang of major yang. When these two yang [qi] join each other, this results in brilliance. Hence in the middle lies 'yang brilliance.'" Fang Yaozhong: " 'The two yang [qi]' refers to major yang and minor yang. 合 refers to the position between major yang and minor yang. That is, yang brilliance resides between major yang and minor yang. Minor yang is 'first yang,' major yang is 'third yang.' Hence yang brilliance is 'second yang.' .. The interpretation of yang brilliance as most abundant yang qi does not agree with the spirit of the *Nei jing*. In contrast, Gao Shishi's interpretation of yang brilliance as being located amidst minor yang and major yang is consistent with the spirit behind the categorization of the three yin and three yang in the *Nei jing*. Hence we follow Gao Shishi's commentary."

267 Zhang Jiebin: "厥 is 盡, 'finished.' 兩陰交盡 is 陰之極, 'the limit of yin.'" *NJCD*: "交 is 都, 'all.'"" Gao Shishi: "Moving from minor to major, yang brilliance is situated in the middle; moving from major to minor, ceasing yin comes at the end. There is the yin of major yin and there is the yin of minor yin. If both yin are equally exhausted (兩陰交盡), then there is ceasing yin." Fang Yaozhong: "交 is 交傳, 'to transmit to each other.' 盡 is 最後, 'the very last.' The meaning of 兩陰交盡 is: Ceasing yin resides behind major yin and minor yin. Major yin is 'third yin,' minor yin is 'second yin.' Ceasing yin resides behind major yin and minor yin; hence ceasing yin is 'first yin.' .. Zhang Jiebin's comment does not reflect the spirit of the *Nei jing*, hence our interpretation is based on Gao Shishi."

Treatment may be light or heavy.
Adaptation to the location [the qi of the drugs is supposed] to reach is the
starting point [of any treatment].[268]

The *Great Essential* states:
'One ruler, two ministers,
that is an uneven composition.

Two rulers, four ministers,
that is an even composition.

Two rulers, three ministers,
that is an uneven composition.

Two rulers, six ministers,
that is an even composition.'[269]

Hence when it is stated:

'Those who are near, [treat] them [with] an uneven [composition],
those who are far away, [treat] them [with] an even [composition];

---

268 Wang Bing: "The positions of the depots [in the body extend from] above to
below; the qi in the palaces is more or less remote [from the depots]; the signs of the
disease appear in the outer or inner [sections of the body]; and the drugs employed are
light or heavy. The amounts of the drugs and the speed of their effects are composed in
a way that the drugs reach the location of the disease. Excess and inadequacy are to be
avoided." 1257/12: "適其至所為故 is: 視其至所為法, that is, 'make it a rule to examine whether the strength of the drugs is able to reach the location of the disease.'"

269 Wang Bing: "奇 is the ancient term for prescriptions with an odd number [of
substances]; 偶 is the ancient term for prescriptions with an even number [of sub-
stances]. Both prescriptions with an odd number [of substances] and those with an
even number [of substances] may vary in the amount [of their ingredients]. Hence is
it said of those with an uneven number that they may consist of one ruler and two
ministers, or two rulers and three ministers, and of those with an even number [of
ingredients] that they may consist of two rulers and four ministers, or two rulers and
six ministers." Gao Shishi: "Those ingredients which are present [in a presription] in
small numbers but large portions, they are called 'rulers'; those which are present in
large numbers but in small portions, they are called 'ministers.' Diseases that are near
[their depots] are yang, and prescriptions with an uneven number [of ingredients]
are to be employed for treating them. Illnesses that are far away [from their depots]
are yin, and prescriptions with an even number [of ingredients] are to be employed
for treating them." Fang Yaozhong: " 'Near' is to say: the disease is not located in the
depth; 'far away' is to say: the disease is located in the depth."

to induce sweating, do not use an uneven [composition],
to purge, do not use an even [composition];²⁷⁰
when supplementing above, when treating above,
employ a relaxing composition;
when supplementing below, when treating below,
employ a tightening composition;
{to achieve a 'tightening' effect, the qi and the flavor [of the drugs must be] strong,
to achieve a 'relaxing' effect, the qi and the flavor [of the drugs must be] weak;}²⁷¹
[the treatment] is to be adapted to the location which [the qi of the drugs is supposed] to reach;'

then [all] this means just the same.

74-529-10
If the location of the disease is far away and qi and flavor go [only] half way,

---

270 Wang Bing: "Prescriptions with even numbers [of ingredients] are not employed as drugs to induce sweating; their qi is insufficient to achieve an effusion towards the outside. Prescriptions with an uneven number [of ingredients] are not employed as drugs to move [the stools] downward because the poison in the drugs might launch an attack and act excessively." Zhang Jiebin: "[Diseases] that are near are those which are located above [in the body] and are yang; hence [for treating them] prescriptions with an uneven number [of ingredients] are employed and [the drugs] used are light [in weight] and relaxed [in their effects]. [Diseases] that are far away are those which are located below [in the body] and are yin; hence [for treating them] prescriptions with an even number [of ingredients] are employed and [the drugs] used are heavy [in weight] and urgent [in their effects]. To induce sweating it is not suitable to employ [prescriptions with] an even number [of ingredients] because they are yin and they are active in the depth. They are unable to proceed to the exterior. For moving [stools] downward it is not suitable to employ [prescriptions with] an uneven number [of ingredients] because they are yang and they rise. They are unable to descend."

271 Wu Kun: "[Prescriptions employed] to supplement above and to treat above are made up from [drugs exerting] relaxed [effects] lest they strike downward. [Prescriptions employed] to supplement below and to treat below are made up from [drugs exerting] tightening [effects] lest they remain in the center. If tightening prescriptions were made up from [drugs with] a weak qi or flavor, their strength would be identical to relaxing [prescriptions]; and if relaxing prescriptions were made up from [drugs with] a strong qi or flavor, their strength would be identical with tightening [prescriptions]. Hence qi and flavor must be strong to achieve tightening [effects] and they must be weak to achieve relaxing [effects]."

food serves to get them across [to where they should be active].²⁷²
Do not exceed the [appropriate] quantities in the composition [of a prescription].²⁷³

Hence
the Way of balancing the qi is such that
when [the location of the disease] is near, [no matter whether] an uneven or
even composition is employed,
the dosage must be small.

When [the location of the disease] is far away, [no matter whether] an uneven
or even composition is employed,
the dosage must be large.

---

272 Fu Weikang & Wu Hongzhou/307: "When the disease is in the upper burner,
[patients] should eat first and take their medication afterwards. When the disease is in
the lower burner, [patients] should take their medication first and eat afterwards, lest
the food blocks the passage of the qi and of the flavors of the drugs thereby causing
the effects of the drugs to vanish on their way."

273 Zhang Jiebin: "That is to say: when the disease is in the depth and far away, the
drugs have to get there from the stomach. If they are applied without pattern, then
the drugs do not reach the disease and it is at half way that their qi and flavors are
received. Hence the placement of the intake of food [before or after the intake of the
drugs] serves to send [the latter] to locations far away or near. This is [meant by] 過之,
'to get them across.' If the intention is to have them move to a location far away, the
drugs are to be taken before the meals; in this case, the food pushes the drugs to reach
a distant location. If the intention is to have them move to a location nearby, the drugs
are to be taken after the meals. In this case, the food blocks the drugs and they remain
where they are. From this it may be deduced that decoctions, pastes, pills, and powders
all have their suitable application. Hence [the text] states: 'do not violate the limits of
the [prescription] compositions.'" Ma Shi: "If the disease is located far away but the
qi and the flavors of drugs and food stop half way, then they accumulate there. For
example, if a kidney drug enters the heart, then the heart, contrary [to the aim of the
treatment], is attacked by the kidney drug. In such a situation it is necessary to move
it beyond half way by means of food." Zhang Zhicong: "'The disease is far away' is to
say: it is high up or below [in the body], i.e., far away from the stomach in the center.
中道氣味之 is to say: the qi and the flavors proceed from the central way and move
upward or downward. Hence drugs and food are to be consumed together to organize
[their movement]. In case the disease is far away from the center because it is high up
[in the body], food is to be consumed first and drugs afterwards. In case the disease is
far away from the center because it is in the lower [sections of the body], the drugs are
to be taken first and meals are consumed afterwards. By consuming meals prior to or
subsequent to the intake of drugs, the flavors of the latter are caused to reach the upper
or lower sections [of the body]." Fang Yaozhong: "過 is 直達, 'through,' 通過, 'to reach
through.' 制度 is 規定, 'stipulation.'" Cheng Shide et al.: "之 is 往, 'to proceed.'"

When [the dosage] is large, then the number [of drugs] is small;
when [the dosage] is small, then the number [of drugs] is large.
{'Large' [number] is: to increase them nine times;
'small' [number] is: to increase them twice.}²⁷⁴

When [a disease is treated with] an uneven [composition] but does not go
away,
then [increase its ingredients to] make it an even [composition].
This is what is called 'to double a prescription.'²⁷⁵

When [a disease is treated with] an even [composition] and does not go away,
then [the treatment] should be assisted with [drugs] contradicting [the regular
norms of treating a disease] to seize it.
This is what is called 'the cold, hot, warm or cool [qi of the drugs in a prescrip-
tion] contrary [to normal approaches] follow the respective disease.' "²⁷⁶

---

274 Wang Bing: "This applies to the amounts [of drugs employed for preparing] all
decoctions and pills. 'Near' and 'far away' refers to the locations of the palaces and
depots. Heart and lung are 'near'; kidneys and liver are 'far away.' Spleen and stomach
are located in the center. Of the three sections of the human body, the upper is 'near,'
the lower is 'far away.'"

275 Wang Bing: "When a doubled (重) prescription is to be given, could it be light?
When a poison is to be given, could it be beneficial? When a large [prescription] is to
be given, could it be small? Hence, if after a treatment with an uneven prescription the
disease does not go away, an even prescription will master the disease." Zhang Jiebin:
"When it is advisable to employ an uneven [composition first] and an even [compo-
sition afterwards], this is called 'doubled prescription' (重方). In later times this was
called 復方, 'repetitive prescription.'" Zhang Zhicong: "重方 is to say: to employ an
even and an uneven [composition] together." Fang Yaozhong: "奇方 is 單方; 偶方 is
復方. Because 重方 is 復方, it can be interpreted here as 偶方."

276 Wang Bing: "If after a treatment with a prescription of an even [composition]
the disease is still present, then, contrary [to the normal approach], the treatment is
assisted with [drugs whose] qi is identical to that of the disease. Heat is opposed to
cold; cold offends heat. Minor heat is reduced by cold; minor cold is diminished by
heat. [However,] cold and heat of extreme strength will certainly fight for victory with
[drugs of] their opposite nature; they will bravely resist any different qi. When [two]
sounds are not identical, they do not echo each other; when [two] qi are not identical,
they do not go along with each other. In such a situation, [one qi] fears [the other]
and does not dare to attack the [other]. When one attacks the [other], then the disease
qi and the drug qi will move into each other frontally, and hence cause cold or heat
to close themselves in and guard themselves firmly." Zhang Jiebin: "反佐者 is to say:
[the nature, i.e, qi of] the drugs parallels that of the disease. For example, when cold
is treated with heat and the cold wards off the heat, then, in contrast [to the regular
approach, drugs of] cold [nature] are added to assist [the heat of the drugs] to enter

74-530-5
[Huang] Di:
"Good!
That a disease emerges at the roots, this I have come to know.[277]
When it emerges at the tip, how to treat it?"[278]

Qi Bo:
"When a disease contradicts its root,
one will get a tip disease.
When a treatment contradicts the root [of the disease],
one will get a prescription directed at the tip."[279]

74-530-7
[Huang] Di:
"Good!
The domination of [any of] the six qi, how can it be examined?"

Qi Bo:
"Take advantage of their arrival.

---

the [cold of the disease], and vice versa. Or, when treating heat by means of cold drugs, [additional drugs of] hot [nature] are used to [help] the cold [drugs] move, and vice versa."

277 Gao Shishi: "The six qi wind, heat, dampness, fire, dryness, and cold are the so-called 'roots.'" Zhang Jiebin: "That from which a disease emerges in the beginning is called 'root.' 生於本者 is to say: the origin of being affected by a disease."

278 Zhang Jiebin: "That to which a disease changes later on is called 'tip.' 生於標者 is to say: the many changes lying ahead [in the development of a disease]." Gao Shishi: "The three yin and the three yang qi are the tip."

279 Wang Bing: "This refers to the two qi of minor yin and major yang. The relationship of root and tip is the same for the remaining four qi." Zhang Zhicong: "病反其本 is: the disease is cold but contrary [to what might be expected] a transformation of the major yang [i.e., cold] to heat appears, or the disease is heat but contrary [to what might be expected a transformation of] minor yin to yin cold appears, or the disease is in the yang [section] but [contrary to what might be expected] a depletion cold appears, (etc.). That is meant by 'When a disease opposes its root, one gets a disease at the tip.' 治反其本 is: in case a disease originated from cold and has then transformed to heat, then, contrary [to a treatment required originally], drugs of a cool nature are to be employed to treat the heat. .. In case a disease is situated in the yang brilliance [section] and transforms to a depletion frigidity, then warmth is to be employed to supplement the [patient's] central qi, (etc.). That is meant by 'When a treatment [is conducted] contrary to [what is required in view of] the root [of the disease], one gets a prescription directed at the tip.'"

When cool qi arrives massively,
that is a domination of dryness [qi].
Wind and wood receive evil [qi].
Liver diseases emerge from this.²⁸⁰

When heat qi arrives massively,
that is a domination of fire [qi].
Metal and dryness receive evil [qi].
Lung diseases emerge from this.²⁸¹

74-531-1
When cold qi arrives massively,
that is a domination of water [qi].
Fire and heat receive evil [qi].
Heart diseases emerge from this.²⁸²

When dampness qi arrives massively,
that is a domination of soil [qi].
Cold and water receive evil [qi].
Kidney diseases emerge from this.²⁸³

When wind qi arrives massively,
that is a domination of wood [qi].
Soil and dampness receive evil [qi].
Spleen diseases emerge from this.²⁸⁴

---

280 Wang Bing: "[This] flows into the gallbladder." Gao Shishi: "When coolness qi arrives massively, this is a domination of dryness and metal. Metal punishes wood, [i.e., all that is associated with] wind and wood receives evil [qi]. Hence liver diseases emerge."

281 Wang Bing: "[This] flows into the bent intestine, the large intestine." Lin Yi et al.: "According to the *Jia yi jing*, the bent intestine is the large intestine." Gao Shishi: "When heat qi arrives massively, fire punishes the metal. Hence lung diseases emerge."

282 Wang Bing: "[This] flows into the triple burner and into the small intestine."

283 Wang Bing: "[This] flows into the bladder." Zhang Jiebin: "Soil qi overcomes water. Hence the kidneys, [i.e.,] water, are affected by evil [qi]. The kidneys fall ill and so does the bladder."

284 Wang Bing: "[This] flows into the stomach." Zhang Jiebin: "Wood qi overcomes soil. Hence the spleen, [i.e.,] soil, receives evil [qi]. The spleen falls ill and so does the stomach."

{This is the so-called
'affection by evil [qi] generating disease.'}[285]

If [the evil qi] takes advantage of the depleted [state] of a year, then the evil is severe.[286]
If there is failure to be in harmony with the season, then, too, the evil is severe.[287]
If [the evil qi] meets with new moon, then, too, the evil is severe.[288]
In case of a multiple affection by evil, the disease is dangerous.[289]

---

285 Wang Bing: "These qi are present outside and the inside detests them. Center and outside are not happy. Hence disease results. This is called 感, ['affected']." Fang Yaozhong: "The five depots can be affected by the qi which they themselves are unable to dominate and then develop a disease. For example, liver diseases can develop when the qi of dryness dominates disproportionately and lung diseases can develop when the qi of heat dominates disproportionately."

286 Wang Bing: "When the wood [qi ruling] a year is insufficient and when [at the same time] a coolness evil is present outside, [or] when the fire [qi ruling] a year is insufficient and when [at the same time] a cold evil is present outside, (etc.,) then this is a 'depleted [state] of the year.' When the annual qi is insufficient, then outside evil accumulates excessively." Zhang Zhicong: "When the wood period is inadequate, then coolness qi dominates it; when the fire period is inadequante, then cold qi dominates it. .. In all these cases, the annual period is inadequate and the dominating qi of the four seasons encroaches on [the annual qi] and humiliates it."

287 Wu Kun: "失時之和 is: the four seasons have lost their regular sequence." Zhang Zhicong: "失時之和 is: the qi of the four seasons are weak. For instance, if the spring qi is insufficient, then the autumn qi dominates it; if the summer qi is insufficient, then the winter qi dominates it; (etc.)." Fang Yaozhong: "Host qi and visitor qi have lost their harmony. For example, the initial qi of the host qi is the ceasing yin [qi, i.e.,] wind and wood. If the initial qi of the visitor qi is the yang brilliance [qi, i.e.,] dryness and metal, then [in spring] it should be warm, but on the contrary it is cool. Spring carries out the orders of autumn. The season of spring and the actual climate contradict each other. This is a situation of visitor qi and host qi having lost harmony. In such a situation the human body can be affected by evil and develop disease. Diseases most easily develop in those depots and palaces dominated by the visitor evil. For example, when spring carries out the orders of autumn, then liver diseases develop easily."

288 Fang Yaozhong: "Chinese medicine assumes that the qi and the blood in the human body are closely associated with the changing size of the moon. That is, when the moon is full, qi and blood in the human body are replete, too. At the time of new moon, qi and blood in the human body are depleted and weak. 遇月之空 means: at a time of new moon, if [people] encounter the evil of a disproportionate domination of any of the six qi they may develop a disease even more easily than usual."

289 Zhang Zhicong: "If it takes advantage of the depleted [state] of a year, if it fails to harmonize with the seasons, and if it meets with new moon, this is called 'three

In case a dominating qi is present, [another qi] must come to take revenge."

74-531-6
[Huang] Di:
"The arrivals of the respective [qi in the] vessels, what are they like?"

Qi Bo:
"When a ceasing yin [qi] arrives, the [movement in the] vessels is string[-like].[290]
When a minor yin [qi] arrives, the [movement in the] vessels is hook[-like].[291]
When a major yin [qi] arrives, the [movement in the] vessels is in the depth.[292]
When a minor yang [qi] arrives, the [movement in the vessels] is big and at the surface.[293]
When a yang brilliance [qi] arrives, the [movement in the vessels] is short and rough.[294]
When a major yang [qi] arrives, the [movement in the vessels] is big and extended.[295]

---

depletions.' If [a person] is affected by evil [in such a situation], then the resulting disease is dangerous."

290 Wu Kun: " 'String[-like]' is to say: the [movement in the] vessels comes pulled straight like a string."

291 Zhang Jiebin: " 'Hook[-like]' is: it comes abounding and leaves weak. It is repleted on the outside and depleted inside; like the hook of a belt."

292 Wang Bing: " 'In the depth' is: below. This [movement] is found below the [movement in the] vessels associated with the [seasonal] position [of that qi]." Wu Kun: " 'In the depth' is: the [movement in the] vessels comes below the flesh."

293 Wang Bing: "浮 is 高, 'high.' 大 is: it is somewhat bigger than the [movement in the] vessels associated with the [seasonal] position [of that qi]." Gao Shishi: "Minor yang is associated with fire. Hence [its movement is] 'big and at the surface.'"

294 Wang Bing: "When the going and coming [of a movement] are not unimpeded, that is called 'rough.' When the going and coming [of a movement] are not spaced, that is called 'short.'" Zhang Jiebin: "When a yang brilliance [qi] arrives, then this is the qi of dryness and metal. The nature of metal is to collect and draw together. Hence the [movement in the] vessels comes short and is rough."

295 Wang Bing: "When the going and coming [of a movement in the vessels] are spaced, that is called 'extended.'" Wu Kun: "The major yang [qi, i.e.,] cold and water, is the final qi. Water has the image of flowing over extended distances. Hence the [movement in the] vessels comes full and big and greatly extended."

When [the qi] that arrives is harmonious, then [the patient is in a state of] balance.²⁹⁶

When [the qi] that arrives is extreme, then [the patient has an] disease.²⁹⁷

When [the qi] that arrives is contrary [to what it should be like], there is a disease.²⁹⁸

When [the qi should] arrive but does not arrive, there is a disease.²⁹⁹

When [the qi] arrives before it [should] arrive, there is a disease.

When yin and yang have exchanged [their positions], that is dangerous."³⁰⁰

74-532-5

[Huang] Di:

"The six qi are not identical in their conforming to tip or root, how is that?"³⁰¹

---

296 Zhang Jiebin: "If the arrival of the six [movements in the] vessels listed above is neither greatly excessive nor inadequate, then this is a harmonious and balanced [movement in the] vessels. If it is not balanced, then this is [a sign of] disease."

297 Wang Bing: "If it is as smooth as a string of pearls, if it is deep [to a degree that it] is attached to the bones, if it is at the surface [to a degree that it] is high up at the skin, if it is rough [to a degree that it] halts, if it is as short as [seeds of] hemp or wheat, if it is as big as a hat-pin, if it is as extended as a rope that is pulled, all these are [conditions] that are called 'excessive arrival.'"

298 Wang Bing: "If it should be string[-like] but, on the contrary, is rough; if it should be big but, on the contrary, is fine; if it should be at the surface but, on the contrary, is in the depth, (etc.,) all these are signs of a qi contrary to what is regular and balanced." Gao Shishi: "If it arrives and is contrary to [that which is associated with] the season, this is [a sign of] disease."

299 Wang Bing: "The [seasonal] position of a qi has arrived but the qi in the vessels fails to correspond."

300 Wang Bing: "When during a [seasonal] position associated with yin a yang [movement in the] vessels appears, or vice versa, then they appear having exchanged their positions."

301 Zhang Jiebin: "The six qi include wind, cold, summerheat, dampness, fire, and dryness. These are the orders issued by heaven. 標, 'tip' is 末, 'end.' 本 is 原, 'origin.' This is like the trees having root and tip. Seen separately, root and tip have different shapes; seen together, the tip emerges from the root." Fang Yaozhong: " 'To conform' refers to the focus in diagnosing and treating a disease. .. Among the six qi, some are tip and some are root. For example, wind is the root, ceasing yin [qi] is the tip; heat is the root, minor yin [qi] is the tip; fire is the root, minor yang [qi] is the tip; dampness is the root, major yin [qi] is the tip; dryness is the root, yang brilliance [qi] is the tip; cold is the root, major yang [qi] is the tip. In diagnosing and treating illnesses, sometimes the focus is on the root, sometimes on the tip." Gao Shishi: "The three yin and the three yang are the 'tip' of the six qi. Wind, fire, dampness, heat, dryness, and cold are the

Qi Bo:

"Among the qi are those conforming to the root;

there are those conforming to the tip and the root;

there are those conforming to neither the tip nor the root."[302]

[Huang] Di:

"I should like to hear this comprehensively."

Qi Bo:

"The minor yang and the major yin conform to the root.[303]

'roots' of the six qi. Tip and root differ in their associations with yin and yang. Hence what they follow differs, too."

302 Fang Yaozhong: " 'Qi' may refer to the climate and it may also refer to the manifestation of a disease. 氣有從本者 is: when analysing the climate or the manifestation of a disease, the focus should be on the 'root.' In terms of the manifestation of a disease, the focus should be on the cause of the disease. 有從標本者 is: when analysing the climate or the manifestation of a disease, one should not only focus on the 'root' but also on the 'tip.' In terms of the manifestation of a disease, one should pay attention not only to the 'root' of the disease and the organs where it emerged originally, but also to its clinical signs and to organs affected secondarily. 有不從標本者 is: under certain circumstances, 'root' and 'tip' are for the time being of secondary significance only. The focus should be on other related pathological changes. To take a liver disease as an example, when the liver [qi, i.e., wood] abounds, it will intrude into the [sphere of] the spleen [i.e., of soil]. Generally speaking, the first thing that should be paid attention to is the problem of the liver and of the ceasing yin [qi]. However, if the spleen disease is too serious already, or if the spleen is about to cease functioning, in such a situation the focus of a clinical treatment must be on the spleen and stomach first."

303 Wang Bing: "The root of minor yang [qi] is fire; the root of major yin [qi] is dampness. Root and tip agree; hence [the text states:] 'they conform to the root.'" Zhang Jiebin: "Of the six qi, minor yang [qi] is the minister fire. That is, minor yang [qi] is a transformation product of fire. Hence fire is the root and minor yang [qi] is the tip. Major yin [qi] is dampness and soil. That is, major yin [qi] is a transformation product of dampness. Hence dampness is the root and major yin [qi] is the tip." Fang Yaozhong: " 'Minor yang' is the minor yang [qi, i.e.,] minister fire. Minor yang [qi] is the tip; the minister fire is the root. 'Major yin' is the major yin [qi, i.e.,] dampness and soil. Major yin [qi] is the tip; dampness and soil are the root. In terms of yin and yang association, minor yang [qi] is associated with yang; and the fire is, in terms of yin and yang, associated with yang, too. Tip and root agree in terms of their yinyang associations. In other words, manifestation and basic nature agree. Minor yang [qi] is called minor yang because the disease it stands for is associated with yang. From the name 'minor yang' it is obvious that its diseases are associated with fire and heat. Hence 'minor yang [qi] conforms with the root.' Major yin [qi] is associated with yin and dampness is associated with yin, too. That is to say, manifestation and basic nature agree. Major yin [qi] is called major yin because the disease it stands for is associated

The minor yin and the major yang conform to the root and the tip.[304]
The yang brilliance and the ceasing yin conform to neither the tip nor the root;
they conform to the center.[305]

---

with yin. From the name 'major yin' it is obvious that its diseases are related to dampness. Hence major yin [qi], too, 'conforms with the root.'"

304 Wang Bing: "The root of the minor yin [qi] is heat; its tip is yin. The root of the
major yang [qi] is cold; its tip is yang. Root and end differ. Hence [the text states:]
'they conform to the root, and they conform to the tip.'" Zhang Jiebin: "Minor yin [qi]
is ruler fire; it is a transformation product of heat. Hence the heat is the root and the
minor yin [qi] is the tip. This is: yin conforms with (i.e., emerges from) yang. Major
yang [qi] is cold and water; it is a transformation product of cold. Hence the cold is
the root and the major yang [qi] is the tip. This is: yang conforms with (i.e., emerges
from) yin." Fang Yaozhong: " 'Minor yin' is the minor yin [qi, i.e.,] ruler fire. Minor
yin [qi] is the 'tip'; the ruler fire is the 'root.' 'Major yang' is the major yang [qi, i.e.,]
cold and water. Major yang [qi] is the 'tip'; cold and water are the 'root.' In terms of
yinyang association, minor yin [qi] is associated with yin, while the ruler fire is associated with yang. The yinyang association of tip and root is not identical. In other words,
the ancients knew from experience that sometimes the manifestations of diseases are
associated with yin while their basic nature is associated with yang. [In this case,] yang
is generated by yin. Minor yin [qi] is associated with a situation of yin outside and
yang inside, or the tip is yin and the root is yang. Because in the case of minor yin [qi]
tip and root, yin and yang are both apparent, in a minor yin [situation it is advisable
to] conform to both the root and the tip. Major yang [qi] is associated with yang,
while cold and water are associated with yin. The yinyang association of tip and root is
not identical. In other words, the ancients knew from experience that sometimes the
manifestations of diseases are associated with yang while their basic nature is associated with yin. [In this case,] yin is generated by yang. Major yang [qi] is associated
with a situation of yang outside and yin inside, or the tip is yang and the root is yin.
Because in the case of major yang [qi] tip and root, yin and yang ar both apparent, in a
major yang [situation it is advisable to] conform to both the root and the tip."

305 Wang Bing: "Within yang brilliance is major yin and within ceasing yin is minor
yang. Root and end differ from what is in the center. Hence [the text states:] 'they
conform to neither the root nor the tip; they conform to the center.' Whether to
conform to the root, to conform to the tip, or to conform to the center, this is always
based on their function as ruler of transformation." Zhang Jiebin: "Yang brilliance [qi]
and major yin [qi] constitute outside and inside. Hence major yin [qi] is considered
the 'central qi'; metal follows the transformation of dampness and soil. Ceasing yin
[qi] and minor yang [qi] constitute outside and inside. Hence minor yang [qi] is
considered the 'central qi'; wood follows the transformation of minister fire. That is,
both 'conform to (i.e., emerge from) the center.'" Fang Yaozhong: " 'Yang brilliance' is
the yang brilliance [qi, i.e.,] dryness and metal. Yang brilliance [qi] is the tip; dryness
and metal constitute the root. 'Ceasing yin' is the ceasing yin [qi, i.e.,] wind and wood.
Ceasing yin [qi] is the tip; wind and wood constitute the root. 'Central' is the qi appearing in the center. This is a qi which appears amidst the root qi. That is, when any of

Hence

when the [qi] conforms to the root, transformations are generated at the root.
When the [qi] conforms to the tip and the root, transformations occur at the
tip and at the root.
When the [qi] conforms to the center, then transformations are caused in the
central qi."

74-533-4
[Huang] Di:
"When the [movement in the] vessels conforms to [the root, the tip, or the
center] while the disease contradicts [the respective root, tip, or center],
how to diagnose this?"

Qi Bo:
"When the arrival of the [movement in the] vessels conforms to [the root, the
tip, or the center],
pressing for it does not [reveal any] drumming.[306]
The same applies to all yang [movements]."

[Huang] Di:
"When any of the yin [movements] contradicts [the root, the tip, or the
center],
what are the [movements in the] vessels like?"

---

the six qi has transformed to a certain degree its opposite qi will result from this transformation. The qi that appears from amidst yang brilliance [qi] is major yin [qi]; the
qi that appears from amidst ceasing yin [qi] is minor yang [qi]. 陽明厥陰不從標本
從乎中 is: even though ceasing yin [qi] is associated with wind and with warmth, one
should nevertheless keep in mind that warmth can transform to heat and that wind
can transform to fire. Even though yang brilliance [qi] is associated with coolness and
with dryness, one should nevertheless keep in mind that coolness can transform to
cold and that dryness can transform to dampness. Generally speaking, with respect to
the six qi it is advisable to pay attention not only to the changes and transformation of
their root qi but also to their transformations among themselves."

306 Wang Bing: "That is, the disease is heat and the [movement in the] vessels
[should be] frequent. If pressing [the vessels] fails to reveal a movement, then this is
a situation where abounding cold blocks the yang and [the movement that] arrives is
not one of heat." Zhang Jiebin: "按之不鼓 is: [the movement in the vessels] has no
strength. It does not indicate [the presence] of true yang. Hence it must not be mistaken for a yang [movement]. All such yang movements appear like yang but are not
yang. Hence there are conditions such as false heat, or blocked yang."

Qi Bo:

"When the arrival of [a yin movement in the] vessels conforms to [the root, the tip, or the center],

pressing for it [shows that it] drums severely and abounds.[307]

74-533-7

Hence

when the one hundred illnesses emerge,

some are generated at the root,

some are generated at the tip, and

some are generated at the qi in the center.

In some cases, one achieves a success by selecting [for treatment] the root;

In some cases, one achieves a success by selecting [for treatment] the tip;

In some cases, one achieves a success by selecting [for treatment] the qi in the center;

In some cases, one achieves a success by selecting [for treatment] tip and root.[308]

In some cases, one achieves a success by selecting [a treatment] that is an opposition;

In some cases, one achieves a success by selecting [a treatment] that is a conformance.

{Opposition is: proper, in accordance [with the nature of a disease.] If [a treatment] is in accordance [with the nature of a disease,] this is an opposing [treatment].}[309]

74-533-11

Hence when it is said:

'[If someone] knows about tip and root,

applying his [knowledge] will not result in failure.

If one is familiar with opposition and compliance

---

307 Wang Bing: "The actual appearance of the disease is cold. [However], pressing [the vessels] reveals that the qi in the vessels drums and beats below the hand. 'Abundance' indicates heat abundance blocking the yin [qi] and generating a disease which is not cold."

308 Zhang Jiebin: "取 is 求, 'to search for.' When a disease is generated by the root, it is essential to search for this root and apply a treatment there."

309 Zhang Jiebin: "If cold is used to treat heat, that is treating true heat. If heat is used to treat cold, that is treating true cold. This is [called] 逆取. If heat is used to treat heat, that is treating false heat. If cold is used to treat cold, that is treating false cold. That is [called] 從取."

proper conduct [comes by itself], without one having to worry about it,'
then this means just the same.

Those who do not know this,
they are not sufficiently [equipped] to discuss diagnosis, they are just sufficiently [equipped] to cause disorder in the conduits.

Hence when the *Great Essential* states:
'Uneducated practitioners smile to themselves;[310]
they assume they are knowledgable.
They say: 'The heat has not ended yet, [but]
a cold disease sets in in addition.'
The qi are identical, the physical appearances differ.[311]
They are confused in their diagnosis and they cause disorder in the conduits,'
then this means just the same.

Now the Way of tip and root,
it is important and farreaching;
[it may seem] small, but it is big.
It is possible to discuss one [example] and
to know the harm caused by the one hundred illnesses.

[If someone] discusses tip and root,
[his treatment will be] easy and does not cause harm;
[If someone] investigates root and tip,
he will be able to regulate the qi.
[If someone is] familiar with domination and revenge,
he will establish a model for all mankind.
The Way of heaven is completed [herewith]."

---

310 Wang Bing: "嘻嘻 is 悅, 'to rejoice.' That is to say, in their hearts they rejoice and
believe they know everything. [However,] in the manifestation of the six qi, crude
practitioners understand only half of what skilled practioners understand. Transformations of ceasing yin [qi] are interpreted by crude practitioners as cold, while in fact
they constitute warmth. Major yang transformations are interpreted by crude practitioners as heat while in fact they constitute cold. Because of these different manifestations, [crude practitioners] miss the correct Way."

311 Fang Yaozhong: "That is, the basic nature of illnesses [in different patients] is
identical, but the clinical manifestations of these diseases differ."

74-534-6
[Huang] Di:
"The changes [resulting from] domination and revenge,
they may be early or late; how is that?"

Qi Bo:
"Now,
as for the dominating [qi],
the dominating [qi] arrives and already the disease sets in.
While the disease gains in strength,
the revenge [qi] already sprouts.³¹²

Now,
as for the revenge [qi],
when the dominating [qi] is exhausted, it rises.
When it occupies its [proper] position [the commands it issues] are severe.
Domination may be slight or severe;
the revenge [qi may respond] in small or large quantities.
When the dominating [qi] is harmonious, [the revenge qi] will be harmonious,
[too].
When the dominating [qi] is depleted, [the revenge qi] will be depleted, [too].
That is the regularity of heaven."³¹³

74-535-3
[Huang] Di:
"When the dominating [qi] or the revenge [qi] are active,
[it may be that their] movement does not occur on their proper position,
or it happens that they arrive late.
What is the reason?"³¹⁴

Qi Bo:
"Now,

---

312 Wang Bing: "In case of revenge, an irritation of the heart is not far away." Wu
Kun: "As soon as the dominating qi arrives, the disease sets in. As soon as the disease
comes to an end, that is, it has been 'brought together, but has not been discarded yet,'
the revenge qi sprouts already." Cheng Shide et al.: "慍慍 carries the idea of 蘊積, 'to
bring together.' 萌 is 萌發, 萌動, 'to break into buds.'"

313 Zhang Jiebin: "Domination and revenge are as inseparable as a physical appearance and its shadow, or sound and echo."

314 Gao Shishi: 動不當位 refers to an early arrival of a qi; 後時而至 refers to a
belated arrival of a qi."

the generation of a qi, and its transformation, may differ between weakness and abundance.³¹⁵
The abundant or weak operation of cold, summerheat, warmth and coolness [can be observed] at the four ropes.³¹⁶

Hence
the movement of the yang [qi]
begins in the warmth and
abounds in the summerheat.

The movement of the yin [qi]
begins in the coolness and
abounds in the cold.

Spring, summer, autumn, and winter,
the length of their [time] sections is always different."³¹⁷

---

315 Zhang Jiebin: " 'Being generated' is to say: the begin of its emergence; 'transformation' is to say: massive qi transformation. Hence [these two states] differ in that [the first is characterized by] weakness, while [the second is characterized by] abundance." Gao Shishi: "The generation and the transformation of things by the qi of the four seasons differs in that there may be abundance or weakness."

316 Zhang Jiebin: "Spring warmth abounds at *chen*. Summerheat abounds at *wei*. Autumn coolness abounds at *xu*. Winter cold abounds at *chou*. These are the manifestations of abundance and weakness in the course of the four seasons." Cheng Shide et al.: " 'Four ropes' refers to the *chen, xu, chou,* and *wei* months." Fang Yaozhong: " 'Four ropes' refers to the third, sixth, ninth, and twelfth months."

317 Wang Bing: "That is to say: the qi of the four proper seasons, i.e., spring, summer, autumn, and winter, are present in the segments of the four ropes. The warmth of spring is present in the *chen* and *si* months. The heat of summer is present in the *wu* and *wei* months. The coolness of autumn is present in the *xu* and *hai* months. The cold of winter is present in the *yin* and *chou* months. Spring begins in the second month of spring; summer begins in the second month of summer; autumn begins in the second month of autumn; winter begins in the second month of winter. .. It is obvious that the qi differs from section to section [of the year. However, while the emergence, effusion, collection, and storage of yin and yang qi parallels the regular pattern, it is obvious that the qi transformations are echoed differently in the human [body] in each of the four seasons. The number of days does not agree with the regular pattern." Zhang Jiebin: " 'Begins in warmth' is the emergence of yang [qi]; 'abounds in summerheat' is the transformation of yang [qi]. 'Begins in coolness' is the emergence of yin [qi]; 'abounds in cold' is the transformation of yin. The arrival of the qi may be weak or strong; hence each of the four seasons gets a different portion (差分)." Cheng Shide et al.: "分 is the 度 of the text further down. 差其分 is: domination and revenge may begin early or belated."

Hence when the *Great Essential* states:
'The gentle warmth of the bygone spring
brings forth the summerheat of summer,
the indignation of a bygone autumn
brings forth the anger of winter;'[318]
Carefully examine the four ropes;
when the scouts all return,
the end is apparent and
the beginning can be known;'
then this means just the same.[319]

74-536-1
[Huang] Di:
"Can the discrepancies [in the lengths of the sections] be quantified?"

Qi Bo:
"Again, they all amount to 30 degrees."[320]

---

318 Fang Yaozhong: "忿 is to describe the coolness of qi here; 怒 is to describe the
cold of qi here. What this means is: autumn coolness is the basis of winter cold; winter
cold is the outcome of a transformation of coolness."

319 Wang Bing: "This refers to a minor or strong presence of qi. When the yang presence is minor, then [the climate] is mild; when its presence is strong, then it is hot as
in summer. When the yin presence is minor, then this is paralleled by irritation; when
its presence is strong, this brings about anger. All these statements here refer to differences [associated with] a minor or strong presence [of qi, i.e., with] an abundance
or weakness in the operations of qi. If only one determines abundance and weakness
at the positions of the four ropes, then one knows all the corresponding operations of
yin and yang [qi] from begin to end." Gao Shishi: "四維 are the intersections of winter
and spring, of spring and sumer, of summer and autumn, and of autumn and winter."
Fang Yaozhong: "斥候 has the meaning of 觀測候望, 'to observe and examine.' 終始
refers to the end and to the begin of a season. E.g., in spring 終 is the third month, 始
is the first month. The meaning of the entire sentence is: one must observe the climatic
changes in the third, the sixth, the ninth, and the twelfth months and on the basis of
this it is possible to examine and understand the climatic changes in each of the four
seasons spring, summer, autumn, and winter of that year." We interpret 斥候 in the
meaning of 'sentry,' 'guards,' 'scouts,' even though the original context of this quotation that gave sense to this metaphor is no longer traceable.

320 Wang Bing: "度 is 日, 'day.'" Lin Yi et al.: "*Su wen* 71 (71-493-6) states: 差有數
乎, and it says further: 後皆三十度而有奇. In the present paragraph [the text] speaks
only of 三十度. The text is corrupt here." Zhang Jiebin: "Early or late arrival of a qi
never exceeds 30 days. '30 degrees' refers to the number of days of one month." Gao
Shishi: "'30 degrees' is one month. If it is the twelfth month and spring qi is present,
if it is the third month and summer qi is present, if it is the sixth month and autumn

[Huang] Di:

"How do the [movements in the] vessels correspond to these [discrepancies]?"

Qi Bo:

"The discrepancies follow the same law [which applies] to the proper [move-
ments in the vessels]. [The movement in the vessels corresponding to the qi of
the previous season] vanishes when its time has come.³²¹

74-536-3
The *Essentials of the Vessels* states:
'If in spring [the movement in the vessels] is not in the depth,
in summer not string[-like],
in winter not rough, and
in autumn not frequent,
this is called "the four obstructions [of the seasonal qi]".'³²²

---

qi is present, if it is the ninth month, and winter qi is present, the qi has arrived early
and the discrepancy [in comparison with the regular pattern] is 30 degrees. If it is the
first month and it is not warm yet and if it appears as if winter qi was still present, if
it is the fourth month and summer has not arrived yet and if it appears as if spring qi
was still present, (etc.), the qi arrive late and the discrepancy [in comparison with the
regular pattern] is 30 degrees, too. Hence [the text] states: 'always 30 degrees.'"

321 Another reading of this passage could hypothesize an original phrasing 差正同
法. In contrast to the phrase 正法, which is not attested elsewhere in the *Su wen*, the
phrase 同法 is attested in the *Su wen* several times. With this reading, the statement
offers a logical response to Huang Di's question. A translation would be "the same law
applies to discrepancies [in the movements in the vessels] and to proper [movements
in the vessels]: When their time has come, they leave." Wang Bing: "The discrepancy
occurs in the [movement in the] vessels, too, corresponding to the [earlier or later
arrival of the seasonal] qi." Zhang Zhicong: "正 is: the proper positions of the four
seasons. That is to say: the [movement in the] vessels agrees with the proper pattern of
the four seasons. At the interaction point of preceding and subsequent seasons, 'when
the time has come it will leave' [is to say: it] will leave after thirty days [of the new
season]. For example, a floating [movement in the] vessels in spring is still associated
with the qi of winter. After thirty days of the first month have passed, the qi of spring
will begin to be in control of its orders alone." Fang Yaozhong: "時 refers to the 'four
ropes' mentioned above, i.e., the third, sixth, ninth, and twelfth months."

322 Wang Bing: "The qi of heaven and earth of the four seasons is obstructed and
cannot move anywhere." Zhang Jiebin: "In spring the [movement in the] vessels
should be string[-like]. However, because it emerges out out winter, the qi of winter
is still present. Hence it should still be in the depth. In summer, the [movement in
the] vessels should be frequent. However, because it emerges out of spring, the qi of
spring is still present. Hence it should be string[-like]. (Etc.) If [the movement in the
vessels] is not in the depth in spring, is not string[-like] in summer, is not frequent

When a [movement] in the depth is severe, this means disease.

When a string[-like movement] is severe, this means disease.

When a rough [movement] is severe, this means disease.

When a frequent [movement] is severe, this means disease.[323]

When [several movements] appear together, this means disease.

When [a movement] appears again, this means disease.[324]

When [a movement] vanishes before it [should have] vanished, this means disease.

When [a movement] does not vanish even though it [should have] vanished, this means disease.

[Movements] contrary [to the season are signs of imminent] death.[325]

74-536-6

Hence when it is said:

'The qi guard and control each other like weight and beam [of a balance] who cannot lose each other.

---

in autumn, and is not rough in winter, these [are signs] that it has lost its host qi. The qi do not interact, hence [the text] speaks of 'four obstructions.'" Zhang Zhicong: "If [the movement in the vessels] is not in the depth in spring, then the qi of winter does not interact with spring. (Etc.) That is, the qi of the four seasons do not interact and are obstructed." Fang Yaozhong: "In spring the [movement in the] vessels is string[-like]. However, because spring builds on the foundation of winter, the string[-like] movement in the] vessels of spring should be accompagnied by a stone[-like movement in the] vessels of winter. That is, it should continue on the basis of a deep [movement in the] vessels. Hence the [movement in the] vessels in spring, in addition to being string[-like] it should also be in the depth. Especially in the first and second months of spring, a manifestation in the depth should be especially obvious. The regular [movement in the] vessels in spring is in the depth, fine, and string[-like]. (Etc. for the three remaining seasons)."

323 Cheng Shide et al.: "The [movement in the] vessels should resemble, to a certain degree, that of the preceding season. However, if [the qi of the preceding season continues to] abound excessively, then the [movement in the] vessels is out of season. Hence it is a [movement in the] vessels indicating disease." Fang Yaozhong: "Slightly in the depth [in spring], slightly string[-like in summer], slightly frequent [in autumn], and slightly rough [in winter], these are the regular appearances of the [movements in the] vessels."

324 Wang Bing: "參 is to say: all qi arrive simultaneously. 復見 is: a qi that had weakened and died is seen again."

325 Wang Bing: "If the [movement] is in the depth in summer, is frequent in autumn, is relaxed in winter, and is rough in spring, that is called 反. If something is generated in opposition to the command of heaven, how could it last for long?"

Now, when the yin qi and the yang qi are clear and calm, then generation and transformation occur orderly. When they are agitated, then severe diseases emerge,'

then this means just the same."³²⁶

74-536-8
[Huang] Di:
"What about 'darkness' and 'brilliance'?"

Qi Bo:
"Both yin [qi] are equally exhausted. Hence one speaks of 'darkness.'³²⁷
The two yang [qi] unite [their] brilliance. Hence one speaks of 'brilliance.'³²⁸

The [varying] pairings of darkness and brilliance [account for] the differences between cold and summerheat."³²⁹

[Huang] Di:
"What about 'divisions' and 'extremes' ? "³³⁰

Qi Bo:
"When the qi is extreme, this is called 'extreme' (i.e., 'solstice');
when the qi is divided, this is called 'division,' (i.e., equinox).
At [the time of] 'extreme,' the qi are homogenous;

---

326 Fang Yaozhong: " 'Clear and calm' refers to the regular processes of interactions between the yin and yang [qi]. 治 refers to normality. 動 refers to changes in the sense of irregular changes in the interactions of the qi, as mentioned above."

327 See 74-529-2. Cheng Shide et al.: "The 'two yin' are major yin and minor yin."

328 See 74-529-1. Cheng Shide et al.: "The 'two yang [qi]' are major yang and minor yang."

329 Zhang Jiebin: " 'Darkness' and 'brilliance' are the images of extreme abundance of yin and yang [qi] respectively. Hence *Ling shu* 41 identifies *chen* and *si* as yang brilliance and *xu* and *hai* as ceasing yin. Now, the qi of *chen* and *si* is summerheat; the qi of *xu* and *hai* is cold. Like night is cold and daytime is hot; winter is cold and summer is hot; the West and the North are cold, the East and the South are hot. Everywhere the qi of *chen*, *si*, *xu*, and *hai* are present. Hence the [varying] combinations of darkness and brilliance account for the differences of cold and summerheat."

330 Gao Shishi: "At 'summer extreme' (i.e., summer solstice), the qi of summer is extreme. At 'winter extreme' [i.e., winter solstice), the qi of winter is extreme. Hence the term 'extreme' in 'qi extreme.' At 'spring division' (i.e., vernal equinox) the division from winter qi has taken place and at 'autumn division' (i.e., autumnal equinox) the division from summer qi has taken place. Hence the term 'division' in 'qi division.'"

at [the time of] 'division,' the qi are heterogenous.³³¹
This is the so-called 'proper arrangement of heaven and earth.' "

[Huang] Di:
"Sir, you have stated that
the qi of spring and autumn start ahead [of their time],
the qi of winter and summer start behind [their time].
This I have come to know by now.

However, in the leaving and returning of the six qi,
[which of them] rules a year, this is irregular.
What about supplementing or draining in such [a situation]?"³³²

74-537-4
Qi Bo:
"The [qi] that rule above and below,³³³
in accordance with what benefits them,
one applies the proper flavors.

---

331 Wang Bing: "At the times of the two solstices of summer and winter, the qi of
heaven and earth ruling a year have reached a peak (至) in their presence. At the times
of the two equinoxes of spring and autumn, the four intervening qi, i.e., the initial, the
second, the fourth, and the fifth [qi], divide (分) their policies in ruling a year to the
right and to the left. Hence [the text] states: 'At the [time of] peak (i.e., solstice) the qi
is homogenous; at the [time of] division (i.e., equinox) the qi is heterogeneous.' "

332 Wang Bing: "[This statement] takes the equinoxes and solstices to clarify the
separate positions occupied [in the course of a year] by the six qi. I.e., the initial and
the fourth qi begin [their presence] fifteen days before [the solar terms] Spring Begins
and Autumn Begins. That is the pattern of their arrangement. The third qi and the
sixth qi begin [their presence] fifteen days after [the solar terms] Summer Begins and
Winter Begins. That is the pattern of their arrangement. Because of the arrangement
of these four qi before and after [Spring, Autumn, Summer, and Winter Begins], the
two solstices occur right in the middle of the third and of the sixth qi. Hence [the
text] states: 'The qi of spring and autumn begin ahead; the qi of winter and summer
begin afterwards.' Now, every 365 days all qi change. With the end of each year, a new
qi sets in. When the new qi arrives, the old qi leaves. The appropriate flavors differ
with respect to [the qi controlling] heaven and [those at the fountain on the] earth. To
compose prescriptions that supplement or drain, it is essential to know the earlier and
later [arrival of the qi]. Hence [Huang Di] raises this question again."

333 Wang Bing: "主 is to say: 主歲, 'ruling a year.' " Cheng Shide et al.: " 'That which
rules above and below' are the qi controlling heaven and at the fountain."

This, then, is the essential [approach required].
The same law applies to [the qi on] the left and right.[334]

The *Great Essential* states:
'When the minor yang rules, first [use] sweet [flavor], later [use] salty [flavor].
When the yang brilliance rules, first [use] acrid [flavor], later [use] sour [flavor].
When the major yang rules, first [use] salty [flavor], later [use] bitter [flavor].
When the ceasing yin rules, first [use] sour [flavor], later [use] acrid [flavor].
When the minor yin rules, first [use] sweet [flavor], later [use] salty [flavor].
When the major yin rules, first [use] bitter [flavor], later [use] sweet [flavor]'.

To assist, use that which is beneficial.
To supply, use that by which it is generated.[335]
This is called 'to get the qi.' "[336]

74-537-10
[Huang] Di:
"Good!

Now,
as for the emergence of the one hundred illnesses,
they all emerge from wind, cold, summerheat, dampness, dryness, and fire,
because of the transformations and changes of these [six qi].

The classic states:
'That which abounds, discharge it;
that which is depleted, supplement it.'

---

334 Zhang Jiebin: "As for the intervening qi to the left and to the right, those above are [to be treated] identically with the [qi] controlling heaven, those below are [to be treated] identically with the [qi] at the fountain. Hence [the text] speaks of 'identical patterns.'"

335 Zhang Jiebin: "資以所生 is: support the sources of their transformations."

336 Wang Bing: "得 is to say: 得其性用, 'to make use of the operation of their nature.' If one is able to make use of the operation of their nature, then rolling and unrolling depends on [the will of] man. If one is unable to make use of the operation of their nature, then movement and generation run counter [one's wishes]. How could one hope to be able to eliminate an evil [qi] in such a situation? This would just suffice to attack the wonderful true qi of heaven! The flavors used 'first' and 'later' is to say: they are all used in case of a disease. First one drains [the evil] and later one supplements [the proper qi]."

I have conferred [this knowledge] upon the prescription gentlemen.[337]
However, when the prescription gentlemen apply it, they are not yet able to
achieve a success in all [cases they treat].
It is my intention to see to it that the Way of the essential will prevail everywhere,
so that [therapeutic success corresponds to treatment just as] the drum responds to the drumstick,
as if one pulled a thorn or cleaned the dirt.[338]
[The therapeutic methods employed by] simple practitioners, skilled [physi-
cians], spirit[-like physicians], and sage[-like physicians],
May [I] hear [of them]?"

Qi Bo:
"[When it is said:]
'[Physicians should] carefully investigate the trigger underlying a disease,
they must not miss what befits a qi,'[339]
then this explains what [you have asked]."

74-538-4
[Huang] Di:
"I should like to hear about the trigger underlying a disease."

Qi Bo:
"All [diseases with] wind [causing] swaying and dizziness,
without exception they are associated with the liver.[340]

All [diseases with] cold [causing] contracting and pulling in,
without exception they are associated with the kidneys.[341]

---

337 Zhang Jiebin: "錫 is 賜, 'to hand to.'"

338 Zhang Jiebin: "由 is 猶, 'as if,' 'like.'"

339 Wang Bing: "If one makes use of the 'trigger,' of the essential, then the movement [required] is small but the effect is big; the operation is shallow but the effect is
deep." Zhang Jiebin: "機 is 要, 'essential,' 變, 'change [to the worse].' It is the origin of
pathological changes."

340 Wang Bing: "The nature of wind is movement; the qi of wood parallels it." Zhang
Jiebin: "眩 is 運, 'vertigo.'" Wu Kun: "There are different types of wind. Hence [the
text] speaks of 諸風, 'all winds.' 眩 is: uncontrolled movement together with darkness
in front of the eyes."

341 Wang Bing: "收 is to say: 斂, 'to contract.' 引 is to say: 急, 'tense.' When things
are cold they shrink, similar to the qi of water." Zhang Jiebin: "The kidneys are associated with water. Their transformation is cold. Whenever yang qi fails to penetrate,

All [diseases with] dammed up qi [resulting in chest] pressure,
without exception they are associated with the lung.³⁴²

All [diseases with] dampness [causing] swelling and fullness,
without exception they are associated with the spleen.³⁴³

All [diseases with] heat [causing] pressure and spasm,
without exception they are associated with fire.³⁴⁴

All pain [diseases with] itch and sores,
without exception they are associated with the heart.³⁴⁵

74-538-8
All recession [diseases with] hardening or outflow,
without exception they are associated with the lower [parts of the body].³⁴⁶

---

then the camp and the guard [qi] freeze and collect. The physical body has a cramp.
All this is called 收引."

342 Wang Bing: "膹 is 膹滿, 'full.' 鬱 is 奔迫, 'to press.' These effects of qi are similar
to [those of] the qi of metal." Zhang Jiebin: "膹 is 喘急, 'to pant hastily'" Fang Yaozhong: "膹 is identical to 膨, in the sense of 脹滿, 'swollen to fullness.' 鬱 is 鬱積; here
it refers to a feeling of pressure and blockage in the chest." 2055/53: "氣 is an error
for 燥, 'dryness.'" Accordingly, the sentence would read: 'All [diseases with] dryness
[resulting in chest] fullness and pressure, without exception they are associated with
the lung.'

343 Wang Bing: "When the soil is thin, then the water is shallow. When the soil is
thick, then the water is deep. When the soil is flat, then it is dry; when it is heaped
up high, then it is damp. The presence of dampness qi is paralleled by the qi of soil."
1798/36: "胕 is not 足, it stands for 浮, 'surface,' 'floating.'"

344 Zhang Jiebin: "When heat evil harms the spirit, then this results in 瞀. When
an overactive yang [qi] harms the blood, then this results in 瘛. Hence both [these
conditions] are associated with fire." Wu Kun: "瞀 is 昏, 'dizziness.' 瘛 is: hands and
feet have a cramp and move." Gao Shishi: "Old editions have 火, 'fire', instead of 心,
'heart.' I have changed this [to 'heart'] now. " (See also the next note.)

345 Wang Bing: "When the heart is quiet, then the pain is minor; when the heart is
vexed, then the pain is severe. Pain, itch, and ulcers emerge from the heart." Zhang
Jiebin: "Severe heat causes ulcers and pain; minor heat causes ulcers and itch. The
heart is associated with fire; its transformation is heat. Hence all ulcers are associated
with the heart." Gao Shishi: "Old editions have 'heart' instead of 'fire.' I have changed
this [to 'fire'] now. All pain, itch, and ulcers are associated with the fire of the hand
minor yang [conduits of the] triple burner."

346 Wang Bing: " 'Lower [parts of the body]' is to say: the lower burner, [i.e.,] the
qi of the liver and of the kidneys. Now, the qi of the kidneys is responsible for guard-

All [cases of] limpness [with] panting and vomiting,
without exception they are associated with the upper [parts of the body].[347]

All [cases of] clenched [teeth], chattering [teeth], and shivering,
as if [the patient] had lost his spirit guard,
without exception they are associated with fire.[348]

All [cases of] tetany and stiff nape,
without exception they are associated with dampness.[349]

All [cases of qi] countermovement rushing upward,
without exception they are associated with fire.[350]

All [cases of] distension and abdominal enlargement,
without exception they are associated with heat.[351]

---

ing what is 'below.' To keep the gates shut is the responsibility of the qi of the liver. Hence, recession, hardening, and outflow, they all are associated with what is below. 厥 is 氣逆, 'countermovement of qi.' 固 is 禁固, 'firmly closed.'" Zhang Jiebin: "厥 is 逆, 'countermovement.' 固 is constipation in front and behind. 泄 is: the two yin [orifices, i.e., for urine and stools] do not close firmly." Fang Yaozhong: "泄 is: urine and stools move unrestrained."

347 Wang Bing: "'Upper [parts of the body]' is to say: the upper burner, [i.e.,] the qi of the heart and of the lung." Lin Yi et al.: "The diseases caused by wilting are not necessarily diseases of what is above. Wang Bing's commentary fails to explain why they should be associated with what is above. This has created controversies among people of later times." Zhang Jiebin: "'Limpness' includes 'sinew limpness,' 'flesh limpness,' 'vessel limpness,' and 'bone limpness.' Hence [the text] speaks of 'all types of limpness.'"

348 Wang Bing: "These are internal effects of heat." Cheng Shide et al.: "禁 is lock-jaw, the mouth cannot be opened. 鼓慄 is: to be excited and to shiver from cold."

349 Wang Bing: "The major yang [section] has been harmed by dampness." Gao Shishi: "瘈 is: hands and feet have a cramp. All such cramps and stiffness of nape and back are illnesses of the foot major yang [section, i.e., of the] bladder. The bladder is the palace of water and dampness. Hence all [these conditions] are associated with dampness."

350 Wang Bing: "This is a manifestation of the rising nature of flames."

351 Zhang Jiebin: "When heat abounds in the lung, then swelling occurs in the upper [section of the body]. When [heat abounds] in the spleen or/and in the stomach, then swelling occurs in the center. When [heat abounds] in the liver and in the kidneys, then swelling occurs in the lower [section of the body]. That is, vexation and fullness result from an arrival of fire evil. Hence [the text] states: 'all [instances of] swelling and enlargement of the abdomen are associated with heat.'"

All [cases of] overexcitement and jumping in craziness,
without exception they are associated with fire.[352]

74-539-3
All [cases of] sudden rigidity,
without exception they are associated with wind.[353]

All diseases accompanied by sounds,
with a beating like the beating of a drum,
without exception they are associated with heat.[354]

All diseases [such as] *fu*-swelling,
pain, soreness, and shock,
without exception they are associated with fire.[355]

---

352 Wang Bing: "Heat abounds in the stomach and in the four extremities." Zhang
Jiebin: "躁 is 'restlessness.' 狂 is 'wild,' 'disorderly.' 越 is 'overly,' 'abnormal.' When heat
abounds in the exterior, then the limbs and the body move uncontrolled. When heat
abounds internally, then the spirit is restless and vexed. The reason is, when fire enters
the lung, this results in vexation; when fire enters the kidneys, this results in restlessness. Vexation is a light [affection] by heat; restlessness is a severe [affection] by heat.
狂 is a yang disease." Fang Yaozhong: "越 is: 'to climb over walls and houses.'"

353 Wu Kun: "Wind causes harm to the large sinews in the yang section. Hence the
sinews are tense and there is sudden stiffness. This is a transformation of strong wind
together with [the qi of] dryness and metal." Gao Shishi: "These are illnesses of the
foot ceasing yin liver conduit. The ceasing yin rules the wind. Hence all [these condi-
tions] are associated with wind."

354 Wang Bing: "That is to say, there are sounds." Zhang Jiebin: "鼓之如鼓 is: the
intestines have sounds." 1585/87: "The first 鼓 should be 鼓. Both characters are very
similar and can easily be mistaken for each other. 鼓 has the meaning of 響, 'sound.' 鼓
之如鼓 has the meaning of 響之如鼓, 'it makes sounds like a drum,' that is, during a
disease the sounds in the intestines are greatly increased." Fang Yaozhong: "'Accompanied by sounds' includes coughing, panting, retching, breaking a wind, abdominal
sounds, etc. The first character 鼓 is to say: to knock at the chest or at the abdomen
comparable to percussion in Western medicine. The second character 鼓 refers to the
sound produced by a drum. The meaning is: if one knocks at the chest or at the abdomen of the patient, this produces a hollow sound."

355 Wu Kun: "When fire is oppressed in the conduits, then this leads to swelling.
This is a yang sign. As for 'pain and soreness,' extreme fire restrains metal. [Hence
metal] cannot level wood. When wood is replete, it causes sores. Internal fire causes
shock. This is a manifestation of the nature of fire which is sudden movement."

All types of contortions and
[all diseases of] watery fluids being turbid,
without exception they are associated with heat.[356]

74-539-6
All diseases of watery fluids
being extremely clear and cool,
without exception they are associated with cold.[357]

All [cases of] vomiting sour [matter],
sudden outpour, and downward pressing,
without exception they are associated with heat."[358]

74-539-7
Hence when the *Great Essential* states:
'Carefully watch the trigger underlying a disease;
in each case control what is associated with it.
Where there is something, search for it;
where there is nothing, search for it, [too].
What abounds, punish it;
what is depleted, punish it, [too].[359]

---

356 Wang Bing: "反戾 is: twisted sinews. 水液 is: urine." Wu Kun: "Extreme fire
restrains metal. [Hence metal] cannot level wood. The wood becomes extreme and
assists the fire. As a result, the sinews become tense, or they are pulled unilaterally.
This causes 'twisting' and 'turning.' This is a 'deviation' (乖戾) from normal. When the
liquids [discharged] are clear, then this is [a sign of] cold; when they are turbid, it is [a
sign of] heat." Cheng Shide et al.: "轉 refers to difficulties in turning the lower back;
反 refers to the back being stretched backwards. 戾 refers to a crouched body. 水液
refers to liquids discharged by the body, including sweat, urine, snivel, tears, etc."

357 Wang Bing: "This includes all discharges through the upper and lower [orifices],
also vomiting and urination."

358 Wang Bing: " 'Sour' refers to sour liquid and flavor." Wu Kun: "Fire manifests
itself flaming upward. Hence [fire in the body results in] vomiting. 'Sour [flavor]'
is the flavor of the liver. Extreme fire restrains metal. [Hence metal] cannot level
wood. When the wood flourishes, it assists the heat. Hence [patients] vomit sour
[liquids/flavor]. When the intestines and the stomach are hot, then transmission and
transformation turn abnormal. Hence there is 'sudden discharge.' This is a manifestation of the quickness in the nature of fire." *Gu dian yi zhu xuan* bianxiezu /39: "下迫
refers to pressure against a closed anus. That is, one wishes to move the bowels but is
unable to do so."

359 Wang Bing: "有無求之虛盛責之 is to say: [make efforts] to understand the ori-
gin/cause [of a disease]. For example, when in case of extreme cold, heat [is employed

First of all, one must [take into account] the five dominations.³⁶⁰
Open [the flow of] blood and qi and
cause their regulation and have them reach [everywhere],
to achieve a harmonious balance,'
then this means just the same."

74-540-1
[Huang] Di:
"Good!
What about the operation of yin and yang among the five flavors?"

Qi Bo:
"Acrid [flavor] and sweet [flavor] are effused and disperse and are yang.
Sour [flavor] and bitter [flavor] cause gushing up and outflow and are yin.

---

to treat the patient but he] fails to turn hot, these are [signs that] there is no fire. If
the heat comes and goes again; if it appears during daytime but is hidden at night;
if it breaks out at night but rests during daytime, or if it is active only intermittingly,
these are [signs that] there is no fire, and it is advisable to assist the [qi of the] heart.
Or, when [a patient suffers from] extreme heat and a cooling [treatment is applied]
to him but he fails to turn cold, these are [signs that] there is no water. If the heat is
active and rests alternately; if its appearance and disappearance is hurried, if at times
it is active and at times not, these are [signs that] there is no water, and it is advisable to assist the [qi of the] kidneys. In case of internal resistance, with vomiting and
countermovement [of qi], so that food cannot enter [the stomach], this is [a sign that]
there is fire. Illnesses such as vomiting and spitting, when the food is thrown up after
some time only, are [signs that] there is no fire. Rapid discharge of [undigested] food
is a [sign that] there is no water. Semiliquid discharge over some time, which stops
and commences again irregularly, is a [sign that] there is no fire. Hence if one [tries to]
cool [a patient] without getting him to turn cold, this is to be blamed on the absence
of water. If one heats [a patient] without getting him to turn hot, this is to be blamed
on the absence of fire. If the heat does not last long, blame it on a depletion of the [qi
of the] heart; if the cold does not last long, blame it on a deficiency of [the qi of] the
kidneys." *Gu dian yi zhu xuan* bianxiezu /57: "有者求之無者求之 is to say: no matter
whether the pathoconditions are obvious or not they are to be examined closely to
discover the nature of what has triggered the disease. 盛者責之虛者責之 is to say: no
matter whether it is a pathocondition of depletion or repletion, in each case its origin
is to be investigated to apply a differential treatment." Wan Lanqing et al./48: "有者
is: if the cause of the disease, the trigger of the disease, underlying pathoconditions
that appear in clinical situations is listed among the preceding 19 paragraphs. 無者 is:
if the cause of the disease, the trigger of the disease, underlying pathoconditions that
appear in clinical situations is not listed among the preceding 19 paragraphs."

360 Wang Bing: "五勝 refers to the mutual domination among the five agents."

Salty flavor causes gushing up and outflow and is yin.
Bland flavor causes seeping and outflow and is yang.³⁶¹

Of these six [flavors]
some contract, some disperse,
some relax, some tighten,
some dry, some moisten,
some soften, some harden.

Use that which is of benefit and apply it.
regulate the [patient's] qi and cause its balance."³⁶²

74-540-4
[Huang] Di:
"If someone contracts [a disease] because his/her qi was unregulated,
how is a treatment to be performed?³⁶³
Some [substances] have poison, others have no poison;
which [are employed] first and which subsequently?
I should like to hear the Way of this."³⁶⁴

---

361 Wang Bing: "涌 is 吐, 'to spit.' 泄 is 利, 'diarrhea.' 滲泄 is urine."

362 Gao Jiwu/253: "所利 is 所宜, '[they are employed according to] what is suited.'"
Yan Hongchen & Gao Guangzhen/25: "A therapy is carried out with drugs that are
of use (所利) in treating the disease."

363 Zhang Jiebin: "非調氣 is: the disease was not contracted because of [a disregulation of] any qi." Wu Kun: "非調氣 is: if the disease was contracted because of a
disregulation of qi" Gao Shishi: "When a disease was contracted because of a disregulation of qi, then it is to be treated with drugs." Cheng Shide et al.: "Zhang Jiebin is
right. Diseases that are not the result of a [disregulated] qi, they are not to be treated
with patterns aiming at a regulation of qi."

364 Wang Bing: "In view of their generation, there are four categories of diseases.
First, internal formation of a disease because of a qi movement. Second, external formation of a disease without a qi movement. Third, internal emergence of a disease
because of a qi movement. Fourth, external emergence of a disease without a qi movement. Examples of [illnesses] that have formed internally because of a qi movement
are the following: accumulations, concretions and conglomerations, goiters and tumors, peak illness and convulsion. Examples of [illnesses] that have formed externally
[because of a qi movement] are the following: abscesses, swelling, ulcers, sores, scabies,
piles, red eyes, *fu*-swellings, and itch. Examples of [illnesses] that emerge internally
without a qi movement are the following: stagnating drink, outflow of [undigested]
food, harm due to hunger, overeating, or exhaustion, food staying in the body over-
night, cholera, sadness, fear, joy, anger, longing and depression. Examples of [illnesses]
that emerge externally without a qi movement are the following: various demonic on-

Qi Bo:
"Whether they have poison or not,
the main [concern in their application] is the [disease] that is to be treated.
In accordance [with the severity of a disease], the composition [of the prescription] should be large or small."³⁶⁵

74-541-1
[Huang] Di:
"Please speak about these compositions."

Qi Bo:
"One ruler, two ministers,
that is a small composition.
One ruler, three ministers, and five assistants,
that is a middle[-size] composition.
One ruler, three ministers, and nine assistants,
that is a large composition.

What is cold, heat it;
what is hot, make it cold.
What is feeble, oppose it;
what is severe, conform to it.³⁶⁶

---

slaughts, beatings and contusion, affections by wind, cold, summerheat and dampness, shots and stabbings, and falls. Among these four categories are those where a cure is achieved through a treatment directed solely at the interior or at the interior too, and those where a cure is achieved through a treatment directed solely at the exterior, or at the exterior too. There are cases which are cured in that first the exterior is treated and then the interior, and there are cases which are cured in that first the interior is treated and then the exterior. In some cases one must rely on poison and launch an attack, and there are other cases where one must not rely on poison and regulate instead. For all these approaches, the prescriptions to be applied may be heavy or light, slow or urgent, contracting or dispersing, moistening or drying, softening or hardening. The views and ideas of the prescription masters differ; everybody has his own ideas."

365 Wang Bing: "A good prescription is one that is able to break an accumulation, to heal a disease, to dissolve tensions, and to ward off death. There is no need in making statements such as 'to use a poison first is correct and to use a poison afterwards is a mistake,' or '[if the drugs] contain no poison, that is incorrect, and [if the drugs] contain poison, that is correct.' All that is required is to assess the severity of the disease in question and to vary the size of the prescription accordingly."

366 Wang Bing: "A minor disease is like a man [made] fire. It lights up when it meets grass; it burns when it is fed with wood. Dampness is able to subdue it; water is able to extinguish it. Hence to break it and to attack it [ways are employed that] confront its

What is firm, cut it;
what has settled, remove it.[367]
What is fatigued, warm it;
what is knotted, disperse it.

What stays in place, attack it.
What is dry, make it soggy.
What is tense, relax it;
what has dispersed, contract it.
What is injured, warm it;[368]
what is idle, move it;
what is scared, calm it.[369]
Raise it,[370] down it;[371]
rub it,[372] wash it;

---

nature. A severe disease is like a dragon fire. When it meets with dampness, it blazes; when it is confronted with water, it roars. If anyone who does not know its nature [attempts] to break its [force] with water or dampness, this will be only sufficient to have its light rise to heaven. Those who know its nature, they will act contrary to the normal principle. They will use fire to subdue it and the burning will be extinguished as a result. To 'confront it' is to say: to employ cold to attack heat, to employ heat to attack cold. To 'conform to it' is to say: by attacking with cold or heat, even though [the nature of the drugs] conforms with/parallels the nature [of the disease], their applications are not necessarily always identical. As the text says further down: 'To confront [the disease] is a regular treatment; to conform to [it] is a treatment contrary to what is normal. [To decide whether] to conform a little or to conform a lot, one [should] see which issue [is at hand].'" Beijing zhongyi xueyuan et al./114: "*Su wen* 5 says: 'Doubled cold turns into heat; doubled heat turns into cold.' In the present statement, 'severe' refers to a false appearance of some serious signs of a disease. 'Conform to them' is: [design your treatment] by conforming with these false appearances. For instance, if extreme cold turns into heat, then cold drugs are added to assist the heat drugs [in a prescription]. If extreme heat turns into cold, then heat drugs are added to assist the cold drugs."

367 *Gu dian yi zhu xuan* bianxiezu /58: "A reference to a treatment designed to remove any evil that has intruded from outside."

368 Zhang Zhicong: "To 'warm' is to 'supplement' because supplementing drugs are often sweet and warming, while draining drugs are often bitter and cold."

369 Zhang Jiebin: "平之 is 安之, 'pacify it.'"

370 Zhang Jiebin: " 'Raise it' is: cause it to be spit out."

371 *Gu dian yi zhu xuan* bianxiezu /58: " 'Down it' refers to treatments causing diarrhea."

372 502/45: "摩之 refers to 藥摩法, the 'method of rubbing drugs into the skin.' This method was first mentioned in the *Wu shi er bing fang* of the Mawangdui manuscripts. It is also recommended in the Han-dynasty bamboo slips of Wuwei, the *Jin*

strike it,³⁷³ rob it;
open it, effuse it.

Adaptation to the issue [at hand] is the starting point [of any treatment]."

74-541-8
[Huang] Di:
"What does that mean: 'oppose' and 'conform?'"

Qi Bo:
"To oppose [a disease] is a normal treatment;
to conform [to it] is a treatment contrary [to normal].
[A decision whether] to conform a little or to conform a lot
[should be based on] an assessment of the issue [at hand]."³⁷⁴

74-541-9
[Huang] Di:
"A 'treatment contrary [to normal],' what does that mean?"

Qi Bo:
"If the cause was heat, one employs cold [to treat it];
if the cause was cold, one employs heat [to treat it.³⁷⁵

---

gui yao lue, the *Zhou hou bei ji fang*, the *Qian jin yao fang*, the *Wai tai bi yao*, and others. When Zhang Jiebin and others explain 摩之 as 'massage,' then this does not reflect the meaning of the classic in its entirety."

373 *Gu dian yi zhu xuan* bianxiezu /58: "薄 is 搏, in the sense of 搏擊, 'to attack.'"

374 Wang Bing: "從少 is to say: one [drug in a prescription] is identical [with the nature of the disease to be treated], two differ [from it]. 從多 is to say: two [drugs in a prescription] are identical [with the nature of the disease to be treated], three differ [from it]. That is to say, if [a prescription corresponds to the nature of a disease] entirely, that is an extraordinary composition."

375 Ma Shi: "When cold is treated with heat, which is assisted by cold drugs, then this is 熱因寒用. When heat is treated with cold, which is assisted by heat drugs, then this is 寒因熱用." Fang Yaozhong: "熱因寒用 should be 熱因熱用, 'when heat is used in case of heat,' 寒因熱用 should be 寒因寒用, 'when cold is used because of cold.'" *Gu dian yi zhu xuan* bianxiezu /60: "To use drugs of hot nature to treat cold illnesses and to consume these drugs [as a decoction that has] cooled, or to use drugs of hot nature to treat cold illnesses and to assist with drugs of cold [nature], all these [patterns] belong to 熱因寒用. To use drugs of cold nature to treat heat illnesses and to consume these drugs as a warm [decoction], or to use drugs of cold nature to treat heat illnesses and to assist with drugs of heat [nature], all these [patterns] belong to 寒因熱用." For a detailed discussion see 2471/13.

If the cause was obstruction, obstructing [drugs] are employed [to treat it];[376]
if the cause was [uncontrolled] passage, [drugs] opening passages are employed
[to treat it].[377]

It is essential to put aside what [a therapy normally] masters and
to pay prime attention to its cause.[378]

In view of their beginning [diseases and treatment are] identical,
in view of their final [symptoms, diseases and treatment] differ.

[This way],
it is possible to break up accumulations; and
it is possible to destruct what is firm.
It is possible to harmonize the qi; and
it is possible to achieve a definite cure."

74-542-3
[Huang] Di:
"Good!
If [a disease] was contracted even though the [patient's] qi was regulated, how
[to treat that]?"[379]

---

376 Beijing zhongyi xueyuan et al./117: "That is, even though there are signs of abdominal fullness, prescriptions that supplement are employed nevertheless. Abdominal
fullness may be associated with repletion or depletion. If abdominal fullness of the depletion type is not treated with warm and supplementing prescriptions but with draining patterns, the result may be only temporary relief. Once the [effects of the] drugs
have subsided, the abdominal fullness will continue as before." *Gu dian yi zhu xuan*
bianxiezu /60: "For example, in case of abdominal distension and fullness caused by qi
depletion, or of dysmenorrhea caused by blood depletion, 'obstructing' therapy patterns
should be employed nevertheless, i.e., supplementing qi and supplementing blood."

377 Beijing zhongyi xueyuan et al./117: "That is, even though there are signs of diarrhea, drugs causing diarrhea are employed nevertheless. When heat evil has accumulated in the intestines, it is drained by [drugs] stimulating a passage downward. As
soon as the heat has left with cold drugs draining it downward, the diarrhea comes
to an end." *Gu dian yi zhu xuan* bianxiezu /60: "For example, [uterine] flooding and
spotting caused by stagnating blood are to be treated by patterns transforming sta-
sis."

378 Zhang Jiebin: "伏其所主 is: check the root of the disease. 先其所因 is: search for
the origin of the disease." Wan Lanqing et al./50: "伏 is 制伏, 'to check,' 'to subdue.' 主
refers to the basic nature of a disease. 因 is the cause of a disease."

379 Zhang Jiebin: "That is to say: if the qi [of a person] is regulated and [that person]
contracts a disease nevertheless."

Qi Bo:
"Oppose the [disease] and conform to it.
While opposing it, conform to it.
While conforming to it, oppose it.[380]

To open [the flow of] the qi to regulate it,
this is the Way of this."

74-543-1
[Huang] Di:
"Good!
When a disease proceeds to the center or to the exterior, how [to treat that]?"

Qi Bo:
"[In case of] those [diseases] proceeding from the interior to the exterior, regulate the [patient's] interior.
[In case of] those [diseases] proceeding from the exterior to the interior, treat
the [patient's] exterior.

[In case of] those proceeding from the interior to the exterior and if they
abound in the exterior, the [patient's] interior is to be regulated first and his
exterior is to be treated afterwards.
[In case of] those proceeding from the exterior to the interior and if they
abound in the interior, the [patient's] exterior is to be regulated first and his
interior is to be regulated afterwards.[381]

If [there are diseases in the] center and in the exterior which do not link up
with each other, then a treatment is to be directed at the main disease."[382]

[Huang] Di:
"Good!
Revenge taken by fire and heat [results in]
an aversion to cold and a development of fever
resembling malaria.

---

380 Wang Bing: " 'To oppose is to say: to oppose the disease qi with a regular treatment. 'To conform to' is to say: to go along with the qi of the disease by applying a
treatment contrary to normal."

381 Wang Bing: "That is to say: always eliminate the root first and then cut its
branches."

382 Wang Bing: "If diseases in the center and in the exterior do not link up with each
other, this is because each is a disease of its own."

Sometimes it breaks out every day,
sometimes it breaks out after skipping several days,
what is the reason?"³⁸³

Qi Bo:
"The qi of domination and revenge,
at the time they meet,
they differ in their quantities

When the yin qi is plentiful while there is only a little yang qi, then the days
when [the fever] breaks out are distant from each other.
When the yang qi is plentiful while there is only a little yin qi, then the days
when [the fever] breaks out are close to each other.

As for this mutual battling of the dominant [qi] and of the revenge [qi] and
the terms of [their] abundance and weakness,
[the outbreaks of] malaria, too, follow the same law."³⁸⁴

74-543-9
[Huang] Di:
"The discourse states:
'Treat the cold with heat;
treat the heat with cold;'
and the prescription gentlemen are unable to leave this marking line and alter
its Way.³⁸⁵

[However,] when someone who has a heat disease is [given] cold [drugs] with
the effect that [further] heat [is generated], or
when someone who has a cold disease is given] heating [drugs] with the effect
that [further] cold [is generated],
[then the old and the new heat or cold] are both present
and a new disease emerges in addition.
How to treat this?"³⁸⁶

---

383 Zhang Zhicong: " 'Fire heat' is: [The patient] has fallen ill because of fire heat.
Now, fire heat harms the qi. That is to say, the disease is in the qi, not in the conduits."

384 2753/63: "薄 is identical to 搏, 'to strike against.' "

385 In contrast, Wang Shaozeng/36-37: "Physicians must not abandon this principle
and resort to another pattern."

386 Wang Bing: "That is to say, the disease is treated but fails to weaken or to retreat.
To the contrary, because the drugs are cold or hot, they subsequently generate new

74-543-12
Qi Bo:
"Whenever cold [is employed for treating heat] but the heat [continues nevertheless], seize it from the yin;

whenever heat [is employed for treating cold] but the cold [continues], seize it from the yang."

That is the so-called 'search for its association.' "387

74-544-1
[Huang] Di:
"Good!

If [a patient] consumes [drugs] of cold [nature] and contrary [to what might be expected] turns hot, or

if [a patient] consumes [drugs] of hot [nature] and contrary [to what might be

---

illnesses of cold or heat. It also happens that [the old illness] is brought to a halt and then breaks out again. Or that [the disease] vanishes as long as the [effects of the] drugs are present and that it breaks out again as soon as the [effects of the] drugs have vanished." Zhang Jiebin: "寒之而熱 is to say: to treat heat with cold, but the heat remains the same as before [the treatment]. .. That is, the old heat is still present and new cold is generated."

387 Wang Bing: "That is to say: support the source of the fire to diminish the darkness of yin; strengthen the generation of water to restrain the light of yang. Hence [the text] states: 'search for its association.' Now, crude practitioners whose knowledge is shallow and has not reached any deaper refinement yet, they resort to heat to attack cold, or they resort to cold to treat heat. Before the heat is eliminated, a cold disease emerges already. They intensify their attacks with cold day after day and the heat disease emerges again. While the heat emerges, the cold is still present in the center. Cold has been generated but the heat in the exterior has not been removed. If [in such a situation a pratitioner] intends to attack the cold he [only] fears that the heat does not advance; if he intends to treat the heat, then his only concern is that the cold might stop on its way. [Cold and heat] move forward and retreat; a battle is waged causing utmost danger. How could they know that the source of the depots and palaces is ruled by cold, heat, warmth, and coolness [simultaneously]? .. Hence sometimes heat is treated with heat and cold is treated with cold. [This way,] a myriad cases treated are a myriad cases cured. Alas, when people die, why is this blamed on fate and not on the ignorance of prescription masters who have killed them?" Zhang Zhicong: "If [heat is] treated with cold but fails to turn cold, this is because the true yin [qi] is present insufficiently. If [cold is] treated with heat but fails to turn hot, this is because the true yang [qi] is present insufficiently. Hence, if the disease is not resolved despite a long-term use of cold or heat, illnesses of disproportionate domination [of cold or heat] will be generated contrary [to one's intentions]. Hence it is essential 'to search for its associations' to weaken a [disease]. 'Take it from the yin, take it from the yang' is to say: supplement the yin [qi], or supplement the yang [qi]."

expected] turns cold,
what is the reason of this?"

Qi Bo:
"Because the treatment focussed on the flourishing qi
[the result] was contrary [to expectations]."388

74-544-3
[Huang] Di:
"If the treatment had not focussed on the flourishing [qi] and such [a result
had occurred nevertheless], why was this?"

Qi Bo:
"An encompassing question, indeed!

---

388 Wang Bing: "A strike against the flourishing qi [only serves] to strengthen its
manifestation." Zhang Jiebin: "治其旺氣 is to say: a disease may be associated with
yin or yang [qi]; a qi [causing a disease] may be weak or strong. A treatment that is not
based on an understanding of what is weak and what is strong, will lead, contrary to
expectations, to a more severe [disease]. For example, in a situation where the yang [qi]
abounds while the yin [qi] is weak, the yin [qi] is depleted and the fire is strong. If this
is treated without a knowledge that a supplementation of yin is to be accompanied by
yang and if only [substances of] bitter [flavor] and cold [qi] are employed to treat the
strength of the fire, how could it be known that bitter [flavor] and cold [qi] descend
[in the body] and that by descending they contribute to the loss of yin [qi]! The more
the yin [qi] is lost, the more the fire abounds. Hence when [a patient] consumes cold
[qi] and turns hot nevertheless, the reason is that it is not permissible in a state of yin
depletion to cause a descent [in the body]. Also, in a situation where the yang [qi] is
weak while the yin [qi] abounds, the [yang] qi is weak and cold is generated. If this is
treated without a knowledge that the yang [qi] is to be supplemented to diminish the
yin [qi] and if only [substances of] acrid [flavor] and warm [qi] are employed to treat
the strength of the yin [qi], how could it be known that acrid [flavor] and warm [qi]
mostly serve to cause dispersion. Dispersion, however, contributes to a loss of yang
[qi]. The more yang [qi] is lost, the more severe turns the cold. Hence when [a patient]
consumes heat [qi] and turns cold nevertheless, the reason is that in a state of yang
depletion it is not permissible to cause a dispersion. In all these cases, the treatment
was directed only against the most flourishing qi; hence the disease, contrary to what
was expected, turned out as [described] here." Wu Kun: "Spring is [associated with
the qi of] wood; summer is [associated with the qi of] fire; autumn is [associated with
the qi of] metal; winter is [associated with the qi of] water. If one intends to move
against any of these [qi] at a time when they flourish, that is to oppose heaven. That
is, in spring it is impossible to attempt to keep the [qi of] wood from being warm; in
summer it is impossible to attempt to keep the [qi of] fire from being hot; in autumn
it is impossible to attempt to keep the [qi of] metal from being cool; and in winter it
is impossible to attempt to keep the [qi of] water from being cold."

This was not a treatment based on the associations of the five flavors.
Now,
the five flavors enter the stomach, [whence]
each of them turns to its preferred [depot].

Hence
sour [flavor] first enters the liver;[389]
bitter [flavor] first enters the heart;
sweet [flavor] first enters the spleen;
acrid [flavor] first enters the lung;
salty [flavor] first enters the kidneys.

If [one flavor is consumed] over an extended period, thereby increasing [its
particular] qi,
this is a regularity in the transformation of things.[390]

If this increase of qi continues over an extended period,
this is the origin of early death."

74-545-1
[Huang] Di:
"Good!
When prescriptions are composed as rulers and ministers, what does that
mean?"

Qi Bo:
"[The drug] which rules the disease is called 'ruler.'
[The drug] which assists the ruler is called 'minister.'
[The drugs] which respond to the minister are called 'messengers.'
This has nothing to do with the three ranks [of drugs as categorized] in the
upper, [middle], and lower [ranks]."[391]

---

389 Gao Shishi exchanged 攻 for 故, 'hence.' 2767/38: "攻 is a mistake for 故."

390 See *Zhuang zi*, ch.13 Tian dao 天道 and 15 Ke yi 刻意, for a usage of 物化 in
the sense of "to die" (Chen Guying p.374 and 435). Wang Bing: "If the increase of [a
particular qi] continues over many years, the qi of [the associated] depot will be unilaterally dominant. When a qi is unilaterally dominant, it will be cut off unilaterally.
Once [the qi of] a depot has been cut off unilaterally, sudden death results. Hence [the
text] says: 'if the increase of qi continues over an extended period, this is the origin of
early death.'"

391 Cheng Shide et al.: "This is a reference to the three ranks, [i.e.,] upper, middle,
and lower [rank], in the *Shen nong ben jing*."

74-545-2
[Huang] Di:
" 'Three ranks,' what does that mean?"

Qi Bo:
"They serve to clarify the differences and parallels between the good and bad
[nature of drugs]."392

[Huang] Di:
"Good!
When a disease is in the center or in the exterior, how is that?"

Qi Bo:
"To establish a [therapeutic] prescription to regulate the qi,
it is necessary to distinguish yin and yang and
to settle [the qi in] the center and the exterior, so that
each keeps its native place.

When a [disease] is in the interior, treat it in the interior;
when a [disease] is in the exterior, treat it in the exterior.
When it is feeble, regulate it.

When it is more [serious], balance it.
When it abounds, remove it.
[Let the patient] sweat it, purge it.

[Regardless of whether a disease was caused by] cold, hot, warm, or cool [qi],
weaken it through what it is associated with,
act in accordance with what benefits it.393

If the Way is carefully observed in accordance with the law [just outlined],
a myriad successes are achieved in a myriad [cases] taken up.
Qi and blood will assume a proper balance and
the mandate of heaven will last long."

74-546-1
[Huang] Di:
"Good!"

---

392 Zhang Zhicong: "That is to say, [they serve] to differentiate between those that
are toxic and others that are not."

393 Gao Jiwu/253: "攸 is 所, 'that which'; 利 is 宜, 'suitable.'"

Chapter 75[1]
Discourse on Making Known the Perfect Teachings[2]

75-547-2
Huang Di sat in the Hall of Light.[3]
He summoned Lei Gong and asked him:
"Do you know the Way of medicine?"

Lei Gong responded:
"When reciting [the texts, I] am not yet[4] able to explain [them].
When explaining [them, I] am not yet able to differentiate [their contents].
When differentiating their [contents, I] am not yet able to understand [them].
When understanding [them, I] am not yet able to elucidate [them].[5]

---

1 2078/20: "The present *Su wen* 75 was the second half of a treatise named 四時病
類論, "On Types of Disease [Associated with] the Four Seasons" in the Quan Yuanqi
edition. The first half appears now in *Su wen* 79."

2 Wu Kun: "著 is 明, 'to clarify.' The teachings of the sages are called 至教, 'perfect
teachings.' Because Huang Di was revered as sage the title of this treatise is 'To make
known the perfect teachings [of the sages].'"

3 Wang Bing: "明堂 is the palace where political decisions were made known. It had
eight windows and four doors; it was round above and square below, located in the
South of the capital. Hence, it was called 'Hall of Light.' Now, since the great sage
aimed his thoughts at bringing to an end the suffering of people and because he felt
pity with them for their plight, he called Lei Gong and asked him for the Way of sav-
ing lives." See also *Su wen* 67, note 2 and 3.

4 Several editions, including the *Tai Su*, 附篇 and the *Lei jing* 13, have 頗, "a
little," instead of 未, "not yet." *TPYL* has 不. 2268 lists 頗 as one of the erroneous
characters in current editions of the *Su wen*. The evidence is contextual. Zhang Jiebin:
"頗能解 is 粗解其義, 'roughly explain its meaning.'"

5 Wang Bing: "He has not fully penetrated yet the miraculous operations of the essential subtleties [of the Way]." Lin Yi et al.: "Yang Shangshan commented: 'To
practice the Way implies five [stages]: First, to recite; second, to explain; third, to differentiate; fourth, to understand; fifth, to demonstrate.'" The terms 誦, "to recite," 解,
"to explain," 別, "to differentiate," 明, "to understand," and 彰, "to manifest," may refer
to a method of learning generally applied in Chinese antiquity (2332/35). "Recitation"
is reading aloud, with the aim of memorizing a text. "To explain" may refer to the
ability of a student to explain what he has learned (252/38), but it may also refer to
the stage, after memorizing the texts, where he requires explanations from his teacher
(2332/25). In this case, the statement would have to be read as "I have recited (the
text) without being able to receive explanations yet." "To differentiate" appears to refer

[My knowledge] is sufficient to treat the common officials;
it is insufficient to treat princes and kings.[6]

75-547-5
I should like to be taught to determine the measures of heaven,[7] and
to match them with the [varying] yin and yang [qi] of the four seasons.[8]

[I should like] to differentiate the light of the stars and of sun and moon,
to elucidate the art of the classics, to contribute to the enlightenment of later
generations, and
<of former times, they shall participate [in the knowledge of] Shen Nong>
to make known the perfect teachings resembling [the teachings][9] of the two
August ones."[10]

---

to the approach mentioned in *Su wen* 76, i.e., to distinguish between what is similar
and what is not. 252/39: " 'To differentiate' is one level higher than 'to explain' in the
hierarchy of learning." "To understand" refers here to a comprehensive penetration of
a field of learning. "To manifest," finally, is to make full use of the abilities one has
acquired.

6 Wang Bing: "[Lei] Gong did not dare to praise himself for his mastering of the
Way. However, the main indications in the treatment of commoners and of those who
consume meat are different, indeed." Zhang Jiebin: "The nature of the common officials is easy to comprehend. The sentiments of princes and kings are difficult to assess.
Hence there is a difference."

7 Wang Bing: "樹天之度 is to say: 'high and distant do not reach limits.'" We
identify 樹 here in the sense of "to establish," in parallel to the use of the term 正, "to
determine" in *Su wen* 9: 所以正天之度, "that by which to determine the measures
of heaven." Gao Shishi and other Chinese commentators have seen a relationship
between the term 樹 and the ancient Chinese method of measuring the course of the
year by planting a vertical stick into the earth and by following the varying length and
circular movement of its shadow. (Cheng Shide et al. 468)

8 Wang Bing: "四時陰陽合之 is to say: 'to follow the sequence of the qi [in the
course of the seasons].'"

9 Wang Bing: "[Lei] Gong wished to make known the patterns of the classics and to
penetrate [the wisdom of] Shen Nong, to let future generations realize it. He suspect-
ed (疑) it represented the teachings of the two August ones." In contrast, Lin Yi et al.:
"The Quan Yuanqi edition and the *Tai su* have 擬, 'to resemble,' instead of 疑." Qian
Chaochen-88/150 regards 擬 as the original and correct character. See also 1978/48,
2520/51, Qian Chaochen-88/150 and 916/53 with a passage from the *Li ji* 禮記, Yan
yi 燕義, where 疑 appears to have been used in the sense of 擬.

10 i.e., Shen Nong and Fu Xi.

75-547-7
[Huang] Di:
"Good!
Do not miss this!¹¹

All this [concerns] the correspondences in the transportation [of qi] among
yin and yang, exterior and interior, above and below, as well as female and male
[regions].¹²

And [to know] the Way is
to know the line patterns in heaven above,
to know the structures of the earth below, and
to know the human affairs in the center.¹³
It can last long.
If taught to the common people,
it will surely not leave any uncertainties and [cause no] dangers.¹⁴

The chapters of the discourses on the Way of medicine,
they can be transmitted to later generations and
they can be regarded as a treasure."¹⁵

Lei Gong:
"Please, teach me the Way.
When reciting [the text] apply explanations."¹⁶

---

11 2568/49 identifies the final 之 as merely a particle employed to express a strong
sentiment. In this case the statement should read: "Good! Certainly not wrong!" Gao
Jiwu/342: " 'Do not forget!' Others: 'Do not lose!'"

12 This statement is identical with a wording in *Su wen* 4 (25-8).

13 See *Su wen* 05-45-3 for an identical wording, presented there, however, as a
quotation from an *Upper Classic*, a text no longer traceable today.

14 Wang Niansun 王念孫 in his *Du shu za zhi* 讀書雜志 quotes the *Shi Ji* 史記
passage "良工取之 拙者疑殆", and states: "This character 殆 is not the 殆 of 危殆,
'danger.' This 殆 has the meaning of 疑, too. In ancient times, authors loved to express
things by doubled expressions. Hence, the meaning here is 'uncertain,' 'doubtful,' 'confused.'"

15 Wang Bing: "Because of their brilliant shine."

16 Wang Bing: "誦 is also [used in the sense of] 諭, 'instructions.' 諷誦, 'to read
aloud,' is the [way] of comparing what is closely related and of offering an analysis
of it."

[Huang] Di:
"You have not listened to the transmission of the yin yang [doctrine]?"[17]

[Lei Gong]:
"I'm not familiar with it."

75-548-1
[Huang Di]:
"Now,
the [qi] in the three yang [conduits], heaven is [responsible for their] operation.[18]
When upward and downward movements lack regularity,
they unite and disease arrives.
Onesidedness harms yin and yang."[19]

Lei Gong:
" 'The [qi] in the three yang [conduits] have nothing to match them,'[20]
Please, may I hear an explanation of this [statement]?"

75-548-3
[Huang] Di:
" 'The [qi] in the three yang [conduits] arrive alone' is:
the [qi] in the three yang [conduits] arrive merged.[21]

---

17 The 1983 *Su wen* edition by Renmin weisheng chubanshe identifies 陰陽傳 as a title of an ancient text (no text of this title is known today). We do not follow this suggestion, because 傳 does not necessarily indicate a written transmission.

18 Wang Bing: "天為業 is to say: the three yang qi move and reside in the upper part of the human body. *Yin yang chuan* is the title of an ancient text." Lin Yi et al.: "The *Tai su* has 太, 'great,' instead of 天, 'heaven'."

19 Wang Bing: "上下無常 is to say, the qi moves disorderly and has no fixed location above or below. 合而病至 is to say, the [qi] in the three yang [conduits] of hand and foot unite and cause a disease to arrive. When the yang (qi) arrive merged, the essence qi is weak. Hence, a onesided [presence of yang qi] harms the operations of yin and yang [qi]." Gao Shishi: "三陽, 'third yang', is the major yang."

20 Wang Bing: "莫當 is to say: the [yang] qi arrive merged and do not fulfill the functions expected of them."

21 Wang Bing: "并至 is to say, the three yang qi of the hand and the three yang qi of the feet merge and arrive together."

They arrive merged like wind and rain.[22]
Above this causes peak illness;
below this causes drip disease.[23]

Outside there is no [sign enabling a] prognosis;
inside there is nothing normal.
They do not meet the normal arrangements.
Diagnosis has no [way to differentiate] rise and descent.
It is by means of the written records that [one can] differentiate."[24]

75-548-5
Lei Gong:
"In performing treatments, [I, your] subject, rarely achieve a healing.
[Please,] explain the meaning [of the records] and [my uncertainties] will end."[25]

[Huang] Di:
"The [merged qi of all] three yang [conduits], that is the extreme yang.[26]
When they have accumulated and merged, then this causes fright.

---

22 Wang Bing: " 'They arrive merged like wind and rain' is to say: their proportions are not fixed."

23 Wang Bing: "漏: blood and pus appear." *Jia yi jing* 4 has 漏血病, "dripping blood disease." Lin Yi et al.: "Yang Shangshan states: 'Drip disease is a disease of a dripping bladder. Stools and urine pass frequently and cannot be stopped.'"

24 Wang Bing: "That is to say, the three yang arrive merged; their rise and descent is irregular. Outside there is no complexion permitting a prognosis; inside there is no proper regularity. The times when the [three yang qi] arrive do not meet the standard arrangement of the [flow through the] conduit vessels. Because the signs of the disease are irregular in that they may appear above or below, they are to be judged by means of written records to enable their differentiation." Ma Shi: "書 refers to the 'Yin Yang Records' mentioned above."

25 Wang Bing: "Lei Gong said that his therapeutic successes are few and he asked [Huang Di] to inform him of the deepest meanings [of healing], thereby to bring to an end the confusion in his heart. 已 stands for 止, 'to bring to an end.' That is to say, after receiving the teaching [by Huang Di], the confusion in [Lei Gong's] heart will come to an end." Sun Yirang: "When Wang Bing read this sentence as 臣治疏愈, this was not the meaning of the classic. The three characters 臣治疏 should be read as one sentence; the five characters 愈說意而已 constitute another sentence. 愈 is another writing of 愉. .. It should be read here as 偷, 'improper,' 'foolish.' .. Hence Lei Gong said: When [I, your] subject treat [diseases], my art is unrefined. All I do is foolishly speak about my intention of healing and that is it." Wang Hongtu et al./158 agrees. Another reading of 而已 might be: "only." In the sense of "Just explain to me the basic meaning."

26 Wang Bing: "The six yang merge, hence this is an extremely (至) abundant yang."

The disease arises [like] swift wind;
it arrives like rolling thunder.²⁷
The nine orifices are all obstructed;
yang qi gushes forth and overflows.
The throat region dries up and the throat is obstructed.

When the [yang qi] merge in the yin [region],
then there is upward and downward movement, without regularity.
When [the yang qi] weakens it causes intestinal flush.²⁸

That is called: the [qi] in the three yang [conduits] confront the heart.
When [the patients] sit they cannot rise;
[only] when they lie down, then their body [feels] intact.²⁹

[These are] diseases of the [qi] in the three yang [conduits].³⁰

---

27 Wang Bing: "積 stands for 重, 'heavy,' 'double.' That is to say, the six yang merge in double intensity; they are present in vast abundance; nothing could impede them. The yang [qi] gush forth and overflow, with no banks stopping them. Hence, the throat is dried up and the orifices are blocked."

28 Wang Bing: "陰 stands for 藏, 'depot.' When the yang [qi] collects in the depots, this causes disease. Here, too, one diagnoses an upwards and downwards movement without permanence, or fixed location. When it is in the lower part, stools and urine pass frequently and are red and white."

29 Wang Bing: "The foot major yang vessel passes along the top of the shoulder to the lower back. Hence, [patients] sit and cannot rise, only when they lie down their body feels intact. The reason is, when one rises, the yang is abundant and drums. Hence, [patients] often desire to lie down. When they lie down, the conduit qi is well distributed and the body feels intact." In contrast, Zhang Jiebin: "All cases where one suffers from an evil that has moved directly to the heart and hence sits and cannot rise, rises and cannot lie down, then this means that the entire body is affected by a disease of the three yang," and "third yang evils often enter [the body] from the outside; hence those who specialize in harm caused by cold often encounter pathoconditions where [the evil] has moved directly to the heart and [the patients] cannot rise or lie down." Lin Yi et al.: "The *Jia yi jing* has 身重 instead of 身全." The *Jia yi jing* does not have the character 便. Yang Shangshan: "The four limbs have lost their functions; regardless of whether one sits or lies, the body [feels] heavy."

30 Li Guoqing/252: Ma Shi, Zhang Jiebin, Zhang Zhicong suggest a different punctuation and separate between 臥者 and 便身. Ma Shi exchanged 全 by 患, "to suffer." Hence Ma Shi: "One sits and cannot rise; one rises and cannot lie down. This is just that someone suffers from a third yang disease."

75-549-1
Also,
to know the world,
how to differentiate yin and yang [qi] as they correspond to the four seasons, and
[how to] match them with the five agents?"³¹

Lei Gong:
"[I can] not differentiate [the meanings of] the word yang;
[I] do not [even] understand the word yin.

Please raise [me from ignorance] by giving me explanations.
[I should] consider them as the perfect Way."³²

75-549-3
[Huang] Di:
"When you receive the transmitted [teaching] and when you do not know how to combine it with the perfect Way, you will be confused by the teachings of the masters.³³

[I] have instructed you in the essentials of the perfect Way.
When a disease harms the five depots,
sinews and bones will wane as a result.
If you do not understand and if you cannot differentiate the words,
then in the present age the major learning has come to an end.³⁴

---

31 Lin Yi et al.: "The Quan Yuanqi edition has the text beginning with 且以知 and ending with 事不殷 as a separate treatise."

32 Wang Bing: "[Huang] Di has not bestowed [Lei Gong] with the most fundamental knowledge yet. Hence, [Lei Gong] asks him again."

33 Wang Bing: "In case the essentials of the [Way] are not known, [these incomplete teachings] will spread without end. When later generations hand their practice on from one to the next, they will be ever more distant from the sages. Students will develop patterns out of their own experiences and they will be confused by their teachers' instructions."

34 Wang Bing: "That is to say, when [you] have no understanding yet and cannot distinguish [the therapeutic principles] in view of serious diseases, when it comes to healing light diseases, how could you have a complete knowledge? If this way there is no knowledge and understanding, then the Way of the major learning in the world comes to an end." Mori interprets 世主 as "ruler of the world;" hence: "in this case the learning of the ruler of the world is exhausted." In Mori's reading, Huang Di identifies himself as "ruler of the world", and the meaning of his statement is "I have taught you in vain; I have nothing else to say."

When the kidneys are about to be cut off [from the movement of qi, this leads to] distress;
{the distress [sets in] in the evening.}[35]
When a natural approach fails to appear,
the human affairs cannot flourish."[36]

35 The *Tai su* has 腎且絕死死日暮, "When the kidneys are cut off [from the movement of qi, the patient] dies. Death occurs in the evening."Zhang Zhicong:"惋惋 stands for 驚嘆, 'to wonder,''be startled.'" 915/58: "惋惋 stands for 'mournful,''grieved.'"

36 Wang Bing: "[Huang Di] raises an issue in connection with the depots that is easily understandable. When the [movement in the] vessels of the kidneys is interrupted, then the spirit of the heart is luminous inside and the sinews, the bones, the vessels, and the flesh experience soreness and emptiness at day's end. 暮 is 晚, 'late.' If, following this example, the qi of all the depots are diminished and fail to appear, then the human affairs are paralysed and do no longer flourish. This situation has come about because of an insufficiency of [qi in] kidneys, not because of an injury." The eight characters 從容不出人事不殷 may be an editorial addition meant both as a conclusion of the preceding statement and as an introduction to the notion of 從容 that shall play a more significant role in the subsequent treatises. 殷 was used by *Zhuang zi* 莊子, Shan mu 山木, in the sense of 大, "great." (See Chen Guying vol. I, p. 572/573.) Also, the *Li ji* 禮記, Zeng zi wen 曾子問, uses 殷 in the sense of "significant", "important", in connection with 事, "business", "affair": 有殷事則之君所, "in case of important affairs, go to the residence of the ruler."(See Ruan Yuan vol. II, 1397 below.) In contrast, Zhang Yizhi et al. quotes Sun Dingyi 孫鼎宜: "殷 should be 安, 'peaceful.' The two sentences beginning with 從容 describe the state of the kidneys. The kidneys prefer quietude. Hence, if a natural approach (從容) fails to appear and if the human affairs are not peaceful, a state of extreme confusion sets in."

Chapter 76
Discourse on Demonstrating a Natural Approach[1]

76-549-8

Huang Di sat leisurely.[2]

He summoned Lei Gong and asked him:

"Having been taught the art and reciting the written records,
it appears you are able
to consider a broad variety of teachings,[3]
to reach [an ability] to compare the likes,[4] and
to penetrate and become one with the structures of the Way.

Speak to me about where you excel.

---

1 Cheng Shide et al.: "示 is 示范, 'to set an example,' 'to demonstrate.'" Ma Shi: "從容 is the title of an ancient classic. This chapter was written to elucidate its contents." In contrast, Gao Shishi: "When the sages treated diseases, they followed the laws and they guarded the standard measures. They argued about beings by analogy and they pursued the Way in a natural manner. [In the present chapter, Huang] Di demonstrated this principle to Lei Gong. Hence, the title is 示從容, 'to demonstrate a natural approach [in the application of the Way].'" The earliest known appearance of the term 從容 is in *Zhuang zi* 莊子, chapter 11 在宥 and 17 秋水. (See Chen Guying p. 299 and 457.) There it carries the meaning of "relaxed, natural behavior". In the present chapter we interpret its usage in the sense of "natural approach" in that it is contrasted, by Huang Di, with its opposite, i.e., an approach to healing entirely based on fixed patterns formulated in the classic texts. Hence, the current chapter bears witness of an awareness of the potential conflict in medicine between an understanding and a treatment of disease based on formularized notions on the one hand and one guided by pragmatism and the empirically guided approach of an expert physician on the other hand.

2 Mori: "燕坐 is identical with 燕居. The *Lun yu* 論語 has 子之燕居, 申申如也, '.. in a relaxed, self-possessed way.'" 916/53: "燕 stands for 晏, 'quiet.'" Zhang Yizhi et al.: "The *Han shu* 漢書, Cai Yi zhuan 蔡義傳 has 愿賜清間之燕. The commentary states: 安息也. Hence, 燕坐 is 安坐, 'to sit quietly.'"

3 Wang Qi: "雜學 is scholarship apart from medicine."

4 Zhang Jiebin: "比類 means 'to compare what is different and to differentiate among what is alike in order to assess the nature of a disease.'" Ma Shi: "The preceding and the following chapters have [the term] 比類; it belongs to an ancient book title. Its actual meaning, though, is 比方相類, 'to classify through comparison.'" Zhang Yizhi et al.: "比方相類 is 觸類旁通, 'to comprehend by analogy.'" Gu Guangguang: "比類 is an ancient book title." Mori: "於 is identical with 為. In ancient records, 於 was frequently written as 為." On the concept of 類 in the *Su wen* see 2800/28 and 1513/4.

The five depots and the six palaces,
the gallbladder, the stomach, the large and the small intestines,
the spleen, the uterus, and the urinary bladder,
the brain, the marrow, the snivel, and the saliva,
weeping, sadness, and grief, as well as
the paths where the water moves,[5]
all these together form the basis of human life.

When mistakes are committed in treating them,[6]
it is your obligation to understand them!
[Only then] you will be able to achieve a success in all [cases you treat].
If you are unable to have this knowledge,
you will incite the grudge of everyone."[7]

Lei Gong:
"[I, your] subject, request [to state the following.]

I have recited the upper and the lower chapters of the *Vessel Classic*[8] very
many times and
I differentiate what is different[9] and I compare the likes.
Still, I am not yet able to achieve a success in all [cases I treat].
Also, how could [my learning] suffice to understand them?"

---

5 Gao Shishi: "The five depots are responsible for the storing of essence. Hence,
[the text] speaks of 'water.'" Zhang Jiebin: " 'Water' refers to the five liquids. This is a
reference to the 14 origins [of the paths] of blood and qi from gallbladder and stomach downwards. Man relies on them for his life. If they are not understood, [therapeu-
tic] activities will result in many mistakes."

6 In contrast, Wang Bing reads the four characters 治之過失 as a final statement
linked to the preceding argument: According to Wang Bing, "those who treated diseases in antiquity considered [treating these palaces] a mistake." Zhang Jiebin: "A
treatment in excess of the [requirements of a] disease, is called 過, 'excess'; a treatment
insufficient vis-a-vis the [requirements of a] disease, is called 失, 'miss.'" The *Li ji* 禮
記, Qiu guan 秋官, Si ci 司刺, has: 一宥曰不識, 二宥曰過失, 三宥曰遺忘, "The
first case for leniency is ignorance, the second case for leniency is [an unintentional]
mistake, the third case for leniency is forgetfulness."

7 Wang Bing: "When the activities of those who are ignorant harm a life, people
will hear discussions and criticisms [of such cases] and as a result they will often develop feelings of deepseated resentments."

8 Gao Shishi: "The *Vessel Classic* (脈經) is the *Ling shu*."

9 2332/35 sees this "differentiation" as one of the five levels in the acquisition of
knowledge referred to in *Su wen* 75.

76-550-4
[Huang] Di:
"You, attempt [to fulfill] another [task].
Provide a detailed survey of
the excesses in the five depots,
the reasons for disharmonies in the six palaces,
[the locations where] needles and [pointed] stones could cause destruction,
[the cases] where toxic drugs are appropriate and
[the situations when to use] decoctions and nourishing substances.[10]

Speak on all these conditions,
speak exhaustively in response [to my request],[11] and,
please, ask [me] about what [you] do not know."

Lei Gong:
"Liver depletion, kidney depletion, spleen depletion,

---

10 Wang Bing: "過 is 過失, 'mistake.' That is to say, [the five depots] do not display the normal signs but have generated a disease. Poisonous drugs attack the evil; nourishing substances complete the diet. [Huang Di] asked these questions to test (試) [Lei] Gong, [to find out] what he knew and what he did not know "

11 Wu Kun: "別 is to say 往時, 'formerly.'" Zhang Zhicong: "別 is to say 'no complete understanding of the heavenly Way yet.'" Tanba: "別試 is to say: [Huang Di requested Lei Gong] to try to discuss his additional knowledge (別有所通) apart from the upper and the lower chapters of the *Vessel Classic*." Lin Yi et al.: "The *Tai su* has 誠別而已 instead of 別試." 2719/8: "This sentence continues the preceding statement of 'Lei Gong states: ... How could [my learning] suffice to understand them?' Hence, Huang Di replied: 'If you are really (當真) able to distinguish (別) what is different and to compare the likes and if you do already (已) understand the excesses in the five depots, the reasons for disharmonies in the six palaces, [the locations where] needles and stones could deliver harm, [the cases] where toxic drugs are appropriate, and [the situations when to use] decoctions and nourishing substances. Speak on all these conditions, speak exhaustively in response [to my request]. If there is anything that you still do not know, or do not understand, please tell.' 誠 is 果真, 'if indeed'; 當真, 'really'; 確實, 'if really.' 別 takes up the meaning expressed in the statement above: 別異比類. With the original wording of the *Tai su*, the text made sense. When Wang Bing erroneously changed this to 別試 and when he added a comment 'Poisonous drugs attack the evil; nourishing substances complete the diet. [Huang Di] asked these questions to test (試) [Lei] Gong, [to find out] what he knew and what he did not know,' interpreting the characters too literally and without understanding, he left the original meaning entirely. To make his statement consistent he had to drop the character 別 [in his comment]. .. He may have omitted the characters 而已 because he considered them a later insertion." Zhang Yizhi et al.: "All commentators disagree on this statement; it awaits further research."

all [these conditions] let a person's body become heavy; they [cause feelings of] vexation and grievance.[12]

[Their treatment] requires an application of toxic drugs, of piercing, cauterization, and pointed stones, as well as of decoctions.

Sometimes [the disease] comes to an end;
sometimes it does not come to an end.
[I] should like to hear an explanation of this."

76-550-8
[Huang] Di:
"Sir, how can it be that while you are old in years you ask like a child?
Truly, I have put my question in a way that I have misled myself!"[13]

I have asked you about enigmatic issues;[14]
you refer to the upper and lower chapters [of the well known *Vessel Classic*] in response.
Why?

Now,
when the [movement in the vessels associated with the] spleen is depleted and near the surface,
it resembles [movements associated with] the lung.

---

12 Zhang Jiebin: "The liver controls the muscles. When the muscles have a disease, they cannot contract. The kidneys control the bones. When the bones have a disease, the movement is restricted. The spleen controls the four limbs. When the four limbs have a disease one is tired and has no strength. Hence, all these [conditions] let man's body [feel] heavy. But all these three depots are yin. When the yin is depleted, the yang is strong. Hence, [these conditions] also let man feel uneasiness and depression."

13 Wang Bing: "That is to say [the question posed by Lei Gong] did not correspond to the question [posed by Huang Di]. Because these questions did not correspond to each other, [Huang Di] stated 'I truly posed a question inviting a meaningless response myself.'" Yu Chang: "問 should be 聞, 'to hear'; [the present 問] is an erroneous repetition of the 問 further down." Zhang Yizhi et al.: "Yu Chang's interpretation of 問 as 聞 is wrong."

14 Wang Bing: "窈冥 refers to that what is invisible, i.e., the physical qi, the camp qi, and the guard qi. .. [Huang] Di stated: 'I have asked you about enigmatic issues.' However, liver depletion, kidney depletion, and spleen depletion are outlined in the Upper and Lower Chapters. Hence, [Huang] Di said: 'You refer to the Upper and Lower Chapters, why?'" Wu Kun: "窈冥 are hidden meanings that are not transmitted as statements in the literature."

When the [movement in the vessels associated with the] kidneys is minor and
at the surface,
it resembles [movements associated with] the spleen.

When the [movement in the vessels associated with the] liver is tense, in the
depth, and dispersed,
it resembles [movements associated with] the kidneys.

All these [conditions] are often confused by the practitioners.
However, with a natural approach one can grasp them.[15]

Now,
that the three depots of soil, wood, and water[16] are located closely together,
this is known by any young boy.
Why would [you] ask such a question?"[17]

Lei Gong:
"Here was a person [with a condition as follows:]
He had headache and sinew cramps.
His bones felt heavy and he was timid.
He was short of qi, [suffered from] hiccup and belching, and

---

15 Wang Bing: "When in case of a spleen depletion the [movement in the] vessels
is at the surface, then this sign makes it appear like [a disease in] the lung. When the
kidney [qi] is minor, at the surface, and rising, then these signs make it appear like [a
disease in] the spleen. When the liver [qi] is hasty, in the depth, and dispersed, then
these signs make it appear like [a disease in] the kidneys. Why is that so? Because
these three depots are located close to each other. Hence, the appearances of [the
movements in] their vessels differ and are still similar. Hence, the confusion of practitioners leads to erroneous treatments. Nevertheless, it is advisable to compare the
likes and to apply a natural approach with a quiet and relaxed mind and to grasp the
physical signs associated with these three depots. How to achieve this? Now, [when
the movement in the vessels is] at the surface and relaxed, this refers to the spleen.
When it is at the surface and short, this refers to the lung. When it is minor, at the
surface, and smooth, this refers to the heart. When it is hasty, tight and dispersed, this
refers to the liver. When it strikes in the depth and is smooth, this refers to the kidneys. Anybody who is unable to compare the likes will be greatly confused." Wu Kun:
"If one follows man's appearance and complexion to search for the nature of a disease,
one will get to it." In contrast 1789/54 and others read 從容 as "quiet," "relaxed."

16 These are spleen, liver, and kidneys.

17 Wang Bing: "The spleen is associated with the soil, the liver is associated with
the wood, the kidneys are associated with the water. These three depots are all located
below the diaphragm; they are situated close to each other."

his abdomen was full.
He was often frightened and had no desire to lie down.
From which depot did this [condition] emerge?

The [movement in the] vessels was at the surface and string[-like].
When I squeezed it, it was firm like a stone.
I do not know the explanation of this.

When I once again ask about the three depots,
it is because [I wish] to know how to compare the likes of them."¹⁸

76-551-6
[Huang] Di:
"Now,
this is what is meant by 'natural approach.'¹⁹

Now,
when [the patient] is of old age, search for [the disease] in the palaces.
When [the patient] is of young age, search for it in the conduits.
When [the patient] is in the prime of his life, search for it in the depots.²⁰

18 Zhang Jiebin: "The following [text] outlines [problems] resembling a kidney disease. When the [movement in the] vessels is at the surface it is categorized as lung
[movement]; when it resembles a string, it is categorized as liver [movement]; and
when it resembles a stone and is hard, it is categorized as a kidney [movement]. These
[conditions] are difficult to differentiate. Hence, [Lei Gong] once again asks about the
comparison and categorization of the three depots."

19 Zhang Jiebin: "He quotes from a classic, as in the following text." Wu Kun:
"[Huang] Di says: In such a case one must follow the appearance of that person and
bring it together with the nature of the disease."

20 Wang Bing: "Those old in years, they may overindulge in food. Those young
in years, they may be exhausted by being employed [by others]. Those in years of
strength, they exaggerate [sexual intercourse] in the inner [quarters], thereby wasting
and harming their essence qi. When [those young in years] are exhausted by being
employed [by others], then wind evil [settles] inside their conduits. When there is no
restraint in what one seeks, then this causes harm in the palaces. Hence, searching
for these [diseases requires] different [approaches]." Zhang Jiebin: "This statement
outlines the method of comparing what is different and of differentiating what is
alike. Those old in years often [have a disease because of] what they eat. Substances
are received [in the organism] by the six palaces. Hence, [in the old] one must search
for [diseases] in the palaces. Those young in years are careless with regard to wind and
cold and fatigue. These affect the conduits. Hence, [in the young] one must search
for [diseases] in the conduits. Those in the years of strength often indulge in sexual
desires. The essence is stored in the five depots. Hence, one must search for [diseases]

In the present case, all your words have missed [the point].
If the eight winds[21] cause what is densely compacted to boil,
the five depots waste away [as if] melting.
They transmit the evil among each other.[22]

76-551-9
Now,
[a movement in the vessels that is] at the surface and string[-like],
this is: kidney insufficiency.[23]
[A movement in the vessels that is] in the depth and stone[-like],
this is: the qi of the kidneys is stuck inside.[24]

When [the patient is] timid and when he is short of qi,
this is: the paths of water are impassable;
the qi of the physical appearance wanes until it is exhausted.[25]

Coughing with vexation and grievance,
this is: a movement of the kidney qi contrary [to its regular course].[26]

---

in the depots. It is essential to examine whether there is depletion or repletion." See also 2179/12 echoing Zhang Jiebin.

21 Mori: "The eight winds are the winds of the eight cardinal directions. This is a general reference to all the evil qi between heaven and earth. That is to say, when evil qi enters [the body], it gradually penetrates deeper. The heat gradually reaches an extreme, until it causes a waning/melting of the five depots. This is the meaning of evil being transmitted among [the depots]." See *Ling shu* 77 for details on the "eight winds."

22 Zhang Jiebin: "[Huang] Di says that [Lei] Gong's question is limited to a description of the disease and that he does not understand its causes."

23 Wang Bing: "When the [movement in the] vessels is at the surface, this indicates a depletion. When it is string[-like], this refers to the qi of the liver. Because the kidney qi is insufficient, hence, [the movement in] the vessels is at the surface and string[-like]."

24 Wang Bing: " 'Stone[-like]' is to say: it is hard. 'Stuck' is to say: the kidney qi collects and is stuck inside and fails to move on."

25 Wang Bing: "When the kidney qi is insufficient, the water fails to pass through its passage ways. The lung depot is attacked, hence, the physical qi wanes through dispersion. 索 stands for 盡, 'exhausted.'" Zhang Jiebin: "The essence generates physical form and it transforms into qi. When the water ways are not passable, the physical form and the qi vanish. Hence, one is scared and short of breath."

26 Wang Bing: "When the kidney qi is stuck inside it rises to turn to the mother [depot] of the [kidneys]."

The qi of the entire human [body was affected]
by a disease in the one depot [of the kidneys].
When you say three depots passed [evil qi] all alike,
this does not agree with the pattern [of diagnosis]."²⁷

76-551-12
Lei Gong:
"Here was a person [with a condition as follows:]
his four limbs were sluggish.
He panted and coughed, and [suffered from] blood outflow.

[I, the] ignoramus, diagnosed the [disease] and
I considered it to be a harmed lung.
When squeezing the [patient's] vessels, [I felt a movement] at the surface, big,
and tight.
[I, the] ignoramus, did not dare to treat [the patient].
An uneducated practitioner applied a pointed stone.
The disease was healed. He let a large amount of blood.
When the bleeding stopped, the body felt light.
What is this?"²⁸

[Huang] Di:
"Those [cases] you are able to treat [successfully],
[I] know that they are very many, too.
With this disease [just described by you] you have missed [the point again].²⁹

---

27 Tanba: "So far no commentator has explained the character 行; it refers to the movement of the disease." Mori: "That is to say, [at first,] the qi disease of the kidneys is present in that one depot. That is, when the qi of the kidneys has a disease, then it must affect the two depots liver and spleen. This is not a sign indicating that the kidneys, the liver, and the spleen all alike have been affected by a disease and pass it on. If one were to say the three depots all alike pass the disease, then this would not correspond to the proper pattern of diagnosing a kidney disease."

28 Gao Shishi: "[This should be:] 此何故, 'what is the reason for this?.'" Tanba: "I do not see any justification for reading 物 as 故." Mori: "物 is 事, 'affair,' 類, 'type.' .. That is to say: of which type is this disease? The *Zuo zhuan* 左傳, 21st year of duke Zhao 昭二十一年, has 是何物也. The commentary explains: 物 is 事."

29 Wang Bing: "When he considered it to be a harmed lung and did not dare to treat it, this was a strange perspective missing the [correct] pattern!" Zhang Jiebin: "That is to say, 'those [diseases] you are able [to treat, I] know that they are many , too. But when you consider the present disease to be a harmed lung, then you have missed the [point].'" Wu Kun: "[Huang] Di said: 'The diseases you know to treat, very many people speak of them." Tanba: "Zhang Jiebin is right."

This is comparable to the flight of the wild swan.
It, too, may [occasionally] soar into heaven.[30]

Now,
when the sages treated a disease,
they followed[31] the pattern and they guarded the standards.[32]
[Still, even] they drew on facts and compared the likes.[33]

The obscure [aspects of] transformation,[34]
they follow [what is] above, to reach [what is] below.[35]

---

30 Wang Bing: "When a wild swan flies to soar into heaven and unexpectedly is successful, how could its [inadequate] feathers have enabled it to achieve this?! When a crude practitioner inserts a pointed stone [and has success], this is the same situation." Gao Shishi: "If an uneducated practitioner carries out his reckless treatments and achieves a cure, this is one win in a thousand plans. This is comparable to a wild swan [trying to] soar into heaven."

31 Gao Jiwu/726: " 循 is identical with 遵, "to follow."

32 Zhang Jiebin: "They honored the guidelines set up by the ancients."

33 1884/1 considers the various expressions 援物比類, 別異比類, and 取類比象 to be terms denoting the method of building a system of correspondences. See also 1373/13 and 2904/33.

34 Wu Kun: "Transformations and changes in the realm of darkness where no measurements can be carried out." Ma Shi: "The character 化 should be 托, 'to push.' [The meaning is:] 'One must push for it into the mysterious, one must not be impeded by traces of physical form.' It really is to say 'to observe its mysteries.'" Mori: " 'The secrets of transformation' is to say: the irregular transmission and transformation of evil qi [in the body]. Its depletion and repletion, cold and heat, true cold and false heat, true heat and false cold are mysterious and difficult to investigate; the text refers to this with the statement: 'rising and descending have no regularity.' Hence, if one sticks to the conditions appearing in the three conduits of the three yang [qi] and applies a treatment, then the resulting mistakes are not a few. Hence, [the text] states: 'why stick to the conduits?' When Ma Shi suggested to read 化 as 托 and when Wu Kun said 'examine the mysteries of creation,' then both were wrong." Various Chinese commentators have interpreted this passage as an exhortation to flexibility, i.e., to always adapt one's theoretical book knowledge to the real and ever changing situations one is confronted with. See, for instance, 1818/45. In contrast, 1373/13: "The *Nei jing* believes that by drawing on facts and comparing the likes the knowledge of things can be lifted to a theoretical level. Hence, *Su wen* 76 states: '[they] drew on the facts, compared the likes and transformed them into mysteries."

35 Zhang Zhicong: "They investigate the secrets of creation." 2469/3: "夫聖人之治病 ... 何必守經, the meaning [of this passage is]: To treat a disease one must follow

Why should it be necessary to cling to the classics?[36]

Now,
as for a [movement in the] vessels that is at the surface, big, and depleted,
this is a situation where the spleen qi has been interrupted in the outside.
It leaves the stomach aside and has turned to the yang brilliance [conduit].[37]

Now,
two fires do not dominate three waters.
It is therefore that the [movement in the] vessels is disorderly and has no
regularity.[38]

---

a specific method; further more, one must consider [the case at hand], then analyse it
and make a flexible application according to the actual condition."

36 In contrast, Wang Bing: "經 refers to 'conduits vessels,' not to any laws in the
classics." Ma Shi: "經 is associated with 經法, 'laws in the classics.'

37 Wang Bing: "A branch of the foot major yin network [vessel] (i.e., of the vessel
associated with the spleen) enters and encircles the intestines and the stomach. It is
therefore that when the [passage of the] spleen qi [through the foot major yin vessel]
is interrupted externally and [when the spleen qi] cannot reach the stomach [by way
of the foot major yin vessel], it turns to the yang brilliance [conduit] (i.e., the vessel
associated with the intestines and the stomach) externally." Zhang Jiebin: "All the vessel [movement] conditions listed in this question refer to diseases in the spleen and
stomach. Now, the spleen belongs to the yin; it is the interior [depot] of the [exterior
palace] stomach. The stomach belongs to the yang; it is the exterior of the spleen.
When the [movement in the] vessels, in the present case now, comes at the surface,
and is large and depleted, then there is an overabundance in the exterior and an insufficiency inside. That is, the spleen qi is cut off outside of the stomach. The spleen [qi]
has already left the stomach. Hence, the qi has turned to the yang brilliance [vessel of
the intestines and of the stomach] and a [movement in the] vessels such as the present
one appears."

38 Wang Bing: " 'Two fires' refers to the two yang depots. 'Three waters' refers to the
three yin depots. The two yang depots are the heart and the lung because they are located above the diaphragm. Now, the qi of the three yin [depots] moves upwards and
dominates the two yang. The yang cannot dominate the yin. Hence, the [movement
in the] vessels is disorderly and has no permanence." Wu Kun: " 'Second fire,' this is
to say: 'second yang,' that is, the stomach. 'Third water,' this is to say: 'third yin,' that is,
the spleen. That is to say, the qi of great yin has turned, outside, to the yang brilliance.
Yang brilliance cannot dominate the great yin. Hence, the [movement in the] vessels
is disorderly and not normal. A normal [movement in the] vessels is at the surface and
slow. Here now it is abnormal and comes at the surface, large and depleted."

That the four limbs were sluggish,
this is [a sign that] the essence of the spleen does not move.[39]

76-552-8
As for the panting and coughing, [this is because] the water qi had merged
with the yang brilliance.[40]

As for the blood outflow, [in this case the movement in the] vessels is tense and
the blood has nowhere to move.[41]

Now,
if you assume this to be a harmed lung,
you started from an error and it is therefore that you arrived at utter confusion.[42]
You did not draw [on the method of] comparing the likes.
Hence, your knowledge has not [reached the level of] understanding yet.[43]

---

39 Wang Bing: "The soil rules the four limbs. Hence, when the four limbs are inactive, [this is a sign indicating that] the spleen essence has not been transformed.
Hence, it causes such [a situation]."

40 Wang Bing: "The kidney qi has moved against [its regular course] into the stomach. Hence, the water qi collects in the yang brilliance [conduit]." Zhang Jiebin: "The
spleen has a disease; it cannot control the water. As a result the water evil is rampant
and collects in the stomach palace. The passage ways of the qi are impassable. Hence,
this causes panting and coughing. The reason is, all the five depots and six palaces can
cause coughing in man."

41 Wang Bing: "泄 is to say 泄出, 'to flow out.' When the qi in the vessels [moves]
frequently and hastily and the blood spills into the center, the blood cannot enter the
conduits and, hence, the blood flows away. Because the [movement in the] vessels
runs hastily and the blood spills, hence, [the text] states 'the blood has nowhere to
move.'" Zhang Jiebin: "The conduit vessels are where the blood and the qi move and
nourish the yin and the yang [regions]. When the [movement in the] vessels is tense
and fast, this is because the [movement of the] qi is disorderly. When the qi [moves]
disorderly, the blood [moves] disorderly. Hence, it flows away into stools and urine. It
has nowhere to move regularly."

42 Mori: "失 is equivalent to 失心, 'to lose one's mind.' When [the text] states 失以
狂, this is to say: 'to have lost one's mind and to make crazy speeches.' The fact is, first
one loses one's mind and then one makes crazy speeches."

43 Zhang Jiebin: "Because panting and cough are [signs of] a harmed lung, [Huang
Di] knew that [Lei Gong] had not reached an understanding [of this case] yet. If one
combines [the signs of cough and panting] with the signs of the [movement in the]
vessels, then a comparative examination shows that the disease is in the spleen, not
in the lung." Gu Guangguang interprets 比類 as a title of a scripture: "This paragraph

Now,
in case of harmed lung,
the spleen qi does not guard [its proper function],
the stomach qi is not clear, and
the conduit qi cannot serve as their messenger.

The true [qi] of the depots is spoiled,
the conduit vessels are ruptured nearby, and
the five depots leak.
If there is no nosebleed, then there is vomiting.

These two are not alike.[44]

This is comparable to [erroneous statements such as]:
heaven having no physical appearance,
the earth having no structures.

They are as distant from each other as black and white.[45]

---

occurs in the [text] *Comparing the Likes*, but Lei Gong was unaware of it and did not quote it. Hence, [Huang] Di thought he had not understood it."

44 Wang Bing: "When the lung qi is harmed, then the spleen grants help from outside. Hence, [the text] states: 'The spleen qi does not guard [its proper location].' When the lung depot is harmed, then the qi fails to move. When it does not move, then the stomach experiences fullness. Hence, [the text] states: 'the stomach qi is not clear.' The lung rules the movement of camp and guard [qi] through yin and yang [regions]. Hence, when the lung is harmed, then the conduit vessels are unable to pass its [qi]. 'True depot' is to say: the lung depot. In case the lung depot is harmed, skin and membranes break open. The conduit vessels are ruptured nearby and there is no flow passing further the qi of the five depots. When [these qi] rise and overflow and when they drip and flow away, if this does not lead to nosebleed, then it leads to vomiting blood. Why? The lung rules the nose; the stomach corresponds to the mouth. Now, the mouth and the stomach are gates of the qi. In the present situation, the lung depot has been injured and the stomach qi is not clear. When [the lung qi] does not rise to cause nosebleed, then it flows down into the stomach. Hence, if there is no nosebleed, then there will be vomiting. That is, a harmed lung and a harmed spleen, nosebleed and blood flowing away, these are appearances of different tips, and the roots they can be traced to are not identical either. Hence, [the text states:] 'these two are not alike.'"

45 Wang Bing: "That is to say, a harmed lung and a harmed spleen are far apart and separate in physical appearance and pathoconditions; they are as far apart as heaven and earth and as different as the images of black and white."

That you missed [the point] in this, this is my mistake.
I assumed you knew this;
hence, I did not instruct you.

[A practitioner with an] understanding draws on [the method of] comparing
the likes and on a natural approach.
Therefore this is called the 'Lightness of Diagnosis.'
This is meant by the perfect Way."[46]

---

46 The *Tai su* has 診經, "Classic on Diagnosis." Wang Bing: "[Practitioners with an]
understanding draw on the signs [of diseases manifested in the patient's] physical
appearance; they compare what falls into one category and match this with the instructions of the [text] The Natural Approach. Hence they do not miss even the most
feeble [signs] (輕微). .. The Natural Approach is the title of a chapter of an ancient
classic. Why do I know this? Because in *Su wen* 79 Lei Gong states: 'I have received
what is transmitted on the conduits and vessels and I have learned, through recitations, the Way of the natural approach to combine it with the [contents of the text]
The Natural Approach.' That makes it clear that there was a text in antiquity with the
title Cong Rong." Zhang Jiebin: "This chapter refers to appearance and pathoconditions and it differentiates between what is different and what is alike, to combine this
with the method of comparing the likes. Hence, it is called 'Classic on Diagnosis.' This
is where the perfect Way is." See also 2719/8: "From *Su wen* 79 it is obvious that the
Cong Rong was a title of a text on pulse diagnosis. .. Wang Bing did not know that
Cong Rong was a book title, hence he erroneously changed 經 to 輕, making this text
passage difficult to understand."

Chapter 77
Discourse on Expounding the Five Faults

77-553-5
Huang Di:
"Alas! How profound!

As unfathomable,[1]
as if one looked into a deep abyss,
as if one faced drifting clouds!

[However,]
when looking into a deep abyss,
it is still possible to measure [its depth];
when facing drifting clouds,
no one knows their farthest extension.[2]

The art of the sages,
it establishes a model for all mankind.
Judgment and mind
must be based on laws and rules.
If one follows the classics and observes the calculations and
accordingly practices medicine,
this will be beneficial to all mankind.[3]

Hence,
the practice [of medicine] has five faulty and four virtuous [ways of therapy].[4]

---

1 Wang Bing: "嗚呼遠哉 is to lament the limitless nature of the perfect Way. 閔閔
乎 refers to the inexhaustible variety of its miraculous operations."

2 *Su wen* 68 has almost identical introductory words, with 極 instead of 際.

3 Yang Shangshan: "副 stands for 助, 'to help.'" Zhang Jiebin agrees. *Su wen* 76
has 循法守度.

4 In contrast, Wang Bing interprets 過 here as "transgression": "To be cautious
of the five transgressions is to honor and follow the virtuous qi of the four seasons.
Virtue is the operation of the Way, it is the master of life. Hence, it must be honored
and followed. The [treatise *Su wen* 1] 上古天真論 states: 'The reason why someone is
able to live through his entire lifespan of one hundred years without weakening in his
activities is that his virtue remains complete and is never endangered.'" Zhang Jiebin:
"In medicine one distinguishes among the ignorant and the sages. The ignorant commit many mistakes; hence, there are the five transgressions [in treatment]. The Way of

Do you know them?"⁵

Lei Gong rose from his seat and paid reverence twice:

"[I, your] subject, am young in years and ignorant and therefore insecure.
[I] have not heard of the five faulty and four virtuous [ways of therapy].

The *To Compare the Likes*⁶ and the *Manifestations and Names [of Diseases]*⁷,
[I] have made use of these classics in vain.
[My] heart is unprepared⁸ to respond [to your question]."⁹

77-554-3
[Huang] Di:
"Whenever a disease has not been diagnosed yet,¹⁰
it is essential to inquire [about the patient's social status].

In case [the patient] was formerly of noble rank and later fell to low rank,
even though he was not hit by an evil [qi from the outside];¹¹

---

the sages is perfect; hence, it embraces the four virtues." Qian Chaochen-90/95: "五
過 is the opposite of 四德. 過 is 'fault,' 'mistake.' 五過 refers to five types of mistakes.
德 is a loan character for the homophone 得, used here in the sense of 'correct medical
procedure.' 德 must not be read here as the 德 of 道德, but as the 得 of 得失, 'gain
and loss,' 'success and failure.' Wang Bing was wrong." Zhang Qi: "The text does not
refer to the 'four virtuous ways of behavior' again. Hence, this text is corrupt. Another
author states: 德 is an error for 失, as can be seen from the title of the next treatise: 征
四失論." Zhang Yizhi et al.: "The two characters 四德 are an erroneous insertion."

5 Wang Bing: "He who carefully avoids the five faults acts in accordance with the
virtuous qi of the four seasons. This virtuous qi is the operation of the Way; it is the
ruler of life. Hence, there is no way but to honor it."

6 For a discussion of the 比類 method, see 2904/32 ff.

7 575/42 interprets 問名 as "ask [the patient] to name his disease signs." See also
note 39. Here we read 比類 and 形名 as ancient book titles.

8 lit.: "has nothing"

9 Wang Bing: "He has not been taught the classics yet, his heart has not developed
any knowledge and his practice is trifling. Hence, he assumes a humble manner and
excuses himself."

10 Zhang Yizhi et al.: "The *Ishimpo* 醫心方, quoting the *Tai su*, does not have the
character 未." In this case the translation should read: "Whenever one diagnoses a
disease, .."

11 The *Ishimpo* 醫心方 added the two characters 于外 to the character 中: "hit by
outside evil."

his disease emerged from within.¹²
It is called lost camp [qi].¹³
In case [the patient] was formerly wealthy and later became poor,
this is called lost essence.¹⁴
The five qi stay for long;
one suffers from something having merged.¹⁵

A medical practitioner diagnosing it [will find the following:]
it is not in the depots and palaces and
it has not changed the [patient's] physical appearance.¹⁶
He [attempts to] diagnose it and remains in doubt.
He does not know the name of the disease.¹⁷

---

12 Wang Bing: "Because the spirit is depressed. The high standing of the noble [has given way to] the disgraced standing of the commoner; the love and longings carried in the heart [have given way to] the fear and alarm knotted to the mind. Hence, even though [the patient] was not hit by an evil [qi from outside], his disease emerged from inside nevertheless."

13 Wang Bing: "The blood in his vessels has decreased to a state of depletion; hence, [the text] speaks of 'lost camp [qi].'" Zhang Jiebin: "Camp [qi] 營 refers to the yin qi. The camp [qi] (營) moves inside the vessels and is controlled by the heart. When heart and mind are not relaxed, no blood can be generated. The vessels are increasingly depleted day by day. Hence, this is called 'lost camp [qi].'" See also 1172/2-3 and 2607/53.

14 Zhang Jiebin: "When someone was wealthy first and has become poor afterwards, his anger increases daily and the support he will be able to give to his parents decreases day by day. Hence, the essence in his five depots decreases and disperses day by day and this is 'lost essence.'"

15 Zhang Jiebin: "When the essence is lost, the qi is weakened. When the qi is weakened, it will not move. Hence, it stays where it is and accumulates and one is ill because 'something has come together.'"

16 In contrast, Gao Shishi: "在 is 察, 'to examine'; 變 is 通, 'to penetrate,' 'to understand.'" In this case the translation should read: "When a physician diagnoses the [disease] without examining the depots and palaces and without penetrating the physical body, his diagnosing the [disease] will leave him in doubt; he does not know the name of the disease."

17 Wang Bing: "That is to say, the disease is at its very beginning. The disease has emerged from changes in the [patient's] thoughts. Hence, it has not settled down yet in any of the depots and palaces. Because it emerged from the emotions, it has not transformed the physical appearance. The physicians do not know this. Hence, their diagnosis results in nothing but confusion."

77-554-6
The [substance of the] body decreases day by day;
its qi is depleted and it has no essence.[18]
When the disease is in the depth and no qi is present,
[the patient] shivers; at times he is frightened.[19]
{When the disease is in the depth, this is because the guard [qi] is diminished
in the outer [regions of the body] and the camp [qi] has been removed from its
inner [region].}[20]

When a good practitioner misses [this],[21] and
does not know the nature of the disease,
this is certainly one fault that may occur in treatment.

77-554-9
Whenever one wishes to diagnose a disease,
it is essential to inquire about
the [patient's] drinking and eating [habits] and his place of living.[22]

---

18 Wang Bing: "That is a reference to the subsequent development of the disease. Qi
and blood press on each other and the physical flesh melts away. Hence, the [substance
of the] body decreases day by day.

19 Wang Bing: "That is to say, the disease is in the depth [of the body now]. The
disease qi has penetrated [the body] deeply and the grain qi is used up. The yang qi
has weakened internally. Hence, [patients] have an aversion to cold and experience
fear." Zhang Yizhi et al.: "The repetition of the character 洒 is an error. All previous
sentences have four characters; this one should not have five characters." Mori: "In
his outer regions [the patient's body] is deprived of guard [qi]; hence, he shivers and
has an aversion to cold. In his inner regions he is deprived of camp [qi]; hence, he
frequently develops fear. .. These are signs of a depletion of the two depots heart and
lung."

20 Wang Bing: "The blood is boiled by the anxiety; the qi decreases in accordance
with the sadness. Hence, the guard [qi] is diminished in the outer [segments of the
body], while the camp [qi] is removed from its inner [segments]. Why the disease was
able to penetrate [the body's] depth? Because [the guard qi was] diminished and [the
camp qi was] removed." Lin Yi et al.: "Instead of 病深者以其 the *Tai su* has 病深以
甚也."2719/9 considers this to be the correct and original wording. It would translate:
"The disease moves deeper and becomes serious. Hence, it destroys the guard ..."

21 Wang Bing: " 'Misses this' means 'fails to inquire about the origins [of the dis-
ease].' "

22 Wang Bing: "Beverages and food and the places of living differ in the five cardinal directions. Hence, one inquires about them."

Whether he has experienced violent[23] joy or violent suffering, or
whether he has experienced an initial joy that was followed by suffering.[24]

All this harms the essence qi.
When the essence qi is exhausted and when [its flow] is interrupted,
the physical body will be destroyed.[25]

Violent anger harms the yin;
violent joy harms the yang.[26]
Receding qi moves upwards;
it fills the vessels and leaves the physical appearance.[27]

If an ignorant physician treats this and
knows neither whether to supplement or to drain,
nor what the nature of the diseases is like,
then the [patient's] bloom of essence is lost day by day, and
evil qi collects.[28]

---

23 In contrast, Wang Shaozeng/84 reads 暴 as 突然, "sudden," "unexpected."

24 Lin Yi et al.: "The *Tai su* has 始樂始苦 instead of 始樂後苦." 2719/9 considers this the original and correct wording: "The physician must ask whether there was any violent joy or violent suffering and if so, whether the joy was first, or the suffering."

25 Wang Bing: "Joy slows down [the flow of] the qi; sadness makes the qi waste away. Now, when sadness and grief move the center, [the essence and the qi] are exhausted and interrupted [in their flow], and fail to provide life. Hence [the text states:] the essence is exhausted, the [flow of the] qi is interrupted, the physical body is destroyed, and the spirit is lost."

26 Wang Bing: "Anger causes the qi to flow contrary [to its normal course]; hence, it harms the yin. Joy slows down the flow of the qi; hence, it harms the yang." In contrast, Beijing zhongyi xueyuan et al./105: "Anger harms the liver; the liver stores the blood. Hence, it harms the yin. Joy harms the heart. The heart stores the spirit. Hence, it harms the yang."

27 Wang Bing: "厥 refers to qi flowing contrary to its normal course. Qi flowing contrary to its normal course moves upwards and fills the conduits and network [vessels]. As a result the spirit qi disperses and leaves the physical appearance and the skeleton." Mori: "滿脈 is to say: all the vessels of the entire body. 去形 is to say: there is no [movement in the] vessels in the entire body. These four statements appear in *Su wen* 05, too; the *Tai su* has them in ch.3, but in the present context it does not have these 16 characters. Hence, they have been moved here by Wang Bing as a commentary written in red ink, as he has stated in his preface. They are not part of the original text." The textus receptus of ch. 3 of the *Tai su* does not have these 16 characters.

28 Zhang Jiebin: "When the yang suffers losses, evil sides with the yin; when the yin suffers losses, evil sides with the yang. Hence, [the text] states: 'evil qi sides with.'"

This is the second fault that may occur in treatment.

77-555-4
Those who are experts in the [movement in the] vessels, for them
it is essential to rely on [such methods as]
comparing the likes,
[comparing] the strange and the normal,[29] and
the natural approach, and
thereby to acquire the respective knowledge.

To be a practitioner and not to know the Way,
this results in a diagnosis of lower value.[30]

This is the third fault that may occur in treatment.

77-555-6
In diagnosis there are three rules [to be observed].[31]

[The patient] must be asked
whether he is of noble or low rank;
whether he was a feudal lord who has been destroyed or harmed; and
whether he aspires to be prince or king.[32]

---

29 In contrast, Wang Bing: "奇恆 is to say: the observation of signs of qi that are
different (奇異) from the normal (恆常) signs. 從容 is to say: to differentiate whether
the qi in the depots is in a state of depletion or repletion, whether the vessels appear high or low. [These two approaches] are quite similar." It is difficult to decide
whether the three terms *bi lei* 必類, *qi heng* 奇恆, and *cong rong* 從容 are meant here
to designate diagnostic and therapeutic methods or whether they are to be read as
book titles in the way as the context forces us to interpret some of them further down
in the present discourse (*qi heng* 奇恆: 557-10) and in *Su wen* 81 (*cong rong* 從容:
571-11). In the latter case, the passage would read as follows: "Those who are experts
in the [movement in the] vessels, for them it is essential to rely on [such texts as] *To
Compare the Likes*, *The Strange and the Normal*, and *The Natural Approach* and thereby
to acquire the respective knowledge." See also above, note 7.

30 lit.: "this is a diagnosis that is not [good] enough to be appreciated." 2568/50
reads 此診之不足貴 as 此診便不足貴.

31 Tanba: "三常 has the meaning of to examine whether someone is of noble or low
rank, whether he is wealthy or poor and whether he suffers or is happy."

32 Wang Bing: "When someone is of noble rank, then his physical appearance is
marked by joy and so is his mind. When someone is a commoner, then his physical
appearance is marked by suffering and so is his mind. Suffering and joy have different implications; hence, one enquires after them first. 封君敗傷 is: a feudal ruler has

The fact is,

when a [man of] noble rank is stripped of his power,

even though he was not struck by an evil [qi from outside],

his essence and spirit have been harmed inside and

[hence] his body must face destruction and death.

If someone was wealthy first and became poor later,

even though he was not harmed by an evil [qi from outside],

his skin is scorched and his sinews [force the body to] bend.

[He suffers from] limpness and an inability to walk; [his limbs] have a cramp.[33]

When a physician is unable to severely [reprove the patient and, hence,]

is unable to move [the patient's] spirit[34] and

when his outer [appearance] is soft and weak,

[so that the patient behaves] disorderly to a degree where he fails [to observe the] regular [pattern],[35] and

his disease cannot be removed,

then no therapeutic activities can be performed.[36]

---

lost his position and has become a [simple] feudal duke or nobleman. 及欲侯王 is to say: his feelings love and long for noble status; but his efforts are futile and lead to nothing." Lin Yi et al.: "The *Tai su* has 公 instead of 欲." 2719/9 considers this to be the correct and original wording. The author argues that a "feudal ruler" is higher in position than a prince or king. When the feudal ruler is "destroyed" he becomes either a 公, or a 侯, or a 王: "[The physician] must ask whether he was a feudal ruler who has been harmed or destroyed, arriving at a status of Duke, Prince, or King.."

33 Wang Bing: "This is because the qi in the five depots stays where it is and one suffers from accumulations."

34 *Ling shu* 29 assumes that a physician's advice, if offered skillfully, will always be accepted: "Man's nature is such that everyone abhors death and loves to live. [If the physician] speaks to the [patient] of what is destructive, if he tells him of what is beneficial, if he guides him by [pointing out] what is convenient for him, and if he explains to him what makes him suffer, why should not even those listen, who are outside the Way?" See also 1500/14.

35 484/44 identifies 亂 as carrying its opposite meaning: 治, 'order:' "Treatment reaches [a point] where it misses the regular pattern."

36 Wang Bing: "嚴 is to say: 戒, 'to warn.' That is that by which one forbids what is wrong; [動] is that by which one makes [the patient] follow orders. 外為柔弱 is to say: docile and obedient. Now, when warnings are not sufficient to make someone avoid what is wrong, when moving [a person's spirit] is not sufficient to make someone follow orders so that he can be employed to shoulder tasks and if he is disorganized to a degree that he fails to carry out the daily routines and if the patient does not move,

This is the fourth fault that may occur in treatment.

77-556-3
Whenever one diagnoses [a disease],
it is essential to know its end and begin,[37] and
one must also know the remaining clues.[38]
Squeeze the vessels, inquire about the name [of the diseases], and
match [your findings] with the male or female [gender of the patient].[39]

Separation and interruption,[40] dense compactness and knotting,[41]
anxiety, fear, joy, and anger,
[whether they let] the five depots be empty and depleted and

---

what medicine could there be to treat him!" Mori: "Whenever a physician is anxious
and unable to remind [a patient] of what is right and wrong, he will also be unable to
terrify the spirit of the patient. If the physician's outer appearance is soft and weak, the
patient will not believe his words."

37 Wu Kun: "That is to say, the current [state of the] disease and the initial disease."
Gao Shishi: "One must know the point of departure and the final end of the conduit
vessels."

38 Mori: "有 is 又, 'also,' 'further.' The two characters were used interchangeably in
antiquity."

39 Wang Bing: "終始 is to say: qi and complexion. 餘緒 is to say: the development
of a disease subsequent to its onset. 切 is to say: to press the vessels with a finger. 問
名 is to say: ask [the patient] how he names the disease signs. When a male has much
yang qi and when the vessels on his left are big, then this is normal. When a female
has much yin qi and when the vessels on her right are big, then this is normal. Hence,
this is to be examined and [the results] are always to be matched [with the patient's
gender] first." Zhang Jiebin: "Males and females differ in their [endowment with] yin
and yang [qi]. The [movement in the] vessels and the complexion may be contrary
to or in accordance with [a normal state]. Hence, [a practitioner] must distinguish
between males and females and he must examine to what degree [their condition]
matches [their gender]." Zhang Qi: "Something is wrong with the phrase 問名. Wang
Bing's commentary ... is not correct. The names of a disease and its signs should be
inquired from a practitioner; why should [a practitioner] ask a patient?" Wu Kun:
"Males and females differ in terms of [their endowment with] qi and blood; it is also
essential to match their [movement in the] vessels with their illness signs."

40 See also *Su wen* 3 where the phrase 離絕 refers to a separation of yin and yang. In
contrast, Zhang Jiebin offers a social interpretation: "離, 'separation,' is to lose one's relatives or loved ones. 絕, 'to be cut off,' is to be separated from what one cherishes." 2235/60
(see there and 2334/18-19 for a more detailed discussion of the concepts involved).

41 For 菀結, 'to accumulate,' see also *Su wen* 2 and *Su wen* 4. In contrast, Zhang
Jiebin interprets this term as a consequence of the preceding: "菀 means one's

[whether they let] blood and qi lose their guardian [function],
if the practitioner fails to know this,
what art is there to speak of?⁴²

77-556-5
When someone who was wealthy in the beginning [and is impoverished now]
is severely harmed,
with his sinews cut and [the movement in] his vessels interrupted,
[even if] the body walks again,
[the injury] does not let his liquids recover.⁴³

Hence,
if as a result one is harmed by destruction and knotting,
[the qi] remains [at one place], presses and turns to the yang.⁴⁴
Pus accumulates, [causing a feeling of] cold and heat.⁴⁵

---

thoughts are severely depressed [after the loss of relatives or loved ones]; 結 refers to deeply felt sentiments that cannot be resolved."

42 Wang Bing: "離 is to say: to leave one's loved ones. 絕 is to say: to part from what one has thought of. 菀 is to say: to focus one's thoughts [on something]. 結 is to say: to contract great hatred. Now, when one is separated from a loved one, the *hun*-soul leaves. When one parts from what one has cherished, the sentiments are mournful. Excessive pondering exhausts the spirit; to contract hatred makes the mind suffer. In case of anxiety [the qi] is blocked and fails to move; fear makes one hesitant and lose control. In case of great anger one is confused and lacks order; in case of joy [the qi] disperses and cannot remain stored. All these eight states are the cause of depletion of the five depots; it is because of them that blood and qi leave their guarded [position]. If a practitioner fails to take this into regard, what else should one speak of!?"

43 Wang Bing: "The body may have been restored to its former condition and be able to move. Nevertheless, this does not let the liquids recover (滋息)... 澤 stands for 液, 'liquid.'" Zhang Jiebin: "澤 is 精液, 'essence liquid.' 息 is 生長, 'come to life and grow.'" Mori: "令澤不息 is: not to allow the glossiness of the facial complexion (色澤) to come to an end (止息).

44 Wang Bing: " 'Yang' refers to all the yang vessels and to the six palaces."

45 Wang Bing: "炅 is to say: 熱, 'heat.' When the qi of both sinews and vessels is destroyed indiscriminately, blood and qi form knottings internally; they stay where they are and do not leave. They collect in the yang vessels and are transformed into pus. When [the pus] has collected in the abdomen for a long time, then [the patient] will feel cold or hot outside." Zhang Jiebin: "故 is 舊, 'old.' That is, if someone was harmed some time ago and if there was destruction and accumulation, blood and qi stay at one place, collect, and do not disperse. As a result there is [local] abundance and this generates heat which turns to the yang section. Hence, pus and blood accumulate and

When an uneducated practitioner treats this and
hastily[46] pierces yin and yang,
the [patient's] body will disintegrate;
the sinews in his four limbs will become twisted and
the day of death will be foreseeable.[47]

If a physician is unable to reach an understanding, and
if he does not inquire how [a disease] developed, and
if he is [able] only to tell the day of [the patient's] death,
then he, too, is an uneducated practitioner.[48]

This is the fifth fault that may occur in treatment.

77-557-1
All these five [faults result from]
not penetrating the art one was taught and from
not understanding the human affairs.[49]

Hence,
it is said:

'When the sages treated a disease,
they certainly knew
the yin and yang [qi] of heaven and earth and
the normal arrangements of the four seasons;

---

let the patient have alternating feelings of cold and heat." Mori: "故傷 corresponds to
the phrase 故貴, 'formerly of noble rank' above."

46 Wang Bing: "數刺陰陽, 'frequently pierces yin and yang.'"

47 Wang Bing: "When [a practitioner] does not know that feelings of cold and heat
result from a collection of pus and believes that this is a disease of ordinary heat and
then applies the respective therapeutic pattern of frequently piercing yin and yang
conduits and vessels, he will remove the qi and increase the severity of the disease.
Hence, the body will disintegrate and can no longer function; the four limbs will cease
moving and the sinews will be twisted. If this way the day of death is foreseeable, how
could anybody blame fate rather than the physician?!"

48 Wang Bing: "That is, one is not necessarily an uneducated practitioner only because of a lack of training."

49 Wang Bing: "That is to say: [as for the reasons of the occurrence of] these five
[faults], those who can only be called adepts who have been taught the art, their
knowledge is insufficient to comprehend the subtleties and they are even more ignorant when it comes to [judging] the human affairs."

the five depots and six palaces,
female and male, exterior and interior,
[as well as] piercing, cauterization, pointed stones, and
toxic drugs with all [the diseases] they master.

Their approach to the human affairs was natural, thereby
understanding the Way laid down in the classics.'⁵⁰

77-557-4
The noble and the common, the poor and the wealthy,
they all [represent] a structure of different ranks,⁵¹
[and the sages] inquired [from the patients] whether they were young or old,
and whether they had a character of courage or timidity.

They investigated [all the] divisions and sections [of the human body] and
they knew the root and the beginning of the diseases [to be treated].⁵²
As for the eight cardinal [turning points]⁵³ and the nine indicators,⁵⁴
in their examinations they were of definite help⁵⁵ [too].

77-557-6
The Way of treating diseases
considers the qi inside⁵⁶ as most valuable.⁵⁷

---

50 An alternative interpretation is: "they understood the regular Way." Fu Weikang & Wu Hongzhou/310.

51 Fu Weikang & Wu Hongzhou/310 interpretes 品 as 品德, "moral character," and 理, as "reason," "cause" of a disease.

52 See 1963/33.

53 These are the qi at "the eight seasonal turning points," i.e., the two solstices, the two equinoxes, and the four first days of the four seasons." See Fu Weikang & Wu Hongzhou/310. Another possible explanation is "the eight cardinal points where diseases causing winds may originate."

54 The movement in the vessels can be felt at the "nine indicators." See *Su wen* 20.

55 副 interpreted here as 福, in the sense of 福利, "profitable." See Fang Wenhui/114. In contrast, Fu Weikang & Wu Hongzhou/311: "副 stands for 全, 'complete.'" ("Diagnosis will be complete").

56 Zhang Jiebin: "The 'qi inside' is the 元氣, the 'principal qi.' Whenever one treats a disease, the first thing to be found out is the strength or weakness of the principal qi."

57 Lin Yi et al.: "*Tai su* has 氣內為實, 'the qi inside is replete.' Yang Shangshan comments: 'The qi between heaven and earth is the external qi. The qi in the human

[One must] search for its structures.
If one is unable to find them,
an excess [is present] in the exterior and in the interior.⁵⁸

Observe the calculations, treat according [to their indications] and
do not miss the structures of the transporters.⁵⁹
If [a physician] is able to apply this art,
he will never encounter failure in his entire life.
If he is not familiar with the structures of the transporters,
what is densely compacted in the five depots will boil.⁶⁰
Yong-abscesses develop in the six palaces.⁶¹

He diagnoses a disease and fails to recognize [it].
This is called to miss the regular [pattern].⁶²
If [a physician] carefully observes these [rules in] treatment,
he is on one level of understanding with the classics.

---

body is the qi inside. The external qi generates all things; hence, it is replete outside. The qi inside, both as camp and guard [qi], manages life. Hence, it is replete inside. For treating diseases, one should be able to search for the patterns of the qi inside. This is a requirement for the treatment of diseases." 2719/10 considers the *Tai su* wording 氣 內為實 as the original and correct version.

58 Wang Bing: "When a practitioner treats a disease, he must search whether there is an excess in the qi of the physical appearance. This is what the sages consider most valuable. If this search does not bring any result, one must examine the qi of the depots and palaces, with respect to its yin and yang [nature] and to its presence outside or inside." Zhang Jiebin: "If a search for a disease of the principal qi does not yield any results, one examines whether the excess is in the outer or inner segments [of the body] and treats it. This way no fault occurs." Zhang Zhicong: "This is a discourse on the Way of piercing. One must regard the internal qi as most valuable and search for the structures of its [movement in the] vessels. If nothing can be found, the disease is in the qi section of outer or inner."

59 Wang Bing: "守數 is to say: the calculation of the quantities of blood and qi, as well as of the depth of piercing. 据治 is to say: the [art of piercing] is to be used on the basis of the therapeutic indications of the transportation holes. Only with these calculations and on the basis of these indications the structures of the transportation points will not be missed."

60 Wang Bing: "菀 is 積, 'to accumulate.' 熟 stands for 熱."

61 Wang Bing: "When heat accumulates in the five depots, the six palaces receive it. When yang [qi] and heat clash, the resulting excess of heat leads to abscesses."

62 Wang Bing: "That is to say: one misses the Way of the proper operation of the classic art [of treatment]."

{*The Upper Classic, The Lower Classic,*[63] *To Estimate and Measure, Yin and Yang, The Strange and The Normal, The Five Inside.*}[64]

[He whose] decisions are based on the Hall of Light,[65] [and who] investigates end and begin,[66]
he is in a position to move across [greatest obstacles]."

---

63 For the interpretation of 上經 and 下經 as titles of ancient books, see *Su wen* 46.

64 For an identification of 揆度, 陰陽, 奇恆, and 五中 as ancient book titles, see also Fu Weikang & Wu Hongzhou/310

65 Zhang Jiebin: "明堂, 'hall of light,' refers to the region of face and nose." Zhang Jiebin assumed that the facial area and the nose are meant here to indicate, through changes in a patient's complexion, the condition of the five depots. 1285/107 agrees: "That is to say, whenever a teacher of medicine has studied the books *Shang jing, Xia jing, Kuei du,* and *Yin yang,* and when he knows how to diagnose from the condition of the nose whether the five depots have a disease or not, and when he is able to fore-see the disease process in its entirety, then he will be able to go everywhere without meeting an opponent."

66 Zhang Jiebin: "終始 is the title of a *Ling shu* treatise." Hence, Zhang Jiebin in-terpretes this phrase as "and investigates [symptoms .. on the basis of the meaning of the treatise] Zhong shi."

Chapter 78
Discourse on Evidence of the Four Failures[1]

78-558-3
Huang Di was in the Hall of Light; Lei Gong sat in attendance.

Huang Di:
"Now,
the written records you have penetrated and the [therapeutic] tasks you have accepted, are many.[2]

Attempt to speak [to me] of
the meaning of achieving or missing [success].
That by which one achieves it.
That by which one misses it."[3]

Lei Gong responded:
"[I have] followed the classics[4] and [I have] received [instructions in medical] practice.[5]
All these [modes of learning] are said to result in success in all [cases treated].
[Nevertheless, I] occasionally commit a mistake.
Please, may I hear an explanation of these matters."[6]

---

1 Lin Yi et al.: "This treatise was titled 方論得失明著 in the Quan Yuanqi edition. "Wang Qi: "徵 is 懲戒, 'to punish somebody as a warning.' This treatise issues a warning against physicians committing the four types of transgressions listed."

2 Cheng Shide et al.: "受事 is 接受的工作, 'the work [you have] accepted.'"

3 2568/49: "所以 is 以所 in the sense of 'why?.'" Cheng Shide et al.: "得 is success; 失 is failure." See also Gao Jiwu/342.

4 Wang Bing: "That is to say, to study from the classics and from teachers and to receive the practical knowledge handed down [from the past], all these [ways of acquiring expertise] are said to lead to ten cures [in ten treatments] when it is applied to people. [However,] when applying the proper art and when spreading the perfect Way, it nevertheless happens that they are lost in the world. Hence, [Lei Gong] asks to have this explained."

5 The *Li ji* 禮記, Tan gong xia 檀弓下, and *Shi ji*, preface by Sima Qian, have 業 in the sense of "learning."

6 Wang Bing repeated this question in his comment as 請聞其解說也. Hence Qian Chaochen-90/85 concluded that the character 事 in the main text was erroneously inserted by a copyist who lived after Wang Bing.

78-558-6
[Huang] Di:
"Is it because you are young in years and
that your wisdom has not reached perfection yet,[7] or
that you combine the words [written in the scriptures] with various
[practices]?[8]

Now,
the twelve conduit vessels and the 365 network vessels, everybody is familiar
with them and
the practitioners follow and employ them [in therapy].[9]

The reasons why there is no success in all [cases treated are the following:]
when the essence spirit is not concentrated and
when the mind lacks understanding,
outside and inside lose mutual correspondence.
Hence,
[practitioners] often encounter uncertainties and dangers.[10]

---

7 Wang Bing: "That is to say: 'Is it because of [your] youth that [your] knowledge
is not yet perfect so that [you] do not achieve ten cures [in ten treatments]?" Cheng
Shide et al.: "邪 is identical here with 耶."

8 Zhang Jiebin: "言以雜合 is to say: oneself does not have a firm opinion yet.
Hence, one combines all types of doctrines without being able to arrive at a decision."
Wu Kun :"That is to say: to grasp all types of doctrines and combine them with one's
personal opinion." Sun Yirang: „雜 should be 離; the shapes of these characters are
very similar, hence they are often erroneously exchanged. .. 言以離合 is to say: to discuss what is appropriate and what is not appropriate." Wang Hongtu et al./159 agrees.
If one were to follow Sun Yirang, this passage should read: "You are young in years
and your wisdom has not reached perfection yet. Shall I discuss what is appropriate
and what is not appropriate?" 2168/5 reads 將 as 抑, "or."

9 Wang Bing: "循用 is to say 循學而用."

10 Wang Bing: " 'Outside' refers to one's complexion; 'inside' refers to the [move-
ment in the] vessels. Hence, when [a patient's] complexion and [his movement in the]
vessels are not brought into mutual agreement, oneself may develop doubts (自疑)
and create danger." Wu Kun: "The external appearance of the disease and the internal
spirit do not agree with each other." Zhang Zhicong: "When someone diagnoses [a
disease], he must guard his essence spirit and he must order his intentions. Internally
this should affect his heart and externally it should be reflected by his hand."

If in diagnosing [a disease a practitioner] does not know the structures of yin and yang and of [movements] contrary to or following [their regular course],[11] this is the first [reason of] therapeutic failure.[12]

78-558-10
If [the instructions] received from a teacher are incomplete,[13]
if one applies heterogeneous arts in an absurd fashion,[14]
if one adopts misleading statements as the Way,
if one exchanges the [correct] names [of the diseases], and [in doing so] is proud of oneself,[15]
and if one absurdly applies pointed stones,
so that one attracts blame on himself for his mistakes,[16]
this is the second [reason of] therapeutic failure.

78-559-1
If one does not take into account whether [a patient's] circumstances are those of poverty or wealth, of noble or low rank,[17]

---

11 In contrast, 126/47 identifies 逆從, following *Su wen* 74, as reference to 正治 and 反治 respectively. Given the general coherence of *Su wen* treatises 75 through 81, it is more likely, though, that the meaning of 逆 and 從 in *Su wen* 80 should be taken as starting point for an interpretation of *Su wen* 78. See there.

12 Wang Shaozeng/24-25: "治療工作中的一個失敗原因."

13 Wu Kun: "卒 is 卒業, 'to complete one's course of study.'"

14 Cheng Shide et al.: "Wu Kun and Zhang Jiebin read 雜 as 離. Wu Kun: '離術 stands for 別術, wayward art.' Zhang Jiebin: 'Those who practice wayward arts, they do not understand the proper art and accept unorthodox principles.'" See also 2332/34.

15 Wu Kun: "更名 is: to make changes in the [proper] doctrine." Yu Chang: "更名 is to appropriate the patterns developed by people in former times and alter their terms." Lin Yi et al.: "The *Tai su* has 巧, 'skillful,' instead of 功." 2719/10: "If 自功 is read as 自 巧, 'to consider one's skill as eminent,' then this is in keeping with the preceding text and it is the direct cause of 'a foolish application of pointed stones, finally endangering the [patient's] body.' Wang Bing changed 巧 to 功; he did not understand [the meaning of this passage]." 道 and 巧 form a rhyme.

16 遺身咎 is a phrase possibly borrowed from *Lao zi Dao de jing* 52: 用其光復歸其 明,無遺身咎,是為習常 "If one uses one's light to return to one's enlightenment, one will not deliver oneself to disaster. This is [meant by] practicing permanence." Cheng Shide et al.: "咎 is 過, 'error.'"

17 Wang Bing: "The poor and those of low rank are tired by work; the rich and those of noble rank have an easy life. Where life is at ease, the evil cannot cause any harm. When [the people] are tired by work, they will easily be harmed." 2289/22: "Wang

whether his seat is thin or thick,[18] and
whether his physical appearance is cold or warm;
[further,] if one fails to take into account whether his drinking and eating
[habits] are appropriate,
if one does not distinguish whether a person is brave or timid,
if one does not know [the method of] comparing the likes,
and if [one's learning] suffices to confuse oneself,
while it does not suffice to enlighten oneself,
this is the third [reason of] therapeutic failure.

When [a practitioner] diagnoses a disease without asking for its beginning,
whether anxiety or suffering,[19] drinking and eating have been immoderate, and
whether [the patient's] rising and resting have exceeded the norm, or
whether he was harmed by poison,[20] and
when [the practitioner] fails to speak about all these [conditions] first, but
hastily grasps the inch opening [to examine the movement in the vessels],[21]
which disease could he hit?[22]

Bing read 適 as 觀, 'to observe,' in the extended meaning of 區別, 'to distinguish.'"
1257: "適 is close in meaning to 別, 'to dinstinguish.'"

18 Zhang Qi: "坐 may be a mistake for 生, 'life.'" Gao Shishi: "坐 stands for 土, 'soil.'"
Zhang Jiebin: "坐 stands for 處, 'place of residence.'" Tanba: "Gao Shishi is correct."
1742/52: "Gao Shishi's suggestion to interpret 坐 as 土 has no basis whatsoever... 坐之
薄厚 refers to the thickness of the bed a person sits or lies on. There is no need to change
坐 to 土." Zhang Yizhi et al.: "The soil [on which people live] may be rich or poor and the
treatment [these people receive] varies [accordingly]. To interpret 坐 as 土 is correct."

19 954/27 reads 始 as 原因, "cause", "origin." Punctuation in this sentence commonly
separates as follows: 不問其始,憂患飲食之失節. Another possibility is to divide this
statement into a sequence of two four and two five character strings and separate after
問 and after 患. A parallel may be seen in *Su wen* 77, 始樂, and in the *Tai su* which has
始樂始苦 as important parameters of diagnostic inquiry. In contrast Zhang Jiebin: "The
Way of diagnosing a disease requires one to examine the cause which led to the disease
and to match this [cause] with the [movement in the] vessels. As a result, the yin or yang
[nature of a disease] and whether it is a case of depletion or repletion, will become clear
by themselves... When sadness and suffering, drinking and eating exceed the appropriate limits, these are internal causes. The extent of activity and rest is an external cause.
Or one may be harmed by poison. This is neither an internal nor an external cause."

20 Wang Bing: "That is, the disease cannot be treated according to the principles of
mutual infringement among the depots and palaces."

21 Zhang Qi: "卒 is identical with 猝, 'abrupt.'"

22 中, "to hit the center," could also be interpreted here as "successful strike against
[a disease]." However, in parallel with the use of 中 in 78-559-8, we prefer, in agreement with *Gu dian yi zhu xuan* bianxiezu /51-52, a translation of "to identify."

To issue absurd statements and to make up [disease] names,[23]
these are activities pursued by uneducated [practitioners] to exhaustion.[24]

This is the fourth [reason of] therapeutic failure.

78-559-6
Therefore,
the speeches of today's people
quickly travel over more than one thousand miles, while [in fact]
they do not understand the discourses on the foot-long section and on the inch,[25] and
in their diagnoses they do not take the human affairs [of their patients] into account.[26]

The Way of calculations in treatment
is a thicket [concealing] a natural approach.[27]

---

23 Yan Hongchen & Gao Guangzhen/205: "作名 is: to identify fictitious disease names."

24 In contrast, Yan Hongchen & Gao Guangzhen/205: "為粗所窮 is: 'the bad effects resulting from uneducated practice.'"

25 Wang Bing: "That is to say, success and failure, slander and praise can travel in the words of people more than a thousand miles. However if [a physician] fails to understand the diagnosis of the foot and inch [sections at the wrist] through what activities could [his] discourse become known to [even a single other] person?" Wu Kun :"That is to say, today's people search for the Way far away. They often travel to places a thousand miles away." Zhang Zhicong: "That is to say, today's people make big words, but they do not even know the subtleties of foot and inch." 386/60 reads "foot and inch" as 大小相稱, "large and small in accordance." Qian Chaochen-90/85: "The main text has 不明尺寸之論診無人之事. Wang Bing writes: 然其不明尺寸之診, 論當以何事知見于人. Obviously the two characters 論 and 診 have been erroneously exchanged in the main text."

26 Cheng Shide et al.: "人事 refers to the living circumstances and family conditions of the patients."

27 The *Shi ji* and further Han sources use 葆 in the sense of 守, "to watch," "to guard," "to maintain." In contrast, Wang Bing: "治 stands for 王, 'to rule.' 葆 stands for 平, 'level.' If one diagnoses the qi that should rule according to the calendar, one must take the high or low level of the qi as the starting point for comparing the likes." Zhang Jiebin: "葆 is 韜藏, 'to conceal.' When knowledge is comprehensive and learning is rich, then this the [coating] concealing a natural approach." Ma Shi: "葆 is 保, 'to guard.'" Zhang Zhicong: "葆 stands for 寶, "treasure," "valuable." That is to say, for

When [a practitioner] at random[28] feels the inch opening,
in his diagnosis fails to [correctly] identify the five [movements in the] vessels,
[and does not find out] where the one hundred diseases emerge,
[such practitioners] at first draw a grudge at themselves,
[then] they put the blame on [their] teachers.

Hence,
in their treatment they do not follow the patterns, and they discard their art on the market.[29]
Absurd treatments may occasionally result in a healing,
and ignorant minds will [regard this as] their own achievement.

78-560-1
Alas!
How subtle,

---

the Way of treatment and diagnosis, only the [Way] of the heavenly principles and of the human affairs is to be considered valuable." Zhang Zhicong's interpretation was supported by Tanba Genken 丹波元堅: "The 之 in 從容之葆 is a term referring to an issue. That is to say, 'the Way of treating and calculating can be obtained in a relaxed and peaceful state. Hence, it is considered to be a treasure (以為寶).'" 2617: "Tanba Genken 丹波元堅 referred to several occurrences of a phrase 為寶 in *Su wen* 17, 77, and *Ling shu* 1, 16, 19, to explain why 之 should be read as 為 and why it constitutes a 'term referring to an issue,' a verb, in the present context." Wu Kun: "The luxuriant growth of herbs and trees is called *bao* 葆. Hence, [this term] refers to inexhaustible vitality. That is, [the *Su wen*] sentence is to be read as follows: If the therapeutic method is in accordance with the Way and if a treatment is applied on the basis of the courageous or cowardish appearance [of the patient], then the patient's vitality will be inexhaustible." *SWTXDS*: "The *Lü lan* 呂覽, Jin shu 盡數, has 五藏之葆. The commentary states: '葆 is 安,'peace.'"

28 Zhang Jiebin: "If one is not familiar with structures and numbers and only feels the inch opening, one will not arrive at [a correct assessment of] the [movements in the] vessels [associated with] the five depots and how could one know the origins of the hundreds of diseases?!" Zhang Zhicong omitted the character 坐. Gao Shishi: "坐 is like 定, 'firm,' 'to settle.'" Cheng Shide et al.: "坐 is 徒然, 'useless,' 'in vain.'" In view of an earlier passage in line 78-559-5, one could also assume that the character 坐 in 坐持寸口 is a mistake for 卒.

29 "To discard on the market," 棄市, is an expression referring to the execution of criminals, a punishment traditionally performed on the market. In this sense, the *Su wen* statement could be read as "one kills one's own art." In contrast, Wang Bing: "If one fails to study diligently and, hence, does not arrive at the principles and yet offers [one's art] for sale at the market, the people will not trust it and will call it empty and false. Hence, [the text] states: 'one's art is discarded [by the people] on the market.'"

how obscure!
Who knows this Way!³⁰

The greatness of the Way
it resembles [the inexhaustible space of] heaven and earth and
it matches the [vastness of the] four seas.³¹

If you do not understand the message of the Way,
what you have received as brilliant will [remain] obscure [to you]."³²

---

30 Wang Bing: "窈窈冥冥 is to say: dark and distant! [That is], the perfect Way is dark and distant; who could get to know it." For 窈窈冥冥 see *Zhuang zi*, Zai you 在宥 (Chen Guying p. 308).

31 Wang Bing: "擬於天地 is to say: its height cannot be measured. 配於四海 is to say: its depth and extension cannot be fathomed."

32 Wang Bing: "However, if one is unable to understand the teachings of the Way, being taught the brilliant Way may but generate obscurity." Zhang Jiebin: "不知道之諭 is: not to grasp the message of the [Way]. When its message is missed then it is unavoidable that confusion harms its meaning. Hence, contrary [to what was to be expected], what was a clear instruction turns into an obscure [message]." Because of the wording of Wang Bing's comment 不能曉諭于道, Qian Chaochen-90/85 concluded that the two characters 道 and 諭 have been erroneously exchanged by a copyist after Wang Bing had written his commentary. Hence the correct meaning should be: "If you do not know the Way of the instructions [you receive], what you have received as brilliant will [remain] obscure [to you]."

Chapter 79
Discourse on Yin and Yang Categories

79-561-2

At the first arrival of the first month of spring,[1]

Huang Di sat leisurely.[2]

While he looked down [from his elevated seat] and observed the eight farthest [regions][3] and

rectified the qi of the eight winds,[4]

he asked Lei Gong:

"The categories of yin and yang and

the Way of the conduit vessels,

---

1 Wang Bing: "孟春始至 refers to 立春之日, 'the day when spring begins.'" Cheng Shide et al.: "孟春 is the begin of spring; this is the first month of the lunar calendar."

2 Wang Bing: "燕 is 安, 'composed.'" Zhang Jiebin: "燕 stands for 閑, 'leisurely.'" Cheng Shide et al.: "燕坐 is: to sit calmly."

3 Zhang Jiebin: "八極 refers to 八方遠際, 'the distant borders of the eight cardinal directions.'"

4 Wang Bing: "正八風 is to say 候八方所至之風, 'he examined the winds coming from the eight cardinal directions.'" Lin Yi et al.: "[The statement] 八風朝太一, 'the eight winds appear at the court of Tai-yi,' appears in the 天元玉冊 *Tian yuan yu ce*. Now, Yang Shangshan has said: 'Heaven is yang, the earth is yin. Man constitutes [their] harmonious [merger]. If there is only yin and no yang, there is weakening and killing without end. If there is only yang and no yin, generation and growth do not stop. When generation and growth do not stop, then this causes harm to the yin. When the yin is harmed, then yin catastrophes emerge. When weakening and killing do not end, then this causes harm to the yang. When the yang is harmed, then yang disasters are generated. Hence it is necessary that the sages between heaven and earth harmonize the qi of yin and yang, thereby letting the myriad beings come to life. The Way of harmonizing the qi is to say: first cultivate the body in virtue, then the qi of yin and yang are harmonized. When yin [qi] and yang qi are harmonized, then the winds of the eight seasonal turning points are regulated. When the winds of the eight seasonal turning points are regulated, then the eight depletion winds stop. As a result, no epidemic diseases emerge and extraordinary happiness sets in plentifully. This, too, is something one does not know why it is so, and yet it is so. Hence Huang Di asked about the noble or low status of the conduit vessels of the body, to regulate them accordingly and cultivate the virtue in the body, in order to 'rectify the qi of the eight winds.'" Zhang Jiebin: "正 is 察, 'to examine.'" Cheng Shide et al.: "正 is 較正, 'to correct.'"

that is what is ruled by the five inside.[5]
Which depot is the most precious?"

Lei Gong responded:
"Spring, [that is] *jia* and *yi*, [that is] green-blue.
Inside it rules the liver.[6]

It governs for 72 days;
this is the season ruling the vessels.

[I, your] subject consider this depot to be the most precious."

79-561-5
[Huang] Di:
"Still,
reading the *Upper [Classic]* and the *Lower Classic*, the *Yin and Yang*, and the *Natural Approach*,[7]
that which you state to be precious
is the most inferior [there]."[8]

Lei Gong devoted himself to fasting for seven days.[9]
In the morning he resumed his seat to attend [Huang Di].

[Huang] Di:
"The third yang is the warp
The second yang is the rope.
The first yang travels between sections.[10]

---

5 Wang Bing: "五中 stands for 五藏, 'the five depots.'" Cheng Shide et al.: "Another opinion identifies 五中 as the title of an ancient treatise."

6 Cf *Su wen* 4: 東方色青，入通于肝, "The Eastern region; green color. Internally it communicates with the liver."

7 Wang Bing: "從容 is to say 安緩比類 'to compare similarities in a relaxed mood.'"

8 693/38: "最 modifies 下."

9 Wang Bing: "His understanding was incorrect. Hence, he devoted himself to fasting to clean his mind."

10 Wang Bing: "經 is to say 經綸, 'warp threads,' 'main structures / principles.' It is that which assists in completing a task. 維 is to say 維持, 'to uphold.' It is that by which the true [qi] of heaven is tied. 游 is to say: 游行, 'to travel.' 部 is to say 身形部分, 'the sections of the physical body.' Hence, that which rules the qi assists in completing a task; that which transforms the grain ties the true [qi of] heaven; that which rules the colors disperses the essential and subtle and makes it travel through all sec-

From this one knows the five depots from end to begin.[11]

The third yang is the exterior;
the second yin is the interior.[12]

---

tions [of the body]." Lin Yi et al.: "Yang Shangshan: The third yang is the foot major
yang vessel. It rises from the inner canthi to the top of the head, separates into four
distinct paths descending via the neck and merges with the courses of the six proper
and branch vessels rising and descending along the spine. To the body it constitutes
a 'warp' (經). The second yang is the foot yang brilliance vessel. It emerges from the
nose, descends via the throat, separates into four distinct paths and merges with the
courses of the six proper and branch vessels rising and descending along the abdomen. It forms a 'net' (綱維) on the body. The first yang is the foot minor yang vessel.
It emerges from the outer canthi and encircles the head. It separates into four distinct
paths, descends into the broken basin, merges with the courses of the six proper and
branch vessels rising and descending [in the organism]. It is responsible for supplying
all junctures and to make the qi flow into the three [body] sections. Hence, [the text
states] 'it [makes it] travel to [all] sections.'" Zhang Jiebin: "經 stands for 大經, 'major
conduit/big warp.' It is a vessel surrounding the entire body. Only the foot major yang
[vessel] occupies such a chief position. It penetrates the peak [of the skull], descends
through the spine and is the sole ruler of the yang section. Hence, [the text] speaks
of 'warp.'" Gao Shishi: "As for 'the third yang is the warp,' the major yang serves as
opener; it follows the body's spine. It is like a large warp passing through the outside.
As for 'the second yang is the weft,' the yang brilliance serves as unifier; if follows the
body's front side. It is like a girdle holding together the interior." Cheng Shide et al.:
" 'First yang' refers to the foot minor yang [conduit]. It passes along the body's sides. It
is tied to the yang brilliance [conduits] on the front and to the major yang [conduits]
on the back. It leaves and enters [the body] between the two vessels of the major
yang and of the yang brilliance [conduits]. Hence, [the text] speaks of it as 'travelling
through [the body's sections].'" 1837/49: "The foot yang brilliance passes through the
body's chest and abdomen. It binds the frontal region." Zhang Zhicong: "游部 is: it
travels between inner and outer [sections], between yin and yang [regions]."

11 Wang Bing: "By observing the meanings of 經綸, 'warp thread,' 維繫, 'rope tie,'
and 游部, 'travel between sections,' [the course of the conduits of] the five depots from
begin to end can be known."

12 Wang Bing: "The third yang is the major yang; the second yin is the minor
yin. The minor yin and the major yang constitute outside and inside [to each other].
Hence, [the text] states: 'The third yang is outside; the second yin is inside.'" Zhang
Jiebin: " 'Third yang' is a mistake and should be 'third yin.' The third yin is the major
yin. The major yin constitutes the outside to all the yin. Hence, [the text states: 'the
third yin is outside.' The second yin refers to the minor yin, i.e., the kidneys. The kidneys belong to the water; their qi is in the depth and it rules the bones. Hence, [the
text] states: 'the second yin is inside.'"

When the arrival of the first yin is interrupted, this is the darkness of the new moon.[13]

Now, combine all this to determine its [underlying] structure."[14]

Lei Gong:
"Receiving instructions [in medical practice] has not enabled [me] to reach an understanding."

[Huang] Di:
"As for the so-called third yang,
the major yang constitutes the warp.

When the third yang [movement in the] vessels arrives at the hand major yin string[-like], at the surface, but not in the depth,
decide on the basis of the [respective] degree [of heaven],
investigate with [your] heart and
combine [your insights] with the discourse on yin and yang.[15]

---

13 Wang Bing: "The first yin is the ceasing yin. 厥 stands for 盡, 'exhausted..'. Now, when the yin is exhausted, this means darkness; when the yin comes to life, this is new moon. 'Ceasing yin' has the meaning of 'exhausted yin.' When this qi emerges, this is new moon. That is to say, when this qi is exhausted, then there is darkness. Hence, one sees the new moon and there is this darkness, too. Hence, [the text] states: 'When the arrival of the first yin is interrupted, this brings about new moon and darkness.'" Lin Yi et al.: "When the commentary [by Wang Bing] states: 'when the yin is exhausted, this means darkness; when the yin emerges, this is new moon,' this might be 'when the yang emerges, this is new moon.'" Zhang Jiebin: "As for the Way of the vanishing and growing of yin and yang, when the yin is exhausted, this is like the darkness of the moon. When the yang emerges, this is like new moon. Hence, 'darkness and then new moon' means interruption and new life."

14 Wang Bing: "This way, one brings together the completely exhausted yin with the developing wood to determine the structures corresponding to the five agents without abandoning their circular course. Hence, [the text] states: 'bring all this to-gether to determine its structure.'"

15 Wang Bing: " 'Major yin' is to say: 寸口, 'inch opening.' The inch opening is the hand major yin. This is the location where the qi in the vessels passes by. Hence, all the vessels arrive at the inch opening. [Usually,] the major yang [movement in the] vessels is vast, large, and extended. Here now it is string[-like], at the surface, and not in the depth. In such a case one must take into account the high or low degree of the four seasons [present] and decide about [their significance]. And this must be combined with an examination of those signs that indicate whether the [status of the] five depots does or does not conform [with the present season]. Once this, in turn, is brought into correspondence with the yin yang doctrine, one knows whether a par-

79-562-6
The so-called second yang, this is yang brilliance.

When it arrives at the hand major yin
string[-like], in the depth, tense, and without drumming,
the disease was caused by extreme heat.[16]
All [such patients] die.[17]

The first yang, this is the minor yang.

When it arrives at the hand major yin,
and at man's facing above,[18] and
when it is string[-like], tense, and suspended without being interrupted,
this is a minor yang disease.[19]

If there is only yin [qi], then death follows.[20]

---

ticular depot's [qi] is present or not." Wu Kun: "The [movement in the] major yang vessels is vast, large, and extended. Here now it is a string, at the surface, and not in the depth. ... One must combine it with the yin yang doctrine, to understand whether it is benign or malign."

16 Wang Bing: "[Usually,] the yang brilliance [movement in the] vessels is at the surface, large and short. Here now it is a string and in the depth, it is tense and does not beat. In this case the yin qi dominates the yang; the wood has come to occupy the soil."

17 Wang Bing: "When the yin qi dominates the yang, when the wood has come to occupy the soil and when contrary [to what one might expect] a heat disease sets in, this is [a situation] of yang qi being weakened to destruction. This is like the flame of a lamp that is about to disappear and is bright nevertheless. Hence, [the text] states 'all [such patients] die.'"

18 Wang Bing: "Man's facing is a [region] where the movement in the vessels can be felt with the hand on both sides of the throat at a distance of one and a half individually standardized inches."

19 Wang Bing: "String refers to the minor yang [movement in the] vessels. Here now it is tense, suspended, but not interrupted. This means that the qi in the conduit is insufficient. Hence, [the text] speaks of 'a minor yang disease.' 'Suspended' is to say 'like the dangling movement of a suspended item.'"

20 Wang Bing: "專 stands for 獨, 'alone.' That is to say, if there is only yin qi and no yang qi, this means death." Zhang Jiebin: "When the yang qi is used up and [when its flow is] interrupted, then the yin evil alone is present in abundance."

79-563-3
The third yin, it rules the six conduits.[21]
They intersect at the major yin.

If there is hidden drumming, and if [the movement is] not at the surface,
this is an evacuation of mind and heart above.[22]

---

21 Wang Bing: "The third yin is the major yin. Why is it that all the vessels come to
the hand major yin? Because [the hand major yin] is the ruler of the six conduits. 'Six
conduits' refers to the three yin and three yang conduit vessels. Why do they come to
the hand major yin? Because the lung is where the qi of all the vessels meet, they all
come together at the qi opening. Hence, the following statement." Zhang Jiebin: "The
depots of the third yin are spleen and lung. The lung controls the qi; it is the meeting
point of all vessels. The spleen is associated with the soil; it is the mother of all beings.
Hence, the third yin is the ruler of the six conduits."

22 Wang Bing: "When the [movement in the] vessels is hidden, beats like a drum,
and does not rise to the surface, then [this indicates that] the qi of the heart is insufficient. Hence, it pulls on the heart above and causes disease. 志心 stands for 小
心, 'minor heart.' *Su wen* 52 states: 'to the side of the seventh vertebra, inside there
is the minor heart.' This is explained by what was said above." Lin Yi et al.: "Yang
Shangshan commented: 'The [movement in the] lung vessel is near the surface and
rough. This is the normal state. Here now it appears beating in the depth. This is a
kidney [movement in the] vessels. The foot minor yin vessel passes through the spine
and touches the spleen. It rises, enters the lung, leaves the lung again and encircles
the heart. The lung qi descends into the kidneys [storing the] will; it rises to enter
the heart [storing the] spirit.' When Wang Bing identified 志心 as 小心, he had not
penetrated the meaning [of this statement]." See the notes accompanying *Su wen* 52
for a further discussion of various attempts in history to identify "minor heart." Qian
Chaochen-88/135 agrees with Wang Bing, pointing out that *Tai su* 19 [知針石] has
志心 where *Su wen* 52 has 小心. Wu Kun: "上空志心 should be 志上控心, 'the mind
moves upwards to pull on the heart.' The will is the qi of the kidneys. The spleen [cor-
responds with the eighth diagram] *kun* and with the soil; it has the image of mother-
ing all beings. Hence, when [all] the six conduits receive their qi from the spleen, they
are in order. This is meant by 六經所主 (sic!).' Here now, this qi moves upwards and
intersects with the major yin at the inch-opening. The [movement in the] vessels arrives beating in the depth. This indicates that the [movement of the] spleen [qi] has
been interrupted. When the [movement of the] spleen [qi] is interrupted, then the
kidneys have nothing to fear. [Their] qi moves upwards to bother the heart. It pulls on
the heart [and causes] pain. The kidneys rule the will; hence, [the text] states: 志上控
心, 'the will moves upwards to pull on the heart.'" Ma Shi: "Basically, the [movement
in the] vessels of the major yin is at the surface and rough. Here now a hidden [move-
ment] appears [in the] vessels; also, it resembles beating and is not at the surface. This

When the second yin arrives at the lung,
its qi turns to the urinary bladder;
externally it connects with spleen and stomach.[23]

When the first yin arrives all alone,
the conduit [movement] is interrupted.
The qi is at the surface and does not drum.
[Its movement is] hook[-like] and smooth.[24]

---

is a [movement associated with the] kidneys at the [location of the] lung. The spirit of the kidneys is the will. When the lung is depleted, the kidneys are depleted too. And their will is also depleted and has nothing to rest on. When [the text] states 上空, 'empty above,' that is to say, the spirit of the kidneys is sparse above. When [the text] states 志心, 'will and heart,' [that is to say,] even though the will is the spirit of the kidneys, in fact it is situated in the heart." Zhang Jiebin: "The lung rules what is light and at the surface; the spleen rules blending and slowness. These are their basic [movements in the] vessels. Here now [the movement] appears hidden, beating, and not at the surface. This indicates that the yin is abundant, while the yang is weak. The [resulting] disease is that the upper warmer is empty and depleted, while the mind of spleen and lung, as well as the spirit of the heart have been harmed by the yin. They all are insufficient. Hence, [the text] states: 'Above, mind and heart are empty.'"

23 Wang Bing: "The second yin is the foot minor yin vessel of the kidneys. Its branch course enters the heel and after having reached further upwards into the thighs, along the edge on its back, touches the spine, associates with the kidneys and encloses the urinary bladder. Its straight course moves upwards from the kidneys, penetrates the liver and the diaphragm and enters into the lung. Hence, above it reaches to the lung and its qi turns to the urinary bladder. On the outside it connects with spleen and stomach." Zhang Jiebin: "When [the text states:] 'the second yin arrives at the inch-opening,' that is a reference to the arrival of a kidneys [movement in the] vessels at the inch-opening. *Su wen* 21 says: 'When the second yin arrives beating, this is [a movement associated with] the kidneys that is in the depth and not at the surface. The upwards movement of the vessels of the kidneys is such that its straight [branch] rises from the kidneys, passes through the liver and the diaphragm, enters into the lung and emerges at the qi opening. This is [meant by] 'the second qin arrives at the lung.' The kidneys rule the water; they receive qi from the lung to carry out the order of downward movement and to penetrate and harmonize the water ways. Its qi turns to the urinary bladder. The lung is above; the kidneys are below. Spleen and stomach are located in the middle. They control the power of rising and descending. Hence, [the text] states: 'Externally it connects with spleen and stomach.'"

24 Wang Bing: "When the first yin arrives alone, the [flow of the] qi of the lung conduit is interrupted internally. In this case the qi is at the surface but does not beat against the hand [examining its movement]. When the qi is not interrupted internally, [its movement resembles] a hook and is smooth." Lin Yi et al.: "Yang Shangshan: The first yin is the ceasing yin." Ma Shi: "The [movement in the] vessels of the ceasing yin is like a string, weak, and extended. Here now it alone arrives at the lung conduit.

79-564-1
These six [movements in the] vessels,
at times they are yin, at times they are yang.[25]
They are tied to and merge with each other.
Crosswise penetrating the five depots
they link up with yin and yang."

<That which arrives first is the host;
that which arrives subsequently is the visitor.>[26]

Lei Gong:
"[I, your] subject, am fully acquainted with the meaning of all of this.

I have received what is transmitted on the conduit vessels and
I have learned, through recitations,[27] the Way of the [text] *Natural Approach*
to become one with the natural approach.

[And, yet,]
I do not know [how to dinstinguish] yin and yang and
I do not know [how to distinguish] female and male."[28]

When the conduit qi is interrupted, then the vessel qi is at the surface and does not
beat. When it is not yet interrupted, then [the movement] resembles a hook and it is
smooth at the same time. In this case, there is still yang qi present." Zhang Jiebin: "The
basic [movement of the] vessels of the ceasing yin should be soft, smooth, like a string,
and extended. In yin there is yang. That is the normal situation. If the first yin arrives
alone, then the [movement in the] conduit is interrupted in the interior and the qi is
at the surface outside. Hence, it cannot beat, [resemble] a hook, and be smooth, but
solely [resembles] a string and has no stomach [qi]. The purpose of life is exhausted."

25 Wang Bing: "Sometimes one notices a yang vessel [movement] in the yin, sometimes one notices a yin vessel [movement] in the yang."

26 Wang Bing: "When the qi in the vessels is such that at times one notices a yang
in the yin, or a yin in the yang, how can this be differentiated? One should identify
that which arrives first as host and that which arrives afterwards as visitor. 'To arrive'
means 'to arrive at the inch opening.'"

27 Wang Bing: "頌 is written 誦, 'to recite,' today".

28 Wang Bing: "[Lei] Gong states: 'I recite the miraculous Way of the natural approach of today, to bring it in agreement with the natural approach of antiquity and
compare the likes of physical appearance and names. Still, I do not know the sequence
of the superior and inferior position of yin and yang and I do not know the meaning
of the differences between something being labelled female or male."

79-564-4
[Huang] Di:
"The third yang is father;²⁹
the second yang is guard;³⁰
the first yang is the beginning of the thread.³¹

The third yin is mother;³²
the second yin is female;³³
the first yin is >solitary< emissary.³⁴

---

29 Wang Bing: "The father directs all the little ones. That is to say, [like a father, the third yang] is revered highly." Zhang Jiebin: "The major yang rules over all the conduits. It alone is revered as great. Hence, it is called 'father.'" 1837/49: "It commands all conduits; hence it is revered as 'father.'"

30 Wang Bing: "The guard drives away and protects against all the evil. That is to say, [like a guard, the second yang] supports life." Ma Shi: "The second yang is the yang brilliance. The yang brilliance is that which holds together the exterior and it protects all sections. Hence, it is the guard." 1837/49: "It can drive away all evils; hence, it is called guard."

31 Wang Bing: "紀 is that by which the physical body and the qi are arranged. That is a reference to its levelling [potential]." Cheng Shide et al.: "紀 is 會, 'to meet.' The minor yang [conduit] appears and enters [the body again] between the major yang and yang brilliance [conduits]. It constitutes the intersection of the yang [conduits]. Hence it is called 紀." 1837/49: "It is the meeting place of all the yang [vessels]; hence, it is called 紀."

32 Wang Bing: "The mother raises all the children. That is to say, [like a mother, the third yin] nourishes life." Wu Kun: "The major yin nourishes all the depots. This is the image of the mother."

33 Wang Bing: "Female is a yin label." Ma Shi: "The second yin is the minor yin. The minor yin is that which holds together the interior. It is here where life commences. Hence, it is female." Zhang Jiebin: "The minor yin belongs to the water. Water can generate the beings."

34 Wang Bing: "The depot of the first yin forms a union on the outside with the triple warmer. The triple warmer is responsible for guiding all the qi. [The triple warmer] is called 'emissary;' hence, [the text] speaks of the 'sole emissary.'" Zhang Jiebin: " 'Emissary' is to say: end and begin of communication. The yin is exhausted and the yang comes to life; only the ceasing yin rules it. Hence, it is the sole emissary." Ma Shi: "The first yin is the ceasing yin. The ceasing yin is that which travels to [all] sections internally. [It helps] the generals make their plans. Hence, it is the sole emissary." 1837/49: "When the yin is at its end, then the yang comes to life. It is only ceasing yin that controls it. Hence, it is also called 'sole emissary.'"

79-564-6
When the second yang [meets with] the first yin,
yang brilliance rules the disease.
When it cannot dominate the first yin,[35]
the vessels are soft and [display] a movement.[36]
The nine orifices have all sunken into the depth.[37]

When the third yang [meets with] the first yin,
the major yang [movement in the] vessels dominates.
The first yin cannot stop [it].
Internally it causes disorder in the five depots.
Externally it causes shock.[38]

---

35 Wang Bing: "The first yin is the ceasing yin; it is the qi of liver and wood. The second yang is the qi of yang brilliance, stomach, and soil. Wood and soil clash at each other; hence, yang brilliance rules the disease. The wood overcomes the soil; the soil does not dominate the wood. Hence, [the text] states: 'does not dominate first yin.'"

36 Wang Bing: " 'Soft' refers to the stomach qi; 'movement' refers to the physical appearance of wood." The term 動, "to move," is not attested anywhere else in the *Su wen* as denoting a special quality of the movement in the vessels; several times it is used to refer to the movement in the vessels in general. Also, it could be interpreted as "made to move" in the sense of "excited."

37 Wang Bing: "When wood and soil hold each other, then the stomach qi cannot turn [things] around. Hence, the nine orifices are blocked and impassable." Zhang Jiebin: "The second yang is the soil, the first yin is the wood. When yang brilliance and ceasing yin strike at each other, then the liver evil turns against the stomach. Hence, the yang brilliance controls the disease. It does not dominate the first yin. When the [movement in the] vessels is soft, this is the qi of the stomach. That which moves/is excited is the liver qi. When soil is affected by the evil of wood, then it is soft and moves/is excited at the same time." Wang Bing's interpretation here of 沉 with the meaning of 沉滯, "blocked," "obstructed," is supported by the use of 沉 in *Su wen* 26.

38 Wang Bing: "The third yang is the qi of the foot major yang. Hence, [the text] states: 'The major yang dominates.' Wood generates fire. Here now, an abundant yang burns the wood. The wood is affected by it repeatedly; the yang qi is vast and abounds. Internally this generates craziness and heat, causing internal confusion among the five depots. The liver qi rules [the affect of] shock. Hence, the external physical appearance offers an image of being affected by shock." Zhang Jiebin: "When the third yang [meets with] the first yin, the urinary bladder and the lung have both a disease. The wood of the liver generates fire and the urinary bladder uses cold water to turn against it. Hence, the major yang [movement in the] vessels dominates. The liver qi of the first yin may be strong, but it is unable to stop [the major yang]. Hence, wind and cold embrace each other and internally they confuse the five depots."

79-565-1

When the second yin [meets with] the second yang,
the disease is in the lung.³⁹
The minor yin [movement in the] vessels is in the depth.
It dominates the lung; it harms the spleen.⁴⁰
Externally it harms the four limbs.

When the second yin arrives all intertwined with the second yang,
the disease is in the kidneys.⁴¹
[The patient] voices insults, making absurd movements.
[He suffers from] peak illness and is crazy.⁴²

---

39 Wang Bing: "The second yin refers to the hand minor yin vessel of the heart.
The second yang refers to the stomach vessel too. When both heart and stomach
have a disease, the evil [qi of both depots] move upwards and downwards and unite
with each other. Hence, there is internal harm to the spleen and on the outside they
dominate the lung. This is so because the stomach has the spleen as its palace. Heart
fire dominates metal. The spleen controls the four limbs. When, therefore, the spleen
is harmed, then the four limbs are harmed externally." Lin Yi et al.: "The second yang
[referred to] here is the hand yang brilliance [of the large intestine vessel]. The large
intestine is the palace of the lung. The minor yin is the heart. Fire dominates the palace
of the metal. Hence, [the text] states: 'The disease is in the lung.' When Mr. Wang
[Bing] states that second yang refers to the stomach, he has not understood the meaning here. ... Also, the Quan Yuanqi edition, the *Jia yi jing*, and the *Tai su*, they all have
'when the second yin [meets] the first yang.'"

40 Gao Shishi: " 'Second yang' should be 'third yang.' The major yang qi is in the
skin and its hair. The skin and its hair are associated with the lung. Hence, when the
second yin and the third yang meet, the disease is in the lung. When the second yin
meets with the third yang and when the disease is in the lung, then the third yang has
a surplus, while the second yin is insufficient. Hence, the minor yin [movement in the]
vessels is in the depth. 'Dominates the lung' should be 'the lung qi dominates.' When
the lung dominates, then the spleen receives harm. This explains clearly, when the
spleen is harmed, this does not mean that the spleen depot of the major yin is harmed,
but the four limbs on the outside."

41 Wang Bing: "The second yin refers to the kidneys, the depot of water. The second yang is the stomach, the palace of the soil. The qi of the soil punishes the water;
Hence, [the text] states: 'they arrive intertwined and the disease is in the kidneys.'"
Wu Kun: " 'The second yin and the second yang all arrive intertwined,' this is to say,
the four qi of the heart, the kidneys, the stomach, and the large intestine all arrived
intertwined at the hand major yin. When these four qi strike against each other, one
water does not suffice to dominate two fires. Hence, the disease is in the kidneys."

42 Wang Bing: "Because the water of the kidneys cannot dominate, the stomach
[qi] is abundant and causes peak [illness] and craziness. " Wu Kun: "The less water

79-565-2
When the second yin [meets with] the first yang,
the disease emerges from the kidneys.[43]
The yin qi travels to the heart as an [uninvited] visitor.[44]
The orifices below the [stomach] duct
are obstructed by a dike and made impassable.[45]
The four limbs are severed.[46]

---

there is, the more the fire flares up. Hence, this causes [the patient] to utter insults and to make absurd movements."

43 Wang Bing: "First yang is to say hand minor yang triple burner, which is the palace of the heart ruler, the fire. [Here] water moves upwards to attack the fire, hence the fire disease emerges from the kidneys."

44 Wang Bing: "The yin qi travels to the heart as an [uninvited] visitor. Why? The vessel of the kidneys moves upwards from the kidneys; it passes through the liver and the diaphragm and enters into the lung. Its branch course leaves from the lung, winds around the heart and pours into the chest. Hence, it is like this."

45 Wang Bing: "The yin visitor in the orifices moves upwards and the stomach can not check [it]. When the stomach cannot check [it, that indicates that] the qi of the soil is weak. Hence, the orifices below the duct are all impassable. [The text] speaks of 堤, 'blocked.' This is like a dike, 堤堰, which does not permit leaking." Ma Shi read 心 脘下 and 空竅堤 as sentences. His commentary: "When the minor yin qi travels as a visitor to below the heart duct, this is water coming to rebel against the fire. Now, when the yin qi travels upwards, the stomach cannot contain it. The opening of intestine and stomach is diked; it is blocked and impassable." Gao Shishi: 空竅 refers to the openings of the sweat. 堤 is like 路, 'pathway.' When minor yin and minor yang merge, the yin dominates the yang. Hence the disease originates in the kidneys of the minor yin. The minor yang triple burner vessel spreads out to encircle the heart enclosure and emerges again at the stomach duct. When, in the present case, the minor yin qi travels as a visitor to below the heart duct, this is yin [qi settling as an unvited] visitor in the yang [section, i.e.,] water dominating its fire. This results in the triple burner being unable to make the qi leave; it warms the muscles and the skin [structures]. It appears as if the pathways of the [sweat] openings were blocked and impassable." Wu Kun: "Second yin is the minor yin qi of the kidneys. First yang is the minor yang qi of the gallbladder. When these two qi clash, water cannot dominate fire. The disease originates from the kidneys. When the kidneys have a disease, their qi moves contrary [to their regular course]. It rises and fills the openings below the heart duct as if there were a dike creating a block in the chest."

46 Wang Bing: "The stomach vessel follows the feet; the heart vessel winds around the hands. Hence, the four limbs are like severed and cannot be used." Lin Yi et al.: "Mr. Wang [Bing] says: 'the stomach vessel follows the feet.' This disease of the second yin [meeting with] the first yang emerges from the kidneys. Instead of 'stomach' it should be 'kidneys.'"

79-565-4
When the first yin [meets with] the first yang, [the movement in the vessels is] intermittent and interrupted.⁴⁷
Here the yin qi has reached the heart.⁴⁸
Upward and downward movements [occur] without regularity.⁴⁹
[One] does not know whether it moves out or in.
Throat and gullet are dry,
the disease is in the spleen, [which is] the soil.⁵⁰

When the second yang [meets with] the third yin,
the extreme yin is all present.⁵¹
The yin does not surpass the yang.
The yang qi cannot stop the yin.
Yin and yang [qi] are both interrupted.
[When the movement in the vessels is] at the surface, this means blood conglomerations;
[when it is] in the depth, this means pus and rotting.⁵²

---

47 Wang Bing: "The first yin is the ceasing yin vessel; the first yang is the minor yang vessel. Both [carry] qi of wood. 'Intermittent and interrupted' is to say it moves and stops in between."

48 Wang Bing: "The qi of wood generates fire. Hence, the disease emerges and the yin qi moves to the heart."

49 Wang Bing: "The qi of liver and gall move upwards to the head and downwards to the lower back and to the feet; in the center it controls the abdomen and the flanks. Hence, when the disease breaks out, it moves upwards and downwards without remaining at a permanent location."

50 Wang Bing: "The back of the throat belongs to the gullet and is the messenger of the gallbladder. Hence, in case of disease, the throat and the gullet are dry. Even though the disease is in the soil of the spleen, it has originated from the liver and the gallbladder."

51 Wang Bing: "The second yang is the yang brilliance. The third yin is the hand major yin. The extreme yin is the spleen. Hence, [the text] states: 'The extreme yin is all present.' However, the yin qi is unable to surpass the yang and the yang qi cannot subdue the heart. In the present situation, yin and yang press against each other; hence all the vessels are interrupted and do not continue each other's [flow]."

52 Wang Bing: "A [movement in the] vessels at the surface indicates that the yang qi strikes against the yin. Hence, there are blood conglomerations. A [movement in the] vessels in the depth indicates that the yin qi strikes against the yang. Hence, pus accumulates and [the flesh] rots."

79-566-1
When both yin and yang are strong,
they reach yin and yang below.[53]

< 'Upper conjunction [results in] luminosity,
lower conjunction [results in] obscurity.' >[54]

When diagnosis includes a decision about the times of death or survival,
in all cases combine it with the begin of the year."[55]

Lei Gong:
"Please, may I ask about shortened times."[56]

Huang Di did not respond.

Lei Gong asked again.

---

53 Wang Bing: "When yin and yang are both strong and strike at each other without end, then [the disease] gradually moves downwards into the yin and yang and this
turns into a severe disease. 'Yin and yang' refer in males to the male member and in
women to the female receptacle." Tanba: "The six sentences beginning with 陰陽皆
壯 do not fit with the rest of the text; also, their meaning is quite obscure and difficult
to understand. They may have been moved here erroneously from another chapter."
Zhang Jiebin has 至, 'to arrive,' 'when it comes to,' instead of 合.

54 Wang Bing: "昭昭 is to say: above the yang brilliance; 冥冥 is to say: inside the
extreme yin, which is the location of mysterious darkness." Zhang Jiebin: "昭昭 is the
visible; 冥冥 is the fathomable. This is where the Way of yin and yang is present." Wu
Kun: "昭昭 is the Way of heaven; 冥冥 is the Way of the earth. That is a reference to
the union of the [movements in the] vessels with heaven and earth." Zhang Yizhi et
al.: "昭昭, 'brilliance,' refers to the yang of heaven; 冥冥 , 'darkness,' refers to the yin of
the earth. This is to say that if [a physician] examines the movement in the vessels and
the pathoconditions [of his patients] together, then he is able to determine whether
[his patients] suffer from depletion or repletion, from true [heat or cold] or false [heat
or cold]. [This phrase] does by no means exclusively refer to the [movement in the]
vessels." 2167/48: "昭昭 refers to heaven, to yang; 冥冥 refers to the earth, to yin. 上
合昭昭,下合冥冥 means: 'the changes of yin and yang in heaven and on earth correspond to each other.' For our translation, see *Su wen* 74-503-4.

55 歲首 was used first in the *Shi ji* 史記 for "first month of the year." See *Shi ji*, Xiao
Wu ji 孝武紀.

56 Yao Shaoyu: "短期, 'shortened times,' stands for 死期, 'times of death.' If one dies
because of disease, one cannot live out a complete life and [one's life] is short." Lin
Yi et al.: "In the Quan Yuanqi edition, beginning from 'Lei Gong' this is a separate
treatise, entitled '四時病類,' "The Four Seasons, Disease Classifications."

Huang Di:
"It is [outlined] in the discourses in the classics."

79-566-4
Lei Gong:
"Please, may I hear about shortened times."

Huang Di:
"[In case of] diseases during the three months of winter,
if the disease is a union with yang,
by the time of spring in the first month of the year,
the [movement in the] vessels will display evidence of death.
All [such patients] pass away after the end of spring.[57]

79-566-6
[In case of] diseases during the three months of winter,[58]
when [the qi] in the interior is exhausted,

---

57 Wang Bing: "病合於陽 is to say: the frontal yin (i.e., the sexual organ) joins
with the yang and this results in a disease. Even though the [movement in the] vessels has signs of death in the first month, the yang has emerged already, and when it
comes to rule there will be no death. Hence, [the moment of death] leaves the third
month of spring and reaches the begin of summer." Zhang Zhicong: "A disease in
the three months of winter is a disease caused by water. 病合於陽 is to say: there is
also a disease because of the major yang qi. When during the first month of spring a
[movement in the] vessels occurs that indicates death, this is always traceable to the
appearance of spring qi. The reason is, the origin of the spring qi is in winter and yang
qi emerges from water. The yang qi already has a disease and in addition something
emerges outside of spring qi. Hence, [these patients] die." Zhang Jiebin: "The three
months of winter are a time of abounding yin. 病合於陽 is to say: yang pathoconditions and a yang [movement in the] vessels. 出春 is the time from the end of spring
to the beginning of summer. Because the disease has united with the yang at the time
when the water rules, [in the beginning of spring], the seasonal qi is insufficient, while
the disease qi is present in surplus. When it comes to the first month of spring, when
the yang qi effuses, then the yang evil dominates ever more, while the yin qi is ever
more exhausted. If the [movement in the] vessels exhibits signs of death, then at the
end of spring and the beginning of summer, the yang [evil] abounds and the yin is
weak. Both have reached their extremes; there is no place where to escape."

58 Obviously, the seasons referred to here correspond to the division of the year
introduced by the calendar of Emperor Taichu 太初 around 100 B.C. Accordingly,
winter includes October through December; spring includes January through March.
See 1457/11.

when all herbs and willow leaves have perished,[59] and
when in spring all the [movements of] yin and the yang [qi] are interrupted,
the time [of death] is during the first month of spring.[60]

[In case of] diseases during the three months of spring,
{one speaks of 'yang kills'}[61]
when all the [movements of] yin and the yang [qi] are interrupted,
the time [of death] is when the herbs [are still] dry.[62]

79-567-1
[In case of] diseases during the three months of summer,
when the [period of] extreme yin has not exceeded ten days,[63] and

---

59 The received text has 理, "structure". We follow Wang Bing. Wang Bing: "裡 is
to say: the second yin; i.e., the qi of the kidneys. However, when the kidneys have a
disease and when the vessels during the first month display signs of death, all [these
patients] will perish at the moment when the dry herbs have turned green again and
when the willow leaves appear again. 理 stands for 裡. 已 stands for 以. In ancient
times [both characters] were used identically." Cheng Shide et al.: "The meaning is,
the disease will lead to death in spring." For a use of 殺 in a botanical context in the
sense of "to weaken", "to perish", see the poem *Fu ju* 賦菊 by Huang Chao 黃巢: 我花
開後百花殺, "after my flower(s) blossomed, all flowers perished."

60 Lin Yi et al.: "The *Tai su* does not have the character 春, 'spring.'"

61 Wang Bing: " 'Yang disease' does not refer to diseases of harm caused by cold,
warmth, or heat. [Yang disease] refers to an untimely heat disease, with a vast, abundant, and frequent [movement in the] vessels. That is, in the third month of spring, the
yang qi is still minor; it should not yet be complete and abundant. If now, in contrast
[to the regular seasonal course], one suffers from heat and the [movement in the]
vessels corresponds to the qi of summer, [this is what] the classic states: 'this [move-
ment in the] vessels will not be seen again.' The summer [movement in the] vessels
should be vast and frequent. [Here now] there is yang externally corresponding [to
the disease and to the movement in the vessels]. Hence, [the patient] must die when
summer begins. He dies at the onset of summer because this is the time when yang qi
kills the beings. Hence, [the text] states: 'yang kills.'" See *Suwen* 05 2-1 and 66 366-4
for wordings of 陽殺 in the sense of "yang kills."

62 Wang Bing: "If no yang disease is present, but both the yin and the yang [move-
ments in the] vessels are suspended and interrupted, [the patient] will die at the time
of [the solar term] hoar frost descends, when the herbs dry." [The solar term "hoar
frost descends" falls into late October].

63 Wang Bing: "This is a heat disease. When the spleen has a heat disease, then the
five depots are in danger. The completion number associated with soil is ten. Hence,
[the patient] will not survive ten days."

when yin and yang interact,
the time [of death] is at 'quiet water.'⁶⁴

[In case of] diseases during the three months of autumn,
when all the three yang arise,
do not treat. They will end by themselves."⁶⁵

79-567-2
<When yin and yang interact to unite,
[the patient] stands being unable to sit, or sits being unable to rise.

When the third yang arrives alone,
the time [of death] is at 'stone water.'⁶⁶

When the second yin arrives alone,
the time [of death] is at 'abundant water.'>⁶⁷

---

64 Lin Yi et al.: "Quan Yuanqi: 'Quiet water' is the seventh month." Yang Shang-shan: "溓 means 'the water is quiet.' The seventh month is the time when water is generated." 1490/46: "溓 refers to the time when the water is clear and cool; this is autumn."

65 Wang Bing: "In autumn, the yang qi is weak and the yin qi slowly emerges. The yang does not dominate the yin. Hence, [the disease] ends by itself."

66 Wang Bing: "There is yang but no yin. Hence, [the text] states: 'arrives alone.' 'Stone water' is to say, this is the time of the winter months when water turns into ice and is like a stone. The fire is buried during the term of *xu* [i.e., the ninth lunar month]. In winter there is very little yang qi. Hence, [such patients] die when water [becomes] stone."

67 Wang Bing: " 'Abundant water' refers to the season when rain and snow all turn to water. This refers exactly to the qi in the first month." Lin Yi et al.: "The Quan Yu-anqi edition has 'third yin' instead of 'second yin.'" 1490/46: " 'Abundant water' refers to the season when the most water and rain are present, that is early spring."

Chapter 80
Discourse on Comparing Abundance and Weakness

80-567-6
Lei Gong requested to ask:
"The large or small amounts of qi,
which [of their movements] are contrary [to their regular course] and
which [of their movements] follow [their regular course]?"

Huang Di answered:
"Yang [qi] follows the [course on the] left;
yin [qi] follows the [course on the] right.[1]

In the old, it follows the [course] above;
in the young, it follows the [course] below.[2]

---

1 Wang Bing: "Yang qi, regardless of whether in large or small [quantities], always
follows [a course on] the left. Yin qi, regardless of whether in large or small quantities,
always follows [a course on] the right. 從 stands for 順, "to comply with". The opposite
is 逆, 'to move contrary [to its regular course].' *Su wen* 5 states: 'Left and right are the
pathways of yin and yang.'" Zhang Jiebin: "Yang qi controls rise; hence, it originates
on the left. Yin qi controls descent; hence, it originates on the right." Zhang Zhicong:
"陽從左者 is to say, the qi of spring and summer originates from the left and moves
to the right. 陰從右者 is to say, the qi of autumn and winter originates from the right
and moves to the left."

2 Wang Bing: "The old consume little solid food; hence, to follow the above is appropriate [for them]. The young have many desires; hence, to follow the below is appropriate [for them]." Zhang Zhicong: "The qi of the old moves downwards from
above. This is like the qi of autumn which originates from above and is then weak
below. The qi of the young moves upwards from below. This is like the qi of spring
which originates from below and is then abundant above." Zhang Jiebin: "The qi of
the old begins to weaken below. Hence, when it originates from above, this is correct.
The qi of the young is first abundant below. Hence, when it originates below, this is
correct." Gao Shishi: "Among the qi of the four seasons, that of autumn and winter is
yin; it originates from above and moves down. [The qi of] spring and summer is yang;
it originates from below and moves up. Hence, [the text states]: in the old, it originates above; in the young, it originates below. The fact is, old stands for the yin [qi]
of autumn and winter; young stands for the yang [qi] of spring and summer." Mori:
"When in old people the spleen and the kidneys have weakened, while the heart and
the lung still abound [with qi], this is the normal state. Hence, [the text says]: 'originates above.' Whenever the feet are weak, the knees are cold, the passage of the stools
is blocked, while urination occurs frequently, and ears and eyes are sharp nevertheless,
then this is the meaning of 'originates above.' In the young, when spleen and kidneys

Hence,
in spring and summer,
an association with yang is life;
an association with autumn or winter, this is death.[3]

80-568-1
In the opposite [case],
an association with autumn or winter is life.[4]

Therefore,
whenever large or small [amounts of] qi move contrary [to their regular course],
in all instances this is recession."[5]

---

abound [with qi], while heart and lung are weak, then this is normal. Hence, [the text] states: 'originates below.' Whenever drinking and eating is doubled, when sexual desires abound, when thoughts and plans are directed at the nearby and when the chest is full resulting in coughing and panting, then this is the meaning of 'originates below.'"

3 Wang Bing: "歸秋冬 is to say: to move contrary [to a regular course] and to associate with the yin. The reason [for death in this case] is that to associate with the yin means to follow the qi of attack and killing." Zhang Jiebin: "Spring and summer are seasons of yang abundance. External signs and the [movement in the] vessels should both be associated with yang, to signal life. If one notices yin indicators, as should be the case in autumn and winter, this is 'moving against [a regular course],' this means death." Ma Shi: "In spring and summer, both in disease and in the [movement in the] vessels, an association with yang is life. If a yin disease or a yin [movement in the] vessels [appear], as if it were autumn or winter, this is death." Yu Chang: "春夏歸陽 should perhaps be 陽歸春夏, 'when yang associates with spring and summer, [this is life].' Hence, the sentence below states: 'when it associates with autumn and winter, this is death.' This would match a sentence 歸春夏為生. Further down the text states: 反之則歸秋冬為生. ... The entire sentence is corrupt; the subsequent text makes no sense either." Shen Zumian: "Something was omitted from this passage."

4 Wang Bing: "反之 refers to autumn and winter. When autumn and winter are associated with yin, this means life." Ma Shi: "When in spring and summer either a disease or a [movement in the] vessels is associated with yang [qi], then this signals life. In case [the patient has] a yin disease or a yin [movement in the] vessels, as [one should expect it to occur] in autum or winter, then this signals death." Wu Kun: "That is to say, during the seasons of spring and summer, the [movement in the] vessels at the inch [section should] be abundant. In cases associated with autumn or winter, the [movement in the] vessels at the foot-long section is abundant. [One] goes along with the [nature of the] yang qi; hence [the patient] survives. [One] moves contrary to the [nature of the] yang qi; hence [the patient] dies."

5 Wang Bing: "When large or small [amounts of] yang qi contrary [to normal] originate from the right, or when large or small [amounts of] yin qi contrary [to what

[Lei Gong] asked:
"What about recession in [situations where there is] surplus?"[6]

[Huang Di] answered:
"Once [the qi] moves up and does not move down,
cold recession reaches to the knees.[7]

The young, they die in autumn or winter.
The old, they survive in autumn or winter.[8]

---

is normal] originate from the left, this is 'no compliance'. Hence, [the text] speaks of qi moving contrary [to its regular course], regardless of whether large or small amounts are concerned. Such instances of originating from the left or of originating from the right that are 'not complying', they are [called] 'recession.' 'Recession' is to say: a qi that moves contrary [to its regular course]." Zhang Qi: "This entire paragraph appears to be corrupt." For detailed discussions of the concept of 厥 see 2619/52, 854/1, 1623/13, and 2225/4.

6 Wang Bing: "That is to say, if a [movement] of diminished [qi] that is 'not complying' is a 'movement contrary [to its regular course],' is it possible that a qi that is present in surplus can generate a disease of recession, i.e., of movement contrary [to its regular course]?'"

7 Wang Bing: "When the qi of all conduits follows a reverse [movement, i.e.] rises in a movement contrary [to what is normal], and if the yang qi fails to descend, how can such [a situation] be differentiated? [The sign] is cold [because of] recession reaching up to the knees. The four limbs are the origins of all yang. They should be warm but they are, in contrast [to what is normal, affected by] cold moving upwards. Hence, [the text speaks of] 'cold [because of] recession.'"

8 Wang Bing: "'Autumn and winter' is to say 'return to the yin.' 'Return to the yin' means that their diseases develop from the right. The young depend in their activities on yang qi. Hence, they die in autumn and winter. The old depend in their activities on yin qi. Hence, they survive in autumn and winter." Lin Yi et al.: Yang Shangshan: "'Depleted' means 厥, 'recession.' When all the yang qi moves upwards into the head and does not move downwards into the feet, the feet and the shinbones are depleted. Hence, cold [because of] recession reaches up to the knees." Zhang Jiebin: "In old people, the yang qi starts from above. Cold knees do not constitute a problem. In youth, the yang qi starts from below and cold knees are a 'movement contrary [to a regular course].' The yang of the youth should not be weak, but if it is weak the season when yin dominates is to be feared most. In old people the yang qi is weak in itself. That is a normal condition. Hence, there is no reason to worry in autumn and winter." Wu Kun: "When the yang qi rises contrary [to its regular course] and does not move down, then the yin accumulates below. Hence the cold reaches to the knees. In old people the yang qi follows [a course] above. Hence it is normal when their knees are cold. In young people the yang qi follows [a course] below. When their knees are cold, this is contrary [to regular]. In autumn and winter when the yang is weak and the yin

80-568-3
When the qi moves up and does not move down,
headache and peak illness [result].⁹

Searching the yang: one does not get [its movement].
searching the yin: one does not recognize it.¹⁰

The five sections are barred; there is no evidence.

As if one lived in a vast wilderness;
as if one [tried to] hide in an empty chamber.

A thin thread; it belongs to [the signs] of early death.¹¹

---

flourishes, cold recession increases. In young people this is contrary [to regular]; hence
they die. In old people this is normal; hence they survive."

9 Wang Bing: " 'Peak' refers to the very top of the body. 'Peak disease' is a disease
of the head." Yao Shaoyu: "That is to say, when qi and blood move upwards, then not
only the feet become cold up to the knees, a disease must develop above too, in the
peak [of the head]." Zhang Jiebin: "Such diseases occur because of repletion above
and depletion below." 2738/14: " 'Peak disease' does not refer here to 癲癇, 'epilepsy,'
or 癲狂, 'madness.' It is a disease of the top [of the head], that is, a type of headache."
Similarly, 1505/2: "巔疾 refers to all diseases in the head."

10 Cf. *Su wen* 23: 夏得秋脈, "when in summer one feels a winter [movement in the]
vessels." In contrast, Gao Jiwu/726: "得 stands for 合適, 'fitting,' 'appropriate.' 審 stands
for 確實, 'reliable.' When the nature of the disease is doubtful, it is difficult to differentiate
its pathoconditions. Hence, 不得 and 不審 have the meaning of 'difficult to define.' "

11 Wang Bing: "When he calls it a yang [movement in the] vessels, then there is
a [movement in the] vessels resembling a yin abundance, and when he calls it a yin
[movement], then there is a [movement in the] vessels resembling a yang abundance.
Hence, [the text] states: 'search for a yang [movement]: one cannot get it; search for
a yin [movement]: one cannot recognize it.' 'The five sections' refers to the sections of
the five depots. 隔 is to say 隔遠, 'far apart.' 無徵 is like 無可信驗, 'nothing that could
be trusted as evidence.' That is, one searches for yang [qi] but cannot feel its heat, one
searches for yin [qi] but cannot recognize its cold and the five sections of the depots
are far apart, with nothing being present that could be trusted as evidence. Hence, [the
text] states: 'search for a yang [movement]: it cannot be felt; search for a yin [move-
ment]: it cannot be recognized. The five sections are separate and there is no evidence.'
Now, such a situation results from qi moving contrary [to its regular course] for a long
time; it does not result from the cold or heat of yin or yang qi. Hence, 'as if one lived
in a vast wilderness' is to say: the spirit of the heart is dispersed beyond its boundaries.
'As if one were to hide in an empty house' is to say: mind and sentiments lie hidden
in the depth. [The spirit of the heart] is dispersed beyond its boundaries because
the qi moves contrary [to its regular course] generating extreme and incessant pain.

80-568-5

It is therefore that
a recession of [the type] being short of qi
lets one have absurd dreams.[12]
In extreme cases, this leads to hallucinations.

{When the [flow of the] [qi] in the three yang [conduits] is interrupted and
when the [flow of the qi] in the three yin [conduits] is feeble,
this is being short of qi.}[13]

80-569-1

Therefore,
when the lung qi is depleted,
then this causes man in his dreams to see white items,[14]
to see people executed,[15] with [their] blood flowing in all directions.[16]

[Mind and sentiments] lie hidden in the depth because the pain was stabilized and
there is fear that it will return. 綿綿乎 is to say: movement and breathing are weak.
Even though the body is extremely weak, it is still present nevertheless. However, the
expectations in his heart are such that he will not live through the end of his days."
Gao Shishi: "With the extreme weakness of each breathing, the prognosis of survival
is such that he will not reach the end of this day."

12 Wang Bing: "A recession of diminished qi, [i.e.,] a movement contrary [to its
regular course], causes a person to develop foolish dreams. When this recession reaches an extreme, the dreams of that person will turn to bewilderment." Zhang Jiebin,
Ma Shi and others have 少陰 instead of 少氣. Zhang Jiebin: "The hand minor yin is
the heart. The heart controls the yang; it stores the spirit. The foot minor yin is the
kidneys; the kidneys control the yin; they store the essence. Hence, when the minor
yin is ceasing and counteracts, then heart and kidneys do not interact and essence as
well as spirit disperse. As a result one has wild dreams. In extreme cases, the respective
person will be confused and benighted."

13 Wang Bing: "When the three yang [movements in the] vessels are suspended
and interrupted and when the three yin [movements in the] vessels are diagnosed as
very subtle, these are indications of diminished qi." Zhang Jiebin: "When the three
yang are separated and interrupted, then the yin vanishes above. When the three yin
are subtle and weak, then the yang vanishes below. [This is a situation where] yin and
yang do not create and transform each other; hence, the qi is diminished and it is
insufficient for breathing." Lin Yi et al.: Yang Shangshan: "Extreme yang and interrupted yin, this is 'diminished qi.'"

14 Wang Bing: "'White items' are images reflecting the color of metal."

15 Wang Bing: "An execution is an operation of metal."

16 Wang Bing: "藉藉 is to dream of dead appearances." Zhang Zhicong: "藉藉 is
狼藉, 'disorder,' 'mixed up.'" *NJCD*: "The *Han shu* 漢書, biography of 燕剌王旦 has

When it is its time,
then he dreams of weapons and combat.[17]

When the kidney qi is depleted,
then this causes man to see boats and drowning people in his dreams.[18]
When it is its time,[19]
then he dreams he was lying in water;
as if there was something to be feared.

When the liver qi is depleted,
then he sees fragrant plants and fresh herbs in his dreams.[20]
When it is its time,[21]
then he dreams he was lying under a tree and did not dare to get up.[22]

When the heart qi is depleted,
then he dreams of stopping a fire and of yang items.[23]
When it is its time,[24]
he dreams of burning.

80-569-5
When the spleen qi is depleted,

籍籍. The commentary explains 籍籍 as 從橫貌, 'in all directions', lit. 'vertically and horizontally'."(See *Han shu* 63, 2757.) 915/59, on the basis of the use of this term in *Han shu* 漢書, biography of Sima Xiangru 司馬相如, first chapter, interprets 藉 as 眾多紛亂, "profuse," "many." The text of the present edition has 借借, a variant of 藉藉.

17 Wang Bing: " 'Its time' are the three months of autumn. Weapons are made of metal. Hence, one dreams of weapons and fighting."

18 Wang Bing: "Boats and drowning people are related to water. The kidneys reflect the water. Hence, [the water] takes shape in one's dreams."

19 Wang Bing: "These are the three months of winter."

20 Wang Bing: "Fragrant plants and fresh herbs belong to the category of herbs and trees. The liver is associated with herbs and trees. Hence, one sees them in his dreams."

21 Wang Bing: "These are the three months of spring."

22 Zhang Zhicong: " 'One does not dare to get up' is to say, even though one is supported by the qi of the seasons, one is unable to gain the upper hand."

23 Wang Bing: "The heart is associated with fire. Hence, one dreams of it. Yang items belong to the category of fire, too." Zhang Zhicong: " 'To put out fire,' this indicates the heart qi is depleted. 'Yang items' are dragons."

24 Wang Bing: "These are the three months of summer."

then he dreams of insufficient drinking and eating.²⁵
When it is its time,²⁶
he dreams of putting up walls and building a house.²⁷

In all these [cases],
the qi of [one of] the five depots is depleted.
The yang qi has a surplus, while
the yin qi is insufficient.²⁸

[How] to combine this with the five diagnostic indicators and
[how] to assess it in view of yin and yang,
this is already [outlined] in the *Conduit Vessels*.²⁹

<A diagnosis includes ten measurements
which measure a person's³⁰
vessel measures,
depot measures,
flesh measures,
sinew measures, and
transporter measures.>³¹

---

25 Wang Bing: "The spleen takes in water and grains. Hence, one dreams of insufficient beverages and food."

26 Wang Bing: " 'Its time' refers to the third, sixth, ninth, and twelfth month. In each of these months [the soil] rules for 18 days."

27 Wang Bing: "To put up walls and to build houses are operations of soil."

28 Wang Bing: "The palaces [are filled with] yang qi; the depots [store] yin qi."

29 Wang Bing: "The *Ling shu* classic has exhausting [discussions] of balancing yin and yang and combines this with the five diagnoses. Hence, it is quoted here as being outlined in the 'Conduit vessels.' 'Conduit vessels' is the title of a *Ling shu* treatise." Qian Chaochen-88/282: "Mr. Wang fails to discuss the character 在. Mr. Gu has stated: '在 stands for 察, to examine.' 在 and 察 were pronounced in ancient times with identical initial consonant and were often used interchangeably. Hence, the *Er ya* states: '在 is 察.'"

30 Zhang Qi: "The two characters 度人 are an insertion."

31 Wang Bing: "Each measurement includes two. Hence, two times five makes ten measurements." Ma Shi: "Basically, diagnosis comprises five measurements. When it speaks of ten measurements here, this is because the vessels, the depots, the flesh, the muscles, and the transportation [holes] are identical left and right. Hence, one may also speak of ten measurements." Zhang Zhicong: " 'Ten measurements' is to measure

80-569-9
If yin and yang qi are exhausted,
a person's disease will fully develop by itself.[32]
The vessel movement is irregular,
with yin dispersed and yang unilaterally [increased].[33]
The [qi in the] vessels is lost and incomplete.
No regular diagnosis can be carried out.

The diagnosis must take high and low [status into account].
Assess whether [the patient] is a commoner, a lord, or an official.[34]

80-570-1
If the [instructions] received from a teacher are incomplete,

---

the [movement in the] human vessels, to measure the depots, to measure the flesh, to measure the sinews, to measure the transportation [holes], to measure yin and yang qi, to measure above and below, to measure the [common] people, to measure the rulers, and to measure the noble." Gao Shishi suggested to move the four characters 度民君卿 behind the characters 陰陽氣盡. and he commented: "As for the ten measurements, the first is to measure man ..., the second is to measure the [movement in the] vessles ..., the third is to measure the depots ..., the fourth is to measure the flesh ..., the fifth is to measure the sinews ..., the sixth is to measure the transportation [holes] ..., the seventh is to measure the exhaustion of yin and yang qi ..., the eighth is to measure the [common] people, the ninth is to measure the rulers, and the tenth is to measure the noble. .. The common people cannot be equated with the noble and the noble cannot be equated with the rulers. [For diagnosis], their different minds must be assessed."

32 Wang Bing: "When a diagnosis takes all the principles of yin and yang depletion and abundance into account, the diseases of the persons [examined] can all be known."

33 Zhang Jiebin: "散陰頗陽 is to say the yin qi is dispersed [散] and lost and the [movement in the] vessels is mostly [頗] to be classified as yang." Wu Kun: "頗 stands for 跛, 'to be partial.'" Gu Guangguang: "頗 should be explained as 偏頗, 'unilaterally strong.'"

34 Wang Bing: "When the diagnosis of the [movement in the] vessels reveals a loss [of qi] that has resulted in an incomplete [presence of qi], there is no basis to carry out a regular diagnosis. To examine such [a patient] it is necessary to assess whether [the patient belongs to one of] the three [social classes, i.e.,] commoner, ruler, or official, because of the differences in their taking care of their life. Why? Because different social ranks are allotted with different shares of grief, joy, and suffering." Zhang Jiebin: "That is to say, the yin is dispersed and only yang is present. The [movement in the] vessels appears mainly as yang and has no root. This is not a true yang [movement in the] vessels. In this case, the [movement in the] vessels has a loss and yin and yang are not complete."

if practicing the art is not enlightened, and
if [a practitioner] fails to investigate whether a movement is contrary to or follows [its regular course],
this is an absurd practice.

[Such a practitioner]
holds onto the female and neglects the male,
discards the yin and attaches himself to the yang and
does not know how to combine [both sides].
His diagnosis, hence, will not be enlightened.[35]
He transmits [this] to later generations,
contradicting the [regular] discourse to make his own light shine.[36]

80-570-3
When the extreme yin is depleted,
the qi of heaven is interrupted;
when the extreme yang abounds,
the qi of the earth is insufficient.[37]

The merging and interacting of yin and yang,
this it what the accomplished man practices.[38]

---

35 See 1254/1 for a discussion of the ethics of diagnosis proposed here.

36 Wang Bing: "章 is 露, 'to expose,' 'to disclose.' Because [the practitioner] has not understood [what he was taught] but hands [his incomplete knowledge] to others nevertheless, the evidence [that this knowledge] contradicts the ancient [teachings] will come to light by itself." Zhang Yizhi et al.: "Judging from Wang Bing's commentary, the character 論 [in today's version] may be an error for 古, 'ancient.'"

37 Wang Bing: "When the extreme yin is depleted, the heavenly qi is interrupted and does not descend. When the extreme yang abounds, the qi of the earth is weak and does not rise. This is meant by 'absence of mutual penetration.' 至 stands for 至盛, 'extreme abundance.'" Zhang Jiebin: "The statement 'the extreme yin is depleted' is to say, the earth qi is weak and does not rise. When it does not rise, then there is nothing that could descend. Hence, the qi of heaven is interrupted. 'The extreme yang is abundant' is to say the qi of heaven is strong and does not descend. When it does not descend, there is nothing that could rise. Hence, the earth qi is insufficient. That is, the two qi of yin and yang contain each other's roots and they depend on each other. There can be no deformation to only one side." Wu Kun: "The extreme yin is the spleen; the qi of heaven is the lung. The extreme yang is manifested in fire. The qi of the earth is the qi of spleen and stomach. That is to say, when the spleen qi is depleted, the lung qi is necessarily interrupted. Metal has soil as its mother. When the mother has a disease, the [activities of the] son will be interrupted."

38 Wang Bing: "交 stands for 交通, 'mutual penetration.'"

As for the merging and interacting of yin and yang,
the yang qi arrives first,
the yin qi arrives second.[39]

Therefore, the Way of diagnosis by feeling [the vessels followed by] the sages
[was such that]
when they felt [the vessels, they examined which comes] first or second, [what
is] yin or yang.

80-570-6
< The features [dealt with in the text] *The Strange and the Normal* [are outlined]
under sixty headings.[40]
To diagnose the circumstances of the union with the subtle.
To pursue the changes of yin and yang, and
to elucidate the nature of the five inside.
The discourses in this [text]
take up the essentials of depletion and repletion and
determine the circumstances of the five measurements.
To know this, then, is sufficient for carrying out a diagnosis.>

Therefore,
if squeezing [the vessels, one only gets] a yin [movement], but does not get a
yang [movement],
the diagnosis is futile.
If one gets a yang [movement], but does not get a yin [movement],
the teaching one clings to is not profound.

[Such practitioners,]
when they know left, they do not know right;
when they know right, they do not know left;

---

39 Wang Bing: "When the qi of yin and yang pass alongside and penetrate each
other at one specific location, then the yang qi must arrive first and the yin qi arrive
second. Why? Because yang is fast and yin is slow."

40 Wang Bing: "[A text with the title] 奇恆勢 with sixty entries is no longer transmitted nowadays," and Ma Shi: " '奇恆' is the title of an ancient treatise. 六十首 refers
to the therapeutic methods of people in antiquity." Wu Kun: "六十首 refers to the
begin of each year in a cycle of 60 years. That is to say, all changes and normal states of
yin and yang occur within a period of 60 years." In the *Nan jing*, 16th difficult issue,
the term 六十首 appears to refer to "sixty indicators" offering hints on the condition
of the organism.

when they know the above, they do not know the below;
when they know what is first, they do not know what is second.
Hence, [the results of] their treatments will not last long.

To know what is bad and to know what is good;
to know what is a disease and to know what is no disease;
to know what is high and to know what is below;
to know about resting and to know about rising;
to know about movement and to know about halting, and
to apply [all] this [knowledge] on the basis of basic rules,
in this case the Way of diagnosis is complete and within a myriad generations
there will be no failure.

Start from that which has surplus and
know what is insufficient.⁴¹
Measure the circumstances above and below.
This will [enable one] to arrive at a proper [diagnosis of the] circumstances of
the vessels.⁴²

80-571-1
Therefore,
when the physical appearance is weak and the qi is depleted, [the patient will]
die.⁴³

---

41 Wang Bing: "*Su wen* 25 states: 內外相得無以形先, 'outer and inner [signs must]
be brought together [in diagnosis]; no priority is to be given to the [condition of the]
physical appearance.' This is to say, start from your own body's having a surplus and
then you will know the patient's insufficiencies." Wu Kun: „起 stands for 'begin of
a disease.' 有余 is: 'an evil has settled and there is surplus.' 不足 is 'insufficiency of
proper qi.' That is to say, when a disease emerges, even though it is said to be related
to surplus, one still will know that [basically] there was depletion which allowed the
evil to be received."

42 Wang Bing: "If one measures what should be present above and below, [in assessing the movement in] the vessels one will arrive at the subtleties. 格 stands for 至,
'to reach,' 'to arrive.'" Wu Kun: "格 stands for 'investigate its principles.' That is to say,
assess the nature of the disease, whether it is above or below, and subsequently investigate its principle through the [movement in the] vessels."

43 Wang Bing: "That is, both the interior and the external have insufficiencies."

When the qi of the physical appearance has a surplus,
while the qi in the vessels is insufficient,
[the patient will] die.[44]

When the qi in the vessels has a surplus,
while the qi of the physical appearance is insufficient,
[the patient will] survive.[45]

Therefore,
diagnosis has an important method.
Resting and rising are to be based on regularity;[46]
leaving and entering should follow a [proper] conduct,[47]
to focus [one's] spirit brilliance on [the patient].[48]

80-571-3
It is essential to be clear and to be pure,
to behold the above and to behold the below,[49]
to control the evils of the eight cardinal [turning points],[50]
to distinguish between the sections of the five inside.[51]

---

44 Wang Bing: "The depots are weak. Hence, insufficiency [shows up] in the [movement in the] vessels."

45 Wang Bing: "The [qi stored in the] depots abounds. Hence, the qi in the vessels is present in surplus."

46 Wang Bing: "When sitting and rising are regular, the force of breathing is balanced. Hence, this [technique] is to be applied at the begin of a diagnosis." See also 1818/45.

47 Zhang Jiebin: "The heart of the phyisician is set at keeping people alive. In all his daily activities, his thoughts must always be true and there should not be a single incidence where he is not careful. As a result, his virtue will be able to move heaven and his sincereness can rectify the minds. Hence, he can move around and practice everywhere and nowhere will he lose his spirit."

48 Zhang Jiebin: " 'To focus spirit brilliance' means one focusses one's own deficient spirit to examine the qi of someone else."

49 Wang Bing: " 'To behold the above' is to say: [behold] the [patient's] complexion. 'To behold the below' is to say: [behold] the [patient's] pysical appearance."

50 Wang Bing: " 'Eight cardinal [turning points]' refers to the regular indicators at the eight seasonal turning points." The eight seasonal turning points include spring begins, summer begins, autumn begins, winter begins, spring equinox, autumn equinox, summer solstice, and winter solstice. "Evil" refers to evil qi.

51 Wang Bing: " 'Five internal sections' refers to the sections of the five depots."

Press the vessels [whether they have] a movement or not,[52] and
pass along the foot-long section to examine whether it is] smooth or rough.
[To understand] the significance of cold or warmth,
observe the [patient's] feces and urine and
combine [all] this with the manifestations of the disease.[53]

Once it is understood whether [a movement] is contrary to or follows [its regular course] and
if further the name of the disease is known,
then diagnosis can bring success in all [cases treated] and
a person's [normal] nature cannot be missed.

<Hence,
in diagnosis occasionally [it is essential] to observe [the patient's] breathing
and to find out [his] sentiments.>[54]

Hence,
if the regular structure [of diagnostic steps] is not missed,[55]
the Way is very clear;
hence, it can last long.

---

52 Wang Bing: "Afterwards press [the vessels in] the inch and foot sections [to find
out whether there is] movement or not and determine [a patient's] death or survival."

53 A comment by the anonymous editors of the *Huang Di nei jing su wen* edition
of 1963/1983 by Renmin weisheng chubanshe interprets 病能 as 病態 because "態
rhymes with 意." However, 能 may rhyme with 意, too, and, more importantly, it is
unclear whether the rhyming of 意 and 能 is relevant here.

54 Zhang Jiebin: " 'To observe the breathing' is to examine inhalation and exhalation to recognize the [patient's] qi. 'To observe the meaning' is to examine the physical appearance and the complexion in order to recognize the [patient's] condition."
In contrast, Gao Jiwu/729: "The first 視 is to be interpreted as 瞻, 'to regard.' The
second 視 is to be intepreted as 審察, 'to examine.' It may also be that 視 equals 示,
'to display.' The meaning is: the breathing of the patient may provide evidence of the
condition of his spirit."

55 Wang Bing: "Count the lengths of [the patient's] breathing and examine the frequency of the arrival [of the movement in his] vessels. Hence, the pattern of diagnosis
occasionally includes an observation of [the patient's] breathing. Once the breathing
and the [movement in the] vessels are known, the location of the disease [in the body]
will be known too. The system underlying the examinations carried out by the sages
was to combine all these [diagnostic steps]."

He who does not know this Way,
he misses the conduits and breaks the [skin] structures;[56]
he [utters] absurd words[57] and offers absurd predictions.

This is called 'to miss the Way.' "

---

56 In contrast, Gao Jiwu/725 interprets 經 here as in *Su wen* 77 as "normal:" "to oppose the normal rules and patterns." 546/43 identifies 絕 as 違背, "to oppose." For the interpretation of 絕理 as "to break [skin] structures", see *Su wen* 25-159-2 where the text speaks of 絕皮, "to break the skin."

57 Zhang Qi: "亡言 should be 妄言, 'foolish speaches.'" Yu Chang agrees.

Chapter 81
Discourse on Explaining the Subtleties of Essence[1]

81-571-11
Huang Di was in the Hall of Light.

Lei Gong requested:
"[I, your] subject, give[2] instructions [in medical practice and thereby] I transmit it.

When I give lessons, they are based on the discourses in the classics, [including]
the *Natural Approach* and the *Patterns of Physical Appearance*,
Yin and Yang and *Piercing and Cauterization*, as well as
the nourishing effects of drugs prepared as decoctions.[3]
When I give treatments, [though,] they show [instances of] exemplary and
[others of] non-exemplary [therapies];[4]
I cannot yet definitely achieve success in all [cases I treat].

81-572-1
When [you] have spoken before of
sadness and grief, joy and anger,
dryness and dampness, cold and summerheat,
yin and yang, women and girls,

---

1 Lin Yi et al.: "In the Quan Yuanqi edition, this treatise was named 方論解."

2 The *Tai su* has 受 instead of 授. Hence some commentators read this character as "[I was] taught."

3 This passage was punctuated differently by various authors. For example, Zhang Yizhi et al. reads it as follows: 臣授業傳之, 行教以經論, 從容形法, 陰陽刺灸, 湯藥所滋. Gu Guanguang: "All these are ancient book titles. *Su wen* 77 refers to the classics *Bi lei* 比類 and *Xing ming* 形名. Maybe, [the] 形法 [referred to here] is the 形名 [referred to there]." Mori: "藥滋 means: liquids produced by boiling drugs... The meaning of 滋 is 津汁, 'liquid juice.'" The *Tai su*, ch. 29, ties 傳之 to the following sentence. It has 傳之以教, 皆以經論. Instead of 藥, it has 液, "liquid"; instead of 所 it has 藥, "drug." Yang Shangshan: "從容 refers to an investigative attitude. In the *Tai su jing* discourse received [by Lei Gong], the patterns of nourishing life, of calming down the physical appearance, and of examination, that is to say: the four arts of yinyang, piercing and cauterizing, of decoctions and drug liquids, all are important."

4 Zhang Yizhi et al. quotes Sun Dingyi 孫鼎宜: "That is as if he had said: sometimes I have sucess; sometimes I do not."

I would have liked to ask why all this is so.
A low position and poverty, wealth and nobility, they
constitute that which the physical body of man adapts himself to.
To have [your] subordinates fulfill [their] tasks, and,
when confronted with an actual case, to make them act in accordance with the art of the Way,[5]
I respectfully [ask to] hear [your] instructions.

Among the questions I should like to ask, some are stupid and vulgar,
[they concern issues] that are not in the classics;[6]
I wish to hear about these conditions."

[Huang] Di:
"This is a large [terrain]."

---

5 Gao Shishi reads this passage as follows: 人之形體, 所從群下, 通使臨事, 以適
道術. He commented: "Lei Gong received his instructions from [Huang] Di; and
[Huang] Di taught him on the basis of discourses in the classics. Hence, [the text]
states: 臣受業傳之行教以經論. Among these [teachings were instructions on] the
patterns of [generating] a relaxed state of one's physical appearance, on piercing and
cauterizing on the basis of yin and yang, and on the nourishment achieved by medicinal decoctions. When earlier it was spoken of inner harm caused by grief, sadness, joy,
and anger, and of external affections caused by dryness, dampness, cold, and summerheat, as well as of the Way of yin and yang, women and girls, and when it was asked,
why all this is so, [Huang Di] discussed the [varying states of the] physical body of
people by referring to their being of lower or higher social status. 所從群下 are people
of a low social position; 通使臨事 are the rich and noble. That is, how the human body
can adapt to the art of the Way, this has been outlined in the discourses of the classics
and [Lei Gong] has attentively listened to [Huang Di's] instructions [on this]. What
[Lei Gong] begs to ask now, these are foolish and vulgar questions. If something is
'foolish,' then the heart is not enlightened; if something is 'vulgar,' then the body is
not in best shape. [The issues raised by Lei Gong] differ from the questions raised in
the ancient classics. Hence, [the text] states: 'of those that are not [dealt with] in the
classics, I should like to hear an outline.'" Tanba: "Gao Shishi's statement shows that
he did not realize that these are words of Lei Gong directed at [Huang] Di. Hence,
所從群下 refers to all officials and the common people; it is a summarizing statement
referring to those of low status and to the rich and noble mentioned above. [The statement in the *Su wen* is] to say: enable the masses [of officials and common people] to
adapt to the art of the Way so that they may nourish what is proper."

6 Zhang Jiebin: "龏 stands for 妄, 'foolish;' 漏 stands for 陋, 'vulgar,' 'rude.' The
questions [raised by Lei Gong] are not in the classics; hence, [he terms them] 'foolish
and vulgar.' This is a self-depreciatory expression."

[Lei] Gong requested to ask:
"When [a person] weeps and no tears leave [the eyes],
or if [tears] leave [the eyes] with only a little snivel,[7]
what is the reason?"[8]

[Huang] Di:
"This is [written] in the classics."[9]

[Lei Gong] asked once again:
"I do not know
where the water originates from,[10]
where the snivel leaves from."

81-572-7
[Huang] Di:
"When you ask such questions,
this is of no benefit to treatment.
The knowledge acquired by practitioners
is generated by the Way.[11]

Now,
as far as the heart is concerned,
it is that of the five depots which concentrates the essence.[12]

---

7 384/57: "In the early Qin era, 涕 carried the meaning of 'tears.' The *Shuo wen jie zi* of the Eastern Han explained 涕 as 'tears.' But beginning with the Han, 涕 was already widespread used to signify 'snivel.'" 1679/25: "The character 涕 was used, in ancient times, for tears. Only beginning with the Han dynasty its meaning was changed to 'snivel.'" For a critique of this passage as "unexplainable" see 2637/48.

8 Wang Bing: "That is to say, which depot is responsible for this?"

9 Gao Shishi: "This is elucidated in *Ling shu* 28."

10 Cheng Shide et al.: " 'Water' refers to tears here."

11 Wang Bing: "That is to say, snivel and water are generated by the pathways of qi. Why should one ask about this?" Gao Shishi: "Even though [you,] practitioner, wish to know this, it is, in fact, present in the Way [of the classics already]." Zhongyi yanjiuyuan...: " 'The Way' refers here to the normal physiological laws of the human body. That is, tears and snivel are produced by man's normal physiological faculties." Mori: "道 is 液道, 'pathways of liquids.' *Ling shu* 28 states: 上液之道開則泣, 'when the upper pathways of the liquids open, then weeping results.'" Ma Shi, Wu Kun, and Gao Shishi have 道之所在, 'it is in the Way,' instead of 道之所生.

12 Wang Bing: "專 stands for 任, 'to be responsible for.' That is to say, the essence qi of the five depots relies on the heart for becoming activated. It is the palace of spirit

The eyes are its orifice.[13]
Effulgence and complexion show its splendor.[14]

Therefore,
when a person makes gains,[15]
then [his] qi [displays] harmony in [his] eyes.[16]
In the case of loss,
anxiety can be noticed in [that person's] complexion.

Therefore,
once there is sadness and grief, then tears flow.
When tears flow, they have originated from the water.

---

brilliance. Hence, it is able to carry out these [tasks]." Zhang Zhicong: "[All] the five depots store essence, but the heart is the ruler of the five depots and six palaces. Hence, among the five depots it is especially [responsible for] the essence." The *Tai su* does not have the character 之 following 藏. Yang Shangshan: "The heart is the overall ruler of the body's five depots. Hence, it 'controls the essence.'"

13 Wang Bing: "When the spirit is guarded internally, brilliance is reflected externally. Hence, the eye is the orifice of the [spirit]." 668/73 considers the identification of the eye as the orifice of the heart as contradicting the general association of the eye with the liver, as, for instance, in *Su wen* 4.

14 Wang Bing: "Effulgence and complexion are the external signs of the spirit brilliance." Gao Shishi: "The essence of the five depots follows the heart qi and manifests itself in the complexion. Hence, effulgence and complexion are its splendor."

15 Lin Yi et al.: "The *Tai su* has 得 instead of 德." Gao Shishi reads 德 as 得. Qian Chaochen-88/149 and 419/4 agree on the basis that 德 and 亡 form a pair of opposites here, with 德 meaning 獲得, 'to obtain,' and 亡 meaning 失掉, 'lost.'" In contrast, Wang Bing: "德, 'virtue,' is the operation of the Way; it is the life of man. Lao zi says: 'The Way creates it; the virtue nourishes it.' The qi is the ruler of life; it is the abode of the spirit. Heaven spreads virtue; the earth transforms the qi. Hence, man comes to life."

16 Wang Bing: "When the qi is in harmony, then the spirit is in peace. When the spirit is in peace, then this is clearly reflected externally. When the qi is not in harmony, then the spirit is not guarded. When the spirit is not guarded, then the external luster decreases. Hence, [the text] states: "When a person has virtue, the eyes offer evidence of his harmonious qi. When it is lost, grief is noticeable in his complexion." Zhang Yizhi et al.: "知 can also be interpreted as 見, 'to see.'" Yang Shangshan: "If one has suffered a personal loss, the [respective] qi will become visible in one's complexion. [Hence,] looking at his complexion one can see a person's grief."

81-573-1
As for the basis of water,[17] that is accumulated water.
As for the accumulated water, that is the extreme yin.
As for the extreme yin, that is the essence of the kidneys.

The reason why the water of basic essence[18] does not come out is that the essence holds it.[19]

It supports it; it wraps it up.
Hence,
the water does not flow.[20]

81-573-3
Now,
the essence of the water is the will;
the essence of the fire is the spirit.[21]
When water and fire affect each other,

---

17 Yang Shangshan: "宗 is 本, 'origin.'" Lin Yi et al.: "The *Jia yi jing* has 眾精 instead of 水宗." Wu Kun: "水宗 is 水之始, 'the origin of water.'" Zhang Jiebin: "水宗 stands for 水之原, 'the source of water.'" Gao Shishi: "宗 stands for 聚, 'to gather.' 水宗 is where the water gathers." Tanba considers the *Jia yi jing* version to be correct.

18 Wu Kun: "宗精 is the essence of the kidneys. The five liquids originate from the kidneys. Hence the kidney essence is called 宗精, 'basic essence.'" Zhang Jiebin: "宗精 is the source of water." Gao Shishi: "精 is like 聚, 'to accumulate.' Accumulations of water form through gradual collection. Hence [the text] states: 'water accumulations are collections of water.'" The *Jia yi jing* has 眾精 instead of 宗精. Tanba considers this as the correct version. Zhongyi yanjiuyuan...: "宗精 is the place where all the essence accumulates; it refers to the eyes. In the *Ling shu*, 大惑論, [it is said:] '精之窠為眼,' 'the nest of the essence is the eye.' Also in the *Ling shu*, 口問, [it is said:] '目者宗脈之所聚也,' 'As for the eye, it is where all the vessels gather.'"

19 Zhongyi yanjiuyuan...: " 'Essence' is here the essence of the five depots and six palaces mentioned above. But because [it is said] in *Su wen* 1 'the kidneys rule the water, they receive the essence of the five depots and six palaces and store it,' the essence stored in the kidneys is most important. The character 持 stands for 主持, 'to control.'"

20 Zhang Jiebin: "All the five liquids originate from the kidneys. Hence it is also called 宗精, 'that which is origin to the essence.' The essence is able to control the passageways of water. Hence it does not let them move irregularly."

21 "Water" and "fire" referring here to kidneys and heart respectively.

both spirit and will are sad.
Therefore, the water of the eyes is generated.[22]

Hence, a saying states:
'Heart sadness is called will sadness.'
The [essence of the] will and the essence of the heart,[23]
they both collect in the eyes.[24]

Therefore,
when both are sad,
then the spirit qi is transmitted to the essence of the heart.
[...]
Above, there is no transmission to the will,
and the will alone is sad.[25]
Hence, tears leave [the eyes].[26]

------

22 Wang Bing: "The eye is the passageway of the upper liquids. Hence, when water
and fire affect each other, spirit and will are both sad. The water-liquid moves upwards
and is generated in the eyes." *Ling shu* 28: "The heart is the ruler of the five depots and
six palaces. The eye is where all the vessels gather. It is the passageway of the liquids
above. .. Hence the heart is moved by grief and sadness. When the heart is moved,
then the five depots and six palaces are excited. When they are excited, then the gathering of all the vessels is affected. When the gathering of all the vessels is affected,
then the passageway of the liquids opens. As a result of the opening of the passageway
of the liquids, tears and snivel appear."

23 The "essence of the heart" is the spirit.

24 Wang Bing: "Both spirit and will ascend. Hence, the will and the heart-spirit
both rush to and collect in the eyes." Gao Shishi: "That is, as outlined earlier, the essence of will and heart pour into the eyes together."

25 Zhang Qi: "The sixteen characters from 則神氣傳 to 而志獨悲 are a later insertion."

26 Zhang Jiebin: "In case of grief the heart connection is tightened. Hence the spirit
qi is transmitted to the heart. When it is transmitted to the heart then the essence
is not transmitted downwards to the will. The essence collects above. The will is depleted below. As a result, the will alone generates grief and the essence has nothing
to control. Hence the water is not stored below and tears appear above." Gao Shishi:
"When the heart qi fails to be transmitted to the will and when the will alone is sad,
the sadness of the will occurs inside. Hence, when tears appear this is because the eyes
generate water, and as a result tears appear outside. Because the eyes generate water,
hence, tears appear outside. When the will in the kidneys is sad alone, then tears appear inside. From this one can know wherefrom the water originates." This passage
is not entirely clear. Wu Kun changed the text to: 身氣上傳于心, 精氣下傳于腎志.
心志俱悲故泣出也, "the spirit qi is transmitted above to the heart, the essence qi is

Tears and snivel are brain.[27]
The brain is yin.[28]
Marrow is what fills the bones.
Hence, when the brain leaks, this generates snivel.[29]

81-573-7
The will is the ruler of the bones.[30]
Therefore, when water[31] flows and snivel follows it,
this is because their passage is of one type.[32]

Now,
snivel and tears,
they are comparable to elder and younger brother among men.
In a critical situation, they both die.
When they survive, they both survive.[33]

---

transmitted below to the will [associated with the] kidneys. Both heart and will are sad. Hence, tears flow."

27 Zhang Yizhi et al.: "The character 泣 is a later insertion. The *Shuo wen* states: "涕 that appear without noise are 泣. Obviously, 涕 and 泣 are identical."

28 The *Tai su*, the *Jia yi jing*, and the Quan Yuanqi edition all have 陽, "yang", instead of 陰, "yin."

29 Wang Bing: "The nose orifice communicates with the brain. Hence, 'when the brain leaks, this is snivel,' and it flows in the nose."

30 The kidneys store the will and the kidneys rule the bones. See *Su wen* 23.

31 "Water" refers here to tears.

32 Wang Bing: "類 is to say 同類, 'same type.'" Gao Shishi: "Whenever one weeps with tears, there will also be snivel. But the origin of the snivel is not identical with that of the tears. Hence, [the text says]: Tears and snivel are brain. The brain is the see of essence and marrow. Hence, the brain is yin. The brain is the sea of the marrow; the marrow is located in the bones. Hence, the marrow is that which fills the bones. Tears and snivel are brain. Hence, when the brain leaks this generates snivel. The marrow is that which fills the bones, and the will, in turn, is ruled by the bones. Hence, when the water flows and the snivel must follow it, this is because their passage is of one type." Zhongyi yanjiuyuan...: "Above it is said that the essence of the water is the will. This explains that the tears are ruled by the kidneys. Here now [the text] says: the will is the ruler of the bones. This explains that tears and snivel are two liquids that are both ruled by the kidneys."

33 Wang Bing: "They are of identical origin; hence, they come to life and die together." The *Tai su* has 出則俱亡, "when they go out [to fight] they both perish", instead of 生則俱生.

81-573-10
Because the will is sad³⁴ first,³⁵
tears and snivel leave [eyes and nose] together and flow³⁶ uncontrolled.³⁷

Now,
when a person's snivel and tears leave [eyes and nose] together and follow each
other, [this is because] of the [identical] type³⁸ of their association."³⁹

Lei Gong:
"This is great!
I should like to ask:
When a person weeps and tears do not leave [the eyes],
or if they leave [the eyes] in small quantities and if the snivel does not follow
them,
why is that?"⁴⁰

---

34 The *Tai su* has 搖, "to incite," instead of 早. Hence, one could read 早悲 as "moved
to sadness."

35 The *Tai su* has 搖, "to shake", "to excite", instead of 早, "early", "first." Yang
Shangshan: "When the will it moved to grief, then tears appear uncontrolled."

36 Wang Bing: "I suspect 行, 'to move,' should be 流, 'to flow.'"

37 Zhang Jiebin: "橫 means 'a lot.'" Wu Kun: "橫行 stands for 橫流, 'a river flowing
out of its usual channel.'"

38 2568/47 reads 之類 as 這一類.

39 Wang Bing: " 'Their association' is to say: [their association] with the brain. Why?
Above the text states: 'Snivel and tears are brain.'"

40 Wang Bing: "[Lei Gong] wonders how their association is the same, while their
movement and their appearance differ." Gao Shishi: "[Lei] Gong asked [earlier]
where the water originates from and where the snivel appears from. The principles of
spirit and will, grief and weeping are extremely essential and extremely subtle. They
are truly part of the Way, they are not something an [ordinary] practitioner would
know. Hence, [Lei Gong] says 'Great!.' In the beginning [he raised] the question of
weeping without the appearance of tears and of when they appear of the presence of
only a little snivel. [Huang] Di replied: 'This is in the classics.' Here now [Lei Gong]
once again asks about weeping without the appearance of tears, why there may be only
a little snivel if they appear. [That is,] there is weeping, but tears and snivel do not
[necessarily] follow it. Why?"

81-573-12
[Huang] Di:
"Now,
when tears do not leave [the eyes],[41]
the weeping is not [caused by] grief.
Absence of tears [indicates] the spirit lacks compassion.
When the spirit lacks compassion,
then the will is not sad.
Yin and yang hold each other.
How could tears come alone?[42]

Now,
when the will is sad, this is distress.[43]
When there is distress, then [it] rushes against the yin.[44]
When it rushes against the yin,
then the will leaves the eye.
When the will has left, then the spirit no longer guards the essence.
When essence and spirit have left the eye,
[then] snivel and tears leave [eyes and nose].[45]

Moreover, are you the only[46] one who has not recited, who has not thought
about the [following] words in the classic:
'In case of recession, the eyes have nothing to see' ?[47]

---

41 The *Tai su* has 下, "to [flow] downwards", instead of 出.

42 Zhang Jiebin: "When the spirit has no compassion, the will is not sad. This is
because the spirit is yin and the will is yang and yin and yang control each other."

43 Zhang Jiebin: "悗 stands for 惨郁, 'sad,' 'distressed.'"

44 Zhongyi yanjiuyuan...: "Above, the text states 'the brain is yin.' Hence, 'it moves
against the yin' means: it ascends and moves against the brain."

45 Wang Bing: "悗 is to say: 内燥, 'internal melting.' 衝 is identical with 升, 'to rise.'
When spirit and will affect each other, tears are generated from this. Hence, when
there is internal melting, then yang qi rises to the yin. Yin is the brain. 去目 is to
say: neither yin nor yang [qi] guard the eyes. The will leaves the eyes, hence, the spirit
moves around disorderly, too. Now, when the will leaves the eyes, then there is no light
that could shine internally. When the spirit fails to guard, then the essence does not
shine externally. Hence, [the text] states: essence and spirit leave the eyes."

46 *NJCD*/343 reads 獨 here as 難道, "is it possible that ..?" If one were to follow this
interpretation, the sentence could be translated as "Moreover, is it possible, Sir, that
you have not read, that you have not considered ..."

47 Gao Shishi: "厥 is like 極, 'apex,' 'peak.'"

81-574-5
Now,
when a person [experiences] recession, then
the yang qi collects[48] above,
the yin qi collects below.
When the yang collects above,
then the fire alone has luster.
When the yin collects below,
then the feet are cold.
When the feet are cold, then they swell.

Now,
one water cannot dominate five fires.[49]
Hence, the eyes and the canthi are blind.[50]
Therefore, when one encounters wind,
tears flow and do not stop.[51]

81-574-7
Now,
when the wind hits the eyes,
the yang qi is internally guarded by the essence.
In this [situation], the fire burns the eye.
Hence, when one meets wind, then tears flow.[52]

---

48 Wang Bing: "并 is to say: each gathers at its original position." Zhang Jiebin: "并 stands for 偏盛, 'unilateral abundance.'"

49 Wang Bing: "'One water' refers to the eyes. 'Five fires' ist to say: the reversely moving yang [qi] of the five depots." The *Tai su* has 兩火, "two fires."

50 Wang Bing: "眥 is 視, 'to behold.'" Zhang Jiebin agrees. Lin Yi et al.: "The *Jia yi jing* does not have the character 盲."

51 Zhang Jiebin: "When wind hits the eyes, the qi of the fire burns internally and the water cannot be guarded. Hence, tears appear."

52 Wang Bing: "When wind hits [a person, his] yang [qi] hides and does not effuse. Hence, it burns internally."

There is something to compare this with.

Now, when [in the event of] fire a swift wind emerges, this can lead to rain.[53]

This is the same type [of phenomena]."[54]

---

53 The *Tai su* has 天之疾風生, "when the rapid wind of heaven emerges", instead of 夫火疾風生.

54 Wang Bing: "Hence, when yang [qi] collects, then the shine of the fire abounds only above; it does not shine below. Now, the eyes are generated from yang [qi]; they are tied to the depots. Hence, when yin and yang [qi] are balanced harmoniously, then the essence shines. When yang [qi] recedes, then the light does not rise; when the yin [qi] recedes, then the feet are cold and swollen. When [the text] states: one water cannot dominate five fires, that is: the yang [qi] of the hands and feet constitute five fires. The yin [qi] below is the qi of the liver. 'To move against wind and to develop incessant tear flow' is to say: the wind strikes against the eyes. In such a situation, the yang qi is guarded by the essence internally. Hence, the yang qi abounds and fire qi burns at the eyes. Wind and heat interact; hence, there is tear flow. Hence, when a rapid fire generates wind, this may result in rain. This is comparable to the tears resulting from wind generated by the heat of a yang fire."

BIBLIOGRAPHY
Vol. 2 *Su wen* Chapters 53-71 and 74-82

The following list of Chinese dictionaries, encyclopedias, monographs, and articles includes data from an encompassing bibliography we have prepared to include close to 3000 articles written by Chinese authors over the past decades and more than 600 Chinese and Japanese monographs from the past 1600 years that appeared to us relevant, and were consulted by us, for a better understanding of the history and contents of the *Huang Di nei jing su wen*. We have excerpted here for easy reference only those titles that we considered sufficiently essential to enter our annotations to our translation of *Su wen* chapters 53-71 and 74-81. Chinese dictionaries and encyclopedias are quoted in the notes by abbreviations combining the first letters of the words constituting their titles. Chinese and Japanese monographs, and those few written by Western authors, are quoted by the names of their authors, or, in cases of anonymous Chinese compilations, by the name of the academic units identified as editors. As for ancient Chinese works, e.g. the dynastic histories, philosophical texts, or ancient medical compilations apart from the *Su wen*, these are identified by their titles. Finally, articles are quoted in the annotations by their number in the comprehensive bibliography. These numbers are also provided in the listing below. Where necessary, references to page numbers follow the names of authors/compilers (in the case of monographs) or the title numbers from the encompassing bibliography (in the case of articles), separated by a slash. All Chinese monographs that examine and annotate the received text of the *Su wen* in the present sequence of its contents are quoted simply by the name of the author/compiler without page numbers. The complete bibliography of articles and monographs, except for commonly known texts such as the Han dynastic history or works by Chinese philosophers with no special reference to the *Su wen*, is added on a CD to the first volume of the present *Su wen* translation.

1. DICTIONARIES AND ENCYCLOPEDIAS

- *CY*: Wu Ziyan 吳澤炎 et al., *Ci yuan (xiu ding ben)* 辭源(修定本). Beijing 北京: Shangwu yinshu guan 商务印书馆 1998

- *GHYZD*: Zhang Yongyan 张永言et al., *Jian ming gu han yu zi dian* 簡明古漢語字典. Chengdu 成都: Sichuan renmin chubanshe 四川人民出版社1986

- *HDNJCD*: Guo Aichun 郭靄春, Li Siyuan 李思源 et al., *Huang Di nei jing ci dian* 黄帝内经辞典. Tianjin 天津: Tianjin Science and Technology Press 天津科学技术出版社1991

- *HYDCD*: Luo Chufeng 罗竹风et al., *Han yu da ci dian* 漢語大詞典. Shanghai上海: *Han yu da ci dian* chubanshe 漢語大詞典出版社1986 - 1994

- *JJZG*: Ruan Yuan 阮元 et al., *Jing ji zuan gu* 經籍纂詁. Beijing: Zhonghua shuju 1982

- *JMZYCD*: Zhongyi da cidian bianji weiyuanhui 中医大辞典编辑委员会, *Jian ming zhong yi ci dian* 简明中医词典. Beijing北京: People's Hygiene Press 人民卫生出版社1986

- *NJCD*: Zhang Dengben 张登本, Wu Changchun 武长春 et al., *Nei jing ci dian* 内经词典. Beijing 北京: People's Hygiene Press 人民卫生出版社1990

- *SWJZ*: Xu Shen 許慎, *Shuo wen jie zi* 說文解字. Beijing 北京: Zhonghua shuju 中华书局1981

- *SWJZGL*: Yang Jialuo 楊家駱 et al., *Shuo wen jie zi gu lin zheng bu he bian* 說文解字詁林正補合編. Taipei 臺北: Ding wen shuju 鼎文書局1983

- *SWJZZ*: Duan Yucai 段玉裁, *Shuo wen jie zi zhu* 说文解字注. Shanghai 上海: Shanghai guji chubanshe yingyin上海古籍出版社影印 1988

- *SWTXDS*: Zhu Junsheng 朱駿声, *Shuo wen tong xun ding sheng* 说文通训定声. Wuhan 武汉: Wuhanshi guji chubanshe 武汉市古籍出版社影印. Cited according to Zhang Yizhi et al.

- *TPYL*: Li Fang 李昉 ed., *Tai ping yu lan* 太平御覽.Taipei 臺北: Taiwan shangwu yinshu guan 臺灣商務印書館1967

- *WLGHYZD*: Wang Li 王力 ed., *Wang Li Gu han yu zi dian* 王力古漢話字典. Beijing 北京: *Zhonghua Shuju*中華書局 2000

- *YHHYZYCD*: Wiseman, Nigel: *Ying-Han/ Han-Ying zhong yi ci dian = English-Chinese/ Chinese-English Dictionary of Chinese Medicine*. Hunan 1995

- *ZGYXDCD*: Xie Guan 謝觀 et al., *Zhong guo yi xue da ci dian* 中國醫學大辭典. Taipei 臺北: Taiwan shangwu yinshu guan 臺灣商務印書館1982

2. MONOGRAPHS

– Beijing zhongyi xueyuan: 北京中医学院, *Nei jing shi yi* 内经释义. Shanghai上海: Shanghai kexue jishu chubanshe 上海科学技术出版社1978

– Beijing zhongyi xueyuan (2): 北京中医学院, *Nei jing xuan du* 内经选读. Shang hai 上海: Shanghai kexue jishu chubanshe 上海科学技术出版社 1978

– Beijing zhongyi xueyuan et al.: 北京中医学院, 北京市中医学校, *Zhong yi yuan zhu xuan du* 中医原著选读. Beijing北京: Beijing renmin chubanshe 北京人民出版社1978

– Chen Guying 陳鼓應, *Zhuang zi jin zhu jin yi* 莊子今註今譯. Taipei 臺北: Taiwan shangwu yinshu guan 臺灣商務印書館本之木1981

– Chen Menglei 陈梦雷, *Yi bu quan lu* 醫部全錄. Beijing 北京: People's Hygiene Press人民卫生出版社1963

– Chen Zhuyou 陈竹友, *Yi yong gu han yu* 医用古汉语. Fuzhou 福州: Fujian renmin chubanshe 福建人民出版社1981

– Cheng Shide 程士德 et al., *Su wen zhu shi hui cui* 素问注释汇粹. Beijing 北京: People's Hygiene Press 人民卫生出版社1982

– Cullen, Christopher: Some Further Points on the Shih. *Early China* 6, 1980-81, p. 39

– Duan Yishan 段逸山, *Yi gu wen* 医古文. Beijing北京: People's Hygiene Press 人民卫生出版社 1986

– Fang Wenhui 方文辉, *Zhong yi gu ji tong jie gu jin zi li shi* 中医古籍通借古今字例释. Guangzhou 广州: 科学普及出版社广州分社 1982

– Fang Yaozhong 方药中 & Xu Jiasong 许家松, *Huang Di nei jing su wen yun qi qi pian jiang jie* 黄帝内经素问运气七篇讲解. Beijing 北京: People's Hygiene Press 人民卫生出版社 1984

– Fu Weikang 傅维康 & Wu Hongzhou 吴鸿洲, *Huang Di nei jing dao du* 黄帝内经导读. Chengdu 成都: Bashu Books 巴蜀书社 1987

– Gao Jiwu 高纪武, *Yi gu wen yu fa yu xiu ci* 医古文语法与修辞. Xining 西宁: Qinghai renmin chubanshe 青海人民出版社1987

– Gao Shishi 高世栻, *Huang Di su wen zhi jie* 黄帝素问直解 (or *Su wen zhi jie* 素问直解). Beijing 北京: Beijing kexue jishu wenxian chubanshe 北京科学技术文献出版社 1980

– *Gu dian yi zhu xuan* bianxiezu: Quanguo zhongdeng weisheng xuexiao shiyong jiaocai *Gu dian yi zhu xuan* bianxiezu 全国中等卫生学校试用教材《古典医著选》编写组, *Gu dian yi zhu xuan* 古典医著选. Chenyang沈阳: Liaoning renmin chubanshe辽宁人民出版社1979

- Gu Guanguang 顾观光, *Su wen jiao kan ji* 素问校勘记. Cited according to Zhang Yizhi et al.

- Gu Yanwu 顧炎武, *Ri zhi lu* 日知錄. Cited according to Zhang Yizhi et al.

- Guan Jisheng 管济生, "*Su wen shang gu tien zhen lun*" *yi shi er ze*《素问·上古天真论》异释二则. *Guo yi lun tan* 国医论坛 1989 期 2(14), 43

- Gui Fu 桂馥, *Shuo wen jie zi yi zheng* 说文解字义证. Cited according to Zhang Yizhi et al.

- Guo Aichun-81: Guo Aichun 郭蔼春, *Huang Di nei jing su wen jiao zhu yu yi* 黄帝内经素问校注语译. Tianjin 天津: Tianjin kexue jishu chubanshe 天津科学技术出版社 1981

- Guo Aichun-92: Guo Aichun 郭蔼春, *Huang Di nei jing su wen jiao zhu* 黄帝内经素问校注. Beijing 北京：People's Hygiene Press 人民卫生出版社 1992

- Guo Tian 郭霭, *Nei jing jiang yi* 内经讲义. Beijing: People's Hygiene Press 人民卫生出版社 1989

- *Han Fei zi*: Shao Zenghua 邵增樺, *Han Fei zi jin zhu jin yi* 韓非子今註今譯. Taipei: Taiwan shangwu yinshu guan 臺灣商務印書館 1983

- *Han shu*: Ban Gu 班固, Han shu 漢書. Beijing: Zhonghua shuju 1987

- Harper 1998: Harper, Donald: *Early Chinese Medical Literature*. London: Kegan Paul International 1998

- Harper 1978-79: Harper, Donald: The Han Cosmic Board. *Early China* 4, p.1–10

- Harper 1980-81: Harper, Donald: The Han Cosmic Board - A Response to Christopher Cullen. *Early China* 6, p. 50 – 51

- *Hou Han shu*: Fan Ye 范曄, *Hou Han shu* 後漢書. Beijing: Zhonghua shuju 1973

- Hsü, Elisabeth: Yinyang and Mao's Dialectics in Traditional Chinese Medicine. *Asiatische Studien/Études Asiatiques*, LII, 2, 1988, p. 438.

- Hu Shu 胡澍, *Su wen jiao yi* 素问校义, *Huang Di nei jing su wen jiao yi* 黄帝内经素问校义. Cited according to Cheng Shide et al. and Zhang Yizhi et al.

- Hu Tianxiong 胡天雄, *Su wen bu shi* 素问补识. Beijing 北京: Chinese Medical and Pharmaceutical Science and Technology Press 中国医药科技出版社 1991

- Hua Shou 滑寿, *Du su wen chao* 读素问钞. Cited according to Cheng Shide et al.

- *Huai nan zi*: Liu An 劉安, *Huai nan zi* 淮南子. *Er shi er zi* 二十二子, *p.* 1204-1308. *Shanghai*: Shanghai guji chubanshe 上海古籍出版社 1986

- Huang Sanyuan 黄三元, *Zhong yi gu wen ji chu* 中医古文基础. Taipei 台北：Bade jiaoyu wenhua chubanshe 八德教育文化出版社 1983

- Hucker, Charles O.: *A Dictionary of Official Titles in Imperial China*. Stanford 1985

- *Jia yi jing*: Huangfu Mi 皇甫謐, *Huang Di zhen jiu jia yi jing* 黄帝針灸甲乙經. Taipei: Tailian guofeng chubanshe yinxing 台聯國風出版社印行 1975

- *Lao zi*: Wang Bi王弼, *Lao zi dao de jing zhu* 老子道德經注. *Wang Bi ji jiao shi* 王弼集校釋, shang ce 上册. Beijing: Zhonghua shuju 1980

- Legge, James: *The Chinese Classics in Five Volumes*. Taipei: SMC Publishing Inc 1991

- Li Guoqing 李国清, *Su wen yi shi* 素问疑识. Harbin 哈尔滨: Heilongjiang renmin chubanshe 黑龙江人民出版社1988

- Li Jinyong 李今庸, *Xin bian Huang Di nei jing gang mu* 新编黄帝内经纲目. Shanghai上海: Shanghai Science and Technology Press 上海科学技术出版社 1988

- Li Zhongzi 李中梓 (= Li Nian'e 李念莪), *Nei jing zhi yao* 内经知要. (Written in 1642.) Shanghai上海：上海商务印书馆 1955

- Lin Yi et al. 林億等 (Song commentators of Wang Bing's *Su wen* edition), *Xin jiao zheng* 新校正. Cited according to our editions of Wang Bing 王冰, *Huang Di nei jing su wen* 黄帝内經素問, see below.

- *Ling shu*: Dai Xinmin 戴新民, *Huang Di nei jing zhang ju suo yin* 黄帝内經章句索引, p. 263-482 Ling shu jing 靈樞經. Taipei台北: Qiye shuju 啓業書局 1987

- Liu Zhenmin et al. 刘振民等, *Yi gu wen ji chu* 医古文基础. *Beijing* 北京：人民卫生出版社1980

- Ma Jixing 马继兴, *Ma wang dui gu yi shu kao shi* 马王堆古医书考释. Changsha 长沙: Hunan kexue jishu chubanshe 湖南科学技术出版社1992

- Ma Kanwen 马堪温, "Classic Chinese Medical Literature in Contemporary China: Texts Selected for Modern Editions, and Problems Associated with this Work". In Paul U. Unschuld, ed., *Approaches to Traditional Chinese Medicine*. Dordrecht: Kluwer Academic Press 1989, p. 7

- Ma Shi 马莳, *Huang Di nei jing su wen zhu zheng fa wei* 黄帝内经素问注证发微. (Written in 1586.) Beijing 北京：科学技术文献出版社1999. Normally cited according to Cheng Shide et al.

- *Mai jing*: Wang Shuhe王叔和, *Mai jing* 脈經. Fuzhou shi renmin yiyuan 副州市人民醫院, *Mai jing jiao shi* 脈經校釋. Beijing: People's Hygiene Press 人民卫生出版社1988

- Mori: Mori Risshi (or Tatsuyuki) 森立之, *Somon Kôchû* 素问考注. Cited according to Zhang Yizhi et al.

- *Nan jing*: Hua Shou 滑壽, *Nan jing ben yi, nan jing gu yi* 難經本義, 難經古義. Taipei: Wenguang tushu youxian gongsi yinxing 文光圖書有限公司印行 1984

- Nanjing zhongyi xueyuan: Nanjing zhongyi xueyuan yijing jiaoyanzu 南京中医学院医经教研组, *Huang Di nei jing su wen yi shi* 黄帝内经素问译释. Shanghai上

海：Shanghai kexue jishu chubanshe 上海科学技术出版社 1959 Cited according to Cheng Shide et al

– Qian Chaochen-88: Qian Chaochen 钱超尘, *Zhongyi guji xungu yanjiu* 中医古籍训诂研究. Guiyang 贵阳：Guizhou renmin chubanshe 贵州人民出版社 1988

– Qian Chaochen-90: Qian Chaochen 钱超尘, *Nei jing yu yan yan jiu* 内经语言研究. Beijing 北京: People's Hygiene Press 人民卫生出版社 1990

– Ruan Yuan 阮元 et al., *Shisanjingzhushu* 十三經注疏. Beijing: Zhonghua shuju 1987

– Shanghai zhongyi xueyuan: Shanghai zhongyi xueyuan yiguwen jiaoyanzu 上海中医学院医古文教研组, *Gu dai yi xue wen xuan* 古代医学文选. Shanghai 上海：Shanghai kexue jishu chubanshe 上海科学技术出版社 1980

– Shanghai zhongyi xueyuan et al.: Shanghai zhongyi xueyuan, Zhejiang zhongyi xueyuan 上海中医学院、浙江中医学院, *Yi gu wen* 医古文. Shanghai 上海：Shanghai kexue jishu chubanshe 上海科学技术出版社 1978

– *Shen Nong ben cao jing*: Wang Jumo 王筠默, Wang Hengfen 王恒芬, *Shen Nong ben cao jing jiao zheng* 神農本草經校證. Changchun 長春: Jilin kexue jishu chubanshe 吉林科学技术出版社 1988

– Shen Zumian 沈祖绵, *Du su wen yi duan* 读素问臆断. Cited according to Zhang Yizhi et al.

– *Shi ji*: Sima Qian 司馬遷, *Shi ji* 史記. Beijing: Zhonghua shuju 1989

– Soothill, W. E.: *The Hall of Light*. New York 1952

– Sun Dingyi 孙鼎宜, *Huang Di nei jing zhang ju* 黄帝内经章句. Cited according to Zhang Yizhi et al., Hu Tianxiong, etc.

– Sun Yirang 孙诒让, *Su wen Wang Bing zhu jiao* 素问王冰注校. Cited according to Zhang Yizhi et al.

– *Tai su*: Yang Shangshan 楊上善 (ed.), *Huang Di nei jing tai su* 黄帝内經太素. Critical edition by Xiao Yanping 萧延平 (1924). Beijing: Renmin weisheng chubanshe yingyin 人民卫生出版社影印 1955-1958

– Tanba: Tanba Genkan 丹波元简, *Somon Shi* 素問識. Beijing 北京：人民卫生出版社 1984

– Tanba Genken 丹波元堅, *Somon Shôshi* 素問紹識. Cited according to Cheng Shide et al. and Zhang Yizhi et al.

– Tang Rongchuan 唐容川, *Yi jing jing yi* 醫經精義. Cited according to Cheng Shide et al.

– Unschuld, Paul U. 2003: *Huang Di nei jing su wen - Nature, Knowledge, Imagery in an Ancient Chinese Medical Text*. Berkeley: University of California Press 2003

– Wan Lanqing 万兰清 et al., *Zhong yi si da jing dian zhu zuo ti jie* 中医四大经典著作题解. Nanchang 南昌: Jiangxi renmin chubanshe 江西人民出版社 1982

– Wang Ang 汪昂, *Su wen ling shu lei zuan yue zhu* 素问灵枢类纂约注, or *Su ling lei zuan* 灵素类纂. Shanghai 上海：上海科学技术出版社1959

– Wang Bing 王冰 (ed.), *Huang Di nei jing su wen* 黄帝内經素問 (ed. 762). Taipei 台北: 国立中国医药研究所影印明嘉靖顾从德本1960

– Wang Bing王冰 (ed.), *Huang Di nei jing su wen* 黄帝内經素問. Beijing 北京：People's Hygiene Press 人民卫生出版社1963/ 1983

– Wang Hongtu 王洪图et al., *Huang Di nei jing yan jiu da cheng* 黄帝内经研究大成. Beijing 北京: Beijing chubanshe 北京出版社1997

– Wang Ji 汪机, *Xu su wen chao* 续素问钞. Cited according to Cheng Shide et al.

– Wang Qi 王琦 et al., *Su wen jin shi* 素问今释. Guiyang 贵阳：Guizhou renmin chubanshe 贵州人民出版社1981

– Wang Shaozeng王绍增, *Yi gu wen yu fa* 医古文语法. Harbin 哈尔滨: Heilongjiang kexue jishu chubanshe 黑龙江科学技术出版社1983

– Wang Shaozeng 王绍增 & Xu Yongnian 徐永年, *Yi gu wen xiu ci* 医古文修辞. Harbin 哈尔滨：Heilongjiang kexue jishu chubanshe 黑龙江科学技术出版社 1985

– Wu Kun 吴崐: *Nei jing su wen Wu zhu* 内经素问吴注. Jinan 济南: Shandong kexue jishu chubanshe 山东科学技术出版社1984

– *Xun zi*: Zhang Shitong 章诗同, *Xun zi jian zhu* 荀子簡注. Shanghai: Shanghai renmin chubanshe上海人民出版社1974

– Xue Xue 薛雪, *Yi jing yuan zhi* 医经原旨. Cited according to Cheng Shide et al.

– Yan Hongchen 阎洪臣 & Gao Guangzhen 高光振, *Nei nan jing xuan shi* 内难经选释. Chang chun 长春：Jilin renmin chubanshe 吉林人民出版社 1979

– Yan Zhenhai 严振海, *Gu yi ji de ju dou biao dian* 古医籍的句读标点. Shanghai上海：Shanghai kexue jishu chubanshe上海科学技术出版社1987

– Yang Shangshan 楊上善 (ed.), *Huang Di nei jing tai su* 黄帝内經太素. Taipei 台北: Wenguang Tushu Ltd. 文光圖書有限公司 1990

– Yao Shaoyu 姚紹虞 (*zi*: Zhi'an 止庵), *Su wen jing zhu jie jie* 素問經注節解. (Written in 1669.) Beijing 北京: Renmin weisheng chubanshe 人民卫生出版社, 1963 . Normally cited according to Cheng Shide et al.

– Yang Weijie 楊維傑, *Huang Di nei jing su wen yi jie* 黄帝内經素問譯解. Taipei: 樂群出版公司1977

– Ye Gang 叶岗, *Zhong yi gu ji yue du tan* 中医古籍阅读谈. Guangzhou 广州：Guangdong keji chubanshe 广东科技出版社 1980

- Yu Chang 于鬯, *Xiang cao xu jiao shu – Su wen jiao* 香草续校书，素问校. Cited according to Zhang Yizhi et al.

- Yu Yue 俞樾, *Nei jing bian yan* 内经辩言. Cited according to Zhang Yizhi et al.

- Yu Zihan et al. 余自汉等, *Nei jing ling su kao* 内经灵素考. Beijing 北京: Zhongguo zhongyiyao chubanshe 中国中医药出版社 1992

- Zhang Canjia 张灿玾, *Huang Di nei jing su wen jiao shi* 黄帝内经素问校释. Beijing 北京: People's Hygiene Press 人民卫生出版社 1980

- Zhang Jiyou 张继有, *Huang Di nei jing su wen Wu zhu ping shi* 黄帝内经素问吴注评释. Beijing 北京: Chinese Ancient Literature Press 中医古籍出版社 1986

- Zhang Jiebin 张介宾, *Lei jing* 類經. Beijing 北京: Renmin weisheng chubanshe 人民卫生出版社 1957

- Zhang Jiebin (2): 张介宾, *Lei jing tu yi* 類經圖翼. Beijing 北京: Renmin weisheng chubanshe 人民卫生出版社 1985

- Zhang Qi 张琦, *Su wen shi yi* 素问释义. Cited according to Cheng Shide et al. and Zhang Yizhi et al.

- Zhang Wenhu 张文虎, *Shu yi shi xu bi – nei jing su wen* 舒艺室续笔·内经素问. 同治十三年金陵冶城刊本. Cited according to Zhang Yizhi et al.

- Zhang Yizhi 张毅之 et al., *"Nei jing su wen" yi nan wen ti zhu du*《内经·素问》疑难问题助读. Beijing 北京: Zhongguo yiyao keji chubanshe 中国医药科技出版社 1993

- Zhang Zhicong 张志聪 (=Zhang Yin'an 张隐庵), *Huang Di nei jing su wen ji zhu* 黄帝内经素问集注, or *Su wen ji zhu* 素问集注. Taipei 台北: Wenguang tushu youxian gongsi yingyin 文光图书有限公司影印 1982

- Zhen Lifen et al. 陈丽芬等, *Yi wen jing hua* 医文精华. Shanghai 上海: Shanghai kexue jishu chubanshe 上海科学技术出版社 1986

- Zhongyi yanjiuyuan: Zhongyi yanjiuyuan zhongyi yanjiushengban 中医研究院中医研究生班, *Huang Di nei jing zhu ping* 黄帝内经注评. Published in Beijing by Research Class in Chinese Medicine of the Academy of Chinese Medicine 1980

- Zhou Fengwu 周凤梧 et al., *Huang Di nei jing su wen bai hua jie* 黄帝内经素问白话解. Beijing 北京: People's Hygiene Press 人民卫生出版社 1958

- Zhou Xuehai 周学海, *Nei jing ping wen* 内经评文. Cited according to Cheng Shide et al.

3. ARTICLES

13. Ban Zhaoxian 班兆贤 1991. *Nei jing* zhong de cuo zong xiu ci fa《内经》中的错综修辞法. *He nan zhong yi* 河南中医 3, 10

15. Ban Zhaoxian 班兆贤 1989. *Nei jing* xiu ci ju yu《内经》修辞举隅. *Shan dong zhong yi xue yuan xue bao* 山东中医学院学报 2, 37-38

16. Ban Zhaoxian 班兆贤 1990. *Nei jing* fen cheng xiu ci fa ju yao《内经》分承修辞法举要. *Shan dong zhong yi xue yuan xue bao* 山东中医学院学报 4, 61

19. Bao Laifa 包来发 1984. Tan tan *Huang Di nei jing* zhong de hu wen 谈谈《黄帝内经》中的互文. *Zhong yi han shou tong xun* 中医函授通讯 4, 141, 144

20. Bao Laifa 包来发 1985. *Huang Di nei jing* zhu shi fen qi yuan yin qian xi《黄帝内经》注释分歧原因浅析. *Zhong yi za zhi* 中医杂志 11, 54-55

25. Bao Xiaodong 鲍晓东 1986. "Shen wei qian wei ti" bian "肾为欠为嚏"辨. *Zhe jiang zhong yi xue yuan xue bao* 浙江中医学院学报 4, 45

26. Bao Xiaodong 鲍晓东 1988. "Si wei" xin gu "四维"新诂. *Zhe jiang zhong yi xue yuan xue bao* 浙江中医学院学报 2, 46-47

29. Bi Fugao 毕福高 1986. "Miu ci" yu "ju ci" tan tao "缪刺"与"巨刺"探讨. *Zhong yi yan jiu* 中医研究 1, 31-33

59. Cao Zhenhua 曹振华 1978. "Shui qi" yu shen bing zong he zheng "水气"与肾病综合征. *Shan dong zhong yi xue yuan xue bao* 山东中医学院学报 增刊, 10-13

63. Chai Ruiji 柴瑞霁 1988. Gan zhu shu xie yuan liu kao 肝主疏泄源流考. *Si chuan zhong yi* 四川中医 8, 2-3

64. Chai Ruiji 柴瑞霁 1986. Gan zhu shu xie zong heng kao 肝主疏泄纵横谈. *Zhong yi yao yan jiu za zhi* 中医药研究杂志 2, 41-43

66. Chang Jianxiu 畅建修 1982. Shi tan zhong yi de "shang bing xia qu, xia bing shang qu" 试谈中医的"上病下取,下病上取". *Shaan xi zhong yi* 陕西中医 4, 4-6

78. Chen Gang 陈钢 1987. Cong "you wu", "you yu bu zu" kan xu shi zheng de han yi 从"有无"、"有余不足"看虚证实证的涵义. *Liao ning zhong yi za zhi* 辽宁中医杂志 8, 42-44

88. Chen Guoxin, Wu Yuanqian 陈国信,吴元黔 1981. Cong lin chuang zhi "qi fan" tan *Nei jing* zhi bing qiu ben de si xiang 从临床治"气反"谈《内经》治病求本的思想. *Yun nan zhong yi xue yuan xue bao* 云南中医学院学报 4, 4-6

94. Chen Junwen 陈俊文 1983. "Qi ben zai shen, qi mo zai fei" jie xi "其本在肾,其末在肺"解析. *Hu bei zhong yi za zhi* 湖北中医杂志 3, 51-52

117. Chen Nong 陈农 1988. "Qu yu chen cuo" xi "去宛陈莝"析. *Shang hai zhong yi yao za zhi* 上海中医药杂志 6, 38-39

126. Chen Shuying 陈淑英 1989. Tan pian yi fu ci zai *Nei jing* zhong de yun yong 谈偏义复词在《内经》中的运用. *He nan zhong yi* 河南中医 5, 46-47

140. Chen Wujiu 陈无咎 1983. *Nei jing* bian huo ti gang 内经辨惑提纲.内经辨惑提纲. *Zhe jiang zhong yi za zhi* 浙江中医杂志 4, 25-32

144. Chen Xianping 陈贤平 1986. "Xiao zhe ju ju, shu zhi qi yao" zhi wo jian "消者瞿瞿,孰知其要"之我见. *Shang hai zhong yi yao za zhi* 上海中医药杂志 1, 33

150. Chen Yiting 陈贻庭 1990. *Nei jing* yi wen ci yu yong fa kao cha《内经》疑问词语用法考察. *Fu jian zhong yi yao* 福建中医药 4, 59-64

155. Chen Yun 陈云 1991. *Nei jing* zhong "nai he", "ru he" (he ru) yong fa chu tan《内经》中"奈何"、"如何"(何如)用法初探. *Yi gu wen zhi shi* 医古文知识 1, 14-16

169. Chen Zhuyou 陈竹友 1981. Zhong yi gu shu jiao du fa 中医古书校读法. *Xin zhong yi* 新中医 12, 51

171. Chen Zongqing 陈宗清 1981. *Nei jing* sheng hua xue shuo chu tan《内经》生化学说初探. *Fu jian zhong yi yao* 福建中医药 6, 1-3

218. Cheng Shide, Guo Xiazhen 程士德, 郭霞珍 1983. *Nei jing* shi ti da an yao dian (xuan zai)《内经》试题答案要点 (选载). *Bei jing zhong yi xue yuan xue bao* 北京中医学院学报 2, 44-45

223. Cheng Zhiqing 程志清 1985. Lu Zhi qing lao zhong yi tan "shang bing xia qu, xia bing shang qu" 陆芷青老中医谈"上病下取,下病上取". *Shaan xi zhong yi* 陕西中医 1, 20-21

234. Chi Huaji 迟华基 1986. Lesson 29: Zang fu zhi jie jing luo lian, zhi bing ke cong tiao jing yan (2) 第二十九讲: 脏腑肢节经络连 治病可从调经言 (下). *Shan dong zhong yi za zhi* 山东中医杂志 , 5, 57-60

240. Chu Xuanren, Wang Tianru 褚玄仁, 王天如 1982. Ye tan "qi zeng er jiu, yao zhi you ye" 也谈"气增而久,夭之由也". *Jiang su zhong yi za zhi* 江苏中医杂志 1, 55-56

241. Chun Xue 春雪 1982. Ou ci miu ci he ju ci (4) 偶刺、缪刺和巨刺 (四). *Cheng du zhong yi xue yuan xue bao* 成都中医学院学报 1, 42

252. Cui Zhongping 崔仲平 1986. *Nei jing* ben wen xun gu chu tan (1)《内经》本文训诂初探(上). *Ji lin zhong yi yao* 吉林中医药 2, 38-30

263. Dang Binglin, Zhang Dengben 党炳琳, 张登本 1985. Wu yun liu qi ru men (1) 五运六气入门(一). *Shaan xi zhong yi han shou* 陕西中医函授 3, 6-18

271. Deng Mingzhong 邓明仲 1963. Shi lun biao ben 試論标本. *Zhong yi za zhi* 中医杂志 12, 30-32

296. Du Xudian 杜煦电 1988. "Yi yuan san qi" zheng yi "一源三歧" 正义. *Zhong yi za zhi* 中医杂志 11, 69

306. Duan Yishan 段逸山 1981. Gu yi jing te shu yu wen xian xiang ju ju 古医经特殊语文现象举隅. *Zhong hua yi shi za zhi* 中华医史杂志 2, 120-123

307. Duan Yishan 段逸山 1981. Gu yi jing te shu yu wen xian xiang ju ju (ctd.) 古医经特殊语文现象举隅 (续). *Zhong hua yi shi za zhi* 中华医史杂志 3, 183-186

314. Fan Xingzhun 范行準 1951. Wu yun liu qi shuo de lai yuan 五運六氣說的來源. *Yi shi za zhi* 醫史雜誌 复刊号, 3

315. Fan Yongsheng 范永升 1984. Yong yao yu shi ling de han re yuan jin bian xi 用药与时令的寒热远近辨析. *Zhe jiang zhong yi xue yuan xue bao* 浙江中医学院学报 5, 7-10

329. Fang Yaozhong 方药中 1981. Qian tan "xiang" he "zang xiang" 浅谈 "象" 和 "脏象". *Liao ning zhong yi za zhi* 辽宁中医杂志 3, 7-9

331. Fang Yaozhong 方药中 1982. Tan "xu er xiang bing" 谈 "虚而相并". *Si chuan zhong yi* 四川中医创刊号, 3-5

338. Fang Yaozhong, Xu Jiasong 方药中, 许家松 1982. *Su wen* "Wu yun xing da lun" jiang jie (1)《素问·五运行大论》讲解 (一). *Shaan xi zhong yi* 陕西中医 3, 41-46

339. Fang Yaozhong, Xu Jiasong 方药中, 许家松 1982. *Su wen* "Wu yun xing da lun pian" jiang jie (2)《素问·五运行大论篇》讲解 (二). *Shaan xi zhong yi* 陕西中医 4, 34-38

343. Fang Yaozhong, Xu Jiasong 方药中, 许家松 1982. *Su wen* "Qi jiao bian da lun" jiang jie (1)《素问·气交变大论》讲解 (一). *Shang hai zhong yi yao za zhi* 上海中医药杂志 1, 31-33

352. Fang Yaozhong, Xu Jiasong 方药中, 许家松 1983. *Su wen* "Qi jiao bian da lun pian" jiang jie (10)《素问·气交变大论篇》讲解 (十). *Shang hai zhong yi yao za zhi* 上海中医药杂志 3, 40-41

353. Fang Yaozhong, Xu Jiasong 方药中, 许家松 1986. Lun zhong yi li lun ti xi de ji ben nei han ji qi chan sheng de wu zhi ji chu 论中医理论体系的基本内涵及其产生的物质基础. *Tian jin zhong yi xue yuan xue bao* 天津中医学院学报 2-3, 14-27

354. Fang Yaozhong, Xu Jiasong 方药中, 许家松 1981. "Liu wei zhi da lun pian" jiang jie (1) 六微旨大论篇讲解 (一). *Xin zhong yi* 新中医 9, 47-49,45

355. Fang Yaozhong, Xu Jiasong 方药中, 许家松 1981. "Liu wei zhi da lun pian" jiang jie (2) 六微旨大论篇讲解 (二). *Xin zhong yi* 新中医 10, 49-52

356. Fang Yaozhong, Xu Jiasong 方药中, 许家松 1981. "Liu wei zhi da lun pian" jiang jie (3) 六微旨大论篇讲解 (三). *Xin zhong yi* 新中医 11, 45-48,55

357. Fang Yaozhong, Xu Jiasong 方药中, 许家松 1981. "Liu wei zhi da lun pian" jiang jie (4) 六微旨大论篇讲解 (四). *Xin zhong yi* 新中医 12, 47-50.19

359. Fang Yaozhong, Xu Jiasong 方药中, 许家松 1984. "Wu yun xing da ji (lun)" ti yao《五运行大记(论)》提要. *Zhong yi han shou tong xun* 中医函授通讯 4, 154-156

360. Fang Yaozhong, Xu Jiasong 方药中, 许家松 1984. Di san pian "Liu wei zhi da lun" ti yao 第三篇《六微旨大论》提要. *Zhong yi han shou tong xun* 中医函授通讯 5, 194

384. Feng Songjie 冯松杰 1986. Cong ci yi bian hua kan *Nei jing* cheng shu nian dai 从词义变化看《内经》成书时代. *Nan jing zhong yi xue yuan xue bao* 南京中医学院学报 3, 57-58

386. Franzini Serge 弗朗齐尼·塞尔日 1988. *Nei jing* zhong chi ji yin chi qian kao《内经》中尺及阴尺浅考. *Zhong yi za zhi* 中医杂志 11, 59

409. Fu Yourong 傅幼荣 1984. Wo dui *Nei jing* cheng shu nian dai de kan fa 我对《内经》成书年代的看法. *Jiang xi zhong yi yao* 江西中医药 1, 2-4

419. Fu Zhenliang 付贞亮 1979. Zen yang xue xi *Nei jing* 怎样学习《内经》. *Shaan xi zhong yi xue yuan xue bao* 陕西中医学院学报 1, 1-7

445. Gao Guangzhen 高光震 1985. *Nei jing ci yu ci dian* yang gao xuan deng (6)《内经词语辞典》样稿选登(六). *Ji lin zhong yi yao* 吉林中医药 5, 36-38

458. Gao Hesheng 高和声 1980. Wo dui *Nei jing* de ji dian ren shi 我对《内经》的几点认识. *Zhe jiang zhong yi xue yuan xue bao* 浙江中医学院学报 2, 10-13

484. Gao Yuemin, Hu Bin 高越敏, 胡滨 1986. Biao ge zi yu xun gu 标格资于诂训. *Zhe jiang zhong yi xue yuan xue bao* 浙江中医学院学报 4, 42-44

490. Gao Zhongzu 高中祖 1987. *Nei jing* ben biao zhong qi lun yu *Shang han lun* liu jing fa bing gui lü《内经》本标中气论与《伤寒论》六经发病规律. *He nan zhong yi* 河南中医 3, 4-7

502. Gong Weixing 宫伟星 1988. *Su wen* "Zhi zhen yao da lun" "mo zhi" shi yi《素问·至真要大论》"摩之"释义. *An mo yu dao yin* 按摩与导引 4, 45

524. Guan Zunhui 管遵惠 1986. *Nei jing* bu xie shou fa tan shu《内经》补泻手法探述. *Yun nan zhong yi za zhi* 云南中医杂志 4, 7-9

528.   Guo Aichun 郭霭春 1985. *Su wen* jiao kan ju li《素问》校勘举例. *Tian jin zhong yi xue yuan xue bao* 天津中医学院学报 1, 18-20,44

546.   Guo Bingneng 郭冰能 1986. *Nei jing* "jue" "jie" er zi yong yi li shi《内经》"绝""竭"二字用义例释. *Bei jing zhong yi xue yuan xue bao* 北京中医学院学报 2, 43

550.   Guo Chunde 郭春德 1986. *Nei jing* "guo" zi han yi ji yong fa ju ju《内经》"过"字含义及用法举隅. *Jiang su zhong yi za zhi* 江苏中医杂志 2, 31

575.   Ha Xiaoxian 哈孝贤 1985. Lüe lun *Nei jing* you guan fu ke de lun shu 略论《内经》有关妇科的论述. *Tian jin zhong yi* 天津中医 2, 42-45

582.   Han Baoxian 韩葆贤 1984. "Qi fan" qiu zhen "气反"求真. *Shan dong zhong yi xue yan xue bao* 山东中医学院学报 1, 6

595.   Hao Baohua 郝保华 1983. *Su wen* "Qi jiao bian da lun" zhong "bian xing" wen ti de tan tao《素问·气交变大论》中"变星"问题的探讨. *Shaan xi zhong yi xue yuan xue bao* 陕西中医学院学报 1, 47-49

597.   Hao Baohua, Wang Jin 郝葆华, 王瑾 1984. *Nei jing* "qi pian da lun" cheng shu nian dai xin lun — ju tian wen lü li li shi liao yuan liu tan《内经》"七篇大论"成书年代新论——据天文律历史料源流探. *Zhong hua yi shi za zhi* 中华医史杂志 1, 46-50

601.   Hao Baohua, Zhang Hongyin 郝葆华, 张宏印 1981. "Er yang zhi bing fa xin pi" xi yi "二阳之病发心脾"析疑. *Shaan xi zhong yi xue yuan xue bao* 陕西中医学院学报 4, 44-45

630.   He Cun 河村 1985. Gu yi ji "hu wen" shuo lüe 古医籍"互文"说略. *He nan zhong yi* 河南中医 3, 39-42

635.   Hong Biliang 洪必良 1989. Shi lun *Lao zi* zhe xue guan dui *Su wen* de ying xiang 试论《老子》哲学观对《素问》的影响. *An hui zhong yi xue yuan xue bao* 安徽中医学院学报 4, 10-12

638.   Hong Menghu 洪梦浒 1985. Guan yu "qi" de yi yi he duo yi wen ti 关于"气"的一义和多义问题. *Cheng du zhong yi xue yuan xue bao* 成都中医学院学报 4, 8-11

639.   Hong Qinguo 洪钦国 1987. Shen ku zao, ji shi xin yi run zhi 肾苦燥, 急食辛以润之. *Guang zhou zhong yi xue yuan xue bao* 广州中医学院学报 2, 56

668.   Hu Tianxiong 胡天雄 1980. Tan tan *Nei jing* jiao xue de wen ti 谈谈《内经》教学的问题. *Hu nan zhong yi xue yuan xue bao* 湖南中医学院学报 , 3, 70

670.   Hu Tianxiong 胡天雄 1982. *Su wen* zha ji (2) Si qi tiao shen da lun pian 素问札记 (二) 四气调神大论篇. *Hu nan zhong yi xue yuan xue bao* 湖南中医学院学报 4, 5-9

674. Hu Tianxiong 胡天雄 1990. *Su wen* wu wen li shi《素问》误文例释. *Hu nan zhong yi xue yuan xue bao* 湖南中医学院学报 3, 160-162

677. Hu Tianxiong 胡天雄 1980. *Su wen* zhong you guan shui qi bing ruo gan wen ti de ping shi《素问》中有关水气病若干问题的评释. *Zhe jiang zhong yi za zhi* 浙江中医杂志 9, 396-397

683. Hu Yongnian 胡永年 1985. *Nei jing* "hu wen" "dao zhi" yi xun ju ju《内经》"互文""倒置"义训举隅. *Hei long jiang zhong yi yao* 黑龙江中医药 2, 49-50

691. Hu Yuankui 胡元奎 1987. Xian qin gu ji yu *Nei jing* zheng ti guan de xing cheng he fa zhan 先秦古籍与《内经》整体观的形成和发展. *Shaan xi zhong yi xue yuan xue bao* 陕西中医学院学报 4, 54-57

692. Hu Zhixi 胡止犀 1986. Yi ji xun gu ju ju (1) 医籍训诂举隅 (一). *Hu bei zhong yi za zhi* 湖北中医杂志 3, 40-41

693. Hu Zhixi 胡止犀 1986. Yi ji xun gu ju ju (2) 医籍训诂举隅 (二). *Hu bei zhong yi za zhi* 湖北中医杂志 4, 37-39

694. Hu Zhixi 胡止犀 1986. Yi ji xun gu ju ju (3) 医籍训诂举隅 (三). *Hu bei zhong yi za zhi* 湖北中医杂志 5, 45-46

696. Hu Zuode 胡作德 1960. Xue xi "yun qi" xue shuo de ti hui 学习 "運气" 学說的体会. *Fu jian zhong yi yao* 福建中医药 4, 38-39

732. Huang Minggui 黄明贵 1987. Qian tan Wan Mizhai dui *Nei jing* "fa shi" li lun de yun yong 浅谈万密斋对《内经》"法时" 理论的运用. *Hu bei zhong yi za zhi* 湖北中医杂志 2, 2-3

849. Ke Xinqiao 柯新桥 1985. *Nei jing* yu xue zheng zhi zhi yan tao《内经》瘀血证治之研讨. *Shaan xi zhong yi* 陕西中医 4, 150-152

852. Kong Lingxu 孔令诩 1981. Dui *Nei jing* zhong "yin qu" yi ci de tan tao 对《内经》中 "隐曲" 一词的探讨. *Guang xi zhong yi yao* 广西中医药 4, 14-15

854. Kong Qingxi 孔庆玺 1981. Jue zheng tan tao (1) 厥证探讨 (上). *Yun nan zhong yi xue yuan xue bao* 云南中医学院学报 1, 1-5

882. Li Bin 李滨 1987. Dui Wang Bing yuan yin *Zhou yi* zhu shi *Huang Di nei jing su wen* de yan jiu 对王冰援引《周易》注释《黄帝内经素问》的研究. *An hui zhong yi xue yuan xue bao* 安徽中医学院学报 4, 5-9

894. Li Congming, Zhou Shucheng 李从明, 周书成 1991. *Su wen* die yin ci lei shi《素问》迭音词类释. *Yi gu wen zhi shi* 医古文知识 4, 15-17

897. Li Dexin 李德新 1983. Lun biao ben zhong qi 论标本中气. *Liao ning zhong yi za zhi* 辽宁中医杂志 5, 7-9

913. Li Fuhan et al. 李富汉 等 1991. *Su wen* "shui yu zhe zhi" bian xi《素问》"水郁折之" 辨析. *Guo yi lun tan* 国医论坛 3, 37

914. Li Gongshu 李攻成 1989. *Nei jing* yun qi xue shuo zhong de biao ben zhong qi li lun chu tan《内经》运气学说中的标本中气理论初探. *Liao ning zhong yi za zhi* 辽宁中医杂志 5, 5-8

915. Li Guang 李广 1981. *Huang Di nei jing su wen* zhong de die zi《黄帝内经素问》中的迭字. *Shan dong zhong yi xue yuan xue bao* 山东中医学院学报 2, 55-59

916. Li Guang 李广 1982. *Nei jing* tong jia zhi yi pie《内经》通假之一瞥. *Shan dong zhong yi xue yuan xue bao* 山东中医学院学报 增刊, 52-54

919. Li Guoqing 李国卿 1986. "Qu yun chen cuo" xin jie "去菀陈莝" 新解. *Zhong yi yao xin xi* 中医药信息 1, 1-2

944. Li Jiakang 李家康 1984. Qian tan *Nei jing* miu ci fa 浅谈《内经》缪刺法. *Gui yang zhong yi xue yuan xue bao* 贵阳中医学院学报 4, 52-53

954. Li Jianyi 李健颐 1958. *Nei jing zhi yao* qian zhu (12) 内經知要淺註 (十二). *Xin zhong yi yao* 新中醫藥 8, 27-29

964. Li Jinyong 李今庸 1984. Zhong yi gu dai bing zheng ming ci kao 中医古代病证名词考. *Hu bei zhong yi za zhi* 湖北中医杂志 2, 1-3

967. Li Jinyong 李今庸 1983. *Huang Di nei jing* jie yi san ze《黄帝内经》揭疑三则. *Ji lin zhong yi yao* 吉林中医药 3, 44-46

969. Li Jinyong 李今庸 1979. *Huang Di nei jing* yue du zhi dao《黄帝内经》阅读指导. *Shan dong zhong yi xue yuan xue bao* 山东中医学院学报 4, 60-64, 57

971. Li Jinyong 李今庸 1977. *Nei jing* xi yi san ze《内经》析疑三则. *Xin zhong yi* 新中医 1, 56-58

972. Li Jinyong 李今庸 1981. *Nei jing* xi yi er ze《素问》析疑二则. *Zhe jiang zhong yi xue yuan xue bao* 浙江中医学院学报 4, 47-48

982. Li Keshao 李克绍 1981. Du *Nei jing* zha ji 读《内经》札记. *Xin zhong yi* 新中医 7, 37-38

1004. Li Shimao, Tian Shuxiao 李士懋, 田淑霄 1985. Lun "huo yu fa zhi" 论 "火郁发之". *Tian jin zhong yi* 天津中医 3, 25-27

1028. Li Weipu 李蔚普 1956. Nan chang xi yi xue xi zhong yi ban *Nei jing* jiang zuo (ctd.) 南昌西医学习中医班内經講座 (續). *Jiang xi zhong yi yao* 江西中医药 12, 2-41

1074. Li Zhenbin 李振彬 1987. Lun *Nei jing* de shi jian ce bing si xiang 论《内经》的时间测病思想. *Liao ning zhong yi za zhi* 辽宁中医杂志 10, 4-6

1099. Liang Mingda 梁明达 1986. Cong *Jin gui* "Fu ren bing" pian kan Zhongjing dui *Nei jing* de xu cheng he fa zhan 从《金匮·妇人病》篇看仲景对《内经》的继承和发展. *Bei jing zhong yi za zhi* 北京中医杂志 3, 40

1109. Liao Qiuyuan 廖秋元 1988. *Su wen* "Biao ben bing chuan lun pian" de yi dian zhi yi《素问·标本病传论篇》的一点质疑. *Hu nan zhong yi xue yuan xue bao* 湖南中医学院学报 1, 28

1110. Liao Yuqun 廖育群 1988. Jin ben *Huang Di nei jing* yan jiu 今本《黄帝内经》研究. *Zi ran ke xue shi yan jiu* 自然科学史研究 4, 367-374

1126. Ling Yaoxing 凌耀星 1981. Jiao xue *Nei jing* de ti hui 教学《内经》的体会. *Shan dong zhong yi xue yuan xue bao* 山东中医学院学报 4, 9-17

1127. Ling Yaoxing 凌耀星 1979. Tan bao yu tiao ci, wen li yu yi li 探宝与挑疵文理与医理. *Shang hai zhong yi yao za zhi* 上海中医药杂志 3, 9-11

1134. Ling Yaoxing 凌耀星 1987. *Huang Di nei jing* ju dou zhi yi《黄帝内经》句读质疑. *Tian jin zhong yi xue yuan xue bao* 天津中医学院学报 2, 4-8

1142. Liu Aimin 刘爱民 1987. "Jing sou bu li" shi "泾溲不利" 释. *Shang hai zhong yi yao za zhi* 上海中医药杂志 2, 43

1150. Liu Chen 刘晨 1991. *Su wen* "jing sou bu li" xin jie《素问》"泾溲不利" 新解. *Guo yi lun tan* 国医论坛 6, 42

1166. Liu Chuanzhen 刘传珍 1989. Shi yue tai yang li zai *Nei jing* zhong de yi ji 十月太阳历在《内经》中的遗迹. *Guo yi lun tan* 国医论坛 3 (15), 14

1167. Liu Daigeng 刘代庚 1988. "Huo yu fa zhi" zhi wo jian "火郁发之"之我见. *Shan dong zhong yi za zhi* 山东中医杂志 2, 19-20

1172. Liu Guanghua 刘光华 1979. Shi tan *Nei jing* xing shen guan xi de lun shu 试探《内經》形神关系的論述. *Cheng du zhong yi xue yuan xue bao* 成都中医学院学报 3, 1-3

1179. Liu Hui 刘辉 1985. *Ling shu jing* tong jie zi li shuo《灵枢经》通借字例说. *Gui yang zhong yi xue yuan xue bao* 贵阳中医学院学报 4, 49-50

1186. Liu Jiayi 刘家义 1984. Shi lun "zhi bing bi qiu yu ben" 试论 "治病必求于本". *Shan dong zhong yi xue yuan xue bao* 山东中医学院学报 4, 19-22

1188. Liu Jiayi 刘家义 1986. "Mu yu da zhi" lun "木郁达之"论. *Shan dong zhong yi xue yuan xue bao* 山东中医学院学报 3, 44-48

1196. Liu Jinwen 刘蓝文 1986. Yun qi xue shuo de bian zheng fa si xiang ji qi yun yong 运气学说的辩证法思想及其应用. *Liao ning zhong yi xue yuan xue bao* 辽宁中医学院学报 1, 5-10

1254. Liu Yaxian 刘亚娴 1985. *Nei jing* suo shi yi de shi ze《内经》所示医德十则. *He bei zhong yi* 河北中医 4, 1-2

1257. Liu Yangyuan 刘养元 1990. "Shi qi mai" bian xi "适其脉" 辨析. *Yi gu wen zhi shi* 医古文知识 2, 11-13

1285. Long Bojian 龙伯坚 1957. *Huang Di nei jing* de zhu zuo shi dai 黄帝内經的著作时代. *Yi xue shi yu bao jian zu zhi* 醫學史与保健組織 2, 106-113

1289. Lou Baiceng 樓百层 1964. Shi lun *Nei jing* zhen ci bu xie (2) 試論《内經》針刺补泻 (下). *Zhe jiang zhong yi za zhi* 浙江中医杂志 4, 15-17

1293. Lu Yuqi 卢玉起 1981. Shi lun jun huo yu xiang huo 试论君火与相火. *Liao ning zhong yi za zhi* 辽宁中医杂志 理论专辑增刊, 15-17

1329. Lü Zhusun 吕竹孙 1983. Xiao yi "huo yu fa zhi" 小议"火郁发之". *Fu jian zhong yi yao* 福建中医药 3, 13-15

1373. Meng Qingyun 孟庆云 1980. *Huang Di nei jing* yu kong zhi lun《黄帝内經》与控制论. *Liao ning zhong yi za zhi* 辽宁中医杂志 6, 11-15

1376. Meng Qingyun 孟庆云 1989. *Huang Di nei jing* zhong de fang fa tan xi《黄帝内经》中的方法论探析. *Zhong yi yan jiu* 中医研究 2, 7-9

1381. Ming Yu 明宇 1988. "Gan zhu shu xie" de li lun yuan chu *Nei jing* ben zhi "肝主疏泄"的理论原出《内经》本旨. *Shang hai zhong yi yao za zhi* 上海中医药杂志 5, 39-40

1391. Nie Lifang, Wei Zixiao 聂莉芳, 魏子孝 1982. Xi "mu yu da zhi" — tan tan gan yu zheng de zhi liao 析"木郁达之"——谈谈肝郁证的治疗. *Liao ning zhong yi za zhi* 辽宁中医杂志 9, 12-14

1397. Niu Zhanhe 牛占和 1981. He wei "shen ji", "qi li"? 何谓"神机"、"气立"? 河南中医. *He nan zhong yi* 河南中医 6, 21-23,41

1399. Ouyang Bing, Meng Lingjun 欧阳兵, 孟令军 1990. *Nei jing* "ni zhi" "cong zhi" "you san yi"《内经》"逆治""从治"有三义. *Cheng du zhong yi xue yuan xue bao* 成都中医学院学报 4, 43-44

1412. Pan Chenglian 潘澄濂 1982. Lüe tan *Nei jing* de xue shu si xiang ji chu 略谈《内經》的學术思想基础. *Hei long jiang zhong yi yao* 黑龙江中医药 2, 1-3,17

1440. Pu Xiaodong 蒲晓东 1988. "Fu he" ti dai "shu xie" wu shi ji yi yi "敷和"替代"疏泄"无实际意义. *Shang hai zhong yi yao za zhi* 上海中医药杂志 9, 38

1457. Qian Chaochen 钱超尘 1986. *Nei jing* han li kao lüe《内经》汉历考略. *Bei jing zhong yi xue yuan xue bao* 北京中医学院学报 1, 10-12

1490. Qin Bowei 秦伯未 1957. *Nei jing* zhi yao qian jie (ctd.) "内經知要" 淺解 (續). *Zhong yi za zhi* 中医雜誌 1, 44-46

1497. Qiu Jianrong 邱建荣 1991. "Huo yu fa zhi" qian shi "火郁发之"浅识. *Zhe jiang zhong yi xue yuan xue bao* 浙江中医学院学报 5, 10-11

1500. Qiu Xingfan 邱幸凡 1982. Cong *Nei jing* kan qing zhi yu ren ti jian kang he ji bing de guan xi 从《内经》看情志与人体健康和疾病的关系. *Fu jian zhong yi yao* 福建中医药 5, 12-14

1505. Qiu Xingfan 邱幸凡 1985. *Nei jing* dian kuang bian xi《内经》癫狂辨析. *Jiang xi zhong yi yao* 江西中医药 4, 2-3

1508. Qiu Xingfan 邱幸凡 1983. *Nei jing duo yi zi ci xi yi*《内经》多义字词析义. *Zhe jiang zhong yi za zhi* 浙江中医杂志 1, 10-11

1513. Qu Feng 曲峰 1984. *Huang Di nei jing de ren shi lun*《黄帝内经》的认识论. *Nan jing zhong yi xue yuan xue bao* 南京中医学院学报 3, 1-4

1524. Qu Yueyun 瞿岳云 1980. *Lüe tan "qi fan" zheng zhi* 略谈 "气反" 证治. *Shaan xi zhong yi* 陕西中医 4, 7-8

1556. Ren Yingqiu 任应秋 1959. *Shen me jiao "yang sha yin cang"?* 什么叫 "陽杀陰藏" ?. *Zhong yi za zhi* 中医杂志 3, 71

1569. Sha Tao, Liu Weiqing 沙涛, 刘维庆 1991. *Shi tan Huang Di nei jing zhong de die yin ci* 试谈《黄帝内经》中的迭音词. *Yi gu wen zhi shi* 医古文知识 1, 17-18

1581. Shen Hongyan 申鸿砚 1982. *Su wen "qiu sha" kao*《素问》"秋杀" 考. *He nan zhong yi* 河南中医 3, 20-21

1585. Shen Hongyan 申鸿砚 1984. *"Yang" "gu" xin yi* "痒" "鼓" 新绎. *Zhe jiang zhong yi za zhi* 浙江中医杂志 2, 87

1610. Shi Guanqing, Wu Mingqin 石冠卿, 武明钦 1979. *Nei jing su wen "biao ben bing chuan lun" shi*《内經·素問·標本病傳論》释. *He nan zhong yi xue yuan xue bao* 河南中医学院学报 3, 48-53

1616. Shi Yulin 石玉麟 1984. *Zhong jing zhen jiu xue shu si xian yu Nei jing zhi guan xi* 仲景针灸学术思想与《内经》之关系. *Zhe jiangzhong yi za zhi* 浙江中医杂志 11, 483

1617. Shi Jiping, Liu Donghan 时吉萍, 刘东汉 1989. *"Qu yun chen cuo" zhi guan jian* "去菀陈莝" 之管见. *Gan su zhong yi xue yuan xue bao* 甘肃中医学院学报 2, 35

1620. Shi Yiren 時逸人 1940. *Shi shi Nei jing xue (xu mai zhen)* 時氏内經學(續脈診). *Fu xing zhong yi* 復興中醫 5, 10

1623. Shi Zhensheng 时振声 1983. *Dui Nei jing jue zheng de tan tao* 对《内经》厥证的探讨. *Hei long jiang zhong yi yao* 黑龙江中医药 1, 13-17

1656. Song Zhixing 宋知行 1983. *Shen ji bian shi* 神机辨识. *Liao ning zhong yi za zhi* 辽宁中医杂志 1, 10-11

1667. Sun Daizong 孙岱宗 1979. *Tan yan zu guo yi xue "zuo gan you fei" zhi shuo* 谈谈祖国医学 "左肝右肺" 之说. *Yun nan zhong yi xue yuan xue bao* 云南中医学院学报 3, 10-11

1673. Sun Hongsheng 孙洪生 1985. *"Si wei xiang dai" shi* "四维相代" 释. *Bei jing zhong yi xue yuan xue bao* 北京中医学院学报 5, 44

1679. Sun Manzhi 孙曼之 1987. *Huang Di nei jing de ci yu te dian ji qi zhu zuo nian dai chu tan*《黄帝内经》的词语特点及其著作年代初探. *Bei jing zhong yi xue yuan xue bao* 北京中医学院学报 5, 25-26

1681.   Sun Qiming 孙启明 1985. *Bo shu "ye" yu Nei jing "zhi"*《帛书》"冶"与
        《内经》"治". *Zhong yi za zhi* 中医杂志 5, 78

1682.   Sun Qingfu 孙庆甫 1982. *Su wen zhong "fu" "fu zhong" shi shi*《素问》
        中"胕""胕肿"试释. *Gui yang zhong yi xue yuan xue bao* 贵阳中医学院
        学报 3, 42-44

1720.   Sun Zhongnian 孙忠年 1988. *Qian xi Nei jing Nan jing lun fu zhen* 浅析
        《内经》《难经》论腹诊. *Shaan xi zhong yi xue yuan xue bao* 陕西中医学
        院学报 4, 11-16

1735.   Tan Baolin 覃保霖 1987. *Huang Di nei jing yu gu dai san Yi yan jiu* 黄帝内
        经与古代三易研究. *Nei meng gu zhong yi yao* 内蒙古中医药 4, 38-41

1742.   Tang Gouyu 唐构宇 1991. *Su wen zhi xiao yi*《素问识》小议. *Hu nan
        zhong yi xue yuan xue bao* 湖南中医学院学报 3, 50-52

1749.   Tang Xuemei 唐雪梅 1990. *Nei jing de shi jian zhi liao xue si xiang tan
        xi*《内经》的时间治疗学思想探析. *Nan jing zhong yi xue yuan xue bao* 南
        京中医学院学报 2, 6-8

1779.   Wang Deyun 汪德云 1986. *Dui "sheng sheng hua hua, pin wu xian zhang"
        de li jie* 对"生生化化,品物咸章"的理解. *Bei jing zhong yi xue yuan xue
        bao* 北京中医学院学报 4, 43

1788.   Wang Hong 汪红 1988. *Fan xun zi ou shi* 反训字偶拾. *Zhe jiang zhong yi
        xue yuan xue bao* 浙江中医学院学报 1, 44-45

1789.   Wang Kemin et al. 汪克敏 等 1985. *Cong pian ming kan Nei jing xin li xue
        si xiang de xi tong xing* 从篇名看《内经》心理学思想的系统性. *Cheng
        du zhong yi xue yuan xue bao* 成都中医学院学报 2, 53-55

1794.   Wang Weidong 汪卫东 1987. *"Qi xue", "qi fu", "gu kong" yi bian* "气
        穴"、"气府"、"骨空"义辨. *Hei long jiang zhong yi yao* 黑龙江中医药
        5, 34

1798.   Wang Changrong 王长荣 1989. *Nei jing "fu" zi wu "zu" yi*《内经》"胕"字
        无"足"义. *Yi gu wen zhi shi* 医古文知识 4, 36

1817.   Wang Guimiao 王贵淼 1983. *"Biao ben" qian shi* "标本"浅释. *Shaan xi
        zhong yi* 陕西中医 1, 37,36

1818.   Wang Guiting 王贵廷 1985. *Nei jing bian zheng lun zhi gai shu* (1)《内
        经》辨证论治概述(上). *Nei meng gu zhong yi yao* 内蒙古中医药 2, 44-45

1833.   Wang Hongtu, Che Baoping 王洪图, 车保平 1983. *Lüe lun Nei jing de yin
        yi er zhi* 略论《内经》的因宜而治. *Bei jing zhong yi za zhi* 北京中医杂志
        4, 16

1837.   Wang Hongtu, Che Baoping 王洪图, 车保平 1984. *Tan Huang Di nei jing
        zhi liu jing* 谈《黄帝内经》之六经. *Bei jing zhong yi za zhi* 北京中医杂志
        4, 49-53

1884. Wang Minghui 王明辉 1986. *Nei jing* xue shu si xiang fang fa qian xi《内经》学术思想方法浅析. *Liao ning zhong yi za zhi* 辽宁中医杂志 10, 1

1892. Wang Niansheng 王年生 1983. Yu Chang dui *Nei jing* de jiao zhu 于鬯对《内经》的校注. *An hui zhong yi xue yuan xue bao* 安徽中医学院学报 4, 45-47

1895. Wang Ping 王平 1987. *Nei jing* xi yi san ze《内经》析疑三则. *Nei meng gu zhong yi yao* 内蒙古中医药 2, 47

1901. Wang Qi et al. 王琦 等 1979. Lüe lun *Nei jing* zhong de yi xue yu qi xiang wen ti 略论《内经》中的医学与气象问题. *Shang hai zhong yi yao za zhi* 上海中医药杂志 5, 44-49

1908. Wang Qingqi 王庆其 1986. *Nei jing* "yi xiang zhi wei" shu yi《内经》"以象之谓" 疏义. *Shang hai zhong yi yao za zhi* 上海中医药杂志 4, 35-36

1911. Wang Qingqi 王庆其 1989. *Nei jing ci dian* xuan zai《内经辞典》选载. *Yi gu wen zhi shi* 医古文知识 2, 10-11

1946. Wang Shiwen 王世文 1991. *Nei jing* lun nao shu lüe《内经》论脑述略. *Zhong yi han shou tong xun* 中医函授通讯 6, 4-5

1963. Wang Xiafang 王霞芳 1984. Shen yu fen bu zhi bing chu — lüe lun *Nei jing* fen bu mian zhen ji qi zai er ke de ying yong 审于分部知病处——略论《内经》分部面诊及其在儿科的应用. *Shang hai zhong yi yao za zhi* 上海中医药杂志 11, 33-35

1978. Wang Yicheng, Guo Huixiong 王义成, 郭辉雄 1988. *Nei jing* zhong gu yin tong jia qian tan《内经》中古音通假浅谈. *Hu bei zhong yi za zhi* 湖北中医杂志 2, 46-48

1979. Wang Yicheng, Wang Shuping 王义成, 王淑萍 1989. "Qin han" xiao yi "寝汗" 小议. *Bei jing zhong yi xue yuan xue bao* 北京中医学院学报 5, 10

2007. Wang Yuchuan 王玉川 1985. Guan yu "san yin san yang" wen ti 关于 "三阴三阳" 问题. *Bei jing zhong yi xue yuan xue bao* 北京中医学院学报 1, 12-15

2016. Wang Yuchuan 王玉川 1988. Wu zang pei wu xing, wu wei ji qi ta (3) 五脏配五行、五味及其它(三). *Bei jing zhong yi xue yuan xue bao* 北京中医学院学报 3, 5-10

2043. Wang Zhi 王志 1986. "Huo yu fa zhi" zai yan ke lin chuang de ying yong "火郁发之" 在眼科临床的应用. *Liao ning zhong yi za zhi* 辽宁中医杂志 11, 20-22

2055. Wang Ziqiang 王自强 1987. "Zhu qi fen yu, jie shu yu fei" zhi "qi" zi zhi yi "诸气膹郁, 皆属于肺" 之 "气" 字质疑. *An hui zhong yi xue yuan xue bao* 安徽中医学院学报 1, 52

2058. Wang Ziqiang 王自强 1982. Shi lun "qi fan" de zhi fa 试论 "气反" 的治法. *Nan jing zhong yi xue yuan xue bao* 南京中医学院学报 1, 12-14

2069. Wei Musen 魏睦森 1988. "Gan zhu shu xie" he hu *Nei jing* ben zhi "肝主疏泄" 合乎《内经》本旨. *Shang hai zhong yi yao za zhi* 上海中医药杂志 6, 45

2078. Wei Yiguang 魏贻光 1984. Wang Bing yu *Su wen ci zhu* 王冰与《素问次注》. *Fu jian zhong yi yao* 福建中医药 6,19-22

2154. Wu Zhengzhi 吴正治 1985. Shi lun sheng jiang chu ru 试论升降出入. *Hu nan zhong yi xue yuan xue bao* 湖南中医学院学报 1, 45-47

2167. Xia Xuechuan 夏学传 1985. *Nei jing* "chong yan ci" qian shi (2)《内经》"重言词" 浅释(下). *Ji lin zhong yi yao* 吉林中医药 2, 48-49

2168. Xia Xuechuan 夏学传 1986. Shi shu Hu Peng jiao gu *Su wen* zhi fang fa 试述胡澎校诂《素问》之方法. *Si chuan zhong yi* 四川中医 12, 5

2171. Xiang Ping 项平 1983. *Nei jing* zhong de wai zhi fa《内经》中的外治法. *Nan jing zhong yi xue yuan xue bao* 南京中医学院学报 3, 13-15

2179. Xiao Xi 蕭熙 1931. *Nei jing* gan zang jin shi (1) 内經肝臟今釋 (上). *Yi jie chun qiu* 醫界春秋 63, 8-10

2186. Xiao Guoshi 肖国士 1982. He wei "xuan fu"? 何謂 "玄府"?. *Cheng du zhong yi xue yuan xue bao* 成都中医学院学报 4, 64-65

2204. Xie Jiguang 谢继光 1986. Lun *Nei jing* zhen jiu shi zhi de xian hou ci xu 论《内经》针灸施治的先后次序. *Shang hai zhen jiu za zhi* 上海针灸杂志 4, 39-41

2225. Xiong Jibo 熊继柏 1985. Lüe tan *Nei jing* zhong "jue" de han yi 略谈《内经》中 "厥" 的含义. *Zhe jiang zhong yi xue yuan xue bao* 浙江中医学院学报 6, 4-6

2235. Xu Lianchun 徐连春 1984. "Bu cang jing" xi "不藏精" 析. *Fu jian zhong yi yao* 福建中医药 2, 60

2264. Xu Xiangting 徐湘亭 1983. Lun *Su wen* kai he shu yu *Tai su* guan he shu zai yi yi shang de cha bie 论《素问》开阖枢与《太素》关阖枢在意义上的差别. *Jiang su zhong yi za zhi* 江苏中医杂志 2, 4-5

2270. Xu Xiangting 徐湘亭 1984. Du yi jing yao bian bie gu zi yi yi 读医经要辨别古字意义. *Shang hai zhong yi yao za zhi* 上海中医药杂志 11, 37-38

2277. Xu Yuxiang et al. 徐余祥 等 1988. Shi lun "gan zhu shu xie" de sheng li yu bing li 试论 "肝主疏泄" 的生理与病理. *Jiang su zhong yi* 江苏中医 11, 41-43

2289. Xu Xuedong 许学东 1991. *Su wen* "shi" "jin" kao shi《素问》"适" "尽" 考释. *Yi gu wen zhi shi* 医古文知识 3, 22-23

2305. Xu Qi 项祺 1989. *Nei jing* zhi ze ji yang sheng xue shuo gai shu《内经》治则及养生学说概述. *Shan xi zhong yi* 山西中医 4, 49-52

2315. Xue Ningsong 薛凝嵩 1958. *Nei jing* sheng hua lun xue shuo de ke xue jing hua chu tan 内經生化論學說的科學精華初探. *Zhe jiang zhong yi za zhi* 浙江中医雜誌 4, 6-14

2317. Xue Tongquan 薛彤权 1988. *Huang Di nei jing* bu fen jing wen zhi yi《黄帝内经》部分经文质疑. *Tian jin zhong yi xue yuan xue bao* 天津中医学院学报 1, 5-7

2332. Yan Hongchen, Cui Zhongping 阎洪臣, 崔仲平 1981. Cong *Huang Di nei jing* kan gu dai yi xue jiao yu 从《黄帝内经》看古代医学教育. *Zhe jiang zhong yi xue yuan xue bao* 浙江中医学院学报 1, 33-35, 27

2334. Yan Huihan 阎惠涵 1981. *Ling shu* "Ben shen" jiao shi《灵枢·本神》校释. *Shaan xi zhong yi xue yuan xue bao* 陕西中医学院学报 3, 15-22, 39

2337. Yan Zili 阎自力 1991. *Nei jing* wu yu yu yi xue qi xiang xue《内经》五郁与医学气象学. *Shan dong zhong yi za zhi* 山东中医杂志 3, 10-11

2414. Ye Youxin 叶又新 1981. Shi shi dong han hua xiang shi shang ke hua de yi zhen 试释东汉画象石上刻划的医针——兼探九针形成过程. *Shan dong zhong yi xue yuan xue bao* 山东中医学院学报 3, 60-68

2417. Yi Zheng'an 衣正安 1979. *Nei jing* xue ye sheng cheng li lun de chu bu tan tao《内经》血液生成理论的初步探讨. *Shang hai zhong yi yao za zhi* 上海中医药杂志 5, 50

2424. Yi Sidi 易斯狄 1955. *Nei jing* shang de ci jiu zhi liao (abstract) — *Nei jing* ci jiu yan jiu zhi wu 内經上的刺灸治療 (摘要)——内經刺灸研究之五. *Xin zhong yi yao* 新中醫藥 3, 24-27

2435. You Shuxian 尤淑贤 1990. Tan *Huang Di nei jing su wen* zhong "...zhe,... ye" ju shi 谈《黄帝内经素问》中 "……者,……也" 句式. *Yi gu wen zhi shi* 医古文知识 4, 13-15

2445. Yu Weidong 于卫东 1983. Shi "yang sheng yin zhang, yang sha yin cang" 释 "阳生阴长, 阳杀阴藏". *He nan zhong yi* 河南中医 2, 22

2469. Yu Changrong 俞长荣 1982. Shi lun *Nei jing* de fang zhi xue si xiang 试论《内经》的防治学思想. *Fu jian zhong yi yao* 福建中医药 1, 2-7

2470. Yu Changrong 俞长荣 1962. Shi lun "qi fan" 試論 "气反". *Zhong yi za zhi* 中医杂志 12, 35-37

2471. Yu Changrong 俞长荣 1979. Lüe lun "shen zhe cong zhi" 略论 "甚者从之". *Zhong yi za zhi* 中医杂志 7, 13 (397)

2493. Zeng Fanfu 曾凡夫 1981. *Su wen* cheng shu nian dai kao《素问》成书年代考. *Zhe jiang zhong yi za zhi* 浙江中医杂志 12, 530-531

2520. Zhang Canjia 张灿玾 1986. Xue xi *Nei jing* bi xu zhu yi de ji ge wen ti 学习《内经》必须注意的几个问题. *Fu jian zhong yi yao* 福建中医药 5, 50-53

2530. Zhang Changcheng 张长城 1991. Lun xiu ci xue zai xun jie *Nei jing* zhong de zuo yong 论修辞学在训解《内经》中的作用. *He nan zhong yi* 河南中医 6, 18-20

2563. Zhang Dengbu 张登部 1984. Ren chong du mai "yi yuan er san qi" chu tan 任冲督脉 "一源而三歧" 初探. *Zhong yi za zhi* 中医杂志 2, 53-55

2566. Zhang Dianxiang 张殿相 1987. Shi lun *Nei jing* "shou jing sui" 试论《内经》"守经隧". *Zhong yi han shou tong xun* 中医函授通讯 3, 13

2568. Zhang Dongda 张东达 1986. *Su wen* zhong "zhi" zi yong fa qian yi《素问》中 "之" 字用法浅议. *Shaan xi zhong yi xue yuan xue bao* 陕西中医学院学报 1, 45-50

2582. Zhang Huiyun, Chen Xuanping 张惠云, 陈选平 1984. *Nei jing* "yin xu sheng nei re" chu yi《内经》"阴虚生内热" 刍议. *Shaan xi zhong yi* 陕西中医 10, 7-8

2607. Zhang Mancheng 张曼诚 1982. Qian xi *Nei jing* she sheng li lun zhong de bian zheng fa si xiang 浅析《内经》摄生理论中的辨证法思想. *Gui yang zhong yi xue yuan xue bao* 贵阳中医学院学报 4, 53-55

2617. Zhang Qicheng 张其枨 1989. Danbo fu zi ji ji xun gu de fang fa 丹波父子医籍训诂的方法. *Yi gu wen zhi shi* 医古文知识 3, 3-5

2619. Zhang Qixian 张启贤 1983. *Nei jing* "jue" zi qian shi《内经》"厥" 字浅识. *Hu bei zhong yi za zhi* 湖北中医杂志 4, 52-53

2623. Zhang Ruqing 张如青 1989. Qing ru yan zhi *Nei jing* ji qi dui zhong ri yi jie de ying xiang 清儒研治《内经》及其对中日医界的影响. *Zhong hua yi shi za zhi* 中华医史杂志 2, 65

2637. Zhang Shanlei 张山雷 1985. Du *Su wen* shi xiao lu (9) 读素问识小录 (九). *Zhe jiang zhong yi xue yuan xue bao* 浙江中医学院学报 1, 48-50

2643. Zhang Shiqing et al. 张士卿 等 1982. Wen ti jie da 问题解答. *Zhong yi za zhi* 中医杂志 5, 60-61

2682. Zhang Zhenyu 张珍玉 1978. *Nei jing* de wu yu ji qi lin chuang yi yi《内经》的五郁及其临床意义. *Shan dong zhong yi xue yuan xue bao* 山东中医学院学报 4, 1 (225)

2683. Zhang Zhenyu 张珍玉 1983. Du *Nei jing* zha ji (1) 读《内经》札记(一). *Shan dong zhong yi xue yuan xue bao* 山东中医学院学报 4, 34

2689. Zhang Zhenyu 张珍玉 1985. Du *Nei jing* zha ji (7) 读《内经》札记(七). *Shan dong zhong yi xue yuan xue bao* 山东中医学院学报 4, 55

2690. Zhang Zhenyu 张珍玉 1986. Du *Nei jing* zha ji (8) 读《内经》札记 (八). *Shan dong zhong yi xue yuan xue bao* 山东中医学院学报 2, 43-46

2694. Zhang Zhihua 张志华 1985. "You gu wu yun, yi wu yun ye" bian xi "有故无殒, 亦无殒也" 辨析. *Bei jing zhong yi za zhi* 北京中医杂志 3, 55

2719. Zhao Huixian 赵辉贤 1980. *Huang Di nei jing tai su* yi wen kao bian《黄帝内经》太素遗文考辨. *Gui yang zhong yi xue yuan xue bao* 贵阳中医学院学报 4, 6-11

2723. Zhao Huixian 赵辉贤 1978. *Tai su* yi pian kao《太素》遗篇考. *Zhe jiang zhong yi xue yuan xue bao* 浙江中医学院学报 3, 3-7

2738. Zhao Mingshan 赵明山 1982. *Nei jing* zhong de shen jing jing shen bing zheng chu tan《内经》中的神经精神病症初探. *Liao ning zhong yi za zhi* 辽宁中医杂志 11, 12-14

2753. Zhao Yifu 赵益夫 1981. Gu yi ji tong jie zi li shi 古医籍通借字例释. *Zhong yi za zhi* 中医杂志 8, 61-63

2766. Zheng Bangben 郑邦本 1985. Zhong jing dui *Nei jing* zhi ze xue shuo de ji cheng yu fa zhan 仲景对《内经》治则学说的继承与发展. *Cheng du zhong yi xue yuan xue bao* 成都中医学院学报 2, 8-9,7

2767. Zheng Bangben 郑邦本 1985. *Nei jing* nei zheng jiao kan ju ju《内经》内证校勘举隅. *Shang hai zhong yi yao za zhi* 上海中医药杂志 4, 38-40

2790. Zheng Shaoxiang 郑少祥 1988. "Dong qu jing xing, chun bu qiu nü" qian xi "冬取井荥, 春不鼽衄" 浅析. *Shaan xi zhong yi* 陕西中医 2, 84

2800. Zheng Shouzeng 郑守曾 1982. *Nei jing* lei gai nian yan jiu (jie lu)《内经》类概念研究 (节录). *Cheng du zhong yi xue yuan xue bao* 成都中医学院学报 1, 28-32

2802. Zheng Xiaochang, Song Ziran 郑孝昌, 宋子然 1984. *Nei jing* chong yan(2)《内经》重言 (下). *Cheng du zhong yi xue yuan xue bao* 成都中医学院学报 4, 45-47,60

2855. Zhu Guangren 朱广仁 1981. *Su wen* jiao shi jie xuan《素问》校释节选. *Jiang su zhong yi za zhi* 江苏中医杂志 6, 53-54

2857. Zhu Guangren, Wang Xiaoju 朱广仁, 王效菊 1981. Lüe lun "miu ci" yu "ju ci" 略论 "缪刺" 与 "巨刺". *Zhong yi za zhi* 中医杂志 5, 49-51

2862. Zhu Renkang 朱仁康 1955. *Nei jing* shang de "sheng li" "bing li" xue shuo 内經上的 "生理" "病理" 學說. *Shang hai zhong yi yao za zhi* 上海中醫藥雜誌 11, 3-4

2889. Zhu Chenyu 祝諶予 1961. Wen yi er ze 問疑二則. *Zhong yi za zhi* 中医杂志 6, 37(237)

2904. Zhuo Tongnian 卓同年 1989. *Nei jing* "bi lei qu xiang" tan xi《内经》"比类取象" 探析. *Xin jiang zhong yi yao* 新疆中医药 1, 32-36